Principles of Object Oriented Modeling and Simulation with Modelica 3.3

IEEE Press
445 Hoes Lane
Piscataway, NJ 08854

Principles of Object Oriented Modeling and Simulation with Modelica 3.3

A Cyber-Physical Approach

Peter Fritzson

IEEE
IEEE PRESS

WILEY

For further information visit: the book web page http://www.DrModelica.org, the Modelica Association web page http://www.modelica.org, the authors research page http://www.ida.liu.se/labs/pelab/modelica, or email the author at petfr@ida.liu.se

Library of Congress Cataloging-in-Publication Data:

Fritzson, Peter A., 1952-
Principles of object oriented modeling and simulation with Modelica 3.3 : a cyber-physical approach / Peter Fritzson. — 2nd edition.
ISBN: 9781118859124
pages cm
Includes bibliographical references and index.
1. Object-oriented methods (Computer science) 2. Computer simulation. 3. Modelica. I. Title.
QA76.64.F758 2015
005.1'17—dc23 2014022271

Printed in the United States of America.

10 9 8 7 6 5 4 3 2 1

Table of Contents

Preface

The Modelica modeling language and technology is being warmly received by the world community in modeling and simulation with major applications in virtual prototyping of complex cyber-physical systems, which mix physical system dynamics with software (cyber) and networks. It is bringing about a revolution in this area, based on its ease of use, visual design of models with combination of lego-like predefined model building blocks, its ability to define model libraries with reusable components, its support for modeling and simulation of complex applications involving parts from several application domains, and many more useful facilities. To draw an analogy—Modelica is currently in a similar phase as Java early on, before the language became well known, but for virtual prototyping instead of Internet programming.

About the Author

Peter Fritzson, PhD, is Professor and Research Director of the Programming Environment Laboratory within Department of Computer and Information Science, Linköping University, Sweden. Prof. Fritzson is also Director of the Open Source Modelica Consortium, Director of the MODPROD Center for Model-Based Product Development, and Vice Chairman of the Modelica Association, all organizations he helped to establish. Previously, he has served as Chairman of the Scandinavian Simulation Society, Secretary of EuroSim, and a Project Leader at Sun MicroSystems California. Prof. Fritzson is one of the world's leading experts on object-oriented equation-based modeling and simulation technology, and is one of the founding fathers of Modelica..

About this Book

This book teaches modeling and simulation of cyber-physical systems and gives an introduction and complete overview of the Modelica language to people who are familiar with basic programming concepts. It gives a basic introduction to the concepts of cyber-physical systems, modeling and simulation, equation-based object-oriented modeling, as well as the basics of object-oriented component-based modeling for the novice, and a comprehensive overview of modeling and simulation in a number of application areas. In fact, the book has several goals:

- Being a useful textbook in introductory courses on modeling and simulation of cyber-physical systems.
- Being easily accessible for people who do not previously have a background in modeling, simulation and object orientation.
- Introducing the concepts of cyber-physical modeling, object-oriented modeling, and component-based modeling.
- Providing a complete yet informal reference for the Modelica 3.3 language including the new synchronous features for embedded system modeling.

- Demonstrating modeling examples from a wide range of application areas.
- Being a reference guide for the most commonly used Modelica libraries.
- Introducing requirement driven model-based system design and verification.
- Giving an introduction to numeric and symbolic techniques used in current Modelica tools.

The book contains many examples of models in different application domains, as well as examples combining several domains. However, it is not primarily intended for the advanced modeler who, for example, needs additional insight into modeling within very specific application domains, or the person who constructs very complex models where special tricks may be needed.

All examples and exercises in this book are available in an electronic self-teaching material called DrModelica, based on this book, which gradually guides the reader from simple introductory examples and exercises to more advanced ones. All of this teaching material can be freely downloaded from the book web site within `www.openmodelica.org`. This site also includes the downloadable free open source tool OpenModelica for modeling and simulation, which is the tool primarily used in this book.

Moreover, the web site contains additional (teaching) material related to this book. The Modelica Standard Library 3.2.1 release August 2013 is used for the examples in this book. The main web site for the Modelica and Modelica libraries, including the most recent versions, is the Modelica Association website, `www.Modelica.org`.

This second edition describes improvements and updates of the Modelica language up to Modelica 3.3. revision 1, including synchronous clocked constructs, examines basic concepts of cyber-physical, equation-based, object-oriented system modeling and simulation. The Modelica class concept and its use in graphical and textual modeling is introduced together with several hundred examples from many application areas and explores modeling methodology for continuous, discrete, and hybrid systems; and more.

Reading Guide

This book is a combination of a textbook for teaching modeling and simulation of cyber-physical systems, a textbook and reference guide for learning how to model and program using Modelica, and an application guide on how to do physical modeling in a number of application areas. The book can be read sequentially from the beginning to the end, but this will probably not be the typical reading pattern. Here are some suggestions:

- Very quick introduction to modeling and simulation of cyber-physical systems – an object-oriented approach: Chapters 1 and 2.
- Basic introduction to the Modelica language: Chapter 2 and first part of Chapter 13.
- Full Modelica language course: Chapters 1–13.
- Emphasis on cyber-physical system modeling: Chapter 12 and Chapter 13.
- Application-oriented course: Chapter 1, and 2, most of Chapter 5, Chapters 12–15. Use Chapters 3–11 as a language reference, and Chapter 16 and appendices as a library reference.
- Teaching object orientation in modeling: Chapters 2–4, first part of Chapter 12.
- Introduction to mathematical equation representations, as well as numeric and symbolic techniques, Chapters 17-18.
- Modelica environments, with three example tools, Chapter 19.

An interactive computer-based self-teaching course material called DrModelica is available as electronic live notebooks at www.openmodelica.org. This material includes all the examples and exercises with solutions from the book, and is designed to be used in parallel when reading the book, with page references, etc.

The reading diagram below is yet another reading guideline, giving a combination of important language concepts together with modeling methodology and application examples of your choice. The selection is of necessity somewhat arbitrary – you should also take a look at the table of contents of other chapters and part of chapters so that you do not miss something important according to your own interest.

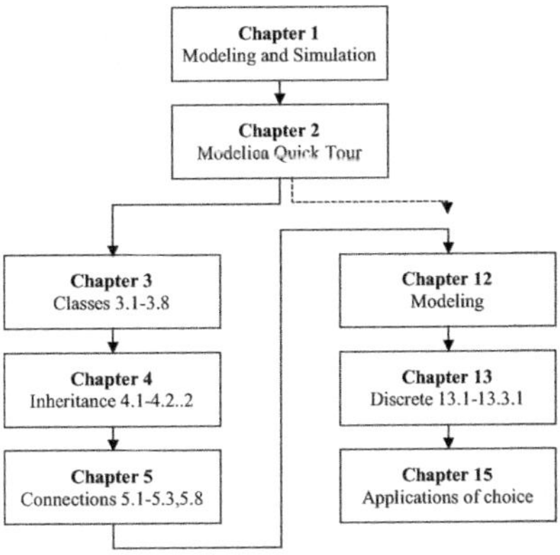

Acknowledgements

The members of the Modelica Association created the Modelica language, and contributed have many examples of Modelica code in the *Modelica Language Rationale* and *Modelica Language Specification* (see http://www.modelica.org), some of which are used in this book. The members who contributed to various versions of Modelica are mentioned further below.

First, thanks to my wife, Anita, who has supported and endured me during this writing effort.

Very special thanks to Peter Bunus for help with model examples, some figures, Microsoft Word formatting, and for many inspiring discussions. Without your help this project might have been too hard, especially considering the damage to my hands from too much typing on computer keyboards.

Many thanks to Hilding Elmqvist for sharing the vision about a declarative modeling language, for starting off the Modelica design effort by inviting people to form a design group, for serving as the first chairman of Modelica Association, and for enthusiasm and many design contributions including pushing for a unified class concept. Also thanks for inspiration regarding presentation material including finding historical examples of equations.

Many thanks to Martin Otter for serving as the second chairman of the Modelica Association, for enthusiasm and energy, design and Modelica library contributions, as well as inspiration regarding presentation material.

Many thanks to Eva-Lena Lengquist Sandelin and Susanna Monemar for help with the first version of the exercises, for help with preparing certain appendices, and for preparing the first version of the DrModelica interactive notebook teaching material which makes the examples in this book more accessible for interactive learning and experimentation.

Thanks to Peter Aronsson, Bernhard Bachmann, Peter Beater, Jan Brugård, Dag Brück, Brian Elmegaard, Hilding Elmqvist, Vadim Engelson, Rüdiger Franke, Dag Fritzson, Torkel Glad, Pavel Grozman, Daniel Hedberg, Andreas Idebrant, Mats Jirstrand, Olof Johansson, Emma Larsdotter Nilsson, Håkan Lundvall, Sven-Erik Mattsson, Iakov Nakhimovski, Hans Olsson, Adrian Pop, Per Sahlin, Levon Saldamli, Hubertus Tummescheit, and Hans-Jürg Wiesmann for constructive comments on the first edition, and in some cases other help, on parts of the book, and to Peter Bunus for help in making Microsoft Word more cooperative.

Thanks to Hans Olsson and Dag Brück, who edited several versions of the Modelica Specification, and to Michael Tiller for sharing my interest in programming tools and demonstrating that it is indeed possible to write a Modelica book.

Thanks to Bodil Mattsson-Kihlström for handling many administrative chores at the Programming Environment Laboratory while I have been focusing on the first edition book writing, to Ulf Nässén for inspiration and encouragement, and to Uwe Assmann for encouragement and sharing common experiences on the hard task of writing books.

Thanks to all members of PELAB and employees of MathCore Engineering, who have given comments and feedback.

Thanks to the staff at Vårdnäs Stiftgård, who have provided a pleasant atmosphere for important parts of this writing effort.

Approximately 95 per cent of the running text of the first edition this book has been entered by voice using Dragon Naturally Speaking. This is usually slower than typing, but still quite useful for a person like me, who has acquired RSI (Repetitive Strain Injury) due to too much typing. Fortunately, I could still do limited typing and drawing, e.g., for corrections, examples, and figures. All Modelica examples are hand-typed, but often with the help of others. All figures except the curve diagrams are, of course, hand drawn.

The first version of this book "Principles of Object-Oriented Modeling and Simulation with Modelica 2.1" was finalized in September 2003.

The second edition, titled "Principles of Modeling and Simulation with Modelica 3.3: A Cyber-Physical Approach" has been updated to Modelica 3.3 rev 1 and extended with more aspects covering modeling of cyber-physical systems with integrated hardware-software and the new clocked synchronous features in Modelica 3.3 especially suitable for embedded systems modeling. A description of stream connectors including several examples has been added, as well as a description of expandable connectors. The chapter on the Modelica standard library and some other open source libraries has been updated to the current status. Moreover, some additional material has been included such as requirements-driven modeling and verification of cyber-physical software/hardware products, meta-modeling with MetaModelica, and a short introduction to FMI – the Functional Mockup Interface for model exchange and/or co-simulation.

Regarding the second edition many people have contributed with feedback—there is a risk of forgetting somebody here. I would especially like to thank Per Östlund for very detailed and expert feedback on nine of the chapters, Bernhard Thiele for detailed feedback regarding the new sections about the clocked synchronous constructs in Chapter 13, Francesco Casella for feedback on stream connectors and modeling style, Rüdiger Franke regarding application models and help to convert the thermodynamic examples in Chapter 15 to stream connector style, Alachew Shitahun for help with updating library and scripting appendices, Arunkumar Palanisamy for help with the grammar appendix update, Adeel Asghar for feedback regarding graphical annotations and the graphical editor. Also thanks to Dirk Zimmer, Elena Shmoylova, Martin Otter, Hilding Elmqvist, and Bernt Lie for feedback. Many thanks to Adrian Pop, Per Östlund, Martin Sjölund, Adeel Asghar, Willi Braun, Lennart Ochel, Vitalij Ruge, and all other developers in the OpenModelica project for support and help when needed. Thanks to Lena Buffoni for additional exercises and collaboration in teaching our Modelica course. Thanks to Adrian Pop and Martin Sjölund regarding MetaModelica and compiler bootstrapping work, and to Wladimir Schamai regarding feedback and collaboration on ModelicaML, requirement verification, and state charts semantics.

The updates for this edition were possible for me to type without voice input. My hands have become better with frequent crawl swimming exercises and a work position using a thin laptop on my lap.

Linköping, July 2014

Peter Fritzson

Contributions to Examples

Many people contributed to the original versions of some of the Modelica examples presented in this book. Most examples have been significantly revised compared to the originals. A number of individuals are acknowledged below with the risk of accidental omission due to oversight. If the original version of an example is from the Modelica Tutorial or the Modelica Specification on the Modelica Association web sites, the contributors usually are the members of the Modelica Association, but in some cases individuals are mentioned also in this case. In addition to the examples mentioned in this table, there are also numerous small example fragments from the Modelica Tutorial and Specification used in original or modified form in the text, which is indicated to some extent in the reference section of each chapter.

Example Models	*Individuals*
`VanDerPol` in Section 2.1.1	Andreas Karström
`SimpleCircuit` in Section 2.7.1	Members of the Modelica Association.
`PolynomialEvaluator` in Section 2.14.3	Members of the Modelica Association.
`LeastSquares` in Section 2.14.4	Mikael Adlers
`Diode` and `BouncingBall` in Section 2.15	Members of the Modelica Association.
`SimpleCircuit` expansion in Section 2.20.1	Martin Otter
`Rocket` in Section 3.5	Peter Bunus
`MoonLanding` in Section 3.5	Peter Bunus
`BoardExample` in Section 3.17.5	Members of the Modelica Association.
`BaseClassExtendsConflict` in Section 4.1.6	Per Östlund
`LowPassFilter` in Section 4.2.10	Members of the Modelica Association.
`FrictionFunction`, `KindOfController` Sec 4.3.12	Members of the Modelica Association.
`Tank` in Section 4.4.5	Peter Bunus
`Oscillator`, `Mass`, `Rigid` in Section 5.4.4	Martin Otter
`SpringDamper` of Figure 5-22 in Section 5.4.5 5.4.4	Dirk Zimmer
`RealInput`, `RealoutPut`, `MISO` in Section 5.5.2	Martin Otter
`MatrixGain`, `CrossProduct` in Section 5.7.5	Members of the Modelica Association.
`Environment` in Section 5.8.1	Members of the Modelica Association.
`CircuitBoard` in Section 5.8.2	Members of the Modelica Association.
`uniformGravity`, `pointGravity` in Section 5.8.3	Members of the Modelica Association.
`ParticleSystem` in Section 5.8.3	Members of the Modelica Association.
`Volume` in Section 5.10.4.1	Rüdiger Franke, Francesco Casella, Martin Otter, Michael Sielemann, Hilding Elmqvist, Sven-Erik Mattsson, Hans Olsson
`WaterVolumeConstant` in Section 5.10.4.1	Per Östlund
`WaterVolumeCompressible` in Section 5.10.4.1	Francesco Casella
`IsoenthalpicFlow` in Section 5.10.4.25.10.4.1	Rüdiger Franke, Francesco Casella, Martin Otter, Michael Sielemann, Hilding Elmqvist, Sven-Erik Mattsson, Hans Olsson
`WaterVolumeConstant` in Section 5.10.4.1	Per Östlund
`WaterVolumeCompressible` in Section 5.10.4.1	Francesco Casella
`IsoenthalpicFlow` in Section 5.10.4.25.10.4.1	Rüdiger Franke, Francesco Casella, Martin Otter, Michael Sielemann, Hilding Elmqvist, Sven-Erik Mattsson, Hans Olsson
`TemperatureSensor` in Section 5.10.4.3	Rüdiger Franke, Francesco Casella, Martin Otter, Michael Sielemann,

	Hilding Elmqvist, Sven-Erik Mattsson, Hans Olsson
`TimeEventTest`, `mySinNoTime` in Section 5.10.4.36.3.3	Per Östlund
`PendulumImplicitL`, `readParameterData` in Section 8.4.4	Sven-Erik Mattsson, Hilding Elmqvist, Martin Otter, Hans Olsson
`ProcessControl1`, `ProcessControl2`, `ProcessControl3`, `ProcessControl4` in Section 8.4.6	Sven-Erik Mattsson, Hilding Elmqvist, Martin Otter, Hans Olsson
`HeatRectangle2D` in Section 8.10.1.4	Levon Saldamli
Material to Figure 8-13 on 2D heat flow using FEM.	Levon Saldamli
`FieldDomainOperators1D` in Section 8.10.5.	Hilding Elmqvist, Jonas Jonasson
`DifferentialOperators1D` in Section 8.10.5.	Jonas Jonasson, Hilding Elmqvist
`HeadDiffusion1D` in Section 8.10.5.	Jonas Jonasson, Hilding Elmqvist
`Diff22D` in Section 8.10.5.1	Hilding Elmqvist
`FourBar1` example in Section 8.5.1.	Martin Otter
`Orientation` in Section 8.5.1.	Martin Otter, Hilding Elmqvist, Sven-Erik Mattsson.
`FixedTranslation` in Section 8.5.3	Martin Otter, Hilding Elmqvist, Sven-Erik Mattsson.
Material to Figure 8-5 on cutting branches in virtual connection graph.	Martin Otter, Hilding Elmqvist, Sven-Erik Mattsson.
`findElement` in Section 9.2.7	Peter Aronsson
`FilterBlock1` in Section 8.3.6	Members of the Modelica Association.
`realToString` in Section 9.3.2.1	Members of the Modelica Association.
`eigen` in Section 9.3.2.3	Martin Otter
`findMatrixElement` in Section 9.3.2.6	Peter Aronsson
`Record2` in Section 9.3.3	Members of the Modelica Association.
`bilinearSampling` in Section 9.4.3	Members of the Modelica Association.
`MyTable, interpolateMyTable` in Section 9.4.8	Members of the Modelica Association.
`Mechanics` in Section 10.3.2.2	Members of the Modelica Association.
`Placement`, `Transformation` in Section 11.4.4	Members of the Modelica Association.
`Line`, `Polygon`, etc. in Section 11.4.5	Members of the Modelica Association.
`Resistor`, `FrictionFunction` in Section 11.5.8.2	Members of the Modelica Association.
`h0`, `h1`, `h2` in Section 11.10.1	Members of the Modelica Association.
`FlatTank` in Section 12.2.1.1	Peter Bunus
`TankPI`, `Tank`, `LiquidSource` in Section 12.2.3	Peter Bunus
`PIContinuousController` in Section 12.2.3	Peter Bunus
`TankPID`, `PIContinuousController` Section 12.2.4	Peter Bunus
`DC-Motor Servo` in Section 12.3	Mats Jirstrand
`SmoothAndEvents` in Section 13.2.5.11	Members of the Modelica Association.
`CountingStateMachine1` in Section 13.3.2.1	Hilding Elmqvist, Fabien Gaucher, Sven Erik Mattsson, Francois Dupont
`ClockedVarWhen` in Section 13.2.6.4	Bernhard Thiele
`PreVsPrevious` in Section Section 13.2.5.14	Bernhard Thiele
`WatchDogSystem` in Section 13.3.2.4	Peter Bunus
`WatchDogSystemStateMachinePack` in Section 13.3.2.5	Bernhard Thiele
`CustomerGeneration` in Section 13.3.4.2	Peter Bunus
`ServerWithQueue` in Section 13.3.4.2	Peter Bunus
`BasicDEVSTwoPort` in Section 13.3.5	Peter Bunus
`SimpleDEVSServer` in Section 13.3.5	Peter Bunus
`Place`, `Transition` in Section 13.3.6.5	Hilding Elmqvist, Peter Bunus
`GameOfLife`, `nextGeneration` in Section 13.3.3.1	Peter Bunus

`PIdiscreteController` in Section 13.4.1	Peter Bunus
`TankHybridPI` in Section 13.4.1	Peter Bunus
`SimpleElastoBacklash` in Section 13.4.2	Peter Bunus
`DCMotorCircuitBacklash` in Section 13.4.2	Peter Bunus
`ElastoBacklash` in Section 13.4.2	Martin Otter
`Philosophers`, `DiningTable` in Section 13.5.1	Håkan Lundvall
`MassWithSpringDamper` in Section 13.6.1	Hilding Elmqvist, Sven-Erik Mattsson, Martin Otter, Bernhard Thiele
`SpeedControlP_MassWithSpringDamper` in Section 13.6.1	Hilding Elmqvist, Sven-Erik Mattsson, Martin Otter, Bernhard Thiele
`ClockedPiEx` in Section 13.6.5	Hilding Elmqvist, Martin Otter, Sven-Erik Mattsson
`BackSampleEx1` in Section 13.6.9.4	Hilding Elmqvist, Martin Otter, Sven-Erik Mattsson
`NoClockVsSampleHold` in Section 13.6.9.5	Bernhard Thiele
`BaseClockPartitionEx` in Section 13.6.13.1	Hilding Elmqvist, Martin Otter, Sven-Erik Mattsson
`ControlledMass` in Section 13.6.13.2	Hilding Elmqvist, Sven-Erik Mattsson, Martin Otter, Bernhard Thiele
`SolverMethodClockedPI` in Section 13.6.15.3	Hilding Elmqvist, Sven-Erik Mattsson, Martin Otter, Bernhard Thiele
`ClockTicks` in Section 13.6.16	Hilding Elmqvist, Martin Otter, Sven-Erik Mattsson
`ClockTicksWithModelica32` in Section 13.6.16	Hilding Elmqvist, Martin Otter, Sven-Erik Mattsson
`StateMachineSemantics` in Section 13.7.4.4	Hilding Elmqvist, Fabien Gaucher, Sven Erik Mattsson, Francois Dupont
`HierarchicalAndParallelStateMachine1` in Section 13.7.5	Hilding Elmqvist, Fabien Gaucher, Sven Erik Mattsson, Francois Dupont
`HierarchicalAndParallelStateMachine2` in Section 13.7.5	Hilding Elmqvist, Fabien Gaucher, Sven Erik Mattsson, Francois Dupont
`BasicVolume` in Section 15.2.2	Mats Jirstrand
`BasicVolume` in Section 15.2.3	Mats Jirstrand
`BasicVolume` in Section 15.2.4	Mats Jirstrand
`BasicVolume` in Section 15.2.4.2	Johan Gunnarsson
`FlowConnectorIn` in Section 15.2.5.1	Francesco Casella
`FlowConnectorOut` in Section 15.2.5.1	Francesco Casella
`FlowConnector` in Section 15.2.5.1	Rüdiger Franke
`IdealGas` in Section 15.2.5.2	Mats Jirstrand, Hubertus Tummescheit
`BasicVolumeFirst` in Section 15.2.5.2	Mats Jirstrand, Hubertus Tummescheit
`BasicVolume` in Section 15.2.5.2	Mats Jirstrand, Hubertus Tummescheit, Rüdiger Franke
`PressureEnthalpySource` in Section 15.2.5.3	Mats Jirstrand
`PressureEnthalpyBoundary` in Section 15.2.5.3	Rüdiger Franke
`SimpleValveFlow` in Section 15.2.5.4	Mats Jirstrand
`ValveFlowFirst` in Section 15.2.5.5	Mats Jirstrand
`ValveFlow` in Section 15.2.5.5	Mats Jirstrand, Rüdiger Franke
`ControlledValveFlowFirst` in Section 15.2.5.6	Mats Jirstrand
`ControlledValveFlow` in Section 15.2.5.6	Mats Jirstrand, Rüdiger Franke
`CtrlFlowSystem` in Section 15.2.5.6	Mats Jirstrand, Rüdiger Franke
`PneumaticCylinderVolume` in Section 15.2.5.7	Hubertus Tummescheit
`PneumaticCylinderVolume` in Section 15.2.5.8	Hubertus Tummescheit

`RoomWithFan` in Section 15.2.6	Hubertus Tummescheit
`RoomInEnvironment` in Section 15.2.6	Hubertus Tummescheit
`HydrogenIodide` in Section 15.3.1	Emma Larsdotter Nilsson
`LotkaVolterra` in Section 15.4.1	Emma Larsdotter Nilsson
`HandyBase` in Section 15.4.2.2	Rodrigo Castro
`HandyEgalitarianBase` in Section 15.4.2.4	Rodrigo Castro
`HandyEquitableBase` in Section 15.4.2.5	Rodrigo Castro
`HandyUnEquitableBase` in Section 15.4.2.6	Rodrigo Castro
`World3` in Section 15.4.2.7	Francois Cellier
`WillowForest` in Section 15.4.3	Emma Larsdotter Nilsson
`TCPSender`, `Loss_link_queue` in Section 15.6.3	Daniel Färnquist et. al., Peter Bunus
`Router21`, `TCPSackvsTCPWestWood` in Section 15.6	Daniel Färnquist et. al., Peter Bunus
`LinearActuator` in Section 15.7	Mats Jirstrand, Jan Brugård
`WeakAxis` in Section 15.8	Mats Jirstrand, Jan Brugård
`WaveEquationSample` in Section 15.9	Jan Brugård, Mats Jirstrand
`FreeFlyingBody` in Section 15.10.2	Vadim Engelson
`doublePendulumNoGeometry` in Section 15.10.7	Vadim Engelson
`doublePendulumCylinders` in Section 15.10.6.2	Vadim Engelson
`PendulumLoop2D` in Section 15.10.7	Vadim Engelson
`ExtForcePendulum` in Section 15.10.9.1	Vadim Engelson
`PendulumRotationalSteering` in Section 15.10.9.3	Vadim Engelson
`PendulumWithPDController` in Section 15.10.9.4	Vadim Engelson
`TripleSprings` in Section `TripleSprings` 5.4.3.2	Martin Otter
`EngineV6` in Section 15.10.10	Martin Otter
`Generator` in Section 17.1.6	Peter Bunus
Material to Figure 17-4, Figure 17-5, and Figure 17-6	Bernhard Bachmann

Contributors to the Modelica Standard Library, Version 3.2.1

Person	*Affiliation*
Marcus Baur	DLR Institute of System Dynamics and Control, Oberpfaffenhofen, Germany
Thomas Beutlich	ITI GmbH, Dresden, Germany
Thomas Bödrich	Technical University of Dresden, Dresden, Germany
Francesco Casella	Politecnico di Milano, Milano, Italy
Christoph Clauß	Fraunhofer Institute for Integrated Circuits, Dresden, Germany
Rüdiger Franke	ABB AG, Mannheim, Germany
Leo Gall	Bausch-Gall GmbH, Munich, Germany
Peter Harmann	CyDesign Ltd., Coventry, U.K.
Anton Haumer	Technical Consulting & Electrical Engineering, St.Andrae-Woerdern, Austria
Andreas Heckmann	DLR Institute of System Dynamics and Control, Oberpfaffenhofen, Germany
Daniel Hedberg	Wolfram MathCore AB, Linköping, Sweden
Philipp Jordan	Technical University of Hamburg-Harburg, Hamburg, Germany
Christian Kral	AIT Austrian Institute of Technology, Vienna, Germany
Kristin Majetta	Fraunhofer Institute for Integrated Circuits, Dresden, Germany
Jesper Mattsson	Modelon AB, Lund, Sweden
Hans Olsson	Dassault Systèmes AB, Lund Sweden
Martin Otter	DLR Institute of System Dynamics and Control, Oberpfaffenhofen, Germany
Bruno Scaglioni	Consorzio MUSP, Piacenza, Italy
Michael Sielemann	DLR Institute of System Dynamics and Control, Oberpfaffenhofen, Germany

Martin Sjölund	Linköpings University, Linköping, Sweden
Bernhard Thiele	DLR Institute of System Dynamics and Control, Oberpfaffenhofen, Germany
Jakub Tobolar	DLR Institute of System Dynamics and Control, Oberpfaffenhofen, Germany
Hubertus Tummescheit	Modelon AB, Lund Sweden
Michael Wetter	Lawrence Berkeley National Laboratory, Berkeley, U.S.A.
Dietmar Winkler	Telemark University College, Porsgrunn, Norway
Stefan Wischhusen	XRG Simulation GmbH, Hamburg, Germany
Johannes Ziske	Technical University of Dresden, Dresden, Germany

Contributors to the Modelica Standard Library, Versions 1.0 to 2.1

Person	*Affiliation*
Peter Beater	University of Paderborn, Germany
Christoph Clauß	Fraunhofer Institute for Integrated Circuits, Dresden, Germany
Martin Otter	German Aerospace Center, Oberpfaffenhofen, Germany
André Schneider	Fraunhofer Institute for Integrated Circuits, Dresden, Germany
Nikolaus Schürmann	German Aerospace Center, Oberpfaffenhofen, Germany
Christian Schweiger	German Aerospace Center, Oberpfaffenhofen, Germany
Michael Tiller	Ford Motor Company, Dearborn, MI, U.S.A.
Hubertus Tummescheit	Lund Institute of Technology, Sweden

Contributors to the Modelica Language, Version 3.3 revision 1

Person	*Affiliation*
Peter Aronsson	Wolfram MathCore AB, Linköping, Sweden
Hilding Elmqvist	Dassault Systèmes, Lund, Sweden
Peter Fritzson	Linköping University, Linköping, Sweden
Christoph Höger	TU Berlin, Berlin, Germany
Gerd Kurzbach	ITI GmbH, Dresden, Germany
Jesper Mattsson	Modelon, Lund, Sweden
Hans Olsson	Dassault Systèmes, Lund, Sweden
Martin Otter	German Aerospace Center (DLR), Oberpfaffenhofen, Germany
Adrian Pop	Linköping University, Sweden
Elena Shmoylova	Maplesoft, Waterloo, Canada
Martin Sjölund	Linköping University, Linköping, Sweden
Stefan Vorkoetter	Maplesoft, Waterloo, Canada

Contributors to the Modelica Language, Version 3.3

Person	*Affiliation*
Peter Aronsson	Wolfram MathCore AB, Linköping, Sweden
Johan Åkesson	Modelon AB, Lund, Sweden
Ingrid Bausch-Gall	Bausch-Gall GmbH, Munich, Germany
Volker Beuter	Kämmerer AG, Germany

Torsten Blochwitz	ITI GmbH, Dresden, Germany
David Broman	Linköping University, Linköping, Sweden
Dag Brück	Dassault Systèmes, Lund, Sweden
Francesco Casella	Politecnico di Milano, Milano, Italy
Christoph Clauss	Fraunhofer, Dresden, Germany
Mike Dempsey	Claytex Services Limited, Leamington Spa, U.K.
Karin Dietl	TU Hamburg-Harburg, Germany
Francois Dupont	Dassault Systèmes, Brest, France
Jonas Eborn	Modelon, Lund, Sweden
Hilding Elmqvist	Dassault Systèmes, Lund, Sweden
Guilioano Fontanella	AIT, Vienna, Austria
Rüdiger Franke	ABB Power Generation, Mannheim, Germany
Peter Fritzson	Linköping University, Linköping, Sweden
Sébastien Furic	LMS International, Roanne. France
Leo Gall	Bausch Gall Gmbh, Munich, Germany
Peter Harmann	deltatheta uk limited, U.K.
Anton Haumer	AIT, Vienna, Austria
Carsten Heinrich	Institut für Luft- und Kältetechnik gGmbH, Dresden, Germany
Dan Henriksson	Dassault Systèmes, Lund, Sweden
Christoph Höger	TU Berlin, Berlin, Germany
Christian Kral	AIT, Vienna, Austria
Gerd Kurzbach	ITI GmbH, Dresden, Germany
Kilian Link	Siemens AB, Erlangen, Germany
Krisitin Majetta	Fraunhofer, Dresden, Germany
Martin Malmheden	Dassault Systèmes, Velicy, France
Jesper Mattsson	Modelon, Lund, Sweden
Sven Erik Mattsson	Dassault Systèmes, Lund, Sweden
Eric Neuber	ITI GmbH, Dresden, Germany
Ramine Nikoukhah	Altair, France
Hans Olsson	Dassault Systèmes, Lund, Sweden
Martin Otter	German Aerospace Center (DLR), Oberpfaffenhofen, Germany
Peter Pepper	Fraunhofer FIRST, Berlin, Germany
Adrian Pop	Linköping University, Sweden
Olena Rogovchenko	Linköping University, Linköping, Sweden
Stefan-Alexander Schneider	BMW, Munich, Germany
Michael Sielemann	German Aerospace Center, Oberpfaffenhofen, Germany
Martin Sjölund	Linköping University, Linköping, Sweden
Kristian Stavåker	Linköping University, Linköping, Sweden
Bernhard Thiele	German Aerospace Center, Oberpfaffenhofen, Germany
Eric Thomas	Dassault Aviation, Paris, France
Michael Tiller	Dassault Systèmes, Velicy, France
Hubertus Tummescheit	Modelon AB, Lund, Sweden
Andreas Uhlig	ITI Gmbh, Dresden Germany
Stefan Vorkoetter	Maplesoft, Waterloo, Canada
Daniel Weil	Dassault Systèmes, Grenoble, France
Hans-Jürg Wiesmann	ABB Switzerland, Corporate Research, Baden, Switzerland
Dietmar Winkler	Telemark University College, Porsgrunn, Norway
Stefan Wischhusen	XRG Simulation, Hamburg, Germany
Dirk Zimmer	German Aerospace Center (DLR), Oberpfaffenhofen, Germany

Contributors to the Modelica Language, Version 3.2

Person	*Affiliation*
Peter Aronsson	MathCore AB, Linköping, Sweden
Johan Åkesson	Lund University and Modelon AB, Lund, Sweden
Bernhard Bachmann	University of Applied Sciences, Bielefeld, Germany
Jonathan Beck	Dassault Systèmes, Paris, France
Torsten Blochwitz	ITI GmbH, Dresden, Germany
David Broman	Linköping University, Linköping, Sweden
Dag Brück	Dynasim, Lund, Sweden
Francesco Casella	Politecnico di Milano, Milano, Italy
Mike Dempsey	Claytex Services Limited, Leamington Spa, U.K.
Karin Dietl	TU Hamburg-Harburg, Germany
Filippo Donida	Politecnico di Milano, Milano, Italy
Hilding Elmqvist	Dassault Systèmes, Lund, Sweden
Rüdiger Franke	ABB Corporate Research, Ladenburg, Germany
Peter Fritzson	Linköping University, Sweden
Sébastien Furic	LMS International, Roanne. France
Manuel Gräber	TU Braunschweig, Germany
Peter Harmann	deltatheta uk limited, U.K.
Anton Haumer	AIT, Vienna, Austria
Carsten Heinrich	Institut für Luft- und Kältetechnik gGmbH, Dresden, Germany
Dan Henriksson	Dassault Systèmes, Lund, Sweden
Fredrik Karlsson,	Linköping University, Sweden
Christian Kral	AIT, Vienna, Austria
Imke Krüger	TU Hamburg-Harburg, Hamburg, Germany
Gerd Kurzbach	ITI GmbH, Dresden, Germany
Kilian Link	Siemens AB, Erlangen, Germany
Sven Erik Mattsson	Dynasim, Lund, Sweden
Eric Neuber	ITI GmbH, Dresden, Germany
Hans Olsson	Dynasim, Lund, Sweden
Martin Otter	German Aerospace Center, Oberpfaffenhofen, Germany
Adrian Pop	Linköping University, Sweden
Katrin Prölß	Modelon AB, Lund, Sweden
Michael Sielemann	German Aerospace Center, Oberpfaffenhofen, Germany
Bernhard Thiele	German Aerospace Center, Oberpfaffenhofen, Germany
Michael Tiller	Emmeskay, Plymouth, MI, U.S.A.
Hubertus Tummescheit	Modelon AB, Lund, Sweden
Stefan Vorkoetter	Maplesoft, Waterloo, Canada
Hans-Jürg Wiesmann	ABB Switzerland, Corporate Research, Baden, Switzerland
Dietmar Winkler	Telemark University College, Porsgrunn, Norway

Contributors to the Modelica Language, Version 3.0

Person	*Affiliation*
Peter Aronsson	MathCore AB, Linköping, Sweden
Bernhard Bachmann	University of Applied Sciences, Bielefeld, Germany
John Batteh	Ford Motor Company, Dearborn, MI, U.S.A.
David Broman	Linköping University, Linköping, Sweden
Dag Brück	Dynasim, Lund, Sweden
Peter Bunus	Linköping University, Linköping, Sweden
Francesco Casella	Politecnico di Milano, Milano, Italy
Christoph Clauß	Fraunhofer Institute for Integrated Circuits, Dresden, Germany
Thomas Doumenc	Dassault Systèmes, Paris, France
Jonas Eborn	Modelon AB, Lund, Sweden
Hilding Elmqvist	Dynasim, Lund, Sweden
Rüdiger Franke	ABB Corporate Research, Ladenburg, Germany
Peter Fritzson	Linköping University, Sweden
Sebastien Furic	Imagine, Roanne, France
Anton Haumer	Tech. Consult. & Electrical Eng., St.Andrae-Woerdern, Austria
Daniel Hedberg	MathCore AB, Linköping, Sweden
Carsten Heinrich	Institut für Luft- und Kältetechnik gGmbH, Dresden, Germany
Olof Johansson	Linköping University, Linköping, Sweden
Roland Kossel	TLK Thermo GmbH, Braunschweig, Germany
Christian Kral	arsenal research, Vienna, Austria
Gerd Kurzbach	ITI GmbH, Dresden, Germany
Kilian Link	Siemens AB, Erlangen, Germany
José Diaz Lopez	Dynasim AB, Lund, Sweden
Karin Lunde	Fachhochschule Ulm, Germany
Håkan Lundvall	Linköping University, Linköping, Sweden
Ludwig Marvan	VA TECH ELIN EBG Elektronik GmbH & Co, Vienna, Austria
Sven Erik Mattsson	Dynasim, Lund, Sweden
Jakob Mauss	Qtronic GmbH, Berlin, Germany
Chuck Newman	Ford Motor Company, Dearborn, MI, U.S.A
Kaj Nyström	Linköping University, Linköping, Sweden
Hans Olsson	Dynasim, Lund, Sweden
Martin Otter	German Aerospace Center, Oberpfaffenhofen, Germany
Markus Plainer	arsenal research, Vienna, Austria
Adrian Pop	Linköping University, Sweden
Katrin Prölß	Technical University Hamburg-Harburg, Germany
Christoph Richter	Technical University of Braunschweig, Braunschweig, Germany
Anders Sandholm	Linköping University, Linköping, Sweden
Christian Schweiger	German Aerospace Center, Oberpfaffenhofen, Germany
Michael Tiller	Ford Motor Company/Emmeskay, Dearborn, MI, U.S.A.
Hubertus Tummescheit	Modelon AB, Lund, Sweden
Hans-Jürg Wiesmann	ABB Switzerland Ltd., Corporate Research, Baden, Switzerland

Contributors to the Modelica Language, Version 2.0

Person	*Affiliation*
Peter Aronsson	Linköping University, Sweden
Bernhard Bachmann	University of Applied Sciences, Bielefeld, Germany
Peter Beater	University of Paderborn, Germany
Dag Brück	Dynasim, Lund, Sweden
Peter Bunus	Linköping University, Sweden
Hilding Elmqvist	Dynasim, Lund, Sweden
Vadim Engelson	Linköping University, Sweden
Rüdiger Franke	ABB Corporate Research, Ladenburg
Peter Fritzson	Linköping University, Sweden
Pavel Grozman	Equa, Stockholm, Sweden
Johan Gunnarsson	MathCore, Linköping, Sweden
Mats Jirstrand	MathCore, Linköping, Sweden
Sven Erik Mattsson	Dynasim, Lund, Sweden
Hans Olsson	Dynasim, Lund, Sweden
Martin Otter	German Aerospace Center, Oberpfaffenhofen, Germany
Levon Saldamli	Linköping University, Sweden
Michael Tiller	Ford Motor Company, Dearborn, MI, U.S.A.
Hubertus Tummescheit	Lund Institute of Technology, Sweden
Hans-Jürg Wiesmann	ABB Switzerland Ltd. Corporate Research, Baden, Switzerland

Contributors to the Modelica Language, up to Version 1.3

Person	*Affiliation*
Bernhard Bachmann	University of Applied Sciences, Bielefeld, Germany
Francois Boudaud	Gaz de France, Paris, France
Jan Broenink	University of Twente, Enschede, the Netherlands
Dag Brück	Dynasim, Lund, Sweden
Thilo Ernst	GMD FIRST, Berlin, Germany
Hilding Elmqvist[1]	Dynasim, Lund, Sweden
Rüdiger Franke	ABB Network Partner Ltd. Baden, Switzerland
Peter Fritzson	Linköping University, Sweden
Pavel Grozman	Equa, Stockholm, Sweden
Kaj Juslin	VTT, Espoo, Finland
David Kågedal	Linköping University, Sweden
Mattias Klose	Technical University of Berlin, Germany
N. Loubere	Gaz de France, Paris, France
Sven Erik Mattsson	Dynasim, Lund, Sweden
P. J. Mosterman	German Aerospace Center, Oberpfaffenhofen, Germany
Henrik Nilsson	Linköping University, Sweden
Hans Olsson	Dynasim, Lund, Sweden
Martin Otter	German Aerospace Center, Oberpfaffenhofen, Germany
Per Sahlin	Bris Data AB, Stockholm, Sweden
André Schneider	Fraunhofer Institute for Integrated Circuits, Dresden, Germany
Michael Tiller	Ford Motor Company, Dearborn, MI, U.S.A.
Hubertus Tummescheit	Lund Institute of Technology, Sweden
Hans Vangheluwe	University of Gent, Belgium

[1] The Modelica 1.0 design document was edited by Hilding Elmqvist.

Modelica Association Member Companies and Organizations 2013

Company or Organization
Austrian Institute of Technology, Vienna, Austria
CyDesign Labs, Inc., Palo Alto, CA, USA
DLR - Institute of Robotics and Mechatronics, Oberpfaffenhofen, Germany
Dassault Systèmes AB, Lund, Sweden
Dassault Systèmes SA, Paris, France
LMS Imagine S.A., Leuven, Belgium
Equa Simulation Technology AB, Stockholm, Sweden
Institut für Thermodynamik, Universität Braunschweig, Braunschweig, Germany
Institute of Thermo-Fluid Dynamics, Hamburg University of Technology, Hamburg, Germany
Linköping University, IDA, Programming Environment Laboratory, Linköping, Sweden
ITI GmbH, Dresden, Germany
Maplesoft, Waterloo, ON, Canada
Modelon AB, Lund, Sweden
Palo Alto Research Center, Palo Alto, CA, USA
Wolfram MathCore AB, Linköping, Sweden
XRG Simulation GmbH, Hamburg, Germany

Funding Contributions

For the first edition (2004) of this book, Linköping University, the Swedish Strategic Research Foundation (SSF) in the ECSEL graduate school, and MathCore AB have supported me for part of this work. Additionally, results in the form of reports and papers produced in a number of research projects at my research group PELAB, the Programming Environment Laboratory, Department of Computer and Information Science, Linköping University, have been used as raw material in writing parts of this book. Support for these research projects have been given by: the Swedish Business Development Agency (NUTEK) in the Modelica Tools project, the Wallenberg foundation in the WITAS project, the Swedish Agency for Innovation Systems (VINNOVA) in the VISP (Virtuell Integrerad Simuleringsstödd Produktframtagning) project, the European Union in the REALSIM (Real-Time Simulation for Design of Multi-physics Systems) project, SSF in the VISIMOD (Visualization, Identification, Simulation, and Modeling) project, and by AB SKF.

The second edition (2014) has been partially supported by Linköping University, by the Swedish Strategic Research Foundation (SSF) in the Proviking HIPo and EDOP projects; by MathCore Engineering AB, by Vinnova in the GridModelica, RTSIM, OPENPROD, and MODRIO projects; by EU in the Lila project; by VR in the Debugging Equation-based languages project, and by ELLIIT.

Part I

Introduction

Chapter 1

Introduction to Modeling and Simulation

It is often said that computers are revolutionizing science and engineering. By using computers, we are able to construct complex engineering designs such as space shuttles. We are able to compute the properties of the universe as it was fractions of a second after the Big Bang. Our ambitions are ever-increasing. We want to create even more complex designs such as better spaceships, cars, medicines, computerized cellular phone systems, and so on. We want to understand deeper aspects of nature. These are just a few examples of computer-supported modeling and simulation. More powerful tools and concepts are needed to help us handle this increasing complexity, which is precisely what this book is about.

This text presents an object-oriented, component-based approach to computer-supported mathematical modeling and simulation through the powerful Modelica language and its associated technology. Modelica can be viewed as an almost-universal approach to high-level computational modeling and simulation, by being able to represent a range of application areas and providing general notation as well as powerful abstractions and efficient implementations. The introductory part of this book, consisting of the first two chapters, gives a quick overview of the two main topics of this text:

- Modeling and simulation
- The Modelica language

The two subjects are presented together since they belong together. Throughout the text, Modelica is used as a vehicle for explaining different aspects of modeling and simulation. Conversely, a number of concepts in the Modelica language are presented by modeling and simulation examples. This first chapter introduces basic concepts such as *system*, *model*, and *simulation*. The second chapter gives a quick tour of the Modelica language as well as a number of examples, interspersed with presentations of topics such as object-oriented mathematical modeling, declarative formalisms, methods for compilation of equation-based models, and so forth.

Subsequent chapters contain detailed presentations of object-oriented modeling principles and specific Modelica features; introductions of modeling methodology for continuous, discrete, and hybrid systems; as well as a thorough overview of a number of currently available Modelica model libraries for a range of application domains. Finally, in the last chapter, a few of the currently available Modelica environments are presented.

1.1 Systems and Experiments

What is a system? We have already mentioned some systems such as the universe, a space shuttle, and so on. A system can be almost anything. A system can contain subsystems that are themselves systems. A possible definition of system might be:

- A system is an object or collection of objects whose properties we want to study.

Our wish to study selected properties of objects is central in this definition. The "study" aspect is fine despite the fact that it is subjective. The selection and definition of what constitutes a system is somewhat arbitrary and must be guided by what the system is to be used for.

What reasons can there be to study a system? There are many answers to this question but we can discern two major motivations:

- Study a system to understand it in order to build it. This is the engineering point of view.
- Satisfy human curiosity; for example, to understand more about nature—the natural science viewpoint.

1.1.1 Natural and Artificial Systems

A system, according to our previous definition, can occur naturally, for example, the universe, or it can be artificial, such as a space shuttle, or a mix of both. For example, the house in Figure 1-1, with solar-heated tap water is an artificial system, that is, it is manufactured by humans. If we also include the sun and clouds in the system, it becomes a combination of natural and artificial components.

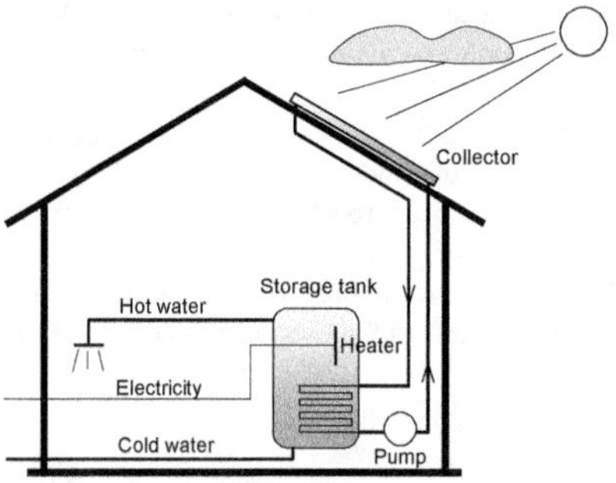

Figure 1-1. A system: a house with solar-heated tap water, together with clouds and sunshine.

Even if a system occurs naturally, its definition is always highly selective. This is made very apparent in the following quote from Ross Ashby [Ashby-56]:

> At this point, we must be clear about how a *system* is to be defined. Our first impulse is to point at the *pendulum* and to say "the system is that thing there." This method, however, has a fundamental disadvantage: every material object contains no less than an infinity of variables, and therefore, of possible systems. The real pendulum, for instance, has not only length and position; it has also mass, temperature, electric conductivity, crystalline structure, chemical impurities, some radioactivity, velocity, reflecting power, tensile strength, a surface film of moisture, bacterial contamination, an optical absorption, elasticity, shape, specific gravity, and so on and on. Any suggestion that we should study all the facts is unrealistic, and actually the attempt is never made. What is necessary is that we should pick out and study the facts that are relevant to some main interest that is already given.

Even if the system is completely artificial, such as the cellular phone system depicted in Figure 1-2, we must be highly selective in its definition, depending on what aspects we want to study for the moment.

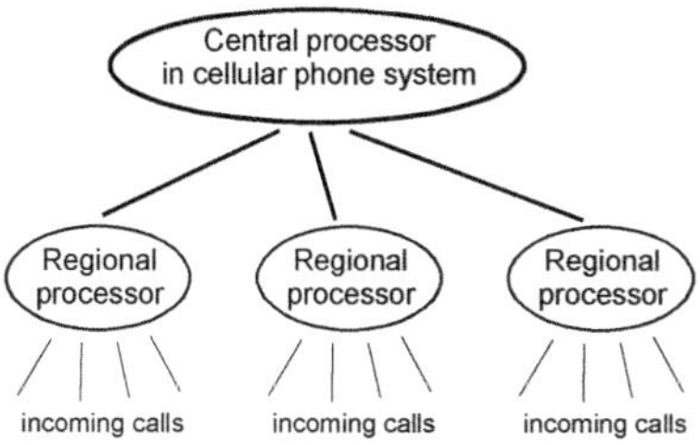

Figure 1-2. A cellular phone system containing a central processor and regional processors to handle incoming calls.

An important property of systems is that they should be *observable*. Some systems, but not large natural systems like the universe, are also *controllable* in the sense that we can influence their behavior through inputs:

- The *inputs* of a system are variables of the environment that influence the behavior of the system. These inputs may or may not be controllable by us.
- The *outputs* of a system are variables that are determined by the system and may influence the surrounding environment.

In many systems, the same variables act as *both inputs and outputs*. We talk about *acausal* behavior if the relationships or influences between variables do not have a causal direction, which is the case for relationships described by equations. For example, in a mechanical system the forces from the environment influence the displacement of an object but, on the other hand, the displacement of the object influences the forces between the object and environment. What is input and what is output in this case is primarily a choice by the observer, guided by what is interesting to study, rather than a property of the system itself.

1.1.2 Experiments

Observability is essential in order to study a system according to our definition of system. We must at least be able to observe some outputs of a system. We can learn even more if it is possible to exercise a system by controlling its inputs. This process is called *experimentation*:

- An *experiment* is the process of extracting information from a system by exercising its inputs.

To perform an experiment on a system it must be both controllable and observable. We apply a set of external conditions to the accessible inputs and observe the reaction of the system by measuring the accessible outputs.

One of the disadvantages of the experimental method is that for a large number of systems many inputs are not accessible and controllable. These systems are under the influence of inaccessible inputs, sometimes called *disturbance inputs*. Likewise, it is often the case that many really useful possible outputs are not accessible for measurements; these are sometimes called *internal states* of the system. There are also a number of practical problems associated with performing an experiment:

- The experiment might be too *expensive*—investigating ship durability by building ships and letting them collide is a very expensive method of gaining information.
- The experiment might be too *dangerous*—training nuclear plant operators in handling dangerous situations by letting the nuclear reactor enter hazardous states is not advisable.
- The *system* needed for the experiment might *not yet exist*—this is typical of systems to be designed or manufactured.

The shortcomings of the experimental method lead us to the model concept. If we make a model of a system, this model can be investigated and may answer many questions regarding the real system if the model is realistic enough.

1.2 The Model Concept

Given the previous definitions of system and experiment, we can now attempt to define the notion of model:

- A *model* of a system is anything an "experiment" can be applied to in order to answer questions about that *system*.

This implies that a model can be used to answer questions about a system *without* doing experiments on the *real* system. Instead, we perform simplified "experiments" on the model, which in turn can be regarded as a kind of simplified system that reflects properties of the real system. In the simplest case, a model can just be a piece of information that is used to answer questions about the system.

Given this definition, any model also qualifies as a system. Models, just like systems, are hierarchical in nature. We can cut out a piece of a model, which becomes a new model that is valid for a subset of the experiments for which the original model is valid. A model is always related to the system it models and the experiments it can be subject to. A statement such as "a model of a system is invalid" is meaningless without mentioning the associated system and the experiment. A model of a system might be valid for one experiment on the model and invalid for another. The term model *validation* (see Section 1.5.3, page 10) always refers to an experiment or a class of experiments to be performed.

We talk about different kinds of models depending on how the model is represented:

- *Mental* model—a statement like "a person is reliable" helps us answer questions about that person's behavior in various situations.
- *Verbal* model—this kind of model is expressed in words. For example, the sentence "More accidents will occur if the speed limit is increased" is an example of a verbal model. Expert systems is a technology for formalizing verbal models.
- *Physical* model—this is a physical object that mimics some properties of a real system to help us answer questions about that system. For example, during design of artifacts such as buildings and airplanes it is common to construct small physical models with same shape and appearance as the real objects to be studied, with respect to their aerodynamic properties and aesthetics.
- *Mathematical* model—a description of a system in which the relationships between variables of the system are expressed in mathematical form. Variables can be measurable quantities such as size, length, weight, temperature, unemployment level, information flow, bit rate, and so on. Most laws of nature are mathematical models in this sense. For example, Ohm's law describes the relationship between current and voltage for a resistor; Newton's laws describe relationships between velocity, acceleration, mass, force, and so on.

The kinds of models that we primarily deal with in this book are mathematical models represented in various ways, for example as equations, functions, and computer programs. Artifacts represented by mathematical models in a computer are often called *virtual prototypes*. The process of constructing and investigating such models is virtual prototyping. Sometimes the term *physical modeling* is used also for the process of building mathematical models of physical systems in the computer if the structuring and synthesis process are the same as when building real physical models.

1.3 Simulation

In the previous section, we mentioned the possibility of performing "experiments" on models instead of on the real systems corresponding to the models. This is actually one of the main uses of models, and is denoted by the term *simulation*, from the Latin *simulare,* which means to pretend. We define a simulation as follows:

- A *simulation* is an experiment performed on a model.

In analogy with our previous definition of *model*, this definition of simulation does not require the model to be represented in mathematical or computer-program form. However, in the rest of this text we will concentrate on *mathematical models*, primarily those that have a computer-representable form. The following are a few examples of such experiments or simulations:

- A simulation of an industrial process, such as steel or pulp manufacturing, to learn about the behavior under different operating conditions in order to improve the process.
- A simulation of vehicle behavior, for example of a car or an airplane, for the purpose of providing realistic operator training.
- A simulation of a simplified model of a packet-switched computer network, to learn about its behavior under different loads in order to improve performance.

It is important to realize that the *experiment description* and *model description* parts of a simulation are conceptually separate entities. On the other hand, these two aspects of a simulation belong together even if they are separate. For example, a model is valid only for a certain class of experiments. It can be useful to define an *experimental frame* associated with the model, which defines the conditions that need to be fulfilled by valid experiments.

If the mathematical model is represented in executable form in a computer, simulations can be performed by *numerical experiments,* or in nonnumeric cases by *computational experiments.* This is a simple and safe way of performing experiments, with the added advantage that essentially all variables of the model are observable and controllable. However, the value of the simulation results is completely dependent on how well the model represents the real system with regard to the questions to be answered by the simulation.

Except for experimentation, simulation is the only technique that is generally applicable for analysis of the behavior of arbitrary systems. Analytical techniques are better than simulation, but usually apply only under a set of simplifying assumptions, which often cannot be justified. On the other hand, it is not uncommon to combine analytical techniques with simulations, that is, simulation is used not alone but in combination with analytical or semianalytical techniques.

1.3.1 Reasons for Simulation

There are a number of good reasons to perform simulations instead of performing experiments on real systems:

- Experiments are too *expensive*, too *dangerous*, or the system to be investigated does *not yet exist.* These are the main difficulties of experimentation with real systems, previously mentioned in Section 1.1.2, page 5.
- The *time scale* of the dynamics of the system is not compatible with that of the experimenter. For example, it takes millions of years to observe small changes in the development of the universe, whereas similar changes can be quickly observed in a computer simulation of the universe.
- Variables may be *inaccessible.* In a simulation, all variables can be studied and controlled, even those that are inaccessible in the real system.

- Easy *manipulation* of models. Using simulation, it is easy to manipulate the parameters of a system model, even outside the feasible range of a particular physical system. For example, the mass of a body in a computer-based simulation model can be increased from 40 to 500 kg at a keystroke, whereas this change might be hard to realize in the physical system.
- Suppression of *disturbances*. In a simulation of a model, it is possible to suppress disturbances that might be unavoidable in measurements of the real system. This can allow us to isolate particular effects and thereby gain a better understanding of those effects.
- Suppression of *second-order effects*. Often, simulations are performed because they allow suppression of second-order effects such as small nonlinearities or other details of certain system components, which can help us to better understand the primary effects.

1.3.2 Dangers of Simulation

The ease of use of simulation is also its most serious drawback: it is quite easy for the user to forget the limitations and conditions under which a simulation is valid and, therefore, draw the wrong conclusions from the simulation. To reduce these dangers, one should always try to compare at least some results of simulation against experimental results from the real system. It also helps to be aware of the following three common sources of problems when using simulation:

- Falling in love with a model—the Pygmalion[2] effect. It is easy to become too enthusiastic about a model and forget all about the experimental frame; the model is not the real world but only represents the real system under certain conditions. One example is the introduction of foxes to the Australian continent to solve the rabbit problem, on the model assumption that foxes hunt rabbits, which is true in many other parts of the world. Unfortunately, the foxes found the indigenous fauna much easier to hunt and largely ignored the rabbits.
- Forcing reality into the constraints of a model—the Procrustes[3] effect. One example is the shaping of our societies after currently fashionable economic theories having a simplified view of reality, and ignoring many other important aspects of human behavior, society, and nature.
- Forgetting the model's level of accuracy. All models have simplifying assumptions and we have to be aware of those in order to correctly interpret the results.

For these reasons, while analytical techniques are generally more restrictive since they have a much smaller domain of applicability, such techniques are more powerful when they apply. A simulation result is valid only for a particular set of input data. Many simulations are needed to gain an approximate understanding of a system. Therefore, if analytical techniques are applicable they should be used instead of simulation or as a complement.

1.4 Building Models

Given the usefulness of simulation in order to study the behavior of systems, how do we go about building models of those systems? This is the subject of most of this book and of the Modelica language, which has been created to simplify model construction as well as reuse of existing models.

There are in principle two main sources of general system-related knowledge needed for building mathematical models of systems:

---

[2] Pygmalion was a mythical king of Cyprus, who also was a sculptor. The king fell in love with one of his works, a sculpture of a young woman, and asked the gods to make her alive.

[3] Procrustes was a robber known from Greek mythology. He was known for the bed where he tortured travelers who fell into his hands: if the victim was too short, he stretched arms and legs until the person fit the length of the bed; if the victim was too tall, he cut off the head and part of the legs.

- The collected *general experience* in relevant domains of science and technology, found in the literature and available from experts in these areas. This includes the *laws of nature*, including Newton's laws for mechanical systems, Kirchhoff's laws for electrical systems, and approximate relationships for nontechnical systems based on economic or sociological theories.
- The *system* itself, that is, observations of and experiments on the system we want to model.

In addition to the above system knowledge, there is also specialized knowledge about mechanisms for handling and using facts in model construction for specific applications and domains, as well as generic mechanisms for handling facts and models:

- *Application expertise*—mastering the application area and techniques for using all facts relative to a specific modeling application.
- *Software and knowledge engineering*—generic knowledge about defining, handling, using, and representing models and software, for example, object orientation, component system techniques, and expert system technology.

What is then an appropriate analysis and synthesis *process* to be used in applying these information sources for constructing system models? Generally, we first try to identify the main components of a system and the kinds of interaction between these components. Each component is broken down into subcomponents until each part fits the description of an existing model from some model library, or we can use appropriate laws of nature or other relationships to describe the behavior of that component. Then we state the component interfaces and make a mathematical formulation of the interactions between the components of the model.

Certain components might have unknown or partially known model parameters and coefficients. These can often be found by fitting experimental measurement data from the real system to the mathematical model using *system identification*, which in simple cases reduces to basic techniques like curve fitting and regression analysis. However, advanced versions of system identification may even determine the form of the mathematical model selected from a set of basic model structures.

1.5 Analyzing Models

Simulation is one of the most common techniques for using models to answer questions about systems. However, there also exist other methods of analyzing models such as sensitivity analysis and model-based diagnosis, or analytical mathematical techniques in the restricted cases where solutions can be found in a closed analytical form.

1.5.1 Sensitivity Analysis

Sensitivity analysis deals with the question how *sensitive* the behavior of the model is to *changes* in model parameters. This is a very common question in design and analysis of systems. For example, even in well-specified application domains such as electrical systems, resistor values in a circuit are typically known only by an accuracy of 5 to 10 percent. If there is a large sensitivity in the results of simulations to small variations in model parameters, we should be very suspicious about the validity the model. In such cases, small random variations in the model parameters can lead to large random variations in the behavior.

On the other hand, if the simulated behavior is not very sensitive to small variations in the model parameters, there is a good chance that the model fairly accurately reflects the behavior of the real system. Such robustness in behavior is a desirable property when designing new products, since they otherwise may become expensive to manufacture if certain tolerances must be kept very small. However, there are also a number of examples of real systems that are very sensitive to variations in specific model parameters. In those cases, that sensitivity should be reflected in models of those systems.

1.5.2 Model-Based Diagnosis

Model based *diagnosis* is a technique somewhat related to sensitivity analysis. We want to find the causes of certain behavior of a system by analyzing a model of that system. In many cases, we want to find the causes of problematic and erroneous behavior. For example, consider a car, which is a complex system consisting of many interacting parts such as a motor, an ignition system, a transmission system, suspension, and wheels. Under a set of well-defined operating conditions, each of these parts can be considered to exhibit a correct behavior if certain quantities are within specified value intervals. A measured or computed value outside such an interval might indicate an error in that component, or in another part influencing that component. This kind of analysis is called model-based diagnosis.

1.5.3 Model Verification and Validation

We have previously remarked about the dangers of simulation, for example, when a model is not valid for a system regarding the intended simulation. How can we verify that the model is a good and reliable model, that is, that it is valid for its intended use? This can be very hard and sometimes we can hope only to get a partial answer to this question. However, the following techniques are useful to at least partially verify the validity of a model:

- Critically review the assumptions and approximations behind the model, including available information about the domain of validity regarding these assumptions.
- Compare simplified variants of the model to analytical solutions for special cases.
- Compare to experimental results for cases when this is possible.
- Perform sensitivity analysis of the model. If the simulation results are relatively insensitive to small variations of model parameters, we have stronger reasons to believe in the validity of the model.
- Perform internal consistency checking of the model, such as checking that dimensions or units are compatible across equations. For example, in Newton's equation $F = ma$, the unit [N] on the left-hand side is consistent with [kg m s^{-2}] on the right-hand side.

In the last case, it is possible for tools to automatically verify that dimensions are consistent if unit attributes are available for the quantities of the model. This functionality, however, is yet not available for most current modeling tools.

1.6 Kinds of Mathematical Models

Different kinds of mathematical models can be characterized by different properties reflecting the behavior of the systems that are modeled. One important aspect is whether the model incorporates *dynamic* time-dependent properties or is *static*. Another dividing line is between models that evolve *continuously* over time, and those that change at *discrete* points in time. A third dividing line is between *quantitative* and *qualitative* models.

Certain models describe *physical distribution* of quantities, such as mass, whereas other models are *lumped* in the sense that the physically distributed quantity is approximated by being lumped together and represented by a single variable such as a point mass.

Some phenomena in nature are conveniently described by stochastic processes and probability distributions, for example noisy radio transmissions or atomic-level quantum physics. Such models might be labeled *stochastic* or *probability-based* models for which the behavior can be represented only in a statistic sense, whereas *deterministic* models allow the behavior to be represented without uncertainty. However, even stochastic models can be simulated in a "deterministic" way using a computer since the random number sequences often used to represent stochastic variables can be regenerated given the same seed values.

The same phenomenon can often be modeled as being either stochastic or deterministic depending on the level of detail at which it is studied. Certain aspects at one level are abstracted or averaged away at the next higher level. For example, consider the modeling of gases at different levels of detail starting at the quantum-mechanical elementary particle level, where the positions of particles are described by probability distributions:

- Elementary particles (orbitals)—stochastic models.
- Atoms (ideal gas model)—deterministic models.
- Atom groups (statistical mechanics)—stochastic models.
- Gas volumes (pressure and temperature)—deterministic models.
- Real gases (turbulence)—stochastic models.
- Ideal mixer (concentrations)—deterministic models.

It is interesting to note the kinds of model changes between stochastic or deterministic models that occur depending on what aspects we want to study. Detailed stochastic models can be averaged as deterministic models when approximated at the next upper macroscopic level in the hierarchy. On the other hand, stochastic behavior such as turbulence can be introduced at macroscopic levels as the result of chaotic phenomena caused by interacting deterministic parts.

1.6.1 Kinds of Equations

Mathematical models usually contain equations. There are basically four main kinds of equations; we give one example of each.

Differential equations contain time derivatives such as $\frac{dx}{dt}$, usually denoted $\dot{x}$:

$$\dot{x} = a \cdot x + 3 \tag{1-1}$$

Algebraic equations do not include any differentiated variables:

$$x^2 + y^2 = L^2 \tag{1-2}$$

Partial differential equations also contain derivatives with respect to other variables than time:

$$\frac{\partial a}{\partial t} = \frac{\partial^2 a}{\partial z^2} \tag{1-3}$$

Difference equations express relations between variables, for example at different points in time:

$$x(t+1) = 3x(t) + 2 \tag{1-4}$$

1.6.2 Dynamic vs. Static Models

All systems, both natural and man-made, are dynamic in the sense that they exist in the real world, which evolves in time. Mathematical models of such systems would be naturally viewed as *dynamic* in the sense that they evolve over time and therefore incorporate time. However, it is often useful to make the approximation of ignoring time dependence in a system. Such a system model is called *static*. Thus, we can define the concepts of dynamic and static models as follows:

- A *dynamic* model includes *time* in the model. The word *dynamic* is derived from the Greek word *dynamis,* meaning force and power, with dynamics being the (time-dependent) interplay between forces. Time can be included explicitly as a variable in a mathematical formula or be present indirectly, for example through the time derivative of a variable or as events occurring at certain points in time.
- A *static* model can be defined *without* involving *time*, where the word *static* is derived from the Greek word *statikos,* meaning something that creates equilibrium. Static models are often used to describe systems in steady-state or equilibrium situations, where the output does not change if the input is the same. However, static models can display a rather dynamic behavior when fed with dynamic input signals.

It is usually the case that the behavior of a dynamic model is dependent on its *previous* simulation history. For example, the presence of a time derivative in a mathematical model means that this derivative needs to be integrated to solve for the corresponding variable when the model is simulated, that is, the *integration* operation takes the previous time history into account. This is the case, for example for models of capacitors where the voltage over the capacitor is proportional to the accumulated charge in the capacitor or integration/accumulation of the current through the capacitor. By differentiating that relation, the time derivative of the capacitor voltage becomes proportional to the current through the capacitor. We can study the capacitor voltage increasing over time at a rate proportional to the current in Figure 1-3.

Another way for a model to be dependent on its previous history is to let preceding events influence the current state, as in a model of an ecological system where the number of prey animals in the system will be influenced by events such as the birth of predators. On the other hand, a dynamic model such as a sinusoidal signal generator can be modeled by a formula directly including time and not involving the previous time history.

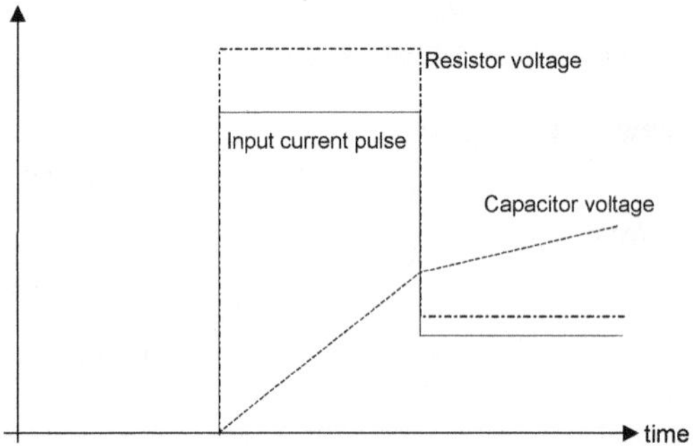

Figure 1-3. A resistor is a static system where the voltage is directly proportional to the current, independent of time, whereas a capacitor is a dynamic system where voltage is dependent on the previous time history.

A resistor is an example of a static model which can be formulated without including time. The resistor voltage is directly proportional to the current through the resistor, as depicted in Figure 1-3, with no dependence on time or on the previous history.

1.6.3 Continuous-Time vs. Discrete-Time Dynamic Models

There are two main classes of dynamic models: continuous-time and discrete-time models. The class of continuous-time models can be characterized as follows:

- *Continuous-time* models evolve their variable values continuously over time.

A variable from a continuous-time model A is depicted in Figure 1-4. The mathematical formulation of continuous-time models includes differential equations with time derivatives of some model variables. Many laws of nature, for example as expressed in physics, are formulated as differential equations.

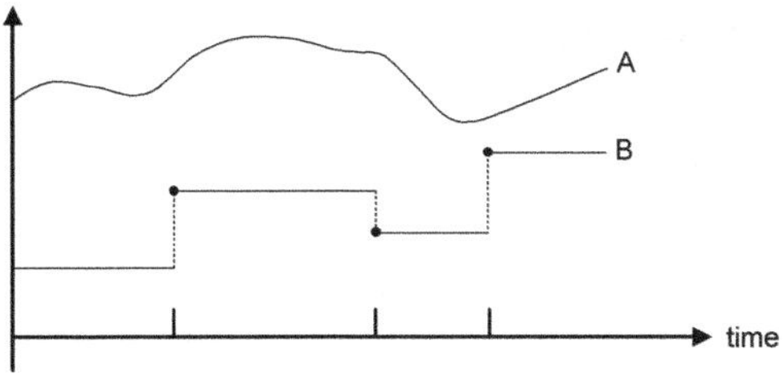

Figure 1-4. A discrete-time system B changes values only at certain points in time, whereas continuous-time systems like A evolve values continuously.

The second class of mathematical models is discrete-time models, as B in Figure 1-4, where variables change value only at certain points in time:

- *Discrete-time* models may change their variable values only at discrete points in time.

Discrete-time models are often represented by sets of difference equations, or as computer programs mapping the state of the model at one point in time to the state at the next point in time.

Discrete-time models occur frequently in engineering systems, especially computer-controlled systems. A common special case is sampled systems, where a continuous-time system is measured at regular time intervals and is approximated by a discrete-time model. Such sampled models usually interact with other discrete-time systems like computers. Discrete-time models may also occur naturally, such as an insect population that breeds during a short period once a year; the discretization period in that case is one year.

1.6.4 Quantitative vs. Qualitative Models

All of the different kinds of mathematical models previously discussed in this section are of a quantitative nature—variable values can be represented numerically according to a quantitatively measurable scale.

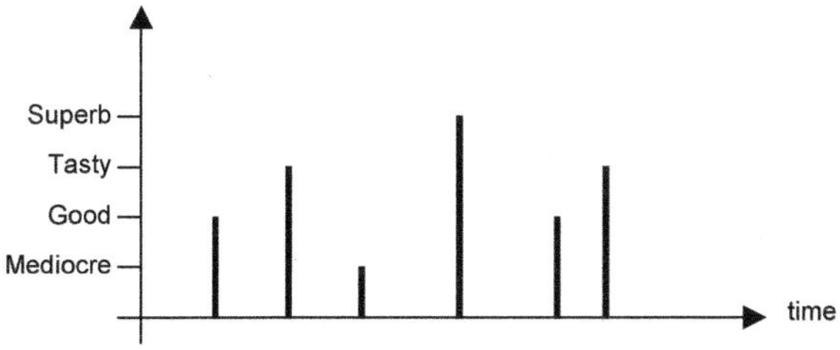

Figure 1-5. Quality of food in a restaurant according to inspections at irregular points in time.

Other models, so-called *qualitative* models, lack that kind of precision. The best we can hope for is a rough classification into a finite set of values, as in the food-quality model depicted in Figure 1-5. Qualitative models are by nature discrete-time, and the dependent variables are also discretized. However, even if the discrete values are represented by numbers in the computer (e.g. mediocre—1, good—2, tasty —3, superb—4), we have to be aware of the fact that the values of variables in certain qualitative models do not necessarily fit a linear measurable scale, for example, tasty might not be three times better than mediocre.

1.7 Using Modeling and Simulation in Product Design

What role does modeling and simulation have in industrial product design and development? In fact, our previous discussion has already briefly touched on this issue. Building mathematical models in the computer—so-called *virtual prototypes*—and simulating those models is a way to quickly determine and optimize product properties without building costly physical prototypes. Such an approach can often drastically reduce development time and time to market while increasing the quality of the designed product.

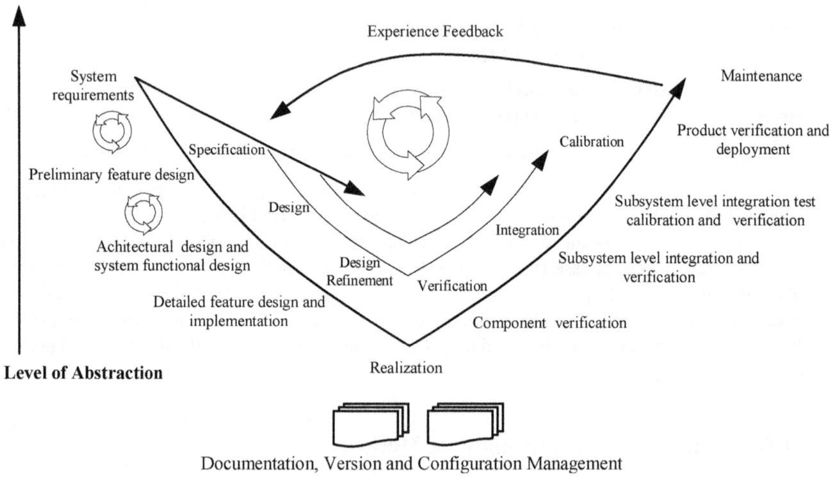

Figure 1-6. The product design-V.

The so-called product *design-V*, depicted in Figure 1-6, includes all the standard phases of product development:

- Requirements analysis and specification.
- System design.
- Design refinement.
- Realization and implementation.
- Subsystem verification and validation.
- Integration.
- System calibration and model validation.
- Product deployment.

How does modeling and simulation fit into this design process?

In the first phase, *requirements analysis*, functional and nonfunctional requirements are specified. In this phase important design parameters are identified and requirements on their values are specified. For example, when designing a car there might be requirements for acceleration, fuel consumption, maximum emissions, and so on. Those system parameters will also become parameters in our model of the designed product.

In the *system-design phase* we specify the architecture of the system—the main components in the system and their interactions. If we have a simulation model component library at hand, we can use these library components in the design phase, or otherwise create new components that fit the designed product. This design process iteratively increases the level of detail in the design. A modeling tool that supports hierarchical system modeling and decomposition can help in handling system complexity.

The *implementation phase* will realize the product as a physical system and/or as a virtual prototype model in the computer. Here a virtual prototype can be realized before the physical prototype is built, usually for a small fraction of the cost.

In the *subsystem verification and validation phase*, the behavior of the subsystems of the product is verified. The subsystem virtual prototypes can be simulated in the computer and the models corrected if there are problems.

In the *integration phase* the subsystems are connected. Regarding a computer-based system model, the models of the subsystems are connected together in an appropriate way. The whole system can then be simulated, and certain design problems corrected based on the simulation results.

The system and model *calibration and validation phase* validates the model against measurements from appropriate physical prototypes. Design parameters are calibrated, and the design is often *optimized* to a certain extent according to what is specified in the original requirements.

During the last phase, *product deployment*, which usually only applies to the physical version of the product, the product is deployed and sent to the customer for feedback. In certain cases this can also be applied to virtual prototypes, which can be delivered and put in a computer that is interacting with the rest of the customer physical system in real time—hardware-in-the-loop simulation.

In most cases, experience feedback can be used to tune both models and physical products. All phases of the design process continuously interact with the model and design database, as depicted at the bottom of Figure 1-6.

1.8 Examples of System Models

In this section, we briefly present examples of mathematical models from three different application areas, in order to illustrate the power of the Modelica mathematical modeling and simulation technology to be described in the rest of this book:

- A thermodynamic system—part of an industrial GTX100 gas turbine model.
- A 3D mechanical system with a hierarchical decomposition—an industry robot.
- A biochemical application —part of the citrate cycle (TCA cycle).

A connection diagram of the power cutoff mechanism of the GTX100 gas turbine is depicted in Figure 1-8 on page 15, whereas the gas turbine itself is shown in Figure 1-7 below. This connection diagram might not appear as a mathematical model, but behind each icon in the diagram is a model component containing the equations that describe the behavior of the respective component. In Figure 1-9, we show a few plots from simulations of the gas turbine, which illustrates how a model can be used to investigate the properties of a given system.

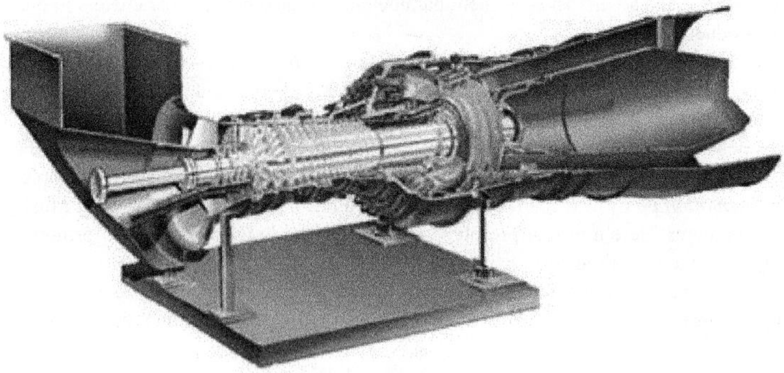

Figure 1-7. A schematic picture of the GTX100 gas turbine. Courtesy Siemens Industrial Turbomachinery AB, Finspång, Sweden.

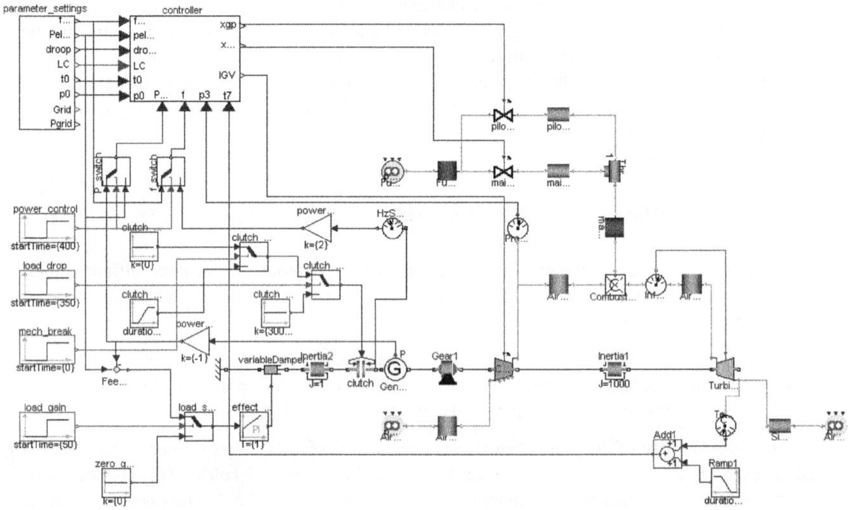

Figure 1-8. Detail of power cutoff mechanism in 40 MW GTX100 gas turbine model. Courtesy Siemens Industrial Turbomachinery AB, Finspång, Sweden.

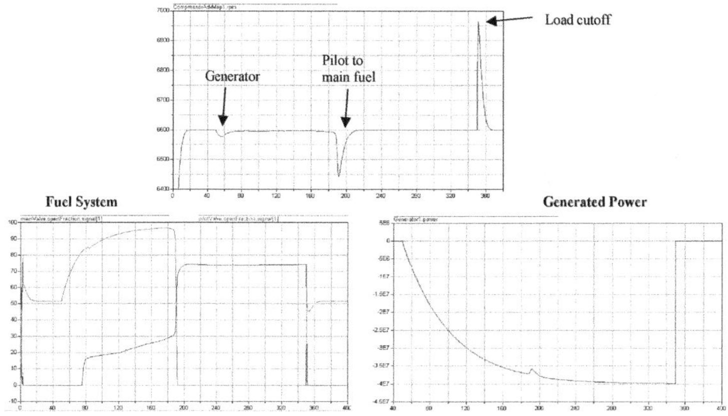

Figure 1-9. Simulation of GTX100 gas turbine power system cutoff mechanism. Courtesy Siemens Industrial Turbomachinery AB, Finspång, Sweden

The second example, the industry robot, illustrates the power of hierarchical model decomposition. The three-dimensional robot, shown to the right of Figure 1-10, is represented by a two-dimensional connection diagram (in the middle). Each part in the connection diagram can be a mechanical component such as a motor or joint, a control system for the robot, and so on. Components may consist of other components, which can in turn can be decomposed. At the bottom of the hierarchy we have model classes containing the actual equations.

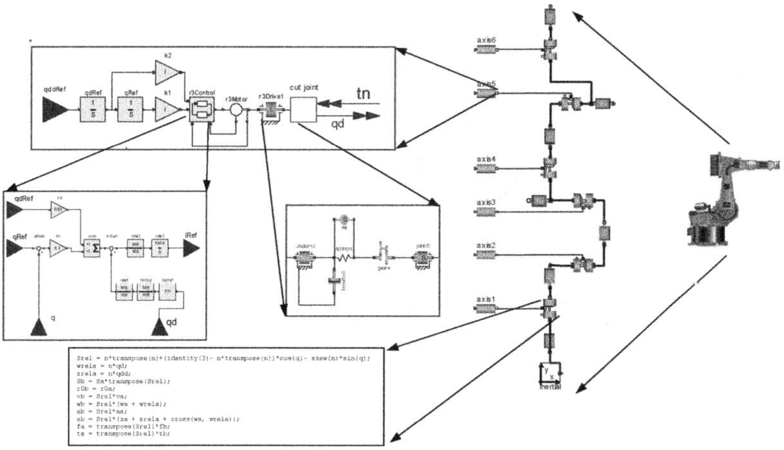

Figure 1-10. Hierarchical model of an industrial robot. Courtesy Martin Otter.

The third example is from an entirely different domain—biochemical pathways describing the reactions between reactants, in this particular case describing part of the citrate cycle (TCA cycle) as depicted in Figure 1-9.

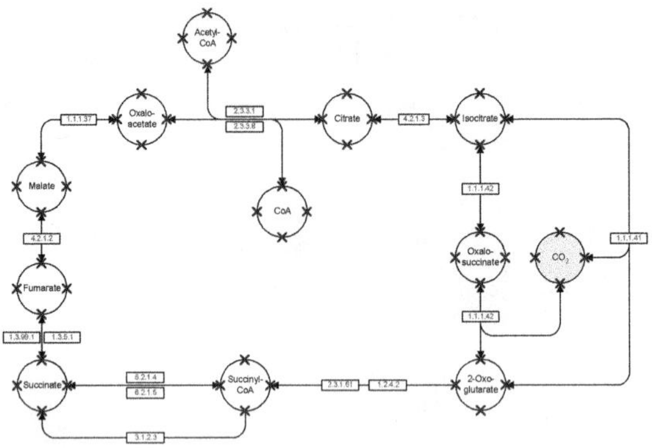

Figure 1-11. Biochemical pathway model of part of the citrate cycle (TCA cycle).

1.9 Summary

We have briefly presented important concepts such as system, model, experiment, and simulation. Systems can be represented by models, which can be subject to experiments, that is, simulation. Certain models can be represented by mathematics, so-called mathematical models. This book is about object-oriented, component-based technology for building and simulating such mathematical models. There are different classes of mathematical models—static versus dynamic models, continuous-time versus discrete-time models, and so on—depending on the properties of the modeled system, the available information about the system, and the approximations made in the model.

1.10 Literature

Any book on modeling and simulation must define fundamental concepts such as system, model, and experiment. The definitions in this chapter are generally available in the modeling and simulation literature, including (Ljung and Glad 1994; Cellier 1991). The quote on system definitions, referring to the pendulum, is from (Ashby 1956). The example of different levels of details in mathematical models of gases presented in Section 1.6 is mentioned in (Hyötyniemi 2002). The product design-V process mentioned in Section 1.7 is described in (Stevens, Brook., Jackson, and Arnold 1998; Shumate and Keller 1992). The citrate cycle biochemical pathway in Figure 1-11 is modeled after the description in (Michael 1999).

Chapter 2

A Quick Tour of Modelica

Modelica is primarily a modeling language that allows specification of mathematical models of complex natural or man-made systems, for example, for the purpose of computer simulation of dynamic systems where behavior evolves as a function of time. Modelica is also an object-oriented, equation-based programming language, oriented toward computational applications with high complexity requiring high performance. The four most important features of Modelica are:

- Modelica is primarily based on equations instead of assignment statements. This permits acausal modeling that gives better reuse of classes since equations do not specify a certain data-flow direction. Thus a Modelica class can adapt to more than one data flow context.
- Modelica has multidomain modeling capability, meaning that model components corresponding to physical objects from several different domains such as electrical, mechanical, thermodynamic, hydraulic, biological, and control applications can be described and connected.
- Modelica is an object-oriented language with a general class concept that unifies classes, generics—known as templates in C++ —and general subtyping into a single language construct. This facilitates reuse of components and evolution of models.
- Modelica has a strong software component model, with constructs for creating and connecting components. Thus the language is ideally suited as an architectural description language for complex physical systems and, to some extent, for software systems.

These are the main properties that make Modelica both powerful and easy to use, especially for modeling and simulation. We will start with a gentle introduction to Modelica from the very beginning.

2.1 Getting Started with Modelica

Modelica programs are built from classes, also called models. From a class definition, it is possible to create any number of objects that are known as instances of that class. Think of a class as a collection of blueprints and instructions used by a factory to create objects. In this case, the Modelica compiler and run-time system is the factory.

A Modelica class contains elements that can be variable declarations and equation sections containing equations. Variables contain data belonging to instances of the class; they make up the data storage of the instance. The equations of a class specify the behavior of instances of that class.

There is a long tradition that the first sample program in any computer language is a trivial program printing the string `"HelloWorld."` Since Modelica is an equation-based language, printing a string does not make much sense. Instead, our Hello World Modelica program solves a trivial *differential equation*:

$$\dot{x} = -a \cdot x \tag{2-1}$$

The variable x in this equation is a dynamic variable (here also a state variable) that can change value over time. The time derivative $\dot{x}$ is the time derivative of x, represented as `der(x)` in Modelica. Since all Modelica programs, usually called ***models***, consist of class declarations, our `HelloWorld` program is declared as a class:

```
class HelloWorld
  Real x(start = 1);
  parameter Real a = 1;
equation
  der(x) = -a*x;
end HelloWorld;
```

Use your favorite text editor or Modelica programming environment to type in this Modelica code[4], or open the DrModelica electronic document (part of OpenModelica) containing most examples and exercises in this book. Then invoke the simulation command in your Modelica environment. This will compile the Modelica code to some intermediate code, usually C code, which in turn will be compiled to machine code and executed together with a numerical ordinary differential equation (ODE) solver or differential algebraic equation (DAE) solver to produce a solution for x as a function of time. The following command in the OpenModelica environment produces a solution between time 0 seconds and time 2 seconds:

```
simulate⁵(HelloWorld,stopTime=2)
```

Since the solution for x is a function of time, it can be plotted by a plot command:

```
plot⁶(x)
```

(or the longer form `plot(x,xrange={0,2})` that specifies the x-axis), giving the curve in Figure 2-1.

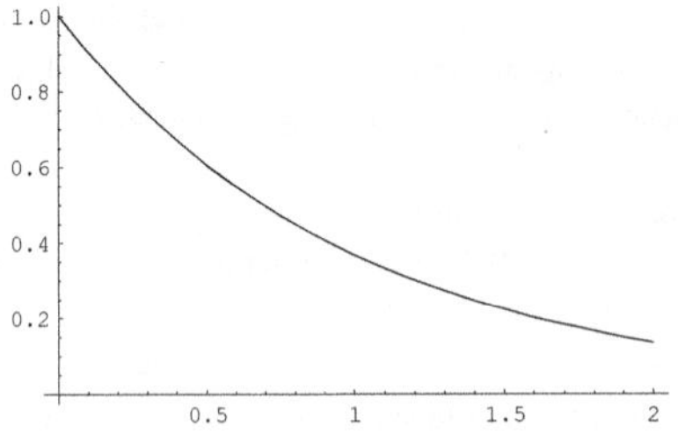

Figure 2-1. Plot of a simulation of the simple `HelloWorld` model.

Now we have a small Modelica model that does something, but what does it actually mean? The program contains a declaration of a class called `HelloWorld` with two variables and a single equation. The first attribute of the class is the variable `x`, which is initialized to a start value of 1 at the time when the simulation starts. All variables in Modelica have a `start` attribute with a default value that is normally set to 0. Having a different start value is accomplished by providing a so-called modifier

[4] There is a downloadable open source Modelica environment OpenModelica from OSMC at www.openmodelica.org, Wolfram SystemModeler is from Wolfram Research (www.mathcore.com or www.wolfram.com), Dymola from Dassault Systems (www.dymola.com), etc.

[5] Before simulating an existing model, you need to open it or load it, e.g. `loadModel(HelloWorld)` in OpenModelica.. The OpenModelica command for simulation is `simulate`. The corresponding Wolfram SystemModeler (WSM) Mathematica-style command for this example, after loading the model into WSM, would be `M1=WSMSimulate["HelloWorld", {0,2}]`, and in Dymola `simulateModel("HelloWorld", stopTime=2)`.

[6] `plot` is the OpenModelica command for plotting simulation results. The corresponding Wolfram SystemModeler Mathematica-style and Dymola commands would be `WSMPlot[M1,"x"]`, and `plot({"x"})` respectively.

within parentheses after the variable name, that is, a modification equation setting the start attribute to 1 and replacing the original default equation for the attribute.

The second attribute is the variable a, which is a constant that is initialized to 1 at the beginning of the simulation. Such a constant is prefixed by the keyword `parameter` in order to indicate that it is constant during simulation but is a model parameter that can be changed between simulations, for example, through a command in the simulation environment. For example, we could rerun the simulation for a different value of a, without recompilation if a is changed through the environment's parameter update facility.

Also note that each variable has a type that precedes its name when the variable is declared. In this case, both the variable x and the "variable" a have the type `Real`.

The single equation in this `HelloWorld` example specifies that the time derivative of x is equal to the constant $-a$ times x. In Modelica, the equal sign = always means equality, that is, establishes an equation, and not an assignment as in many other languages. The time derivative of a variable is indicated by the pseudofunction `der( )`.

Our second example is only slightly more complicated, containing five rather simple equations (2-2):

$$
\begin{aligned}
m\dot{v}_x &= -\frac{x}{L}F \\
m\dot{v}_y &= -\frac{y}{L}F - mg \\
\dot{x} &= v_x \\
\dot{y} &= v_y \\
x^2 + y^2 &= L^2
\end{aligned}
\tag{2-2}
$$

This example is actually a mathematical model of a physical system, a planar pendulum, as depicted in Figure 2-2.

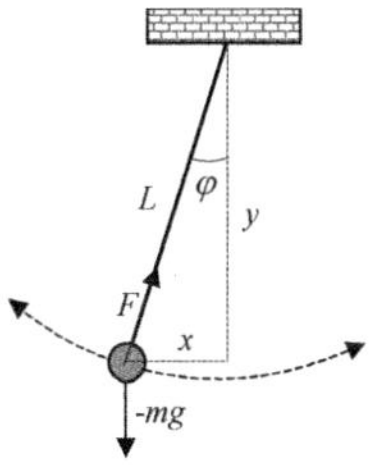

Figure 2-2. A planar pendulum.

The equations are Newton's equations of motion for the pendulum mass under the influence of gravity, together with a geometric constraint, the fifth equation $x^2 + y^2 = L^2$, that specifies that its position (x,y) must be on a circle with radius L. The variables v_x and v_y are its velocities in the x and y directions, respectively. A Modelica model of the pendulum appears below:

```
class Pendulum  "Planar Pendulum"
  constant  Real PI=3.141592653589793;
  parameter Real m=1, g=9.81, L=0.5;
  Real F;
  output    Real x(start=0.5),y(start=0);
  output    Real vx,vy;
equation
  m*der(vx)=-(x/L)*F;
  m*der(vy)=-(y/L)*F-m*g;
  der(x)=vx;
```

```
    der(y)=vy;
    x^2+y^2=L^2;
end Pendulum;
```

The interesting property of this model, however, is the fact that the fifth equation is of a different kind: a so-called *algebraic equation* only involving algebraic formulas of variables but no derivatives. The first four equations of this model are differential equations, as in the `HelloWorld` example. Equation systems that contain both differential and algebraic equations are called *differential algebraic equation systems* (DAEs).

We simulate the `Pendulum` model and plot the x-coordinate, as shown in Figure 2-3. You can also write down DAE equation systems without physical significance, with equations containing formulas selected more or less at random, as in the class `DAEexample` below:

```
simulate(Pendulum, stopTime=4)
plot(x);
```

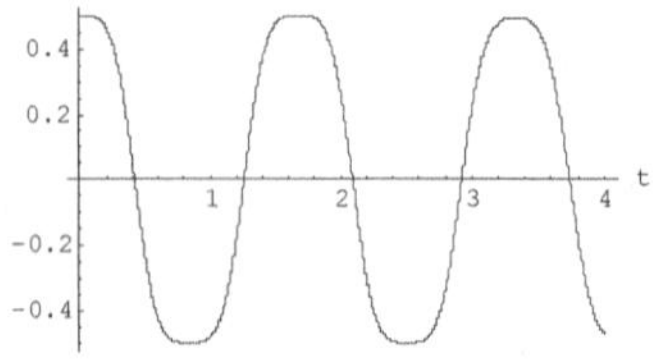

Figure 2-3. Plot of a simulation of the Pendulum DAE (differential algebraic equation) model.

```
class DAEexample
  Real x(start=0.9);
  Real y;
equation
  der(y) + (1+0.5*sin(y))*der(x) = sin(time);
  x-y = exp(-0.9*x)*cos(y);
end DAEexample;
```

This class contains one differential and one algebraic equation. Try to simulate and plot it yourself, to see if any reasonable curve appears!

Finally, an important observation regarding Modelica models:

- The number of *variables* must be equal to the number of *equations*!

This statement is true for the three models we have seen so far, and holds for all solvable Modelica models. By variables we mean something that can vary, not named constants and parameters to be described in Section 2.1.3, page 24.

2.1.1 Variables and Predefined Types

This example shows a slightly more complicated model, which describes a Van der Pol[7] oscillator. Notice that here the keyword `model` is used instead of `class` with almost the same meaning:

```
model Van,DerPol  "Van der Pol oscillator model"
  Real x(start = 1)  "Descriptive string for x";  // x starts at 1
  Real y(start = 1)  "Descriptive string for y";  // y starts at 1
  parameter Real lambda = 0.3;
```

[7] Balthazar van der Pol was a Dutch electrical engineer who initiated modern experimental dynamics in the laboratory during the 1920's and 1930's. Van der Pol investigated electrical circuits employing vacuum tubes and found that they have stable oscillations, now called limit cycles. The van der Pol oscillator is a model developed by him to describe the behavior of nonlinear vacuum tube circuits

```
equation
  der(x) = y;                        // This is the first equation
  der(y) = -x + lambda*(1 - x*x)*y;  /* The 2nd differential equation */
end VanDerPol;
```

This example contains declarations of two dynamic variables (here also state variables) `x` and `y`, both of type `Real` and having the start value 1 at the beginning of the simulation, which normally is at time 0. Then follows a declaration of the parameter constant lambda, which is a so-called model parameter.

A parameter is a special kind of constant which is implemented as a static variable that is initialized once and never changes its value during a specific execution. A `parameter` is a constant variable that makes it simple for a user to modify the behavior of a model; for example, changing the parameter lambda, which strongly influences the behavior of the Van der Pol oscillator. By contrast, a fixed Modelica constant declared with the prefix `constant` never changes and can be substituted by its value wherever it occurs.

Finally, we present declarations of three dummy variables just to show variables of data types different from `Real`: the boolean variable `bb`, which has a default start value of `false` if nothing else is specified; the string variable `dummy`, which is always equal to `"dummy string"`; and the integer variable `fooint`, which is always equal to `0`:

```
Boolean bb;
String dummy  = "dummy string";
Integer fooint = 0;
```

Modelica has built-in "primitive" predefined data types to support floating-point, integer, boolean, and string values. These predefined primitive types contain data that Modelica understands directly, as opposed to class types defined by programmers. There is also the `Complex` type for complex-numbers computations, which is predefined in a library. The type of each variable must be declared explicitly. The predefined basic data types of Modelica are:

`Boolean`	either `true` or `false`
`Integer`	32-bit two's complement, usually corresponding to the C int data type
`Real`	64-bit floating-point usually corresponding to the C double data type
`String`	string of text characters
`enumeration(...)`	enumeration type of enumeration literals
`Clock`	clock type for clocked synchronous models
`Complex`	for complex number computations, a basic type predefined in a library

Finally, there is an equation section starting with the keyword `equation`, containing two mutually dependent equations that define the dynamics of the model.

To illustrate the behavior of the model, we give a command to simulate the Van der Pol oscillator during 25 seconds starting at time 0:

```
simulate(VanDerPol, stopTime=25)
```

and a phase plane plot of the state variables for the Van der Pol oscillator model (Figure 2-4):

```
plotParametric(x,y, stopTime=25)
```

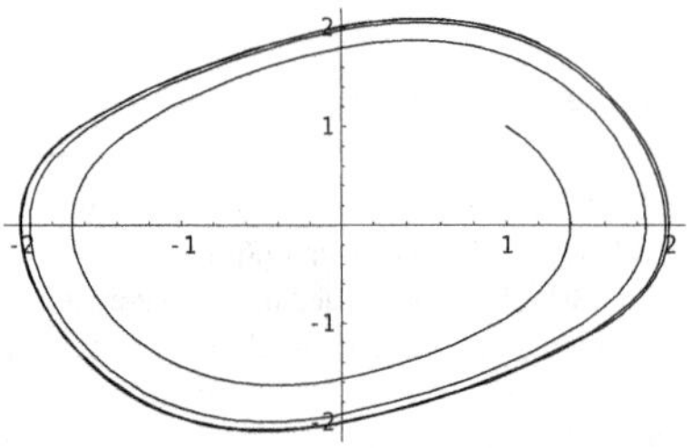

Figure 2-4. Parametric plot of a simulation of the Van der Pol oscillator model.

The names of variables, functions, classes, and so on are known as identifiers. There are two forms in Modelica. The most common form starts with a letter, followed by letters or digits, for example, `x2`. The second form starts with a single quote, followed by any characters, and terminated by a single quote, for example, `'2nd*3'`.

2.1.2 Comments

Arbitrary descriptive text, for example, in English, inserted throughout a computer program, are comments to that code. Modelica has three styles of comments, all illustrated in the previous `VanDerPol` example.

Comments make it possible to write descriptive text together with the code, which makes a model easier to use for the user, or easier to understand for programmers who may read your code in the future. That programmer may very well be yourself, months or years later. You save yourself future effort by commenting your own code. Also, it is often the case that you find errors in your code when you write comments since when explaining your code you are forced to think about it once more.

The first kind of comment is a string within string quotes, for example, "`a comment`," optionally appearing after variable declarations or at the beginning of class declarations. Those are "definition comments" that are processed to be used by the Modelica programming environment, for example, to appear in menus or as help texts for the user. From a syntactic point of view, they are not really comments since they are part of the language syntax. In the previous example, such definition comments appear for the `VanDerPol` class and for the `x` and `y` variables.

The other two types of comments are ignored by the Modelica compiler, and are just present for the benefit of Modelica programmers. Text following `//` up to the end of the line is skipped by the compiler, as is text between `/* and the next */`. Hence, the last type of comment can be used for large sections of text that occupies several lines.

Finally we should mention a construct called `annotation`, a kind of structured "comment" that can store information together with the code, described in Section 2.17.

2.1.3 Constants

Constant literals in Modelica can be integer values such as 4, 75, 3078; floating-point values like 3.14159, 0.5, 2.735E-10, 8.6835e+5; string values such as `"hello world,"` `"red"`; and enumeration values such as `Colors.red`, `Sizes.xlarge`.

Named constants are preferred by programmers for two reasons. One reason is that the name of the constant is a kind of documentation that can be used to describe what the particular value is used for. The other, perhaps even more important reason, is that a named constant is defined at a single place in the program. When the constant needs to be changed or corrected, it can be changed in only one place, simplifying program maintenance.

Named constants in Modelica are created by using one of the prefixes `constant` or `parameter` in declarations, and providing a declaration equation as part of the declaration. For example:

```
constant  Real    PI = 3.141592653589793;
constant  String  redcolor = "red";
constant  Integer one = 1;
parameter Real    mass = 22.5;
```

Parameter constants (often called *parameters*) can usually be accessed and changed from Modelica tool graphical user interfaces. Most Modelica tools support resimulating a model without recompilation after changing a parameter, which usually makes the time waiting for results much shorter.

Parameters can be declared without a declaration equation (but a default start value is recommended) since their value can be defined, e.g., interactively or by reading from a file, before simulation starts. This is not possible for constants with prefix `constant`. For example:

```
parameter Real mass, gravity, length;
```

A parameter with a default start value, as shown below, means that the parameter has a value, but that this value is expected to be replaced by a more realistic value, for example, by the user, at a real simulation:

```
parameter Real mass(start=0), gravity(start=0), length(start=0);
```

Constants and parameters are very similar, but also have some differences (Section 3.11.2, page 99). Parameters are typically much more common in application models. When in doubt whether to use `constant` or `parameter`, use `parameter`, except when declaring a constant in a package/library where `constant` is allowed but not `parameter`.

2.1.4 Variability

We have seen that some variables can change value at any point in time whereas named constants are more or less constant. In fact, there is a general concept of four levels of variability of variables and expressions in Modelica (see also Section 6.9, page 279):

- Expressions or variables with *continuous-time variability* can change at any point in time.
- *Discrete-time variability* means that value changes can occur only at so-called events; see Section 13.2, page 593. There are two kinds: *unclocked discrete-time variability* and *clocked discrete-time variability*. In the latter case the value can only change at clock tick events.
- *Parameter variability* means that the value can be changed at initialization before simulation but is fixed during simulation.
- *Constant variability* means the value is always fixed. However, a named constant definition equation can be replaced by a so-called redeclaration or modification.

2.1.5 Default start Values

If a numeric variable lacks a specified definition value or `start` value in its declaration, it is usually initialized to zero at the start of the simulation. Boolean variables have `start` value `false`, and string variables the `start` value empty string `""` if nothing else is specified.

Exceptions to this rule are function *results* and *local* variables in functions, where the default initial value at function call is *undefined*. See also Section 8.4, page 363.

2.2 Object-Oriented Mathematical Modeling

Traditional object-oriented programming languages like Simula, C++, Java, and Smalltalk, as well as procedural languages such as Fortran or C, support programming with operations on stored data. The stored data of the program include variable values and object data. The number of objects often changes dynamically. The Smalltalk view of object orientation emphasizes sending messages between (dynamically) created objects.

The Modelica view on object orientation is different since the Modelica language emphasizes *structured* mathematical modeling. Object orientation is viewed as a structuring concept that is used to handle the complexity of large system descriptions. A Modelica model is primarily a declarative mathematical description, which simplifies further analysis. Dynamic system properties are expressed in a declarative way through equations.

The concept of *declarative* programming is inspired by mathematics, where it is common to state or declare what *holds*, rather than giving a detailed stepwise *algorithm* on *how* to achieve the desired goal, as is required when using procedural languages. This relieves the programmer from the burden of keeping track of such details. Furthermore, the code becomes more concise and easier to change without introducing errors.

Thus, the declarative Modelica view of object orientation, from the point of view of object-oriented mathematical modeling, can be summarized as follows:

- Object orientation is primarily used as a *structuring* concept, emphasizing the declarative structure and reuse of mathematical models. Our three ways of structuring are hierarchies, component connections, and inheritance.
- Dynamic model properties are expressed in a declarative way through *equations*[8].
- An object is a collection of *instance* variables and equations that share a set of data.

However:

- Object-orientation in mathematical modeling is *not* viewed as dynamic message passing.

The declarative object-oriented way of describing systems and their behavior offered by Modelica is at a higher level of abstraction than the usual object-oriented programming since some implementation details can be omitted. For example, we do not need to write code to explicitly transport data between objects through assignment statements or message-passing code. Such code is generated automatically by the Modelica compiler based on the given equations.

Just as in ordinary object-oriented languages, classes are blueprints for creating objects. Both variables and equations can be inherited between classes. Function definitions can also be inherited. However, specifying behavior is primarily done through equations instead of via methods. There are also facilities for stating algorithmic code including functions in Modelica, but this is an exception rather than the rule. See also Chapter 3, page 79 and Chapter 4, page 135 for a discussion regarding object-oriented concepts.

2.3 Classes and Instances

Modelica, like any object-oriented computer language, provides the notions of classes and objects, also called instances, as a tool for solving modeling and programming problems. Every object in Modelica has a class that defines its data and behavior. A class has three kinds of members:

- Data variables associated with a class and its instances. Variables represent results of computations caused by solving the equations of a class together with equations from other

[8] Algorithms are also allowed, but in a way that makes it possible to regard an algorithm section as a system of equations.

classes. During numeric solution of time-dependent problems, the variables store results of the solution process at the current time instant.

- Equations specify the behavior of a class. The way in which the equations interact with equations from other classes determines the solution process, that is, program execution.
- Classes can be members of other classes.

Here is the declaration of a simple class that might represent a point in a three-dimensional space:

```
class Point "Point in a three-dimensional space"
 public
  Real x;
  Real y, z;
end Point;
```

The Point class has three variables representing the x, y, and z coordinates of a point and has no equations. A class declaration like this one is like a blueprint that defines how instances created from that class look, as well as instructions in the form of equations that define the behavior of those objects. Members of a class may be accessed using dot (.) notation. For example, regarding an instance myPoint of the Point class, we can access the x variable by writing myPoint.x.

Members of a class can have two levels of visibility. The public declaration of x, y, and z, which is the default if nothing else is specified, means that any code with access to a Point instance can refer to those values. The other possible level of visibility, specified by the keyword protected, means that only code inside the class as well as code in classes that inherit this class, are allowed access.

Note that an occurrence of one of the keywords public or protected means that all member declarations following that keyword assume the corresponding visibility until another occurrence of one of those keywords or the end of the class containing the member declarations has been reached.

2.3.1 Creating Instances

In Modelica, objects are created implicitly just by declaring instances of classes. This is in contrast to object-oriented languages like Java or C++, where object creation is specified using the new keyword when allocating on the heap. For example, to create three instances of our Point class we just declare three variables of type Point in a class, here Triangle:

```
class Triangle
  Point  point1;
  Point  point2;
  Point  point3;
end Triangle;
```

There is one remaining problem, however. In what context should Triangle be instantiated, and when should it just be interpreted as a library class not to be instantiated until actually used?

This problem is solved by regarding the class at the *top* of the instantiation hierarchy in the Modelica program to be executed as a kind of "main" class that is always implicitly instantiated, implying that its variables are instantiated, and that the variables of those variables are instantiated, and so on. Therefore, to instantiate Triangle, either make the class Triangle the "top" class or declare an instance of Triangle in the "main" class. In the following example, both the class Triangle and the class Foo1 are instantiated.

```
class Foo1
  ...
end Foo1;

class Foo2
  ...
end Foo2;
```

```
...
class Triangle
  Point  point1;
  Point  point2;
  Point  point3;
end Triangle;

class Main
  Triangle  pts;
  Foo1      f1;
end Main;
```

The variables of Modelica classes are instantiated per object. This means that a variable in one object is distinct from the variable with the same name in every other object instantiated from that class. Many object-oriented languages allow class variables. Such variables are specific to a class as opposed to instances of the class, and are shared among all objects of that class. The notion of class variables is not yet available in Modelica.

2.3.2 Initialization

Another problem is initialization of variables. As mentioned previously in Section 2.1.4, page 25, if nothing else is specified, the default start value of all numerical variables is zero, apart from function results and local variables where the initial value at call time is unspecified. Other start values can be specified by setting the `start` attribute of instance variables. Note that the start value only gives a suggestion for initial value—the solver may choose a different value unless the `fixed` attribute is true for that variable. Below, a start value is specified in the example class `Triangle`:

```
class Triangle
  Point  point1(start=Point(1,2,3));
  Point  point2;
  Point  point3;
end Triangle;
```

Alternatively, the start value of `point1` can be specified when instantiating `Triangle`, as below:

```
class Main
  Triangle  pts(point1.start=Point(1,2,3));
  Foo1      f1;
end Main;
```

A more general way of initializing a set of variables according to some constraints is to specify an equation system to be solved in order to obtain the initial values of these variables. This method is supported in Modelica through the `initial equation` construct.

An example of a continuous-time controller initialized in steady-state, that is, when derivatives should be zero, is given below:

```
model Controller
  parameter Real a=1, b=2;
  Real y;
equation
  der(y)  = a*y + b*u;
initial equation
  der(y)=0;
end Controller;
```

This has the following solution at initialization:

```
der(y)  = 0;
y = -(b/a)*u;
```

For more information, see Section 8.4, page 363.

2.3.3 Specialized Classes

The class concept is fundamental to Modelica and is used for a number of different purposes. Almost anything in Modelica is a class. However, in order to make Modelica code easier to read and maintain, special keywords have been introduced for specific uses of the class concept. The keywords `model`, `connector`, `record`, `block`, `type`, `package`, and `function` can be used to denote a class under appropriate conditions, called restrictions. Some of the specialized classes also have additional capabilities, called enhancements. For example, a `function` class has the enhancement that it can be called, whereas a `record` is a class used to declare a record data structure and has the restrictions that it may not contain equations and may only contain public declarations:

```
record Person
  Real   age;
  String name;
end Person;
```

A `model` is almost the same as a `class`, that is, those keywords are completely interchangeable. A `block` is a class with fixed causality, which means that for each connector variable of the class it is specified whether it has input or output causality. Thus, each `connector` variable in a `block` class interface must be declared with a causality prefix keyword of either `input` or `output`.

A `connector` class is used to declare the structure of "ports" or interface points of a component, may not contain equations, and has only public sections, but has the additional property to allow `connect(...)` to instances of connector classes. A `type` is a class that can be an alias or an extension to a predefined type, enumeration, or array of a type. For example:

```
type vector3D = Real[3];
```

The idea of specialized classes has some advantages since they re-use most properties of the general *class concept*. The notion of specialized classes also gives the user a chance to express more precisely what a class is intended for, and requires the Modelica compiler to check that these usage constraints are actually fulfilled.

Fortunately, the notion of specialized class is quite uniform since all basic properties of a class, such as the syntax and semantics of definition, instantiation, inheritance, and generic properties, are identical for all kinds of specialized classes. Furthermore, the construction of Modelica translators is simplified since only the syntax and semantics of the general class concept has to be implemented along with some additional checks on restrictions and enhancements of the classes.

The `package` and `function` specialized classes in Modelica have much in common with the class concept but also have many additional properties, so-called enhancements. Especially, functions have quite a lot of enhancements—they can be called with an argument list, instantiated at run-time, and so on. An `operator` class is similar to a `package` that is like a container for other definitions, but may only contain declarations of functions and is intended for user-defined overloaded operators. See also Section 3.8, page 87, regarding specialized classes.

2.3.4 Reuse of Classes by Modifications

The class concept is the key to reuse of modeling knowledge in Modelica. Provisions for expressing adaptations or modifications of classes through so-called modifiers in Modelica make reuse easier. For example, assume that we would like to connect two filter models with different time constants in series.

Instead of creating two separate filter classes, it is better to define a common filter class and create two appropriately modified instances of this class, which are connected. An example of connecting two modified low-pass filters is shown after the example low-pass filter class below:

```
model LowPassFilter
  parameter Real T=1  "Time constant of filter";
  Real u, y(start=1);
equation
  T*der(y) + y = u;
end LowPassFilter;
```

The model class can be used to create two instances of the filter with different time constants and "connecting" them together by the equation `F2.u = F1.y` as follows:

```
model FiltersInSeries
  LowPassFilter F1(T=2), F2(T=3);
equation
  F1.u = sin(time);
  F2.u = F1.y;
end FiltersInSeries;
```

Here we have used modifiers—attribute equations such as `T=2` and `T=3`—to modify the time constant of the low-pass filter when creating the instances `F1` and `F2`. The independent time variable is a built-in, predefined variable denoted `time`. If the `FiltersInSeries` model is used to declare variables at a higher hierarchical level, for example, `F12`, the time constants can still be adapted by using hierarchical modification, as for `F1` and `F2` below:

```
model ModifiedFiltersInSeries
  FiltersInSeries F12(F1(T=6), F2.T=11);
end ModifiedFiltersInSeries;
```

See also Chapter 4, page 135.

2.3.5 Built-in Classes

The built-in predefined type classes of Modelica correspond to the types `Real`, `Integer`, `Boolean`, `String`, `enumeration(...)`, and `Clock`, and have most of the properties of a class, for example, they can be inherited, modified, and so on. Only the value attribute can be changed at run time and is accessed through the variable name itself, not through dot notation, that is, use `x` and not `x.value` to access the value. Other attributes are accessed through dot notation.

For example, a `Real` variable has a set of default attributes such as unit of measure, initial value, and minimum and maximum value. These default attributes can be changed when declaring a new class, for example:

```
class Voltage = Real(unit= "V", min=-220.0, max=220.0);
```

See also Section 2.1.1, page 22, and Section 3.9, page 93.

2.4 Inheritance

One of the major benefits of object-orientation is the ability to extend the behavior and properties of an existing class. The original class, known as the *superclass* or *base class*, is extended to create a more specialized version of that class, known as the *subclass* or *derived class*. In this process, the behavior and properties of the original class in the form of variable declarations, equations, and other contents are reused, or inherited, by the subclass.

Let us look at an example of extending a simple Modelica class, the class `Point` introduced previously. First, we introduce two classes named `ColorData` and `Color`, where `Color` inherits the data variables to represent the color from class `ColorData` and adds an equation as a constraint. The new class `ColoredPoint` inherits from multiple classes, that is, it uses multiple inheritance, to get the position variables from class `Point`, and the color variables together with the equation from class `Color`.

```
record ColorData
  Real red;
  Real blue;
  Real green;
end ColorData;

class Color
  extends ColorData;
equation
  red + blue + green = 1;
end Color;

class Point
 public
  Real x;
  Real y, z;
end Point;

class ColoredPoint
  extends Point;
  extends Color;
end ColoredPoint;
```

See also Chapter 4, page 135, regarding inheritance and reuse.

2.5 Generic Classes

In many situations, it is advantageous to be able to express generic patterns for models or programs. Instead of writing many similar pieces of code with essentially the same structure, a substantial amount of coding and software maintenance can be avoided by directly expressing the general structure of the problem and providing the special cases as *parameter* values.

Such generic constructs are available in several programming languages, for example, templates in C++, generics in Ada, and type parameters in functional languages such as Haskell or Standard ML. In Modelica the class construct is sufficiently general to handle generic modeling and programming in addition to the usual class functionality.

There are essentially two cases of generic class parameterization in Modelica: *class parameters* can either be *instance parameters*, that is, have instance declarations (components) as values, or be *type parameters*, that is, have types as values. Note that by class parameters in this context we do not usually mean model parameters prefixed by the keyword `parameter`, even though such "variables" are also a kind of class parameter. Instead we mean *formal parameters to the class*. Such formal parameters are prefixed by the keyword `replaceable`. The special case of replaceable local functions is roughly equivalent to virtual methods in some object-oriented programming languages.

See also Section 4.4, page 168.

2.5.1 Class Parameters Being Instances

First, we present the case when class parameters are variables, that is, declarations of instances, often called components. The class `C` in the example below has three class parameters *marked* by the keyword `replaceable`. These class parameters, which are components (variables) of class `C`, are declared as having the (default) types `GreenClass`, `YellowClass`, and `GreenClass`, respectively. There is also a red object declaration that is not replaceable and therefore not a class parameter (Figure 2-5).

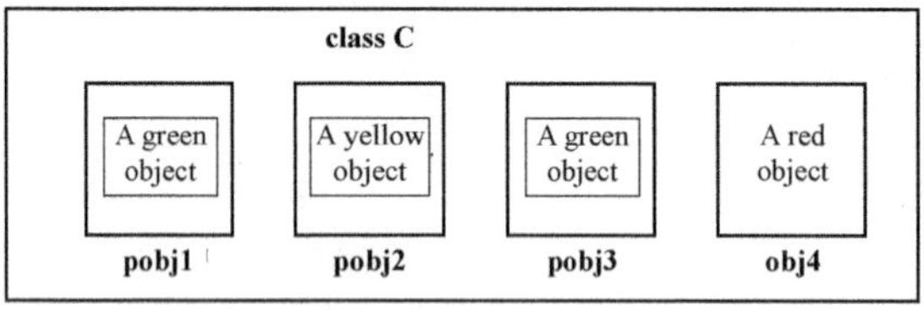

Figure 2-5. Three class parameters `pobj1`, `pobj2`, and `pobj3` that are instances (variables) of `class C`. These are essentially slots that can contain objects of different colors.

Here is the `class C` with its three class parameters `pobj1`, `pobj2`, and `pobj3`, and a variable `obj4` that is not a class parameter:

```
class C
  replaceable GreenClass  pobj1(p1=5);
  replaceable YellowClass pobj2;
  replaceable GreenClass  pobj3;
  RedClass    obj4;
equation
  ...
end C;
```

Now a class `C2` is defined by providing two declarations of `pobj1` and `pobj2` as actual arguments to class `C`, being `red` and `green`, respectively, instead of the defaults `green` and `yellow`. The keyword `redeclare` must precede an actual argument to a class formal parameter to allow changing its type. The requirement to use a keyword for a redeclaration in Modelica has been introduced in order to avoid accidentally changing the type of an object through a standard modifier.

In general, the type of a class component cannot be changed if it is not declared as `replaceable` and a redeclaration is provided. A variable in a redeclaration can replace the original variable if it has a type that is a subtype of the original type or its type constraint. It is also possible to declare type constraints (not shown here) on the substituted classes.

```
class C2 = C(redeclare RedClass pobj1, redeclare GreenClass pobj2);
```

Such a class `C2`, obtained through redeclaration of `pobj1` and `pobj2`, is, of course, equivalent to directly defining `C2` without reusing class `C`, as below.

```
class C2
  RedClass   pobj1(p1=5);
  GreenClass pobj2;
  GreenClass pobj3;
  RedClass   obj4;
equation
  ...
end C2;
```

2.5.2 Class Parameters Being Types

A class parameter can also be a type, which is useful for changing the type of many objects. For example, by providing a type parameter `ColoredClass` in class `C` below, it is easy to change the color of all objects of type `ColoredClass`.

```
class C
  replaceable class ColoredClass = GreenClass;
  ColoredClass           obj1(p1=5);
  replaceable YellowClass obj2;
  ColoredClass           obj3;
  RedClass               obj4;
equation
  ...
end C;
```

Figure 2-6 depicts how the type value of the `ColoredClass` class parameter is propagated to the member object declarations `obj1` and `obj3`.

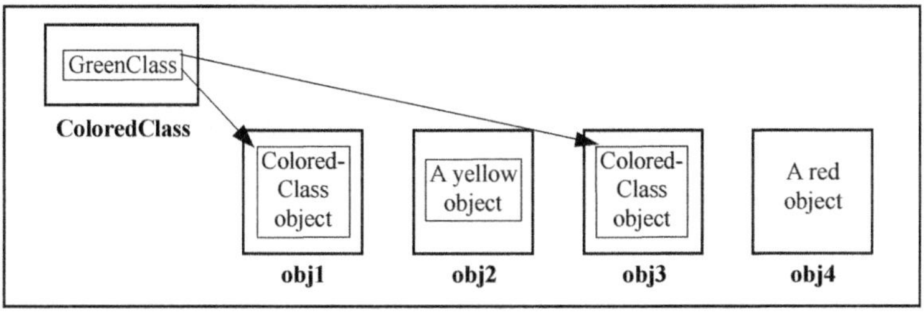

Figure 2-6. The class parameter `ColoredClass` is a type parameter that is propagated to the two member instance declarations of `obj1` and `obj3`.

We create a class `C2` by giving the type parameter `ColoredClass` of class `C` the value `BlueClass`.

```
class C2 = C(redeclare class ColoredClass = BlueClass);
```

This is equivalent to the following definition of `C2`:

```
class C2
  BlueClass   obj1(p1=5);
  YellowClass obj2;
  BlueClass   obj3;
  RedClass    obj4;
equation
  ...
end C2;
```

2.6 Equations

As we already stated, Modelica is primarily an equation-based language in contrast to ordinary programming languages, where assignment statements proliferate. Equations are more flexible than assignments since they do not prescribe a certain data flow direction or execution order. This is the key to the physical modeling capabilities and increased reuse potential of Modelica classes.

Thinking in equations is a bit unusual for most programmers. In Modelica the following holds:

- Assignment statements in conventional languages are usually represented as equations in Modelica.
- Attribute assignments are represented as equations.
- Connections between objects generate equations.

Equations are more powerful than assignment statements. For example, consider a resistor equation where the resistance `R` multiplied by the current `i` is equal to the voltage `v`:

```
R*i = v;
```

This equation can be used in three ways corresponding to three possible assignment statements: computing the current from the voltage and the resistance, computing the voltage from the resistance and the current, or computing the resistance from the voltage and the current. This is expressed in the following three assignment statements:

```
i := v/R;
v := R*i;
R := v/i;
```

Equations in Modelica can be informally classified into four different groups depending on the syntactic context in which they occur:

- *Normal equations* occurring in equation sections, including the connect equation, which is a special form of equation.
- *Declaration equations*, which are part of variable or constant declarations.
- *Modification equations*, which are commonly used to modify attributes.
- *Initial equations*, specified in initial equation sections or as start attribute equations. These equations are used to solve the initialization problem at startup time.

As we already have seen in several examples, normal equations appear in equation sections started by the keyword `equation` and terminated by some other allowed keyword:

```
equation
  ...
  <equations>
  ...
<some other allowed keyword>
```

The above resistor equation is an example of a normal equation that can be placed in an equation section. Declaration equations are usually given as part of declarations of fixed or parameter constants, for example:

```
constant Integer one = 1;
parameter Real mass = 22.5;
```

An equation always holds, which means that the mass in the above example never changes value during simulation. It is also possible to specify a declaration equation for a normal variable:

```
Real speed = 72.4;
```

However, this does not make much sense since it will constrain the variable to have the same value throughout the computation, effectively behaving as a constant. Therefore, a declaration equation is quite different from a variable initializer in other languages since it always holds and can be solved together with other equations in the total system of equations.

Concerning attribute assignments, these are typically specified using modification equations. For example, if we need to specify an initial value for a variable, meaning its value at the start of the computation, then we give an attribute equation for the start attribute of the variable:

```
Real speed(start=72.4);
```

See also Chapter 8, page 347, for a complete overview of equations in Modelica.

2.6.1 Repetitive Equation Structures

Before reading this section, you might want to take a look at Section 2.13 about arrays, page 47, and Section 2.14.2 about statements and algorithmic for-loops, page 50.

Sometimes there is a need to conveniently express sets of equations that have a regular, that is, repetitive structure. Often this can be expressed by array equations, including references to array elements denoted using square bracket notation[9]. However, for the more general case of repetitive equation structures Modelica provides a loop construct. Note that this is not a loop in the algorithmic sense of the word—it is rather a shorthand notation for expressing a set of equations.

For example, consider an equation for a polynomial expression:

```
y = a[1]+a[2]*x + a[3]*x^2 + ... + a[n+1]*x^n
```

The polynomial equation can be expressed as a set of equations with regular structure in Modelica, with `y` equal to the scalar product of the vectors `a` and `xpowers`, both of length `n+1`:

```
xpowers[1]  = 1;
xpowers[2]  = xpowers[1]*x;
xpowers[3]  = xpowers[2]*x;
...
xpowers[n+1]  = xpowers[n]*x;
y = a * xpowers;
```

The regular set of equations involving `xpowers` can be expressed more conveniently using the `for` loop notation:

```
for i in 1:n loop
  xpowers[i+1]  = xpowers[i]*x;
end for;
```

In this particular case, a vector equation provides an even more compact notation:

```
xpowers[2:n+1]  = xpowers[1:n]*x;
```

Here the vectors `x` and `xpowers` have length `n+1`. The colon notation `2:n+1` means extracting a vector of length `n`, starting from element 2 up to and including element `n+1`.

2.6.2 Partial Differential Equations

Partial differential equations (abbreviated PDEs) contain derivatives with respect to other variables than time, for example, of spatial Cartesian coordinates such as *x* and *y*. Models of phenomena such as heat flow or fluid flow typically involve PDEs. At the time of this writing, PDE functionality is not yet part of the official Modelica language. See Section 8.10, page 400, for an overview of the most important current PDE design proposals, which to some extent have been evaluated in test implementations, as well as one language construct (`spatialDistribution`, Section 8.10.3, page 412) for 1D PDEs that is part of the Modelica language standard.

[9] For more information regarding arrays see Chapter 7, page 207.

2.7 Acausal Physical Modeling

Acausal modeling is a declarative modeling style, meaning modeling based on equations instead of assignment statements. Equations do not specify which variables are inputs and which are outputs, whereas in assignment statements variables on the left-hand side are always outputs (results) and variables on the right-hand side are always inputs. Thus, the causality of equation-based models is unspecified and becomes fixed only when the corresponding equation systems are solved. This is called *acausal modeling*. The term *physical modeling* reflects the fact that *acausal modeling* is very well suited for representing the *physical structure* of modeled systems.

The main advantage with acausal modeling is that the solution direction of equations will adapt to the data flow context in which the solution is computed. The data flow context is defined by stating which variables are needed as *outputs* and which are external *inputs* to the simulated system.

The acausality of Modelica library classes makes these more reusable than traditional classes containing assignment statements where the `input-output` causality is fixed.

2.7.1 Physical Modeling vs. Block-Oriented Modeling

To illustrate the idea of acausal physical modeling, we give an example of a simple electrical circuit (Figure 2-7). The connection diagram[10] of the electrical circuit shows how the components are connected. It may be drawn with component placements to roughly correspond to the physical layout of the electrical circuit on a printed circuit board. The physical connections in the real circuit correspond to the logical connections in the diagram. Therefore the *term physical modeling* is quite appropriate.

The Modelica `SimpleCircuit` model below directly corresponds to the circuit depicted in the connection diagram of Figure 2-7. Each graphic object in the diagram corresponds to a declared instance in the simple circuit model. The model is acausal since no signal flow, that is, cause-and-effect flow, is specified. Connections between objects are specified using the connect-equation construct, which is a special syntactic form of equation that we will examine later. The classes `Resistor`, `Capacitor`, `Inductor`, `VsourceAC`, and `Ground` will be presented in more detail on pages 43 to 46.

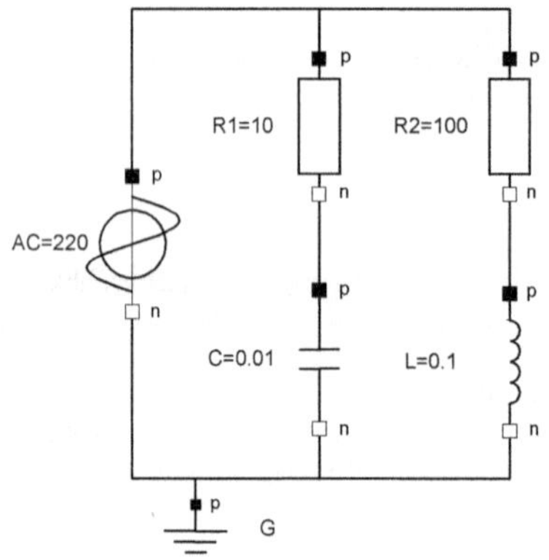

Figure 2-7. Connection diagram of the acausal `SimpleCircuit` model.

```
model SimpleCircuit
```

[10] A connection diagram emphasizes the connections between components of a model, whereas a composition diagram specifies which components a model is composed of, their subcomponents, and so on. A class diagram usually depicts inheritance and composition relations.

```
    Resistor  R1(R=10);
    Capacitor C(C=0.01);
    Resistor  R2(R=100);
    Inductor  L(L=0.1);
    VsourceAC AC;
    Ground    G;
  equation
    connect(AC.p, R1.p);      // Capacitor circuit
    connect(R1.n, C.p);
    connect(C.n, AC.n);
    connect(R1.p, R2.p);      // Inductor circuit
    connect(R2.n, L.p);
    connect(L.n,  C.n);
    connect(AC.n, G.p);       // Ground
  end SimpleCircuit;
```

As a comparison we show the same circuit modeled using causal block-oriented modeling depicted as a diagram in Figure 2-8. Here the physical topology is lost—the structure of the diagram has no simple correspondence to the structure of the physical circuit board.

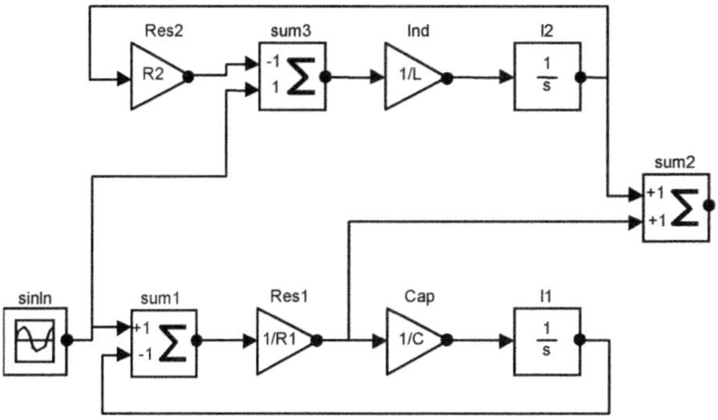

Figure 2-8 The simple circuit model using causal block-oriented modeling with explicit signal flow.

This model is causal since the signal flow has been deduced and is clearly shown in the diagram. Even for this simple example, the analysis to convert the intuitive physical model to a causal block-oriented model is nontrivial. Another disadvantage is that the resistor representations are context dependent. For example, the resistors `R1` and `R2` have different definitions, which makes reuse of model library components hard. Furthermore, such system models are usually hard to maintain since even small changes in the physical structure may result in large changes to the corresponding block-oriented system model.

2.8 The Modelica Software Component Model

For a long time, software developers have looked with envy on hardware system builders, regarding the apparent ease with which reusable hardware components are used to construct complicated systems. With software, there seems too often to be a need or tendency to develop from scratch instead of reusing components. Early attempts at software components include procedure libraries, which unfortunately have too limited applicability and low flexibility. The advent of object-oriented programming has stimulated the development of software component frameworks such as CORBA, the Microsoft COM/DCOM component object model, and JavaBeans. These component models have considerable success in certain application areas, but there is still a long way to go to reach the level of reuse and component standardization found in the hardware industry.

The reader might wonder what all this has to do with Modelica. In fact, Modelica offers quite a powerful software component model that is on par with hardware component systems in flexibility and potential for reuse. The key to this increased flexibility is the fact that Modelica classes are based on equations. What is a software component model? It should include the following three items:

1. Components
2. A connection mechanism
3. A component framework

Components are connected via the connection mechanism, which can be visualized in connection diagrams. The component framework realizes components and connections, and ensures that communication works and constraints are maintained over the connections. For systems composed of acausal components, the direction of data flow, that is, the causality, is automatically deduced by the compiler at composition time.

See also Chapter 5, page 187, for a complete overview of components, connectors, and connections.

2.8.1 Components

Components are simply instances of Modelica classes. Those classes should have well-defined interfaces, sometimes called ports, in Modelica called connectors, for communication and coupling between a component and the outside world.

A component is modeled independently of the environment in which it is used, which is essential for its reusability. This means that in the definition of the component including its equations, only local variables and connector variables can be used. No means of communication between a component and the rest of the system, apart from going via a connector, should be allowed. However, in Modelica access of component data via dot notation is also possible. A component may internally consist of other connected components, that is, hierarchical modeling.

2.8.2 Connection Diagrams

Complex systems usually consist of large numbers of connected components, of which many components can be hierarchically decomposed into other components through several levels. To grasp this complexity, a pictorial representation of components and connections is quite important. Such graphic representation is available as connection diagrams, of which a schematic example is shown in Figure 2-9. We have earlier presented a connection diagram of a simple circuit in Figure 2-7.

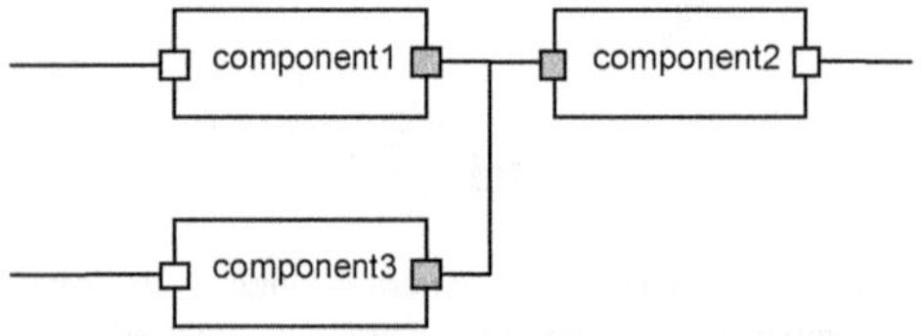

Figure 2-9. Schematic picture of a connection diagram for components.

Each rectangle in the diagram example represents a physical component—a resistor, a capacitor, a transistor, a mechanical gear, a valve, and so on. The connections represented by lines in the diagram correspond to real, physical connections. For example, connections can be realized by electrical wires, by the mechanical connections, by pipes for fluids, by heat exchange between components, and so on.

The connectors (interface points) are shown as small square dots on the rectangle in the diagram. Variables at such interface points define the interaction between the component represented by the rectangle and other components.

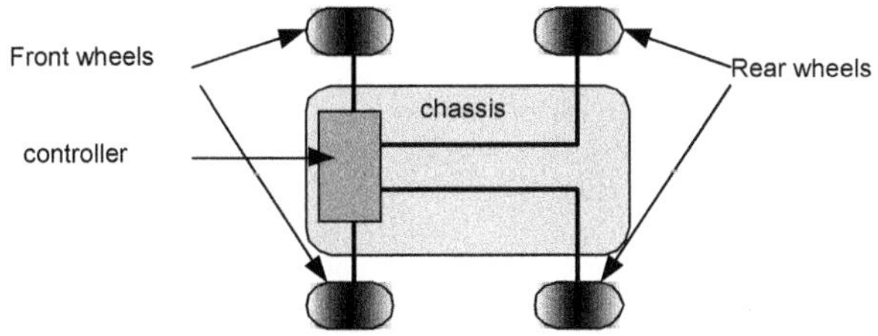

Figure 2-10. A connection diagram for a simple car model.

A simple car example of a connection diagram for an application in the mechanical domain is shown in Figure 2-10. The simple car model below includes variables for subcomponents such as wheels, chassis, and control unit. A "comment" string after the class name briefly describes the class. The wheels are connected to both the chassis and the controller. Connect equations are present, but are not shown in this partial example.

```
class Car  "A car class to combine car components"
  Wheel          w1,w2,w3,w4  "Wheel one to four";
  Chassis        chassis      "Chassis";
  CarController  controller   "Car controller";
  ...
end Car;
```

2.8.3 Connectors and Connector Classes

Modelica connectors are instances of connector classes, which define the variables that are part of the communication interface that is specified by a connector. Thus, connectors specify external interfaces for interaction.

For example, `Pin` is a connector class that can be used to specify the external interfaces for electrical components (Figure 2-11) that have pins. The types `Voltage` and `Current` used within `Pin` are the same as `Real`, but with different associated units. From the Modelica language point of view, the types `Voltage` and `Current` are similar to `Real`, and are regarded as having equivalent types. Checking unit compatibility within equations is optional.

```
type Voltage = Real(unit="V");
type Current = Real(unit="A");
```

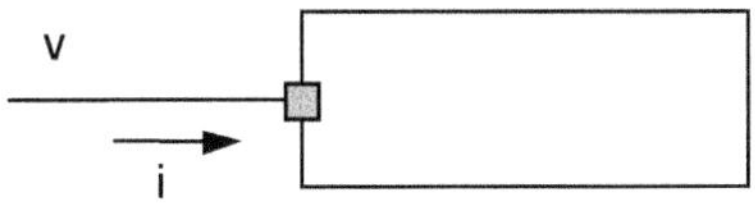

Figure 2-11. A component with one electrical `Pin` connector.

The `Pin` connector class below contains two variables. The `flow` prefix on the second variable indicates that this variable represents a flow quantity, which has special significance for connections as explained in the next section.

```
connector Pin
  Voltage        v;
```

```
   flow Current  i;
end Pin;
```

2.8.4 Connections

Connections between components can be established between connectors of equivalent type. Modelica supports equation-based acausal connections, which means that connections are realized as equations. For acausal connections, the direction of data flow in the connection need not be known. Additionally, causal connections can be established by connecting a connector with an `output` attribute to a connector declared as `input`.

Two types of coupling can be established by connections, depending on whether the variables in the connected connectors are potential (default) or declared using the `flow` prefix:

1. Equality coupling, for potential variables, according to Kirchhoff's first law.
2. Sum-to-zero coupling, for flow variables, according to Kirchhoff's current law.

For example, the keyword `flow` for the variable `i` of type `Current` in the `Pin` connector class indicates that all currents in connected pins are summed to zero, according to Kirchhoff's current law.

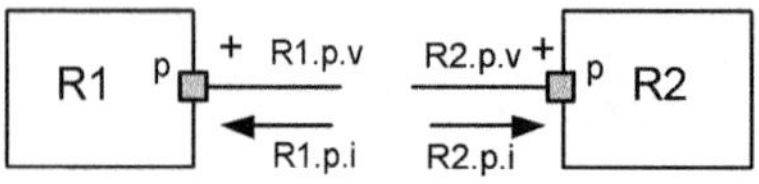

Figure 2-12. Connecting two components that have electrical pins.

Connection equations are used to connect instances of connection classes. A connection equation `connect(R1.p,R2.p)`, with `R1.p` and `R2.p` of connector class `Pin`, connects the two pins (Figure 2-12) so that they form one node. This produces two equations, namely:

```
R1.p.v = R2.p.v
R1.p.i + R2.p.i = 0
```

The first equation says that the voltages of the connected wire ends are the same. The second equation corresponds to Kirchhoff's second law, saying that the currents sum to zero at a node (assuming positive value while flowing into the component). The sum-to-zero equations are generated when the prefix `flow` is used. Similar laws apply to flows in piping networks and to forces and torques in mechanical systems.

See also Section 5.3, page 190, for a complete description of this kind of explicit connections. We should also mention the concept of *implicit connections*, useful for modeling force fields, which is represented by the Modelica `inner/outer` construct and described in more detail in Section 5.8, page 224.

2.8.5 Implicit Connections with inner/outer

So far we have focused on explicit connections between connectors, where each connection is explicitly represented by a `connect`-equation and a corresponding line in a connection diagram. However, when modeling certain kinds of large models with many interacting components this approach becomes rather clumsy because of the large number of potential connections—a connection might be needed between each pair of components. This is especially true for system models involving *force fields*, which lead to a maximum of $n \times n$ connections between the n components influenced by the force field or $1 \times n$ connections between a central object and n components if intercomponent interaction is neglected.

For the case of $1 \times n$ connections, instead of using a large number of explicit connections, Modelica provides a convenient mechanism for *implicit connections* between an object and n of its components through the `inner` and `outer` declaration prefixes.

A rather common kind of implicit interaction is where a *shared attribute* of a single environment object is *accessed* by a number of components within that environment. For example, we might have an environment including house components, each accessing a shared environment temperature, or a circuit board environment with electronic components accessing the board temperature.

A Modelica environment-component example model along these lines is shown below, where a shared environment temperature variable `T0` is declared as a *definition declaration* marked by the keyword `inner`. This declaration is implicitly accessed by the *reference declarations* of `T0` marked by the prefix `outer` in the components `comp1` and `comp2`. For more details, see Section 5.8, page 224.

```
model Environment
  inner Real T0;              //Definition of actual environment temperature T0
  Component comp1, comp2; //Lookup match comp1.T0 = comp2.T0 = T0
  parameter Real k=1;
equation
  T0 = sin(k*time);
end Environment;

model Component
  outer Real T0; // Reference to temperature T0 defined in the environments
  Real T;
equation
  T = T0;
end Component;
```

2.8.6 Expandable Connectors for Information Buses

It is common in engineering to have so-called information buses with the purpose of transporting information between various system components, for example, sensors, actuators, and control units. Some buses are even standardized (e.g., IEEE), but are usually rather generic to allow many kinds of different components.

This is the key idea behind the `expandable connector` construct in Modelica. An expandable connector acts like an information bus since it is intended for connection to many kinds of components. To make this possible, it automatically expands the expandable connector type to accommodate all the components connected to it with their different interfaces. If an element with a certain name and type is not present, it is added.

All fields in an expandable connector are seen as connector instances even if they are not declared as such, that is, it is possible to connect to a `Real` variable for example.

Moreover, when two expandable connectors are connected, each is augmented with the variables that are only declared in the other expandable connector. This is repeated until all connected expandable connector instances have matching variables, that is, each of the connector instances is expanded to be the union of all connector variables. If a variable appears as an input in one expandable connector, it should appear as a non-input in at least one other expandable connector instance in the connected set. The following is a small example:

```
expandable connector EngineBus
end EngineBus;

block Sensor
  RealOutput speed;
end Sensor;

block Actuator
  RealInput speed;
```

```
end Actuator;

model Engine
  EngineBus bus;
  Sensor sensor;
  Actuator actuator;
equation
  connect(bus.speed, sensor.speed); // provides the non-input
  connect(bus.speed, actuator.speed);
end Engine;
```

There are many more issues to consider when using expandable connectors, see for example Section 5.9, page 238.

2.8.7 Stream Connectors

In thermodynamics with fluid applications where there can be bi-directional flows of matter with associated quantities, it turns out that the two basic variable types in a connector—potential variables and flow variables—are not sufficient to describe models that result in a numerically sound solution approach. Such applications typically have bi-directional flow of matter with convective transport of specific quantities, such as specific enthalpy and chemical composition

If we would use conventional connectors with flow and potential variables, the corresponding models would include nonlinear systems of equations with Boolean unknowns for the flow directions and singularities around zero flow. Such equation systems cannot be solved reliably in general. The model formulations can be simplified when formulating two different balance equations for the two possible flow directions. This is, however, not possible using only flow and potential variables.

This fundamental problem is addressed in Modelica by introducing a third type of connector variable, called *stream variable*, declared with the prefix `stream`. A stream variable describes a quantity that is carried by a flow variable, that is, a purely convective transport phenomenon.

If at least one variable in a connector has the `stream` prefix, the connector is called a *stream connector* and the corresponding variable is called a *stream variable*. For example:

```
connector FluidPort
  ...
  flow   Real m_flow     "Flow of matter; m_flow>0 if flow into component";
  stream Real h_outflow "Specific variable in component if m_flow < 0"
end FluidPort

model FluidSystem
  ...
  FluidComponent m1, m2, ..., mN;
  FluidPort      c1, c2, ..., cM;
equation
  connect(m1.c, m2.c);
  ...
  connect(m1.c, cM);
  ...
end FluidSystem;
```

For more details and further explanations, see Section 5.10, page 245, together with an extensive example developed from first principles in Section 15.2, page 800.

2.9 Partial Classes

A common property of many electrical components is that they have two pins. This means that it is useful to define a "blueprint" model class, called `TwoPin`, that captures this common property. This is a *partial class* since it does not contain enough equations to completely specify its physical behavior, and is therefore prefixed by the keyword `partial`. Partial classes are usually known as *abstract classes* in other object-oriented languages. Since a partial class is incomplete it cannot be used as a class to instantiate a data object.

```
partial class TwoPin11 "Superclass of elements with two electrical pins"
  Pin      p, n;
  Voltage  v;
  Current  i;
equation
  v = p.v - n.v;
  0 = p.i + n.i;
  i = p.i;
end TwoPin;
```

The `TwoPin` class has two pins, `p` and `n`, a quantity `v` that defines the voltage drop across the component, and a quantity `i` that defines the current into pin `p`, through the component, and out from pin `n` (Figure 2-13). It is useful to label the pins differently, for example, `p` and `n`, and using graphics such as filled and unfilled squares, respectively, to obtain a well-defined sign for `v` and `i`, although there is no physical difference between these pins in reality.

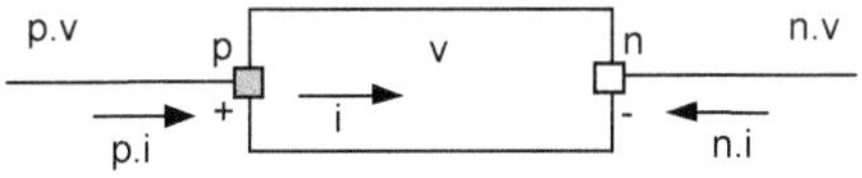

Figure 2-13. Generic `TwoPin` class that describes the general structure of simple electrical components with two pins.

The equations define generic relations between quantities of simple electrical components. In order to be useful, a constitutive equation must be added that describes the specific physical characteristics of the component.

2.9.1 Reuse of Partial Classes

Given the generic partial class `TwoPin`, it is now straightforward to create the more specialized `Resistor` class by adding a constitutive equation:

```
R*i = v;
```

This equation describes the specific physical characteristics of the relation between voltage and current for a resistor (Figure 2-14).

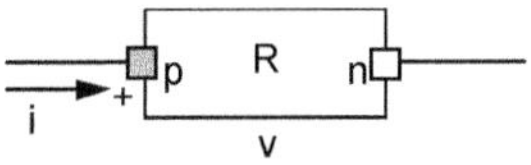

Figure 2-14. A resistor component.

[11] This `TwoPin` class is referred to by the name `Modelica.Electrical.Analog.Interfaces.OnePort` in the Modelica standard library since this is the name used by electrical modeling experts. Here we use the more intuitive name `TwoPin` since the class is used for components with two physical ports and not one. The `OnePort` naming is more understandable if it is viewed as denoting composite ports containing two subports.

```
class Resistor "Ideal electrical resistor"
  extends TwoPin;
  parameter Real R(unit="Ohm") "Resistance";
equation
  R*i = v;
end Resistor;
```

A class for electrical capacitors can also reuse `TwoPin` in a similar way, adding the constitutive equation for a capacitor (Figure 2-15).

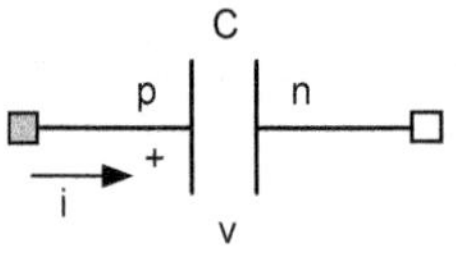

Figure 2-15. A capacitor component.

```
class Capacitor "Ideal electrical capacitor"
  extends TwoPin;
  parameter Real C(Unit="F") "Capacitance";
equation
  C*der(v) = i;
end Capacitor;
```

During system simulation, the variables `i` and `v` specified in the above components evolve as functions of time. The solver of differential equations computes the values of $v(t)$ and $i(t)$ (where t is `time`) such that $C \cdot \dot{v}(t) = i(t)$ for all values of t, fulfilling the constitutive equation for the capacitor.

2.10 Component Library Design and Use

In a way similar to how we previously created the resistor and capacitor components, additional electrical component classes can be created, forming a simple electrical component library that can be used for application models such as the `SimpleCircuit` model. Component libraries of reusable components are actually the key to effective modeling of complex systems.

2.11 Example: Electrical Component Library

Below we show an example of designing a small library of electrical components needed for the simple circuit example, as well as the equations that can be extracted from these components.

2.11.1 Resistor

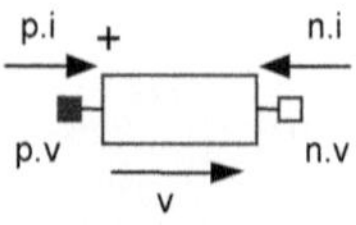

Figure 2-16. Resistor component.

Four equations can be extracted from the resistor model depicted in Figure 2-14 and Figure 2-16. The first three originate from the inherited `TwoPin` class, whereas the last is the constitutive equation of the resistor.

```
0 = p.i + n.i
v = p.v - n.v
i = p.i
v = R*i
```

2.11.2 Capacitor

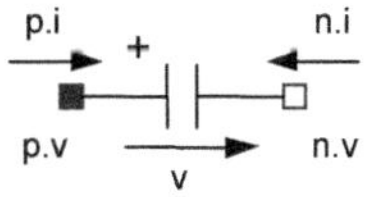

Figure 2-17. Capacitor component.

The following four equations originate from the capacitor model depicted in Figure 2-15 and Figure 2-17, where the last equation is the constitutive equation for the capacitor.

```
0 = p.i + n.i
v = p.v - n.v
i = p.i
i = C * der(v)
```

2.11.3 Inductor

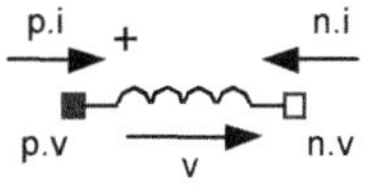

Figure 2-18. Inductor component.

The inductor class depicted in Figure 2-18 and shown below gives a model for ideal electrical inductors.

```
class Inductor "Ideal electrical inductor"
  extends TwoPin;
  parameter Real L(unit="H") "Inductance";
equation
  v = L*der(i);
end Inductor;
```

These equations can be extracted from the inductor class, where the first three come from `TwoPin` as usual and the last is the constitutive equation for the inductor.

```
0 = p.i + n.i
v = p.v - n.v
i = p.i
v = L * der(i)
```

2.11.4 Voltage Source

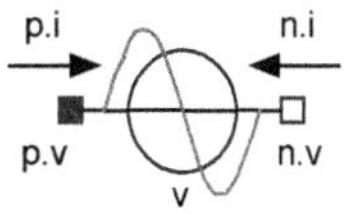

Figure 2-19. Voltage source component `VsourceAC`, where `v(t) = VA*sin(2*PI*f*time)`.

A class `VsourceAC` for the sine-wave voltage source to be used in our circuit example is depicted in Figure 2-19 and can be defined as below. This model as well as other Modelica models specify behavior that evolves as a function of time. Note that the built-in predefined variable `time` is used. In order to keep the example, simple the constant `PI` is explicitly declared even though it is usually imported from the Modelica standard library.

```
class VsourceAC "Sin-wave voltage source"
  extends TwoPin;
  parameter Voltage  VA              = 220 "Amplitude";
  parameter Real     f(unit="Hz")    = 50  "Frequency";
  constant  Real     PI              = 3.141592653589793;
equation
  v = VA*sin(2*PI*f*time);
end VsourceAC;
```

In this `TwoPin`-based model, four equations can be extracted from the model, of which the first three are inherited from `TwoPin`:

```
0 = p.i + n.i
v = p.v - n.v
i = p.i
v = VA*sin(2*PI*f*time)
```

2.11.5 Ground

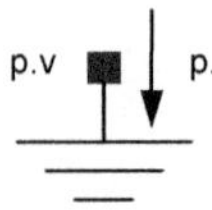

Figure 2-20. Ground component.

Finally, we define a class for ground points that can be instantiated as a reference value for the voltage levels in electrical circuits. This class has only one pin (Figure 2-20).

```
class Ground "Ground"
  Pin p;
equation
  p.v = 0;
end Ground;
```

A single equation can be extracted from the `Ground` class.

```
p.v = 0
```

2.12 The Simple Circuit Model

Having collected a small library of simple electrical components, we can now put together the simple electrical circuit shown previously and in Figure 2-21.

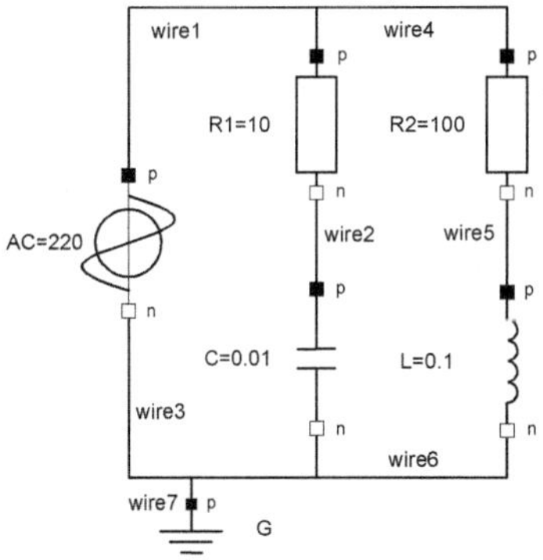

Figure 2-21. The `SimpleCircuit` model.

The two resistor instances `R1` and `R2` are declared with modification equations for their respective resistance parameter values. Similarly, an instance `C` of the capacitor and an instance `L` of the inductor are declared with modifiers for capacitance and inductance respectively. The voltage source `AC` and the ground instance `G` have no modifiers. Connect equations are provided to connect the components in the circuit.

```
class SimpleCircuit
  Resistor  R1(R=10);
  Capacitor C(C=0.01);
  Resistor  R2(R=100);
  Inductor  L(L=0.1);
  VsourceAC AC;
  Ground    G;
equation
  connect(AC.p, R1.p);     // Wire1, Capacitor circuit
  connect(R1.n, C.p);      //    Wire 2
  connect(C.n, AC.n);      //    Wire 3
  connect(R1.p, R2.p);     // Wire4, Inductor circuit
  connect(R2.n, L.p);      //    Wire 5
  connect(L.n,  C.n);      //    Wire 6
  connect(AC.n, G.p);      // Wire7, Ground
end SimpleCircuit;
```

2.13 Arrays

An array is a collection of variables all of the same type. Elements of an array are accessed through simple `Integer` indexes ranging from a lower bound of 1 to an upper bound being the size of the respective dimension, or by `Boolean` indexes from `false` to `true`, or by enumeration indexes. An array variable can be declared by appending dimensions within square brackets after a class name, as in Java, or after a variable name, as in the C language. For example:

```
Real[3]     positionvector = {1,2,3};
Real[3,3]   identitymatrix = {{1,0,0}, {0,1,0}, {0,0,1}};
Real[3,3,3] arr3d;
```

This declares a three-dimensional position vector, a transformation matrix, and a three-dimensional array. Using the alternative syntax of attaching dimensions after the variable name, the same declarations can be expressed as:

```
Real  positionvector[3] = {1,2,3};
Real  identitymatrix[3,3] = {{1,0,0}, {0,1,0}, {0,0,1}};
Real  arr3d[3,3,3];
```

In the first two array declarations, declaration equations have been given, where the array constructor {} is used to construct array values for defining `positionvector` and `identitymatrix`. Indexing of an array `A` is written `A[i,j,...]`, where 1 is the lower bound and `size(A,k)` is the upper bound of the index for the *k*th dimension. Submatrices can be formed by utilizing the : notation for index ranges, for example, `A[i1:i2, j1:j2]`, where a range `i1:i2` means all indexed elements starting with `i1` up to and including `i2`.

Array expressions can be formed using the arithmetic operators +, -, *, and /, since these can operate on either scalars, vectors, matrices, or (when applicable) multidimensional arrays with elements of type `Real` or `Integer`. The multiplication operator * denotes scalar product when used between vectors, matrix multiplication when used between matrices or between a matrix and a vector, and element-wise multiplication when used between an array and a scalar. As an example, multiplying `positionvector` by the scalar `2` is expressed by:

```
positionvector*2
```

which gives the result:

```
{2,4,6}
```

In contrast to Java, arrays of dimensionality > 1 in Modelica are always rectangular as in Matlab or Fortran.

A number of built-in array functions are available, of which a few are shown in the table below.

`transpose(A)`	Permutes the first two dimensions of array A.
`zeros(n1,n2,n3,...)`	Returns an n_1 x n_2 x n_3 x... zero-filled integer array.
`ones(n1,n2,n3,...)`	Returns an n_1 x n_2 x n_3 x ... one-filled integer array.
`fill(s,n1,n2,n3, ...)`	Returns the n_1 x n_2 x n_3 x ... array with all elements filled with the value of the scalar expression s.
`min(A)`	Returns the smallest element of array expression A.
`max(A)`	Returns the largest element of array expression A.
`sum(A)`	Returns the sum of all the elements of array expression A.

A scalar Modelica function of a scalar argument is automatically generalized to be applicable also to arrays element-wise. For example, if `A` is a vector of real numbers, then `cos(A)` is a vector where each element is the result of applying the function `cos` to the corresponding element in `A`. For example:

```
cos({1, 2, 3})  =  {cos(1), cos(2), cos(3)}
```

General array concatenation can be done through the array concatenation operator `cat(k,A,B,C,...)` that concatenates the arrays `A,B,C,...` along the `k`th dimension. For example, `cat(1,{2,3}, {5,8,4})` gives the result `{2,3,5,8,4}`.

The common special cases of concatenation along the first and second dimensions are supported through the special syntax forms `[A;B;C;...]` and `[A,B,C,...]` respectively. Both of these forms can be mixed. In order to achieve compatibility with Matlab array syntax, being a de facto standard, scalar and vector arguments to these special operators are promoted to become matrices before performing the concatenation. This gives the effect that a matrix can be constructed from scalar expressions by separating rows by semicolons and columns by commas. The example below creates an $m \times n$ matrix:

```
[expr11, expr12, ... expr1n;
expr21, expr22, ... expr2n;
...
exprm1, exprm2, ... exprmn]
```

It is instructive to follow the process of creating a matrix from scalar expressions using these operators. For example:

```
[1,2;
 3,4]
```

First each scalar argument is promoted to become a matrix, giving

```
[{{1}}, {{2}};
 {{3}}, {{4}}]
```

Since [... , ...] for concatenation along the second dimension has higher priority than [... ; ...], which concatenates along the first dimension, the first concatenation step gives

```
[{{1, 2}};
 {{3, 4}}]
```

Finally, the row matrices are concatenated giving the desired 2×2 matrix:

```
{{1, 2},
 {3, 4}}
```

The special case of just one scalar argument can be used to create a 1×1 matrix. For example:

```
[1]
```

gives the matrix:

```
{{1}}
```

See also Chapter 7, page 311, for a complete overview of Modelica arrays.

2.14 Algorithmic Constructs

Even though equations are eminently suitable for modeling physical systems and for a number of other tasks, there are situations where nondeclarative algorithmic constructs are needed. This is typically the case for algorithms, that is, procedural descriptions of how to carry out specific computations, usually consisting of a number of statements that should be executed in the specified order.

2.14.1 Algorithm Sections and Assignment Statements

In Modelica, algorithmic statements can occur only within algorithm sections, starting with the keyword `algorithm`. Algorithm sections may also be called algorithm equations, since an algorithm section can be viewed as a group of equations involving one or more variables, and can appear among equation sections. Algorithm sections are terminated by the appearance of one of the keywords `equation`, `public`, `protected`, `algorithm`, `end`, or `annotation`.

```
algorithm
  ...
  <statements>
  ...
  <some other keyword>
```

An algorithm section embedded among equation sections can appear as below, where the example algorithm section contains three assignment statements.

```
equation
  x = y*2;
  z = w;
algorithm
```

```
    x1 := z+x;
    x2 := y-5;
    x1 := x2+y;
  equation
    u = x1+x2;
    ...
```

Note that the code in the algorithm section, sometimes denoted algorithm equation, uses the values of certain variables from outside the algorithm. These variables are called *input variables* to the algorithm—in this example `x`, `y`, and `z`. Analogously, variables assigned values by the algorithm define the *outputs of the algorithm*—in this example `x1` and `x2`. This makes the semantics of an algorithm section quite similar to a function with the algorithm section as its body, and with `input` and `output` formal parameters corresponding to inputs and outputs as described above.

See also Chapter 9, page 421, regarding algorithms and functions.

2.14.2 Statements

In addition to assignment statements, which were used in the previous example, a few other kinds of "algorithmic" statements are available in Modelica: `if-then-else` statements, for-loops, while-loops, return statements, and so on. The summation below uses both a while-loop and an if-statement, where `size(a,1)` returns the size of the first dimension of array `a`. The elseif- and else-parts of if-statements are optional.

```
sum := 0;
n := size(a,1);
while n>0 loop
  if a[n]>0 then
    sum := sum + a[n];
  elseif a[n] > -1 then
    sum := sum - a[n] -1;
  else
    sum := sum - a[n];
  end if;
  n := n-1;
end while;
```

Both for-loops and while-loops can be immediately terminated by executing a break-statement inside the loop. Such a statement just consists of the keyword `break` followed by a semicolon.

Consider once more the computation of the polynomial presented in Section 2.6.1 on repetitive equation structures, page 35:

```
y := a[1]+a[2]*x + a[3]*x^1 + ... + a[n+1]*x^n;
```

When using equations to model the computation of the polynomial, it was necessary to introduce an auxiliary vector `xpowers` for storing the different powers of `x`. Alternatively, the same computation can be expressed as an algorithm including a for-loop as below. This can be done without the need for an extra vector—it is enough to use a scalar variable `xpower` for the most recently computed power of `x`.

```
algorithm
  y := 0;
  xpower := 1;
  for i in 1:n+1 loop
    y := y + a[i]*xpower;
    xpower := xpower*x;
  end for;
  ...
```

See Section 9.2.3, page 425, for descriptions of statement constructs in Modelica.

2.14.3 Functions

Functions are a natural part of any mathematical model. A number of mathematical functions like abs, sqrt, mod,sin, cos, exp, and so on are both predefined in the Modelica language and available in the Modelica standard math library Modelica.Math. The arithmetic operators +, -, *, / can be regarded as functions that are used through a convenient operator syntax. Thus it is natural to have user-defined mathematical functions in the Modelica language. The body of a Modelica function is an algorithm section that contains procedural algorithmic code to be executed when the function is called. Formal parameters are specified using the input keyword, whereas results are denoted using the output keyword. This makes the syntax of function definitions quite close to Modelica block class definitions.

Modelica functions are *mathematical functions*, that is, without global side-effects and with no memory (except impure Modelica functions marked with the keyword impure). A Modelica function always returns the same results given the same arguments. Below we show the algorithmic code for polynomial evaluation in a function named polynomialEvaluator.

```
function polynomialEvaluator
  input  Real a[:];        // Array, size defined at function call time
  input  Real x := 1.0;    // Default value 1.0 for x
  output Real y;
protected
  Real   xpower;
algorithm
  y := 0;
  xpower := 1;
  for i in 1:size(a,1) loop
    y := y + a[i]*xpower;
    xpower := xpower*x;
  end for;
end polynomialEvaluator;
```

Functions are usually called with positional association of actual arguments to formal parameters. For example, in the call below the actual argument {1,2,3,4} becomes the value of the coefficient vector a, and 21 becomes the value of the formal parameter x. Modelica function formal parameters are read-only, i.e., they may not be assigned values within the code of the function. When a function is called using positional argument association, the number of actual arguments and formal parameters must be the same. The types of the actual argument expressions must be compatible with the declared types of the corresponding formal parameters. This allows passing array arguments of arbitrary length to functions with array formal parameters with unspecified length, as in the case of the input formal parameter a in the polynomialEvaluator function:

```
p = polynomialEvaluator({1, 2, 3, 4}, 21);
```

The same call to the function polynomialEvaluator can instead be made using named association of actual arguments to formal parameters, as in the next example. This has the advantage that the code becomes more self-documenting as well as more flexible with respect to code updates.

For example, if all calls to the function polynomialEvaluator are made using named parameter association, the order between the formal parameters a and x can be changed, and new formal parameters with default values can be introduced in the function definitions without causing any compilation errors at the call sites. Formal parameters with default values need not be specified as actual arguments unless those parameters should be assigned values different from the defaults:

```
p = polynomialEvaluator(a={1, 2, 3, 4}, x=21);
```

Functions can have multiple results. For example, the function f below has three result parameters declared as three formal output parameters r1, r2, and r3:

```
function f
```

```
    input Real x;
    input Real y;
    output Real r1;
    output Real r2;
    output Real r3;
    ...
  end f;
```

Within algorithmic code, multiresult functions may be called only in special assignment statements, as the one below, where the variables on the left-hand side are assigned the corresponding function results:

```
(a, b, c) := f(1.0, 2.0);
```

In equations a similar syntax is used:

```
(a, b, c) = f(1.0, 2.0);
```

A function is returned from by reaching the end of the function or by executing a return-statement inside the function body.

See also Section 9.3, page 438, for more information regarding functions.

2.14.4 Operator Overloading and Complex Numbers

Function and operator overloading allow several definitions of the same function or operator, but with a different set of input formal parameter types for each definition. This allows one, for example, to define operators such as addition and multiplication of complex numbers, using the ordinary + and * operators but with new definitions, or provide several definitions of a `solve` function for linear matrix equation solution for different matrix representations such as standard dense matrices, sparse matrices, and symmetric matrices.

In fact, overloading already exists predefined to a limited extent for certain operators in the Modelica language. For example, the plus (+) operator for addition has several different definitions depending on the data type:

- 1+2— means integer addition of two integer constants giving an integer result, here 3.
- 1.0+2.0— means floating point number addition of two `Real` constants giving a floating-point number result, here 3.0.
- "ab"+"2"— means string concatenation of two string constants giving a string result, here "ab2."
- {1,2}+{3,4}— means integer vector addition of two integer constant vectors giving a vector result, here {4,6}.

Overloaded operators for user-defined data types can be defined using `operator record` and `operator function` declarations. Here we show part of a complex numbers data type example:

```
operator record Complex "Record defining a Complex number"

  Real re "Real part of complex number";
  Real im "Imaginary part of complex number";

  encapsulated operator 'constructor'
   import Complex;

    function fromReal
      input  Real re;
      output Complex result = Complex(re=re, im=0.0);
        annotation(Inline=true);
    end fromReal;
  end 'constructor';
```

```
  encapsulated operator function '+'
   import Complex;
    input  Complex c1;
    input  Complex c2;
    output Complex result  "Same as: c1 + c2";
      annotation(Inline=true);
  algorithm
    result := Complex(c1.re + c2.re, c1.im + c2.im);
  end '+';

end Complex;
```

In the above example we start as usual with the real and imaginary part declarations of the `re` and `im` fields of the `Complex` operator record definition. Then comes a *constructor definition* `fromReal` with only one input argument instead of the two inputs of the default `Complex` constructor implicitly defined by the `Complex` record definition, followed by overloaded operator definition for `'+'`.

How can these definitions be used? Take a look at the following small example:

```
Real    a;
Complex b;
Complex c = a + b;   // Addition of Real number a and Complex number b
```

The interesting part is in the third line, which contains an addition `a+b` of a `Real` number `a` and a `Complex` number `b`. There is no built-in addition operator for complex numbers, but we have the above overloaded operator definition of `'+'` for two complex numbers. An addition of two complex numbers would match this definition right away in the lookup process.

However, in this case we have an addition of a real number and a complex number. Fortunately, the lookup process for overloaded binary operators can also handle this case if there is a constructor function in the `Complex` record definition that can convert a real number to a complex number. Here we have such a constructor called `fromReal`.

Note that the `Complex` is already predefined in a Modelica record type called `Complex`. This is distributed as part of the standard Modelica library (MSL) but defined at the top level outside of MSL. It is referred to as `Complex` or `.Complex`. and is automatically preloaded by most tools, enabling direct usage without the need for any import statements (except in encapsulated classes). There is a library ComplexMath with operations on complex numbers (Section 16.3, page 923). See Section 9.5, page 481 for more information regarding this topic.

The following are some examples of using the predefined type `Complex`:

```
Real a = 2;
Complex j = Modelica.ComplexMath.j;
Complex b = 2 + 3*j;
Complex c = (2*b + a)/b;
Complex d = Modelica.ComplexMath.sin(c);
Complex v[3] = {b/2, c, 2*d};
```

2.14.5 External Functions

It is possible to call functions defined outside of the Modelica language, implemented in C or Fortran. If no external language is specified, the implementation language is assumed to be C. The body of an external function is marked with the keyword `external` in the Modelica external function declaration:

```
function log
  input Real x;
  output Real y;
external
end log;
```

The external function interface supports a number of advanced features such as in–out parameters, local work arrays, external function argument order, and explicit specification of row-major versus column-major array memory layout. For example, the formal parameter `Ares` corresponds to an in–out parameter in the external function `leastSquares` below, which has the value `A` as input default and a different value as the result. It is possible to control the ordering and usage of parameters to the function external to Modelica. This is used below to explicitly pass sizes of array dimensions to the Fortran routine called `dgels`. Some old-style Fortran routines like `dgels` need work arrays, which is conveniently handled by local variable declarations after the keyword `protected`.

```
function leastSquares "Solves a linear least squares problem"
  input Real A[:,:];
  input Real B[:,:];
  output Real Ares[size(A,1),size(A,2)] := A;
    //Factorization is returned in Ares for later use
  output Real x[size(A,2),size(B,2)];
protected
  Integer lwork = min(size(A,1),size(A,2))+
                  max(max(size(A,1),size(A,2)),size(B,2))*32;
  Real work[lwork];
  Integer info;
  String transposed="NNNN"; // Workaround for passing CHARACTER data to
                            // Fortran routine
  external "FORTRAN 77"
  dgels(transposed, 100, size(A,1), size(A,2), size(B,2), Ares,
        size(A,1), B, size(B,1), work, lwork, info);
end leastSquares;
```

See also Section 9.4, page 466, regarding external functions.

2.14.6 Algorithms Viewed as Functions

The function concept is a basic building block when defining the semantics or meaning of programming language constructs. Some programming languages are completely defined in terms of mathematical functions. This makes it useful to try to understand and define the semantics of algorithm sections in Modelica in terms of functions. For example, consider the algorithm section below, which occurs in an equation context:

```
algorithm
  y := x;
  z := 2*y;
  y := z+y;
  ...
```

This algorithm can be transformed into an equation and a function as below, without changing its meaning. The equation equates the output variables of the previous algorithm section with the results of the function `f`. The function `f` has the inputs to the algorithm section as its input formal parameters and the outputs as its result parameters. The algorithmic code of the algorithm section has become the body of the function `f`.

```
(y,z) = f(x);
...
function f
  input Real x;
  output Real y,z;
algorithm
  y := x;
  z := 2*y;
```

```
    y := z+y;
end f;
```

2.15 Discrete-Event and Hybrid Modeling

Macroscopic physical systems in general evolve continuously as a function of time, obeying the laws of physics. This includes the movements of parts in mechanical systems and current and voltage levels in electrical systems, chemical reactions. Such systems are said to have continuous dynamics.

On the other hand, it is sometimes beneficial to make the approximation that certain system components display discrete behavior, that is, changes of values of system variables may occur instantaneously and discontinuously at specific points in time.

In the real physical system, the change can be very fast, but not instantaneous. Examples are collisions in mechanical systems, for example, a bouncing ball that almost instantaneously changes direction, switches in electrical circuits with quickly changing voltage levels, and valves and pumps in chemical plants. We talk about system components with discrete-time dynamics. The reason to make the discrete approximation is to simplify the mathematical model of the system, making the model more tractable and usually speeding up the simulation of the model several orders of magnitude.

For this reason it is possible to have variables in Modelica models of *discrete-time variability*, that is, the variables change value only at specific points in time, so-called *events*. There are two kinds of discrete-time variables: *unclocked discrete-time variables,* which keep their values constant between events, and *clocked discrete-time variables,* which are undefined between associated clock-tick events; see Figure 2-22. Examples of discrete-time variables are `Real` variables declared with the prefix `discrete`, clock variables and clocked variables, or `Integer`, `Boolean`, and `enumeration` variables, which are discrete-time by default and cannot be continuous-time.

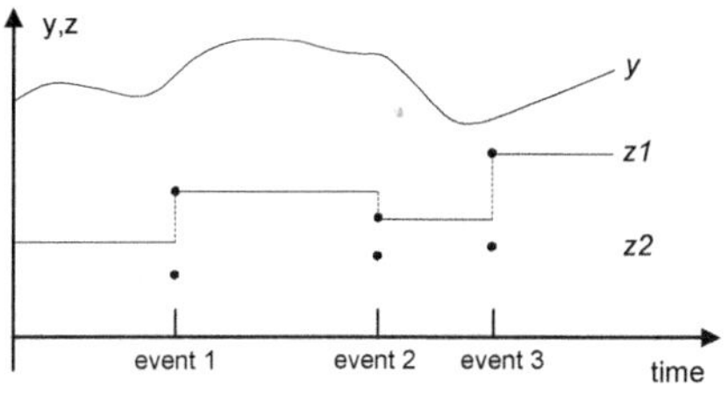

Figure 2-22. Discrete-time variables *z1* and *z2* change value only at event instants, whereas continuous-time variables like *y* may change value both between and at events. An unclocked discrete-time variable *z1* is defined also between events, whereas a clocked discrete-time variable *z2* is defined only at associated clock-tick events.

Since the discrete-time approximation can only be applied to certain subsystems, we often arrive at system models consisting of interacting continuous and discrete components. Such a system is called a *hybrid system* and the associated modeling techniques *hybrid modeling*. The introduction of hybrid mathematical models creates new difficulties for their solution, but the disadvantages are far outweighed by the advantages.

Modelica provides four kinds of constructs for expressing hybrid models: conditional expressions or equations to describe discontinuous and conditional models, when-equations to express equations that are valid only at discontinuities (e.g., when certain conditions become true), clocked synchronous constructs, and clocked state machines. For example, if-then-else conditional expressions allow modeling of phenomena with different expressions in different operating regions, as for the equation describing a limiter below:

```
y = if v > limit then limit else v;
```

A more complete example of a conditional model is the model of an ideal diode. The characteristic of a real physical diode is depicted in Figure 2-23 and the ideal diode characteristic in parameterized form is shown in Figure 2-24.

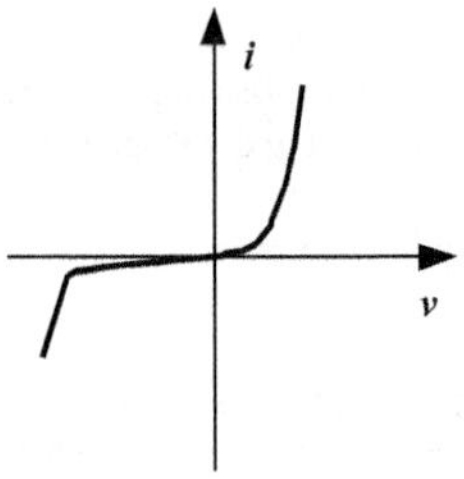

Figure 2-23. Real diode characteristic.

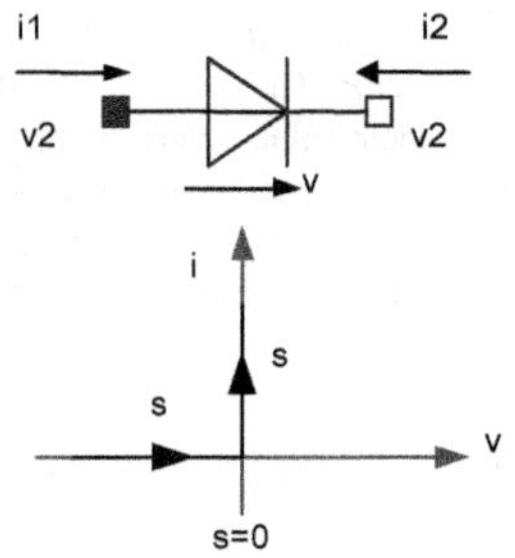

Figure 2-24. Ideal diode characteristic.

Since the voltage level of the ideal diode would go to infinity in an ordinary voltage-current diagram, a parameterized description is more appropriate, where both the voltage v and the current i, same as i1, are functions of the parameter s. When the diode is off, no current flows and the voltage is negative, whereas when it is on there is no voltage drop over the diode and the current flows.

```
model Diode "Ideal diode"
  extends TwoPin;
  Real s;
  Boolean off;
equation
  off = s < 0;
  if off
    then v=s;
    else v=0;    // conditional equations
  end if;
  i = if off then 0 else s;    // conditional expression
end Diode;
```

When-equations have been introduced in Modelica to express instantaneous equations, equations that are valid only at certain points in time that, for example, occur at discontinuities when specific conditions become true, so-called *events*. The syntax of when-equations for the case of a vector of conditions is shown below. The equations in the when-equation are activated when at least one of the conditions becomes true, and remain activated only for a time instant of zero duration. A single condition is also possible.

```
when {condition1, condition2, ...} then
  <equations>
end when;
```

A bouncing ball is a good example of a hybrid system for which the when-equation is appropriate when modeled. The motion of the ball is characterized by the variable `height` above the ground and the vertical `velocity`. The ball moves continuously between bounces, whereas discrete changes occur at bounce times, as depicted in Figure 2-25. When the ball bounces against the ground its velocity is reversed. An ideal ball would have an elasticity coefficient of 1 and would not lose any energy at a bounce. A more realistic ball, as the one modeled below, has an elasticity coefficient of 0.9, making it keep 90 percent of its speed after the bounce.

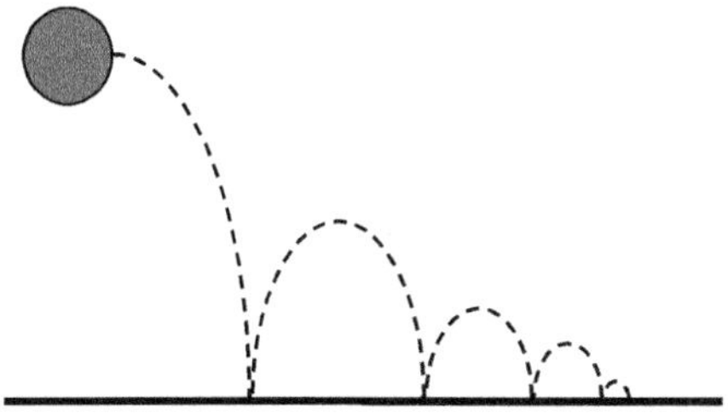

Figure 2-25. A bouncing ball.

The bouncing ball model contains the two basic equations of motion relating height and velocity as well as the acceleration caused by the gravitational force. At the bounce instant, the velocity is suddenly reversed and slightly decreased—`velocity` (after bounce) = `-c*velocity` (before bounce)—which is accomplished by the special `reinit` syntactic form of instantaneous equation for reinitialization: `reinit(velocity,-c*pre(velocity))`, which in this case reinitializes the `velocity` variable.

```
model BouncingBall "Simple model of a bouncing ball"
  constant  Real g = 9.81      "Gravity constant";
  parameter Real c = 0.9       "Coefficient of restitution";
  parameter Real radius=0.1    "Radius of the ball";
  Real height(start = 1)       "Height of the ball center";
  Real velocity(start = 0)     "Velocity of the ball";
equation
  der(height) = velocity;
  der(velocity) = -g;
  when height <= radius then
    reinit(velocity,-c*pre(velocity));
  end when;
end BouncingBall;
```

Note that the equations within a when-equation are active only during the instant in time when the condition(s) of the when-equation become `true`, whereas the conditional equations within an if-equation are active as long as the condition of the if-equation is true.

If we simulate this model long enough, the ball will fall through the ground. This strange behavior of the simulation, called shattering or the Zeno effect (explained in more detail in Section 18.2.5.6, page 1015), is due to the limited precision of floating-point numbers together with the event-detection mechanism of the simulator, and occurs for some (unphysical) models where events may occur infinitely close to each other. The real problem in this case is that the model of the impact is not realistic—the law `new_velocity = -c*velocity` does not hold for very small velocities. A simple fix is to state a condition when the ball falls through the ground and then switch to an equation stating that the ball is lying on the ground. A better but more complicated solution is to switch to a more realistic material model.

See also Section 8.3.4, page 355; Section 9.2.10, page 433; and Chapter 13, page 591, regarding discrete and hybrid issues.

2.15.1 Synchronous Clocks and State Machines

Starting from Modelica version 3.3, two main groups of discrete-time and hybrid modeling features are available in the language: built-in synchronous clocks with constructs for clock-based modeling and synchronous clock-based state machines.

As depicted in Figure 2-22, clocks and clocked discrete-time variable values are only defined at clock-tick events for an associated clock and are undefined between clock ticks.

Synchronous clock-based modeling gives additional advantages for real-time and embedded system modeling in terms of higher performance and avoidance and/or detection of certain kinds of errors.

To give a very simple example, in the model below the clock variable `clk` is defined with an interval of 0.2 seconds. This clock is used for sampling the built-in `time` variable, with result put in `x` and defined only at clock ticks. Finally the variable `y` is defined also between clock ticks by the use of the `hold` operator.

```
model BasicClockedSynchronous
  Clock          clk  "A clock variable";
  discrete Real   x   "Clocked discrete-time variable";
  Real            y   "Unclocked discrete-time variable";
equation
  clk = Clock(0.2);         // Clock with an interval of 0.2 seconds
  x = sample(time,clk);     // Sample the continuous time at clock ticks
  y = hold(x)+1;            // Hold value is defined also between clock ticks
end BasicClockedSynchronous;
```

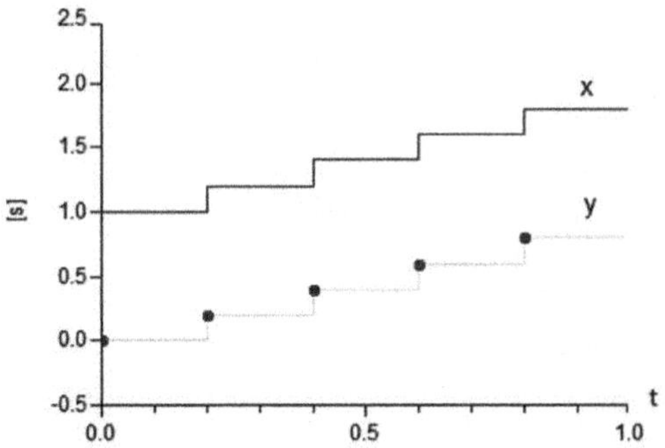

Figure 2-26. Simulation of model `BasicClockedSynchronous` showing clocked discrete-time variable x and unclocked discrete-time variable y.

2.16 Packages

Name conflicts are a major problem when developing reusable code, for example, libraries of reusable Modelica classes and functions for various application domains. No matter how carefully names are chosen for classes and variables, it is likely that someone else is using some name for a different purpose. This problem gets worse if we are using short descriptive names since such names are easy to use and therefore quite popular, making them quite likely to be used in another person's code.

A common solution to avoid name collisions is to attach a short prefix to a set of related names, which are grouped into a package. For example, all names in the X-Windows toolkit have the prefix Xt, and most definitions in the Qt GUI library are prefixed with Q. This works reasonably well for a small number of packages, but the likelihood of name collisions increases as the number of packages grows.

Many programming languages, for example, Java and Ada as well as Modelica, provide a safer and more systematic way of avoiding name collisions through the concept of *package*. A package is simply a container or name space for names of classes, functions, constants, and other allowed definitions. The package name is prefixed to all definitions in the package using standard dot notation. Definitions can be *imported* into the name space of a package.

Modelica has defined the package concept as a restriction and enhancement of the class concept. Thus, inheritance could be used for importing definitions into the name space of another package. However, this leads to conceptual modeling problems since inheritance for import is not really a package specialization. Instead, an `import` language construct is provided for Modelica packages. The type name `Voltage` together with all other definitions in `Modelica.SIunits` is imported in the example below, which makes it possible to use it without prefix for declaration of the variable `v`. By contrast, the declaration of the variable `i` uses the fully qualified name `Modelica.SIunits.Ampere` of the type `Ampere`, even though the short version also would have been possible. The fully qualified long name for `Ampere` can be used since it is found using the standard nested lookup of the `Modelica` standard library placed in a conceptual top-level package.

```
package MyPack
  import MyTypes.*;
  import Modelica.SIunits.*;

  class Foo;
    Voltage  v;
    Modelica.SIunits.Ampere  i;
  end Foo;

end MyPack;
```

Importing definitions from one package into another class as in the above example has the drawback that the introduction of new definitions into a package may cause name clashes with definitions in packages using that package. For example, if a type definition named `Voltage` is introduced into the package `MyTypes`, a compilation error would arise in the package `MyPack` since it is also defined in the package `Modelica.SIunits`.

An alternative solution to the short-name problem that does not have the drawback of possible compilation errors when new definitions are added to libraries is introducing short, convenient name aliases for prefixes instead of long package prefixes. This is possible using the renaming form of `import` statement as in the package `MyPack` below, where the package name `SI` is introduced instead of the much longer `Modelica.SIunits`.

Another disadvantage of the above package is that the `Ampere` type is referred to using standard nested lookup and not via an explicit `import` statement. Thus, in the worst case we may have to do the following in order to find all such dependencies and the declarations they refer to:

- Visually scan the whole source code of the current package, which might be large.
- Search through all packages containing the current package, that is, higher up in the package hierarchy, since standard nested lookup allows used types and other definitions to be declared anywhere above the current position in the hierarchy.

Instead, a *well-designed package* should state all its dependencies *explicitly* through `import` statements that are easy to find. We can create such a package, for example, the package `MyPack` below, by adding the prefix `encapsulated` in front of the `package` keyword. This prevents nested lookup outside the package boundary (unfortunately with one exception—names starting with a dot . , see Section 3.17.3, page 112), ensuring that all dependencies on other packages outside the current package have to be explicitly stated as `import` statements. This kind of encapsulated package represents an independent unit of code and corresponds more closely to the package concept found in many other programming languages such as Java or Ada.

```
encapsulated package MyPack
  import SI = Modelica.SIunits;
  import Modelica;

  class Foo;
    SI.Voltage v;
    Modelica.SIunits.Ampere i;
  end Foo;
  ...

end MyPack;
```

See Chapter 10, page 495, for additional details concerning packages and import.

2.17 Annotations

A Modelica annotation is extra information associated with a Modelica model. This additional information is used by Modelica environments for supporting documentation or graphical model editing. Most annotations do not influence the execution of a simulation—the same results should be obtained even if the annotations are removed—but there are exceptions to this rule. The syntax of an annotation is as follows:

```
annotation(annotation_elements)
```

where *annotation_elements* is a comma-separated list of annotation elements that can be any kind of expression compatible with the Modelica syntax. The following is a resistor class with its associated annotation for the icon representation of the resistor used in the graphical model editor:

```
model Resistor
  ...
  annotation(Icon(coordinateSystem(preserveAspectRatio = true,
    extent = {{-100,-100},{100,100}}, grid = {2,2}),
    graphics = {
      Rectangle(extent = {{-70,30},{70,-30}}, lineColor = {0,0,255},
        fillColor = {255,255,255}, fillPattern = FillPattern.Solid),
      Line(points = {{-90,0},{-70,0}}, color = {0,0,255}),
      Line(points = {{70,0},{90,0}}, color ={0,0,255}),
      Text(extent = {{-144,-40},{142,-72}}, lineColor = {0,0,0},
        textString = "R=%R"),
      ...
  ));
end Resistor;
```

Another example is the predefined annotation `choices`, used to generate menus for the graphical user interface:

```
annotation(choices(choice=1 "P",  choice=2 "PI",  choice=3 "PID"));
```

The annotation `Documentation` is used for model documentation, as in this example for the `Capacitor` model:

```
annotation(
  Documentation(info = "<HTML>
    <p>
```

```
    The linear capacitor connects the branch voltage <i>v</i> with the
    branch current <i>i</i> by <i>i = C * dv/dt</i>.
    The Capacitance <i>C</i> is allowed to be positive, zero, or negative.
    </p>
    </HTML>
)
```

The external function annotation `arrayLayout` can be used to explicitly give the layout of arrays, e.g., if it deviates from the defaults `rowMajor` and `columnMajor` order for the external languages C and Fortran 77 respectively.

This is one of the rare cases of an annotation influencing the simulation results, since the wrong array layout annotation obviously will have consequences for matrix computations. An example:

```
annotation(arrayLayout = "columnMajor");
```

See also Chapter 11, page 519.

2.18 Naming Conventions

You may have noticed a certain style of naming classes and variables in the examples in this chapter. In fact, certain naming conventions, described below, are being adhered to. These naming conventions have been adopted in the Modelica standard library, making the code more readable and somewhat reducing the risk for name conflicts. The naming conventions are largely followed in the examples in this book and are recommended for Modelica code in general:

- Type and class names (but usually not functions) always start with an uppercase letter, for example, `Voltage`.
- Variable names start with a lowercase letter, e.g., `body`, with the exception of some one-letter names such as T for temperature.
- Names consisting of several words have each word capitalized, with the initial word subject to the above rules, for example, `ElectricCurrent` and `bodyPart`.
- The underscore character is only used at the end of a name, or at the end of a word within a name, often to characterize lower or upper indices, for example, `body_low_up`.
- Preferred names for connector instances in (partial) models are `p` and `n` for positive and negative connectors in electrical components, and name variants containing `a` and `b`, for example, `flange_a` and `flange_b`, for other kinds of otherwise-identical connectors often occurring in two-sided components.

For more details on naming conventions see Appendix D, page 1095, and the documentation inside the package.

2.19 Modelica Standard Library

Much of the power of modeling with Modelica comes from the ease of reusing model classes. Related classes in particular areas are grouped into packages to make them easier to find.

A special package, called `Modelica`, is a standardized predefined package that together with the Modelica Language is developed and maintained by the Modelica Association. This package is also known as the *Modelica Standard Library*, abbreviated MSL. It provides constants, types, connector classes, partial models, and model classes of components from various application areas, which are grouped into subpackages of the `Modelica` package, known as the Modelica standard libraries.

The following is a subset of the growing set of Modelica standard libraries currently available:

`Modelica.Constants`	Common constants from mathematics, physics, etc.
`Modelica.Icons`	Graphical layout of icon definitions used in several packages.
`Modelica.Math`	Definitions of common mathematical functions.
`Modelica.SIUnits`	Type definitions with SI standard names and units.
`Modelica.Electrical`	Common electrical component models.
`Modelica.Blocks`	Input/output blocks for use in block diagrams.
`Modelica.Mechanics.Translational`	1D mechanical translational components.
`Modelica.Mechanics.Rotational`	1D mechanical rotational components.
`Modelica.Mechanics.MultiBody`	MBS library—3D mechanical multibody models.
`Modelica.Thermal`	Thermal phenomena, heat flow, etc. components.
...	...

Additional libraries are available in application areas such as thermodynamics, hydraulics, power systems and data communication.

The Modelica Standard Library can be used freely for both noncommercial and commercial purposes under the conditions of *The Modelica License* as stated in the front pages of this book. The full documentation as well as the source code of these libraries appear at the Modelica web site.

So far the models presented have been constructed of components from single-application domains. However, one of the main advantages with Modelica is the ease of constructing multidomain models simply by connecting components from different application-domain libraries. The DC (direct current) motor depicted in Figure 2-27 is one of the simplest examples illustrating this capability.

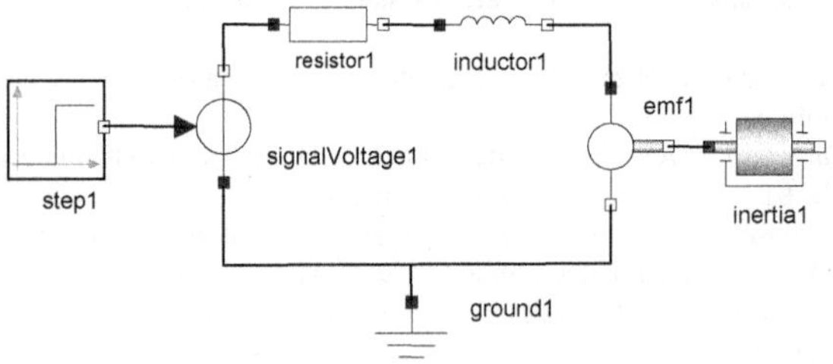

Figure 2-27. A multidomain `DCMotorCircuit` model with mechanical, electrical, and signal block components.

This particular model contains components from the three domains, mechanical, electrical, and signal blocks, corresponding to the libraries `Modelica.Mechanics`, `Modelica.Electrical`, and `Modelica.Blocks`.

Model classes from libraries are particularly easy to use and combine when using a graphical model editor, as depicted in Figure 2-28, where the DC-motor model is being constructed. The left window shows the `Modelica.Mechanics.Rotational` library, from which icons can be dragged and dropped into the central window when performing graphic design of the model.

See Chapter 16, page 909, for an overview of many of the current Modelica libraries, and Appendix D, page 1095, for samples of source code.

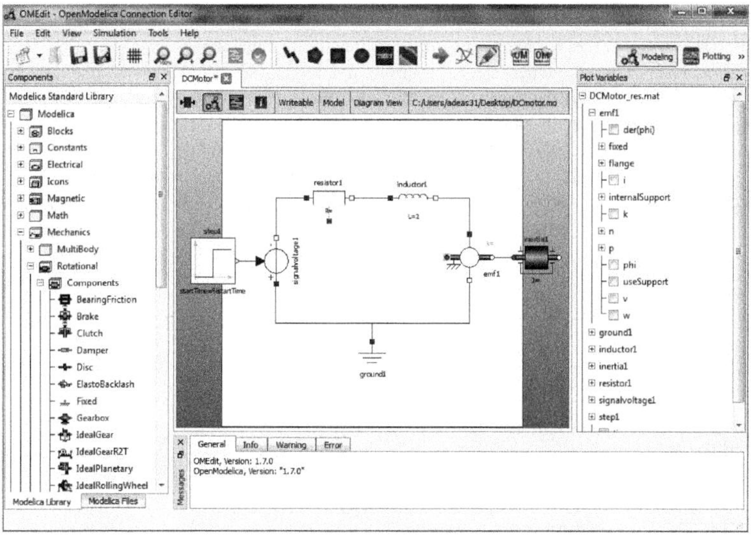

Figure 2-28. Graphical editing of an electrical DC-motor model, with part of the model component hierarchy at the right and icons of the `Modelica` standard library in the left window.

2.20 Implementation and Execution of Modelica

In order to gain a better understanding of how Modelica works, it is useful to take a look at the typical process of translation and execution of a Modelica model, which is sketched in Figure 2-29. Note that this is the typical process used by most Modelica tools. There are alternative ways of executing Modelica, some of which are currently at the research stage, that often keep more of the object-oriented structure at the later stages of translation and execution.

First the Modelica source code is parsed and converted into an internal representation, usually an abstract syntax tree. This representation is analyzed, type checking is done, classes are inherited and expanded, modifications and instantiations are performed, connect equations are converted to standard equations, and so on. The result of this analysis and translation process is a flat set of equations, constants, variables, and function definitions. No trace of the object-oriented structure remains, apart from the dot notation within names.

After flattening, all of the equations are topologically sorted according to the data-flow dependencies between the equations. In the case of general differential algebraic equations (DAEs), this is not just sorting, but also manipulation of the equations to convert the coefficient matrix into block lower triangular form, a so-called BLT transformation. Then an optimizer module containing algebraic simplification algorithms, symbolic index reduction methods, and so on, eliminates most equations, keeping only a minimal set that eventually will be solved numerically.

Then independent equations in explicit form are converted to assignment statements. This is possible since the equations have been sorted and an execution order has been established for evaluation of the equations in conjunction with the iteration steps of the numeric solver. If a strongly connected set of equations appears, this set is transformed by a symbolic solver, which performs a number of algebraic transformations to simplify the dependencies between the variables. It can sometimes solve a system of differential equations if it has a symbolic solution. Finally, C code is generated, and linked with a numeric equation solver that solves the remaining, drastically reduced, equation system.

The approximations to initial values are taken from the model definition or are interactively specified by the user. If necessary, the user also specifies the parameter values. A numeric solver for differential-algebraic equations (or in simple cases for ordinary differential equations) computes the values of the variables during the specified simulation interval $[t_0, t_1]$. The result of the dynamic system simulation is a set of functions of time, such as `R2.v(t)` in the simple circuit model. Those functions can be displayed as graphs and/or saved in a file.

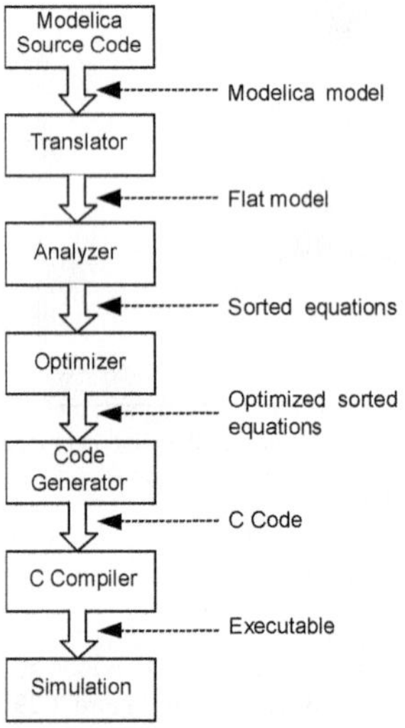

Figure 2-29. The typical stages of translating and executing a Modelica model.

In most cases (but not always) the performance of generated simulation code (including the solver) is similar to handwritten C code. Often Modelica is more efficient than straightforwardly written C code, because additional opportunities for symbolic optimization are used by the system, compared to what a human programmer can manually handle.

2.20.1 Hand Translation of the Simple Circuit Model

Let us return once more to the simple circuit model, previously depicted in Figure 2-7, but for the reader's convenience also shown below in Figure 2-30. It is instructive to translate this model by hand, in order to understand the process.

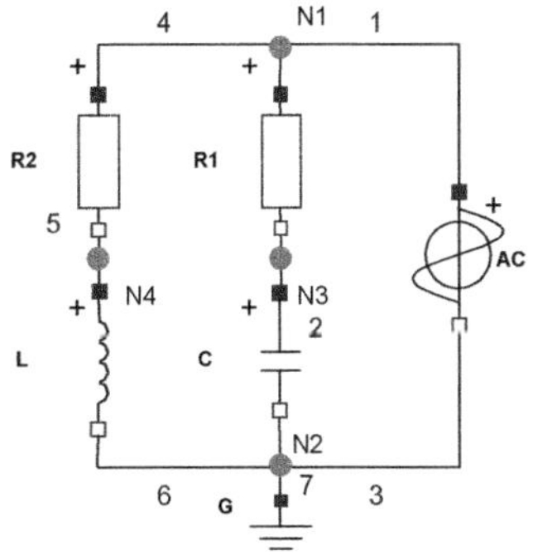

Figure 2-30. The `SimpleCircuit` model once more, with explicitly labeled connection nodes N1, N2, N3, N4, and wires 1 to 7.

Classes, instances, and equations are translated into a flat set of equations, constants, and variables (see the equations in Table 2-1), according to the following rules:

1. For each class instance, add one copy of all equations of this instance to the total differential algebraic equation (DAE) system or ordinary differential equation system (ODE)—both alternatives can be possible, since a DAE in a number of cases can be transformed into an ODE.
2. For each connection between instances within the model, add connection equations to the DAE system so that potential variables are set equal and flow variables are summed to zero.

The equation `v=p.v-n.v` is defined by the class `TwoPin`. The `Resistor` class inherits the `TwoPin` class, including this equation. The `SimpleCircuit` class contains a variable `R1` of type `Resistor`. Therefore, we include this equation instantiated for `R1` as `R1.v=R1.p.v-R1.n.v` into the system of equations.

The wire labeled `1` is represented in the model as `connect(AC.p, R1.p)`. The variables `AC.p` and `R1.p` have type `Pin`. The variable `v` is a *potential* variable representing voltage potential. Therefore, the equality equation `R1.p.v=AC.p.v` is generated. Equality equations are always generated when potential variables are connected.

Notice that another wire (labeled `4`) is attached to the same pin, `R1.p`. This is represented by an additional connect-equation: `connect(R1.p.R2.p)`. The variable `i` is declared as a flow variable. Thus, the equation `AC.p.i+R1.p.i+R2.p.i=0` is generated. Zero-sum equations are always generated when connecting flow variables, corresponding to Kirchhoff's second law.

The complete set of equations (see Table 2-1) generated from the `SimpleCircuit` class consists of 32 differential-algebraic equations. These include 32 variables, as well as `time` and several parameters and constants.

Table 2-1. The equations extracted from the simple circuit model—an implicit DAE system.

AC	`0 = AC.p.i+AC.n.i`
	`AC.v = Ac.p.v-AC.n.v`
	`AC.i = AC.p.i`
	`AC.v = AC.VA* sin(2*AC.PI* AC.f*time);`
		L	`0 = L.p.i+L.n.i`
			`L.v = L.p.v-L.n.v`
			`L.i = L.p.i`
			`L.v = L.L*der(L.i)`

R1	`0 = R1.p.i+R1.n.i`
	`R1.v = R1.p.v-R1.n.v`
	`R1.i = R1.p.i`
	`R1.v = R1.R*R1.i`
		G	`G.p.v = 0`

R2	`0 = R2.p.i+R2.n.i`	wires	`R1.p.v = AC.p.v // wire 1`

	R2.v = R2.p.v-R2.n.v
	R2.i = R2.p.i
	R2.v = R2.R*R2.i
			C.p.v = R1.n.v // wire 2
			AC.n.v = C.n.v // wire 3
			R2.p.v = R1.p.v // wire 4
			L.p.v = R2.n.v // wire 5
			L.n.v = C.n.v // wire 6
			G.p.v = AC.n.v // wire 7

C	0 = C.p.i+C.n.i
	C.v = C.p.v-C.n.v
	C.i = C.p.i
	C.i = C.C*der(C.v)
		flow at node	0 = AC.p.i+R1.p.i+R2.p.i // N1
			0 = C.n.i+G.p.i+AC.n.i+L.n.i // N2
			0 = R1.n.i + C.p.i // N3
			0 = R2.n.i + L.p.i // N4

Table 2-2 gives the 32 variables in the system of equations, of which 30 are algebraic variables since their derivatives do not appear. Two variables, `C.v` and `L.i`, are dynamic variables since their derivatives occur in the equations. In this simple example, the dynamic variables are state variables, since the DAE reduces to an ODE (also see Section 18.2.6, page 1016).

Table 2-2. The variables extracted from the simple circuit model.

R1.p.i	R1.n.i	R1.p.v	R1.n.v	R1.v
R1.i	R2.p.i	R2.n.i	R2.p.v	R2.n.v
R2.v	R2.i	C.p.i	C.n.i	C.p.v
C.n.v	C.v	C.i	L.p.i	L.n.i
L.p.v	L.n.v	L.v	L.i	AC.p.i
AC.n.i	AC.p.v	AC.n.v	AC.v	AC.i
G.p.i	G.p.v			

2.20.2 Transformation to State-Space Form

The implicit differential algebraic system of equations (DAE system) in Table 2-1 should be further transformed and simplified before applying a numerical solver. The next step is to identify the kind of variables in the DAE system. We have the following four groups:

1. All constant variables which are model parameters, thus easily modified between simulation runs and declared with the prefixed keyword `parameter`, are collected into a parameter vector p. All other constants can be replaced by their values, thus disappearing as named constants.
2. Variables declared with the input attribute, that is, prefixed by the `input` keyword, that appears in instances at the highest hierarchical level, are collected into an input vector u.
3. Variables whose derivatives appear in the model (dynamic variables), that is, the `der()` operator is applied to those variables, are collected into a state vector x (for exceptions see Section 18.2.6, page 1016).
4. All other variables are collected into a vector y of algebraic variables, that is, their derivatives do not appear in the model.

For our simple circuit model these four groups of variables are the following:

```
p = {R1.R, R2.R, C.C, L.L, AC.VA, AC.f}
u = {AC.v}
x = {C.v,L.i}
y = {R1.p.i, R1.n.i, R1.p.v, R1.n.v, R1.v, R1.i, R2.p.i, R2.n.i,
R2.p.v, R2.n.v, R2.v, R2.i, C.p.i, C.n.i, C.p.v, C.n.v, C.i, L.n.i, L.p.v,
L.n.v, L.v, AC.p.i, AC.n.i, AC.p.v, AC.n.v, AC.i, AC.v, G.p.i, G.p.v}
```

We would like to express the problem as the smallest possible ordinary differential equation (ODE) system (in the general case a DAE system) and compute the values of all other variables from the solution of this minimal problem. The system of equations should preferably be in explicit state space form as below:

$$\dot{x} = f(x,t) \tag{2-3}$$

That is, the derivative $\dot{x}$ with respect to time of the state vector x is equal to a function of the state vector x and time. Using an iterative numerical solution method for this ordinary differential equation system, at each iteration step, the derivative of the state vector is computed from the state vector at the current point in time.

For the simple circuit model we have the following:

x = `{C.v,L.i}`, u = `{AC.v}` (with constants: `R1.R,R2.R,C.C,L.L,` `AC.VA,AC.f,AC.PI`) (2-4)

$\dot{x}$ = `{der(C.v), der(L.i)}`

2.20.3 Solution Method

We will use an iterative numerical solution method. First, assume that an estimated value of the state vector x =`{C.v,L.i}` is available at `t=0` when the simulation starts. Use a numerical approximation for the derivative $\dot{x}$ (`der(x)`) at time `t`:

```
der(x) = (x(t+h)-x(t))/h                                   (2-5)
```

giving an approximation of x at time `t+h`:

```
x(t+h) = x(t) + der(x)*h                                   (2-6)
```

In this way, the value of the state vector x is computed one step ahead in time for each iteration, provided `der(x)` can be computed at the current point in simulated time. However, the derivative `der(x)` of the state vector can be computed from $\dot{x} = f(x,t)$ by selecting the equations involving `der(x)` and algebraically extracting the variables in the vector x in terms of other variables, as below:

```
der(C.v) = C.i/C.C                                         (2-7)
der(L.i) = L.v/L.L
```

Other equations in the DAE system are needed to calculate the unknowns `C.i` and `L.v` in the above equations. Starting with `C.i`, using a number of different equations together with simple substitutions and algebraic manipulations, we derive equations (2-8) through (2-10) below.

```
C.i = R1.v/R1.R                                            (2-8)
  using: C.i = C.p.i = -R1.n.i = R1.p.i = R1.i = R1.v/R1.R

R1.v = R1.p.v - R1.n.v = R1.p.v - C.v
  using: R1.n.v = C.p.v = C.v+C.n.v = C.v + AC.n.v = C.v + G.p.v   (2-9)
                = C.v + 0 = C.v

R1.p.v = AC.p.v = AC.VA*sin(2*AC.f*AC.PI*t)
  using: AC.p.v = AC.v+AC.n.v = AC.v+G.p.v =               (2-10)
                = AC.VA*sin(2*AC.f*AC.PI*t)+0
```

In a similar fashion we derive equations (2-11) and (2-12) below:

```
L.v = L.p.v - L.n.v = R1.p.v - R2.v
  using: L.p.v = R2.n.v = R1.p.v-R2.v                      (2-11)
  and: L.n.v = C.n.v = AC.n.v = G.p.v = 0
```

```
R2.v = R2.R*L.p.i
  using: R2.v  =  R2.R*R2.i  =  R2.R*R2.p.i  =  R2.R*(-R2.n.i)  =
  R2.R*L.p.i = R2.R*L.i
```
(2-12)

Collecting the five equations together:

```
C.i    = R1.v/R1.R
R1.v   = R1.p.v - C.v
R1.p.v = AC.VA*sin(2*AC.f*AC.PI*time)
L.v    = R1.p.v - R2.v
R2.v   = R2.R*L.i
```
(2-13)

By sorting the equations in data-dependency order, and converting the equations to assignment statements—this is possible since all variable values can now be computed in order—we arrive at the following set of assignment statements to be computed at each iteration, given values of `C.v`, `L.i`, and `t` at the same iteration:

```
R2.v       := R2.R*L.i
R1.p.v     := AC.VA*sin(2*AC.f*AC.PI*time)
L.v        := R1.p.v - R2.v
R1.v       := R1.p.v - C.v
C.i        := R1.v/R1.R
der(L.i)   := L.v/L.L
der(C.v)   := C.i/C.C
```

These assignment statements can be subsequently converted to code in some programming language, for example, C, and executed together with an appropriate ODE solver, usually using better approximations to derivatives and more sophisticated forward-stepping schemes than the simple method described above, which, by the way, is called the *Euler integration* method. The algebraic transformations and sorting procedure that we somewhat painfully performed by hand on the simple circuit example can be performed completely automatically, and is known as *BLT partitioning*—conversion of the equation system coefficient matrix into block lower triangular form (Figure 2-31).

	R2.v	R1.p	L.v	R1.v	C.i	L.i	C.v
`R2.v = R2.R*L.i`	1	0	0	0	0	0	0
`R1.p.v = AC.VA*sin(2*AC.f*AC.PI*time)`	0	1	0	0	0	0	0
`L.v = R1.p.v - R2.v`	1	1	1	0	0	0	0
`R1.v = R1.p.v - C.v`	0	1	0	1	0	0	0
`C.i = R1.v/R1.R`	0	0	0	0	1	0	0
`der(L.i) = L.v/L.L`	0	0	1	0	0	1	0
`der(C.v) = C.i/C.C`	0	0	0	0	1	0	1

Figure 2-31. Block lower triangular form of the `SimpleCircuit` example.

The remaining 26 algebraic variables in the equation system of the simple circuit model that are not part of the minimal 7-variable kernel ODE system solved above can be computed at leisure for those iterations where their values are desired—this is not necessary for solving the kernel ODE system.

It should be emphasized that the simple circuit example is trivial. Realistic simulation models often contain tens of thousands of equations, nonlinear equations, hybrid models, and so on. The symbolic transformations and reductions of equation systems performed by a real Modelica compiler are much more complicated than what has been shown in this example, including index reduction of equations and tearing of subsystems of equations.

```
simulate(SimpleCircuit,stopTime=5)]
```

```
plot(C.v, xrange={0,5})
```

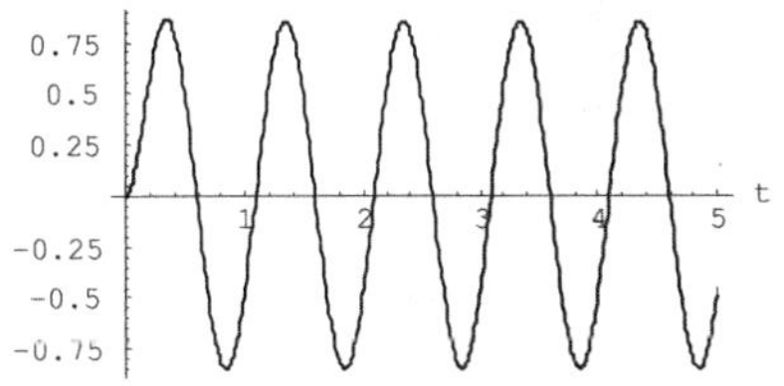

Figure 2-32. Simulation of the `SimpleCircuit` model with a plot of the voltage `C.v` over the capacitor.

2.21 Tool Interoperability through Functional Mockup Interface

Even though Modelica is a universal modeling language that covers most application domains, there are many established existing modeling and simulation tools in various application domains. There is a strong industrial need for interoperability and model interchange between tools. The Functional Mockup Interface standard (FMI, `www.fmi-standard.org`) has been developed to fulfill this need. It allows exporting models compiled into C-code combined with XML-based descriptors, which can be imported and simulated in other tools, both Modelica and non-Modelica tools. The standard also supports co-simulation between tools and is already supported by a number of tool vendors. For more information, see Appendix G, page 1165.

2.22 History

In September 1996, at the initiative of Hilding Elmqvist, Lund, Sweden, a group of tool designers, application experts, and computer scientists joined forces to work together in the area of object-oriented modeling technology and applications. The group included specialists behind the object-oriented modeling languages Dymola, Omola, ObjectMath, NMF (Neutral Modeling Format), Allan-U.M.L, SIDOPS+, and Smile, even though not all were able to attend the first meeting. Initially the goal was to write a white paper on object-oriented modeling language technology including possible unification of existing modeling languages, as part of an action in the ESPRIT project Simulation in Europe Basic Research Working Group (SiE-WG).

However, the work quickly focused on the more ambitious goal of creating a new, unified object-oriented modeling language based on the experience from the previous designs. The designers made an effort to unify the concepts to create a common language, starting the design from scratch. This new language is called *Modelica*.

Figure 2-33. The Modelica Design group at the time of releasing Modelica 1.0.
Photo during Modelica design meeting at DLR, Oberphaffenhofen, Germany.
Upper row from left: Mattias Klose, Peter Fritzson, Dag Brück, Jan Broenink, Kaj Juslin, Hilding Elmqvist, Alexandre Jeandel, Thilo Ernst, Pieter Mosterman, Hans Vangheluwe;
lower row from left: André Schneider, Sven-Erik Mattsson, Hubertus Tummescheit, Martin Otter.

The group soon established itself as Technical Committee 1 within EuroSim, and as the Technical Chapter on Modelica within Society for Computer Simulation International (SCS). In February 2000, Modelica Association was formed during a Modelica Design meeting in Linköping, Sweden, as an independent nonprofit international organization for supporting and promoting the development and dissemination of the Modelica Language and the Modelica Standard Libraries.

The first Modelica language description, version 1.0, was put on the web in September 1997, by a group of proud designers (Figure 2-33), after a number of intense design meetings.

In 2014, at the date of this writing, the Modelica 3.3 specification has been released with Modelica 3.3 revision 1 on the way—the result of a large amount of work including 82 three-day design meetings. Nine complete (or mostly complete) commercial tools supporting textual and graphical model design and simulation with Modelica are currently available, as well as two rather complete open-source implementations, and several partial university prototypes. A large and growing Modelica Standard Library is also available. The language is quickly spreading both in industry and in academia.

If we trace back a few steps and think about the Modelica technology, two important points become apparent:

- Modelica includes *equations,* which is unusual in most programming languages.
- The Modelica technology includes *graphical* editing for application model design based on predefined components.

In fact, concerning the first point, equations were used very early in human history—already in the third millennium B.C. At that point, the well-known equality sign for equations was not yet invented. That happened much later—the equation sign was introduced by Robert Recorde in 1557, in a form depicted in Figure 2-34. However, it took a while for this invention to spread in Europe. Even a hundred years later, Newton (in his *Principia*, vol. 1, 1686) still wrote his famous law of motion as text in Latin, as shown in Figure 2-35. Translated to English this can be expressed as: "The change of motion is proportional to the motive force impressed."

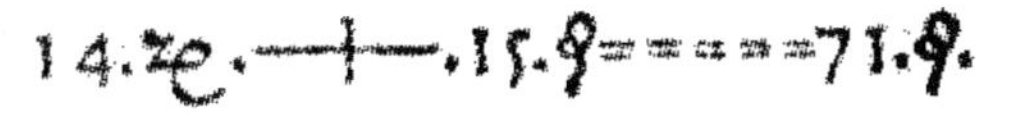

Figure 2-34. Equation sign invented by Robert Recorde 1557. Reproduced from Figure 4.1-1 on page 81 in (Gottwald, Gellert, Kuestner 1989), courtesy Thompson Inc.

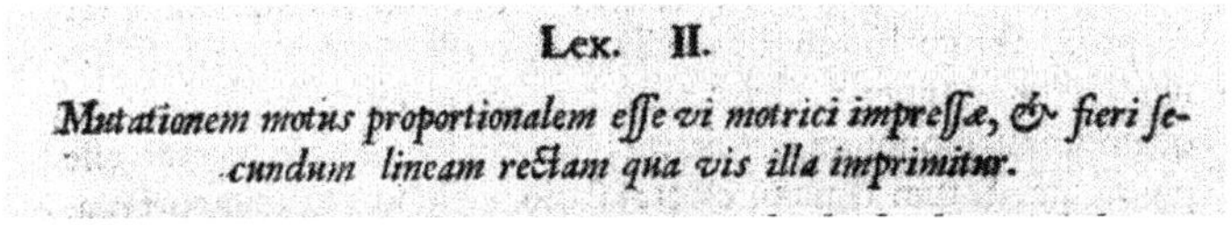

Lex. II.

Mutationem motus proportionalem eſſe vi motrici impreſſæ, & fieri ſecundum lineam rectam qua vis illa imprimitur.

Figure 2-35. Newton's famous second law of motion in Latin. Translated to English this becomes "The change of motion is proportional to the motive force impressed". Reproduced from Figure "Newton's laws of motion" on page 51 in (Fauvel, Flood, Shortland, and Wilson 1990), courtesy Oxford University Press.

In modern mathematical syntax, Newton's law of motion appears as follows:

$$\frac{d}{dt}(m \cdot v) = \sum_i F_i \tag{2-14}$$

This is an example of a differential equation. The first simulators to solve such equations were analog. The idea is to model the system in terms of ordinary differential equations and then make a physical device that obeys the equations. The first analog simulators were mechanical devices, but from the 1950s electronic analog simulators became predominant. A number of electronic building blocks such as adders, multipliers, and integrators, could be interconnected by cables, as depicted in Figure 2-36.

Concerning the further development, for a long time equations were quite rare in computer languages. Early versions of Lisp systems and computer algebra systems were being developed, but mostly for formula manipulation rather than for direct simulation.

However, a number of simulation languages for digital computers soon started to appear. The first equation-based modeling tool was Speed-Up, a package for chemical engineering and design introduced in 1964. Somewhat later, in 1967, Simula 67 appeared—the first object-oriented programming language, with profound influence on programming languages and somewhat later on modeling languages. The same year, the CSSL (Continuous System Simulation Language) report unified existing notations for expressing continuous system simulation models and introduced a common form of causal "equation":

$$\begin{aligned} &variable = expression \\ &v = \mathrm{INTEG}(F)\,/\,m \end{aligned} \tag{2-15}$$

The second equation is a variant of the equation of motion: the velocity is the integral of the force divided by the mass. These are not general equations in the mathematical sense since the causality is from right to left, that is, an equation of the form *expression* = *variable* is not allowed. However, it is still a definite step forward toward a more general executable computer representation of equation-based mathematical models. ACSL, first introduced in 1976, was a rather common simulation system initially based on the CSSL standard.

An important pioneering predecessor to Modelica is Dymola (*Dynamic Modeling Language*—not today's Dymola tool meaning Dynamic Modeling Laboratory), described in Hilding Elmqvist's PhD thesis in 1978. This was the first work to recognize the importance of modeling with acausal equations together with hierarchical submodels and methods for automatic symbolic manipulation to support equation solution. The GASP-IV system in 1974, followed by GASP-V a few years later, introduced integrated continuous-discrete simulation. The Omola language (1989) is a modeling language with full object orientation including inheritance as well as hybrid simulation. The Dymola language was later (1993) enhanced with inheritance, as well as with mechanisms for discrete-event handling and more efficient symbolic-numeric equation system solution methods.

Other early object-oriented acausal modeling languages include NMF (Neutral Model Format, 1989), primarily used for building simulation; Allan-U.M.L, SIDOPS+, supporting bond graph modeling; and Smile (1995)—influenced by Objective C. Two other important languages that should be mentioned are ASCEND (1991) and gPROMS (1994).

This author's acquaintance with equation-based modeling and problem solving started in 1975 by solving the Schrödinger equation for a very specific case in solid-state physics, using the pseudopotential approximation. Later, in 1989, I initiated development of a new object-oriented modeling language called ObjectMath together with my brother, Dag Fritzson. This was one of the earlier object-oriented computer algebra and simulation systems, integrated with Mathematica and with a general parameterized generic class concept, as well as code generation to C++ for efficient simulation of industrial applications. The fourth version of ObjectMath was completed in the fall of 1996 when I decided to join the Modelica effort instead of continuing with a fifth version of ObjectMath. Later, 1998, we did the first formal executable specification (in Operational Semantics using the RML tool) of part of the Modelica language, which eventually developed into the OpenModelica open source effort. We eventually designed a Modelica version of the RML language called MetaModelica. This was used starting from fall 2006 for the OpenModelica effort. In December 2007, this author initiated the creation of the Open Source Modelica Consortium with, initially, 7 members, which has expanded to 46 members in 2014. Several research efforts in the Modelica community were pioneered within OpenModelica, including compilation of equation models to parallel code, meta-modeling, and requirement modeling, and integration of UML-Modelica for cyber-physical hardware–software system modeling.

Concerning the second aspect mentioned earlier—graphical specification of simulation models—Figure 2-36 is tells an interesting story. The left part of the figure shows the circuitry of an analog computer with its building blocks connected by cables. The right figure is a block diagram of very similar structure, directly inspired by the analog computing paradigm but executed on digital computers. Such block diagrams are typically constructed by common tools available today such as Simulink or SystemBuild. Block diagrams represent causal equations since there is a specified data-flow direction.

The connection diagrams used in Modelica graphical modeling include connections between instances of classes containing acausal equations, as first explored in the Hibliz system. This is a generalization inspired by the causal analog computing circuit diagrams and block diagrams. The Modelica connection diagrams have the advantage of supporting natural physical modeling since the topology of a connection diagram directly corresponds to the structure and decomposition of the modeled physical system.

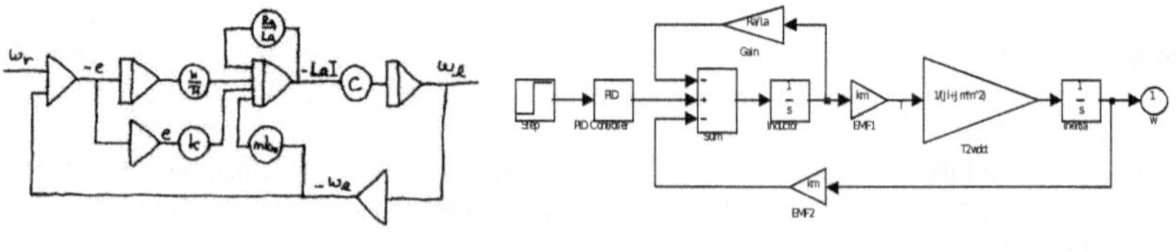

Figure 2-36. Analog computing vs. graphical block diagram modeling on modern digital computers. Courtesy Karl-Johan Åström and Hilding Elmqvist.

2.23 Summary

This chapter has given a quick overview of the most important concepts and language constructs in Modelica. However, Chapter 3 to Chapter 11 together with Chapter 13 give a much more complete description of the language, with many examples including a number of language and usage aspects not covered by this quick tour. We have also defined important concepts such as object oriented mathematical modeling and acausal physical modeling, and briefly presented the concepts and Modelica language constructs for defining components, connections, and connectors. The chapter concludes with an in-depth example of the translation and execution of a simple model, and a short history of equations and mathematical modeling languages up to and including Modelica from ancient times until today.

2.24 Literature

Many programming language books are organized according to a fairly well-established pattern of first presenting a quick overview of the language, followed by a more detailed presentation according to the most important language concepts and syntactic structures. This book is no exception to that rule, where this chapter constitutes the quick overview. As in many other texts, we start with a `HelloWorld` example, as in the Java programming language book (Arnold and Gosling 1999), but with a different contents since printing an "Hello World" message is not very relevant for an equation-based language.

The most important reference document for this chapter is the Modelica tutorial (Modelica Association 2000), of which the first version, including a design rationale (Modelica Association 1997), was edited primarily by Hilding Elmqvist. Several examples, code fragments, and text fragments in this chapter are based on similar ones in the tutorial, for example the `SimpleCircuit` model with the simple electrical components, the `polynomialEvaluator`, the low pass filter, the ideal `Diode`, and the `BouncingBall` model. Figure 2-8 on block oriented modeling is also from the tutorial. Another important reference document for this chapter is the Modelica language specification (Modelica Association 2012) Some formulations from the Modelica specification regarding operator overloading and stream connectors are reused in this chapter in order to state the same semantics.

The hand translation of the simple circuit model is inspired by a similar but less elaborated example in a series of articles by Martin Otter *et al.* (Otter 1999). The recent history of mathematical modeling languages is described in some detail in (Åström, Elmqvist, and Mattsson 1998), whereas bits and pieces of the ancient human history of the invention and use of equations can be found in (Gottwald, Gellert, and Kuestner 1989), and the picture of Newton's second law in latin in (Fauvel, Flood, Shortland, and Wilson 1990). Early work on combined continuous/discrete simulation is described in (Pritsker 1974) followed by (Cellier 1979). A very comprehensive overview of numeric and symbolic methods for simulation is available in (Cellier and Kofman 2006). This author's first simulation work involving solution of the Schrödinger equation for a particular case is described in (Fritzson and Berggren 1976).

Current versions of several Modelica tools are described in Chapter 19, including OpenModelica, Wolfram SystemModeler (called MathModelica before 2012), and Dymola (meaning the Dynamic Modeling Laboratory). The predecessors of the Modelica language are briefly described in Appendix F, including Dymola (meaning the Dynamic Modeling Language): (Elmqvist 1978; Elmqvist, Brück, and Otter 1996), Omola: (Mattsson, Andersson, and Åström 1993; Andersson 1994), ObjectMath: (Fritzson, Viklund, Herber, Fritzson 1992), (Fritzson, Viklund, Fritzson, and Herber 1995; Viklund and Fritzson 1995), NMF: (Sahlin, Bring, Sowell 1996), Smile: (Ernst, Jähnichen, and Klose 1997).

Speed-Up, the earliest equation-based simulation tool, is presented in (Sargent and Westerberg 1964), whereas Simula-67—the first object-oriented programming language—is described in (Birtwistle, Dahl, Myhrhaug, and Nygaard 1974). The early CSSL language specification is described in (Augustin, Fineberg, Johnson, Linebarger, Sansom, and Strauss 1967), whereas the ACSL system is described in (Mitchell and Gauthier 1986). The Hibliz system for an hierarchical graphical approach to modeling is presented in (Elmqvist 1982).

Software component systems are presented in (Assmann 2002; Szyperski 1997).

The Simulink system for block oriented modeling is described in (MathWorks 2001), whereas the MATLAB language and tool are described in (MathWorks 2002).

The DrModelica electronic notebook with the examples and exercises from this book has been inspired by DrScheme (Felleisen, Findler, Flatt, and Krishnamurthi 1998) and DrJava (Allen, Cartwright, and Stoler 2002), as well as by Mathematica (Wolfram 1997), a related electronic book for teaching mathematics (Davis, Porta, and Uhl 1994), and the MathModelica (renamed to Wolfram SystemModeler in 2012) environment (Fritzson, Engelson, and Gunnarsson 1998; Fritzson, Gunnarsson, and Jirstrand 2002; Fritzson 2006). The first version of DrModelica is described in (Lengquist-Sandelin and Monemar 2003; Lengquist-Sandelin, Monemar, Fritzson, and Bunus 2003).

The OpenModelica version of notebook, called OMNotebook, is described in (Fernström, Axelsson, Fritzson, Sandholm, and Pop 2006; Asghar, Tariq, Torabzadeh-Tari, Fritzson, Pop, Sjölund, Vasaiely, and Schamai 2011). Applications and extensions of this notebook concept are presented in (Sandholm, Fritzson, Arora, Delp, Petersson, and Rose 2007; Torabzadeh-Tari, Fritzson, Pop, and Sjölund 2010; Torabzadeh-Tari, Sjölund, Pop, and Fritzson 2011; Torabzadeh-Tari, Remala, Sjölund, Pop, and Fritzson 2011; Torabzadeh-Tari, Hossain, Fritzson, and Richter 2011).

General Modelica articles and books: (Elmqvist and Mattsson 1997; Fritzson and Engelson 1998; Elmqvist, Mattson, and Otter 1999), a series of 17 articles (in German) of which (Otter 1999) is the first, (Tiller 2001; Fritzson and Bunus 2002; Elmqvist, Otter, Mattsson, and Olsson 2002; Fritzson 2004; Fritzson 2011).

The proceedings from the following conferences, as well as several conferences not listed here, contain a number of Modelica related papers: the International Modelica Conference: (Fritzson 2000; Otter 2002; Fritzson 2003, Schmitz 2005; Kral and Haumer 2006; Bachmann 2008; Casella 2009; Clauß 2011; Otter and Zimmer 2012) and the Equation-Based Object-Oriented Languages and Tools (EOOLT) workshop series: (Fritzson, Cellier, Nytsch Geusen 2007; Fritzson, Cellier, Broman 2008; Fritzson, Lee, Cellier, Broman 2010; Cellier, Fritzson, Lee, Broman 2011; Nilsson 2013). the Scandinavian Simulation Conference, e.g.: (Fritzson 1999) and some later conferences in that series, two special conferences with focus on biomedical (Fritzson 2005a) and safety issues (Fritzson 2005b), respectively.

2.25 Exercises

Exercise 2-1:

Question: What is a class?

Creating a Class: Create a class, `Add`, that calculates the sum of two parameters, which are `Integer` numbers with given values.

Exercise 2-2:

Question: What is an instance?

Creating Instances:

```
class Dog
  constant Real legs = 4;
  parameter String name = "Dummy";
end dog;
```

- Create an instance of the class `Dog`.
- Create another instance and give the dog the name "Tim".

Exercise 2-3:

Write a function, `average`, that returns the average of two `Real` values.

Make a function call to `average` with the input 4 and 6.

Exercise 2-4:

Question: What do the terms `partial`, `class,` and `extends` stand for?

Exercise 2-5:

Inheritance: Consider the `Bicycle` class below.

```
record Bicycle
  Boolean has_wheels = true;
  Integer nrOfWheels = 2;
end Bicycle;
```

Define a record, `ChildrensBike`, that inherits from the class `Bicycle` and is meant for kids. Give the variables values.

Exercise 2-6:

Declaration Equations and Normal Equations: Write a class, `Birthyear`, which calculates the year of birth from this year together with a person's age.

Point out the declaration equations and the normal equations.

Modification Equation: Write an instance of the class `Birthyear` above. The class, let's call it `MartinsBirthyear`, shall calculate Martin's year of birth, call the variable `martinsBirthyear`, who is a 29-year-old. Point out the modification equation.

Check your answer, e.g. by writing as below[12]

```
val(martinsBirthday.birthYear,0)
```

Exercise 2-7:

Classes:

```
class Ptest
  parameter Real x;
  parameter Real y;
  Real z;
  Real w;
equation
  x + y = z;
end Ptest;
```

Question: What is wrong with this class? Is there something missing?

Exercise 2-8:

Create a record containing several vectors and matrices:

- A vector containing the two `Boolean` values `true` and `false`.
- A vector with five `Integer` values of your choice.
- A matrix of three rows and four columns containing `String` values of your choice.

[12] In OpenModelica, the expression `val(martinsBirthday.birthYear,0)` means the `birthYear` value at time=0, at the beginning of the simulation. Interpolated values at other simulated time points can also be obtained. Constant expressions such as 33+5, and function calls, can also be evaluated interactively.

- A matrix of one row and five columns containing different `Real` values, also those of your choice.

Exercise 2-9:

Question: Can you really put an algorithm section inside an equation section?

Exercise 2-10:

Writing an Algorithm Section: Create the class, `Average`, which calculates the average between two integers, using an algorithm section.

Make an instance of the class and send in some values.

Simulate and then test the result of the instance class by writing
`instanceVariable.classVariable`.

Exercise 2-11: (A harder exercise)

Write a class, `AverageExtended`, that calculates the average of 4 variables (`a, b, c,` and `d`).

Make an instance of the class and send in some values.

Simulate and then test the result of the instance class by writing
`instanceVariable.classVariable`.

Exercise 2-12:

If-equation: Write a class `Lights` that sets the variable switch (integer) to one if the lights are on and zero if the lights are off.

When-equation: Write a class `LightSwitch` that is initially switched off and switched on at time 5.

Tip: `sample(start, interval)` returns true and triggers time events at time instants and `rem(x, y)` returns the integer remainder of `x/y`, such that `div(x,y) * y + rem(x, y) = x`.

Exercise 2-13:

Question: What is a Package?

Creating a Package: Create a package that contains a division function (that divides two `Real` numbers) and a constant `k = 5`.

Create a class, containing a variable `x`. The variable gets its value from the division function inside the package, which divides 10 by 5.

Part II

The Modelica Language

Chapter 3

Classes, Types, Declarations, and Lookup

The fundamental unit of modeling in Modelica is the class. Classes provide the structure for objects, also known as instances, and serve as templates for creating objects from class definitions. Classes can contain equations that provide the basis for the executable code that is used for computation in Modelica. Conventional algorithmic code can also be part of classes. Interaction between objects of well-structured classes in Modelica is usually done through so-called connectors, which can be seen as "access ports" to objects. All data objects in Modelica are instantiated from classes, including the basic data types—`Real`, `Integer`, `String`, `Boolean`—and enumeration types, which are built-in classes or class schemata.

A class in Modelica is essentially equivalent to a type. Declarations are the syntactic constructs needed to introduce classes and objects.

This chapter is organized into two parts. The first part comprising Sections 3.1 to 3.6 gives a tutorial introduction to the Modelica class concept using the moon landing example as well as the contract idea. The rest of the chapter is presented in a somewhat more formal style, giving a complete description of most aspects of Modelica classes, types, declarations, and lookup, except inheritance, covered in Chapter 4, and component aspects, covered in Chapter 5.

3.1 Contract between Class Designer and User

Object-oriented modeling languages try to separate the notion of *what* an object is from *how* its behavior is implemented and specified in detail. The "what" of an object in Modelica is usually described through documentation including graphics and icons, together with possible public connectors, variables, and other public elements, and their associated semantics. For example, the "what" of an object of class `Resistor` is the documentation, that it models a "realistic" ideal resistor coupled with the fact that its interaction with the outside world is through two connectors `n`, `p` of type `Pin`, and their semantics. This combination—documentation, connectors and other public elements, and semantics—is often described as a *contract* between the designer of the class and the modeler who uses it, since the "what" part of the contract specifies to the modeler what a class represents, whereas the "how" provided by the class designer implements the required properties and behavior.

An incorrect, but common, assumption is that the connectors and other public elements of a class (its "signature") specify its entire contract. This is not correct since the intended semantics of the class is also part of the contract even though it might only be publicly described in the documentation, and internally modeled through equations and algorithms. Two classes e.g., a `Resistor` and a temperature-dependent `Resistor`, may have the same "signature" in terms of connectors but still not be equivalent since they have different semantics. The contract of a class includes both the signature and the appropriate part of its semantics together.

The "how" of an object is defined by its class. The implementation of the behavior of the class is defined in terms of equations and possibly algorithmic code. Each object is an instance of a class. Many objects are composite objects, that is, they consist of instances of other classes.

3.2 A Class and Instance Example

The basic properties of a class are given by:

- Data contained in variables declared in the class.
- Behavior specified by equations together with possible algorithms.

Here is a simple class called `CelestialBody` that can be used to store data related to celestial bodies such as the earth, the moon, asteroids, planets, comets, and stars:

```
class CelestialBody
  constant  Real   g = 6.672e-11;
  parameter Real   radius;
  parameter String name;
  Real             mass;
end CelestialBody;
```

The declaration of a class starts with a keyword such as class or model, followed by the name of the class. A class declaration creates a *type name* in Modelica, which makes it possible to declare variables of that type, also known as *objects* or *instances* of that class, simply by prefixing the type name to a variable name:

```
CelestialBody moon;
```

This declaration states that `moon` is a *variable* containing an *object/instance* of type `CelestialBody`. The declaration actually creates the object, that is, it allocates memory for the object. This is in contrast to a language such as Java where an object declaration just creates a reference to an object.

This first version of `CelestialBody` is not very well designed. This is intentional since we will demonstrate the value of certain language features for improving the class in this and the following two chapters.

3.3 Variables

The variables belonging to a class are sometimes called record fields or attributes; the `CelestialBody` variables `radius`, `name`, and `mass` are examples. Every object of type `CelestialBody` has its own instances of these variables. Since each separate object contains a different instance of the variables, this means that each object has its own unique state. Changing the `mass` variable in one `CelestialBody` object does not affect the `mass` variables in other `CelestialBody` objects.

Certain programming languages, for example, Java and C++, allow so-called static variables, also called class variables. Such variables are shared by all instances of a class. However, this kind of variable is not available in Modelica.

A declaration of an instance of a class, for example `moon` being an instance of `CelestialBody`, allocates memory for the object and initializes its variables to appropriate values.

In Modelica, variables store results of computations performed when solving the equations of a class together with equations from other classes. During solution of time-dependent problems, the variables store results of the solution process at the current time instant.

As the reader may have noted, we use the terms *object* and *instance* interchangeably with the same meaning; we also use the terms *record field*, *attribute*, and *variable* interchangeably. Sometimes the *term* variable is used interchangeably with *instance* or *object*, since a variable in Modelica always contains an instance of some class.

3.3.1 Constants

Three of the variables in the class `CelestialBody` have special status. The gravitational *constant* `g` is a `constant` that never changes and can be substituted by its value.

The *simulation parameters* `radius` and `name` are examples of a special kind of "constant" denoted by the keyword `parameter` in Modelica. Such simulation parameter "constants" are assigned their values only at the start of the simulation and keep their values constant during simulation. Most simulation tools provide functionality to make it easy for users to change such simulation parameters before simulation.

3.3.2 Duplicate Variable Names or Type Names

Duplicate variable names or type names are not allowed in class declarations. The name of a declared element, for example a variable or a local class, must be *different* from the names of all other declared elements in the class. For example, the following class is illegal:

```
class IllegalDuplicate
  Real     duplicate;
  Integer duplicate;     // Error! Illegal duplicate variable name
end IllegalDuplicate;
```

3.3.3 Identical Variable Names and Type Names

The name of a variable is *not allowed* to be identical to its type specifier. Consider the following erroneous class:

```
class IllegalTypeAsVariable
  Voltage Voltage;    // Error! Variable name must be different from type
  Voltage voltage;    // Ok! Voltage and voltage are different names
end IllegalTypeAsVariable;
```

The first variable declaration is illegal since the variable name is identical to the type specifier of the declaration. The reason this is a problem is that the `Voltage` type lookup from the second declaration would be hidden by a variable with the same name. The second variable declaration is legal since the lowercase variable name `voltage` is different from its uppercase type name `Voltage`.

3.3.4 Initialization of Variables

The suggested default (the solver may choose otherwise, if not `fixed`) initial variable values are the following, if no explicit start values are specified (see Section 2.3.2, page 28, and Section 8.4, page 363):

- The value zero as the default initial value for numeric variables.
- The empty string `""` for String variables.
- The value `false` for `Boolean` variables.
- The lowest enumeration value in an enumeration type for enumeration variables.

However, *local variables* to functions have *unspecified* initial values if no defaults are explicitly given. Initial values can be explicitly specified by setting the `start` attributes of instance variables equal to some value, or providing initializing assignments when the instances are local variables or formal parameters in functions. For example, explicit start values are specified in the class `Rocket` shown in the next section for the variables `mass`, `altitude`, and `velocity`.

3.4 Behavior as Equations

Equations are the primary means of specifying the behavior of a class in Modelica, even though algorithms and functions also are available. The way in which the equations interact with equations from other classes determines the solution process, that is, program execution, where successive values of variables are computed over time. This is exactly what happens during dynamic system simulation. During solution of time-dependent problems, the variables store results of the solution process at the current time instant.

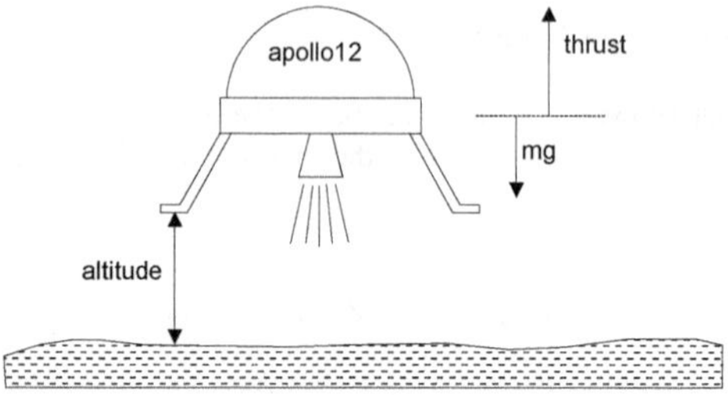

Figure 3-1. Apollo12 rocket for landing on the moon.

The class `Rocket` embodies the equations of vertical motion for a rocket (as depicted in Figure 3-1), which is influenced by an external gravitational force field `gravity`, and the force `thrust` from the rocket motor, acting in the opposite direction to the gravitational force, as in the expression for acceleration below:

$$acceleration = \frac{thrust - mass \cdot gravity}{mass}$$

The following three equations are first-order differential equations stating well-known laws of motion between altitude, vertical velocity, and acceleration:

$$mass' = -massLossRate \cdot abs(thrust)$$
$$altitude' = velocity$$
$$velocity' = acceleration$$

All these equations appear in the class `Rocket` below, where the mathematical notation (') for derivative has been replaced by the pseudo function `der()` in Modelica. The derivative of the rocket `mass` is negative since the rocket fuel mass is proportional to the amount of `thrust` from the rocket motor.

```
class Rocket "rocket class"
  parameter String name;
  Real mass(start=1038.358);
  Real altitude(start= 59404);
  Real velocity(start= -2003);
  Real acceleration;
  Real thrust;      // Thrust force on the rocket
  Real gravity;     // Gravity forcefield
  parameter Real massLossRate=0.000277;
equation
  (thrust-mass*gravity)/mass = acceleration;
```

```
    der(mass)   = -massLossRate * abs(thrust);
    der(altitude) = velocity;
    der(velocity) = acceleration;
  end Rocket;
```

The following equation, specifying the strength of the gravitational force field, is placed in the class `MoonLanding` in the next section since it depends on both the mass of the rocket and the mass of the moon:

$$gravity = \frac{g_{moon} \cdot mass_{moon}}{\left(altitude_{apollo} + radius_{moon}\right)^2}$$

The amount of thrust to be applied by the rocket motor is specific to a particular class of landings, and therefore also belongs to the class `MoonLanding`:

$$\begin{aligned} thrust = {} & if\ (time < thrustDecreaseTime)\ then \\ & \quad force1 \\ & else\ if\ (time < thrustEndTime)\ then \\ & \quad force2 \\ & else\ 0 \end{aligned}$$

3.5 Access Control

Members of a Modelica class can have two levels of visibility: `public` or `protected`. The default is `public` if nothing else is specified, for example regarding the variables `force1` and `force2` in the class `MoonLanding` below. The `public` declaration of `force1`, `force2`, `apollo`, and `moon` means that any code with access to a `MoonLanding` instance can read or update those values.

The other possible level of visibility, specified by the keyword `protected` for example, for the variables `thrustEndTime` and `thrustDecreaseTime`, means that only code *inside* the class as well as code in classes that inherit this class are allowed access. Code inside a class includes code from local classes; see Section 3.7.2 on page 86. However, only code inside the class is allowed access to the *same* instance of a protected variable; classes that extend the class will naturally access another instance of a protected variable since declarations are "copied" at inheritance. This is different from corresponding access rules for Java.

Note that an occurrence of one of the keywords `public` or `protected` means that all member declarations following that keyword assume the corresponding visibility until another occurrence of one of those keywords.

The variables `thrust`, `gravity`, and `altitude` belong to the `apollo` instance of the `Rocket` class and are therefore prefixed by `apollo` in references such as `apollo.thrust`. The gravitational constant `g`, the `mass`, and the `radius` belong to the particular celestial body called `moon` on which surface the `apollo` rocket is landing.

```
class MoonLanding
  parameter Real force1 = 36350;
  parameter Real force2 = 1308;
protected
  parameter Real thrustEndTime = 210;
  parameter Real thrustDecreaseTime = 43.2;
public
  Rocket         apollo(name="apollo12");
  CelestialBody  moon(name="moon",mass=7.382e22,radius=1.738e6);
equation
  apollo.thrust = if (time<thrustDecreaseTime) then force1
                  else if (time<thrustEndTime) then force2
```

Also see pg 143

```
                    else 0;
  apollo.gravity = moon.g * moon.mass / (apollo.altitude + moon.radius)^2;
end MoonLanding;
```

For more details on access control, see Section 3.11.1, page 98.

3.6 Simulating the Moon Landing Example

We simulate the `MoonLanding` model during the time interval `{0,230}` by the following command, using the OpenModelica simulation environment:

```
simulate(MoonLanding, stopTime=230)
```

Alternatively, we click on the simulation button in the graphic user interface. Since the solution for the altitude of the Apollo rocket is a function of time, it can be plotted in a diagram (Figure 3-2). It starts at an altitude of 59404 (not shown in the diagram) at time zero, gradually reducing it until touchdown at the lunar surface when the altitude is zero. Note that an OpenModelica `plot` command refers to the results of the most *recent* simulation. If there is need to plot results of some previous simulation, for example, from a Mars landing, the values returned by previous simulation commands can accessed for plotting, both in OpenModelica OMEdit and in several other tools. The range of the x-axis in the plot is set to the interval {0,208}.

```
plot(apollo.altitude, xrange={0,208})
```

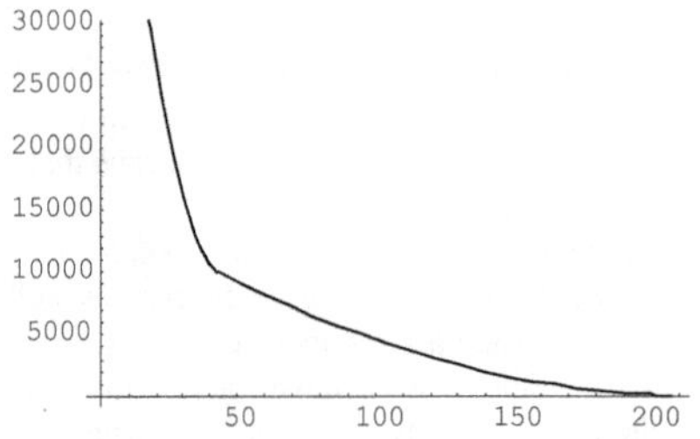

Figure 3-2. Altitude of the Apollo rocket over the lunar surface.

The thrust force from the rocket is initially high but is reduced to a low level after 43.2 seconds, that is, the value of the simulation parameter `thrustDecreaseTime`, as shown in Figure 3-3.

```
plot(apollo.thrust, xrange={0,208})
```

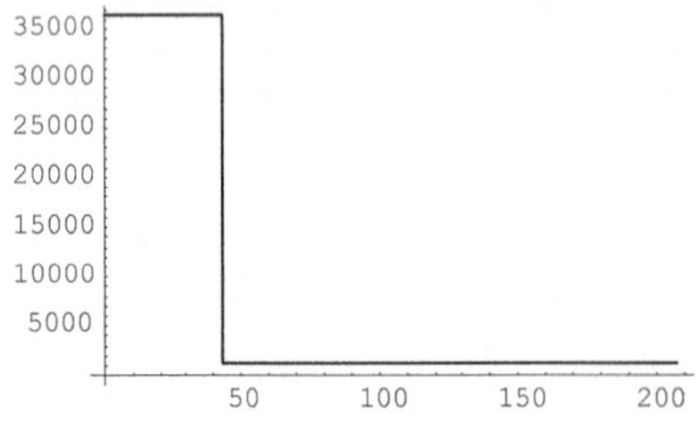

Figure 3-3. Thrust from the rocket motor, with an initial high thrust `f1` followed by a lower thrust `f2`.

The mass of the rocket decreases from initially 1038.358 to around 540 as the fuel is consumed (Figure 3-4).

```
plot(apollo.mass, xrange={0,208})
```

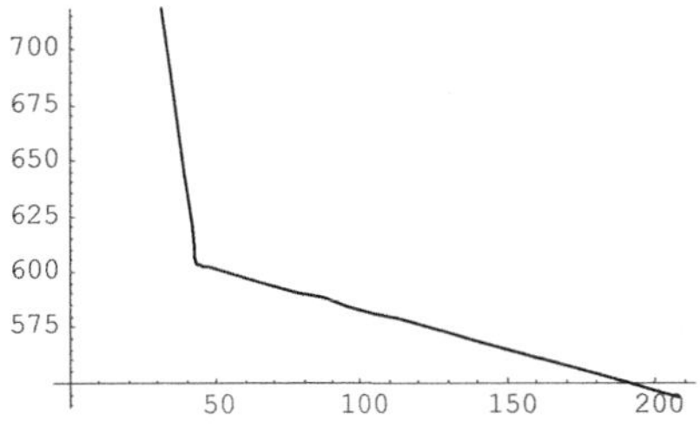

Figure 3-4. Rocket mass decreases when the fuel is consumed.

The gravity field increases when the rocket gets closer to the lunar surface, as depicted in Figure 3-5, where the gravity has increased to 1.63 after 200 seconds.

```
plot(apollo.gravity, xrange={0,208})
```

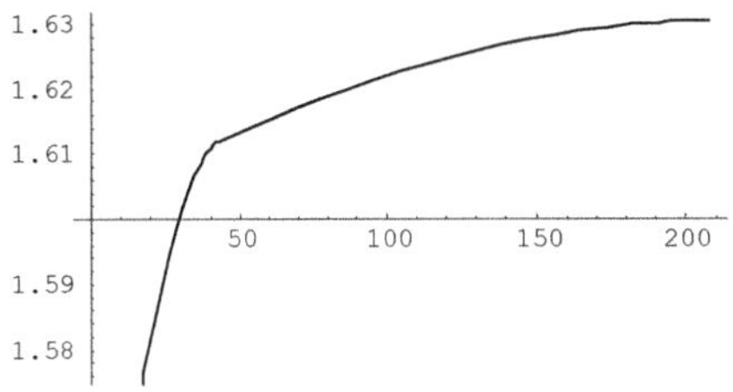

Figure 3-5. Gradually increasing gravity when the rocket approaches the lunar surface.

The rocket initially has a high negative velocity when approaching the lunar surface. This is reduced to zero at touchdown, giving a smooth landing, as shown in Figure 3-6.

```
plot(apollo.velocity, xrange={0,208})
```

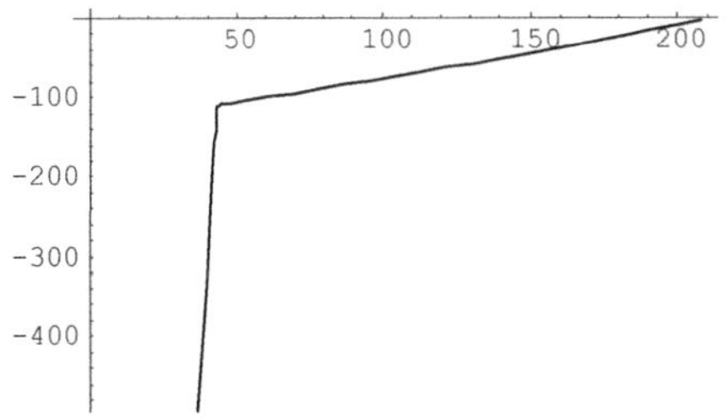

Figure 3-6. Vertical velocity relative to the lunar surface.

When experimenting with the `MoonLanding` model, the reader might notice that the model is nonphysical regarding at least one important aspect of the landing. After touchdown, when the speed has been reduced to zero, if the simulation is allowed to continue the speed will increase again and the lander will accelerate toward the center of the moon. This is because we have left out the ground contact force from the lunar surface acting on the lander after it has landed, which will prevent this from happening. It is left as an exercise to introduce such a ground force into the `MoonLanding` model.

3.6.1 Object Creation Revisited

As already pointed out, objects are created implicitly in Modelica just by declaring instances of classes. This is done simply by prefixing the type name to the variable name, for example, the variable `apollo` of type `Rocket` below. This is in contrast to object-oriented languages like Java or C++, where object creation on the heap is specified using the `new` keyword.

```
Rocket apollo;
```

There is one remaining problem, however. In what context, that is, within which class, should the `apollo` object be instantiated, and how do we ensure that it actually becomes instantiated? It could be that the `MoonLanding` class is just a library class, which is not instantiated if not part of some existing instance.

As explained previously (Section 2.3.1 on page 27), this problem is solved by regarding the class specified in the simulation command as a kind of "main" class that is always instantiated, implying that its variables are instantiated, and that the variables of those variables are instantiated, and so on. Therefore, to instantiate `Rocket` as an object called `apollo`, it is declared as a variable in the simulation model to be simulated, which in this example happens to be `MoonLanding`.

3.7 Short Classes and Nested Classes

Modelica also has a very concise way of declaring classes, called *short class definition*. Moreover, it is possible to declare classes locally within another class, so-called *nested classes*.

3.7.1 Short Class Definitions

There is a short syntax using equality for defining classes in terms of other classes, commonly used to introduce more informative type names for existing classes, which, for example, is similar to the typedef construct in the C language. For example:

```
class Voltage = Real;
```

It is possible to use any other specialized class, including `type`, instead of class:

```
type Voltage = Real;
```

The short class definition is the only way of introducing a "class" name for an array type, for example:

```
type Matrix10 = Real[10,10];
```

When using class in the short class definition

```
class MyClass = ExistingModel;
```

If the inherited class (on the right-hand side) is partial, the new class will also be partial:

```
class MyPartialClass = ExistingPartialModel;
```

3.7.2 Local Class Definitions—Nested Classes

In Modelica, it is possible to define local classes nested inside a class, to an arbitrary level of nesting if desired. For example, the classes `Lpin` and `Voltage` below are locally defined:

```
class C1
  class Lpin
    Real p;
  end Lpin;
```

```
    class Voltage = Real(unit="kV");

    Voltage v1, v2;
    Lpin    pn;
  end C1;
```

All declarations of a class, even protected ones, are accessible from within a local nested class, except when that local class or a class enclosing that class is encapsulated. For more details, see the rules for scoping and lookup described in Section 3.16 on page 108.

3.8 Specialized Classes

The class concept is fundamental to Modelica, and is used for a number of different purposes. Almost anything in Modelica is a class. However, in order to make Modelica code easier to read and maintain, special keywords have been introduced for specific uses of the class concept. The keywords model, connector, record, block, type, package, operator, operator record, operator function, and function can be used under appropriate conditions.

For example, a record is a class used to declare a record data structure and may not contain equations. A block is a class with fixed causality, that is, each part of its interface must have causality equal to input or output. A connector class is used to declare the structure of connection points and may not contain equations. A type is a class that can be an alias or an extension to a predefined type, record, or array. A function is a kind of class, but has quite a number of restrictions and enhancements, which makes it quite different from the usual class concept. For example, a function has the enhancement that it can be called.

A class that inherits a specialized class needs to be of the same specialized class kind, or have the same or more restrictions than the parent class, which is described in more detail in Chapter 4, page 145.

The idea of specialized classes is useful since the modeler does not have to learn several completely different concepts, but only one: the class concept. Many properties of a class, such as the syntax and semantics of definition, instantiation, inheritance, and generic properties, are identical to all kinds of specialized classes. Furthermore, the construction of Modelica translators is slightly simplified because only the syntax and semantics of the class concept have to be implemented along with some additional checks on restrictions and enhancements of specialized classes.

Below we briefly summarize the typical usage, restrictions, and enhancements for each kind of specialized class compared to the generic Modelica class construct, as well as give a few simple examples.

3.8.1 Specialized Class: model or class

The model specialized class is the most commonly used kind of class for modeling purposes. Its semantics is the same as the basic Modelica class concept specified with the class keyword except its inheritance properties (Section 4.1.4, page 139). Any specialized class including model can inherit from class, whereas only model can inherit from model. The previous example classes CelestialBody, Rocket, and MoonLanding could very well have been defined as models. A trivial example:

```
model Resistor "Electrical resistor"
  Pin p, n  "positive and negative pins";
  Voltage v;
  Current i;
  parameter Real R(unit="Ohm")          "Resistance";
equation
  v = i*R;
end Resistor;
```

3.8.2 Specialized Class: record

A `record` is a class for specifying data without behavior. Its restrictions are the following:

No equations or algorithms—no `equation`, `algorithm`, `initial equation`, `initial algorithm` sections—are allowed in the definition of a record or in any of its elements, for example, in local classes or record fields.

Only public sections are allowed in the record definition or in any of its elements, that is, protected sections are not allowed. Instances (record fields) declared in a record may only be of specialized classes `record` or `type`. For example, all basic types Real, Integer, and so on, are special cases of `type`.

The elements of a record may not have prefixes `input`, `output`, `inner`, `outer`, `stream` or `flow`, since otherwise a record instance could not, for example, be passed as argument to a function. The restrictions also apply to classes that inherit a record, since classes with fewer restrictions are not allowed to inherit a record class.

The enhancements include the implicitly available record constructor function, see Section 9.3.8, page 452. Additionally, record variables can be referenced in expressions and in the left-hand side of assignments, subject to normal type compatibility rules. An example:

```
record Person
  Real age;
  String name;
end Person;
```

3.8.3 Specialized Class: type

The `type` specialized class is typically used to introduce new type names using short class definitions, even though short class definitions can be used to introduce new names also for other kinds of classes.

The restrictions are that a `type` specialized class may only be identical or an extension to one of the *predefined types*, *enumerations*, *arrays* of `type`, or classes extending from `type`. Note that all kinds of classes define types in Modelica, not only those using the `type` keyword, but only types defined with the `type` keyword have the corresponding restrictions and enhancements. Its enhancement is that it can extend from predefined types. This is unique, since no other specialized class has this property.

The general concepts of Modelica types and type checking are described in Section 3.18 on page 115. Example:

```
type Matrix = Real[3,3];
```

3.8.4 Specialized Class: connector

Connector classes are typically used as templates for connectors, i.e., a kind of "port" for communicating data between objects. Therefore *no equations or algorithm sections* are allowed in the definition of a `connector` class or within any of its elements. Only public declarations are allowed since connector clases are used to define interfaces. The declarations in a connector class may not have the prefixes `inner` or `outer`. Instances declared in a connector class may only be of specialized class `connector`, `record` and `type`.

The `connector` specialized class is enhanced to allow `connect(...)` between instances of connector classes.

We examine connector classes, connectors, and connections more closely in Chapter 5. The following connector class, called `Flange`, is from the standard Modelica mechanical library for translational motion:

```
connector Flange
  Position    s;
```

```
  flow Force  f;
end Flange;
```

3.8.5 Specialized Class: block

A `block` is a class for which the causality, that is, data-flow direction being either input or output, is known for each of its variables. Thus, blocks are typically used for signal-related modeling since in that case the data-flow direction is always known. The prefixes `input` and `output` define that the corresponding connectors can only be connected according to block-diagram semantics (Section 5.7.3, page 211 or Section 12.5, page 582); for example, a connector with an `output` variable can only be connected to a connector for which the corresponding variable is declared as `input`.

The main restriction of a block is that all *variables* declared in a block must have one of the *prefixes* `input` or `output`. A trivial example:

```
block Multiply
  input  Real x;
  input  Real y(start=0);
  output Real result;
equation
  result = x*y;
end Multiply;
```

3.8.6 Specialized Class: function

The `function` concept in Modelica corresponds to mathematical functions without external side effects, and can be regarded as a specialized class with some enhancements. Its syntax and semantics are somewhat related to that of the `block` specialized class. Function results are returned by those formal parameters prefixed by the keyword `output`. A `function` has the following restrictions (see also Section 9.3.15, page 464) compared to a `class`:

- Each input formal parameter of the function must be *prefixed* by the keyword `input`, and each result formal parameter by the keyword `output`. All public variables are formal parameters.
- Input formal parameters are read-only after being bound to the actual arguments or default values, that is, they may not be assigned values in the body of the function.
- A function may *not be used in connections*, may have *no equations*, may have *no initial algorithm*, and can have at most *one algorithm* section, which, if present, is the body of the function.
- A function may have zero or one external function interface, which, if present, is the external definition of the function.
- For a function to be called, its output formal parameters must be assigned either in declaration assignments (Section 9.3.1, page 438) or in an algorithm section, or it must have an external function interface as its body or be defined as a function partial derivative (Section 9.3.10, page 459), and it may not be partial, that is, may not have the `partial` prefix.
- A function *cannot contain* calls to the Modelica *built-in operators* `der`, `initial`, `terminal`, `sample`, `Subtask.activated`, `Subtask.lastInterval`, `pre`, `edge`, `change`, `reinit`, `delay`, `cardinality`, `inStream`, `actualStream`, the operators of the built-in package `Connections`, and is not allowed to contain when-statements.
- The dimension *sizes* not declared with `(:)` of each array result or array local variable of a function must be either given by the input formal parameters, or given by constant or parameter expressions, or by expressions containing combinations of those (Section 9.3.2.8, page 445).

- The local variables of a function are *not* automatically initialized to the implicit default values of the corresponding data types (Section 3.9.1, page 94 and Section 9.3.15, page 464; for example, 0.0 for `Real` and 0 for `Integer`) for performance reasons. It is the responsibility of the user to provide explicit defaults or to define the values of such variables before they are referenced.
- Local variables and formal parameters of a function will behave inside the function as though they have discrete-time variability.
- A subtype of a function type must be almost type equivalent to the function type itself, that is, fulfill *function subtyping* (Section 3.19.6, page 130). This is more restrictive than the usual subtyping rules (Section 3.19.3, page 125) between Modelica classes.

A Modelica `function` has the following enhancements compared to a general Modelica `class`:

- A function may be called using the conventional *positional calling syntax* for passing arguments.
- A function can be *recursive*.
- A formal parameter or local variable may be initialized through an *assignment* (`:=`) of a default value in its declaration. Initialization through an equation is not possible.
- A function is dynamically instantiated, creating an activation record when it is called, rather than being statically instantiated by an instance declaration, which is the case for other kinds of classes.
- A function may have an external function interface specifier as its body.
- A function may be defined in a short function definition to be a function partial derivative.
- A function allows dimension sizes declared with (`:`) to be resized for array results or array local variables, see Section 9.3.2.8, page 445.

The above `Multiply` example is shown below reformulated as a function, where we have changed the name to `multiply`, following the convention that a function name should start with a lowercase letter:

```
function multiply
  input  Real x;
  input  Real y := 0;
  output Real result;
algorithm
  result := x*y;
end multiply;
```

Additional information regarding Modelica functions is available in Chapter 8, page 438.

3.8.7 Specialized Class: package

A `package` is a specialized and enhanced class that is primarily used to manage name spaces and organize Modelica code. A package has the restrictions of only *containing* declarations of *classes* including all kinds of specialized classes, and *constants*, that is, no variable declarations. A package has the enhancement of being allowed to *import* from. The prefix `encapsulated` makes a package an independent unit of code, where dependencies to definitions in other packages are explicitly visible through `import` clauses. A trivial example package:

```
package SmallPack
  import OtherPackage;
  constant Real mypi = 3.14159;

  connector Pin
    ...
  end Pin;

  function multiply
```

```
    ...
  end multiply;
end SmallPack;
```

More information on packages is available in Chapter 10.

3.8.8 Specialized Class: operator record

The `operator record` specialized class is similar to a `record` class except that definition of user-defined overloaded operators is possible, which makes the typing rules different from ordinary records (Section 3.8.2, page 88).

It is not legal to extend from an `operator record`, except as a short class definition modifying the default attributes for the record fields declared directly inside the operator record. Moreover, it is currently not legal to extend from any of its enclosing scopes, that is, scopes containing the operator record definition. A short example is given below:

```
operator record Complex
  Real re;
  Real im;
  ...
  encapsulated operator function '*'
    import Complex;

    input  Complex c1;
    input  Complex c2;
    output Complex result
      annotation(Inline=true);
 algorithm
     result = Complex(re=c1.re*c2.re - c1.im*c2.im,
                      im=c1.re*c2.im + c1.im*c2.re);
  end '*';
end Complex;

// Allowed inheritance via a short class definition
operator record ComplexVoltage" =
  operator record Complex(re(unit="V"),im(unit="V"));

// Disallowed inheritance from an enclosing scope
record MyComplex
  extends Complex;  // not allowed, since extending from enclosing scope
  Real k;
end MyComplex;
```

The restrictions on `extends` are intended to avoid combining two variants inheriting from the same operator record but with possibly different operations; thus `ComplexVoltage` and `ComplexCurrent` still use the operations from `Complex`. The restriction that it is not legal to extend from any of its enclosing scopes also implies the following:

```
package A
  extends Icon; // Ok.
  operator record B … end B;
end A;

package A2
  extends A(…); // Not legal
end A2;
```

```
package A3=A(…); // Not legal
```

More information on user-defined, overloaded operators with the `operator record` specialized class is available in Section 9.5, page 481.

3.8.9 Specialized Class: operator

The `operator` specialized class is similar to `package` but may only contain declarations of functions or operators. It is used for user-defined overloaded operators. An `operator` definition may only be placed within a record or a package. It is currently not legal to extend from any scope containing an operator definition. For example:

```
encapsulated operator '+'
  import Complex;

  function add  "Binary addition, e.g. c1+c2"
    input  Complex c1;
    input  Complex c2;
    output Complex result  "Same as: c1 + c2";
      annotation(Inline=true);
  algorithm
    result := Complex(c1.re + c2.re, c1.im + c2.im);
  end add;

end '+';
```

More information on user-defined overloaded operators with the operator specialized class is available in Section 9.5, page 481.

3.8.10 Specialized Class: operator function

The `operator function` specialized class is shorthand for an `operator` class with exactly one function. The same restrictions as for function class apply. Moreover, it may only be placed inside a record or package and it is not legal to extend from any of its enclosing scopes. This example is from within the `Complex` example in the previous section:

```
encapsulated operator function '*'
  import Complex;

  input  Complex c1;
  input  Complex c2;
  output Complex result
    annotation(Inline=true);
algorithm
  result = Complex(re=c1.re*c2.re - c1.im*c2.im,
                   im=c1.re*c2.im + c1.im*c2.re);
end '*';
```

In general, the operator function definition has the following form:

```
encapsulated operator function 'op'
  ...
end 'op';
```

Such a definition is conceptually the same as, for example, the following:

```
encapsulated operator 'op'
  function foo
    ...
  end foo;
```

```
end 'op';
```

More information on the `operator function` declaration is available in Section 9.5.2.1, page 485.

3.9 Predefined Types/Classes

The basic predefined, built-in types of Modelica are `Real`, `Integer`, `Boolean`, `String`, `Clock`, and the basic enumeration type. These types have some of the properties of a class, that is, they can be inherited, modified, and so on, but, on the other hand, have a number of restrictions and somewhat different properties compared to normal classes. At type checking, variables of these types are regarded as scalar types. Only the *value* attribute can be changed at run-time, and is accessed through the variable name itself, not through dot notation; for example, use `x` and not `x.value` to access the value of the variable `x`. There is also a type `Complex`, predefined in a library and thus not a built-in type.

The primitive types of the machine representations of the *values* of these predefined types have the following properties:

`Real`	IEC 60559:1989 (ANSI/IEEE 754-1985) double format, at least 64-bit floating point precision.
`Integer`	Typically two's-complement 32-bit integer.
`Boolean`	`true` or `false`.
`String`	String of Unicode characters.
Enumeration types	Distinct from `Integer` but values are internally represented as a positive integers.
`Clock`	Built-in clock type for clocked synchronous models.

Note that for argument passing of values when calling external functions in C from Modelica, `Real` corresponds to `double` and `Integer` corresponds to `int`. Below, we use '`RealType`', '`BooleanType`', '`IntegerType`', '`StringType`', and '`EnumType`' as mnemonics corresponding to the above-mentioned primitive types. These mnemonics are enclosed in single quotes to emphasize that they are not available in the Modelica language.

Apart from being built-in types containing machine representations of values, the predefined Modelica types can also be inherited and modified similarly to ordinary Modelica classes, but with the restrictions that variable declarations and equations *cannot be added* in the *derived class*, that is, the class that inherits/extends some other class. See Section 4.1.6, page 141, for a detailed presentation of these restrictions. Another restriction is that attributes cannot be redeclared (see Section 4.3, page 156, regarding redeclaration). Apart from the `value` attribute, the predefined types also have a number of additional attributes that are parameters, that is, cannot be modified at run-time during simulation. These parameter attributes are accessed through ordinary dot notation, for example, `x.unit` for the attribute unit of the variable `x`. The only way to define a subtype of a predefined Modelica type is through inheritance into a specialized `type` class, usually expressed as modifications.

For example, a `Real` variable has a set of attributes such as unit of measure, initial value, and minimum and maximum value. Some of these attributes can be modified when declaring a new type, for example, through a short type definition:

```
type Voltage = Real(unit= "V", min=-220.0, max=220.0);
```

The same definition can also be expressed using the standard inheritance syntax (see Chapter 4 for more details):

```
type Voltage
  extends Real(unit= "V", min=-220.0, max=220.0);
end Voltage;
```

The attributes (the class attributes) of the predefined variable types are described below with Modelica syntax as part of pseudo-type class declarations. These are "pseudo declarations" since they cannot be declared and processed by standard Modelica. Also, as already stated, redeclaration of any of the predefined attributes is not allowed. If the values of these attributes are not explicitly specified, the defaults given below are used.

3.9.1 Real Type

The predefined `Real` type is described by the following pseudo class declaration:

```
type Real "Pseudo class declaration of predefined Real type"
  'RealType'    'value';         // Accessed without dot-notation
  parameter 'StringType'  quantity    = "";
  parameter 'StringType'  unit        = ""  "Unit used in equations";
  parameter 'StringType'  displayUnit = ""  "Default display unit";
  parameter 'RealType'    min=-Inf, max=+Inf; //Inf denotes a large value
  parameter 'RealType'    start = 0;      // Initial value
  parameter 'BooleanType' fixed = true,   // default for parameter/constant
                                = false;  // default for other variables
  parameter 'RealType'    nominal;        // Nominal value equation
  parameter StateSelect   stateSelect = StateSelect.default;
equation
  assert('value' >= min and 'value' <= max,"Variable value out of limit");
  assert(nominal >= min and nominal <= max, "Nominal value out of limit");
end Real;
```

The attributes of the `Real` predefined type have the following meaning:

- *'value'*—not a class attribute in the usual sense but rather the scalar value of a variable declared as having the type `Real`. The value is accessible directly via the variable name and is not accessible using dot notation, which is indicated by enclosing this attribute within single quotes. Thus, use `x` and not `x.value` to access the value of the variable `x`.
- *quantity*—a string describing what physical quantity the type represents. Example quantities could be "force," "weight," "acceleration," and so on.
- *unit*—a string describing the physical unit of the type. Examples are `"kg"`, `"m"`, `"m/s"`, and so on. See also Section 11.16.1, page 559.
- *displayUnit*—gives the default unit used by a Modelica tool for interactive input/output. For example, the `displayUnit` for angle might be `"deg"`, but the `unit` might be `"rad"`. Values interactively input or output as `"deg"` are then automatically converted to/from `"rad"`. See also 11.16.1, page 559.
- *min*—the minimum scalar value representable by the type.
- *max*—the maximum scalar value representable by the type.
- *start*—the initial value of a variable declared as being an instance of the type. The start value is assigned to the variable before starting time-dependent simulation. See also Section 8.4, page 363.
- *fixed*—determines whether the `start` value of a variable having this type is fixed or can be adjusted by the simulator before actually starting the simulation. The default for the attribute `fixed` is `true` for constants and parameters but `false` for other variables, which in practice means (unless `fixed` is explicitly set to `true`) that the specified start value is treated as an initial guess for the variable that can be changed by the simulator in order to find a consistent set of start values before proceeding with dynamic simulation forward in time. See also Section 3.13, page 105.
- *nominal*—a nominal value of the "typical" value type that can be used, for example, by a simulation tool to determine appropriate tolerances or for scaling purposes by giving a hint of the order of magnitude for typical values. The user need not set this value even though a default value

is not specified. The reason is that in cases such as `a=b`, where `b` has a nominal value but not `a`, the nominal value can be propagated to the other variable.

- *stateSelect*—this attribute is used for manual control of which variables should be selected as state variables for numerical solution of equation systems (see Section 18.2.6.1, page 1016, for more information). The default value for this attribute is the enumeration value `StateSelect.default`, which gives automatic state variable selection. This usually works well in almost all applications and the user should therefore normally not need to set this attribute.

3.9.2 Integer, Boolean, and String Types

Analogously to the `Real` predefined type, pseudo class declarations for the types `Integer`, `Boolean`, and `String` are given below:

```
type Integer "Pseudo class declaration of predefined Integer type"
  'IntegerType' 'value';                    // Accessed without dot-notation
  parameter 'StringType'  quantity = "";
  parameter 'IntegerType' min=-Inf, max=+Inf;
  parameter 'IntegerType' start = 0;        // Initial value
  parameter 'BooleanType' fixed = true,     // default for parameter/constant;
                                = false;    // default for other variables
equation
  assert('value'= min and 'value'<= max, "Variable value out of limit");
end Integer;

type Boolean "Pseudo class declaration of predefined Boolean type"
  'BooleanType' 'value';                    // Accessed without dot-notation
  parameter 'StringType'  quantity = "";
  parameter 'BooleanType' start = false;    // Initial value
  parameter 'BooleanType' fixed = true,     // default for parameter/constant
                                = false;    // default for other variables
end Boolean;

type String "Pseudo class declaration of predefined String type"
  'StringType' 'value';                     // Accessed without dot-notation
  parameter 'StringType' quantity = "";
  parameter 'StringType' start = "";        // Initial value
end String;
```

3.9.3 Enumeration Types

Conceptually, an enumeration type is a type whose values can be enumerated using a finite enumeration. In theory, finite ranges of integers are also enumeration types.

However, in Modelica we reserve the concept of *enumeration type* for types defined using a special enumeration-type construct, in which each possible enumeration value of the type is explicitly named. For example, an enumeration type `ShirtSizes` can be defined as follows:

```
type ShirtSizes = enumeration(small, medium, large, xlarge);
```

Enumeration types are regarded as *simple predefined types* with many properties in common with integers apart from the fact that their values, so-called enumeration literals, are explicitly named.

An optional comment string can be specified with each enumeration literal in the enumeration type declaration as follows:

```
type ShirtSizes = enumeration(small "1st", medium "2nd", large "3rd",
                              xlarge "4th");
```

Here the enumeration literals are `ShirtSizes.small`, `ShirtSizes.medium`, `ShirtSizes.large`, and `ShirtSizes.xlarge`.

To show a simple example of using this type we declare a variable `my_shirtsize` of enumeration type `ShirtSizes` and set its start value to the constant enumeration literal value `ShirtSizes.medium`:

```
ShirtSizes my_shirtsize(start = ShirtSizes.medium);
```

Values of enumeration types can be used in many ways analogous to integer values for indexing, comparison, and so on, but excluding arithmetic operations. Iteration over ranges of enumeration values is especially useful (Section 9.2.5, page 427). Arrays indexed by enumeration values can currently only be used in two ways: array element indexing (Section 7.4.1.1, page 322) or in array declaration equations or assignments (Section 7.6.1, page 327). Enumeration values can be stored as array elements. It is possible to use an enumeration type name to represent the possible index elements of array dimensions in declarations (see Section 7.6.1, page 327 and this example):

```
Real w[ShirtSizes]  "Weight of shirts depending on size";
```

There exists an unspecified enumeration type that is a supertype of all possible enumeration types:

```
type SuperEnumeration = enumeration(:);
```

The only practical uses of the unspecified enumeration supertype `enumeration(:)` are as a constraining type of replaceable enumeration types (see Section 4.3.7, page 162) and in enumeration subtyping rules. Thus it can be used as a replaceable enumeration type that can be freely redeclared to any other enumeration type. There can be no enumeration variables declared using `enumeration(:)` in a simulation model. In general we declare an enumeration type `E` as follows:

```
type E = enumeration(e1, e2, ..., en);
```

Here the enumeration literals *e1*, *e2*, ... *en* must have different names within the enumeration type. The names of the enumeration literals are defined inside the scope of the enumeration type *E*. Each enumeration literal in the list has type *E*.

The enumeration type *E* can be viewed as conceptually defined according to the following predefined type schema:

```
type E    "Pseudo class declaration of any enumeration type E"
  'EnumType' 'value';                          // Accessed without dot-notation
  parameter 'StringType'  quantity  = "";
  parameter 'EnumType'    min=e1, max=en;
  parameter 'EnumType'    start = e1;     // Initial value
  parameter 'BooleanType' fixed = true,   // default for parameter/constant;
                                = false;  // default for other variables
  constant  'EnumType'    e1 =...;
  ...
  constant  'EnumType'    en =...;
equation
  assert('value' >= min and 'value' <= max, "Variable value out of limit");
end E;
```

However, even though the above enumeration type schema is similar to an ordinary class declaration, enumeration types are *sub-range types* that do not follow the usual subtyping rules for classes (see Section 3.18.2, page 117, and Section 3.19, page 123, for more details).

One can obtain the ordinal integer value of an enumeration value by using `Integer` as a conversion function. The call `Integer(e)` returns the ordinal number of the enumeration value `E.enumvalue` to which `e` is evaluated, where `Integer(E.e1)=1` and `Integer(E.en)=n`, for an enumeration type *E* = `enumeration(e1, e2, ..., en)`. Referring to our previous example, `Integer(ShirtSizes.Medium) = 2`.

There is also a conversion function `String` that returns the string representation of an enumeration value. For example, `String(ShirtSizes.Large) = "Large"`.

3.9.4 Clock Type

The predefined `Clock` type is used for synchronous clock-based system modeling and is described in detail in Section 13.6, page 694.

3.9.5 Other Predefined Types

The predefined `StateSelect` enumeration type is the type of the `stateSelect` attribute of the `Real` type. It is used to control state selection, and is defined and explained in Section 18.2.6.1, page 1016.

The predefined partial class `ExternalObject` is used to define opaque references to data structures created outside Modelica (see Section 9.4.8, page 476).

A number of "predefined" record types and enumeration types for graphical annotations are described in Chapter 11. However these types are not predefined in the usual sense since they cannot be referenced in ordinary Modelica code, only within annotations.

The `Complex` type is predefined, but not in the Modelica language. Instead it is predefined in a Modelica record type called `Complex`. This is distributed as part of the standard Modelica library (MSL) but defined at the top-level outside of MSL. It is referred to as `Complex` or `.Complex.` and is automatically preloaded by most tools, enabling direct usage without the need for any import statements (except in encapsulated classes). There is a library ComplexMath with operations on complex numbers (Section 16.3, page 923). See also Section 9.5, page 481.

The following are some examples of using the predefined type `Complex`:

```
Real a = 2;
Complex j = Modelica.ComplexMath.j;
Complex b = 2 + 3*j;
Complex c = (2*b + a)/b;
Complex d = Modelica.ComplexMath.sin(c);
Complex v[3] = {b/2, c, 2*d};
```

3.9.6 Types for Symbolic Programming

Data types such as trees and lists used for symbolic programming and modeling in Modelica are described in Section 6.15, page 296. These constructs are at the time of this writing not part of the Modelica Language standard but are available implemented in the MetaModelica language extension, which is supported by the OpenModelica compiler.

3.10 Structure of Variable Declarations

A Modelica variable, that is, a class instance, is always a member of some other class instance or function instance. The declaration of a variable states the type, access, variability, data flow, and other properties of the variable. A declaration can be divided into three parts: zero or more *prefixes*, followed by a *type*, and followed by a list of *variable specifiers*. A variable specifier can be a single *identifier*, or an identifier optionally followed by a *modifier* and/or an array dimension descriptor, optionally followed by an *initializer* or *declaration equation* right-hand side, optionally followed by an *ifcondition* for conditional instance declarations, that is, the keyword `if` and a Boolean expression. Thus, the structure of a *declaration* is as follows:

<prefixes> <type-specifier> <variable specifier list>

A *variable specifier* has the following structure, where all elements apart from the identifier are optional:

<identifier> <array dimension descriptor> <modifiers> <declaration equation/initializer> <ifcondition>

The type specifier part of a declaration describes the kind of values that can be represented by the declared variable(s). It consists of a type name optionally followed by an array dimension descriptor.

There is no difference between variables declared in a single declaration or in multiple declarations. For example, regard the following single declaration of two matrix variables:

```
Real[2,2]  A, B;
```

That declaration has the same meaning as the following two declarations together:

```
Real[2,2]  A;
Real[2,2]  B;
```

The array dimension descriptors may instead be placed after the variable name in the variable specifier, giving the two declarations below, with the same meaning as in the previous example:

```
Real  A[2,2];
Real  B[2,2];
```

The following declaration is different, meaning that the variable `a` is a scalar and `B` is a matrix as above:

```
Real  a, B[2,2];
```

3.11 Declaration Prefixes

Both class and variable declarations can contain various qualifier prefixes. These prefixes associate certain properties with the declaration and are placed at the beginning of the declaration. The following sections give an overview of the Modelica declaration prefixes.

3.11.1 Access Control by Prefixes: public and protected

As was already described in the introductory Section 3.5 on access control, page 83, an optional *access prefix* may be specified at the beginning of a declaration. The access prefixes available in Modelica are `public` and `protected`, giving two possible levels of visibility for Modelica variables. This is illustrated by the class `AccessDemo` below.

Note that an access prefix is implicitly *applied* to all *subsequent declarations* without access prefix following the current declaration until the next declaration with an access prefix in the same scope. This makes it natural to view an access prefix as a *heading* for a *section* of declarations. The initial default is `public` if nothing yet has been specified within the current scope. Thus, the variables `a`, `x`, `y`, `z`, `u3` are `public`, whereas `w`, `u`, `u2` and class `Clocal` are `protected`.

```
class AccessDemo "Illustration of access prefixes"
  Real a;
public
  Real x;
  Real y, z;
protected
  Real w, u[3];
  Real u2;

  class Clocal
  end Clocal;

public
  Real u3;

  class Caccess
```

```
    Clocal c; // Legal use of protected class Clocal from enclosing scope
  end Caccess;

end AccessDemo;

class AccessDemoUse
  AccessDemo a;
  Real x2 = a.x;              // Legal use of public x through dot notation
  Real x3illegal = a.w;       // Illegal use of protected w through dot notation
end AccessDemoUse;
```

The `public` declaration of variables `a`, `x`, `y`, `z`, `u3` means that any code with access to, directly within the current scope or via dot notation, an `AccessDemo` instance can read or update those variables. The other possible level of visibility, specified by the keyword `protected`, means that only code inside the class `AccessDemo` as well as code in classes that inherit this class are allowed access to the variables `w`, `u`, and `u2`. In fact, only code inside the class `AccessDemo` has access to the same instances of the protected variables `w`, `u`, and `u2`.

Elements are inherited with their own protection, that is, `public` and `protected` elements keep being `public` and `protected`, respectively, after being inherited into another class. However, the access prefixes `public` and `protected` from a parent class are not inherited as elements themselves and can therefore never influence the protection status of the declarations in a child class.

To summarize, a protected class or instance `P`, which is part of a class or instance, may not be accessed via dot-notation as in the illegal examples `A.P`, `a.P`, `a[1].P`, `a.b.P`, `.A.P`, but there is no restriction on using `P` or `P.x` for a protected element `P` in a scope where `P` is visible.

Regarding inheritance of protected elements see also Section 4.1.11, page 145, and regarding their modification see Section 4.2.9, page 154.

3.11.2 Variability Prefixes: constant, parameter, and discrete

The prefixes `constant`, `parameter`, `discrete` of a variable declaration are called *variability prefixes* and define in which situations the value of variable may change and when it is kept constant. The term *variability* here should be interpreted as *time variability*. See also Section 6.8.1.3, page 278 for more details regarding variability. The variability prefixes can be used to define the following four kinds of variables (see Figure 3-7):

- Named *constants*—variables with the `constant` prefix that *never change value* once they have been defined. They can, for example, be used to define mathematical constants. The derivative of a constant is zero. A constant definition can be modified using a modifier (Section 4.2.3, page 149) if it is not `final` (Section 3.11.6, page 103). A named constant can be defined in a package, can be imported from a package (Section 10.2.1, page 497), and can be accessed by nested lookup (Section 3.16.1, page 109) from inside a subclass to the class where the constant is defined. See also Section 6.9.1, page 280, regarding constant variability expressions.
- Named constant *parameters*—variables with the `parameter` prefix, that *remain constant* during time-dependent simulation and have time derivative equal to zero. These "constants" may be assigned values, for example, during the initialization phase or interactively by the user via a simulation tool immediately before time-dependent simulation starts. Interactive setting of simulation parameters is usually done very conveniently via the graphical user interface of the simulation tool. The built-in `der(...)` derivative operator need not be applied to such variables since the result is always zero. A parameter cannot be defined in a package, it cannot be imported from a package, and cannot be accessed implicitly from a scope inside the model where it is defined. See also Section 6.9.2, page 281, regarding parameter variability of expressions.
- *Discrete-time* variables with the optional associated prefix `discrete` change their values only at event instants during simulation (see Section 13.2.2 in Chapter 13), and have time derivative equal

to zero. However, it is illegal to apply the `der()` operator to a discrete-time variable. There are two kinds of discrete-time variables: unclocked discrete time and clocked discrete time. Unclocked discrete-time variables are *piecewise constant* signals that change only at event instants, whereas clocked discrete-time variables are defined and changed only at clock tick events for an associated clock (Section 13.2.5.5, page 603 and Section 13.6, page 694 regarding clocks) and are undefined between clock ticks. `Boolean`, `Integer`, `String`, and `enumeration` variables are unclocked discrete time by default and cannot be continuous time according to the Modelica language rules. A `Real` variable with the prefix `discrete` is a discrete-time variable. Any variable defined only at ticks of a clock is a clocked discrete-time variable. However, note that a `Real` variable *without* the `discrete` prefix but assigned a value in a when-statement or when-equation is an unclocked discrete-time variable. See also Section 6.9.3, page 281, regarding discrete-time variability of expressions.

- *Continuous-time* variables evolve their values continuously during simulation. This is default for `Real` variables if no variability prefix is specified and they are not assigned in a when-equation or when-statement. This is the most common kind of variable in continuous models.

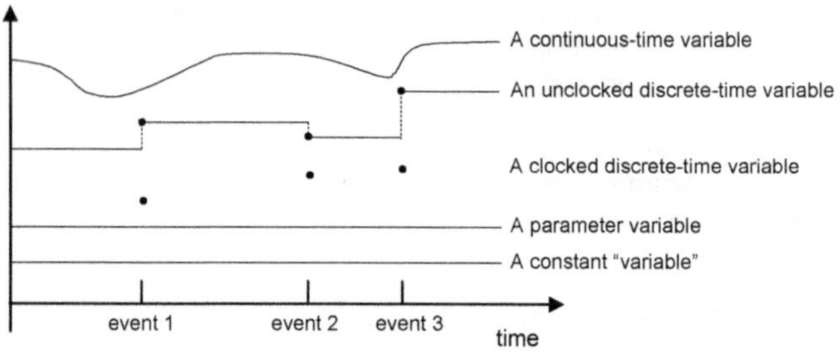

Figure 3-7. Illustrating variables with different variability.

Named constants can be defined in Modelica by using the prefixes `constant` or `parameter` in declarations and providing declaration equations as part of the declarations. For example:

```
constant  Real    PI = 4*arctan(1);
constant  String  redcolor = "red";
constant  Integer one = 1;
parameter Real    mass = 22.5;
constant  Real    tobespecified; // to be given value through a modification
```

A constant or parameter cannot be defined to cyclically depend on itself; the definition must be acyclic (Section 8.2.3, page 350). The following illegal declaration is cyclic:

```
parameter Real x = 3*exp(x);  // Illegal, since x = 3*exp(x) is cyclic
```

Parameter "constants" can be declared without a declaration equation containing a default value since their value can be defined, for example, by reading from a file, before simulation starts. For example:

```
parameter Real  mass, gravity, length;
```

Parameter "constants" may also be used as *structural parameters*, parameters whose values influence the structure of the model, that is, the set of active equations. For example, in the model `Inertia` below, two equations are effectively removed from influencing the simulation if the user sets `condflg` to `false` before simulation starts.

```
model Inertia
  parameter Boolean condflg;
  ...
```

```
equation
  J*a = t1 - t2;
  if condflg then
    der(v) = a;      // Two conditional equations,
    der(r) = v;      // deactivated if condflg=false
  end if
  ...
end Inertia;
```

Variables of type `Real` are normally continuous-time variables as the default, without explicit declaration of a more restrictive variability prefix. Piecewise constant (`discrete`) `Real` variables can be declared but are rarely needed. However, unclocked `Real` variables that are explicitly assigned in when-statements or implicitly assigned values through solution of equations in when-equations are also `discrete`, that is, piecewise constant.

Variables of type `Integer`, `Boolean`, `String`, or `enumeration` have data types that change value in discrete steps. Such variables may change their values only at events (or during function evaluation for local variables in functions), which makes the default variability `discrete` natural.

Variables and expressions in functions behave as though they were discrete-time expressions since a function is always called and evaluated at some point in time that is, time does not go forward during evaluation of a function call, similar to the evaluation of a when-equation at an event. Function calls can, however, occur at any point in time, not only at events.

3.11.3 Causality Prefixes: input and output

One of the major advantages of an equation-based language such as Modelica is that acausal mathematical models can be specified since equations do not prescribe a certain data-flow direction. However, certain model components such as functions and blocks have specified causality. When calling a function, data are supplied as actual input arguments and results are returned from the function. The same is true for blocks since a `block` is a kind of specialized Modelica class with specified causality for all variables in its interface.

The prefixes `input` and `output` are mainly available for specifying, thus restricting the direction of data flow for declared variables. This is required for interface variables of blocks and functions but can be used for a variable in any class, for example, to simplify the solution process when the data-flow direction is known. However, the data-flow direction is allowed to be reversed in equation-based models, including blocks, if that enables solution. A simple `block` with one `input` and one `output` variable is shown below:

```
block SquareDance
  input  Real x;
  output Real squared;
equation
  squared = x*x;
end SquareDance;
```

The prefixes `input` and `output` when used on a variable which is structured, e.g., a record variable, are also applied to the elements (e.g. record fields) of the variable. This is done after verifying that the prefixes occurring on the elements of the variable are correct. The `input` and `output` prefixes shall only be applied to a structured variable if no element of the variable has a prefix which is `input` or `output`.

The prefixes `input` and `output` have slightly varying semantic meanings depending on the context in which they are used:

- In *functions,* these prefixes define the *computational causality* of the function body, that is, given the variables declared as `input`, the variables declared as `output` are computed in the function body (Section 9.3.1, page 438).
- At the *top level of a model* that is to be *simulated,* these prefixes define the *interaction with the environment* in which the *simulation model* is used, that is, data from environment provided as

input to the simulated model, or output data from the simulation provided to the environment. Thus the `input` prefix defines those values for such a variable that have to be provided from the simulation environment and the `output` prefix defines that the values of the corresponding variable can be directly utilized in the simulation environment. See also the notion of globally balanced in Section 8.9.2.5, page 393.

- In *model instances,* the `input` prefix defines that a binding equation, that is, a declaration equation or modifier, *has to be provided* to define the input value of the corresponding variable when the instance is used in order to guarantee a *locally balanced model*; that is, the number of local equations is identical to the local number of unknowns (Section 8.9.2.1, page 389). The `output` prefix does not have any effect in a model instance and is ignored. Note that in model instances the `input` or `output` prefixes do not necessarily specify causality since causality can be reversed even in block models because they contain equations (see comment in Section 8.9.3.4, page 398, regarding computational causality). A binding equation is shown here:

```
block Fum
  input Real x;      // An input variable x in a model
end Fum;

model UseFum
  Fum fum(x=time); // A binding equation x=time for x in instance fum
end UseFum;
```

- In *connectors* the prefixes `input` and `output` define that the corresponding connectors can only be connected according to block diagram semantics, that is, a connector with an `output` variable can only be connected to a connector where the corresponding variable is declared as `input`, and vice versa (Section 5.7.3, page 211). There is also the restriction that connectors that have at least one variable declared as `input` must be externally connected in order to get a locally balanced model, where the number of local unknowns is identical to the number of unknown equations (Section 8.9.2, page 389). Together with the block diagram semantics rule, this means that such connectors must be connected exactly once externally.
- In *records* the prefixes `input` and `output` are not allowed, since otherwise a record could not be, for example, passed as input argument to a function.

3.11.4 Flow Prefix: flow

The `flow` prefix when used on a variable which is structured, e.g. a record variable, is also applied to the elements (e.g. record fields) of the variable. This is done after verifying that the prefixes occurring on the elements of the variable are correct; e.g. the `flow` prefix can be used on a record field and all the record fields will generate zero-sum equations, even if elements of a record may not be declared with the `flow` prefix. The `flow` prefix shall only be applied to a structured variable if no element of the variable has a prefix which is `flow` or `stream`. For more in-depth information concerning the `flow` prefix including examples, see Chapter 5, page 190. A small example of a `flow` variable declaration inside a connector class:

```
connector Pin
  Voltage v;
  flow Current i;
end Pin;
```

3.11.5 Stream Prefix: stream

The `stream` prefix is required in front of *stream variables* in *stream connector* definitions, see Section 5.10, page 245, which are useful in models with reversible flows. Stream variables must be a subtype of Real. The `stream` prefix when used on a variable which is structured, e.g. a record variable, is also applied to the elements (e.g., record fields) of the variable. This is done after verifying that the prefixes occurring on the elements of the variable are correct. The `stream` prefix shall only be applied to a structured variable if no element of the variable has a prefix which is `flow` or `stream`. A small example of a `stream` variable declaration inside a stream connector class is:

```
connector FluidPort
  AbsolutePressure         p;
  flow    MassFlowRate     m_flow;
  stream SpecificEnthalpy  h_outflow;
end FluidPort;
```

3.11.6 Modification Prefixes[13]: replaceable, redeclare, and final

Modification prefixes control modification of declared elements in classes. What is a modifier? It can be regarded as a kind of (incomplete) declaration that is used to change certain declarations from an inherited class. We have already seen several examples of simple modifiers that are used to change default class attribute values. For example, the following type declaration contains three modifiers to the built-in class `Real` that modifies the attributes `unit`, `min`, and `max`.

```
type Voltage = Real(unit="V", min=-220.0, max=220.0);
```

The `final` prefix used at the front of a declaration or modifier prevents all modifications of a declared element and further modifications of a modified element. The motivation behind the `final` prefix is to prevent users from unknowingly introducing certain errors, which can be avoided by forbidding modifications of sensitive elements. The use of `final` also prevents interactive setting of parameter variables in the simulation environment since this is a kind of modification. The `final` prefix prohibits further modification of the `unit` attribute in the next example:

```
type Angle = Real(final unit = "rad");
Angle a1(unit="deg");           // Error, since unit declared as final!
```

The modification prefix `replaceable` used in front of a declaration enables modification in the form of a redeclaration of that declaration. The following is an example of a replaceable declaration from the class C below of the example variable `pobj1`, where `pobj1` also has a local modifier `p1=5`:

```
replaceable GreenClass  pobj1(p1=5);
```

However, modification of the default attribute *value* of a declared element is allowed also without the `replaceable` prefix, as for the `unit` attribute in the above `Voltage` declaration.

The `class C`, also presented previously in Chapter 2, Section 2.5.1, page 32.

```
class C
  replaceable GreenClass  pobj1(p1=5);
  replaceable YellowClass pobj2;
  replaceable GreenClass  pobj3;
  RedClass    obj4;
equation
  ...
end C;
```

When a modifier contains a complete declaration including type and/or prefixes, the `redeclare` prefix is required at the front of the modifier, which then replaces the original declaration. Such a modifier is called a *redeclaration*, and usually (but not always—see Chapter 4, page 156) requires the original declaration to be declared with the prefix `replaceable`. For example:

```
class C2 = C(redeclare RedClass pobj1);
```

The modification prefix `replaceable` when used in a modifier enables *further* modification of the resulting modified element. For example, in class `C3` this is used to enable further modification of `pobj1` when creating `C4`:

[13] The reader who wants a more accessible and in-depth treatment of this topic should read Chapter 4 instead of the short presentation in this section.

```
class C3 = C(redeclare replaceable RedClass pobj1);
class C4 = C3(redeclare YellowClass pobj1);  // OK, since replaceable
class C4 = C2(redeclare YellowClass pobj1);  // Error, not replaceable
```

Modelica classes and packages can be parameterized in a general way, corresponding to generic classes or packages (see Chapter 2, page 31, and Chapter 10, page 508). Both classes and variables that are members of some class can be used as a kind of class parameter by attaching the prefix `replaceable` in front of their declarations. It is *required* to have the prefix `replaceable` in an element declaration to allow replacing the declaration, except when only changing the default attribute value, and/or restricting the variability and possible dimension sizes.

For more details and examples regarding modifiers, see Chapter 4, page 148, regarding redeclaration and generic classes see Chapter 4, page 156 and page 168 respectively, and on the semantics of `final` see page 161 in the same chapter.

3.11.7 Class Prefix: partial

The class prefix `partial` is used to indicate that a class is incomplete such that it cannot be instantiated. The keyword is optional—a class can be incomplete without having the prefix `partial`. On the other hand, the `partial` prefix is required for those partial classes for which type checking of the class declaration cannot be performed without generating type errors, for example, because a type used by the partial class might not be available where the class is declared, only where it is used. Partial classes are aimed at reuse through inheritance (see Chapter 4, page 173 for more details). The common terminology for partial class in other programming languages is *abstract* class.

3.11.8 Class Encapsulation Prefixes: encapsulated

The class encapsulation prefix `encapsulated` is used to achieve lookup encapsulation of classes, that is, the lookup stops at the class boundary. This mechanism is primarily intended for Modelica packages, since the common concept of packages entails an independent software unit used for organization of large software systems. An encapsulated package (or class) has no implicit dependencies on the declaration context within which it is placed. All dependencies are explicit via `import` clauses. See Chapter 10 on packages, page 497, for more information.

3.11.9 Instance Hierarchy Lookup Prefixes: inner and outer

Lookup of names in Modelica is normally done in the usual way for lexically scoped languages with nested scopes. First the current scope containing the name reference is searched for a definition of the name; if not found, the next outer scope is searched, and so on.

However, *lookup through the instance hierarchy* instead of through the class nesting hierarchy is more suitable when a pervasive object property such as a *force field* or an *environment* temperature should affect all parts of the object. In Modelica such a common property can be declared as a *definition declaration* using the `inner` prefix, and subsequently accessed by *reference declarations* using the `outer` prefix. The lookup is performed through the instance hierarchy instead of through the nested class declaration hierarchy.

See Section 5.8 on page 224 for a comprehensive description of applications of this concept and Section 3.17.5 on page 113 in this chapter for a presentation of the instance hierarchy lookup mechanism.

3.11.10 Ordering and Placement of Prefixes

The *ordering* of Modelica declaration prefixes within a declaration is strictly specified according to the list below. Not all combinations of prefixes are meaningful; for example, a `constant input` variable is not very interesting since it can never change value. The modification prefix `redeclare` may occur in modifiers or in declarations (Section 4.3.1, page 157), whereas the access prefixes `public` and `protected` may never occur in a modifier.

The prefixes `encapsulated` and `partial` may be used only for classes, whereas `flow, stream, discrete, parameter, constant, input,` and `output` may be used only in variable declarations.

The prefixes are placed at the beginning of a declaration element and should be used in the following order whenever more than one prefix occurs in the same declaration:

1. Access prefixes `public` and `protected`.
2. Modification prefix `final`.
3. Instance hierarchy lookup prefixes `inner` and `outer`.
4. Modification prefix `redeclare`.
5. Modification prefix `replaceable`.
6. Class encapsulation prefix `encapsulated`.
7. Class prefix `partial`.
8. The flow prefix `flow` or the stream connector prefix `stream`.
9. Variability prefixes `constant`, `parameter`, and `discrete`.
10. Causality prefixes `input` and `output`.

A subset of the prefixes are denoted *type prefixes* i.e., `flow, stream, discrete, parameter, constant, input, output,` and are considered part of the class type when type checking. See also Section 3.18.7, page 120, in this chapter.

3.12 Variable Specifiers

After having discussed declaration prefixes in detail in the previous sections, it is useful to recall the structure of a declaration:

<prefixes> <type> <variable specifier list>

Each *variable specifier* also has a structure, where all parts apart from the identifier are optional:

<identifier> <array dimension descriptor> <modifiers> <declaration equation/initializer> <ifcondition>

As previously stated, an array dimension descriptor can either be part of the type or be put directly after the identifier in the variable specifier. The modifiers should always be placed after the array dimension descriptor if present, otherwise directly after the identifier. More information on modifiers is available in Chapter 4, page 148. The next section shows examples of modifications of start values for specifying default initial values of variables.

The optional *ifcondition* is used in conditional instance declarations, see Section 3.14, page 107.

3.13 Initial Values of Variables

A Modelica variable is either statically allocated and instantiated, which is normally the case for instantiations of models, or is dynamically instantiated, as is the case for function formal parameters and local variables. The `start` value of a variable is the default initial value of the variable normally used at the beginning of a simulation. The simulation tool, the solver, is, however, free (unless specifically prohibited in each declaration by setting the built-in attribute `fixed` to `true`) to choose another start value for the variable if this is necessary to be able to solve the systems of equations.

If nothing else is specified, the default start value of all statically allocated numerical variables is zero or an array containing elements of the value zero, apart from function results and local variables, where the initial value is unspecified. Start values other than the default zero can be specified by setting the `start` attribute of instance variables. For example, a start value can be specified in the class `MyPoints`:

```
class MyPoints
  Point  point1(start={1,2,3});
  Point  point2;
  Point  point3;
end MyPoints;
```

Alternatively, the start value of `point1` can be specified when instantiating `MyPoints` as below:

```
class Main
  MyPoints  pts(point1.start={1,2,3});
  foo1      f1;
end Main;
```

Note that the `start` attribute of an array variable has the same dimensionality as the variable itself. Single elements of the `start` value can be modified by indexing the attribute in the modification equation, for example, `start[2,1]` in the array `A5` example. Below are a few declarations with different combinations of array dimension descriptors and modifiers.

```
Real  A3[2,2];                          // Array variable
Real  A4[2,2](start={{1,0},{0,1}}); // Array with explicit start value
Real  A5[2,2](start[2,1]=2.3); // Array with single element modification
```

Do not make the mistake of using declaration equations for specifying initial values since this will set the variable equal to a constant value throughout the simulation. This is fine for constants or parameters since their values should be fixed during simulation, but is usually not what is expected for a normal variable. For example:

```
class test2
  parameter Real x1 = 35.2;       /* OK, since x1 has a fixed value */
  Real x2 = 99.5;                 /* Probably a mistake */
end test2;
```

No equations are present in functions, not even equations for start values, since functions can contain only algorithmic code. Instead, assignment statements can be used to specify default initial values of formal parameters, function results, or local variables. Consider the example function `f2` below:

```
function f2
  input  Real x;
  input  Real y := 2;
  output Real r1;
  output Real r2 := 3;
algorithm
  r1 := 2*x;
  if r1>5 then r2 := 2*y;
end f2;
```

A call to `f2` using positional parameter passing always requires specifying values of all the arguments, which leaves the default value of `y` unused:

```
(z1,z2) := f2(33.3,44.4);
```

On the other hand, a call to `f2` using named parameter passing as below can leave out the second argument since the default is available for this argument. Note that because the conditional assignment to `r2` will never take place as a result of the call below, the default result of `3` will be used for the second result `r2`:

```
(z1,z2) := f2(x=1);
```

3.14 Conditional Instance Declarations

A variable/instance declaration can be made *conditional* by attaching the keyword `if` followed by a condition that is a Boolean parameter expression. This expression must be possible to evaluate at compile time.

If the condition is `false`, the instance, its modifiers, and any connect equation involving the instance are removed.

For example, the following model instantiates either `R1` or `R2` and selects the relevant connection:

```
model ConditionalResistorCircuit
  parameter connectR1 = false;
  Resistor R1(R=100) if connectR1;
  Resistor R2(R=200) if not connectR1;
  Resistor R3(R=300);
equation
  connect(R1.p, R3.p);  // Selected if connectR1 = true
  connect(R2.p, R3.p);  // Selected if connectR1 = false
end ConditionalResistorCircuit;

model R1Circuit =
  ConditionalResistorCircuit(connectR1=true);

model R2Circuit =
  ConditionalResistorCircuit(connectR1=false);
```

If `connectR1=true`, the flattened `R1Circuit` would appear as follows:

```
model R1CircuitFlat
  parameter connectR1 = true;
  Resistor R1(R=100) if connectR1;
  Resistor R3(R=300);
equation
  connect(R1.p, R3.p);  // Selected if connectR1 = true
end R1CircuitFlat;
```

If the condition is true for a public conditional connector containing flow variables the connector must be connected from the outside. The reason for this restriction is that the default flow equation is probably incorrect (since it could otherwise be an unconditional connector) and the model cannot check that the connector is connected.

An instance declared with a condition attribute can *only* be modified and/or *used* in *connections*. Thus, the following equation, which directly refers to the conditional instance `R1`, is illegal:

```
R1.p.v = w; // Illegal since conditional instance R1 only in connections
```

Regarding redeclaration of conditional instances, see Section 4.3.8, page 165. The following example shows issues regarding modifiers and conditional instances:

```
  parameter Integer level(min=1)=1;
  Motor  motor;
  Level1 instance1(J=J)            if level==1 "Conditional instance";
  Level2 instance2                 if level==2 "Conditional instance";
  Level3 instance3(J=instance1.J) if level<2  "Conditional instance";
// Illegal modifier on instance3 since instance1.J is conditional
// Even if we can see that instance1 always existx if instance3 existx
equation
  connect(instance1..., ...) "Connection to conditional instance 1";
  connect(instance2.n, motor.n) "Connection to conditional instance 2";
  connect(instance3.n, motor.n) "Connection to conditional instance 3";
  instance1.u=0; // Illegal
```

3.15 Declaration Order and Use before Declaration

In Modelica, as well as for classes in Java, variables and classes can be used *before* they are declared. This gives maximum flexibility in organizing the code to achieve logical structuring and maximum readability. For example, the well-known top-down design methodology emphasizes the major building blocks at the top level of the system structure and puts less emphasis on low-level details. A declaration before use constraint, common in several older programming languages, would force the low-level model components to be declared first, making it harder to use top-down design.

In fact, in Modelica declaration order is significant only in the following two cases:

- Declaration order is significant for input or output formal parameter declarations in *functions* with more than one input formal parameter or more than one result. The reason is that functions may be called with positional parameter passing, for example, as in the examples in the previous section.
- Declaration order is significant for the variable declarations within *record* classes. The reason is that any record can be passed as an argument to an external function, in which case the variable ordering in the Modelica record is reflected in the variable ordering of the corresponding external record data structure.

In the example class below, which is perfectly legal, the types `Voltage` and `Current` are used before they are declared, and variable `x` can use a reference to variable `y` before it is declared:

```
class UseBeforeDecl
  Voltage v1;
  Current i1;
  Voltage v2;
  type Voltage = Real(unit="kV");
  type Current = Real(unit="mA");
  Real x = y;
  Real y = x;
end UseBeforeDecl;
```

3.16 Introduction to Scoping and Name Lookup

The scope of a name in Modelica is the region of the code where the name has a meaning corresponding to its intended use. For example, we may have declared a `Real` variable `x` in a class `RC` and an `Integer` variable `x` in another class `IC`:

```
class RC
  Real x;
  class IC
    Integer x;
  equation
    x = 2;
  end IC;
  class BC
    Real y;
  equation
    x = y;
  end BC;
equation
  x = 3.14;
end RC;
```

The scope of the `Real` variable `x` includes the whole class `RC` apart from the class `IC` where the `Real x` is hidden by a local declaration of an `Integer` variable `x` within `IC`, which has a scope that is precisely `IC`. Thus, scopes usually correspond to class declarations.

3.16.1 Simple Nested Name Lookup

Modelica uses nested lookup of names like most other programming languages. The lookup procedure searches for declarations of names within local nested scopes before going out to enclosing scopes. This is the reason why the `Real x` is hidden within `IC`—the search procedure finds the declaration of the integer `x` first; it does not even need to investigate the declarations within `RC`.

However, even if there was no local declaration of the variable `x`, it would still be illegal to refer to the `Real x` in the enclosing scope `RC`—*references* to *variables and parameters in enclosing scopes is illegal* in Modelica. Such nested lookup is only allowed for names of constants and declared classes. For example:

```
package A
  constant Real z = 2;
  model B
    Real z;
    function foo
      output Real y
    algorithm y := z; // Illegal since reference to non-constant z in B
    ...
```

It is not only classes that introduce declarations with local scopes. The iteration variable in Modelica for-loops has a scope that extends throughout the for-loop, and hides declarations of variables with the same name in enclosing scopes. For example:

```
function PolynomialEvaluator3
  input  Real a[:];
  input  Real x;
  output Real y;
protected
  Real    xpower;
  Integer i;   (* Declared local variable i *)
algorithm
  y := 0;
  xpower := 1;
  for i in 1:size(a, 1) loop   (* Iteration variable i *)
     y := y + a[i]*xpower;
     xpower := xpower*x;
  end for;
end PolynomialEvaluator3;
```

The iteration variable `i` introduced by the for-loop in the body of the function `PolynomialEvaluator3` has a scope that extends throughout that for-loop, thus preventing access to the declared local variable `i` from within the for-loop.

3.16.2 Scope Preprocessing Needed for Lookup

Some preprocessing/flattening needs to be done on declarations and other elements in each enclosing scope/class before lookup can be performed in that scope. Modifiers and redeclarations, when present, are applied to the declarations where they appear. *Extends clauses* are processed by lookup and copying of inherited class contents into the current class. The detailed procedure is described in Section 4.1.7, page 143.

For example, the following class `TemperatureDepResistorCircuit` is expanded/flattened into the class `TempDepResistorCircuitFlattened` below. The contents of `GenericResistorCircuit` is copied and the two redeclarations are performed, giving a class scope where all named elements are explicitly available for lookup. This example is explained in more detail in Section 4.4.2, page 169.

```
model GenericResistorCircuit
  replaceable Resistor R1(R=100);
```

```
    replaceable Resistor R2(R=200);
    replaceable Resistor R3(R=300);
  equation
    connect(R1.p, R2.p);
    connect(R1.p, R3.p);
  end GenericResistorCircuit;

  model TemperatureDepResistorCircuit
    Real Temp;
    extends GenericResistorCircuit(
      redeclare TempResistor R1(RT=0.1, Temp=Temp),
      redeclare TempResistor R2
    );
  end TemperatureDepResistorCircuit;
```

The following is the expanded/flattened version of `TemperatureDepResistorCircuit`:

```
  model TempDepResistorCircuitFlattened
    Real Temp;
    TempResistor R1(R=100, RT=0.1, Temp=Temp);
    TempResistor R2(R=200);
    replaceable Resistor R3(R=300);
  equation
    connect(R1.p, R2.p);
    connect(R1.p, R3.p);
  end TempDepResistorCircuitFlattened;
```

3.17 Nested Lookup Procedure in Detail

The following stepwise procedure specifies the semantics of lookup for a name used within some piece of Modelica code. The lookup starts in the innermost scope containing the code, usually a class, and proceeds through the sequence of enclosing scopes until the outermost scope or an encapsulated package or class is encountered. The notion of class should be interpreted in the general sense, that is, it can also be a function or package.

Implicitly defined names of record constructor functions are ignored during *type name lookup*, since a record and its implicitly created record constructor function (Section 9.3.8, page 452) have the same name. Names of record classes are ignored during *function name lookup*.

Certain language constructs referred to below such as `import` clauses, `encapsulated` packages, and `encapsulated` classes are explained in more detail in Chapter 10, page 495. To summarize, regarding the following clause:

```
  import A.B.Myclass;
```

This clause makes it possible to access `Myclass` using the short name `Myclass` instead of `A.B.Myclass`. A more concise way of importing several definitions is the following:

```
  import A.B.{Myclass1,Myclass2,Myclass3};
```

This unqualified import makes it possible to refer to the classes only using the short names `Myclass1`, `Myclass2`, `Myclass3` instead of long names such as `A.B.Myclass1`.

Qualified import of a whole package `A.B` can be done as below:

```
  import A.B;
```

This qualified package import makes it possible to use the name `B.Myclass` with a short package prefix `B` for access, whereas the following unqualified import has a different effect:

```
  import A.B.*;
```

Such an unqualified import allows the use of short names such as `Myclass` for all classes in `A.B`.

3.17.1 Lookup of Simple Names

The lookup procedure for simple unqualified names (without dot notation) is as follows, excluding lookup of names with the prefix `outer`, which is described in Section 3.17.5, page 113:

1. First look for implicitly declared iteration variables in possible enclosing for-equations (Section 8.3.2, page 352) or for-statements (Section 9.2.5, page 427) if the analyzed code is inside the body of a for-construct, or within iterator expressions in array constructors (Section 7.2.2, page 316), or reduction expressions (Section 7.9.4, page 337).
2. When a piece of Modelica code is analyzed, for example, a class or variable declaration, an `extends` clause, an equation or algorithm, encountered names in the code are looked up. Each such name is looked up in the sequence of enclosing scopes starting at the innermost scope. The search continues until a match is found or the outermost scope or a scope corresponding to an encapsulated class or encapsulated package has been reached. (However, even if found, it is illegal to reference a variable or parameter declaration in an enclosing scope, whereas constants and classes can be accessed, similar to the rules for definitions in packages.)

   If not found, the lookup continues in the global scope containing the predefined Modelica types, functions, and operators. (For example, the predefined function `abs` is searched upwards in the hierarchy as usual. If an encapsulated boundary is reached, `abs` is searched for in the global scope instead. The operator `abs` cannot be redefined in the global scope, because an existing class cannot be redefined at the same level.) Certain operators are denoted by reserved words or special characters and therefore do not need lookup (see the Modelica Grammar in Appendix B, page 1073).

As stated above, references to variables successfully looked up in an enclosing class are only allowed for variables declared as constant, illustrated by the example in Section 3.16.1, page 109. The values of identifiers in modifier expressions (Section 4.2.1, page 148) are thus resolved in the scope in which the modifier appears.

The lookup in each scope is performed in the following order until a match is found:

- Search among *declared* named elements, that is, *classes and variables* declared in the scope, including elements inherited from other classes. Note that import clauses are not inherited from other classes. Regarding inheritance see Chapter 4, and concerning `import` see Chapter 10, page 497.
- Search among the import names of *single or multiple definition import clauses* in the scope. Such an import name may refer only to an imported package, class, or constant. The *import name* of the single definition import clause `import A.B.C;` is `C` and the import name of the *renaming* import clause `import D=A.B.C;` is `D`. The import names of the multiple definition `import A.B.{Def1,Def2,...};` are `Def1`, `Def2`, and `Def3`. In all cases, `A.B` must be a package. Regarding the special case `import E;`, `E` can be any class or package as an element of the unnamed top-level package.
- Search among the public members of packages imported via *unqualified import clauses* in the current scope e.g., `import A.B.*;`. It is an error if this step produces matches from several unqualified imports. Unqualified import clauses may only import from packages, that is, `A.B` must be a package in the clause `import A.B.*;`.

Lookup of the name of an imported package or class e.g., `A.B.C` in the import clauses `import A.B.C;` `import D=A.B.C;` `import A.B.{Def1,Def2,...};` `import A.B.C.*;` deviates from the normal lookup by starting the lookup of the first part of the package/class name at the top level of the hierarchy.

3.17.2 Lookup of Qualified Names

The lookup procedure for *qualified names*, that is, names like `C.x` and `A.B.D.y` with dot notation, is a somewhat more involved procedure. The lookup for the first part of a name, such as `C` in `C.x`, or `A` in `A.B.D.y`, proceeds as described above, starting with the current scope. If no matching variable declaration is found, the first part of the name is assumed to be a package name.

For a qualified name of the form `A.B`, or `A.B.C`, etc., lookup is performed as follows:

1. The first part of the name e.g., `A`, is looked up as defined in lookup of simple names above.
2. If the first part of the name matches the name of a *declared variable*, the rest of the name, for example, `B` or `B.C`, is looked up among the named attributes (variables) of that variable, since the variable must be an instance of a record or other kind of class.
3. If not found, and if the first identifier denotes a scalar instance and if the composite name is used as a function call, the lookup is also performed among the declared named class elements of the scalar instance and *must find a nonoperator function*. All identifiers of the rest of the name (e.g., `B` and `B.C`) must be classes of which the last one must denote a function. Note that this is a *member function call* via dot notation, for example, `inst.func(arg1,arg2)`. See also Section 9.3.2.4, page 443.
4. If the first part of the name denotes a class, typically *a package*, that class declaration is analyzed and partially flattened, that is, flattened without any modifiers on that class. Partially flattening means performing inheritance and modifications of the class in the lookup context of the hierarchy of enclosing classes of that class. The rest of the name, for example, `B` or `B.C`, is looked up among the declared named elements of that partially flattened class declaration.

In case 4, if the class is not a package or does not fulfill the requirements for a package, the lookup of the rest of the name is restricted to elements that are encapsulated packages or encapsulated classes of any kind of restricted class. Such lookup can be used, e.g. to access a local version of the Modelica library embedded within a `model` specialized class that is not a package. See also Chapter 10, page 514.

Morover, the class within which lookup is performed may *not be a partial class* when compiling a *simulation model*, that is, a model that is assumed to be compiled to executable simulation code and not just inherited. This check on simulation models is needed, for example in class extends, as mentioned at the end of Section 4.6.5, page 180.

The top level of the package/class hierarchy referred to above can be viewed as an unnamed package containing declared elements loaded into the current workspace together with packages stored in the file system at positions specified by `MODELICAPATH`. See Chapter 10, page 506, for more information on `MODELICAPATH`.

3.17.3 Absolute Global Name Lookup

A special case of qualified name lookup involves names starting with a dot, which denote absolute global names at the top level of the package/class hierarchy mentioned in the previous section. For such names, for example, `.A`, *or* `.A.B`, `.A.B.C`, lookup is performed in the following way:

- The first identifier (`A`) in the name is looked up in the global scope. This is possible even if the current class is encapsulated. Import clauses are not considered in this kind of lookup. If there does not exist a class `A` in the global scope this is an error.
- If the name is simple then the class `A` is the result of lookup.
- If the name is a qualified name then the class `A` is temporarily flattened with an empty lookup context (i.e., no modifiers) and using the enclosing classes of the denoted class `A`. The rest of the name, for example, `B` or `B.C`, is looked up among the declared named elements of the temporary flattened class `A`. If the class `A` does not satisfy the requirements for a package, the lookup is

restricted to encapsulated elements only. The class we look inside may not be partial. The package restriction ensures that global name lookup of variables can only find global constants.

3.17.4 Imported Name Lookup

Lookup of imported simple names is described in the above Section 3.17.1, page 111. A complete description of imported name lookup, both simple and qualified, is available in Section 10.2.1, page 497.

3.17.5 Instance Hierarchy Lookup Using inner and outer

As we already stated briefly in Section 3.11.9, standard nested lookup as described in the previous sections is not convenient in some situations where a pervasive object property should be accessible to all components of the object. For example:

- The components of a planetary system influenced by a common gravitational field.
- Electrons influenced by an electromagnetic field.
- An environmental temperature or pressure influencing the components of the system in question.

Section 5.8, page 224, contains a more thorough discussion of such applications, including the modeling of gravitational fields.

As an example, the temperature of a circuit board (see the example below) should be accessible to all components on the board even though the classes of those components are not declared inside, that is, nested inside, the class of the board itself.

Regarding the circuit board model, it is not practical to place the class definitions of the components inside a specific board class, since they should be usable also for models of other boards. Rather, the common property belongs to the object which contains the components in question. This leads us to the concept of *lookup within the instance hierarchy.*

Based on these considerations, the `inner`/`outer` concept has been introduced in Modelica to provide access to common properties by specific *definition* and *reference* declarations, with lookup through the instance hierarchy that *overrides* the usual nested lookup:

- A declaration with the prefix `inner` is a *definition declaration* of an element that *defines* an object property or element in common to the components of the object, and therefore should be accessible from within those components.
- A declaration with the prefix `outer` is a *reference declaration* of an element that *references* a common property or element defined by a definition declaration in the enclosing instance hierarchy.
- A declaration with both `inner outer` prefixes combines definition and reference declarations under the same name, which is more concise than two separate declarations. This is used in complex systems with several levels of nested subsystems. See Section 5.8.3, page 228 for more details.

Note that the enclosing instance hierarchy is the hierarchy of parts/instances that the current instance is a member of.

The following holds for an *instance hierarchy lookup* of the name of a reference declaration:

- The search for a matching *definition* declaration (`inner`) with the same name as in the *reference* declaration (`outer`) is from the current instance to containing instances within the *instance hierarchy* of the reference declaration, not necessarily within the *class nesting hierarchy*.
- The definition declaration (`inner`) can be shadowed by nested declarations with the same name.

- The item declared in the definition declaration (`inner`) should be a subtype (see Section 3.18, page 115 in this chapter) of the type of the corresponding reference declaration (`outer`) or a subtype of an explicitly given constraining type. Also, the reference declaration should not have any modifications.
- The reference declaration instance (`outer`) may be of a *partial* class, but the referenced definition declaration instance (`inner`) must be of a *nonpartial* class.
- A modeler can use the `missingInnerMessage` annotation to provide a good error message if the lookup fails, see Section 536, page 536.

Note that instance hierarchy lookup is more selective than conventional lookup of global variables found in many other programming languages, since the search is only in the hierarchy starting at a specific instance.

We give a simple example in terms of an electric circuit board `CircuitBoard1` containing temperature-dependent components that depend on a common board temperature.

The two kinds of hierarchies, the usual *class nesting hierarchy* as well as the *instance hierarchy*, are depicted in Figure 3-8 for the `BoardExample` class shown in the following.

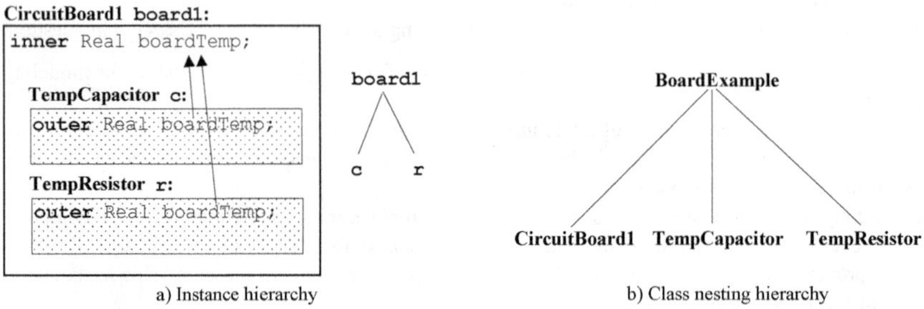

Figure 3-8. Instance hierarchy (a) and class nesting hierarchy (b) for the electric circuit board example.

All components in the electric circuit board should reference exactly the same board temperature variable `boardTemp`, which is defined by an `inner` declaration within the `CircuitBoard1` class. Each component contains an `outer` reference declaration referring to the board temperature `boardTemp`, which is found during the *instance hierarchy lookup* to be the `inner` board temperature `boardTemp` of `CircuitBoard1` since the components `c` and `r` belong to `board1`.

```
class BoardExample

  class CircuitBoard1
    inner Real BoardTemp;   // Definition of the board temperature variable
    TempCapacitor c    "Component within CircuitBoard1 instance";
    TempResistor  r    "Component within CircuitBoard1 instance";
  end CircuitBoard1;

  class TempCapacitor
    outer Real BoardTemp;   // Reference to the board temperature variable
    Real T;
  equation
    T = BoardTemp;
  end TempCapacitor;

  class TempResistor
    outer Real BoardTemp;   // Reference to the board temperature variable
    Real T;
  equation
    T = BoardTemp;
```

```
    end TempResistor;

    CircuitBoard1 board1   "CircuitBoard1 instance";
  end BoardExample;
```

For additional examples on how to use this facility see Section 5.8.5 in Chapter 5, page 233.

3.18 The Concepts of Type and Subtype

What is a type and what is it useful for? This is a relevant question in the context of programming languages. We are talking about the type of variables, of values, of classes, and so on, making it important to convey some intuition about the concept. Types have primarily two main uses in Modelica:

- Checking type *compatibility*—checking compatibility of data and objects in many situations for example binary arithmetic operations on two data objects which need to be of compatible type, or assignment of an expression value to a variable. For example, it is typically not allowed to add a Boolean value to a real number.
- Checking *substitutability*, that is, when an object or class can be used instead of another object or class, such as `TempResistor` being used instead of `Resistor`. This is the case when using replaceable classes (Section 4.4, page 168), which is the main mechanism in Modelica for creating very flexible parameterized classes. Another example is implicit connections using `inner-outer` (Section 5.8, page 224).

The uses of types are discussed in more detail in Section 3.19, page 123.

A *type* can conceptually be viewed as a *set of values*. When we say that the variable `x` has the type `Real`, we mean that the value of `x` belongs to the set of values represented by the type `Real`, that is, roughly the set of floating point numbers representable by `Real`, for the moment ignoring the fact that `Real` is also viewed as a class with certain attributes. Analogously, the variable `b` having `Boolean` type means that the value of `b` belongs to the set of values {`false`, `true`}. The built-in types `Real`, `Integer`, `String`, `Boolean` are considered to be distinct types.

The *subtype* relation between types is analogous to the *subset* relation between sets. A type `Asub` being a subtype of type `A` means that the set of values corresponding to type `Asub` is a subset of the set of values corresponding to type `A`.

The type `Integer` is not a subtype of `Real` in Modelica even though the set of primitive integer values is a subset of the primitive real values since there are some attributes of `Real` that are not part of `Integer` (Section 3.9.2, page 95).

A common way to define a *subtype* (subset), for example, called `Asub` in relation to another type `A`, is by requiring that the elements of the set corresponding to `Asub` is a subset of the set corresponding to `A`. Such a subset can be characterized by the elements having additional attributes or properties.

Thus the type `TempResistor` from the class declared below is a subtype of `Resistor` since the set of temperature-dependent resistors is the subset of resistors having the additional variables (attributes) `RT`, `Tref`, and `Temp`.

The type `Integer` is not a subtype of `Real` in Modelica even though the set of primitive integer values is a subset of the primitive real values since there are some attributes of `Real` that are not part of `Integer` (see Figure 3-9).

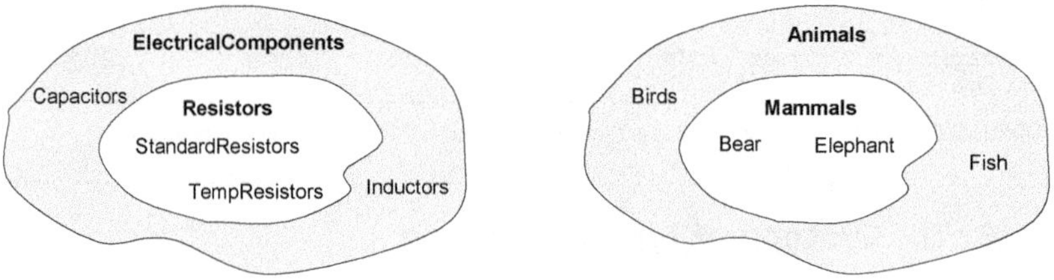

Figure 3-9. Relation between the concepts of subtype and subset in the domains of electrical components and animals.

The *supertype* relation is the inverse of the subtype relation. Since `TempResistor` is a subtype of `Resistor`, then `Resistor` is a supertype of `TempResistor`.

```
model Resistor  "Electrical resistor"
  Pin p, n  "positive and negative pins";
  Voltage v;
  Current i;
  parameter Real R(unit="Ohm")           "Resistance";
equation
  v = i*R;
end Resistor;

model TempResistor "Temperature dependent electrical resistor"
  Pin p, n  "positive and negative pins";
  Voltage v;
  Current i;
  parameter Real R(unit="Ohm")          "Resistance at reference Temp.";
  parameter Real RT(unit="Ohm/degC")=0  "Temp. dependent Resistance.";
  parameter Real Tref(unit="degC")=20   "Reference temperature.";
  Real           Temp=20                "Actual temperature";
equation
  v = i*(R + RT*(Temp-Tref));
end TempResistor;
```

The definitions of `Pin`, `Voltage`, and `Current` that are used in the resistor classes above were previously defined in Section 2.8.3, page 39.

3.18.1 Types and Subtypes Characterized by Public Interfaces

In the previous section we defined the notion of *type* as a set of values, and the *subtype* relation as a subset relation. A convenient way of characterizing such a set (a type) is by describing the essential common properties of all elements that belong to the set. These properties can be viewed as the *public interface* of the elements. In this way, one can think of a *type* as an *interface descriptor*.

For example, the record type `X` depicted in Figure 3-10 is characterized by its public fields `x` and `b`, which define the data access interface to instances of this record type. Moreover, the record `Xs` is a *subtype* of the record `X` since it has the same fields `x` and `b`, augmented by the additional field `w`. This is analogous to the previous case of `TempResistor` being a subtype of `Resistor` since instances of `TempResistor` have the same fields augmented by the additional attributes `RT`, `Tref`, and `Temp`. The records `X` and `Xs` as well as a few instances of these are declared below.

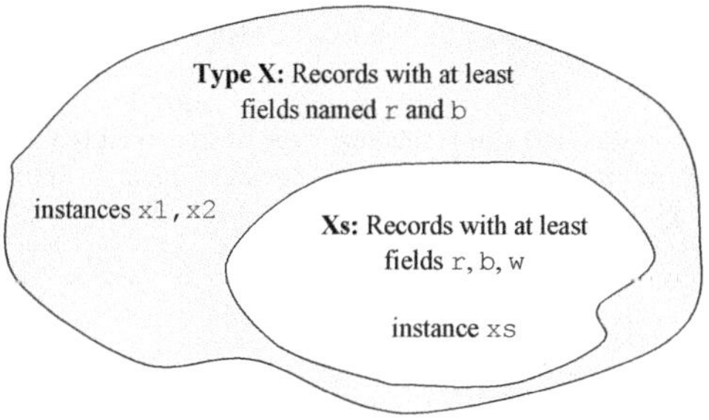

Figure 3-10. The type X can be defined as the set of record values containing r and b. The subtype Xs is the subset of values (instances) that contain r, b, and w.

```
record X
  Real r;
  Boolean b;
end X;

record Xs
  Real r;
  Boolean b;
  Real w;
end Xs;

X x1,x2;   // Instances x1 and x2

Xs xs;     // Instance xs
```

Returning to the set interpretation of types, the type X can be viewed as the set of all record values containing the attributes defined by X, for example, the infinite set {X(r=2.1,b=true), X(r=3.4,b=true), X(r=2.5,b=false), Xs(r=2.1,b=false,w=2), Xs(r=2.2,b=false, w=3),...}. The statement that x1 has the type X means that the value x1 belongs to this infinite set.

The type Xs is a subtype of X since its instances fulfill the additional property of having the attribute Real w; in all its values. Only a subset of values fulfills this property, as depicted in Figure 3-10.

3.18.2 Inheritance Type versus Object Type

It is relevant to distinguish between the so-called *object type* of a class and its *inheritance type*. The inheritance type is also called *class type* in certain literature but we do not use that term here because of confusion with the type of a class. The *object type* is based on the public attributes of a class, that is, its public interface, and used in situations related to data access, whereas the *inheritance type* also includes the protected attributes since both public and protected attributes are inherited. Thus a class declaration will give rise to two different types.

3.18.3 Conceptual Subtyping of Subranges and Enumeration Types

Conceptually, a subrange is a subset of an ordered set of elements, defined as the ordered set of all elements from the first to the last element in the subrange. A number of programming languages, including

Ada and Pascal, allow the user to define subrange types of enumerable types, for example integer, subranges that appear as follows in Pascal:

```
2..10
```

This subrange is conceptually a subtype of `Integer` and also a subrange type of integers from 2 to 10. The general idea of subrange subtypes as subsets of ordered enumerable elements is illustrated in Figure 3-11, where `SmallSizes` is a subtype of `AllSizes`, `Int_1_2` is a subtype of `Int_1_4`, and `FalseBoolean` a subtype of `Boolean`.

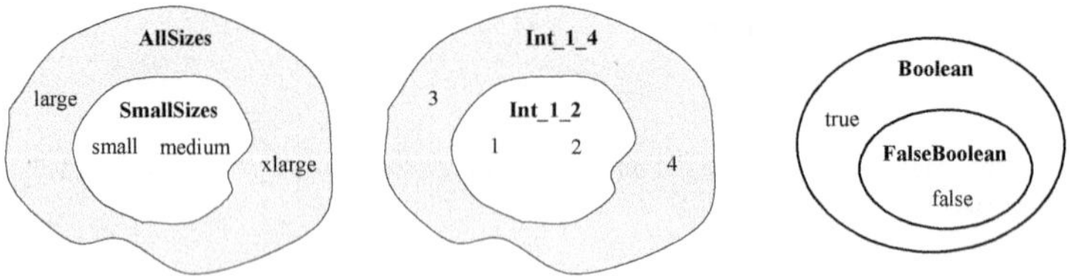

Figure 3-11. Conceptual subtyping examples of enumeration types, Integer ranges, and Boolean ranges. However, general subrange subtyping as illustrated in this figure is not in the current version of Modelica.

In Modelica we can define enumeration types e.g., as follows:

```
type AllSizes   = enumeration(small, medium, large, xlarge);
type SmallSizes = enumeration(small, medium);
```

According to the examples in Figure 3-11 and general subset relations, `SmallSizes` should be a subtype of `AllSizes`. However, this is not the case in the current version of Modelica, which does not support definition of subrange subtypes.

Instead, subtyping of enumeration types usually requires type equivalence (Section 3.19, page 123), based on the fact that two identical sets are subsets of each other. This restrictive subtyping rule might be extended in the future, but that will require enhancements in several places of the Modelica language. There is also a special enumeration type `enumeration(:)`, which is a supertype of all possible enumeration types. For example:

```
S1 = enumeration(small,medium);         // S1 not subtype of S2
S2 = enumeration(small,medium,large);   // S2 is not a supertype of S1
S3 = enumeration(small,medium,large);   // S3 is a subtype of S2
S4 = enumeration(:);                    // S1, S2, S3 are subtypes of S4
```

3.18.4 Tentative Type Representation of Records/Classes

As just mentioned, a *record type* in Modelica is conceptually the (possibly infinite) set of all possible record values of that record type, where each value contains named values for the variables (also known as fields or attributes) of that record. Thus, both the *record field names* and the *record field types* are significant when defining a record type. Duplicate field names in a type are not allowed. In general, a tentative representation of the type of a record/class with N elements can be given by a descriptor that is a set of pairs of the form (*field-name*, *field-type*) where field ordering is unspecified, analogous to several type systems for object-oriented languages by Abadi and Cardelli:

{*name1*:type1, *name2*:type2, ... *nameN*:typeN}

We will gradually develop this tentative type representation into a more general type representation suitable for all type aspects of the Modelica language. However, returning to the view of a record type as a set of record values, consider the `Person` record declaration below:

```
record Person
  String name;
  Real   weight;
  Real   length;
end Person;
```

A set of `Person` values might appear as follows, using pseudo syntax for record values (not conforming to Modelica syntax), where both the field name tag and the field data value are part of a `Person` value:

```
{{name:"Eve", weight:65, length:170},
 {name:"Adam", weigth:80, length:180}, ... }
```

In general, the ordering between the variables of a class is not considered significant except in two cases:

1. The ordering within the two sets: function formal parameters and function results.
2. The ordering between the variables of a record being passed to an external function.

However, except for the case of function types, the ordering between variables (fields) is not considered significant for type checking. Therefore the following record value is also considered compatible with type `Person`:

```
{weight:65, length:170, name:"Carl"}
```

3.18.5 Array Type

An *array type* is conceptually a set of array values, where each array value can be considered as a *set* of pairs (*array-element-index*, *array-value*), analogous to the set of pairs (record-field-name, record-field-value) that make up a record value. Thus, for a vector type with four elements, with the possible array indices '1', '2', '3', '4', where the array index is used as a name instead of the field name in a record, a set of three or more array values with labeled array elements could appear as follows in pseudo code:

```
{ {'1':35.1, '2':77, '3':38, '4':96},
  {'1':5.1,  '2':11, '3':305,'4':83},
  {'1':4.2,  '2':10, '3':55, '4':44}, ... }
```

Following our informal definition of array type, each possible index value for an array should also be part of the array type in the same way as all variable names of a record are significant. However, this is impractical or impossible when there is a large number of array elements and in cases where the number of array elements is unknown. Instead, we will soon turn to a *more compact type representation*.

Unspecified dimension sizes is generally the case for library functions operating on arrays. For example, the library function for inverting a matrix should work on any size of matrix and therefore has the dimension sizes unspecified, causing the number of array elements to be unspecified. It would not make sense to have a separate inverting function for 2 × 2 matrices, another for 3 × 3 matrices, and so on. Thus it must be possible to define array types for which certain array dimension sizes are unspecified. Two vector types in Modelica are shown below:

```
type Vec2 = Real[2];    // Vector type with specified dimension size
type Vec  = Real[:];    // Vector type with unspecified dimension size
```

We now replace our informal set definition of *array type* above with a more compact type descriptor still with the same form as the one used for record types. This descriptor is a set containing a single pair (*index-specifier*, *element-type*), which can be used since all array elements share the same element type, in contrast to records where variables (fields) usually have different types. In this array type representation, the *element-type* is the type of the array elements and the *index-specifier* represents all possible legal indices for the array where each dimension in an index is represented by a nonnegative size expression for the maximum index value of that the dimension, or a colon (:) representing unspecified dimension size:

```
{ (index-specifier, element-type), ...}
```

The array type descriptors for the two types `Vec2` and `Vec` would then become the following:

```
{ ('2', Real) }
{ (':', Real) }
```

Turning to the problem of representing multidimensional arrays, we observe that in Modelica as well as in many programming languages a multidimensional array is defined as an array of arrays. Thus a 2 × 3 matrix type is viewed as a 2-sized vector of 3-sized vectors. For example:

```
type Mat23 = Real[2,3]; // Matrix type with specified dimension size
type Mat   = Real[:,:]; // Matrix type with unspecified dimension size
```

These two matrix types will have the following type representation given the array of arrays representation:

```
{ ('2', {('3', Real)} ) }
{ (':', {(':', Real)} ) }
```

The subtype relation between two array types, `Asub` subtype of `A`, requires that the element-type of `Asub` is a subtype of the element-type of `A` and each corresponding dimension specifier in the index-specifier is either identical size or the dimension specifier of `A` is a colon (:). Thus, `Mat23` is a subtype of `Mat`. This is reasonable since arrays of type `Mat23` can be used in places where type `Mat` is required, but not vice versa.

3.18.6 Tentative Function Type

The definition of a *function type* is analogous to our previous definition of general class type with the additional properties that the *ordering* between the fields (variables), that is, the formal parameters of the function, is significant and that the prefixes `input` and `output` for each formal parameter are also part of the type of each formal parameter and thus part of the function type. A function with three input formal parameters and one result is actually quite different from a function with two input formal parameters and two results, even if the names and types of the formal parameters are the same in both cases.

3.18.7 Complete Type Representation for Classes and Instances

Regarding function types, in the previous section we concluded that the prefixes `input` and `output` are also part of the type of each element and thus part of the function type. In fact, all *type prefixes* when present in the variable declarations within a class declaration—`flow`, `stream`, `discrete`, `parameter`, `constant`, `input`, `output`, as well as the `final` element prefix—are considered part of the class type not only for functions but for all kinds of classes in Modelica. The variability prefixes `discrete`, `parameter`, `constant` are considered part of the type since they influence the semantics and type checking of assignment statements and equations. The `flow` and `stream` prefixes are part of the type since they affect the semantics of connection equations. Also, the `final` prefix influences the semantics of inheritance and modifications, described in more detail in Chapter 4.

Thus, our tentative representation of the type of a class or instance is *generalized* to be a *tuple* of a *set of attributes* and a *sequence of pairs* (*element-name*, *element-prefixes&type*) for all N public elements in the class, where *element ordering* is part of the type but not used in type checking except in certain situations such as regarding functions, and *index-specifier* is used instead of element-name for array types:

(type-attributes, {*name1*: prefixes1&type1, *name2*: prefixes2&type2, ... *nameN*: prefixesN&typeN})

Given the simple example function `multiply` below:

```
function multiply;
  input  Real x;
  input  Real y;
```

```
  output Real result;
algorithm
  result := x*y;
end multiply;
```

Using our general definition of type to represent this function, we obtain the following tuple:

({*specialized-class*: function, *is-class*: true, *is-replaceable*: false, ... },
{*x*: input&Real, *y*: input&Real, *result*: output&Real)

Regarding the general type attributes of `multiply`, it is a function and a class (not an instance) so it is not replaceable. Moreover, it contains a number of named elements that comprise two input formal parameters of type Real and one output result of type Real.

3.18.7.1 Type Representation in Detail

Below we show the type representation of a class or instance in even more detail, represented as a tuple:

(*type-attributes*, *name-type-pairs*)

The first part of the type representation, the *type attributes*, contains the following information:

- Whether it is an instance or a class.
- The kind of specialized class.
- Whether it is replaceable or not.
- The `flow` or `stream` prefix, if present.
- Declared variability prefix, `constant`, `parameter`, `discrete`, if present.
- The prefixes `input` and `output`.
- The prefixes `inner` and/or `outer`.
- Whether the declaration is `final`, and in that case its contents represented in a way that avoids dependence on minor syntactic variations.
- Array sizes (if any).
- The condition(s) of conditional instance declarations (if any).
- For an enumeration type or instance of enumeration type the names of the enumeration literals in order.
- Whether it is a built-in type and in that case the built-in type name, one of (`RealType`, `IntegerType`, `StringType` or `BooleanType`.
- Whether the class itself or the class of the instance is transitively nonreplaceable (Section 3.18.7.3, page 122), and if not, a reference to the replaceable class (Section 4.4, page 168) it refers to.
- Only for an `operator record` class and (subclasses of) classes derived from `ExternalObject`: the full name of the `operator record` base-class, that is, the one containing the definition of the operations, or the class derived from `ExternalObject`, respectively. The second part of the type representation, the name-type pair sequence, is empty for an `operator record` class or a class derived from `ExternalObject`, since the type is already uniquely defined by the full name of the `operator record` or the class derived from `ExternalObject`, respectively. This is sometimes called nominal typing. See also Section 9.5, page 481, regarding operator overloading and Section 9.4.8, page 476, regarding `ExternalObject`.
- Only needed for inheritance types: visibility (`public` or `protected`).

The second part of the type representation consists of *name-type pairs*, a sequence containing one pair for each named public element defined in the class or instance. This kind of type representation is often called structural typing. This part is not needed and is empty for the type of `operator record` classes.

The type contains a sequence of name-type pairs, one for each named element of the class or instance, including both local and inherited named elements. For object types, only include the `public` elements. For inheritance types needed for inheritance of classes, also include `protected` elements. Each pair (tuple) contains the following:

- The name of the element.
- The type of the element as defined in this section and, regarding functions, also Section 9.3, page 438; also see subtyping of functions in Section 3.19.6, page 130. This might have been modified by modifiers and is thus not necessarily identical to the type of the original declaration.

Note that the public elements do not contain all of the information about the class or instance. When using a class as an inherited base class, we also need `protected` elements for the *inheritance type*, and for internal type checking we need, for example, `import` elements. However, the public information is sufficient for checking type compatibility of instances.

3.18.7.2 Constraining Type

Replaceable declarations in a class can be replaced by so-called redeclare operations to give a new modified class (Section 4.3, page 156). All replaceable declarations have a constraining type (Section 4.3.7, page 162), which can be given explicitly after the `constrainedby` keyword, if present, or use otherwise defined as the type of the replaceable element itself.

3.18.7.3 Transitively Nonreplaceable Classes

In several cases, it is important to avoid that new elements can be added to the type of a class during redeclaration, especially considering short class definitions. Such classes are called *transitively nonreplaceable*.

If it were possible to add an element to a replaceable class that is redeclared, that element when inherited from the replaceable class could in some cases conflict with an element with the same name in the enclosing class (Section 4.1.5.1, page 140). Being transitively nonreplaceable prevents such errors.

See also the definition of transitively nonreplaceable in Section 4.3.10, page 166, and some usage examples and motivation for this feature in Section 4.1.5, page 140. Replaceable declarations are briefly explained in Section 3.11.6, page 103, and redeclarations are presented in detail in Section 4.3, page 156.

A *class reference* is transitively nonreplaceable if and only if *all parts* of its name satisfy the following:

- If the class definition is long it is transitively nonreplaceable if *not declared replaceable* (Section 4.3.10, page 166).
- If the class definition is short (e.g., `class A=P.B`) it is transitively nonreplaceable if it is nonreplaceable and equal to a class reference (`P.B`) that is transitively nonreplaceable.

According to Section 4.1.5, page 140, for a hierarchical name reference, *all parts* of the name must be transitively nonreplaceable, that is, in `extends A.B.C` this implies that `A.B.C` must be transitively nonreplaceable, as well as `A` and `A.B`, with the exception of the `class extends` redeclaration mechanism, (Section 4.6, page 175) where the class reference must always be replaceable.

3.18.8 Discussion on Types of Classes that Contain Local Classes

So far we have primarily shown examples of classes that only contain attributes or fields (variables) that can contain data ("data fields"), similar to a classical record type. However, in Modelica it is possible to declare local classes inside a class, as, for example, the classes `IC` and `BC` inside the class `RC2` below.

```
class RC2
  Real x;      // field x
  class IC
    Integer x;
  equation
    x = 2;   // Refers to local x inside IC
  end IC;
```

```
    class BC
      Real y;
    equation
      x = y;  // Refers to x in RC2
    end BC;
    IC ix;      // field ix, instance of IC
    BC bx;      // field bx, instance of BC
  equation
      x = 3.14;
  end RC2;

  ...
  RC2  z;
  ...
```

The three variables ("data fields") of class `RC2` are `x`, `ix`, and `bx`. There are also two local classes (not "data fields") `IC` and `BC` inside `RC2`. They can be referred to only within the local scope of `RC2`, but in principle they could be moved outside `RC2` with some changes of names. An outside class `BC` could appear as follows:

```
class RC2_BC    // Hypothetical BC outside RC2
  Real y;
equation
  z.bx.x = y;   // Refers to x in the z instance of RC2
end RC2_BC;
```

A version of `RC2` referring to such external classes would appear as follows:

```
class RC2_v2    // Hypothetical RC2 referring to outside IC and BC
  Real x;       // field x

  RC2_IC ix;    // field ix, instance of RC2_IC
  RC2_BC bx;    // field bx, instance of RC2_BC
equation
  x = 3.14;
end RC2_v2;
```

From this perspective it would be natural to include only the three "data fields" `x`, `ix`, and, `bx` in the type of `RC2`. Operations on and use of data objects of type `RC2` involve only these three "data fields."

On the other hand, the class `RC2_BC` is not very general since it refers only to the `z` instance of `RC2` in its equation `z.bx.x = y`. The hypothetical notation `RC2.bx.x` in that equation is not possible since that would imply that `bx` is a class variable (see page 80), which is not the case. Also, class variables are not currently allowed in Modelica.

Furthermore, one might argue that a class containing local classes is different from a class without local classes, and that the local types `IC` and `BC` need to be included anyway since they are referred to by `ix` and `bx`. These considerations have led to the design decision that in Modelica local classes are considered as elements of the type of the class within which they are declared. The "*field name*" of such a local class is the class name, and the type is the type representation of the local class as a tuple of attributes and a set of pairs according to our general type representation, but for brevity denoted by names such as `RC2.IC` and `RC2.BC`. The general type representation of class `RC2` then becomes as follows, with unspecified type attributes:

(type-attributes, {*x*: Real, *IC*: RC2.IC, *BC*: RC2.BC, *ix*: RC2.IC, *bx*: RC2.IC})

3.19 Use of Subtyping and Type Compatibility

Having defined the notion of type for the different kinds of classes and objects that can occur in Modelica, we need to turn to the issue of how and when are used.

Type equivalence is needed to ensure compatibility of data objects in different situations such as equality between the left-hand side and the right hand-side in equations, ensuring that the types of all arguments to the array constructor are equivalent since the types of all elements in array must be the same, and so on.

We have informally defined the notion of *subtype* as analogous to the notion of subset, for example, with the example of `TempResistor` being a subtype of `Resistor`. The notion of subtype is usually associated with the idea of specialization and *substitutability*: if T2 is a subtype of T1, then an object or class of type T2 should usually be allowed to be substituted instead of an object of T1, or assigned to a variable of type T1 e.g., a `TempResistor` being substituted for a `Resistor`.

Below we will discuss the use of subtyping and type equivalence, and provide more precise definitions of those notions.

3.19.1 Uses of Type Compatibility of Expressions

Type compatibility (equivalence) has the following main uses:

- The types of the left- and right-hand sides of equations (e.g., $x = y$) must be equivalent after first doing type coercion, for example, an `Integer` expression at one side of an equation is automatically converted to a `Real` expression if the other side has type `Real`. Regarding the variability properties (Section 6.8.1.3, page 278) which are part of the type of the variable *a* and expression *expr* in declaration equations or modifier equations such as $a = expr$, the variability of *expr* must be equal or lower compared to that of *expr*, the same rule as for assignments below. The variability of *expr* is converted to be the same as that of *a*, to make their types equivalent.
- *Assignment statements*. In an assignment statement e.g., $a := expr$, the type T2 of the right-hand side must be equivalent to the type T1 of the left-hand side after possible type coercions. For example, type conversions makes assignments such as `Real[:] vec := {1,2}` possible, where the right-hand side has type `Real[2]`, and the left side has type `Real[:]`, where the type of the left-hand side is coerced into `Real[2]`. Additionally, the standard coercion rule of converting an `Integer` expression to a `Real` expression when it occurs at the right-hand side of an assignment to a `Real` variable is automatically applied in order to satisfy type equivalence. Moreover, the *variability* (Section 6.8.1.3, page 278) of the expression *expr* must be equal or lower than that of variable *a*, (e.g., an *expr* of parameter variability can be assigned to a variable of continuous-time variability, but not vice versa) and is converted to the variability of variable *a*.
- The types of the arguments to the array construction function {} as well as to the relational operators (==, <>, <=, >=, <, >) must be equivalent. `Integer` arguments are converted to `Real` arguments when needed to achieve type equivalence. Relational operators are defined only for scalar arguments, that is, not for arrays and user-defined class types.

3.19.2 Checking Type Compatibility of Expressions

Certain expressions consist of an operator applied to two or more type compatible subexpressions (here denoted A and B), including binary operators, e.g. A + B, B * A, if-expressions, e.g. `if x then A else B`, and array expressions, e.g. `{A,B}`. The resulting type of the expression in case of two type compatible subexpressions A and B is defined as follows:

- If A is a record-expression B must also be a record-expression with the same named elements. The type compatible expression is a record comprised of named elements that are compatible with the corresponding named elements of both A and B.

- If A is an array expression then B must also be an array expression, and `ndims`(A)=`ndims`(B). The type compatible expression is an array expression with elements compatible with the elements of both A and B. If both `size`(A) and `size`(B) are known and `size`(A)=`size`(B) then this defines the size of the type compatible expression, otherwise the size of the expression is not known until the expression is about to be evaluated. In case of an if-expression, the size of the type compatible expression is defined based on the branch selected, and for other cases `size`(A)=`size`(B) must hold at this point.
- If A is a scalar expression of a simple type B must also be a scalar expression of a simple type.
- If A is a Real expression then B must be a Real or Integer expression and the type of the resulting expression is Real.
- If A is an Integer expression then B must be a Real or Integer expression and the type of the resulting expression is Real or Integer (same as B).
- If A is a Boolean expression then B must be a Boolean expression and the type of the resulting expression is Boolean.
- If A is a String expression then B must be a String expression and the type of the resulting expression is String.
- If A is an enumeration expression then B must be a enumeration expression and the resulting expression is an enumeration expression, and all enumeration expressions must be defined in terms of an enumeration type with the same enumeration literals in the same order.
- If A has an `operator record` (Section 9.5.2, page 483) base class then B must also have an `operator record` base class, and the base class must be the same for both A and B. Otherwise neither A nor B may have an `operator record` base-class. This is also the `operator record` base class for the expression, for example, for `if (cond) then A else B`.
- If A is derived from (is a subclass of, inheriting) `ExternalObject` (Section 9.4.8, page 476) then B must also be derived from `ExternalObject` and they must have the same full name. Otherwise neither A nor B may be derived from `ExternalObject`. The common full name also defines the type of the expression, for example, for `if (cond) then A else B`.

3.19.3 Uses of Subtyping

Subtyping has the following uses, assuming that T2 is a subtype of T1:

- *Redeclarations*. For explanations of redeclaration, modification, and inheritance see Chapter 4, page 135. The type of a class member can be changed through a redeclaration when the class is inherited through a modification. In a `replaceable` declaration, there can be an optional constraining type. In a redeclaration of a `replaceable` element the type T2 of the variable must be a subtype of the constraining type T1. Furthermore, the constraining type of a `replaceable` redeclaration, that is, a redeclaration that can be further redeclared, must be a subtype of the constraining type of the declaration it redeclares.
- *Instance hierarchy lookup*. The type of a definition declaration with prefix `inner` must be a subtype of the type of the corresponding reference declaration with prefix `outer` that references the definition declaration.
- *Argument passing at function calls*. The type T2 of an argument passed to a formal parameter (of type T1) of some function needs to be a subtype of the type T1 after possible type coercions. For example, a subtype of a record with additional fields can be passed to a parameter having the record type. An array of specific size can be passed to a parameter with unspecified dimension size. Passing a 2D array where a 1D array is expected is not allowed. However, a 1D array slice, for example, a row or column, can be extracted from the 2D array and passed in that case.

A class T2 that inherits a class T1 naturally becomes a subtype of T1. However, inheritance is not required for subtyping. In one of our previous examples, `TempResistor` is a subtype of `Resistor` even though it does not inherit `Resistor`.

3.19.4 Checking Subtyping

As mentioned in the previous section, checking subtyping is needed where a class or instance `Asub` is substituted for another class or instance `A` in redeclarations, instance hierarchy lookup, and argument passing. Intuitively, for this to hold, all relevant elements of `A` must be present in `Asub` since all operations applied to `A` must automatically work also for `Asub`.

A type of a class or instance `Asub` is a *subtype* of a class or instance `A` (or the constraining type of `A`), if and only if the type properties (Section 3.18.7.1, page 121) of `A` and `Asub` are identical, except in the following cases where additional considerations hold:

- If `A` is not replaceable then `Asub` may not be replaceable. See Section 4.4, page 168 regarding the replaceable concept.
- If `A` is transitively nonreplaceable (Section 3.18.7.3, page 122) then `Asub` must be transitively nonreplaceable. For each element in the inheritance type of `A` there must exist a type compatible (subtype of) element with the same name and visibility in the inheritance type of `Asub`. The type of `Asub` may not contain any other elements. We might even extend this to say that `Asub` and `A` should have the same contents, as in the additional restrictions below.
- If `A` is replaceable then for all elements of the object type of `A` there must exist a plug-compatible element with the same name in the object type of `Asub`.
- If `A` is neither transitively nonreplaceable (Section 3.18.7.3, page 122) nor replaceable then `Asub` must be linked to the same class, and for all elements of the object type of `A` there must thus exist a plug-compatible element with the same name in the object type of `Asub`.
- If `A` is a nonreplaceable long class definition, `Asub` must also be a long class definition.
- If `Asub` has an `operator record` (Section 9.5.2, page 483) base-class then `A` must also have one and it must be the same. If `Asub` does not have an operator record base-class then `A` may not have one.
- If `Asub` is derived from (is a subclass of, is inheriting) `ExternalObject` (Section 9.4.8, page 476), then `A` must also be derived from `ExternalObject` and have the same full name. If `Asub` is not derived from `ExternalObject` then `A` may not be derived from `ExternalObject`.
- Variability is ordered `constant` < `parameter` < `discrete` < (no prefix: *continuous-time* for Real), and `Asub` is only a subtype of `A` if the declared variability in `Asub` is less than or equal the variability in `A`. For a redeclaration of an element the variability prefix is by default inherited by the redeclaration. For example, there is no need to repeat parameter when redeclaring a parameter to be a parameter.
- The `input` and `output` prefixes must be matched. This ensures that the rules regarding inputs/outputs for matching connectors and (nonconnector inputs) are preserved, as well as the causality restriction on blocks. For a redeclaration of an element the `input` or `output` prefix is inherited from the original declaration.
- The `inner` and/or `outer` prefixes must be matched. For a redeclaration of an element the `inner` and/or `outer` prefixes are inherited from the original declaration since it is not possible to have `inner` and/or `outer` as part of a redeclare.
- The number of array dimensions in `Asub` and `A` must be matched. Furthermore, the following must be valid for each array dimension: either the array size in `A` is unspecified (":") or the content of the corresponding array dimension in `Asub` is identical to the one in `A`.

- A conditional instance can only be a subtype of a conditional instance. The condition must have equivalent contents, analogous to array sizes, except there is no ":" for conditional instances. For a redeclaration of an element the conditional part is inherited from the original.
- `A` and `Asub` must have identical specialized class for `function`, `package`, `connector`. Moreover, a `model` or `block` class can only be a subtype of a `model` or `block` class, and a `type` or `record` class only a subtype of a `type` or `record` class.
- If `A` is an enumeration type `Asub` must also be an enumeration type and vice versa. If `A` is an enumeration type not defined as (:) then `Asub` must have the same enumeration literals in the same order, whereas if `A` is an enumeration type defined as (:) then there is no restriction on to enumeration type `Asub`.

For a replaceable declaration or modifier, the default class must be a subtype of the specified constraining class, if present. For a modifier, the following must apply:

- The modified element should exist in the element being modified.
- The modifier should be a subtype of the element being modified, and in most cases also fulfill plug-compatible subtyping (Section 3.19.5, page 127).

If the original constraining class is legal, that is, there are no references to unknown elements, no illegal use of class/instance, and all modifiers are legal as above, then the resulting flat class will be legal, that is, there are no references to unknown elements and no illegal use of class/instance, the type is a subtype of the original constraining class, and references refer to similar entities.

Moreover, plug-compatible subtyping (Section 3.19.5, page 127) is a further restricted variant of the above subtyping, whereas function subtyping (Section 3.19.6, page 130) is a further restricted version used for functions.

3.19.5 Plug-Compatible Subtyping

Plug-compatible subtyping is stricter than standard subtyping and is used to prevent undefined connection errors when "plugging in" a model, that is, passing a class or model instance (`Asub`) with connectors as an argument to a parameterized model (`A`). Declaring such formal model parameters is done using the `replaceable` construct (Section 4.4.1, page 169), whereas the argument passing is done using `redeclare`. A simple example of passing model instances as arguments is presented in Section 4.4.2, page 169.

Regarding plug-compatible subtyping, in the model example below the `Clutch` model is a subtype, but not a plug-compatible subtype, of `FrictionElement` since it introduces a `pressure` connector not present in `FrictionElement` at the top instance level within `Clutch`.

If a connector instance declared within another instance is *redeclared* (Section 4.3, page 156) it is not allowed to connect it to any new connector. The *reason* is that it is not allowed to connect to a connector more than one level down in the instance hierarchy (Section 5.3.2, page 191). Therefore it should not be allowed to introduce such a connector at a level where a connection is not possible.

To avoid accidentally introducing such illegal connectors when performing redeclarations, we introduce the notion of *plug-compatible subtyping*, which is stricter than standard subtyping and requires the use of default connections. All connector instances with `input` prefix must be connected. Therefore all public declared connector instances which are present in `Asub` but are not present in `A` must be connected by default.

The type of `Asub` is a *plug-compatible subtype* of the type of `A` (or the constraining type of `A`) if and only if:

- `Asub` is a subtype of `A`.

- All public components which are present in `Asub` but not in `A` must be *default connectable* (defined below).

An instance is *default connectable* if and only if:

- All of its instance elements are default connectable.
- The connector instance must not be an input, otherwise a connection to the input will be missing.
- The connector instance must not be of an expandable connector class since an expandable connector potentially has inputs.
- A parameter, constant, or nonconnector input must either have a binding declaration equation or all of its subinstances must have binding equations.

Based on the above definitions, there are the following rules:

- Case 1: A redeclaration of an *inherited top-level instance* declaration must be *a subtype of* the constraining type of the element being redeclared.
- Case 2, the *main case*: In *all other cases* redeclarations must have *plug-compatible subtypes* of the constraining types of the elements being redeclared.

The reason for the difference is that for an inherited top-level instance it is possible to connect this instance to the additional connectors, either in this class or in a derived class. However, for instances further down in instance hierarchies this is not possible and we have to rely on default connections guaranteed by plug-compatible subtyping.

For example, in the example below `Clutch` is a subtype, but not a plug-compatible subtype of `FrictionElement`, since it introduces the input connector `pressure`.

The example uses `extends`, `replaceable`, and `redeclare` which are introduced in Chapter 4, page 135. A flattened version of the same example is provided further below to make it easier to follow the effects of inheritance and redeclarations. Take special notice of the classes `FlatDriveLine` and `FlatUseDriveLine` compared to `DriveLine` and `UseDriveLine`.

```
partial model TwoFlanges
  Modelica.Mechanics.Rotational.Interfaces.Flange_a flange_a;
  Modelica.Mechanics.Rotational.Interfaces.Flange_b flange_b;
end TwoFlanges;

partial model FrictionElement
  extends TwoFlanges;
...
end FrictionElement;

model Clutch "Subtype - but not plug-compatible subtype of FrictionElement"
  Modelica.Blocks.Interfaces.RealInput pressure; // An input, not a flow var
  extends FrictionElement;
...
end Clutch;

model DriveLineBase
  extends TwoFlanges;
  Inertia J1;
  replaceable FrictionElement friction;
equation
  connect(flange_a, J1.flange_a);
  connect(J1.flange_b, friction.flange_a);
  connect(friction.flange_b, flange_b);
end DriveLineBase;

model DriveLine    "Case 1, Clutch must be subtype of FrictionElement"
  extends DriveLineBase(redeclare Clutch friction); // Redeclaration OK
```

```
  Constant const; //Introduced and used in the connection
equation
  connect(const.y, friction.pressure);  // Legal connection to new
   // input connector pressure because inherited from top-level of DriveLine
end DriveLine;

model UseDriveLine "Illegal model"
      // Case 2, Clutch must be a plug-compatible subtype but is not
      // Hierarchical connection to base.friction.pressure would be illegal
  DriveLineBase base(redeclare Clutch friction); // Redeclaration not OK
  Constant const;                  //Introduced and used in the connection
equation
  connect(const.y, base.friction.pressure); // Illegal hierarchical connect
end UseDriveLine;
```

The above model has been partially flattened below, where all inheritance (`extends`) and redeclarations have been expanded.

```
partial model FrictionElement
  Modelica.Mechanics.Rotational.Interfaces.Flange_a flange_a;
  Modelica.Mechanics.Rotational.Interfaces.Flange_b flange_b;
end FrictionElement;

model Clutch "Subtype - but not plug-compatible subtype of FrictionElement"
  Modelica.Mechanics.Rotational.Interfaces.Flange_a flange_a;
  Modelica.Mechanics.Rotational.Interfaces.Flange_b flange_b;
  Modelica.Blocks.Interfaces.RealInput pressure; // An input, not a flow var
end Clutch;

model DriveLineBase
  Modelica.Mechanics.Rotational.Interfaces.Flange_a flange_a;
  Modelica.Mechanics.Rotational.Interfaces.Flange_b flange_b;
  Inertia J1;
  replaceable FrictionElement friction;
equation
  connect(flange_a, J1.flange_a);
  connect(J1.flange_b, friction.flange_a);
  connect(friction.flange_b, flange_b);
end DriveLineBase;

model FlatDriveLine   "Redeclaration of friction in Driveline done"
  Modelica.Mechanics.Rotational.Interfaces.Flange_a flange_a;
  Modelica.Mechanics.Rotational.Interfaces.Flange_b flange_b;
  Inertia J1;
  Clutch friction;
  Constant const;    //Introduced and used in the connection
equation
  connect(const.y, friction.pressure);  // Legal connection to new
   // input connector pressure because inherited from top-level of DriveLine
end Flat DriveLine;

model FlatUseDriveLine "Redeclaration of friction component done, needing
                        a flattened class DriveLineBaseClutch for base"
  DriveLineBaseClutch base;
  Constant const;     //Introduced and used in the connection
equation
  connect(const.y, base.friction.pressure); // Illegal hierarchical connect
end FlatUseDriveLine;

model DriveLineBaseClutch  "Introduced class needed in FlatUseDriveLine"
  Modelica.Mechanics.Rotational.Interfaces.Flange_a flange_a;
```

```
  Modelica.Mechanics.Rotational.Interfaces.Flange_b flange_b;
  Inertia J1;
  Clutch friction;
equation
  connect(flange_a, J1.flange_a);
  connect(J1.flange_b, friction.flange_a);
  connect(friction.flange_b, flange_b);
end DriveLineBaseClutch;
```

To summarize, if a declared subinstance is redeclared, it is impossible to connect it to any new connector introduced by the redeclaration since connecting to a connector more than one level down is illegal (Section 5.3.2, page 191). Thus any new connectors must work without being connected, that is, use the default connection of flow-variables. That fails for inputs, and expandable connectors may contain inputs.

For parameters and nonconnector inputs, it would be possible to provide bindings in a derived class, but that would require hierarchical modifiers and this would be bad modeling practice because a hierarchical modifier (with several levels of dot-notation) must be used in order to make a model valid.

A replaceable class might be used as the class for a subinstance; therefore plug-compatibility is required not only for replaceable subcomponents, but also for replaceable classes in a class. For constraints on redeclarations in general, see Section 4.3.7, page 162 and Section 4.3.11, page 166.

3.19.6 Function Subtyping

Functions may be called with either named or positional arguments, and thus both the names and the order of the arguments are significant. If a function (`A`) is *redeclared* to another function (`Asub`) (Section 4.3, page 156), any new formal parameters (in `Asub`) must have declaration assignments to default values and be placed at the end of the formal parameter list in order to preserve the meaning of existing calls without arguments passed to these new formal parameters.

The (type of) a function class `Asub` is *a function subtype of* a function class `A` if and only if:

- The type of `Asub` is a subtype of `A` according to the general class subtyping (Section 3.19.4, page 126).
- All input formal parameters of `A` have correspondingly named input formal parameters of `Asub` in the same order and preceding any additional input formal parameters of `Asub`.
- All result formal parameters of `A` have correspondingly named result formal parameters of `Asub` in the same order and preceding any additional result formal parameters of `Asub`.
- An input formal parameter of `Asub` must have a declaration assignment to a default value if the corresponding input formal parameter has a declaration assignment to a default value in `A`.
- An input formal parameter of `Asub` not present in `A` must have a declaration assignment to a default value.

Based on the above definition the following subtyping restriction holds for redeclaration of functions:

- The type of a function (`Asub`) supplied in a redeclaration must be *a function subtype of* the constraining type of the function (`A`) being redeclared.

The following example demonstrates the use of function subtyping. In the `PlanetSimulation` model the gravitational force field function `gravity`, declared in model `Body`, is redeclared to two variants of force field functions which must be function subtypes of `GravityInterface`.

```
partial function GravityInterface
  input  Modelica.SIunits.Position     position[3];
  output Modelica.SIunits.Acceleration acceleration[3];
end GravityInterface;

function PointMassGravity
```

```
  extends GravityInterface;
  input Modelica.SIunits.Mass m;
algorithm
  acceleration:= -Modelica.Constants.g*m*position/(position*position)^1.5;
end PointMassGravity;

model Body
  Modelica.Mechanics.MultiBody.Interface.Frame_a frame_a;
  replaceable function gravity=GravityInterface; // NOTE: gravity must be a
                                                 // subtype of GravityInterface.
equation
  frame_a.f = gravity(frame_a.r0); // or gravity(position=frame_a.r0);
  frame_a.t = zeros(3);
end Body;

model PlanetSimulation
   function sunGravity = PointMassGravity(m=2e30);
   Body planet1(redeclare function gravity=sunGravity);
   Body planet2(redeclare function gravity=PointMassGravity(m=2e30));
     ...
end PlanetSimulation;
```

Note that `PointMassGravity` by itself is not a function subtype of `GravityInterface` since there is no default binding assignment for `m`. However, `PointMassGravity(m=2e30)` is a function subtype of `GravityInterface` since it has a default value for m through the modification `m=2e30`. Moreover, `sunGravity` inside `PlanetSimulation` is a function subtype of `GravityInterface` since it has a default value for `m`.

3.20 Summary of Type Concepts

In this section the most important type concepts introduced in previous sections are summarized.

Term	*Description*
type	The notion of *type* can be defined as a set of values (objects). A convenient way of characterizing such a set (a type) is by describing the essential common properties of all elements which belong to the set, e.g., the set of all Integer values or all Real values. These properties can be viewed as the *public interface* of the elements. In this way one can think of a *type* as an *interface descriptor*. Thus, a type (sometimes called object type) used to describe the objects which can be created from a certain class can be defined by the public declarations of that class. Note that certain elements of a class such as import clauses do not belong to the essential public declarations. The "essential" public declarations of a class are those elements needed to decide whether a class `Asub` can be used instead of a class `A`. For example, a declaration `Real x` is part of the type but an import clause such as `import Foo` is not. See also Section 3.18, page 115.
inheritance type	The inheritance type of a class is defined by the *public and protected* declarations of a class that are needed to decide whether `Asub` can be used instead of `A`. The *inheritance type*, also known as *class type* in the literature, is used when inheritance takes place since both protected and public declarations are inherited. See also Section 3.18.2, page 117.
subtype	The *subtype* relation is basically a subset relation between types

	defined as sets. Since a type is usually defined by the common interface property of all objects in the type, `Asub` is a *subtype* of `A`, if the public declarations of `A` are also available in `Asub`. For example, if `A` has a declaration `Real x`, this declaration must also be present in `Asub`. If `Asub` has a declaration `Real y`, this declaration need not be present in `A`. When subtyping between *inheritance types* is determined, both the public and protected declarations must be considered. See also Sections 3.18.1, 3.18.7 and 3.19.
plug-compatible subtype	`Asub` is a *plug-compatible subtype* of `A`, if `Asub` is a subtype of `A` and if connector instances in `Asub` that are not in `A`, are default connectable. For example, it is not allowed that such connectors have variables with the `input` prefix, because then they must be explicitly connected. A model or block `Asub` containing additional connectors cannot be used instead of `A` if the particular situation does not allow making a connection to these additional connectors. In such a case the stricter plug-compatible subtyping requirement is required for a redeclaration. See also Section 3.19.5, page 127.
function subtype	`Asub` is a *function subtype* of `A`, if `Asub` is a subtype of `A` and if the additional formal parameters of function `Asub` that are not in function `A` are defined in such that `Asub` can be called at places where `A` is called. For example each additional formal parameter in `Asub` compared to `A` must have a default value. See also Section 3.19.6, page 130.

3.21 Summary

This chapter has its focus on the most important structuring concept in Modelica: the class concept. We started with a tutorial introduction of the idea of contract between designer user together with the basics of Modelica classes as exemplified by the moon landing model, but excluding inheritance, which is presented in Chapter 4. We continued by presenting the idea of specialized classes, the predefined types in Modelica, and the structure of declarations—both class declarations and variable declarations. We concluded with a presentation of the two kinds of lookup in Modelica: nested lookup and instance hierarchy lookup, followed by a description of the typing and subtyping concepts of Modelica and their usage.

3.22 Literature

The primary reference document for this chapter is the Modelica language specification (Modelica Association 2012), (Modelica Association 2013). Several examples in this chapter are based on similar examples in that document, and in (Modelica Association 2000). Some formulations and pieces of text from the Modelica specification are reused in this chapter in order to state the same semantics.

At the beginning of this chapter, we mention the idea of a contract between software designers and users. This is part of methods and principles for object-oriented modeling and design of software described in (Rumbaugh 1991; Booch 1991; Booch 1994; Meyer 1997). The moon landing example is based on the same formulation of Newton's equations as in the lunar landing example in (Cellier 1991).

The typing and subtyping concepts of Modelica are inspired by some of the simpler type systems described in the introductory part of (Abadi and Cardelli 1996). The concepts of inheritance type vs. object type in the Modelica context were first described in (Broman, Fritzson, Füric 2006). Type safety in general for such languages is discussed in (Broman and Fritzson 2006). Dimensional inference and unit checking is presented in (Broman, Aronsson, and Fritzson 2008).

3.23 Exercises

Exercise 3-1:

Creating a Class: Create a class, `Multiply`, that calculates the product of two variables, which are `Real` numbers with given values.

Make the previous class into a model.

Exercise 3-2:

Creating a Function and Making a Function Call: Write a function, `AddTen`, that adds 10 to the input number. Make a function call to `AddTen` with the input `3.5`.

Exercise 3-3:

Creating a Local Class: Here you should test that local classes are possible. For example, given the trivial class `Add` below, create a new empty class `AddContainer`, and place `Add` as a local class inside `AddContainer`.

```
class Add
  Real x = 1;
  Real y = 2;
  Real z;
equation
  x + y = z;
end Add;
```

Exercise 3-4:

Creating Instances: Consider the class `Student` below:

```
class Student
  constant  Real   legs = 2;
  constant  Real   arms = 2;
  parameter Real   nrOfBooks;
  parameter String name = "Dummy";
end Student;
```

Create an instance of the class `Student`.

Create another instance and give the student the name `Alice`. This student has 65 books.

You also want to create a student called `Burt` who owns 32 books.

Exercise 3-5:

Question: What is a variable?

Question: Which are the two kinds of variables and what is the difference between them?

Question: What is a parameter?

Exercise 3-6:

Declaring Variables: Define a class `Matrices` that declares the variables `m1`, `m2`, `m3`, `m4` all being matrices with `Integer` respectively `Real` numbers. Make at least one of them an array. Let `m1` and `m2` be parameters, `m3` a regular variable, and `m4` a constant.

Exercise 3-7:

Question: How can a variable be initialized?

Initializing Variables: Declare the variables `length1`, `length2`, and `length3` of type `Real` with different initial values. One of the variables should have the value 0. Name the class `Variables`.

Exercise 3-8:

Creating a Record: Create a record `Dog` with the value `nrOfLegs` which is an `Integer`, and `name` which is a `String`. Give the variables some values.

Exercise 3-9:

Question: What is a type?
Question: What is a subtype?
Question: What is a supertype?

Subtype and Supertype:

```
class House
  Real length;
  Real width;
end House;
```

Define a class `Room` that is a subtype of the class `House`. This also means that `House` is a supertype of `Room`. Also give some values to the variables.

Exercise 3-10:

Access Control: Complete the classes `Access` and `AccessInst` below by adding simple equations. The variable `acc` is an instance of the class `Access`, which contains the variables `a`, `b`, `c`, `d` and `e`, of which `d` and `e` are protected. Where can the variables be referenced e.g., in equations setting them equal to some numeric constant values? (Set `a = 7.4` in the class `AccessInst`.)

```
class Access
  ...
equation
  ...
end Access;

class AccessInst
  Acc acc;
end AccessInst;
```

Exercise 3-11:

Introduce a ground force into the classes of the `MoonLanding` model to make the lander stand still after the landing, thus avoiding accelerating toward the center of the moon.

Chapter 4

Inheritance, Modifications, and Generics

One of the major benefits of object orientation is the ability to *extend* the behavior and properties of an existing class. The original class, known as the *base class* or *superclass*, is extended to create a more specialized version of that class, known as the *derived class* or *subclass*. In this process, the data and behavior of the original class in the form of variable declarations, equations, and certain other contents are reused, or *inherited*, by the subclass. In fact, the inherited contents is copied from the superclass into the subclass, but before copying certain operations, such as type expansion, checking, and modification, are performed on the inherited contents when appropriate.

In Chapter 2, page 30, we briefly described how classes can be extended through inheritance using the `extends` clause in Modelica. For example, a class `Point` was extended to a more specialized class called `ColoredPoint` containing additional variables and equations dealing with the color aspects. Classes can also be extended through modifications in Modelica, which is just a variant of inheritance by which the contents of the superclass is copied in "expanded" form into the subclass apart from certain elements that are modified or replaced.

In Chapter 3 we defined the notion of contract between the designer of the class and the modeler/programmer who uses it. The contract is essentially what the class designer has promised that the class will do, that is, its semantics. This is described by documentation as well as by connectors, variables, and other public elements of the class. The equations of a class together with possible algorithmic parts define the behavior and are therefore an important part of its semantics.

When a class is extended/inherited by adding new variables and additional behavior, for example, through extra equations, a new class is created with an extended contract. However, one should avoid changing the part of the contract the subclass inherits from the superclass since otherwise an instance of the subclass cannot be used in place of an instance of the superclass—the subclass would not be a true specialization (and thus subtype) of the superclass. It is reasonable to change the way the superclass's contract is implemented but we should avoid making changes that violate the contract of the superclass.

Violating the contract of the superclass usually does not occur when extending a Modelica class using `extends` clauses that add new variables and equations. Still, it is possible to add equations in a subclass that invalidate the behavior of a superclass, for example, by creating an unsolvable system of equations. Also, when using inheritance through modification, it is even possible to change the type of inherited members of the superclass, provided that those members have been declared `replaceable` by the superclass designer. Therefore, to make visible for the user the possible danger that the semantics of the subclass may not be compatible with the superclass, it is required to use the special keyword `redeclare` in such modifications.

In the rest of this chapter we first examine the basic method of inheritance in Modelica, including application to moon landing and other examples, followed by a description of the concept of modification and inheritance through modification. Then we present how to do generic parameterized classes in Modelica. Finally, we discuss how a class should be designed to be extended.

4.1 Inheritance

Inheritance from a *superclass* (also called base class) into a *subclass* (derived class) is specified by an `extends` clause containing a superclass identifier and possibly modifiers (Section 4.2.6, page 152):

extends *<superclass identifier>* *<optional modifiers>*;

The `extends` clause is placed within some subclass:

class *<subclass identifier>*
  extends *<superclass identifier>* *<optional modifiers>*;
end *<subclass identifier>*;

As mentioned, the inherited contents is copied from the superclass *into* the subclass at the *place* of the `extends` clause. However, before copying certain operations, such as type expansion, checking, and modification, might be performed on the inherited contents.

Let us regard an example of extending a very simple Modelica class, for example, the class `ColorData` introduced in Chapter 2, Section 2.4 on page 30. We show two classes named `ColorData` and `Color`, where the derived class (subclass) `Color` inherits the variables to represent the color from the base class (superclass) `ColorData` and adds an equation as a constraint on the color values.

```
record ColorData
  Real   red;
  Real   blue;
  Real   green;
end ColorData;

class Color
  extends ColorData;
equation
  red + blue + green = 1;
end Color;
```

In the process of inheritance, the data and behavior of the superclass in the form of variable and attribute declarations, equations, and certain other contents, excluding import clauses, are copied into the subclass. However, as already mentioned, before the copying is done certain type expansion, checking, and modification operations are performed on the inherited definitions. The contents of the expanded inherited class are copied into the subclass at the position of the extends clause. The expanded `Color` class is equivalent to the following class:

```
class ExpandedColor
  Real red;
  Real blue;
  Real green;
equation
  red + blue + green = 1;
end ExpandedColor;
```

4.1.1 Inheritance of Elements with the Same Name as an Existing Element

What happens if a variable or attribute declaration is inherited which has the *same name* as a local variable or other element already present in the derived class? This is *illegal* if the local variable or attribute declaration and the inherited declaration are *different*, for example, have different types, different protection level `public` or protected, or some other difference. However, this is legal if the local declaration and the inherited one are identical, in which case they are subsumed into a single declaration, i.e., one is discarded since they are identical.

For example, the locally declared variable `blue` in the class `ErrorColor` is identical to the inherited variable `blue`, which is no problem since they are identical and are subsumed into a single `blue` variable. On the other hand, the local variable `red` conflicts with the inherited variable `red` since one is a `Real` and the other is an `Integer`, which is impossible to have within the same class.

```
class ErrorColor
  extends ColorData;
  Real    blue;   // Legal, since identical to the inherited variable blue
  Integer red;    // Illegal, since same name but different type
equation
  red + blue + green = 1;
end ErrorColor;
```

4.1.2 Inheritance of Equations

In the previous section we mentioned that inherited equations are copied from the superclass or base class and inserted into the subclass or derived class. What happens if there already is an *equivalent equation* locally declared in the derived class? Then we may obtain an underdetermined system of equations which makes the system unsolvable if there are not enough additional equations for the variables. Remember that there must be the same number of *independent* equations as the number of variables, in order to solve a system of equations.

```
class Color2
  extends Color;
equation
  red + blue + green = 1;
end Color2;
```

The inherited class `Color` already contains an equation, which makes `Color2` contain two identical equations. A Modelica tool may give a warning when an identical equation is inherited, for example, as below.

```
red + blue + green = 1;
red + blue + green = 1;
```

4.1.3 Multiple Inheritance

Multiple inheritance, that is, several `extends` clauses, is supported in Modelica. This is useful when a class wishes to include several orthogonal kinds of behavior and data, for example, combining geometry and color.

For example, the new class `ColoredPoint` inherits from multiple classes, that is, uses multiple inheritance, to get the *position* variables from class `Point`, as well as the color variables together with the equation from class `Color`.

```
class Point
  Real x;
  Real y, z;
end Point;

class ColoredPoint
  extends Point;
  extends Color;
end ColoredPoint;
```

In many object-oriented programming languages multiple inheritance causes problems when the same definition is inherited twice, but through different intermediate classes. A well-known case is so-called diamond inheritance (Figure 4-1):

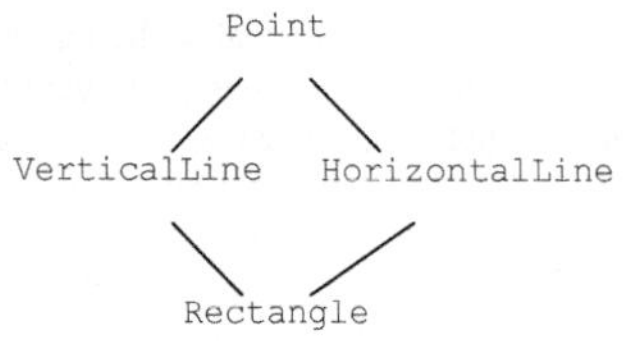

Figure 4-1. Diamond inheritance.

The class `Point` contains a coordinate position defined by the variables `x` and `y`. The class `VerticalLine` inherits `Point` but also adds the variable `vlength` for the line length. Analogously, the class `HorizontalLine` inherits the position variables `x`, `y` and adds a horizontal length. Finally, the class `Rectangle` is intended to have position variables `x`, `y`; a vertical length, and a horizontal length.

```
class Point
  Real x;
  Real y;
end Point;

class VerticalLine
  extends Point;
  Real vlength;
end VerticalLine;

class HorizontalLine
  extends Point;
  Real hlength;
end HorizontalLine;

class Rectangle
  extends VerticalLine;
  extends HorizontalLine;
end Rectangle;
```

The potential problem is that we have diamond inheritance since the coordinate position defined by the variables `x` and `y` is inherited twice: both from `VerticalLine` and from `HorizontalLine`. Should the position variables from `VerticalLine` be used, or the ones from `HorizontalLine`? Is there some way to resolve the problem?

In fact, there is a way. In Modelica, diamond inheritance is usually not a problem since there is a rule stating that if several identical declarations are inherited, only one of them is kept. Thus, there will be only one set of position variables in the class `Rectangle`, making the total set of variables in the class the following: `x`, `y`, `vlength`, and `hlength`. The same is true for the classes `Rectangle2` and `Rectangle3` below.

```
class Rectangle2
  extends Point;
  extends VerticalLine;
  extends HorizontalLine;
end Rectangle;

class Rectangle3
  Real x, y;
  extends VerticalLine;
  extends HorizontalLine;
end Rectangle;
```

The reader might perhaps think that there could be cases where the result depends on the relative order of the `extends` clauses. However, this is in fact not possible in Modelica, which we shall see in Section 4.1.8 below.

4.1.4 Restrictions on the Kind of Inherited Base Class

Since specialized classes of different kinds have different properties (Section 3.8, page 87) only specialized classes that are "in some sense compatible" to each other can be derived from each other via inheritance. Table 4-1 shows which kind of specialized class can be used in an extends clause of another kind of specialized class (the "grey" cells mark the few exceptional cases, where a specialized class can be derived from a specialized class of another kind).

Table 4-1. Allowed combinations of base classes and derived classes.

	Base Class										
Derived Class	package	operator	function	operator function	type	record	operator record	expandable connector	connector	block	model
package	yes										
operator		yes									
function			yes								
operator function			yes	yes							
type					yes						
record						yes					
operator record							yes				
expandable connector								yes			
connector					yes	yes		yes	yes		
block						yes				yes	
model						yes				yes	yes

Some specialized classes can also be derived from, that is, inherit from, other kinds of classes. Those cases of inheritance are marked with a grey background in the table. If a derived class is inherited from another type of specialized class, then the result is a specialized class of the derived class type. For example, if a `block` inherits from a `record`, then the result is a `block`.

All specialized classes can be derived from `class`, provided the resulting class fulfills the restriction(s) of the specialized class. It is recommended to use the most specific specialized class.

The specialized classes `package`, `operator`, `function`, `type`, `record`, `operator record`, and `expandable connector` can only be derived from their own kind. For example, a package can only be a base class for packages. All other kinds of classes can use the import clause to use the contents of a package and from `class`.

Below we show some examples of inheritance.

```
record RecordA
  ...
end RecordA;

package PackageA
  ...
end PackageA;

package PackageB
  extends PackageA;   // Fine, a package can inherit a package.
end PackageB;

model ModelA
  extends RecordA;    // Fine, a model can inherit a model.
end ModelA;
```

```
model ModelB
  extends PackageA;   // Error, a model cannot inherit a package!
end ModelB;
```

4.1.5 Restrictions on Base Classes and Constraining Types to be Transitively Nonreplaceable

The *class name* used after `extends` for base classes and after `constrainedby` for constraining classes (Section 4.3.7, page 162) must use a class reference considered ***transitively nonreplaceable*** (see definition in Section 3.18.7.3, page 122), meaning approximately that there are *no replaceable elements* in the referenced class or any of its base classes or constraining types transitively at any level

For example, in this `extends` clause `BaseClass` must be transitively non-replaceable:

```
extends BaseClass;
```

In this example from Section 4.3.7, page 162, the constraining type `TwoPin` must be transitively nonreplaceable:

```
replaceable type CompType = Resistor constrainedby TwoPin;
```

For a replaceable variable declaration without constraining clause the class must use a class reference considered transitively nonreplaceable. For example, here the class `Voltage` must be transitively nonreplaceable.

```
replaceable Voltage u;
```

Constraining classes are *always* transitively nonreplaceable, either if given explicitly after a `constrainedby` keyword or derived implicitly as in the above `Voltage` example.

However the rule regarding transitively nonreplaceable does not apply to `class extends`, where the inherited class must be replaceable (Section 4.6, page 175).

4.1.5.1 Motivation for Transitively Nonreplaceable

What is the motivation for the restriction of being transitively nonreplaceable? The main reason is to avoid errors/conflicts with existing elements in an enclosing class if an inherited class would be redeclared to contain additional elements with the same name(s) as existing elements in that enclosing class.

On the other hand, one might argue that the special restriction for transitively nonreplaceable is unnecessary since an inheritance conflict is detected anyway by the requirement that an inherited element with the same name must have identical type (Section 4.1.1, page 136). This is the case for the variable `y` in the example below.

However, there is one remaining reason for keeping the restriction of transitively nonreplaceable: *early detection of errors*. Errors such as the inheritance conflict can be prevented just by checking a library containing models such as `A` below, rather than waiting for some future usage of the library to trigger an error.

Consider the following example:

```
model A
  extends M;  // Inherits replaceable M below - Error!
              // since M is not transitively non-replaceable

  replaceable model M    // Inherited into A
    Real x;
  end M;

  Real y = 1.0; // Element y in the enclosing scope of M
end A;
```

```
model B
  A a1;
  A a2(redeclare model M = M2); // Not OK, creates an inheritance conflict
                                // between Integer y and Real y

  model M2          // M2 is a subtype of M
    Real    x;
                    // Avoid conflict: must be the same when inherited
    Integer y;      // M2.y will conflict with A.y when inherited into A
                    // M2.y has Integer type, A.y has Real type
   // Real y = 1.0;   // This would be OK, A.y is the same as M2.y
  end M2;
end B;
```

The instance a1 will contain:

```
Real x;
Real y = 1.0;
```

The instance a2 will contain:

```
Real x;
Integer y;          // Inheritance conflict!, two different definitions of y
Real    y = 1.0;
```

4.1.6 Restrictions on Combining Inherited Classes and other Declarations

Predefined simple types such as Real, Integer, and so on (Section 3.9, page 93), and arrays of those are allowed to be inherited in a limited way, for example:

```
type Voltage
  extends Real(unit= "V", min=-220.0, max=220.0);
end Voltage;
```

Here we just changed the default values of the attributes unit, min, and max for the new subtype called Voltage.

Another example of allowed inheritance from simple predefined types or arrays of simple types is the declaration of an overdetermined type such as Orientation (Section 8.5.1, page 374):

```
type Orientation   "Transformation matrix rotating frame 1 into frame 2"
  extends Real[3,3];

  function equalityConstraint
    input  Orientation R1  "Rotation of inertial frame to frame 1";
    input  Orientation R2  "Rotation of inertial frame to frame 2";
    output Real            residue[3];
    ...
  end equalityConstraint;
    ...
end Orientation;
```

On the other hand, when creating subtypes of the simple types it is important that the basic properties of the types are preserved. For example, it should always be possible to map a subtype of Real to a double precision floating point variable.

This would be *violated* if we allow the combination of inherited predefined types with additional variable declarations. Such a resulting subtype might need several floating point variables, integer variables, or other data structures, which would violate several of the assumptions about the Real type, for example, performance, size, and numerical behavior. Therefore such a combination is disallowed.

Another case that is not allowed because of undefined semantics is a combination of a class with a nonempty type prefix such as `flow`, `stream`, `discrete`, `parameter`, `constant`, `input`, or `output`.

To summarize, it is *not allowed* within the same class to combine *variable declarations* or *inheritance* from other classes with *inheritance from the following*:

1. A simple type (`Real`, `Boolean`, `Integer`, `String` and enumeration types).
2. An array type.
3. A class with non-empty type prefix.
4. Any class transitively inheriting from cases 1 to 3.

The following is an illegal model that combines inheritance from a simple type and another class.

```
model IllegalCombinedExtends    // Illegal combination of extends
  extends Real;       // Inheritance from a simple type
  extends MyClass;  // Inheritance from another class
end IllegalCombinedExtends;
```

The illegal models below illustrate cases 1, 2, and 3 mentioned above.

```
model Foo2
  Real x1, x2;
end Foo2;

model Foo2Input = input Foo2;

model Real3 = Real[3];

connector IllegalModel1   // Case 1
   extends Real;
   Real y; // Illegal combination of variable and inherited simple type
end IllegalModel1;

model IllegalModel2  // Case 2
  extends Real3;
  Real x; // Illegal combination of variable and inherited array class
end IllegalModel2;

model IllegalModel3  // Case 3
  extends Foo2Input;
  Real x; // Illegal combination of variable and inherited prefixed class
end IllegalModel3;
```

Another restriction is that a name of an inherited class (such as `C` below) may not be inherited from any base class (such as `B` below):

```
class BaseClassExtendsConflict
  class B
    class C end C;
  end B;

  class C end C;

  class D
    extends B;
    extends C; // Incorrect, since the name C is inherited from B
  end D;
end BaseClassExtendsConflict;
```

4.1.7 Processing Declaration Elements and Use Before Declare

In order to guarantee that declared elements can be used before they are declared and that they do not depend on their order of declaration, the lookup and analysis of element declarations within a class proceeds as follows:

1. The *names* of declared local classes, variables, and other attributes are found. Also, modifiers are merged with the local element declarations, and redeclarations are applied.
2. *Extends clauses* are processed by lookup and expansion of inherited classes. Their contents is expanded and inserted into the current class. The lookup of the inherited classes should be *independent*, that is, the analysis and expansion of one `extends` clause should not be dependent on another.
3. All element declarations are expanded and type checked.
4. A check is performed that all elements with the same name are identical.

The reason that all the names of local types, variables, and other attributes need to be found first is that a *use* of an element can come before its *declaration*. Therefore the names of the elements of a class need to be known before further expansion and type analysis are performed.

For example, the classes `Voltage` and `Lpin` are used before they are declared within the class C2:

```
class C2
  Voltage v1, v2;
  Lpin    pn;

  class Lpin
    Real p;
  end Lpin;
  class Voltage = Real(unit="kV");
end C2;
```

4.1.8 Declaration Order of extends Clauses

We have already stated in Chapter 2 and in the previous section that in Modelica the *use* of declared items is independent of the order in which they are declared, except for function formal parameters and record fields (variables). Thus variables and classes can be used before they are declared. This also applies to `extends` clauses. The order in which `extends` clauses are stated within a class does not matter with regards to declarations and equations inherited via those `extends` clauses.

4.1.9 The MoonLanding Example Using Inheritance

In the `MoonLanding` example from Chapter 3, page 83, the declaration of certain variables like `mass` and `name` were repeated in each of the classes `CelestialBody` and `Rocket`. This can be avoided by collecting those variable declarations into a generic body class called `Body`, and reusing these by inheriting `Body` into `CelestialBody` and `Rocket`. This restructured `MoonLanding` example appears below. We have replaced the general keyword `class` by the specialized class keyword `model`, which has the same semantics as `class`. The reason is that it is more common practice to use the keyword `model` for modeling purposes than to use the keyword `class`. The first model is the generic `Body` class designed to be inherited by more specialized kinds of bodies.

```
model Body  "generic body"
  Real   mass;
  String name;
end Body;
```

The CelestialBody class inherits the generic Body class and is in fact a specialized version of Body. Compare with the version of CelestialBody without inheritance previously presented in Chapter 3, page 83.

```
model CelestialBody "celestial body"
  extends Body;
  constant  Real g = 6.672e-11;
  parameter Real radius;
end CelestialBody;
```

The Rocket class also inherits the generic Body class and can of course be regarded as another specialized version of Body.

```
model Rocket "generic rocket class"
  extends Body;
  parameter Real massLossRate=0.000277;
  Real altitude(start= 59404);
  Real velocity(start= -2003);
  Real acceleration;
  Real thrust;
  Real gravity;
equation
  thrust - mass * gravity = mass * acceleration;
  der(mass)   = -massLossRate * abs(thrust);
  der(altitude) = velocity;
  der(velocity) = acceleration;
end Rocket;
```

The MoonLanding class below is identical to the one presented in Chapter 3, page 83, apart from the change of keyword from class to model.

```
model MoonLanding
  parameter Real force1 = 36350;
  parameter Real force2 = 1308;
  parameter Real thrustEndTime = 210;
  parameter Real thrustDecreaseTime = 43.2;
  Rocket     apollo(name="apollo12", mass(start=1038.358) );
  CelestialBody moon(mass=7.382e22,radius=1.738e6,name="moon");
equation
  apollo.thrust = if (time<thrustDecreaseTime) then force1
                  else if (time<thrustEndTime) then force2
                       else 0;
  apollo.gravity = moon.g*moon.mass /(apollo.altitude+moon.radius)^2;
end Landing;
```

We simulate the restructured MoonLanding model during the time interval {0, 230}:

```
simulate(MoonLanding, stopTime=230)
```

The result is identical to the simulation of MoonLanding in Chapter 3, page 84, which it should be. See, for example, the altitude of the Apollo rocket as a function of time, plotted in Figure 4-2.

```
plot(apollo.altitude, xrange={0,208})
```

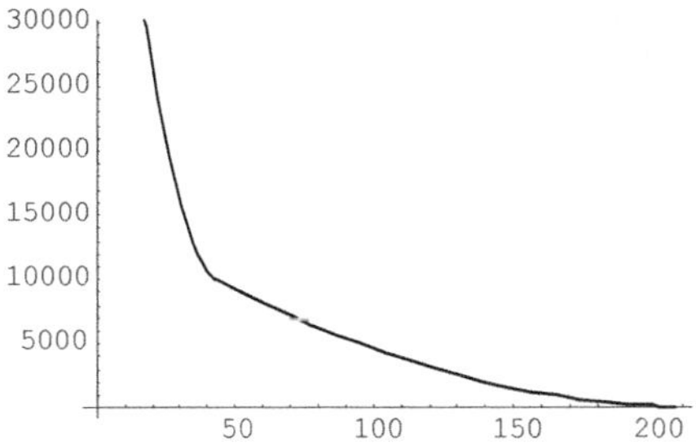

Figure 4-2. Altitude of the Apollo rocket over the lunar surface.

4.1.10 Inheritance and Subtyping

As we already remarked in Chapter 3, inheritance is not the basic mechanism for defining *subtype* relationships in Modelica. On the other hand, inheritance in the form of a modification or an `extends` clause (almost) always *creates* a subtype relationship between a derived class and a base class by inheriting all declared elements of the base class with their original types.

The only exception to the rule that a derived class is a subtype is when the derived class contains redeclarations of replaceable elements with explicit constraining types in the base class. For example, the replaceable type might be a `Resistor`, the constraining type a `TwoPin`, and the new type a `Capacitor` that is not a subtype of `Resistor`. This is explained in more detail in the section on generalizing constraining types of class parameters on page 170.

A subtype relationship can also be created without inheritance. As has already been covered in detail in Chapter 3, an arbitrary class `B`, for example, a temperature-dependent resistor class, is defined to be a *subtype* of a class `C`, for example, a resistor class, *if and only if* the class `B` contains all the public elements of class `C`. In other words, class `C` contains a *subset* of the elements declared in class `B`.

To conclude, an inheritance relationship between two classes (almost) always gives rise to a subtype relationship between the classes. On the other hand, a subtype relationship can exist between two classes without an inheritance relationship between these classes.

4.1.11 Inheritance of Protected Elements

If an `extends` clause is used preceded by the `protected` keyword (Section 3.11.1, page 98), all inherited elements from the superclass become protected elements of the subclass. If an `extends` clause is a `public` element, all elements of the superclass are inherited with their own protection. For example:

```
class Point2
public Real x;
protected Real y, z;
end Point2;

class ColoredPoint2
protected
  extends Color;
public
  extends Point2;
end ColoredPoint2;
```

The color variables `red`, `green`, `blue` that are inherited from `Color` via an `extends` clause preceded by the `protected` keyword become protected variables of `ColoredPoint2`. On the other hand, the inherited variables from `Point2` keep their protection status since that `extends` clause is preceded by `public`.

The possible prefixes `protected` and `public` used within the superclass do not affect the consequent elements of the subclass, that is, the prefixes `protected` and `public` are *not* inherited.

A protected element cannot be accessed via dot notation from outside its scope—this is the essence of being protected. Additionally, protected elements may not be modified or redeclared in class modifications (except elements directly declared within an inherited base class, see Section 4.2.9, page 154), since otherwise this would be a way to get around the access restrictions of protected elements.

4.1.12 Short Class Definition as Inheritance

The short class definition in Modelica provides a concise way of defining classes based on inheritance, often used to introduce more descriptive type names for already existing classes. For example:

```
class SpecialReal = Real;
```

One may apply modifiers (see page 148) in short class definitions to adapt the type for a specific use, as for the types `Current` and `Voltage` defined below:

```
type Current = Real(unit="A");
type Voltage = Real(unit="V", min=-220.0, max=220.0);
```

In fact, a short class definition is in most cases just a shorter syntax for defining a class that could just as well be defined using an ordinary class definition containing an `extends` clause. Thus, the same `Voltage` definition as above could also be expressed using the standard inheritance syntax:

```
type Voltage
  extends Real(unit= "V", min=-220.0, max=220.0);
end Voltage;
```

In general, given a short class definition of the following form:

```
class <class identifier> = <superclass identifier> <modifiers>;
```

Such a class definition is usually identical to the longer form that uses a standard `extends` clause:

```
class <class identifier>
  extends  <superclass identifier> <modifiers>;
end <class identifier>;
```

The only differences are that in the short class definition the identifier *<superclass identifier>* may be replaceable and regarding modifiers where the short class definition does not introduce an additional lexical scope for modifiers which is the case in the longer form.

Regarding array types, this does not work since the short type definition is the *only* way in Modelica to define a *named array type*, which in its general form has the following structure:

```
type TN = T[n1,n2,n3,…](optional modifiers);
```

Here *n1*,*n2*,*n3*,… represents arbitrary array dimensions, *T* represents a type name, that is, the superclass identifier, and *TN* the name of the type to be defined. Even though this is not correct Modelica, such a type definition could *conceptually* be expanded to a kind of array class with the keyword `array and` exactly one anonymous variable, here denoted by the placeholder <*arr*>:

```
array TN    // A conceptual array class, not correct Modelica
  T[n1,n2,n3,…]  <arr>(optional modifiers);
end TN;
```

The type of a variable declared using a type defined via a short type definition (e.g., `Force3` below) is identical to the type of a variable declared with the same base type (e.g., `Real` below), array dimensions, and optional modifiers as in the short type definition. Thus the type of the variable `v1` is the same as the type of the variable `v2`.

```
type Force3 = Real[3](unit={"N","N","N"});
Force3  v1;
Real    v2[3](unit={"N","N","N"});
```

4.1.13 Extending Predefined Types/Classes

The predefined Modelica types `Real`, `Integer`, `Boolean`, and `String` can be inherited and modified similarly to ordinary Modelica classes, but with certain restrictions:

- Variables/attributes and equations cannot be added in a derived class that inherits a predefined class.
- Variables/attributes cannot be redeclared.

The *only* way to define a subtype of a *predefined* Modelica class is through inheritance, usually expressed as a set of modifications. For example, a `Real` variable has a set of attributes such as unit of measure, initial value, minimum and maximum value. A complete list of these attributes is available in Chapter 3, page 98. It is possible to modify these attributes when declaring a new type, for example, through a short `type` definition with modifiers. This is exemplified by the type `Voltage` in the previous section.

4.1.14 Redefining Declared Elements at Inheritance

In most object-oriented languages, including Java, the default rule is to allow redefinition of declared elements at inheritance. A locally declared element in a Java class overrides an inherited element with the same name. This is not the case in Modelica. A locally declared element that is different from an inherited element with the same name obtained through an `extends` clause constitutes an error, as in the example below.

```
class BaseB1
  Real b1;
end BaseB1;

class ErroneousExtends
  extends BaseB1;
  Integer b1;    // Error! Local b1 clashes with inherited b1
end ErroneousExtends;
```

The only way in Modelica to locally redefine an inherited element is to use inheritance through *modification*, which is described in detail in Section 4.2.

4.1.15 The class extends Inheritance Mechanism

The `class extends` inheritance mechanism has been introduced to simplify adapting and extending libraries to different usage situations.

The general structure of a `class extends` declaration is as follows, where the `class` keyword can be replaced by any of the specialized class keywords `model`, `block`, `type`, `function`, `package`, etc.:

class extends *className class_modification*$_{opt}$ *class_body*

See Section 4.6, page 175, for a detailed description of `class extends` including examples.

4.2 Inheritance through Modification

The class concept with inheritance is the key to reuse of modeling knowledge in Modelica. However, in contrast to many other object-oriented languages, Modelica also provides *inheritance through modification* via so-called modifiers. This makes reuse even easier, and can be expressed very concisely. In fact, the three operations; inheritance, specialization through modifications, and object instantiation, can be expressed within a single Modelica declaration.

There are three kinds of constructs in the Modelica language in which modifications can occur:

- Variable declarations.
- Short class declarations.
- `extends` clauses.

What does a modifier do? It modifies one or more declarations from an (implicitly) inherited class by changing some aspect(s) of the (implicitly) inherited declarations. The most common kind of modifier just changes the *default value* or the *start value* in a declaration equation. We have already seen many examples of such modifiers, for example, modifying the default `start` value of the `altitude` variable from the `Rocket` class:

```
Real altitude(start= 59404);
```

A more dramatic change is to modify the *type* and/or the *prefixes* and possibly the *dimension sizes* of a declared element. This kind of modification is called a *redeclaration* and requires the special keyword `redeclare` to be used in the modifier in order to reduce the risk for accidental programming errors. In most cases a declaration that can be redeclared must include the prefix `replaceable`. Section 4.3.4 about redeclaration (page 160) covers this topic in quite some detail. This mechanism is often used to create generic classes with formal parameters, see Section 4.4, page 169 and Section 2.5, page 31.

There is also a general restriction about what can be modified:

- Any element declared `final` (Section 3.11.6, page 103) is not allowed to be modified.

4.2.1 Modifiers in Variable Declarations

Before getting into more details concerning modifiers in *variable declarations* it is useful to recall the structure of such a declaration:

<prefixes> <type> <variable specifier list>

Each *variable specifier* has the following structure, where all elements apart from the identifier are optional:

<identifier> <array dimension descriptor> <modifiers> <declaration equation/initializer>

As stated in Chapter 2, an array dimension descriptor can either be part of the type or be put directly after the identifier in the variable specifier. The *modifiers* should always be placed after the array dimension descriptor if present, otherwise directly after the identifier.

Modifiers change the type of a declared variable by modifying specified member declarations of the unmodified type. This can be regarded as conceptually creating an unnamed modified child class used only for the instance(s) created by the variable declaration. For example, the `Real` type of the variable `A2` has its default declaration equations for its members `unit` and `fixed` replaced by those given by the modifiers `unit="Voltage", fixed=true`.

```
Real  A1;  // Scalar variable
Real  A2(unit="Voltage",fixed=true); // Scalar with modifiers
```

One apparent difficulty regarding a modification as a special short syntactic form of class inheritance might be the absence of an explicit named child class. However, we can view a modification as conceptually creating an invisible anonymous (unnamed) child class. In most cases, but not all, a declaration of an instance (such as `A2`) of a modified class can be expressed by the introduction of an explicit intermediate modified child class (such as `ModifiedReal`), for example:

```
ModifiedReal = Real(unit="Voltage",fixed=true);
ModifiedReal A2;
```

4.2.2 Modifiers for Continuous-time or Discrete-time Variables

Are there any restrictions regarding which kinds of variables can be modified? There are several examples in the previous and the following sections of modifications of constants, parameters, and attributes with parameter *variability* (Section 3.11.2, page 99 and Section 6.8.1.3, page 278), for example, attributes `start`, `unit`, and `fixed` in predefined types (Section 3.9, page 93). For such variables and attributes there are no restrictions, apart from the general restriction that elements declared `final` (Section 3.11.6, page 103) can never be modified.

However, for variables with higher levels of variability such as continuous-time or unclocked discrete-time we have the following restriction:

- A (noninput) variable with continuous-time or unclocked discrete-time variability without a declaration binding equation is not allowed to be modified.

The reason is that if there is not already a declaration equation for a variable in a model with balanced equation count (Section 8.9, page 387), adding a new equation via a modifier will increase the number of equations and thus destroy the balancing of the modified model. This does not apply to constants and parameters which are not variables to be solved for during simulation, have defaults of value zero and anyway always have to be defined at compile-time for a model to be compiled and simulated. It does not apply to variables with an `input` prefix since they are assumed to be defined by some connection or actual parameter passed at function calls. For example:

```
model Vars
  parameter x0;
  Real x1;
  discrete Real x2;
  Real x3 = 35.7;
end Vars;

model VarsModify
  Vars y0(x0=8.33); // Legal modification, x0 is a parameter
  Vars y1(x1=7.1);  // Illegal modification, x1 is without binding equation
  Vars y2(x2=3.77); // Illegal modification, x2 is without binding equation
  Vars y3(x3=55.1); // Legal modification, x3 has a binding equation
end VarsModify;
```

4.2.3 Modifiers for Constant Declarations

Modifiers for named constants declared with the `constant` keyword are allowed in Modelica. This might appear as a contradiction since a constant always keeps the same value. However, the apparent contradiction is resolved if we remember that modification is a form of inheritance. What is modified is not the original "parent" class definitions but rather the inherited definitions in the new conceptual "child" class, as for the named constants `unit` and `fixed` in the examples of the previous section.

Moreover, modifier equations for constants and parameters must be acyclic (Section 8.2.3, page 350).

4.2.4 Modifiers for Array Variables

Regarding modifiers for array variables, it is important to be aware of the fact that each *attribute* or *variable* has the *same dimensionality and extent* as the array itself, possibly combined with the extent of the attribute if it is an array. See also Section 7.4.3 on page 323 regarding such array *record field slices* for arrays of records. The second line in the example below modifies the start value for the whole array. It is illegal to modify an indexed element of an array.

```
Real A3[2,2];                           // Array variable
Real A4[2,2](start={{1,0},{0,1}}); // Array with modifier
Real A5[2,2](unit={{"Voltage","Voltage"},{"Voltage","Voltage"}});
```

Modification of an indexed element of an array is illegal:

```
Real A6[2,2](start[2,1]=2.3); // Illegal! single element modification
```

4.2.4.1 Iterative Array Element Modification Using each

In the previous section we noted that an attribute of the element type of an array is itself an array of the same extent as the array itself. This is apparent in the *whole array attribute modifier* for the above array `A4`, repeated below. The `start` attribute of the `Real` type which is the element type for array `A4` has the same extent as `A4` itself, i.e., a 2×2 array. It is modified as a whole:

```
Real A4[2,2](start={{1,0},{0,1}}); // Array with modifier
```

However, there are cases where this scheme is too inflexible and clumsy. Consider the array `A7` with extent 2×3, containing records of type `Crec`:

```
record Crec
  Real b[4];
end Crec;

model B
  Crec A7[2,3](b = { {{1,2,3,4},{1,2,3,4},{1,2,3,4}},
                     {{1,2,3,4},{1,2,3,4},{1,2,3,4}} } );
end B;
```

The array denoted by `A7.b`, or only by `b` inside the modifier, has an extent of $2 \times 3 \times 4$, since the extent 2×3 of the array `A7` is augmented by the size 4 of the single dimension of the vector `b` declared as an attribute or field of the record `Crec`. We wish to give each instance of the vector `b` inside all `Crec` record elements of the array `A7` the value `{1,2,3,4}`. To write down the whole array value as in the above example is rather clumsy and would be quite impractical for large arrays of records.

However, by using *iterative array element modification* specified by the `each` keyword as a prefix to the modified attribute, the modifier value will be set equal to *each* array element individually:

```
model C1
  Crec A7[2,3](each b = {1,2,3,4});
end C;
```

In this way, we do not need to repeat the desired array element value in the array modifier as in the previous example. The same effect can be achieved by using an *array constructor with iterators*, see Section 7.2.2 on page 316, which creates the whole array value:

```
model D
  Crec A7[2,3](b = { {1,2,3,4} for i in 1:size(A7,1), j in 1:size(A7,2) };
end D;
```

The disadvantage of this solution is the verbose syntax needed for the iteration variable range expressions with the size functions, or analogous verbosity using other array construction variants. This verbosity has motivated the introduction of the `each` facility into the Modelica language.

The each keyword only applies to the modified element it is a prefix for. In the example below each instance of b is individually set equal to the modifier value, whereas e without the each keyword is set equal to the array d.e as a whole.

```
model Drec
  Real b[4];
  Real e;
end Drec;

model E
  Drec d[5](each b ={1,2,3,4}, e={1,2,3,4,5});
end E;
```

A common use of the each facility is to assign a common parameter value for each element of an array, for example, in a connector array as described in Section 5.7.5, page 214

If the modified element is a vector and the modifier does not contain the each-attribute, the modification is split such that the first element in the vector is applied to the first element of the vector of elements, the second to the second element, until the last element of the vector-expression is applied to the last element of the array; it is an error if these sizes do not match. Matrices and general arrays of elements are treated by viewing those as a vectors of vectors and so on.

If the modified element is a vector with subscripts the *subscripts must be Integer literals*.

If a nested modifier is split, the split is propagated to all elements of the nested modifier, and if they are modified by the each-keyword the split is inhibited for those elements. It is illegal if the nested modifier that is split in this way contains redeclarations that are split.

4.2.4.2 Modification of Arrays with Non-constant Sizes of Array Dimensions

An apparent problem might be the modification of arrays of nonconstant extent (sizes of array dimensions). Remember that modification is a short syntactic form of inheritance which is a compile-time operation. The extent of an array, however, need not be fixed at compile-time, but is fixed after the array has been created, for example, at run-time. The following are more flexible variants of the above array examples A4 and A6 where the arrays are not instantiated until run-time:

```
Real  A4b[n,n](start=identity(n));
Real  A6b[n,n](start={{i+j+1.3 for j in 1:n} for i in 1:n});
```

In example A4b we call the function identity (Section 7.9.3, page 336) to create an identity matrix of the right size. The array declaration for A6b uses an array constructor with iterators (Section 7.2.2, page 316) to create a matrix containing element values i+j+1.3 where i and j are row and column indices, respectively.

4.2.5 Modifiers in Short Class Definitions

Modifiers may occur in short class definitions after the optional array dimension descriptor if present, otherwise directly after the superclass identifier. The class keyword can either be class or one of the keywords for specialized classes. The general structure of short class definitions with modifiers is as follows:

<class keyword> <identifier> = <superclass identifier> <array dimension descriptor> <modifiers>

A few simple examples of short class definitions with modifiers are shown below, all being modifications of the superclass Real:

```
class Current  = Real(unit="mA");
type Force3    = Real[3](unit={"N","N","N"});
type Voltage   = Real(unit="V", min=-220.0, max=220.0);
```

The mechanism of modifiers in a class definition is to *replace* inherited element declarations with the same *names* as in the modifiers by appropriately modified element declarations, where the modifications are merged with the original declarations. We show an example based on the class `LowPassFilter1` below.

```
model LowPassFilter1
  constant  Real ystart = 1;
  parameter Real T = 1;
  Real u, y(start=ystart);
equation
  T*der(y) + y = u;
end LowPassFilter1;
```

The contents of the class `LowPassFilter1` is inherited into `LowPassFilter20`, for which the declarations of `ystart` and `T` are modified.

```
model LowPassFilter20 = LowPassFilter1(ystart=0, T=20);
```

The resulting class `LowPassFilter20` is equivalent to the class `LowPassFilter20B`.

```
model LowPassFilter20B
  constant  Real ystart = 0;
  parameter Real T = 20;
  Real u, y(start= ystart);
equation
  T*der(y) + y = u;
end LowPassFilter20B;
```

4.2.6 Modifiers in extends Clauses

Modifiers may also occur in `extends` clauses, and are applied to inherited element declarations in a similar way as modifiers in short class definitions. Consider the previous example class `LowPassFilter1`. We inherit the contents of this class into the class `LowPassFilter20C` below, and give the same modifiers as in the short class definition of `LowPassFilter20` above. The result is the same, and is equivalent to the class `LowPassFilter20B`.

```
model LowPassFilter20C
  extends LowPassFilter1(ystart=0, T=20);
end LowPassFilter20C;
```

Another example demonstrates that modifiers in `extends` clauses can be applied to elements that are *local classes* such as `Voltage` within the class `LowVoltage` below.

```
class LowVoltage
  type Voltage = Real(unit="V");
  Voltage v1;
  Voltage v2;
end LowVoltage;

class HighVoltage
  extends LowVoltage(Voltage(unit="kV"));
end HighVoltage;

HighVoltage vhigh;
```

The class `HighVoltage` has a local type `Voltage` with unit `"kV"`, since it was modified compared to the original version of `Voltage` in class `LowVoltage`. Thus, both variables `vhigh.v1` and `vhigh.v2` have the unit `"kV"`.

4.2.7 Modification of Nested extends Clauses

The possibilities to apply modifiers are not limited to declared elements that are variables or local classes. In the example below we have a modifier in an `extends` clause:

```
class A
  parameter Real a;
  parameter Real b;
end A;

class B
  extends A(b=3);
end B;
```

The class `B` inherits the class `A` and applies the modifier `b=3` in the `extends` clause. The result is equivalent to the class `Bexpanded`.

```
class Bexpanded
  parameter Real a;
  parameter Real b=3;
end Bexpanded;
```

It is actually possible to modify elements that are *extends clauses* in superclasses, so-called nested `extends` clauses, even though such clauses disappear in the expanded subclass, as shown below in Section 4.2.8, page 153.

4.2.8 Priority of Modifications including extends Clauses

The more recent "outermost" modifications in a chain of modifications have priority over earlier modifications.

However, consider the class `C` below with the modifier `A(b=2)` that modifies the *nested extends clause* `extends A(b=3)`of class `B` from the previous section, which can be considered to be nested one level down in the inheritance chain where `C` inherits `B`, which inherits `A`. The modified `extends` clause then becomes `extends A(b=2)`, giving a class `C` that is equivalent to `Cexpanded` with `b=2`.

The most recent, that is, "*outermost*", modifiers in the inheritance chain have priority over previous modifiers. In other words, the "*innermost*" extensions are expanded first.

```
class C
  extends B(a=1, A(b=2));
end C;

class Cexpanded
  parameter Real a=1;
  parameter Real b=2;
end Cexpanded;
```

The class `C1` below illustrates the rule that the most recently applied "*outermost*" modifications like `b=1` override "inner" modifications such as `A(b=2)` of a nested `extends` clause, since `b=2` is further down in the modification chain. The instance `bcomp` has `bcomp.b=1`, which overrides `b=2` from the nested modifier.

```
class C1
  B bcomp(b=1, A(b=2));
end C1;
```

Another example: the "*outermost*" modifier in the chain, `b=66` in the class `C4 below`, overrides the nested modification of `b` in `extends C2(b=6)`. Thus, merging the modifications (`b=66`), (`b=6`) gives the result (`b=66`).

```
class C2
```

```
    parameter Real b;
    parameter Real c;
  end C2;

  class C3
    extends C2(b=6,c=77);      // Inherited b gets default value 6
  end C3;

  class C4
    extends C3(b=66);          // The most recent modification of b
  end C4;
```

4.2.9 Modification of Protected Elements

Protected elements may not be modified or redeclared in class modifications, despite the fact that protected elements are inherited. Consider the class `D` below, inherited by class `D1`, which is correct. On the other hand, the definition of class `D2` is illegal since it tries to modify the declaration of the variable `b`, which is `protected`.

```
class D
  Real a=0;     // a is a public element
protected
  Real b=0;     // b is a protected element
end D;

class D1 = D(a=10); // Ok, since a is public

class D2 = D(b=20); // Illegal since b is protected, access outside D!
```

A protected class or instance may *not* be modified or redeclared *except* for the following. It is allowed to have modifiers applied to protected classes or instances directly within an inherited base class, but not inside any instance or class within that base class. Modifiers on the declaration of the protected element are also allowed. Further examples are shown below.

```
package A

  model B
   protected
    parameter Real x;
  end B;

 protected

  model C end C;
 public

  model D
    C c; // Legal use of protected class C from enclosing scope
    extends A.B(x=2); // Legal modifier for x in inherited base class A.B
                      // also x.start=2 and x(start=2) are legal.
    Real y=x; // Legal use of x in derived class
  end D;

  model E
    A.B a(x=2);   // Illegal modifier, also x.start=2 and x(start=2) illegal
    A.C c;        // Illegal use of protected class C

    model F=A.C; // Illegal use of protected class C
  end E;

end A;
```

4.2.10 Hierarchical Modification

Hierarchical modification means that elements one or more levels down in the *instantiation hierarchy* are modified. Such modifiers can use nested notation using parentheses or dot notation. We use a slightly enhanced version of the low-pass filter model from Section 2.3.4 on page 29 as an example.

```
model LowPassFilter
  parameter Real T=1;
  parameter Real k=1;
  Real u, y(start=1);
equation
  T*der(y) + y = k*u;
end LowPassFilter;
```

Two instances of the filter with different time constants `T` are put together to form the class `FiltersInSeries`:

```
model FiltersInSeries
  LowPassFilter F1(T=2), F2(T=3);
equation
  F1.u = sin(time);
  F2.u = F1.y;
end FiltersInSeries;
```

Finally, two different instances `F12` and `F34` of `FiltersInSeries` are created in the class `ModifiedFiltersInSeries` with modified time constants. Both instances have identical time constants, but the first uses nested notation and the second uses dot notation for hierarchical modification.

```
model ModifiedFiltersInSeries
  FiltersInSeries F12(F1(T=6), F2(T=11, k=2));    // nested notation
  FiltersInSeries F34(F1.T=6, F2.T=11, F2.k=2);   // dot notation
end ModifiedFiltersInSeries;
```

Another example of hierarchical modification is shown for the class `C5`, where the instance `anest` uses nested syntax and the instance `adot` dot notation. Both of them produce identical results.

```
class C5
  Real x;
end C5;

C5 anest(x(unit = "V", displayUnit="mV") = 5.0));

C5 adot(x.unit = "V", x.displayUnit="mV", x=5.0);
```

When using qualified names, the different qualified names starting with the *same* identifier are merged into one modifier during analysis of the modifiers. In the above example this would have the effect of converting the modifiers with dot notation in the declaration of `adot` to the nested notation used in the declaration of `anest`.

4.2.11 Single Modification Rule

Two arguments of a modification are not allowed to denote and modify the same element, attribute, or string comment. This is usually self-evident, but in the context of classes with record variables one may sometimes forget that the variable name denotes a record. Moreover, when using qualified names the different qualified names starting with the same identifier are merged into one modifier.

For example, the first modifier argument to `C1` below, `x=Foo(1,1,1)`, means that all three record elements `x.x1`, `x.x2`, `x.x3` are set equal to 1, which is in conflict with the second modifier `x.x2=2`.

```
record Foo
  Real x1;
```

```
  Real x2;
  Real x3;
end Foo;

class C1
  Foo x = Foo(0,0,0);
end C1;

class C2 = C1(x=Foo(1,1,1), x.x2=2);  // Error: x.x2 designated twice

class C3
  class C4
    Real x = 0;
  end C4;
  C4 a(x.unit = "V", x.displayUnit="mV",  x=5.0);  // OK, different
                   // attributes designated (unit, displayUnit and value)
  C4 b(x(unit = "V", displayUnit="mV") = 5.0)); // Identical to the above
end C3;
```

More examples of incorrect multiple modifications follow:

```
m1(r=1.5, r=1.6)  // Multiple modifier for r (its value)
m1(r=1.5, r=1.5)  // Multiple modifier for r (its value) - even if identical
m1(r.start=2, r(start=3)) // Multiple modifier for r.start
m1(x.r=1.5 "x", x.r(start=2.0) "y")) // Multiple string-comment for x.r
m1(r=R(), r(y=2))  // Multiple modifier for r.y - both direct value and part of record
```

Some modifications that are correct follow:

```
m1(r=1.5, r(start=2.0))
m1(r=1.6, r "x")
m1(r=R(), r(y(min=2)))
```

4.3 Redeclaration

So far we have primarily dealt with modifiers that change the default value in a declaration. A more dramatic change is to modify the *type* and/or the *prefixes* of a declared element, that is, the original declaration is actually *replaced* by the "new declaration" given in the modifier merged with the modifiers of the original declaration if such modifiers are present.

This kind of modification is called a *redeclaration* and requires the special keyword `redeclare` to be used in the corresponding modifier in order to reduce the risk for accidental modeling errors. There also exists a kind of redeclaration that appears as an element directly in a class; see Section 4.3.1, page 157.

The element to be redeclared has to be declared `replaceable`, except for the rather specific case where the only change is to restrict its variability (e.g. from continuous-time to parameter variability; see Section 4.3.4 on page 160) and/or dimension sizes. Redeclaration with an element which is the same type is possible to restrict variability and/or array dimension sizes. The following contrived example illustrates a redeclaration. The used definitions of `Resistor` and `TempResistor` are available on page 115 in Chapter 3.

```
class MiniCircuit
  replaceable discrete Resistor R1;
end MiniCircuit;

MiniCircuit tempcircuit1(redeclare parameter TempResistor R1);
```

The redeclaration of the `R1` element changes its type from `Resistor` to `TempResistor` and its prefix from `discrete` to `parameter`. The resulting anonymous modified class, which is the type of `tempcircuit1`, is equivalent to `MiniCircuit2`.

```
class MiniCircuit2
  parameter TempResistor R1;
```

```
end MiniCircuit2;
```

The element that is provided in a redeclaration must have a type that is a *subtype* of the corresponding replaceable element in the modified class or a subtype of an explicitly given (optional) constraining type. This is fulfilled in the above example since `TempResistor` is a subtype of `Resistor`., Regarding subtyping and other restrictions on redeclarations, see Section 4.3.11, page 166, and how to check subtyping in general, see Section 3.19.4, page 126.

The next example illustrates a redeclaration `redeclare A2 z(y=2)` used in an *extends clause* to replace the original declaration `A z(x=1)` from class `B`, but merging the original nested modifier `(x=1)` with the modifiers in the redeclaration to effectively get `A2 z(x=1,y=2)`. The type of the redeclared variable `z` in class `B` is changed from `A` to `A2` in class `B2`, which is correct since `A2` is a subtype of `A`.

```
class A
  parameter Real x;
end A;

class A2                      // A2 is a subtype of A
  parameter Real x=3.14;
  parameter Real y;
end A2;

class B
  replaceable A z(x=1);
end B;

class B2
  extends B(redeclare A2 z(y=2));
end B2;
```

The class B2 is equivalent to the class `B2expanded` below:

```
class B2expanded
  A2 z(x=1,y=2);
end B2expanded;
```

4.3.1 Redeclaration as an Element in a Class

At the beginning of Section 4.3, page 156, we stated that a redeclaration is a kind of modifier with a `redeclare` keyword. This is the main case and the most common form of redeclaration.

However, it is also possible to have a *redeclare clause directly within a class*. Such a redeclaration requires that the redeclared element is inherited, and cannot be combined with a modifier of the same redeclared element in the extends-clause. For example:

```
class C5Base
  replaceable Real y2=10;
end C5Base;

class C6
  extends C5Base;
  redeclare Integer y2=5;
end C6;

class C6expanded
  Integer y2=5;
end C6expanded;
```

This redeclaration replaces the inherited `Real y2` declaration with an `Integer y2` declaration. However, the following example is illegal since it combines a modifier in the extends clause with a redeclaration of the same element `y2`:

```
class C7illegal
  extends C5Base(y2=5);   // Illegal y2 redeclare. Cannot be combined
  redeclare Integer y2;   // with modifier of y2 in extends clause
end C7illegal;
```

A redeclaration clause directly in a class is particularly useful in combination with `class extends`; see Section 4.3.9, page 165.

4.3.2 Redeclaration of Elements not Declared Replaceable

Redeclarations usually require the modified element to be declared with the `replaceable` prefix. There are only *two* kinds of *redeclarations* that do not require the modified element to be declared `replaceable`:

1. Restricting the variability of a declared variable, e.g., from `parameter` to `constant`.
2. Restricting array dimension sizes, e.g., from (:) to a specified size.

The following example demonstrates these kinds of redeclarations:

```
class C3
  Real    x1;
  Real[:] vec;
end C3;

class C4 = C3(redeclare parameter Real x1, redeclare Real vec[20]);
```

The class `C4` is equivalent to the class `C4expanded` below. The variable `x1` has been restricted from *continuous-time* to *parameter* variability.

```
class C4expanded
  parameter Real  x1;
  Real[20]        vec;
end C4expanded;
```

4.3.3 Preserving Properties from Redeclared Original Declarations

Some properties from the original declaration are *preserved* if they are not explicitly changed in the redeclared version of the declaration. This feature is intended to make it easier to write redeclarations by not having to repeat many of the original declaration properties in the redeclaration.

For example, given two declarations:

```
replaceable input flow Real y3 = 15.3;
replaceable type InVoltage = input Real;
```

Below we give redeclarations of both of these, excluding modifier syntax and the enclosing class:

```
redeclare Current y3 = 22;      // Allowed, since Current is a subtype of Real
redeclare InVoltage = Voltage; // and Voltage is a subtype of Real
```

Then the result will be as follows, since properties such as the `flow` and `input` prefixes are preserved:

```
input flow Current y3 = 22;
type InVoltage = input Voltage;
```

Preservation of declaration properties applies to declaration prefixes which must be identical (excluding variability prefixes) according to the subtyping rules (Section 3.19.4, page 126) and the redeclaration restrictions (Section 4.3.11, page 166).

- The *general rule* is that if no property within one of the following groups is present in the new declaration the old properties of the same kind are preserved.

- Preserving properties only applies to the declaration *itself* and *not* to elements of the declaration.

The following groups of properties are preserved for both *class* and *variable* redeclarations:

- public, protected
- inner, outer
- constraining type according to Section 4.3.7, page 162.

These groups of properties are *only* preserved for *variable* declaration redeclarations:

- flow, stream
- discrete, parameter, constant
- input, output
- array dimensions

The above rules ensure that parts in /*...*/ in the example below are automatically added to the redeclared elements in HeatExchanger2 from the original declarations in HeatExhanger.

```
model HeatExchanger
  replaceable parameter GeometryRecord geometry;
  replaceable input Real u[2];
end HeatExchanger;

model HeatExchanger2 = HeatExchanger(
  redeclare replaceable /*parameter */ GeoHorizontal geometry,
  redeclare /* input */ Modelica.SIunits.Angle u /*[2]*/ );
```

Remember that preserving array dimensions only applies to variable declarations, not to classes. Thus, if the original declaration was a *short class definition* with array dimensions the *array dimensions are not automatically preserved*, and thus have to be repeated in those cases they are used.

```
class C8Base
  replaceable type OrigType = input Real[4];
end C8Base;

class C8
  type newType = C8Base(redeclare OrigType = Real);
end C8;

class C8expanded
  type newType = input Real;   // Array dimensions not preserved!
class C8expanded;
```

In order to preserve the array dimensions for the redeclared type, they would need to be supplied explicitly as below:

```
type NewTypeComplete = C8Base(redeclare OrigType = Real[4]);
```

Moreover, note that preservation of properties is always *from* the *original declaration*, not from replaced ones. This is a strange language rule which is different from essentially all other rules in Modelica where the most recent definition of a property is always referred to.

In most cases replaced or original does not matter. However, it does matter for example if a user redeclares a variable to be a parameter and then subsequently redeclares it without parameter.

```
class C9Base
  replaceable discrete Real x = 10.2;
end C9Base;

class C9A = C9Base(redeclare parameter Real x);

class C9Aexpanded
  parameter Real x = 10.2;
end C9Aexpanded;
```

If we subsequently redeclare C9A without parameter, it will get the discrete prefix of the original declaration in C9Base, not the replaced one in C9A:

```
class C9B = C9A(redeclare Real x);

class C9Bexpanded
  discrete Real x = 10.2;
end C9Bexpanded;
```

There is ongoing discussion whether to remove this special nonintutive rule from the language. However, if the rule to preserve properites of the original declaration is removed and instead merge properties when merging modifiers (Section 4.2.8, page 153) there can be certain properties that cannot be removed by a modifier. That issue may have to be resolved. For example, if we redeclare a variable to be parameter we cannot add another modifier that removes that parameter property:

```
model C13
  extends C12(redeclare parameter Real b=2, c=C.PARAMETER);
end C13;

model C14
  extends C13(redeclare Real b=4, d=4);
end C14;
```

If these modifiers are merged, where the most recent is to the left:

```
((redeclare Real b=4, d=4), (redeclare parameter Real b=2, c=C.PARAMETER))
```

then we obtain the following where the parameter property is still present despite the redeclaration without parameter in model C14.

```
(redeclare parameter Real b=4, d=4, c=C.PARAMETER)
```

4.3.4 Modification Prefix: replaceable

In the introduction to the topic of redeclaration, we mentioned that the prefix replaceable usually must be attached at the front of those declarations in a superclass that are enabled for *redeclaration* in a subclass. This corresponds to *virtual* in some other object-oriented languages like C++ and Simula. Note that, for example, in Java, the default rule is to allow redeclaration of all members at inheritance, that is, all members are replaceable. Only members declared final in Java are not allowed to be redeclared.

In Modelica the *default* is to *disallow redeclaration* of class members unless they have been explicitly declared as replaceable, apart from the exceptions mentioned in Section 4.3.1, page 157. The main motivation for this rule is that a class needs to be *designed* for inheritance that includes redeclaration. Otherwise unexpected errors may occur.

We have previously stated that the element that is provided in a redeclaration must have a type that is a *subtype* of the corresponding replaceable element in the modified class or a subtype of an explicitly given (optional) constraining type (see Section, 4.3.7, page 162). The motivation to this rule is similar to the above—to prevent errors. An element that fulfills the subtype condition has a reasonable chance of keeping the contract of the original element to be replaced.

Summarizing the main points of the replaceable prefix:

- A declared element of a class must have the prefix replaceable in order to be *redeclared*, apart from redeclarations that only change the attribute value and/or restrict the variability and possibly the dimension sizes.

A trivial example of a class with a replaceable element is:

```
class MicroCircuit
  replaceable Resistor R1;
end MicroCircuit;
```

Replaceable elements of a class can be regarded as a kind of *formal parameters* of that class. The use of such class parameters is described in more detail in Section 4.4 regarding generic classes on page 168.

The keyword `replaceable` in a modification automatically adds a `redeclare` if not present. See Section 4.3.5, page 161.

4.3.5 Modification Prefix: redeclare

The modification prefix `redeclare` is used only in *modifiers* and is needed when a *whole declaration* is included in the modifier. Those modifiers that use the prefix `redeclare` are known as *redeclarations*. To summarize the main points:

- The `redeclare` prefix is used at the front of a modifier containing a new variable or type declaration that *replaces* the original variable or type declaration element in the modified class.

The reason for requiring a special keyword like `redeclare` to be used in a redeclaration is to reduce the risk for accidental programming errors that otherwise might occur when whole declarations are replaced by declarations of different types. A correct example is shown below where the variable `R1` of type `Resistor` is redeclared as a `TempResistor`, which is a subtype of `Resistor`, obtaining a temperature-dependent circuit:

```
TempMicroCircuit = MicroCircuit(redeclare TempResistor R1);
```

In order to allow *further redeclaration* of a redeclared element the `replaceable` prefix should be present also in the modifier:

```
TempMicroCircuit2 = MicroCircuit(redeclare replaceable TempResistor R1);
```

A modifier with the keyword `replaceable` implicitly adds a `redeclare` keyword if not present, which makes the following somewhat shorter redeclaration equivalent:

```
TempMicroCircuit2 = MicroCircuit(replaceable TempResistor R1);
```

Modifiers prefixed with `replaceable` allow further redeclaration as below, which otherwise would not be possible:

```
SuperTempMicroCircuit = TempMicroCircuit2(redeclare SuperTempResistor R1);
```

Redeclarations can sometimes be regarded as a kind of *actual arguments* to classes when modifying generic classes in order to create more specialized classes; see Section 4.4 regarding generic classes on page 168.

4.3.6 Modification Prevention Prefix: final

The class designer may wish to *prevent* certain modifications since the correct semantics of a class can be dependent on details of its declared members. A user who is not aware of those details can otherwise unknowingly introduce errors. The `final` prefix can be used to prevent such modifications.

A variable declared as `final` in a member modification cannot be further modified by another modification. All members of a `final` member are also `final`, e.g., the variables of a `final` member that is a record are `final`. To summarize the rules for `final`:

- The `final` prefix in front of a variable, a constant, or class declaration prevents modification and redeclaration of the variable, the constant, the class, and the members of the class.
- The `final` prefix in a modifier prevents further modifications of the modified element.

In the example with the type `Angle` below, the members `quantity` and `unit` are declared `final` and cannot be further modified, whereas it is fine to modify the declaration of the variable `displayUnit`.

```
type Angle = Real(final  quantity = "Angle",
                  final  unit     = "rad",
                  displayUnit     = "deg");

Angle a1(unit="deg");  // Error, since unit declared as final!
Angle a2(displayUnit="rad");   // Fine!
```

Another slightly more advanced example of the use of `final` involves a model that is used as a transfer function within a `PI` controller. The numerator and denominator coefficient vectors `b` and `a` of the transfer block instance `tf` in the `PI` controller cannot be modified since they have been declared `final`. For a detailed explanation of the array notation see Chapter 7.

```
block TransferBlock  // works like a transfer function
  parameter Real b[:] = {1}    "numerator coefficient vector";
  parameter Real a[:] = {1,1} "denominator coefficient vector";
protected
  constant Integer nb(max=na) = size(b,1);
  constant Integer na         = size(a,1);
  constant Integer n          = na-1;
  Real[n]          x    "State vector";
  Real[na]         b0 = cat(1,zeros(na-nb), b);
 equation
  ...
end TransferBlock;

model PI  "PI controller"
  parameter Real k=1 "gain";
  parameter Real T=1 "time constant";
  TransferBlock tf(final b={T,1}, final a={T,0});
end PI;

model Test
  PI c1(k=2, T=3);    // Fine!
  PI c2(tf.b={1});    // Error, b is declared as final
end Test;
```

A `final` declaration of a variable also has implications for *interactive* setting of parameter variables in the simulation environment, since setting of the value of a parameter in a simulation environment is conceptually treated as a modification. This implies that a `final` declaration or modification of a parameter *cannot* be changed in a simulation environment.

4.3.7 Constraining Type of Replaceable Elements

A declaration of a *replaceable* element of a class can have one of the following two forms, where the *element declaration* represents either a variable or a local class declaration.

1. `replaceable` *<element declaration>*
2. `replaceable` *<element declaration>* `constrainedby` *<constraining type>*

So far, we have only seen examples of the first form of replaceable element. However, it will soon be apparent that the second form is quite useful in certain situations. It is, however, recommended to avoid modifiers in the constraining type. Regarding modifications the following holds:

- Any modifications following the constraining type name are applied both for the purpose of defining the actual constraining type and they are automatically applied in the declaration and in any subsequent redeclaration. The precedence order is that declaration modifiers override constraining type modifiers.

We state once more the subtyping condition of a redeclaration:

- The *element declaration* that is provided in a *redeclaration* must have a type that is a *subtype* of the type of the corresponding *replaceable element* in the modified class or a subtype of an explicitly given (optional) *constraining type*.
- Moreover, in many cases the declaration element must fulfill the stricter plug-compatible subtyping condition (Section 3.19.5, page 127), instead of just standard subtyping. Plug-compatible subtyping often is needed for classes or instances containing connectors.

Thus, the constraining type is either stated explicitly or otherwise defined as the type of the replaceable element. Being a subtype of the replaceable element is fulfilled in the example below, for example, when replacing the resistor component `comp1` with a temperature-dependent resistor:

```
class MicroCircuit
  replaceable Resistor comp1;
end MicroCircuit;

TempMicroCircuit = MicroCircuit(redeclare TempResistor comp1);
```

We turn `MicroCircuit` into a more generic circuit called `GenMicroCircuit`. The type `CompType` of the component `comp1` has been made `replaceable`.

```
class GenMicroCircuit
  replaceable type CompType = Resistor;
  replaceable  CompType comp1;
end GenMicroCircuit;
```

The idea is to be able to specialize the generic circuit into a circuit that can use types of components other than resistors, for example, capacitors or inductors. We try to define an inductor circuit class below, but this fails since `Inductor` is not a subtype of `CompType`, which currently is `Resistor`!

```
// Type error! Inductor is not subtype of Resistor!

class InductorMicroCircuit =
  GenMicroCircuit(redeclare type CompType = Inductor);
```

The problem is that the constraining type of `CompType` is too restrictive just using its current default value, which is `Resistor`. Instead, we would like to express that `CompType` can be any electrical component type with two pins—`CompType`—should be a subtype of `TwoPin`. Here the *second* form of replaceable element declaration comes into play, which allows us to express the *constraining type* explicitly by adding `constrainedby TwoPin`.

```
class GenMicroCircuit
  replaceable type CompType = Resistor  constrainedby TwoPin;
  // No inheritance!
  replaceable  CompType comp1;
end GenMicroCircuit;
```

After this change, there is no problem to define a more specific circuit, for example, using the component type `Capacitor`:

```
class CapacitorMicroCircuit =
  GenMicroCircuit(redeclare type CompType = Capacitor);
```

However, this capacitor circuit has no replaceable `CompType` declaration left since the original replaceable declaration was replaced. To keep `CompType` replaceable, we need to perform a redeclaration with `redeclare replaceable` as in the class below. In this case, we might want to set the constraining type to `GenCapacitor` in order to have a more specific constraint than `TwoPin`.

```
class GenCapacitorMicroCircuit = GenMicroCircuit(
  redeclare replaceable type CompType =
    Capacitor constrainedby GenCapacitor);
```

Further redeclaration is now possible, for example, using a temperature-dependent capacitor:

```
class TempCapacitorMicroCircuit =
  GenCapacitorMicroCircuit(redeclare type CompType = TempCapacitor);
```

There is also a subtyping condition for the constraining type optionally provided in a replaceable redeclaration:

- The constraining type of a *replaceable redeclaration* must be a subtype of the constraining type of the declaration it redeclares.

This condition is fulfilled for `GenCapacitorMicroCircuit` above since the constraining type `GenCapacitor` is a subtype of `TwoPin`.

The following rule applies to modifications of replaceable elements with constraining types:

- In an element *modification* of a replaceable element the modifications are applied to the *actual type* and also to the *constraining type* provided the modified attribute exists in the constraining type.

Thus the modifier `R=20` in the definition of `MicroCircuit3` is propagated to both the declaration and the constraining type, which is apparent in the class `MicroCircuit3expanded`.

```
class MicroCircuit2
  replaceable TempResistor R1 constrainedby Resistor;
end MicroCircuit2;

class MicroCircuit3 = MicroCircuit2(R1(R=20));

class MicroCircuit3expanded
  replaceable TempResistor R1(R=20) constrainedby Resistor(R=20);
end MicroCircuit3expanded;
```

There is one additional rule concerning propagation of modifiers for the case of modifiers in the constraining type:

- In an element redeclaration of a replaceable element the modifiers of the replaced constraining type are merged both to the new declaration and to the new constraining type, using the normal rules where the most recent "outermost" modifiers override earlier modifiers (see Section 4.2.8).

The modifier `R=30` for the constraining type `Resistor` is merged into `R1`, see `MicroCircuit5expanded` below.

```
class MicroCircuit4
  replaceable TempResistor R1 constrainedby Resistor(R=30);
end MicroCircuit4;

class MicroCircuit5 = MicroCircuit4(
  redeclare replaceable TempResistor2 R1 constrainedby Resistor2);

class MicroCircuit5expanded
  replaceable TempResistor2 R1(R=30) constrainedby Resistor2(R=30);
end MicroCircuit5expanded;
```

This rule concerns the use of a class as a constraining type, in case the class contains replaceable elements:

- When a class is elaborated as a constraining type, the elaboration of its replaceable elements will use the constraining type and not the actual default types.

The following two rules regarding array dimensions are just special cases and follow directly from the previously mentioned subtyping rules of constrained elements, their constraining types, and the types of elements in redeclarations:

- The number of array dimensions of a constraining type (`T2`) must be the same as the number of dimensions of the type (`T1[n]`) of the constrained element.

- The type (T3) used in a redeclaration must have the same number of array dimensions as the type (T1[n]) of the redeclared element.

In the examples below the number of array dimensions of the types T1[n], T2, and T3 must be equal.

```
replaceable T1 x[n] constrainedby T2;
replaceable type T=T1[n] constrainedby T2;
replaceable T1[n] x constrainedby T2;

redeclare T3 x;
redeclare type T=T3;
```

Note that the variable declarations of the form T1 x[n] and T1[n] x are two syntactic variations of array declarations with the same meaning (Section 7.1, page 311). In both cases the type of x is T1[n].

4.3.8 Redeclaration of Conditional Instance Declarations

A conditional instance declaration (Section 3.14, page 107), can be redeclared just like any other instance declaration. However, the redeclaration cannot supply a new condition and the existing condition from the original declaration is kept.

For example, in the following model we can choose either R1 or R2 to be instantiated. Only connections to existing instances are kept. The Resistor is changed to a TempResistor by the redeclaration.

```
model ConditionalResistorCircuit2
  parameter connectR1 = false;
  replaceable Resistor R1(R=100) if connectR1;
  replaceable Resistor R2(R=200) if not connectR1;
  replaceable Resistor R3(R=300);
equation
  connect(R1.p, R3.p);  // Selected if connectR1 = true
  connect(R2.p, R3.p);  // Selected if connectR1 = false
end ConditionalResistorCircuit2;

model R1Circuit2 =
  ConditionalResistorCircuit2(connectR1=true, redeclare TempResistor R1);

model R2Circuit2 =
  ConditionalResistorCircuit2(connectR1=false, redeclare TempResistor R2);
```

If connectR1=true, the expanded partially flattened R1Circuit2 would appear as follows:

```
model R1Circuit2Expanded
  parameter connectR1 = true;
  TempResistor R1(R=100) if connectR1;
  replaceable Resistor R3(R=300);
equation
  connect(R1.p, R3.p);  // Selected since connectR1 = true
end R1Circuit2Expanded;
```

4.3.9 class extends Redeclarations

The class extends mechanism has been created to simplify adapting a library to a usage situation without changing the original library itself by allowing modifications and redeclarations to be conveniently applied to an implicit copy of the inherited library.

The general structure of a class extends declaration is as follows, where the class keyword can be replaced by any of the specialized class keywords model, block, type, function, package, and so on:

```
class extends className class_modificationopt class_body
```

The `class extends` construct can be used by itself, but is very often combined with `redeclare`:

```
redeclare class extends className class_modificationopt class_body
```

See Section 4.6, page 175, for a detailed description of `class extends` including examples.

4.3.10 Transitively Nonreplaceable Classes

In several cases, it is important that *no new elements* can be added to the *type* of a class *during redeclaration*, especially considering short class definitions.

The main reason for this requirement is *early prevention of errors/conflicts* with existing elements in the type or class if an inherited class would be redeclared to contain additional elements with the same name(s) as existing elements in that class.

Such classes are called *transitively nonreplaceable*. See Section 4.1.5, page 140, for some examples and detailed motivation. See also Section 3.18.7.3, page 122, for the same definitions as this section.

Either the class is declared *without* the `replaceable` keyword (thus being nonreplaceable) or defined using a short class definition to be the same as another class which also must be nonreplaceable transitively to any level.

More formally, a class reference is *transitively nonreplaceable* if and only if all parts of its name satisfy the following:

- If the class definition is long it is transitively nonreplaceable if *not declared replaceable*.
- If the class definition is short (e.g., `class A=P.B`) it is transitively nonreplaceable if it is *nonreplaceable* and equal to a class reference (`P.B`) that is transitively nonreplaceable.

According to Section 4.1.5, page 140, for a hierarchical name reference *all parts* of the name must be transitively nonreplaceable. In `extends A.B.C` this implies that `A.B.C` must be transitively nonreplaceable, as well as `A` and `A.B`, with the exception of the `class extends` redeclaration mechanism, (Section 4.6, page 175) where the class reference must always be replaceable.

4.3.11 Summary of Restrictions on Redeclarations

The following is a summary of the constraints that apply to redeclarations apart from the restrictions related to constraining types and redeclarations described in the previous section. Several constraints are stated explicitly for clarity even though they follow automatically from the subtyping constraint, given the general definition of type described in Chapter 3, page 115. How to check subtyping is described in Section 3.19.4, page 126.

- Only classes and instances declared as `replaceable` can be redeclared with a different type, which must be a *subtype* of the *constraining type* of the original declaration. To allow further redeclarations of the redeclared element one must use `redeclare replaceable.` Redeclaration of elements not declared as `replaceable` is allowed with the same type and the same or more restrictive *variability* and array *dimension sizes*.
- Moreover, in many cases (when the element contains connectors) the element provided in the redeclaration must fulfill the stricter plug-compatible subtyping condition (Section 3.19.5, page 127), instead of just standard subtyping. Plug-compatible subtyping usually makes a difference for classes or instances containing connectors. Very briefly stated: *plug-compatible subtyping requires that additional connectors in the subtype interface must be default connectable*.
- A replaceable class used in an *extends clause*, for example, the `ResistorModel` below, must contain only `public` elements. If the replaceable class were to contain `protected` elements, for

example, the protected variables of the replaceable default class, it cannot be guaranteed that those variables would be kept after redeclaration.

```
class GenResistor
   replaceable class ResistorModel=Resistor;
   extends ResistorModel;
 end GenResistor;
```

- An element declared as `constant` or `final` cannot be redeclared.
- The *variability* of a declared element must be *kept the same or decrease* at redeclaration, for example, `parameter` may change to `parameter` or `constant`; `discrete` may change to `discrete`, `parameter`, or `constant`; *continuous-time* may change to *continuous-time*, `discrete`, `parameter`, or `constant`.
- A `function` can only be redeclared as a `function`.
- The `flow` properties of an element cannot be changed at redeclaration.
- The *access properties* of an element, i.e., `public` or `protected`, cannot be changed at redeclaration.
- A class redefined by `class extends` must be replaceable. See Section 4.6.2, page 177 for detailed restrictions.

4.3.12 Annotation Choices for Redeclarations

Apart from textual Modelica programming, redeclarations may also be specified through a graphical user interface (GUI) of a Modelica modeling tool, for example, via menu choices. The user interface can suggest reasonable redeclarations, where the string comment in the choice declaration can be used as a textual explanation of a choice. Based on the interactions with the user, the GUI then generates the appropriate Modelica code. The annotation can also be used as a hint to the user doing textual Modelica programming.

In order to support this mode of operation, an `annotation` (see Section 11.5.8, page 541) called `choices` containing `choice` elements is predefined to be recognized with certain semantics in Modelica, including recognition of redeclaration statements in the annotation.

Choices menus of replaceable elements can be automatically constructed showing the names of all classes that are either directly or indirectly derived by inheritance from the constraining class of the declaration. This can be recommended by having **annotation** `choicesAllMatching = true`; and disabled by having **annotation** `choicesAllMatching = false`. The behavior when `choicesAllMatching` is not specified; ideally it should present (at least) the same choices as for `choicesAllMatching = true`; but if it takes (too long) time to present the list it is better to have `choicesAllMatching = false`.

For example, consider the following `replaceable` model with a `choices` annotation:

```
replaceable model MyResistor=Resistor
  annotation(choices(
  choice(redeclare MyResistor=lib2.Resistor(a={2}) "..."),
  choice(redeclare MyResistor=lib2.Resistor2 "...")));
```

If the user would choose the first alternative, the following code might be produced if `MyResistor` is part of the class `MyCircuit` and the chosen name of the instantiated component is `x`:

```
MyCircuit x(redeclare MyResistor=lib2.Resistor(a={2}))
```

Additional examples of `replaceable` class declarations with redeclaration `choices` are shown below:

```
replaceable Resistor Load(R=2) extends TwoPin
  annotation(choices(
            choice(redeclare lib2.Resistor Load(a={2}) "..."),
            choice(redeclare Capacitor Load(L=3) "...")));

replaceable FrictionFunction a(func=exp) extends Friction
  annotation(choices(
            choice(redeclare ConstantFriction a(c=1) "..."),
```

```
                choice(redeclare TableFriction a(table="...") "..."),
                choice(redeclare FunctionFriction a(func=exp) "...")));

replaceable package Medium                              =
Modelica.Media.Water.ConstantPropertyLiquidWater
  constrainedby Modelica.Media.Interfaces.PartialMedium
                                 annotation (choicesAllMatching=true);
```

The choices annotation is not restricted to replaceable elements. It is also applicable to nonreplaceable elements, simple variables, and types used for enumerations. For a Boolean variable, a choices annotation may contain the definition checkbox = true, meaning to display a checkbox to input the values false or true in the graphical user interface.

For example, consider the following Integer type called KindOfController used to represent a choice of *controller* in the modeling process out of the following enumeration of three recommended alternatives:

```
type KindOfController = Integer(min = 1,max = 3)
   annotation(choices(
              choice = 1 "P",
              choice = 2 "PI",
              choice = 3 "PID"));
```

Assume that KindOfController is used in a model A as below:

```
model A
  KindOfController x;
end A;
```

An interactive choice of the third alternative from a menu containing the alternatives {"P","PI","PID"} would result in the default value 3 for the instantiated variable x in the following code for an instance a2 of the model A:

```
A a2(x=3 "PID");
```

It can also be applied to Boolean variables to define a check box.

```
parameter Boolean useHeatPort=false annotation(choices(checkBox=true));
```

4.4 Parameterized Generic Classes

In many situations it is advantageous to be able to express *generic* patterns for models or programs. Instead of writing many similar pieces of code with essentially the same structure, a substantial amount of coding and software maintenance can be avoided by directly expressing the general structure of the problem and providing the specific information as parameters.

Such *generic* constructs are available in several programming languages, for example, templates in C++, generics in Ada, functions and packages with type parameters in functional languages such as Haskell or Standard ML. Similar capability is provided in Modelica. In fact, the Modelica class concept is sufficiently general to handle both *generic programming* and *object-oriented modeling* within a single construct.

There are essentially two main cases of generic class parameterization in Modelica:

1. *Instance* formal parameters, for which *variable declarations* are supplied as actual arguments.
2. *Type* formal parameters, for which *classes* are supplied as actual arguments.

Interface parameterization of a class is a natural consequence where the class formal parameters are connector classes or connector variables belonging to the class.

Note that by class parameterization in this context we do not mean simulation parameter variables prefixed by the keyword parameter, even though such variables can also be class formal parameters. Instead we mean formal parameters to the class. Such *formal parameters* are prefixed by the keyword replaceable. The special case of replaceable local functions is roughly equivalent to virtual methods in some object-oriented programming languages.

4.4.1 Class Parameterization Using Replaceable and Redeclare

Modelica classes and packages can be parameterized in a general way, corresponding to generic classes or packages. Both classes and variables which are members of some class can be used as a kind of *formal class parameter* by attaching the prefix `replaceable` in front of their declarations.

As we have seen in the previous Section 4.3 about *redeclaration* on page 156 in this chapter, a declared variable can be *replaced by a variable* of a different type that must be a subtype of the constraining type of the replaced variable. Additionally, a locally declared type can be *replaced by another type*. The `replaceable` prefix must be put in front of declared elements that can be replaced. To summarize:

- *Formal class parameters* are *replaceable* variable or type declarations within the class (usually) marked with the prefix `replaceable`.
- *Actual arguments* to classes are modifiers, which when containing whole variable declarations or types are preceded by the prefix `redeclare`.

In Section 2.5, page 31, we gave two examples of parameterized classes: in the first case the formal parameters were colored objects, that is, class parameters being components or variables. In the second example, the color type itself was the class parameter.

Here we use the simple `ResistorCircuit` of three resistors connected at one node, (see Figure 4-3), as an example of a class that can be *converted* into different variants of *generic classes*. More details about the connections semantics of this class is available in Section 5.4.3, page 198.

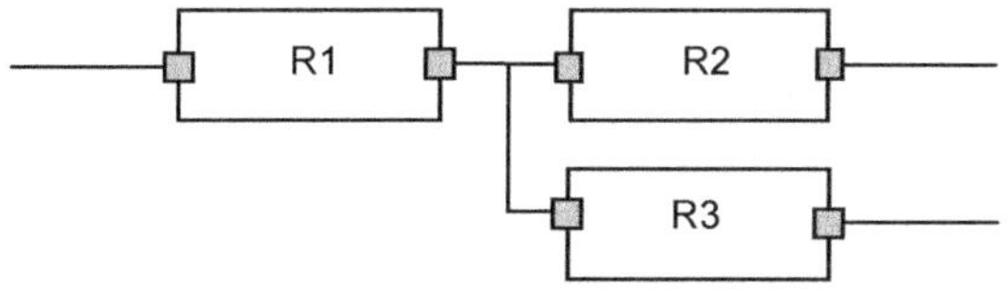

Figure 4-3. Schematic picture of the `ResistorCircuit`.

```
model ResistorCircuit  // Circuit of 3 resistors connected at one node
  Resistor R1(R=100);
  Resistor R2(R=200);
  Resistor R3(R=300);
equation
  connect(R1.p, R2.p);
  connect(R1.p, R3.p);
end ResistorCircuit;
```

In the next two sections, the two main kinds of class parameterization are discussed, using the resistor circuit as the primary example.

4.4.2 Class Parameters Being Instances

First we present the case when class parameters are components, that is, instances or objects, also called variables. Also compare this to the color class example in Section 4.1 on page 136. The class `ResistorCircuit` has been converted into a parameterized generic class `GenericResistorCircuit` in the example below with three *formal class parameters* `R1`, `R2`, `R3` marked by the keyword `replaceable`. These class parameters are declared as having the default type `Resistor`.

```
model GenericResistorCircuit    // The resistor circuit made generic
  replaceable Resistor R1(R=100);
  replaceable Resistor R2(R=200);
  replaceable Resistor R3(R=300);
equation
  connect(R1.p, R2.p);
  connect(R1.p, R3.p);
end GenericResistorCircuit;
```

Subsequently, a more specialized class `TemperatureDependentResistorCircuit` is created by changing the types of `R1` and `R2` to `TempResistor`, which is a subtype of `Resistor`, by supplying `TempResistor` declarations of `R1` and `R2` as *actual arguments* when creating a modified class out of `GenericResistorCircuit`. The keyword `redeclare` must precede a whole declaration actual argument to a formal class parameter:

```
model TemperatureDependentResistorCircuit =
  GenericResistorCircuit( redeclare TempResistor R1,
                          redeclare TempResistor R2
  );
```

We also add a temperature variable `Temp` for the temperature of the resistor circuit, and modifiers for the component `R1`, which now is a `TempResistor`, to set the temperature-dependent resistance parameter `RT` to `0.1` and the resistor temperature `Temp` to the circuit temperature `Temp`. The standard class syntax is used rather than the previous short class definition.

```
model TemperatureDependentResistorCircuit
  Real Temp;
  extends GenericResistorCircuit(
    redeclare TempResistor R1(RT=0.1, Temp=Temp),
    redeclare TempResistor R2
  );
end TemperatureDependentResistorCircuit;
```

This class is equivalent to the class below. The prefix `replaceable` has been lost for `R1` and `R2`, since we did not use `redeclare replaceable`.

```
model TempDepResistorCircuitInherited
  Real Temp;
  TempResistor R1(R=100, RT=0.1, Temp=Temp);
  TempResistor R2(R=200);
  replaceable Resistor R3(R=300);
equation
  connect(R1.p, R2.p);
  connect(R1.p, R3.p);
end TempDepResistorCircuitInherited;
```

4.4.3 Generalizing Constraining Types of Class Parameters

Sometimes, it can be useful to allow a more general *constraining type* of a class parameter, for example, `TwoPin` instead of `Resistor` for the formal class parameters and components `comp1` and `comp2` below. This allows replacement by another kind of electrical component than a resistor in the circuit.

```
model GeneralResistorCircuit
  replaceable Resistor comp1(R=100) constrainedby TwoPin;
  replaceable Resistor comp2(R=200) constrainedby TwoPin;
  replaceable Resistor R3(R=300);
equation
  connect(R1.p, R2.p);
  connect(R1.p, R3.p);
end GeneralResistorCircuit ;
```

Here, the resistors R1 and R2 can be replaced by any electrical component which is a subtype of model TwoPin, as in the following redeclaration.

The generalized parameterization properties of GeneralResistorCircuit are used below when replacing the circuit components comp1 and comp2 with components of the types Capacitor and Inductor that are subtypes of TwoPin.

```
model RefinedResistorCircuit
  extends GeneralResistorCircuit(redeclare Capacitor comp1(C=0.003),
                                 redeclare Inductor comp2(L=0.0002) );
end RefinedResistorCircuit;
```

4.4.4 Class Parameters Being Types

A *formal class parameter* can also be a *type*, which is useful for changing the type of many objects. For example, by providing a type parameter ResistorModel in the generic class below it is easy to change the resistor type of all objects of type ResistorModel, for example, from the default type Resistor to the temperature-dependent type TempResistor. The class GenericResistorCircuit2 is denoted as generic since it is valid for many possible values of the class parameter ResistorModel. Also compare to the ColoredClass class parameter example in Section 2.5.2 on page 33.

```
model GenericResistorCircuit2    // A generic resistor circuit
  replaceable model ResistorModel = Resistor;
  ResistorModel R1(R=100);
  ResistorModel R2(R=200);
  ResistorModel R3(R=300);
equation
  connect(R1.p, R2.p);
  connect(R1.p, R3.p);
end GenericResistorCircuit2;
```

A more specialized temperature-dependent circuit RefinedResistorCircuit2 (which is not generic) can be created where the resistor type TempResistor is supplied as an actual argument value for the formal class parameter ResistorModel:

```
model RefinedResistorCircuit2 =
  GenericResistorCircuit2(redeclare model ResistorModel = TempResistor);
```

This class is equivalent to the following "expanded" class:

```
model RefinedResistorCircuit2expanded   // A generic resistor circuit
  TempResistor R1(R=100);
  TempResistor R2(R=200);
  TempResistor R3(R=300);
equation
  connect(R1.p, R2.p);
  connect(R1.p, R3.p);
end RefinedResistorCircuit2expanded;
```

4.4.5 Parameterization and Extension of Interfaces

External interfaces to component classes are defined primarily through the use of connectors. The topic of connectors and connections is primarily dealt with in Chapter 5, but here we describe parameterization and extensions of such interfaces.

For example, assume that we have a definition of a Tank model in a model library. The Tank model is depicted in Figure 4-4 and as the class Tank declared below. The model has an external interface in terms of the connectors `inlet` and `outlet`, as well as a formal class parameter `TankStream`, which is a connector class with its default class value being the `Stream` connector class .

Figure 4-4. A tank with connectors inlet and outlet.

```
model Tank
  parameter Real Area=1;
  replaceable connector TankStream = Stream; // Class parameterization
  TankStream inlet, outlet; // The connectors
  Real level;
equation
  // Mass balance
  Area*der(level) = inlet.volumeFlowRate + outlet.volumeFlowRate;
  outlet.pressure = inlet.pressure;
end Tank;

connector Stream    // Connector class
  Real pressure;
  flow Real volumeFlowRate;
end Stream;
```

We would like to extend the `Tank` model to include temperature-dependent effects, analogous to how we extended a resistor to a temperature-dependent resistor. This involves *extension* both of the *connector-based external interface* of the class `Tank` and of its model equations. The result is the temperature-dependent `Tank` model called `HeatTank`. A new connector class `HeatStream` is defined as an extension of the previous connector class `Stream`, and provided as an actual argument, i.e., redeclaration, when defining the class `HeatTank`.

```
model HeatTank
  extends Tank(redeclare connector TankStream = HeatStream);
  Real temp;
equation
  // Energy balance for temperature effects
  Area*level*der(temp) = inlet.volumeFlowRate*inlet.temp +
                         outlet.volumeFlowRate*outlet.temp;
  outlet.temp = temp;   // Perfect mixing assumed.
end HeatTank;

connector HeatStream
  extends Stream;
  Real temp;
end HeatStream;
```

The definition of `HeatTank` is equivalent to the following class definition:

```
model HeatTankExpanded
  parameter Real Area=1;
  TankStream inlet, outlet;
  Real level;
  Real temp;

  connector TankStream
    Real pressure;
    flow Real volumeFlowRate;
```

```
    Real temp;
  end TankStream;

equation
  // Mass balance:
  Area*der(level) = inlet.volumeFlowRate + outlet.volumeFlowRate;
  outlet.pressure = inlet.pressure;  // Energy balance:
  Area*level*der(temp) = inlet.volumeFlowRate * inlet.temp +
                         outlet.volumeFlowRate * outlet.temp;
  outlet.temp = temp;
end HeatTankExpanded;
```

4.5 Designing a Class to Be Extended

At this stage, it should be apparent to the reader that a class needs to be *carefully designed* to be extended. Otherwise, it will often be misused by derived classes, or may not be possible to extend at all. One example is our by now well-known `Resistor` class, also shown below. It has a lot in common with the `TempResistor` class, also shown below. Unfortunately, `Resistor` cannot be inherited by `TempResistor` since the constitutive resistor equation `v=i*R` would still be kept together with the new temperature-dependent `Resistor` equation if we try to inherit from `Resistor`, giving conflicts between the two equations and an overdetermined system of equations.

The conclusion is that the `Resistor` class should be designed for extending only its data declarations since the behavior in terms of equation(s) creates problems, or otherwise be designed to allow replacement also of the behavior. Thus there are at least two design goals when designing a class to be extended:

- Reuse of data, i.e., variable declarations.
- Reuse of behavior, i.e., equations.

We will explore both of these possibilities.

Another aspect to consider is that any non-`final` class, i.e., any class *not* declared `final`, has two interfaces. The *public interface* is for code *referring* to the class, for example, through its connectors or other public elements. The *protected interface* is for code *inheriting* the class since protected declarations are inherited. Both interfaces are real *contracts* between the class designer and user, and should be designed carefully.

If a class can be extended we should also design its `protected` parts carefully and especially consider whether protected elements really are necessary. The result might be to have no protected elements in the superclass, if it does not need any special access.

4.5.1 Reuse of Variable Declarations from Partial Base Classes

One way of getting around the problems of inheriting and specializing behavior, exemplified with the `Resistor` class below, is to create incomplete, that is, `partial`, base classes that can be inherited.

```
model Resistor "Electrical resistor"
  extends TwoPin; // TwoPin, see Section 2.8.5, page 40.
  parameter Real R(unit="Ohm")          "Resistance";
equation
  v = i*R;
end Resistor;

model TempResistor "Temperature dependent electrical resistor"
  extends TwoPin; // TwoPin, see Section 2.8.5, page 40.
  parameter Real R(unit="Ohm") "Resistance at reference Temp.";
  parameter Real RT(unit="Ohm/degC")=0  "Temp. dependent Resistance.";
  parameter Real Tref(unit="degC")=20    "Reference temperature.";
```

```
  Real            Temp=20                 "Actual temperature";
equation
  v = i*(R + RT*(Temp-Tref));
end TempResistor;
```

Such `partial` base classes can be made to contain only the data declarations that can be reused.

```
partial model BaseResistor "Electrical resistor"
  Pin p, n;   "positive and negative pins";
  Voltage v;
  Current i;
  parameter Real R(unit="Ohm") "Resistance";
end BaseResistor;
```

This is a `partial` class since it does not contain enough equations to completely specify its physical behavior, and is therefore prefixed by the keyword `partial`. The keyword is optional when items referred to by the class are available. Partial classes are usually known as *abstract* classes in other object-oriented languages.

Using the `BaseResistor` partial class the two classes `Resistor2` and `TempResistor2`, equivalent to the `Resistor` and `TempResistor` above, can be defined to reuse all common variable declarations in the base class.

```
model Resistor2 "Electrical resistor"
  extends BaseResistor;
equation
  v = i*R;
end Resistor2;

model TempResistor2 "Temperature dependent electrical resistor"
  extends BaseResistor;
  parameter Real RT(unit="Ohm/degC")=0  "Temp. dependent Resistance.";
  parameter Real Tref(unit="degC")=20    "Reference temperature.";
  Real           Temp=20                 "Actual temperature";
equation
  v = i*(R + RT*(Temp-Tref));
end TempResistor;
```

The *drawback* of this approach is that we have essentially given up on reuse and inheritance of behavior when part of the behavior needs to be *redefined*. In the next section, we examine a way to get around that problem.

4.5.2 Extending and Redefining Behavior

Redefining behavior when classes are extended is not a problem in standard object-oriented languages such as Java and C++ since behavior is contained in *named* methods. One named method of a class can be replaced by another method with the same name in the extended class.

This solution is not possible in Modelica since behavior is primarily represented by *unnamed equations*. There is no general simple mechanism to name equations in Modelica, but fortunately there are two ways to indirectly associate a name with equation(s):

- A declaration equation named by its variable.
- A group of equations stored in a named replaceable local class.

The first possibility is to use the fact that a declaration equation is implicitly named by the variable that is declared in the declaration. However, such equations are seldom useful for general representation and specialization of behavior since they are closely tied to the declaration of the variable that is declared, for example, the variable might be declared in an inherited class but the equation may refer to variables in the current class.

The second method is to put the *class's* equation(s) that might need replacement into a *replaceable local class* that is inherited into the *class* itself. The local class ResistorEquation within the class Resistor3 below is an example of this technique. Resistor3 has the same variables and behavior as Resistor, but allows redeclaration of its equations since they are defined in the replaceable class ResistorEquation.

```
model Resistor3 "Electrical resistor"
  Pin p, n;  "positive and negative pins";
  parameter Real R(unit="Ohm")      "Resistance";
  replaceable class ResistorEquation
    Voltage v;
    Current i;
   equation
    v = i*R;
  end ResistorEquation;
  extends ResistorEquation;
end Resistor3;
```

The temperature-dependent resistor class TempResistor3, essentially equivalent to the previous TempResistor, can inherit Resistor3 by declaring its temperature-dependent equation in a redeclaration class ResistorEquation that replaces the original local class ResistorEquation. Note that in this case we have supplied a *whole* new class declaration within the redeclaration

```
model TempResistor3 "Temperature dependent electrical resistor"
  extends Resistor3( redeclare class ResistorEquation
         Voltage v;
         Current i;
       equation
         v = i*(R + RT*(Temp-Tref));
       end ResistorEquation;
  );
  parameter Real RT(unit="Ohm/degC")=0  "Temp. dependent Resistance.";
  parameter Real Tref(unit="degC")=20    "Reference temperature.";
  Real           Temp=20                 "Actual temperature";
end TempResistor3;
```

The described method of redefining behavior at inheritance by collecting equations into replaceable local classes works, but is somewhat clumsy. It is possible to allow further redefinition of the behavior of a derived class such as TempResistor3 by using redeclare replaceable in the redeclaration instead of just redeclare. A more elegant approach of extending and redefining behavior of classes and libraries is provided by the class extends mechanism described in Section 4.6 below.

4.6 Adapting and Extending Libraries by class extends

A common problem when using libraries is that they often need to be adapted somewhat before they fit a particular application. A brute force approach would be to copy the library and make the necessary changes and additions. However, this creates maintenance problems when new versions of the same library appear. Manually redoing the same changes and enhancements over and over again for each new version of the library is time consuming, tedious, and error prone.

The Modelica class extends mechanism has been created to simplify adapting a library to a usage situation without changing the original library itself by allowing modifications and redeclarations to be applied to an implicit copy of the inherited library.

The general structure of a class extends declaration is as follows, where the class keyword can be replaced by any of the specialized class keywords model, block, type, function, package, and so on:

```
class extends className class_modificationopt class_body
```

Expressed somewhat formally, a `class extends` declaration has the following effect:

- A class declaration of the form `class extends Bclass(`*class_modification*$_{opt}$`)` replaces a replaceable inherited class (`Bclass`) with another declaration with the same name (`BClass`) that inherits the optionally modified original inherited class `Bclass(`*class_modification*$_{opt}$`)`. Since all definitions are inherited with modifiers already applied, they need not be applied later.

The `class extends` can be used by itself, but is very often combined with redeclare:

```
redeclare class extends className class_modificationopt class_body
```

As usual, a redeclaration (Section 4.3, page 156) of a definition is applied within an implicit copy of the class/package containing the definition; in this case a copy of the inherited class/package where the definition named `className` is originally defined.

When should we use `class extends` and when should we use `redeclare class extends`? These are approximate guidelines:

- Use `class extends` to add new definitions to an existing inherited library after it is inherited.
- Use `redeclare class extends` to replace definitions in an existing inherited library in an implicit copy of the library before it is inherited.

The `class extends` mechanism might appear to be rather abstract and complicated. Below we give some examples of its use to make it easier to understand. Note that it is rather easy to use.

4.6.1 A Simple Example of Adding Definitions to an Inherited Library

Regard the following simple `class extends` example without modifiers, where we have replaced the `class` keyword by `package`:

```
package extends InheritedLib ...
```

Assume that we have the following definition of `InheritedLib` inside `BasePackage`:

```
package BasePackage

  replaceable package InheritedLib
    model A1 ... end A1;  model A2 ... end A2;
  end InheritedLib;

end BasePackage;
```

`InheritedLib` is inherited by some other class, e.g.:

```
class OtherClass

  extends BasePackage;

  package extends InheritedLib
    model C3 ... end C3;  model D4 ... end D4; model E5 ... end E5;
  end InheritedLib;

end OtherClass;
```

The `class extends` mechanism gives the following result when all inheritance has been expanded, since it replaces the original `InheritedLib` containing `A1` and `A2` with the new `InheritedLib` which inherits the original `InheritedLib` but also contains `C3`, `D4`, and `E5`.

```
class OtherClassExpanded
  package InheritedLib
    model A1 ... end A1;  model A2 ... end A2;
    model C3 ... end C3;  model D4 ... end D4;  model E5 ... end E5;
```

```
  end InheritedLib;
end OtherClassExpanded;
```

The following PowerTrain example is very similar. The clause `package extends Gearboxes` adds new definitions to the already inherited subpackage `Gearboxes`. Note that `GearBoxes` *must* have been declared `replaceable`.

```
package PowerTrain        // Library from someone else
  replaceable package GearBoxes
    ... // Some library classes
  end GearBoxes;
end PowerTrain;

package MyPowerTrain
  extends PowerTrain;     // Inherit all classes from PowerTrain
                          // including the sublibrary GearBoxes

  package extends GearBoxes    // Add more classes to the sublibrary
    model G5 ... end G5;       // Here G5 and G6 are added to GearBoxes
    model G6 ... end G6;
    ...
  end GearBoxes;
end MyPowerTrain;
```

4.6.2 General Mechanism and Restrictions for Class Extends

As already shown, a `class extends` declaration has the following form:

`class extends` *`InheritedClass class_modification`*$_{opt}$ *`class_body`*

The following general rules and restrictions apply to `class extends` declarations:

- `InheritedClass` is a class that has been inherited from some base class.
- `InheritedClass` is subject to the same restrictions, for example constraining type, as a standard redeclare of `InheritedClass`.
- `InheritedClass` should always be declared replaceable.
- The new inherited class is only replaceable if the `class extends` definition has been declared as replaceable, for example `replaceable class extends` *InheritedClass class_modification*$_{opt}$ *class_body*.
- The restriction in short class definitions, e.g., `class Aclass=Bclass`, that `Bclass` should be transitively nonreplaceable (Section 3.18.7.3, page 122), i.e., that no new elements can be added to the interface of a class, does not apply to an `InheritedClass` inherited via `class extends` since `InheritedClass` is required to be replaceable.

Conceptually, a Modelica compiler implementing support for the `class extends` mechanism has to perform the following steps:

- Step 1. Make a copy of the inherited enclosing class/package containing `InheritedClass` with the enclosing class modifiers applied.
- Step 2. Before inheriting, if there are any `redeclare extends class` definitions, redeclare those in the copy.
- Step 3. After inheriting, replace the inherited definitions by their corresponding `extends class` definitions if present.

4.6.3 Redeclarations with redeclare class extends in a Parameterized Inherited Class

We continue with a more advanced example which demonstrates a combination of parameterization of an inherited class and redeclarations of definitions within that class. The `A` model is parameterized by the `Integer` constant `n`. The replaceable model `M` is replaced both using `class extends` and `redeclare class extends` to demonstrate the difference.

```
model A
  constant Integer n=1;
  replaceable model M
    Real x;
  end M;

  M[n] mA;
end A;
```

The `UserB` model inherits a copy of `A` where the modifier `n=2` has been applied to replace `n=1` by `n=2`.

```
model UserB
  extends A(n=2);

  model extends M  // This will not change M in the modified A
    VoltageB x;
  end M;
  M[n]  mB;
end UserB;
```

This results in the expanded/flattened model below, where we use dot notation like `mA.x` to show that this is the `x` from the inherited `A` model, and `mB.x` to show that this `x` originates from the `mB` instance in `UserB`.

The `UserB` model inherits a copy of `A` where with the modifiers (here `n=2`) have been applied. This copy contains `mA` of type `M[n]` where `M` contains x of type `Real`. The effect of `model extends M` in `UserB` is to *locally* replace the *inherited* `M` by an `M` containing `VoltageB` which is used by the `mB` instance, giving the following expanded result. Arrays are shown without expansion to scalar elements.

```
model UserB_Expanded
  Real[2]        mA.x;
  VoltageB[2]   mB.x;
end UserB_Expanded;
```

The `UserC` model inherits `A` with a `redeclare model extends` clause referring to the inherited `M`. The difference compared to the previous case is that we have a `redeclare` in front of the `model extends M` declaration.

```
model UserC
  extends A(n=3);

  redeclare model extends M  // This will replace M in the modified A
    VoltageC x;
  end M;
  M[n]  mC;
end UserC;
```

The `redeclare` has the effect of redefining `M` in a copy of the modified package `A` *before* it is inherited into `UserC`. The applied modification is `n=3`. The redefined `M` is used by the `mA` instance declared in `A` as well as by `mC` in `UserC`, resulting in the following expanded/flattened model, here shown with arrays not expanded:

```
model UserC_Expanded
  VoltageC[3]  mA.x;
  VoltageC[3]  mC.x;
```

```
end UserC_Expanded;
```

Similarly, the `UserD` model also inherits the modified `A`, but with a different modification `n=4`, with a `redeclare model extends` clause referring to the inherited `M`:

```
model UserD
  extends A(n=4);

  redeclare model extends M
    VoltageD x;
  end M;
    M[n]  mD;
end UserD;
```

This will result in the following expanded/flattened model, here shown with arrays not expanded:

```
model UserD_Expanded
  VoltageD[4]  mA.x;
  VoltageD[4]  mD.x;
end UserD_Expanded;
```

4.6.4 Redeclarations with redeclare class extends in a Media Application

The following example is an advanced type of package structuring typical in media applications.

First we show a generic but incomplete partial package called `PartialMedium` which is defined containing both a partial model for the basic properties of the medium and a partial function that defines the dynamic viscosity of the medium.

```
partial package PartialMedium  "Generic medium interface"
  constant Integer nX "number of substances";

  replaceable partial model BaseProperties
    Real X[nX];
    ...
  end BaseProperties;

  replaceable partial function dynamicViscosity
    input  Real p;
    output Real eta;
    ...
  end dynamicViscosity;
end PartialMedium;
```

We use the `PartialMedium` package as a basis for creating our own specialized package for the moist air medium, `MoistAir`, where `BaseProperties` has been specialized according to its `redeclare model extends` definition.

Note that since `MostAir` extends from `PartialMedium` in the example below, the constant definition `nX = 2`, the model `BaseProperties`, and the function `dynamicViscosity` are present in `MoistAir`.

By the following definitions, the available partial `BaseProperties` model is replaced by the given definition which inherits the original modified partial `BaseProperties` model that has been temporarily constructed during the inheritance of `PartialMedium` from the package `MostAir`.

The redeclared `BaseProperties` model references the constant `nX` which is 2, since by construction the redeclared `BaseProperties` model is in the modified `PartialMedium` package with `nX` = 2, where the modification has been applied before the package is inherited.

```
package MoistAir "Special type of medium"
```

```
  extends PartialMedium(nX = 2);   // Inherits BaseProperties and
                                   // dynamicVisosity redeclared below

  redeclare model extends BaseProperties(T(stateSelect=StateSelect.prefer))
    // Replaces BaseProperties by this new definition and extends from
    // the previous partial BaseProperties with a modification on T
    // Note that nX = 2 since BaseProperties is inherited as an element in
    // the PartialMedium which is inherited with modifier nX = 2
  equation
    X = {0, 1};
    ...
  end BaseProperties;

  redeclare function extends dynamicViscosity
    // Replaces partial dynamicViscosity by this new implementation and
    // extends from the previous partial dynamicViscosity
  algorithm
    eta = 2*p;
  end dynamicViscosity;
end MoistAir;
```

The above definition is compact but perhaps a bit difficult to understand. However, a possible alternative approach is impractical and/or erroneous, which is explained below (Section 4.6.5, page 180).

4.6.5 A Conventional Approach with Erroneous Modifiers

At a first glance, an alternative modeling approach with conventional redeclarations might exist that could be more straightforward and easier to understand. The `MostAir2` example demonstrates this approach.

```
partial package PartialMedium  "Generic medium interface"
  constant Integer nX "number of substances";

  replaceable partial model BaseProperties
    Real X[nX];
    ...
  end BaseProperties;

  replaceable partial function dynamicViscosity
    input  Real p;
    output Real eta;
    ...
  end dynamicViscosity;
end PartialMedium;


package MoistAir2  "Alternative definition with duplicate definitions"
  extends PartialMedium(    // Standard modifiers/redeclarations:
    nX = 2,
    redeclare model BaseProperties = MoistAir_BaseProperties,
    redeclare function dynamicViscosity = MoistAir_dynamicViscosity );

  model MoistAir_BaseProperties // Additional BaseProperties model
    extends PartialMedium.BaseProperties(nX = 2);
      // Error! Modifier nX is not declared in BaseProperties
  equation
    X = {1,0};
  end MoistAir_BaseProperties;
```

```
  function MoistAir_dynamicViscosity    // Used in above redeclaration
    extends PartialMedium.dynamicViscosity(nX = 2);
      // Modifier nX=2 is duplicated
  algorithm
    eta :=p;
  end MoistAir_dynamicViscosity;
end MoistAir2;
```

Here the usual approach is used to inherit, for example from `PartialMedium`, where all redeclarations are performed in the modifiers. In order to perform these redeclarations, the corresponding implementations of all elements of `PartialMedium`, e.g. `BaseProperties`, `dynamicViscosity`, etc., have to be given under different names, such as `MoistAir2.MoistAir_BaseProperties`, and so on, since `BaseProperties` already exists as a local class since it has been inherited via `extends PartialMedium`. Then it is possible in the modifier to redeclare `PartialMedium.BaseProperties` to `MoistAir2.MoistAir_BaseProperties` through a short class definition.

One drawback is that the *namespace is polluted* by elements that have different names but the same implementation, for example `MoistAir2.BaseProperties` is identical to `MoistAir2.MoistAir_BaseProperties`, and `MoistAir2.dynamicViscosity` is identical to `MoistAir2.MoistAir_dynamicViscosity`.

However more *serious* is that the whole construction *does not work* if arrays are present that depend on constants in `PartialMedium`, for example, `X[nX]` that depends on the value of the constant `nX`.

The problem is that `MoistAir_BaseProperties` extends from `PartialMedium.BaseProperties` where the constant `nX` does not yet have a value and cannot be give a value through a modification since `nX` has no definition inside `MoistAir_BaseProperties`. This means that the dimension of the array `X` is undefined and the model `MoistAir_BaseProperties` is *wrong*.

Thus, with this construction, all constant definitions have to be repeated whenever these constants are to be used, especially in `MoistAir_BaseProperties` and `MoistAir_dynamicViscosity`.

For larger models it is not very practical to repeat definitions of the same constants for reasons of maintainability. Therefore the preferred practically useful approach is the construction used in the previous example with `redeclare model extends BaseProperties`.

To detect the issue of erroneous lookup in partial packages such as for `PartialMedium.dynamicViscosity`, the rule of lookup of composite names (Section 3.17.2, page 112) has an extra condition that the class within which lookup is done may not be a partial class when we are performing the lookup in the context of compiling a simulation model, i.e., a model being compiled to executable code.

4.7 Summary

In this chapter, we presented the Modelica version of one of the major benefits of object orientation: the ability to inherit behavior and properties from an existing class. The presentation started by reorganizing the previous moon landing example to use inheritance, and thereby achieving a certain degree of reuse. We continued by presenting the concepts of modification and redeclaration in Modelica, which provide particularly concise and elegant ways of expressing inheritance in many situations. We concluded by describing how to define and use generic classes in Modelica, as well as designing a class to be extended.

4.8 Literature

The primary reference documents for this chapter are the Modelica language specification (Modelica Association 2012), (Modelica Association 2013), and tutorial (Modelica Association 2000). Modelica inheritance is quite similar to Java inheritance, e.g. as described in (Arnold and Gosling 1999). Diamond inheritance is mentioned, e.g. in (Szyperski 1997). Inheritance in conjunction with the idea of a contract between a software designer and user is discussed in for example (Booch 1994; Meyer 1997).

4.9 Exercises

Exercise 4-1:

Inheritance:

```
class Animal
  Boolean isAlive = true;
  Boolean talks = false;
end Animal;
```

Define a class, `Bird`, that inherits from the class `Animal`. Give the variables values.

Question: What value has the variable talks in the class `Bird`?

Exercise 4-2:

Create Subclasses and Superclasses: In this exercise you should create a partial class `Vehicle` with the variable speed. You should also create four classes; `Car`, `Boat`, `Train`, and `Bicycle`, which inherit from `Vehicle`. Remember the variables for each subclass, which you can see in the figure below.

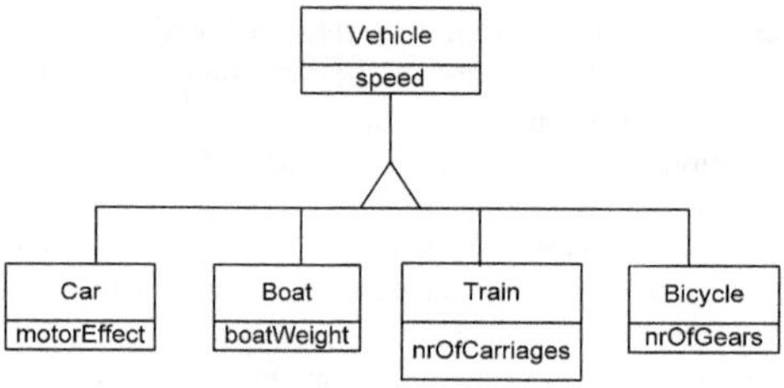

Let's write an instance of Train!

Exercise 4-3:

Using Inheritance and Access Control: Write a class, `Person`, with the variables name, weight, and ID, where ID should be protected. The next class `Employed` should inherit from `Person` and have a protected variable, salary. The last class, Programmer, contains the variables `favProgLang` (favorite programming language) and `drinksJoltCola`.

Question: Which protected variable(s) does the class `Employed` have?

Use the same class `Person`, but use this changed class `Employed` below:

```
class Employed2
protected
  extends Person;
protected
  Real salary;
end Employed2;
```

Now which protected variable(s) does the class `Employed` have?

Exercise 4-4:

Question: What does a modifier do?

Easy Modifying Example: Modify

- the start value to 3,
- the min value to −22 and
- the fixed value to true

of the variable test in the class `Test` below.

```
class Test
  parameter Integer test;
end Test;
```

Exercise 4-5:

Modifiers for Array Values: In this exercise you should modify different values of the following variables:

- Set fixed to true in A1.
- Set the start value to false in `truthvalues`.
- Set unit to "`kV`" in the position: first row and second column of `A2`.
- Set the start value on the first row in `A3` to the values 3, 5, and 8. In the second row of the matrix the values should be set to 3, 10, and 22.
- Set the matrix elements to "`Pippi`" in `A4`.

```
class ModArray
  Integer A1[5];
  Boolean truthvalues[2];
  Real A2[2,2];
  Integer A3[2,3];
  Real A4[2,2];
end ModArray;
```

Tip: Remember that each attribute has the same dimensionality as the array itself. Read more about predefined types/classes in Section 3.9. Read more about array construction in Chapter 7.

Exercise 4-6:

Modification and Access Control: The class `Mod`, below, contains five variables. Are you allowed to modify all of them? Why or why not?

```
class Mod
  parameter Real x;
  parameter Real y;
  parameter Real z;
protected
  parameter Real w;
  parameter Real s;
end Mod;
```

Exercise 4-7:

Inheritance Through Modification: Declare a `Real` variable temp with the unit "`degC`" in the class `Temperature`.

```
class Temperature

end Temperature;
```

Use short class definition and create a new class `Temp20` that modifies the variable temp in `Temperature` to be equal to 20.

Do the same thing as in `Temp20`, but this time `Temp20` should inherit from `Temperature`.

Tip: The variable `temp` must be a parameter so it can be modified in the short class definition.

Exercise 4-8:

Applying Hierarchical Modification: Today you are going on a lunch date! To help you, several classes are created below.

The first class is DayName, contains the parameter nameOfDay, a certain day written as a String.

The second class, LunchAppointment, contains the variables lunchTime (what time you are going to lunch) and lunchDate (whom you are going to lunch with).

And finally, the class Date, with parameters dayName (where you can set the variable in the class DayName; for fun it is now Funday) as well as date, month, and year.

```
class DayName
  parameter String nameOfDay;
end DayName;

class LunchAppointment
  parameter Integer lunchTime;
  parameter String lunchDate;
end LunchAppointment;

class Date
  DayName dayName(nameOfDay = "Funday");
  parameter Integer date;
  parameter String month;
  parameter Integer year;
end Date;
```

Now create a class, Today, in which you can modify the values in the class Date as well as in the class LunchAppointment. First, write the class using nested notation.

Now write the class, Tomorrow, going with another date, using dot notation.

Exercise 4-9:

Using Replaceable and Redeclare on Class *Point*: Point is a built-in type in Modelica.

```
class Point
  parameter Real x;
  parameter Real y;
  parameter Real z;
end Point;
```

Create a class Redeclaration, containing a Point P as a variable. You should set the values of x, y, and z as well.

In the class below you should redeclare P as the type myPoint, which is a subtype of Point (you can write myPoint further below).

```
class PointRed

end PointRed;
```

You can declare the class myPoint.

*Tip:*The variable P must be declared replaceable in class Redeclaration.

Question: If you instead had a class MyPoint with z as an Integer, would that work?

```
class MyPoint
  parameter Real x;
  parameter Real y;
  parameter Integer z = 4;
end MyPoint;
```

Exercise 4-10:

Using the Extends Clause in Redeclarations: The next exercise will test if you know how to use an `extends` clause when redeclaring.

First write a class `A` with a `Real` parameter `salt`. We also need a class `Asub` , extending `A` and having two `Real` parameters: `pepper` and `basil`. The parameter `salt` shall be set to 20. Then we need a class `AInst`, containing a variable a, which is an instance of `A`, in which you should set salt to 100.

Write a class `AIred`, extending `AInst`. Also, change the type of the component a to `AIsub` and set the pepper parameter to 200.

Write a similar class `AIred2` that instead of extending `AInst`, declares a component of type `AInst`. As above, the type of component a should be changed to `AIsub`.

Exercise 4-11:

More on Redeclaration: Write a class `MoreRed` that declares two variables `v1` and `v2` being vectors and one variable `x` being an `Integer`. Set x to a value.

Use the class above to redeclare the dimension sizes of v1 and v2 and the type of x.

Tip: In the redeclaration-statement of the variables, you have to include the term "parameter" so that they, as parameters, can be modified.

Exercise 4-12:

Prefix Final: We have a type `Banana`. Imagine you want to make two instances of this banana, `lightBanana` and `swedishBanana`.

```
type Banana = Real(unit = "kg",final fixed = false);
```

Is this allowed? Why or why not?

```
class Bananas
  Banana lightBanana(unit = "hg");
  Banana swedishBanana(fixed = true);
end Bananas;
```

Tip: Attribute `fixed` is declared `final`.

Exercise 4-13:

Question: What is a generic parameterized class? Why is that good?

Chapter 5

Components, Connectors, and Connections

For a long time, software developers have looked with envy on hardware system builders, regarding the apparent ease with which reusable hardware *components* are used to construct complicated systems. With software, there seems too often to be a need or tendency to develop from scratch instead of reusing components. Early attempts at *software components* include procedure libraries, which unfortunately have too limited applicability and low flexibility. The advent of object-oriented programming has stimulated the development of software component *frameworks* such as CORBA, the Microsoft COM/DCOM component object model, and JavaBeans. These component models have considerable success in certain application areas, but there is still a long way to go to reach the level of reuse and component standardization found in the hardware industry.

5.1 Software Component Models

What have software component models to do with Modelica? In fact, as we already stated in Section 2.8, Modelica offers quite a powerful *software component model* that is on par with hardware component systems in flexibility and potential for *reuse*. The key to this increased flexibility is the fact that Modelica classes are based on equations. What is a software component model? It should include the following three items:

- Components.
- A connection mechanism.
- A component framework.

Components are connected via the *connection mechanism* realized by the Modelica system, which can be visualized in connection diagrams. The *component framework* realizes components and connections, and ensures that communication works over the connections. For systems composed of *acausal* components the direction of data flow, that is, the *causality*, is initially unspecified for connections between those components. Instead the causality is automatically deduced by the compiler when needed. Components have well-defined *interfaces* consisting of ports, also known as *connectors*, to the external world. These concepts are illustrated in Figure 5-1.

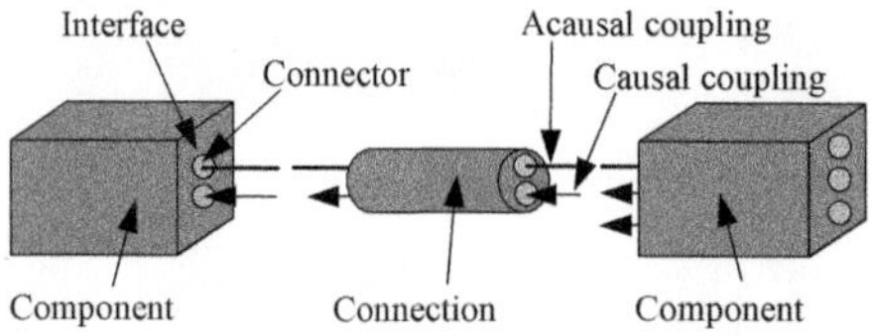

Figure 5-1. Connecting two components within a component framework.

Modelica uses a slightly different terminology compared to most literature on software component systems: *connector* and *connection*, rather than *port* and *connector* respectively in software component literature.

5.1.1 Components

In the context of Modelica *class libraries*, software components are Modelica classes. However, when building particular models, components are *instances* of those Modelica classes. Classes should have well-defined communication interfaces, sometimes called *ports*, in Modelica called *connectors*, for communication between a component and the outside world.

A component class should be defined *independently of the environment* where it is used, which is essential for its *reusability*. This means that in the definition of the component including its equations, only local variables and connector variables can be used. No means of communication between a component and the rest of the system, apart from going via a connector, is allowed. A component may internally consist of other connected components, that is, *hierarchical* modeling.

5.1.2 Connection Diagrams

Complex systems usually consist of large numbers of *connected* components, of which many components can be hierarchically decomposed into other components through several levels. To grasp this complexity, a pictorial representation of components and connections is quite important. Such graphic representation is available as *connection diagrams*, of which a schematic example is shown in Figure 5-2. We have already (e.g., on page 38 in Chapter 2) seen connection diagrams of simple electrical circuits and as well as a few models from other domains.

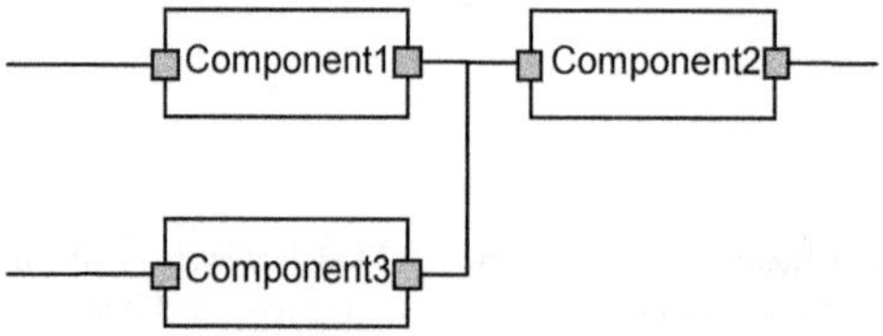

Figure 5-2. Schematic picture of a connection diagram for components.

5.2 Connectors and Connector Classes

Modelica *connectors* are instances of *connector classes*, that is, classes with the keyword `connector`. See Figure 5-3 to Figure 5-5. Such *connectors* declare variables that are part of the communication *interface* of a component defined by the connectors of that component. Thus, connectors specify the interface for interaction between a component and its surroundings. For example, the by now well-known class `Pin` is a connector class that can be used to specify the external interface for electrical components that have pins as interaction points:

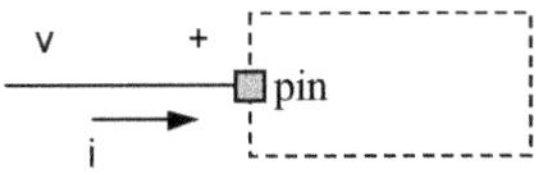

Figure 5-3. A component with an electrical pin connector.

```
connector Pin
  Voltage      v;
  flow Current i;
end Pin;    // From Modelica.Electrical.Analog.Interfaces
```

```
Pin pin;   // An instance pin of class Pin
```

Connector classes have certain restrictions (Section 3.8.4, page 88) compared to other classes. Only public variables and other public declaration elements may be declared within a connector class. No equations or algorithm sections are allowed within a connector class. The declarations in a connector class may not have the prefixes `inner` or `outer`.

Since Modelica is a multidomain language, connector classes can be formulated for a number of different application domains. The `Flange` connector class below, analogous to `Pin`, is used to describe interfaces for one-dimensional interaction in the mechanical domain by specifying the position `s` and force `f` at a point of interaction.

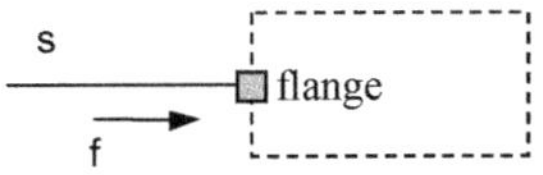

Figure 5-4. A component with a mechanical flange connector.

```
connector Flange
  Position   s;
  flow Force f;
end Flange; // From Modelica.Mechanical.Translational.Interfaces
```

```
Flange flange;    // An instance flange of class Flange
```

Most examples of connector classes previously presented in this book are aimed at *acausal* modeling. *Causal* connections usually arise when there is a *signal* flowing in a specified *direction*. For example, the connector class `RealInput` when instantiated as `u` is a signal `input` port that can be connected to receive signals.

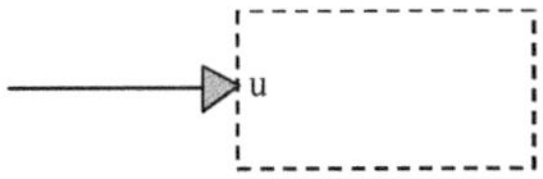

Figure 5-5. A component with an `u` input connector for signals.

```
connector RealInput = input Real; // RealInput is subtype of Real
// From Modelica.Blocks.Interfaces
```

```
RealInput u;  // An instance u with one signal
```

Connector classes often use special types for standard physical quantities represented by `Real` values, for example, `Voltage`, and so on, used above. The types `Voltage`, `Current`, `Position`, `Force` and `Distance` shown below and used in this chapter are just five of the classes available in the Modelica standard library Modelica.SIunits. This library contains more than four hundred predefined types comprising the complete set of ISO standard units.

```
type Voltage  = Real(final quantity="ElectricPotential", final unit="V");
type Current  = Real(final quantity="ElectricCurrent", final unit= "A");
type Position = Real(final quantity="Length", final unit="m");
type Force    = Real(final quantity="Force", final unit="N");
type Distance = Length(min=0);
```

5.3 Connections

There are two general kinds of connections that can be represented in Modelica:

- *Explicit connections* between pairs of connectors that are represented by lines in connection diagrams and connect-equations (see Section 5.3.2) in Modelica code.
- *Implicit connections* between a declared element in an object and corresponding elements in components of the object. This is useful in cases when too many explicit connections would be needed, for example, when modeling implicit interaction between bodies and a force field, or access of common shared object properties.

In the following sections, when we speak about connections we just refer to explicit connections, until Section 5.8, page 224, where implicit connections are introduced.

Explicit connections between components can be established only between *connectors* of *equivalent type* and *compatible causality*. Relying on our definition of Modelica type from Chapter 3, the typing constraints for allowing connections can be formulated approximately as follows:

- The *names* must be identical and corresponding *types* of declared *variable members* in the classes of the explicitly connected connectors *must* be equivalent, but the ordering between the member declarations in the connector classes need not be the same.

The typing constraints are actually slightly more *relaxed* than the above when connecting connectors containing arrays, but are *stricter* concerning array subscripts (Section 5.7.4, page 214).

There are also special restrictions (Section 5.7.3, page 211) regarding connections of causal connectors with input/output prefix (Section 5.3.5, page 193) and connections involving expandable connectors (Section 5.9, page 238) as well as stream connectors (Section 5.10, page 245).

It is important to note that explicit connections can be established only between connectors, that is, instances of connector classes. Instances of class or the specialized classes record, block, model, operator, operator record, operator function, function, and package are not allowed in explicit connections.

5.3.1 The flow Prefix and Kirchhoff's Current Law

As we have already noted in the above example, there are basically two kinds of variables in connectors:

- *Potential variables* representing some kind of "*potential*" or energy level, for example, voltage, pressure, or position.
- *Flow variables* prefixed by the keyword flow that represent some kind of flow, for example, electrical current, force, or fluid flow.

Two different types of *coupling* are established by *connections* depending on whether the variables in the connected connectors are potential variables (default) usually representing some kind of potential, or flow variables declared using the flow prefix:

- *Equality coupling*, for potential (also called effort) variables.

- *Sum-to-zero coupling*, for flow variables, according to Kirchhoff's current law in the electrical domain, i.e., conservation of charge makes the sum of all charge flows into a point be zero..

Analogous laws apply in other domains, for example, for hydraulic systems the sum of mass flows into a point is zero (conservation of mass), for mechanical systems Newton's third law (action and reaction).

In order to ensure that sum-to-zero coupling always works for flow variables we need a rule for consistent assignment of *flow direction* or *sign* to flow variables in a connector:

- The value of a flow variable is *positive* when the current or the flow is *into* the component to which the connector belongs.

One might question the exact meaning of the term "*flow into* a component" for flow variables. This is fairly obvious for charge, mass, or energy flow. However, what does "flow *into*" mean for forces and torques? In such cases the connector should contain variables that represent forces and torques *applied to* the component and not reaction forces and torques. This topic is discussed to some extent in Section 5.4.5, page 201.

5.3.2 Connect-Equations and General Restrictions

Connections between connectors are realized as *equations* in Modelica. These equations are specified by `connect`-equations, and are stated in an `equation` section of a class as for other kinds of equations. Note that connect-equations are regarded as equations despite the fact that the syntax is different from normal equations. The reason is that connect-equations are eventually expanded into normal equations. The general form of a connect-equation is as follows:

connect(*connector1*, *connector2*)

The two arguments *connector1* and *connector2* of the connect-equation must be references to *connectors*, and are restricted to one of the following two forms:

- Structured (nested) connector references $c_1.c_2.c_3. \ldots .c_n$, where c_1 is a connector of the class containing the connect-equation, n>=1 and c_{i+1} is a connector element of c_i for i=1:(n-1). For example, if `c1` contains the connector `c2` which contains the connector `c3`, we may use a connector reference such as `c1.c2.c3`. The simplest and most common case is when there is just a simple unstructured connector, for example, `connector1`, immediately within the class instance.

- Local element connectors, `m.d`, where `m` is a non-connector element instance within the class and `d` is a connector element of `m`. This means that it is not allowed to connect to a connector which belongs to an instance more than one level down in the hierarchy of non-connector instances, see Figure 5-6, where `m` is one level down.

There may optionally be array subscripts on any of the instances within the class instance; the array subscripts must be parameter expressions or the symbol colon ":". The arguments *connector1* and *connector2* can be arrays of connectors, see Section 5.7.5, page 214. There are additional restrictions and detailed semantics of connections, see Section 5.7, page 208.

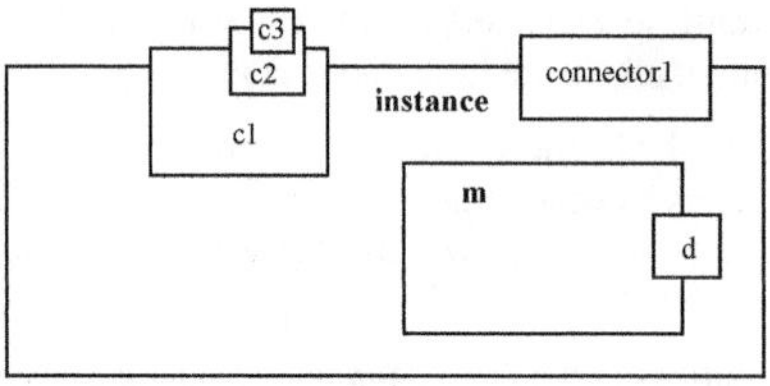

Figure 5-6. Different forms of allowed connectors of a class instance. A direct `connector1`, a local element `m` containing a connector `d1`, referred to as `m.d1`, and a connector `c3` within a connector `c2` within a connector `c1`, referred to as `c1.c2.c3`.

5.3.3 Electrical Connections

In Figure 5-7, there is an example of two connected electrical pins `pin1` and `pin2`. The connectors `pin1` and `pin2` are instances of the connector class `Pin`.

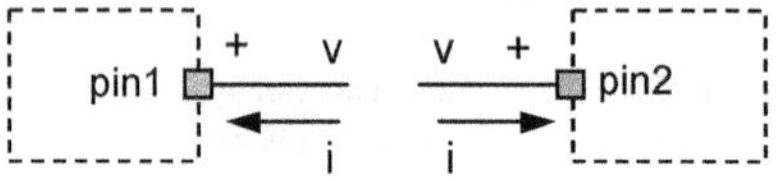

Figure 5-7. Connecting two electrical pins. The connected voltages are equal, and the sum of the currents is zero.

The connection equation:

```
connect(pin1,pin2)
```

connects the two pins so that they form one node. This produces two equations, namely:

```
pin1.v = pin2.v
pin1.i + pin2.i = 0
```

The first equation says that the voltages at the connected wire ends are the same, leading to *equality coupling*.

The second equation corresponds to Kirchhoff's current law saying that the currents *sum to zero* at a node (assuming positive value while flowing into the component), that is, *sum-to-zero coupling*, since the keyword `flow` is used for the variable `i` of type `Current` in the `Pin` connector class.

Since connectors are instances of connector classes they can be declared anywhere a declaration is allowed, for example, as above. However, connectors define the *interfaces* of components and are therefore usually declared inside those components. This has consequences for the naming of the connectors, but does not change anything else. Instead of `pin1` and `pin2` as above, we would, for example, have `E1.pin` and `E2.pin` as names for two connectors of type `Pin` in the electrical components `E1` and `E2`, when referring to those components from the outside.

5.3.4 Mechanical Connections

Connecting mechanical components, as in Figure 5-8 below, is somewhat different but still quite similar to the previous examples with electrical components. The *filled* and *nonfilled squares* on a mechanical component represent identical *mechanical flanges*.

The only difference is the sign of the flange variables in relation to the current coordinate system (see also Section 5.4.2 on page 196), analogous to positive and negative electrical pins for electrical components, but with the difference that in 1D translational mechanics there is also a global coordinate system in which displacements *s* and forces *f* are defined. Regarding why forces are flow quantities, flow of momentum in mechanical systems, see Section 5.4.5, page 201.

Drawing a line between such squares means that the corresponding flanges are *rigidly attached* to each other. The instances of classes in the Modelica *mechanical translational library* used here as examples (from `Modelica.Mechanical.Translational`) can usually be connected together in an arbitrary way.

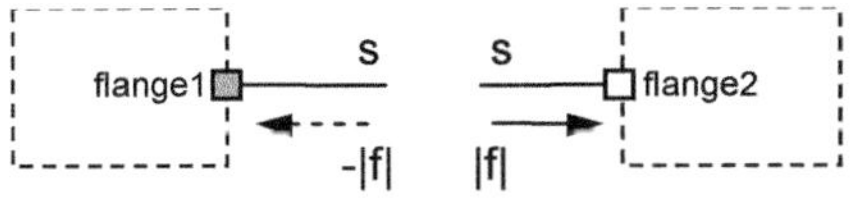

Figure 5-8. Connecting two mechanical flanges. The positions at the connection point are identical, and the sum of the forces is zero since the connection point has no mass. The displacement `s` is defined relative to the global 1D coordinate system. The force `f` is usually viewed as a vector quantity in that system, here positive in the direction into flange2. The two force values get opposite signs to make their sum equal zero.

Given instances `flange1` and `flange2` of the connector class `Flange`:

```
Flange flange1;
Flange flange2;
```

We connect these flanges using a connect-equation so that they form one node:

```
connect(flange1, flange2)
```

This produces two equations, namely:

```
flange1.s = flange2.s        // Identical positions
flange1.f + flange2.f = 0    // Sum of forces is zero
```

These equations are analogous to the corresponding equations for the electrical pins apart from the fact that they deal with positions (`s`) and forces (`f`).

5.3.5 Acausal, Causal, and Composite Connections

There are actually two *basic* and one *composite* kind of connection in Modelica:

- *Acausal connections*, for which the data flow in the connection is not explicitly specified.
- *Causal connections*, also called *signal* connections, where the *direction* of data flow is specified using the prefixes `input` or `output` in the declaration of at least one of the connectors in the connection.
- *Composite connections*, also called structured connections, composed of basic or composite connections.

Most examples of connections so far in this book have been acausal. Causal connections usually arise when there is a *signal* flowing in a specified *direction*. For example, the connector class `RealOutput` below when instantiated in a signal generator connected to an electrical circuit as in the `DCMotorCircuit` example in Section 5.6, page 207, creates a *causal connection* since the signal flows from the signal generator into the circuit.

```
connector RealOutput = output Real; // From Modelica.Blocks.Interfaces
```

The third kind of connection is the *composite connection*, where composite connectors, also called structured connectors, composed of several subconnectors, are connected. Such a structured connection can consist of several basic connections, both acausal and causal.

5.4 Connectors, Components, and Coordinate Systems

Many components have a kind of internal *coordinate system* to which the connectors of the components need to *relate*. This is very apparent for mechanical components, but is also present in components from other domains like the electrical domain.

The coordinate direction is by convention defined from "left" to "right" for simple two-connector components such as resistors and compressed springs as shown in Figure 5-9. A *positive flow*, for example, current `i` or force `|f|`, is propagated from left to right through the component. How can a force be a flow? For explanation see Section 5.4.5, page 201. The flow leaves the component from the right connector.

This is true for electrical components, because they cannot store net charge; even a capacitor has positive and negative charges on its two plates, that is, no storage of net charge. Thus `p.i + n.i = 0`, (Section 5.3.3, page 192). However, this is not true in general for mechanical components with mass since `flange_a.f+flange_b.f = m*der(v)`. In such as case the "flow of force" entering from the right is in general different from the "flow of force" going out from the other side, unless the component is at rest, or has no mass, like a spring.

The compressed massless spring (Figure 5-9) exerts a force with absolute value `|f|` from its right "driven" flange to some other component that is placed at its right side.

Note that the labels "left" and "right" are somewhat arbitrary. We could turn around the electrical component and it would still work the same and have the same current values. Regarding the mechanical component, the situation is slightly different. For 1D translational mechanical systems, all positions and forces are defined relative to a global 1D coordinate system. Thus, if we turn the spring around, the force `f`, which is a vector quantity in that system, would change sign. However, the rules with positive flow values for flows into a component still apply also for the mechanical system; therefore we use the absolute value `|f|` of the force vector `f` in Figure 5-9. The flange forces can be defifned as vectors in that global coordinate system.

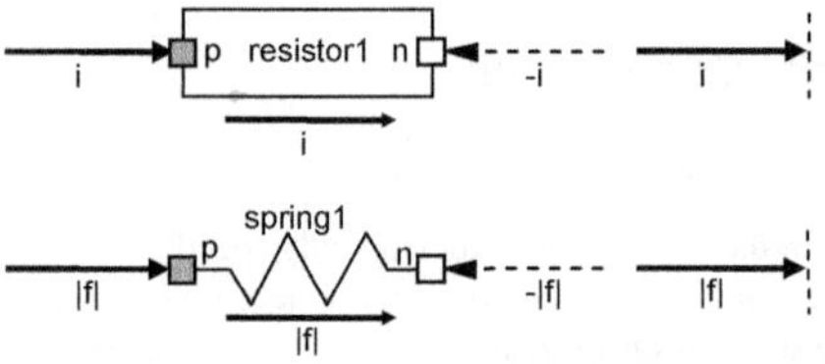

Figure 5-9. Positive values of current flow `i` and force flow `f` means propagation from left to right through the resistor and the compressed spring respectively. Solid arrows indicate the direction of actual flow transmitted through the component; dashed arrows positive flow direction into the component but opposite to the transmitted flow. 1D mechanical systems have a global reference coordinate system in which positions s and forces f are defined, with f as a vector quantity.

The *positive direction* of the *flow* variables directly belonging to the resistor and spring is indicated by the arrow from *left to right* under each component. Regarding connectors, we have earlier stated that positive flow direction of connectors is always *into* the component where they belong, which is indicated by the arrows into the connectors. Since positive flow direction for the right-hand side connectors is in the *opposite* direction, that is, from right to left, the values of the right-hand side connector flow variables are negative, for example, `-i` and `-|f|`. However, as we shall soon see, the conventions for flow direction of mechanical components are somewhat different from the electrical counterparts.

5.4.1 Coordinate Direction for Basic Electrical Components

In the electrical domain, several idealized electrical components extend the base class `TwoPin`, which has two connectors `p` and `n` for positive and negative pins respectively (Figure 5-10). The "coordinate system" or coordinate *direction* here is that the positive direction of current flow `i` for a component is defined to be from `p` to `n`, with `i=p.i`.

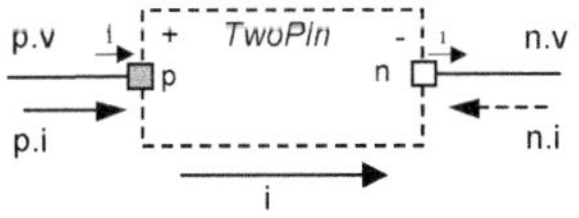

Figure 5-10. `TwoPin` base class for simple electrical components with two pins. Solid arrows indicate the direction of actual current flow; dashed arrows positive direction into the component but opposite to the flow through the component.

The connector classes `PositivePin` and `NegativePin` are identical to `Pin` apart from having different icons (see `Modelica.Electrical.Analog.Interfaces`) and can be used in electrical components to help distinguish positive and negative pins. Disregarding the icons they can be defined as follows:

```
connector PositivePin = Pin;  // Current p.i flowing into positive pin
connector NegativePin = Pin;  // Current n.i flowing into negative pin
```

The `partial` base class `TwoPin`, known from Chapter 2, is stated below in a form that uses the connector classes `PositivePin` and `NegativePin`:

```
partial model TwoPin
  "Component with two electrical pins p and n and current i from p to n"
  Voltage     v    "Voltage drop between the two pins (= p.v - n.v)";
  Current     i    "Current flowing from pin p to pin n";
  PositivePin p;
  NegativePin n;
equation
  v = p.v - n.v;
  0 = p.i + n.i;
  i = p.i;
end TwoPin;
// Same as OnePort in Modelica.Electrical.Analog.Interfaces
```

The familiar idealized resistor class is depicted in Figure 5-11. The "coordinate system", that is, the direction of current flow in the resistor, is from `p` to `n` as inherited from `TwoPin`. Four equations are present in the resistor model. The first three originate from the inherited `TwoPin` class, whereas the last is the constitutive equation for ideal resistors `v=R*i`, which is specific for the resistor class.

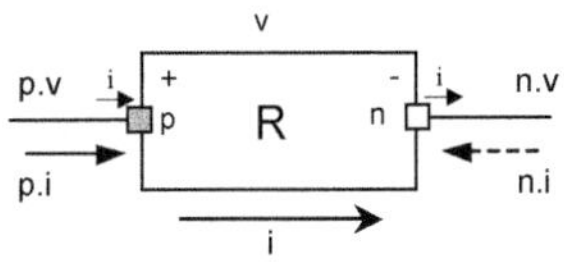

Figure 5-11. Resistor component including the resistor equation `v=R*i`.

```
model Resistor
  extends TwoPin;
  parameter Real R(unit="Ohm")  "Resistance";
equation
  v = R*i;      // Resistor equation
end Resistor;
```

5.4.2 Mechanical Translational Coordinate Systems and Components

Each mechanical component has an associated *coordinate system*, called *frame*. This is relevant especially for frames in 3D mechanical systems. Regarding the *flanges* in the 1D mechanical translational domain, this is possible, especially for the flange forces, but not very practical, for example, the position value would always be zero in that system.

For the simple 1D mechanical translational domain, there is always a global coordinate system in which positions `s` and forces `f` can be defined

The connector classes `Flange_a` and `Flange_b` used for flanges in the 1D translational mechanical domain are identical but have slightly different roles, somewhat analogous to the roles of `PositivePin` and `NegativePin` in the electrical domain.

A `flange_a` connector is used at the "left" side of a component represented by the *filled* square in Figure 5-12, whereas a `flange_b` connector is used at the "right" side of the component, represented by the *empty* square. Each flange could be interpreted as having an internal coordinate system characterized by the unit vector *n* from left to right, depicted by a small arrow above each flange in Figure 5-12. Internal vectors such as position and forces could be interpreted in the positive direction along the unit vector. However, a simpler approach is to regard the flange positions and forces as defined in the global 1D coordinate system, see also the discussion in Section 5.4.5, page 201.

```
// From Modelica.Mechanical.Translational.Interfaces

connector Flange_a = Flange;     // "left" flange class
connector Flange_b = Flange;     // "right" flange class
```

The `partial` base class `PartialCompliant` depicted below is extended by classes for compliant flexible mechanical components with two flanges, for example, springs and dampers. It can be regarded as a 1D mechanical analogue of the `TwoPin` base class from the electrical domain. However, `PartialCompliant` is not the only base class for two-flange components—there is also, for example, the `partial` class `Rigid` for rigid mechanical components. The coordinate system used in components instantiated from classes extended from `PartialCompliant` is characterized by the unit vector N from `flange_a` (the driving flange) to `flange_b` (the driven flange) shown in Figure 5-12 and Figure 5-14.

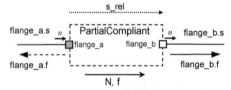

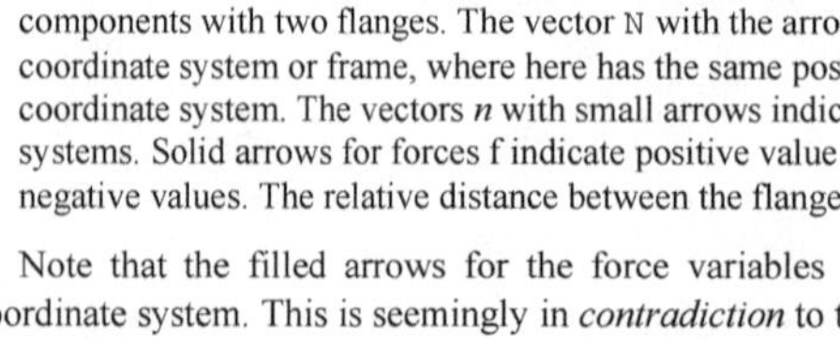

Figure 5-12. `PartialCompliant` is a base class for simple compliant (flexible) 1D mechanical components with two flanges. The vector `N` with the arrow indicates positive direction in the component coordinate system or frame, where here has the same positive direction unit vectors as the global 1D coordinate system. The vectors *n* with small arrows indicate positive direction in the flange coordinate systems. Solid arrows for forces f indicate positive value in the associated coordinate system; dashed arrow negative values. The relative distance between the flanges is represented by `s_rel`.

Note that the filled arrows for the force variables have positive direction according to the global coordinate system. This is seemingly in *contradiction* to the *rule* that positive flow direction is always into the component, see discussion in Section 5.4.5, page 201. However, the choice of flow variable is in some sense somewhat arbitrary. If we instead would choose –f as our force variable, the arrows would change direction and the rule of positive flow direction into the component would be satisfied.

The designers of the 1D mechanical translational library have defined the force variable `f` of models derived from `PartialCompliant` is equal to the force in the right flange, that is, `f=flange_b.f`. This is different from the design choice of the electric library, where the current `i` of the component is equal to the current into its left connector, that is, i=p.i. However, as long as this new design choice is used consistently for mechanical components it works fine since the original rule for connectors can always be fulfilled by multiplying forces by −1 when forming the connection equations. The base class PartialCompliant for flexible 1D two-flange mechanical components is available below.

```
partial model PartialCompliant
  "Compliant connection of two translational 1D flanges"
  Flange_a flange_a "Left flange of compliant 1-dim. translation component"
  Flange_b flange_b "Right flange of compliant 1-dim. translation component"
  SI.Position s_rel(start=0) "Relative distance (= flange_b.s-flange_a.s)";
  SI.Force f "Force between flanges (positive direction of flange axis R)";
equation
  s_rel = flange_b.s - flange_a.s;
  flange_b.f = f;
  flange_a.f = -f;
end PartialCompliant;   // from Modelica.Mechanics.Translational.Interfaces
```

Springs are one kind of compliant component with two flanges. Figure 5-13 shows a spring in three different configurations: compressed (a), neutral (b), and stretched (c). In the compressed configuration a force f applied at the left "driving" flange called flange_a in Figure 5-14 propagates through the spring, and leaves the spring at the right "driven" flange, called flange_b.

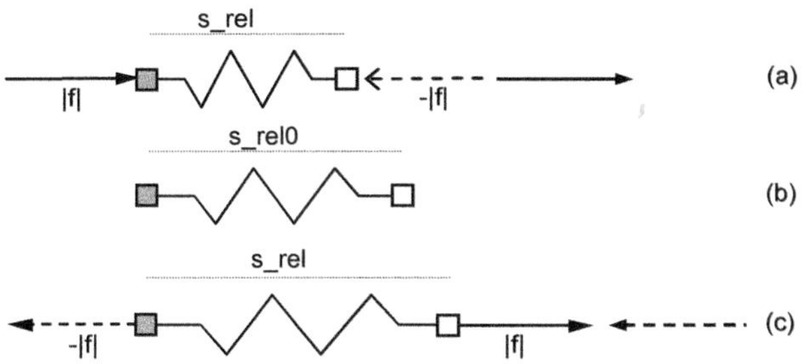

Figure 5-13. Compressed (a), neutral (b), and stretched (c) spring. The flange arrows indicate the actual direction of forces applied to flanges. Solid arrows represent positive values in the global and component coordinate systems; dashed arrows negative values.

For the *compressed* spring the external *force applied at the left flange*, flange_a.f = |f|, has positive sign since it is directed from left to right in the same direction as the normal vector of the global coordinate system, whereas the force exerted on the *right* flange, flange_b.f = -|f|, has negative sign since it points in the opposite direction, as indicated by the dashed arrow.

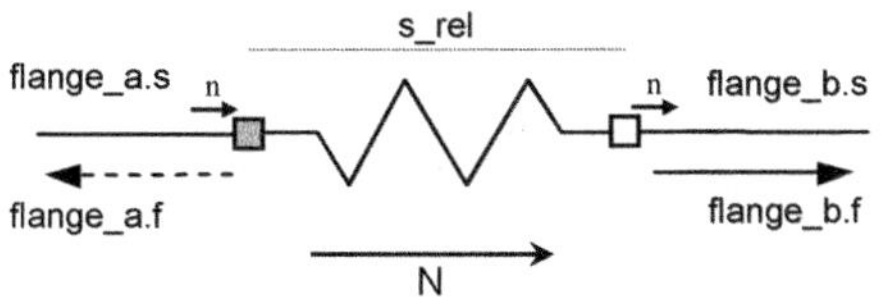

Figure 5-14. Linear 1D translational spring.

When the spring is stretched its actual length, s_rel becomes greater than s_rel0, which is its length in the neutral state when the applied forces are zero. In the stretched state, the force direction is reversed compared to the compressed state. The force variable f = c*(s_rel-s_rel0) is positive, and since flange_b.f = f, the right flange is dragged by the component attached at the right side in the positive coordinate direction to the right. The external force applied at the left flange, flange_a.f = -f, is negative since it drags the left flange in the opposite compared to the normal vector *n*. The `Spring` class below inherits all equations apart from the constitutive spring equation from its base class `PartialCompliant`.

```
model Spring    "Linear 1D translational spring"
  extends Translational.Interfaces.PartialCompliant;
  parameter SI.TranslationalSpringConstant c(final min=0, start = 1)
                                             "Spring constant";
  parameter SI.Distance s_rel0=0 "Unstretched spring length";
equation
  f = c*(s_rel - s_rel0);  // spring equation
end Spring;
```

5.4.3 Multiple Connections to a Single Connector

In almost all previous examples, we connected only two connectors. In fact, there is in general no limitation to the number of connections that can be made to a single connector. Two examples of multiple connections to the same node are shown below, where three components are being connected. The first example is a resistor circuit, and the second consists of three mechanical springs connected together.

5.4.3.1 ResistorCircuit

The class `ResistorCircuit` connects three resistors at one node using two connect-equations (Figure 5-15).

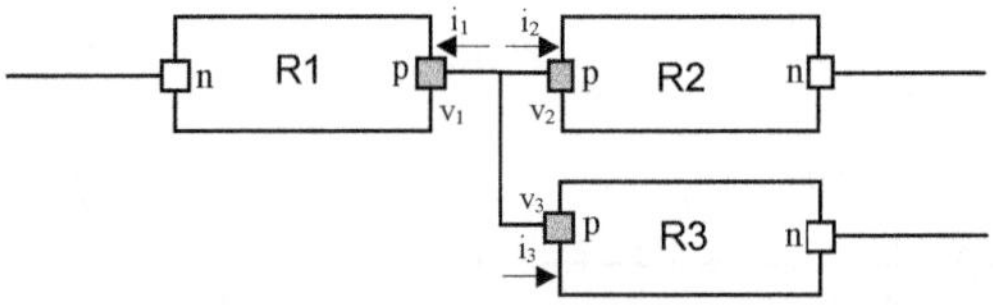

Figure 5-15. Schematic picture of the `ResistorCircuit` containing three resistors connected at one node. The connection laws on voltages `v` and currents `i` at that node give `v1=v2=v3` and `i1+i2+i3=0`.

```
model ResistorCircuit   "Three connected resistors"
  Resistor R1(R=100);
  Resistor R2(R=200);
  Resistor R3(R=300);
equation
  connect(R1.p, R2.p);
  connect(R1.p, R3.p);
end ResistorCircuit;
```

As usual, the special operator *connect* produces equations by taking into account what kind of variables, `flow` or potential, are involved. The generated equations, based on equal potentials at a connection point and Kirchhoff's current law, are as follows for this particular example:

```
R1.p.v = R2.p.v;
R1.p.v = R3.p.v;
R1.p.i + R2.p.i + R3.p.i = 0;
```

Moreover, equations are automatically generated for unconnected flow variables which always have zero flow:

```
R1.n.i = 0;
R2.n.i = 0;
R3.n.i = 0;
```

5.4.3.2 TripleSprings

The `TripleSprings` model connects three springs at one node using two connect-equations (Figure 5-16). This model is quite similar in structure to the `ResistorCircuit` model presented in the previous section.

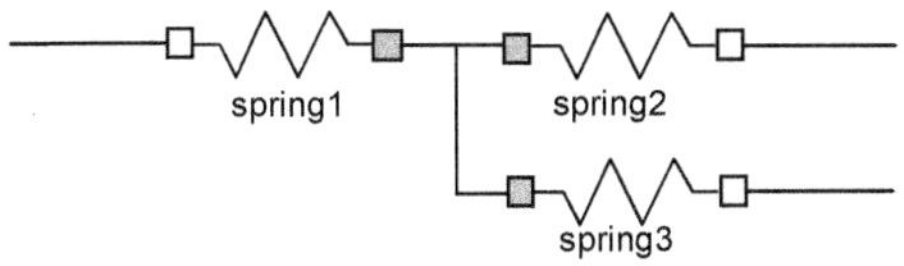

Figure 5-16. Schematic picture of the mechanical connection of three springs.

```
model TripleSprings  "Three connected springs"
  Spring  spring1(c=1, s_rel0=0.1);
  Spring  spring2(c=1, s_rel0=0.1);
  Spring  spring3(c=1, s_rel0=0.1);
equation
  connect(spring1.flange_a, spring2.flange_a);
  connect(spring1.flange_a, spring3.flange_a);
end TripleSprings;
```

Also the equations generated from the two connect-equations in the `TripleSprings` model are analogous to the corresponding equations from the `ResistorCircuit` model. We have the connector `flange_a` instead of the connector `p`, position `s` instead of voltage `v`, and force `f` instead of current `i`.

Identical positions of the connected flanges of the three springs give the first two equations. The last equation is force equilibrium where the sum all forces applied at the connection node is zero.

```
spring1.flange_a.s = spring2.flange_a.s;
spring1.flange_a.s = spring3.flange_a.s;
spring1.flange_a.f + spring2.flange_a.f + spring3.flange_a.f = 0;
```

Moreover, equations are automatically generated for unconnected flow variables which always have zero flow:

```
spring1.flange_b.f = 0;
spring2.flange_b.f = 0;
spring3.flange_b.f = 0;
```

5.4.4 An Oscillating Mass Connected to a Spring

The following model is a somewhat more interesting example from the 1D mechanical domain since it gives rise to some dynamic movement when simulated. A *mass* is hanging in a *spring*, which is connected to a *fixed* housing. Those objects are instances of the classes `Mass`, `Spring`, and `Fixed`, respectively, which are declared farther down. The mass `mass1` is subject to the gravitational force `-mg` and the force from the spring. It is given an initial position `s=-0.5`, which is offset from the equilibrium position and therefore starts an oscillating movement up and down.

```
model Oscillator
  Mass    mass1(L = 1, s(start = -0.5));
  Spring  spring1(s_rel0 = 2, c = 10000);
  Fixed   fixed1(s0 = 1.0);
equation
  connect(spring1.flange_b, fixed1.flange_b);
  connect(mass1.flange_b, spring1.flange_a);
end Oscillator;
```

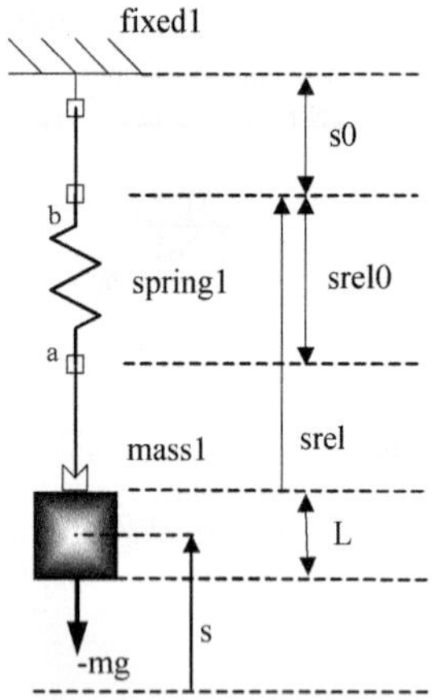

Figure 5-17. The oscillator model contains a mass hanging in an ideal spring which is fixed at a housing. The mass which is subject to the gravitational force -mg performs an oscillating movement up and down. Positive coordinate direction is upward.

The model with its three components `mass1`, `spring1`, and `fixed1` is depicted in Figure 5-17, including certain absolute and relative positions and the gravitational force `-mg`. The positive coordinate direction is upward in the figure, which applies to both positions and forces.

The absolute position of the center of mass for the `mass1` component is represented by the variable `mass1.s`, which is plotted in Figure 5-18. The model is idealized since there is no damping, causing the amplitude of the oscillations to remain the same instead of the gradual decrease that would occur in a more realistic model.

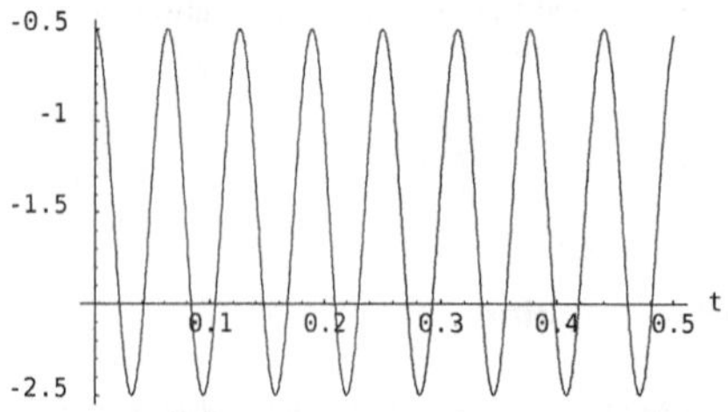

Figure 5-18. Plot of the absolute position `mass1.s(t)` of the center of the hanging mass.

The velocity `mass1.v` of the hanging mass is plotted in Figure 5-19. It is the same as the derivative of `s`. Both `s` and `v` are declared in the class `Mass` below.

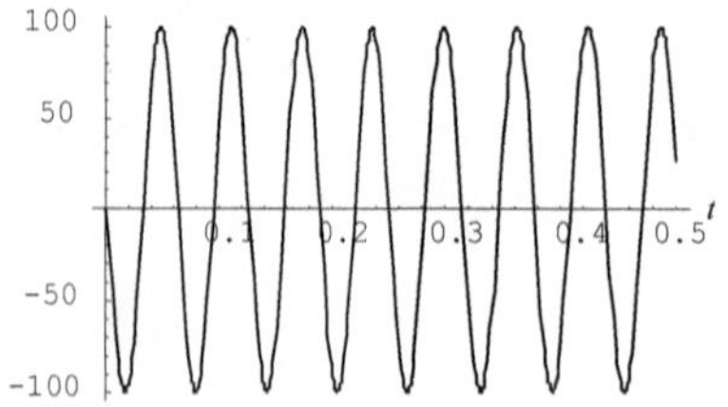

Figure 5-19. Plot of the absolute velocity `mass1.v(t)` of the hanging mass.

In addition to the previous declarations of `Spring`, `Oscillator`, and so on, the following three classes are needed to simulate the `Oscillator` model. The class `Mass` is a specialization of the class `Rigid`, which is a base class for rigid objects of fixed length `L`. The class `Fixed` represents a housing with a fixed position and a flange where other objects can be attached.

```
model Mass    "Hanging mass object"
  extends PartialRigid;
  parameter Real  m = 1    "mass of the hanging mass";
  constant  Real  g = 9.81 "gravitational acceleration";
  Real            v        "absolute velocity of component";
  Real            a        "absolute acceleration of component";
equation
  v = der(s);
  a = der(v);
  flange_b.f - m*g = m*a;
end Mass;

partial model PartialRigid "Rigid connection of two translational 1D
                             flanges"
  Real            s     "absolute position s of center of component
                         (s = flange_a.s + L/2 = flange_b.s - L/2)";
  parameter Real L = 0 "length  L of component from left to right flange
                         (L = flange_b.s - flange_a.s)";
  Flange_a  flange_a;
  Flange_b  flange_b;
equation
  flange_a.s = s - L/2;
  flange_b.s = s + L/2;
end PartialRigid; // From Modelica.Mechanics.Translational.Interfaces

model Fixed  "Fixed flange at a housing"
  parameter Real s0 = 0  "fixed offset position of housing";
  Flange          flange_b;
equation
  flange_b.s = s0;
end Fixed;  // From Modelica.Mechanics.Translational
```

5.4.5 Coordinate Systems and Forces with Spring-Damper Example

In the previous discussion, the reader might have been slightly confused by the two rules or abstractions:

- The rule that there is a positive flow direction into a connector.
- The rule for 1D mechanical systems that the forces (i.e., flows) are defined in a global 1D coordinate system, where the positive direction is defined by that coordinate system.

The problem is simply that levels of abstraction might interfere with each other (in the reader's head). In Modelica, *flows* in mechanical systems (here forces) from different directions in a model diagram *do not mean* forces acting in different directions in the geometry of the resulting system. This is what is creating the potential misunderstanding.

In this section, we try to eliminate such possible confusion, and also explain why forces are flow quantities.

In an electrical system the flow variable is the current which describes a flow of charge. What is then *flow* in a mechanical system?

The flow in mechanical systems is represented by a flow of momentum $p(t) = m \cdot v(t)$:

$$\frac{d}{dt}p(t) = \frac{d}{dt}(m \cdot v(t)) = \frac{dm}{dt} \cdot v(t) + m \cdot \frac{d}{dt}v(t) \qquad (5\text{-}1)$$

As can be seen by this equation, the flow of momentum has two parts. In fluid systems, where the mass contents of a component can change, both parts can be relevant. In a rigid body system, the mass of a component is constant and only the second part remains. This is equal to the force *f(t)* according to Newton's law:

$$m \cdot \frac{d}{dt} v(t) = f(t) \tag{5-2}$$

In 1D translational mechanics the flow is also pointing into the component. A positive flow of momentum (a positive force) means an increase in velocity. It does not matter if there flow is coming by a "left" or a "right" connector. A positive sum of flows (sum of forces) leads to a positive acceleration of mass.

Consider the following system: a body hanging on a spring damper. The following diagram depicts the geometry of the system for two possible states. The first state (a) represents the initial point at time=0 when the body is released at the resting length of the spring. The second state (b) represents the final state. Here the body is at rest again and the spring forces are in equilibrium with the gravity force of –10N.

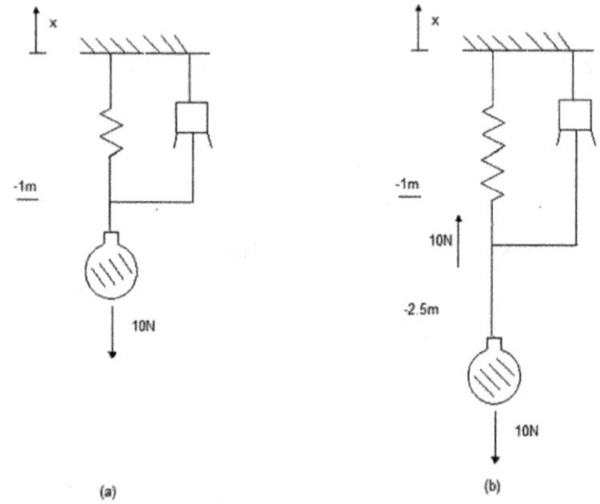

Figure 5-20. A body hanging on a spring damper. The first state (a) represents the initial point at time=0 just when the body is released. The second state (b) represents the final state when the body is at rest and the spring forces are in equilibrium with the gravity force of –10N.

The plot below (Figure 5-21) depicts the trajectory of the body leading from state (a) to state (b). The body performs a damped oscillation until it comes to a final resting state.

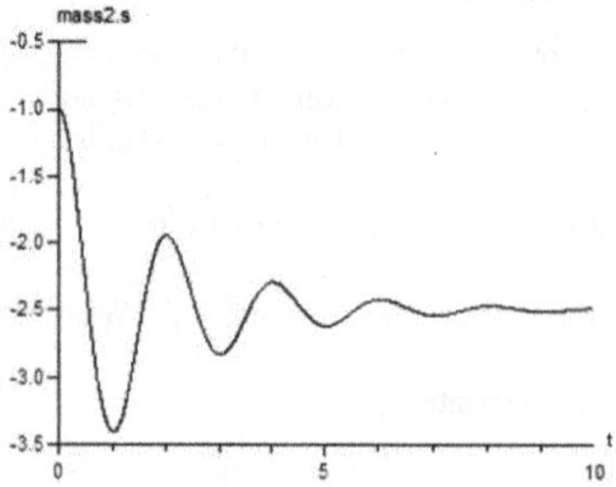

Figure 5-21. Plot of body hanging on a spring-damper, performing damped oscillations.

To model this system behavior we create model diagram of Figure 5-22 in Modelica. As shown before, the *potential* variable of the connector is *position* and the *force* represents a *flow of momentum*. The flow of momentum is therefore always defined to *flow into* the component.

This means that the forces in the positive x direction acting on a component remain with a positive sign whereas the corresponding reaction forces get a negative sign.

This is sometimes confusing but best explained by means of an example. The two diagrams in Figure 5-23 include the values of all force variables in the connectors for state (a) and (b). The forces values are always defined in the positive x-coordinate direction acting on the component. Thus, the connector of the force that is pulling with 10N in the negative x direction contains a positive force value. This is strange in the first place but absolutely in accordance with the rule.

The force that is acting on the body is found at the bodies connector and is correctly –10N. The connector of the force model component must thus represent the reactive part and this is +10N. In this way, the balance of flows is maintained.

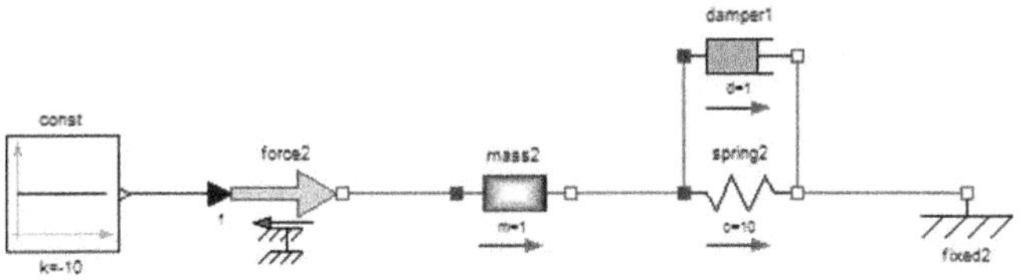

Figure 5-22. Connection diagram of the spring-damper system.

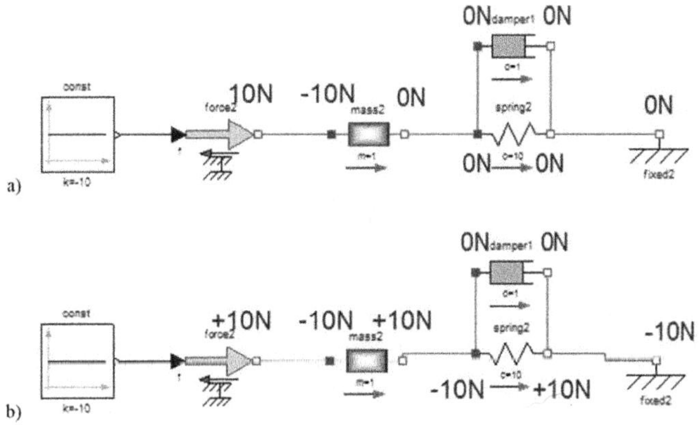

Figure 5-23. Force values at the connectors in state (a) just before the spring is released, and in the final state (b) when damped oscillations have stopped and the gravity force and the spring force are in equilibrium.

5.5 Design Guidelines for Connector Classes

So far, the above-mentioned connector classes have always consisted of a *pair* of one *potential* variable and one *flow* variable, apart from the `RealOutput` class briefly mentioned in the context of causal connections. One might ask whether this is a coincidence or a general pattern for connector class design.

We shall soon see that this is no coincidence; but on the other hand there exist many connector classes that do not follow this pattern for various reasons.

More important is to identify the basic *requirements* behind the design of *component interfaces*, that is, connector classes which influence their structure. These requirements can be briefly stated as follows:

1. It should be *easy* and *natural* to connect components provided this is possible for the corresponding physical components.
2. Component interfaces should facilitate *reuse* of existing model components in class libraries.

Fulfilling these requires careful design of connector classes. The number of connector classes should be kept small in order to avoid unnecessary mismatches between connectors due to different names and types of variables in the connectors.

Experience shows that it is surprisingly difficult to design connector classes that satisfy these requirements. There is a tendency for extraneous details that are created during software (model) development for various computational needs to creep into the interfaces, thereby making them harder to use and preventing component reuse. Therefore one should keep the connector classes as simple as possible, and try to avoid introducing variables that are not really necessary.

A good rule of thumb when designing connector classes for models of physical components is to identify the characteristics of (acausal) interaction in the physical real world between these components. The interaction characteristics should be simplified and abstracted to an appropriate level and reflected in the design of the connector classes. For nonphysical components, for example, signal blocks and software components in general, one has to work hard on finding the appropriate level of abstraction in the interfaces and trying these in practice for feedback on ease of use and reusability. The Modelica standard library contains a large number of well-designed connector classes which can serve as inspiration when designing new interfaces.

There are basically three different kinds of connector classes, reflecting three design situations:

1. Often, but not always, if there is some kind of interaction between two *physical* components involving *energy flow*, a combination of potential and flow variables in the appropriate domain should be used for the connector class. In some cases other combinations may be more natural, e.g., the choice of temperature and heat flow in the `Modelica.Thermal.HeatTransfer` library.
2. If information or *signals* are exchanged between components of clearly defined causality, `input/output` signal variables should be used in the connector class.
3. For complex interactions between components, involving several interactions of type (1) and (2) above, a hierarchically structured *composite connector* class is designed that includes one or more connectors of the appropriate type (1), (2), or (3).

When all the connectors of a component have been designed according to the three principles above, the formulation of the rest of the component class follows partly from the constraints implied by these connectors. However, these guidelines should not be followed blindly. There are several examples of domains with special conditions that deviate slightly from the above rules. In the next three sections we will discuss the basic design situations for connector classes in more detail.

5.5.1 Physical Connector Classes

The first design situation with interaction between physical components usually based on some kind of generalized *energy flow* leads to the following generic structure of a connector class:

```
connector <class name>      "Physical connector class"
  Real        <e>    "potential variable";
  flow Real   <f>    "flow variable";
end <class name>;
```

This structure corresponds to the physical connectors presented so far, for example, the `Pin` connector class for the electrical domain from the library `Modelica.Electrical.Analog.Interfaces` with the voltage variable `v` as the potential variable and the current `i` as the flow variable, or the `Flange_a` connector class from the library `Modelica.Mechanics.Translational.Interfaces` for the translational mechanical domain with the position `s` as the potential variable, and the force `f` as the flow variable.

We talk about this design method being based on energy or energy flow. Energy flow is the change of energy per time unit, i.e., power $p=e*f$, the product of the potential or effort variable e and the flow variable f. In electrical systems the power $p=v*i$. In translational mechanical systems the energy $E=s*f$. These correspond to our choices of variables in the previously presented connector classes. Another choice of potential variable in translational mechanical systems is the velocity v, which, however, can be easily obtained by differentiating s. The *kind* of potential variable *must* always be chosen in such a way that at energy flow *connection points* all potential variables of connected components are equal.

Energy is always transported using some carrier, which in the case of electrical current is charged particles, and in the case of translational or rotational mechanical systems is linear or angular momentum respectively.

When energy flows together at a certain point, without storing energy at that point, the sum of all energy *flows* into that point is zero. This is the explanation for the *sum-to-zero rule* for flow variables at connection points, which thus is based on the principle of *conservation of energy*. In the electrical domain this corresponds to Kirchhoff's current law, and in the mechanical domain Newton's law that the sum of all forces acting at a specific point is zero.

Table 5-1 describes possible choices for potential, flow, and energy carrier for some common physical domains, as well as the names of certain corresponding Modelica libraries, which should be prefixed by the name Modelica. Connectors for these domains are available in the `Interfaces` part of the corresponding Modelica library. There are also libraries for additional domains, e.g., the MBS (multibody systems) library described in Section 15.10, page 877, for mechanical bodies in three dimensions.

Table 5-1. Common physical domains with appropriate connector quantities. (See also Table 14-1)

Domain Type	**Potential**	**Flow**	**Carrier**	**Modelica Library**
Electrical	Voltage	Current	Charge	Electrical
Translational	Position	Force	Linear momentum	Mechanical.Translational
Rotational	Angle	Torque	Angular momentum	Mechanical.Rotational
Magnetic	Magnetic potential	Magnetic flux rate	Magnetic flux	Magnetic.Fluxtubes
Hydraulic, thermo-hydraulic	Pressure	Volume flow rate	Volume	OpenHydraulics, Fluid
Heat	Temperature	Heat flow rate	Heat	Thermal
Chemical	Chemical potential	Particle flow rate	Particles	

Regarding the mechanical rotational domain it should be mentioned that in addition to the previously presented translational `Flange_a` there is also a rotational `Flange_a` connector class, shown renamed below, from the library called `Modelica.Mechanics.Rotational.Interfaces` for one-dimensional rotational mechanical systems (drive trains). This class has the rotation angle `phi` as a potential variable and the torque `tau` as a flow variable. To avoid confusion with the translational `Flange_a` connector class we have renamed it `RotFlange_a` in this text.

```
connector RotFlange_a    "1D rotational flange"
  Angle         phi     "Absolute rotation angle";
  flow Torque   tau     "Cut torque in the flange";
end rotFlange_a;

type Angle  = Real(final quantity="Angle", final unit="rad",
                   displayUnit="deg");
type Torque = Real(final quantity="Torque", final unit="N.m");
```

Returning to the question posed at the beginning of this section—whether all physical connector classes consist of the same number of *acausal* potential and flow variables—the answer is *yes*, in Modelica 3.0 and later versions all connector classes must be balanced (Section 5.7.7, page 217).

However, the following three situations make it necessary to have different numbers of potential and flow variables. In order to fulfill the balancing restrictions for the acausal connector variables some of them can be made causal by attaching an `input` or `output` prefix.

- The *same* energy *carrier* for several associated domains. For example, the energy flow of a one-dimensional compressible fluid, $P = dE/dt = m'(h + 0.5*v^2)$, where m' is the mass flow being the same energy carrier, h the enthalpy, and v the fluid velocity. Here m' is the flow variable. In this case stream connectors (Section 5.10, page 245) is the best choice with h being a stream variable, i.e., a domain property carried with the flow. There are also older connector variants with causal `input/output` prefixes, for exmaple, in the ThermoPower library (Section 5.10.3.2, page 249).
- Singularities of *variable sets*, e.g., rotation matrices. For example, the orientation of a 3D mechanical connector can be described by a 3×3 rotation matrix, which causes singularities at certain orientations based on transformations using three separate rotations. This problem can be solved, for example, by introducing 4×4 transformation matrices through Euler parameters or Quaternions (see Section 14.8), but this adds at least one extra potential variable in the connector class.
- Singularities caused by *connections*, for example, in so-called higher index systems (see Chapter 18). In some cases the connection of components leads to higher index systems that cannot be transformed to solvable (state space) form using only algebraic transformations. For example, in 3D mechanical systems almost all connections lead to higher index systems. The solution is to differentiate the equations, causing differentiated variables to be added as extra variables. Sometimes it is practical to store some of these extra variables in the connectors, thereby increasing the number of potential variables. Examples of such connector classes, for example, the illegal one presented below, can be found in the old Modelica MBS library.

The connector class `Frame_illegal` below renamed from `Frame_b` in an old simpler version (`ModelicaAdditions` from MSL 2.2) of the Modelica multibody systems (MBS) library without overdetermined connectors is an example of a connector class of the kind that contains extra potential variables to get around problems caused by connections that cause higher index systems. Several extra potential variables, e.g., velocity and acceleration, are derivatives of the basic potential variables. There are six potential variables, `r0`, `S`, `v`, `w`, `a`, and `z`, whereas there are only two flow variables, `f` and `t`.

```
connector Frame_illegal    "Frame b of a 3D mechanical element, old version"
  import Modelica.SIunits;
  output SIunits.Position r0[3]    "Frame origin in inertial system";
  Real                    S[3,3]   "Transformation matrix";
  SIunits.Velocity        v[3]     "Absolute velocity of frame origin";
  SIunits.AngularVelocity w[3]     "Absolute angular velocity of frame a";
  SIunits.Acceleration   a[3]      "Absolute acceleration of frame origin";
  SIunits.AngularAcceleration z[3] "Absolute angular acceleration";
  flow SIunits.Force      f[3];
  flow SIunits.Torque     t[3];
end Frame_illegal;  // From ModelicaAdditions.MultiBody.Interfaces
```

However, the `Frame_Illegal` connector is *illegal* since the number of flow and potential variables do not match. The solution is to create two connector classes, where two 3-vectors (e.g., `a` and `z`) are acausal `Real[3]` vectors and the other variables are matching pairs of `input` and `output`. See Section 5.7.7, page 217 for a solution with balanced connector classes.

5.5.2 Signal-based Connector Classes

Signal-based connector classes are very simple. All that is needed is a vector of input signals or output signals. Most application models where signal connectors are needed can be satisfied with the connector classes `RealInput` and `RealOutput` below, both from the library `Modelica.Blocks.Interfaces`.

```
connector RealInput  = input Real;
connector RealOutput = output Real;
```

The `RealInput` and `RealOutput` connector classes can be specialized to different numbers of signals when instantiated, as in the class `MISO` below. This is a `partial` block that captures the generic features of multiple-input-single-output continuous control blocks (Figure 5-24).

The definition of this block reflects the fact that any connection with a set of only inside connectors can contain exactly one output and zero or more inputs (Section 5.7.3.1, page 213).

Figure 5-24. A `MISO` block with an input signal type `RealInput` and an output signal `RealOutput`.

```
partial block MISO
  "Multiple Input Single Output continuous control block"
  parameter Integer  nin=1    "Number of inputs";
  input   RealInput  u[nin]   "Connector of Real input signals";
  output  RealOutput y        "Connector of Real output signal";
end MISO;   // From Modelica.Blocks.Interfaces
```

Signal connector types for other basic types are available in `Modelica.Blocks.Interfaces`:

```
connector BooleanInput   = input  Boolean;
connector BooleanOutput  = output Boolean;
connector IntegerInput   = input  Integer;
connector IntegerOutput  = output Integer;
```

5.5.3 Composite Connector Classes

A *composite connector* class is an aggregation of one or more connectors, not just variables as in simple connectors. Such connector classes can represent more complex interactions by combinations of a number of simple connectors. Here it is especially important to choose an appropriate level of abstraction.

For example, consider the interface between the mechanical body of an aircraft and the aircraft engine. This might be represented as a composite connector class containing a connector for the rigid coupling between the aircraft body and the engine, a hydraulic connector for the fuel flow between the aircraft tank and the engine, and a signal connector for controlling the engine from the cockpit.

5.6 Connecting Components from Multiple Domains

So far most of the presented models have been of the single domain type being constructed of components from a single application domain. However, one of the main advantages with Modelica is the ease of constructing multidomain models simply by connecting components from different domains. A DC (direct current) motor as depicted in Figure 5-25 is one of the simplest examples illustrating this capability.

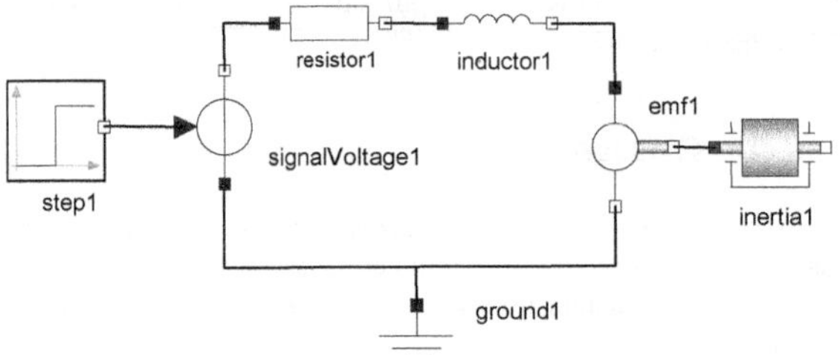

Figure 5-25. A multidomain `DCMotorCircuit` model with mechanical, electrical, and signal block components.

This particular model contains components from the three domains discussed previously in this chapter: mechanical components such as `inertia1`, the electrical components `resistor1`, `inductor1`, `signalVoltage1`, and `ground1`, as well as pure signal components such as `step1`. The `DCMotorCircuit` model together with several of the needed Modelica classes is presented in detail in Chapter 15, page 793, together with a simulation of the model.

5.7 Detailed Connection Semantics

At the beginning of this chapter we introduced the concepts of *connector class*, *connector*, and *connection*, primarily by means of examples from the electrical and mechanical domains. The general form and restrictions on connections, i.e., connect-equations, were given in Section 5.3.2, page 191. However, some details regarding the meaning of connections, generation of connection equations, and certain special situations have not yet been specified. The rest of this chapter fills this gap and gives a rather complete and somewhat more formal description of connection semantics.

5.7.1 Hierarchically Structured Components with Inside and Outside Connectors

Complex systems are naturally described as hierarchical structures of components which internally consist of components, and so on, often many levels deep. Components that have an internal structure of other components are called *structured components*. Those are natural for modeling large reusable components.

Let us return to the `DCMotorCircuit` example. We would like to create a structured library component class that captures most of the essentials of the DC motor circuit and allows us to connect different signal generators and different loads when instantiating a real DC motor. This library class is shown in Figure 5-26 and as the declaration of the class `DCMotorKernel`. It is of course incomplete and nonphysical since no real motor is without inertia.

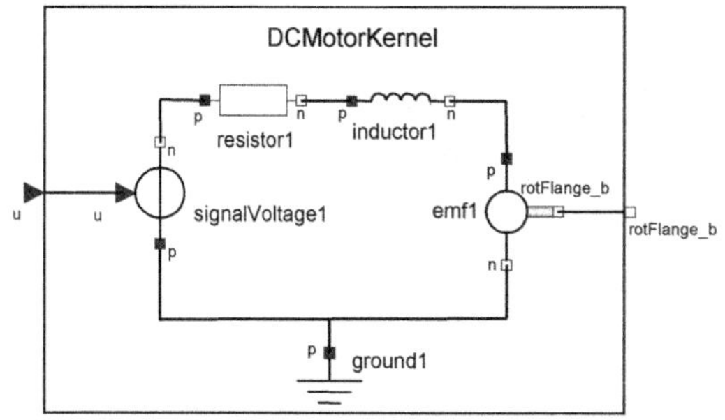

Figure 5-26. A DC motor kernel packaged as a structured component class with the outside connectors `u` and `rotFlange_b`. (Note that in the Modelica standard library the rotational flange class is called `Rotational.Flange_b` and the connector is named `flange_b`, which we here call `rotFlange_b` to avoid confusion with other kinds of flanges.)

```
model DCMotorKernel
  RealInput     u;              // Outside signal connector
  RotFlange_b   rotFlange_b;    // Outside rotational flange connector
  Inductor      inductor1;
  Resistor      resistor1;
  Ground        ground1;
  EMF           emf1;
  SignalVoltage signalVoltage1;
equation
  connect(u,              signalVoltage1.voltage);
  connect(signalVoltage1.n, resistor1.p);
  connect(resistor1.n,      inductor1.p);
  connect(signalVoltage1.p, ground1.p);
  connect(ground1.p,        emf1.n);
  connect(inductor1.n,      emf1.p);
  connect(emf1.rotFlange_b, rotFlange_b);
end DCMotorKernel;
```

The class `DCMotorKernel` has the internal components `inductor1`, `resistor1`, `ground1`, `emf1`, and `signalVoltage1`. Connectors belonging to the internal components or any non-connector top-level component are called *inside* connectors, whereas connectors that constitute the external interface of a structured component class are called *outside* connectors.

- An *outside connector* is a connector that is part of the *external interface* of a structured class instance.

  Note that all connectors declared at the hierarchical level *directly within* that class instance are *outside connectors* with respect to that instance. Connectors directly within outside connectors are also outside connectors, recursively.

- An *inside connector* is a connector that does *not* belong to the external interface of a structured class instance.

  Connectors belonging to an *internal component* that is not connector of a structured component class instance are *inside*. Any connector that is hierarchically inside a class instance is an *inside connector* if it is not an outside connector.

The classification of connectors as *inside* or *outside* is done before mapping `outer` connectors to corresponding `inner` connectors, see Section 5.8.5, page 233, regarding `inner/outer`.

Regarding the class `DCMotorKernel`, its outside connectors are `u` and `rotFlange_b`, whereas its inside connectors are `signalVoltage1.voltage`, `emf1.rotFlange_b`, `signalVoltage1.n`, `resistor1.p`, `resistor1.n`, `inductor1.p`, etc.

Using this class it is trivial to construct a full DC motor circuit called `DCMotorCircuit2` as in Figure 5-27, for example, by connecting a step signal generator block `step1` and an inertia instance called `inertia1`.

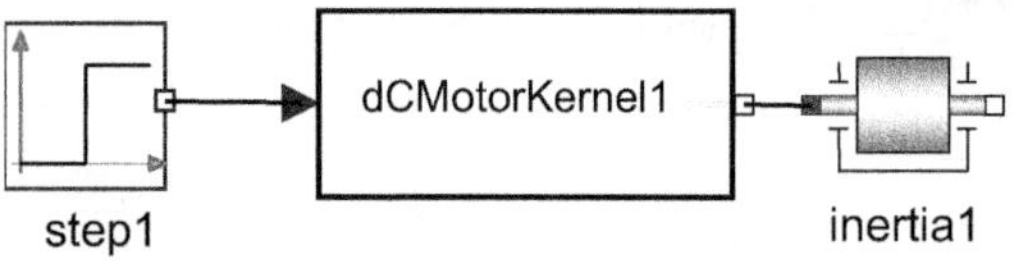

Figure 5-27. Connecting the structured component `dCMotorKernel1` to a signal generator called `step1` and an inertial load called `inertia1` to form the complete `DCMotorCircuit2` model.

```
model DCMotorCircuit2
  Step          step1;
  DCMotorKernel dCMotorKernel1;
  Inertia       inertia1;
equation
  connect(step1.y, dCMotorKernel1.u);
  connect(dCMotorKernel1.rotFlange_b, inertia1.rotFlange_a);
end DCMotorCircuit2;
```

5.7.2 Restrictions for Connect-Equations

Here we first give a short overview of the restrictions on where and how connect-equations can be used. More detailed explanations with examples are presented in subsequent sections.

The *connector references* in connect-equations can take two *syntactic forms*:

- The connect-equation construct only accepts the two forms of connector references, structured and local connector references, as previously described in Section 5.3.2, page 191.

There is a general restriction on *compatible types* of connected connectors:

- In a connect-equation the two connectors must have the same named instance elements with the same dimensions; recursively down to the instances of primitive type. The primitive elements with the same name are matched and belong to the same connection set.
- In a connect-equation the corresponding primitive elements of the two connectors must have the *same* basic built-in types (Section 5.3.2, page 191), flow-variables may only connect to other flow-variables, and causal variables (`input`/`output`) only to other causal variables (`input`/`output`).

Moreover, there are restrictions regarding the *use* of connect-equations in *if-equations* and *when-equations*:

- Connect-equations *cannot* be used inside if-equations with Boolean conditions that do not have parameter or constant variability, or in when-equations. The same restrictions apply for overconstrained equation operators (Section 8.5.3, page 379)

The reason for this restriction is that connect-equations have to be expanded during the process of generating connection equations (Section 5.7.8, page 219), which takes place at compile time. It is fine to for example have connect-equations inside for-equations since they always have parameter expressions for their array range expression and are expanded into normal equations at compile time.

The following restriction *forbids* the connection of `outer` elements:

- A connect-equation may not (*directly* or *indirectly*) connect two connectors of `outer` elements.

The meaning of the term *indirectly* connect is similar to stating that the connectors are being part of the same connection set. However, there is the difference that connections to `outer` elements are "moved up"

(Section 5.8.5, page 233) before forming connection sets. Otherwise the connection sets could contain "redundant" information breaking the equation count for locally balanced models (Section 5.7.7, page 217).

There are constraints on connection sets of causal variables:

- A connection set of *causal variables* (variables with `input/output` prefix) must contain at most *one source of a signal*, see Section 5.7.3.1, page 213.

The quantity attribute must be the same for the elements within a connection set:

- In a connection set all variables having non-empty quantity attribute must have the same quantity attribute.

There are also restrictions regarding *variables* from `protected` *outside* connectors. Such a variable may not be an implicitly defined part of an expandable connector (Section 5.9, page 238):

- Variables from a `protected` *outside* connector must be part of a connection set containing at least one *inside* connector or one declared public *outside* connector. That is, such a variable may *not* be an implicitly defined part of an expandable connector—otherwise it would not be possible to deduce the causality for the expandable connector element.

The following holds regarding the connection of *arrays of connectors* or array elements which are connectors:

- Array subscripts in a connector reference must be parameter expressions or the special operator ":", see Section 5.7.4.1, page 214 for more explanations and details.

Regarding restrictions for *conditional connectors*, i.e., connectors declared with an `if` keyword followed by a conditional expression, see Section 3.14, page 107 and Section 5.7.6, page 216.

5.7.3 Connection Restrictions on Input/Output, Inside/Outside Connectors

The introduction of structured instances with *inside* and *outside* connectors described in Section 5.7.1, page 208, introduces some additional complexity in the rules for connecting causal connectors with `input` or `output` causality, that is, connectors declared with the `input` or `output` type prefix. Examples are instances of the connector classes `RealInput` and `RealOutput`.

In this section we first give a *simplified* intuitive description that covers most cases, excluding some cases of connections to connectors hierarchically within connectors and expandable connectors (Section 5.9, page 238) and connection set related rules (Section 5.7.3.1, page 213). If we temporarily ignore the *inside/outside* issues the following rules apply:

- Two *acausal* connectors can be connected to each other (Section 5.3.2, page 191).
- An `input` connector can be only connected to one `output` connector, but an `output` connector can be connected to many `input` connectors, except when *inside/outside* aspects are taken into account (see below).
- An `input` or `output` connector *cannot* be connected to an *acausal* connector, i.e., a connector without `input/output` prefixes. The reason is balanced connectors (Section 8.9, page 387, and Section 5.7.7, page 217).

It is not possible to connect an `input` to an `input` or an `output` to an `output`, except when *outside* connectors are involved. The reason is data-flow consistency. A variable with an `input` prefix on one side of an equation will eventually be on the receiving side of an assignment statement (or receive a value as a result of solving an equation system) when causality analysis has been performed on the total system of equations.

Therefore, connecting an `input` *inside* connector to another `input` *inside* connector is not possible since then only one of the two input connectors would be on the receiving side in the data flow.

Analogously, connecting an `output` *inside* connector to another `output` *inside* connector is not allowed. In more general terms, one can say that there should be a *single source* when connecting a set of causal connectors, see also Section 5.7.3.1, page 213.

The situation is somewhat different with *outside* connectors since they play different roles in *outside* and *inside* connections. This is especially apparent for outside connectors that have `input` or `output` causality, for which the following rules apply for ***internal*** use inside a structured model instance:

- An *outside* `input` connector behaves approximately like an `output` connector internally.
- An *outside* `output` connector behaves approximately like an `input` connector internally.

This might at first glance appear rather strange, but is easy to understand when examining the simple example in Figure 5-28.

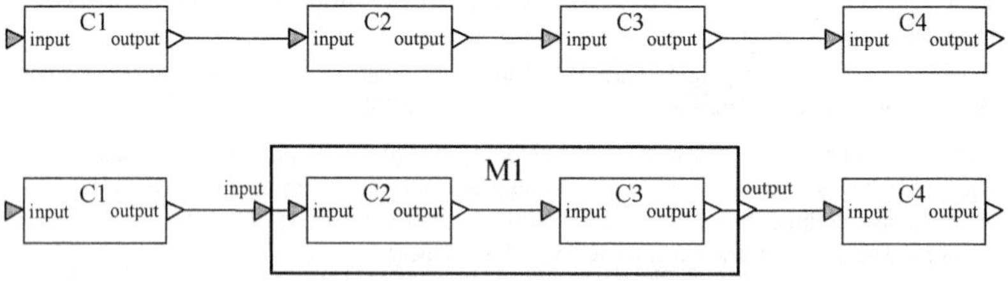

Figure 5-28. Two essentially equivalent example circuits of four connected components with connectors of input or output causality, in the figure labeled `input` and `output`, but in most signal connectors named `u` and `y`. Within the lower circuit two components have been embedded in the structured component `M1`.

The figure shows two almost-identical circuits of four connected components `C1`, `C2`, `C3`, and `C4`, which are instances of the class `C` declared below. The signal connectors, usually named `u` and `y` but in the figure marked `input` and `output`, are instances of `RealInput` and `RealOutput` which have `input` and `output` causality respectively.

```
connector RealInput   = input Real;    // subtype of input Real;
connector RealOutput  = output Real;   // subtype of output Real;

class C
  RealInput  u;    // input connector
  RealOutput y;    // output connector
end C;

class CInst
  C  C1, C2, C3, C4; // Instances of C
equation
  connect(C1.y, C2.u);
  connect(C2.y, C3.u);
  connect(C3.y, C4.u);
end CInst;

class M   "Structured class M"
  RealInput  u;     // Outside input connector
  RealOutput y;     // Outside output connector
  C  C2;
  C  C3;
end M;

class MInst
  M  M1;                       // Instance M1 of M
equation
  connect(C1.y, M1.u);     // Normal connection of y to u
  connect(M1.u, C2.u);     // Outside u connected to inside u
  connect(C2.y, C3.u);     // Inside y connected to inside u
  connect(C3.y, M1.y);     // Inside y connected to outside y
  connect(M1.y, C4.u);     // Normal connection of y to u
end MInst;
```

Data flow is from left to right in both circuits. In fact, the only difference in the lower circuit compared to the upper is that the middle components `C2` and `C3` have been placed inside a structured component `M1` to which two outside connectors `M1`.u and `M1.y` have been attached.

The "input" connection from `C1` *into* `C2` in the upper circuit:

```
connect(C1.y, C2.u)
```

is therefore equivalent to:

```
connect(C1.y, M1.u)
  // Normal connection of y to u
connect(M1.u, C2.u)
  // Outside u connected to inside u
```

Analogous rules apply to "output" connections. The connection *out of* `C3` to `C4` in the upper circuit:

```
connect(C3.y, C4.u)
```

is equivalent to:

```
connect(C3.y, M1.y) // Inside y to outside y
connect(M1.y, C4.u)
  // Normal connection of y to u
```

We are now ready to formulate the *approximate* connection constraints for `input` and `output` connectors. The first two rules state the approximate *special circumstances* when an input can be connected to an input and an output can be connected to an output:

- The "only case" when it is allowed to connect an `input` connector to an `input` connector is when one of them is an *inside* connector and the other is an *outside* connector.
- The "only case" when it is allowed to connect an `output` connector to an `output` connector is when one of them is an *inside* connector and the other is an *outside* connector.

Note that these two rules are intuitive but *approximate* connection restrictions. The *precise* restrictions are formulated below in terms of connection sets, see Section 5.7.3.1, page 213.

This is a special case of data-flow consistency constraint mentioned previously, which here is expressed more generally:

- A set of connected causal connectors may contain at most one source of a signal.

This restriction is elaborated in more detail in the next section (Section 5.7.3.1, page 213).

5.7.3.1 Single-Source Restriction of Connected Causal Connectors

In order to more precisely express the constraint that a set of connected causal connectors may contain at most one source of a signal, we need to use the concept of *connection set*, which can be thought of as the set of variables connected through a set of connected connectors, and is more precisely defined in Section 5.7.8.1, page 219.

The *single-source restriction* is stated more precisely by explicitly mentioning the different cases of connected sources. Two common cases of sources are *inside* `output` connectors or *outside* `input` connectors (see also examples in Figure 5-28, page 212).

Remember that all connectors declared at the hierarchical level directly within a class instance are outside connectors (part of the external interface), whereas

- A connection set of causal variables (`input`/`output`) may at most contain variables from one *inside* `output` connector or one public *outside* `input` connector.

This rule means that there may be ***at most one such source in a connection set***. This also applies to connection sets from partial models.

Furthermore, at least one of the following must hold for a connection set containing causal variables and originating from a non-partial model:

- The connection set includes variables from an *outside* public expandable connector.
- The connection set contains variables from protected *outside* connectors.
- The connection set contains either (a) variables from one *inside* `output` connector, or (b) from one public *outside* `input` connector, or (c) the set is comprised solely of variables from an *inside* `input` connector that is not part of an expandable connector.

The last item (c) covers the case where a connector of the block is left unconnected and the source given textually as an equation.

5.7.4 Connection Constraints Regarding Arrays, Subscripts, and Constants

As stated earlier in this chapter in the first section on connections, the main constraint between connected connectors is that they should have equivalent type.

5.7.4.1 Constant/Parameter or Colon Subscript Constraint

In order to simplify the analysis of connections and make the generation of connection equations possible at compile time, the following constraint applies:

- *Subscripts* in a connector reference must be *constant* or *parameter* expressions, or the special symbol ":" (colon).

For example:

```
class ConnectTest
  Pin   x[3];
  Pin   y[3];
  Integer i=2;
equation
  connect(x[2],y[2]);   // Ok! Constant subscripts.
  connect(x[i],y[2]);   // Error! Non-constant subscript.
end ConnectTest;
```

5.7.4.2 Connecting Connectors with Constant Elements

Connectors with constant or parameter primitive elements (fields) can be declared and connected. In such connections, connection equations need not and are not generated. Instead, appropriate assert statements are generated by the Modelica compiler to check that the connected values are the same. Moreover, parameter elements can only be connected to parameters and constant elements only to constants.

Constants and parameters are not allowed to have `flow` or `stream` prefix.

5.7.4.3 No Parameter of Constant Connectors

Connectors may not be declared with `parameter` or `constant` prefix.

5.7.5 Connecting Arrays of Connectors

As mentioned in Section 5.7.4, page 214, connections between scalar connectors are automatically vectorized, which for example is quite useful when using components from the `Modelica.Blocks` library, which can be used in both scalar and vector contexts.

The `connect` construct can be used to directly connect arrays of connectors. For such *array connections* the following holds:

- The array dimensions of the connected arrays of connectors must match.
- Each corresponding pair of elements is connected as a pair of scalar connectors.

We demonstrate this functionality in the `ArrayConnects` class below, for which the connections are graphically depicted in Figure 5-29.

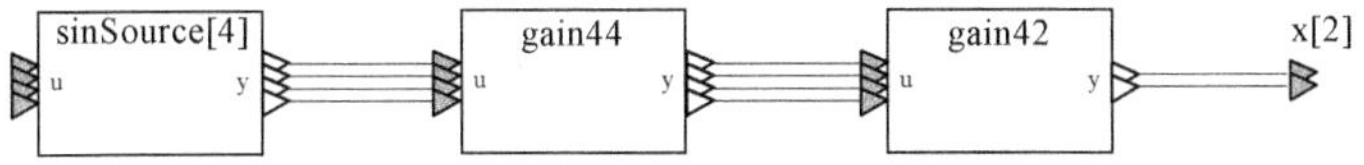

Figure 5-29. Example of connections between arrays of connectors.

The `sinSource` signal generator produces a vector of 4 sinusoidal signals, which are connected to the input vector `gain44.u` of the `gain44` block. This gain block multiplies the signal by its gain factor, here 5, which is present in the diagonal elements of the matrix `gain44.A`.

$$\texttt{gain44.A:} \begin{pmatrix} 5 & 0 & 0 & 0 \\ 0 & 5 & 0 & 0 \\ 0 & 0 & 5 & 0 \\ 0 & 0 & 0 & 5 \end{pmatrix}, \quad \texttt{gain42.A:} \begin{pmatrix} 1 & 1 & 1 & 1 \\ 1 & 1 & 1 & 1 \end{pmatrix} \tag{5-3}$$

Moreover, we connect the output vector `gain44.y` of length four to the input vector `gain42.u` of the `gain42` block. This block transforms its input signals into the two output signals `gain42.y`, which we finally connect to the vector `x[2]`.

The corresponding Modelica code follows:

```
connector RealInput  = input Real;
connector RealOutput = output Real;

block MatrixGain
  parameter Real      A[:,:] = [1];
  input RealInput     u[size(A,1)];
  output RealOutput   y[size(A,2)]
equation
  y=A*u;
end MatrixGain;

model ArrayConnects
  import Modelica.Math.sin;
  sin          sinSource[4];
  MatrixGain gain44(A=5*identity(4)); // 4x4 identity matrix * 7
  MatrixGain gain42(A=ones(4,2));     // 4x2 matrix of ones
  RealOutput     x[2];                // 2-vector
equation
  connect(sinSource.y, gain44.u);
  connect(gain44.y,    gain42.u);
  connect(gain42.y,    x);
end ArrayConnects;
```

Quite often when symbolically instantiating models with arrays of connectors there is a need to modify a common attribute of each array element to a single value. The iterative array element modification construct with the `each` keyword, described in Section 4.2.3.1, page 150, has been designed with such applications in mind.

We show an example below with the `frequency` attribute of the source vector elements being modified to the common value 50 in the `ConnectUseEach` model.

```
model ConnectUseEach
  import Modelica.Blocks.Sources.Sine;
  Sine          base[3];
  Sine          source[3](each frequency=50, phase={0,2,-2});
  CrossProduct a;

  block CrossProduct
    import Modelica.Blocks.Interfaces.MI2MO;
    extends MI2MO(final n=3); // Two multiple input to multiple output block
  equation
    y = cross(u1,u2);
  end CrossProduct;

equation
  connect(source.y, a.u1);
  connect(base.y,   a.u2);
end ConnectUseEach;
```

5.7.6 Connecting Conditional Instances

Variables and instances, including connectors, can be declared conditionally on the value of a Boolean expression being true, as described in Section 3.14, page 107. If the Boolean expression is false, the instance is *not present* in the flattened system of equations to be simulated, and connections to/from associated connector(s) are removed.

The Boolean expression must have parameter variability so that the conditional instance with associated connections can be removed during compilation of the model.

There are also restrictions regarding connection of conditional connectors.

- If the *condition* is *true* for a public *conditional connector* containing flow variables the connector must be *connected from the outside*. The reason for this restriction is that the default flow equation is probably incorrect (since it could otherwise be an unconditional connector) and the model cannot check that the connector is connected..

In Figure 5-30 we have adapted the previous `ResistorCircuit` model (Section 5.4.3.1, page 198) to contain a conditional component `R3Cond`. The conditionally active connection to `R3Cond` is shown as a dashed line.

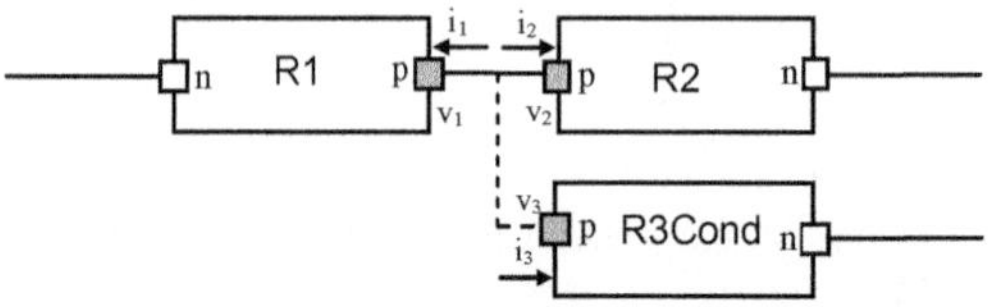

Figure 5-30. A `ResistorCircuitCond` containing three resistors connected at one node. One of the resistors, `R3Cond`, is declared conditionally, with the conditional connection shown as a dashed line.

```
model ResistorCircuitCond
  parameter Integer control = 1;
  Resistor R1(R=100);
  Resistor R2(R=200);
  Resistor R3Cond(R=300) if control == 2;
equation
  connect(R1.p, R2.p);
  connect(R1.p, R3Cond.p);
end ResistorCircuitCond;

model ResistorCondTest
```

```
  ResistorCircuitCond  circuit1;            // This circuit has 2 resistors
  ResistorCircuitCond  circuit2(control=2); // This circuit has 3 resistors
end ResistorCondTest;
```

The `ResistorCondTest` example contains two instances, `circuit1` and `circuit2`. The first has two resistors, since the `control` parameter has a default value 1, making the conditional expression in the `R3Cond` component declaration false. The second circuit instance, `circuit2`, has three resistors and one additional connection, since the Boolean expression in that case has the value true.

5.7.7 Balancing Restrictions on Connector Classes

The model balancing restrictions (Section 8.9, page 387) of Modelica 3.0 and later versions of the language have special implications for connector classes, described in more detail in Section 8.9.2.3, page 392. For a model to be balanced, its connector classes must have the *same* number of acausal flow variables and potential variables. This can be expressed more precisely as follows:

- For each nonpartial connector class the number of variables with prefix `flow` must be *equal to* the number of variables which have neither of the prefixes `parameter`, `constant`, `input`, `output`, `stream`, nor `flow`. As usual the number of variables is counted in the connector class after expanding all records and arrays to a set of scalars of basic types as described in Section 8.9.2.1, page 389.

Note that stream variables work almost like output variables which is why they are not counted in the balancing counts: "A model using a stream connector must expose the outflow value, which is known from internal storage or from inflow values of other connectors, independently of the flow direction. The inflow value can be obtained by a model on demand by using the operator `inStream(h_outflow)`".

For example, the following unbalanced connector class is illegal in Modelica 3.0 but was legal in Modelica 2.2:

```
connector NotValid  // Illegal connector, one flow and two potential
  Real r1;
  Real r2;
  flow Real r3;
end NotValid;
```

It is not easy to understand how the above connector class restriction can make the model balanced. We need to invoke another rule (Section 5.7.8.2, page 221) to make that happen:

- *A connection set is added* for each primitive (unconnected) flow variable as an *inside* (Section 5.7.1, page 208) connector.

A balancing example including the use of this rule is presented in Section 8.9.2.3, page 392. Several examples of balanced and unbalanced connector classes are shown below:

```
connector Pin   // A connector class from Modelica.Electrical.Analog
  Real      v;
  flow Real i;
end Pin;

connector Plug  // A connector class from Modelica.Electrical.MultiPhase
  parameter Integer m=3;
  Pin p[m];
end Plug;

connector InputReal = input Real;   // A causal input connector class

connector OutputReal = output Real; // A causal output connector class
```

```
connector FrameIllegal // Illegal connector class since not balanced
  Modelica.SIunits.Position         r0[3]  "Position vector of frame origin";
  Real                              S[3,3] "Rotation matrix of frame";
  Modelica.SIunits.Velocity         v[3]    "Abs. velocity of frame origin";
  Modelica.SIunits.AngularVelocity w[3]    "Abs. angular velocity of frame";
  Modelica.SIunits.Acceleration     a[3]    "Abs. acc. of frame origin";
  Modelica.SIunits.AngularAcceleration z[3] "Abs. angular acc. of frame";
  flow Modelica.SIunits.Force       f[3]    "Cut force";
  flow Modelica.SIunits.Torque      t[3]    "Cut torque";
end FrameIllegal;
```

The `FrameIllegal` connector, which is used in the earlier Modelica 2.2 compatible MultiBody package without over-determined connectors, is illegal in Modelica 3.0 and later versions of the language since the number of flow and potential variables do not match.

The current Modelica.MultiBody package uses the `Frame` connector class defined below. It is inherited into the two classes `Frame_a` and `Frame_b`, which are identical except having different icons. The Frame connector class contains a basic definition of a coordinate system that is fixed to a mechanical component. The cut-force and the cut-torque are acting at the origin of the coordinate system.

```
connector Frame
  "Coordinate system fixed to the component with one cut-force & cut-torque"
  import SI = Modelica.SIunits;
  SI.Position          r_0[3] "Position vector from world frame to the
                               connector frame origin, resolved in world frame";
  Frames.Orientation R       "Orientation object to rotate the world frame into
                               the connector frame";
  flow SI.Force f[3]   "Cut-force resolved in connector frame"
  flow SI.Torque t[3] "Cut-torque resolved in connector frame";
end Frame;

connector Frame_a
  "Coordinate system fixed to the component with one cut-force and
   cut-torque (filled rectangular icon)"
  extends Frame;
end Frame_a;

connector Frame_b
  "Coordinate system fixed to the component with one cut-force and
   cut-torque (non-filled rectangular icon)"
  extends Frame;
end Frame_b;
```

The subsequent connector classes `PlugExpanded` and `PlugExpanded2` are correct, but `PlugExpandedIllegal` can be illegal since the number of potential and flow variables are different if `n` and `m` become different through a redeclaration of n to something else.

It is not clear how a Modelica tool in general at an early stage can detect that connectors such as `PlugExpandedIllegal` can become illegal. However, it is always possible to detect this defect after actual values of parameters and constants are provided in the simulation model.

```
connector PlugExpanded   // Correct connector class
   parameter Integer m=3;
   Real      v[m];
   flow Real i[m];
end PlugExpanded;

connector PlugExpanded2   // Correct connector class
   parameter Integer m=3;
   final parameter Integer n=m;
   Real      v[m];
   flow Real i[n];
end PlugExpanded2;
```

```
connector PlugExpandedIllegal   // Connector class can become illegal
   parameter Integer m=3;
   parameter Integer n=m;       // Not illegal if n=m, but illegal if n#m
   Real      v[m];
   flow Real i[n];
end PlugExpandedIllegal;
```

5.7.8 Generation of Connection Equations

By *generating connection equations* we mean the *conversion* of connect-equations to the two different forms of normal equations to be used for potential and flow variables respectively, even though the connect-equation itself is a kind of equation. This was described to some extent in Section 5.3 on page 190 but is presented here in more detail. The process of converting connect-equations can be divided into two steps:

- Building *connection setss* from connect-equations.
- Generating *connection equations* for the complete model.

Connection sets and generation of connection equation for "normal" connections and connectors are described here, whereas the corresponding for implicit connections with `inner/outer` matching is presented in Section 5.8.5, page 233, and for stream connectors in Section 5.10.5, page 254.

Constants or parameters in connected instances give rise to the appropriate *assert* equations/statements asserting equality (or sum-to-zero) of such connected constants or parameters—connection equations are not generated.

5.7.8.1 Connection Sets from Connect-Equations

Connections sets are needed to generate the connection equations of a model. They are formed for every usage of a connect-equation, such as the following:

```
connect(a, b);
```

Connection sets are sets of *variables* of built-in type from expanded connector instance arguments in connec- equations, e.g. `a` and `b` from the above connect-equation:

- A *connection set* is a set of variables *connected* by means of connect-equations. Each variable in the set needs to have associated information indicating if it is from an *inside* or *outside* connector.
- If there are variables having *structured connector types*, those variables are *expanded* into their primitive elements until all variables have primitive built-in Modelica types, except variables of `operator record` types. This means that an instance of an `operator record` type is not split into its parts.
- All variables in one connection set will *either* be flow variables or potential variables due to the restriction on connect-equations that flow connects to flow and potential connects to potential.

The fact that connection sets are formed from the primitive elements, that is, variables of basic type and not from the connectors, handles connections to parts of hierarchical connectors and also makes it easier to generate equations directly from the connection sets.

There are special rules regarding the generation of connection sets in the presence of `inner` or `outer` prefixes on connected objects; see Section 5.8.5, page 233.

A practical way to represent the associated information is to use pairs/tuples consisting of the variable name together with an indication whether the variable is from an *inside* or an *outside* connector (Section 5.7.1, page 208), for example, (*variablename*, *inside*) or (*variablename*, *outside*). For simple models without structured components all connectors can be regarded as *inside*.

These sets are generated by first creating a number of small connection sets from the expanded two arguments to each connect-equation. Arguments which are not of basic type such as `Real`, `Integer`, and so on, except `operator record` types, are expanded into its elements of basic type. In the second step, if any of the elements are also members of other connection sets, the corresponding connection sets are merged. We demonstrate this on the small `ResistorCircuit` example.

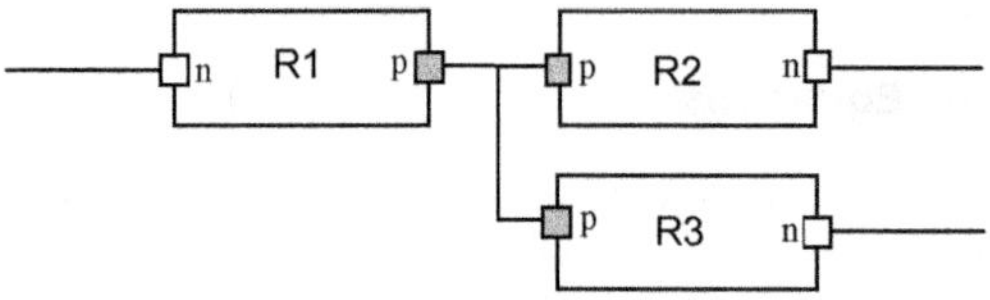

Figure 5-31. Schematic picture of `ResistorCircuit`, also in Figure 5-15.

```
model ResistorCircuit
  Resistor  R1,R2,R3;
equation
  connect(R1.p,R2.p);
  connect(R2.p,R3.p);
end ResistorCircuit;
```

For example, the connection sets corresponding to the connect-equations in the `ResistorCircuit` model in Figure 5-31 are the following, where each connector contains a current `i` and a voltage `v`:

```
{ (R1.p.v, inside), (R2.p.v, inside) } // from first connect
{ (R1.p.i, inside), (R2.p.i, inside) } // from first connect
{ (R2.p.v, inside), (R3.p.v, inside) } // from second connect
{ (R2.p.i, inside), (R3.p.i, inside) } // from second connect
```

There are also single-element connection sets for unconnected flow variables, since the flow for such variables eventually must be set to zero by generated equations:

```
{ (R1.n.i, inside) } // from unconnected port R1.n
{ (R2.n.i, inside) } // from unconnected port R2.n
{ (R3.n.i, inside) } // from unconnected port R3.n
```

These sets are merged into the following connection sets, for potential and flow variables respectively:

```
{ (R1.p.v, inside), (R2.p.v, inside), (R3.p.v, inside) } // potential
{ (R1.p.i, inside), (R2.p.i, inside), (R3.p.i, inside) } // flow

{ (R1.n.i, inside) } // flow into unconnected port R1.n
{ (R2.n.i, inside) } // flow into unconnected port R2.n
{ (R3.n.i, inside) } // flow into unconnected port R3.n
```

The connected variables in the set are reachable in a graph defined by the three connector nodes and the two connect-equations `connect(R1.p,R2.p)` and `connect(R2.p,R3.p)` given in the model.

The situation is somewhat different regarding the `ECircuit` model in Figure 5-32 since it contains a structured component `E1` that contains both *inside* and *outside* connectors (Section 5.7.1, page 208).

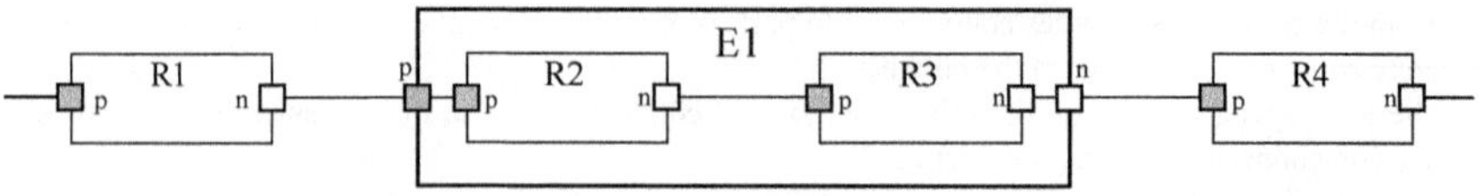

Figure 5-32. The `ECircuit` model.

```
class E
  Resistor R2;
  Resistor R3;
equation
```

```
    connect(E1.p, R2.p);
    connect(R2.n, R3.p);
    connect(R3.n, E1.n);
  end E;

  model ECircuit;
    Resistor R1;
    Resistor R4;
    E        E1;
  equation
    connect(R1.n,E1.p);
    connect(E1.n,R4.p);
  end ECircuit;
```

The `ECircuit` model contains three components `R1`, `E1`, and `R4` at the topmost hierarchical level of the model. All connectors in `ECircuit` have the type `Pin` with the two members; `v` of type `Voltage`, and `i` which is a flow variable of type `Current`. The two connections at the topmost level of the model between `R1.n` and `E1.p` as well as between `E1.n` and `R4.p` give rise to the following connection sets.

```
{ (R1.n.v, inside),  (E1.p.v, inside) }
{ (R1.n.i, inside),  (E1.p.i, inside) }

{ (E1.n.v, inside),  (R4.p.v, inside) }
{ (E1.n.i, inside),  (R4.p.i, inside) }
```

On the other hand, the structured component `E1` with three *internal* connect-equations gives rise to the following connection sets that also include variables from the *outside* connectors `E1.p` and `E1.n`:

```
{ (E1.p.v, outside),  (E1.R2.p.v, inside) }
{ (E1.p.i, outside),  (E1.R2.p.i, inside) }

{ (E1.R2.n.v, inside),  (E1.R3.p.v, inside) }
{ (E1.R2.n.i, inside),  (E1.R3.p.i, inside) }

{ (E1.R3.n.v, inside),  (E1.n.v, outside) }
{ (E1.R3.n.i, inside),  (E1.n.i, outside) }
```

Since all tuples occur only in one connection set, the merged sets are the same as these sets.

5.7.8.2 Connection Sets from Inside or Augmented Flow Variables

Recall our `ResistorCircuit` example shown in the previous section and in Figure 5-31. Single-element connection sets for *unconnected inside flow variables* are also generated since the flow for such variables is zero which must be represented as an equality to zero in generated equations:

```
{ (R1.n.i, inside) } // from unconnected port R1.n
{ (R2.n.i, inside) } // from unconnected port R2.n
{ (R3.n.i, inside) } // from unconnected port R3.n
```

In general, the following connection sets with just one member should also be generated and merged:

- Each primitive (unconnected) flow-variable as an *inside* (Section 5.7.1, page 208) connector.
- Each flow variable *added* during augmentation of expandable connectors (Section 5.9.6, page 242), both as *inside* and as *outside*.

Instead of adding sets only for unconnected flow variables, it is possible to add sets for all *inside* connector flow variables from the start. The connected ones will then disappear (be merged) during the merging process, and only the unconnected ones will be left as they are initially, giving the same result.

Regarding connection sets for flow variables that are added to an expandable connector during augmentation (Section 5.9.6, page 242), this refers to flow variables which are elements in structured connectors since it is not possible (Section 5.9.4, page 241) to explicitly declare flow variables as members of expandable connectors.

5.7.8.3 Restrictions on Connection Sets Containing Causal Variables

There are special restrictions on connection sets containing causal (`input/output`) variables since a connection set may contain at most contain one source of a signal; see Section 5.7.3.1, page 213.

5.7.8.4 Generating Connection Equations for Potential Variables

Each primitive connection set of potential variables (a_i) is used to generate equations of the form:

```
a1 = a2 = ... an;
```

There are five primitive connection sets of potential variables from the model `ECircuit`, generating the following equations:

```
R1.n.v = E1.p.v;          E1.p.v = E1.R2.p.v;
E1.R2.n.v = E1.R3.p.v;
E1.R3.n.v = E1.n.v;       E1.n.v = R4.p.v;
```

Regarding the `ResistorCircuit` model, the connection equations for potential variables become:

```
R1.p.v = R2.p.v = R3.p.v
```

5.7.8.5 Generating Connection Equations for Flow Variables

Each primitive connection set of flow variables (z_i) is used to generate *sum-to-zero* equations of the form:

```
z1 + z2 + ... + (-zk) + ... + zn = 0;
```

In order to generate equations for flow variables, the sign used for the connector variable z_i above is +1 for *inside* connectors and –1 for *outside* connectors, for example, z_k in the above equation.

For each flow variable z_j in a connector that is *not* connected as an *inside* connector in any element instance belonging to the model, the following *zero-equation* is generated:

```
zj = 0;
```

The bold-face **0** represents a scalar zero or a zero-valued array of appropriate dimensions (i.e., the same dimensionality and size as z_j).

Regarding the model `ECircuit`, the following sum-to-zero equations with flow variables are generated:

```
R1.n.i + E1.p.i  = 0;        (-E1.p.i) + E1.R2.p.i = 0;
E1.R2.n.i + E1.R3.p.i = 0;
E1.R3.n.i + E1.n.i = 0;      (-E1.n.i) + R4.p.i
```

The reason that a *negative* sign is used for *outside* connector variables such as `E1.p.i` and `E1.n.i` is rather apparent when looking at Figure 5-32 of the `ECircuit` model. The positive flow *into* the `E1` component via the connector `E1.p` continues in the same direction *out* of `E1.p` when used internally as an outside connector in `E1`. Since the positive flow direction is into a component and the actual flow is in the opposite direction out of `E.p`, a *negative* sign has to be used.

If we expand the structured component `E1` into its parts, that is, effectively remove its component boundary, this will eliminate the outside connectors. Such a transformation corresponds to merging equations, e.g., adding the first two flow equations above:

```
R1.n.i + E1.p.i  +  (-E1.p.i) + E1.R2.p.i = 0;
```

This equation is easily simplified using the negative sign of the flow variable from the outside connector. The resulting *merged* equation below closely corresponds to a situation where the resistors `R1` and `R2` would be directly connected to each other without the existence of the structured component `E1`:

```
R1.n.i + E1.R2.p.i = 0;
```

Returning to the matter of zero-equations, there are two connectors `R1.p` and `R4.n` in `ECircuit` that are not connected anywhere. The following zero-equations are generated for the flow variables in those connectors. The flow will of course be zero since nothing will flow into an unconnected port. Another example of this rule is presented in Section 15.2.5.4, page 817:

```
R1.p.i = 0;
R4.n.i = 0;
```

This also means that it is not possible to have additional equations (would be too many equations!) that define unconnected flow variables like `R1.p.i` and `R4.n.i` since they are already equal to zero. Returning to the `ResistorCircuit` model once more, the connection equation and the zero-equations for the flow variables become:

```
R1.p.i + R2.p.i + R3.p.i  =  0;
R1.n.i = 0;
R2.n.i = 0;
R3.n.i = 0;
```

5.7.8.6 Generating Connection Equations for Constants and Parameters

Constants and parameters sometimes occur in connectors, e.g., the `parameter n` declared in the connector classes `RealInVec` and `RealOutVec`. It does not make much sense to generate constant connection equations to be solved by an equation solver. On the other hand, it must be guaranteed that corresponding constants or parameters have the same value. This can be done through `assert` statements instead of connection equations:

- *Constants* or *parameters* in connected connectors produce `assert` statements instead of connection equations.

For example, the following class has the connectors `ip` and `op`, which both contain the parameter `n`:

```
class ConnectedParameter   "Example class with parameter connectors"
  RealOutVec op;     // connector with parameter n
  RealInVec  ip;     // connector with parameter n
equation
  connect(op,ip);
end ConnectedParameter;

connector RealInVec "Vector Integer input connector"
  parameter Integer n = 1;
  input Real        vec[n];
end TestRealInput;

connector RealOutVec "Vector Integer input connector"
  parameter Integer n = 1;
  output Real       vec[n];
end TestRealInput;
```

The equation `connect(op,ip)` generates the usual connection equation for the variables `op` and `ip`:

```
op = ip;
```

However, regarding the parameter `n` the following `assert` statement is produced:

```
assert(op.n=ip.n, "");
```

5.7.9 Cardinality and Direction of Connections

Note that the *cardinality operator has been deprecated* (removed) from Modelica language releases after Modelica 3.1 for the following reasons: such a reflective operator may make early type checking more difficult, it is almost always abused in strange ways, and it is not used for Bond graphs even though it was originally introduced for that purpose.

In old versions of Modelica, it was possible to let the behavior of a model be dependent on the number of connections to certain connectors of the model. This can be achieved by using a built-in function `cardinality` that returns the number of connections that have been made to a connector. This is an example of a self-inspecting (reflecting) language construct.

The cardinality is counted after removing conditional components. and may not be applied to expandable connectors, elements in expandable connectors, or to arrays of connectors, but can be applied to the scalar elements of an array of connectors. The cardinality operator should only be used in the condition of assert and if-statements – that do not contain connect and similar operators.

- The function `cardinality`(*c*) with formal parameter *c* returns the total number of (internal and external) occurrences of the connector *c* in connect-equations in the total model.

For example, a model library might be built with the assumption that only one connection can be made to each connector. Another example is to specify *connection-dependent equations* in a model, for example, as in the model `CardinalityResistor` below, where each case with no connections to a connector or a group of connectors is treated in a special way.

```
model CardinalityResistor
  extends TwoPin;
  parameter Real R(unit="Ohm")   "Resistance";
equation
// Handle cases if pins are not connected
  if cardinality(p) == 0 and cardinality(n) == 0 then
  p.v = 0; n.v = 0;
  elseif cardinality(p) == 0 then
    p.i = 0;
  elseif cardinality(n) == 0 then
    n.i = 0;
  end if;
  // Resistor equation
  v = R*i;
end CardinalityResistor;
```

5.7.9.1 The Direction of a Connection

Note that the `direction` *operator has been deprecated* (removed) from Modelica language releases after Modelica 1.4 for the same reasons as for the `cardinality` operator.

In very old versions of Modelica it was possible to get information about the *direction* of a connection by using the built-in function `direction(c)` on a connector `c`, provided that `cardinality(c) = 1`, i.e., the connector `c` is involved in exactly one connection.

Given a connection of the following form:

```
connect(c1,c2);
```

calls passing the two connector arguments give the following results:

```
direction(c1) returns  -1
direction(c2) returns   1
```

The `cardinality` and `direction` operators were intended to be used when building certain kinds of libraries, for example, libraries of bond graph components or components for modeling discrete event systems. However, it turned out that they were not actually used for that purpose.

5.8 Implicit Connections with the inner/outer Construct

So far in we have focused on explicit connections between connectors where each connection is explicitly represented by a connect-equation and a corresponding line in a connection diagram. However, when modeling certain kinds of large models with many interacting components this approach becomes rather clumsy because of the large number of potential connections—a connection might be needed between each pair of components. This is especially true for system models involving *force fields*, which lead to a maximum of $n \times n$ connections between the n components influenced by the force field or $1 \times n$ connections between a central object and n components if intercomponent interaction is neglected.

For the case of $1 \times n$ connections, instead of using a large number of explicit connections, Modelica provides a convenient mechanism for *implicit connections* between an object and n of its components through the `inner` and `outer` declaration prefixes.

These language constructs force lookup for implicit connections through the *instance hierarchy* instead of the usual nested lookup in the class hierarchy, as described briefly in the next section and more formally in Section 3.17.5, page 113. Another difference compared to explicit connections is that the `inner/outer` mechanism can be applied to *any declared element* in a class, not only to connectors.

5.8.1 Access of Shared inner Environment Variables

A rather common kind of implicit interaction is where a *shared attribute* of a single environment object is *accessed* by a number of components within that environment. For example, we might have an environment including house components, each accessing a shared environment temperature, or a circuit board environment with electronic components accessing the board temperature.

A Modelica environment-component example model along these lines is shown below, where a shared environment temperature variable `T0` is declared as a *definition declaration* marked by the keyword `inner`. This declaration is implicitly accessed by the *reference declarations* of `T0` marked by the prefix `outer` in the components `comp1` and `comp2`.

```
model Environment
  inner Real T0;          // Definition of actual environment temperature T0
  Component comp1, comp2; // Lookup match makes comp1.T0 = comp2.T0 = T0
  parameter Real k=1;
equation
  T0 = sin(k*time);
end Environment;

model Component
  outer Real T0; // Reference to temperature T0 defined in the environments
  Real T;
equation
  T = T0;
end Component;

model EnvironmentInstances
  Environment env1(k=1);
  Environment env2(k=4);
end EnvironmentInstances
```

The instance hierarchy lookup is from an `outer` reference declaration to a matching `inner` definition declaration with the same name. The search is upward in the instance hierarchy starting from the current instance. In this example, the search starts at the components `comp1` or `comp2` upward to the `Environment` instances `env1` or `env2` where the matching `inner` definition declaration of `T0` is found, as depicted in Figure 5-33.

Note that there exists only one actual instance of `T0` in each environment, marked by the prefix `inner`. All `outer` reference declarations of `T0` within the components of an environment are just references to this single instance.

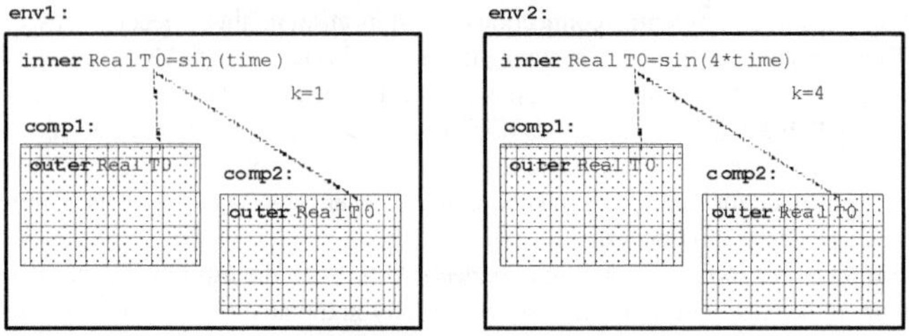

Figure 5-33. Two Environment instances `env1` and `env2`, each containing a definition of a temperature `T0` which is implicitly accessed by the reference declarations of `T0` in the components `comp1` and `comp2`.

A nice property of the instance hierarchy lookup mechanism provided by the `inner/outer` language feature is its selectiveness. Thus we can have several simultaneously existing environment hierarchies as shown in Figure 5-33, with independent lookup within each hierarchy.

We simulate the `EnvironmentInstances` model containing the two environments `env1` and `env2`:

```
simulate(EnvironmentInstances, stopTime=2)
plot({env1.comp1.T0, env2.comp1.T0})
```

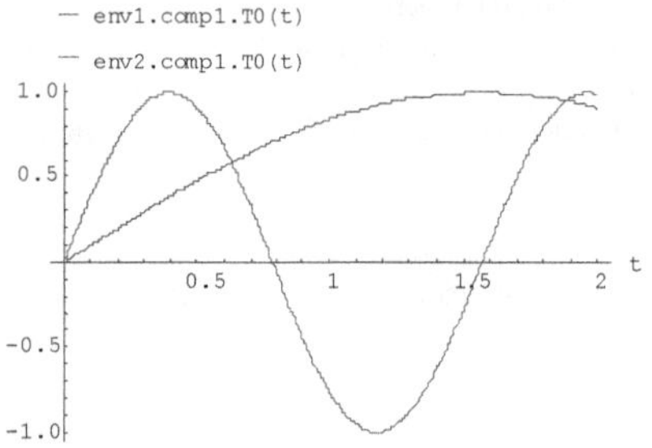

Figure 5-34. Plot of `env1.T0` and `env2.T0` for the two environments `env1` and `env2` respectively.

Both environments have a sine-shaped temperature profile `T0` as a function of time (Figure 5-34), but the second environment temperature is varying faster in time since the coefficient `k=4` compared to `k=1` for the first environment.

5.8.2 Implicit versus Explicit Connection Structures

As mentioned above, the `inner/outer` mechanism can be applied to any kind of element, not only to connectors. However, this mechanism is especially useful when applied to connectors to establish *implicit connections* between a single environment object and their components, i.e., a case of $1 \times n$ interaction.

An implicit connection structure has the nice property that additional components can be added to the structure without the need for additional explicit connections. A new component becomes *automatically connected* to the system.

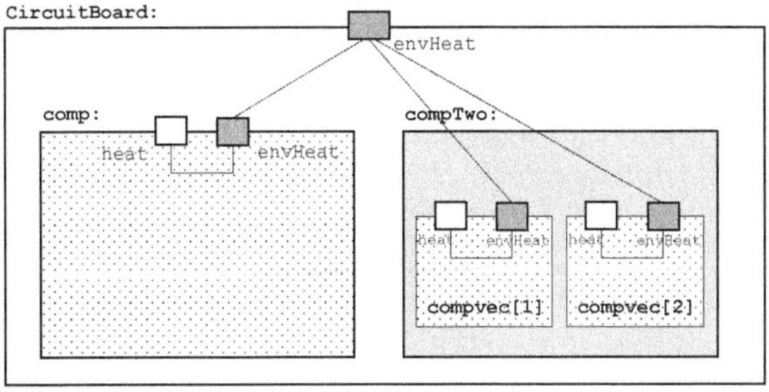

Figure 5-35. `CircuitBoard` heat exchange with implicit connections between inner/outer connectors shown as dotted lines.

Consider the `CircuitBoard` example depicted in Figure 5-35, with Modelica code below. New components added to the `compvec` vector within the `compTwo` model instance become automatically connected. The reason is that all `outer envHeat` connectors within the `compvec` vector automatically reference the `inner envHeat` definition connector declared in the `CircuitBoard`.

```
connector HeatPort
  Modelica.SIunits.Temp_K           T  "Temperature in [K]";
  flow  Modelica.SIunits.HeatFlux  q  "Heat flux";
end HeatPort;

model Component  "Component within a circuit board in an environment"
  outer HeatPort envHeat;  // Reference to environment heat interface
  HeatPort       heat;     // Local heat connector of component
equation
  connect(heat, envHeat);
end Component;

model TwoComponents  "Two Components together"
  Component compvec[2];
end TwoComponents;

model CircuitBoard
  inner HeatPort  envHeat;  // Definition of environment heat interface
  Component       comp;
  TwoComponents   compTwo;
end CircuitBoard;
```

As a comparison, we show the same example modeled using traditional *explicit connections* depicted in Figure 5-36, with corresponding Modelica code below.

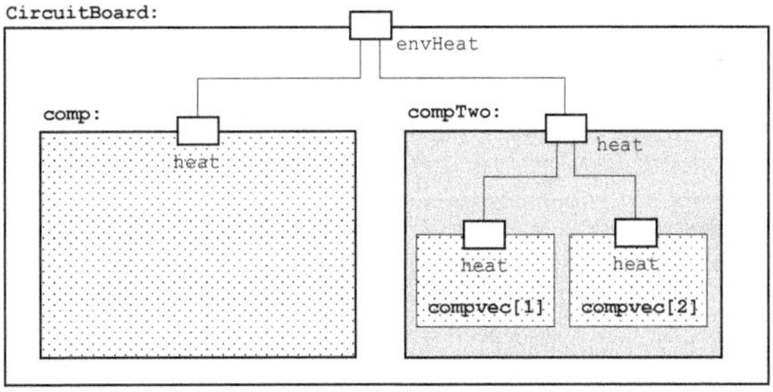

Figure 5-36. `CircuitBoard` heat exchange model with explicit connections.

Each time we add a new component to the compvec vector in the compTwo instance, an additional explicit connection has to be added into the TwoComponents class as a connect-equation.

```
connector HeatPort
  Modelica.SIunits.Temp_K          T   "Temperature in [K]";
  flow Modelica.SIunits.HeatFlux   q   "Heat flux";
end HeatPort;

model Component
  HeatPort  heat;
end Component;

model TwoComponents
  Component  compvec[2];
  HeatPort   heat;
equation
  connect(compvec[1].heat, heat);
  connect(compvec[2].heat, heat);
end TwoComponents;

model CircuitBoard
  HeatPort        envHeat;
  Component       comp;
  TwoComponents   compTwo;
equation
  connect(comp.heat, envHeat);
  connect(compTwo.heat, envHeat);
end CircuitBoard;
```

5.8.3 Nested Hierarchical Subsystems with Simultaneous inner/outer

The previous sections show how inner definition declarations, for example in the Environment model, are implicitly connected to and propagated to outer reference declarations, e.g. in components of the environment.

What happens if we have a more complex system structure, with possibly several levels of nested subsystems? Can we propagate across the subsystem boundaries? The answer is yes, but it is a bit clumsy. We would need to have different inner and outer declarations for the same entity in each subsystem, introduce a new name for each additional declaration, and couple these through additional equations. This is complicated and makes model re-use harder.

To avoid these drawbacks when modeling with nested subsystems, the *simultaneous inner-outer declaration* has been introduced. This eliminates the need for extra names and equations, and increases reusability, e.g. as needed by libraries such as Modelica.Stategraph. The declaration has both keywords inner and outer as depicted below:

```
inner outer <Type> <variable>;
```

This declaration conceptually introduces two declarations with the same name, both an inner and an outer declaration:

- An *element* declared with *both* the *prefixes* inner and outer conceptually introduces two declarations with the same name: one that follows the above rules for inner and another that follows the rules for outer.
- *Local uses* of elements in declarations with simultaneous prefixes inner and outer use the outer element. That in turn references the corresponding inner definition declaration in an enclosing scope.
- Simultaneous inner/outer declarations may have *modifications*, including declaration equations in the modifier. Those modifications are *only* applied to the inner part of the declaration. Modifiers or declaration equations on pure outer declarations are not allowed.
- Outer class declarations should be defined using the short class definition. Modifiers to such outer class declarations are only allowed if the inner keyword is also present, i.e., a simultaneous inner outer class declaration.

The last point is illustrated by the following erroneous model:

```
class A
  outer parameter Real p=2; // Error, since declaration equation needs inner
end A;
```

To demonstrate the use of simultaneous `inner outer` declarations we have introduced a subsystem level, `SubEnvironment`, with instance `subEnv`, in the previous `Environment` model. The new model is called `EnvironmentsWithSubsystem` and is shown below and in Figure 5-37.

The model contains two environment instances env1 and env2, each containing an inner definition of a temperature `T0` and a subsystem `subEnv`. The top-level environment temperatures `env1.T0` and `env2.T0` respectively are picked up by the reference (`outer`) part of the simultaneous `inner outer T0` in `subEnv`, transferred to its definition (`inner`) `T0` part which is implicitly accessed by the reference declarations of `T0` in the components `comp1` and `comp2`.

```
model Environment
  inner Real T0;           // Definition of actual environment temperature T0
  SubEnvironment subEnv; // Lookup makes subEnv.comp1.T0=subEnv.comp2.T0=T0
  parameter Real k=1;
equation
  T0 = sin(k*time);
end Environment;

model SubEnvironment
  inner outer T0;    // Inner T0 used by comp1,comp2; outer ref to env1/2.T0
  Component comp1, comp2; // Lookup makes comp1.T0 = comp2.T0 = subEnv.T0
equation
end SubEnvironment;

model Component
  outer Real T0; // References temperature T0 defined in the subenvironment
  Real T;
equation
  T = T0;
end Component;

model EnvironmentsWithSubsystem
  Environment env1(k=1);
  Environment env2(k=4);
end EnvironmentsWithSubsystem;
```

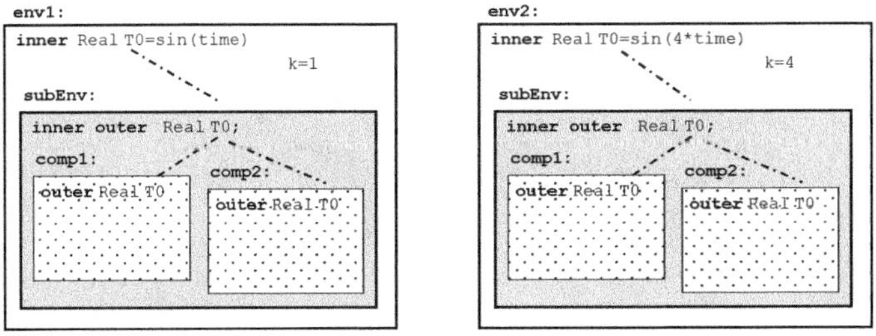

Figure 5-37. The structure of the `EnvironmentsWithSubSystem` model. Two Environment instances, `env1` and `env2`, each containing an inner definition of a temperature `T0` and a ***subsystem*** `subEnv`. The `env1.T0` and `env2.T0` are picked up by the reference (`outer`) part of the simultaneous `inner outer T0` in `subEnv`, transferred to its definition (`inner`) `T0` part which is implicitly accessed by the reference declarations of `T0` in the components `comp1` and `comp2`.

We simulate the `EnvironmentsWithSubsystem` model containing the two environments `env1` and `env2`:

```
simulate(EnvironmentsWithSubsystem, stopTime=2)
plot({env1.subEnv.comp1.T0, env2.subEnv.comp1.T0})
```

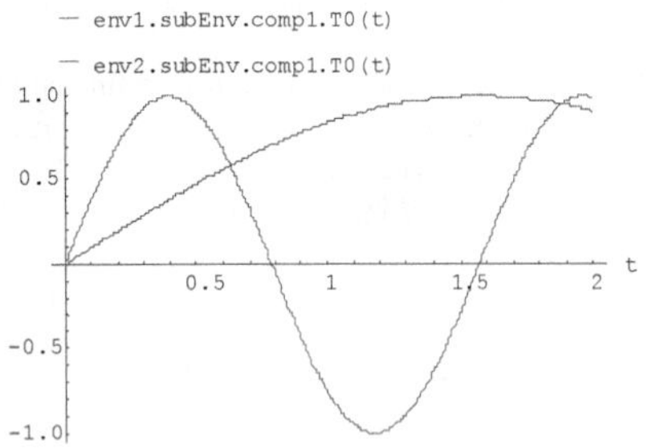

Figure 5-38. Plot of `env1.subEnv.comp1.T0` and `env2.subEnv.comp1.T0` for the two environments `env1` and `env2`, respectively, where the `T0` is propagated via `subEnv` to `comp1` and `comp2`.

The plots for the simulation of the `EnvironmentsWithSubsystem` model in Figure 5-38 are the same, as they should be, compared to the previous `EnvironmentInstances` simulation in Figure 5-34. Propagating the temperature T0 via the simultaneous `inner outer` declaration in subsystem `subEnv` to the components `comp1` and `comp2` works just as well as direct propagation to `comp1` and `comp2` in the previous example.

5.8.4 Implicit Interaction within a Gravitational Force Field

An interesting case of implicit interaction is when a force field interacts with a number of components. In some cases the exact nature of the force field is unknown when the components are described. For example, we might not know a priori whether a uniform gravity field or a central gravity field should be applied as depicted in Figure 5-39.

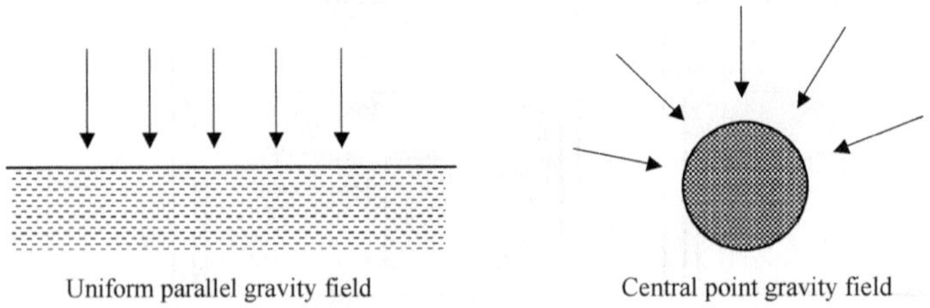

Figure 5-39. Uniform gravity field and point gravity field.

To model this situation, we start by defining a generic gravity field through the partial function `gravityInterface`, for which only the interface to the function is defined. Since the function is partial it cannot be called. Instead it is used as a superclass for other functions with the same interface, in particular the functions `uniformGravity` and `pointGravity` defined below.

```
partial function gravityInterface
  input  Real r[3] "position";
  output Real g[3] "gravity acceleration";
end gravityInterface;

function uniformGravity
  extends gravityInterface;
algorithm
  g := {0, -9.81, 0};
end uniformGravity;

function pointGravity
  extends gravityInterface;
  parameter Real k=1;
protected
   Real n[3];
algorithm
  n := -r/sqrt(r*r);
  g := k/(r*r) * n;
end pointGravity;
```

We would like to compute the position and velocity of a particle moving in a gravity field, as depicted in Figure 5-40. However, at this stage we do not yet know the exact form of the gravity field. The idea is to use the partial function `gravityInterface` as an interface for gravity fields when defining a general model of a particle moving in an unspecified gravity field.

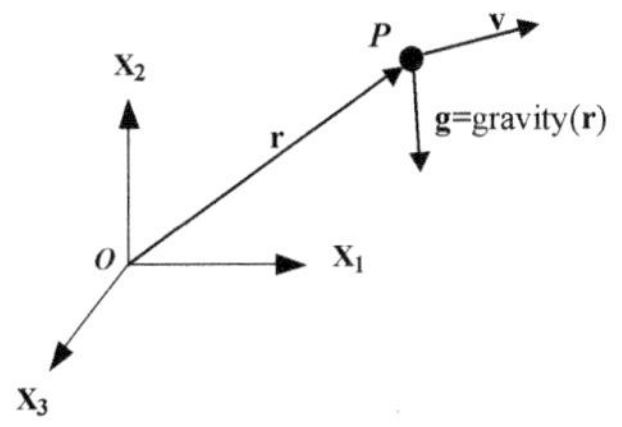

Figure 5-40. Position r, velocity v, and gravitational acceleration g for a point mass *P* with respect to a Cartesian coordinate system.

Here we can use the `inner/outer` mechanism by defining an interface function as an `outer` reference function `gravity`, being type compatible with its default `gravityInterface`, and intended to match a corresponding `inner` function definition that specifies the actual gravity field:

```
model Particle
  parameter Real m = 1;
  outer function gravity = gravityInterface;
  Real r[3](start = {1,1,0}) "position";
  Real v[3](start = {0,1,0}) "velocity";
equation
    der(r) = v;
  m*der(v) = m*gravity(r);
end Particle;
```

In the following models of a particle in a point gravity field or a uniform gravity field, we specify `inner` definitions of the `gravity` function as a `pointGravity` or a `uniformGravity` function respectively. The `outer` reference function declaration in the `Particle` model will refer to one of these `inner` definitions.

```
model ParticlesInPointGravity
```

```
  inner function gravity = pointGravity(k=1);
  Particle p1, p2(r(start={1,0,0}));
end ParticleInPointGravity;

model ParticlesInUniformGravity
  inner function gravity = uniformGravity;
  Particle p1, p2(v(start={0,0.9,0}));
end ParticleInUniformGravity;

model ParticleSystem
  ParticlesInPointGravity   pP;
  ParticlesInUniformGravity pU;
end ParticleSystem;
```

We simulate the ParticleSystem model containing two particle pairs. The pP.p1 and pP.p2 particles move in a point source gravity field whereas the pU.p1 and pU.p2 particles move in a uniform field.

```
simulate(ParticleSystem, stopTime=0.2)
```

First we show a plot of the two particles that move in a uniform field (Figure 5-41). The pU.p1 particle has a default start velocity vector of {0,1,0} specified in class Particle, whereas pU.p2 has a start velocity vector {0,0.9,0} given by the modification of p2 in the ParticlesInUniformGravity class. We can see that the particle pU.p1 with the slightly higher start velocity moves a bit farther than pU.p2 before it falls down, which is to be expected.

```
plot({pU.p1.r[2], pU.p2.r[2]} )
```

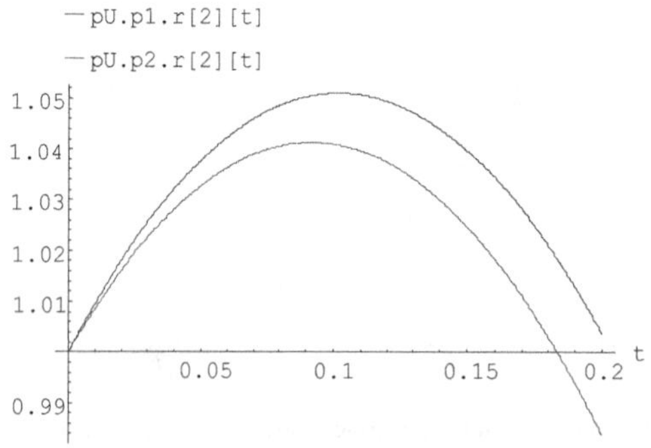

Figure 5-41. Two parabolic trajectories of particles moving in a uniform gravitational field, where the particle pU.p1 represented by the higher curve has a slightly higher initial velocity than pU.p2.

In our second simulation, we are interested in studying the two particles pP.p1 and pP.p2 moving in a central gravity field, which is typical of satellites in orbits around the earth. The simulation is during a longer time period, 25 seconds, to cover full orbital periods for the particles.

Both particles have a default start velocity vector {0,1,0} specified in the Particle class. However, they have different start positions: the r vectors are {1,1,0} and {1,0,0} for pP.p1 and pP.p2 specified in the classes Particle and ParticlesInPointGravity respectively.

We perform the simulation and show plots of the second position coordinate r[2] of both particles in Figure 5-42.

```
simulate(ParticleSystem, stopTime=25)
plot({pP.p1.r[2], pP.p2.r[2]} )
```

We can see that the particle pP.p1 has a longer orbital period than pP.p2 partly because its initial position is farther away from the gravity point source.

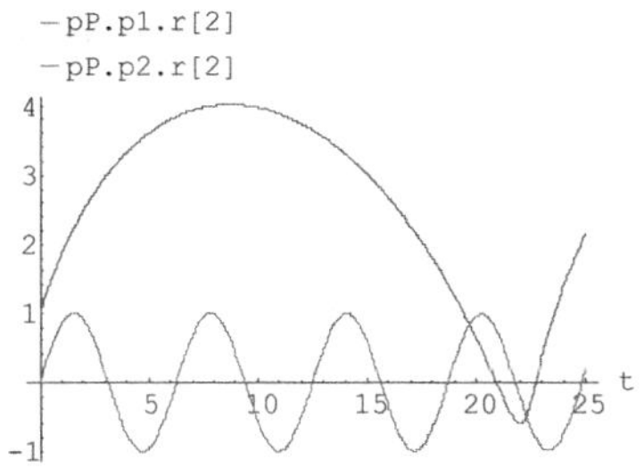

Figure 5-42. Particles moving in a central gravity field. The particle pP.p1 has a longer orbital period than pP.p2 since it initially had a position farther away from the gravity point source.

We perform parametric plots of the particle trajectories based on the x (=r[1]) and y (=r[2]) coordinates of the particles as a function of time, shown in Figure 5-43. This gives a better visual display of the shape of the trajectories than the previous plots. The time periods for the plots have been chosen to be slightly less than the orbital periods of the particles, which causes small gaps in the plotted trajectories.

```
parametricPlot({pP.p1.r[1], pP.p1.r[2]}, xrange={0,23.3})
parametricPlot({pP.p2.r[1], pP.p2.r[2]}, xrange={0,6.2})
```

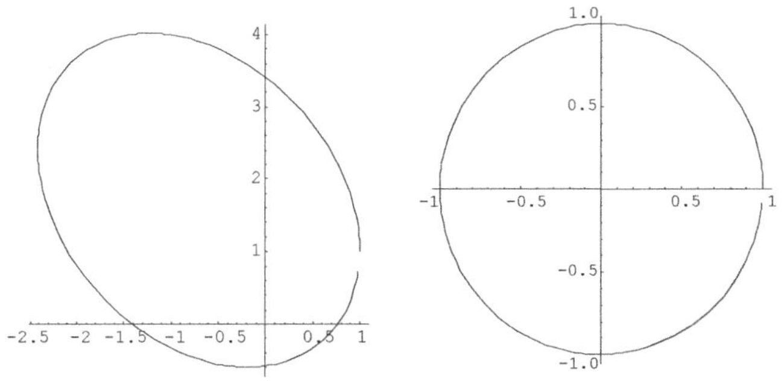

Figure 5-43. Elliptic and circular particle trajectories around a central gravitational point source for the particles pP.p1 and pP.p2 respectively.

The first particle (pP.p1) has an elliptic orbit around the central gravitational point source for two reasons: the particle's initial position {1,1,0} is a bit further away from the point source, and its initial velocity vector {0,1,0} is not perpendicular to its position vector relative the point source. However, the second particle is at the appropriate distance and has a perpendicular initial velocity vector, resulting in a circular orbit.

We conlude that implicit $1 \times n$ interaction with an unspecified force field acting on n bodies can be conveniently modeled using the inner/outer language mechanism applied to functions that represent the actual shape and type of force interaction.

5.8.5 Generating Connection Equations Involving inner/outer Connectors

Certain connectors might have been declared with one of the prefixes inner and outer, which are described in detail in Section 5.8, page 224, and in the section on reference lookup using inner and `outer` (Section 3.17.5, page 113). A connector declared as `outer` is essentially just a reference to a corresponding connector declared as `inner` higher up in the instance hierarchy.

However, recall the locality constraint on connected connectors, that both connector arguments are *hierarchically contained within the class of the current instance* (Section 5.3.2, page 191).

This constraint has implications for the interpretation of connect-equations where one or more of the arguments are connectors with the `outer` prefix. Since a connector declared as `outer` is just a reference to a corresponding `inner` connector declared higher up in the instance hierarchy, the connect-equation has to be conceptually *moved up in the instance hierarchy* until the locality constraint is fulfilled. This has to be done *before* generating the connection sets and the connection equations. To summarize:

- `outer` *objects* (that are *not* connectors) are handled by mapping the objects to the corresponding `inner` objects higher up in the instance hierarchy. (5-4)
- `outer` *connectors* are handled by mapping the connectors to the corresponding `inner` connectors. They are treated as *outside* connectors before being *moved up* since they refer to (via an `outer` reference) to a corresponding `inner` connector outside and above the current hierarchy level. (5-5)
- The mapping from an `outer` to an `inner` element must occur *before* merging the connection sets in order to get one zero-sum equation. (5-6)

A simple `LoadCircuitInnerOuter` model presented further below will be used to demonstrate generation of connection equations in conjunction with connectors and `inner/outer` matching. As a comparison, we first demonstrate generation of connection equations for almost the same model without `inner/outer`, called `LoadCircuit`.

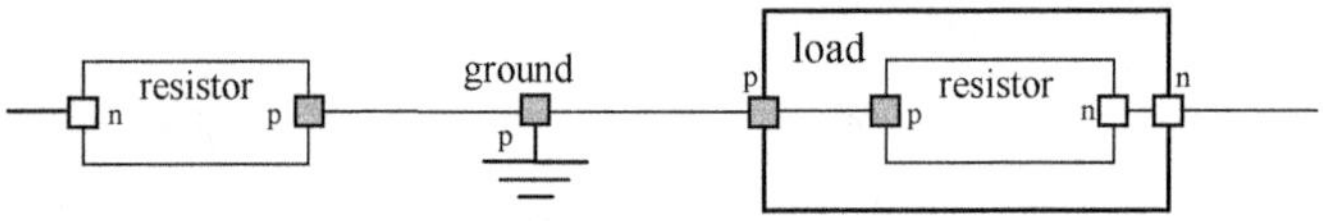

Figure 5-44. The `LoadCircuit` model without inner/outer. The `resistor.n` and the `load.n` are unconnected.

```
model Load
  extends TwoPin;  // TwoPin, Resistor are defined in Section 5.4.1, page
195
  Resistor resistor;
equation
  connect(p, resistor.p);
  connect(resistor.n, n);
end Load;

model LoadCircuit
  Ground   ground;
  Load     load;
  Resistor resistor;
equation
  connect(load.p    , ground.p);
  connect(resistor.p, ground.p);
end LoadCircuit;
```

The connection sets before merging are shown below. Note that the connector `load.n` and the connector of the resistor, `resistor.n`, are not connected to anything and thus give rise to connection sets with just one member.

```
{ (load.p.i, outside), (load.resistor.p.i, inside) }  // flow
{ (load.p.v, outside), (load.resistor.p.v, inside) }  // potential
```

```
{ (load.n.i, outside), (load.resistor.n.i, inside) }  // flow
{ (load.n.v, outside), (load.resistor.n.v, inside) }  // potential
{ (load.p.i, inside), (ground.p.i, inside) }       // flow
{ (load.p.v, inside), (ground.p.v, inside) }       // potential
{ (resistor.p.i, inside), (ground.p.i, inside) }  // flow
{ (resistor.p.v, inside), (ground.p.v, inside) }  // potential

{ (load.n.i, inside) }       // flow
{ (resistor.n.i, inside) } // flow
```

After merging, these sets are obtained:

```
{ (load.p.i, outside), (load.resistor.p.i, inside) } // flow
{ (load.p.v, outside), (load.resistor.p.v, inside) } // potential
{ (load.n.i, outside), (load.resistor.n.i, inside) } // flow
{ (load.n.v, outside), (load.resistor.n.v, inside) } // potential

{ (load.p.i, inside), (ground.p.i, inside), (resistor.p.i, inside) } // flow
{ (load.p.v, inside), (ground.p.v, inside), (resistor.p.v, inside) } //potential

{ (load.n.i, inside) }       // flow
{ (resistor.n.i, inside) } // flow
```

The following equations are generated from the sets, equality equations for potential connection sets, and sum-to-zero equations for connection sets of flow variables. Negative sign (-) is used for *outside* flow variables, whereas *inside* flow variables have positive sign (+).

```
load.p.v = load.resistor.p.v;             // potential
load.n.v = load.resistor.n.v;             // potential
load.p.v = ground.p.v;                    // potential
load.p.v = resistor.p.v;                  // potential

0 = (-load.p.i) + load.resistor.p.i;      // flow
0 = (-load.n.i) + load.resistor.n.i;      // flow
0 = load.p.i + ground.p.i + resistor.p.i;  // flow

0 = load.n.i;              // flow default equation for unconnected port
0 = resistor.n.i;          // flow default equation for unconnected port
```

The example is now changed to use `inner/outer` and renamed to `LoadCircuitInnerOuter`. The `load.resistor` has become an `outer resistor` component that is mapped to the corresponding `inner resistor` at the next level up in the instance hierarchy. This means that what is actually being connected is the `inner resistor`. We still have the unconnected connectors `inner resistor.n` and `load.n`, as well as the now unconnected `inner resistor.p` that was previously connected to `ground.p`.

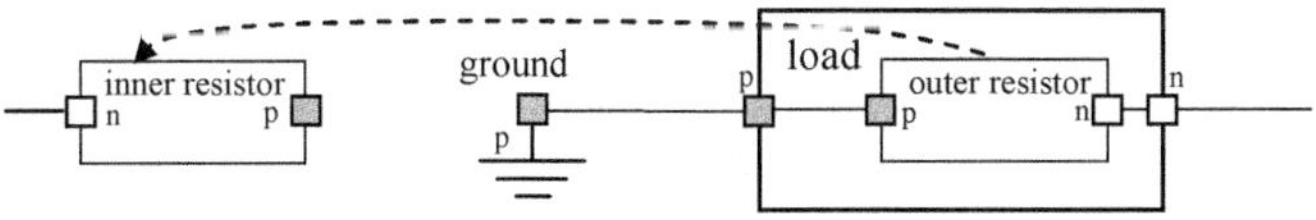

Figure 5-45. The `LoadCircuitInnerOuter` model, with an `outer resistor` hierarchically within the `load` mapped to an `inner resistor` higher up in the hierarchy, and the connection `resistor.p` to `ground.p` removed.

Below is the Modelica code for the `LoadCircuitInnerOuter` model:

```
model Load
  extends TwoPin;
  outer Resistor resistor;
equation
```

```
    connect(p, resistor.p);
    connect(resistor.n, n);
  end Load;

  model LoadCircuitInnerOuter   "Load circuit with outer mapping to inner"
    Ground ground;
    Load   load;
    inner Resistor resistor;
  equation
    connect(load.p, ground.p);
  end LoadCircuitInnerOuter;
```

The internal instance hierarchy of the `LoadCircuitInnerOuter` model is shown in Figure 5-46.

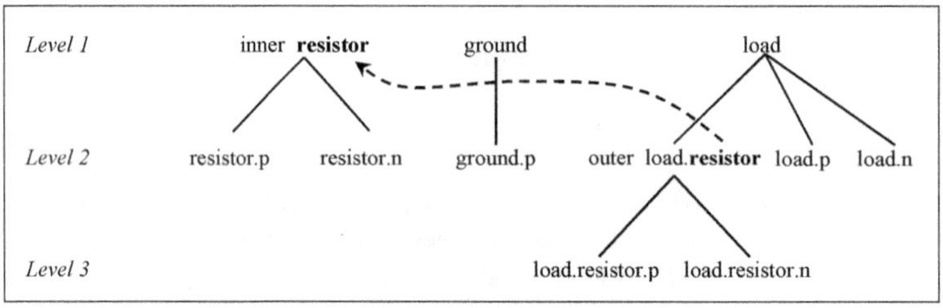

Figure 5-46. The `LoadCircuitInnerOuter` model together with its instance hierarchy. The outer resistor at Level 2 is mapped to the inner resistor at Level 1 through instance hierarchy lookup, and the previous connection of `resistor.p` to `ground.p` has been removed .

An `inner resistor` instance is first added to the instance hierarchy at Level 1 when creating an instance of the `LoadCircuitInnerOuter` model, based on the following declaration within that model:

```
inner Resistor resistor;
```

Subsequently, the `ground` and `load` instances are added at Level 1. Note that the `Load` class contains the following connect-equations:

```
connect(p, resistor.p);
connect(resistor.n, n);
```

When the `load` instance is created from `Load`, we first generate the following preliminary sets of *virtual* `outer` connections from the connected variables inside `load`. By the term *virtual*, we indicate that these connections are not the final ones, since the mapping of the `outer load.resistor` to the `inner resistor` is not yet done.

The connectors `load.resistor.p` and `load.resistor.n` are labeled *outside* because of the rule (5-5), page 234, that `outer` connectors are labeled as *outside* since they define an interface referring to something outside the current model level. The connectors `load.p` and `load.n` are *outside* since they constitute the external interface to `load`.

```
{ (load.p.v, outside),    (load.resistor.p.v, outside /* because outer */) }
{ (load.p.i, outside),    (load.resistor.p.i, outside /* because outer */) }

{ (load.resistor.n.v, outside /* because outer */),    (load.n.v,outside) }
{ (load.resistor.n.i, outside /* because outer */),    (load.n.i,outside) }
```

Via lookup in the instance hierarchy, Figure 5-46, we find the `inner resistor` corresponding to the `outer load.resistor`. Therefore the connection set is moved up from Level 2 where `load.resistor` is found to Level 1 where we find the `inner resistor`, and references to `load.resistor` are replaced by `resistor`.

At the same time the "moved up" `outer` *outside* connector references are changed to *inside* since they now refer to connectors of a component (the `inner resistor`) at the same hierarchical level and not something outside (above) the current level. We need to switch *outside* to *inside only* for `outer` components; all the other components stay the same as before, either *inside* or *outside*.

```
{ (load.p.v, outside),    (resistor.p.v, inside /* because moved up to same level */) }
{ (load.p.i, outside),    (resistor.p.i, inside /* because moved up to same level */) }

{ (resistor.n.v, inside /* because moved up to same level */),    (load.n.v, outside) }
{ (resistor.n.i, inside /* because moved up to same level */),    (load.n.i, outside) }
```

Note that *no connection sets* are generated for `load` any longer because connections involving the `outer` components and connectors in `load` do not belong in `load`! They belong to the hierarchy level of the corresponding `inner` component, and the connection set has been moved up as in the current example.

The `LoadCircuitInnerOuter` model has only one connect-equation at its own hierarchy level:

```
connect(load.p, ground.p);
```

That connect-equation generates the following two connection sets.

```
{ (load.p.v, inside), /* inside because load.p is qualified; i.e., load.p is not an external interface */
  (ground.p.v, inside)  /* inside because ground.p is qualified */ }

{ (load.p.i, inside),   /* inside because load.p is qualified */ }
  (ground.p.i, inside) /* inside because ground.p is qualified */ }
```

The connectors `load.p` and `ground.p` have qualified names so they are not interface connectors, that is, they are *inside* connectors.

Now we merge the previous connection set originating from the *virtual* outer components of the `load` instance with the local connection set inside `LoadCircuitInnerOuter` and obtain:

```
{ (load.p.v, outside),    (resistor.p.v, inside /* because moved up to same level */) }
{ (load.p.i, outside),    (resistor.p.i, inside /* because moved up to same level */) }

{ (resistor.n.v, inside /* because moved up to same level */), (load.n.v, outside) }
{ (resistor.n.i, inside /* because moved up to same level */), (load.n.i, outside) }

{ (load.p.v, inside),   /* inside because load.p is qualified */
  (ground.p.v, inside)  /* inside because ground.p is qualified */ }

{ (load.p.i, inside),   /* inside because load.p is qualified */ }
  (ground.p.i, inside) /* inside because ground.p is qualified */ }
```

Now we can generate the equations. The potential `v` stays the same as in the same connection set, the flow `i` sums to zero in the same connection set and depending on *inside/outside* has + sign for *inside* and – sign for *outside*. First the potential equations:

Set:

```
{ (load.p.v, inside),    /* inside because load.p is qualified */
  (ground.p.v, inside)   /* inside because ground.p is qualified */ }
```

Generates equation:

```
load.p.v = ground.p.v;
```

Set:

```
{ (load.p.v, outside),   /* Interface connector in Load */
  (resistor.p.v, inside)   /* outer moved one level up */ }
```

Generates equation:

```
load.p.v = resistor.p.v;
```

Set:

```
{ (resistor.n.v, inside   /* outer moved one level up */ ),
  (load.n.v, outside) /* Interface  connector in Load */ }
```

Generates equation:

```
resistor.n.v = load.n.v;
```

Then we generate the flow equations originating from the connect-equations:

Set:

```
{ (load.p.i, inside), /* inside because load.p is qualified */
  (ground.p.i, inside) /* inside because ground.p is qualified */ }
```

Generates equation:

```
load.p.i + ground.p.i = 0;
```

Set:

```
{ (load.p.i, outside), /* Interface connector in Load */
  (resistor.p.i, inside)    /* outer moved one level up  */ }
```

Generates equation:

```
(-load.p.i) + resistor.p.i = 0;
```

Set:

```
{(resistor.n.i, inside)    /* outer moved one level up */,
 (load.n.i, outside)       /* Interface connector in Load */ }
```

Generates equation:

```
(-load.n.i) + resistor.n.i = 0;
```

To summarize, in the final system of equations, the potential connection equations are:

```
load.p.v = ground.p.v;
load.p.v = resistor.p.v;
resistor.n.v = load.n.v;
```

The flow equations generated by the connections are:

```
load.p.i + ground.p.i = 0;
(-load.p.i) + resistor.p.i = 0;
(-load.n.i) + resistor.n.i = 0;
```

As a final phase we go through all the connectors, fetch the *unconnected inside flow* variables and set them to zero:

```
load.n.i = 0;
```

Remember that the basic idea of handling explicit connections to `inner/outer` connectors is that `connect`(*outerComponent*, *localConnector*); does *not* generate a connection set in the local scope, but is "*moved up*" to the corresponding *innerComponent* scope higher up in the instance hierarchy where there is an *innerComponent* with the same name as the *outerComponent*. This will generate a connection set in the *innerComponent* scope.

5.9 Expandable Connectors for Information Buses

It is common in engineering to have so-called information buses with the purpose of transporting information between various system components, e.g. sensors, actuators, control units. Some buses are even standardized (e.g., IEEE 488), but are usually rather generic to allow many kinds of different components.

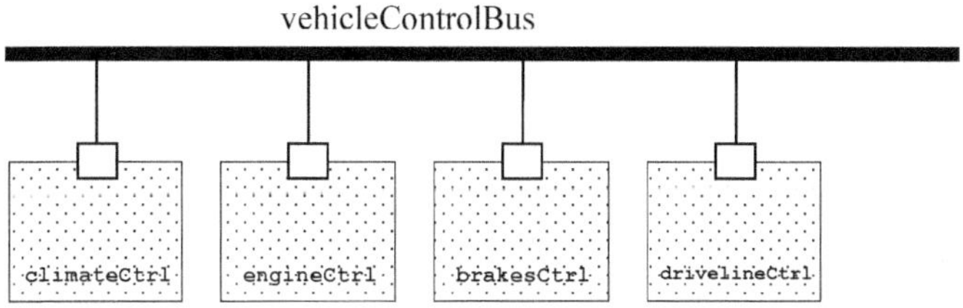

Figure 5-47. Example of a conceptual vehicle control bus, with connected components such as climate control unit, engine control, brakes control, driveline control, etc.

The main motivation behind expandable connectors is to be able to easily control complex hierarchical systems. For example, given a hierarchically structured system with many control signals—dozens, hundreds, or more. If the system is structured so that the physical components and the control components are located in different models, then an unbelievable tangle of individual connections would be needed to be carried around in the model. This would be very complex and totally unpractical. With expandable connectors it is possible to use a single data bus to carry around all the required signals through complex hierarchies.

Flexible construction of information buses is the key idea behind the `expandable connector` construct. An expandable connector acts like an information bus since it is intended for connection to many kinds of components. To make this possible it automatically expands the expandable connector type to accommodate all the components connected to it with their different interfaces. If an element with a certain name and type is not present, it is added. All variables/fields in an expandable connector are seen as connector instances even if they are not declared as such, i.e., it is possible to connect to, for example, a `Real` variable.

The syntax of an expandable connector class declaration is simple, just put the `expandable` keyword in front of the `connector` keyword:

```
expandable connector MyExpandableConnectorClass
  ...
end MyExpandableConnectorClass;
```

If the `expandable` prefix is present on a connector definition, for example, as above, all instances of that connector class are referred to as *expandable connectors*. Instances of connector classes without the `expandable` keyword are called *non-expandable connectors*.

There are two categories of connections in the context of expandable connectors:

- Connections between expandable connector instances, see Section 5.9.1 below.
- Connections between variables within expandable connector instances and other connectors or variables, for example, see Sections 5.9.2, 5.9.3, and 5.9.6.

5.9.1 Connecting Expandable Connector Instances

When two or more expandable connectors are connected, each is *augmented* with the variables that are only declared in the other expandable connector. The added new variables are neither input nor output even if the original variable has an input/output prefix.

This is repeated until all connected expandable connector instances have matching variables. The final effect is that each of the connector instances will be expanded to contain the union of all sets of variables from the declarations of the corresponding expandable connector classes. Each union set of variables without attached `input` or `output` prefixes is called an *augmentation set*. For example:

```
expandable connector Bus1
  Real x;
  Integer y;
end Bus1;

expandable connector Bus2
  Real z;
end Bus2;

expandable connector Bus3
  Real w;
end Bus3;

model CombiningBuses
  Bus1 bus1;
  Bus2 bus2;
  Bus3 bus3;
  connect(bus1, bus2);
  connect(bus2, bus3);
end CombiningBuses;
```

After the connection in the `CombiningBuses` example has been processed, `bus1`, `bus2`, and `bus3` will contain variables `x`, `y`, `z` and `w`. The corresponding so-called *augmentation sets* are as follows:

set1: {`bus1.x`, `bus2.x`, `bus3.x`}
set2: {`bus1.y`, `bus2.y`, `bus3.y`}
set3: {`bus1.z`, `bus2.z`, `bus3.z`}
set4: {`bus1.w`, `bus2.w`, `bus3.w`}

5.9.2 Connecting Simple Variables in Expandable Connectors

All variables/fields in an expandable connector are treated as connector instances even if they are not declared as such, i.e., it is possible to connect to, for example, a `Real` variable such as `speed`. For example:

```
expandable connector EngineBus   // EngineBus has predefined signals: speed,T
  import SI=Modelica.SIunits;
  SI.AngularVelocity speed;
  SI.Temperature T;
end EngineBus;

block Sensor
  RealOutput speed;
end Sensor;

model Engine
  EngineBus bus;
  Sensor sensor;
equation
  // connection to non-connector speed is possible in expandable connectors
  connect(bus.speed, sensor.speed);
end Engine;
```

5.9.3 Connecting Inputs and Non-Inputs

If a variable appears as an *input* in one expandable connector or in a component connected to it, it should appear as a *non-input* in at least one other expandable connector associated with a variable in the same augmentation set. See Section 5.9.1 for *augmentation* when connecting expandable connectors themselves, and Section 5.9.6 when connecting variables in expandable connectors. For example, in the augmentation set related to the `speed` variable, {`bus.speed`, `sensor.speed`, `actuator.speed`}, `actuator.speed` is the input and `sensor.speed` the non-input. The causality of `bus.speed`, *input* or *output*, is according to Section 5.9.6, page 242.

```
connector RealOutput = output Real;
connector RealInput = input Real;

expandable connector EngineBus  // Initially empty expandable connector
end EngineBus;

block Sensor
  RealOutput speed; // Non-input since it is an output
end Sensor;

block Actuator
  RealInput speed;  // Input
end Actuator;

model Engine
  EngineBus bus;
  Sensor sensor;
  Actuator actuator(speed=10);
equation
  connect(bus.speed, sensor.speed);    // sensor.speed provides the non-input
  connect(bus.speed, actuator.speed); // actuator.speed is the input
end Engine;
```

The `Engine` model can be simulated , with the not so surprising result that the `speed` has been propagated to the expandable connector `bus`, giving `bus.speed` the constant value 10.

```
simulate(Engine, stopTime=1)
plot(bus.speed)
```

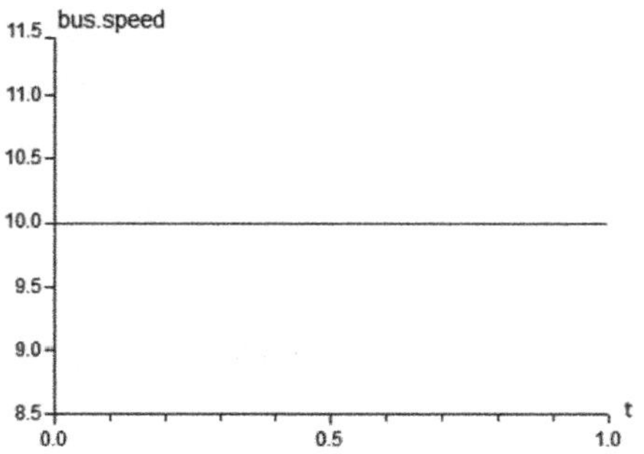

Figure 5-48. The sensor and actuator have been connected via the expandable connector `bus`, and both `actuator.speed` and `sensor.speed` are connected via that expandable connector which has expanded to include `speed`.

5.9.4 No Flow Variables Directly in Expandable Connectors

An expandable connector may not contain a variable declared with the prefix `flow`, but may contain non-expandable connectors that contain `flow` variables. For example, the connectors `p42` and `n42` in the `Battery` model are non-expandable connectors that contain flow variables:

```
import Interfaces=Modelica.Electrical.Analog.Interfaces;

expandable connector ElectricalBus
  Interfaces.PositivePin p12, n12; // OK, non-expandable connectors
  flow Modelica.SIunits.Current i; // flow variable not allowed
end ElectricalBus;

model Battery
  Interfaces.PositivePin p42, n42; // p42, n42 are non-expandable connectors
  ElectricalBus bus;
equation
  connect(p42, bus.p42); // Adds new electrical pin p42 to expandable conn
  connect(n42, bus.n42); // Adds another pin n42 to expandable connector
end Battery;
```

5.9.5 Potentially Present Variables and Restrictions

Variables that are not parameters and are declared in an expandable connector are only *potentially present*. This means that they will not be present in the final compiled model if there are no connections to them. For example, if there are no connections to any element of the vector `x` or to the scalar `y` in the example below, they will not be present in the compiled model used for simulation. The parameters `z` and `v` will however be present even if there are no connections to them.

```
expandable connector C
  Real x[:];
  Real y;
  parameter Real z;
  parameter Real v[10]
end C;
```

However, note the following restrictions:

- It is an error if there are *modifiers* for potentially present variables or array elements.
- It is an error if there are expressions referring to *potentially present* variables or array elements that are not actually present, since the expressions can only access variables from the bus that are actually declared in the connector, in order that the types of the variables can be determined in the local scope. This elaboration implies that expandable connectors can be connected even if they do not contain the same variables.

Note that the introduction of potentially present variables, as described above, is conceptual and does not necessarily impact the flattening hierarchy in any way.

5.9.6 Augmentation when Connecting Declared and Undeclared Variables

One connector of the two connectors in a connect-equation involving expandable connector(s) must reference a declared variable. The (other) undeclared variable is handled as follows:

- The expandable connector instance is automatically *augmented* with a new variable having the used *name* and corresponding *type*. For example, `connect(speed,bus1.speed)` below introduces the new variable `speed` in `bus1`.
- If the undeclared variable is subscripted, an array variable is created, and a connection to the specific array element is performed. For example, `connect(speed,bus2.speed[2])` below introduces a `speed` vector in `bus2`.
- If the variable on the other side of the connect-equation is `input` or `output` the new variable will be either `input` or `output` to satisfy the restrictions in Section 5.7.2, page 210. If the existing side

of the connect-equation refers to an *inside* connector (i.e., a connector belonging to the instance in which class the connect-equation occurs) the new variable will *copy its causality*, i.e., `input` if input and `output` if output, since the expandable connector must always be an *outside* connector. For an array the `input/output` property can be deduced separately for each array element.

If a connect-equation references a *potentially present variable* or variable element in an expandable connector, the variable or variable element is marked as being *present*, and due to the above paragraph it is possible to deduce whether the bus variable shall be treated as `input` or `output` in the connect-equation. For example:

```
expandable connector EmptyBus
end EmptyBus;

model Controller
  EmptyBus bus1;
  EmptyBus bus2;
  RealInput speed;
equation
  connect(speed, bus1.speed);                // OK, only one undeclared and it is unsubscripted
  connect(bus1.pressure, bus2.pressure);     // Not allowed, since both are undeclared
  connect(speed, bus2.speed[2]);             // introduces speed array (with element speed[2]).
end Controller;
```

After this elaboration, the expandable connectors are treated as normal connector instances, and the connections as normal connections.

All *potentially present* variables and array elements that are not actually present are undefined. A Modelica compiler may remove them or set them to their default value, for example zero for `Real` variables.

5.9.7 Issues with Modifiers, Inside/Outside, Nesting, and Protected

Furthermore, it is important to note that the elaboration/expansion rules for expandable connectors must consider the following:

- Expandable connectors which are nested hierarchically. This means that both *outside* and *inside* connectors must be included at every level of the hierarchy in the elaboration process.
- When processing an expandable connector that possesses the `inner` scope qualifier, all `outer` instances must also be taken into account during elaboration.
- A variable from a `protected` *outside* connector may *not* be an implicitly defined part of an expandable connector, see Section 5.7.2, page 210.

5.9.8 Engine System Example with Nested Buses

The following is an `EngineSystem4` model example with sensors, controllers and actuator as part of the ignition system for each cylinder, and a plant (the spark plug) that exchange information via a bus, that is, an engine bus created using expandable connectors.

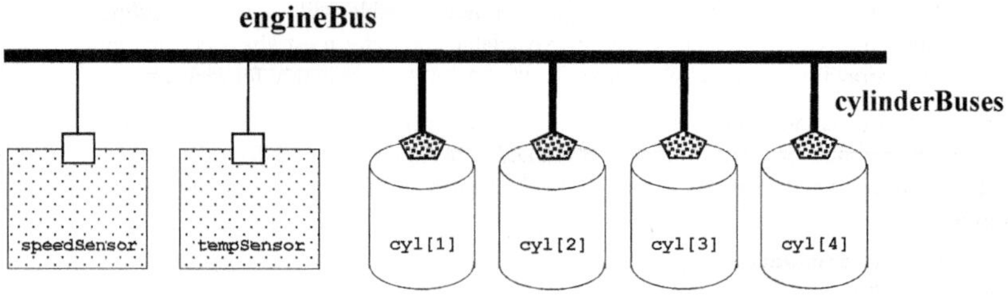

Figure 5-49. Engine system with `engineBus`, `speedSensor`, `tempSensor` and four nested cylinder buses which connect the cylinders with the `engineBus` Each cylinder contains a spark plug.

The following is the engine system model:

```
import SI=Modelica.SIunits;
import Modelica.Blocks.Interfaces.*;

// Plant Side
model SparkPlug
  Real sparkAdvance;
  ...
end SparkPlug;

expandable connector EngineBus
end EngineBus;

expandable connector CylinderBus
  Real sparkAdvance;
end CylinderBus;

model Cylinder
  CylinderBus cylinderBus;
  SparkPlug sparkPlug;
  ...
equation
  connect(sparkPlug.sparkAdvance, cylinderBus.sparkAdvance);
end Cylinder;

model EngineSystem4
  EngineBus engineBus;
  Modelica.Mechanics.Rotational.Sensors.SpeedSensor speedSensor;
  Modelica.Thermal.Sensors.TemperatureSensor tempSensor;
  parameter Integer nCylinder = 4  "Number of cylinders";
  Cylinder cyl[nCylinder];
equation
  connect(speedSensor.w, engineBus.engineSpeed);// add engineSpeed (as output)
  connect(tempSensor.T, engineBus.engineTemp);  // add engineTemp (as output)
  for i in 1:nCylinder loop                     // add cylinderBus[i] (a nested bus)
    connect(cyl[i].cylinderBus, engineBus.cylinderBus[i]);
  end for;
end EngineSystem4;
```

Due to the connections in the above model, conceptually a connector consisting of the *union of all connectors* is introduced. Thus, the `engineBus` contains the following variable declarations:

```
RealOutput engineSpeed;
RealOutput engineTemp;
CylinderBus cylinderBus[1];
CylinderBus cylinderBus[2];
```

```
CylinderBus cylinderBus[3];
CylinderBus cylinderBus[4];
```

5.10 Stream Connector Concept for Fluid Systems

Previously, we have introduced two basic variable types in a connector—potential variables and flow variables (Section 5.3.1, page 190), with associated Kirchhoff's laws (known under other names in nonelectrical domains) how to generate connection equations. This works well for a number of application domains (Section 5.5.1, page 204).

However, for some applications involving bidirectional flows of matter with associated properties the standard connector approach gives rise to problematic nonlinear systems of equations with `Boolean` unknowns for the flow directions and singularities around zero flow that so far, despite substantial efforts, have proven not possible to solve reliably. An example application in the thermohydraulic domain with such properties can be found in Figure 5-50 below.

As an example of discontinuous change, the temperature at a certain point can change discontinuously for a flowing fluid that reverses its flow direction, that is, the flow is changing continuously but it passes through zero, at some point in time to the opposite direction in an idealized model.

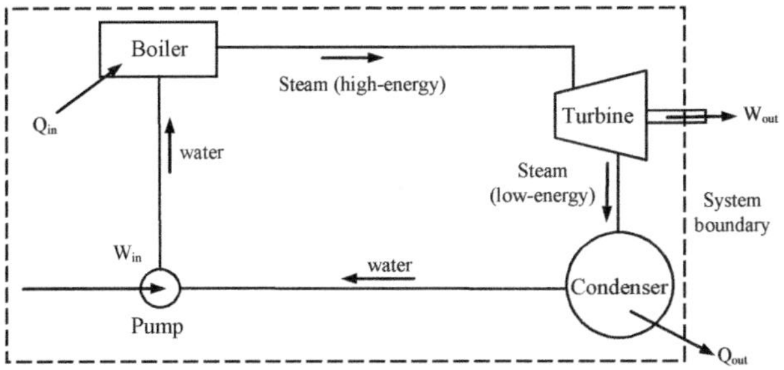

Figure 5-50. A schematic picture (not a connection diagram) of a power plant system consisting of four control volumes: `pump boiler`, `turbine`, and `condenser`. Some arrows denote flow of matter, others flow of energy.

5.10.1 Stream Variables and Operators inStream() and actualStream()

To solve the abovementioned problems, the concept of *stream connector* has been introduced in Modelica. It introduces a third kind of variable in connectors, so-called *stream variables*, in addition to flow and potential variables.

For a discussion of the background to stream connectors and comparison to the classical approach, see below (Section 5.10.3, page 247). A comprehensive example in two variants using either classical connectors or stream connectors is presented in Section 15.2, page 800.

The following three language elements are introduced for the stream connector concept:

- A prefix keyword `stream`, only used in front of *stream variables* in *stream connector* definitions (see below).
- A built-in operator `inStream(c.v)`, which when applied to a stream variable `c.v` in a stream connector `c`, returns its value close to the connection point for `c` provided that the associated mass flow is *positive* in the direction *into* the component.

- A built-in operator `actualStream(c.v)`, which when applied to a stream variable `c.v` returns its value close to the connection point for `c` regardless of the direction of the associated mass flow `c.m_flow`. It is equivalent to the expression `if c.m_flow > 0 then inStream(c.v) else c.v` where `c.v` belongs to the same connector `c` as the mass flow variable `c.m_flow`.

We define *stream connector* and *stream variable* concepts as follows:

- A *stream variable* is a variable with the `stream` prefix declared in a stream connector class.
- A *stream connector* is an instance of a stream connector class. Such a class has *at least one stream variable* and *exactly* one *flow variable* that must be a scalar, i.e., a variable with the `flow` prefix.

The idea is that the stream variables in the connector are associated with the *flow variable* which usually specifies a *mass flow*. The stream variables are used for additional properties of the flowing mass, e.g., enthalpy and chemical composition. The flowing mass is of some kind of medium, e.g., a certain kind of gas, fluid, etc., with associated medium properties. An example stream connector class definition is the `FluidPort` class from the `Modelica.Fluid` package shown below:

```
connector FluidPort
  replaceable package Medium = Modelica.Media.Interfaces.PartialMedium;
  Medium.AbsolutePressure          p           "Pressure in connection point";
  flow   Medium.MassFlowRate       m_flow      "> 0, if flow into component";
  stream Medium.SpecificEnthalpy h_outflow   "h close to port if m_flow<0";
  stream Medium.MassFraction       X_outflow[Medium.nX] "X close to port if m_flow<0";
end FluidPort;
```

`FluidPort` is a stream connector class, because some connector variables have the `stream` prefix. The `Medium` definition and the stream variables are associated with the only flow variable (`m_flow`) that defines a fluid stream. The `Medium` mass flow and the stream variables (i.e., the properties they represent) are transported with this flow variable.

The stream variables `h_outflow` (specific enthalpy flow) and `X_outflow` (mass fraction flow for medium number `nX`) are the *stream properties* inside the component close to the component boundary at the connection point, assuming that matter flows *out* of the component into the connection point/volume. In other words, it is the value the carried quantity/property *would* have if the fluid was flowing out of the connector, irrespective of the actual flow direction. One can also say that a stream variable describes a quantity that is carried by a flow variable, i.e., a mass flow transport phenomenon where the quantities of the stream variables are carried by the mass flow.

As mentioned, the stream properties for the opposite flow direction, that is, *into* the component, can be inquired using the built-in operator `inStream()`.

For example, in Figure 5-51, the three stream connectors `c1`, `c2`, and `c3` are connected via a small triangular control volume (Section 5.10.2) where mass flows are mixed. Then the stream property specific enthalpy for the connector `c2` can be computed by `inStream(c2.h_outflow)` according to the above definition since there is positive mass flow from the control volume into the connector `c2`. For the connectors `c1` and `c2`, the values of the specific enthalpy are given by `c1.h_outflow` and `c2.h_outflow` since the mass flows are in the negative direction out of the components.

Regardless of the flow direction, the value of the stream variable corresponding to the actual flow direction can be inquired through the built-in operator `actualStream()`, however, see Section 5.10.4.4, page 254, for advice regarding its usage.

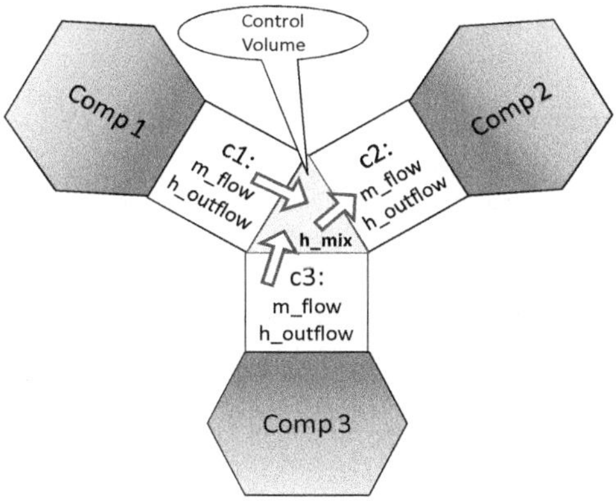

Figure 5-51. Three stream connectors `c1`, `c2`, and `c3` connected together via an infinitesimally small control volume. The flow is out of the components `Comp1` and `Comp3`, and *into* the component `Comp2`. Thus, the stream variable value can be obtained by `inStream(c2.h_outflow)` for connector `c2`, and by `c1.h_outflow` and `c2.h_outflow` for `c1` and `c2` respectively.

5.10.2 Control Volumes and Basic Thermodynamics

Thermodynamics is a part of natural science in which the storage of energy, the transformation of energy between different forms, and the transfer of energy (and mass) between subsystems is studied. For more details see Section 14.7.1, page 759. One of the primary energy forms dealt with in thermodynamics is *thermal energy*. Mass flows and transformation and transfer of energy are often part of thermodynamic models. In thermodynamics we speak about thermodynamic *systems*, their *surroundings*, and *control volumes* embedded in systems, as depicted in an abstract way in Figure 5-52 below.

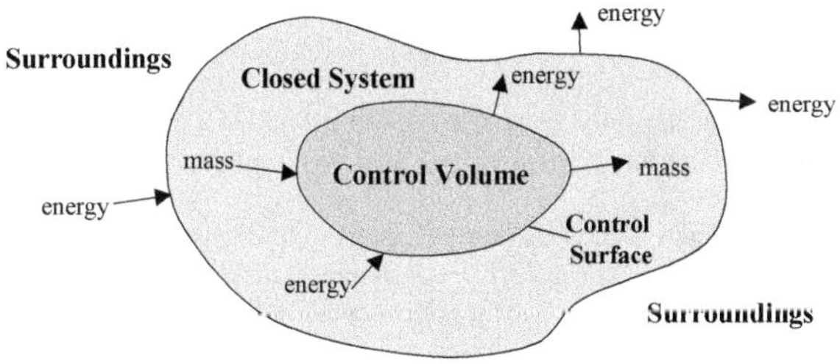

Figure 5-52. A control volume allows transfer of energy and mass across its boundaries, whereas a closed system contains a definite quantity of matter and only allows energy transfer to and from its surroundings.

Basic laws regarding conservation of mass and energy hold for control volumes, see Section 14.7.5.4, page 766. Only energy is allowed to cross the boundaries of a *closed system*, whereas both mass and energy can cross the boundaries of a *control volume*.

5.10.3 Classical Fluid Connectors and their Problems

In Section 15.2.5.1, page 811, we introduce a classical style mass flow connector based on potential and flow variables. For this we need a connector class containing the variables that describe interaction at the *mass flow* inlets and outlets of the control volume. In that same section we also discuss a version of that model with stream connectors.

5.10.3.1 Basic Fluid Connectors

Not only *mass* is flowing, the flowing substance also has some *energy* content represented by its *enthalpy*. Moreover, the *pressure* influences the interactions of the flowing substance at the inlets and outlets. Therefore the following variables need to be included in the interface:

- *Mass flow* rate $\dot{m}$, represented by the Modelica variable `m_flow`.
- *Specific enthalpy* h, a measure of the energy content per mass unit in the substance, represented by the Modelica variable `h`, see also Section 14.7.5.2, page 764.
- *Pressure* P, represented by the Modelica variable `P`.

The first attempt at a corresponding connector class for mass flow, called `FlowConnector`, appears as follows, but is unfortunately unbalanced with two acausal potential variables and one flow variable:

```
connector FlowConnector   "Unbalanced flow connector, illegal!"
  import Modelica.SIunits.*;
  Pressure              P;
  SpecificEnthalpy      h;
  flow MassFlowRate     m_flow;
end FlowConnector;
```

We can make it balanced by splitting it into two connector classes, for inflow and outflow respectively:

```
connector FlowConnectorIn "connector with incoming flow"
  import Modelica.SIunits.*;
  Pressure P;
  input SpecificEnthalpy  h;
  flow MassFlowRate       m_flow(min = 0);
end FlowConnector;

connector FlowConnectorOut "connector with outgoing flow"
  import Modelica.SIunits.*;
  Pressure P;
  output SpecificEnthalpy h;
  flow MassFlowRate       m_flow(max = 0);
end FlowConnector;
```

However, here is a limitation in that you can only have one `FlowConnectorOut` connector in a connection set, that is, one outflow can fan out into several inputs, but several outflows at a connection point cannot mix.

The application model in Section 15.2.6, page 825, is also further prepared for thermal interaction with its environment using a connector class from the `Modelica.Thermal` library. This connector is for purely thermal interaction between components without a convective mass flow and is defined as:

```
connector HeatPort "Thermal port for 1-dim. heat transfer"
  import Modelica.SIunits;
  SIunits.Temperature         T       "Port temperature";
  flow SIunits.HeatFlowRate   Q_flow  "Heat flow rate (positive if flowing"+
                                      "from outside into the component)";
end HeatPort;
```

Classical connectors such as the `FlowConnectorIn` and `FlowConnectorOut` can work for models of simple systems, which do not allow arbitrary connections, sometimes avoids mass flows as in the above `HeatPort`, and do not involve reverting flows (i.e., changing flow direction).

5.10.3.2 Requirements on a General Fluid Library vs. Previous Approaches

For a long time there has been work in the Modelica community to create a general easy-to-use fluid modeling library that fulfills the following conditions:

- Single definition of one general fluid connector class.
- Intuitive semantics for hierarchical, device oriented modeling, for example, the outer connectors of a functional unit model (e.g., a steam generator) should correspond to physical flanges of the unit.
- Numerical robustness at zero and reversing flows.
- Arbitrary connections between multiple fluid connectors should be possible; automatically generated connection equations represent idealized flow junctions.

No fluid library before the introduction of stream connectors fulfills these conditions. First we take a look at the ThermoPower library from 2003. It provides rather robust signal-oriented fluid modeling. Its connector has the following definition; there is also a corresponding `FluidPort_SignalB` variant:

```
connector FluidPort_SignalA
  import SI = Modelica.SIunits;
  SI.Pressure                p;
  flow SI.MassFlowRate       m_flow;
  input SI.SpecificEnthalpy  hBA;
  output SI.SpecificEnthalpy hAB;
end FluidPort_SignalA;

connector FluidPort_SignalB
  import SI = Modelica.SIunits;
  SI.Pressure                p;
  flow SI.MassFlowRate       m_flow;
  output SI.SpecificEnthalpy hBA;
  input SI.SpecificEnthalpy  hAB;
end FluidPort_SignalA;
```

However, the use of signals for physical modeling restricts the connection semantics and complicates the device-oriented modeling of fluid systems. Another approach is used in an early version (2003) of the Modelica_Fluid library where transported quantities such as specific enthalpy are modeled as potential variables, complemented by an enthalpy flow rate variable as in the following connector class:

```
connector FluidPort_Potential
  import SI = Modelica.SIunits;
  SI.Pressure               p;
  flow SI.MassFlowRate      m_flow;
  SI.SpecificEnthalpy       h_mix;
  flow SI.EnthalpyFlowRate H_flow;
end FluidPort_Potential;
```

This does not have restrictions of connecting components together as in the signal-oriented approach. However, there are problems with the mixing enthalpy `h_mix` in solving the resulting connection equations for the control volume, as we shall soon see.

5.10.3.3 Mixing Enthalpy in Connector Definitions Gives Unstable Solutions

In order to illustrate the problems with the classical approach with a common mixing enthalpy `h_mix` in solving the resulting connection equations for the control volume, we consider a connection set with n connectors which can be regarded as a very small mixing control volume for matter entering and exiting that volume. An example with three connected components is shown in Figure 5-53 below. The specific enthalpy `h_mix` from the above `FluidPort_Potential` connector class is the mixing enthalpy for arbitrary flow directions in this control volume.

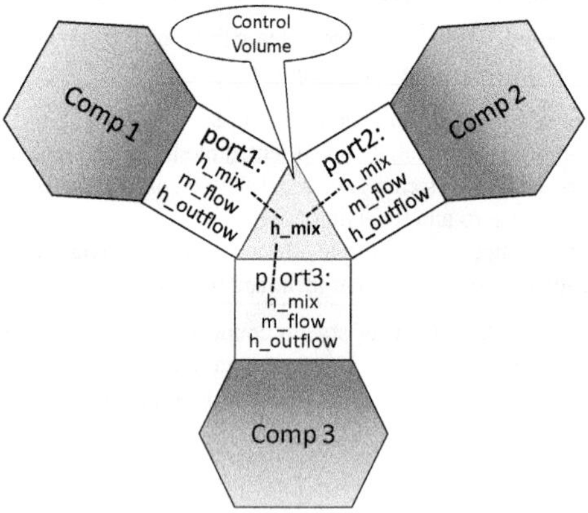

Figure 5-53. Example connection set with three connected components and a *common* mixing enthalpy for *all flow directions* using the classical approach, which in the general case gives rise to numerical problems during simulation due to discontinuous residual equations with reversing flows.

The mass balance equation (5-7) and the energy balance (5-8) follow from the Modelica connection semantics for the flow variables `m_flow` ($\dot{m}_j$) and `H_flow` ($\dot{H}_j$). The mixing enthalpy h_{mix} can be obtained by solving the equation system containing equations (5-7), (5-8), and (5-9).

$$0 = \sum_{j=1...n} \dot{m}_j \tag{5-7}$$

The energy balance where enthalpy flows $\dot{H}_j$ are summed to zero:

$$0 = \sum_{j=1...n} \dot{H}_j \tag{5-8}$$

Each enthalpy flow is defined depending on the mass flow direction, positive or negative:

$$\dot{H}_j = \dot{m}_j \begin{cases} h_{mix} & \text{if} \quad \dot{m}_j > 0 \\ h_{outflow\,j} & \text{if} \quad \dot{m}_j \le 0 \end{cases} \tag{5-9}$$

Here, mass flow rates $\dot{m}_i$ are *positive* for flow *entering* models, that is, exiting the connection set for the infinitesimally small control volume. Since the flow in that case is from the control volume into the component, the mixing enthalpy h_{mix} defined for that control volume is used.

The other case, $\dot{m}_j \le 0$ represents *outflow* from the component, using the specific enthalpy $h_{outflow}$ that represents the specific enthalpy inside the component close to the connector boundary.

Expressed with variables used in the balance equations we arrive at

$$h_{outflow,j} = \begin{cases} \dfrac{\dot{H}_j}{\dot{m}_j} & \text{if} \quad \dot{m}_j < 0 \\ \text{arbitrary} & \text{if} \quad \dot{m}_j \ge 0 \end{cases} \tag{5-10}$$

While these equations are suitable for device-oriented and signal oriented modeling, the straightforward usage of this definition leads to models with *discontinuous residual equations*, which violates the prerequisites of several solvers for nonlinear equation systems.

This is the *reason* why the actual mixing enthalpy should *not* be modeled directly in the model equations. The stream connectors provide a suitable alternative.

5.10.4 Usage of Stream Connectors

Stream connectors are used extensively, for example in the Modelica.Fluid library that has been included in the Modelica Standard Library starting from version 3.1. In that library, stream connectors are used to model the convective transport of energy and substances. Generally, Modelica.Fluid provides interfaces and basic components for the device-oriented modeling of one-dimensional thermo-fluid flow in networks containing vessels, pipes, fluid machines, valves, and fittings. The medium models are treated separately in Modelica.Media.

Thermo-fluid models are built from model components each representing a control volume. There are two basic kinds of such models:

- *Volume models* that define the thermodynamic state for a lumped medium, i.e., in a lumped medium the medium state is approximated by a single value, thus ignoring its physical distribution.
- *Transport or flow models* that serve to connect volume models.

Such models do not define their own thermodynamic state. Instead they define the transport of fluid for thermodynamic states given at their ports. Multiple volume and transport models can be assembled to build component models hierarchically. The following examples use the `FluidPort` connector definition:

```
connector FluidPort = Modelica.Fluid.Interfaces.FluidPort;

connector FluidPort  // from MSL 3.2.1 Modelica.Fluid.Interfaces.FluidPort
  "Interface for quasi one-dimensional fluid flow in a piping network
   (incompressible or compress, one or more phases, one or more substances)"
  replaceable package Medium = Modelica.Media.Interfaces.PartialMedium
    "Medium model"
  flow Medium.MassFlowRate     m_flow
    "Mass flow rate from the connection point into the component";
  Medium.AbsolutePressure  p "Thermodynamic pressure in the connection point";
  stream Medium.SpecificEnthalpy h_outflow
    "Specific thermodynamic enthalpy close to the connection point if m_flow<0";
  stream Medium.MassFraction    Xi_outflow[Medium.nXi]
    "Independent mixture mass fractions m_i/m close to the connection point
     if m_flow < 0";
  stream Medium.ExtraProperty  C_outflow[Medium.nC]
    "Properties c_i/m close to the connection point if m_flow < 0";
end FluidPort;
```

5.10.4.1 Volume Model with actualStream()

A basic example model of an ideally mixed lumped volume is defined below:

```
model Volume "Generic Lumped volume, e.g. vessel"
  replaceable package Medium = Modelica.Media.Interfaces.PartialMedium;
  parameter Integer                   nPorts=0 "Number of ports";
  Modelica.Fluid.Interfaces.FluidPort[nPorts] ports;
  parameter Modelica.SIunits.Volume   V "Volume of device";
  Modelica.SIunits.Mass               m(start=0.01) "Mass in device";
  Modelica.SIunits.Energy             U "Inner energy in device";
  Medium.BaseProperties               medium;
equation
  // Definition of port variables
  for i in 1:nPorts loop
    ports[i].p = medium.p;
    ports[i].h_outflow = medium.h;
  end for;
  // Mass and energy balance
  m = V*medium.d;
  U = m*medium.u;
```

```
  der(m) = sum(ports.m_flow);
  der(U) = ports.m_flow*actualStream(ports.h_outflow);
end Volume;

// The generic volume specialized to a constant incompressible
// liquid water medium
model WaterVolumeConstant = Volume(nPorts=1, V = 1e-3,
                Medium = Modelica.Media.Water.ConstantPropertyLiquidWater);
```

We try to simulate the model with an incompressible constant water medium:

```
simulate(WaterVolumeConstant, endTime=1);
```

However, a Modelica compiler typically will give the message:

```
"The model is structurally singular …"
```

The reason is that `ConstantPropertyLiquidWater.BaseProperties` has constant density which means that `m` is constant, thus `der(m)` is identically zero. Therefore the mass balance equation `der(m) = sum(ports.m_flow)` becomes `0 = 0`, which of course is singular.

If we instead use a compressible medium model, e.g., `Modelica.Media.CompressibleLiquids.LinearColdWater`, as in the model below, simulation works fine.

```
// The generic volume specialized to a compressible liquid water medium
model WaterVolumeCompressible = Volume(nPorts=1, V = 0.001,
    redeclare Medium = Modelica.Media.CompressibleLiquids.LinearColdWater);
```

A simulation of `WaterVolumeCompressible` is shown below:

```
simulate(WaterVolumeCompressible,endTime=1);
plot({medium.p,medium.T})
```

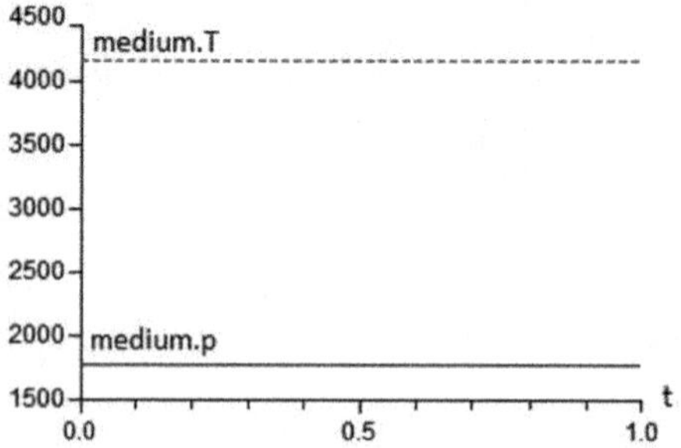

Figure 5-54. Simulation of `WaterVolumeCompressible` with plot of pressure `medium.p` and temperature `medium.T`.

However, despite the above problems with the `WaterVolumeConstant` model, the problem is not the model itself, nor the `ConstantPropertyLiquidWater` medium. If this volume is connected to, for example, a flow source on one port, a valve on the other port, it would simulate. The problem is that if an insulated stand-alone volume is desired a compressible fluid model is needed, otherwise the mass balance equation becomes singular. In other words, if the fluid is compressible, then the value of the mass allows determining the pressure from the equations, but if it is incompressible, the pressure remains undetermined.

In principle, the volume model can be used with an arbitrary medium model out of `Modelica.Media`. The mass balance and the energy balance sum up the contribution of flows going through `nPorts` fluid ports.

Alternatively, the volume model could be defined with only one fluid port as multiple connections can be made to it. Then, however, ideal mixing would take place in the port outside the volume. Using unary connections to multiple ports ensures that the mixing takes place inside the volume. This is the generally intended behavior for multi-way connections to a volume. Nonlinear systems of mixing equations are avoided.

The `actualStream()` operator used to define the energy balance is a shorthand notation for:

```
actualStream(port.h_outflow) ==
  if port.m_flow > 0 then inStream(port.h_outflow) else port.h_outflow;
```

Note that with stream variables the `Boolean` unknown for the flow direction appears in the energy balance, where the flow dependent value of the specific enthalpy is multiplied with the mass flow rate. This is why a reversing flow, that is, `m_flow` crossing zero, does not cause jumping values in the model equations.

5.10.4.2 IsoenthalpicFlow Transport Model with inStream()

The flows are defined with transport models. A basic model for isenthalpic flow, that is, with fixed enthalpy, is given below:

```
model IsoenthalpicFlow  "Flow model without storage of mass or energy,
                         e.g. a fitting or valve"
  replaceable package Medium = Modelica.Media.Interfaces.PartialMedium;
  FluidPort                      port_a, port_b:
  Medium.ThermodynamicState  state_a  "State at port_a if inflowing";
  Medium.ThermodynamicState  state_b  "State at port_b if inflowing";
equation
 // Medium states for inflowing fluid
  state_a = Medium.setState_phX(port_a.p, inStream(port_a.h_outflow));
  state_b = Medium.setState_phX(port_b.p, inStream(port_b.h_outflow));

 // Mass balance
  0 = port_a.m_flow + port_b.m_flow;

 // Isoenthalpic energy balance
  port_a.h_outflow = Medium.specificEnthalpy(state_b);
  port_b.h_outflow = Medium.specificEnthalpy(state_a);

 // (Regularized) Momentum balance
  port_a.m_flow = f(port_a.p, port_b.p, Medium.density(state_a),
    Medium.density(state_b));
end IsoenthalpicFlow;
```

The flow model does not define own thermodynamic states as it has no storage of mass or energy. Instead, the mass flow rate is defined for thermodynamic states seen through the ports for the case of inflow.

These are generally the (transformed) states defined by connected volume models. The flow model defines steady-state mass, energy, and momentum balances. The function `f` gives the relationship between pressure drop and mass flow rate.

The use of the `ThermodynamicState` records `state_a` and `state_b` also ensures that appropriate equation systems are generated by a Modelica tool for medium models that do not use pressure and enthalpy as independent variables, such as gas models often using pressure and temperature instead.

5.10.4.3 TemperatureSensor Model with inStream()

Ideal sensor models are used to pick up fluid properties, such as temperatures. They do not contribute to the fluid flow. A basic model for a temperature sensor is given below.

```
model TemperatureSensor  "Ideal temperature sensor"
  replaceable package Medium = Modelica.Media.Interfaces.PartialMedium;
```

```
  FluidPort  port(m_flow(min=0)) "Port with no outflow ever since min=0";
  Modelica.Blocks.Interfaces.RealOutput T "Upstream temperature";
equation
  T = Medium.temperature(Medium.setState_phX(port.p,
        inStream(port.h_outflow));
  port.m_flow = 0;
  port.h_outflow = Medium.specificEnthalpy(Medium.setState_pTX(
    Medium.reference_p,Medium.reference_T));
end TemperatureSensor;
```

The mass flow rate in the port is defined to be nonnegative with its min value set to 0. This tells the translation tool that the outflow enthalpy defined by the sensor must not be used in any mixing equations, as outflow never happens; see also Figure 5-57, page 262, showing an attached sensor.

5.10.4.4 Operator actualStream—Definition and Usage

The `actualStream(v)` operator is provided for convenience, in order to return the actual value of the stream variable, depending on the actual flow direction. The only argument of this built-in operator needs to be a *reference to a stream variable*. The operator is vectorizable, in the case of vector arguments. For the following definition it is assumed that an (inside or outside) connector `c` contains a stream variable `h_outflow` which is associated with a flow variable `m_flow` in the same connector `c`:

```
actualStream(port.h_outflow) =
  if port.m_flow > 0 then inStream(port.h_outflow) else port.h_outflow;
```

The `actualStream`(v) operator is typically used in two contexts:

```
der(U)  = c.m_flow*actualStream(c.h_outflow);     // Energy balance            (5-11)

h_port  = actualStream(port.h);         // Monitoring the enthalpy at a port   (5-12)
```

In the case of equation (5-11), although the `actualStream()` operator is discontinuous by construction when the flow is zero, the product with the flow variable is not. Therefore, a tool might infer that the expression is `smooth`(0, ...) automatically, and decide whether or not to generate an event. If a user wants to avoid events entirely, he/she may enclose the right-hand side of (5-11) with the `noEvent`() operator.

Equations like (5-12) might be used for monitoring purposes (e.g. plots), in order to inspect what the "actual" enthalpy of the fluid flowing through a port is. In this case, the user will probably want to see the change due to flow reversal at the exact instant, so an event should be generated.

If the user does not bother, then he/she should enclose the right-hand side of (5-12) with `noEvent`(). Since the output of `actualStream`() will be discontinuous, it should *not be used* by itself to model physical behavior, for example, to compute densities used in momentum balances. Instead, `inStream`() should be used for that purpose. The operator `actualStream`() should be used to model physical behavior only when multiplied by the corresponding flow variable, like in the above energy balance equation, because this removes the discontinuity.

5.10.5 Generating Connection Equations for Stream Connectors

If at least one variable in a connector has the `stream` prefix, the connector is called *stream connector* and the corresponding variable is called *stream variable*. The following definitions hold:

- For every *outside* connector, Section 5.7.1, page 208, one equation is generated for every variable with the `stream` prefix in order to describe the propagation of the stream variable along a model hierarchy. For the exact definition, see Section 5.10.7, page 257.
- For *inside* connectors, Section 5.7.1, page 208, variables with the `stream` prefix do not lead to connection equations.

- *Connection equations* with stream variables are generated in a model when using the `inStream()` operator, Section 5.10.6, page 255, or the `actualStream()` operator, see Section 5.10.4.4, page 254.

5.10.6 Generation of inStream() Connection Equations for Inside/Outside

This section describes the generation of connection equations of `inStream()` for hierarchical *inside/outside* connections involving stream connectors. The definitions below are only for the *inside/outside* interaction, and are dependent on the equation-based definition of `inStream()` described in Section 5.10.7, page 257.

As already mentioned, in combination with the stream variables of a connector, the `inStream()` operator is designed to describe the bi-directional transport of specific quantities carried by a flow of matter in a way that makes the solution of resulting equations numerically stable.

The operator `inStream(v)` is only allowed to be used on stream variables, i.e., variables with the `stream` prefix, and is informally the flow value of the stream variable assuming that the flow is from the connection point *into* the component. This value is computed from the stream connection equations of the flow variables and of the stream variables.

For the following definition of `inStream()` it is assumed that we have `3` inside connectors m_j`.c` `(j=1,2,3)` which can be generalized to `N` connectors for the general case, and `2` outside connectors c_k `(k=1,2)` which can be generalized to `M` connectors. These belong to the same connection set and are connected together. A stream variable `h_outflow` is associated with a flow variable `m_flow` in the connector `c`.

See also the definition of *connection set*, Section 5.7.8.1, page 219, as a set of variables connected by means of connect-equations, containing either only flow variables or only potential variables.

```
connector FluidPort
  flow   Real m_flow     "Flow of matter; m_flow > 0 if flow into component";
  stream Real h_outflow "Specific variable in component if m_flow < 0"
end FluidPort

model FluidSystem
  FluidComponent m1, m2, m3;
  FluidPort      c1, c2, c3;
equation
  connect(m1.c, m2.c);
  connect(m1.c, m3.c);
  connect(m1.c, c1);
  connect(m1.c, c2);
end FluidSystem;
```

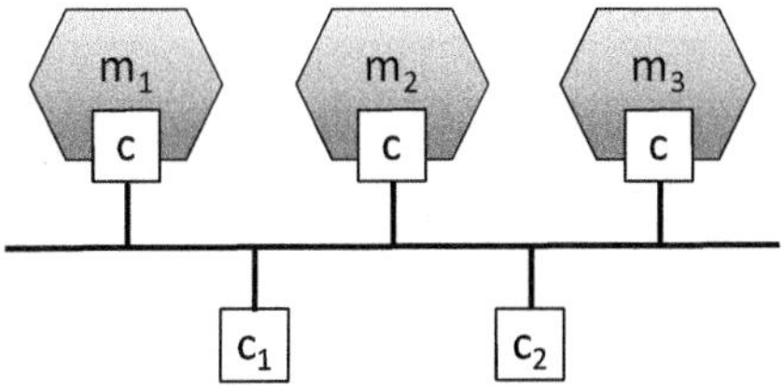

Figure 5-55. Example `FluidSystem` model with three (N=3) inside connectors m_1.c, m_2.c, m_3.c and two (M=2) outside connectors c_1 and c_2.

The connection set represents an infinitesimally small control volume, for which the stream connection equations are equivalent to the mass and energy balance equations.

With these prerequisites, the semantics of the expression `inStream(m_i.c.h_outflow)` is given implicitly by defining an additional variable `h_mix_in_i`, and by adding to the model the conservation equations for mass and energy corresponding to the infinitesimally small volume spanning the connection set. The connection equation for the flow variables has already been added to the system according to the standard connection semantics of flow variables, that is, the sum of all flows into a point are summed to zero, as defined in Section 5.7.8.5, page 222.

Thus, the standard connection equation for flow variables is generated as follows for `N` inside connectors and `M` outside connectors (Figure 5-55):

```
0 = sum(m_j.c.m_flow for j in 1:N) + sum(-c_k.m_flow for k in 1:M);
```

Whenever the `inStream()` operator is applied to a stream variable of an inside connector, the balance equation of the *transported property* must be added under the assumption of flow going into the connector.

The implicit definition below of the `inStream()` operator corresponds to the balance equation of the transported quantity at the connection point, where for example the transported quantity can be energy for the specific enthalpy stream variables or mass of single chemical components for composition stream variables.

The following is an *implicit definition* of the `inStream()` operator applied to the inside connector `i`:

```
0 = sum(m_j.c.m_flow*(if m_j.c.m_flow > 0 or j==i then h_mix_in_i else
       m_j.c.h_outflow) for j in 1:N) +
    sum(-c_k.m_flow* (if -c_k.m_flow > 0 then h_mix_in_i else
       inStream(c_k.h_outflow) for k in 1:M);

inStream(m_i.c.h_outflow) = h_mix_in_i;
```

Note that the result of the `inStream(m_i.c.h_outflow)` operator is different for each port `i`, because the assumption of flow entering the port is different for each port.

Additional implicit equations need to be generated for the stream variables of *outside* connectors:

```
for q in 1:M loop // Additional implicit connection equations for outside
  0 = sum(m_j.c.m_flow*(if m_j.c.m_flow > 0 then h_mix_out_q else m_j.c.h_outflow)
        for j in 1:N) +
          sum(-c_k.m_flow *(if -c_k.m_flow > 0 or k==q then h_mix_out_q else
            inStream(c_k.h_outflow) for k in 1:M);
  c_q.h_outflow = h_mix_out_q;
end for;
```

Neglecting zero flow conditions, the *solution* of the above-defined implicit *stream connection equations* for `inStream` values of *inside* connectors and *outflow* stream variables of *outside* connectors is the following (for a derivation, see Section 5.10.7, page 257).

The solution equation is a mixing rule that only weights in flows entering the connection point, i.e., negative flows from the point of view of inside connectors and positive flows from the point of view of outside connectors, and assumes that the flow is entering the connector to which `inStream()` is applied.

```
inStream(m_i.c.h_outflow) :=
         (sum(max(-m_j.c.m_flow,0)*m_j.c.h_outflow for j in cat(1,1:i-1, i+1:N)
          + sum(max( c_k.m_flow,0)*inStream(c_k.h_outflow) for k in 1:M))/
            (sum(max(-m_j.c.m_flow,0) for j in cat(1,1:i-1, i+1:N)
          + sum(max( c_k.m_flow  ,0) for k in 1:M));
```

Additional explicit solution equations to be generated for outside connectors `q`:

```
for q in 1:M loop
   c_q.h_outflow :=
         (sum(max(-m_j.c.m_flow,0)* m_j.c.h_outflow for j in 1:N)
          + sum(max(c_k.m_flow,0)*inStream(c_k.h_outflow) for k
              in cat(1,1:q-1, q+1:M))/(sum(max(-m_j.c.m_flow,0) for j in 1:N)
```

```
            + sum(max( ck.m_flow  ,0) for k in cat(1,1:q-1, q+1:M)));
end for;
```

Note that `inStream(ck.h_outflow)` is computed from the connection set that is present one hierarchical level above. At this higher level `ck.h_outflow` is no longer an outside connector, but an inside connector and then the formula from above for inside connectors can be used to compute it.

If the argument of `inStream()` is an array, the implicit equation system holds element-wise, i.e., `inStream()` is vectorizable.

Note that the stream connection equations have singularities and/or multiple solutions if one or more of the flow variables become zero. See Section 5.10.7, page 257 below, regarding how equations are handled in that case.

5.10.7 Definition of inStream() Using Basic Equations

Here we describe in detail how the uses of `inStream()` can be defined in terms of generated "normal" basic equations, in the context of a general connection, see Figure 5-55, with N inside and M outside connectors. This section can be skipped by the reader who is mainly interested in application modeling. The mathematical derivation for the general case is presented further below in Section 5.10.8, page 259, and in Section 5.10.9, page 261, for some special cases.

Remember that the solution equation for `inStream()` below is a mixing rule that only weights in flows entering the connection point, i.e., negative flows from the point of view of inside connectors and positive flows from the point of view of outside connectors, and assumes that the flow is entering the connector to which `inStream()` is applied.

The stream connection equations have singularities and/or multiple solutions if one or more of the flow variables become zero. When all the flows are zero, a singularity is always present, so it is necessary to approximate the solution in an open neighborhood of that point. For example assume that `mj.c.m_flow = ck.m_flow = 0`, then all equations above are identically fulfilled and `inStream()` can have any value. It is required that the `inStream()` operator is appropriately approximated in that case and the approximation must fulfill the following requirements:

- `inStream(mi.c.h_outflow)` and `inStream(ck.h_outflow)` must be unique with respect to all values of the flow and stream variables in the connection set, and must have a continuous dependency on them.
- Every solution of the implicit equation system above must fulfill the equation system up to the usual numerical accuracy, provided the absolute value of every flow variable in the connection set is greater as a small value (`|m1.c.m_flow| > eps and |m2.c.m_flow| > eps and ... and |cM.m_flow| > eps`).

Based on the above requirements, the following definition of `inStream()` is recommended:

Case where N = 1, M = 0:

```
inStream(m1.c.h_outflow) = m1.c.h_outflow;
```

Case where N = 2, M = 0:

```
inStream(m1.c.h_outflow) = m2.c.h_outflow;
inStream(m2.c.h_outflow) = m1.c.h_outflow;
```

Case where N = 1, M = 1:

```
inStream(m1.c.h_outflow) = inStream(c1.h_outflow);
```

Additional equation to be generated for this case:

```
c1.h_outflow = m1.c.h_outflow;
```

All other cases:

```
if mj.c.m_flow.min >= 0 for all j = 1:N with j <> i and
     ck.m_flow.max <= 0 for all k = 1:M
then
  inStream(mi.c.h_outflow) = mi.c.h_outflow;
else
  si = sum(max(-mj.c.m_flow,0) for j in cat(1,1:i-1, i+1:N) +
       sum(max( ck.m_flow   ,0) for k in 1:M);
  inStream(mi.c.h_outflow) =
   (sum(positiveMax(-mj.c.m_flow,si)*mj.c.h_outflow) +
    sum(positiveMax(ck.m_flow,si)    *inStream(ck.h_outflow)))/
   (sum(positiveMax(-mj.c.m_flow,si)) +
    sum(positiveMax(ck.m_flow,si)))
                        for j in 1:N and i <> j and mj.c.m_flow.min < 0,
                        for k in 1:M            and ck.m_flow.max > 0
```

Additional equations to be generated for all other cases:

```
for q in 1:M loop
  if mj.c.m_flow.min >= 0 for all j = 1:N and
       ck.m_flow.max <= 0 for all k = 1:M and k <> q
  then
     cq.h_outflow = 0;
  else
     sq = (sum(max(-mj.c.m_flow,0) for j in 1:N) +
           sum(max( ck.m_flow   ,0) for k in cat(1,1:q-1, q+1:M)));
     cq.h_outflow = (sum(positiveMax(-mj.c.m_flow,sq)* mj.c.h_outflow) +
          sum(positiveMax(ck.m_flow,sq)* inStream(ck.h_outflow)))/
                    (sum(positiveMax(-mj.c.m_flow,sq)) +
                     sum(positiveMax(ck.m_flow,sq)))
                          for j in 1:N and mj.c.m_flow.min < 0,
                          for k in 1:M and k <> q and ck.m_flow.max > 0
end for;
```

The operator `positiveMax(-mj.c.m_flow,si)` should be defined such that:

- `positiveMax(-mj.c.m_flow,si)` = `-mj.c_m_flow if -mj.c.m_flow>eps1j>=0`, where `eps1j` are small flows, compared to typical problem-specific values.
- All denominators should be > `eps2` > 0, where `eps2` is also a small flow, compared to typical problem-specific values.

The following trivial definition of `positiveMax` guarantees the continuity of `inStream()`:

`positiveMax(-mj.c.m_flow, si) = max(-mj.c.m_flow, eps1);` // so `si` is not needed

A more sophisticated definition is given below, with a smooth approximation that is applied only when *all* flows are small:

Define a "small number" `eps` where `nominal`(v) is the nominal value of v:

```
eps := relativeTolerance*min(nominal(mj.c.m_flow));
```

Define a smooth curve, such that `alpha(si>=eps)=1` and `alpha(si<=0)=0`

```
alpha := smooth(1, if si > eps then 1 else
                   if si > 0   then (si/eps)^2*(3-2*(si/eps)) else 0);
```

Define the function `positiveMax(v,si)` as a linear combination of `max(v,0)` and of `eps` along `alpha`

```
positiveMax((-mj.c.m_flow, si) := alpha*max(-mj.c.m_flow,0) + (1-alpha)*eps;
```

Note that in the cases N = 1, M =0 (unconnected port, physically corresponding to a plugged-up flange), and N = 2, M=0 (one-to-one connection), the result of `inStream()` is trivial and no non-linear equations are left in the model, despite the fact that the original definition equations are nonlinear.

The following properties hold for this definition:

- `inStream(...)` is continuous and differentiable, provided that `mj.c.h_outflow, mj.c.m_flow, ck.h_outflow,` and `ck.m_flow` are continuous and differentiable.
- A division by zero can no longer occur (since `sum(positiveMax(-mj.c.m_flow,si))>=eps2 > 0`), so the result is always well-defined.
- The balance equations are exactly fulfilled if the denominator is not close to zero (since the exact formula is used, if `sum(positiveMax(-mj.c.m_flow,si) ) > eps)`.
- If all flows are zero, `inStream(mi.c.h_outflow) = sum(mj.c.h_outflow for j<>i and mj.c.m_flow.min < 0)/Np`, that is, it is the mean value of all the `Np` variables `mj.c.h_outflow`, such that `j<>i and mj.c.m_flow.min < 0`. This is a meaningful approximation, considering the physical diffusion effects that are relevant at small flow rates in a small connection volume (thermal conduction for enthalpy, mass diffusion for mass fractions).

The value of `relativeTolerance` should be larger than the relative tolerance of the nonlinear solver used to solve the implicit algebraic equations.

As a final remark, further symbolic simplifications could be carried out by taking into account equations that affect the flows in the connection set (i.e., equivalent to `mj.c.m_flow = 0`, which then implies `mj.c.m_flow.min >= 0`). This is interesting, e.g., in the case of a valve when the stem position is set to closed by its controller.

5.10.8 Mathematical Derivation of Stream Equations and inStream()

This section contains a derivation of the equations for stream connectors shown in Section 5.10.5, page 254. *It could be skipped* by the reader not interested in this mathematical background.

For simplicity, the derivation of the `inStream()` operator is shown at hand for 3 model components that are connected together. The case for N connections follows correspondingly.

By using the energy (5-8) and mass (5-7) balance equations in Section 5.10.3.3, page 249, and substituting (5-9) into (5-8), we arrive at the following two balance equations for the *connection set* for three connected components according to Figure 5-56:

$$
\begin{aligned}
0 = \dot{m}_1 \cdot &\begin{cases} h_{mix} & \text{if} \quad \dot{m}_1 > 0 \\ h_{outflow,1} & \text{if} \quad \dot{m}_1 \le 0 \end{cases} \\
+ \dot{m}_2 \cdot &\begin{cases} h_{mix} & \text{if} \quad \dot{m}_2 > 0 \\ h_{outflow,2} & \text{if} \quad \dot{m}_2 \le 0 \end{cases} \\
+ \dot{m}_3 \cdot &\begin{cases} h_{mix} & \text{if} \quad \dot{m}_3 > 0 \\ h_{outflow,3} & \text{if} \quad \dot{m}_3 \le 0 \end{cases}
\end{aligned} \tag{5-13}
$$

$$
0 = \dot{m}_1 + \dot{m}_2 + \dot{m}_3 \tag{5-14}
$$

The balance equations can also be expressed using the `max()` operator in place of the piecewise expressions, taking care of the different flow directions:

$$\begin{aligned}0 &= \max(\dot{m}_1,0)h_{mix} - \max(-\dot{m}_1,0)h_{outflow,1} \\ &+ \max(\dot{m}_2,0)h_{mix} - \max(-\dot{m}_2,0)h_{outflow,2} \\ &+ \max(\dot{m}_3,0)h_{mix} - \max(-\dot{m}_3,0)h_{outflow,3}\end{aligned} \tag{5-15}$$

$$\begin{aligned}0 &= \max(\dot{m}_1,0) - \max(-\dot{m}_1,0) \\ &+ \max(\dot{m}_2,0) - \max(-\dot{m}_2,0) \\ &+ \max(\dot{m}_3,0) - \max(-\dot{m}_3,0)\end{aligned} \tag{5-16}$$

Equation (5-15) is solved for h_{mix}

$$h_{mix} = \frac{\max(-\dot{m}_1,0)h_{outflow,1} + \max(-\dot{m}_2,0)h_{outflow,2} + \max(-\dot{m}_3,0)h_{outflow,3}}{\max(\dot{m}_1,0) + \max(\dot{m}_2,0) + \max(\dot{m}_3,0)} \tag{5-17}$$

Using (5-16), the denominator can be changed to:

$$h_{mix} = \frac{\max(-\dot{m}_1,0)h_{outflow,1} + \max(-\dot{m}_2,0)h_{outflow,2} + \max(-\dot{m}_3,0)h_{outflow,3}}{\max(-\dot{m}_1,0) + \max(-\dot{m}_2,0) + \max(-\dot{m}_3,0)} \tag{5-18}$$

Above, it was shown that an equation of this type does not yield properly formulated model equations. In the *streams concept* we therefore decide to *split the energy balance*, which consists of *different branches* depending on the *mass flow direction*.

Note that the energy balance is *split for every single connector*, assuming the flow is entering in that specific connector, according to the semantics of the `inStream()` operator. This is the basic mechanism to *avoid discontinuities and undeterminacy* at zero or reversing flows

Consequently, separate energy balances are the result; each valid for specific flow directions, for each connector.

In a model the governing equations have to establish the specific enthalpy $h_{outflow,i}$ of fluid leaving the model based on the specific enthalpy of fluid flowing into it. Whenever the mixing enthalpy is *used* in a model it is therefore the mixing enthalpy under the assumption of fluid flowing into said model.

We establish this quantity by defining a dedicated operator $inStream(h_{outflow,i}) = h_{mix}(\dot{m}_i \geq 0)$. This leads to three different incarnations of h_{mix} (*n* incarnations in the general case). This is illustrated in Figure 5-56 below. For the present example of three components in a connection set, this means the following:

$$\begin{aligned}inStream(h_{outflow,1}) &= \frac{\max(-\dot{m}_2,0)h_{outflow,2} + \max(-\dot{m}_3,0)h_{outflow,3}}{\max(-\dot{m}_2,0) + \max(-\dot{m}_3,0)} \\ inStream(h_{outflow,2}) &= \frac{\max(-\dot{m}_1,0)h_{outflow,1} + \max(-\dot{m}_3,0)h_{outflow,3}}{\max(-\dot{m}_1,0) + \max(-\dot{m}_3,0)} \\ inStream(h_{outflow,3}) &= \frac{\max(-\dot{m}_1,0)h_{outflow,1} + \max(-\dot{m}_2,0)h_{outflow,2}}{\max(-\dot{m}_1,0) + \max(-\dot{m}_2,0)}\end{aligned} \tag{5-19}$$

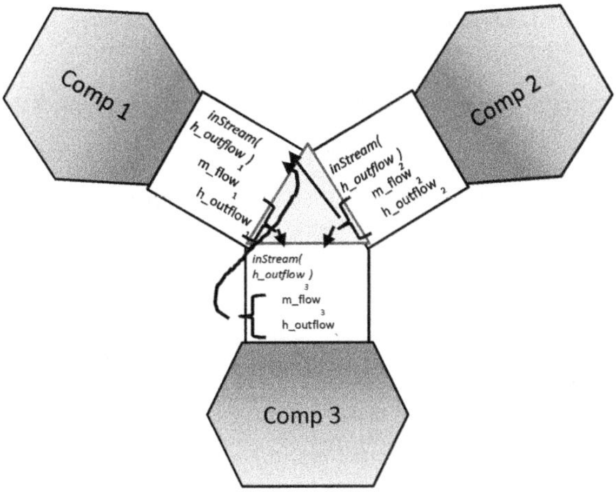

Figure 5-56. Example connection set with three connected components, where inflow into one port is computed via `inStream()` from the quantities and outflows from the other two connected ports, shown for port 1 at Comp 1 and port 3 at Comp 3.

In the general case of a connection set with *n* components, similar considerations lead to the following.

$$inStream\left(h_{outflow,i}\right) = \frac{\sum\limits_{j=1,\ldots,n;\,j\neq i} \max\left(-\dot{m}_j, 0\right) h_{outflow,j}}{\sum\limits_{j=1,\ldots,n;\,j\neq i} \max\left(-\dot{m}_j, 0\right)} \tag{5-20}$$

5.10.9 Derivation of Special Cases of the inStream() Definition

The following are common special cases where the definition of `inStream()` can be simplified. This mathematical derivation can be skipped by the reader primarily interested in the modeling aspects.

5.10.9.1 Stream Connector is NOT Connected

In this case, N=1, only one connector, i.e., unconnected. For this case, the return value of the `inStream()` operator is arbitrary. Therefore, it is set to the outflow value.

5.10.9.2 Connection of Two Stream Connectors, One-to-one Connections

In this case N=2, two connected connectors.

$$\begin{aligned} inStream\left(h_{outflow,1}\right) &= \frac{\max\left(-\dot{m}_2, 0\right) h_{outflow,2}}{\max\left(-\dot{m}_2, 0\right)} = h_{outflow,2} \\ inStream\left(h_{outflow,2}\right) &= \frac{\max\left(-\dot{m}_1, 0\right) h_{outflow,1}}{\max\left(-\dot{m}_1, 0\right)} = h_{outflow,1} \end{aligned} \tag{5-21}$$

In this case, `inStream()` is continuous (contrary to h_{mix}) and does not depend on flow rates. The latter result means that this transformation may remove nonlinear systems of equations, which requires that either simplifications of the form "`a*b/a = b`" must be provided, or that this case is treated directly.

5.10.9.3 Connection of Three Stream Connectors where One Mass Flow Rate is Zero

In this case, N=3 and $\dot{m}_3 = 0$ if we select the third mass to have zero mass flow rate. This case occurs when a one-port sensor (like a temperature sensor) is connected to two connected components. For the sensor, the min attribute of the mass flow rate $\dot{m}_3$ has to be set to zero since no fluid is exiting or entering the component via this connector. The suggested modeling results in the following equations, assuming $\dot{m}_1 = -\dot{m}_2$ since $\dot{m}_3 = 0$:

$$\begin{aligned}
inStream(h_{outflow,1}) &= \frac{\max(-\dot{m}_2,0)h_{outflow,2} + \max(-\dot{m}_3,0)h_{outflow,3}}{\max(-\dot{m}_2,0)+\max(-\dot{m}_3,0)} = h_{outflow,2} \\
inStream(h_{outflow,2}) &= \frac{\max(-\dot{m}_1,0)h_{outflow,1} + \max(-\dot{m}_3,0)h_{outflow,3}}{\max(-\dot{m}_1,0)+\max(-\dot{m}_3,0)} = h_{outflow,1} \\
inStream(h_{outflow,3}) &= \frac{\max(-\dot{m}_1,0)h_{outflow,1} + \max(-\dot{m}_2,0)h_{outflow,2}}{\max(-\dot{m}_1,0)+\max(-\dot{m}_2,0)} \\
&= \begin{cases} h_{outflow,2} & \text{if } \dot{m}_1 \ge 0 \\ h_{outflow,1} & \text{if } \dot{m}_1 < 0 \end{cases}
\end{aligned} \tag{5-22}$$

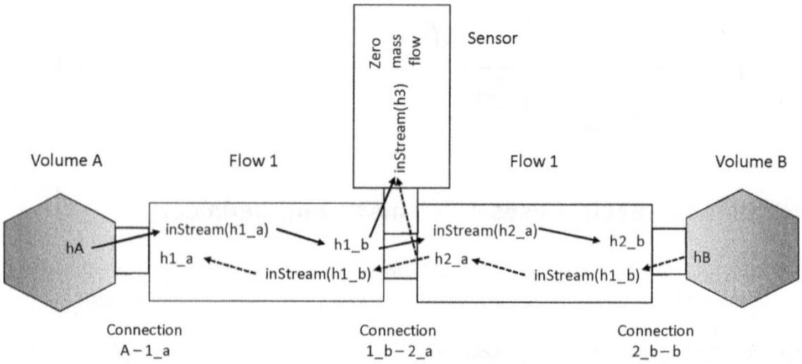

Figure 5-57. Example series connection of multiple models with stream connectors.

For the two components with finite mass flow rates (not the sensor), the properties discussed for two connected components still hold. The connection set equations reflect that the sensor does not have any influence by discarding the flow rate of the latter. In several cases a non-linear equation system is removed by this transformation. However, `inStream()` results in a discontinuous equation for the sensor, which is consistent with modeling the convective phenomena only. The discontinuous equation is not critical if the sensor variable is not used in a feedback loop with direct feed through, since the discontinuous equation is then not part of an algebraic loop. Otherwise, it is advisable to regularize or filter the sensor signal.

5.10.9.4 Connection of Three Stream Connectors where Two Mass Flow Rates are Positive

This is an ideal splitting junction for unidirectional flow. If unidirectional flow is present and an ideal splitter is modeled, the required flow direction should be defined in the connector instance with the "`min`" attribute (the "`max`" attribute could also be defined, however it does not lead to simplifications):

```
model m2
   Fluidport c(m_flow(min=0));
   ...
end m2;
```

Consider the case of $\dot{m}_1 < 0$ and all other mass flow rates positive (with the `min` attribute set accordingly). Connecting `m1.c` with `m2.c` and `m3.c`, such that

```
m2.c.m_flow.min = 0;     // Note that max(-m2.c.m_flow,0) = 0
m3.c.m_flow.min = 0;     // Note that max(-m3.c.m_flow,0) = 0
```

results in the following equation:

$$inStream\left(h_{outflow,1}\right) = \frac{\max\left(-\dot{m}_2,0\right)h_{outflow,2} + \max\left(-\dot{m}_3,0\right)h_{outflow,3}}{\max\left(-\dot{m}_2,0\right) + \max\left(-\dot{m}_3,0\right)} = \frac{0}{0} \tag{5-23}$$

Thus, the `inStream()` operator cannot be evaluated for a connector on which the mass flow rate has to be negative by definition. The reason is that the value is arbitrary, which is why it is instead defined as (5-24) below:

$$inStream\left(h_{outflow,1}\right) := h_{outflow,1} \tag{5-24}$$

For the remaining connectors the `inStream()` operator reduces to a simple result.

$$\begin{aligned} inStream\left(h_{outflow,2}\right) &= \frac{\max\left(-\dot{m}_1,0\right)h_{outflow,1} + \max\left(-\dot{m}_3,0\right)h_{outflow,3}}{\max\left(-\dot{m}_1,0\right) + \max\left(-\dot{m}_3,0\right)} \\ inStream\left(h_{outflow,3}\right) &= \frac{\max\left(-\dot{m}_1,0\right)h_{outflow,1} + \max\left(-\dot{m}_2,0\right)h_{outflow,2}}{\max\left(-\dot{m}_1,0\right) + \max\left(-\dot{m}_2,0\right)} \end{aligned} \tag{5-25}$$

Again, the previous non-linear algebraic system of equations is removed. This means that utilizing the information about unidirectional flow is very important.

To summarize, if all mass flow rates are zero, the balance equations (5-13) and (5-14) for stream variables and for flows (5-15), (5-16) are identically fulfilled. In such a case, any value of `h_mix` fulfills (5-13), (5-14), that is, a unique mathematical solution does not exist. This specification only requires that a solution fulfills the balance equations. Additionally, a recommendation is given to compute all unknowns in a unique way, by providing an explicit formula for the `inStream()` operator.

Due to the definition, that only flows where the corresponding `min` attribute is neither zero nor positive enter this formula, a meaningful physical result is always obtained, even in the case of zero mass flow rate. As a side effect, non-linear equation systems are automatically removed in special cases, like sensors or unidirectional flow, without any symbolic transformations (no equation must be analyzed; only the "min"-attributes of the corresponding flow variables).

5.11 Overconstrained Connection Graphs

Depending on the formulation of connector classes, certain connection graphs that represent fairly common physical systems may give rise to overdetermined equation systems, i.e., systems with more equations than variables. One example is multibody system models with so-called kinematic loops, see Section 15.10.8, page 894.

For this reason, Modelica includes equation operators for overconstrained connection-based equation systems (Section 8.5, page 374), which can be used to state information that allows a Modelica environment to deduce which equations resulting from an overconstrained connection graph are superfluous and should be removed.

5.12 Summary

In this chapter we presented how the basic object oriented mathematical modeling concept in Modelica is enhanced with mechanisms for defining, using, and connecting components, thereby promoting even more reuse than is possible by just inheritance.

We started with a general overview of software component models, followed by a presentation of components, connectors and connector classes, as well as connections defined using an equation based semantics. Then we gave examples of both electrical and mechanical components and connectors to show the ability of Modelica to handle multiple application domains.

We gave a short presentation of design guidelines for connector classes together with some physical quantities used when defining connector classes in a some common physical domains. We also discussed connecting components from different domains, hierarchical connections, and the generation of equations from the `connect` construct.

We presented connection semantics in detail, e.g. including hierarchical connections, and how to define implicit connection structures for force fields such as gravitational fields with the inner outer constructs.

Finally we concluded by a presentation of expandable connectors for information buses and a detailed presentation of stream connectors for fluid systems.

5.13 Literature

The book on invasive software composition (Assmann 2002) gives a comprehensive overview of many aspects of software components, composition, and component systems. The component software book (Szyperski 1997) discusses software component technology, but mostly conventional component systems like CORBA, COM, and Java Beans.

The main Modelica related reference documents are the Modelica language specification (Modelica Association 2003), (Modelica Association 2013) and tutorial (Modelica Association 2003) concerning language properties and several examples, e.g. including the circuit board example in Section 5.8.2 and the gravitational field examples in Section 5.8.3. Tables comparing energy flow and potential quantities for different application domains can for example be found in (Cellier 1991; Ljung and Glad 1994; Otter 1999). Francesco Casella gave important feedback which led to revision of Section 5.4. Dirk Zimmer contributed most of the contents of Section 5.4.5.

Expandable connectors were initially proposed by Michael Tiller, developed by several people and described in (Modelica Association 2003) and (Modelica Association 2010) from which most of the text in Section 5.9 has been cited and adapted. Applications of expandable connectors are described e.g. in (Batteh and Tiller 2009).

Stream connectors were proposed, designed, and implemented as described in (Franke, Casella, Otter, Sielemann, Elmqvist, and Olsson 2009). The design conditions for a general Fluid library in Section 5.10.3.2 as well as the three example models in Section 5.10.4 and some associated text have been cited from that paper. A detailed review and analysis of this and earlier thermo-fluid connectors appears in (Sielemann 2012). Stream connectors have been used for improvement and standardization of the Modelica.Fluid library as described in (Franke, Casella, Sielemann, Proelss, Otter, and Wetter 2009), which is a collective effort where 17 persons have contributed over 6 years, 2003-2009. Most of the text in

Section 5.10 has been cited from (Modelica Association 2013) and slightly adapted, with some more explanations added.

Regarding earlier approaches, the ThermoPower library is described in (Casella and Leva 2003) and in more detail especially the connector design (Casella and Leva 2006), whereas early versions of libraries such as Modelica_Fluid and Modelica_Media are presented in (Elmqvist, Tummescheit, and Otter 2003), and more developed versions of Modelica Fluid and Media Libraries are described in (Casella, Otter, Proelss, Richter, and Tummescheit 2006).

5.14 Exercise

Exercise 5-1:

Question: How can connections between components be established in Modelica? What are requirements for connections? How many connectors can you connect?

Exercise 5-2:

For the model below:

- Name the inside and outside connectors for M.
- *Question*: What connection equations are generated when components `C1`, `C2`, and `C3` are connected?

```
connector RealInput = input RealSignal;
connector RealOutput = output RealSignal;

model C
  RealInput u;
  RealOutput y;
end C;

model M
  RealInput u;
  RealOutput y;
  C C1, C2, C3;
equation
  connect(C1.y, C3.u);
  connect(C1.y, C2.u);
end M;

model  System
  M M1; // Instance M1 of M
  C C4, C5, C6;
equation
  connect(C4.y, M1.C1.u);
  connect(M1.C2.y, C6.u);
  connect(M1.C3.y, C5.u);
end System;
```

Exercise 5-3:

Inner/outer

- By relying on the inner/outer mechanism, define a class `NResistors`, which contains `n` Resistors connected in parallel.
- Create two instances of the class with 5 and 6 resistors in parallel, respectively, without having to modify the connections.

Exercise 5-4:

Expandable connectors:

- What are expandable connectors?
- What are they used for?
- Can expandable connectors contain flow variables?

Chapter 6

Literals, Operators, and Expressions

This chapter describes several of the basic building blocks of Modelica such as characters and lexical units, including identifiers, literals, and operators. Without question, the smallest building blocks in Modelica are single characters belonging to a character set. Characters are combined to form lexical units, also called tokens. These tokens are detected by the lexical analysis part of the Modelica translator. Examples of tokens are literal constants, identifiers, and operators. Comments are not really lexical units since they are eventually discarded. On the other hand, comments are detected by the lexical analyzer before being thrown away.

The lexical units are combined to form even larger building blocks such as expressions according to the rules given by the expression part of the Modelica grammar. Expressions may occur in many places in Modelica classes, for example, in the equation part or in the declaration part.

The rest of this chapter describes the evaluation rules for expressions, type conversions, the concept of expression variability, built-in mathematical operators and functions, and, finally, the set of built-in special Modelica operators with function syntax.

Additional information regarding certain kinds of expressions is available in some other chapters. Array expressions are described in more detail in Chapter 7. A thorough description of the meaning of names and name lookup is available in Chapter 3.

6.1 Character Set

The character set of the Modelica language is Unicode, but restricted to the Unicode characters corresponding to 7-bit ASCII characters in several places, such as keywords and identifiers; for details see Appendix B.

Modelica files are UTF-8 encoded (see the Unicode Consortium; `http://www.unicode.org`), and can start with the UTF-8 encoded byte order mark (0xef 0xbb 0xbf) to indicate that it may contain UTF-8 characters; this is treated as white-space in the Modelica grammar which defined in Appendix B.

6.2 Comments

There are two kinds of comments in Modelica that are not lexical units in the language and therefore are treated as white-space by a Modelica translator. The white-space characters are space, tabulator, and the line separators carriage-return and line-feed.

White-space cannot occur inside tokens such as operators, identifiers and numbers; for example, a <= must be written as two characters without space or comments between them. The comment syntax is identical to that of Java and C++. The following comment variants are available:

`// comment`	Characters from `//` to the end of the line are ignored.
`/* comment */`	Characters between `/*` and `*/` are ignored, including line terminators.

Modelica comments do not nest, that is, `/* */` cannot be embedded within `/* */`. The following is *invalid*:

```
/* Commented out - erroneous comment, invalid nesting of comments!
  /* This is a interesting model */
  model interesting
  ...
  end interesting;
*/
```

There is also a kind of "documentation comment," really a *documentation string*, that is part of the Modelica language and therefore not ignored by the Modelica translator. Such "comments" may occur at the ends of declarations or at the beginnings of class definitions. For example:

```
model TempResistor  "Temperature dependent resistor"
  ...
  parameter Real R  "Resistance for reference temp.";
  ...
end TempResistor;
```

There is also a `Documentation` annotation (Section 11.911.8.2, page 545), which is often used for more detailed documentation of models.

6.3 Identifiers, Names, and Keywords

Identifiers are sequences of letters, digits, and other characters such as underscore, which are used for *naming* various items in the language. Certain combinations of letters are *keywords* represented as *reserved* words in the Modelica grammar and are therefore not available as identifiers.

6.3.1 Identifiers

Modelica *identifiers*, used for naming classes, variables, constants, and other items, are of two forms. The first form always start with a letter or underscore (_), followed by any number of letters, digits, or underscores. Case is significant, that is, the names `Inductor` and `inductor` are different.

The second form (`Q-IDENT`) starts with a single quote, followed by a sequence of any characters, where a possible single quote must be preceeded by a backslash, and terminated by a single quote, for example, `'12H'`, `'13\'H'`, `'+foo'`. The single quotes are part of the identifier, i.e., 'z' and z are distinct identifiers.

The following BNF-like rules define Modelica identifiers, where curly brackets {} indicate repetition zero or more times, and a vertical bar | indicates alternatives. A full BNF definition of the Modelica syntax and lexical units is available in Appendix B.

```
IDENT     = NONDIGIT { DIGIT | NONDIGIT }  |  Q-IDENT
Q-IDENT   = "'" { Q-CHAR | S-ESCAPE } "'"
NONDIGIT  = "_" | letters "a" to "z" | letters "A" to "Z"
DIGIT     = 0 | 1 | 2 | 3 | 4 | 5 | 6 | 7 | 8 | 9
Q-CHAR   = NONDIGIT | DIGIT | "!" | "#" | "$" | "%" | "&" | "(" | ")" | "*" |
            "+" | "," | "-" | "." | "/" | ":" | ";" | "<" | ">" | "=" | "?" |
            "@" | "[" | "]" | "^" | "{" | "}"  | "|" | "~" | " "
S-ESCAPE = "\'" | "\"" | "\?" | "\\" |
            "\a" | "\b" | "\f" | "\n" | "\r" | "\t" | "\v"
```

6.3.2 Names

A *name* is an identifier with a certain interpretation or meaning. For example, a name may denote an `Integer` variable, a `Real` variable, a function, a type, and so on. A name may have different meanings in different parts of the code, that is, different scopes. The interpretation of identifiers as names is described in more detail in Chapter 3, page 81. Package names are described in more detail in Chapter 10.

6.3.3 Built-in Predefined Variable time

All declared variables are functions of the independent variable `time`. This is a built-in predefined variable that can be referenced in the specialized classes `model`, `class`, and `block`. The variable `time` is from the Modelica language point of view treated as an `input` variable. It is implicitly defined as:

```
input Real time (final quantity = "Time", final unit = "s");
```

The value of the `start` attribute of `time` is initially set to the time instant at which the simulation is started. The variable `time` can be used to trigger events a specific time points after the start of simulation. In the example below an event is triggered at time 0.5 seconds of simulated time.

The `TimeEventTest` example model has a variable `x` with an initial value of 1.0. At the time point 0.5s, the when-equation (Section 8.3.5, page 357, and Section 13.2.6, page 613) is triggered and the equation x = 2.0 becomes active. Note that the event happens at the time point 0.5s, not after 0.5s of simulation (unless the simulation started at 0s).

```
model TimeEventTest
  Real x(start = 1.0, fixed = true);
equation
  when time >= 0.5 then
    x = 2.0;
  end when;
end TimeEventTest;
```

We simulate and plot:

```
simulate(TimeEventText, startTime = 0.2, stopTime = 0.6);
plot({x, time})
```

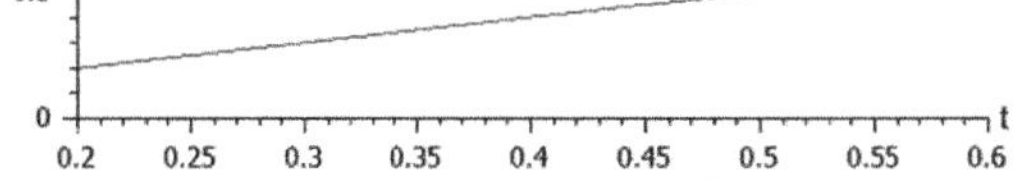

Figure 6-1. The variable `x` gets the value 2.0 when `time` reaches the value 0.5 causing the when-equation to be triggered which makes the variable `x` get the value 2.0.

The variable `time` is not available in functions since Modelica functions are mathematical functions, that is, the same input should always give the same output. This means that `time` is not allowed to be accessed inside a function, but can still be passed as a function argument as in the call to `mySinNoTime` in the model `SinTest` below:

```
function mySinNoTime
  input Real x;
  output Real y;
algorithm
  y := sin(x*10);   // sin(time) would be an error here.
end mySinNoTime;

model SinTest
  Real z = mySinNoTime(time);
end SinTest;
```

We simulate and plot:

```
simulate(SinTest, stopTime=2);
plot(z)
```

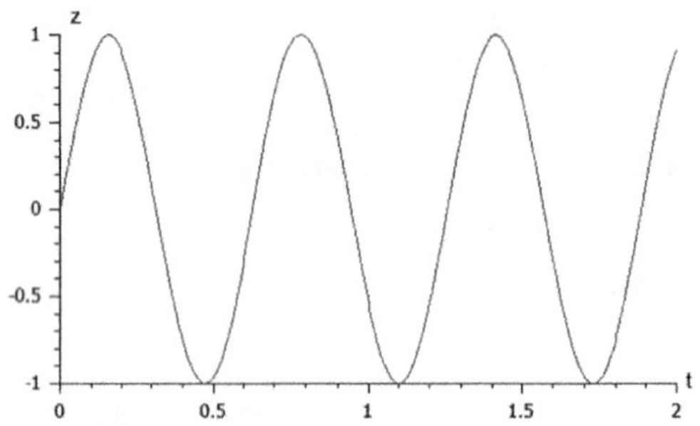

Figure 6-2. The built-in variable `time` cannot be referenced directly within a function but can be passed as an argument to a function as in the model `SinTest`.

6.3.4 Modelica Keywords

The following Modelica *keywords* are reserved words and may not be used as identifiers:

algorithm	each	final	model	record
and	else	flow	not	redeclare
annotation	elseif	for	operator	replaceable
block	elsewhen	function	or	return
break	encapsulated	if	outer	stream
class	end	import	output	then
connect	enumeration	impure	package	true
connector	equation	in	parameter	type
constant	expandable	initial	partial	when
constrainedby	extends	inner	protected	while
der	external	input	public	within
discrete	false	loop	pure	

6.4 Predefined Types

The predefined built-in types of Modelica are `Real`, `Integer`, `Boolean`, `String`, and `enumeration`, which are presented in more detail in Section 3.9 of Chapter 3, page 93. These types have some of the properties of a class—can be inherited, modified, and so on—but, on the other hand, have a number of restrictions and somewhat different properties compared to normal classes.

Redeclaration of any of these predefined types is an error, and the type names are reserved such that it is illegal to declare something using these names.

At type checking, variables of these types are treated similarly to variables with nonclass scalar types in other programming languages. Only the *value* attribute can be changed at run-time, and is accessed through the variable name itself, and not through dot notation; for example, use `x` and not `x.value` to access the value of the variable `x`. The machine representations of the *values* of these predefined types typically have the following properties:

`Real`	IEC 60559:1989 (ANSI/IEEE 754-1985) double format, at least 64-bit precision.
`Integer`	typically two's-complement 32-bit integer.
`Boolean`	`true` or `false`.
`String`	string of unicode characters, UTF-8 encoded.
`enumeration`	Enumeration values represented internally as integers.

Note that for argument passing of values when calling external functions in C from Modelica, `Real` corresponds to `double` and `Integer` corresponds to `int`.

6.5 Literal Constants

Literal constants are unnamed constants that have different forms depending on their type. Each of the predefined types in Modelica has a way of expressing unnamed constants of the corresponding type, which is presented in the ensuing subsections. Additionally, array constant values and record constant values can be expressed.

6.5.1 Floating Point Numbers

A floating point number is expressed as a decimal number in the form of an optional sign (+ or –), a sequence of decimal digits optionally followed by a decimal point and one or more digits, optionally followed by an exponent. At least one digit must be present. The exponent is indicated by an E or e, followed by an optional sign (+ or –) and one or more decimal digits. The range is that of IEEE double precision floating point numbers, for which the largest representable positive number is 1.7976931348623157E+308 and the smallest positive number is 2.2250738585072014E–308. For example, the following are floating point number literal constants:

```
22.5,  3.141592653589793, 1.2E-35, -56.08
```

The same floating point number can be represented by different literals. For example, all of the following literals denote the same number:

```
13.0,  13E0,  1.3e1,  0.13E2
```

The following numbers are illegal:

```
13.,   .13E2
```

6.5.2 Integers

Literals of type `Integer` are sequences of decimal digits, for example, as in the integer numbers `33`, `0`, `100`, and `30030044`, or negative numbers such as `-998`. The range depends on the C compiler implementation of integers (Modelica compiles to C), but typically is from –2,147,483,648 to +2,147,483,647 for a two's-complement 32-bit integer implementation.

6.5.3 Booleans

The two `Boolean` literal values are `true` and `false`.

6.5.4 Strings

String literals appear between double quotes as in `"between"`. Any character in the Modelica language character set apart from double quote (") and backslash (\), but including nonprintable characters like new-line, backspace, null, etc., can be *directly* included in a string without using an escape code. Certain characters in string literals are represented using escape codes, i.e., the character is preceded by a backslash (\) within the string. Those characters are:

`\'`	single quote—may also appear without backslash in string constants.
`\"`	double quote
`\?`	question mark—may also appear without backslash in string constants.
`\\`	backslash itself
`\a`	alert (bell, code 7, ctrl-G)
`\b`	backspace (code 8, ctrl-H)
`\f`	form feed (code 12, ctrl-L)
`\n`	new-line (code 10, ctrl-J)
`\r`	return (code 13, ctrl-M)
`\t`	horizontal tab (code 9, ctrl-I)
`\v`	vertical tab (code 11, ctrl-K)

For example, a string literal containing a tab, the words: `This is`, double quote, space, the word: `between`, double quote, space, the word: `us`, and new-line, would appear as follows:

```
"\tThis is\" between\" us\n"
```

Concatenation of string literals in certain situations (see the Modelica grammar) is denoted by the + operator in Modelica, for example, `"a" + "b"` becomes `"ab"`. This is useful for expressing long string literals that need to be written on several lines.

6.5.5 Enumeration Constant Values

Enumeration value constants are introduced by declaration of an enumeration type:

```
type Color = enumeration(red, blue, green);
```

This makes the enumeration literal values `Color.red`, `Color.blue`, and `Color.green` available for use.

6.5.6 Array Constant Values

Array values can be expressed using the array constructor { } or the array concatenation operator [ ]. For example, the following are one-dimensional array constants, that is, vector literals:

```
{1,2,3},        {3.14, 58E-6}
```

Two-dimensional array constants, that is, matrix literals, may appear as below, where the same constant matrix is expressed in two ways:

```
{{1,2},{3,4}}    or    [1,2; 3,4]
```

More information concerning arrays and array values is available in Section 7.2, page 315, and in Section 7.11.1 concerning empty array values.

6.5.7 Record Constant Values

Record values can be expressed using the record constructor functions automatically defined as a consequence of record declarations (Section 3.18.4, page 118). Below is an example record value of a complex number based on the record `Complex`:

```
Complex(1.3, 4.56)
Complex();          // Use argument default values of the constructor function
```

6.6 Operator Precedence and Associativity

Operator precedence determines the order of evaluation of operators in an expression. An operator with higher precedence is evaluated before an operator with lower precedence in the same expression. For example, relational operators have higher precedence than logical operators:

```
Xwithin := x>35.3 and x<=999.6;
```

Assuming x has the value 55.0, then both relational terms are first evaluated to `true`, eventually giving the value `true` to be assigned to the variable `Xwithin`. The multiplication operator * has higher precedence than the subtraction operator, causing the following expression to have the value 45, not zero:

```
10 * 5 - 5
```

Parentheses can be used to override precedence, e.g. causing the expression below to evaluate to zero:

```
10 * (5 - 5)
```

The associativity determines what happens when operators with the same precedence appear next to each other. Left-associative operators evaluate the leftmost part first, for example, the expression:

```
x + y + w
```

is equivalent to

```
(x + y) + w
```

The following table presents all the operators in order of precedence from highest to lowest. All operators are binary except the postfix operators and those shown as unary together with *expr*, the conditional operator, the array construction operator {} and concatenation operator [], and the array range constructor which is either binary or ternary. Operators with the same precedence occur at the same line of the table:

Table 6-1. Operators.

Operator Group	Operator Syntax	Examples
postfix array index operator	`[]`	`arr[index]`
postfix access operator	`.`	`a.b`
postfix function call	funcName(function-arguments)	`sin(4.36)`
array construct/concat	{expressions} [expressions]	`{2,3}  [5,6]`
	[expressions; expressions...]	`[2,3; 7,8]`
exponentiation	`^`	`2^3`
multiplicative and array	`*  /  .*  ./`	`2*3  2/3`
elementwise multiplicative		`[1,2;3,4].*[2,3;5,6]`
additive and array	`+  -  `*+expr* *-expr*	`a+b,  a-b,  +a,  -a`
elementwise additive	`.+ .-`	`[1,2;3,4].+[2,3;5,6]`
relational	< <= > >= == <>	`a<b,  a<=b,  a>b,  ...`
unary negation	`not` *expr*	`not b1`
logical and	`and`	`b1 and b2`
logical or	`or`	`b1 or  b2`
array range	expr : expr	`1:5`
	expr : expr : expr	`start:step:stop`
conditional	`if` *expr* `then` *expr* `else` *expr*	`if b then 3 else x`
named argument	ident = expr	`x = 2.26`

Equation equality = and assignment := are not expression operators since they are allowed only in equations and in assignment statements respectively. All binary expression operators are left associative, except exponentiation which is non-associative. The array range operator is also non-associative. For example:

```
x^y^z                 // Not legal, use parentheses to make it unambiguous
a:b:c:d:e:f:g         // Not legal, use parentheses to make it unambiguous
```

The unary plus and minus operators may not be directly combined with arithmetic operators in Modelica without intervening spaces or parentheses, whereas this is allowed in some languages, such as Mathematica and MATLAB. For example:

```
3*-3   // = -9 in Mathematica/MATLAB is illegal in Modelica; instead: 3*(-3)
--3    // =  3 in Mathematica/MATLAB is illegal in Modelica; instead: -(-3)
++3    // =  3 in Mathematica/MATLAB is illegal in Modelica; instead: +(+3)
3--3   // =  6 in Mathematica/MATLAB is illegal in Modelica; instead: 3-(-3)
```

6.7 Order of Evaluation

A Modelica tool is free to solve equations, to reorder expressions, and to avoid evaluating expressions if their values do not influence the result. For example, a tool can choose to evaluate only the first argument of the `and`-operator in the following expression, the so-called short-circuit evaluation:

```
false and true
```

Alternatively, both arguments can be evaluated. Therefore, the order of evaluation, for example, regarding variable references and function calls in expressions, cannot be guaranteed. This is normally not a problem since Modelica is a declarative language. However, the user should be careful *not* to call external functions with *side-effects* where the order of evaluation of such function calls may influence the simulation result. Typical side effects might be storing values in global variables, or performing output, that will later influence the value of some function call.

Constructs such as if-statements and if-expressions, however, guarantee that their then- or else-parts are only evaluated if the corresponding *condition* is true. Except for the operators `and`, `or`, and `if-then-else` (to be described later in this chapter), every operand of an operator will always be evaluated *before* the operation is performed.

Of course, the usual rules for arithmetic expressions are observed, where operators with higher precedence are evaluated before those with lower precedence, and where the laws of commutativity and associativity are obeyed. In algorithmic code, that is, code within algorithm sections or function bodies, assignment statements are usually present, giving more constraints for code rearrangements. In all cases of code transformations the data-flow dependencies between all parts of the code have to be preserved to keep the same meaning of the code.

6.7.1 Guarding Expressions Against Incorrect Evaluation

Only constructs like if-statements and if-expressions can be used to *guard* expressions against evaluation since the bodies of these constructs are evaluated only if the corresponding *condition* is `true`.

Boolean operators such as logical `and` cannot be used for evaluation protection, since there is no prescribed short-circuit evaluation of Boolean expressions, for example, as in Java. The reason is that a Modelica compiler should be free to perform advanced symbolic manipulation of logical expressions. Code corresponding to short-circuit evaluation can be produced by the compiler, but this is not required.

The first equation in the class `GuardTest` below can generate an error such as *index out of bounds*. Even if the boolean expression `(I>=1 and I<=n)` evaluates to `false`, the evaluation of `v[I]` is not necessarily prevented.

The second equation is correct since the use of an if–expression guarantees that the condition `(I>=1 and I<=n)` is always evaluated before then- or else-parts of the if-expression.

```
class GuardTest
  Boolean v[n];
  Boolean x;
  Integer I;
equation
  x = v[I] and (I>=1 and I<=n);                    // Invalid
  x = if (I>=1 and I<=n) then v[I] else false;    // Correct
end GuardTest;
```

6.7.1.1 Guards with Discrete-Time Conditions

The condition (`I>=1` and `I<=n`) in the `GuardTest` class example contains only so-called discrete variables, that is, variables that change value only at specific points in time when events are handled. `Boolean`, `Integer`, `String`, and `enumeration` variables are always discrete-time and cannot be continuous. We say that these variables have discrete-time variability (see also Section 6.8.1.3 about variability on page 278 in this chapter and Section 3.11.2 about variability prefixes on page 99 in Chapter 3).

6.7.1.2 Guards with Continuous-Time Conditions

Variables that can change value continuously at any time during the simulation are said to have *continuous-time* variability. When such variables are used in conditions, for example, `h` in `h>0` below, the Modelica simulator needs to find the exact value for which `h` performs a zero-crossing (see Section 18.2.5.5, page 1015) that causes the expression to change between `false` and `true`. This is a *discontinuous* change that might cause a discontinuous change of `der(h)` and/or its derivatives according to the first equation in the class `GuardContinuousVar` below.

An *event* (see Chapter 13, page 591) is normally generated at a zero-crossing to help the simulator to efficiently handle possible discontinuities. In the iterative process of finding the exact value of `h` for which an event should be generated, h will be varied both above and below the possible point of zero crossing. One problem with the iterative zero-crossing search is that if-expressions in Modelica do ***not*** behave exactly as most people expect based on experience with conventional programming languages. During this iterative process, small negative values of h can be actually supplied to the body of the if-expression, for example, c*sqrt(h) below, causing an attempt to compute the square root of a negative number, which is an error.

To guard sqrt against a negative argument one can use the built-in pseudofunction noEvent (see Section 6.14, page 291) that prevents generation of events (see Section 13.2.5.10, page 606) for argument expressions. In this way it is possible to use if-expressions to *guard* against taking the square root of a negative number. The only drawback of avoiding generating an event is that an adaptive equation solver will temporarily perform its computations substantially slower if there is a discontinuity since the numerical solver must switch to a much smaller step size when encountering a discontinuity.

Discontinuities, events, and similar issues are discussed in more detail in Chapter 13.

```
class GuardContinuousVar
  Real h, c;
equation
  der(h) = if h>0 then -c*sqrt(h) else 0;             // Incorrect
  der(h) = if noEvent(h>0) then -c*sqrt(h) else 0;    // Correct
end GuardContinuousVar;
```

6.8 Expression Type and Conversions

All expressions have a *type*. The expression type is obtained from the types of its constituent parts, for example, variables, constants, operators, and function calls in an expression. Recall the definition of the notion of type in Modelica, previously presented in Chapter 3 page 115. For example, an addition of two Integer variables gives a result of type Integer. Similarly, a multiplication of two Real values gives a result of type Real.

If either operand of an arithmetic operator has Real type, the operation is performed in double precision floating point arithmetic. Integer operands in such cases are converted to Real before the floating point operation is performed. If either operand is an array, the result is an array. The detailed typing rules when array operands are involved are explained in more detail in Chapter 7.

6.8.1 Type Conversions

Modelica is a strongly typed language. This means that type compatibility is checked at compile time in almost all cases, and at run-time in the remaining cases. Modelica prevents incompatible left-hand and right-hand sides in equations as well as incompatible assignments by not allowing anything questionable.

The language also provides a few checking and *type conversion* operations for cases when the compatibility of a type can be determined only at run-time, for example, to check the size of a variable-length array, or when we want to explicitly convert a type, for example, when assigning a Real value to an Integer variable. We discuss these conversions in terms of assignment, sometimes called *assignment conversion*, but what is said here is also applicable to conversions between left-hand sides and right-hand sides of equations, and conversions when passing actual arguments to formal parameters at function calls.

6.8.1.1 Implicit Type Conversions

Sometimes a type can be converted without any explicit action from the Modelica modeler or programmer. The only case in Modelica when this happens is *implicit conversion* of integer operands when used together with floating point operands in an expression. For example, consider the following expression where x has the type Real, being added together with the integer 66:

```
x + 66
```

In this case the integer `66` is converted to the floating point number `66.0`, which in turn is added to `x` using floating point addition.

6.8.1.2 Functions for Explicit Conversion

Explicit (type) conversions are needed when implicit conversions are not enough or are not available, for example, when converting from a `Real` to an `Integer`. Then there are two options: rounding to the integer value *closest above* the current value, or rounding to the integer value *closest below* the current value. Using the built-in conversion functions below the first alternative is achieved by `integer(ceil(x))` for a real value `x`, and the second alternative is obtained by just using `integer(x)`.

`ceil(x)`	Returns the smallest integer not less than `x`, i.e., the closest integer above `x`. Result and argument have type `Real`. Note that outside of a when-clause or clocked discrete-time partition state events are triggered when the return value of this function changes discontinuously.
`floor(x)`	Returns the largest integer not greater than `x`, i.e., the closest integer below `x`. Result and argument have type `Real`. Note that outside of a when-clause or clocked discrete-time partition state events are triggered when the return value of this function changes discontinuously.
`integer(x)`	Returns the largest integer not greater than `x`, i.e., the closest integer below `x`. The argument has type `Real`. The result has type `Integer`. Note that outside of a when-clause or clocked discrete-time partition state events are triggered when the return value of this function changes discontinuously.
`Integer(e)`	Returns the ordinal integer value corresponding to the enumeration value e which evaluates to `E.ev` of the enumeration type `E = enumeration(..., ev, ...)`. For example, if `E=enumeration(e1,e2,e3)`, then `Integer(E.e2)` is 2.
`String(e)`	Returns the string `"ev"` corresponding to the enumeration value e which evaluates to `E.ev` of the enumeration type `E = enumeration(..., ev, ...)`. This is just a special case of the `String` function described below:
String(b, <options>) String(i, <options>) String(r, significantDigits=d, <options>) String(r, format=s) String(e, <options>)	Convert a scalar non-`String` expression to a `String` representation. The first argument maybe a `Boolean b`, an `Integer i`, a `Real r`, or an `Enumeration e` (see above). The other arguments must use named arguments. The optional arguments <options> are: • `Integer minimumLength=0`: minimum length of the resulting string. If necessary, the blank character is used to fill up unused space. • `Boolean leftJustified=true`: if true, the converted result is left justified in the string; if false it is right justified in the string. For Real expressions the output shall be according to the Modelica grammar. Integer `significantDigits=6`: defines the number of significant digits in the result string. For example: "`12.3456`", "`0.0123456`", "`12345600`", "`1.23456E-10`". The format string corresponding to options is: • for Reals: `(if leftJustified then "-" else "")+String(minimumLength)+"."+`

	`String(signficantDigits)+"g"`, • for Integers: `(if leftJustified then "-" else "")+String(minimumLength)+"d"`. *Format string*: According to ANSI-C (Section 6.8.1.3 below) the format string specifies one conversion specifier (excluding the leading %), may not contain length modifiers, and may not use `"*"` for width and/or precision. For all numeric values the format specifiers `f`, `e`, `E`, `g`, `G` are allowed. For integral values it is also allowed to use the `d`, `i`, `o`, `x`, `X`, `u`, and `c`-format specifiers (for non-integral values a tool may round, truncate or use a different format if the integer conversion characters are used). • The `x`,`X`-formats (hexa-decimal) and `c` (character) for Integers does not lead to input that agrees with the Modelica-grammar.

6.8.1.3 ANSI-C Format String for String Explicit Conversion

The Modelica `String(…)` conversion function described above accepts an optional format string according to the ANSI-C standard, of which the applicable parts are described below.

Formatting takes place via *placeholders* within the *format string*. For example, if a program wanted to print out a person's age, it could present the output by prefixing it with `"Your age is "`. To denote that we want the integer for the age to be shown immediately after that message, we may use the format string:

```
"Your age is %d."
```

The syntax for a *format placeholder* in the format string is:

```
%[parameter][flags][width][.precision][length]type
```

The *`type`* part at the end must be present and can be one of the following single format characters:

- '`d`', '`i`' – a integer value as a signed decimal number. '`%d`' and '`%i`' have the same meaning for numeric to string conversion.
- '`u`' – produce a string with a decimal unsigned integer.
- '`f`', '`F`' – real number in normal (fixed-point) notation. '`f`' and '`F`' only differs in how the strings for an infinite number or NaN are produced ('`inf`', '`infinity`' and '`nan`' for '`f`', '`INF`', '`INFINITY`' and '`NAN`' for '`F`').
- '`e`', '`E`' – a real value in standard form `([-]d.ddd e[+/-]ddd)`. An `E` conversion uses the letter `E` (rather than `e`) to introduce the exponent. The exponent always contains at least two digits; if the value is zero, the exponent is 00. In Windows, the exponent contains three digits by default, for example, `1.5e002`, but this can be altered by Microsoft-specific `_set_output_format` function.
- '`g`', '`G`' – a real number in either normal or exponential notation, whichever is more appropriate for its magnitude. '`g`' uses lower-case letters, '`G`' uses upper-case letters. This type differs slightly from fixed-point notation in that insignificant zeroes to the right of the decimal point are not included. Also, the decimal point is not included on whole numbers.
- '`o`' – unsigned integer in octal.
- '`s`' – null-terminated string.
- '`a`', '`A`' – real value produced in hexadecimal notation, starting with `"0x"` or `"0X"`. '`a`' uses lower-case letters, '`A`' uses upper-case letters.
- '`%`' – a literal '`%`' character (this *`type`* doesn't accept any flags, width, precision or length).

The *`parameter`* part can be omitted or can be `n$`. For Modelica, `n` is always 1 since `String()` only accepts one numeric argument.

In `n$`, `n` is the number of the *`parameter`* to display using this format specifier, allowing the arguments provided to be output multiple times, using varying format specifiers or in different orders. If any single placeholder specifies a parameter, all the rest of the placeholders *must* also specify a parameter. For example:

```
String(16, format="%1$d %1$#x; %1$d %1$#x")
```

produces

```
"16 0x10; 16 0x10"
```

The `flags` part can be zero or more (in any order) of the single characters '+', ' ', '-', '#', '0':

- '+' – always denote the sign '+' or '-' of a number (the default is to omit the sign for positive numbers). This is only applicable to numeric types.
- ' ' – space prefixes non-negative signed numbers with a space.
- '-' – left-align the output of this placeholder (the default is to right-align the output).
- '#' – Alternate form. For 'g' and 'G', trailing zeros are not removed. For 'f', 'F', 'e', 'E', 'g', 'G', the output always contains a decimal point. For 'o', 'x', and 'X', a `0`, `0x`, and `0X`, respectively, is prepended to non-zero numbers.
- '0' – use 0 instead of spaces to pad a field when the width option is specified. For example, `String(3, format="%2d")` results in `" 3"`, while `String(3,format="%02d", 3)` results in `"03"`.

The `width` part specifies a minimum number of characters to output, and is typically used to pad fixed-width fields in tabulated output, where the fields would otherwise be smaller, although it does not cause truncation of oversized fields. A leading zero in the width value is interpreted as the zero-padding flag mentioned above, and a negative value is treated as the positive value in conjunction with the left-alignment '–' flag also mentioned above.

The `precision` part usually specifies a maximum limit on the output, depending on the particular formatting type. For floating point numeric types, it specifies the number of digits to the right of the decimal point that the output should be rounded. For the `String` type, it limits the number of characters that should be output, after which the string is truncated.

The `length` part is omitted since it is not relevant for Modelica.

6.9 Variability of Expressions

We have already briefly encountered the concept of *variability* in the above section on guarding expressions against incorrect evaluation in Section 6.7.1 on page 275 in this chapter, and in the section on variability prefixes in Section 3.11.2, page 99. See also Section 13.2.2, page 595, regarding this matter.

The variability of an expression essentially means the *freedom* of the expression to *change* value during simulation. There are four degrees of *expression variability* in Modelica from the lowest to the highest degree of variability:

- *constant* variability
- *parameter* variability
- *discrete-time* variability in two forms: *unclocked discrete-time* and *clocked discrete-time*.
- *continuous-time* variability

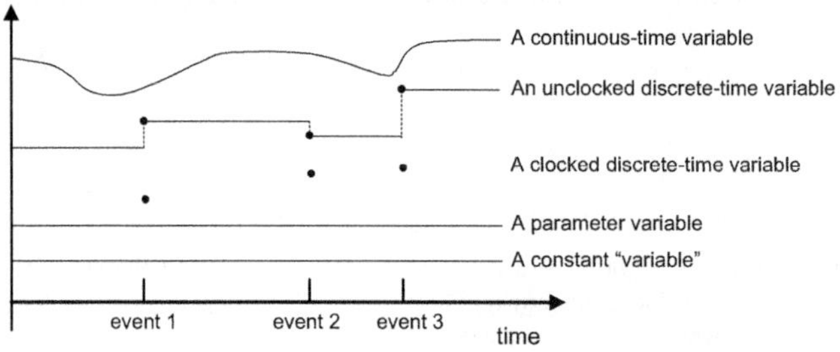

Figure 6-3. Illustrating expressions with different variability. See also Figure 3-7.

Regarding assignments such as `v:=expr` (Section 9.2.3, page 425) or declaration and modifier equations such as `v=expr` (Section 8.2, page 349), the variable `v` must have the same or higher variability than `expr`. This is described in more detail below in Section 6.9.5, page 283.

6.9.1 Constant Expressions

Constant expressions have constant variability, that is, *never change value* (but the definition of a non-final named constant can be redeclared, see below) and have time derivative equal to zero. For example, constant expressions can include literal constant expressions such as `3+5`, `false`, `"hello!"`, constant "variables" that have been declared with the prefix `constant`, enumeration values, and applications of operators or functions with constant expressions as arguments, where parameter variable declarations may not be present in those functions.

Additionally, applications of the following special operators (with function syntax) `initial`, `terminal`, `der`, `edge`, `change`, `sample`, `pre`, are not allowed in constant expressions since those operators imply discrete-time or continuous-time variability.

To summarize, a constant expression is one of the following:

- Real, Integer, Boolean, String, and enumeration literals.
- Variables declared as constant.
- A function or operator with constant subexpressions as argument (and no parameters defined in the function) is a constant expression, except for applications of the special built-in operators `initial`, `terminal`, `der`, `edge`, `change`, `sample`, and `pre`.

Examples of constant expressions:

```
3.14 - 27 * 83
sin(35.6)
false or true
"this is a constant string literal"
one + 2   // one from the declaration:  constant Real one = 1;
Color.red // from the declaration Color = enumeration(red,blue,green)
```

Variables declared as `constant` (*constant variable*, Section 3.11.2, page 99) must have an associated declaration equation with a constant expression if the constant is directly in the simulation model or used in the simulation model. The value of a declared constant can be modified after it has been given a value, unless the constant is declared `final` or modified with a final modifier. A constant declared without an associated declaration equation can be given one by using a modifier.

A named constant can be defined in a package, can be imported from a package (Section 10.2.1, page 497), and can be accessed by nested lookup (Section 3.16.1, page 109) from inside a subclass to the current class where the constant is defined

6.9.2 Parameter Expressions

Parameter expressions have parameter variability, ***remain constant*** during time-dependent simulation, and have time derivative equal to zero. Parameter expressions may include constant expressions or parameter variables declared with the prefix `parameter`, or applications of operators and functions with parameter expressions as arguments. Parameter variables may be assigned values immediately before time-dependent simulation starts, either in a declaration equation or interactively through a simulation tool. This implies that the value of a parameter expression becomes available immediately before simulation starts and remains constant throughout the simulation.

However, in *contrast to* named constants, a named parameter cannot be defined in a package, cannot be imported from a package (Section 10.2.1, page 497), and cannot be accessed by nested lookup (Section 3.16.1, page 109) from inside a subclass to the class where the parameter is defined.

Analogous to constant expressions, applications of the special operators `initial`, `terminal`, `der`, `edge`, `change`, `sample`, `pre` are not allowed in parameter expressions since those operators imply discrete-time or continuous-time variability.

To summarize, expressions with parameter variability can be the following:

- Constant expressions. (This may appear as a contradiction since constant and parameter expressions have different variability but means that a constant expression can be used in a context that requires parameter variability.)
- Variables declared as parameter.
- A function or operator with parameter subexpressions is a parameter expression, e.g. `4+n`, except for the special built-in operators `initial`, `terminal`, `der`, `edge`, `change`, `sample`, and `pre`.

Example of an expression with parameter variability:

```
3 + n    // Where n comes from:  parameter Integer n = 10;
```

Example of a named parameter variable:

```
parameter Real  height = 186;
```

See Section 3.11.2, page 99 for restrictions regarding the definition and use of named parameters.

6.9.3 Discrete-Time Expressions

Discrete-time expressions have discrete-time variability, may *change* their values *only at event instants* during simulation (see also Chapter 13 about hybrid modeling, starting on page 591), and have time derivative equal to zero. However, it is not allowed to apply the `der`-operator to a discrete-time variable. Discrete-time expressions may include *constant* or *parameter* expressions, discrete-time variables, as well as applications of operators and functions with discrete-time arguments.

There are two kinds of discrete-time expressions:

- *Unclocked discrete-time expressions* which have unclocked discrete-time variability and keep defined values between events (i.e., are piecewise constant).
- *Clocked discrete-time expressions* which have defined values only at clock tick events for an associated clock. See Section 13.6.15.1, page 722 and Section 13.6.3, page 697.

`Boolean`, `Integer`, `String`, and `enumeration` variables are discrete-time by default and cannot be continuous-time according to the language rules. However, note that there is no mathematical necessity behind the decision that such variables must be discrete-time in Modelica, it would be perfectly possible to have a different language rule which lets integer variables change value at any point in time.

An unclocked `Real` variable declared with the prefix `discrete` has discrete-time variability and must be assigned in some when-statement or be on the left-hand side of an equation inside a when-equation. Additionally, an unclocked `Real` variable without the `discrete` prefix but assigned a value in a when-equation or when-statement, either through an assignment statement or by being on the left-hand side of an equation in a when-equation, is a discrete-time variable.

Expressions in unclocked when-equations and when-statements have unclocked discrete-time variability. This is a natural consequence of the fact that when-equations and when-statements are executed only at event instants, causing expressions inside the when constructs to change value only at events.

Applications of the functions `pre`, `edge`, and `change` are always unclocked discrete-time expressions. Provided that they do not occur within argument expressions to the special function `noEvent()`, relational expressions involving the relational operators (>, <, >=, <=) as well as applications of the functions `ceil`, `floor`, and operators `div`, `mod`, and `rem` are discrete-time expressions, even if their argument expressions have continuous-time variability. This follows from the fact that the result of these relational operators and special functions remain piecewise constant and cause events to be generated when they change value, that is, they change value only at events. However, remember that relational expressions and function applications when enclosed by `noEvent()` are continuous-time rather than discrete-time expressions; for example, `x<2` is a discrete-time expression whereas `noEvent(x<2)` is a continuous-time expression.

Expressions in functions behave as though they were discrete-time expressions since a function is always called and evaluated at some point in time, that is, time does not go forward during evaluation of a function call, similar to the evaluation of a when-equation or a when-statement at an event. Function calls can, however, occur at any point in time, not only at events.

To summarize, discrete-time expressions can be either:

- *Clocked discrete-time expressions* (Section 13.6.15.1, page 722).
- *Unclocked discrete-time expressions.*

Unclocked discrete-time expressions can be one of the following:

- Parameter expressions. (It might appear as a contradiction that parameter expressions can be part of discrete-time expressions even though they do not change during simulation. However, this is fine, since a discrete-time expression *may* change at event instants, it does not necessarily have to change.)
- Unclocked discrete-time variables, that is, `Integer`, `Boolean`, `String` variables and `enumeration` variables, as well as `Real` variables assigned in when-clauses
- Function calls where all input arguments of the function are unclocked discrete-time expressions.
- Expressions where all the subexpressions are unclocked discrete-time expressions.
- Expressions in the body of a when-clause, initial equation, or initial algorithm.
- Unless inside `noEvent`: Ordered relations (>,<,>=,<=) if at least one operand is a subtype of Real (i.e., Real elementary relations, see Section 6.11.1, page 287) and the functions `ceil`, `floor`, `div`, `mod`, `rem`. These will generate events if at least one sub-expression is not a discrete-time expression. In other words, relations inside `noEvent()`, such as `noEvent(x>1)`, are not discrete-time expressions.
- The functions `pre`, `edge`, and `change` result in unclocked discrete-time expressions.
- Expressions in functions behave as though they were discrete-time expressions.

These are some examples of unclocked discrete-time expressions:

```
y >= 35.2
div(x,2) + 5
b2 and b3      // Where b2 and b3 are booleans:    Boolean b2, b3;
```

Moreover, inside an if-expression, if-clause, while-statement, or for-clause, that is controlled by a non-discrete-time (i.e., a continuous-time expression that is not discrete-time) condition or range expression and not in the body of a when-clause, it is not legal to have assignments to unclocked discrete-time variables, equations between unclocked discrete-time expressions, or real elementary relations/functions that should generate events. This restriction is necessary in order to guarantee that all equations for unclocked discrete-time variables are unclocked discrete-time expressions, and to ensure that crossing functions do not become active between events.

6.9.4 Continuous-Time Expressions

Continuous-time expressions have continuous-time variability and may *change* their *values* continuously during simulation.

Continuous-time expressions may include constant, parameter, unclocked discrete-time expressions as well as continuous-time `Real` variables and applications of operators and functions.

Note that expressions involving continuous-time variables like `x` are still continuous-time even when combined with constant or parameter expressions; for example if `x` is continuous-time, then `2*x` is also continuous-time. The fact that a variable has continuous-time variability does not mean that it will necessarily change, only that it has the *possibility to change*. For example, if there is an equation `x=2` in the model then `x` will have a constant value but still keeps its continuous-time variability property.

Variables declared as `Real` have the default variability continuous-time if no variability prefix is specified and they are *not* assigned values in any when-statement or on the left-hand side of any equation in a when-equation.

Examples of continuous-time expressions:

```
x + y - 2      // Where x, y are continuous-time:   Real  x, y;

noEvent(z+2 >= 37)
```

6.9.5 Variability and Subtyping

We have learned that the variability of an expression governs the degree of freedom with which the expression may vary during simulation. Variability is a specific property but has clear connections with the notion of data type, for example, variables of the built-in type `Real` have default variability continuous-time whereas `Integer`, `Boolean`, and `String` variables have default variability unclocked discrete-time.

The question is whether variability should be considered as part of a total type concept. In fact, we have already included variability as part of the notion of type in our definition of general class type on page 118 in Chapter 3. There are clear advantages of including variability in a total type concept, as well as being necessary for class types since variability prefixes can occur in declarations of class members.

The rules regarding assignment of expressions with different variability as well as inheritance relations between classes containing members of different variability become special cases of the general subtyping rules (Section 3.19, page 123) about the definition and use of subtyping.

According to these rules for definition and use of type equivalence, type coercion, and variability in an assignment statement, e.g. *a* := *expr*, or a declaration equation, for example, *a* = *expr*, the following holds:

- The type T2 of the right-hand side (*expr*) must be equivalent to the type T1 of the left-hand side (*a*) after type coercion.
- The variability of type T2 is lower than or equal to the variability of type T1, where *constant* is the lowest variability and *continuous-time* is the highest.

For example, this has the consequence that the right-hand side expression (*expr*) in a declaration equation of a `parameter` variable (*a*, and its attributes such as `start`) need to be of parameter variability (which also includes constant variability). If the left-hand side (*a*) would have unclocked discrete-time variability, the right-hand side (*expr*) must also have unclocked discrete-time variability (which also includes constant and parameter variability).

For normal equations *expr1* = *expr2*, type equivalence holds between both sides of the equation as defined in Section 3.19.1, page 124. This poses no special constraints on variability. However, there is one additional rule regarding variability in equations stemming from the existence of the `noEvent` operator and the fact that `Integer`, `Boolean`, `String`, and `enumeration` expressions are never allowed to have continuous-time variability:

- For an equation *expr1* = *expr2* where the two expressions have a type derived from `Integer`, `Boolean`, `String`, or `enumeration`, both expressions must be either unclocked discrete-time expressions or clocked discrete-time expressions.

For equations involving expressions of records or other user-defined types, the above rule is applied to each element equation, where, for example, a record has been broken down into elements corresponding to its fields with built-in basic types. This rule prevents the use of the `noEvent` operator on one side of `Integer`, `Boolean`, `String`, and `enumeration` equations outside of a when-equation, since otherwise one of the two expressions would not have unclocked discrete-time variability.

The example classes below illustrate the subtyping and variability rules for declaration equations and normal equations.

```
model ParConstants
  parameter Real p1 = 1;
  // constant  Real c1 = p1 + 2; // Error! - not a constant expression.
  parameter Real p2 = p1 + 2;    // Fine!  - p1+2 has same variability.
end ParConstants;

model TestEquations
  ParConstants c1(p1=3);       // Fine!
  ParConstants c2(p2=7);       // Fine, declaration equation can be modified.
  Boolean b;
  Real    x;
equation
  b = noEvent(x > 1);       // Error, since b is a discrete-time and
  // noEvent(x > 1) is a continuous-time expression.
end TestEquations;
```

6.10 Arithmetic Operators

Modelica supports five binary arithmetic operators that operate on any numerical type:

^	Exponentiation
*	Multiplication
/	Division
+	Addition
-	Subtraction

Some of these operators can also be applied to a combination of a scalar type and an array type, which means an operation between the scalar and each element of the array. Addition and subtraction are also defined between two arrays. In the case of multiplication the operation is also defined between two arrays being interpreted as matrix multiplication. More details about the array versions of these operators are available in Chapter 7.

Unary versions of the addition and subtraction operators are available, for example, as in –35 and +84.

6.10.1 Element-Wise Arithmetic Operators

Modelica also supports five element-wise binary arithmetic operators that operate on arrays of any numerical type, as well as on scalars:

`.*`	Element-wise multiplication
`./`	Element-wise division
`.+`	Element-wise addition
`.-`	Element-wise subtraction
`.^`	Element-wise exponentiation.

See Section 7.8 , page 329, for more details.

6.10.2 Integer Arithmetic

When Modelica is compiled into C, integer arithmetic in Modelica is the same as in the ISO C language standard. However, even though compiling into C is quite common this is not required since Modelica can also be compiled into other languages. The most common representation of integers is 32-bit two's complement (e.g. see a definition in *C—A Reference Manual*, Section 5.1.1 (Harbison and Steele 1991)). This representation is used on widespread modern microprocessors such as Pentium, Sparc, and so on. In Modelica, at least a minimum representable value of –2,147,483,648 and a maximum value of 2,147,483,647 must be supported. Note, however, that other Integer representations are also allowed according to the ISO C standard.

For certain arithmetic operations, regarding both integer and floating point numbers, it can be the case that the true mathematical result of the operation cannot be represented as a value of the expected result type. This condition is called *overflow*, or in some cases *underflow*.

In general, neither the Modelica language nor the C language specify the consequences of overflow of an arithmetic operation. One possibility is that an incorrect value (of the correct type) is produced. Another possibility is that program execution is terminated. A third possibility is that some kind of exception or trap is generated that could be detected by the program in some implementation-dependent way.

For the common case of two's complement representation, integer arithmetic is modular—meaning that integer operations are performed using a two's-complement integer representation, but if the result exceeds the range of the type it is reduced modulo the range. Thus, such integer arithmetic never overflows or underflows but only wraps around.

Integer division, that is, division of two integer values, truncates toward zero with any fractional part discarded (e.g., `div(5,2)` becomes `2`, `div(-5,2)` becomes `-2`). This is the same as in the C language according to the C99 standard. According to the earlier C89 standard, integer division for negative numbers was implementation dependent.

Division by zero in Modelica causes unpredictable effects, that is, the behavior is undefined.

6.10.3 Floating Point Arithmetic

Floating point arithmetic in Modelica is specified as double precision floating point arithmetic. Since Modelica can be compiled into different languages, the only formal requirement by the Modelica language specification is that the minimal recommended `Real` number range corresponds to the range of IEEE double precision floating point numbers, for which the largest representable positive number is 1.7976931348623157E+308 and the smallest positive number is 2.2250738585072014E–308.

When compiled into C, values of the Modelica `Real` type are represented as values of the `double` type in ISO C, and floating point operations in Modelica are compiled into corresponding double precision floating point operations in C. Even if not strictly required by the ISO C standard, most C implementations have adopted the IEEE standard for binary floating point arithmetic (ISO/IEEE Std 754-1985), which completely dominates the scene regarding C implementations as well as floating point instructions provided by modern microprocessors. Thus, we can for practical purposes assume that Modelica follows ISO/IEEE Std 754-1985. Real values are then represented as 64-bit IEEE floating point numbers. The largest representable positive number in that representation is 1.7976931348623157E+308, whereas the smallest positive number is 2.2250738585072014E–308.

The effects of arithmetic overflow, underflow, or division by zero in Modelica are implementation dependent, depending on the C compiler and the Modelica tool in use. Either some value is produced and execution continues, or some kind of trap or exception is generated which can terminate execution if it is not handled by the application or the Modelica run-time system.

6.11 Equality, Relational, and Logical Operators

Modelica supports the standard set of relational and logical operators, all of which produce the standard boolean values `true` or `false`:

>	greater than
>=	greater than or equal
<	less than
<=	less than or equal to
==	equality within expressions
<>	inequality

The equality and relational operators apply only to scalar arguments. Currently there is a restriction in Modelica models (but not in functions) that the equality == and inequality <> operators may not be directly applied to arguments that have a type which is `Real` or a subtype of `Real`.

The reason for this rule is that relations with `Real` arguments are transformed to state events (see events, Section 13.2.4.4, page 600, and crossing functions, Section 18.2.5.5, page 1015) and this transformation becomes unnecessarily complicated for the == and <> relational operators, for example, two crossing functions instead of one crossing function needed. Even inside functions where these operations are allowed testing of equality of Real variables is questionable on machines where the number length in registers is different to the number length in main memory.

These operations, e.g. `x==y`, `x<>y`, however, can for example be reformulated as `abs(x-y)<1e-10`, `abs(x-y)>1e-10` respectively or using some other small number instead of `1e-10`.

Relational operators are typically used within if-statements or if-equations, or to compute the value of a `Boolean` variable, for example:

```
if v1<v2 then ...  ;
boolvar2 := v3 >= v35;
```

A single equality sign = is never used in relational expressions, only in equations and in function calls using named parameter passing.

=	equality within equations
=	single assignment of named arguments at function call

The following logical operators are defined:

`not`	negation, unary operator
`and`	logical and
`or`	logical or

As stated in the section about evaluation order on page 274, Modelica is free to use *any order* in evaluation of expression parts as long as the evaluation rules for the operators in the expression are fulfilled.

Concerning the logical operators `and`, `or` in boolean expressions, one possibility is short-circuit evaluation, that is, the expression is evaluated from left to right and the evaluation is stopped if evaluation of further arguments is not necessary to determine the result of the boolean expression. Thus, if the variable `b1` in the expression below has the value `true`, then evaluation of `b2` and `b3` would not be necessary since the result will be `true` independent of their values. On the other hand, we cannot rely on this order—evaluation might start with `b3` and involve all three variables. However, this does not really matter for the user since Modelica is a declarative language, and the result of evaluation is the same in all these cases. See also Section 6.7.1, page 275, for guarding evaluation.

```
boolvar   :=  true and false;
boolvar2  :=  not boolvar;
boolvar3  :=  b1 or b2 or b3;
```

6.11.1 Real Elementary Relations

Relations of the form `v1 rel_op v2`, where `v1` and `v2` are variables and `rel_op` a relational operator (Section 6.11, page 286) are called elementary relations. If either `v1` or `v2` or both variables are a subtype of Real, the relation is called a Real elementary relation.

See also `noEvent(...)` (Section 0, page 293) which suppresses event generation at Real elementary relations; dicrete-time expressions and event generation (Section 6.9.3, page 281);

The numerical solution process is halted and an event occurs whenever a Real elementary relation, for example, `x > 2`, changes its value (Section 18.2.5.4, page 1014).

6.12 Miscellaneous Operators

All operators are not arithmetic or logical operators. There also exist a string concatenation operator, a conditional operator for conditional expressions, and a member access operator for accessing fields of variables. There is also `time`, which is a built-in variable, that is, not an operator.

6.12.1 String Concatenation

The + operator is also a built-in string concatenation operator in Modelica, both for string variables and literal string constants. For example, long comment strings can be constructed using the + operator for concatenation of string constants, for example:

```
Real longval = 1.35E+300  "This is" + " a " + "rather " + " long comment";
```

Another example using string variables and string literals in expressions returning string values:

```
String val1 = "This is";
String val2 = " a ";
String concatvalue = val1 + val2 +"rather " + " long string";
// The value becomes: "This is a rather long string"
```

Element-wise concatenation of arrays of strings is also available using the + operator (see Section 7.3, page 318).

6.12.2 The Conditional Operator—if-expressions

The conditional if-expression operator in Modelica provides a single expression that computes one out of two expressions dependent on the value of the condition. The general syntactic form is shown below:

if *condition* **then** *expression1* **else** *expression2*

Both the `then`-part and the `else`-part of the conditional if-expression must be present. Conditional if-expressions can be nested, that is, *expression2* can itself be an if-expression.

A conditional if-expression is evaluated as follows:

- First the *condition* is evaluated, which must be a Boolean expression. If *condition* is true, then *expression1* is evaluated and becomes the value of the if-expression. Otherwise *expression2* is evaluated and becomes the value of the if-expression.
- The result expressions, i.e., *expression1* and *expression2*, must have assignment-compatible types. This means that the type of one result expression must be assignable to the type of the other result expression, which defines the type of the conditional expression.

The following equation contains a conditional if-expression operator on the right-hand side:

```
value = (if a+b<5 then firstvalue else secondvalue);
```

This is equivalent to the following conditional equation (see also Chapter 8, page 347, and Section 13.2.6, page 613):

```
if (a+b<5) then
  value = firstvalue;
else
  value = secondvalue;
end if;
```

It is a matter of taste as to which form is used. Whether to use parentheses around the conditional if-expression operator is a matter of personal style since this is not required by the language.

A nested conditional if-expression can have one of the following two equivalent forms:

if *condition1* **then** *expression2* **else if** *condition2* **then** *expression3* **else** *expression4*
if *condition1* **then** *expression2* **elseif** *condition2* **then** *expression3* **else** *expression4*

In the second form, the keywords `else if` have been replaced by the single keyword `elseif`, which also is the case in the second variant in the example below:

```
Integer i;
Integer sign_of_i_v2 = if i<0 then -1 else if i==0 then 0 else 1;
Integer sign_of_i_v1 = if i<0 then -1 elseif  i==0 then 0 else 1;
```

The conditional if-expression operator is one of the two ternary operators in Modelica—the operator basically has three arguments (regarding `elseif` as nested application). The other ternary operator is the range operator *expr* : *expr* : *expr*.

Moreover, inside an if-expression that is controlled by a non-discrete time (i.e., a continuous-time expression that is not discrete-time) switching expression and not in the body of a when-clause, it is not legal to have real elementary relations/functions that should generate events, see Section 6.8.1.3, page 278.

6.12.3 Member Access Operator

It is possible to access members of a class instance using dot notation, that is, the `.` operator, as in `R1.R` for accessing the resistance field `R` of resistor `R1`. Local types and inner classes which are members of a class can of course also be accessed using dot notation on name of the class, not on instances of the class.

6.12.4 User-Defined Overloaded Operators

Mechanisms to define the standard Modelica operators for user-defined data types are described in Section 9.5, page 481.

6.13 Built-in Intrinsic Mathematical Functions

The following are built-in intrinsic mathematical functions in Modelica. Their result(s) are in principle dependent only on the value(s) of the input argument(s), apart from possible unwanted effects such as square root of negative numbers or division by zero caused by the combination of event generation and unguarded use of `sqrt` or division operators. See the section on guarding expressions against incorrect evaluation on page 275 to avoid such problems.

Passing `Integer` arguments to functions requiring `Real` argument type is of course possible: the `Integer` arguments are automatically promoted to `Real` type. Most of these standard mathematical functions are also available in the standard Modelica library `Modelica.Math` (Section 16.2, page 920). In fact, most functions defined in `Modelica.Math` behave as built-in functions (Section 6.13.2, page 291) and can be called using the short function names without package prefix. There are also a few, e.g., `atan3`, `asinh`, `acosh`, etc., which are in `Modelica.Math` but are not built-in functions.

There are three groups of built-in intrinsic mathematical functions, of which two are listed further below:

- Functions that may give rise to state events (Section 6.13.1, page 289).
- Continuous functions (Section 6.13.2, page 291) which never give rise to state events.
- Type conversion functions, e.g., `Integer` and `String`, (Section 6.8.1.2, page 277).

6.13.1 Special and/or Event Generating Intrinsic Mathematical Functions

When used outside when-equations, when-statements, or clocked discrete-time partitions (Section 13.6, page 694) and not within Modelica function bodies, certain built-in mathematical functions in the table below will cause events to be triggered at points where the function or its derivative are *discontinuous*, for example, at zero crossings of the argument. This is stated explicitly for each such function. Some functions do not generate events but have special properties, for example, `sqrt` which is not defined for negative arguments.

It is possible to avoid generating events by enclosing the function call by `noEvent()`, for example, `noEvent(abs(x))`, at the cost of less efficient operation of the numerical equation solver. On the other hand, if an expression or function together with its derivatives to an appropriate degree is known to be continuous despite containing event-generating constructs, it will be more efficient to enclose the expression or function within `noEvent()` since in that particular case unnecessary event-handling code will be avoided.

`abs(v)`	Gives the absolute value of expression v. Expanded into "`noEvent(if v >= 0 then v else -v)`", i.e. no events are triggered. The argument must have `Integer` or `Real` type. If the argument has `Integer` type, then the result has

	`Integer` type; otherwise, if the argument has `Real` type, then the result has `Real` type.
`sign(v)`	Gives the sign of the expression v. Expanded into "`noEvent(if v > 0 then 1 else if v < 0 then -1 else 0)`." The argument must have `Integer` or `Real` type. The result has `Integer` type. No events are triggered. Examples: `sign(-1.7)=-1, sign(5.1)=1, sign(0)=0`
`sqrt(v)`	Returns the *square root* of `v` if `v>=0`, otherwise an error occurs. Result and argument have type `Real`. No events are triggered.
`div(x,y)`	Returns the *algebraic quotient* `x/y` with any *fractional part discarded* (also known as truncation toward zero). Result and arguments have type `Real` or `Integer`. If any of the arguments have type `Real`, the result is a `Real`, otherwise an `Integer`. Note that outside of a when-clause or clocked discrete-time partition state events are triggered when the return value of this function changes discontinuously. Examples: `div(10,2)=5, div(10,3)=3, div(-2,3)=0, div(-4,3)=-1, div(10.2,3)=3.0, div(-7.1,2)=-3.0`

`mod(x,y)`	Returns the *integer modulus* of `x/y`, i.e., `mod(x,y)=x-floor(x/y)*y`. Result and arguments shall have type `Real` or `Integer`. If either of the arguments has type `Real`, the result is a `Real`, otherwise an `Integer`. Note that outside of a when-clause or clocked discrete-time partition state events are triggered when the return value of this function changes discontinuously.
	Examples: `mod(7,5)=2, mod(13,5)=3, mod(10,5)= 0,`
	`mod(-7,5) = -7-(-2)*5 = 3,`
	`mod(7,-5) = 7-(-2)*(-5) = -3,`
	`mod(2,0.9)=0.2, mod(-2,0.9)=0.7, mod(2,-0.9)=-0.7`

`rem(x,y)`	Returns the *integer remainder* of `x/y`, such that `div(x,y) * y + rem(x,y) = x`. Result and arguments shall have type `Real` or `Integer`. If either of the arguments have type `Real`, the result is a `Real`, otherwise an `Integer`. Note that outside of a when-clause or clocked discrete-time partition state events are triggered when the return value of this function changes discontinuously. Examples: `rem(10,2)=0, rem(11,2)=1,` `rem(2,0.8) = 0.4, rem(-3,1.4)=-0.2.`
`ceil(x)`	Returns the smallest integer not less than `x` as a floating point number, i.e., the closest integer above `x`. Result and argument have type `Real`. Note that outside of a when-clause or clocked discrete-time partition state events are triggered when the return value of this function changes discontinuously. Examples: `ceil(3)=3.0, ceil(3.5)=4.0, ceil(-1.7)=-1.0`
`floor(x)`	Returns the largest integer not greater than `x` as a floating point number, i.e., the closest integer below `x`. Result and argument have type `Real`. Note that outside of a when-clause or clocked discrete-time partition state events are triggered when the return value of this function changes discontinuously. Examples: `floor(3)=3.0, floor(3.5)=3.0,` `floor(-1.7)=-2.0`

`integer(x)`	Returns the largest integer not greater than `x` as an *integer*, i.e., the closest integer below `x`. The argument has type `Real`. The result has type `Integer`. Note that outside of a when-clause or clocked discrete-time partition state events are triggered when the return value of this function changes discontinuously. Examples: `integer(3.5)=3, integer(-1.7)=2`

6.13.2 Continuous Intrinsic Mathematical Functions

The following are the continuous built-in common mathematical functions which do not generate events:

`sin`(*u*)	sine
`cos`(*u*)	cosine
`tan`(*u*)	tangent (*u* shall not be: ..., $-\pi/2,\ \pi/2,\ 3\pi/2, \ldots$)
`asin`(*u*)	inverse sine $(-1 \le u \le 1)$
`acos`(*u*)	inverse cosine $(-1 \le u \le 1)$
`atan`(*u*)	inverse tangent
`atan2`(*u1*,*u2*)	The atan2(*u1*,*u2*) function calculates the principal value of the arc tangent of *u1*/*u2*, using the signs of the two arguments to determine the quadrant of the result.
`sinh`(*u*)	hyperbolic sine
`cosh`(*u*)	hyperbolic cosine
`tanh`(*u*)	hyperbolic tangent
`exp`(*u*)	exponential, base *e*
`log`(*u*)	natural (base *e*) logarithm $(u > 0)$
`log10`(*u*)	base 10 logarithm $(u > 0)$

6.14 Built-in Special Operators and Functions

The following built-in special operators in Modelica have the same syntax as a function call. However, they do *not* behave as mathematical functions since the result depends not only on the input arguments but also on the status of the simulation. The non-event-related operators are described below in Section 6.14.1 and the event-related special operators are given further below in Section 0, page 293. Several operators are vectorized for non-scalar arguments according to Section 7.10, page 340.

6.14.1 Non-Event-Related Special Operators and Functions

This table describes a number of special operators and functions which are not specifically event related.

`der(`*`expr`*`)`	The time derivative of expression *`expr`*. The expression *`expr`* must have a type which is a subtype of `Real`, and cannot have discrete-time variability, i.e., it must have *continuous-time* variability. For example, `der(m*h)` is interpreted as `der(m)*h + m*der(h)`. The expression and all its subexpressions must be differentiable. If `x` is an array, the operator is applied to all elements of the array. For a `Real` argument *`expr`* with parameter or constant variability, the result is a zero-valued scalar or zero-valued array of the same size as `x`.

`delay(expr, delayTime, delayMax)`
 	
`delay(expr, delayTime)`
	Returns the value of `expr` at the time `(time-delayTime)` for `time > time.start + delayTime` and the value of `expr` at the time `time.start` for `time <= time.start + delayTime`.
	The arguments, i.e. `expr`, `delayTime` and `delayMax`, need to be subtypes of `Real`. The expression `delayMax` must be a parameter expression, and is used to avoid excessive storage requirements and enhance efficiency by storing the delayed expression for a maximum delay time given by `DelayMax`.
	The following relation must hold: `0 <= delayTime <= delayMax`, otherwise an error occurs. If `delayMax` is not supplied in the argument list, `delayTime` needs to be a parameter expression.
	For more details, see Section 13.2.5.17, page 612.

`cardinality(c)`	Returns the number of (internal and external) occurrences of connector instance *c* in connect-equations of the current model as an `Integer` number. For an example on the use of `cardinality`, see Section 5.7.9, page 223. *Note: this construct should no longer be used since it is deprecated in the current Modelica version.*
`direction(c)`	The function `direction(c)` gives information about the direction of the connection, provided that `cardinality(c)== 1`, i.e., the connector `c` is involved in exactly one connection. For a connection clause `connect(c1,c2)` fulfilling that constraint, `direction(c1)` returns `-1` and `direction(c2)` returns `1`. See also Section 5.7.9.1 on page 224. *Note: this construct should no longer be used since it is deprecated in the current Modelica version.*
`semiLinear(x, positiveSlope, negativeSlope)`	Returns: `if x>=0 then positiveSlope*x else negativeSlope*x`. The result is of type Real. For more details, especially for the case when x = 0, see Section 8.8.1, page 386. For non-scalar arguments the function is vectorized according to Section 7.10, page 340.
`homotopy(actual=actual, simplified=simplified)`	The scalar expressions `actual` and `simplified` are subtypes of Real. A Modelica translator should map this operator into either of the two forms: 1. Returns `actual` (i.e., a trivial implementation). 2. In order to solve algebraic systems of equations, the operator might during the solution process return a combination of the two arguments, ending at actual, e.g., `actual*lambda + simplified*(1-lambda),` where `lambda` is a homotopy parameter going from 0 to 1. The solution must fulfill the equations for homotopy returning `actual`. For a more detailed explanation, see Section 8.4.7, page 372. For non-scalar arguments the function is vectorized according to Section 7.10, page 340.
`inStream(v)`	The operator `inStream(v)` is only allowed on stream variables `v` defined in stream connectors, and is the value of the stream variable v close to the connection point assuming that the *flow* is from the connection point *into*

	the component. This value is computed from the stream connection equations of the flow variables and of the stream variables. The operator is vectorizable. For more details see Section 5.10.1, page 245.
`actualStream(v)`	The `actualStream(v)` operator is provided for convenience, and returns the actual value of the stream variable v for any flow direction. It is equivalent to the expression `if c.m_flow > 0 then inStream(v) else v` where `v` belongs to the same stream connector `c` as the flow variable `c.m_flow`. The operator is vectorizable. For more details see Section 5.10.1, page 245.
`spatialDistribution(in0, in1, x, pv, iP, iV)`	The `spatialDistribution(...)` operator allows modeling of 1D PDEs especially for transport phenomena, see Section 8.10.3, page 412.
`getInstanceName()`	The `getInstanceName()` operator is called with no input arguments and returns a string with the name of the model that is simulated (subject to the simulation command), appended with the fully qualified name of the instance in the simulated model within which this function is called. For example, if a `Vehicle` model is simulated, and this function is called within the controller instance which is part of the engine instance, the string `"Vehicle.engine.controller"` is returned. For more details see Section 6.14.1.1, page 293.

6.14.1.1 getInstanceName

The `getInstanceName()` is called with no arguments. It returns a string with the name of the model that is simulated, for example, subject to a simulation command, appended with the fully qualified name within that model of the instance within which the `getInstanceName` function is called.

```
package MyLib
  model Vehicle
    Engine engine;
    ...
  end Vehicle;

  model Engine
    Controller controller;
    ...
  end Engine;

  model Controller
  equation
    Modelica.Utilities.Streams.print("Info from: " + getInstanceName());
  end Controller;
end MyLib;
```

If `MyLib.Vehicle` is simulated, the call `getInstanceName()` returns `"Vehicle.engine.controller"` since `Vehicle` is the model subject to simulation and `engine.controller` is the fully qualified name within `Vehicle` of the instance within which `getInstanceName` is called.

If the `getInstanceName` function is not called inside a model or block, for example, the function is called in a function or within an expression used in a constant definition in a package, the return value is not specified.

Moreover, the Modelica language standard requires that the simulation result *should not* depend on the return value of this function. It is primarily intended for information messages or error messages.

6.14.2 Event-Related Special Operators

The following event-related special operators with function syntax are available. Note that there are even more operators and functions that are event-related in the sense that they generate events; see Section 6.13.1, page 289. The operators `noEvent`, `pre`, `edge`, and `change` are vectorized if applied to a non-scalar argument, see Section 7.10, page 340.

A *clocked discrete-time* equation partition may not contain calls to these event-related special operators with the exception of `noEvent`, see Section 13.6.15.1, page 722.

`initial()`	An `initial()` call returns `true` at the beginning of the simulation (when `time` is equal to `time.start`, the start time of the simulation) and returns `false` otherwise. This is during the initialization phase. See also Section 13.2.5.1, page 601.
`terminal()`	Returns `true` at the end of a successful simulation. See also Section 13.2.5.2, page 601.
`noEvent(expr)`	By placing `noEvent` around *expr*, no events are generated from *expr*. Relational expressions involving real variables or function calls within *expr* are evaluated exactly as stated, i.e., no events are triggered at possible discontinuities of *expr* or its derivatives, thus avoiding generating events and event iteration. The operator is vectorized if applied to a non-scalar argument. See below in Section 6.14.2.1, page 296, about event iteration, or (Section 13.2.6.7, page 623, and Section 18.2.5, page 1012), for more detailed information regarding events and event-iteration.
`smooth(p, expr)`	By placing a call to smooth around *expr*, we state that *expr* is continuous and its derivatives up to order *p* are continuous. This information can be used by the Modelica environment to avoid event generation and thus increase performance. However, `smooth` does not prohibit event generation from *expr*. If p>=0, then `smooth(p, expr)` returns *expr*, and declares that *expr* is *p* times continuously differentiable, i.e., *expr* is continuous in all real variables appearing in the expression and all partial derivatives with respect to all appearing real variables *exist* and are continuous up to order *p*. The argument p should be a scalar integer parameter expression. The only allowed types for *expr* in `smooth` are Real expressions, arrays of allowed expressions, and records only containing components of allowed expressions. For more details see Section 13.2.5.11, page 608.
`sample(start, interval)`	Returns `true` and triggers time events at time instants *start* + `i*`*interval* `(i=0,1,...)`. During a numerical solution of the continuous part of the equation system, i.e., between the time events, the operator always returns `false`. The starting time *start* and the sample interval *interval* need to be parameter expressions and need to have types which are subtypes of `Real` or `Integer`. See also Section 13.2.5.4, page 602.

`pre(y)`	Returns the "left limit" $y(t^{pre})$ of variable y(t) at a time instant t. The left limit is the value immediately before the event is triggered. At an event instant, $y(t^{pre})$ is the value of *y* after the most recent *event iteration* at time instant *t*. The value `pre(y)` can be thought of as the "predecessor value" of y. The argument *y* must be a variable and not a general expression. The operator is vectorized if applied to a non-scalar argument. Regarding event iteration see Section 6.14.2.10, page 296 below, or (Section 13.2.6.7, page 623, and Section 18.2.5, page 1012) for more detailed information. The `pre` operator can only be applied if the following three conditions are fulfilled simultaneously: (a) the variable *y* has a type which is record type, or a subtype of `Boolean`, `Integer`, `Real`, or `String`, or an array type of one of those subtypes. (b) the variable *y* has unclocked discrete-time variability, (c) the `pre` operator is *not* used within a function. At the initial time `pre(y) = y.start`, i.e. the left limit of y is identical to the start value. See Chapter 13, especially Section 13.2.5.12, page 609, for more information regarding `pre`, event iteration and events.
`edge(b)`	The expression `edge(b)` is expanded into `(b and not pre(b))` for the `Boolean` variable *b*. The same three restrictions as for the `pre()` operator apply. The argument b must be a `Boolean` variable and not a general expression. The operator is vectorized if applied to a non-scalar argument. See also Section 13.2.5.15, page 611.
`change(v)`	The expression `change(v)` is expanded into `(v<>pre(v))`. The same three restrictions as for the `pre()` operator apply. The argument *v* must be a variable and not a general expression. The operator is vectorized if applied to a non-scalar argument. See also Section 13.2.5.16, page 611.
`reinit(x,expr)`	In the body of a when-equation reinitializes the state variable *x* with *expr* at an event instant, i.e., a kind of assignment. The argument *x* is a `Real` (or subtype of Real) variable or an array of `Real` variables, which is implicitely defined to have `StateSelect.always`, i.e., it must be selected as a state, (or states), respectively. It is an error if it is not possible to select x as a state. It can *only* be applied within a when-equation. A variable is a state variable if the `der`-operator is applied to it somewhere in the model, or it is selected by `stateSelect` (Section 18.2.6.1, page 1018). The second argument *expr* must be an `Integer` or `Real` expression (or array of such expressions, respectively). The `reinit` operator can only be used once on the same variable *x*, i.e., single assignment, either to an individual variable or to a part of an array of variables. The `reinit` operator does not break the single assignment rule for equations since `reinit(x,expr)` makes the previously known state variable *x* unknown and has the same effect as introducing a new state variable x with the equation `x = expr`. For a simple example of the use of `reinit`, see the bouncing ball example in Chapter 2, page 57. For more details on the use of `reinit` among equations, see Section 8.3.6, page 359.

6.14.2.1 Event Iteration and the pre Function

Regarding *event iteration*, a new event is triggered automatically if *at* the time instant *t* of the current event it is the case that for at least one variable v, "`pre(v)<>v`" after the active model equations have been evaluated. Typically a discontinuity causes the value of a discontinuous variable `v` to be different from its predecessor value `pre(v)`. In this case the model equations are reevaluated, until for *all* variables `v` used in `pre`-operators it is the case that "`pre(v)=v`." This evaluation sequence is called *event iteration*. After such an evaluation sequence, the solution process for the continuous part of the equation system is resumed, also known as "continuous integration." More detailed information regarding this subject is available in Section 13.2.6.7, page 623, but especially in Chapter 18, Section 18.2.5, page 1012.

6.15 Match-Expressions and Symbolic Programming

General computational modeling and programming languages often have the ability to perform both numeric and symbol computations. Examples are computer algebra languages such as Mathematica, Maple, and Macsyma, which can mix numeric and symbolic computations.

Such powerful capabilities are also relevant for Modelica now and in the future, to be able to address problems that may be both numerical and symbolic in character.

An important motivation is to extend the expressive power of Modelica with functional programming features for scripting as well as control algorithms. The latter would introduce safe programming constructs especially for embedded software, that is, complement the declarative constructs for physical modeling with corresponding constructs for advanced embedded control software.

Such extensions can also provide symbolic programming and modeling constructs needed to model some of the Modelica language semantics using symbolic transformations or elaborations from those constructs to lower level primitives by Modelica functions. Match-expressions discussed in this section can be used to build and process models represented as symbolic data structures such as trees and lists.

Note that, at the time of this writing, all constructs discussed in this section are non-standard Modelica, they have not yet been standardized by Modelica Association. The MetaModelica language extension supports all of these constructs and a few more, and has been in regular use since 2006. OpenModelica provides an efficient implementation of these constructs. About three hundred thousand lines of code has so far been written in MetaModelica (see also Section 19.3.1.1, page 1038).

6.15.1 Case Records and Union Types for Tree Data Structures

The most common data type used to represent programs and models in compilers are tree structures. Typical operations are transformations of such trees into other trees during the translation process. Lists are a special case of tree data types, but are typically given special support in many symbolic programming languages. Tree data types typically have two interesting properties:

- Union type – the type of a tree data type is typically the union of a number of node types, each representing a tree node.
- Recursive type – the children of a tree node may have a type which is the tree data type itself.

A small arithmetic expression tree, of the expression 12+5*13, is depicted in Figure 6-4. Using the record constructors `PLUSop`, `MULop`, `RCONST`, this tree can be constructed by the expression `PLUSop(RCONST(12), MULop( RCONST(5), RCONST(13)))`. Such trees are usually called abstract syntax trees.

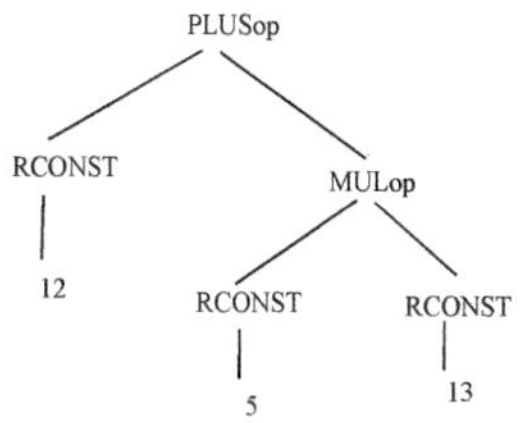

Figure 6-4. Abstract syntax tree of the expression 12+5*13.

Recursive types are currently missing from the Modelica language, which so far has been a conscious decision in order to avoid heap-allocated objects.

The MetaModelica 1.0 language introduced the `uniontype` restricted class construct. The example below declares a small expression tree type `Exp` containing 6 different node types represented as ordinary Modelica record types.

```
uniontype Exp    // Note: Non-standard Modelica
  record RCONST Real rval; end RCONST;
  record INTconst Integer int; end INTconst;
  record PLUSop  Exp exp1; Exp exp2; end PLUSop;
  record SUBop   Exp exp1; Exp exp2; end SUBop;
  record MULop   Exp exp1; Exp exp2; end MULop;
  record DIVop   Exp exp1; Exp exp2; end DIVop;
  record NEGop   Exp exp1;          end NEGop;
end Exp;
```

A similar but slightly different design would be to introduce a parent class that denotes the tree data type. All record types that belong to that union type must inherit this class. This approach is called *case classes*, which is used in the Scala language. Thus we introduce the language construct `case record`.

It is important to introduce a `case record` or `uniontype` construct in order that the compiler gets information to check which member records are allowed and to compile such record structures internally using references/pointers which are needed for efficient internal implementations of such tree data structures.

In the following, we will interchangeably use the constructs `uniontype` that are implemented in current MetaModelica, and `case record`, which is inspired by Scala. Both are currently discussed for standardization in Modelica, but at most one will be chosen. Each has pros and cons.

```
case record Exp   // Note: Non-standard Modelica
end Exp;

record RCONST extends Exp;
  Real rval;
end RCONST;

record INTconst extends Exp;
  Integer int;
end INTconst;

record PLUSop extends Exp;
  Exp exp1; Exp exp2;
end PLUSop;

record SUBop extends Exp;
  Exp exp1; Exp exp2;
end SUBop;

record MULop extends Exp;
  Exp exp1; Exp exp2;
```

```
end MULop;

record DIVop extends Exp;
  Exp exp1; Exp exp2;
end DIVop;

record NEGop extends Exp;
  Exp exp1;
end NEGop;
```

The case record or uniontype construct currently has the following properties:

- Such record types can be *recursive*, i.e., reference themselves. That is the case in the above `Exp` example, where `Exp` is referenced inside its member record types.
- A member record type may only belong to *one* case record (uniontype) type. This restriction may be removed in the future.
- The typing rules for a case record is similar to operator records, i.e., nominal typing comparing type names. To check subtyping of two member records, it is tested whether they belong to a subtype with the same name.

This is very similar to corresponding constructs in functional languages such as Haskell, Standard ML, OCaml, and Scala.

To provide a type-safe implementation, case records or uniontype records internally in their implementation need an extra hidden record field (here called `tag`) to identify which record it belongs to. For example:

```
// Internal implementation approach:

record PLUSop Tagtype tag; Exp exp1; Exp exp2;  end PLUSop;
record NEGop Tagtype tag; Exp exp1;  end PLUSop;
```

6.15.2 Match Expressions for Processing Complex Data

Pattern matching and transformation of structured data representations such as trees is one of the central facilities in symbolic modeling and programming languages. The matching provided by the match-expression construct is very close to similar facilities in many functional languages, but is also related to switch statements in C or Java. It has two important advantages over traditional switch statements:

- A match-expression can appear in any of the three Modelica contexts: expressions, statements, or in equations.
- The selection in the case branches is based on pattern matching, which reduces to equality testing (Section 6.15.2.1, page 301) or switch in simple cases, but is much more powerful in the general case.

A very simple example of a match-expression is the following code fragment, which returns a number corresponding to a given input string. The pattern matching is very simple – just compare the string value of `s` with one of the constant pattern strings `"one"`, `"two"` or `"three"`, and if none of these matches return 0 since the wildcard pattern value `any` matches anything. In MetaModelica an underscore (_) usually used as wildcard pattern.

```
  String s;   // Note: Non-standard Modelica
  Real   x;
algorithm
  x := match s
    case "one"   then 1;
    case "two"   then 2;
    case "three" then 3;
    case  any    then 0;
```

```
    end match;
```

Alternatively, an else-branch can be used instead of the wildcard pattern:

```
    String s;
    Real   x;
  algorithm
    x := match s
      case "one"   then 1;
      case "two"   then 2;
      case "three" then 3;
      else              0;
    end match;
```

Another example with named integer constants is:

```
    Integer i;
    Real   x;
    constant Integer One=1, Two=2, Three=3;
  algorithm
    x := match i
      case One   then 10;
      case Two   then 20;
      case Three then 30;
      else 0;
    end match;
```

The keyword `any` (or _) is used to match one item, it is part of the so-called pattern expression language. The above simple examples are trivial special cases of match expressions.

The general structure of match-expressions starting with the `match` keyword is indicated by the outline below. The else-branch is optional and is identical to a `case any` branch. The `<opt-local-decl>` can be left out if there are no local declarations, e.g. `local Real`. The equations `<opt-local-equations>` are also optional.

```
  match <m-expr>  <opt-local-decl>
      ...
    case <pat-expr>
      <opt-local-equations>
      then <expr>;
      ...
    case <pat-expr>
      <opt-local-equations>
      then <expr>;
      ...
    else
      <opt-local-equations>
      then <expr>;

  end match;
```

A set of optional local equations `<opt-local-equations>` start with the `equation` keyword followed by local algebraic single-assignment equations. This example shows a case branch with three local equations:

```
      case BINARY(e1,binop,e2)
        equation
          v1 = eval(e1);
          v2 = eval(e2);
          v3 = applyBinop(binop, v1, v2);
        then v3;
```

The above match-expression outline without local equations:

```
match <m-expr>  <opt-local-decl>
  ...
  case <pat-expr>
    then <expr>;
    ...
  case <pat-expr>
    then <expr>;
    ...
  else
    <expr>;
end match;
```

A slightly more advanced usage of match-expressions compared to the above trivial cases with constant case patterns is in a small expression evaluator, the function `eval` below. The first version binds the variable x (which as a very short name) to the result of the match in each case branch. However, in MetaModelica 2.0, instead of the equality sign in `x = RCONST(),` the syntax `x as RCONST()` is currently used:

```
function eval "Small expression evaluator"  // Note: Non-standard Modelica
  input  Exp  inExpression;
  output Real result;
algorithm
  result := match inExpression
    case x = RCONST() then x.rval;
    case x = ADDop() then eval(x.exp1) + eval(x.exp2);
    case x = SUBop() then eval(x.exp1) - eval(x.exp2);
    case x = MULop() then eval(x.exp1) * eval(x.exp2);
    case x = DIVop() then eval(x.exp1) / eval(x.exp2);
    case x = NEGop() then -eval(x.exp);
  end match;
end eval;
```

Alternatively, binding `x` to `inExpression` in the match expression:

```
function eval "Small expression evaluator"  // Note: Non-standard Modelica
  input  Exp inExpression;
  output Real result;
algorithm
  result := match x = inExpression
    case RCONST() then x.rval;
    case PLUSop() then eval(x.exp1) + eval(x.exp2);
    case SUBop() then eval(x.exp1) - eval(x.exp2);
    case MULop() then eval(x.exp1) * eval(x.exp2);
    case DIVop() then eval(x.exp1) / eval(x.exp2);
    case NEGop() then -eval(x.exp);
  end match;
end eval;
```

Alternatively have a short named variable `x` as an input formal parameter:

```
function eval "Small expression evaluator"  // Note: Non-standard Modelica
  input  Exp  x;
  output Real result;
algorithm
  result := match x
    case RCONST() then x.rval;
    case PLUSop() then eval(x.exp1) + eval(x.exp2);
    case SUBop() then eval(x.exp1) - eval(x.exp2);
    case MULop() then eval(x.exp1) * eval(x.exp2);
    case DIVop() then eval(x.exp1) / eval(x.exp2);
    case NEGop() then -eval(x.exp);
```

```
    end match;
  end eval;
```

Alternatively, using pattern variables (Section 6.15.2.2, page 301) `rv`, `x` and `y` which become bound to the arguments of the constructor during the matching:

```
  function eval "Small expression evaluator"  // Note: Non-standard Modelica
    input  Exp  inExpression;
    output Real result;
  algorithm
    result := match inExpression
     local Exp x,y; Real rv;
      case RCONST(rv) then rv;
      case PLUSop(x,y) then eval(x) + eval(y);
      case SUBop(x,y) then eval(x) - eval(y);
      case MULop(x,y) then eval(x) * eval(y);
      case DIVop(x,y) then eval(x) / eval(y);
      case NEGop(x) then -eval(x);
    end match;
  end eval;
```

6.15.2.1 Simple Implementation of Pattern Matching

A match with simple patterns as above can be expanded to if-then-else as below. However, this example is not type correct Modelica, it just shows a low-level implementation approach.

```
  if tag(x) == Exp_RCONST then x.rval
  else if tag(x) == Exp_PLUSop then eval(x.exp1) + eval(x.exp2)
  else if tag(x) == Exp_SUBop then eval(x.exp1) - eval(x.exp2)
  ...
```

A more complicated pattern is `CALL(IDENT("sin"),{any})`:

```
  case x = CALL(IDENT("sin"),{any})
        then MUL(CALL(IDENT("cos"),{x.e2[1]}), ...
```

This can be expanded to the following not type correct Modelica:

```
if tag(x) == Exp_CALL and tag(x.exp1) == Exp__IDENT and x.exp1.id=="sin" and
size((x.exp2.args),1)==1 then MUL(CALL(IDENT("cos"),{x.e2[1]}),...
```

6.15.2.2 Pattern Variables

Most the examples shown so far are without pattern variables. What then is a pattern variable? Such a variable can occur inside a pattern expression and will be bound to a value during pattern matching. This feature is present in almost all languages with pattern matching, including OCaml, Haskell, RML, MetaModelica, Scala, and often enables rather compact notation. The main alternative to pattern variables is to use standard dot notation to extract field values.

The following is an example of a case with a `PLUSop` pattern without pattern variables:

```
  case x=PLUSop() then eval(x.exp1) + eval(x.exp2);
```

This is an example of a `PLUSop` pattern with pattern variables `e1` and `e2` which become bound to values during matching:

```
  case PLUSop(e1,e2) then eval(e1) + eval(e2);
```

This is an example of a `PLUSop` ***named pattern*** mentioning field names `exp1` and `exp2` with pattern variables `e1` and `e2` which become bound to values during matching:

```
  case PLUSop(exp1=e1,exp2=e2) then eval(e1) + eval(e2);
```

Named pattern variable arguments are slightly more verbose, but have advantages when a program is updated such as being not sensitive to changes in the argument order or to adding extra arguments. They are usually more readable and self-documenting, especially for constructors with long argument lists.

Pattern variables, both positional and named patterns, are implemented in MetaModelica, and are also available in most functional languages.

6.15.2.3 Guarded Patterns

A pattern can also include an optional Boolean conditional expression preceded by the `guard` keyword as specified by the following grammar rule for a pattern expression:

```
<pat-expr> ::=  <pattern-no-guard> [guard <bool-expr>]
```

The matching process of such a pattern first performs structural matching of the part without guard, the `<pattern-no-guard>`. If that is successful, the guard conditional expression, `<bool-expr>`, is evaluated. If it evaluates to `true`, the whole pattern is considered matching successfully, otherwise the matching fails.

For example, regard the following two cases with guarded patterns obtained from the function `numberAbs` below:

```
case REAL() guard x.value >  0 then  x.value;
case REAL() guard x.value <= 0 then -x.value;
```

Given a constructor `REAL(-3.14)` containing a Real number –3.14. This is passed in the call `numberAbs(REAL(-3.14))`. The first case will match OK structurally but the guard expression `x.value>0` will evaluate to `false` which makes the matching fail. Therefore the next case is tried which matches structurally and also has a guard expression `x.value<=0` which evaluates to `true`, making the match succeed.

```
function numberAbs "Returns the absolute value of a Number as a Real."
  input Number x;
  output Real result;
algorithm
  result := match x
    case INT() then abs(x.int);
    case RATIONAL() then abs(x.dividend/x.divisor);
    case REAL() guard x.value>0 then x.value;
    case REAL() guard x.value<=0 then -x.value;
    case COMPLEX() then abs(sqrt(x.im^2+x.re^2));
  end match;
end numberAbs;
```

6.15.3 Additional Data Structures

Apart from the tree data structures already discussed there also lists, tuples, and option data structures.

6.15.3.1 List Data Structures

Lists are common data structures in declarative languages since they conveniently allow representation and manipulation of sequences of elements. Elements can be efficiently (in constant time) added to beginning of lists in a declarative way. Lists are immutable meaning that the list is not updated. When an element is added a new list is created. All elements of a list have the same type. The following basic list construction operators are available, presented below through several examples.

In the examples, on the first line the expression to be evaluated is shown, on the following line the evaluated result.

```
{} // The empty list
```

```
{}

{1, 2, 3} // The list constructor
{1, 2, 3}

1 :: {2, 3} // The cons :: operator to add an element to a list
{1, 2, 3}

1 :: "2" :: {} // An illegal expression

OMC-ERROR:
"Error: Failed to match types of cons expression 1::"2"::{}. The head has
type Integer and the tail list<String>.
"
```

Appending lists is expensive; it uses the `cons` operation once for each element in the first argument since the contents of the first argument is copied:

```
listAppend( {1, 2, 3}, {4})
{1, 2, 3, 4}
```

The types of lists often need to be specified. Named list types can be declared using MetaModelica type declarations, e.g.:

```
type StringList = List<String>;
```

An example of a list type for lists of `Real` elements:

```
type RealList    = List<Real>;
```

The most readable and convenient way of accessing elements in an existing list or constructing new lists is usually through pattern matching operations, used in the `stringDelimitList` function below.

```
function stringDelimitList
  input StringList stringList;
  input String delimiter;
  output String outString;
algorithm
  outString := match stringList
    local
      String head;
      StringList tail;
    // Remember to match the empty list
    case {} then "" ;
    // The last element does not need the delimiter
    case {head} then head;
    // Pattern-matching using the cons operator
    case head::tail then head + delimiter +
                         stringDelimitList(tail,delimiter);
  end match;
end stringDelimitList;
```

Calling the function:

```
stringDelimitList( {"1", "2", "3", "4"}, "," )
```

with result

```
"1,2,3,4"
```

6.15.3.2 Tuples

Tuples are represented by parenthesized, comma-separated sequences of items each of which may have a different type. For example:

```
( 1, 2.0, "3" )
( 12, 2.6, "mine" )
```

Named tuple types can be declared explicitly through the type declaration using the tuple type constructor.

```
type ThreeTup = Tuple<Integer,Real,String>;
```

A tuple data type can be viewed as a kind of light-weight record type, where names of the fields do not need to be declared. The values of a tuple are easiest accessed through pattern-matching.

```
function threeTupString
  input ThreeTup tup;
  output String str;
algorithm
  str := match tup
    local Integer int; Real real; String string;
    case (int,real,string)
      then stringAppendList({"(", String(int), ", ",
                             String(real), ", ", string, ")"});
  end match;
end threeTupString;
```

Calling the function:

```
threeTupString( ( 1, 2.5, "3" ) )
"(1, 2.5, 3)"
```

6.15.3.3 Option Types

Option types have been introduced in MetaModelica to provide a type-safe way of representing the common situation where a data item is optionally present in a data structure.

The constructor `NONE()` is used to represent the case where the optional data item is not present, whereas the constructor `SOME()` is used when the data item is present in the data structure.

We start by defining an `Option` type and a function using it:

```
type StringOption = Option<String>;

function stringOrDefault
  input StringOption strOpt;
  input String default;
  output String str;
algorithm
  str := match strOpt
    case SOME(str) then str;
    else default;
  end match;
end stringOrDefault;
```

Calling the function a few times:

```
stringOrDefault(NONE(),"default")
"default"

stringOrDefault(SOME("string"),"default")
"string"
```

6.15.4 Parameterized Data Structures

A *parameterized data type* in MetaModelica is a type that may have another type as a formal parameter. A parameterized type available in most programming languages is the array type which is usually parameterized in terms of its array element type. For example, we can have integer arrays, string arrays, or real arrays, and so on, depending on the type of the array elements. The size of an array may also be regarded as a formal parameter or attribute of the array.

The MetaModelica language extension provides three basic kinds of parameterized types as well as user-defined parameterized union types and record types.

- Lists – the `List` built-in predefined type constructor, parameterized in terms of the type of the list elements (Section 6.15.3.1, page 302). For example, the type of a list of integers is denoted `List<Integer>`.
- Arrays – parameterized in terms of the array element type.
- Option types – the `Option` built-in predefined type constructor, parameterized in terms of the type of the optional value (Section 6.15.3.3, page 304). An example of an option type is `Option<String>`.
- Parameterized user-defined union types and record types.

Note that all basic parameterized types in MetaModelica are ***monomorphic***: all elements must have the same type, that is, you cannot mix elements of type `Real` and type `String` within the same array or list. Certain languages provide *polymorphic* arrays, i.e., array elements may have different types.

However, arrays of elements of "different" types in MetaModelica can be represented by arrays of elements of union types, where each "type" in the union type is denoted by a different record constructor.

6.15.4.1 Parameterized Union Types and Record Types

Records and other classes in standard Modelica 3.2 are parameterizable using the replaceable and redeclare constructs. For example, we could make the above `INTconst` record in Section 6.15.1, page 296, parameterized by adding a type variable `IntType`, where `Any` is a built-in supertype of all types:

```
record INTconst  "Version with replaceable syntax"
  replaceable type IntTypeVar constrainedby Any;
  IntType int;
end INTconst;
```

In Modelica, by using `INTconst(redeclare IntTypeVar=Integer)` we will get a result which is equivalent to the previous `INTconst` class with a field `int` of type `Integer`. If instead we would use `INTconst(redeclare IntTypeVar=LongInt)` the result would be equivalent to:

```
record INTconst
  LongInt int;
end INTconst;
```

In MetaModelica we can use the more concise angle-bracket syntax < > to express type variables in parameterized classes. The following short syntax version is equivalent to the above `INTconst` record with replaceable:

```
record INTconst<IntTypeVar>  "Version with short angle-bracket syntax"
  IntType int;
end INTconst;
```

It is also possible to parameterize union types. The above `Number` union type parameterized by a type variable `IntTypeVar` appears as follows:

```
uniontype Number<IntTypeVar>
  record INTconst  IntTypeVar int;  end INT;
  record RATIONAL  IntTypeVar int1;  IntTypeVar int2;  end RATIONAL;
  record REAL      Real re;  end REAL;
  record COMPLEX   Real re;  Real im;  end COMPLEX;
end Number;
```

6.15.5 Example of Symbolic Differentiation

Symbolic differentiation of expressions is a translational mapping that transforms expressions into differentiated expressions. The following `Exp` record type is used, first declared using the `case record` syntax variant, then using the `uniontype`:

```
case record Exp   // Note: Non-standard Modelica
end Exp;

record RCONST extends Exp;    Real e1;                   end RCONST;
record PLUS   extends Exp;     Exp e1; Exp e2;           end PLUS;
record SUB    extends Exp;     Exp e1; Exp e2;           end SUB;
record MUL    extends Exp;     Exp e1; Exp e2;           end MUL;
record DIV    extends Exp;     Exp e1; Exp e2;           end DIV;
record NEG    extends Exp;     Exp e1;                   end NEG;
record IDENT  extends Exp;     String name;              end IDENT;
record CALL   extends Exp;     Exp id; Exp[:] args;      end CALL;
record AND    extends Exp;     Exp e1; Exp e2;           end AND;
record OR     extends Exp;     Exp e1; Exp e2;           end OR;
record LESS   extends Exp;     Exp e1; Exp e2;           end LESS;
record GREATER extends Exp;    Exp e1; Exp e2;           end GREATER;
```

Here using the union type syntax:

```
uniontype Exp
  record RCONST   Real e1;                   end RCONST;
  record PLUS      Exp e1; Exp e2;           end PLUS;
  record SUB       Exp e1; Exp e2;           end SUB;
  record MUL       Exp e1; Exp e2;           end MUL;
  record DIV       Exp e1; Exp e2;           end DIV;
  record NEG       Exp e1;                   end NEG;
  record IDENT     String name;              end IDENT;
  record CALL      Exp id; Exp[:] args;      end CALL;
  record AND       Exp e1; Exp e2;           end AND;
  record OR        Exp e1; Exp e2;           end OR;
  record LESS      Exp e1; Exp e2;           end LESS;
  record GREATER   Exp e1; Exp e2;           end GREATER;
end Exp;
```

An example function `difft` performs symbolic differentiation of the expression `expr` with respect to the variable `time`, returning a differentiated expression. In the patterns, `any` is a reserved word that can be used as a placeholder instead of a pattern variable when the particular value in that place is not needed later as a variable value. The equations such as `e1prim = difft(x.e1,timevars)` in the fourth case-branch is used to bind the additional identifiers `e1prim` and e2prim to the relevant expressions.

We can recognize the following well-known derivative rules represented in the match-expression code:

- The time-derivative of a constant `RCONST()` is zero.
- The time-derivative of the `time` variable is one.
- The time-derivative of a time dependent variable `id` is `der(id)`, but is zero if the variable is not time dependent, i.e., not in the list `timevars`.
- The time-derivative of the sum `ADD(x.e1,x.e2)` of two expressions is the sum of the expression derivatives.
- The time-derivative of `sin(x)` is `cos(x)*x'` if `x` is a function of time, and `x'` its time derivative.
- etc...

In the following example we use the `any` keyword as a placeholder of any argument in one of the patterns, `CALL(IDENT("sin"),{any})`. This is a function call to `sin` with the argument list being an array of exactly one element `{any}`. We also use constructors with empty parentheses like `ADD()` to match for zero or more arguments. Some arithmetic operator nodes have been excluded in the `difft` example below in order to make it more compact.

```
function difft "Symbolic differentiation of expression with respect to time"
  input  Exp expr;              // Note: Non-standard Modelica
  input  String[:] timevars;
  output Exp diffexpr;
algorithm
  diffexpr := match x = expr
   local Exp e1prim, e2prim;  // Two variables local to the match expression
    // der of constant
    case RCONST() then RCONST(0.0);
    // der of a variable
    case IDENT()
      then
      if x.id == "time" then RCONST(1.0)  // der of time variable
      else if member(x.id,timevars)          // der of any variable id
        then CALL(IDENT("der"),{x.id})
      else RCONST(0.0);
    // (x.e1 + x.e2)' => x.e1' + x.e2'
    case ADD()
      then ADD(difft(x.e1,timevars), difft(x.e2,timevars));
   // (x.e1 - x.e2)' => x.e1' - x.e2'
    case SUB()
      equation  // introducing local single-assignment equations
        e1prim = difft(x.e1,timevars);
        e2prim = difft(x.e2,timevars);
      then SUB(e1prim,e2prim);
    // (x.e1 * x.e2)' => x.e1' * x.e2 + x.e1 * x.e2'
    case MUL()
      then PLUS(MUL(difft(x.e1,timevars),x.e2), MUL(x.e1,
              difft(x.e2,timevars);));
    // (x.e1 / x.e2)' => (x.e1' * x.e2 - x.e1 * x.e2') / x.e2 * x.e2
    case DIV()
      equation
        e1prim = difft(x.e1,timevars);
        e2prim = difft(x.e2,timevars);
      then DIV(SUB(MUL(e1prim,x.e2), MUL(x.e1,e2prim)), MUL(x.e2,x.e2));
    // (-x.e1)' => -x.e1'
    case NEG()
      then NEG(difft(x.e1,timevars);
    // sin(x.e1)' => cos(x.e1) * x.e1'
    case CALL(IDENT("sin"),{any})
      then MUL(CALL(IDENT("cos"),{x.e2[1]}),
           difft(x.e2[1],timevars)); //pick first elem from 2nd arg, an array
    // (x.e1 and x.e2)' => x.e1'and x.e2'
    case AND()
      then AND(difft(x.e1,timevars), difft(x.e2,timevars));
    // (x.e1 or x.e2)' => x.e1' or x.e2'
    case OR()
      then OR(difft(x.e1,timevars), difft(x.e2,timevars));
    // (x.e1<x.e2)' => x.e1' < x.e2'
    case LESS()
      then LESS(difft(x.e1,timevars), difft(x.e2,timevars));
    // (x.e1 > x.e2)' => x.e1' > x.e2'
    case GREATER()
      then GREATER(difft(x.e1,timevars), difft(x.e2,timevars));
    // etc...

  end match;
end difft;
```

6.16 Summary

We have presented the structure of expressions in Modelica, together with the building blocks used to construct expressions. These building blocks include literal constants, names, and operators. We have briefly described properties of operators, the order of evaluation, guarding against incorrect evaluation, and the rules for deriving expression types and performing type conversions. This chapter also includes tables of the Modelica built-in intrinsic mathematical functions together with the built-in special operators and functions, excluding built-in array functions which are described in Section 7.9, page 335. Moreover, we have also briefly described the MetaModelica language extensions for symbolic programming and modeling.

6.17 Literature

The main reference document for this chapter is the Modelica Language Specification (Modelica Association 2012) and (Modelica Association 2013), whereas expressions and the style of presentation is common to many other programming language books, e.g. for the C language in (Harbison and Steele 1991). The tables describing intrinsic functions and operators are close to those in the Modelica Language Specification, but have been slightly improved, and some examples have been added. The text in Section 6.8.1.3 about ANSI-C format string specifiers is from (Wikipedia 2013) and has been slightly adapted for Modelica use.

The MetaModelica language extension is presented in more detail in (Fritzson, Pop, and Aronsson 2005; Pop and Fritzson 2006; Fritzson and Pop 2011; Fritzson, Pop, and Sjölund 2011). The compilation of the whole OpenModelica compiler using itself (i.e., bootstrapping) is described in (Sjölund, Fritzson, and Pop 2011; Sjölund, Fritzson, and Pop 2014). Haskell is described in (Hudak 2000), Standard ML in (Milner, Tofte, Harper, and MaQueen 1997), OCaml in (OCaml 2010), and Scala in (Odersky, Spoon, Venners 2008).

6.18 Exercises

Exercise 6-1:

Quiz:

- What is a keyword?
- What is so special about them?
- Name some Modelica keywords that you have come across.
- Certainly by now you have come across some of the predefined types of Modelica, if not all of them. Which are they?
- What is a literal constant?
- Give an example of a literal constant.
- Describe what the variability of an expression means.
- Which are the degrees of expression variability? Describe the properties of the expressions having the different degrees.

Exercise 6-2:

Variability and Subtyping: What is wrong with this class?

```
class Happy
  boolean right(fixed = true);
  parameter Integer h = 15;
```

```
  constant Integer m = h + 28;
  parameter Real k = 32;
end Happy;
```

Exercise 6-3:

Are the following initializations allowed in Modelica?

- a) `Real r1 = i +5;`
- b) `Integer i1 = r +5;`

Here `r` and `i` are `Real` and `Integer` parameters respectively.

- Explain why/why not.
- What needs to be changed to make both initializations correct?

Exercise 6-4:

What is a conditional expression?
Rewrite the conditional equation below in the form of a conditional expression:

```
if (a > 0) then
  der(x) = x;
elseif (a == 0) then
  der(x) = 0;
else
  der(x) = -x;
end if;
```

Chapter 7

Arrays

An array can be regarded as a collection of scalar variables all of the same type. Modelica arrays can be multidimensional and are "rectangular," which in the case of matrices has the consequence that all rows in a matrix have equal length, and all columns have equal length. This is also the case for languages like FORTRAN, C, and MATLAB, permitting efficient implementation for computational numeric applications. However, this is in contrast to Java arrays, which can be ragged, that is, different rows of a Java array need not contain the same number of elements.

Each array has a certain dimensionality, that is, number of dimensions. The degenerate case of a scalar variable is not really an array, but can be regarded as an array with zero dimensions. Vectors have one dimension; matrices have two dimensions, and so on. So-called row vectors and column vectors do not exist in Modelica and cannot be distinguished since vectors have only one dimension. If distinguishing these is desired, row matrices and column matrices are available, being the corresponding two-dimensional entities. However, in practice this is seldom needed since the usual matrix arithmetic and linear algebra operations have been defined to give the expected behavior when operating on Modelica vectors and matrices.

Modelica is a strongly typed language, which also applies to array types. The number of dimensions of an array is fixed and cannot be changed at run-time in order to permit strong type checking and efficient implementation. However, the sizes of array dimensions can be computed at run-time, allowing fairly generic array manipulation code to be written as well as interfacing to standard numeric libraries implemented in other programming languages.

An array is allocated by declaring an array variable or calling an array constructor. Elements of an array can be indexed by `Integer`, `Boolean`, or `enumeration` values.

7.1 Array Declarations and Types

An array variable can be declared by appending dimension size and index type information within square brackets after a type name or after a variable name. The dimension information is a comma-separated list of elements, where each element is an `Integer` expression, a colon (:), or a type name denoting a `Boolean` type, or an `enumeration` type. Colon (:) means that the dimension upper bound is unknown and is a subtype of Integer. Each integer expression specifies the size of the dimension where it occurs. For example:

```
Real[3]         positionvector = {1,2,3};
Real[3,3]       identitymatrix = {{1,0,0}, {0,1,0}, {0,0,1}};
Integer[n,m,k]  arr3d;
```

```
Voltage[10]      voltagevector;
String[3]        str3 = {"one", "two", "blue"};
```

This declares a three-dimensional position vector, a transformation matrix, a three-dimensional array, a `Boolean` vector, a vector of `Voltage` values where `Voltage` is a specialization of the `Real` type, and a `String` vector. Using the alternative syntax of attaching dimensions after the variable name, the same declarations can be expressed as:

```
Real       positionvector[3] = {1,2,3};
Real       identitymatrix[3,3] = {{1,0,0}, {0,1,0}, {0,0,1}};
Real       arr3d[n,m,k];
Boolean    truthvalues[2] = {false,true};
Voltage    voltagevector[10]
String     str3[3] = {"one", "two", "blue"};
```

Four of the array declarations contain declaration equations, where the array constructor {} is used to construct array values for defining `positionvector`, `identitymatrix`, `truthvalues`, and `str3`. More information about array constructors is available in Section 7.2, page 315, and Section 7.3, page 318.

It is possible to mix the two declaration forms, but the code becomes less readable. For example:

```
Real[3,2]  A[4,5];      // A has type  Real[4,5,3,2];
```

Column matrices and row matrices can be declared, for example as below, but are seldom needed since the common matrix operations work well with vectors. Note that both column matrices and row matrices are 2D data structures, i.e., have two dimensions of which one has size 1, whereas vectors are 1D data structures with just one dimension.

```
Real[n,1]  colmat;      // Column matrix
Real[1,n]  rowmat;      // Row matrix
```

Declaration of empty arrays is allowed in Modelica. An empty array has at least one dimension of size 0 and contains no array elements. One might question whether there is any use for such a strange language feature. Surprisingly enough, the answer is yes; see Section 7.11 on page 341 for more information on the usage of empty arrays.

```
Real[0,3]  M;           // An empty matrix M
Integer    x[0];        // An empty vector x
```

An array can be declared to be indexed by values of an `enumeration` or by `Boolean` values. The index range is implicitly specified by an `enumeration` type name or the type `Boolean`. For example:

```
type Sizes = enumeration(small, medium, large);

Real[Sizes]    sz = {1.2, 3.5, 7};
Real[Boolean]  bv = {3.1, 3.2};
```

7.1.1 Array Dimension Lower and Upper Index Bounds

The lower and upper index bounds for a dimension of an array indexed by `Integer`, `Boolean`, or `enumeration` values are as follows:

- An array dimension indexed by integers has a lower bound of 1 and an upper bound being the size of the dimension.
- An array dimension indexed by `Boolean` values has the lower bound `false` and the upper bound `true`.
- An array dimension indexed by `enumeration` values of the type `E=enumeration(e1, e2, ..., en)` has the lower bound `E.e1` and the upper bound `E.en`.

7.1.2 Flexible Array Sizes

The possibility to declare arrays with unspecified dimension sizes is quite important in order to design flexible models that can adapt to different problem sizes. This is absolutely necessary for implementing general numeric procedure libraries involving arrays, or for interfacing to existing libraries in other languages such as C or Fortran through the Modelica external function mechanism.

An unspecified dimension size is stated by using a colon (`:`) instead of the usual expression, and means that the dimension size is unknown and that its type is a subtype of `Integer` (i.e., not an `enumeration` value). In the third example we call the built-in function `size` that returns the size of an array dimension. For example:

```
Real[:,:]  Y;                  // A matrix with two unknown dimension sizes
Real[:,3]  Y2;                 // A matrix where the number of columns is known
Real       M[:,size(M,1)]      // A square matrix of unknown size
```

Several arrays with unknown sizes can of course be declared in the same declaration:

```
Real[:]  v1, v2;               // Vectors v1 and v2 have unknown sizes
```

The actual sizes of `v1` and `v2` need not be the same even though they are part of the same declaration, since the above declaration is equivalent to two separate declarations:

```
Real[:]  v1;
Real[:]  v2;
```

The unspecified dimension sizes will eventually be determined when the array variable is bound to some value, for example by passing an array value to a Modelica function having an array formal parameter with unspecified size, or assigning an array value to an array variable in a function. Moreover, function array results and local variables with dimension sizes declared with (`:`) can be resized. See Section 9.3.2.8, page 445, for examples and more details regarding arrays with flexible sizes in functions.

Array variables in classes (not functions) that are instantiated in order to be used in a simulation must have known sizes, that is, sizes must be defined by expressions of constant or parameter variability, or by a declaration equation (declaration assignment in an algorithm section) setting the variable equal to (or assigned to, respectively) an array expression of known size, for example:

```
Real[:]  v3 = fill(3,14, n);    // A vector v3 of size n filled with 3.14
```

An array variable in a partial class can however use unspecified dimension sizes given by colon (`:`) without a defining declaration equation, since the size will eventually be defined by a modification or redeclaration of the array variable before it is used.

7.1.3 Array Types and Type Checking

It is possible to declare user-defined array types analogously to other user-defined types. For example, a type `ColorPixel` can be defined as a three-element vector representing the three base colors, and a variable `image` declared as a matrix of such pixels:

```
type ColorPixel = Real[3];

ColorPixel[512,512]  image;
```

However, for the purpose of type checking and selecting the right version of overloaded array operators and functions it is important to determine the expanded type of a variable. The term *overloaded* means that the same (or similar) operation, for example, "*" is defined for several different types. The variable `image` can superficially be regarded as a matrix of pixels but since each pixel is a vector its expanded type is really `Real[512,512,3]`.

The *expanded type* of an array of arrays is the multidimensional array, which is constructed by taking the first dimensions from the variable declaration and subsequent dimensions from the *maximally expanded* array element type of the declaration. A type is maximally expanded, if it is either one of the built-in types (`Real`, `Integer`, `Boolean`, `String`, `enumeration`) or not defined by a `type` definition.

Consider this definition of the notion of expanded type in the example below. The user-defined types `Voltage` and `Current` are defined using `type` definitions, whereas `Pin` is defined through the declaration of a `connector`, which is a specialized class.

```
type Voltage = Real(unit = "V");
type Current = Real(unit = "A");

connector Pin
  Voltage      v;  // Type of v is Voltage, expanded type of v is Real
  flow Current i;  // Type of i is Current, expanded type of i is Real
end Pin;

type MultiPin = Pin[5];
MultiPin[4] p;  // Type of p is MultiPin[4], expanded type is Pin[4,5]
```

The types of the variables `v` and `i` in this example are `Voltage` and `Current` respectively, whereas the expanded types of those variables are both `Real` since the expansion continues through `type` definitions. Concerning the variable `p`, its type is `MultiPin[4]`, whereas its expanded type is `Pin[4,5]` according to the above rules. `Pin` is not expanded further since it is a class definition.

```
type Point = Real[3];
Point[10]    p1;
Real[10,3]   p2;
```

The array variables `p1` and `p2` have identical expanded types of `Real[10,3]` which makes the two equations below type correct. The colon notation, e.g. `p2[5,:]` denoting the fifth row of `p2`, is further explained in Section 7.4.2 on array slices, page 322.

```
p2[5]  = p1[2]+ p2[4];   // equivalent to    p2[5,:] = p1[2,:] + p2[4,:]
Real r[3] = p1[2];       // equivalent to    r[3] = p1[2,:]
```

7.1.4 Modifiers for Array Variables and the each Operator

Array variables can be initialized using modifiers. See Section 4.2.4, page 150 for a detailed description of array modifiers. Note that every array *attribute* or *variable* has the *same dimensionality and extent* as the array itself, possibly combined with the extent of the attribute if it is an array. See also Section 7.4.3 on page 323 regarding such array *record field slices* for arrays of records.

The second line in the example below modifies the `start` value for the whole array.

```
Real A3[2,2];                              // Array variable
Real A4[2,2](start={{1,0},{0,1}}); // Array with modifier
Real A5[2,2](unit={{"Voltage","Voltage"},{"Voltage","Voltage"}});
```

Modification of an indexed element of an array is illegal:

```
Real A6[2,2](start[2,1]=2.3); // Illegal! indexed element modification
```

The `each` operator can only be used inside modifiers, e.g., as in the modifier `A7[2,3](each b = {1,2,3,4})` in the model `C1` below . This gives a more compact syntax for certain kinds of initializations and/or declaration equations. Consider the array `A7` with extent 2×3, containing records of type `Crec`:

```
record Crec
  Real b[4];
end Crec;

model B
```

```
  Crec A7[2,3](b = { {{1,2,3,4},{1,2,3,4},{1,2,3,4}},
                     {{1,2,3,4},{1,2,3,4},{1,2,3,4}} } );
end B;
```

An equivalent, more compact, way is the following, where each instance of the vector `b` inside all `Crec` record elements of the array `A7` gets the value `{1,2,3,4}`:

```
model C1
  Crec A7[2,3](each b = {1,2,3,4});
end C;
```

A more detailed description and explanation is available in Section 4.2.4.1, page 150.

7.2 General Array Construction

An *array constructor* provides a convenient way of constructing array values, giving concise and readable code. The clumsier alternative is to declare an extra array variable, write code for assignment of values to this array, and then use it as the needed array value.

An array constructor is just a function accepting scalar or array arguments and returning an array result. The array constructor function `array(A,B,C,...)`, with short-hand notation {A, B, C, ...}, constructs an array from its arguments according to the following rule:

- Each application of this constructor function adds a dimension to the left in the result array compared to the dimensions of the arguments. The size of this dimension is equal to the number of arguments to {}. For example, {1,2} has dimensionality 1 with dimension size 2, {{1,2}} has dimensionality 2 with dimension extents 1×2, {{{1,2}}} has dimensionality 3 with dimension extents $1\times1\times2$. In general, `ndims(array(A))` = `ndims(A)`+1, where `ndims(A)` gives the number of dimensions of A.

Thus, it is straightforward to construct multidimensional arrays as arrays of arrays by repeated application of the array constructor {}.

The following conditions must be fulfilled for the arguments to the array constructor function:

- Equal dimensionality of arguments, i.e., all arguments must have the same number of dimensions and sizes of dimensions, e.g. `size(A)` = `size(B)` = `size(C)` = ..., where `size(A)` is a vector containing the dimension sizes of A. For example, `size({{1},{2},{3}})` is {3,1}.
- All arguments must be *type equivalent*, requiring the expanded types of the arguments to be equivalent. For example, the expanded type of a subtype of `Real` such as `Angle` below is `Real`. Arguments to {} with `Real` and `Integer` subtypes can be mixed, resulting in a `Real` result array with `Real` elements where the `Integer` numbers have been converted to `Real` numbers. This is the case for {1, 2, 3.0}, which has an expanded type `Real[3]` since it is converted to {1.0, 2.0, 3.0}.
- There must currently be at least one argument, i.e., `array()` and {} are not defined at the time of this writing, but might be defined as an empty array literal (see also Section 7.11.1, page 342) in a future version of Modelica.

```
{1,2,3}                         // A 3-vector of type Integer[3]
array(1.0,2.0,3)                // A 3-vector of type Real[3]

{{11,12,13}, {21,22,23}}        // A 2x3 matrix of type Integer[2,3]
{{{1.0, 2.0, 3.0}}}             // A 1x1x3 array of type Real[1,1,3]
{ {1}, {2,3} }                  // Illegal, arguments have different size

Real[3] v = array(1, 2, 3.0);   // The vector v is equal to {1.,2.,3.}

type Angle = Real(unit="rad");  // The type Angle is a subtype of Real
parameter Angle alpha = 2.0;    // The expanded type of alpha is Real
```

```
array(alpha, 2, 3.0)           // A 3-vector of type Real[3]
Angle[3] A = {1.0,alpha,4};    // The expanded type of A is Real[3]
```

7.2.1 Range Vector Construction

A *range vector* is a vector containing a range of numeric values increasing or decreasing by a fixed increment or decrement value for each additional element. For example, `{1,2,3}` is an `Integer` range vector starting at `1` and increasing by `1` for each element. Such ranges are useful, for example in iterative constructs such as algorithmic for-loops, or in for-equations when expressing regular sets of equations.

A colon operator expression in one of its two forms, *startexpr* : *endexpr*, or *startexpr* : *deltaexpr* : *endexpr*, is a convenient way of constructing `Real`, `Integer`, `Boolean`, or `enumeration` range vectors. The colon operator is defined as follows:

- The range vector *j* : *k* is the `Integer` vector {j, j+1, ..., k}, if j and k are of type `Integer`, or the `Real` vector {j, j+1.0, ... j+n}, with n = `floor`(k-j), if j or k are of type `Real`.
- The range vector *j* : *d* : *k* is the `Integer` vector {j, j+d, ..., j+n*d}, with n = `div`((k – j),d), if j, d, and k are of type `Integer`, or the `Real` vector {j, j+d, ..., j+n*d}, with n = `floor`((k-j)/d), if j, d, or k are of type `Real`.
- The range vector `false` : `true` is the Boolean vector {`false`, `true`}.
- The range vector `j` : `j` is {`j`} if `j` is of type `Real`, `Integer`, `Boolean`, or `enumeration`.
- The range vector `E.ei` : `E.ej` is the enumeration type vector {`E.ei`, ... `E.ej`} where `E.ej`> `E.ei`, and `ei` and `ej` belong to some enumeration type `E=enumeration(`...`ei`, ...`ej`, ...`)`.

In the following cases, the range vector constructor gives rise to an empty vector without any elements:

- The range vector *j* : *k* is an empty `Real`, `Integer`, `Boolean`, or `enumeration` vector containing no elements if j > k.
- The range vector *j* : *d* : *k* is an empty `Real` or `Integer` vector containing no elements if d > 0 and j > k, or if d < 0 and j < k.

For example:

```
Real v1[5] = 2.7 : 6.8;    // v1 is {2.7,3.7,4.7,5.7,6.7}
Real v2[5] = {2.7, 3.7, 4.7, 5.7, 6.7};  // v2 is equal to v1

Integer v3[3] = 3 : 5;        // v3 is {3,4,5}
Integer v4empty[0] = 3 : 2;  // v4empty is an empty Integer vector

Real     v5[4]  = 1.0 : 2  : 8;    // v5 is {1.0,3.0,5.0,7.0}
Integer v6[5]  = 1    : -1 : -3;  // v6 is {1,0,-1,-2,-3}
Real[0] v7none = 2.0 : -1 : 3;    // v7none is an empty Real vector

Boolean b1[2]  = false:true;
Colors ec[3]   = enumeration(red,blue,green);
Colors ec[3]   = Colors.red : Colors.green;
```

7.2.2 Set Formers—Array Constructors with Iterators

Set formers are common in the area of mathematics that deals with sets. The following mathematical notation allows declarative specification of the creation of a set of expressions:

$\{\ expr_i\ \mid\ i \in A\}$

This expression can be read as follows: create a set of values of $expr_i$ for all i such that i belongs to A. Assuming the set $A = \{1, 3, 4, 6...\}$, this specifies the creation of the following set:

{ $expr_1$, $expr_3$, $expr_4$, $expr_6$, ... }

In Modelica we do not have sets in the usual mathematical sense. However, sets can be represented as arrays, which in the mathematical sense are ordered multisets. Modelica has an *array constructor with iterators*, which is quite similar to the above mathematical notation, but with the vertical bar | replaced by the keyword `for` and the symbol ∈ replaced by the keyword `in`. In functional programming languages this kind of construct is usually known as an *array comprehension*.

{ $expr_i$ `for` *i* `in` *A*}

We can have multiple iterators in the same array constructor:

{ $expr_{ij}$ `for` *i* `in` *A*, *j* `in` *B* }

The general syntax is as follows:

{ *expression* `for` *iterators* }

where *iterators* is a comma-separated list of items, each of which is an *iterator*. As we have seen from the above examples, an iterator has the following structure:

ident `in` *range-expression*

The *range-expression* inside an iterator should be a vector expression where elements can have a subtype of Real, Integer, Boolean, enumeration or be of a record type. The *range-expression* can alternatively be an enumeration type name or the Boolean type, Section 9.2.5, page 427. It is evaluated once for each array constructor in the local scope immediately enclosing the array constructor.

The scope of the iterator variable *ident* is the *expression* inside {*expression* `for` *iterators*}. The iterator variable *ident* has the same type throughout all iterations and may hide variables with the same name in enclosing scopes, analogous to for-loops or for-equations.

If only one iterator is present, the result is a vector of values constructed by evaluating the *expression* for each value of the iterator variable. For example:

```
{r for r in 1.0 : 1.5 : 5.5} // The vector 1.0:1.5:5.5={1.0, 2.5, 4.0, 5.5}
{i^2 for i in {1,3,7,6}}     // The vector {1, 9, 49, 36}
{b for b in Boolean}         // The vector {false, true}
{not b for b in Boolean}     // The vector {true, false}
```

There is an alternative syntax for an array constructors with iterators, using the `array()` function style syntax instead of curly brackets:

```
array(i for i in 1:10)       // The vector 1:10={1,2,3,...,10}
```

The *rangeexpression* in an iterator may be left out if the range can be implied from the use of the iteration variable *ident* in an index position of an array with known dimension size (see the example below, or Section 9.2.5.1, page 428 for more information).

```
Real x[3]  = {2,1,4};
Real s1[3] = {x[i]*3 for i in 1:size(x,1)}; // result is {6,3,12}
Real s2[3] = {x[i] for i};  // result is {2,1,4}, range deduced to be 1:3
```

Multiple iterators in an array constructor, for example as in the first example below, have the advantage of having the iterators appear in the same order as the dimensions of the constructed array. When using *nested constructors* (as in the second example below), the iterators appear in the opposite order. The following two definitions are equivalent:

```
 {(1/(i+j-1) for i in 1:m, j in 1:n};        // Multiple iterators
{{(1/(i+j-1) for j in 1:n} for i in 1:m}     // Nested constructors
```

In fact, by first reversing the order of the iterators and then replacing each comma between the iterators by '`} for`' together with putting a left curly bracket '{' to the left of the whole array constructor, we can convert the multiple iterators form as in the example in the first line above, to the nested form used in the second example.

One can, of course, use an array constructor with iterators in any place where an array expression is allowed, for example, as in the right-hand side of a declaration equation for an array:

```
Real hilb[:,:]= {(1/(i+j-1) for i in 1:n, j in 1:n};
```

Array constructors with iterators are useful for defining special matrices. The following defines a matrix with 1 on the diagonal and the rest of the elements equal to the sum of row and column index.

```
{if i=j then 1 else i+j for i in 1:size(A,1), j in 1:size(A,2) }
```

Such an array of dimensions 4×4 appears as follows:

$$\begin{pmatrix} a_{11} & a_{12} & a_{13} & a_{14} \\ a_{21} & a_{22} & a_{23} & a_{24} \\ a_{31} & a_{32} & a_{33} & a_{34} \\ a_{41} & a_{42} & a_{43} & a_{44} \end{pmatrix} \text{ or with values: } \begin{pmatrix} 1 & 3 & 4 & 5 \\ 3 & 1 & 5 & 6 \\ 4 & 5 & 1 & 7 \\ 5 & 6 & 7 & 1 \end{pmatrix}$$

Array constructors with iterators can be useful for initialization of special matrices:

```
Integer[n,m] A := {if i==1 or i==n or j==1 or j==m then 0 else 3
                   for i in 1:n, j in 1:m};
```

which gives the array `A` the following value for `n=4` and `m=4`:

$$\begin{pmatrix} 0 & 0 & 0 & 0 \\ 0 & 3 & 3 & 0 \\ 0 & 3 & 3 & 0 \\ 0 & 0 & 0 & 0 \end{pmatrix}$$

An array constructor with iterators can of course also be used in equations, for example, as in the right-hand side of an equation for a discretized partial differential equation in one dimension:

```
model DiscretePDE1D
  Real U[15](start={0,0.7,...});
equation
  U[1]=0;
  der(U[2:14]) = {196*(U[i-1] - 2*U[i] + U[i+1] for i in 2:14}
  U[15]=0;
end DiscretePDE1D;
```

The same equation expressed as a for-equation appears as follows:

```
for i in 2:14 loop
  der(U[i])=196*(U[i-1] - 2*U[i] + U[i+1]);
end for;
```

7.3 Array Concatenation and Construction

General array concatenation can be done through the array concatenation operator `cat`(k,A,B,C,...) that concatenates the arrays A,B,C,... along the *k*th dimension. For example:

```
cat(1, {1,2}, {10,12,13} )           // Result: {1,2,10,12,13}
cat(2, {{1,2},{3,4}}, {{10},{11}} )  // Result: {{1,2,10},{3,4,11}}
```

The common special cases of concatenation along the first and second dimensions are supported through the special syntax forms [A;B;C;...] and [A,B,C,...] respectively. Both of these forms can be mixed.

In order to achieve compatibility with MATLAB array syntax, being a de facto standard, scalar and vector arguments to these special operators are promoted to become matrices before performing the concatenation. This gives the effect that a matrix can be constructed from scalar expressions by separating rows by semicolon and columns by comma. The example below constructs an $m \times n$ matrix assuming that all expressions are scalar:

```
[expr11, expr12, ... expr1n;
 expr21, expr22, ... expr2n;
 ...
 exprm1, exprm2, ... exprmn]
```

The previous example of concatenation along the second dimension can then be expressed:

```
[ [1,2; 3,4], [10; 11] ]           // Result: [1,2,10; 3,4,11]
cat(2, [1,2; 3,4], [10; 11] )      // Same result: {{1,2,10}, {3,4,11}}
```

It is instructive to follow the process of creating a matrix from scalar expressions using these operators. For example:

```
[1,2;
 3,4]
```

Since `[...,...]` for concatenation along the second dimension has higher priority than `[...;...]`, which concatenates along the first dimension, this is parsed as follows:

```
[[1,2];
 [3,4]]
```

Then each scalar argument is promoted to become a matrix, giving:

```
[[{{1}},{{2}}];
 [{{3}},{{4}}]]
```

Evaluating the first concatenation step along the second dimension gives:

```
[{{1, 2}};
 {{3, 4}}]
```

Finally, the row matrices are concatenated along the first dimension, giving the desired 2×2 matrix:

```
{{1, 2},
 {3, 4}}
```

The special case of just one scalar argument can be used to create a 1×1 matrix. For example:

```
[2]
```

This gives the matrix:

```
{{2}}
```

7.3.1 Type Rules for Concatenation

The function `cat(k,A,B,C,...)` concatenates arrays `A,B,C`,... along dimension `k`. The type and size constraints for the arguments to the concatenation function are expressed by the following rules:

- Arrays `A, B, C`, ... must have the same number of dimensions n, i.e., n = `ndims(A)` = `ndims(B)` = `ndims(C)`, etc.
- The concatenation dimension k must exist, i.e., 1 <= k <= `ndims(A)`, where k shall be an integer number.
- Size matching: arrays `A, B, C`, ... must have identical dimension sizes with the exception of the size of dimension k, i.e., `size(A,j) = size(B,j) = size(C,j) =` ..., for 1 <= j <= n and j <> k.

- Argument arrays `A, B, C, ...` must have equivalent maximally expanded element types. The element type of the result array is the element type of the maximally expanded type of the arguments. `Real` and `Integer` subtypes can be mixed, resulting in a `Real` result array where the `Integer` numbers have been transformed to `Real` numbers.

The above rules make it possible to mix integers and real numbers as in the example below:

```
Real[2,3]  r1 = cat(1, {{1.0, 2.0, 3}}, {{4, 5, 6}});
Real[2,6]  r2 = cat(2, r1, r1);
```

The sizes of the dimensions of the result array R = `cat(k,A,B,C,...)` are the same as in each of the array arguments, apart from the *k*th dimension where `size(R,k) = size(A,k) + size(B,k) + size(C,k) +...`, and so on. For example, concatenating along the 3rd dimension and adding the sizes of that dimension:

```
Real[1,1,1]  A = {{{1}}};
Real[1,1,2]  B = {{{2,3}}};
Real[1,1,3]  C = {{{4,5,6}}};

Real[1,1,6]  R = cat(3,A,B,C);  // Result value:  {{{1,2,3,4,5,6}}}
```

7.3.2 More on Concatenation Along the First and Second Dimensions

Earlier in this chapter, we introduced special operators for concatenation along the first and second dimensions. Below is a more precise definition of these operators in terms of the general `cat` function. The function *promote* used below is a pseudo function that keeps the contents of its array argument unchanged but increases its dimensionality by adding one-sized dimensions to the right in the list of dimensions, for example, if M has dimension `Real[3,4]` then *promote*(M,4) has the type `Real[3,4,1,1]`. The function *promote*(A,n) cannot be a function in Modelica since the number of dimensions of the returned array is not known at compile time when n is variable.

- Concatenation along the first dimension:

  `[A; B; C; ...] = cat(1, promote(A,n), promote(B,n), promote(C,n), ...)`

  where

  `n = max(2, ndims(A), ndims(B), ndims(C), ....).`

- *Concatenation along the second dimension*:

  `[A, B, C, ...] = cat(2, promote(A,n), promote(B,n), promote(C,n), ...)`

  where

  `n = max(2, ndims(A), ndims(B), ndims(C), ....).`

The following additional rules apply to these operators:

- The two forms can be mixed. The form [...,...] has higher precedence than [...;...]; e.g. [a, b; c, d] is parsed as [[a,b]; [c,d]].
- The form [A] with just one argument is allowed. The argument A is promoted to at least two dimensions, i.e., `[A]` = *promote*(A,n) where n = `max(2,ndims(A))`.
- There must currently be at least one argument, i.e., [] is not yet defined, but it may soon be defined and will then be equivalent to {{}}, i.e., with dimensionality 1×0.

7.3.2.1 Examples

```
Real s1, s2;                                    // Scalars
Real v1[n1], v2[n2];                            // Vectors
Real M1[m1,n], M2[m2,n], M3[n,m1], M4[n,m2];    // Matrices
Real K1[m1,n,k], K2[m2,n,k];                    // 3-dimensional arrays
```

```
[v1;v2]   // A matrix of type Real[n1+n2, 1]
[M1;M2]   // A matrix of type Real[m1+m2, n]
[M3,M4]   // A matrix of type Real[n, m1+m2]

[K1;K2]   // An array of type Real[m1+m2, n, k]
[s1;s2]   // A matrix of type Real[2, 1]
[s1,s1]   // A matrix of type Real[1, 2]

[s1]      // A matrix of type Real[1, 1]
[v1]      // A matrix of type Real[n1, 1]

Real[3]    v1 = {1, 2, 3};
Real[3]    v2 = {4, 5, 6};
Real[3,2] K1 = [v1, v2];
Real[3,2] K2 = [v1, [4;5;6]];    // Indentical values in K1 and K2

Real[2,3] K3 = [1, 2, 3; 4, 5, 6];
Real[1,3] K4 = [1, 2, 3];
Real[3,1] K5 = [1; 2; 3];
```

7.4 Array Indexing

The array indexing operator ...[...] , for example, as in `arr[4,2]`, is used to access array elements for retrieval of their values or for updating these values. An indexing operation is assumed to take constant time, that is, largely independent of the size of the array. The indexing operator takes two or more operands, where the first operand is the array to be indexed and the rest of the operands are index expressions:

arrayname[*indexexpr1*, *indexexpr2*, ...]

For example:

```
Real[2,2] A = {{2,3},{4,5}};   // Definition of Array A
A[2,2]                         // Retrieves the array element value 5
A[1,2] := ...                  // Assignment to the array element A[1,2]
```

Index expressions can be either scalar integer, Boolean, or enumeration expressions; or integer, Boolean, or enumeration vector expressions. The type of an index expression must be the same as the type of the array dimension it is indexing. For example, if an array is declared with a dimension that is an enumeration as in the `Real[Sizes]` example below, the index expression must have the same enumeration type.

Scalar index expressions is the common case and is usually used to access single array elements, whereas vector index expressions are always used to access array slices, i.e., subsections of arrays.

The array indexing operator is currently restricted to array variables and cannot be applied to general array expressions. For example, consider a function `f` returning an array:

```
f(x)[2]      // Illegal, indexing is only allowed for array variables!
```

Arrays can be indexed by integers as in the above examples, or Booleans and enumeration values, for example:

```
type Sizes = enumeration(small, medium);

Real[Sizes]   sz = {1.2, 3.5};
Real[Boolean] bb = {2.4, 9.9};

sz[Sizes.small]     // Ok, gives value 1.2
bb[true]            // Ok, gives value 9.9
```

7.4.1 Indexing with Scalar Index Expressions

Array indexing using scalar integer index expressions is usually used to retrieve or update single array elements. The value of the index expression for the *i*th dimension of an array `X` must be within the bounds of the size of that dimension, that is, 1 <= *indexvalue* <= `size(X,i)`. For example:

```
Real[2,3] B = {{1,2,3},{4,5,6}}
Real[3]   v = {10,11,12};

B[1,3]          // Retrieves the value 3
v[2]            // Retrieves the value 11
v[4]            // Error, index out of range!
```

However, since multidimensional arrays are defined as arrays of arrays in Modelica it is also possible to access sub-arrays using simple scalar indexing. For example, the array `B` in the previous example can also be regarded as a one-dimensional array of vectors:

```
B[2]            // Retrieve B[2] giving {4,5,6}
B[1] := v;      // Update B to become {{10,11,12},{4,5,6}}
```

7.4.1.1 Indexing with Boolean or Enumeration Values

As already mentioned above, arrays can be indexed using values of enumeration types or the `Boolean` type, not only by integers. For example:

```
type ShirtSizes = enumeration(small, medium, large, xlarge);
Real[ShirtSizes] w;
Real[Boolean]     b2;

w[ShirtSizes.large] := 2.28;  // Assign a value to an element of w
b2[true]            := 10.0;
b2[ShirtSizes.xlarge] := 5; // Error, b2 was declared with Boolean dimension
w[2]                := 8; // Error, w was declared with ShirtSizes dimension
```

7.4.1.2 Indexing with end

We observe that array index expressions involving calls to the built-in function `size(...)` are fairly common. Such expressions, e.g. `A[size(A,1)-1,size(A,2)]` when indexing the matrix `A`, can sometimes become rather complicated and hard to read.

To enable more concise and readable notation, the `end` keyword in Modelica can also be used as a scalar *expression* within array subscripts, equivalent to a call to `size(...)`, under the following conditions:

- The expression `end` may only appear inside array subscript expressions.
- If used within the *i*th subscript of an array `A`, `end` is equivalent to `size(A,i)`, provided the *i*th subscript index type is a subtype of *Integer*.
- If `end` is used inside nested array subscripts, it refers to the most closely nested array.

For example:

```
A[end-1,end]    // Same as:  A[size(A,1)-1,size(A,2)]
A[v[end],end]   // Same as:  A[v[size(v,1)],size(A,2)]
```

The second line in the example contains an `end` inside a nested array subscript `v[end]`, where `end` refers to the most closely nested array `v` and therefore is equivalent to `size(v,1)`.

7.4.2 Accessing Array Slices with Index Vectors

When at least one of the index expressions in an array indexing operation is a vector expression, a slice or subsection of the array is accessed rather than a single element. Such an index vector must be a vector of integer, Boolean, or enumeration values, where each value must be within the size bounds for the particular array dimension. An index vector can be constructed in any way but it is often convenient to use the colon operator to construct a range vector of index values. A single colon without operands (:) used as an index expression at a dimension `k` of an array of `X` denotes all indices of that dimension and is equivalent to the index vector `1:size(X,k)`.

The number of dimensions and dimension sizes of the returned array slice is determined by how many index expressions are vectors rather than scalars, and the sizes of those vectors. For example:

```
Real[3,2] X = {{1,2},{3,4},{8,9}};
Real[4]   w = {15,16,17,18};

X[2,1]        // Retrieves the value 3
X[:,1]        // Gets the first column of X as the vector {1,3,8}
X[2,:]        // Gets the second row of X as the vector {3,4}

X[2,1:2]      // Same as above, i.e. {3,4}
X[2,{1,2}]    // Same as above, i.e. {3,4}
X[2,{2}]      // Half of the above vector, i.e. {4}

X[:,1:1]      // Gets the first column of X as column matrix {{1},{2},{8}}
X[{2},:]      // Gets the second row of X as the row matrix {{3,4}}
X[{2,3},{1,2}]  // Extract submatrix giving {{3,4},{8,9}}

w[2:4]        // Get the 2:nd through 4:th elements as {16,17,18}
w[{1,3}]      // Get the 1:st and 3:rd elements as {15,17}
w[1:2:4]      // Get the 1:st to 4:th step 2 elements as {15,17}

w[3:4] := {1,2};  // Assignment causing w to become {15,16,1,2}
```

7.4.3 Array Record Field Slices of Record Arrays

If A is an array of records and m is a field of that record type, the expression $A.m$ is interpreted as an array *field slice* operation of that record array. It returns the array of fields: $\{A[1].m, A[2].m, A[3].m, \ldots\}$.

For example, assume a record `Person` with three fields: `name`, `age`, and `children`:

```
record Person
  String     name;
  Integer    age;
  String[2]  children;
end Person;
```

For the purpose of this example, we use the record constructor function `Person`(*name*, *age*, *children*) returning a `Person` record, which in Modelica is automatically defined as a byproduct of the `Person` record declaration (see Section 3.18.4, page 118). This function is used to define the contents of a small array `persons` consisting of `Person` records.

```
Person[3] persons =
  {Person("John",   35, {"Carl",   "Eva"} ),
   Person("Karin",  40, {"Anders","Dan"}),
   Person("Lisa",   37, {"John","Daniel"})
  };
```

The record field slices `persons.name` and `persons.age` contain the following results:

```
persons.name       // Returns:  {"John","Karin","Lisa"}
persons.age        // Returns:  {35,40,37}
```

If the field m is an array, the slice operation is valid only if `size`(A[1].m)=`size`(A[2].m)=... to ensure that the returned array is rectangular. This is fulfilled for the array field slice `persons.children` since:

```
size(persons[1].children) = size(persons[2].children) = {2}
```

The field slice evaluates as follows:

```
persons.children   // Returns:  {{"Carl", "Eva"},
```

```
//                {"Anders","Dan"},
//                {"John","Daniel"})
```

It is also possible to mix slicing and indexing:

```
persons.children[1]  // Returns: {"Carl", "Anders", "John"}
```

7.5 Using Array Concatenation and Slices

In order to properly use Modelica arrays and array operations, especially concatenation and slices, it is useful to review some of the existing properties of Modelica arrays and compare with other languages often used for array computation, with emphasis on MATLAB.

The Modelica array concatenation and slice operations have been designed for multidimensional arrays and therefore can produce arrays of various dimensions, from one-dimensional vectors to matrices and multidimensional arrays. The special-purpose [..., ...] and [...; ...] concatenation operators are applicable to multidimensional arrays but are primarily intended for matrices and always produce arrays of at least two dimensions. Row vectors and column vectors do not exist in Modelica since vectors are one-dimensional entities. However, most array operators have been defined to implicitly treat a vector as a column vector since this is common in matrix algebra, with the exception of *vector*matrix*, where the vector is treated as a row vector.

7.5.1 Advice for Users with MATLAB Background

Modelica arrays and array operations have been carefully designed to provide a rather high degree of MATLAB compatibility in syntax and semantics, while still conforming quite well to mainstream strongly typed programming languages. However, there are important differences stemming from the fact that Modelica has strongly typed multidimensional arrays, whereas MATLAB was designed for matrix computation:

- MATLAB scalars and vectors are in reality matrices, and behave as such. So-called row vectors are in fact row matrices (matrices with one row), and column vectors are column matrices. MATLAB does not have strong type checking. Array slices always produce matrices.
- Modelica has strongly typed multidimensional arrays. Scalars are true zero-dimensional entities, vectors are one-dimensional entities, matrices are two-dimensional entities, and so on. Array slices produce vectors, matrices, or multidimensional arrays depending on the form of the slice operation. This is standard for strongly typed programming languages, for example, Fortran90 or C++, with array data types and/or libraries.

The following properties give a high degree of MATLAB compatibility:

- Vectors are implicitly treated as column vectors with the exception of *vector*matrix* where *vector* is treated as a row vector.
- The special-purpose [..., ...] and [...; ...] square bracket concatenation operators primarily intended for matrices promote scalar arguments to 1×1 matrices and vector arguments to column matrices. This allows the use of MATLAB notation for creating matrices from scalar arguments.

The user with a MATLAB background should watch out for the following language differences that can cause mistakes:

- The {...} curly bracket operator is an array constructor—not a concatenation operator. It always increases the dimensionality of the result by 1 compared to its arguments. Thus it can be used to create vectors from scalar arguments, e.g. {1,2,3}, but *not* to concatenate vectors since application of {} on vectors will create a matrix.

- The [*v1*,*v2*] and [*v1*;*v2*] concatenation operators *cannot* be used to concatenate two vectors *v1* and *v2* into a result vector since a matrix always will be returned. Instead use `cat`(1,*v1*,*v2*), which returns a vector.
- The array slice operator when used on a matrix can return a matrix, a vector, or a scalar depending on whether two of its arguments are vectors, one argument is a vector, or no arguments are vectors. It is advisable to make sure that all arguments to an array slice operation used together with the special-purpose concatenation operators [...] are vectors since the slice then will return an array instead of a vector that unintentionally might be promoted to a column matrix. For example, use [M2[{2},:]; M3[{3},:] or [M2[2:2,:]; M3[3:3,:] rather than [M2[2,:]; M3[3,:] to concatenate row matrices from M2 and M3. Alternatively use the `cat`(...) function.

Certain notation in MATLAB, for example, the apostrophe ' operator has not been introduced in Modelica since it has a different meaning in mathematics (differentiation) and is easy to miss when reading code. Instead a built-in `transpose` function is available in Modelica.

7.5.2 Usage Examples

The following usage examples show a few common programming situations where both array concatenation and array slices are involved, and how to do this correctly in order to avoid certain mistakes.

7.5.2.1 Appending an Element to Vectors and Row/Column Matrices

The first equations set `XA1`, `XA2`, `XA3`, and `XA4` equal to row matrices and `XB1`, `XB2` equal to column matrices respectively, created by appending an additional element to row/column matrices `PA` and `PB`.

```
Real[1,3]     PA = [1,2,3];      // A row matrix value
Real[3,1]     PB = [1;2;3];      // A column matrix value
Real[3]       q  = {1,2,3};      // A vector value
Real[1,4]     XA1,XA2,XA3,XA4;   // Row matrix variables
Real[4,1]     XB1,XB2;           // Column matrix variables
Real[4]       y;                 // Vector variable

equation
  XA1 = [PA, 4];             // Append OK, since 4 is promoted to {{4}}
  XA2 = cat(2,PA,{{4}});     // Append OK, same as above but not promoted

  XB1 = [PB; 4];              // Append OK, result is {{1},{2},{3},{4}}
  XB2 = cat(1,PB,{{2}});      // Append OK, same result

  y   = cat(1,q,{4});         // Vector append OK, result is {1,2,3,4}
  //y   = {q,4};              ERROR! {...} not a concatenation operation

  XA3 = [-1,zeros(1,2),1];  // Append OK. result:  {{-1,0,0,1}}
  XA4 = cat(2,{{-1}},zeros(1,2),{{1}});
  // Append OK result:  {{-1,0,0,1}}

  //XA4 = {-1,zeros(1,2),1};  Error!  args have incompatible dimensions
```

7.5.2.2 Composing a Blocked Matrix from Sub-matrices

The following example shows three very similar ways of constructing a blocked matrix from sub-matrices. The first two variants follow the rule of always making sure that returned array slices as arguments to the special-purpose concatenation operators are matrices. The third variant breaks this rule, since two of the array slices return vectors, causing an error. The first vector `-Q[1:3,3]` happens to be promoted to a column matrix according to the default promotion rules for [...,...], which is fine. However, the second vector `-Q[3,1:3]` is also promoted to column matrix, which is wrong since a row matrix was intended, causing the error.

```
Real[3,3]  P = [1,2,3;
                4,5,6;
                7,8,9];  // A 3x3 matrix value

Real[6,6]  Q;    // Q consists of four 3x3 matrix blocks
                 // to be defined by P apart from sign

equation                  // Variant 1 - OK
  Q[1:3, 1:3] = P;                               // Upper left block
  Q[1:3, 4:6] = [Q[1:3,1:2], -Q[1:3, {3}]];      // Upper right block
  Q[4:6, 1:3] = [Q[1:2,1:3]; -Q[{3}, 1:3]];      // Lower left block
  Q[4:6, 4:6] = P;                               // Lower Right block

equation                  // Variant 2 - OK
  Q[1:3, 1:3] = P;                               // Upper left block
  Q[1:3, 4:6] = [Q[1:3,1:2], -Q[1:3, 3:3]];      // Upper right block
  Q[4:6, 1:3] = [Q[1:2,1:3]; -Q[3:3, 1:3]];      // Lower left block
  Q[4:6, 4:6] = P;                               // Lower Right block

equation                  // Variant 3 - ERROR!
  Q[1:3, 1:3] = P;                               // OK!
  Q[1:3, 4:6] = [Q[1:3,1:2], -Q[1:3, 3]];        // OK, correct promotion
  Q[4:6, 1:3] = [Q[1:2,1:3]; -Q[3, 1:3]];        // ERROR!
  Q[4:6, 4:6] = P;                               // OK!
```

7.5.2.3 Cyclic Permutation of Matrix Rows or Columns

Cyclic permutation can be achieved by a combination of concatenation operations and array slices or just array slices using a permutation vector.

```
Real[1,3]  W0 = [1,2,3];              // Row matrix
Real[2,3]  X0 = [1,2,3; 4,5,6];       // Matrix with two rows

Real[1,3]  W;                         // Permuted Row matrix
Real[2,3]  X;                         // Permuted Matrix with two rows

Integer[3] p = {2,3,1};               // Permutation vector

algorithm
  W := [[2,3], 1];                    // OK, result: [2,3,1] = {{2,3,1}}
  W := [{{2,3}}, {{1}}];              // OK, same result: {{2,3,1}}

  W := [W0[{1},2:3], W0[{1},{1}]]; // OK, result: {{2,3,1}}
  W := [W0[1:1,2:3], W0[1:1,1:1]]; // OK, same result: {{2,3,1}}

  W := W0[:,p];                       // OK, same result: {{2,3,1}}

  W := cat(2, W0[1:1,2:3], W0[1:1,1:1]); // OK, same result {{2,3,1}}
  //W := [W0[1,2:3], W0[1,1]];        ERROR, since W0[1,2:3] is a vector

  X := [X0[:,2:3], X0[:,{1}]];        // OK, X becomes [2,3,1; 5,6,4]
  X := X0[:,p];                       // OK, X becomes [2,3,1; 5,6,4]

  X[{1},:] := [X0[{1},2:3],X0[{1},{1}]];
          // OK, X becomes [2,3,1; 4,5,6]
  //X[1,:]   := [X0[1,2:3],X0[1,1]];
                // ERROR! Incompatible dimensions
```

7.6 Array Equality and Assignment

Both of the operators denoting equation equality (=) and assignment (:=) are defined for arrays as well as for scalars. These operators are defined elementwise for arrays, that is, corresponding elements in the array operands are set equal or assigned. The dimensionality and size of the operands must be identical, and the element types must be equivalent. The element types can be simple built-in types and all types satisfying the requirements for a record. In case of record array elements the operations are applied element-wise for each declared record field element of the records.

Note that *relational operators* such as ==, <>, <=, etc. for use in Boolean expressions are *not defined for arrays*, only for scalars. The table below indicates the definitions of the operators = and := for various combinations of scalar and array types. The notation = / := means one of the operators = or :=.

Table 7-1. Equality and assignment of arrays and scalars.

Equality/Assignment: = / :=	*Scalar* `b`	*Array* `b[n,m,...]`
Scalar `a`	*Scalar*: `a = / := b`	–
Array `a[n,m,...]`	–	*elementwise*: `a[j,k,...] = / := b[j,k,...]` `j=1:n, k=1:m, ...`

Type of `a`	*Type of* `b`	*Result of* `a = b` or `a := b`	*Operation* (j=1:n, k=1:m)
Scalar	*Scalar*	*Scalar*	a = b or a := b
Vector[n]	*Vector*[n]	*Vector*[n]	a[j] = b[j] or a[j] := b[j]
Matrix[n, m]	*Matrix*[n, m]	*Matrix*[n, m]	a[j, k] = b[j, k] (also :=)
Array[n, m, ...]	*Array*[n, m, ...]	*Array*[n, m, ...]	a[j, k, ...] = b[j, k, ...] (also :=)

The example below contains a vector equation for `v1` and a vector assignment for `v2`:

```
Real[3] v1,v2;
equation
  v1 = {1,2,3};
algorithm
   v2 := {4,5,6};
```

The above vector equation and vector assignment are equivalent to the expanded scalar version below:

```
Real[3] v1,v2;
equation
  v1[1] = 1;
  v1[2] = 2;
  v1[3] = 3;
algorithm
  v2[1] := 4;
  v2[2] := 5;
  v2[3] := 6;
```

7.6.1 Declaration Equations and Assignments for Arrays Indexed by Enumerations and Booleans

Arrays with the same element type, dimensionality, and dimension sizes can be used in declaration equations or declaration assignments, independent of whether the index types of dimensions are subtypes of `Integer`, `Boolean`, or `enumeration` types. Necessary type conversions of index types are done automatically. These are the *only* kind of equations and assignments allowed for *whole arrays* indexed by `enumeration` and `Boolean` values. However, array elements of such arrays can still be used in any kind of equation or statement.

In the following example the vector `x`, indexed by `Booleans`, is set equal to the value `{22.4, 33.5}`:

```
Real[Boolan] x = {22.4, 33.5};
```

The vectors `w`, `w2`, `w3`, and `y` are all indexed by values of the enumeration type `ShirtSizes`. For example, the vector `w`, indexed by `ShirtSizes`, is set equal to the vector expression `ones(4)`, which is indexed by integers (analogously for the other vectors).

```
type ShirtSizes = enumeration(small, medium, large, xlarge);
Real[ShirtSizes] w  =  ones(4);
Real[ShirtSizes] w2 := ones(4); // Ok, declaration assignment (in function)
Real[ShirtSizes] y  =  {1.4, 3.5, 2.8, 3.1};
Real[ShirtSizes] w3,w4;

w3  = ones(4);  // Error, equation only allowed in declaration equations
w4  = ones(4);  // Error, assignment only allowed in declaration assignments
```

7.7 String Concatenation Array Operator

Elementwise string concatenation operations on scalars or arrays of strings is available through the standard plus (+) operator or the element-wise plus (.+) operator. The (.+) operator is equivalent to (+) when both operands are scalars.

The dimensionality and dimension sizes of both arguments must be the *same*. Elementwise concatenation of a scalar string with an array of strings is *not* defined with the (+) operator which is indicated by the tables below. A vector is a 1-dimensional array and a matrix is a 2-dimensional array.

Table 7-2. Concatenation of strings and arrays of strings.

String Concatenation: +	*Scalar* b	*Array* b[n,m,...]
Scalar a	*scalar*: a + b	–
Array a[n,m,...]	–	*elementwise*: a[j,k,...] + b[j,k,...] j=1:n, k=1:m, ...

Type of a	*Type of* b	*Result of* a + b	*Operation* c := a + b (*j=1:n, k=1:m*)
Scalar	*Scalar*	*Scalar*	c := a + b
Vector[n]	*Vector*[n]	*Vector*[n]	c[j] := a[j] + b[j]
Matrix[n, m]	*Matrix*[n, m]	*Matrix*[n, m]	c[j, k] := a[j, k] + b[j, k]
Array[n, m, ...]	*Array*[n, m, ...]	*Array*[n, m, ...]	c [j, k, ...] := a[j, k, ...] + b[j, k, ...]

Examples:

```
{"a","b","c"} + "d"              // Not allowed!
{"a","b","c"} + {"d","d","d"}    // Result: {"ad","bd","cd"}
{"a","b","c"} + {"a","b"}        // Not allowed, different array sizes!
```

However, elementwise concatenation of a scalar string with an array of strings is *defined* with the (.+) operator:

Table 7-3. Element-wise concatenation of strings and arrays of strings.

String Concatenation: .+	*Scalar* b	*Array* b[n,m,...]
Scalar a	*scalar*: a .+ b	*elementwise*: a .+ b[j,k,...] j=1:n, k=1:m, ...

Array a[n,m,...]	*elementwise*: a[j,k,...] .+ b j=1:n, k=1:m, ...	*Elementwise*: a[j,k,...] .+ b[j,k,...] j=1:n, k=1:m, ...

Type of a	*Type of* b	*Result of* a .+ b	*Operation* c := a .+ b *(j=1:n, k=1:m)*
Scalar	*Scalar*	*Scalar*	c := a .+ b
Vector[n]	*Vector*[n]	*Vector*[n]	c[j] := a[j] .+ b[j]
Matrix[n, m]	*Matrix*[n, m]	*Matrix*[n, m]	c[j, k] := a[j, k] .+ b[j, k]
Array[n, m, ...]	*Array*[n, m, ...]	*Array*[n, m, ...]	c [j, k, ...] := a[j, k, ...] .+ b[j, k, ...]

Examples:

```
{"a","b","c"} .+ "d"                // Result: {"ad","bd","cd"}
"d" .+ {"a","b","c"}                // Result: {"da","db","dc"}
{"a","b","c"} .+ {"d","d","d"}      // Result: {"ad","bd","cd"}
{"a","b","c"} .+ {"a","b"}          // Not allowed, different array sizes!
```

7.8 Arithmetic Array Operators and Elementwise Operators

Arithmetic operations on arrays and certain combinations of arrays and scalars are available through the standard arithmetic operators, addition (+), subtraction (–), division (/), and multiplication (*), as well as through the exponentiation (^) operator. The semantics of the array versions of these operators are of course different from the scalar case.

Moreover, there are also five special elementwise arithmetic operators which are always performed elementwise: elementwise addition (.+), elementwise subtraction (.–), elementwise division (./), elementwise multiplication (.*), and elementwise exponentiation (.^).

Addition (+) , subtraction(-) , and division (/) are defined as elementwise operations on elements of array operands. Elementwise operations for the combination of an array and a scalar operand are defined for multiplication (*) and division (/) but not for addition (+) and subtraction (-) where we instead have to use elementwise addition (.+) and elementwise subtraction (.–).

The array multiplication operator (*) is defined only for vectors and matrices and is overloaded, that is, has several different definitions depending on the type of its arguments, see also Section 7.8.3, page 332. If both operands are vectors, then array multiplication means scalar product; otherwise, if the operands are vectors or matrices, then it means matrix multiplication. If one of the operands is a scalar, then the multiplication operation is defined as elementwise multiplication, which, however, is not available when both operands are arrays despite the fact that analogous elementwise operations are defined for addition and subtraction. The reason is that we have already used the multiplication notation (*) for the more common operation of matrix multiplication. Instead we can use (.*) for elementwise multiplication.

Array exponentiation (^) is the same as repeated matrix multiplication and is therefore defined only when the first operand is a square matrix and the second operand is a nonnegative integer. Elementwise array exponentiation (.^) is however available.

7.8.1 Array Addition and Subtraction

Elementwise addition and subtraction of scalars and/or arrays can be done with the (+), (.+), and (–), (.–) operators. The operators (.+) and (.–) are defined for combinations of scalars with arrays, which is not the case for (+) and (–). The (.+) operator is equivalent to (+) and the (.–) operator is equivalent to (–) when both operands are scalars.

Table 7-4. Array addition and subtraction.

Addition/Subtraction: `+ / -`	*Scalar* `b`	*Array* `b[n,m,...]`
Scalar `a`	*Scalar*: `a +/- b`	–
Array `a[n,m,...]`	–	*elementwise*: `a[j,k,...] +/- b[j,k,...]` `j=1:n, k=1:m, ...`

Type of `a`	*Type of* `b`	*Result of* `a +/- b`	*Operation* `c := a +/- b` *(j=1:n, k=1:m)*
Scalar	*Scalar*	*Scalar*	c := a +/- b
Vector[n]	*Vector*[n]	*Vector*[n]	c[j] := a[j] +/- b[j]
Matrix[n, m]	*Matrix*[n, m]	*Matrix*[n, m]	c[j, k] := a[j, k] +/- b[j, k]
Array[n, m, ...]	*Array*[n, m, ...]	*Array*[n, m, ...]	c [j, k, ...] := a[j, k, ...] +/- b[j, k, ...]

Examples:

```
{1,2,3} + 1                    // Not allowed!
{1,2,3} - {1,2,0}              // Result: {0,0,3}
{1,2,3} + {1,2}                // Not allowed, different array sizes!
{{1,1},{2,2}} + {{1,2},{3,4}}  // Result: {{2,3},{5,6}}
```

Table 7-5. Elementwise array and scalar addition and subtraction.

Addition/Subtraction: `.+ / .-`	*Scalar* `b`	*Array* `b[n,m,...]`
Scalar `a`	*scalar*: `a .+/.- b`	*elementwise*: `a .+/.- b[j,k,...]` `j=1:n, k=1:m, ...`
Array `a[n,m,...]`	*elementwise*: `a[j,k,...] .+/.- b` `j=1:n, k=1:m, ...`	*elementwise*: `a[j,k,...] .+/.- b[j,k,...]` `j=1:n, k=1:m, ...`

Type of `a`	*Type of* `b`	*Result of* `a .+/.- b`	*Operation* `c := a .+/.- b` *(j=1:n, k=1:m)*
Scalar	*Scalar*	*Scalar*	c := a .+/.- b
Scalar	*Array*[n, m, ...]	*Array*[n, m, ...]	c[j, k, ...] := a .+/.- b[j, k, ...]
Array[n, m, ...]	*Scalar*	*Array*[n, m, ...]	c[j, k, ...] := a[j, k, ...] .+/.- b
Array[n, m, ...]	*Array*[n, m, ...]	*Array*[n, m, ...]	c [j, k, ...] := a[j, k, ...] .+/.- b[j, k, ...]

Examples:

```
{1,2,3} .+ 1                    // Result: {2,3,4}
1 .+ {1,2,3}                    // Result: {2,3,4}
{1,2,3} .- {1,2,0}              // Result: {0,0,3}
{1,2,3} .+ {1,2}                // Not allowed, different array sizes!
{{1,1},{2,2}} .+ {{1,2},{3,4}}  // Result: {{2,3},{5,6}}
```

7.8.2 Array Division

Element-wise division between scalars and/or arrays can be done with the (`/`) and (`./`) operators. The (`./`) operator is equivalent to (`/`) when both operands are scalars. The operator (`./`) is defined for all combinations of scalars with arrays, which is not the case for (`/`).

Table 7-6. Array and scalar division.

Division: /	*Scalar* b	*Array* b[n,m,...]
Scalar a	*scalar*: a / b	–
Array a[n,m,...]	*elementwise*: a[j,k,...] / b j=1:n, k=1:m, ...	–

Type of a	*Type of* s	*Result of* a / s	*Operation* c := a / s (*j=1:n, k=1:m*)
Scalar	*Scalar*	*Scalar*	c := a / s
Vector[n]	*Scalar*	*Vector*[n]	c[k] := a[k] / s
Matrix[n, m]	*Scalar*	*Matrix*[n, m]	c[j, k] := a[j, k] / s
Array[n, m, ...]	*Scalar*	*Array*[n, m, ...]	c[j, k, ...] := a[j, k, ...] / s

Examples:

```
{2,4,6} / 2                          // {1,2,3}
6 / {1,2,3}                          // Not allowed!
{1,2,3} / {1,2,2}                    // Not allowed!
```

Table 7-7. Elementwise array and scalar division.

Division: ./	*Scalar* b	*Array* b[n,m,...]
Scalar a	*Scalar*: a ./ b	*elementwise*: a ./ b[j,k,...] j=1:n, k=1:m, ...
Array a[n,m,...]	*elementwise*: a[j,k,...] ./ b j=1:n, k=1:m, ...	*elementwise*: a[j,k,...] ./ b[j,k,...] j=1:n, k=1:m, ...

Type of a	*Type of* b	*Type of* a ./ b	*Operation* c:=a ./ b (j=1:n, k=1:m)
Scalar	*Scalar*	*Scalar*	c := a / b
Scalar	*Array*[n, m, ...]	*Array*[n, m, ...]	c[j, k, ...] := a ./ b[j, k, ...]
Array[n, m, ...]	*Scalar*	*Array*[n, m, ...]	c[j, k, ...] := a[j, k, ...] ./ b
Array[n, m, ...]	*Array*[n, m, ...]	*Array* [n, m, ...]	c[j, k, ...] := a[j, k, ...] ./ b[j, k, ...]

Examples:

```
{2,4,6} ./ 2                         // Result: {1,2,3}
12 ./ {2,4,6}                        // Result: {6,3,2}
{2,4,6} ./ {1,2,2}                   // Result: {2,2,3}
{1,2,3} ./ {1,2}                     // Not allowed, different array sizes!
```

Sometimes an extra space is needed before an elementwise operator to clarify the difference compared to a number with a decimal point.

Example:

```
4./ [1,2;2,4]  // Error, the dot in 4. makes: 4.0 / [1,2;3,4], not allowed!
4 ./[1,2;2,4]  // Fine, element-wise division, result: [4,2;2,1]
```

7.8.3 Linear Algebra Array Multiplication

The multiplication operator (*) is interpreted as scalar product or matrix multiplication depending on the dimensionality of its array arguments.

Table 7-8. Linear algebra array multiplication.

Multiplication: *	*Scalar* b	*Array* b[n,m,...] or b[m,p]
Scalar a		
Array a[n,m,...]		*scalar product* a*b: *Vector*[n]**Vector*[n]: SUM$_k$(a[k]*b[k]), k=1:n *matrix multiplication* c := a*b *Vector*[m] := *Vector*[n]**Matrix*[n,m]: c[k] := SUM$_j$(a[j]*b[j,k]), j=1:n, k=1:m *Vector*[n] := *Matrix*[n,m]**Vector*[m]: c[j] := SUM$_k$(a[j,k]*b[k]), j=1:n, k=1:m *Matrix*[n,p] := *Matrix*[n,m]**Matrix*[m,p]: c[j,r] := SUM$_k$(a[j,k]*b[k,r]), j=1:n, k=1:m, r=1:p

Type of a	*Type of* b	*Type of* a* b	*Operation* c := a*b
Vector [n]	*Vector* [n]	*Scalar*	c := sum$_k$(a[k]*b[k]), k=1:n
Vector [n]	*Matrix* [n, m]	*Vector* [m]	c[j] := sum$_k$(a[k]*b[k, j]), j=1:m, k=1:n
Matrix [n, m]	*Vector* [m]	*Vector* [n]	c[j] := sum$_k$(a[j, k]*b[k])
Matrix [n, m]	*Matrix* [m, p]	*Matrix* [n, p]	c[i, j] = sum$_k$(a[i, k]*b[k, j]), i=1:n, k=1:m, j=1:p

Examples:

```
{1,2,3} * {1,2,2}                   // Scalar product:    11

{{1,2},{3,4}} * {1,2}               // Matrix mult:       {5,11}
{1,2,3} * {{1},{2},{10}}            // Matrix mult:       {35}
{1,2,3} * [1;2;10]                  // Matrix mult:       {35}

{{1,2},{3,4}} * {{1,2},{2,1}}       // Matrix mult:       {{5,4},{11,10}}
[1,2; 3,4] * [1,2; 2,1]             // Matrix mult:       {{5,4},{11,10}}
{{1,2},{3,4}} * {1,2,3}             // Error, incompatible array sizes!
```

7.8.4 Elementwise Array Multiplication

Elementwise multiplication between scalars and/or arrays can be done with the (*) and (.*) operators. The (.*) operator is equivalent to (*) when both operands are scalars. The elementwise operator (.*) is defined for all combinations of scalars with arrays, and also between arrays, which is not the case for (*).

Table 7-9. Scalar and scalar to array multiplication with *.

Multiplication: *	*Scalar* b	*Array* b[n,m,...]
Scalar a	*Scalar*: a*b	*elementwise*: a*b[j,k,...] j=1:n, k=1:m, ...
Array a[n,m,...]	*elementwise*: a[j,k,...] * b j=1:n, k=1:m, ...	–

Type of s	*Type of* a	*Type of* s*a *and* a*s	*Operation* c := s*a or c := a*s (j=1:n, k=1:m)
Scalar	*Scalar*	*Scalar*	c := s * a
Scalar	*Vector* [n]	*Vector* [n]	c[j] := s* a[j]
Scalar	*Matrix* [n, m]	*Matrix* [n, m]	c[j, k] := s* a[j, k]
Scalar	*Array*[n, m, ...]	*Array* [n, m, ...]	c[j, k, ...] := s*a[j, k, ...]

Examples:

```
{1,2,3} * 2                    // Result: {2,4,6}
2 * {1,2,3}                    // Result: {2,4,6}
```

Table 7-10. Elementwise array and scalar multiplication with .*.

Multiplication: .*	*Scalar* b	*Array* b[n,m,...]
Scalar a	*Scalar*: a .* b	*elementwise*: a .* b[j,k,...] j=1:n, k=1:m, ...
Array a[n,m,...]	*elementwise*: a[j,k,...] .* b j=1:n, k=1:m, ...	*elementwise*: a[j,k,...] .* b[j,k,...] j=1:n, k=1:m, ...

Type of a	*Type of* b	*Type of* a .* b	*Operation* c:=a .* b (j=1:n, k=1:m)
Scalar	*Scalar*	*Scalar*	c := a .* b
Scalar	*Array*[n, m, ...]	*Array*[n, m, ...]	c[j, k, ...] := a.* b[j, k, ...]
Array[n, m, ...]	*Scalar*	*Array*[n, m, ...]	c[j, k, ...] := a[j, k, ...].* b
Array[n, m, ...]	*Array*[n, m, ...]	*Array* [n, m, ...]	c[j, k, ...] := a[j, k, ...].* b[j, k, ...]

Examples:

```
{1,2,3} .* 2                   // Result: {2,4,6}
2 .* {1,2,3}                   // Result: {2,4,6}
{2,4,6} .* {1,2,2}             // Result: {2,8,12}
{1,2,3} .* {1,2}               // Not allowed, different array sizes!
```

7.8.5 Square Matrix Array Exponentiation

Array exponentiation of a square matrix with an integer exponent is defined as repeated matrix multiplications.

Exponentiation of two scalars a and b, a^b, is defined as equivalent to pow(double a, double b) in the ANSI C library if both a and b are Real scalars. A Real scalar value is returned. If a or b are Integer scalars, they are automatically promoted to Real.

The consequences of exceptional situations, such as `a==0.0` and `b<=0.0`, `a<0` and `b` is not an integer, or overflow, are undefined.

Table 7-11. Square matrix array and scalar exponentiation.

Exponentiation: `^`	*Scalar* `b`	*Array* `b[n,n]`
Scalar `a`	*Scalar*: `a ^ b`	–

Array `a[n,n]`
`(square matrix)`
	`a ^ b = a*a*a*...`
	`b` multiplications, `b>=0`
	`a^0 = identity(size(a,1))`
	`a^1 = a`
		–

Examples:

```
{{1,2},{1,2}}  ^ 0          // Result: {{1,0},{0,1}}
[1,2; 1,2]     ^ 1          // Result: {{1,2},{1,2}}
[1,2; 1,2]     ^ 2          // Result: {{3,6},{3,6}}
[1,2; 1,2]     ^ 2.5        // Error, non-integer exponent!
[1,2,3; 1,2,3] ^ 2          // Error, non-square array!
a^3 = a*a*a;
a^0 = identity(size(a,1));
assert(size(a,1)==size(a,2),"Matrix must be square");
a^1 = a;
```

Elementwise exponentiation between scalars and/or arrays can be done with the (`.^`) operator. The (`.^`) operator is equivalent to (`^`) when both operands are scalars. The element-wise operator (`.^`) is defined for all combinations of scalars with arrays, and arrays with arrays, which is not the case for (`^`).

Table 7-12. Elementwise array and scalar exponentiation.

Exponentiation: `.^`	*Scalar* `b`	*Array* `b[n,m,...]`
Scalar `a`	*Scalar*: `a .^ b`	*elementwise*: `a .^ b[j,k,...]` `j=1:n, k=1:m, ...`

Array `a[n,m,...]`	*elementwise*:
	`a[j,k,...] .^ b`
	`j=1:n, k=1:m,`
	`...`
		elementwise:
		`a[j,k,...] .^ b[j,k,...]`
		`j=1:n, k=1:m,`
		`...`

Type of a	*Type of* b	*Type of* a .^ b	*Operation* c:=a .^ b (j=1:n, k=1:m)
Scalar	*Scalar*	*Scalar*	c := a .^ b
Scalar	*Array*[n, m, ...]	*Array*[n, m, ...]	c[j, k, ...] := a .^ b[j, k, ...]
Array[n, m, ...]	*Scalar*	*Array*[n, m, ...]	c[j, k, ...] := a[j, k, ...] .^ b
Array[n, m, ...]	*Array*[n, m, ...]	*Array* [n, m, ...]	c[j, k, ...] := a[j, k, ...] .^ b[j, k, ...]

Examples:

```
{2,4,6} .^ 2               // Result: {4,16,36}
2 .^ {1,2,3}               // Result: {2,4,8}
{2,4,6} .^ {1,2,2}         // Result: {2,16,36}
{1,2,3} .^ {1,2}           // Not allowed, different array sizes!
```

Sometimes an extra space is needed before the elementwise exponentiation operator to clarify the difference compared to a number with a decimal point.

Examples:

```
2.^ [1,2;2,4]  // Error, the dot in 2. makes: 2.0 ^ [1,2;3,4], not allowed!
2 .^ [1,2;2,4] // Fine, element-wise exponentiation, result: [2,4;4,16]
```

7.9 Built-in Array Functions

A number of built-in functions for array expressions are provided in Modelica. These functions are directly available and need not be imported from some package in the standard library before being used. The built-in array functions can be divided into six groups:

- Dimension and size functions.
- Conversion functions for changing the dimensionality of scalars and arrays.
- Constructor functions for creating array values.
- Reduction functions for computing scalar values from arrays.
- Matrix and vector algebra functions.
- Array concatenation functions.

In the following subsections we use boldface for built-in array function names in examples for visibility, even if this is not according to the Modelica code formatting conventions.

7.9.1 Array Dimension and Size Functions

The following built-in functions return the number of dimensions of an array, the sizes of its dimensions, or the size of a specific dimension.

`ndims(A)`	Returns the number of dimensions `k` of array `A`, with `k >= 0`.
`size(A,i)`	Returns the size of dimension `i` of array `A` where `1 <= i <= ndims(A)`.
`size(A)`	Returns a vector of length `ndims(A)` containing the dimension sizes of `A`.

Examples:

```
Real[4,1,6] x;
ndims(x);                   // returns 3
size(x,1);                  // returns 4
size(x);                    // returns the vector {4, 1, 6}
size(2*x+x) = size(x);      // this equation holds
```

7.9.2 Dimensionality Conversion Functions

The following conversion functions convert scalars, vectors, and arrays to scalars, vectors, or matrices by adding or removing one-sized dimensions.

`scalar(A)`	Converts the array `A` containing a single element to a scalar by returning this element. All dimensions of array `A` must have size 1, i.e., `size(A,i) = 1` for `1 <= i <= ndims(A)`. The operation removes all those dimensions.
`vector(A)`	Converts `A` to a vector. If `A` is a scalar, then returns the one element vector `{A}`. Otherwise, if `A` is an array with at most one dimension of `size > 1`, then returns a vector containing all the elements of the array.
`matrix(A)`	Converts `A` to a matrix. If `A` is a scalar, then returns `{{A}}`. If `A` is a vector `{a,b,c,...}`, then returns the column matrix `{{a},{b},{c},...}`. Otherwise, if `A` is an array for which all but the first two dimensions must have size 1, i.e., `size(A,i) = 1 for 3 <= i <= ndims(A)`, then returns a matrix obtained by eliminating all but the first two dimensions of `A`. This matrix contains all the elements

	of A.

Examples:

```
Real[3]       v1  = {1.0, 2.0, 3.0};
Real[3,1]     m1  = matrix(v1);      // m1 contains {{1.0}, {2.0}, {3.0}}
Real[3]       v2  = vector(m1);      // v2 contains {1.0, 2.0, 3.0}

Real[1,1,1] m2  = {{{4.0}}};
Real        s1  = scalar(m2);      // s1 contains 4.0
Real[2,2,1] m3  = {{{1.0},{2.0}}, {{3.0},{4.0}}}
Real[2,2]   m4  = matrix(m3)       // m4 contains {{1.0,2.0}, {3.0,4.0}}
```

7.9.3 Specialized Constructor Functions

An array constructor function constructs and returns an array computed from its arguments. Most of the constructor functions in the table below construct an array by filling in values according to a certain pattern, in several cases just giving all array elements the same value. The general array constructor with syntax `array` (...) or {...} is described elsewhere in this chapter in more detail, and is just included here for completeness.

Note that even though the functions `zeros`(...), `ones`(...), and `identity`(...) return `Integer` arrays, they can also be used in a context requiring `Real` arrays, since the integer elements of the returned array then will be converted to real numbers.

`array(x1,x2,...)` {x1,x2,...}	This is the general array constructor function described in the separate section on array constructors, with the alternative syntax {x1,x2,...}, constructing an array containing the elements `x1`, `x2`, etc. Repeated application of this function constructs multidimensional arrays.
`zeros`($n_1,n_2,n_3,...$)	Constructs and returns an $n_1 \times n_2$ x $n_3 \times$ ... integer array with all elements equal to zero (n_i >= 0). The function has at least one argument.
`ones`($n_1,n_2,n_3,...$)	Constructs and returns an $n_1 \times n_2 \times n_3 \times$ ... integer array with all elements equal to 1 (n_i >=0). The function has at least one argument.
`fill`($s,n_1,n_2,n_3, ...$)	Creates and returns the $n_1 \times n_2 \times n_3 \times$ ... array (n_i >= 0) with all elements equal to the value of the expression s, which can have any simple type, record type, or array type. The returned array has the same element type as s. A recursive definition of fill is: `fill`(s,n_1,n_2,n_3, ...)= `fill`(`fill`(s,n_2,n_3, ...), n_1); `fill`(s,n)={s,s,..., s}. The function has at least two arguments.
`identity`(n)	Creates and returns the n × n integer identity matrix, with ones on the diagonal and zeros at all other places.
`diagonal`(v)	Constructs and returns a square matrix with the elements of vector v on the diagonal and all other elements zero.
`linspace`(x1,x2,n)	Constructs and returns a `Real` vector with n equally spaced elements, such that if v : =`linspace`(x1,x2,n), then v[i] = x1 + (x2-x1)*(i-1)/(n-1) for 1 <= i <= n, n >= 2.

Examples of using the specialized array constructor functions in the above table:

```
zeros(2,3)                        // Constructs the matrix {{0,0,0}, {0,0,0}}
ones(3)                           // Constructs the vector {1,1,1}
fill(2.1,2,2)                     // Constructs the matrix
{{2.1,2.1},{2.1,2.1}}
Boolean check[3,4] = fill(true, 3, 4);  // Fills a Boolean matrix
identity(3)                       // Creates the matrix {{1,0,0}, {0,1,0},
{0,0,1}}
diagonal({1,2,3})    // Creates the matrix {{1,0,0}, {0,2,0}, {0,0,3}}
```

```
linspace(0.0,8.0,5)   // Computes the vector {0.0, 2.0, 4.0, 6.0, 8.0}
```

7.9.4 Array Reduction Functions and Operators

An *array reduction function* "reduces" an array to a scalar value, that is, computes a scalar value from the array. The only allowed Modelica array reduction functions are the four built-in functions specified in the table below, based on the corresponding associative elementary arithmetic operations (+, *) and functions (`min`, `max`). Note that none of these four reduction functions give rise to events, even though arguments to the functions could do that.

`min(A)`	Returns the smallest element of array `A` as defined by the < operator.
`max(A)`	Returns the largest element of array `A` as defined by the > operator.
`sum(A)`	Returns the sum of all the elements of array `A`.
`product(A)`	Returns the product of all the elements of array `A`.

Below are a few example calls to these functions returning scalar results:

```
min({1,-1,7})                    // Gives the value -1
max([1,2,3; 4,5,6])              // Gives the value 6
sum({{1,2,3},{4,5,6}})           // Gives the value 21
product({3.14, 2, 2})            // Gives the value 12.56
```

7.9.4.1 Array Reduction Operators with Iterators

The array reduction functions `min`, `max`, `sum`, and `product` mentioned in the previous section are not just ordinary functions; they can also be used in a more general form as reduction operators with iterators:

The general syntax for a *reduction operator* is as follows:

functionname (*expression* `for` *iterators*)

where *iterators* is a comma-separated list of elements, each of which is an *iterator*, and *functionname* is either `min`, `max`, `sum`, or `product`, each representing an associative operator as in these examples:

```
min(i^2 for i in {1,3,7})       // min(min(1, 9), 49)) = 1
max(i^2 for i in {1,3,7})       // max(max(1, 9), 49)) = 49
sum(i^2 for i in {1,3,7})       // 1+9+49 = 59
product(i^2 for i in {1,3,7})   // 1*9*49 = 441
```

The evaluation order of the expressions (`i^2` in the above examples) is not specified and should not matter. The result is of the same type as *expression*, and is constructed by evaluating *expression* for each value of the iterator variable and computing the `sum`, `product`, `min`, or `max` of the computed elements.

The syntax and evaluation rules for the iterators are identical to those for array constructors with iterators (see Section 7.2.2, page 316).

As we have seen from the above examples, an *iterator* has the following structure:

ident `in` *range-expression*

The *range-expression* inside an iterator should be a vector expression, that is, a one-dimensional array, (or be a vector deduced from a type or the context, see comment at the end of this section), and is evaluated once for each reduction operator in the local scope immediately enclosing the reduction operator. The reason it needs to be a vector expression is because the value of the iterator needs to be a scalar. The scope of the iterator variable *ident* is the *expression* inside the reduction operator. The iterator variable *ident* may hide variables with the same name in enclosing scopes, analogous to for-loops or for-equations.

By expanding the *iterators* inside the reduction operator syntax we obtain:

functionname (*expression* for *ident* in *range-expression*, ...)

where the following restrictions and conditions apply depending on the values of *expression* and *range-expression*:

Function name	*Restriction on expression*	*Result if range-expression is an empty vector*
`min`	Scalar enumeration, Boolean, Integer, or Real.	Maximum value of the type (e.g. `Modelica.Constants.inf` for Real)
`max`	Scalar enumeration, Boolean, Integer, or Real.	Minimum value of the type (e.g. `-Modelica.Constants.inf` for Real)
`sum`	Real or Integer.	`0 or zeros(...)`
`product`	Scalar Integer or Real.	`1`

We show a few additional examples. A standard sum of the variable *i* for *i* in the range 1 to 10,

$$\sum_{i=1}^{10} i = 1+2+...+10 = 55$$

can be expressed as the following sum reduction operator expression:

```
sum(i for i in 1:10)
```

A sum of the squares of *i* for *i* in the set {1,3,7,5},

$$\sum_{i\in\{1,3,7,5\}} i^2 = 1+9+49+25 = 84$$

is represented as follows:

```
sum(i^2 for i in {1,3,7,5})
```

A product of expressions like $(a \cdot b_{i1} - b_{i2})$,

$$\prod_{i=1}^{n}(a \cdot b_{i1} - b_{i2}) = (a \cdot b_{11} - b_{12}) + (a \cdot b_{21} - b_{22}) + ... + (a \cdot b_{n1} - b_{n2})$$

can be expressed as a product reduction expression:

```
product(a*b[i,1]-b[i,2] for i in 1:n)
```

We can combine the product reduction operator and the array constructor {} for collecting products into a vector. Note that the product for an empty iteration vector `1:0` is 1 according to the above table.

```
{product(j for j in 1:i) for i in 0:4}   // Gives {1,1,2,6,24}
```

The range expression in an iterator may be *left out* if the range can be *deduced* from the use of the iteration variable `ident` in an index position of an array with known dimension size, e.g.:

```
Real x[5] = {1,2,3,4,10};
Real xsum1 = sum(x[i] for i in 1:size(x,1));   // result is 20
Real xsum2 = sum(x[i] for i);    // same result, range deduced to be 1:5
```

See Section 9.2.5.1, page 428, for more details regarding automatic deduction of iteration ranges. Boolean or enumeration types can also be used as ranges, see Section 9.2.5, page 427.

7.9.5 Matrix and Vector Algebra Functions

The following set of functions are rather common in matrix and vector algebra, but are not associated with any Modelica operator symbol. The function `transpose` can be applied to any matrix. The functions `outerProduct`, `symmetric`, `cross` and `skew` require Real/Integer vector(s) or matrix as input(s) and returns a Real vector or matrix.

`transpose(A)`	Permutes the first two dimensions of array `A`. It is an error if array `A` does not have at least two dimensions.
`outerProduct(v1,v2)`	Returns the outer product of vectors `v1` and `v2` equal to `matrix(v1)*transpose(matrix(v2))`.
`symmetric(A)`	Returns a matrix where the diagonal elements and the elements above the diagonal are identical to the corresponding elements of matrix A and where the elements below the diagonal are set equal to the elements above the diagonal of `A`, i.e., `B` := `symmetric(A)` → `B`[i,j] := `A`[i,j], if i <= j, `B`[i,j] := `A`[j,i], if i > j.
`cross(x,y)`	Returns the 3-vector cross product of the 3-vectors x and y, i.e., `cross(x,y)` = {`x`[2]*`y`[3]-`x`[3]*`y`[2], `x`[3]*`y`[1]-`x`[1]*`y`[3], `x`[1]*`y`[2]-`x`[2]*`y`[1]}
`skew(x)`	Returns the 3 × 3 skew symmetric matrix associated with a 3-vector, i.e., `skew(x)` = {{0, -`x`[3], `x`[2]}, {`x`[3], 0, -`x`[1]}, {-`x`[2], `x`[1], 0}} and `cross(x,y)` = `skew(x)*y`

Examples:

```
transpose([1,2; 3,4])           // Gives [1,3; 2,4] of type Integer[2,2]
transpose( {{{1},{2}}, {{3},{4}}} )
                                // Gives {{{1},{3}}, {{2},{4}}} of type Integer[2,2,1]
outerProduct({2,1}, {3,2})      // Gives {{6,4}, {3,2}}
symmetric ( {{1,2}, {3,1}} )    // Gives {{1,2}, {2,1}}

cross ( {1,0,0}, {0,1,0} )      // Gives {0,0,1}
skew ( {1,2,3} )                // Gives {{0,-3,2}, {3,0,-1}, {-2,1,0}}
```

7.9.6 Array Concatenation Functions Once More

The Modelica array concatenation functions have been described in detail in Section 7.3 on page 318 in this chapter and are mentioned in this section on built-in functions only for completeness.

`cat(k,A,B,...)`	General concatenation function that concatenates arrays `A,B,...` along the *k*th dimension.
`[A,B,...]`	Concatenation of arrays `A,B,...` along the second dimension.
`[A;B,...]`	Concatenation of arrays `A,B,...` along the first dimension.

```
cat(1,{1,2},{3,4})        // Concatenates two vectors into {1,2,3,4}

[{{1},{2}}, {{3},{4}}]     // Concatenates two column matrices into
                           // the square matrix {{1,3},{2,4}}
                           // which is the same as [1,3; 2,4]
```

7.10 Vectorization via Application of Scalar Functions to Arrays

In certain situations it is useful to be able to apply a function to array values even if it has not been defined for such arguments. This is possible if an obvious generalization/vectorization to elementwise application of the function is possible.

Modelica functions with one scalar return value can be applied to arrays elementwise, for example, if v is a vector of reals, then `sin(v)` is a vector where each element is the result of applying the function `sin` to the corresponding element in v. For example:

```
sin({a,b,c})      // Vector argument, result: {sin(a),sin(b),sin(c)}
sin([1,2; 3,4])  // Matrix argument, result: [sin(1),sin(2); sin(3),sin(4)]
```

Functions with more than one argument can be generalized/vectorized to elementwise application. If more than one argument is generalized to an array, all of the arguments have to be of the same size, and they are traversed in parallel. This is the case in the example with the function `atan2`(*x*,*y*) below:

```
atan2({a,b,c},{d,e,f})      // Result: {atan2(a,d), atan2(b,e), atan2(c,f)}
```

All function arguments need not be generalized to arrays, only those that are actually applied to arrays of higher dimension than the declared types of the corresponding formal function parameters. Consider the function `atan2Add`(*w*,*x*,*y*) = *w*+`atan2`(*x*,*y*) that adds a value *w* to each application of `atan2`, for example:

```
atan2Add(2,{a,b},{d,e}) // Result: {2+atan2(a,d), 2+atan2(b,e)}
```

Formal function parameters that are generalized to higher dimension arrays need not necessarily be scalars. For example, the function `atan2SumVec(v1,v2)=atan2(sum(v1),sum(v2))` used below has two formal parameters v1 and v2 of type `Real[:]`, computing `atan2` on the sums of the argument vectors. Applying this function on a matrix which is a vector of vectors gives a result which is a vector. Calling this function with two matrices `M1` and `M2` as arguments gives the following result:

```
Real[3]    v1,v2,v3,v4;
Real[2,3] M1 = {v1,v2};
Real[2,3] M2 = {v3,v4};

atan2SumVec(M1,M2) // is:   atan2SumVec({v1,v2},{v3,v4})
                   // is: {atan2(sum(v1),sum(v2)), atan2(sum(v3),sum(v4))}

atan2SumVec({{1,2},{3,4}}, {{6,7},{8,9}})
 // which is: {atan2(sum({1,2}),sum({3,4})), atan2(sum({6,7}),sum({8,9}))}
 // which is: {atan2(3,7), atan2(13,17) }
```

7.10.1 General Formulation of Elementwise Function Application

Consider the expression `f`(*arg1*,...,*argn*). Then an application of the function `f` to the arguments *arg1*, ..., *argn* is defined as follows.

For each passed argument, the type of the argument is checked against the type of the corresponding formal parameter of the function.

1. If the types match, nothing is done.
2. If the types do not match, and a type conversion can be applied, it is applied and then continued with step 1.
3. If the types do not match, and no type conversion is applicable, the passed argument type is checked to see if it is an array of the formal parameter type. If it is not, the function call is invalid. If it is, we call this a *foreach* argument.

4. For all foreach arguments, the number and sizes of dimensions must match. If they do not match, the function call is invalid. If no foreach argument exists, the function is applied in the normal fashion, and the result has the type specified by the function definition.
5. The result of the function call expression is a multidimensional array with the same dimension sizes as the foreach arguments, that is, arguments generalized to arrays. Each element $e_{i,...,j}$ is the result of applying `f` to arguments constructed from the original arguments in the following way.
    - If the argument is not a foreach argument, it is used as-is.
    - If the argument is a foreach argument, the element at index [i,...,j] is used.

7.11 Empty Arrays

It might appear ridiculous to have empty arrays, that is, arrays that do not contain any elements. However, there is actually some use for such strange creatures. They can function as a kind of null element for certain general operations, such as, for example, concatenation operations or general formulations of certain kinds of equation systems. It makes sense to have empty arrays when representing sets as arrays in order to represent the empty set.

An empty array cannot at the time of this writing be constructed in Modelica by {} or [] since in those cases the type of the array would be unknown, for example, it would not be known whether the empty array is an array of integers, of real numbers, or of some other type. One idea would to automatically infer the type from the surrounding context, which however has not yet been formally accepted in the Modelica language standard. Instead, an empty array is created using some other array constructor, for example, `fill`, from which the type can be deduced, or explicitly declared as a variable. For example:

```
fill(1., 0)       // An empty vector of type Real[0] since 1. is Real
Real x[0];        // An empty vector variable x of type Real[0]

Real[0,3] A;                    // An empty matrix variable A
Real B[5,0], C[0,0];            // Empty matrices B and C
```

Array variables of unspecified size can be set equal to or assigned empty array values, for example:

```
Real    A[:,:]   = fill(0.0, 0, 1)        // A Real 0 x 1 matrix
Boolean B[:,:,:] = fill(false, 0, 1, 0)   // A Boolean 0 x 1 x 0 array
```

It is not possible to perform an indexing operation, for example, `A[i,j]`, on an empty array since it does not contain any elements that can be accessed and returned by the indexing operation.

Many array operations require certain constraints to be fulfilled by their operands. Built-in array operators such as elementwise addition (+), subtraction (–), equation equality (=), and assignment (:=) require that the operands have the same dimensionality and size of dimensions. Matrix multiplication (*) requires that the size of the second dimension of the first operand is equal to the size of the first dimension of the second operand. These size and dimensionality constraints also apply to array operands which are empty arrays. For example:

```
Real[3,0] A, B;
Real[0,0] C;

A + B    // Fine, the result is an empty matrix of type Real[3,0]
A + C    // Error, incompatible types Real[3,0] and Real[0,0]
```

Concerning matrix multiplication, the above-mentioned constraints on operands together with the size and dimensionality of the result can be expressed as follows:

- *Matrix*[n,m]**Matrix*[m,p] giving a result matrix of size and dimension *Matrix*[n,p]

For the case of empty arrays this definition gives the following result:

- *Matrix*[n,0]**Matrix*[0,p] giving a result matrix of size and dimension *Matrix*[n,p]

What is remarkable here is that matrix multiplication of two empty arrays sometimes gives rise to a nonempty array filled with zero values, which is somewhat counterintuitive but according to a general definition of matrix multiplication. The behavior of matrix multiplication of empty matrices and vectors is summarized in the following table.

Table 7-13. Matrix multiplication of empty arrays.

Type of arg1	*Type of arg2*	*Type of arg1*arg2*	*Value*
Real[0]	Real[0,m]	Real[m]	zeros(m)
Real[n]	Real[n,0]	Real[0]	empty vector
Real[0,m]	Real[m]	Real[0]	empty vector
Real[m,0]	Real[0]	Real[m]	zeros(m)
Real[0,m]	Real[m,n]	Real[0,n]	empty matrix
Real[m,0]	Real[0,n]	Real[m,0]	empty matrix
Real[m,0]	Real[0,n]	Real[m,n]	zeros(m,n)

One might ask why such a general and somewhat nonintuitive definition of matrix multiplication should be allowed. Is there some practical usage for this feature? Surprisingly, the answer is yes. Consider the following linear ordinary differential equation system model formulated in A-B-C-D matrix form with a state vector x, an input vector u, and an output vector y:

```
model ABCDsystem
  Real u[p], x[n], y[q];
  Real A[n,n], B[n,p], C[q,n], D[q,p];
equation
  der(x) = A*x + B*u;
  y = C*x + D*u;
end ABCDsystem;
```

Assume that `n=0`, that is, the state vector is empty, the input vector `u` is nonempty with size `p>0`, and the output vector `y` is empty with size `q>0`. Using the definitions in the above table, the first equation will disappear since `x` is empty, causing `der(x)` to be an empty vector with type `Real[0]`, with `A*x` and `B*u` also being empty vectors with type `Real[0]`. In the second equation the term `C*x` becomes a vector `zeros(m)` of type `Real[m]` containing `m` zero-valued elements. Since zero-valued elements can be eliminated in addition operations the second equation simplifies to

```
y = D*u
```

7.11.1 Empty Array Literals

As mentioned in the previous section, empty array literals can be constructed by the `fill` array constructor function:

- The call `fill`(*constelem*, *n1*, *n2*, *n3*, ...) returns an empty array literal of dimension *n1* × *n2* × *n3* × etc., provided at least one of the dimensions *ni* is zero, with element type being the type of *constelem*, which can be of any Modelica type expressible as a constant literal.

For example:

```
fill(0.0, 0, 1)        // A Real 0 x 1 matrix
fill(false, 0, 1, 0)   // A Boolean 0 x 1 x 0 array
fill(Person("Jane", 54.5, 170), 1, 0) // A Person 1 x 0 array
```

Two other possibilities, which, however, are not part of the Modelica language standard at the time of this writing (but might be included later), would be:

- `{}`—denoting an empty array of dimension size 0, where the element type is inferred from the context. As a consequence, `{{}}` would be an 0 × 1 matrix of inferred element type.
- `[]`—denoting an empty array identical to `{{}}`, i.e. an 0 × 1 matrix of inferred element type. This is natural since `[x]` is the same as `{{x}}` which has dimensions 1 × 1.

Such a notation would be somewhat more concise and readable compared to using `fill`, for example:

```
  Person x[:];
equation
  x = {};
```

7.12 Summary

This chapter has presented most aspects of arrays in Modelica, starting with the declaration of arrays and array types, arrays sizes, and type checking for arrays. We continued by presenting the general array construction operator, the special array constructor for range vector construction, array constructors with iterators, and the MATLAB compatible combined array concatenation and construction operator. We also presented array indexing with different kinds of arguments, as well as accessing and constructing array slices. One section gave special advise for users with MATLAB background regarding the use of array concatenation and slices, including the construction of block matrices. We presented the four common arithmetic operators and their interpretation when used on arrays as well as on combinations of arrays and scalars. A set of built-in array functions were described, including four array reduction operators that can have iterator arguments. The chapter was concluded by presenting how scalar functions are automatically promoted to work for arrays, and how empty arrays can be declared and array literals created.

7.13 Literature

The description of arrays given here is directly based on the Modelica Language Specification (Modelica Association 2012), including most examples. The array design of Modelica has primarily been influenced by MATLAB (MathWorks 2002), Fortran90 (Adams, Brainerd, Martin, Smith, and Wagener 1992), C (Harbison and Steele 1991), and Mathematica (Wolfram 1997). Array constructors with iterators in Modelica are analogous to array comprehensions in several functional languages, e.g. Haskell (Hudak 1989), Standard ML (Myers, Clack, and Poon 1993), or the `Table` array constructor in Mathematica (Wolfram 1997).

7.14 Exercises

Exercise 7-1:

Constructing Arrays: Create a record containing several vectors and matrices. It is your choice what types and values the variables should have:

- a vector with seven values,
- a matrix of four rows and two columns,
- a matrix of one row and five columns,
- two unspecified matrices,
- and an empty matrix.

Exercise 7-2:

Expanded Type: Consider the classes `Student`, `Class` and `GraduateClass` below. Which is the expanded type of `GraduateClass`?

```
class Student
```

```
    constant Real legs = 2;
    constant Real arms = 2;
    parameter Real nrOfBooks;
    parameter String name = "Dummy";
  end Student;

  type Class = Student[35];

  class GraduateClass
    Class[42] c;
  end GraduateClass;
```

Exercise 7-3:

Question: What is a range vector? Give an example of a range vector with 5 Integers with increasing by 5 for each additional element.

Exercise 7-4:

Considering Array Ranges: Which result do the `v1`, `v2`, `v3`, `v4` and `v5` have below?

```
  class RangeVectors
    Integer v1[6] = 3 : 8;
    Integer v2[10] = -20 : -11;
    Real    v3[5] = 11.3 : 15.3;
    Integer v4[0];
    Real    v5[3]      = 1.1 : 3.1;
  end RangeVectors;
```

Wider Ranges: How can you construct the range vectors below?

```
  {15.0, 18.0, 21.0, 24.0, 27.0},
  {-6.5, -8.5, -10.5}
```

and an empty `Integer` vector.

Exercise 7-5:

Question: Which are the type rules for concatenation?

Considering Array Concatenation: What will be the result of the arrays below?

```
  class ArrayConcatenation
    Real[2, 3] array1 = cat(2, [22, 34; 66, 78], [15; 52]);
    Real[2, 3] array2 = cat(2, {{22, 34}, {66, 78}}, {{15}, {52}});
    Real[2, 2] array3 = cat(1, {{11, 12}}, {{13, 14}});
    Real[3, 2] array4 = cat(1, {{7, 2}, {5, 42}}, {{24, 74}});
    Real[3, 2] array5 = cat(1, [7, 2; 5, 42], [24, 74]);
    Real[4, 2] array6 = cat(1, {{1, 2}, {11, 12}}, {{13, 14}, {3, 4}});

    Real[2, 4] array7 = cat(2, {{1, 2}, {72, 51}}, {{35, 73}, {12, 23}});
  end ArrayConcatenation;
```

Using cat: Now it is your turn to concatenate arrays using cat:

- Concatenate two 1×2-arrays along the first dimension.
- Concatenate the arrays you just concatenated, but along the second dimension.
- Concatenate one 2×3-array with a 2×1-array along the second dimension.
- Concatenate two 2×2-arrays along the first dimension.

What are the results of the array concatenations?

```
  class MyArrayConcat

  end MyArrayConcat;
```

Exercise 7-6:

More Dimensions: The final thing you should do now is concatenate three arrays with higher dimension.

So, the arrays you should concatenate are of size 1×2×1, 1×2×2 and 1×2×3 and they should be concatenated along the first dimension. Do the concatenation in the class `MoreConcat` below.

What is the result after the concatenations?

```
class MoreConcat

end MoreConcat;
```

Exercise 7-7:

Array Indexing: In the class `ArrayIndexing` below, you should first define a 2×3-array and set values to every position in the array. Also define a second array while you're at it, with the same size but with different values. The final thing you should do is to change a few values in each array. Then you're done!

Oh, one more thing; what are the results after changing the values?

```
class ArrayIndexing

end ArrayIndexing;
```

Tip: When you set the values in the arrays you can use the fill function to fill a whole array with a value. `fill(value, nrOfRows, nrOfColumns).`

Indexing with Scalar Expressions: In the class `ArrayIndexing2` below you should first define a 2×2-array and set values to every position in the array. Then define a second 2×4-array with different values. This time you should change a whole row in each array.

What are the results after changing the values?

```
class ArrayIndexing2

end ArrayIndexing2;
```

Accessing Array Slices with Index Vectors: What is the result of the vectors v1, v2, v3, v4, v5, v6, v7, v8 and v9 below?

```
class Slice
  Real[3, 3] V = {{22, 14, 71}, {33, 41, 17}, {44, 11, 77}};
  Real[3, 2] W = {{12, 13}, {23, 88}, {99, 43}};
  Real[5]          Y = {23, 24, 25, 26, 27};

  Real v1[3]  = V[:, 1];
  Real v2[3]  = V[3, :];
  Real v3[1]  = V[3, {2}];
  Real v4[3]  = W[:, 2];

  Real v5[2]  = Y[{1, 2}];
  Real v6[2]  = W[3, {1, 2}];
  Real v7[2]  = V[3, 1:2];

  Real v8[2]  = Y[3:4];
  Real v9[3]  = Y[1:2:5];
end Slice;
```

Exercise 7-8:

Concatenate: Complete the class, `Concatenate`, like this:

(i) Create a new variable V1 in which you append 60 to A.

(ii) Append 50 to V1.

(iii) If you didn't use the cat-operator before, use this to append 60 to A.

(iv) Append the set of 60 to B.

(v) If you didn't use the cat-operator before, use this to append 60 to B.

(vi) Append the set of 18 to v, using the cat-operator.

```
class Concatenate
  Real[1, 2]              = [50, 32];
  Real[2, 1]              = [3; 7];
  Real[5]                 = {4, 9, 7, 5, 2};
end Concatenate;
```

Question: Which are the results of your newly created variables?

Exercise 7-9:

Question: Is this allowed? If not, why not? If it is, what is the result?

```
class Add1
  Real A1[2] = {2, 3} + 1;
end Add1;
```

Is this allowed? If not, why not? If it is, what is the result?

```
class Sub5
  Real A5[3] = {3, 45, 6} - 5;
end Sub5;
```

Is this allowed? If not, why not? If it is, what is the result?

```
class Mult2
  Real A2[3] = {11, 14, 12} * 2;
end Mult2;
```

Exercise 7-10:

Matrix Multiplication: Write a class that multiplies two matrices using the multiplication operator for matrices.

Exercise 7-11:

Question: Is this allowed? If not, why not? If it is, what is the result?

```
class MultMany
  Real mult1 = {1, 1, 1, 1} * {1, 1, 1, 1};
  Real mult2[2] = {{2, 2}, {2, 2}} * {2, 2};
  Real mult3[2, 2] = {{1, 1}, {1, 1}} * {{2, 2}, {2, 2}};
  Real mult4[1] = {1, 3, 5, 7} * {{1}, {3}, {5}, {7}};
end MultMany;
```

Is this allowed? If it is, what is the result?

```
class Div4
  Real A4[5] = {16, 14, 10, 18, 12} / 4;
end Div4;
```

Is this allowed? If it is, what is the result?

```
class Div7
  Real A4[5] = 7 / {16, 14, 10, 18, 12};
end Div7;
```

How would you write `{{1, 3}, {4, 5}}^2` in Modelica? Write the expression in a class. What is the result?

Chapter 8

Equations

Equations are the foundation of Modelica. This should be rather apparent to the reader at this stage, with equations and equation-based class examples appearing in each of the previous chapters. As already has been emphasized, equations are more flexible than traditional programming constructs such as assignment statements since they do not prescribe a certain data-flow direction. This is the key to the physical modeling capabilities and increased reuse potential of Modelica classes.

The goal of this chapter is to give an overview in one place of all kinds of equations that can occur in Modelica models. Certain kinds of equations are primarily described here, whereas other equation types are treated in more detail in other parts of this book. For example, declaration equations and modification equations are described extensively in Chapter 3 and Chapter 4, respectively, whereas the topic of connection equations occupies a large part of Chapter 5. Conditional equations like if-equations and when-equations are only briefly covered here but are presented in more detail in Chapter 13.

8.1 General Equation Properties

Equations are different in many ways compared to traditional programming constructs such as assignment statements and control structures. Equations are used in several different ways and are rather expressive. There are also certain necessary conditions for the total system of equations to be solvable, such as having the same number of variables and equations. Some of these aspects are discussed briefly below.

8.1.1 Equation Categories and Uses

Thinking in equations is a bit unusual for most programmers. The reason is that equations express relations and constraints in a declarative way, rather than forcing the programmer to handle control flow and data flow more or less explicitly as in conventional imperative and object-oriented languages. In Modelica equations are used for many tasks:

- Assignment statements in conventional languages are usually represented as equations in Modelica.
- Attribute assignments are represented as equations.
- Connections between objects generate equations.

Equations in Modelica can informally be classified into three different categories depending on the syntactic context in which they occur:

- *Normal equations* occurring in equation sections, including connect-equations and other equation types of special syntactic form.
- *Declaration equations*, which are part of variable, parameter, or constant declarations.
- *Modification equations*, which are commonly used to modify attributes of classes.
- *Initial equations*, which are used to express equations for solving initialization problems.

Each of these equation types will be covered in separate sections in this chapter.

Equations are declarative and express relations between expressions. Therefore, they are not allowed in algorithm sections and functions that contain only algorithmic imperative code, that is, sequences of statements that are "commands." Conversely, assignment operations (:=) are allowed in algorithm sections and in functions, but not in equation sections.

8.1.2 Expressivity of Equations

Equations are more *expressible* than assignment statements. For example, consider the well-known resistor equation once more, where the resistance `R` multiplied by the current `i` is equal to the voltage `v`:

```
R*i = v;
```

This equation can be used in three ways corresponding to three possible assignment statements: computing the current from the voltage and the resistance, computing the voltage from the resistance and the current, or computing the resistance from the voltage and the current. This is expressed in the following three assignment statements:

```
i := v/R;
v := R*i;
R := v/i;
```

8.1.3 Single-Assignment Rule for Equations

All of the equations of a Modelica model to be simulated form a total system of equations. These equations usually come from a number of classes that comprise the total system model, and only in very simple cases from a single class. It is essential that this system of equations can be solved; otherwise, the model cannot be simulated. One important prerequisite for solution is that the system is neither underdetermined nor overdetermined, that is, the number of equations is equal to the number of unknowns. This can be formulated as the single-assignment rule for equations, which can be understood as having one equation assigned to each unknown:

- *Single-assignment rule for equations*: the total number of "equations" is identical to the total number of "unknown" variables to be solved for.

By counting "equations" according to this rule we mean counting both equations and assignment statements, including assignments within when-equations and when-statements. Multiple assignments to a variable within the same algorithm section is counted as a single assignment. Assignment statements within function bodies are not counted.

If the equations in the system are "unique", that is, not trivial combinations of each other, the system is not underdetermined and there are usually good chances for solution. This rule also prevents a variable from being defined by two equations, which would give rise to conflicts or nondeterministic behavior.

The single-assignment rule is valid for all Modelica models of systems to be simulated, including hybrid models that contain conditional equations, where certain equations are typically activated or deactivated dynamically during simulation. Modelica imposes certain constraints on the form of such conditional equations in order to guarantee that this rule is always obeyed. This is discussed briefly here and in more detail in Chapter 13 on hybrid and discrete event modeling. Note that the single-assignment rule need not apply to single classes, since these might require combination with other classes to form a model that can be simulated.

8.1.4 Synchronous Data-flow Principle for Modelica

The single-assignment rule is a necessary but not sufficient condition for the solvability of a system of equations. Another principle, called the *synchronous data-flow principle*, is the basis for the design of the hybrid part of the Modelica language, that is, the handling of events and interaction between the continuous and the discrete parts of a model during simulation. This principle together with the single-assignment rule makes it possible for the Modelica compiler to perform compile-time consistency checks that, for example, usually can prevent deadlocks caused by cyclic dependencies from occurring during a Modelica simulation. The drawback is that certain "asynchronous" models cannot be expressed. The synchronous data-flow principle can be expressed in the following way for Modelica:

- All variables keep their actual values until these values are explicitly changed. Variable values can be accessed at any point in time during "continuous integration" (i.e., numerical solution of the continuous part of the system of equations), and at event instants.
- At every point in time, during "continuous integration" and at event instants, the *active* equations express relations between variables which have to be fulfilled *concurrently*. Equations are not active if the corresponding if-branch or when-equation in which the equation is present is not active because the corresponding branch condition currently evaluates to `false`.
- Computation and communication at an event instant does not take time. (If computation or communication time has to be simulated, this property has to be explicitly modeled.)

It is useful to keep this principle in mind when understanding hybrid models containing conditional equations, as, for example, in the sections on conditional equations with if-equations and when-equations below. The principle is just stated here as background information, and is explained in more detail in Section 13.2.3 on page 597 in Chapter 13 on discrete-event and hybrid modeling.

8.2 Equations in Declarations

There are two kinds of equations that occur as parts of declarations: *declaration equations* and *modifier equations*, where redeclaration equations are classified as a kind of modifier equations. The term *binding equation* is sometimes used to denote both declaration equations and modifier equations. Additional aspects of declaration equations are described in Section 3.10, page 97, and modifier equations in Section 4.2, pagc 148.

8.2.1 Declaration Equations

Declaration equations (see also Section 3.10, page 97) are usually given as part of declarations of constants or parameters, of the form *variable* = *expression*, for example:

```
constant Integer one = 1;
parameter Real mass = 22.5;
```

Such equations are actually required for constants if the constant is used in a model, but are optional for parameters. However, if is allowed to declare a constant without a declaration equation if it is associated with a value by a modifier equation (Section 8.2.2, page 350).

An equation always holds, which means that the `mass` in the above example never changes value during simulation. It is also possible to specify a declaration equation for a normal variable, for example:

```
Real speed = 72.4;
```

However, this does not make much sense since it will constrain the variable to have the same value throughout the computation, effectively behaving as a kind of constant. Therefore, a declaration equation is quite different from a variable initializer in other programming languages.

The types of the left-hand-side and right-hand sides of a declaration equation must be equivalent after type coercion (Section 3.19.1, page 124) and the variability (Section 6.8.1.3, page 278) of the left-hand-side must be greater or equal to the variability of the right-hand side.

8.2.2 Modifier Equations

Modifier equations (Section 4.2, page 148) occur, for example, in a variable declaration when there is a need to modify or specify the default value of an attribute of the variable. A modifier equation replaces the declaration equation, if present, for an attribute of the type in question. A common usage is modifier equations for the `start` attribute of variables, for example:

```
Real speed(start=72.4);
```

Modifier equations also occur in type definitions, for example as below:

```
type Voltage = Real(unit="V", min=-220.0, max=220.0);
```

Note that it is possible to replace a whole declaration equation involving the modified variable.

The types of the left-hand-side and right-hand sides of a declaration equation must be equivalent after type coercion (Section 3.19.1, page 124) and the variability (Section 6.8.1.3, page 278) of the left-hand-side must be greater or equal to the variability of the right-hand side.

Modifier equations for constants and parameters must be acyclic (Section 8.2.3, page 350).

8.2.3 Acyclic Declaration Equations for Constants and Parameters

Declaration equations for parameters and constants in a translated model must be acyclic after flattening, except that cycles are allowed if the cycles disappear when evaluating parameters having the annotation `Evaluate=true` that are not part of the cycle. Thus it is not possible to introduce equations for constants or parameters which have cyclic dependencies except in that special case. For example, consider the following two declarations:

```
constant Real p=3*q;
constant Real q=cos(p); // Illegal since p=2*q, q=sin(p) are cyclical
```

The second declaration equation is erroneous since `p` has already been defined to depend on `q`, and now `q` is defined to depend on an expression containing `p`.

The following example illustrates that a cyclic dependency between the dimension size parameter `m` in the declaration of matrix `A` and the size of the same matrix obtained through the `size()` call is not allowed.

```
model Amat
  parameter Real A[m,m];
  parameter Integer m=size(A,1);
end Amat;

Amat a;
// Illegal since there are cyclic dependencies between size(a.A,1) and a.m
Amat b(redeclare Real A[2,2]=[1,2;3,4]);
// Legal since size of A is no longer dependent on m.
Amat c(m=2); // Legal since m is no longer dependent on the size of A.
```

A cyclic dependency within the same equation is of course not allowed, as in the example below:

```
parameter Real w = 2*sin(w);  // Illegal, since w = 2*sin(w) is cyclic
```

The following cyclic dependency is allowed since it disappears when evaluating `use_T_start` (`Evaluate=true`):

```
partial model PartialLumpedVolume
  parameter Boolean use_T_start = true
    "= true, use T_start, otherwise h_start"
      annotation(Dialog(tab = "Initialization"), Evaluate=true);
  parameter Medium.Temperature T_start = if use_T_start
    then system.T_start else Medium.temperature_phX(p_start,h_start,X_start)
      annotation(Dialog(tab = "Initialization", enable = use_T_start));
  parameter Medium.SpecificEnthalpy h_start = if use_T_start then
    Medium.specificEnthalpy_pTX(p_start, T_start, X_start) else
    Medium.h_default
   annotation(Dialog(tab = "Initialization", enable = not use_T_start));
end PartialLumpedVolume;
// This is a cycle for T_start and h_start, but ok since it disappears
// when evaluating use_T_start
```

8.3 Equations in Equation Sections

As stated previously, *normal equations* appear in equation sections started by the keyword `equation` and terminated by one of the keywords or keyword combinations `end`, `equation`, `algorithm`, `protected`, `public`, or `initial equation`. Thus, the general structure of an equation section appears as follows:

equation
  ...
  equations
  ...
some other allowed keyword

The following kinds of equations can be present in equation sections:

- Simple equality equations.
- Repetitive equation structures with for-equations.
- Connect-equations.
- Conditional equations with if-equations.
- Conditional equations with when-equations.
- The `reinit` equation.
- `assert` and `terminate`.
- Overconstrained equation operators, see Section 8.5.3, page 379.

Simple equality equations containing an equal sign (=) are the most basic and common kinds of equations in Modelica models, and the only ones known from mathematics. In fact, the other syntactic forms of equations (except for the last) are transformed by the Modelica compiler to this basic kind of simple equation often combined with some event-handling code.

8.3.1 Simple Equality Equations

Simple equality equations are the traditional kinds of equations known from mathematics that express an equality relation between two expressions. There are two syntactic forms of such equations in Modelica. The first form below is *equality* equations between two expressions, whereas the second form is used when calling a function with *several* results.

- `expr1 = expr2;`
- `(out1, out2, out3, ...) = function_name(inexpr1, inexpr2, ...);`

The second form is equivalent to several simple equations setting the variables *out1*, *out2*, *out3*, etc. in the parenthesized list equal to the results of the function call in that order. No expressions are allowed in the parenthesized list on the left-hand side, only variables.

For example, the first equation in the class `EqualityEquations` below involving the function `f` with two inputs and three results is correct, whereas the second equation is illegal since there are expressions in the left-hand side:

```
class EqualityEquations
  Real x,y,z;
equation
  (x, y, z)        = f(1.0, 2.0);   // Correct!
  (x+1, 3.0, z/y)  = f(1.0, 2.0);   // Illegal!  Not a list of variables
                                    // on the left-hand side
end EqualityEquations;
```

Type equivalence is required between the expressions on the left-hand side and the right-hand side of equations (Section 3.19.1, page 124). Variability can be different on the two sides. However, for equations where both the left-hand side and the right-hand side are of subtypes of `Integer`, `Boolean`, `enumeration`, or `String`, the variability of both sides cannot be higher than *discrete-time* (see also Section 6.8.1.3 on variability, page 278). For equations involving record or array expressions, this rule is applied to corresponding parts of these data structures broken down to elements of built-in types.

8.3.2 Repetitive Equation Structures with for-Equations

Repetitive equation structures can be expressed rather compactly with the special syntactic form of equation called a *for-equation*. Such a structured equation can be expanded to a sometimes large number of simple equations. The syntactic form of a for-equation with a single iterator is as follows:

```
for iteration-variable in range-expression loop
   equation1
   equation2
   ...
end for;
```

The *iteration-variable* ranges over the set of values in the *range-expression*, which must be a *vector expression* with *parameter or constant variability*, and has the same type as the elements in the *range-expression*. This expression is evaluated once in each for-equation, and is evaluated in the scope immediately enclosing the for-equation. Such a scope can typically be the scope of an enclosing class definition or the scope of an enclosing for-equation.

The *iteration-variable* is defined within the scope of the for-equation itself. One copy of the equations in the body of the for-equation is effectively generated for each value of the iteration variable. Consider the following simple class example with a for-equation:

```
class FiveEquations
  Real[5]  x;
equation
  for i in 1:5 loop
    x[i] = i+1;
  end for;
end FiveEquations;
```

That class is equivalent in behavior to the class below, where the for-equation has been unrolled into five simple equations:

```
class FiveEquationsUnrolled
  Real[5]  x;
equation
  x[1]  = 2;
  x[2]  = 3;
  x[3]  = 4;
  x[4]  = 5;
  x[5]  = 6;
end FiveEquationsUnrolled;
```

Nested for-equations can be represented by a single for-equation with multiple iterators:

`for` *iteration-variable*$_1$ `in` *range-expression*$_1$, *iteration-variable*$_2$ `in` *range-expression*$_2$, ... `loop`

```
  ...
end for
```

The range expression can be an `Integer` or `Real` vector, a vector of enumeration values of some enumeration type, or a `Boolean` vector. In the case of a vector of enumeration or `Boolean` values, the type name (e.g. `Boolean` or `Sizes` in the example below) can be used to denote the range expression, meaning the full range from the lowest to the highest value of the type in question. For example:

```
type Sizes = enumeration(small, medium, large);

for e in Sizes loop // e takes values Sizes.small, Sizes.medium, Sizes.large
for e in Sizes.small : Sizes.large loop  // Same sizes as above
for e in Boolean loop  // e takes the values false, true
```

Since the scope of the iteration variable is the enclosing for-equation, it may hide other variables with the same name, for example, the constant `k` declared in the class `HideVariable`. Note that the `k` used in the iteration expression `1:k+1` is the constant `k` declared in the class, whereas the `k` used in the equations inside the for-equation is the iteration variable `k`. One should avoid this style of modeling even if it is legal since it is confusing and hard to read such code.

```
class HideVariable
  constant Integer k=4;
  Real     x[k+1];
equation
  for k in 1:k+1 loop // The iteration variable k gets values 1,2,3,4,5
    x[k]=k;           // Uses of the iteration variable k
  end for;
end HideVariable;
```

8.3.2.1 Implicit Iteration Ranges

The iteration range of a loop variable may sometimes be inferred from its use as an array index, as in the example below. See Section 9.2.5.1, page 428, for more information on iteration range inference.

```
Real x[n],y[n];
for i loop            // Same as:  for i in 1:size(a,1) loop
  x[i] = 2*y[i];
end loop;
```

8.3.2.2 Polynomial Equations Using for-Equations

Consider a polynomial equation:

$$y = \sum_{i=1}^{n+1} c_i x^{i-1}$$

This equation can be used to obtain the value of a polynomial, given a set of coefficients c_i in a vector `c` of length n+1, where c[i] = c_i. The powers of x are stored in a vector `xpowers`, where `xpowers`[i]= x^{i-1}.

```
xpowers:   {1, x, x^2, ... x^n}
```

The contents of the vector `xpowers` is defined by the following set of equations:

```
xpowers[1]   = 1;
xpowers[2]   = xpowers[1]*x;
xpowers[3]   = xpowers[2]*x;
...
xpowers[n+1] = xpowers[n]*x;
```

This can be expressed more compactly as a simple equation together with a for-equation:

```
xpowers[1] = 1;
for i in 1:n loop
  xpowers[i+1] = xpowers[i]*x;
end for;
```

Finally, the polynomial equation can be expressed using a scalar product between the vectors:

```
y = c * xpowers;
```

Everything is packaged into the class `PolynomialEvaluator` below. This can be a specialized class of the `block` kind since both public variables have specified causality `input` or `output`.

```
block PolynomialEvaluator
  parameter Real c[:];
  input     Real x;
  output    Real y;
protected
  parameter Integer n = size(c,1)-1;
  Real xpowers[n+1];
equation
  xpowers[1] = 1;
  for i in 1:n loop
    xpowers[i+1] = xpowers[i]*x;
  end for;
  y = c * xpowers;
end PolynomialEvaluator;
```

We can, for example, use this class to evaluate a simple polynomial in terms of the built-in variable `time`, by instantiating the class with the coefficient vector `c={1,2,3,4}`:

```
class PolyEvaluate1
  Real p;
  PolynomialEvaluator polyeval(c = {1,2,3,4});
equation
  polyeval.x = time;
  p = polyeval.y;
end PolyEvaluate1;
```

An alternative way is to bind the inputs and the outputs using modifier equations in the declaration of the `polyeval` instance of `PolynomialEvaluator`:

```
class PolyEvaluate2
  Real p;
  PolynomialEvaluator polyeval(c ={1,2,3,4}, x=time, y=p);
end PolyEvaluate2;
```

8.3.3 Connect-Equations

In Modelica, we use connect-equations to establish connections between variables via connectors. The general form of a connect-equation is as follows:

```
connect(connector1,connector2)
```

The following constraints apply to the two arguments *connector1* and *connector2* of a connect-equation:

- The two arguments of a connect-equation must be references to *connectors*, each of which either has to be declared directly *within* the *same class* where the connect-equation occurs, or has to be a *member* of one of the declared variables in that class.

This implies a locality constraint on connections: it is not possible within a class to connect connectors declared outside a class to connectors within the class. This is natural since the connectors of a class should be the external interface of that class, implying that external connections should be via that interface.

Connect-equations can be placed inside for-equations and if-equations provided the indices of the for-loop and conditions of the if-equation are parameter expressions that do not depend on `cardinality`, `rooted`, `Connections.rooted`, or `Connections.isRoot`. The for-equations/if-equations are expanded by the compiler during model elaboration.

The `ResistorCircuit` class example below (also in Figure 5-15 on page 198 in Chapter 5) connects connectors called `p` belonging to variables `R1`, `R2`, and `R3`. This fulfills the locality constraint mentioned above.

```
model ResistorCircuit
  Resistor R1(R=100);
  Resistor R2(R=200);
  Resistor R3(R=300);
equation
  connect(R1.p, R2.p);
  connect(R1.p, R3.p);
end ResistorCircuit;
```

Connect-equations are described in more detail in Chapter 5. See also Section 8.5, page 374, regarding equation operators for overconstrained connections.

8.3.3.1 Repetitive Connection Structures

We can also use connect-equations together with the for-equation construct described previously to establish *repetitive connection structures* consisting of a number of connections between connectors belonging to array elements. This is a very important use of for-equations in combination with connect-equations. For example, in the class `RegVariables` below there is an array called `variables` in which each element *outlet* has been connected to an *inlet* from its neighbor element, apart from the outlet of the *n*th element, which is still free for external connections:

```
class RegVariable
  Variable variables[n];
equation
  for i in 1:n-1 loop
    connect(variables[i].Outlet, variables[i+1].Inlet);
  end for;
end RegVariable;
```

8.3.4 Conditional Equations with if-Equations

Modelica can be used for expressing hybrid models, that is, models with mixed continuous and discrete parts. One can use two kinds of equation constructs for such models: conditional equations with if-equations and conditional equations with when-equations. How can we know which one to use in different hybrid modeling situations? The following guidelines are useful:

- *If-equations* (see also Section 13.2.6, page 613) or *if*-expressions (see Section 6.12.2, page 288) are used for conditional models with different behavior in *different operating regions*. The conditional equations may contain *continuous-time* expressions.
- *When-equations* are used to express instantaneous equations that are valid (become active) only *at events*, for example, at discontinuities or when certain conditions become `true`. The conditional equations automatically contain only *discrete-time* expressions since they become active only at event instants.

The general form of the if-equation is specified below. The elseif-part is optional and can occur zero or more times. The else-part is also optional and can occur at most once.

```
if <condition> then
  <equations>
elseif <condition> then
```

```
   <equations>
else
   <equations>
end if;
```

For example, the if-equation below specifies different equations for the variable `y` in three *different operating regions*, limiting values of `y` such that: `uMin` <= `y` <= `uMax`:

```
if u > uMax then
  y = uMax;
elseif u < uMin then
  y = uMin;
else
  y = u;
end if;
```

During solution of the continuous part of the equation system ("continuous integration"), the same branch of the if-equation with its equations is always included in the total equation system. The solution process is temporarily halted whenever `u-uMax` or `u-uMin` crosses zero. When this happens an event is generated. At the event instant the conditions are reevaluated, the correct if-branch is selected, and continuous integration is restarted.

There is also a constraint regarding the number of equations in each part of an if-equation:

- *If-equations* for which the conditions have higher variability than `constant` or `parameter` must have the *same number of equations* in each branch (then-, elseif-, and else-parts). A missing else-part is counted as zero equations and the number of equations is defined after the compiler has expanded the equations to scalar equations.

This constraint is a consequence of the *single-assignment rule* stated previously. If this constraint is violated the number of equations might change during simulation when different then-, elseif-, and else-parts become active even though the number variables remain the same.

This constraint need *not* be fulfilled if the conditions in the if-equation have at most `parameter` variability since then the active branch of the if-equation is selected before simulation starts, allowing the number of variables and the number of equations to be kept the same.

Below is an example class (also shown in Section 5.7.9) containing a conditional if-equation with a *condition* that is a parameter expression (the built-in function `cardinality` has parameter variability), that is, the *condition* does not change during simulation:

```
model CardinalityResistor
extends TwoPin;
  parameter Real R(unit="Ohm")   "Resistance";
equation
  // Handle cases if pins are not connected
  if cardinality(p) == 0 and cardinality(n) == 0 then
    p.v = 0; n.v = 0;
  elseif cardinality(p) == 0 then
    p.i = 0;
elseif cardinality(n) == 0 then
    n.i = 0;
end if;
  // Resistor equation
    v = R*i;
end CardinalityResistor;
```

Moreover, inside an if-equation that is controlled by a nondiscrete time (i.e., a continuous-time expression that is not discrete-time) *condition* expression and not in the body of a when-clause, it is *not* legal to have equations between discrete-time expressions (Section 6.9.3, page 281), or real elementary relations/functions that should *generate events*.

The use of if-equations, events, and related topics is described in more detail in Chapter 13, page 591.

8.3.5 Conditional Equations with when-Equations

In the previous section, we stated that when-equations are used when we need to specify what should hold *at event instants* through conditional *equations*:

- *When-equations* are used to express instantaneous equations that are valid (become active) only *at events*, for example, at discontinuities or when certain conditions become `true`. The conditional equations automatically contain only *discrete-time* expressions since they become active only at event instants.

The structure of an *unclocked when-equation* is specified below, where *conditions* is a `Boolean` scalar or vector expression which automatically has variability discrete-time because of its type. The elsewhen-part is optional and can be repeated zero or more times.

- There is also a *clocked when-equation* (Section 13.6.6, page 700), without the optional elsewhen-part, in which the <*conditions*> is replaced by a clock expression.

The equations within the when-part are activated when the scalar condition expression becomes `true`, or in the case of a `Boolean` vector expression, when at least one of the vector elements becomes `true`.

The equations in a subsequent elsewhen-part are activated if at least one of the associated *conditions* becomes `true` and no preceding when- or elsewhen-part of the same when-equation has been activated.

```
when <conditions> then
  <equations>
elsewhen <conditions> then
  <equations>
end when;
```

For example, the two equations in the when-equation below become active at the event instant when the `Boolean` expression `x > 2` becomes `true`.

```
when x > 2 then
  y1 = sin(x);
  y3 = 2*x + y1+y2;
end when;
```

If we instead use a `Boolean` vector expression containing three elements as the *conditions*, then the two equations will be activated at event instants when either of the three conditions: `x > 2`, `sample(0,2)`, or `x < 5` becomes `true`. Typically, each condition in the vector gives rise to its own event instants.

```
when {x > 2, sample(0,2), x < 5} then
  y1 = sin(x);
  y3 = 2*x + y1+y2;
end when;
```

Special behavior can be specified by when-equations when a simulation starts and finishes by testing the built-in predicates `initial()` and `terminal()`. The predicate `initial()` returns `true` during initialization at the beginning of the simulation (or before) when `time` is equal to `time.start`, and the predicate `terminal()` returns `true` at the end of the simulation. For example:

```
when initial() then
  ...      // Equations to be activated during initialization at beginning.
end when;
...
when terminal() then
  ...      // Equations to be activated at the end of the simulation.
end when
```

Additional events are *not* generated from relations or discontinuous functions within when-equations, for example, from the use of relations in if-expressions or if-equations within when-equations. This is unnecessary since we are already at an event by being in a when-equation.

8.3.5.1 Restrictions on Equations within Unclocked when-Equations

How should equations within unclocked when-equations be solved together with all other discrete and continuous equations in the total system of equations of a model? This is possible by first locally solving the system of equations within a when-equation at the event, and then keeping the *result variables* from this local solution *constant* during solution of the continuous part of the rest of the system of equations, i.e., during "continuous integration." Thus, it is essential to know *which variables* are *results* from the local solution of equations within a when-equation. Such result variables will of course have variability *unclocked discrete-time*.

To make it possible both for a Modelica tool and a person to determine which variables are results from a when-equation, and to guarantee an effective and simple solution process for such results, Modelica *restricts* the *allowed equations* within an unclocked when-equation to the forms below, except for the clocked when-equation described in Section 13.6.6, page 700.

The result variables on the left-hand side of the equation forms shown below, for example, *variable*, *out1*, *out2*, and so on, are immediately obvious:

- *variable* = *expression*,
- (*out1*, *out2*, *out3*, ...) = *function_name*(*inexpr1*, *inexpr2*, ...),
- Special equation forms: `assert` (), `terminate` (), `reinit`(),
- Repetitive and conditional structured equations such as for-equations and if-equations if the equations within the for-equations and if-equations satisfy these requirements.

Regarding the variables on the left hand side, for example, `variable`, `out1`, and so on, if they are array elements, the array indices must be parameter expressions.

The need for this restriction on the form of equations in unclocked when-equations is especially obvious in the following example:

```
model WhenNotValid
  Real x, y;
equation
  x + y = 5;
  when sample(0,2) then
    2*x + y = 7;           // Error: not valid Modelica.
  end when;
end WhenNotValid;
```

When the equations within the when-equation are not active, it is not clear which variable, either x or y, is a "result" from the when-equation to keep constant outside the when-equation. A corrected version of this when-equation appears in the class `WhenValidResult` below:

```
model WhenValidResult
  Real x,y;
equation
  x + y = 5;               // Equation to be used to compute x.
  when sample(0,2) then
    y = 7 - 2*x;   // Correct, y is a result variable from the when!
  end when;
end WhenValidResult;
```

Here it is clear that `y` is a result variable from the when-equation since it appears alone at the left-hand side of an equation. The variable `y` is kept constant when the when-equation is deactivated. This allows computing `x` from the first equation during "continuous integration" as (`5-y`) using the value of `y` computed at the previous event instant.

The following restrictions also apply to when-equations:

- When-equations are not allowed in initial equation sections, but when initial() is possible.
- When-equations are not allowed to be nested.

For example:

```
model ErrorNestedWhen
  Real x,y1,y2;
equation
  when x > 2 then
    when y1 > 3 then    // Error! when-equations cannot be nested
      y2 = sin(x);
    end when;
  end when;
end ErrorNestedWhen;
```

8.3.5.2 Application of the Single-Assignment Rule on when-Equations

Two when-equations may *not* define the same variable. Without this rule that may actually happen for the erroneous model `DoubleWhenConflict` below, since there are two equations (`close = true; close = false;`) defining the same variable `close`. A conflict between the equations will occur if both conditions would become `true` at the same time instant.

```
model DoubleWhenConflict
  Boolean close;    // Erroneous model: close defined by two equations!
equation
  ...
  when condition1 then
    close = true;
  end when;
  when condition2 then
    close = false;
  end when;
  ...
end DoubleWhenConflict
```

One way to resolve the conflict would be to give one of the two when-equations higher priority. This is possible by rewriting the when-equation using `elsewhen`, as in the `WhenPriority` model below or using the algorithmic version of the when-construct shown in Chapter 9, Section 9.2.10, page 433.

The when-equation involving an elsewhen-part resolves the conflict since the first of the two event handlers is given higher priority:

```
model WhenPriority
  Boolean close;    // Correct model: close defined by two equations!
equation
  ...
  when condition1 then
    close = true;
  elsewhen condition2 then
    close = false;
  end when;
  ...
end WhenPriority;
```

Here it is well defined what happens if both conditions become `true` at the same time instant since *condition1* with associated conditional equations has a higher priority than *condition2*.

8.3.6 reinit

The following is a rather special form of equation (also available as an operator, see Table 6-1, page 274 in Chapter 6), and also briefly mentioned in Section 13.2.5.18, page 613.

The `reinit` equation can only be used within the body of a when-equation. It reinitializes the first argument *`statevariable`* with the value of *`valueexpression`* at an event instant The `reinit` equation has the following form:

reinit(*statevariable*, *valueexpression*);

The first argument, *`statevariable`*, is a `Real` (or subtype of Real) continuous-time variable (or an array of such variables), which must be selected as a state (or states, respectively). Note that `reinit` on *`statevariable`* implies `stateSelect=StateSelect.always` for *`statevariable`*. In general, a variable is a state variable if the `der`-operator is applied to it somewhere in the model, or it is selected by `stateSelect`, see Section 18.2.6.1, page 1014.

The second argument, *`valueexpression`*, must be an `Integer` or `Real` expression (or array of such expressions, respectively), and be type compatible with the first argument *`statevariable`*.

This "equation" effectively "removes" (deactivates) the previously active equation defining *`statevariable`* and "adds" a new instantaneous equation *`statevariable`* = *`valueexpression`* that gives a new definition to *`statevariable`*, which is valid at the current event instant and is used to reinitialize the variable.

The `reinit` operator does not break the single assignment rule, because `reinit(`*`statevariable`*`,` *`valueexpression`*`)` in equations evaluates *`valueexpression`* to a value, then at the end of the current event iteration step it assigns this value to *`statevariable`*. This copying from values to reinitialized state(s) is done after all other evaluations of the model and before copying *`statevariable`* to `pre(`*`statevariable`*`)`.

Neither the number of variables nor the number of equations is changed. The single-assignment rule is therefore not violated.

The `reinit` equation can for the same variable (or array of variables) only be applied in one equation, but having `reinit` of the *same* variable in `when` and `elsewhen` is allowed.

The `BouncingBall` example already seen in Figure 2-25, page 57 in Chapter 2 illustrates the use of `reinit`:

```
model BouncingBall    "The bouncing ball model"
  parameter Real g=9.81;    // gravitational acceleration
  parameter Real c=0.90;    // elasticity constant of ball
  Real height(start=0);     // height above ground
  Real v(start=10);         // velocity
equation
  der(height) = v;
  der(v)      = -g;
  when height<0 then
    reinit(v, -c*v);
  end when;
end BouncingBall;
```

For the benefit of the critical reader; note that the behavior of `reinit` is suspiciously close to an assignment statement even if it is not one.

If instead of `reinit` we would have used an equation section containing the equation "`v = -c*v`" there would have been an error message of too many equations since the previous equation was not removed. The following class `BouncingBallError` gives rise to an error since the equation `v=-c*v` is used instead of `reinit(v,-c*v)`, thereby creating an over-determined system of equations.

```
model BouncingBallError  "Bouncing ball model with error"
  parameter Real g=9.81  "since reinit is not used";
  parameter Real c=0.90;
  Real height(start=0);
  Real v(start=10);
equation
  der(height) = v;
  der(v)      = -g;
```

```
  when height<0 then
    v = -c*v;    // Error, old "equation" not "removed" leads to
  end when;  // an overdetermined system of equations
end BouncingBallError;
```

Another example of the use of `reinit` is in the self-initializing block class `FilterBlock1` below, which at initialization time when `initial()` becomes `true` defines `x` to be `u`, which causes `der(x)` to initially be zero according to its defining equation:

```
block FilterBlock1  "First order filter block"
  parameter Real T  "Time constant";
  parameter Real k  "Gain ";
  input  Real u;
  output Real y;
  protected
  Real x;
equation
  der(x) = (u - x) / T;
  y  = k*x;
  when initial() then
    reinit(x, u);      // Initialize such that der(x) becomes 0 if x is u
  end when             // since der(x) = (u-x)/T;
end FilterBlock1;
```

Finally, if a higher index (Section 18.2.3, page 1003) system of equations is present in the model, that is, constraints between state variables, some state variables need to be redefined to nonstate variables. During simulation, nonstate variables should be chosen in such a way that variables with an applied `reinit` operator are selected as states at least when the corresponding when-equations become active. If this is not possible, an error occurs, since otherwise the `reinit` operator would be applied to a non-state variable.

8.3.7 assert and terminate

The special equation clauses `assert` and `terminate` are not really equations in the usual sense, but are declarative since they do not cause side-effects such as updates or input/output to variables. Therefore they can still be used among equations in equation sections.

8.3.7.1 assert

The intention behind `assert` is to provide a convenient means for specifying checks on model validity within a model. There is also a statement version of `assert` (Section 9.2.11, page 445). It can be called as a function with three formal parameters and may refer to values of the predefined type `AssertionLevel`:

```
type AssertionLevel = enumeration(warning, error);
```

An `assert` equation has the following structure:

assert(*assert-expression*, *message-string*); // Uses level=AssertionLevel.error   *or*
assert(*assert-expression*, *message-string*, *assertionlevel*);   *or*
assert(*assert-expression*, *message-string*, *level* = *assertionlevel*);

The *`assert-expression`* in an `assert` equation should normally evaluate to `true`, in which case the *`message-string`* argument is not evaluated and the procedure call to `assert` is ignored. A failed assertion, that is, when the *`assert-expression`* evaluates to `false`, should be reported back to the user in some way which is dependent on the third argument to assert, called `level`, which has a default value `level = AssertionLevel.error`.

In that case, `AssertionLevel.error`, the default behavior is to report some problem back to the user, stop the simulation, and then possibly (which is tool-dependent) continue simulation, for example, after some adjustment such as choosing smaller step-size for numerical solution (if an adaptive solver that will adjust step sizes automatically was not already used). The default `AssertionLevel.error` case can, for example, be used to avoid evaluating a model outside its limits of validity. The following class `AssertTest2` contains an example of the use of `assert`:

```
class AssertTest2
  parameter Real lowlimit = -5;
  parameter Real highlimit = 5;
  Real x;
algorithm
  assert(x >= lowlimit and x <= highlimit, "Variable x out of limit");
end AssertTest2;
```

Alternatively, if the input variable `level = AssertionLevel.warning`, the current evaluation is not aborted. Instead, `message` indicates the cause of the warning. The warning is reported only once when the *`assert-expression`* becomes `false`, and it is also be reported that the *`assert-expression`* is no longer violated when it returns to true. In all cases, the `assert(...)` equation must not have any influence on the behavior of the model.

The `AssertionLevel.warning` case can be used when the boundary of validity is not hard. For example, a fluid property model based on a polynomial interpolation curve might give accurate results between the temperatures 240 K and 380 K, but still give reasonable results in the range 200 K and 500 K. When the temperature gets out of the smaller interval, but still stays in the larger one, the user should be warned, but the simulation should continue without any further action. The corresponding `assert` equations would be:

```
assert(T > 240 and T < 380, "Medium model outside full accuracy range",
       AssertionLevel.warning);
assert(T > 200 and T < 500, "Medium model outside feasible region");
```

8.3.7.2 terminate

The `terminate` equation successfully terminates the current simulation, that is, no error condition is indicated. A string argument is used to indicate the reason for successful termination, which can be reported back to the user in some appropriate way by the simulation tool.

The most common usage of `terminate` is to give more appropriate stopping criteria for terminating a simulation than a fixed point in time, such as when a certain fixed simulation duration time is supplied to a simulation command.

Recall the `MoonLanding` model from Chapter 4, page 143. We can use `terminate` to stop the simulation when the lander touches the surface in order to avoid the lander descending into the interior of the moon. This is the case for the version of the `MoonLanding` class below.

```
model MoonLanding
  parameter Real force1 = 36350;
  parameter Real force2 = 1308;
  parameter Real thrustEndTime = 210;
  parameter Real thrustDecreaseTime = 43.2;
  Rocket     apollo(name="apollo13", mass(start=1038.358) );
  CelestialBody moon(mass=7.382e22,radius=1.738e6,name="moon");
equation
  apollo.thrust = if (time<thrustDecreaseTime) then force1
                  else if (time<thrustEndTime) then force2
                  else 0;
  apollo.gravity = moon.g * moon.mass /(apollo.height + moon.radius)^2;
  when apollo.height < 0 then        // termination condition
    terminate("The moon lander touches the ground of the moon");
  end when;
end MoonLanding;
```

8.4 Initialization and Initial Equation

A dynamic model describes how model variables evolve over time. For the model to be well specified it must be possible to define the variable values at the initial time, for example, $time = 0$, in order to compute their values at a $time > 0$, dependent on these initial values.

This *initialization phase* takes place at the initial time but before the actual simulation starts, and assigns consistent initial values to all variables in the model, including derivative "variables" `der(x)` and pre-"variables" `pre(v)` for continuous-time `Real` variables x and unclocked discrete-time variables v respectively. Note that during this initialization phase `der(x)` and `pre(v)` are treated as variables with unknown values. Initialization requires an *initialization equation system* to be solved, including all equations and algorithm sections used during the simulation as well as special initial constraints.

Previously, for example, in Section 2.3.2, page 28, we have shown a way of specifying initial constraints as initial values of variables through the `start` attribute available for all kinds of variables in Modelica. However, this is not enough to cover all situations. The `initial equation` construct described in Section 8.4.2 shows us a way of specifying initial values, for example, for derivatives, which is not possible by just giving start values. In fact, we have three ways of specifying initial constraints necessary to solve certain initialization problems:

- Specifying initial values through the `start` attribute, often together with the `fixed` attribute.
- Specifying initial constraints as equations in `initial equation` sections.
- Specifying initial values through assignments in `initial algorithm` sections.

The first two methods are shown further below; whereas `initial algorithm` sections are briefly described in Section 9.2.2, page 424. However, all special considerations mentioned for initial equations also apply analogously for initial algorithms.

Moreover, the following equations are implicitly added to the initialization equation system:

- For all non-discrete continuous-time Real variables `vc`, the equation `pre(vc) = vc` is added to the initialization equations. If `pre(vc)` is not present in the flattened model, a Modelica compiler may choose not to introduce this equation, or if it was introduced it can eliminate it to avoid the introduction of many dummy variables `pre(vc)`.

8.4.1 Initialization Constraints and Hints through the start Attribute

As pointed out earlier, the `start` attribute available for any variable can be used to specify initial value information. For example:

```
parameter Real x0 = 0.5;
Real x(start = x0);
```

The modification equation `start=x0` gives a hint that `x0` is a good guess value when solving the initialization problem. It does *not* specify that `x` must have the initial value `x0`. Moreover, the value of a `start` attribute must be a parameter or constant expression.

On the other hand, we also have an attribute called `fixed` available for all variables. If `fixed` is `true` for a continuous-time variable (see example below), it *must* have the specified start value at the initial time, i.e., a constraint equivalent to an equation at the initial time. The default is `fixed=false` for all variables except for parameters and constants which have the default `fixed=true`. For variables declared as constant it is an error to have `fixed = false`. For example:

```
Real x(start = x0, fixed=true);
```

This declaration with the attribute `fixed=true` for a continuous-time variable implies that the following equation is added to the initialization equation system to be solved:

```
x = x0
```

Taking a look at a slightly larger model:

```
model Init2
  constant  Real a  = 2;
  parameter Real x0 = 0.5;
  Real x(start = x0, fixed = true);
```

```
equation
  der(x) = a*x;
end Init2;
```

We make a separate group of definition equations for parameters and constants since they have `fixed=true` by default, already have defined values, and need not be part of the initial equation system:

```
a  = 2
x0 = 0.5
```

Thus, the following initial equation system is obtained:

```
x    = x0;
der(x) = a*x;
```

The solution for initialization at the initial time is as follows:

```
x      = x0        // = 0.5
der(x) = a*x       // = 2*x0 = 1
```

Regarding *unclocked discrete-time variables* the situation is slightly different. Here a start value equation for `pre(xd)` is added to the initialization equation system for each unclocked discrete-time variable `xd`. For example:

```
Boolean b(start=false, fixed=true);
Integer k(start=3,     fixed=true);
```

This implies the following initialization equations for enforcing start-value constraints:

```
pre(b) = false;
pre(k) = 3;
```

Thus, the unclocked discrete-time variable itself does not get the start value, only the `pre`-value of the variable is defined. However, for any unclocked discrete-time variable `xd` the following equation holds, keeping its value constant, except when the instantaneous equations defining that variable are active:

```
pre(xd) = xd
```

This will in practice define the value also for the variable `xd` itself except when a defining equation such as `xd=`*expression* is active during the initialization phase, for example, inside a when-equation during initialization, which then instead will define the value (see Section 8.4.2 below). For a more thorough discussion of events, instantaneous equations, and when-equations see Section 13.2.6, page 613.

To summarize, by using the attribute modifiers `start=`*value* and `fixed=true` in the declaration of variables, we get the following initialization equations:

- For any non-discrete continuous-time `Real` variable `v`, the equation `v=`*start_expression* is added to the system of initialization equations, if the modifier equations `start=`*start_expression* and `fixed=true` are present for the variable v.
- For any unclocked discrete-time variable `vd`, the equation `pre(vd)=`*start_expression* is added to the system of initialization equations, if the modifier equations `start=`*start_expression* and `fixed=true` are present for the variable `vd`.
- For any variable declared as constant and parameter, with `fixed = true`, no equation is added to the initialization equations.

For constants and parameters, the attribute `fixed` is by default `true`. For other variables `fixed` is by default `false`.Non-discrete continuous-time Real variables `vc` have exactly one initialization value since the rules assure that during initialization `vc` = `pre(vc)` = `vc.startExpression` if `fixed`= `true`.

8.4.1.1 Recommended Selection of non-fixed start-Values by Modelica Tools

Start-values of variables having `fixed` = `false` can be used as initial guesses in case iterative solvers are used by the simulator in the initialization phase. In case of iterative solver failure, it is recommended for a Modelica simulator to specially report those variables for which the solver needs an initial guess, but which only have the default value of the start attribute since the lack of appropriate initial guesses is a likely cause of the solver failure.

In general many variables have `start` values that are not fixed. Selecting an appropriate subset of these start values as guess values can provide a consistent set of start values close to user expectations.

- Each instance within a model can be given a unique instance hierarchy level number. The top level model has a level number of 1. The level number increases by 1 for each level down in the model instance hierarchy.
- The model instance hierarchy level number is used to give start values a confidence number, where a lower number means that the `start` value is more confident. Roughly stated, if the `start` value is set or modified at level `i` then the confidence number is `i`.
- If a `start` value is set by a possibly hierarchical modifier at the top level, then this `start` value has the highest confidence, namely 1 irrespectively at what level the variable itself is declared.

8.4.2 Initialization Constraints through initial equation

The syntax of an initial equation section is the same as for an equation section (see Section 8.3, page 351) apart from using the keywords `initial equation` instead of just `equation`:

initial equation
  <equations>
<some other allowed keyword>

The following holds for an initial equation section:

- Any kind of equation is allowed inside an initial equation section, *except* for when-equations.
- In the equations inside an initial equation section `der(`*x*`)` and `pre(`*v*`)` are treated as variables with unknown values in the initialization system of equations.
- All expressions inside an initial equation section have unclocked discrete-time variability (Section 6.9.3, page 281).

However, certain when-equations outside an initial equation section can contribute to the initialization system of equations (see Section 8.4.3 below.)

We can use an initial equation section to specify the initialization constraint for a derivative:

```
initial equation
  der(x) = 0;
```

This is useful when we want to investigate and initialize a system in steady state, i.e., variables do not change with time (their derivatives are zero) if the system inputs do not change. For example:

```
model ContinuousController   "Continuous Proportional Controller"
  Real y(fixed = false);   // fixed=false is redundant since it is default
equation
  der(y) = a*y + b*u;
initial equation
  der(y) = 0;
end ContinuousController
```

The start value from `y` gives no additional constraint since `fixed=false`. The extracted equations for the initialization problem are as follows:

```
der(y) = a*y + b*u;
der(y) = 0;
```

This system has the following solution for initialization:

```
der(y) = 0;
y      = -b/a * u;
```

8.4.3 Using when-Equations during Initialization

During the initialization phase, the equations inside a when-equation are included in the initialization system of equations only if they fulfill the following condition:

- The equations inside a when-equation are included in the initialization equation system *if and only if* they are explicitly enabled with the `initial()` operator, either in the scalar predicate form `when initial()`, or in the array predicate form `when {..., initial(), ...}`:

Thus, even if a when-equation is active during simulation at an initial `time=0`, its equations are not included if the `initial()` operator is not used among the predicates of the when-equation. The initialization phase is actually executed before simulation starts at `time=0`.

In case of a `reinit(x,expr)` being active during initialization by being inside `when initial()`, this is interpreted as adding `x=expr`, i.e., the reinit-equation, as an initial equation.

For example, the following when-equation from the `ProcessControl2` model below explicitly enables its equations for initialization by its use of the `initial()` operator:

```
when {initial(), sample(0,Ts)} then
  xd = pre(xd) + Ts/T*(xref-x);
   u = k*(xd + xref - x);
end when
```

Note that this when-equation is also active during the simulation phase at the initial `time=0` by its use of `sample(0,Ts)`, which generates its first sample at `time=0`.

If the `initial()` is removed from the when-equation predicate, its equations are not included in the initialization system of equations. Instead the two default equations related to the variables defined in the when-equation are used. These equations hold when the when-equation is not active:

```
xd = pre(xd);
u  = pre(u);
```

8.4.4 Explicit and Implicit Specification of Parameter Values for Initialization

By far the most common way of specifying parameter values is through *explicit* declaration equations, where the right-hand sides are literal constants or parameter expressions, for example, `g`, `m`, and `L` in the `Pendulum` model below:

```
model Pendulum
  import Modelica.Math.*;
  parameter Real g = 9.81;
  parameter Real m = 1       "mass";
  parameter Real L = 1       "Pendulum Length;
  Real           phi         "Angle";,
  Real           w           "Angular velocity";
  Real           x,y         "Point mass coordinates";
equation
  der(phi) = w;
  m*der(w) = -(m*g/L)*sin(phi);
  x = L*sin(phi);
  y = -L*cos(phi)
end Pendulum;
```

The pendulum is depicted in Figure 8-1.

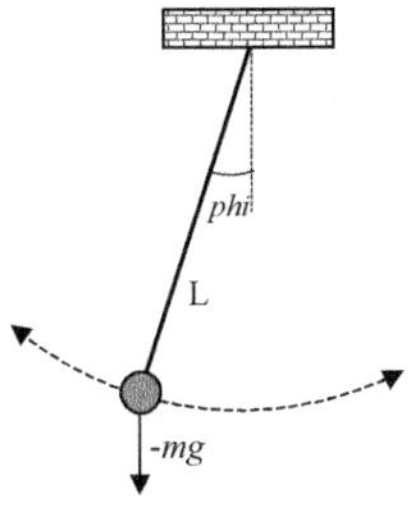

Figure 8-1. A simple planar pendulum.

The variables x and y are not independent since the pendulum point mass coordinates x and y are constrained to positions on a circular path, fulfilling the following Pythagorean condition:

$$x^2 + y^2 = L^2 \tag{8-1}$$

Now consider that we would like to specify the initial position of the point mass, for example, as follows:

```
Real x(start = 0.3, fixed = true);
Real y(start = 0.4, fixed = true);
```

The length L, computed according to equation (8-1), becomes $\sqrt{0.3^2 + 0.4^2} = 0.09 + 0.16 = 0.25 = 0.5$, which contradicts the specified initial value L=1, which cannot be changed since its default attribute fixed=true according to the above model.

However, if we let its attribute fixed=false, the initial value of the length L is *implicitly* computed from the initial values of x and y in the following variant of the model:

```
model PendulumImplicitL
  import Modelica.Math.*;
  parameter Real g = 9.81;
  parameter Real m = 1              "mass";
  parameter Real L(fixed=false);    "Pendulum Length;
  Real           phi                "Angle";,
  Real           w                  "Angular velocity";
  Real           x(start = 0.3, fixed = true);
  Real           y(start = 0.4, fixed = true);
equation
  der(phi)  = w;
  m*der(w)  = -(m*g/L)*sin(phi);
  x = L*sin(phi);
  y = -L*cos(phi)
end PendulumImplicitL;
```

Implicit specification of a parameter value may appear strange. However, recall the definition of a parameter variable in Modelica: a parameter is a variable that is constant during simulation.

Letting the parameter value depend on the initial values of time-dependent variables does not violate this definition.

This feature is actually quite useful in certain modeling situations. For example, when modeling power systems it is common to specify initial conditions such as power dissipation levels, which then implicitly may specify parameter values such as resistance that are related to the power dissipation.

Parameter values may also be specified by reading from a file, e.g. as in the ReadParameterData model below.

```
model ReadParameterData
  parameter Real A(fixed=false);
  parameter Real w(fixed=false);
  Real x;
```

```
initial equation
  (A,w) = readSineData("init.txt");
equation
  der(x) = -A*sin(w*x);
end ReadParameterData;
```

Single start attribute values can also be read directly from a file, for example:

```
parameter Real A(start = readAdata("initA.txt"));
```

All variables declared as parameters having `fixed = false` are treated as unknowns during the initialization phase, i.e., there must be additional equations for them and the start-value can be used as a guess-value during initialization.

In the case in which a parameter has both a declaration equation and `fixed = false`, diagnostics from the Modelica tool is recommended. However, the parameter should still be solved using the declaration equation.

8.4.4.1 Default Parameter start-values for Preliminary Test Simulations

There is often a need for users to investigate and test library models by quickly combining library models and performing preliminary test simulations. If all parameters would be required to be specified during such a preliminary stage this would be rather cumbersome for the user. To simplify preliminary exploratory simulation using libraries, a mechanism is provided to let the library author specify preliminary parameter expressions through the following mechanism:

- If a parameter has a `start`-expression, it does not have `fixed=false`, and neither has a declaration equation nor is part of a record having a binding equation, the `start`-expression can be used during simulation as a parameter-expression.

However, it is recommended that a Modelica tool issues a diagnostic message when initializing the model without setting the parameter value to make it apparent for the user that a parameter expression should eventually be provided for that parameter.

This is used in libraries to give non-zero defaults so that users can quickly combine library models and do preliminary test simulations without explicitly setting parameters; but still easily find the parameters that eventually need to be set for the real simulations. String parameters are also covered by this rule, since they lack a `fixed`-attribute they can never have `fixed=false`.

8.4.5 The Number of Equations Needed for Initialization

How many equations are needed to solve an initialization problem?

In general, for the case of a pure ordinary differential equation (ODE) system with n state variables and m output variables, explained in more detail in Section 2.20.2, page 66, or in Section 12.6, page 584, we will have n+m unknowns in the *simulation* problem. The ODE *initialization* problem has n additional unknowns corresponding to the derivative variables. At initialization of an ODE we will need to find the values of 2n+m variables, in contrast to just n+m variables to be solved for during simulation.

Consider the following simple equation system:

```
der(x1) = f1(x1);
der(x2) = f2(x2);
y = x1+x2+u;
```

Here we have three variables with unknown values: two dynamic variables that also are state variables, `x1` and `x2`, i.e., n=2, one output variable `y`, i.e., m=1, and one input variable `u` with known value. A consistent solution of the initial value problem providing initial values for `x1`, `x2`, `der(x1)`, `der(x2)`, and `y` needs to be found. Two additional initial equations thus need to be provided to solve the initialization problem.

Regarding differential algebraic equation systems (DAEs, see Section 12.7.3, page 586, and Section 17.1, page 979), the situation concerning the number of equations needed for initialization is more complex than for ODEs in whcih exactly *n* additional equations are required for *n* state variables. Here we can assert only that at most *n* additional equations are needed to arrive at $2n+m$ equations in the initialization system. The reason is that in a so-called higher index DAE problem (see 18.2.3, page 1003), the number of dynamic continuous-time state variables might be less than the number of state variables *n*.

For complex models it might be hard for the user to know how many initial equations should be added. This is especially true since a Modelica tool usually performs index reduction (see Section 18.2.4, page 1007) on the equations of high index problems, thereby producing additional equations. Fortunately, the Modelica environment is usually able help the user to correct a mistake by giving helpful hints, or by automatically adjusting the number of active initial equations to the desired number.

8.4.6 System Initialization Examples—Discrete Controller Models

It is quite instructive to apply the above rules to extract initialization systems of equations from a series of similar models. Here we use models of an extremely simple industrial process coupled to an unclocked discrete-time proportional-integrating (PI) controller in four variants.

To find these examples useful for illustration of initialization you need not actually understand the concept of a PI-controller. However, if you would like to read about that topic before continuing, continuous PI controllers are discussed in detail in Section 12.2.3, page 573, whereas discrete PI controllers in a Hybrid Tank system are covered in Section 13.4.1, page 676. Simple periodic sampled systems like the process control models corresponding to Figure 8-2 are described in Section 13.3.1, page 625.

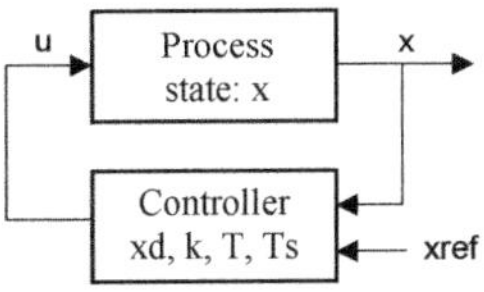

Figure 8-2. An industrial process with state x coupled to a discrete sampling PI controller.

In the first model variant, called `ProcessControl1`, the initial values are given explicitly through start values with the `fixed` attribute being `true`, giving rise to explicit initialization equations.

```
model ProcessControl1  "Initial values given Explicitly"
  parameter Real k = 10, T = 1          "PI controller parameters k, T, Ts";
  parameter Real Ts = 0.01              "Sample time";
            Real x( fixed=true, start=2) "Process state";
  input     Real xref                   "Reference input";
  discrete  Real xd(fixed=true, start=0) "Controller state";
  discrete  Real u (fixed=true, start=0) "Process input";
equation
  // Process model:
  der(x) = -x + u;
  // Discrete PI controller:
  when sample(0,Ts) then
    xd = pre(xd) + Ts/T*(xref-x);
     u = k*(xd + xref - x);
  end when;
end ProcessControl1;
```

The equations inside the when-equation are not included in the initialization since the enabling condition `initial()` is missing. Instead the two default equations that hold when the when-equation is not active are included:

```
xd = pre(xd);
u  = pre(u);
```

Thus the initialization system of equations becomes the following, excluding the parameters `k`, `T`, and `Ts`:

```
x       = x.start    // = 2
pre(xd) = xd.start   // = 0
pre(u)  = u.start    // = 0
xd      = pre(xd)    // = 0
u       = pre(u)     // = 0
der(x)  = -x + u     // = -2
```

The obtained solution of the initial variable values is indicated in the comments to the right.

In the second model variant, `ProcessControl2`, the when-equation is enabled by the presence of the `initial()` predicate. Initial values are still given explicitly through start values.

```
model ProcessControl2  "Enabled when-equation and explicit start values"
  parameter Real k = 10, T = 1               "PI controller parameters k, T, Ts";
  parameter Real Ts = 0.01                    "Sample time";
            Real x( fixed=true, start=2)     "Process state";
  input     Real xref                         "Reference input";
  discrete  Real xd(fixed=true, start=0)     "Controller state";
  discrete  Real u (fixed=true, start=0)     "Process input";
equation
  // Process model:
  der(x) = -x + u;
  // Discrete PI controller:
  when {initial(), sample(0,Ts)} then       // initial() added
    xd = pre(xd) + Ts/T*(xref-x);
     u = k*(xd + xref - x);
  end when;
end ProcessControl2;
```

The extracted initialization system of equations becomes as follows, with solutions at the right:

```
x       = x.start         // = 2
pre(xd) = xd.start        // = 0
pre(u)  = u.start         // = 0
xd      = pre(xd) + Ts/T*(xref-x)   // = 0+0.01/1*(xref-2) = 0.01*(xref-2)
u       = k*(xd + xref - x)         // = 10*(0.01*(xref-2)+xref-2)
der(x)  = -x + u                    // = -2 + u
```

The third process control model, `ProcessControl3`, is similar to the second but uses two equations in an `initial equation` section to define the initial values of `xd` and `u` instead of the start value definitions we used in the previous variants.

```
model ProcessControl3  "Enabled when-equation and initial equation section"
  parameter Real k = 10, T = 1             "PI controller parameters k, T, Ts";
  parameter Real Ts = 0.01                  "Sample time";
            Real x(fixed=true, start=2)    "Process state";
  input     Real xref                       "Reference input";
  discrete  Real xd                         "Controller state";
  discrete  Real u                          "Process input";
equation
  // Process model:
  der(x) = -x + u;
  // Discrete PI controller:
  when {initial(), sample(0,Ts)} then
    xd = pre(xd) + Ts/T*(xref-x);
```

```
    u = k*(xd + xref - x);
  end when;
initial equation
  pre(xd) = 0;
  pre(u)  = 0;
end ProcessControl3;
```

The system of initialization equations from the ProcessControl3 model is almost the same as in the second variant. The only difference is the presence of the two equations from the initial equation section.

```
x        = x.start       // = 2
pre(xd)  = 0             // = 0
pre(u)   = 0             // = 0
xd       = pre(xd) + Ts/T*(xref-x)  // = 0+0.01/1*(xref-2) = 0.01*(xref-2)
u        = k*(xd + xref - x)        // = 10*(0.01*(xref-2)+xref-2)
der(x)   = -x + u                   // = -2 + u
```

In the fourth model, ProcessControl4, we give initialization constraints using the following *steady-state* conditions within an initial equation section:

```
der(x)  = 0
pre(xd) = xd
```

These conditions imply that the system should be in a state where the state variables x and xd do not change with time, that is, steady-state.

```
model ProcessControl4  "Enabled when-equation and steady state init"
  parameter Real k = 10, T = 1    "PI controller parameters k, T, Ts";
  parameter Real Ts = 0.01        "Sample time";
            Real x(start=2)       "Process state";
  input     Real xref             "Reference input";
  discrete  Real xd               "Controller state";
  discrete  Real u                "Process input";
equation
  // Process model:
  der(x) = -x + u;
  // Discrete PI controller:
  when sample(0,Ts) then;
    xd = pre(xd) + Ts/T*(xref-x);
     u = k*(xd + xref - x);
  end when
initial equation
  der(x)  = 0;      // Steady state condition
  pre(xd) = xd;
end ProcessControl4;
```

The obtained system of when-equations for initialization is as follows:

```
der(x)  = 0
pre(xd) = xd
xd      = pre(xd) + Ts/T*(xref-x)
u       = k*(xd + xref - x)
der(x)  = -x + u
```

The stationary initialization system is a linear system of equations in the following unknowns: der(x), xd, pre(xd), u, and x. Simplifying by using der(x)=0, pre(xd)=xd, and 0=-x+u, we obtain:

```
der(x)  = 0
x       = xref
u       = xref
xd      = xref/k
pre(xd) = xd
```

By using the numerical values `k=10` and the guess value `x.start=2` we obtain `xref=2`, `xd=2/10`, which when substituted gives a consistent stationary solution of the initialization problem:

```
der(x)   = 0
x        = 2
u        = 2
xd       = 0.2
pre(xd)  = 0.2
```

8.4.7 Initialization of Nonlinear Systems Using the homotopy Operator

During the initialization phase of a dynamic simulation problem, it often happens that large nonlinear systems of equations must be solved by means of an iterative solver. The convergence of such solvers critically depends on the choice of initial guesses for the unknown variables. The process can be made more robust by providing an alternative, *simplified version of the model*, such that convergence is possible even without accurate initial guess values, and then by continuously transforming the simplified model into the *actual model*. This transformation has the following syntax and is usually called a `homotopy` transformation. The syntax is as follows:

```
homotopy(actual=actual, simplified=simplified)
```

The operator can also be called using positional calling syntax:

```
homotopy(actual, simplified)
```

The types of the scalar expressions *actual* and *simplified* are subtypes of Real. The following usage example is from the `IdealDiode` model further below:

```
Goff2 = homotopy(actual=Goff, simplified=Goff_flat);
```

A Modelica translator should map this operator into either always returning *actual* (the trivial implementation) or alternatively the operator might during the solution process return a combination of the two arguments as below, where `lambda` is a homotopy parameter going from 0 to 1. When `lambda`=1 the homotopy operator should return *actual*, e.g.:

```
lambda*actual + (1-lambda)*simplified
```
(8-2)

If the *simplified* expression is chosen carefully, the solution of the problem changes continuously with `lambda`, so by taking small enough steps it is possible to eventually obtain the solution of the actual problem. The `homotopy` operator can be called with positional parameter passing or preferably with named arguments for improved readability.

It is recommended that a Modelica tool (conceptually) performs one homotopy iteration over the whole model, and not several homotopy iterations over the respective non-linear algebraic equation systems that might be present. The reason is that the following structure can be present in the total system of equations:

$$\begin{aligned} \mathbf{w} &= \mathbf{f}_1(\mathbf{x}) \quad \text{// has homotopy operator} \\ \mathbf{0} &= \mathbf{f}_2(\text{der}(\mathbf{x}), \mathbf{x}, \mathbf{z}, \mathbf{w}) \end{aligned} \tag{8-3}$$

Here, a nonlinear equation system $\mathbf{f}_2$ is present. The `homotopy` operator is, however, used on a variable that is an "input" to the non-linear algebraic equation system, and modifies the characteristics of the non-linear algebraic equation system. Thus, the only meaningful way is to perform the homotopy iteration over $\mathbf{f}_1$ and $\mathbf{f}_2$ together.

The suggested approach is "conceptual", because more efficient implementations are possible, e.g. by determining the smallest iteration loop that contains the equations of the first BLT (Section 17.1.6, page 984) block in which a `homotopy` operator is present and all equations up to the last BLT block that describes a non-linear algebraic equation system.

A trivial implementation of the homotopy operator by a Modelica tool can be obtained by making the following function predefined in the global scope:

```
function homotopy
  input Real actual;
  input Real simplified;
  output Real y;
algorithm
  y := actual;
  annotation(Inline = true);
end homotopy;
```

Example 1:

In electrical systems it is often difficult to solve nonlinear algebraic equations if switches are part of an algebraic loop in the system of equations. An idealized diode model might be implemented in the following way, by starting with a "flat" diode characteristic and then move with the homotopy operator to the desired "steep" characteristic:

```
model IdealDiode
  ...
  parameter Real Goff = 1e-5;
protected
  Real Goff_flat = max(0.01, Goff);
  Real Goff2;
equation
  off   = s < 0;
  Goff2 = homotopy(actual=Goff, simplified=Goff_flat);
  u = s*(if off then 1     else Ron2) + Vknee;
  i = s*(if off then Goff2 else 1   ) + Goff2*Vknee;
  ...
end IdealDiode;
```

Example 2:

In electrical systems it is often useful that all voltage sources start with zero voltage and all current sources with zero current, since steady state initialization with zero sources can easily be obtained. A typical voltage source would then be defined as:

```
model ConstantVoltageSource
  extends Modelica.Electrical.Analog.Interfaces.OnePort;
  parameter Modelica.SIunits.Voltage V;
equation
  v = homotopy(actual=V, simplified=0.0);
end ConstantVoltageSource;
```

Example 3:

In fluid system modeling, the pressure/flowrate relationships are highly nonlinear due to the quadratic terms and due to the dependency on fluid properties. A simplified linear model, tuned for the nominal operating point, can be used to make the overall model less nonlinear and thus easier to solve without accurate start values. Named arguments are used here in order to further improve the readability.

```
model PressureLoss
  import SI = Modelica.SIunits;
  ...
  parameter SI.MassFlowRate m_flow_nominal "Nominal mass flow rate";
  parameter SI.Pressure     dp_nominal     "Nominal pressure drop";
  SI.Density                rho            "Upstream density";
  SI.DynamicViscosity       lambda         "Upstream viscosity";
equation
  ...
```

```
  m_flow = homotopy(actual     = turbulentFlow_dp(dp, rho, lambda),
                    simplified = dp/dp_nominal*m_flow_nominal);
  ...
end PressureLoss;
```

Example 4:

Note that the homotopy operator *shall not* be used to combine expressions which are not related, since this can generate singular systems from combining two well-defined systems. The following is an example of such illegal usage of homotopy:

```
model DoNotUse
  Real x;
  parameter Real x0 = 0;
equation
  der(x) = 1-x;
initial equation
  0 = homotopy(der(x), x - x0);
end DoNotUse;
```

The initial equation is expanded into

```
0 = lambda*der(x) + (1-lambda)*(x-x0)
```

and you can solve the two equations

```
der(x) = 1-x;
0 = lambda*der(x) + (1-lambda)*(x-x0)
```

by substituting `der(x) = 1-x` and rearranging terms to give

```
x = (lambda+(lambda-1)*x0)/(2*lambda - 1)
```

which has the correct value of `x0` at `lambda` = 0 and of 1 at `lambda` = 1, but unfortunately has a singularity at `lambda` = 0.5.

8.5 Equation Operators for Overconstrained Connection-Based Equation Systems

There is a special problem regarding equation systems resulting from *loops* in connection graphs in which the connectors contain potential variables *dependent* on each other. When a loop structure occurs in such a graph, the resulting equation system will be *overconstrained*, that is, have more equations than variables, since there are implicit constraints between certain potential variables in the connector in addition to the connection equations around the loop. At the current state of the art, it is not possible to automatically eliminate the unneeded equations from the resulting equation system without additional information from the model designer.

The purpose of this section is to describe a set of equation operators for such overconstrained connection-based equation systems which makes it possible for the model designer to specify enough information in the model to allow a Modelica environment to automatically remove the superfluous equations.

8.5.1 An Example of an Overconstrained Connection Loop

We first take a look at the typical case of a connector containing dependent potential variables. For example, the `Frame` connector class for three-dimensional mechanical systems defined in the Modelica multi-body library (see also Section 15.10.5.1, page 884), and shown below, contains a rotation matrix `R` in the `Frame` connector class of type `Orientation`—basically a `Real[3,3]` matrix type.

```
connector Frame "3-dimensional mechanical connector"
  import SI = Modelica.SIunits;
  SI.Position    r_0[3] "Vector from inertial frame to Frame";
  Orientation    R      "Rotation matrix from inertial frame to Frame";
  flow SI.Force  f[3]   "Cut-force resolved in Frame";
  flow SI.Torque t[3]   "Cut-torque resolved in Frame";
end Frame;
```

This matrix contains nine elements that are potential variables in the connector. However, the matrix can be completely defined by three independent variables as shown in Section 14.8.4.2, page 776, meaning that there are six implicit constraint equations between the nine variables, in addition to the nine equation equality equations between `R` matrices from two connected connectors, that is, more equations than variables if no other variables were available.

Let us investigate a realistic physical example of a mechanical pendulum-like system of four connected bars in a loop, described by the model `MultiBody.Examples.Loops.Fourbar1` shown in Figure 8-3.

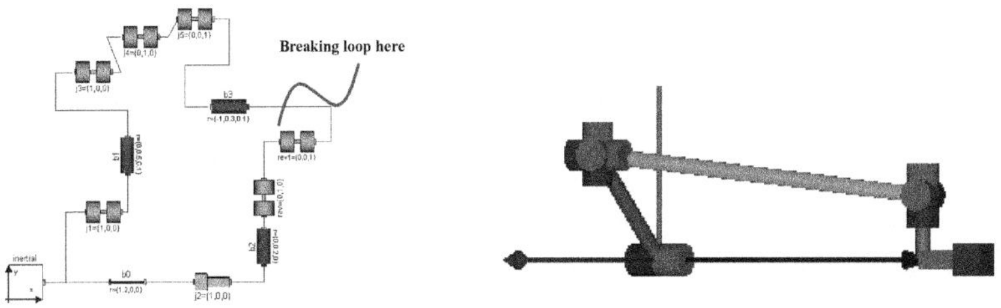

Figure 8-3. Loop in the connection graph (left) of model `MultiBody.Examples.Loops.Fourbar1`, (see also Section 15.10.8, page 894) with overdetermined connectors, and 3D visualization (right) of the loop structure of the mechanical mechanism. The loop can be automatically broken at the connection between bar `b3` and the joint to the right in the connection graph, to eliminate superfluous equations and create a tree.

In the *virtual connection graph* shown in Figure 8-4, we have marked each `connect(...)` equation with a *dotted* arrow, and each bar or joint with a *filled* arrow, indicated by the presence of a `Connections.Branch()` in the equation section of each bar or joint.

There are basically two ways of arriving at the branch *position* in the loop where we have indicated that the loop dependency chain could be *broken* (there might also be other possible places to cut branches) to obtain the desired tree structure that would eliminate the overconstraining problems. The sequence of transformation matrices $\mathbf{R}_i$ can be computed successively, starting at the inertial world frame root node at the lower left with $\mathbf{R}_1$ and following the graph at the left and at the top, arriving at $\mathbf{R}_{13}$, through a sequence of equalities at connections and via bars, and rotations by angles φ_1, φ_2, φ_3, φ_4 at revolute joints:

$\mathbf{R}_1$=`identity`(3); $\mathbf{R}_2=\mathbf{R}_1$; $\mathbf{R}_3=\mathbf{R}_{32}(\varphi_1)\,\mathbf{R}_2$; $\mathbf{R}_4=\mathbf{R}_3$; $\mathbf{R}_5=\mathbf{R}_4$; $\mathbf{R}_6=\mathbf{R}_5$; $\mathbf{R}_7=\mathbf{R}_{76}(\varphi_2)\,\mathbf{R}_6$; $\mathbf{R}_8=\mathbf{R}_7$;

$\mathbf{R}_9=\mathbf{R}_{98}(\varphi_3)\,\mathbf{R}_8$; $\mathbf{R}_{10}=\mathbf{R}_9$; $\mathbf{R}_{11}=\mathbf{R}_{11,10}(\varphi_4)\,\mathbf{R}_{10}$; $\mathbf{R}_{12}=\mathbf{R}_{11}$; $\mathbf{R}_{13}=\mathbf{R}_{12}$

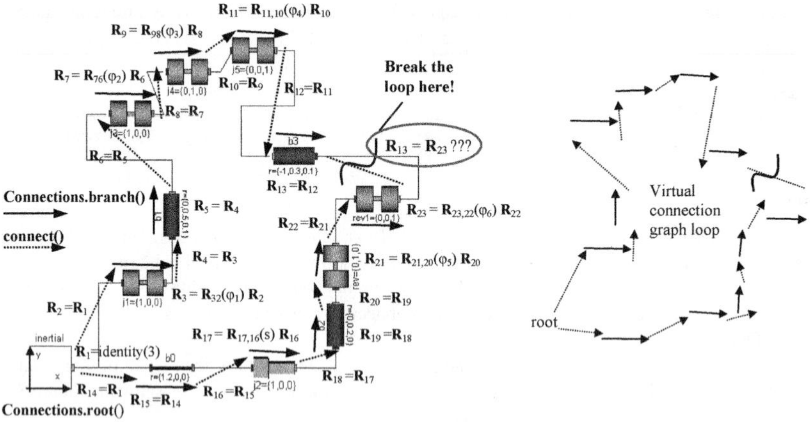

Figure 8-4. Kinematic loop (left) in model `MultiBody.Examples.Loops.Fourbar1`, (see also Section 15.10.8, page 894) with an overdetermined connection, rotation matrices, and connection graph, and the virtual connection graph with only arrows (right) for clarity. Each dotted arrow represents a `connect()`, and each solid line a `Connections.branch()`. The inertial frame has a `Connections.root()`, whereas each joint or bar contains a `Connections.branch()`. Rotation matrices $\mathbf{R}_n$ are shown at joints and bars.

If we perform a similar exercise starting from the inertial root but in the other direction around the loop starting at the bottom, and then to the right, we transform $\mathbf{R}_1$ into $\mathbf{R}_{23}$ through the following sequence:

$\mathbf{R}_1$=`identity`(3); $\mathbf{R}_{14}=\mathbf{R}_1$; $\mathbf{R}_{15}=\mathbf{R}_{14}$; $\mathbf{R}_{16}=\mathbf{R}_{15}$; $\mathbf{R}_{17}=\mathbf{R}_{17,16}(s)\,\mathbf{R}_{16}$; $\mathbf{R}_{18}=\mathbf{R}_{17}$; $\mathbf{R}_{19}=\mathbf{R}_{18}$; $\mathbf{R}_{20}=\mathbf{R}_{19}$;

$\mathbf{R}_{21}=\mathbf{R}_{21,20}(\varphi_5)\,\mathbf{R}_{20}$; $\mathbf{R}_{22}=\mathbf{R}_{21}$; $\mathbf{R}_{23}=\mathbf{R}_{23,22}(\varphi_6)\,\mathbf{R}_{22}$

The final connection, the one we indicate as the candidate to break, results in the following equation containing 9 scalar equations (from the 3 × 3 matrix), where we have indicated that the transformation matrices are functions of certain variables:

$$\mathbf{R}_{13}(\varphi_1,\varphi_2,\varphi_3,\varphi_4)=\mathbf{R}_{23}(s,\varphi_5,\varphi_6) \qquad (8\text{-}4)$$

Thus we have nine scalar algebraic equations, and seven scalar variables ($\varphi_1,\varphi_2,\varphi_3,\varphi_4,s,\varphi_5,\varphi_6$), that is, an overconstrained equation system! Moreover, there are also differential equations implying constraints.

However, the nine matrix elements are not independent of each other. In fact, as we remarked previously, there are three "real" equations and six "redundant" equations since the transformation matrix can be computed from just three variables.

- Solution: At the connection to be broken, replace the nine equality equations by the three essential equations using a function with the predefined name `equalityConstraint`!

To perform this replacement, we need to find the three essential scalar equations. This is possible by using the fact that the matrices `R13` and `R23` are equal or almost equal at the connection and expressing the equation by a user-defined function with the predefined name `equalityConstraint` returning a vector residue (i.e., a kind of difference or rest value which is a vector of zeroes at equality) between the two sets of variables to be able to express their equality. This is a local function declared within the type of the variables (here the `Orientation` data type, essentially a matrix) to be set equal to a vector of zeroes:

```
{0,0,0} = Orientation.equalityConstraint(R13,R23);
```
(8-5)

The declaration of the example matrix type `Orientation` including the local function `equalityConstraint` follows below. Declaring such a type which inherits from a basic type or an array of a basic type is allowed according to Section 4.1.6, page 141.

```
type TransformationMatrix = Real[3,3];

type Orientation "Orientation from frame 1 to frame 2"
  extends TransformationMatrix;

  function equalityConstraint
    input  Orientation R1 "Rotation from inertial frame to frame 1";
    input  Orientation R2 "Rotation from inertial frame to frame 2";
    output Real residue[3];
  protected
    Orientation R_rel "Relative Rotation from frame 1 to frame 2";
  algorithm
    R_rel = R2*transpose(R1);
    /* If frame_1 and frame_2 are identical, R_rel must be
       the unit matrix. If they are close together, R_rel can be
       linearized yielding:
         R_rel = [     1,  phi3, -phi2;
                   -phi3,     1,  phi1;
                    phi2, -phi1,     1 ];
       where phi1, phi2, phi3 are the small rotation angles around
       axis x, y, z of frame 1 to rotate frame 1 into frame 2.
       The atan2 is used to handle large rotation angles, but does not
       modify the result for small angles.
    */
    residue := { Modelica.Math.atan2(R_rel[2, 3], R_rel[1, 1]),
                 Modelica.Math.atan2(R_rel[3, 1], R_rel[2, 2]),
                 Modelica.Math.atan2(R_rel[1, 2], R_rel[3, 3])};
  end equalityConstraint;
end Orientation;

connector Frame "3-dimensional mechanical connector"
  import SI = Modelica.SIunits;
  SI.Position    r[3] "Vector from inertial frame to Frame";
  Orientation    R    "Orientation from inertial frame to Frame";
  flow SI.Force  f[3] "Cut-force resolved in Frame";
  flow SI.Torque t[3] "Cut-torque resolved in Frame";
end Frame;
```

A fixed translation from a frame `A` to a frame `B` may be defined as:

```
model FixedTranslation
  parameter Modelica.SIunits.Position r[3];
  Frame frame_a, frame_b;
equation
  Connections.branch(frame_a.R, frame_b.R);
  frame_b.r = frame_a.r + transpose(frame_a.R)*r;
  frame_b.R = frame_a.R;
  zeros(3)  = frame_a.f + frame_b.f;
  zeros(3)  = frame_a.t + frame_b.t + cross(r, frame_b.f);
end FixedTranslation;
```

Since the transformation matrix `frame_a.R` is algebraically coupled with `frame_b.R`, a branch in the virtual connection graph has to be defined. At the inertial system, the orientation is consistently initialized and therefore the orientation in the inertial system connector has to be defined as root:

```
model InertialSystem
  Frame frame_b;
equation
```

```
    Connections.root(frame_b.R);
    frame_b.r = zeros(3);
    frame_b.R = identity(3);
  end InertialSystem;
```

8.5.2 Overdetermined Types and Variables

Regarding types such as the `Orientation` type described above in Section 8.5.1, in general the following applies:

- A type class with an `equalityConstraint` function declaration is called *overdetermined type*.
- A record class with an `equalityConstraint` function definition is called *overdetermined record*.
- A connector that contains instances of overdetermined type and/or record classes is called *overdetermined connector*.
- An instance of an overdetermined type class is called an *overdetermined variable*.
- An overdetermined type or record may neither have flow variables nor may be used as a type of flow variables.

Thus, in general, a `type` or `record` declaration may contain an optional definition of the function `equalityConstraint(...)` which must have the form shown below. The `residue` output of the `equalityConstraint` function must have known size, here defined by the constant `n`.

```
type Type  // Overdetermined type
  extends <base type>;

  function equalityConstraint  // Equality without redundant equations
    input  Type T1;
    input  Type T2;
    output Real residue[ n ];
  algorithm
    residue := ...
  end equalityConstraint;
end Type;

record Record
  <declaration of record fields>

  function equalityConstraint  // Equality without redundant equations
     input  Record R1;
     input  Record R2;
     output Real residue[ n ];
  algorithm
    residue := ...
  end equalityConstraint;
end Record;
```

If the elements of a record, e.g., `Record`, are not independent of each other, the equation `R1 = R2` contains redundant scalar equations, which would make it hard to solve the system of equations.

By instead using a function such as `equalityConstraint` the `R1 = R2` can be transformed into a form with `n` independent variables.

The function `equalityConstraint` must be able to express the equality between the two type instances `T1` and `T2` or two record instances `R1` and `R2`, respectively, using a number $n \geq 0$ of equations, which should be the same as the number of independent unknowns. In this way redundancy is eliminated and the subsystem of equations becomes nonredundant.

The residues of these equations, that is, differences between equation left-hand sides and right-hand sides, are returned in a vector (here called `residue`) of size `n` as the result of the function.

The set of `n` nonredundant equations stating equality between the records `R1` and `R2` is given by the equation **0** = `Record.equalityConstraint(R1,R2)`, where **0** characterizes a vector of zeros of appropriate size `n`. Inside a model this might appear as follows:

```
  Record R1, R2;
equation
  0 = Record.equalityConstraint(R1,R2);
```

8.5.3 Overconstrained Equation Operators for Connection Graphs

The *overconstrained equation operators* for connection graphs, with the prefix `Connections`, should be used to *specify* additional model *information* that allows a Modelica environment to break loops in a virtual connection graph for converting it into a tree structure that can be compiled into efficient simulation code.

Below we assume that there are variables `A.R` and `B.R` of connector instances `A` and `B`, and that the type of `R` is an overdetermined type. In the above example we have used the following overconstrained equation operators, which can be placed in the *equation section* of a model containing the connector instances `A` and/or `B`.

However, remember the following important fact: overconstrained equation operators should *only* be used when needed to specify information to be used for breaking of dependency loops of *relevant* overdetermined variables. For example, if the dependency loop is mechanical, an operator such as `Connections.branch` should *only* be used if there is an algebraic equation in the loop involving relevant overdetermined mechanical variables, and not if there are only equations for other purposes, for example, equations within an electronic controller unit that is connected to the mechanical structure.

- `Connections.root(A.R);`. Put this definition in a model where the *relevant* overdetermined variable `A.R` is (*consistently*) *assigned*, e.g. from a parameter expression. This is true for our previous example where `A.R` is set equal to the identity matrix. This definition states that `A.R` is a (definite) *root node* in a virtual connection graph
- `Connections.branch(A.R,B.R);` Put this definition in a model where there is an *algebraic equation* between *relevant* overdetermined variables `A.R` and `B.R`, e.g. of the form `B.R` = f(`A.R`, ...). This defines a *non-breakable branch* from `A.R` to `B.R` in a virtual connection graph, and can be used at all places where a `connect(...)` equation is allowed, e.g. not in a when-equation and not in an if-equation with more than parameter variability..
- `connect(A,B);` This is used as usual for *standard connections* between connectors. In the virtual connection graph such connections are represented as *breakable branches* between corresponding variables in the connectors `A` and `B`.

There are also three additional operators available that we have not yet used in our example:

- `Connections.potentialRoot(A.R, priority = prioexpr);` where the `priority` argument is an optional nonnegative `Integer` parameter expression (default 0). Use this definition if a *relevant* overdetermined variable `A.R` appears *differentiated* (i.e., `der(A.R)`) in an equation. In a virtual connection subgraph without a `Connections.root` definition, one of the potential roots with the lowest priority number is selected as root.
- `b = Connections.isRoot(A.R);` Returns true if `A.R` is selected as a root in the virtual connection graph.
- `b = Connections.rooted(A.R)` or the deprecated older version `b = rooted(A.R)`. If the operator `Connections.rooted(A.R)` is used, or the equivalent but deprecated operator

`rooted(A.R)`, then there must be exactly one statement `Connections.branch(A.R,B.R)` involving `A.R` (the argument of `Connections.rooted` must be the first argument of `Connections.branch`). In that case `Connections.rooted(A.R)` returns true, if `A.R` is closer to the root of the spanning tree than `B.R`; otherwise false is returned. This operator can be used to avoid equation systems by providing analytic inverses, see for example `Modelica.Mechanics.MultiBody.Parts.FixedRotation`.

Overconstrained equation operators are not allowed to be used in certain contexts:

- Overconstrained equation operators cannot be used inside if-equations with Boolean conditions that do *not* have parameter or constant variability, or in when-equations. Use in for-equations is fine since the array range expression has parameter variability. The same restrictions apply for connect-equations (Section 5.7.2, page 210).

Note that `Connections.branch`, `Connections.root`, and `Connections.potentialRoot` do ***not*** generate equations. They only generate nodes and branches in the virtual graph, and thereby indirectly influence the generation of equality equations from `connect(...)` equations.

Below we give two simple examples of using the `Connections.root` and `Connections.branch` operators in model classes.

In the inertial system model, the variable `frame_b.R` is consistently initialized and is also an instance of the overdetermined connector type `Orientation` (see also the class `Frame`, Section 15.10.5.1, page 884). Therefore the orientation matrix `R` in the inertial system connector `frame_b` has to be defined as *root*:

```
model InertialSystem
  Frame frame_b;
equation
  Connections.root(frame_b.R); // Use of connection operator!
  frame_b.r_0 = zeros(3);
  frame_b.R   = identity(3);    // Always consistent initialization => root
end FixedTranslation;
```

A model for fixed 1D mechanical translational motion from a frame `A` to a frame `B` is defined as follows:

```
model FixedTranslation
  import SI = Modelica.SIunits;
  parameter SI.Position r_rel[3]    "Vector from A to B, resolved in A";
  Frame           frame_a, frame_b;
equation
  Connections.branch(frame_a.R, frame_b.R);    // Use of connection operator!
  frame_b.r_0 = frame_a.r_0 + transpose(frame_a.R)*r_rel;
  frame_b.R   = frame_a.R;
  zeros(3)    = frame_a.f + frame_b.f;
  zeros(3)    = frame_a.t + frame_b.t + cross(r_rel, frame_b.f);
end FixedTranslation;
```

Since the transformation matrices `frame_a.R` and `frame_b.R` are related through the algebraic equation `frame_b.R = frame_a.R`, a *branch* in the virtual connection graph is defined by using the `Connections.branch()` equation operator.

8.5.4 Converting the Connection Graph into Trees and Generating Connection Equations

After having built a virtual connection graph based on connect-equations and overdetermined connection operators as described previously, the Modelica environment converts the graph into one or more trees:

- Break `connect()` branches in the graph until the graph has been converted into trees.

When the trees have been obtained, equality equations are generated from the `connect()` equations:

- A `connect()` branch (i.e., not broken) in a tree is converted to ordinary equality equations according to the usual rules, see Section 5.7.8, page 219.
- A `connect(A.R,B.R)` branch that has been broken, with `A` and `B` containing a variable `R` that is an instance of an overdetermined connector type, is converted to equations of the form `0=equalityConstraint(A.R,B.R)` where **0** is a vector of zeroes, e.g. as equation (8-5) in our previous example. However, if `R` is an ordinary type, standard equality equations such as `A.R=B.R` are generated.

The process of cutting `connect()` branches from the virtual connection graph is illustrated by Figure 8-5.

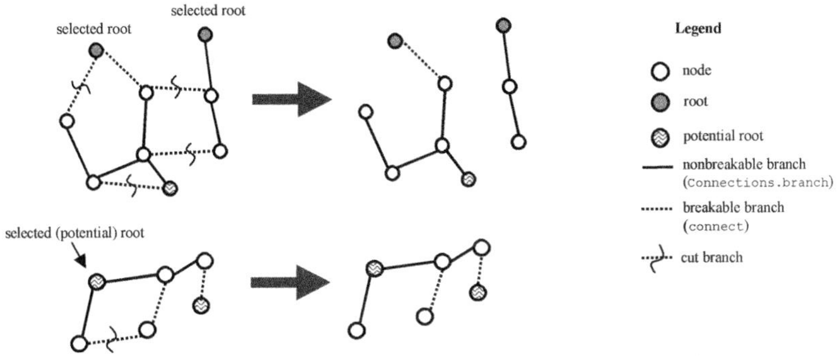

Figure 8-5. Cutting breakable branches in virtual connection graphs to obtain trees.

The following additional considerations apply to the conversion of the virtual connection graph into a *set* of *trees*:

1. Every root node defined via a `Connections.root()` operator is a *definite* root of one tree.
2. The virtual connection graph may consist of sets of unconnected sub-graphs, each of which should have at least one root node or one potential root node. If a graph of this set does not contain any root node, then *one potential root* node in this sub-graph with the lowest priority number is selected to be the root of that sub-graph. The selection can be inquired in a class with the function `Connections.isRoot()`.
3. If there are *n* selected roots in a sub-graph, then *breakable branches* have to be *broken* such that the result becomes a set of *n* trees with the selected root nodes as roots.

8.6 Synchronous Clock-Based Equations

This section briefly summarizes language elements for describing synchronous clock-based equations. The full description is available in Section 13.6, page 694. However, to get the full picture including several examples, start reading from the beginning of Chapter 13, page 591.

As depicted in Figure 8-6, clocks and clocked discrete-time variable values are only defined at clock tick events for an associated clock and are undefined between clock ticks.

To give a very simple example of a model with clock-based equations, in the model below the clock variable `clk` is defined with an interval of 0.2 seconds. This clock is used for sampling the built-in `time` variable, with result put in `x` and defined only at clock ticks. Finally, the variable `y` is defined also between clock ticks by the use of the `hold` operator.

```
model BasicClockedSynchronous
  Clock          clk  "A clock variable";
  discrete Real   x   "Clocked discrete-time variable";
  Real            y   "Unclocked discrete-time variable";
equation
  clk = Clock(0.2);        // Clock with an interval of 0.2 seconds
  x = sample(time,clk);   // Sample the continuous time at clock ticks
  y = hold(x)+1;           // Hold value is defined also between clock ticks
end BasicClockedSynchronous;
```

We simulate and plot:

```
simulate(BasicClockedSynchronous, stopTime=1.0)
plot({x,y})
```

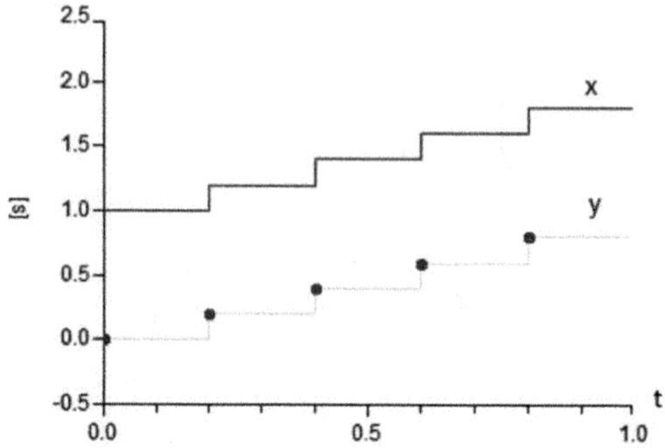

Figure 8-6. Simulation of model `BasicClockedSynchronous` showing clocked discrete-time variable `x` and unclocked discrete-time variable `y`.

How is it possible to know whether an equation is clocked or unclocked? The *clocked when-equation* (Section 13.6.6, page 700) is one simple case. It is itself a clocked equation and all equations inside a clocked when-equation are clocked with the same clock.

For other equations, it is more complicated. It is necessary to look inside the equation regarding to occurrence of clocked-based operators such as `Clock`, `sample`, `subsample`, etc. If such operators occur the equation is clocked, otherwise unclocked.

In fact, the analysis is even more involved. All clocked equations and variables belong to different *clocked partitions* depending on their clock frequency, where all in the same partition are synchronized to the same base clock frequency. Unclocked variables and equations belong to the *unclocked continuous-time partition*. The precise rules (Section 13.6.14.2, page 719) are as follows:

- A variable `u` in `sample(u)` and a variable `y` in `y=hold(ud)` is in a continuous-time partition.
- Correspondingly, variables `u` and `y` in `y = sample(uc)`, `y = subSample(u)`, `y = superSample(u)`, `y = shiftSample(u)`, `y = backSample(u)`, `y = previous(u)`, are in a clocked partition. Equations in a *clocked when-equation* are also in a clocked partition.
- Other partitions where none of the variables in the partition are associated with any of the operators above have an unspecified partition kind and are considered continuous-time partitions.
- Finally, for the resulting final partitioning all continuous-time partitions are collected together and form "the" single continuous-time partition.

8.7 Equation Operators for Clocked State Machines

This section briefly summarizes equation operators for synchronous clocked state machines. The full description is available in Section 13.7, page 729. Several usage examples of clocked state machines are presented in Chapter 13, starting from Section 13.3.2, page 635.

The following equation operators for clocked state machines are available, described in Section 8.7.2 below:

- `transition(...)`
- `initialState(...)`
- `activeState(...)`

8.7.1 States for State Machines

Any Modelica *block* instance *without* continuous-time equations or algorithms can potentially be a state of a state machine. All equations in such a state have to be clocked; a continuous-time clock is not allowed.

A *state* in a state machine might contain *clocked* or *clocked discretized continuous-time* equations. In the latter case the equations are numerically solved between the previous and the next clock tick if the corresponding state is active.

This section is essentially the same as Section 13.7.1, page 729.

8.7.2 Transitions and State Operators for State Machines

A cluster of instances that are coupled by `transition` equations makes a *state machine*. All parts of a state machine must have the *same* clock. All transitions leaving one state must have different priorities. One and only *one instance* in each state machine must be marked as *initial* by appearing in an `initialState` equation.

This section is essentially the same as Section 13.7.2, page 729.

The following special kinds of state machine equations are used to define transitions between states and to define the initial state:

Equation Operators to define a state machine	
`transition`*(from, to, condition, immediate, reset, synchronize, priority)*	The arguments *`from`* and *`to`* are block instances and *`condition`* is a Boolean argument. The optional arguments *`immediate`*, *`reset`*, and *`synchronize`* are of type Boolean, have parameter variability and default values `true`, `true`, `false` respectively. The optional argument *`priority`* is of type Integer, has parameter variability, and a default value 1. The `transition(...)` operator defines a transition from instance *`from`* to instance *`to`*. The *`from`* and *`to`* instances become states of a state machine. The transition fires when *`condition`* = `true` if *`immediate`* = `true` (this is called an "*`immediate`* transition") or `previous(`*`condition`*`)` when *`immediate`*`=false` (this is called a "*delayed* transition"). The argument *`priority`* defines the priority of firing when several transitions could fire. *`priority`*`=1` is the highest priority. If `reset=true`, the states of the target state are reinitialized, i.e., state machines are restarted in initial state and state variables are

	reset to their start values. If *synchronize*=true, any transition is disabled until all state machines of the from-state have reached final states, i.e., states without outgoing transitions. For the precise details about firing a transition, see Section 13.7.4, page 732.
initialState(*state*)	The argument *state* is the block instance that is defined to be the initial state of a state machine. At the first clock tick of the state machine, this state becomes active.

The transition and initialState equation operators may not be used inside if-equations with nonparametric conditions, or in when-equations.

It is possible to query the status of the state machine by using the following operators:

activeState(*state*)	The argument *state* is a block instance. The operator returns true if this instance is a state of a state machine and this state is active at the actual clock tick. If it is not active, the operator returns false. It is an error if the instance is not a state of a state machine.
ticksInState()	The operator returns the number of clock ticks since a transition was made to the currently active state. This function can only be used in transition conditions of state machines not present in states of higher level state machines.
timeInState()	The operator returns the time duration as Real in [s] since a transition was made to the currently active state. This function can only be used in transition conditions of state machines not present within states of higher level state machines.

An example state machine model in textual form (without graphical annotations) is shown below. This is exactly the same model as presented in Section 13.7.5, page 735, where its graphical representation is also shown.

```
block HierarchicalAndParallelStateMachine

  inner Integer v(start=0);

  State1 state1;
  State2 state2;
equation
  initialState(state1);
  transition(state1,state2,activeState(state1.stateD) and
    activeState(state1.stateY), immediate=false);
  transition(state2,state1,v >= 20, immediate=false);

public
  block State1
    inner Integer count(start=0);
    inner outer output Integer v;

    block StateA
      outer output Integer v;
    equation
      v = previous(v) + 2;
    end StateA;
    StateA stateA;

    block StateB
      outer output Integer v;
    equation
      v = previous(v) - 1;
```

```
    end StateB;
    StateB stateB;

    block StateC
      outer output Integer count;
    equation
      count = previous(count) + 1;
    end StateC;
    StateC stateC;

    block StateD
    end StateD;
    StateD stateD;

  equation
    initialState(stateA);
    transition(stateA, stateB, v >= 6, immediate=false);
    transition(stateB, stateC, v == 0, immediate=false);
    transition(stateC, stateA, true, immediate=false, priority=2);
    transition(stateC, stateD, count >= 2, immediate=false);

  public
    block StateX
      outer input Integer v;
      Integer i(start=0);
      Integer w; // = v;
    equation
      i = previous(i) + 1;
      w = v;
    end StateX;
    StateX stateX;

    block StateY
      Integer j(start=0);
    equation
      j = previous(j) + 1;
    end StateY;
    StateY stateY;

  equation
    initialState(stateX);
    transition(stateX, stateY, stateX.i > 20, immediate=false, reset=false);
  end State1;

  block State2
    outer output Integer v;
  equation
    v = previous(v) + 5;
  end State2;
end HierarchicalAndParallelStateMachine;
```

8.8 Special Operators for Enabling Equation System Solution

In addition to the special operators for overconstrained connection graphs described in Section 8.5, page 374, there are other special operators which have been introduced into Modelica in order to enable modeling in a way that supports symbolic transformations of models as well as stable and efficient simulation during the solution process. One such operator is `semiLinear` which is used to model fluid system applications in a way that enables handling reversing flows. The `homotopy` operator is another case, which, however, is used for initialization and therefore is described in Section 8.4.7, page 372. See also the table in Section 6.14, page 291, which includes brief descriptions of these operators.

8.8.1 semiLinear for Handling Reversing Flows in Fluid Systems

The built-in function `semiLinear(...)`, see also a short definition in Section 6.14, page 291, is intended for modeling fluid system applications, for example, the Modelica `Fluid` library, in a way that enables handling reversing flows in a mathematically clean way. To achieve this, the `semiLinear` function is used to define characteristics with two slopes and a set of rules for symbolic transformations. These rules are especially relevant when the function becomes underdetermined. The syntax is as follows:

```
semiLinear(x,positiveSlope, negativeSlope)
```

The function effectively returns the value of this expression:

```
if x>=0 then positiveSlope*x else negativeSlope*x
```

The result is of type Real. For nonscalar arguments, the function is vectorized according to Section 7.10, page 340. An example of using the `semiLinear` function for reversing flows in fluid systems is the following:

```
H_flow = semiLinear(m_flow, port.h, h);
```

Here the enthalpy flow rate `H_flow` is computed from the mass flow rate `m_flow` and the upstream specific enthalpy depending on the flow direction. Another example can be found in Section 8.9.3.5, page 399. Using `semiLinear` works well for one-to-one connections. For connections with more than two flows the stream connector (Section 5.10, page 245) leads to more robust solutions and is recommended for use instead of `semiLinear`.

In some situations, equations with the `semiLinear()` function become underdetermined if the first argument (`x`) becomes zero, that is, there is an infinite number of solutions. It is recommended that the following rules are used by a Modelica tool to transform the equations during the translation phase in order to select one meaningful solution in such cases:

Rule 1:

The equations

```
y = semiLinear(x, sa, s1);
y = semiLinear(x, s1, s2);
y = semiLinear(x, s2, s3);
  ...
y = semiLinear(x, sN, sb);
  ...
```

may be replaced by

```
s1 = if x >= 0 then sa else sb
s2 = s1;
s3 = s2;
  ...
sN = sN-1;
y = semiLinear(x, sa, sb);
```

Rule 2:

The equations

```
x = 0;
y = 0;
y = semiLinear(x, sa, sb);
```

may be replaced by

```
x = 0
y = 0;
sa = sb;
```

For symbolic transformations, the following property is useful (this follows from the definition):

```
semiLinear(m_flow, port_h, h);
```

It is identical to

```
-semiLinear(-m_flow, h, port_h);
```

8.9 Balanced Model Equation Systems

A basic property of Modelica models is that each Modelica model that can be simulated can be transformed into a *system* of equations with the *same* number of equations and variables/unknowns. Such a system is called *balanced.* Being balanced is a necessary but not always sufficient condition for an equation system being *structurally nonsingular* and solvable. A system of equations with more equations than variables is called *over-constrained,* whereas a system of equations with fewer equations than variables is called *under-constrained.*

A basic approach to checking whether a model is balanced is to expand the model into a flat system of equations and variables, count the number of equations and variables, and check if they are equal. We always count scalar variables and equations. Array variables and equations will need to be expanded into their scalar variants.

However, if the system contains thousands of equations it can be very hard for the modeler to determine the root cause(s) of a system being unbalanced and how to correct such a problem. The difficulty partially comes from the many symbolic transformations including inheritance and substitution operations on the way from the original model to the expanded version. It can be very hard to recognize original equations in the expanded form, and even harder to realize the appropriate way to convert an unbalanced model into a balanced one.

Specialized debugging tools (Section 18.3.1, page 1016) have been developed to help localize and correct sources of balancing problems. Even better would be to prevent these problems from ever occurring, at least for large models where it is difficult to understand and correct the causes of being unbalanced. It would be good if balancing problems were detected and reported early during the analysis of a model instead of at a late stage when the model has been expanded into a system of equations that is not very recognizable in terms of the original model.

One simple idea is based on the fact that *if all model components* in a large model *are balanced,* the *whole model* will also be *balanced.* Having balanced model components would also simplify combining separately compiled model components into a correct total model. A possible drawback of balanced models may be less freedom in expressing models and decreased reuse of models, since the balancing condition will put constraints on the forms of allowed models. However, one kind of model component that should be excluded from the balancing requirement is *partial models,* since they are anyway meant to be incomplete.

Balanced models *and* model components is a requirement of Modelica 3.0 and later versions of the language. Modelica 2.2 and earlier versions allow unbalanced model components but still (of course) require that the final simulation model always must be balanced.

This section including several subsequent subsections describes the concept of balanced models and specifies the rules which are necessary to ensure that the resulting simulation model is balanced.

8.9.1 Problems Detecting Causes of Unbalanced Models

As mentioned in the introduction, the causes(s) of a model being unbalanced are often hard to understand for large models. However, even for small parameterized models it can be a bit tricky as demonstrated in the following very simple examples.

```
partial model BaseCorrelation  // Unbalanced but correct since partial
  input Real x;
  Real y;
end BaseCorrelation;

model SpecialCorrelation  // Correct in both Modelica 2.2 and Modelica 3.0
  extends BaseCorrelation(x=2);
equation
   y = 2/x;
end SpecialCorrelation;

model SpecialCorrelationExpanded
  input Real x=2;
  Real y;
equation
  y = 2/x;
end SpecialCorrelationExpanded;
```

The first model, `BaseCorrelation`, is a partial model and obviously unbalanced with two variables and no equations.

The second model, `SpecialCorrelation`, inherits `BaseCorrelation` and is balanced since it adds one declaration equation `x=2` through the modifier and another one `y=2/x` in the equation section, giving two equations and two variables. The balanced property of two equations and two variables becomes even more clear when looking at the expanded model `SpecialCorrelationExpanded`.

We now turn to a model called `UseCorrelation` containing a replaceable model which by default is `BaseCorrelation`.

```
model UseCorrelation   // Correct according to Modelica 2.2
                       // Not valid according to Modelica 3.0
   replaceable model Correlation=BaseCorrelation;
   Correlation correlation;
equation
   correlation.y = time;
end UseCorrelation;

model UseCorrelationExpanded
  input Real correlation.x;
  Real correlation.y;
equation
  correlation.y = time;
end UseCorrelationExpanded;
```

The `useCorrelation` model inherits `BaseCorrelation` with two variables as a default for its replaceable model `Correlation`. It adds one equation, giving a total of one equation and two variables which is *unbalanced*. This model is correct in Modelica 2.2 if it is not used as a simulation model. It is *incorrect* in Modelica 3.0 which requires that all nonpartial models are balanced irrespective of whether they are used as simulation models or not.

However, the model `Broken` below gives an error in both Modelica 2.2 and Modelica 3.0:

```
model Broken // After redeclaration there is one equation too much in both Modelica 2.2 and 3.0
   UseCorrelation example(redeclare Correlation=SpecialCorrelation);
end Broken;

model BrokenExpanded
  input Real example.correlation.x=2;
```

```
  Real example.correlation.y;
equation
  example.correlation.y = 2/x;
  example.correlation.y = time;
end BrokenExpanded;
```

Where is the error? The redeclaration seems to be correct since `SpecialCorrelation` is a subtype of `BaseCorrelation` which acts as the constraining type of `Correlation` at redeclarations (Section 4.3, page 156).

In Modelica 2.2, the model `Broken` will work with some models provided in the redeclaration but not with others. Just by redeclaring it to the model `SpecialCorrelation` an error will occur. It will be very difficult to find the source of such an error in a large model.

Thus, by combining correct models in Modelica 2.2 in a correct way one can still produce an incorrect model which is very unsatisfactory.

By introducing strict language rules about balanced models in Modelica 3.0 and later versions the model `UseCorrelation` is no longer allowed and will be indicated as erroneous by a Modelica tool. In fact, those rules now guarantee that a redeclaration cannot give rise to an unbalanced model any more.

8.9.2 Conditions for Balanced Models

Certain conditions must be fulfilled by a model in order to be balanced. These conditions apply after partial model expansion, that is, inherited variables are included and possibly modified by modification equations. The following concepts explained in subsequent sections are needed to precisely express the conditions for balanced models:

- Local number of variables/unknowns
- Local equation size
- Locally balanced model
- Balancing restriction for connector classes

8.9.2.1 Local Number of Unknowns

In the following, we only consider counting scalar variables. Array variables, record variables, and operator record variables are expanded into sets of scalar variables of primitive basic types before counting. The number of counted variables of an overdetermined type or record class (Section 8.5.2, page 378) is the size of the output result vector of the corresponding `equalityConstraint()` function.

```
function equalityConstraint  // Equality without redundant equations
  input  Type T1;
  input  Type T2;
...
  output Real residue[n];  // Output vector of size n
algorithm
  residue := ...
end equalityConstraint;
```

The *local number of* scalar *unknowns* in a model, that is, in a `class`, `model`, or `block` specialized class, the sum is based on counting the variables directly or indirectly (via local instances) declared in the class according to the following rules:

- Count scalar variables without the `outer` prefix declared as (parts of) *basic types*, *arrays*, *records*, and subtypes of those e.g. defined using the Modelica `type` construct. Basic types include `Real`, `Integer`, `String`, `Boolean`, and enumeration. Parameters and constants are *excluded* in the counting since they are not unknowns in the system of equations to be solved and get their values through declaration equations or modifiers.

- *Ignore* `outer` variables of basic types, arrays, records, and subtypes of those. The reason is that variables with prefix `outer` are treated as known since they are just references to `inner` variables (Section 5.8, page 224) and will get their values through these corresponding `inner` variables.
- Count variables declared inside `connector` instances, excluding parameters and constants.
- Count variables with prefixes `input` or `flow` which belong to public (top level) *connectors* within *local instances* of `model`, `class`, or `block`. See for example the connectors `p1` and `p2` in the `Upart` model below. Top level means that only connectors directly within the local instances are considered, *not* connectors within connectors or further down in the instance hierarchy. The reason that only such inputs and flow variables are counted is that these are unknowns of the local instances within the current instance.

Examples:

```
type Voltage = Real(unit="V");

record Rec1
  Real a1;
  constant Boolan b2;
end Rec1;

connector Pin1
  Real v;
  flow Real i;
end Pin1;

connector Pin2     // Illegal unbalanced connector class
  input Real v;
  flow Real i;
end Pin2;

model Upart
  Pin1 p1;    // Count 1 scalar from the flow variable in p1
  Pin2 p2;    // Count 2 from the input and the flow variables in p2
end Upart;

model U1
  Real        x1;  // Counted as 1 scalar
  Voltage     x2;  // Counted as 1 scalar
  Integer[3] x3;   // Counted as 3 scalars
  outer Integer x4;   // Not counted since it is outer
  parameter Real x5; // Not counted since it is a parameter
  Upart x6;          // Counted as 3; 1 from p1 and 2 from p2 in Upart
  Rec1  x7;          // Counted as 1 since the record contains one constant
end U1;
```

8.9.2.2 Local Equation System Size

In the following, we only consider counting *scalar equations*. Array or record equations will have to be expanded into scalar equations for counting. The *local equation system size* of a `model`, `class`, or `block` class is the sum of the equation counts from the class according to the following rules:

- Count the number of *equations directly defined* at the top-level in the class, that is, *not in* any *local model* or block instance within the class. This includes counting equations in equation sections—both simple equations and the contents of structured equations typically containing several simple equations, declaration equations, and inherited modifier equations.

  The count also includes equations generated from connect-equations with standard connectors (Section 5.2, page 188, and Section 5.7, page 208), expandable connectors (Section 5.9, page 238), and stream connectors (Section 5.10, page 245). when-equations (Section 8.3.5, page 357) and when-statements (Section 9.2.10, page 433) are counted according to the number of variables which are defined by the equations or statements in their bodies. The equation count of an *algorithm section* (see below) is also according to the number of variables it defines.

- Count the number of *input* and *flow variables* present *in* each (top-level) public *connector instance* declared in the class. This represents the number of connection equations that will be generated when the class is used, since inputs will be connected to outputs and flow variables will always give rise to equations even when they are not connected—in the latter case default zero-flow equations are generated.
- Count the number of (top level) *public input variables* that are *not connectors* and do *not* have *binding equations*. The concept of *binding equations* is explained below. Top-level input variables are treated as known variables since they represent the number of binding equations that must be provided to define values for these input variables when the class is used.

A *binding equation* for a variable can appear directly as a declaration equation, but also includes the case when a binding equation is provided as a modifier. For example, this is the case if another model inherits or uses the model M below and has a modifier on u that specifies the value of u.

```
model M
  input Real u;      // u is a top-level input since defined directly in M
  input Real u2=2;   // u2 is another top-level input variable
end M;
```

Here u and u2 are *top-level public input variables* in the model M and not connectors. The variable u2 has a declaration equation u2=2, but u does not have a declaration equation. However, in the equation count it is *assumed* that an equation for u is supplied when using the model. Thus the equation count for the model M is considered as two, even though only one equation is visible in the example.

Another issue briefly mentioned above is *counting equations in algorithm sections*. An algorithm section does not contain equations even though it *behaves* as if it contains equations, and can be mixed with equation sections. Variables assigned values by the algorithm define the *outputs of the algorithm*—in the example below, y and z. This makes the semantics of an algorithm section quite similar to an equation section calling a function with the algorithm section as its body, with input and output function formal parameters corresponding to inputs and outputs of the algorithm section. For example, consider the algorithm section below which occurs in a model intermixed with equation sections:

```
algorithm
  y := x;
  z := 2*y;
  y := z+y;
  ...
```

This algorithm can be transformed into an equation section and a function as below, without changing its meaning. The equation equates the output variables of the above algorithm section with the results of the function f. The function f has the inputs to the algorithm section as its input formal parameters and the outputs as its result parameters. The algorithmic code of the algorithm section has become the body of the function f.

```
equation
  (y,z) = f(x);
  ...

function f
  input  Real x;
  output Real y,z;
algorithm
  y := x;
  z := 2*y;
  y := z+y;
end f;
```

How do we count equations regarding computation of array elements, that is, the number of assigned-to array elements, inside an algorithm section? There might for example be if-statements containing conditional assignments to array elements with indices that are evaluated at run-time, making it impossible to statically determine if a particular array element is assigned. However, there is the rule regarding assigned-to variables in algorithm sections (Section 9.2.1, page 423) that all continuous-time variables are (conceptually) initialized to their start values and all discrete-time variables to their pre-values or previous-values at the beginning of the algorithm section. Thus the whole array is always considered to be assigned if it cannot be statically determined that assignments to the array elements in the algorithm section are always to certain fixed indices or within array slice(s) with specific lower and upper index bounds.

8.9.2.3 Connector Class Balancing Restrictions

What happens if there are several connectors with flow variables and all of these are connected to generate a single sum-to-zero equation based on Kirchhoff's current law (Section 5.7.8.5, page 222)? Then we have several flow variables but only one sum-to-zero equation. Would not this make the model unbalanced?

Fortunately, as we explain further below, the model will still be balanced if all *connector classes* obey the following *balancing* rule:

- For each non-partial connector class the number of variables with prefix `flow` must be *equal to* the number of variables which have neither of the prefixes `parameter`, `constant`, `input`, `output`, `stream`, nor `flow`. As usual the number of variables is counted in the connector class after expanding all records, operator records, and arrays to a set of scalars of basic types.

For example, the following connector class is illegal in Modelica 3.0 and later versions but was legal in Modelica 2.2:

```
connector NotValid  // Illegal connector, one flow and two potential
  Real r1;
  Real r2;
  flow Real r3;
end NotValid;
```

The connector class balancing restriction is discussed in more *detail* in Section 5.7.7, page 217, including several larger examples.

It is still not easy to understand how the above connector class restriction can make the model balanced. We need to invoke another rule (Section 5.7.8.2, page 221) to make that happen:

- *A connection set is added* for each primitive (unconnected) flow variable as an *inside* (Section 5.7.1, page 208) connector.

A connection set for an unconnected *inside* flow variable will give rise to a set-to-zero equation. If the variable is connected there will be a connection equation. In any case there will be an equation for each flow variable, *n* equations if there are *n* flow variables. There will also be one zero-sum equation for all outside flows according to Kirchhoff's current law. Finally there will be *n*-1 equations corresponding to the n-1 connections between the n potential variables, giving a total of 2*n* equations for the 2*n* variables, *n* flow and *n* potential. This is demonstrated in the following example model.

```
// C10 must have the same number of potential and flow variables.
connector C10
  Real e;
  flow Real f;
end C10;

model M10
  C10 c1, c2, c3, c4;
equation
  connect(c1, c2);
  connect(c2, c3);
```

```
    connect(c3, c4);
  end M10;
```

The model M10 will expand into the following:

```
  class M10expanded  // 8 variables and 8 equations
    Real c1.e;
    Real c1.f;
    Real c2.e;
    Real c2.f;
    Real c3.e;
    Real c3.f;
    Real c4.e;
    Real c4.f;
  equation
    // Unconnected inside connector flows
    c1.f = 0.0;
    c2.f = 0.0;
    c3.f = 0.0;
    c4.f = 0.0;
    // Equality equations for potential variables
    c1.e = c2.e;
    c1.e = c3.e;
    c1.e = c4.e;
    // Zero-sum equation for flows, in this case all outside connectors
    -c1.f + -c2.f + -c3.f + -c4.f = 0.0;
  end M10expanded;
```

The model M10 is not a simulation model, that is, it cannot be simulated. This is not surprising since it just consists of four connectors connected in series, with two open endings. Moreover, it is not connected to a ground-like model instance. The model has three equations involving the four potential variables and five equations involving the four flow variables, which makes the model unsolvable.

8.9.2.4 Locally Balanced

A model or block class is *locally balanced* if the *local number of unknowns* is identical to the *local equation size* for all *legal* values of constants and parameters. The legal values of constants and parameters (which are always constant during simulation) must obey possible `final` prefixes and min/max-restrictions of those declarations.

Modelica tools should verify the *locally balanced* property for the *actual values* of parameters and constants in the particular simulation model being checked.

It is a quality of implementation for a Modelica tool how well this property is verified in general for arbitrary legal constant and parameter values, due to arrays of (locally) undefined sizes, conditional declarations, for-loops, and so on.

8.9.2.5 Globally Balanced

The property of a model being *globally balanced* is similar to being locally balanced, but includes *all unknowns and equations* from *all instances* in the model.

The *global number of unknowns* is computed by expanding all unknowns, excluding parameters and constants, into a set of scalar variables of primitive types. It is defined as the sum of the following items below, but could also be done by summing the local number of unknowns and the local equation system sizes for all model instances in the model.

- The number of equations defined, including equations in *any model instance* and equations generated from connect-equations.
- The number of input and flow-variables present *in* each (top-level) public connector variable.

- The number of (top level) public input variables that *neither* are connectors *nor* have binding equations, i.e., such top-level input are treated as known variables that are assumed to be set by the environment (Section 3.11.3, page 101).

The number of unknowns and the number of equations should be equal globally for the whole model. The following restrictions hold for globally balanced models:

- In a nonpartial model, all *non-connector variables* with prefix `input` within model instances *must* have *binding equations* (Section 8.9.2.2, page 390). For example, if the model contains an instance, e.g., `inst`, and `inst` contains `input Real u`, then there must be a binding equation for `inst.u`. This is because input variables are assumed to have known values, and these values must be defined somewhere using binding equations.
- An instance declared with the `inner` or `outer` prefix must not be an instance of a class having top-level public connectors containing inputs. This restriction is present to avoid introducing complex semantic rules for the combination of `input` and `inner/outer`, for which no use-case yet has been found.
- A nonpartial model may *not* contain an instance of a partial model.
- In a declaration of an instance of a record, connector, or simple type, *modifiers* can be applied to any element. These modifiers are also considered for the equation count since they are equations. For example: `Flange support(phi=phi2, tau=torque1+torque2) if useSupport;` If the condition `useSupport=true` there are two equations for `support.phi` and `support.tau` provided via the modifiers.
- In *other cases*, that is, declaration of an instance of a model or block type, modifiers on extends, and modifier on short-class-definitions: modifiers for instances shall only contain redeclarations of replaceable elements and binding equations. The binding equations in modifiers for instances may in these cases only be for parameters, constants, inputs, and variables having a default binding equation.
- *All nonpartial model and block classes must be locally balanced*, that is, the local number of unknowns equals the local equation size.

Based on the above restrictions, the following statement can be given for simulation models (see also Section 3.11.3, page 101, regarding simulation models):

- *All simulation models are globally balanced.*

Therefore, the number of unknowns is equal to the number of equations of a simulation model. Moreover, without being globally balanced it would not simulate.

8.9.3 Balanced Model Examples

Below we present three examples of balanced models and how the balancing conditions are checked by counting variables and equations in the models. The models are presented roughly in order of increasing complexity:

- `Capacitor` model
- `Circuit` model
- `SimpleAir` medium model
- `DynamicVolume` medium model
- `FixedBoundary_pTX` medium model

8.9.3.1 Balancing Analysis for Capacitor

The following is a very simple `Capacitor` model which illustrates the basics of performing checks on model balancing.

```
connector Pin
  Real v;
  flow Real i;
end Pin;

model Capacitor
  parameter Real C;
  Pin  p, n;
  Real u;
equation
  0 = p.i + n.i;
  u = p.v - n.v;
  C*der(u) = p.i;
end Capacitor;
```

The model `Capacitor` is a locally balanced model according to our analysis below. These five local variables can be found in the model:

```
p.i, p.v, n.i, n.v, u
```

The following three local equations can be extracted from the equation section:

```
0 = p.i + n.i;
u = p.v - n.v;
C*der(u) = p.i;
```

Two equal-to-zero equations as below are implicitly generated from the connection sets of the two (unconnected) *inside* flow-variables `p.i` and `n.i`. If they would be connected there would also be two equations, but different. In either case there will be two equations.

```
p.i = 0;
n.i = 0;
```

Thus, there are five equations and five unknowns in the model which makes it locally balanced.

If the equation `u = p.v - n.v` would be missing in the `Capacitor` model, there would be four equations and five unknowns and the model would be *locally unbalanced*. Simulation models in which such a model is used would usually not be solvable.

If the equation `u = p.v - n.v` would be replaced by the equation `u = 0` and the equation `C*der(u) = p.i` would be replaced by the equation `C*der(u) = 0`, there would be five equations and five unknowns, i.e., the equation system would be *locally balanced*. However, the system of equations would be *singular* (not solvable) regardless of how the equations corresponding to the flow-variables are constructed because the two equations would be two variants of almost the same equation setting `u` equal to a constant value, that is, since integrating `der(u)=0` would give `u` = some constant value.

8.9.3.2 Balancing Analysis for Circuit

The second example, the `Circuit` model, is also very simple. It contains a `Capacitor` as previously but also adds a `Circuit`, inheritance from the partial model `TwoPin`, connections between connectors, and an instance `tp` within `Circuit`. Note that `tp` is an instance of a *replaceable partial model*.

```
connector Pin
  Real v;
  flow Real i;
end Pin;

partial model TwoPin
```

```
  Pin p,n;
end TwoPin;

model Capacitor
  parameter Real C;
  extends TwoPin;
  Real u;
equation
  0 = p.i + n.i;
  u = p.v - n.v;
  C*der(u) = p.i;
end Capacitor;

model Circuit
  extends TwoPin;
  replaceable TwoPin tp;
  Capacitor c(C=12);
equation
  connect(p, tp.p);
  connect(tp.n, c.p);
  connect(c.n, n);
end Circuit;
```

Since `tp` in `Circuit` is an instance of a partial model it is not possible to check whether `Circuit` is a *globally balanced model*. The reason is that it does not fulfill all the conditions for globally balanced models in Section 8.9.2.5.

However, we can still check whether the model is *locally balanced*, and count variables and equations. Regarding variables, there are eight local variables according to the following analysis:

- Four variables from the connectors `p` and `n`: `p.i, p.v, n.i, n.v`—according to the rule "count variables declared inside `connector` instances".
- Two flow variables for `tp`: `tp.p.i, tp.n.i`—according to the rule "count variables, with prefixes `input` or `flow` which belong to public (top level) *connectors* within local instances of `model`, `class`, or `block`", here the connectors `p` and `n` in the local instance `tp`.
- Two flow variables *for* `c`: `c.p.i, c.n.i`—according to the rule "count variables with prefixes `input` or `flow` which belong to public (top level) *connectors* within local instances of `model`, `class`, or `block`," here connectors `p` and `n` in the local instance `c`.

There are eight local equations in the `Circuit` model according to the following analysis:

- Six equations from the expanded connect-equations:

```
  p.v = t.p.v;           // from connect(p, tp.p);
    0 = p.i-t.p.i;

c.p.v = load.n.v;        // from connect(tp.n, c.p)
    0 = c.p.i+load.n.i;

  n.v = c.n.v;           // from connect(c.n, n)
    0 = n.i-c.n.i;
```

- Two implicitly generated equal-to-zero equations from the (unconnected) flow variables `p.i, n.i` or alternatively two expanded connection equations if they are connected.

```
p.i = 0
n.i = 0
```

In total we have eight scalar unknowns and eight scalar equations, that is, this is a *locally balanced model*. It is quite nice that the local balancing property holds in general for *any* model used for the replaceable instance `tp`.

8.9.3.3 Balancing Analysis for the SimpleAir Medium Model

The third example is slightly more complex. It is a medium model containing a partial model `BaseProperties` which is inherited by `SimpleAir` being a special case of a medium.

```
import SI = Modelica.SIunits;

partial model BaseProperties
  "Interface of medium model for all types of media"

  connector InputAbsolutePressure = input SI.AbsolutePressure;
  connector InputSpecificEnthalpy = input SI.SpecificEnthalpy;
  connector InputMassFraction = input SI.MassFraction;

  parameter Boolean preferredMediumStates=false;
  constant  Integer nXi "Number of independent mass fractions";
  InputAbsolutePressure      p;        // input
  InputSpecificEnthalpy      h;        // input
  InputMassFraction          Xi[nXi];  // input;  The sum of fractions is 1
  SI.Temperature             T;
  SI.Density                 d;
  SI.SpecificInternalEnergy u;
end BaseProperties;
```

The use of connectors in the `BaseProperties` model is an example of a special *modeling pattern* which can be useful in many similar cases.

The instances `p`, `h`, and `Xi` are marked as `input` to get the correct equation count. Since they are connectors they should neither be given binding equations in derived classes inheriting `BaseProperties` nor when using `BaseProperties` to create instances.

The *idea* behind the modeling pattern is to give textual equations for them (as below). Using connect-equations for these connectors would be possible (and would work) but is not part of this modeling pattern.

This partial model defines that `T,d,u` can be computed from the medium model, provided that `p,h,Xi` are given. Each medium with one or more substances and one or more phases, including incompressible media, has the property that `T,d,u` can be computed from `p,h,Xi`, or from `p`, `h` if there is only one substance/phase and `nXi=0`. We use `nXi=0` below for one substance to get fewer equations but the same result. Using `nXi=1` would just involve `Xi[1]=1`, i.e., a factor 1 that can be eliminated anyway.

A particular medium may have different "independent variables" from which all other intrinsic thermodynamic variables can be recursively computed. For example, a simple air model could be defined as follows:

```
model SimpleAir "Medium model of simple air. Independent variables: p,T"
  extends BaseProperties(nXi = 0,
       p(stateSelect = if preferredMediumStates then StateSelect.prefer
                                                 else StateSelect.default),
       T(stateSelect = if preferredMediumStates then StateSelect.prefer
                                                 else StateSelect.default));
  constant SI.SpecificHeatCapacity R  = 287;
  constant SI.SpecificHeatCapacity cp = 1005.45;
  constant SI.Temperature          T0 = 298.15;
equation
  d = p/(R*T);
  h = cp*(T-T0);
  u = h - p/d;
end SimpleAir;
```

The local number of unknowns in the `SimpleAir` model after expansion is `5+nXi` as follows:

- Three variables—the `T`, `d`, `u` variables defined in `BaseProperties` and inherited into `SimpleAir`.
- 2+`nXi` variables—the `p`, `h`, `Xi[nXi]` variables in connectors defined in `BaseProperties` and inherited into `SimpleAir`.

The local equation count below is 5+`nXi` which is the same as the obtained variable count:

- Three equations—the equations defined in the equation section of `SimpleAir`.
- `2+nXi` equations—implicitly generated from the input variables in the connectors inherited from `BaseProperties`.

Therefore the model `SimpleAir` is locally balanced.

What about possible global balancing of this model (Section 8.9.2.5, page 393)? The connector variables `p`, `T`, and `Xi[nXi]` in `SimpleAir` which are inherited from `BaseProperties` are all inputs. Input variables are expected to implicitly obtain their values from the environment if not given explicitly.

However, to obtain a model that can be simulated we explicitly provide the properties of air at a given temperature and pressure in the model `AirProperties1` using explicit equations and in `AirProperties2` using modifier equations.

```
model AirProperties1
  SimpleAir air;
  SI.Temperature T_amb   "Ambient temperature";
  SI.Pressure p_amb      "Ambient pressure";
equation
  T_amb = 273.15 + 20;
  p_amb = 101325;
  air.p = p_amb;
  air.T = T_amb;
end AirProperties1;
```

The model `AirProperties2` provides ambient temperature and pressure through modifier equations.

```
model AirProperties2
  SimpleAir air(p = p_amb, T = T_amb);
  SI.Temperature T_amb   "Ambient temperature";
  SI.Pressure p_amb      "Ambient pressure";
equation
  T_amb = 273.15 + 20;
  p_amb = 101325;
end AirProperties2;
```

8.9.3.4 Balancing Analysis for the DynamicVolume Medium Model

The generic medium model `BaseProperties` can be used as a *replaceable* model in different usage models, like a dynamic volume or a fixed boundary condition.

These use cases are exemplified by the parameterized model `DynamicVolume`, shown in this section, and the model `FixedBoundary_pTX` presented below in Section 8.9.3.5, page 399. Both models are parameterized in terms of the choice of medium with the default medium being defined by the partial model `BaseProperties`.

Such models can be checked for local balancing but not for global balancing since they contain the instance `medium` of the partial model `Medium`.

```
import SI = Modelica.SIunits

connector FluidPort
  replaceable model Medium = BaseProperties;

  SI.AbsolutePressure  p;
  flow SI.MassFlowRate m_flow;

  SI.SpecificEnthalpy      h;
  flow SI.EnthalpyFlowRate H_flow;

  SI.MassFraction       Xi      [Medium.nXi] "Independent mixture mass fractions";
```

```
  flow SI.MassFlowRate mXi_flow[Medium.nXi] "Independent subst. mass flow rates";
end FluidPort;

model DynamicVolume
  parameter SI.Volume V;
  replaceable model Medium = BaseProperties;
  FluidPort port(redeclare model Medium = Medium);
  Medium    medium(preferredMediumStates=true); // No modifiers for p,h,Xi
  SI.InternalEnergy U;
  SI.Mass           M;
  SI.Mass           MXi[medium.nXi];
equation
  U   = medium.u*M;
  M   = medium.d*V;
  MXi = medium.Xi*M;
  der(U)   = port.H_flow;    // Energy balance
  der(M)   = port.m_flow;    // Mass balance
  der(MXi) = port.mXi_flow;  // Substance mass balance

// Equations binding to medium (inputs)
  medium.p  = port.p;
  medium.h  = port.h;
  medium.Xi = port.Xi;
end DynamicVolume;
```

The local number of unknowns of `DynamicVolume` is `8+4nXi` given from the following:

- `4+2*nXi` variables—from inside the `port` connector.
- `2+nXi` variables—the variables `U`, `M` and `MXi[nXi]`.
- `2+nXi` variables—the input variables in the connectors of the `medium` model.

The number of local equations is also `8+4nXi` as follows:

- `6+3*nXi` equations from the equation section.
- `2+nXi` implicitly generated equations from the flow variables in the `port` connector.

`DynamicVolume` is therefore a *locally balanced* model.

An interesting observation can be made for this example regarding state selection (Section 18.2.6, page 1014) and *computational causality* (Section 2.7, page 36, and Section 3.11.3, page 101).

When the `DynamicVolume` is used and the replaceable `Medium` model is redeclared to a concrete model such as `SimpleAir`, then a Modelica tool will try to select `p` and `T` as states. The reason is that these variables have the `StateSelect.prefer` property in the `SimpleAir` model which implies that the default states `U,M` are derived quantities. If this state selection is performed all intrinsic `medium` variables will be computed from `medium.p` and `medium.T`, although `medium.p` and `medium.h` are the arguments with `input` prefix in the medium model instance called `medium` in `DynamicVolume`.

This demonstrates that in Modelica `input` and `output` prefixes do not always necessarily define the *computational causality*. Instead they require that equations have to be provided here for `p,h,Xi` in order for the equation count to be correct and the model properly balanced. The actual computational causality can be different from the prefixes in certain situations which is demonstrated with the `SimpleAir` model.

8.9.3.5 Balancing Analysis for the FixedBoundary_pTX Medium Model

The model `FixedBoundary_pTX` defines fixed boundary conditions for the medium by defining pressure `p`, temperature `T`, and mass fractions `Xi`, thereby the suffix `pTX` in the model name. The model is parameterized in terms of the choice of medium and can be *checked* for *local balancing* but *not* for *global balancing* since it contains the instance `medium` of the partial model `Medium`.

Regarding the use of semiLinear (Section 8.8.1, page 386), this is used to handle reversing flows in a numerically stable way. If the mass flow port.m_flow is positive (into the connector), then semiLinear will return port.m_flow*port.h, whereas if the flow is negative it returns port.m_flow*medium.h. This works well for one-to-one connections. For connections with more than one connector connected the use of stream connectors (Section 5.10, page 245) is more robust.

```
model FixedBoundary_pTX
  parameter SI.AbsolutePressure p "Predefined boundary pressure";
  parameter SI.Temperature      T "Predefined boundary temperature";
  parameter SI.MassFraction    Xi[medium.nXi] "Predefined boundary mass fraction";
  replaceable model Medium = BaseProperties;
  FluidPort port(redeclare model Medium = Medium);
  Medium medium;
equation
  port.p          = p;
  port.H_flow     = semiLinear(port.m_flow, port.h , medium.h);
  port.MXi_flow = semiLinear(port.m_flow, port.Xi, medium.Xi); // Vector eq

// Equations binding parameters to medium (note: T is not an input)
  medium.p  = p;
  medium.T  = T;
  medium.Xi = Xi;    // Vector equation
end FixedBoundary_pTX;
```

The number of local variables in FixedBoundary_pTX is 6+3*nXi:

- 4+2*nXi variables—from inside the port connector.
- 2+nXi variables—the input variables in the connectors of the medium model.

The number of local equations in the model is 6+3*nXi, the same as the number of variables, based on the following:

- 4+2*nXi equations from the equation section—4 scalar equations and 2 array equations involving (some of) the vectors Xi, medium.Xi, port.Xi, and port.MXi_flow.
- 2+nXi implicitly generated equations from the flow variables in the port connector.

Therefore, FixedBoundary_pTX is a *locally balanced* model. The predefined boundary variables p and Xi are provided via equations to the input arguments medium.p and medium.Xi. Additionally, there is an equation for T in the same way, even though T is not an input.

Depending on the flow direction, either the specific enthalpy in the port (port.h) or h is used to compute the enthalpy flow rate H_flow. The variable h is provided in a binding equation to the medium. With the equation medium.T = T, the specific enthalpy h of the reservoir is indirectly computed via the medium equations.

Once more this demonstrates that inputs often just define the number of equations that have to be provided, but not necessarily define the computational causality.

8.10 Partial Differential Equations[14]

Before reading this section you should be aware of that parts of this section present Modelica design work in progress. There is a new Modelica indomain construct mentioned in this section that is not part of standard Modelica. Consult the book web page for the current status, since this preliminary design of

[14] This section includes the usage of a generalized indomain operator that at the time of this writing is not accepted in the Modelica language specification. See the book web page at www.openmodelica.org for future updates.

PDEs in Modelica will change. However, the `spatialDistribution` operator described in Section 8.10.3, page 412, is part of the Modelica language since version 3.3.

The kind of equations that can be directly represented in Modelica models in the current version of the language are hybrid differential algebraic equations, hybrid DAEs (see Chapter 17, page 979), containing algebraic relations and differential equations with time derivatives that might be conditionally active. The quantities in such models are just functions of time, and do not vary depending on spatial position.

On the other hand, many physical phenomena are dependent on quantities that are physically distributed and therefore functions of spatial coordinates. Typical examples of such quantities are temperature distributions in a material, electromagnetic field strength, material density, tension, and so on. In fact, the kind of variables that have no spatial variation are typically approximations of distributed real variables, for example, by computing the mean value of the quantity over some region.

Equations expressing relations involving variations of quantities over spatial coordinates, for example, x and y, usually involve derivatives with respect to those coordinates, so-called partial derivatives. Systems of equations including both *partial differential equations* and hybrid DAEs can be denoted *hybrid PDAEs* or even *HPDAEs*.

Partial derivatives of both space variables and time appear in the heat flow equation (8-6) below:

$$\frac{\partial u}{\partial t} - c\left(\frac{\partial^2 u}{\partial x^2} + \frac{\partial^2 u}{\partial y^2}\right) = f \qquad (x,y) \in \Omega \tag{8-6}$$

Here the quantity u, denoting the temperature at the position $\{x,y\}$ in the material, is a dependent variable being a function of the time t and the independent 2D spatial coordinate variables x and y, that is, $u(t, x, y)$. Such a function defined over a certain region is called a *field*.

The quantities `c` and `f` are constant model parameters in the following models but could also be functions of x and y. The derivatives occurring in the equation include a time derivative, $\partial u / \partial t$, and two second-order partial derivatives $\partial^2 u / \partial x^2$ and $\partial^2 u / \partial y^2$ with respect to the independent space variables x and y of the field. By introducing the `pder()` partial differentiation operator as an ordinary user-defined function, partial derivatives can be represented in Modelica according to Table 6-1. Using this notation, equation (8-6) will appear as follows:

```
der(u)-c*(pder(u,D.x2)+pder(u,D.y2)) = f
```

Ideally, we would have preferred a Modelica notation such as `pder(u,x,1)` and `pder(u,x,2)` for $\partial u / \partial x$ and $\partial^2 u / \partial x^2$, respectively. Since this is not possible in the current Modelica language, we instead use `pder(u,D.x)` and `pder(u,D.x2)` or `pder(u,x=1)` and `pder(u,x=2)`, which come quite close in terms of notation.

Table 8-1. Partial differentiation operators applied to the 2D field u up to the second degree. Since a notation such as pder(u,x,2) cannot be realized in the current Modelica language, we use pder(u,D.x2) or pder(u,x=2) instead. The first representation is used here, and the second in Section 8.10.5.

Operator	Modelica Representation 1	Modelica Representation 2
$\partial u / \partial x$	`pder(u,D.x)`	`pder(u,x=1)`
$\partial^2 u / \partial x^2$	`pder(u,D.x2)`	`pder(u,x=2)`
$\partial u / \partial y$	`pder(u,D.y)`	`pder(u,y=1)`
$\partial^2 u / \partial y^2$	`pder(u,D.y2)`	`pder(u,y=2)`
$\partial^2 u / \partial x \partial y$	`pder(u,D.xy)`	`pder(u,x=1,y=1)`
$\partial u / \partial t$	`der(u) or pder(u,D.t)`	`der(u)`

In the first `pder()` representation we use literal constants from `D=enumeration(x,x2,y,y2,xy,t)` to indicate the order and variable for differentiation. In the second variant, used in Section 8.10.5, the function `pder(fieldname,x,y)` lets the two integer formal parameters x and y specify the differentiation order of the derivative with regards to the first and second independent space variable x and y of the field u. The formal parameters to `pder()` should have the *same* names as the *independent space variables* of the field.

Equation (8-6) holds on a region with some geometric shape. Such a region is called the *domain* of the PDE problem. In the two-dimensional heat flow problem depicted in Figure 8-7 the domain has rectangular shape.

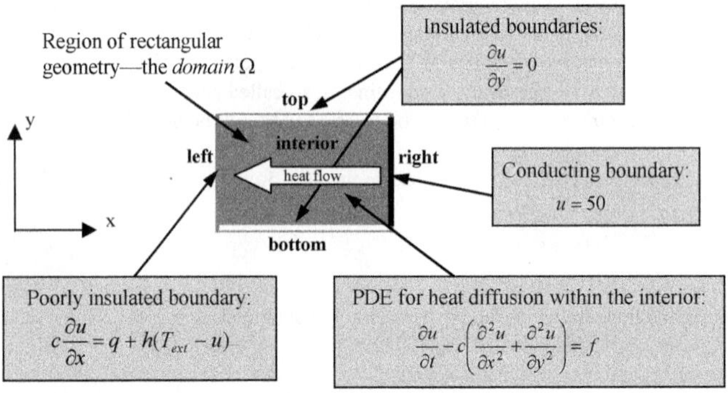

Figure 8-7. A PDE defined on the rectangular domain Ω, i.e., a rectangular geometry for the region where the PDE is defined, with insulated boundaries at the top and bottom, a poorly insulated boundary to the left, and a conducting boundary to the right. The PDE refers to the temperature field *u(time,x,y)* and *c*, *q*, *h*, *f*, and T_{ext}. which in this example are constant parameters, but in general could be functions of *x* and *y*. Heat flows from right to left since the external temperature T_{ext} is only 20°C, i.e., cooler than the right boundary.

In Figure 8-7 we observe that certain equations, so-called *boundary conditions*, apply at the four different boundary segments of the domain. The *top* and *bottom* boundaries are insulated, that is, there is no heat flow through the boundaries, and $\partial u / \partial y = 0$. The *right* boundary is conducting. It keeps a fixed temperature $u = 50$ °C at the boundary. The left boundary is poorly insulated and therefore allows some heat leakage through the boundary, since the external temperature T_{ext} has the lower value 20°C compared to the 50°C of the right boundary. We should also mention that equation (8-6) can be stated somewhat more compactly using the *gradient* (∇) and *divergence* ($\nabla\cdot$) differential operators defined in (8-7) below:

$$\frac{\partial u}{\partial t} - \nabla\cdot(c\nabla u) = f \qquad \text{in } \Omega \tag{8-7}$$

This equation coul be represented in Modelica using the functions `gradient()` and `divergence()`:

```
der(u) - divergence(c*gradient(u)) = f          indomain  Omega;
```

Here we have used the 2D vector definitions of the gradient and divergence differential operators:

$$\nabla \equiv \begin{pmatrix} \partial/\partial x \\ \partial/\partial y \end{pmatrix} \text{ gradient} \qquad \nabla\cdot \equiv \begin{pmatrix} \partial/\partial x & \partial/\partial y \end{pmatrix} \text{ divergence} \tag{8-8}$$

8.10.1 Structuring a PDE Problem

After the introductory example in the previous section we are now ready to define the structure of a PDE problem in general. We have a *result* to be computed based certain *problem elements*:

- Compute a *field*—that is, a function of time and the independent (spatial) coordinates, returning a real number—a *scalar* field, or multiple real numbers—e.g. a *vector* field.

- The field computation is based on the following PDE *problem elements*:

1. A partial differential equation (PDE).
2. A *domain*, i.e., the region on which interior the PDE is defined.
3. *Boundary conditions*, defined on the boundary of the domain.
4. Initial conditions.

Our PDE heat diffusion problem on a rectangular domain, previously depicted in Figure 8-7, can be formulated as follows according to this structure:

- *Field*: $u(t,x,y)$ to be solved for.

- $PDE: \dfrac{\partial u}{\partial t} - c\left(\dfrac{\partial^2 u}{\partial x^2} + \dfrac{\partial^2 u}{\partial y^2}\right) = f \qquad (x,y) \in \Omega_{\text{interior}}$

- A *domain* Ω, in this case the interior of a rectangle: $(0 < x < L_x,\ \ 0 < y < L_y)$.

- *Boundary conditions*:

$$\begin{array}{lll} \text{left}: & c\dfrac{\partial u}{\partial x} = q + h(T_{ext} - u) & x = 0 \\ \text{right}: & u = 50 & x = L_x \\ \text{top}: & \dfrac{\partial u}{\partial y} = 0 & y = L_y \\ \text{bottom}: & \dfrac{\partial u}{\partial y} = 0 & y = 0 \end{array}$$

- Initial condition: $u(t,x,y) = 0 \qquad t = 0,\ \ (x,y) \in \Omega$

The obvious question is how such a problem could be expressed in Modelica. We will first show the boundary conditions:

```
c*pder(u,D.x) = q + h*(T_ext - u);      // left
u = 50,                                 // right
pder(u,D.y) = 0;                        // top
pder(u,D.y) = 0;                        // bottom
```

In the next section, we turn to the problem of how to represent the geometry information of the domain as well as the field itself. We will *include* the *boundaries* in the full domain representation, since both boundaries and the interior then can be extracted by simple subset operations. The main PDE equation is however only applied at the interior of the domain as it should be.

8.10.1.1 Basic Definitions of Domain, Field, Boundary, and Interior

We recapitulate some definitions:

- *Domain*—region (with some geometry) on which the whole PDE *problem* is defined.
- *Field*—function of time (except for stationary problems) and independent spatial variables. This function is the desired solution to the PDE problem.

- *Boundary*—subset of the domain (usually with one dimension less than the domain) on which the boundary conditions are defined.
- *Interior*—subset of the domain on which the "main PDE" is defined.

It is desirable to have a general approach for constructing domains, applicable to 1D, 2D, or 3D regions, with one, two, or three independent spatial variables respectively.

A domain is a geometrical object that can be constructed in various ways. For example:

- Defining a domain from a *mesh* data structure, e.g. created by some external tool.
- Defining a domain using a discrete *grid* (i.e., array) representation— where a set of points on the grid belong to the domain.
- Defining a domain as the region enclosed by two points (the 1D case), by a *parametric curve* (the 2D case), or a *parametric surface* (the 3D case). If we want to specify both the interior points and the boundaries, a *parametric function* with 1, 2, or 3 arguments, for the 1D, 2D, or 3D cases respectively, can be used to generate all points in the interior or on the boundary. The geometric shape of a domain often needs a *composition* of several parts or segments to be completely defined.

The first approach is typically used by finite-element method (FEM) tools that solve PDE problems on domains represented by meshes usually consisting of triangles (2D, see Figure 8-13, page 414) or pyramidal shapes (3D). The second approach is commonly used by tools and solution schemes based on finite difference PDE solution methods, shown in several of the following examples.

The third approach is often used when domains have simple shapes that are easy to describe mathematically, e.g. lines, rectangles, circles, cubes, spheres, etc., or regions consisting of a combination of those. It is also used when high-accuracy scalable (to arbitrary resolution) domain definitions are needed, for example, in high resolution 3D graphics. Arbitrary scalable shapes can be described by parametric spline polynomials (called Nurbs in the OpenGL graphic standard). When needed, grids or meshes can be generated automatically based on parametric function domain definitions, and discretization parameters.

- We should emphasize that our *final goal* is to allow the definition of domains and fields in Modelica models to be completely *independent* of low level implementation details such as grids or meshes, even though this is only partially (or not at all) realized for the examples in the following.

8.10.1.2 The Method of Lines Approach to Spatial Discretization

In the so-called *method of lines* the PDE equations and boundary conditions are discretized on a grid over the independent spatial variables, but not over the independent time variable. Thus each remaining variable is a function of time only:

- All partial derivatives are expanded and approximated by sets of algebraic equations and differential equations at discrete points in space, yielding a set of DAEs that usually can be solved (for well-posed problems) using the current Modelica language.

See also the discretization example with a PDE solution for pressure distribution in 1D ducts described in Section 15.9, page 875, as another example of using the method of lines.

As an example, regard the boundary condition at the bottom of the rectangular region previously shown in Figure 8-7:

$$\frac{\partial u(t)}{\partial y} = 0 \qquad y = 0 \qquad (8\text{-}9)$$

We would like to solve the PDE problem described in Section 8.10.1, for example, by discretizing the domain and the equations on a grid as shown in Figure 8-8.

The boundary condition (8-9) can be discretized along the bottom boundary, by expressing the condition at several discrete points (u is still time-dependent, but not shown in the formulas):

$$\frac{\partial u(x=x_1)}{\partial y}=0, \quad \frac{\partial u(x=x_2)}{\partial y}=0, \quad \frac{\partial u(x=x_3)}{\partial y}=0, \quad \ldots \quad \frac{\partial u(x=x_{nx})}{\partial y}=0 \tag{8-10}$$

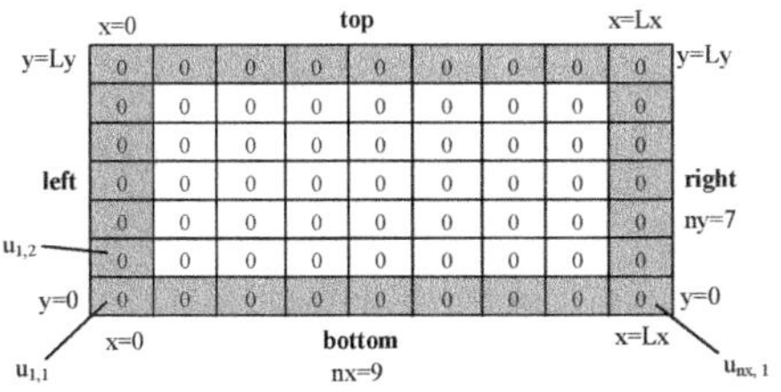

Figure 8-8. DomainRectangle2D is a rectangular domain spanned by rect2Dfunc. We also show a grid discretization with `nx=9`, `ny=7`, on which a field containing zeroes is defined. The elements u_{11}, u_{12}, and $u_{nx,1}$ of the discretized field represented as a matrix are specially marked. The boundary elements of the grid are shown in grey color.

The derivatives in (8-10) can for example be approximated using the following simple first-order differences:

$$\frac{u_{12}-u_{11}}{\Delta y}=0, \quad \frac{u_{22}-u_{21}}{\Delta y}=0, \quad \frac{u_{32}-u_{31}}{\Delta y}=0, \quad \ldots \quad \frac{u_{nx,2}-u_{nx,1}}{\Delta y}=0 \tag{8-11}$$

For example, here $u_{12}-u_{11}$ is the field value difference between the two vertically adjacent elements at the lower left corner, and Δy is the difference in y-coordinate between those elements. The resulting variables $u_{11}, u_{12}, \ldots$ in equation (8-11) are all functions of time, as is it should be using the method of lines.

One should be aware of the fact that numerical stability problems can occur for certain combinations of PDEs, boundary conditions, step sizes, and numerical approximation method. Consult the literature concerning relevant results for the method-of-lines. See also the comment on numerical diffusion in Section 8.10.3, page 412.

However, 1D PDEs have already been used successfully in Modelica libraries since several years, e.g. in the `Modelica.Fluid` library (Section 16.12, page 957), using method-of-lines approximations similar in style to the example in Section 15.9, page 875. The 1D problem formulations shown here look much nicer, but expands to the same kind of discretized equations.

8.10.1.3 Range and Domain Geometry Types and Generalized *indomain* Operator

We will need range types that are used in the following models to represent parameter ranges of arguments to shape functions that define the boundary (and interior) points of a domain.

```
type Range1D = Real[2]   "Defines 1D ranges {{x1,x2}}";
type Range2D = Real[2,2] "Defines 2D ranges {{x1,x2},{y1,y2}}";
type Range3D = Real[3,2] "Defines 3D ranges {{x1,x2},{y1,y2},{z1,z2}}";
```

The following unspecified types represent the data structures used for discretized domains (e.g., meshes or grids) in 1, 2, and 3 dimensions respectively.

```
type DomainGe1D = ... "Domain Geometry representation for 1D domains";
type DomainGe2D = ... "Domain Geometry representation for 2D domains";
type DomainGe3D = ... "Domain Geometry representation for 3D domains";
```

We sometimes also need a generalized `indomain` operator to express that an equation holds on a domain or on a subset of a domain. For example, the equation below holds on `omega.interior` which is a subset of `omega`:

```
der(u) = pder(u,D.x2)+ pder(u,D.y2)      indomain omega.interior;
```

8.10.1.4 Summary of Operators and Types Needed for PDEs in Modelica

We have in the preceding sections introduced several operators and types needed for PDE representation in Modelica, and demonstrated their application to a 2D heat diffusion problem on a rectangular domain. It can be useful to summarize the needed features (Table 8-2):

Table 8-2. Operators and data structures, their usage and realization for PDEs in Modelica.

Operators and Data structures	*Usage*	*Modelica Realization*
`pder()`	Partial derivatives.	User defined Modelica function with inline semantics.
Generalized `indomain` operator	Mathematical style syntax for expressing on which domain or part of a domain a PDE or boundary condition applies to.	Not yet standard. Language extension needed.
Grid functions	Grid or mesh dependent alternative to the `indomain` operator for expressing on which domain or part of a domaina PDE or boundary condition applies to.	User defined Modelica functions with inline semantics.
`Domain` data structures	Geometry of region or boundaries on which a PDE problem is defined.	Record or array data structure.
`Field` data structure	Representation of the solution to the PDE problem as a "function" of independent spatial variables and time.	Record or array data structure.
Shape functions	Define the geometry of a domain with boundaries in a way that is independent of low-level grid or mesh approximations.	User defined Modelica functions.
`spatialDistribution`	Modeling of 1D PDE problems for variable-speed transport of properties.	Part of Modelica 3.3 or later.

Note that *inline semantics* is needed for the `pder()` function and the grid functions. This means that the functions compute results in exactly the same way as any Modelica function, but is expanded inline, that is, the function call is replaced by the returned expression. This makes it possible to put calls to such a function at places where function calls are usually not allowed. Most Modelica environments support inline semantics for functions where the function body is a single assignment with the inlined expression as its right hand side.

8.10.2 Modelica PDE Examples of Domains, Fields, and Models in 1D, 2D, and 3D

In the following four subsections we will show partial examples of PDE problem definitions in Modelica for 2D, 1D, 2D, and 3D problems, respectively. We start with our familiar heat diffusion problem on a rectangular domain.

8.10.2.1 Modelica Heat Diffusion Model on a Rectangular Domain

We are now ready to formulate a Modelica model of the heat diffusion PDE problem described in Section 8.10.1, page 403, and in Figure 8-7. The model instantiates a domain `omega` and a field `u` defined on this domain. The domain and field have the types `DomainRectangle2D` and `FieldRectangle2D`, respectively.

```
model HeatRectangle2D
  // Uses non-standard Modelica indomain operator
  import SI= Modelica.SIunits;
  replaceable package DifferentialOperators = DifferentialOperators2D;
  import DifferentialOperators.pder;
  parameter Integer nx = 50, ny = 50;
  parameter Real    Lx = 2, Ly = 1;
  parameter DomainRectangle2D  omega(nx=nx, ny=ny, Lx=Lx,  Ly=Ly,
                                     FieldValueType=SI.Temperature);
  parameter Real    c = 1;
  parameter Real    q = 1;
  parameter Real    h = 1;
  parameter Real    T_ext = 20  "External temperature";
  FieldRectangle2D  u(domain=omega);
equation
  der(u) = pder(u,D.x2)+ pder(u,D.y2)    indomain omega.interior;
  c*pder(u,D.x) = q + h*(T_ext-u);       indomain omega.left;
  u = 50;                                indomain omega.right;
  pder(u,D.y) = 0;                       indomain omega.top;
  pder(u,D.y) = 0;                       indomain omega.bottom;
end HeatRectangle2D;
```

The model is still incomplete since the package `DifferentialOperators2D` is not yet available, (one operator is however shown in Section 8.10.5.1, page 418), and the record `GeomRect` for shape parameters is not declared.

The domain type `DomainRectangle2D` for rectangular geometries can be defined as a record:

```
record DomainRectangle2D
  parameter Integer nx = 50, ny = 50;
  parameter Real    Lx = 2, Ly = 1;
  replaceable function shapeFunc = rect2Dfunc;
  replaceable record Ge = GeomRect "Record with rect geometry information";
  DomainGe2D bottom(shape=shapeFunc,range={{0,Lx},{0,0}},
                    geom=Ge(nx,ny,Lx,Ly));
  DomainGe2D right( shape=shapeFunc, range={{Lx,Lx},{0,Ly}},
                    geom=Ge(nx,ny,Lx,Ly));
  DomainGe2D top(   shape=shapeFunc, range={{0,Lx},{Ly,Ly}},
                    geom=Ge(nx,ny,Lx,Ly));
  DomainGe2D left(  shape=shapeFunc, range={{0,0},{0,Ly}},
                    geom=Ge(nx,ny,Lx,Ly));
  DomainGe2D interior(shape=shapeFunc, range={{0,Lx},{0,Ly}},
                    geom=Ge(nx,ny,Lx,Ly));
end DomainRectangle2D;
```

The boundaries as well as the interior are represented by instances of the DomainGe2D data structure. The parametric shape function returning {x,y} can generate all points in the domain or in subsets of the domain such as the interior and the boundary segments bottom, right, top, and left, by letting the inputs vary over the specified ranges for the function arguments v1 and v2. In this case the shape function is the trivial identity function rect2Dfunc, but in other cases the mapping can be nontrivial.

```
function rect2Dfunc  "2D Identity function to span rectangular region"
  input  Real v1, v2;
  output Real x := v1;
  output Real y := v2;
algorithm
end rect2Dfunc;
```

Finally, we define the field type FieldRectangle2D used for the field u in the above HeatRectangle2D model. The actual field values, being subtypes of Real, are stored in the val attribute, here a matrix. The field is initially zero over the whole domain.

```
record FieldRectangle2D
  parameter DomainRectangle2D domain;
  replaceable type FieldValueType = Real;
  replaceable type FieldType = FieldValueType[domain.nx,domain.ny];
  parameter FieldType  start = zeros(domain.nx,domain.ny);
  FieldType            val;  // Actual field values
end FieldRectangle2D;
```

In the following three sections we will show simple examples of a heat diffusion models with temperature fields defined on 1D, 2D, and 3D domains respectively. We also assume that the following import clause is present for these models.:

```
import SI = Modelica.SIunits;
```

For simplicity, we use grid representations of the domains in these examples. However, other data structures could be used. For example, the 2D and 3D models could instead be formulated based on an external mesh representation.

8.10.2.2 One-dimensional Domains

A 1D domain is can be specified by its length, for example, as depicted in Figure 8-9.

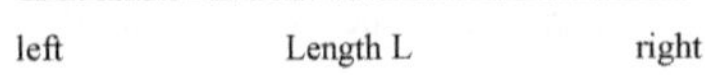

Figure 8-9. DomainLine1D can be used for one-dimensional domains like rods.

The domain data structure DomainLine1D is defined using a shape function over a range, but in this case specialized to a grid representation. An instance rod with length L=2, and nx=100 discretization intervals is declared:

```
DomainLine1D rod(L=2, nx=100);
```

The heat diffusion PDE with boundary conditions can be stated in the following way:

$$
\begin{aligned}
&\frac{\partial u}{\partial t} = \frac{\partial^2 u}{\partial x^2} && x \in \Omega_{\text{interior}} \\
&u = 20\sin(\pi \cdot t/12) + 300 && x \in \Omega_{\text{left}} \qquad (8\text{-}12) \\
&\frac{\partial u}{\partial x} = 0 && x \in \Omega_{\text{right}}
\end{aligned}
$$

The corresponding Modelica heat diffusion model is defined on the 1D line geometry of a rod, where we use `rod` instead of `omega` for the domain name:

```
model HeatLine1D
  import DifferentialOperators1D.pder;
  parameter DomainLine1DGrid rod;
  FieldLine1DGrid           u(domain=rod, FieldValueType=SI.Temperature);
equation
  der(u)   = pder(u,D.x2)           indomain  rod.interior;
  u = 20*sin(PI*time/12)+300        indomain  rod.left;
  pder(u,D.x) = 0                   indomain  rod.right;
end HeatLine1D;
```

The Modelica model `DomainLine1DGrid` with `interior` and two boundaries `left` and `right`:

```
record DomainLine1DGrid   "Domain being a line segment region"
  parameter SI.Length  L   = 1;
  parameter Integer    nx  = 100;
  replaceable function shapeFunc = line1Dfunc  "Span 1D line region";
  replaceable record Ge = GeomLine "Record with geometry information";
  DomainGe1D  interior(shape=shapeFunc,range={{0,L}},geom=Ge(nx,L));
  DomainGe1D  left(shape=shapeFunc,range={{0,0}},geom=Ge(nx,L));
  DomainGe1D  right(shape=shapeFunc,range={{L,L}},geom=Ge(nx,L));
end DomainLine1DGrid;
```

The trivial identity parametric function that spans a line region:

```
function line1Dfunc  "1D identity function to span line region"
  input  Real v;
  output Real x := v;
algorithm
end line1Dfunc;
```

The field `FieldLine1DGrid` with a grid representation (a vector) of the field values:

```
record FieldLine1DGrid
  parameter DomainLine1DGrid domain(L=1, nx=100);
  replaceable type FieldValueType = Real;
  replaceable type FieldType  = FieldValueType[domain.nx];
  parameter FieldType  start  = zeros(domain.nx);
  FieldType            val;  // Actual field values
end FieldLine1DGrid;
```

8.10.2.3 Two-dimensional Domains

Two-dimensional domains have two independent spatial variables, for example, x and y if Cartesian coordinates are used. A simple 2D domain is the circular region depicted in Figure 8-10. Mapping to polar coordinates would have been natural in this special case. However, here we just want to illustrate the shape function approach using a simple 2D domain, and keep the Cartesian coordinates for simplicity.

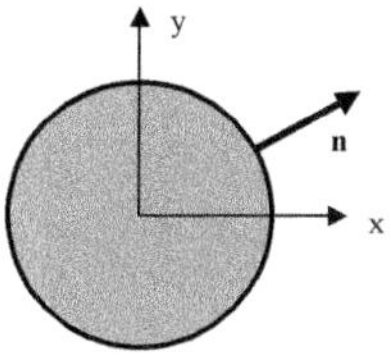

Figure 8-10. DomainCircular2D domain spanned by the shape function circular2Dfunc. The normal vector **n** of the boundary is used for the normal vector derivative operator `nder()`.

We state the two-dimensional version of the heat diffusion equation, with the boundary condition expressed as the partial derivative along the normal vector **n** perpendicular to the boundary:

$$
\begin{aligned}
&\frac{\partial u}{\partial t} = \frac{\partial^2 u}{\partial x^2} + \frac{\partial^2 u}{\partial y^2} && (x, y) \in \Omega_{\text{interior}} \\
&\frac{\partial u}{\partial \mathbf{n}} = 0 && (x, y) \in \Omega_{\text{boundary}}
\end{aligned}
\tag{8-13}
$$

This problem can be specified in a model, using the operators `pder()` and `nder()` imported from the package `DifferentialOperators2D`:

```
model HeatCircular2D
  // Uses non-standard Modelica indomain operator
  import DifferentialOperators2D.*;
  parameter DomainCircular2DGrid   omega;
  FieldCircular2DGrid       u(domain=omega, FieldValueType=SI.Temperature);
equation
  der(u)   = pder(u,D.x2)+ pder(u,D.y2)    indomain omega.interior;
  nder(u)  = 0                              indomain omega.boundary;
end HeatCircular2D;
```

The shape of the circular domain is defined by a general parametric shape function `circular2Dfunc`. This selects a circular subset of the grid representation of the domain.

```
record DomainCircular2DGrid  "Domain being a circular region"
  parameter Real radius    = 1;
  parameter Integer nx     = 100;
  parameter Integer ny     = 100;
  replaceable function shapeFunc = circular2Dfunc  "2D circular region";
  DomainGe2D  interior(shape=shapeFunc,range={{0,radius},{0,1}},geom=...);
  DomainGe2D  boundary(shape=shapeFunc,range={{radius,radius},{0,1}},geom=);
  function shapeFunc = circular2Dfunc    "Function spanning circular region";
end DomainCircular2DGrid;
```

The parametric shape function spanning a circular region:

```
function circular2Dfunc  "Spanned circular region for v in range 0..1"
  input  Real r,v;
  output Real x,y;
algorithm
  x := r*cos(2*PI*v);
  y := r*sin(2*PI*v);
end circular2Dfunc;
```

Finally, we declare the field type using a grid representation of values on the circular domain. Note that we are not using polar coordinates in this particular grid example.

```
record FieldCircular2DGrid
  parameter DomainCircular2DGrid domain;
  replaceable type FieldValueType = Real;
  replaceable type FieldType = Real[domain.nx,domain.ny,domain.nz];
  parameter FieldType  start = zeros(domain.nx,domain.ny,domain.nz);
  FieldType            val;  // Actual field values
end FieldCircular2DGrid;
```

8.10.2.4 Three-dimensional Domains

The third example illustrates the heat diffusion problem on a three-dimensional domain. We choose a spherical domain for simplicity, but keep Cartesian coordinates instead of switching to spherical coordinates, since this shape could be replaced by a shape with more complicated geometry.

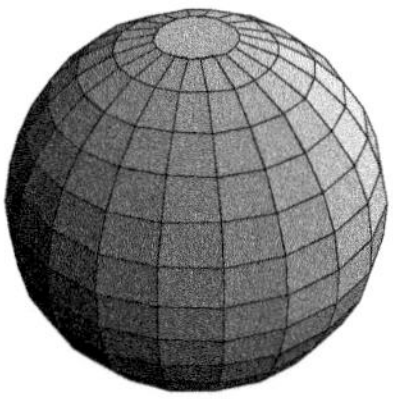

Figure 8-11. The spherical DomainSphere3D domain is spanned by the shape function sphere3Dfunc. The normal vector `n` of the boundary is used to define the normal vector derivative operator `nder()`.

The PDE is similar to the 2D case, but with three partial derivative since there are three independent spatial variables of this domain:

$$
\begin{aligned}
&\frac{\partial u}{\partial t} = \frac{\partial^2 u}{\partial x^2} + \frac{\partial^2 u}{\partial y^2} + \frac{\partial^2 u}{\partial z^2} && (x,y,z) \in \Omega_{\text{interior}} \\
&\frac{\partial u}{\partial \mathbf{n}} = 0 && (x,y,z) \in \Omega_{\text{boundary}}
\end{aligned}
\qquad (8\text{-}14)
$$

The 3D heat diffusion problem in a sphere expressed in the `HeatSphere3D` Modelica model:

```
model HeatSphere3D
  import DifferentialOperators3D.*;
  parameter DomainSpherical3DGrid   omega;
  FieldSphere3DGrid        u(domain=omega, FieldValueType=SI.Temperature);
equation
  der(u)  = pder(u,D.x2)+pder(u,D.y2)+pder(u,D.z2)   indomain omega.interior;
  nder(u) = 0                                         indomain omega.boundary;
end HeatSphere3D;
```

The interior and boundary parts of the spherical domain are characterized as follows:

- Interior: $0 \le r < radius$
- Boundary: $r = radius$

The corresponding domain type declaration is:

```
record DomainSphere3DGrid  "Domain spanning a sphere, with grid parameters"
  parameter Real radius   = 1;
  parameter Real nx    = 100; // Gives x discretization, for fields on grid
  parameter Real ny    = 100; // Gives y discretization, for fields on grid
  parameter Real nz    = 100; // Gives z discretization, for fields on grid
  function shapeFunc = sphere3Dfunc "Function spanning the sphere";
  DomainGe3D  interior(shape=shapeFunc,{{0,radius},{0,1},{0,1}},geom=...);
  DomainGe3D  boundary(shape=shapeFunc,{{radius,radius},{0,1},{0,1}},geom=);
end DomainSphere3DGrid;
```

And the parametric shape function spanning the spherical domain is:

```
function sphere3Dfunc  "Span a Sphere for u,v in range 0..1, r in 0..R"
  input  Real r,u,v;
  output Real x,y,z;
algorithm
  x := r*sin(2*PI*v)*cos(2*PI*u);
  y := r*sin(2*PI*v)*sin(2*PI*u);
  z := r*cos(2*PI*v);
end sphere3Dfunc;
```

Finally, we declare the field on the spherical domain as a Modelica data structure, using a grid representation of the field data:

```
record FieldSphere3DGrid  "Field on a Sphere with Cartesian grid"
  parameter DomainSphere3DGrid domain;
  replaceable type FieldValueType = Real;
  replaceable type FieldType=FieldValueType[domain.nx,domain.ny,domain.nz];
  parameter FieldType  start=zeros(domain.nx,domain.ny,domain.nz);
  FieldType            val;  // Actual field values
end FieldSphere3DGrid;
```

8.10.3 PDEs on 1D Domains Using the spatialDistribution Operator

Many applications involve the modeling of variable-speed transport of properties. One option to model this one-dimensional PDE system is to approximate it by an ODE using the method of lines described in Section 8.10.1.2, page 404, but this requires a large number of state variables and in some cases might introduce either numerical diffusion (reference in Section 8.12, page 418) or numerical oscillations. Numerical diffusion tends to create more diffusion in the simulation than in the real physical system due to the constraint that the computed quantity has to be represented on a finite grid.

Another option is to use a built-in operator that keeps track of the spatial distribution of *z(y, t)*, by suitable sampling, interpolation, and shifting of the stored distribution. In this case, the internal state of the operator is hidden from the ODE solver.

The Modelica `spatialDistribution()` operator allows to efficiently approximate the solution of the following 1D PDE problem:

$$\begin{aligned}
&\frac{\partial z(y,t)}{\partial t} + v(t)\frac{\partial z(y,t)}{\partial y} = 0.0 \\
&z(0.0,t) = in_0(t)\ if\ v \geq 0 \\
&z(1.0,t) = in_1(t)\ if\ v < 0
\end{aligned} \tag{8-15}$$

Here *z(y, t)* is the transported quantity, *y* is the normalized spatial coordinate ($0.0 \leq y \leq 1.0$), *t* is the time, *v*(*t*)=`der`(*x*) is the normalized transport velocity and the boundary conditions are set at either $y = 0.0$ or $y = 1.0$, depending on the sign of the velocity. The calling syntax is as follows:

```
(out0, out1) = spatialDistribution(in0, in1, x, positiveVelocity
                                   initialPoints = {0.0, 1.0},
                                   initialValues = {0.0, 0.0});
```

Here `in0`, `in1`, `out0`, `out1`, `x`, `v` are all Real or subtypes of Real, `positiveVelocity` is a Boolean, `initialPoints` and `initialValues` are equal-sized arrays of Real elements, containing the y coordinates and the *z* values of a finite set of points describing the initial distribution of *z*(*y, t0*). The `out0` and `out1` are given by the solutions at *z(0.0, t)* and *z(1.0, t)*; and `in0` and `in1` are the boundary conditions at *z(0.0, t)* and *z(1.0, t)* (at each point in time only one of `in0` and `in1` is used).

Elements in the `initialPoints` array must be sorted in nondescending order, that is, elements increasing or equal in value. The operator cannot be vectorized according to the vectorization rules described in Section 7.10, page 340. It can be vectorized only with respect to the arguments `in0` and `in1` (which must have the same size), returning vectorized outputs `out0` and `out1` of the same size; the arguments `initialPoints` and `initialValues` are vectorized accordingly.

The solution, z(...), can be described in terms of a characteristics *z(y,t)*, for all β, as long as staying inside the domain:

$$z(y,t) = z(y + \int^{t+b} v(a)da, t + b) \tag{8-16}$$

This allows us to directly compute the solution based on interpolating the boundary conditions. The `spatialDistribution` operator can be described in terms of the pseudo-code given as a block:

```
block spatialDistribution
  input Real in0;
  input Real in1;
  input Real x;
  input Boolean positiveVelocity;
  parameter Real initialPoints(each min=0, each max=1)[:] = {0.0, 1.0};
  parameter Real initialValues[:] = {0.0, 0.0};
  output Real out0;
  output Real out1;
protected
  Real points[:];
  Real values[:];
  Real x0;
  Integer m;
algorithm
  if positiveVelocity then
    out1:=interpolate(points, values, 1-(x-x0));
    out0:=values[1];   // similar to in0 but avoiding algebraic loop
  else
    out0:=interpolate(points, values, (x-x0));
    out1:=values[end]; // similar to in1 but avoiding algebraic loop
  end if;
  when acceptedStep then
    if x>x0 then
      m:=size(points,1);
      while (if m>0 then points[m]+(x-x0)>=1 else false) then
        m:=m-1;
      end while;
      values:=cat(1, {in0}, values[1:m],
                     {interpolate(points, values,1-(x-x0))} );
      points:=cat(1, {0}, points[1:m] .+ (x1-x0), {1} );
    elseif x<x0 then
      m:=1;
      while (if m<size(points,1) then points[m]+(x-x0)<=0 else false) then
        m:=m+1;
      end while;
      values:=cat(1,
        {interpolate(points, values, 0-(x-x0))}, values[m:end],{in1});
      points:=cat(1, {0}, points[m:end] .+ (x1-x0), {1});
    end if;
    x0:=x;
  end when;
initial algorithm
  x0:=x;
  points:=initialPoints;
  values:=initialValues;
end spatialDistribution;
```

The PDE problem stated above can then be formulated in the following way:

```
der(x) = v;
(out0,out1) = spatialDistribution(in0, in1, x, v>=0, initialPoints,
                                                     initialValues);
```

Events are generated at the exact instants when the velocity changes sign. If this is not needed, `noEvent()` can be used to suppress event generation. If the velocity is known to be always positive, then `out0` can be omitted, for example, as follows:

```
der(x) = v;
```

```
(,out1) = spatialDistribution(in0, 0, x, true, initialPoints,initialValues);
```

Technically relevant use cases for the use of the spatialDistribution() operator are modeling of electrical transmission lines, pipelines and pipeline networks for gas, water and district heating, sprinkler systems, impulse propagation in elongated bodies, conveyor belts, and hydraulic systems. Vectorization is needed for pipelines where more than one quantity is transported with velocity v in the example above.

8.10.4 A PDE on a 2D Domain with General Shape and FEM Solution

Many realistic domains have more complicated shapes (see Figure 8-12) than the simple lines, circles, spheres, rectangles, and so on, presented in the previous sections. Such shapes are usually specified by a mesh in two or three dimensions (e.g., left part of Figure 8-13), which has been created by a special mesh-generating tool.

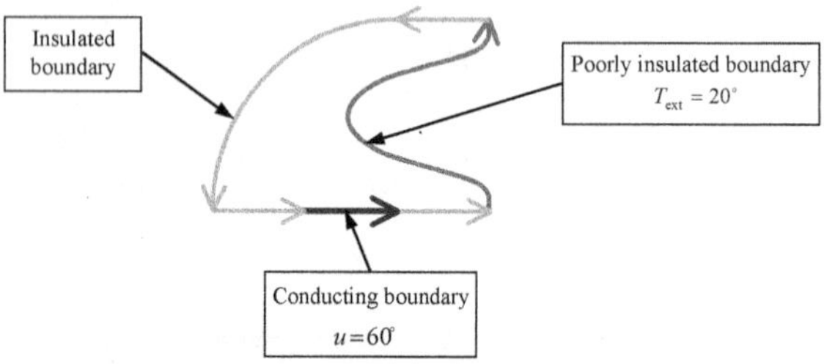

Figure 8-12. Heat diffusion problem on a 2D domain with complicated geometry, and boundary sections which are insulated, poorly insulated, or conducting.

The heat diffusion problem has been modeled in a PDE extension of Modelica similar to the approach outlined in the previous sections, but with an external mesh defining the geometry. An external PDE solver using the finite element method (FEM) was employed to produce the solution depicted in Figure 8-13 (right).

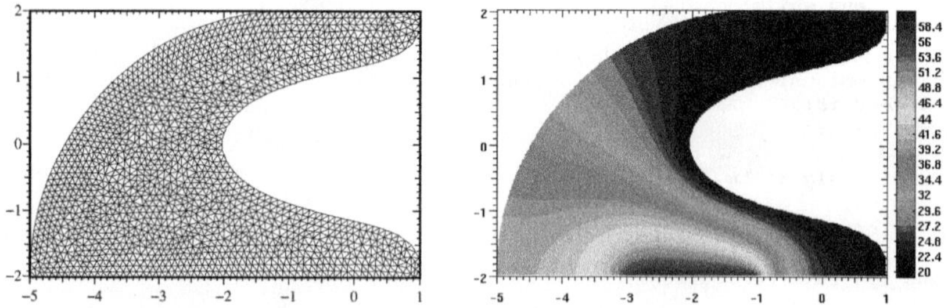

Figure 8-13. Solution of a 2D heat flow problem specified in a PDE extension of Modelica on a domain with complicated shape. The shape is defined by an external mesh (left). The problem is solved using a version of the finite element method (FEM). The solution is shown to the right.

8.10.5 Grid Function Finite Difference Approach to 1D Heat Diffusion

In the previous Modelica PDE examples we have relied on an extension called `indomain` related to the `in` operator in Modelica to express which part of the domain an equation applies to (here using the second `pder()` representation in Table 4-1), e.g., using the non-standard `indomain` operator:

```
der(u)   = pder(u,x=2)               indomain  rod.interior; //non-standard
u = 20*sin(PI*time/12)+300           indomain  rod.left;
pder(u,x=1)  = 0                     indomain  rod.right;
```

Another approach is to use so-called *grid functions*, common in many finite difference packages. A grid function applies some operation to a field defined on a grid, including arithmetic operations and selection operations such as `left`, `right`, or `interior`, that return part of a field. Using grid functions, the above equations can be expressed as follows:

```
interior(der(u.val)) = interior(4*pder(u.val,x=2));
left(u.val) = 20*sin(PI/12*time) + 300;
right(pder(u.val,x=1)) = 0;
```

Here we need to use `u.val` instead of `u`, since the `der()` operator currently is not defined for records. The use of overloaded function and operator definitions (Section 9.5, page 481) would remove that restriction.

The whole model appears as follows, and can be executed in ordinary Modelica using function inlining:

```
model HeatDiffusion1D
  import SI=Modelica.SIunits;
  parameter SI.Length L=1;
  import Fields.*;
  import Domains.*;
  import FieldDomainOperators1D.*;
  import DifferentialOperators1D.*;
  constant Real PI=Modelica.Constants.PI;
  Domain1D rod(left=0, right=L, n=50);
  Field1D  u(domain=rod,
             redeclare type FieldValueType = SI.Temperature,
             start={20*sin(PI/2*x) + 300 for x in rod.x});
equation
  interior(der(u.val)) = interior(4*pder(u,x=2));
  left(u.val) = 20*sin(PI/12*time) + 300;
  right(pder(u,x=1)) = 0;
end HeatDiffusion1D;
```

The drawback is that part of the model has to be formulated in terms of the grid, and therefore is dependent on the domain and field data structures.

The grid functions `left`, `right`, and `interior` for field selection on the grid, are defined below:

```
package FieldDomainOperators1D  "Selection operators of field on 1D domain"

  function left "Returns the left value of the field vector v1"
    input  Real[:] v1;
    output Real    v2;
  algorithm
    v2:= v1[1];
  end left;

  function right "Returns the right value of the field vector v1"
    input  Real[:] v1;
    output Real    v2;
  algorithm
    v2 := v1[end];
  end right;
```

```
  function interior "Returns the interior values of the field as a vector"
    input  Real v1[:];
    output Real v2[size(v1,1)-2];
  algorithm
    v2 := v1[2:end - 1];
  end interior;

end FieldDomainOperators1D;
```

The domain and field definitions are:

```
package Domains
  import SI = Modelica.SIunits;
  record Domain1D "1D spatial domain"
    parameter SI.Length left=0.0;
    parameter SI.Length right=1.0;
    parameter Integer   n=100;
    parameter SI.Length dx   = (right-left)/(n-1);
    parameter SI.Length x[n] = linspace(right, left, n);
  end Domain1D;
end Domains;

package Fields
  record Field1D "Field over a 1D spatial domain"
    replaceable type  FieldValueType = Real;
    parameter Domains.Domain1D   domain;
    parameter FieldValueType  start[domain.n] = zeros(domain.n);
    FieldValueType            val[domain.n](start=start);
  end Field1D;
end Fields;
```

The differential operators for numerical approximations to the partial derivatives. Both first and second-order versions are available:

```
package DifferentialOperators1D  "Finite Difference differential operators"

  function pder "Returns vector of spatial derivative values of a 1D field"
    input  Fields.Field1D  f;
    input  Integer         x=1  "Diff order - first or second derivative";
    output Real            df[size(f.val, 1)];
  algorithm
    df := if x == 1 then SecondOrder.diff1(f.val, f.domain.dx)
          else SecondOrder.diff2(f.val, f.domain.dx);
  end pder;

  package FirstOrder  "First order polynomial derivative approximations"

    function diff1  "First derivative"
      input  Real u[:];
      input  Real dx;
      output Real du[size(u,1)];
    algorithm          //  Left, central, and right differences
      du := cat(1, {(u[2] - u[1])/dx}, (u[3:end] - u[1:end-2])/2/dx,
                   {(u[end] - u[end-1])/dx});
    end diff1;
  end FirstOrder;

  package SecondOrder  "Second order polynomial derivative approximations"

    function diff1 "First derivative"
      input  Real u[:];
      input  Real dx;
      output Real du[size(u,1)];
    algorithm
```

```
      du := cat(1, {(-3*u[1] + 4*u[2] - u[3])/2/dx },
                   (u[3:end]- u[1:end-2])/2/dx,
                   {(3*u[end] - 4*u[end-1] + u[end-2])/2/dx} );
    end diff1;

    function diff2  "Second derivative"
      input  Real u[:];
      input  Real dx;
      output Real du2[size(u,1)];
    algorithm
      du2 := cat(1, {(2*u[1] - 5*u[2] + 4*u[3] - u[4])/dx/dx },
                     (u[3:end] - 2*u[2:end-1] + u[1:end-2])/dx/dx,
                    {(2*u[end] - 5*u[end-1] + 4*u[end-2] - u[end-3])/dx/dx} );
    end diff2;
  end SecondOrder;
end DifferentialOperators1D;
```

We simulate and plot the `HeatDiffusion1D` model using the Mathematica command mode available in the Wolfram SystemModeler, with results as interpolation functions (Section 19.4.5.1, page 1052). The plot of the temperature profile is as follows at the fourth grid point (i.e., `x=0.08`), out of a total of `n=50` grid points.

```
res = WSMSimulate["HeatDiffusion1D",{0,1}];

uVal = res[{
"u.val[1]","u.val[2]", "u.val[3]", "u.val[4]", "u.val[5]", "u.val[6]",
"u.val[7]", "u.val[8]", "u.val[9]", "u.val[10]",
"u.val[11]","u.val[12]", "u.val[13]", "u.val[14]", "u.val[15]", "u.val[16]",
"u.val[17]", "u.val[18]", "u.val[19]", "u.val[20]",
"u.val[21]","u.val[22]", "u.val[23]", "u.val[24]", "u.val[25]", "u.val[26]",
"u.val[27]", "u.val[28]", "u.val[29]", "u.val[30]",
"u.val[31]","u.val[32]", "u.val[33]", "u.val[34]", "u.val[35]", "u.val[36]",
"u.val[37]", "u.val[38]", "u.val[39]", "u.val[40]",
"u.val[41]","u.val[42]", "u.val[43]", "u.val[44]", "u.val[45]", "u.val[46]",
"u.val[47]", "u.val[48]", "u.val[49]", "u.val[50]"
}];

Plot[uVal[[4]][t], {t, 0, 1}]
```

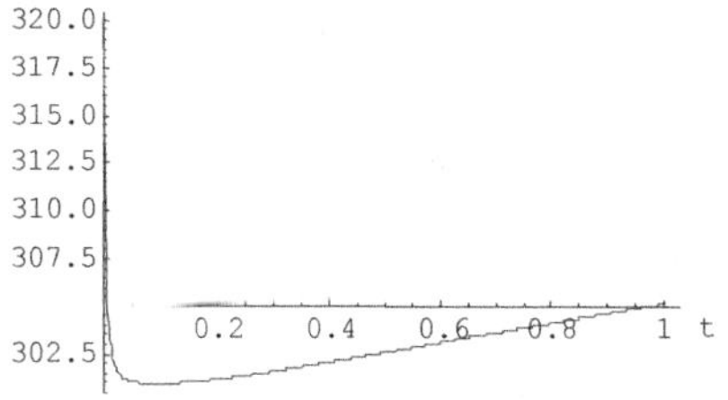

Figure 8-14. Plot of the temperature field u at fourth grid point for the HeatDiffusion1D model.

By forming an interpolated polynomial from the matrix representation of the solution, we can create a continuous 3D-plot of the solution as a function of both `x` and `time`, as depicted in Figure 8-15.

```
intp=Interpolation[
  Flatten[Table[{k,t,uVal[[k]][t]},{k,1,50,1},{t,0,1,0.1}],1]];

Plot3D[intp[x,t],{x,1,50},{t,0,1},PlotPoints->30,
  AxesLabel->{"x","t","u(x,t)"},ViewPoint->{-4,2.4,2}]
```

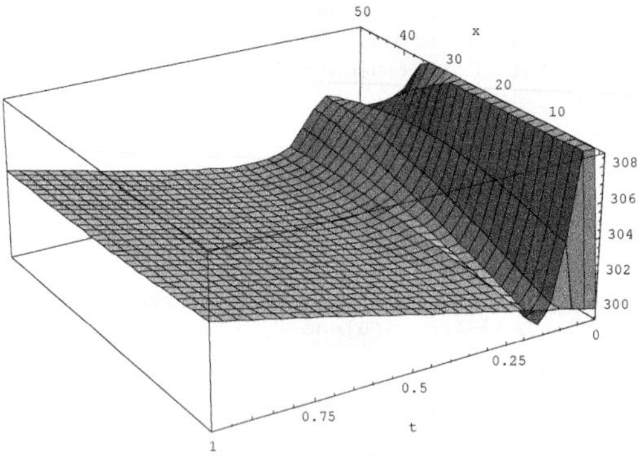

Figure 8-15. The temperature distribution field of the rod as a function of time and the spatial x coordinate—a solution to the HeatDiffusion1D problem.

8.10.5.1 2D Grid Functions

The grid function approach to modeling PDEs can of course be generalized to grids in two and three dimensions, grids for polar coordinates, etc. As an illustration, we show a 2D finite difference operator as a grid function for a 2D grid:

```
function diff22D "Second order finite difference operator on 2D grid"
  input Real u[:,:];
  input Real dx;
  output Real du2[size(u, 1), size(u, 2)];
algorithm
  du2 := cat(1, {(2*u[1,:] - 5*u[2,:] + 4*u[3,:] - u[4,:])/dx/dx},
                 (u[3:end,:] - 2*u[2:end-1, :] + u[1:end-2, :])/dx/dx,
            {(2*u[end,:] - 5*u[end-1,:] + 4*u[end-2,:] - u[end-3,:])/dx/dx});
end diff22D;
```

8.11 Summary

Equations are the foundation of Modelica. In this chapter we have presented the different forms of equations that can be expressed in Modelica, including normal mathematical equations, declaration equations, modification equations, and initial equations that are used to state equations for solving initialization problems. We have described several ways of specifying the initialization equation system together with some examples. We have also presented equation operators for overconstrained connection based equation systems that allows elimination of superfluous equations which would otherwise result from certain kinds of connection graphs, for example, certain graphs involving connection loops.

8.12 Literature

Equations can be found in any Mathematics textbook, whereas they are quite rare in programming language books. The description of Modelica equations in this chapter is primarily based on the Modelica language specification (Modelica Association 2003; Modelica Association 2013).

The description of initialization and the initial equation construct in Section 8.4 is to a large extent based on (Mattsson, Elmqvist, Otter, and Olsson 2002) both regarding the presentation and the examples.

Moreover, (Casella 2012) gives a description of steady-state initialization problems in object-oriented models of closed thermo-hydraulic systems, and (Sielemann 2012) presents robust initialization using homotopy. (Bachmann, Aronsson, and Fritzson 2006) presents a method for robust initialization of DAEs.

The presentation of overconstrained connection operators is based on (Otter, Elmqvist, and Mattsson 2003) and (Otter 2003).

The summary description in Section 8.7, page 383, (a more detailed version is available in Section 13.6, page 694), of the approach to synchronous clock-based equations and state machines in Modelica 3.3 is directly based on the text in Chapters 16 and 17 of (Modelica Association 2012) and was developed by Hilding Elmqvist, Martin Otter, Sven-Erik Mattson, Fabien Gaucher, Francois Dupont and Bernhard Thiele, as well as additional contributions, see (Elmqvist, Otter, and Mattsson 2012; Elmqvist, Gaucher, Mattsson, and Dupont 2012; Otter, Thiele, and Elmqvist 2012). It is based on the clock calculus and inference system proposed by (Colaco and Pouzet 2003) that was implemented in Lucid Synchrone version 2 and 3 (Pouzet 2006). However, the Modelica approach also uses multi-rate periodic clocks based on rational arithmetic introduced by (Forget et. al. 2008) as an extension to the Lucid Synchrone semantics. These approaches belong to the class of synchronous languages (Benveniste et al 2002).

The current Modelica approach to balanced model checking which required a rather large language change, is described in (Olsson, Otter, Mattsson, and Elmqvist 2008). A slightly earlier approach addressing almost the same issue, keeping track on the degree of balancing through the notion of structural constraint delta, is described in (Broman, Nyström, and Fritzson 2006).

Modelica PDE extensions and related work is presented in (Wrangsjö, Fritzson, and Sheshadri 1999; Saldamli and Fritzson 2001; Sheshadri and Fritzson 2001; Saldamli, Fritzson, and Bachmann 2002; Saldamli 2002; Elmqvist 2003a; Saldamli and Fritzson 2004; Saldamli, Bachmann, Wiesmann, and Fritzson 2005; Saldamli 2006). A method to import FEM-based PDE solvers into Modelica using FMI is presented in (Stavåker, Ronnås, Wlotzska, Heuveline, and Fritzson 2013). Automatic generation of inlined PDE solvers using explicit and implicit finite difference schemes together with a short discussion of stability criteria is presented in (Sheshadri and Fritzson 2003a; Sheshadri and Fritzson 2003b; Sheshadri and Fritzson 2011), whereas a similar approach using FEM is presented in (Sheshadri and Fritzson 2003c). Object oriented PDE software is described in (Mossberg, Otto, and Thuné 1997; Åhlander 1999; Langtangen 1999). The grid function approach is used in the Cogito system (Mossberg, Otto, and Thuné 1997), in the Overture system (Henshaw 2000), and recently in some Modelica examples (Jonasson, Elmqvist, Mattson, and Olsson 2003; Elmqvist 2003b). The topic of PDE numerical methods in general including stability criteria is presented in several books, e.g. (Gustafsson, Kreiss, and Oliger 1995) and (Ames 1992). Numerical diffusion mentioned for finite difference schemes used in method-of-lines is described in (Glover 2002).

8.13 Exercises

Exercise 8-1:

Question:

- What is specific about equations in Modelica?
- What is a declaration equation?
- What is a modifier equation?

Exercise 8-2:

Using the for-Loop: Write a class `Repetitive`, with an array rep, with 7 `Integer` values. The class should set all values in the array to 15, using a for-loop.

Without Using the for-Loop: Write the class `RepetitiveWithoutFor`, doing the same thing as `Repetitive` above, though not using a for-loop.

Exercise 8-3:

Using the for-Loop: This time write a class `Repeat`, with an array repeater containing 4 `Real` values. The values in the array shall be set to 1, 4, 7, 10, using a for-loop.

Function with for-Loop: Write a function, `Rapper`, which calculates the sum of the values in the array.

Write an instance, where the values of that array shall be set. Then simulate the instance class and plot the result.

Exercise 8-4:

Question: Why is it better not to have the same name on the variable in the iteration expression as a variable inside the for-clause in an equation?

Exercise 8-5:

Question: What is a hybrid model? What do hybrid models have to do with if- and when-equations?

Exercise 8-6:

Nested for-Loop: Write a function, `MatrixAddition`, for adding two two-dimensional matrices. Do a function call to `MatrixAddition` with two arrays. Then simulate the class with the function call and plot the result.

Chapter 9

Algorithms and Functions

Equations are very well suited for physical modeling, but there are situations in which computations are more conveniently expressed as algorithms, that is, sequences of instructions, also called statements. In this chapter, we describe the algorithmic constructs that are available in Modelica as well as the Modelica function concept.

Since this is the first point at which we introduce nondeclarative algorithmic constructs in Modelica, apart from the short introduction in Chapter 2, we start this chapter with a section containing a somewhat philosophical discussion about the difference between declarative and nondeclarative constructs and their pros and cons.

9.1 Declarative versus Nondeclarative Constructs

An algorithm is a recipe or stepwise procedural description containing instructions on *how* to achieve a certain goal. This is in contrast to declarative constructs such as equations and declarations, which describe *what* holds, for example, by stating relations and properties.

- An *algorithm* describes *how* to reach a certain goal.
- A *declarative* construct states and describes *what* the goal is.

So far, we have emphasized the advantages of declarative constructs such as equations in Modelica. It is usually more concise and understandable to use declarative constructs than algorithmic ones, which is why equations have a prominent role in mathematics. Algorithms have the disadvantage of often bringing a clutter of details. Also, it is usually not immediately clear what is the exact result of an algorithm, that is, what holds after the execution of an algorithm. Being declarative implies another important advantage:

- Declarative constructs are *referentially transparent*, that is, keep the same semantics or meaning independently of where they are referenced.

For example, a declarative construct such as an equation or an expression states a fact or computation that holds independently of where the construct is placed or referenced (for the moment ignoring details such as name scoping), that is, it is *transparent* with respect to where it is referenced. For example, it is possible to change the ordering within a set of equations without changing their meaning since they are referentially transparent. Consider the following systems of three equations:

```
x   = y+2;
z-3 = x+5;
```

```
y+8  = z;
```

The meaning, that is, the solution of this system of equations, is unchanged even if the equations are reordered as below since equations are referentially transparent. The solution is the same in both cases.

```
y+8  = z;
x    = y+2;
z-3  = x+5;
```

By contrast, if we change the placement order of nonreferentially transparent constructs like assignment statements, this usually changes their meaning and thereby introduces errors. For example, consider the following two assignment statements, where we assume that all variables have well-defined initial values before the statements are executed:

```
y := x-8;
x := y+2;
```

The result of executing these assignment statements is different if the order is changed, that is, the semantics or meaning of the group of statements has changed:

```
x := y+2;
y := x-8;
```

What is the case regarding the declarativity of functions in Modelica? Functions can be called from within expressions which are declarative. Therefore function calls must be declarative. On the other hand, a Modelica function can internally within its function body contain locally nondeclarative algorithmic constructs. We have the following situation:

- Modelica functions without the `impure` keyword (Section 9.3.14, page 462) are *call declarative*[15], that is, from the caller's point of view behave as *mathematical functions* meaning that the same function results are always returned given the same input argument values.

Thus, function calls are *referentially transparent*, whereas the statements inside a function body are not referentially transparent. The declarative behavior of function calls implies that functions have no memory (not being able to store values that can be retrieved in subsequent calls) and no side effects (e.g., no update of global variables and no input/output operations). The declarative behavior of function calls is actually a necessary (but not sufficient) prerequisite for guaranteeing the continuity and differentiability conditions required by the solver for solution of the continuous part of the total system of equations (see Section 9.3, page 438, regarding functions for further details).

After this list of disadvantages of algorithmic constructs, why bother introducing them in the Modelica language? After all, Modelica is supposed to be a mathematical modeling language.

The reason is that certain computations of algorithmic character are hard to express using only equations. This is typically the case for many numerical algorithms, whereas equations work well for modeling physical phenomena. We have earlier remarked that mathematics is mostly declarative. However, there is a branch of mathematics called constructive mathematics which has algorithmic flavor. Also, numerical analysis to a large extent deals with numerical algorithms for computation.

On the other hand, there exist declarative programming languages, for example, the pure functional language Haskell, in which any kind of algorithm can be expressed in a declarative way. Why does not Modelica incorporate the same facilities? The reasons are twofold. There is currently a performance penalty in implementations of pure functional languages that is not acceptable for Modelica since it is intended for large engineering applications where maximum performance is essential. The second reason

[15] There is currently an exception to this rule: impure Modelica functions called in when-equations/when-statements or during some parts of initialization are allowed to return different values at different calls. In certain when-equations/when-statements this is needed for communication with external systems, e.g. during hardware-in-the-loop simulation, but may eventually be replaced by a cleaner declarative construct. See also Section 9.3.14, page 41, regarding impure functions.

is that the special programming styles needed for pure functional algorithmic programming are not yet well-known in the intended user community for Modelica.

Despite not being a pure declarative language, Modelica still enjoys most of the advantages of a declarative language since function calls are declarative. In fact, a function call returning *n* result values can be viewed as a coupled subsystem of *n* equations and thus fits well together with the equation part of the Modelica language.

9.2 Algorithms and Statements

Algorithms are expressed as sequences of commands or instructions, henceforth called statements. Such statements may occur in algorithm sections and in function bodies.

9.2.1 Algorithm Sections

In Modelica, algorithmic statements can occur only within algorithm sections, starting with the keyword `algorithm`. Algorithm sections could also be called algorithm equations, since an algorithm section externally is treated as a group of equations involving one or more variables, and can appear among equation sections. An algorithm section is terminated by the appearance of one of the five keywords `equation`, `public`, `protected`, `algorithm`, `initial`, or `end`.

```
algorithm
  ...
  <statements>
  ...
<some keyword>
```

An algorithm section embedded among equation sections can appear as below, where the example algorithm section contains three assignment statements.

```
equation
  x = y*2;
  z = w;
algorithm
  x1 := z+x;
  x2 := y-5;
  x1 := x2+y;
equation
  u = x1+x2;
  ...
```

Note that the code in the algorithm section uses the values of certain variables from outside the algorithm section. These variables are so-called *inputs* to the algorithm section—in this example `x`, `y`, and `z`. Analogously, variables assigned values by the algorithm section define the *outputs* of the algorithm section—in this example `x1` and `x2`. This makes the semantics of an algorithm section quite similar to a function with the algorithm section as its body, and with `input` and `output` formal parameters corresponding to inputs and outputs as described above. Such inputs and outputs from operations on arrays and records are obtained by expanding them into scalars.

Regarding the size of the conceptual system of equations created by an algorithm section, see also the discussion in Section 8.9.2.2, page 390.

9.2.1.1 Execution of an Algorithm Section

An algorithm section is conceptually a code fragment that remains together. The statements of an algorithm section are executed in the order of appearance. This applies to algorithm sections in both models and functions.

However, for algorithm sections in models (not in functions) the following also applies: whenever an algorithm section is invoked, all variables appearing on the left hand side of the assignment operator := in assignment statements are initialized (at least conceptually):

- A non-discrete continuous-time variable is initialized with its start value (i.e., the value of the start-attribute).
- An unclocked discrete-time variable `v` is initialized with `pre(v)`.
- A clocked discrete-time variable `v` is initialized with `previous(v)`.
- If at least one element of an array appears on the left hand side of the assignment operator, then the complete array is initialized in this algorithm section.

Initialization of variables in an algorithm section *in a function* is not done automatically for performance reasons; if needed this must be done explicitly in the function.

Regarding algorithm sections *in models* (not in functions) the following also applies:

- Initialization of an algorithm section is performed in order that an algorithm section cannot introduce "memory" from one numerical solver iteration step to the next (except in the case of discrete states which are explicitly given), which could invalidate the assumptions of a numerical integration algorithm. Note that a Modelica tool may change the evaluation of an algorithm section provided the result is identical to the case as if the above conceptual processing is performed.
- To be more precise, from the point of view of the equational part of Modelica an algorithm section with *n* outputs is treated as an indivisible subsystem of *n* equations that are dependent on each other, i.e., each equation directly or indirectly depends on all inputs and all outputs of the algorithm section. This is identical to the treatment of an equation with a function call with *n* results, e.g.: `(lhs1, lhs2, ...) = someFunction(nonLhs1, nonLhs2, ...)` where `lhs` are the variables assigned by statements in the algorithm section and `nonLhs` are other appearing variables. See also Section 17.6 regarding BLT.

Below an example of initialization of algorithm sections based on start values:

```
model AlgTest  // wrong Modelica model; it has 4 equations for 2 unknowns
   Real x[2] (start={-11, -22});
algorithm
   x[1] := 1;     // conceptually: x becomes {1,-22}
algorithm
   x[2] := 2;     // conceptually: x becomes {-11,2}
end AlgTest;
```

9.2.1.2 Usage Constraints Related to Statements and Special Operators

All the statement types in Modelica can be used within algorithm sections, that is, simple assignment statements, assignment statements calling functions with multiple results, for-statements, while-statements, if-statements, when-statements, and the special statements `assert() and terminal()`. Multiple assignments to the same variable are allowed. Function bodies may not contain when-statements. Nested when-statements are not allowed, that is, when-statements may not contain when-statements. For additional details regarding constraints on when-statements, see Section 9.2.10, page 433.

One difference between algorithm sections and functions is that the following special operators and functions; `der()`, `edge()`, `change()`, `sample()`, `pre()`, `initial()`, `terminal ()`, `noEvent()`, and `smooth()`, as well as when-statements, which can be used in algorithm sections are *disallowed* in functions.

9.2.1.3 Local Initialization and Output Consistency

It is guaranteed that the outputs of an algorithm section always have well-defined values. This is achieved by initializing all conditionally assigned variables to their start-values (to initial default values regarding variables in functions) whenever the algorithm is invoked. For local variables or formal parameters to functions the initialization is instead given by the default initialization assignment of the corresponding variable declaration. Even if the conditional assignments are not executed, the variables will always have well-defined values. This eliminates the possibility of writing a function that uses some kind of memory from previous calls, which is one of the requirements of declarative function calls.

9.2.2 initial algorithm Sections

An *initial algorithm section* contains statements that are executed only during initialization, at the initial time, just before simulation starts. It is strongly related to initial equation sections, described in detail in Section 8.4, page 363. In fact, since most of the rules for initial algorithms are analogous to those for initial equations, we just give a short presentation here and refer the reader to the description of initial equations for remaining issues.

The syntax of an *initial algorithm section* is the same as for an algorithm section apart from using the keywords `initial algorithm` instead of just `algorithm`:

```
initial algorithm
  ...
  <statements>
  ...
<some allowed keyword>
```

The following holds for an initial algorithm section:

- Any kind of statement is allowed inside an initial algorithm section, *except* for when-statements.
- In the statements inside an initial algorithm section `der(x)` and `pre(v)` are treated as variables.
- All expressions inside an initial algorithm section have unclocked discrete-time variability (Section 6.9.3, page 281).

However, when-statements outside an initial algorithm section, but with `initial()` in the list of predicates, can contribute to the initialization (see Section 8.4.3, page 366, for analogous examples).

Below we show the use of an initial algorithm section to specify the initial value for a derivative, for a pre-value of a variable, and an ordinary variable. However, the first model `InitAlg1` is incorrect since `der()` and `pre()` are not allowed on left-hand sides of assignments. This restriction is not present for initial equation sections, as exemplified in the model `InitAlg2`.

```
model InitAlg1  "Erroneous initial algorithm model"
  Real  x, x2;
  discrete Real xd;
initial algorithm
  der(x)   := 0;  // Error! only variables on left-hand side of :=
  pre(xd)  := 5;  // Error! only variables on left-hand side of :=
  x2       := der(x)-10;
end InitAlg1;
```

This model has a correct initial algorithm section with variables on left-hand sides of assignments.

```
model InitAlg2  "Correct initial algorithm model"
  Real  x, x2;
  discrete Real xd;
initial algorithm
  x2      := der(x)-10;
initial equation
  der(x)   = 0;
  pre(xd)  = 5;
end InitAlg2;
```

9.2.3 Simple Assignment Statements

Simple assignment statements are probably the most common kind of statements in algorithm sections. use the term *simple* to distinguish from assignments of called functions with multiple results, which described in the next section.

The assignment operator `:=` is used to denote assignment to distinguish from the equation operato which is used in equations, and the equality operator `==` used for comparisons in `Boolean` expressions. assignment statement has the structure depicted below, where the value of an expression (*expr*) on right-hand side is assigned to a variable (*v*) on the left-hand side.

```
v := expr;
```

The causality is from the right-hand side to the left-hand side since data flows in that direction. One make several assignments to a variable within the same algorithm section.

The type constraint of assignment statements is that the type of the right-hand side (*expr*) must be a subtype of the type of the left-hand side (*v*). Additionally, `Integer` expressions are automatically converted to `Real` expressions when needed to fulfill the subtyping constraints. Thus one can assign an `Integer` value to a `Real` variable. More details regarding subtyping and assignment are available in Section 3.18 on page 115 in Chapter 3.

A few examples of assignment statements are shown below:

```
x       := 35 - y + 5;
y[3]    := sin(x)-14.31;
z.name  := "Maria";
x       := y[3]-1;
onoff   := false;
...
```

Assignment statements may also occur as initializers in the declaration of local variables (after the keyword `protected`) or formal parameters of Modelica functions. In the case of formal parameters the value of the expression on the right-hand side is just a default value that is used only if the corresponding argument is not supplied at the function call. Below is an example function `foo` containing a declaration of the local variable `y1` with an initializing assignment and the formal parameter `x` with a default value assignment:

```
function foo;
  input Real x := 2.0;
protected
  Real y1 := cos(1.84) + x - 1.2E-2;
end foo;
```

9.2.4 Assignments from Called Functions with Multiple Results

There is a special form of assignment statement that is used only when the right-hand side contains a call to a function with multiple results. The left-hand side contains a parenthesized, comma-separated list of variables receiving the results from the function call. A function with *n* results can have at most *n* receiving variables on the left-hand side; receiving variables can be omitted (Section 9.3.2.3, page 442).

```
(out1, out2, out3, ...) := function_name(in1, in2, in3, in4, ...);
```

For example, the function `f` called below has three results and two inputs:

```
(a, b, c) := f(1.0, 2.0);
(x[1], x[2], x[3]) := f(3,4);
```

The example function `f` has three results declared as three `output` formal parameters `r1`, `r2`, and `r3`:

```
function f
  input Real x;
  input Real y;
  output Real r1;
  output Real r2;
  output Real r3;
algorithm
  r1 := x;
  r2 := y;
  r3 := x*y;
end f;
```

9.2.5 Iteration Using for-statements

The *for-statement*, also called *for-loop*, is a convenient way of expressing iteration. This fits well when we know how to express the range of values, the *range-expression*, over which the *iteration-variable* should iterate. The general structure of a for-statement with a single iterator is shown below.

```
for iteration-variable in range-expression loop
  statements
end for;
```

The *range-expression* is a vector expression which is first evaluated *once* before the loop iteration starts and is evaluated in the scope immediately enclosing the for-loop. This scope is typically the class or function containing the algorithm section with the for-loop. The enclosing scope can also be another for-loop in case of nested loops. The rest of the for-loop is executed in the following way:

1. The *iteration-variable* is assigned the next element from the *range-expression* vector
2. The body (*statements*) of the for-loop is executed.
3. If there are no more elements in the range expression (or if a `break` statement, see Section 9.2.7, page 430, or `return` statement, see Section 9.3.2.6, page 444, is executed) the loop is exited, otherwise execution continues at step 1.

A very simple for-loop summing the five elements of the vector `z` within the class `SumZ`:

```
class SumZ
  parameter Integer n = 5;
  Real[n]  z(start = {10,20,30,40,50});
  Real sum;
algorithm
  sum := 0;
  for i in 1:n loop      // 1:5 is {1,2,3,4,5}
    sum := sum + z[i];
  end for;
end SumZ;
```

Below are some examples of for-loop headers with different range expressions:

```
for k in 1:10+2 loop            // k takes the values 1,2,3,...,12
for i in {1,3,6,7} loop         // i takes the values 1, 3, 6, 7
for r in 1.0 : 1.5 : 5.5 loop // r takes the values 1.0, 2.5, 4.0, 5.5
```

The *range-expression* can be any vector, i.e., a one-dimensional vector of elements of any type. For example, a vector of `String` values is allowed.

If the range-expression is created using a colon-based *range vector* constructor (Section 7.2.1, page 316) as in the above examples, it can be an `Integer` or `Real` vector, a vector of enumeration values of some enumeration type, or a `Boolean` vector. In the case of a vector of enumeration or `Boolean` values, the *type name* (e.g., `Boolean` or `Colors` in the example below) can be used to denote the range expression, meaning the full range from the `min`-to the `max`-value of the type in question. For example:

```
type Colors = enumeration(red, green, blue);
Real c[Colors];

for e in Colors loop // e takes values Colors.red, Colors.green, Colors.blue
for e in Colors.red : Colors.blue loop  // Same colors as previous
for e in Boolean loop  // e takes the values false, true
```

The example below uses the type name to represent the range vector as the range expression. We also demonstrate the conversion function `Integer`, converting from enumeration value to ordinal value. In this example the numbers `Integer(e)` become 1, 2, and 3, corresponding to `red`, `green`, and `blue`:

```
for e in Colors loop
```

```
    c[e] := 1.2 + 0.2*Integer(e);
  end loop;
```

The scope of the iteration variable is inside the for-statement. One may *not* make an assignment to such an iteration variable. For example:

```
  for i in 1:n loop       // Illegal for-loop, since
    sum := sum + z[i];
    i := i+1;            // the iteration variable i may not be assigned to!
  end for;
```

Since the scope of the iteration variable is the body of the for-statement, it may hide other variables with the same name, for example, the constant `k` declared in the class `HideVariable2`. Note that the `k` used in the iteration expression `1:k+1` is the constant `k` declared in the class, whereas the `k` used in the statements inside the for-loop is the iteration variable `k`. It is recommended to avoid this style of programming even if it is legal since it is confusing and hard to read such code.

```
  class HideVariable2
    constant Integer k=4;
    Real      z[k+1];
  equation
    for k in 1:k+1 loop // The iteration variable k gets values 1,2,3,4,5
      z[k] := k;        // Uses of the iteration variable k
    end for;
  end HideVariable2;
```

Moreover, inside a for-statement that is controlled by a non-discrete-time (i.e., a continuous-time expression that is not discrete-time) range expression and not in the body of a when-statement, it is not legal to have assignments to unclocked discrete-time variables, or real elementary relations/functions that should generate events. This restriction is necessary in order to guarantee that all equations for unclocked discrete-time variables only contain unclocked discrete-time expressions, and to ensure that crossing functions do not become active between events. See also Section 6.9.3, page 281.

9.2.5.1 Implicit Iteration Ranges

The standard for-loop presented in the previous section has an explicit iteration *range-expression*, as follows:

for *ident* **in** *range-expression* **loop**

However, Modelica also allows a *short form* of the loop header with *implicit* iteration range:

for *ident* **loop**

where the range-expression is *inferred* from the use of the iteration variable *ident* inside the loop body. The iteration range-expression is inferred according to the following method:

- For an iteration variable *ident* that occurs *alone* as an index of an array in the loop body, e.g. *arr*[..., *ident*, ...], the *range-expression* of the iteration variable is *inferred* to be `1:size`(*arr*,*indexpos*) if the indices are a subtype of `Integer`, or as `E.e1:E.en` if the indices are of an `enumeration` type `E=enumeration(e1`, ..., `en)`, or as `false:true` if the indices are of type `Boolean`. The inferred range is the full range of the indexed array dimension.
- If the iteration variable is used as an index to several arrays within the loop body, their ranges must be identical; otherwise the range expression must be given explicitly.
- The iteration variable can be used in the loop body without being an index. Such a usage does not contribute to inferring its range expression.

For example:

```
  Real a[n],b[n],c[n+1];
```

```
for i loop            // Same as:  for i in 1:size(a,1) loop
  a[i] := 2*b[i];
end loop;

for i loop            // Illegal since a and c have different dimension sizes
  a[i] := 2*c[i];     // Instead use: for i in 1:size(a,1) loop
end loop;
```

Some examples of range inference for arrays indexed by enumerations:

```
type FourEnums = enumeration(one,two,three,four);
Real x[4];

Real xe[FourEnums] = x;
Real xsquared1[FourEnums] = {xe[i]*xe[i] for i};
Real xsquared2[FourEnums] = {xe[i]*xe[i] for i in FourEnums};
Real xsquared3[FourEnums] = {x[i]*x[i] for i};
```

Implicit iteration ranges can be used in for-statements (Section 9.2.5, page 427), for-equations (Section 8.3.2, page 352), array constructors with iterators (Section 7.2.2, page 316), and reduction operator expressions with iterators (Section 7.9.4.1, page 337).

9.2.5.2 Nested for-loops with Multiple Iterators

A nested for-loop may be expressed compactly using multiple iterators in the same loop:

```
for iterators loop
   statements
end for;
```

where *iterators* is a comma-separated list of iterators. Each iterator has the structure:

iteration-variable `in` *range-expression*

For example, regard a standard nested for-loop where each loop has a single iterator:

```
Real[n,m]  A,B;

for i in 1:size(A,1) loop
  for j in 1:size(A,2) loop
      A[i,j] := B[i,j]^3;
  end for;
end for;
```

This can be represented more compactly using a nested for-loop with two iterators:

```
for i in 1:size(A,1), j in 1:size(A,2) loop
  A[i,j] := B[i,j]^3;
end for;
```

The loop can be made *very* compact using implicit iteration ranges in the iterators:

```
for i,j loop
  A[i,j] := B[i,j]^3;
end for;
```

9.2.6 Iteration Using while-statements

When using the for-loop for iteration we must be able to express the range of values over which the iteration variable should iterate in a *closed* form as an iteration expression. For cases where this is not feasible there is also a while-loop iteration construct in Modelica where the termination condition is just a `Boolean` expression and the range of iteration values need not be expressed in closed form as an expression. One must declare the iteration variable separately if such a variable is used, as well as handle the increment or decrement of this variable. The general structure of a while-loop is shown below:

```
while condition loop
  statements
end while
```

where the *condition* expression must be of `Boolean` type. The while-statement has the following meaning:

1. The *condition* of the while-statement is evaluated.
2. If the *condition* is `false`, the execution continues after the while-statement.
3. If the *condition* is `true`, the entire body (*statements*) of the while-statement is executed (except if a `break` statement, see Section 9.2.7, page 430, or `return` statement, see Section 9.3.2.6, page 444, is executed), after which execution continues at step 1.

The example class `SumSeries` shows the while-loop construct used for summing a series of exponential terms until the loop condition is violated, that is, the terms become smaller than `eps`. In this case it would be quite impractical to use a for-loop.

```
class SumSeries
  parameter Real eps = 1.E-6;
  Integer i;
  Real sum;
  Real delta;
algorithm
  i := 1;
  delta := exp(-0.01*i);
  while delta>=eps loop
    sum := sum + delta;
    i := i+1;
    delta := exp(-0.01*i);
  end while;
end SumSeries;
```

Moreover, inside a while-statement that is controlled by a non-discrete-time (i.e., a continuous-time expression that is not discrete-time) condition and not in the body of a when-statement, it is not legal to have assignments to unclocked discrete-time variables or real elementary relations/functions that should generate events. This restriction is necessary in order to guarantee that all equations for unclocked discrete-time variables are unclocked discrete-time expressions, and to ensure that crossing functions do not become active between events. See also Section 6.9.3, page 281.

9.2.7 Breaking Iteration Using break-statements

When executing for-statements or while-statement the iteration can be terminated by executing a break-statement somewhere within the loop:

- A break-statement executed within an iteration statement such as a for- or while-statement terminates the enclosing iteration immediately without executing the rest of the iteration statement body. In the case of a while-loop, the loop is terminated without executing the while-predicate.

A break-statement has the following syntax, and is only allowed inside a for-loop or a while-loop:

```
break;
```

For example, the following function `findElement` searches an `Integer` array for a specific element. The search is done by a for-loop, which is terminated by a break-statement when the correct index position has been found and assigned to the result variable called `position`.

```
function findElement
```

```
  input  Integer element;
  input  Integer v[:];
  output Integer position;
algorithm
  for i in 1:size(v,1) loop
    if v[i] == element then
      position := i;
      break;
    end if;
  end for;
end findElement;
```

9.2.8 Returning from Functions Using return-statements

It is possible to return from a function using a return-statement of the following form:

```
return;
```

The return-statement is described in more detail in Section 9.3.2.7, page 444.

9.2.9 if-statements

The general structure of if-statements is given below, where the elseif-part is optional and can occur zero or more times whereas the optional else-part can occur at most once.

```
if <condition> then
  <statements>
elseif <condition> then
  <statements>
else
  <statements>
end if
```

The semantics of an if-statement is as follows: if the *condition* after the keyword `if` evaluates to `true` the statements after `then` are executed; otherwise if there are one or more elseif-parts their *conditions* are evaluated in order. The first that evaluates to `true` causes the corresponding *statements* to be executed; otherwise, if present, the *statements* in the else-part are executed.

Below is an example of an if-statement used in the class `SumVector`, which performs a combined summation and computation on a vector `v`.

```
class SumVector
  Real sum;
  parameter Real v[5] = {100,200,-300,400,500};
  parameter Integer n = size(v,1);
algorithm
  sum := 0;
  for i in 1:n loop
    if v[i]>0 then
      sum := sum + v[i];
    elseif v[i] > -1 then
      sum := sum + v[i] -1;
    else
      sum := sum - v[i];
    end if;
  end for;
end SumVector;
```

9.2.9.1 Assignments within if-statements

There is a special feature regarding *conditional assignments*, that is, assignment statements inside if-statements. Modelica guarantees that all the outputs of an algorithm section always have well-defined values, and that an algorithm section does *not* have memory of previous invocations. This is achieved by *initializing* all *conditionally assigned variables* to their start-values whenever the algorithm is invoked.

Remember that a function or algorithm section is said to have memory if its results are dependent not only on the inputs but also on some value(s) that may have been stored away during some previous call. Since conditionally assigned variables are not always assigned they could preserve memory from previous calls or be undefined if it were not for this rule of automatically giving such variables their start-value on entry. Thus it is impossible for a Modelica function or algorithm section to have memory.

For example, the algorithm section in the class `CondAssign` below automatically assigns the start values 35 and 45 to the variables x and y respectively when entering the algorithm section since these variables are *conditionally assigned* within the algorithm section. This means that the condition `x>5` becomes 35>5 which is always `true`. On the other hand, the variable `z` is not given its start value when entering the algorithm section since it is not conditionally assigned; it is actually an *input* to the algorithm section.

```
class CondAssign
  Real x(start=35);
  Real y(start=45);
  Real z(start=0)  = time;
algorithm
  if x>5 then
    x := 80;       // The condition x>5 will always be true
  end if;          // since 35>5
  if z>10 then
    y := 100;
  end if;
end CondAssign;
```

We simulate for 30 seconds and plot (see Figure 9-1).

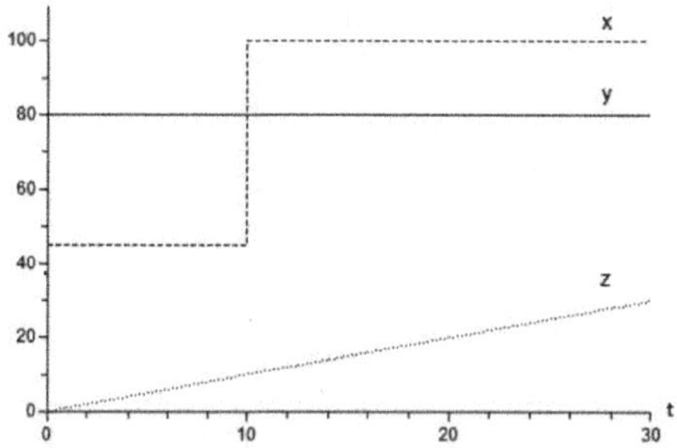

Figure 9-1. Simulation of the `CondAssign` model.

The function `CondAssignFunc` below behaves similarly; here the local variables `x` and `y` are automatically assigned the default initial values 35 and 45 on entry to the algorithm section that comprises its function body.

```
function CondAssignFunc
  input Real z;
protected
  Real x := 35;
  Real y := 45;
```

```
algorithm
  if x>5 then
    x := 80;
  end if;
  if z>10 then
    y := 100;
  end if;
end CondAssignFunc;
```

9.2.9.2 Restriction Regarding Unclocked Discrete-Time Variables and Events

Inside an if-statement that is controlled by a non-discrete-time (i.e., a continuous-time expression that is not discrete-time) condition and not in the body of a when-statement, it is *not legal* to have assignments to unclocked discrete-time variables or real elementary relations/functions that should generate events. This restriction is necessary in order to guarantee that all equations for unclocked discrete-time variables only include unclocked discrete-time expressions, and to ensure that crossing functions do not become active between events. See also Section 6.9.3, page 281.

9.2.10 when-statements

When-statements are used to express *actions at event instants* and are closely related to when-equations earlier described in Section 8.3.5, page 357. An obvious difference is that when-statements are statements containing other statements (actions) and can be used only in algorithm sections (but not in functions) whereas when-equations are equations which are allowed only in equation sections.

- *When-statements* are used to express actions (statements) that are executed only at events, for example, at discontinuities or when certain conditions become true. The executed statements contain *unclocked discrete-time* expressions since they are computed only at event instants, even expressions that otherwise would be classified as continuous-time.

The general structure of a when-statement is given below where the elsewhen-part is optional and can be repeated zero or more times. The conditional expression *conditions* is a `Boolean` scalar or vector expression which automatically has variability unclocked discrete-time because of its type. The statements within the when-statement are executed when the scalar *conditions* expression *becomes* `true`, or in the case of a `Boolean` vector expression, when at least one of the vector elements *becomes* `true`. The statements in a subsequent elsewhen-part are executed if at least one of the associated *conditions* becomes `true` and no preceding when- or elsewhen-part of the same when-statement was executed.

```
when <conditions> then
  <statements>
elsewhen <conditions> then
  <statements>
end when
```

For example, the two statements in the when-statement below are executed at the event instant when the `Boolean` expression `x > 2` *becomes* `true`. We should note that this is different from an if-statement with the same condition which executes its body each time when invoked provided that the condition of the if-statement *is* `true`. This difference is easier to understand if we consider the definition of when-statements in terms of if-statements and the `edge` operator in the section below.

```
when x > 2 then
  y1 := sin(x);
  y3 := 2*x + y1 + y2;
end when;
```

If we instead use a `Boolean` vector expression containing three elements as the *conditions*, then the two statements will be executed at event instants when at least one of the three conditions: `x > 2`, `sample(0,2)`, or `x < 5` becomes `true`. Typically each condition in the vector generates its own event instants.

```
when {x > 2, sample(0,2), x < 5} then
  y1 := sin(x);
  y3 := 2*x + y1 + y2;
end when;
```

The order between the statements in the body of the when-statement is of course significant. If we would put the assignment to `y3` before the assignment of `y1` we would get a different result and thus different model behavior.

In general, it is advisable to try to put only one assignment within each when-statement and instead have several when-statements with identical conditions. This has been done in the example below, allowing the solver the flexibility to arrange the computation in data-dependency order. We should note, however, that this is not an absolute requirement. There are situations where several assignment statements within the same when-statement is more convenient.

```
algorithm
  when x > 2 then
    y1 := sin(x);
  end when;
equation
  y2 = sin(y1);
algorithm
  when x > 2 then
    y3 := 2*x + y1 + y2;
  end when;
```

9.2.10.1 Defining when-statements by if-statements

A when-statement can be defined as a combination of the following:

- An if-statement.
- `Boolean` variables with appropriate start-values.
- Calls to the `edge` operator in the conditional expressions (i.e., *conditions*) of the if-statement.

We can easily understand the mapping from when-statement to if-statement by regarding the following schematic when-statement example:

```
algorithm
  when {x>1, ..., y>p} then
    ...
  elsewhen x > y.start then
    ...
  elsewhen x+3 < z then
    ...
  end when;
```

This when-statement is equivalent to the following special if-statement. The `Boolean` variables `b1`, `b2`, and `b3` are necessary since the `edge` operator can be applied only to `Boolean` variables. Each conditional expression of the when-statement is assigned to a `Boolean` variable which becomes the argument to one of the `edge` operators in the conditional expressions of the if-statement.

```
  Boolean[N] b1(start = {x.start>1, ..., y.start>p.start});
  Boolean    b2(start = x.start > y.start);
  Boolean    b3(start = x.start+3 < z.start);
algorithm
```

```
b1 := {x>1, ..., y>p};
b2 := x > y.start;
b3 := x+3 < z;
if edge(b1[1]) or edge(b1[2]) or ... edge(b1[N]) then
  ...
elseif edge(b2) then
  ...
elseif edge(b3) then
  ...
end if;
```

Remember the definition of `edge` as "`edge(x)= x and not pre(x).`" See also the table of special operators and functions in Section 6.14 on page 291. The `edge` operators in the *conditions* of the if-statement ensure that the statements within the if-statements are executed only when the original conditions *become* `true`, that is, these statements are evaluated only at event instants.

9.2.10.2 Avoiding Multiple-Definition Conflicts for when-statements

Recall the erroneous model `DoubleWhenConflict` in Section 8.3.5.2, page 359, where two when-equations try to define the same variable. A similar model `DoubleWhenConflict2` using when-statements in separate algorithm sections instead of when-equations is shown below.

Two when-statements in different algorithm sections may define the same variable, but this is not recommended modeling practice since the simulation may become dependent on the choice of execution order between the when-statements. See the model below, where there are two assignments (`close := true; close := false;`) defining the same variable `close`.

```
model DoubleWhenConflict2
  Boolean close;   // not recommended: close defined by two statements!
algorithm
  when condition1 then
    close := true;
end when;

algorithm
  when condition2 then
    close := false;
  end when;
end DoubleWhenConflict2;
```

One possible way to resolve the conflict would be to put both when-statements within the same algorithm section, as in the `DoubleWhenSequential` model below. The sequential execution semantics of algorithm sections allow several assignments to the same variable.

If there are several when-statements with assignments active at the same time instant, they will be executed in sequential order, and the result of the last assignment will prevail. However, this method is not recommended since the modeling style is less clear than the alternative method presented in the next section. Another disadvantage is the nondeclarative style of using when-constructs by relying on multiple sequential assignments.

```
model DoubleWhenSequential
  Boolean close;   // Possible conflicting definitions resolved by
algorithm          // sequential assignments in an algorithm section
  when time<=2 then
    close := true;
  end when;
  when time<=2 then
    close := false;
  end when;
end DoubleWhenSequential;
```

A more explicit and therefore *better* way to resolve the conflict would be to give one of the two event handlers higher priority, which is possible using the `elsewhen` construct, for example, as shown below:

```
model WhenPriority
  ...
algorithm
  when condition1 then
    close := true;
  elsewhen condition2 then
    close := false;
  end when;
  ...
end WhenPriority;
```

Here it is well defined what happens if both conditions become `true` at the same time instant since *condition1* has a higher priority than *condition2*.

9.2.10.3 Restrictions on when-statements

The following restrictions apply to when-statements:

- when-statements are not allowed in functions.
- when-statements cannot be nested.
- when-statements are not allowed in initial algorithm sections, but when initial() can be used outside initial algorithm or initial equation sections.

The reader might find it strange that when-statements are allowed in algorithm sections but not allowed in functions since algorithm sections can be seen as a special case of functions. The main reason is that the analysis to determine when events should be generated would be very complicated, in certain cases infeasible, since functions can be recursive, functions can call other functions, and the same function can be called from many places. The special case of algorithm sections is much simpler and can be handled, since an algorithm section can be "called" from only one place, cannot be called from functions, and is nonrecursive. The restriction of not nesting when-statements is both to keep it closer to the allowable forms of when-equations, and to simplify the analysis needed for event generation.

9.2.11 assert

The `assert` statement provides a convenient means for specifying checks on model validity within a model. There is also an equation version of `assert` (see Section 8.3.7.1, page 361). An `assert` statement has the following structure:

```
assert(assert-expression, message-string);          or
assert(assert-expression, message-string, , level = assertionlevel);
```

The *assert-expression* in an `assert` statement should normally evaluate to `true`, in which case the `message-string` argument is not evaluated and the procedure call to `assert` is ignored. A failed assertion, that is, when the `assert-expression` evaluates to `false`, should be reported back to the user in some way that is dependent on the third argument to assert, called `level`, which has a default value `level = AssertionLevel.error`. In that case the default behavior is to report some problem back to the user, stop the simulation, and then possibly (which is tool-dependent) continue simulation, for example, after some adjustment such as choosing smaller step-size for numerical solution. The default `AssertionLevel.error` case can for example be used to avoid evaluating a model outside its limits of validity. The following class `AssertTest2` contains an example of the use of `assert`:

```
class AssertTest2
  parameter Real lowlimit = -5;
  parameter Real highlimit = 5;
  Real x;
```

```
algorithm
  assert(x >= lowlimit and x <= highlimit, "Variable x out of limit");
end AssertTest2;
```

Alternatively, if the input variable `level = AssertionLevel.warning`, the current evaluation is not aborted. Instead, `message` indicates the cause of the warning. The warning is reported only once when the `assert-expression` becomes `false`, and it should also be reported that the `assert-expression` is no longer violated when it returns to true. In all cases, the `assert(...)` statement must not have any influence on the behavior of the model.

The `AssertionLevel.warning` case can be used when the boundary of validity is not hard. For example, a fluid property model based on a polynomial interpolation curve might give accurate results between the temperatures 240 K and 380 K, but still give reasonable results in the range 200 K and 500 K. When the temperature gets out of the smaller interval, but still stays in the larger one, the user should be warned, but the simulation should continue without any further action. The corresponding `assert` statements would be:

```
assert(T > 240 and T < 380, "Medium model outside full accuracy range",
       AssertionLevel.warning);
assert(T > 200 and T < 500, "Medium model outside feasible region");
```

9.2.12 terminate

The `terminate` statement successfully terminates the current simulation, that is, no error condition is indicated. There is also an equation version of `terminate` (see Section 8.3.7.2, page 362). A string argument is used to indicate the reason for successful termination, which can be reported back to the user in some appropriate way by the simulation tool. The structure of a `terminate` statement is as follows:

terminate(*message-string*);

The most common usage of `terminate` is to give more appropriate stopping criteria for terminating a simulation than a fixed point in time. This is exemplified in the `terminate` statement within the `when` statement below, which is a slightly modified version of the termination code of the `MoonLanding` model in Section 3.5, page 83.

```
algorithm
  when apollo.height < 0 then       // termination condition
    terminate("The moon lander touches the ground of the moon");
  end when;
```

9.2.13 Print Statements

As mentioned earlier (Section 9.1, page 421), Modelica functions are pure, that is, given the same arguments will always return the same value(s), and are not allowed to have side effects that influence the simulation state.

However, calls to impure functions (Section 9.3.14, page 462) are allowed in some special cases if the side effects of these calls do not influence the simulation state.

Two cases which are sometimes useful in algorithmic code are print functions (Section 16.4.3, page 926) and timing functions for performance measurements. Some calls like that can be without arguments (Section 9.3.2.5, page 444).

9.3 Functions

Functions are a natural part of any mathematical model. A small number of standard mathematical functions like abs, sqrt, sin, cos, exp, etc. are predefined in the Modelica language. Most of these functions and a few more, including sin, cos, exp, and so on, are also available in the Modelica standard math library Modelica.Math, (Section 16.2, page 920), which also makes it possible to associate graphical annotations with these functions. The arithmetic operators +, -,*, / can be regarded as functions that are referred to through a convenient operator syntax. Thus it is natural to have user-defined mathematical functions in the Modelica language.

At the beginning of this chapter (Section 9.1, page 421), we discussed the issues as well as pros and cons of *declarative* versus *nondeclarative* algorithmic constructs including functions. Modelica functions are declarative *mathematical functions*, that is, a Modelica function always returns the same results given the same argument values. Thus a function call is *referentially transparent*, which means that it keeps the same semantics or meaning independently of from where the function is referenced or called.

The declarative behavior of function calls implies that functions have *no memory* (not being able to store values that can be retrieved in subsequent calls) and *no side effects* (e.g., no update of global variables and no input/output operations). This is actually a prerequisite for guaranteeing the continuity and differentiability conditions required by the solver for solution of the continuous part of the total system of equations. However, it is possible that external functions could have side effects or input/output operations. If we call such a function the simulation will still work well if the external function behaves as a mathematical function, that is, the same inputs always give rise to the same results[16].

On the other hand, whereas functions behave in a declarative way, that is, are *call declarative*, the statements inside the function body are algorithmic and therefore non-declarative. The nondeclarativeness of statements is, however, local, and does not influence the global properties of Modelica functions.

9.3.1 Function Declaration

The body of a Modelica function is a kind of algorithm section that contains procedural algorithmic code to be executed when the function is called. A function body can alternatively consist of an external function specifier (Section 9.4, page 466). Formal parameters are specified using the input keyword, whereas results are denoted using the output keyword. This makes the syntax of function definitions quite close to Modelica class definitions, but using the keyword function instead of class.

The structure of a typical function declaration is sketched by the following schematic function example:

```
function <functionname>
  input  TypeI1 in1;
  input  TypeI2 in2;
  input  TypeI3 in3 := <default expr> "Comment" annotation(...);
  ...
  output TypeO1 out1;
  output TypeO2 out2 := <default expr>;
  ...
protected
  <local variables>
  ...
algorithm
  ...
  <statements>
```

[16] There is an exception to this rule for external functions called in when-equations or when-statements. See the footnote in Section 9.1, page 3.

```
  ...
end <functionname>;
```

Optional explicit default values can be associated with any input or output formal parameter as well as local variable through declaration assignments. Such defaults are shown for the third input parameter and the second output parameter in our example.

Initialization of output formal parameters and local variables from associated default values in *declaration assignments*, for example, the assignment `in3 := ...` above, is done at the start of the function invocation before the function algorithm section or associated external function is evaluated. Such initializations must be executed in an acyclic order where a variable is not used before its declaration assignment has been executed. It is an error if such an acyclic execution order does not exist.

Comment strings and annotations can be given for any formal parameter declaration, as usual in Modelica declarations.

All internal parts of a function are optional; that is, the following is also a legal function:

```
function <functionname>
end <functionname>;
```

9.3.1.1 Ordering of Formal Parameters

The relative ordering between *input* formal parameter declarations is important since that determines the matching between actual arguments and formal parameters at function calls with positional parameter passing. Likewise, the relative ordering between the declarations of the *outputs* is significant since that determines the matching with receiving variables at function calls of functions with multiple results. However, the declarations of the inputs and outputs can be intermixed as long as these internal orderings are preserved. Mixing declarations in this way is not recommended, however, since it makes the code hard to read. For example:

```
function <functionname>
  output TypeO1 out1; // Intermixed declarations of inputs and outputs
  input  TypeI1 in1;  // not recommended since code becomes hard to read
  input  TypeI2 in2;
  ...
  output TypeO2 out2;
  input  TypeI3 in3;
  ...
end <functionname>;
```

9.3.2 Function Call

There are two basic forms of argument to formal parameter association in Modelica function calls:

- Positional association of actual arguments to formal parameters.
- Named association of actual arguments to formal parameters.

These two forms can be mixed:

- Mixed positional and named association of actual arguments to formal parameters.

As an example we will use the function `polynomialEvaluator` that computes the value of a polynomial given two arguments: a coefficient vector `A` and a value of `x`.

```
function polynomialEvaluator
  input  Real A[:];        // Array, size defined at function call time
  input  Real x := 1.0;    // Explicit default value 1.0 for x
  output Real sum;
protected
```

```
  Real   xpower;           // Local variable xpower
algorithm
  sum := 0;
  xpower := 1;
  for i in 1:size(A,1) loop
    sum := sum + A[i]*xpower;
    xpower := xpower*x;
  end for;
end polynomialEvaluator;
```

A function call with *positional association* of actual arguments to formal parameters is the most common form of function call in Modelica as well as in other programming languages. The actual arguments are associated with the formal parameters according to their position in the argument list. Thus, the *n*th actual argument is passed to the *n*th input formal parameter based on the ordering of the input formal parameter declarations in the function definition. However, formal parameters with default values need not be given actual arguments unless those parameters should be assigned values different from the defaults.

The number of actual arguments can be less than the number of formal parameters in such a function call if the remaining formal parameters have specified default values. Otherwise the number of actual arguments and the number of formal parameters must be the same.

Using positional association, in the call below the actual argument `{1,2,3,4}` becomes the value of the coefficient vector `A`, and `21` becomes the value of the formal parameter `x`.

```
p := polynomialEvaluator({1, 2, 3, 4}, 21);
```

The same call to the function `polynomialEvaluator` can instead be made using *named association* of actual arguments to formal parameters, as in the next example. Here the actual argument is associated with the formal parameter through an equation in the argument list with the name of the formal parameter on the left-hand side and the actual argument on the right-hand side:

```
p := polynomialEvaluator(A={1, 2, 3, 4}, x=21);
```

or, since the order of named arguments does not matter:

```
p := polynomialEvaluator(x=21, A={1, 2, 3, 4});
```

Named association has the advantage that the code becomes more self-documenting as well as more flexible with respect to code updates, but the drawback is less concise code. For example, assume that we make all calls to the function `polynomialEvaluator` using named parameter association. Then we can change the order between the formal parameters `A` and `x` and introduce new formal parameters with default values in the function definition without causing any compilation errors at the call sites.

The default value of `1.0` for the `x` input formal parameter makes the following three calls equivalent:

```
p := polynomialEvaluator({1, 2, 3, 4}, 1.0);
p := polynomialEvaluator({1, 2, 3, 4};
p := polynomialEvaluator(A={1, 2, 3, 4});
```

For both kinds of function argument passing, type compatibility of arguments and formal parameters applies:

- The types of the actual argument expressions at a function call must be *compatible* with the declared types of the corresponding formal parameters, except where the standard type conversions can be used to make the types agree. See also Section 3.19, page 124, regarding type compatibility for argument passing, and the section on applying scalar functions to arrays, Section 9.3.2.8 on page 445, in this chapter.

9.3.2.1 Mixed Positional and Named Function Argument Passing

We mentioned briefly that the positional and named argument passing styles can be mixed in a function call. The placement of the positional and named arguments must adhere to the following rule:

- A function application has optional positional arguments followed by zero or more named arguments.

Such a mixed call to some example function `f` might appear as follows:

```
f(3.5, 5.76, arg3=5, arg6=8.3);
```

or in the case of our well-known `polynomialEvaluator` function:

```
p := polynomialEvaluator({1, 2, 3, 4}, x=21);
```

We are now ready to state the complete rules for binding values to the input formal parameters of a Modelica function based on a combination of *positional* arguments, *named* arguments, and explicitly given *default* values:

1. First, a list of unfilled "slots" is created corresponding to all formal input parameters, where the order of the slots is given by the order of the formal input parameter declarations in the function definition.
2. If there are *n* positional arguments, they are placed in the first *n* slots, which thereby become filled.
3. Next, for each named argument "*identifier* = *expression*," the *identifier* is used to determine the corresponding slot. This slot must be unfilled, otherwise an error occurs. The value of the argument is placed in this slot, thereby filling it.
4. When all arguments have been processed, the slots that are still unfilled are filled with the corresponding explicit default values (if present) of the function definition. The default values may depend on other inputs; these dependencies must be acyclical in the function. The values for those other inputs will then be substituted into the default values. This process may be repeated if the default value for that input depend on another input. The default values for inputs may not depend on non-input variables in the function.
5. At this stage there must not be any remaining unfilled slots, otherwise an error occurs. The contents of the complete list of filled slots can now be used as the input formal parameter values for the call.

We illustrate this procedure with an example. Assume that a function `realToString` is defined as follows for converting a `Real` number to a `String`:

```
function realToString
  input  Real   number            "Real value to be converted to a string";
  input  Real   precision := 6    "Number of significant digits";
  input  Real   length    := 0    "Minimum length of field";
  output String string            "Result number as a string";
  ...
end realToString;
```

Then the following function calls are equivalent:

```
String ns;
ns := realToString(2.0);
ns := realToString(2.0, 6, 0);
ns := realToString(2.0, 6);
ns := realToString(2.0, precision=6);
ns := realToString(2.0, length=0);
```

As stated in the argument-passing procedure, it is an error to pass the same argument twice. We show an erroneous example call below where the argument value 6 is passed twice to the `precision` formal parameter, first using positional association and then using named association:

```
ns := realToString(2.0, 6, precision=6); // Error: precision passed twice
```

9.3.2.2 Returning Single or Multiple Function Results

A function with one output formal parameter always returns a *single result*. Our previously presented example functions `polynomialEvaluator` and `realToString` are single result functions.

However, a function with *more* than one output formal parameter has *multiple results*. An example is the function `pointOnCircle` below, which computes the Cartesian coordinates of a point located at a certain angle on a circle with a specific radius. The Cartesian coordinates are returned via the two result variables x and y.

```
function pointOnCircle  "Computes cartesian coordinates of a point"
  input  Real angle  "angle in radians";
  input  Real radius;
  output Real x;     // 1:st result formal parameter
  output Real y;     // 2:nd result formal parameter
algorithm
  x := radius*Modelica.Math.cos(phi);
  y := radius*Modelica.Math.sin(phi);
end pointOnCircle;
```

If we call a function with just one result we can put the call anywhere within an expression. This is also the case when calling a function with multiple results if we only want to access its first result.

On the other hand, if we wish to call a Modelica function with multiple results and want to obtain more than the first result, there are just two syntactic forms to choose from depending on whether the function call should occur in an equation section or in an algorithm section: one equation form and one statement form, as specified below:

```
(out1,out2,out3,...) = function_name(in1, in2, in3, in4, ...);  // Equation
(out1,out2,out3,...) := function_name(in1, in2, in3, in4, ...); // Statement
```

The left-hand side of both the equation and the assignment statement contains a parenthesized, comma-separated list of variables receiving the results from the function call. A called function with *n* results can have at most *n* receiving variables on the left-hand side. Fewer than *n* receiving variables means that some function results are discarded.

For example, when calling our example function pointOnCircle with two receiving variables px and py on the left-hand side, such calls can appear as follows:

```
(px,py)  = pointOnCircle(1.2, 2);     // Equation form
(px,py) := pointOnCircle(1.2, 2);     // Statement form
```

Any kind of variable of compatible type is allowed in the list on the left-hand side, e.g. array elements:

```
(arr[1],arr[2]) := pointOnCircle(1.2, 2);
```

However, the parenthesized list on the left-hand side must contain variables, not general expressions:

```
(a+3, b/c) := pointOnCircle(1.2, 2); // Error! Should be variables
                                     // on the left-hand side
```

To summarize, the following rules apply when returning results from a multiple-result function:

- The variables in the list on the left-hand side of the equation or assignment containing the call are associated with the returned function results according to the order of the variables in the list and the corresponding declaration order of the output result variables in the function.
- Only the first result is returned when calling a function with multiple results from inside an expression not being the right-hand side of a statement or equation.
- As in any standard equation or assignment, the type of each variable on the left-hand side must be compatible with the type of the corresponding function result on the right-hand side, with or without type coercion.

9.3.2.3 Optional Function Results

In the previous section we mentioned briefly that selected results from a multiple-result function can be discarded depending on the form of the function call. This is useful since we might not always be interested in all results returned from a function call.

By leaving out variables in the comma-separated list on the left-hand side of a multiple-result call equation or assignment, or calling a multiple-result function within an expression context, we can control which results are actually obtained according to the following rules:

- A multiple-result function can be called as a *single-result function* within an expression. In such a case the value and type of the function call are given by the value and type of the *first result*, and the rest of the results are discarded.
- Selected function results can be discarded by *leaving out* the corresponding *variables* in the comma-separated list on the left-hand side of multiple-result function call equation or assignment. Enough commas must be retained to determine the position of each variable, counting from the left.

A typical case is the following example function `eigen`, which computes both eigenvalues and eigenvectors, whereas the user would like to obtain only one or two of these results.

```
function eigen "calculate eigenvalues and eigenvectors"
  discrete Integer n = size(A,1);
  input     Real    A[:,n];
  output    Real    eigenValues[n,2];           // 1st result
  output    Real    leftEigenVectors [n,n];     // 2nd result
  output    Real    rightEigenVectors[n,n];     // 3rd result
algorithm
  // The function body computes eigenvalues, right and left eigenvectors
  // An optimizing Modelica compiler may recognize that the result variables
  // can be computed separately (and not, e.g., by one
  // single call to an external Fortran function) in order to remove
  // unnecessary computations if one or more output arguments are missing.
  // 1. compute eigenvalues
  // 2. compute right eigenvectors using the computed eigenvalues
  // 3. compute left eigenvectors using the computed eigenvalues
end eigen;
```

This function may be called in different ways depending on which results should be returned or discarded, e.g. as in the example calls below:

```
(evalues,vleft,vright) := eigen(A);    // Return all results
       (evalues,vleft) := eigen(A);    // Eigenvalues and left eigenvectors
               evalues := eigen(A);    // Only eigenvalues
                     X := 2*eigen(A);  // Eigenvalues in an expression
     (evalues,,vright) := eigen(A);    // Eigenvalues and right eigenvectors
              (,vleft) := eigen(A);    // Only left eigenvectors
```

An optimizing Modelica compiler having access to both the actual function calls and the Modelica source code of the called multiple-result function, for example, `eigen`, may avoid computing unused results by doing analysis of the code and compiling the multiple-result function to special optimized versions that avoid computation of unused results depending on the function call context.

9.3.2.4 Call via an Instance Name

A *function* declared in a class can be called via a reference to an *instance* of that class using *dot notation*. Such locally declared functions are sometimes called member functions. An example of such a call is `foo.func(33.5)` below. Regarding the lookup rules to find the definition of such a function, see Section 3.17.2, page 112.

```
model Foo
  Real x1;

  function func
    input  Real x;
```

```
    output Real y;
  algorithm
    y := 3*x;
  end func;
end Foo;

model FuncTest
  Real z;
  Foo  foo(x1=5);
equation
  z = foo.func(33.5);   // Call to function func via instance foo
end FuncTest;
```

9.3.2.5 Empty Function Calls

An "empty" function call is a call that does not return any results. An empty call is not of much use in equation-based Modelica models since a function call without results does not contribute to the simulation, and is not allowed to have side-effects that influence the simulation state.

However, this degenerate case of function call is still allowed and can be of use for calls to impure functions (Section 9.3.14, page 462) called from algorithmic code, e.g., calls to print functions (Section 16.4.3, page 926) or timing functions for performance measurements. It can occur either as a kind of "null" equation or "null" statement, for example, as in the empty calls to `eigen()` in the example below:

```
equation
  eigen(A);    // Empty function call as an equation
algorithm
  eigen(A);    // Empty function call as a statement
```

9.3.2.6 Scalar Functions Applied to Array Arguments

In certain situations, it is useful to be able to apply a function to array values even if it has not been defined for such arguments. This can be done if an obvious generalization to elementwise application of the function is possible.

Modelica functions with one scalar return value can be applied to arrays elementwise, for example, if *v* is a vector of reals, then `cos(v)` is a vector where each element is the result of applying the function `cos` to the corresponding element in *v*. For example:

```
cos({a,b,c})      // Vector argument, result: {cos(a),cos(b),cos(c)}
cos([1,2; 3,4]) // Matrix argument, result: [cos(1),cos(2); cos(3),cos(4)]
```

Functions with more than one argument can be generalized to elementwise application. If more than one argument is generalized to an array, all of the arguments have to be of the same size, and they are traversed in parallel.

For more information regarding the application of scalar functions to array arguments, see Section 7.10 on page 340 in Chapter 7.

9.3.2.7 Function return-statement

A function is returned from when reaching the end of the function body. However, immediate return from anywhere inside a function body can be done by executing a return-statement with the following syntax (Also mentioned in Section 9.2.8, page 431):

```
return;
```

For example, the following function `findMatrixElement` searches an `Integer` matrix for a specific element. The search is done by a doubly nested for-loop, which is immediately exited when the function is returned from by executing a return-statement. At this point, the correct index position has been found and assigned to the result variables `row` and `column`.

```
function findMatrixElement
  input  Integer element;
  input  Integer M[:,:];
  output Integer column;
  output Integer row;
algorithm
  for r in 1:size(M,1) loop
    for c in 1:size(M,2) loop
      if M[r,k]== element then
        row:=r;
        column:=c;
        return;
      end if;
    end for;
  end for;
end findMatrixElement;
```

9.3.2.8 Flexible Array Sizes and Resizing of Arrays in Functions

In Section 7.1.2, page 313, we briefly discussed flexible array dimension sizes. For example, a dimension size of an input array formal parameter specified with a colon(`:`) is flexible—it is unknown and becomes known when an argument is bound to such a formal parameter during a function call. Moreover, a function array result variable or local variable with a dimension size specified with a colon(`:`) needs to get its size defined through an array assignment.

A dimension size not specified with colon(`:`) for an array variable declared in a function must be given by an expression only dependent on the input formal parameters and/or constants. For example:

```
function concatFourVectors  "Concatenate four Real vectors of any length"
  input  Real v1[:],v2[:],v3[:],v4[:];
  output Real vres[ size(v1,1)+size(v2,1)+size(v3,1)+size(v4,1) ];
algorithm
  vres := cat(1,v1,v2,v3,v4);
end concatFourVectors;
```

The following example function concatenates three vectors which must be of equal length:

```
function concatThreeEqualSizeVectors "Concatenate 3 vectors of equal length"
  input  Real v1[:],v2[size(v1,1)],v3[size(v1,1)];
  output Real vres[size(v1,1)+size(v2,1)+size(v3,1)];
algorithm
  vres := cat(1,v1,v2,v3);
end concatThreeEqualSizeVectors;
```

Certain arrays declared in functions can even be resized one or more times. An array result variable or local variable declared in a function with a flexible dimension size specified by colon(`:`) and no declaration assignment, can change size according to the following:

- Prior to execution of the function algorithm the flexible dimension size(s) of such an array is (are) defined to be zero.
- The entire array (array variable without any subscripts) may be assigned a corresponding array with arbitrary dimension size. This will cause the array variable to be resized if its size is different from the array assigned to it.

These rules also apply if the array variable is an element of a record variable in a function. The following example shows a function that collects the negative elements in a vector and resizes the result vector each time a new element is added to the result:

```
function collectNegative
  input Real x[:];
  output Real xneg[:];
algorithm
  for i in 1:size(x,1) loop
    if x[i]<0 then
      xneg := cat(1,xneg,x[i:i]);
    end if;
  end for;
end collectNegative;
```

9.3.3 Extending Base Functions

Since a function is a specialized class, that is, a restricted and enhanced kind of class (see Section 3.8.6 on page 89 in Chapter 3), it is possible to inherit an existing function declaration in the declaration of a new function. In this way we can declare the common structure of a set of functions as a *partial base function* (analogous to base class) which we subsequently inherit into the functions we want to define. The drawback to this approach is that the number of formal parameters as well as their types are not immediately visible when reading the code of a function that inherits another function. In the example below, the common structure of having one input parameter and one result is declared as a base function which is extended and reused by several functions:

```
partial function oneArgBaseFunction
  input  Real x;              // Base function with one argument
  output Real result;         // and one result.
end oneArgBaseFunction;

function myTan
  extends oneArgBaseFunction; // Inherits a base function.
algorithm                     // The code becomes harder to read
  result := sin(x)/cos(x);    // since the formal parameter list is not
end myTan;                    // available in the function.

function addTen
  extends oneArgBaseFunction;
algorithm
  result := x+10;
end addTen;
```

There is clearly some benefit of reuse of `oneArgBaseFunction` in the above example. On the other hand, we will find the code harder to read as we just explained. The drawbacks are probably greater than the benefits in this case.

9.3.4 Functional Input Arguments to Functions

Allowing functions to be passed as arguments to a function is a useful feature that allows greater generality and re-use. For example, a sorting function may have a comparison function as a formal parameter. This makes the sorting function more general and reusable, since it can adapt to different comparison schemes. For example, the `sort` function below sorts an array in decreasing or increasing order depending on the passed `compare` function:

```
function sort  "Sorting function using the bubblesort algorithm"
  input Real[:] arr;
  input CompareFunc compare;
  output Real[size(arr,1)] sortedarr;
  protected Real t;
algorithm
```

```
    sortedarr := arr;
    for i in 1:size(arr,1) loop
      for j in 1:size(arr,1) loop
        if not compare(sortedarr[i], sortedarr[j]) then
          t:= sortedarr[i];  sortedarr[i]:= sortedarr[j]; sortedarr[j]:= t;
        end if;
      end for;
    end for;
  end sort;

  partial function CompareFuncType  "Function type of the comparison function"
    input Real x;  input Real y;  output Boolean comp;
  end CompareFuncType;

  function greaterThan
    input Real x;  input Real y;  output Boolean comp := x>y;
  end greaterThan;

  function lessThan
    input Real x;  input Real y;  output Boolean comp := x<y;
  end lessThan;

  model SortApplication   "Example calls of the sort function"
    parameter Real[:] ax = {4.0,6.0,2.0,5.0,8.0};
    Real[size(ax,1)] xGt;
    Real[size(ax,1)] xLt;
  equation
    xGt = sort(ax, lessThan);     // Decreasing order: {8.0,6.0,5.0,4.0,2.0}
    xLt = sort(ax, greaterThan);  // Increasing order: {2.0,4.0,5.0,6.0,8.0}
  end SortApplication;
```

From the above `sort` function example we can observe the following:

- A formal parameter of function type, that is, a functional argument, is declared in the usual syntax with a type (e.g., `CompareFunc`) followed by the formal parameter name (e.g., `compare`).
- The type of a function, that is, its interface or signature with input and output formal parameters, is declared using a partial function. (e.g., `CompareFunc`).
- A function (e.g., `lessThan`) can be passed to a formal parameter at a function call just by mentioning its function name (e.g., as in the call: `sort(ax,lessThan)`).

There are some restrictions on function types that are allowed to be used in this context:

- The declared type of an input formal parameter of function type must be the name of a partial function that has no replaceable elements.
- The function type name cannot be the name of a record constructor function automatically obtained from the declaration of a record type. This is because of ambiguity: a record type name is usually interpreted as the type of record data objects.

Moreover:

- When placing a type prefix such as `input` in a variable declaration of function type, e.g. a formal parameter, this `input` prefix is not applied to the elements of the function variable and is allowed even if the elements of the function variable have `input` or `output` prefixes.

What happens when a function is passed as a functional argument in a function call? Since function calls usually occur at run-time, some representation of the function needs to be passed efficiently. This cannot be the function type, since the representation of types (currently) is only handled at compile-time. A common solution is that a "function instance" is created in addition to the function type when a function is declared. A pointer to this "function instance," sometimes referred to as a "function pointer" can then be passed as an argument to the called function. This technique is also used by low-level languages such as C.

An input formal parameter of function type can also have an optional function default value in the form of a short class definition with = replaced by `:=`. The assignment `:=` is used since it is a default, not a binding that always holds which would be the case with the equality sign. For example:

```
  function quadrature "Integrate function y=integrand(x) from x1 to x2"
```

```
    input Real x1;
    input Real x2;
    input Integrand integrand := Modelica.Math.sin;  // With default integrand
    // Case without default:   input  Integrand integrand;
    output Real integral;
  algorithm
    integral :=(x2-x1)*(integrand(x1) + integrand(x2))/2;  // Approximate
  end quadrature;

  partial function Integrand  "Function type of Integrand functions"
    input  Real x;
    output Real y;
  end Integrand;
```

The function `parabola` is passed as an input positional input argument in the call to `quadrature` below:

```
  function parabola
     extends Integrand;
  algorithm
     y = x*x;
  end parabola;

  model IntegrateParabola1
    Real area;
  equation
    area = quadrature(0, 1, parabola);   // Integration of area under parabola
  end IntegrateParabola1;
```

9.3.4.1 Forms of Functional Arguments to Functions

There are four possible forms of functional arguments in function calls:

a) a function name (as in the above `sort` and `IntegrateParabola1` examples),
b) a function partial application (see examples in Section 9.3.4.2 below),
c) a function that has been declared as an instance (see the example `IntegrateParabola2` below),
d) a function partial application of a function that has been declared as an instance (see example `quadratureOnce` in Section 9.3.4.2 below).

In all cases, the provided function must have a type which is a function subtype (Section 3.19.6, page 130) of the corresponding function formal parameter.

The `IntegrateParabola2` example below uses a function `integrand` that is a declared function instance, i.e., `integrand`, as an input argument according to case (c) above:

```
  function IntegrateParabola2 "Integrate func y=integrand(x) from x1 to x2"
    input  Real x1;
    input  Real x2;
    input  Integrand integrand;    // Integrand is a partial function type
    output Real integral;
  algorithm
     // Approximate integration by quadrature over two intervals
     integral := quadrature(x1, (x1+x2)/2, integrand)+
                 quadrature((x1+x2)/2, x2, integrand);
  end IntegrateParabola2;
```

9.3.4.2 Function Partial Application

A *function partial application* has the form of a function call with certain formal parameters bound to expressions. A function partial application returns a *partially evaluated function* that is also a function, with the remaining not bound formal parameters still present in the same order as in the original function declaration. A function partial application is specified by the `function` keyword followed by a function call to `func_name` giving named formal parameter associations for the formal parameters to be bound:

```
function func_name(..., formal_parameter_name = expr, ...)
```

Note that the keyword `function` in a function partial application differentiates the syntax from a normal function call where some parameters have been left out and instead are supplied via default values.

The function created by the function partial application acts as the original function but with the bound formal input parameters(s) removed, that is, they cannot be supplied arguments at function call. The binding occurs when the partially evaluated function is created. A partially evaluated function is type compatible (see section 6.5) to the same function with all bound arguments removed.

The following examples show a function partial application `function Sine(A=2,w=3)` with the two extra arguments `A` and `w` bound and thus eliminated, that is, the resulting function is type compatible to `Integrand` with only formal parameters `x` and `y` left. The first example below, `QuadratureSine1`, has a call with a named input argument, according to case (b) in Section 9.3.4.1.

```
function Sine  "y = Sine(A,w,x)"
  input  Real A;
  input  Real w;
  input  Real x; // Note: x is currently last in the argument list.
  output Real y;
algorithm
  y:=A*Modelica.Math.sin(w*x);
end Sine;

partial function Integrand  "Function type of Integrand functions"
  input  Real x;
  output Real y;
end Integrand;

model QuadratureSine1  "Coarse approximation with one quadrature call"
  Real area;
equation
  area = quadrature(0, 1, integrand = function Sine(A=2, w=3));
end QuadratureSine1;
```

Instead of repeating the declaration of input formal parameter `x` and output formal parameter `y`, they can be inherited from `Integrand`, which is fine despite `A` and `w` now being at the end of the parameter list:

```
function Sine  "y = Sine(x,A,w)"
  extends Integrand;
  input Real A;
  input Real w;
algorithm
  y:=A*Modelica.Math.sin(w*x);
end Sine;
```

The second example, `QuadratureSine2`, shows a function partial application being passed as a positional argument. The numeric approximation of the integral will be better since a number of calls to quadrature on many short intervals are summed. The quadrature approximation that the integrated function is a straight line is typically more true over a short interval.

```
model QuadratureSine2  "Finer approximation, N quadrature calls"
  parameter Integer N;
  Real area;
algorithm
  area := 0;
  for i in 1:N loop
    area  := area + quadrature(0, 1, function Sine(A=2, w=i*time));
  end for;
end QuadratureSine2;
```

Below is an example of a function partial application of the function `integrand` which is an *instance*, according to case (d) above:

```
partial function SurfaceIntegrand
  input Real x;
  input Real y;
  output Real z;
end SurfaceIntegrand;

function quadratureOnce
  input Real x;
  input Real y1;
  input Real y2;
  input SurfaceIntegrand integrand;
  output Real z;
algorithm
  z := quadrature(y1, y2, function integrand(y=x));
  // This is according to case (d) and needs to bind the 2nd argument y in
  // order to be type compatible to Integrand
end quadratureOnce;

function surfaceQuadrature
  input Real x1;
  input Real x2;
  input Real y1;
  input Real y2;
  input SurfaceIntegrand integrand;
  output Real integral;
algorithm
  integral := quadrature(x1, x2,
    function quadratureOnce(y1=y1, y2=y2, integrand=integrand);
    // Case (b) and (c)
end surfaceQuadrature;
```

9.3.4.3 Nested Functional Arguments and Propagation of Function Arguments

The following example demonstrates *nested* functional arguments, that is, functional arguments in functional arguments, and *propagation* of functional arguments through two call levels.

In this example the goal is to solve the equation `sin(x) = x` to obtain a solution for `x`. This is performed by calling the generic function `solveScalarEquation` with the function `sineEqualX` as input argument, in which the desired equation is present:

```
x = solveScalarEquation(f=sineEqualX, x0=1);

function sineEqualX  "residue = sin(w*x) - x"
  extends ScalarEquationType;
  input Real w=1;
algorithm
  residue := Modelica.Math.sin(w*x) - x;
end sineEqualX;

partial function ScalarEquationType "Type for residue=f(x)"
  input  Real x        "Independent variable";
  output Real residue "Residue (should be zero)";
end scalarEquationType;
```

The generic function `solveScalarEquation` is implemented by using a general iterator function `iterate` that iterates over `NewtonStep`:

```
function solveScalarEquation "solve  0 = fi(x) for scalar x"
  input  ScalarEquationType fi;  // The scalar equation to solve
```

```
    input  Real x0;
    output Real x;
  protected
    Real x;
  algorithm
     x := iterate(f=function NewtonStep(g=fi), x0=x0);
    // g=fi is function propagation where the supplied fi is bound
    // to g in NewtonStep
  end solve;

  function iterate "Iterate until recursive function call converges"
    input  IteratorType f  "Iterator function"
    input  Real  x0    "Initial value of independent variable x";
    input  Real  defaultRelativeTolerance := 100*Modelica.Constants.eps;
    output Real  x     "Solution (final value of x)";

  protected
    Boolean converged;
    Real    x_last, err;
  algorithm
    converged := false;
    x_last    := x0;
    while not converged loop
      x      := f(x_last);
      err    := abs(x - x_last)/max(1, abs(x_last));
      x_last := x;
      converged := err < getRelativeTolerance(defaultRelativeTolerance);
    end while;
  end iterate;

  partial function IteratorType "Type of the iteration function"
    input  Real x_last  "Last value of x in the iteration";
    output Real x       "New value of x in the iteration";
  end IteratorType;

  function NewtonStep "Perform one Newton step to solve g(x)=0 for x"
    extends IteratorType;
    input ScalarEquationType g;
  protected
    Real h = 1e-5;
  algorithm
    x := x_last - h*g(x_last) / (g(x_last + h) - g(x_last));
  end NewtonStep;
```

9.3.5 Ways of Defining Functions

Apart from the standard way of declaring a Modelica function described in Section 9.3.1, functions can also be defined (or be predefined) in some other ways. Below we summarize the different ways a function can be defined (or be predefined) in Modelica:

- Standard function definitions, described previously in Section 9.3.1, page 438.
- Function definition through short class definition, Section 9.3.6, page 452.
- Built-in functions, Section 9.3.7, page 452.
- Record constructor functions, Section 9.3.8, page 452.
- Defining function derivatives of functions, Section 9.3.9, page 455
- Defining partial derivatives of functions, Section 9.3.10, page 459.
- Defining inverses of functions, Section 9.3.11, page 459.

- External functions, Section 9.4, page 466.

The additional ways of defining functions are described in the following sections.

9.3.6 Short Function Definition

Since functions have many properties in common with general Modelica classes, they can be defined using a short function definition in the same way as a short class definition (Section 3.7.1, page 86), which also can contain modifications or redeclarations. For example, we can define our own `sin` function called `mySin` to be identical to `sin`:

```
function mySin = sin;
```

9.3.7 Built-in Functions

Certain functions are built into the Modelica language and need not be made available for example, by being imported from some package. There are basically four groups of built-in functions in Modelica:

- Conversion functions.
- Intrinsic mathematical functions.
- Special operators and functions.
- Built-in Array functions.

It is possible to declare built-in functions as external `"builtin"` functions as described in Section 9.4.1.1 on page 467. This is already done in the Modelica Standard Library for all Modelica built-in functions, giving the benefit for the user of being able to access function signature and comment information in a Modelica browser.

Functions for explicit conversion of values of built-in types are described in Section 6.8.1.2, page 277. These functions include `ceil` and `floor` for converting from an integer to a real value, `integer()` for converting from real to integer, the `Integer` function for getting the ordinal integer value of an enumeration value, and the `String()` function for converting the built-in data types into string values.

The following intrinsic mathematical functions are built into Modelica: `abs`, `sign`, `sqrt`, `div`, `mod`, `rem`, `ceil`, `floor`, and `integer`, as well as `sin`, `cos`, `exp`, and so on. These functions are described in Section 6.13 on page 289 in Chapter 6. All functions in the standard Modelica library `Modelica.Math` behave as built-in functions and can be called using short names such as `sin`, `cos`, `exp`, and so on.

The special operators and functions have function syntax even though many of these are not really functions in the usual sense. They are described in Section 6.14 on page 291 in Chapter 6 and include e.g. the following: `der`, `initial`, `terminal`, `noEvent`, `smooth`, `sample`, `pre`, `edge`, `change`, `reinit`, `delay`, and so on.

The built-in array functions are described in Section 7.9 starting on page 335 in Chapter 7. These include dimension and size functions such as `size` and `ndims`, conversion functions for changing the dimensionality of scalars and arrays, for example, `vector` and `matrix`, constructor functions for creating array values, reduction functions for computing scalar values from arrays, matrix and vector algebra functions, and array concatenation functions.

See also Chapter 16, page 909, for a list of the built-in functions and operators.

9.3.8 Record Constructor Functions

A *record constructor function* is a function that creates and returns a record. For example, consider a record called `Person` with three fields: `name`, `age`, and `children`:

```
record Person
  String     name;
  Integer    age;
  String[2]  children;
end Person;
```

We would like to have a record constructor function `Person`(*name*, *age*, *children*) returning a `Person` record. However, it is normally illegal in Modelica to declare a function with the same name as a record type within the same scope. If declared, it might be something similar to the following:

```
function Person
  input  String     name;
  input  Integer    age;
  input  String[2]  children;
  output Person     p;
algorithm
  p.name  := name;
  p.age   := age;
  p.children := children;
end Person;
```

Fortunately we do not need to declare a `Person` constructor function explicitly in Modelica since such a function is ***automatically defined*** as a byproduct of the `Person` record declaration. In this special case, both a record and a function with the same name is allowed. The name `Person` is overloaded with two different meanings.

The different uses of the `Person` record ***type name*** and the `Person` ***function name*** can be distinguished since the first is used in a type context and the second in a function call context. See also Section 7.4.3, page 323, where we compute record field slices of arrays of `Person` records.

We declare a `Person` instance called `john` where its value is created by a call to the `Person` constructor function:

```
Person john = Person("John",  35, {"Carl", "Eva"});
```

Another use of record constructors is to create complex numbers, as in the example model `AddComplex` below. The declaration of the record `Complex` also gives rise to a record constructor function, which in the `add` function is called to create and return a value for the `w` output formal parameter. It is also called in the equation involving the variable `c2`:

```
model AddComplex

  record Complex "Complex number"
    Real re  "real part";
    Real im  "imaginary part";
  end Complex;

  function add
    input  Complex u, v;
    output Complex w = Complex(re = u.re+v.re, im = u.im+v.re);
  end add;

  Complex c1, c2;

equation
  c2 = add(c1, Complex(sin(time), cos(time));
end AddComplex;
```

A third example of using record constructors is in the package `Motors` below. Here records are used to define a data sheet library for use in motor components. The record constructor functions represent data sheets used for creation of the different motor instances: `motor1`, `motor2`, and `motor3`.

```
encapsulated package Motors
  record MotorData  "Generic data sheet of a motor"
```

```
    parameter Real inertia;
    parameter Real maxSpeed;
  end MotorData;

  model Motor "Motor model"
    MotorData data;    // Using the generic MotorData
  equation  // Realistic motor model would need more variables and equations
  end Motor;

  // Data sheets for motors I123 and I145
  record MotorDataI123 = MotorData(inertia = 0.0010, maxSpeed = 2800)
  record MotorDataI145 = MotorData(inertia = 0.0015, maxSpeed = 3600)
end Motors

model Robot
  import Motors.*;  // Just refer to data sheets as constructor functions
  Motor motor1(data = MotorDataI123());
  Motor motor2(data = MotorDataI123(inertia=0.0012));
  Motor motor3(data = MotorDataI145());
end Robot;
```

After these introductory examples we are ready to formulate the general rules for automatic creation of record constructor functions from corresponding record declarations.

Whenever a record is defined, a record constructor function with the *same* name and in the *same scope* as the record class is implicitly defined according to the following rules:

1. The declaration of the record is first elaborated and expanded. This includes inheritance, modifications, redeclarations, and expansion of all names referring to declarations outside of the scope of the record to their fully qualified names.
2. All record elements, i.e., record fields and local class definitions, of the expanded record declaration are used as declarations in the record constructor function. All `public` record *fields* become *input formal parameters* except fields which do not allow modifications, that is, `constant` and `final` declarations as well as `protected` declarations, which all become `protected` declarations in the function. The detailed conversion procedure is specified below.
3. An *output result formal parameter* is declared using the record as its type and a name that is not used by any of the other elements in the record. The result formal parameter has modifiers, which set the record variables to the corresponding input formal parameters of the function.

The detailed rules according to (2) above for converting record field declarations to input formal parameters or local protected variables and constants within the constructor function are as follows:

1. Record field declarations which do not allow modifications, for example, `final parameter Real`, as well as `protected` declarations, are declared as `protected` local variables and constants in the record constructor function.
2. Prefixes (e.g., `constant`, `parameter`, `discrete`, ...) of the remaining record fields (being public and modifiable) are removed.
3. The prefix `input` is added to the `public` variables declared in the record constructor function.

In the above examples, we show several uses of such constructor functions converted from records. For example, the function `add` in the `AddComplex` example has an elegant use of modifiers in its result parameter of type `Complex`.

The following rather contrived `Demo` package contains two records, `RecordBase1` and `Record2`, which illustrate most of the situations that may occur in implicit record constructor function creation according to the above rules.

```
encapsulated package Demo;
  record RecordBase1;
    parameter Real r0 = 0;
  end RecordBase1;
```

```
    record Record2
      import Modelica.Math.*;
      extends RecordBase1;
      constant  Real        c1 = 2.0;
      constant  Real        c2;
      parameter Integer     n1 = 5;
      parameter Integer     n2;
      parameter Real        r1    "comment";
      parameter Real        r2 = sin(c1);
      final parameter Real  r3 = cos(r2);
      Real                  r4;
      Real                  r5 = 5.0;
      Real                  r6[n1];
      Real                  r7[n2];
    end Record2;
  end Demo;
```

From the above declarations of the records `RecordBase1` and `Record2`, the following record constructor functions are implicitly defined within the same `Demo` package:

```
  encapsulated package Demo;
    ...
    function RecordBase1
      input  Real     r0 := 0;
      output Record1 result(r0 = r0);
    end RecordBase1;

    function Record2
      input  Real      r0  := 0;
      input  Real      c2;
      input  Integer   n1  := 5;
      input  Integer   n2;
      input  Real      r1 "comment";  // The comment is also copied from record
      input  Real      r2  := Modelica.Math.sin(c1);
      input  Real      r4;
      input  Real      r5  := 5.0;
      input  Real      r6[n1];
      input  Real      r7[n2];
      output Record2   result(r0=r0,c2=c2,n1=n1,n2=n2,r1=r1,r2=r2,
                              r4=r4,r5=r5,r6=r6,r7=r7);
    protected
      constant         Real  c1 := 2.0;  // Referenced from r2
      final parameter  Real  r3 := Modelica.Math.cos(r2);
    end Record2;
  end Demo;
```

For example, the `Demo.Record2` constructor function can be called as below to construct a value for the instance `r1`, where we have used mixed positional and named parameter passing:

```
Demo.Record2 r1 = Demo.Record2(1, 2, 2, n2=3, r1=1, r2=2,
                               r4=5, r5=5, r6=1:5, r7={1,2,3});
```

However, the use of a record constructor function in the special case of declaring `r1` is not very meaningful since it would have been simpler to use modifiers directly on `r1` to specify its field values.

9.3.9 Function Derivatives

A Modelica compiler usually needs to differentiate functions called in equations and expressions of a model when transforming the model into a form that is better suited (performance, numeric accuracy) for execution. A function defined in Modelica can be automatically differentiated based on symbolic differentiation of the statements in the body of the function. However, this option is not possible for external functions, for which the only alternative for the system usually is to resort to numerical approximations of the derivatives. Also, even for Modelica functions the automatically obtained symbolic derivatives may sometimes (but rather seldom) be inefficient or have numerical instabilities.

For these reasons, an annotation called `derivative` (also briefly mentioned in Section 11.13.1, page 554) with associated optional attributes `order`, `noDerivative`, and `zeroDerivative` is available for Modelica functions, that is, for both external functions and functions implemented in Modelica. This allows us to explicitly state the computation of the derivatives of a function to any desired order.

A derivative annotation can state that it is only valid under certain conditions on the input arguments. These restrictions are defined using the following optional attributes: `order` (only a restriction if `order>1`, the default for `order` is 1), `noDerivative`, and `zeroDerivative`. The given derivative-function can only be used to compute the derivative of a function call if these restrictions are satisfied. There may be multiple restrictions on the derivative, in which case they must all be satisfied. The restrictions also imply that some derivatives of certain inputs are excluded from the call of the derivative (since they are not necessary). A function may supply multiple derivative functions subject to different restrictions.

We should point out that the `derivative` annotation is seldom needed, but is useful in certain cases where accuracy and/or performance need to be improved. For example, the function `h0` below specifies its time derivative to be given by the function `h1`, which in turn specifies its derivative (of order 2) to be computed by the function `h2`.

```
function h0 annotation(derivative=h1);
  ...
end h0;
function h1 annotation(derivative(order=2)=h2);
  ...
end h1;
function h2
  ...
end h2;
```

The formal parameter list of a `derivative` function of order 1 is constructed as follows:

- First comes all the input formal parameters of the original function. After those we will in order append one derivative input formal parameter for each input formal parameter containing `Real`-typed values, for example, scalars, arrays, or records.
- The outputs are constructed by starting with an empty list and then in order appending one derivative formal parameter for each output containing reals.

The formal parameter list of a `derivative` function of order n+1 >1 is defined as follows:

- If the Modelica function for which the derivative function is specified is an *n*th derivative (n>=1), the `derivative` annotation should indicate the (n+1)th derivative by setting the attribute `order`=n+1.
- The list of input formal parameters is amended by the (n+1)th derivative formal parameters, which are constructed in order from the *n*th `order` derivatives.
- The output formal parameters are similar to the output formal parameters for the *n*th derivative function, but each output is one higher in derivative order.

An input or output formal parameter to a function with a `derivative` annotation may be of any predefined type (`Real`, `Boolean`, `Integer`, and `String`) or a record, or array thereof, provided the record does not contain fields of both `Real` and non-`Real` predefined types. The function must have at least one input formal parameter containing reals. The set of output formal parameters of the derivative function may not be empty.

We apply this construction to a function `h0` with three formal parameters: the `Integer`-valued `i1`, the `Real`-valued `x` (implicitly a function x(t) of time as all `Real` variables), and the `Boolean`-valued `b`. Let y(t) be the return value of `h0`:

$$y(t) = h_0(i_1, x(t), b) \tag{9-1}$$

By differentiating twice, using inner derivatives, we obtain:

$$\begin{aligned} \frac{dy(t)}{dt} &= h_1(i_1, x(t), b, \frac{dx(t)}{dt}) \\ \frac{d^2y(t)}{dt^2} &= h_2(i_1, x(t), b, \frac{dx(t)}{dt}, \frac{d^2x(t)}{dt^2}) \end{aligned} \tag{9-2}$$

Applying this to the example function $y(t) = h0(t) = exp(x(t)) + i1$ when specifying the first- and second-order derivative functions gives the following definitions of `h0`, `h1`, and `h2`:

```
function h0          // exp(x(t)+i1)
  annotation(derivative=h1);
  input  Integer i1;
  input  Real    x;
  input  Boolean linear;   // not used
  output Real    y;
algorithm
  y := exp(x)+i1;
end h0;

function h1          // (d/dt)(exp(x(t))
  annotation(derivative(order=2)=h2);
  input  Integer i1;
  input  Real    x;
  input  Boolean linear;
  input  Real    der_x;
  output Real    der_y;
algorithm
  der_y := exp(x)*der_x;
end h1;

function h2          // (d/dt)(exp(x(t)*der_x(t))
  input  Integer i1;
  input  Real    x;
  input  Boolean linear;
  input  Real    der_x;
  input  Real    der_2_x;
  output Real    der_2_y;
algorithm
  der_2_y := exp(x)*der_x*der_x + exp(x)*der_2_x;
end h1;
```

The `noDerivative` optional annotation attribute is:

- `noDerivative=input_var1`

The derivative of `input_var1` is excluded from the argument list of the derivative-function. This relies on assumptions on the arguments to the function and the function should document these assumptions. However, it is not always straightforward to verify such assumptions. In many cases even the undifferentiated function will only behave correctly under these assumptions.

Assume for example that the function `fg` is defined as a composition `f(x, g(x))`. When differentiating `f` it is useful to give the derivative under the assumption that the second argument is defined in this way:

```
function fg
  input Real x;
  output Real z;
algorithm
   z := f(x, g(x));
end fg;

function f
  input Real x;
  input Real y;
  output Real z;
  annotation(derivative(noDerivative=y)) = f_der);
algorithm
  ...
end f;

function f_der
  input Real x;
  input Real x_der;
  input Real y;
  output Real z_der;
algorithm
  ...
end f_der;
```

This is useful if `g` represents the major computational effort of `fg`.

The `zeroDerivative` optional annotation attribute has the following form:

- `zeroDerivative=input_var1`

This attribute states the condition that the derivative function is only valid if `input_var1` is independent of the variables the function call is differentiated with respect to (i.e., that the derivative of `input_var1` is "zero"). The derivative of `input_var1` is excluded from the argument list of the derivative-function.

For example, assume that a function `f` has a matrix `y` and a scalar `x` as arguments. Since in this particular example the matrix argument `y` usually is a parameter expression (i.e., constant during simulation) it is then useful to define the function as follows. The additional derivative = `f_general_der` is optional and can be used when the derivative of the matrix is nonzero.

```
function f "Simple table lookup"
  input Real x;
  input Real y[:, 2];
  output Real z;
  annotation(derivative(zeroDerivative=y) = f_der,
             derivative=f_general_der);
algorithm
  ...
end f;

function f_der "Derivative of simple table lookup"
  input Real x;
  input Real y[:, 2];
  input Real x_der;
  output Real z_der;
algorithm
  ...
end f_der;

function f_general_der "Derivative of table lookup taking into account varying tables"
  input Real x;
  input Real y[:, 2];
```

```
  input Real x_der;
  input Real y_der[:, 2];
  output Real z_der;
algorithm
  ...
end f_general_der;
```

9.3.10 Function Partial Derivatives

A function defined using a short function definition can be defined by a partial derivative of another function with respect to one or more variables:

```
function func1 = der(func2, id1, id2, ...) "optional comment"
```

This means that the function `func1` is defined to be the *partial derivative* of the function `func2` with respect to the variables `id1`, `id2`, etc., in order, starting with the first variable. The variables `id1`, `id2`, etc., must have type `Real` or a subtype of `Real`.

For example, the specific enthalphy (function `specificEnthalpy`) can be computed from a `Gibbs` function by a partial derivative with respect to the temperature `T` as below:

```
function Gibbs
  input Real p,T;
  output Real g;
algorithm
  ...
end Gibbs;

function Gibbs_T = der(Gibbs, T);

function specificEnthalpy
  input Real p,T;
  output Real h;
algorithm
  h: = Gibbs(p,T) - T*Gibbs_T(p,T);
end specificEnthalpy;
```

9.3.11 Function Inverses

Inverses of functions are sometimes useful in symbolic processing, for example, during solution of systems of equation. Therefore it is possible for every Modelica function with one output (result) formal parameter to have one or more `inverse` annotations to define inverses of this function:

```
function f1
  input A1 u1;
  ...
  input T1 uk;
  ...
  input Am um = am;
  ...
  input An un;
  output T2 y;
  annotation(inverse(uk = f2(..., y, ....), ui = f3(..., y, ...), ...));
  annotation(inverse(up = f4(..., y, ....), ...));
algorithm
  ...
end f1;
```

The meaning is that function f_2 is an inverse to function f_1 where the previous output y is now an input and the previous input u_k is now an output. More than one inverse can be defined within the same inverse annotation. Several inverses are separated by commas.

For example, function f_3 is an inverse to function f_1 where the previous output y is now an input and the previous input u_i is now an output, and function f_4 is an inverse to function f_1 where the previous output y is now an input and the previous input u_p is now an output.

The inverse requires that for all valid values of the input arguments of f_2(...,y, ...) and u_k being calculated as $u_k := f_2(..., y, ...)$, this implies that the equality $y = f_1(..., u_k, ...,)$ should be valid to a certain precision as computed by the function f_1 .

The function f_1 can have any number and types of formal parameters with and without default value. The restriction is that the number of unknown variables (i.e., the number of array elements in the case of an array, record components in the case of a record, or just 1 in the case of a single scalar) in the output formal parameter of both f_1 and f_2 must be the same and that f_2 must have exactly the same formal parameters as f_1 (with the same defaults, if an argument u_m has a default) excluding the `input/output` prefixses, but the order of the formal parameters may be permuted. For example:

```
function h_pTX
  input  Real p     "pressure";
  input  Real T     "temperature";
  input  Real X[:] "mass fractions";
  output Real h     "specific enthalpy";
  annotation(inverse(T = T_phX(p,h,X)));
algorithm
   ...
end h_pTX;

function T_phX
  input  Real p     "pressure";
  input  Real h     "specific enthalpy";
  input  Real X[:] "mass fractions";
  output Real T     "temperature";
algorithm
   ...
end T_phX;
```

See also Section 11.13.2, page 555 for a short summary.

9.3.12 Function Inlining

Function inlining is a technique that replaces each function call with a copy of its function body with the actual arguments substituted for the formal function parameters. The advantage is more efficient execution because the function call overhead is eliminated. This can be noticeable for small functions which are called many times. The disadvantage is code expansion, since a copy of the function body is inserted for each call.

Function inlining is controlled by setting the `Inline`, `LateInline`, or `InlineAfterIndex-Reduction` annotations to `true` or `false`. All three annotations only have effect within function declarations and should be stated at the end of the function.

If `Inline=true`, the model developer proposes to inline the function. This means that the function call is replaced by the body of the function at all places where the function is called. This makes the execution more efficient by avoiding the overhead of a function call but increases memory usage since the function body is duplicated at each call site. If `Inline=false`, the model developer proposes not to inline the function.

The setting `Inline=true` is for example used in `Modelica.Mechanics.MultiBody.Frames` and in functions of `Modelica.Media` to have no overhead for function calls such as resolving a vector in a different coordinate system. At the same time the inlined function can be analytically differentiated, e.g., for index reduction needed for mechanical systems.

If `LateInline=true`, the model developer proposes to inline the function after all symbolic transformations have been performed, especially symbolic differentiation and inversion of functions. For efficiency reasons it is then useful to replace all function calls with identical input arguments by one function call, after the late inlining.

If `LateInline=false`, the model developer proposes to not inline the function after symbolic transformations have been performed.

The `LateInline` annotation is used in certain models to provide, in combination with common subexpression elimination, the automatic caching of function calls. One such model is `Modelica.Media.Water.IF97_Utilities.T_props_ph`. Furthermore, it is used in order to enable Modelica compilers to propagate specific enthalpy over connectors in the `Modelica.Fluid` library.

A function is only inlined once, either early or late. `LateInline` has priority over (early) `Inline`, since if a function is inlined early, there are no function calls left to be inlined by `LateInline`. This has the following consequences regarding combinations of the `Inline` and `LateInline` annotations:

- The combination `Inline=true, LateInline=false` is identical to `Inline=true`.
- The combination `Inline=true, LateInline=true` is identical to `LateInline=true`.
- The combination `Inline=false, LateInline=true` is identical to `LateInline=true`.

The `Inline` or `LateInline` annotations are stated at the end of the function definition as in the following examples:

```
function homotopy
  input Real actual;
  input Real simplified;
  output Real y;
algorithm
  y := actual;
  annotation(Inline = true);
end homotopy;

function fromReal
  input  Real re;
  input  Real im := 0;
  output Complex result(re=re, im=im);
  annotation(Inline=true);
end fromReal;
```

If `InlineAfterIndexReduction = true`, the model developer proposes to inline the function after the function is differentiated for index reduction, and before any other symbolic transformations are performed. This annotation *cannot* be combined with annotations `Inline` and `LateInline`.

This annotation is for example used in `Modelica.Mechanics.Rotational.Sources.Move` to define that an input signal is the derivative of another input signal.

See also Section 11.13.3, page 555 for a short summary of these annotations.

9.3.13 smoothOrder for Continuous Function Differentiation

Sometimes it is very useful for a Modelica compiler to have access to information about how many times a function is continuously differentiable, for example when the derivative of a function is needed for index reduction or to compute an analytic Jacobian,

The `smoothOrder` annotation can be used to state such information. The `smoothOrder=`*number* annotation within a function states that the function can be symbolically differentiated with continuous results at least *number* times, which defines the maximum number of differentiations of the function for which it is guaranteed that all of its differentiated outputs are continuous provided all input arguments and their derivatives up to order `smoothOrder` are continuous.

This means that the function is at least $C^{smoothOrder}$, that is, differentiable with continuous results at least `smoothOrder` times. The setting `smoothOrder=1` means that the function can be differentiated at least once and still keep all its output arguments continuous, provided that the input arguments are continuous. If a Modelica compiler needs the derivative of a function, e.g. for index reduction or to compute an analytic Jacobian, the function can be differentiated analytically at least `smoothOrder` times. Examples:

```
annotation(smoothOrder=2)
annotation(smoothOrder(normallyConstant=FARG)=1)
annotation(smoothOrder(normallyConstant=FARG1,normallyConstant=FARG2)=2)
```

The optional argument `normallyConstant` of `smoothOrder` defines that the function argument `FARG` is usually constant.

A Modelica compiler might check whether the actual argument to `FARG` is a parameter expression at the place where the function is called. If this is the case, the derivative of the function might be constructed under the assumption that the corresponding argument is constant, to enhance efficiency.

Typically, a tool would generate at most two different derivative functions of a function: One, under the assumption that all `normallyConstant` arguments are actually constant. And one, under the assumption that all input arguments are time varying.

Based on the actual arguments of the function call either of the two derivative functions is used.

This annotation is used by many functions of the `Modelica.Fluid` library, such as `Modelica.Fluid.Dissipation.PressureLoss.StraightPipe.dp_laminar_DP`, since geometric arguments to these functions are usually constant.

See also Section 11.13.4, page 555 for a short summary.

9.3.14 Impure Functions

It is possible to declare an *impure*, that is, nondeclarative, Modelica function by prefixing a Modelica function by the `impure` keyword. This is in contradiction to the properties of a typical Modelica function which is declarative—"*pure*" (see Section 9.1, page 421) by default. A *pure* function has the following properties:

- It is a mathematical function, i.e., calls with the same input arguments always give the same output results.
- It is side-effect free with respect to the internal Modelica simulation state—the set of all Modelica variables in a total simulation model. Specifically, the ordering of function calls and the number of calls to a function shall not influence the simulation state.

The declarative "pure" property makes it possible for Modelica compilers to freely perform algebraic manipulation of expressions containing function calls while still preserving their semantics. For example, a Modelica compiler may use common subexpression elimination to eliminate all except one of the calls to the same function with identical input arguments.

A Modelica translator is responsible for maintaining the purity property for *pure* non-external Modelica functions, that is, functions without the `impure` keyword written in the Modelica language. Regarding external functions, the external function implementer is responsible for maintaining the purity property. Note that *impure* external functions can have side-effects as long as they do not influence the internal Modelica simulation state, for example, caching variables for performance or printing trace output to a log file.

A Modelica compiler is not allowed to perform certain optimizations on function calls to an *impure* function. For example, reordering calls or common subexpression elimination is not allowed.

The following are examples of typical *use cases* for using *impure* functions:

- Functions doing *input-output*. Such functions typically return different results in different calls despite having the same input arguments (Section 16.4.3, page 926). Calls to such functions can typically not be reordered.
- Functions for *communication* with external systems, e.g., during hardware-in-the-loop simulation.
- Functions doing *data caching*, e.g., for performance. Some results is computed in one call, and stored for re-use in a later call.

Where in a Modelica model can then *impure* functions be *called* and where should they *not* be *called*?

- Except for the case of when-equations/when-statements, *impure* functions should *not* be called within equation sections or algorithm sections. For example, such sections can be re-ordered (sorted) relative to each other, and equations re-ordered with respect to each other.
- An *impure* function can be called from within when-equations/when-statements. In such cases the point of execution is determined by an event.
- *Impure* functions can be called from a function marked with the `impure` prefix.
- *Impure* functions can be called from within a function with the `pure` prefix if the side-effects from the called *impure* functions cancel out before returning from the *pure* function.

For example, if two *impure* functions are being called from a function with the `pure` prefix, a temporary side-effect by the first function call may be restored by the second function call.

By using the `pure` prefix, the modeler guarantees that the function is *pure*, despite calling *impure* functions or using external objects. Moreover, a function inheriting an *impure* function must be marked `impure` or `pure` by the modeler. To summarize:

- An *impure* function must be marked with the `impure` prefix.
- It is only allowed to call an *impure* function from within another function marked `impure` or `pure`, or from within a when-equation or when-statement.
- The prefix `pure` is used to state that a function is *pure* even though it may call *impure* functions.

The following are two example functions, one *pure* and one *impure*:

```
function evaluateLinear  // pure function, the standard Modelica case
   input  Real a0;
   input  Real a1;
   input  Real x;
   output Real y;
algorithm
   y = a0 + a1*x;
end evaluateLinear;

impure function receiveRealSignal    // impure function
   input  HardwareDriverID id;
   output Real y;
   external "C" y = receiveSignal(id);
end receiveRealSignal;
```

9.3.14.1 Impure Functions as Function Arguments

Furthermore, note that *functions* can be *passed as arguments* to other functions, as described in Section 9.3.3, page 446. A natural question is under what conditions can an *impure* function be passed as an argument?

To allow such argument passing we require that the corresponding *function formal parameter* is marked `impure` to make its *impure* properties visible in the context (i.e., the function body) where the *impure* function parameter is called.

Moreover, a function having a formal function parameter marked `impure` must itself be marked `pure` or `impure`. The reason is that the modeler must take a conscious decision regarding the purity of the function itself. The first case (`pure`) means that the modeler guarantees that the side-effects of the function parameter cancel out; in the second case (`impure`) they don't. For example:

```
partial function Functype
  input Real a;
  output Real b;
end FuncType;

pure function foo
  input Real x;
  input impure FuncType formalFunc;
  output Real res;
algorithm
  res := formalFunc(x+2);
end foo;
```

Call 1, pass a pure function `sin`:

```
w := foo(5.1, sin);
```

Call 2, pass an impure function `sinTrace`:

```
w := foo(9.4, sinTrace);
```

9.3.15 Additional Function Properties, Restrictions, and Enhancements

A number of additional properties and issues of Modelica functions also need be pointed out. We start by comparing functions to general Modelica classes and continue with a discussion on how algorithm sections can be viewed as functions.

9.3.15.1 Comparison of Functions with General Modelica Classes

The `function` concept in Modelica is a specialized class with some restrictions and enhancements, for example, see the section on specialized classes in Section 3.8 on page 87 in Chapter 3, which contains a shortened description compared to the one below. The syntax and semantics of a function have many similarities to those of the `block` specialized class. A `function` also has many of the properties of a general class, for example, being able to inherit other functions, or to redeclare or modify elements of a function declaration. However, a `function` has the following restrictions compared to a general Modelica `class`:

- Each input formal parameter of the function must be *prefixed* by the keyword `input`, and each result formal parameter by the keyword `output`. All public variables are formal parameters.
- Input formal parameters are read-only after being bound to the actual arguments or default values, i.e., they may not be assigned values in the body of the function.
- A function may *not be used in connections*, may have *no equations*, may have *no initial algorithm*, and can have at most *one algorithm* section, which, if present, is the body of the function.
- A function may have zero or one external function interface, which, if present, is the external definition of the function.
- For a function to be called in a simulation model, it must have an algorithm section or an external function interface as its body or be defined as a function partial derivative (Section 9.3.10, page 459), and it may not be partial. Moreover, the output variables must be assigned inside the function either in declaration assignments or in an algorithm section, or via an external function body or function partial derivative.
- Function output variables should be computed. It is a quality of implementation to what degree a Modelica tool can perform analysis to determine if an output variable is computed.

- A function may only contain variables/instances of the restricted classes `type`, `record`, `operator record`, and `function`; i.e., no `model` or `block` instances.
- The elements of a function may not have prefixes `inner`, or `outer`.
- A function *cannot contain* calls to the Modelica *built-in operators* `der`, `initial`, `terminal`, `sample`, `pre`, `edge`, `change`, `reinit`, `delay`, `cardinality`, `inStream`, `actualStream`, the operators of the built-in package `Connections`, the synchronous operators (Section 13.6, page 694, the state machines operators (Section 13.7, page 729), and is not allowed to contain when-statements.
- The dimension *sizes* not declared with `(:)` of each array result or array local variable of a function must be either given by the input formal parameters, or given by constant or parameter expressions, or by expressions containing combinations of those. See also Section 8.2.3, page 350 and Section 9.3.2.8, page 445, regarding dimension sizes of arrays in functions.
- The local variables of a function are not automatically initialized to the implicit default start values of the data type (Section 3.9, page 93); e.g. 0.0 for `Real`, 0 for `Integer`, and `false` for `Boolean`) for performance reasons. It is the responsibility of the user to provide explicit defaults or to define the values of such variables before they are referenced.
- Local variables and formal parameters of a function will inside the function behave as though they have discrete-time variability.
- A subtype of a function type must fulfill the rules for function subtyping (Section 3.19.6, page 130). This is more restrictive than the usual subtyping rules between Modelica classes.

A Modelica `function` has the following enhancements compared to a general Modelica `class`:

- A function may be called using the conventional *positional calling syntax* for passing arguments, as well as mixed positional and named calling.
- A function may be called through a reference to an instance name, see Section 9.3.2.4, page 443.
- A function can be *recursive.*
- A formal parameter or local variable may be initialized through an *assignment* `(:=)` of a default value in its declaration. Initialization through an equation is not possible.
- A function is dynamically instantiated, that is, creating an activation record when it is called, rather than being statically instantiated by an instance declaration, which is the case for other kinds of classes.
- A function may have an external function interface specifier as its body.
- A function may be defined in a short function definition to be a function partial derivative.
- A function allows dimension sizes declared with `(:)` to be resized for array results or array local variables, see Section 9.3.2.8, page 445.

9.3.15.2 Viewing Algorithms as Functions

The function concept is a basic building block when defining the semantics or meaning of programming language constructs. Some programming languages are completely defined in terms of mathematical functions. This makes it useful to try to understand and define the semantics of algorithm sections in Modelica in terms of functions. We have already mentioned several times in this chapter that algorithm sections are special cases of functions.

For example, consider the algorithm section below, which occurs in an equation context:

```
algorithm
  y := x;
  z := 2*y;
  y := z+y;
  ...
```

This algorithm can be transformed into an equation and a function as below, without changing its meaning. The equation equates the output variables of the previous algorithm section with the results of the function `f`. The function `f` has the *inputs* to the algorithm section as its input formal parameters and the *outputs* as its result parameters. The algorithmic code of the algorithm section has become the body of the function `f`.

```
(y,z) = f(x);
...
function f
  input  Real x;
  output Real y,z;
algorithm
  y := x;
  z := 2*y;
  y := z+y;
end f;
```

9.4 External Functions

It is possible to call functions defined outside of the Modelica language, implemented in C or Fortran 77, in the C subset of C++, or in the Fortran 77 subset of Fortran 90. Other languages, for example, Java, may be supported in the future. If no external language is specified, the implementation language for the external function is assumed to be C. The body of an external function is marked with the keyword `external` in the Modelica external function declaration, for example:

```
function log
  input Real x;
  output Real y;
external
end log;
```

The external function interface supports a number of advanced features:

- Support for external functions written in C and FORTRAN 77. Other languages, for example, C++ and Fortran 90, may be supported in the future.
- Mapping of argument types from Modelica to the target language and back.
- Natural type conversion rules in the sense that there is a mapping from Modelica to standard libraries of the target language.
- Arbitrary formal parameter order for the external function.
- Passing arrays to and from external functions where the dimension sizes are passed as explicit integer parameters.
- External function formal parameters which are used both for input and output.
- Explicit specification of row-major versus column-major array memory layout.
- Local work arrays.

9.4.1 Structure of External Function Declarations

The standard structure of a Modelica external function declaration is basically the same as that of a standard Modelica function. The only difference is that we have replaced the algorithm body of the function with the keyword `external` possibly followed by any of the *optional* items *language_spec*, *external_function_call_spec*, *external_call_spec_annotation*, and *external_function_annotation*. The structure is as follows:

```
function <functionname>
  <formal parameters>
protected
```

```
  <local variables>
external <language_spec> <external_function_call_spec>
           <external_call_spec_annotation>;
  <external_function_annotation>;
end <functionname>;
```

The local variables in the optional `protected` part allow for temporary storage, for example, work arrays needed for certain Fortran library routines.

If we just use the keyword `external` without any of the optional items, a number of default rules apply. If there is no *language_spec*, the external implementation language is assumed to be C. If there is no *external_function_call_spec*, a *default call structure mapping*, see below, from the Modelica function formal parameters to the external function parameters and return value applies.

The *language_spec* in an external function specification gives the implementation language of the external function and must currently be one of the following strings if specified:

- `"C"`
- `"FORTRAN 77"`
- `"builtin"`
- `"Java"` // Currently not part of the Modelica standard, but supported by some implementations.

Note that uppercase letters and one space character must be used in the string `"FORTRAN 77"`. Otherwise, if the language is not specified, the default external language `"C"` is assumed.

9.4.1.1 The "builtin" External Language Specification

The `"builtin"` specification is only used for functions that are defined to be built-in in Modelica. The external-function call mechanism for `"builtin"` functions is implementation-defined. Typically, for functions from the standard C-library, the prototype of the function is provided but no library annotation. Currently, there are no other builtin functions defined in Modelica. For example:

```
package Modelica
  package Math
    function sin
      input Real x;
      output Real y;
      external "builtin"  y=sin(x);
    end sin;
  end Math;
end Modelica;

model UserModel
  parameter Real p=Modelica.Math.sin(2);
end UserModel;
```

9.4.1.2 Default Call Structure Mapping

The following *default mapping* rules apply if no *external_function_call_spec* is provided:

- The default external function *name* is the same as the Modelica function name.
- The default *ordering* of the formal parameters in the external function prototype in the external programming language is the same as the ordering of the Modelica function input and output formal parameter declarations. There is one exception, however. If there is just one Modelica output parameter, the default assumption is that it corresponds to the return value of the external function and not to an output formal parameter.
- An array argument is passed by default for both C and Fortran 77 as the address of the array followed by the array dimension sizes.

- The default array layout mapping is conversion to "rowMajor" when calling a C function and to "columnMajor" when calling a Fortran 77 function. This can be overridden by the arrayLayout annotation (Section 9.4.6, page 475).
- Automatic mapping of Modelica types to C or Fortran 77 and back, according to the table in Section 9.4.2 on page 470.

The function tan2 below is a very simple external function specification just using the single keyword external, which implies that the default mapping rules apply.

```
function tan2
  input  Real x1;
  input  Real x2;
  output Real y;
external
end tan2;
```

This Modelica external function specification gives rise to the following C function prototype, shown below together with an example call in Modelica and the corresponding translated call.

C-prototype:	`double tan2(double, double);`
Example call in Modelica:	`z := tan2(5.5, 4);`
Translated call in C:	`z = tan2(5.5, 4);`

We will now illustrate the default mapping of array arguments to external C and Fortran 77 functions according to the type translation table in Section 9.4.2 on page 470. First we show a simple Modelica external function that maps to an external C function:

```
function foo
  input   Real       a[:,:,:];
  output  Real       x;
external;
end foo;
```

This corresponds to the following C function prototype and example calls:

C-prototype:	`double foo(double *, size_t, size_t, size_t);`
Example call in Modelica:	`w := foo( {{{1,2},{3,4}},{{5,6},{7,8}}} );`
Translated call in C:	`double temp[][][] = {{{1,2},{3,4}},{{5,6},{7,8}}};` `w = foo(&temp, 2,2,2);`

The same external function foo can instead be specified as mapping to a Fortran 77 function:

```
function foo
  input   Real       a[:,:,:];
  output  Real       x;
external "FORTRAN 77";
end foo;
```

The default mapping corresponds to a Fortran 77 function defined as below:

```
FUNCTION foo(a, n1, n2, n3)
  DOUBLE PRECISION    a(n1,n2,n3)
  INTEGER             n1
  INTEGER             n2
  INTEGER             n3
  DOUBLE PRECISION    foo
  ...
END
```

9.4.1.3 Explicit Call Structure Mapping

The *external_function_call_spec* allows calling external functions that do not match the default mappings of function name, external formal parameter ordering, input or output parameters, return value, and array arguments. The structure of the *external_function_call_spec* is one of the following two variants:

1. externalfuncname(argumentlist)
2. output_parameter = externalfuncname(argumentlist)

The only kinds of expressions allowed in the *argumentlist* are variable references, scalar constants, and the function `size(`*arr,i*`)` applied to an array and a constant array dimension number. A reference to a variable that is part of an input or output, e.g. reference to a record field that is part of a record variable, is treated the same way as a top-level input or output in the external call.

The optional *external_function_annotation* is used to pass additional information to the compiler when necessary. Currently the only supported annotation is `arrayLayout`, which can be either `"rowMajor"` or `"columnMajor"`, being defaults for C and Fortran array layout respectively.

We use the simple external C function `joinThreeVectors` below as an example of the first variant of *external_function_call_spec*. A Modelica implementation `joinThreeVectorsM` of the same function is shown as a comparison.

```
function joinThreeVectorsM    "Modelica version"
  input Real v1[:],v2[:],v3[:];
  output Real vres[size(v1,1)+size(v2,1)+size(v3,1)];
algorithm
  vres := cat(1,v1,v2,v3);
end joinThreeVectorsM;
```

The external C function in this case happens to have a different name `join3vec` in C compared to its Modelica name `joinThreeVectors`. The parameter list of the C function does not follow the default mapping rules, and returns its result in an output parameter and not as a return value. Therefore an *external_function_call_spec* of the first of the above two variants is appropriate. The array layout annotation is really not needed here since `"rowMajor"` is default for C. It is just shown as an example.

```
function joinThreeVectors    "Modelica external function version"
  input Real v1[:],v2[:],v3[:];
  output Real vres[size(v1,1)+size(v2,1)+size(v3,1)];
external "C" join3vec(v1,v2,v3,vres,size(v1,1),size(v2,1),size(v3,1));
           annotation(arrayLayout = "rowMajor");
end joinThreeVectors;
```

The above Modelica external function version of `joinThreeVectors` corresponds to the following C-prototype with example calls, where the predefined C type `size_t` is the same as the C type `unsigned int`, and is used to pass array dimension sizes.

C-prototype:	`void join3vec(double*, double*, double*, double*,size_t, size_t, size_t);`
Example call in Modelica:	`vjoined := joinThreeVectors(va,vb,vc);`
Translated call in C:	`join3vec(&va, &vb, &vc, &vjoined, n1, n2, n3);`

The next example shows how arrays can be passed an external Fortran 77 function using explicit call structure mapping.

```
function fum
  input   Real      x[:];
  input   Real      y[size(x,1),:];
  input   Integer   i;
  output  Real      u1[size(y,1)];
  output  Integer   u2[size(y,2)];
external "FORTRAN 77" myfum(x, y, size(x,1), size(y,2), u1, i, u2);
end fum;
```

The corresponding Fortran 77 subroutine would be declared as follows:

```
SUBROUTINE myfum(x, y, n, m, u1, i, u2)
  DOUBLE PRECISION(n)   x
  DOUBLE PRECISION(n,m) y
  INTEGER               n
  INTEGER               m
  DOUBLE PRECISION(n)   u1
  INTEGER               I
  DOUBLE PRECISION(m)   u2
  ...
END
```

The *second form* of *external_function_call_spec* is *output_parameter* = *externalfuncname*(*argumentlist*). It is needed in situations where additional information about how to map the external function value is required. The following external function returns two results: one function value and one output parameter value. Both are mapped to Modelica function results as specified. This situation requires the second form of external function call specification.

```
function dualResults
  input  Real     x;
  input  Integer  y;
  output Real     funcvalue;
  output Integer  out1;
external "C" funcvalue = doubleresults(x, y, out1);
end dualResults;
```

This corresponds to the following:

C-prototype:	`double doubleresults(double, int, int *);`
Example call in Modelica:	`(z1,i2) := dualResults(2.4, 3);`
Translated call in C:	`z1 = doubleresults(2.4, 3, &i2);`

9.4.2 Argument and Result Type Mapping

Arguments and result values are mapped from Modelica types to corresponding C or Fortran 77 types and back when calling an external function from Modelica. The table shows the mapping of argument and result types at external function calls between Modelica, and C or FORTRAN 77. Here *T*, *TC*, and *TF* denote corresponding Modelica, C, and Fortran array element types respectively; see further explanations in the table below.

There are two ways for an external function to return results:

1. Through output formal parameters.
2. As a function return value.

The external types for output parameters are indicated in the table when different from the input parameter types. The external types for function return values should be declared in the same way in the external function as for input formal parameters of the same type, except for arrays where array dimension sizes are to be left out.

If there is a single output parameter and no *external_function_call_spec*, or if there is an explicit *external_function_call_spec*, in which case the left-hand side must be one of the output formal parameters, the external routine is assumed to be a value-returning function. Otherwise, the external function is assumed not to return anything, i.e., it is a `void`-function in C or a subroutine in Fortran.

Modelica	C	FORTRAN 77
`Real`	`double (double* for output)`	`DOUBLE PRECISION`
`Integer`	`int (int* for output)`	`INTEGER`
`Boolean`	`int (int* for output)`	`LOGICAL`

`String`	`const char*`
	`(const char** for output,`
	may need `ModelicaAllocateString)`
		`CHARACTER`
		(Not yet in the Modelica standard; tool dependent availability)

`Enumeration type`	`int (int* for output)`	`INTEGER`
T`[`d_1`, …, `d_n`]` *Input or output formal parameter*	*TC* `*, size_t` d_1`, …, size_t` d_n This is the default argument mapping of an array including dimension sizes used if no *external_function_call_spec* is present. If such a call specification is present only the address of the array, of type *TC*`*`, is passed since we explicitly specify dimension size arguments in the *external_function_call_spec*.	*TF*`,` `INTEGER` d_1`, …, INTEGER` d_n Default mapping of an array including dimension sizes used if no *external_function_call_spec* is present. If such a call specification is present only the address of the array is passed since we explicitly specify dimension size arguments in the *external_function_call_spec*.
T`[`d_1`, …, `d_n`]` *Return value*	*TC* `*` No dimension sizes are included when mapping return types since the sizes are already known by the caller.	*TF*
`record` *Only* records with `Real`, `Integer`, `Boolean`, enumeration fields, or record fields. Array fields are not allowed.	`struct * (struct** for output)` Each Modelica record field is mapped into a C struct field with the same field ordering. The mapping is according to the translation of types in this table.	Not available for Fortran.

The following general and simple-type related considerations apply for argument- and return-type mapping at external function calls:

- Formal parameters of the *primitive* C *types* `double` and `int` are declared as `double*` and `int*` for output formal parameters in C function prototypes, since addresses of receiving variables are needed for output.
- If we call an external Fortran function or subroutine, addresses are passed for both input and output formal parameters since Fortran always uses call by reference.
- When an argument in a C *external_function_call_spec* is of the form `size(…, …)`, then the corresponding C formal parameter type is `size_t`, usually defined as `unsigned int`, instead of the usual `int`.
- Values of *enumeration types* used as *arguments* are mapped to type `int` when calling an external C function, and to type `INTEGER` when calling an external Fortran function. The *i*th enumeration

literal is mapped to integer value i, starting at 1. *Return enumeration values* in integer form are mapped to enumeration types analogously: the integer value 1 is mapped to the first enumeration literal, 2 to the second, etc. Returning a value which does not map to an existing enumeration literal for the specified enumeration type is an error.

The following applies to strings passed and returned to/from external functions:

- Modelica *string* arguments can be passed to input formal parameters in C and for certain Modelica implementations to Fortran 77 even if not yet officially in the Modelica standard. Strings are `NULL`-terminated, i.e., ending with a null character `'\0'`, to simplify calling of C functions.
- When *returning* a nonliteral *string* as an output formal parameter or return value, the memory for this string can be allocated with the function `ModelicaAllocateString` (see Section 9.4.7, page 475). The C `malloc` function should not be used because a Modelica simulation environment may have its own allocation scheme, e.g. a special stack for local variables of a function. After return of the external function the Modelica environment is responsible for the memory allocated with `ModelicaAllocateString`, e.g. to free this memory when appropriate. It is not allowed to access memory that was allocated using `ModelicaAllocateString` in a previous call of the external function since it might have become deallocated.

Regarding arrays and records we have the following considerations:

- *Array arguments* of type $T[d_1, ..., d_n]$ can be passed as input as well as output formal parameters, where the element type T is one of the basic Modelica types `Real`, `Integer`, `Boolean`, `String` as well as `record` (but `record` is not supported for Fortran 77) and d_1, ..., d_n are the sizes of the 1st to the *n*th array dimensions. TC and TF are the corresponding C and Fortran 77 versions of the element type according to the above table. An array is generally passed as the address of the array followed by *n* integers for the *n* dimension sizes. In the case of C these integer formal parameters are declared with the type `size_t` which normally is the same as `unsigned int`.
- An *array or record* can also be returned as a *function return value*. In that case only the address of the array or record is returned since storage for the returned data must be preallocated by the caller. Dimension sizes are not returned since the dimensions of a preallocated returned array are set by the caller. A record can be returned from a C function but not from a Fortran 77 function.
- When we *pass* record, array, and string arguments or *return* records and arrays, these are passed or returned *by reference*, i.e., a pointer to each argument is passed or returned, which is evident from the above type translation table.

As an example, a Modelica record `Rec` below is mapped to a corresponding C `struct`:

```
record Rec                                         struct Rec {
  Real      z;            mapped to                  double  z;
  Boolean   b;                                       int     b;
end Rec;                                           };
```

9.4.3 A Large Example

The external function interface supports a number of advanced features such as in/out parameters and declaration of temporary work variables, which are illustrated by the following rather complicated example. For example, the formal parameters `Ares`, `Bres`, `Cres`, and `Dres` correspond to in/out parameters in the external function `bilinearSampling` below, which has the values `A`, `B`, `C`, and `D` as input defaults and different values as results. The ordering and usage of formal parameters to the external Fortran function is handled through explicit call structure mapping. This is used below to explicitly pass sizes of array dimensions to the Fortran routine called `ab04md`. Some old-style Fortran routines like `ab04md` need work arrays, which are conveniently handled by local variable declarations after the keyword `protected`. A string constant is also passed to the Fortran function, even though passing strings to Fortran functions is not yet officially in the Modelica standard. In fact, almost all Fortran functions or subroutines available in common numerical libraries require at least one string argument.

```
function bilinearSampling
  "Function for Discrete-time <--> continuous-time systems conversion by a
bilinear transformation."
  input Real alpha := 1, beta := 1;
  input Real A[:,size(A,1)], B[size(A,1),:],
             C[:,size(A,1)], D[size(C,1),size(B,2)];
  input Boolean isContinuous := true;
  output Real Ares[size(A,1), size(A,2)] := A, // Ares is in-out
  Bres[size(B,1), size(B,2)] := B, // to the Fortran function
  Cres[size(C,1), size(C,2)] := C,
  Dres[size(D,1), size(D,2)] := D;
  output Integer info;
protected
  Integer iwork[size(A,1)];   // Work arrays
  Real    dwork[size(A,1)];
  String  c2dstring := if isContinuous then "C" else "D";
external "FORTRAN 77" ab04md(c2dstring,size(A,1),size(B,2),size(C,1),
  alpha,beta,Ares,size(Ares,1),Bres,size(Bres,1),
  Cres,size(Cres,1),Dres,size(Dres,1),
  iwork,dwork,size(dwork,1),info);
end bilinearSampling;
```

The following Modelica class contains an example call to `bilinearSampling`, which via the external function interface is transformed to a call to `ab04md`.

```
class BilinearSamplingTest
  parameter Real alpha=1, beta=1;
  parameter Real A[:,:] = [0, 1; 2, 4],        // Coefficients
                 B[:,:] = [5, 6; 7, 8],
                 C[:,:] = [9, 10; 11,12],
                 D[:,:] = [13,14; 15,16];
  Real Ares[size(A,1), size(A,2)],          // Results
       Bres[size(B,1), size(B,2)],
       Cres[size(C,1), size(C,2)],
       Dres[size(D,1), size(D,2)];
  Integer info;
equation
   (Ares,Bres,Cres,Dres,info) = bilinearSampling(alpha,beta,A,B,C,D,true);
end BilinearSamplingTest;
```

If the external function `ab04md` would have been a C function instead of a Fortran function the corresponding C function prototype would become:

```
void ab04md(const char *, size_t, size_t, size_t, double, double,
            double *, size_t, double *, size_t, double *, size_t,
            double *, size_t, int *, double *, size_t, int *);
```

9.4.4 Preventing External Functions from Changing their Inputs

Modelica functions disallow changing input formal parameters. An external function called from Modelica must behave in the same way as if the function had been implemented in Modelica. Therefore an external function is not allowed to internally change its inputs, even if they are restored before the end of the function. For efficiency reasons, for example, to avoid copying of large arrays, the Modelica function formal parameters are mapped directly to the external function formal parameters. When calling Fortran functions all arguments are passed by reference, and when calling C functions arrays and records are passed by reference. Such input arguments could theoretically be changed by the external function and thus violate the above rule. If the external function interface programmer suspects that the external function may change some of its inputs, those inputs should be copied in the interface function to prevent any problems on the Modelica side.

For example, consider the following Modelica function `f`, which calls an external Modelica function `efunc` that is mapped to the external Fortran function `forfunc`.

```
function f
  input  Real a;
  output Real b;
algorithm
  b:=efunc(a,a);
  b:=efunc(b,2*b);
end f;
```

The Modelica compiler will usually translate the function `f` to the C function `f` below, which in turn calls the external function `efunc` that has been mapped from `forfunc`. The extra underscore in `forfunc_` is usually added when calling a Fortran function from C.

```
double f(double a) {
  extern void forfunc_(double*,double*,double*);
  double b,temp1,temp2;
  forfunc_(&a,&a,&b);
  temp1=2*b;
  temp2=b;
  forfunc_(&b,&temp1,&temp2);
  return temp2;
}
```

A straightforward external function declaration of `efunc` being mapped to `forfunc` can appear as follows:

```
function efunc       "Straightforward version of interface function"
  input Real x;
  input Real y;
  output Real z:=x;
  external "FORTRAN 77" forfunc(x,y,z);
end efunc;
```

If the first input is changed internally within `forfunc`, the designer of the interface would have to change the interface function `efunc` to the following by inserting a copying operation in order to protect against unwanted change of that input formal parameter:

```
function efunc  "Version that protects first argument against change"
  input Real x;
  input Real y;
  output Real z;
protected
  Real xtemp:=x; // Temporary since forfunc changes 1:st input
  external "FORTRAN 77" forfunc(xtemp,y,z);
end efunc;
```

9.4.5 External Function Formal Parameter Aliasing

Variable aliasing means that two variables may refer to the same memory area. Thus, if two variables x and y are aliased, if the variable x is changed, the variable y will also be changed. Such changes are sometimes unintentional, which is a source of programming errors.

Modelica does not allow aliasing between variables. However, this may occur in languages such as C or Fortran. When calling external functions from Modelica, there is a small danger that there is aliasing between the external function formal parameters, which is not allowed when called from Modelica. If there is uncertainty about the aliasing properties of certain external function formal parameters it is possible to do copying of such parameters to avoid the problems, as described in Section 9.4.4.

9.4.6 External Function Array Layout rowMajor columnMajor

Regarding specific annotations only for external function declarations, there is an optional `arrayLayout` annotation, which can have one of the values `"rowMajor"` or `"columnMajor"`. These are the defaults for C and Fortran 77 array layouts, respectively. This annotation causes additional information to be passed to the compiler when necessary. It is needed only when the array storage layout deviates from the default for the external language. This is the case for the function `joinThreeVectors2` below where the C function uses column-major array representation, which is different from the default row-major layout that normally is used for C. A summary of this feature is given in Section 11.13.5, page 556.

```
function joinThreeVectors2 "External C function with column-major arrays"
  input Real v1[:],v2[:],v3[:];
  output Real vres[size(v1,1)+size(v2,1)+size(v3,1)];
external "C" join3vec(v1,v2,v3,vres,size(v1,1),size(v2,1),size(v3,1));
  annotation(arrayLayout = "columnMajor");
end joinThreeVectors2;
```

9.4.7 Utility Functions Callable in External Functions

Within external functions called from Modelica we often need access to the following two kinds of generic mechanisms:

- *Reporting errors* in a way compatible with the Modelica error-handling mechanism.
- *Allocating memory* for variable-sized results such as strings that are passed back from the external function for use by Modelica code and therefore need to be Modelica-managed data. This is not needed for known-size results, e.g. arrays, since that memory is preallocated by the caller.

This kind of functionality is different from most other user-defined external code in that it needs to be compatible with and interact closely with the Modelica run-time system, which usually is not accessible to the user. However, note that the `getInstanceName` function, Section 6.14.1.1, page 293, useful for some error reporting, is only callable within Modelica code, not within external functions.

For these reasons the following utility functions are provided. They can be called within external Modelica functions implemented in C if `ModelicaUtilities.h` is included into the C-file.

`ModelicaMessage`	`void ModelicaMessage(const char* string)` Output the message `string` as is without format control.
`ModelicaFormatMessage`	`void ModelicaFormatMessage(const char* fstring, ...)` Output the message using the same format control as used by the C-function `printf`, with `fstring` as the format control string and `...` representing the arguments to be printed.
`ModelicaVFormatMessage`	`void ModelicaVFormatMessage(const char*string,va_list)` Output the message under the same format control as the C-function `vprintf`.
`ModelicaError`	`void ModelicaError(const char* string)` Output the error message `string` as is without format control. This function never returns to the calling function, but handles the error similarly to an `assert` in Modelica code.
`ModelicaFormatError`	`void ModelicaFormatError(const char* fstring, ...)`

	Output the error message using the same format control as the C-function `printf`, with `fstring` as the format control string and `...` representing the arguments to be printed. This function never returns to the calling function, but handles the error similarly to an `assert` in Modelica code.
`ModelicaVFormatError`	`void ModelicaVFormatError(const char* string, va_list)` Output the error message under the same format control as the C-function `vprintf`. This function never returns to the calling function, but handles the error similarly to an assert in the Modelica code.
`ModelicaAllocateString`	`char* ModelicaAllocateString(size_t n)` Allocate memory for a Modelica string of length `n`, which is used as a result formal parameter or a return function value of an external Modelica function. An extra byte for a terminating NUL-character is automatically allocated. Note that the storage for string arrays (i.e., pointer to string array) is still provided by the calling program, as for any other array. If an error occurs, this function does not return, but calls `ModelicaError`.
`ModelicaAllocateStringWithErrorReturn`	`char* ModelicaAllocateStringWithErrorReturn(size_t len)` Same as `ModelicaAllocateString`, except that in case of error, the function returns 0. This allows the external function to close files and free other open resources in case of error. After cleaning up resources use `ModelicaError` or `ModelicaFormatError` to signal the error.

We illustrate the use of one of these utility functions by the following example. A Modelica external function `fillString` returns a string filled with characters of the specified 8-bit ASCII-code:

```
function fillString
  input  Integer charCode(min=0,max=255);
  input  Integer n(min=0);
  output String  result;
  external "C"
    result = fillString(charCode,n);
end fillString;
```

The C code for the `fillString` external function might be written as follows:

```
#include "ModelicaUtilities.h"

char* fillString(int charCode, int n)
  /* Create and return string with n characters of code charCode */
  char* str =  ModelicaAllocateString(n);
  int i;
  for (i=0; i<n; i++)
    str[i] = (char)charCode;
  str[n] = '\0';   /* Terminate string with a NUL character */
  return str;
};
```

Note that the Modelica interface provides extra checking, for example, that `n>0` and `0<=charCode<=255`, which therefore need not be done by the C-function.

9.4.8 External Data Structures—External Objects

External functions sometimes need to access and manipulate external data structures without being forced to expose the details of those data structures to Modelica. We say that such data structures are *opaque* from the Modelica point of view—the internal structure of the data is not accessible from Modelica, only from the external code. The Modelica *external objects* facility allows the user to define and access such external data structures, satisfying the following three requirements:

- *Passing opaque references*: references to external data can be passed to Modelica and back to the external code as argument values in external function calls.
- *Data preserved between calls*: an important requirement of external data structures—to be preserved between external function calls—is satisfied by the above facility. As long as the reference to the external object exists in Modelica the data structure is kept.
- *Limited updating*: for efficiency reasons we would also like to allow limited updating of the external data structure, for example, for caching purposes, as long as the external function behaves as a mathematical function that returns the same outputs given the same inputs.

Our simple example model `TestInterpolate` below demonstrates all of these properties:

- An opaque reference to an external table data structure is returned by `MyTable`, which reads table data from a file in a user-defined format and creates the table instance. The reference is of type `MyTable`, a subclass of `ExternalObject`.
- The table data structure is preserved between calls since it is kept by the `table` variable in the model. It is passed to external functions, e.g. to `interpolateMyTable`.
- The table data structure caches/preserves the most recent row index (by updating the variable `lastIndex`) to speed up the interpolation computation for the case when the current call to the interpolation function accesses the same table row as in the previous call.

The Modelica code of `TestInterpolate` is as follows, referring to the subclass `MyTable` and the external function `interpolateMyTable` defined further below:

```
model TestInterpolate  "Define a new table and interpolate in it"
  Real     y;
  MyTable table=MyTable(fileName  = "testTables.txt",
                        tableName = "table1");  // Call initMyTable below
equation
  y = interpolateMyTable(table, time);
end TestInterpolate;
```

An `ExternalObject` ***subclass*** such as `MyTable` should be a subclass of (derived from) the predefined class `ExternalObject` according to the following rules:

- The class definition for the user-defined external data type should directly inherit the predefined partial class `ExternalObject`. Since the `ExternalObject` class is partial, it is not possible to define an instance of that class.
- Classes derived from `ExternalObject` can be used ***neither*** in `extends` clauses ***nor*** in short class definitions.

An `ExternalObject` subclass contains exactly two local functions, `constructor` and `destructor`:

- Classes derived from `ExternalObject` should have exactly two local external function definitions, named `constructor` and `destructor` respectively, and should not contain any other elements. The functions `constructor` and `destructor` must not be replaceable.
- The `constructor` external function is called by the Modelica run-time system exactly once before the first use of the object. The `constructor` should have exactly one output formal parameter in which the constructed instance of a type derived from `ExternalObject` is returned. Only the `constructor` function may return external objects.
- For each completely constructed object, the `destructor` is called exactly once after the last use of the object, even if an error has occurred. The `destructor` should have no output formal parameters. The only input formal parameter of the `destructor` should be the external object of a

type derived from `ExternalObject`. It is not legal to explicitly call the `constructor` and `destructor` functions.

Moreover:

- An external object can only be bound in instance declarations and can neither be modified later nor assigned to.
- In addition to the usual type prefixes such as `input`, `output`, `flow`, etc., variables declared in classes extending from `ExternalObject` may also have prefixes `parameter` and `constant`,

The following applies to external functions referring to instances of subclasses of `ExternalObject`:

- External functions may be defined which update the internal memory of instances of subclasses of `ExternalObject`, as long as the external functions behave as mathematical functions that return the same outputs given the same inputs.
- External functions should declare their input formal parameters as well as result formal parameters and return values of subclasses of `ExternalObject` using the C-type `void*` in their C code.

The user-defined table class `MyTable` mentioned above can be defined in the following way as a subclass of the predefined class `ExternalObject`, including definitions of its `constructor` and `destructor` functions:

```
class MyTable
  extends ExternalObject;

  function constructor
    input  String  fileName = "";
    input  String  tableName = "";
    output MyTable table;
    external "C" table = initMyTable(fileName, tableName);
  end constructor;

  function destructor "Release storage of table"
    input  MyTable table;
    external "C" closeMyTable(table);
  end destructor;
end MyTable;
```

The above `TestInterpolate` model calls the function `interpolateMyTable` defined below that performs interpolation in the table created by the `constructor` function of the class `MyTable`:

```
function interpolateMyTable "Interpolate in table"
  input  MyTable table;
  input  Real  u;
  output Real  y;
  external "C" y = interpolateMyTable(table, u);
end interpolateTable;
```

The external C-functions referred to in the above Modelica code could be defined in the following way:

```
typedef struct {  /* User defined data structure of the table */
  double* array;      /* nrow*ncolumn vector        */
  int     nrow;       /* number of rows             */
  int     ncol;       /* number of columns          */
  int     type;       /* interpolation type         */
  int     lastIndex;  /* most recent row index for search */
} MyTable;

void* initMyTable(char* fileName, char* tableName) {
  MyTable* table = malloc(sizeof(MyTable));  /* Allocate Table! */
  if ( table == NULL ) ModelicaError("Not enough memory");
  // read table from file and store all data in *table
  return (void*) table;
};
```

```
void closeMyTable(void* object) { /* Release table storage */
  MyTable* table = (MyTable*) object;
  if ( object == NULL ) return;
  free(table->array);            /* Free table storage */
  free(table);
}

double interpolateMyTable(void* object, double u) {
  MyTable* table = (MyTable*) object;
  double y;
  // Interpolate using "table" data (compute y)
  return y;
};
```

9.4.9 External Libraries and Include Files

There are several useful annotations for specifying external libraries and include files in the context of calling external functions from Modelica. These annotations are called `Library`, `Include`, `IncludeDirectory`, and `LibraryDirectory` and should occur on the external clause and no other standard annotations should occur on the external-clause. They have the following meaning:

- The `annotation(Library="libraryName")` is used to give information to the linker to include the library file where the compiled external function is available.
- The `annotation(Library={"libraryName1","libraryName2"})` is used to give information to the linker to include the library files where the compiled external function is available and additional libraries which are used to implement it.
- The `annotation(Include="includeDirective")`, used to include source files, for example, header files or source files that contain the functions referenced in the external function declaration, needed for calling the external function in the code generated by the Modelica compiler.
- The `annotation(IncludeDirectory="modelica://`*`LibName`*`/Resources/Include")` can be used to specify a location for header files. The location `"modelica://`*`LibName`*`/Resources/Include"` is the default and need not be specified. However, another location could be specified by using an URI name (Section 11.15, page 556) for the include directory.
- The `annotation(LibraryDirectory="modelica://`*`LibName`*`/Resources/Library")` can be used to specify a location for library files. The location `"modelica://`*`LibName`*`/Resources/Library"` is the default and need not be specified. However, another location could be specified by using an URI name (Section 11.15, page 556) for the library directory. Different versions of an object library can be provided, e.g. one for Windows and one for Linux, by providing a "platform" directory below the `LibraryDirectory`. If no `platform` directory is present, the object library must be present in the `LibraryDirectory`. The following `platform` directory names are standardized:

  `win32` (Microsoft Windows 32 bit)
  `win64` (Microsoft Windows 64 bit)
  `linux32` (Linux Intel 32 bit)
  `linux64` (Linux Intel 64 bit)

The `LibraryName` used for `IncludeDirectory` and `LibraryDirectory` indicates the top-level class where the annotation is found in the Modelica source code. The example below shows the use of external functions together with object libraries.

The function `ExternalFunc1` is defined by the external C function `ExternalFunc1_ext` in the statically linked library `ExternalLib1` together with the header file `ExternalFunc1.h`.

`ExternalFunc2` is defined by the C function `ExternalFunc2_ext` in the dynamically linked library `ExternalLib2` together with the header file `ExternalFunc2.h`.

The function `ExternalFunc3` is defined in the C source include file `ExternalFunc3.c`.

```
package ExternalFunctions
  model Example
    Real x(start=1.0),y(start=2.0),z(start=3.0);
  equation
    der(x)=-ExternalFunc1(x);
    der(y)=-ExternalFunc2(y);
    der(z)=-ExternalFunc3(z);
  end Example;

  function ExternalFunc1
    input  Real x;
    output Real y;
  external "C"
    y=ExternalFunc1_ext(x) annotation(Library="ExternalLib1",
                               Include="#include \"ExternalFunc1.h\"");
  end ExternalFunc1;

  function ExternalFunc2
    input  Real x;
    output Real y;
  external
    y=ExternalFunc2_ext(x) annotation(Library="ExternalLib2",
                               Include="#include \"ExternalFunc2.h\"");
  end ExternalFunc2;

  function ExternalFunc3
    input  Real x;
    output Real y;
    external "C" annotation(Include="#include \"ExternalFunc3.c\"");
  end ExternalFunc3;

end ExternalFunctions;
```

The following directory structure:

```
ExternalFunctions  // Dir,
  package.mo      // File, contains the Modelica code from above
  Resources       // Dir, contains include files and library resources
    Include       // Dir, contains the include files
      ExternalFunc1.h    // C-header file
      ExternalFunc2.h    // C-header file
      ExternalFunc3.c    // C-source file
    Library      // Dir, contains the object libraries for different platforms
      win32      // Dir, contains Windows versions of libraries
        ExternalLib1.lib    // statically linked library for VisualStudio
        ExternalLib2.lib    // statically linking the dynamic linked library
        ExternalLib2.dll    // dynamically linked library (with manifest)
      linux32  // Dir, contains Linux versions of libraries
        libExternalLib1.a    // statically linked library
        libExternalLib2.so  // shared library
```

Below is the header file `ExternalFunc2.h` e.g. for the function `ExternalFunc2` in the dynamically linked / shared library `ExternalLib2` so that the desired functions are defined to be exported for the Microsoft VisualStudio C compiler and for the GNU C compiler. Regarding the GNU compiler on Linux it is recommended to use the compiler option "`-fPIC`" to build shared libraries or object libraries that are later transformed to a shared library.

```
// File ExternalFunc2.h
#ifdef __cplusplus
extern "C" {
#endif

#ifdef _MSC_VER
#ifdef EXTERNAL_FUNCTION_EXPORT
```

```
#  define EXTLIB2_EXPORT  __declspec( dllexport )
#else
#  define EXTLIB2_EXPORT  __declspec( dllimport )
#endif
#elif  __GNUC__ >= 4
  /* In gnuc, all symbols are by default exported. It is still often useful
     to not export all symbols but only the needed ones */
#  define EXTLIB2_EXPORT  __attribute__  ((visibility("default")))
#else
#  define EXTLIB2_EXPORT
#endif

EXTLIB2_EXPORT void ExternalFunc2(<function arguments>);

#ifdef  __cplusplus
}
#endif
```

The `Library` name and the `LibraryDirectory` name specified in the function annotation are mapped to a linkage directive in a compiler-dependent way thereby selecting the object library suited for the respective computer platform.

A short summary of these library and include file annotations is also given in Section 11.14, page 556.

9.5 User-Defined Overloaded Operators and Constructor Functions

What does it mean to have overloading of operators and functions in a language, and why do we need it? The main reason to have this mechanism in a programming language is economy of notation—overloading allows us to reuse well-known notation and names for more than one kind of data structure. This is convenient and gives more concise and readable code. The concept of overloading can be defined roughly as follows:

- A function or operator is *overloaded* if it has several definitions, each with a different type signature.

The concept of Modelica function type signature is the same as the Modelica class type of the function (see Section 3.18.6, page 120), and can be defined roughly as follows:

- A Modelica function type signature consists of the set of input formal parameter and result types together with the names of the formal parameters and results, in the order they are defined. To avoid certain lookup and type resolution difficulties, overloading is defined based on the input formal parameters only.

In fact, overloading already exists predefined to a limited extent for certain operators in the Modelica language as described elsewhere in this book. For example, the plus (+) operator for addition has several different definitions (see also Section 6.10, page 284, and Section 6.12.1, page 287) depending on the data type:

- 1+2— means integer addition of two integer constants giving an integer result, here 3.
- 1.0+2.0— means floating point number addition of two `Real` constants giving a floating-point number result, here 3.0.
- "ab"+"2"— means string concatenation of two string constants giving a string result, here "ab2".
- {1,2}+{3,4}— means integer vector addition of two integer constant vectors giving a vector result, here {4,6}.

Overloading of certain built-in functions also exists. For example, the `size` function is defined for arrays of different functionality and occurs in two variants: with one or two arguments (see Section 7.9.1, page 335). Scalar functions of one or more (scalar) arguments are implicitly defined also for arrays, see Section 7.10, page 340.

However, the above examples are just special cases. In some situations it is very desirable for the user to be able to define the standard operators as overloaded for user-defined data structures of choice. One prime example is operations on complex numbers, which will be presented further down. However, remember that operator overloading is only a short-hand notation for function calls.

In the following subsections, we will describe mechanisms for user-defined overloaded constructors and operators:

- Overloaded binary operations (`'+'`, `'-'` (subtraction), `'*'`, `'/'`, `'^'`,`'=='`, `'<>'`, `'>'`, `'<'`, `'>='`, `'<='`, `'and'`, `'or'`), Section 9.5.3.2, page 486.
- Overloaded unary operations (`'-'` (negation), `'not'`), Section 9.5.3.3, page 487.
- Overloaded constructors (`'constructor'`, `'0'`), Section 9.5.3.4, page 488.
- Overloaded string conversions, `String`, Section 9.5.3.6, page 488.

9.5.1 Allowed Overloaded Operators and Constructors

The mechanism for overloading operators is only defined for the standard operators mentioned in Table 9-1 below. Adding arbitrary new operators is not possible. The full set of Modelica operators, including precedence and associativity, is described in Section 6.6, page 273, Table 6-1.

Note that equality = and assignment := are not expression operators since they are allowed only in equations and in assignment statements respectively. Equality and assignment are automatically available between values of the same record type, which makes overloading definitions for those operators unnecessary. Overloading of the array indexing operator `[]` would have been useful e.g. for specialized array libraries, but this is not yet available in Modelica.

Table 9-1. Overloaded operators.

Operator	Operator Example
+	a+b
–	a-b
–	-a
*	a*b
/	a/b
^	a^b
<	a<b
<=	a<=b
==	a==b
>=	a>=b
>	a>b
<>	a<>b
and	a and b
or	a or b
not	not a

9.5.1.1 Overloaded Constructor Functions

Overloaded constructor functions are allowed in the following two cases:

- For any user-defined record type it is possible to define additional overloaded constructors with the same name (but different input formal parameters) compared to the default record constructor.
- The `String` constructor (also viewed as a data conversion function) can be given additional definitions within a user-defined record type.

This is also summarized in Table 9-2, where we can see examples of using an overloaded definition of the `Complex(...)` constructor with only one real valued argument, compared to the standard constructor with two arguments automatically derived from the `Complex` record type.

Table 9-2. Overloaded constructor functions.

Constructor	Constructor Example
record name	`Complex(3.2)`
`String`	`String(Complex(2.1))`
`'0'`	`Complex.'0'()`

9.5.2 Definition of Overloaded Operators and Constructors

Overloaded operator definitions can only be given inside declarations of a new specialized class called `operator` (See also the short description in Section 3.8.9, page 92). The `operator` specialized class is similar to a package, but may only contain function definitions. Moreover, *operator classes may only be defined inside operator records*, for example, as in the definition of the `Complex` operator record below..

The `operator` keyword in the new specialized class declaration is followed by the *name* of the operation within *single quotes*:

```
'constructor', '+', '-', '*', '/', '^', '==', '<>', '>', '<', '>=', '<=',
'and', 'or', 'not', 'String', '0'.
```

The properties of overloaded operators are summarized below:

- Function definitions for overloaded operators can only be given inside an `operator` class.
- Operator classes can only be defined *inside* an `operator record`, which also may contain additional functions and fields/variables of the record.
- The functions defined inside an operator class must have one formal output parameter and at least one formal input parameter with type being the operator record type, except the constructor functions which must have exactly one output result of the corresponding operator record type.
- It is sufficient to define overloading for operator records. Overloaded operations on arrays of operator records are automatically derived from the overloaded operator record operations by vectorization (Section 7.10, page 340).
- It is not legal to extend from an operator record except as a short class definition modifying the default attributes of the record fields directly inside the operator record.. (This restriction is currently in place because all implications of extending from an operator record have not yet been analyzed by the Modelica language design group). See Section 3.8.8, page 91, for an example.
- If an operator record is derived by a short class definition, the overloaded operators of this operator record are the operators that are defined in its base class. For information on subtyping in this case see Section 3.19.4, page 126.
- The precedence and associativity of an overloaded operator is identical to what is defined in Table 6-1 in Section 6.6, page 273.
- The functions defined in an operator class must be encapsulated.
- A function defined in an operator class can either be called as shown in this section, or can be called directly using its full hierarchical name.

- There is a shorthand notation called `operator function` for defining an operator with only one function.

We start with a small example extracted from the Complex numbers example:

```
operator record Complex "Record defining a Complex number"

  Real re "Real part of complex number";
  Real im "Imaginary part of complex number";

  encapsulated operator 'constructor'
    import Complex;

    function fromReal
      input  Real re;
      output Complex result = Complex(re=re, im=0.0);
        annotation(Inline=true);
    end fromReal;
  end 'constructor';

  encapsulated operator '+'
    import Complex;

    function add  "Binary addition, e.g. c1+c2"
      input  Complex c1;
      input  Complex c2;
      output Complex result  "Same as: c1 + c2";
        annotation(Inline=true);
    algorithm
      result := Complex(c1.re + c2.re, c1.im + c2.im);
    end add;
  end '+';

  encapsulated operator '-'
    import Complex;

    function negate  "Unary negation, e.g. -c"
      input  Complex c;
      output Complex result  "Same as: -c";
        annotation(Inline=true);
    algorithm
      result := Complex(-c.re, -c.im);
    end negate;

    function subtract  "Binary subtraction, e.g. c1-c2"
      input  Complex c1;
      input  Complex c2;
      output Complex result  "Same as: c1 - c2";
        annotation(Inline=true);
      algorithm
        result := Complex(c1.re - c2.re, c1.im - c2.im);
      end subtract;
    end '-';

  ...

end Complex;
```

In the above example, we start as usual with the real and imaginary part declarations of the `re` and `im` fields of the `Complex` operator record definition. Then comes a *constructor definition* `fromReal` with only one input argument instead of the two inputs of the default `Complex` constructor implicitly defined by the `Complex` record definition, followed by overloaded operator definitions for `'+'` and `'-'`, where `'-'` has both a binary and a unary definition.

How can these definitions be used? Take a look at the following small example:

```
Real    a;
Complex b;
Complex c = a + b;    // Addition of Real number a and Complex number b
```

The interesting part is in the third line, which contains an addition `a+b` of a `Real` number `a` and a `Complex` number `b`. There is no built-in addition operator for complex numbers, but we have the above overloaded operator definition of `'+'` for two complex numbers. An addition of two complex numbers would match this definition right away in the lookup process.

However, in this case we have an addition of a real number and a complex number. Fortunately, the lookup process for overloaded binary operators (Section 9.5.3.1, page 486) can also handle this case if there is a constructor function in the `Complex` record definition that can convert a real number to a complex number. Here we have such a constructor called `fromReal`.

Since we are using the `Inline` annotation, the expression `a+b` is transformed in the following way:

```
a+b => Complex.'+'.add(Complex.'constructor'.fromReal(a), b);
    => Complex.'+'.add(Complex(re=a,im=0), b)
    => Complex(re=a+b.re, im=b.im);
```

If we insert this into the record equation `c=a+b` and expand into equations for each record field according to the usual rules for record equations, we obtain:

```
c.re = a + b.re;
c.im = b.im;
```

These equations have thus been converted into the standard form which only uses built-in types, and can be further symbolically processed by the Modelica compiler in the usual way for equations. This example should also work without the `Inline` annotation, but with some more function call overhead.

9.5.2.1 The Operator Function Short-Hand Notation

Instead of introducing the function `add` as in the above example, one can use the `operator function` short-hand two-keyword notation to define the + operator since it only contains one function. In general, for any operator `op` with a single function definition the following short-hand notation can be used:

```
encapsulated operator function 'op'
  ...
end 'op';
```

Such a definition is conceptually the same as, for example:

```
encapsulated operator 'op'
  function foo
    ...
  end foo;
end 'op';
```

Using this short-hand notation for the above operator +, its definition can be expressed as follows:

```
encapsulated operator function '+'
  import Complex;
  input  Complex c1;
  input  Complex c2;
  output Complex result  "Same as: c1 + c2";
    annotation(Inline=true);
algorithm
  result := Complex(c1.re + c2.re, c1.im + c2.im);
end '+';
```

9.5.3 Lookup and Evaluation of Overloaded Operators

As mentioned in Section 9.5.2, page 483, all functions defined inside one operator class must have exactly one output, but may also include optional arguments with default values, e.g., `in3` and `in4` below:

```
function f
  input  TypeI1 in1;
  input  TypeI2 in2;
  input  TypeI3 in3  := <default expr1>;
  input  TypeI4 in4  := <default expr2>;
  ...
  output TypeO1 out1;
algorithm
  ...
end f;
```

9.5.3.1 Matching Lookup of Operators

A constructor function call or operator application converted to function syntax is *equivalent* to a function call which can have positional or named arguments, or a mix of positional and named arguments, for example:

```
f(expr1, expr2, ..., in3 = value1, in4 = value2, ...)
```

At lookup, the overloaded operator application or constructor function call is *matched* against the function definitions inside the corresponding operator definition.

- The *matching succeeds* if the types of the call arguments are the same as the types of the corresponding formal parameters (treating `Integer` and `Real` as equivalent types), and the named arguments in the call (e.g., `in3`, `in4` in the above call to `f`) are defined.
- At most one matching function definition for the same operator is allowed

As we have seen in the case of the `Complex` example, it is possible to have a match even if some arguments are not type compatible if there is a constructor that can provide implicit type conversion to the needed type.

In general, a valid call requires that all inputs have some value given by a positional argument, named argument, or default value (and that positional and named arguments do not overlap). This corresponds to the normal treatment of function calls with named arguments (Section 9.3.2, page 439).

9.5.3.2 Overloaded Binary Operators

There are special considerations for binary operators. The following restrictions apply, i.e., *a function is allowed for a binary operator* if and only if:

- It has at least two input formal parameters; at least one of which is of the operator record type.
- The first two input formal parameters shall not have default values.
- All input formal parameters after the first two must have default values.

Let `op` denote a binary operator and consider an expression `a op b` where `a` is of type `Atype` and `b` is of type `Btype`.

1. If `Atype` and `Btype` are *basic types*, e.g. `Integer`, `Real`, `Boolean`, `String`, or an enumeration, or arrays of such types (Section 7.10 on page 340), then the corresponding built-in basic type operation is performed.
2. Otherwise, if there exists *exactly one* function `f` in the union of the sets of function definitions in the operator classes `Atype.op` and `Btype.op` such that `f(a,b)` is a valid match for the function `f`, then `a op b` is evaluated using this function. It is an error if multiple functions match. If `Atype` is not an operator record type, `Atype.op` is regarded as an empty set of functions, and similarly for

`Btype`. Note that having a union of the sets of functions from the operator classes ensures that if `Atype` and `Btype` are the same, each function only appears once in the resulting union set.

3. Otherwise, if there is *no direct match* of `a op b`, then it is tried to find a direct match by automatic type casts of `a` or `b`, by converting either `a` or `b` to the needed type using an appropriate constructor function from one of the operator record types of the arguments of the overloaded `op` functions.

   For example using the `Complex` definition (below and in Section 9.5.4) a multiplication is tried between a real number `a` and a complex number `b`. Fortunately there is a constructor `fromReal` that can convert the real number `a` to a Complex, thereby matching the `multiply` function between two complex numbers:

   ```
   Real    a;
   Complex b;
   Complex c = a*b;
   ```

   The multiplication `a*b` is interpreted as:

   ```
   // Complex.'*'.multiply(Complex.'constructor'.fromReal(a),b);
   ```

4. If `Atype` or `Btype` is an *array type*, then the expression is conceptually evaluated according to the rules for application of scalar functions to array arguments (Section 7.10 on page 340), with the following exceptions concerning the array multiplication table in Section 7.8.3, page 332:
   (a) `vector*vector` must be left undefined, since the scalar product defined by the array multiplication table does not generalize to the expected linear and conjugate linear scalar product of complex numbers. The reason is that scalar product of two complex vectors, c := sum_k(a[k]*conj(b[k]), k=1:n, involve conjugates of complex numbers, where conj(a+i*b)=a-i*b.
   (b) `vector*matrix` must be left undefined since the corresponding definition of the array multiplication table does not generalize to complex numbers in the expected way, analogous to case (a).
   (c) If the inner dimension for `matrix*vector` or `matrix*matrix` is zero, this uses the overloaded `'0'` operator of the result array element type. If the operator `'0'` is not defined for that operator record class it is an error.

5. Otherwise, if the expression `a op b` does not match any of the above cases, it is erroneous.

9.5.3.3 Overloaded Unary Operators

There are also special rules for unary operators. A *function is allowed for a unary operator* if and only if:

- It has at least one input formal parameter, which has to be of the operator record type.
- The first input formal parameters must not have a default value.
- All input formal parameters after the first must have default values.
- If the operator is used both as a unary and a binary operator (such as `'-'`), the operator class must contain definitions of corresponding functions for both the unary and the binary operator.

Regarding the evaluation of a unary operator application `op a`, (e.g. `-a`), where a is of type `Atype`, the following applies:

1. If `Atype` is a *basic type*, e.g. `Integer`, `Real`, `Boolean`, , `String`, or an enumeration, then the corresponding built-in operation for this type is performed.
2. If `Atype` is an `operator record` *type* and there exists a *unique* function `f` in `Atype.op` such that `Atype.op.f(a)` is a valid match, then `op a` is evaluated to `Atype.op.f(a)`. It is an error if there are multiple valid matches.
3. If `Atype` is an *array type,* then the expression is conceptually evaluated according to the rules of Section 7.10 on page 340.
4. Otherwise the expression is erroneous.

9.5.3.4 Overloaded Record Constructors

Let `Ctype` denote an operator record type and consider a constructor call such as below:

```
Ctype(expr1, expr2, ..., in3=value1, in4=value2, ...)
```

Then the following rules apply:

1. If there exists a unique function `f` in `Ctype.'constructor'` such that the argument list to `Ctype` is a valid match for the formal parameter types of function `f`, then the call to `Ctype` is resolved to a call to `Ctype.'constructor'.f`.
2. If there is no operator `Ctype.'constructor'` the automatically generated record constructor is called.
3. Otherwise the expression is erroneous.

The following restrictions apply to overloaded record constructors:

- The operator definition of `Ctype.'constructor'` must only contain *functions that declare one output formal parameter* of the operator record type `Ctype`.
- For an operator record type there must not exist any possible call that leads to multiple matches in (1) above.
- For a pair of operator record types `Ctype` and `Dtype` and variables c and d of these types, the calls `Ctype.'constructor'(d)` and `Dtype.'constructor'(c)` cannot simultaneously be legal, i.e., one of the two constructor definitions must be removed.

The last restriction avoids the following problem for binary operators.

Assume that there are two operator records types `Ctype` and `Dtype` which both have a constructor `fromReal`. If we want to extend `c+c` and `d+d` to support mixed operations `c+d` and `d+c`, one variant would be to define special operations for `c+d` and `d+c`; but then `c+2.0` becomes ambiguous, since it is not clear to which type `Ctype` or `Dtype` the `Real` constant 2.0 should be converted.

Instead, without mixed operations, `c+2.0` is converted to `c+fromReal(2.0)`. However, in that case expressions such as `c+d` are only ambiguous if both conversion from `Ctype` to `Dtype` and back from `Dtype` to `Ctype` are both available. This possibility is not allowed by the above restriction.

9.5.3.5 Zero-Element '0' Record Constructor

There is also a record constructor operator `'0'` which can be used to defined a zero-value for an operator record. This can also be used to construct an element.

The operator '0' for an operator record `Ctype` can contain only one function, having no inputs and exactly one output of type `Ctype`, making the lookup of the called function `'0'` unambiguous. It should return the identity element of addition, and is used for generating flow-equations for connect-equations and zero elements for matrix-multiplication.

Below is an example zero-element constructor for the `Complex` operator record:

```
encapsulated operator function '0'
  import Complex;
  output Complex c;
algorithm
  c := Complex(0,0);
    annotation(Inline=true);
end '0';
```

9.5.3.6 Overloaded String Constructor / Data Converter

Consider an expression `String(aexpr1, expr2, ..., in3=value1, in4=value2, ...)`, where the first argument `aexpr1` in the *argument list* is of type `Atype`:

1. If `Atype` is a basic type, that is, `Boolean`, `Integer`, `Real`, `String` or an enumeration, or a type derived from these, then the corresponding built-in `String` operation is performed.
2. If `Atype` is an operator record type and there exists a unique function `f` in `Atype.'String'` such that the argument list in the above call to `String` is a valid match for `f`, then the call to `String` is evaluated to the call `Atype.'String'.f`.
3. Otherwise the expression is erroneous.

The following restrictions apply:

- The operator `Atype.'String'` must only contain functions that declare one output formal parameter, which must be of the `String` type, and the first input argument must be of the operator record type `Atype`.
- For an operator record type there shall not exist any call that leads to multiple matches in (2) above.

9.5.4 The Complete Complex Numbers Example

Below we show the complete definition of the Complex numbers example including a simple use case:

```
operator record Complex "Record defining a Complex number"

  Real re "Real part of complex number";
  Real im "Imaginary part of complex number";

  encapsulated operator 'constructor'

    function fromReal
      import Complex;
      input  Real re;
      input  Real im := 0.0;
      output Complex result(re=re, im=im);
        annotation(Inline=true);
    end fromReal;
  end 'constructor';

  encapsulated operator function '+'  // See the above Section 9.5.2.1

  encapsulated operator '-'           // See the above Section 9.5.2

  encapsulated operator function '*'
    import Complex;
    input  Complex c1;
    input  Complex c2;
    output Complex result "i.e., = c1 * c2";
   algorithm
     result := Complex(c1.re*c2.re - c1.im*c2.im, c1.re*c2.im +c1.im*c2.re);
       annotation(Inline=true);
  end '*';

  encapsulated operator function '/'
    import Complex;
    input  Complex c1;
    input  Complex c2;
    output Complex result "i.e., = c1 / c2";
  algorithm
    result := Complex(( c1.re*c2.re + c1.im*c2.im)/(c2.re^2 + c2.im^2),
                      (-c1.re*c2.im + c1.im*c2.re)/(c2.re^2 + c2.im^2));
      annotation(Inline=true);
```

```
    end '/';

    encapsulated operator function '=='
      input  Complex c1;
      input  Complex c2;
      output Boolean result "= c1 == c2";
    algorithm
      result := c1.re == c2.re and c1.im == c2.im;
        annotation(Inline=true);
    end '==';

    encapsulated operator function 'String'
      import Complex;
      input  Complex c;
      input  String name="j"
                     "Name of variable representing sqrt(-1) in the string";
      input  Integer significantDigits=6
                     "Number of significant digits to be shown";
      output String s;
    algorithm
      s := String(c.re, significantDigits=significantDigits);
      if c.im <> 0 then
        s := if c.im > 0 then s + " + " else s + " - ";
        s := s + String(abs(c.im), significantDigits=significantDigits) +
               name;
      end if;
    end 'String';

    encapsulated function j
      import Complex;
      output Complex c;
        annotation(Inline=true);
     algorithm
       c := Complex(0,1);
    end j;

    encapsulated operator function '0'
      import Complex;
      output Complex c;
    algorithm
      c := Complex(0,0);
        annotation(Inline=true);
    end '0';

  end Complex;
```

The above is the complete definition of `Complex`, including its operators, constructors, and additional functions such as the function `j`. Now we turn to the simple use case.

```
  function eigenValues
    input  Real    A[:,:];
    output Complex eigenComplex[size(A, 1)];
  protected
    Integer nx=size(A,1);
    Real    eigenValues[nx,2];
    Integer i;
  algorithm
    eigenValues := Modelica.Math.Matrices.eigenValues(A);
    for i in 1:nx loop
      eigenComplex[i] := Complex(eigenValues[i,1], eigenValues[i,2]);
    end for;
```

```
end eigenValues;
```

The function `eigenValues` in the use case below returns a vector of complex numbers defining the eigenvalues of the input matrix argument `A`.

```
// Use case of Complex numbers:
   Complex j  = Complex.j(); // Variable j to avoid clumsy expr Complex.j()
   Complex c1 = 2 + 3*j;
   Complex c2 = 3 + 4*j;
   Complex c3 = c1 + c2;
   Complex c4[:] = eigenValues([1,2; -3,4]);
algorithm
  Modelica.Utilities.Streams.print("c4 = " + String(c4));
```

This results in the following printed output string showing a vector of the two eigenvalues computed from the example matrix `[1,2; -3,4]`:

```
c4 = {2.5 + 1.93649j, 2.5 - 1.93649j}
```

Complex can also be used in a connector:

```
operator record ComplexVoltage = Complex(re(unit="V"), im(unit="V"));
operator record ComplexCurrent = Complex(re(unit="A"), im(unit="A"));

connector ComplexPin
  ComplexVoltage v;
  flow ComplexCurrent i;
end ComplexPin;

  ComplexPin p1,p2,p3;
equation
  connect(p1,p2);
  connect(p1,p3);
```

The two connect-equations `connect(p1,p2)` and `connect(p1,p3)` expand into the following equations:

```
p1.v = p2.v;
p1.v = p3.v;
p1.i + p2.i + p3.i = Complex.'0'();
// Complex.'+'(p1.i, Complex.'+'(p2.i, p3.i)) = Complex.'0'();
```

Note that the `Complex` type is already predefined in a Modelica record type called `Complex`. This is distributed as part of the standard Modelica library (MSL) but defined at the top-level outside of MSL. It is referred to as `Complex` or `.Complex.` and is automatically preloaded by most tools, enabling direct usage without the need for any import statements (except in encapsulated classes). There is a library ComplexMath with operations on complex numbers (Section 16.3, page 923).

The following are some examples of using the predefined type `Complex`:

```
Real a = 2;
Complex j = Modelica.ComplexMath.j;
Complex b = 2 + 3*j;
Complex c = (2*b + a)/b;
Complex d = Modelica.ComplexMath.sin(c);
Complex v[3] = {b/2, c, 2*d};
```

9.6 Summary

As indicated by the title, this chapter is approximately equally divided between the topics of algorithms and functions, even though functions is a special case of algorithms. We started by a discussion of the pros and cons of declarative versus non-declarative constructs. Then followed a description of algorithm sections and initial algorithm sections, together with descriptions of the kinds of statements allowed in Modelica. Subsequently we presented the function concept in Modelica, how to declare and call functions, positional and named argument passing, returning single or multiple results, as well as optional function results. We also described empty function calls, the function return statement, as well as record constructor functions. We discussed how to inherit base functions, as well as the similarity between the algorithm and function concepts in Modelica. Finally we presented the Modelica external function concept with possible mapping to C or Fortran 77, the mechanism for declaring external data structures accessed via opaque references, and user-defined overloaded operators and record constructors including a complex number example.

9.7 Literature

The idea of declarative programming language constructs and the notion of referential transparency discussed at the beginning of the chapter can be found in many functional language textbooks as well as in the survey article (Hudak 1989).

The rest of the description including many examples is mostly based on the Modelica language specification (Modelica Association 2013) even though the `bilinearSampling` external function example is from (Modelica Association 2000).

9.8 Exercises

Exercise 9-1:

Using Algorithm Sections: Write a function, `Sum`, which calculates the sum of numbers, in an array of arbitrary size. Write a function, `Average`, which calculates the average of numbers, in an array of arbitrary size. `Average` should make a function call to `Sum`.

Write a class, `LargestAverage`, that has two arrays and calculates the average of each of them. Then it compares the averages and sets a variable to true if the first array is larger than the second and otherwise false.

Exercise 9-2:

Using Algorithm Sections: Write a class, `FindSmallest`, that finds the value and position of the smallest element in an arbitrary array. Write a class that makes an instance of the `FindSmallest` class and give the array values.

Exercise 9-3:

while-statements: Write a class that calculates the sum: $\frac{1}{1*1}+\frac{2}{2*2}+\frac{3}{3*3}+\frac{4}{4*4}+\frac{5}{5*5}+\frac{6}{6*6}$

Follow the algorithm:

- Initialize the sum to 0 and the first term to 1.
- If the absolute value of next term >= 0.000001, do the next two steps:
- 1. Add next term to the sum.

- 2. Calculate a new next term.

Tip: Every term in the sum is of the form `1/(k*k)`, where `k` increases by one for each step. Set a variable to keep track of whether the next term is negative or positive. When the program is run the sum will be 0.82247.

Exercise 9-4:

When-statement: Let us go back to the class `LightSwitch`, (Exercise 2-12), which is initially switched off and switched on at time 5. Change this class to contain a when-statement instead of a when-equation.

Now change the `LightSwitch` class so that in the time interval 5—20 it turns the light on every fifth second for one second and then it is switched off again.

Tip: `sample(start, interval)` returns `true` and triggers time events at time instants and `rem(x, y)` returns the integer remainder of `x/y`, such that `div(x,y) * y + rem(x, y) = x`.

Exercise 9-5:

reinit: Write a model `BilliardBalls` with two billiard balls that are rolling from opposite directions and bounce into each other.

Tip: `reinit(x, value)` is the same thing as `x := value`, but `reinit` reinitializes the value of `x` at a specific time and the equations still holds.

Exercise 9-6:

Functions: Write a function faculty, such that `faculty(n) = 1*2*3*4*....*n`.

Write a class that contains a function call to `faculty`.

Exercise 9-7:

Functions: We want to search through an array of names and find the position of a particular name. The function should have two arguments, an array of names and the name we are looking for. The output will be the index where the name was found, or an error will occur if the name was not found.

Write a class that tests the previous function.

Tip: Assert can be used to check whether the result has been found, and, if it has not been found, the message in the second argument will be shown otherwise.

Exercise 9-8:

Vector Orthogonality: Write a function, `ScalarProduct`, that calculates the scalar product of two arbitrary vectors `(u1, u2, u3, ..., un)` and `(v1, v2, v3, ... , vn)`. The result should be: `u1*v1 + u2*v2 + ... + un*vn`.

Two vectors `(u1, u2, u3, ..., un)` and `(v1, v2, v3, ... , vn)` are orthogonal if the scalar product is equal to 0.

Write a class, `Orthogonal`, that decides if two integer vectors are orthogonal. The vectors must have the same number of elements, but the number of elements should be arbitrary.

Tip: Applying the multiplication operator between two vectors gives the scalar product.

Chapter 10

Packages

Packages in Modelica may contain definitions of constants and classes including all kinds of specialized classes, functions, and subpackages. By the term *subpackage* we mean that the package is declared inside another package and no inheritance relationship is implied. Parameters and variables cannot be declared in a package. The definitions in a package should be related in some way, which is the main reason they are placed in a particular package. Packages are useful for a number of reasons:

- Definitions that are related to some particular topic are typically grouped into a package. This makes those definitions easier to find and the code more understandable.
- Packages provide encapsulation and coarse-grained structuring that reduces the complexity of large systems. An important example is the use of packages for construction of (hierarchical) class libraries.
- Name conflicts between definitions in different packages are eliminated since the package name is implicitly prefixed to names of definitions declared in a package.
- Information hiding and encapsulation can be supported to some extent by declaring `protected` classes, types, and other definitions that are available only inside the package and therefore inaccessible to outside code.
- Modelica defines a method for locating a package by providing a standard mapping of package names to storage places, typically file or directory locations in the file system.
- Identification of packages. A package stored separately for example, in a file, can be (uniquely) identified.

We will gradually cover all these aspects throughout the chapter. First we present a simple example of a package with related definitions and discuss the notions of information hiding and abstract data types in relation to Modelica packages.

10.1 Packages as Abstract Data Types

The notion of a package is related to and partly originates from the notion of abstract data type. The classical definition of a data type, for example, `Real` with its associated operations `+`,`-`,`*`, `/`, `==`, is as a data structure together with operations on that data structure. An abstract data type is just like an ordinary data type, that is, definitions of data and operations, together with a method for collecting the implementations of the operations in one place and hiding the details of those implementations.

As an example, consider the package `ComplexNumbers` below, which contains a data structure declaration, the record `Complex`, and associated operations such as `Add`, `Multiply`, `MakeComplex`, and so on. The package is declared as `encapsulated`, (Section 3.11.8, page 104), which is the recommended software engineering practice to keep our software well structured as well as being easier to understand and maintain.

```
encapsulated package ComplexNumbers
```

```
record Complex
  Real re;
  Real im;
end Complex;

function Add
  input  Complex x;
  input  Complex y;
  output Complex z;
algorithm
  z.re := x.re + y.re;
  z.im := x.im + y.im
end Add;

function Multiply
  input  Complex x;
  input  Complex y;
  output Complex z;
algorithm
  z.re := x.re*y.re - x.im*y.im;
  z.im := x.re*y.im + x.im*y.re;
end Multiply;

function MakeComplex
  input  Real    x;
  input  Real    y;
  output Complex z;
algorithm
  z.re := x;
  z.im := y;
end MakeComplex;

// Declarations of Subtract, Divide, RealPart, ImaginaryPart, etc.
// (not shown here)
end ComplexNumbers;
```

How can we make use of the package `ComplexNumbers`? We can find one example in the class `ComplexUser` below, where both the type `Complex` and the operations `Multiply` and `Add` are referenced by prefixing them with the package name `ComplexNumbers`.

```
class ComplexUser
  ComplexNumbers.Complex  a(re=1.0, im=2.0);
  ComplexNumbers.Complex  b(re=1.0, im=2.0);
  ComplexNumbers.Complex  z,w;
equation
  z = ComplexNumbers.Multiply(a,b);
  w = ComplexNumbers.Add(a,b);
end ComplexUser;
```

What about information hiding in the package? The type `Complex` must be made available for use in classes and packages for allocation and initialization of variables of that type, for example, the variables `a`, `b`, `z`, and `w` in `ComplexUser`. The implementation details of `Complex` are exposed and used, for example, to initialize the variables `a` and `b` via their fields `x` and `y`. It would not work if we declared x and y `protected` in `Complex` since then these fields would not be available for the implementation of `Add` and `Multiply`, and so on. However, by declaring the operations on `Complex` inside the class `Complex` itself as in the `operator record` version of `Complex` in Section 9.5.4, page 489, these fields can be accessed even if they are protected.

We can increase the degree of data abstraction by using the function `MakeComplex` for initialization instead of modifiers, for example, as in `ComplexUser2` below, thus avoiding exposing the fields `x` and `y`. If we apply the programming convention that all direct access to these fields is avoided in user code it would be possible to change the internal implementation, for example, to polar coordinates, without changing any of the user code. However, avoiding such internal access to the fields is not checked by Modelica.

```
class ComplexUser2
  ComplexNumbers.Complex  a=MakeComplex(1.0,2.0);
```

```
  ComplexNumbers.Complex  b=MakeComplex(1.0,2.0);
  ComplexNumbers.Complex  z,w;
equation
  z = ComplexNumbers.Multiply(a,b);
  w = ComplexNumbers.Add(a,b);
end ComplexUser2;
```

10.2 Package Access

There are essentially two ways of accessing the definitions of a package:

- Direct reference by prefixing the package name to definition names.
- Importing definitions from the package.

We have already used the first method in the previous examples. It is usually more convenient and often necessary to use the `import` mechanism, which is the subject of the next section.

The two access levels in Modelica, `public` and `protected`, also apply to definitions declared in a package since `package` is a specialized class that shares most properties of general Modelica classes. Protected definitions of a package cannot in general be accessed by other packages and classes, except for local packages and classes, and packages inheriting the current package. For discussions of these exceptions, see the sections on *local packages* on page 514 and *inheriting packages* on page 509 in this chapter.

10.2.1 Importing Definitions from a Package

The `import` statement makes public classes and other public definitions declared in some package available for use in a class or a package. It is also the only way of referring to definitions declared in some other package for use inside an encapsulated package or class. To summarize, `import` statements in a package or class fill the following two needs:

- Making definitions from other packages available for use in a package or class without needing to prefix the definitions with the full names of the packages where they are defined.
- Explicit declaration of usage dependences on other packages. This is important for reducing the complexity of understanding and maintaining large systems consisting of many packages.

An `import` statement can occur in one of the following six syntactic forms which are explained in more detail in the following sections:

import *packagename*;	(qualified import)
import [*packagename*.]*definitionname*;	(single definition import)
import *packagename*.{*def1*,*def2*,*def3*,...};	(multiple definition import)
import *packagename*.*;	(unqualified import)
import *shortpackagename* = *packagename*;	(renaming import)
import *shortdefname* = [*packagename*.]*definitionname*;	(renaming single def. import)

The parts within [...] are optional. Here *packagename* is the fully qualified name of the imported package including possible dot notation. For example, if the package `ComplexNumbers` would have been declared as a subpackage inside the package `Modelica.Math`, its fully qualified name would be `Modelica.Math.ComplexNumbers`. *Definitionname* is the simple name without dot notation of a single definition that is imported. A *shortpackagename* is a simple name without dot notation that can be used to refer to the package after import instead of the presumably much longer *packagename*.

The six forms of `import` are exemplified below assuming that we want to access the addition operation (in one case also the subtraction operator) of the package `Modelica.Math.ComplexNumbers`:

```
import Modelica.Math.ComplexNumbers;          // Access by ComplexNumbers.Add
import Modelica.Math.ComplexNumbers.Add;      // Access by Add
import Modelica.Math.ComplexNumbers.{Add,Subtract}; // Access by Add,Subtract
```

```
import Modelica.Math.ComplexNumbers.*;              // Access by Add
import Co = Modelica.Math.ComplexNumbers;           // Access by Co.Add
import MyAdd = Modelica.Math.ComplexNumbers.Add;    // Access by MyAdd
```

The following rules also apply to `import` statements:

- Import statements are *not* inherited.
- Import statements are not named elements of a class or package. This means that `import` statements cannot be changed by modifiers or redeclarations.
- The *order* of `import` statements does not matter.
- One can only import *from* packages, not from other kinds of classes. Packages and all other forms of (specialized) classes can be imported *into*, that is, they may contain `import` statements.
- An imported package or definition should always be referred to by its fully qualified name in the `import` statement.

10.2.1.1 Qualified Import

The *qualified import* statement `import` *optpackageprefix.simplepackagename*`;` imports all definitions in a package, which subsequently can be referred to by (usually shorter) names *simplepackagename* and *definitionname*, where the simple package name is the full package name without its (optional) prefix. For example, if the package `ComplexNumbers` would have been a subpackage of `Modelica.Math`, the `import` statement in the package `ComplexUser1` would appear as `import Modelica.Math.ComplexNumbers;` but the rest would be the same, that is, we write `ComplexNumbers.Add` for the addition operation. This is the most common form of `import` that eliminates the risk for name collisions when importing from several packages.

```
encapsulated package ComplexUser1
  import ComplexNumbers;

class User
  ComplexNumbers.Complex  a(x=1.0, y=2.0);
  ComplexNumbers.Complex  b(x=1.0, y=2.0);
  ComplexNumbers.Complex  z,w;
equation
  z = ComplexNumbers.Multiply(a,b);
  w = ComplexNumbers.Add(a,b);
end User;

end ComplexUser1;
```

10.2.1.2 Single Definition Import

The *single definition import* of the form `import` *packagename.definitionname*`;` allows us to import a single specific definition (a constant, (specialized) class, or function) from a package and use that definition referred to by its *definitionname* without the package prefix. The statement `import ComplexNumbers.Add;` allows us to just write `Add` for the addition operation as in the class `User` within `ComplexUser2` below. The drawback is that we have to write an `import` statement for each imported definition which can be a bit cumbersome. There is no risk for name collision as long as we do not try to import two definitions with the same short name.

```
encapsulated package ComplexUser2
  import ComplexNumbers.Complex;
  import ComplexNumbers.Multiply;
  import ComplexNumbers.Add;

class User
  Complex  a(x=1.0, y=2.0);
  Complex  b(x=1.0, y=2.0);
  Complex  z,w;
equation
  z = Multiply(a,b);
```

```
    w = Add(a,b);
  end User;

end ComplexUser2;
```

10.2.1.3 Multiple Definition Import

The *multiple definition import* of the form `import` *packagename*.{*def1*,*def2*,*def3*,...}; allows us to import multiple specific definitions (constants, (specialized) classes, functions, or subpackages) from a package and use those definitions referred to by their short names *def1*, *def2*, *def3*, etc., without the package prefix. The statement `import ComplexNumbers.{Add,Multiply,Complex};` allows us to just write `Add` for the addition operation as in the class `User` within `ComplexUser2` below. Similarly for `Multiply` and `Complex`. This is more concise and convenient than having to write an `import` statement for each imported definition which can be a bit cumbersome. The multiple definition import is equivalent to multiple single definition imports with corresponding packagename and definition names. There is no risk for name collision as long as we do not try to import two definitions with the same short name.

```
encapsulated package ComplexUser2
  import ComplexNumbers.{Complex,Multiply,Add};

  class User
    Complex  a(x=1.0, y=2.0);
    Complex  b(x=1.0, y=2.0);
    Complex  z,w;
  equation
    z = Multiply(a,b);
    w = Add(a,b);
  end User;

end ComplexUser2;
```

10.2.1.4 Unqualified Import

The unqualified import statement of the form `import` *packagename*.* imports all definitions from the package using their short names without qualification prefixes. This might appear convenient for the lazy programmer but has a high risk for name collisions when importing from several packages. Another problem is that future compilation errors may occur if new definitions are added to the imported packages. For example, if a new definition named `w` would be added to the package `ComplexNumbers` there would be a name collision causing a compilation error in the class `ComplexUser3` below since there is already an imported variable `w` with the same name. For these reasons, the unqualified `import` statement is not recommended for code that is intended to be stable and maintainable. Its main use is in small examples where conciseness is important. None of the other forms of import has these problems. This example also shows direct `import` into a class instead of into an enclosing package.

```
class ComplexUser3
  import wpackage.w;   // Importing w from a package with a constant called w
  import ComplexNumbers.*;
  Complex  a(x=1.0, y=2.0);
  Complex  b(x=1.0, y=2.0);
  Complex  z;
equation
  z = Multiply(a,b);
  w = Add(a,b);
end ComplexUser3;
```

10.2.1.5 Renaming Import

The *renaming import* statement has two forms. The first of the form `import` *shortpackagename* = *packagename*; imports a package and renames it locally to *shortpackagename*. The second variant: `import` *shortdefname* = *packagename.definitionname*; imports a definition and renames it locally to *shortdefname*.

One can refer to imported definitions using *shortpackagename* as a presumably shorter package prefix. For example, the statement `import Co = ComplexNumbers;` in the class `ComplexUser4` below, allows us to refer to the addition operation by `Co.Add`. There is also the variant with renaming the operation to `MyAdd`. Both of these are as safe as qualified import but give more concise code.

```
class ComplexUser4
  import Co = ComplexNumbers
  import MyAdd = ComplexNumbers.Add;
  Co.Complex  a(x=1.0, y=2.0);
  Co.Complex  b(x=1.0, y=2.0);
  Co.Complex  z,w,w2;
equation
  z = Co.Multiply(a,b);
  w = Co.Add(a,b);
  w2 = MyAdd(w,b);
end ComplexUser4;
```

10.3 Package and Library Structuring

A well-designed package structure is one of the most important aspects that influences the complexity, understandability, and maintainability of large software systems. There are many factors to consider when designing a package, for example:

- The name of the package
- Structuring of the package into subpackages
- Reusability and encapsulation of the package
- Dependencies on other packages

Modelica defines a standard mapping of hierarchical package structures onto file systems or other storage mechanisms such as databases, which provides us with a simple and unambiguous way of locating a package. The Modelica library path mechanism makes it possible to make multiple packages and package hierarchies simultaneously available for lookup.

All of these mechanisms give us considerable flexibility and power in structuring a package. This freedom should, however, be used in an appropriate way.

10.3.1 Package Naming and Subpackages

The name of a package should be descriptive and relate to the topic of the definitions in the package. The name can be chosen to be unique within a project, within an organization, or sometimes in the whole world, depending on the typical usage scope of the package.

Since classes can be placed in packages, and packages is a specialized form of class, Modelica allows packages to contain *subpackages* i.e., packages declared within some other package. This implies that a package name can be composed of several simple names appended through dot notation, for example, "*Root package*"." *Package level two*"." *Package level three*", and so on. Typical examples can be found in the Modelica standard library, where all level-one subpackages are placed within the root package called `Modelica`. This is an extensive library containing predefined subpackages from several application domains as well as subpackages containing definitions of common constants and mathematical functions. See also Chapter 16, page 909, for a more complete description of the Modelica standard libraries, and Section 2.17 on page 60 in Chapter 2 for naming conventions in general recommended for Modelica code. A few examples of names of subpackages in this library follow here:

```
Modelica.Mechanics.Rotational.Interfaces    // Four levels of packages
Modelica.Electrical.Analog.Basic            // Basic electrical definitions
Modelica.Blocks.Interfaces                  // Interfaces to Blocks library
```

Choosing meaningful and unique names for packages within a large organization can be a problem. Sometimes one can choose the name by the help of an internal arbiter in an organization to ensure that two projects will not pick conflicting names.

However, in the world at large this approach is insufficient. One way to ensure unique package names over the whole world is to use an Internet domain name as a prefix. For example, for a company with a domain name `xcompany.com`, the prefix would be `org.xcompany`. The use of uppercase letters in the first part of the name further reduces the risk for name conflicts. Regarding the Modelica Association having the domain name `modelica.org`, this kind of package prefix becomes `org.modelica`. For example, the `Mechanics` part of the Modelica standard library could be denoted:

```
org.modelica.library.Modelica.Mechanics
```

Package names can become quite long using this method, but it is relatively safe against name conflicts. No one else using this scheme will take the same name as us, and for those who do not follow these conventions it is very unlikely that they will choose the first part of the name containing only uppercase letters.

10.3.2 Subpackages and Hierarchical Libraries

The main use for Modelica packages and subpackages is to structure hierarchical model libraries, of which the standard Modelica library is a good example. Below is a small example of a hierarchical package structure which has been extracted and adapted from the Modelica standard library. We have taken the liberty of making all subpackages encapsulated, which corresponds to good software engineering practice. This library consists of a number of subpackages like `Modelica.Blocks`, `Modelica.Mechanics`, `Modelica.Electrical`, and so on, which in turn usually are divided into subpackages to an appropriate level. The `Modelica.Mechanics` subpackage is divided into subpackages corresponding to different kinds of mechanical model components, for example, rotational components are in `Modelica.Rotational`, translational components in `Modelica.Translational`, etc.

The example is a bit misleading since these packages are quite large and are normally stored on separate files and directories and not seen as a single piece of code as below. The fully qualified names of each package or model component are shown as comments.

```
encapsulated package Modelica           // Modelica
  encapsulated package Mechanics        // Modelica.Mechanics
    encapsulated package Rotational // Modelica.Mechanics.Rotational
      model Inertia // Modelica.Mechanics.Rotational.Inertia
        ...
      end Inertia;
      model Torque   // Modelica.Mechanics.Rotational.Torque
        ...
      end Torque;
      ...
    end Rotational;
    ...
  end Mechanics;
  ...
end Modelica;
```

Public components in hierarchical libraries can be accessed through their fully qualified name. As pointed out previously, the Modelica standard library is always available for use, for example, as in the contrived model `InertiaUser` below, where we instantiate an `Inertia` component where the type is directly referred to by its fully qualified name `Modelica.Mechanics.Rotational.Inertia`.

```
model InertiaUser
  Modelica.Mechanics.Rotational.Inertia  w;
  ...
end InertiaUser;
```

10.3.2.1 Encapsulated Packages and Classes

An `encapsulated` package or class for example, the model `TorqueUser` below, *prevents* direct reference to `public` definitions *outside* itself, (with one exception, names starting with a dot (Section 3.17.3, page 113)), but as usual allows access to public subpackages and classes inside itself. Instead used packages from outside must be *imported*. As we have already emphasized in the preceding sections and examples, this is standard practice for *packages* in order to eliminate the possibility of implicit dependencies. However, sometimes it is also useful to have `encapsulated` *models* where there is no danger of implicit dependencies, e.g., application examples that are intended to be self-consistent and might be sent around to other users and developers.

```
encapsulated model TorqueUserExample1
  import Modelica.Mechanics.Rotational;   // Import package Rotational
  Rotational.Torque  t2;                  // Use Torque, OK!
  Modelica.Mechanics.Rotational.Inertia  w2;
       //Error! No direct reference
  ...   // to outside an encapsulated class
end TorqueUserExample1;
```

10.3.2.2 Name Lookup in Hierarchically Structured Packages

Name lookup in a hierarchical package structure follows the same rules as for general name lookup in (nested) Modelica classes that are described in Section 3.16.1 on page 109 in Chapter 3. Since you might find that description rather detailed and technical, it can be useful to point out the main issues of name lookup in package structures.

A name to be looked up consists of one or more parts, for example, `Modelica.Blocks.Interfaces` consists of the three parts `Modelica`, `Blocks`, and `Interfaces`. The first part of the name in this case is simply `Modelica`. The procedure for lookup of such a name consists of the following phases:

- Search for the first part of the name until it is found, starting in the innermost scope and upward recursively through the package and class hierarchy until we reach the top or an encapsulated package or class boundary. If not found, search the roots of other package hierarchies in the `MODELICAPATH` (see Section 10.3.4 in this chapter); otherwise, if not found, it is an error "missing declaration."
- If the first part of the name matches an `import` statement, locate the corresponding imported package or definition.
- Locate the rest of the name, if necessary, within the found package, class, or other kind of definition.

We apply this lookup algorithm for the lookup of `Interfaces.Flange_a` in the declaration of `a1` within the model `Inertia` in the package hierarchy below. Note that `Inertia` is declared within the package `Modelica.Mechanics.Rotational`. We search for the first part of the name, which is `Interfaces`, and find it declared within the same package, that is, within `Rotational`. The rest of the name, that is, `Flange_a`, is subsequently found as a connector class declared within `Interfaces`.

```
encapsulated package Modelica              // Modelica
  encapsulated package Blocks              // Modelica.Blocks
     encapsulated package Interfaces        // Modelica.Blocks.Interfaces
        ...
     end Interfaces;
  end Blocks;

  encapsulated package Mechanics         // Modelica.Mechanics
    encapsulated package Rotational   // Modelica.Mechanics.Rotational
     import Modelica;          // Import Modelica

     encapsulated package Interfaces
     // Modelica.Mechanics.Rotational.Interfaces
        connector Flange_a
        // Define Modelica.Mechanics.Rotational.Interfaces.Flange_a
          ...
```

```
        end Flange_a;
      end Interfaces;

       model Inertia
          Interfaces.Flange_a a1;
          // Use Modelica.Mechanics.Rotational.Interfaces.Flange_a
          Modelica.Mechanics.Rotational.Interfaces.Flange_a  a2;
          // Same type
       end Inertia;

       ...
      end Rotational;
    end Mechanics;
  end Modelica;
```

The declaration of a2 uses the same connector class Flange_a as a1, but the lookup is a bit different since it refers to Modelica.Mechanics.Rotational.Interfaces.Flange_a. The first part of the name in this case is Modelica, which is found in the import statement import Modelica; before hitting the boundary of the encapsulated package Rotational. The rest of the name, that is, Mechanics.Rotational.Interfaces.Flange_a, is located within the found Modelica package by searching from the root and downward. First Mechanics is located within Modelica, then Rotational is located within Mechanics, then Interfaces is located within Rotational, and finally Flange_a is found within Interfaces.

10.3.3 Mapping Package Structures to a Hierarchical File System

Packages and classes are usually stored in a file system, or sometimes, but this is less common, in a database. Each Modelica file in the file-system is stored in UTF-8 format (defined by The Unicode Consortium; http://www.unicode.org) and may start with the UTF-8 encoded byte order mark (0xef 0xbb 0xbf); this is treated as white-space in the grammar, see Appendix B. Modelica defines a mapping that unambiguously locates the storage place of a package or class from its fully qualified name. This gives us the following advantages:

- From its fully qualified name we can easily find the file and directory where the definition of a package or class is stored, for example, when you need to edit it.
- The Modelica environment can automatically locate and load referenced packages and classes from the file system into the simulation environment when needed.

A package can be stored either as a file or as a directory, whereas classes are stored either as separate files or as part of a package file. This gives more flexibility than the related storage scheme for Java where classes are always stored on separate files and packages are always represented by directories.

10.3.3.1 The within Statement

The Modelica syntax does not allow a package or class to use its fully qualified name with dot notation when declaring the package or class in question, for example, on a separate file or storage unit. Therefore the within statement has been introduced, which states the *prefix* needed to form the fully qualified name, and thereby provides a "unique" identification of the declared package or class. Note that the within statement is effective only for a package or class stored at the corresponding place in the package hierarchy, that is, it cannot be used to introduce a modified package or class without actually storing it. The within statement has the following syntax:

within *packageprefix*;

For example, the subpackage Rotational declared within Modelica.Mechanics has the fully qualified name Modelica.Mechanics.Rotational, which is formed by concatenating the *packageprefix* with the short name of the package. The declaration of Rotational is given below as it appears stored on a file:

```
within Modelica.Mechanics;
```

```
    encapsulated package Rotational    // Modelica.Mechanics.Rotational

    encapsulated package Interfaces
       import ...;
       connector Flange_a;
         ...
       end Flange_a;
       ...
    end Interfaces;

    model Inertia
       ...
    end Inertia;
    ...
  end Rotational;
```

Note that a `within` statement always appears *first* in a file containing a package or class declaration.

10.3.3.2 Mapping a Package Hierarchy into a Directory Hierarchy

A Modelica package hierarchy can be mapped into a corresponding directory hierarchy in the file system. The most visible part of this mapping is the translation of package or class names into similar or identical directory or file names. A package can be stored either as a directory or as a file:

- A *package* can be stored as a *directory* with the *same* short name as the package. This directory *must* contain a file named `package.mo` which starts with a `within` statement (see the previous section), and a (possibly empty) declaration of the package in question, for example, "`encapsulated package Modelica  end Modelica;`" exemplified by the package `Modelica`. The file `package.mo` typically contains documentation and graphical information for the package but may also contain `import` statements and declarations of constants and classes in the package.
- The classes (including functions) or subpackages in a package mapped as a directory are usually stored as their own *files* with extension `.mo` or *subdirectories* within this directory. Such files or subdirectories *must not* correspond to classes or packages with identical names, for example, there should *not* be a file `Rotational.mo` and a subdirectory `Rotational` within the same directory.
- A *package* or *class* can be stored as a *file* with the same *short name* as this package or class, and with the extension `.mo`. This file must start by a `within` statement (see above), stating where the package or class belongs. A class or subpackage can of course also be stored within some package file.
- The *ordering* of classes, constants, and subpackages within the package mapped to a directory can be specified by a file called `package.order` within the directory. Each line of that file contains the name of one class, subpackage, or constant. The file `package.order` may be automatically created by a modeling and simulation tool. It is recommended to create this file, since without it, the order of classes and constants in the package is file system and tool dependent, and may change from time to time. The classes and constants stored in `package.mo` are also mentioned in `package.order`, but their relative order should be the same as in `package.mo` to ensure that the relative order is preserved between classes and constants stored in different ways.

In order to give the reader some visual intuition about this mapping, a small part of the Modelica standard library is depicted below, both graphically as a package hierarchy, and as an example file directory hierarchy using directory syntax from Microsoft Windows file systems. It appears almost the same using Unix or Linux, just replace backslashes with slashes and remove "`C:`".

The packages `Modelica`, `Blocks`, `Examples`, and `Mechanics` are all represented as directories containing the required file `package.mo`. The packages `Continuous`, `Interfaces`, and `Rotational` are stored as the corresponding files `Continuous.mo`, `Interfaces.mo`, and `Rotational.mo`. The class `Example1` is stored in its own file `Example1.mo` within the package subdirectory `Examples`.

In this example, the directory corresponding to the root package `Modelica` happens to be placed within the directory `C:\library`. A root directory such as `Modelica` can be placed anywhere—the system will be able to find it through the `MODELICAPATH` as explained in the next section.

Directory and file structure:

```
C:\library
     \Modelica
         package.mo
         \Blocks
            package.mo
            Continuous.mo
            Interfaces.mo
         \Examples
            package.mo
            Example1.mo
          \Mechanics
            package.mo
            Rotational.mo
            ...
```

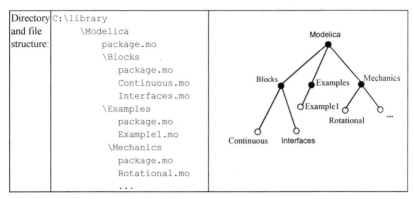

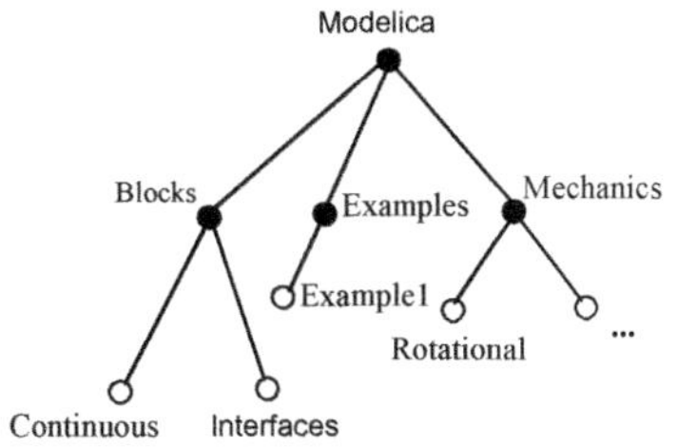

Below we show the contents and names of a few files resulting from this mapping. First is the file `package.mo` within the root package directory `C:\library\Modelica`. It contains an empty `Modelica` package declaration since all subpackages under `Modelica` are represented as subdirectories of their own. The empty `within` statement can be left out if desired.

File: `C:\library\Modelica\package.mo`

Contents:

```
within;
encapsulated package Modelica  "Modelica root package";
end Modelica;
```

Below is the file `package.mo` in the directory `C:\library\Modelica\Blocks\Examples` that stores the `Examples` package. It might be convenient to place `import` statements in the package declaration that can be used by example classes like `Example1` that are stored as separate files in the directory.

File: `C:\library\Modelica\Blocks\Examples\package.mo`

Contents:

```
within Modelica.Blocks;
encapsulated package Examples "Examples for Modelica.Blocks";
  import ...;
end Examples;
```

Here is the class `Example1` stored in a separate file `Example1.mo`.

File: `C:\library\Modelica\Blocks\Examples\Example1.mo`

Contents:

```
within Modelica.Blocks.Examples;
model Example1   "Usage example 1 for Modelica.Blocks";
  ...
end Example1;
```

Finally, we show the subpackage `Rotational` stored as the file `Rotational.mo`. Note that `Rotational` contains the subpackage `Interfaces`, which also is stored in the same file since we chose not to represent `Rotational` as a directory.

File: `C:\library\Modelica\Mechanics\Rotational.mo`

Contents:

```
within Modelica.Mechanics;
encapsulated package Rotational
   // Modelica.Mechanics.Rotational

  encapsulated package Interfaces
    import ...;
```

	``
	    connector Flange_a;
	      ...
	    end Flange_a;
	      ...
	  end Interfaces;
	
	  model Inertia
	    ...
	  end Inertia;
	  ...
	
	end Rotational;
	``

10.3.3.3 Mapping a Package Hierarchy or Class into a Single File

A complete package hierarchy can be stored as a single file according to the rules described in the previous sections. It is possible, but not very common, to store the whole Modelica standard library as a single file, as shown in the example below. One reason could be to package a special version of the standard library into a file that can be easily distributed to other users, for example, for debugging purposes.

File: `C:\lib3\Modelica.mo`

Contents:

```
within ;
encapsulated package Modelica
  encapsulated package Blocks
    ...
  end Blocks;

  encapsulated package Mechanics
    ...
  end Mechanics;
  ...
end Modelica;
```

Below is a small application model that refers to the `Inertia` class in the `Rotational` subpackage of the above Modelica standard library. It does not contain a `within` statement since it is not placed within any package. First it has to be loaded into the Modelica environment in order to be used.

File: `C:\applications\InertiaUser.mo`

Contents:

```
model InertiaUser
  Modelica.Mechanics.Rotational.Inertia  w;
  ...
end InertiaUser;
```

10.3.4 The Modelica Library Path—MODELICAPATH

The Modelica environment has an unnamed top-level scope which contains classes and packages that have been loaded into the Modelica workspace. Models to be simulated can refer to such classes or packages since they can be accessed through the normal lookup rules. For classes with version information, see also Section 11.10.1, page 547.

However, Modelica also provides a facility to access libraries stored externally as package hierarchies. This facility is called the `MODELICAPATH`, which on a typical computer system is an *environment variable* containing a string with a semicolon-separated ordered list of names of directories where package hierarchies corresponding to Modelica model libraries are stored.

If during lookup a top-level name is not found in the unnamed top-level scope, the search continues in the package hierarchies stored in these directories. Figure 10-1 shows an example `MODELICAPATH = "C:\library; C:\lib1; C:\lib2"`, with three directories containing the roots of the package hierarchies `Modelica`, `MyLib`, and `ComplexNumbers`. The first two are represented as the subdirectories `C:\library\Modelica` and `C:\lib1\MyLib`, whereas the third is stored as the file `C:\lib2\ComplexNumbers.mo`.

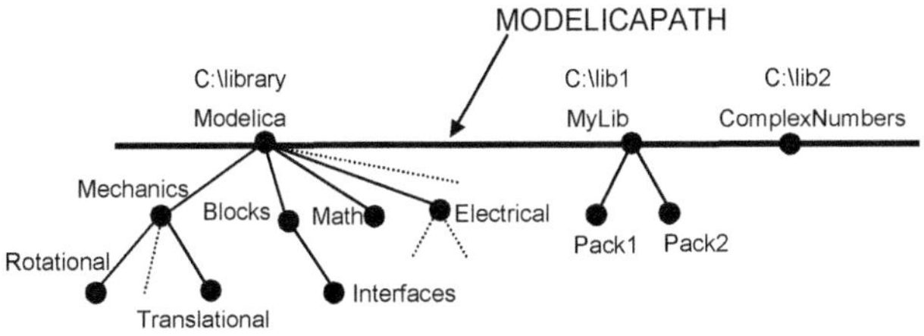

Figure 10-1. Roots of package hierarchies, e.g., `Modelica`, `MyLib`, and `ComplexNumbers` in `MODELICAPATH = "C:\library; C:\lib1; C:\lib2"`.

Assume that we want to access the package `MyLib.Pack2` in Figure 10-1, for example, through an `import` statement `import MyLib.Pack2;`. During lookup we first try to find a package `MyLib` corresponding to the first part of the import name. It is not found in the top-level scope since it has not previously been loaded into the environment.

Since the name was not found in the top-level scope the search continues in the directories in the `MODELICAPATH` in the specified order. For the search to succeed, there must be a subdirectory `MyLib` or a file `MyLib.mo` in one of the directories mentioned in the `MODELICAPATH`. If there is no such subdirectory or file, the lookup fails. If `MyLib` is found in one of the directories, the rest of the name, in this case `Pack2`, is located in `MyLib`. If that fails, the entire lookup fails without continuing the search in possibly remaining directories.

In this example the name matches the subdirectory named `MyLib` in the second directory "`C:\lib1`" mentioned in the `MODELICAPATH`. This subdirectory must have a file `package.mo` containing a definition of the package `MyLib`, according to the Modelica rules on how to map a package hierarchy to the file system. The subpackage `Pack2` is stored in its own subdirectory or file in the subdirectory `MyLib`. In this case the search succeeds and the package `MyLib.Pack2` is loaded into the environment.

10.3.5 Packages versus Classes

In the preceding sections we have mostly discussed various properties of packages. In fact, many of these properties also apply to classes in general, e.g. the possibility of mapping to storage places such as directories or files in the file system. This follows from the fact that a package is a specialized class that is largely a restricted form of class in Modelica, apart from the enhancement of being imported from. This does not imply that we should use classes instead of packages just because there are few restrictions in Modelica. Use packages for libraries and coarse-grained structuring of systems, and classes for models and model components.

10.4 Package Variants and Operations

In the following sections we will examine certain variants of packages that can be created through operations such as instantiation of generic packages, inheritance of packages, and manual editing. In addition we will examine two special types of packages local packages and non-encapsulated packages, as well as their usage and some associated inherent problems.

10.4.1 Generic Packages

Generic packages are packages with some kind of formal parameter, e.g. a replaceable type. They are really a special case of parameterized generic classes described in Section 4.4 on page 168, where several examples of parameterized models are given.

In the beginning of this chapter we presented the view of a package as an abstract data type containing a data structure with associated operations. Generic packages can often be regarded as parameterized abstract data types, for example, the package `GeneralStack` below, which is parameterized in terms of the type of the elements in the stack—the *type parameter* `Element`. This example is rather algorithmic in contrast to the parameterized generic models presented in Chapter 4.

```
package GeneralStack

replaceable class Element
end Element;

record Stack
  parameter Integer maxsize = 0;
  Integer           size = 0;
  Element[maxsize]  vec;
end Stack;

function Push
  input  Stack   si;
  input  Element e;
  output Stack   so;
algorithm
  so := si;
  so.size := so.size+1;
  so.vec[so.size] := e;
end Push;

function Pop
  input  Stack   si;
  output Stack   so;
algorithm
  so := si;
  so.size := so.size-1;
end Pop;

function Top
  input  Stack   si;
  output Element e;
algorithm
  e := si.vec[si.size];
end Top;

end GeneralStack;
```

By "instantiating" the package `GeneralStack` with different values of the type parameter `Element` we can create specialized stack packages containing elements of a specified type. This is a different meaning of *instantiation* compared to our previous use of the term for creating data instances from classes. In this case instantiation means the creation of a more *specialized package*. For example, below we have instantiated `GeneralStack` with a type argument `Integer` creating the specialized stack called `IntegerStack`, and with `Real` giving the stack `RealStack`.

```
package IntegerStack = GeneralStack(redeclare type Element = Integer);

package RealStack    = GeneralStack(redeclare type Element = Real);
```

Finally, the package `IntegerStack` is used in the class `IntStackUser` into which it is imported. A stack with room for a maximum of two hundred integers is allocated. Some stack operations are performed such as pushing three numbers on the stack, getting the top element, and popping the top element.

```
class IntStackUser
  import IS = IntegerStack;
```

```
  IS.Stack    stk(maxsize = 200);
  Integer     item;
algorithm
  stk  := IS.Push(stk,35);    // Push three numbers on the stack
  stk  := IS.Push(stk,400);
  stk  := IS.Push(stk,44);
  item := IS.Top(stk);        // Get the top element, i.e. 44
  stk  := IS.Pop(stk);        // Pop the top element from the stack
end IntStackUser;
```

10.4.2 Inherited Packages

Since packages are specialized classes they can be inherited and specialized in the same way as classes in general. For example, a double-ended queue, sometimes called *deque*, is an (abstract) data type that combines the actions of a stack and a queue. To create a package for this data type, we can inherit all stack operations together with the data structure declaration `Element` from `GeneralStack`, and add operations to insert, remove, and access a data element at the other end of the stack/queue, i.e. at the bottom, as in the example package `DoubleEndedQueue` below.

```
encapsulated package DoubleEndedQueue    "Combined stack and queue"

extends GeneralStack;

function AddBottom             "Add element at the bottom / the end"
  input  Stack   si;
  input  Element e;
  output Stack   so;
algorithm
  so.size := si.size+1;
  for i in 1:si.size loop
     so.vec[i+1] := si.vec[i]
  end loop;
  so.vec[1] := e;
end AddBottom;

function RemoveBottom          "Remove element at the bottom / the end"
  input  Stack   si;
  output Stack   so;
algorithm
  so.size := si.size-1;
  for i in 1:so.size loop
     so.vec[i] := si.vec[i+1]
  end loop;
end RemoveBottom;

function Bottom                "Get bottom element"
  input  Stack   si;
  output Element e;
algorithm
  e := si.vec[1];
end Bottom;

end DoubleEndedQueue;
```

Below is an "instantiation" of the double-ended queue together with a small usage example. Two integers are inserted at the beginning of the queue and one integer at the end of the queue. Then the end element is accessed and the first element is removed.

```
package IntDeQueue = DoubleEndedQueue(redeclare type Element = Integer);

class DeQueueUser
  import ID = IntDeQueue;
  ID.Stack    q(maxsize = 200);
  Integer     item;
algorithm
```

```
    q  := ID.Push(q,65);        // Insert two numbers at the beginning
    q  := ID.Push(q,500);
    q  := ID.AddBottom(q,455)  // Insert at the end of the queue
    item := ID.Bottom(q);       // Get the end element, i.e. 445
    q  := ID.Pop(q);            // Remove the first element from the queue
  end DeQueueUser;
```

10.4.3 Local Packages

A *local package* in Modelica is simply a package that is declared directly inside a *class* that is not a package. This is in contradiction to the usual role of packages as coarse-grained independent structuring units. However, there are situations where it can be convenient to have access to a local package which has been adapted to the specific needs within a certain model. For example, in the model `MyCircuit` below we use a local specialized version of the package `Electrical.Components` which is parameterized in terms of the type `ResistorModel` being replaced by the local type `MyResistorModel` in `MyCircuit`. Several classes from this local package `MyComponents` are subsequently used for instantiating variables.

```
model MyCircuit
  model MyResistorModel
  extends Electrical.Interfaces.ResistorModel;
     ...  // My special declarations and equations
  end MyResistorModel;

  encapsulated package MyComponents =
     Electrical.Components(redeclare ResistorModel = MyResistorModel);

  MyComponents.Transformer tr1
  MyComponents.Transducer  td2;
  ...
end MyCircuit;
```

In a similar way, the class `DeQueueLocalUser` below uses the local package `P` that is a version of the package `DoubleEndedQueue` from the previous section parameterized by the local type `VerySecret`.

```
class DeQueueLocalUser
  protected
  type VerySecret = Integer;
  package P = DoubleEndedQueue(redeclare type Element = VerySecret);
  P.Stack   q(maxsize = 200);
  Integer   item;
algorithm
  q  := P.Push(q,65);        // Insert two numbers at the beginning
  q  := P.Push(q,500);
  q  := P.AddBottom(q,455)  // Insert at the end of the queue
  item := P.Bottom(q);       // Get the end element, i.e. 445
  q  := P.Pop(q);            // Remove the first element from the queue
end DeQueueLocalUser;
```

10.4.4 Nonencapsulated Packages

A nonencapsulated package is a package declared without the prefix `encapsulated`. Such a package has the disadvantage of being implicitly dependent on packages in the environment through nested lookup, as discussed in the next section. However, there is one case where nonencapsulated packages are useful. Large encapsulated packages containing `protected` declarations can internally be structured into nonencapsulated subpackages. This is the only way `protected` declarations of a parent package can be accessed by subpackages since declarations imported into encapsulated subpackages have to be `public`.

For example, below the encapsulated package `Blocks` has been internally structured into three nonencapsulated packages `Interfaces`, `Continuous`, and `Examples` that all can access the protected type `MySecret`.

```
encapsulated package Modelica
  encapsulated package Blocks
     protected
        type MySecret = ...;

     public
        package Interfaces
          ...
         end Interfaces;

        package Continuous
           MySecret x;
           ...
        end Continuous

        package Examples
           ...
        end Examples;
    end Blocks;
end Modelica;
```

It might be argued that it is against the principle of information hiding and the concept of packages as independent code units to let other packages access protected variables. This is true, but the damage is hopefully limited if nonencapsulated packages are seldom used and used only for internal structuring of large packages, at most one level down in the package hierarchy.

You might think that non-encapsulated packages are more convenient than encapsulated ones since one avoids some typing, that is, the keyword `encapsulated` and certain `import` statements. However, this is not true in general, since experience shows that people spend much more time reading code than writing it, and implicit dependencies implied by nonencapsulated packages makes the code harder to understand.

10.4.4.1 Problems with Nonencapsulated Packages

We have already noted that nonencapsulated packages may create problems of understanding and maintaining code. This is caused by implicit dependencies on declarations in the environment. The usual nested lookup rules for classes apply to nonencapsulated packages and classes, rather than explicit, easily visible, `import` dependencies. In fact, in order to find a name used in a nonencapsulated package we may have to do the following:

- Visually scan the whole source code of the current package, which might be quite large.
- Search through all packages containing the current package, that is, higher up in the package hierarchy, since standard nested lookup allows used types and other definitions to be declared anywhere above the current position in the hierarchy. This amount of code is even larger.

The following example consisting of three levels of nested non-encapsulated packages illustrates these problems:

```
package MyModelica
  package Mechanics
     package Rotational
        model Inertia
           MyType x;
           ...
        end Inertia;
     end Rotational;
  end Mechanics;
  package Blocks
    ...
  end Blocks;
end MyModelica;
```

The type MyType used inside the Inertia model can be declared anywhere within the package Rotational, the package Mechanics, or the package MyModelica, or be one of the classes already loaded into the current workspace.

10.4.5 Moving Packages

Copying or moving a nonencapsulated subpackage such as MyModelica.Mechanics.Rotational in the above example might be a bit problematic since used declarations, for example, MyType declared in MyModelica, may not be available in the new location for Rotational, if for example we place it within the package YourModelica that probably lacks MyType.

The situation is much better for encapsulated (i.e., self-contained) packages since all dependencies are explicit through import statements:

- When copying or moving an encapsulated package or class, at most the import statements inside this package or class, including subpackages and local classes, need to be updated.

The reason this works is that lookup stops at the package or class boundary for encapsulated packages and classes, and all internal references to declarations in other packages and classes are via import statements. In the example below, the subpackage Modelica.Blocks.Interfaces is imported into Rotational, which uses Interfaces.InPort:

```
encapsulated package Modelica
  encapsulated package Blocks
     encapsulated package Interfaces
        connector InPort
           ...
        end InPort;
    end Interfaces;
  end Blocks;

  encapsulated package Mechanics
     encapsulated package Rotational
        import Modelica.Blocks.Interfaces;    // Import
       model Torque
           Interfaces.InPort inPort;           // Use
           ...
        end Torque;
        ...
       end Rotational;
  end Mechanics;
end Modelica;
```

If we move the package Rotational inside YourModelica as below, it will continue to work without changes since its import statement still refers to Modelica.Blocks.Interfaces. If we would like it to instead refer to the package YourModelica.Blocks.Interfaces, just update the import statement as we have done below:

```
encapsulated package YourModelica
  encapsulated package Blocks
     encapsulated package Interfaces
        connector InPort
           ...
        end InPort;
       end Interfaces;
  end Blocks;

  encapsulated package Mechanics
     encapsulated package Rotational
        import YourModelica.Blocks.Interfaces;    // Updated import
       model Torque
```

```
            Interfaces.InPort inPort;                 // Use
            ...
        end Torque;
        ...
      end Rotational;
    end Mechanics;
  end YourModelica;
```

10.5 A Comparison Between Java and Modelica Packages

You might find it useful to do a brief comparison between the Java package concept and the Modelica counterpart. The Java package concept is without question currently the best-known package concept, and the Java programming language is taught in many, perhaps the majority, of introductory programming courses around the world. It might be the case that you have been acquainted with the Java language before learning Modelica. The Modelica package concept has been considerably influenced by Java—it can almost be considered as a superset of the corresponding Java concept. There are a number of differences between the two concepts with regard to the following aspects:

- Import
- Subpackages
- Encapsulation and independence of packages
- Local packages
- Inheritance of packages
- Lookup
- Mapping to the file system
- Identification of packages

We briefly compare and discuss each of these aspects.

10.5.1 Import

Java has two forms of `import` statement: single definition import and unqualified import, whereas Modelica also provides qualified import of whole packages, multiple definition import, and renaming import.

10.5.2 Subpackages

Java packages are always "independent" entities. Even a subpackage in Java has to be explicitly imported or its definitions referenced by their fully qualified names in order to be used within its parent package or by some other package. The subpackage relation is just a relation between the names of two packages and an organizational tool for storage in the file system, for example, `java.lang.reflect` is a subpackage of `java.lang`, but this does not imply any special access rights between those packages. By contrast, a nested subpackage in Modelica can actually be placed inside its parent package and can in its *non-encapsulated* form use nested lookup for access of definitions in its parent package or higher up in the hierarchy. This may create implicit dependencies between packages, for example, `Modelica.Blocks.Interfaces` may implicitly use definitions in `Modelica.Blocks`.

Encapsulated Modelica packages are close to the Java notion of packages as independent entities. In fact, an `encapsulated` Modelica package is somewhat more "independent" and "encapsulated" than a corresponding Java package, since all use of other packages declared outside itself must be via `import` statements. Direct use of definitions via fully qualified names is not allowed in that case in Modelica. This makes package dependencies very clear. However, a Modelica package can use definitions declared in its own subpackages without `import`, for example, code in `Modelica.Blocks`, which can use definitions in `Modelica.Blocks.Interfaces` without explicit `import`.

10.5.3 Encapsulation and Independence of Packages

Java packages are more independent than Modelica packages in the sense that no other Java package, not even a subpackage, can access protected or private definitions of a Java package. A non-encapsulated Modelica subpackage may access protected definitions in its parent package—there is no way a parent package can prevent that.

On the other hand, an `encapsulated` Modelica package always requires `import` for access of definitions in other packages that are not subpackages. Therefore such Modelica package dependences become cleaner and more visible than in Java where direct references using fully qualified names of definitions in other packages often occur.

10.5.4 Local Packages

Local packages are packages that are declared inside a class and not directly inside a package. Such packages are allowed in Modelica but are disallowed in Java and most other programming languages.

10.5.5 Inheritance of Packages

Modelica packages can be specialized and extended through inheritance, whereas Java packages cannot. Using inheritance on packages can be quite useful and encourages reuse, as we saw in the example where a stack was extended to become a double-ended queue.

10.5.6 Lookup

In Java there are only two modes of lookup of definitions from other packages: lookup via `import` statements or lookup through direct references using fully qualified names. The Modelica package concept supports both of those mechanisms. Additionally, in Modelica nested lookup is possible from non-encapsulated packages. Also, definitions in subpackages can be used or imported without giving fully qualified names. Thirdly, local packages can be defined inside classes in Modelica, which is not allowed in Java.

10.5.7 Mapping to the File System

Java has a simpler convention for mapping packages and classes to storage places in the file system, whereas Modelica's mapping gives increased flexibility. In fact, the Modelica mapping is approximately a superset of the Java mapping. A Java class is always mapped to a file and Java packages to different levels of directories corresponding to the dot notation in the package name, e.g. `java.util.Date` is mapped to a two-level directory structure such as `C:\java\util\` containing the file `Date.j` with the class `Date`.

In Modelica we have the choice of either mapping each class to a separate file as in Java, or storing whole packages including all their classes, and possibly subpackages, on a single file. For example, the package `Modelica.Blocks.Interfaces` might be stored on the single file `C:\Modelica\Blocks\Interfaces.mo`, be part of some file, for example, `C:\Modelica\Blocks.mo`, or be represented as the directory `C:Modelica\Blocks\Interfaces\` containing a number of files, one for each class.

10.5.8 Identification of Packages

This property concerns the ability to (unambiguously) identify a class or package from its declaration, for example, as stored on a file. A Java class file always contains a `package` statement that identifies which package the class belongs to and in which directory it is stored in the file system. For example, the Java class `BitSet` in the package `java.util` can be declared on a file as follows:

```
package java.util;
class BitSet {
  ...
}
```

A corresponding declaration in Modelica with the `Util` package represented as a directory and `BitSet` as a file `BitSet.mo` could be:

```
within Modelica.Util;      // The file BitSet.mo
class BitSet
  ...
end BitSet;
```

If the `Util` subpackage is instead represented as a whole file `Util.mo`, we will have:

```
within Modelica;           // The file Util.mo
package Util;

  class BitSet
    ...
  end BitSet;

  ...
end Util;
```

10.5.9 Remarks

The Modelica package concept is an improvement over the Java package concept by being more flexible and powerful. On the other hand, the Java concept is simpler—simplicity versus power. It is almost the case that the Modelica package concept is a superset of the Java concept. The Modelica import mechanism is more convenient and solves some problems often caused by unqualified import in Java. The file mapping algorithm in Modelica is slightly more complicated but gives possibilities for better structuring by allowing the grouping of classes, and even subpackages, on the same file in addition to the usual directory mapping. The concept of non-encapsulated packages in Modelica can provide some increased flexibility in internal structuring of encapsulated packages, but can on the other hand easily be misused to create package structures and hierarchies with many implicit dependencies that are hard to understand and maintain.

This matter to some extent depends on personal taste, but if we want to keep most of the simplicity and style of Java packages and still get the advantages of Modelica packages, the following coding conventions might be a good compromise:

- Avoid unqualified import and use the increased possibilities of qualified and renaming import in Modelica.
- Always use `encapsulated` packages with explicit `import` of used packages even including subpackages. The extra typing will be paid off by increased readability through easily visible and unambiguous package dependencies.
- Avoid the use of nonencapsulated packages if there are not very strong reasons to use them.

Remember that saving a few keystrokes of typing is not the most important factor. Experience has shown that code is read approximately 10 times more often than written. Structuring our models in a way that reduces complexity is one of the most important design goals, for which the package mechanism is a quite valuable tool.

10.6 External Resources and Libraries

Models may reference external resources and call functions defined in external libraries.

10.6.1 External Resources in Packages

Modelica models may reference external *resources* such as files or documents accessed via internet links, identified by so-called *Uniform Resource Identifiers* (URIs). Moreover, a Modelica related URI scheme called `modelica` is defined for accessing resources associated with a certain package. See Section 11.15, page 556, for more information regarding this topic.

10.6.2 External Library Packages and Include Files

Functions in another programming language defined in external libraries and/or include files may be called by referring to that library or include file as described in Section 9.4, page 466.

10.7 Summary

This chapter is mainly devoted to the Modelica package concept, which is used for constructing libraries of reusable model definitions. We started by discussing packages as abstract data types, followed by a description of different mechanisms for accessing packages and importing definitions from packages. We also described the structuring of packages and libraries, as well as the notion of encapsulated packages and classes. The mapping of package structures to a hierarchical file systems was described, as well as the Modelica library path for searching externally stored package hierarchies. We presented generic packages, inherited packages, local packages, non-encapsulated packages and gave a comparison between the Java and Modelica package concepts. Finally, the chapter was concluded by a presentation how resources identified by URIs can referred to in Modelica models.

10.8 Literature

Further reading on the topic of abstract data types and their relation to the module and package concept can for example be found in (Louden 1993). A classic article on information hiding is (Parnas 1972).

The package presentation briefly relates to the Modelica language specification (Modelica Association 2003), but with a substantially expanded explanatory text. The example of a package structure has been adapted from the `Modelica.Mechanics.Rotational` example in (Modelica Association 2000) and the corresponding part of the Modelica standard library. The comparison between Modelica packages and Java packages relates to the Java package presentation in (Arnold and Gosling 1999) concerning the Java language. Information about Uniform Resource Identifiers (URIs) can be found in (Wikipedia-URI 2011), and the concept of resource in (Wikipedia-Resource 2011).

10.9 Exercises

Exercise 10-1:

Question: Packages are nice to use in Modelica, but what exactly is a package? Why use the word encapsulated when creating packages?

Exercise 10-2:

Creating a Package: Create a package that contains a constant `PI`, a type `Distance`, a function `RectangleArea`, a function `TriangleArea`, a function `CirclePerimeter`, and a function `CircleArea`.

Write a class, `GeometryUser`, which uses the package and calls the functions.

Exercise 10-3:

Question: What is important to consider before designing a package?

Exercise 10-4:

Question: There are different kinds of packages. What is a generic package? What is a local package? Is there something called a non-encapsulated package? If so, explain it. Why might it be a problem to move packages?

Exercise 10-5:

Question: Is it really possible to inherit packages?

Inheriting Packages: Inherit the package `Geometry` into a class `GeometryUser`, which is calling functions from `Geometry`.

```
class GeometryUser

end GeometryUser;

package Geometry
  constant Real PI = 3.1415926536;
  type Distance = Real(unit = "m");

  function RectangleArea
    input Distance B;
    input Distance H;
    output Distance area;
  algorithm
    area := B*H;
  end RectangleArea;

  function TriangleArea
    input Distance B;
    input Distance H;
    output Distance area;
  algorithm
    area := RectangleArea(B, H)/2;
  end TriangleArea;

  function CirclePerimeter
    input Distance radius;
    output Distance perimeter;
  algorithm
    perimeter := 2*PI*radius;
  end CirclePerimeter;

  function CircleArea
    input Distance radius;
    output Distance area;
  algorithm
    area := PI*radius^2;
  end CircleArea;
end Geometry;
```

Chapter 11

Annotations, Units, and Quantities

This chapter presents some additional constructs and attributes that are not really part of the Modelica core language but still belong to Modelica in a broad sense, and therefore are part of the Modelica language definition. Here we will present the following features:

- Annotations
- Units and quantities

What is an *annotation*? It can be understood as an attribute or property containing information associated with some element of a Modelica model. Examples are model documentation and graphical layout information concerning icons and connections associated with models. This is needed, for example, by graphical connection editors used to combine Modelica model components. The graphical view usually makes models easier to understand as we have seen in many examples earlier in this book. The Modelica `annotation` construct is similar to the concept of *pragma* known from the Ada programming language. It has the following syntactic structure:

annotation (*annotation_elements*)

where *annotation_elements* is a comma-separated list of annotation elements that can be any kind of expression compatible with the Modelica syntax. In the rest of this chapter we will present a number of predefined standard annotations that should be recognized by Modelica environments.

Below is an example of an `annotation` containing information about documentation and the graphical layout of both the icon and the diagram layer representing a capacitor model (`Modelica.Electrical.Analog.Basic.Capacitor`):

```
model Capacitor "Ideal linear electrical capacitor"
  extends Interfaces.OnePort;
  parameter SI.Capacitance C(start = 1) "Capacitance";
equation
  i = C * der(v);
  annotation(
   Documentation(info = "<HTML>
    <p>
    The linear capacitor connects the branch voltage <i>v</i> with the
    branch current <i>i</i> by <i>i = C * dv/dt</i>.
    The Capacitance <i>C</i> is allowed to be positive, zero, or negative.
    </p>
    </HTML>
    ", revisions = "<html>
    <ul>
    <li><i> 1998   </i>
           by Christoph Clauss<br> initially implemented<br>
```

```
          </li>
      </ul>
      </html>"),
    Icon(coordinateSystem(preserveAspectRatio = true,
      extent = {{-100,-100},{100,100}}, grid = {2,2}),
      graphics = {
        Line(points={{-14,28},{-14,-28}}, thickness = 0.5,color = {0,0,255}),
        Line(points={{14,28},{14,-28}}, thickness = 0.5,color = {0,0,255}),
        Line(points = {{-90,0},{-14,0}},color = {0,0,255}),
        Line(points = {{14,0},{90,0}},color = {0,0,255} ),
        Text(extent = {{-136,-60},{136,-92}}, textString = "C=%C",
                     lineColor={0,0,0} ),
        Text(extent = {{-150,85},{150,45}}, textString = "%name",
                     lineColor = {0,0,255}) } ),
    Diagram(coordinateSystem(preserveAspectRatio = true,
      extent = {{-100,-100},{100,100}}, grid = {2,2}),
      graphics = {
        Line(points={{-20,40},{-20,-40}}, thickness=0.5, color = {0,0,255}),
        Line(points={{20,40},{20,-40}}, thickness=0.5, color = {0,0,255}),
        Line(points={{-96,0},{-20,0}}, color = {0,0,255}),
        Line(points={{20,0},{96,0}}, color = {0,0,255}) }
      ));
  end Capacitor;
```

The annotations in this example have the names `Documentation`, `Icon`, and `Diagram`. The `Icon` and `Diagram` annotations contain instances of the graphical annotation elements `Text`, `Line`, and so on. The whole annotation is expressed using Modelica *modifier* syntax.

Neither the majority of annotations (except a few) nor the above-mentioned units and quantities are supposed to influence the *simulation* of a Modelica model. Apart from some exceptional cases such as the external function `arrayLayout` annotation described later, one should in theory be able to remove both annotations and unit and quantity information from a model and be able to rerun the simulation of the model *without* any change of results. In practice, certain annotations are necessary to give information to the Modelica compiler and simulator to make the symbolic manipulation and simulation efficient enough.

Annotations are needed primarily by *tools* such as programming environments for Modelica, which access the annotation information associated with models. A typical example of a tool in a Modelica environment is the already-mentioned graphical connection editor, which reads the model together with graphical annotations about the layout including icons and arrows, allows the user to graphically edit the model, and saves the edited result, including possibly changed values of the annotations.

The usual *strong type checking* of Modelica models is *not* applied to annotations. This is motivated by the fact that annotations are automatically generated and read by tools, and not manually edited by humans. Therefore the information is presumably correct. Another reason for avoiding type checking in this case is to make it simple for tools to support and extend their own annotation notation without undue constraints.

Apart from annotations, the rest of this chapter deals with the topic of *units* and *quantities*. The `unit` attribute of a variable can be seen as some kind of more precise type information, whereas the `quantity` attribute defines the physical category of the variable, like `Length`, `Mass`, and `Pressure`. Several units are possible for the same `quantity`, for example, a variable measuring `Length` could have one of the units "m" (meter), "mm," or "km." A Modelica tool is not required to do any unit analysis based on the `unit` information. Certain tools may offer dimension analysis, including unit checking, which is an analysis related to type checking that may help the user to find certain modeling errors based on inconsistent use of quantities and units, for example, in equations or expressions.

11.1 Standard Annotations

In order to maintain portability of models, all Modelica tools should recognize a *minimum set* of annotations, that is, the annotations described in this chapter. All Modelica tools are free to add their own annotations, but other tools may not recognize these.

However, all tools are able to parse annotations of any kind since they follow the Modelica *modifier syntax*, including attribute values that are Modelica expressions. The following are the names of the predefined standard Modelica annotations, annotation elements, and annotation attributes, to be described in more detail in subsequent sections. First we show the standard *annotation* names:

`absoluteValue`	`Evaluate`	`License`
`arrayLayout`	`experiment`	`missingInnerMessage`
`Authorization`	`HideResult`	`obsolete`
`choices`	`Icon`	`Protection`
`conversion`	`IconMap`	`revisionId`
`dateModified`	`Include`	`singleInstance`
`defaultComponentName`	`IncludeDirectory`	`smoothOrder`
`defaultComponentPrefixes`	`Inline`	`unassignedMessage`
`defaultConnection-StructurallyInconsistent`	`InlineAfterIndexReduction`	`uses`
`derivative`	`inverse`	`version`
`Diagram`	`LateInline`	`versionBuild`
`DiagramMap`	`Library`	`versionDate`
`Dialog`	`LibraryDirectory`	
`Documentation`		

The following predefined graphical *annotation elements* are typically used within the `graphics` attribute of `Icon` or `Diagram` annotation elements:

```
Line, Polygon, Rectangle, Ellipse, Text, Bitmap
```

A few additional graphical annotation elements:

```
Placement, transformation, iconTransformation
```

11.2 Annotation Syntax

The syntax of a Modelica annotation is the keyword `annotation` followed by a parenthesized comma-separated list of elements. These elements have the same syntax as Modelica modifiers. There are two kinds of annotation elements:

- Simple annotation elements.
- Redeclaration annotation elements.

Simple annotation elements have the same syntax as simple modifiers described in more detail in Section 11.2.1, and redeclaration annotation elements comply with the syntax of redeclaration modifiers described in Section 11.2.2. Both forms of annotation elements can be nested to any level.

11.2.1 Simple Annotation Elements

An annotation with simple annotation elements consists of pairs associating a name with an expression, for example, according to the following structure where possible prefixes and other details are left out:

```
annotation(name1 = expr1, name2 = expr2, ...)
```

An example derivative annotation containing a simple annotation element:

```
annotation(derivative=foo1);
```

Annotations can be nested to any level. The following is a common structure for two-level simple annotations:

```
annotation(name(name1 = expr1, name2 = expr2, ...), ...)
```

Here is an example of a two-level simple annotation called choices, where the elements on the second level contain string comments that can be used by tools to generate menu alternatives:

```
annotation(choices(choice=1 "P", choice=2 "PI", choice=3 "PID"));
```

11.2.2 Redeclaration Annotation Elements

Annotation elements also can be structured as redeclarations, e.g. as in the example structure below containing a redeclaration of a short class definition:

```
annotation(Name1(Name2(redeclare class Name3 = Name2, ...)))
```

Here is an example of a level-three nested choices redeclaration annotation using short class definitions in the redeclarations:

```
annotation(choices(
  choice(redeclare MyResistor=lib2.Resistor(a={2}) "..."),
  choice(redeclare MyResistor=lib2.Resistor2 "...")));
```

The choices annotation in this case is used to generate menus with redeclaration alternatives for replaceable models. The user interface can suggest reasonable redeclarations, where the string comment in a choice annotation element is used as a textual explanation of the choice alternative. Based on the interactions with the user, the graphical user interface then generates the appropriate Modelica code. For more details, see Section 11.5.8.2, page 542.

Redeclaration annotations also can be like variable declarations:

```
annotation(name(redeclare Type1 variable1));
```

11.3 Annotation Placement

Annotations can be placed at the end of class definitions, and at the end of variable declarations, import clauses, extends clauses, equations, and statements.

11.3.1 Class Annotations

A *class annotation* contains information associated with a class. One class annotation may be placed at the end of the list of elements in a long class declaration. Remember that the class can contain elements such as local classes, variable declarations, import statements, extends statements, equation sections, and algorithm sections.

Icon, Diagram, and Documentation annotations are only allowed directly in classes, for example, not on instances or connections. The allowed annotations for a short class definition is the union of the allowed annotations in classes and on extends-clauses.

For example here is a Documentation annotation inside a long class declaration:

```
<class keyword> <class identifier>
  <element1>;
  <element2>;
  ...
  annotation(Documentation(info = " ... "))
end < class identifier>;
```

This also can be used to attach documentation information to a package:

```
package Modelica
   ...
   annotation(Documentation(info = " ... "))
end Modelica;
```

The `Resistor2` example below illustrates that a class level annotation element can only occur at the end of a class:

```
model Resistor2
  Pin p;
  Pin n;
  parameter R "Resistance in [Ohm]";
equation
  R*p.i = p.v - n.v;
  n.i = p.i;
public
  annotation(Icon(
    graphics = {Rectangle(extent={{-70,30},{70,-30}}, lineColor={0,0,255},
     ... }, ...
  ));
end Resistor2;
```

Class annotations for declarations, including *long* and *short* class definitions, are always placed at the *end* of the declaration, for example, first a short class definition:

```
<class keyword> <identifier1> = < identifier2> <array dims> <modifiers> <comment> <annotation>
```

and a long class declaration:

```
<class keyword> <identifier1>
  ...
  <annotation>
end <identifier1>
```

For example, the `Icon` annotation is placed at the end of the `Velocity` declaration below, after the optional string comment:

```
type Velocity = Real[3](unit="m/s") "a comment" annotation(Icon(...));
```

A class level annotation at the end of a class within an algorithm or equation section is not associated with that section, instead it is associated with the class as a whole. However, an equation or statement can have its own associated annotation if the annotation occurs before the semicolon that marks the end of the respective equation or statement.

11.3.2 Variable Annotations

A *variable annotation* associates information with a declared variable. Such an annotation is placed at the end of the variable declaration after the optional string comment. For example:

```
Pin p annotation(Placement(transformation(extent = {{-110,-10},{-90,10}},
                                          rotation = 0)));
```

11.3.3 Import Annotations

Analogous to variable annotations, *import annotations* are placed in the end of the `import` statement after the optional string comment, for example, as below. Such an annotation can be any annotation for which it is meaningful to associate it with an `import` statement.

```
import Modelica.Mechanics.Rotational "Rotational import" annotation(...);
```

11.3.4 Equation Annotations

Any equation can have an associated annotation. The most common form of *equation annotation* is annotations to connection equations. It is natural to associate graphical attributes such as lines with a certain position, length, and color to such equations. As in the previous cases, the annotation is placed at the end, after the optional comment. For example:

```
connect(p1.n,p2.p) "comment" annotation(Line(points=[-90, 0; -70, 0]));
```

11.3.5 Statement and Algorithm Annotations

Statements can also be annotated, even though the need is less obvious than for connection equations. As for equations, *statement* annotations are placed at the end of the statement after the optional string comment, for example:

```
name := x+2*y   "comment"  annotation( );
```

11.4 Graphical Annotations

Graphical annotations is the most common form of annotation in typical Modelica models. All models created using a graphic model editor and saved as Modelica text usually contain annotations that describe the graphical layout of the model components, including positions and sizes of icons and lines representing connections between the components.

The predefined graphical annotations, annotation elements, and annotation attributes in Modelica provides a notation to express and save this kind of graphical information.

The description given here specifies the meaning for a subset of standard graphic annotations that should be supported by all Modelica environments.

Remember that a Modelica environment is free to define and use other annotation attributes in addition to those defined here. The only requirement is that any environment must be able to save files with all attributes intact, including those that are not used. To ensure this, annotations must be represented with constructs according to the Modelica syntax.

11.4.1 Graphical Representation of Models

Graphical annotation information is normally given together with five different kinds of Modelica entities. We have the following cases where graphical annotations can appear:

- Annotations of a *class* to specify the graphical representation of its icon as a diagram and common properties such as a local coordinate system.
- Annotations associated with an *instance* of a class, typically to specify the position and size of the graphical representation of the instance.

- Annotations of *connectors*.
- Annotations of *extends clauses*.
- Annotations associated with a *connection*, that is, its `line` representation, the `color` of the connection line, etc.

The example below shows the use of such graphical attributes in the form of annotations to define the different parts of the `Resistor` icon in Figure 11-1.

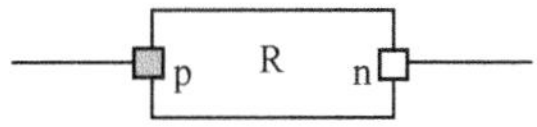

Figure 11-1. A Resistor icon defined by graphical annotations.

The *class annotation* named `Icon` in the `Resistor` model below defines the graphical layout of its icon, which in this case is a *rectangle*. This rectangle is specified by the `Rectangle` annotation element in which its two opposite corners are given by the `extent` attribute, and its visual pattern by the `fillPattern` attribute (see the graphical annotation attributes described in a subsequent section).

Additionally, the resistor icon contains a *text* label given by the `Text` annotation elements with its attributes `extent` and `string`. The resistor also has two *line* segments, given by the two `Line` annotation elements, to visually emphasize its pins.

The resistor has two `Pin` connectors represented by the two small squares. The left filled square represents the `p` connector whereas the right unfilled square represents the `n` connector. This square is the graphical icon for the `Pin` class.

The icon image for `Pin` is positioned and scaled to the right size by the `Placement` annotation for the component, for example, `p` and `n` in Figure 11-1 and in the code below. The icon is first drawn in the master coordinate system specified in the component's class, for example, `Pin`. The graphical image is subsequently rotated and translated so that the coordinate system is mapped to the region defined by the `transformation` or `iconTransformation` attributes in the components declaration.

```
model Resistor
  Pin p  annotation(Placement(
             transformation(extent = {{-110,-10},{-90,10}}, rotation = 0)));
  Pin n  annotation(Placement(
             transformation(extent = {{110,-10},{90,10}}, rotation = 0)));
  parameter Real R "Resistance in [Ohm]";
equation
  R*p.i = p.v - n.v;
  n.i = p.i;
public
 annotation(
 Icon(coordinateSystem(preserveAspectRatio = true,
   extent = {{-100,-100},{100,100}}, grid = {2,2} ),
   graphics = {
     Rectangle(extent = {{-70,30},{70,-30}}, lineColor = {0,0,255},
          fillColor = {255,255,255}, fillPattern = FillPattern.Solid),
     Line(points = {{-90,0},{-70,0}}, color = {0,0,255}),
     Line(points = {{70,0},{90,0}}, color = {0,0,255}),
     Text(extent={{-144,-40},{142,-72}},textString = "R=%R",
       lineColor = {0,0,0}),
     Text(extent={{-152,87},{148,47}},textString="%name",
       lineColor ={0,0,255})}));
end Resistor;
```

11.4.1.1 Icon and Diagram Layers of Graphical Annotations

The graphical representation abstraction of a class consists of two graphical layers:

- The *icon* graphical layer.

- The *diagram* graphical layer.

Both representations show graphical objects such as icons to represent class instances, connectors, and connection lines.

- The icon representation typically visualizes an instance by hiding hierarchical details.
- The diagram graphical layer typically describes the hierarchical decomposition by showing icons of subcomponents.

A graphical layer description is represented as an `Icon` or a `Diagram` annotation element. The structure of an `Icon` annotation element is given by one of these expressions:

Icon(*coordsys_specification*, *graphics*)
Icon(*graphics*)

A `Diagram` annotation element has one of the following two analogous forms:

Diagram(*coordsys_specification*, *graphics*)
Diagram(*graphics*)

Here is an example of a simple icon with a *coordsys_specification* element and a *graphics* element defining the appearance through a list of two graphical primitives:

```
annotation (
  Icon(coordinateSystem(extent={{-100,-100}, {100,100}}),
       graphics={Rectangle(extent={{-100,-100}, {100,100}}),
                    Text(extent={{-100,-100},{100,100}}, textString="Icon")}));
```

The graphics of an icon is specified as an ordered sequence of graphical primitives, which are described further in Section 11.4.5 below. Note that such an ordered sequence is a syntactically valid Modelica annotation, although there is currently no mechanism in Modelica for defining an array of elements of heterogeneous types.

`Icon`, `Diagram`, and `Documentation` annotations are only allowed directly in classes, for example, not on instances or connections. The allowed annotations for a short class definition is the union of the allowed annotations in classes and on extends-clauses.

11.4.2 Graphical Annotation Attributes

There are a number of predefined graphical *annotation attributes*, which can be divided into basic attributes; attributes to classes, instances, and connections; and attributes that are graphical elements to specify the appearance of class icons.

The attributes represent component positions, connections, and various graphical primitives for building icons as shown below. The attribute structures are described through Modelica classes. Points are denoted by vectors, and extents (two opposite points) are described using vectors of two points.

11.4.3 Basic Graphical Attributes

These definitions of basic graphical attributes are used for the specification of the graphical annotation elements in the subsequent sections.

```
type DrawingUnit  = Real(final unit="mm");
type Point        = DrawingUnit[2]    "{x, y}";
type Extent       = Point[2] "Defines a rectangular area {{x1, y1}, {x2, y2}}";
```

The interpretation of `unit` is with respect to printer output in natural size (not zoomed). On the screen, one mm in "natural size" is typically mapped to some pixels for a common value of screen resolution.

All graphical entities inherit the partial record `GraphicItem` that has a `visible` attribute which indicates if the entity should be displayed or not.

```
partial record GraphicItem
  Boolean visible = true;
  Point origin = {0, 0};
  Real rotation(quantity="angle", unit="deg")=0;
end GraphicItem;
```

The `origin` attribute specifies the origin of the graphical item in the coordinate system of the layer in which it is defined. The origin is used to define the geometric information of the item and for all transformations applied to the item. All geometric information is given relative the `origin` attribute, which by default is {0, 0}.

The `rotation` attribute specifies the rotation of the graphical item around the point defined by the `origin` attribute.

11.4.3.1 Coordinate Systems for Icon and Diagram Graphical Layers

Each graphical layer is a graphical object that has its own coordinate system.

A coordinate system is defined by the coordinates of two points: the lower-left corner and the upper-right corner, where the coordinates of the first point shall be less than the coordinates of the second point, implying a first quadrant coordinate system.

This is represented by the `extent` attribute, of type `Extent=Point[2]`, where each `Point` is a two-dimensional coordinate.

The attribute `preserveAspectRatio` specifies a constraint on the shape of components of the class. If `preserveAspectRatio` is `true`, changing the extent of components shall preserve the aspect ratio of the coordinate system of the class.

The attribute `initialScale` specifies the default component size as `initialScale` times the size of the coordinate system of the class. An application may use a different default value of `initialScale`.

The attribute `grid` specifies the spacing between grid points which can be used by tools for alignment of points in the coordinate system, for example, "snap-to-grid". Its use and default value is tool dependent.

```
record CoordinateSystem "Attribute to graphical layer"
  Extent extent;
  Boolean preserveAspectRatio=true;
  Real initialScale = 0.1;
  DrawingUnit[2] grid;
end CoordinateSystem;
```

For example, a coordinate system for an icon could be defined as:

```
CoordinateSystem(extent = {{-10, -10}, {10, 10}});
```

that is, a local coordinate system extent with width 20 units and height 20 units, with the local x coordinate from –10 to 10 and the local y from –10 to 10. The exact interpretation of the units is to a certain extent tool dependent.

The coordinate systems for `Icon` and `Diagram` are by default defined as follows. The `graphics` attribute being an array of `GraphicItem` represents an ordered list (a sequence) of graphical primitives.

```
record Icon       "Representation of Icon graphical layer"
  CoordinateSystem  coordinateSystem(extent = {{-10, -10}, {10, 10}});
  GraphicItem[:]    graphics;
end Icon;

record Diagram    "Representation of Diagram graphical layer"
  CoordinateSystem  coordinateSystem(extent = {{-100, -100}, {100, 100}});
  GraphicItem[:]    graphics;
end Diagram;
```

For example, a coordinate system with extent for a connector icon could be defined as:

```
CoordinateSystem(extent = {{-1, -1}, {1, 1}});
```

11.4.3.2 Color and Appearance of Graphical Objects

Color and pattern properties of graphical objects and connection lines are described using the following attribute types:

```
type Color = Integer[3](min=0, max=255)    "RGB representation";

constant Color Black = zeros(3);  // Default color

type LinePattern = enumeration(None, Solid, Dash, Dot, DashDot, DashDotDot);

type FillPattern = enumeration(None, Solid, Horizontal, Vertical,
                               Cross, Forward, Backward, CrossDiag,
                               HorizontalCylinder, VerticalCylinder, Sphere);

type BorderPattern = enumeration(None, Raised, Sunken, Engraved);

type Smooth = enumeration(None, Bezier);
```

The `FillPattern` attribute values `Horizontal, Vertical, Cross, Forward, Backward,` and `CrossDiag` specify fill patterns drawn with the border `lineColor` over the `fillColor.`

The attributes `HorizontalCylinder, VerticalCylinder,` and `Sphere` specify color intensity gradients that represent a horizontal cylinder, a vertical cylinder, and a sphere, respectively.

The border pattern attributes `Raised`, `Sunken` and `Engraved` represent frames which are rendered in a tool-dependent way.

The `smooth` attribute specifies that a line can be drawn as straight line segments (`None`) or using a spline (`Bezier`), where the line's points specify control points of a quadratic Bezier curve. For lines with only two points, the `smooth` attribute has no effect.

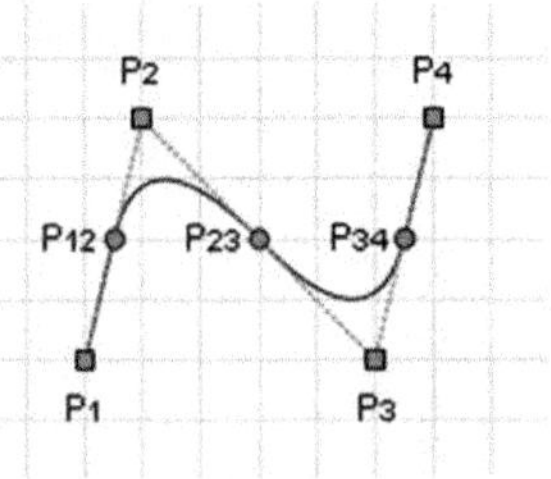

Figure 11-2. Bezier curve with control points.

For lines with three or more points (P_1, P_2, ..., P_n), the middle point of each line segment (P_{12}, P_{23}, ..., $P_{(n-1)n}$) becomes the starting point and ending points of each quadratic Bezier curve. For each quadratic Bezier curve, the common point of the two line segment becomes the control point. For instance, point P_2 becomes the control point for the Bezier curve starting at P_{12} and ending at P_{23}. A straight line is drawn between the starting point of the line and the starting point of the first quadratic Bezier curve, as well as between the ending point of the line and the ending point of the last quadratic Bezier curve.

In the illustration in Figure 11-2, the square points (P_1, P_2, P_3, and P_4) represent the points that define the line, and the circle points (P_{12}, P_{23}, and P_{34}) are the calculated middle points of each line segment. Points P_{12}, P_2, and P_{23} define the first quadratic Bezier curve, and the points P_{23}, P_3, and P_{34} define the second quadratic Bezier curve. Finally a straight line is drawn between points P_1 and P_{12} as well as between P_{34} and P_4.

```
type Arrow = enumeration(None, Open, Filled, Half);

type TextStyle = enumeration(Bold, Italic, UnderLine);

type TextAlignment = enumeration(Left, Center, Right);
```

Filled-shape graphical objects, for example; rectangle, polygon, and ellipse, inherit the record `FilledShape` that has the following attributes for the border and the interior:

```
record FilledShape    "Style attributes for filled shapes"
  Color       lineColor     = Black              "Color of border line";
  Color       fillColor     = Black              "Interior fill color";
  LinePattern pattern       = LinePattern.Solid "Border line pattern";
  FillPattern fillPattern   = FillPattern.None  "Interior fill pattern";
  DrawingUnit lineThickness = 0.25               "Border line thickness"
end Style;
```

When a color gradient is specified, the color fades from the specified fill color to white and black using the hue and saturation of the specified color.

11.4.4 Graphical Representation of Certain Model Elements

So far we have primarily discussed the graphical representation of a whole class in the icon or diagram graphical layer, as well as a set of basic graphical attributes. Now we turn to the graphical representation of certain elements appearing in classes, such as instances, extends clauses, connectors, and connections.

11.4.4.1 Components

Graphical representations of components, i.e., class instances, can be placed within a diagram or icon graphical layer. Each kind of graphical element has an annotation with a `Placement` modifier to describe its placement.

```
record Placement
  Boolean visible = true;
  Transformation transformation "Placement in the diagram layer";
  Transformation iconTransformation "Placement in the icon layer";
end Placement;
```

Placements are defined in terms of coordinate system transformations, defining the position and orientation of a graphic object with its local coordinate system, relative to the coordinate system of the graphic object associated with the enclosing class.

For example, icon placement is defined by the record `Transformation` so that the actual coordinates of the icon of a model instance are defined in the class where the instance is declared.

```
record Transformation
  Point origin = {0, 0};
  Extent extent;
  Real rotation(quantity="angle", unit="deg")=0;
end Transformation;
```

The origin attribute defines the position of the component in the coordinate system of the enclosing class. The `extent` defines the position, size, and flipping of the component, relative to the `origin` attribute.

The `extent` is defined relative to the `origin` attribute of the component instance. Given an `extent` `{{x1,y1}, {x2,y2}}`, `x2<x1` defines horizontal flipping and `y2<y1` defines vertical flipping around the point defined by the `origin` attribute. The `rotation` attribute specifies rotation of the `extent` around the point defined by the `origin` attribute.

The graphical operations are applied in the order: scaling, flipping and rotation. If no `iconTransformation` is given the `transformation` is also used for placement in the icon layer. Figure 11-3 illustrates scaling and rotation of a rectangle.

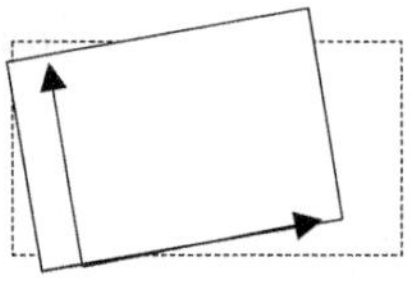

Figure 11-3. Scaling and rotation coordinate system transformations on a rectangular object.

11.4.4.2 Connectors

A connector can be displayed in both an icon graphical layer and a diagram graphical layer of a class. Since the coordinate systems typically are different, placement information needs to be given using two different coordinate systems. More flexibility than just using scaling and translation is needed since the abstraction views might need different visual placement of the connectors.

The `transformation` attribute of a `Placement` annotation element gives the placement in the diagram graphical layer and the `iconTransformation` attribute gives the placement in the icon graphical layer. For example:

```
Pin p annotation(Placement(
  transformation(extent = {{-110,-10},{-90,10}}, rotation = 0),
  iconTransformation(extent = {{-110,-10},{-90,10}}, rotation = 0);
```

Recall that if no `iconTransformation` is given the `transformation` is also used for placement in the icon layer, as in the connector `p2` below:

```
Pin p2 annotation(Placement(transformation(extent = {{-110,-10},{-90,10}},
                                            rotation = 0)));
```

When a connector is shown in a diagram graphical layer, its diagram graphical layer is displayed to facilitate opening up a hierarchical connector to allow connections to its internal subconnectors.

For connectors, the icon graphical layer is used to represent a connector when it is displayed in the icon graphical layer of the enclosing model. The diagram graphical layer of the connector is used to represent it when shown in the diagram graphical layer of the enclosing model.

Protected connectors are shown only in the diagram graphical layer. Public connectors are shown in both the diagram graphical layer and the icon graphical layer. Nonconnector components are shown only in the diagram graphical layer.

11.4.4.3 Extends Clause

Each `extends` clause may have layer specific annotations, i.e., for the `Icon` or `Diagram` layer, which describe the rendering of the base class' icon and diagram layers in the subclass.

```
record IconMap
  Extent extent = {{0, 0}, {0, 0}};
  Boolean primitivesVisible = true;
end IconMap;

record DiagramMap
  Extent extent = {{0, 0}, {0, 0}};
  Boolean primitivesVisible = true;
end DiagramMap;
```

All graphical objects are by default inherited from a base class. If the `primitivesVisible` attribute is `false`, components and connections are visible but graphical primitives are not.

The base class coordinate system is mapped to the region specified by the attribute `extent`. If the `extent` defines a null region (the default), the base class coordinate system shall be fitted to the derived class coordinate system with center alignment and respected `preserveAspectRatio` of the base class. For example:

```
model A
  extends B annotation(
    IconMap(extent={{-100,-100}, {100,100}},primitivesVisible=false),
    DiagramMap(extent={{-50,-50}, {0,0}},primitivesVisible=true)
  );
end A;

model B
  extends C annotation(DiagramMap(primitivesVisible=false));
  ...
end B;
```

In this example the diagram of `A` contains the graphical primitives from `A` and `B`, but not from `C` since they were hidden in `B`. The ones from `B` are rescaled, and the icon of `A` contains the graphical primitives from `A`, but neither from `B` nor from `C`.

11.4.4.4 Connections

A connection is specified with an annotation containing a `Line` primitive, and optionally a Text-primitive, as exemplified below:

```
connect(a.x, b.x)
  annotation(Line(points={{-25,30}, {10,30}, {10, -20}, {40,-20}}));
```

The optional Text-primitive defines a text that will be written on the connection line. It has the following definition. However, it is not the same as the Text-primitive (Section 11.4.5.5, page 533) that is part of the graphics, the differences are marked as bold lines:

```
record Text
  extends GraphicItem;
  extends FilledShape;
  Extent extent;
  String string;
  Real fontSize = 0 "unit pt";
  String fontName;
  TextStyle textStyle[:];
  TextAlignment horizontalAlignment = if index<0 then TextAlignment.Right
                                      else TextAligment.Left;
  Integer index;
end Text;
```

The `index` is one of the points of `Line` (numbered 1, 2, 3, ... where –1 can be used to indicate the last one). The `string` may use the special symbols "`%first`" and "`%second`" to indicate the connectors in the the connect-equation. For example:

```
connect(controlBus.axisControlBus1, axis1.axisControlBus) annotation (
  Text(string="%first", index=-1, extent=[-6,3; -6,3]),
  Line(points={{-80,-10},{-80,-14.5},{-79,-14.5},{-79,-17},
              {-65,-17},{-65,-65}, {-25,-65}}));
```

This draws a connection line and adds the text ”`axisControlBus1`” ending at {-6, 3}+{-25, -65}.

11.4.5 Definitions of Graphical Elements

The following predefined graphical elements are used as graphical annotation elements when describing the appearance of graphical objects in annotations. This includes annotation attributes used when defining the appearance of class icons. The `Line` graphical element can also be used for connection lines.

A list of such graphical elements whose types are subtypes of `GraphicItem` occur as the value of the `graphics` attribute. The following elements are available:

- `Line`
- `Polygon`
- `Rectangle`
- `Ellipse`
- `Text`
- `Bitmap`

In the subsequent sections we specify the structure of each graphical element in more detail.

11.4.5.1 Line

The properties of a line are described by the following record definition:

```
record Line
  extends GraphicItem;
  Point[:]       points;
  Color          color      = Black;
  LinePattern    pattern    = LinePattern.Solid;
  DrawingUnit    thickness = 0.25;
  Arrow[2]       arrow = {Arrow.None, Arrow.None}; "{start arrow, end arrow}"
  DrawingUnit    arrowSize = 3;
  Smooth         smooth = Smooth.None                "Spline";
end Line;
```

Remember that the `Line` primitive is also used to directly specify the graphical representation of a connection, as described in Section 11.4.4.4 above.

11.4.5.2 Polygon

The properties of a polygon are specified by the following record definition:

```
record Polygon
  extends GraphicItem;
  extends FilledShape;
  Point[:]  points;
  Smooth    smooth = Smooth.None             "Spline outline";
end Polygon;
```

A polygon is closed by definition. This is obvious if the first and the last points are the same. However, if the first and the last points are not identical, the polygon is automatically closed by generating a line segment between these two points.

11.4.5.3 Rectangle

A rectangle is described as follows:

```
record Rectangle
  extends  GraphicItem;
  extends  FilledShape;
  BorderPattern  borderPattern = BorderPattern.none;
  Extent         extent;
  DrawingUnit    radius = 0   "Corner radius";
```

```
end Rectangle;
```

The `extent` attribute specifies the bounding box of the rectangle. If a nonzero `radius` value is specified, the rectangle is drawn with rounded corners of the given radius.

11.4.5.4 Ellipse

An ellipse graphic element is specified by the following record type:

```
record Ellipse
  extends  GraphicItem;
  extends  FilledShape;
  Extent   extent;
  Real     startAngle(quantity="angle", unit="deg")=0;
  Real     endAngle(quantity="angle", unit="deg")=360;
end Ellipse;
```

The `extent` attribute of the record specifies the bounding box of the ellipse. For elliptic arcs, `startAngle` and `endAngle` specify the arc prior to the stretch and rotate operations. The arc is drawn counter-clockwise from `startAngle` to `endAngle`, where `startAngle` and `endAngle` are defined counter-clockwise from "3 o'clock".

11.4.5.5 Text

The graphical properties of a text string are described by the `Text` record:

```
record Text
  extends GraphicItem;
  extends FilledShape;
  Extent          extent;
  String          textString;
  Real            fontSize = 0  "unit pt";
  String          fontName;
  TextStyle       textStyle[:];
  Color           textColor=lineColor;
  TextAlignment horizontalAlignment = TextAlignment.Center;
end Text;
```

The `textColor` attribute defines the color of the text. The text is drawn with transparent background and no border around the text (and without outline). The contents inherited from `FilledShape` is deprecated.

There are a number of common macros that can be used in the text, and they should be replaced by the tool when displaying the text as follows:

- `%par` replaced by the value of the parameter `par`. The intent is that the text is easily readable, thus if `par` is of an enumeration type, replace `%par` by the item name, not by the full name. For example: if `par="Modelica.Blocks.Types.Enumeration.Periodic"`, then `%par` should be displayed as `Periodic`.
- `%%` replaced by `%`.
- `%name` replaced by the name of the instance, i.e., the identifier for it in the enclosing class.
- `%class` replaced by the name of the class.

The style attribute `fontSize` specifies the font size. If the `fontSize` attribute is 0 the text is scaled to fit its `extent`. Otherwise, the `fontSize` specifies the absolute size in `pt`. The text is vertically centered in the `extent`.

If the string `fontName` is empty, the tool may choose a font. The style attribute `textStyle` specifies variations of the font.

11.4.5.6 Bitmap

A bitmap image is specified as follows:

```
record Bitmap
  extends GraphicItem;
  Extent  extent;
  String  fileName                "Name of bitmap file";
  String  imageSource             "Base64 representation of bitmap";
end Bitmap;
```

The `Bitmap` primitive renders a graphical bitmap image. The data of the image can either be stored on an external file or in the annotation itself. The image is scaled to fit the extent. Given an extent {{x1, y1}, {x2, y2}}, x2<x1 defines horizontal flipping and y2<y1 defines vertical flipping around the point defined by the origin attribute.

When the attribute `fileName` is specified, the string refers to an external file containing image data. The mapping from the string to the file is specified for some URIs (Section 11.15, page 556). The supported file formats include `PNG`, `BMP`, and `JPEG`. Other supported file formats are unspecified.

When the attribute `imageSource` is specified, the string contains the image data. The image is represented as a Base64 encoding of the image file format (see RFC 4648, `http://tools.ietf.org/html/rfc4648`).

The image is uniformly scaled to preserve aspect ratio so that it exactly fits within the `extent`, touching the `extent` along one axis. The center of the image is positioned at the center of the `extent`.

11.4.6 Variable Graphics and Schematic Animation using DynamicSelect

Any value (coordinates, color, text, etc.) in graphical annotations can be dependent on class variables using the `DynamicSelect` expression. `DynamicSelect` has the syntax of a function call with two arguments, where the first argument specifies the value of the editing state and the second argument the value of the non-editing state. The first argument must be a literal expression. The second argument may contain references to variables to enable a dynamic behavior.

For example, the level of a tank could be animated by a rectangle expanding in vertical direction and its color depending on a variable overflow:

```
annotation (
  Icon(graphics={Rectangle(
    extent=DynamicSelect({{0,0},{20,20}},{{0,0},{20,level}}),
    fillColor=DynamicSelect({0,0,255},
                            if overflow then {255,0,0} else {0,0,255}))}
);
```

11.4.7 User Input and Interaction

It is possible to interactively modify variables during a simulation. The variables may either be parameters, discrete variables, or states. New numeric values can be given, a mouse click can change a `Boolean` variable, or a mouse movement can change a `Real` variable. Input fields may be associated with a `GraphicItem` or a component as an array named `interaction`. The `interaction` array may occur as an attribute of a graphic primitive, an attribute of a component annotation, or as an attribute of the layer annotation of a class.

11.4.7.1 Mouse Input

A `Boolean` variable can be changed when the cursor is held over a graphical item or component and the selection button is pressed if the interaction annotation contains `OnMouseDownSetBoolean`:

```
record OnMouseDownSetBoolean
  Boolean variable  "Name of variable to change when mouse button pressed";
  Boolean value     "Assigned value";
end OnMouseDownSetBoolean;
```

For example, a button can be represented by a rectangle changing color depending on a `Boolean` variable `on` and toggles the variable when the rectangle is clicked on:

```
annotation(Icon(graphics={Rectangle(
  extent=[0,0; 20,20]),
  fillColor = if on then {255,0,0} else {0,0,255},
  interaction = { OnMouseDownSetBoolean (on, not on)} ) }
);
```

In a similar way, a variable can be changed when the mouse button is *released*:

```
record OnMouseUpSetBoolean
  Boolean variable  "Name of variable to change when mouse button released";
  Boolean value     "Assigned value";
end OnMouseUpSetBoolean;
```

Note that several interaction objects can be associated with the same graphical item or component, for example:

```
    interaction={OnMouseDownSetBoolean(on,true), OnMouseUpSetBoolean(on,false)};
```

The `OnMouseMoveXSetReal` interaction object sets the variable to the position of the cursor in the X direction in the local coordinate system mapped to the interval defined by the `minValue` and `maxValue` attributes.

```
record OnMouseMoveXSetReal
  Real xVariable    "Name of variable to change when the cursor is moved
                     in the x direction";
  Real minValue;
  Real maxValue;
end OnMouseMoveXSetReal;
```

The `OnMouseMoveYSetReal` interaction object works in a similar way to the `OnMouseMoveXSetReal` object but in the Y direction.

```
record OnMouseMoveYSetReal
  Real yVariable    "Name of variable to change when the cursor is moved
                     in the y direction";
  Real minValue;
  Real maxValue;
end OnMouseMoveYSetReal;
```

11.4.7.2 Edit Input

The `OnMouseDownEditInteger` interaction object presents an input field when the graphical item or component is clicked on. The field shows the actual value of the variable and allows changing the value. If a too small or a too large value according to the `min` and `max` parameter values of the variable is given, the input is rejected.

```
record OnMouseDownEditInteger
  Integer variable  "Name of variable to change";
end OnMouseDownEditInteger;
```

The `OnMouseDownEditReal` interaction object presents an input field when the graphical item or component is clicked on. The field shows the actual value of the variable and allows changing the value. If a too small or too large value according to the `min` and `max` parameter values of the variable is given, the input is rejected.

```
record OnMouseDownEditReal
  Real variable     "Name of variable to change";
end OnMouseDownEditReal;
```

The `OnMouseDownEditString` interaction object presents an input field when the graphical item or component is clicked on. The field shows the actual value of the variable and allows changing the value.

```
record OnMouseDownEditString
  String variable  "Name of variable to change";
end OnMouseDownEditString;
```

11.5 Annotations for Customizing Library GUIs

A class, that is, in most cases a library package, may use special annotations to define a customized graphical user interface for that particular library.

11.5.1 defaultComponentName Annotation

One such annotation called `defaultComponentName` can be used when creating a component of the given class by default, where the recommended *default component name* is *name*, as specified below:

```
annotation(defaultComponentName = "name")
```

11.5.2 defaultComponentPrefixes Annotation

Moreover, the annotation `defaultComponentPrefixes` can be used to set the *default prefixes*:

```
annotation(defaultComponentPrefixes = "prefixes")
```

When creating a component, it is recommended for the tool to generate a declaration of the form:

```
prefixes class-name component-name
```

The following prefixes may be included in the *prefixes* string: `inner`, `outer`, `replaceable`, `constant`, `parameter`, `discrete`.

In combination with the `defaultComponentName` the `defaultComponentPrefixes` annotation can be used to make it easy for users to create `inner` components matching the `outer` declarations. See also the `World` model example below.

11.5.3 missingInnerMessage Annotation

During instance hierarchy lookup (Section 3.17.5, page 113), when an `outer` component of the class does not have a corresponding `inner` component, this is an error. In such cases the string `"message"` in the `missingInnerMessage` annotation may be used as a diagnostic message to the modeler. Moreover, the tool may also temporarily automatically add the corresponding `inner` component during translation, visible to all of the outer components.

```
annotation(missingInnerMessage = "message")
```

For example, consider the following `World` model:

```
model World
  annotation(defaultComponentName      = "world",
             defaultComponentPrefixes = "inner replaceable",
             missingInnerMessage      = "The World object is missing");
```

```
  ...
end World;
```

When an instance of `World` model is dragged into the diagram layer the following declaration is generated:

```
inner replaceable World world;
```

11.5.4 unassignedMessage Annotation

A declaration may also have an `unassignedMessage` annotation:

```
annotation(unassignedMessage = "message");
```

This is used when the variable to which this annotation is attached in the declaration cannot be computed due to the structure of the equations. In such cases the string `"message"` can be used as a presumably informative diagnostic message to the modeler.

When the Modelica compiler uses BLT partitioning (Section 17.1.6, page 984), this means that if a variable `x` or one of its aliases `y=x`, `y=-x`, cannot be assigned, the message is displayed. This annotation is used to provide library specific error messages in such cases.

For example:

```
connector Frame "Frame of a mechanical system"
  ...
  flow Modelica.SIunits.Force f[3] annotation(unassignedMessage =
   "All Forces cannot be uniquely calculated. The reason could be that the
    mechanism contains a planar loop or that joints constrain the
    same motion. For planar loops, use in one revolute joint per loop
    the option PlanarCutJoint=true in the Advanced menu.
   ");
end Frame;
```

11.5.5 absoluteValue Annotation

A simple type or variable of a simple type may have:

```
annotation(absoluteValue=false);
```

If `false`, then the variable defines a relative quantity, and if true an absolute quantity. When converting between units (in the user-interface for plotting and entering parameters), the offset must be ignored, for a variable defined with annotation `absoluteValue=false`. This annotation is used in the Modelica Standard Library for example in `Modelica.SIunits` for the type definition `TemperatureDifference`.

11.5.6 defaultConnectionStructurallyInconsistent Annotation

A model or block definition may contain:

```
annotation(defaultConnectionStructurallyInconsistent=true);
```

If true, it is stated that a default connection will result in a structurally inconsistent model or block. For a definition of structurally inconsistent, see (Pantelides 1988).

A "default connection" is constructed by instantiating the respective `model` or `block` and for every input `u` providing an equation `0=f(u)`, and for every (potential,flow) pair of the form `(v,i)`, providing an equation of the form `0=f(v,i)`.

It is useful to be able to check all models/blocks of a Modelica package in a simple way. One check is to default connect every model/block and to check whether the resulting class is structurally consistent (= a stronger requirement than "balanced").

This is rarely needed; but is for example used in `Modelica.Blocks.Math.InverseBlockConstraints` in order to prevent a wrong error message. Additionally, when a user-defined model is structurally inconsistent, a Modelica tool should try to pinpoint in which class the error is present. This annotation avoids then to show a wrong error message.

11.5.7 The Dialog Annotation and the connectorSizing Attribute

The `Dialog` annotation allows a tool to produce customized dialogs in the graphic user interface for specifying parameter values. An example is shown below in Figure 11-4 for the `DialogDemo` model. A *parameter dialog* is a sequence of tabs, where each tab may contain a sequence of groups.

When clicking on an instance of the model `DialogDemo`, a menu pops up that may have the following layout. Other layouts are possible since the layout is tool specific.

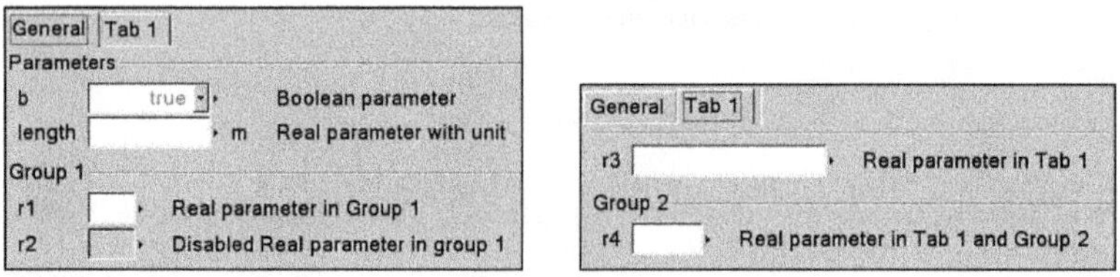

Figure 11-4. Possible menu layout for interaction with the `DialogDemo` model.

The `DialogDemo` example model that uses the `Dialog` annotation appears as follows:

```
model DialogDemo
  parameter Boolean                  b   = true   "Boolean parameter";
  parameter Modelica.SIunits.Length  length       "Real parameter with unit";
  parameter Integer   nInports=0   annotation(Dialog(connectorSizing=true));

  StepIn              stepIn[nInports]            "Vector of input ports";

  parameter Real r1 "Real parameter in Group 1"
                     annotation(Dialog(group="Group 1"));

  parameter Real r2 "Disabled Real parameter in group 1"
                     annotation(Dialog(group="Group 1", enable = not b));

  parameter Real r3 "Real parameter in Tab 1"
                     annotation(Dialog(tab="Tab 1"));

  parameter Real r4 "Real parameter in Tab 1 and Group 2"
                     annotation(Dialog(tab="Tab 1", group="Group 2"));
  ...
end DialogDemo;
```

An example of the `Dialog` annotation with possible attribute values is shown below:

```
annotation(Dialog(
  enable    = true,
  tab       = "General",
  group     = "Parameters",
  showStartAttribute = false,
  colorSelector = false,

  groupImage          = "modelica://MyPackage/Resources/Images/switch.png",
```

```
  connectorSizing     = false));
```

The `Dialog` annotation *attributes* including default values are defined by the following record:

```
record Dialog
  parameter String  tab                   = "General";
  parameter String  group                 = "Parameters";
  parameter Boolean enable                = true;
  parameter Boolean showStartAttribute    = false;
  parameter Boolean colorSelector         = false;
  parameter Selector loadSelector;
  parameter Selector saveSelector;
  parameter String  groupImage            = "";
  parameter Boolean connectorSizing       = false;
end Dialog;
```

The annotation attributes `tab` and `group` define the *placement* of the component or of variables in a dialog with optional *tab* and *group* specifications.

If `enable = false`, the input field is disabled, and no input can be given (read-only).

If `showStartAttribute = true`, the dialog should allow the user to set the `start` value and the `fixed` attribute for the variable instead of the usual value attribute. This is primarily intended for non-parameter values and avoids introducing a separate parameter for the `start` value of the variable.

If `colorSelector=true`, it indicates that an rgb-value selector can be presented for a vector of three elements and generate values 0..255. The annotation should be useable both for vectors of integers and vectors of reals.

The annotation attribute `groupImage` references an image using an URI, see Section 11.15, page 556. The image is intended to be shown together with the parameter group. Only one image per group is supported. Disabling the input field will not disable the image.

The parameter `nInports` is *not visible* in the menu example in Figure 11-4 since it has the `connectorSizing` annotation attribute (see below Section 11.5.7.1, page 539) and therefore should not be modified by the user. An alternative is to show the `parameter nInports` in the menu but as a read-only field disabled for input.

```
record Selector
  parameter String filter="";
  parameter String caption="";
end Selector;
```

A `Selector` displays a file dialog to select a file. Setting `filter` only shows files that fulfill the given pattern defined by `"text1 (*.ext1);;text2 (*.ext2) "` to show only files `*.ext1` and `*.ext2` and displaying a description text `"text1"` and `"text2"`, respectively. Parameter `caption` is the text displayed in the dialog menu. The parameter `loadSelector` is used to select an existing file for reading, whereas the parameter `saveSelector` is used to define a file for writing.

11.5.7.1 connectorSizing Annotation Attribute

The `connectorSizing` annotation attribute is used in cases where connections to a vector of connectors are made and a new connection requires resizing of the vector and to connect to the new index (unary connections). This annotation attribute allows a tool to perform these two actions automatically in many cases. This is for example very useful for state machine models and for certain models of fluid libraries.

The value of the `connectorSizing` annotation attribute must be one of the literal values `false` or `true`. If the value would be allowed to be an expression, the `connectorSizing` functionality would be conditional and this could easily lead to erroneous models.

If `connectorSizing = false`, it has no effect, i.e., the same as if the attribute would not be present.

If `connectorSizing = true`, the *variable* to which the corresponding `Dialog` annotation is attached must be declared with the `parameter` prefix, must be a subtype of `Integer` and must have a literal default value of zero. The reason for the zero default value of the parameter *variable* is that the `connectorSizing` annotation attribute is designed for a parameter that is used as a vector dimension. The default dimension of the vector should be zero when the component is dragged or redeclared, since if a tool does not support the `connectorSizing` annotation attribute dragging should still result in a correct model because the default size is zero.

If `connectorSizing = true`, a Modelica tool may automatically set the dimension size parameter value in a modifier when used as a dimension size of a vector of connectors.

11.5.7.2 Rules for Handling the connectorSizing Attribute

The following example describes a useful way for a tool to handle the `connectorSizing` annotation attribute of the dimension size of a vector of connectors. However, tools may use other strategies and/or may handle other cases than those described below. The recommended rules are clarified by the use of the following example which represents a connector and a model from the `Modelica.StateGraph` library:

```
connector StepIn // Only 1:1 connections are possible since input used
  output Boolean occupied;
  input  Boolean set;
end StepIn;

model Step
  // nIn cannot be set in the parameter dialog (but maybe shown)
  parameter Integer nIn=0 annotation(Dialog(connectorSizing=true));
  StepIn inPorts[nIn];
  ...
end Step;
```

If the parameter is used as a *dimension size* of a *vector of connectors* it is automatically updated according to the following rules:

- *Rule* 1. If a *new outside* connection line is drawn to the connector dimensioned with the `connectorSizing` associated parameter, the parameter is incremented by one and the connection is performed for the new highest index. For example, assume that three connections are present and a new connection is performed. The result is:

  ```
    Step step1(nIn=4); // index changed from nIn=3 to nIn=4
  equation
    connect(.., step1.inPorts[4]); // new connect-equation
  ```

  In some applications, like state machines, the vector index is used as a priority, for example, to define which transition is firing if several transitions become active at the same time instant. It is then not sufficient to only provide a mechanism to always connect to the last index. Instead, some mechanism to select an index conveniently should be provided.

- *Rule* 2. If an existing *outside* connection line is *deleted*, then the `connectorSizing` associated parameter is decremented by one and all connections with index above the deleted connection index are also decremented by one. For example, assume that there are four connections:

  ```
    Step step1(nIn=4);
  equation
    connect(a1, step1.inPorts[1]);
    connect(a2, step1.inPorts[2]);
    connect(a3, step1.inPorts[3]);
    connect(a4, step1.inPorts[4]);
  ```

  Further, assume that the connection from `a2` to `step1.inPorts[2]` is deleted, resulting in:

  ```
    Step step1(nIn=3);
  equation
    connect(a1, step1.inPorts[1]);
  ```

```
  connect(a3, step1.inPorts[2]);
  connect(a4, step1.inPorts[3]);
```

- *Rule* 3. If a *new inside connection line* is drawn between two vectors of connectors dimensioned with the `connectorSizing` associated parameters, a connection between the two vectors is performed and the `connectorSizing` associated parameter is propagated. Other types of inside connections do not lead to an automatic update of a `connectorSizing` associated parameter. For example, assume that there is a connector vector `inPorts` and a component `step1`:

```
  parameter Integer nIn=0 annotation(Dialog(connectorSizing=true));

  StepIn inPorts[nIn];
  Step   step1(nIn=0);
```

Drawing a connection line between the connector vectors `inPorts` and `step1.inPorts` results in the following:

```
  parameter Integer nIn=0 annotation(Dialog(connectorSizing=true));

  StepIn inPorts[nIn];
  Step   step1(nIn=nIn);   // nIn=0 changed to nIn=nIn
equation
  connect(inPorts, step1.inPorts);   // new connect-equation
```

- *Rule* 4. If an *inside* connection line between two vectors of connectors dimensioned with the `connectorSizing` associated parameters is *deleted*, the connect-equation is removed and the `connectorSizing` associated parameter of the component is set to zero or the modifier is removed. For example, assume that the connection line in drawn according to rule 3 is removed, which results in:

```
  parameter Integer nIn=0 annotation(Dialog(connectorSizing=true));

  StepIn inPorts[nIn];
  Step   step1;   // modifier nIn=nIn is removed
```

- *Rule* 5. If a *new inside or outside* connection line is drawn to the connector dimensioned with the `connectorSizing` associated parameter and this connector is defined in a *superclass*, then rule 1 and rule 3 are correspondingly applied in the subclass. For example, assume that `step1` is defined in the superclass `CompositeStep` with three connections, and a new connection is performed in a subclass. The result is as follows:

```
  extends CompositeStep(step1(nIn=4));     // new modifier nIn=4

equation
  connect(..., step1.inPorts[4]);          // new connect-equation
```

11.5.8 Annotations Defining Interactive Menus

Most Modelica environments allow us to specify simulation parameter values through interactive graphical menus and forms. This is commonly used to interactively assign numerical values for parameters of model components before a specific simulation run, for example, to give a resistance parameter value for a certain resistor component.

In certain situations, e.g. when there is a small number of predefined choices of a simulation parameter, it is more user-friendly to be able to choose among alternatives in a menu containing easy-to-understand descriptive menu items. For example, we might have a parameter that specifies the kind of controller to be used, where alternative 1 is a proportional controller, the second alternative is a proportional and integrating controller, and the third alternative is a PID controller. Instead of giving the number 2 to choose the second alternative, we interactively choose the PI alternative in a menu containing the three items: P, PI, and PID.

In order to specify such menus Modelica supports a standard annotation called choices. This annotation can be associated either directly with a parameter declaration or with a declaration of a type in some class or package. The choices annotation contains a number of choice annotation elements, one for each menu item.

11.5.8.1 Choices Annotations for Variables and Enumeration Types

The choices annotation is applicable to both replaceable and nonreplaceable elements. Examples of the latter are simple parameter variables and types used for enumerations.

For a Boolean variable, a choices annotation may contain the definition checkbox = true, meaning to display a checkbox to input the values false or true in the graphical user interface.

An an example, consider the following Integer type called KindOfController used to represent a choice of *controller* in the modeling process. This choice is made from the following enumeration of three recommended alternatives:

```
type KindOfController=Integer(min=1,max=3)
  annotation(choices(
                  choice=1 "P",
                  choice=2 "PI",
                  choice=3 "PID"));
```

Assume that KindOfController is used in a model A as below:

```
model A
  parameter KindOfController x;
end A;
```

Without the choices annotation an interactive Modelica environment would present us with an integer value field for x in the parameter menu of model A. Instead, the choices annotation makes it possible for the environment to present a choice selection menu with the entries "P","PI","PID". If we interactively choose the third alternative from the menu this corresponds to giving the default value 3 for the instantiated variable x in the following code for an instance a2 of the model A:

```
A a2(x=3 "PID");
```

It can also be applied to Boolean variables to define a check box.

```
parameter Boolean useHeatPort=false annotation(choices(checkBox=true));
```

11.5.8.2 Choices Annotations for Replaceable Model Elements

The choices annotation also can be used to generate menus with redeclaration alternatives for replaceable models. The user interface can suggest reasonable redeclarations, where the string comment in a choice annotation element is used as a textual explanation of the choice alternative. Based on the interactions with the user, the graphical user interface then generates the appropriate Modelica code.

Choices menus of replaceable elements can be automatically constructed showing the names of all classes that are either directly or indirectly derived by inheritance from the constraining class of the declaration. This can be recommended by having annotation choicesAllMatching = true; and disabled by having annotation choicesAllMatching = false.

See also Section 4.3.12 in Chapter 4 concerning redeclarations. For example, consider the following replaceable model with a choices annotation:

```
replaceable model MyResistor=Resistor
  annotation(choices(
    choice(redeclare MyResistor=lib2.Resistor   "Resistor 1"),
    choice(redeclare MyResistor=lib2.Resistor2 "Resistor 2")));
```

If the user would choose the first alternative, the following code might be produced if `MyResistor` is part of the class `MyCircuit` and the chosen name of the instantiated component is `x`:

```
MyCircuit x(redeclare MyResistor=lib2.Resistor)
```

Additional examples of `replaceable` class declarations with redeclaration `choices` are shown below. In the first example we can choose between a resistor and a capacitor as choices of components with two pins, and in the second example a friction function is implemented as a constant, a table, or defined as an exponentiation function depending on our choice.

```
replaceable Resistor Load(R=2) extends TwoPin
  annotation(choices(
     choice(redeclare lib2.Resistor Load(a={2}) "Resistor"),
     choice(redeclare Capacitor Load(L=3)       "Capacitor")));

replaceable FrictionFunction a(func=exp) extends Friction
  annotation(choices(
      choice(redeclare ConstantFriction a(c=1)   "Friction-constant"),
      choice(redeclare TableFriction    a(table="...") "Friction-table"),
      choice(redeclare FunctionFriction a(func=exp)"Friction-exp"))));

replaceable package Medium =Modelica.Media.Water.ConstantPropertyLiquidWater
                constrainedby Modelica.Media.Interfaces.PartialMedium
                                    annotation (choicesAllMatching=true);
```

11.6 Annotations for Simulation Experiments

Usually, the user explicitly gives the start time and stop time, and sometimes the relative tolerance (precision) for simulation experiments. This can be done either through a command line interface using commands such as `simulate()`, or through the graphical user interface of a Modelica tool.

However, for many models it can be useful to associate meaningful default values for start time, stop time, or tolerance, since the user might not know the values which are valid for a particular model. This is the purpose of the `experiment` annotation

The `experiment` annotation defines the default start time (`StartTime`) in seconds, the default stop time (`StopTime`) in seconds, the suitable time resolution for the result value grid (`Interval`) in seconds, and the default relative integration tolerance (`Tolerance`) for simulation experiments to be carried out with a model. For example:

```
annotation(experiment(StartTime=0, StopTime=100, Interval=0.1,
                      Tolerance=1.0E-4))

annotation(experiment(StartTime=-5, StopTime=10))
```

11.7 Annotation for Single Use of a Class

For state machines (Section 13.7, page 729) it is useful to have single instances of local classes. This can be specified using the `singleInstance` annotation:

```
annotation(singleInstance=true)
```

The `singleInstance` annotation in a class indicates that there should only be one instance of the class, and it should be in the same scope where the class is defined. The intent is to automatically remove the class when the instance is removed and to prevent duplication of the instance.

11.8 Annotations Influencing Code Generation

Several annotations influence the code generation of the Modelica compiler, that is, the way the model code is translated to executable code. This typically has consequences for the performance of the generated code, visibility of results, or compatibility with certain external function code.

- `Inline`—function calls are replaced by corresponding function bodies with actual parameters substituted, see Section 11.13.3, page 555.
- `LateInline`—function calls are replaced by corresponding function bodies with actual parameters substituted after symbolic optimizations. Calls with the same arguments may be replaced by a call to a generated specialized function for these arguments. See Section 11.13.3, page 555.
- `InlineAfterIndexReduction`—the function should be inlined after the function is differentiated for index reduction, and before any other symbolic transformations are performed, see Section 11.13.3, page 555.
- `arrayLayout` with `rowMajor` and `columnMajor`—determines generated code calling external functions with different array layouts. See Section 11.13.5, page 556.
- `Evaluate`—evaluate a parameter expression to a value, see Section 11.8.1, page 544.
- `HideResult`—controls whether simulation results for a certain variable should be accessible, see Section 11.8.2, page 544.

11.8.1 Annotations for Parameter Evaluation

The `Evaluate` annotation allows the model developer to state that a parameter expression should be evaluated, which can give rise to more efficient code. It only has effect for variable declarations with the `parameter` prefix.

The annotation `Evaluate` can occur in a variable declaration, its type declaration, or a base-class of the type-declaration. In the case of multiple conflicting annotations it is handled in a similar way as modifiers, i.e., an `Evaluate`-annotation on the variable declaration takes precedence.

If `Evaluate=true`, the model developer proposes to utilize the value for the symbolic processing. This means that the parameter name is replaced by its value during symbolic processing which can give opportunities to generate more efficient code. In that case it is not possible to change the parameter value after symbolic preprocessing.

If `Evaluate=false`, the model developer proposes to *not* utilize the value of the corresponding parameter for symbolic processing.

`Evaluate` is for example used for the axis of rotation parameters in the `Modelica.Mechanics.MultiBody` library in order to improve the efficiency of the generated code.

11.8.2 Annotations for Variable Visibility

The attribute `HideResult=true` defines that the model developer proposes to not show the simulator results of the corresponding variable, e.g., it will not be possible to plot this variable.

`HideResult=false` defines that the developer proposes to show the corresponding variable. If a variable is declared in a protected section, a tool might not include it in a simulation result. By setting `HideResult=false`, the modeler would like to have the variable in the simulation result, even if in the protected section.

`HideResult` is for example used in the connectors of the `Modelica.StateGraph` library not to show variables to the modeler that are of no interest and would be confusing.

11.9 Documentation Annotations

Documentation is important for any kind of software including Modelica models. The additional documentation information helps understanding and reusing code, as well as providing hints for its use in different kind of applications.

Regarding the form of Modelica documentation, we have already mentioned string comments that can be associated with various constructs in Modelica and are displayed by most Modelica browser tools. Standard Modelica comments can be given everywhere but are not processed by Modelica tools.

Modelica also defines a `Documentation` annotation for classes and packages, where information can be structured in key-value pairs, for example:

```
annotation(Documentation(
  info = "Text string",
  revisions = "Text string",
  userdefined_key1 = "Text string",   // Not standardized user defined key
  userdefined_key2 = "Text string"    // Not standardized user defined key
));
```

Currently there is no Modelica standard for the categories (e.g. represented as key-value pairs) in this kind of documentation, except the “standard” `info` attribute described in the next section, which is used for general documentation of packages and classes in the Modelica standard library, and the `revisions` attribute used for a log of the revisions (may be left out in printout) of Modelica classes. It is expected that most organizations will specify their own documentation guidelines.

We give the following hints for categories of information that typically should be part of good documentation:

- Revision (development) history and author information.
- Literature references.
- Validation information regarding model behavior and comparison with measurement data.
- Explanations and schematic drawings of models.
- User advice for reuse and application of models.

11.9.1 Information and HTML Documentation

In the Modelica Standard Library and generally in Modelica code the `Documentation` annotation with the `info` attribute is a standardized way to define documentation. A Modelica environment should recognize documentation annotations of the following form:

```
Documentation(info = string)
```

For example, the documentation of the Modelica standard library package is expressed as the following annotation:

```
annotation(Documentation(info = "
<HTML>
 <p> Package <b>Modelica</b> is a <b>standardized</b> and <b>pre-defined</b>
 package that is developed together with the Modelica language from the
 Modelica Association, see
 <a href=\"http://www.Modelica.org\">http://www.Modelica.org</a>.
 It is also called <b>Modelica Standard Library</b>.
 It provides constants, types, connectors, partial models and model
 components in various disciplines.</p>
 ...
<HTML>" ) );
```

As we can see from the above example, `HTML` tags can be present in the `info` text. When extracting documentation information from a model, a Modelica tool should store this part of the documentation as an HTML-file that, for example, can be displayed by an appropriate HTML-browser.

11.9.1.1 HTML Links to External Resources and Modelica Classes

External resources can be linked from the HTML text in the `info` attribute, see Section 11.15, page 556.

Links to Modelica classes may be defined with the HTML link command using the URI scheme `modelica` (Section 11.15.1 page 557) for example:

```
<a href="modelica://MultiBody.Tutorial">MultiBody.Tutorial</a>
```

Together with the URI scheme `modelica` the (URI) fragment specifiers: `#diagram`, `#info`, `#text`, `#icon` may be used to reference different layers. For example:

```
<a href="Modelica://MultiBody.Joints.Revolute#info">Revolute</a>
```

11.9.1.2 Preferred Documentation View of a Class

When viewing a class through a tool there is a need to specify the default view of the class. Certain classes have only a textual definition whereas others are easiest to understand using the diagram view. Some classes may have a preferred view using the `Documentation` annotation `info` attribute contents. Such a default view can be specified using the `preferredView` annotation, which can have one of the three values `"info"`, `"diagram"`, or `"text"`.

The `preferredView` annotation defines the default view when selecting the class. The annotation attribute value `"info"` means the `info` layer, that is, the documentation of the class, `"diagram"` means the diagram layer, and `"text"` means the Modelica text layer. The annotation can be stated in the following ways:

```
annotation(preferredView = "info")
```

or

```
annotation(preferredView = "diagram")
```

or

```
annotation(preferredView = "text")
```

11.9.1.3 DocumentationClass Annotation

The `DocumentationClass` annotation can be used as follows:

```
annotation(DocumentationClass=true)
```

It is only allowed as a class annotation on any kind of class and implies that this class and all classes within it are treated as having the annotation `preferredView="info"`. If the annotation `preferredView` is explicitly set for a class, it has precedence over a `DocumentationClass` annotation.

A Modelica tool may display such classes in special ways. For example, the description texts of the classes might be displayed instead of the class names, and if no icon is defined, a special information default icon may be displayed in the package browser.

11.10 Version Handling Annotations

A top level package or model can specify the version of top level classes it uses, its own version number, and if possible how to convert from previous versions. This can be used by a Modelica environment to guarantee that consistent versions are used, and if possible to automatically upgrade usage from an earlier version to the current one.

11.10.1 Version Numbering

Version numbers are of the following forms, where the notation `{}` means repetition zero of more time (see Appendix B for interpretation of `UNSIGNED_INTEGER` and `S-CHAR`):

- *Main release versions*: `"""  UNSIGNED_INTEGER  {  "."  UNSIGNED_INTEGER  }  """`, e.g. `"3.2"`.
- *Pre-release versions*: `"""  UNSIGNED_INTEGER  {  "."  UNSIGNED_INTEGER  }  "  "  {S-CHAR}  """`, e.g. `"3.2 Beta 1"`.
- *Unordered versions*: `"""  NON-DIGIT  {S-CHAR}  """`, e.g. `"Test 1"`.

The main release versions are ordered using hierarchical numerical names, and follow the corresponding prerelease versions. The prerelease versions of the same main release version are internally alphabetically ordered.

11.10.2 Version Handling

In a top-level class, the version number and the dependency to earlier versions of this class are defined using one or more of the following annotations:

- The annotation `version` = *current-version-number* defines the version number (in string form) of the model or package. All classes within this top level class have this version number.
- The annotation `conversion(noneFromVersion =` ***version-number***`)` defines that user models using the *version-number* can be upgraded to the *current-version-number* of the current class without any changes.
- The annotation `conversion(from(version =` ***version-number***`, script = "...")) ` defines that user models using the *version-number* can be upgraded to the *current-version-number* of the current class by applying the given script. The semantics of the conversion script is not defined.
- `conversion(from(version =` ***version-number***`, script = "...") )` or `conversion(from(version = {` ***version-number***`,` ***version-number***`,...}, script = "..."))` Defines that user models using the *version-number* or any of the given *version-number* can be upgraded to the *current-version-number* of the current class by applying the given script. The semantics of the conversion script is not defined.
- The annotation `uses(`*ident*`(version =` ***version-number***`))` defines that classes within this top-level class uses version *version-number* of classes within the top-level class `IDENT`.

The annotations `uses` and `conversion` may contain several different subentries. For example:

```
package Modelica
  annotation(version="3.1",
             conversion(noneFromVersion="3.1 Beta 1",
                        noneFromVersion="3.1 Beta 2",
                        from(version={"2.1", "2.2", "2.2.1"},
                             script="convertTo3.mos"),
                        from(version="1.5",
                             script="convertFromModelica1_5.mos")));
    ...
end Modelica;

model A
```

```
  annotation(version="1.0", uses(Modelica(version="1.5")));
  ...
end A;

model B
  annotation(uses(Modelica(version="2.1 Beta 1")));
  ...
end B;
```

In this example, the model `A` uses an older version of the Modelica library and can be upgraded using the given script, and model `B` uses an older version of the Modelica library but no changes are required when upgrading.

11.10.3 Mapping of Versions to the File System

A top-level class, named *ident*, with version *version-number* can be stored in one of the following ways in a file system directory given in the `MODELICAPATH`:

- The file *ident*+`".mo"`, e.g. `"Modelica.mo"`.
- The file *ident*+`" "`+ *version-number* +`".mo"`, e.g. `"Modelica 2.1.mo"`.
- The directory *ident*, e.g. `"Modelica"`, with the file `package.mo` directly inside it.
- The directory *ident*+`" "`+ *version-number*, e.g. `"Modelica 2.1"`, with the file `package.mo` directly inside it.

This allows a Modelica environment to access multiple versions of the same package.

11.10.4 Version Date and Build Information

Besides version information (the annotation `version`, Section 11.10.2, page 547), a top-level class can have the following top level annotations to specify information associated to the version number:

- The string `versionDate` which is the UTC date of the first version build in the format: `YYYY-MM-DD`.
- The integer `versionBuild` where a bigger number denotes a more recent maintenance update.
- The string `dateModified` which is the UTC date and time of the latest change to the package in the following format, with one space between date and time: `YYYY-MM-DD hh:mm:ssZ`.
- The string `revisionId` which is the revision identifier of the version management system used to manage this library. It marks the latest submitted change to any file belonging to the package.

For example:

```
package Modelica
 annotation(version      = "3.0.1",
            versionDate  = "2008-04-10",
            versionBuild = 4,
            dateModified = "2009-02-15 16:33:14Z",
            revisionId   = "$Id:: package.mo 2566 2009-05-26 13:25:54Z #$");
 ...
end Modelica;

model M1
  annotation(uses(Modelica(version = "3.0.1")));  // Common case
end M1

model M2
   annotation(uses(Modelica(version = "3.0.1", versionBuild = 4)));
```

```
end M2
```

The meaning of the annotation attributes in the above example for the library package Modelica is explained in more detail as follows.

- The `version` is the version number of the released library, in this case the library package Modelica.
- The `versionDate` is the date in UTC format (according to ISO 8601) when the library was released. This string is updated by the library author to correspond with the version number.
- The `versionBuild` is the optional build number of the library. When a new version is released `versionBuild` should be omitted or `versionBuild =1`. There might be bug fixes to the library that do not justify a new library version. Such maintenance changes are called a "build" release of the library. For every new maintenance change, the `versionBuild` number is increased. A `versionBuild` number `A1` that is higher than the `versionBuild` number `A2` is a newer release of the library. There are no conversions between the same versions with different build numbers.

  Two releases of a library with the same `version` but different `versionBuild` are in general assumed to be compatible. In special cases, the `uses` annotation (Section 11.10.2, page 547) of a model may specify `versionBuild` and/or `dateModified`. In such a case the tool is expected to give a warning if there is a mismatch between the library and the model using the library.
- The `dateModified` is the UTC date and time (according to ISO 8601) of the most recent modification of the package. The intention is that a Modelica tool updates this annotation whenever the package or part of it was modified and saved on persistent storage such as a file or database.
- The `revisionId` is a tool specific revision identifier possibly generated by a source code management system (e.g. Subversion or CVS). This information allows exact identification the library source code in the source code management system.

The `versionBuild` and `dateModified` annotation attributes can also be specified in the `uses` annotation together with the `version` number. The recommendation is that they are not automatically stored in the `uses` annotation by a tool.

11.11 Tool Specific Annotations

Sometimes there is a need for a Modelica tool vendor to add information in a model for a specific purpose. One example is an experimental early version of a construct which in some form might become a standardized part of the language in the future. Another case is to turn on specific functionality which never will be standardized but is useful for a specific purpose, perhaps asked for by a certain customer.

To fulfill this need, it is possible to introduce nonstandard, so called *tool* or *vendor specific annotations*, anywhere within an annotation expression. Such annotations are identified by the first characters being double underscore concatenated with a vendor name as prefix of the vendor specific annotation identifier, for example, a new vendor specific annotation attribute `__NameOfVendor_shadow`.

Vendor specific annotations need not be documented and are not intended to be interpreted by other Modelica tools. However, any tool shall save files with all standard annotations and all vendor-specific annotations intact. This has the advantage is that a typo in nonvendor annotations can be detected and marked as an error.

There are two variants of vendor specific annotations, one *simple* variant and one *hierarchical*.

The following example introduces a *simple* vendor specific annotation attribute called `__NameOfVendor_shadow` to be used within the `Rectangle` primitive.

```
annotation (
  Icon(coordinateSystem(extent={{-100,-100}, {100,100}}),
```

```
        graphics={Rectangle(extent={{-5,-5},{7,7}},
                                __NameOfVendor_shadow=2)})
);
```

The second example shows a *hierarchical* vendor specific graphical primitive called `Circle` which is embedded in an expression prefixed by `__NameOfVendor`.

```
annotation (
  Icon(coordinateSystem(extent={{-100,-100}, {100,100}}),
       graphics={__NameOfVendor(Circle(center={0,0}, radius=10))})
);
```

11.12 Annotations for Access Control to Protect Intellectual Property

This section presents annotations to define the protection and the licensing of packages. The goal is to unify basic mechanisms to control the access to a package in order to protect the intellectual property contained in it. This information is used to encrypt a package and bind it optionally to a particular target machine, and/or restrict the usage for a particular period of time.

Protecting the intellectual property of a Modelica package is considerably more difficult than protecting code from a programming language. The reason is that a Modelica tool needs the model equations in order that it can process the equations symbolically, as needed for acausal modeling. Furthermore, if a Modelica tool generates C-code of the processed equations, this code is then potentially available for inspection by the user. Finally, the Modelica tool vendors have to be trusted, that they do not have a backdoor in their tools to store the (internally) decrypted classes in human readable format. The only way to protect against such misuse are legally binding warranties of the tool vendors.

The intent of this section is to enable a library vendor to maintain one source version of their Modelica library that can be encrypted and used with several different Modelica tools, using different encryption formats.

These terms are used in the following two subsections.

- `Protection`— defines what parts of a class are visible.
- `Obfuscation`— this means changing a Modelica class or generated code so that it is difficult to inspect and understand by a user, e.g. by automatically renaming variables to non-meaningful names.
- `Encryption` —encoding of a model or a package in a form so that the modeler cannot inspect any content of a class without an appropriate key. An encrypted package that has the `Protection` annotation is read-only. The only way to modify it is to generate a new encrypted version.
- `Licensing`— restrict the use of an encrypted package for particular users for a specified period of time.

Annotations are defined for `Protection` and `Licensing`. Obfuscation and encryption are not standardized. `Protection` and `Licensing` are both defined inside the `Protection` annotation.

```
annotation(Protection(...));
```

11.12.1 Protection of Classes

A class may have the following annotations to define what parts of a class are visible. If a class is encrypted and no `Protection` annotation is defined, the `access` annotation has the default value `Access.documentation`):

```
type Access = enumeration(hide, icon, documentation,
```

```
                          diagram, nonPackageText, nonPackageDuplicate,
                          packageText, packageDuplicate);
annotation(Protection(access = Access.documentation));
```

The items of the `Access` enumeration have the following meaning:

- `Access.hide`
  Do not show the class anywhere (it is not possible to inspect any part of the class)
- `Access.icon`
  The class definition can be flattened, and public parameter, constant, input, and output variables as well as public connectors can be accessed, as well as the `Icon` annotation (Section 11.4.1, page 524). The declared information of these elements can be shown. Moreover, the class name and its description text can be accessed.
- `Access.documentation`
  This is analogous to `Access.icon`. Moreover, the documentation annotation (Section 11.9, page 545) can be accessed. HTML-generation in the documentation annotation is normally performed before encryption, but the generated HTML is intended to be used with the encrypted package. Thus the HTML-generation should use the same access as the encrypted version, even before encryption.
- `Access.diagram`
  This is similar to `Access.documentation`. Additionally the diagram annotation and all components and connect-equations that have a graphical annotation can be accessed.
- `Access.nonPackageText`
  This is the same as `Access.diagram` with the additional capability that if it is not a package: the whole class definition can be accessed, but cannot be copied.
- `Access.nonPackageDuplicate`
  This is the same as `Access.nonPackageText` with the additional capability that if it is not a package: the class, or part of the class, can be copied and pasted.
- `Access.packageText`
  This is the same as `Access.diagram` (but *not* including all rights of `Access.nonPackageDuplicate`) with the additional capability the whole class definition can be accessed, but cannot be copied.
- `Access.packageDuplicate`
  This is the same as `Access.packageText` with the additional capability that the class, or part of the class, can be copied and pasted.

The `access` annotation holds for the respective class and all classes that are hierarchically on a lower level, unless overridden by a `Protection` annotation with `access`. For example, if the annotation is given at the top level of a package and at no other class in this package, then the annotation holds for all classes in this package. Overriding `access=Access.hide` and `access=Access.packageDuplicate` has no meaningful effect.

It is currently not standardized which result variables of encrypted package that are accessible for plotting. It seems natural to not introduce new flags for this, but instead reuse the `Access.XXX` definition, for example, for `Access.icon` only the variables can be stored in a result file that can also be inspected in the class, and for `Access.nonPackageText` all public and protected variables can be stored in a result file, because all variables can be inspected in the class.

```
package CommercialFluid      // Access icon, documentation, diagram

  package Examples           // Access icon, documentation, diagram

    model PipeExample        // Access everything, can be copied
    end PipeExample;

    package Circuits         // Access icon, documentation, diagram
```

```
      model ClosedCircuit // Access everything, can be copied
      end ClosedCircuit;
    end Circuits;

    model SecretExample    // No access
      annotation(Protection(access=Access.hide));
    end SecretExample;

    annotation(Protection(access=Access.nonPackageDuplicate));
  end Examples;

  package Pipe              // Access icon
    model StraightPipe      // Access icon
    end StraightPipe;
    annotation(Protection(access=Access.icon));
  end Pipe;

  package Vessels           // Access icon, documentation, diagram
    model Tank              // Access icon, documentation, diagram, text
    end Tank;
  end Vessels;

  annotation(Protection(access=Access.nonPackageText));
end CommercialFluid;
```

11.12.2 Licensing

Annotations within the `Protection` annotation are defined to restrict the usage of an encrypted package.

```
record Protection
   ...
   String features[:]=fill("", 0) "Required license features";
   record License
      String libraryKey;
      String licenseFile="" "Optional, default mapping if empty";
   end License;
end Protection;
```

The `License` annotation only has effect at the top of an encrypted class, usually a package, and is then valid for that whole package hierarchy. The `libraryKey` is a secret string from the library vendor and is the protection mechanism so that a user cannot generate his/her own authorization file since the `libraryKey` is unknown to the user.

The `features` annotation defines the required license options. If the features vector has more than one element, then at least a license feature according to one of the elements must be present. As with the other annotations, the `features` annotation holds for the respective class and for all classes that are hierarchically at a lower level, unless further restricted by a corresponding annotation. If no license according to the `features` annotation is provided in the authorization file, the corresponding classes are not visible and cannot be used, not even internally in the package.

For example:

```
// Requires license feature "LicenseOption"
annotation(Protection(features={"LicenseOption"}));

// Requires license features "LicenseOption1" or "LicenseOption2"
annotation(Protection(features={"LicenseOption1", "LicenseOption2"}));

// The following requires license features ("LicenseOption1" and
   "LicenseOption2") or "LicenseOption3"
annotation(Protection(features={"LicenseOption1 LicenseOption2",
"LicenseOption3"}));
```

In order that the protected class can be used either a tool specific license manager, or a license file (called `licenseFile`) must be present. The license file is standardized. It is a Modelica package without classes that has a `Protection` annotation of the following form which specifies a sequence of target records, which makes it natural to define start/end dates for different sets of targets individually.

```
record Authorization
  String licensor=""  "Optional string to show information about the
                       licensor";
  String  libraryKey  "Matching the key in the class. Must be encrypted and
                       not visible";
  License license[:]  "Definition of the license options and of the access
                       rights";
end Authorization;

record License
  String licensee=""   "Optional string to show information about the
                        licensee";
  String id[:]          "Unique machine identifications, e.g. MAC addresses";
  String features[:]=fill("",0) "Activated library license features";
  String startDat =""   "Optional start date in UTCformat YYYY-MM-DD";
  String expirationDate="" "Optional expiration date in UTCformat YYYY-MM-DD";
  String operations[:]=fill("",0) "Library usage conditions";
end License;
```

The format of the strings used for `libraryKey` and `id` are not specified since they are vendor specific. The `libraryKey` is a secret of the library developer. The `operations` define the usage conditions and the following are default names:

- `ExportBinary`—Binary code generated from the Modelica code of the library can be can be included in binaries produced by a simulation tool.
- `ExportSource`—Source code generated from the Modelica code of the library can be included in sources produced by a simulation tool.

Additional tool-specific names can also be used. To protect the `libraryKey` and the target definitions, the authorization file must be encrypted and must never show the `libraryKey`.

All other information, especially licensor and license should be visible, in order that the user can get information about the license. It is useful to include the name of the tool in the authorization file name with which it was encrypted. Note, it is not useful to store this information in the annotation, because only the tool that encrypted the Authorization package can also decrypt it.

An example before encryption:

```
// File MyLibrary\package.mo
package MyLibrary
  annotation(Protection(License(libraryKey="15783-A39323-498222-444ckk411",
                        licenseFile="MyLibraryAuthorization_Tool.mo_lic",
                        operations={"ExportBinary"}), …));
end MyLibrary;

// File MyLibrary\MyLibraryAuthorization_Tool.mo
// (authorization file before encryption)
package MyLibraryAuthorization_Tool
  annotation(Authorization(
             libraryKey="15783-A39323-498222-444ckk411",
               licensor  ="Organization A\nRoad, Country",
               license={
               License(licensee="Organization B, Mr.X",
                       id      ={"lic:1269"}),       // tool license number
               License(licensee="Organization C, Mr. Y",
                       id      ={"lic:511"}, expirationDate="2010-06-30"),
```

```
                License(licensee="Organization D, Mr. Z",
                        id       ={"mac:0019d2c9bfe7"})  // MAC address
              }));
end MyLibraryAuthorization_Tool;
```

11.13 Function Annotations

Several rather special annotations are defined for functions. These annotations enable the Modelica compiler to generate more efficient code or to perform more efficient symbolic manipulation in certain situations.

These annotations are the function `derivative` annotation, the function `inverse` annotation, the function `Inline`, `LateInline`, and `InlineAfterIndexReduction` annotations, the function `smoothOrder` annotation, and the external function `arrayLayout` annotation. The function `derivative` annotation allows us to explicitly specify the computation of the derivatives of a function to any order, e.g., in order to gain performance and/or numerical accuracy.

The function `inverse` annotation can be used to specify inverses of functions, sometimes useful in symbolic processing and solution of equation systems. The `Inline`, `LateInline`, and `InlineAfterIndexReduction` annotations allow replacing function calls by corresponding function bodies. The `smoothOrder` annotation states that symbolic differentiation can be performed on the function up to a certain order. The external function annotation `arrayLayout` can be used to explicitly give the layout of arrays, e.g. if it deviates from the default `rowMajor` and `columnMajor` order for the external languages C and Fortran 77, respectively.

11.13.1 Function Derivative Annotation

A Modelica compiler usually needs to differentiate functions called in equations and expressions of a model when transforming the model into a form that is better suited for execution. A function defined in Modelica can be automatically differentiated based on symbolic differentiation of the statements in the body of the function. However, this option is not possible for external functions, for which the only alternative for the system usually is to resort to numerical approximations of the derivatives. Also, even for Modelica functions the automatically obtained symbolic derivatives may sometimes (but rather seldom) be inefficient or have numerical instabilities.

For these reasons, an annotation called `derivative`, with an associated optional annotation attribute `order`, is available for Modelica functions, i.e., for both external functions and functions implemented in Modelica. This allows us to explicitly state the computation of the derivatives of a function to any desired order. We should point out that the `derivative` annotation is seldom needed, but is useful in certain cases where accuracy and/or performance need to be improved. For example, the function `h0` below specifies its time derivative to be given by the function `h1`, which in turn specifies its derivative (of order 2) to be computed by the function `h2`.

```
function h0 annotation(derivative=h1);
  ...
end h0;

function h1 annotation(derivative(order=2)=h2);
  ...
end h1;

function h2
  ...
end h2;
```

The function derivative annotation is described in more detail in Section 9.3.9, page 455.

11.13.2 Function Inverse Annotation

Inverses of functions are sometimes useful in symbolic processing, e.g. during solution of systems of equation. Therefore it is possible for every Modelica function with one output argument to have one or more `inverse` annotations to define inverses of this function:

```
function f1
  input  A1 u1;
  ...
  input  T1 uk;
  ...
  input  Am um = am;
  ...
  input  An un;
  output T2 y;
 annotation(inverse(uk = f2(..., y, ....), ui = f3(..., y, ...), ...));
algorithm
  ...
end f1;
```

The meaning is that function f_2 is an inverse to function f_1 where the previous output `y` is now an input and the previous input u_k is now an output.

See Section 9.3.11, page 459, for more details including examples, of function inverse annotations.

11.13.3 Function Inline, LateInline, InlineAfterIndexReduction Annotations

There are three annotations that control possible inlining of function calls, called `Inline`, `LateInline`, and `InlineAfterIndexReduction` respectively. All three annotations only have effect within function declarations.

If `Inline=true`, the model developer proposes to inline the function. This means that the function call is replaced by the body of the function at all places where the function is called. This makes the execution more efficient by avoiding the overhead of a function call at each place but increases memory usage since the function body is duplicated at each call site. If `Inline=false`, the model developer proposes not to inline the function.

If `LateInline=true`, the model developer proposes to inline the function after all symbolic transformations have been performed, especially symbolic differentiation and inversion of functions.

Since a function call can only be inlined at most once, `LateInline` has priority over `Inline`, giving the following combination results:

- The combination `Inline=true, LateInline=false` is identical to `Inline=true`.
- The combination `Inline=true, LateInline=true` is identical to `LateInline=true`.
- The combination `Inline=false, LateInline=true` is identical to `LateInline=true`.

If `InlineAfterIndexReduction = true`, the model developer proposes to inline the function after the function is differentiated for index reduction, and before any other symbolic transformations are performed. This annotation cannot be combined with annotations `Inline` and `LateInline`

See Section 9.3.12, page 460, for a more detailed description with examples of function inlining.

11.13.4 Function smoothOrder Annotation

The `smoothOrder` annotation set to an unsigned integer value gives the number of differentiations of the function for which it is guaranteed that all of its differentiated outputs are continuous provided all input arguments and their derivatives up to order `smoothOrder` are continuous. This information is useful for a

Modelica compiler when performing certain symbolic transformations. For a more detailed description, see Section 9.3.13, page 461.

11.13.5 External Function Annotation arrayLayout with rowMajor and columnMajor

Regarding specific annotations only for external function declarations there is an optional `arrayLayout` annotation, which can have one of the values `"rowMajor"` or `"columnMajor"`. These are the defaults for C and Fortran 77 array layout, respectively. This annotation causes additional information to be passed to the compiler when necessary. It is needed only when the array storage layout deviates from the default for the external language. This is the case for the function `joinThreeVectors2` below where the C function uses column-major array representation, which is different from the default row-major layout that normally is used for C. For more information on external functions, see Section 9.4, page 466, specifically Section 9.4.6, page 475.

```
function joinThreeVectors2 "External C function with column-major arrays"
  input  Real v1[:],v2[:],v3[:];
  output Real vres[size(v1,1)+size(v2,1)+size(v3,1)];
external "C" join3vec(v1,v2,v3,vres,size(v1,1),size(v2,1),size(v3,1));
  annotation(arrayLayout = "columnMajor");
end joinThreeVectors2;
```

11.14 Annotations for External Libraries and Include Files

There are several useful annotations for specifying external libraries and include files in the context of calling external functions from Modelica. See Section 9.4.9, page 479, for a more detailed description with examples on how to use these annotations. Below is a short summary:

- The `annotation(Library="libraryName")` is used to give information to the linker to include the library file where the compiled external function is available.
- The `annotation(Library={"libraryName1","libraryName2"})` is used to give information to the linker to include the library files where the compiled external function is available as well as additional libraries used to implement it. For shared libraries it is recommended to include all non-system libraries in this list.
- The `annotation(Include="includeDirective")` is used to include source files, e.g., header files or source files that contain the functions referenced in the external function declaration and are needed for calling the external function in the code generated by the Modelica compiler.
- The `annotation(IncludeDirectory="modelica://`*`LibName`*`/Resources/Include")` can be used to specify a location for header files. See also Section 11.15.1, page 557, regarding Modelica URIs.
- The `annotation(LibDirectory="modelica://`*`LibName`*`/Resources/Library")` can be used to specify a location for library files.

11.15 URI References to External Resources

Modelica models may reference external *resources* such as files or documents accessed via internet links, identified by so-called *Uniform Resource Identifiers* (URIs).

An URI is a more general concept than URL (Uniform Resource Locator) or URN (Uniform Resource Name). A URI can be classified as either a URL or a URN or both. For example, an ISBN number that refers to a book (e.g. urn:isbn:0-486-27557-4) is a typical case of a URN, whereas a URL could be used to locate where a .pdf file of the book can be found. If the file is stored on a local file system, the URL might appear as follows: file:///home/username/BookFileName.

In the internet literature the term ***resource*** has a general meaning, i.e., whatever that might be identified by a URI, including more abstract things like services, relationships, and operators. However, in Modelica models we limit the term resource to mean files and/or documents.

Examples of URI references in Modelica models can be found in html documentation annotations (Section 11.9, page 545), for example:

```
annotation(Documentation(info = "
  ...
  <a href=\"http://www.Modelica.org\">
  ...
```

Another example of Modelica related URI references are names of files storing bitmaps, referenced in the fileName attribute of BitMap records in graphical annotations (Section 11.4.5.6, page 534):

```
record BitMap
  extends GraphicItem;
  Extent  extent;
  String  fileName                "Name of bitmap file, specified by URI";
  String  imageSource             "Base64 representation of bitmap";
end BitMap;
```

How does a URI look like? A URI to locate a file, i.e., a URL, takes the following form:

```
file://<host>/<path>
```

Here file is a so-called scheme, <host> is the name of the server where the file resides, and <path> is the full path-name of the file on the file system. If it resides on the file system of the local computer the <host> can be omitted, but the third slash must be kept. For files with special characters in their names, such as spaces in "the file.txt", the percent % sign is used as an escape code. A URI to locally access that file on the C: disk in a Windows file system can appear as follows:

```
file:///c:/path/to/the%20file.txt
```

If instead a resource is obtained from the server at example.org through the http protocol, http (hyper text transfer protocol) becomes our access scheme, with the following example of a possible URI:

```
http://example.org/absolute/path/to/resource.txt
```

In general the syntax of most URI variants follows this template:

```
<scheme>://[<authority>]/<path_to_resource>[?<query>][#<fragment>]
```

The URI starts by a scheme name such as http, ftp, mailto, file, or modelica, followed by a colon and then by a scheme-specific part, which has its own syntax and semantics. The parts within [], i.e., <authority>, ?<query>, and #<fragment> are optional. When <authority> is present, the <path> must either be empty or preceded by a slash (/) character, whereas if <authority> is not present, the <path> is not allowed to be preceded by two slash characters (//).

11.15.1 The modelica URI Scheme for Package Related Resources

As a complement to the common standard URI schemes, a Modelica related URI scheme called modelica is defined for accessing resources associated with a certain package. Note that even though scheme names are case insensitive, lower-case is preferred. For example, the URI prefix modelica:// is preferred over Modelica://.

The main advantage of the modelica scheme is its ability to reference a hierarchical structure of resources associated with packages. The same structure can be used for all kind of resource references, independent of use (external file, image in documentation, bitmap in icon layer, and link to external file in the documentation), and regardless of the storage mechanism.

Consider a top-level package Modelica with a class Electrical inside. A modelica scheme URI for referencing the resource D.jpg associated with that package can appear as follows:

```
modelica://Modelica.Electrical/D.jpg
```

The general structure of modelica scheme URIs is given by this template:

```
modelica://<authority>/<path>
```

The following rules apply to modelica scheme URIs:

- The <authority> portion of the URI is interpreted as a fully qualified package name.
- The <path> portion of the URI is interpreted as the path (relative to the package) of the resource.
- Any modelica scheme URI containing a slash after the package name is interpreted as a reference to a resource.
- Each storage method can define its own interpretation of the path, but care should be taken when converting from one storage method to another, or when restructuring packages for which resource references resolve to the same resource.
- Any storage method should be constrained such that a resource with a given <path> should be *unique* for any package name that precedes it.
- The *first part* of the <path> may not be the name of a class in the *package* given by the <authority>.
- In case the class-name contains quoted identifiers, the single-quote (') and any reserved characters (:, /, ?, #, [,], @, !, $, &, (,), *, +, ",", ;, =) should be percent-encoded as normal in URIs.

For example, the following is a legal reference to the resource D.jpg within the Modelica.Electrical class:

```
modelica://Modelica.Electrical/D.jpg        // this is legal
```

This reference is incorrect since Modelica/Electrical is not a legal class name in Modelica:

```
modelica://Modelica/Electrical/D.jpg        // this is illegal
```

The above uniqueness property that resource should be unique for any package name that precedes it, means that the following resource reference

```
modelica://Modelica.Mechanics/D.jpg
```

must refer to a different resource than this one:

```
modelica://Modelica/D.jpg
```

11.16 Units and Quantities

What is the meaning of *unit* and *quantity*? These notions are often used in the literature of natural sciences, e.g. in physics and chemistry. We speak about measuring physical *quantities,* and the *unit* by which we are measuring those quantities. Unfortunately the literature is sometimes confusing. Some texts use the terms unit, quantity, and dimension more or less interchangeably. Nonetheless one can discern some kind of consensus regarding the definition of unit and quantity based on the majority of scientific texts in the area:

- *Quantity*, also called *dimension,* is *what* we measure, i.e., any measurable extent or magnitude such as length, mass, time, and so on.

- A *unit* is a "yardstick" by which we *express* our measurements. For example, a measurement of the length quantity can be expressed as a number of meter units.

As we just stated, quantity can be interpreted as the basic notion of *what* we measure. There is a set of seven *base* quantities defined in the ISO SI system, stated below. The associated measurement *unit* is given within parentheses:

- Length (m).
- Mass (kg).
- Time (s).
- ElectricCurrent (A).
- Temperature (K).
- Amount of substance (mol).
- Luminosity (Cd).

However, the set of base quantities is not enough for engineering application modeling. For example, `Angle` is not included among the SI system base quantities—it is regarded as dimensionless. A number of derived quantities are quite important, e.g. Force (N), Torque (N.m), ElectricPotential (V), Voltage (V), Velocity (m/s), AngularVelocity (rad/s), etc.—the list is quite long. Applications in areas such as information technology may require additional quantities, for example, information flow with an associated unit of bit/second.

The choice of the SI system base quantities above is somewhat arbitrary, partly influenced by practical considerations regarding the complexity of common unit expressions. Some unit systems use ElectricCharge as a base quantity instead of ElectricCurrent, since this can be considered as somewhat more basic from a physical modeling point of view. However, that leads to longer unit expressions in many practical cases when converting to base units.

Modelica provides somewhat more precise definitions of `quantity` and `unit` compatible with the above guidelines, as well as a formal syntax of unit expressions according to guidelines found in the ISO SI unit standard.

11.16.1 Quantity, Unit, and displayUnit in Modelica

The Modelica notions of `quantity` and `unit` correspond to the definitions given in the previous section, but with a concrete representation as string attributes to the `Real` predefined class (see below and in Section 3.9 on page 93 in Chapter 3).

```
type Real "Pseudo class declaration of predefined Real type"
  ...
  parameter 'StringType'  quantity    = ""  "Physical quantity";
  parameter 'StringType'  unit        = ""  "Unit used in equations";
  parameter 'StringType'  displayUnit = ""  "Default display unit";
  ...
end Real;
```

The `quantity`, `unit`, and `displayUnit` attributes of the `Real` predefined type have the following meaning:

- `quantity`—a string describing *what* physical quantity the type represents. Example quantities are: "`Mass`," "`Force`," "`Torque`," "`Acceleration`," etc. The `quantity` attribute defines the category of a variable. It is used as a grouping mechanism for different units belonging to the same physical quantity.
- `unit`—a string describing the physical *measurement unit* of the type. Examples are "`kg`", "`m`", "`m/s`", "`N.m`", "`kg.m/s2`", "`kg.m.s-2`", "`1/rad`", etc. The `unit` attribute defines the unit of

variable values as used for computation in expressions and equations. The numeric values of variables are interpreted with respect to their associated units.

- `displayUnit`—gives the default *unit* used by a Modelica tool for *interactive input/output*. For example, the display unit for angle might be "`deg`," but the unit might be "`rad`." Values interactively input or output as "`deg`" are then automatically converted to/from "`rad`."

Below are examples of definitions and uses of types corresponding to some physical quantities. Remember that the `final` prefix on `quantity` and `unit` means that these attributes cannot be changed by further modification of the types `Force` and `Angle`.

```
// Define quantity types
type Force = Real(final quantity="Force", final unit="N");
type Angle = Real(final quantity="Angle", final unit="rad",
                                                  displayUnit="deg");
// Use the quantity types
Force  f1;
Force  f2(displayUnit="kp");
Angle  alpha;
Angle  beta(displayUnit="rad");
```

As stated above, the `quantity` attribute can be used as a grouping mechanism in interactive Modelica environments. The quantity name is needed because it is in general not possible to determine just from the `unit` whether two different units belong to the same physical quantity. For example, consider the following two types:

```
type Torque = Real(final quantity="MomentOfForce", final unit="N.m");

type Energy = Real(final quantity="Energy"       , final unit="J");
```

The units of type `Torque` and type `Energy` both can be transformed to the same combination of base units, that is, "`kg.m2/s2`". However, the two types still characterize different physical quantities. In an interactive Modelica environment with a menu prompting for a choice of `displayUnit` for an instantiated component of the `Torque` type, the unit "`J`" should not appear in the menu. If only the `unit` of the variable is given without any `quantity information`, it is not possible for the Modelica environment to produce a correct list of alternatives in the menu for using a display unit.

The Modelica standard library package `Modelica.SIunits` contains *predefined* quantity and connector types in the form shown in the above examples. This library contains approximately 450 predefined types comprising the complete set of ISO SI standard units, which is quite helpful when defining the interfaces of a model. Some additional examples from this library are shown below:

```
type ElectricCurrent    = Real(final quantity="ElectricCurrent",
                                final unit= "A");
type Current            = ElectricCurrent;
type Resistance         = Real(final quantity="Resistance",
                                final unit="Ohm", min=0);
type Inductance         = Real(final quantity="Inductance",
                                final unit="H", min=0);
type Time     = Real(final quantity="Time",    final unit="s" );
type Length   = Real(final quantity="Length",  final unit="m" );
type Position = Real(final quantity="Length",  final unit="m");
type AngularVelocity      = Real(final quantity="AngularVelocity",
                                  final unit="rad/s",
                                  displayUnit="rev/min");
type AngularAcceleration = Real(final quantity="AngularAcceleration",
                                  final unit="rad/s2");
type MomentOfInertia      = Real(final quantity="MomentOfInertia",
                                  final unit="kg.m2");
```

11.16.2 Unit Conversion

Automatic conversion between units is not required by a conforming Modelica language implementation. This is a facility that can be provided by separate tools such as unit and dimension checkers, or special high-quality Modelica implementations. Not requiring automatic unit conversion simplifies a Modelica translator considerably, partly because it is hard to define a complete unit database with conversion rules.

As a consequence, the semantics of a correct Modelica model is independent of the `unit` and `quantity` attributes, which are ignored during code generation. It is even the case that the `unit` attributes are not checked for connections, that is, connected variables may have different units and quantities. However, an interactive Modelica environment, for example, a model connection editor, is free to provide support for such automatic unit conversion when two interfaces are connected. If there are conflicting units a warning will be issued since this is not really considered an error. As a general rule it will always be allowed to connect any variable to a variable without `unit` and `quantity` information.

11.16.2.1 Dimension and Quantity Checking

The more common term *dimension checking* refers to consistency checking regarding compatible *quantities* and *units* in expressions and equations. For example, a Modelica environment may optionally check the consistency of the `quantity` and `unit` attributes between the left-hand side and the right hand side of an equation.

Dimension checking is done by transforming the `quantity` and `unit` information into combinations of the seven base quantities with associated units. For example, consider the equation:

$$f = m \cdot a \qquad (11\text{-}1)$$

The quantity of the right-hand side is initially `Mass*Acceleration`, which is reduced to `Mass*Length^2/Time^2` in terms of base quantities. The corresponding units are converted to "`kg.m2/s2`". If the left-hand side has the quantity `Force` with the unit "`N`", this can be converted to the same base quantities as in the right-hand side. However, if, for example, the unit of f instead would have been "`N.m`", a unit inconsistency warning should be issued.

11.16.3 Unit Expression Syntax

The Modelica syntax rules for unit expressions determine the structure of Modelica `unit` attributes represented as strings, for example, as in the following example unit strings: "`kg`", "`m`", "`m/s`", "`N.m`", "`kg.m/s2`", "`kg.m.s-2`", "`1/rad`".

These rules are conformant with the international standards ISO 31/0-1992, "General principles concerning quantities, units and symbols" and ISO 1000-1992 "SI units and recommendations for the use of their multiples and of certain other units." Unfortunately, neither these standards nor any other previous standard define a *formal syntax* for unit expressions. However, Modelica *defines* a formal syntax for unit expressions based on recommendations in the above standards. These formal syntax rules can be found in Appendix B.

Below we informally describe the Modelica syntax rules for unit expressions together with a few examples:

- The unit of a dimension-free quantity is denoted by "1".
- The only permitted operators in unit expressions are division, represented by "/", and multiplication, represented by a dot "`.`".
- Implied multiplication between units in unit expressions is not allowed, e.g. "`Nm`" is incorrect, instead "`N.m`" should be used.

- There is no operator symbol for exponentiation. Instead a possibly signed number immediately after a unit operand is interpreted as an exponent. There should be no space between the operand and the exponent, for example, for square meter, m^2, write "`m2`".
- The ISO standard recommends at most one division where the expression to the right of "`/`" either contains no multiplications or is enclosed within parentheses. It is also possible to use negative exponents, for example, "`J/(kg.K)`" may be written as "`J.kg-1.K-1`".
- A unit symbol is a string of letters, for example, "kg", "Ohm", etc. A basic support of units in a Modelica tool should know the basic and derived units of the SI system. It should be possible to support user-defined unit symbols. In the base version, Greek letters are not supported, but full names must then be written, for example "Ohm".
- A unit operand expression should first be analyzed with an interpretation as a unit symbol. Only if not successful the second alternative assuming a prefixed operand should be investigated. There should be no spacing between the unit symbol and a possible unit prefix. The possible value of the prefix is according to the ISO standard, that is, one of Y, Z, E, P, T, G, M, k, h, da, d, c, m, u, p, f, a, z, y. The letter u is used as a symbol for the prefix *micro*.

Below are some examples of combinations of prefixes, unit symbols, and possible exponents. Prefixes have a higher priority than exponents, and may not be used in isolation.

- The unit expression "`m`" means meter and not milli (10^{-3}), since prefixes cannot be used in isolation. For millimeter use "`mm`" and for square meter, m^2, write "`m2`".
- The expression "`mm2`" means $mm^2 = (10^{-3}m)^2 = 10^{-6}m^2$. Note that exponentiation includes the prefix.
- The unit expression "`T`" means Tesla, but note that the letter "`T`" is also the symbol for the prefix *tera*, which has a multiplier value of 10^{12}.

11.17 Summary

In this chapter, we presented the Modelica annotation concept followed by a short overview of units and quantities in Modelica. First we described annotation syntax and placement, including annotation elements for redeclarations, classes, variables, imports, equations, and algorithms. Then followed a description of graphical annotations, which comprise a large part of the predefined annotations in Modelica. We subsequently presented the layered structuring of graphical annotations and the different graphical annotation attributes. We also defined the graphical annotation elements as record structures in Modelica, as well as annotations defining interactive menus, documentation annotations, and different kinds of function annotations. Finally we presented the concepts of units and quantities with associated attributes, unit conversion, and unit expression syntax.

11.18 Literature

The Modelica language specification (Modelica Association 2011) and the tutorial (Modelica Association 2000) specify the rules for annotations in Modelica, and give the basics of units and quantities.

More information concerning the general principles of quantities, units and symbols and their use can be found in (ISO 31/0-1992; ISO 1000-1992). Information on units and unit conversion is available in (Cardarelli 1997).

11.19 Exercises

Exercise 11-1:

Define a type `Acceleration` with the associated SI unit `m/s2`.

Exercise 11-2:

To which Modelica elements can annotations be applied?

Part III

Modeling and Applications

Chapter 12

Cyber-Physical System Modeling Methodology

So far in this text we have primarily discussed the principles of object-oriented mathematical modeling, a number of Modelica language constructs to support high-level model representation and a high degree of model reuse, and presented many model examples that demonstrate the use of these language constructs. However, we have not yet presented any systematic method on how to create a model of a system to be investigated, nor have we previously presented the underlying mathematical state-space equations in any detail. These are the topics of the current chapter. However, the state-space representation presented here covers only the simple case for continuous systems. The background for discrete event and hybrid continuous-discrete system modeling is explained in Chapter 13, whereas the complete hybrid DAE representation that also handles discrete events and hybrid systems is defined in Chapter 17.

12.1 Building System Models

A basic question is: How do we arrive at reasonable mathematical models of the systems we want to study and possibly simulate? That is, what is an effective modeling process?

The application domain is of primary importance in all kinds of modeling. We talk about *physical modeling* when the systems to be modeled are described by natural laws in physics, chemistry, biology, mechanical and electrical engineering, and so on, and these laws can be represented directly in the mathematical model we are constructing. However, it does not really matter whether the application domain is "physical" or not. There are laws governing economic systems, data communication, information processing, and so on that should be more or less directly expressible in the model we are building when using a high-level modeling approach. All of these laws are given by the universe in which we exist (but formulated by human beings), and can be regarded as basic laws of nature. An overview of common laws for a number of application domains is given in Chapter 14.

At the start of a modeling effort we first need to identify which application domains are involved in the system we want to model, and for each of these domains find out the relevant governing laws that influence the phenomena we want to study.

In order to be able to handle the complexity of large models and to reduce the effort of model building by reusing model components, it is quite useful to apply hierarchical decomposition and object-oriented component-based techniques such as those advocated in this text. To make this more clear, we will briefly contrast the traditional physical modeling approach to the object-oriented, component-based approach.

However, one should be aware that even the traditional approach to physical modeling is "higher-level" than certain other approaches such as block-oriented modeling or direct programming in common imperative languages, where the user has to manually convert equations into assignment statements or blocks and manually restructure the code to fit the data and signal flow context for a specific model use.

12.1.1 Deductive Modeling versus Inductive Modeling

So far we have dealt almost exclusively with the so-called *deductive modeling* approach, also called *physical modeling* approach, by which the behavior of a system is *deduced* from the application of natural laws expressed in a model of the system. Such models are created based on an understanding of the "physical" or "artificial" processes underlying the system in question, which is the basis for the term "physical modeling."

However, in many cases, especially for biological and economic systems, accurate knowledge about complex systems and their internal processes may not be available to an extent that would be needed to support physical modeling. In such application areas, it is common to use an entirely different approach to modeling. You make observations about the system under study and then try to fit a hypothetical mathematical model to the observed data by adapting the model, typically by finding values of unknown coefficients. This is called the *inductive modeling* approach.

Inductive models are directly based on measured values. This makes such models difficult to validate beyond the observed values. For example, we would like to accommodate mechanisms in a system model is such a way that disasters can be predicted and therefore possibly prevented. However, this might be impossible without first observing a real disaster event (that we would like to avoid by all means) in the system. This is a clear disadvantage of inductive models.

Also notice that just by adding sufficiently many parameters to an inductive model it is possible to fit virtually any model structure to virtually any data. This one of the most severe disadvantages of inductive models since in this way one can be easily fooled concerning their validity.

In the rest of this book, we will mainly deal with the deductive or physical modeling approach, except for a few biological application examples where we present models that are partly inductive and partly have some physical motivation.

12.1.2 Traditional Approach

The traditional methodology for physical modeling can be roughly divided into three phases:

1. Basic structuring in terms of variables
2. Stating equations and functions
3. Converting the model to state space form

The *first* phase involves identification of which variables are of interest, for example, for the intended use of the model, and the roles of these variables. Which variables should be considered as *inputs*, for example, external signals, as *outputs*, or as internal *state* variables? Which quantities are especially important for describing what happens in the system? Which are time varying and which are approximately *constant*? Which variables influence other variables?

The *second* phase involves stating the basic equations and formulas of the model. Here we have to look for the governing laws of the application domains that are relevant for the model, for example, *conservation equations* of quantities of the *same kind* such as power in related to power out, input flow rate related to output flow rates, and conservation of quantities such as energy, mass, charge, information, and so on. Formulate *constitutive equations* that relate quantities of *different kind*, for example, relating voltage and current for a resistor, input and output flows for a tank, input and output packets for a communication link, and so on. Also formulate relations, for example, involving material properties and other system properties. Consider the level of precision and appropriate approximation trade-offs in the relationships.

The *third* phase involves converting the model in its current form consisting of a set of variables and a set of equations to a *state space* equation system representation (see page 588 in this chapter) that fits the numeric solver to be used. A set of state variables needs to be chosen, their time derivatives (for dynamic variables) expressed as functions of state variables and input variables (for the case of state space equations in explicit form), and the output variables expressed as functions of state variables and input variables. If a few unnecessary state variables are included, this causes no harm, just some unnecessary computation. This phase is completely eliminated when using Modelica since the conversion to state space form is performed automatically by the Modelica compiler.

12.1.3 Object-Oriented, Component-Based Approach

When using the object-oriented, component-based approach to modeling we first try to understand the system structure and decomposition in a hierarchical top-down manner. When the system components and interactions between these components have been roughly identified, we can apply the first two traditional modeling phases of identifying variables and equations on each of these model components. The object-oriented approach has the following phases:

1. *Define* the system briefly. What kind of system is it? What does it do?
2. *Decompose* the *system* into its most important *components*. Sketch model classes for these components, or use existing classes from appropriate libraries.
3. Define *communication*, that is, determine interactions and communication paths between these components.
4. Define *interfaces*, that is, determine the external ports/*connectors* of each component for communication with other components. Formulate appropriate connector classes that allow a high degree of connectivity and reusability, while still allowing an appropriate degree of type checking of connections.
5. Recursively *decompose tentative model components* of assumed "high complexity" further into a set of "smaller" subcomponents by restarting from phase 2, until all components have been defined as instances of predefined types, library classes, or new classes to be defined by the user.
6. *Formulate new model classes* when needed, both base classes and derived classes:
    a. Declare new *model classes* for all model components that are not instances of existing classes. Each new class should include variables, equations, functions, and formulas relevant to define the behavior of the component, according to the principles already described for the first two phases of the traditional modeling approach.
    b. Declare possible *base classes* for increased reuse and maintainability by extracting common functionality and structural similarities from component classes with similar properties.

To get more of a feeling for how the object-oriented modeling approach works in practice, we will apply this method to modeling a simple tank system described in Section 12.2 on page 570, and to a DC motor servo in Section 12.3 on page 578.

12.1.4 Top-Down versus Bottom-Up Modeling

There are two related approaches to the structuring process when arriving at a model:

- *Top-down modeling*. This is useful when we know the application area rather well, and have an existing set of library component models available. We start by defining the top-level system model at a high level of abstraction. The level of detail of the system model is gradually increased by adding subsystems to the model, possibly hierarchically at several levels of abstraction, until we arrive at subsystems that correspond to the component models in our library.
- *Bottom-up modeling*. This approach is typically used when the application is less well known, or when we do not have a ready-made library at hand. First we formulate the basic equations and design small experimental models on the most important phenomena to gain a basic understanding of the application area. After some experimentation we have gained some understanding of the

application area, we can then add more details and restructure our model fragments into a set of of low-level model components which can be used as building blocks for further modeling. These component models might have to be restructured several times if they turn out to have problems when used for applications. We gradually build more complex application models based on our component models, and finally arrive at the desired application model.

Section 12.3, page 578, on modeling of a DC-motor from predefined components gives a typical example of top-down modeling. The small tank modeling example described in Section 12.2 has some aspects of bottom-up modeling since we start with a simple flat tank model before creating component classes and forming the tank model. A better example is the thermodynamic application described in Section 15.2, page 800, which is gradually developed, starting from scratch with very simple model examples. These examples gradually grow into a set of components that are used for the final application models.

12.1.5 Simplification of Models

It is sometimes the case that models are not precise enough to accurately describe the phenomena at hand. Too extensive approximations might have been done in certain parts of the model.

On the opposite side, even if we create a reasonable model according to the above methodology, it is not uncommon that parts of the model are too complex, which might lead to problems, e.g.:

- Too time-consuming simulations.
- Numerical instabilities.
- Difficulties in interpreting results due to too many low-level model details.

Thus, there are usually good reasons to consider simplification of a model. It is sometimes hard to get the right balance between simplicity and preciseness of models. This is more an art than a science and requires substantial experience. The best way to acquire such experience, however, is to keep on designing models together with performing analysis and evaluation of their behavior. The following are some hints of where to look for model simplifications, e.g. reduction of the number of state variables:

- *Neglect* small effects that are not important for the phenomena to be modeled.
- *Aggregate* state variables into fewer variables. For example, the temperatures at different points in a rod might sometimes be represented by the mean temperature of the whole rod.

Focus modeling on phenomena whose *time constants* are in the interesting range, that is:

- Approximate subsystems with very slow dynamics with constants.
- Approximate subsystems with very fast dynamics with static relationships, i.e. not involving time derivatives of those rapidly changing state variables.

An advantage of ignoring the very fast and the very slow dynamics of a system is that the order of the model, that is, the number of state variables, is reduced. Systems having model components with time constants of the same order of magnitude are numerically simpler and more efficient to simulate. On the other hand, certain systems have the intrinsic property of having a great spread of time constants. Such systems give rise to stiff systems of differential equations, which require certain adaptive numerical solvers for simulation (see also Chapter 18).

12.2 Modeling a Tank System

Regarding our exercise in modeling methodology, let us consider a simple tank system example containing a level sensor and a controller that is controlling a valve via an actuator (Figure 12-1). The liquid level `h` in the tank must be maintained at a fixed level as closely as possible. Liquid enters the tank through a pipe from a source, and leaves the tank via another pipe at a rate controlled by a valve.

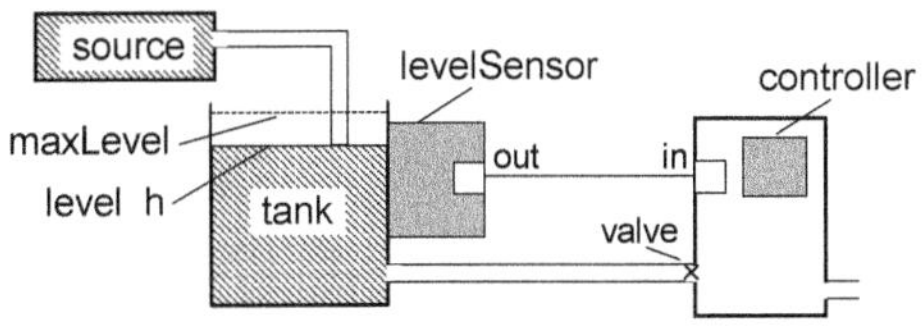

Figure 12-1. A tank system with a tank, a source for liquid, and a controller.

12.2.1 Using the Traditional Approach

We first show the result of modeling the tank system using the traditional approach. A number of variables and equations related to the tank system have been collected into the flat model presented in the next section. At this stage we do not explain how the equations have been derived and what exactly certain variables mean. This is described in detail in subsequent sections where the object-oriented approach to modeling the tank system is presented.

12.2.1.1 Flat Tank System Model

The `FlatTank` model is a "flat" model of the tank system with no internal hierarchical "system structure" visible, that is, just a collection of variables and equations that model the system dynamics. The internal system structure consisting of components, interfaces, couplings between the components, and so on, is not reflected by this model:

```
model FlatTank
  // Tank related variables and parameters
  parameter Real flowLevel(unit="m3/s")=0.02;
  parameter Real area(unit="m2")       =1;
  parameter Real flowGain(unit="m2/s") =0.05;
  Real           h(start=0,unit="m")    "Tank level";
  Real           qInflow(unit="m3/s")   "Flow through input valve";
  Real           qOutflow(unit="m3/s")  "Flow through output valve";
  // Controller related variables and parameters
  parameter Real K=2                     "Gain";
  parameter Real T(unit="s")= 10         "Time constant";
  parameter Real minV=0, maxV=10;     // Limits for flow output
  Real           ref = 0.25  "Reference level for control";
  Real           error       "Deviation from reference level";
  Real           outCtr      "Control signal without limiter";
  Real           x;          "State variable for controller";
equation
  assert (minV>=0,"minV must be greater or equal to zero");//
  der(h) = (qInflow-qOutflow)/area;    // Mass balance equation
  qInflow  = if time>150 then 3*flowLevel else flowLevel;
  qOutflow = LimitValue(minV,maxV,-flowGain*outCtr);
  error  = ref-h;
  der(x) = error/T;
  outCtr = K*(error+x);
end FlatTank;
```

A limiter function is needed in the model to reflect minimum and maximum flows through the output valve:

```
function LimitValue
  input  Real pMin;
  input  Real pMax;
  input  Real p;
  output Real pLim;
algorithm
  pLim := if p>pMax then pMax
          else if p<pMin then pMin
          else p;
end LimitValue;
```

Simulating the flat tank system model and plotting the results (Figure 12-2):

```
simulate(FlatTank, stopTime=250)
plot(h, stopTime=250)
```

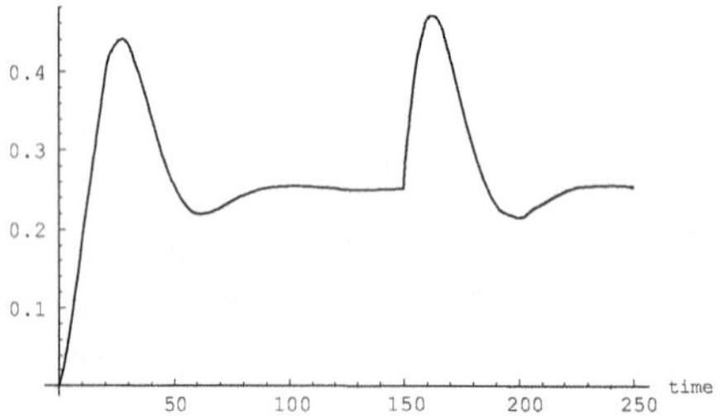

Figure 12-2. Simulation of the `FlatTank` model with plot of the tank level.

12.2.2 Using the Object-Oriented, Component-Based Approach

When using the object-oriented, component-based approach to modeling, we first look for the internal structure of the tank system. Is the tank system naturally decomposed into certain components? The answer is yes. Several components are actually visible in the structure diagram of the tank system in Figure 12-3, for example, the tank itself, the liquid source, the level sensor, the valve, and the controller.

Thus it appears that we have five components. However, since we will choose very simple representations of the level sensor and the valve, i.e. just a single scalar variable for each of these two components, we let these variables be simple `Real` variables in the tank model instead of creating two new classes containing a single variable each. Thus we are left with three components that are to be modeled explicitly as instances of new classes: the tank, the source, and the controller.

The next stage is to determine the interactions and communication paths between these components. It is fairly obvious that fluid flows from the source to the tank via a pipe. Fluid also leaves the tank via an outlet controlled by the valve. The controller needs measurements of the fluid level from the sensor. Thus a communication path from the sensor of the tank to the controller needs to be established.

Communication paths need to be connected somewhere. Therefore, connector instances need to be created for those components which are connected, and connector classes declared when needed. In fact, the system model should be designed so that the only communication between a component and the rest of the system is via connectors.

Finally we should think about reuse and generalizations of certain components. Do we expect several variants of a component to be needed? In that case it is useful to collect the basic functionality into a base class, and let each variant be a specialization of that base class. In the case of the tank system we expect to plug in several variants of the controller, starting with a continuous PI controller. Thus it is useful for us to create a base class for tank system controllers.

12.2.3 Tank System with a Continuous PI Controller

The structure of the tank system model developed using the object-oriented component-based approach is clearly visible in Figure 12-3. The three components of the tank system—the tank, the PI controller, and the source of liquid—are explicit in Figure 12-3 and in the declaration of the class `TankPI` below.

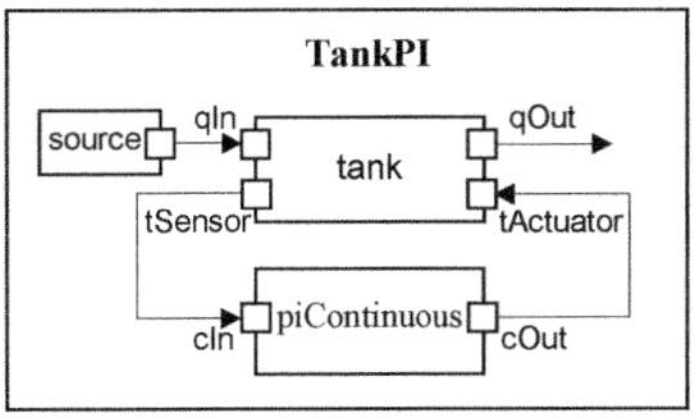

Figure 12-3. A tank system with a continuous PI controller and a source for liquid. Even though we have used arrows for clarity there need not be a signal direction—there are only physical connections represented by equations.

```
model TankPI
  LiquidSource              source(flowLevel=0.02);
  PIcontinuousController    piContinuous(ref=0.25);
  Tank                      tank(area=1);
equation
  connect(source.qOut, tank.qIn);
  connect(tank.tActuator, piContinuous.cOut);
  connect(tank.tSensor, piContinuous.cIn);
end TankPI;
```

Tank instances are connected to controllers and liquid sources through their connectors. The tank has four connectors: `qIn` for input flow, `qOut` for output flow, `tSensor` for providing fluid level measurements, and `tActuator` for setting the position of the valve at the outlet of the tank. The central equation regulating the behavior of the tank is the *mass balance* equation, which in the current simple form assumes constant pressure. The output flow is related to the valve position by a `flowGain` parameter, and by a limiter that guarantees that the flow does not exceed what corresponds to the open/closed positions of the valve.

```
model Tank
  ReadSignal  tSensor   "Connector, sensor reading tank level (m)";
  ActSignal   tActuator "Connector, actuator controlling input flow";
  LiquidFlow  qIn    "Connector, flow (m3/s) through input valve";
  LiquidFlow  qOut   "Connector, flow (m3/s) through output valve";
  parameter Real area(unit="m2")        = 0.5;
  parameter Real flowGain(unit="m2/s") = 0.05;
  parameter Real minV=0, maxV=10; // Limits for output valve flow
  Real h(start=0.0, unit="m") "Tank level";
equation
  assert (minV>=0,"minV - minimum Valve level must be >= 0 ");//
  der(h)       = (qIn.lflow-qOut.lflow)/area;    // Mass balance
equation
  qOut.lflow  = LimitValue(minV,maxV,-flowGain*tActuator.act);
  tSensor.val = h;
end Tank;
```

As already stated, the tank has four connectors. These are instances of the following three connector classes:

```
connector ReadSignal  "Reading fluid level"
```

```
  Real val(unit="m");
end ReadSignal;

connector ActSignal    "Signal to actuator for setting valve position"
  Real act;
end ActSignal;

connector LiquidFlow   "Liquid flow at inlets or outlets"
  Real lflow(unit="m3/s");
end LiquidFlow;
```

The fluid entering the tank must come from somewhere. Therefore, we have a liquid source component in the tank system. The flow increases sharply at time=150 to factor of three of the previous flow level, which creates an interesting control problem that the controller of the tank has to handle.

```
model LiquidSource
  LiquidFlow qOut;
  parameter Real flowLevel = 0.02;
equation
  qOut.lflow = if time>150 then 3*flowLevel else flowLevel;
end LiquidSource;
```

The controller needs to be specified. We will initially choose a PI controller but later replace this by other kinds of controllers. The behavior of a continuous PI (*proportional and integrating*) controller is primarily defined by the following two equations:

$$\begin{aligned} \frac{dx}{dt} &= \frac{error}{T} \\ outCtr &= K*(error + x) \end{aligned} \tag{12-1}$$

Here x is the controller state variable, *error* is the difference between the reference level and the actual level of obtained from the sensor, T is the time constant of the controller, *outCtr* is the control signal to the actuator for controlling the valve position, and K is the gain factor. These two equations are placed in the controller class `PIcontinuousController`, which extends the `BaseController` class defined later.

```
model PIcontinuousController
  extends BaseController(K=2,T=10);
  Real  x  "State variable of continuous PI controller";
equation
  der(x) = error/T;
  outCtr = K*(error+x);
end PIcontinuousController;
```

By integrating the first equation, thus obtaining x, and substituting into the second equation, we obtain the following expression for the control signal, containing terms that are directly proportional to the error signal and to the integral of the error signal respectively, i.e. a PI (proportional and integrating) controller.

$$outCtr = K*(error + \int \frac{error}{T} dt) \tag{12-2}$$

Both the PI controller and the PID controller to be defined later inherit the partial controller class `BaseController`, containing common parameters, state variables, and two connectors: one to read the sensor and one to control the valve actuator.

In fact, the `BaseController` class also can be reused when defining discrete PI and PID controllers for the same tank example in Section 13.4.1, page 676. Discrete controllers repeatedly sample the fluid level and produce a control signal that changes value at discrete points in time with a periodicity of `Ts`.

```
partial model BaseController
  parameter Real Ts(unit= "s") = 0.1 "Time period between discrete samples";
  parameter Real K=2                 "Gain";
  parameter Real T(unit = "s") = 10  "Time constant";
```

```
  ReadSignal      cIn             "Input sensor level, connector";
  ActSignal       cOut            "Control to actuator, connector";
  parameter Real  ref             "Reference level";
  Real            error           "Deviation from reference level";
  Real            outCtr          "Output control signal";
equation
  error    = ref-cIn.val;
  cOut.act = outCtr;
end BaseController;
```

We simulate the TankPI model and obtain the same response as for the FlatTank model, which is not surprising given that both models have the same basic equations (Figure 12-4).

```
simulate(TankPI, stopTime=250)
plot(tank.h)
```

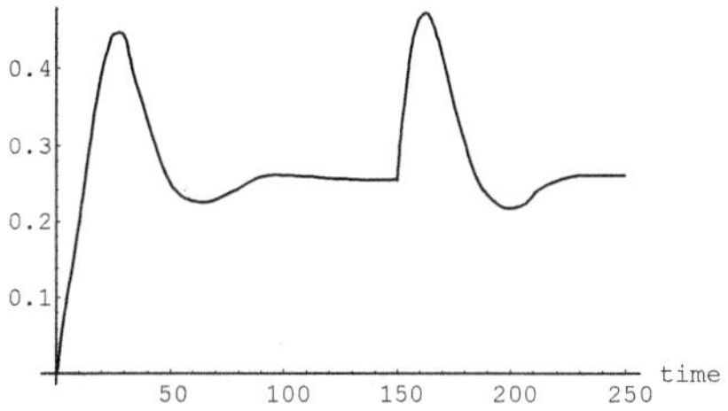

Figure 12-4. The tank level response for the TankPI system containing a PI controller.

12.2.4 Tank with Continuous PID Controller

We define a TankPID system which is the same as the TankPI system except that the PI controller has been replaced by a PID controller. Here we see a clear advantage of the object-oriented, component-based approach over the traditional modeling approach, since system components can be easily replaced and changed in a plug-and-play manner (Figure 12-5).

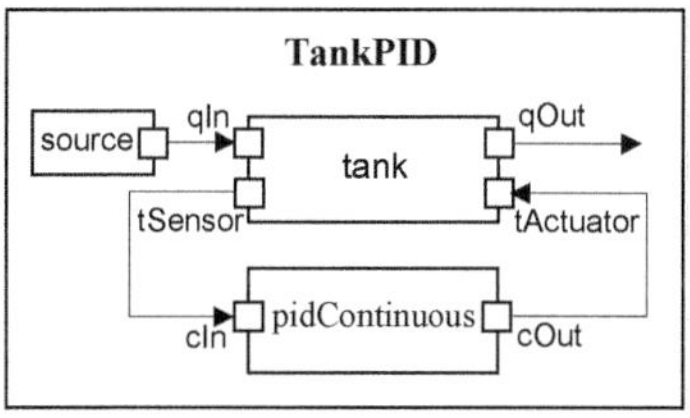

Figure 12-5. The tank system with the PI controller replaced by a PID controller.

The Modelica class declaration for the TankPID system appears as follows:

```
model TankPID
  LiquidSource                source(flowLevel=0.02);
  PIDcontinuousController pidContinuous(ref=0.25);
  Tank                        tank(area=1);
equation
  connect(source.qOut, tank.qIn);
  connect(tank.tActuator, pidContinuous.cOut);
  connect(tank.tSensor, pidContinuous.cIn);
end TankPID;
```

A PID (*proportional, integrating, derivative*) controller model can be derived in a similar way as was done for the PI controller. PID controllers react quicker to instantaneous changes than PI controllers due to the term containing the derivative. A PI controller on the other hand puts somewhat more emphasis on compensating slower changes. The basic equations for a PID controller are the following:

$$\begin{aligned}\frac{dx}{dt} &= \frac{error}{T} \\ y &= T\frac{d\,error}{dt} \\ outCtr &= K*(error + x + y)\end{aligned} \tag{12-3}$$

We create a `PIDcontinuousController` class in Modelica containing the three defining equations:

```
model PIDcontinuousController
  extends BaseController(K=2,T=10);
  Real  x; // State variable of continuous PID controller
  Real  y; // State variable of continuous PID controller
equation
  der(x)  = error/T;
  y       = T*der(error);
  outCtr  = K*(error + x + y);
end PIDcontinuousController;
```

By integrating the first equation and substituting x and y into the third equation, we obtain an expression for the control signal which contains terms directly proportional, proportional to the integral, and proportional to the derivative of the error signal, that is, a proportional integrating derivative (PID) controller.

$$outCtr = K*(error + \int \frac{error}{T}dt + T\frac{d\,error}{dt}) \tag{12-4}$$

We simulate the tank model once more but now including the PID controller (Figure 12-6). The tank level as a function of time of the simulated system is quite similar to the corresponding system with a PI controller, but with somewhat faster control to restore the reference level after quick changes of the input flow.

```
simulate(TankPID, stopTime=250)
plot(tank.h)
```

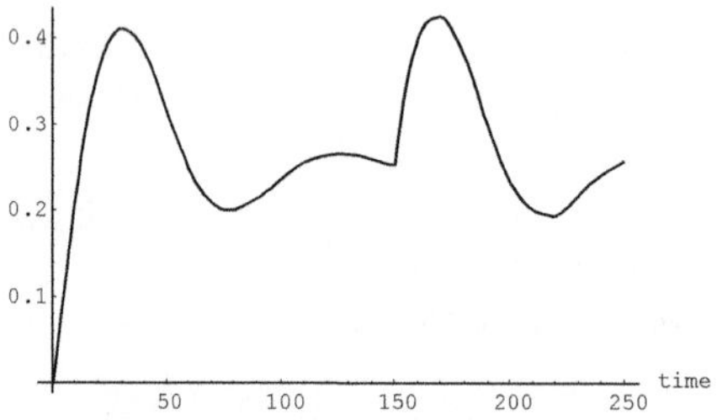

Figure 12-6. The tank level response for the `TankPID` system containing a `PID` controller.

The diagram in Figure 12-7 shows the simulation results from both `TankPI` and `TankPID` plotted in the same diagram for comparison.

```
simulate(compareControllers, stopTime=250)
plot({tankPI.h,tankPID.h})
```

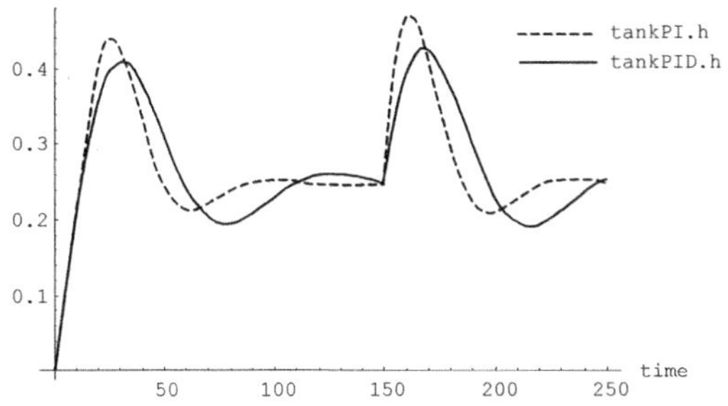

Figure 12-7. Comparison of `TankPI` and `TankPID` simulations.

12.2.5 Two Tanks Connected Together

The advantages of the object-oriented, component-based approach to modeling become even more apparent when combining several components in different ways, as in the example depicted in Figure 12-8, where two tanks are connected in series, which is not uncommon in process industry.

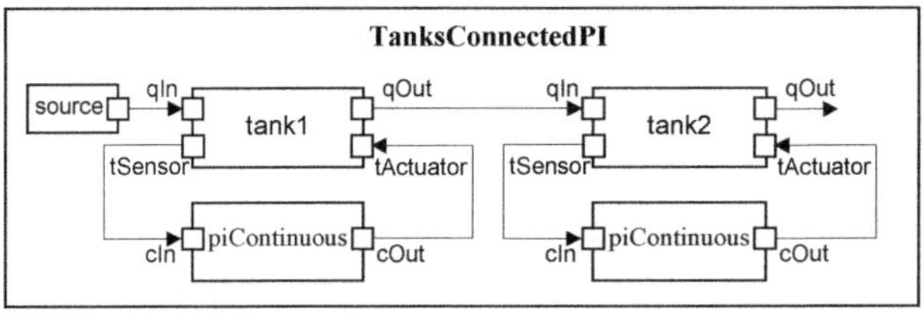

Figure 12-8. Two connected tanks with PI controllers and a `source` for liquid connected to the first tank.

The Modelica model `TanksConnectedPI` corresponding to Figure 12-8 appears as follows:

```
model TanksConnectedPI
  LiquidSource    source(flowLevel=0.02);
  Tank            tank1(area=1);
  Tank            tank2(area=1.3);
  PIcontinuousController piContinuous1(ref=0.25);
  PIcontinuousController piContinuous2(ref=0.4);
equation
  connect(source.qOut,tank1.qIn);
  connect(tank1.tActuator,piContinuous1.cOut);
  connect(tank1.tSensor,piContinuous1.cIn);
  connect(tank1.qOut,tank2.qIn);
  connect(tank2.tActuator,piContinuous2.cOut);
  connect(tank2.tSensor,piContinuous2.cIn);
end TanksConnectedPI;
```

We simulate the connected tank system. We clearly see the tank level responses of the first and second tank to the changes in fluid flow from the source, where the response from the first tank of course appears earlier in time than the response of the second tank (Figure 12-9).

```
simulate(TanksConnectedPI, stopTime=400)
plot({tank1.h,tank2.h})
```

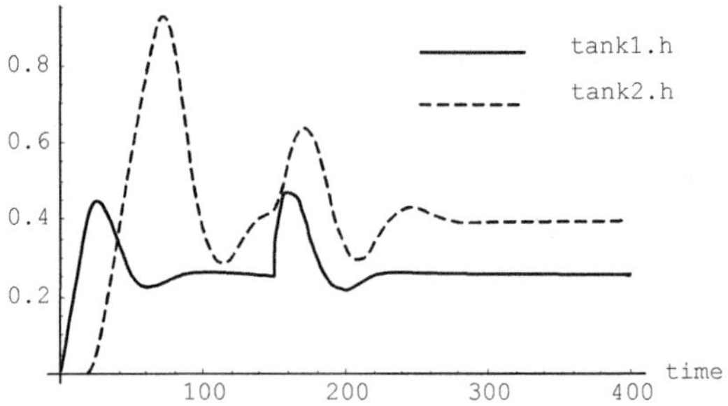

Figure 12-9. The tank level responses for two tanks connected in series.

12.3 Modeling of a DC-Motor Servo from Predefined Components

In this section, we illustrate the object-oriented, component-based modeling process when using predefined library classes by sketching the design of a DC motor servo model. We do not go into any detail since the majority of the used classes are described in the context of the DC motor application presented in Section 15.1, page 794, and the previous tank example was presented in quite some detail.

12.3.1 Defining the System

What does a DC motor servo do? It is a motor, the speed of which can be controlled by some kind of regulator (Figure 12-10). Since it is a servo, it needs to maintain a specified rotational speed despite a varying load. Presumably it contains an electric motor, some mechanical rotational transmissions and loads, some kind of control to regulate the rotational speed, and some electric circuits since the control system needs electric connections to the rest of the system, and there are electric parts of the motor. The reader may have noticed that it is hard to define a system without describing its parts, i.e., we are already into the system decomposition phase.

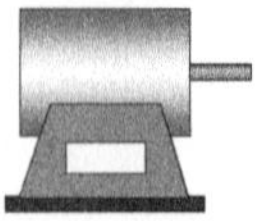

Figure 12-10. A DC motor servo.

12.3.2 Decomposing into Subsystems and Sketching Communication

In this phase we decompose the system into major subsystems and sketch communication between those subsystems. As already noted in the system definition phase, the system contains rotational mechanical parts including the motor and loads, an electric circuit model containing the electric parts of the DC motor together with its electric interface, and a controller subsystem that regulates the speed of the DC motor by controlling the current fed to the motor. Thus there are three subsystems as depicted in Figure 12-11: controller, an electric circuit, and a rotational mechanics subsystem.

Regarding the communication between the subsystems, the controller must be connected to the electric circuit since it controls the current to the motor. The electric circuit also needs to be connected to the rotational mechanical parts in order that electrical energy can be converted to rotational energy. Finally, a feedback loop including a sensor of the rotational speed is necessary for the controller to do its job properly. The communication links are sketched in Figure 12-11.

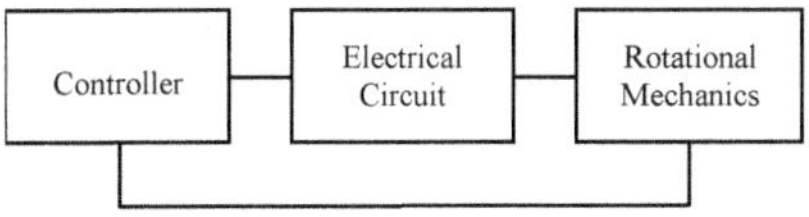

Figure 12-11. The subsystems and their connections.

12.3.3 Modeling the Subsystems

The next phase is to model the subsystems by further decomposition. We start by modeling the controller and manage to find classes in the standard Modelica library for a feedback summation node and a PI controller. We also add a step function block as an example of a control signal. All these parts are shown in Figure 12-12.

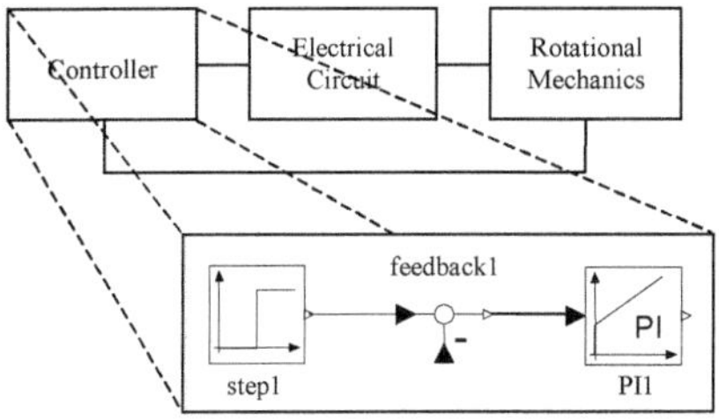

Figure 12-12. Modeling the controller.

The second major component to decompose is the electric circuit part of the DC motor (Figure 12-13). Here we have identified the standard parts of a DC motor such as a signal-controlled electric voltage generator, a ground component needed in all electric circuits, a resistor, an inductor representing the coil of the motor, and an electromotoric force (EMF) converter to convert electric energy to rotational movement.

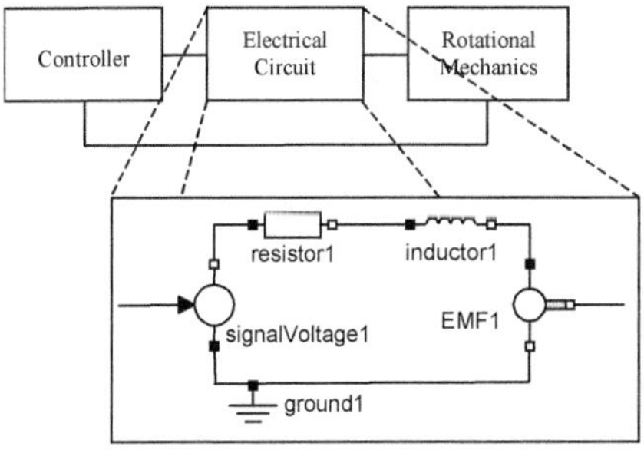

Figure 12-13. Modeling the electric circuit.

The third subsystem, depicted in Figure 12-14, contains three mechanical rotational loads with inertia, one ideal gear, one rotational spring, and one speed sensor for measuring the rotational speed needed as information for the controller.

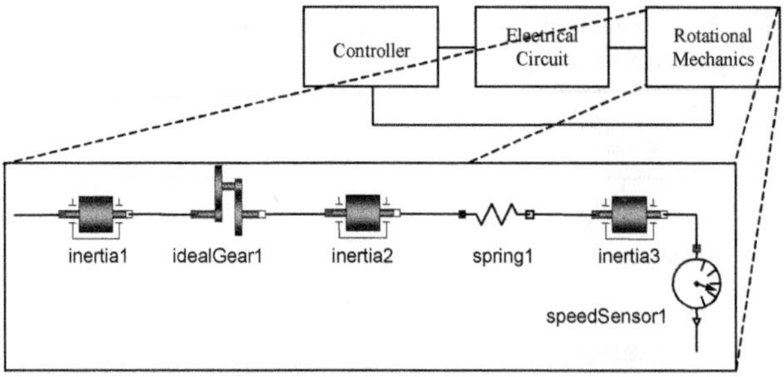

Figure 12-14. Modeling the mechanical subsystem including the speed sensor.

12.3.4 Modeling Parts in the Subsystems

We managed to find all the needed parts as predefined models in the Modelica class library. If that would not have been the case, we would also have needed to define appropriate model classes and identified the equations for those classes, as sketched for the parts of the control subsystem in Figure 12-15, the electric subsystem in Figure 12-16, and the rotational mechanics subsystem in Figure 12-17.

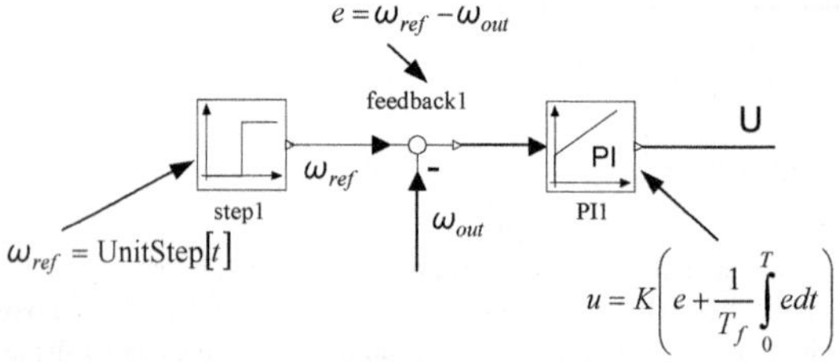

Figure 12-15. Basic equations and components in the control subsystem.

The electric subsystem depicted in Figure 12-16 contains electrical components with associated basic equations, for example, a resistor, an inductor, a signal voltage source, and an electromotoric force (EMF) component.

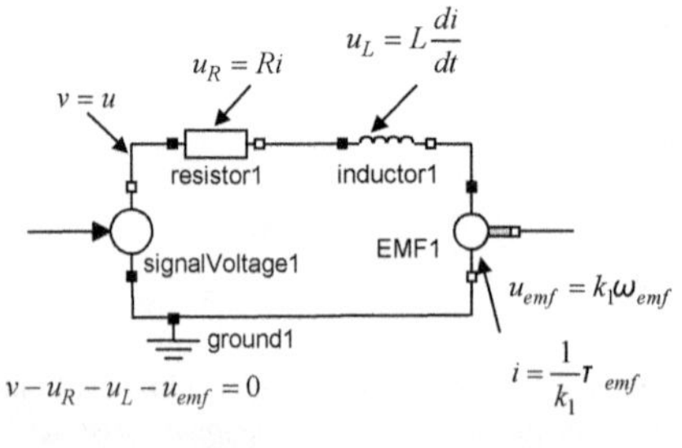

Figure 12-16. Defining classes and basic equations for components in the electric subsystem.

The rotational mechanics subsystem depicted in Figure 12-16 contains a number of components such as inertias, a gear, a rotational spring, and a speed sensor.

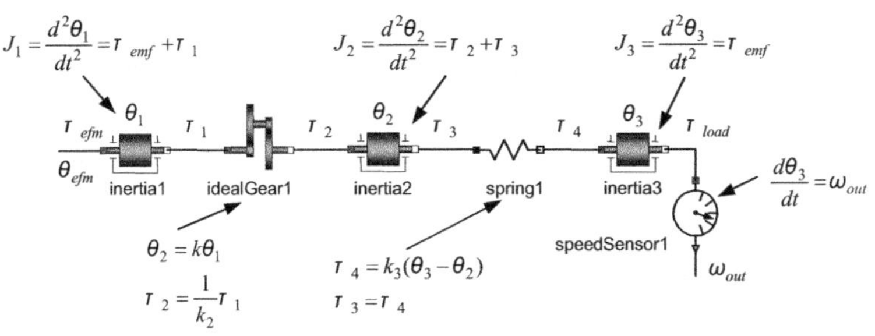

Figure 12-17. Defining classes and basic equations for components in the rotational mechanics subsystem.

12.3.5 Defining the Interfaces and Connections

When each subsystem has been defined from predefined models, the interfaces to the subsystem are given by the connectors of those components that interact with other subsystems. Each subsystem has to be defined to enable communication with the other subsystems according to the previously sketched communication structure. This requires the connector classes to be carefully chosen to be type compatible. Actually, the selection and definition of these connector interfaces is one of the most important steps in the design of a model.

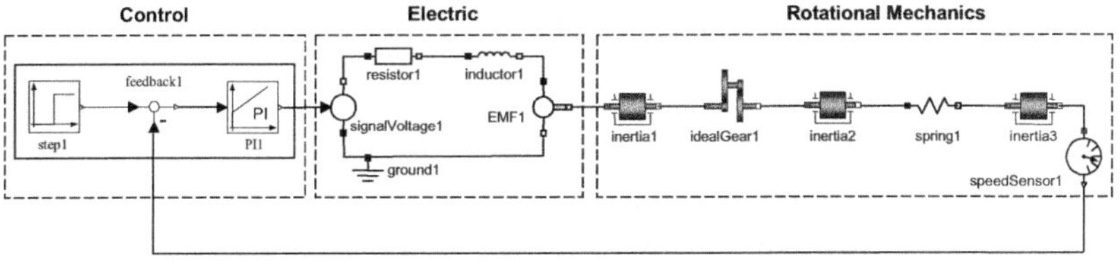

Figure 12-18. Finalizing the interfaces and connections between the subsystems, including the feedback loop.

The completed model of the DC motor servo is depicted in Figure 12-18, including the three subsystems and the feedback loop.

12.4 Designing Interfaces—Connector Classes

As in all system design, defining the interfaces between the components of a system model is one of the most important design tasks since this lays the foundation for the communication between the components, thereby also heavily influencing the decomposition of the model.

Most important is to identify the basic *requirements* behind the design of component interfaces, i.e., connector classes, that influence their structure. These requirements can be briefly stated as follows:

- It should be *easy* and *natural* to connect components. For interfaces to models of physical components it must be physically possible to connect those components.
- Component interfaces should facilitate *reuse* of existing model components in class libraries.

Fulfilling these goals requires careful design of connector classes. The number of connector classes should be kept small in order to avoid unnecessary mismatches between connectors due to different names and types of variables in the connectors.

Experience shows that it is surprisingly difficult to design connector classes that satisfy these requirements. There is a tendency for extraneous details that are created during software (model) development for various computational needs to creep into the interfaces, thereby making them harder to use and preventing component reuse. Therefore one should keep the connector classes as simple as possible, and try to avoid introducing variables that are not really necessary.

A good rule of thumb when designing connector classes for models of physical components is to identify the characteristics of (acausal) interaction in the physical real world between these components. The interaction characteristics should be simplified and abstracted to an appropriate level and reflected in the design of the connector classes. For nonphysical components, for example, signal blocks and software components in general, one has to work hard on finding the appropriate level of abstraction in the interfaces and trying these in practice for feedback on ease-of-use and reusability. The Modelica standard library contains a large number of well-designed connector classes which can serve as inspiration when designing new interfaces.

There are basically three different kinds of connector classes, reflecting three design situations:

1. If there is some kind of interaction between two *physical* components involving *energy flow*, a combination of one potential and one `flow` variable in the appropriate domain should be used for the connector class.
2. If information or *signals* are exchanged between components, `input/output` signal variables should be used in the connector class.
3. For complex interactions between components, involving several interactions of type (1) and (2) above, a hierarchically structured *composite connector* class is designed that includes one or more connectors of the appropriate type (1), (2), or (3).

When all the connectors of a component have been designed according to the three principles above, the formulation of the rest of the component class follows partly from the constraints implied by these connectors. However, these guidelines should not be followed blindly. There are several examples of domains with special conditions that deviate slightly from the above rules.

The topic of designing connector classes is discussed in more detail, including a number of examples, in Section 5.5 on page 203 in Chapter 5.

12.5 Block Diagram Models

A block diagram model can be regarded as a special case of model for which the *causality* of each interface variable has been fixed to either *input* or *output*. Such models for example, can be represented by Modelica models which have the prefixes `input` or `output` on all their connector variables, and thereby fulfill the requirements for the restricted `block` class in Modelica.

Before digital computers became common, analog computers were used for simulation. These were a physical realization of block diagrams in terms of building blocks such as multipliers, adders, integrators, etc., as depicted in Figure 12-19. These are graphical representations, for example, of basic mathematical operations like multiplication, addition, integration, and so on, that also can be expressed in textual programming language syntax. The well-known Simulink® product realizes block diagrams on digital computers and provides a graphical user interface where block diagrams can be specified, as well as an environment where block diagram models can be simulated.

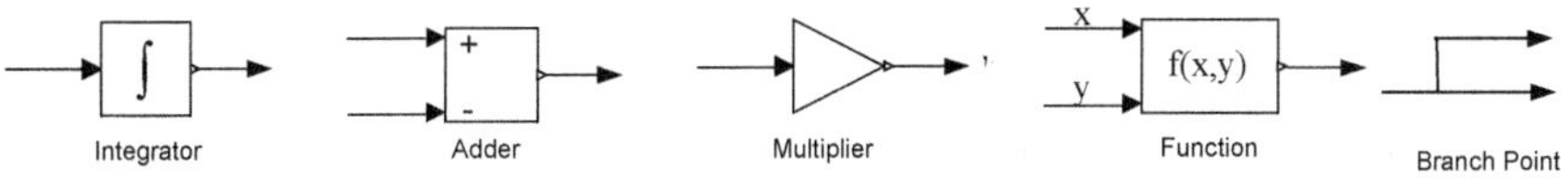

Figure 12-19. Examples of common block diagrams.

A block diagram is a more *primitive* model concept than general Modelica classes in the sense that it is valid only for specific data-flow context and thereby is less reusable. It represents a signal-oriented way of thinking, where the signal direction in terms of data flow is always known.

Block diagrams consist of blocks that are connected by arrows. A block is a transducer that transforms the incoming signals to one or more output signals. A block can represent simple arithmetic operations or functions without memory, but also operations whose results are dependent on previous input to the block, that is, with memory. Hierarchical decomposition is supported since connected blocks forming a block diagram can itself be treated as a block. While a block diagram clearly depicts the data flow in a system, it does not preserve any of the structure of the system itself, as can be seen in the block diagram model of the DC motor servo in Figure 12-20.

A small change in the model or in the set of variables we want to study may force us to rearrange the entire structure of the block diagram, which may have little similarity to the previous version. This is a clear disadvantage of a block diagram that forces many engineers in industry to redesign the block diagram models over and over again.

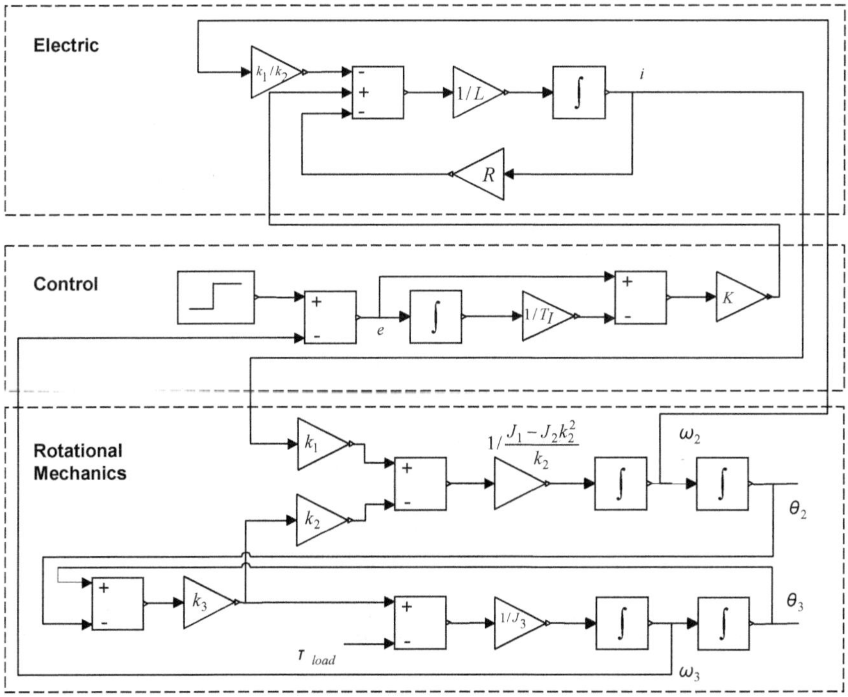

Figure 12-20. A block diagram model of the DC motor servo.

These disadvantages are not as noticeable in control engineering, where block diagrams are quite popular. The reason is that control engineers force their circuits to behave in such a way that the signal flow structure and the topological structure coincide, for example, by effectively decoupling stages and using feedback loops. A number of common block classes, for example, for use in control applications, are available in the Modelica library `Modelica.Blocks`, see Section 16.8, page 936).

12.6 Categories of Variables and Constants in Mathematical Models

It is rather obvious from the previous discussions of mathematical models and presented examples that several different categories of variables and constants can be present in those models. For a certain model under some experimental conditions, some variables play roles as inputs, others as outputs, others are internal state variables, and some are not variables but constants since they keep the same value over time.

12.6.1 Input, Output, State Variables, and Constants

The following is a list of definitions concerning variables and constants having different roles in mathematical models (see also Section 17.1.3, page 981). These roles are usually not a property of the model or the modeled system as such, but rather a consequence of a combination of a model, some experiments, or simulation, and conditions given by what we want to study. However, we should be aware that models can be formulated in more or less general or reusable ways. An acausal equation-based model fits many different data-flow contexts with different roles of variables, for example, as inputs or outputs, whereas a model for which the variables have been fixed in either input or output roles only fits a few experimental settings.

- *Constant*—a quantity in the model that does not vary with time. Such a quantity is declared with the `constant` prefix in Modelica.
- *Model parameter*—a constant in the model that is determined by the system, that is, a *system parameter*, or a constant that can be changed in order to give the system different properties, that is, a *design parameter*. It is declared with the `parameter` prefix in Modelica, and is constant during a simulation run, but can be modified between simulation runs.
- *Variable*—a quantity in the model that varies with time, sometimes also called *signal*.
- *Output variable*—a variable whose behavior we want to observe. Usually denoted by $y(t)$. Whether a variable is an output variable is not a property of the modeled system, but is determined by what we want to study. However, it is often the case that we also want to observe a few state variables (see below).
- *Input variable*—a variable that affects the model behavior without being affected by the model's other variables, that is, an *external signal*, and whose time variations we *can* control, usually denoted by $u(t)$.
- *Disturbance signal*—an external signal whose time variations we cannot affect, usually denoted by $w(t)$, but usually $u(t)$ and $w(t)$ are grouped together into a single input vector denoted $u(t)$.
- *Internal variable*—a model variable that is neither an output, an input, nor a disturbance signal.
- *State variable*—for continuous-time ODE models: an internal variable whose time derivative appears in the model, usually denoted by $x(t)$, and its time derivative by $\dot{x}(t)$. A state variable must be of type `Real` or a subtype of `Real` in Modelica. If we want to study some state variable $x_i(t)$, we can always introduce a corresponding output variable $y_j(t)$ together with an equation $y_j(t)=x_i(t)$, or directly observe the state variable. For hybrid models containing discrete-time variables, a more general but less precise definition might be appropriate: a variable that needs to be stored and updated during the simulation in order to compute the output. For DAEs the set of state variables is

a selection of some dynamic variables $x(t)$ together with some algebraic variables $y(t)$ (see also Section 18.2.6, page 1016).

- *Algebraic variable*—a variable that appears in algebraic equations, but whose derivative does not appear in the model, usually included in the set of variables denoted by $y(t)$ even if we are not interested in observing that variable.

Any of the above-mentioned model variables—$y(t)$, $u(t)$, $w(t)$, $\dot{x}(t)$ and $x(t)$—can denote a scalar if there is just one variable of that kind in the model, but usually a vector, i.e.:

$$x(t) = \begin{pmatrix} x_1(t) \\ \vdots \\ x_n(t) \end{pmatrix}, \quad y(t) = \begin{pmatrix} y_1(t) \\ \vdots \\ y_r(t) \end{pmatrix}, \quad u(t) = \begin{pmatrix} u_1(t) \\ \vdots \\ u_m(t) \end{pmatrix}, \text{ etc.} \tag{12-5}$$

A block diagram model of a generic system with outputs $y(t)$, internal state variables $x(t)$, controllable inputs $u(t)$, and disturbance inputs $w(t)$ is depicted in Figure 12-21. In the following we group $u(t)$ and $w(t)$ together into a single input vector denoted $u(t)$.

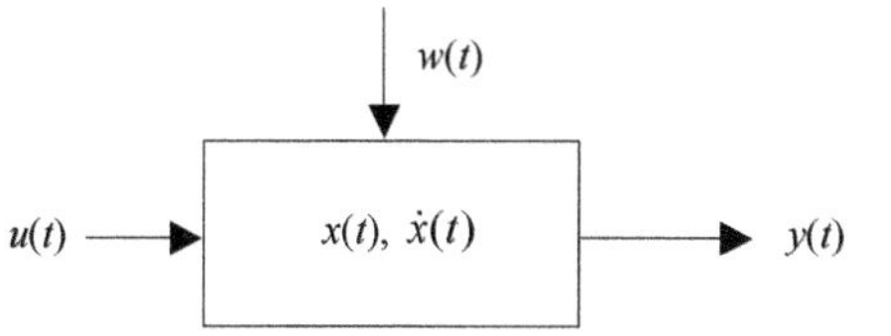

Figure 12-21. A simple block diagram model of a generic system.

12.7 Types of Equations in Mathematical Models

So far, we have seen many examples of equations in Modelica models. One might ask what is a natural classification of different categories of equations in mathematical models intended for simulation, and what subset of those categories can be represented in the Modelica language? The form of equations derived from simple Modelica models was briefly discussed in Chapter 2, Section 2.20.1, page 64.

In this section we will give a short overview of different types of equations and their relation to Modelica, whereas in Chapter 17, page 979, we will go into more depth concerning the general form of the hybrid DAE representation that is used to represent the full range of mathematical models expressible in Modelica. We exclude integral equations from this overview.

12.7.1 Ordinary Differential Equations—ODEs

Ordinary differential equations (ODEs), arise in most mathematical models of continuous dynamic systems since the time dependency in those systems usually is reflected by the presence of time derivatives of state variables of the corresponding models. Newton's force law that the force F is equal to the mass m times the second-derivative $\ddot{s}$ of the position s with respect to time (i.e., the acceleration) is a simple example of a second order ODE:

$$m\ddot{s}(t) = F(t) \tag{12-6}$$

By introducing an additional variable $v(t)$, we can get rid of the second derivative. After a slight rearrangement of the first equation we have all derivatives on the left-hand side (in explicit form) and they are all first-order derivatives. This means that we have transformed the system into a first-order ODE system in explicit form:

$$\dot{v}(t) = \frac{F(t)}{m}$$
$$\dot{s}(t) = v(t) \tag{12-7}$$

An ODE system in this form is especially efficient to solve numerically. The general structure of an ODE system in explicit state space form is the following, with inputs $u(t)$, outputs $y(t)$, and state variables $x(t)$:

$$\dot{x}(t) = f(x(t), u(t))$$
$$y(t) = g(x(t), u(t)) \tag{12-8}$$

Here we have also introduced outputs $y(t)$ that are directly computable from the state variables and the inputs but do not influence the solution for the state variables $x(t)$.

12.7.2 Algebraic Equations

Algebraic equations are relations between variables not involving derivatives of any variables. Such equations arise naturally in models of natural and artificial systems, especially when some kind of constraint is involved. For example, the Cartesian coordinates $\{x_1, x_2\}$ of the mass in the pendulum system depicted in Figure 2-2 fulfill the following algebraic equation that the length of the pendulum is L according to Pythagoras's law:

$$x_1^2 + x_2^2 = L^2 \tag{12-9}$$

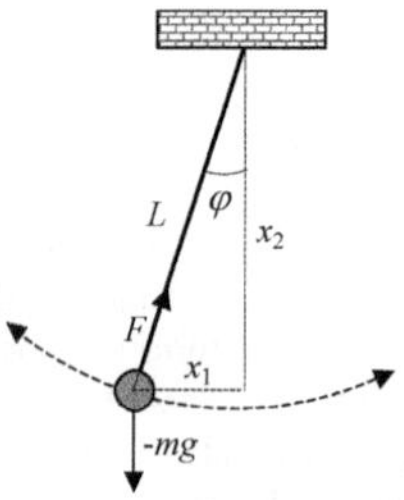

Figure 12-22. A planar pendulum.

Variables that are defined by algebraic equations and whose derivatives do not appear in the model are called algebraic variables. Some of those variables may also be output variables.

The *general implicit form* of a system of *algebraic equations* (not including differential equations) is as follows:

$$g(x(t), u(t), y(t)) = 0 \tag{12-10}$$

12.7.3 Differential Algebraic Equations—DAEs

A system of differential and algebraic equations (DAEs), include both differential and algebraic equations. For example, the pendulum model equations below are a DAE system of five differential and two algebraic equations, involving the variables x_1,x_2,v_1,v_2,φ,ω,F, and the constants L, m, g. We have replaced the previous Pythagoras-style algebraic equation by two algebraic equations involving x_1 and x_2 respectively, which still preserve the length constraint of the pendulum.

$$\begin{aligned}
m\dot{v}_1 &= -F\sin(\varphi) \\
m\dot{v}_2 &= F\cos(\varphi) - mg \\
\dot{x}_1 &= v_1 \\
\dot{x}_2 &= v_2 \\
\dot{\varphi} &= \omega \\
x_1 &= L\sin(\varphi) \\
x_2 &= -L\cos(\varphi)
\end{aligned} \tag{12-11}$$

The general *implicit form of a DAE system* is as follows, of which the above example is a special case where $x = \{ x_1, x_2, v_1, v_2, \varphi \}$, $u = \{\}$, and $y = \{\omega, F\}$.

$$\begin{aligned}
f(x(t), \dot{x}(t), u(t), y(t)) = 0 \\
g(x(t), u(t), y(t)) = 0
\end{aligned} \tag{12-12}$$

12.7.4 Difference Equations

Difference equations occur in discrete-time models and typically relate values of quantities at different discrete points in time, e.g. between the times t_k and t_{k+1}. The general explicit form of a system of difference equations can be expressed as

$$x(t_{k+1}) = f(x(t_k), u(t_k), t_k) \tag{12-13}$$

Difference equations are treated in more detail in Chapter 13.

12.7.5 Conditional Equations and Hybrid DAEs

Conditional equations include equations that become active only at certain points in time, or during certain time periods. This kind of equation is used to define the notion of event, and is treated in more detail in Chapter 13. Hybrid DAEs are DAEs which also may include some conditional equations. The hybrid DAE equation form is the basic equation representation behind Modelica, and is described in detail in Chapter 17, page 979.

12.7.6 Partial Differential Equations—PDEs

Partial differential equation (PDE)-based models allow derivatives also by space coordinate variables and not only by time, as in ordinary differential equations. Typical space coordinates are x, y, and z in a three-dimensional Cartesian coordinate system. Phenomena modeled by PDEs are distributed in space in one or more dimensions, for example, heat diffusion, fluid flows, and so on. The following is the one-dimensional diffusion equation along the z coordinate:

$$\frac{\partial a}{\partial t} = \sigma \frac{\partial^2 a}{\partial z^2} \tag{12-14}$$

The current version of Modelica cannot directly represent models containing PDEs. However, ongoing work is extending Modelica to handle PDEs, see Section 8.10, page 400. Still, simple one-dimensional PDEs can rather easily be handled in the current version of Modelica by explicit discretization along a space coordinate (see Section 15.9, page 875).

12.8 Statespace Equations for Continuous Systems

We have earlier made a general definition of a *state variable* as a variable that needs to be stored and updated during the simulation in order to compute the output of the model. For continuous-time system models, these variables are those whose time derivatives appear in the model. There is a standard formulation of the equations of certain mathematical models of dynamic systems called explicit state space models, based on the derivatives of state variables (in the discrete-time case the state variable values for the next time step) being *explicit* on the left side of the equations.

These models are attractive as a basic mathematical representation since they usually are easier and more efficient to solve and to analyze than more complicated models, while being able to represent a fairly large spectrum of application models. However, we should be aware that many models cannot be transformed into an explicit state space form. This simple form is not a requirement of the Modelica language, which is based on the more general implicit hybrid DAE form described in Chapter 17, page 979.

12.8.1 Explicit State Space Form

The basic ODE *state space explicit* form of the continuous *equations* of a model is presented below, where $x(t)$ is the set of state variables, i.e., the variables for which time derivatives occur in the model, $u(t)$ represents the input variables, and $y(t)$ represents the output variables and/or algebraic variables. The model is said to be in explicit state space form if only the derivatives are present on the left-hand side of the first equation.

$$\begin{aligned} \dot{x}(t) &= f(x(t), u(t)) \\ y(t) &= g(x(t), u(t)) \end{aligned} \qquad (12\text{-}15)$$

Here $x(t)$, $u(t)$, and $y(t)$ are vectors and $f(t)$ and $g(t)$ are vector-valued functions. State space models that have not been manipulated into this form are in an implicit form. The *semi-explicit* form of a DAE appears as follows:

$$\begin{aligned} \dot{x}(t) &= f(x(t), y(t), u(t)) \\ y(t) &= g(x(t), u(t)) \end{aligned} \qquad (12\text{-}16)$$

Discrete and hybrid versions of DAEs are defined in Section 17.1, page 979.

12.8.2 Linear Models

A *linear model* is an explicit state space model for which the functions $f(x,u)$ and $g(x,u)$ can be expressed as linear functions of their arguments. This enables a matrix formulation of those functions as expressed below, where A, B, C, and D are matrices:

$$\begin{aligned} f(x(t), u(t)) &= A x(t) + B x(t) \\ g(x(t), u(t)) &= C x(t) + D u(t) \end{aligned} \qquad (12\text{-}17)$$

The dimensions of these matrices are as follows, A: $n \times n$, B: $n \times m$, C: $r \times n$, and D: $r \times m$, which is compatible with $x(t)$ being an n-dimensional vector, $u(t)$ being an m-dimensional vector, and $y(t)$ being an r-dimensional vector.

12.9 Summary

In this chapter, we have presented an object-oriented, component-based process on how to arrive at mathematical models of the systems we are interested in, and compared this to the traditional modeling approaches, e.g. based on programming language or block diagram representation. We have also made a short overview of different kinds of notation and equations in mathematical models, as well as presenting the state space model representation for continuous systems.

12.10 Literature

General principles for object-oriented modeling and design are described in (Rumbaugh 1991; Booch 1991). A general discussion of block oriented model design principles can be found in (Ljung and Glad 1994), whereas (Andersson 1994) describes object-oriented mathematical modeling in some depth. Simulink®, described in (MathWorks 2001), is the currently most well-known tool for block-oriented modeling.

Many concepts and terms in software engineering and in modeling/simulation are described in the standard software engineering glossary: (IEEE Std 610.12-1990) together with the IEEE Standard glossary of modeling and simulation (IEEE Std 610.3-1989).

12.11 Exercises

Exercise 12-1:

What is the difference between top-down and bottom-up modeling?

Exercise 12-2:

What are the rules to follow when defining connector interfaces?

Exercise 12-3:

What are the advantages of a component-based model over a flat model?

Chapter 13

Discrete Events and Hybrid and Embedded System Modeling

Physical systems evolve continuously over time, whereas certain man-made systems evolve by discrete steps between states. For example, a binary digital computer internally switches between many instances of the discrete states 0 and 1. This discrete approximation enormously simplifies the understanding and use of a computer, since otherwise one would have to deal with the physics of transistors continuously changing voltage between the level representing 0 and the level representing 1.

These discrete changes, or *events*—when something happens—occur at certain points in time. We talk about *discrete event dynamic systems* as opposed to *continuous dynamic systems* directly based on the physical laws derived from first principles, for example, from conservation of energy, matter, or momentum.

A *hybrid* system contains both discrete parts and continuous parts. A typical example is a digital computer system interacting with the external physical world, as depicted schematically in Figure 13-1. This is, however, a very simplified picture since the discrete parts usually are distributed together with physical components in many technical systems. For example, consider a paper mill where local digital controllers are integrated as parts in the paper-making machines.

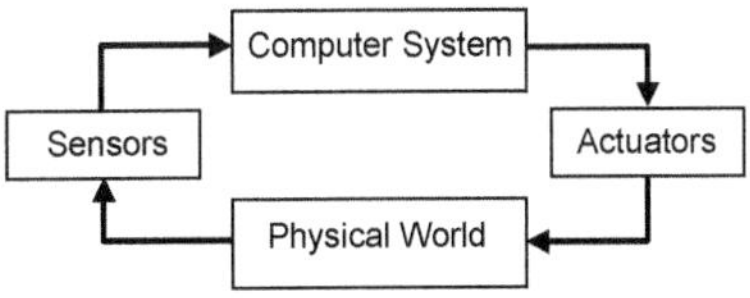

Figure 13-1. A hybrid system in which a discrete computer senses and controls the continuous physical world.

Since hybrid models contain both discrete and continuous components, they are very hard to treat analytically. Computer simulation is usually the only way to understand such systems, apart from certain simplified cases.

This chapter gives an introduction to modeling and simulating discrete event dynamic systems and hybrid dynamic systems using Modelica. First, the notions of events, use events, and event-based formalisms are informally introduced for modeling a number of discrete systems as well as relating several well-known discrete event-modeling formalisms to equivalent forms in Modelica. Both clocked and unclocked modeling styles are presented, including several model examples presented in clocked and unclocked versions. We continue by presenting a few hybrid model examples based on the *hybrid DAE* mathematical representation (differential, algebraic, and discrete equations) used for hybrid models in

Modelica. Finally, a detailed presentation of Modelica clocked modeling constructs and clocked state machines is given.

Before going into the details about discrete modeling concepts such as events, we will in the next section say a few words about the general characteristics of an important class of discrete event dynamic systems that can be modeled using Modelica.

13.1 Real-Time and Reactive Systems

Reactive system is an important subclass of real-time computer systems with discrete characteristics, usually with a general structure roughly corresponding to that depicted in Figure 13-1. Such systems continuously *react* to their environment at a speed or rate determined by that environment, that is, the computer system is subject to *time constraints* of the environment. *Reactive* systems differ from ordinary *batch* computational software systems that compute certain results based on some input data without any time constraints, and *interactive* systems that continuously react to users and to the environment, but subject to their own constraints, for example, load sharing in an operating system, and without sharp time constraints from the environment. Most industrial real-time systems are reactive, for example, control systems and supervision and signal processing systems, but also certain communication protocols and man-machine interfaces.

We can generally characterize reactive systems by the following major features:

- *Concurrency.* Reactive systems are at least subject to concurrency between the environment and the computer system itself. Additional concurrency is usually the case since it is both natural and convenient to regard such systems as a number of parallel interacting subsystems that cooperate to achieve the desired behavior. Reactive systems are usually decomposed into logically concurrent components without this being reflected into an implementation on concurrent hardware, even though implementations on such hardware sometimes occur, for example, to achieve increased reliability or performance.
- *Time constraints.* These systems are subject to strict time requirements that concern both the input data rates and the required output response times. These constraints need to be taken into account during the system design and expressed in the system specifications, as well as being checked with regard to the final implementation. Efficient implementations are often required to fulfill tight time constraints.
- *Determinism.* The output of a reactive system is entirely determined by the input values and by the occurrence times of these inputs, that is, it is deterministic. By contrast, interactive systems such as operating systems are usually nondeterministic since their behavior also depends on factors such as CPU load.
- *Reliability.* Reactive systems are often subject to high reliability requirements. For example, control systems for high-speed trains or nuclear reactors cannot be allowed to fail. For certain applications formal verification methods should be considered, which usually require the use of clean declarative system specification formalisms.
- *Hardware/software.* Reactive systems are often realized by a combination of hardware and software, for reasons of performance, cost-effectiveness, and flexibility. For example, a modeled control system or modeled physical subsystem can interact directly in real time with hardware components together with the surrounding physical environment.

One might ask how well the Modelica modeling formalism matches these requirements. There is quite a good match, as we will see in the rest of this chapter. Concurrency is natural since modeled objects evolve concurrently over time. Time aspects can be efficiently modeled, and specified behavior is deterministic. Since Modelica is a declarative formalism, models should hopefully be somewhat amenable to formal verification techniques for enhancing reliability. Modeled subsystems can be realized as efficient implementations of reactive computer systems that interact directly with the physical environment in real time. Alternatively, both the reactive system and the surrounding physical environment can be modeled and simulated. A third alternative is to mix simulated subsystems with hardware components, that is, hardware-in-the-loop simulation.

13.2 Events

What is an *event*? Using everyday language an event is simply *something that happens*. This is also true for events in the abstract mathematical sense. An event in the real world, for example, a train departure, is always associated with a point in time. However, abstract mathematical events are not always associated with time but they are usually ordered, that is, an event ordering is defined. By associating an event with a point in time, for example, as in Figure 13-2 below, we will automatically obtain an ordering of events to form an event history. Since this is also the case for events in the real world we will in the following always associate a point in *time* to each event. However, such an ordering is *partial* since several events can occur at the same point in time. To achieve a total ordering we can also use causal relationships between events, priorities of events, or, if these are not enough, simply pick an order based on some other event property.

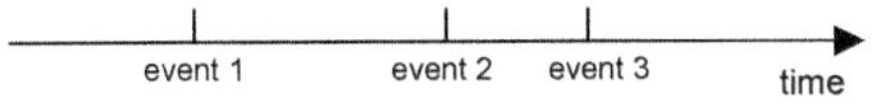

Figure 13-2. Events are ordered in time and form an event history.

The next question is whether the notion of event is a useful and desirable abstraction, that is, do events fit into our overall goal of providing an object-oriented declarative formalism for modeling the world? There is no question that events actually exist, for example, a cocktail party event, a car collision event, or a voltage transition event in an electrical circuit. A set of events without structure can be viewed as a rather low-level abstraction—an unstructured mass of small low-level items that just happen.

The trick to arrive at declarative models about *what is*, rather than imperative recipes of how things *are done*, is to focus on *relations* between events, and between events and other abstractions. Relations between events can be expressed using declarative formalisms such as equations. The object-oriented modeling machinery provided by Modelica can be used to bring a high-level model structure and grouping of variables affected by events, relations between events, conditions for events, and behavior in the form of equations associated with events. This brings order into what otherwise could become a chaotic mess of low-level items.

Our abstract "mathematical" notion of event is an approximation compared to real events. For example, events in Modelica *take no time*—this is the most important abstraction of the *synchronous* principle to be described later. This abstraction is not completely correct with respect to our cocktail party event example since there is no question that a cocktail party actually takes some time. However, experience has shown that abstract events that take no time are more useful as a modeling primitive than events that have duration. Instead, our cocktail party should be described as a model class containing variables such as the number of guests that are related by equations active at primitive events like opening the party, the arrival of a guest, ending the party, serving the drinks, etc.

To conclude, an event in Modelica is something that happens that has the following four properties:

- A *point* in time that is instantaneous, that is, has zero duration.
- A clock variable or `Boolean` *event condition* that changes value for the event to happen.
- A set of *variables* that are associated with the event, that is, are referenced or explicitly changed by equations associated with the event.

- Some *behavior* associated with the event, expressed as *conditional equations* that become active or are deactivated at the event. *Instantaneous equations* is a special case of conditional equations that are active only *at* events.

Here we speak about event behavior expressed as equations in a wide sense, since algorithm sections containing assignment statements also can be viewed as a kind of equation systems. In the next section, we will further motivate the choice of conditional equations to express behavior at events.

13.2.1 Basing Event Behavior on Conditional Equations

One of the key issues concerning the use of events for modeling is how to express behavior associated with events. The traditional imperative way of thinking about behavior at events is a piece of code that is activated when the event condition becomes `true` and then executes certain actions, for example, as in the when-statement skeleton below:

```
when event-conditions then
   event-action1 ;
   event-action2 ;
   ...
end when;
```

However, this contradicts our ambitions to provide a declarative mathematical equation-based way of thinking about modeling. Let us instead try to use equations to express what happens at an event.

If we recapitulate the continuous modeling case, the occurrence of time derivatives in equations, that is, differential equations, is enough to provide the modeling power to describe a continuous system, relating the past, present, and future, for example, as in the extremely simple one-equation example below where the time derivative of x is equal to the constant 1:

$$\dot{x} = 1 \tag{13-1}$$

If instead we want to model a similar discrete system example, for example, with a time-discretization of one second between events, we will instead of the differential equation need to use a difference equation as the one below that relates the current value of x, $x_k = x(t_k)$, to the value one second ago, $x_{k-1} = x(t_{k-1})$:

$$x_k = x_{k-1} + 1 \tag{13-2}$$

This difference equation is valid only at the periodic events. Between the events the value of x is constant, i.e., its time derivative is zero, as expressed by the equation below:

$$\dot{x} = 0 \tag{13-3}$$

We thus have the situation for the discrete system model that *different* sets of equations are valid at different points in time: the difference equation is valid only at events, whereas the equation $\dot{x} = 0$ is valid between events, as depicted in Figure 13-3.

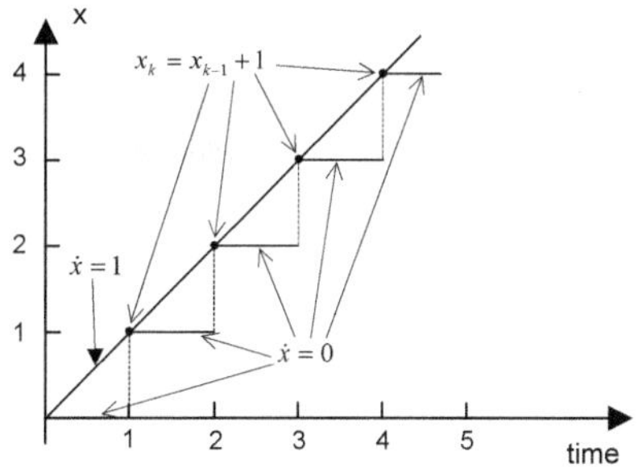

Figure 13-3. A continuous-time model giving a straight line versus a discrete-time model where different sets of equations are active during different time periods.

Through this example we have arrived at the idea of *conditional equations* as the basis of defining behavior at events. Different sets of equations can be active during different time periods as defined by the *condition* associated with each conditional equation or alternatively by clocks defining which equations are conditionally active at clock ticks of *clocked partitions* (Section 13.6.8, page 705).

To conclude, the *behavior* of an event can be defined as a combination of:

- Sets of equations associated with the event, that become active or are deactivated at the event
- An activation time period determined by the event condition

This topic is further discussed in the context of specific Modelica language constructs for expressing event behavior as presented in Section 13.2.5 on page 600 in this chapter.

These considerations lead us to the notions of discrete-time variables versus continuous-time variables, together with the synchronous data-flow principle for Modelica. These ideas are presented in the following two sections.

Regarding the simple example above, it is easy to see the connection between the discrete-time model and the corresponding continuous-time model. Let us use a shorter period of h seconds between events and modify the difference equation as follows:

$$x_k = x_{k-1} + h \tag{13-4}$$

After a slight rearrangement of the terms in the difference equations, dividing by h on each side, and letting $h \to 0$, we arrive at a numerical approximation of the derivative $\dot{x}$ of the continuous-time equation at the left-hand side of the difference equation:

$$\dot{x} \approx \frac{x_k - x_{k-1}}{h} = 1 \tag{13-5}$$

13.2.2 Discrete-Time versus Continuous-Time Variables

As already mentioned in Section 2.15, page 55, and in Section 6.9.3, page 281, so-called *discrete-time* variables in Modelica only change value at discrete points in time, i.e., at event instants. There are two kinds of discrete-time variables: *unclocked discrete-time* variables keep their values constant between events (implicit hold), whereas *clocked discrete-time* variables (Section 13.6.3, page 697) only have defined values at clock tick events for their associated clocks and are undefined between events. This is in contrast to continuous-time variables, which usually evolve continuously over time. To summarize:

- An *unclocked discrete-time variable* is defined at any point in time, changes value only at events.

- A *clocked discrete-time variable* is defined and changes value only at clock tick events for the clock associated to the variable. Such a clock has built-in type `Clock`.
- A *continuous-time variable* is defined and may change value at any point in time.

Figure 13-4 shows a graph of an unclocked discrete-time variable, Figure 13-5 shows a clocked discrete-time variable, whereas Figure 13-6 shows two evolving continuous-time variables.

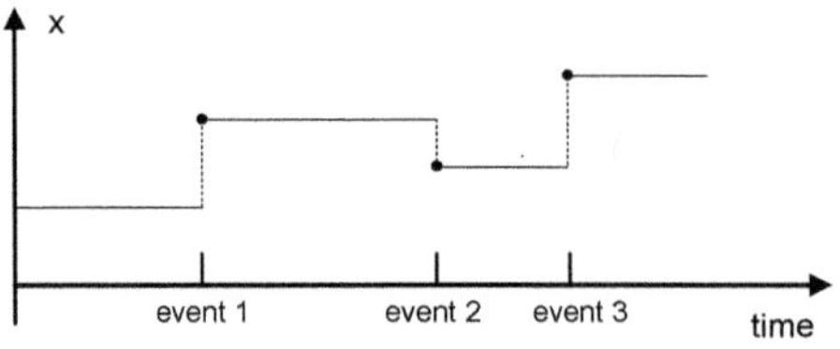

Figure 13-4. An unclocked discrete-time variable `x` changes value only at event instants and keeps its value between events.

Figure 13-5 shows a clocked discrete-time variable which is defined and may change value only at clock tick events for its associated clock (here an aperiodic clock). Note that discrete-time variables obtain their new values at an event instant by solving the equations (together with algorithm sections viewed as sets of equations) active at the event. The previous values can be obtained via the `pre` function (Section 13.2.5.11) for unclocked discrete-time variables and via the `previous` function (Section 13.2.5.13) for clocked discrete-time variables.

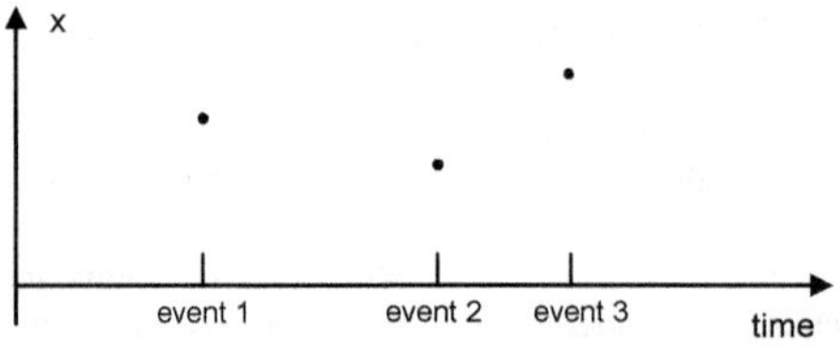

Figure 13-5. A clocked discrete-time variable `x` is defined and changes value only at clock tick event instants and is undefined between events.

Variables in Modelica are discrete-time if they are declared using the `discrete` prefix, e.g. `discrete Real y`, or if they are of type `Boolean`, `Integer`, or `String`, or of types constructed from discrete types or if they are clocked (Section 13.6.3, page 697). A Real unclocked variable assigned in a when-statement or being on the left-hand side of an equation in a when-equation is an unclocked discrete-time variable even if it is not declared with the discrete prefix, which is somewhat strange. See also in Section 3.11.2, page 99, for more information regarding discrete-time and continuous-time variables and expressions.

A Real variable not assigned in any when-statement and not being on the left-hand side of an equation inside a when-equation and not related to a clock is continuous-time. It is not possible to have continuous-time Boolean, Integer, or String variables.

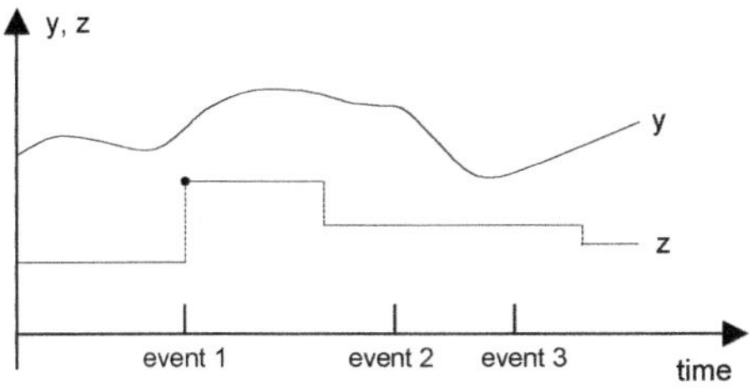

Figure 13-6. Continuous-time variables like y and z may change value both between and at events. The z variable looks like a discrete-time variable, but is continuous-time since it also changes between events.

In Figure 13-6, both y and z are classified as continuous-time variables and are allowed to change at any point in time. The y variable is a continuous function of time whereas z is discontinuous at several points in time. Two of those points where z is discontinuous are not associated with any events, which will create some extra work and possibly numerical difficulties for the numerical equation solver. In this case, it would have been better to have z as a discrete-time variable with events at all its points of discontinuity.

13.2.3 Synchronous Data-flow Principle for Modelica

Many of the considerations discussed so far in this chapter can be summarized into a few rules as the *synchronous data-flow principle* for Modelica, consisting of the following principles:

- The synchronous principle that events take no time.
- The single assignment principle for variables and equations/assignments, also enforced by data-flow programming languages.
- The continuous-discrete unification and concurrency principle.

The synchronous principle is the basis for the event concept, whereas the single assignment rule ensures that the variables are always defined by the system of equations. The continuous-discrete unification and concurrency principle states how discrete-time and continuous-time variables and behavior are unified in the same framework. A more detailed description of the Modelica language rules in this matter is available below in Section 13.2.3.3, page 598 in this chapter.

13.2.3.1 Synchronous Principle

The synchronous principle has been invented to make modeling and programming of time-related systems easier and less error prone, as well as giving more efficient implementations. It can be stated as follows:

- Computation and communication at an event instant does *not* take time, i.e., is instantaneous. If computation or communication time has to be simulated, this property has to be explicitly modeled.

This principle is the same as used by typical synchronous languages for real-time applications, which allow programs to be considered as instantaneously reacting to external events. Each internal or output event of the program is precisely dated with respect to the flow of input events. The consequence is that the behavior of the program is fully *deterministic*, that is, gives the same behavior when reexecuted with the same inputs occurring at the same times, both from the functional and from the timing point of view.

The synchronous hypothesis is the same as assuming that the program reacts quickly enough to handle all external events in the right order, which, for example, is essential for hardware-in-the-loop simulations.

This hypothesis is often quite realistic, and can be checked by a combination of measurements and analysis.

As a counterexample and comparison, consider a small application in the Ada programming language which has asynchronous parallel processes. A process `A` signals "minutes" to a process `B` by counting 60 "seconds":

```
loop    // Small Ada program. Process A is signaling process B
   delay 60; B.Minute;
end;
```

This program does not give the intended behavior of letting process `B` precisely count minutes, since process `A` first waits 60 seconds, and then signals process `B`, which eventually receives the `Minute` signal. The total time is more than 60 seconds since the communication to process `B` takes some time. The program is nondeterministic, that is, nonrepeatable, since the communication time is dependent on external factors such as operating system load. An additional disadvantage is that the interprocess communication overhead in such a language usually is substantial.

Finally we should not forget that modeling and simulation without real-time constraints also benefits considerably from the synchronous principle by simpler and less errorprone modeling, as well as more efficient simulation.

13.2.3.2 Single Assignment Principle

The *single assignment principle*, stated below, is the same as you might remember from basic mathematics courses: the number of variables and the number of equations must be the same for a system of equations to be solvable. This applies to any Modelica model to be simulated, since the model first needs to be converted to a total system of equations before simulation. The single assignment principle is also adhered to by all pure functional and data-flow languages: *a variable can be assigned at most once*.

- *Single assignment principle for equations*: the total number of "equations" is identical to the total number of "unknown" variables to be solved for.

There are a number of special considerations in Modelica on how to count equations within conditional equations, and how to count assignment statements as equations, that is, within algorithm sections but not within function bodies. These rules are described in Section 8.1.3, page 348.

The single assignment principle also prevents a variable, for example, from being defined by two "equations," which would give rise to conflicts (overconstrained, e.g., $x = 2$ and $x = 3$) or nondeterministic behavior. Moreover, this principle is the basis for the declarative properties of Modelica by allowing only a single defining "equation" for each variable.

13.2.3.3 Continuous-Discrete Unification and Concurrency Principle

The following two rules state how the unclocked discrete and continuous parts of a model are unified, that is, how the discrete part interprets the continuous part and vice versa. Additionally, the second rule states that concurrent behavior can be represented by concurrently active equations.

- *Variables*: All variables keep their actual values until these values are explicitly changed. Unclocked variable values can be accessed at any point in time during "continuous integration" (i.e., during numerical solution of the continuous part of the system of equations), and at event instants, whereas clocked variable values can be accessed only at clock tick event instants and are not accessible between such event instants except by applying the hold operator to the variables.

- *Behavior*: At every point in time, during solution of the continuous part of the equation system between events, and at event instants, the *active* equations express relations between variables which have to be fulfilled *concurrently*. Equations are not active if the corresponding if-branch, when-equation, or clocked partition in which the equation is present is not active because the corresponding condition currently evaluates to `false` or the clock is not currently at a tick point.

13.2.4 Creating Events

After this initial discussion of events, the synchronous data-flow principle, and behavior based on conditional equations, as well as discrete-time variables that change values at events, a natural question remains: How are events *created*? In fact, we already have the answer from the previous discussion and from earlier chapters: events may occur naturally, created in the physical world external to the modeled system, or are created internally in the simulated computer model through various mechanisms.

Events can be classified according to where they come from, that is, *external* and *internal* events, or how they are created internally in a simulated model, that is, *time events*, *clock-based events*, and *state events*.

13.2.4.1 External versus Internal Events

The question of external versus internal events should be stated relative to a modeled subsystem. An external event can be triggered by signals in the external world, as in Figure 13-7 below, or by another modeled subsystem in the total system model. Internal events are triggered by changes in `time`, state variables, or output variables of the subsystem in question.

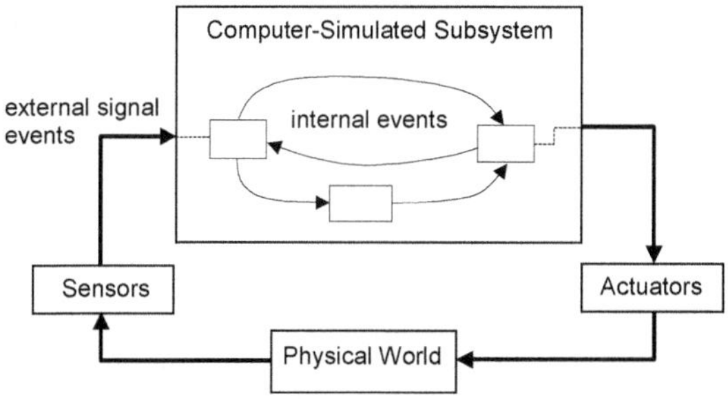

Figure 13-7. External events are related to external input variables whereas internal events are related to internal model variables.

Thus, to summarize:

- External events are related to the input variables of a subsystem.
- Internal events are related to internal state variables or output variables of a subsystem, internal clock variables, or the built-in `time` variable.

13.2.4.2 Scheduled Time Events

Time events are directly related to value changes of the built-in continuous evolving variable `time` in a way that makes it possible to predict the point in time for the event some time in advance, before it actually happens. Such events can be handled more efficiently by the simulator since they can be *scheduled* in advance.

A time event can be created by a conditional discrete-time expression involving `time` which is used in an unclocked when-equation or when-statement, or in some other context, for example, expressions of the form:

```
time >= discrete-time expression
time <  discrete-time expression
```

The whole conditional expression apart from the variable `time` needs to have unclocked discrete-time variability, that is, contain constants, parameters, and/or unclocked discrete-time variables, in order to be able to predict the event ahead of time.

For example, the condition `time>=10.0` in the when-equation below will cause a time-event at `time=10.0` since it becomes `true` at approximately (floating-point numbers might not be exact) that time instant:

```
when time>=10.0 then
  ...
end when;
```

Another way to cause a time event is to pass a time expression as an argument to one of the built-in mathematical functions with discontinuities described in Section 13.2.5.19, page 613 in this chapter, for example, as in the function call `sign(time-10)`. The built-in functions `sample`, `initial`, and `terminal` described in Section 13.2.5, page 600, can also be used to create time events since they become `true` at well-specified instants in time. Time events are primarily used for model related reasons.

13.2.4.3 Clock-Based Events

Clock-based events (Section 13.6, page 694) are directly related to the ticks of clock variables. Thus they are similar to time events in the sense that it is usually possible to predict the next clock tick before it actually happens, at least for repetitive synchronous clocks. This makes it possible for the simulator to efficiently handle repetitive clocked events since they can also be *scheduled* in advance.

For example, a clocked when-equation (Section 13.6.6, page 13.6.6) which activates at clock tick events from `clock` can appear as follows:

```
when clock then
  ...
end when;
```

13.2.4.4 State Events

State events usually cannot be scheduled in advance, and are related to value changes in the state variables of a model in a wide sense, also including input and output variables. A state event can be induced by a conditional expression involving at least one state variable, for example, as in the when-equation below where an event is generated and handled each time `sin(x)` becomes greater than 0.5 as a result of value changes in the state variable `x`:

```
when sin(x)>0.5 then
  ...
end when;
```

A state-event can also be induced by passing an expression containing a reference to a state variable to one of the built-in functions described in Section 13.2.5.19, for example, as in `mod(x-5,2)`.

The Modelica simulator is continually watching event-inducing expressions, for example, the above examples `sin(x)>0.5` and `mod(x-5,2)`, during the numerical solution of the continuous part of the system of equations. For more details, see Section 18.2.5.4, page 1014.

State events can be created for modeling reasons as in the above when-equation. However, a more common use is automatic triggering of state events to get better performance and to avoid numerical difficulties for the solver at discontinuities.

13.2.5 Event-Related Built-in Functions and Operators

Modelica provides a number of built-in functions and operators related to events and time, which you will find quite useful in discrete and hybrid modeling. Some functions generate events, some generate clocks or convert between clocked values and unclocked values, some can be used to express conditions for triggering events, one function prevents events, and some operators and functions provide access to variable values before the current event as well as causing discontinuous change of variable values at an event.

All clocked event-related operators and functions are not presented here. Some are described in the detailed overview of clock-based modeling in Section 13.6, page 694.

13.2.5.1 Initialization Actions Triggered by initial()

The function call `initial()` returns `true` at an instant immediately before the beginning of the simulation, when `time` still is equal to `time.start` (usually `time`=0). By using `initial()` somewhere in the code we can generate a fictitious event immediately before the start of the simulation, for example, as depicted in Figure 13-8.

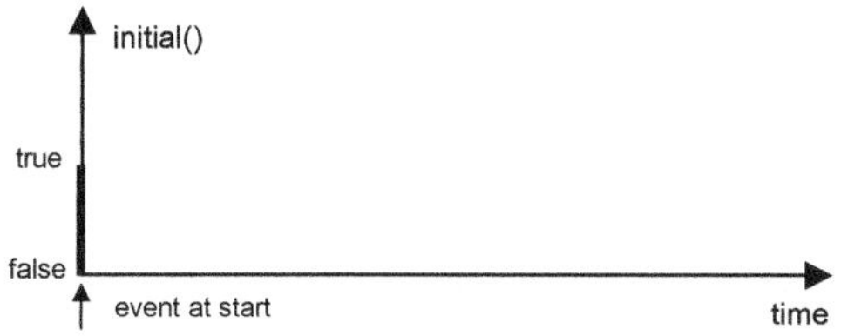

Figure 13-8. The function `initial()` returns `true` at an event at the start of the simulation.

The typical use of `initial()` is in conditions for unclocked when-equations, for example, as below. This is sometimes used for possibly needed additional initialization of discrete-time variables in addition to the initial values provided by the `start` attributes of those variables. It can be used for possibly needed more elaborate initialization equations for discrete-time variables in addition to the alternative possibility of providing initial values by setting the start attribute of variables. Note that setting a start value, if it is `"fixed"`, and additionally providing an initial equation for that variable leads to an overdetermined system of equations.

```
when initial() then
  ...  // some initialization or other actions
end;
```

In fact, if `initial()` is part of the conditions of a when-equation or when-statement, the equations within the when-equation or statements within the when-statement become part of the initialization equation system to be solved before start of simulation. Another way of specifying behavior at the initial time is by the `initial equation` construct.

A more thorough discussion of initialization based on `initial equation`, `initial()`, and the `start` attribute can be found in Section 8.4, page 363.

13.2.5.2 Using terminal() to Trigger Actions at the End of a Simulation

The function call `terminal()` returns `true` at an instant at the end of a successful simulation. If it is used somewhere in the code it can trigger an event as depicted in Figure 13-9.

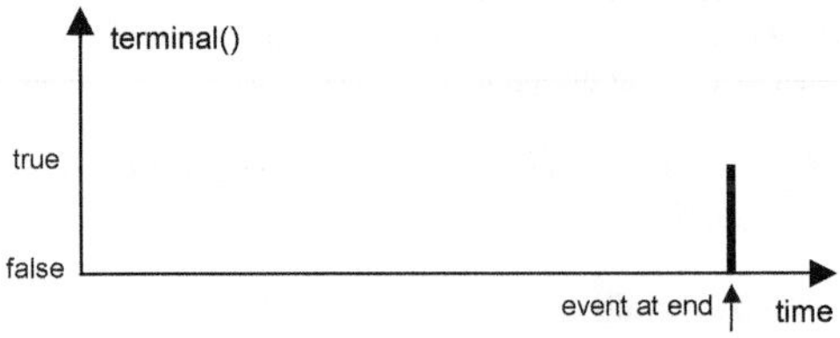

Figure 13-9. The function `terminal()` returns `true` at an event at the end of the simulation.

This is typically used to trigger actions at the end of a simulation, for example, calling an external function to store some data on the file system. If the simulation is not successful it will be aborted prematurely, and `terminal()` will never return `true` during this simulation.

```
when terminal() then
  ...  // some action at the end of the simulation
end when;
```

13.2.5.3 Terminating a Simulation Using terminate()

Since we have been discussing the termination of a simulation in the previous section, it can be useful to briefly recapitulate `terminate`, which is described in more detail in Section 9.2.12 on page 437 in Chapter 9. The statement `terminate(`*message*`)` causes a successful termination of the simulation and passes the *message* string to the simulation environment in order to inform the user. The reason might be that it is no longer relevant to continue the simulation, for example, as in the moon landing example on page 82 in Chapter 3 when the moon lander is starting to sink below the surface because the simulation has gone outside the domain where the model is valid.

If you would like to check for conditions that when violated should cause abortion of the simulation, that is, unsuccessful termination, you should instead use the `assert()` statement, which is described in more detail in Section 9.2.11 on page 436 in Chapter 9.

13.2.5.4 Generating Repeated Events Using Unclocked sample ()

The unclocked function `sample(`*first, interval*`)` returns `true` and can be used to trigger events at time instants *first* + i**interval* (i=0,1,...), where *first* is a Real number specifying the time of the first event and *interval* is a Real number specifying the time interval between the periodic events. It is typically used in models of periodically sampled systems. However, see also the clocked version of `sample()` in Section 13.2.5.6, page 604, which is even better for modeling sampled systems.

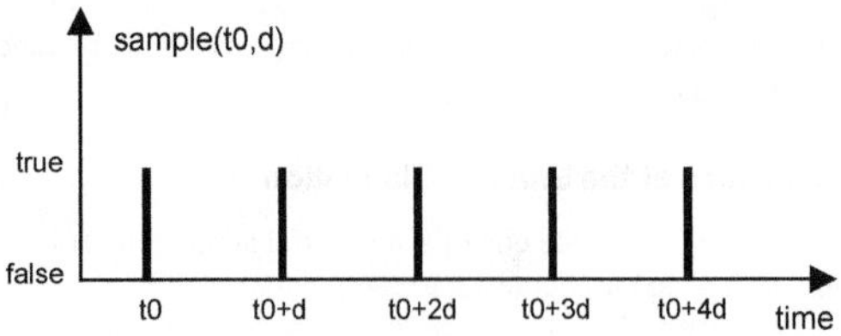

Figure 13-10. The call `sample(t0,d)` returns true and triggers events at times `t0+i*d`, where `i=0,1`, etc.

The function acts as a kind of clock that returns `true` at periodically occurring time instants (Figure 13-10), which in the `SquareWave` model is stored in the Boolean variable `clk`. We can use this behavior in combination with a when-equation to periodically trigger events, for example, when creating a square wave:

```
class SquareWave
  parameter Modelica.SIunits.Time  first=0, interval=1;
  Boolean clk;  // A Boolean variable representing a kind of clock
  Real x(start=1);
equation
  clk = sample(first,interval);
  when clk then
    x = -pre(x);
  end when;
end SquareWave;
```

We simulate and plot:

```
simulate(SquareWave, stopTime=5)
plot(x)
```

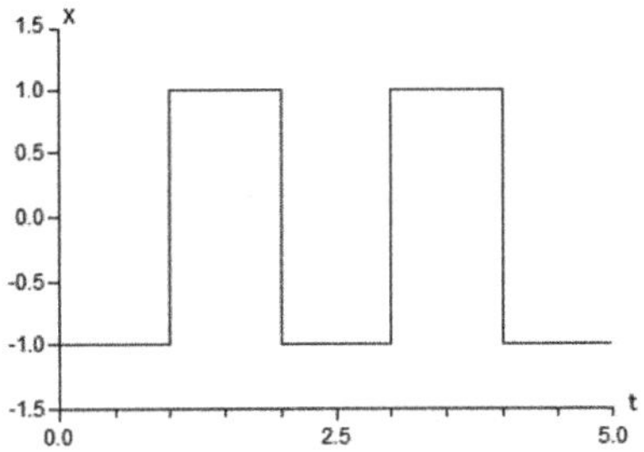

Figure 13-11. The generated square wave.

You should note that the unclocked function `sample` always returns `false` between the events it generates, that is, during the solution of the continuous part of the equation system that is going on as part of the simulation between events. The starting time *start* and the sample *interval* need to be `parameter` expressions, that is, they are constant during simulation, and need to have `Real` or `Integer` types, or subtypes of those types, for example, `Modelica.SIunits.Time`, which is a subtype of `Real`.

13.2.5.5 Generating Clock Tick Events Using Clock()

The following variants of the `Clock(...)` constructor for generating clock tick events are available:

- `Clock( )` – inferred clock (Section 13.6.7.2, page 702).
- `Clock(intervalCounter, resolution)` – clock with Integer quotient (rational number) interval (Section 13.6.7.3, page 703).
- `Clock(interval)` – clock with a Real value interval (Section 13.6.7.4, page 703).
- `Clock(condition, startInterval)` – Boolean condition clock (Section 13.6.7.5, page 704).
- `Clock` – solver clock (Section 13.6.7.6, page 705).

For more details including several examples, see Section 13.6.7, page 701. A simple example is presented below.

```
class ClockTicks
  // Integer quotient rational number interval clock
  Clock c1 = Clock(3,10);          // ticks: 0, 3/10, 6/10, ..
  // Clock with real value interval between ticks
  Clock c2 = Clock(0.2);           // ticks: 0.0, 0.2, 0.4, ...
end ClockTicks;
```

We simulate and plot, see Figure 13-13.

```
simulate(ClockTicks, stopTime=1)
```

```
plot({c1,c2})
```

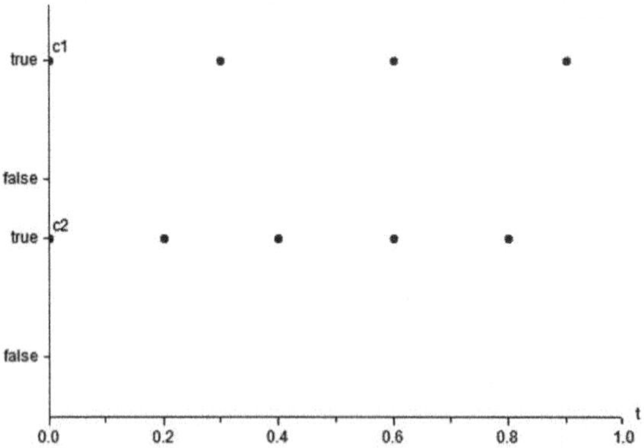

Figure 13-12. The clocks `c1` and `c2` from model `ClockTicks`, where clock c1with a rational number (integer quotient) interval ticks at 0, 3/10, 6/10, ... seconds, and clock `c2` with a real number interval ticks at 0.0, 0.2, 0.4, etc.

13.2.5.6 Sampling Values at Clock Ticks Using Clocked sample(...)

The clocked version of `sample(...)` is quite different from the unclocked version generating events, which was described in the previous section. The clocked version of the operator samples a continuous-time expression at the ticks of a clock and returns a clocked expression.

The input argument `u` to `sample(u,c)` is a continuous-time expression (Section 6.9.4, page 283). The optional input argument `c` is of type `Clock`.

The clocked version, `sample(u,c)` or `sample(u)`, see also Section 13.6.8.1, page 705, returns a *clocked variable value* that has the associated clock `c` and the value of the left limit of `u` when the clock `c` is active. This is the *value* of `u` *immediately before* the event of `c` is triggered. If the optional argument `c` is not provided the clock is inferred (Section 13.6.14.4, page 721).

Below a very simple example model using `sample` is given where the variable x is sampled at 5 Hz.

```
class SampleTime
  parameter Modelica.SIunits.Time  interval=1;
  Clock clk;                     // A clock variable
  discrete Real stime(start=1);  // A clocked variable for the sample result
  Real x=time;
equation
  clk = Clock(1,5);            // Clocked equation, interval=1/5 s, freq 5Hz
  stime = sample(x, clk);      // Clocked equation to perform the sampling
end SampleTime;
```

We simulate and plot, see Figure 13-13:

```
simulate(SampleTime, stopTime=1)
plot(stime)
```

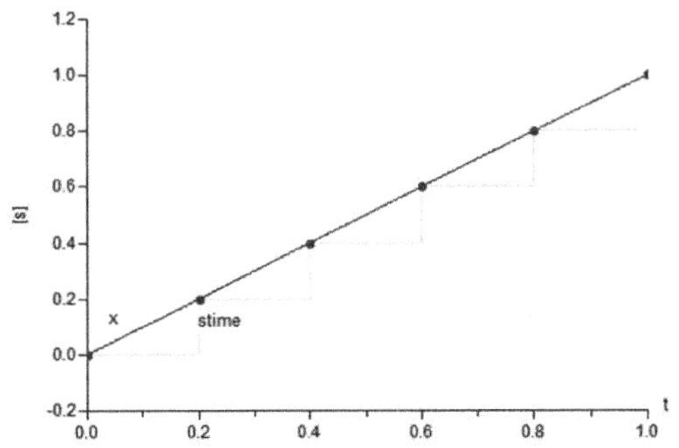

Figure 13-13. The clocked variable `stime` showing the sampled value of `x=time`.

Since the `sample(...)` operator returns the *left limit* of `u` it introduces an *infinitesimally small delay* between the continuous-time and the clocked partition. This corresponds to the reality where a sampled data system cannot act infinitely fast and even for a very idealized simulation, an infinitesimal small delay is present.

The input argument `u` can be a general expression since the argument has continuous-time variability and therefore always has a value. It can also be a constant, a parameter, or a piecewise constant expression.

To summarize, there are three variants of `sample()`:

- Unclocked `sample(u,r)` has *two input* arguments where the second argument `r` is of *type Real*. This is the traditional unclocked `sample(...)` operator described in Section 13.2.5.4, page 602.
- Clocked `sample(u)` has *one input* argument u which is converted to a clocked value according to a clock inferred from the context.
- Clocked `sample(u,c)` has *two input* arguments where the second argument if of *type* `Clock`. It returns a clocked version of the input argument u according to the above description.

13.2.5.7 Accessing Clocked Values Between Clocked Events Using hold(...)

Unclocked discrete-time variables are piece-wise constant, may change at events, and have defined values also between events. This is however *not* the case for *clocked variables,* which are only *defined* and may only change *at clock ticks* for their associated clock.

The `hold(...)` operator (Section 13.6.8.2, page 706) makes clocked values available also in unclocked equations and expressions. The operator effectively converts a clocked discrete-time expression into an unclocked discrete-time expression which is piece-wise constant and accessible between clock tick events.

The `hold(...)` operator is used in the `SquareWaveClocked` model below to make the variable `x` defined between clock ticks. This model is a clocked version of the previous unclocked `SquareWave` model in Section 13.2.5.4, page 602. In the `SquareWaveClocked` model we instead use Modelica synchronous clocks where the clock variable `clk` is declared using the builtin `Clock` type, the clock interval is specified using the `Clock` constructor, and we have introduced a synchronous *clocked discrete-time* variable `xclocked` which is only defined at clock ticks.

```
class SquareWaveClocked
  parameter Modelica.SIunits.Time  interval=1;
  Clock clk;  // A clock variable
  discrete Real xclocked(start=1);  // A clocked variable
  Real x;
equation
  clk = Clock(interval);  // Clocked equation
  when clk then
```

```
    xclocked = -previous(xclocked);   // Clocked equation
  end when;
  x = hold(xclocked);  // Unclocked equation
end SquareWaveClocked;
```

We simulate and plot:

```
simulate(SquareWaveClocked, stopTime=5)
plot(x);   plot(xclocked)
```

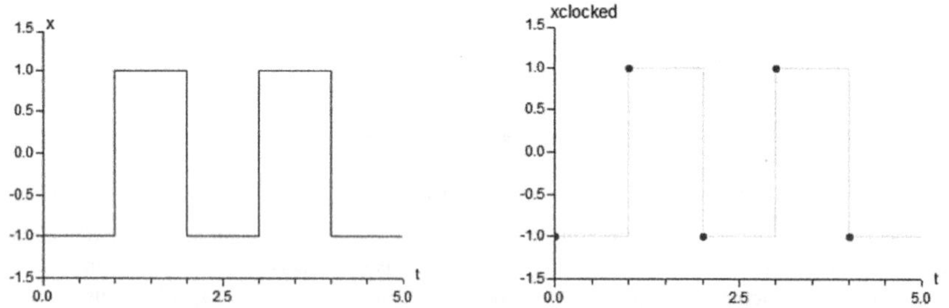

Figure 13-14. The generated square wave using a clocked when-equation. The variable `x` is an unclocked discrete-time real variable also defined between clock points by the use of `hold()`, whereas the variable `xclocked` is a clocked discrete-time real variable only defined at clock points.

The plots in Figure 13-14 clearly shows the difference between the clocked variable `xclocked` only defined at clock ticks and the unclocked variable `x` defined also between clock ticks and obtained by the call `hold(xclocked)`.

13.2.5.8 Generating Clock Tick Events Using subSample, superSample, shiftSample, backSample

There are additional clock tick generation operators to generate clock ticks based on some existing clock or Boolean condition. These operators are mentioned briefly here but described in more detail including examples in Section 13.6.9, page 707.

- `subSample`—generate a slower (lower frequency) clock based on an existing clock. See Section 13.6.9.1, page 707.
- `superSample`—generate a faster (higher frequency) clock based on an existing clock. See Section 13.6.9.2, page 708.
- `shiftSample`—generate a clock based on an existing clock, where the ticks of the generated clock are shifted forward in time. See Section 13.6.9.3, page 709.
- `backSample`—generate a clock based on an existing clock, where the ticks of the generated clock are shifted backward (earlier) in time. See Section 13.6.9.4, page 710.

13.2.5.9 Accessing the Time Difference Between Clocked Events Using interval()

The `interval(u)` operator returns the *interval* between the *previous* and *present tick* of the clock of the expression within which this operator is called and the clock of the optional argument `u`. For more details including an example see Section 13.6.5, page 699.

13.2.5.10 Preventing Events Using noEvent(...)

The function `noEvent(`*expr*`)` evaluates and returns the expression *expr* in a way that prevents generating events in unclocked parts of a model.

Suppressing events for an expression is useful, e.g. to prevent expressions like `log(x)` and `sqrt(x)` protected by guards like `x>0` from going outside their domain of validity—in this case to prevent negative values of `x`.

The expression `x>0` is an unclocked discrete-time expression with possible values `true` and `false`. We need to search for the value of `x` for which the event will occur, that is, when `x>0` switches between `false` and `true`. This occurs at the zero-crossing of the expression `x-0`, that is, when the expression switches from negative to positive value or vice versa.

To perform this zero-crossing search for an expression, e.g. for `sqrt(x)`, it is necessary to evaluate the expression also for small negative values of `x`, which will cause problems for the above type of expressions. By contrast, `noEvent(x>0)` is an example of a continuous-time expression that does not generate events and therefore avoids these problems by not performing any zero-crossing search. See Section 18.2.5.5, page 1015, for a more thorough discussion regarding zero-crossing functions.

Another use for `noEvent` is to slightly improve performance for expressions that are continuous despite the fact that they normally generate events, for example, as in the example below (Figure 13-15). However, to improve performance for continuous expressions it is better to call `smooth()` (see Section 13.2.5.11).

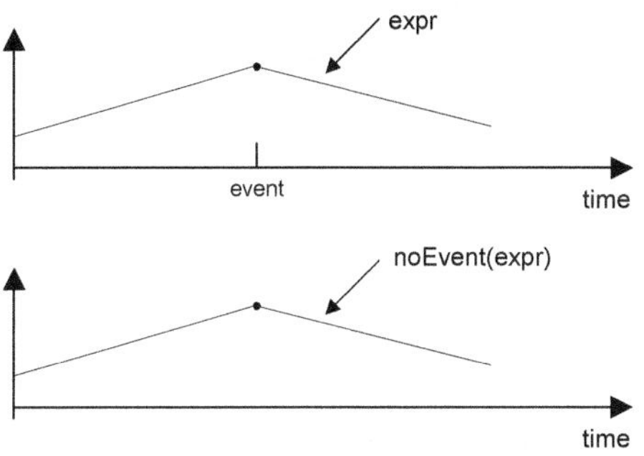

Figure 13-15. The expression `noEvent(`*expr*`)` avoids generating events that otherwise would be triggered by *expr*.

For example, consider the equation:

```
equation
  z = if x<0 then -x^3 else x^3;
```

The conditional expression at the right-hand side together with its derivatives is continuous at x=0. However, the condition `x<0` will implicitly generate an event since a conditional expression is a suspect case that normally gives rise to a discontinuity. To avoid generating an unnecessary event in this case, and thereby slightly improving performance, the condition or the whole conditional expression can be enclosed within `noEvent` as below or within `smooth` as described in the next section:

```
equation
  z = if noEvent(x<0) then -x^3 else x^3;
```

However, you should avoid using `noEvent` on an expression that has a genuine discontinuity, since that would force the continuous numerical solver to use a very small step size to handle the discontinuity, thereby incurring a substantial overhead.

The `noEvent` operator can never be used in equations in a way that tries to change the value of a `Boolean`, `Integer`, or `String` variable outside of an event since by definition such variables are only changed at events. Therefore the equation below is invalid, since `b` is discrete-time but the `noEvent`-expression on the right-hand side is continuous-time and can change at any time:

```
  Boolean b;
  Real x;
equation
  b = noEvent(x<0);   // Invalid equation!
```

13.2.5.11 Preventing Events Using smooth (...) for Continuous Expressions

The function `smooth(`*p*`,`*expr*`)` evaluates and returns the value of the expression *expr* in a way that can avoid event generation. This is similar to `noEvent()`, but with the difference that `smooth()` does not guarantee preventing events—it lets the Modelica environment decide what is appropriate.

By placing a call to `smooth()` around *expr*, we state that *expr* is continuous and its derivates up to order *p* are continuous. This information can be used by the Modelica environment to avoid event generation and thus increase performance.

Note that `smooth()` is intended to be used instead of `noEvent()` in order to avoid events for efficiency reasons. Since `smooth()` does not guarantee prevention of events it can be necessary to use `noEvent()` inside `smooth()` to guard subexpressions against erroneous evaluation. The example below avoids negative argument values to `sqrt()` in the expression on the right-hand side of the equation for `z`:

```
model SmoothAndEvents
  Real x,y,z;
  parameter Real p;
equation
  x = if time<1 then 2 else time-2;                // time<1 generates events
  y = smooth(0, if time<0 then 0 else time);  // may avoid events
  z = smooth(1,noEvent(if x<0 then 0 else sqrt(x)*x)); // noEvent is necessary
end SmoothAndEvents;
```

We can summarize the properties of `smooth()` as follows:

- A call such as `smooth(`*p*`,`*expr*`)`, for $p \geq 0$, evaluates *expr* in a way that can avoid generating events. The call also informs the Modelica environment that *expr* is *p* times continuously differentiable, i.e., *expr* is continuous in all real variables appearing in the expression, and all partial derivatives with respect to all appearing real variables exist and are continuous up to order *p*.
- The only allowed types for *expr* in `smooth(`*p*`,`*expr*`)` are `Real`, arrays of `Real`, and record types with fields having allowed types.
- The `smooth(`*p*`,`*expr*`)` function call does not guarantee a smooth result *if* any of the occurring variables in *expr* changes discontinuously.
- For `smooth(`*p*`,`*expr*`)` the liberty to possibly use events in evaluation is propagated to all subrelations within *expr*, but the smooth-property itself is not propagated—it applies only to *expr* as a whole.

Regarding the difference between `noEvent()` and `smooth()`, compare the following three examples:

```
x1 = if noEvent(u > uMax) then uMax        // Events are not generated
     elseif noEvent(u < uMin) then uMin
     else u;

x2 = noEvent(if u > uMax then uMax         // Events are not generated
             elseif u < uMin then uMin
             else u);

x3 = smooth(0, if u > uMax then uMax       // Events might be generated
               elseif u < uMin then uMin
               else u);
```

In this case the values of the expressions are the same, i.e., `x1=x2=x3`, but a Modelica environment is allowed to generate events when computing the right-hand side of the `x3` equation, but not for `x1` and `x2`.

13.2.5.12 Obtaining Predecessor Values of a Variable Using pre(...)

The function call `pre(y)` gives the "predecessor value" of `y`. For an unclocked discrete-time variable `y` *at an event*, `pre(y)` is the *value* of `y` *immediately preceding* the event, also called the *left limit* of the value of y at the event, that is, taking the limit value of `y` while letting time t approach time t_{event} from the left, as depicted in Figure 13-16, This holds except for what happens at event propagation through event iterations when several events occur at the same point in time, when the value is obtained from the event iteration immediately preceding the current one. The argument `y` to `pre(y)` must be a variable and not a general expression.

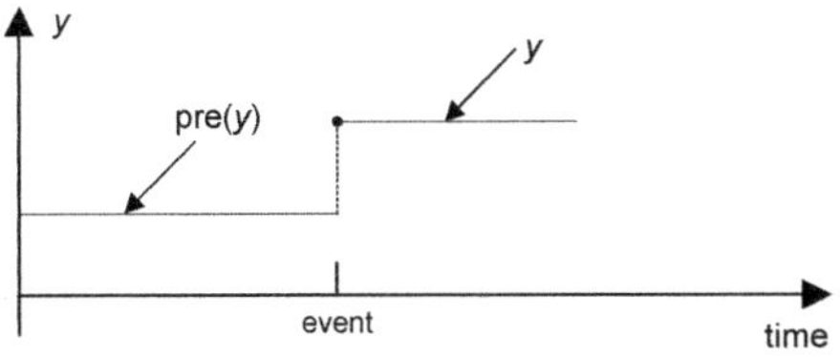

Figure 13-16. At an event, `pre(y)` gives the previous value of `y` immediately before the event, except for event iteration of multiple events at the same point in time when the value is from the previous iteration.

The `pre` operator can be applied only to a variable `y`, for example, as in the expression `pre(y)`, if the following three conditions are fulfilled:

- The variable `y` has one of the basic types `Boolean`, `Integer`, `Real`, or `String`, a subtype of those, or an array type of one of those basic types or subtypes.
- The variable `y` is an unclocked discrete-time variable.
- The operator is *not* used within a function.

At the initial time when simulation starts, `pre(y) = y.start`, that is, it is identical to the start attribute value of its argument, for example, as depicted in Figure 13-17. For a constant or parameter variable `c` it is always the case that `c=pre(c)`.

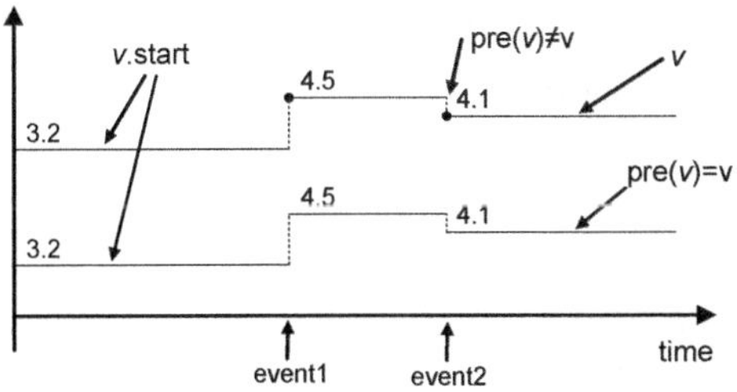

Figure 13-17. Between events, `pre(v)` gives the value of **v** obtained at the most recent event that updated `v`, i.e., the *same* as `v`. At an event, `v` and `pre(v)` can be different, e.g. at `event2` in the current figure `v=4.1` and `pre(v)=4.5`.

Immediately *after an event* when a variable such as `v` in Figure 13-17 has obtained a new value, the expression `pre(v)` returns the value of the variable `v` at the most recent event that updated `v`. This means that:

- *Between* events `pre(v)` returns the *same* value as `v`.
- The expressions `v` and `pre(v)` can only be *different at* an event.

This behavior of `pre` outside when-clauses is different from the corresponding behavior of the `previous` operator, see Section 13.2.5.14, page 610.

13.2.5.13 Obtaining Predecessor Values of a Clocked Variable Using previous(...)

The function call `previous(y)` gives the "predecessor value" of a *clocked discrete-time variable* `y`. For a clocked discrete-time variable `y` at a clock tick event `previous(y)` is the value of `y` immediately preceding the event, as depicted in Figure 13-18. The argument `y` to `previous(y)` must be a variable that fulfills the conditions of an instance expression (i.e., roughly an instance of a class without equations, see Section 13.6.11, page 713) and not a general expression.

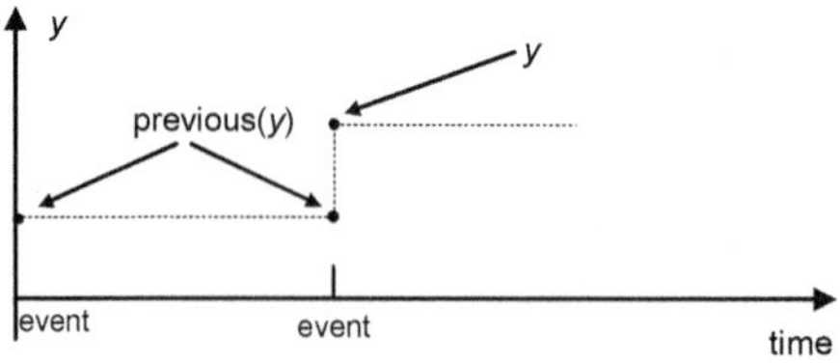

Figure 13-18. At a clock tick event, `previous(y)` gives the previous value (its value at the previous clock tick) of a clocked variable `y` at the current clock tick.

The `previous` operator can be applied only to a variable `y`, for example, as in the expression `previous(y)`, if the following three conditions are fulfilled:

- The variable `y` is an instance expression (Section 13.6.11, page 713), that is, it has one of the basic types `Boolean`, `Integer`, `Real`, or `String`, a subtype of those, a record of those, or an array type of one of those basic types or subtypes, no associated equations, and a defined initial value.
- The variable `y` is a clocked discrete-time variable.
- The operator is *not* used within a function.

At the initial time when simulation starts, `previous(y) = y.start`, that is, it is identical to the start attribute value of its argument. It is also described in Section 13.6.4, page 699. Note that `hold(previous())` is different from `pre()` outside when-clauses, see Section 13.2.5.14, page 610.

13.2.5.14 Different Behavior of pre and previous

Outside when-clauses the behavior of `pre()` and `hold(previous())` is very different:

- `pre(y)` is the same as `y`, i.e., the value of `y` at the most recent event
- `hold(previous(y))` is the value of `y` at the clock tick *before* the most recent clock tick

Consider the following model which compares `xpre` with `yprevious`:

```
model PreVsPrevious
  Real x(start=0,fixed=true);
  Real xpre;
  Real y(start=0);
  Real yprevious;
equation
   xpre = pre(x);
   when sample(0,0.1) then
     x = pre(x) + 1;
   end when;

   yprevious = hold(previous(y));
   when Clock(0.1) then
```

```
        y = previous(y) + 1;
    end when;
end PreVsPrevious;
```

Figure 13-19 shows the difference in behavior.

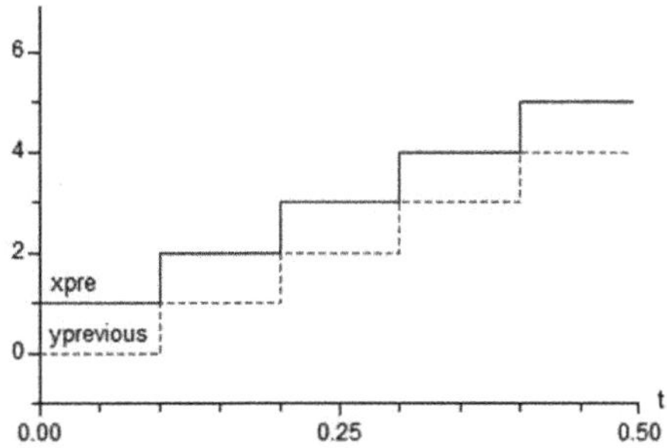

Figure 13-19. Outside events, the behavior of `xpre=pre(x)` and `yprevious=hold(previous(y))` is different since `xpre==pre(x)==x`, whereas `yprevious` has the value of `y` at the previous tick, not the most recent tick.

13.2.5.15 Detecting Changes of Boolean Variables Using edge()

The expression `edge(b)` for the `Boolean` variable *b* is expanded into `(b and not pre(b))` for the `Boolean` variable *b*. It becomes `true` for an instant when the variable *b* changes value from `false` to `true` (Figure 13-20). To detect a change from `true` to `false`, introduce a variable equal to `not b`.

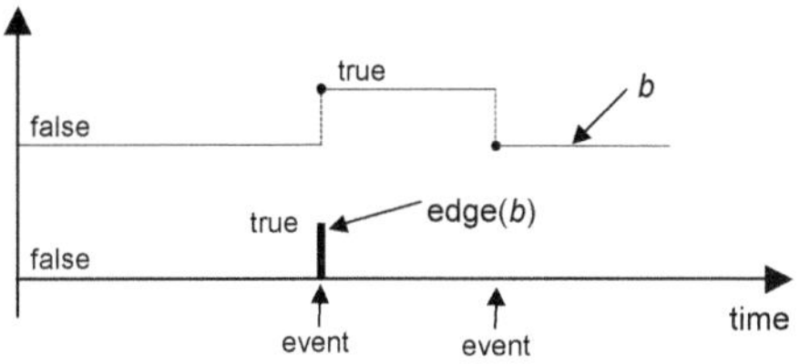

Figure 13-20. The expression `edge(b)` is `true` at events when `b` switches from `false` to `true`.

The argument *b* must be an unclocked discrete-time `Boolean` variable and not a general expression. The function `edge` may not be called within Modelica functions.

13.2.5.16 Detecting Changes of Unclocked Discrete-Time Variables Using change()

The expression `change(v)` is expanded into `(v<>pre(v))` for an unclocked `non-Real` discrete-time variable *v*. It returns `true` for an instant when the variable *v* changes value (Figure 13-21).

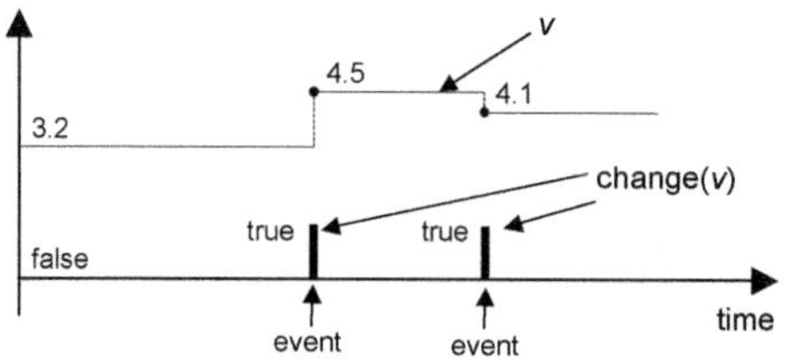

Figure 13-21. The expression `change(v)` is `true` at instants when `v` changes value.

The argument *v* must be an unclocked discrete-time variable and not a general expression, and should be declared as a variable of type `Boolean`, `Integer`, or `String`, or a subtype of those. The function `change` may not be called within Modelica functions. The argument may not be `discrete Real` since `change` is dependent on the inequality operation that sometimes has spurious behavior for floating point numbers due to roundoff errors.

13.2.5.17 Creating Time-Delayed Expressions Using delay(...)

The function `delay` is used to create time-delayed expressions, that is, to obtain the value of an expression as it was at an earlier point in time. In fact, applying `delay` to an expression enables access of values from the value history of that expression.

There are two variants of the `delay` function, `delay(`*expr*, *delayTime*, *delayMax*`)` and `delay(`*expr*, *delayTime*`)`. Both variants return the value of *expr* at the time `(time-`*delayTime*`)`, that is, its value at a point in time *delayTime* earlier compared to the value of the current simulated time represented by the built-in `time` variable.

During an initial period of length *delayTime* at the beginning of the simulation when `time.start <= time < time.start +` *delayTime*, the function `delay` returns the start value of *expr*, that is, the value it had at time = `time.start`, since otherwise the function value would be undefined. This is, for example, indicated by the initial dashed section of the graph for `delay(v,d)` in Figure 13-22.

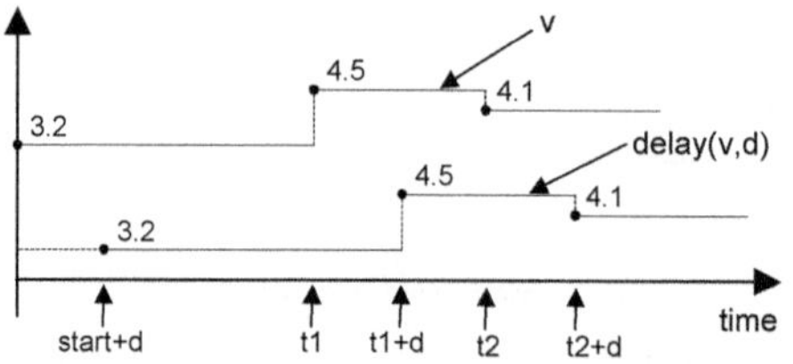

Figure 13-22. The expression `delay(v,d)` is `v` delayed by a delay time `d`.

The Modelica run-time system must in principle store the most recent value history of the expression *expr* for the length of time indicated by *delayTime*. To allow for an efficient implementation, and since *delayTime* is allowed to vary over time, a third optional argument *delayMax* to `delay` is provided which specifies the maximum delay allowed for *delayTime*. The argument *delayMax* must be a `parameter` expression, that is, constant over the simulation, to enable efficient implementation e.g. by allowing preallocation of the needed storage.

From the numerical point of view an implementation of `delay` can be achieved by interpolating in the internal polynomials of the continuous equation solver, or alternatively using the simpler approach of linear interpolation in a buffer containing past values of the expression `expr`.

If *delayMax* is specified then `0` <= *delayTime* <= *delayMax*, otherwise an error occurs. If the third argument *delayMax* is not supplied in the argument list, then *delayTime* needs to be a `parameter` expression, that is, constant for the duration of the simulation.

13.2.5.18 Reinitialization of Variables at Events Using reinit(...)

The `reinit`(*x*,*expr*) construct is briefly recapitulated here for the sake of completeness of presentation regarding the event-related constructs. It reinitializes the state variable *x* with *expr* at an event instant, that is, a kind of "assignment," but not quite the same since it simultaneously *deactivates* any existing defining equation or assignment to *x*. Therefore it does not break the single assignment rule (see Section 8.1.3, page 348 and Section 13.2.3.2, page 598), since the number of defining equations is still the same. The second argument *expr* must be an `Integer` or `Real` expression, and is computed from the values of variables referenced in *expr* as they were immediately before the event. The first argument *x* in a call to `reinit` must be a state variable which also fulfills the following properties:

- The type of *x* is `Real` or a subtype of `Real`.
- The `der`-operator needs to be applied to *x* somewhere in the model.

For a simple example of the use of `reinit`, see the bouncing ball example on page 57 in Chapter 2. Regarding the use of `reinit` among equations, see Section 8.3.6, page 359.

13.2.5.19 Mathematical Functions Implicitly Causing Events

The built-in functions `abs`, `sign`, `div`, `mod`, `rem`, `ceil`, `floor`, and `integer`, previously described in Section 6.13, page 289, may implicitly trigger events since they themselves or their derivatives are discontinuous at certain points. Such events are triggered at the points of discontinuity when an argument to the function in question contains a continuous-time subexpression and the call to the function is made *outside* of a when-equation or when-statement. When a function call is *inside* a `when` construct a new event is not triggered since an event is already being processed.

Remember that Modelica functions cannot cause events even if they contain calls to these functions, since the body of a Modelica function is treated as if `noEvent()` is applied to it.

13.2.6 Handling Events

Events arise naturally external to a simulated system or are generated internally in the simulation model. These events need to be handled, that is, some behavior should be executed associated with each event. Previously we have come to the conclusion that the notion of conditional equations is an appropriate declarative formalism to express such behavior. To give you a clear picture, we provide a brief summary of the different constructs used to express event-related behavior in Modelica even though the syntax and semantics of these constructs is treated in more detail in Chapters 8 and 9.

13.2.6.1 Expressing Event Behavior in Modelica

The conditional equations associated with an event become active when the *condition* of the equations switches from the value `false` to `true`, or when the clock controlling a set of equations arrives at a clock tick There are basically three groups of conditional equation constructs in Modelica:

- *if-equations* (Section 8.3.4, page 355), *if-statements* (Section 9.2.8, page 431), and *if-expressions* embedded in equations or statements (Section 6.12.2, page 288) are used for conditional models with different behavior in *different operating regions*. The conditional equations may contain both *continuous-time* and *discrete-time* expressions.
- unclocked *when-equations* (Section 8.3.5, page 357) and *when-statements* (Section 9.2.10, page 433) are used to express instantaneous equations that are valid only (become active) *at events*, for

example, at discontinuities or when certain conditions become `true`. The conditional equations automatically contain only *discrete-time* expressions since they become active only at event instants.

- clocked equations in clocked partitions (Section 13.6.13, page 715) which become active at clock ticks of the associated clocks.

The if-constructs are more fundamental than the when-constructs, since unclocked when-clauses can be expressed in terms of if-constructs as we shall see in Section 13.2.6.3.

The if-equations are conditional equations with the following general structure, of which the elseif-parts are optional. The if-statements are similar, but contain statements instead of equations.

```
if condition then
  equations
elseif condition then
  equations
else
  equations
end if;
```

The if-expressions have the general structure: `if` *condition* `then` *expr1* `else` *expr2*, and can be used to express conditional equations when embedded in an equation, for example:

```
expr = if condition then expr1 else expr2;
```

For example, the if-equation in the ideal diode example below from Chapter 2, page 56, specifies different equations for the variable `v` in two *different operating regions*: the equation `v=s` in the region `s<0` and the equation `v=0` in the region `s>=0`.

```
model Diode "Ideal diode"
  extends TwoPin;
  Real s;
  Boolean off;
equation
  off = s < 0;
  if off then                       // conditional if-equation
    v=s
  else
    v=0;
  end if;
  i = if off then 0 else s;         // equation with conditional expression
end Diode;
```

During solution of the continuous part of the equation system ("continuous integration"), the same branch of the if-equation with its constituent equations is always included in the total equation system. The then-branch of the if-equation in the `Diode` model has the condition `off`, whereas the else-branch implicitly has the condition `not off`. The solution process is temporarily halted whenever `s` crosses zero, that is, `off` changes value. When this happens an event is generated. At the event instant the conditions are reevaluated, the correct if-branch is selected, and continuous integration is restarted. This process is described in more detail in Chapter 18.

The second group of constructs consists of when-equations and when-statements that are used to express *instantaneous* conditional "equations", that is, equations that are active only at events.

The unclocked when-equation is a conditional equation of the following general form, which can be used in equation sections together with other equations. The elsewhen-part is optional.

```
when conditions then
  equations
elsewhen conditions then
  equations
```

```
end when;
```

For example, the two equations in the when-equation below become active at the event instant when the `Boolean` expression `x > 2` becomes `true`. The variables `y1` and `y3` have their values defined by the when-equation and therefore must have unclocked discrete-time variability. The variables `y1` and `x` are only referenced. When the when-equation is not active, the equations `y3=pre(y3)` and `y1=pre(y1)` hold, keeping the number of equations the same and therefore avoiding violation of the single assignment principle.

```
when x > 2 then
  y3 = 2*x + y1+y2;
  y1 = sin(x);
end when;
```

The when-statement is a statement construct, which therefore can be used only in algorithm sections. Furthermore, functions cannot contain when-statements. The when-statements have the following general structure where the elsewhen-part is optional:

```
when conditions then
  statements
elsewhen conditions then
  statements
end when;
```

The two statements inside the when-statement example below are executed at the event instant when the `Boolean` expression `x > 2` *becomes* `true`. You should note that this is different from an if-statement with the same condition which executes its body each time when invoked provided that the condition of the if-statement *is* `true`. This difference is easier to understand if you look at the definition of when-statements in terms of if-statements and the `edge` operator in Section 13.2.6.3.

The execution order of the statements within the when-statement is important: the variable `y1` must be computed first since it is used to compute `y3`. Such ordering does not matter for the previous when-equation variant of the same example.

```
when x > 2 then
  y1 := sin(x);
  y3 := 2*x + y1 + y2;
end when;
```

The clocked when-equation (Section 13.6.6, page 700) is a conditional equation of the following general form, which also can be used in equation sections together with other equations.

```
when clock then
  equations
end when;
```

Equations can be in a clocked partition (Section 13.6.13, page 715) and can be governed by a clock even without the use of clocked when-equations. If clock-related operators are used, a Modelica tool can determine which equations are activated by a certain clock by the use of clock inferencing.

13.2.6.2 Unclocked versus Clocked Discrete-time Modeling

Several models with discrete-time parts are presented in this chapter with both unclocked and clocked modeling styles. The reader might wonder which modeling style should be chosen in a particular situation. This is partly a matter of taste, but some subjective guidelines can be given:

- If your application contains a digital subsystem controlled by a digital clock, the clocked modeling style is the most natural.
- If your model is mainly continuous-time, the unclocked style might fit better.

- If your model mainly uses and interacts with unclocked libraries, the unclocked style might be better.
- If your application needs maximum performance and contains clocked digital parts, the clocked style is recommended since the continuous-time numeric solver need not be involved when solving the clocked equations.

The two modeling styles also have different properties:

- The unclocked style is more flexible since it allows access and solution/assignment of any unclocked variables.
- The clocked style will cause all equations to be put into groups/partitions: an *unclocked partition* as well as a number of *clocked partitions*, one for each clock rate. Only equations with the same clock rate are placed in the same partition.
- Clocked variables of a certain clock rate can *only* be *solved for/assigned to* in the *clocked partition* with that clock rate; in *other partitions* these variables can *not be written only read* using the appropriate clock operator (`sample`, `hold`, `subSample`, `superSample`, `noClock`, ...).
- The clocked style is more strict in compile-time checks since only equations with the same clock-rate can be solved in the same partition; this is an advantage to avoid certain errors, but also sometimes a disadvantage since it puts more constraints in the way the model can be constructed.

13.2.6.3 Defining Unclocked when-equations by if-equations

An unclocked when-equation can be defined as a combination of the following:

- An if-equation.
- `Boolean` variables with appropriate start values.
- Calls to the `edge` operator in the *conditions* of the if-equation.

An analogous mapping from when-statements to if-statements can be specified (see Chapter 9, Section 9.2.10.1 on page 434, for a more elaborate example). You can easily understand the mapping from when-equations to if-equations by regarding the following schematic when-equation example:

```
equation
  when x > y.start then
    ...
  end when;
```

This when-equation is equivalent to the following special if-equation. The `Boolean` variable `b2` is necessary since the `edge` operator can be applied only to `Boolean` variables. Each *condition* of the when-equation is set equal to a `Boolean` variable, which becomes the argument to one of the `edge` operators in the *conditions* of the if-equation.

```
Boolean b2(start = x.start > y.start);
equation
  b2 = x > y.start;
  if edge(b2) then
    ...
  end if;
```

Remember the definition of `edge` as "`edge(x)= x and not pre(x)`." The `edge` operators in the *conditions* of the if-equation ensure that the equations within the if-equation are activated only when the original conditions *become* `true`, that is, at event instants.

13.2.6.4 Discontinuous Changes to Variables at Events

It is often the case that variables change discontinuously at events. Furthermore, the behavior of an event often inflicts further *direct discontinuous* changes to certain variables. Depending on the kind of variable, you can choose between two mechanisms to inflict a direct change to a variable in a when-equation or when-statement:

- The value of an *unclocked discrete-time* variable can be changed by placing the variable on the left-hand side in an equation within a when-equation, or on the left-hand side of an assignment statement in a when-statement.
- The value of a *clocked discrete-time* variable can be changed by placing the variable in an equation within a clocked when-equation (Section 13.6.6, page 700), or in an equation that will solve for the variable within a clocked partition (Section 13.6.14, page 719).
- The value of a *continuous-time* state variable that also is a dynamic variable, i.e., a variable whose derivative appears in the model by having the `der()` operator applied to it, can be instantaneously changed by a `reinit()` equation within a when-equation (Section 8.3.6, page 359).

Section 13.2.6.1 contains several examples of the first case. The second case shows that equations in clocked when-clauses are just normal equations so that a variable solved for during the solution process can also be on the right hand side, like in the following model:

```
model ClockedVarWhen
  Real x;
equation
  when Clock(0.1) then
    3 = x;
  end when;
end ClockedVarWhen;
```

An example of the third case can be found below, taken from our old friend, the bouncing-ball model, first presented on page 57 in Chapter 2. The `reinit()` equation instantaneously reinitializes the variable `v` to a new initial value, which is used as the start value when the continuous equation solver restarts after the when-equation has been handled, i.e., after a bounce.

```
equation
  der(height)  = v;
  der(v)       = -g;
  when height<0 then
    reinit(v, -c*v);
  end when;
```

13.2.6.5 Using Event Priority to Avoid Erroneous Multiple Definitions

Two separate unclocked when-equations or when-statements in different algorithm sections may *not* define the same variable, as pointed out e.g. in Section 8.3.5.2, page 359. Without this rule a conflict between the equations would occur if both conditions would become `true` at the same time instant. This would happen for the erroneous model `WhenConflictX` below if we would have the same condition, for example, `time>=1`, in both when-equations since there are two equations, `x = pre(x)+1.5` and `x = pre(x)+1`, that define the same variable `x`.

In this particular case it would be possible to avoid the conflict by analyzing the conditions since they are of a particular simple form for which the time of the events can be predicted in advance. However, in the general case it is impossible to perform a compile time analysis that determines whether two or more conditions will trigger events at the same time instant. Therefore Modelica *always* enforces the *single assignment* principle, that is, at most one equation defining a variable, irrespective of the form of the conditions in when-equations and `when`-statements.

```
model WhenConflictX    // Erroneous model: two equations define x
  discrete Real x;
equation
  when time>=2 then    // When A: Increase x by 1.5 at time=2
    x = pre(x)+1.5;
```

```
  end when;
  when time>=1 then       // When B: Increase x by 1 at time=1
    x = pre(x)+1;
  end when;
end WhenConflictX;
```

The multiple-assignment conflict in the above example can be avoided by giving a higher *priority* to one of the defining equations through the `elsewhen` construct, as in the same example in converted form below. We have put both equations within the same when-equation and ordered the conditions in decreasing priority (Figure 13-23).

```
model WhenPriorityX
  discrete Real x;
equation
  when time>=2 then           // Higher priority
    x = pre(x)+1.5;
  elsewhen time>=1 then       // Lower priority
    x = pre(x)+1;
  end when;
end WhenPriorityX;
```

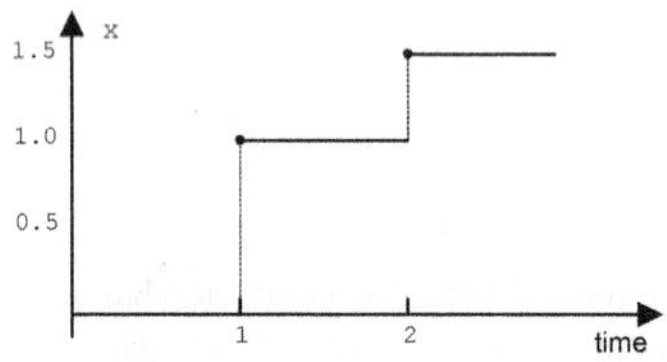

Figure 13-23. Eliminating the double definition conflict between equations in different when-equations in the `WhenPriority` model by giving the event at `time=2` higher priority than the event at `time=1` through the use of `elsewhen` in the `WhenPriorityX` model.

However, note that multiple assignments to the same variable within an *algorithm* section are allowed since only the last assignment to the same variable in an algorithm section is counted according to the single assignment principle explained in more detail in Section 8.1.3, page 348, for example:

```
algorithm
  when time>=2 then
    x := pre(x)+0.75; // multiple assignments within the same
    x := x+0.75; // when-statement or algorithm section is allowed
  elsewhen time>=1 then
    x := pre(x)+1;
  end when;
```

13.2.6.6 Event Synchronization and Propagation

Events often need to be *synchronized* and propagated. However, Modelica gives *no guarantee* that two different independent events occur at *exactly* the same time instant if they are not explicitly synchronized, for example, via equations or clocks of the built-in type `Clock`. This has to do with the fact that Modelica deals with both continuous and discrete system modeling, in contrast to certain purely discrete modeling languages that may provide implicit synchronization of all events using a central clock.

For example, events triggered by independent calls to the unclocked version of `sample`, for example, `sample(0,3.3)`, may not necessarily occur at exactly the same time instants as those triggered by `sample(0,1.1)`. Numerical roundoff errors can create small differences in the time values even though the first sample period appears to be a multiple of the second one. Of course, two or more independent events may actually occur at the same time instant, but Modelica gives no guarantee of synchronization if the events are not coupled by equations or precise clocks of type `Clock`.

To achieve *guaranteed synchronization* between two events, we use the *synchronous principle* that computation at an event takes no time. An event can instantaneously via one or more equations change the values of certain discrete-time variables used for the synchronization, typically `Boolean` or `Integer` variables. These changes may trigger other events without any elapsed time, which thereby are synchronized.

For example, it is possible to synchronize counters performing their counting behavior at different frequencies, for example, as in the `SynchCountersUnclocked` example below. The equation involving `slowPulses` and `count` synchronizes the two counters, that is, `slowPulses = mod(count,2)==0`.

With the introduction of built-in synchronized clock variables in Modelica it has become much easier and less error-prone to model clocked event synchronization, for example, as in the `SynchCountersClocked` example further below. Moreover, this gives more efficient simulation. This is now the *recommended* way to model applications involving *synchronized clocks* in Modelica. However, below the old unclocked modeling style is first shown. If you are more interested in the clocked version, skip to the next example.

```
model SynchCountersUnclocked   "Two unclocked synchronized counters"
  Boolean slowPulses;
  Boolean fastPulses;
  Integer count, slowCount;
equation
  fastPulses = sample(1,1);
  when fastPulses then         // Count every second
    count      = pre(count)+1;
    slowPulses = mod(count,2)==0;      // true when count=2,4,6,...
  end when;
  when slowPulses then         // Count every 2nd second
    slowCount  = pre(slowCount)+1;
  end when;
end SynchCountersUnclocked;
```

Figure 13-24 shows the two synchronized counters `count` and `slowCount` in a simulation of the `SynchCountersUnclocked` model. The `slowPulses` when-equation is evaluated at every 2nd occurrence of the `fastPulses` when-equation.

The single assignment rule and the requirement to explicitly model the synchronization of events in Modelica allow a certain degree of model checking and error detection already at compile time. For example, a kind of "deadlock" between different when-equations is present if there are mutual dependencies, a so-called "algebraic loop," between the equations of the when-equations, as in the `DeadLock` example model on page 622 below. This case should be detected by a Modelica compiler.

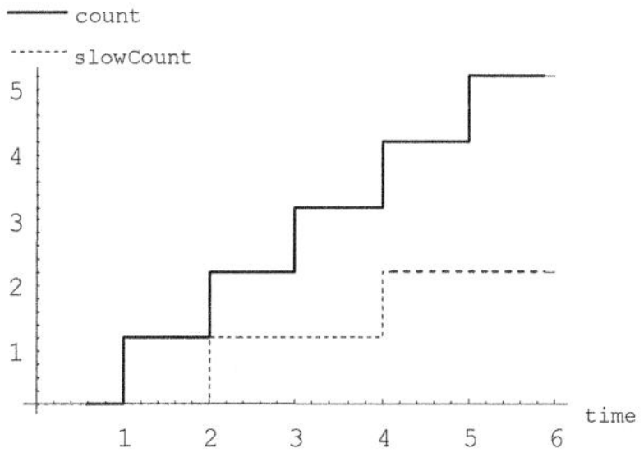

Figure 13-24. Simulation of the model `SynchCountersUnclocked` with two unclocked synchronized counters, where the slow counter is incremented every 2nd pulse of the fast counter.

Below is a version of the previous model using clocked synchronous language primitives (Section 13.6, page 694). The new model called `SynchCountersClocked` has a structure that is very similar to the previous model. The unclocked when-equations have been replaced by clocked when-equations. The `pre()`

calls in the difference equations have been replaced by calls to `previous()`. The `slowPulses` and `fastPulses` variables have been changed from `Boolean` to the built-in `Clock` type. The clock constructor call `Clock(1)` now returns a clock with interval 1 second used for `fastPulses`. For `slowPulses` we use the built-in `subSample()` operator to obtain every second clock tick giving an interval of 2 seconds. Finally, we have introduced two unclocked "hold" variables `hcount` and `hslowCount` which are defined also between clock ticks, whereas the clocked variables `count` and `slowCount` are only defined at clock ticks.

```
model SynchCountersClocked   "Two clocked synchronized counters"
  Clock slowPulses;             // Clock variables
  Clock fastPulses;
  discrete Integer count, slowCount;  // Clocked variables
  Integer hcount, hslowCount;
equation
  fastPulses = Clock(1);
  when fastPulses then           // Count every second
    count      = previous(count)+1;
  end when;
    slowPulses = subSample(fastPulses,2); // Slow down clock by a factor 2
  when slowPulses then           // Count every 2nd second
     slowCount = previous(slowCount)+1;
  end when;
  hcount = hold(count);          // Hold variables also defined between ticks
  hslowCount = hold(slowCount);
end SynchCountersClocked;
```

The plot is identical to the plot for the previous model, as it should be.

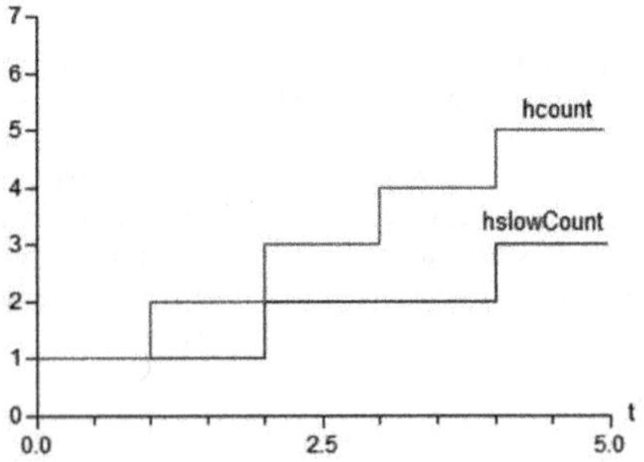

Figure 13-25. Simulation of the model `SynchCountersClocked` with two explicit hold versions of clocked synchronized counters, `hcount` with an interval of 1 second and `hslowCount` with an interval of 2 seconds.

There is an alternative way of writing this model without clocked when-equations if we make the difference equations clocked by other means, as shown in the shorter model `SynchCounters-ClockedShort` below. The clocked version of `sample()` with call `sample(1,fastPulses)` takes a clock as its second argument and returns the value 1 of the first argument only at the clock ticks. This is an example of overloading since the unclocked version of `sample()` also has two arguments but the second argument in that case is a real number.

Since the call `sample(1,fastPulses)` returns a clocked value, clock inference makes the whole equation including the variable count clocked with the same rate. The clocked equation is solved only at clock tick events, for example, the same as using the clocked when-equation.

Moreover, it is possible to declare `slowPulses = Clock(2)` and still have it synchronized with `fastPulses` without using subsampling since *clocks* of type `Clock` which are related by an *exact* integer or rational number factor are *automatically synchronized*. Clocked variables of type `Integer` are automatically synchronized when possible but not clocked variables of type `Real`. This is different from the unclocked variables in the model `SynchCountersUnclocked`, which always must be related by equations to be synchronized.

```
model SynchCountersClockedShort  "Two clocked synchronized counters"
  Clock fastPulses = Clock(1) "Clock tick every second";
  Clock slowPulses = Clock(2) "Clock tick every 2 seconds";
  discrete Integer count, slowCount;
  Integer hcount, hslowCount;
equation
  // Sample the constant value 1 at clock ticks of fastPulses or slowPulses
  // The count equation gets updated at every tick of fastPulses
  // Clock inference associates the fastPulses clock to count
  count      = previous(count) + sample(1,fastPulses);
  slowCount  = previous(slowCount) + sample(1,slowPulses);
  hcount     = hold(count);     // Hold variables also defined between ticks
  hslowCount = hold(slowCount);
end SynchCountersClockedShort;
```

The simulation results of `SynchCountersClockedShort` are identical to those of `SynchCountersClocked`. The plots in Figure 13-26 to the left show the clocked `count` and `slowCount` variables represented by round dots overlaid on top of the `hcount` and `hslowCount` variables. The clock variables are shown to the right.

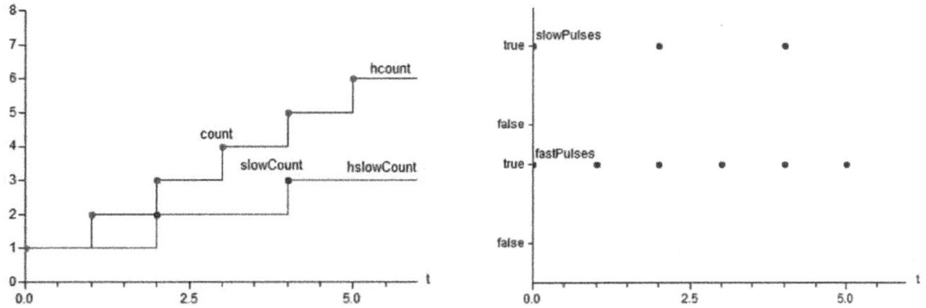

Figure 13-26. *Left*: two synchronized counters, `count` with an interval of 1 second and `slowCount` with an interval of 2 seconds, shown as round dots at clock ticks, together with the hold variables `hcount` and `hslowCount` which also have values between clock ticks. *Right*: the two clock variables, `slowPulses` with an interval of 2 seconds, and `fastPulses` with an interval of 1 second.

If we change the slow clock to make it even slower, with a tick every fourth second, the declaration of `slowPulses` is changed as follows:

```
  Clock slowPulses = Clock(4) "Clock tick every 4 seconds";
```

Simulation results and plots with the factor four difference in counter frequency appear in Figure 13-27 below.

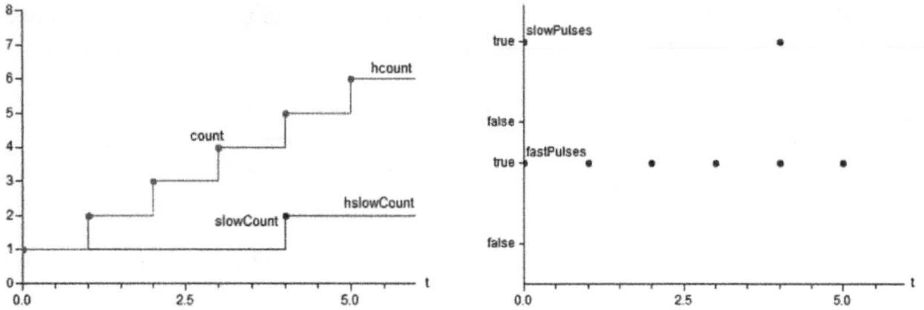

Figure 13-27. The same simulation and plots as in Figure 13-26, except that `slowCount` is now a factor of 4 slower than `count` instead of as previously a factor of 2.

In general, as is well known from process programming theory, deadlocks can occur between mutually dependent parallel processes competing for the same resource. In Modelica each when-equation can be thought of as specifying a kind of parallel process. However, the great advantage here is that the deadlock is detected at compile time in contrast to asynchronous parallel programming languages where deadlocks often cause problematic bugs first noticed at run time.

```
model DeadLock
  Boolean b1,b2;  // by a more realistic example
equation
  when b1 then
     b2 = true;
  end when;
  when b2 then
     b1 = true;
  end when;
end DeadLock;
```

After having focused on event synchronization for a while, we will now turn to general *propagation* of events of which synchronization is a special case. Furthermore, we should not forget that an event also might involve the change of continuous variables, which might be used in equations and conditions of other models and when-equations. Propagation of events thus might require evaluation of both continuous equations and conditional equations.

Regarding simple propagation of events, `Boolean` variables are quite useful. For example, a level sensor in a tank may generate a `tank.level` measurement value. If the `tank.level` variable exceeds a certain `tank.maxLevel`, an overflow event should be generated and propagated (Figure 13-28).

For propagation of the overflow event we declare a variable called `overflowing` in the connector `out` belonging to the level sensor, and define the variable by a `Boolean` equation, for example:

```
levelSensor.out.overflowing = tank.level > tank.maxLevel;
```

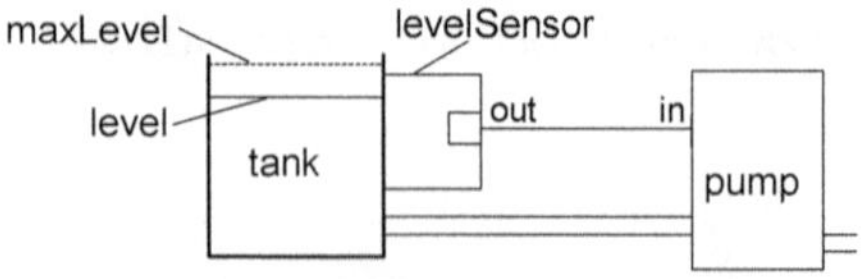

Figure 13-28. A level sensor in a tank may set the variable `overflowing` to `true`, causing an event which propagates to the pump via the connection between the connectors `out` and `in`.

Furthermore, we connect the level sensor to a pump to be able to automatically start pumping when an overflow happens in order to reduce the level. This is modeled by connecting the `levelSensor.out` connector to the `pump.in` connector as below:

```
connect(levelSensor.out, pump.in);
```

This connection generates an equation for the `Boolean` variable `overflowing`, which enables propagation of overflow events from the level sensor to the pump:

```
levelSensor.out.overflowing = pump.in.overflowing;
```

The pump might react on such events by testing its corresponding variable `in.overflowing` from its connector `pump.in`. The condition for starting pumping, for example, could be either tank overflow or the user pushing a start button on the pump:

```
startPumping = in.overflowing or startPushed;
```

For simulation, these equations need to be solved for the variable `pump.startPumping`. Equations that define boolean variables usually need to have a simple form in order to be solvable. There should be a single `Boolean` variable on the left-hand side or on the right-hand side of such equations.

13.2.6.7 Multiple Events at the Same Point in Time and Event Iteration

Multiple events may actually occur at the same point in time, as hinted at in the previous section about event synchronization. Two or more independent events may just happen to be fired at the same time instant, or additional events may be fired at the time instant as a consequence of handling one of the events at that time instant.

The discussion below concerns *unclocked events*. Clocked events are handled specially when solving equations in the clocked partition of the equation system and do not need event iteration (Section 18.2.5, page 1012).

It is useful to maintain a well-defined ordering between events also if they occur at the same time instant when time ordering is not possible. An important reason is to provide a deterministic execution, that is, the simulation will always give the same results given the same input data. Two rules can be used to define this ordering, where the first is mandatory and the second is somewhat arbitrary since it is *not supported* by the Modelica language specification:

- Data dependency order.
- Declaration order.

The *data dependency order* is determined by data-flow dependencies from defining equations to event conditions. For example, in the model `MultipleEvents` below the event handler `C` gives the new value `2` to the variable `x`, which in turn causes the event condition `x==2` of the event handler `A` to become `true`, thereby generating an additional event at the same time instant. The handler A subsequently gives `x` the value `3`, which triggers the event `B`. This gives the ordering: C→A→B.

Note that when *several events* are generated at the *same time instant*, the value of the `pre` function, for example, `pre(x)` in the example below, refers to the value of `x` previous to the current event according to the event ordering, and not to the value of `x` immediately before the current time instant.

The declaration order or some other deterministic ordering rule could in principle be used to order the independent events `C` and `D`, which both occur at the same time instant when `time`=2. However, since declaration order is *not* supported by Modelica we need to use `elsewhen` for priorities. Using "declaration order" and `elsewhen`, we obtain the ordering `C`→`D`, since the event handler for `C` occurs before the one for `D` in the elsewhen-sequence in the Modelica code below.

```
model MultipleEvents
  discrete Integer x(start=1);
  Boolean          signal(start=false);
equation
```

```
    when x==2 then           // Event handler A
      x = pre(x)+1;            // x becomes 2+1 = 3
    elsewhen x==3 then       // Event handler B
      x = pre(x)+5;            // x becomes 3+5 = 8
    end when;

    when time>=2 then        // Event handler C
      x = 2;                     // x becomes 2
    elsewhen time>=2 then    // Event handler D
      signal = true;
    end when;

  end MultipleEvents;
```

The second issue concerns the *event-handling order* in the queue of events pending at the same time instant. For example, the ordered set of events {C,D} is initially pending at time=2. According to the above ordering rules, C is serviced first. What happens next is dependent on the event-handling ordering algorithm.

The simplest algorithm would always service the first event according to the event ordering. In theory, but not in this example, C might cause the C event to be triggered once more and thereby be serviced first again since it comes first in the event ordering, giving the C event unfair advantages. A servicing algorithm that is more *fair* would handle the remaining events in the queue *before* coming back to the first event. Such an algorithm is sketched below, where steps 1–4 are *repeated* until you exit from the algorithm:

1. Determine the ordered set of pending events.
2. If this set is empty, that is, no conditions for conditional equations are `true`, exit this algorithm and continue continuous simulation and/or future time-event handling.
3. Otherwise handle the first event in the ordered set of pending events.
4. For each of the remaining events in the ordered set, check if the event condition is still `true`, and if this is the case, handle the event.

It is possible to formulate models for which this algorithm never terminates. However, in practice, for most practical models the algorithm terminates within a few iterations. This kind of iterative procedure is also known as *event iteration*, see also Section 18.2.5, page 1012. Note that according to step 2 in the algorithm all event conditions (e.g., typical edge conditions for when-equations) are `false` at exit. This kind of algorithm also assumes that it is possible to compute a consistent state after handling each event. If we apply the algorithm to the above `MultipleEvents` example, the following sets of ordered pending events are created and serviced in order:

1. The initial ordered set of pending events is determined to be {C,D} at time = 2. First service C, then D.
2. The next set of pending events is {A}, since event C triggers A.
3. The next set becomes {B}, since A triggers B.
4. The final set is {}, that is, empty, causing exit from the algorithm and continuation of continuous simulation and handling of future events.

This is just an example of an event-servicing algorithm. The Modelica language specification does not prescribe any special algorithm, thereby giving freedom to the Modelica language implementor to invent even better algorithms.

13.3 Discrete Model Examples and Related Formalisms

The purpose of this section is to provide you with a number of model examples of different kinds of discrete systems, and to compare with several well-known discrete modeling formalisms. You will see that the modeling power of Modelica is quite sufficient to conveniently represent models based on these formalisms. A number of examples are presented in two variants, using either unclocked or clocked (Section 13.6, page 694) modeling styles. Clocked modeling is especially suitable for sampled systems which usually contain digital system parts with built-in digital clocks.

13.3.1 Sampled Systems

A simple type of discrete-time model is the *sampled* data model often used in applications because of its simplicity and favorable analytical properties. A sampled model is characterized by its ability to periodically *sample* continuous input variables $u(t)$, calculate new *outputs* y that can influence the physical world as well as continuous parts of the model, and update discrete-time state variables x. Both the output variables y and the state variables x keep their values between the sample events since they are discrete-time variables. Such a sampled system model is schematically depicted in Figure 13-29. A sampled system model has only one kind of event, the *sample event*, and can be represented by the following state space equations:

$$\begin{aligned} x_{k+1} &= f(x_k, u_k, t_k, t_{k+1}) \\ y_k &= h(x_k, u_k, t_k) \end{aligned} \qquad (13\text{-}6)$$

Here x_k is a sequence of state vectors or scalars, u_k is a sequence of sampled input vectors or scalars, and y_k is a sequence of output vectors or scalars at points in time $t = t_0, t_1, ..., t_k, t_{k+1}, ...$, and so on. In a real-time environment, periodic sampling is usually assumed with $t_k = kT, k = 0,1,2,3,...$, where T is the fixed sample interval. At any sample event occurring at time t_k, the model should compute x_{k+1} and y_k depending on u_k and x_k. It is important that the input u_k can propagate through the system without any time delay, since the input might be the output of another subsystem.

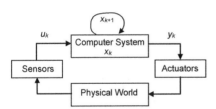

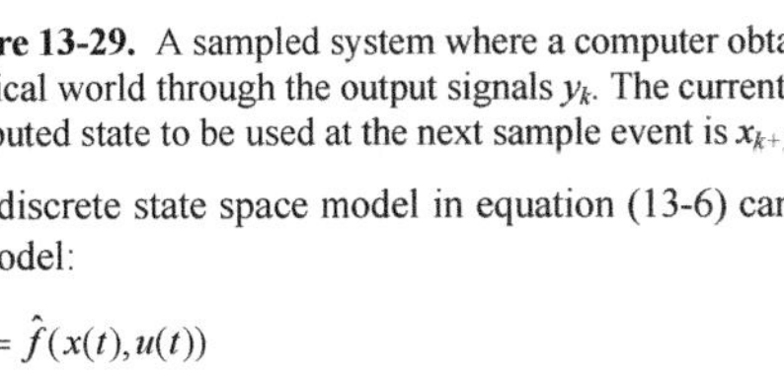

Figure 13-29. A sampled system where a computer obtains sampled inputs u_k and controls the continuous physical world through the output signals y_k. The current discrete state is represented by x_k, and the computed state to be used at the next sample event is x_{k+1}.

The discrete state space model in equation (13-6) can be derived from the usual continuous-time state space model:

$$\begin{aligned} \dot{x}(t) &= \hat{f}(x(t), u(t)) \\ y(t) &= h(x(t), u(t)) \end{aligned} \qquad (13\text{-}7)$$

using the Euler approximation of the derivative $\dot{x}(t)$:

$$\dot{x}(t_k) \approx \frac{x(t_{k+1}) - x(t_k)}{t_{k+1} - t_k} \qquad (13\text{-}8)$$

By substituting the above approximation for $\dot{x}(t_k)$ into the continuous state space model equations and doing a few rearrangements, we obtain the following approximate state space equations on a difference equation form:

$$x(t_{k+1}) \approx f(x(t_k), u(t_k), t_k, t_{k+1}) = x(t_k) + (t_{k+1} - t_k)\hat{f}(x(t_k), u(t_k)) \tag{13-9}$$
$$y(t_k) = h(x(t_k), u(t_k))$$

Using the definitions below for x_k, x_{k+1}, u_k, and y_k we obtain the previously presented state space equations for sampled systems. In the following Modelica models of sampled systems we will use the notation `u`, `y`, `x`, and `pre(x)` (or `previous(x)`) as defined below:

$$\begin{aligned}
\mathrm{u} &= u_k = u(t_k) \\
\mathrm{y} &= y_k = y(t_k) \\
\mathrm{x} &= x_{k+1} = \lim_{\varepsilon \to 0} x(t_{k+1} - \varepsilon) \\
\mathrm{pre}(x) &= x_k = \lim_{\varepsilon \to 0} x(t_k - \varepsilon) \\
\mathrm{f} &= f
\end{aligned} \tag{13-10}$$

Figure 13-30 illustrates the relationships between the input u_k, output y_k, and state variables x_k at and between sampling points t_k in a sampled system model.

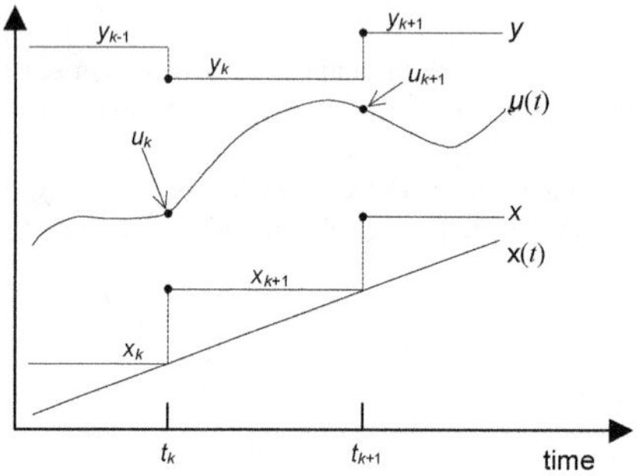

Figure 13-30. At a sample point t_k, the sampled value u_k of $u(t)$ together with the value x_k of the discrete state variable x are used to compute the output value y_k and the next state value x_{k+1}. The discrete-time variable x is an approximation to the continuous-time variable $x(t)$.

13.3.1.1 Simple Periodic Sampler

The following model is a simple periodic sampler with a sampling period `T` that is constant and defined as a parameter that can be changed by the model user. As we remarked previously, this model has only one kind of event, the sampling event. We use the built-in function `sample` in the when-condition `sample(0,T)` to periodically generate sampling events with a period time `T`. This is a simple model using the state space equations that were defined in the previous section.

```
model SimplePeriodicSamplerUnclocked
  parameter Real T=1   "Sample period";
  input     Real u     "Input used at sample events";
  discrete output Real y  "Output computed at sample events";
protected
  discrete Real x;      // discrete-time state variable
equation
  when sample(0,T) then
    x = f(pre(x),u);   // state update expression
    y = h(pre(x),u);   // output expression
  end when;
end SimplePeriodicSamplerUnclocked;
```

A clocked version of the same model appears as follows. A clocked output variable `y1` had to be introduced since only equations for clocked variables are allowed inside a clocked when-equation. The equation for the unclocked variable `y` which is just a hold version of `y1`, had to be placed outside the clocked when-equation.

```
model SimplePeriodicSamplerClocked
  parameter Real T=1  "Clock period";
  input     Real u    "Input used at sample events";
  discrete output Real y1   "Output only defined at sample events";
  output    Real y   "hold output y also defined between sample events";
protected
  discrete Real x     "clocked discrete-time state variable";
equation
  when Clock(T) then
    x = f(previous(x),sample(u));    // state update expression
    y1 = h(previous(x),sample(u));  // output updated at clock events
  end when;
  y = hold(y1);       // hold output y also defined between events
end SimplePeriodicSamplerClocked;
```

We simplify even further by replacing the calls to the functions `f` and `h` by simple example expressions, removing the `protected` keyword to make the state variable `x` accessible for plotting, and setting `u=time` as an example instead of a real input signal:

```
model VerySimplePeriodicSamplerClocked
  parameter Real T=1  "Clock period";
            Real u=time    "Use time as input at sample events";
  discrete output Real y1  "Output only defined at sample events";
  output    Real y   "hold output y also defined between sample events";
  discrete  Real x(start=0)    "clocked discrete-time state variable";
equation
  when Clock(T) then
    x = previous(x) + sample(u);   // state update expression
    y1 = previous(x)+ 3*sample(u);  // output updated at clock events
  end when;
  y = hold(y1);       // hold output y also defined between events
end VerySimplePeriodicSamplerClocked;
```

Simulating `VerySimplePeriodicSamplerClocked` for five seconds appears as shown in Figure 13-31.

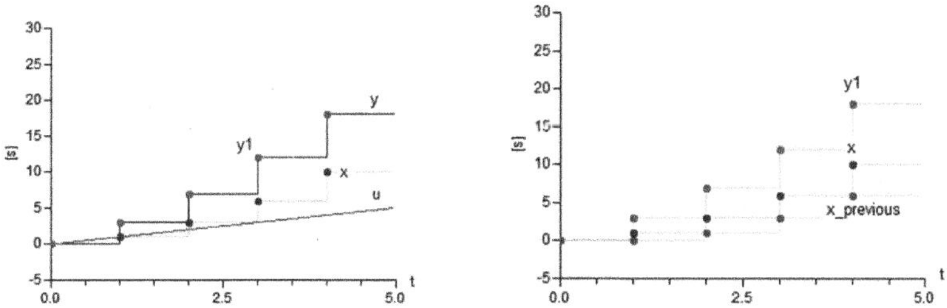

Figure 13-31. *Left*: Plot of the clocked `y1` and unclocked `y` output variables on top of each other, state variable `x` and input `u=time`. *Right*: Clocked variables `y1`, `x`, and `previous(x)`.

As a comparison, we show an unclocked version of `VerySimplePeriodicSampler`:

```
model VerySimplePeriodicSamplerUnclocked
  parameter Real T=1  "Sample period";
            Real u=time   "Input used at sample events";
  discrete output Real y  "Output computed at sample events";
```

```
  discrete Real x;      // discrete-time state variable
equation
  when sample(0,T) then
    x = pre(x) + u;     // state update expression
    y = pre(x) + 3*u;   // output y updated at sample events
  end when;
end VerySimplePeriodicSamplerUnclocked;
```

As expected, when simulating the unclocked model `VerySimplePeriodicSamplerUnclocked` the output variable `y` and state variable `x` to the left in Figure 13-32 appear to be the same as the previously simulated clocked model with `x`, `y` and `y1` in the right diagram of Figure 13-32 and in Figure 13-31, apart from the usual difference between clocked and unclocked variables.

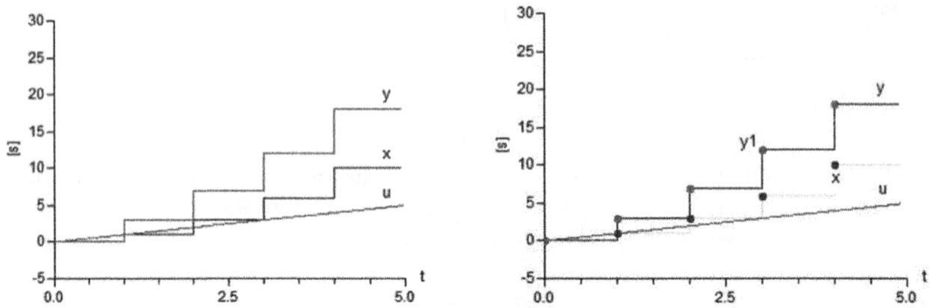

Figure 13-32. *Left*: Plot of the simulation of the unclocked model with output variable `y`, state variable `x`, and input `u=time`. *Right*: Plot from Figure 13-31 of corresponding variables from the clocked model.

13.3.1.2 Base Classes for Sampling Models

It is possible to formulate base classes for scalar sampling models using the previously presented state-space equations. Two base classes are presented, one for unclocked and one for clocked models. The general classes `BaseSamplerUnclocked` and `BaseSamplerClocked` can, for example, be specialized to either periodic or aperiodic sampler models and have replaceable functions `f` and `h` to adapt their behavior. In the unclocked model a `Boolan` variable is used to represent a clock, whereas the clocked model uses a `Clock` variable.

```
partial class BaseSamplerUnclocked
  Real  u    "Input used at sample events";
  discrete output Real y;
  Boolean   doSample;
  replaceable function f = Modelica.Math.atan2; // atan2 used as dummy
  replaceable function h = Modelica.Math.atan2; // default function
  discrete   Real x(start=0);
equation
  when doSample then
    x = f(pre(x),u);  // state update expression
    y = h(pre(x),u);  // output expression
  end when;
end BaseSamplerUnclocked;
```

The clocked base sample model uses a clock variable `doSample` of built-in type `Clock`:

```
partial model BaseSamplerClocked
  Real u     "Input used at clock events";
  discrete output Real y1    "Output only defined at sample events";
  output     Real y     "hold output y also defined between sample events";
  Clock   doSample;
  replaceable function f = Modelica.Math.atan2; // atan2 used as dummy
```

```
  replaceable function h = Modelica.Math.atan2; // default function
  discrete Real x(start=0)  "clocked discrete-time state variable";
equation
  when doSample then
    x = f(previous(x),sample(u));    // state update expression
    y1 = h(previous(x),sample(u));  // output updated at clock events
  end when;
  y = hold(y1);       // hold output y also defined between clock events
end BaseSamplerClocked;
```

We use two very simple example functions `f2` and `h2` for the redeclarations:

```
  function f2
    input Real u1;
    input Real u2;
    output Real y;
  algorithm
     y :=  u1+u2;
  end f2;

  function h2
    input Real u1;
    input Real u2;
    output Real y;
  algorithm
     y := u1 + 5*u2;
  end h2;
```

The base models are extended to periodic sampling models `PeriodicSamplerUnclocked` and `PeriodicSamplerClocked` with a fixed period time `T`:

```
model PeriodicSamplerUnclocked
  extends BaseSamplerUnclocked(u=time,redeclare function f=f2,
                                      redeclare function h=h2);
  parameter Real T=1 "sample period";
equation
  doSample = sample(0, T);
end PeriodicSamplerUnclocked;

model PeriodicSamplerClocked
  extends BaseSamplerClocked(u=time,redeclare function f=f2,
                                    redeclare function h=h2);
  parameter Real T=1 "sample period";
equation
  doSample = Clock(T);
end PeriodicSamplerClocked;
```

Plots of simulations of these two models for five seconds are shown in Figure 13-33 below.

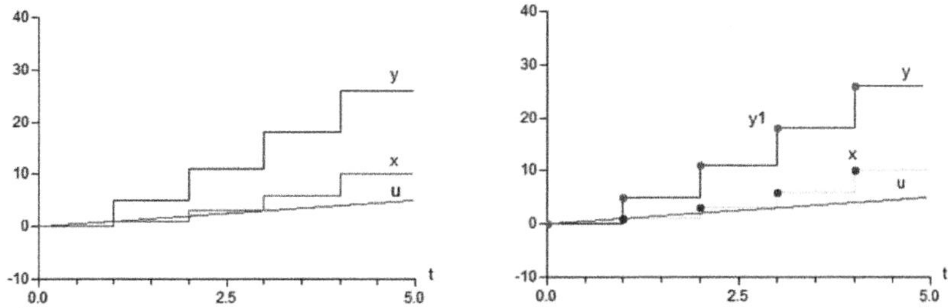

Figure 13-33. *Left*: Plot of a simulation of the unclocked model `PeriodicSamplerUnclocked`. *Right*: Plot of a simulation of an "equivalent" clocked model `PeriodicSamplerClocked`.

13.3.1.3 Aperiodic Sampler

Besides the above periodic sampler, an *aperiodic* sampling model with a time-varying sample period can be obtained by specializing the base class.

A variable `nextSampling` is used for the next sampling time, which is *current time* + `periodTime` when the current time has reached the previous value of `nextSampling`. In these examples we increase the period time by the logarithm of the current time just to have a time-varying period time.

As before, a Boolean `doSample` is used in the unclocked model:

```
model APeriodicSamplerUnclocked
  extends BaseSamplerUnclocked(u=time,redeclare function f=f2,
                                redeclare function h=h2);
  discrete Real nextSampling(start=0);
  discrete Real periodTime(start=2)   "time-varying sample period";
equation
  doSample  = time>pre(nextSampling);
  when doSample then
    nextSampling  = pre(nextSampling) + periodTime;
    periodTime    = pre(periodTime) + log(pre(periodTime)); // example
  end when;
end APeriodicSamplerUnclocked;
```

In the clocked model, the clock with a varying increasing interval is created by the expression `Clock(`*`condition`*`, `*`startInterval`*`)` gives a *clock triggered* by the *`condition`* expression (Section 13.6.7.5, page 704), with an optional *`startInterval`* having default 0.0. In the model below only the first argument is supplied. The variable `doSample` has `Clock` type.

Note that the clocked model uses `Clock(time>hold(nextSampling))` and not `Clock(time>hold(previous(nextSampling)))`, whereas the unclocked model uses `time>pre(nextSampling))`. See Section 0, page 631, for an explanation.

```
model APeriodicSamplerClocked
  extends BaseSamplerClocked(u=time,redeclare function f=f2,
                              redeclare function h=h2);
  discrete Real nextSampling(start=0);
  discrete Real periodTime(start=2)   "time-varying sample period";
equation
  doSample  = Clock(time>hold(nextSampling));
  when doSample then
    nextSampling  = previous(nextSampling)+periodTime;
    periodTime    = previous(periodTime) +log(previous(periodTime));
  end when;
end APeriodicSamplerClocked;
```

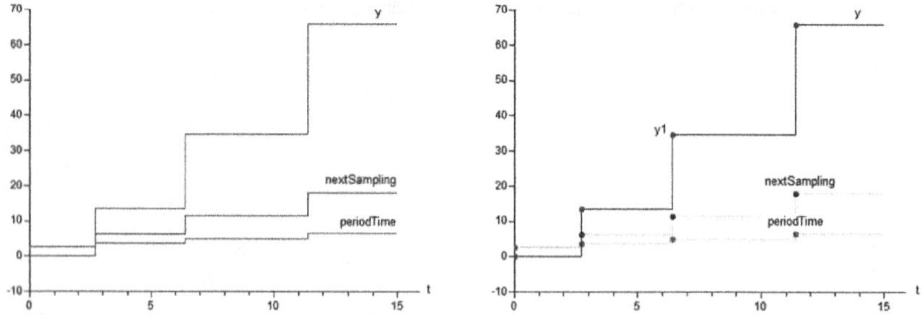

Figure 13-34. *Left*: Plot of a simulation of the unclocked model `APeriodicSamplerUnclocked`. *Right*: Plot of a simulation of an "equivalent" clocked model `APeriodicSamplerClocked`. In both cases the time interval `periodTime` between events slowly increases over time.

Simulations and plots of the `APeriodicSamplerUnclocked` and `APeriodicSamplerClocked` models are shown in Figure 13-34.

13.3.1.4 Analysis of pre versus previous in Clocked and Unclocked APeriodicSampler

There is a difference between the clocked and unclocked models. `APeriodicSamplerClocked` uses `doSample = Clock(time>hold(nextSampling))` and not `doSample = Clock(time>hold(previous(nextSampling)))`. The unclocked model uses `doSample = time>pre(nextSampling))`.

This is due to the different behavior of `pre()` and `hold(previous())` outside when-clauses (Section 13.2.5.14, page 610). Let us analyze what is happing with the expression:

```
Clock(time > hold(previous(nextSampling)))
```

At `time == 0 + eps` we have:

```
hold(previous(nextSampling)) == 0
(time > hold(previous(nextSampling))) ==  true   // clock tick when true
nextSampling = 0 + periodTime                    // updated nextSampling
```

After the clock tick we still have the value zero from the previous tick, before the most recent tick:

```
hold(previous(nextSampling)) == 0
```

Now, let us analyze the unclocked example. The expression `pre(nextSampling)` *outside of* a when-clause just refers to the *left limit* (Section 13.2.5.12, page 609) of `nextSampling` which is the *same* as `nextSampling` between events. It is *not* the value `nextSampling` had at the previous event.

```
time == 0+eps:
pre(nextSampling) == 0
(time > pre(nextSampling)) == true      // event is generated when true
nextSampling = 0 + periodTime;          // updated nextSampling
```

After the event at time zero:

```
pre(nextSampling) == nextSampling  // pre(nextSampling) same as nextSampling
time > pre(nextSampling) == false => no event
```

At time `0+nextSampling`:

```
time == 0+nextSampling+eps:
time > pre(nextSampling)  ==  true   // generates event
```

Since `pre(nextSampling)` and `nextSampling` are the same outside when-clauses we can change the model:

```
model APeriodicSamplerUnclocked2
  extends BaseSamplerUnclocked(u=time,redeclare function f=f2,
                                      redeclare function h=h2);
  discrete Real nextSampling(start=0);
  discrete Real periodTime(start=2)  "time-varying sample period";
equation
  doSample = time>pre(nextSampling);  // changed here
  when doSample then
    nextSampling = pre(nextSampling) + periodTime;
    periodTime   = pre(periodTime) + log(pre(periodTime)); // example
  end when;
end APeriodicSamplerUnclocked2;
```

The simulation of `APeriodicSamplerUnclocked2` is the same as `APeriodicSamplerUnclocked` in Figure 13-34, page 630.

13.3.1.5 Discrete Scalar State Space Sampling Model

A discrete first-order scalar state space model with periodic sampling can be formulated as follows, essentially being a special case of the `BaseSampler` models (Section 13.3.1.2, page 628) even though they do not inherit from the base classes in this case. Similar models are in Section 13.3.1.1, page 626.

```
model DiscreteScalarStateSpaceUnclocked
  parameter Real a=1, b=1, c=1, d=3;
  parameter Real T=1   "Clock period;
            Real u=time;  // an external input, here replaced with time
  discrete output Real y;
  discrete Real x;
equation
  when sample(0,T) then
    x = a*pre(x) + b*u;
    y = c*pre(x) + d*u;
  end when;
end DiscreteScalarStateSpaceUnclocked;
```

The clocked model version is:

```
model DiscreteScalarStateSpaceClocked
  parameter Real a=1, b=1, c=1, d=3;
  parameter Real T=1  "Clock period";
            Real u=time    "Use time as input at sample events";
  discrete output Real y1  "Output only defined at sample events";
  output    Real y   "hold output y also defined between sample events";
  discrete  Real x(start=0)   "clocked discrete-time state variable";
equation
  when Clock(T) then
    x  = a*previous(x) + b*sample(u);  // state update expression
    y1 = b*previous(x) + d*sample(u);  // output updated at clock events
  end when;
  y = hold(y1);      // hold output y also defined between events
end model DiscreteScalarStateSpaceClocked;
```

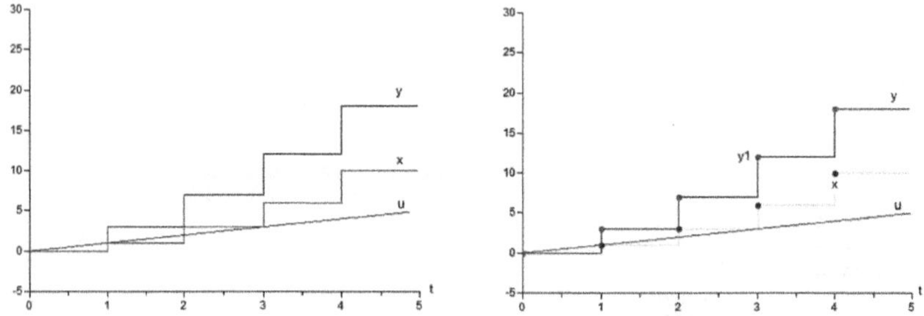

Figure 13-35. *Left*: Plot of a simulation of the unclocked `DiscreteScalarStateSpaceUnclocked`. *Right*: Plot of a simulation of an "equivalent" clocked model `DiscreteScalarStateSpaceClocked`.

Alternatively, the discrete scalar state space model can be expressed by extending the `BaseSampler` model for periodic sampling and redeclaring the functions `f` and `g` as below. However, in this case the result is not shorter or more readable since the syntax for expressing the local functions `f1` and `h1` is not very concise. On the other hand, if the functions `f1` and `h1` instead would be used in several places, the modeling style based on replaceable functions is preferable.

```
model DiscreteScalarStateSpace2Unclocked
  extends BaseSamplerUnclocked(u=time,redeclare function f=f1,
                                      redeclare function h=h1);
  constant Real a=1, b=1, c=1, d=7;
  constant Real T=1 "sample period";

  function f1
    input  Real x1;
    input  Real x2;
    output Real y1;
  algorithm
    y1 := a*x1 + b*x2;
  end f1;

  function h1
    input  Real x1;
    input  Real x2;
    output Real y1;
  algorithm
    y1 := c*x1 + d*x2;
  end h;
equation
  doSample = sample(0,T);
end DiscreteScalarStateSpace2Unclocked;
```

A simulation and plot of the model is shown in Figure 13-34 below.

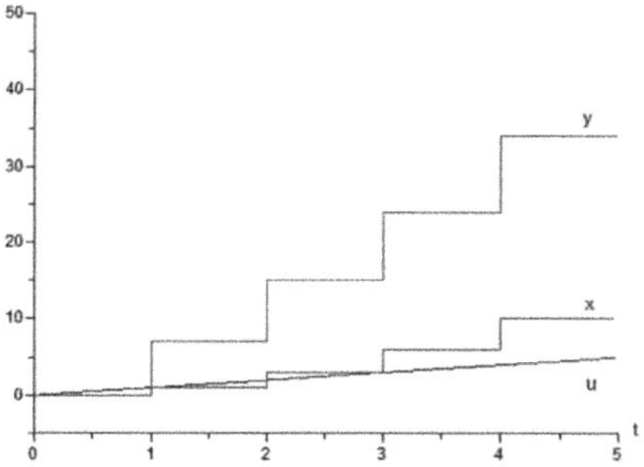

Figure 13-36. Simulation and plot of the unclocked model `DiscreteScalarStateSpace2Unclocked`.

13.3.1.6 Discrete Vector State Space Sampling Model

Usually, state space models are expressed using the more general vector form, as in the `DiscreteVectorStateSpace` periodic sampling model below:

```
model DiscreteVectorStateSpace
  parameter Integer n,m,p;
  parameter Real A[n,n], B[n,m], C[p,n], D[p,m];
  parameter Real T=1;
  input     Real u[m];
  discrete output Real y[p];
protected
  discrete Real x[n];
equation
  when sample(0,T) then
    x = A*pre(x) + B*u;
    y = C*pre(x) + D*u;
  end when;
end DiscreteVectorStateSpace;
```

13.3.1.7 Two-rate Sampling Model

A rather general structure for many sampled systems is a common clock together with one or more subsystems that are synchronized by this common clock. The sample events are synchronized and the sampling frequencies are integer fractions of the common clock frequency (Figure 13-37).

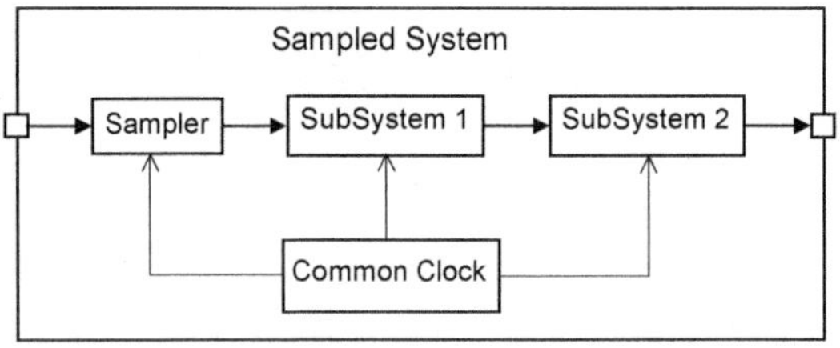

Figure 13-37. A sampled system consisting of a sampler and two subsystems, all synchronized by a common clock.

One of the simplest examples of this structure is a two-rate sampler with a fast sampling system coupled to a fast clock, and a slow sampling system with a sampling frequency that is an integer fraction of the frequency of the fast clock. At every 5th activation of the `fastSample` when-equation is the `slowSample` when-equation evaluated.

For example, in the `TwoRateSamplerUnclocked` and `TwoRateSamplerClocked` models below, the slow sampler is five times slower than the fast sampler, i.e., the `slowSample` when-equation is evaluated at every fifth activation of the `fastSample` when-equation.

This model and similar models are very natural to model using the clocked language primitives (Section 13.6, page 694) which have the property that clocks related by an integer or rational number or by the `subSample` or `superSample` operators are automatically synchronized.

```
model TwoRateSamplerClocked  "Two clocked synchronized counters"
  Clock slowPulses;             // Clock variable of type Clock
  Clock fastPulses;             // Clock variable of type Clock
  discrete Real x,y;            // Clocked variables for sampled values
  Real        hx,hy;            // Hold variables also defined between ticks
  Integer hcount, hslowCount;
equation
  fastPulses = Clock(1);        // Define the fast clock
  slowPulses = subSample(fastPulses,5); // Slow down clock by a factor 5
  when fastPulses then          // Sample sin every second
    x = sin(sample(time)+1);
  end when;
  when slowPulses then          // Sample log every 5th second
    y = log(sample(time)+1);
  end when;
  hx = hold(x);         // Hold variables are also defined between ticks
  hy = hold(y);
end TwoRateSamplerClocked;
```

In the unclocked version of the model, `TwoRateSamplerUnclocked`, the two samplers are synchronized in a more complicated way via equations involving the `cyCounter` variable. This is an example of the synchronization method earlier described in Section 13.2.6.6, page 618.

```
model TwoRateSamplerUnclocked
  discrete Real x,y;             // Variables for sampled values
  Boolean fastSample;
  Boolean slowSample;
  Integer cyCounter(start=0);   // Cyclic count 0,1,2,3,4, 0,1,2,3,4,...
equation
```

```
    fastSample = sample(0,1);     // Define the fast sampling interval
    when fastSample then
      cyCounter  = if pre(cyCounter) < 4 then pre(cyCounter)+1 else 0;
      slowSample = pre(cyCounter) == 0;   // Define the slow clock
    end when;
  equation
    when fastSample then         // Sample sin every second
      x = sin(time+1);
    end when;
  equation
    when slowSample then         // Sample log every 5th second
      y = log(time+1);
    end when;
  end TwoRateSamplerUnclocked;
```

Both models are simulated for 20 seconds and plotted in Figure 13-38. Even though the sampling is very coarse-grained, the `sin` and `log` function shapes can be recognized in the sampled variable curves.

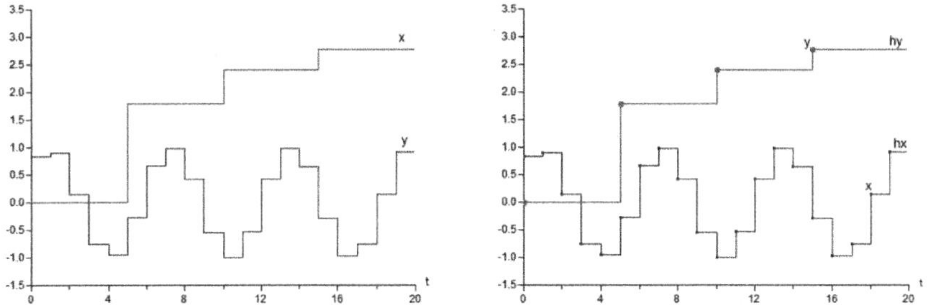

Figure 13-38. *Left*: Plot of a simulation of the unclocked `TwoRateSamplerUnclocked`. *Right*: Plot of a simulation of an "equivalent" clocked model `TwoRateSamplerUnclocked`. The fast sampler samples the `sin` function 5 times per second, whereas the slow sampler samples the `log` function once per second.

13.3.2 Finite State Automata and State Machines

Finite state automata is a simple and often-used formalism for modeling the behavior of certain discrete systems. Applications include digital circuits such as control units, neural networks, lexical analysis of text input to compilers, and so on. A finite state automaton consists of the following components:

- A finite set of *states*, often denoted $Q = \{q_1, q_2, ...\}$.
- A finite set or alphabet of values, corresponding to *event types*, denoting state transitions. An event is the arrival of a value e in this finite set.
- A *next state* function δ mapping a state q and a transition value e to a set of states. A *deterministic* finite automaton maps to a set containing a single state, making the choice of the next state unambiguous.
- A set of initial states and a set of final states.

A pure finite state automaton has no notion of time. However, it is often used as a model component in a continuous-time dynamic system where time is relevant. In this case each state transition *value* corresponds to an event type. A specific event is the arrival of a certain *value* at some point in time.

A finite state automaton can be viewed as a kind of control unit that always is in some state, denoted q, belonging to a finite set of states Q. It continuously receives values, denoted e, thereby switching to new states as specified by the next state function δ (q,e). The automaton moves from a state q to a state q', where $q' \in \delta'(e,q)$. The automaton is *deterministic* provided that the following two conditions hold:

- The next state function $\delta'(e,q) = \{q'\}$, i.e., the target set contains only one state.
- There is only one initial state.

The arrival of values in the alphabet can be viewed as inputs, as outputs, as external control signals, or as internal events, depending on how the finite state automaton interacts with the rest of the system.

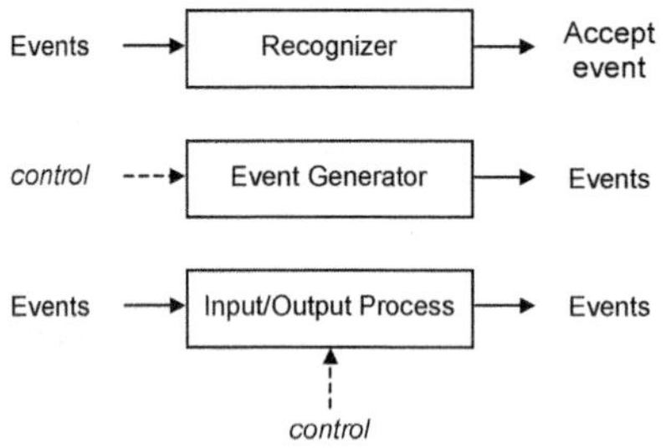

Figure 13-39. Three common uses of finite state automatons as model components.

There are at least three common uses of finite state automatons as model components which are depicted in Figure 13-39:

- In the first configuration, the finite state automaton works as a *recognizer* for certain sequences of input events. A very common application is as a *string acceptor* in lexical analysis of text, typically in compiler frontends. Input events are the arrival of characters in an input stream. For example, in Figure 13-40 the arrival of the character values ":" and "=" are accepted and recognized as the symbol "assignment operator," generating an output accept ":=" event. The automaton moves into a final state when a sequence of characters has arrived that is recognized as the string that should be accepted.
- The second configuration is that the finite state automaton works as a *generator*, that is, it generates a sequence of output events. It is controlled by the environment, for example, via input variables or input control events. This control influences the selection of events from the set of possible transitions, and the time when a transition should occur.
- In the third configuration, the finite state automaton works as an input/output process. Certain events are considered to be input events generated by the environment, some are output events, and some are internal events. The process can be controlled by the environment through external input variables or control events.

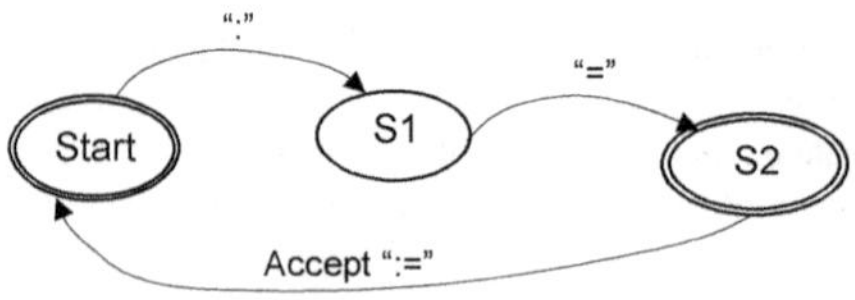

Figure 13-40. A finite state automaton that recognizes the assignment operator ":=" from its two characters colon and equal sign.

Several examples of finite state automata are presented below, including an introduction to clocked state machines with a counting state machine example in Section 13.3.2.1, page 637, a simple server model in Section 13.3.2.2, page 639, and an assignment operator (:=) recognizer related to Figure 13-40 above in Section 13.3.2.3, page 642.

13.3.2.1 Clocked State Machines

Starting with the Modelica language version 3.3, constructs for directly creating state machines to model finite state automata applications are available in the Modelica language. This section gives a short introduction to the use of such clocked state machines. A more complete description is available in Section 13.7, page 729.

There are many similarities between finite state automata and clocked state machines, but also some differences:

- *Self-transitions are not needed in Modelica clocked state machines*. The reason is that a clocked state machine stays in its current state if the transition conditions to other states are not fulfilled.
- *Transitions in state machines are made at clock ticks,* whereas transitions in finite state automata happen at the *arrival of events*. However, events can be modeled by Boolean transition conditions which may become true and cause a transition at the next clock tick.

The following equation operators are available to define state machines:

- `initialState(`*`state`*`)`. This equation operator makes the instance *`state`* be the initial state in the state machine. Only *one* initial state is allowed in a state machine.
- `transition(`*`from, to, condition, immediate, reset, synchronize, priority`*`)`. This equation operator defines a transition from instance *`from`* to instance *`to`*. These instances become states in the state machine.

  The transition fires when *`condition`* = `true` if *`immediate`* = `true` (this is called an "*`immediate`* transition," graphically depicted by a mark close to the arrow tip) or `previous(`*`condition`*`)` when *`immediate`*`=false` (this is called a "*delayed* transition," graphically depicted by a mark close the beginning of the arrow).

  If *`reset`* = `true`, graphically depicted as a filled arrow tip, the local states of the target state are reinitialized, that is, state machines are restarted in initial state and local state variables are reset to their start values. Global `inner` state variables declared as `outer` variables in the target states are not affected by `reset`.

  If *`synchronize`* = `true`, the transition is disabled until all state machines hierarchically within the `from` state have reached the final states, i.e., states without outgoing transitions.

These restrictions and properties currently apply:

- The state machine constructs are *only* applicable to *clocked* models which are *input-output blocks* only using clocked equations. No unclocked equations are allowed. Any instances of such blocks can be states of a state machine.
- A state machine is defined by a number of block instances instances at the same hierarchical level connected by `transition(...)` equations.
- A state without outgoing transitions is a *final state*.
- All parts of the state machine must have the *same clock*.
- If no clock is explicitly specified, a default clock starting at 0 with interval 1 is used.

The *restrictions* that all parts of a state machine have the *same clock* and that *no unclocked equations* are allowed are planned to be removed in a future Modelica language version.

We first define a simple state machine model called `CountingStateMachine1`. It has two states, the initial state `state1` and a second state `state2`. The default clock with interval 1 applies since there is no explicit clock declaration.

It has a counting variable `cn`, initially zero, which is declared `inner` at the model level, and `outer` in each state so that it can be referred to locally within each state. In `state1`, `cn` is increased by 1 at each clock tick, whereas in `state2`, `cn` is decreased by 3 at each clock tick.

When the transition condition for the first transition fulfills `previous(cn>7)=true` (since `immediate=false`) there is a transition to `state2` according to the `transition(...)` equation.

In `state2`, when the condition `previous(cn<3)=true` is fulfilled, there is a transition back to `state1`. The textual version of the model is shown immediately below, followed by the graphical version of the model in Figure 13-41 and a plot from the simulation in Figure 13-42.

```
model CountingStateMachine1
  inner Integer cn(start=0);

  block State1  "The initial state"
    outer output Integer cn;
  equation
    cn = previous(cn) + 1;   // Increase at each clock tick
  end State1;
  State1 state1;

  block State2
    outer output Integer cn;
  equation
    cn = previous(cn)  - 3;  // Decrease at each clock tick
  end State2;
  State2 state2;

equation
  initialState(state1);   // Make state1 the initial state starting at time 0
  transition(state1, state2, cn > 7, immediate=false); //transfer to state2
  transition(state2, state1, cn < 3, immediate=false);  //transfer to state1
end CountingStateMachine1;
```

The graphical version of the model is depicted in Figure 13-41. As usual, the textual version is automatically generated from the graphical one, but often with a different order of the declarations.

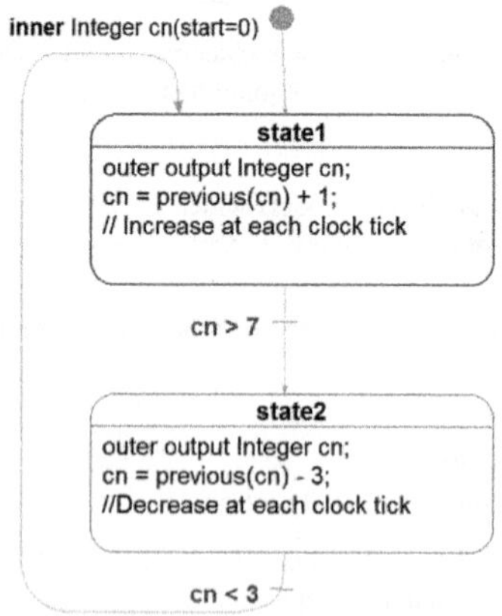

Figure 13-41. Connection diagram of the simple clocked state machine model `CountingStateMachine1`, except that `reset=true` in the transitions. This does not affect the behavior since `cn` is an `outer` variable.

We simulate the model `CountingStateMachine1` for 18 seconds and plot some results (Figure 13-42). Note that if the transition arguments are changed by setting `reset=true` the behavior is not changed since reset only affects local state variables and not the outer variable cn which is an alias of the global inner variable cn.

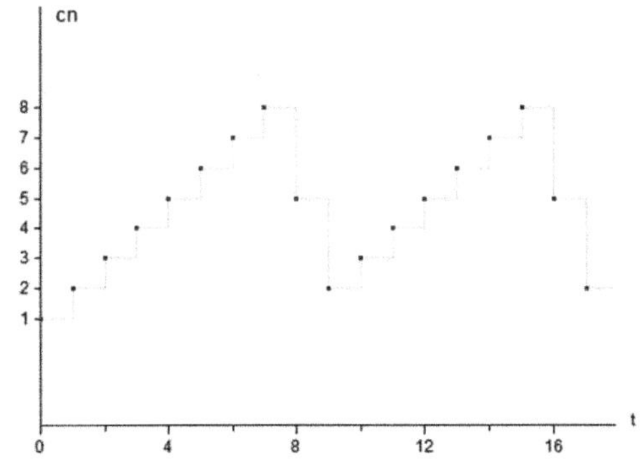

Figure 13-42. Plot of the counter cn from a simulation of the simple state machine model CountingStateMachine1.

13.3.2.2 Simple Server

One of the simplest possible examples of an input/output process modeled as a finite state automaton is the simple server whose state transition diagram is depicted in Figure 13-43.

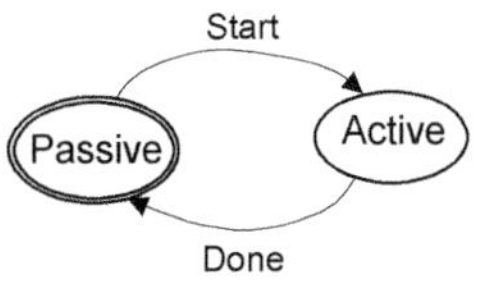

Figure 13-43. A finite state automaton model of a simple server system—an example of an input/output process with Start as input event and Done as output event.

The simple server finite automaton has two states, denoted Active and Passive, and a set of values {Start, Done} which is an alphabet of two symbols. The system becomes active and provides some service after receiving a Start event. After finishing the service item, the system emits a Done event and returns to the Passive state. This can be described by a next-state mapping function: δ(Passive, Start) = Active, δ(Active,Done) = Passive.

A graphical view of a clocked Modelica state machine model of the simple server automaton is depicted in Figure 13-44, whereas the textual version shown further below.

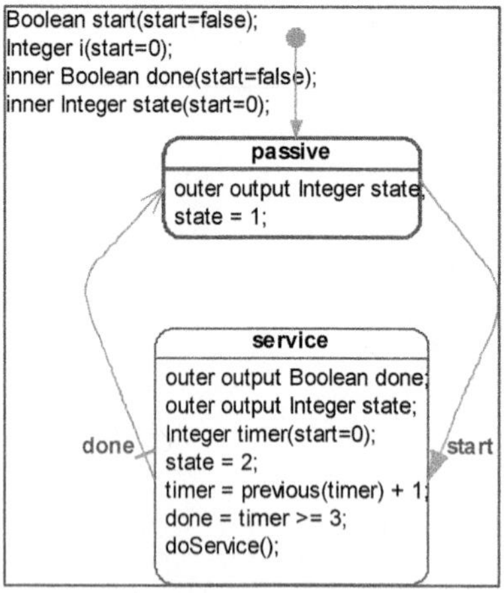

Figure 13-44. The simple server automaton starts in the `passive` state (state=1), transfers to the `service` state (`state`=2) at the event when the `start` variable becomes true. The filled arrow indicates a `reset` transition, the local variables (including `timer`) within the `service` state are reset to their start values. When the service is completed (`done` becomes true) a transition is done to the final state `passive`.

The variables `state` and `i` have been introduced to illustrate the operation of the simple server automaton shown in Figure 13-45 even though they are not needed for correct operation of the automaton. The `passive` state is encoded by `state=1` and the `service` state is encoded by `state=2`. A local `timer` variable in the `service` state counts the service time, the default clock is 1 Hz since no clock rate is specified. When the service activity in the `service` state is completed, the variable `done` is set to `true`.

```
model SimpleServer

  function doService "Dummy function to perform service"
  protected
    Integer i,sum := 0;
  algorithm
    for i in 1:10 loop
      sum :=  sum+i;
    end for;
  end doService;

  Boolean start(start=false);
  Integer i(start=0);
  inner Boolean done(start=false);
  inner Integer state(start=0);

  model Passive "State Passive"
    outer output Integer state;
  equation
    state = 1;  // indicate passive state
  end Passive;
  Passive passive;

  model Service "State Service"
    outer output Boolean done;
    outer output Integer state;
    Integer timer(start=0);
  equation
    state = 2;  // indicate service state
```

```
      timer = previous(timer) + 1;
      done = timer >= 3;
      doService();
    end Service;
    Service service;

  equation
    transition(passive, service, start, immediate=true,
               reset=true, synchronize=false, priority=1);
    transition(service, passive, done, immediate=false,
               reset=false, synchronize=false, priority=1);
    i = previous(i) + 1;
    start = (mod(i,2) == 0); // Generate a start service event every 2 ticks
    initialState(passive);
  end SimpleServer;
```

The `initialState(passive)` equation makes the `passive` state the initial state. There are two transition equations, the first from `passive` to `service` and the second back from `service` to `passive` which is both the initial and the final state.

The transition to the `service` state takes place when the `start` Boolean variable become true. The transition is immediate, and has `reset=true` which ***resets*** the ***local state variables*** (e.g., `timer`) in the target state `passive`. However, the `outer` variables `done` and `state` which are aliases of the same `inner` ***global*** variables are not reset since they are not local state variables. The transition back to the `passive` state is not immediate in order to avoid an algebraic loop.

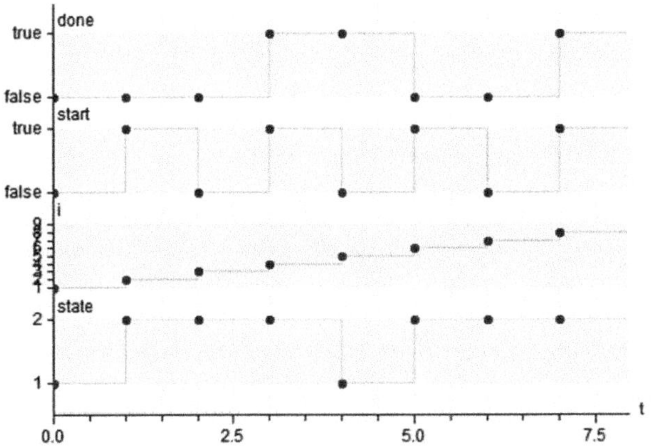

Figure 13-45. The automaton starts in `state=1` (`passive`) and transfers to `state=2` (`service`) at the event when `start` becomes true. The service in the `service` state is ongoing until `done` becomes true, when there is a transition back to the final `state=1`, the `passive` state. The cycle repeats when `start` again becomes true.

It can be useful to point out some modeling alternatives which do not work in this example using state machines. When-clauses with Boolean conditions are not allowed in clocked partitions (Section 13.6.15.1, page 722), especially not in state machines which currently only allow clocked equations. Thus, introducing a variable `event` and using a when-equation `when time>3 then event=Eventtype.done end when` would not work in the `service` state. Moreover, if we replace the when-equation with an if-equation to conditionally set `event=Eventtype.done` or `event=Eventtype.start`, there will be problems violating the single assignment rule. The solution in the above model is to introduce two separate clocked Boolean variables `done` and `start`, with the equation `done = timer >= 3` in the `service` state.

13.3.2.3 Assignment Recognizer

The assignment regocnizer is an example of a common application, a *string acceptor* in lexical analysis of text, typically in compiler frontends. Input events are the arrival of characters in an input stream. For example, in Figure 13-46 the arrival of the character values ":" and "=" are accepted and recognized as the symbol "assignment operator," generating an output accept ":=" event. The automaton moves into a final state when a sequence of characters has arrived that is recognized as the string that should be accepted.

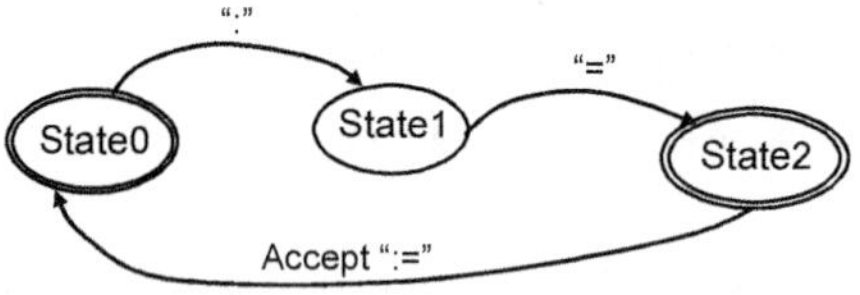

Figure 13-46. A finite state automaton that recognizes the assignment operator ":=" from its two characters colon and equal sign.

The `AssignmentRecognizer` model below is an example of using Modelica state machines to represent the finite state automaton that recognizes the ":=" assignment symbol. It is somewhat simplified for practical reasons; the characters represented as enumeration values are picked from the `chars` array instead of an input stream.

```
model AssignmentRecognizer
  type Chartypes = enumeration(colon, equals, space);
  constant Chartypes chars[:] = {Chartypes.colon, Chartypes.equals,
                                 Chartypes.space};
  inner Integer i(start=0);

  block State0 "The initial state"
    outer output Integer i;
  equation
    i = 0;
  end State0;
  State0 state0;

  block State1 "State1, colon has been seen"
    outer output Integer i;
  equation
    i = 1;
  end State1;
  State1 state1;

  block State2 "The final state, := has been recognized"
    outer output Integer i;
  equation
    i = 2;
  end State2;
  State2 state2;

equation
  initialState(state0);  // Make state0 the initial state starting at time 0
  transition(state0, state1, chars[i+1]==Chartypes.colon,
             immediate=false);  // transfer to state1, seen colon
  transition(state1, state2, chars[i+1]==Chartypes.equals,
             immediate=false);  // transfer to final state2, seen equal sign
  transition(state2, state0, true,
             immediate=false);  // transfer back to initial state0
```

```
end AssignmentRecognizer;
```

The model appears as follows (Figure 13-47) using state machine graphical modeling facilities in a Modelica tool:

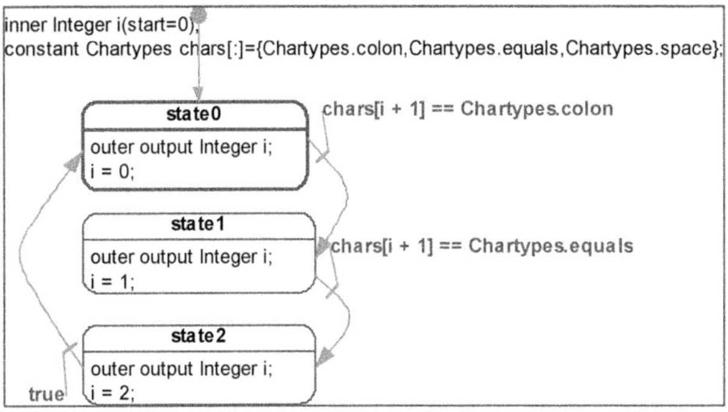

Figure 13-47. A graphical view of the `AssignmentRecognizer` state machine model in a Modelica tool.

We simulate for 6 seconds and plot the variable `i` which indicates the current state (see Figure 13-48).

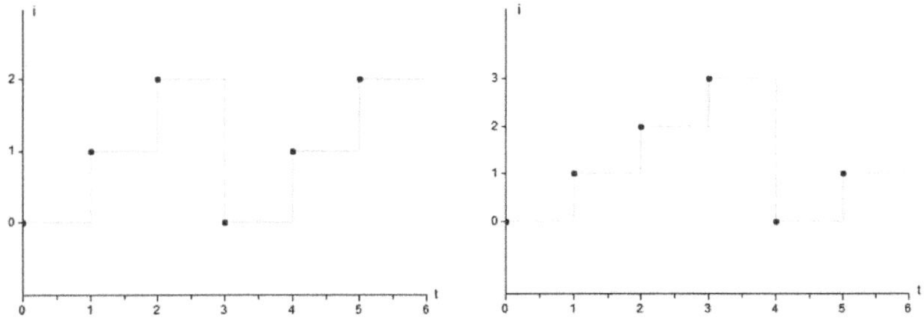

Figure 13-48. *Left*: A plot of the state transistion of the `AssignmentRecognizer` model. The := has been recognized in the final `state2`, after which a transition back to the initial `state0` is done at the next tick. *Right*: The same model augmented by an additional `state3`, which is reached after one more character.

The above model directly transfers back to the initial `state0` at the next clock tick. Another way to model is to transfer to a final state when another character, e.g. a space, has been seen. This approach can be modeled by adding a fourth state (`state3`), and another transition.

```
// A modified version of the model with a 4th state3 added
  block State3
    "The final state, := has been recognized followed by another character"
    outer output Integer i;
  equation
    i = 3;
  end State3;
  State3 state3;

equation
  ...
  transition(state2, state3, chars[i+1]==Chartypes.space,
    immediate=false); // transfer to final state3 when another char is seen
  transition(state3,state0,true,immediate=false); // transfer back to state0
end AssignmentRecognizer;
```

13.3.2.4 Watchdog System

A watchdog system is a slightly more elaborate example of an input/output process than the simple server. It has two basic states, `Passive` and `Active`, but can also enter a third state `Alarmed` when receiving a `deadlineSignal` event. When entering this third state the watchdog immediately emits an `Alarm` event. In general the function of a watchdog in its active state is to emit an alarm when a deadline is passed.

Thus, the finite state automaton of the watchdog system in Figure 13-49 has a set of three states `{Passive, Active, Alarmed}` and a set of four values `{Off, On, deadlineSignal, Alarm}`, of which the arrival of any of the first three are *input* or *control* events, and emitting the last value is an *output* event.

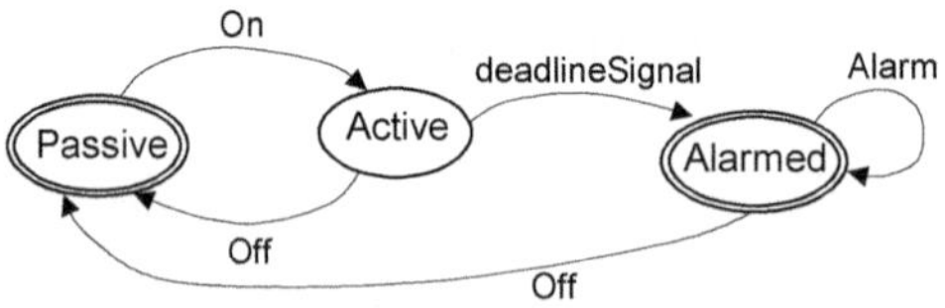

Figure 13-49. A finite state automaton of a watchdog system.

The watchdog system shown in Figure 13-50 consists of the watchdog itself and three event generators, emitting `On` events, `Off` events, and `deadlineSignal` events.

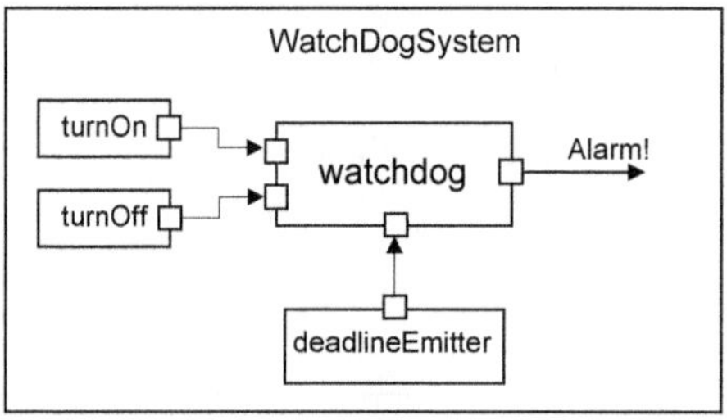

Figure 13-50. A watchdog system.

An unclocked Modelica model of the watchdog system follows below, consisting of the watchdog itself and the three event generators. The watchdog is formulated using an algorithm section since otherwise the multiple when-equations would cause multiple assignments to be reported for the variable `watchdogActive`.

```
model WatchDogSystem
  EventGenerator  turnOff(eventTime=0.25);
  EventGenerator  turnOn(eventTime=1);
  EventGenerator  deadlineEmitter(eventTime=1.5);
  WatchDog        watchdog;
equation
  connect(turnOn.dOutput,  watchdog.dOn);
  connect(turnOff.dOutput, watchdog.dOff);
  connect(deadlineEmitter.dOutput, watchdog.dDeadline);
end WatchDogSystem;

model WatchDog
  EventPortInput dOn;
  EventPortInput dOff;
  EventPortInput dDeadline;
  EventPortOutput dAlarm;
```

```
  Boolean watchdogActive(start=false); // Initially turned off
algorithm
  when dOn then // Event watchdog on
    watchdogActive := true;
  end when;
  when dOff then  // Event watchdog off
    watchdogActive := false;
    dAlarm  := false;
  end when;
  when dDeadline and watchdogActive then // Event Alarm!
    dAlarm := true;
  end when;
end WatchDog;

// Event ports also defined in CustomerGeneration, Section 13.3.4.2
connector EventPortInput = input Boolean;
connector EventPortOutput = output Boolean;

model EventGenerator
  parameter Real eventTime=1;
  EventPortOutput dOutput;
equation
  dOutput = time>eventTime;
end EventGenerator;
```

We simulate the `WatchDogSystem` and plot the alarm signal in Figure 13-51, letting `true` be represented by `1` and `false` by `0` in the diagram. The watchdog receives an `Off` event at time = 0.25 and an `On` event at time = 1.0, which causes it to be in the `Active` state to emit an `Alarm` at time = 1.5, when the `deadlineEmitter` component generates its "deadline reached" event.

```
simulate(WatchDogSystem, stopTime=2.6)
plot(watchdog.dAlarm)
```

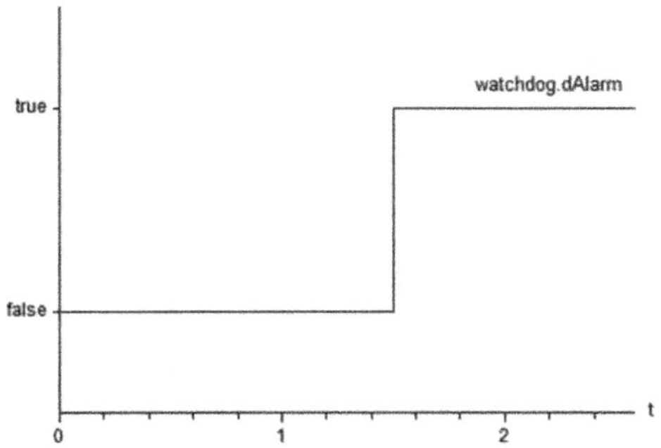

Figure 13-51. Simulating the unclocked watchdog system which emits an alarm event at time = 1.5.

A clocked version of the model called `WatchDogSystemClocked`, is shown below. The main difference is that a global clocked `timer` variable has been introduced, and that the event generator detects when to emit a clocked signal synchronized with the clock ticks of the global clock by the equation `dOutput = timecmp==true and previous(timecmp)==false`. An if-then-else statement is used instead of the when-statements in the unclocked version since clocked when-statements are currently not available in the Modelica language.

```
model WatchDogSystemClocked  "Clocked with synchronous global clocked timer"
  parameter Integer clockfrequency = 5;
```

```
    inner discrete Real timer(start=-1.0/clockfrequency);
    EventGenerator  turnOff(eventTime=0.25);
    EventGenerator  turnOn(eventTime=1);
    EventGenerator  deadlineEmitter(eventTime=1.5);
    WatchDogClocked watchdog;

    model WatchDogClocked
      EventPortInput dOn;
      EventPortInput dOff;
      EventPortInput dDeadline;
      EventPortOutput dAlarm(start=false);
      Boolean watchdogActive(start=false); // Initially turned off
    algorithm
      if dOn then // Event watchdog on
        watchdogActive :=true;
      elseif dOff then // Event watchdog off
        watchdogActive :=false;
        dAlarm :=false;
      elseif dDeadline and previous(watchdogActive) then //Event Alarm!
        dAlarm :=true;
      end if;
    end WatchDogClocked;

    connector EventPortInput = input Boolean;

    connector EventPortOutput = output Boolean;

    model EventGenerator
      parameter Real eventTime=1;
      outer discrete Real timer;
      EventPortOutput dOutput;
      Boolean timecmp(start=false);
    equation
      timecmp = timer > eventTime; // Detect change from false to true
      dOutput = timecmp==true and previous(timecmp)==false;
    end EventGenerator;

  equation
      connect(turnOn.dOutput,  watchdog.dOn);
      connect(turnOff.dOutput, watchdog.dOff);
      connect(deadlineEmitter.dOutput, watchdog.dDeadline);
      timer = sample(time, Clock(1,clockfrequency)); // timer interval 1/freq

//Alt2: timer = previous(timer)+
          sample(1.0/clockfrequency,Clock(1,clockfrequency));

//Alt3: when Clock(1,clockfrequency) then // interval 1/clockfrequency sec
//Alt3:   timer = previous(timer) + 1.0/clockfrequency;
//Alt3: end when; */

  end WatchDogSystemClocked;
```

There are several ways to define the clocked variable `timer`. In the model `WatchDogSystemClocked`, it is currently defined by an equation to sample the built-in variable `time`. Another option (`Alt2`) would be to add a delta `1/clockfrequency`, for example, 0.2 for 5Hz, at each tick, which may give rise to numerical roundoff errors after many such additions. The reason for sampling the delta value is to make the timer variable be clocked via clock inferencing. Yet another option is to use a clocked when-equation (`Alt3`).

The model is simulated for 2.6 seconds and results are shown in Figure 13-52 below. When the clock frequency is low, 5Hz, this is a rather coarse-grained approximation causing the alarm to be delayed until the next tick at 1.6 seconds, instead of 1.5 seconds as in the unclocked model. If the clock frequency is increased to 100Hz, the behavior is much closer to the unclocked model.

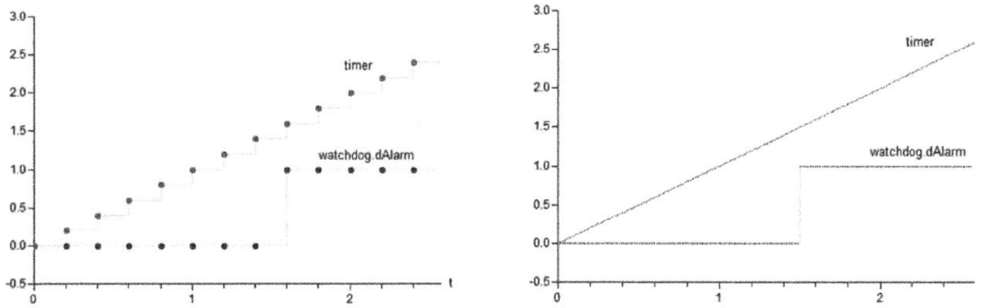

Figure 13-52. Simulation and plot of the `WatchDogSystemClocked` model. At the low sampling frequency 5Hz the deadline is detected and the alarm given at the next clock tick at 1.6 sec. At the higher frequency 100Hz the alarm is given much closer to the real deadline time at 1.5 sec.

The algorithm section in `WatchDogClock` can be replaced by an if-equation as in the model below:

```
model WatchDogClocked  "Version with equation section, if-then-else"
  EventPortInput dOn;
  EventPortInput dOff;
  EventPortInput dDeadline;
  EventPortOutput dAlarm(signal(start=false));
  Boolean watchdogActive(start=false); // Initially turned off
equation
  if dOn then // Event watchdog on
    watchdogActive =true;
    dAlarm = previous(dAlarm);
  elseif dOff then // Event watchdog off
    watchdogActive =false;
    dAlarm =false;
  elseif dDeadline and previous(watchdogActive) then //Event Alarm!
    watchdogActive = previous(watchdogActive);
    dAlarm =true;
  else
    watchdogActive = previous(watchdogActive);
    dAlarm = previous(dAlarm);
  end if;
end WatchDogClocked;
```

A more concise but perhaps less readable version can be formulated using if-expressions:

```
model WatchDogClocked  "Shorter Version, equation section, if-expressions"
  EventPortInput dOn;
  EventPortInput dOff;
  EventPortInput dDeadline;
  EventPortOutput dAlarm(signal(start=false));
  Boolean watchdogActive(start=false); // Initially turned off
equation
  watchdogActive =
    if dOn then true
    elseif dOff then false
    else previous(watchdogActive);
  dAlarm =
    if dDeadline and watchdogActive then true
    elseif dOff then false
    else previous(dAlarm);
end WatchDogClocked;
```

13.3.2.5 Watchdog System—Graphical State Machines Model

The Watchdog system finite state automaton can also be modeled using the clocked Modelica state machines constructs which are quite natural to use for such an application since the concepts of finite state automaton and state machines are almost the same.

We replicate the watchdog system finite state automaton from Figure 13-49 in Figure 13-53 below for easy comparison to the state machine diagram in Figure 13-54. It is easy to see that both diagrams have the same structure, that is, the same states and transitions.

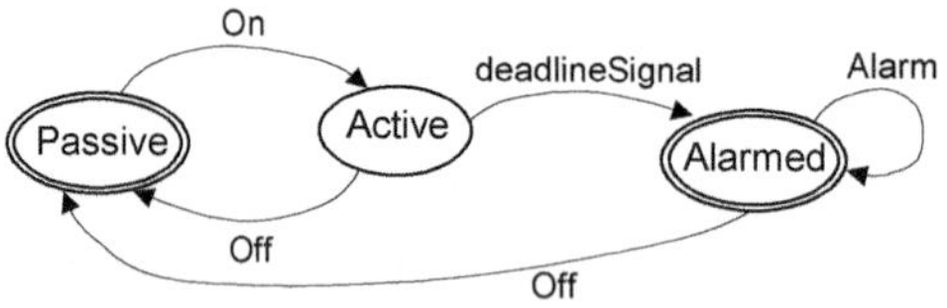

Figure 13-53. The finite state automaton of the watchdog system, the same as in Figure 13-49.

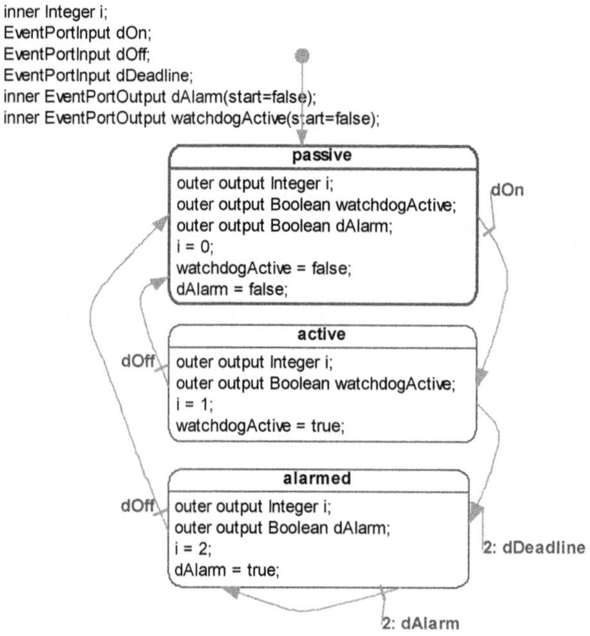

Figure 13-54. State machine diagram of the `WatchDogSystemStateMachine` model.

The whole model in textual form without graphical annotations is packaged into the `WatchDogSystemStateMachinePack` package shown below. Since each state is represented by its own model and model instance, the `inner outer` construct is needed to make the counter `i` and the Boolean condition variables `dOn`, `dOff`, `dDeadline`, and `dAlarm` accessible from all parts of the state machine model including the transition equations.

```
package WatchDogSystemStateMachinePack
  model WatchDogSystemStateMachine
    parameter Integer clockfrequency = 5;
    inner discrete Real timer(start=-1.0/clockfrequency);
    EventGenerator turnOff(eventTime=0.25);
    EventGenerator turnOn(eventTime=1);
    EventGenerator deadlineEmitter(eventTime=1.5);
    WatchDogStatemachine watchdog;
  equation
    connect(turnOn.dOutput, watchdog.dOn);
    connect(turnOff.dOutput, watchdog.dOff);
    connect(deadlineEmitter.dOutput, watchdog.dDeadline);
    timer = sample(time, Clock(1,clockfrequency)); // timer interval
                                                   // 1/clockfrequency sec
  end WatchDogSystemStateMachine;

  model WatchDogStatemachine
    inner Integer i;
    EventPortInput dOn;
    EventPortInput dOff;
    EventPortInput dDeadline;
    inner EventPortOutput dAlarm(start=false);
    inner EventPortOutput watchdogActive(start=false);

    model Passive
      outer output Integer i;
      outer EventPortOutput watchdogActive;
      outer EventPortOutput dAlarm;
    equation
      i = 0;
      watchdogActive = false;
      dAlarm = false;
    end Passive;
    Passive passive;

    model Active
    outer output Integer i;
    outer EventPortOutput watchdogActive;
    equation
      i = 1;
      watchdogActive = true;
    end Active;
    Active active;

    model Alarmed
      outer output Integer i;
      outer EventPortOutput dAlarm;
    equation
      i = 2;
      dAlarm = true;
    end Alarmed;
    Alarmed alarmed;

  equation
    initialState(passive);
    transition(passive, active, dOn, immediate=false);
    transition(active, passive,
      dOff, immediate=false, reset=true, synchronize=false, priority=1);
    transition(active, alarmed, dDeadline, immediate=true, priority=2);
    transition(alarmed, passive, dOff, immediate=false);
    transition(alarmed, alarmed, dAlarm, immediate=false, priority=2);
```

```
  end WatchDogStatemachine;

  connector EventPortInput  = input Boolean;
  connector EventPortOutput = output Boolean;

  model EventGenerator
    parameter Real eventTime=1;
    outer discrete Real timer;
    Boolean timecmp(start=false);
    EventPortOutput dOutput(start=false);
  equation
    timecmp = timer > eventTime;
    dOutput = timecmp == true and previous(timecmp) == false;
  end EventGenerator;

end WatchDogSystemStateMachinePack;
```

However, there are some differences between finite state automata and Modelica state machines, as well as compared to state machines expressed using Modelica if-equations:

- *Self-transitions are not needed in Modelica clocked state machines.* The arc from the state `Alarmed` back to itself is not actually needed since a clocked state machine stays in the current state if the transition conditions to other states are not fulfilled. However, to make the diagram identical to the finite state automaton we added a self-transition with a trivial condition `dAlarm=true`.
- *Transitions in state machines are made at clock ticks* whereas transitions in finite state automata happen at the *arrival of events*. In the `WatchDogSystemStateMachine` model we modeled the events by Boolean transition conditions which may become true and cause a transition at the next clock tick.
- *The equation counts of explicit equations in each state of a state machine need not be the same.* The reason this works and does not violate the single assignment principle (the same number of equations as variables) is that state variables automatically keep the same value if not updated by an equation or assignment. Thus, equations like `dAlarm = previous(dAlarm)` are not needed since they are generated automatically.

Regarding the third point, compare to the clocked watchdog state machine modeled using if-then-else equations below extracted from the second version of the `WatchDogClocked` model in Section 13.3.2.4, page 644. Here the Modelica language rules require the same number of explicit equations in each branch of the if-then-else equation, that is, no default equations generated. This is an example of some inconsistency in the design of the Modelica language.

```
if dOn then // Event watchdog on
  watchdogActive =true;
  dAlarm = previous(dAlarm);
elseif dOff then // Event watchdog off
  watchdogActive =false;
  dAlarm =false;
elseif dDeadline and previous(watchdogActive) then //Event Alarm!
  watchdogActive =previous(watchdogActive);
  dAlarm =true;
else
  watchdogActive = previous(watchdogActive);
  dAlarm = previous(dAlarm);
end if;
```

The `WatchDogStatemachine` model in `WatchDogSystemStateMachinePack` is simulated for 2.6 seconds. The results are plotted in Figure 13-55 below and are identical to the results in Figure 13-52.

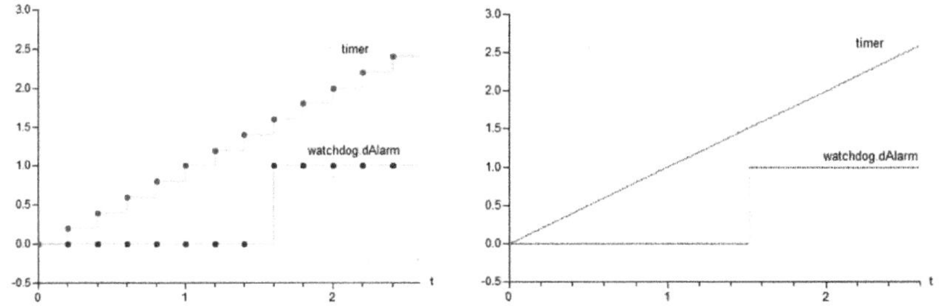

Figure 13-55. Simulation and plot of the `WatchDogSystemStateMachine` model. At the low sampling frequency 5Hz the deadline is detected and the alarm given at the current clock tick at 1.6 sec. At the high sampling frequence 100Hz the alarm is given close to the deadline overrun at 1.5 sec.

13.3.3 Cellular Automata

A cellular automaton is a regular spatial array of cells that interact with one another, each of which can be in any one of a finite number of states. Thus it is related to finite state automatons. The cells are arranged in a configuration, e.g. a one-dimensional line of cells, a 2-dimensional grid, or a 3-dimensional array. Other configurations are also possible, such as a honeycomb array of hexagonal cells. Each cell has a neighborhood which includes neighboring cells according to a well-defined pattern, which may or may not include the cell itself. The following are examples of 1-dimensional and 2-dimensional neighborhoods to the cell `C` marked by the letter `n`:

```
             n        n n n        n n n
   n C n   n C n    n C n      n C n n
             n        n n n      n n n
```

The state of each cell in the array is updated according to a transition mapping which may depend on the state of the cell and its neighbors at the previous time step. Each cell in a cellular automaton could be considered to be a finite state machine that takes its neighbors' states as input and outputs its own state. To summarize, a finite state automaton is characterized by the following properties:

- *State*. Each cell is assigned one of a finite set of state values, e.g. integer values.
- *Neighborhood*, which is the set of cells interacting with the cell according to a well-defined pattern. The neighborhood of *border* cells in the array of cells may or may not be determined according to "wraparound" semantics, for example, top and bottom cells, and left and right cells respectively in a 2-dimensional grid may be treated as "touching" each other.
- A *transition* mapping, usually expressed as *transition rules* and a *transition function* that take as input the present states, that is, the present values, of all of the cells in a given cell's neighborhood and generate the next state, that is, the next value, of the given cell. In some cases it is possible for different groups of cells in the automaton to have different transition rules and functions.

For example, regard a very simple cellular automaton consisting of a linear sequence of cells, with the neighborhood being the left and right cells, and wraparound semantics for defining the border cells. The transition function is simply the sum of the state values of the neighborhood cells, here the border cells and the cell itself.

Step 1: Create the initial state:

0 0 0 1 1 0 0 0

Step 2: Compute the transition function, i.e., the sum, for each cell:

0 0 1 2 2 1 0 0

Step 3: Apply the following transition rules ($0 \to 1,\ \ 1 \to 0,\ \ 2 \to 1,\ \ 3 \to 0$):

1 1 0 1 1 0 1 1

13.3.3.1 The Game of Life

An example of cellular automata in Modelica is a simple model representing Conway's game of life (Figure 13-78). Life is played on a grid of square cells where a cell can be alive or dead. In our example, we represent the grid of square cells as a matrix and a live cell is indicated by placing the value 1 on the corresponding element in the matrix. Obviously, each cell in the grid has a neighborhood consisting of the eight cells in every direction including the diagonals. We simulate the game of life over a limited time, on a grid of 10×10 with the help of the following model:

```
model GameOfLife
  parameter Integer n=10;
  parameter Integer initialAlive[:,2]={{2,2},{2,1},{1,2},{3,3},{3,2}};
  Integer lifeHistory[n,n](start=zeros(n,n));
  Boolean init = initial();
equation
 when {init, sample(0.1,0.1)} then
   if edge(init) then
      lifeHistory = firstGeneration(pre(lifeHistory), initialAlive);
   else
     lifeHistory = nextGeneration(pre(lifeHistory));
   end if;
 end when;
end GameOfLife;
```

We simulate for 1 second, using the `WSMSimulate[]` command input to the Mathematica frontend, which is further sent to Wolfram SystemModeler, with results as interpolation functions (Section 19.4.5.1, page 1054), and plot using the Mathematica function `PlotGameOfLife`, creating a new generation every 0.1th second as specified by the `sample(0.1,0.1)` expression in the above model.

```
res = WSMSimulate["GameOfLife",{0,1}];

{lifeHistory} = res[{"lifeHistory"}]

PlotGameOfLife[lifeHistory]

PlotGameOfLife[table_] := For[z=0, z<1, s={};
  For[i=1,i<=10, s1={};
     For[j=1,j<=10, s1=Append[s1,table[[j,i]][z]];j++ ];  s=Append[s,s1];
  i++];
  s=Reverse[ReplaceAll[s,{0.->1.,1.->0.}]];
  ListDensityPlot[s,Frame->False,AspectRatio->Automatic];
z=z+0.1]
```

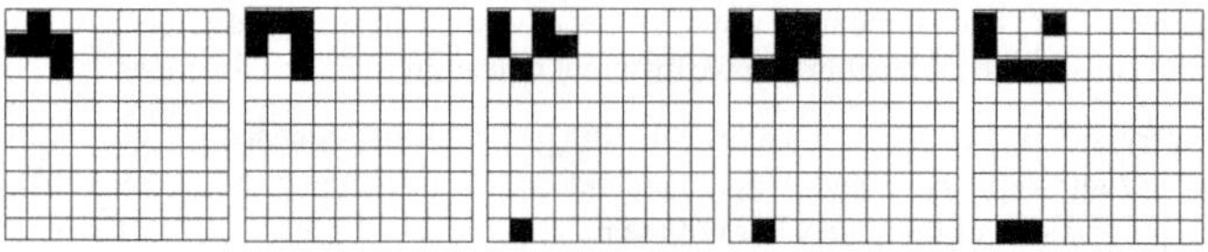

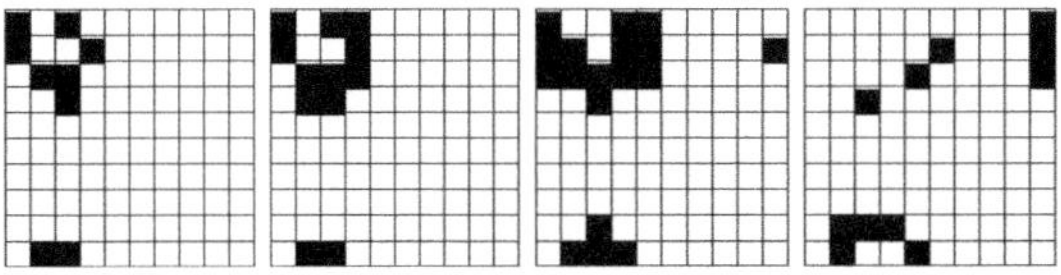

Figure 13-56. The first eight generations from the simulation of the `GameOfLife` model.

The simulation starts with an initial generation represented by the `initialAlive` parameter which updates the `lifeHistory` variable in the `initial equation` section. This is done by calling the function `firstGeneration`.

```
function firstGeneration
  input Integer M[:,:];
  input Integer I[:,2];
  output Integer G[size(M,1),size(M,1)] := M;
algorithm
  for i in 1:size(I,1) loop
    G[I[i,1],I[i,2]] := 1;
  end for;
end firstGeneration;
```

At each event, generated by the `sample` statement, the `nextGeneration` function is called, which applies the rules of the game to each cell of the grid. To apply one step of the rule we count the number of live neighbors for each cell. The value of the cell depends on the number of live neighbors according to the following rules:

- A dead cell with exactly three live neighbors becomes a live cell (birth).
- A live cell with two or three live neighbors stays alive (survival).
- In all other cases, a cell dies or remains dead (overcrowding or loneliness).

The rules of the life game are illustrated by the `nextGeneration` function, which uses wraparound semantics (indices computed by the `mod` function) for determining neighbors of cells on the border:

```
function nextGeneration
  input  Integer M[:,:];
  output Integer G[size(M,1),size(M,1)];
protected
  Integer borderSum,iW,iE,jN,jS;  // West,East,North,South
  parameter Integer n=size(M,1);
algorithm
  for i in 1:n loop
    for j in 1:n loop
       iW := mod(i-2+n,n)+1; iE := mod(i+n,n)+1;
       jS := mod(j-2+n,n)+1; jN := mod(j+n,n)+1;
       borderSum := M[iW,j] + M[iE,j] + M[iW,jS] + M[i,jS] +
         M[iE,jS] + M[iW,jN] + M[i,jN] + M[iE,jN];
       if borderSum==3 then
         G[i,j] := 1;            // Alive
       elseif borderSum==2 then
         G[i,j] := M[i,j];       // Unchanged
       else
         G[i,j] := 0;            // Dead
       end if;
    end for;
  end for;
end nextGeneration;
```

The behavior of the GameOfLife model is dependent on the start configuration. Certain configurations, for example, as in Figure 13-57, reach steady state already after a few generations. Other configurations never reach a steady state.

```
model GameOfLife2 = GameOfLife(initialAlive =
  {{1,1}, {2,2},{3,3},{4,4},{5,5},{6,6},{7,7},{8,8},{9,9},{10,10},
   {1,10},{2,9},{3,8},{4,7},{5,6},{6,5},{7,4},{8,3},{9,2},{10,1}});

res2 = WSMSimulate["GameOfLife2", {0,1}]

{lifeHistory} = res2[{"lifeHistory"}]

PlotGameOfLife[lifeHistory]
```

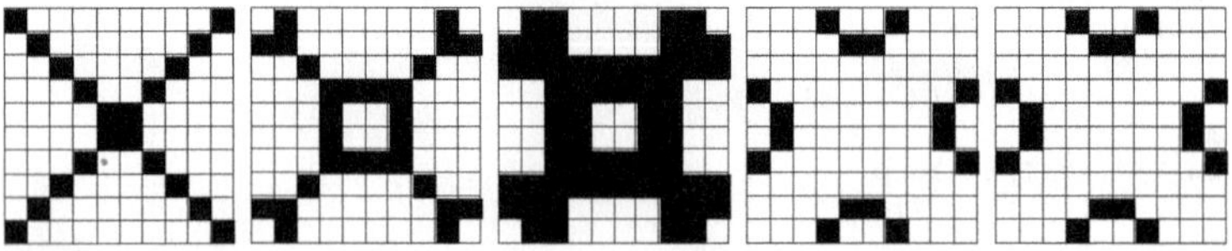

Figure 13-57. With another initialAlive start configuration the behavior of the GameOfLife model reaches steady state already at the third generation.

It is not necessary to employ user-written functions like nextGeneration as an aid to model the game of life in Modelica, as shown below by GameofLife3, which is equivalent to the previous GameOfLife model but is considerably shorter and uses only equations to model its behavior. The borderSum is computed by applying the sum reduction function with iterators over each neighborhood including its center element, which subsequently is subtracted.

```
model GameOfLife3  "Game of Life model only based on equations"
  parameter Integer n=10;
  parameter Integer initialAlive[:,2]={{2,2},{2,1},{1,2},{3,3},{3,2}};
  Integer lifeHistory[n,n](start=zeros(n,n));
  Integer M[n,n];
  Integer borderSum[n,n];//borderSum array because of single assigment
initial equation
  for i in 1:size(initialAlive,1) loop
    lifeHistory[initialAlive[i,1],initialAlive[i,2]] = 1;
  end for;
equation
  when sample(0.1,0.1) then
    M = pre(lifeHistory);
    for i in 1:n loop
      for j in 1:n loop
        borderSum[i,j] = -M[i,j] +  //  West/south, center, east/north
          sum(M[k,p] for k in {mod(i-2+n,n)+1, i, mod(i+n,n)+1},
                         p in {mod(j-2+n,n)+1, j, mod(j+n,n)+1});
          lifeHistory[i,j] =  if  borderSum[i,j]==3 then 1     // Alive
                  else (if borderSum[i,j]==2 then M[i,j] // Unchanged
                        else 0);                         // Dead
      end for;
    end for;
  end when;
end GameOfLife3;
```

13.3.4 Models for Event-based Stochastic Processes

If we generalize a finite state automaton by letting the time between two events be stochastic, and possibly also letting the choice of the next state be stochastic, we obtain a model for event-based stochastic processes. Such models have many applications, of which one are queuing systems.

13.3.4.1 Generalized Semi-Markov Processes

Generalized semi-Markov processes is one model for stochastic processes often used for queuing systems in manufacturing industry, or for server models in general with stochastic customer arrival. Such processes are generalized in the following major ways compared to finite state automatons:

- The time between two events is stochastic.
- The choice of the next state might be stochastic.
- The set of states to choose from can be an infinite enumerable set instead of a finite set.

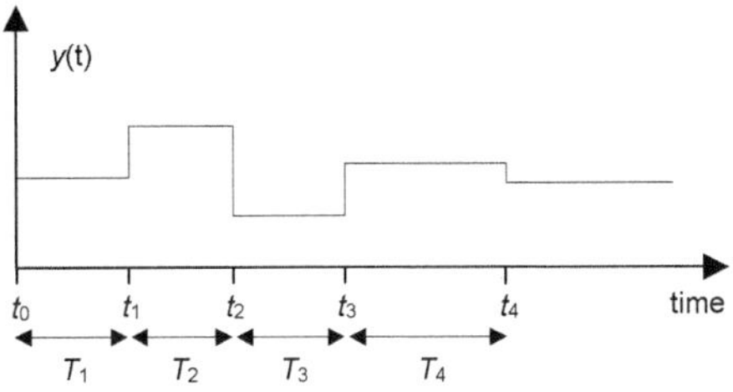

Figure 13-58. An output variable generated by a generalized semi-Markov process.

We show an example of an output variable from a semi-Markov process in Figure 13-58. The level of the output variable $y(t)$ changes in discrete steps between values in an enumerable set of discrete values. The changes occur at events at times $t = t_0$, t_1, t_2, and so on. Both the output level and the time of the events may depend on random variables. The time intervals $T_i = t_i - t_{i-1}$ between two successive events are stochastic variables with some random distribution. The choice of the output value may depend on stochastic variables. This is typical for a queuing system where customers arrive and leave at discrete points in time, increasing or decreasing state variables such as the number of customers in the system.

We regard the output sequence of values y_n as being generated from some internal sequence X_n of state variable values together with random variables R_n:

$$
\begin{aligned}
X_{n+1} &= f(R_{n+1}, X_n) \\
X_0 &- f_0(R_0) \\
y_n &= h_1(X_n) \\
T_n &= h_2(X_n)
\end{aligned}
\qquad (13\text{-}11)
$$

13.3.4.2 Server with Queue

As a simple example of discrete-time stochastic process simulation we can consider a simple server model with a queue. We first start by defining a model which generates customers at random points in time. The time delay until the next customer arrival is assumed to be the absolute value of a normally distributed stochastic variable `Tdiff`, here computed by calling the random number function `normalvariate` (in Appendix D, page 1095, `Modelica.Math.Random` library), where the negative part is folded back on the positive side using `abs(Tdiff)` to avoid unrealistic negative service times. Since this function is side-effect free as all Modelica functions, it returns a `randomSeed` value to be used at the next call to normalvariate. The CustomerGeneration model contains an output connector outCustomer that transmits the customer arrival events to the rest of the system.

```
model CustomerGeneration
  import Random;  // See Math.Random package in Appendix D
  EventPortOutput outCustomer;
  BoolView bv;  // Only for plotting to see events
  parameter Real mean = 0;
  parameter Real stDeviation = 1;
  discrete Real Tdiff;  // Its absolute value is timediff to next customer
  discrete Real nextCustomerArrivalTime(start=0);
  discrete Random.Seed randomSeed(start={23,87,187});
  Boolean changeflg(start=false);
equation
  when pre(nextCustomerArrivalTime)<time then  // Customer arrives
    (Tdiff,randomSeed) =
       Random.normalvariate(mean,stDeviation,pre(randomSeed));
    nextCustomerArrivalTime = pre(nextCustomerArrivalTime) + abs(Tdiff);
    changeflg = not pre(changeflg); // Changes at each customer arrival
  end when;
  outCustomer = change(changeflg);  // Signal true only at event
  bv.inv = outCustomer;  // Only for plotting, widening event peaks

// real value comparison to zero not reliable for short durations at events:
// outCustomer = edge(nextCustomerArrivalTime >
//         pre(nextCustomerArrivalTime) ); -- wrong, wsignal always false
end CustomerGeneration;

// Eventport connectors also defined in WatchDogSystem, Section 13.3.2.4
connector EventPortInput = input Boolean;

connector EventPortOutput = output Boolean;


model BoolView "Increase width of Boolean event signal for plotting"
  Boolean inv,outv;
  parameter Real width=0.0001;
  discrete  Real T0;
equation
  when inv then
    T0=time;
  end when;
  outv =(time>=T0) and (time<T0+width);
end BoolView;
```

We simulate the CustomerGeneration model for a while to observe the customer arrival times (Figure 13-59).

```
simulate(CustomerGeneration, stopTime=10)
plot({nextCustomerTime, timediff})   plot({nextCustomerTime, bv.outv})
```

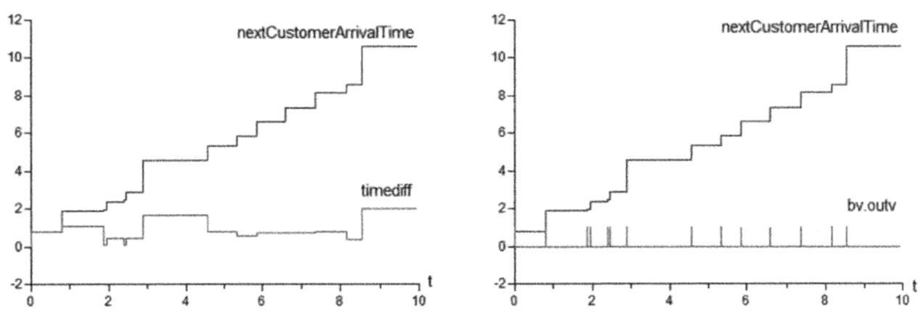

Figure 13-59. *Left*: next customer arrival time for customers arriving at random points in time, and time difference between arrivals; ***right***: the same together with the actual arrivals shown as small peaks.

We can now design a server model `ServerWithQueue` which through its `inCustomer` port will accept the arriving customers from the `CustomerGeneration` model.

The `nrOfCustomersInQueue` represents the current number of customers in the queue. Other state variables of interest are `nrOfArrivedCustomers`, the number of customers that have so far arrived, and `nrOfServedCustomers`, the number of customers that have so far been served. The first when-equation services the arrival of a new customer, whereas the second when-equation handles the event when a customer is serviced and is ready to leave the queue.

There are three kinds of events in the `ServerWithQueue` model:

- The arrival of a new customer.
- Starting servicing a customer.
- Completing service for a customer.

The event when `readyCustomer` becomes `true` represents completed service for the current customer. The time needed to serve a customer is `serveTime`, which is constant in this model but could be varying according to some formula or be randomly distributed. The variable `recentServeStart` represents the starting time for servicing the most recently serviced customer.

```
model ServerWithQueue
  EventPortInput inCustomer;
  parameter Real    custServeTime=0.1 "Time needed to service a customer";
  discrete  Real    nrOfArrivedCustomers;
  discrete  Real    nrOfServedCustomers;
  discrete  Real    nrOfCustomersInQueue(start=0);
  discrete  Boolean readyCustomer(start=false);
  discrete  Boolean serveCustomer(start=false);
  Real     lastServeStart  "Most recent start servicing";
 equation
  readyCustomer = serveCustomer and (custServeTime < time-lastServeStart);
  nrOfCustomersInQueue = nrOfArrivedCustomers - nrOfServedCustomers;
  when inCustomer then      // Event: New customer arrives
    nrOfArrivedCustomers = pre(nrOfArrivedCustomers)+1;
  end when;
  when readyCustomer then           // Event: Customer finished service
    nrOfServedCustomers = pre(nrOfServedCustomers)+1;
  end when;
  when (pre(nrOfCustomersInQueue)==0 and inCustomer) or
   (pre(nrOfCustomersInQueue)>=1 and pre(readyCustomer)) then
    serveCustomer = true;
    lastServeStart = time;
  end when;
end ServerWithQueue;
```

The simulation of the whole system can be done by defining a test model which connects the `CustomerGeneration` model with the `ServerWithQueue` model (Figure 13-60).

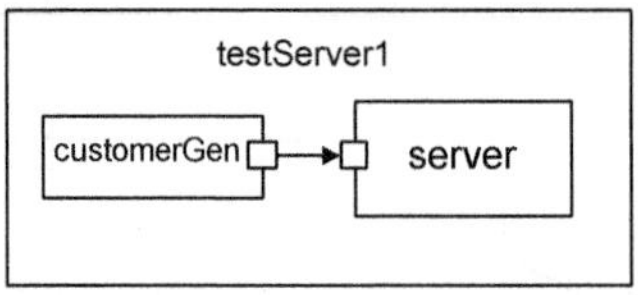

Figure 13-60. The `testServer1` model connecting a customer generator to a server.

```
model testServer1
  CustomerGeneration   customerGen;
  ServerWithQueue      server(serveTime=0.4);
equation
  connect(customerGen.outCustomer, server.inCustomer);
end testServer1;
```

We simulate the model for 10 seconds with the customer service time `serveTime = 0.4` seconds (Figure 13-61).

```
simulate(testServer1, stopTime=10)
plot({server.nrOfArrivedCustomers,
  server.nrOfServedCustomers, server.nrOfCustomersInQueue})
plot(customer.bv.outv)
```

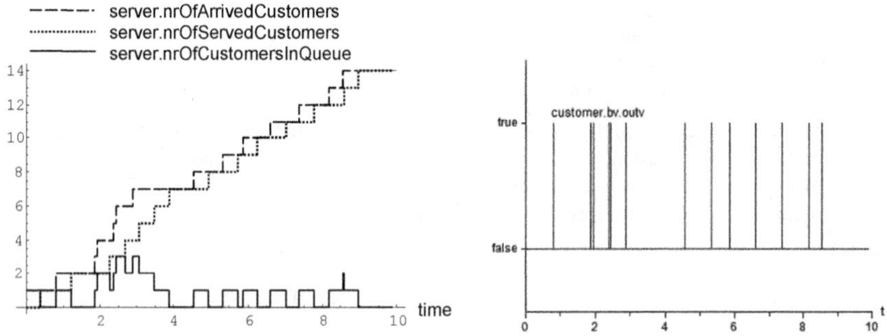

Figure 13-61. *Left*: number of arrived customers, number of served customers, and number of customers waiting in the queue or being serviced; *right*: the actual customers arrivals shown as small peaks.

13.3.5 Discrete Event System Specification (DEVS)

The discrete event system specification formalism (DEVS), is a modeling style and mathematical formalism that has found use in representing and analyzing models for discrete event simulation, for example, in job shop manufacturing system applications.

In a formal mathematical sense, DEVS is closely related to the previously presented generalized semi-Markov processes, but with two enhancements:

- In DEVS the state space *can* also include an infinite *uncountable* set of `Real` values—it need not be restricted to a countable enumerable set of values.
- The DEVS formalism also supports *hierarchical* internal structuring of models. The composition of two DEVS models is still a DEVS model.

In the following, we will see that DEVS models can be conveniently represented in Modelica, with the hierarchical structuring properties preserved and enhanced by Modelica.

State changes in DEVS models are mathematically represented by transition functions as previously done for finite state automatons. For DEVS models we talk about two transition functions: δ_{int}—the internal transition functions, and δ_{ext}—the external transition function. Analogous to the case for finite state automatons, transition functions are usually represented by equations or assignments, only in complicated cases by explicit Modelica functions. Models designed according to the DEVS style distinguish two types of events:

- *Internal events* are time scheduled. As an example, an internal event can be the completion of the current processing of a job in a job shop. State changes at internal events are defined by the internal transition function δ_{int}.
- *External events* occur upon the arrival of an input value at one of the input ports. For example, an external event could be the arrival of a job at a job shop. State changes at external events are defined by the external transition function δ_{ext}.

From the mathematical point of view, a basic DEVS model has the following elements, where we use the subscript k to denote the state or other properties at event k in a sequence of events, $k = 0,1,2,...,$ and have adapted the notation slightly to make it easier to understand compared to the original DEVS notation:

- The *state* x_k at time t_k. In addition there is a local timer variable t_{local} which is reset to zero at each event, and continuously increases between events. The set of states can be finite, infinite countable, or infinite uncountable.
- *Inputs* u_k belonging to a finite set of input data values, and *outputs* y_k belonging to a finite set of output data values.
- A *time residual* function $T_R(x_k,\ t_{local})$, defining the time span from the current time to the next internal event, i.e., $t_{k+1}=t_k+T_R(x_k,0)$ if the next event is an internal event. If no internal event is scheduled in state x_k, then $T_R(x_k,0) = inf$, i.e., some value representing infinity.
- An *internal transition* function δ_{int} used to compute the next state $x_{k+1} = \delta_{int}(x_k)$ if at an input event.
- An *external transition* function δ_{ext} used to compute the next state $x_{k+1} = \delta_{ext}(x_k,\ u_k,\ t_{local})$ if at an external event.
- An *output function* λ to compute output values $y_k=\lambda(\ x_k)$.

The interpretation of these elements is depicted in Figure 13-62, and can be summarized as follows.

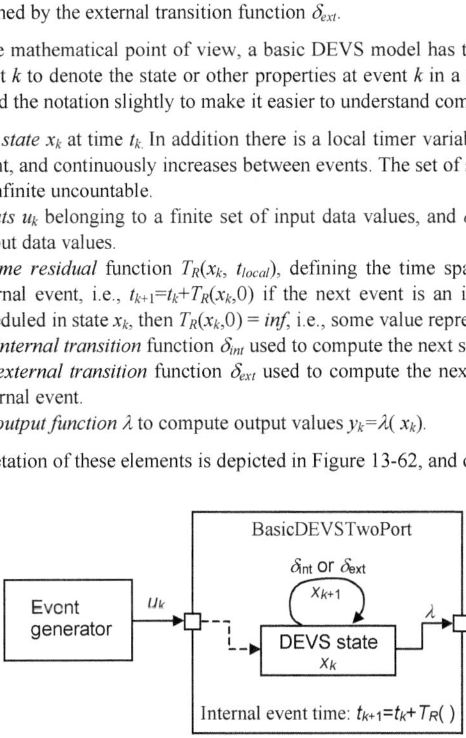

Figure 13-62. The base class `BasicDEVSTwoPort` captures many common properties of basic (atomic) DEVS classes. Inputs uk arrive and/or are available at time t_k. The current state at event time t_k is represented by x_k, and the computed state to be used at the next event is $x_{k+1} = \delta_{int}(x_k)$ if at an input event, or $x_{k+1} = \delta_{ext}(x_k, u_k, t_{local})$ if at an external event. The output event value is computed: $y_k=\lambda(\ x_k)$.

At any time the system is in some state x_k, where k denotes the most recent event. If no input value u is received at the input port the system will stay in state x_k for the time $T_R(x_k,\ t_{local})$. When this residual time expires the output function λ determines the output $y_k=\lambda(\ x_k)$, and the state changes to $x_{k+1} = \delta_{int}(x_k)$. If the arrival of an input u_k causes an external event before the expiration time $T_R(x_k, t_{local})$ reaches 0 or at any other time, the external transition function δ_{ext} will specify the next state of the model $x_{k+1} = \delta_{ext}(x_k, u_k, t_{local})$, after which t_{local} is reset to zero. Notice that between events only the local timer t_{local} is changing and increasing at a constant rate.

We will now describe a fairly comprehensive example of how DEVS models can be represented in Modelica. One difference in Modelica is that we have a built-in `time` variable for absolute time rather than a local timer `tlocal` that is reset at the most recent event. This local timer is not really needed for modeling purposes since `time` is available, but is included to show the relation to traditional DEVS models. The facilities for model structuring and reuse are in general much greater in Modelica due to its object-oriented properties compared to traditional DEVS. In order to simplify comparisons this example connects model components such as servers or generators in a way that is analogous to traditional DEVS.

The base class `BasicDEVSTwoPort` describes most common properties of DEVS components with two ports. It has two connectors, `inp` and `outp`, for receiving and emitting `Boolean` signals. Many DEVS components need to keep track of whether they are active or not—this is represented by the state variable `DEVSactive`, sometimes known by the more cryptic name *phase*. We also have the local timer `tlocal` (t_{local}) and the residual time function represented by `tResidual` (T_R), often labeled *e* and *sigma*, respectively, using traditional DEVS notation.

We also need the discrete real variable `tNextEvent`—the time of the next internal event or some value < the current `time` if there is no scheduled internal event, and `tLastEvent`—the time of the most recent event, in order to define `tResidual` and `tlocal`. There is one slight difference compared to the above theoretical model: the model behaves better if we represent the case where `tNextEvent` is undefined by some value < `time` instead of the infinite value (`inf`).

```
partial model BasicDEVSTwoPort
  import Modelica.Constants.inf;
  input EventPortInput  inp;          // Input port for external events
  output EventPortOutput  outp;        // Output port for emitted events
  Boolean DEVSactive(start=false); // Start in non-active mode (phase)
  Real tResidual(start=inf);    // Time until internal event (sigma)
  Real tlocal(start=0);         // Local timer reset at events (e)
  discrete Real tNextEvent(start=0); // Time of next internal event
  discrete Real tLastEvent(start=0);  // Time of most recent event
equation
  tResidual = if tNextEvent<time then  inf  else  tNextEvent-time;
  tlocal = if inp or tNextEvent<time
             then 0 else time - tLastEvent;
  when {inp, pre(tNextEvent)<time} then
    tLastEvent = time;          // Save the time of this event
  end when;
end BasicDEVSTwoPort;

// Eventport connectors also defined in WatchDogSystem, Sec 13.3.2.4

connector EventPortInput = input Boolean;

connector EventPortOutput = output Boolean;
```

13.3.5.1 A DEVS Job Shop Model

A simple job shop model illustrates DEVS based modeling. A generator for arriving jobs is connected to a simple DEVS-based server (Figure 13-63).

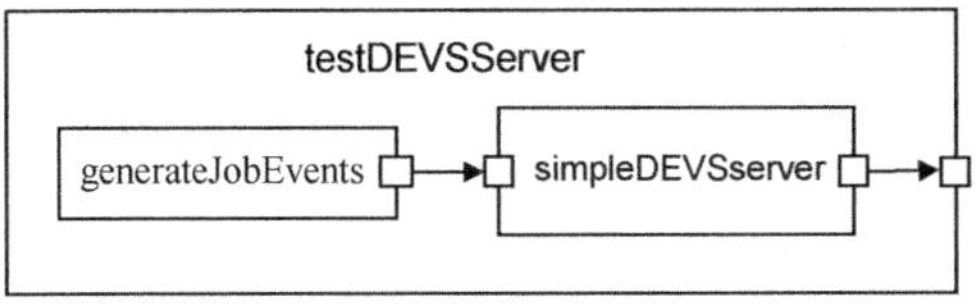

Figure 13-63. The `testDEVSServer` model connects a job generator to a simple DEVS-based server.

The `testDEVSServer` model contains two main items: a `generateJobEvents` generator component that generates arriving jobs at regular intervals, and a `simpleDEVSServer` server component being a very simple model of a job shop system that services arriving jobs with a normally distributed service time. The `SignalView` class instances are needed to widen sharp peaks for plotting.

```
model testDEVSServer
  GenerateJobEvents  generateJobEvents(period=1.5,startTime=3) "generator";
  SimpleDEVSServer   simpleDEVSServer                          "server";
  SignalView         viewSignal1;    // Just for plotting
  SignalView         viewSignal2;    // Just for plotting
equation
  connect(generateJobEvents.outp, simpleDEVSServer.inp);
  connect(simpleDEVSServer.outp, viewSignal2.inp);    // Just for plotting
  connect(generateJobEvents.outp, viewSignal1.inp);   // Just for plotting
end testDEVSServer;

model GenerateJobEvents   "Generates Job events periodically"
  EventPortOutput outp; // Output port
  parameter Real startTime = 0;
  parameter Real period = 2;
equation
  outp = sample(startTime,period);
end GenerateJobEvents;
```

The `SimpleDEVSServer` class is a fairly straightforward extension of the basic DEVS class `BasicDEVSTwoPort`. A randomly distributed service time variable `servTime` has been added with a normal distribution determined by parameters `mean` and `stdev`. The discrete `randomSeed` variable is needed to store the seed between calls to `normalvariate`, which as in all Modelica functions is a mathematical function whose value is completely determined by its inputs. The absolute value of `servTime` is used to guarantee positive service times.

The class also contains three when-equations that model what happens when a job arrives and at completion of the servicing of a job. There are two cases of arriving job external events:

- If the server is not busy (`DEVSactive` = `false`), servicing the job is started immediately.
- On the other hand, if the server is already busy (`DEVSactive = true`), the job is ignored—the only thing that happens is that `tlocal` is reset to zero by the equation inherited from the `BasicDEVSTwoPort` class.

The internal event of competing service of a job means that the server should not be busy any longer, no completion event should be scheduled (`tNextEvent < time`), and a completed service event is generated as an output event via `outp`.

```
model SimpleDEVSServer
  extends BasicDEVSTwoPort;
  Boolean   internalEvent;
  Boolean   externalEvent;
  parameter Real  mean  = 2.0  "mean of job service time";
  parameter Real  stdev = 0.5;
```

```
    discrete  Real   servTime      "time needed to service current job";
    discrete  Random.Seed randomSeed(start={23,87,187});
  equation
    internalEvent = pre(tNextEvent)<time;
    externalEvent = inp;
    outp = edge(internalEvent) and  pre(DEVSactive);
    when {externalEvent,internalEvent} then
      (servTime,randomSeed) = Random.normalvariate(mean,stdev,
                                                 pre(randomSeed));
      // * External event - job arrives, start service
      if edge(externalEvent) and not pre(DEVSactive) then

        DEVSactive = true;
        tNextEvent = time + abs(servTime);//abs of normal distr servTime
        // * External event - job arrives but is not serviced since busy
        elseif edge(externalEvent) and pre(DEVSactive) then
          DEVSactive = true;
          tNextEvent = pre(tNextEvent); // Next internal event unchanged

      // * Internal event - servicing current job finished
      else   // Here effectively: edge(internalEvent)
        DEVSactive = false;
        tNextEvent = pre(tNextEvent); // time now >= tNextEvent
      end if;
    end when;
  end SimpleDEVSServer;

  model SignalView  "Increase width of sample trigger signals"
    EventPortInput      inp;
    EventPortOutput     outp;
    parameter Real width=0.001;
    discrete  Real T0;
  equation
    when inp then
      T0 = time;
    end when;
    outp = (time>=T0) and (time<T0+width);
  end SignalView;
```

Remember the following two connect-equations from the `testDEVSServer` model:

```
connect(simpleDEVSServer.outp, viewSignal2.inp);
connect(generateJobEvents.outp, viewSignal1.inp);
```

When using the currently available Modelica tools, it is necessary to employ some kind of `SignalView` peak-widening facility in order to plot sharp peaks that have zero width, that is, have no time duration. Otherwise these peaks would not be visible in the diagram.

We simulate the `testDEVSServer` model to be able to view some of the input and output signals. The plot agrees with the specification of the `generateJobEvents` instance, where the first event is generated at `time` = 3 and subsequent events are generated with a periodicity 1.5 seconds (Figure 13-64).

```
simulate(testDEVSServer, stopTime=10)
plot(viewSignal1.outp)
```

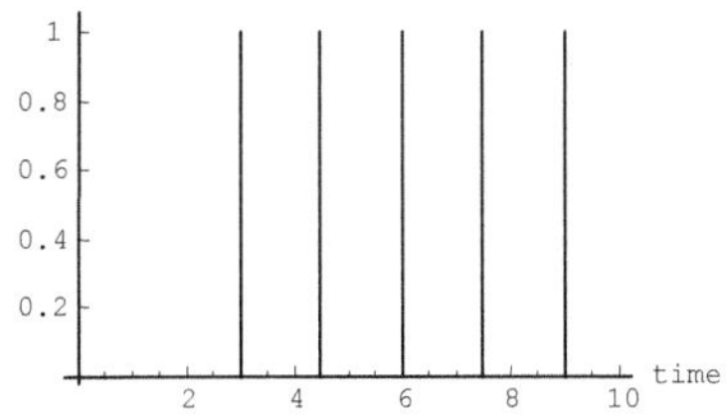

Figure 13-64. The output signal `outp` of the `generateJobEvents` generator component in `testDEVSServer`, with `startTime=3` and `period=1.5` as specified.

The output signal `testDEVSServer.simpleDEVSServer.outp` of the simple DEVS server instance is generated when completing the servicing of a job. Here such events occur only for the first and third jobs during this simulation, since the second and fourth jobs arrive while the server is busy and therefore are ignored. Servicing the fifth job was not completed before the end of the simulation interval at `time` = 10 (see Figure 13-65).

```
plot(viewSignal2.outp, stopTime=10)
```

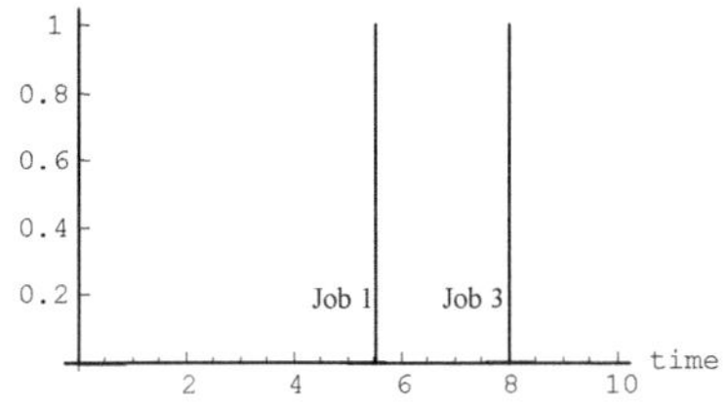

Figure 13-65. A signal is emitted through `testDEVSServer.simpleDEVSServer.outp` when completing service of a job, here Job 1 and Job 3.

The time periods when the server is active are represented by the variable `DEVSactive` being `true`, represented by the value 1 in Figure 13-66. Since the service times are drawn from a random distribution the widths of the bars in the diagram will vary somewhat. Servicing the first job takes a little bit longer than servicing the third arriving job (remember that the second job was ignored). The fifth job is started but not finished before the end of the simulation.

```
plot(simpleDEVSServer.DEVSactive)
```

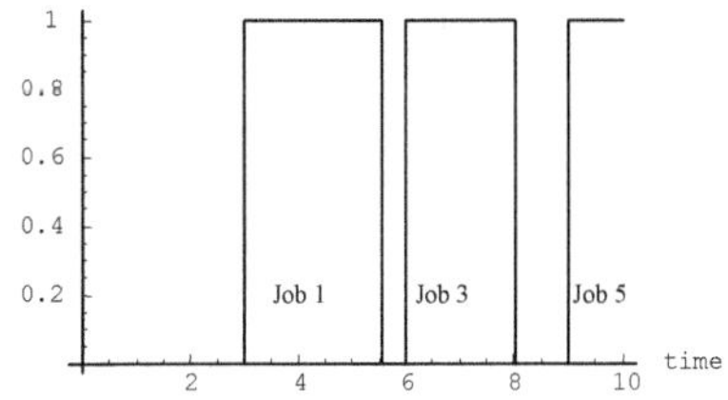

Figure 13-66. The variable `testDEVSServer.simpleDEVSServer.DEVSactive` is true while a job is being serviced.

The service time variable `testDEVSServer.simpleDEVSServer.servTime` shown in Figure 13-67 has unclocked discrete-time variability, that is, changes only at events when it is given a new value picked from the random distribution. The only events in this model are the arrival and completion of jobs.

```
plot(simpleDEVSServer.servTime)
```

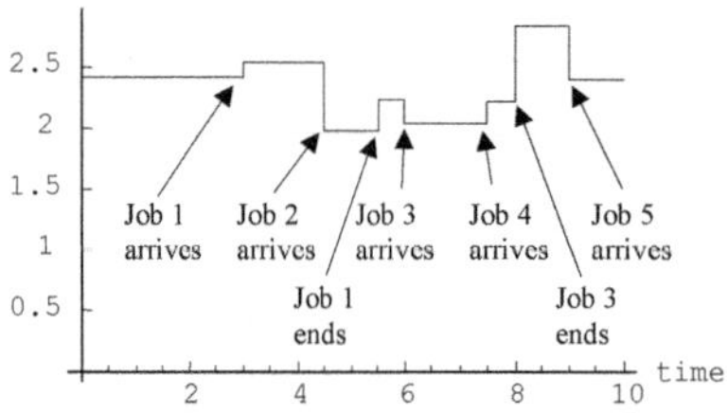

Figure 13-67. The service time variable `testDEVSServer.simpleDEVSServer.servTime` obtains new values at events.

Finally, we take a look at the `simpleDEVSServer.internalEvent` variable in Figure 13-68, which becomes `true` when completing the servicing of a job. It is reset to `false` at the next job arrival event, i.e., not a service completion event. The variable is initially `true`.

```
plot(simpleDEVSServer.internalEvent)
```

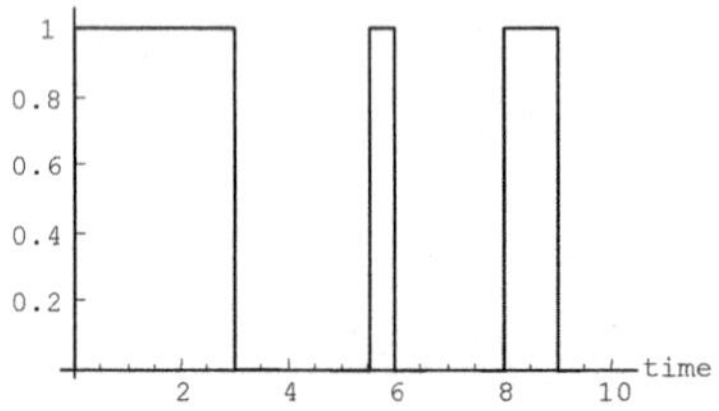

Figure 13-68. The output signal `testDEVSServer.simpleDEVSServer.internalEvent`.

13.3.5.2 A Coupled Pipelined DEVS Model

Several basic DEVS model components can be connected together to form a coupled model, which itself is a DEVS model. This is illustrated by the Modelica realization of a simple DEVS coupled model by placing three simple servers in series to form a three-server pipeline (Figure 13-69). In the `testPipeline` model further down, the job generator has been attached to the three-server pipeline (of class `ThreeServerPipeline`). The generator outputs events which are considered to be jobs that need some time to be processed by the server. Inside the basic server model only the time needed to complete a job is represented, not the detailed manner in which the processing is done. When a server receives a job it goes into busy mode (`DEVSactive` = `true`). Since the server has no buffering capabilities, if it is already busy, it ignores incoming jobs. When a server has finished processing a job, a *job completed* event is emitted and the server returns to passive mode (`DEVSactive` = `false`).

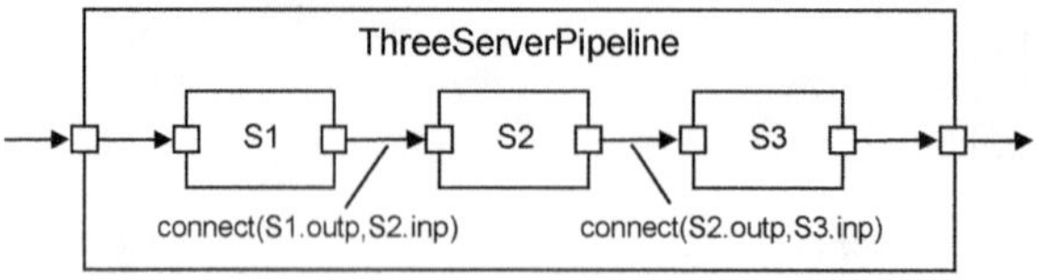

Figure 13-69. Coupled model consisting of three servers `S1`, `S2`, and `S3`, connected in a pipeline.

The coupled pipelined DEVS model class represented in Modelica can be described as follows:

```
model ThreeServerPipeline
  EventPortInput       extInSignal;
```

```
    EventPortOutput     outSignal;
    SimpleDEVSServer    S1(mean=2.0);
    SimpleDEVSServer    S2(mean=2.5);
    SimpleDEVSServer    S3(mean=1.5);
  equation
    connect(extInSignal,S1.inp);
    connect(S1.outp, S2.inp);
    connect(S2.outp, S3.inp);
    connect(S3.outp, outSignal);
  end ThreeServerPipeline;
```

The three-server coupled DEVS pipeline model can be tested using the following model. Plots of incoming jobs, DEVSactived, and output signals of the three servers in the simulated model are given in Figure 13-70.

```
  model testPipeline
    ThreeServerPipeline   pipeLine;
    GenerateJobEvents     jobgenerator(period=4);
    SignalView            viewJobGen; // Just for plotting
    SignalView            viewS1;     // Just for plotting
    SignalView            viewS2;     // Just for plotting
    SignalView            viewS3;     // Just for plotting
  equation
    connect(jobgenerator.outp, pipeLine.extInSignal);
    connect(jobgenerator.outp, viewJobGen.inp); // Just for plotting
    connect(pipeLine.S1.outp, viewS1.inp);   // Just for plotting
    connect(pipeLine.S2.outp, viewS2.inp);   // Just for plotting
    connect(pipeLine.S3.outp, viewS3.inp);   // Just for plotting
  end testPipeline;
```

We simulate the model and plot a number of variables:

```
  simulate(testDEVSServer, stopTime=10 )
```

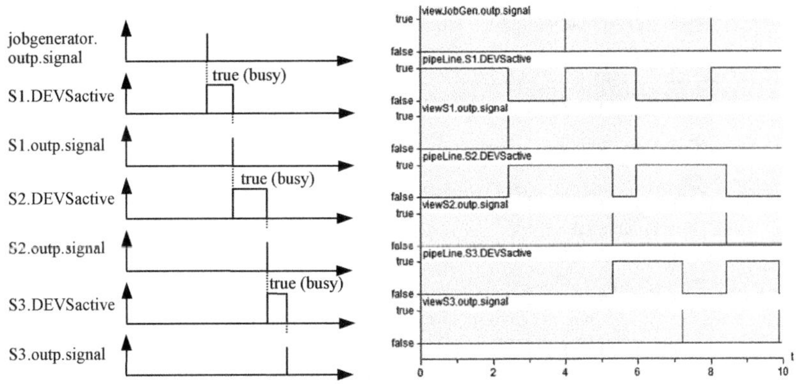

Figure 13-70. Signals for the testPipeline model including a ThreeServerPipeline containing the servers S1, S2 and S3. The jobgenerator generates job events starting at time=0 with a period of 4 seconds. After servicing by S1 in the pipeline, an output event is generated (S1.outp) which is fed to S2 for further processing, etc., until S3. Plots are shown from two different tools.

13.3.6 Petri Nets

Petri nets is a widely used formalism[17] for modeling and analyzing discrete event systems, with an associated intuitive visual representation. Application areas include modeling computer hardware, computer software, physical systems, social and economic systems, and so on. Petri nets are primarily used to model the occurrence of various events and activities within a system, in particular the flow of information or other resources.

In this section we give a basic introduction to Petri nets within the context of Modelica. More advanced Petri nets, for example, including stochastic Petri nets, are available in the Modelica library PNLib, see Section 16.18, page 965.

We demonstrate that the Petri net modeling primitives can be represented as Modelica classes, and that discrete model parts represented as Modelica Petri nets can be conveniently connected to continuous model parts.

13.3.6.1 Modeling of Events and Conditions with Petri Nets

The fundamental Petri net modeling view of a system is based on the two primitive concepts of *events* and *conditions*. As previously mentioned in this chapter, events can be viewed as actions that take place in a system. The state of the system is represented by a set of state variables. The state can also be viewed as a set of conditions, where a condition is a predicate or logical formula expressed in terms of state variables, that may either hold (be true) or not hold (be false).

Since events are actions they may or may not happen. For an event to occur it might be necessary that certain conditions, *preconditions*, are true. The event, when it occurs, may change certain state variables and thereby cause some preconditions to not hold any longer, but on the other hand cause other conditions, *postconditions*, to become true.

As an example, consider a variant of a job shop system, which, for example, can be a batch computer system that is processing jobs, or a machine shop for processing machine part manufacturing orders. The interesting conditions for this job shop system are:

- C1: the job shop is idle, waiting for work.
- C2: a job is waiting.
- C3: the job is being processed.
- C4: a finished job is waiting to be output.

The events, that is, actions in the system, would be:

- E1: a job arrives.
- E2: start processing a job.
- E3: a job is completed.
- E4: a finished job is delivered

The preconditions of event E2, start processing a job, are rather obvious: C2—a job needs to be waiting, and C1—the job shop needs to be idle, to start processing a new job. The postcondition of event E2 is C3—the job is being processed by the job shop system. In a similar way, we can define the preconditions and postconditions for other events in the system, which are collected in the table below.

0. Event	1. Preconditions	2. Postconditions

[17] StateCharts is another widely used formalism with a visual representation, not covered here, but has a Modelica implementation in ModelicaML (Section 13.7.6, page 714). Synchronous state charts can be translated to equation-based models in Modelica, whereas asynchronous state charts currently need to be translated to algorithmic Modelica code due to their nondeclarative style. Clocked synchronous state machines are available in Modelica since version 3.3 (Section 13.7, page 703).

E1	—	C2
E2	C1, C2	C3
E3	C3	C4, C1
E4	C4	—

The job shop system is graphically depicted in Figure 13-71, using the Petri net visual formalism to be explained in the next section. The black dots within the circles at conditions C1 and C2 means that these conditions are currently enabled, that is, the preconditions for event E2 hold.

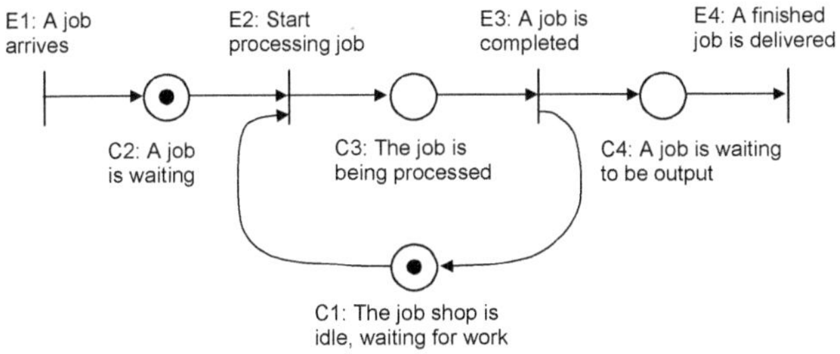

Figure 13-71. A job shop system modeled as a Petri net, with a job waiting and the shop idle.

13.3.6.2 Basic Primitives and Mathematical Definition of Petri Nets

A Petri net can be thought of as a graph containing two kinds of nodes:

- *Places*—visually depicted by circles.
- *Transitions*—visually depicted by vertical bars.

Thus, a Petri net contains a finite set of places and a finite set of transitions. Examples of places and transitions are shown in Figure 13-72, a Petri net graph modeling the job shop system. Places within a Petri net can have markings consisting of one or more *tokens*, visually represented by black dots. One of the most common kinds of Petri net, *normal Petri nets*, allows at most one token to be contained within a *place*. In the following discussion we restrict ourselves to such Petri nets, with the additional constraints (to be explained in more detail in the following and in Section 13.3.6.7) of *deterministic* execution and of immediate *firing* of enabled transitions without delay. These properties are natural when Petri nets are used to model discrete parts of control systems, as well as for many other applications.

The nodes of a Petri net are connected by arrows. An arrow into a node denotes an *input* to the node, whereas an arrow out of a node denotes an *output* from the node. A Petri net is a bipartite graph since places and transitions appear alternatingly and nodes of the same kind are not allowed to be directly connected. Places may be connected only to transitions, and transitions only to places—never places to places or transitions to transitions. The execution model of Petri nets maps the state represented as a *marking* (an attribute that represents the number of tokens in each place) to a new state, that is, to a new marking. The arrows of a Petri net can be represented by a few functions. Thus a Petri net also needs the following items to have a complete mathematical definition:

- An *input* function, mapping each transition to a set of input places, and each place to set of input transitions.
- An *output* function, mapping each transition to a set of output places, and each place to set of output transitions.
- A *marking*, defining the state of the system as the number of tokens associated with each place. Normal Petri nets is a subclass that allows only at most one token per place.
- A *transition* function, δ, defining an execution model for Petri nets, mapping a state, that is, a marking, to a new state.

A Petri net executes by *firing* transitions, that is, removing tokens from the input places of a transition and creating new tokens which are distributed to its output places. A transition can fire only if its input places are *enabled* and its output places are *free*. The fact that its input places are enabled means that they contain a sufficient number of tokens, which is one token per place in *normal* Petri nets. The output places being free means that none of them contain any token so that all of them are able to receive a token during the next execution step.

To understand this execution model consider the example of Petri net execution in Figure 13-72.

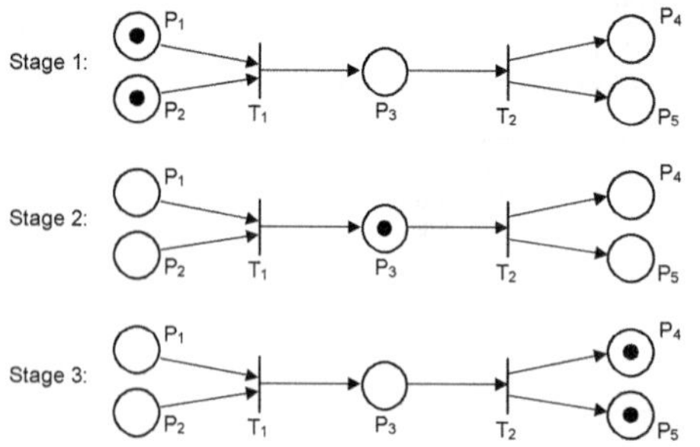

Figure 13-72. An example with three stages of a Petri net execution.

In Stage 1, both input places P_1 and P_2 to transition T_1 are enabled and its output place P_3 is free, making it possible for the transition to fire. When the transition fires, the tokens are removed from its input places and a token is placed in its output place P_3, mapping the state to the situation shown in Stage 2. In the next phase, transition T_2 fires, putting tokens in its output places P_4 and P_5, and removing a token from its input place P_3, as shown in Stage 3 of Figure 13-72.

13.3.6.3 Petri Net Primitives for Parallelism and Synchronization

We can easily use Petri nets to model the basic *fork* and *join* primitives for parallelism and synchronization. The transition T_1 in Figure 13-74 is a *synchronization* primitive, the *join* operation, for the parallel processes represented by P_1 and P_2. Execution is not allowed to proceed until tokens have arrived in both P_1 and P_2, i.e., when the executions of both processes have reached the desired points.

Conversely, the transition T_2 in Figure 13-74 is a *parallelism* or *concurrency* primitive, the *fork* operation. It splits the current thread of execution into two parallel processes represented by P_4 and P_5.

13.3.6.4 Equation-Based Hybrid Semantics of Places and Transitions

Here we present an equation-based execution semantics of places and transitions, which is useful when defining our small Modelica library of Petri net modeling primitives. We also extend the basic Petri net *transition* primitive with a *continuous-§ condition C*, which can be used to link the discrete Petri net parts of a system model with its continuous parts.

As previously mentioned, the *state* of a Petri net model is maintained as markings in the *places*, here represented by `Boolean` state variables called *state*, while decisions to *change* the state are made in the *transitions*.

With every connection between a place and a transition we also associate two `Boolean` variables: *is* and *if* for input connections or *os* and *of* for output connections, for example, as in Figure 13-73, where input and output places are connected to a transition T. The letter *s* in this notation represents setting, and *f* represents firing. The variables is_n and os_k report the state of connected input places IP_n and output places OP_k to the transition so that it can determine if it should fire.

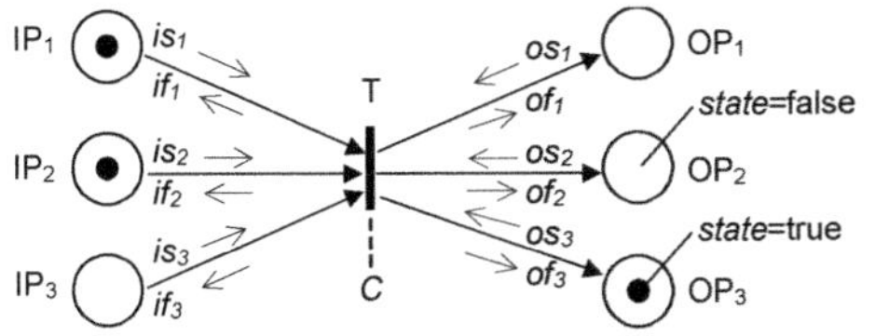

Figure 13-73. A transition `T` with three input places `IPn`, three output places `OPn`, and a condition `C`.

Recall that the decision to fire a transition is dependent on tokens being present in all its input places (represented by *state* and variables is_n having the value `true`), all its output places being free (represented by *state* and variables os_k having the value `false`), and sometimes also on a *condition* C associated with the transition. The availability of this *condition* is an extension provided by the Modelica version compared to the standard version of the Petri net transition primitive. Thus the firing condition for the transition T in Figure 13-73 can be expressed by the following equation:

$$fire = C \text{ and } (is_1 \text{ and } is_2 \text{ and } is_3) \text{ and not } (os_1 \text{ or } os_2 \text{ or } os_3) \tag{13-12}$$

When the transition fires this must be reported to all input places via the variables if_n so that they can remove their tokens, i.e., set their *state* to `false`, and to all output places via the variables of_n so that they can set their *state* to `true`. These variables are also defined by equations, e.g.:

$$if_1 = if_2 = if_3 = of_1 = of_2 = of_3 = fire \tag{13-13}$$

We now turn to the problem of describing the execution semantics of a place by equations. Remember that we have chosen a deterministic execution semantics for our Petri nets. Deterministic execution is achieved by assigning a priority ordering to transitions so that only the transition with the highest priority may fire if several are enabled simultaneously. This is necessary since a place can hold at most one token, requiring synchronization of the transition connections to ensure that at most one token is moved to the place and at most one token is removed from it. In Figure 13-74, the transition IT_1 has higher priority than IT_2, which in turn has higher priority than IT_3.

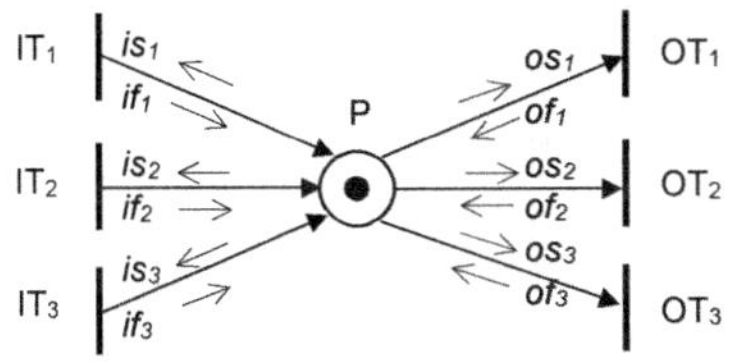

Figure 13-74. A place `P` connected to three input transitions $\texttt{IT}_n$ and three output transitions $\texttt{OT}_n$.

The synchronization and priorities of the transitions connected to the place are represented by the equations below, which specify the removal and placement of tokens in the place, as well as reporting to the input and output transitions.

Since the input transition IT_1 has the highest priority, we start its evaluation first. The *state* of place P in Figure 13-74 is reported to this transition through the variable is_1 in the first equation. Only if *state*=`false`, i.e., the place is free, is there a possibility for the transition IT_1 to fire and thereby set if_1 to `true`, which in turn will prevent transition IT_2 from firing by the presence of if_1 in the right-hand side of the second equation.

$$\begin{aligned}
is_1 &= state \\
is_2 &= is_1\ or\ if_1 \\
is_3 &= is_2\ or\ if_2 \\
dummy_1 &= is_3\ or\ if_3 \\
os_1 &= state \\
os_2 &= os_1\ and\ not\ of_1 \\
os_3 &= os_2\ and\ not\ of_2 \\
dummy_2 &= os_3\ and\ not\ of_3 \\
newstate &= (state\ and\ not\,(of_1\ or\ of_2))\ or\ (if_1\ or\ if_2)
\end{aligned} \qquad (13\text{-}14)$$

This will cause is_2 to be `true`, which in turn prevents firing IT_3, and so on. Thus, at most one of the input transitions will fire, and they are evaluated in priority order with the first transition having the highest priority. The equation involving the $dummy_1$ variable is not needed to define the semantics of the place, but is included anyway since it enables a concise formulation of these input transition equations in terms of the two vectors *is* and *if* of length 3, and the scalars *state* and $dummy_1$, as shown in the definition of the class `Place` in the next section.

There is an analogous situation regarding the three equations that report the *state* to the output transitions through the variables os_1, os_2, and os_3. In order to avoid nondeterminism and letting at most one output transition fire, each output transition in order gets the chance to fire, starting with OT_1, which thus gets the highest priority. A precondition for firing is that state=`true`, which is reported to the first output transition through os_1. If this transition fires, then of_1 will become `true`, which through the right-hand side of the equation defining os_2 will cause os_2 to be `false`. This avoids firing OT_2 and trying to remove a token from place P since that token already was removed because transition OT_1 already fired. An analogous reasoning applies to transition OT_3 through the equation defining os_3.

Finally, the last equation defines the new state *newstate* of the place P in the next iteration of the Petri net execution. This new state becomes `true` if the current state is `true` and the token is not removed, that is, none of the of_n variables are `true`. It can also become `true` if one of the input transitions fires and sets an if_n variable to `true`.

13.3.6.5 Classes for Connectors, Places, and Transitions

Based on the above equation-based semantics for the execution taking place at places and transitions, we can now define Modelica classes for these entities. Also, the variables is_n and if_n are collected into input connectors, whereas os_n and of_n are put into output connectors. Both are intended to be used for connections between places and transitions.

In principle it would be enough with one connector class for these connectors. However, Petri nets are bipartite graphs that allow connection only of different kinds of nodes, places to transitions or transitions to places. The Modelica type system can ensure that only legal connections are made if we define two different connector classes, one class `PTPort` for places to transitions (with class prefix and variable suffixes `PT`), and another class `TPPort` for transitions to places (with class prefix and variable suffixes `TP`). Since the variable names are different, the connector types are different in the Modelica type system, even though the connector classes in both cases represent the same kind of variables: state and firing information.

In order to have slightly different connector icons for the input version (filled triangle) and the output version (unfilled triangle), we also define otherwise-identical input and output versions of these connector classes (see below). There is also a `ConditionPort` connector class for specifying an optional input condition to a `Transition`.

```
connector PTPort "Connecting Places to Transitions"
  Boolean sPT    "state information";
```

```
  Boolean fPT    "firing information";
end PTPort;

connector PTPortIn  = PTPort;  // Input version of PTPort
connector PTPortOut = PTPort;  // Output version of PTPort

connector TPPort "Connecting Transitions to Places"
  Boolean sTP    "state information";
  Boolean fTP    "firing information";
end TPPort;

connector TPPortIn  = TPPort;  // Input version of PTPort
connector TPPortOut = TPPort;  // Output version of PTPort

connector ConditionPort "Optional condition to a Transition"
  Boolean c(start=true);
end ConditionPort;
```

We now define `Place` and `Transition` classes, using the previously described equations generalized to an arbitrary number of input and output ports.

```
class Place
  constant Integer nIn  = 1  "Number of input transition ports";
  constant Integer nOut = 1  "Number of output transition ports";
  TPPortIn  inTrans[nIn]   "Vector of input transition connectors";
  PTPortOut outTrans[nOut] "Vector of output transition connectors";
  Boolean   state;
  Boolean   d1, d2;  // Dummy variables
equation
  ostate = pre(state);  // ostate is the current state
    // Report state to input transitions, vector equation
  cat(1,inTrans.sTP,{d1}] = cat(1,{ostate},inTrans.sTP or inTrans.fTP);
    // Report state to output transitions, column matrix equation
  [outTrans.sPT,{d2}] = [{ostate}, outTrans.sPT and not outTrans.fPT];
    // Compute new state for next Petri net iteration
  state = (ostate and not anyTrue(outTrans.sPT)) or
    (anyTrue(inTrans.sTP));
end Place;

class Transition
  ConditionPort condition "Optional condition";
  constant Integer nIn  = 1;
  constant Integer nOut = 1;
  PTPortIn  inPlaces[nIn]   "Vector of input place connectors";
  TPPortOut outPlaces[nOut] "Vector of output place connectors";
  Boolean   fire;
equation
  fire = condition and allTrue(inPlaces.sPT) and not
         anyTrue(outPlaces.sTP);
    // Report firing info to input places, vector equation
  inPlace.fPT = fill(fire,nIn);
    // Report firing info to output places, vector equation
  outPlace.fTP = fill(fire,nOut);
end Transition;
```

We also need utility `Boolean` reduction functions `anyTrue` and `allTrue`:

```
function anyTrue  "True, if at least one element is true in a vector"
  input  Boolean inp[:];
  output Boolean result;
algorithm
  result := false;
  for i in 1:size(inp,1) loop
    result := result or inp[i];
```

```
    end for;
  end anyTrue;

  function allTrue  "True, if all elements are true in a vector"
    input  Boolean inp[:];
    output Boolean result;
  algorithm
    result := true;
    for i in 1:size(inp,1) loop
      result := result and inp[i];
    end for;
  end allTrue;
```

All classes and functions are collected into a package called `NormalPetriNet`:

```
encapsulated package NormalPetriNet
  connector PTPort ...;
  connector PTPortIn ...;
  connector PTPortOut ...;
  connector TPPort ...;
  connector TPPortIn ...;
  connector TPPortOut ...;
  connector ConditionPort ...;
  class Place ...;
  class Transition ...;
  function anyTrue ...;
  function allTrue ...;
end NormalPetriNet;
```

13.3.6.6 A Modelica Petri Net Model and Simulation of a Job Shop System

We now return to our job shop system example. Its Petri net graph is shown once more below in Figure 13-75, with the difference that the token has advanced, representing the condition C3, that a job is currently being processed.

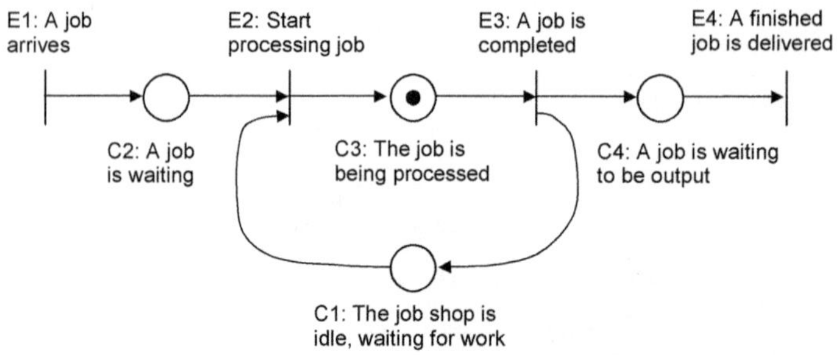

Figure 13-75. The job shop system Petri Net graph once more. The job has now advanced to the stage of being processed.

We would now like to build a Modelica Petri net model of the job shop system, using our recently developed `NormalPetriNet` package. We need modified instances of the general `Place` and `Transition` classes in order to reflect the different numbers of input and output ports. The `JobShopSystem` model follows below, containing these modified instances of places and transitions, as well as connection equations.

```
model JobShopSystem
  import NormalPetriNet.*;
  // Need to generate some jobs; coupled to time condition in Transitions.
  Transition arrival(nIn=0,nOut=1);       // E1
  Place      inwait(nIn=1,nOut=1);        // C2
  Transition synchronize(nIn=2,nOut=1);   // E2
  Place      processing(nIn=1,nOut=1);    // C3
  Transition parallel(nIn=1,nOut=2);      // E3
  Place      idle(nIn=1,nOut=2);          // C1
  Place      outwait(nIn=1,nOut=1);       // C4
  Transition delivery(nIn=1,nOut=0);      // E4
equation
  connect(arrival.inPlaces, inwait.inTrans);
  connect(inwait.outTrans[1], synchronize.inPlaces[1]);
  connect(idle.outTrans[1], synchronize.inPlaces[2]);
  connect(synchronize.outPlaces[1], processing.inTrans[1]);
  connect(processing.outTrans[1], parallel.inPlaces[1]);
  connect(parallel.outPlaces[1], outwait.inTrans[1]);
  connect(parallel.outPlaces[2], idle.inTrans[1]);
  connect(outwait.outTrans[1], delivery.inPlaces[1]);
end JobShopSystem;
```

The connection diagram in Figure 13-76 corresponds to the Modelica Petri Net model of the job shop system example. It is quite close to the usual Petri net graphic diagram style that has been used in previous figures of the job shop system. Input connectors are clearly depicted as filled triangles, whereas output connectors are represented by unfilled triangles.

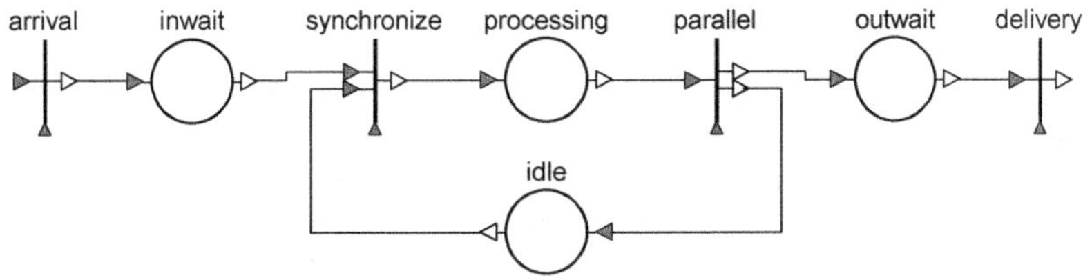

Figure 13-76. A connection diagram of the Modelica Petri Net Job Shop System Example.

Finally, we simulate the job shop system model using the above default settings, for a job that passes through the system and is processed (Figure 13-77).

```
simulate(JobShopSystem, stopTime=1)

plot(S1.state)
plot(P1.state)
plot(P2.state)
plot(P3.state)
```

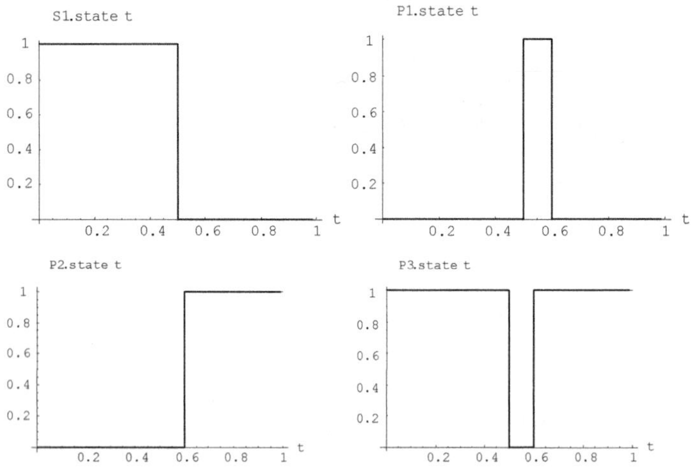

Figure 13-77. Petri Net job shop system.

13.3.6.7 Finite State Automata Represented as Petri Nets

It is actually possible to represent finite state automata, previously described in Section 13.3.2, as Petri nets. One problem that has to be solved when performing this mapping is to represent communication with the outside world. This can be handled by representing each kind of input token as an input place to the Petri net, and each kind of output token as an output place. The arrival of an input token to a finite state automaton corresponds to putting a token in an input place of the Petri net. An alternative approach not used in this example is to use input and output transitions instead of input and output places. The rest of the mapping rules from automatons to Petri nets are as follows:

- Each state in the automaton is represented by a place in the Petri net. The current state is marked by a token, whereas all other places corresponding to automaton states are empty.
- State changes and generating outputs are represented by transitions. For each pair of state and input symbol, we define a transition whose input places are the two places corresponding to the state and input symbol, and whose output places correspond to the next state and the output.

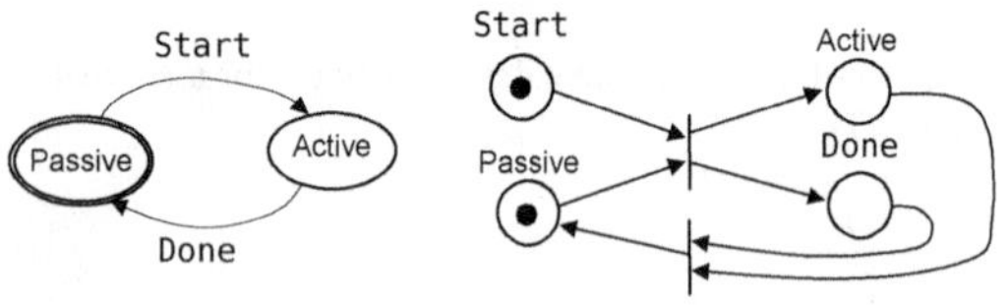

Figure 13-78. A finite state automaton model and the corresponding Petri net to the right.

We apply this mapping to the finite state automaton model of the simple server system model, which has `Start` as input event and `Done` as output event. The result is shown in Figure 13-78.

13.3.6.8 Flowcharts Represented as Petri Nets

A flowchart is a common graphic formalism, often used to represent the control structure of programs or workflow systems. It is possible to conveniently map flowcharts into Petri nets, including our Modelica-based Petri nets, as shown in Figure 13-79.

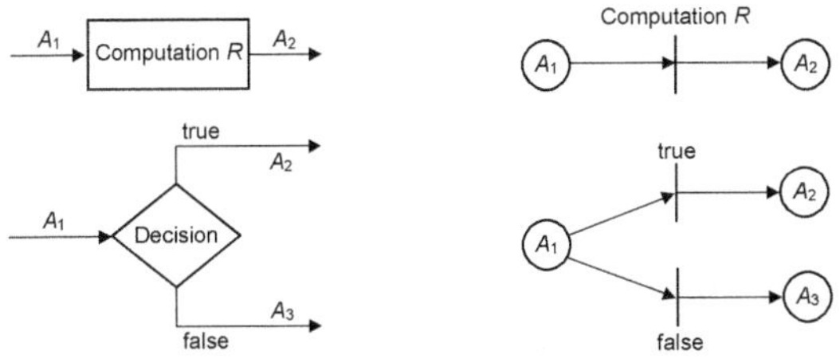

Figure 13-79. The mapping of computation and decision nodes of a flowchart into Petri net transition nodes.

A convenient way to execute a flowchart translated into a Petri net is to introduce a token which represents the current instruction, that is, a kind of program counter. As instructions execute, the token moves around in the Petri net. Note that when translating flowcharts into Petri nets, we replace the nodes of the flowcharts by transitions and the arcs by places. This is natural, since in the Petri net model, the transitions model actions, whereas in the flowchart model, the nodes model actions. What is the meaning of the places in the translated Petri net model? The easiest interpretation is to consider the program counter role of the token. This means that a token residing in a place corresponds to the program counter being positioned ready to execute the next instruction.

13.3.6.9 Short Overview of Different Petri Net Variants

As we have already briefly hinted, there are many variants of Petri nets with different properties. The kind of *Normal Petri nets* described previously is only one variant, albeit a rather useful one. There are Petri nets where several tokens are allowed to reside in place. It is possible to have multiple arrows between the same nodes. If a place is connected to several output transitions and execution is nondeterministic, then it is in general not possible to determine which of these transitions should fire—the Petri net is nondeterministic. Below we briefly describe a few different kinds of Petri nets with different semantics:

- *Bounded Petri nets*. This kind of Petri net enforces an upper bound of the number of tokens that can reside in place. This requires a modification of the firing rule, since the transition can fire only when the updated number of tokens in each of its output places would not exceed the upper bound of the place.
- *Normal Petri nets* are bounded Petri nets with an upper bound of at most one token in a place.
- *Inhibitor Petri nets* are a kind of Petri net that can contain a special kind of arc from place to transition, which can inhibit the transition from firing.
- *Priority Petri nets* allow assigning priorities to transitions. If several transitions are enabled, the one with the highest priority will fire. This can be used to eliminate nondeterminism and achieve deterministic execution of Petri nets.
- *Maximal firing Petri nets* require transitions to fire maximally, that is, *immediately*, as soon as they are enabled. This *must fire* semantics is different from the *may fire* semantics of a number of other forms of Petri nets.
- *Colored Petri nets* assign attributes, for example, color, to transitions and tokens. Transitions can fire depending on the presence of tokens with specific attributes in their input places.
- *Time Petri nets* associate upper and lower time bounds with each transition. A transition may fire as soon as time exceeds its lower bound. It must fire before time exceeds its upper time bound unless it has been disabled before that time.
- *Timed Petri nets* associate a length of time with each transition. When a transition fires, tokens are removed from the input places as usual. However, there is a time delay of specified length until tokens are moved into the output places of the transition.
- *Stochastic Petri nets*—see the Modelica library PNLib, Section 16.18, page 965.

Using the above definitions, the kind of normal Petri nets described previously and represented in our Modelica library, `NormalPetriNets`, can be more precisely characterized as *normal priority maximal firing Petri nets*.

Note that further generalized Petri nets in Modelica, also including stochastic Petri nets, have become available in the Modelica library PNLib, see Section 16.18, page 965.

13.4 Hybrid System Modeling and Simulation

At the beginning of this chapter we mentioned the notion of hybrid systems, i.e., systems that contain both continuous-time and discrete-time subsystems. There are a number of reasons why such systems and models are both appropriate and practical. The following cases of hybrid models and systems are quite common:

- *Discrete* computer-based components such as discrete-time controllers that interact with *continuous* physical systems.
- *Mode switching* systems containing components that have different behavior in different operating regions.

In the following we discuss examples of each of these kinds of hybrid systems.

13.4.1 Hybrid Tank Model with Clocked and Unclocked Discrete Controllers

Let us once again consider the tank system example previously presented in Chapter 12, page 573, containing a proportional-integral (PI) controller (Figure 13-80).

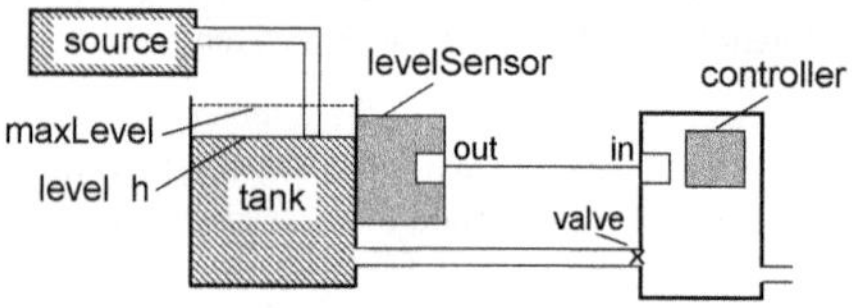

Figure 13-80. A tank system with a tank, a source for liquid, and a controller.

For convenience the `TankPI` and `Tank` models together with three connector classes from Section 12.2.3, page 573, are also shown below:

```
model TankPI
  LiquidSource            source(flowLevel=0.02);
  PIcontinuousController piContinuous(ref=0.25);
  Tank                    tank(area=1);
equation
  connect(source.qOut, tank.qIn);
  connect(tank.tActuator, piContinuous.cOut);
  connect(tank.tSensor, piContinuous.cIn);
end TankPI;

model Tank
  ReadSignal  tSensor   "Connector, sensor reading tank level (m)";
  ActSignal   tActuator "Connector, actuator controlling input flow";
  LiquidFlow  qIn       "Connector, flow (m3/s) through input valve";
  LiquidFlow  qOut      "Connector, flow (m3/s) through output valve";
  parameter Real area(unit="m2")        = 0.5;
```

```
  parameter Real flowGain(unit="m2/s") = 0.05;
  parameter Real minV=0, maxV=10; // Limits for output valve flow
  Real h(start=0.0, unit="m") "Tank level";
equation
  assert(minV>=0,"minV - minimum Valve level must be >= 0 ");//
  der(h)      = (qIn.lflow-qOut.lflow)/area;    // Mass balance
equation
  qOut.lflow  = LimitValue(minV,maxV,-flowGain*tActuator.act);
  tSensor.val = h;
end Tank;

connector ReadSignal   "Reading fluid level"
  Real val(unit="m");
end ReadSignal;

connector ActSignal    "Signal to actuator for setting valve position"
  Real act;
end ActSignal;

connector LiquidFlow   "Liquid flow at inlets or outlets"
  Real lflow(unit="m3/s");
end LiquidFlow;
```

The fluid level h in the tank must be maintained at a fixed level as closely as possible. Fluid can enter the tank through a pipe at a rate controlled via a valve, and leaves the tank via another pipe. In the previous tank model a continuous controller was used, shown below once more, which we now will replace by a discrete controller to illustrate this kind of common hybrid system.

```
model PIcontinuousController
  extends BaseController(K=2,T=10);
  Real  x; // State variable of continuous controller
equation
  der(x) = error/T;
  outCtr = K*(x+error);
end PIcontinuousController;
```

The behavior of the continuous PI controller is defined by the following two equations:

$$\begin{aligned} \frac{dx}{dt} &= \frac{error}{T} \\ outCtr &= K*(x+error) \end{aligned} \tag{13-15}$$

Here x is the controller state variable, *error* is the difference between the reference level and the actual level obtained from the sensor, T is the time constant of the controller, *outCtr* is the control signal to the actuator for controlling the valve position, and K is the gain factor. Both the continuous controller and the discrete controller to be defined inherit the partial controller class BaseController (also defined in Section 12.2.3, page 573), containing common parameters, state variables, and two connectors: one to read the sensor and one to control the valve actuator.

```
partial model BaseController
  parameter Real Ts(unit="s")=0.1  "Time between samples";
  parameter Real K=2               "Gain";
  parameter Real T(unit="s")=10    "Time constant";
  ReadSignal      cIn              "Input sensor level, connector";
  ActSignal       cOut             "Control to actuator, connector";
  parameter Real ref               "Reference level";
  Real            error            "Deviation from reference level";
  Real            outCtr           "Output control signal";
equation
  error    = ref-cIn.val;
  cOut.act = outCtr;
end BaseController;
```

In order to define the discrete PI controller, we first discretize the above equations to obtain difference equations, assuming a sampling period *dt*, below denoted *Ts*, and a difference approximation $dx = x_k - x_{k-1}$. After some rearrangements we obtain:

$$x_k = \frac{x_{k-1} + error * Ts}{T} \qquad (13\text{-}16)$$
$$outCtr = K * (x_k + error)$$

These difference equations are reflected in the class definition of the discrete PI controller below, with x_k replaced by `x`, and x_{k-1} = `pre(x)` or `previous(x)` within a when-equation to obtain the desired discrete sampling behavior. First an unclocked controller model:

```
model PIdiscreteControllerUnclocked
  extends BaseController(K=2,T=10);
  discrete Real x; // State variable of discrete controller
equation
  when sample(0,Ts) then
    x = pre(x)+error*Ts/T;
    outCtr = K*(x+error);
  end when;
end PIdiscreteControllerUnclocked;
```

A first version of a clocked controller model has `x` as a clocked state variable but still keeps the unclocked state variables `error` and `outCtr` inherited from `BaseController`.

```
model PIdiscreteControllerClockedV1 "Hybrid version, clocked PI controller"
  extends BaseController(K=2,T=10);
  discrete Real x; // State variable of discrete controller
equation
  when Clock(Ts) then
    x = previous(x)+sample(error*Ts/T);
  end when;
  outCtr = K*(hold(x)+error);
end PIdiscreteControllerClockedV1;
```

This version `V1` of the clocked controller can be simulated together with the tank model, showing the results in Figure 13-82, page 680. However, there is a *serious problem* with this controller model.

One of the main goal with the clocked language constructs is to be able to write clocked controller models that can be downloaded and efficiently executed on clocked digital hardware.

The desired structure of such a system is depicted in Figure 13-100, page 695, with the following typical model parts:

- A discrete controller—periodically executed control software on clocked digital hardware.
- A sampling device—an electronic hardware device, typically an analog-digital converter.
- A hold device—an electronic hardware device, typically a digital-analog converter.
- The (continuous-time) plant model—here the tank.

Since the `PIdiscreteControllerClockedV1` controller model contains a mix of clocked and unclocked state variables and internally converts between them, it cannot be compiled for efficient direct execution on real-world clocked digital hardware.

In a real-world implementation the *sensor signals are sampled* and the *actuator signals are held constant* during one sample period. The sensor input to the model is `cIn.val` which should therefore be sampled before entering the discrete controller model that constitutes the software on the controller. The actuator output is `cOut` which therefore should converted from digital to analog using `hold` after leaving the control software model.

Below we have made a second version of the clocked controller model with *clean separation* between the clocked controller and the unclocked controlled (physical) tank system. Here all controller state variables are clocked by making a new `BaseControllerClocked` base class. Figure 13-100 in Section 13.6.1, page 694, shows such a clean separation between controller and plant.

The external connector interface is still continuous-time, but a sampler (an analog-digital converter) immediately converts the input sensor signal into a clocked value `dCinval`, whereas a hold (a digital-analog converter) converts the output control signal into an unclocked value `cOut.act`.

```
model PIdiscreteControllerClocked  "Pure clocked version of PI controller"
  extends BaseControllerClocked(K=2,T=10);
  discrete Real x; // State variable of discrete controller
equation
  when Clock() then  // clock frequency inferred from the variable error
    x = previous(x) + error*Ts/T;
  end when;
  outCtr = K*(x+error);
end PIdiscreteControllerClocked;

partial model BaseControllerClocked  "Controller with clocked states"
  parameter Real Ts(unit="s")=0.1 "Time between samples";
  parameter Real K=2              "Gain";
  parameter Real T(unit="s")=10   "Time constant";
  ReadSignal     cIn              "Input sensor level, connector";
  ActSignal      cOut             "Control to actuator, connector";
  parameter Real ref              "Reference level";
  discrete Real  error            "Deviation from reference level";
  discrete Real  outCtr           "Output control signal";
  discrete Real  dCinval          "Sampled sensor level";
equation
  dCinval  = sample(cIn.val, Clock(Ts)); // sampling of sensor Cin.val
  error    = ref - dCinval;
  cOut.act = hold(outCtr);        // hold clocked output control signal
end BaseControllerClocked;
```

Finally, we put together the hybrid tank system by simply replacing the continuous PI controller with the discrete one, called `piDiscrete`, as depicted in Figure 13-81.

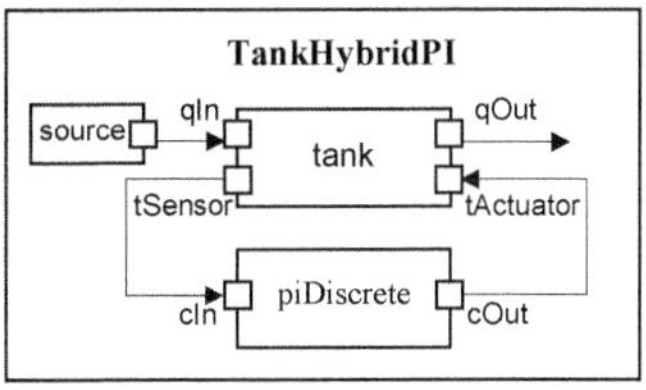

Figure 13-81. A hybrid tank system consisting of a continuous tank model connected to a source for liquid and a discrete `PI` controller.

The `TankHybridPI` models (unclocked and clocked versions) connect a discrete PI controller to a liquid source and a tank (Figure 13-81), both defined by continuous models previously presented in Section 12.2.3, page 573.

```
model TankHybridPIUnclocked
  LiquidSource                  source(flowLevel=0.02);
  PIdiscreteControllerUnclocked piDiscrete(ref=0.25);
  Tank                          tank(area=1);
equation
  connect(source.qOut, tank.qIn);
  connect(tank.tActuator, piDiscrete.cOut);
  connect(tank.tSensor, piDiscrete.cIn);
end TankHybridPIUnclocked;
```

```
model TankHybridPIClocked
  LiquidSource                     source(flowLevel=0.02);
  PIdiscreteControllerClocked  piDiscrete(ref=0.25);
  Tank                             tank(area=1);
equation
  connect(source.qOut, tank.qIn);
  connect(tank.tActuator, piDiscrete.cOut);
  connect(tank.tSensor, piDiscrete.cIn);
end TankHybridPIClocked;
```

The hybrid tank system with a discrete PI controller is simulated (Figure 13-82), obtaining essentially the same result as when using the continuous PI controller (compare to Figure 12-4 on page 575). The same result is obtained from the unclocked and clocked versions. The response shown in the curve is the reaction of the controller to an instantaneous increase in the input flow from the source at time t=150. The only difference compared to the continuous controller case are a few small squiggles in the curve, probably caused by the discrete approximation.

```
simulate(TankHybridPIUnclocked, stopTime=250);  plot(tank.h)
simulate(TankHybridPIClocked, stopTime=250);  plot(tank.h)
```

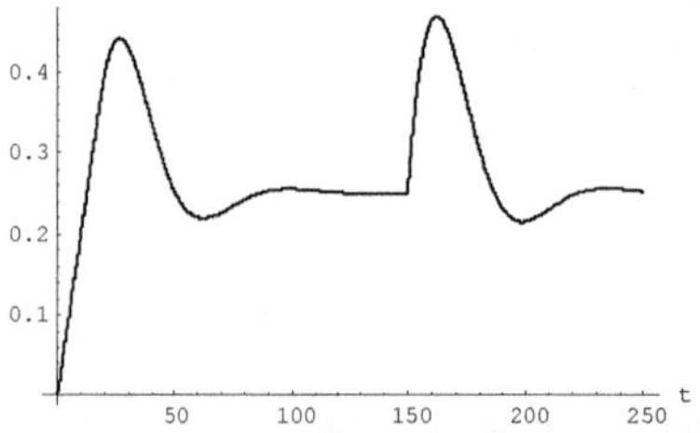

Figure 13-82. The tank level from a simulation of the `TankHybridPIUnclocked` and `TankHybridPI-Clocked` models, both with a discrete `PI` controller (unclocked and clocked versions). The same simulation results are obtained from the clocked and unclocked versions.

The discrete PID (proportional integrating derivative) controller models below can be derived in a similar way as was done for the discrete PI controller. A PID controller can react quicker to instantaneous changes than a PI controller.

```
model PIDdiscreteControllerUnclocked
  extends BaseController(K=2,T=10);
  discrete Real x; // State variable of discrete controller
  discrete Real y; // State variable of discrete controller
equation
  when sample(0,Ts) then
    x = pre(x)+error*Ts/T;
    y=T*(error-pre(error));
    outCtr = K*(x+error+y);
  end when;
end PIDdiscreteControllerUnclocked;

model PIDdiscreteControllerClocked  "Clocked PID controller"
  extends BaseControllerClocked(K=2,T=10);
  discrete Real x; // Clocked state variable of discrete controller
  discrete Real y; // Clocked state variable of discrete controller
equation
  when Clock() then
    x = previous(x)+error*Ts/T;
    y=T*(error-previous(error));
```

```
    end when;
    outCtr = K*(x+error+y);
  end PIDdiscreteControllerClocked;
```

We define a `TankHybridPID` system which is the same as the `TankHybridPI` system except that the discrete `PI` controller has been replaced by the discrete `PID` controller (Figure 13-83).

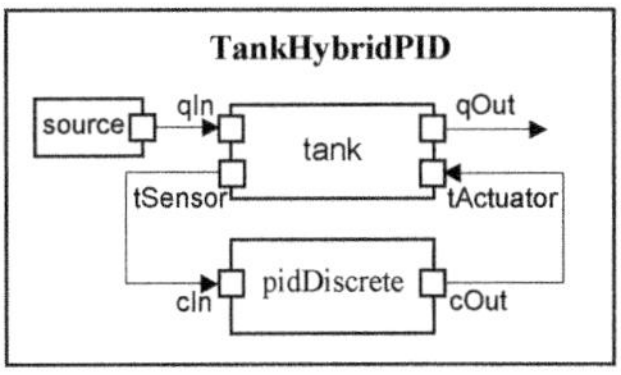

Figure 13-83. A hybrid tank system consisting of a continuous tank model connected to a `source` for liquid and a discrete `PID` controller.

The source code of the `TankHybridPID` models (both unclocked and clocked) appear as follows:

```
model TankHybridPIDUnclocked
  LiquidSource                     source(flowLevel=0.02);
  PIDdiscreteControllerUnclocked   pidDiscrete(ref=0.25);
  Tank                             tank(area=1);
equation
  connect(source.qOut,     tank.qIn);
  connect(tank.tActuator, pidDiscrete.cOut);
  connect(tank.tSensor,    pidDiscrete.cIn);
end TankHybridPIDUnclocked;

model TankHybridPIDClocked
  LiquidSource                   source(flowLevel=0.02);
  PIDdiscreteControllerClocked   pidDiscrete(ref=0.25);
  Tank                           tank(area=1);
equation
  connect(source.qOut, tank.qIn);
  connect(tank.tActuator, pidDiscrete.cOut);
  connect(tank.tSensor, pidDiscrete.cIn);
end TankHybridPIDClocked;
```

The tank level of the simulated system is quite similar to the corresponding system with a PI controller, but with faster control to restore the reference level after quick changes of the input flow (Figure 13-84).

```
simulate(TankHybridPIDUnclocked, stopTime=250);  plot(tank.h)
simulate(TankHybridPIDClocked, stopTime=250);  plot(tank.h)
```

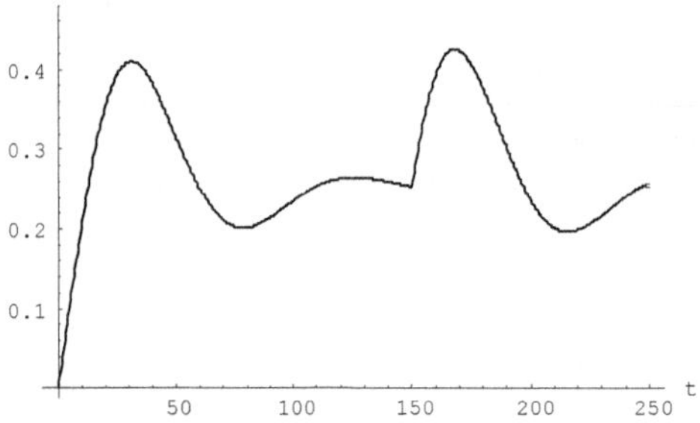

Figure 13-84. The tank level from a simulation of the `TankHybridPIDUnclocked` and `TankHybridPID-Clocked` models, both with a discrete `PID` controller (unclocked and clocked versions). The same simulation results are obtained from the clocked and unclocked versions.

Figure 13-85 shows the simulation results from both `TankHybridPI` and `TankHybridPID` plotted in the same diagram.

```
plot({tankm1.h,tankm2.h})
```

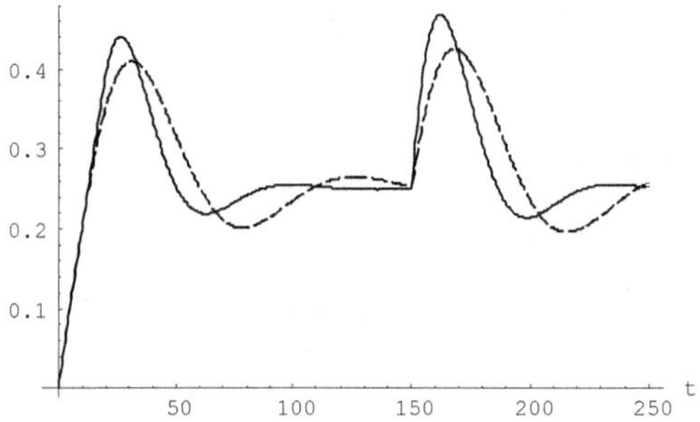

Figure 13-85. Comparison of `TankHybridPI` (solid) and `TankHybridPID` (dashed) simulations.

13.4.2 A Mode-Switching Model—DCMotor Transmission with Elastic Backlash

Certain hybrid systems consist of components that are primarily continuous but have different behavior in different operating regions, and discontinuously change between these regions. Such systems are called *mode-switching systems* since each operating region can be represented by a specific operating mode, and switching between the regions is often modeled by changing value of discrete mode state variables.

We will illustrate a typical mode-switching system by an example of an elastic transmission with slack, connecting a motor with a rotating shaft via an elastic transmission to a driven shaft coupled to a load, as depicted in Figure 13-86.

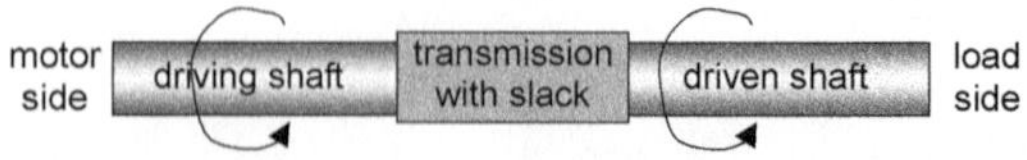

Figure 13-86. Two rotating shafts connected via an elastic transmission with slack.

The elastic transmission with slack transmits torque between the shafts via an elastic spring. For small values of the relative angle deviation `phi_dev` between the shafts, the transmission exhibits *slack*, i.e., the shafts can rotate freely relative to each other without transmitting any torque. The transmission has three basic operating modes:

- The *Forward* mode, when the motor side is ahead of the load side (angle deviation `phi_dev` > `b/2`) and transmitting positive torque, i.e., driving the load side.
- The *Backward* mode, when the motor side is behind the load side (angle deviation `phi_dev` < -`b/2`) and transmitting negative torque, i.e., braking the load side.
- The *Slack* mode, when the motor and the load can rotate freely relative to each other within the limits `-b/2` < `phi_dev` < `b/2`, without transmitting any torque.

The three operating modes of the transmission can be discerned in the three different parts of the torque characteristics of the transmission, that is, the torque as a function of the relative angle deviation `phi_dev` between the shafts as depicted in Figure 13-87.

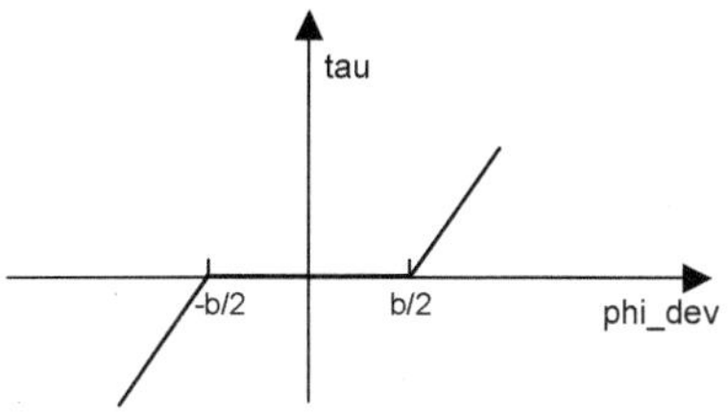

Figure 13-87. The characteristics of the elastic transmission with slack. The torque `tau` between the flanges of the shafts is zero in the slack state, and a linear function `tau = c*phi_dev` outside the slack region provided that zero damping `(d=0)` holds.

The three operating modes of the elastic transmission can be modeled by a finite state automaton, as in Figure 13-88. The state transitions between the modes are caused by detecting when continuous changes of the relative angle `phi_dev` cause the system to enter or leave the *Slack* region.

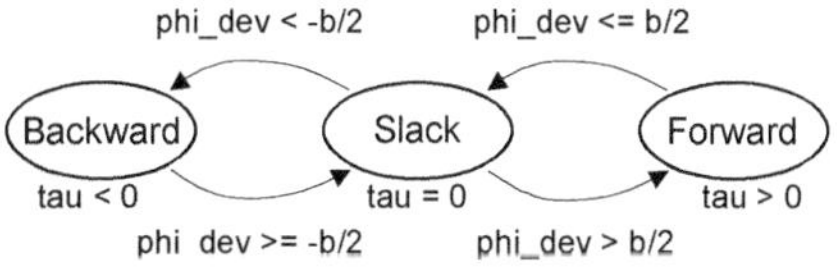

Figure 13-88. A finite state automaton illustrates the transitions between the three discrete modes of the `SimpleElastoBacklash` model. In the `Backward` mode when the relative angle deviation, `phi_dev`, between the rotating shafts is less than `-b/2`, negative torque `tau` is transmitted. In the `Forward` mode when `phi_dev > b/2`, positive torque is transmitted. When `Slack` holds, no torque is transmitted.

Most properties of the elastic transmission with backlash, both continuous and discrete, are represented in the partial model `SimpleElastoBacklash` below. This is a typical hybrid mode-switching model, with the finite state automaton represented by the equations for the `Boolean` variables `backward`, `forward`, and `slack`, and the conditional equation for the torque `tau` having different right-hand side expressions in the three operating modes.

```
partial model SimpleElastoBacklash
  Boolean backward, slack, forward;  // Mode variables
  parameter Real  b              "Size of backlash region";
```

```
  parameter Real  c = 1.e5       "Spring constant (c>0), N.m/rad";
  Flange_a        flange_a       "(left) driving flange - connector";
  Flange_b        flange_b       "(right) driven flange - connector";
  parameter Real  phi_rel0 = 0 "Angle when spring exerts no torque";
  Real            phi_rel        "Relative rotation angle betw. flanges";
  Real            phi_dev        "Angle deviation from zero-torque pos";
  Real            tau            "Torque between flanges";
equation
  phi_rel    = flange_b.phi - flange_a.phi;
  phi_dev    = phi_rel - phi_rel0;
  backward   = phi_rel < -b/2;     // Backward angle gives torque tau<0
  forward    = phi_rel > b/2;      // Forward angle gives torque tau>0
  slack      = not (backward or forward);// Slack angle gives no torque
  tau = if forward then                  // Forward angle gives
          c*(phi_dev - b/2)              // positive driving torque
        else (if backward then           // Backward angle gives
                c*(phi_dev + b/2)        // negative braking torque
              else                       // Slack gives
                0);                      // zero torque
end SimpleElastoBacklash;
```

We now employ the elastic transmission with backlash for the small application shown in Figure 13-89, where the DC motor circuit described in Section 5.6, page 207 and Section 15.1, page 794, is connected to a load denoted `inertia2` via the `elastoBacklash` instance of the transmission.

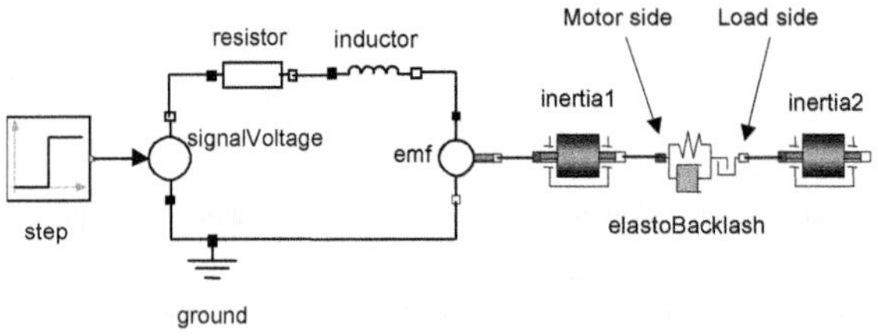

Figure 13-89. A `DCMotorCircuitBacklash` model including a transmission with elastic backlash.

The Modelica model corresponding to Figure 13-89 is as follows, using classes from the Modelica standard library:

```
model DCMotorCircuitBacklash
  import Modelica.Mechanics.Rotational;
  import Modelica.Electrical.Analog;
  import Modelica.Blocks;
  Rotational.Inertia              inertia1(J=1);
  Rotational.Inertia              inertia2(J=6);
  Rotational.ElastoBacklash       elastoBacklash(b=3,c=10,d=0.8);
  Analog.Basic.Inductor           inductor;
  Analog.Basic.Resistor         resistor;
  Analog.Basic.Ground           ground;
  Analog.Basic.EMF              emf;
  Analog.Sources.SignalVoltage signalVoltage;
  Blocks.Sources.Step           step;
equation
  connect(step.y,    signalVoltage.v);
  connect(signalVoltage.n, resistor.p);
  connect(resistor.n,      inductor.p);
  connect(signalVoltage.p, ground.p);
  connect(ground.p,        emf.n);
  connect(inductor.n,      emf.p);
```

```
    connect(emf.flange_b,     inertia1.flange_a); // rotFlange
    connect(inertia1.flange_b, elastoBacklash.flange_a); // rotFlange
    connect(elastoBacklash.flange_b,inertia2.flange_a);  // rotFlange
  end DCMotorCircuitBacklash;
```

The elastic transmission with backlash that we have used here is an instance of the `ElastoBacklash` model from the `Mechanics.Rotational.Components` package in the Modelica standard library.

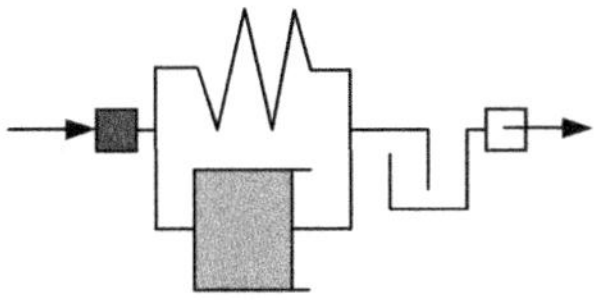

Figure 13-90. The `ElastoBacklash` model—a backlash connected in series with a linear spring and a damper.

The `ElastoBacklash` model consists of a backlash element connected in series to a spring and damper element, which are connected in parallel (Figure 13-90). This is a slight extension compared to the previous `SimpleElastoBacklash` model since we have introduced a damping element with a damping constant `d`. The damping element contributes to the torque `tau` equation by the expression `d*w_rel` that is nonzero provided `d` is nonzero. The spring constant must be nonzero, otherwise the model cannot be used. Another extension compared to the simple model is that a constant `bEps` for minimum backlash has been introduced. The backlash behavior of the model is available only if `abs(b) > bEps`, since if `b` is too small or zero, numeric problems with too many generated state events will occur.

The following `ElastoBacklash` model is from the Modelica standard library version MSL3.2.1, `Mechanics.Rotational.Components` package, but slightly reformatted to increase readability.

```
model ElastoBacklash
  "Backlash connected in series to linear spring and damper
   (backlash is modeled with elasticity)"
  parameter SI.RotationalSpringConstant c(final min=Modelica.Constants.
            small, start=1.0e5)  "Spring constant (c > 0 required)";
  parameter SI.RotationalDampingConstant d(final min=0, start=0)
                                "Damping constant";
  parameter SI.Angle  b(final min=0) = 0 "Total backlash";
  parameter SI.Angle  phi_rel0=0         "Unstretched spring angle";
  extends   Modelica.Mechanics.Rotational.
            Interfaces.PartialCompliantWithRelativeStates;
  extends   Modelica.Thermal.HeatTransfer.Interfaces.
            PartialElementaryConditionalHeatPortWithoutT;
protected
  final parameter SI.Angle bMax=b/2
    "Backlash in range bMin <= phi_rel - phi_rel0 <= bMax";
  final parameter SI.Angle bMin=-bMax
    "Backlash in range bMin <= phi_rel - phi_rel0 <= bMax";
  SI.Torque tau_c;
  SI.Torque tau_d;
  SI.Angle phi_diff = phi_rel - phi_rel0;
  // A minimum backlash bEps is defined in order to avoid an infinite
  // number of state events if backlash b is set to zero.
  constant SI.Angle bEps=1e-10 "Minimum backlash";
equation
  if initial() then
  /* During initialization the characteristic is modified, in order that
     it is a strict monoton rising function. Otherwise, initialization might
     result in a singular system when the characteristic has to be
     inverted. The characteristic is modified in the range
     1.5*bMin <= phi_rel - phi_rel0 <= 1.5 bMax,
```

```
      so that in this range a linear characteristic is present that
      approaches the original function continuously at its limits, e.g.,
           original:  tau(1.5*bMax) = c*(phi_diff - bMax)
                                    = c*(0.5*bMax)
           initial :  tau(1.5*bMax) = (c/3)*phi_diff
                                    = (c/3)*(3/2)*bMax
                                    = (c/2)*bMax
     */
     tau_c = if phi_diff > 1.5*bMax then c*(phi_diff - bMax) else if
       phi_diff < 1.5*bMin then c*(phi_diff - bMin) else (c/3)*phi_diff;
     tau_d = d*w_rel;
     tau = tau_c + tau_d;
     lossPower = tau_d*w_rel;
   else
     if abs(b) <= bEps then        // Less than minimum backlash to avoid
         tau_c = c*phi_diff;       // infinite number of state events
         tau_d = d*w_rel;
         tau   = tau_c + tau_d;
      elseif phi_diff > bMax then   // Forward angle gives positive torque
         tau_c = c*(phi_diff - bMax);
         tau_d = d*w_rel;
         tau   = smooth(0, noEvent(if tau_c + tau_d <= 0 then 0
                                   else tau_c + min(tau_c,tau_d)));
      elseif phi_diff < bMin then   // Backward angle gives negative torque
         tau_c = c*(phi_diff - bMin);
         tau_d = d*w_rel;
         tau   = smooth(0, noEvent(if tau_c + tau_d >= 0 then 0
                                   else tau_c + max(tau_c,tau_d)));
      else
         tau_c = 0;                 // Slack gives zero torque
         tau_d = 0;
         tau   = 0;
     end if;
 end ElastoBacklash;
```

The class `ElastoBacklash` extends `Rotational.Interfaces.PartialCompliant`, which is a general base class for flexible, that is, compliant, connection of two rotational one-dimensional flanges. One example is the flanges in the `ElastoBacklash` model. Inertial effects between the two flanges are neglected, that is, structures such as springs used for connections are assumed to have negligible mass compared to the rest of the rotating system. The torques of the two flanges sum to zero, i.e., they have the same absolute value but opposite sign: `flange_a.tau` + `flange_b.tau` = 0. This base class is usually inherited when defining models of rotational connecting elements such as springs, dampers, friction elements, etc., and is different from the translational version of `PartialCompliant`, e.g. shown in Figure 5-12 on page 196.

The connector classes `Flange_a` and `Flange_b` used in the class `PartialCompliant` are from the library `Modelica.Mechanics.Rotational.Interfaces` and are identical to `RotFlange_a` and `RotFlange_b`, respectively, described in Section 5.5.1, page 204.

```
partial model PartialCompliant  "Partial model for the compliant connection
                          of two rotational 1-dim. shaft flanges"
  Flange_a  flange_a "Left flange of compliant 1-dim. rotational component"
  Flange_b  flange_b "Right flange of compliant 1-dim. rotational component"
  Modelica.SIunits.Angle    phi_rel(start=0)
    "Relative rotation angle (= flange_b.phi - flange_a.phi)";
  Modelica.SIunits.Torque  tau "Torque between flanges (= flange_b.tau)";
equation
  phi_rel = flange_b.phi - flange_a.phi;
  flange_b.tau = tau;
  flange_a.tau = -tau;
end PartialCompliant;  // from Modelica.Mechanics.Rotational.Interfaces
```

Now it is time to simulate the `DCMotorCircuitBacklash` model. Remember that the model has a backlash parameter `b` = 3, i.e., not to the default value 0, otherwise we would not get the backlash phenomena demonstrated by the plots in the figures below. We simulate for 25 seconds, and first plot the relative rotational speed in Figure 13-91. There are quick changes back and forth in the relative rotation speed as the rotating masses hit the boundary of the slack region and recoil.

```
simulate(DCMotorCircuitBacklash, stopTime=25)
plot(elastoBacklash.w_rel)
```

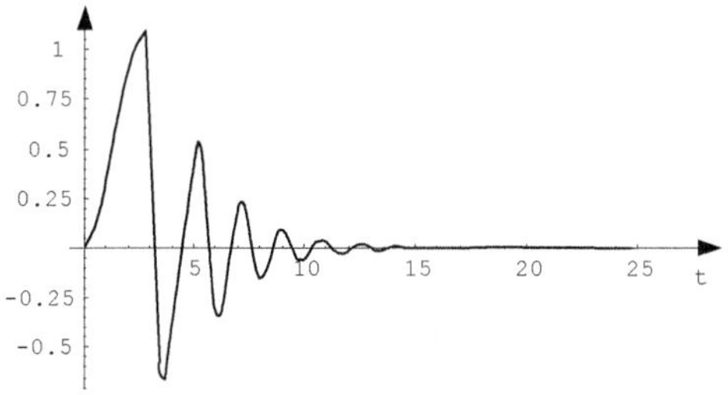

Figure 13-91. Relative rotational speed between the flanges of the `Elastobacklash` transmission.

We also take a look at the relative angle `phi_rel`, in Figure 13-92. Initially, the driving flange is ahead by a positive angle. Later, the relative angle becomes negative since the driven load tries to continue rotating due to inertial effects.

```
plot(elastoBacklash.phi_rel)
```

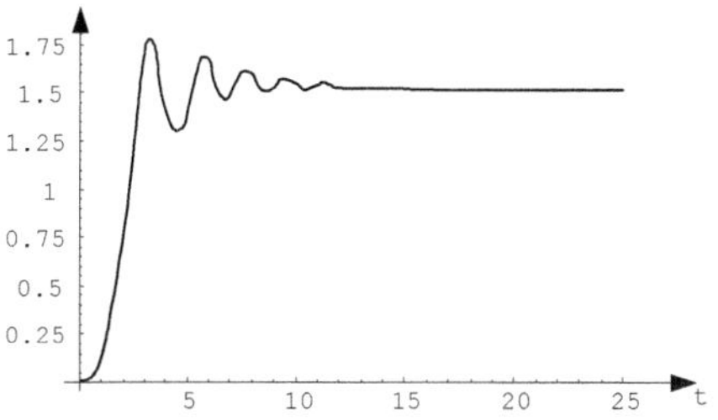

Figure 13-92. Relative angle between the flanges of the transmission.

Finally we plot the rotational speeds of both masses (Figure 13-93a).

```
plot({inertia1.w,inertia2.w})
```

For comparison, we define a model with less mass in inertia2 (`J=1`), no damping `d`, and weaker string constant `c`, to show more even more dramatic backlash phenomena (Figure 13-93b).

```
model DCMotorCircuitBacklash2 = DCMotorCircuitBacklash(inertia1(J=1),
                                  inertia2(J=1), elastoBacklash(b=1,c=1e-5,d=0));


simulate(DCMotorCircuitBacklash2, stopTime=25)
plot({inertia1.w,inertia2.w})
```

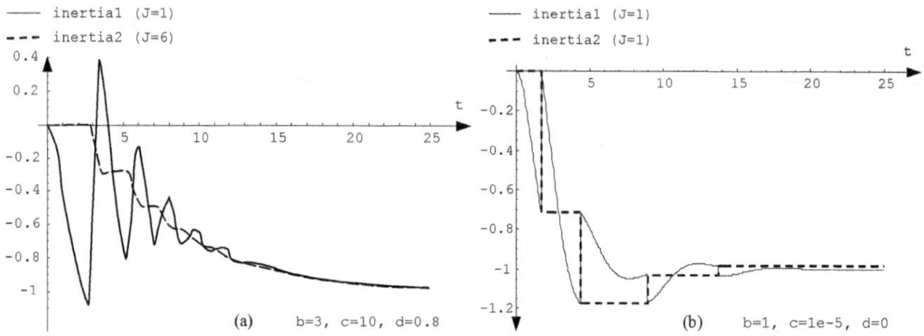

Figure 13-93. Two sets of rotational speeds for the two flanges of the transmission with elastic backlash.

13.5 Concurrent Access to Shared Resources

Modelica is an inherently concurrent language in the sense that objects with behavior specified by equations evolve in parallel, concurrently in time. Equations specify how objects evolve and interact, as well as giving constraints for the parallel behavior. We can view each object as some kind of parallel process. Regarding objects described by discrete events, when-equations and when-statements can be viewed as server processes for these objects which evolve their state at discrete points in time.

As always in parallel activities, concurrent access of shared common resources can lead to problems. We will exemplify these resource access and synchronization aspects through the dining philosophers problem, and their solution through access via a shared `Mutex` (mutual exclusion) instance.

13.5.1 The Dining Philosophers Problem

The dining philosophers problem is considered to be a classic synchronization problem. This is not because of its practical importance—philosophers are not very common in real life. The reason this problem is interesting is that it represents a large class of concurrency problems. It is a simple example of allocation of resources among several concurrent processes. This needs to be done in a deadlock and starvation-free manner.

Let us now describe our dining philosophers, schematically depicted in Figure 13-94.

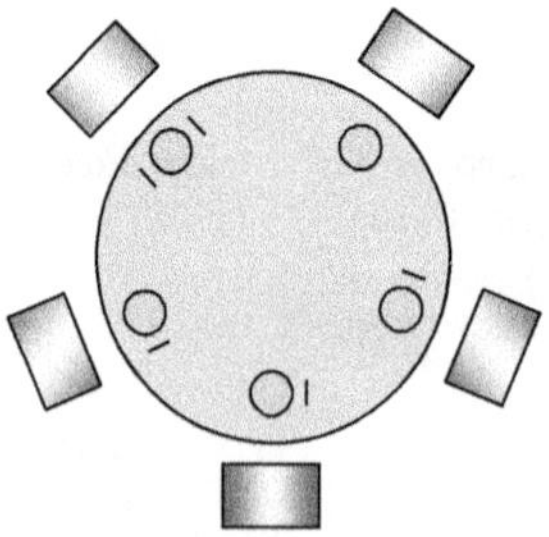

Figure 13-94. Five dining philosophers around a table. Only philosophers with two forks can eat.

There are five dining philosophers who are sitting around a table thinking and eating during their whole life. Five plates and five forks are available on the table. A philosopher is either thinking or eating, and can eat only if he has two forks in his hands.

Now and then a philosopher gets hungry and tries to pick up the two forks closest to him. If one of the forks is already in the hand of neighbor, he cannot take it. When a hungry philosopher has *both forks* in his hands, he eats without releasing the forks. When he has finished eating, he puts down both forks and starts thinking again. The crucial observation is that the philosopher can eat only if he has access to two neighboring forks out of the common resource of five forks.

There are two potential problems associated with the dining philosophers:

- Deadlock—philosophers wait indefinitely on each other without ever being able to grab two forks.
- Starvation—certain philosophers are never able to eat because their neighbors always grab the forks ahead of them.

In the next section as we will present a Modelica model of the dining philosophers. The model is deadlock free through access via the mutual exclusion `Mutex` instance, but not starvation free in its current form. However, it is possible to improve the model even further to become starvation free.

13.5.1.1 The Philosopher and DiningTable Models

Figure 13-95 shows the connection structure of a Modelica model with five philosophers, five forks, and a `Mutex` instance providing mutually exclusive access to the two forks needed for a philosopher to eat.

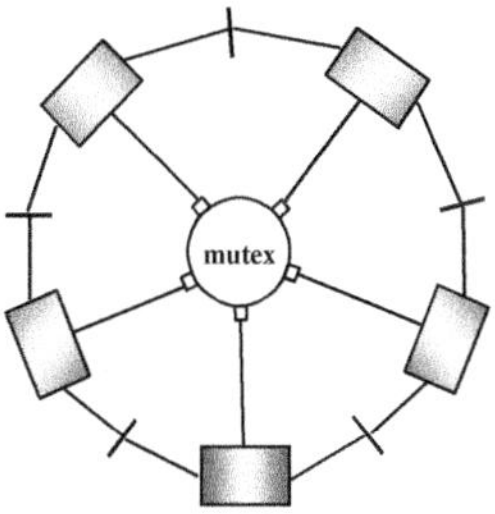

Figure 13-95. Connection structure of the dining philosophers model, alternating philosophers and forks, together with a central mutex.

Each philosopher in the `DiningTable` model is connected to the two forks on his left and right sides. He can pick up those forks only if they are not occupied by his left and right neighbor philosophers.

Each philosopher is connected to the shared `mutex`. This connection is used to signal if he wants to get access to two forks in order to eat, to possibly get OK if the forks are not occupied, and to deny other philosophers access to the same forks while he is eating.

```
model DiningTable
  parameter Integer n = 5  "Number of philosophers and forks";
  parameter Real sigma = 5 " Standard deviation for the random function";
  // Give each philosopher a different random start seed
  // Comment out the initializer to make them all hungry simultaneously.
  Philosopher phil[n](startSeed=[1:n,1:n,1:n], sigma=fill(sigma,n));
  Mutex       mutex(n=n);
  Fork        fork[n];
equation
  for i in 1:n loop
    connect(phil[i].mutexPort, mutex.port[i]);
    connect(phil[i].right, fork[i].left);
    connect(fork[i].right, phil[mod(i, n) + 1].left);
  end for;
end DiningTable;
```

A philosopher is connected to his left and right neighboring forks via `ForkPhilosopherConnection` ports.

```
connector ForkPhilosopherConnection
  Boolean pickedUp(start=false);
  Boolean busy;
end ForkPhilosopherConnection;

model Fork
  ForkPhilosopherConnection left "Connection to the philosopher to the "+
                                 "left of the fork";
  ForkPhilosopherConnection right "Connection to the philosopher to the "+
                                 "right of the fork";
equation
  // If one philosopher picks up the fork then
  // tell the other it is busy
  right.busy = left.pickedUp;
  left.busy  = right.pickedUp;
end Fork;
```

Each philosopher is connected to the shared mutex through a `mutexPort` instance of the `MutexPortOut` connector class.

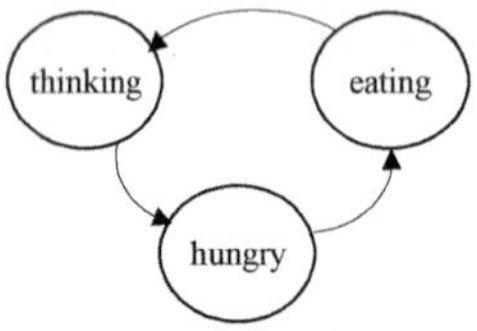

Figure 13-96. Switching between three different states: thinking, hungry, and eating.

All philosophers are initially in the `thinking` state without any forks picked up, as specified by the `when initial()` clause. The variable `timeOfNextChange` determines when something is going to happen and is increased compared to the current time by `abs()` of a normal distributed value.

The equations at the beginning of the equation section define condition variables used in the conditions for state changes. From the initial `thinking` state, a philosopher can move to a `hungry` state, then to an `eating` state, and finally back to the `thinking` state, as depicted in Figure 13-96.

A philosopher moves from the `thinking` state to the `hungry` state when `timeToGetHungry` becomes true. However, he can move from the `hungry` state to the `eating` state only when `canEat` is true, which is dependent on the condition that the forks on both the left-hand and the right-hand side are not busy. When `canEat` becomes true he requests the `mutex` in order to reserve both neighboring forks. However, the forks might not be available if another philosopher in the meantime has grabbed one of them.

To be sure that both forks are available the philosopher waits for `mutexPort.ok` to become true, which means that the forks are free and have been reserved for us. At this point the philosopher grabs both forks and starts eating, specified by the `if pre(canEat) statement`. Eventually he stops eating when `doneEating` becomes true, and puts down the forks by setting `left.pickedUp` and `right.pickedUp` to false.

```
connector MutexPortOut  "Application mutex port connector for access"
  output Boolean request   "Set this to request ownership of the mutex";
  output Boolean release   "Set this to release ownership of the mutex";
  input  Boolean ok        "This signals that ownership was granted";
end MutexPortOut;

model Philosopher    "A Philosopher, connected to forks and a mutex"
  import Random; // Regarding Random library see Appendix D
  MutexPortOut           mutexPort   "Connection to the global mutex";
  parameter Random.Seed startSeed = {1,2,3};
  parameter Real         mu        = 20.0 "mean value";
  parameter Real         sigma     = 5.0  "standard deviation";
```

```
    discrete Integer      state "1==thinking, 2==hungry, 3==eating";
    ForkPhilosopherConnection left;
    ForkPhilosopherConnection right;
  protected
    constant Integer     thinking=0;
    constant Integer     hungry=1;
    constant Integer     eating=2;
    discrete Real        T;
    discrete Real        timeOfNextChange;
    discrete Random.Seed randomSeed;
    Boolean              canEat;
    Boolean              timeToChangeState;
    Boolean              timeToGetHungry;
    Boolean doneEating;
  equation
    timeToChangeState = timeOfNextChange <= time;
    canEat            = (state == hungry) and  not (left.busy or right.busy);
    timeToGetHungry   = (state == thinking) and timeToChangeState;
    doneEating        = (state == eating)   and timeToChangeState;
  algorithm
    when initial() then  // Philosophers are initially thinking, have no forks
      state := thinking;
      left.pickedUp  := false;
      right.pickedUp := false;
      (T,randomSeed) := Random.normalvariate(mu, sigma, startSeed);
      timeOfNextChange := abs(T);
    elsewhen pre(timeToGetHungry) then
      state := hungry;
    end when;
    // Request the mutex to be able to grab the forks
    when pre(canEat) then
      mutexPort.release := false;
      mutexPort.request := true;
    end when;
    // Got the mutex
    when pre(mutexPort.ok) then
      // If the forks are still available
      // then grab them and decide for how long to eat
      if pre(canEat) then
        left.pickedUp  := true;
        right.pickedUp := true;
        (T,randomSeed) := Random.normalvariate(mu, sigma, pre(randomSeed));
        timeOfNextChange := time + abs(T);
        state := eating;
      end if;
      // Release the mutex
      mutexPort.release := true;
      mutexPort.request := false;
    end when;
    // When done eating lay down the forks and set a new time to get hungry
    when pre(doneEating) then
      state          := thinking;
      left.pickedUp  := false;
      right.pickedUp := false;
      (T,randomSeed) := Random.normalvariate(mu, sigma, pre(randomSeed));
      timeOfNextChange := time + abs(T);
    end when;
  end Philosopher;
```

In this model, the time between events is randomly distributed as abs() of Random.normalvariate. (see Appendix D, page 1095, Modelica libraries, subpackage Math.Random, at the end of the Modelica.Math package).

13.5.1.2 Mutual Exclusion with the Mutex Model

An instance of the Mutex class provides clients with mutually exclusive access to a shared resource. The Mutex instance can be configured for different numbers of clients—in Figure 13-97 it is depicted with five access ports corresponding to five clients. In the dining philosophers case the shared resource is five forks, of which the two neighboring forks need to be grabbed in order for a philosopher to eat.

Figure 13-97. Class Mutex for mutual exclusion of a common resource, here configured with 5 mutex ports of type MutexPortIn.

The Mutex class operates in the following way. Three of the local variables are always equal to the corresponding port variables through the for-equation. The first when-statement is activated when one of the philosophers signals that he wants to eat.

If the mutex is not occupied, then the philosopher is set waiting. If the mutex is still not occupied when waiting[i] becomes true, the mutex is reserved, that is, occupied=true, and the port[i].ok is set to true to signal to the philosopher that the forks can be picked up. Finally, when the philosopher sets release[i] to false, the mutex is freed.

```
connector MutexPortIn  "Mutex port connector for receiveing requests"
  input  Boolean request   "Set by application to request access";
  input  Boolean release   "Set by application to release access";
  output Boolean ok        "Signal that ownership was granted";
end MutexPortIn;

model Mutex     "Mutual exclusion of shared resource"
  parameter Integer n = 5  "The number of connected ports";
  MutexPortIn[n] port;
protected
  Boolean request[n];
  Boolean release[n];
  Boolean ok[n];
  Boolean waiting[n];
  Boolean occupied     "Mutex is locked if occupied is true";
equation
  for i in 1:n loop  // Locals equal to port variables
    port[i].ok = ok[i];
    request[i] = port[i].request;
    release[i] = port[i].release;
  end for;
algorithm
  for i in 1:n loop
    when request[i] then  // Client requests mutex to get the forks
      if not occupied then
        ok[i] := true;         // Got fork access
        waiting[i] := false;
      else
        ok[i] := false;        // Denied fork access
        waiting[i] := true;
      end if;
```

```
      occupied := true;
    end when;
    //  If a client is waiting it gets access when not occupied
    when pre(waiting[i]) and not occupied then
      occupied   := true;
      ok[i]      := true;
      waiting[i] := false;
    end when;
    when pre(release[i]) then  // Release the forks
      ok[i] := false;
      occupied := false;
    end when;
  end for;
end Mutex;
```

13.5.1.3 Simulating the Philosophers

As mentioned previously, the philosophers switch between the three states `thinking`, `hungry`, and `eating`. The three states with transitions are depicted in Figure 13-96.

We simulate the `DiningTable` model containing instances of five philosophers, five forks, one five-port mutex, and some connector classes for the used ports. Some Mathematica scripting code is used to get the diagrams and labels the way we want (Figure 13-98). Results are represented as interpolation functions (Section 19.4.5.1, page 1054), for example, `n[0]` is the value of `n` at time 0.

```
res = WSMSimulate["DiningTable", {0,500}];

{philState} = res[{"phil[1].state", "phil[2].state phil[3].state",
   "phil[4].state", "phil[5].state"A}];
{n} = res[{"n"}];

expl = Apply[Join,
  {Map[Function[i, Text["Thinking", {550, 4*i}, {-1, 0}]],Range[n[0]]],
   Map[Function[i, Text["Eating", {550, 2 + 4*i}, {-1, 0}]],Range[n[0]]]}];
 Map[Function[i, philState[[i]][t] + 4*i ] , Range[n[0]]];
Plot(expl,{t,0,500}, Legend->False, Axes->{False,False},Epilog->expl)
```

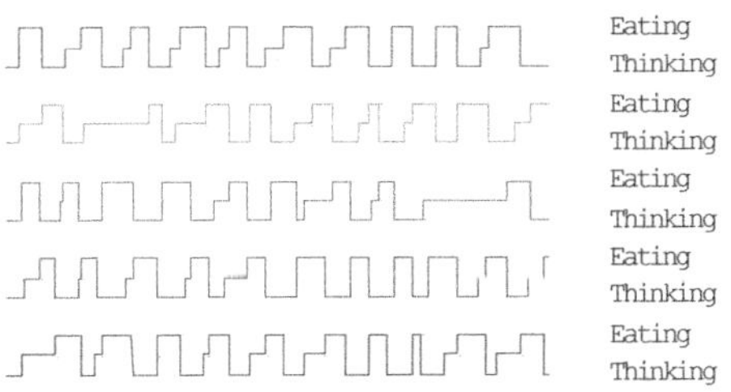

Figure 13-98. Activity diagrams of the five dining philosophers—eating or thinking, and hungry in between.

No deadlock occurs—this cannot happen since we use the mutex for resource access. In this case, with normally distributed thinking times, each philosopher gets a chance to eat.

However, if the thinking times are constant, starvation can easily occur. For example, one of the philosophers will never get any food since a pattern arises where two pairs of philosophers alternate between thinking and eating. By setting the `sigma` parameter to zero all thinking and eating times become constant and starvation occurs (Figure 13-99). Here we use the Mathematica command interface to Wolfram SystemModeler with scripting functionality in terms of the Mathematica language.

```
res2 = WSMSimulate["DiningTable", {0,500}, WSMParameterValues -> {sigma ->
0}];

{philState} = res2[{"phil[1].state", "phil[2].state phil[3].state",
   "phil[4].state", "phil[5].state"}];
{n} = res2[{"n"}];

expl = Apply[Join,
  {Map[Function[i, Text["Thinking", {550, 4*i}, {-1, 0}]],Range[n[0]]],
   Map[Function[i, Text["Eating", {550, 2 + 4*i}, {-1, 0}]],Range[n[0]]]}];
 Map[Function[i, philState[[i]][t] + 4*i ] , Range[n[0]]];
Plot(expl,{t,0,500}, Legend->False, Axes->{False,False},Epilog->expl)
```

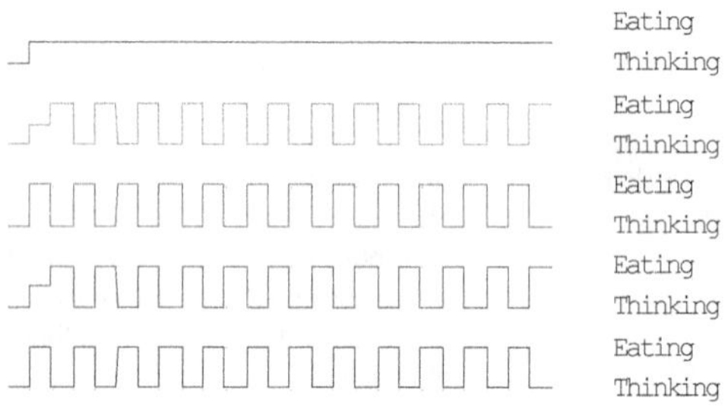

Figure 13-99. Activity diagrams of the five dining philosophers where one is starving.

13.6 Clock-Based Modeling in Detail

Synchronous clock-based modeling gives additional advantages for real-time and embedded system modeling in terms of higher performance and avoidance and/or detection of certain kinds of errors.

We already introduced several of the most important clock-based features in Section 13.2.5, page 600, a number of clock-based example models in Section 13.3, page 624, and briefly compared clocked versus unclocked modeling in Section 13.2.6.2, page 615.

In this section, we give a more detailed presentation including a complete overview of all the Modelica clock-based language features.

13.6.1 Introductory Example – Controller and Plant

A major application area for the clocked language constructs is the modeling and implementation of systems with a discrete-time digital controller coupled to a continuous-time "plant" subsystem, as depicted below in Figure 13-100 for a small application. This is an instance of the typical general hybrid system shown in Figure 13-1, page 591. See also examples of clocked sampled systems in Section 13.3, page 624, and clocked controller-plant models in Section 13.4, page 676, e.g., `PIdiscreteControllerClocked`.

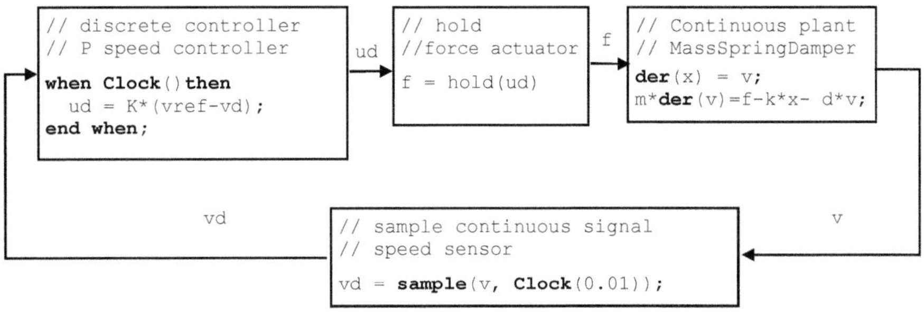

Figure 13-100. A continuous plant and a sampled data controller connected together with `sample` and `hold` elements. This is an instance of a general hybrid system as depicted in Figure 13-1. A model with clean separation between controller `PIdiscreteControllerClocked` and plant is available in Section 13.4.1.

The plant part of the system model is defined by the `MassWithSpringDamper` model which is incomplete since the force `f` is unknown, making it a partial model. This partial model is also used by the more advanced `ControlledMass` model in Section 13.6.13.2, page 717.

```
partial model MassWithSpringDamper
  parameter Modelica.SIunits.Mass  m=1;
  parameter Modelica.SIunits.TranslationalSpringConstant   k=1;
  parameter Modelica.SIunits.TranslationalDampingConstant  d=0.1;
  Modelica.SIunits.Position  x(start=1,fixed=true) "Position";
  Modelica.SIunits.Velocity  v(start=0,fixed=true) "Velocity";
  Modelica.SIunits.Force     f "Force";
equation
  der(x) = v;
  m*der(v) = f - k*x - d*v;
end MassWithSpringDamper;
```

The force `f` is controlled by the output `ud` of the proportional digital controller in the model `SpeedControlP_MassWithSpringDamper` with a control to make the speed close to the reference velicity `vref`.

```
model SpeedControlP_MassWithSpringDamper
  extends MassWithSpringDamper;
  parameter Real  K = 20   "Gain of P proportional speed controller";
  parameter Modelica.SIunits.Velocity  vref = 100 "Speed reference";
  discrete Real vd;
  discrete Real ud(start=0);
equation
  // speed sensor
  vd = sample(v, Clock(0.01));

  // P Proportional speed controller
  when Clock() then
    ud = K*(vref-vd);
  end when;

  // force actuator
  f = hold(ud);
end SpeedControlP_MassWithSpringDamper;
```

The velocity `v` of the mass `m` in the `MassWithSpringDamper` subsystem is sampled at the clock ticks by the *speed sensor* into the clocked variable `vd` at a clock frequency of 100 Hz, i.e., a sampling interval of 0.01 seconds, using the `sample(v,Clock(0.01))` operator. For details see Section 13.6.7, page 697.

The digital proportional *speed controller* works with the clocked variables `ud` and `vd` and outputs the clocked control signal `ud`.

Clocked variables such as `vd` and `ud` in the speed controller are uniquely associated with a clock and can only be directly accessed when the associated clock is active. Since all variables in a clocked equation must belong to the same clock it is possible to detect clocking errors at compile time. If variables from different clocks are used in an equation then explicit conversion operators such as `sample(...)` must be used to convert from continuous-time to clocked discrete-time, or `sample(hold(...))` to convert from a clocked variable of a different frequency.

For a when-equation with an associated clock (Section 13.6.6, page 700), all equations inside the when-equation are clocked with the given clock. When no argument is defined for `Clock()`, as in the speed controller when-equation, the clock is deduced by *clock inference*. The clock is defined by the call `Clock(0.01)` in the speed sensor and inferred and transferred to the variable ud and the when-equation argument `Clock()`. This clock inference is based on the requirement that all expressions and equations solved together must be on the same clock except arguments to some special operators. Such clock inference has the advantage that the clock only needs to be defined in a few places and automatically propagated by inference, but also the disadvantage that it sometimes can be hard to understand from where the clock is propagated.

General equations can be used within such clocked when-equations, whereas unclocked when-equations (Section 13.2.6.1, page 613) with Boolean conditions require a variable reference on the left-hand side of an equation and therefore do not allow general equations.

Note that in the speed controller the when-equation can be removed and replaced with the single clocked equation `ud = K*(vref-vd)`. All equations on an associated clock are treated together and in the same way regardless of whether they are inside a when-equation or not.

The force actuator uses `hold(...)` to convert the clocked value `ud` to a continuous-time force `f` acting on the mass `m`. We simulate the model for 0.2 seconds:

```
simulate(SpeedControlP_MassWithSpringDamper, stopTime=0.2)
plot({vref,vd,v});    plot({f,ud})
```

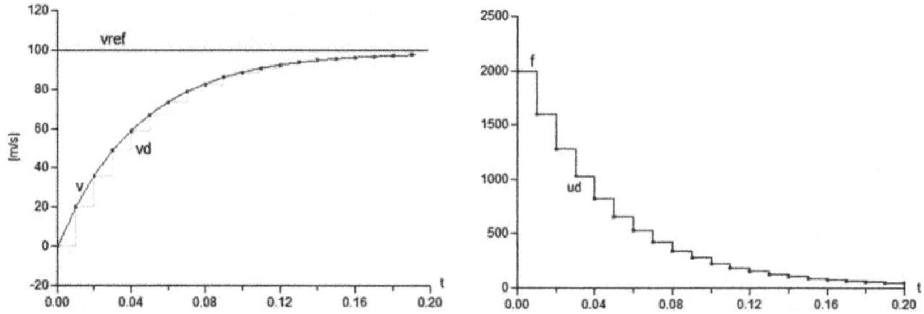

Figure 13-101. Simulation of `SpeedControlP_MassWithSpringDamper` model. *Left*: the velocity `v` of the mass `m`, the sampled clocked velocity `vd`, and the reference velocity `vref`. *Right*: the clocked controller output `ud` and the actuator force `f`.

13.6.2 Built-in Type Clock, Clock Variables, Clocked Expressions, and Partitions

The built-in type `Clock` is available for clocked synchronous modeling. *Clock variables* (Section 13.6.3.2, page 698) of type `Clock` can be defined which have certain attributes such as clock `interval`. Both periodic and aperiod clocks are possible.

Associated to a clock there are typically *clocked expressions* and *variables* (Section 13.6.3, page 697) which only have defined values at the ticks of their associated clock, as well as *clocked equations* which are only defined and solved at the clock ticks of their clock.

Variables and equations which are defined at the ticks of a certain clock are said to belong to the *clocked partition* (Section 13.6.13, page 715) associated to that clock.

There are *clock constructors* (Section 13.6.7, page 701) which create clocks with different properties such as interval, phase, etc.

For example, below is a declaration of the clock variable `clk` of type `Clock` which is defined to have a clock of `interval` 0.1 seconds (i.e., frequency 10 Hz), by the clock constructor `Clock(0.1)`.

```
Clock clk = Clock(0.1);
```

13.6.3 Unclocked and Clocked Discrete-Time Variables

Modelica defines the concept of expression variability (Section 6.8.1.3, page 278) which essentially means the *freedom* of the expression to *change* value during simulation. There are several levels of variability.

In this section, two kinds of discrete-time expressions/variables are defined that are associated to clocks and are therefore called *clocked discrete-time expressions.*

There are three kinds of discrete-time expressions in Modelica, one unclocked and two kinds of clocked discrete-time expressions. Clocked discrete-time variables have recently been introduced in Modelica 3.3.

- Piecewise constant *unclocked discrete-time variables*, see Section 6.9.3, page 281.
- *Clock variables*, see below, Section 13.6.3.2, page 698.
- *Clocked variables*, see below, Section 13.6.3.3, page 698.

13.6.3.1 Piecewise Constant Unclocked Discrete-Time Variables

These are the traditional discrete-time variables available in Modelica, called *unclocked discrete-time* variables, see Section 6.9.3, page 281.

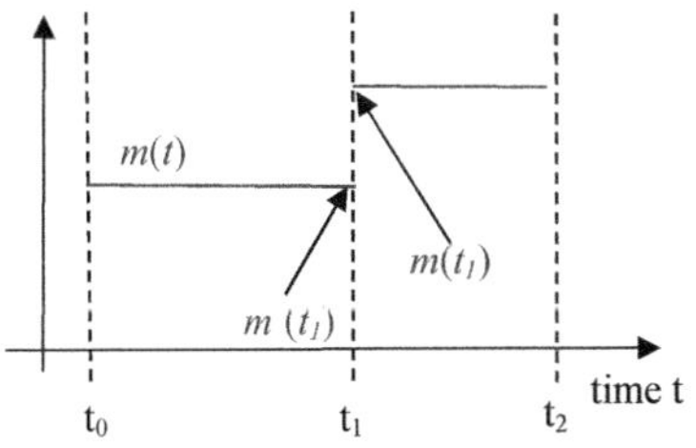

Figure 13-102. Piecewise constant unclocked discrete-time variables may change at events and are defined also between events.

Variables $m(t)$ of base type Real, Integer, Boolean, enumeration, and String that have *constant* value inside each interval $t_i \leq t < t_{i+1}$, i.e., piecewise constant unclocked discrete-time variables. In other words, $m(t)$ *changes* value *only at events*. This means that $m(t) = m(t_i)$, for $t_i \leq t < t_{i+1}$. Such variables are defined at all points during the simulation time interval and have unclocked discrete-time variability.

13.6.3.2 Discrete-Time Clock Variables

Clock variables $c(t_i)$ are of base type `Clock`, and have clocked discrete-time variability. A clock is either defined by a constructor call, such as `Clock`(3), which defines when the clock ticks are active at a particular time instant, or it is defined with clock operators relative to other clocks, see Section 13.6.9, page 707. For example:

```
Clock c1 = Clock(...);
Clock c2 = c1;
Clock c3 = subSample(c2,4);
```

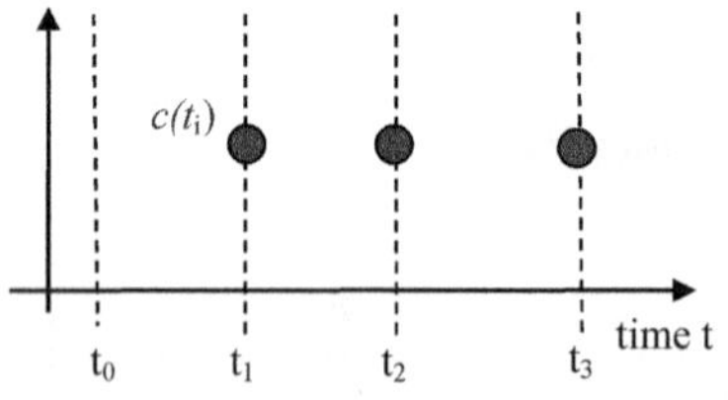

Figure 13-103. Discrete-time *clock variables* $c(t_i)$ are only defined at clock tick events.

13.6.3.3 Discrete-Time Clocked Variables

The elements of *clocked variables $r(t_i)$* are of base type Real, Integer, Boolean, enumeration, or String that are uniquely associated with a clock *$c(t_i)$*. A *clocked variable* is clocked discrete-time and can only be directly accessed at the event instant where the associated clock is *active*. A constant and a parameter can always be used at a place where a clocked variable is required.

At time instants where the associated clock is not active, the value of a clocked variable can be inquired by using an explicit cast operator, see below. In such a case a "hold" semantics is used, in other words the value of the clocked variable from the most recent event instant is used. This is visualized in Figure 13-104 with the dashed horizontal lines.

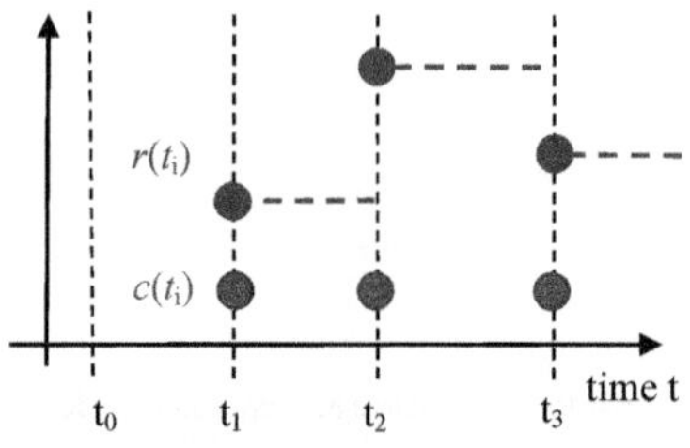

Figure 13-104. Discrete-time *clock variables* $c(t_i)$ as well as *clocked variables* $r(t_i)$ which may be accessed between events using the `hold` operator, indicated by the horizontal dashed line.

13.6.4 Clocked State Variable by the previous() Operator

The *previous value* of a *clocked variable* such as `u` can be accessed with the `previous(u)` operator. Such a *variable* is also called a *clocked state variable*. The previous operator has the following properties (see also Section 13.2.5.13, page 610, for additional explanations):

- The input argument `u` to `previous(...)` is an *instance expression* (Section 13.6.11, page 713) or a parameter expression.
- The returned result has the same type as the input argument.
- The input argument and the returned result are on the same clock.
- At the first tick of the clock of `u` or after a `reset` transition (Section 13.7.4.2, page 733) the `start` value of `u` is returned, see Section 13.6.12, page 715. At subsequent activations of the clock of `u`, the value of `u` from the previous clock activation is returned.

For a simple example of using `previous(...)`, see for example the model `SquareWaveClocked` further below in Section 13.6.6, page 700.

13.6.5 The interval(u) Operator

The `interval(u)` operator returns the *interval* between the *previous* and *present tick* of the clock of the expression within which this operator is called and the clock of the optional argument `u`. At the *first tick* of the clock the following is returned:

- If the specified clock interval has parameter variability, this value is returned.
- Otherwise the start value of the variable specifying the interval is returned.
- For an event clock the additional `startInterval` argument to the event clock constructor is returned.

The returned interval is returned as a Real number. The following model example `ClockedPiEx` uses the `interval(...)` operator.

A discrete PI controller is parameterized with the parameters of a continuous PI controller in order that the discrete model should be adaptable in terms of the sample period. This is achieved by discretizing a continuous PI controller using the implicit Euler method (Section 18.2.1.1, page 998).

Also compare to a very similar clocked PI controller model, `PIdiscreteControllerClocked`, (Section 13.4.1, page 676). Regarding the model `ClockedPIEx` below, a clocked when-equation is used in this example. It is described in the next section (Section 13.6.6, page 700) using the clock constructor `Clock()` with inferred clock (Section 13.6.7.2, page 702).

```
model ClockedPIEx
  parameter Real T=10   "Time constant of continuous PI controller";
  parameter Real k=2    "Gain of continuous PI controller";
 // input  Real u       "Clocked external input variable u -- commented out";
  Real u = sample(2.0*sign(sin(time)),Clock(0.4))  "Clocked square-wave
                                                    variable u instead of input";
  output Real y         "Clocked result variable y";
  Real x(start=0)       "Clocked state variable x";
protected
  Real Ts = interval(u);    // Obtain interval of clocked variable u
equation
  /* Continuous PI equations:  der(x) = u/T;    y = k*(x + u);
     Discretization equation:  der(x) = (x - previous(x))/Ts;
  */
  when Clock() then    // Clock() means the clock is inferred
    x = previous(x) + Ts/T*u;
    y = k*(-x + u);
```

```
    end when;
  end ClockedPIEx;
```

In the model, we have commented out the external input clocked variable u and replaced it with an internal clocked variable u in order to conveniently simulate the model without connecting to external sources.

```
  simulate(ClockedPIEx, stopTime=10)
  plot({u,y});
```

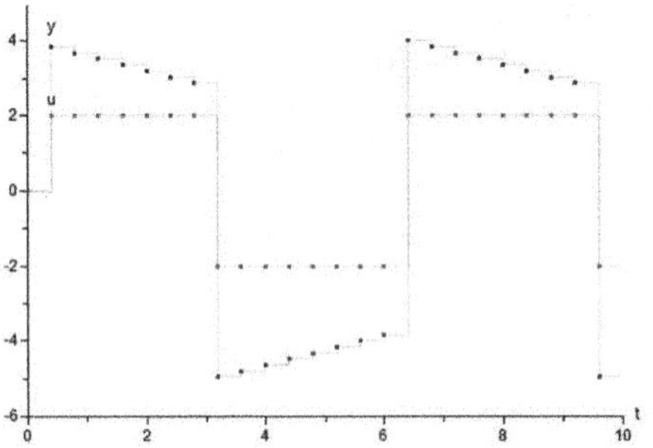

Figure 13-105. Simulation of `ClockedPIEx` model, with square wave signal u and controlled output variable y (uppermost and lowest).

13.6.6 Clocked When-Equation

In addition to the traditional conditional *when-equation* (Section 8.3.5, page 357) or *when-statement* (Section 9.2.10, page 433), a *clocked when-equation* is available:

```
  when clock-expression then
    clocked-equation
    ...
  end when;
```

The clocked when-equation cannot be nested and does *not* have any elsewhen-part. It cannot be used inside an algorithm section, i.e., there is no clocked when-statement. *General equations are allowed* in a clocked when-equation, that is, the restrictions described in Section 8.3.5.1, page 358, do not apply.

Regarding a clocked when-equation, all equations inside the when-equation are clocked with the same clock as given by the *clock-expression*.

See also Section 13.3.1, page 625, which contains a number of examples using clocked when-equations. Below we give a very simple example, also in Section 13.2.5.7, page 605.

```
  class SquareWaveClocked
    parameter Modelica.SIunits.Time  interval=1;
    Clock clk;                         // A clock variable
    discrete Real xclocked(start=1);   // A clocked variable
    Real x;
  equation
    clk = Clock(interval);   // Clocked equation
    when clk then
      xclocked = -previous(xclocked);   // Clocked equation
    end when;
    x = hold(xclocked);   // Unclocked equation
  end SquareWaveClocked;
```

We simulate and plot:

```
simulate(SquareWaveClocked, stopTime=5)
plot(x);    plot(xclocked)
```

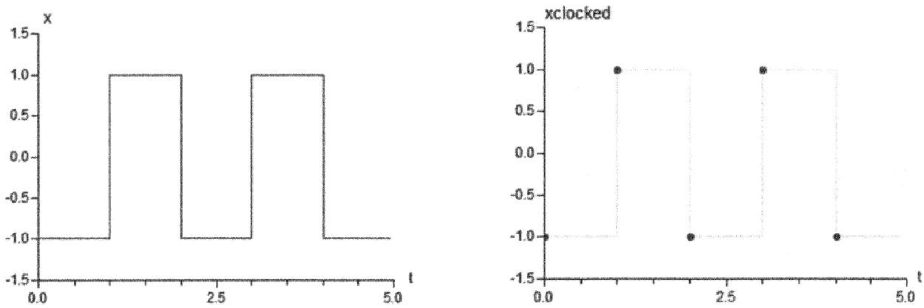

Figure 13-106. The generated square wave using a clocked when-equation. The variable `x` is an unclocked discrete-time real variable also defined between clock points by the use of `hold()`, whereas the variable `xclocked` is a clocked discrete-time real variable only defined at clock points.

13.6.7 Clock Constructors

The following overloaded `Clock` constructors are available to generate clocks:

- `Clock( )`—inferred clock (Section 13.6.7.2, page 702).
- `Clock(intervalCounter, resolution)`—clock with Integer quotient (rational number) interval (Section 13.6.7.3, page 703).
- `Clock(interval)`—clock with a Real value interval (Section 13.6.7.4, page 703).
- `Clock(condition, startInterval)`—Boolean conditional clock (Section 13.6.7.5, page 704).
- `Clock`—solver clock (Section 13.6.7.6, page 705).

Besides inferred clocks and solver clocks, *one* of the following mutually exclusive associations of clocks are possible in *one base partition*:

- One or more Integer quotient interval clocks, provided they are consistent with each other, see Section 13.6.14.4, page 721.
  For example, assume `y=subSample(u)`, `Clock(1,10)` is associated to `u`, `Clock(2,10)` is associated to `y`, then this is correct, but it would be an error if `y` is associated to a `Clock (1,3)`.
- Exactly one Real interval clock. For example, assume `Clock c = Clock(2.5)`, then variables in the same base partition can be associated multiple times with `c` but not multiple times with `Clock(2.5)`.
- Exactly one condition-based clock.
- A default clock, if neither a Real interval nor an Integer interval nor a condition-based clock is associated with each base partition. In this case the default clock is associated with the fastest sub-clock partition. Typically, a Modelica tool will use `Clock(1.0)` as a default clock and will raise a warning that it selected a default clock.

Clock variables can be used in a restricted form of expressions. Generally, *every* expression containing clock variables must have parametric variability in order that clock analysis can be performed when translating a model. Otherwise, the following kinds of expressions are allowed:

- Declaring arrays of clocks, e.g. `Clock c1[3] = {Clock(1), Clock(2), Clock(3)}`
- Array constructors of clocks: `{}`, `[]`, `cat(...)`.

- Array access of clocks, e.g. `sample(u, c1[2])`
- Equality of clocks. Example: `c1 = c2`.
- If-expressions of clocks in equations, e.g. `Clock c2 = if f>0 then subSample(c1, f) elseif f < 0 then superSample(c1, f) else c1`.
- Clock variables can be declared in models, blocks, connectors, and records,. A Clock variable can be declared with the prefixes `input`, `output`, `inner`, `outer`, but *not* with the prefixes `flow`, `stream`, `discrete`, `parameter`, or `constant`.
  Example: `connector ClockInput = input Clock;`

13.6.7.1 Exact Periodic Clocks are Automatically Synchronized

Periodic clocks with intervals *exactly defined* by integers or integer quotients, i.e., rational numbers, are *automatically synchronized* if they have the *same* frequency and phase, whereas clocks defined by inexact floating point numbers are not synchronized. For example:

```
model ClockSynch
  Clock c1a = Clock(1,10);              // period = 1/10
  Clock c2a = superSample(c1a,3);  // period = 1/30
  Clock c3a = Clock(1,30);              // period = 1/30
end ClockSynch;
```

We simulate and plot for 0.5 seconds:

```
simulate(ClockSynch, stopTime=0.5)
plot({c1a,c2a,c3a})
```

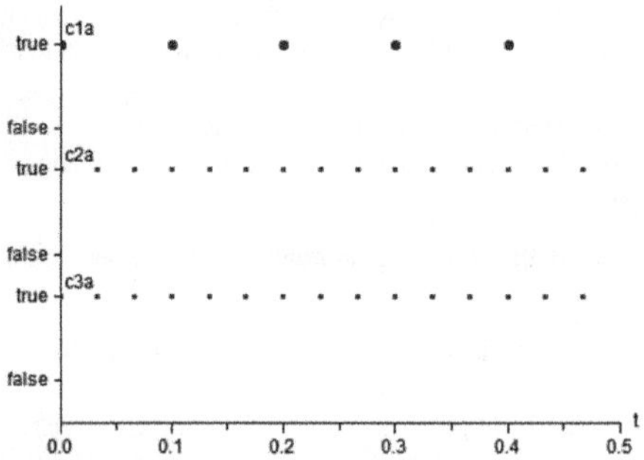

Figure 13-107. Clocks `c2a` and `c3a` are automatically synchronized since they are exactly defined by rational number intervals and have the same frequency and phase.

Clocks defined by inexact Real number intervals are not synchronized:

```
Clock c1b = Clock(0.1);
Clock c2b = superSample(c1,3);
Clock c3b = Clock(0.1/3);  // Not synchronized with c2b
```

13.6.7.2 Inferred Clock

The `Clock()` expression returns an clock inferred from the context. For example, since all equations inside the clocked when-equation have the same clock, the `Clock()` expression and the whole when-equation will get the clock of variable `x`:

```
when Clock() then   // equations are with the same clock
  x = A*previous(x) + B*u;
  Modelica.Utilities.Streams.print(
```

```
    "clock ticks at = " + String(sample(time)) );
end when;
```

Note that in most cases the `Clock()` operator is not needed and the equations could be written without a when-equation, but not in the above example, since the "print" statement is otherwise not associated to a clock which is needed for the expression `sample(time)`. This style is useful if a modeler would clearly like to mark the equations that must belong to one clock, which also enhances readability and understandability.

However, a Modelica tool could deduce this information as well even if the when-clause is not present, but at the cost of a less readable model. To understand such a model the reader would also have to perform this deduction using his/her brain, which is an extra effort.

13.6.7.3 Clock with Integer Quotient Interval

The clock expression `Clock(intervalCounter,resolution)` specifies a clock with an exact Integer quotient (rational number) interval.

The first input argument, `intervalCounter`, is a *clocked instance expression* (Section 13.6.11, page 713) or a parameter expression of type Integer with `min=0`. The optional argument `resolution` (default=1) is a parameter expression of type Integer with `min=1` and `unit="Hz"`. The interval of the clock is defined as `previous(intervalCounter)/resolution` seconds.

If `intervalCounter` is zero, the period of the clock is derived by clock inference (Section 13.6.14.4, page 721). The output argument is of base type `Clock` that ticks when time becomes t_{start}, t_{start}+`interval1`, t_{start}+`interval1`+`interval2`, ...

The clock starts at the start of the simulation t_{start} or when the controller is switched on. Here the next clock tick is scheduled at:

```
interval1 = previous(intervalCounter)/resolution =interval.start/resolution
```

At the second clock tick at time t_{start}+`interval1`, the next clock tick is scheduled at `interval2` = `previous(intervalCounter)/resolution`, and so on. If `interval` is a parameter expression, the clock defines a periodic clock on which `interval` must be defined.

Note that the clock is defined by `previous(intervalCounter)`. Therefore, for equation *sorting* in data dependency order (Section 17.1.6, page 984) performed by a Modelica tool, the first input argument, `intervalCounter`, is treated as known. The given interval and time shift can be modified by using the `subSample`, `superSample`, `shiftSample` and `backSample` operators on the returned clock, see Section 13.6.9, page 707. For example:

```
  Integer nextInterval(start=2);     // first interval = 2/100
equation
  when Clock(2,1000) then
     // periodic clock that ticks at 0, 0.002, 0.004, ...
  end when;

  when Clock(nextInterval, 100) then
    // interval clock that ticks at 0, 0.02, 0.05, 0.09, ...
    nextInterval = previous(nextInterval) + 1;
    y = previous(y) + 1;
  end when;
```

13.6.7.4 Clock with Real Value Interval

The expression `Clock(interval)` gives a clock with a real-valued clock interval.

The input argument, `interval`, is a clocked instance expression (Section 13.6.11, page 713) or a parameter expression of type Real with `min=0.0` and unit `"s"`. The output argument is of base type `Clock` that ticks when time becomes t_{start}, t_{start}+`interval1`, t_{start}+`interval1+interval2`, ... The clock starts at the start of the simulation t_{start} or when the controller is switched on. Here the next clock tick is scheduled at `interval1 = previous(interval) = interval.start`. At the second clock tick at time t_{start}+interval1, the next clock tick is scheduled at `interval2 = previous(interval)`, and so on. If interval is a parameter expression, the clock defines a periodic clock.

Note that the clock is defined with `previous(interval)`. Therefore, for equation sorting (Section 17.1.6, page 984) performed by a Modelica tool the input argument, `interval`, is treated as known. The given interval and time shift can be modified by using the `subSample`, `superSample`, `shiftSample`, and `backSample` operators on the returned clock, see Section 13.6.9, page 707. There are restrictions where this operator can be used, see `Clock` expressions below.

13.6.7.5 Condition-Based Clock

The expression `Clock(condition, startInterval)` gives a *clock triggered* by the `condition` expression. The first input argument, `condition`, is a continuous-time expression of type Boolean.

The optional `startInterval` argument (default = 0.0) is the value to be returned by the operator `interval()` (Section 13.6.5, page 699) at the first tick of the clock.

The output result of the base type `Clock` ticks when `edge(condition)` becomes `true`.

This clock is used to trigger a clocked partition due to a *state event*, i.e., a zero-crossing of a Real variable in a continuous-time partition, or due to a *hardware interrupt* that is modeled as a Boolean in the simulation model. For example:

```
Clock c = Clock(angle > 0, 0.1)    // before first tick of c:
                                   // interval(c) = 0.1
```

The implicitly given interval and time shift can be modified by using the `subsample`, `superSample`, `shiftSample` and `backSample` operators on the returned clock, see Section 13.6.9, page 707, provided the base interval is not smaller than the implicitly given interval.

A simple example is given below, whereas a slightly more advanced example can be found in Section 13.3.1.3, page 630.

```
model SinConditionClock
  Real xsin = sin(4*Modelica.Constants.pi*time);
  Clock w = Clock(xsin > 0, startInterval=0); // ticks: 0, 0.5, 1.0, 1.5,
end SinConditionClock;

simulate(SinConditionClock, 1.6)
plot({w,xsin})
```

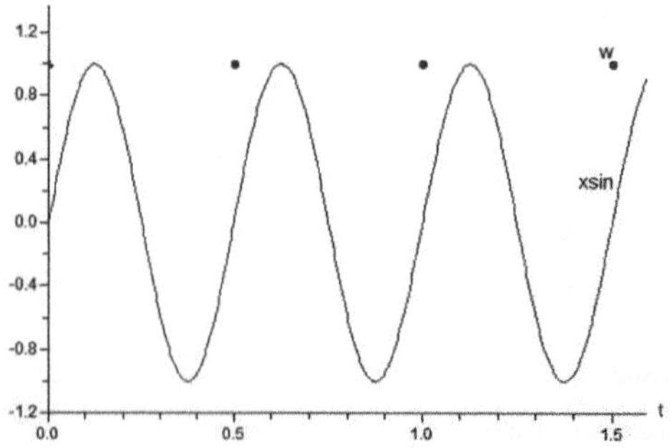

Figure 13-108. Boolean condition clock `w` and Boolean condition `xsin`.

In the model `SinConditionClock` the Boolean *condition clock* `w` ticks when `xsin` passes zero from negative to positive.

13.6.7.6 Solver Clock

A so-called solver clock can be specified by the expression `Clock(c, solverMethod)`.

The first input argument `c` is a clock and the operator returns this clock. The returned clock is associated with the second input argument of type String containing the name of a numeric solver, e.g., `"solverMethod"`. The meaning of `solverMethod` is defined in Section 13.6.15.2, page 723, including an example. If the second input argument `solverMethod` is an empty String, then no integrator is associated with the returned clock. Below are some examples:

```
Clock c1 = Clock(1,10)                      // 1/10 sec =100 ms, no solver
Clock c2 = Clock(c1,"ImplicitTrapezoid"); // 100 ms,ImplicitTrapezoid solver
Clock c3 = Clock(c2, "");                   // 100 ms,no solver ]
```

13.6.8 Base-Clock Partitioning Conversion Operators

A set of *clock conversion operators* together act as *boundaries* between different *clock partitions*.

The following operators convert between a continuous-time and a clocked-time representation and vice versa:

- `sample`(*u*, *c*)—converts from continuous-time variable u to a clocked version according to the clock *c*.
- `hold`(*u*)—converts from a clocked *u* to a continuous-time version that is defined between the clock ticks.

13.6.8.1 sample(u, c) and sample(u)

The operator `sample(...)` is an overloaded operator with function syntax. The input argument `u` to `sample(u,c)` is a continuous-time expression (Section 6.9.4, page 6.9.4). The optional input argument `c` is of type `Clock`. See also Section 13.2.5.6, page 604 for an example.

The clocked `sample` operator returns a *clocked variable value* that has the associated clock `c` and the *value of the left limit* of `u` when the clock `c` is active. This is the *value* of `u` *immediately before* the event of `c` is triggered, see also Figure 13-16, page 609. If the optional argument `c` is not provided the clock is inferred (Section 13.6.14.4, page 721).

Since the operator returns the left limit of `u` it introduces an *infinitesimally small delay* between the continuous-time and the clocked partition. This corresponds to the reality where a sampled data system cannot act infinitely fast and even for a very idealized simulation, an infinitesimal small delay is present. The consequences for the *sorting* (Section 17.1.7, page 989) of equations performed by Modelica tools are discussed below.

The input argument `u` can be a general expression since the argument has continuous-time variability and therefore always has a value. It can also be a constant, a parameter, or a piecewise constant expression.

Thus, there are three variants of `sample()`:

- Unclocked `sample(u,r)` has *two input* arguments where the second argument `r` is of *type Real*. This is the traditional unclocked `sample(...)` operator described in Section 13.2.5.4, page 602.
- Clocked `sample(u)` has *one input* argument `u` which is converted to a clocked value according to a clock inferred from the context.
- Clocked `sample(u,c)` has *two input* arguments where the second argument if of *type* `Clock`. It returns a clocked version of the input argument `u` according to the above description.

The model `SampleEx` below illustrates both kinds of clocked `sample`. The call `sample(time,clk)` samples the `time` variable according to the clock `clk`, and `sample(time)` samples according to the inferred clock of the equation, inferred from the clocked variable `xclocked` which has clock `clk`.

```
model SampleEx "Examples of using clocked sample"
  Clock clk = Clock(0.2) "Clock variable";
  Real xclocked          "Clocked variable";
  Real yclocked          "Clocked variable, inferred clock";
equation
  xclocked = 1.5 + sample(time,clk);          // Clock of xclocked is clk
  yclocked = 0.5 + xclocked + 2*sample(time); // Clock of yclocked inferred
end SampleEx;

simulate(SampleEx, 1.0);
plot({clk,xclocked,yclocked})
```

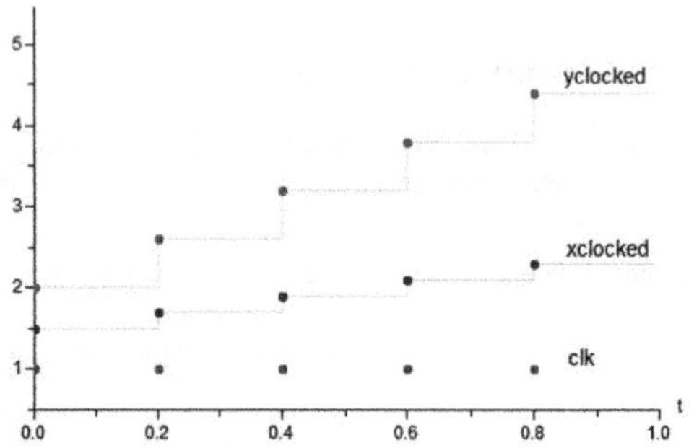

Figure 13-109. Simulation of `SampleEx` model with clock variable `clk` lowest, the clocked variable `xclocked` in the middle with explicitly specified clock, and at the top `yclocked` with inferred clock.

13.6.8.2 hold(u)

The input argument `u` to `hold(u)` is a clocked *instance expression* (Section 13.6.11, page 713) or a parameter expression. The operator returns a piecewise constant signal of the same type of `u`. When the clock of `u` ticks, the operator returns `u` and otherwise returns the value of `u` from the most recent clock activation. Before the first clock activation of `u` the operator returns the start value of `u`, see Section 13.6.12, page 715.

Since the input argument `u` is not defined before the first tick of the clock of `u`, there is a restriction that it must be an *instance expression* or a parameter expression, to enable the initial value of `u` to be defined and used in such a case.

The `HoldEx` example model shows the application of the `hold` operator on the clocked variable `xclocked`, giving an unclocked variable `hx` that is defined between clock ticks.

```
model HoldEx "Example of using hold"
  Clock clk = Clock(0.2) "Clock variable";
  Real  xclocked         "Clocked variable";
  Real  hx               "Unclocked hold variable";
equation
  xclocked = 1.5 + sample(time, clk);  // Clock of xclocked is clk
  hx = hold(xclocked); // Unclocked hx, also defined between ticks
end HoldEx;

simulate(HoldEx, 1.0);
plot({clk,hx})
```

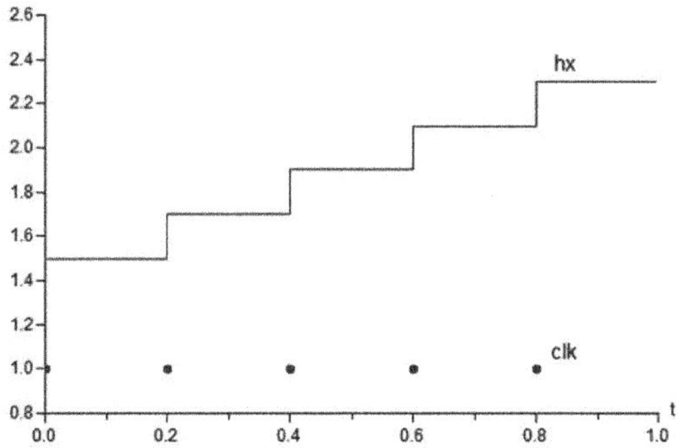

Figure 13-110. Simulation of the `HoldEx` model with clock variable `clk` lowest and the unclocked variable `hx` at the top.

13.6.9 Subclock Conversion Operators

The following operators with function syntax convert between synchronous clocks:

- `subsample(u, factor)`
- `superSample(u, factor)`
- `shiftSample(u, shiftCounter, resolution)`
- `backSample(u, backCounter, resolution)`
- `noClock(u)`

These operators have the following common properties:

- The input argument `u` is a *clocked expression* (Section 13.6.15.1, page 722) or an expression of type `Clock`. Note that these operators can operate on all kinds of clock variables and expressions. If `u` is a *clocked expression*, the operator returns a clocked variable that has the same type as the expression. If `u` is an expression of type `Clock`, operator returns a `Clock`.
- The optional input arguments `factor` (default=0, min=0), and `resolution` (default=1, min=1) are parameter expressions of type `Integer`.
- The input arguments `shiftCounter` and `backCounter` are parameter expressions of type `Integer` (min=0).

13.6.9.1 subSample(u, factor) and subSample(u)

The clock of `y` = `subSample(u,factor)` is `factor` times slower than the clock of `u`. At each `factor` tick of the clock of `u` the operator returns the value of `u`. For example, if `factor=3`, the value of `u` is returned at every third tick of the clock of `u`. The variable `u` can be either a clock variable or a clocked variable.

The first activation of the clock of `y` coincides with the first activation of the clock of `u`. If the second argument `factor` is not provided or is equal to zero it is inferred, see Section 13.6.14.4, page 721.

The example model `SubSampleEx` shows an explicitly subsampled variable `xsub`, which samples every third sample of `xbase`, and a subsampled variable `xsubinf` with an inferred factor 3.

```
model SubSampleEx "Examples of using clocked subsample"
  Clock clk = Clock(0.1) "Clock variable";
  Real xbase          "Base clocked variable";
```

```
  Real xsub          "Subsampled clocked variable, explicit clock factor";
  Real xsubinf       "Subsampled clocked variable, inferred clock factor";
equation
  xbase  = sample(time,clk);
  xsub   = 1 + subSample(xbase, 3);         // Subsampling, explicit factor 3
  xsubinf = 0.5 + xsub + 2*subSample(xbase);//Subsampling, inferred factor 3
end SubSampleEx;
```

```
simulate(SubSampleEx, 1.0)
plot({xbase,xsub,xsubinf})
```

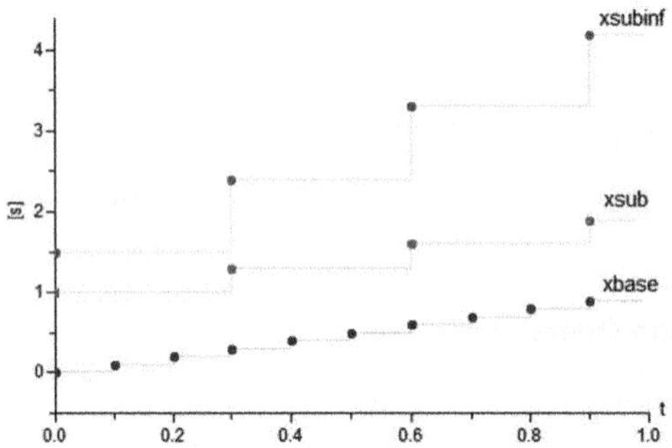

Figure 13-111. At the bottom is the clocked variable xbase, middle is an explicitly subsampled variable xsub subsampling factor 3, and at the top the variable xsubinf with an inferred subsampling factor 3.

13.6.9.2 superSample(u, factor) and superSample(u)

The clock of y = superSample(u,factor) is factor times faster than the clock of u. At every tick of the clock of y, the operator returns the value of u from the most recent tick of the clock of u. The first activation of the clock of y coincides with the first activation of the clock of u. The variable u can be either a clock variable or a clocked variable.

If the argument factor is not provided or is equal to zero it is inferred, see Section 13.6.14.4, page 721.

The model SuperSampleEx illustrates several aspects of supersampling. First, the clock clk1 is defined with a clock interval which is a rational number, i.e., an integer quotient. Second, the clock clk2 is defined by supersampling clk1. Finally, xsuper and xsuperinf are defined by supersampling the clocked variable xbase with an explicit or implicit clock factor respectively. The example shows supersampling both of a clock and of a clocked variable.

```
model SuperSampleEx "Examples of using clocked supersample"
  Clock clk1 = Clock(1,2) "Clock with ticks at 0, 1/2, 2/2, …";
  Clock clk2 = superSample(clk1,2) "Clock with ticks at 0, 1/4, 2/4, …";
  Real xbase     "Base clocked variable";
  Real xsuper    "Supersampled clocked variable, explicit clock factor 4";
  Real xsuperinf "Supersampled clocked variable, inferred clock factor 4";
equation
  xbase = sample(time,clk2);
  xsuper   = 1 + superSample(xbase, 4); // Supersampling, explicit factor 4
  xsuperinf = 0.5 + xsuper + 2*superSample(xbase); //Inferred factor 4
end SuperSampleEx;
```

```
simulate(SuperSampleEx, 1.0);
plot({xbase,xsuper,xsuperinf});  plot({clk1,clk2})
```

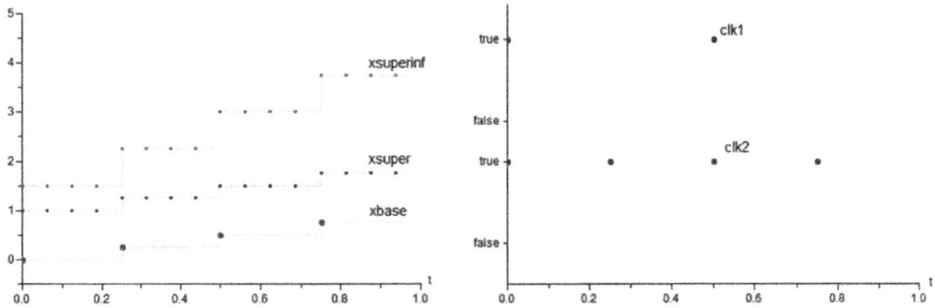

Figure 13-112. *Left*: At the bottom is the clocked variable `xbase`, middle is an explicitly supersampled variable `xsuper` supersampling factor 4, and at the top the variable `xsuperinf` with an inferred supersampling factor 4. *Right*: The two clocks `clk1` and `clk2`.

If a Boolean condition clock (Section 13.6.7.5, page 704), for example, `Clock(x>0)`, is associated to a base-clock partition all its subclock partitions must have resulting clocks that are subsampled with an Integer factor with respect to this base clock. For example:

```
Clock u  = Clock(x > 0); // A clocked defined by a Boolean condition
Clock y1 = subSample(u,4);
Clock y2 = superSample(y1,2);  // fine. Same as y2 = subSample(u,2)
Clock y3 = superSample(u ,2);  // error
Clock y4 = superSample(y1,5);  // error
```

13.6.9.3 shiftSample(u,shiftCounter,resolution) and shiftSample(u,shiftCounter)

The first activation of the clock of y = `shiftSample(u,shiftcounter,resolution)` is shifted forward in time `shiftCounter/resolution*interval(u)` compared to the first activation of the clock of `u`. Conceptually, the operator constructs a clock `cBase`:

```
Clock cBase = subSample(superSample(u,resolution),shiftCounter)
```

Here the clock of `y` = `shiftSample(...)` starts at the second clock tick of `cBase`. At every tick of the clock of `y` the operator returns the value of `u` from the most recent tick of the clock of `u`.

The call `shiftSample(u,shiftCounter)` shifts forward `shiftCounter*interval(u)`, with a default value `resolution=1`.

Note that due to the restriction of `superSample` on Boolean condition clocks (Section 13.6.7.5, page 704) , `shiftSample` can only shift the number of ticks of the Boolean condition clock, but cannot introduce new ticks.

In the example below, the clock `u1` will tick at 0, 3/10, 6/10, etc. The shift introduced by `shiftSample(u1,1,3)` according to the above formula is 1/3*(3/10) = 1/10, with `shiftCounter=1`, `resolution=3`, `interval=3/10`.

The Boolean condition clock `u2` ticks when `xsin` passes zero from negative to positive.

```
model ShiftSampleEx
  // Integer quotient rational number interval clock
  Clock u1 = Clock(3,10);          // ticks: 0, 3/10, 6/10, ..
  Clock y1 = shiftSample(u1,1,3); // ticks: 1/10, 4/10, ...

  // Boolean condition clock
  Real xsin = sin(4*Modelica.Constants.pi*time);
  Clock u2  = Clock(xsin > 0, startInterval=0.0);
                                   // ticks: 0.0, 0.5, 1.0, 1.5, ...

  Clock y2 = shiftSample(u2,2);  // ticks: 1.0, 1.5, ...
```

```
  // Clock y3 = shiftSample(u2,2,3);// error - clock resolution must be 1
end ShiftSampleEx;

simulate(ShiftSampleEx, 1.2)
plot({u1,y1,u2,y2});   plot({u2,xsin})
```

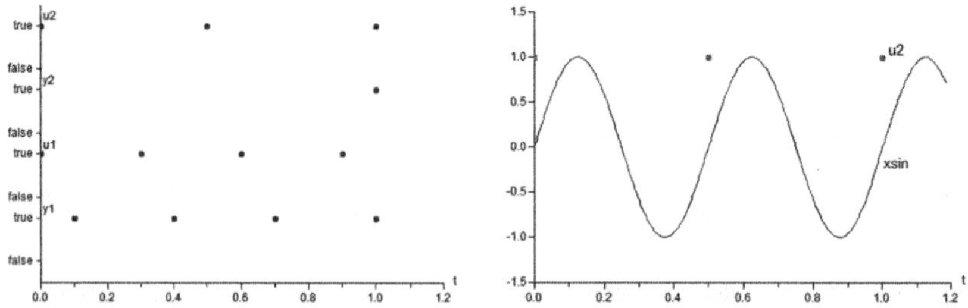

Figure 13-113. *Left*: the clock u1 at 0, 3/10, etc., the clock y1 shifted 1/10 at 1/10, 4/10, etc., the condition-based clock u2 and the clock y2 which is u2 shifted two intervals of length 0.5. *Right*: The state variable xsin which triggers the condition-based clock u2 when it passes through zero from negative to positive.

13.6.9.4 backSample(u,backCounter,resolution)

The first activation of the clock of y = backSample(u,backCounter,resolution) is shifted backwards in time backCounter/resolution*interval(u) before the first activation of the clock of u. The input argument u must either be an *instance expression* (Section 13.6.11, page 713) or an expression of type Clock. Conceptually, the operator constructs a clock cBase:

```
Clock cBase = subSample(superSample(u, resolution), backCounter)
```

The clock of y = backSample(u,backCounter,resolution) is *shifted backwards* a time duration before the clock of u, such that this duration is identical to the duration between the first and second clock tick of cBase. It is an error, if the clock of y starts before the base clock of u.

The call backSample(u,shiftCounter) shifts backwards shiftCounter*interval(u), with a default value resolution=1.

At every tick of the clock of y, the operator returns the value of u from the most recent tick of the clock of u. If u is a clocked instance expression, the operator returns the start value of u (Section 13.6.12, page 715) before the first tick of the clock of u.

For example, in the model BackSampleEx1 below for backsampling of integer quotient clocks, clock y1 is shifted forward 3 whole intervals, y2 is shifted backward 2 intervals compared to y1, y4 is shifted forward 2/3 interval, whereas y5 is shifted backward 1/3 interval compared to y4.

```
model BackSampleEx1 "Backsampling of integer quotient clock"
  // Rational number integer quotient interval clock
  Clock u =  Clock(3, 10);          // ticks: 0, 3/10, 6/10, ..
  Clock y1 = shiftSample(u,3);      // ticks: 9/10, 12/10, ..
  Clock y2 = backSample(y1,2);      // ticks: 3/10, 6/10, ...
  //Clock y3 = backSample(y1,4);  // error; ticks before u not allowed
  Clock y4 = shiftSample(u,2,3);  // ticks: 2/10, 5/10, ..
  Clock y5 = backSample(y4,1,3);  // ticks: 1/10, 4/10, ..
end BackSampleEx1;


simulate(BackSampleEx1, 1.3)
plot({u, y4,y5, y1,y2})
```

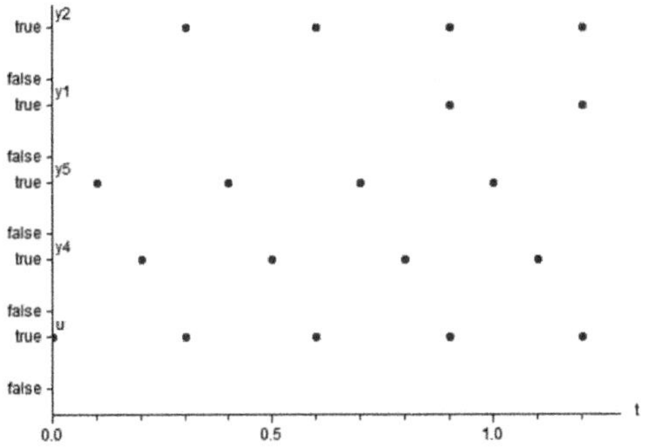

Figure 13-114. Five clocks from model `BackSampleEx1`, with `u` ticking at 0, 3/10, 6/10, etc., `y4` shifted forward 2/3 interval, `y5` shifted backward 1/3 relative to that, `y1` shifted forward 3 whole intervals, `y2` shifted backward 2 intervals relative to that.

The model `BackSampleEx2` below shows examples of backSampling Boolean conditional clocks.

```
model BackSampleEx2 "BackSample of Boolean Condition Clock";
  Real xsin = sin(4*Modelica.Constants.pi*time);
  Clock w =  Clock(xsin > 0, startInterval=0);
                                    // ticks: 0, 0.5, 1.0, 1.5, ...
  Clock z1 = shiftSample(w,2); // ticks: 1.0, 1.5, ...
  Clock z2 = backSample(z1,1); // ticks: 0.5, 1.0, ...
end BackSampleEx2;

simulate(BackSampleEx2, 1.6)
plot({w,z1,z2});  plot({w,xsin})
```

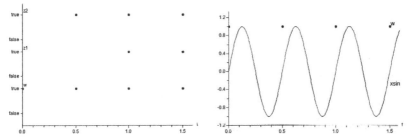

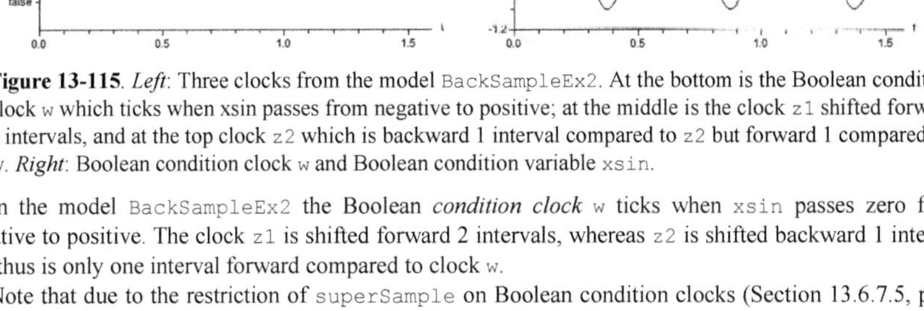

Figure 13-115. *Left*: Three clocks from the model `BackSampleEx2`. At the bottom is the Boolean condition clock `w` which ticks when xsin passes from negative to positive; at the middle is the clock `z1` shifted forward 2 intervals, and at the top clock `z2` which is backward 1 interval compared to `z2` but forward 1 compared to w. *Right*: Boolean condition clock `w` and Boolean condition variable `xsin`.

In the model `BackSampleEx2` the Boolean *condition clock* `w` ticks when `xsin` passes zero from negative to positive. The clock `z1` is shifted forward 2 intervals, whereas `z2` is shifted backward 1 interval and thus is only one interval forward compared to clock `w`.

Note that due to the restriction of `superSample` on Boolean condition clocks (Section 13.6.7.5, page 704), `backSample` can only shift a whole number of ticks of the Boolean condition clock, but cannot introduce new ticks.

13.6.9.5 noClock(u)

The clock of `y=noClock(u)` is always inferred. At every tick of the clock of `y`, the operator returns the value of `u` from the most recent tick of the clock of `u`. If `noClock(u)` is called before the first tick of the clock of `u`, the start value of `u` is returned. Consider the following model `NoClockEx` where the value of `y1+1` at clock `u1` is returned at ticks of clock `u2` using either `noClock(...)` or `sample(hold(...))`.

```
model NoClockEx
  // Integer quotient rational number interval clock
  Clock u1 = Clock(3,10);           // ticks: 0, 3/10, 6/10, ..
  Clock u2 = shiftSample(u1,1,3); // ticks: 1/10, 4/10, ...

  discrete Real y1 = sample(time+2, u1);

  discrete Real ynoClock = noClock(y1+1) + sample(0.0,u2);
  discrete Real ysamphold = sample(hold(y1+1)) + sample(0.0,u2);
end NoClockEx;
```

We first simulate the above `NoClockEx` model:

```
simulate(NoClockEx, stopTime=1.0);
plot({u2,y1,ynoClock})    plot({u1,u2,y1,ysamphold})
```

When inspecting Figure 13-116 one might come to the conclusion that the expressions `noClock(u)` and `sample(hold(u))` are equivalent since the variables `ynoClock` and `ysamphold` look the same.

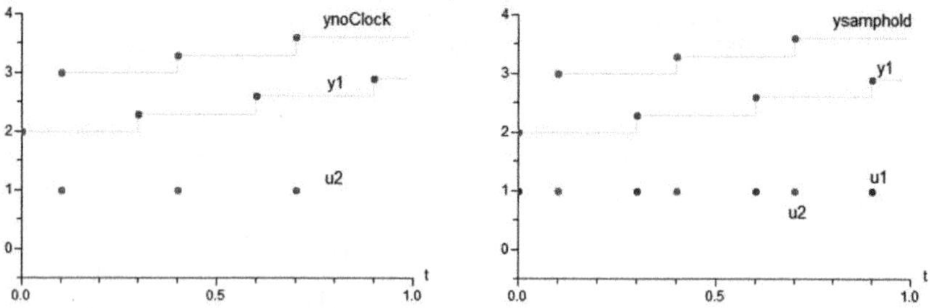

Figure 13-116. Simulation of `noClockEx`. *Left*: `u2` at the bottom, `y1` in the middle with clock `u1`, `ynoClock` at the top with clock `u2`. *Right*: `u1` and `u2` at the bottom, `y1` in the middle with clock `u1`, `ysamphold` at the top with clock `u2`. The variables `ynoClock` and `ysamphold` look identical.

Surprisingly, the expressions `noClock(u)` and `sample(hold(u))` are not equivalent in all cases. They have slightly different semantics due to the infinitesimal delay of `sample` at the actual sampling. According to Section 13.6.8.1 the semantics of `y=sample(u,c)` is as follows: "The clocked `sample` operator returns a *clocked variable value* that has the associated clock `c` and the *value of the left limit* of `u` when the clock `c` is active. This is the *value* of `u` *immediately before* the event of `c` is triggered". Consider following model:

```
model NoClockVsSampleHold
  Clock clk1 = Clock(0.1);
  Clock clk2 = subSample(clk1,2);
  Real x(start=0), y(start=0), z(start=0);
equation
  when clk1 then
    x = previous(x) + 0.1;
  end when;
  when clk2 then
    y = noClock(x);          // most recent value of x
```

```
    z = sample(hold(x)); // Left limit of x (infinitesimally delayed) value!
  end when;
end NoClockVsSampleHold;
```

Due to the infinitesimal delay of `sample`, that is, the delay between the time of taking the left limit value and the event time, `z` will not show the current value of `x` at the current event/tick as `clk2` ticks, but will show its previous value, the left limit. However, `y` will show the current value at the current clock tick, since it has no infinitesimal delay because it does not use `sample`. This is depicted in Figure 13-117 below.

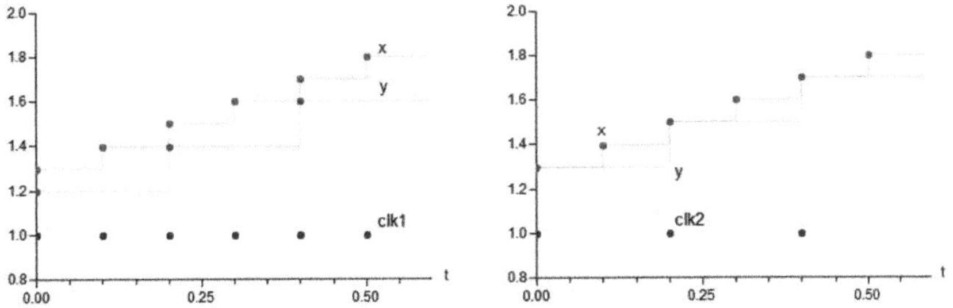

Figure 13-117. Simulation of `NoClockVsSampleHold`. *Left*: `clk1` at the bottom, `z` in the middle, `x` at the top, where `z=sample(hold(x))` shows the previous value of `x` at clock `clk2`. *Right*: `clk2` at the bottom, `x` and `y` in the middle, where `y=noClock(x)` shows the current value of `x` at clock `clk2`.

We could instead define `clk2` as an independent base clock, i.e., with *no synchronization* with `clk1`:

```
Clock clk2 = Clock(0.2);
```

In this case it is *not guaranteed* whether `y=noClock(x)` will hold the "current" value of `x` or the "previous" value since *no synchrony is guaranteed*. The value depends on which of the partitions is executed first, Section 13.6.10 below: "Different base-clock partitions can be associated to separate tasks for asynchronous execution".

13.6.10 Base-Clock and Subclock Partitions

The following concepts are used:

- A *base-clock partition* identifies a set of equations and a set of variables which must be solved together in one task. Different base-clock *partitions* can be associated to *separate tasks* for *asynchronous execution*.
- A *subclock partition* identifies a subset of equations and a subset of variables of a base-clock partition which are partially synchronized with other sub-clock partitions of the same base-clock partition, that is, synchronized when the ticks of the respective clocks are simultaneous.

13.6.11 Instance Expression and Operator Argument Restrictions

The built-in clock-related operators with function syntax defined in the following sections have some restrictions on their input arguments that are not present for standard Modelica functions. To define these restrictions the notion of *instance expression* is introduced, also known under the name *component expression* in (Modelica Association 2012):

- An *instance expression* is an expression with some restrictions, i.e., it does not refer to instances of models with equations.

An *instance expression* is an *instance* of one of the following:

- A base type
- A derived type
- A record type
- An array of such an instance, i.e., of a base type, derived type, or record type
- One or more elements, for example, indexed elements or slices, of such an array indexed by index expressions which are parameter expressions (see below)
- An element of a record

The essential features are that *one or more values* are associated with the instance, that *start values* can be defined on these values, and that *no equations* are associated with the instance. An *instance expression* can be constant or can vary with time.

The notions of instance expression, parameter expression, and ordinary expression is used to describe argument restrictions in the definition of the clock-based operators:

- The input argument is an *instance expression*
  The meaning is that the input argument when calling the operator must be an *instance expression*. The reason for this restriction is that the start value of the input argument is returned before the first tick of the clock of the input argument and this is not possible for a general expression. For example:

```
Real u1;
Real u2[4];
Complex c;
Resistor R;
 ...
y1 = previous(u1);     // fine
y2 = previous(u2);     // fine
y3 = previous(u2[2]); // fine
y4 = previous(c.im);   // fine
y5 = previous(2*u);// Error, general expression, no instance expression
y6 = previous(R); // Error, instance, no instance expression
```

- The input argument is a *parameter expression*
  The meaning is that the input argument when calling the operator must have parameter variability, i.e., the argument must depend directly or indirectly only on parameters, constants or literals, see Section 6.8.1.3, page 278.
  The reason for this restriction is that the value of the input argument needs to be evaluated during translation in order that clock analysis can be performed during translation. Examples:

```
Real u;
parameter Real p=3;
...
y1 = subSample(u, factor=3);          // fine (literal)
y2 = subSample(u, factor=2*p - 3);   // fine (parameter expression)

y3 = subSample(u, factor=3*u);        // error (general expression)
```

- The input argument is an *ordinary expression*
  There is no restriction on the input argument when calling the operator. This notation is used to emphasize the case when a standard function call can be used ("is an expression"), instead of restricting the input ("is an *instance expression*").

13.6.12 Initialization of Clocked Partitions

The standard scheme for initialization of Modelica models does not apply for clocked discrete-time partitions. Instead, initialization is performed in the following way:

- Clocked discrete-time variables *cannot* be used in initial equation or initial algorithm sections.
- The attribute "`fixed`" cannot be applied to clocked discrete-time variables. The attribute `fixed` is `true` for variables to which the `previous` operator is applied, otherwise `false`.

13.6.13 Clock Inference, Clocked Partitions, and Evaluation Order

This section briefly describes how *clocked partitions* and *clocks* associated with equations are *inferred* in a *clock inference* process. Typically *clock partitioning* is performed by the Modelica tool *before sorting* the equations in data dependency order. Sorting by hand is described in Section 2.20.1, page 64, and the sorting algorithm in Section 17.1.7, page 989. The benefit is that clocking and symbolic transformation errors are separated. The following holds:

- Every *clocked variable* is uniquely associated with exactly *one clock*.
- After model flattening, *every equation* in an equation section, *every expression*, and *every algorithm* section is either *unclocked* containing continuous-time and/or unclocked discrete-time parts or is *clocked* with unique association to exactly one clock.

In the latter case it is called a *clocked equation*, a *clocked expression*, or *clocked algorithm section* respectively. The associated clock is either explicitly defined by a *clocked when-equation* (Section 13.6.6, page 700) or is implicitly defined.

- The *implicitly derived clock* is *defined* by the requirement that a *clocked equation*, a *clocked expression* and a *clocked algorithm section* must have the *same clock* as the *variables* used in them with exception of the expressions used as first arguments in the conversion operators of Section 13.6.8, page 705 and Section 13.6.9, page 707.
- *Clock inference* means to *infer the clock* of a variable, an equation, an expression, or an algorithm section if the clock is not explicitly defined and is deduced from the required properties in the previous two paragraphs.
- All variables in an expression without clock conversion operators must have the same clock to infer the clocks for each variable and expression.

The clock inference works both forward and backwards regarding the data flow and is also being able to handle algebraic loops. The clock inference method uses the set of variable incidences of the equations, that is, which variables that appear in each equation.

Note that incidences of the first argument of clock conversion operators of Section 13.6.8, page 705 and Section 13.6.9, page 707, are handled specially.

13.6.13.1 Evaluation Order, Event Handling, and Possible Sorting of Clocked Partitions

As recently mentioned in Section 13.6.8, page 705, `sample` acts as an input boundary and `hold` as an output boundary from a clocked partition versus the continuous-time partition. Since `sample(u)` returns the left limit of `u`, and the left limit of `u` is a known value, all *inputs* to a clocked base-clock partition are treated as *known* during equation sorting (Section 17.1.6, page 984) performed by a Modelica tool. Similarly, the first argument to a `Clock` constructor is treated as known for a clock with integer quotient (Section 13.6.7.3, page 703) or with real value interval (Section 13.6.7.4, page 703).

Since a periodic and/or interval clock can tick at most once at each time instant, and since the left limit of a variable does not change during event iteration, *base-clock partitions* (Section 13.6.14.2, page 719) *need not to be sorted with respect to each other* by the Modelica tool. However, the *equations within* each base-clock partition still *need* to be *sorted.*

The reason for this is that the `sample(u)` inputs do not change and therefore need not be re-evaluated, i.e., re-evaluating a base-clock partition associated with a condition clock always gives the same result.

Thus, at an event instant, equations and algorithm sections in active base-clock partitions can be solved first, just once, in *any order*.

Afterwards the continuous-time partition is evaluated. *Event iteration* takes place *only* over the *continuous-time partition*. In such a scenario, accessing the *left limit* of `u` in `sample(u)` just means to pick the latest available value of `u` when the partition is entered, storing it in a local variable of the partition and only using this local copy during evaluation of the equations in this partition.

As an illustration, the two base-clock partitions in the model `BaseClockPartitionEx` can be evaluated independently in any order.

```
model BaseClockPartitionEx
  Real x(start=0.1, fixed=true);
  Real xd1(start=-0.1);
  Real xd1_hold;
  Real xd2;
  Real xd3;
equation
   der(x) = 1;                    // Continuous partition
   when Clock(0.1) then           // Base-clock partition 1
     xd1 = sample(x);
   end when;
   xd1_hold = hold(xd1);
   when Clock(0.2) then           // Base-clock partition 2
     xd2 = sample(xd1_hold);
   end when;
   xd3 = subSample(xd1,1);
end BaseClockPartitionEx;
```

We simulate for 0.8 seconds and plot.

```
simulate(BaseClockPartitionEx, stopTime=0.8);
plot({xd1, xd2})
```

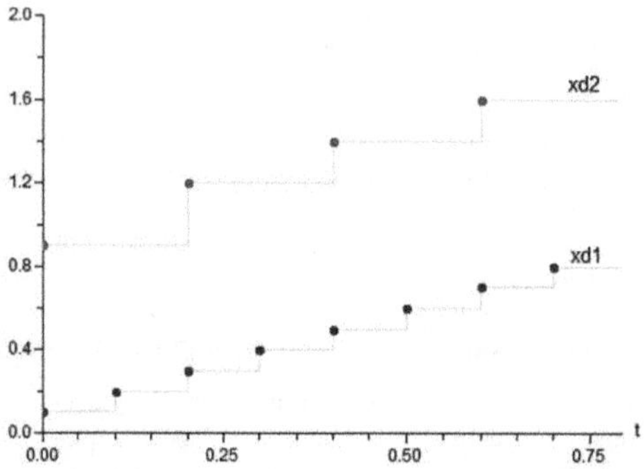

Figure 13-118. Simulation of the `BaseClockPartitionEx` model with plots of variables `xd1` and `xd2`. The two base-clock partitions can be evaluated in any order at a clock tick event. The variable `xd2` (uppermost curve) shows the previous value of `xd1`, initially -0.1, increased by 1.0 .

13.6.13.2 Partitioning Example—ControlledMass

Below we give an example model, `ControlledMass`, which illustrates the clock inference (Section 13.6.13, page 715) and clock partitioning (Section 13.6.14, page 719). The model inherits the `MassWithSpringDamper` model which was described in Section 13.6.1, page 694.

```
model ControlledMass
  extends MassWithSpringDamper(k=100);
  parameter Real KOuter = 10 "Gain of position PI controller";
  parameter Real KInner = 20 "Gain of speed P controller";
  parameter Real Ti     = 10 "Integral time for pos. PI controller";
  parameter Real xref   = 10 "Position reference";

  discrete Real xd;
  discrete Real eOuter;
  discrete Real intE(start=0);
  discrete Real uOuter(start=0);

  discrete Real xdFast;
  discrete Real vd;
  discrete Real vref;
  discrete Real uInner(start=0);

  Clock cControl = Clock(0.01);                           // 100Hz, delay 0
  Clock cOuter= subSample(shiftSample(cControl,2,3),5); // 20Hz, delay 2/300
  Clock cFast = superSample(cControl, 2);               // 200 Hz
equation
  // position sensor
  xd = sample(x, cOuter);   // Clock 20 Hz, delay 2/300 = 4/600

  // outer PI controller for position
  eOuter = xref-xd;                   // Clock 20 Hz, delay 4/600
  intE = previous(intE) + eOuter;     // Inferred clock of xref, eOuter,
  uOuter = KOuter*(eOuter + intE/Ti); // intE, and uOuter

  // speed estimation
  xdFast = sample(x, cFast);                                  // 200 Hz
  vd = subSample((xdFast-previous(xdFast))/interval(), 2);    // 100 Hz
                                                        // Inferred interval()

  // inner P controller for speed
  vref = backSample(superSample(uOuter,5), 2, 3);          // 100 Hz, delay 0
  uInner = KInner*(vref-vd);   // Inferred uInner, KInner // 100 Hz, delay 0

  // force actuator
  f = hold(uInner);
end ControlledMass;
```

We simulate for 0.26 seconds and plot, first the clocks in Figure 13-119 and then a few variables in Figure 13-120.

```
simulate(ControlledMass, stopTime=0.26);
plot({eControl, cOuter, cFast})
```

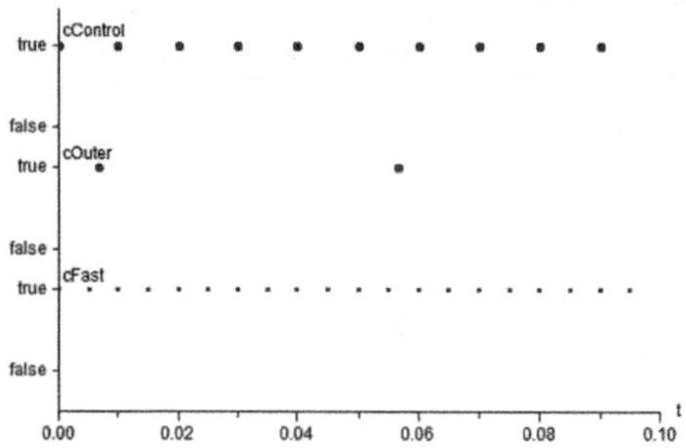

Figure 13-119. Simulation of the `ControlledMass model` model only showing its declared clocks. The clock `cControl` is 100 Hz, delay 0, `cFast` 200 Hz, delay 0, and `cOuter` 20 Hz, delay 4/600.

```
plot({xd, xdFast})
plot({uOuter, vref})
```

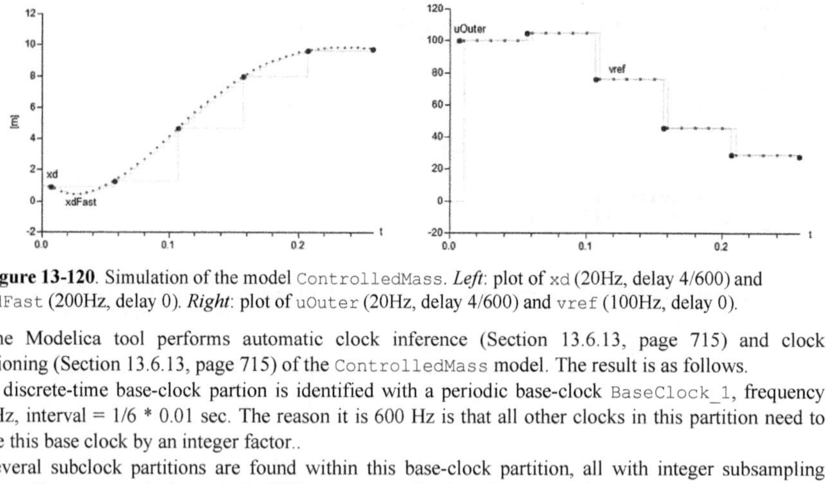

Figure 13-120. Simulation of the model `ControlledMass`. *Left*: plot of `xd` (20Hz, delay 4/600) and `xdFast` (200Hz, delay 0). *Right*: plot of `uOuter` (20Hz, delay 4/600) and `vref` (100Hz, delay 0).

The Modelica tool performs automatic clock inference (Section 13.6.13, page 715) and clock partitioning (Section 13.6.13, page 715) of the `ControlledMass` model. The result is as follows.

A discrete-time base-clock partion is identified with a periodic base-clock `BaseClock_1`, frequency 600 Hz, interval = 1/6 * 0.01 sec. The reason it is 600 Hz is that all other clocks in this partition need to divide this base clock by an integer factor..

Several subclock partitions are found within this base-clock partition, all with integer subsampling factors with respect to the base clock. This means that all subclocks are synchronized with the base clock, which is a requirement to be in the same base-clock partition. The following partitions are found:

- Continuous-time partition:

```
der(x)  = v;         // First two equations inhertied from MassWithSpringDamper
m*der(v)  = f - k*x - d*v;

  f = hold(uInner);
```

- Subclock partition with `BaseClock_1.SubClock_1`, 100 Hz, subsampling factor 6, start delay 0

```
vd = subSample(vd_temp1, 2);                          // 100 Hz, delay 0
vref = backSample(superSample(uOuter,5), 2, 3); // 100 Hz, delay 0
uInner = KInner*(vref-vd);                            // 100 Hz, delay 0
```

- Subclock partition with `BaseClock_1.SubClock_2`, 200 Hz, subsampling factor 3, delay 0 sec. A temporary variable `vd_templ` clocked at 200Hz has been introduced.

```
xdFast = sample(x, cFast);                          // 200 Hz, delay 0
vd_templ = (xdFast-previous(xdFast))/interval(); // 200 Hz, delay 0
```

- Subclock partition with `BaseClock_1.SubClock_3`, 20Hz, subsampling factor 30, delay 4/600

```
xd = sample(x, cOuter);                            // Clock 20 Hz, delay 4/600
eOuter = xref-xd;
intE = previous(intE) + eOuter;
uOuter = KOuter*(eOuter + intE/Ti);
```

13.6.14 Clock Partitioning in Detail

The *clock partitioning* is *conceptually performed* by the Modelica tool after model flattening, that is, redeclarations have been elaborated, arrays of model instances expanded into scalar model instances, and overloading resolved. Furthermore, function calls to inline functions have been inlined.

This is called "conceptually," because a Modelica compiler might do this more efficiently in a different way provided the result is the same as if everything is flattened. For example, array and matrix equations and records do not need to be expanded if they have the same clock.

Furthermore, each nontrivial expression $expr_i$ (nonliteral, nonconstant, nonparameter, nonvariable), appearing as first argument of any clock conversion operator is recursively replaced by a unique variable, v_i, and the equation $v_i = expr_i$ is added to the equation set.

13.6.14.1 Connected Components of the Equations and Variables Graph

Consider the set E of equations and the set V of unknown variables (not constants and parameters) in a flattened model, that is, M = <E, V>. The partitioning is described in terms of an undirected graph <N, F> with the nodes N being the set of equations and variables, N = E + V.

The set `incidence(e)` for an equation `e` in E is a subset of V, in general it consists of the unknowns which lexically appear in `e`. There is an edge in F of the graph between an equation, `e`, and a variable, `v`, if `v = incidence(e)`:

$$F = \{(e, v) : e \in E, v \in \text{incidence}(e)\} \tag{13-17}$$

A set of clock partitions is the "*connected components*" of this graph with appropriate definition of the incidence operator below (Section 13.6.14.2, page 719).

13.6.14.2 Base-clock Partitioning

The goal is for the Modelica tool to *identify* all *clocked equations and variables* that should be solved together in the same task, as well as to identify the unclocked continuous-time partition.

The base-clock partitioning is performed with base-clock inference, which uses the following incidence (occurrence) definition (see also a different incidence matrix in Section 17.1.7, page 989):

`incidence(e)` = the set of *unknown* variables, as well as all variables `x` in `der(x)`, `pre(x)`, and `previous(x)`, which lexically appear in equation `e` except as first argument of the base-clock conversion operators `sample()` and `hold()`.

The resulting set of connected elements (equations, variables) defines the initial partitioning of the equations and variables, $B_i = <E_i, V_i>$, according to having a base-clock or being in a continuous-time partition.

The base clock partitions are identified as *clocked partitions* or as *unclocked continuous-time partitions* according to the following properties:

- A variable `u` in `sample(u)` and a variable `y` in `y=hold(ud)` is in a continuous-time partition.
- Correspondingly, variables `u` and `y` in `y = sample(uc)`, `y = subSample(u)`, `y = superSample(u)`, `y = shiftSample(u)`, `y = backSample(u)`, `y = previous(u)`, are in a clocked partition. Equations in a *clocked when-equation* are also in a clocked partition.
- Other partitions where none of the variables in the partition are associated with any of the operators above have an unspecified partition kind and are considered continuous-time partitions.
- Finally, for the resulting final partitioning all continuous-time partitions are collected together and form "the" single continuous-time partition.

For example, perform base-clock partitioning of the following small model:

```
// Controller 1
ud1 = sample(y,c1);
  0 = f1(yd1, ud1, previous(yd1));

// Controller 2
ud2 = superSample(yd1,2);
  0 = f2(yd2, ud2);

// Continuous-time system of equations
u = hold(yd2);
0 = f3(der(x1), x1, u);
0 = f4(der(x2), x2, x1);
0 = f5(der(x3), x3);
0 = f6(y, x1, u);
```

After base clock partitioning, the following partitions are identified:

```
// Base partition 1 // clocked partition
ud1 = sample(y,c1);                       // incidence(e) = {ud1}
0   = f1(yd1, ud1, previous(ud1));        // incidence(e) = {yd1,ud1}
ud2 = superSample(yd1,2);                 // incidence(e) = {ud2, yd1}
0   = f2(yd2, ud2);                       // incidence(e) = {yd2, ud2}

// Base partition 2 // continuous-time partition
u = hold(yd2);                     // incidence(e) = {u}
0 = f3(der(x1), x1, u);            // incidence(e) = {x1,u}
0 = f4(der(x2), x2, x1);           // incidence(e) = {x2,x1}
0 = f6(y, x1, u);                  // incidence(e) = {y,x1,u}
  // Identified as separate partition, but belonging to partition 2
0 = f5(der(x3), x3);               // incidence(e) = {x3}
```

13.6.14.3 Subclock Partitioning

For each clocked partition B_i, identified in Section 13.6.14.2, page 719, the subclock partitioning is performed with sub-clock inference which uses the following `incidence` definition:

`incidence`(e) = the *unknown* variables, as well as variables x in `der`(x), `pre`(x), and `previous`(x), which lexically appear in `e` except as first argument of sub-clock conversion operators: `subSample`, `superSample`, `shiftSample`, `backSample`, and `noClock`.

The resulting set of connected components, is the partitioning of the equations and variables, $S_{ij} = \langle E_{ij}, V_{ij} \rangle$, according to subclocks.

It can be noted that:

$$E_{ij} \cap E_{kl} = \varnothing \quad \forall \quad i \neq k, j \neq l \tag{13-18}$$

$$V_{ij} \cap V_{kl} = \varnothing \ \forall \ i \neq k, j \neq l \tag{13-19}$$

$$V = \bigcup V_{ij} \tag{13-20}$$

$$E = \bigcup E_{ij} \tag{13-21}$$

For example, after subclock partitioning of the above example from Section 13.6.14.2, page 719, the following partitions are identified:

```
// Base partition 1 (clocked partition)

   // Sub-clock partition 1.1
   ud1 = sample(y,c1);                  // incidence(e) = {ud1}
   0   = f1(yd1,ud1,previous(yd1)); // incidence(e) = {yd1,ud1}

   // Sub-Clock partition 1.2
   ud2 = superSample(yd1,2);            // incidence(e) = {ud2}
   0   = f2(yd2,ud2);                   // incidence(e) = {yd2,ud2}

// Base partition 2, no sub-clock partitioning, since continuous-time
   u = hold(yd2);
   0 = f3(der(x1), x1, u);
   0 = f4(der(x2), x2, x1);
   0 = f5(der(x3), x3);
   0 = f6(y, x1, u);
```

13.6.14.4 Subclock Inferencing

For each *base-clock partition*, the *base clock interval* needs to be determined and for each *subclock partition*, the *subsampling factors* and *shift* need to be determined.

For each subclock partition, the interval might be rational or Real type and known or parametric or being unspecified.

The subclock partition intervals are constrained by `subSample` and `superSample` sampling factors which might be known, be parameters, or unspecified and by `shiftSample`, `shiftCounter`, and `resolution` or `backSample`, `backCounter`, and `resolution`. This constraint set is used to solve for all intervals and subsampling factors and shift of the subclock partitions. The model is erroneous if no solution exists.

Note that it must be possible to determine that the constraint set is valid at compile time. However, in certain cases, it could be possible to defer providing actual numbers until run time.

It is required that accumulated sub- and super-sampling factors in the range of 1 to 2^{63} can be handled.

A 64 bit internal representation of numerator and denominator with sign can be used and gives a minimum resolution 1.08E-19 seconds and maximum range 9.22E+18 seconds = 2.92E+11 years.

13.6.15 Continuous-Time Equations in Clocked Partitions

The goal of allowing continuous-time equations in clocked partitions is that continuous-time Modelica models can be utilized in a clocked sampled data control system applications. This can be achieved by solving the continuous-time equations with a defined integration method between clock ticks. With this feature, it is for example possible to invert the nonlinear dynamic model of a plant (see reference in Section 13.9, page 742) and use it in a feed forward path of an advanced control system that is associated with a clock.

The feature of continuous-time equations in clocked partitions also allows definition of *multirate clocked systems*. This means that different parts of a continuous-time model are associated to different clocks and are solved with different integration methods between clock ticks. For example, a very fast subsystem could be solved with an implicit solver with a small step size and a slow subsystem with an explicit solver with a large step size.

With the language elements defined in this section, continuous-time equations can also be used within clocked partitions. Thereby the continuous-time equations are solved with the defined integration method between clock ticks.

From the point of *view of the continuous-time partition*, the *clock ticks are not interpreted as events*, but as *step sizes of the integrator that the integrator must exactly hit*. This is the same assumption as for manually discretized controllers, such as the z-transform. Thus, no event handling is triggered at clock ticks (provided an explicit event is not triggered from the model at this time instant).

It is not defined how events are handled that appear when solving the continuous-time partition. For example, a tool could handle events exactly in the same way as for a usual simulation. Alternatively, relations might be interpreted literally, so that events are no longer triggered in order that the time for an integration step is always the same, as needed for hard real-time requirements.

From the point of *view of the clocked partition*, the continuous-time partition is discretized and the discretized continuous-time variables only have values at clock ticks. Therefore, such a partition is handled in the same way as any other clocked partition. Especially, operators such as `sample`, `hold`, `subSample` must be used to communicate signals of the discretized continuous-time partition with other partitions. Thereby a *discretized continuous-time partition* is seen as a clocked partition.

13.6.15.1 Clocked Discrete-Time and Clocked Discretized Continuous-Time Partition

The concept of variability of expressions in general is defined in Section 6.8.1.3, page 278. Here the concept of *clocked discrete-time expressions* is defined more precisely, closely related to *clocked discrete-time variables* defined in Section 13.6.3, page 697.

- If not explicitly stated otherwise, an expression with a variability such as *continuous-time* or *unclocked discrete-time* means that the expression is inside a partition that is not associated to a clock.
- If an expression is present in a partition that is *not* a *continuous-time partition*, it is a *clocked expression* and has *clocked discrete-time variability*.

After subclock inferencing (Section 13.6.14.4, page 721) every *partition* that is *associated* to a *clock* has to be categorized as *clocked discrete-time* or *clocked discretized continuous-time* partition according to the following rules:

- *Clocked discrete-time partition*. If a clocked partition does not contain the operators `der`, `delay`, `spatialDistribution`, no event-related operators (`initial`, `terminal`, `pre`, `edge`, `change`, `noEvent`, `sample`, `smooth`, `reinit`, see Section 0, page 293) with the exception of `noEvent(...)`, and no `when`-clause with a Boolean condition, it is a *clocked discrete-time* partition, i.e., it is a standard sampled data system that is described by difference equations.
- *Clocked discretized continuous-time partition*. If a clocked partition is *not* a *clocked discrete-time* partition and it contains *neither* the operator `previous(...)` (Section 13.6.4, page 699) nor the operator `interval(...)` (Section 13.6.5, page 699), it is a *clocked discretized continuous-time* partition. Such a partition has to be solved with a "solver method" of section 13.6.15.2, page 723.

It is an *error* if *none* of the two properties hold, e.g., if the operators `previous(...)` and `der(...)` are both used in the same partition.

In a clocked discrete-time partition *none* of the *event generating* mechanisms apply. For example, neither relations nor any of the event triggering mathematical functions (Section 6.13.1, page 289) will trigger an event.

13.6.15.2 Solver Methods

The *integration method* associated with a *clocked discretized continuous-time partition* is defined by specifying a string which is the name of the chosen integration method. A predefined type `ModelicaServices.Types.SolverMethod` defines the methods supported by the respective tool by using the `choices` annotation.

The `ModelicaServices` package contains tool specific definitions. Each solver method is denoted by a string. The following names of solver methods are standardized:

```
type SolverMethod = String annotation(choices(
      choice="External"              "Solver specified externally",
      choice="ExplicitEuler"         "Explicit Euler method (order 1)",
      choice="ExplicitMidPoint2"     "Explicit midpoint rule (order 2)",
      choice="ExplicitRungeKutta4"   "Explicit Runge-Kutta method (order 4)",
      choice="ImplicitEuler"         "Implicit Euler method (order 1)",
      choice="ImplicitTrapezoid"     "Implicit trapezoid rule (order 2)"
  ))
  "Type of integration method to solve differential equations in a clocked"+
  "discretized continuous-time partition."
```

If a tool supports one of the numeric solvers of `SolverMethod` it must use one of the above solver method names. A Modelica tool may also support other integrators. Typically, a tool supports at least the methods "`External`" and "`ExplicitEuler`". If a tool does not support the integration method defined in a model, typically a warning message is printed and the method is changed to "`External`".

If the solver method is `"External"`, then the equations in the partition associated with this method are numerically solved during an interval of length of `interval()` using a numeric solution method selected and provided by the simulation tool.

For example, one possibility is to have a table of the clocks that are associated with discretized continuous-time partitions and a method selection per clock. In such a case, the solution method might be a variable step solver with step-size control that numerically solves equations between two clock ticks.

The simulation tool might also combine all partitions associated with method `"External"`, as well as all continuous-time partitions, and solve the equations from all these partitions together using the solver selected by the simulation tool.

If the solver method is *not* `"External"`, then the equations in the partition are numerically solved using the given method with the numeric step size being `interval()`. For a periodic clock, the numeric solution is thus performed with fixed step size.

The solvers are defined with respect to the underlying ordinary differential equation in state space form to which the continuous-time partition can be transformed, at least conceptually (t is time, $\mathbf{u}(t)$ is the real vector of input variables, $\mathbf{x}(t)$ is the real vector of states, and $\mathbf{y}(t)$ is the real vector of algebraic and/or output variables). See Section 17.1, page 979 for a more detailed description of the underlying ODE or DAE system of equations.

$$\begin{aligned} \dot{\mathbf{x}} &= \mathbf{f}(\mathbf{x}, \mathbf{u}, t) \\ \mathbf{y} &= \mathbf{g}(\mathbf{x}, \mathbf{u}, t) \end{aligned} \tag{13-22}$$

The solver methods below (with exception of `"External"`) performs numerical solution of the equations from clock tick t_{i-1} to clock tick t_i and computing the desired variables at t_i, with $h = t_i - t_{i-1} =$ `interval(u)` and $\mathbf{x}_i = \mathbf{x}(t_i)$. See Section 18.2.1, page 998, for more details regarding solver methods.

SolverMethod	*Solution method* (for all methods: $\mathbf{y}_i = \mathbf{g}(\mathbf{x}_i, \mathbf{u}_i, t_i)$)
`ExplicitEuler`	$\mathbf{x}_i := \mathbf{x}_{i-1} + h \cdot \dot{\mathbf{x}}_{i-1}$ $\dot{\mathbf{x}}_i := \mathbf{f}(\mathbf{x}_i, \mathbf{u}_i, t_i)$
`ExplicitMidPoint2`	$\mathbf{x}_i := \mathbf{x}_{i-1} + h \cdot \mathbf{f}(\mathbf{x}_{i-1} + \tfrac{1}{2} \cdot h \cdot \dot{\mathbf{x}}_{i-1}, \frac{\mathbf{u}_{i-1} + \mathbf{u}_i}{2}, t_{i-1} + \tfrac{1}{2} \cdot h)$ $\dot{\mathbf{x}}_i := \mathbf{f}(\mathbf{x}_i, \mathbf{u}_i, t_i)$
`ExplicitRungeKutta4`	$\mathbf{k}_1 := h \cdot \dot{\mathbf{x}}_{i-1}$ $\mathbf{k}_2 := h \cdot \mathbf{f}(\mathbf{x}_{i-1} + \tfrac{1}{2}\mathbf{k}_1, \frac{\mathbf{u}_{i-1} + \mathbf{u}_i}{2}, t_{i-1} + \tfrac{1}{2}h)$ $\mathbf{k}_3 := h \cdot \mathbf{f}(\mathbf{x}_{i-1} + \tfrac{1}{2}\mathbf{k}_2, \frac{\mathbf{u}_{i-1} + \mathbf{u}_i}{2}, t_{i-1} + \tfrac{1}{2}h)$ $\mathbf{k}_4 := h \cdot \mathbf{f}(\mathbf{x}_{i-1} + \mathbf{k}_3, \mathbf{u}_i, t_i)$ $\mathbf{x}_i := \mathbf{x}_{i-1} + \tfrac{1}{6} \cdot (\mathbf{k}_1 + 2 \cdot \mathbf{k}_2 + 2 \cdot \mathbf{k}_3 + \mathbf{k}_4)$ $\dot{\mathbf{x}}_i := \mathbf{f}(\mathbf{x}_i, \mathbf{u}_i, t_i)$
`ImplicitEuler`	$\mathbf{x}_i = \mathbf{x}_{i-1} + h \cdot \dot{\mathbf{x}}_i$ // equation system with unknowns: $\mathbf{x}_i, \dot{\mathbf{x}}_i$ $\dot{\mathbf{x}}_i = \mathbf{f}(\mathbf{x}_i, \mathbf{u}_i, t_i)$
`ImplicitTrapezoid`	$\mathbf{x}_i = \mathbf{x}_{i-1} + \tfrac{1}{2} h \cdot (\dot{\mathbf{x}}_i + \dot{\mathbf{x}}_{i-1})$ // equation system with unknowns: $\mathbf{x}_i, \dot{\mathbf{x}}_i$ $\dot{\mathbf{x}}_i = \mathbf{f}(\mathbf{x}_i, \mathbf{u}_i, t_i)$

For the implicit integration methods the efficiency can be enhanced by utilizing the solver discretization formula to expand the equations to the discretized forms such as the above during the symbolic transformation of the equations. This method is also known as inline integration. For example, linear differential equations are then mapped to linear and not non-linear algebraic equation systems, and also the structure of the equations can be utilized.

It might be necessary to associate additional data for an implicit integration method, for example, the relative tolerance to solve the non-linear algebraic equation systems, or the maximum number of iterations in case of hard real-time requirements. This data is tool specific and is typically either defined with a vendor annotation or is given in the simulation environment.

13.6.15.3 Associating a Solver to a Partition

A `solverMethod` can be associated to a clock with the overloaded `Clock` constructor `Clock(c, solverMethod)`, see also Section 13.6.7.6, page 705. If a clock is associated with a clocked partition and a `solverMethod` is associated with this clock, then the continuous-time equations in that clocked partition are numerically solved using that solver.

We show the model `SolverMethodClockedPI` which uses the numeric solver `"ImplicitEuler"` for solving its continuous-time equations because they refer to the variable `e` which is clocked according to clock `c` with associated `solverMethod = "ImplicitEuler"`.

```
model SolverMethodClockedPI
  parameter Real k=1;
  parameter Real T=1;
//  input Real y_ref;    // reference value
//  input Real y_mes;    // measured value
  Real y_ref = 3;                   // dummy reference value
  Real y_mes = 3+sign(sin(time)); // dummy measured value
  Real e;
  Real x(start=0,fixed=true);
  Real ud;
```

```
  output Real u(start=0.0);
  Clock c = Clock(Clock(0.4), solverMethod="ImplicitEuler");
equation
  // Sampling the inputs
  e = sample(y_ref,c) - sample(y_mes);

  // Continuous-time PI controller in a clocked partition
  der(x) = e/T;
  ud = k*(x + e);

  // Holding the output
  u = hold(ud);
end SolverMethodClockedPI;
```

The variable x, which first appears to be continuous-time because `der()` is applied to it, is automatically discretized according to the solver method difference equations with a numeric step-size being the clock interval of the clocked partition. Thus `x` has become a discrete clocked variable.

We simulate and plot. Note that `x` is now a clocked discrete-time variable.

```
simulate(SolverMethodEx, stopTime=10.0);
plot({y_ref,y_mes, u})
plot({e, x})
```

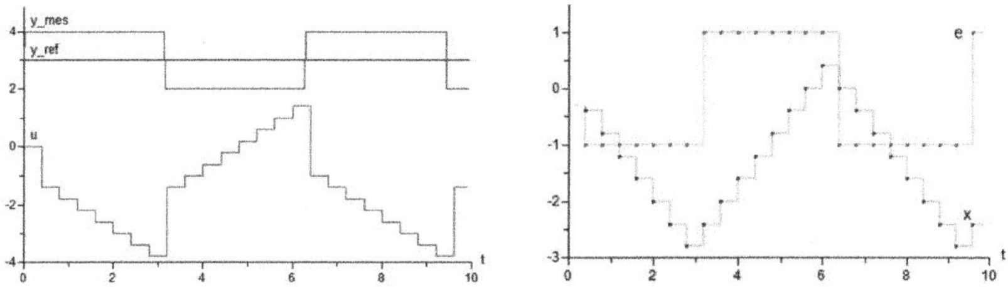

Figure 13-121. Simulation of the model `SolverMethodClockedPI`. Note that `x` in the right diagram has become a clocked discrete-time variable due to discretization according to the chosen `solverMethod`.

13.6.15.4 Automatic Choice of solverMethod

If a `solverMethod` is not explicitly associated with a partition, the choice of solver is inferred with a similar mechanism as for sub-clock inferencing (Section 13.6.14.4, page 721). The inferencing mechanism is defined using the operator `solverExplicitlyDefined(c)` which returns `true` if a `solverMethod` is explicitly associated with the clock `c` and returns `false` otherwise.

For every partitioning operator of Section 13.6.8, page 705 and Section 13.6.9, page 707, two clocks `c1` and `c2` are defined for the input arguments and the output results of the operator, respectively. Furthermore, for every equation or assignment statement of clocks, e.g., `c1=c2` or `c1 := c2`, two clocks are defined as well. In all these cases, the following if-then-else equation (or statement) is implicitly introduced:

```
if solverExplicitlyDefined(c1) and solverExplicitlyDefined(c2) then
  // o.k. (no action)

elseif not solverExplicitlyDefined(c1) and not solverExplicitlyDefined(c2)
then
  assert(c1.solverMethod == c2.solverMethod);

elseif solverExplicitlyDefined(c1) <> solverExplicitlyDefined(c2) then
  c1.solverMethod = c2.solverMethod

end if;
```

This introduced set of potentially underdetermined or overdetermined constraints has to be solved. If no solution exists or if a solution is contradictory on some clocks that are associated with clocked discrete-time partitions, then this is ignored, since no `solverMethod` is needed for such partitions. For example:

```
model InferenceTest "Specific clocks set on all partitions.
                     Decouple constraint"
  ...
equation
  // Physical model
  der(x1) = -100*x1 + hold(z2);

  // Controller submodels
  der(z1) = -100*z1 + sample(x2,
    Clock(Clock(1,100), solverMethod="ImplicitEuler") );
  w = 0.9*previous(w) + superSample(z1, 3);
  when Clock(Clock(1,20), solverMethod="ExplicitEuler") then
    ww = superSample(w);
  end when
  der(z2) = -z2 + ww;
end InferenceTest;
```

13.6.16 Semantics of Subpartition Clock Synchronization

The execution of subpartitions requires exact time management for proper synchronization. The implication is that testing a Real valued time variable to determine sampling instants is not possible. One possible method is to use counters to handle sub-sampling scheduling.

```
Clock_i_j_ticks = if pre(Clock_i_j_ticks) < subSamplingFactor_i_j then 1+pre
(Clock_i_j_ticks) else 1;
```

and to test the counter to determine when the sub-clock is ticking:

```
Clock_i_j_activated =  BaseClock_i_activated and Clock_i_j_ticks >= subSampl
ingFactor_i_j;
```

The `Clock_i_j_activated` flag is used as the guard for the sub-partition equations.

Consider the following example:

```
model ClockTicks
  Integer second = sample(1, Clock(1));
  Integer seconds(start=-1) = mod(previous(seconds) + second, 60);
  Integer milliSeconds(start=-1)=
      mod(previous(milliSeconds) + superSample(second, 1000), 1000);
  Integer minutes(start=-1)=
      mod(previous(minutes) + subSample(second, 60), 60);
end ClockTicks;
```

A possible implementation model is shown below using the Modelica 3.2 language. The base-clock is determined to 0.001 seconds and the subsampling factors to 1000 and 60000.

```
model ClockTicksWithModelica32
  Integer second;
  Integer seconds(start = -1);
  Integer milliSeconds(start = -1);
  Integer minutes(start = -1);

  Boolean BaseClock_1_activated;
  Integer Clock_1_1_ticks(start=59999);
  Integer Clock_1_2_ticks(start=0);
```

```
    Integer Clock_1_3_ticks(start=999);
    Boolean Clock_1_1_activated;
    Boolean Clock_1_2_activated;
    Boolean Clock_1_3_activated;

  equation
  // Prepare clock tick
    BaseClock_1_activated =  sample(0, 0.001);
    when BaseClock_1_activated then
      Clock_1_1_ticks = if pre(Clock_1_1_ticks) < 60000 then 1+pre(Clock_1_1_t
icks) else 1;
      Clock_1_2_ticks = if pre(Clock_1_2_ticks) < 1 then 1+pre(Clock_1_2_ticks
) else 1;
      Clock_1_3_ticks = if pre(Clock_1_3_ticks) < 1000 then 1+pre(Clock_1_3_ti
cks) else 1;
    end when;
    Clock_1_1_activated =  BaseClock_1_activated and Clock_1_1_ticks >= 60000;
    Clock_1_2_activated =  BaseClock_1_activated and Clock_1_2_ticks >= 1;
    Clock_1_3_activated =  BaseClock_1_activated and Clock_1_3_ticks >= 1000;

  // ----------------------------------------------------------------------------
  // Sub partition execution
    when {Clock_1_3_activated} then
      second = 1;
    end when;
    when {Clock_1_1_activated} then
      minutes = mod(pre(minutes)+second, 60);
    end when;
    when {Clock_1_2_activated} then
      milliSeconds = mod(pre(milliSeconds)+second, 1000);
    end when;
    when {Clock_1_3_activated} then
      seconds = mod(pre(seconds)+second, 60);
    end when;
  end ClockTicksWithModelica32;
```

13.6.17 Clocked versus Unclocked Modeling

The clocked language constructs are especially motivated by their applications in periodically sampled control systems. However, such control systems can also be modeled with standard unclocked when-equations (Section 8.3.5, page 357), and the unclocked `sample` operator (Section 13.2.5.4, page 602). For example:

```
when sample(0,3) then
   xd = A*pre(xd) + B*y;
    u = C*pre(xd) + D*y;
end when;
```

Examples of both unclocked and clocked sampled system models are given in Section 13.3.1, page 625. Remember that equations *inside* an unclocked when-clause with a Boolean condition have the following properties:

- Variables on the left hand side of the equal sign in equations or `:=` in assignments are assigned a value when the when-condition becomes true and otherwise hold their value.
- Variables not assigned in the when-clause are directly accessed, i.e., automatic `sample` semantics.
- Variables assigned to or solved for in the when-clause can be directly accessed outside of the when-clause, automatic `hold` semantics.

Modeling with unclocked discrete-time constructs like unclocked when-clauses has some advantages:

- There are few unclocked discrete-time language constructs to learn and understand, whereas there are many constructs needed for clocked modeling.
- The sampling condition has to be propagated explicitly which might be tedious and some models clumsy but on the other hand makes the dependencies within the model more explicit and thus probably easier to follow and understand.
- There is no clock inference that can depend on low-level information distributed over different parts of the model. Depending on the tool, the clock inference can give cryptic and hard-to-understand error messages when it fails because of some problem in the model.
- The constraint that all equations need to be grouped into partitions with the same clock, where only equations with the same clock can be solved together, imposes some constraints in modeling.

On the other hand, modeling with clocked language constructs have a number of *clear advantages* for modeling *periodically sampled data systems*, especially when digital clocks are present. The use of unclocked when-clauses to model such sampled systems has the following drawbacks that are not present using clocks and clocked equations:

- It is not possible for the Modelica tool to automatically detect sampling errors in unclocked models due to the automatic sample and hold semantics of unclocked when-clauses. Examples:
  (a) If when-clauses in different blocks should belong to the same controller part, but by accident different when-conditions are given, then this is accepted by the Modelica tool, that is, no error is detected.
  (b) If a sampled data library such as the `Modelica_LinearSystems2.Controller` library is used, at every block the sampling of the block has to be defined as an integer multiple of a base sampling rate. If several blocks should belong to the same controller part, and different integer multiples are given, then the translator has to accept this, that is, no error is detected.
- Due to the automatic sample and hold semantics, all unclocked discrete-time variables solved for or assigned in an unclocked when-clause must have an initial value because they might be used before they are assigned a value the first time. As a result, all these variables are "discrete-time states" although in reality only a small subset of them need an initial value.
- Only a restricted form of equations can be used in an unclocked when-clause since the left hand side has to be a variable in order to identify the variables that are assigned in the unclocked when-clause. This restriction is not present for clocked equations.
- All equations belonging to an unclocked discrete controller must be within a single unclocked when-clause. If the controller is built-up of several building blocks then the clock condition (the sampling) must be explicitly propagated to all blocks. This is sometimes tedious and somewhat error prone. With clocked equations, the clock condition needs to be defined only at one place and is automatically propagated to other places by clock inference.
- It is not possible to use a continuous-time model in unclocked when-clauses. For example, this would be desirable in applications where some advanced controllers use an inverse model of a plant in the feedforward path of the controller, see Section 13.9, page 742. When using the unclocked part of Modelica, a nonlinear plant model in a controller would require to export the continuous-time model with an embedded integration method and then import it in an environment where the rest of the controller is defined. With clocked equations, clocked controllers with continuous-time models can be directly defined in Modelica.
- At a sample event instant an event iteration occurs as for any other event. A clocked partition, as well as a clocked when-clause with a `sample(...)` call is evaluated exactly once at such an event

instant. However, the continuous-time model to which the sampled data controller is connected will be evaluated several times when the overall system is simulated.

When using unclocked when-clauses the continuous-time part is typically evaluated three times at each sample instant. Once, when the sample instant is reached, once to evaluate the continuous equations at the sample instant, and once when an event iteration occurs since a discrete variable v is changed and `pre`(v) appears in the equations.

With clocked equations no event iteration is triggered if a clocked variable v is changed and `previous`(v) appears in the equations because the event iteration cannot change the value of v. As a result, typically the simulation model is evaluated twice at each sample instant and therefore the simulation is more efficient with clocked equations.

13.7 Clocked State Machines in Detail

This section gives a more detailed description of clocked state machines including all the current Modelica language elements that can be used to define clocked state machines.

Such state machines have the important feature that at each clock tick there is only a *single assignment* to every variable. For example, it is an error if state machines are executed in parallel and assign to the same variable at the same clock tick. Such errors are detected and prevented by the compiler during translation.

Furthermore, it is possible to activate and deactivate clocked equations and models at a clock tick. An efficient implementation will *only* evaluate the equations and models that are active *at the current clock tick*, which is not available with unclocked Modelica language elements.

Parallel state machines can be explicitly synchronized using the `activeState` function (Section 13.7.2, page 729). The detailed semantics of the state machine constructs is defined in Section 13.7.4, page 732.

Since these state machines are based on clocked synchronous language constructs, an appropriate application is modeling safety critical control software, for example, for aircraft applications, since the models can be statically checked.

13.7.1 State Machine States

Any Modelica block instance *without* continuous-time equations or algorithms can potentially be a state of a state machine. All equations in such a state have to be clocked, where a continuous-time clock is not allowed. A state might contain clocked or clocked discretized continuous-time equations. In the latter case the equations are numerically solved between the previous and the next clock tick if the corresponding state is active.

13.7.2 Transitions and State Operators

A cluster of instances which are coupled by `transition` equations makes a *state machine*. All parts of a state machine must have the *same* clock. All transitions leaving one state must have different priorities. One and only one instance in each state machine must be marked as *initial* by appearing in an `initialState` equation. The following special kinds of connect-equations are used to define transitions between states and to define the initial state:

	Equation Operators to define a state machine
transition(*from, to, condition, immediate, reset, synchronize, priority*)	The arguments *from* and *to* are block instances and *condition* is a Boolean argument. The optional arguments *immediate*, *reset*, and *synchronize* are of type Boolean, have parameter variability and default values true, true, false respectively. The optional argument *priority* is of type Integer, has parameter variability, and a default value 1. The transition(...) operator defines a transition from instance *from* to instance *to*. The *from* and *to* instances become states of a state machine. The transition fires when *condition* = true if *immediate* = true (this is called an "*immediate* transition", graphically shown with a mark close to the arrow) or previous(*condition*) when *immediate*=false (this is called a "*delayed* transition", graphically shown with a mark at the beginning of the arrow). The argument *priority* defines the priority of firing when several transitions could fire. *priority*=1 is the highest priority. If reset=true, graphically shown as a filled transition arrow, the states of the target state are reinitialized, i.e., state machines are restarted in initial state and local state variables are reset to their start values. If *synchronize*=true, any transition is disabled until all state machines of the from-state have reached final states, i.e., states without outgoing transitions. For the precise details about firing a transition, see Section 13.7.4, page 732.
initialState(*state*)	The argument *state* is the block instance that is defined to be the initial state of a state machine. At the first clock tick of the state machine, this state becomes active.

The transition and initialState equation operators may not be used inside if-equations with non-parametric conditions or in when-equations.

It is possible to query the status of the state machine by using the following operators:

activeState(*state*)	The argument *state* is a block instance. The operator returns true if this instance is a state of a state machine and this state is active at the actual clock tick. If it is not active, the operator returns false. It is an error if the instance is not a state of a state machine.
ticksInState()	The operator returns the number of clock ticks since a transition was made to the currently active state. This function can only be used in transition conditions of state machines not present in states of higher level state machines.
timeInState()	The operator returns the time duration as Real in [s] since a transition was made to the currently active state. This function can only be used in transition conditions of state machines not present within states of higher level state machines.

13.7.3 State Machine Graphic Representation

The recommended layout of state machines is shown below for a simple state machine with five transitions.

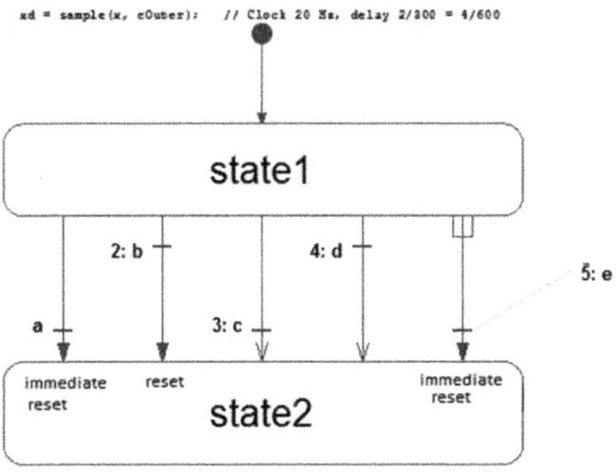

Figure 13-122. A simple state machine with five transitions.

For the five transitions in Figure 13-122 above, the settings are as follows, from left to right:

```
immediate   = true, false, true, false, true;
reset       = true, true, false, false, true;
synchronize = false, false, false, false, true;
priority    = 1, 2, 3, 4, 5.
```

The recommended color is {95, 95, 95} for states and for transition text and {175,175,175} for transition lines.

The annotation for the graphic representation of `transition()` has the following structure: `annotation(Line(...), Text(...));` and for `initialState(): annotation(Line(...));` with `Line` and `Text` annotations defined in Section 11.4.5, page 532. For example:

```
transition(state2, state1, x < 10, immediate=true, reset=true,
           synchronize=false, priority=1)
  annotation(
    Line(
      points={{-40,-16},{-36,-4},{-32,8},{-40,26},{-40,32},{-46,50}},
      color={175,175,175},
      thickness=0.25,
      smooth=Smooth.Bezier),
    Text(
      string="%condition",
      extent={{4,-4},{4,-10}},
      fontSize=10,
      textStyle={TextStyle.Bold},
      textColor={95,95,95},
      horizontalAlignment=TextAlignment.Left),
  );
```

The `Text` annotation representing the transition condition can use the notation `%condition` to refer to the condition expression.

The extent of the `Text` is interpreted relative to either the first point of the `Line`, in the case of `immediate=false`, or the last point (`immediate=true`).

In addition to the line defined by the points of the `Line` annotation, a *perpendicular line* is used to represent the transition. This line is closer to the first point if `immediate=false` otherwise closer to the last point.

If the `condition` text is somewhat distant from the perpendicular line, a dimmed straight line joins the transition text and the perpendicular line. For example, see the rightmost transition above.

If `reset=true`, a *filled arrow head* is used otherwise an open arrow head. For `synchronize=true`, an inverse "fork" symbol is used in the beginning of the arrow. See the rightmost transition in Figure 13-122 above.

The value of the `priority` attribute is prefixing the condition text followed by a colon if `priority>1`.

The `initialState` line has a filled arrow head and a bullet at the opposite end of the initial state as shown above.

13.7.4 Precise State Machine Semantics

For the purpose of defining the semantics of state machines precisely, assume that the data of all transitions are stored in an array of records:

```
record Transition
  Integer from;
  Integer to;
  Boolean immediate = true;
  Boolean reset = true;
  Boolean synchronize = false;
  Integer priority = 1;
end Transition;
```

The transitions have been sorted with lowest priority number last in the array. The states are enumerated from 1 and up. The transition conditions are stored in a separate array `c[:]` since they are time varying.

The semantics model is a discrete-time system with inputs {`c[:]`, `active`, `reset`} with `t` being an array corresponding to the inputs to the `transition` operator, outputs {`activeState`, `activeReset`, `activeResetStates[:]`} and states {`nextState`, `nextReset`, `nextResetStates[:]`}. State machines can be nested in a hierarchy, and can contain state machines called substate machines.

For a top-level state machine, `active` is always true. For substate machines, `active` is true only when the parent state is active. For a top level state machine, `reset` is true at the first activation only. For a substate machine, `reset` is propagated down from the state machines higher up in the hierarchy.

13.7.4.1 State Activation

The state `update` starts from `nextState`, i.e., what has been determined to be the next state at the previous time. The variable `selectedState` takes into account if a reset of the state machine is to be done.

```
output Integer selectedState = if reset then 1 else previous(nextState);
```

The integer `fired` is calculated as the index of the transition to be fired by checking that `selectedState` is the `from`-state and the `condition` is true for an immediate transition or `previous(condition)` is true for a delayed transition. The `max` function returns the *index of the transition with highest priority or 0*.

```
Integer fired = max(if (if t[i].from == selectedState then (if t[i].immediat
e then c[i] else previous(c[i])) else false) then i else 0
                              for i in 1:size(t,1));
```

The start value of `c` is false. This definition would require that the previous value is recorded for all transition conditions. Below is described an equivalent semantics which just require to record the value of one integer variable `delayed`.

The integer `immediate` is calculated as the index of the immediate transition to potentially be fired by checking that `selectedState` is the `from`-state and the condition is true. The `max` function returns the *index of the transition with true condition and highest priority or 0*.

```
Integer immediate = max(if (if  t[i].immediate and t[i].from == selectedStat
e then c[i] else false) then i else 0 for i in 1:size(t,1));
```

In a similar way, the integer `delayed` is calculated as the index for a potentially *delayed transition*, i.e., a *transition taking place at the next clock tick*. In this case the `from`-state needs to be equal to `nextState`:

```
Integer delayed =  max(if (if not t[i].immediate and t[i].from == nextState
 then c[i] else false) then i else 0 for i in 1:size(t,1));
```

The transition to be fired is determined as follows, taking into account that a delayed transition might have higher priority than an immediate transition:

```
Integer fired = max(previous(delayed), immediate);
```

The variable `nextState` is set to the found transitions `to`-state:

```
Integer nextState = if active then (if fired > 0 then t[fired].to else selec
tedState) else previous(nextState);
```

In order to define synchronized transitions, each state machine must determine which are the *final states*, that is, *states without from-transitions* and to determine if the state machine currently is in a final state:

```
Boolean finalStates[nStates] = {max(if t[j].from == i then 1 else 0 for
  j in 1:size(t,1)) == 0 for i in 1:nStates};
Boolean stateMachineInFinalState = finalStates[activeState];
```

To enable a `synchronize` transition, all the `stateMachineInFinalState` conditions of all state machines within the meta state must be true. An example is given below (Section 13.7.4.4, page 734) in the semantic example model.

13.7.4.2 Reset Handling

A state can be *reset* for two reasons:

- The *whole state machine* has been *reset* from its context. In this case, *all states* must be *reset*, and the initial state becomes active.
- A `reset` *transition* has been fired. Then, its target state is *reset*, but not other states.

The first *reset* mechanism is handled by the `activeResetStates` and `nextResetStates` vectors. The state machine `reset` flag is propagated and maintained to each state individually:

```
output Boolean activeResetStates[nStates]= {if reset then true else previous
(nextResetStates[i]) for i in 1:nStates};
```

until a state is eventually executed, then its corresponding `reset` condition is set to false:

```
Boolean nextResetStates[nStates] = if active then {if activeState == i then
false else activeResetStates[i] for i in 1:nStates}
```

The second reset mechanism is implemented with the `selectedReset` and `nextReset` variables. If no `reset` transition is fired, the `nextReset` is set to `false` for the next cycle.

13.7.4.3 Activation handling

The execution of a substate machine has to be suspended when its enclosing state is not active. This activation flag is given as a Boolean input `active`. When this flag is `true`, the substate machine maintains its previous state by guarding the equations of the state variables `nextState`, `nextReset` and `nextResetStates`.

13.7.4.4 State Machines Semantics Summary

The entire semantics of the state machines constructs is given by the model below:

```
model StateMachineSemantics "Semantics of state machines"
  parameter Integer nStates;
  parameter Transition t[:] "Array of transition data sorted in priority";
  input Boolean c[size(t,1)] "Transition conditions sorted in priority";
  Boolean active "true if the state machine is active";
  Boolean reset  "true when the state machine should be reset";

  Integer selectedState = if reset then 1 else previous(nextState);
  Boolean selectedReset = if reset then true else previous(nextReset);

// For strong (immediate) and weak (delayed) transitions
  Integer immediate = max(if (if t[i].immediate and t[i].from ==
    selectedState then c[i] else false) then i else 0 for i in 1:size(t,1));
  Integer delayed = max(if (if not t[i].immediate and t[i].from == nextState
    then c[i] else false) then i else 0 for i in 1:size(t,1));
  Integer fired = max(previous(delayed), immediate);
  output Integer activeState = if reset then 1 elseif fired > 0 then
    t[fired].to else selectedState;
  output Boolean activeReset = if reset then true elseif fired > 0 then
    t[fired].reset else selectedReset;

// Update states
  Integer nextState = if active then activeState else previous(nextState);
  Boolean nextReset = if active then false else previous(nextReset);

// Delayed resetting of individual states
  output Boolean activeResetStates[nStates] = {if reset then true else
    previous(nextResetStates[i]) for i in 1:nStates};
  Boolean nextResetStates[nStates] = if active then {if selectedState == i
    then false else activeResetStates[i] for i in 1:nStates}
    else previous(nextResetStates);

  Boolean finalStates[nStates] = {max(if t[j].from == i then 1 else 0
    for j in 1:size(t,1)) == 0 for i in 1:nStates};
  Boolean stateMachineInFinalState = finalStates[activeState];
end StateMachineSemantics;
```

13.7.4.5 Merging Variable Definitions

When a state class uses an `outer output` declaration, the equations have access to the corresponding variable declared `inner`. Special rules are then needed to maintain the single assignment rule since multiple definition of such outer variables in different mutually exclusive states needs to be merged.

In each state, the outer output variables are solved for, and for each such variable a single definition is formed:

```
v := if activeState(state1) then expre1
      elseif activeState(state2) then expre2
      elseif ...
      else last(v)
```
(13-23)

The operator `last()` is special internal semantic operator which just returns its input. It is used to mark for the sorting (Section 17.1.7, page 989) that the incidence/occurrence of its argument should be ignored. A start value must be given to the variable if not assigned in the initial state.

A new assignment equation is formed which might be merged on higher levels in nested state machines.

13.7.4.6 Merging Connections from Multiple Outputs to an Input

Since instances of blocks can be used as states of a state machine it is natural to *extend* the connection semantics of Modelica to *allow several outputs to be connected to one input.*

It is possible to *connect several outputs to an input* if all the outputs comes from states of the same state machine. In such cases, we get the following constraint equations:

$$u_1 = u_2 = \ldots = y_1 = y_2 = \ldots \tag{13-24}$$

with u_i inputs and y_i outputs. The semantics is defined as follows. Introduce a variable v representing the signal flow and rewrite the equation above as a set of equations for u_i and a set of assignment equations for v:

```
v := if activeState(state1) then y1 else last(v);
v := if activeState(state2) then y2 else last(v);
...
u1 = v
u2 = v
...
```
(13-25)

The merge of the variable definitions of v is then made according to Section 13.7.4.5, page 734. The result is as follows after simplification:

```
v := if activeState(state1) then y1 elseif activeState(state2)
then y2 elseif ... else last(v)
u1 = v
u2 = v
...
```
(13-26)

13.7.5 Example of an Hierarchical State Machine

Consider the hierarchical state machine model in Figure 13-123. The hierarchical state machine model demonstrates the following properties:

- The state `state1` is a meta state with two parallel state machines inside it.
- The state `stateA` declares `v` as an `outer output` variable. The state `state1` is at an intermediate level and declares `v` as `inner outer output`, that is, matches the lower level `outer v` by being `inner` and also matches the higher level `inner v` by being `outer`. The top level declares `v` as `inner` and gives the start value.
- The variable `count` is defined with a start value in `state1`. It is reset when a `reset` transition (v>=20) is made to `state1`.
- The state `stateX` declares the local variable `w` to be equal to `v` declared as `inner input`.
- The state `stateY` declares a local counter `j`. It is reset at start and as a consequence of the `reset` transition (`v>=20`) to `state1` as follows: When the `reset` transition (`v>=20`) fires, then the variables of the active states are reset immediately, i.e., `count` from `state1`, and `i` from `stateX`. The variables of other states are only reset at the time instants when the states become active. Thus `j` in `StateY` is reset to 0, when the transition `stateX.i>20` fires (after `state1` became active again, that is, after the reset transition `v>=20`).
- Synchronizing the exit from the two *parallel* state machines of `state1` is done by checking that `stateD` and `stateY` are active using the `activeState` function (Section 13.7.2, page 729).

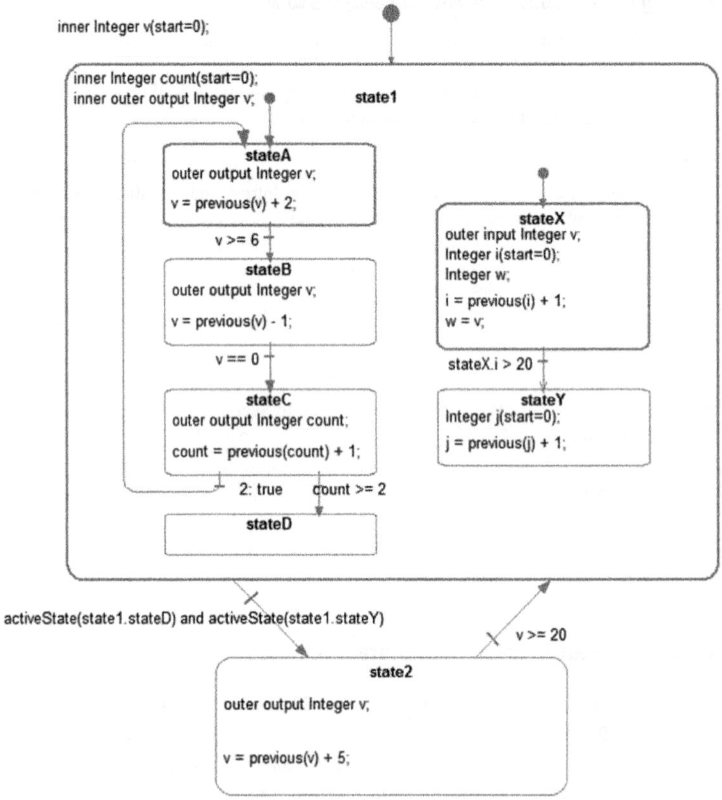

Figure 13-123. An hierarchical state machine model.

The Modelica code (without annotations) is:

```
block HierarchicalAndParallelStateMachine1

  inner Integer v(start=0);

  State1 state1;
  State2 state2;
equation
  initialState(state1);
  transition(state1,state2,activeState(state1.stateD) and
    activeState(state1.stateY), immediate=false);
  transition(state2,state1,v >= 20, immediate=false);

public
  block State1
    inner Integer count(start=0);
    inner outer output Integer v;

    block StateA
      outer output Integer v;
```

```
      equation
        v = previous(v) + 2;
      end StateA;
      StateA stateA;

      block StateB
        outer output Integer v;
      equation
        v = previous(v) - 1;
      end StateB;
      StateB stateB;

      block StateC
        outer output Integer count;
      equation
        count = previous(count) + 1;
      end StateC;
      StateC stateC;

      block StateD
      end StateD;
      StateD stateD;

    equation
      initialState(stateA);
      transition(stateA, stateB, v >= 6, immediate=false);
      transition(stateB, stateC, v == 0, immediate=false);
      transition(stateC, stateA, true, immediate=false, priority=2);
      transition(stateC, stateD, count >= 2, immediate=false);

    public
      block StateX
        outer input Integer v;
        Integer i(start=0);
        Integer w; // = v;
      equation
        i = previous(i) + 1;
        w = v;
      end StateX;
      StateX stateX;

      block StateY
        Integer j(start=0);
      equation
        j = previous(j) + 1;
      end StateY;
      StateY stateY;

    equation
      initialState(stateX);
      transition(stateX, stateY, stateX.i > 20, immediate=false, reset=false);
    end State1;

    block State2
      outer output Integer v;
    equation
      v = previous(v) + 5;
    end State2;
  end HierarchicalAndParallelStateMachine1;
```

The behavior of the hierarchical state machine can be seen in the plots of *v* in Figure 13-124.

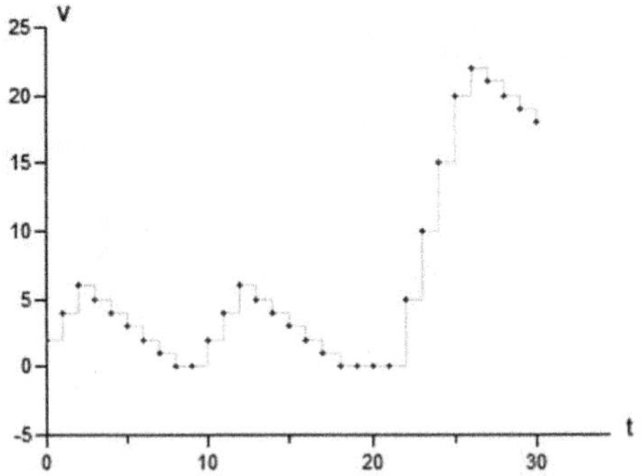

Figure 13-124. Plot of hierarchical state machine behavior.

The transition from `state1` to `state2` could have been done with a `synchronize` transition with `condition=true` instead. The semantically equivalent model is shown below:

```
block HierarchicalAndParallelStateMachine2

  extends StateMachineSemantics(
    nStates=2,
    t={Transition(from=1, to=2, immediate=false, synchronize=true),
       Transition(from=2, to=1, immediate=false)},
    c={true, v >= 20});
  Boolean init(start=true) = sample(false);

  block State1
    Boolean active;
    Boolean reset;

    outer input Integer v_previous;
    inner output Integer v;

    inner Integer count(start=0);
    inner Integer count_previous = if reset then 0 else previous(count);


    block StateMachineOf_stateA
      extends StateMachineSemantics(
        nStates=4,
        t={Transition(from=1, to=2, immediate=false),
           Transition(from=2, to=3, immediate=false),
           Transition(from=3, to=1, immediate=false),
           Transition(from=3, to=4, immediate=false)},
        c={v >= 6, v==0, true, count >= 2});

    outer input Integer v_previous;
    outer output Integer v;

    outer input Integer count_previous;
    outer output Integer count;

    equation
      inFinalState = true; // no macro states
      if activeState == 1 then
        // equations for stateA
```

```
        v = v_previous + 2;
        count = count_previous;
      elseif activeState == 2 then
        // equations for stateB
        v = v_previous - 1;
        count = count_previous;
      elseif activeState == 3 then
        // equations for stateC
        v = v_previous;
        count = count_previous + 1;
      else // if activeState == 4 then
        // equations for stateD
        v = v_previous;
        count = count_previous;
      end if;
    end StateMachineOf_stateA;

    StateMachineOf_stateA stateMachineOf_stateA(active=active, reset=reset);


    block StateMachineOf_stateX
      extends StateMachineSemantics(
        nStates=2,
        t={Transition(from=1, to=2, immediate=false, reset=false)},
        c={i>25});
      outer input Integer v;
      Integer i(start=0);
      Integer i_previous;
      Integer j(start=0);
      Integer j_previous;
      Integer w;
    equation
      inFinalState = true; // no macro states
      if activeState == 1 then
        // equations for stateX
        i_previous = if activeReset or activeResetStates[1] then 0
                     else previous(i);
        j_previous = previous(j);
        i = i_previous + 1;
        w = v;
        j = j_previous;
      else // if activeState == 2 then
        // equations for stateY
        i_previous = previous(i);
        j_previous = if activeReset or activeResetStates[2] then 0
                     else previous(j);
        i = i_previous;
        w = previous(w);
        j = j_previous + 1;
      end if;
    end StateMachineOf_stateX;

    StateMachineOf_stateX stateMachineOf_stateX(active=active, reset=reset);


    Boolean inFinalState = stateMachineOf_stateA.stateMachineInFinalState
                          and stateMachineOf_stateX.stateMachineInFinalState;

  end State1;

  State1 state1;
```

```
  Integer v(start=0);
  inner Integer v_previous = if reset then 0 else previous(v);
equation
  active = true;
  reset = previous(init);

  if activeState == 1 then
    // equations for state1
    inFinalState = state1.inFinalState;
    state1.active = true;
    state1.reset = activeReset or activeResetStates[1];
    v = state1.v;
  else // if activeState == 2 then
    // equations for state2
    inFinalState = true; // not macro state
    state1.active = false;
    state1.reset = false;
    v = previous(v) + 5;
  end if;

end HierarchicalAndParallelStateMachine2;
```

13.7.6 Comparison to other State Machine Approaches

The Modelica state machine constructs have a similar modeling power as Statecharts (Harel 1987). The design is inspired by mode automata and is basically the one from Lucid Synchrone 3.0 (Pouzet 2006), (Pouzet 2013). The following properties are different compared to Lucid Synchrone 3.0:

- Lucid Synchrone has two kinds of transitions: "*strong*" and "*weak*" transitions. Strong transitions are executed before the actions of a state are evaluated and weak transitions are executed after the actions of a state are evaluated. This can lead to surprising behavior, because the actions of a state are skipped if it is activated by a weak transition and exited by a true strong transition.
  For this reason the Modelica state machines use `immediate` (the same as "strong") and `delayed` transitions. Delayed transitions are `immediate` transitions where the condition is automatically delayed with an implicit `previous(...)`.
- Parallel state machines can be explicitly synchronized using the `activeState` function (Section 13.7.2, page 729), similarly to parallel branches in Sequential Function Charts. This often occurring operation can also be defined in Statecharts or in Lucid Synchrone state machines but only indirectly with appropriate conditions on transitions.

In comparison to Statecharts, the Modelica state machines have the following similarities and differences:

For interlevel transitions, there will still be an issue: entry/exit actions for states at different hierarchies has to be executed in a specific order. This will need algorithmic code in contrast to equations.

- Hierarchical decomposition of states, i.e., state machines within states, is present in both.
- State entry/exit actions are present in Statecharts but not yet in Modelica state machines. They may be introduced in a future version. However, for inter-level transitions there will be a need for entry/exit actions for states at different hierarchies to be executed in a specific order, to be specified by algorithmic code or some other mechanism.
- Decision/Junction/Fork/Join/History pseudo states in Statecharts are partly supported. In Modelica state machines history is kept as long as the `reset` operation is not used. There is a Join functionality called `synchronize` with two parallel state machines joining before leaving a

substate. They both have to go to a final state before leaving, see the example in Section 13.7.5, page 735. Fork can be done if you encapsulate two initial states in a substate. Regarding Decision/Junction, these might be added in a future version after more analysis of consequences, e.g., in relation to compound transitions.

- Compound transitions, that is, groups of simple transitions that involve decision or junction pseudo states, and so on. This might be added a future version after more analysis. For example, what happens when continuous states are introduced? If there is an event iteration, is it possible that the state machine switches to a substate within the same clock cycle? All issues with extension to continuous-time equations are not yet analyzed.
- Inter-level transitions, that is, transitions that cross states hierarchy borders. This is not present in Modelica state machines since it would make the semantics more complex and hard to check. It is not present in Lucid Synchrone either. This is a powerful feature that is useful for certain kinds of modeling, but prevents compositionality of state machine models, that is, composing state machines, and so on. Thus, a trade-off between expressiveness and compositionality.

Regarding Statecharts, a list of general issues and challenges as well as a summary of the then existing Statechart variants is presented in (Beeck 1994). In (Crane and Dingel 2005), it is pointed out that different UML Statechart variants are usually not compatible even though their graphical syntax is the same, and that execution semantics of the different variants strongly depends on implementation decisions.

Several issues with UML State Machines semantics are discussed and resolved in (Schamai, Pohlmann, Fritzson, Paredis, Helle, Strobel 2010; Schamai, Fritzson, Paredis 2013; Schamai 2013), which also contains a rather complete translation of UML State Machines to algorithmic Modelica. This is implemented in the ModelicaML (Section 18.3.3, page 1022) extension to Modelica, allowing unified UML-Modelica modeling.

An important objective with the current design of Modelica clocked state machines is to provide standardized syntax and semantics to support model portability.

13.8 Summary

This chapter presented the important concepts of discrete events, hybrid continuous-discrete modeling, and modeling of concurrent systems. We started by discussing real-time systems and defining the notion of event based on conditional equation semantics as well as clock ticks. Then we again described the difference between discrete-time and continuous-time variables, and made an in-depth presentation of the synchronous data flow principle for Modelica.

We showed how events are created internally or externally to Modelica followed by presentations of a number of event-related built-in functions and operators. The notion of discrete-time was presented, both unclocked and clocked discrete-time. We explained how to handle events, for example, using if-equations or when-equations, and described when to use event priority, event synchronization and propagation, and how to handle multiple events at the same point in time.

A number of formalisms and model examples for discrete systems were presented, together with their Modelica representations. These included sampled systems—both periodic and aperiodic, finite state automata, cellular automata modeling the game of life, models for stochastic processes applied to a server with a queue, the discrete event systems specification formalism (DEVS) expressed in Modelica and applied to a job shop model, as well as Petri nets expressed in Modelica and modeling a job shop system. Many of the models were shown in both unclocked and clocked versions.

We described hybrid system modeling and simulation together with two examples: a hybrid tank model with a discrete controller and a mode switching model comprising a DC motor transmission with elastic backlash. Concurrent access to shared resources was exemplified by the dining philosophers problem.

Finally we made a detailed presentation of the clocked synchronous language features, followed by a presentation of clocked synchronous Modelica state machines.

13.9 Literature

Synchronous data flow languages and the corresponding synchronous data flow principle are described in (Halbwachs 1993). A short overview of a number of discrete and hybrid formalisms and their relation to the object-oriented modeling language Omola can be found in (Andersson 1994).

Petri nets are described in (Peterson 1981), the first Modelica library representing Petri Nets is presentented in (Mosterman, Otter, and Elmqvist 1998). The currently most comprehensive and general Modelica Petri Net library, called PNLib, is described in (Proß and Bachmann 2012).

The first DEVS representation in Modelica is presented briefly in (Bunus and Fritzson 2000), traditional DEVS in (Zeigler 1984; Zeigler 1990), whereas hybrid Modeling in Modelica based on the synchronous data flow principle is described in (Otter, Elmqvist, and Mattsson, 1999).

Stephen Wolfram presents cellular automata and their use as a general representation (Wolfram 2002).

The method of inline integration, that is, inline expansion of numeric solver difference equations, is described in (Elmqvist, Otter, and Cellier, 1995). A later usage of inline integration is for improved parallel multi-core numeric solution of equations (Lundvall, Stavåker, Fritzson, and Kessler 2008).

Synchronous state charts can be translated to equation-based Modelica (Ferreira and de Oliveira 1999), and asynchronous state charts to algorithmic Modelica (Pereira-Remelhe 2002), (Schamai, Pohlmann, Fritzson, Paredis, Helle, Strobel 2010), (Schamai, Fritzson, and Paredis 2013), and (Schamai 2013).

Section 13.7.6, page 740, gives a *comparison* including literature references between the Modelica 3.3 *state machines* and other state machine approaches.

As mentioned in Section 13.6.15, page 721, a continuous-time Modelica model can be utilized in a sampled data control system by solving the continuous-time equations with a defined integration method between clock ticks, e.g., to be used for inverting the nonlinear dynamic model of a plant (Looye, Thümmel, Kurze, Otter, and Bals, 2005).

The clocked synchronous Modelica approach described in Section 13.6 is based on the clock calculus and inference system proposed by (Colaco and Pouzet 2003) and implemented in Lucid Synchrone version 2 and 3 (Pouzet 2006). However, the Modelica approach also uses multirate periodic clocks based on rational arithmetic introduced by (Forget, Boniol, Lesens, and Pagetti 2008), as an extension of the Lucid Synchrone semantics. These approaches belong to the class of synchronous languages (Benveniste, Caspi, Edwards, Halbwachs, Guernic, and Simone 2003).

Almost all the text in Section 13.6 about clocked synchronous modeling is from Chapter 16 in MLS2013—the Modelica Language Specification 2013 (Modelica Association 2013), and almost all text in Section 13.7 is from Chapter 17 in MLS2013. The version in this book has been slightly rearranged and improved for readability, including adding more examples.

The Modelica language elements for describing clocked synchronous behavior, described in Chapter 16 of MLS2013, was mainly developed by Hilding Elmqvist, Martin Otter, and Sven Erik Mattsson. Hilding Elmqvist wrote a detailed tutorial abouit this design. Sven Erik Mattsson developed a test implementation of the language elements and the needed new algorithms. Based on the prototype, tests and feedback have mainly been provided by Martin Otter and Bernhard Thiele. Additional feedback on the clocked synchronous language design was given by Albert Beneviste and Marc Pouzet.

The language elements to define clocked synchronous state machines, described in Chapter 17 of MLS2013, were mainly developed by Hilding Elmqvist with contributions from Francois Dupont, Sven Erik Mattsson and Fabien Gaucher. Hilding Elmqvist wrote a tutorial on the design. Sven Erik Mattsson and Carl-Fredrik Abelson developed a test implementation. Based on the prototype, tests and feedback have mainly been provided by Alain Thura, Emmanuel Ledinot, Claire Campan, and Martin Malmheden.

13.10 Exercises

Exercise 13-1:

a) What is the single assignment principle in Modelica?
b) What are over-constrained and nondeterministic systems?

Exercise 13-2:

Write a model that emits a signal that increases by 2 every 3 ticks using the unclocked `sample` function. Rewrite this model using clock-based constructs.

Exercise 13-3:

Explain the functionality of `pre()` and `previous()`, including their similarities and differences.

Exercise 13-4:

We want to design a model which during the first 20 seconds emits a signal, stops for 20 seconds, and then continues to emit the signal.

- Is the model below correct?
- If not, what should be changed?

```
model MultipleEvents
  discrete Integer x(start=1);
  Boolean signal(start=false);
equation
  when time =< 20 then
    signal = true;
  end when;
  when time > 20 then
    signal = false ;
  end when;
  when time > 40 then
    signal = true;
  end when;
end MultipleEvents;
```

Exercise 13-5:

Write a model that emits a signal `s` with Boolean value `true` from time `t`= 20 to `t` = 80 but only if the value of `y` is above a certain level, otherwise it emits `s=false`.

Exercise 13-6:

- What are hybrid systems?
- Give an example of such a system.

Chapter 14

Basic Laws of Nature

When modeling a system, it is essential to use the appropriate laws of nature that govern the behavior of the different parts of the system. These laws are often expressed as equations that can be stated in Modelica classes. However, even if application models usually are built by combining model components from libraries of predefined classes and functions, it can be useful to expose the basic equations of each application domain to gain an increased understanding of the basic mechanisms behind the behavior. This is the purpose of this chapter.

14.1 Energy Conservation

The principle of *conservation of energy* is one of the most fundamental laws of nature. It can be formulated as follows:

- The amount of energy in a closed system can neither be created nor destroyed.

Here we talk about energy in the general sense, since matter is equivalent to energy according to Einstein's famous law:

$$E = mc^2 \tag{14-1}$$

where E is the energy, m is the mass, and c is the speed of light. A consequence of the principle of *conservation of energy* (or similarly for charge, mass, etc.) for a *closed* system is the following:

- When energy (or charge, mass, etc.) flows together at a certain point, without storage at that point, the sum of all *flows* into that point is zero.

This is the background for the Modelica *sum-to-zero rule* for flow variables at connection points. In the electrical domain this corresponds to Kirchhoff's current law, and in the mechanical domain Newton's second law that the sum of all forces acting at a specific point is zero if there is no acceleration.

Energy is always transported using some carrier, which in the case of electrical current is charged particles, and in the case of translational or rotational mechanical systems is linear or angular momentum respectively. Different domains will usually have different flow quantities, since they normally use different carriers.

The concept of *potential* is a measure of the level of energy. The *choice* of a *potential* quantity for a particular domain *must* always be such that at *connection points* all *potential* variables of connected components are equal. This is essential for the *equality rule* regarding potential variables in Modelica, that the variable values are equal at a connection.

Table 14-1 summarizes possible choices of energy carrier together with associated potential and flow quantities for a few common physical domains, as well as a selection of corresponding Modelica libraries.

Table 14-1. Energy carriers with associated potential and flow quantities for a set of common physical domains.

Domain Type	Potential	Flow	Carrier	Modelica Library
Electrical	Voltage	Electric current	Charge	Electrical
Translational 1D	Position	Force	Linear momentum	Mechanical.Translational
Rotational 1D	Angle	Torque	Angular momentum	Mechanical.Rotational
Mechanical 3D	Position (3D) and Rotation angle (3D)	Force (3D) and Torque (3D)	Linear and angular momentum	Mechanical.MultiBody
Magnetic	Magnetic potential	Magnetic flux rate	Magnetic flux	–
Flow, Hydraulic	Pressure	Volume flow rate	Volume	OpenHydraulics, etc.
Heat	Temperature	Heat flow rate	Heat	Thermal, etc.
Chemical	Chemical potential	Particle flow rate	Particles	Fluid

In the rest of this chapter, we will present a selection of the basic laws of nature for the above-mentioned physical domains as well as for some additional domains.

14.2 Analog Electrical Circuits

Analog electrical circuits consist of passive components such as resistors, capacitors, inductors, transformers, and so on, as well as active components such as transistors and amplifiers. Here we give the basic equations governing some of the simpler components in electrical circuits. Several of these components were introduced already in Section 2.11, page 44. The corresponding Modelica library, called `Modelica.Electrical.Analog`, is presented in Section 16.6.1, page 929.

The basic analog electrical quantities are the *voltage* quantity $v(t)$ (V—volt) for potential and the flow rate quantity *current* $i(t)$ (A—ampere). These are used in the basic equations of analog electrical systems as well as in interfaces in the form of connector classes.

An ideal linear resistor is described by Ohm's law, where the constant R is the resistance (ohm) of the component:

$$v(t) = R \cdot i(t) \tag{14-2}$$

An ideal capacitor is defined by the equation below, where the voltage change is proportional to the current through the capacitor, and the constant C (F—farad) is its capacitance:

$$i(t) = C \cdot \frac{d}{dt} v(t) \tag{14-3}$$

or using the shorter notation $\dot{v}(t)$ for time derivative:

$$i(t) = C\,\dot{v}(t) \tag{14-4}$$

The voltage over an ideal inductor is proportional to the change in current $i(t)$, with the constant L (henry):

$$v(t) = L \cdot \frac{d}{dt} i(t) \tag{14-5}$$

A nonlinear resistor can be described as follows:

$$v(t) = h_1(i(t)) \tag{14-6}$$

or

$$i(t) = h_2(v(t)) \tag{14-7}$$

The power dissipation (in some cases also including conversion to electromagnetic field energy) of an electrical component is defined by the product of the voltage drop over the component and the current through the component:

$$P(t) = v(t) \cdot i(t) \tag{14-8}$$

Kirchhoff's laws describe connected components in electrical circuits. The sum of the voltages (both positive and negative) around a loop is zero:

$$\sum_k v_k(t) = 0 \tag{14-9}$$

Kirchhoff's current law states that the sum of all currents (with sign) into a node is zero:

$$\sum_k i_k(t) = 0 \tag{14-10}$$

Both relationships are illustrated in Figure 14-1.

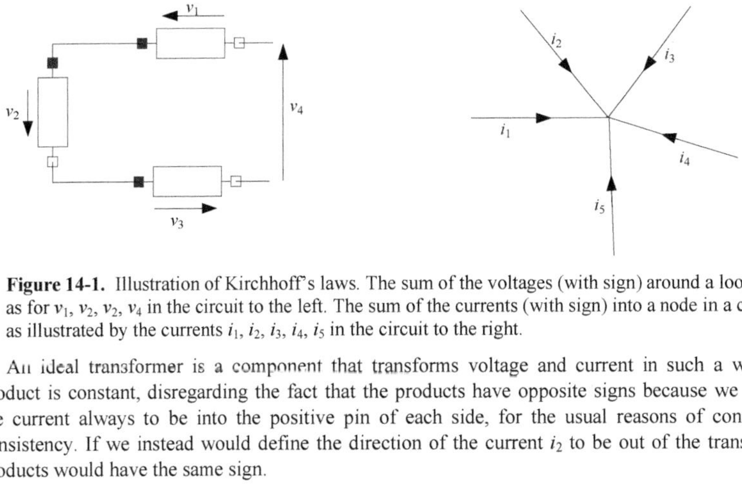

Figure 14-1. Illustration of Kirchhoff's laws. The sum of the voltages (with sign) around a loop is zero, e.g. as for v_1, v_2, v_2, v_4 in the circuit to the left. The sum of the currents (with sign) into a node in a circuit is zero, as illustrated by the currents i_1, i_2, i_3, i_4, i_5 in the circuit to the right.

An ideal transformer is a component that transforms voltage and current in such a way that their product is constant, disregarding the fact that the products have opposite signs because we have defined the current always to be into the positive pin of each side, for the usual reasons of connectivity and consistency. If we instead would define the direction of the current i_2 to be out of the transformer, both products would have the same sign.

$$v_1 \cdot i_1 = v_2 \cdot i_2 \tag{14-11}$$

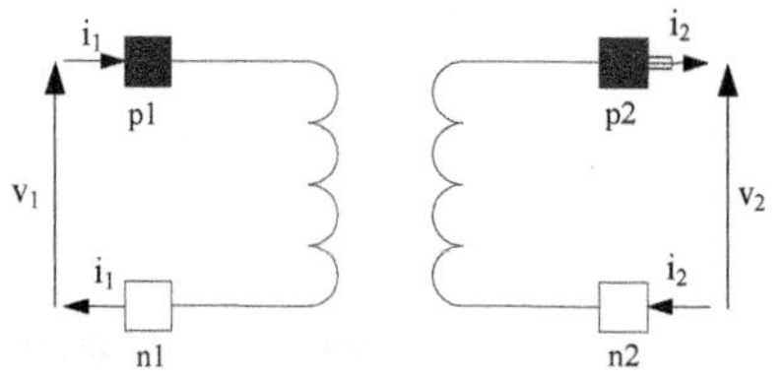

Figure 14-2. An ideal transformer.

The transformer is ideal since we assume that properties such as resistance, stray inductance, and so on are negligible, which is often the case for many practical purposes. The relationships between the voltages and the currents are given by the two equations below. The voltage v_2 is decreased by a factor n, whereas the current i_2 is increased a factor of n compared to v_1 and i_1 respectively. The factor n is a real number (really a rational number) called the *turns ratio*, being the relation between the number of turns in the two coils of the transformer.

$$v_2 = \frac{1}{n} \cdot v_1 \qquad (14\text{-}12)$$
$$i_2 = n \cdot i_1$$

The current directions shown in Figure 14-2 make a positive current i_1 cause a positive current i_2, which is common in most textbook presentations of transformers. However, the corresponding Modelica library component `IdealTransformer` shown in Section 16.6.1.4, page 933, has the opposite direction of the current i_2 since we have defined the current to be always into the positive pin of each side, for the usual reasons of connectivity and consistency. This causes a minus sign to appear in the equations involving i_2 in the Modelica class.

A transformer with finite inductance is a more realistic model since the coils in a transformer typically behave as inductors:

$$v_1 = L_1 \cdot \frac{d}{dt} i_1 + M \cdot \frac{d}{dt} i_2 \qquad (14\text{-}13)$$
$$v_2 = M \cdot \frac{d}{dt} i_1 + L_2 \cdot \frac{d}{dt} i_2$$

Here L_1, L_2, and M are the primary, secondary, and coupling inductances respectively. The corresponding Modelica model appears below:

```
model Transformer "Transformer with inductance"
  extends Modelica.Electrical.Analog.Interfaces.TwoPort;
  parameter SIunits.Inductance L1=1 "Primary inductance";
  parameter SIunits.Inductance L2=1 "Secondary inductance";
  parameter SIunits.Inductance M=1  "Coupling inductance";
equation
  v1 = L1*der(i1) + M*der(i2);
  v2 = M*der(i1) + L2*der(i2);
end Transformer;   // from Modelica.Electrical.Analog.Basic.Transformer
```

The `EMF` (*Electro Motoric Force*) converter is one of the more interesting components in the electrical library since it is a transducer that converts electrical energy to mechanical rotational energy (Figure 14-3). This class is an idealized model of the most important properties of a voltage-to-rotation converter excluding resistance, inductance, and inertia. It is both electrical and mechanical, but is placed in the `Electrical.Analog.Basic` library.

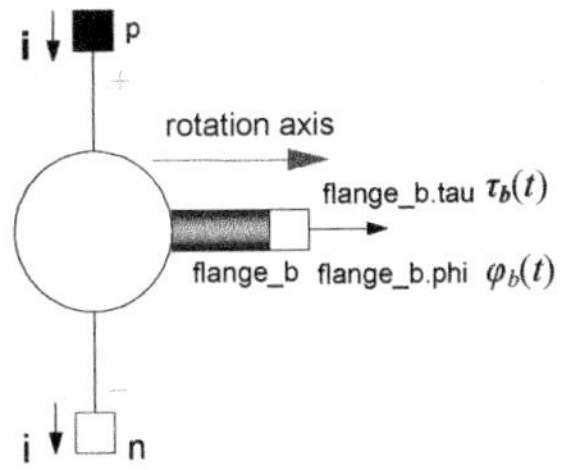

Figure 14-3. EMF—Electro Motoric Force converter.

The three most important equations of the `EMF` class are given below. The rotational speed $\omega(t)$ is of course equal to the derivative of the rotation angle $\varphi_b(t)$. The voltage $v(t)$ is proportional to the rotational speed $\omega(t)$. The torque $\tau_b(t)$ is proportional to the current $i(t)$ through the coil. The `EMF` class has two `Pin` type connectors that transmit voltage $v(t)$ and current $i(t)$, and a `rotFlange_b` connector that transmits absolute angle $\varphi_b(t)$ and torque $\tau_b(t)$.

$$\begin{aligned} \omega(t) &= \dot{\varphi}_b(t) \\ v(t) &= k \cdot \omega(t) \\ \tau_b(t) &= -k \cdot i(t) \end{aligned} \tag{14-14}$$

The Modelica `EMF` class from the `Electrical.Analog.Basic` library is shown below. It is used, for example, in the DC motor application described in Section 15.1, page 794.

```
model EMF "Electromotoric force (electric/mechanic transformer)"
  import Modelica.Electrical.Analog.Interfaces;
  import Modelica.Mechanics.Rotational.Interfaces.Flange_b;
  parameter Real       k(final unit="N.m/A")=1 "Transformation coefficient";
  SIunits.Voltage      v     "Voltage drop between the two pins";
  SIunits.Current      i     "Current flowing from positive to negative pin";
  SIunits.AngularVelocity     w "Angular velocity of flange_b";
  Interfaces.PositivePin      p;
  Interfaces.NegativePin      n;
  Flange_b                    flange_b;
equation
  v = p.v-n.v;
  0 = p.i+n.i;
  i = p.i;
  w = der(flange_b.phi);
  k*w = v;
  flange_b.tau = -k*i;
end EMF;   // from Modelica.Electrical.Analog.Basic.EMF
```

14.3 Mechanical Translational 1D

The dynamics of mechanical translational systems in one dimension are described by the equations covering this application domain. These equations are Newton's laws together with a few additional laws for specific translational components like springs, dampers, etc. The corresponding library is `Modelica.Mechanical.Translational`, described in Section 16.11.3, page 951. The basic concepts for this library together with a few important classes are presented in detail in Chapter 5, page 196. Note that the generalization to three dimensions, that is, the dynamics of mechanical systems consisting of multiple bodies moving in three dimensions, is discussed in Section 14.8, page 770.

This domain uses the following basic quantities: force $f(t)$ (N—newton) as the flow rate quantity and position $s(t)$ (m—meter) as the potential quantity. These two quantities are used both in a number of equations, as well as in interfaces defined by connector classes.

The common quantities *velocity* $v(t)$ (m/s—meter/second) and *acceleration* $a(t)$ (m^2/s—$meter^2/$ second,) are defined as follows:

$$v(t) = \dot{s}(t)$$
$$a(t) = \dot{v}(t) \tag{14-15}$$

Newton's second law applies— the sum of all forces on a *rigid body* is equal to the constant mass of the body multiplied with its acceleration:

$$m \cdot a(t) = \sum_i f_i(t) \tag{14-16}$$

This law is used, for example, by the `SlidingMass` class in the `Mechanics.Translational` library, and can be reformulated as follows:

$$\frac{d}{dt}(m \cdot v(t)) = \sum_i f_i(t) \tag{14-17}$$

The term $m \cdot v(t)$ is often called the *momentum* or *impulse* of the rigid body.

In an equilibrium situation when the body is at rest there is no acceleration, making it possible to simplify Newton's second law so that the sum of the forces is zero:

$$\sum_i f_i(t) = 0 \tag{14-18}$$

The force $f(t)$ exerted by an ideal *elastic spring* is defined by the following equation:

$$f(t) = c \cdot (s(t) - s_0) \tag{14-19}$$

where c is the spring constant, $s(t)$ is the spring length, usually expressed as the position of one of the spring flanges, and s_0 is the length of the spring at rest when it exerts no force. This equation occurs in the `Spring` class described in Chapter 5, page 197, and belongs to the `Mechanics.Translational` library presented in Section 16.11.3, page 951.

The *friction* force between a body and a surface on which the body is sliding in the general case can be expressed as a function h of the velocity:

$$f(t) = h(v(t)) \cdot f_N \tag{14-20}$$

where $v(t)$ is the relative velocity between the surfaces sliding against each other, and f_N is the normal force to these surfaces. In machines the normal force is often constant and therefore known, for example, due to pre-tension of bearings or because the normal force f_N is the controlled pressure force of a clutch or brake. The simple case of *dry friction* force between a body and a surface is described by the following version of the function h:

$$h(v(t)) = \begin{cases} +\mu(|v|) & if\, v(t) > 0 \\ f_0(t) & if\, v(t) = 0 \\ -\mu(|v|) & if\, v(t) < 0 \end{cases} \tag{14-21}$$

Here the force $f_0(t)$ is the frictional force at rest, usually the negative of the sum of the other forces applied to the body given by Newton's second law, force equilibrium for a body which is not accelerating $(\dot{v}(t) = 0)$. If $v(t) \neq 0$, then h is computed as a function of v, and is often a constant.

Viscous friction occurs, for example, in dampers. See for example the model presented in 15.10.9.2, page 898, using `SpringDamper`. Viscous friction is described by the function h below, where the force is proportional to the speed of the body through the viscous medium:

$$h(v(t)) = k \cdot v(t) \tag{14-22}$$

Power lost as heat through friction is expressed by the equation defining the power $P(t)$:

$$P(t) = f(t) \cdot v(t) \tag{14-23}$$

The power transmitted to/from a moving body is

$$P(t) = f(t) \cdot v(t) = m\,\dot{v}(t) \cdot v(t) \tag{14-24}$$

By integrating this expression we obtain the kinetic energy of a moving body:

$$E(t) = \frac{1}{2} m v(t)^2 \tag{14-25}$$

14.4 Mechanical Rotational 1D

The mechanical rotational domain defines the dynamic rotational behavior of mechanical components that rotate along one axis of rotation. Examples are rotating shafts and wheels, torsion springs, gears, and so on. Such components occur in drive trains that are used to transport rotational energy from motors to loads, for example, in cars. The corresponding Modelica library is `Modelica.Mechanics.Rotational`, described in Section 16.11.2, page 948, and certain key concepts and classes are explained in Chapter 5, page 196.

This domain uses the following interface quantities: *torque*, $\tau(t)$ (Nm—newtonmeter), as the flow quantity, and *angular postion*, $\varphi(t)$ (radians), as the potential quantity. The quantity *angular velocity*, $\omega(t)$ (1/s—radians/second), is defined by the following equation:

$$\omega(t) = \dot{\varphi}(t) \tag{14-26}$$

The *rotational version of Newton's second law* states that the sum of all torques exerted on a (rotating) rigid body equals the moment of inertia (J) multiplied by the angular acceleration $\dot{\omega}(t)$:

$$J \cdot \dot{\omega}(t) = \sum_i \tau_i(t) \tag{14-27}$$

This law is used, for example, in the `Inertia` class in the `Rotational` library and is depicted in Figure 14-4. It can be reformulated as follows, where the term $J \cdot \omega(t)$ is often called the *angular momentum* of the body:

$$\frac{d}{dt}(J \cdot \omega(t)) = \sum_i \tau_i(t) \tag{14-28}$$

In an equilibrium situation when the rotational mechanical system is at rest, that is, nonrotating, the sum of the torques is zero:

$$\sum_i \tau_i(t) = 0 \tag{14-29}$$

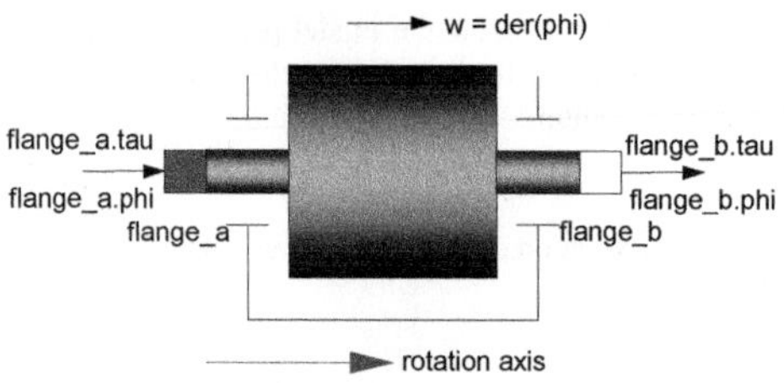

Figure 14-4. A rotating mechanical body with inertia.

The equation for an *elastic torsion spring* is the rotational counterpart of the previously presented translational spring:

$$\tau(t) = c \cdot (\varphi(t) - \varphi_0) \tag{14-30}$$

where c is the torsion spring constant. The applied torque $\tau(t)$ is proportional to the difference between the current angle $\varphi(t)$ and the equilibrium angle φ_0 when no torque is applied.

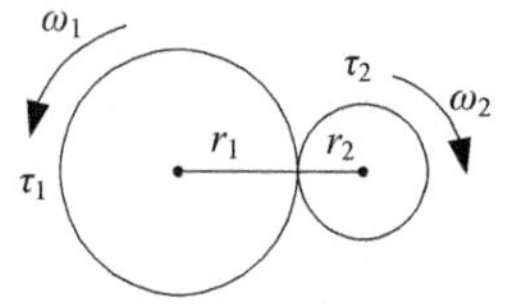

Figure 14-5 A mechanical gear, with gear ratio = r_2/r_1.

An *ideal mechanical gear* transforms torque and rotational movement. The approximation that the gear is *ideal* means that the wheels have no inertia and that no elasticity, friction, damping, or backlash has been taken into account. See the `IdealGear` class in the `Mechanics.Rotational` library, in which the direction of the torque flow quantity τ_2 is opposite to what is shown in Figure 14-4 due to flow direction into the flange. The following equations apply:

$$\begin{aligned} \varphi_1 &= ratio \cdot \varphi_2 \\ \tau_1 &= \frac{1}{ratio} \tau_2 \end{aligned} \tag{14-31}$$

Here the *gear ratio* = r_2/r_1 according to Figure 14-5 is the same as the relation between the circumferences of the gear wheels. By differentiating the first equation and multiplying with the second equation, we obtain:

$$\begin{aligned} \omega_1 &= ratio \cdot \omega_2 \\ \tau_1 \cdot \omega_1 &= \tau_2 \cdot \omega_2 \end{aligned} \tag{14-32}$$

14.5 Flow **Systems and Hydraulics**

Flow systems consist of components containing a flowing substance such as fluid or gas, with typical applications in hydraulics and process industry. In this section we are treating only incompressible fluids for which the volume is not affected by the pressure. Gases are excluded since they are compressible, as well as compressible fluids which are more complicated to model mathematically. In the following we will discuss volume flows. For incompressible fluids, mass flows can be obtained from volume flows by multiplying with the density ρ.

The basic quantities are the *pressure* $p(t)$ (N/m^2) potential quantity and the *volume flow rate* quantity $q(t)$ (m^3/s). These are used in flow equations as well as in interfaces in the form of connector classes. Usually, the pressure difference between ports of a component is used rather than the absolute pressure. The pressure difference $p(t)$:

$$p(t) = p_1(t) - p_2(t) \tag{14-33}$$

between the two ports of a flow component such as a flow resistance, where p_1 and p_2 are the input and output pressures, respectively.

A flow resistance component with laminar (not turbulent) fluid flow of incompressible fluid through a thin tube with friction against the walls is depicted in Figure 14-6.

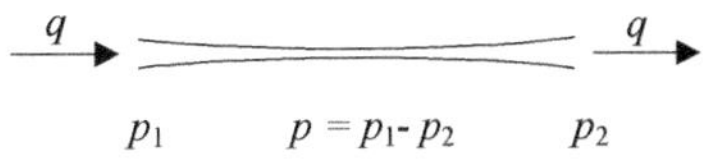

Figure 14-6. Linear flow resistance component with laminar flow. The flow rate is denoted by q, the pressure difference by p, the input and output pressures by p_1 and p_2 respectively.

The relation between pressure and flow rate for a flow resistance with laminar flow is approximately given by d'Arcy's law:

$$p(t) = R_f \cdot q(t) \tag{14-34}$$

Here R_f (s.Pa/m^3—second·pascal/meter^3) is called the flow resistance. In case of steady laminar flow, Hagen-Poiseuille's relation is valid for cylindrical pipes, for which R_f can be obtained as follows:

$$R_f = \frac{128\eta L}{\pi D^4} \tag{14-35}$$

Here D is the diameter, L is the length of the pipe, whereas η is the dynamic viscosity of the fluid. The laminar flow resistor equation is often formulated using flow conductance $Q_f = 1/R_f$ ($m^3/(s \cdot Pa)$) as in the class `LamResNoStates`:

$$q(t) = Q_f \cdot p(t) \tag{14-36}$$

For a tube that contains a sudden change in area, for example, an orifice as in Figure 14-7, the flow becomes turbulent, which happens when Reynolds number *Re* is greater than $Re_{crit} \approx 2300$. For turbulent flow, the pressure difference is approximated by:

$$p(t) = H \cdot q(t)^2 \operatorname{sgn}(q(t)) \tag{14-37}$$

where H is a constant.

Figure 14-7. Nonlinear flow resistance from turbulent flow caused by a sudden change of the area of the tube, e.g. an orifice, a bend, or a valve.

Consider flow through a tube of length l with a rather wide cross-section area A, as depicted in Figure 14-8. In this case we make the approximation of no flow resistance against the walls of the tube. The pressure difference $p(t)$ between the ends of the tube will create a force $p(t) \cdot A$ that accelerates the liquid, which has a mass $\rho \cdot l \cdot A$, where ρ is the density. Newton's second law gives:

$$p(t)\cdot A=\rho\cdot l\cdot A\cdot\frac{d}{dt}v(t) \tag{14-38}$$

where $v(t)$ is the velocity of the liquid, which corresponds to a fluid flow rate $q(t) = v(t) \cdot A$ (m^3/s). Thus we obtain:

$$p(t)=L_f\cdot\frac{d}{dt}q(t) \tag{14-39}$$

where $L_f = \rho \cdot l/A$. This relation is the flow counterpart of the electrical inductor equation. The constant L_f is called the inertance of the tube, with units (kg/m^4).

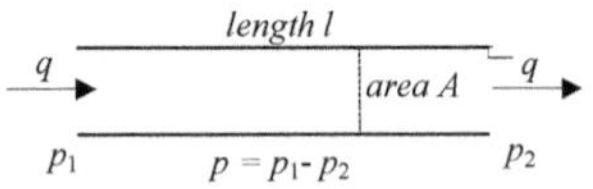

Figure 14-8. Frictionless flow rate $q(t)$ through a tube of length l and cross-section area A, with pressure difference $p(t)$.

A tank is a component that stores fluid, being the flow domain counterpart of an electrical capacitor that is a storage place for charge. The volume of the liquid in the tank depicted in Figure 14-9 is $h{\cdot}A$, with a gravity force $\rho{\cdot}h{\cdot}A{\cdot}g$ acting on the mass of the fluid, giving a pressure $p(t)= \rho{\cdot}h{\cdot}g$ at the bottom of the tank. Differentiating this equation, and using $q(t)=\dot{h}(t)\cdot A$, we obtain:

$$q(t)=C_f\cdot\frac{d}{dt}p(t) \tag{14-40}$$

where $C_f= A/\rho{\cdot}g$ (m^4s^2/kg) is the *fluid capacitance* of the tube.

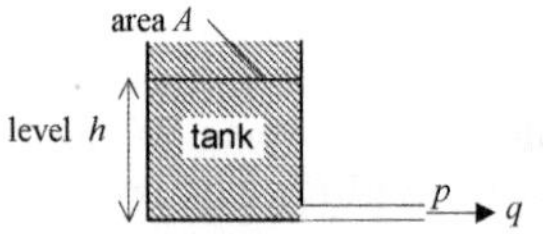

Figure 14-9. A tank works as a fluid store, here with capacity $h{\cdot}A$, analogous to an electrical capacitor which behaves as a charge store.

There are laws analogous to Kirchhoff's laws in the electrical domain that describe the connection of flow components. The sum of the pressure changes (positive and negative) around a flow system loop is zero:

$$\sum_k p_k(t)=0 \tag{14-41}$$

This is illustrated by the flow system example shown in Figure 14-10.

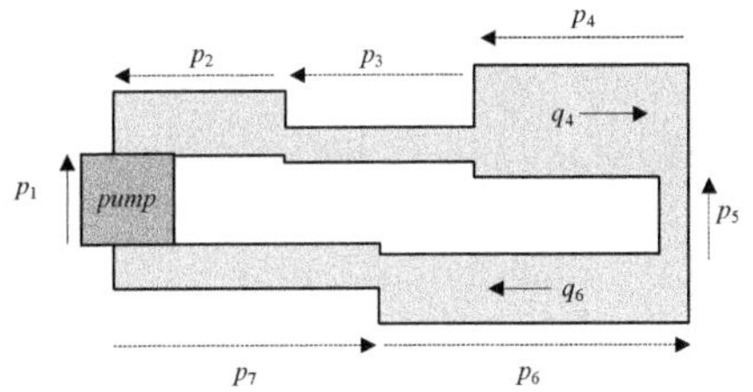

Figure 14-10. Pressure changes p_1 to p_7 over a series of connected flow subsystems. The sum of all pressure changes (with sign) around a complete loop is zero.

Likewise, the sum of all flows (with signs) into a node is zero since matter is neither created nor destroyed:

$$\sum_k q_k(t) = 0 \tag{14-42}$$

Figure 14-11 shows five flows into the same junction.

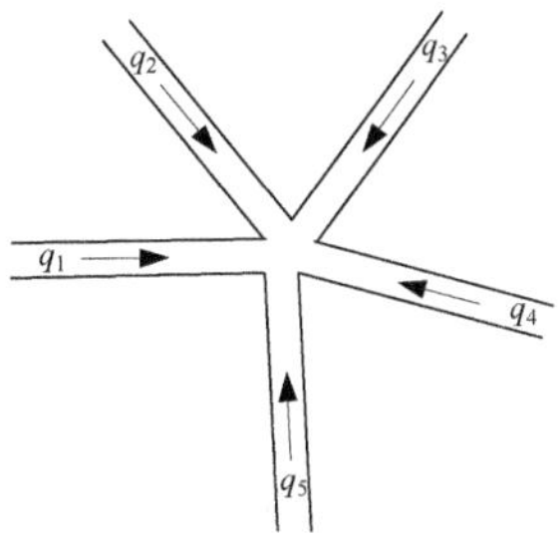

Figure 14-11. Fluid flows q_1 to q_5 at the junction of several pipes. The sum of all flows (with sign) into one junction is zero.

Analogous to the well-known electrical transformer, there are *flow transformers* that can transform a pair of pressure and flow rate quantities into another pair of pressure and flow rate quantities. An ideal flow transformer, e.g. as depicted in Figure 14-12 makes this transformation without loss of energy.

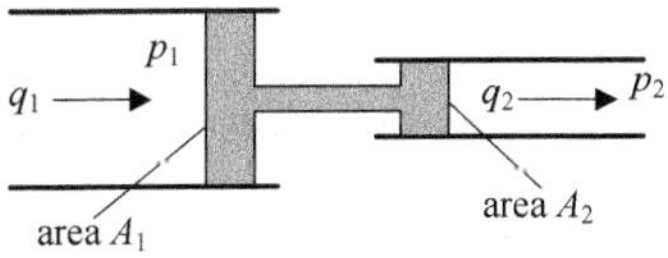

Figure 14-12. A flow transformer.

An ideal flow transformer preserves the product of pressure and flow rate, and is described by the following equations:

$$\begin{aligned} p_1(t)\cdot q_1(t) &= p_2(t)\cdot q_2(t) \\ p_1(t) &= \alpha \cdot p_2(t) \\ q_1(t) &= \frac{1}{\alpha}\cdot q_2(t) \end{aligned} \tag{14-43}$$

where the quotient α defined below determines the relation between the pressures and flows before and after the transformer.

$$\alpha = \frac{A_2}{A_1} \tag{14-44}$$

Transducers translate between pairs of quantities from different domains. A *flow transducer* such as a hydraulic pump depicted in Figure 14-13 translates between the mechanical quantities force and velocity to pressure and flow quantities, or vice versa:

$$\begin{aligned} f_1(t) &= A \cdot p_2(t) \\ v_1(t) &= A \cdot q_2(t) \end{aligned} \tag{14-45}$$

where A is the area of the piston.

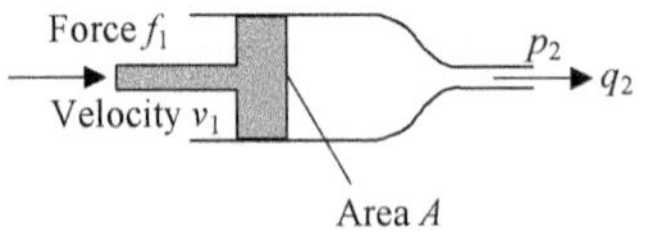

Figure 14-13. A hydraulic pump, a transducer between mechanical quantities and flow quantities.

14.6 Thermal Systems

Thermal systems involve the storage and transport of thermal energy, which is internal kinetic energy in the form of microscopic movements and oscillations of particles such as atoms and molecules in a material. For example, the heating or cooling of a house involves transport of thermal energy and are influenced by the conduction of heat through the walls, radiation from the radiators, and convection of air in the rooms of the house. The laws describing these phenomena usually involve the *temperature* quantity $T(t)$ (K—kelvin) and the *heat flow rate* quantity $q(t)$ (W—watt, or J/s—joule/second). Modelica libraries for thermal system components are mentioned in Chapter 16, page 909.

The temperature $T(t)$ of an object influences the amount of thermal energy $E_T(t)$ stored in the object. The following equation describes the heat flow rate into or out of an object:

$$q(t) = C \cdot \frac{d}{dt} T(t) \tag{14-46}$$

where $C = m \cdot c$ is the heat capacity of the object, c is the *specific heat capacity* of the material, and m is the mass of the object. Normally c is temperature dependent, but can be regarded as constant over limited temperature ranges for most materials.

Equation (14-47) describes a *heat capacitance* and is the thermal counterpart of the equation that describes electric charge flow rate (current) into an electric capacitor.

By integrating this equation we obtain an equation for the thermal energy $E_T(t)$ in the object

$$E_T(t) = \int (C \cdot \frac{d}{dt} T(t)) dt \tag{14-47}$$

For the cases where C is approximately constant we obtain:

$$E_T(t) = C \cdot T(t) \tag{14-48}$$

There are basically three ways of transporting thermal energy or heat: *conduction*, *convection*, and *radiation*. The mechanism behind heat conduction is *diffusion*, that is, heat transfer that is caused by the microscopic motion of individual particles such as molecules or atoms. Heat conduction does not imply macroscopic motion of the particles themselves—rather the propagation of local motion (vibration) between microscopic particles which on the average (in solids) remain at the same place.

Heat transfer can also take place on a macroscopic scale, by moving heated matter. This process is called *convection*. The third way of transporting heat is through thermal *radiation*, i.e., the emission and absorption of light.

14.6.1 Conduction

Within solid matter heat is transported by conduction, which is based on the microscopic process of diffusion. In the case of one-dimensional heat flow this process is described by the *heat equation*, which is a well-known partial differential equation giving the temperature $T(x,t)$:

$$\frac{\partial T}{\partial t} = \frac{\lambda}{\rho \cdot c} \cdot \frac{\partial^2 T}{\partial x^2} \tag{14-49}$$

where λ is the heat conductivity of the material, c is the specific heat capacity, and ρ is the density.

For a homogeneous block of solid material such as a rod, depicted in Figure 14-14, the solution to this equation can be used to obtain the stationary heat flow rate through the object, given a temperature difference T caused by the temperatures T_1 and T_2 at each end of the object:

$$q(t) = \frac{\lambda \cdot A}{d}(T_1(t) - T_2(t)) = W \cdot T(t) \tag{14-50}$$

where $W = \lambda \cdot A/d$ is the heat transfer coefficient (J/(K·s)), A is the cross-section area, and d the distance between the ends of the rod.

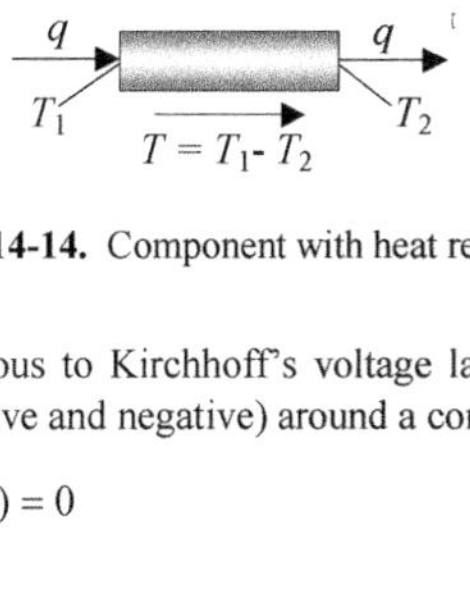

Figure 14-14. Component with heat resistance/conduction, with temperature difference T and heat flow rate q.

Analogous to Kirchhoff's voltage law for electrical systems, the sum of all temperature differences (both positive and negative) around a complete path within a system is zero:

$$\sum_k T_k(t) = 0 \tag{14-51}$$

Since energy cannot be destroyed, the sum of all heat flows (with sign) into a node without energy storage is zero:

$$\sum_k q_k(t) = 0 \tag{14-52}$$

Both relationships are illustrated in Figure 14-15.

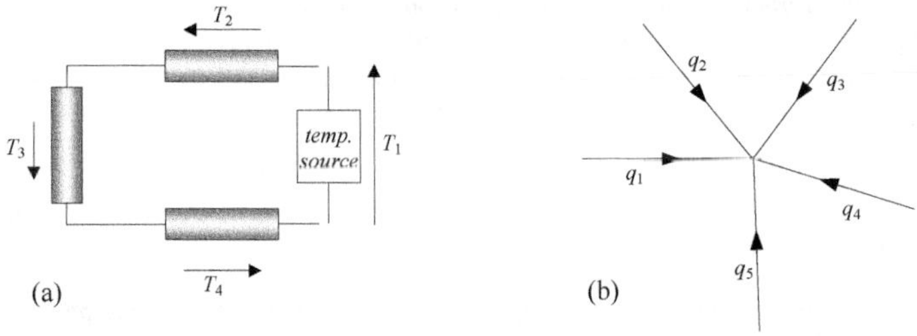

Figure 14-15. The sum of the temperature differences (with sign) along a path around a system is zero, e.g. as for T_1,T_2,T_3, and T_4 on the left. The sum of the heat flows (with sign) into the same node is zero, as illustrated by q_1, q_2, q_3, q_4, q_5 on the right.

14.6.2 Convection

Thermal convection is heat flow on the macroscopic scale based on the fact that heat stored in any moving piece of matter moves together with that object. This process describes transfer of heat as a result of macroscopic movements rather than microscopic movements, which was the case for thermal conduction.

For example, consider a room in a house. If we heat the floor of the room, the air close to the floor will be heated up through conduction. Its density will be reduced because it is warmer; therefore it will rise to the ceiling and transfer part of its heat to the ceiling. Colder air will move down to the floor to replace the air that moved up. This is a typical convection phenomenon. For buildings in general, convection takes place between the air and the walls, floors and ceilings inside buildings as well as outside. Convection is described by the following equation:

$$q(t) = \alpha \cdot A \cdot T(t) \tag{14-53}$$

where $T(t) = T_1(t)$-$T_2(t)$, that is, the temperature difference between the two objects or surfaces, α is the convective heat transfer coefficient, and A is the area perpendicular to the heat flow where the heat flow takes place.

14.6.3 Radiation

The third way of transporting thermal energy is through radiation. The atoms and molecules of a material in solid, fluid, or gas form continuously emit and absorb radiation. For example, the walls of a house absorb some solar radiation, become heated up, and emit radiation. There is emission from radiators and continuous heat exchange between walls. The Stephan-Boltzmann Law governs the radiation, that is, energy flow, emitted from a surface with the temperature $T(t)$:

$$q_{rad}(t) = \sigma \cdot \varepsilon \cdot A \cdot T^4 \tag{14-54}$$

where σ is the Stephan-Boltzmann constant, ε is the emission coefficient of the surface, and A is the surface area. A dark surface has higher emission coefficient than a white one. The radiation exchange between a surface (1) of area A and a fictitious ideal black body (2) with the same surface becomes:

$$q_{rad}(t) = \sigma \cdot \varepsilon_1 \cdot \varepsilon_2 \cdot A \cdot (T_1^4 - T_2^4) \tag{14-55}$$

For an ideal black body the emission coefficient $\varepsilon_2 = 1$. A fictitious black body is useful, for example, when modeling a room using the so-called two-star approximation: instead of explicitly modeling all combinations of radiation interactions between a number of objects, e.g. all walls and other objects in a room, all radiating surfaces are connected to and interact with a fictitious massless black body.

14.7 Thermodynamics

Thermodynamics is a part of natural science in which the storage of energy, the transformation of energy between different forms, and the transfer of energy (and mass) between subsystems is studied. One of the primary energy forms dealt with in thermodynamics is *thermal energy*, also mentioned in the preceeding Section 14.6, page 756, about *thermal systems*. Mass flows are often part of thermodynamic models, involving model components such as those described in Section 14.5, page 752, regarding *flow systems*. The transformation and transfer of the following four main forms of energy is typically studied in thermodynamics:

- Internal *thermal energy*, associated with temperature and due to microscopic random motion of constituent particles such as atoms and molecules.
- Macroscopic *kinetic energy*, due to macroscopic motion of chunks of material.
- *Potential energy*, for example, due to the position of a subsystem in a gravitational or electromagnetic field, or due to internal pressure in a subsystem, and so on.
- *Chemical energy*, due to internal molecular and atomic bonds in the material.

In thermodynamics we formulate equations that relate transformations and transfers of energy to certain material properties. These properties include *temperature*, *pressure*, or *enthalpy* which is a property specifying a combination of thermal energy and pressure-related potential energy of the material. The engineer's goal when studying thermodynamics is usually to design some large-scale system, anything from a refrigerator to a power plant. The materials in such large systems can be regarded as continuums where the individual motion of molecules and atoms is averaged into quantities such as temperature, pressure, etc. The *continuum* approximation *used here* is made in *macroscopic thermodynamics*, in contrast to statistical thermodynamics where the individual motion of molecules is important.

14.7.1 Thermodynamic Systems and Control Volumes

In thermodynamics we speak about thermodynamic *systems*, their *surroundings*, and *control volumes* embedded in systems, as depicted in an abstract way in Figure 5-52 below.

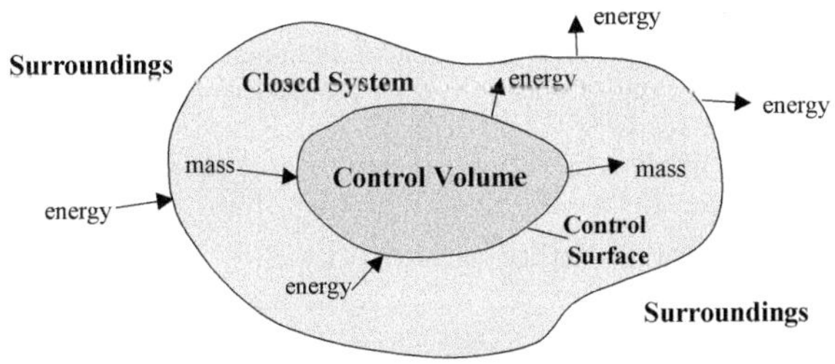

Figure 14-16. A control volume allows transfer of energy and mass across its boundaries, whereas a closed system contains a definite quantity of matter and only allows energy transfer to and from its surroundings.

We have the following definitions:

- A thermodynamic *system* is a definite quantity of matter, usually contained within some closed boundary. An example is a cylinder containing a gas or fluid. A system can usually exchange energy and matter with its surroundings, and can be either *open* or *closed*.
- An *open system* can exchange both energy and matter with its surroundings.
- A *closed system* can only exchange energy with its surroundings.
- An *isolated system* does not exchange energy or matter with its surroundings.
- A *system* may contain *subsystems*.
- The *surroundings* of a system is all matter (and radiation) external to the system.

A control volume is a simple open system defined as follows:

- A *control volume* is a volume in space consisting of a single *phase* or *pseudo-phase* (see below). The boundary can be physical or imaginary.
- A *control surface* is the boundary surface that completely surrounds the control volume.

Note that a system can contain several control volumes. When modeling a particular problem we must decide whether a *control volume* or an open/closed *system* is appropriate. If there is a mass flow across the boundary of a region consisting of a single phase, a control volume should be used, otherwise a system.

14.7.1.1 Continuum Postulate and System Properties

As mentioned briefly above, in *engineering thermodynamics*, also called *macroscopic thermodynamics*, we use the continuum postulate that the material is continuously distributed throughout the region, and as a consequence has uniform properties in this region. This allows us to characterize the material in a system or control volume by only a few measurable quantities such as temperature, pressure, volume, average position, velocity, and so on.

The matter in a system or control volume can exist in several phases: *solid*, *liquid*, or *gas*.

- A *phase* is a quantity of matter that has the same homogenous chemical composition throughout the region in question, that is, with spatially uniform *intensive* properties (see below).

Sometimes we generalize phase to *pseudo phase* where properties are not completely uniform but are represented by averaged intensive properties for the purpose of simplified modeling. Regarding the properties of the matter, in thermodynamics we have two general classes of thermodynamic properties: *intensive* and *extensive*, as well as *specific* properties:

- An *intensive property* does not depend on the mass of the system. Temperature, pressure, density, and velocity are examples of such quantities. Intensive properties cannot be summed when subsystems are brought together into single system.
- An *extensive property* depends on the mass of the system. Volume, kinetic energy, and momentum are examples. Extensive properties are summed when several subsystems are brought together to a single system.
- A *specific property* is obtained by dividing an extensive property by the mass, thus becoming independent of the mass of the system.

For example, the specific volume v is obtained by dividing the volume V by the mass:

$$v = \frac{V}{m} \tag{14-56}$$

Extensive properties (apart from the mass m) are usually denoted by uppercase letters, whereas lowercase letters are used for the corresponding specific properties.

14.7.2 Thermodynamic Equilibrium and Thermodynamic Processes

The continuum postulate mentioned in the previous section allows us to characterize a system by a few property values. This assumption is dependent on thermodynamic equilibrium of a system:

- *Thermodynamic equilibrium* of a system means that its thermodynamic properties such as temperature, pressure, etc. are uniform throughout the system. The properties may change with time as long as this uniformity or homogeneity is preserved.
- A system being in *nonequilibrium* means that the system has a spatial nonuniformity of some of its properties, which also may change with time. For example, if the temperature is suddenly increased at the corner of a region, spontaneous redistribution is assumed to occur until all parts of the region are at the same temperature, which means that the system has returned to an equilibrium state.

The system undergoes a *thermodynamic process* when it changes from one equilibrium state to another through a series of successive states:

- A *quasiequilibrium process* occurs when the system is passing from state to state at most has infinitesimal deviations from equilibrium, that is, each successive state can be regarded as being in equilibrium. For example, expansion and compression of gases in an internal combustion engine can be approximated well by quasiequilibrium processes.
- A *nonequilibrium process* occurs when the system goes from one equilibrium state to another through a series of nonequilibrium states. A typical example is combustion for which very fast changes occur nonuniformly at a reaction surface that propagates throughout the region. The uniformity assumption cannot be maintained at all times.

The basic assumption behind a quasiequilibrium process is that the spontaneous redistribution of quantities such as temperature and pressure after a small change is much faster than the changes of quantity values caused by the process itself, which means that the uniformity approximation is still reasonably valid.

The surroundings play no part in the notion of equilibrium. However, it is possible that the surroundings do work on the system, for example, via friction. Also in that case, to be a quasiequilibrium process it is only required that the properties of the system be uniform at any instant. A system that undergoes a quasiequilibrium process that returns to the same state is called a *cycle*:

- A thermodynamic *cycle* is a process consisting of series of quasiequilibrium processes for which the system from an initial state after going through the cycle will return to the same state.

A typical cycle is depicted in Figure 14-17.

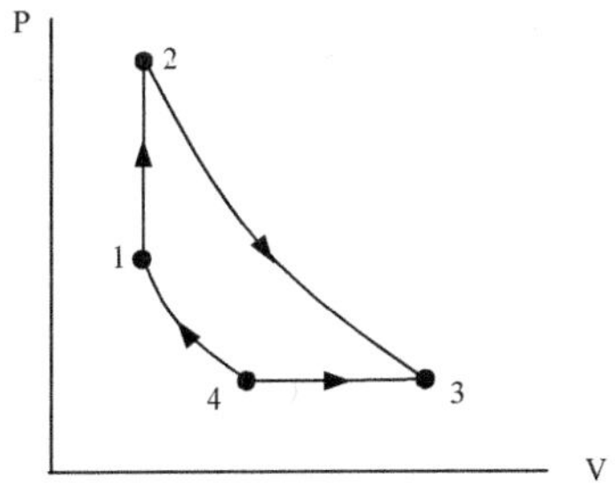

Figure 14-17. A thermodynamic cycle.

It is common that a process cycle has a subprocess in which one of the thermodynamic quantities remains unchanged. Such a subprocess is labeled by the prefix *iso*:

- An *isothermal* process is one in which the temperature is held constant.
- In an *isobaric* process the pressure is held constant.
- An *isometric* process is a constant-volume process.

We will now take a look at the properties of so-called pure substances, that is, with homogenous composition.

14.7.3 Compressible Pure Substances

A *pure substance* is homogeneous, that is, has the same chemical composition throughout a region. It may exist in more than one phase: solid, liquid or gas, but all phases must have the same chemical composition. For example, water is a pure substance, that is, it has only one kind of molecule, but air is nonpure— a mixture of different kinds of gas molecules. Air is homogeneous in its gas phase but not necessarily in its liquid and solid phases.

14.7.3.1 Ideal and Nonideal Gases

When the vapor of a substance has relatively low density the interaction between the molecules is low enough to fulfill the conditions of an ideal gas, meaning that the well-known ideal gas law holds:

$$P \cdot V = n \cdot \overline{R} \cdot T \tag{14-57}$$

where P is the pressure, V is the volume, n is the number of moles[18] of the substance, T is the temperature and $\overline{R}$ is the *universal gas constant*, which has the same value 8.314 [kJ/(kmol.K)] for all gases. The ideal gas law can also be expressed as follows:

$$P \cdot V = m \cdot R \cdot T \tag{14-58}$$

where m is the mass of the system, and R is the *gas constant* for the particular gas:

$$R = \frac{\overline{R}}{M} \tag{14-59}$$

Here M is the molar mass, that is, the mass of a mole of the substance:

$$M = \frac{m}{n} \tag{14-60}$$

For example, for standard air the value of M is 28.97 (kg/kmol), and R is 287 (J/kg).

When the pressure is high enough, the assumptions behind the ideal gas law are not fulfilled since other kinds of interactions between the gas molecules come into play. For example, the *van der Waals equation of state* is intended to account for the volume occupied by the gas molecules and for the attractive forces between the molecules. This law is an example of a *nonideal gas law*:

$$P = \frac{R \cdot T}{v - b} - \frac{a}{v^2} \tag{14-61}$$

where P is the pressure, R is the gas constant, v is the specific volume as defined by equation (14-56), and a and b are constants which are related to properties of the particular gas. There are other forms of gas laws that are more accurate, for example, for higher pressure.

[18] A mole of a substance is $6.0225 \cdot 10^{23}$ entities, typically molecules, that make up the substance.

14.7.4 Work and Heat

Work and *heat* are two forms of energy that can flow across a system boundary. A common and simple definition of work W, with energy units (Nm—newtonmeter) or (J—joule), is the following:

$$W = F \cdot l \tag{14-62}$$

where W is the work done by moving an object a distance l against a force F. In thermodynamics we use the convention that *work done by a system* on its surroundings is *positive*[19], that is, energy is flowing from the system into the surroundings. For example, a system consisting of a cylinder containing a gas expanding against a piston is doing positive work, whereas negative work is the case if the piston is compressing the gas.

14.7.4.1 Quasiequilibrium Work

There are many kinds of work that can occur in different systems for different engineering situations. One example is the work done to move a boundary against a pressure force, e.g. as depicted in Figure 14-18 below. We have quasiequilibrium work if the movement is slow enough compared to molecular movements so that the system is approximately at equilibrium at all times.

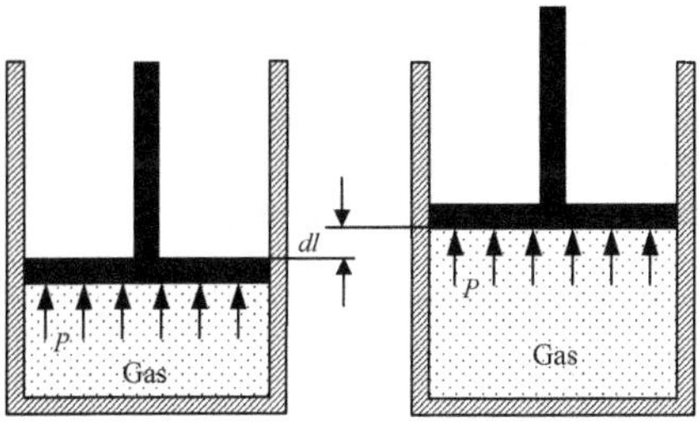

Figure 14-18. A system consisting of a gas filled cylinder doing work on the surroundings by pushing up a piston.

The infinitesimal work dW done by the system when the gas expands is the force $P \cdot A$ multiplied by the distance dl:

$$dW = P \cdot A \cdot dl \tag{14-63}$$

where P is the pressure, A is the piston area, and dl is the distance moved by the piston. Since the infinitesimal change in volume is $dV = A \cdot dl$, we get the total work by integrating $P \cdot dV$:

$$W_{1-2} = \int_{V_1}^{V_2} P \cdot dV \tag{14-64}$$

Thus the work exerted by the system when expanding from volume V_1 to volume V_2 is the integral of the pressure as a function of volume.

14.7.4.2 Nonequilibrium Work

It must be emphasized that *only* the work done by a quasiequilibrium process can be computed by the integral in equation (14-64). In the nonequilibrium case the work must be obtained using other relations, e.g. conservation of energy, to be discussed in the next section.

[19] Note that this is opposite to the definition of positive flow for Modelica connector quantities of a component, where positive value of a connector flow variable is into the component. However, the internal quantities of a system component are usually defined independent of the connectors.

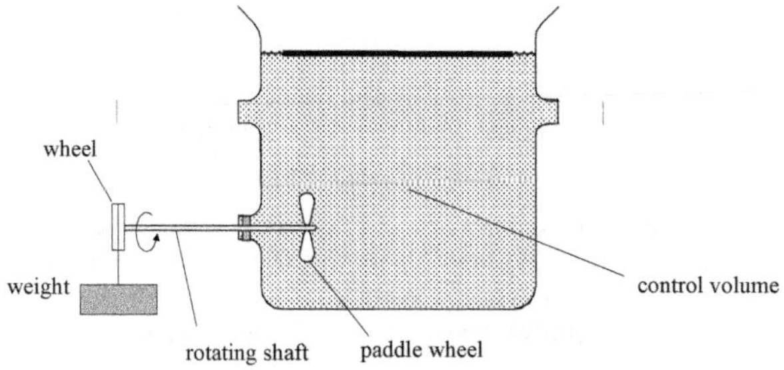

Figure 14-19. A thermodynamic example system with a control volume and a rotating shaft with an attached paddle wheel that performs nonequilibrium work on the system when the weight attached by the wire around the wheel causes the shaft to rotate.

An example of a system with nonequilibrium work is a paddle wheel rotating in a control volume filled with a gas or fluid, as depicted in Figure 14-19. The homogeneity assumption is not fulfilled around the rotating paddle wheel, where there is turbulence and local variations in pressure and velocity of the substance. For the system depicted in Figure 14-19 the work done by the paddle wheel can be found from the distance the weight is lowered multiplied by the gravity force together with the principle of conservation of energy, where we neglect the rotational energy of the rotating shaft and paddle.

14.7.5 First Law of Thermodynamics—Conservation of Energy

One of the fundamental laws of nature is the law of *conservation of energy*. In the context of thermodynamics, when the effects of heat transfer and internal energy changes are included, this is called the *first law of thermodynamics*. This means that in a cycle the heat energy transfer ΔQ is equal to the work ΔW done for the system, that is, no change in total energy:

$$\sum \Delta W - \sum \Delta Q = 0 \tag{14-65}$$

In our example with the falling weight in Figure 14-19, a direct consequence of the first law is that the heat transfer to the gas or fluid in the control volume is exactly equal to the work done by the falling weight.

14.7.5.1 Main Energy Forms

In the beginning of Section 14.7.1 we briefly mentioned the most important forms of energy dealt with in thermodynamic system models. Of those, thermal energy and chemical energy are two forms of internal energy. We summarize the three main energy forms:

- *Internal energy*, denoted U or specific internal energy $u = U / m$ for a system with mass m (we include possible nonnegligible radiation in the notion of mass).
- *Kinetic energy*, e.g. $m \cdot v^2 / 2$ for a substance of mass m moving with macroscopic speed v.
- *Potential energy*, e.g. $m \cdot g \cdot z$ due to the elevation z of a substance with mass m in the gravitational field .

14.7.5.2 Enthalpy

Enthalpy, denoted H, is an energy term that is a combination of internal energy U and work done by an expanding volume of a substance in a constant pressure situation. The enthalpy of a substance has physical relevance since it occurs in models of many engineering situations. The specific enthalpy $h=H/m$ is actually a property that has been measured and tabulated for many common substances. The *enthalpy* H of a system, typically being a substance in fluid or gas form, is defined as follows:

$$H = U + P \cdot V \tag{14-66}$$

where U is the internal energy of the substance in the system, P is the pressure, and V is the volume. The *specific enthalpy* h is obtained by dividing by the mass m of the system:

$$h = u + P \cdot v \tag{14-67}$$

where u is the specific internal energy, and $v = V / m$ is the specific volume of the substance.

Consider a system for which the kinetic energy changes and potential energy changes are neglected and all other kinds of work are absent. An example of such a system is the cylinder containing a gas depicted in Figure 14-20 to which heat is slowly added under constant pressure, that is, a quasiequilibrium process. Then the first law of thermodynamics, i.e., conservation of energy, gives:

$$\Delta Q - \Delta W = U_2 - U_1 \tag{14-68}$$

where ΔQ is the added heat, ΔW is the work done on the piston by the volume expanding against constant pressure, U_1 is the internal energy before the process of adding heat and the volume expansion, and U_2 is the internal energy after the process has finished.

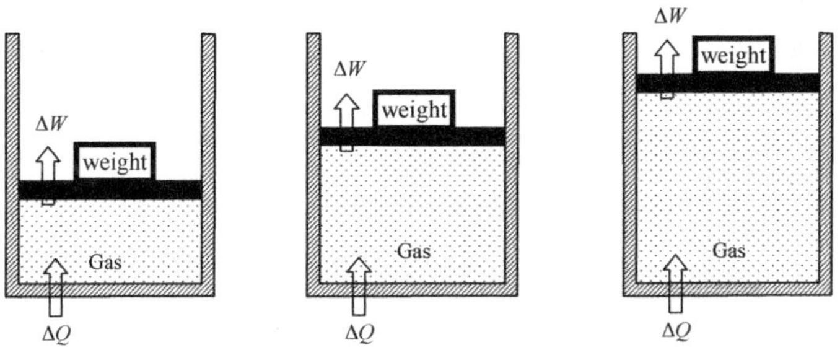

Figure 14-20. A system where heat is added under constant pressure. The increase in enthalpy equals the added heat energy for the system.

The cylinder system with expanding volume performs work in raising the piston a distance z against the force, given by $P \cdot A$, created by the constant pressure P acting on the piston surface area A:

$$\Delta W = P \cdot A \cdot z \tag{14-69}$$

By observing that the change in volume $(V_2 - V_1) = A \cdot z$, where V_2 is the volume after the expansion and V_1 is the volume before the expansion, and substituting into the previous equation, we obtain the following expression for the work ΔW :

$$\Delta W = P \cdot (V_2 - V_1) \tag{14-70}$$

By slightly rewriting the first law of thermodynamics from (14-68) we obtain:

$$\Delta Q = \Delta W + U_2 - U_1 \tag{14-71}$$

which reformulated using (14-70) becomes:

$$\Delta Q = (U + P \cdot V)_2 - (U + P \cdot V)_1 \tag{14-72}$$

We note that the energy expressions on the right hand side before and after the expansion are identical to the definition of enthalpy according to (14-66). Thus we obtain the equation for *conservation of energy* stated for a system going through a *constant-pressure equilibrium process*:

$$\Delta Q = H_2 - H_1 \tag{14-73}$$

where ΔQ is the *heat energy* added to the system. For a variable-pressure process, the difference in enthalpy loses its physical significance. However, enthalpy as an energy term is still useful in engineering applications and remains a property as defined by equations (14-66) and (14-67). In a nonequilibrium constant-pressure process $H_2 - H_1$ would not equal the heat transfer.

14.7.5.3 Latent Heat and Steam Tables

The amount of heat energy that must be added to a substance at constant pressure in order that a phase change should occur is called the *latent heat*. For an equilibrium process, according to equation (14-73), it is equal to the change in enthalpy of the substance before and after the phase change. The substance must be in saturated conditions in the two phases. The specific latent heat is a material property that has been measured and tabulated for many common substances. For example, the specific *melting heat* is the heat necessary to melt a unit mass of the substance:

$$\Delta Q_{sl} = m \cdot (h_l - h_s) \tag{14-74}$$

where h_l is the enthalpy of the saturated liquid and h_s is the enthalpy of the saturated solid. Likewise, the *heat of a vaporization* is the heat required to completely vaporize a unit mass of saturated liquid:

$$\Delta Q_{lg} = m \cdot (h_g - h_l) \tag{14-75}$$

where h_g is the enthalpy of the saturated gas and h_l is the enthalpy of the saturated liquid. When a solid changes phase directed to a gas, *sublimation* occurs. The melting heat and the heat of sublimation are rather insensitive to temperature or pressure changes. However, the heat of vaporization and related properties is strongly pressure dependent, and has been measured and tabulated into so-called *steam tables* for water and many other common substances.

14.7.5.4 Mass and Energy Conservation in Control Volumes

Recall our previous definitions of thermodynamic systems and control volumes respectively, in Section 14.7.1 on page 759. Only energy is allowed to cross the boundaries of a *closed system*, whereas both mass and energy can cross the boundaries of a *control volume*. The restriction that only energy crosses the boundaries of a closed system is acceptable for many practical problems of interest, including a simplified analysis of the power plant system schematically depicted in Figure 14-21 below.

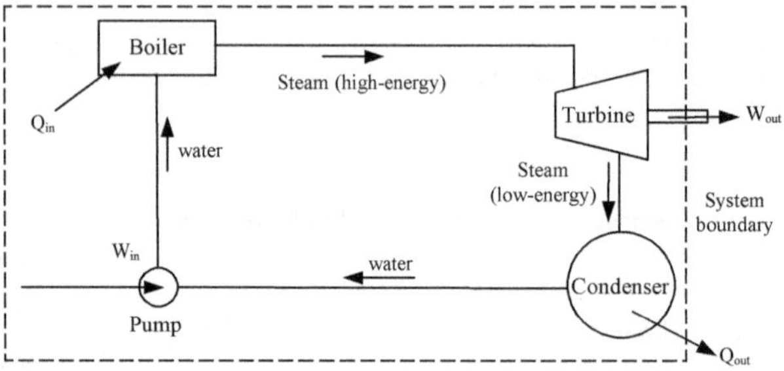

Figure 14-21. A schematic picture (not a connection diagram) of a power plant system consisting of four control volumes: pump, boiler, turbine, and condenser. Some arrows denote flow of matter, others flow of energy.

However, for a more complete analysis we need to study the components of the power plant. These are *control volumes* and not closed systems in the thermodynamic sense since mass flows into and out of these components, and they can be described by a single phase (i.e., one set of intensive thermodynamic properties).

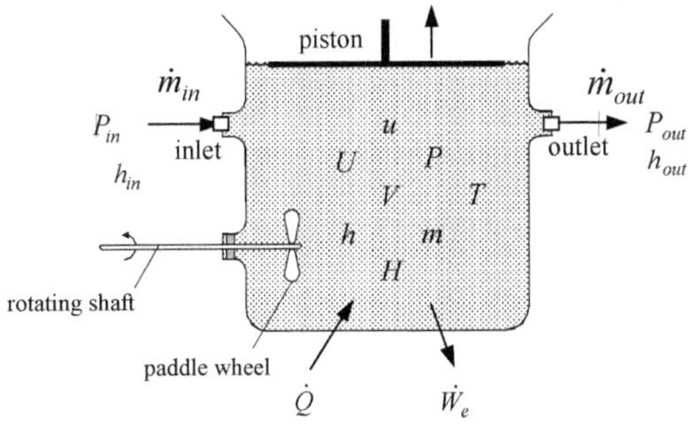

Figure 14-22. A generic control volume with mass flows and energy flows.

A rather generic control volume that represents the properties of many specific control volumes is depicted in Figure 5-52. We will develop relations involving mass flow rate and the common thermodynamic quantities for this control volume based on conservation of mass and conservation of energy. More details regarding this control volume are available in Section 15.2.4 on page 804.

Conservation of mass means that the change of mass Δm in the control volume must equal the difference between the mass Δm_{in} entering the system and the mass Δm_{out} leaving the system since no mass can disappear:

$$\Delta m = \Delta m_{in} - \Delta m_{out} \tag{14-76}$$

By observing the mass change during a finite time increment Δt we obtain the average mass flow rate $\Delta m / \Delta t$. If we let the time increment become infinitely short, $\Delta t \to dt$, we obtain the relation for the mass flows of the control volume:

$$\frac{dm}{dt} = \dot{m}_{in} - \dot{m}_{out} \tag{14-77}$$

The principle of *conservation of energy* for the *control volume*, abbreviated *c.v.*, can be stated as follows:

$$\begin{array}{ccccccc} \text{Change of} & & \text{Energy} & & \text{Energy} & & \text{Net energy} \\ \text{energy in } c.v. & = & \text{entering } c.v. & - & \text{leaving } c.v. & + & \text{transferred to } c.v. \\ \Delta E_{c.v.} & & \Delta E_{in} & & \Delta E_{out} & & \Delta Q - \Delta W \end{array} \tag{14-78}$$

where ΔQ is the heat energy transferred to the control volume and ΔW is the net work done by the control volume on the surroundings. Remember that the total energy E of a system is composed of kinetic energy E_{kin}, potential energy E_{pot}, and internal energy U:

$$E = E_{kin} + E_{pot} + U \tag{14-79}$$

Thus, the terms for energy changes ΔE_{in} and ΔE_{out} during a certain time increment Δt are composed of terms for kinetic energy $mv^2/2$, potential energy mgz, and internal energy mu:

$$\begin{aligned} \Delta E_{in} &= \frac{\Delta m_{in} v_{in}^2}{2} + \Delta m_{in}\, g\, z_{in} + \Delta m_{in}\, u_{in} \\ \Delta E_{out} &= \frac{\Delta m_{out} v_{out}^2}{2} + \Delta m_{out}\, g\, z_{out} + \Delta m_{out}\, u_{out} \end{aligned} \tag{14-80}$$

where Δm_{in} is the inflowing mass—fluid or gas—during the time increment Δt, v_{in} is the velocity of the inflowing mass, g is the gravitational constant, z_{in} is the vertical position of the inflowing mass, and u_{in} is the specific internal energy for the inflowing substance. Analogous definitions apply to the quantities for the outflowing mass used in the second equation of (14-80).

The work ΔW that the control volume performs on its surroundings during the time increment Δt is composed of two parts: the work due to the pressure needed to move the fluid or gas into and out of the control volume, sometimes called *flow work*, ΔW_{flow}, and other forms of *external work*, ΔW_e, done by the expanding control volume to move the piston as well as work done by the rotating shaft, sometimes denoted *shaft work*, ΔW_s, included in ΔW_e. This can be expressed as:

$$\Delta W = \Delta W_{flow} + \Delta W_e \tag{14-81}$$

or in the following form where the expression for the flow work is stated explicitly:

$$\Delta W = P_{out} A_{out} v_{out} \Delta t - P_{in} A_{in} v_{in} \Delta t + \Delta W_e \tag{14-82}$$

where $P_{out} A_{out}$ is the pressure force caused by the pressure P_{out} against which the outflowing fluid or gas is moving through the output pipe with cross-section area A_{out} and the term $v_{out} \cdot \Delta t$ is the distance the fluid or gas is moving with velocity v_{out} during the time increment Δt.

The following equation relates fluid or gas flow velocity to mass flow rate:

$$A \cdot v = \frac{A \cdot dx}{dt} = \frac{dV}{dt} = \frac{dm/dt}{dm/dV} = \frac{\dot{m}}{\rho} \tag{14-83}$$

where A is the cross-section area of the pipe, v is the fluid or gas velocity, dx is the distance increment covered during the time increment dt, the volume increment dV corresponds to the distance increment, dm is the mass within the volume increment transported during the time increment dt, ρ is the density, and $\dot{m}$ is the mass flow rate.

By substituting the above expression into (14-82) we obtain the desired form of the equation for the work ΔW:

$$\Delta W = \frac{P_{out}}{\rho_{out}} \dot{m}_{out} \Delta t - \frac{P_{in}}{\rho_{in}} \dot{m}_{in} \Delta t + \Delta W_e \tag{14-84}$$

Recall the energy conservation equation (14-78) for a control volume:

$$\Delta E_{c.v.} = \Delta E_{in} - \Delta E_{out} + \Delta Q - \Delta W \tag{14-85}$$

By substituting the derived expressions for energy and work we obtain the *complete energy conservation equation* relating the energy change $\Delta E_{c.v.}$ for a control volume during a time increment Δt to inflows and outflows of mass and energy:

$$\begin{aligned}\Delta E_{c.v.} &= \Delta m_{in}\left(\frac{v_{in}^2}{2} + g z_{in} + u_{in}\right) - \Delta m_{out}\left(\frac{v_{out}^2}{2} + g z_{out} + u_{out}\right) \\ &\quad - \frac{P_{out}}{\rho_{out}} \dot{m}_{out} \Delta t + \frac{P_{in}}{\rho_{in}} \dot{m}_{in} \Delta t + \Delta Q - \Delta W_e\end{aligned} \tag{14-86}$$

14.7.5.5 Energy Flow, Internal Energy, and Enthalpy

The previously derived energy conservation equation (14-86) is easily converted into the *energy equation* for control volumes that relates energy and mass flows, by dividing both sides by Δt and letting the time increment become infinitesimally small, that is, $\Delta t \rightarrow dt$:

$$\frac{dE_{c.v.}}{dt}=\dot{m}_{in}\left(\frac{v_{in}^2}{2}+g\,z_{in}+u_{in}+\frac{P_{in}}{\rho_{in}}\right)-\dot{m}_{out}\left(\frac{v_{out}^2}{2}+g\,z_{out}+u_{out}+\frac{P_{out}}{\rho_{out}}\right)+\dot{Q}-\dot{W}_e \quad (14\text{-}87)$$

Using our previous definition (14-66) for the *enthalpy* H we obtain the *specific enthalpy* h:

$$h=\frac{H}{m}=\frac{U+P\cdot V}{m}=u+\frac{P}{m/V}=u+\frac{P}{\rho} \quad (14\text{-}88)$$

Substituting the specific enthalpy into (14-87), we obtain the *enthalpy form of the energy equation*:

$$\frac{dE_{c.v.}}{dt}=\dot{m}_{in}\left(\frac{v_{in}^2}{2}+g\,z_{in}+h_{in}\right)-\dot{m}_{out}\left(\frac{v_{out}^2}{2}+g\,z_{out}+h_{out}\right)+\dot{Q}-\dot{W}_e \quad (14\text{-}89)$$

For many control volumes, such as the one depicted in Figure 14-22, there are negligible changes of kinetic and potential energy since the fluid or gas does not move or change level very much within the control volume. Thus the *energy equation* can be simplified by *eliminating* the terms for changes in *kinetic* and *potential* energy:

$$\frac{dE_{c.v.}}{dt}=\dot{m}_{in}\,h_{in}-\dot{m}_{out}\,h_{out}+\dot{Q}-\dot{W}_e \quad (14\text{-}90)$$

The total energy in the control volume is the sum of the kinetic energy E_{kin}, the potential energy E_{pot}, and the internal energy U:

$$E_{c.v.}=E_{kin}+E_{pot}+U \quad (14\text{-}91)$$

If we assume that the *changes* in kinetic energy and potential energy are zero and use the above equations (14-90) and (14-91), we obtain an equation for the *internal energy of the control volume* assuming negligible changes of kinetic and potential energy:

$$\frac{dU}{dt}=h_{in}\,\dot{m}_{in}-h_{out}\,\dot{m}_{out}+\dot{Q}-\dot{W}_e \quad (14\text{-}92)$$

The specific internal energy can be expressed as follows assuming the specific heat capacity of the substance is constant within a temperature range close to some constant temperature T_0:

$$u=\frac{U}{m}$$
$$u=u_0+c_v(T-T_0) \quad (14\text{-}93)$$

where u_0 is the specific internal energy at some constant temperature T_0 and c_v is the specific heat capacity of the substance at that temperature.

For *steady flow*, which is a very common situation when a gas or a vapor is flowing, we have no change of energy and no storage of mass inside the control volume:

$$\frac{dE_{c.v.}}{dt}=0$$
$$\dot{m}=\dot{m}_{in}=\dot{m}_{out} \quad (14\text{-}94)$$

simplifying (14-89) into the *energy equation for steady state flow*:

$$\dot{W}_e-\dot{Q}=\dot{m}\left(h_{in}-h_{out}+g(z_{in}-z_{out})+\frac{(v_{in}^2-v_{out}^2)}{2}\right) \quad (14\text{-}95)$$

where we have *not* assumed negligible potential and kinetic energy changes.

Regarding a control volume through which liquid flows it is better to use the previously developed form (14-87) of the energy equation. For *steady state liquid flow* with $\rho_{out} = \rho_{in} = \rho$, neglecting the heat flow rate $(\dot{Q} = 0)$ and internal energy changes $(\dot{U} = 0)$, we obtain:

$$\dot{W}_e = \dot{m}\left(\frac{P_{in} - P_{out}}{\rho} + g(z_{in} - z_{out}) + \frac{(v_{in}^2 - v_{out}^2)}{2}\right) \tag{14-96}$$

which is the form of the energy equation commonly used for a pump or a hydroturbine. If the heat flow rate $\dot{Q}$ or the internal energy changes $\dot{U}$ are not negligible, just include them in the above equation.

14.8 Multibody Systems

What is a multibody system? It can be defined as a system consisting of a number of interacting bodies or substructures (Figure 14-23 and Figure 14-24). A multibody system can be almost anything from an atom containing a nucleus and electrons, to star systems with gravitational interaction between bodies, as well as man-made three-dimensional mechanical systems such as vehicles, airplanes, and industry robots. In the following, we restrict ourselves to multibody systems subject to Newtonian physics, that is, excluding microscopic quantum mechanical systems such as atoms. We also restrict ourselves to rigid bodies and thereby exclude deformable bodies that may change shape and size. Our goal in this section is to explain the basic concepts and derive the most important equations for multibody systems in the form they appear in the Modelica MBS library.

Figure 14-23. A vehicle such as a bus is a multibody system with a number of moving and fixed parts.

The basic quantities associated with the bodies in the multibody system are the following three-vector valued quantities (shown in bold font): potential quantities position **s**, velocity **v**, and acceleration **a**, angular position or degree of rotation **θ**, angular velocity **ω**, and angular acceleration $\dot{\boldsymbol{\omega}}$, also denoted **α** or **z**, as well as the flow quantities force **f** and torque **τ**. These quantities are defined precisely and explained in the following sections.

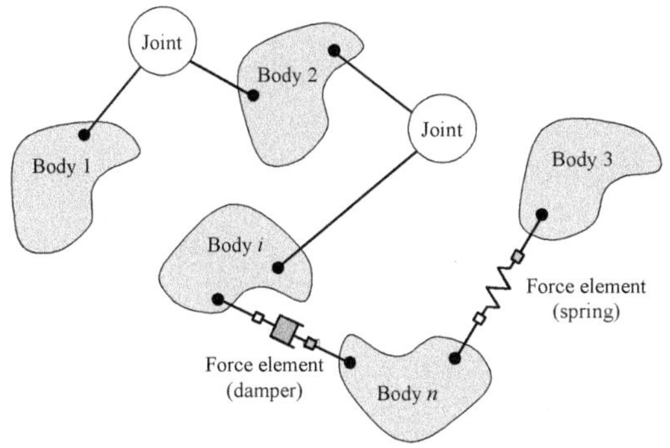

Figure 14-24. Example of a multibody system with force elements and joints constraining movements and transmitting forces between the bodies.

The motion of the bodies (or subsystems) is fundamental to the understanding of a multibody system. The field of mechanical multibody systems can be divided into three areas: *rigid-body mechanics* being briefly presented here, *structural mechanics*, and *continuum mechanics*. The term *rigid-body* implies that the distance between any two particles of the body remains constant at all times. The motion of a rigid body moving freely in space can be completely described by six generalized coordinates, three positions and three rotations, whereas for a deformable body a large number of coordinates (large dimensionality) is needed. Structural mechanics might be seen as a subtopic of continuum mechanics primarily dealing with deformation, whereas continuum mechanics in general deals with general body motion, often resulting in mathematical models with problems such as nonlinearity and large dimensionality.

14.8.1 Reference Frames and Coordinate Systems

The configurations of the bodies in the multibody system are characterized by values of measurable quantities such as positions, velocities, and accelerations. These values must be related to some coordinate system or frame of reference, for example, as described by classes such as `Frame`, `Frame_a` and `Frame_b` in the `Interfaces` sublibrary of the Modelica MBS library. Figure 14-25 shows two coordinate systems. The ***reference frame*** $\mathbf{X}_1\mathbf{X}_2\mathbf{X}_3$ to the lower left consists of the orthogonal axes $\mathbf{X}_1$, $\mathbf{X}_2$, and $\mathbf{X}_3$ based in the origin point O of the system. The orientation of the axes is defined by the unit vectors $\mathbf{i}_1$, $\mathbf{i}_2$, and $\mathbf{i}_3$ pointing along the respective axes. An arbitrary vector, e.g. $\mathbf{r}_p^i$ depicted in Figure 14-25, can be expressed in this coordinate system using its three components $r_{1\text{p}}^i, r_{2\text{p}}^i, r_{3\text{p}}^i$ along the respective axes:

$$\mathbf{r}_p^i = r_{1\text{p}}^i \cdot \mathbf{i}_1 + r_{2\text{p}}^i \cdot \mathbf{i}_2 + r_{3\text{p}}^i \cdot \mathbf{i}_3 \tag{14-97}$$

In a cartesian coordinate system this can be stated using mathematical vector notation:

$$\mathbf{r}_p^i = \begin{pmatrix} r_{1\text{p}}^i \\ r_{2\text{p}}^i \\ r_{3\text{p}}^i \end{pmatrix} \tag{14-98}$$

or using the more compact curly braces vector notation:

$$\mathbf{r}_p^i = \{r_{1\text{p}}^i, r_{2\text{p}}^i, r_{3\text{p}}^i\} \tag{14-99}$$

Note, however, that even though equations (14-97) and (14-98) appear equivalent, there is a subtle difference. Equation (14-97) is always true as stated, whereas (14-98) is relative to a particular cartesian coordinate system and might look different if another coordinate system is chosen.

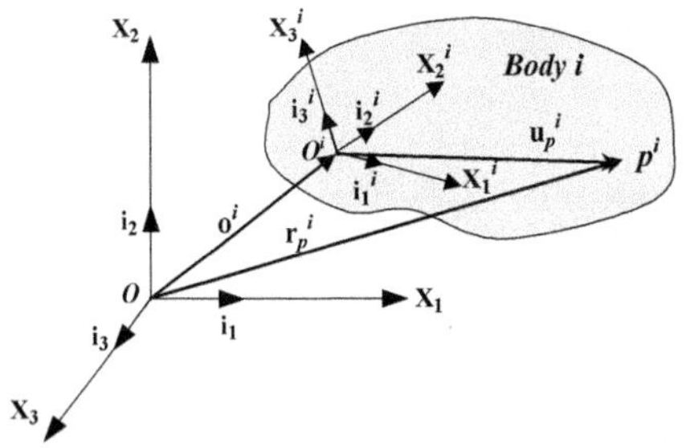

Figure 14-25. Reference frame $\mathbf{X}_1\mathbf{X}_2\mathbf{X}_3$, also called the inertial coordinate system, and the body coordinate system $\mathbf{X}_1\mathbf{X}_2\mathbf{X}_3$ for body i, conceptually consisting of arbitrary point-like particles P^i.

In general, two types of coordinate systems are needed in multibody systems:

- A *global* or *inertial frame* of reference, also called the inertial coordinate system or inertial frame. The inertial frame can be represented by an instance of the class `InertialSystem` in the Modelica MBS library. The unit vectors $\mathbf{i}_1$, $\mathbf{i}_2$, and $\mathbf{i}_3$ of the inertial frame depicted in Figure 14-25 are fixed in time, that is, they have constant magnitude and direction, and the origin O of the system does not move.
- A *body coordinate system*, or *body frame* of reference, attached to each body in the system, that translates and rotates with the body. Such frames can be represented by instances of the classes `Frame_a` and `Frame_b` in the Modelica MBS library. The unit vectors $\mathbf{i}_1^i$, $\mathbf{i}_2^i$, and $\mathbf{i}_3^i$ of the body coordinate system of body i have changeable orientations, and the origin O^i is subject to translational movement.

The reason to have a body coordinate system attached to each body is that many local relationships and formulas related to the body become much simpler when expressed in the body coordinate system. The vectors expressed in the body frame can always be transformed into the global inertial coordinate system through translational and rotational coordinate transformations, which is needed when quantities from different bodies are related to each other.

14.8.2 Particle Mechanics with Kinematics and Kinetics

The subject of dynamics involves the study of the motion of particles and bodies, and can be divided into two subareas:

- *Kinematics* studies motion without regard to the forces that cause it, that is, with focus on geometric aspects. Kinematic quantities are translational and angular *position*, *velocity*, and *acceleration*, which become "potential" variables in Modelica models.
- *Kinetics* deals with motion including the forces that produce it. Force-related kinetic or dynamic quantities are *force* and *torque*, which are represented by flow variables in Modelica models.

In order to understand the kinematics and dynamics of bodies in a multibody system, it is important to understand the motion of the particles that comprise the body. Therefore we start with a short discussion of the kinematic and dynamic properties of particles.

14.8.2.1 Particle Kinematics

A particle has no dimensions and therefore can be represented by a point in three-dimensional space. Therefore, the motion of a particle can be treated as translational motion of a point relative to a frame of reference. The position vector **r** of a point ***p*** in a coordinate system as depicted in Figure 5-40 can be expressed as follows:

$$\mathbf{r} = r_1 \cdot \mathbf{i}_1 + r_2 \cdot \mathbf{i}_2 + r_3 \cdot \mathbf{i}_3 \qquad (14\text{-}100)$$

which in a cartesian coordinate system can be stated using vector notation:

$$\mathbf{r} = \{r_1, r_2, r_3\} \qquad (14\text{-}101)$$

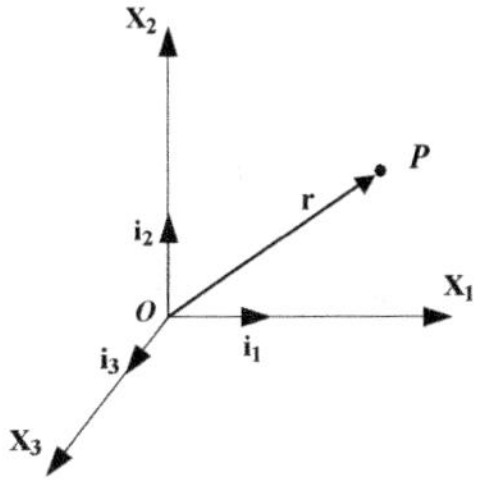

Figure 14-26. Position of a particle *P* with respect to a coordinate system.

The velocity **v** of a particle represented as a point is the time derivative of the position vector of that point. This can be expressed as follows in an inertial coordinate system where the unit vectors $\mathbf{i}_1$, $\mathbf{i}_2$, and $\mathbf{i}_3$ have constant magnitude and direction:

$$\mathbf{v} = \dot{\mathbf{r}} = \frac{d}{dt}\mathbf{r} = \dot{r}_1 \cdot \mathbf{i}_1 + \dot{r}_2 \cdot \mathbf{i}_2 + \dot{r}_3 \cdot \mathbf{i}_3 \qquad (14\text{-}102)$$

The acceleration of the particle becomes:

$$\mathbf{a} = \dot{\mathbf{v}} = \frac{d}{dt}\mathbf{v} = \ddot{r}_1 \cdot \mathbf{i}_1 + \ddot{r}_2 \cdot \mathbf{i}_2 + \ddot{r}_3 \cdot \mathbf{i}_3$$

14.8.2.2 Particle Dynamics

The motion of a particle is determined by Newton's second law:

$$\mathbf{f} = \dot{\mathbf{p}} = \frac{d}{dt}(m \cdot \mathbf{v}) \qquad (14\text{-}103)$$

where **f** is the applied force and **p** is the momentum. For nonrelativistic cases where the mass m is constant, this can be expressed as an equation relating the force vector **f** to the acceleration vector **a**:

$$\mathbf{f} = m \cdot \mathbf{a} \qquad (14\text{-}104)$$

This corresponds to the following three scalar component equations:

$$f_1 = m \cdot a_1,\ f_2 = m \cdot a_2,\ f_3 = m \cdot a_3 \qquad (14\text{-}105)$$

14.8.3 Rigid-Body Mechanics

Rigid bodies have masses that are distributed in space, that is, not just point masses. A rigid body can be thought of as consisting of a very large number of particles, all related by fixed relative translations and rotations. Therefore a rigid body as a whole can be characterized by three translational and three rotational coordinates, six in total. Figure 14-25 depicts a rigid body i in three-dimensional space, together with the global inertial coordinate system $\mathbf{X}_1\mathbf{X}_2\mathbf{X}_3$ and a body local coordinate system $\mathbf{X}_1^i\mathbf{X}_2^i\mathbf{X}_3^i$ whose origin O^i is rigidly attached to some point in the body, and which translates and rotates with the body. The position of an arbitrary point P_p^i of the body can be defined by the vector $\mathbf{r}_p^i = \{r_{1p}^i, r_{2p}^i, r_{3p}^i\}$ in the global coordinate system as depicted in Figure 14-25, and defined as the sum of two vectors:

$$\mathbf{r}_p^i = \mathbf{o}^i + \mathbf{u}_p^i \tag{14-106}$$

where $\mathbf{o}^i = \{o_1^i, o_2^i, o_3^i\}$ is the position of the origin O^i of the body i system, and the relative position vector $\mathbf{u}_p^i = \{u_{1p}^i, u_{2p}^i, u_{3p}^i\}$, both expressed in the global coordinate system. However, the relative position is more conveniently obtained as the fixed vector $\bar{\mathbf{u}}^i = \{\bar{u}_1^i, \bar{u}_2^i, \bar{u}_3^i\}$ in the local body coordinate system since it denotes a fixed rigid vector relative to the origin O^i. If the local system unit vectors $\mathbf{i}_1^i$, $\mathbf{i}_2^i$, and $\mathbf{i}_3^i$ are expressed in the global coordinate system, we obtain $\mathbf{u}_p^i$ as follows:

$$\mathbf{u}_p^i = \bar{u}_{1p}^i \cdot \mathbf{i}_1^i + \bar{u}_{2p}^i \cdot \mathbf{i}_2^i + \bar{u}_{3p}^i \cdot \mathbf{i}_3^i \tag{14-107}$$

The rotational transformation from the local coordinate system to the global inertial coordinate system can be represented by a rotation matrix $\mathbf{S}^i$, as further discussed in Section 14.8.4. Since $\mathbf{u}_p^i$ is relative to the origin O^i and we keep the same scale, only the rotational transformation remains and we obtain:

$$\mathbf{u}_p^i = \mathbf{S}^i \cdot \bar{\mathbf{u}}_p^i \tag{14-108}$$

Putting everything together, with the translation taken care of by the vector $\mathbf{o}^i$:

$$\mathbf{r}_p^i = \mathbf{o}^i + \mathbf{S}^i \cdot \bar{\mathbf{u}}_p^i \tag{14-109}$$

14.8.4 Rotation Matrix

The rotation matrix $\mathbf{S}^i$ is used to perform rotational transformations of vectors expressed in the local body i coordinate system to the global inertial system. There are several different ways of deriving this rotation matrix, including Euler angles or Euler parameters. Such methods have computational and modeling advantages but will not be described here since they are more complicated than the simple method of direction cosines which is used by the Modelica MBS library and presented in the next section.

14.8.4.1 Direction Cosines

Consider the local body i coordinate system or frame and the global inertial frame. The origins of both frames have been placed at the same point to eliminate translation as depicted in Figure 14-27. We want to derive the coordinate transformation of a point $\mathbf{u}^i = \{u_1^i, u_2^i, u_3^i\}$ expressed in the *global frame* of reference to the same point $\bar{\mathbf{u}}^i = \{\bar{u}_1^i, \bar{u}_2^i, \bar{u}_3^i\}$ expressed in the *local frame*, and vice versa.

Let $\mathbf{i}_1^i$, $\mathbf{i}_2^i$, and $\mathbf{i}_3^i$ be the orthogonal unit vectors of the local body i frame $\mathbf{X}_1^i\mathbf{X}_2^i\mathbf{X}_3^i$, and $\mathbf{i}_1$, $\mathbf{i}_2$, and $\mathbf{i}_3$ the orthogonal unit vectors of the inertial frame $\mathbf{X}_1\mathbf{X}_2\mathbf{X}_3$.

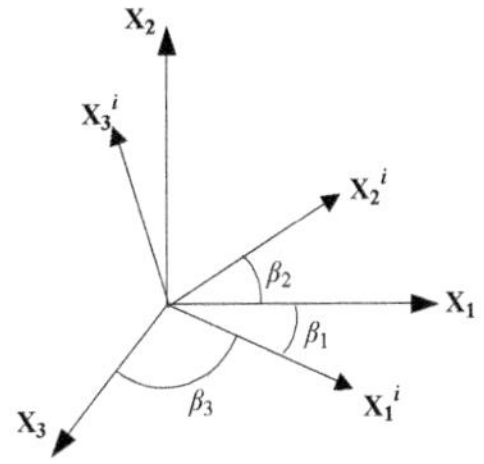

Figure 14-27. Angles for direction cosines between the X_1^i axis and the three inertial system axes.

Let β_1, β_2, and β_3 be the angles between the $\mathbf{X}_1^i$ axis and the three inertial frame axes $\mathbf{X}_1$, $\mathbf{X}_2$, and $\mathbf{X}_3$ respectively, as depicted in Figure 14-27. The direction cosines c_{11}, c_{12}, and c_{13} of the $\mathbf{X}_1^i$ axis with respect to the three inertial frame axes $\mathbf{X}_1$, $\mathbf{X}_2$, and $\mathbf{X}_3$ can be obtained as follows by taking the cosines of the angles or the scalar product between the unit vectors:

$$\begin{aligned} c_{11} &= \cos(\beta_1) = \mathbf{i}_1^i \cdot \mathbf{i}_1 \\ c_{12} &= \cos(\beta_2) = \mathbf{i}_1^i \cdot \mathbf{i}_2 \\ c_{13} &= \cos(\beta_3) = \mathbf{i}_1^i \cdot \mathbf{i}_3 \end{aligned} \tag{14-110}$$

In a similar way, the direction cosines c_{21}, c_{22}, and c_{23} of the $\mathbf{X}_2^i$ axis and c_{31}, c_{32}, and c_{33} of the $\mathbf{X}_3^i$ axis with respect to the inertial frame axes $\mathbf{X}_1$, $\mathbf{X}_2$, and $\mathbf{X}_3$ can be computed. Using these relations one can define the unit vectors $\mathbf{i}_1^i$, $\mathbf{i}_2^i$, and $\mathbf{i}_3^i$ in terms of the unit vectors $\mathbf{i}_1$, $\mathbf{i}_2$, and $\mathbf{i}_3$:

$$\begin{aligned} \mathbf{i}_1^i &= c_{11}\mathbf{i}_1 + c_{12}\mathbf{i}_2 + c_{13}\mathbf{i}_3 \\ \mathbf{i}_2^i &= c_{21}\mathbf{i}_1 + c_{22}\mathbf{i}_2 + c_{23}\mathbf{i}_3 \\ \mathbf{i}_3^i &= c_{31}\mathbf{i}_1 + c_{32}\mathbf{i}_2 + c_{33}\mathbf{i}_3 \end{aligned} \tag{14-111}$$

We now consider the three-dimensional vector $\mathbf{u}^i$ with components u_1^i, u_2^i, u_3^i in the inertial frame and $\bar{u}_1^i$, $\bar{u}_2^i$, $\bar{u}_3^i$ in the local frame:

$$\begin{aligned} \mathbf{u}^i &= u_1^i\mathbf{i}_1 + u_2^i\mathbf{i}_2 + u_3^i\mathbf{i}_3 \\ &= \bar{u}_1^i\mathbf{i}_1^i + \bar{u}_2^i\mathbf{i}_2^i + \bar{u}_3^i\mathbf{i}_3^i \end{aligned} \tag{14-112}$$

Using the fact that the product between orthogonal unit vectors is 0 if they are different and 1 if they are identical, we obtain:

$$\begin{aligned} \bar{u}_1^i &= \mathbf{u}^i \cdot \mathbf{i}_1^i = c_{11}u_1^i + c_{12}u_2^i + c_{13}u_3^i \\ \bar{u}_2^i &= \mathbf{u}^i \cdot \mathbf{i}_2^i = c_{21}u_1^i + c_{22}u_2^i + c_{23}u_3^i \\ \bar{u}_3^i &= \mathbf{u}^i \cdot \mathbf{i}_{13}^i = c_{31}u_1^i + c_{32}u_2^i + c_{33}u_3^i \end{aligned} \tag{14-113}$$

which in matrix notation appears as:

$$\begin{pmatrix} \bar{u}_1^i \\ \bar{u}_2^i \\ \bar{u}_3^i \end{pmatrix} = \begin{pmatrix} c_{11} & c_{12} & c_{13} \\ c_{21} & c_{22} & c_{23} \\ c_{31} & c_{32} & c_{33} \end{pmatrix} \begin{pmatrix} u_1^i \\ u_2^i \\ u_3^i \end{pmatrix} \tag{14-114}$$

that is:

$$\bar{\mathbf{u}}^i = \mathbf{C}\mathbf{u}^i \tag{14-115}$$

Since for orthogonal matrices such as **C**, the inverse of a matrix $\mathbf{C}^{-1} = \mathbf{C}^{\mathrm{T}}$, is equal to the transpose of the matrix, we obtain:

$$\mathbf{u}^{i} = \mathbf{C}^{\mathrm{T}}\overline{\mathbf{u}}^{i} \tag{14-116}$$

Thus, our desired rotational transformation matrix **S**, also denoted $\mathbf{R}^{-1}$, for transformations from the local body *i* frame to the global inertial frame is:

$$\mathbf{S} \quad \mathbf{C}^{\mathrm{T}} \tag{14-117}$$

The opposite transformation, the rotation matrix **R** for transformations of vectors from the global inertial frame to the local body *i* frame, used in the new Modelica multi-body library (see Section 15.10, page 877), then becomes:

$$\mathbf{R} = \mathbf{C} = \mathbf{S}^{-1} \tag{14-118}$$

The function *v2*=`MultiBody.Frames.resolve2`(**R**, *v1*) for transforming a vector *v1* from frame 1 to frame 2 is intended for vector transformations in this direction, for example, from the inertial frame to the local body frame.

14.8.4.2 Euler and Cardan Angles

In the previous section we formulated a rotation matrix based on direction cosines of the angles β_1, β_2, and β_3 between the local body frame axes and the three inertial frame axes.

However, from a physical modeling and application point of view it is usually more natural to express the rotational transformation as a series of successive rotations around the local body coordinate axes. This approach to constructing the rotation matrix is called Euler or Cardan angles, depending on the order these rotations are applied. These angles are different from the angles used in the direction cosine formulation described in the previous section since the a rotation around one local coordinate axis causes the direction of the other two local coordinate axes to change.

Assume that the axes of the local body frame are initially aligned with the global inertial frame, and that the body is then rotated, described by a vector $\{\varphi_1,\varphi_2,\varphi_3\}$ for the three successive rotation angles.

To rotate the local body frame coordinate system from its initial configuration aligned with the inertial frame to some arbitrary desired orientation using the Cardan angle approach—rotation sequence {1,2,3}, we first rotate around the x axis (the first axis) by an angle φ_1, then around the resulting y axis (the second axis) by an angle φ_2, and finally around the resulting z axis (the third axis) by an angle φ_3. The third step is shown in Figure 14-28 assuming the first two rotations are zero. The Euler angle rotation sequence is {3,1,3}.

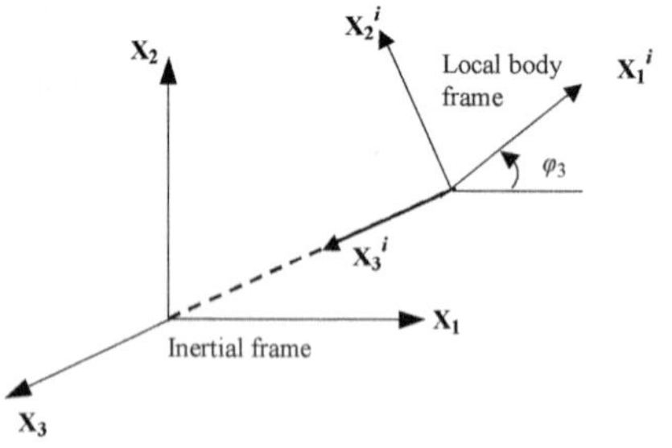

Figure 14-28. Rotating the x_1^{i} and x_2^{i} axes in the local coordinate frame by an angle φ_3 around the x_3^{i} axis as a step in the Cardan/Euler angle rotation sequences.

The respective rotation matrices denoted $\mathbf{R}_1$, $\mathbf{R}_2$, and $\mathbf{R}_3$, are defined as follows using Cardan angles:

$$\mathbf{R}_1: \begin{pmatrix} 1 & 0 & 0 \\ 0 & \cos\varphi_1 & \sin\varphi_1 \\ 0 & -\sin\varphi_1 & \cos\varphi_1 \end{pmatrix}, \mathbf{R}_2: \begin{pmatrix} \cos\varphi_2 & 0 & -\sin\varphi_2 \\ 0 & 1 & 0 \\ \sin\varphi_2 & 0 & \cos\varphi_2 \end{pmatrix}, \mathbf{R}_3: \begin{pmatrix} \cos\varphi_3 & \sin\varphi_3 & 0 \\ -\sin\varphi_3 & \cos\varphi_3 & 0 \\ 0 & 0 & 1 \end{pmatrix} \quad (14\text{-}119)$$

Each of these three rotation matrices can be obtained by applying the MBS library function `MultiBody.Frames.axisRotation(i,angle)` to the arguments $(1, \varphi_1)$, $(2, \varphi_2)$, or $(3, \varphi_3)$ respectively.

The total rotational transformation matrix $\mathbf{R}$ $\mathbf{R}_3$ $\mathbf{R}_2$ $\mathbf{R}_1$ (which is defined in the MBS class `MultiBody.Parts.Body`) for rotating the local body frame to its desired orientation then becomes:

$$\mathbf{R}: \begin{pmatrix} \cos\varphi_2\cos\varphi_3 & \cos\varphi_1\sin\varphi_3 + \sin\varphi_1\sin\varphi_2\cos\varphi_3 & \sin\varphi_1\sin\varphi_3 - \cos\varphi_1\sin\varphi_2\cos\varphi_3 \\ -\cos\varphi_2\sin\varphi_3 & \cos\varphi_1\cos\varphi_3 - \sin\varphi_1\sin\varphi_2\sin\varphi_3 & \sin\varphi_1\cos\varphi_3 + \cos\varphi_1\sin\varphi_2\sin\varphi_3 \\ \sin\varphi_2 & -\sin\varphi_1\cos\varphi_2 & \cos\varphi_1\cos\varphi_2 \end{pmatrix} \quad (14\text{-}120)$$

This rotation matrix R is based on Cardan angles, that is, the rotation sequence {1, 2, 3}.

An absolute vector $\mathbf{u}^i$ expressed in the inertial frame can be transformed into the relative vector $\overline{\mathbf{u}}^i$ expressed in the local body frame using the rotation matrix $\mathbf{R}$:

$$\overline{\mathbf{u}}^i = \mathbf{R}\cdot\mathbf{u}^i = \mathbf{R}_3\mathbf{R}_2\mathbf{R}_1\cdot\mathbf{u}^i \quad (14\text{-}121)$$

This rotation is used, for example, in the Modelica MBS library, in class `MultiBody.Parts.Body`.

The rotation matrix in the other direction, rotating the local body frame back to the orientation of the inertial frame, is obtained as usual by taking the inverse (i.e., the transpose) of the orthogonal matrix $\mathbf{R}$:

$$\mathbf{S} = \mathbf{R}^{-1} = \mathbf{R}^{\mathrm{T}} \quad (14\text{-}122)$$

The inverse transformation applied to a local body vector, i.e., of the vector $\overline{\mathbf{u}}^i$ expressed in the local body frame into its representation $\mathbf{u}^i$ in the inertial frame, is obtained by applying $\mathbf{R}^{-1}$ or by successively applying the 3 inverse rotations, starting with $\mathbf{R}_3^{-1}$.

$$\mathbf{u}^i = \mathbf{R}^{-1}\overline{\mathbf{u}}^i = \mathbf{R}_1^{-1}\mathbf{R}_2^{-1}\mathbf{R}_3^{-1}\overline{\mathbf{u}}^i \quad (14\text{-}123)$$

14.8.4.3 Euler Parameters and Quaternions

The singularities that occur when computing derivatives of rotations for certain Euler angles can be avoided if a 4-vector representation $\mathbf{q} = \{q_1, q_2, q_3, q_4\}$ of four *interdependent* variables is introduced instead of our previous 3-vector Euler angle representation. These 4 variables are dependent on each other since a rotation matrix represents 3 degrees of freedom. This representation is known under two names: *Euler parameters* or *Quaternions*—note that the Euler *angles* presented in the previous section is a different representation. The rotation matrix $\mathbf{R}$ can be computed as follows in terms of these four parameters:

$$\mathbf{R} = \begin{pmatrix} 2(q_1^2+q_4^2)-1 & 2(q_1q_2+q_3q_4) & 2(q_1q_3-q_2q_4) \\ 2(q_1q_2-q_3q_4) & 2(q_2^2+q_4^2)-1 & 2(q_2q_3+q_1q_4) \\ 2(q_1q_3+q_2q_4) & 2(q_2q_3-q_1q_4) & 2(q_3^2+q_4^2)-1 \end{pmatrix} \quad (14\text{-}124)$$

or expressed using matrix and vector operations:

$$\mathbf{R} = (2q_4^2-1)\mathbf{I} + 2\mathbf{q}_{1\text{-}3}\mathbf{q}_{1\text{-}3}^{\mathrm{T}} - q_4\mathbf{Q}_{1\text{-}3}^{w} \quad (14\text{-}125)$$

where $\mathbf{I}$ is the 3x3 identity matrix, $\mathbf{q}_{1-3}$ is a column vector of elements 1-3 of the $\mathbf{q}$ vector, and $\mathbf{Q}_{1-3}^{w}$ is the skew matrix (see (14-138) , page 780) formed from the vector $\mathbf{q}_{1-3}$. These definitions are available in the function `MultiBody.Frames.fromQ` in the Modelica MBS library, see Section 15.10, page 877.

We will not further discuss this representation, and refer the reader to appropriate literature. The Modelica MBS library has an option to use quaternions, see the note in Section 15.10.11, page 902.

14.8.5 The 4 × 4 Transformation Matrix

Previously we showed (14-109) that the position $\mathbf{r}^i$ of an arbitrary point P on the rigid body could be expressed in the global inertial frame as:

$$\mathbf{r}^i = \mathbf{o}^i + \mathbf{S}^i \cdot \overline{\mathbf{u}}^i \tag{14-126}$$

where $\mathbf{o}^i$ is the position for the origin of the local body i coordinate system or frame, $\mathbf{S}^i$ is the matrix for rotational transformations from the local frame to the global frame, and $\overline{\mathbf{u}}^i$ is the position of the point P expressed in the local body i frame relative to the origin O^i. This transformation can be expressed compactly using a 4 × 4 transformation matrix $\mathbf{S}_4^i$ that takes care of both rotation and translation, where we introduce the 4-vectors $\mathbf{r}_4^i$ and $\overline{\mathbf{u}}_4^i$:

$$\mathbf{r}_4^i \quad \mathbf{S}_4^i \quad \overline{\mathbf{u}}_4^i \tag{14-127}$$

This equation is shown in component form below where the matrix $\mathbf{S}_4^i$ is constructed from $\mathbf{S}^i$ and $\mathbf{o}^i$:

$$\begin{pmatrix} r_1^i \\ r_2^i \\ r_3^i \\ 1 \end{pmatrix} = \begin{pmatrix} S_{11}^i & S_{12}^i & S_{13}^i & o_1^i \\ S_{21}^i & S_{22}^i & S_{23}^i & o_2^i \\ S_{31}^i & S_{32}^i & S_{33}^i & o_3^i \\ 0 & 0 & 0 & 1 \end{pmatrix} \begin{pmatrix} \overline{u}_1^i \\ \overline{u}_2^i \\ \overline{u}_3^i \\ 1 \end{pmatrix} \tag{14-128}$$

The inverse equation is:

$$\overline{\mathbf{u}}_4^i = (\mathbf{S}_4^i)^{-1} \cdot \mathbf{r}_4^i \tag{14-129}$$

The inverse matrix $(\mathbf{S}_4^i)^{-1}$ is not equal to the transpose $(\mathbf{S}_4^i)^{\mathrm{T}}$ since it is not orthogonal, but can be constructed as follows:

$$(\mathbf{S}_4^i)^{-1} = \begin{pmatrix} \left(\mathbf{S}^i\right)^{-1} & -\left(\mathbf{S}^i\right)^{-1}\mathbf{o}^i \\ \{0,0,0\} & 1 \end{pmatrix} \tag{14-130}$$

where the inverse rotation matrix $\left(\mathbf{S}^i\right)^{-1} = \left(\mathbf{S}^i\right)^{T}$ since it is orthogonal. The 4 × 4 transformation matrix formulation is common in virtual reality software packages and in certain multibody system packages, but currently not used by the Modelica MBS library.

14.8.5.1 Coordinate System Kinematics

In this section we develop the equations for frame or coordinate system kinematics. These equations relate the kinematic quantities position $\mathbf{r}$, velocity $\mathbf{v}=\dot{\mathbf{r}}$, and acceleration $\mathbf{a}=\ddot{\mathbf{r}}$ between an arbitrary local frame and the inertial frame of reference. The developed equations are used in a slightly different form to relate quantities between two local frames, which, for example, is common for mechanical elements such as joints that consist of two parts. Two frames are related by a translation vector, for example, $\mathbf{o}$ in Figure 14-29, and a rotation about some axis that can be expressed in the inertial frame.

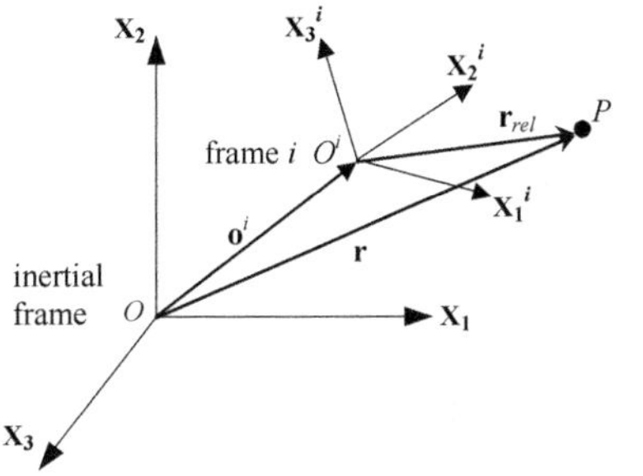

Figure 14-29. A local frame related to the inertial frame by a translation vector o^i and a rotation matrix S^i, with the relative position vector r_{rel} of the point P expressed in the inertial frame.

Since the expressions for position, velocity, and acceleration of an arbitrary point P can be easily obtained just by adding the corresponding relative and frame quantities expressed in the inertial frame according to the equations below, we will for a while ignore the vector $\mathbf{o}$ and focus on the relative vector $\mathbf{r}_{rel}$.

$$\begin{aligned} \mathbf{r} &= \mathbf{o}^i + \mathbf{r}_{rel} \\ \dot{\mathbf{r}} &= \dot{\mathbf{o}}^i + \dot{\mathbf{r}}_{rel} \\ \ddot{\mathbf{r}} &= \ddot{\mathbf{o}}^i + \ddot{\mathbf{r}}_{rel} \end{aligned} \tag{14-131}$$

The rotational transformation matrix S transforms the relative vector $\overline{\mathbf{r}}_{rel}$ expressed in the local frame i to the global inertial frame:

$$\mathbf{r}_{rel} = \mathbf{S}^i \cdot \overline{\mathbf{r}}_{rel} \tag{14-132}$$

By taking the time derivative we obtain the relative velocity vector $\mathbf{v}_{rel}$:

$$\mathbf{v}_{rel} = \dot{\mathbf{r}}_{rel} = \dot{\mathbf{S}}^i \cdot \overline{\mathbf{r}}_{rel} + \mathbf{S}^i \cdot \dot{\overline{\mathbf{r}}}_{rel} \tag{14-133}$$

The rotation matrix $\mathbf{S}^i$ describes the change in orientation, that is, relative angles, of the local frame compared to the inertial frame. The derivative $\dot{\mathbf{S}}^i$ describes the angular change in orientation per unit time, that is, rotational movement. Rotation is always around some axis. The direction of that axis is defined by introducing the *angular velocity vector* $\boldsymbol{\omega}^i$, which can change orientation over time (Figure 14-30).

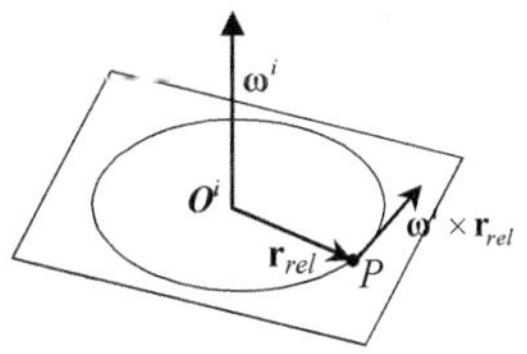

Figure 14-30. Rotational part of the movement of point P expressed as cross product $\boldsymbol{\omega}^i \times \mathbf{r}_{rel}$ between the angular velocity vector and the relative position vector.

One can show that the part $\dot{\mathbf{S}}^i \cdot \overline{\mathbf{r}}_{rel}$ of the velocity vector $\mathbf{v}_{rel}$ caused by rotation of the frame around an axis through the origin O^i can be expressed as the cross product between an angular velocity vector $\boldsymbol{\omega}^i$ expressed in the inertial frame ($\overline{\boldsymbol{\omega}}^i$ in the local frame) and the relative vector $\mathbf{r}_{rel}$ (or $\overline{\mathbf{r}}_{rel}$ expressed in the local frame):

$$\dot{\mathbf{S}}^i \cdot \overline{\mathbf{r}}_{rel} = \boldsymbol{\omega}^i \times \mathbf{r}_{rel} = \mathbf{S}^i \cdot (\overline{\boldsymbol{\omega}}^i \times \overline{\mathbf{r}}_{rel}) \tag{14-134}$$

Thus, the total relative velocity vector of the point P expressed in the inertial frame becomes:

$$\mathbf{v}_{rel} = \dot{\mathbf{r}}_{rel} = \boldsymbol{\omega}^i \times \mathbf{r}_{rel} + \mathbf{S}^i \cdot \dot{\bar{\mathbf{r}}}_{rel} \tag{14-135}$$

The *velocity vector* expressed using vectors in the local body frame after some rearrangement:

$$\mathbf{v}_{rel} = \dot{\mathbf{r}}_{rel} = \mathbf{S}^i \cdot (\dot{\bar{\mathbf{r}}}_{rel} + \bar{\boldsymbol{\omega}}^i \times \bar{\mathbf{r}}_{rel}) \tag{14-136}$$

Here $\dot{\bar{\mathbf{r}}}_{rel}$ denotes change of the vector $\bar{\mathbf{r}}_{rel}$ not related to rotation around the origin since that rotation is already expressed by the rotation of the local frame itself. It is rather, e.g. change of length. Now we want to derive the expression for the acceleration, and for this purpose will need to transform the cross products in terms of matrix multiplications by skew symmetric matrices.

A general mathematical result is that any cross product, for example, $\boldsymbol{\omega} \times \mathbf{r}$, can be expressed as a matrix multiplication by a so-called *skew symmetric matrix* $\mathbf{W}$:

$$\boldsymbol{\omega} \times \mathbf{r} = \mathbf{W} \cdot \mathbf{r} \tag{14-137}$$

where

$$\mathbf{W} = \begin{pmatrix} 0 & -\omega_3 & \omega_2 \\ \omega_3 & 0 & -\omega_1 \\ -\omega_2 & \omega_1 & 0 \end{pmatrix} \tag{14-138}$$

Applying this result to the cross product with the rotation vector $\boldsymbol{\omega}^i$:

$$\boldsymbol{\omega}^i \times \mathbf{r}_{rel} = \mathbf{W}^i \cdot \mathbf{r}_{rel} = \mathbf{W}^i \cdot \mathbf{S}^i \cdot \bar{\mathbf{r}}_{rel} \tag{14-139}$$

Substituting into the equation for the velocity vector:

$$\mathbf{v}_{rel} = \dot{\mathbf{r}}_{rel} = \boldsymbol{\omega}^i \times \mathbf{r}_{rel} + \mathbf{S}^i \cdot \dot{\bar{\mathbf{r}}}_{rel} = \mathbf{W}^i \cdot (\mathbf{S}^i \cdot \bar{\mathbf{r}}_{rel}) + \mathbf{S}^i \cdot \dot{\bar{\mathbf{r}}}_{rel} \tag{14-140}$$

Differentiating the above equation:

$$\mathbf{a}_{rel} = \ddot{\mathbf{r}}_{rel} = \dot{\mathbf{W}}^i \cdot (\mathbf{S}^i \cdot \bar{\mathbf{r}}_{rel}) + \mathbf{W}^i \cdot (\dot{\mathbf{S}}^i \cdot \bar{\mathbf{r}}_{rel}) + \mathbf{W}^i \cdot (\mathbf{S}^i \cdot \dot{\bar{\mathbf{r}}}_{rel}) + \dot{\mathbf{S}}^i \cdot \dot{\bar{\mathbf{r}}}_{rel} + \mathbf{S}^i \cdot \ddot{\bar{\mathbf{r}}}_{rel} \tag{14-141}$$

Analogous to the previous (14-134) result $\dot{\mathbf{S}}^i \cdot \bar{\mathbf{r}}_{rel} = \boldsymbol{\omega}^i \times \mathbf{r}_{rel}$ we obtain $\dot{\mathbf{S}}^i \cdot \dot{\bar{\mathbf{r}}}_{rel} = \boldsymbol{\omega}^i \times \dot{\mathbf{r}}_{rel}$, which can be expressed as:

$$\dot{\mathbf{S}}^i \cdot \dot{\bar{\mathbf{r}}}_{rel} = \boldsymbol{\omega}^i \times \dot{\mathbf{r}}_{rel} = \mathbf{W}^i \cdot \dot{\mathbf{r}}_{rel} = \mathbf{W}^i \cdot \mathbf{v}_{rel} \tag{14-142}$$

After substitution into the previous acceleration equation, using $\mathbf{r}_{rel} = \mathbf{S}^i \cdot \bar{\mathbf{r}}_{rel}$, $\mathbf{v}_{rel} = \mathbf{S}^i \cdot \bar{\mathbf{v}}_{rel}$, $\dot{\mathbf{S}}^i \cdot \dot{\bar{\mathbf{r}}}_{rel} = \mathbf{W}^i \cdot \mathbf{v}_{rel}$, and $\dot{\mathbf{S}}^i \cdot \bar{\mathbf{r}}_{rel} = \mathbf{W}^i \cdot \mathbf{r}_{rel}$ and rearranging terms we obtain:

$$\mathbf{a}_{rel} = \ddot{\mathbf{r}}_{rel} = \mathbf{S}^i \cdot \ddot{\bar{\mathbf{r}}}_{rel} + 2\mathbf{W}^i \cdot \mathbf{v}_{rel} + \dot{\mathbf{W}}^i \cdot \mathbf{r}_{rel} + \mathbf{W}^i \cdot \mathbf{W}^i \cdot \mathbf{r}_{rel} \tag{14-143}$$

We obtain the desired form of the equation for the *relative acceleration vector* by converting back from matrix multiplication by $\mathbf{W}^i$ to cross product by $\boldsymbol{\omega}^i$:

$$\mathbf{a}_{rel} = \ddot{\mathbf{r}}_{rel} = \mathbf{S}^i \cdot \ddot{\bar{\mathbf{r}}}_{rel} + 2\boldsymbol{\omega}^i \times \mathbf{v}_{rel} + \dot{\boldsymbol{\omega}}^i \times \mathbf{r}_{rel} + \boldsymbol{\omega}^i \times (\boldsymbol{\omega}^i \times \mathbf{r}_{rel}) \tag{14-144}$$

To summarize, the vector equations for the absolute position $\mathbf{r}$, velocity $\mathbf{v}$, and acceleration $\mathbf{a}$ for an arbitrary point P appears as follows expressed in the inertial frame related to the relative vectors in the local frame when the translational part has been added and the relative vectors together with the rotation vector are expressed in the local body i frame:

$$
\begin{aligned}
\mathbf{r} &= \mathbf{o}^i + \mathbf{S}^i \cdot \overline{\mathbf{r}}_{rel} \\
\mathbf{v} &= \dot{\mathbf{o}}^i + \mathbf{S}^i \cdot (\dot{\overline{\mathbf{r}}}_{rel} + \overline{\boldsymbol{\omega}}^i \times \overline{\mathbf{r}}_{rel}) \\
\mathbf{a} &= \ddot{\mathbf{o}}^i + \mathbf{S}^i \cdot (\ddot{\overline{\mathbf{r}}}_{rel} + 2\overline{\boldsymbol{\omega}}^i \times \overline{\mathbf{v}}_{rel} + \dot{\overline{\boldsymbol{\omega}}}^i \times \overline{\mathbf{r}}_{rel} + \overline{\boldsymbol{\omega}}^i \times (\overline{\boldsymbol{\omega}}^i \times \overline{\mathbf{r}}_{rel}))
\end{aligned} \qquad (14\text{-}145)
$$

We should mention that the special notation $\boldsymbol{\alpha}$ is often used in the literature for the *angular acceleration vector* $\dot{\boldsymbol{\omega}}$, but $\mathbf{z}$ is employed in the Modelica MBS library:

$$
\boldsymbol{\alpha} = \mathbf{z} = \dot{\boldsymbol{\omega}} \qquad (14\text{-}146)
$$

14.8.5.2 Equations Relating Two Local Frames

Why would you need to relate quantities in two different local frames? A common case is that a body in a multibody system itself consists of several bodies that can move in relation to each other, each with its own frame of reference. Another case is the existence of two or more frames on the same rigid body. In both cases we need to relate quantities such as positions, velocities, and accelerations of one frame to the corresponding quantities in another frame. There is also a need to transform dynamic quantities such as forces and torques when applied to one part of a body to the equivalent forces and torques if applied to another part. The goal of this section is to develop the general form of the equations relating two local frames as they appear e.g. in several Modelica MBS library classes such as `Interact`, `Interact2`, and `TreeJoint` in the sublibrary `Interfaces`, and in the class `FreeMotion` in the `Joint` sublibrary. These relations are relevant for all `Joint` classes, since those classes describe objects containing two coupled parts, each with its own frame of reference (Figure 14-31).

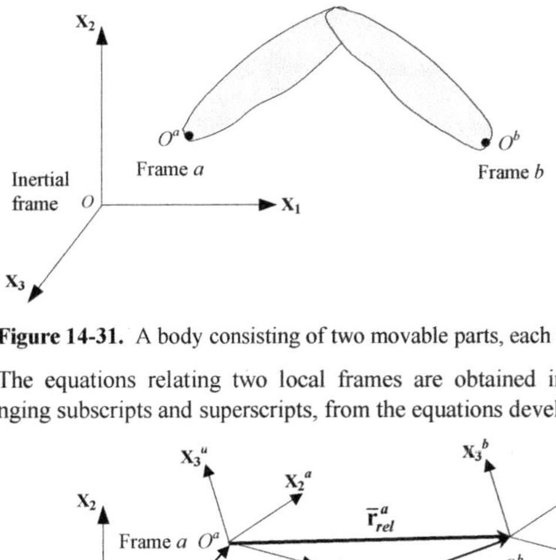

Figure 14-31. A body consisting of two movable parts, each with its own frame of reference.

The equations relating two local frames are obtained in a very straightforward way, e.g. just by changing subscripts and superscripts, from the equations developed in the previous section.

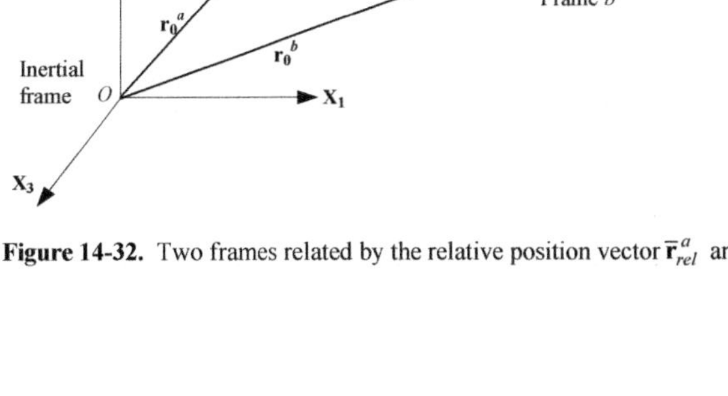

Figure 14-32. Two frames related by the relative position vector $\overline{\mathbf{r}}^{a}_{rel}$ and the relative rotation matrix $\mathbf{S}_{rel}$.

The relative rotation matrix $\mathbf{S}_{rel}$ transforms a vector expressed in frame a to frame b:

$$\mathbf{S}_{rel} = (\mathbf{S}^b)^{-1} \cdot \mathbf{S}^a \tag{14-147}$$

This is easy to see since an arbitrary vector $\overline{\mathbf{u}}^a$ in frame a is transformed into the inertial frame by $\mathbf{S}^a \cdot \overline{\mathbf{u}}^a$, and is transformed back from the inertial into frame b by the inverse of $\mathbf{S}^b$. The kinematic relationships relating the origins of the two frames [from (14-109)] to the inertial frame are:

$$\mathbf{r}_0^b = \mathbf{r}_0^a + \mathbf{S}^a \cdot \overline{\mathbf{r}}_{rel}^a \tag{14-148}$$

where $\mathbf{r}_0^b$ is the vector for the absolute position of the origin of frame b expressed in the inertial frame, $\mathbf{r}_0^b$ is the absolute position of the origin of frame a, and $\overline{\mathbf{r}}_{rel}^a$ is the relative vector from frame a to frame b expressed in frame a, as depicted in Figure 14-32. The relative translational motions between the origins of two frames are:

$$\begin{aligned} \overline{\mathbf{v}}_{rel}^a &= \dot{\overline{\mathbf{r}}}_{rel}^a \\ \overline{\mathbf{a}}_{rel}^a &= \ddot{\overline{\mathbf{r}}}_{rel}^a \end{aligned} \tag{14-149}$$

where $\overline{\mathbf{r}}_{rel}^a$ is the relative vector from the origin of frame a to the origin of frame b expressed in frame a, and $\overline{\mathbf{v}}_{rel}^a$ together with $\overline{\mathbf{a}}_{rel}^a$ are the corresponding velocity and acceleration vectors.

The equations relating the *absolute velocities* $\mathbf{v}$ and the *rotational velocities* $\boldsymbol{\omega}$ of the two frames are:

$$\begin{aligned} \overline{\mathbf{v}}^b &= \mathbf{S}_{rel} \cdot (\overline{\mathbf{v}}^a + \overline{\mathbf{v}}_{rel}^a + \overline{\boldsymbol{\omega}}^a \times \overline{\mathbf{r}}_{rel}^a) \\ \overline{\boldsymbol{\omega}}^b &= \mathbf{S}_{rel} \cdot (\overline{\boldsymbol{\omega}}^a + \overline{\boldsymbol{\omega}}_{rel}^a) \end{aligned} \tag{14-150}$$

where $\overline{\mathbf{v}}^b$ is the velocity of the origin of frame b expressed in frame b, $\overline{\mathbf{v}}^a$ is the velocity of frame a expressed in frame a, $\overline{\mathbf{v}}_{rel}^a$ is the relative velocity vector from the origin of frame a to frame b expressed in frame a, $\overline{\boldsymbol{\omega}}^a$ is the rotational velocity vector of frame a expressed in frame a, $\overline{\boldsymbol{\omega}}^b$ is the rotation velocity vector of frame b expressed in frame b, $\overline{\boldsymbol{\omega}}_{rel}^a$ is the relative angular velocity (rotation) vector between frame b and frame a corresponding to the rotation matrix $\mathbf{S}_{rel}$ and expressed in frame a.

Next we state the equations relating the absolute acceleration $\mathbf{a}$ and the angular acceleration $\dot{\boldsymbol{\omega}}$ (denoted by $\mathbf{z}$ in the Modelica MBS library) of the two frames, expressed in frame b on the left-hand side and in frame a on the right-hand side:

$$\begin{aligned} \overline{\mathbf{a}}^b &= \mathbf{S}_{rel} \cdot (\overline{\mathbf{a}}^a + \overline{\mathbf{a}}_{rel}^a + 2\overline{\boldsymbol{\omega}}^a \times \overline{\mathbf{v}}_{rel}^a + \dot{\overline{\boldsymbol{\omega}}}^a \times \overline{\mathbf{r}}_{rel}^a + \overline{\boldsymbol{\omega}}^a \times (\overline{\boldsymbol{\omega}}^a \times \overline{\mathbf{r}}_{rel}^a)) \\ \dot{\overline{\boldsymbol{\omega}}}^b &= \mathbf{S}_{rel} \cdot (\dot{\overline{\boldsymbol{\omega}}}^a + \dot{\overline{\boldsymbol{\omega}}}_{rel}^a + \overline{\boldsymbol{\omega}}^a \times \overline{\boldsymbol{\omega}}_{rel}^a) \end{aligned} \tag{14-151}$$

derived from (14-145) and (14-150) using $\overline{\mathbf{v}}_{rel}^a = \dot{\overline{\mathbf{r}}}_{rel}^a$ and $\overline{\mathbf{a}}_{rel}^a = \ddot{\overline{\mathbf{r}}}_{rel}^a$. The following two equations relate the vectors representing the dynamic quantities *force* and *torque* applied at the origins of frame a and frame b respectively:

$$\begin{aligned} \overline{\mathbf{f}}^b &= \mathbf{S}_{rel} \cdot \overline{\mathbf{f}}^a \\ \overline{\boldsymbol{\tau}}^b &= \mathbf{S}_{rel} \cdot (\overline{\boldsymbol{\tau}}^a - \overline{\mathbf{r}}_{rel}^a \times \overline{\mathbf{f}}^a) \end{aligned} \tag{14-152}$$

where $\overline{\mathbf{f}}^a$ and $\overline{\boldsymbol{\tau}}^a$ are the force and torque applied at the origin of frame a expressed in frame a and $\overline{\mathbf{f}}^b$ and $\overline{\boldsymbol{\tau}}^b$ are the same force and torque transformed to be applied at the origin of frame b expressed in frame b. The same equations apply for transforming forces and torques in the opposite direction, from frame b to frame a.

14.8.5.3 3D Rigid-body Kinematics

Here we develop the kinematic equations needed to state the dynamic equations of rigid bodies in the next section. It was previously shown [equations (14-145)] that the global position vector $\mathbf{r}$ and the corresponding velocity **v** and acceleration **a** of an arbitrary point *P* of a body *a* (previously denoted body *i*) with a reference frame *a*, e.g. as in Figure 14-33, are given by:

$$\begin{aligned}\mathbf{r} &= \mathbf{o}^a + \mathbf{S}^a \cdot \overline{\mathbf{r}}^a_{rel} \\ \mathbf{v} &= \dot{\mathbf{o}}^a + \mathbf{S}^a \cdot (\overline{\mathbf{v}}^a_{rel} + \overline{\boldsymbol{\omega}}^a \times \overline{\mathbf{r}}^a_{rel}) \\ \mathbf{a} &= \ddot{\mathbf{o}}^a + \mathbf{S}^a \cdot (\overline{\mathbf{a}}^a_{rel} + 2\overline{\boldsymbol{\omega}}^a \times \overline{\mathbf{v}}^a_{rel} + \dot{\overline{\boldsymbol{\omega}}}^a \times \overline{\mathbf{r}}^a_{rel} + \overline{\boldsymbol{\omega}}^a \times (\overline{\boldsymbol{\omega}}^a \times \overline{\mathbf{r}}^a_{rel}))\end{aligned} \tag{14-153}$$

where $\overline{\mathbf{r}}^a_{rel}$ is the relative vector from the origin O^a to point *P*, $\mathbf{o}^a$ is the position of the origin O^a in the inertial frame, $\mathbf{S}^a$ is the rotational transformation matrix from frame *a* to the inertial frame, and $\overline{\boldsymbol{\omega}}^a$ is the rotation vector of frame *a* expressed in frame *a*.

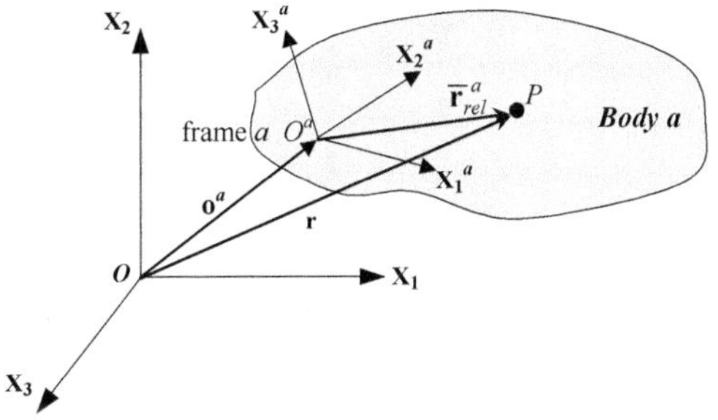

Figure 14-33. Rigid body with a point P relative to a coordinate frame *a* with origin O^a fixed in body *a*.

However, for all points *P* in a *rigid* body the relative vector $\overline{\mathbf{r}}^a_{rel}$ expressed in frame *a* is fixed since the essential property of a rigid body is that it does not change shape, i.e., $\overline{\mathbf{v}}^a_{rel} = \dot{\overline{\mathbf{r}}}^a_{rel} = 0$ and $\overline{\mathbf{a}}^a_{rel} = \ddot{\overline{\mathbf{r}}}^a_{rel} = 0$, giving the following simplified equations:

$$\begin{aligned}\mathbf{r} &= \mathbf{o}^a + \mathbf{S}^a \cdot \overline{\mathbf{r}}^a_{rel} \\ \mathbf{v} &= \dot{\mathbf{o}}^a + \mathbf{S}^a \cdot (\overline{\boldsymbol{\omega}}^a \times \overline{\mathbf{r}}^a_{rel}) \\ \mathbf{a} &= \ddot{\mathbf{o}}^a + \mathbf{S}^a \cdot (\dot{\overline{\boldsymbol{\omega}}}^a \times \overline{\mathbf{r}}^a_{rel} + \overline{\boldsymbol{\omega}}^a \times (\overline{\boldsymbol{\omega}}^a \times \overline{\mathbf{r}}^a_{rel}))\end{aligned} \tag{14-154}$$

where **r**, **v**, and **a** are the absolute position, velocity, and acceleration vectors of point *P* in the inertial system. This also can be expressed as:

$$\begin{aligned}\mathbf{r} &= \mathbf{o}^a + \mathbf{r}^a_{rel} \\ \mathbf{v} &= \dot{\mathbf{o}}^a + \boldsymbol{\omega}^a \times \mathbf{r}^a_{rel} \\ \mathbf{a} &= \ddot{\mathbf{o}}^a + \dot{\boldsymbol{\omega}}^a \times \mathbf{r}^a_{rel} + \boldsymbol{\omega}^a \times (\boldsymbol{\omega}^a \times \mathbf{r}^a_{rel})\end{aligned} \tag{14-155}$$

with all quantities defined in the inertial system.

14.8.5.4 3D Rigid-body Dynamics

Now we want to express Newton's equations governing the dynamics of a rigid body, which, for example, are stated in the old Modelica MBS library class `BodyBase` in the sublibrary `Interfaces`, inherited, for example, by the classes `Body` and `Body2` in the sublibrary `Parts`, or in the new MBS library stated directly in the class `MultiBody.Parts.Body`. First recall (14-154) for the acceleration **a** of an arbitrary point *P* in a rigid body. We express this equation in the local frame *a*, using $\mathbf{a} = \mathbf{S}^a \cdot \overline{\mathbf{a}}^a$ and $\ddot{\mathbf{o}}^a = \mathbf{S}^a \cdot \overline{\mathbf{a}}^a_0$. After eliminating $\mathbf{S}^a$ we obtain:

$$\overline{\mathbf{a}}^a_{\text{cm}} = \overline{\mathbf{a}}^a_0 + \dot{\overline{\boldsymbol{\omega}}}^a \times \overline{\mathbf{r}}^a_{rel} + \overline{\boldsymbol{\omega}}^a \times (\overline{\boldsymbol{\omega}}^a \times \overline{\mathbf{r}}^a_{rel}) \tag{14-156}$$

where $\overline{\mathbf{a}}^a$ is the acceleration of the point *P*, which in the following is chosen to be the center of mass of the body, denoted cm, and $\overline{\mathbf{a}}_0^a$ is the (translational) acceleration vector of the origin of frame *a*, both expressed in frame *a*.

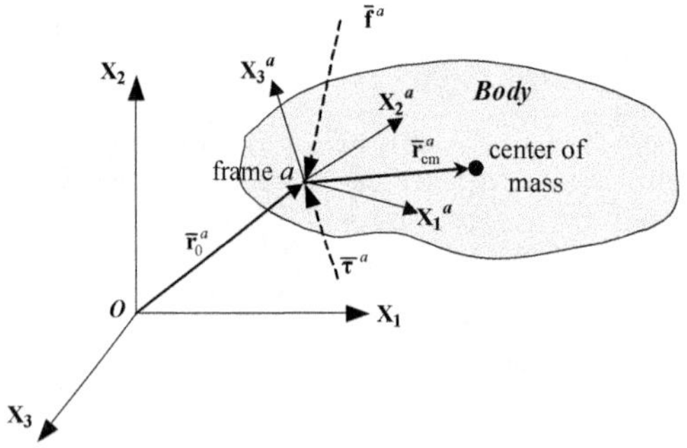

Figure 14-34 Body with mass *m*, coordinate frame *a* as well as external force $\overline{\mathbf{f}}^a$ and torque $\overline{\boldsymbol{\tau}}^a$ being applied at the origin point of frame *a*, and a relative vector $\overline{\mathbf{r}}_{cm}^a$ from the origin of frame *a* to the center of mass of the body.

According to Newton's second law of motion applied to rigid bodies, a force (conceptually) applied at the center of mass of a rigid body equals its mass multiplied by the acceleration of the center of mass:

$$\overline{\mathbf{f}}_{cm}^a = m \cdot \overline{\mathbf{a}}_{cm}^a \tag{14-157}$$

The force vector (but not the torque) is the same translated to be applied at the origin of frame *a* on the rigid body, that is, $\overline{\mathbf{f}}_{cm}^a = \overline{\mathbf{f}}^a$, as depicted in Figure 14-34. Using equation (14-156) for the acceleration $\overline{\mathbf{a}}_{cm}^a$ we obtain:

$$\overline{\mathbf{f}}^a = m \cdot (\overline{\mathbf{a}}^a + \dot{\overline{\boldsymbol{\omega}}}^a \times \overline{\mathbf{r}}_{cm}^a + \overline{\boldsymbol{\omega}}^a \times (\overline{\boldsymbol{\omega}}^a \times \overline{\mathbf{r}}_{cm}^a)) \tag{14-158}$$

where $\overline{\mathbf{f}}^a$ is the force vector applied at frame *a*, $\overline{\mathbf{a}}^a$ is the acceleration of frame *a*, $\overline{\boldsymbol{\omega}}^a$ is the rotation vector of frame *a*, and $\overline{\mathbf{r}}_{cm}^a$ is the vector from the origin of frame *a* to the center of mass, where all these quantities are expressed in frame *a*.

The next issue is to derive the *rotational part* of the equation of motion for a rigid body, also called the *Euler equation*, that is, the relation between the *torque* $\overline{\boldsymbol{\tau}}^a$ around a point O^a, the *angular acceleration* vector $\dot{\overline{\boldsymbol{\omega}}}^a$, the rotation vector $\overline{\boldsymbol{\omega}}^a$, the *moment of intertia* matrix **I**, etc., all expressed in the local body frame *a*:

$$\overline{\boldsymbol{\tau}}^a = \mathbf{I} \cdot \dot{\overline{\boldsymbol{\omega}}}^a + \overline{\boldsymbol{\omega}}^a \times \mathbf{I} \cdot \overline{\boldsymbol{\omega}}^a + \overline{\mathbf{r}}_{cm}^a \times \overline{\mathbf{f}}^a \tag{14-159}$$

Let us for a while return to the basic definitions. Since a rigid body can be viewed as consisting of many particles we will recall certain relations valid for particles. The torque $\boldsymbol{\tau}$ around a point *O* created by a force **f** applied to a particle at a distance **r** is defined as:

$$\boldsymbol{\tau} = \mathbf{r} \times \mathbf{f} \tag{14-160}$$

where $\boldsymbol{\tau}$, **f**, and **r** as usual are vector quantities. Next we introduce the notion of the *angular momentum* vector **L** with respect to a point *O* for a particle of mass *m* moving with velocity **v** as depicted in Figure 14-35, and therefore having momentum $\mathbf{p} = m \cdot \mathbf{v}$. The angular momentum is defined by a vector cross product:

$$\mathbf{L} = \mathbf{r} \times \mathbf{p} = m \cdot \mathbf{r} \times \mathbf{v} \tag{14-161}$$

where **r** is the position vector of the particle relative to the point *O*.

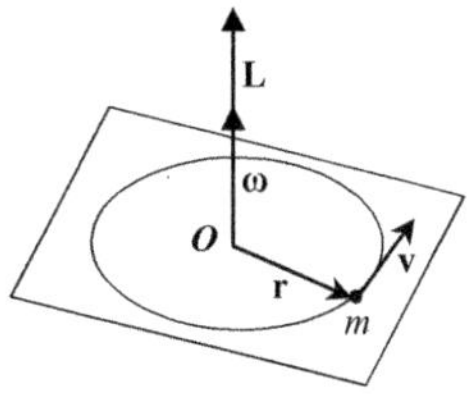

Figure 14-35. Vector relation between angular velocity ω and angular momentum L for a particle. A rigid body can be viewed as consisting of many such particles.

The following relation holds between the torque and the angular momentum:

$$\boldsymbol{\tau} = \dot{\mathbf{L}} \tag{14-162}$$

This relation is just a consequence of Newton's second law of motion $\mathbf{f} = \dot{\mathbf{p}}$, as shown below:

$$\dot{\mathbf{L}} = \frac{d}{dt}\mathbf{L} = \frac{d}{dt}(\mathbf{r}\times\mathbf{p}) = \dot{\mathbf{r}}\times\mathbf{p} + \mathbf{r}\times\dot{\mathbf{p}} = \mathbf{v}\times(m\cdot\mathbf{v}) + \mathbf{r}\times\mathbf{f} = \mathbf{r}\times\mathbf{f} = \boldsymbol{\tau} \tag{14-163}$$

Here we have used the fact that the cross product of a vector to itself is zero, $\mathbf{v}\times\mathbf{v} = 0$, the above definition of torque $\boldsymbol{\tau} = \mathbf{r}\times\mathbf{f}$, and Newton's second law of motion $\mathbf{f} = \dot{\mathbf{p}}$. Next we generalize from a particle to a *rigid body* based on its definition as a system of particles with fixed relative positions. The total angular momentum vector **L** of a rigid body:

$$\mathbf{L} = \sum_i \mathbf{L}_i = \sum_i \mathbf{r}_i \times \mathbf{p}_i = \sum_i m_i \cdot \mathbf{r}_i \times \mathbf{v}_i \tag{14-164}$$

where $\mathbf{L}_i$ is the angular momentum of one of its particles. Using (14-155) and noting that only the rotational part $\boldsymbol{\omega}\times\mathbf{r}_i$ of $\mathbf{v}_i$ which is perpendicular to $\mathbf{r}_i$ contributes to the cross product, we obtain:

$$\mathbf{L} = \sum_i m_i \cdot \mathbf{r}_i \times (\boldsymbol{\omega}\times\mathbf{r}_i) = \sum_i m_i \cdot \mathbf{r}_i \times (-\mathbf{r}_i \times \boldsymbol{\omega}) = \sum_i m_i \cdot \mathbf{R}_i \cdot (-\mathbf{R}_i \cdot \mathbf{W}) = \mathbf{I}\cdot\boldsymbol{\omega} \tag{14-165}$$

where **W** and $\mathbf{R}_i$ are skew matrices corresponding to the vectors $\boldsymbol{\omega}$ and $\mathbf{r}_i$. Here we have used standard mathematical identities for vectors and skew matrices:

$$\begin{aligned} \boldsymbol{\omega}\times\mathbf{r}_i &= -\mathbf{r}_i \times \boldsymbol{\omega} \\ \mathbf{r}_i \times \boldsymbol{\omega} &= \mathbf{R}_i \cdot \mathbf{W} \\ -\mathbf{R}_i &= \mathbf{R}_i^{\mathrm{T}} \end{aligned} \tag{14-166}$$

The matrix **I**, called the *moment of inertia* matrix or *mass matrix* of the body, is defined as:

$$\mathbf{I} = \sum_i m_i \cdot \mathbf{R}_i^{\mathrm{T}} \cdot \mathbf{R}_i \tag{14-167}$$

or as an integral by taking the limit of many small particles, and substituting $m_i = \rho \cdot dV$. The integral form of the *moment of inertia* matrix becomes:

$$\mathbf{I} = \int \rho \cdot \mathbf{R}_i^{\mathrm{T}} \mathbf{R}_i dV \tag{14-168}$$

The matrix **I** is constant for a rigid body, depending only on its shape and mass density. The following relation holds also for a rigid body defined as a system of particles:

$$\boldsymbol{\tau} = \dot{\mathbf{L}} \tag{14-169}$$

where $\boldsymbol{\tau} = \boldsymbol{\tau}_1 + \boldsymbol{\tau}_2 + \boldsymbol{\tau}_3 + \ldots$ is the total external torque relative to the same point exerted by the external forces acting on the particles of the body. The reason is that the internal forces between any pair of particles have the same (or opposite) direction as the relative position vector between the particles, which means that their cross product is zero. Since **I** is constant, we obtain:

$$\boldsymbol{\tau} = \dot{\mathbf{L}} = \frac{d}{dt}(\mathbf{I} \cdot \boldsymbol{\omega}) = \mathbf{I} \cdot \dot{\boldsymbol{\omega}} \tag{14-170}$$

This equation can be expressed in quantities of $\overline{\boldsymbol{\tau}}^a$ and $\overline{\mathbf{L}}^a$ in the local body frame a:

$$\mathbf{S}^a \cdot \overline{\boldsymbol{\tau}}^a = \frac{d}{dt}(\mathbf{S}^a \cdot \overline{\mathbf{L}}^a) = \mathbf{S}^a \cdot \dot{\overline{\mathbf{L}}}^a + \dot{\mathbf{S}}^a \cdot \overline{\mathbf{L}}^a = \mathbf{S}^a \cdot \mathbf{I} \cdot \dot{\overline{\boldsymbol{\omega}}}^a + \dot{\mathbf{S}}^a \cdot \overline{\mathbf{L}}^a = \mathbf{S}^a \cdot \mathbf{I} \cdot \dot{\overline{\boldsymbol{\omega}}}^a + \mathbf{S}^a \cdot (\overline{\boldsymbol{\omega}}^a \times \overline{\mathbf{L}}^a) \tag{14-171}$$

where we have used the relations $\boldsymbol{\tau} = \mathbf{S}^a \cdot \overline{\boldsymbol{\tau}}^a$ and $\mathbf{L} = \mathbf{S}^a \cdot \overline{\mathbf{L}}^a$, and have applied (14-134) to the vector $\overline{\mathbf{L}}^a$ giving $\dot{\mathbf{S}}^a \cdot \overline{\mathbf{L}}^a = \mathbf{S}^a \cdot (\overline{\boldsymbol{\omega}}^a \times \overline{\mathbf{L}}^a)$. By removing the rotation matrix $\mathbf{S}^a$ and using $\overline{\mathbf{L}}^a = \mathbf{I} \cdot \overline{\boldsymbol{\omega}}^a$ we obtain:

$$\overline{\boldsymbol{\tau}}^a = \mathbf{I} \cdot \dot{\overline{\boldsymbol{\omega}}}^a + \overline{\boldsymbol{\omega}}^a \times (\mathbf{I} \cdot \overline{\boldsymbol{\omega}}^a) \tag{14-172}$$

Finally, we add the term $\overline{\mathbf{r}}^a_{\text{cm}} \times \overline{\mathbf{f}}^a$ since the force $\overline{\mathbf{f}}^a$ is applied at a position $\overline{\mathbf{r}}^a_{\text{cm}}$ relative to the center-of-mass

$$\overline{\boldsymbol{\tau}}^a = \mathbf{I} \cdot \dot{\overline{\boldsymbol{\omega}}}^a + \overline{\boldsymbol{\omega}}^a \times (\mathbf{I} \cdot \overline{\boldsymbol{\omega}}^a) + \overline{\mathbf{r}}^a_{\text{cm}} \times \overline{\mathbf{f}}^a \tag{14-173}$$

To summarize, the *Newton-Euler equations of motion* for a rigid body as expressed in a local frame a attached to a rigid body of mass m are as follows:

$$\begin{aligned} \overline{\mathbf{f}}^a &= m \cdot (\overline{\mathbf{a}}^a + \dot{\overline{\boldsymbol{\omega}}}^a \times \overline{\mathbf{r}}^a_{\text{cm}} + \overline{\boldsymbol{\omega}}^a \times (\overline{\boldsymbol{\omega}}^a \times \overline{\mathbf{r}}^a_{\text{cm}}) \\ \overline{\boldsymbol{\tau}}^a &= \mathbf{I} \cdot \dot{\overline{\boldsymbol{\omega}}}^a + \overline{\boldsymbol{\omega}}^a \times (\mathbf{I} \cdot \overline{\boldsymbol{\omega}}^a) + \overline{\mathbf{r}}^a_{\text{cm}} \times \overline{\mathbf{f}}^a \end{aligned} \tag{14-174}$$

where $\overline{\mathbf{f}}^a$ is the force vector applied at the origin of frame a, $\overline{\mathbf{a}}^a$ is the acceleration of frame a, $\overline{\boldsymbol{\omega}}^a$ is the rotation vector of frame a, $\dot{\overline{\boldsymbol{\omega}}}^a$ is the angular acceleration vector (also denoted **z**) of frame a, and $\overline{\mathbf{r}}^a_{\text{cm}}$ is the vector from the origin of frame a to the center of mass. These quantities are all expressed in frame a. The matrix **I** is the moment of inertia of the body with respect to its center of mass.

These equations appear in the same form in the old `ModelicaAdditions.MultiBody` library class `BodyBase` in the `Interfaces` sublibrary. That class is the base class for rigid bodies and is inherited by the class `Body` in the old `Parts` sublibrary:

```
fa = m*(aa + cross(za, rCM) + cross(wa, cross(wa, rCM)));
ta = I*za + cross(wa, I*wa) + cross(rCM, fa);
```

where `fa, aa, za, rCM, wa, ta, I` correspond to $\overline{\mathbf{f}}^a, \overline{\mathbf{a}}^a, \dot{\overline{\boldsymbol{\omega}}}^a, \overline{\mathbf{r}}^a_{\text{cm}}, \overline{\boldsymbol{\omega}}^a, \overline{\boldsymbol{\tau}}^a, \mathbf{I}$ respectively. In the current `Modelica.Mechanics.MultiBody` library briefly described in Section 15.10, page 877, the corresponding equations appear at the end of the `Modelica.Mechanics.MultiBody.Parts.Body` class in the following form:

```
frame_a.f = m*(Frames.resolve2(frame_a.R, a_0 - g_0) +
            cross(z_a, r_CM) + cross(w_a, cross(w_a, r_CM)));

frame_a.t = I*z_a + cross(w_a, I*w_a) + cross(r_CM, frame_a.f);
```

The call `Frames.resolve2(frame_a.R, a_0 - g_0)` is just an application of the rotation matrix `R`, expanding to `frame_a.R*(a_0-g_0)`, which transforms the acceleration vector `a_0-g_0` from the inertial frame to the local frame.

14.8.6 Constrained Motion

In general, each body in a multibody system has six coordinates or degrees of freedom, three translational and three rotational. Thus, a multibody system consisting of n bodies will have $6n$ degrees of freedom. However, the motion of bodies in a multibody system is often constrained by couplings such as mechanical joints between bodies. In theory such constraints can be expressed as algebraic equations relating state variables from both bodies connected by the joint in addition to the usual set of equations of motion.

However, because of these constraints our "standard" state variables are no longer independent. For reasons of computational effectiveness and numerical stability as well as mathematical conciseness, it is in practice usually a good strategy to express the variables as functions of a number of "generalized coordinates" or variables, where the number corresponds to the actual number of degrees of freedom for a multibody system.

For example, consider a small multibody subsystem consisting of two bodies. This system has $6 \cdot 2 = 12$ degrees of freedom when each part can move independently. However, consider a system of two bodies connected via a *revolute joint* as depicted in Figure 14-36. Part 2 can move only according to one rotational degree of freedom relative to part 1, which gives a total of 7 degrees of freedom for this minimal multibody system.

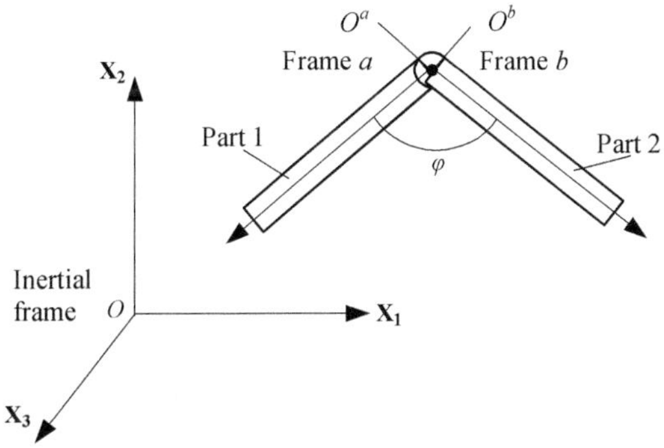

Figure 14-36. A multibody subsystem consisting of two movable parts connected via a revolute joint that just adds 1 degree of freedom, giving this subsystem a total of 7 degrees of freedom. The origins of frame a and frame b coincide.

In the multibody system with two bodies connected by a revolute joint there is only one "generalized coordinate" or variable relating part 2 to part 1, namely the angle φ. All the rest is fixed. We place the origins of frame a and frame b at the same point, giving:

$$\begin{aligned}
\mathbf{r}_0^b &= \mathbf{r}_0^a \\
\overline{\mathbf{r}}_{rel}^a &= 0 \\
\overline{\mathbf{v}}_{rel}^a &= 0 \\
\overline{\mathbf{a}}_{rel}^a &= 0
\end{aligned} \tag{14-175}$$

where we use the notation from Section 14.8.5.2, page 781. The placement of the origins at the same point considerably simplifies equations (14-150), (14-151), and (14-152), which appear as below in simplified form:

$$\begin{aligned}
\overline{\mathbf{v}}^b &= \mathbf{S}_{rel} \cdot \overline{\mathbf{v}}^a \\
\overline{\boldsymbol{\omega}}^b &= \mathbf{S}_{rel} \cdot (\overline{\boldsymbol{\omega}}^a + \overline{\boldsymbol{\omega}}^a_{rel}) \\
\overline{\mathbf{a}}^b &= \mathbf{S}_{rel} \cdot \overline{\mathbf{a}}^a \\
\dot{\overline{\boldsymbol{\omega}}}^b &= \mathbf{S}_{rel} \cdot (\dot{\overline{\boldsymbol{\omega}}}^a + \dot{\overline{\boldsymbol{\omega}}}^a_{rel} + \overline{\boldsymbol{\omega}}^a \times \overline{\boldsymbol{\omega}}^a_{rel}) \\
\overline{\mathbf{f}}^b &= \mathbf{S}_{rel} \cdot \overline{\mathbf{f}}^a \\
\overline{\boldsymbol{\tau}}^b &= \mathbf{S}_{rel} \cdot \overline{\boldsymbol{\tau}}^a
\end{aligned} \tag{14-176}$$

The above equations appear in the Modelica class `Revolute` that belongs to the `Joint` sublibrary of the old ModelicaAdditions MBS library:

```
r_rela = zeros(3);
v_rela = zeros(3);
a_rela = zeros(3);
r0b = r0a;
vb = S_rel*va;
wb = S_rel*(wa + w_rela);
ab = S_rel*aa;
zb = S_rel*(za + z_rela + cross(wa, w_rela));
fa = transpose(S_rel)*fb;
ta = transpose(S_rel)*tb;
```

where $\mathbf{z} = \dot{\overline{\boldsymbol{\omega}}}$ and $(\mathbf{S}_{rel})^{-1} = (\mathbf{S}_{rel})^{\mathrm{T}}$. Corresponding, but slightly different equations appear in the current MBS library in `Modelica.Mechanics.MultiBody.Joints.Internal.Revolute`. The relative rotation vector $\overline{\boldsymbol{\omega}}^a_{rel}$ is determined by the relative angle φ between the two frames and a unit vector $\overline{\mathbf{n}}^a$ that defines the axis of rotation:

$$\begin{aligned}
\overline{\boldsymbol{\omega}}^a_{rel} &= \dot{\varphi} \cdot \overline{\mathbf{n}}^a \\
\dot{\overline{\boldsymbol{\omega}}}^a_{rel} &= \ddot{\varphi} \cdot \overline{\mathbf{n}}^a
\end{aligned} \tag{14-177}$$

As previously, the relative rotation matrix $\mathbf{S}_{rel}$ transforms a vector expressed in frame a to frame b:

$$\mathbf{S}_{rel} = (\mathbf{S}^b)^{-1} \cdot \mathbf{S}^a \tag{14-178}$$

If the angle φ=0 the frames will coincide completely and $\mathbf{S}_{rel}$ becomes the identity matrix. The relative rotation matrix can be expressed in terms of the angle φ and the normal vector for the rotation axis:

$$\mathbf{S}_{rel} = \overline{\mathbf{n}}^a \cdot (\overline{\mathbf{n}}^a)^{\mathrm{T}} + (\mathbf{E} - \overline{\mathbf{n}}^a \cdot (\overline{\mathbf{n}}^a)^{\mathrm{T}}) \cdot \cos(\varphi - \varphi_0) - \overline{\mathbf{N}}^a \cdot \sin(\varphi - \varphi_0) \tag{14-179}$$

where $\mathbf{E}$ is the identity matrix, φ_0 is a rotation angle offset (usually selected to be zero), and $\overline{\mathbf{N}}^a$ is the skew matrix of $\overline{\mathbf{n}}^a$. In the class `ModelicaAdditions.MultiBody.Revolute` of the old MBS library this appears approximately as:

```
qq    = q - q0*PI/180;
S_rel = [nn]*transpose([nn]) + (identity(3)-[nn]*transpose([nn]))*cos(qq) -
          skew(nn)*sin(qq);
```

where the angles `q` and `qq` are in radians and the parameter offset angle `q0` is measured in degrees. The column matrix `[nn]` derived from the vector `nn` represents $\overline{\mathbf{n}}^a$. The skew matrix $\overline{\mathbf{N}}^a$ is represented by `skew(nn)`.

Let us derive the above equation (14-179) for the relative rotation matrix defined by a given normal vector $\overline{\mathbf{n}}^a$ and a relative angle φ, where we temporarily ignore φ_0. By the definition of relative rotation the position $\overline{\mathbf{r}}^b$ of point b is obtained by rotating point a:

$$\overline{\mathbf{r}}^b = \mathbf{S}_{rel} \cdot \overline{\mathbf{r}}^a \tag{14-180}$$

The vectors $\overline{\mathbf{r}}^b$ and $\overline{\mathbf{r}}^a$ are depicted in Figure 14-37:

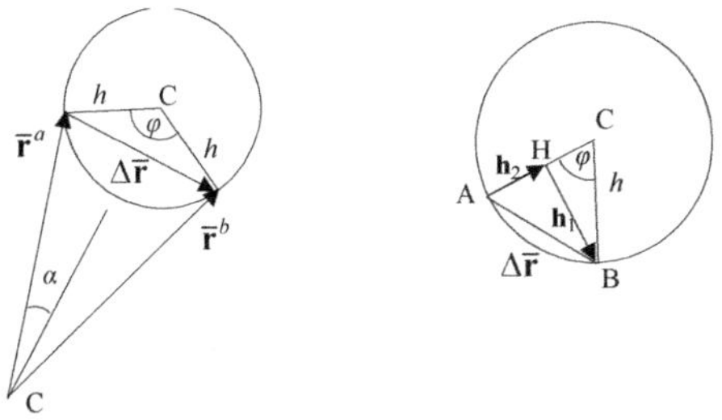

Figure 14-37. Vectors and angles related to a revolute joint.

We can also express $\overline{\mathbf{r}}^b$ by adding the relative vector $\Delta\overline{\mathbf{r}}$:

$$\overline{\mathbf{r}}^b = \Delta\overline{\mathbf{r}} + \overline{\mathbf{r}}^a \tag{14-181}$$

The $\Delta\overline{\mathbf{r}}$ vector can always be represented as a sum of two orthogonal vectors $\overline{\mathbf{h}}_2$ and $\overline{\mathbf{h}}_1$:

$$\Delta\overline{\mathbf{r}} = \overline{\mathbf{h}}_2 + \overline{\mathbf{h}}_1 \tag{14-182}$$

The radius of rotation h can be calculated as follows:

$$h = \left|\overline{\mathbf{r}}^a\right| \cdot \sin(\alpha) = \left|\overline{\mathbf{n}}^a\right| \cdot \left|\overline{\mathbf{r}}^a\right| \cdot \sin(\alpha) = \left|\overline{\mathbf{n}}^a \times \overline{\mathbf{r}}^a\right| \tag{14-183}$$

By construction (cross product) $\overline{\mathbf{h}}_1$ is orthogonal to both $\overline{\mathbf{n}}^a$ and its direction is given by the unit vector $\overline{\mathbf{n}}^a \times \overline{\mathbf{r}}^a / \left|\overline{\mathbf{n}}^a \times \overline{\mathbf{r}}^a\right|$. The length $\left|\overline{\mathbf{h}}_1\right|$ can be found from the right-angled triangle *BCH* as $h \cdot \sin(\varphi)$. By combining the relations for the direction and length we obtain:

$$\overline{\mathbf{h}}_1 = \frac{\overline{\mathbf{n}}^a \times \overline{\mathbf{r}}^a}{\left|\overline{\mathbf{n}}^a \times \overline{\mathbf{r}}^a\right|} \cdot h \cdot \sin(\varphi) = \left(\overline{\mathbf{n}}^a \times \overline{\mathbf{r}}^a\right) \cdot \sin(\varphi) \tag{14-184}$$

Similarly, vector $\overline{\mathbf{h}}_2$ is orthogonal to both $\overline{\mathbf{n}}^a$ and $\overline{\mathbf{h}}_1$, which are orthogonal to each other. The length $\left|\overline{\mathbf{h}}_2\right|$ is given by:

$$\left|\overline{\mathbf{h}}_2\right| = h - h \cdot \cos(\varphi) = h \cdot (1 - \cos(\varphi)) \tag{14-185}$$

Therefore $\overline{\mathbf{h}}_2$ is given by:

$$\overline{\mathbf{h}}_2 = \frac{\overline{\mathbf{n}}^a \times \left(\overline{\mathbf{n}}^a \times \overline{\mathbf{r}}^a\right)}{h} \cdot h \cdot (1 - \cos(\varphi)) = \overline{\mathbf{n}}^a \times \left(\overline{\mathbf{n}}^a \times \overline{\mathbf{r}}^a\right) \cdot (1 - \cos(\varphi)) \tag{14-186}$$

At this point, we need to recall the relations for a skew matrix $\overline{\mathbf{N}}^a$, for any vector $\overline{\mathbf{a}}$:

$$\begin{aligned} &\overline{\mathbf{n}}^a \times \overline{\mathbf{a}} = \overline{\mathbf{N}}^a \cdot \overline{\mathbf{a}} \\ &\overline{\mathbf{N}}^a = -\left(\overline{\mathbf{N}}^a\right)^{\mathrm{T}} \end{aligned} \tag{14-187}$$

Let us now summarize the relations derived so far:

$$\begin{aligned} &\overline{\mathbf{r}}^b = \overline{\mathbf{r}}^a + \Delta\overline{\mathbf{r}} = \overline{\mathbf{r}}^a + \overline{\mathbf{h}}_1 + \overline{\mathbf{h}}_2 \\ &\overline{\mathbf{h}}_1 = \left(\overline{\mathbf{n}}^a \times \overline{\mathbf{r}}^a\right) \cdot \sin(\varphi) = \overline{\mathbf{N}}^a \cdot \overline{\mathbf{r}}^a \cdot \sin(\varphi) \\ &\overline{\mathbf{h}}_2 = \overline{\mathbf{n}}^a \times \left(\overline{\mathbf{n}}^a \times \overline{\mathbf{r}}^a\right) \cdot (1 - \cos(\varphi)) = \overline{\mathbf{N}}^a \cdot \overline{\mathbf{N}}^a \cdot \overline{\mathbf{r}}^a \cdot (1 - \cos(\varphi)) \end{aligned} \tag{14-188}$$

By combining the three equations above we obtain:

$$\begin{aligned}\bar{\mathbf{r}}^b &= \overline{\mathbf{N}}^a \cdot \bar{\mathbf{r}}^a \cdot \sin(\varphi) + \overline{\mathbf{N}}^a \cdot \overline{\mathbf{N}}^a \cdot \bar{\mathbf{r}}^a \cdot (1-\cos(\varphi)) + \bar{\mathbf{r}}^a \\ &= \left(\overline{\mathbf{N}}^a \cdot \sin(\varphi) + \overline{\mathbf{N}}^a \cdot \overline{\mathbf{N}}^a \cdot (1-\cos(\varphi)) + \mathbf{E}\right) \cdot \bar{\mathbf{r}}^a\end{aligned} \tag{14-189}$$

The term in front of $\bar{\mathbf{r}}^a$ is the relative rotation matrix $\mathbf{S}_{rel}$. To derive the relation (14-179) used in the MBS library we just need to utilize the fact that for a unit vector $|\bar{\mathbf{n}}^a| = 1$ the relation below can be verified:

$$\overline{\mathbf{N}}^a \cdot \overline{\mathbf{N}}^a = \bar{\mathbf{n}}^a \cdot \left(\bar{\mathbf{n}}^a\right)^{\mathrm{T}} - \mathbf{E} \tag{14-190}$$

We substitute (14-190) into (14-189) and obtain the desired relation (14-179) apart from the positive sign on $\sin(\varphi)$ caused by the opposite angle direction of φ in this derivation:

$$\begin{aligned}\mathbf{S}_{rel} &= \overline{\mathbf{N}}^a \cdot \sin(\varphi) + (\bar{\mathbf{n}}^a \cdot \left(\bar{\mathbf{n}}^a\right)^{\mathrm{T}} - \mathbf{E}) \cdot (1-\cos(\varphi)) + \mathbf{E} \\ &= \overline{\mathbf{N}}^a \cdot \sin(\varphi) + \bar{\mathbf{n}}^a \cdot \left(\bar{\mathbf{n}}^a\right)^{\mathrm{T}} - \mathbf{E} - \bar{\mathbf{n}}^a \cdot \left(\bar{\mathbf{n}}^a\right)^{\mathrm{T}} \cdot \cos(\varphi) + \mathbf{E} \cdot \cos(\varphi) + \mathbf{E} \\ &= \bar{\mathbf{n}}^a \cdot \left(\bar{\mathbf{n}}^a\right)^{\mathrm{T}} + (\mathbf{E} - \bar{\mathbf{n}}^a \cdot (\bar{\mathbf{n}}^a)^{\mathrm{T}}) \cdot \cos(\varphi) + \overline{\mathbf{N}}^a \cdot \sin(\varphi)\end{aligned} \tag{14-191}$$

The correct formula is as follows, after substitution $\varphi \rightarrow \varphi - \varphi_0$ (the last term should be negative):

$$\mathbf{S}_{rel} = \bar{\mathbf{n}}^a \cdot (\bar{\mathbf{n}}^a)^{\mathrm{T}} + (\mathbf{E} - \bar{\mathbf{n}}^a \cdot (\bar{\mathbf{n}}^a)^{\mathrm{T}}) \cdot \cos(\varphi - \varphi_0) - \overline{\mathbf{N}}^a \cdot \sin(\varphi - \varphi_0) \tag{14-192}$$

14.9 Summary

This chapter presents an overview of a selection of well-known laws of nature, starting with energy conservation, in order to provide an easily accessible physics background to the equations found in many Modelica examples in this book and in a number of Modelica libraries.

We started by describing the law of conservation of energy (or of charge, mass, etc.), followed by a table of energy carriers and quantities for a selection of common application domains. After this introduction we presented sets of basic equations relating to the following domains: analog electrical circuits; one-dimensional mechanical systems—both translational and rotational; flow systems including some hydraulics; simple thermal systems with phenomena such as conduction, convection, and radiation; basic thermodynamics with the notions of systems and control volumes, equilibrium, work, heat, conservation of energy, but excluding entropy and the second law of thermodynamics due to limited space in this book; and finally multibody systems, that is, three-dimensional mechanical systems consisting of rigid bodies, reference frames and coordinate systems, coordinate transformations, and equations for constrained motion e.g. in mechanical joints.

14.9.1 Literature

This chapter presents some of the basic laws of nature described as equations. A very comprehensive overview of equations and mathematical models of diverse areas of physics and engineering is given in (Thomas 1999), whereas a short overview of common relations is presented in (Ljung and Glad 1994). The book (Shabana 1998) gives a comprehensive presentation of most aspects of multi-body systems, regarding both rigid and flexible bodies. Further reading is also available in (Pfeiffer and Glocker 1996). Some multi-body system relations, especially relevant for the Modelica multibody system library to be presented in Chapter 15, are briefly presented in (Otter 1995; Otter, Elmqvist, and Cellier 1996). Further reading on rotational mechanics, especially rotor dynamics, is available in (Olsson and Wettergren 2000). The basic relations in thermodynamics, with many engineering examples, are given in (Potter and Somerton 1993), whereas further reading on thermodynamics, heat, and flow, is available in (Fuchs 1996; Holman 1997). Basic relations in biochemistry are described in (Voit 2000). Biological pathways in biochemistry are discussed in (Michael 1999; SBML 2003).

Chapter 15

Application Examples

This chapter contains a number of examples of Modelica models from a wide range of application areas. The idea is to illustrate the modeling power of Modelica, as well as helping the reader to get started in his or her special area of interest. The following applications or areas are covered:

- Mechatronic systems—illustrated by a DC-motor model.
- Thermodynamic systems—an air-filled generic control volume representing a gas turbine or pump.
- Chemical reactions—a simple hydrogen-iodine reaction.
- Biological and ecological systems—population dynamics and energy forest models.
- Economic systems—Keynesian national economy.
- Internet communication—TCP packet communication protocols.
- Design optimization—improving the response of a linear actuator.
- Fourier analysis of simulation data—vibrations in a rotating weak axis.
- Solving wave equations by discretized PDEs—pressure dynamics in 1D ducts.
- Mechanical multibody systems—overview and 3D pendulum examples.
- Employing CAD systems for designing mechanical Modelica models.

Three of these sections are a bit special since they convey more than just an application example from a particular area:

- The mechatronic DC-motor example is one of the simplest cases of multidomain systems—in this case combining electrical and mechanical parts.
- The thermodynamic example illustrates bottom-up development of a model which eventually becomes a small library, starting from a very simple model and gradually adding more details.
- The multibody section gives a general introduction to the Modelica multibody system (MBS) library, apart from showing a number of examples.

In addition to the above, some application examples are presented in other chapters of this book. For example, several examples related to discrete-event, hybrid, or real-time application models are shown in Chapter 13. The following is a partial list of examples in other chapters:

- Moon lander—Section 3.4, page 82, and Section 4.1.9, page 143.
- Compliant 1D translational coupling—Section 5.4.2, page 196.
- Oscillating mass connected to a spring—Section 5.4.4, page 199.
- Partial DC motor for hierarchical embedding—Section 5.7.1, page 208.
- Circuit board with environment heat interaction—Section 5.8.2, page 226.
- Gravitational force fields with implicit interaction—Section 5.8.3, page 228.
- Tank system—Section 12.2, page 570.

- Modeling a DC motor servo from predefined components—Section 12.3, page 578.
- Clocked and unclocked synchronized counters—Section 13.2.6.6, page 618.
- Clocked and unclocked sampled systems—Section 13.3.1, page 625.
- Clocked and unclocked discrete state space sampled systems—Section 13.3.1.5, page 632.
- Clocked and unclocked two-rate sampled systems—Section 13.3.1.7, page 634.
- Clocked, unclocked, and state machine versions of watchdog system—Section 13.3.2.4, page 644.
- Clocked and unclocked finite state automata and state machine examples—Section 13.3.2, page 635.
- The game of life—Section 13.3.3.1, page 652.
- Clocked and unclocked server with queue—Section 13.3.4.2, page 655.
- Clocked and unclocked DEVS job shop model—Section 13.3.5.1, page 660.
- A three-server pipeline—Section 13.3.5.2, page 664.
- Petri-net-style job shop model—Section 13.3.6.6, page 672.
- Hybrid tank model with clocked and unclocked discrete controller—Section 13.4.1, page 676.
- DC motor transmission with elastic backlash—Section 13.4.2, page 682.
- Dining philosophers—Section 13.5.1, page 688.
- Clocked controller and plant—controlled mass model—Section 13.6.1, page 694.
- Clocked PI controller—Section 13.6.5, page 699.
- State event or interrupt driven clocked model—Section 13.6.7.5, page 704.
- Subsampling, supersampling, shiftsampling, backsampling models—Section 13.6.9, page 707.
- `ControlledMass` clock partitioning example model—Section 13.6.13.2, page 717.
- Clocked PI controller with own choice of solver method—Section 13.6.15.3, page 724.

We start the application examples in this chapter with a simple mechatronic multidomain system, since combining parts from different application domains is one of the strong points of Modelica that we would like to illustrate.

15.1 Mechatronic Systems—A DC Motor

The term *mechatronic* is commonly used for systems consisting of both mechanical and electrical parts, i.e., a special kind of multidomain system. An electric motor is a common example of such a system, and a DC motor (DC = direct current) is the simplest kind of electrical motor. Before continuing, we would like to point out that some of the components and connector interfaces used in the DC motor model are discussed in some detail in Chapter 5, Section 5.6, page 207.

Modeling a DC motor illustrates the ease of constructing multidomain models in Modelica simply by connecting components from different domains. This particular model contains components from three domains: *mechanical* components such as `inertial`, the *electrical* components `resistor1`, `inductor1`, `signalVoltage1`, and `ground1`, as well as pure *signal* components such as `step1` (see 16.6.1.6, page 934).

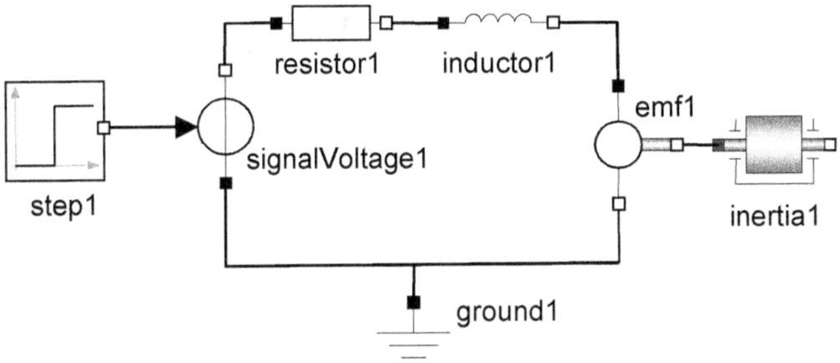

Figure 15-1. A multidomain `DCMotorCircuit` model with mechanical, electrical, and signal block components.

The `DCMotorCircuit` class is declared below. As usual, each component in the model is declared as a variable, and connections are represented by connect statements. What is different from previous examples is that certain connections couple components from different domains, for example, the signal block `step1` is connected to the electrical component `signalVoltage1` and the electrical component `emf1` is connected to the mechanical component `inertia1`. The model parameters are defined in the subsystems and given default unity values, including the moment of intertia `J` in `Intertia`, the coefficient `k` in `EMF`, the resistance `R` in `Resistor`, the inductance `L` in `Inductor`, and the step input signal parameters in `Step`.

```
model DCMotorCircuit
  Inertia      inertia1;
  Inductor     inductor1;
  Resistor     resistor1;
  Ground       ground1;
  EMF          emf1;
  Step         step1(startTime=1.0);
  SignalVoltage signalVoltage1;
equation
  connect(step1.y,       signalVoltage1.voltage);
  connect(signalVoltage1.n, resistor1.p);
  connect(resistor1.n,       inductor1.p);
  connect(signalVoltage1.p, ground1.p);
  connect(ground1.p,         emf1.n);
  connect(inductor1.n,       emf1.p);
  connect(emf1.rotFlange_b, inertia1.rotFlange_a);
end DCMotorCircuit;
```

To avoid confusion with the translational `Flange_a` connector class, we have renamed the rotational flange connector class to be called `RotFlange_a` in this example, even though it is called `Flange_a` in the `Mechanics.Rotational.Interfaces` library. Connectors have the same names as their classes apart from the first letter being lowercase, and a number being appended at the end.

In the following we present the `DCMotorCircuit` model including its parts and used classes in roughly a top-down manner, with the most interesting parts first. This gives the best overview and is also fine from a Modelica language point of view since classes can be used before they are defined.

15.1.1 Physics of the DCMotorCircuit

The combination of the `step1` and `signalVoltage1` components is a voltage generator that feeds a step voltage into the rest of the circuit. The components `resistor1` and `inductor1` represent the resistance and inductance respectively in the DC motor coil.

The instance emf1 of class EMF (electromotive force) is probably the most interesting component in the circuit since it converts electrical energy to mechanical rotational energy. This class is an idealized model of the most important properties of a voltage-to-rotation converter excluding resistance, inductance, and inertia.

The three most important equations of the EMF class are given below, first in mathematical syntax and then in Modelica syntax.

$$\begin{aligned} k\omega &= v \\ \tau_b &= -k\,i \\ \omega &= \dot{\varphi}_b \end{aligned} \tag{15-1}$$

The rotational speed w is proportional to the voltage v according to the equation k*w=v. The torque tau is proportional to the current i through the coil according to the equation rotFlange_b.tau=-k*i, where k is the transformation coeficient. The rotational speed w is of course equal to the derivative of the rotation angle phi. The emf1 component has Pin-type connectors that transmit voltage v and current i, and a rotFlange_b connector that transmits absolute angle phi and torque tau.

```
k*w = v;                        // Equations from class EMF
rotFlange_b.tau = -k*i;         // Electrical: voltage v, current i
w = der(rotFlange_b.phi);       // Mechanical: angle phi, rotational speed w
```

The component inertia1 represents the total inertia of the rotating coil and shaft of the motor together with the connected rotating load. The angular acceleration a is of course equal to the derivative of the angular velocity w, and the sum of the torques through the flanges is equal to J*a, where J is the moment of inertia of the total rotating mass. Two equations inherited from the class MechanicsRotational.Interfaces.PartialRigid (shown in Section 15.1.2 below) simply sets the rotation angle phi equal to the rotation angles of the flanges.

The equations in mathematical syntax, with connectors rotFlange_a and rotFlange_b indicated by suffixes a and b:

$$\begin{aligned} \omega &= \dot{\varphi} \\ a &= \dot{\omega} \\ J \cdot a &= \tau_a + \tau_b \\ \varphi_a &= \varphi \\ \varphi_b &= \varphi \end{aligned} \tag{15-2}$$

The equations in Modelica syntax are:

```
w = der(phi);                   // Equations from class Inertia
a = der(w);
J*a = rotFlange_a.tau + rotFlange_b.tau;
rotFlange_a.phi = phi;          // Equations inherited from class PartialRigid
rotFlange_b.phi = phi;
```

15.1.2 DCMotorCircuit Component Classes

The DCMotorCircuit model contains instances of mechanical, electrical, and signal classes, which are declared below.

15.1.2.1 Mechanical Component Classes: Inertia, PartialRigid

The `Inertia` class models the behavior of rotating masses. It inherits some properties from the base class `PartialRigid`, first mentioned in Section 5.4.4, page 199.

```
model Inertia    "1D-rotational component with inertia"
  extends PartialRigid;
  parameter MomentOfInertia  J=1 "Moment of inertia";
  AngularVelocity       w    "Absolute angular velocity of component";
  AngularAcceleration a    "Absolute angular acceleration of component";
equation
  w = der(phi);
  a = der(w);
  J*a = rotFlange_a.tau + rotFlange_b.tau;
end Inertia;   //  From Mechanics.Rotational

partial model PartialRigid  // Rotational class PartialRigid
  "Base class for the rigid connection of two rotational 1D flanges"
  Angle         phi       "Absolute rotation angle of component";
  RotFlange_a rotFlange_a"(left) driving flange (axis directed into plane)";
  RotFlange_b rotFlange_b "(right) driven flange (axis directed out
                            of plane)";
 equation
  rotFlange_a.phi = phi;
  rotFlange_b.phi = phi;
end Rigid;   //  Adapted From Mechanics.Rotational.Interfaces
```

15.1.2.2 Electrical Component Classes: EMF, TwoPin, Resistor, Inductor, Ground

The `EMF` class below converts electrical energy to rotational mechanical energy. The physics of this class was briefly presented above in the section on the physics of the `DCMotorCircuit`. The rest of the declared classes are the usual simple electrical components, which are presented once more for completeness.

```
model EMF "Electromotoric force (electric/mechanic transformer)"
  parameter Real  k(unit="N.m/A") = 1  "Transformation coefficient";
  Voltage          v  "Voltage drop between the two pins";
  Current          i  "Current flowing from positive to negative pin";
  AngularVelocity w  "Angular velocity of rotFlange_b";
  PositivePin      p;
  NegativePin      n;
  RotFlange_b      rotFlange_b;  // rotational Flange_b
equation
  v = p.v - n.v;
  0 = p.i + n.i;
  i = p.i;
  w = der(rotFlange_b.phi);
  k*w = v;
  rotFlange_b.tau = -k*i;
end EMF;  // From Modelica.Electrical.Analog.Basic

partial model TwoPin  // Same as OnePort in Electrical.Analog.Interfaces
  "Component with two electrical pins p and n and current i from p to n"
  Voltage      v    "Voltage drop between the two pins (= p.v - n.v)";
  Current      i    "Current flowing from pin p to pin n";
  PositivePin p;
  NegativePin n;
equation
  v = p.v - n.v;
  0 = p.i + n.i;
  i = p.i;
```

```
end TwoPin;    // From Modelica.Electrical.Analog.Interfaces

model Resistor "Ideal linear electrical resistor"
  extends TwoPin;  // Same as OnePort
  parameter Resistance R=1 "Resistance";
equation
  R*i = v;
end Resistor;  // From Modelica.Electrical.Analog.Basic

model Inductor "Ideal linear electrical inductor"
  extends TwoPin;  // Same as OnePort
  parameter Inductance L=1 "Inductance";
equation
  L*der(i) = v;
end Inductor;  // From Modelica.Electrical.Analog.Basic

model Ground "Ground node"
  Pin p;
equation
  p.v = 0;
end Ground;  // From Modelica.Electrical.Analog.Basic
```

15.1.2.3 Signal and Signal Voltage Classes: SignalVoltage, SO, Step

The `SignalVoltage` class converts an input signal to a voltage. This is used in the `DCMotorCircuit` to convert a step signal generated by the `step1` instance of the simplified `Step` class below to a step voltage. The `partial` class `SO` is simply a base class inherited by `Step`.

```
model SignalVoltage
  "Generic voltage source using the input signal as source voltage"
  extends TwoPin;   // Same as OnePort
  RealInput u;
equation
  u = v;
end SignalVoltage;  // From Modelica.Electrical.Analog.Sources

partial block SO "Single Output continuous control block"
  extends BlockIcon;
  output RealOutput y;
end SO; //from Modelica.Blocks.Interfaces

block Step "Generate step signals of type Real"
  extends SO;
  parameter Real  height=1     "Height of steps";
  parameter Real  offset=0     "Offset of output signals";
  parameter Time  startTime =0 "Output = offset for time < startTime";
equation
  y = offset + (if time < startTime then 0 else height);
end Step;
```

15.1.3 DCMotorCircuit Connector Classes

The connector classes used by the `DCMotorCircuit` are declared below, in the order mechanical, electrical, and signal (causal) connector classes. All except the mechanical ones have already been described in detail. The mechanical connector classes `RotFlange_a` and `RotFlange_b` are used for rotational mechanical couplings, e.g. between shafts in drive trains. As mentioned above, they have been renamed compared to their original names `Flange_a` and `Flange_b` in the 1D rotational Modelica standard library called `Modelica.Mechanical.Rotational.Interfaces` in order to prevent confusion when compared to the translational flange classes with the same names used previously in this chapter. The rotational flanges contain the potential variable `phi` for the absolute rotation angle of the flange, and the `flow` variable `tau` for the torque transmitted by the flange.

15.1.3.1 Mechanical Connector Classes: RotFlange_a, RotFlange_b

```
connector RotFlange_a "1D rotational flange (filled square)"
  Angle        phi    "Absolute rotation angle of flange";
  flow Torque  tau    "Torque in the flange";
end RotFlange_a;  // from Modelica.Mechanical.Rotational.Interfaces

connector RotFlange_b "1D rotational flange (non-filled square)"
  Angle        phi    "Absolute rotation angle of flange";
  flow Torque  tau    "Torque in the flange";
end RotFlange_b;  // from Modelica.Mechanical.Rotational.Interfaces
```

15.1.3.2 Electrical Connector Classes: PositivePin, NegativePin, Pin

```
connector PositivePin "Positive pin of an electric component"
  Voltage      v  "Potential at the pin";
  flow Current i  "Current flowing into the pin";
end PositivePin;  // From Modelica.Electrical.Analog.Interfaces

connector NegativePin "Negative pin of an electric component"
  Voltage      v  "Potential at the pin";
  flow Current i  "Current flowing into the pin";
end NegativePin;  // From Modelica.Electrical.Analog.Interfaces

connector Pin "Pin of an electrical component"
  Voltage      v  "Potential at the pin";
  flow Current i  "Current flowing into the pin";
end Pin;          // From Modelica.Electrical.Analog.Interfaces
```

15.1.3.3 Block/Signal Connector Classes: RealInput, RealOutput

These are almost identical (slightly simplified) versions of the connector classes from the library `Modelica.Blocks.Interfaces`:

```
connector RealInput = input Real "Connector with input signals of type Real"
// from Modelica.Blocks.Interfaces

connector RealOutput = output Real "Connector with output signals of Real"
// from Modelica.Blocks.Interfaces
```

15.1.4 Types from Modelica.SIunits

The following are the different types from the library `Modelica.SIunits` used by the `DCMotorCircuit` model. All 450 SI units are available in `Modelica.SIunits`.

```
// Electrical units
type ElectricPotential = Real;
type ElectricCurrent = Real(quantity="ElectricCurrent", unit="A");
type Resistance = Real(quantity="Resistance", unit="Ohm", min=0);
type Inductance = Real(quantity="Inductance", unit="H", min=0);
type Voltage = ElectricPotential ;
type Current = ElectricCurrent ;

// Mechanical units
type Force  = Real(quantity="Force", unit="N");
type Angle  = Real(quantity="Angle", unit="rad", displayUnit="deg");
type Torque = Real quantity="Torque", unit= "N.m");
```

```
type AngularVelocity = Real(quantity="AngularVelocity", unit="rad/s",
                            displayUnit="rev/min");
type AngularAcceleration = Real(quantity="AngularAcceleration",
                                unit="rad/s2");
type MomentOfInertia = Real(quantity="MomentOfInertia", unit="kg.m2");

// Other units
type Length   = Real(quantity="Length", unit="m" );
type Time     = Real(quantity="Time", unit="s" );
type Distance = Length(min=0);
type Position = Length;
```

15.1.5 DCMotorCircuit Simulation

Finally we simulate the `DCMotorCircuit` model and plot a few of its variables (Figure 15-2).

```
simulate(DCMotorCircuit,stopTime=25); plot({step1.y,inertia1.flange_a.tau})
```

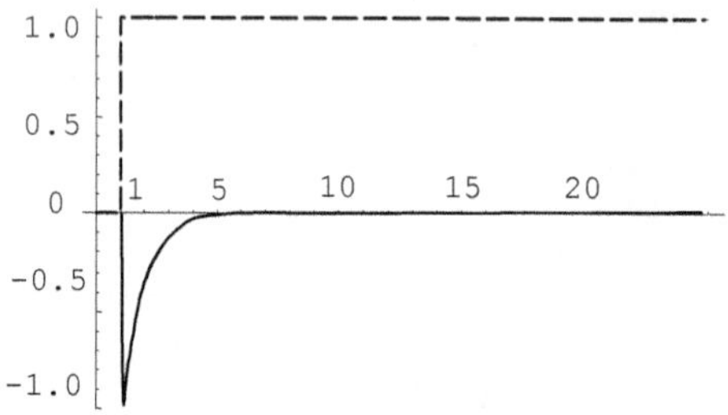

Figure 15-2. `DCMotorCircuit` simulation with plot of input signal voltage step and the flange angle.

15.2 Thermodynamics—An Air-filled Control Volume Interacting with Subsystems

In this section, we develop a model of a macroscopic thermodynamic system in a bottom-up way, starting from the basic notions and equations as defined in Section 14.7, page 759, gradually adding additional equations to the example system model. In this way the model becomes increasingly realistic in the physical sense. The model also becomes more well-structured, since the first versions of the model are without explicit interfaces in the form of connectors which are added after a few design iterations. When connectors have been added it is possible to define the system model by connecting model instances of its constituent parts.

The example model illustrates many aspects of the dynamics of thermodynamic systems with relation to conservation of energy and mass, modeling control volumes, decomposition into subsystems, and interaction between subsystems. However, readers without a strong background in thermodynamics are advised to study Section 14.7 before continuing. Even for readers well acquainted with thermodynamics it can be useful to take a quick look at that section since many of the equations used in this example are developed into the mathematical form they appear in the examples.

The *bottom-up* design approach used to develop this example is also a good example on how to approach modeling in an application area without a finished model library, notwithstanding the fact that there already exist Modelica libraries in this area. In the last example (Section 15.2.6, page 825) we actually use a few components from the `Modelica.Thermal` library, and in the example of Section

15.2.5.7, page 822, a model from `Modelica.Mechanics.Translational`. We basically use the following strategy:

1. Study the system to identify components and physical relationships.
2. Model and simulate each kind of component using the simplest relationships.
3. Put the components together into a complete system.
4. Add additional relationships to make the models more realistic. Simulate the models to gain experience.
5. When you have got a basic understanding of the application area including standard components and interactions between those components, try to identify standard interfaces and define connector classes for those interfaces.
6. Restructure your model using connectors and connections between the components.
7. Evaluate the result. Are the interfaces general enough but still simple to use? Do they capture the needed interaction between the components? If there are problems, go back to step 5 for a redesign, followed by step 6 and 7. It can be tricky to get the connector and subsystem design right the first time.

We will now take a quick look at the example system.

15.2.1 An Example System

Our thermodynamic example system with its components is schematically depicted in Figure 15-3.

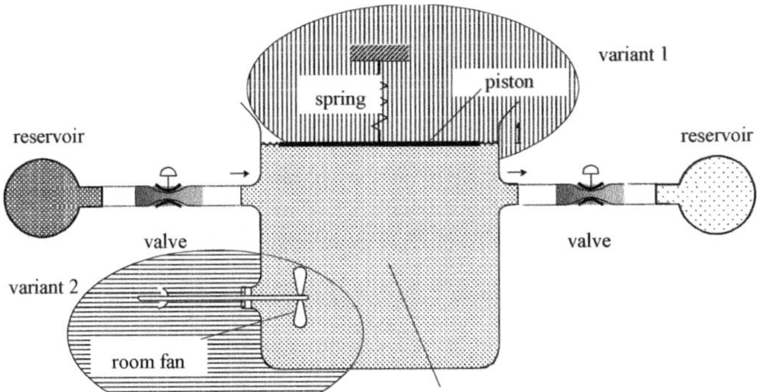

Figure 15-3. A thermodynamic example system with the following subsystems: control volume, reservoirs, and valves. The basic control volume model is extended and used in two different applications: the first variant develops the model into a pneumatic cylinder with a piston, the second reuses the model in a room with a fan to demonstrate heat transfer and dissipation.

The central part of the system is a control volume. Substance in the form of liquid or gas—in our case air—can flow from a reservoir via an inlet pipe with a valve into the control volume. There is also an outlet pipe attached to another valve and reservoir. These flows are useful for modeling mass flows into and out of a control volume. The basic version of the control volume is kept flexible to use it in two different models later on:

1. A model of a pneumatic cylinder with a variable size control volume.
2. A model of a room in a building with a fan.

In both cases we assume that the air in the control volume follows the equation of state for an ideal gas. We start by presenting the simplest possible model of a control volume and gradually add additional equations as well as other details.

15.2.2 Control Volume Model

Recall the equation of state for an ideal gas, previously presented as equation (14-58) on page 762:

$$P \cdot V = m \cdot R \cdot T \tag{15-3}$$

where P is the pressure, V is the volume of the control volume, m is the mass, R is the *gas constant* for the particular gas—not the universal gas constant, and T is the temperature.

In Modelica syntax the ideal gas law appears as follows, to be inserted into the `BasicVolume` Modelica model:

```
P*V=m*R*T
```

Our simplified control volume is schematically depicted in Figure 15-4.

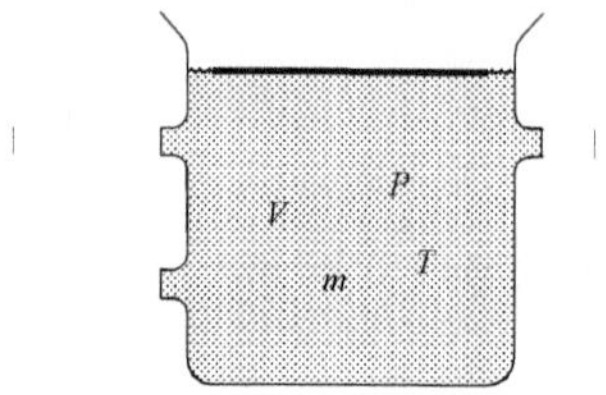

Figure 15-4. A simplified control volume containing air modeled as an ideal gas with the quantities pressure P, volume V, temperature T, and mass m.

The Modelica code for our first simple version of the control volume is given in the `BasicVolume` model below. The complete equation of state for an ideal gas appears in this model. However, the "boundary conditions" are very simplistic and restrictive, restricting all variables except the pressure `P` to constant values. Our control volume contains 1 liter of air with a mass of 0.00119 kg at the constant temperature of 20 degrees Celsius, i.e., 293 degrees Kelvin.

It is possible to make the model somewhat more readable and descriptive by using some of the common "physical types" defined in the Modelica standard library `SIunits` as subtypes of `Real`.

```
package SIunits
type Mass     = Real(final quantity="Mass", final unit="kg", min=0);
type Pressure = Real(final quantity="Pressure",
                     final unit="Pa", displayUnit="bar");
type Volume   = Real(final quantity="Volume", final unit="m3");
...
```

Using such type definitions gives the following advantages:

- More understandable code.
- Constraint values are defined for attributes such as `min`, `max` and `quantity`, which can be used for additional consistency checking.
- Unit attributes specific to the physical type are defined

This is a simple `BasicVolume` model using physical types to declare its variables:

```
model BasicVolume  "First version with physical types"
  parameter Real              R = 287;
  Modelica.SIunits.Pressure   P;
  Modelica.SIunits.Volume     V;
```

```
  Modelica.SIunits.Mass          m;
  Modelica.SIunits.Temperature T;
equation    // "Boundary" conditions
  V=1e-3;       // volume is 1 liter
  T=293;        // 20 deg Celsius
  m=0.00119;  // mass of 1 liter air at K=293
  // Equation of state (ideal gas)
  P*V=m*R*T;
end BasicVolume;
```

15.2.3 Conservation of Mass in Control Volume

The next step is to make the boundary conditions somewhat more flexible and realistic by allowing varying inflow and outflow of gas. The principle of conservation of mass, previously stated as (14-77) on page 767, gives a mass balance equation:

$$\frac{dm}{dt} = \dot{m}_{in} - \dot{m}_{out} \qquad (15\text{-}4)$$

where dm/dt is the net change rate of mass in the control volume, $\dot{m}_{in}$ is the inflow rate of mass, and $\dot{m}_{out}$ is the outflow of mass from the control volume. These variables appear as `der(m)`, `m_flow_in`, and `m_flow_out` in the Modelica syntax version of the mass balance equation:

```
der(m)=m_flow_in-m_flow_out;
```

The control volume with varying mass flows is depicted in Figure 15-5 below:

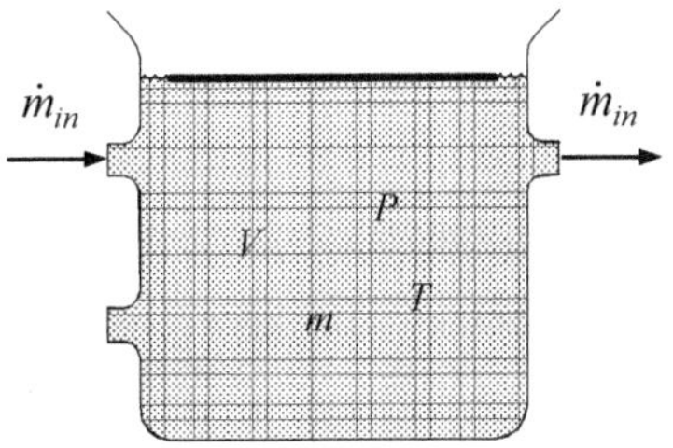

Figure 15-5. The simplistic control volume with varying mass flows added.

In this version of the `BasicVolume` model we specify a `start` attribute for the mass `m` instead of an equation. This allows the mass to vary during the simulation. We have also added the mass flow variables `m_flow_in` and `m_flow_out` as well as three new equations – the inflow of mass, the outflow of mass, and the mass balance equation (15-4).

In the following, all *changed* lines or parts of lines in the model classes compared to the previous versions (as well as Modelica keywords as usual) are marked with **bold**-face and the comment `//Added`.

```
model BasicVolume   "Conservation of Mass"
  import Modelica.SIunits.*;
  parameter SpecificHeatCapacity R = 287;
  Pressure         P;
  Volume           V;
  Mass             m(start=0.00119);           // Added: start value
  Temperature      T;
  MassFlowRate     m_flow_in;                  // Added: mass inflow
  MassFlowRate     m_flow_out;                 // Added: mass outflow
equation
  // Boundary conditions
  V=1e-3;
```

```
  T=293;
  m_flow_in=0.1e-3;                          // Added!
  m_flow_out=0.01e-3;                        // Added!
  // Conservation of mass
  der(m)  = m_flow_in - m_flow_out;          // Added!
  // Equation of state (ideal gas)
  P*V = m*R*T;
end BasicVolume;
```

We simulate and plot:

```
simulate(BasicVolume, stopTime=1);
plot(m);  plot(P);
```

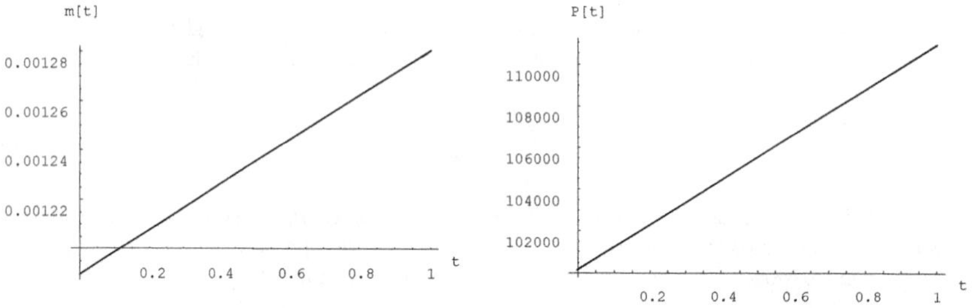

Figure 15-6. Plots of mass m and pressure P for the simplistic control volume with constant inflow, constant outflow, and a mass balance equation added.

Since there is a constant inflow of mass that is greater than the outflow according to the equations in the model (Figure 15-6), the amount of gas in the control volume as well as the pressure steadily increases.

15.2.4 Conservation of Energy in Control Volume

We recall the principle of *conservation of energy* for a *control volume*, abbreviated *c.v.*, previously stated as equation (14-78) on page 767:

Change of energy in *c.v.*	=	Energy entering *c.v.*	–	Energy leaving *c.v.*	+	Net energy transferred to *c.v.*	(15-5)
$\Delta E_{c.v.}$		ΔE_{in}		ΔE_{out}		$\Delta Q - \Delta W$	

where ΔQ is the heat energy transferred to the control volume and ΔW is the net total work done by the control volume on its surroundings. The mass flows and energy flows are schematically depicted in Figure 15-7.

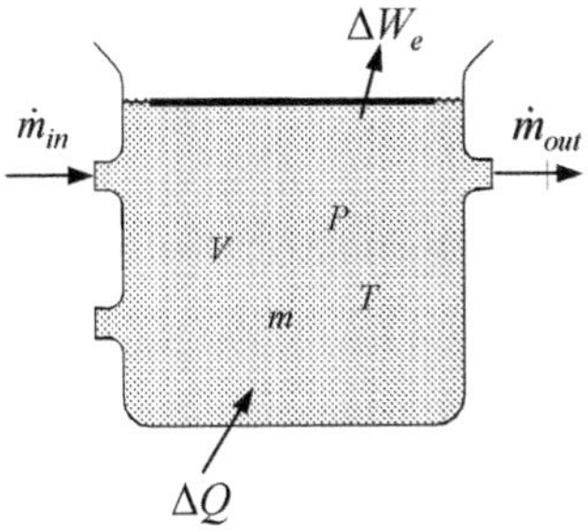

Figure 15-7. A control volume with inflow Q of thermal energy and outflow W_e of external work and of external flow work W_{flow} by the flowing fluid or gas into the inlet and out of the outlet, performed during a time increment t.

Also consider the fact that the total work ΔW that the control volume performs on its surroundings during a time increment Δt is composed of two parts: the work due to the pressure needed to move the fluid or gas into and out of the control volume through the inlet and outlet pipes, sometimes called *flow work*, ΔW_{flow}, and other forms of *external work*, ΔW_e. This can be expressed as:

$$\Delta W = \Delta W_{flow} + \Delta W_e \tag{15-6}$$

To simplify our presentation in the next section we will temporarily assume that both ΔQ and ΔW are zero. This approximation will shortly be removed in Section15.2.4.2, page 807, where the corresponding terms are put back into the energy equation.

15.2.4.1 Energy Flow, Internal Energy, and Enthalpy for Control Volume

In Section 14.7.5.2, page 764, we defined an energy term called enthalpy, H:

$$H = U + P \cdot V \tag{15-7}$$

where U is the internal energy of the substance in the control volume, P is the pressure, and V is the volume. The *change of enthalpy* for a system has the physical significance in being equal to the heat added to a system going through a constant-pressure equilibrium process, see once more Section 14.7.5.2. The *specific enthalpy h* is a useful property of fluids and gases. Specific enthalpy is a measure for how much work can be extracted from the fluid, for example, in a turbine, and is obtained by dividing H by the mass m:

$$h = \frac{H}{m} \tag{15-8}$$

By using the principle of energy conservation for a control volume, and assuming that the kinetic and potential energy changes are negligible, we can derive (see (14-92), page 769) an equation for the rate of change of the internal energy of the control volume:

$$\frac{dU}{dt} = h_{in}\,\dot{m}_{in} - h_{out}\,\dot{m}_{out} + \dot{Q} - \dot{W}_e \tag{15-9}$$

We will temporarily assume that there is no inflow of heat, $\dot{Q} = 0$, and no external work, $\dot{W}_e = 0$, giving:

$$\frac{dU}{dt} = h_{in}\,\dot{m}_{in} - h_{out}\,\dot{m}_{out} \tag{15-10}$$

Assuming that the specific heat capacity of the substance is constant within a temperature range close to some constant temperature T_0, the *specific internal energy* can be expressed as follows:

$$u = \frac{U}{m}$$
$$u = u_0 + c_v(T - T_0) \tag{15-11}$$

where u_0 is the specific internal energy at the temperature T_0 and c_v is the specific heat capacity of the substance at that temperature.

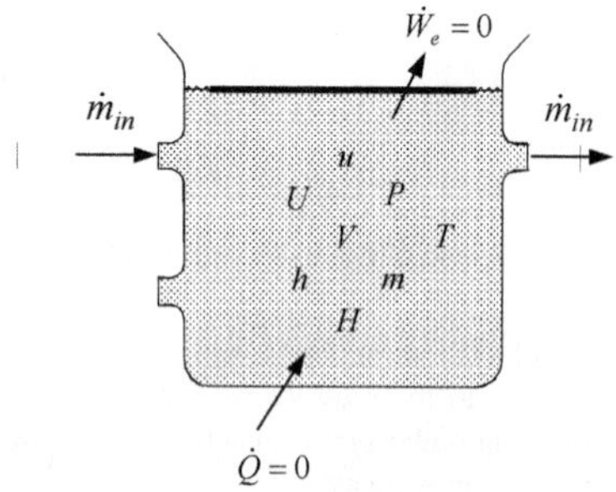

Figure 15-8. Control volume with energy represented as internal energy U, specific internal energy u, enthalpy H, specific enthalpy h, as well as inflow of heat energy Q and outflow of external work W_e, where Q and W_e are temporarily assumed to be zero.

We refine our previous `BasicVolume` model class by adding the equations (14-66), (15-8), (15-10), and (15-11), resulting in the new version of `BasicVolume` presented below. We also fix (for testing purposes, to be changed in a later version of the model) the specific enthalpy for the inflowing gas to a constant value by using the measured value h_{in} = 300190 [J/kg] for air at T = 300 [K] – not exactly at T = 293 [K] but almost – and give values for the following parameters: specific internal energy u_0 = 209058 [J/kg], specific heat capacity c_v = 717 [J/(kg K)], and mass m_0 for 1 liter of air, where all three parameters are valid for air at the temperature T_0 = 293 [K].

In the model below, dU/dt appears as `der(U)`, h_{in} as `h_in`, $\dot{m}_{in}$ as `m_flow_in`, h_{out} as `h_out`, $\dot{m}_{out}$ as `m_flow_out`, etc.

```
model BasicVolume
  import Modelica.SIunits.*;
  parameter SpecificInternalEnergy u_0 = 209058;  // Added!  Air at T=293K
  parameter SpecificHeatCapacity   c_v = 717;     // Added!
  parameter Temperature            T_0 = 293;     // Added!
  parameter Mass                   m_0 = 0.00119; // Added!
  parameter SpecificHeatCapacity   R   = 287;
  Pressure             P;
  Volume               V;
  Mass                 m(start=m_0);              // Added part!
  Temperature          T;
  MassFlowRate         m_flow_in, m_flow_out;
  SpecificEnthalpy     h_in, h_out;               // Added!
  SpecificEnthalpy     h;                         // Added!
  Enthalpy             H;                         // Added!
  SpecificInternalEnergy u;                       // Added!
  InternalEnergy       U(start=u_0*m_0);          // Added!
equation
  // Boundary conditions
  V          = 1e-3;
  m_flow_in  = 0.1e-3;
  m_flow_out = 0.01e-3;
```

```
    h_in       = 300190;                          // Added: Air at T = 300K
    h_out      = h;                               // Added!
    // Conservation of mass
    der(m)     = m_flow_in-m_flow_out;
    // Conservation of energy
    der(U)     = h_in*m_flow_in - h_out*m_flow_out;  // Added!
    // Specific internal energy (ideal gas)
    u = U/m;                                      // Added!
    u = u_0+c_v*(T-T_0);                          // Added!
    // Specific enthalpy
    H = U+P*V;                                    // Added!
    h = H/m;                                      // Added!
    // Equation of state (ideal gas)
    P*V = m*R*T;
end BasicVolume;
```

A simulation of the control volume model is performed below. The simulated temperature of the air as a function of time is depicted in Figure 15-9:

```
simulate(BasicVolume, stopTime=10);
plot(T);
```

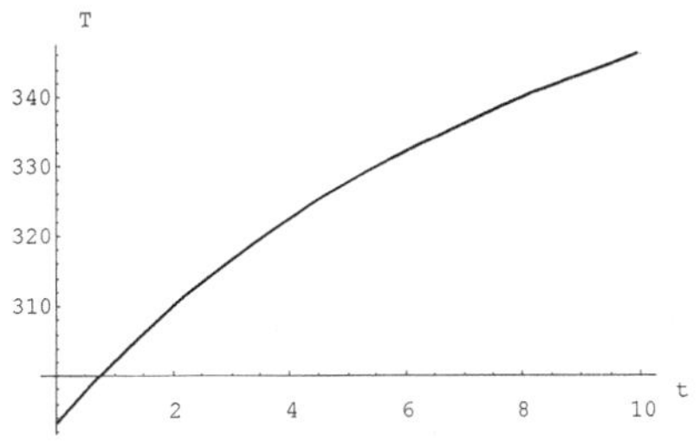

Figure 15-9. The temperature in a control volume increases with fixed inflow of constant enthalpy air.

15.2.4.2 Heat Transfer and Work in Control Volume

In this section we further refine the control volume model by taking into account heat transfer into the volume and work done on the surroundings by the control volume, for example, through the movement of the piston at the top, as shown in Figure 15-10.

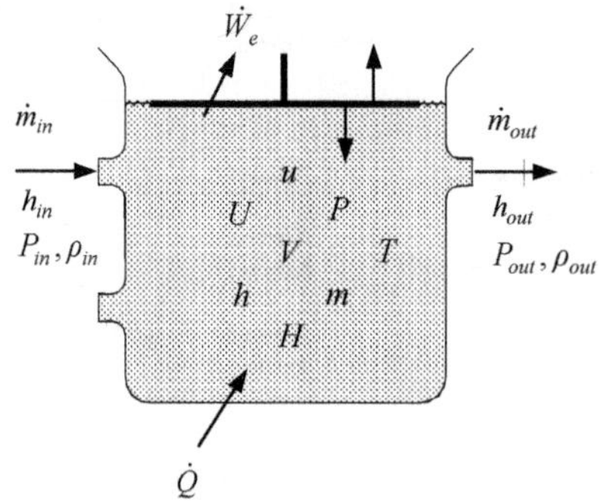

Figure 15-10. A control volume with inflow rate $\dot{Q}$ of thermal energy and external work done on the surroundings at the rate $\dot{W}_e$ consisting of ***flow work*** done by the flowing fluid or gas, and piston work done by the piston, as well as work done by the rotating shaft to be introduced later.

We now return to equation (14-82) for the total work consisting of flow work, ΔW_{flow}, as well as other forms of external work, ΔW_e, done during a time increment Δt. By dividing both sides by Δt and letting the time increment become infinitesimally small, that is, $\Delta t \rightarrow dt$, we obtain the equation for the corresponding power quantities, that is, work per time unit:

$$\dot{W} = \dot{W}_{flow} + \dot{W}_e \tag{15-12}$$

where $\dot{W}_{flow}$ is flow work per time unit done by the flowing fluid or gas, and $\dot{W}_e$ is work per time unit done by the expanding control volume to move the piston as well as work done by for example a rotating *shaft* with a fan rotor, often denoted *shaft work*, W_s, giving:

$$\dot{W}_e = \dot{W}_{piston} + \dot{W}_s \tag{15-13}$$

Regarding the shaft work per time unit, $\dot{W}_s$, there are two common applications:

- *Turbines*, for which $\dot{W}_s > 0$, that is, the flowing gas or fluid transfers energy *out of* the control volume into an external system via the shaft.
- *Compressors*, including our fan rotor example, for which $\dot{W}_s < 0$, that is, the shaft transfers energy *into* the control volume via the rotor blades.

The shaft work is introduced here but temporarily set to zero. It will be used and redefined later when a shaft that can be connected to a fan rotor is added to our example control volume model; see Section 15.2.6, page 825.

The other part of the external work includes work done by the piston when expanding the volume of air an increment dV against a pressure P during a time dt, which is $P \cdot dV$, giving:

$$\begin{aligned} \dot{W}_{piston} &= P \cdot \dot{V} \\ \dot{W}_s &= 0 \end{aligned} \tag{15-14}$$

By some formula manipulations, previously shown in Section 14.7.5.4, page 766, we obtain the following form of equation [approximately (14-84), page 768, but divided by $\Delta t \rightarrow 0$] for the total power $\dot{W}$ exerted by the control volume, i.e., the work per time unit:

$$\dot{W} = \frac{P_{out}}{\rho_{out}} \dot{m}_{out} - \frac{P_{in}}{\rho_{in}} \dot{m}_{in} + \dot{W}_e \tag{15-15}$$

where P_{in}, ρ_{in} and P_{out}, ρ_{out} are the pressures and densities of the fluid or gas at the inlet pipe and outlet pipe of the control volume, respectively.

That form is used in the previous (Section 15.2.4.1, page 805) derivation of the energy equation (15-9) for conservation of energy, where we now have put back the terms for heat flow $\dot{Q}$, and external work, $\dot{W}_e$:

$$\frac{dU}{dt} = h_{in}\,\dot{m}_{in} - h_{out}\,\dot{m}_{out} + \dot{Q} - \dot{W}_e \tag{15-16}$$

The control volume model is further refined by inserting the equations (15-14) and (15-16) describing work and energy balance. Furthermore, an equation for the heat flow rate $\dot{Q} = 0$ is inserted, as well as an equation creating a change of the volume V at time $t = 0.5$ to illustrate the work done on the piston when the volume changes:

$$V = \begin{cases} 10^{-3} & ,t \le 0 \\ 10^{-3}(1+t-0.5) & ,t > 0.5 \end{cases} \tag{15-17}$$

In the refined model below, $\dot{Q}$ is represented by `Q_flow`, $\dot{W}_e$ by `W_flow_e`, and $\dot{W}_s$ by `W_flow_s`:

```
model BasicVolume
  import Modelica.SIunits.*;
  parameter SpecificInternalEnergy u_0 = 209058;   // Air at T=293K
  parameter SpecificHeatCapacity   c_v = 717;
  parameter Temperature            T_0 = 293;
  parameter Mass                   m_0 = 0.00119;
  parameter SpecificHeatCapacity     R = 287;
  Pressure            P;
  Volume              V;
  Mass                m(start=m_0);
  Temperature         T;
  MassFlowRate        m_flow_in, m_flow_out;
  SpecificEnthalpy    h_in, h_out;
  SpecificEnthalpy    h;
  Enthalpy            H;
  SpecificInternalEnergy u;
  InternalEnergy      U(start = u_0*m_0);
  HeatFlowRate        Q_flow=0;                         // Added!
  Power               W_flow_e, W_flow_s=0;             // Added!
equation
  // Boundary conditions
  V = 1e-3 + 0.1e-3*(if time>0.5 then time else 0);     // Added part
  m_flow_in  = 0.1e-3;
  m_flow_out = 0.01e-3;
  h_in       = 300190;    // Air at T=300K
  h_out      = h;
  // Conservation of mass
  der(m)=m_flow_in - m_flow_out;
  // Conservation of energy
  der(U)=h_in*m_flow_in-h_out*m_flow_out+Q_flow-W_flow_e;     // Added part
  W_flow_e - W_flow_s = P*der(V);                              // Added
  // Specific internal energy u (ideal gas)
  u=U/m;
  u=u_0 + c_v*(T-T_0);
  // Specific enthalpy h
  H=U+P*V;
  h=H/m;
  // Equation of state (ideal gas)
  P*V=m*R*T;
end BasicVolume;
```

We simulate the model and plot the mass `m` and pressure `P` as functions of time:

```
simulate(BasicVolume, stopTime=1);
plot(m);  plot(P);
```

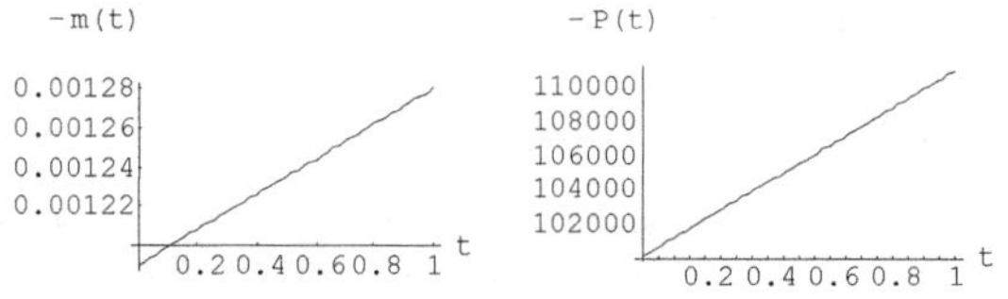

Figure 15-11. The mass steadily increases due to a constant inflow that is greater than the constant outflow, whereas there is a discontinuous drop in pressure at t=0.5 due to the instantaneous change in volume at that time.

We also plot the temperature `T` as a function of time:

```
plot(m);
```

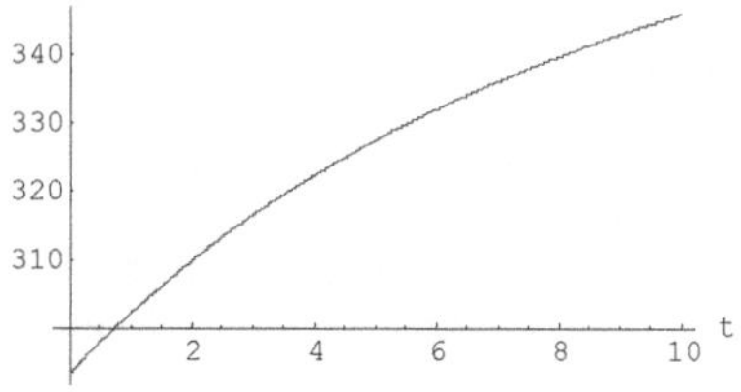

Figure 15-12. Temperature T for the control volume.

15.2.5 Connector Interfaces to the Control Volume

So far we have been increasing the realism of our control volume model by gradually adding additional equations. However, the model is not a system in the sense that the total amount of mass in the system is conserved.

We need to add some external components that should interact with the control volume, that is, build a *system model* that includes the control volume model. However, a well structured system model should have *explicit interfaces* between the components of the system. The interfaces of the control volume should reflect interaction with the surroundings, typically involving the following quantities:

- Mass/energy flow
- Mechanical work
- Heat

Note that some variables are internal to a component, e.g. P, V, U, u, T, H, h, m, and so on, while other variables such as P_{in}, $\dot{m}_{in}$, h_{in}, and so on, are used to exchange information at interfaces by interacting with the surroundings including other connected components.

Take a look at our control volume model once more, as depicted in Figure 15-13.

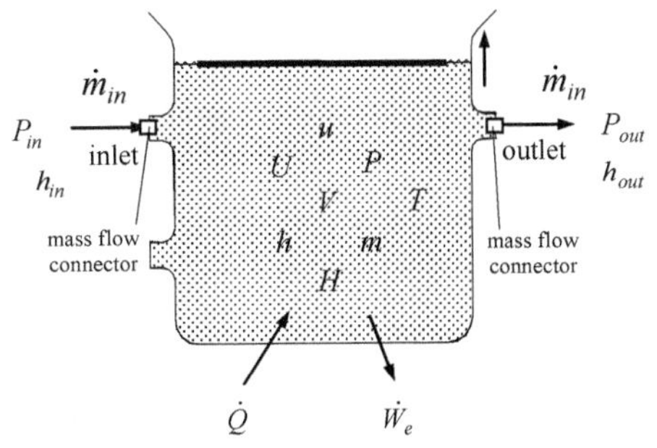

Figure 15-13. The control volume model with explicit mass flow connectors added at the inlet and the outlet.

A slight change has been made compared to the previous figures: two small squares representing *mass flow connectors* have been added at the inlet and the outlet. In this way the interfaces for mass flow between the control volume and the surroundings have been made explicit, thus allowing better structuring of *systems* containing the control volume.

15.2.5.1 Mass Flow Connector Class

In order to introduce mass flow connectors we need a connector class containing the variables that describe interaction at the *mass flow* inlets and outlets of the control volume.

Not only *mass* is flowing, the flowing substance also has some *energy* content represented by its enthalpy. Moreover, the *pressure* influences the interactions of the flowing substance at the inlets and outlets. Therefore the following variables need to be included in the interface:

- *Mass flow* rate $\dot{m}$, represented by the Modelica variable `m_flow`.
- *Specific enthalpy h*, a measure of the energy content per mass unit in the substance, represented by the Modelica variable `h`.
- *Pressure P*, represented by the Modelica variable `P`.

Our first attempt at a corresponding connector class for mass flow, called `FlowConnector`, appears as follows:

```
connector FlowConnector "Illegal unbalanced connector, no stream connector"
  import Modelica.SIunits.*;
  Pressure           P;
  flow MassFlowRate  m_flow;
  SpecificEnthalpy   h_outflow;
end FlowConnector;
```

However, this is an unbalanced connector class which is not allowed in Modelica 3.0 or later versions. For systems which never change flow direction we can split into two balanced connectors, one for inflow and one for outflow:

```
connector FlowConnectorIn  "Old connector style, incoming flow, no stream"
   Pressure P;
   flow MassFlowRate m_flow(min = 0);
   input SpecificEnthalpy h_inflow;
end FlowConnector;

connector FlowConnectorOut "Old connector style, outgoing flow, no stream"
   Pressure P;
   flow MassFlowRate m_flow(max = 0);
   output SpecificEnthalpy h_outflow;
```

```
end FlowConnector;
```

Such classical connectors only work for models of simple systems, which do not allow arbitrary connections, sometimes avoid mass flows as in the above `HeatPort`, and do not involve reverting flows (i.e., changing flow direction, `m_flow` crossing zero). If at all used, such connectors should be used only at the first modeling attempt.

When arbitrary connections might be needed, there is a risk of reverting flows, or a general and numerically robust model is desired, a stream connector version of the `FlowConnector` should be used as defined below.

See Section 5.10.3, page 247, for a comparison of stream connectors to classical connectors and why stream connectors are needed for general and reliable flow modeling in thermo-fluid applications.

In stream connector classes additional variables with the prefix `stream` are introduced (Section 5.10.2, page 247), so-called *stream variables*. These variables are used for additional properties of the flowing mass, which are carried with the flow, e.g., enthalpy/energy and chemical composition.

In fact, specific enthalpy is neither a potential nor a flow variable. It expresses the heat content of the fluid. The heat is transferred by convection as fluid flows through the connector. *Stream* variables for such properties that are *transported* with flows.

In thermo-fluid applications the *flow variable* usually specifies a *mass flow*. The *potential variable* is usually the *pressure*. At connection points, the flowing mass from several connected elements is mixed (Figure 5-51, page 247).

The stream variable `h_outflow` (specific enthalpy flow) is a *stream property* inside the component close to the component boundary at the connection point, assuming that matter flows *out* of the component into the connection point/volume. In other words, it is the value the carried quantity/property *would* have if the fluid was flowing out of the connector, irrespective of the actual flow direction.

Two built-in operators are available that can be applied to stream variables:

- A built-in operator `inStream(c.v)`, which when applied to a stream variable `c.v` in a stream connector `c`, returns its value close to the connection point for `c` provided that the associated mass flow is *positive* in the direction *into* the component.
- A built-in operator `actualStream(c.v)`, which when applied to a stream variable `c.v` returns its value close to the connection point for `c` *regardless of the direction* of the associated mass flow `c.m_flow`.

The operator `actualStream(c.v)` = `if c.m_flow > 0 then inStream(c.v) else c.v`, where `c.v` belongs to the same connector `c` as the mass flow variable `c.m_flow`. That operator is quite convenient since it works irrespective of the flow direction.

An improved version of the flow connector defined as a *stream connector* (Section 5.10, page 245) appears as follows. This is the recommended connector style.

```
connector FlowConnector  "Stream connector style"
  import Modelica.SIunits.*;
  Pressure                   P;
  flow MassFlowRate          m_flow;
  stream SpecificEnthalpy    h_outflow;
end FlowConnector;
```

To allow consistent signs at connections we also need the sign convention for flow variables in connector class instances that belong to a model component:

- Sign convention: *positive flow is into a component*!

It should be pointed out that this definition of a connector only allows *one-directional* flows, that is, the flow at such an interface *may not change its direction* during simulation.

15.2.5.2 Basic Control Volume with Mass Flow Connectors and Separate Ideal Gas Model

In order to create a control volume model with mass flow connectors, the new connectors `inlet` and `outlet` have been added to the control volume model below together with equations relating the internal variables in the control volume to the interface variables in the new connectors. Note that the sign convention for flow variables in connectors is apparent in the following equation:

```
m_flow_out = -outlet.m_flow;
```

The reason for the minus sign is that the flow direction for variables in a connector, for example, `outlet`, is always *into* the component to which it is attached, whereas positive values of the variable `m_flow_out` means flow *out of* the control volume.

In order to improve the modularity and reusability of the model we are also going to separate the equations which are specific to the assumption of ideal gas from the other thermodynamic equations. Easy replacement of the physical property model requires more elaborate schemes, but this separation gives an idea what kind of decisions help in making a model more reusable. This form of the ideal gas model is slightly modified compared to the equations before, because we want to make the model independent from the mass and volume of the control volume. We introduce the specific volume, v :

$$v = \frac{V}{m} \tag{15-18}$$

which is used in the ideal gas law in the model below:

```
partial model IdealGas   "Property model for a simple ideal gas"
  import Modelica.SIunits.*;
  parameter SpecificInternalEnergy u_0=209058;   // Air at T=293K
  parameter SpecificHeatCapacity   c_v = 717;
  parameter SpecificHeatCapacity   R = 287;
  parameter Temperature            T_0 = 293;
  Pressure                         P;
  SpecificVolume                   v;
  Temperature                      T;
  SpecificInternalEnergy           u;
equation
  u=u_0+c_v*(T-T_0);     // Linear model for inner energy
  P*v=R*T;               // Equation of state: ideal gas
end IdealGas;
```

Below is a first preliminary version of `BasicVolume` using *classical flow connectors*:

```
partial model BasicVolumeFirst "Control Volume with Mass Flow Interfaces
                                old version without stream connectors"
  import Modelica.SIunits.*;
  extends IdealGas;                              // Added!
  FlowConnectorIn         inlet;                 // Added!
  FlowConnectorOut        outlet;                // Added!
  parameter Mass          m_0 = 0.00119;
  Mass                    m(start=m_0);
  Volume                  V;
  MassFlowRate            m_flow_in, m_flow_out;
  SpecificEnthalpy        h_in, h_out;
  SpecificEnthalpy        h;
  Enthalpy                H;
  InternalEnergy          U(start=u_0*m_0);
  HeatFlowRate            Q_flow;
  Power                   W_flow_e, W_flow_s;
equation
  // Interface relations
  m_flow_in   = inlet.m_flow;                    // Added!
  inlet.h_inflow = h_in;                         // Added!  Classical approach
```

```
    inlet.P     = P;                          // Added!
    m_flow_out = -outlet.m_flow;              // Added! Note the sign convention!
    outlet.h_outflow = h_out;                 // Added!  Classical approach
    outlet.P    = P;                          // Added!
    h_out       = h;                          // Added!
  // Conservation of mass
    der(m) = m_flow_in-m_flow_out;
  // Conservation of energy
    der(U )= h_in*m_flow_in-h_out*m_flow_out+Q_flow-W_flow_e;
    W_flow_e = P*der(V)+W_flow_s;
    H = U+P*V;
    u = U/m;    // Specific internal energy (ideal gas)
    v = V/m;    // Specific Volume
    h = H/m;    // Specific enthalpy
  end BasicVolumeFirst;
```

Below is an improved version of `BasicVolume` using *stream connectors*, where we use `actualStream` to obtain the property `h_outflow` of the stream connectors `inlet` and `outlet`.

```
partial model BasicVolume "Control Volume with Mass Flow Interfaces,
                          improved version using stream connectors"
    import Modelica.SIunits.*;
    extends IdealGas;                                 // Added!
    FlowConnector            inlet, outlet;           // Added!
    parameter Mass           m_0 = 0.00119;
    Mass                     m(start=m_0);
    Volume                   V;
    MassFlowRate             m_flow_in, m_flow_out;
    SpecificEnthalpy         h_in, h_out;
    SpecificEnthalpy         h;
    Enthalpy                 H;
    InternalEnergy           U(start=u_0*m_0);
    HeatFlowRate             Q_flow;
    Power                    W_flow_e, W_flow_s;
  equation
    // Interface relations
    m_flow_in         = inlet.m_flow;                     // Added!
    h_in          = actualStream(inlet.h_outflow);        // Added! Stream approach
    inlet.h_outflow = h;                                  // Added! Stream approach
    inlet.P           = P;                                // Added!
    m_flow_out        = -outlet.m_flow;      // Added! Note the sign convention!
    h_out         = actualStream(outlet.h_outflow);       // Added! Stream approach
    outlet.h_outflow = h;                                 // Added! Stream approach
    outlet.P          = P;                                // Added!
    // Conservation of mass
    der(m)=m_flow_in - m_flow_out;
    // Conservation of energy
    der(U)=h_in*m_flow_in - h_out*m_flow_out + Q_flow-W_flow_e;
    W_flow_e=P*der(V)+W_flow_s;
    H = U+P*V;
    u = U/m;    // Specific internal energy (ideal gas)
    v = V/m;    // Specific Volume
    h = H/m;    // Specific enthalpy
  end BasicVolume;
```

Note that `BasicVolume` with stream connectors has eight interface equations and is completely symmetric whereas the previous `BasicVolumeFirst` with seven equations is unsymmetric and assigns the specific enthalpy from within the component to the output `outlet.h_outflow`.

The stream variable of each port appears twice in the symmetric stream connector version of `BasicVolume`: as `h_outflow` for flow leaving the component and as `inStream(h_outflow)` for flow entering the component through the respective port.

The difference between seven and eight equations is no problem for checking equation counts in balanced models (Section 8.9, page 387), since stream variables work almost like output variables. That is why they are not counted in the balancing counts. "A model using a stream connector must expose the outflow value, which is known from internal storage or from inflow values of other connectors, independently of the flow direction. The inflow value can be obtained by a model on demand by using the operator `inStream(h_outflow)`.

Now we have constructed a bare-bones control volume that contains all the physics which is needed in a simple control volume model, but in doing so we have a model that can not be simulated as it stands, the model is underspecified. This is typical for object-oriented modeling: in order to improve the reusability of a model, some details have to be left open. For testing the above control volume model, we have to specify the volume `V`, the heat transfer from/to the environment `Q_flow` and the work `W_flow_s`. If a model is underspecified and three equations are missing, it is common to say that the model has three degrees of freedom. Three additional equations are needed to make the equation system solvable so that the model can be simulated.

Unspecified variables in the connectors are treated differently depending on their prefix. Unconnected flow variables are automatically set to zero (Section 5.7.8.5, page 222). This is useful for testing complex flow sheets, because it makes it possible to simulate flow sheets as they are developed when a some connections are still missing. Our test model for the basic control volume model now becomes:

```
model BasicVolumeTest "testing our general volume"
  extends BasicVolume;
equation
  // Specifying the remaining 3 degrees of freedom
  V = 1e-3 + 0.1e-3*(if time > 0.5 then time - 0.5 else 0);
  Q_flow = 0.0;
  W_flow_s = 0.0;
end BasicVolumeTest;
```

We plot the temperature `T` and the pressure `P` as functions of time:

```
simulate(BasicVolumeTest, stopTime=10)
plot({T, U}, xrange={0,2})
```

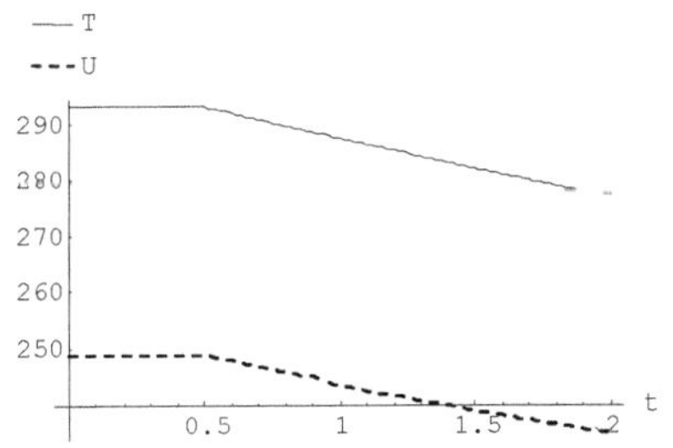

Figure 15-14. Plot of the temperature and internal energy variables of the control volume component of the system.

Now we have a reusable, tested, basic control volume. The next step is to create models for the boundary conditions, we call them sources and sinks, or just boundary objects, and to create models that determine the mass flow between different control volumes, for example a valve or orifice.

15.2.5.3 Pressure Source and Pressure Sink or Pressure Boundary

In this section, we introduce pressure source and pressure sink classes or, alternatively, a general `PressureBoundary` class (see further below), which act as either source or sink depending on the flow direction. The `PressureEnthalpySource` class has constant output pressure and constant specific enthalpy for the flowing substance, and the `PressureSink` class specifies constant input pressure.

Both of these two kinds of sources and sinks use the `FlowConnector` class (Section 15.2.5.1, page 811) to specify their interfaces, containing pressure P and specific enthalpy h, and mass flow rate $\dot{m}$ as a flow variable.

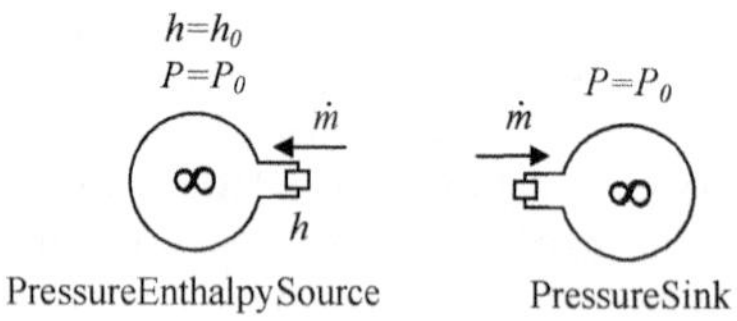

Figure 15-15. The `PressureEnthalpySource` class specifies sources that produce mass flow at constant pressure and specific enthalpy, whereas `PressureSink` specifies flow sinks at constant pressure.

The Modelica code for the `PressureEnthalpySource` and `PressureSink` classes is as follows:

```
model PressureEnthalpySource "Constant pressure and enthalpy source"
  import Modelica.SIunits.*;
  FlowConnector outlet;
  parameter Pressure           P_0 =1.0e5;
  parameter SpecificEnthalpy  h_0 =300190;
equation
  outlet.P = P_0;
  outlet.h_outflow = h _0;
end PressureEnthalpySource;

model PressureSink "Pressure sink, constant pressure"
  FlowConnector inlet;
  parameter Modelica.SIunits.Pressure  P_0=1.0e5;
equation
  inlet.P=P_0
end PressureSink;
```

A more general approach which is more robust against situations with back flow uses a single boundary model `PressureEnthalpyBoundary` for sources/sinks. This is the model that will be used in the following.

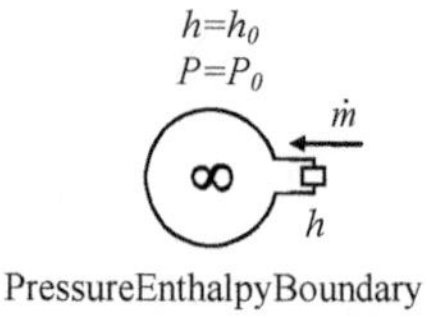

Figure 15-16. The `PressureEnthalpyBoundary` class specifies sources or sinks that produce/receive mass flow at constant pressure and specific enthalpy. The flow direction determines whether it is a source or a sink.

The Modelica code for the `PressureEnthalpyBoundary` class is as follows:

```
model PressureEnthalpyBoundary "Constant pressure and enthalpy: source/sink"
  import Modelica.SIunits.*;
  FlowConnector                port;
  parameter Pressure           P_0 =1.0e5;
```

```
  parameter SpecificEnthalpy  h_0 =300190;
equation
  port.P = P_0;
  port.h_outflow = h_0;
end PressureEnthalpyBoundary;
```

15.2.5.4 Simple Valve Flow Model

This first version of the valve model, depicted in Figure 15-17, has just three variables: the input pressure P_{in}, the output pressure P_{out}, and the mass flow rate $\dot{m}$.

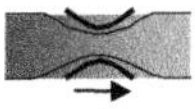

Figure 15-17. Very simple valve flow model.

The model in its current form is unusable as a model building block since both the input and the output pressure are fixed to constant values in the model. Also, the model does not yet have any connector interfaces. The following constitutive equation relates the pressure difference over the valve to the mass flow, only valid when $P_{in} > P_{out}$:

$$\beta \cdot A^2 \cdot (P_{in} - P_{out}) = \dot{m}^2 \tag{15-19}$$

where β is a constant, A is the cross section area of the inlet and outlet, P_{in} is the pressure on the inlet side, P_{out} is the outlet pressure, and $\dot{m}$ is the mass flow rate. The Modelica code for the model appears as follows:

```
model SimpleValveFlow
  import Modelica.SIunits;
  parameter SIunits.Area A = 1e-4;
  parameter Real          beta = 5.0e-5;
  SIunits.Pressure        P_in, P_out;
  SIunits.MassFlowRate    m_flow;
equation  // Boundary conditions
  P_in  = 1.2e5;
  P_out = 1.0e5;
  // Constitutive relation
  beta*A^2*(P_in - P_out) = m_flow^2;
  annotation(experiment(stopTime=1));
end SimpleValveFlow;
```

We simulate the model and plot the mass flow $\dot{m}$, which is not very exciting since the constant pressure difference gives rise to a constant mass flow.

```
simulate(SimpleValveFlow, stopTime=1);
plot(m_flow);
```

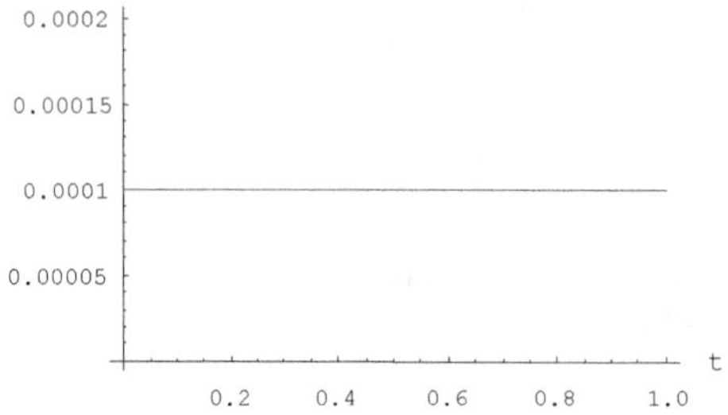

Figure 15-18. Simulation of the very simple valve flow model.

15.2.5.5 Basic Valve Flow Model with Connector Interfaces and Conservation of Mass and Energy

The second version of the valve model extends the simple model with explicit connector interfaces and adds equations for conservation of mass and energy, which represent the fact that there is no mass and energy storage within the valve. This basic valve flow model, depicted in Figure 15-19, is more realistic than the previous version and good enough to be used for simple flow system modeling applications.

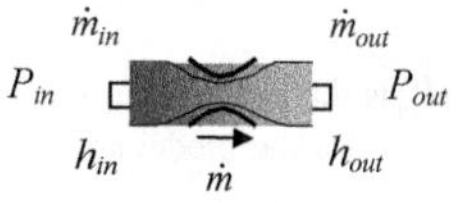

Figure 15-19. Complete valve flow model with conservation of mass and energy. In this case, there is no storage of mass and energy within the valve.

The equation for conservation of mass with no mass storage within the valve component:

$$0 = \dot{m}_{in} + \dot{m}_{out} \tag{15-20}$$

or expressed in Modelica syntax:

```
0 = inlet.m_flow + outlet.m_flow;
```

where $\dot{m}_{in}$ represented as `inlet.m_flow` is the flow into the inlet (positive sign) and $\dot{m}_{out}$ represented as `outlet.m_flow` is the flow out of the outlet (negative sign), that is, it would be positive sign for flow in the opposite direction into the outlet connector.

Analogously, the equation for conservation of energy (15-10) combined with the fact that there is no storage of internal energy U within the valve, $(dU/dt = 0)$, can thus be simplified to the following form:

$$0 = \dot{m}_{in} \cdot h_{in} + \dot{m}_{out} \cdot h_{out} \tag{15-21}$$

or in Modelica syntax:

```
0 = inlet.m_flow*inlet.h_outflow + outlet.m_flow*outlet.h_outflow;
```

where we have the same mass flow quantities as in the mass balance equation (15-20), h_{in} represented as `inlet.h_outflow` is the specific enthalpy of the substance flowing into the inlet, and h_{out} represented as `outlet.h_outflow` is the specific enthalpy of the substance flowing out of the outlet.

By taking the square root on both sides of the constitutive relation from `SimpleValveFlow` we obtain:

```
A*sqrt(beta*(P_in - P_out)) = m_flow;  // Constitutive relation
```

By including flow connectors together with equations (15-20) and (15-21) we obtain a more realistic and configurable valve flow model with connector interfaces and conservation of mass and energy. First a preliminary version not using stream connectors:

```
model ValveFlowFirst  // Preliminary version without stream connectors
  import Modelica.SIunits;
  FlowConnectorIn         inlet;                          // Added!
  FlowConnectorOut        outlet;                         // Added!
  parameter SIunits.Area A     = 1e-4;
  parameter Real          beta = 5.0e-5;
  SIunits.Pressure        P_in, P_out;
  SIunits.MassFlowRate    m_flow;
equation  // Interface relations
  P_in   = inlet.P;                                       // Added!
  P_out = outlet.P;                                       // Added!
  m_flow = inlet.m_flow;                                  // Added!
  0 = inlet.m_flow + outlet.m_flow; //Added:Conservation of mass, no storage
  // Conservation of energy (no storage)
  0 = inlet.m_flow*inlet.h_inflow + outlet.m_flow*outlet.h_outflow;//Added!
  A*sqrt(beta*(P_in - P_out)) = m_flow;  // Constitutive relation
  assert(P_in - P_out>0,"Error: model not valid for backflow"); // Added!
end ValveFlowFirst;
```

We have also added an `assert` at the end of the model. This construct is syntactically an equation since it is allowed in an equation section, but does not add any equation to the system of equations to be solved. It is just used to assert certain conditions that must hold for the valid region of operation of the model, that is, expressing the fact that the model is only valid if `P_in-P_out>0` which means that the flow direction must be *into* the inlet and *out* of the outlet, not in the opposite direction.

Alternatively, to make the model robust against back flow, we can replace `sqrt` with the `regRoot` function, which approximates `sqrt(abs(x))*sgn(x)` such that the derivative is finite and smooth at x=0. This would replace the following constitutive relation and the assert:

```
A*sqrt(beta*(P_in - P_out)) = m_flow; // Constitutive relation
assert(P_in - P_out>0,"Error: model not valid for backflow");
```

by a constitutive relation that is valid for flow in both directions:

```
A*Modelica.Fluid.Utilities.regRoot(beta*(P_in - P_out)) = m_flow;
```

Unfortunately, the combined energy balance equation becomes *singular* when `m_flow` = 0:

```
0 = inlet.m_flow*inlet.h_outflow + outlet.m_flow*outlet.h_outflow;
```

The stream connector concept replaces this with separate energy balances for positive and negative flow as explained in the following derivation. We first express the same combined energy balance using the `actualStream` operator:

```
0 = inlet.m_flow*actualStream(inlet.h_outflow) +
    outlet.m_flow*actualStream(outlet.h_outflow);
```

This expands to:

```
0 = inlet.m_flow*(if inlet.m_flow > 0 then inStream(inlet.h_outflow) else
  inlet.h_outflow) + outlet.m_flow * (if outlet.m_flow > 0 then
  inStream(outlet.h_outflow) else outlet.h_outflow)
```

Considering the mass balance, `outlet.m_flow = -inlet.m_flow`, then `outlet.m_flow` can be eliminated in the energy balance:

```
0 = inlet.m_flow*(if inlet.m_flow > 0 then inStream(inlet.h_outflow) else
  inlet.h_outflow) - inlet.m_flow*(if inlet.m_flow > 0 then outlet.h_outflow
  else inStream(outlet.h_outflow))
```

which simplifies to:

```
0 = inlet.m_flow*(if inlet.m_flow > 0 then inStream(inlet.h_outflow) -
outlet.h_outflow else inlet.h_outflow - inStream(outlet.h_outflow))
```

Division by `inlet.m_flow` != 0 gives:

```
0 = if inlet.m_flow > 0 then inStream(inlet.h_outflow) - outlet.h_outflow
else inlet.h_outflow - inStream(outlet.h_outflow)
```

This equation can be split into two independent equations (not correct Modelica syntax) for forward and reverse flow:

```
0 = inStream(inlet.h_outflow) - outlet.h_outflow if inlet.m_flow > 0;
0 = inlet.h_outflow - inStream(outlet.h_outflow) if inlet.m_flow < 0;
```

It is expressed in the `ValveFlow` model with the following two equations:

```
outlet.h_outflow = inStream(inlet.h_outflow);  // if inlet.m_flow > 0;
inlet.h_outflow  = inStream(outlet.h_outflow); // if inlet.m_flow < 0;
```

The Modelica connection semantics with the `inStream` operator for connected volume models with storage determine which equation takes effect in the simulation at a given point in time, depending on the flow direction.

Alternatively, we could still keep the use of `actualStream` since `actualStream(c.v) = if c.m_flow > 0 then inStream(c.v) else c.v`.

The following version of the `ValveFlow` model uses stream connectors and has a constitutive relation that is valid for flow in both directions, which makes it robust against back flow:

```
model ValveFlow  // Version with stream connectors, robust against back flow
  import Modelica.SIunits;
  FlowConnector               inlet, outlet;          // Added!
  parameter SIunits.Area      A = 1e-4;
  parameter Real              beta = 5.0e-5;
  SIunits.Pressure            P_in, P_out;
  SIunits.MassFlowRate        m_flow;
equation // Interface relations
  P_in   = inlet.P;                                   // Added!
  P_out  = outlet.P;                                  // Added!
  m_flow = inlet.m_flow;                              // Added!
  0 = inlet.m_flow + outlet.m_flow; // Added: Conserv. of mass (no storage)
  // Conservation of energy (no storage)
  outlet.h_outflow = inStream(inlet.h_outflow);  // Added!
  inlet.h_outflow  = inStream(outlet.h_outflow); // Added!
  A*Modelica.Fluid.Utilities.regRoot(beta*(P_in - P_out)) = m_flow;
end ValveFlow;
```

15.2.5.6 System and Valve Model with Interfaces and Externally Controlled Flow

There is still something missing in our previous valve model from Section 15.2.5.5 above: the ability to control the valve. Without the ability to control the opening in the valve, thus controlling the flow through the valve, it is not very useful. Even the simplest water tap can control its flow. Therefore, we introduce an input port `u` on the valve for a control signal as depicted in Figure 15-20.

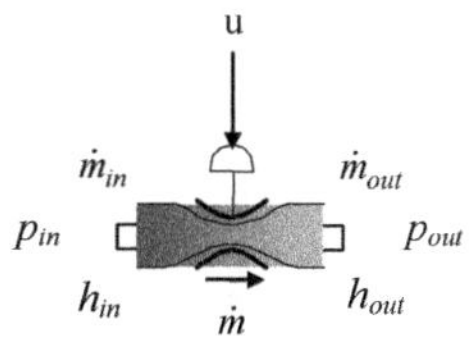

Figure 15-20. Valve with controlled flow via an external input signal u influencing the cross-section area of the opening.

The Modelica code for the `ControlledValveFlow` model appears below, where we have introduced the u connector for a control signal that influences the cross-section area of the opening in the valve and thereby the flow through the valve. First we show a preliminary version without stream connectors:

```
model ControlledValveFlowFirst "Prel version without stream connectors"
  import Modelica.SIunits;
  import Modelica.Blocks.Interfaces;
  FlowConnectorIn        inlet;
  FlowConnectorOut       outlet;
  Interfaces.RealInput              u;                     // Added!
  parameter Modelica.SIunits.Area A = 1e-4;
  parameter Real                    beta = 5.0e-5;
  SIunits.Pressure                  P_in, P_out;
  SIunits.MassFlowRate              m_flow;
equation
  // Interface relations
  P_in  = inlet.P;
  P_out = outlet.P;
  m_flow = inlet.m_flow;
  // Conservation of mass (no storage)
  0 = inlet.m_flow + outlet.m_flow;
  // Conservation of energy (no storage)
  0 = inlet.m_flow*inlet.h_outflow + outlet.m_flow*outlet.h_outflow;
  // Constitutive relation
  (A*u)*sqrt(beta*(P_in - P_out)) = m_flow;              // Added part!
  assert(P_in - P_out>0, "Error: model not valid for backflow");
end ControlledValveFlowFirst;
```

The following version of the `ControlledValveFlow` model uses stream connectors and has a constitutive relation that is valid for flow in both directions which makes it robust against back flow:

```
model ControlledValveFlow // Version with stream connectors and back flow
  import Modelica.SIunits;
  import Modelica.Blocks.Interfaces;
  FlowConnector                     inlet, outlet;
  Interfaces.RealInput              u;                    // Added!
  parameter Modelica.SIunits.Area A = 1e-4;
  parameter Real                    beta = 5.0e-5;
  SIunits.Pressure                  P_in, P_out;
  SIunits.MassFlowRate              m_flow;
equation
  // Interface relations
  P_in = inlet.P;
  P_out = outlet.P;
  m_flow = inlet.m_flow;
  // Conservation of mass (no storage)
  0 = inlet.m_flow + outlet.m_flow;
```

```
  // Conservation of energy (no storage)
  outlet.h_outflow = inStream(inlet.h_outflow);           // Added!
  inlet.h_outflow  = inStream(outlet.h_outflow);          // Added!
  // Constitutive relation
  A*u*Modelica.Fluid.Utilities.regRoot(beta*(P_in-P_out))=m_flow;//Added
end ControlledValveFlow;
```

Now we want to make a small test of our recently developed models of pressure source, sink, and controlled valve components. We put together a test system model called `CtrlFlowSystem`, consisting of a `ctrlFlowModel` with an attached pressure source, a pressure sink, and a step signal component producing the control signal.

```
model CtrlFlowSystem
  import Modelica.Blocks.Sources;
  PressureEnthalpyBoundary  pressureEnthalpySource(P_0=1.2e5);
  Sources.Step              step(offset=1,startTime=0.5,height=-0.5);
  ControlledValveFlow       ctrlFlowModel;  // Negative step signal
  PressureEnthalpyBoundary  pressureSink;
equation
  connect(pressureEnthalpySource.port, ctrlFlowModel.inlet);
  connect(ctrlFlowModel.outlet,        pressureSink.port);
  connect(step.y,                      ctrlFlowModel.u);
  annotation(experiment(stopTime=1));
end CtrlFlowSystem;
```

We simulate the test system and plot the flow through the valve:

```
simulate(CtrlFlowSystem, stopTime=1);
plot(ctrlFlowModel.m_flow)
```

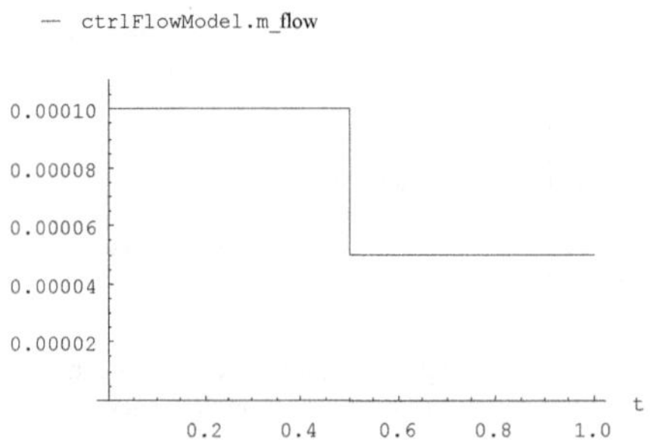

Figure 15-21. Simulation of a controlled flow valve attached to a step control signal.

The simulated and plotted result flow depicted in Figure 15-21 is correct but not very interesting since the flow through the valve is directly proportional to the input step signal.

This version of the valve flow model with external control is used in the pneumatic cylinder system with external valve control described in the next section.

15.2.5.7 Reusing the Control Volume Model in a Pneumatic Cylinder

In the previous section, we added external interfaces for mass flow interaction between the control volume and the surroundings. However, there are other possible interactions between the control volume and external components:

- The piston at the top of the control volume can move up or down, i.e., use a translational connector.
- A rotating shaft with an attached rotor can rotate, i.e., use a rotational connector.

Since both the translational and rotational movements usually are performed against some force or torque, work is done and energy is transferred into or out of the control volume. In this example, we only look at translational movement.

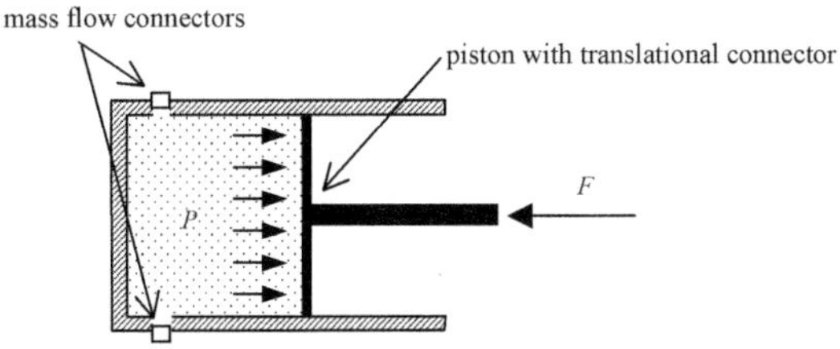

Figure 15-22. The control volume with three external interfaces: two mass flow connectors and one mechanical translational connector to the piston.

Regarding the translational movement of the piston as a consequence of changing volume, we add an equation for the volume in the control volume model and add an equation for the translation force transmitted to the piston:

$$\begin{aligned} V &= V_0 + A \cdot s_{trans} \\ f_{trans} &= -(P - P_0) \cdot A \end{aligned} \tag{15-22}$$

where V is the volume of the control volume, V_0 is the initial volume, A is the area of the piston, P is the pressure inside the cylinder, P_0 is the pressure in the environment, s_{trans} is the vertical translational movement and f_{trans} is the force on the piston. The corresponding equations in Modelica syntax appear as follows:

```
V = V_0 + A*flange_trans.s;
(P - P_0)*A  = flange_trans.f;
```

where s_{trans} is represented by `flange_trans.s`, which is the position variable in the `flange_trans` connector of type `Translational.Interfaces.Flange_a` from the `Modelica.Mechanics` library, and f_{trans} is represented by the force `flange_trans.f` in the same connector. The cylinder volume model that inherits from the previously developed `BasicVolume` model with these additions included appears as follows:

```
model PneumaticCylinderVolume "a simple model of a pneumatic cylinder"
  import Modelica.SIunits.*;
  import Modelica.Mechanics.Translational;
  // Modified states P and T
  extends BasicVolume(P(stateSelect=StateSelect.prefer, start=P_0),
                      T(stateSelect=StateSelect.prefer, start=T_0));
  Translational.Interfaces.Flange_a  flange_trans;
  parameter Area      A  =1e-2 "cylinder cross section area";
  parameter Volume    V_0=1e-3 "cylinder volume in home position";
  parameter Pressure  P_0=1.0e5 "environment pressure";
equation
  V             = V_0 + A*flange_trans.s;
  (P - P_0)*A   = -flange_trans.f;
  W_flow_s      = 0.0;                     // No dissipative work here
  Q_flow        = 0.0;                     // No heat flow
end PneumaticCylinderVolume;
```

Most of the additions to the model are straightforward: the volume is now variable and depends on the piston position, the force in the piston rod is related to the pressure difference inside and outside the cylinder (we use absolute pressures inside the volume), and we neglect dissipative work and heat loss.

Note the modification to the basic control volume: for the pneumatic cylinder it is more natural to have the pressure and temperature as initial conditions and dynamic states. This is achieved via the modification `P(stateSelect=StateSelect.prefer, start=P_0)`— see Section 18.2.6, page 1016, concerning `StateSelect`, and the equivalent modification for `T`.

15.2.5.8 System with a Pneumatic Cylinder—Combined Thermodynamic and Mechanical System, Extracting Mechanical Work from the Control Volume

The cylinder volume model with three connector interfaces—one mechanical and two mass flow connectors—that was defined in the previous section can now be connected to external components to create a pneumatic cylinder system, as depicted in Figure 15-23.

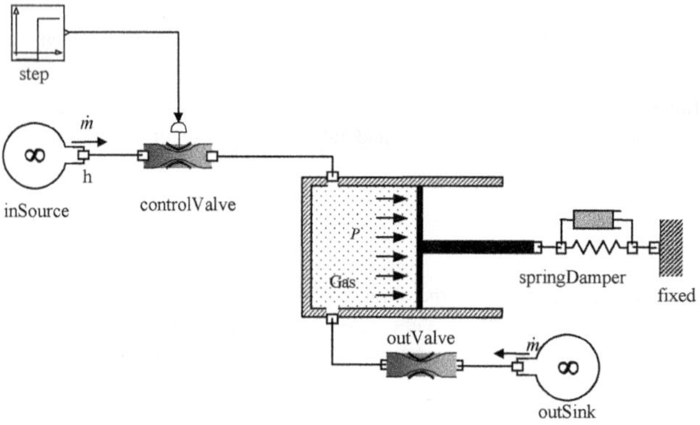

Figure 15-23. A pneumatic cylinder system consisting of a gas filled cylinder doing work on the spring/damper by pushing against a piston. The air comes from a high-pressure reservoir and is released to lower pressure through the controlled valve.

The corresponding Modelica code for the pneumatic cylinder system appears as follows:

```
model PneumaticCylinderSystem "System to test the pneumatic cylinder model"
  import Modelica.SIunits.*;
  import Modelica.Mechanics.Translational.Components;
  import Modelica.Blocks.Sources;
  PneumaticCylinderVolume  cylinder(V_0=1e-2,P_0=2.0e5, T_0=340.0);
  PressureEnthalpyBoundary outSink(P_0=1.0e5);
  ValveFlow                outValve(A=1e-2);
  PressureEnthalpyBoundary inSource(P_0=3.0e5);
  Components.Fixed         fixed(s0=1.0);
  Components.Mass          pistonMass(L=0.1,
                             s(stateSelect=StateSelect.always, start=1.55));
  Components.SpringDamper  springDamper(d=500, s_rel0=0.5, c=5000.0);
  ControlledValveFlow      controlValve(A=1e-2);
  Sources.Step             step(offset=1, startTime=5,height=-0.99);
equation
  connect(outValve.outlet,       outSink.port);
  connect(cylinder.outlet,       outValve.inlet);
  connect(cylinder.flange_trans, pistonMass.flange_b);
  connect(pistonMass.flange_a,   springDamper.flange_b);
```

```
    connect(springDamper.flange_a, fixed.flange);
    connect(inSource.port,          controlValve.inlet);
    connect(controlValve.outlet,    cylinder.inlet);
    connect(step.y,                 controlValve.u);
    annotation(experiment(stopTime=15));
  end PneumaticCylinderSystem;
```

The composition of a translational mechanical model, the piston, that by itself requires two states to model its dynamic behavior, position and velocity, and a variable-volume control volume that requires three states, in this example pressure, temperature and volume, poses numerical problems unless index reduction is performed on the model and the right states are chosen for the numerical integration, see Section 18.2.3, page 1005, concerning the notion of index and index reduction. The volume of the control volume depends on the piston position (`pistonMass.s`) and therefore one of the two states (volume and position) depends on the other one. This is the reason for the `s(stateSelect = StateSelect.always, start=1.55)` modification of the piston mass. All other modifications in the model are to set the parameters and start values to reasonable values for a pneumatic cylinder.

```
  simulate(PneumaticCylinderSystem, stopTime=15);
  plot(pistonMass.s); plot(cylinder.W_flow_e); plot(cylinder.P);
```

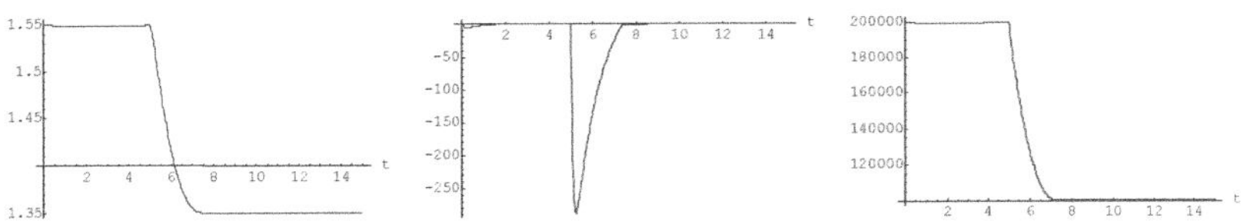

Figure 15-24. Simulation of a pneumatic cylinder system with a controlled flow valve attached to a step-control signal.

15.2.6 System with Dissipation and Heat Sources—A Room with Heat- and Mass Transfer to the Environment

Now we are ready for the second extension to our basic control volume—transforming it into a room with convective heat transfer to the environment. We are also going to look at the effect of dissipative shaft work, including mechanical work done by a rotating shaft, that is, shaft work W_s. In our case the work is dissipated and ultimately transformed into heat. When the work is not dissipated, the shaft work represents a "*turbine*" system for the case when the control volume fluid or gas causes the shaft to turn and perform work, that is, $W_s > 0$, or might be a "*compressor*" when the rotating shaft causes the rotor wheel to turn and move the gas, that is, $W_s < 0$.

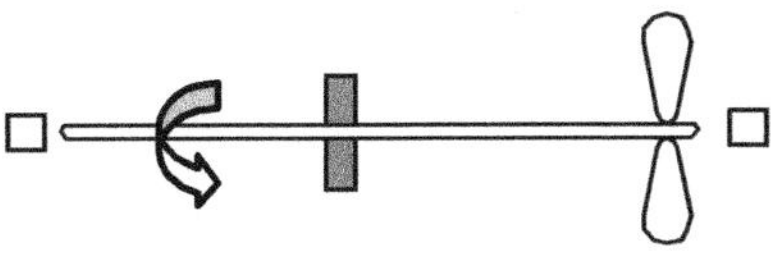

Figure 15-25. A rotor wheel attached to a rotating shaft. In our room example, the work of the fan accelerates the air, but the air dissipates the kinetic energy via turbulence to heat. The model is simplified and directly transforms the electric input power to the fan into heat. The cooling effect of the fan comes not

from the temperature, which is actually increased slightly by the fan, but through increased evaporative cooling due to higher air speed.

The energy transfer aspect of the fan out of or into the control volume through the shaft work done by the rotating fan wheel has already been taken into account in the control volume model previously described in Section 15.2.5.2, page 813 with the shaft work variable `W_flow_s`. The complete system of the room including the fan is depicted in Figure 15-26 below:

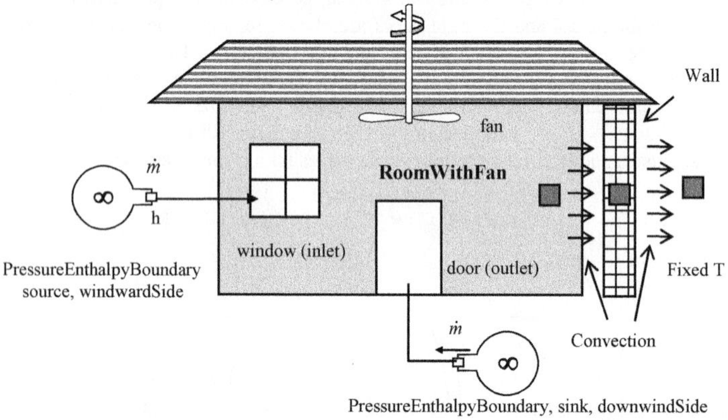

Figure 15-26. House with fan, air flow input through window, and air outflow through door. The room air is also in thermal contact with the wall, which in turn is in contact with the environment. The pressure at the window and the door can be different depending on the wind direction.

The Modelica code for the modified control volume, the `RoomWithFan` model, appears below. New parameters are introduced to compute the room volume and switch on and off the heating loads, e.g. a computer, and the fan. The model is also prepared for thermal interaction with its environment using a connector from the `Modelica.Thermal` library. This connector is for purely thermal interaction between components without a convective mass flow and is defined as:

```
connector HeatPort "Thermal port for 1-dim. heat transfer"
  import Modelica.SIunits;
  SIunits.Temperature        T        "Port temperature";
  flow SIunits.HeatFlowRate  Q_flow   "Heat flow rate (positive if flowing"+
                                      "from outside into the component)";
end HeatPort;
```

Using this connector, we can model interaction between the room air, the room wall, and the environment. Because the time constants of temperature changes in buildings are very slow, we introduce a new time variable to observe time in hours. With this model we could investigate how many hours it takes to cool down the room to almost environment temperature. We also introduce variables for the time when we switch on heat loads or the fan. The connectors in the original model are now reused for the air leakage through the window and the door.

```
model RoomWithFan "Simple room model, built on top of BasicVolume"
  import SI=Modelica.SIunits;
  extends BasicVolume(P(stateSelect=StateSelect.prefer, start=1.0e5),
                      T(stateSelect=StateSelect.prefer, start=T_0));
  HeatPort            heatPort            "heat interaction with environment";
  parameter SI.Power  maxHeatLoad = 400.0 "max power value of heat sources";
  parameter SI.Power  fanPower = 200      "power of fan in Watts";
```

```
  parameter Real         etaFan    = 0.75    "fan efficiency";
  parameter SI.Length length    = 5.0     "room length";
  parameter SI.Length width     = 4.0     "room width";
  parameter SI.Length height    = 2.5     "room height";
  parameter SI.Time    fanOn     = 3600.0 "time when fan is switched on";
  parameter SI.Time    heatOn    = 7200.0 "time heat source is turned on";
  Boolean                heatPowerOn  "on/off flag for heat load";
  Boolean                fanPowerOn   "on/off flag for fan";
  SI.Conversions.NonSIunits.Time_hour  time_hour "time measured in hours";
equation
  heatPort.T = T;
  time_hour  = SI.Conversions.to_hour(time) ;
  V = length*width*height;
  heatPowerOn = if time > heatOn then true else false;
  fanPowerOn  = if time > fanOn then true else false;
  Q_flow = (if heatPowerOn then maxHeatLoad else 0.0) +
        (if fanPowerOn then (1-etaFan)*fanPower else 0.0) + heatPort.Q_flow;
  W_flow_s = if fanPowerOn then -etaFan*fanPower else 0.0;
end RoomWithFan;
```

Now we have a modified control volume, but we are lacking models for the heat capacity of the wall, and the convective heat transfer from the room air to the wall and from the wall to the environment. All the models we need in this case are already available in the `Modelica.Thermal` library. It is always useful to have an idea about the magnitudes of the model parameters that determine the dynamic model behavior. In the case of our room model for example, it is helpful to know where most of the heat is stored. An approximate computation reveals the heat capacity for the air in the room is:

$$C = V\rho c_v \approx 50 \times 1.2 \times 717 = 43020 \frac{J}{K} \tag{15-23}$$

Assuming that the room wall consists of brick stone and the floor is concrete, both with heat capacities of $c \approx 2000$, and we estimate the total weight of the brick wall and floor that are thermally connected to the room at approx. 1000 kg, we realize the heat capacity of the air is only around 2% of the total heat capacity. This clearly indicates that we can not hope to capture the thermal behavior of the room without adding a simple model of the wall heat capacity. The model in the the `Modelica.Thermal` library is a simple, lumped model of a heat capacity:

$$C\frac{dT}{dt} = \sum \dot{Q} \tag{15-24}$$

where the summation of the heat flows is accomplished automatically via the flow semantics, see equation (14-52), page 757, and the sum-to-zero flow summation rule for flows described in Section 5.3.1, page 190. In this case the heat capacity C is a property of a solid body and computed as.

$$C = m \cdot c \tag{15-25}$$

with the mass m and the specific heat capacity c. Another simple thermal model that we need is for the convective heat transfer. It establishes a linear relation between the temperature gradient between a solid body and a fluid, and the heat flow Q_{dot}:

$$Q_{dot} = G_c \cdot T_{solid} - T_{fluid} \tag{15-26}$$

The thermal conductance G_c is determined via an external signal and can be set to a constant or derived form a detailed heat transfer model.

The main remaining task is to compose the system model from our new room model and to determine the coefficients in the components correctly. This is not an easy task for real buildings, because it is often difficult to get reliable values for the mass and specific heat capacity of the materials in the wall. Heat transfer coefficients are also difficult to determine. The external heat transfer coefficient vary substantially depending on the wind conditions. We are going to use estimates which are roughly at the right order of magnitude—values also vary a great deal in reality.

```
model RoomInEnvironment "Room in environment, pressure-driven air flows"
  import Modelica.Thermal.HeatTransfer;
  RoomWithFan                           room(P(start=1.022e5));
  ValveFlow                             window(A=1e-3, beta=0.5);
  ValveFlow                             door(A=1e-3, beta=0.5);
  PressureEnthalpyBoundary              downwindSide(P_0=0.995e5);
  PressureEnthalpyBoundary              windwardSide(P_0=1.05e5, h_0=3.102e5);
  HeatTransfer.Components.Convection       room_wall;
  HeatTransfer.Components.HeatCapacitor wall(T(start=290.0), C=2.5e3*800.0);
  HeatTransfer.Components.Convection       wall_env;
  HeatTransfer.Sources.FixedTemperature T_env(T=310);
  Modelica.Blocks.Sources.Constant         k_inner(k=30);
  Modelica.Blocks.Sources.Constant         k_outer(k=300);
equation
  connect(window.outlet,         downwindSide.port);
  connect(window.inlet,          room.outlet);
  connect(door.outlet,           room.inlet);
  connect(windwardSide.port,     door.inlet);
  connect(room_wall.solid,       room.heatPort);
  connect(room_wall.fluid,       wall.port);
  connect(wall_env.solid,        wall.port);
  connect(k_outer.y,             wall_env.Gc);
  connect(k_inner.y,             room_wall.Gc);
  connect(wall_env.fluid,        T_env.port);
  annotation(experiment(stopTime=14));
end RoomInEnvironment;
```

We can now perform a number of simulation experiments with this model and look at the system variables. In order to get a realistic feeling for the speed of the processes, we chose hours as the units of time for plotting. With the given initial conditions, we can first expect the room temperature to approach the environment temperature of 310 K. Even after five hours, the equilibrium temperature is not yet reached. We can also see that the fan with 200 W of power causes about half of the temperature rise in the room as the heating load of 400 W. The dissipated mechanical power and the direct addition of heat have the same result on the system temperature.

```
simulate(RoomInEnvironment,stopTime=14);
plot(room.T, xrange={0,14});
plot(room.P, xrange={9,12});
```

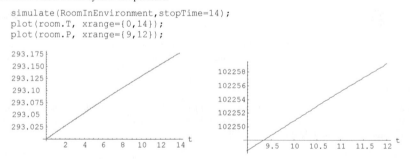

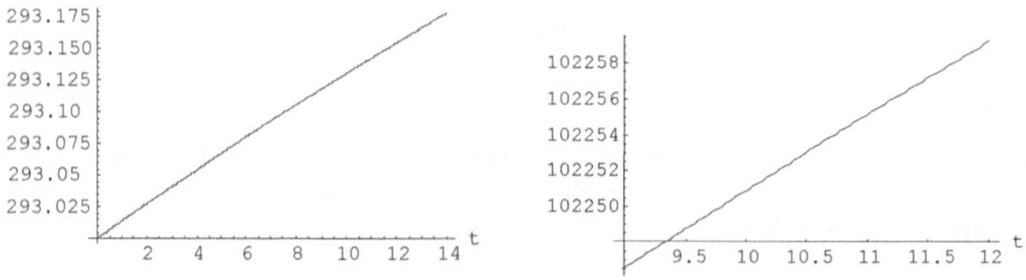

Figure 15-27. Simulation of a room in a house with fan, air flow input through window, air outflow through door, and convection through wall. Plot of temperature (left) and pressure (right)

Another observation from the pressure plot is that the pressure disturbances are very small. The temperature gradients cause the pressure to rise for a short time, but then the pressure flows of to the environment and the pressure always returns to the equilibrium pressure of ≈ 1.02208 bar.

To get more of a feeling for this system, the reader is encouraged to plot additional variables and experiment a bit with the model.

15.3 Chemical Reactions

We have previously presented simple thermodynamic systems (Section 14.7 and Section 15.2), governed by mass balance and energy balance equations. In such systems the amount of matter in each species is preserved even though phase transitions may occur.

However, when dealing with *chemical reactions*, molecules of one species of matter may react with the molecules of a second species, thus forming a third species, that is, a different substance. This has a number of implications for the behavior of systems including chemical reactions.

Traditionally, the literature of chemical reaction dynamics has been divided into two main areas (not mentioning the large number of different application areas in chemistry):

- Chemical reaction kinetics
- Chemical thermodynamics

Chemical reaction kinetics traditionally deals with substance concentrations and their time derivatives. It typically ignores energy conservation, even though internal microscopic energy, that is, chemical potential usually has a large influence on the probability of a reaction to occur.

On the other hand, the literature on chemical thermodynamics concentrates on the energy balance in chemical reactions, but usually covers only equilibrium thermodynamics and ignores dynamic behavior.

In this short example of modeling chemical reactions using Modelica, we will focus on the chemical reaction kinetics and ignore energy conservation. However, in large realistic models, especially when chemical reactions interact with other modeled phenomena, it is usually necessary to include energyrelated terms.

15.3.1 Chemical Reaction Kinetics of Hydrogen Iodine

The dynamics of a chemical reaction are a roughly governed by three factors:

- Mass balance
- Reactant concentration
- Energy conservation

As stated in the previous section, in the following we will just deal with chemical reaction kinetics and ignore energy conservation. First we will focus on conservation of mass, and later on the effects of concentrations.

A chemical reaction represented by a reaction formula transforms the chemical species on the left-hand side of the arrow, called *reactants*, to the species on the right-hand side of the arrow, called *products*:

$$\text{reactants} \rightarrow \text{products} \tag{15-27}$$

Consider a chemical reaction between hydrogen gas and iodine gas to form hydrogen iodine:

$$\mathrm{H_2 + I_2 \leftrightarrow 2HI} \tag{15-28}$$

The double-sided arrow indicates the presence of reactions in both directions, which can be written as two separate reaction formulas:

$$\begin{aligned} &\mathrm{H_2 + I_2 \rightarrow 2HI} \\ &\quad \mathrm{2HI \rightarrow H_2 + I_2} \end{aligned} \tag{15-29}$$

The first reaction states that one molecule of hydrogen together with one molecule of iodine can react. In this reaction the atoms may regroup to form two molecules of hydrogen iodine. The second reaction is the reverse: two molecules of hydrogen iodine are transformed to one molecule of hydrogen and one molecule of iodine.

In both reactions the mass balance is preserved. The number of atoms of each type on both sides of the arrow is the same. An integer number of molecules is involved in the reaction since no fractional molecules exist.

The second issue concerns how frequently a reaction occurs on the microscopic level. In order for a reaction to take place, all involved molecules must be at the same place at the same time. The probability of a molecule of a certain species being in a small volume of space is proportional to the concentration of the species. Thus, assuming statistical independence, the probability of all involved molecules being in the same small volume at the same time is proportional to the product of their concentrations.

Thus, for the reaction between hydrogen gas and iodine gas, the reaction rate is as follows:

$$k_1 \cdot [H_2] \cdot [I_2] \tag{15-30}$$

where the notation $[H_2]$ and $[I_2]$denotes the respective concentrations of hydrogen and iodine molecules, and k_1 is the reaction rate proportionality constant. Analogously, the reaction rate for the reverse reaction of two molecules of HI is given by (15-31) below:

$$k_2 \cdot [HI]^2 \tag{15-31}$$

The reaction rate proportionality constant is often written above the arrow of the reaction it represents, as in (15-32) and (15-33):

$$H_2 + I_2 \xrightarrow{k_1} 2HI \tag{15-32}$$

$$2HI \xrightarrow{k_2} H_2 + I_2 \tag{15-33}$$

Putting the reaction rate expressions in (15-30) and (15-31) together, we can formulate the differential equations for the whole reaction system:

$$\begin{aligned}
\frac{d}{dt}[H_2] &= k_2 \cdot [HI]^2 - k_1 \cdot [H_2] \cdot [I_2] \\
\frac{d}{dt}[I_2] &= k_2 \cdot [HI]^2 - k_1 \cdot [H_2] \cdot [I_2] \\
\frac{d}{dt}[HI] &= 2k_1 \cdot [H_2] \cdot [I_2] - 2k_2 \cdot [HI]^2
\end{aligned} \tag{15-34}$$

Note that the reaction rates are influenced only by the concentrations of reactants in each reaction, not by the products.

Concerning the first equation, the production rate of H_2 from HI is given by $k_2 \cdot [HI]^2$ according to (15-31), whereas the consumption rate of H_2 to HI in the reverse reaction is $k_1 \cdot [H_2] \cdot [I_2]$ according to (15-30). The second equation is almost identical, based on the same reasoning.

The third equation gives the rate of forming HI from H_2 and I_2. The term $2k_1 \cdot [H_2] \cdot [I_2]$ includes a factor of two since a pair of molecules H_2 and I_2 gives rise to two molecules of HI. Analogous reasoning applies to the second term.

We finally put the three reaction rate equations from (15-34) into a Modelica class to prepare for simulation (Figure 15-28).

```
type Concentration = Real(final quantity = "Concentration",
                          final unit = "mol/m3");

class HydrogenIodide
  parameter Real k1 = 0.73;
```

```
  parameter Real k2 = 0.04;
  Concentration  H2(start=5);
  Concentration  I2(start=8);
  Concentration  HI(start=0);
equation
  der(H2) = k2*HI^2 - k1*H2*I2;
  der(I2) = k2*HI^2 - k1*H2*I2;
  der(HI) = 2*k1*H2*I2 - 2*k2*HI^2;
end HydrogenIodide;
```

We simulate for 100 seconds and plot the results.

```
simulate(HydrogenIodide, stopTime=100)
plot({H2, I2, HI}, xrange={0,5})
```

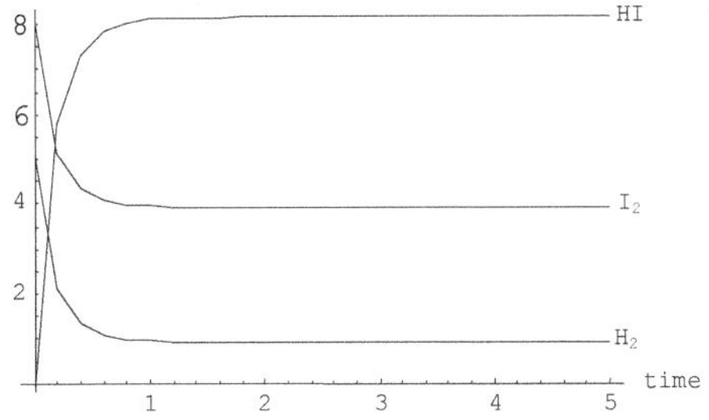

Figure 15-28. Concentrations of hydrogen, iodine, and hydrogen iodine based on the chemical reaction between the involved reactants.

It is easy to observe that after an initial transition phase, a steady-state condition is reached when the concentrations are constant. In steady-state all derivatives are zero. We substitute zero for the derivative in the first equation of (15-34), obtaining:

$$0 = k_2 \cdot [\mathrm{HI}]^2 - k_1 \cdot [\mathrm{H}_2] \cdot [\mathrm{I}_2] \tag{15-35}$$

After a slight rearrangement:

$$\frac{[\mathrm{HI}]^2}{[\mathrm{H}_2] \cdot [\mathrm{I}_2]} = \frac{k_1}{k_2} = \text{constant} \tag{15-36}$$

Thus, the relation between the concentrations in steady state is constant, irrespective of the initial concentrations.

15.4 Biological and Ecological Systems

In this section we will present a few examples of models of biological and ecological systems. As we previously stated in the section on deductive versus inductive modeling (Section 12.1.1, page 568), biological systems are usually quite complex. Normally little exact knowledge is available about such systems, which would be needed for detailed physical modeling. This forces researchers to use inductive models based on experimental observations rather than physical intuition of system dynamics, which has the disadvantage that the models are difficult to validate for predictions outside the observed range.

A combined approach is possible, where some approximate physical knowledge is combined with adapting model coefficients based on experimental observations. Such an approach will be explored in the subsequent models where we will investigate a continuous-time model for population dynamics and a discrete-time cyclic growth model for the energy forest.

15.4.1 Population Dynamics

In this example we will study the dynamics of populations of animals in an idealized ecological system. We assume that a population contains P individuals. In general, the change rate of the number of animals in a population is the difference between the population growth rate or birth rate and its death rate:

$$\dot{P} = growthrate - deathrate \tag{15-37}$$

where $\dot{P}$ is the rate of change of the number of individuals in the population. It is natural to assume that the growth rate and the death rate are proportional to the size of the current population:

$$\begin{aligned} growthrate &= g \cdot P \\ deathrate &= d \cdot P \end{aligned} \tag{15-38}$$

where g is the growth factor and d the death factor for the population. These factors can be assumed to be constant if the same amount of food per individual is available independent of the size of the population, and no sudden lethal illnesses affect the population. These assumptions are of course valid only for a reasonable size of the population, since the food supply is never infinite in a closed system and illnesses sometimes occur. Putting (15-37) and (15-38) together gives:

$$\dot{P} = (g - d) \cdot P \tag{15-39}$$

Solutions to this equation give an exponentially increasing population if $(g - d) > 0$ or exponentially decreasing if $(g - d) < 0$. We represent this equation in the model class `PopulationGrowth` below:

```
class PopulationGrowth
  parameter Real g = 0.04      "Growth factor of population";
  parameter Real d = 0.0005    "Death factor of population";
  Real            P(start=10)  "Population size, initially 10";
equation
  der(P) = (g-d)*P;
end PopulationGrowth;
```

The model is simulated and the population size P plotted:

```
simulate(PopulationGrowth, stopTime=100)
plot(P)
```

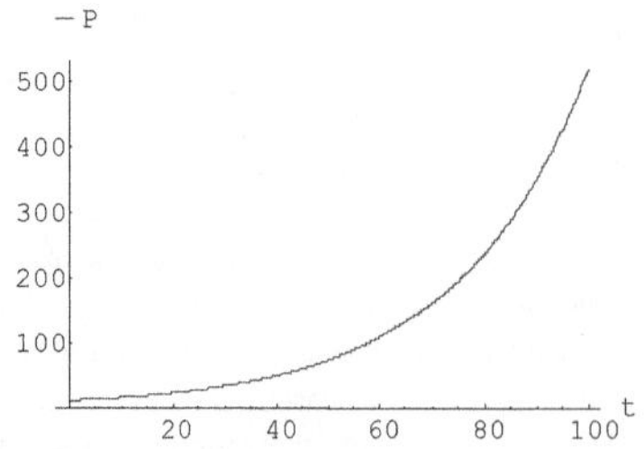

Figure 15-29. Exponential growth of a population with unlimited food supply.

As expected, Figure 15-29 shows an exponentially increasing population. We should, however, remember that exponential growth can never persist indefinitely in a closed system with a limited food supply.

15.4.1.1 A Predator-Prey Model with Foxes and Rabbits

Now we would like to study a more interesting system consisting of two interacting populations of predators and prey animals. The simplest model of this kind is the so-called Lotka-Volterra model. In this case, the predators are foxes and the prey animals are rabbits. The rabbit population of size R is assumed to have an unlimited food supply. Therefore equation (15-39) applies regarding the birth-related growth rate of the rabbit population, giving a positive growth term $g_r \cdot R$, where g_r is the growth factor for rabbits.

On the other hand, the fox population of size F feeds on the rabbits. The rate of rabbit deaths can be assumed to be proportional to the number of foxes due to increased hunting pressure, and to the number of rabbits due to the higher probability of success in hunting, giving a rabbit death rate due to foxes of $d_{rf} \cdot F \cdot R$, where d_{rf} is the death factor of rabbits due to foxes. Putting the growth and death rates together gives the total rabbit population change rate $\dot{R}$ as defined by equation (15-40) below:

$$\dot{R} = g_r \cdot R - d_{rf} \cdot F \cdot R \tag{15-40}$$

The growth of the fox population of size F is proportional to the rate of rabbits consumed, that is, those that die because they were hunted by foxes—which is the death rate term $d_{rf} \cdot F \cdot R$ mentioned in the previous equation. The efficiency of growing foxes from rabbits is determined by the growth factor g_{fr}, giving a fox population growth rate term $g_{fr} \cdot d_{rf} \cdot R \cdot F$. The fox population also has an intrinsic death rate $d_f \cdot F$ proportional to the size of the fox population by the fox death factor d_f. By combining these two terms we obtain equation (15-41):

$$\dot{F} = g_{fr} \cdot d_{rf} \cdot R \cdot F - d_f \cdot F \tag{15-41}$$

where $\dot{F}$ is the total change rate of the fox population.

We have made a Modelica class below called `LotkaVolterra`, which includes both equations (15-40) and (15-41), together with all variables and constant proportionality factors. The two state variables R and F for the sizes of the rabbit and fox populations respectively are represented by the Modelica variables `rabbits` and `foxes`:

```
class LotkaVolterra
  parameter Real g_r =0.04         "Natural growth rate for rabbits";
  parameter Real d_rf=0.0005       "Death rate of rabbits due to foxes";
  parameter Real d_f =0.09         "Natural deathrate for foxes";
  parameter Real g_fr=0.1          "Efficency in growing foxes from rabbits";
  Real      rabbits(start=700) "Rabbits,(R) with start population 700";
  Real      foxes(start=10)    "Foxes,(F) with start population 10";
equation
  der(rabbits) = g_r*rabbits - d_rf*rabbits*foxes;
  der(foxes)   = g_fr*d_rf*rabbits*foxes - d_f*foxes;
end LotkaVolterra;
```

The model is simulated and the sizes of the rabbit and fox populations as a function of time are plotted in Figure 15-30:

```
simulate(LotkaVolterra, stopTime=3000);
plot({rabbits, foxes}, xrange={0,1000});
```

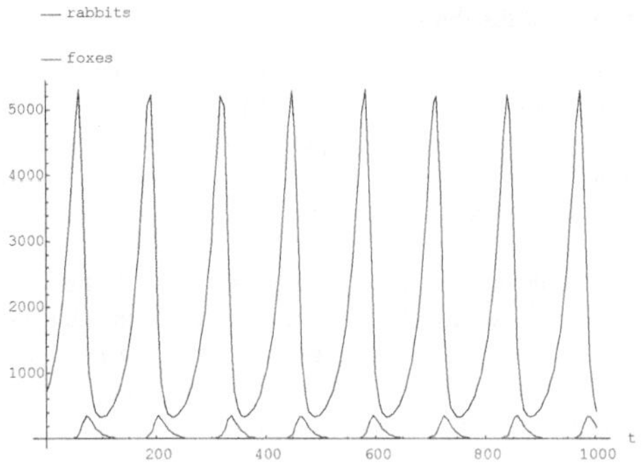

Figure 15-30. Number rabbits—prey animals, and foxes—predators, as a function of time simulated from the `PredatorPrey` model.

The Lotka-Volterra model has a rather special property: the solution variables, that is, the rabbit and fox population sizes, do not approach steady-state values as time goes by. Instead, they approach periodic steady-state values—the solution oscillates. The shape of the oscillation is very characteristic for Lotka-Volterra models and corresponds rather well to several experimental population studies of predators and prey animals. However, this does not prove our partly inductive model equations to be correct, only that they seem to have certain approximate physical significance.

15.4.2 Population Dynamics in World Models with Human–Nature Interaction

Population dynamics modeling can also be applied to the human race living on and interacting with the earth, our world. Such models are often called world models.

Perhaps the most influential modern studies indicating that human population could reach limits are those presented by Richard Malthus in 1798 with his famous work, *An Essay on the Principle of Population*. A catastrophe in the form of population collapse was considered as a feasible consequence of uncontrolled growth, which would hit the limits of food production causing massive famine.

A series of simulation models were developed mainly during the 1970's, with some later updates, aiming at understanding the complexity of the interactions between global societies with their physical environment, searching for the conditions that would lend to a collapse and the possible measures to avoid it. They formed a category of so-called world models (Section 15.4.2.7, page 846). One characteristic was their generality and complexity, spanning several subsystems (demographic, energy, economy, industry, agriculture, minerals, etc.) with varied levels of detail.

15.4.2.1 A Simplified Human–Nature Dynamics Model with Rich and Poor

Simplified approaches to World models can describe an interesting set of behaviors while keeping model complexity at a minimum. One such very simplified model is the `Handy` model, an acronym for Human And Nature Dynamical model.

This model has many similarities to the above `LotkaVolterra` model (Section 15.4.1.1, page 833), but has four differential equations with four state variables: poor population (`commoners`), rich population (`elite`), the earth ecological resource (`nature`), and accumulated wealth (`wealth`), instead of just two (`foxes` and `rabbits`) as in the `LotkaVolterra` model. Human beings play the role of the predators (the foxes) and nature is the preyed resource. An interesting feature of this model is that it introduces the accumulation of economic wealth and divides the human population into rich and poor. Inequality between rich and poor is not only explicitly considered but also plays a key role in the sustainability analyses of this model. Such capability is seldom found in most well-known world models.

However, note that this model is a very strong simplification of the human-nature system, which gives many limitations. Thus the `Handy` model is useful only as a general framework that allows carrying out thought experiments for the phenomenon of collapse and to test changes that would avoid it. Despite its limitations such a simplified model is quite useful since it is easy to understand and gives a more intuitive grasp of the issues and phenomena involved.

A much more advanced and realistic world model called `World3` is briefly introduced in Section 15.4.2.7, page 846. This model (the compiled version) has 41 state variables and 245 algebraic variables, and captures many aspects of humanity and ecology in our world. It has been calibrated against measured data.

15.4.2.2 Handy Model Equations, Description, and Modeled Societies

In the `Handy` model, the total population is divided between two groups: commoners and elite, of population sizes `commoners` and `elite` respectively. The population grows through birth rates `birthRComm` and `birthRElite`, which are constants. The population shrinks through death rates `deathRComm` and `deathRElite` which are in turn defined as functions of `wealth`.

The main state variables of the model are described in Table 15-1, additional variables in The parameters of the model are described in Table 15-3.

Table 15-2, and the parameters of the model in Table 15-3.

Natural renewable and nonrenewable resources are aggregated into a single type of stock represented by the variable `nature`.

The main dynamics part of the model is defined by the following four differential equations:

$$\begin{aligned}
commoners' &= birthRComm \cdot commoners - deathRComm \cdot commoners \\
elite' &= birthRElite \cdot elite - deathRElite \cdot elite \\
nature' &= natureRegen \cdot nature \cdot (natureCap - nature) - depletFactor \cdot nature \\
wealth' &= depletFactor \cdot commoners \cdot nature - consRComm - consRElite
\end{aligned} \qquad (15\text{-}42)$$

which in Modelica are expressed as:

```
der(commoners) = birthRComm*commoners - deathRComm*commoners;
der(elite) = birthRElite*elite - deathRElite*elite;
der(nature) = natureRegen*nature*(natureCap-nature) - depletFactor*nature;
der(wealth) = depletFactor*commoners*nature - consRComm - consRElite;
```

The equation for `nature` includes a regeneration term `natureRegen*nature*(natureCap-nature)` and a depletion term `depletFactor*commoners*nature` for its reduction caused by pollution.

The regeneration term is synthetic (i.e., not directly physical) with an s-shaped form, and designed to give a physically realistic result. It has a regeneration factor `natureRegen`, exponential regrowth for low values of `nature`, because then `(natureCap-nature)` is almost constant and saturation when `nature` approaches `natureCap` (maximum size of `nature` in absence of depletion, i.e., pollution), since then `(natureCap-nature)` goes towards zero. Due to the synthetic form the maximum rate of regeneration takes place when `nature=natureCap/2`. The depletion of `nature` is considered to include the reduction of `nature` due to pollution.

The depletion term includes a rate of depletion (pollution) per worker `depletFactor` making it proportional to both `nature` and the number of commoners represented by the variable `commoners`. The economic activity of elite is modeled to represent supervisory functions with no direct influence on the extraction of resources or the production of wealth. The underlying concept is that "only commoners produce". The model is assumed to be insensitive to technological change, considering that technology through history has proven to produce both increments and decrements in resource use efficiency. Thus a simplification can consider that these effects cancel each other out.

Accumulated wealth (`wealth`) increases with production (`depletFactor*commoners*nature`) and decreases according the consumption rates of the elite and the commoners, `consRComm` and `consRElite` respectively.

Table 15-1. Main state variables of the Handy model.

Name	*Description*	*Unit*	*Typical start value(s)*
`commoners`	Commoner population size	Number of people	100
`elite`	Elite population size	Number of people	0, 1, 25
`nature`	Nature's stock, renewable and non-renewable	EcoDollars	`natureCap` = 100
`wealth`	Accumulated wealth	EcoDollars	0

The additional variables of the model are described in The parameters of the model are described in Table 15-3.

Table 15-2. Two of these variables describe consumption. The consumption of the commoners, `consRComm`, is the result of a subsistence salary per capita `subsSal` times the working population. An elite person gets a salary `ineqFactor` times larger than a commoners, which serves the purpose of measuring the inequality among classes, and is considered to be constant throughout time for any given scenario. This is reflected in the following equations:

$$\begin{aligned} consRComm &= \min(1, wealth / wealthMin) \cdot subsSal \cdot commoners \\ consRElite &= \min(1, wealth / wealthMin) \cdot subsSal \cdot elite \cdot ineqFactor \end{aligned} \tag{15-43}$$

which in Modelica are expressed as

```
consRComm  = min(1, wealth/wealthMin) * subsSal*commoners;
consRElite = min(1, wealth/wealthMin) * subsSal*elite*ineqFactor;
```

Both consumption rates `consRComm` and `consRElite` are subject to a minimum threshold for "accumulated wealth before famine", `wealthMin`. The consumption rates are linearly reduced down to zero by the `min()` terms in the above equations, when `wealth` falls below `wealthMin`.

The death rates of the commoners and the elite are defined by the following equations:

$$\begin{aligned} deathRComm &= deathRnormal + \max(0, 1 - consRComm / (subsSal \cdot commoners)) \cdot \\ &\quad (deathRfamine - deathRnormal) \\ deathRElite &= deathRnormal + \max(0, 1 - consRElite / (subsSal \cdot elite)) \cdot \\ &\quad (deathRfamine - deathRnormal) \end{aligned} \tag{15-44}$$

The carrying capacity (`carryingCap`) of nature and its corresponding maximum carrying capacity (`carryingCapMax`) attainable under certain conditions, are defined by these equations:

$$\begin{aligned} carryingCap &= natureRegen / depleteFactor \cdot (natureCap - subsSal \cdot eta / depletFactor) \\ carryingCapMax &= natureRegen / (eta \cdot subsSal) \cdot (natureCap / 2)^2 \end{aligned} \tag{15-45}$$

The minimum wealth (`wealthMin`), the total population, and a dimensionless quotient `eta` used above are defined as follows:

$$\begin{aligned} wealthMin &= consWorkerMin \cdot commoners + ineqFactor \cdot consWorkerMin \cdot elite \\ eta &= (deathRfamine - birthRComm) / (deathRfamine - deathRnormal) \\ totalPopulation &= elite + commoners \end{aligned} \tag{15-46}$$

The parameters of the model are described in Table 15-3.

Table 15-2. Additional variables of the `Handy` model for human and nature dynamics.

Name	*Description*	*Unit*
`deathRComm`	Commoners death rate	Number of people/year
`deathRElite`	Death rate for elite	Number of people/year
`consRComm`	Consumption rate of a commoner	EcoDollars/year
`consRElite`	Consumption rate of an elite person	EcoDollars/year
`eta`	Dimensionless derived quotient	
`carryingCap`	Carrying capacity of the world	Number of people
`carryingCapMax`	Maximum carrying capacity	Number of people
`totalPopulation`	The total population	Number of people

Table 15-3. Parameters of the `Handy` model for human and nature dynamics.

Name	*Description*	*Typical value(s)*
`deathRnormal`	Healthy normal (minimum) death rate	0.01
`deathRfamine`	Famine (maximum) death rate	0.07
`birthRComm`	Commoner birth rate	0.03, or 0.065
`birthRElite`	Elite birth rate	0.03, or 0.02
`subsSal`	Subsistence salary per person	0.0005
`consWorkerMin`	Minimum required consumption per worker	0.005
`natureRegen`	Nature's regeneration rate	0.01
`natureCap`	Nature's carrying capacity	100
`ineqFactor`	Inequality factor between elite and commoners	1, 10, or 100
`depletFactor`	Depletion (production) factor	0.00000667, or 0.00000635, or 0.000013

There are three dimensions for quantities in the model: `Population` (either commoner or elite), in units of people, `Nature/Wealth`, in units of `EcoDollars`, and `Time`, in units of years. All other parameters and functions in the model carry units that are compatible with these dimensions.

All of the above definitions appear in the `HandyBase` Modelica model below which is a partial model that is inherited by the following actual simulated models.

```
partial model HandyBase "Equations, variables, and parameters for Handy"
  // All parameters, default values for egalitarian society
  parameter Real birthRComm = 0.03 "Birth Rate of Commoners No people/year";
  parameter Real birthRElite = 0.03 "Birth Rate of Elite. No of people/yr";
  parameter Real natureRegen = 0.01 "Nature's regeneration factor. Unit
    1/ecoDollars*year";
  parameter Real natureCap = 100.0 "Nature's capacity. ecoDollars";
  parameter Real subsSal=0.0005 "Subsistence Salary/Worker. Dollars/worker";
  parameter Real consWorkerMin = 0.005 "Minimum required Consumption per
    Worker. Dollars/worker";
  parameter Real depletFactorEq = 0.00000667
   "Rate of depletion (pollution) per worker at Equilibrium. 1/Worker*year";
  parameter Real deathRnormal = 0.01 "Healthy Death Rate. people/year";
  parameter Real deathRfamine = 0.07 "Famine Death Rate. people/year";
  parameter Real ineqFactor = 0 "Inequality in consumption level for Workers
```

```
      and Non-Workers. Does not play a role when elite=0 (as in all Egal
      scenarios). Dimensionless";
    Real depletFactor "Rate of depletion per worker. 1/Worker*year";
    Real commoners "Population of Commoners. Number of people";
    Real elite "Population size of Elite. Number of people";
    Real nature "Natural stock (renewable and nonrenewable). ecoDollars";
    Real wealth "Accumulated wealth. EcoDollars";
    Real wealthMin "Minimum threshold accum wealth before famine. EcoDollars";
    Real deathRComm "Death Rate for Commmoners. Number of people/year";
    Real deathRElite "Death Rate for Elite. Number of people/year";
    Real consRComm "Consumption Rate of Commoners. Dollars/year";
    Real consRElite "Consumption Rate of Elite. Dollars/year";
    Real eta "Derived quotient expression. Dimensionless";
    Real carryingCap "Carrying Capacity. Number of people";
    Real carryingCapMax "Maximum Carrying Capacity. Number of people";
    Real totalPopulation "Total population: elite and commoners. No people";

    // Scaled helper variables for graph drawing purposes
    Real nature_, wealth_, carryingCap_, carryingCapMax_,commoners_,
         elite_,totalPopulation_;

  equation
    der(commoners) = birthRComm*commoners - deathRComm*commoners;
    der(elite) = birthRElite*elite - deathRElite*elite;
    der(nature) = natureRegen*nature * (natureCap-nature) -
      depletFactor*commoners*nature;
    der(wealth) = depletFactor*commoners*nature - consRComm - consRElite;

    deathRComm = deathRnormal + max(0, 1-consRComm / (subsSal*commoners)) *
      (deathRfamine-deathRnormal);
    deathRElite = deathRnormal + max(0, 1-consRElite / (subsSal*elite)) *
      (deathRfamine-deathRnormal);

    consRComm = min(1, wealth/wealthMin) * subsSal*commoners;
    consRElite = min(1, wealth/wealthMin) *ineqFactor*subsSal*elite;
    wealthMin = consWorkerMin*commoners + ineqFactor*consWorkerMin*elite;

    eta = (deathRfamine - birthRComm) / (deathRfamine-deathRnormal);
    carryingCap = natureRegen / depletFactor * (natureCap - subsSal* eta /
      depletFactor);
    carryingCapMax = natureRegen / (eta*subsSal) * (natureCap/2)^2;
    totalPopulation = elite + commoners;

  initial equation
    nature = natureCap;
    wealth = 0;

  end HandyBase;
```

15.4.2.3 Types of Societies, Simulation Methodology, and Scenarios

The `Handy` model can be used to define three types of societies:

- *Egalitarian society*—no elite, that is, the elite population `elite = 0`. Scenario models `HandyEgal1` to `ModelEgal4`.
- *Equitable society*—commoners and elite, both groups earn the same per person, that is, `ineqFactor=1`. Scenario models `HandyEquit1` to `HandyEquit5`.
- *Unequal society*—commoners and elite, an elite person earns more than a commoner; `ineqFactor>=1`. Scenario models `HandyUnEq1` to `HandyUnEq4`.

Several scenarios will be studied for each kind of society. The default initial values for parameters and initial start values for state variables used in these scenarios are those presented in Table 15-1 and Table 15-3.

The thought experiments are performed as simulations and presented in Section 15.4.2.4, Section and Section 15.4.2.6. Within each type of society, different scenarios are studied by varying the rate of depletion per worker called `depletFactor` (short for depletion factor), caused by pollution.

For each type of society simulations should be done until equilibrium is reached, whenever equilibrium can be reached. This means a system state in which all derivatives reach zero value and consequently all the system's variables settle into a stable steady state.

Under that condition, the carrying capacity can be maximized if nature's regeneration rate is maximal. According to the equation for `nature`, the latter is satisfied when `nature=carryingCap/2`.

This requires the depletion factor `depletFactor` to be at the equilibrium (or optimum) value `depletFactorEq`. Under such a situation a steady state with a maximum sustainable population should be achieved.

The scenarios below explore the consequences of different types of societies as they behave optimally or suboptimally, which is measured in terms of the natural depletion factors.

15.4.2.4 Simulation Scenarios of an Egalitarian Society

For this type of society, the optimal value for the depletion factor that maximizes the carrying capacity (`carryingCap`) is `depletFactorEq`=6.67E-6, which has been derived analytically (Motesharrei, Rivas, and Kalnay 2013). Below is the `HandyEgalitarianBase` model which is inherited by all `Egal` models.

```
partial model HandyEgalitarianBase
  "Egal - Scenarios with Egalitarian Society (No-Elite)"
  extends HandyBase;
initial equation
  elite = 0;  // For All "Egal" scenarios: elite=0
  commoners = 100.0;
equation  // Graph scaling
  carryingCapMax_ = carryingCapMax;
  carryingCap_ = carryingCap;
  commoners_ = commoners;
  elite_ = elite;
  totalPopulation_ = totalPopulation;
end HandyEgalitarianBase;
```

Scenario Model HandyEgal1: "Soft landing to Equilibrium"

```
model HandyEgal1 "Scenario Egal1: Soft Landing to Equilibrium"
  extends HandyEqalitarianBase;
equation
  depletFactor = depletFactorEq * 0.8;
  // Graph scaling
  nature_ = nature * 80000 / 100;
  wealth_ = wealth * 80000 / 400;
end HandyEgal1;
```

By making `depletFactor=depletFactorEq` the results in Figure 15-31 below are obtained:

```
simulate(HandyEgal1, stopTime=1000)
plot({commoners_, elites_, nature_, wealth_, carryingCap_, carryingCapMax_})
```

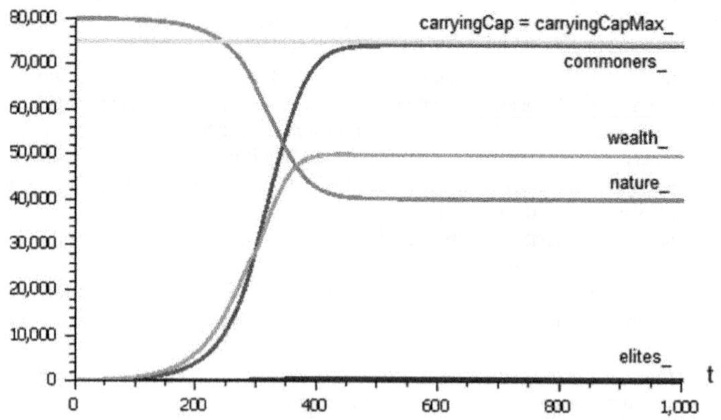

Figure 15-31. Population, nature and wealth. Soft landing to equilibrium, with optimal nature depletion factor (variables rescaled for better visualization). Simulation of `HandyEgal1`.

In this example, the maximum nature regeneration can support a maximum sustainable depletion (pollution) rate and a maximum population number (`commoners`) equal to the carrying capacity (`carryingCap`).

Scenario Model HandyEgal3: "Cycles of Prosperity and Collapse"

In this scenario we increase the depletion intensity by selecting `depletFactor` = 4 * `depletFactorEq`.

```
model HandyEgal3 "Scenario Egal3: Cycles of Prosperity and Collapse"
  extends HandyEgalitarianBase;
equation
  depletFactor = 4 * depletFactorEq;
  // Graph scaling
  nature_ = nature * 100000 / 100;
  wealth_ = wealth * 100000 / 2000;
end HandyEgal3;
```

The results obtained are shown in Figure 15-32 below:

```
simulate(HandyEgal3, stopTime=450)
plot({commoners_, elites_, nature_, wealth_, carryingCap_, carryingCapMax_})
```

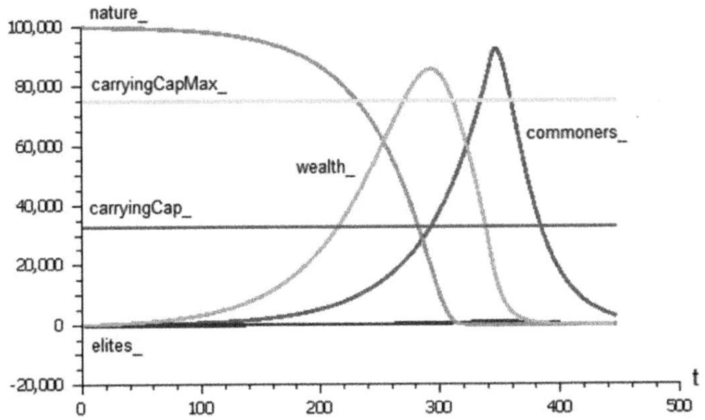

Figure 15-32. Cycles of Prosperity and Collapse. Simulation of HandyEgal3.

The oscillatory mode is can be named as one of "reversible collapses." This scenario can be seen as belonging to a "limit boundary" for the values of the depletion factor. Should depletFactor be increased even further, the system changes into a different mode, one of "irreversible collapse," with only one overshoot-and-collapse cycle. This is obtained in the scenario HandyEgal4.

Additional Scenarios in the Egalitarian Type of Society

There are also scenarios models HandyEgal2 "Oscillatory Approach to Equilibrium" and HandyEgal4 "Full Collapse", which correspond to setting depletFactor = 2.5*depletFactorEq and depletFactor = 5.5*depletFactorEq, respectively. The reader is encouraged to test these models.

15.4.2.5 Simulation Scenarios of an Equitable Society—Elite and Commoners with equal Wealth

In addition to the class of workers called commoners, we now add a new class of population, an elite. The elite has an equitable access to the produced wealth, that is, ineqFactor = 1. Their privilege is that they get access to wealth without being engaged in the production process, that is, without doing work. The initial population for the elite (the group of non-workers) is elite = 25.

As before we look for an equilibrium situation where the depletion factor is set to its optimal value which for this society is depletFactor = depletFactorEq = 8.33E-6. This produces the first scenario HandyEquit1 model shown further below, an adaptation of the HandyEquitableBase model which is inherited by all Equit scenario models.

```
partial model HandyEquitableBase
  "Equit Scenarios: Equitable society (with Workers and Non-Workers)"
  extends HandyBase(ineqFactor = 1, depletFactorEq = 0.00000833);
initial equation
  commoners = 100.0;
equation // Graph scaling
  // Graph scaling
  carryingCap_ = carryingCap;
  carryingCapMax_ = carryingCapMax;
  commoners_ = commoners;
  elites_ = elites;
  totalPopulation_ = totalPopulation;
```

```
end HandyEquitableBase;
```

Scenario HandyEquit1: "Soft Landing to Optimal Equilibrium"

```
model HandyEquit1
  "Equitable society Scenario Equit1: Soft Landing to Optimal Equilibrium"
  extends HandyEquitableBase;
initial equation
  elite = 25;
equation
  depletFactor = depletFactorEq;
  // Graph scaling
  nature_ = nature * 80000 / 100;
  wealth_ = wealth * 80000 / 400;
end HandyEquit1;
```

We simulate and plot:

```
simulate(HandyEquit1, stopTime=1000)
plot({commoners_, elites_, nature_, wealth_, carryingCap_, carryingCapMax_})
```

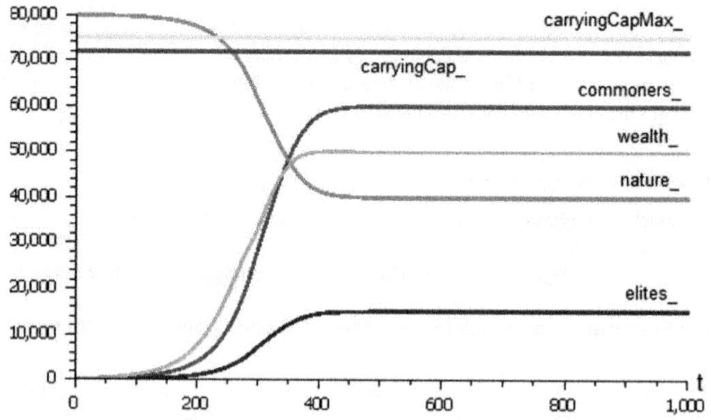

Figure 15-33. Equilibrium in the presence of workers (commoners) and non-workers (an elite) with equal income per person. Simulation of `HandyEquit1`.

In Figure 15-33 it can be seen that the elite and the commoners coexist. Their sum reaches the carrying capacity. The optimal depletion factor in this society is bigger than that of an egalitarian society analyzed in the previous section. This is due to an increased amount of production required from the commoners to sustain the nonworking elite.

Scenario HandyEquit2: "Oscillatory Approach to Equilibrium"

If the depletion factor is further incremented by making `depletFactor` = 2.64 * `depletFactorEq` we obtain an oscillatory behavior. The results are shown in Figure 15-34.

```
model HandyEquit2
  "Equitable society Scenario Equit2: Oscillatory Approach to Equilibrium"
  extends HandyEquitableBase;
initial equation
  elite = 25;
equation
```

```
    depletFactor = 2.64 * depletFactorEq;
    // Graph scaling
    nature_ = nature * 80000 / 100;
    wealth_ = wealth * 80000 / 2000;
  end HandyEquit2;
```

We simulate and plot:

```
simulate(HandyEquit2, stopTime=1000)
plot({commoners_, elites_, nature_, wealth_, carryingCap_, carryingCapMax_})
```

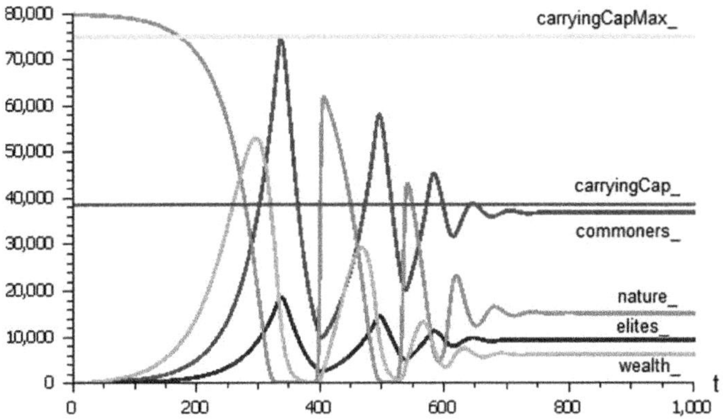

Figure 15-34. Oscillatory convergence to equilibrium with tolerable overshoot. Simulation of `HandyEquit2`.

Now the actual carrying capacity (`carryingCap`) is lower than the maximum carrying capacity, but the total population approaches its value after an oscillatory phase.

Additional Scenarios in an Equitable Type of Society

There are also scenarios `HandyEquit3` "Cycles of Prosperity, Overshoot and Collapse," `HandyEquit4` "Full Collapse," and `HandyEquit5` "Preventing a Full Collapse by Decreasing Average Depletion per Capita."

The reader is encouraged to also try these models, which include experimenting with different values of the depletion factor and for the case of `HandyEquit5` also increasing the ratio of non-workers (`elite`) to workers (`commoners`).

15.4.2.6 Simulation Scenarios of an Unequal Society—Elite and Commoners with Different Income

The unequal society appears to be closer to the status of our current world. The inequality factor `ineqFactor` is made to range from 10 to 100 in the unequal scenarios.

We will reproduce a pair of experiments intended to show the effect of birth control as a means for moving from an unsustainable into a sustainable mode of behavior.

```
partial model HandyUnEquitableBase
    "Uneq Scenarios: Unequal Society (with Elite and Commoners)"
  extends HandyBase(ineqFactor = 100, depletFactorEq = 0.00000667,
    birthRComm = 0.03, birthRElite = 0.03);
```

```
equation
  // Graph scaling
  carryingCap_  = carryingCap;
  carryingCapMax_  = carryingCapMax;
  commoners_  = commoners;
  totalPopulation_  = totalPopulation;
end HandyUnEquitableBase;
```

Scenario HandyUneq2: "Full Collapse"

In this scenario the inequality factor is set very high: `ineqFactor` = 100. Also an initial seed for the population of the elite is set to `elite` = 0.2 and a large depletion factor (including pollution effects) `depletFactor` = `1E-4` are selected. The result is a full collapse with no recovery, as shown in Figure 15-35 below.

```
model HandyUnEq2
  "UnEquitable society Scenario UnEq2: Type-II Collapse (Full Collapse)"
  extends HandyUnEquitableBase(ineqFactor = 100,
    depletFactorEq = 0.00000667, birthRComm = 0.03, birthRElite = 0.03);
initial equation
  elite = 0.2;
  commoners = 100.0;
equation
  depletFactor = 15 * depletFactorEq;
  // Graph scaling
  nature_ = nature * 80000 / 100;
  wealth_ = wealth * 80000 / 4000;
  elites_ = elites * 100;
end HandyUnEq2;
```

```
simulate(HandyUnEq2, stopTime=500)
plot({commoners_, elites_, nature_, wealth_, carryingCap_, carryingCapMax_})
```

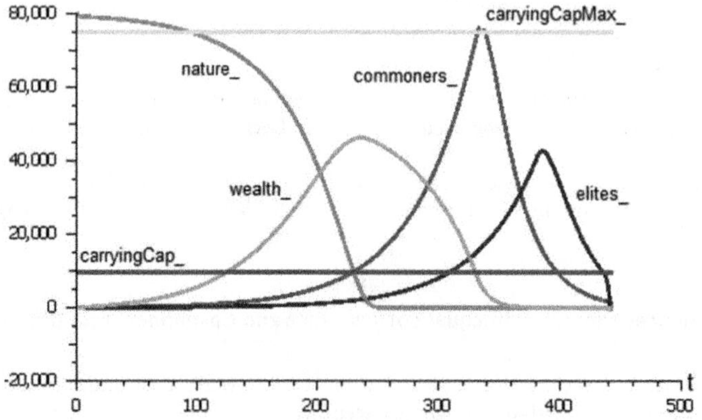

Figure 15-35. Full collapse due to over-depletion and high levels of inequality (`ineqFactor`=100). Simulation of `HandyUnEq2`.

As soon as the commoner's population surpasses the carrying capacity, `wealth` starts to decline and never again recovers. Before disappearing, the elite remains insensitive to the wealth fast decrease during a long period after the commoner's population start their massive die-off. This is possible due to the unequal access to wealth, which is a hundred times larger than that of the commoners.

Scenario HandyUneq3: "Soft Landing to Optimal Equilibrium"

In this scenario several parameters and initial values are changed with respect to the previous case.

- Inequality is reduced a factor ten, yielding `ineqFactor` = 10.
- The depletion factor is set to its equilibrium value, derived analytically: `depletFactor` = `depletFactorEq` = 6.35E-6, much lower than the previous scenario.
- The initial values for the population are set as `commoners`=10 000 and `elite`=3000.
- The birth rates are assumed to be controllable and selected as `birthRComm`=0.065 and `birthRElite`=0.02.

The results are shown below:

```
model HandyUnEq3
    "UnEquitable society UnEquit3: Soft Landing to Optimal Equilibrium"
  extends HandyUnEquitableBase(ineqFactor = 10, depletFactorEq = 0.00000635,
    birthRComm = 0.065, birthRElite = 0.02);
initial equation
  elite = 3000.0;
  commoners = 10000.0;
equation
  depletFactor = depletFactorEq;
  // Graph scaling
  nature_ = nature * 600000 / 100;
  wealth_ = wealth * 600000 / 400;
  elites_ = elites * 10;
  commoners_ = commoners;
end HandyUnEq3;
```

```
simulate(HandyUnEq3, stopTime=500)
plot({commoners_, elites_, nature_, wealth_, carryingCap_, carryingCapMax_})
```

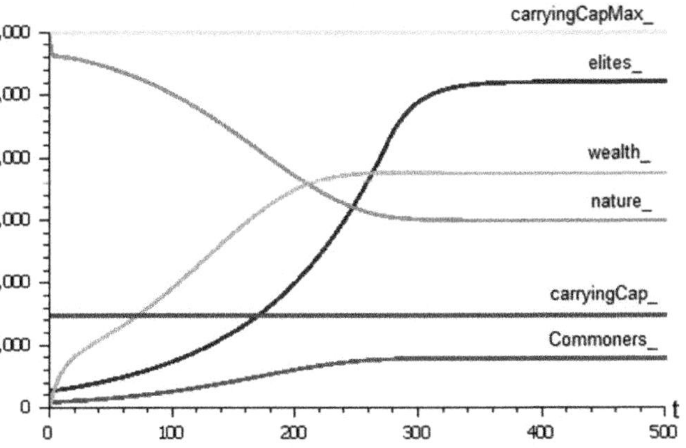

Figure 15-36. Sustainable society reaching equilibrium with moderate inequality (`ineqFactor`=10) and birth rate control. Simulation of `HandyUnEq3`.

The new set of parameters produced a sustainable equilibrium in an unequal society. It represents an example of implementation of policies that simultaneously limit inequality and in parallel enforce birth rates to remain below critical levels. In this model inequality and birth rate are separate but simultaneous measures. In fact, in the real world high birth rates in poor societies are often a consequence of inequality.

Additional Scenarios for an Unequal Type of Society

There are also scenarios `HandyEquit1` "Collapse with Recovery of Nature" and `HandyEquit4` "Oscillatory Approach to Equilibrium," which perform experiments with different values of the depletion factor, birth rates, and values of initial populations.

15.4.2.7 A Short Look at the World3 Model

The `World3` model is a much more complex and realistic world model than the very simple `Handy` model presented in the previous sections. The compiled version contains 41 state variables and 245 algebraic variables, with the same number of equations, representing many facets of human life and world ecological factors.

The model is available as part of the `SystemDynamics.WorldDynamics` library (Section 16.21.1, page 972) or standalone, developed in Modelica by François Cellier and his students. They made a documented Modelica version of the `World3` model by translating the original model from the version in Stella.

The `SystemDynamics.WorldDynamics.World3` model is represented as a Modelica package that implements Meadows et al. World3 model as described in their 1972 book *Limits to Growth: A Report for the Club of Rome's Project on the Predicament of Mankind*. The book has seen two later editions, one published in 1992 (20-year edition), and the most recent one published in 2004 (30-year edition). Each of these new editions was accompanied by an updated model. The model in this Modelica `World3` version is the newest model discussed in the 2004 edition *Limits to Growth: The 30-Year Update*.

Whereas Jay Forrester listed his entire mathematical model in his book *World Dynamics*, Meadows et al. in *Limits to Growth* only discussed about the results obtained using their model. The mathematical model itself was not listed. The main reason was to make the book more accessible to a wider public. Another reason is that the World3 model is considerably more complex than the World2 model, and consequently, a thorough discussion of all aspects of the model would have taken much more space in the book. Instead he published a separate book in 1974: Dynamics of Growth in a Finite World of 637 pages that describes all facets of the model.

Since the World3 model is fairly complex it was subdivided into 13 different sectors (i.e., submodels) describing aspects of the following:

1. arable land dynamics,
2. food production,
3. Mathis Wackernagel's human ecological footprint,
4. human fertility,
5. human welfare index,
6. industrial investment,
7. labor utilization,
8. land fertility,
9. life expectancy,
10. non-recoverable resource utilization,
11. pollution dynamics,
12. population dynamics, and

13. service-sector investment.

For example, one of the submodels, the `World3.Arable_Land_Dynamics` model, is depicted in Figure 16-41. In the main model one submodel of each type is put onto the screen and connected appropriately.

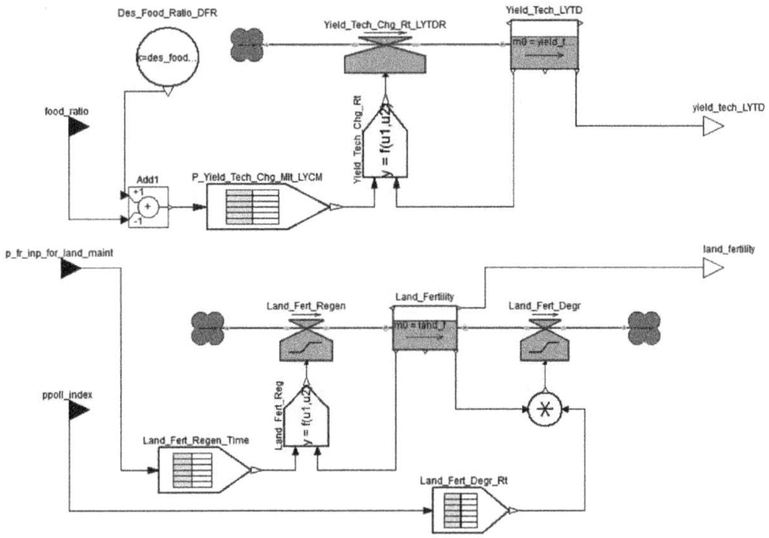

Figure 15-37. The `SystemDynamics.World3.Arable_Land_Dynamics` submodel.

Whereas the `World2` model lumped the entire population into a single state variable, the `World3` model offers a demographic population dynamics model that distinguishes between children and adolescents, young adults of child-bearing age, older adults who are still integrated into the work force, and the retired population.

The capital investment is subdivided into investments in the military/industrial complex, in the service sector, and in agriculture.

Both the natural resources and pollution models have been upgraded by including changes in technology as factors influencing the depletion of resources and the release of pollutants. This is meaningful as improved technology may enable us to use the available resources more efficiently, and may also make it possible to produce goods in a cleaner fashion.

Scenarios with World3

The book *Limits to Growth: The 30-Year Update*, describes eleven scenarios based of different sets of assumptions. These scenarios are also part of the Modelica `World3` model. We will briefly discuss three of these scenarios:

- `Scenario1` is the so-called "Standard Run." This is the original `World3` model with basic assumptions and without any adjustments.
- `Scenario2` is the same as `Scenario1`, but with twice as much non-recoverable resources available, for example, more oil, coal, metal, etc.
- `Scenario9` is based on `Scenario2` but applies a number of measures to avoid collapse and to try to transform the human society into a sustainable one.

The three scenarios are simulated between year 1900 and 2200.

Unfortunately both Scenario1 and Scenario2 rather quickly lead to population collapse, as depicted in Figure 15-38. Doubling the nonrenewable resources in Scenario2 does not help very much. The population increases a little bit more, but the collapse is even quicker, primarily due to increased levels of pollution. The current developments in our world unfortunately seem to be rather close to Scenario2.

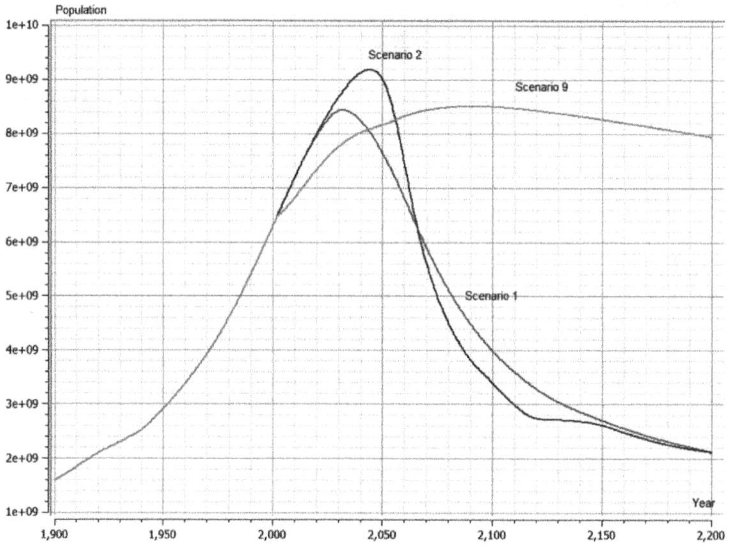

Figure 15-38. The world population according to Scenarios 1, 2, and 3 in the World3 model.

If a collapse will occur, will it be as quick as depicted in Figure 15-38? That may not be the case. The World3 model assumptions may not be completely valid during such a stressful transition period. Political decisions, rationing policies, etc., may lead to decreasing resource consumption and create a slower more controlled contraction to a sustainable level of consumption.

How can a collapse be avoided? Scenario9 applies the following aggressive technology development plan to avoid collapse:

- Increased industrial resource efficiency, that is, less uses of non-renewable material and energy, 4% resource decrease per year.
- Arable land protection, for example, to decrease and prevent land erosion, and to preserve existing land.
- Agricultural yield enhancement, 4% per year.
- Pollution reduction, 4% per year.

Additionally, it is assumed that a program for birth control with an average number of two children per family, that there is a certain capital cost to implement these technologies and that 20 years are required for their full implementation.

The Scenario9 simulation to year 2200 shows a sustainable society. However, if the simulation is extended to year 2500 it is hard to keep sustainability with the large human population combined with high standards of living. If the size of the population is gradually decreased to the level that was present only about a hundred years ago, the chances are much better.

Another issue is model validity. A number of assumptions behind the World3 model may not be valid that far into the future. However, one fact is absolutely certain: the human race must in the long run live sustainably on the earth because of limitations in resources, energy, and space. Consumption overshoots like the current one can only be temporary.

15.4.2.8 Discussion of Human-Nature Models and their Capabilities

The Handy model, in its first version, has the remarkable feature of presenting a structure simple enough for intuitive understanding while rich enough for producing a variety of modes with non-trivial behavior. This combination is seldom found in most well-known earth system (or global, or world) models, where usually the quest for including more details comes at the price of lack of intuitiveness.

Handy is very useful as a "conceptual" model that can trigger varied interpretations and discussions comparing qualitatively different scenarios. Also, as mentioned before, the explicit stratification of social classes guides the interpretations to an essential playground needed to discuss the fate of human population. Nevertheless, its manifest simplicity prevents assigning to results any quantitative soundness.

Also worth mentioning is the fact that human societies developed a degree of cultural and technological complexity that prevents treating it as simply another species. It has been recognized by several senior modelers that it is not reasonable to expect that any model can predict what the trends would be in a situation when collapses start to develop, as unpredictable social disruption and/or restructure are expectable that would invalidate most of the model's parameters and even structures that might have described pre-collapse phases in a credible way. For sure, such social reshaping will have its dynamics determined by interactions between different social classes, and in that regard, again, the Handy approach of disaggregating them in at least two strata is a valuable step.

Moreover, we want to draw the reader's attention to the aggregation made in `Handy` of natural renewable and non-renewable resources, into a single variable. It paves the way for attaining scenarios that look sustainable in the very long run (i.e., "to infinity").

Based on the principles of thermodynamics it is easy to show that in the long run the maximum carrying capacity of supporting humans on earth will be determined only by the remaining renewable resources, once we have depleted all the nonrenewable ones for good.

If renewable and nonrenewable resources were modeled independently (along with the commoners, the elite and their inequality factor) the elements would be given to investigate scenarios that tried to answer an utterly important question: How should we use best the non-renewable resources to reach a society with minimum inequalities, for when the time invariably comes that humanity must rely on renewable resources exclusively? To investigate such a goal, the inequality factor should be shifted from a constant parameter into a variable, or even to a state variable.

Regarding our quick comparison with the World3 model which is more complex and much more realistic than the Handy model, the conclusions are similar. In the long run, not so far into the future, humanity must change to living sustainably on the earth. This change can either be a planned gradual change that preserves a well-functioning society, or a more catastrophic unplanned transition resulting in a less pleasant society and a reduced and less supportive natural ecological system.

15.4.3 An Energy Forest Annual Growth Model for Willow Trees

An energy forest is another example of an ecological system for which it is interesting to study growth and mortality. In particular, in the case of energy forest models we would like to simulate and predict the biomass output of the system depending on solar radiation and other growth factors. In the example to be described shortly we will study a small willow (*Salix spp.*) forest. Research on such forests as a renewable energy source has been conducted in Sweden since the 1970s.

Traditionally, purely inductive statistically based models have been used to make predictions of forest productivity. Such models are problematic since they are site and condition specific, and usually cannot be used at new sites or under new conditions.

The modeling style used for this example is partly an inductive modeling approach based on experimental observations of factors for growth, mortality, radiation absorption, and so on, and partly deductive physical modeling based on approximate physical relations for transformation of energy from solar radiation to stored chemical energy in terms of biomass in the willow forest. This requires fewer and more easily assembled input data than in the statistical approach, but still represents the interaction between environmental factors and forest growth in a realistic way. The simple basis for the willow forest growth model to be described shortly is an assumed linear relationship between the solar radiation absorbed by the forest and the produced biomass:

$$w = \varepsilon \cdot \alpha \cdot R \tag{15-47}$$

where w is the biomass produced by the willow forest, ε is the efficiency with which the forest uses the absorbed radiation to grow wood, α is the fraction of the solar radiation absorbed by the forest, and R is the incoming solar radiation.

15.4.3.1 Model Description

The productivity of a forest of willow can be fairly well described by a discrete-time model in Modelica, with a time resolution of one year. This is a more realistic model than would be a continuous-time one since growth primarily occurs periodically during the summer season of the year, and not continuously all the time. The model includes the following aspects:

- Annual growth proportional to the incoming solar radiation.
- Constant annual mortality fraction as well as additional mortality caused by fungi certain year(s).
- Radiation use efficiency and absorption factors depending on the willow shoot age.
- Periodic harvesting.

First we formulate the difference equations that are the basis for the model, and later the Modelica model including these equations.

The annual increment in stem biomass for a willow forest equals the difference between the growth and the removal of biomass:

$$w_t - w_{t-1} = w_t^{Growth} - w_t^{Mort} - w_t^{Harvest} \tag{15-48}$$

where w_t is the standing living stem biomass at the end of the year, t denotes the current year, and t-1 the previous year. The increase in biomass is the *annual stem growth* (w_t^{Growth}) and the removal of biomass is the *annual stem mortality* (w_t^{Mort}) combined with the stem biomass removed by *harvest* ($w_t^{Harvest}$).

We also need to consider the time (in years) from when the willow shoots appear until they are harvested. The *cyclic shoot age* (c) in years is the age of the shoots that appeared at the plantation or after the most recent harvest:

$$c = 1,2,\ 1,2,3,4,\ 1,2,3,4,\ \ldots \tag{15-49}$$

Harvest occurs at the end of a growth cycle, that is, two years after plantation or after each four-year growth period starting at the most recent harvest. The shoot age is increasing until harvest, after which new shoots appear. In our model the time *condition for harvest* is expressed as follows:

$$c = 1 \textit{ and } t > 1 \tag{15-50}$$

which, strictly speaking, indicates the immediate beginning of the next growth cycle except the first. However, the time difference between the end of the previous cycle and the immediate beginning of the next cycle is essentially zero, which makes it possible to use this condition formulation as the time condition for harvest.

As mentioned previously, the annual stem growth (w_t^{Growth}) of the willow forest is proportional to the fraction of global radiation (R_c^{Absorb}) absorbed by the leaves during a growth season and the efficiency by which this energy is used:

$$w_t^{Growth} = \varepsilon_c \cdot R_c^{Absorb} \tag{15-51}$$

where ε_c, which is dependent on the cyclic shoot age c, is the efficiency with which the willow forest utilizes the absorbed radiation in production of new wood. The efficiency decreases somewhat as the shoots grow older.

The fraction (α_c) of the solar radiation absorbed by the leaves is also dependent on the shoot age c. As the shoots grow older they are able to absorb a slightly larger fraction of the incoming radiation.

$$R_c^{Absorb} = \alpha_c \cdot R_t \tag{15-52}$$

Every year a mortality fraction (m_t) of the forest dies (w_t^{Mort}) due to a certain level of shoot mortality. The shoots that die make the willow forest less dense.

$$w_t^{Mort} = \begin{cases} m_t \cdot (1-h) \cdot (w_{t-1} + w_t^{Growth}) & , c = 1 \text{ and } t > 1 \\ m_t \cdot (w_{t-1} + w_t^{Growth}) & , \text{otherwise} \end{cases} \tag{15-53}$$

Remember that the cyclic shoot age c is defined in relation to the most recent harvest, except before the first harvest when the shoot age is defined in relation to the plantation year. The harvest usually takes place every fourth year. A fraction (h) of the standing stem biomass w_{t-1} at the end of the previous year, along with the dead biomass ($w_{t-1}^{MortAcc}$) accumulated since last harvest, is then removed from the system:

$$w_t^{Harvest} = \begin{cases} h \cdot w_{t-1} + w_{t-1}^{MortAcc} & , c = 1 \text{ and } t > 1 \\ 0 & , \text{otherwise} \end{cases} \tag{15-54}$$

where dead wood has been accumulating until it is harvested:

$$w_t^{MortAcc} = \begin{cases} w_t^{Mort} & , c = 1 \text{ and } t > 1 \\ w_{t-1}^{MortAcc} + w_t^{Mort} & , \text{otherwise} \end{cases} \tag{15-55}$$

The `WillowForest` Modelica model embodying all these equations appears below:

```
class WillowForest
  parameter Real h = 0.95                         "Harvest fraction";
  parameter Real[4] e = {.73,.80,.66,.55} "Radiation efficiency fraction";
  parameter Real[4] a = {.59,.73,.76,.74} "Intercepted radiation fraction";
  parameter Integer[10] growthCycles = {1,2,1,2,3,4,1,2,3,4};
  parameter Integer[10] r = {2097, 2328, 1942, 2359, 2493,
        2290, 2008, 2356, 2323, 2540}    "Solar radiation(MJ/m²) 1985-1994";
  parameter Real[10] m = {.1, .1, .5, .1, .1,
                           .1, .1, .1, .1, .1}  "Mortality fraction 1985-1994";
  parameter Integer[10] mbiomasses = {786, 1091, 539, 980, 1139,
              589, 723, 1457, 1004, 845} "Measured biomass 1985-1994";
  Integer t (start = 0)          "Years since the forest was planted";
  Integer c                      "Year in growth cycle";
  Real w(start = 60)             "Total standing biomass in forest (g/m²)";
  Real wGrowth, wMort, wHarvest "Biomass for growth, mortality and harvest";
  Real wMortAcc (start = 0)      "Accumulated dead biomass by mortality";
  Real wBiomass                  "Biomass produced during a year";
  Integer mbiomass               "Measured biomass for current year";
equation
  when sample(0, 1) then
    t = pre(t)+1;
    mbiomass = mbiomasses[t];
    // Harvest first time after two years, then every fourth year
    c = growthCycles[t];
    w = pre(w)+(wGrowth - wMort - wHarvest);
```

```
      wBiomass = wGrowth - wMort;
      wGrowth = e[c] * a[c] * r[t];
      // A fraction m of the forest dies every year
      wMort = if (c == 1 and t > 1) then (1-h) * m[t] * (pre(w) + wGrowth)
              else m[t] * (pre(w) + wGrowth);
      // A fraction of the forest is removed at harvest

      wHarvest = if (c == 1 and t > 1) then h*pre(w) + pre(wMortAcc)
                 else 0;
      // Dead biomass accumulates by mortality
      wMortAcc = if(c == 1 and t > 1) then wMort
                 else pre(wMortAcc) + wMort;
    end when;
  end WillowForest;
```

15.4.3.2 Model Application and Simulation

The model was calibrated against measured annual data on living stem biomass of Modellskogen, located in Uppsala, Sweden. The data used in the simulation cover the period 1985—1994 (plantation year 1984) and include three harvests (Table 15-4a). Since the forest was not cut back during the plantation year the biomass value given for 1985 also includes the biomass produced during 1984. Biomass at plantation was 60 g/m^2.

The measured fraction of global radiation absorbed by the forest (α), the radiation use efficiency (ε) and the different mortality and harvest factors used in the simulation are shown in Table 15-4b. The mortality fraction (m) is in a normal year 0.10, but in 1987 the forest was infected by fungus and there was a calibrated extra mortality fraction of 0.40. Beginning at the end of 1986, a fraction h (90%) of the forest was harvested every fourth year.

Table 15-4. (a) Annual values for shoot age, incoming solar radiation, and stem biomass for Modellskogen forest. (b) Model inputs for the simulation of Modellskogen forest productivity.

Year	Shoot Age	Solar Radiation (MJ/m^2)	Stem Biomass (g m^{-2})
1985	I[1] [a]	2097	846[a]
1986	II[1]	2328	1091
1987	I[2]	1942	539
1988	II[2]	2359	980
1989	III[2]	2493	1139
1990	IV[2]	2290	589
1991	I[3]	2008	723
1992	II[3]	2356	1457
1993	III[3]	2323	1004
1994	IV[3]	2540	845

[a] The year after plantation. [1,2,3] First, second and third cutting cycle.

Parameter	Value	Unit
Radiation use efficiency		
ε; $t_{Age} = 1$	0.73	G d. w. MJ^{-1}
ε; $t_{Age} = 2$	0.80	G d. w. MJ^{-1}
ε; $t_{Age} = 3$	0.66	G d. w. MJ^{-1}
ε; $t_{Age} = 4$	0.55	G d. w. MJ^{-1}
Intercepted radiation		
α; $t_{Age} = 1$	0.59	-
α; $t_{Age} = 2$	0.73	-
α; $t_{Age} = 3$	0.76	-
α; $t_{Age} = 4$	0.74	-

The `WillowForest` model was simulated and certain results were plotted as depicted in Figure 15-39:

```
simulate(WillowForest,stopTime=9.99})
plot({w,wGrowth})
plot({w,wHarvest,wMortAcc})
Plot({wBiomass,mbiomass}, xrange={0,10), yrange={0,1400))
```

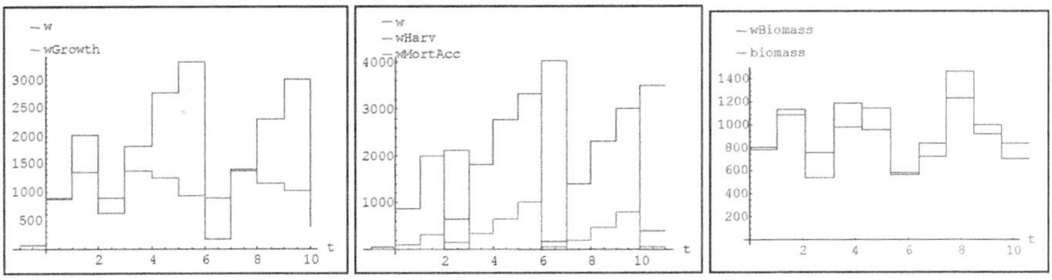

Figure 15-39. (a) The total biomass and the annual increase in biomass plotted against time. (b) The total biomass, harvested biomass, and the annual accumulation of dead biomass plotted against time. (c) The annual net production of biomass and annual measured biomass plotted against time.

Figure 15-39c shows a fairly good correspondence between the biomass production computed by the simulation and actual measured values. In Figure 15-39a can we observe the effects of accumulation of biomass due to growth, effects of harvesting, as well as the fact that biomass growth seems to be highest the year directly after a harvest event.

15.5 Economic Systems

Economic systems are abstractions of physical systems with human beings where only so-called economic aspects are studied, for example, money flow, monetary value, production, consumption, etc. Complete economic systems are intrinsically quite complex, especially since they to a large extent depend on human behavior.

On the other hand, since exact knowledge about the mechanisms in such systems is hard to obtain, many simplifying assumptions are usually made, resulting in very simple models. Such models can never be more than approximately valid and therefore have limited prediction power. However, it is not uncommon that simple economic models are used for predictions outside their area of validity.

The subject area denoted *national economy* deals with the economic behavior of nations. Models of national economies often include variables such as *GNP* (Gross National Product), the *total consumption* of a nation, the *total investments*, and the *government expenses* of the nation.

In particular, according to the simple Keynesian multiplier-accelerator model, the following approximate relation holds:

$$GNP_t \quad consumption_t \quad investments_t \quad expenses_t \tag{15-56}$$

where t denotes the current year. We also assume that the consumption for the current year (t) is proportional to the GNP for the previous year (t-1):

$$consumption_t \quad a \; GNP_{t \; 1} \tag{15-57}$$

Moreover, the investments of the current year are assumed to be proportional to the increase in consumption compared to the previous year:

$$investments_t \quad b \; (consumption_t \quad consumption_{t \; 1}) \tag{15-58}$$

As we remarked previously, one can discuss the validity of these rather simple assumptions. However, there are also certain arguments in favor of these assumptions. We refer the reader to national economic literature for more detailed study.

It is easy to make a simple Modelica model based on equations (15-56) to (15-58):

```
class KeynesianModel
  parameter Real a = 0.5     "Consumption fraction";
  parameter Real b = 0.5     "Investment fraction of consumption increase";
  Real       GNP(start=0)        "Gross National Product";
```

```
  Real      consumption(start=0) "Consumption";
  Real      investments(start=0) "Investments";
  Real      expenses(start=0)    "Government expenses";
equation
  when sample(0, 1) then
    GNP         = consumption + investments + expenses;
    consumption = a * pre(GNP);
    investments = b * (consumption - pre(consumption));
  end when;
  when time >= 1.0 then     // Increase expenses by 1 at year 1
    expenses = pre(expenses)+1;
  end when;
end KeynesianModel;
```

Here we have made the rather unrealistic assumption that GNP, consumption, investments, and government expenses are all zero at the beginning of the first year. However, this can be easily changed and does not matter for the result when studying annual changes instead of absolute values. After one year we suddenly increase government expenses by 1. The proportionality factors for the consumption and investments are assumed to be 0.5, that is, at a level of half of the GNP.

We simulate the model and observe the effects on the other economic variables:

```
simulate(KeynesianModel, stopTime=11)
plot({GNP,consumption}, xrange={0,10})
```

A plot of the simulated GNP and the consumption is depicted in Figure 15-40.

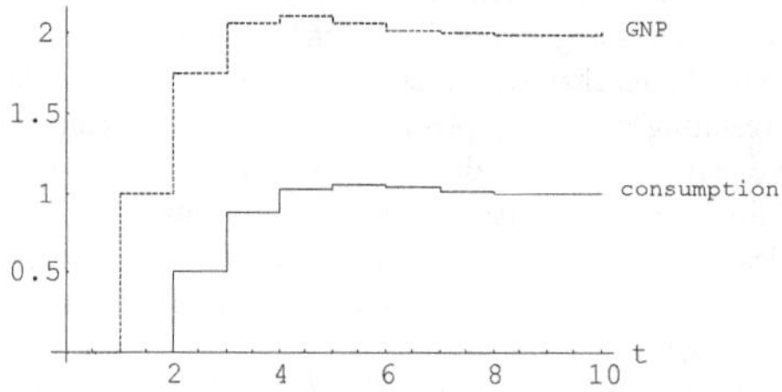

Figure 15-40. The GNP and the consumption after an increase of government expenses by 1 after 1 year.

It is interesting to observe the effects on the GNP and the consumption after the increase in state expenditures. After a few years the GNP has increased to a factor of 2 of the increase of government expenses, which is the so-called *multiplier effect* exhibited by this model.

The immediate effect of the expense increase is that the GNP increases by the same amount. As a consequence, investments increase the year later. This causes a further increase in GNP and consumption. Eventually we arrive at a steady-state GNP level of 2 and a consumption level of 1.

15.6 Packet-Switched Communication Networks

Packet-switched communication networks play a very important role in modern society since they provide the basis for transport of data in widely used networks such as the Internet, local area networks, and a number of special-purpose networks.

A packet-switched network can be described by a directed graph. The nodes in this graph represent routers, which are computers that forward information packets on their way from senders to receivers. The edges between the nodes in the network are either wired or wireless communication links. A sender is a computer that sends information packets into the network with a destination of some receiver computer node.

Figure 15-41 schematically depicts a simple network that provides a connection between a sender and a receiver via a number of routers and communication links.

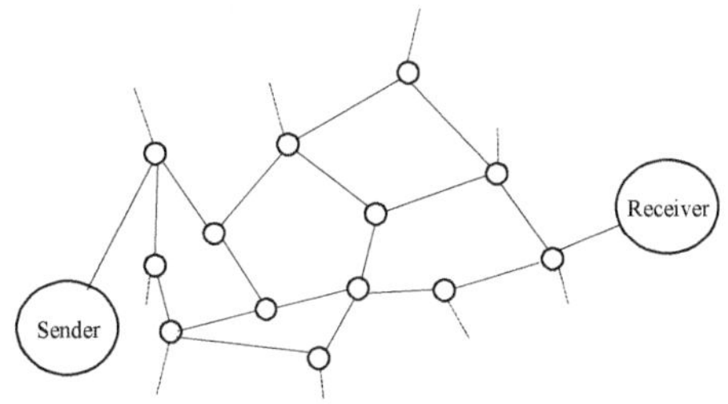

Figure 15-41. Schematic packet-switched communication network, with router nodes connected by communication links, together with a sender and a receiver.

The links between the nodes in the network have limited bandwidth, which can lead to traffic congestion. To handle minor traffic congestion the routers in the network have buffer storage capacity in order to store packets in case more packets are entering than leaving a router. However, if too many packets are entering a router during a short period of time, the buffer capacity may not be enough, which will lead to packets being dropped.

Dropping packets is inefficient since information has to be resent. The congestion problem might be an indication that the sender is transmitting information at a higher rate than what the communication network can handle. The problem is solved if the sender adapts its rate of sending information through some control mechanism. On the Internet a control mechanism denoted the *Transmission Control Protocol* (TCP) is used by the sender to regulate the send rate.

15.6.1 End-to-End Communication Protocols

There exist several variants of the TCP protocol with different properties concerning congestion handling, transmission efficiency, etc.

All TCP protocol versions are *end-to-end* communication protocols, meaning that the network is regarded as a black box from the sender's point of view. Each package is sent all the way to a receiver node, which returns a small acknowledgment package for each received package. If a package is dropped due to congestion or some other reason, this will be eventually detected by the sender due to a missing acknowledgment package.

In order to use the network resources more efficiently and thereby allow higher transmission rates, the TCP sender transmits w number of packages before waiting for acknowledgments for these packages. Therefore w corresponds to the number of unacknowledged packets the sender may have in the network. The w variable is called the TCP *window size* and controls the sending rate—a large value of the window size w means a higher sending rate. When the sender has received acknowledgments for all w packages, w is increased by 1.

If a packet is dropped, meaning that no acknowledgment for that packet has been received by the sender, the TCP protocol assumes that some congestion has occurred, that is, the currently estimated bandwidth and window size values are too high. The algorithm tries to eliminate the congestion by reducing the sending rate. The reduction depends on which variant of the TCP protocol is used. In the following we will focus on two variants:

- TCP SACK—Selective ACKnowledgment—a common protocol variant for wired links, where the receiver of data informs the sender about all packets that have arrived successfully.
- TCP Westwood—a more recent protocol variant very similar to TCP SACK introduced to better handle communication over lossy wireless links where random or sporadic losses are fairly common. This protocol uses bandwidth estimation for quick recovery after sporadic losses.

The TCP SACK protocol provides congestion avoidance, that is, recovery after congestion, by decreasing the window size w by a factor of 2 each time a packet drop occurs, as depicted in the simple transition diagram of Figure 15-42, where we use the notation w_f to indicate that there might be several packet flows between a sender and a receiver, here denoted by the subscript f.

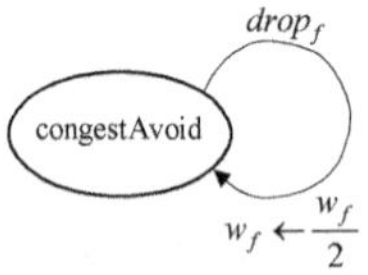

Figure 15-42. Simplified transition diagram of congestion avoidance used in TCP SACK for which the window size w_f is reduced by a factor of 2 when there is a packet drop.

The TCP Westwood protocol has another way of updating the window size w_f after congestion or transmission loss. Instead of dividing the window size by a factor of 2, it is set to a new value based on the bandwidth estimate (`BWE`) for the link. This provides quicker recovery and better use of the available bandwidth after a packet drop.

Both TCP protocols have congestion-control algorithms that use packet loss to detect congestion. Moreover, during a startup phase the TCP senders investigate the network capacity by gradually increasing the size of the window of packets that are outstanding in the network until the network becomes congested and drops packets. A TCP sender initially quickly grabs available bandwidth by exponentially increasing the window size. When the window size reaches a certain value called the *slow start threshold*, `ssth`, the increase becomes linear, which gives a gentler probing of the network bandwidth capacity. It is desirable to keep this threshold at a value that approximates the connection's "fair share" of the total bandwidth.

15.6.2 Types of Communication Network Models

There are basically three classes of mathematical models used for simulating traffic flow based on TCP protocols on the Internet:

- *Discrete models*, which directly implement the Internet protocols and simulate individual packets. Such models give accurate simulation results but rather slow simulation speed, and are therefore limited to smaller networks.
- Continuous-flow models, which approximate the packet transmission with a continuous flow and basically eliminate the network protocols. Such models describe average transmission rates at steady state well but ignore events such as packet drops, and are thus less suitable for studying transient phenomena.
- *Hybrid models*, which use continuous-flow modeling for average rates but also take transient events such as packet drops into account.

Hybrid models can capture the network behavior on time scales between discrete models and continuous flow models. They can be efficiently simulated for large networks and high traffic loads, but can still represent transient phenomena such as traffic congestion and packet drops. In the following we will give a short overview of a hybrid Modelica model of a simple packet-switched network in which two different TCP send protocols are compared.

15.6.3 A Hybrid Network Model Comparing Two TCP Send Protocols

Our simple packet-switched network example is specified in Modelica using the hybrid modeling approach mentioned in the previous section. We would like to simulate the model to compare the congestion behavior of such a network using two different TCP protocol variants: TCP SACK and TCP Westwood. The simple network, depicted in Figure 15-43, contains the following components:

- Two packet senders, using the TCP SACK and the TCP Westwood protocol variants, respectively.
- One router connecting both senders to a wireless lossy communication link.
- Another router connecting the wireless link to two receivers.
- Two receiver components.

The communication ports used for connecting the model components are defined in the next section.

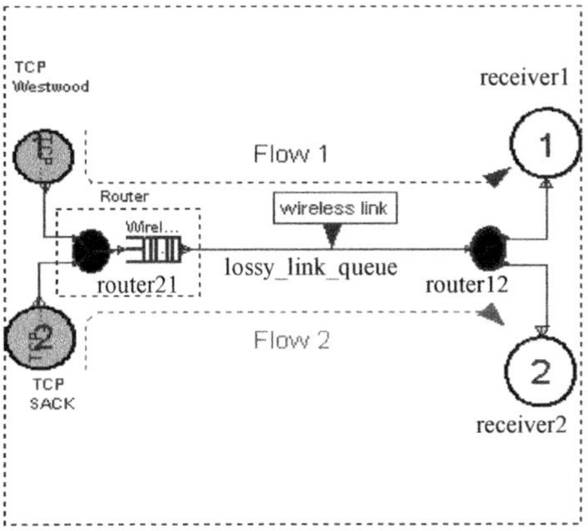

Figure 15-43. Simple network with two senders (TCP Westwood, TCP SACK), two receivers, a wireless link, and two routers.

The Modelica code of the simple TCP communication network model appears below. It is modeled using Modelica version 2.1, which does not require balanced models (Section 5.7.7, page 217) that was introduced in Modelica 3.0. We have configured the system with a packet length `L=500`, a maximum total bandwidth `B_tot` of `500*1250*2`, i.e., max `1250` packets for each of the two flows, and a maximum buffer capacity `q_max` of `50` packets.

```
model TCPSACKvsTCPWestwood  "TCP SACK versus TCP Westwood"
  Router21          router21;
  Router12          router12;
  Lossy_link_queue  lossy_link_queue(B_tot=500*1250*2, q_max=50*500, L=500);
  TCP_Westwood      aTCPWestwood(L=500, send_f_to=1);               // sender 1
  TCP_SACK          aTCPSACK(L=500, send_f_from=2, send_f_to=2); // sender 2
  Receiver          receiver1;
  Receiver          receiver2;
equation
  connect(aTCPSACK.o,  router21.i2);
  connect(aTCPWestwood.o, router21.i1);
  connect(router21.o,  lossy_link_queue.i);
  connect(router12.i,  lossy_link_queue.o);
  connect(router12.o1, receiver1.i);
  connect(router12.o2, receiver2.i);
end TCPSACKvsTCPWestwood;
```

A simulation of this model is available in Section 15.6.9, page 868.

15.6.4 Communication Port Classes

The `Inport` and `Outport` classes shown below define the interfaces used for connections between instances of the components in the TCP network model. All components need at least one `Inport` or one `Outport` connector instance. Some components have several ports, e.g. the routers and the queue, whereas the senders and the receivers have only one `Port` each.

The following variables declared in the `Port` class are propagated throughout the network model:

- The number of packet flows, `n`, in the network.
- The packet round-trip times, `RTT`, from the sender to the receiver and back for each flow.
- The drop-event indicator, `d`, for each flow.
- The flow rates, `r` [bytes/s], sending or incoming rates, for each flow.
- The bandwidth estimates, `BWE`, for each flow.

The Modelica code for the `Inport` and `Outport` classes appear below.

```
connector Inport "Input Port for connector instances in the network"
  parameter Integer n=2 "Number of flows";
  input Real    r[n]   "r[f] - flow rate bytes/sec for flow f in connector";
  input Boolean d[n]   "d[f] - true when drop occurred in flow f";
  input Real    RTT[n] "RTT[f] - Round Trip Time for flow f";
  input Real    BWE[n] "BWE[f] - BandWidth Estimation for sender, flow f";
end Inport;

connector Outport "Output Port for connector instances in the network "
  parameter Integer n=2 "Number of flows";
  output Real    r[n]   "r[f] - flow rate bytes/sec for flow f in connector";
  output Boolean d[n]   "d[f] - true when drop occurred in flow f";
  output Real    RTT[n] "RTT[f] - Round Trip Time for flow f";
  output Real    BWE[n] "BWE[f] - BandWidth Estimation for sender, flow f";
end Outport;
```

We will now turn to the network sender components, each having one `Outport` instance.

15.6.5 Senders

The two hybrid TCP sender models, TCP SACK and TCP Westwood, have four different discrete states, as depicted in Figure 15-44.

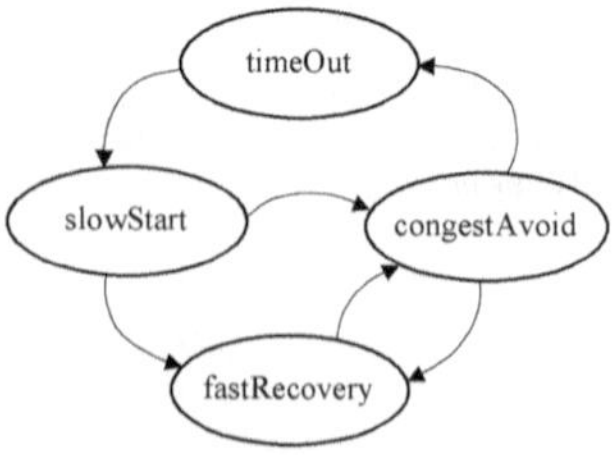

Figure 15-44. State transition diagram for the TCP SACK and TCP Westwood protocol variants.

The states for each flow are the following:

- *Slow start*—the sender is initially in this state, in which the window size quickly increases exponentially up to the slow-start window threshold level, `ssth`, after which a state transition to the congestion-avoidance state occurs.
- *Congestion avoidance*—in this state the window size increases at the slower additive rate specified by equation (15-60), and the system is prepared to handle congestion if it occurs.
- *Fast recovery*—when entering this state we try to recover quickly from a congestion event, by dividing the window size in half according to TCP SACK, or compute it from a bandwidth estimate according to TCP Westwood.
- *Time out*—this state is entered when a timeout occurs in the congestion-avoidance or slow-startup states. The window size is reduced to the very low value of 1 and a transition to the slow-start state is performed.

In all states except the timeout state, the transmission rate r_f for flow f is given by the following equation:

$$r_f = \frac{w_f \cdot L}{RTT_f} \tag{15-59}$$

where w_f is the window size in packets, L is the packet length in bytes, and RTT_f is the round-trip time for flow f. The formula just states that the transmission rate is the number of currently pending transmitted bytes divided by the round-trip time.

The round-trip time is the time between sending a packet and receiving the corresponding acknowledgment. It is the sum of the physical propagation time and the queuing times, and is defined in the lossy link model described in Section 15.6.7, page 863.

We will not discuss all the details of this model, but rather focus more on the important congestion-avoidance state, which specifies additive increase of the window size w_f according to equation (15-60) for probing the available bandwidth:

$$\dot{w}_f = \frac{1}{RTT_f} \tag{15-60}$$

where $\dot{w}_f$ is the additive window size increase rate. A simplified state diagram for congestion avoidance was previously shown in Figure 15-42, whereas the more realistic version of the state diagram is depicted in Figure 15-45.

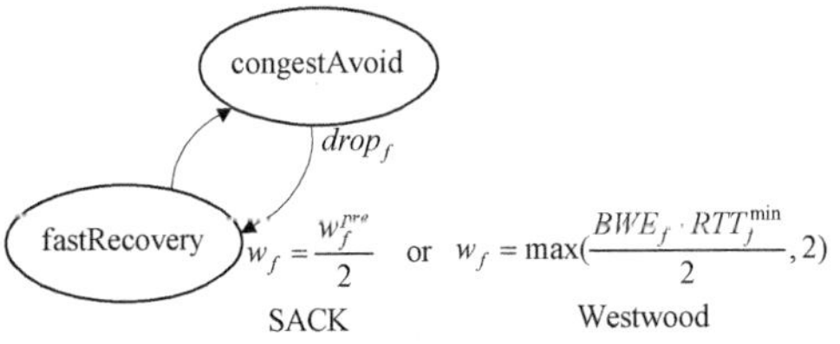

Figure 15-45. State transitions in the congestion-avoidance state after a packet drop for the TCP SACK and TCP Westwood protocol variants.

When a packet drop is detected, the state is changed from congestion avoidance to fast recovery. When entering the fast recovery state in the TCP SACK variant, the instantaneous equation (15-61) is activated that reduces the window size by a factor of 2 compared to the previous value:

$$w_f = \frac{w_f^{pre}}{2} \tag{15-61}$$

As mentioned previously, the TCP Westwood model is the TCP sender variant designed for lossy wireless links. This variant of the TCP protocol is quite similar to TCP SACK, except that the window size is not halved when packet drops occur.

Instead the window size is set to a more realistic value using a bandwidth estimate, BWE_f, for flow f specified by the instantaneous equation (15-62). This enables fast recovery after a drop since a correct setting of the window size is obtained very quickly. The instantaneous equation is activated only at the transition to the fast recovery state, and appears as follows:

$$w_f = \max(\frac{BWE_f \cdot RTT_f^{\min}}{2}, 2) \qquad (15\text{-}62)$$

where $RTT_f^{\min}$ is the minimum round-trip time computed so far for flow f. $RTT_f^{\min}$ is a measure of the fastest possible round-trip with minimum delays from queuing in intermediate routers and other disturbances. The slow-start threshold `ssth` is also updated when entering the fast recovery state.

The Modelica code for both the hybrid TCP SACK and the hybrid TCP Westwood model variants appears merged as a single `TCPSender` class below; there are very small differences between the two variants. When the Boolean variable `tcpSACK` is `true`, that variant is enabled; otherwise the TCP Westwood variant is active.

```
model TCPSender   "Hybrid Transmission Control Protocol, two variants:
                    TCP_Westwood or TCP_SACK Selective ACKnowledgement"
  Outport    o;
  constant  Integer slowStart=1;
  constant  Integer fastRecov=2;
  constant  Integer congestAvoid=3;
  constant  Integer timeOut=4;
  parameter Boolean tcpSACK = true "false means TCP_Westwood";
  parameter Integer n=o.n           "Number of flows";
  parameter Integer a=1             "Additive increase";
  parameter Real    L=1             "Packet size in bytes";
  parameter Integer send_f_from=1   "This sender's first flow";
  parameter Integer send_f_to=n     "This sender's last flow ";
  parameter Real    timeout_th=4.0 "Window threshhold for entering timeout";
  parameter Real    m[n]={2,2}      "log m in Slow-start";
  //       {1.5, 1.7, 2, 2.5, 2.7} "log m in Slow-start";
  parameter Real RTO[n]=fill(0.200,n) "Retransmission TimeOut 200 ms";
  discrete  Integer state[n](start=fill(slowStart, n));
  Real       ssth[n](start=fill(65535.0/L, n)) "Slow start thresholds";
  Real       w[n](start=ones(n)) "Communication window sizes, no of packets";
  Real       d_tim[n](start=zeros(n)) "Drop timer";
  Real       t_tim[n](start=zeros(n)) "Retransmission timer";
  Boolean    DelayD[n](start=fill(false,n))" Delay induced Drop detected";
  //TCP Westwood variables
  Real       RTT_min[n](start=fill(1.0, n)) "Minimum Round-Trip Time";
  Real       BWE[n]  "BandWidth Estimation for each flow";
equation
  for f in 1:n loop
    if (f >= send_f_from and f <= send_f_to) then
   // Instantaneous equations immediately after state transitions
      when ((pre(state[f]) == slowStart or pre(state[f]) ==congestAvoid) and
            state[f] == fastRecov) then
        reinit(t_tim[f], o.RTT[f]);
        if tcpSACK then
           reinit(ssth[f], w[f]/2);
           reinit(w[f], w[f]/2);
         else // TCP Westwood
           reinit(ssth[f], BWE[f]*RTT_min[f]/L);
           reinit(w[f], max(BWE[f]*RTT_min[f]/L, 2));//window size using BWE
```

```
      end if;
    end when;
    when ((pre(state[f]) == slowStart or pre(state[f]) ==congestAvoid) and
          state[f] == timeOut) then
      reinit(t_tim[f], RTO[f]);
      if tcpSACK then
         reinit(ssth[f], w[f]/2);
      else // TCP Westwood
          reinit(ssth[f], max(BWE[f]*RTT_min[f]/L, 2));
      end if;
      reinit(w[f], 1);
    end when;

    // Equations for the 4 different states
    if state[f] == congestAvoid then
      der(w[f]) = a/o.RTT[f];  // additive increase
      o.r[f] = w[f]*L/o.RTT[f];
      der(t_tim[f]) = 0;
    elseif state[f] == fastRecov then
      der(w[f]) = 0;
      o.r[f] = w[f]*L/(o.RTT[f]);
      der(t_tim[f]) = -1;
    elseif state[f] == timeOut then
      der(w[f]) = 0;
      o.r[f] = 0.001;
      der(t_tim[f]) = -1;
      // otherwise RTT will be 0 in queue
    else // state[f] == slowStart
      der(w[f]) = Modelica.Math.log(m[f])*w[f]/o.RTT[f]; //exponential inc
      o.r[f] = w[f]*L/o.RTT[f];
      der(t_tim[f]) = 0;
    end if;

    der(d_tim[f]) = if d_tim[f] > 0 then -1.0 else 0.0;
    DelayD[f] = if d_tim[f] < 0 then true else false;

    when (o.d[f] and d_tim[f] <= 0) then
      reinit(d_tim[f], o.RTT[f]);
    end when;
    der(ssth[f]) = 0;

    // 3 eqs used only by TCP_Westwood:
    BWE[f] = delay(o.BWE[f], o.RTT[f]);
    der(RTT_min[f]) = 0;
    when (RTT_min[f] > o.RTT[f]) then
      reinit(RTT_min[f], o.RTT[f]);
    end when;

  else // Unused flows
    when initial() then
      reinit(w[f], 0);
    end when;
    o.r[f] = 0;
    der(w[f]) = 0;
    der(ssth[f]) = 0;
    der(d_tim[f]) = 0;
    der(t_tim[f]) = 0;
    DelayD[f] = false;
    // 2 eqs used only by TCP_Westwood:
    BWE[f] = 0;
    der(RTT_min[f]) = 0;
```

```
      end if;
    end for;

  algorithm // State transitions
    for f in 1:n loop
      if (f >= send_f_from and f <= send_f_to) then
        when (edge(DelayD[f]) and w[f] >= timeout_th and
              (state[f] == slowStart or state[f] == congestAvoid)) then
           state[f] := fastRecov;
        elsewhen (w[f] >= ssth[f] and state[f] == slowStart) then
           state[f] := congestAvoid;
        elsewhen (w[f] < timeout_th and edge(DelayD[f]) and
                  (state[f] == slowStart or state[f] == congestAvoid)) then
          state[f] := timeOut;
        elsewhen (t_tim[f] < 0 and state[f] == fastRecov) then
          state[f] := congestAvoid;
        elsewhen (t_tim[f] < 0 and state[f] == timeOut) then
          state[f] := slowStart;
        end when;
      else
        state[f] := 0;
      end if;
    end for;
  end TCPSender;
```

Having presented the sender models, we will now turn to the quite simple receiver model.

15.6.6 Receivers

A receiver, for example, as depicted in Figure 15-46, has the sole function of receiving a stream of packets and returning acknowledgments. It has a single input port.

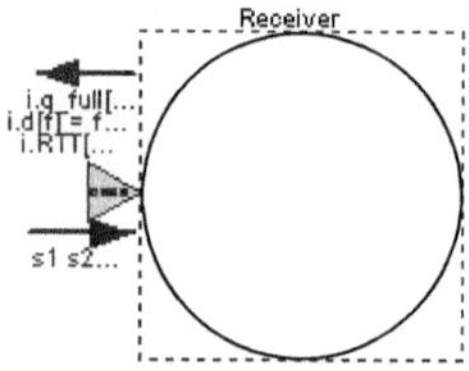

Figure 15-46. Receiver with one `Inport`.

The Modelica code for the `Receiver` model appears below:

```
model Receiver "Receiver"
  Inport i;
  parameter Integer n=i.n;
  parameter Boolean d[n]=fill(false,n) "Drop d[f] true/false for flow f";
  parameter Real RTT[n]=zeros(n)       "Round Trip Times";
  Real received[n](start=zeros(n))     "received[f] bytes for flow f";
  Real received_tot             "Rotal received bytes, all input flows";
  Real r_tot_in                 "Total reception rate bytes/s, all input flows";
equation
  der(received) = i.r;
  r_tot_in = sum(i.r);
  received_tot = sum(received);
  i.d = d;
  i.RTT = RTT;
  i.BWE = i.r;
```

```
end Receiver;
```

The receiver is a very simple model class, which is not quite true for the communication link model to be described in the next section.

15.6.7 Lossy Wireless Communication Link Model

We now arrive at one of the most important components of our network model, namely the intermediate lossy wireless communication link that represents both the physical links and the intermediate routers with queues for temporary packet storage, for example, as schematically depicted in Figure 15-41, page 855. Several communication flows can be accommodated within the same physical network.

Thus, our lossy link model needs to represent packet transmission and transmission delays over physical links and queuing of packets in intermediate routers, as well as stochastic sporadic transmission losses and bandwidth disturbances.

In the following treatment of a mathematical model for the communication link we will make the simplification of a single router queue per flow instead of multiple queues, with no great loss of precision.

We will treat the queue sizes, packet flow transmission rates, as well as a number of other quantities as continuous-time real-valued variables in our hybrid network communication model. However, even though the queues are stored in the routers of real physical systems, in the `TCPSACKvsTCPWestwood` model we have put the queuing mechanism in the communication link model for practical reasons.

The variable q_f is the number of bytes in flow *f stored* in the router queue for that flow, s_f is the input *send rate* (bytes/s) of bytes sent *into* the queue of flow *f*, and r_f is the output *receive rate* (bytes/s) of bytes received from flow *f* of the communication link by some external node(s).

We can express these quantities summed over all flows as follows:

$$
\begin{aligned}
q_{tot} &= \sum_f q_f \\
s_{tot} &= \sum_f s_f \\
r_{tot} &= \sum_f r_f
\end{aligned}
\qquad (15\text{-}63)
$$

where q_{tot} is the total number of bytes summed over all flows for packets queued in the network, s_{tot} is the input total send rate over all flows sending bytes into the network, and r_{tot} is the output total receive rate over all flows receiving bytes from the network.

The behavior of the communication link is dependent on whether the *queue is full*, $q_{tot} = q_{\max}$, or is *not full*, $0 \le q_{tot} < q_{\max}$, which is reflected in the state transition diagram depicted in Figure 15-47.

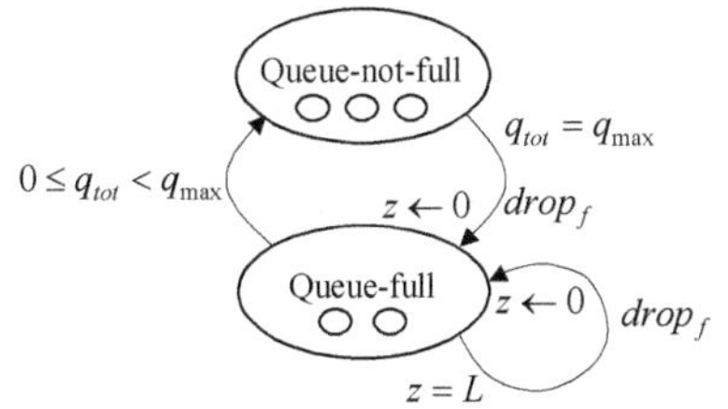

Figure 15-47. Two-state transition diagram of lossy communication link, where the not-full state contains three substates and the full state two substates.

The total bandwidth of the outgoing link is equal to the constant B_{tot}. If the total send rate into the input link $s_{tot} > B_{tot}$, then a fraction of the packets must be temporarily stored in the queue of the communication link at the rate $\dot{q}_f$, which is nonzero when the output rate is defined by the second or third equation that defines r_f in (15-64).

The variable z is the number of input bytes of the currently received packet that have been dropped. When the queue is not full, no bytes need to be dropped since they can be stored in the queue. However, when the queue is full, the drop rate is the amount that the total input rate exceeds the output transmission rate, as defined by the first equation of (15-65). A packet drop is generated when the variable z has accumulated a byte flow amount equal to the packet length L.

The following equations represent the relations between the main quantities of the model for the two main states:

- The *queue not full* state, $0 \le q_{tot} < q_{\max}$:

$$\dot{z} = 0$$

$$\dot{q}_f = s_f - r_f$$

$$r_f = \begin{cases} s_f & , q_{tot} = 0 \; and \; s_{tot} \le B_{tot} \\ \dfrac{s_f}{s_{tot}} B_{tot} & , q_{tot} = 0 \; and \; s_{tot} > B_{tot} \\ \dfrac{q_f}{q_{tot}} B_{tot} & , otherwise \end{cases} \tag{15-64}$$

where the condition $q_{tot} = 0$ is represented as (`q_tot <= eps`) for a small constant `eps` in the Modelica model. In the queue full state the output rate r_f is the fraction q_f / q_{tot} of the total output bandwidth:

- The *queue full* state, $q_{tot} = q_{\max}$:

$$\dot{z} = s_{tot} - B_{tot}$$

$$\dot{q}_f = \begin{cases} s_f - r_f & , s_{tot} \le B_{tot} \\ s_f - \dfrac{q_f}{q_{tot}} s_{tot} & , s_{tot} > B_{tot} \end{cases} \tag{15-65}$$

$$r_f = \frac{q_f}{q_{tot}} B_{tot}$$

The following Modelica class `Lossy_link_queue` represents the previous relations and includes the following aspects of the lossy link:

- Packet flows, including reception of packages sent into the link and transmission of packages to be received by a node at the output.
- Queue handling, including queue storage rates, transmission rates, and the different states when the queue is full or not full.
- Drop regeneration, when the queue is full and input rates exceed the maximum transmission rates.
- Random generation of good state and bad state transmission quality intervals. In the bad state the probability for packet drops is fairly high.
- Computation of the round-trip timing RTT_f and bandwidth estimate BWE_f for each flow.

These properties are in most cases modeled by separate groups of equations in the class. However, the modeling of the two main states with their substates and conditional equations is somewhat more implicit. The Modelica code for the class `Lossy_link_queue` follows below:

```
model Lossy_link_queue  "Wireless transmission link queue"
  Inport i                         "Port for flows from router into queue";
```

```
  Outport o;                          "Port for flows from queue into router";
  parameter Integer n=max(size(i.r))"Number of flows";
  parameter Real    B_tot=10^7/8000 "Default Total Bandwidth";
  parameter Real    q_max=57        "Max total queue size";
  parameter Integer L=500           "Packet size";
  parameter Real    T=0.02          "Physical propagation delay for trip";
  parameter Real    eps=0.01        "Threshold to avoid division by zero";
  parameter Real    loss_factor_good=0.00001 "Absolute loss level";
  parameter Real    loss_factor_bad=0.10     "If bad, fraction lost";
  parameter Real    lg=8;
  parameter Real    lb=4;

  Real    q_tot(start=0) "Total number of bytes in queue";
  Real    s_tot "Sent from router to link - incoming total byte flow rate";
  Real    r_tot "Received from link to ext router - noloss total byte rate";
  Real    s_tot_acc(start=0) "Total no of sent incoming bytes accumulated";
  Boolean q_full(start=false);  // true if queue full

  Integer u_flow(start=1) "1 if underflow - integer used as fake boolean";
  Integer o_flow(start=0) "1 if input overflow - int used as fake boolean";
  Real    q[n](start=zeros(n)) "Number of elements from flow f in queue";
  Real    rand                 "Random variable for drop decision";
  Real    z(start=0)           "Drop detection, dropped bytes";
  Real    RTT_initial "Initial RTT to prevent singularity at init time";

  // To get a lower sending rate than the bandwidth
  Real    s[n]    "s[f] send rate from router into link, flow f";
  Real    r[n]    "r[f] no loss receive rate into router from link, flow f";
  Real    r_acc[n](start=zeros(n)) "Received bytes from link accumulated";
  Boolean loss[n]                  "loss[f] true if loss in flow f";
  Real    rand_loss[n](start=fill(0.5, n));

  Boolean GOOD_STATE  "Good commlink state with low loss factor";
  Boolean BAD_STATE   "Bad commlink state with high loss factor";
  Real    g_tim(start=1)  "Timer for good state duration";
  Real    b_tim(start=-1) "Timer for bad state duration";
  Real    loss_factor(start=0.001);
equation
  s = i.r;                     // Send rate from router at input
  o.r = (1 - loss_factor)*r;   // Lossy receive rate to router at output
  s_tot = sum(s);
  r_tot = sum(r);
  q_tot = sum(q);
  der(s_tot_acc) = s_tot;
  o_flow = if s_tot > B_tot then 1 else 0; // 1 if incoming traffic rate>max
  u_flow = 1 - o_flow;                     // 1 if s_tot <= B_tot
  q_full = (q_tot > q_max);
// Note: Two main states in figure contains substates
// States dependent on: q_full/not full o_flow/u_flow, q_notempty/empty
  for f in 1:n loop
    r[f]   = if (q_tot > eps) then B_tot*q[f]/q_tot    // Queue not empty
                  else o_flow*B_tot*s[f]/s_tot + u_flow*s[f]; // q empty
    der(q[f]) = if q_tot < q_max then s[f] - r[f]      // Queue not full
          else o_flow*(s[f]-q[f]/q_tot*s_tot) + u_flow*(s[f]-r[f]); //full
  end for;

  // Losses independent of queue size
  // Timers for when good state and bad state start and stops
  when edge(GOOD_STATE) then
    reinit(g_tim, -lg*log(randomUniform(time)));//Modelica.Math, Appendix F
  end when;
```

```
    when edge(BAD_STATE) then
      reinit(b_tim, -lb*log(randomUniform(time))); //lb=4
    end when;
    GOOD_STATE = (b_tim < 0);  // Initially true when b_tim= -1
    BAD_STATE  = (g_tim < 0);  // Initially false when g_tim =1
    der(g_tim) = if g_tim > 0 then -1.0 else 0.0;  // If positive, decrease
    der(b_tim) = if b_tim > 0 then -1.0 else 0.0;  // If positive, decrease

    loss_factor = if GOOD_STATE then loss_factor_good else loss_factor_bad;
    for f in 1:n loop
      der(r_acc[f]) = r[f];
      der(rand_loss[f]) = 0;
      loss[f] = (r_acc[f] > rand_loss[f]*2*L/loss_factor);
      when r_acc[f] > rand_loss[f]*2*L/loss_factor then
         reinit(r_acc[f], 0);
      end when;
      when pre(loss[f]) then
        reinit(rand_loss[f], rand);
      end when;
    end for;


    // Compute packet drops uniformly distributed among flows
    // Drop rate der(z) is send rate above total bandwidth when q_full
    der(z) = if q_full then s_tot - B_tot else 0.0;
    rand = randomUniform(time);
    // If q_full becomes true or z>L the generate drop in a flow and set z=0
    if ((z > L and q_tot > eps) or edge(q_full)) then
      i.d[1] = if (0 <= rand and rand < q[1]/q_tot) then true else o.d[1];
      for f in 1:n - 1 loop
        i.d[f + 1] = if (sum(q[1:f])/q_tot <= rand and
                         rand < sum(q[1:f+1])/q_tot) then true
                     else o.d[f + 1];
      end for;
      reinit(z, 0.0);
    else
      i.d = o.d or loss;
    end if;

    // Calculating Round Trip Times and available BandWidth Estimates
    RTT_initial = if initial() then T else 0;
    for f in 1:n loop
      i.RTT[f] = if s[f] <> 0 then T + q_tot/B_tot + o.RTT[f] //<>0 compare
                                else RTT_initial;
      i.BWE[f] = r[f]*B_tot/(r_tot + 0.01);
    end for;
  end lossy_link_queue;
```

Next we will present rather simple router models, since the queuing has already been taken care of.

15.6.8 Routers

In physical communication networks routers are computers that forward information packets on their way from senders to receivers. Routers usually have a limited queuing and storage capacity, which is used when the rate of packets sent to the router exceeds the maximum transmission rate from the router. In general, a router may have several alternative links to choose from when forwarding packets to their destination. Such choices are usually done dynamically at run time.

However, the packet flows in the special case of our simplified hybrid network model are fixed. This means that there are no dynamic routing decisions made in the routers, which just direct the flows to predetermined target nodes. Internally the routers have equations connecting the incoming packet flows to the correct outgoing link(s).

15.6.8.1 Router21 with One Outgoing and Two Incoming Links

The Router21 router model, depicted in Figure 15-48, performs static routing of two packet flows on two incoming links to one outgoing link, essentially merging the flows.

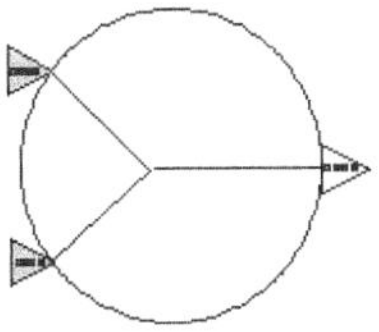

Figure 15-48. Router21 merging two input links to one output link.

The Modelica code for the model class appears below. The equations sum the input packet rates to give the output packet rate o.r. However, other variables such as round-trip time RTT, drop indication d, and bandwidth estimation BWE are just set equal to the output o for both inputs i1 and i2.

```
model Router21  "Two incoming links and one outgoing link"
  parameter Integer n=o.n "number of flows";
  Inport i1 ;
  Inport i2 ;
  Outport o ;
equation
  // RTT and drops must be propagated
  o.r = i1.r + i2.r;
  i1.RTT = o.RTT;         // RTT Round Trip Times
  i2.RTT = o.RTT;
  i1.d = o.d;             // true if dropped packet
  i2.d = o.d;
  i1.BWE = o.BWE;         // BandWidths
  i2.BWE = o.BWE;
end Router21;
```

15.6.8.2 Router12 with One Incoming and Two Outgoing Links

The following router model, depicted in Figure 15-49, performs static routing of two packet flows on one incoming link to two outgoing links, where the packets in flow 1 are directed to output port o1, and the packets in flow 2 are directed to output port o2.

In our simple network model an instance of this router is used to connect the lossy communication link to two receiver nodes.

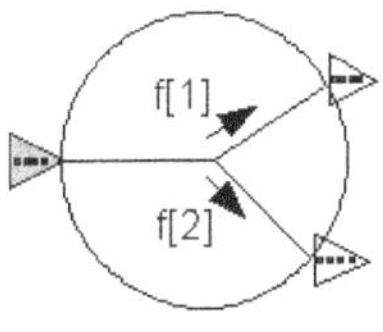

Figure 15-49. Router12 with one incoming and two outgoing links.

The Modelica code for the `Router12` class follows below. Round-trip-time estimates are combined. A packet-drop indication is propagated between one of the outputs and the input. The input bandwidth estimate `i.BWE` is the sum of the bandwidths for the outgoing links.

```
model Router12 "One incoming link and two outgoing links, for 2 flows"
  parameter Integer n=i.n "number of flows";
  Inport  i;
  Outport o1 ;
  Outport o2 ;
equation
  // You must know which flow(s) that should go on which link
  // Implementing that flow 1 should be sent to o1 and flow 2 to o2
  // This router is ok only for 2 flows
  o1.r[1]  = i.r[1];                    // Rates r of flows
  o1.r[2]  = 0;
  o2.r[1]  = 0;
  o2.r[2]  = i.r[2];
  i.RTT    = o1.RTT + o2.RTT;          // RTT Round Trip Times
  i.d      = o1.d or o2.d;             // true if dropped packet
  i.BWE    = o1.BWE + o2.BWE;          // BandWidths
end Router12;
```

15.6.9 Simulation

Below we simulate the `TCPSACKvsTCPWestwood` network model for 25 seconds, with a maximum queue size of `q_max=50`, as specified in the model.

```
simulate(TCPSACKvsTCPWestwood, stopTime=25);
plot({aTCPWestwood.w[1],aTCPSACK.w[2]} )
```

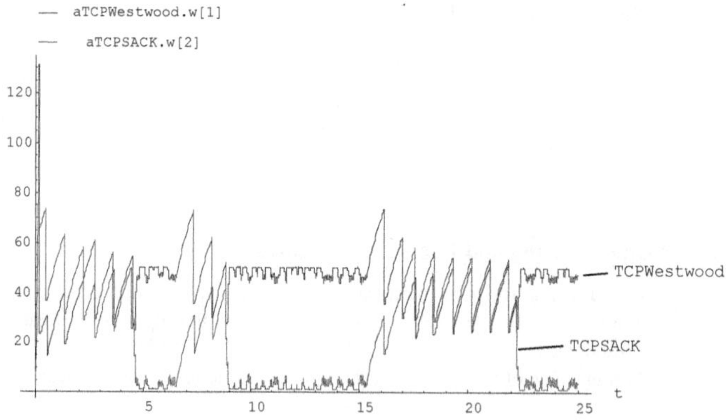

Figure 15-50. TCP SACK versus TCP Westwood communication packet window sizes *w*, related to packet throughput.

Figure 15-50 shows a plot of the simulated packet window size `w` for our small network model, containing a TCP Westwood sender on flow channel 1, and a TCP SACK sender on flow 2.

Both protocol variants show the typical TCP sawtooth shape where the window size is gradually increased until the bandwidth limit is hit and congestion occurs, after which the window size is reduced in half and again increased approximately linearly.

However, during the lossy disturbance phase between time=5 and time=14, as well as between time=17 and time=22, the TCP Westwood protocol grabs the available bandwidth quickly due to its fairly accurate estimate of the available bandwidth. During this phase the TCP SACK protocol performs poorly since it reduces its window estimate too quickly to a very low window size value w=1. After this reduction the window size grows linearly, which during the lossy phase is too slow to get a reasonable increase since there soon will be another disturbance causing the window size to again be reduced.

15.7 Design Optimization

An important use for modeling and simulation is to improve a system design, usually before it is physically realized and manufactured. In this process it is customary to perform a number of simulations for different values of the design parameters, until a design has been obtained that best fulfills a given set of design criteria. To automate this process it is very useful if the simulation environment has programmable scripting facilities that provide the glue between optimization algorithms, executing simulations, and various computational functions. The process of design optimization usually consists of the following steps:

1. Define a parameterized model of the system to be optimized.
2. Define an optimization criterion, usually expressed as a goal function that is minimized.
3. Give values to the design parameters.
4. Perform a simulation of the system for the given set of design parameters.
5. Compute the goal function value based on the results from the simulation.
6. Call the optimization function, which will determine if the minimum value of the goal function has been found. Otherwise the function will compute the next set of design parameter values for getting closer to the optimal set of values, and continue with step 4. Alternatively, first compute the goal function for a number of design parameter values, and call the optimization function to directly find the minimum.

The following example demonstrates the solution of a small but nontrivial design optimization problem containing dynamic system simulations. First we define a Modelica model of a linear actuator with a spring-damped stopping, as well as a first-order system that will be used to generate a kind of "reference" response. The *goal* is to find a damping for the translational spring-damper that minimizes the deviation between the step response of the linear actuator system and the step response from our "reference" first-order system.

In this example, we use the Wolfram SystemModeler environment with Mathematica as the scripting language providing the built-in optimization function `FindMinimum`.

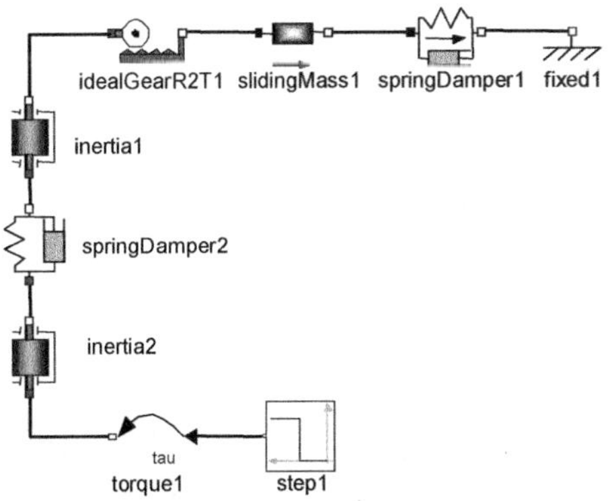

Figure 15-51. A `LinearActuator` model containing a spring-damped connection to an anchoring point.

Consider the following model of a linear actuator, depicted in Figure 15-51, with a spring-damped connection to an anchoring point:

```
model LinearActuator
  import Modelica.Mechanics.Translational;
  import Modelica.Mechanics.Rotational;
  import Modelica.Blocks.Sources;
  Translational.Components.Mass            slidingMass1(m=0.5);
  Translational.Components.SpringDamper springDamper1(d=3, c=20);
  Translational.Components.Fixed           fixed1;
  Rotational.Components.IdealGearR2T       idealGearR2T1;
  Rotational.Components.Inertia            inertia1(J=0.1);
  Rotational.Components.SpringDamper       springDamper2(c=15, d=2);
  Rotational.Components.Inertia            inertia2(J=0.1);
  Rotational.Sources.Torque                torque1;
  Sources.Step step1;
equation
  connect(step1.y,                  torque1.tau);
  connect(idealGearR2T1.flangeT,    slidingMass1.flange_a);
  connect(springDamper2.flange_b,   inertia2.flange_a);
  connect(torque1.flange,           inertia1.flange_a);
  connect(slidingMass1.flange_b,    springDamper1.flange_a);
  connect(springDamper1.flange_b,   fixed1.flange);
  connect(inertia1.flange_b,        springDamper2.flange_a);
  connect(inertia2.flange_b,        idealGearR2T1.flangeR);
end LinearActuator;
```

We first make a simulation of the step response (Figure 15-52) for the above linear actuator with damping `d=2`, and store the result in the scripting language variable called `resLinActFirst`, using the Mathematica command interface to Wolfram SystemModeler, with results as interpolation functions (Section 19.4.5.1, page 1054). Then the simulated position of the sliding mass is plotted as a function of time to have a closer look at the response. However, before running these commands you need to load the model into Wolfram SystemModeler.

```
Needs["WSMLink`"];                    (* Note: first load the model into WSM *)
WSMModelCenter["optionalmodelname"]      Can be done in GUI or using this *)

resLinActFirst = WSMSimulate["LinearActuator", {0,5}]
WSMPlot[resLinActFirst, {"slidingMass1.s"}, PlotRange -> All]
```

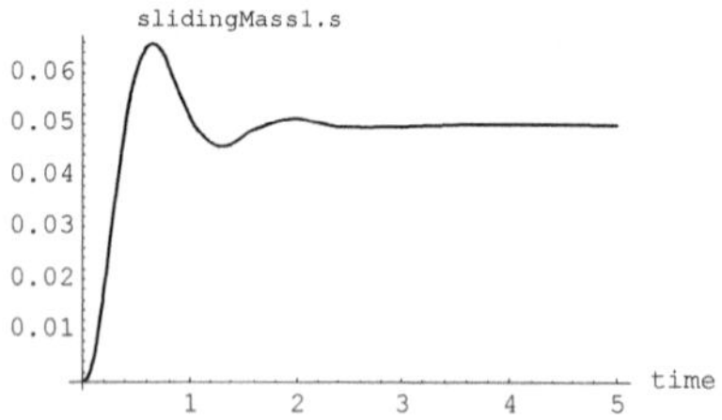

Figure 15-52. Plot of step response from the linear actuator.

Assume that we have some freedom in choosing the damping in the translational spring-damper. A number of simulation runs show what kind of behavior we have for different values of the damping parameter `d`. Using the Mathematica command interface to Wolfram SystemModeler (Section E.3, page 1143), the Mathematica `Table[]` function is used to collect the results from calls to `Simulate[]` into an array res. This array then contains the results from simulations of LinearActuator with a damping of 2 to 14 in increments of 2; i.e., seven simulations are performed (Figure 15-53).

```
res = Table[WSMSimulate["LinearActuator", {0,4},
        WSMParameterValues ->{"springDamper1.d" -> s}], {s,2,14,2}]

WSMPlot[res, "slidingMass1.s", {0, 4}, PlotRange -> All, Legend -> False]
```

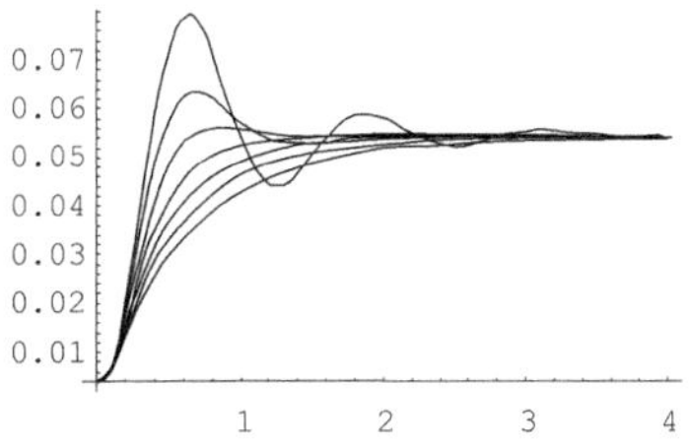

Figure 15-53. Plots of step responses from seven simulations of the linear actuator with different damping coefficients.

Now assume that we would like to choose the damping parameter d so that the resulting linear actuator system behaves as closely as possible to the following "reference" first-order system response, obtained by solving a first-order ODE using the Mathematica differential equation solver NDSolve:

```
resReference = NDSolve[{0.2*y'[t]+y[t] == 0.05, y[0] == 0}, {y}, {t,0,4}]
```

We make a plot to compare the step response we simulated first for a damping value d=2 and the response from the "reference" first-order system (Figure 15-54).

```
Show[Plot[y[t] /. resReference, {t, 0, 4}, PlotRange -> All,
  PlotStyle -> {Red, Dashed, Thick}],
  WSMPlot[resLinActFirst, {"slidingMass1.s"}, PlotRange -> All]]
```

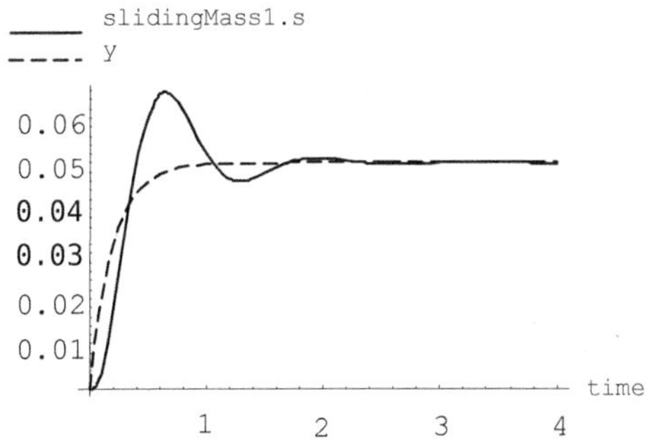

Figure 15-54. Comparison plot between the step response of the linear actuator and the "reference" first-order system.

Now, let us make things a little more automatic. Simulate and compute the integral of the square deviation from t=0 to t=4. This integral is a measure of the deviation from the "reference" response, and is thus suitable as a goal function to be minimized. The expression (y[t] /. resReference) retrieves the interpolating function representing the variable y[t], i.e., the reference response.

```
resLinAct2nd = WSMSimulate["LinearActuator", {0,4},
```

```
  WSMParameterValues -> {"springDamper1.d" -> 3}];
{slidingMass1s} = resLinAct2nd[{"slidingMass1.s"}];
NIntegrate[(First[(y[t] /. resReference)] - slidingMass1s[t])^2, {t, 0, 4}]
```

```
0.000162505
```

We define a Mathematica function, `f[a]`, doing the same thing as above, but for different values of the spring-damper design parameter `d`. The function contains three local variables `res`, `t`, and `localSlidingMass1s`.

```
f[a_] := Module[{res, t, localSlidingMass1s},
       res = WSMSimulate["LinearActuator", {0, 4},
          WSMParameterValues -> {"springDamper1.d" -> a}];
       {localSlidingMass1s} = res[{"slidingMass1.s"}];
       NIntegrate[(First[(y[t] /. resReference)] - localSlidingMass1s[t])^2,
           {t, 0, 4}]
         ]
```

We tabulate some results for $2 \leq d \leq 10$ into an array `resDeviations`:

```
resDeviations = Table[{d, f[d]}, {d, 2, 10, 0.5}]
```

```
{{2,0.000317667},
{2.5,0.000221484}, {3.,0.000162505},{3.5,0.000125513}, {4.,0.000102749},
{4.5,0.0000898832}, {5.,0.000084067}, {5.5,0.0000836711}, {6.,0.0000874586},
{6.5,0.0000945743}, {7.,0.000104399}, {7.5,0.000116464}, {8.,0.000130394},
{8.5,0.000145922}, {9.,0.000162819}, {9.5,0.000180894}, {10.,0.000200008}}
```

The tabulated values are interpolated into a Mathematica interpolating function (Figure 15-55). The default interpolation order is 3.

```
fpre = Interpolation[resDeviations];
Plot[fpre[d], {d, 2, 10}]
```

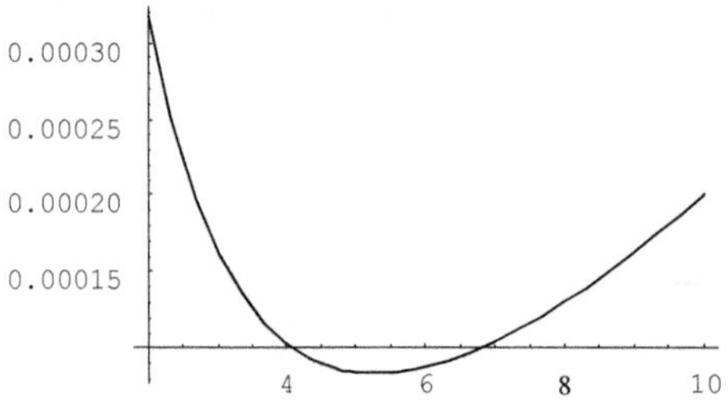

Figure 15-55. Plot of the deviation function for finding the value of the damping parameter that gives a minimum deviation from the reference response.

The minimizing value of `d` can be computed using `FindMinimum`:

```
FindMinimum[fpre[d], {d, 4}]
```

```
{0.0000832564180689619 5, {s -> 5.286423245854051}}
```

A simulation with the optimal parameter value:

```
resLinActOpt = WSMSimulate["LinearActuator", {0, 4},
  WSMParameterValues -> {"springDamper1.d" -> 5.28642}];
```

```
{slidingMass1s} = resLinActOpt[{"slidingMass1.s"}]
```

A plot comparing the "reference" first-order system and linear actuator system responses together with a plot of the squared deviation amplified by a factor 100 is given in Figure 15-56.

```
Plot[{ slidingMass1s[t],
       y[t] /. resReference,
       100*(slidingMass1s[t] - (y[t] /. resReference))^2
     },
       {t, 0, 4}, PlotRange->All, Legend->False]
```

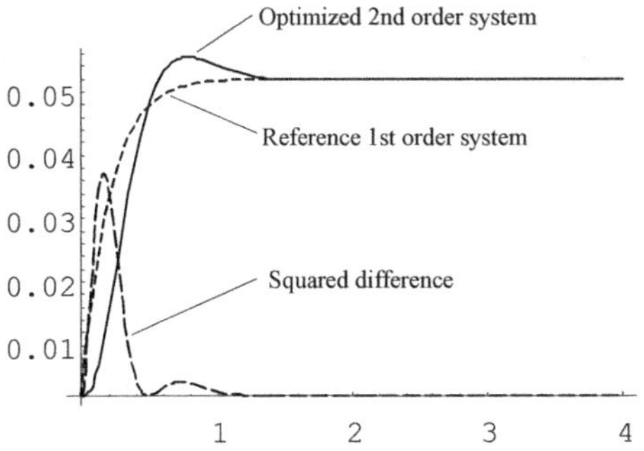

Figure 15-56. Comparison plot of the first- and second-order system step responses together with the squared error.

15.8 Fourier Analysis of Simulation Data

A simulation of a system may indicate the presence of periodic phenomena such as vibrations. Fourier analysis on the simulation results transforms the data from the time domain into the frequency domain, which makes frequency-dependent characteristics very explicit. For example, the main modes of oscillation become visible as peaks in a plot, for example, as in Figure 15-58 below.

For example, consider a weak axis (a nonrigid flexible axis containing springs) excited by a torque pulse train. The axis is modeled by three segments joined by two torsion springs, depicted in Figure 15-57.

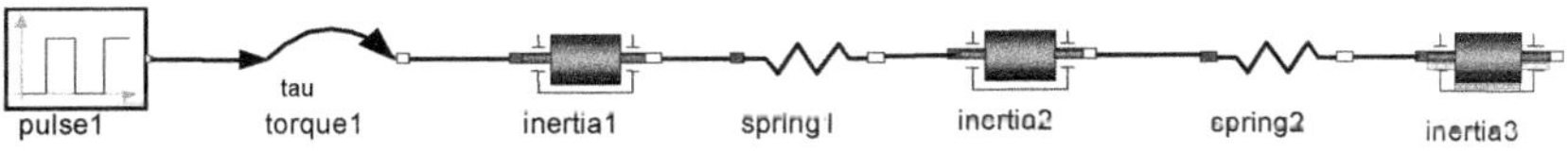

Figure 15-57. A `WeakAxis` model excited by a torque pulse train.

The corresponding Modelica code:

```
model WeakAxis
  import Modelica.Mechanics.Rotational.Components;
  import Modelica.Blocks.Sources;
  Components.Inertia  inertia1;
  Components.Spring   spring1(c=0.7);
  Components.Inertia  inertia2;
  Components.Spring   spring2(c=1);
  Components.Inertia  inertia3;
  Modelica.Mechanics.Rotational.Sources.Torque torque1;
  Sources.Pulse       pulse1(width=1, period=200);
equation
  connect(pulse1.y,            torque1.tau);
```

```
    connect(torque1.flange,     inertia1.flange_a);
    connect(inertia1.flange_b, spring1.flange_a);
    connect(spring1.flange_b,   inertia2.flange_a);
    connect(inertia2.flange_b, spring2.flange_a);
    connect(spring2.flange_b,   inertia3.flange_a);
  end WeakAxis;
```

We simulate the model during 200 seconds:

```
Needs["WSMLink`"];  (* Note: first load the model into WSM *)

resWeakAxis = WSMSimulate["WeakAxis", {0,200}];
{inertia3w} = resWeakAxis[{"inertia3.w"}];
```

The plot of the angular velocity of the rightmost axis segment appears as in Figure 15-58, indicating the presence of oscillation frequencies in the result.

```
WSMPlot[resWeakAxis, "inertia3.w", {0, 200}]
WSMPlot[resWeakAxis, "torque1.tau", {0, 200}]
```

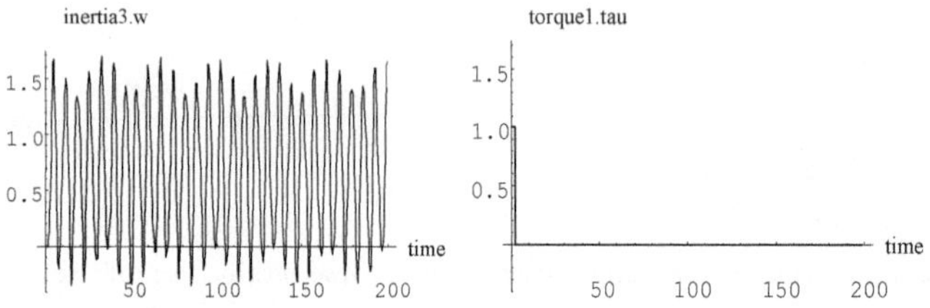

Figure 15-58. Plot of the angular velocity of the rightmost axis segment of the `WeakAxis` model.

Now, let us sample the interpolated function (Section 19.4.5.1, page 1054) `Inertia3w` using a sample frequency of 4Hz, and put the result into an array using the Mathematica `Table` array constructor:

```
data1 = Table[inertia3w[t], {t, 0, 200, 0.25}]
```

Compute the absolute values of the discrete Fourier transform of `data1` with the mean removed:

```
fdata1 = Abs[Fourier[data1 - MeanValue[data1]]]
```

Plot the first 80 points of the data (Figure 15-59).

```
ListPlot[fdata1[[Range[80]]], PlotStyle -> {Red, PointSize[0.015]}];
```

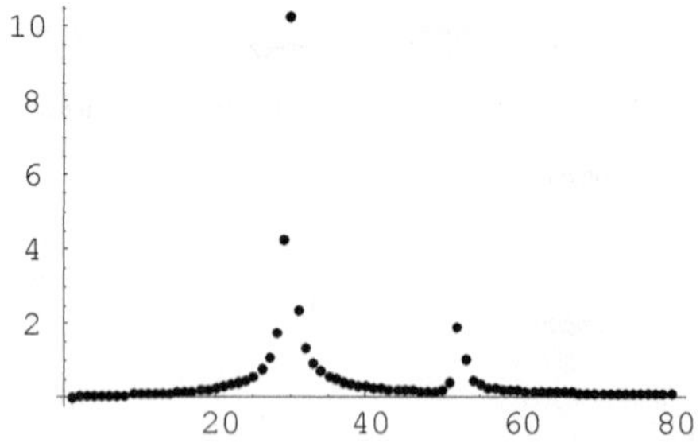

Figure 15-59. Plot of the data points of the Fourier-transformed angular velocity.

A simple Mathematica function `FourierPlot` can be written that repeats the above operations. `FourierPlot` also scales the axes such that amplitude of trigonometric components are plotted against frequency (Hz) (Figure 15-60).

```
FourierPlot[inertia3w[t], {t, 0, 200}, 0.5,
            PlotJoined -> True, PlotStyle -> Red]
```

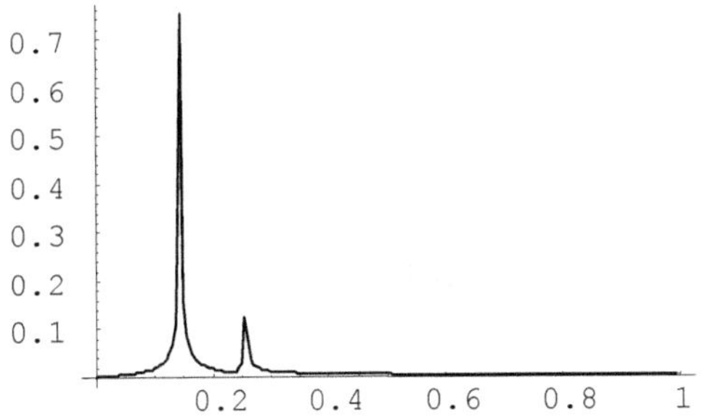

Figure 15-60. Plot of the data points of the Fourier-transformed angular velocity.

15.9 Pressure Dynamics in 1D Ducts—Solving Wave Equations by Discretized PDEs

Currently, Modelica cannot handle partial differential equations (however, language extensions are on the way—see Section 8.10, page 400) directly since there is only the notion of differentiation with respect to time built into the language. However, in many cases derivatives with respect to other variables (such as, for example, spatial dimensions) can be handled by simple discretization schemes represented using the array capabilities in Modelica. Here we will give an example of how the one-dimensional wave equation can be represented in Modelica and how Mathematica and Wolfram SystemModeler can be used for simulation and display of the results, as well as representing the result as a 2D interpolating function.

The one-dimensional wave equation is given by a partial differential equation of the following form:

$$\frac{\partial^2 p}{\partial t^2} = c^2 \frac{\partial^2 p}{\partial x^2} \tag{15-66}$$

where $p = p(x,t)$ is a function of both space and time. As a physical example let us consider a duct of length 10 where we let $-5 \leq x \leq 5$ describe its spatial dimension. Since Modelica can handle time only as the independent variable, we need to discretize the problem in the spatial dimension and approximate the spatial derivatives using difference approximations using the approximation:

$$\frac{\partial^2 p}{\partial t^2} \approx \frac{p_{i-1} + p_{i+1} - 2p_i}{\Delta x^2} \tag{15 67}$$

where $p_i = p(x_1 + (i\text{-}1) \times \Delta x)$ on an equidistant grid. Utilizing this approach a Modelica model of a duct whose pressure dynamics is given by the wave equation can be written as follows, where the pressure function p to be computed is represented as a one-dimensional array `p` of size `n`, where the array index is the discretized space coordinate along the x-coordinate, and the time dependence is implicit as usual for a continuous-time Modelica variable:

```
model WaveEquationSample
  import Modelica.SIunits;
  parameter SIunits.Length   L=10 "Length of duct";
  parameter Integer          n=30 "Number of sections";
  parameter SIunits.Length   dL=L/n "Section length";
  parameter SIunits.Velocity c=1;
  SIunits.Pressure[n]  p(start=initialPressure(n));
```

```
  Real[n]                  dp(start=fill(0,n));
equation
  p[1]=exp(-(-L/2)^2);
  p[n]=exp(-(L/2)^2);
  dp=der(p);
  for i in 2:n-1 loop
    der(dp[i]) = c^2*(p[i+1]-2*p[i]+p[i-1])/dL^2;
  end for;
end WaveEquationSample;
```

Here we are using a Modelica function `initialPressure` (defined further below) to specify the initial value of the pressure along the duct. Assume that we would like an initial pressure profile in the duct of the form e^{-x^2}, depicted in Figure 15-61 by the following plot command:

```
Plot[e^(-x^2), {x, -5, 5}];
```

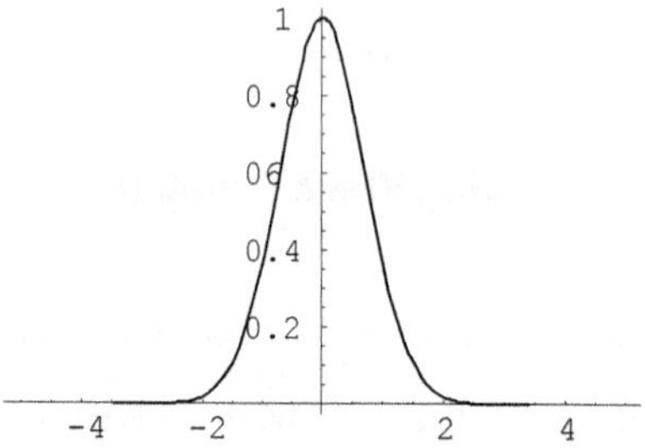

Figure 15-61. The initial pressure profile of the duct.

The function `initialPressure` returns the initial pressure profile function in discretized form as an array.

```
function initialPressure
  input Integer n;
  output Real p[n];
protected
  parameter Modelica.SIunits.Length L=10;
algorithm
  for i in 1:n loop
    p[i]:=exp(-(-L/2+(i-1)/(n-1)*L)^2);
  end for;
end initialPressure;
```

We simulate the `WaveEquationSample` model:

```
resWave = WSMSimulate["WaveEquationSample", {0, 10}]
```

The simulation result, i.e., the array p, shows how the pressure evolves at equidistant positions in the duct as functions of time. This is represented by the array p of 1D interpolation functions of time, which has to be retrieved by specifying each array element since Wolfram SystemModeler currently does not support direct retrieval of arrays. The array p elements are packed into a Mathematica 2D interpolation function (Section 19.4.5.1, page 1054) and plotted using the following two commands (Figure 15-62):

```
p = resWave[{"p[1]","p[2]","p[3]","p[4]","p[5]","p[6]","p[7]","p[8]","p[9]",
"p[10]","p[11]","p[12]","p[13]","p[14]","p[15]","p[16]","p[17]","p[18]",
"p[19]","p[20]","p[21]","p[22]","p[23]","p[24]","p[25]","p[26]","p[27]",
"p[28]","p[29]","p[30]"}];

intp = Interpolation[Flatten[Table[{-5. + ((k - 1)/29)*10, t, p[[k]][t]},
                     {k, 1, 30}, {t, 0, 10, 0.2}], 1]];
```

```
Plot3D[intp[x,t],{x,-5,5},{t,0,10}, PlotPoints->30, PlotRange->{-1,1},
       AxesLabel->{"x","t","p(x,t)"}]
```

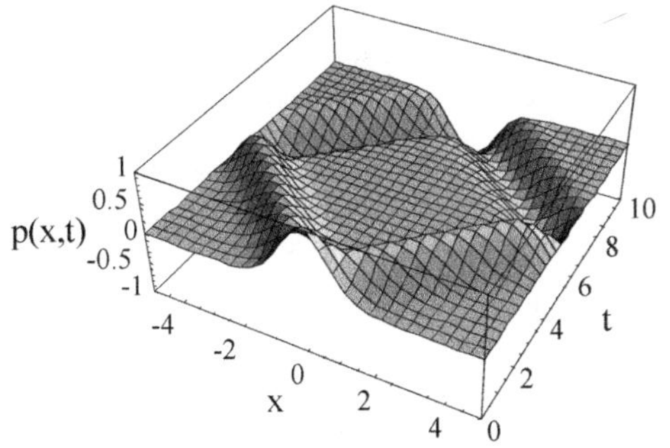

Figure 15-62. A 3D plot of the pressure distribution in the duct.

Let us also plot the wave as a function of position x for a fixed point in time (t=1.2) to observe the pressure distribution in more detail (Figure 15-63):

```
Plot[intp[x,1.2], {x, -5, 5}];
```

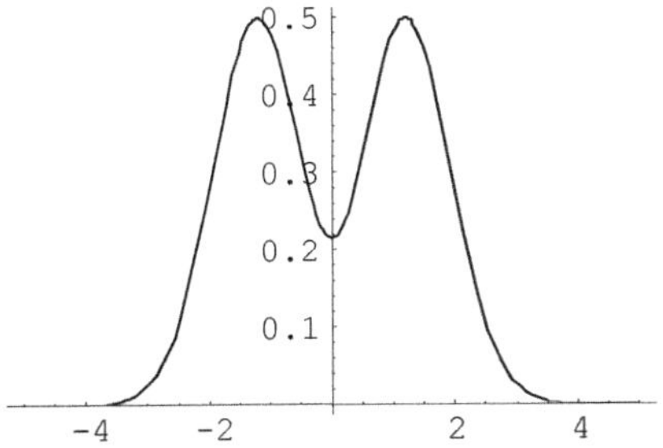

Figure 15-63. The wave as a function of position at `time=1.2`.

15.10 Mechanical Multibody Systems and the MBS Library

A mechanical multibody system can be defined as a system consisting of a number of interacting mechanical bodies or substructures. Previously (Section 14.8, page 770) we gave an introduction to the topic of multibody systems for rigid (nonflexible) bodies, explained the basic concepts, and presented the basic equations including Newton's laws in a form that is used by the *Modelica multibody system* (MBS) library.

The goal of this section is to give a short introduction on how to *use* the Modelica MBS library to model 3D mechanical applications, as well as presenting a short overview of the library itself.

The main goal of the Modelica MBS library is to simplify modeling and dynamic analysis of mechanical systems including mechanical subsystems that are part of larger multidomain systems. Given an idealized model of a mechanical multibody system and external forces influencing this system, a Modelica simulation can compute the position and orientation of each body as a function of time. The most typical use of such a model is to analyze the movements of bodies resulting from the application of certain forces and torques, as well as influences from other changes in the environment. The forces and torques can have different origins: these can be produced by drive trains, electrical motors, controlling devices, and so on, or from a combination of such elements.

Newton's laws are expressed in the MBS library class `MultiBody.Parts.Body`, which also is used in other models. Equations of motion and coordinate transformations are formulated in the library, both for free bodies and for connected bodies related by some constraints. Each body has one or more local *coordinate systems*, also denoted *frames of reference*, or just *frames*. Coordinate transformations are used to relate quantities expressed in these frames. The library works with rigid bodies that have some geometric extent, that is, have not been simplified to point masses. The rotation of bodies relative to the inertial coordinate system is taken into account, being represented by quantities such as angular velocity and angular acceleration vectors.

The MBS library described here is the most comprehensive Modelica multibody system library for three-dimensional mechanical rigid bodies. It has a unique technical feature compared to other MBS libraries in its very efficient treatment of joint locking and unlocking. This allows, for example, easy and efficient modeling of friction elements or brakes in joints. Another rather unique feature is to allow connection of all kinds of object in physically meaningful ways, including designs consisting only of force elements such as springs. The major area that the MBS library currently does not handle is multibody systems consisting of *general* flexible bodies, that is, bodies that may undergo deformations. However, extensions in this direction are available in the FlexibleBodies library.

15.10.1 New and Old Version of the MBS Library

A current version of the Modelica MBS library (`Modelica.Mechanics.Multibody`) was initially released Nov 2003 when it was added to MSL, and has since then been maintained and extended. This library has a number of advantages compared to the old version (before 2003) of the MBS library `ModelicaAdditions.Multibody`. However, the old version of the library is still used by some applications and mentioned in a number of published papers—therefore we will also briefly describe some properties of the old library in this overview, even though we primarily present the *current* library. The current library has the following advantages compared to the old one:

- The current library is much easier to use—all physically meaningful connections between library components are supported, even including direct connections between pure force elements. The old library has several restrictions on how to connect different kinds of objects, which makes it harder to use.
- The current library has automatic removal of superfluous equations resulting from so-called kinematic loop connection structures (except for planar kinematic loops, see Section 15.10.8, page 894)—in the old library kinematic loops have to be broken manually by inserting so-called cutjoints, which can be tricky.
- Built-in animation properties are available for all components, such as joints, forces, bodies, sensors. Animation can easily be turned on or off. The old library has less convenient and less comprehensive support for animation.
- A number of other improvements are available in the current library such as better documentation, structuring, and understandability including a set of vector and matrix expression functions (in `MultiBody.Frames`) that are inlined in equations, definitions of inverse models, initialization via menus, better help messages, automatic selection of states from both joints and bodies, analytic solution of many kinematic loops, force components may be connected directly together, and so on.

If not explicitly stated otherwise, the following description applies to current MBS library, even though a number of general properties also hold for the old MBS library.

15.10.2 Connecting Force Elements—a Triple Springs Model

This example demonstrates that three-dimensional line force elements (e.g., `MultiBody.Forces.Spring` instances) can be connected together in series and in parallel without having a body with mass at the connection point, which would be required by the old MBS library and by most multi-body simulation programs. Besides the modeling inconvenience, a small mass between the springs would have the disadvantage of causing the resulting equation system to become stiff (see Section 18.2.1.5, page 1001). The connection structure and 3D view of the model are shown in Figure 15-64.

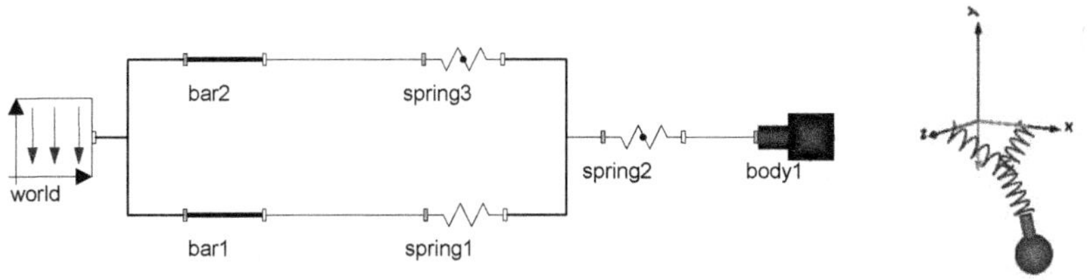

Figure 15-64. Connection diagram (left) and 3D animation view (right) of the `TripleSprings` model with three springs directly connected in series and in parallel.

The `TripleSprings` model, (essentially `MultiBody.Examples.Elementary.ThreeSprings`) appears below with an animation parameter. If the animation attributes are not specified, bodies and bars are animated by default, but not springs. If `animation=false` for the model, there will be no animation at all.

```
encapsulated model TripleSprings "3-dim. springs in series and parallel"
  import Modelica.Mechanics.MultiBody.Parts;
  import Modelica.Mechanics.MultiBody.Forces;
  parameter Boolean animation=true "= true, if animation shall be enabled";
  inner Modelica.Mechanics.MultiBody.World  world(animateWorld=animation);
  Parts.Body                body1(animation=animation,
                                  r_CM={0,-0.2,0}, r_0_start={0.5,-0.3,0},
                                  m=0.8, I_11=0.1, I_22=0.1, I_33=0.1,
                                  startValuesFixed=true, useQuaternions=false,
                                  sphereDiameter=0.2);
  Parts.FixedTranslation    bar1(animation=animation, r={0.3,0,0});
  Parts.FixedTranslation    bar2(animation=animation, r={0,0,0.3});
  Forces.Spring             spring1(s_unstretched=0.1, width=0.1,
                                    coilWidth=0.005, numberOfWindings=5,
                                    c=20, animation=animation);
  Forces.Spring             spring2(s_unstretched=0.1, width=0.1,
                                    coilWidth=0.005, numberOfWindings=5,
                                    c=40, animation=animation);
  Forces.Spring             spring3(s_unstretched=0.1, width=0.1,
                                    coilWidth=0.005, numberOfWindings=5,
                                    c=20, animation=animation);
equation
  connect(world.frame_b,    bar1.frame_a);
  connect(world.frame_b,    bar2.frame_a);
  connect(bar1.frame_b,     spring1.frame_a);
  connect(bar2.frame_b,     spring3.frame_a);
  connect(spring2.frame_b, body1.frame_a);
  connect(spring3.frame_b, spring1.frame_b);
  connect(spring2.frame_a, spring1.frame_b);
end TripleSprings;
```

15.10.3 Main MBS Object Classes

The main *parts* of a multibody system model expressed using the MBS library are primarily constructed from the following three kinds of objects:

- *Frames*—frames of reference, that is, *coordinate systems*. One or more frames are attached to specific points at each body, depending on its geometry. The *inertial system* or *world* object, an instance of the `MultiBody.World` model, is a special global frame of reference which always has to be present in a model. All other frames must be able to relate to this frame through a sequence of coordinate transformations. Frames are described in more detail in Section 14.8.1, page 771, and in Section 15.10.5.1, page 884.
- *Bodies*—rigid bodies with mass and inertia. Each body has one or more *frames* attached at certain points.
- *Joints*—mechanical connections between pairs of bodies including constraints for the relative movements of the two bodies connected via a joint.

All objects in the current MBS library have geometry and color attributes needed for visualization and animation.

Certain types of bodies may have more than one frame attachment point where additional elements can be connected. Such rigid bodies need to be constructed by rigidly connecting a basic body to additional frames via instances of fixed-frame coordinate transformation classes such as `FrameTranslation`, `FrameRotation`, and so on.

The local frames of a body *must* be related to the world object (inertial coordinate system) through the Modelica implicit force-field inner/outer connection mechanism (in the old library through explicit connections via joints). In this way, coordinate system transformations between the current frame and the inertial system are automatically obtained, and the *gravity acceleration* defined in the inertial system is automatically propagated to the body. The basic state variables (sometimes called generalized coordinates) are defined in either bodies or joints.

Additionally, there are two kinds of objects of somewhat less importance that can be attached to a multibody system model:

- *Forces*—these classes are modeling 3-D vector versions of external force objects such as springs, torsion springs, dampers, etc., that can be connected to bodies and joints.
- *Sensors*—these classes are sometimes useful to compute and observe certain variables that may not be directly available in the model classes.

The different kinds of model classes are packaged into the sublibraries to be presented in the next section. Before going into more detail about the structure of the MBS library it can be instructive to take a look at a very simple example: the `FreeFlyingBody` model.

15.10.4 A Simple Free-Flying Body Model

A free-flying body model is one of the simplest models possible to construct using the MBS library. It is useful to construct this kind of simple model in the MBS library for reasons of comparison with the simple point mass model we described in Section 5.8.3, page 228. Still, this is substantially more complicated than Newton's equations for a point mass in a gravity field, since the rotation of the body need to be taken into account. The connection structure of the model is depicted in Figure 15-65.

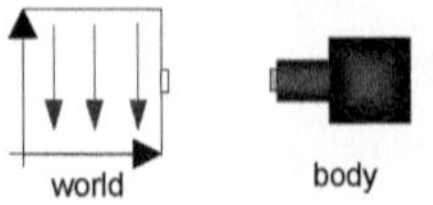

Figure 15-65. Connection diagram for the free-flying body model using the MBS library.

The model, expressed using the current MBS library, needs only two objects: the free-flying *body* itself, and the *world* object or *inertial system* that must be present in all models. The Modelica inner/outer implicit connection mechanism for force fields relates the body with its coordinates to the world coordinate system, which also enables the gravity force to act on the body. The gravity force is obtained by multiplying the body mass with the gravity acceleration defined in the world instance.

```
model FreeFlyingBody
   import Modelica.Mechanics.MultiBody.Parts;
   inner Modelica.Mechanics.MultiBody.World world;
   Parts.Body body(v_0_start={0,5,0});
end FreeFlyingBody;
```

We also show the same model in the old version of the MBS library for comparison (Figure 15-66).

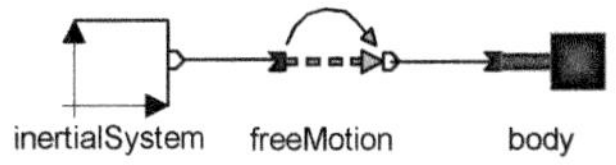

Figure 15-66. Connection diagram for the free-flying body model using the old Modelica 2.2 `Modelica.Additions` MBS library.

That model needs three objects: the free-flying body itself, the inertial system, and a `MultiBody.Joints.FreeMotion` "*joint*" that relates the body coordinates to the inertial system, and enables the gravity force defined in the inertial system instance to act on the body. This joint in the old library is quite strange since it does not impose any movement constraints on the body. However, it is still needed for the above-mentioned reason.

```
model FreeFlyingBody    "Version using the old MBS library"
  import ModelicaAdditions.MultiBody.Parts.*;
  import ModelicaAdditions.MultiBody.Joints.*;
  InertialSystem     inertialSystem;
  FreeMotion         freeMotion(v_rela(start={0,5,0}));
  Body               body(m=1);
equation
  connect(inertialSystem.frame_b, freeMotion.frame_a);
  connect(freeMotion.frame_b,      body.frame_a);
end FreeFlyingBody;
```

A simulation of the `FreeFlyingBody` model computes the altitude above ground as a function of time, as shown in Figure 15-67.

```
simulate(FreeFlyingBody, stopTime=1);
plot(body.r_0[2]);
```

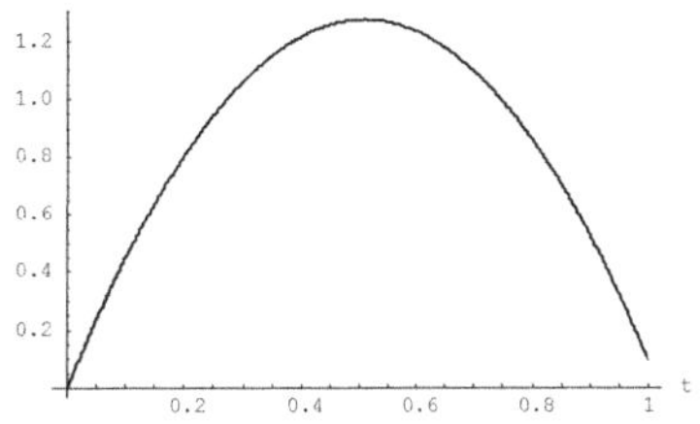

Figure 15-67. Altitude above ground for a free-flying body modeled and simulated using the MBS library.

15.10.4.1 Free-flying Body in Point Gravity

It is easy to construct a model of one or more non-interacting free-flying bodies in a point gravity field, by setting `gravityType=GravityTypes.PointGravity` for the `world` object. The connection structure of such a model with two bodies is depicted in Figure 15-68.

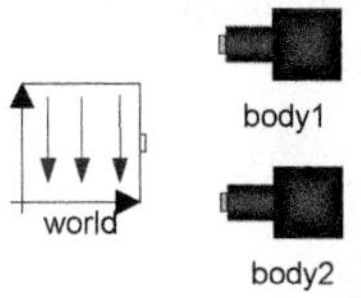

Figure 15-68. Connection diagram for two free-flying bodies in the `PointGravity` model.

The model needs only three objects: the two free-flying *bodies* and the *world* object (the global *inertial system*):

```
model PointGravity
   import Modelica.Mechanics.MultiBody.Parts;
   inner Modelica.Mechanics.MultiBody.World world(gravityType=2,mue=1,
                                             gravitySphereDiameter=0.1);
   Parts.Body  body1(m=1,r_0_start={0,0.6,0},
     v_0_start={1,0,0},sphereDiameter=0.1,I_11=0.1,I_22=0.1,I_33=0.1);
   Parts.Body  body2(m=1,r_0_start={0.6,0.6,0},
     v_0_start={0.6,0,0},sphereDiameter=0.1,I_11=0.1,I_22=0.1,I_33=0.1);
end PointGravity;
```

A simulation of the `PointGravity` model with default animation enabled for the two bodies is shown in Figure 15-69.

```
simulate(PointGravity, stopTime=4); animate(PointGravity);
```

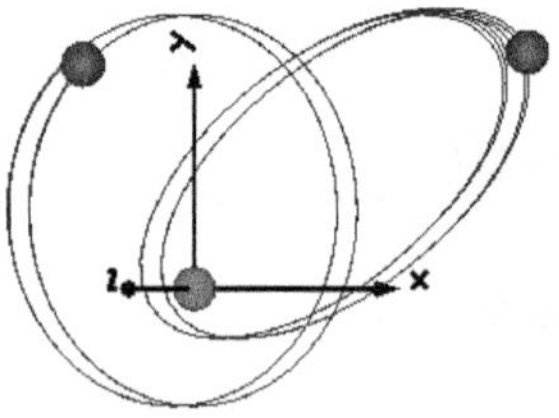

Figure 15-69. Animation of the `PointGravity` model with two bodies in a point gravity field using the MBS library.

15.10.5 Structure of the MBS Library

The classes in the MBS library are grouped into several *sublibraries* or *packages*, from which components can be picked when designing an MBS application model, as depicted in Figure 15-70.

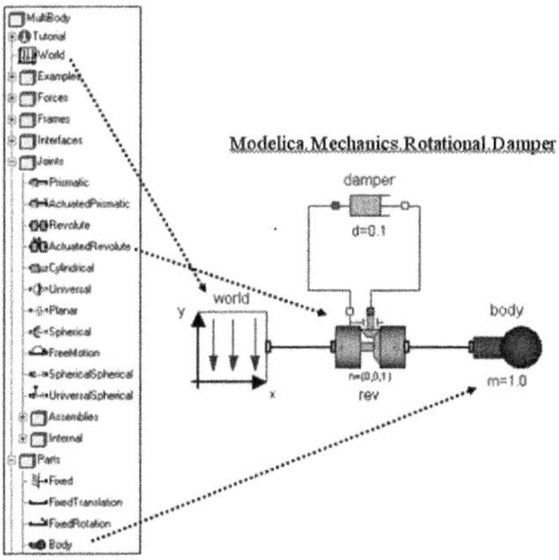

Figure 15-70. Picking objects from the MBS sublibraries for use in an application model.

The MBS library is structured into the following sublibraries:

- `MultiBody.World`—this is a single class, not a package, defining the global inertial system model. Exactly one instance of `World` is necessary in each MBS application model to be simulated.
- `MultiBody.Examples`—a set of examples on how to use the MBS library.
- `MultiBody.Forces`—these are classes modeling 3D force elements such as springs and dampers.
- `MultiBody.Frames`—contains type definitions (e.g., orientation object types) and functions (inlined) to transform rotational frame quantities.
- `MultiBody.Interfaces`—this subpackage contains classes (`Frame`, `Frame_a`, `Frame_b`) for coordinate system *frames*, as well as partial base classes used by the other MBS sublibraries.
- `MultiBody.Joints`—classes describing *joints* connecting two mechanical parts. Different kinds of joints have different constraints on the relative movements of the two connected parts. Also includes the subpackage `MultiBody.Joints.Assemblies`, which contains aggregated joint components for analytic solution of kinematic loops, and `MultiBody.Joints.Internal`, which has components used internally for analytic solution of kinematic loops, and which should not be directly referred to by the user.
- `MultiBody.Parts`—this subpackage primarily contains classes for defining rigid *bodies* which have mass and inertia. The package also contains massless *fixed-frame transformation* classes.
- `MultiBody.Sensors`—this subpackage contains classes for computing relative kinematic quantities between pairs of frames on bodies or joints.
- `MultiBody.Types`—definitions of types and constants that are used in the `MultiBody` library. The types have additional annotation choices definitions that define the menus to be built up in the graphical user interface when the type is used as parameter in a declaration.
- `MultiBody.Visualizers`—the classes in this subpackage support animation of shape objects that can be connected to frame connectors.
- `MultiBody.Icons`—icons for the `MultiBody` package.

Moreover, classes from the following Modelica packages are often used together with the MBS library when modeling MBS applications:

- `Modelica.Mechanical.Rotational.Interfaces`
- `Modelica.Mechanical.Translational.Interfaces`
- `Modelica.Blocks.Interfaces`

The subsequent sections contain a more detailed overview that covers the most important classes of the MBS library. Most mechanical system models can be constructed from these. Several other classes are variations and optimized combinations of the basic classes. At this stage, the reader who is more interested in application examples may skip to Section 15.10.7, page 891, and if needed go back to this section later.

15.10.5.1 MultiBody.Interfaces

This sublibrary contains connector classes and base classes of the MBS library. Most of the base classes are superclasses of models defined in the other sublibraries, and are therefore not used directly by the modeler. In the old MBS library some of the base classes contain basic formulations of Newton's laws, previously described in Section 14.8.5.4, page 783. In the current MBS library these laws are instead stated in `MultiBody.Parts.Body`. The most important connector classes in `MultiBody.Interfaces` are `Frame_a` and `Frame_b`, which describe coordinate systems, i.e., frames of reference.

- Frame connector classes: `Frame`, `Frame_a`, `Frame_b`, and `Frame_resolve`

Each instance of `Frame` (or `Frame_a` or `Frame_b`, which are identical to `Frame`) describes a local coordinate system object. Instances of `Frame_a` are in the following often called frame *a*, and in Modelica code denoted by `frame_a`. Instances of `Frame_b` are denoted `frame_b`. The cut-force `f` (connector force applied at the connector) and cut-torque `t` (connector torque) vectors are resolved relative to the local coordinate system instance, for example, `frame_a`, whereas `r_0` is resolved relative to the global inertial system (the `world` frame). The Modelica code of the `Frame` class appears as follows:

```
connector Frame   "Frame of a mechanical system"
  import SI = Modelica.SIunits;
  SI.Position          r_0[3] "Position vector from world frame to the connector
                               frame origin, resolved in world frame";
  Frames.Orientation R        "Orientation object to rotate the world frame
                               into the connector frame";
  flow SI.Force          f[3] "Cut-force resolved in connector frame";
  flow SI.Torque         t[3] "Cut-torque resolved in connector frame";
end Frame;
```

The cut-force (connector force) and cut-torque (connector torque) are applied at the connector position. As apparent from the above definition, `Frame` contains the following potential variables:

- The vector `r_0[3]` from the inertial frame to the origin of the local connector frame.
- The orientation object `R` (a rotation matrix `R[3,3]` computed from Euler/Cardan angles, see Section 14.8.4.2, page 776, or from quaternions, see Section 14.8.4.3, page 777) for rotating the inertial frame to the same orientation as the local connector frame. All orientation objects are instances of `MultiBody.Frames.Orientation`, see Section 15.10.5.2 below.

The rotation matrix can be used for transformation of vectors between frames:

- To map a vector **v** expressed in the local connector frame to the global inertial frame, we need to apply the inverse $\mathbf{R}^{-1} = \mathbf{R}^{T}$, i.e., $\mathbf{R}^{T}\mathbf{v}$ expressed in the global inertial frame. This is the same as calling `resolve1(R,v)`, transforming from frame 2 (the local frame) to frame 1 (the global inertial frame). `R` is often available in the local frame (`frame_a.R`). See also Section 15.10.5.2.
- To map a vector **x** from the inertial frame to the local frame, apply **R**, i.e. $\mathbf{Rx}$. This is the same as calling `resolve2(R,w)`, transforming from frame 1 (the global inertial frame) to frame 2 (the local frame). `R` is often available in the local frame (`frame_a.R`). See also Section 15.10.5.2.

According to Modelica semantics, if connectors from several objects are *connected*, the potential variables with the same name become constrained to have identical values through equality equations. This corresponds to a common local coordinate system used by all model components connected at the same frame instance. The `Frame_a` connector class also contains two flow variables:

- The resultant force vector `f[3]` acting at the origin of frame *a*.
- The resultant torque vector `t[3]` acting at the origin of frame *a*.

According to the Modelica semantics, if *n* connectors from several objects are connected together, the sum of all flow variables is equal to zero, i.e., the sum of the resultant forces connected at a specific point is zero: $f_1+f_2+...+f_n=0$.

For comparison we also show the `Frame_a` definition from the old MBS library:

```
connector Frame_a  "Frame a of a mechanical element, from old MBS library"
  input SIunits.Position        r0[3] "Position vector from inertial system to
                                   frame origin, resolved in inertial system";
  Real                          S[3,3] "Transformation matrix from frame_a to
                                        inertial system";
  SIunits.Velocity              v[3]   "Absolute velocity of frame origin,
                                        resolved in frame_a";
  SIunits.AngularVelocity       w[3]   "Absolute angular velocity of frame_a,
                                        resolved in frame_a";
  SIunits.Acceleration          a[3]   "Absolute acceleration of frame origin,
                                        resolved in frame_a";
  SIunits.AngularAcceleration z[3]     "Absolute angular acceleration of
                                        frame_a, resolved in frame_a";
  flow SIunits.Force            f[3];
  flow SIunits.Torque           t[3];
end Frame_a;
```

The definition of `Frame_a` from the old library also contains translational and angular velocities and accelerations, which in the current MBS library are defined in the `Body` class. The rotation matrix `R` of the current library is the inverse (i.e., transpose for an orthogonal matrix) of the rotation matrix `S` from old library, that is, $\mathbf{R} = \mathbf{S}^{-1} = \mathbf{S}^{\mathrm{T}}$ (see also Section 14.8.4.1, page 774).

Apart from the frame classes just presented, there are also partial superclasses of joints, force elements, sensors, and visualizers.

To summarize, the following classes are available in the `MultiBody.Interfaces` sublibrary:

- `Frame`, `Frame_a`, `Frame_b`, `Frame_resolve`, `FlangeWithBearing`, `FlangeWithBearingAdaptor`, `PartialElementaryJoint`, `PartialForce`, `PartialLine-Force`, `PartialAbsoluteSensor`, `PartialRelativeSensor`, `PartialVisualizer`, `PartialTwoFrames`, `PartialTwoFramesDoubleSize`, `PartialOneFrame_a`, `PartialOneFrame_b`, `ZeroPosition`

15.10.5.2 MultiBody.Frames

The subpackage `MultiBody.Frames` contains type definitions and functions to transform rotational frame quantities. The basic idea is to hide the actual definition of an orientation in this package by providing the type `Orientation` together with functions operating on instances of this type. These functions typically are inlined by most Modelica environments, and therefore give no call overhead. See The MultiBody library documentation in the Modelica Standard Library for a complete list with examples of all transformation functions.

15.10.5.3 MultiBody.Parts

This package mainly contains classes for defining rigid bodies which have mass and inertia. It is often quite convenient to use the `BodyBox` or `BodyCylinder` model classes, since their geometries are rather simple and the inertia matrix is automatically computed from the size parameters of the box or cylinder. Additionally, the geometry and color properties of the box or cylinder can be used to automatically obtain 3D graphic animations of simulated multibody systems.

The package also contains massless frame transformation elements. The following classes are available:

- `Body`—a rigid body with one `frame_a` connector, as well as mass, inertia tensor, and relative center-of-mass properties, and default geometry with a cylinder and a sphere at the center of mass, see Figure 15-71 for different shapes. This class is the *basic body class*, containing Newton's equations of motion expressed in the body local coordinate system, as well as appropriate coordinate transformations. See Section 14.8.5.4, page 783, for a derivation of some of the formulations of Newton's equations used in this class.
- `BodyShape`—same as `Body`, but also containing both `frame_a` and `frame_b` connectors, and a fixed distance vector `r` between those frames. This body can have a more general shape, e.g. user-defined as a DXF[20]-file or selected from a set of predefined shapes according to the setting of the parameter `shapeType: "box", "sphere", "cylinder", "cone", "pipe", "beam", "gearwheel"`, or `"spring"`, see Figure 15-71.
- `BodyBox`—similar to `BodyShape`, but has a box-shaped geometry and color properties. The inertia matrix, sometimes called the inertia tensor, is automatically defined from the density and the shape of the box, which also may be hollow—see Figure 15-71.
- `BodyCylinder`—similar to `BodyBox`, but with cylindrical geometry. The cylinder may also have a hole, i.e., a pipe—see Figure 15-71 and Figure 15-72.
- `Fixed`—frame fixed in the `world` frame at a given position. Default geometry is a cylinder if `shapeType="cylinder"`.
- `FixedTranslation`—fixed relative translation denoted by the parameter vector `r[3]` from `frame_a` to `frame_b`, resolved in `frame_a`. An object of this class can be viewed as a massless bar between these two points. Default geometry is a cylinder.
- `FixedRotation`—fixed translation and fixed rotation of `frame_b` with respect to `frame_a`. Default geometry is `shapeType="cylinder"`.
- `PointMass`—rigid body where body rotation and inertia tensor is neglected (6 potential states).
- `Mounting1D`—Propagate 1-dimensional support torque to 3-dimensional system, provided `world.driveTrain Mechanics3D=true`.
- `Rotor1D`—1D inertia attachable on 3-dimensional bodies. 3D dynamic effects are taken into account if `world.driveTrainMechanics3D=true`.
- `BevelGear1D`—1D gearbox with arbitrary shaft directions and 3-dim. bearing frame. 3D dynamic effects are taken into account provided `world.driveTrainMechanics3D=true`.
- `RollingWheel`—ideal rolling wheel on flat surface z=0, 5 positional, 3 velocity degrees of freedom.
- `RollingWheelSet`—ideal rolling wheel set consisting of two ideal rolling wheels connected together by an axis.

The default shapes for `Body`, `BodyShape`, `BodyBox`, and `BodyCylinder` are shown in Figure 15-71.

Figure 15-71. Default visualization shapes for `Body`, `BodyShape`, `BodyBox`, and `BodyCylinder` respectively.

Different shapes depending on the value of the parameter `shapeType` are depicted in Figure 15-72.

[20] AutoCad geometry file format.

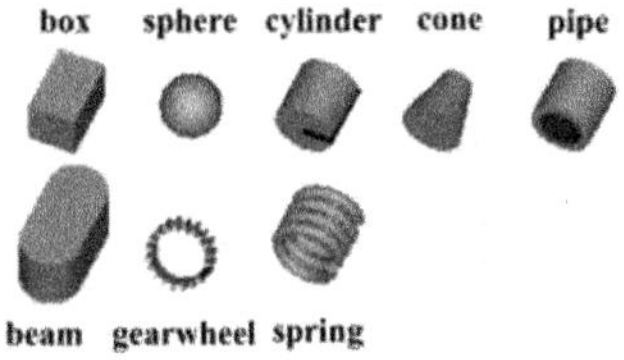

Figure 15-72. Visualization body shapes for `BodyShape` depending on the value of `shapeType`.

15.10.5.4 MultiBody.Joints

The `MultiBody.Joints` package contains model classes describing joints connecting two mechanical bodies with various constraints on the relative movements of the connected bodies.

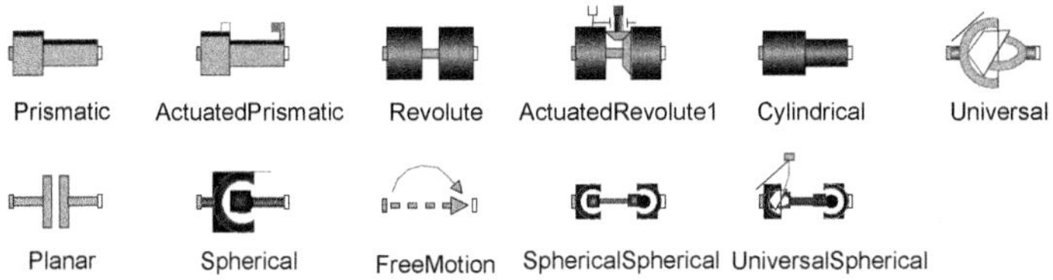

Figure 15-73. Schematic pictures of the 11 different kinds of joints available in the MBS library.

The following is a complete list of the joint classes provided by the `MultiBody.Joints` sublibrary, starting from those with one degree of freedom up to the `FreeMotion` joint with six degrees of freedom and no motion constraints at all.

- `Prismatic`—a joint for *sliding* translational motion in one direction, giving one translational degree of freedom and two potential state variables. This class has connectors `frame_a` and `frame_b`, as well as a `Real` parameter vector `n[3]` (fixed in `frame_a`) that defines the direction of translation when frame *b* moves relative to frame *a*. The variable `s` contains the relative distance between frame *b* and frame *a*.
- `Revolute`—a joint that allows *rotation* relative to one axis (see Figure 14-36, page 787, and Figure 14-30, page 779). The basic state variable is the rotation angle `phi`, which gives one rotational degree of freedom and two potential states, i.e., potential state variables without the flow prefix. This class has the connectors `frame_a` and `frame_b`, as well as a `Real` parameter vector `n[3]`. This unit vector defines the direction of the axis of rotation when frame *b* rotates around frame *a*.
- `RevolutePlanarLoopConstraint`—Revolute joint that is described by two positional constraints for usage in a planar loop. The ambiguous cut-force perpendicular to the loop and the ambiguous cut-torques are set arbitrarily to zero.
- `Cylindrical`—a joint for independent rotation and sliding motions, with two degrees of freedom and four potential states (that is, potential state variables). The `frame_b` rotates around and translates along axis `n` which is fixed in `frame_a`.
- `Universal`—a joint that allows rotation relative to two rotation axes giving two degrees of freedom, and four potential states.
- `Planar`—a joint for arbitrary translational and rotational motion on a plane, with three degrees of freedom and six potential states.
- `Spherical`—a joint for arbitrary rotational motion around a fixed point. This joint has three degrees of freedom, three constraints, and no potential states.

- `FreeMotion`—a joint that allows relative motion with no constraints, as if there were no joint at all, giving six degrees of freedom and twelve potential states from the attached two frames.
- `FreeMotionScalarInit`—free motion joint with scalar initialization and state selection (6 degrees of freedom, 12 potential states).
- `SphericalSpherical`—a spherical aggregated joint consisting of two spherical joints connected by a rod with an optional point mass in the middle.
- `UniversalSpherical`—a spherical aggregated joint with a universal joint at `frame_a` and a spherical joint at `frame_b` which are connected together with a rigid rod.
- `GearConstraint`—ideal three-dimensional gearbox with arbitrary shaft directions.
- `RollingWheel`—joint with no mass and no inertia that describes an ideal rolling wheel rolling on the plane z=0.
- `RollingWheelSet`—joint with no mass and no inertia that describes an ideal rolling wheel set, that is, two ideal rolling wheels connected together by an axis.

The one-degree-of-freedom joints, that is, `Revolute`, `Prismatic`, and so on, can be dynamically locked and unlocked during the movement of the bodies in a multibody system. This facility can be used to model brakes, clutches, stops, or sticking friction. Locking is modeled using classes such as `Clutch` or `Friction` of the `Modelica.Mechanics.Rotational` library. Instances of these classes can be attached to joints at the `axis` connector of type `Flange_a`.

15.10.5.5 MultiBody.Joints.Assemblies, Constraints, Internal

The `Assemblies` subpackage of `MultiBody.Joints` contains aggregations of joints for analytic loop handling. These joints are primarily designed to be used in kinematic loop structures. Every component consists of three elementary joints. These joints are combined such that the kinematics of the three joints between `frame_a` and `frame_b` are computed from the movements of `frame_a` and `frame_b`, i.e., there are no constraints between `frame_a` and `frame_b`. This requires solving a nonlinear system of equations, which here is performed analytically, that is, when an analytic solution exists, it is computed efficiently and reliably.

The assembly joints in this package are named `JointXYZ`, where `XYZ` are the first letters of the elementary joints used in the component, in particular: `P`—prismatic joint, `R`—revolute joint, `S`—spherical joint, and `U`—universal joint. The currently available joints are: `JointUPS`, `JointUSR`, `JointUSP`, `JointSSR`, `JointSSP`, `JointRRR`, and `JointRRP`.

There is also a `Constraints` subpackage with components such as `Prismatic`, `Revolute`, `Spherical`, and `Universal`, that define joints by constraints.

The `Internal` subpackage contains components used for analytic solution of kinematic loops. Use them only if you know what you are doing.

15.10.5.6 MultiBody.Forces

Force elements, such as springs and dampers, can be attached between two frame connectors of arbitrary MBS objects such as bodies, joints, or other elements. The following 3D force elements are available in the `Multibody.Forces` sublibrary:

- `WorldForce`, `WorldTorque`, `WorldForceAndTorque`, `Force`, `Torque`, `ForceAndTorque`, `LineForceWithMass`, `LineForceWithTwoMasses`, `Spring`, `Damper`, `SpringDamperParallel`, `SpringDamperSeries`.

Gravitational forces for all bodies are taken into account by having the gravitational acceleration of the `world` object (the inertial system), i.e., an instance of `MultiBody.World`, as a nonzero value. The default is the gravitational acceleration at the surface of the earth. The propagation to all objects with mass is via implicit connections via the Modelica inner/outer mechanism (see Section 5.8, page 224).

It is easy for a user to introduce new force elements as subclasses, e.g. from the model class `MultiBody.Interfaces.PartialLineForce`. Moreover, one-dimensional force elements from other (non-MBS) libraries such as the `Modelica.Mechanics.Translational` can also be used.

15.10.5.7 MultiBody.Sensors

This subpackage contains measurement components to determine absolute and relative kinematic quantities, as well as cut-forces, cut-torques and power. All measured quantities can be provided in every desired coordinate system. The following classes are available:

- `AbsoluteSensor`, `RelativeSensor`, `AbsolutePosition`, `AbsoluteVelocity`, `AbsoluteAngles`, `AbsoluteAngularVelocity`, `RelativePosition`, `RelativeVelocity`, `RelativeAngles`, `RelativeAngularVelocity`, `Distance`, `CutForce`, `CutTorque`, `CutForceAndTorque`, `TransformAbsoluteVector`, `TransformRelativeVector`, `Power`

For example, the `RelativeSensor` class can compute any relative kinematic quantity (position, velocity, acceleration, angular velocity, angular acceleration) between two frames, whereas the `Power` class measures power flowing from `frame_a` to `frame_b`.

15.10.5.8 MultiBody.Types

This subpackage defines types and constants that are used in the MultiBody library. The types have additional annotation choices definitions that define the menus to be built up in the graphical user interface when the type is used as a parameter in a declaration.

15.10.5.9 MultiBody.Visualizers

The subpackage `Visualizers` contains definitions needed for visualizing three-dimensional shapes. These definitions are the basis for the animation features of the MultiBody library, and include the shape types depicted in Figure 15-72.

15.10.6 Using the MBS Library

There are several approaches to the construction of an MBS model of a multibody system using a collection of Modelica classes. The following are three common approaches:

- Automatic translation from a CAD model to Modelica code.
- Traditional manual stepwise refinement, starting from a kinematic outline, and gradually developing a complete MBS model.
- A physical component top-down design approach starting with the main system structure including bodies and joints picked from the MBS library, and gradually introducing additional details, visualization aspects, and sensor elements.

If a CAD-to-Modelica translator is used (Section 15.11, page 903), there is no need for manual construction of the MBS model. In general, the construction process depends on the context, in particular what type of analysis should be applied to the model, and whether simulation efficiency should be allowed to influence the model structure. Here we advocate the top-down physical component approach, previously described in Section 15.10.6.2, page 890.

15.10.6.1 Kinematic Outline Approach

Most traditional textbooks in multibody system design suggest a process of stepwise refinement of an MBS model, first using a so-called *kinematic outline* (kinematic skeleton), and later introducing details of model dynamics and visualization based on this outline. This approach is also possible using the Modelica MBS library, but is harder to use than the approach described in the next section.

The *kinematic outline* is a graph consisting of *nodes*, with one or more connectors belonging to each node, and *edges* drawn between the connectors.

The nodes of a kinematic outline of a multibody system consist of the *inertial world frame*, massless *elements* (remember that we have not yet added dynamic properties such as mass and inertia), coordinate *frame transformations*, and *joints* that define the kinematic features of the system. The edges of the outline are connections between those nodes attached at coordinate frame connectors. Given the angles of rotation for revolute joints and the length of translation for prismatic joints, or a combination of those in other joints, the Modelica MBS library classes can compute the position of any frame connector using the coordinate transformations between adjacent frame connectors.

15.10.6.2 Top-down Physical Component Approach

The *top-down physical component approach* is similar to the kinematic outline approach, with the difference that here we can use real body models with mass and inertia, including dynamic aspects such as forces and their influence. This approach is the most straightforward since there already exist several easy-to-use body classes in the Modelica MBS library.

15.10.6.3 Multibody System Graph

The *multibody system graph* is a graph consisting of *nodes* with connection points (e.g., frame connectors) and *edges* drawn between the connectors. The nodes of the graph correspond to the global reference frame, the bodies of the system, and the elements defining coordinate frame transformations. The edges of the graph represent interactions between the bodies, in particular joints. In many cases these graphs are acyclic, and represent a tree structure. However, there are models that give rise to graphs with loops, so-called kinematic loops. These are in most cases handled automatically, but sometimes may require special treatment, for example, see Section 15.10.8, page 894.

15.10.6.4 Connection Rules for the Old MBS Library

The elements of the *old* multibody library *cannot* be connected together in an arbitrary way. The reason is to allow the Modelica translator to generate very efficient simulation code by forming a tree-structured connection graph implying an well-defined efficient computation order for equation solution. This is not needed in current MBS library.

The following connection rules apply to the old Modelica 2.2 Modelica.Additions MBS library, which makes that library much harder to use than the current library where these restrictions have been removed:

- Ordinary joint objects (also called *tree* joints, not cutjoints), body objects, and the inertial system object have to be connected together so that the `frame_a` of an object (filled with blue color) is always connected to a `frame_b` of another object (unfilled color). The connection structure has to form a *tree* with the inertial system as root, for example, as depicted in Figure 15-74.
- *CutJoint* (special joints to break kinematic loops when using the old MBS library), force, and sensor objects always have to be connected between two frames of a tree joint, a body, or an inertial system object. For example, in the old MBS library it is not allowed to connect two force objects together.

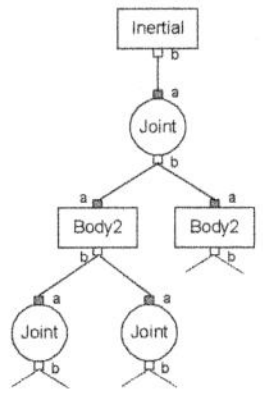

Figure 15-74. Joints in a tree-shaped connection structure implied by the connection rules of the *old* MBS library.

Fortunately, we need not consider these complicated rules when using the current MBS library. The reason is that the current library uses the Modelica equation operators for overconstrained connection-based equation systems as described in Section 8.5, page 374.

15.10.7 Developing an Example Model—a 3D Double Pendulum

In this section, an idealized model of a double pendulum is developed. This pendulum consists of two arms linked by a hinge. The upper box is linked by a hinge to a nonmovable platform, that is, an inertial system. Both arms can move in the *x*-*y* plane. The corresponding kinematic outline consists of two revolute joints, one frame translation and one inertial system, as depicted in Figure 15-75.

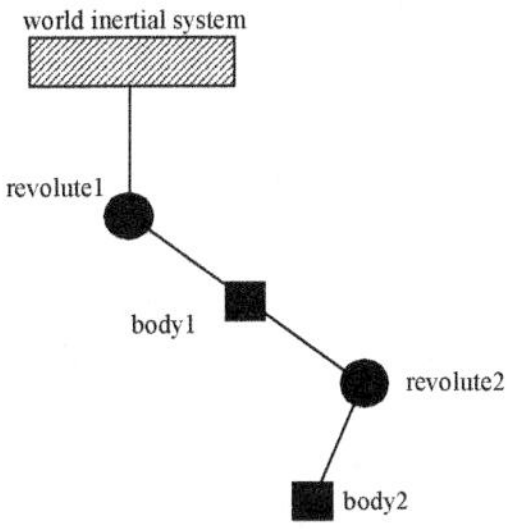

Figure 15-75. Mechanical structure of the double pendulum, where `body2` is an instance of `Body` and `body1` is an instance of a body class with two connectors (`BodyShape`, `BodyBox`, or `BodyCylinder`).

The motion of a dynamic system cannot be defined just by its kinematic outline, since an outline does not contain objects with mass. Fortunately, the body classes in the MBS library have been designed to represent mechanical objects with mass. The `Body` class (instance `body2` in Figure 15-75) has the single connector `frame_a`, whereas the classes `BodyShape`, `BodyBox`, and `BodyCylinder` have two connectors: `frame_a` and `frame_b`, which is apparent for the instance `body1` in Figure 15-75. The following parameters also need to be supplied by the modeler:

- The mass `m` of the body.
- The vector `r_CM[3]` denoting the position of the center of mass with respect to `frame_a`.
- Elements `I_11`, `I_22`, `I_33`, `I_21`, `I_31`, `I_32` of the inertia matrix with respect to the center of mass, with default values 0 if not specified, except for the diagonal elements `I_11`, `I_22`, `I_33` which have default values `1.e-3`.
- The parameter vector `r[3]` from the origin of `frame_a` to `frame_b` with respect to `frame_a`, for instances of the body classes with two frame connectors.

The inertia matrix `I[3,3]` is declared as a variable in all body classes, and defined from the above inertia matrix elements through a matrix equation. This 3×3 matrix containing nine elements is defined by the previously mentioned six inertia matrix numbers since it is symmetric:

$$\begin{pmatrix} I_{11} & I_{21} & I_{31} \\ I_{21} & I_{22} & I_{32} \\ I_{31} & I_{32} & I_{33} \end{pmatrix}$$

In the double pendulum example, two bodies can be added to the kinematic outline.

Since the description of class `Body` contains the distance between its `frame_a` and its center of mass, such objects can be directly connected to the connector `frame_b` of revolute joints `revolute1` and `revolute2`, as depicted in Figure 15-75.

Modelica class instances, such as `body1`, `body2`, `revolute1`, and so on, have attributes that can be modified. For instance, `Body` has attributes that define mass, inertia tensor, and the location of its center of mass relative to the local coordinate system (`r_CM`). Instances of `Revolute` (revolute joint rotating around an axis) have an attribute `n` that defines the direction of axis of rotation. Instances of `Prismatic` (prismatic joint for sliding motion) have an attribute that specifies the direction of the allowed translation. For a `FrameTranslation` instance, the relative position vector from `frame_a` to `frame_b` is specified by the vector `r`.

Several important parameters need to be defined for a double pendulum: `L1` and `L2` are the lengths of the arms. Their masses are `M`. The center of mass of the first arm is located at the distance `L1/2` from the first rotation point. The rotation axes of the revolute joints are directed along the z-axis defined by the direction unit vector `{0,0,1}`.

15.10.7.1 Adding Geometrical Shapes: Cylindrical Bodies

To produce visualizations including 3-D animations we need geometry and color attributes to the bodies in a multibody system model in addition to those necessary for simulation. The MBS library contains the classes `BodyBox`, `BodyShape`, and `BodyCylinder` with associated geometry and color information.

In the following examples we will use the class `BodyCylinder` which describes a body with cylindrical shape. It has a connector `frame_a` which *indirectly* is attached (via implicit connections, see Section 5.8, page 224) to an instance of `World`, and a `frame_b` connector which does not always need to be attached. The class also introduces the following parameters that specify the geometry and color of the cylinder needed for visualization. As usual all position parameters are relative to the local `frame_a` coordinate system, except `r_0` which is expressed in the inertial (`world`) coordinate system. The following is a subset of the available parameters for `BodyCylinder`:

- The parameter vector `r[3]` from the origin of `frame_a` to `frame_b` expressed in `frame_a`. By default the cylinder has two circular surfaces with centers in `frame_a` and `frame_b`, placed perpendicular to the line between `frame_a` and `frame_b`.
- The parameter vector `r_shape[3]` from the origin of `frame_a` to the origin of the cylinder, i.e. the center of the left circular surface of the cylinder.
- The parameter `diameter` specifies the radius of the cylinder (0.1 [m] by default). There is also an `innerDiameter` parameter (usually 0), for cylinders with holes, i.e., pipes.
- The parameter `density` specifies the density of the cylinder (7.7 [g/cm^3] by default—a common value for steel).
- The parameter `m` specifies the mass of the cylinder, automatically computed from the density and volume given by the length and diameter(s)of the cylinder.

- The parameter array `color[3]` (of type `MultiBody.Types.Color=Integer[3]`) specifies the color of the shape, using values for red, green, blue components (RGB). All coefficients are between 0 and 255. Different shapes have different default colors.
- The parameter `length`, which is the length of the cylinder, and `length_direction` , which is a vector (`r - r_shape`) in the direction of the cylinder axis. Both of these are defined from the above parameters by equations.

15.10.7.2 A Double Pendulum Consisting of Two Cylinders

A double pendulum in which the two arms have cylindrical shape is depicted in Figure 15-76 below.

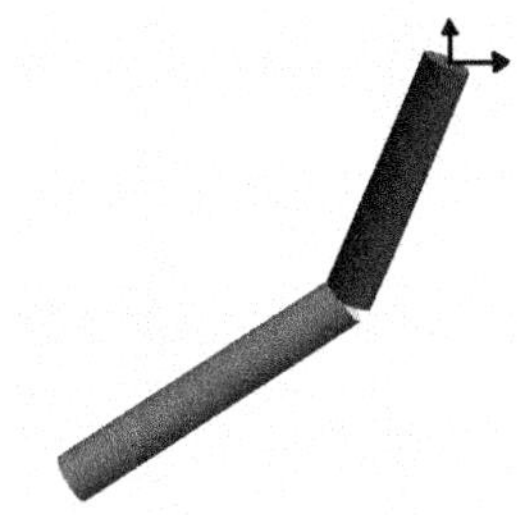

Figure 15-76. A 3D visualization from a 3D animation of the double pendulum with cylindrical geometries of the bodies. The inertial system frame (world object) is shown at the top.

The corresponding Modelica model `DoublePendulumCylinders` for the double pendulum with cylindrical bodies uses an instance of `BodyCylinder` instead of `Body` for the second pendulum arm. This is apparent in the connection diagram of the model shown in Figure 15-77.

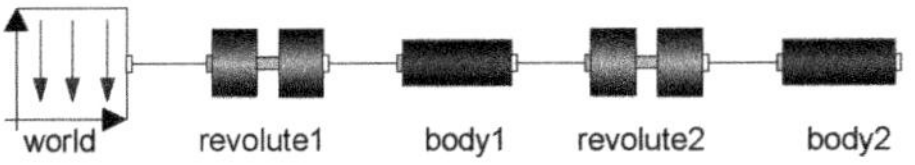

Figure 15-77. The Modelica diagram for the double pendulum consisting of two cylinders.

The `DoublePendulumCylinders` class follows below, including the declaration of the pendulum arms as instances of `BodyCylinder`:

```
model DoublePendulumCylinders
   import Modelica.Mechanics.MultiBody.Parts;
   import Modelica.Mechanics.MultiBody.Joints;
   import Modelica.Mechanics.MultiBody.Types;
   parameter Real L1=0.3 "length of 1st arm";
   parameter Real L2=0.4 "length of 2nd arm";
   parameter Real D=0.1 "diameter";
   inner Modelica.Mechanics.MultiBody.World world;
   Joints.Revolute revolute1;
   Joints.Revolute revolute2;
   Parts.BodyCylinder body1(r={L1,0,0},diameter=D);
   Parts.BodyCylinder body2(r={L2,0,0},diameter=D,color={255,255,0});
equation
   connect(world.frame_b, revolute1.frame_a);
   connect(revolute1.frame_b, body1.frame_a);
   connect(revolute2.frame_b, body2.frame_a);
   connect(body1.frame_b, revolute2.frame_a);
end DoublePendulumCylinders;
```

We simulate and plot the example:

```
simulate(DoublePendulumCylinders, stopTime=1)
plot({body2.body.frame_a.r_0[2], body2.frameTranslation.frame_b.r_0[2]})
```

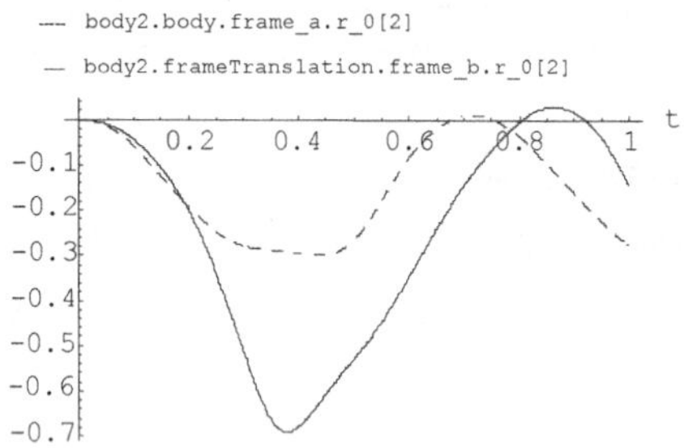

Figure 15-78. Vertical positions of two parts of the double pendulum connected by a joint (variable `body2.frame_a.r_0[2]`) and the tip of the second body (variable `body2.frame_b.r_0[2]`).

15.10.8 Kinematic Loops

A connection chain consisting of joints, bodies, and coordinate transformations may form a circular dependency loop, also called *closed kinematic loop*.

The `PendulumLoop2D` example in Figure 15-79 below, with connection diagram in Figure 15-81, shows a system with a single closed kinematic loop. The upper rod (a cylinder with small radius) is fixed, whereas the three other rods are connected by revolute joints. The whole system behaves like a kind of pendulum.

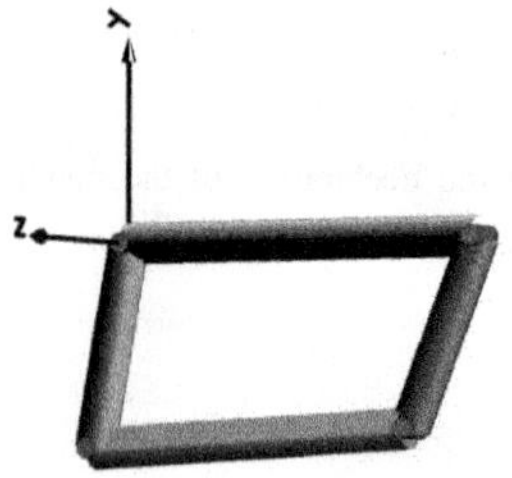

Figure 15-79. 3D visualization and animation of the `PendulumLoop2D` example.

The Modelica MBS library uses equation operators for overconstrained connection-based equation systems (see Section 8.5, page 374) to allow Modelica environments to automatically determine where to "break" the kinematic loop, that is, to remove superfluous equations for cases when there otherwise would be more equations than variables. This is illustrated for the four-bar mechanism depicted in Figure 15-80, which is a kinematic loop consisting of 6 revolute joints, 1 prismatic joint, and 4 bars, that is often used as basic construction unit. The example demonstrates that usually no special knowledge of the user is needed to handle kinematic loops. Just connect the joints and bodies together corresponding to the real physical system.

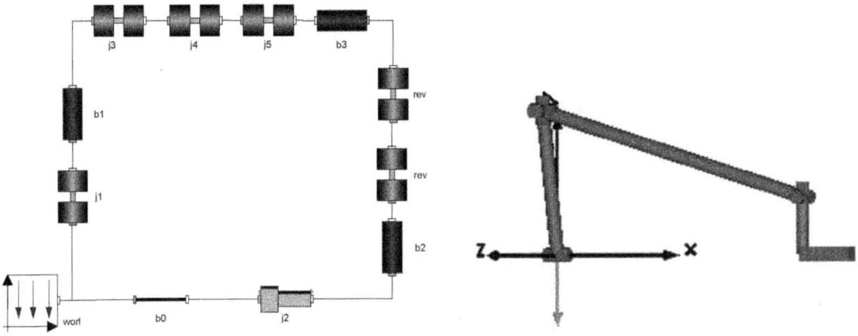

Figure 15-80. Connection diagram and 3D animation visualization of the four-bar kinematic loop example from `MultiBody.Examples.Loops.Fourbar1`.

However, at the current state of the art this analysis cannot be made automatically for *two-dimensional* (planar) kinematic loops (such as the `PendulumLoop2D` example). Planar loops have the difficulty that by infinitesimal changes of parameters such as the axis of rotation of a revolute joint in the loop, the loop has fewer degrees of freedom and is usually locked. The symbolic algorithms currently used to transform the equations are based on structural information and do usually not utilize numerical values. Therefore, these algorithms cannot distinguish the "planar" loop case from the "three-dimensional locked" loop case.

In order to model such loops correctly, the user needs to supply a hint by setting the attribute `planarCutJoint` to true through a modification for one revolute joint that is used to break the circular dependency (also available in the `Advanced` menu of the revolute joint). The `revolute4` instance is an example of such a joint, visible in the connection diagram of `PendulumLoop2D` depicted in Figure 15-81 below. This option sets the connector-force in the direction of the axis of rotation, as well as setting the connector-torques perpendicular to the axis of rotation at this joint to zero and thereby makes the problem mathematically well-formed.

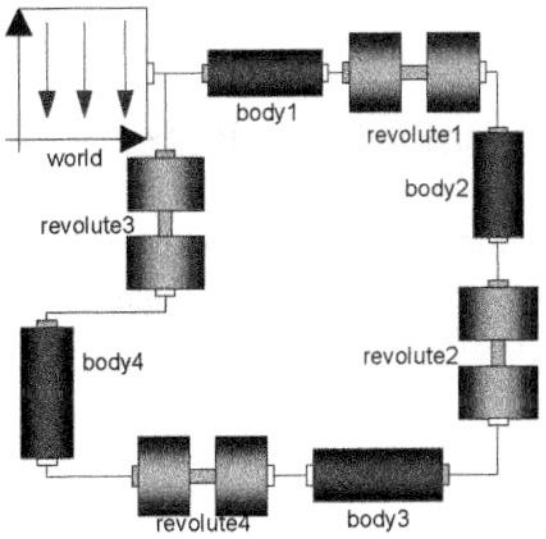

Figure 15-81. Connection diagram for the `PendulumLoop2D` model.

Specifying the initial state can also be tricky for a mechanical system with circular dependencies. In order to specify a valid initial state for a mechanical system that is a planar kinematic loop, a hint needs to be given to the Modelica simulator by selecting a joint with a state variable that has an *independent* start value. The parameter `startValueFixed` is set to `true` to mark this joint (`revolute1`), for which an appropriate `start` value also should be supplied.

The Modelica code of the `PendulumLoop2D` model with these attributes specified follows below.

```
model PendulumLoop2D
   import Modelica.Mechanics.MultiBody.Parts;
   import Modelica.Mechanics.MultiBody.Joints;
   import Modelica.Mechanics.MultiBody.Types;
```

```
    inner Modelica.Mechanics.MultiBody.World  world;
    Parts.BodyCylinder  body1(r={1,0,0},diameter=0.1,color={125,125,125});
    Parts.BodyCylinder  body2(r={0.5,0,0},diameter=0.1);
    Parts.BodyCylinder  body3(r={-0.9,0,0},diameter=0.1,color={0,255,0});
    Parts.BodyCylinder  body4(r={0.5,0,0},diameter=0.1);
    Joints.Revolute     revolute1(startValuesFixed=true,phi_start=-60);
    Joints.Revolute     revolute2;
    Joints.Revolute     revolute3;
    Joints.Revolute     revolute4(planarCutJoint=true);
equation
    connect(world.frame_b, body1.frame_a);
    connect(body1.frame_b, revolute1.frame_a);
    connect(revolute1.frame_b, body2.frame_a);
    connect(world.frame_b, revolute3.frame_a);
    connect(revolute3.frame_b, body4.frame_a);
    connect(body2.frame_b, revolute2.frame_a);
    connect(body3.frame_a, revolute2.frame_b);
    connect(revolute4.frame_b, body3.frame_b);
    connect(body4.frame_b, revolute4.frame_a);
end PendulumLoop2D;
```

We simulate and plot the example:

```
simulate(PendulumLoop2D, stopTime=1)
plot(revolute1.angle)
```

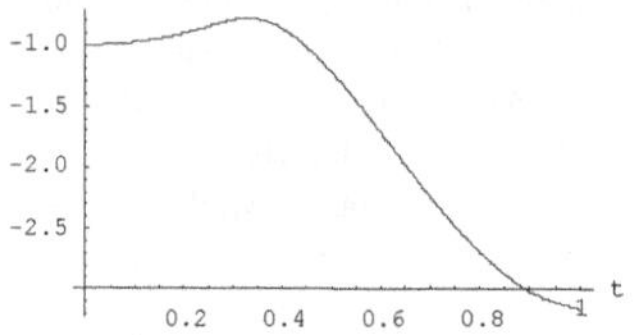

Figure 15-82. The relative angle (in radians) of the joint `revolute1` stored in variable `revolute1.q`.

15.10.9 Interfacing to Non-MBS Models and External Force Elements

When constructing a model of a multidomain system that includes a mechanical multibody subsystem as well as parts from other application domains, all these parts need to be connected through appropriate interfaces. The MBS library provides three main kinds of connector classes:

- Connector classes `Multibody.Interfaces.Frame_a` and `Frame_b`, for connecting external forces described by 3D force elements from `Multibody.Forces`.
- Connector classes `Rotational.Interfaces.Flange_a` and `Flange_b`, for connecting 1D rotational elements from the `Modelica.Rotational` library.
- Connector classes `Translational.Interfaces.Flange_a` and `Flange_b`, for connecting 1D translational elements from the `Modelica.Translational` library.

In the following sections, we give examples of interfacing a multibody model to external force elements and model elements using these three kinds of connector classes.

15.10.9.1 Pendulum with Applied External Forces

Any MBS object with coordinate system connectors of types `Multibody.Interfaces.Frame_a` or `Frame_b`, can be connected to an instance of an external force or torque element from the set of model classes in `Multibody.Forces`. Such an external force or torque element is applied to a corresponding point on the relevant body. The `ExtForcePendulum` example model depicted in Figure 15-83 below includes a force acting at the end of the pendulum in the direction of the local y-axis, that is, perpendicular to the pendulum rod. When a force is applied to the pendulum it does not oscillate; it rotates instead.

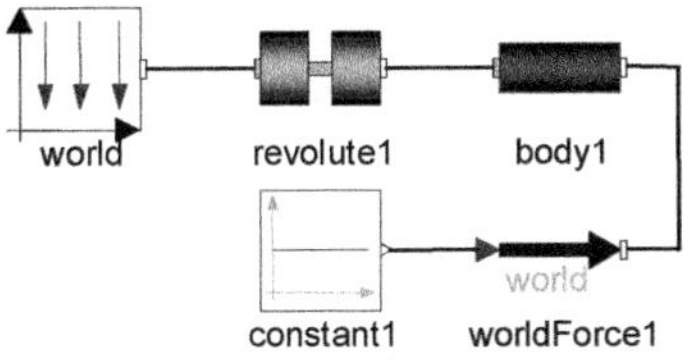

Figure 15-83. Connection diagram for the `ExtForcePendulum` example model of an external force acting on a pendulum.

The Modelica class `ExtForcePendulum` includes an external force element instance `worldForce1` acting on the pendulum. The size and direction of the external force is determined by the constant vector `constant1` here given in the body local coordinate system of the `frame_b` connector. This constant vector must be transformed into the inertial world coordinate system before setting equal to `worldForce1.inPort` and thus determining the external force vector. This is done by applying the inverse `R`$^{-1}$ of the rotational transformation matrix `worldForce1.frame_b.R` to the vector `constant1.y` via the call to the function `Frames.resolve1`.

```
model ExtForcePendulum
   import Modelica.Mechanics.MultiBody.Parts;
   import Modelica.Mechanics.MultiBody.Joints;
   import Modelica.Mechanics.MultiBody.Forces;
   import Modelica.Mechanics.MultiBody.Frames;
   import Modelica.Blocks.Sources;
   inner MultiBody.World world;
   Joints.Revolute      revolute1;
   Parts.BodyCylinder   body1(r={1,0,0},diameter=0.2);
   Forces.WorldForce    worldForce1;
   Sources.Constant     constant1(k={0,1190,0});
equation
   connect(world.frame_b,       revolute1.frame_a);
   connect(revolute1.frame_b, body1.frame_a);
   connect(body1.frame_b,       worldForce1.frame_b);
   worldForce1.force = Frames.resolve1(worldForce1.frame_b.R,constant1.y);
end ExtForcePendulum;
```

We simulate and plot the example:

```
simulate(ExtForcePendulum, stopTime=7);
plot(revolute1.w);
```

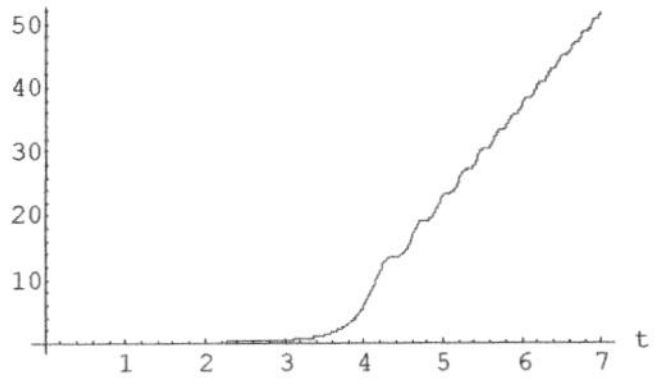

Figure 15-84. The angular velocity of the pendulum caused by the sudden application of a constant force. The force vector is attached to the pendulum tip.

15.10.9.2 Pendulum with Damped Torsion Spring Connected via 1D Rotational Flanges

The `Modelica.Rotational` library describes a number of modeling elements for one-dimensional rotational motion. These elements can be attached to the `Revolute` joint from the `MultiBody` library. A torque, a torsion spring, a torsion damper, or any other rotational component can be attached to one of the connectors of type `Rotational.Flange_a` or `Flange_b` of the revolute joint.

The example in Figure 15-85 illustrates a one-dimensional damped torsion spring (`springDamper1`) from the `Rotational` library attached to the revolute joint (`revolute1`) of a simple pendulum.

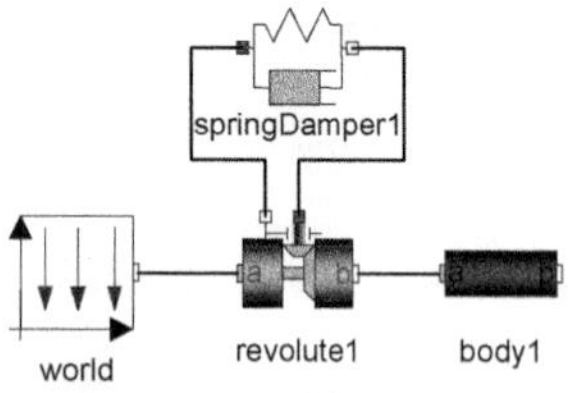

Figure 15-85. Connection Diagram for a pendulum with a non-MBS external force element `springDamper1`.

The `flange_b` connector of the `springDamper1` damped torsion spring is attached to the `axis` connector of the `revolute1` joint of the `PendulumWithDampedSpring` model. The parameter `springDamper1.phi_rel0` describes the unstretched spring angle. In this model the pendulum performs oscillations with gradually decreasing amplitude and converges to the position corresponding to the angle 1 [Rad], which is the default value of `phi_rel0`.

```
model PendulumWithDampedSpring
   import Modelica.Mechanics.MultiBody.Parts;
   import Modelica.Mechanics.MultiBody.Joints;
   import Modelica.Mechanics.MultiBody.Forces;
   import Modelica.Blocks.Sources;
   import Modelica.Mechanics.Rotational;
   inner Modelica.Mechanics.MultiBody.World  world;
   Parts.BodyCylinder        body1(r={1,0,0},diameter=0.2);
   Joints.ActuatedRevolute   revolute1;
   Rotational.SpringDamper   springDamper1(c=500,phi_rel0=1,d=170);
equation
   connect(world.frame_b,           revolute1.frame_a);
   connect(springDamper1.flange_a,  revolute1.bearing);
   connect(springDamper1.flange_b,  revolute1.axis);
   connect(revolute1.frame_b,       body1.frame_a);
end PendulumWithDampedSpring;
```

We simulate and plot the example:

```
simulate(PendulumWithDampedSpring, stopTime=3);
plot(body1.frame_b.r_0[2]);
```

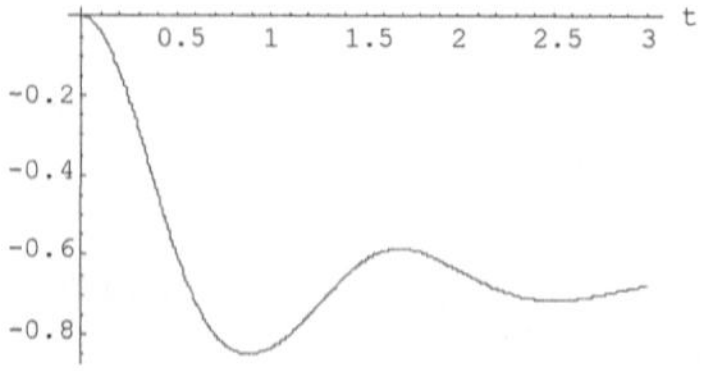

Figure 15-86. The oscillation of the vertical position (`body1.frame_b.r_0[2]`) of the pendulum tip is gradually reduced due to the effect of the springdamper.

15.10.9.3 Pendulum with Rotation Angle Steering

Sometimes there is a need to rotate the body connected to the joint to a certain desired angular position. This can be done by the use of an instance of the class `Rotational.Position`. In the example pendulum with rotation angle steering depicted in Figure 15-87, the specified value of the angle is given by the `step1` instance of the `Step` signal source from the `Modelica.Block.Sources` sublibrary. This value is converted to an angular position by the `position1` component.

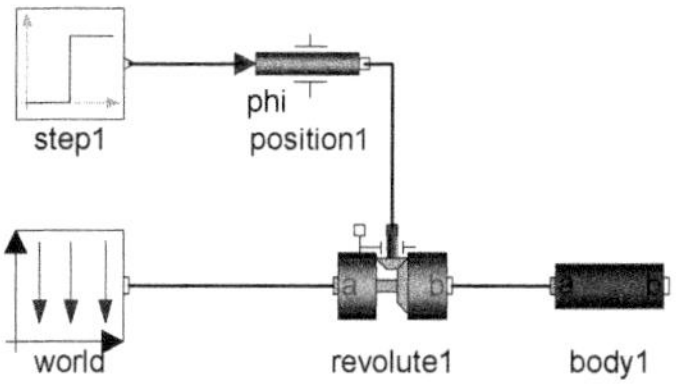

Figure 15-87. Connection Diagram for the `PendulumRotationalSteering` example.

The `Position` class from the `Modelica.Rotational` library filters the input reference angle signal to become smooth. This is needed since the second derivative of the filtered curve is used to compute the reference acceleration of the flange. The angular position of the joint is (partly) computed from this acceleration. For filtering, the `Position` class uses a second order Bessel filter. The critical frequency (also called cut-off frequency, in [Hz]) of the filter is defined via the parameter `f_crit`. This value should be selected to be higher than the essential low frequencies of the signal to preserve its main characteristics while eliminating irrelevant higher frequency noise.

```
model PendulumRotationalSteering
  import Modelica.Mechanics.MultiBody.Parts;
  import Modelica.Mechanics.MultiBody.Joints;
  import Modelica.Modelica.Blocks.Sources;
  import Modelica.Mechanics.Rotational;
  inner Modelica.Mechanics.MultiBody.World    world;
  Parts.BodyCylinder         body1(r={1,0,0});
  Joints.ActuatedRevolute    revolute1;
  Sources.Step               step1(startTime={0.5});
  Rotational.Position        position1(f_crit=5);  // Filter cut-off f_crit
equation
  connect(revolute1.frame_b,   body1.frame_a);
  connect(world.frame_b,       revolute1.frame_a);
  connect(step1.y,             position1.u);
  connect(position1.flange_b,  revolute1.axis); // Connect position1 to axis
end PendulumRotationalSteering;
```

We simulate and plot the example:

```
simulate(PendulumRotationalSteering, stopTime=1);
plot(body1.frame_b.r_0[2]);
```

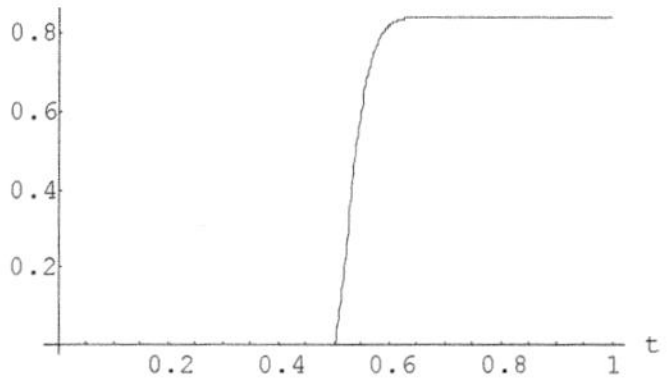

Figure 15-88 The vertical position (`body1.frame_b.r_0[2]`) of the pendulum tip. At `time=0.5` the desired angular position of the revolute joint becomes 1.0 radian.

15.10.9.4 Computational Steering of a Pendulum through a PD controller

Another way to steer the rotational behavior of a joint is to set up a *Proportional Derivative* (PD) controller. Instead of computing a specified angular position as in the pendulum rotational steering class of the previous section, the rotational PD controller creates a torque, which acts on the joint. It actually behaves like a motor-driven actuator. The parameters `k` and `d` of the PD controller can be tuned in order to adjust the reaction speed and power.

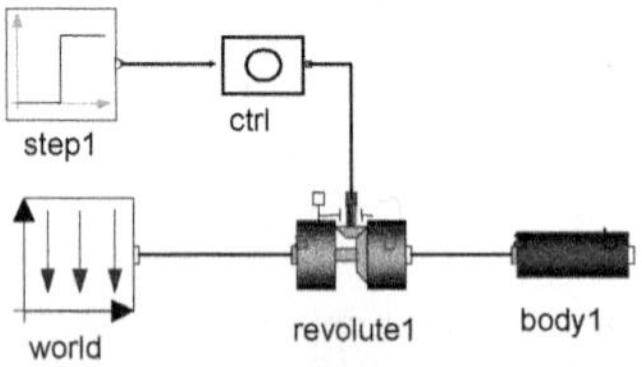

Figure 15-89. The `PendulumWithPDController` connection diagram, including a proportional derivative (PD) controller denoted `ctrl`.

The `PendulumWithPDController` class together with the `RotationalPDController` class used for controlling rotational movement:

```
model PendulumWithPDController
   import Modelica.Mechanics.MultiBody.Parts;
   import Modelica.Mechanics.MultiBody.Joints;
   import Modelica.Blocks.Sources;
   inner Modelica.Mechanics.MultiBody.World  world;
   Parts.BodyCylinder         body1(r={1,0,0},diameter=0.2);
   Joints.ActuatedRevolute    revolute1;
   Sources.Step               step1(startTime={0.5});
   RotationalPDController     ctrl(k=5000,d=500);
equation
   connect(revolute1.frame_b, body1.frame_a);
   connect(step1.y,         ctrl.u);
   connect(ctrl.flange_b, revolute1.axis);
   connect(world.frame_b, revolute1.frame_a);
end PendulumWithPDController

model RotationalPDController "Input signal acting as reference value for
                              angle, gives external torque on a flange"
   import Modelica.Blocks;
   import Modelica.Mechanics.Rotational;
   parameter Real k=1;
   parameter Real d=1;
   Blocks.Interfaces.RealInput      u;
   Rotational.Interfaces.Flange_b  flange_b;
equation
   flange_b.tau = k*(flange_b.phi-u)+d*der(flange_b.phi);
end RotationalPDController;
```

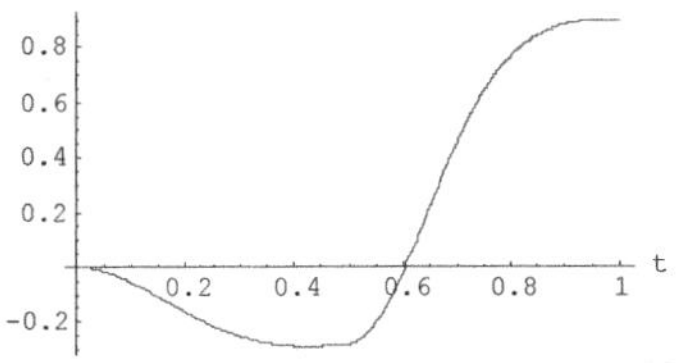

Figure 15-90. The vertical position (`body1.frame_b.r_0[2]`) of the pendulum tip of the controlled pendulum. At `time=0.5` the desired angular position of the revolute joint becomes 1.0 radian and the pendulum smoothly rotates to this position.

15.10.10 V6 Engine

We show a simple model of a V6 engine with six cylinders, `MultiBody.Examples.Loops.EngineV6`, to give an example of a slightly more complex application model using the MBS library than the previous examples. A simple model of the combustion process is used, given by an empirical formula.

The model, `MultiBody.Examples.Loops.EngineV6`, is from the `MultiBody.Examples` sublibrary, and uses the `Cylinder` model (not shown here) from the `Modelica.Mechanics.MultiBody.Examples.Loops.Utilities` sublibrary.

Each cylinder in the engine is modeled solely by revolute and prismatic joints, forming a planar kinematic loop. As was described in Section 15.10.8, page 894, we have to break a planar loop by setting the attribute `planarCutJoint` to true for one of the revolute joints in the loop. This is done in the `Cylinder` model, not in the `EngineV6` model. The connection structure and 3D view of the model are shown in Figure 15-91.

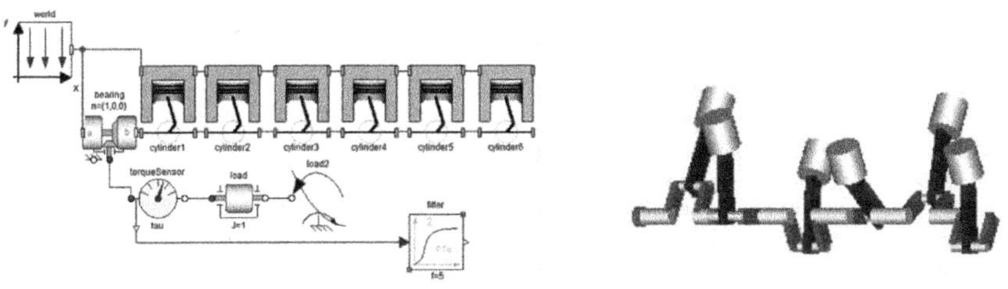

Figure 15-91. Connection diagram (left) and 3D animation view (right) of the V6 engine model, from `MultiBody.Examples.Loops.EngineV6`.

The Modelica code of the `EngineV6` model with one degree-of-freedom and six cylinders, each containing a planar loop, and animation turned on:

```
model EngineV6
  "V6 engine with 6 cylinders, 6 planar loops and 1 degree-of-freedom"
  import Cv = Modelica.SIunits.Conversions;
  import Modelica.Mechanics.MultiBody.Examples.Loops.Utilities;
  import Modelica.Mechanics.MultiBody.Joints;
  extends Modelica.Icons.Example;
  parameter Boolean  animation=true "= true, if animation shall be enabled";
  inner Modelica.Mechanics.MultiBody.World  world(animateWorld=false,
                                                   animateGravity=false);
  Joints.ActuatedRevolute  bearing(n={1,0,0}, cylinderLength=0.02,
                           cylinderDiameter=0.06, animation=animation);
  Modelica.Mechanics.Rotational.Inertia  inertia(
```

```
                    phi(stateSelect=StateSelect.always, fixed=true, start=0),
                    w(stateSelect=StateSelect.always, fixed=true, start=10));
  Utilities.Cylinder  cylinder1(crankAngleOffset=Cv.from_deg(-30),
                   cylinderInclination=Cv.from_deg(-30), animation=animation);
  Utilities.Cylinder  cylinder2(crankAngleOffset=Cv.from_deg(90),
                    cylinderInclination=Cv.from_deg(30), animation=animation);
  Utilities.Cylinder  cylinder3(crankAngleOffset=Cv.from_deg(-150),
                    cylinderInclination=Cv.from_deg(-30), animation=animation);
  Utilities.Cylinder cylinder4(crankAngleOffset=Cv.from_deg(-90),
                    cylinderInclination=Cv.from_deg(30), animation=animation);
  Utilities.Cylinder cylinder5(crankAngleOffset=Cv.from_deg(300),
                    cylinderInclination=Cv.from_deg(-30), animation=animation);
  Utilities.Cylinder cylinder6(crankAngleOffset=Cv.from_deg(150),
                    cylinderInclination=Cv.from_deg(30), animation=animation);
equation
  connect(bearing.frame_b,       cylinder1.crank_a);
  connect(cylinder1.crank_b,     cylinder2.crank_a);
  connect(cylinder2.crank_b,     cylinder3.crank_a);
  connect(cylinder3.crank_b,     cylinder4.crank_a);
  connect(cylinder4.crank_b,     cylinder5.crank_a);
  connect(cylinder5.crank_b,     cylinder6.crank_a);
  connect(cylinder5.cylinder_b, cylinder6.cylinder_a);
  connect(cylinder4.cylinder_b, cylinder5.cylinder_a);
  connect(cylinder4.cylinder_a, cylinder3.cylinder_b);
  connect(cylinder3.cylinder_a, cylinder2.cylinder_b);
  connect(cylinder2.cylinder_a, cylinder1.cylinder_b);
  connect(inertia.flange_b,      bearing.axis);
  connect(world.frame_b,         cylinder1.cylinder_a);
  connect(world.frame_b,         bearing.frame_a);
end EngineV6;
```

15.10.11 Cardan/Euler Angles or Quaternions/Euler Parameters

This rather advanced topic concerns two alternatives for construction of the rotation matrix R. The first approach is to use three independent variables—including the Euler and Cardan angle approaches, whereas the second is based on four variables dependent on each other—the Quaternion/Euler parameter approach. This is discussed in more detail in Sections 14.8.4.2, page 776 and 14.8.4.3, page 777.

Since the rotation matrix represents three degrees of freedom, in principle three independent variables (i.e., states) would suffice. However, if these variables are chosen to be successive rotations around body local coordinate axes—the Euler and Cardan angle approaches—a division by zero may occur in one of the differential equations if the second angle φ_2 becomes $\pm\pi/2$, since there is a division by $\cos(\varphi_2)$ in the right hand side of that equation.

In the MBS library this is prevented by instead transforming relative to an intermediate frame `T_fix`, which is a coordinate system available in each body (class `MultiBody.Parts.Body`), and is fixed relatively to the `world` frame. Whenever the Cardan angles (the `phi` vector) come close to their singular configuration (a condition when `phi[2]` passes the value `phi2_critical`, generating a state event), the frame `T_fix` is changed such that the new Cardan angles are far away from their singularity, i.e., a singular configuration will never occur. The initial values of the Cardan angle states are automatically computed from the initial values given via the `sequence_start` and `angles_start` values. Since the Cardan angles are defined relative to a frame `T_fix` that is changing during simulation, these variables are not very descriptive. It is better to use the rotation matrix `frame_a.R` to get information about the body orientation.

The rotation matrix for transforming a vector from the inertial frame to the local `frame_a` (i.e., `R`) is constructed from the 3 Cardan angles in three steps: first rotate around the x axis of frame `T_fix` with an angle `phi[1]`, then around the y axis with an angle `phi[2]`, and finally around the z axis with an angle phi[3], arriving at frame_a. The Euler angle approach applies these rotations in a different order. See Section 14.8.4.2, page 776.

As an alternative, 4 dependent variables can be used as rotational body states. These are called quaternions or Euler parameters (see Section 14.8.4.3, page 777). They can be used instead of the 3 Cardan/Euler angles, by setting the parameter useQuaternions (also available in the Advanced menu of the MBS library) to true. Quaternions do not have a singular configuration and therefore no state events will occur during simulation, which it is necessary when the Cardan angles need to change their base frame T_fix.

The disadvantage of quaternions is that there is a non-linear constraint equation between the 4 quaternions. Therefore, at least one nonlinear equation has to be solved per body during simulation. In most cases, the Cardan angle choice will be more efficient than the quaternion choice, but there may be cases where quaternions are better suited, e.g. when generation of state-events should be avoided to get continuous derivatives.

15.11 Mechanical CAD Model Simulation and Visualization

The two-dimensional graphic modeling paradigm provided by the connection editors available in most Modelica environments, for example, see Chapter 5, page 187 and Chapter 19 page 1031, provides graphic user interfaces for combining reusable model components. However, for certain applications such as the design of 3D mechanical parts and assemblies of such parts, the two-dimensional connection graph is not very intuitive and sometimes is hard to understand. It would be more natural to use a 3D graphic representation for the design of mechanical application systems consisting of three-dimensional mechanical components. Fortunately, such 3D graphic representations and geometry modeling tools already exist. These are available in CAD systems for design of mechanical applications.

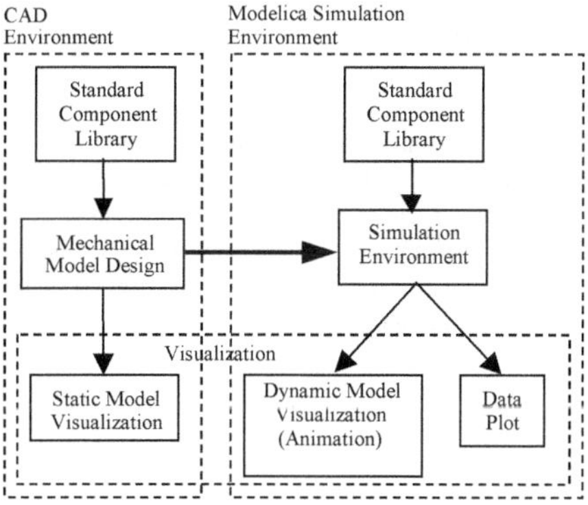

Figure 15-92. Functional structure of the information flow between the Modelica simulation environment, the 3D visualizer, and the CAD environment.

Therefore, it is natural to employ a mechanical CAD system as the interactive user interface to design the geometry, constraints, and connection structure of a mechanical application (Figure 15-92). However, consider the case that we want to simulate the dynamics of a mechanical application, and to do this using Modelica since we are interested in multidomain simulation with the possibility of simulating systems containing both mechanical and nonmechanical parts, for example, attaching control, electric, or hydraulic components.

To perform such a simulation we need a Modelica model that defines the dynamics of the mechanical application designed in the CAD systems. Component classes from the Modelica mechanical multibody system (MBS) library can be used to model the dynamics of a mechanical system consisting of interconnected mechanical parts, provided that the interacting parts are rigid (nonflexible) bodies.

Fortunately, the information needed for simulating a multibody system of interacting mechanical bodies is already available in the CAD design. This includes the geometry, mass, inertia matrix, interconnections, movement constraints, and so on, of the bodies. We just need to translate this information into a Modelica model consisting of appropriately selected instances of certain MBS library classes, connected according the constraints and geometry of the CAD design and design rules of the MBS library.

The translation from CAD design information to a Modelica model for dynamic system simulation can be automated, provided that the CAD design is complete enough. To date, at least two automatic translators exist; for the SolidWorks and the AutoDesk Mechanical Desktop CAD systems, but more will probably follow. Both translators have been designed as CAD system plug-ins that extract geometry, mass, inertia, and constraint information using the CAD system programmable API, and translate this information into Modelica model code. This code can be subsequently combined with other models, for example, control system models, and simulated.

One advantage of the CAD-based model design approach, apart from its ease of use, is that information needed for 3D visualization and animation of the simulated multibody system can be obtained from the same CAD design. The geometry is already available in the 3D design, and if appropriate surface colors and patterns are specified, 3D visualizations of the bodies can be created automatically. Combined with a simulation of the model that computes the coordinates of all the moving bodies as functions of time, 3D animations can be produced automatically based on the CAD model.

Figure 15-93 shows the process of designing a mechanical model using a CAD tool, serving as the starting point for the specification of a virtual prototype with dynamic properties. In the AutoCAD Mechanical Desktop-based translator, the model is first represented in the DWG format, which contains all the information, including connections and mates constraints, related to the geometrical properties of the parts and the whole mechanical assembly.

The geometry of each part is exported in an appropriate geometry format. At the same time, the mass and inertia of the parts are extracted together with mates information from the mechanical assembly. The translator uses this information to generate a corresponding set of Modelica class instances coupled by connections, which contain a set of dynamic equations of motion. This automatically generated Modelica code is processed by the Modelica simulation environment. The simulation code can be enhanced by adding components from other Modelica libraries or by adding externally defined program code, for example, in the C programming language. In this phase, electrical, control, or hydraulics components can be added to the generated mechanical model, thus providing multidomain simulation. The solution of the model equations during simulation computes the dynamic response to a given set of initial conditions including force and/or torque loads, which might even be functions of time.

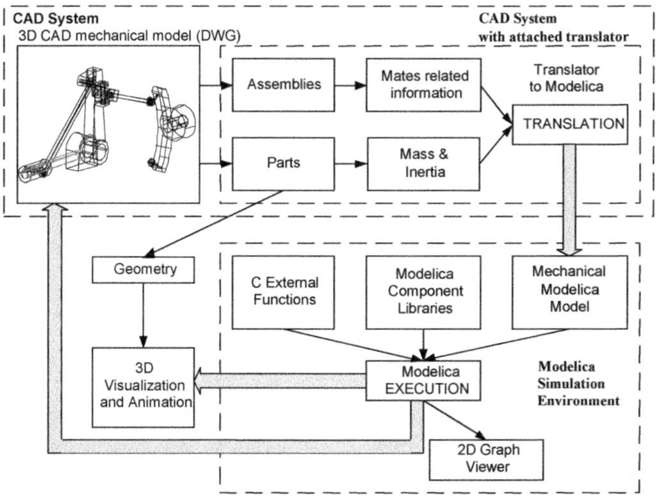

Figure 15-93. The process from a static CAD model to a dynamic system simulation and visualization.

15.12 Summary

Aiming to show different modeling styles and know-how for various domains, we presented application examples from the following areas: mechatronic systems, thermodynamic systems, chemical reactions, biological and ecological systems, economic systems, internet communication, design optimization, Fourier analysis, pressure dynamics with discretized PDEs, mechanical multibody systems, and mechanical CAD systems.

However, important additional goals of this chapter were to illustrate multidomain modeling as in the DC-motor example, bottom-up design of a library as in the thermodynamic example, and to give an introduction to using the Modelica multibody library for 3D mechanical rigid bodies.

15.13 Literature

The literature references for this chapter are grouped according topic, as follows:

- The simple multi-domain DC motor model is discussed in detail in (Andersson 1994). Advanced multidomain systems are discussed in (Clauss and Beater 2002). Hybrid electric vehicles is another example of multi-domain system, described in (Hellgren 2002). Electrical brushless motors is yet another example, presented in (Ferretti, Magnani, Rocco, Bonometti, and Maraglino 2002).
- Thermodynamic theory and systems for engineering applications is presented in (Potter and Somerton 1993). Further reading on changing flow directions in thermodynamic flow systems: (Elmqvist, Otter, Mattsson, and Olsson 2002). Advanced thermodynamics, thermo-hydraulics and chemical reaction modeling is discussed in (Tummescheit 2002; Tummescheit, Eborn 2002). Thermodynamics with models of moving boundaries for dynamic simulation of two-phase flows is described in (Jensen and Tummescheit 2002). Modeling thermodynamic applications in Modelica using stream connectors is described in (Franke, Casella, Otter, Sielemann, Elmqvist, Mattson, and Olsson 2009) from where the quote on equation counting with stream connectors has been fetched.

The Fluid library for such applications is presented in (Franke, Casella, Sielemann, Proelss, Otter, and Wetter 2009).

- Chemical processes with the simple hydrogen-iodine reaction can be found in most chemistry textbooks, but also in (Cellier 1991). Further reading on object oriented modeling of chemical processes can be found in (Nilsson 1993).

  Biological and ecological systems—population dynamics for animals, and for humans with World models that include human-nature interaction. The predator-prey population dynamics is from (Lotka 1956; Volterra 1928). Rodrigo Castro wrote most of the text in Section 15.4.2 on population dynamics with the Handy model, and also developed, mostly based on the paper on Handy1.0 mentioned below, the first Modelica model version of Handy which then was slightly adapted by this author. (Malthus 1798) wrote the first essay on the limits of human population. The 1.0 version of the Handy (Human and Nature Dynamical) model is described in (Motesharrei, Rivas, and Kalnay 2013). An article referring to Handy appeared in Guardian March 26, 2014 (Ahmed 2014). The first version, Handy1.0, is based on a predator-prey Lotka-Volterra type of model, and was introduced as an extension of the Brander-Taylor (BT) model (Brander and Taylor, 1998). Inequality between Elite and Commoners is perhaps the most unique feature of Handy1.0. It is not only explicitly considered but also plays a key role in the sustainability analyses of Handy; this capability is seldom found in the most well known World Models, with few exceptions as, e.g., in (Linnemann, De Hoogh, Keyzer, and van Heemst 1979).

  More than half of the text in Section 15.4.2.7 on the World3 model is cited from the SystemDynamics library documentation (Section 16.21.1, page 972) written by Francois Cellier, and shortened and adapted for presentation in this book. The World3 system dynamics model in Modelica available in the SystemDynamics library is also described in (Cellier 2008). It is a Modelica translation made by Cellier from the original model in STELLA by Meadows et al described in detail in (Meadows, Behrens II, Meadows, Naill, Randers 1974). The limits of growth and interpretations of simulations of the World3 model are presented in (Meadows, Meadows, Randers, Behrens III 1972; Meadows, Randers, and Meadows 2004).
- Biological and ecological systems—energy forest models such as willow growth: (Larsdotter-Nilsson and Fritzson 2003; Sannervik, Eckersten, Verwijst, and Nordh 2002),. A related application in nitrogen processes in treatment wetlands is described in (Edelfeldt and Fritzson 2008). Basic relations in biochemistry are described in (Voit 2000). Biological pathways in biochemistry are discussed in (Michael 1999; SBML 2003).
- Economic systems—Keynesian national economy is presented in detail by (Lipsey 1997).
- Internet communication—TCP packet communication protocols (Färnqvist, Strandemar, Johansson, Hespanha 2002; Mascolo, Casetti, Gerla, Lee, and Sanadidi 2001; Jacobsson and Braden 1988).
- Design optimization—improving the response of a linear actuator. Further reading on design optimization using Modelica can be found in (Franke 2002; Elmqvist, Otter, Mattsson, and Olsson 2002).
- Fourier analysis of simulation data—vibrations in a rotating weak axis. No reference.
- Solving wave equations by discretized PDEs—pressure dynamics in 1D ducts. No reference.
- Mechanical multi-body systems in general are described in (Shabana, 1998), whereas (Otter 1995; Otter, Elmqvist, and Cellier 1996) describes the theory behind the first version of the Modelica multibody library.
- Employing CAD systems for designing mechanical Modelica models as well as generating visualizations based on OpenGL is described in (Engelson 2000), CAD Mechanical translation, Visualization: (Bunus, Engelson, and Fritzson 2000; Engelson, Larsson, and Fritzson 1999; Engelson 2000).

There are many more application areas in which Modelica is being employed. The following are references to some additional applications:

- Car applications, for example, automatic gear boxes: (Otter, Schlegel, and Elmqvist 1997; Pelchen, Schweiger, and Otter 2002). Driveline vibrations in cars is presented in (Tiller, Tobler, and Kuang 2002). Tyre modeling for cars is described in (Andreasson and Jarlmark 2002). Spark-ignited combustion engine simulation is presented in (Newman, Batteh, and Tiller 2002).
- Further reading on parameter estimation/identification using Modelica can be found in (Sjöberg, Fyhr, and Grönstedt 2002).
- Thermal building behavior modeling and simulation is presented in (Sahlin 1996; Felgner, Agustina, Cladera Bohigas, Merz, and Litz 2002).
- An example of the integration of genetic algorithms using a Simulink interface to Modelica is given in (Hongesombut, Mitani, and Tsuji 2002).

Chapter 16

Modelica Library Overview

As we have emphasized earlier in this book, much of the power of modeling with Modelica comes from the ease of reusing model classes. Related classes in particular areas are grouped into packages, also called libraries, which make them easier to find. This chapter gives a *quick overview* of some common Modelica packages. Definitions of a selection of these packages, including source code, are available in the appendices of this book. Explanations on how to use classes from certain commonly used packages are given in Chapter 15, page 793, whereas Chapter 5, page 187, covers the issues of connecting instances of models from different application areas.

A special package, called `Modelica`, is a standardized predefined package that, together with the Modelica Language, is developed and maintained by the Modelica Association. This package is also known as the *Modelica Standard Library*. It provides constants, types, connector classes, partial models, and model classes of components from various application areas, which are grouped into subpackages of the `Modelica` package.

The Modelica Standard Library can be used freely for both noncommercial and commercial purposes under the conditions of *The Modelica License,* as stated in the front pages of this book. The full documentation as well as the source code of these libraries appear at the Modelica web site: `https://www.modelica.org/libraries/`. These libraries are often included in Modelica tool distributions.

Version 3.2.1 of the Modelica Standard Library from August 2013 contains about 1340 models and blocks, and 1000 functions in the sublibraries listed in Table 16-1.

Table 16-1. Main sublibraries of the Modelica Standard Library version 3.2.1, August 2013.

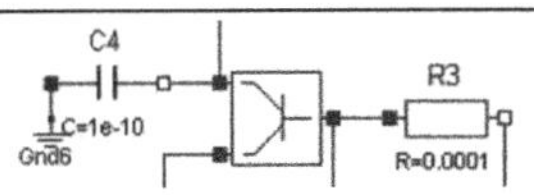	**Modelica.Electrical.Analog** Analog electrical and electronic components such as resistor, capacitor, transformers, diodes, transistors, transmission lines, switches, sources, sensors
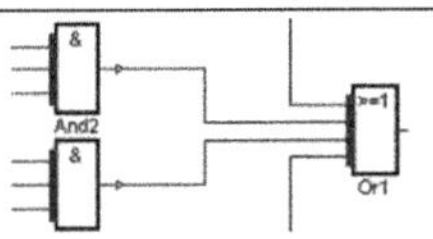	**Modelica.Electrical.Digital** Digital electrical components based on VHDL with nine valued logic. Contains delays, gates, sources, and converters between 2-, 3-, 4-, and 9-valued logic.

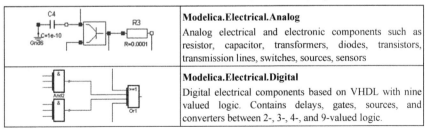

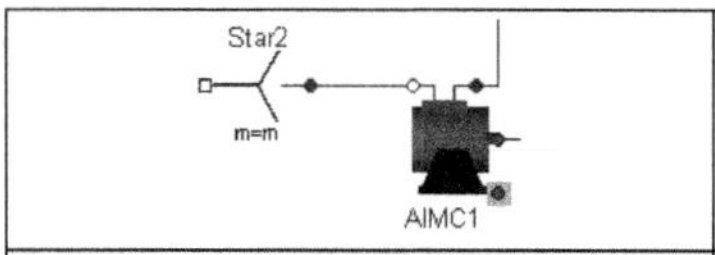	**Modelica.Electrical.Machines** Uncontrolled, electrical machines, such as asynchronous, synchronous and direct current motors and generators.
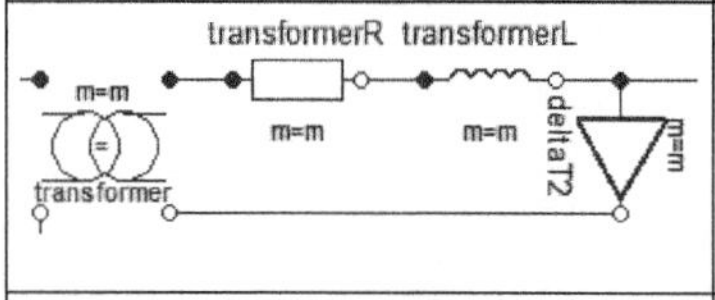	**Modelica.Electrical.MultiPhase** Electrical multiphase componennts to ease the modeling of multiphase circuits. This package has basically the same components as Modelica.Electrical.Analog, but with multiphase connectors.
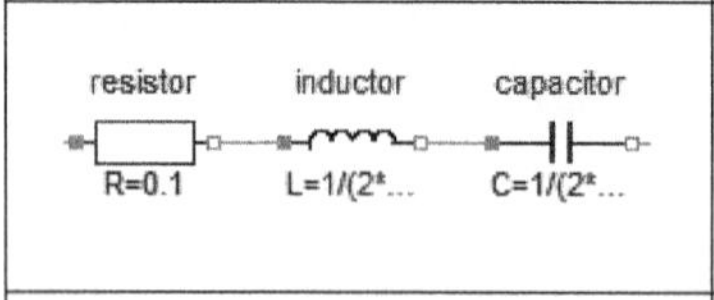	**Modelica.Electrical.QuasiStationary** Very efficient components for electrical circuits with purely sinusoidal voltages and currents. Transients are neglected. The internal description is with Complex numbers
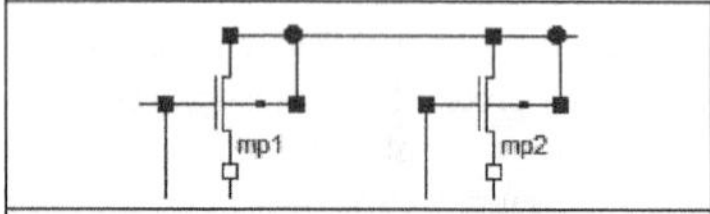	**Modelica.Electrical.Spice3** Detailed semiconductor models, such as MOS, BJT, transformed from Spice3 level 1 and level 2 to Modelica.
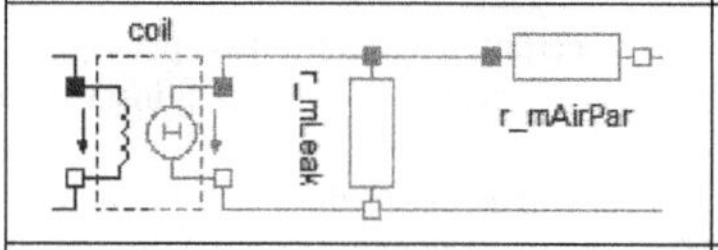	**Modelica.Magnetic.FluxTubes** Modeling of lumped magnetic networks with the fluxtubes concept, especially to model translatory electromagnetic and electrodynamic actuators
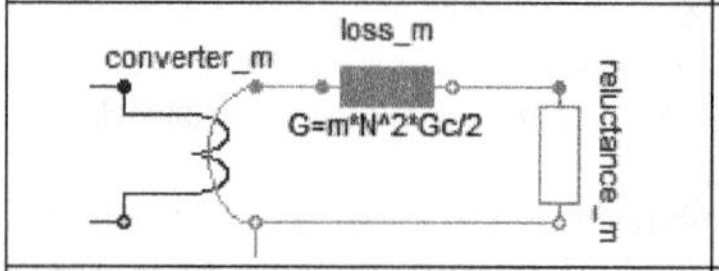	**Modelica.Magnetic.FundamentalWave** Modeling of electromagnetic fundamental wave models for the application in multi phase electric machines.
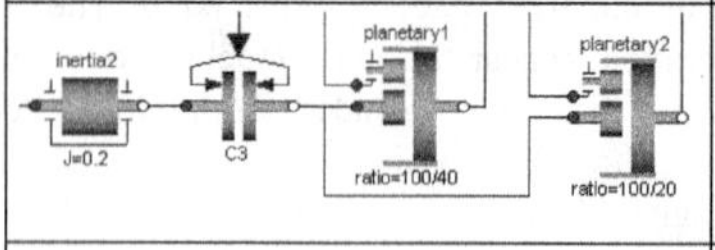	**Modelica.Mechanics.Rotational** 1-dim. rotational mechanical systems, such as drive trains, planetary gear. Contains inertia, spring, gear box, bearing friction, clutch, brake, backlash, torque, etc.
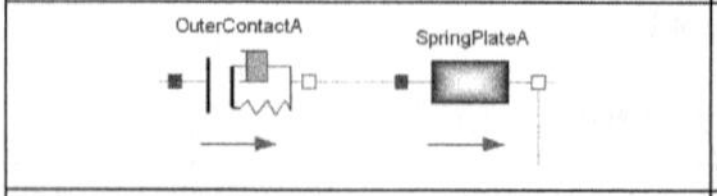	**Modelica.Mechanics.Translational** 1-dim. translational mechanical systems, such as mass, stop, spring, backlash, force
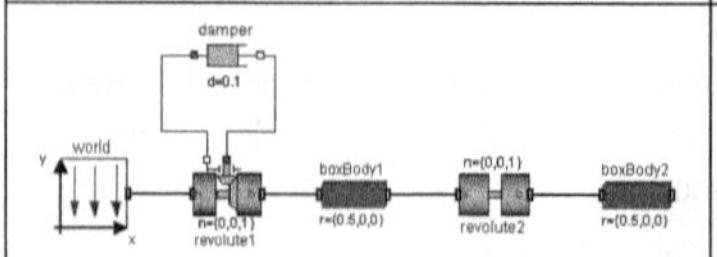	**Modelica.Mechanics.MultiBody** 3-dim. mechanical systems consisting of joints, bodies, force and sensor elements. Joints can be driven by elements of the Rotational library. Every element has a default animation. See Section 15.10, page 877, for an overview description of this library including some hints and examples how to use it.

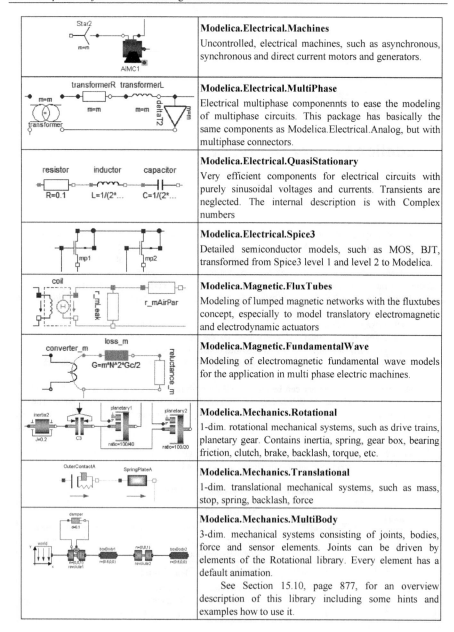

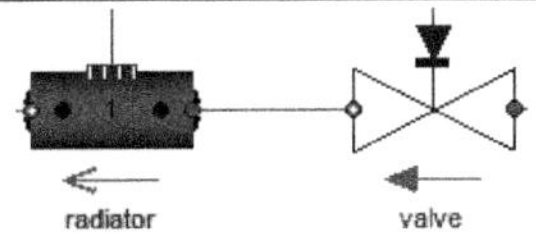	**Modelica.Fluid** Components for 1-dimensional thermo-fluid flow in networks of vessels, pipes, fluid machines, valves and fittings. All components are implemented such that they can be used for media from the Modelica.Media library.
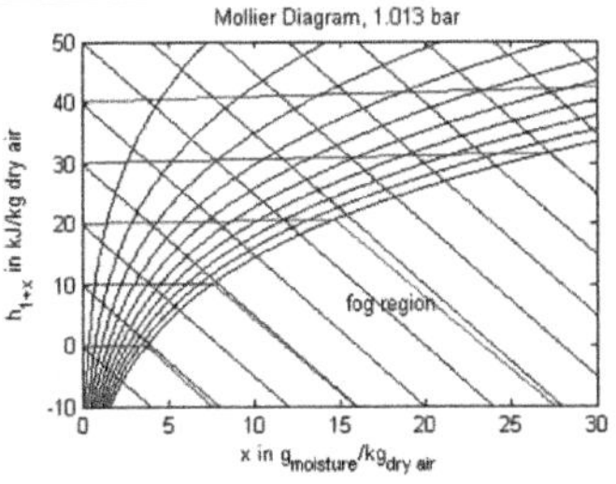	**Modelica.Media** Large media library for single and multiple substance fluids with one and multiple phases: • High precision gas models based on the NASA Glenn coefficients + mixtures between these gas models • Simple and high precision water models (IAPWS/IF97) • Dry and moist air models • Table based incompressible media. • Simple liquid models with linear compressibility
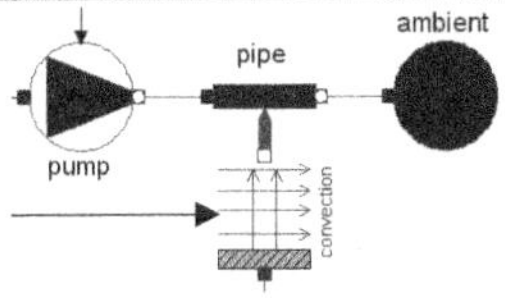	**Modelica.Thermal** Simple thermo-fluid pipe flow, especially for machine cooling systems with water or air fluid. Contains pipes, pumps, valves, sensors, sources etc. Furthermore, lumped heat transfer components are present, such as heat capacitor, thermal conductor, convection, body radiation, etc.
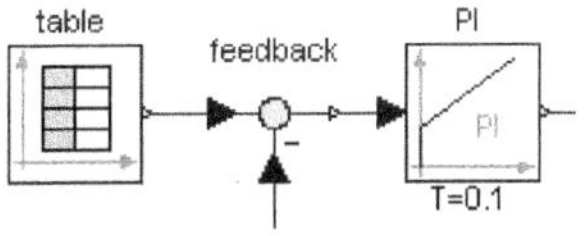	**Modelica.Blocks** Continuous and discrete input/output blocks. Contains transfer functions, linear state space systems, non-linear, mathematical, logical, table, source blocks.
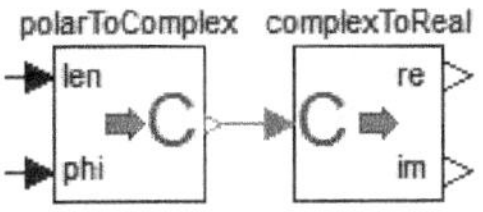	**Modelica.ComplexBlocks** Continuous input/output blocks with Complex signals. Contains algebraic blocks and sources for Complex signals.
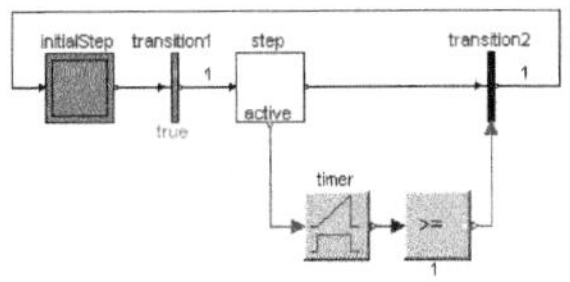	**Modelica.StateGraph** Hierarchical state diagrams with similar modeling power as Statecharts. Modelica is used as synchronous "action" language. Deterministic behavior is guaranteed.
import Modelica.Math.Matrices; A = [1,2,3; 3,4,5; 2,1,4]; b = {10,22,12}; x = Matrices.solve(A,b); Matrices.eigenValues(A);	**Modelica.Math / Modelica.Utilities** Functions operating on scalars, vectors and matrices, e.g. to solve linear systems and compute eigen and singular values, or solve Riccati equations. Functions to operate on nonlinear equations to solve algebraic loops and for adaptive quadrature computation. Also functions are provided to operate on strings, streams and files
import Modelica.ComplexMath;	**Modelica.ComplexMath**

Complex j = ComplexMath.j; Complex a = 2 + 3*j; Complex b = 4 – 5*j; Complex c = 2*a + b;	Functions operating on complex numbers, such as sin, cos, conjugate, as well as vectors of complex numbers.
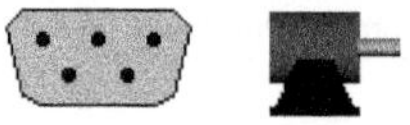 type Angle = Real (final quantity = "Angle", final unit = "rad", displayUnit = "deg");	**Modelica.Constants, Modelica.Icons, Modelica.SIunits** Utility libraries to provide • often used constants such as e, π, R • a library of icons that can be used in models • about 450 predefined types, such as Mass, Angle, Time, based on the international standard on units
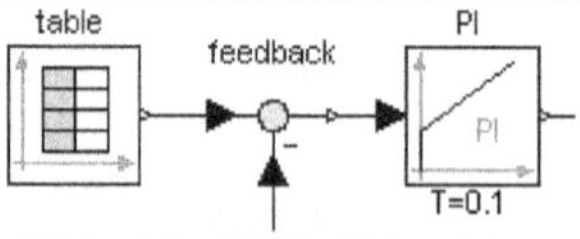	**Modelica.Blocks** Continuous and discrete input/output blocks. Contains transfer functions, linear state space systems, non-linear, mathematical, logical, table, source blocks.
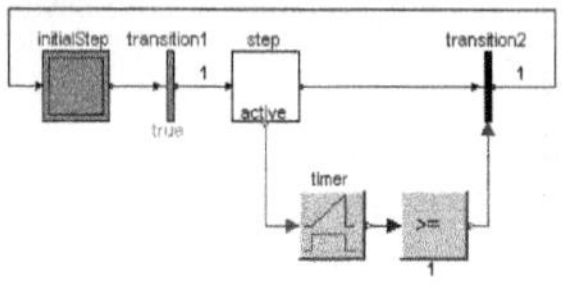	**Modelica.StateGraph** Hierarchical state diagrams with similar modeling power as Statecharts. Modelica is used as synchronous "action" language. Deterministic behavior is guaranteed.

`import Modelica.Math.Matrices;`
`A = [1,2,3;`
`     3,4,5;`
`     2,1,4];`
`b = {10,22,12};`
`x = Matrices.solve(A,b);`
`Matrices.eigenValues(A);`
	Modelica.Math.Matrices / Modelica.Utilities
	Functions operating on matrices, e.g. to solve linear systems and compute eigen and singular values. Moreover, functions are provided to operate on strings, streams and files.

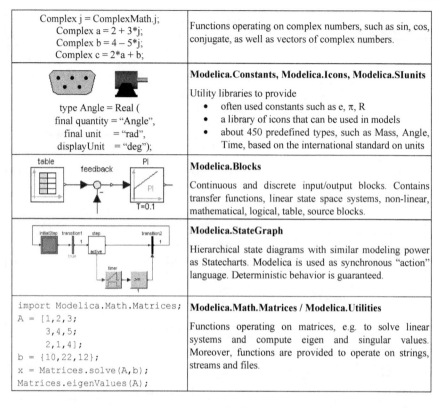

A subpackage named `Interfaces` occurs as part of several packages. It contains *interface definitions* in terms of connector classes for the application area covered by the package in question, as well as *commonly used partial classes* to be reused by the other subpackages within that package.

Also, a subpackage `Examples` contains *example models* on how to use the classes of the package in question occurs in many libraries.

Some MSL libraries with sublibraries are shown in Table 16-2.

Table 16-2. Selected MSL libraries with examples of sublibraries **`Interfaces`** and **`Examples`**.

`Complex`	Complex number record definition, distributed as part of MSL but defined at the top-level outside of MSL. Referred to as `Complex` or `.Complex`. Preloaded by most tools.
`Modelica`	Standard library from the Modelica Association including the following sublibraries:

`Blocks`
`  Interfaces`
`  Continuous`
	Input/output blocks for use in block diagrams.
	Interfaces sublibrary to Blocks.
	Continuous control blocks with internal states

`...`	
`Electrical`	Common electrical component models
`Analog`	Analog electrical component models
`Interfaces, Basic, Ideal,`	Analog electrical sublibraries.
`Sensors, Sources,`	Analog electrical sublibraries.
`Examples,`	Analog electrical sublibraries.
`Lines, Semiconductors`	Analog electrical sublibraries.
`Digital`	Digital electrical components.
`...`	
`Mechanics`	General mechanical library.
	1D rotational mechanical component models.
`Rotational`	Rotational sublibraries.
`Interfaces, Sensors,`	1D translational mechanical components.
`Examples, ...`	Translational sublibraries.
`Translational`	3D mechanical systems – MultiBody library.
`Interfaces, Sensors,`	MultiBody sublibraries.
`Examples`	MultiBody sublibraries.
	MultiBody sublibraries.
`...`	...

There are more libraries than MSL developed by Modelica Association. Table 16-3 presents the Modelica Language standard conforming libraries from Modelica Association including MSL, as of August 2013. Conforming means that they conform to the Modelica Language standard without dependence on vendor-specific language extensions.

Table 16-3. Standard conforming libraries developed by Modelica Association.

Name	*Description*	*Last Release 2013*
`ModelicaStandardLibrary (MSL)`	Free (standard conforming) library from the Modelica Association to model mechanical (1D/3D), electrical (analog, digital, machines), thermal, fluid, control systems and hierarchical state machines. Also numerical functions and functions for strings, files and streams are included.	v3.2.1 (Aug 2013)
`Modelica_DeviceDrivers`	Free (standard conforming) library for interfacing hardware drivers to Modelica models. There is support for joysticks, keyboards, UDP, shared memory, AD/DA converters and other devices.	v1.1build2 (May 2013)
`Modelica_Synchronous`	Free (standard conforming) library to precisely define and synchronize clocked sampled data systems with different sampling rates. It provides convenient to use blocks to utilize the clocked synchronous language elements introduced in Modelica 3.3. This library is planned to eventually	v0.91 (July 2012)

	become part of MSL.	

Table 16-4 lists some other libraries developed by Modelica Association, which are not yet part of MSL or never will be.

Table 16-4. Other libraries developed by Modelica Association.

Name	*Description*	*Last Release 2013*
`ExternalMedia`	The ExternalMedia library provides a framework for interfacing external codes computing fluid properties to `Modelica.Media`-compatible component models.	N/A
`Modelica_EnergyStorages`	Free library that contains models with different complexity for simulating of electric energy storages like batteries (single cells as well as stacks) interacting with loads, battery management systems, loads and charging devices.	N/A
`Modelica_LinearSystems2`	Free library providing different representations of linear, time invariant differential and difference equation systems, as well as typical operations on these system descriptions.	v2.3 (August 2012)
`Modelica_StateGraph2`	Free library providing components to model discrete event, reactive and hybrid systems in a convenient way with deterministic hierarchical state diagrams. Modelica_StateGraph2 is not fully Modelica compliant and will never be, since a better solution with clocked Modelica State Charts is now available with Modelica 3.3	v2.0.1 (August 2010)
`PowerSystems`	The library is intended to model electrical power systems at different levels of detail both in transient and steady-state mode. This library might eventually become part of MSL.	v0.2 (April 2013)

Table 16-5 lists some old libraries earlier developed by Modelica Assocation. The libraries are in most cases replaced by more recent libraries.

Table 16-5. Old deprecated libraries developed earlier by Modelica Association.

Name	*Description*	*Last Release 2013*
`ModelicaAdditions` with sublibraries: `Blocks` `Discrete` `Logical` `Multiplexer`	All components of this library have been incorporated in an improved form into the Modelica Standard Library in version 2.1 and later.	v1.5 (2002)

PetriNets Tables HeatFlow1 MultiBody		
Modelica_Fluid	Free library from the Modelica Association providing components to model 1-dimensional thermo-fluid flow in networks of vessels, pipes, fluid machines, valves and fittings. This library is included in the Modelica Standard Library since version 3.1.	v1.0 (2008)
Modelica_FundamentalWave	Free library for the modeling of spatial fundamental wave effects of electro magnetic quantities in electric machines. (Still using Modelica Standard Library 2.2.2!) This library is included in the Modelica Standard Library since version 3.1.	v0.6 (2009)
Modelica_Magnetic	Free library for modelling of electromagnetic devices with lumped magnetic networks. This library is included in the Modelica Standard Library since version 3.1.	v1.0 (2007)
Modelica_Quasistationary	Free library for the analysis of electrical circuits with purely sinusoidal voltages and currents. With this library single and multi phase circuits can be modelled. (Still uses Modelica Standard Library 2.2.2!) This library is included in the MSL starting from version 3.2.	v0.9.3 (2009)

There are also many free Modelica libraries devoped and contributed by users. These libraries are not (yet) part of the Modelica Standard Library, and have not yet been "certified" by the Modelica Association. The quality of these libraries is varying. Some are well documented and tested, whereas this is not the case for certain other libraries. The number libraries available at the Modelica Association web site is growing rapidly. Table 16-6 is a snapshot of the status in August 2013.

Table 16-6. Free libraries developed and provided by users.

Name	*Description*	*Last Release 2013*
ADGenKinetics	Modeling biochemical reaction networks with generalized kinetic formats with capabilities for computing parameter sensitivities using algorithmic differentiation techniques.	v1.0+r23 (March 2013)
ATplus	Free library for Building Simulation and Building Control, fuzzy control library included. (unlicensed)	v2.1 (2005)
BioChem	Free library for biochemical modeling and simulation, including graphical support for pathway modeling.	v1.0.1 (April 2013)
BondGraph	Free library for graphical Bond Graph modelling that contains common standard linear elements,	v1.0

	sensors, and specific non-linear elements, especially for hydraulic networks.	(February 2013)
BondLib	Free library to model physical systems with bond graphs.	v2.3 (2007)
Buildings	Modelica Buildings library	v1.4_build1 (May 2013)
ComplexLib	Free library for steady-state analysis of AC circuits within phasor domain.	v1.0 (2008)
DESLib	Free library for Parallel DEVS and Process-Oriented Modeling in Modelica	v1.6.1 (February 2013)
ExtendedPetriNets	Free library to model Petri nets and state transition diagrams (extended version). Superseeded by PNLib.	v1.0 (2002)
FCSys	Modelica library of fuel cell models	N/A
FuelCellLib	Free library to model fuel cells (unlicensed)	v1.0 (2004)
FuzzyControl	Free library for fuzzy control (unlicensed)	v1.0 (2002)
HelmholtzMedia	Fluid properties for Modelica, for pure fluids that can be described by a Helmholtz energy equation of state	v0.9.3 (August 2013)
IndustrialControlSystems	Modelica Industrial Control Systems Library by Politecnico di Milano	v1.0 (August 2012)
LinearMPC	Library for model-based predictive controllers with linear process models.	v1.0 (April 2013)
Modelica3D	Library for 3D visualization of objects, primarily together with the MultiBody library.	v0.1 (March 2013)
ModelicaDEVS	A free library for discrete-event modeling using the DEVS formalism. (unlicensed)	v1.0 (2007)
MotorcycleDynamics	Free library for the dynamic simulation of a motorcycle, and tailored to test and validation of active control systems for motorcycle dynamics.	v0.7.0 (2011)
MotorcycleLib	Free Modelica library for the purpose of simulation, analysis and control of bicycles and motorcycles (single-track vehicles, uses BondLib)	v1.0 (2009)
MultiBondLib	Free library to model physical systems with multi-bond graphs.	v1.3 (2007)
NCLib	Free library for combined simulation of networks and controllers in the domain of automation systems.	v0.82 (2009)
NeuralNetwork	Free library that provides a neural network mathematical model. (unlicensed)	v1.0 (2006)

OpenHydraulics	A free Modelica package providing components describing 1-dimensional fluid flow in hydraulic circuits.	v1.0.1 (March 2013)
PDELib	A free library for modeling systems described by 1D partial differential equations. (unlicensed)	v1.0 (2007)
PlanarMechanics	A free library for 2D mechanics.	(2013)
PNlib	Free library for Modeling Petri Nets including extensions (xHPN) such as stochastic Petri Nets, state charts, etc. This library won first prize in the Modelica Library award 2012. See also Section16.18, page 965.	v1.0 (2012)
QSSFluidFlow	Free library for quasi steady-state fluid pipe flow.	v1.0 (2011)
RealTimeCoordination Library	Enables modeling asynchronous and synchronous communication and rich real-time constraints for complex coordination protocols.	v1.0.2 (March 2013)
SPICELib	Free library with some of the modeling and analysis capabilities of the electric circuit simulator PSPICE.	v1.1 (2003)
SPOT	Free library providing components to model power systems both in transient and steady-state mode. This library will be superseded by the new PowerSystems library. There is also a commercial version developed from SPOT.	v0.706 (2007)
SystemDynamics	Free library (also part of Bondlib) for modeling according to the principles of system dynamics of J. Forrester.	v2.0 (2007)
TechThermo	Free library for technical thermodynamics.(unlicensed)	v1.0 (2006)
ThermoBondLib	Free library library that is designed as a graphical library for modeling convective flows using the thermo-bond graph metaphor (uses BondLib)	v2.1 (2007)
ThermoPower	Free library to model thermal power plants (based on Modelica.Media)	v2.1+msl.2.2.2 (2009) v3.0+msl3.2.1 (late fall 2013)
Verif	A free library for verifying the ModelicaSpice library (part of BondLib).	v2.2 (2007)
WasteWater	Free library for modelling and simulation of waste water treatment plants.	v2.0.1 (2003)
WheelsAndTires	Free Modelica package providing the easily modifiable tire models. (uses BondLib and MultiBondLib)	v1.0 (2009)

Several commercial libraries, usually not free of charge, are also available.

When developing an application or a library in some application area, it is wise to use the standardized quantity types available in `Modelica.SIunits` and the standard connectors available in the corresponding `Interfaces` subpackage e.g. `Modelica.Blocks.Interfaces` of the Modelica Standard Library, in order that model components based on the same physical abstraction have compatible interfaces and can be connected together.

The elementary connector classes in Table 16-7 are defined where potential variables are connector variables without the flow prefix and flow variables have the `flow` prefix.

Table 16-7. Basic connector classes for commonly used Modelica libraries.

Domain	*Potential variables*	*Flow Variables*	*Connector Definition*	*Icons*
electrical analog	electrical potential	electrical current	Modelica.Electrical.Analog.Interfaces .Pin, .PositivePin, .NegativePin	
electrical multi-phase	vector of electrical pins		Modelica.Electrical.MultiPhase.Interfaces .Plug, .PositivePlug, .NegativePlug	
electrical sphace phasor	2 electrical potentials	2 electrical currents	Modelica.Electrical.Machines.Interfaces SpacePhasor	
quasi stat. single-phase	complex electrical potential	complex electrical current	Modelica.Electrical.QuasiStationary. SinglePhase.Interfaces.Pin, .PositivePin	
quasi stat. multi-phase	vector of quasi stationary single phase pins		Modelica.Electrical.QuasiStationary. MultiPhase.Interfaces.Pin, .PositivePin	
electrical digital	Integer (1..9)	---	Modelica.Electrical.Digital.Interfaces .DigitalSignal, .DigitalInput, .DigitalOutput	
magnetic flux tubes	magnetic potential	magnetic flux	Modelica.Magnetic.FluxTubes.Interfaces .MagneticPort, .PositiveMagneticPort	
magnetic fundamental wave	complex magnetic potential	complex magnetic flux	Modelica.Magnetic.FundamentalWave. Interfaces.MagneticPort, .PositiveMagneticPort	
translational	distance	cut-force	Modelica.Mechanics.Translational.Interfaces .Flange_a, .Flange_b	
rotational	angle	cut-torque	Modelica.Mechanics.Rotational.Interfaces .Flange_a, .Flange_b	
3-dim. mechanics	position vector orientation object	cut-force vector cut-torque vector	Modelica.Mechanics.MultiBody.Interfaces .Frame, .Frame_a, .Frame_b, .Frame_resolve	
simple fluid flow	pressure specific enthalpy	mass flow rate enthalpy flow rate	Modelica.Thermal.FluidHeatFlow.Interfaces .FlowPort, .FlowPort_a, .FlowPort_b	
thermo fluid flow	pressure	mass flow rate	Modelica.Fluid.Interfaces .FluidPort, .FluidPort_a, .FluidPort_b	
	stream variables (if $m_{flow} < 0$): spec. enthalpy, mass fractions (m_i/m) extra property fractions (c_i/m)			

heat transfer	temperature	heat flow rate	Modelica.Thermal.HeatTransfer.Interfaces .HeatPort, .HeatPort_a, .HeatPort_b	
block diagram	Real, Integer, Boolean		Modelica.Blocks.Interfaces .RealSignal, .RealInput, .RealOutput .IntegerSignal, .IntegerInput, .IntegerOutput .BooleanSignal, .BooleanInput, .BooleanOutput	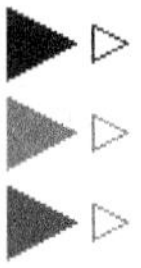
state machine	Boolean variables (occupied, set, available, reset)		Modelica.StateGraph.Interfaces .Step_in, .Step_out, .Transition_in, .Transition_out	

In all domains two equivalent connectors are usually defined, .e.g. `DigitalInput`—`DigitalOutput`, `HeatPort_a`—`HeatPort_b`, and so on. The variable declarations of these connectors are *identical*, only the icons are different in order that it is easy to distinguish two connectors of the same domain that are attached at the same component model.

In the following *a few selected libraries* will be described in some more detail.

16.1 Modelica.Constants Library

The `Modelica.Constants` package provides often needed constants from mathematics, machine dependent constants, and constants from nature.

```
package Constants
  "Library of mathematical constants and constants of nature (e.g., pi, eps, R, sigma)"
  import SI = Modelica.SIunits;
  import NonSI = Modelica.SIunits.Conversions.NonSIunits;
  extends Modelica.Icons.Package;

  // Mathematical constants
  final constant Real e=Modelica.Math.exp(1.0);
  final constant Real pi=2*Modelica.Math.asin(1.0); // 3.14159265358979;
  final constant Real D2R=pi/180 "Degree to Radian";
  final constant Real R2D=180/pi "Radian to Degree";
  final constant Real gamma=0.57721566490153286060
    "see http://en.wikipedia.org/wiki/Euler_constant";

  // Machine dependent constants
  final constant Real eps=ModelicaServices.Machine.eps
    "Biggest number such that 1.0 + eps = 1.0";
  final constant Real small=ModelicaServices.Machine.small
    "Smallest number such that small and -small are representable on the machine";
  final constant Real inf=ModelicaServices.Machine.inf
    "Biggest Real number such that inf and -inf are representable on the machine";
  final constant Integer Integer_inf=ModelicaServices.Machine.Integer_inf
    "Biggest Integer number such that Integer_inf and -Integer_inf are representable
     on the machine";

  // Constants of nature
  // (name, value, description from http://physics.nist.gov/cuu/Constants/)
  final constant SI.Velocity c=299792458 "Speed of light in vacuum";
  final constant SI.Acceleration g_n=9.80665
    "Standard acceleration of gravity on earth";
  final constant Real G(final unit="m3/(kg.s2)") = 6.6742e-11
    "Newtonian constant of gravitation";
  final constant SI.FaradayConstant F = 9.64853399e4 "Faraday constant, C/mol";
  final constant Real h(final unit="J.s") = 6.6260693e-34 "Planck constant";
  final constant Real k(final unit="J/K") = 1.3806505e-23 "Boltzmann constant";
  final constant Real R(final unit="J/(mol.K)") = 8.314472 "Molar gas constant";
  final constant Real sigma(final unit="W/(m2.K4)") = 5.670400e-8
    "Stefan-Boltzmann constant";
  final constant Real N_A(final unit="1/mol") = 6.0221415e23   "Avogadro constant";
  final constant Real mue_0(final unit="N/A2") = 4*pi*1.e-7 "Magnetic constant";
```

```
    final constant Real epsilon_0(final unit="F/m") = 1/(mue_0*c*c)  "Electric constant";
    final constant NonSI.Temperature_degC T_zero=-273.15   "Absolute zero temperature";
  end Constants;
```

16.2 Modelica.Math Library

This package (Table 16-8) contains basic mathematical functions [such as sin(..)], as well as functions operating on vectors, matrices, nonlinear functions, and Boolean vectors.

Table 16-8. Sublibraries and mathematical functions in `Modelica.Math`.

Name	*Description*
`Icons`	Icons for Math
`Vectors`	Library of functions operating on vectors
`Matrices`	Library of functions operating on matrices
`Nonlinear`	Library of functions operating on nonlinear equations
`BooleanVectors`	Library of functions operating on Boolean vectors
`isEqual`	Determine if two Real scalars are numerically identical
`isPowerOf2`	Determine if the integer input is a power of 2
`sin`	Sine
`cos`	Cosine
`tan`	Tangent (u shall not be -pi/2, pi/2, 3*pi/2, ...)
`asin`	Inverse sine (-1 <= u <= 1)
`acos`	Inverse cosine (-1 <= u <= 1)
`atan`	Inverse tangent
`atan2`	Four quadrant inverse tangent
`atan3`	Four quadrant inverse tangent (select solution that is closest to given angle y0)
`sinh`	Hyperbolic sine
`cosh`	Hyperbolic cosine
`tanh`	Hyperbolic tangent
`asinh`	Inverse of sinh (area hyperbolic sine)
`acosh`	Inverse of cosh (area hyperbolic cosine)
`exp`	Exponential, base e
`log`	Natural (base e) logarithm (u shall be > 0)
`log10`	Base 10 logarithm (u shall be > 0)

16.2.1 Modelica.Math.Vectors Library

This library provides functions operating on vectors:

- `toString(v)`—returns the string representation of vector v.
- `isEqual(v1,v2)`—returns true if vectors v1 and v2 have the same size and the same elements.

- `norm(v,p)`—returns the p-norm of vector v.
- `length(v)`—returns the length of vector v (= norm(v,2), but inlined and therefore usable in symbolic manipulations)
- `normalize(v)`—returns vector in direction of v with lenght = 1 and prevents zero-division for zero vector.
- `reverse(v)`—reverses the vector elements of v.
- `sort(v)`—sorts the elements of vector v in ascending or descending order.
- `find(e,v)`— returns the index of the first occurrence of scalar e in vector v.
- `interpolate(x,y,xi)`— returns the interpolated value in (x,y) that corresponds to xi.
- `relNodePositions(nNodes)`— returns a vector of relative node positions (0..1).

16.2.2 Modelica.Math.Matrices Library

This library provides functions operating on matrices. Below, the functions are ordered according to categories and a typical call of the respective function is shown. Most functions are solely an interface to the external LAPACK library. Note: A* is a short hand notation of transpose(A):

Basic Information

- `toString(A)` - returns the string representation of matrix A.
- `isEqual(M1,M2)` - returns true if matrices M1 and M2 have the same size and the same elements.

Linear Equations

- `solve(A,b)`—returns solution x of the linear equation A*x=b (where b is a vector, and A is a square matrix that must be regular).
- `solve2(A,B)`—returns solution X of the linear equation A*X=B (where B is a matrix, and A is a square matrix that must be regular)
- `leastSquares(A,b)`—returns solution x of the linear equation A*x=b in a least squares sense (where b is a vector and A may be non-square and may be rank deficient)
- `leastSquares2(A,B)`—returns solution X of the linear equation A*X=B in a least squares sense (where B is a matrix and A may be non-square and may be rank deficient)
- `equalityLeastSquares(A,a,B,b)`—returns solution x of a linear equality constrained least squares problem: min|A*x-a|^2 subject to B*x=b
- `(LU,p,info)=LU(A)`—returns the LU decomposition with row pivoting of a rectangular matrix A.
- `LU_solve(LU,p,b)`—returns solution x of the linear equation L*U*x[p]=b with a b vector and an LU decomposition from "LU(..)".
- `LU_solve2(LU,p,B)`—returns solution X of the linear equation L*U*X[p,:]=B with a B matrix and an LU decomposition from "LU(..)".

Matrix Factorizations

- `(eval,evec)=eigenValues(A)`—returns eigen values "eval" and eigen vectors "evec" for a real, nonsymmetric matrix A in a Real representation.
- `eigenValueMatrix(eval)`—returns real valued block diagonal matrix of the eigenvalues "eval" of matrix A.
- `(sigma,U,VT)=singularValues(A)`—returns singular values "sigma" and left and right singular vectors U and VT of a rectangular matrix A.
- `(Q,R,p)=QR(A)`—returns the QR decomposition with column pivoting of a rectangular matrix A such that Q*R = A[:,p].
- `(H,U)=hessenberg(A)`—returns the upper Hessenberg form H and the orthogonal transformation matrix U of a square matrix A such that H = U'*A*U.
- `realSchur(A)` - returns the real Schur form of a square matrix A.

- `cholesky(A)`—returns the cholesky factor H of a real symmetric positive definite matrix A so that A = H'*H.
- `(D,Aimproved)=balance(A)`—returns an improved form Aimproved of a square matrix A that has a smaller condition as A, with Aimproved = inv(diagonal(D))*A*diagonal(D).

Matrix Properties

- `trace(A)`—returns the trace of square matrix A, i.e., the sum of the diagonal elements.
- `det(A)`—returns the determinant of square matrix A (using LU decomposition; try to avoid det(..))
- `inv(A)`—returns the inverse of square matrix A (try to avoid, use instead "solve2(..) with B=identity(..))
- `rank(A)`—returns the rank of square matrix A (computed with singular value decomposition)
- `conditionNumber(A)`—returns the condition number norm(A)*norm(inv(A)) of a square matrix A in the range 1..∞.
- `rcond(A)`—returns the reciprocal condition number 1/conditionNumber(A) of a square matrix A in the range 0..1.
- `norm(A)`—returns the 1-, 2-, or infinity-norm of matrix A.
- `frobeniusNorm(A)`— returns the Frobenius norm of matrix A.
- `nullSpace(A)`—returns the null space of matrix A.

Matrix Exponentials

- `exp(A)`—returns the exponential e^A of a matrix A by adaptive Taylor series expansion with scaling and balancing
- `(phi,gamma)=integralExp(A,B)`—returns the exponential phi=e^A and the integral gamma=integral(exp(A*t)*dt)*B as needed for a discretized system with zero order hold.
- `(phi,gamma,gamma1)=integralExpT(A,B)`—returns the exponential phi=e^A, the integral gamma=integral(exp(A*t)*dt)*B, and the time-weighted integral gamma1 = integral((T-t)*exp(A*t)*dt)*B as needed for a discretized system with first order hold.

Matrix Equations

- `continuousLyapunov(A,C)`—returns solution X of the continuous-time Lyapunov equation X*A + A'*X = C
- `continuousSylvester(A,B,C)`—returns solution X of the continuous-time Sylvester equation A*X + X*B = C
- `continuousRiccati(A,B,R,Q)`—returns solution X of the continuous-time algebraic Riccati equation A'*X + X*A - X*B*inv(R)*B'*X + Q = 0
- `discreteLyapunov(A,C)`—returns solution X of the discrete-time Lyapunov equation A'*X*A + sgn*X = C
- `discreteSylvester(A,B,C)`—returns solution X of the discrete-time Sylvester equation A*X*B + sgn*X = C
- `discreteRiccati(A,B,R,Q)`—returns solution X of the discrete-time algebraic Riccati equation A'*X*A - X - A'*X*B*inv(R + B'*X*B)*B'*X*A + Q = 0

Matrix Manipulation

- `sort(M)`—returns the sorted rows or columns of matrix M in ascending or descending order.
- `flipLeftRight(M)`—returns matrix M so that the columns of M are flipped in left/right direction.
- `flipUpDown(M)`—returns matrix M so that the rows of M are flipped in up/down direction.

16.2.3 Modelica.Math.Nonlinear Library

This package (Table 16-9) contains functions to perform tasks such as numerically integrating a function, or solving a nonlinear algebraic equation system. The common feature of the functions in this package is that the nonlinear characteristics are passed as user definable functions.

Table 16-9. Sublibraries and mathematical functions in `Modelica.Math.Nonlinear`.

Name	*Description*
`Examples`	Examples demonstrating the usage of the functions in package Nonlinear
`Interfaces`	Interfaces for functions
`quadratureLobatto`	Return the integral of an integrand function using an adaptive Lobatto rule
`solveOneNonlinearEquation`	Solve f(u) = 0 in a very reliable and efficient way (f(u_min) and f(u_max) must have different signs)

16.2.4 Modelica.Math.BooleanVectors Library

This library (Table 16-10) provides functions operating on vectors that have a Boolean vector as input argument.

Table 16-10. Boolean vector functions in `Modelica.MathBooleanVectors`.

Name	*Description*
`allTrue`	Returns true, if all elements of the Boolean input vector are true ('and')
`anyTrue`	Returns true, if at least on element of the Boolean input vector is true ('or')
`countTrue`	Returns the number of true entries in a Boolean vector
`enumerate`	Enumerates the true entries in a Boolean vector (0 for false entries)
`firstTrueIndex`	Returns the index of the first true element of a Boolean vector
`index`	Returns the indices of the true entries of a Boolean vector

16.3 Modelica.ComplexMath Library

The functions operating on Complex numbers are listed in Table 16-11.

Table 16-11. Mathematical functions in `Modelica.ComplexMath`.

Name	*Description*
`j=Complex(0, 1)`	Imaginary unit
`Vectors`	Library of functions operating on complex vectors, see below
`sin`	Sine of complex number
`cos`	Cosine of complex number

`tan`	Tangent of complex number
`asin`	Arc-sine of complex number
`acos`	Arc-cosine of complex number
`atan`	Arc-tangent of complex number
`sinh`	Hyperbolic-sine of complex number
`cosh`	Hyperbolic-cosine of complex number
`tanh`	Hyperbolic-tangent of complex number
`asinh`	Area-hyperbolic-sine of complex number
`acosh`	Area-hyperbolic-cosine of complex number
`atanh`	Area-hyperbolic-tangent of complex number
`exp`	Exponential of complex number
`log`	Logarithm of complex number
`'abs'`	Absolute value of complex number
`arg`	Phase angle of complex number
`conj`	Conjugate of complex number
`real`	Real part of complex number
`imag`	Imaginary part of complex number
`fromPolar`	Complex from polar representation
`'sqrt'`	Square root of complex number
`'max'`	Return maximum element of complex vector
`'min'`	Return minimum element of complex vector
`'sum'`	Return sum of complex vector
`'product'`	Return product of complex vector

16.3.1 Modelica.ComplexMath.Vectors library

The functions on Complex vectors available in the `ComplexMath.Vectors` sublibrary are listed in Table 16-12.

Table 16-12. Mathematical functions on complex vectors in `Modelica.ComplexMath.Vectors`.

Name	*Description*
`norm`	Returns the p-norm of a complex vector
`length`	Return length of a complex vector
`normalize`	Return normalized complex vector such that length = 1 and prevent zero-division for zero vector
`reverse`	Reverse vector elements (e.g., v[1] becomes last element)
`sort`	Sort elements of complex vector

16.4 Modelica.Utilities Library

This package (Table 16-13) contains Modelica functions that are especially suited for scripting. The functions might be used to work with strings, read data from file, write data to file or copy, move and remove files. It contains the following sublibraries:

Table 16-13. Sublibraries in `Modelica.Utilities`.

Name	*Description*
`Examples`	Examples to demonstrate the usage of package Modelica.Utilities
`Files`	Functions to work with files and directories
`Streams`	Read from files and write to files
`Strings`	Operations on strings
`System`	Interaction with environment
`Types`	Type definitions used in package Modelica.Utilities

16.4.1 Modelica.Utilities.Examples

This package contains examples that demonstrate how to use the functions of package Modelica.Utilities. In particular, the following examples are present:

- The function `calculator` is an interpreter to evaluate expressions consisting of +,-,*,/,(),sin(), cos(), tan(), sqrt(), pi. For example: calculator("1.5*sin(pi/6)");
- The function `expression` is the basic function used in "calculator" to evaluate an expression. It is useful if the expression interpreter is used in a larger scan operation (such as readRealParameter below).
- The function `readRealParameter` reads the value of a parameter from file, given the file and the parameter name. The value on file is interpreted with the Examples.expression function and can therefore be an expression.
- The model `readRealParameterModel` is a test model to demonstrate the usage of "readRealParameter". The model contains 3 parameters which are read from file "Modelica.Utilities/data/Examples_readRealParameters.txt".

16.4.2 Modelica.Utilities.Files

This package (Table 16-14) contains functions to work with files and directories. As a general convention of this package, '/' is used as directory separator both for input and output arguments of all functions. For example:

```
exist("Modelica/Mechanics/Rotational.mo");
```

The functions provide the mapping to the directory separator of the underlying operating system. Note, that on Windows system the usage of '\' as directory separator would be inconvenient, because this character is also the escape character in Modelica and C Strings.

Table 16-14. File and directory functions in `Modelica.Utilities.Files`.

Function/type	*Description*
`list(name)`	List content of file or of directory.

`copy(oldName, newName)` `copy(oldName, newName, replace=false)`	Generate a copy of a file or of a directory.
`move(oldName, newName)` `move(oldName, newName, replace=false)`	Move a file or a directory to another place.
`remove(name)`	Remove file or directory (ignore call, if it does not exist).
`removeFile(name)`	Remove file (ignore call, if it does not exist)
`createDirectory(name)`	Create directory (if directory already exists, ignore call).
`result = exist(name)`	Inquire whether file or directory exists.
`assertNew(name,message)`	Trigger an assert, if a file or directory exists.
`fullName = fullPathName(name)`	Get full path name of file or directory name.
`(directory, name, extension) = splitPathName(name)`	Split path name in directory, file name kernel, file name extension.
`fileName = temporaryFileName()`	Return arbitrary name of a file that does not exist and is in a directory where access rights allow to write to this file (useful for temporary output of files).
`fileReference = FileSystem.loadResource(uri);`	Return the absolute path name of a URI or local file name

16.4.3 Modelica.Utilities.Streams

The package `Streams` (Table 16-15) contains functions to input and output strings to a message window or on files. Note that a string is interpreted and displayed as html text (e.g., with `print(..)` or `error(..)`) if it is enclosed with the Modelica html quotation, e.g.,

```
string = "<html> first line <br> second line </html>".
```

It is a quality of implementation, whether (a) all tags of html are supported or only a subset, (b) how html tags are interpreted if the output device does not allow to display formatted text.

Table 16-15. Functions for input/output and file operations in `Modelica.Utilities.Streams`.

Function/type	*Description*
`print(string)` `print(string,fileName)`	Print string "string" or vector of strings to message window or on file "fileName".
`stringVector = readFile(fileName)`	Read complete text file and return it as a vector of strings.
`(string, endOfFile) = readLine(fileName, lineNumber)`	Returns from the file the content of line lineNumber.
`lines = countLines(fileName)`	Returns the number of lines in a file.
`error(string)`	Print error message "string" to message window and cancel all actions
`close(fileName)`	Close file if it is still open. Ignore call if file is already closed or does not exist.

16.4.4 Modelica.Utilities.Strings

The subpackage `Modelica.Utilities.Strings` (Table 16-16) contains functions to manipulate strings.

The functions `compare`, `isEqual`, `count`, `find`, `findLast`, `replace`, `sort` have the optional input argument `caseSensitive` with default `true`. If `false`, the operation is carried out without taking into account whether a character is upper or lower case.

Table 16-16. String manipulation functions in `Modelica.Utilities.Strings`.

Function	*Description*
`len = length(string)`	Returns length of string
`string2 = substring(string1,startIndex,endIndex)`	Returns a substring defined by start and end index
`result = repeat(n)` `result = repeat(n,string)`	Repeat a blank or a string n times.
`result = compare(string1, string2)`	Compares two substrings with regards to alphabetical order
`identical = isEqual(string1,string2)`	Determine whether two strings are identical
`result = count(string,searchString)`	Count the number of occurrences of a string
`index = find(string,searchString)`	Find first occurrence of a string in another string
`index = findLast(string,searchString)`	Find last occurrence of a string in another string
`string2 = replace(string, searchString,replaceString)`	Replace one or all occurrences of a string
`stringVector2 = sort(stringVector1)`	Sort vector of strings in alphabetic order
`(token, index) = scanToken(string,startIndex)`	Scan for a token (Real/ Integer/ Boolean/ String/Identifier/Delimiter/NoToken)
`(number, index) = scanReal(string,startIndex)`	Scan for a Real constant
`(number, index) = scanInteger(string,startIndex)`	Scan for an Integer constant
`(boolean, index) = scanBoolean(string,startIndex)`	Scan for a Boolean constant
`(string2, index) = scanString(string,startIndex)`	Scan for a String constant
`(identifier, index) = scanIdentifier(string,startIndex)`	Scan for an identifier
`(delimiter, index) = scanDelimiter(string,startIndex)`	Scan for delimiters
`scanNoToken(string,startIndex)`	Check that remaining part of string consists solely of white space or line comments ("// ...\n").
`syntaxError(string,index,message)`	Print a "syntax error message" as well as a string and the index at which scanning detected an error

The sublibrary `Strings.Advanced` also contain these fundamental scanning functions:

```
(nextIndex, realNumber)    = scanReal(string, startIndex, unsigned=false);
(nextIndex, integerNumber) = scanInteger(string, startIndex,
  unsigned=false);
(nextIndex, string2)       = scanString(string, startIndex);
(nextIndex, identifier)    = scanIdentifier(string, startIndex);
 nextIndex                 = skipWhiteSpace(string, startIndex);
 nextIndex                 = skipLineComments(string, startIndex);
```

16.4.5 Modelica.Utilities.System Library

This package (Table 16-17) contains functions to interact with the environment.

Table 16-17. Environment and directory functions in `Modelica.Utilities.System`.

Name	*Description*
`getWorkDirectory`	Get full path name of work directory
`setWorkDirectory`	Set work directory
`getEnvironmentVariable`	Get content of environment variable
`setEnvironmentVariable`	Set content of local environment variable
`command`	Execute command in default shell
`exit`	Terminate execution of Modelica environment

16.4.6 Modelica.Utilities.Types Library

This package (Table 16-18) contains type definitions used in Modelica.Utilities.

Table 16-18. Type definitions used in `Modelica.Utilities`.

Name	*Description*
`Compare`	Enumeration defining comparison of two strings
`FileType`	Enumeration defining the type of a file
`TokenType`	Enumeration defining the token type
`TokenValue`	Value of token

16.5 Modelica.SIUnits Library

This package provides predefined types, such as *Mass*, *Length*, *Time*, based on the international standard on units:

- ISO 31-1992 "General principles concerning quantities, units and symbols"
- ISO 1000-1992 "SI units and recommendations for the use of their multiples and of certain other units".

The following conventions are used in this package:

- Modelica quantity names are defined according to the recommendations of ISO 31. Some of these names are rather long, such as `ThermodynamicTemperature`. Shorter alias names are defined, e.g. `type Temp_K = ThermodynamicTemperature`.
- Modelica units are defined according to the SI base units without multiples (only exception "kg").
- For some quantities, more convenient units for an engineer are defined as `displayUnit`, i.e. the default unit for display purposes (e.g., `displayUnit="deg"` for `quantity="Angle"`).
- The type name is identical to the quantity name, following the convention of type names.
- All quantity and unit attributes are defined as `final` in order that they cannot be redefined to another value.
- Synonyms for identical quantities, for example, `Length`, `Breadth`, `Height`, `Thickness`, `Radius` are defined as the same quantity (here: `Length`).
- The ordering of the type declarations in this package follows ISO 31, that is, 1) Space and Time, 2) Periodic and Related Phenomena, 3) Mechanics, 4) Heat, 5) Electricity and Magnetism, 6) Light and Related Electro-Magnetic Radiations, 7) Acoustics, 8) Physical Chemistry, 9) Atomic and Nuclear Physics, 10) Nuclear Reactions and Ionizing Radiations, 11) (not defined in ISO 31-1992), 12) Characteristic Numbers, 13) Solid State Physics.

Type definitions in the package `Modelica.SIUnits` have the following appearance:

```
type Angle = Real(final quantity="Angle", final unit="rad",
                                            displayUnit="deg");
type SolidAngle = Real(final quantity="SolidAngle", final unit= "sr");
type Length = Real(final quantity="Length", final unit="m" );
type PathLength = Length;
etc...
```

The full set of type definitions of `Modelica.SIUnits` can be found in Appendix D.

16.6 Modelica.Electrical Library

This library contains electrical components to build up analog and digital circuits. The library is currently structured in the following sublibraries:

- `Analog`
- `Digital`
- `Machines`
- `MultiPhase`
- `QuasiStationary`
- `Spice3`

Explanations on how to use several basic electrical components such as resistors, capacitors, and so on, and how to combine them with mechanical components, can be found in Chapter 2, page 19, Chapter 5, page 187, and Chapter 15, page 793. Source code for a selection of classes in the `Modelica.Electrical` library is available in Appendix D.

16.6.1 Modelica.Electrical.Analog Library

This is a library of analog electrical models, containing subpackages for different kinds of analog electrical components:

- Examples: examples that demonstrate the usage of the Analog electrical components.
- Interfaces: connectors and partial models for Analog electrical components.
- Basic: basic components, for example, resistor, capacitor, conductor, inductor, transformer, gyrator.
- Semiconductors: semiconductor devices, for example, diode, bipolar and MOS transistors.
- Lines: lossy and lossless segmented transmission lines, and LC distributed line models.
- Ideal: ideal elements, including switches, diode, transformer, idle, short, and so on.
- Sources: time-dependent and controlled voltage and current sources.
- Sensors: sensors to measure potential, voltage, current, and power.

16.6.1.1 Modelica.Electrical.Analog.Examples

This package contains examples that demonstrate the usage of the components of the Electrical.Analog library. The examples are simple to understand (see Figure 16-1 and Table 16-19). They will show a typical behavior of the components, and they will give hints to users.

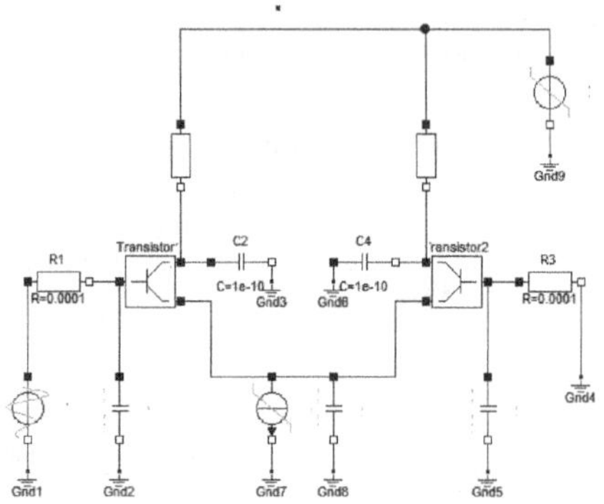

Figure 16-1. An Analog DifferenceAmplifier example model.

Table 16-19. Example models in Modelica.Electrical.Analog.Examples.

Name	*Description*
CauerLowPassAnalog	Cauer low pass filter with analog components
CauerLowPassOPV	Cauer low pass filter with operational amplifiers
CauerLowPassSC	Cauer low-pass filter with operational amplifiers and switched capacitors
CharacteristicIdealDiodes	Characteristic of ideal diodes
CharacteristicThyristors	Characteristic of ideal thyristors
ChuaCircuit	Chua's circuit, ns, V, A
DifferenceAmplifier	Simple NPN transistor amplifier circuit
HeatingMOSInverter	Heating MOS Inverter
HeatingNPN_OrGate	Heating NPN Or Gate
HeatingResistor	Heating resistor
HeatingRectifier	Heating rectifier

NandGate	CMOS NAND Gate (see Tietze/Schenk, page 157)
OvervoltageProtection	Example for Zener diodes
Rectifier	B6 diode bridge
ShowSaturatingInductor	Simple demo to show behaviour of SaturatingInductor component
ShowVariableResistor	Simple demo of a VariableResistor model
SwitchWithArc	Comparison of switch models both with and without arc
ThyristorBehaviourTest	Thyristor demonstration example
AmplifierWithOpAmpDetailed	Simple Amplifier circuit which uses OpAmpDetailed
CompareTransformers	Transformer circuit to show the magnetization facilities
ControlledSwitchWithArc	Comparison of controlled switch models both with and without arc
SimpleTriacCircuit	Simple triac test circuit
IdealTriacCircuit	Ideal triac test circuit
AD_DA_conversion	Conversion circuit
Utilities	Utility components used by package Examples

16.6.1.2 Modelica.Electrical.Analog.Interfaces

This subpackage contains the interface definitions in terms of connector classes, as well as partial models for analog electrical components. The names and icons of the classes appear in Figure 16-1.

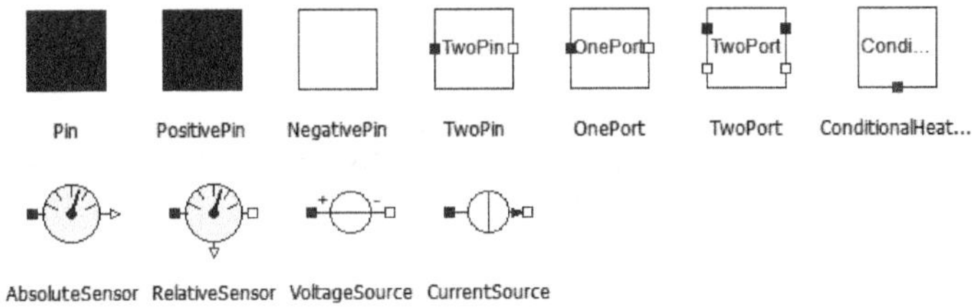

Figure 16-2. Connector and partial model icons in the electrical analog interfaces sublibrary.

Detailed explanations of some classes such as `Pin`, `PositivePin`, etc. is presented in Chapter 5, page 188. Source code for these classes is available in Appendix D.

16.6.1.3 Modelica.Electrical.Analog.Basic

This package (Table 16-20) contains very basic analog electrical components such as resistor, conductor, condensator, inductor, and the ground which is needed in each electrical circuit description. Furthermore, controlled sources, coupling components, and some improved, but nevertheless basic models, are in this package.

Table 16-20. Basic electrical component models in `Modelica.Electrical.Analog.Basic`.

Name	*Description*
Ground	Ground node
Resistor	Ideal linear electrical resistor

HeatingResistor	Temperature dependent electrical resistor
Conductor	Ideal linear electrical conductor
Capacitor	Ideal linear electrical capacitor
Inductor	Ideal linear electrical inductor
SaturatingInductor	Simple model of an inductor with saturation
Transformer	Transformer with two ports
M_Transformer	Generic transformer with free number of inductors
Gyrator	Gyrator
EMF	Electromotoric force (electric/mechanic transformer)
TranslationalEMF	Electromotoric force (electric/mechanic transformer)
VCV	Linear voltage-controlled voltage source
VCC	Linear voltage-controlled current source
CCV	Linear current-controlled voltage source
CCC	Linear current-controlled current source
OpAmp	Simple nonideal model of an OpAmp with limitation
OpAmpDetailed	Detailed model of an operational amplifier
VariableResistor	Ideal linear electrical resistor with variable resistance
VariableConductor	Ideal linear electrical conductor with variable conductance
VariableCapacitor	Ideal linear electrical capacitor with variable capacitance
VariableInductor	Ideal linear electrical inductor with variable inductance

The basic natural laws used in these models are briefly described in Section 14.2, page 746. An application example in terms of a DCMotor model using many of these components, including an EMF (Electro Motoric Force) converter, is presented in Section 15.1, page 794.

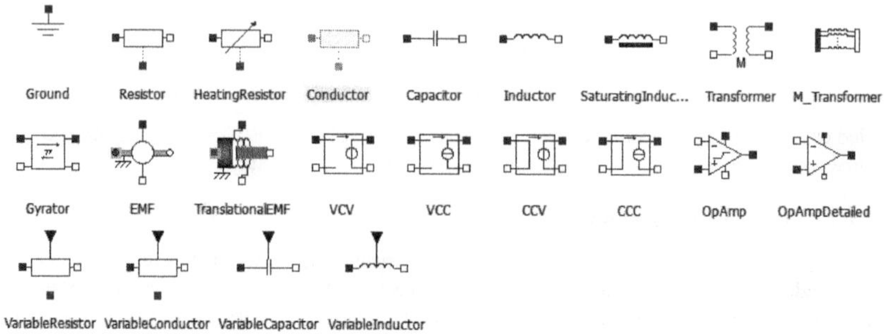

Figure 16-3. Icons for basic electrical analog components.

Source code for these classes is available in Appendix D.

16.6.1.4 Modelica.Electrical.Analog.Ideal

This package (Table 16-21) contains electrical components with idealized behaviour. To enable more realistic applications than it is possible with pure realistic behavior some components have been improved with additional features. For example, the switches have resistances for the open or close case which can be parametrized.

Table 16-21. Ideal component models in `Modelica.Electrical.Analog.Ideal`.

Name	*Description*
`IdealThyristor`	Ideal thyristor
`IdealGTOThyristor`	Ideal GTO thyristor
`IdealCommutingSwitch`	Ideal commuting switch
`IdealIntermediateSwitch`	Ideal intermediate switch
`ControlledIdealCommutingSwitch`	Controlled ideal commuting switch
`ControlledIdealIntermediateSwitch`	Controlled ideal intermediate switch
`IdealOpAmp`	Ideal operational amplifier (norator-nullator pair)
`IdealOpAmp3Pin`	Ideal operational amplifier (norator-nullator pair), but 3 pins
`IdealOpAmpLimited`	Ideal operational amplifier with limitation
`IdealDiode`	Ideal diode
`IdealTransformer`	Ideal transformer core with or without magnetization
`IdealGyrator`	Ideal gyrator
`Idle`	Idle branch
`Short`	Short cut branch
`IdealOpeningSwitch`	Ideal electrical opener
`IdealClosingSwitch`	Ideal electrical closer
`ControlledIdealOpeningSwitch`	Controlled ideal electrical opener
`ControlledIdealClosingSwitch`	Controlled ideal electrical closer
`OpenerWithArc`	Ideal opening switch with simple arc model
`CloserWithArc`	Ideal closing switch with simple arc model
`ControlledOpenerWithArc`	Controlled ideal electrical opener with simple arc model
`ControlledCloserWithArc`	Controlled ideal electrical closer with simple arc model
`IdealTriac`	Ideal triac, based on ideal thyristors
`AD_Converter`	Simple n-bit analog to digital converter
`DA_Converter`	Simple digital to analog converter

The ideal diode model mentioned in the list is discussed in Section 2.15, page 55.

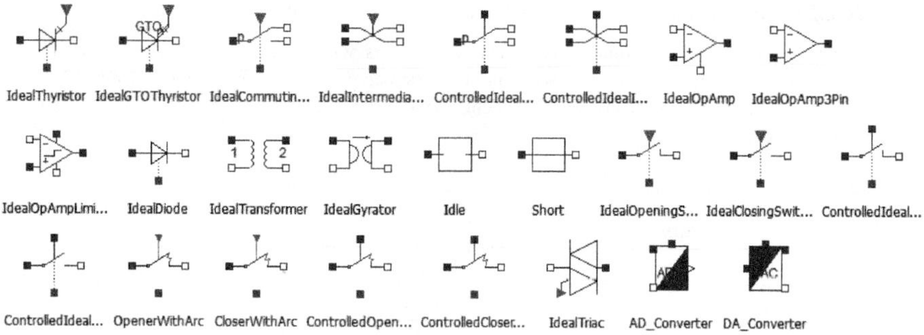

Figure 16-4. Icons for ideal electrical analog components.

Source code for some of these classes is available in Appendix D.

16.6.1.5 Modelica.Electrical.Analog.Sensors

This package contains potential, voltage, and current sensors.

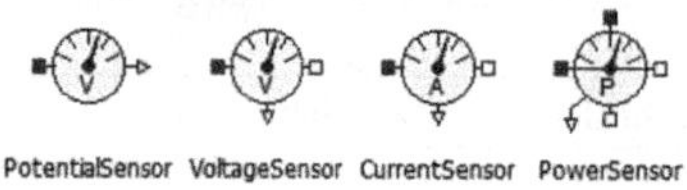

Figure 16-5. Icons for electrical analog sensors, for sensing voltages and currents.

Source code for these classes is available in Appendix D.

16.6.1.6 Modelica.Electrical.Analog.Sources

This package contains time-dependent and controlled voltage and current sources, as depicted in Figure 16-6. Step signals are used in a number of models, e.g. the DCMotor model described in Section 15.1, page 794.

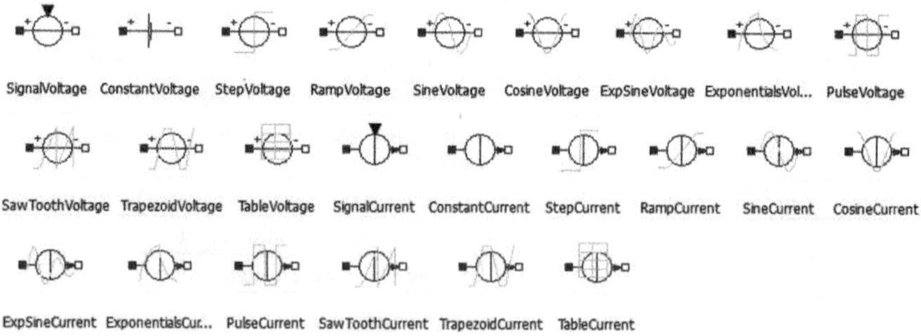

Figure 16-6. Icons for electrical analog voltage and current sources, with generated signals of various forms.

Source code for these classes is available in Appendix D.

16.6.1.7 Modelica.Electrical.Analog.Lines

This package contains models for lossy and lossless analog transmission lines.

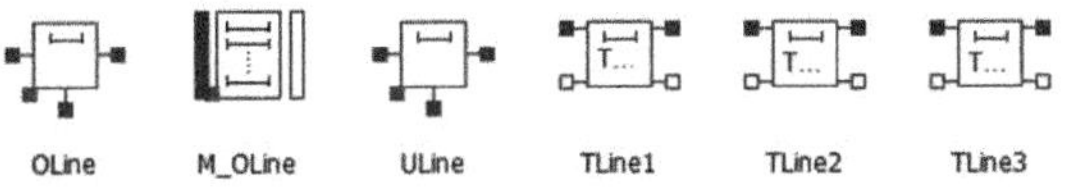

Figure 16-7. Icons for lossy and lossless electrical analog transmission lines.

Source code for these classes is available in Appendix D.

16.6.1.8 Modelica.Electrical.Analog.Semiconductors

This package contains a few common analog semiconductor devices:

- diodes
- MOS transistors
- bipolar transistors
- thyristor and simpletriac

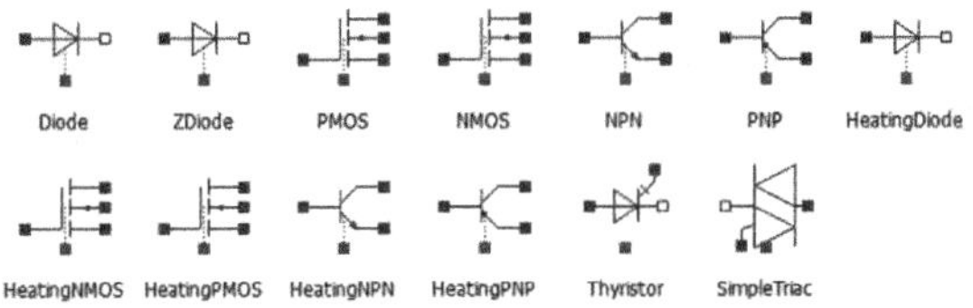

Figure 16-8. Icons for common electrical analog semiconductors such as diodes and transistors.

The diode model is explained in Section 2.15, page 55. Source code for these classes is available in Appendix D.

16.7 Modelica.Electrical.Digital Library

This is a library for digital electrical components based on the VHDL standard with 9-valued logic and conversion to 2-,3-,4-valued logic. It consists of the following parts.

- `Interfaces`: Definition of signals and interfaces
- `Tables`: All truth tables needed
- `Delay`: Transport and inertial delay
- `Basic`: Basic logic without delay
- `Gates`: Basic gates composed by basic components and inertial delay
- `Tristate`: (not yet available)
- `FlipFlops`: D-Flip-Flops
- `Latches`: D-Latches
- `TransferGates`: (not yet available)
- `Multiplexers` (not yet available)
- `Memory`: Ram, Rom, (not yet available)
- `Sources`: Time-dependent signal sources
- `Converters`

- `Examples`

An example model `Adder4` in the `Digital.Examples` sublibrary is shown below:

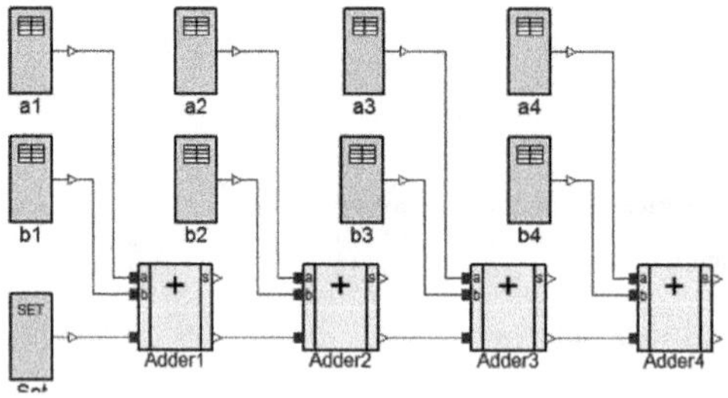

Figure 16-9. The `Adder4` model from `Electrical.Digital.Examples`.

16.8 Modelica.Blocks Library

The `Blocks` library (Table 16-22) contains input/output blocks to build up block diagrams. See Section 12.5, page 582, for description of the notion of block diagrams. The library is structured into the following sublibraries:

Table 16-22. Sublibraries with input/output blocks in `Modelica.Blocks`.

Name	*Description*
`Examples`	Library of examples to demonstrate the usage of package Blocks
`Continuous`	Library of continuous control blocks with internal states
`Discrete`	Library of discrete input/output blocks with fixed sample period
`Interaction`	Library of user interaction blocks to input and to show variables in a diagram animation
`Interfaces`	Library of connectors and partial models for input/output blocks
`Logical`	Library of components with Boolean input and output signals
`Math`	Library of Real mathematical functions as input/output blocks
`MathInteger`	Library of Integer mathematical functions as input/output blocks
`MathBoolean`	Library of Boolean mathematical functions as input/output blocks
`Nonlinear`	Library of discontinuous or non-differentiable algebraic control blocks
`Routing`	Library of blocks to combine and extract signals
`Sources`	Library of signal source blocks generating Real and Boolean signals
`Tables`	Library of blocks to interpolate in one and two-dimensional tables
`Types`	Library of constants and types with choices, especially to build menus
`Icons`	Icons for Blocks

Source code for part of the Modelica.Blocks library is available in Appendix D.

16.8.1 Modelica.Blocks.Examples

This subpackage contains example models to demonstrate the usage of package blocks. An example model `RealNetWork1` is shown in Figure 16-10.

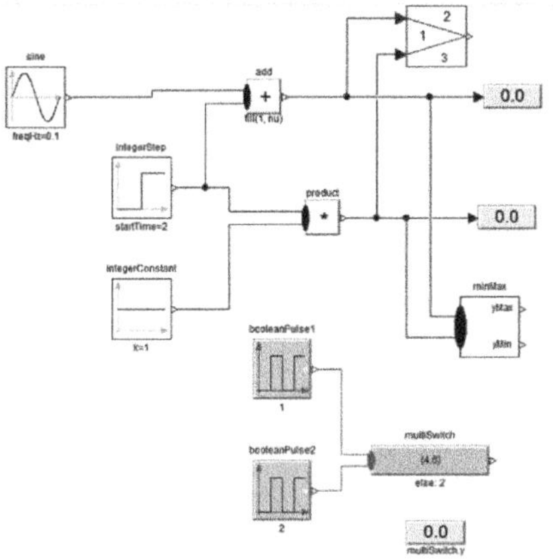

Figure 16-10. The `RealNetwork1` model from `Electrical.Blocks.Examples`.

An example model `LogicalNetwork1` in the `Examples` sublibrary is shown in Figure 16-11.

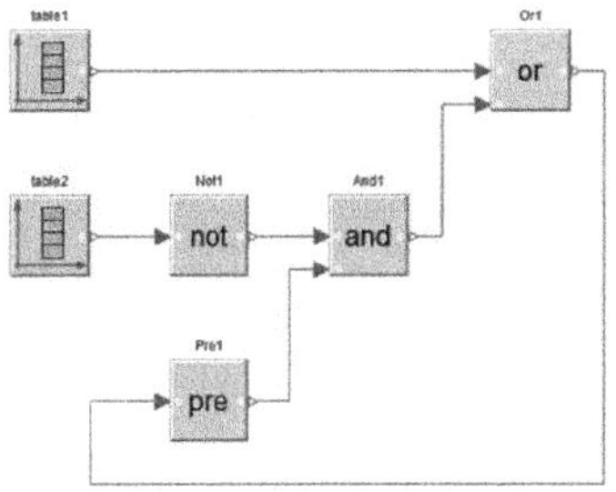

Figure 16-11. The `LogicalNetwork1` model from `Electrical.Blocks.Examples`.

16.8.2 Modelica.Blocks.Interfaces

This package (Table 16-23) contains interface definitions for *continuous* input/output blocks. In particular it contains the following *connector* classes:

Table 16-23. Connector classes in `Modelica.Blocks.Interfaces`.

Name	*Description*
`RealInput`	'input Real' as connector
`RealOutput`	'output Real' as connector

`BooleanInput`	'input Boolean' as connector
`BooleanOutput`	'output Boolean' as connector
`IntegerInput`	'input Integer' as connector
`IntegerOutput`	'output Integer' as connector
`RealVectorInput`	Real input connector used for vector of connectors
`IntegerVectorInput`	Integer input connector used for vector of connectors
`BooleanVectorInput`	Boolean input connector used for vector of connectors

The icons corresponding to these classes are depicted in Figure 16-12.

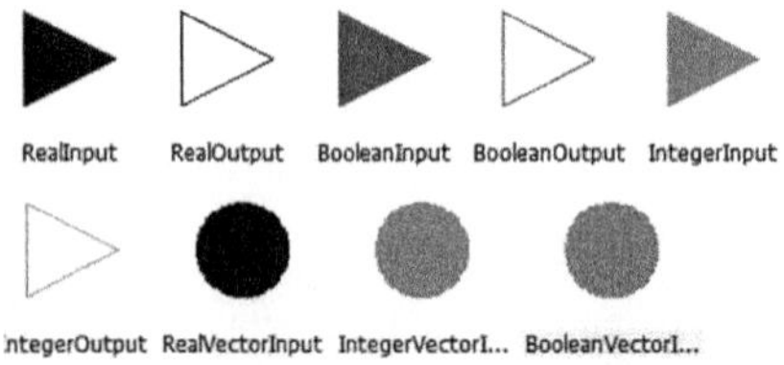

Figure 16-12. Icons for some connector classes used by the Modelica Blocks library.

Of the above, the use of `RealInput` and `RealOutput` is explained in some detail in Section 5.2, page 188. The following partial block classes are provided to model *continuous* control blocks (Table 16-24).

Table 16-24. Partial continuous control block classes in `Modelica.Blocks.Interfaces`.

Name	*Description*
`SO`	Single Output continuous control block
`MO`	Multiple Output continuous control block
`SISO`	Single Input Single Output continuous control block
`SI2SO`	2 Single Input / 1 Single Output continuous control block
`SIMO`	Single Input Multiple Output continuous control block
`MISO`	Multiple Input Single Output continuous control block
`PartialRealMISO`	Partial block with a `RealVectorInput` and a `RealOutput` signal
`MIMO`	Multiple Input Multiple Output continuous control block
`MIMOs`	Multiple Input Multiple Output continuous control block with same number of inputs and outputs
`MI2MO`	2 Multiple Input / Multiple Output continuous control block
`SignalSource`	Base class for continuous signal source
`SVcontrol`	Single-Variable continuous controller
`MVcontrol`	Multi-Variable continuous controller

The partial block classes in Table 16-25 are provided to model *discrete* and *Boolean* control blocks:

Table 16-25. Partial discrete and `Boolean` control block classes in `Modelica.Blocks.Interfaces`.

Name	*Description*
`DiscreteBlock`	Base class of discrete control blocks

DiscreteSISO	Single Input Single Output discrete control block
DiscreteMIMO	Multiple Input Multiple Output discrete control block
DiscreteMIMOs	Multiple Input Multiple Output discrete control block
SVdiscrete	Discrete Single-Variable controller
MVdiscrete	Discrete Multi-Variable controller
BooleanSISO	Single Input Single Output control block with signals of type Boolean
BooleanMIMOs	Multiple Input Multiple Output continuous control block with same number of inputs and outputs of Boolean type
MI2BooleanMOs	2 Multiple Input / Boolean Multiple Output block with same signal lengths
SI2BooleanSO	2 Single Input / Boolean Single Output block
BooleanSignalSource	Base class for Boolean signal sources
IntegerSO	Single Integer Output continuous control block
IntegerMO	Multiple Integer Output continuous control block
IntegerSignalSource	Base class for continuous Integer signal source
IntegerSIBooleanSO	Integer Input Boolean Output continuous control block
IntegerMIBooleanMOs	Multiple Integer Input Multiple Boolean Output continuous control block with same number of inputs and outputs
PartialIntegerSISO	Partial block with a IntegerInput and an IntegerOutput signal
PartialIntegerMISO	Partial block with an IntegerVectorInput and an IntegerOutput signal
partialBooleanSISO	Partial block with 1 input and 1 output Boolean signal
partialBooleanSI2SO	Partial block with 2 input and 1 output Boolean signal
partialBooleanSI3SO	Partial block with 3 input and 1 output Boolean signal
partialBooleanSI	Partial block with 1 input Boolean signal
partialBooleanSO	Partial block with 1 output Boolean signal
partialBooleanSource	Partial source block (has 1 output Boolean signal and an appropriate default icon)
partialBooleanThresholdComparison	Partial block to compare the Real input u with a threshold and provide the result as 1 Boolean output signal
partialBooleanComparison	Partial block with 2 Real input and 1 Boolean output signal (the result of a comparison of the two Real inputs)
PartialBooleanSISO_small	Partial block with a BooleanInput and a BooleanOutput signal and a small block icon
PartialBooleanMISO	Partial block with a BooleanVectorInput and a BooleanOutput signal
Adaptors	Obsolete package with components to send signals to a

	bus or receive signals from a bus (only for backward compatibility)
`PartialConversionBlock`	Partial block defining the interface for conversion blocks

Source code for a selection of these classes is available in Appendix D.

16.8.3 Modelica.Blocks.Continuous

This package contains the basic continuous input/output blocks shown in Figure 16-13.

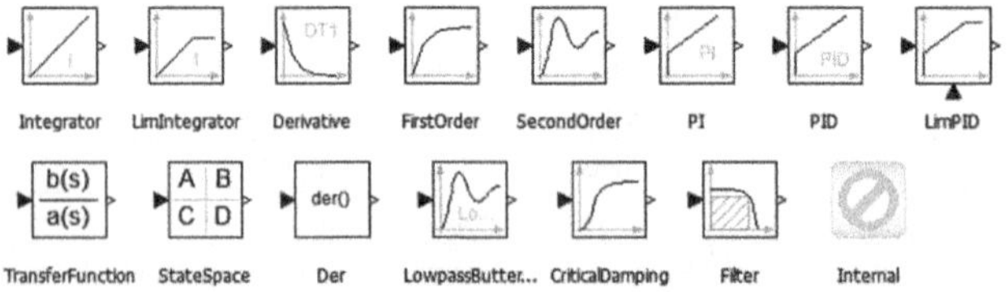

Figure 16-13. Icons for basic continuous input/output blocks in `Modelica.Blocks.Continuous`.

Source code for a selection of these classes is available in Appendix D.

16.8.4 Modelica.Blocks.Nonlinear

This package contains the *discontinuous* and *nondifferentiable*, *algebraic* input/output blocks shown in Figure 16-14.

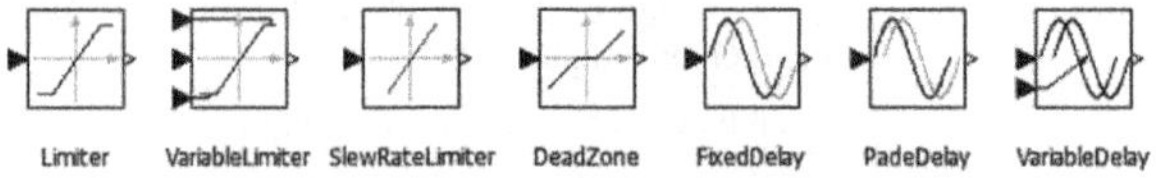

Figure 16-14. Icons for discontinuous and nondifferentiable input/output blocks.

Source code for these classes is available in Appendix D.

16.8.5 Modelica.Blocks.Math

This package contains basic mathematical operations, such as summation and multiplication, and basic mathematical functions, such as `sqrt` and `sin`, as input/output blocks. All blocks of this library can be either connected with continuous blocks or with sampled-data blocks. In particular, the operations and functions shown in Table 16-26 are provided.

Table 16-26. Mathematical operations and functions as blocks in `Modelica.Blocks.Math`.

Name	*Description*
`UnitConversions`	Conversion blocks to convert between SI and non-SI unit signals
`InverseBlockConstraints`	Construct inverse model by requiring that two inputs and two outputs are identical (replaces the

	previously, unbalanced, TwoInputs and TwoOutputs blocks)
`Gain`	Output the product of a gain value with the input signal
`MatrixGain`	Output the product of a gain matrix with the input signal vector
`MultiSum`	Sum of Reals: y = k[1]*u[1] + k[2]*u[2] + ... + k[n]*u[n]
`MultiProduct`	Product of Reals: y = u[1]*u[2]* ... *u[n]
`MultiSwitch`	Set Real expression that is associated with the first active input signal
`Sum`	Output the sum of the elements of the input vector
`Feedback`	Output difference between commanded and feedback input
`Add`	Output the sum of the two inputs
`Add3`	Output the sum of the three inputs
`Product`	Output product of the two inputs
`Division`	Output first input divided by second input
`Abs`	Output the absolute value of the input
`Sign`	Output the sign of the input
`Sqrt`	Output the square root of the input (input >= 0 required)
`Sin`	Output the sine of the input
`Cos`	Output the cosine of the input
`Tan`	Output the tangent of the input
`Asin`	Output the arc sine of the input
`Acos`	Output the arc cosine of the input
`Atan`	Output the arc tangent of the input
`Atan2`	Output atan(u1/u2) of the inputs u1 and u2
`Sinh`	Output the hyperbolic sine of the input
`Cosh`	Output the hyperbolic cosine of the input
`Tanh`	Output the hyperbolic tangent of the input
`Exp`	Output the exponential (base e) of the input
`Log`	Output the natural (base e) logarithm of the input (input > 0 required)
`Log10`	Output the base 10 logarithm of the input (input > 0 required)
`RealToInteger`	Convert Real to Integer signal
`IntegerToReal`	Convert Integer to Real signals
`BooleanToReal`	Convert Boolean to Real signal
`BooleanToInteger`	Convert Boolean to Integer signal
`RealToBoolean`	Convert Real to Boolean signal

`IntegerToBoolean`	Convert Integer to Boolean signal
`RectangularToPolar`	Convert rectangular coordinates to polar coordinates
`PolarToRectangular`	Convert polar coordinates to rectangular coordinates
`Mean`	Calculate mean over period 1/f
`RectifiedMean`	Calculate rectified mean over period 1/f
`RootMeanSquare`	Calculate root mean square over period 1/f
`Harmonic`	Calculate harmonic over period 1/f
`Max`	Pass through the largest signal
`Min`	Pass through the smallest signal
`MinMax`	Output the minimum and the maximum element of the input vector
`LinearDependency`	Output a linear combination of the two inputs
`Edge`	Indicates rising edge of Boolean signal
`BooleanChange`	Indicates Boolean signal changing
`IntegerChange`	Indicates integer signal changing

The icons for these input/output blocks of basic mathematical functions are depicted in Figure 16-15.

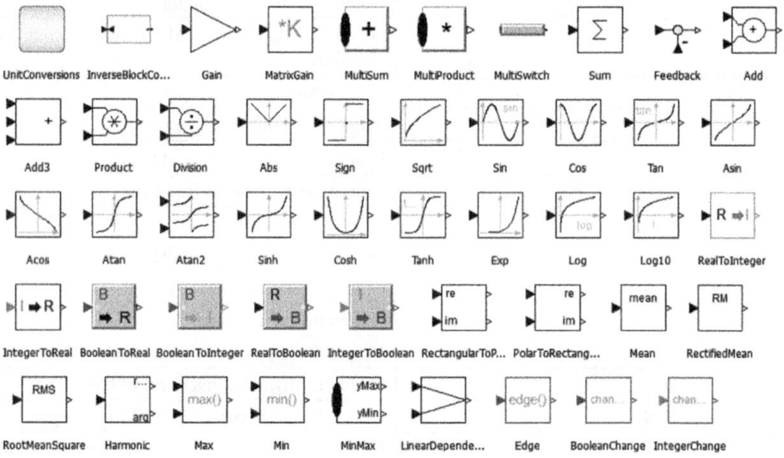

Figure 16-15. Icons for blocks corresponding to basic mathematical operations and functions.

Source code for some of these classes is available in Appendix D.

16.8.6 Modelica.Blocks.MathInteger

This package contains basic mathematical operations on Integer signals (Table 16-27 and Figure 16-16).

Table 16-27. Basic mathematical operations on `Integer` signals in `Modelica.Blocks.MathInteger`.

Name	*Description*
MultiSwitch	Set Integer expression that is associated with the first active input signal
Sum	Sum of Integers: y = k[1]*u[1] + k[2]*u[2] + ... + k[n]*u[n]
Product	Product of Integer: y = u[1]*u[2]* ... *u[n]
TriggeredAdd	Add input to previous value of output, if rising edge of trigger port

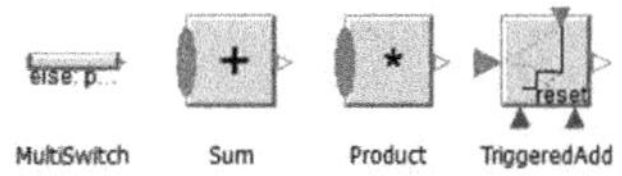

Figure 16-16. Icons for blocks corresponding to basic mathematical operations and functions.

Source code for some of these classes is available in Appendix D.

16.8.7 Modelica.Blocks.MathBoolean

This package (Table 16-28 and Figure 16-17) contains basic mathematical operations on Boolean signals. The package `MathBoolean` is a new design that shall replace in the future the `Logical` package. The new features are:

- If useful, blocks may have an arbitrary number of inputs (e.g., `And` block with 2,3,4,... Boolean inputs). This is based on the `connectorSizing` annotation which allows a tool to conveniently handle vectors of connectors.
- The blocks are smaller in size, so that the diagram area is better utilized for trivial blocks such as `And` or `Or`.

Table 16-28. Basic mathematical operations on `Boolean` signals in `Modelica.Blocks.MathBoolean`.

Name	*Description*
MultiSwitch	Set Boolean expression that is associated with the first active input signal
And	Logical 'and': y = u[1] and u[2] and ... and u[nu]
Or	Logical 'or': y = u[1] or u[2] or ... or u[nu]
Xor	Logical 'xor': y = oneTrue(u) (y is true, if exactly one element of u is true, otherwise it is false)
Nand	Logical 'nand': y = not (u[1] and u[2] and ... and u[nu])
Nor	Logical 'nor': y = not (u[1] or u[2] or ... or u[nu])
Not	Logical 'not': y = not u
RisingEdge	Output y is true, if the input u has a rising edge, otherwise it is false (y = edge(u))
FallingEdge	Output y is true, if the input u has a falling edge, otherwise it is false (y = edge(not u))
ChangingEdge	Output y is true, if the input u has either a rising or a falling edge and otherwise it is false (y=change(u))
OnDelay	Delay a rising edge of the input, but do not delay a falling edge.

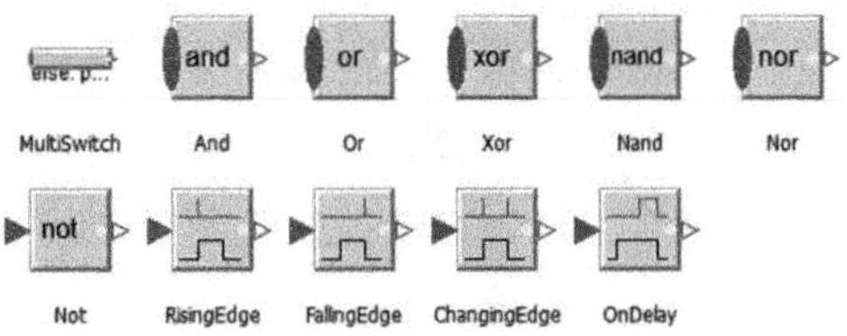

Figure 16-17. Icons for blocks corresponding to basic Boolean operations and functions.

Source code for some of these classes is available in Appendix D.

16.8.8 Modelica.Blocks.Sources

This package (Table 16-29) contains *signal source* components, that is, blocks which only have output signals. These blocks are used as signal generators. For example, a `Step` signal generator is used in the examples in Section Chapter 5, page 187 and Section 15.1, page 794.

Table 16-29. Signal source component models in `Modelica.Blocks.Sources`.

Name	*Description*
`RealExpression`	Set output signal to a time varying Real expression
`IntegerExpression`	Set output signal to a time varying Integer expression
`BooleanExpression`	Set output signal to a time varying Boolean expression
`Clock`	Generate actual time signal
`Constant`	Generate constant signal of type Real
`Step`	Generate step signal of type Real
`Ramp`	Generate ramp signal
`Sine`	Generate sine signal
`Cosine`	Generate cosine signal
`ExpSine`	Generate exponentially damped sine signal
`Exponentials`	Generate a rising and falling exponential signal
`Pulse`	Generate pulse signal of type Real
`SawTooth`	Generate saw tooth signal
`Trapezoid`	Generate trapezoidal signal of type Real
`KinematicPTP`	Move as fast as possible along a distance within given kinematic constraints
`KinematicPTP2`	Move as fast as possible from start to end position within given kinematic constraints with output signals q, qd=der(q), qdd=der(qd)
`TimeTable`	Generate a (possibly discontinuous) signal by linear interpolation in a table
`CombiTimeTable`	Table look-up with respect to time and linear/periodic extrapolation methods (data from matrix/file)
`BooleanConstant`	Generate constant signal of type Boolean
`BooleanStep`	Generate step signal of type Boolean
`BooleanPulse`	Generate pulse signal of type Boolean
`SampleTrigger`	Generate sample trigger signal

`BooleanTable`	Generate a Boolean output signal based on a vector of time instants
`RadioButtonSource`	Boolean signal source that mimics a radio button
`IntegerConstant`	Generate constant signal of type Integer
`IntegerStep`	Generate step signal of type Integer
`IntegerTable`	Generate an Integer output signal based on a table matrix with [time, yi] values

All sources are automatically vectorized when needed, and works either for connecting scalars or vectors of signals.

All `Real` source signals (with the exception of the `Constant` source) have at least the following two parameters:

`offset`	Value which is added to all signal values.
`startTime`	Start time of signal. For `time` < `startTime`, the output is set to offset.

The `offset` parameter is especially useful in order to shift the corresponding source such that at initial time the system is stationary. To determine the corresponding value of `offset` usually requires a trimming calculation.

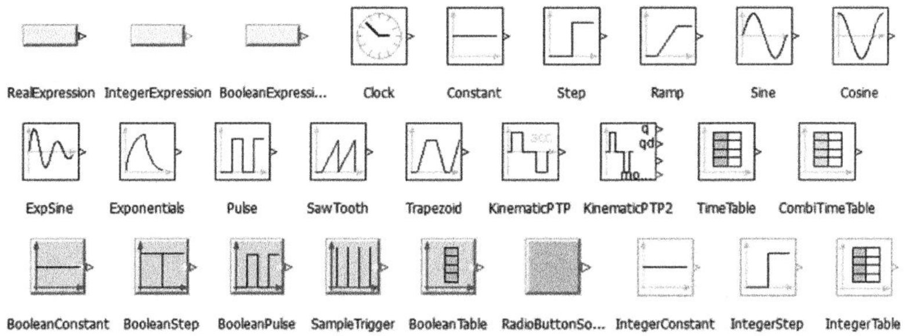

Figure 16-18. Icons for signal sources of various forms.

Source code for some of these classes is available in Appendix D.

16.9 Modelica_StateGraph2 Library

The library `Modelica_StateGraph2` is a free Modelica package providing components to model discrete event, reactive and hybrid systems in a convenient way with deterministic hierarchical state diagrams. An example model constructed with this library is shown in Figure 16-19.

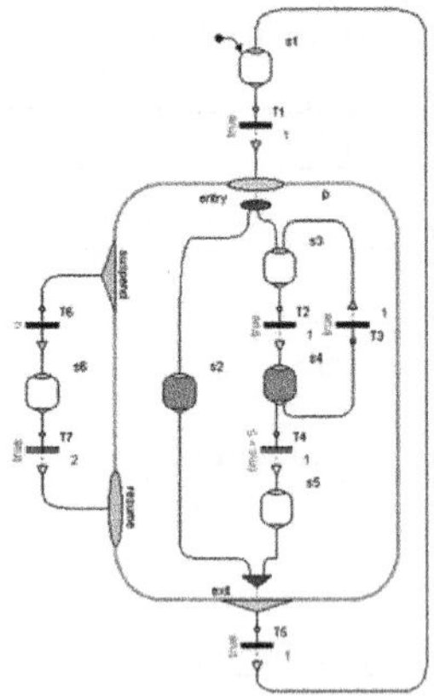

Figure 16-19. An example `Modelica_StateGraph2` model.

This library is inspired by Grafcet/Sequential Function Charts (SFC), Statecharts, Safe State Machines (SSM) and Mode Automata, and utilizes Modelica as action language. It has a similar modeling power as these formalisms, e.g. synchronization of parallel executing branches as in SFC (not easy in Statecharts), or suspending a hierarchical subgraph with one transition and resuming at the same states afterwards when entering it again, as in Statechart (not possible in SFC). A `StateGraph2` model is always deterministic due to Modelicas "single assignment rule." Via special blocks in subpackage `Blocks`, actions can be defined in a graphical way depending on the active step.

This library is implemented with Modelica 3.1 and utilizes non-standard extensions to Modelica 3.1.

Eventually at some point in the future the `StateGraph2` library will be effectively replaced by a library based on the Modelica clocked state machines that were introduced in Modelica 3.3, probably a future version of the Modelica_Synchronous library (Section 16.10, page 947).

The `StateGraph2` library contains the sublibraries listed in Table 16-30.

Table 16-30. Sublibraries in `Modelica_StateGraph2`.

Name	*Description*
`UsersGuide`	User's Guide
`Examples`	Examples to demonstrate the usage of the Modelica_StateGraph2 library
`Step`	Step (optionally with initial step and/or activePort)
`Transition`	Transition between steps (optionally with delayed transition and/or condition input port)
`LoopBreakingTransition`	Transition to break loops by introducing an artificial time delay (immediately fire and then wait)
`Parallel`	Composite or parallel step
`PartialParallel`	Partial compont to construct a parallel submodel via inheritance
`Blocks`	Input/output blocks that are designed for StateGraph2 but shall be included in the Modelica Standard Library
`Internal`	Internal utility models (should usually not be used by user)

16.10 Modelica_Synchronous Library

The `Modelica_Synchronous` library contains basic clocked synchronous input/output control blocks. See Chapter 13 for a detailed presentation regarding these concepts, especially Section 13.6, page 694, regarding the clocked features used in this library. The version of the library described here is preliminary—it is not yet part of the Modelica Standard Library, but is expected to be in the near future.

This library allows precise definition and synchronization of sampled data systems with different sampling rates. The library has elements to define periodic clocks and event clocks that trigger elements to sample, sub-sample, super-sample, or shift-sample partitions synchronously.

Optionally, quantization effects, computational delay or noise can be simulated. Continuous-time equations can be automatically discretized and utilized in a sampled data system. The sample rate of a partition need to be defined only at one location. All Modelica libraries designed so far for sampled systems, such as `Modelica.Blocks.Discrete` or `Modelica_LinearSystems2.Controller` are gradually becoming obsolete. Instead `Modelica_Synchronous` should be utilized in the future.

The library contains the sublibraries listed in Table 16-31.

Table 16-31. Sublibraries in `Modelica_Synchronous`.

Name	*Description*
`UsersGuide`	User's Guide
`Examples`	Library of examples to demonstrate the usage of package Modelica_Synchronous
`ClockSignals`	Library of blocks for clocked signals
`RealSignals`	Library of clocked blocks for Real signals
`IntegerSignals`	Library of clocked blocks for Integer signals
`BooleanSignals`	Library of clocked blocks for Boolean signals
`Types`	Library of types with choices, especially to build menus

The `Examples.SimpleControlledDrive` model in Figure 16-20 shows a simple sampled data system in which the borders of the discrete-time partition are marked by the sample and hold operators, a clocked PI controller is used in the partition and the sample rate is defined at one location with a clock.

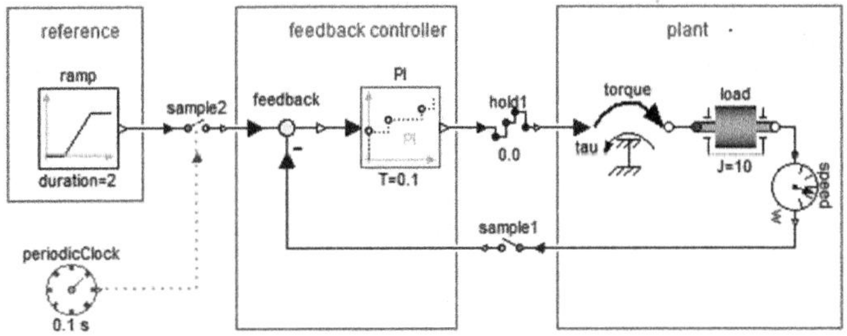

Figure 16-20. The `Examples.SimpleControlledDrive` model from the `Modelica_Synchronous` library.

16.11 Modelica.Mechanics Library

This package contains components to model *mechanical systems*. Currently the following subpackages are available:

- `MultiBody` 3-dimensional mechanical components
- `Rotational` 1-dimensional rotational mechanical components.
- `Translational` 1-dimensional translational mechanical components.

Source code for some models in these sublibraries is available in Appendix D.

16.11.1 Modelica.Mechanics.MultiBody Library

The Mechanics.MultiBody library contains model components for (rigid bodies) three-dimensional mechanical systems consisting of joints, bodies, force and sensor elements. Joints can be driven by elements of the Rotational library. Every element has a default animation.

See Section 15.10, page 877, for an overview description of this library including some hints and examples how to use it. Figure 16-21 below shows some examples of models built using the MultiBody library.

Figure 16-21. Examples of three-dimensional visualizations of models using the MultiBody library.

16.11.2 Modelica.Mechanics.Rotational Library

This package contains components to model one-dimensional *rotational* mechanical systems, including different types of gearboxes, shafts with inertia, external torques, spring/damper elements, frictional elements, backlash, elements to measure angle, angular velocity, angular acceleration and the torque transmitted at a flange. A simple example with explanation of using a few rotational elements from this library is presented in Section 15.1, page 794. A discussion of the hybrid mode switching `ElastoBacklash` model is given in Section 13.4.2, page 682. A selection of the basic equations used in this library is described in Section 14.4, page 751.

In the `Examples` sublibrary several examples are present to demonstrate the usage of the elements. Just open the corresponding example model and simulate the model according to the provided description.

A unique feature of this library is the component-oriented modeling of Coulomb friction elements, such as friction in bearings, clutches, brakes, and gear efficiency. Even (dynamically) coupled friction elements, for example, as in automatic gearboxes, can be handled without introducing stiffness, leading to fast simulations.

The underlying theory is rather new and is based on the solution of mixed continuous/discrete systems of equations, that is, equations where the unknowns are of type `Real`, `Integer`, or `Boolean`. Provided appropriate numeric algorithms for the solution of such types of systems are available in the simulation tool, the simulation of (dynamically) coupled friction elements of this library is efficient and reliable.

In version 3.0 of the Modelica Standard Library, the basic design of the library has changed: Previously, bearing connectors could or could not be connected. In 3.0, the bearing connector is renamed to "`support`" and this connector is enabled via parameter "`useSupport`". If the support connector is enabled, it must be connected, and if it is not enabled, it must not be connected.

In version 3.2 of the Modelica Standard Library, all dissipative components of the Rotational library got an optional `heatPort` connector to which the dissipated energy is transported in form of heat. This connector is enabled via parameter "`useHeatPort`". If the `heatPort` connector is enabled, it must be connected, and if it is not enabled, it must not be connected. Independently, whether the heatPort is enabled or not, the dissipated power is available from the new variable "`lossPower`" (which is positive if heat is flowing out of the `heatPort`). For an example, see `Examples.HeatLosses`.

The library is structured into several sublibraries, shown in Table 16-32.

Table 16-32. Sublibraries in `Modelica.Mechanics.Rotational`.

Name	*Description*
`UsersGuide`	User's Guide of Rotational Library
`Examples`	Demonstration examples of the components of this package
`Components`	Components for 1D rotational mechanical drive trains
`Sensors`	Sensors to measure variables in 1D rotational mechanical components
`Sources`	Sources to drive 1D rotational mechanical components
`Interfaces`	Connectors and partial models for 1D rotational mechanical components
`Icons`	Icons for Rotational package

16.11.2.1 Modelica.Mechanics.Rotational.Components

The `Mechanics.Rotational.Components` sublibrary contains the component models listed in Table 16-33.

Table 16-33. Component models in `Modelica.Mechanics.Rotational.Components`.

Name	*Description*
`Fixed`	Flange fixed in housing at a given angle
`Inertia`	1D-rotational component with inertia
`Disc`	1-dim. rotational rigid component without inertia, where right flange is rotated by a fixed angle with respect to left flange
`Spring`	Linear 1D rotational spring
`Damper`	Linear 1D rotational damper
`SpringDamper`	Linear 1D rotational spring and damper in parallel
`ElastoBacklash`	Backlash connected in series to linear spring and damper (backlash is modeled with elasticity)
`BearingFriction`	Coulomb friction in bearings
`Brake`	Brake based on Coulomb friction
`Clutch`	Clutch based on Coulomb friction
`OneWayClutch`	Series connection of freewheel and clutch
`IdealGear`	Ideal gear without inertia
`LossyGear`	Gear with mesh efficiency and bearing friction (stuck/rolling possible)
`IdealPlanetary`	Ideal planetary gear box
`Gearbox`	Realistic model of a gearbox (based on LossyGear)
`IdealGearR2T`	Gearbox transforming rotational into translational motion
`IdealRollingWheel`	Simple 1-dim. model of an ideal rolling wheel without inertia

`InitializeFlange`	Initializes a flange with pre-defined angle, speed and angular acceleration (usually, this is reference data from a control bus)
`RelativeStates`	Definition of relative state variables
`TorqueToAngleAdaptor`	Signal adaptor for a Rotational flange with angle, speed, and acceleration as outputs and torque as input (especially useful for FMUs)
`AngleToTorqueAdaptor`	Signal adaptor for a Rotational flange with torque as output and angle, speed, and optionally acceleration as inputs (especially useful for FMUs)

The icons corresponding to the rotational model components are depicted in Figure 16-22 below.

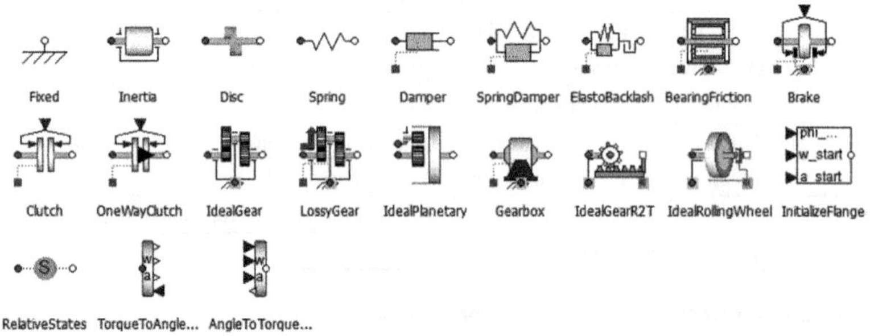

Figure 16-22. Icons for components in the `Mechanical.Rotational.Components` sublibrary.

Source code for some of these classes is available in Appendix D.

16.11.2.2 Modelica.Mechanics.Rotational.Interfaces

This `Rotational.Interfaces` package contains connector classes and partial models (i.e., base classes) for 1D rotational mechanical components. The use of the connector classes `Flange_a` and `Flange_b` for rotational connections is mentioned in Section 15.1, page 794. The icons corresponding to models in the `Interfaces` subpackage are depicted in Figure 16-23.

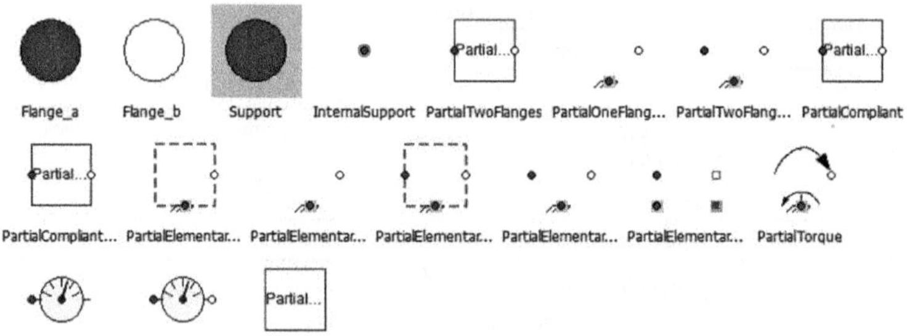

Figure 16-23. Icons for connector classes and partial classes in the mechanical rotational sublibrary.

Source code for these classes is available in Appendix D.

16.11.2.3 Modelica.Mechanics.Rotational.Sensors

The `Sensors` sublibrary for sensors of mechanical rotational quantities such as angle, angular speed, angular acceleration, torque, and so on, can be used to measure certain variables in 1D rotational mechanical components.

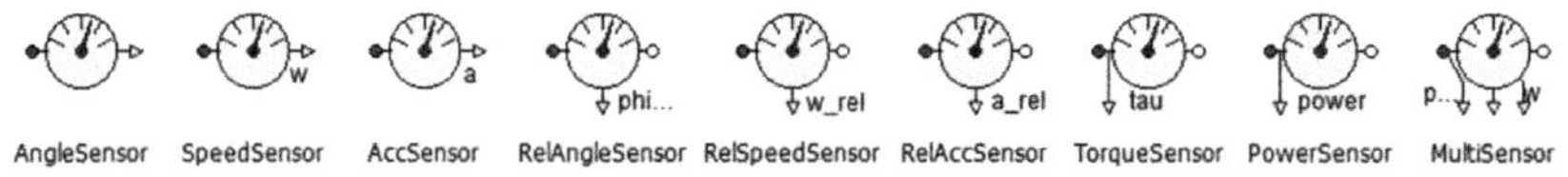

Figure 16-24. Icons for sensor components in the mechanical rotational sensor sublibrary.

Source code for these classes is available in Appendix D.

16.11.2.4 Modelica.Mechanics.Rotational.Examples

This package contains example models to demonstrate the usage of the one-dimensional mechanical rotational library. The example models present are shown in Table 16-34.

Table 16-34. Rotational example models in `Modelica.Mechanics.Rotational.Examples`.

Name	*Description*
`First`	First example: simple drive train
`FirstGrounded`	First example: simple drive train with grounded elements
`Friction`	Drive train with clutch and brake
`CoupledClutches`	Drive train with 3 dynamically coupled clutches
`LossyGearDemo1`	Example to show that gear efficiency may lead to stuck motion
`LossyGearDemo2`	Example to show combination of LossyGear and BearingFriction
`LossyGearDemo3`	Example that failed in the previous version of the LossyGear version
`ElasticBearing`	Example to show possible usage of support flange
`Backlash`	Example to demonstrate backlash
`RollingWheel`	Demonstrate coupling Rotational - Translational
`HeatLosses`	Demonstrate the modeling of heat losses
`SimpleGearShift`	Simple Gearshift
`GenerationOfFMUs`	Example to demonstrate variants to generate FMUs (Functional Mockup Units)
`Utilities`	Utility components used by the example models

Source code for some these classes is available in Appendix D.

16.11.3 Modelica.Mechanics.Translational Library

This package contains components to model 1-dimensional *translational* mechanical systems. In Section 14.3, page 749, we describe the basic equations governing such translational motion. A more detailed presentation concerning many issues of one-dimensional translational mechanical models was earlier given in Sections 5.3 and 5.4 , pages 190 and 194.

The *filled* and *nonfilled green squares* at the left and right side of a component represent translational *mechanical flanges*. Drawing a line between such squares means that the corresponding flanges are *rigidly attached* to each other. The components of this library can usually be connected together in an arbitrary way. For example, it is possible to directly connect two springs or two sliding masses with inertia.

The only connection restriction is that the Coulomb friction elements (e.g., `MassWithStopAndFriction`) should be only connected together provided a compliant element, such as a spring, is in between. The reason is that otherwise the frictional force is not uniquely defined if the elements are stuck at the same time instant (i.e., there does not exist a unique solution) and some simulation systems may not be able to handle this situation, since this leads to a singularity during simulation. It can only be resolved in a "clean way" by combining the two connected friction elements into one component and resolving the ambiguity of the frictional force in the stuck mode.

Another restriction arises if the hard stops in model `MassWithStopAndFriction` are used, that is, the movement of the mass is limited by a stop at `smax` or `smin`. This requires the states `Stop.s` and `Stop.v`. If these states are eliminated during the index reduction stage (Section 18.2.4, page 1009) of the total equation system solution process the model will not work. To avoid this any inertias should be connected via springs to the `Stop` element—other sliding masses, dampers or hydraulic chambers must be avoided.

In the *icon* of every component an *arrow* is displayed in grey color. This arrow characterizes the coordinate system in which the vectors of the component are resolved. It is directed into the positive translational direction (in the mathematical sense). In the flanges of a component, a coordinate system is rigidly attached to the flange. It is called *flange frame* and is directed in parallel to the component coordinate system. As a result, e.g., the positive flange-force of a "left" flange (`flange_a`) is directed into the flange, whereas the positive flange-force of a "right" flange (`flange_b`) is directed out of the flange.

See Section 5.4, page 194, for further discussion of coordinate systems and flanges of one-dimensional translational model components.

As already stated in Section 5.2, page 188, a one-dimensional mechanical translational flange is described by a Modelica connector containing the following variables:

```
Modelica.SIunits.Position s        "absolute position of flange";
flow Modelica.SIunits.Force f      "flange-force at the flange";
```

This library is designed in a general way in order that components can be connected together in every meaningful combination, for example, including direct connections of two springs or two shafts with inertia.

As a consequence, most models lead to a system of differential-algebraic equations (DAEs) of *index 3* (i.e., constraint equations have to be differentiated twice in order to arrive at a state space representation, see also Section 18.2.3, page 1005) and the Modelica translator or the simulator has to cope with this system representation.

According to our present knowledge, this requires that the Modelica translator is able to symbolically differentiate equations—otherwise it is, for example, not possible to provide consistent initial conditions. However, even if consistent initial conditions are present most numerical DAE integrators can handle at most index 2 DAEs.

In version 3.2 of the Modelica Standard Library, all dissipative components of the `Translational` library got an optional `heatPort` connector to which the dissipated energy is transported in form of heat. This connector is enabled via parameter `useHeatPort`. If the `heatPort` connector is enabled, it must be connected, and if it is not enabled, it must not be connected. Independently, whether the `heatPort` is enabled or not, the dissipated power is available from the new variable `lossPower`, which is positive if heat is flowing out of the `heatPort`. For an example, see `Examples.HeatLosses`.

The `Mechanics.Translational library` is structured into the sublibraries listed in Table 16-35.

Table 16-35. Sublibraries in `Modelica.Mechanics.Translational`.

Name	*Description*
`Examples`	Demonstration examples of the components of this package
`Components`	Components for 1D translational mechanical drive trains
`Sensors`	Sensors for 1-dim. translational mechanical quantities
`Sources`	Sources to drive 1D translational mechanical components

`Interfaces`	Interfaces for 1-dim. translational mechanical components

16.11.3.1 Modelica.Mechanics.Translational.Components

The `Translational.Components` sublibrary (Table 16-36 and Figure 16-25) contains basic components for one-dimensional mechanical translational drive trains.

Table 16-36. Basic 1D translational models in `Modelica.Mechanics.Translational.Components`.

Name	*Description*
`Fixed`	Fixed flange
`Mass`	Sliding mass with inertia
`Rod`	Rod without inertia
`Spring`	Linear 1D translational spring
`Damper`	Linear 1D translational damper
`SpringDamper`	Linear 1D translational spring and damper in parallel
`ElastoGap`	1D translational spring damper combination with gap
`SupportFriction`	Coulomb friction in support
`Brake`	Brake based on Coulomb friction
`IdealGearR2T`	Gearbox transforming rotational into translational motion
`IdealRollingWheel`	Simple 1-dim. model of an ideal rolling wheel without inertia
`InitializeFlange`	Initializes a flange with pre-defined position, speed and acceleration (usually, this is reference data from a control bus)
`MassWithStopAndFriction`	Sliding mass with hard stop and Stribeck friction
`RelativeStates`	Definition of relative state variables

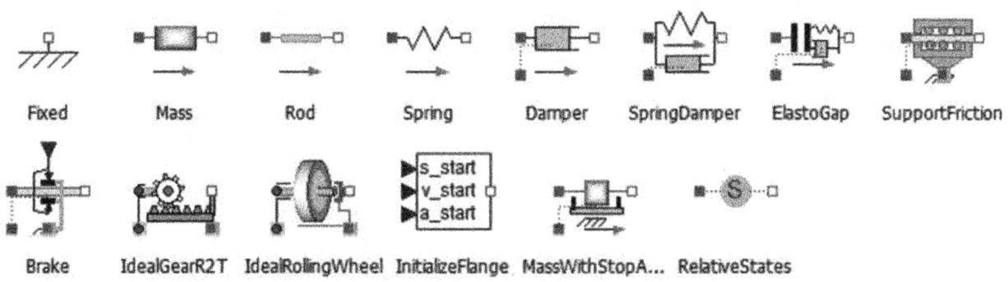

Figure 16-25. Icons for components in the mechanical translational sublibrary.

Some source code for `Mechanics.Translational` classes is available in Appendix D.

16.11.3.2 Modelica.Mechanics.Translational.Sources

Sources for one-dimensional translational mechanical quantities such as position, speed, acceleration, etc., belong to this sublibrary, for which the icons are depicted in Figure 16-26 below.

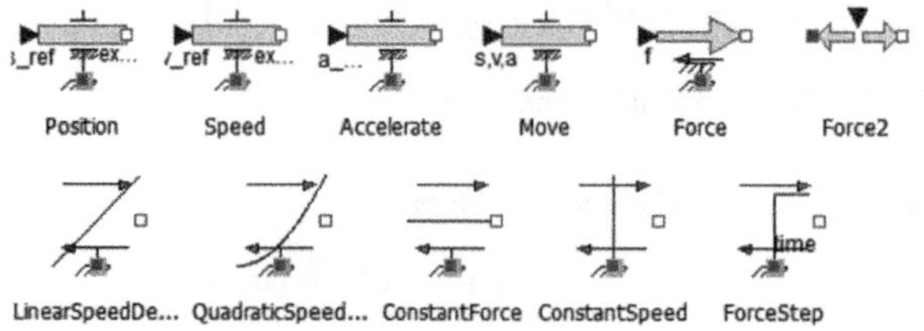

Figure 16-26. Icons for source models in the mechanical translational sources sublibrary.

16.11.3.3 Modelica.Mechanics.Translational.Interfaces

Interfaces for one-dimensional translational mechanical components, that is, the connector classes `Flange_a` and `Flange_b`, as well as base classes such as `PartialRigid` and `PartialCompliant` belong to this library (Table 16-37). The icons are depicted in Figure 16-27 below. The class `PartialCompliant` is presented in some detail in Section 5.4.2, page 196, whereas `PartialRigid` is used in the hanging mass oscillator model in Section 5.4.4, page 199.

Table 16-37. Connector and base classes in `Modelica.Mechanics.Translational.Interfaces`.

Name	*Description*
`Flange_a`	(left) 1D translational flange (flange axis directed INTO cut plane, e. g. from left to right)
`Flange_b`	(right) 1D translational flange (flange axis directed OUT OF cut plane)
`Support`	Support/housing 1D translational flange
`InternalSupport`	Adapter model to utilize conditional support connector
`PartialTwoFlanges`	Component with two translational 1D flanges
`PartialOneFlangeAndSupport`	Partial model for a component with one translational 1-dim. shaft flange and a support used for graphical modeling, i.e., the model is build up by drag-and-drop from elementary components
`PartialTwoFlangesAndSupport`	Partial model for a component with two translational 1-dim. shaft flanges and a support used for graphical modeling, i.e., the model is build up by drag-and-drop from elementary components
`PartialRigid`	Rigid connection of two translational 1D flanges
`PartialCompliant`	Compliant connection of two translational 1D flanges
`PartialCompliantWithRelativeStates`	Base model for the compliant connection of two translational 1-dim. shaft flanges where the relative position and relative velocities are used as states
`PartialElementaryOneFlangeAndSupport`	Obsolete partial model. Use `PartialElementaryOneFlangeAndSupport2`.
`PartialElementaryOneFlangeAndSupport2`	Partial model for a component with one translational 1-dim. shaft flange and a support used for textual

	modeling, i.e., for elementary models
`PartialElementaryTwoFlangesAndSupport`	Obsolete partial model. Use `PartialElementaryTwoFlangesAndSupport2`.
`PartialElementaryTwoFlangesAndSupport2`	Partial model for a component with one translational 1-dim. shaft flange and a support used for textual modeling, i.e., for elementary models
`PartialElementaryRotationalToTranslational`	Partial model to transform rotational into translational motion
`PartialForce`	Partial model of a force acting at the flange (accelerates the flange)
`PartialAbsoluteSensor`	Device to measure a single absolute flange variable
`PartialRelativeSensor`	Device to measure a single relative variable between two flanges
`PartialFriction`	Base model of Coulomb friction elements

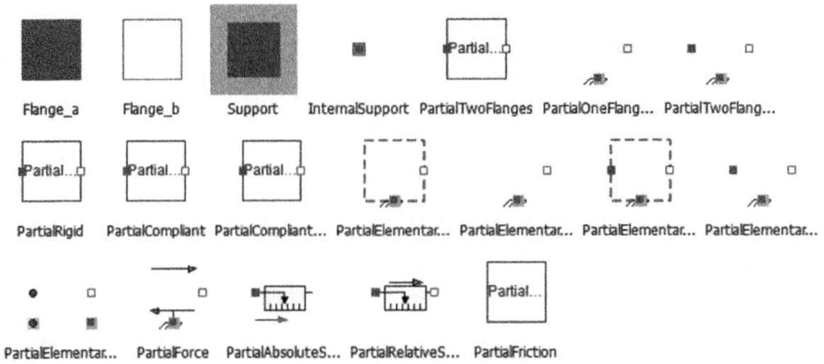

Figure 16-27. Icons for connector classes and partial classes for the mechanical translational sublibrary.

16.11.3.4 Modelica.Mechanics.Translational.Sensors

Sensors for one-dimensional translational mechanical quantities such as force, position, speed, and acceleration belong to this sublibrary, for which the icons are depicted in Figure 16-28 below.

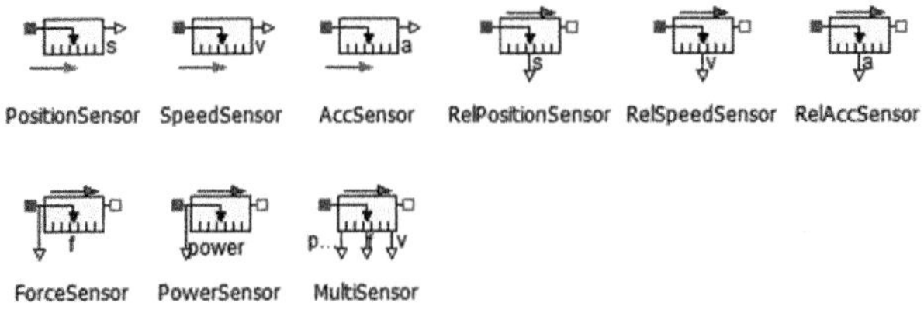

Figure 16-28. Icons for sensor components in the mechanical translational sensor sublibrary.

16.11.3.5 Modelica.Mechanics.Translational.Examples

This package contains example models to demonstrate the usage of the `Mechanics.Translational` package, including instructions on how to simulate them. A variant of the oscillator example is explained in detail in Section 5.4.4, page 199. The example models present in this sublibrary are listed in Table 16-38.

Table 16-38. Translational example models in `Modelica.Mechanics.Translational.Examples`.

Name	*Description*
`SignConvention`	Examples for the used sign conventions.
`InitialConditions`	Setting of initial conditions
`WhyArrows`	Use of arrows in Mechanics.Translational
`Accelerate`	Use of model accelerate.
`Damper`	Use of damper models.
`Oscillator`	Oscillator demonstrates the use of initial conditions.
`Sensors`	Sensors for translational systems.
`Friction`	Use of model Stop
`PreLoad`	Preload of a spool using ElastoGap models.
`ElastoGap`	Demonstrate usage of ElastoGap
`Brake`	Demonstrate braking of a translational moving mass
`HeatLosses`	Demonstrate the modeling of heat losses
`Utilities`	Utility classes used by the Example models

The example model in Figure 16-29 below demonstrates how to model the dissipated power of a `Translational` model by enabling the `heatPort` of all components and connecting these heatPorts via a convection element to the environment. The total heat flow generated by the elements and transported to the environment is present in variable `convection.fluid`.

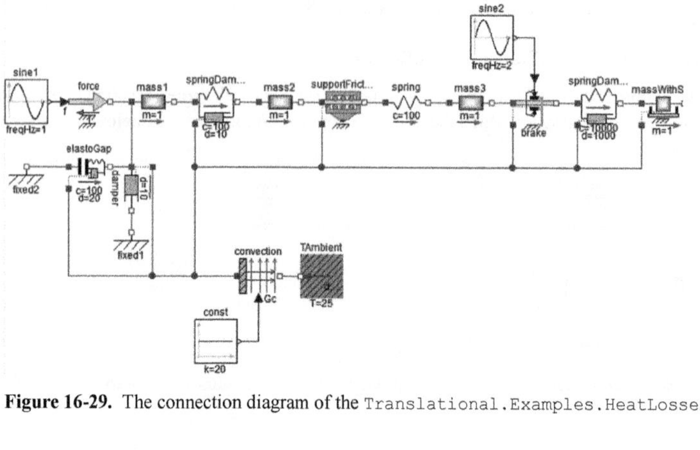

Figure 16-29. The connection diagram of the `Translational.Examples.HeatLosses` model.

16.12 Modelica.FLuid Library

The library `Modelica.Fluid` provides components for one-dimensional thermo-fluid flow in networks of vessels, pipes, fluid machines, valves and fittings.

A unique feature is that the component equations and the media models as well as pressure loss and heat transfer correlations are decoupled from each other.

All components are implemented such that they can be used for media from the `Modelica.Media` library. This means especially that an incompressible or compressible medium, a single or a multiple substance medium with one or more phases might be used.

The `Fluid` library contains the sublibraries listed in Table 16-39.

Table 16-39. Sublibraries in `Modelica.Fluid`.

Name	*Description*
`UsersGuide`	User's Guide
`Examples`	Demonstration of the usage of the library
`System`	System properties and default values (ambient, flow direction, initialization)
`Vessels`	Devices for storing fluid
`Pipes`	Devices for conveying fluid
`Machines`	Devices for converting between energy held in a fluid and mechanical energy
`Valves`	Components for the regulation and control of fluid flow
`Fittings`	Adaptors for connections of fluid components and the regulation of fluid flow
`Sources`	Define fixed or prescribed boundary conditions
`Sensors`	Ideal sensor components to extract signals from a fluid connector
`Interfaces`	Interfaces for steady state and unsteady, mixed-phase, multi-substance, incompressible and compressible flow
`Types`	Common types for fluid models
`Dissipation`	Functions for convective heat transfer and pressure loss characteristics
`Utilities`	Utility models to construct fluid components (should not be used directly)
`Icons`	

In Figure 16-30 below, several features of the `Fluid` library are demonstrated with a simple heating system example with a closed flow cycle. By just changing one configuration parameter in the system object the equations can be changed between steady-state and dynamic simulation with fixed or steady-state initial conditions.

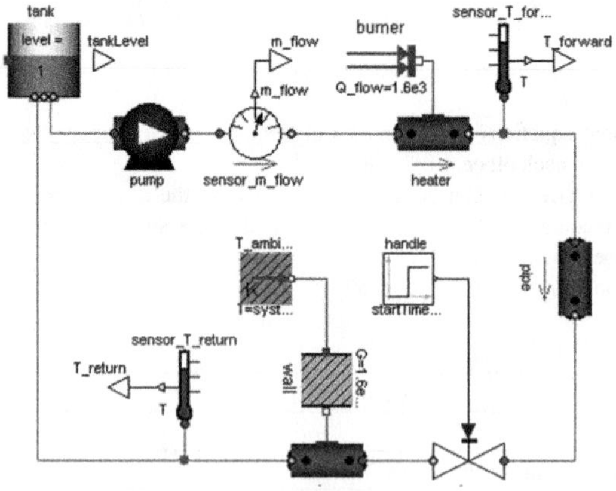

Figure 16-30. The connection diagram of the `Modelica.Fluid.Examples.HeatingSystem` model.

16.13 Modelica.Media Library

The `Modelica.Media` library contains interface definitions for media and the following property models for single and multiple substance fluids with one and multiple phases:

- *Ideal gases*: 1241 high precision gas models based on the NASA Glenn coefficients, plus ideal gas mixture models based on the same data.
- *Water models*: ConstantPropertyLiquidWater, WaterIF97—high precision water model according to the IAPWS/IF97 standard.
- *Air models*: SimpleAir, DryAirNasa, ReferenceAir, MoistAir, ReferenceMoistAir.
- *Incompressible media*: TableBased incompressible fluid models where properties are defined by tables rho(T), HeatCapacity_cp(T), etc.
- *Compressible liquids*: Simple liquid models with linear compressibility, Refrigerant Tetrafluoroethane (R134a).

The following parts are useful to study when starting to use this library:

- `Modelica.Media.UsersGuide`.
- `Modelica.Media.UsersGuide.MediumUsage` describes how to use a medium model in a component model.
- `Modelica.Media.UsersGuide.MediumDefinition` describes how a new fluid medium model has to be implemented.
- `Modelica.Media.UsersGuide.ReleaseNotes` summarizes the changes of the library releases.
- `Modelica.Media.Examples` contains examples that demonstrate the usage of this library.

The Media library contains the sublibraries listed in Talbe 16-40.

Table 16-40. Sublibraries in `Modelica.Media`.

Name	*Description*
`UsersGuide`	User's Guide of Media Library

Examples	Demonstrate usage of property models (currently: simple tests)
Interfaces	Interfaces for media models
Common	Data structures and fundamental functions for fluid properties
Air	Medium models for air
CompressibleLiquids	Compressible liquid models
IdealGases	Data and models of ideal gases (single, fixed and dynamic mixtures) from NASA source
Incompressible	Medium model for T-dependent properties, defined by tables or polynomials
R134a	R134a: Medium model for R134a
Water	Medium models for water

16.14 Modelica.Thermal Library

The Modelica.Thermal library contains thermal system components to model heat transfer and simple thermo-fluid pipe flow. It contains two sublibraries: FluidHeatFlow and HeatTransfer. This library is not as general and comprehensive as the Modelica.Fluid and Modelica.Media libraries and was developed almost ten years before those libraries.

16.14.1 Modelica.Thermal.FluidHeatFlow

This package contains very simple-to-use components to model coolant flows as needed to simulate cooling, for example, of electric machines. It is structured into the following sublibraries:

- Components: components like different types of pipe models
- Examples: some test examples
- Interfaces: definition of connectors and partial models (containing the core thermodynamic equations)
- Media: definition of media properties
- Sensors: various sensors for pressure, temperature, volume and enthalpy flow
- Sources: various flow sources

Variables used in connectors:

- Pressure p
- flow MassFlowRate m_flow
- SpecificEnthalpy h
- flow EnthalpyFlowRate H_flow

EnthalpyFlowRate means the Enthalpy = $cp_{constant}$ * m * T that is carried by the medium's flow.

Limitations and assumptions:

- Splitting and mixing of coolant flows (media with the same cp) is possible.
- Reversing the direction of flow is possible.
- The medium is considered to be incompressible.
- No mixtures of media is taken into consideration.
- The medium may not change its phase.
- Medium properties are kept constant.

- Pressure changes are only due to pressure drop and geodetic height difference rho*g*h (if h > 0).
- A user-defined part (0..1) of the friction losses (V_flow*dp) are fed to the medium.

Note: Connected flowPorts have the same temperature (mixing temperature)! Since mixing may occur, the outlet temperature may be different from the connector's temperature. Outlet temperature is defined by variable T of the corresponding component.

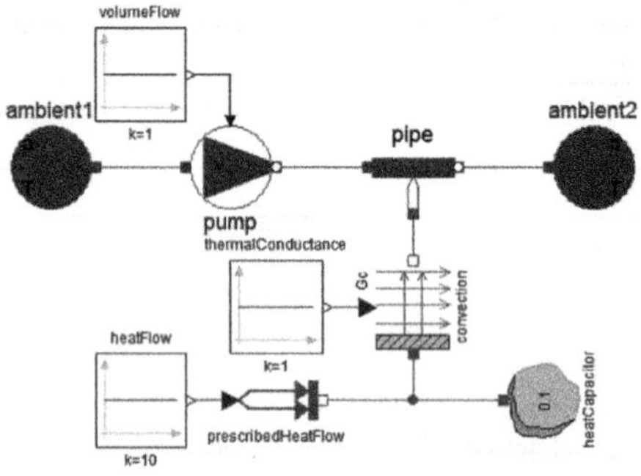

Figure 16-31. The `Modelica.Thermal.FLuidHeatFlow.Examples.SimpleCooling` example model.

16.14.2 Modelica.Thermal.HeatTransfer

The `Thermal.HeatTransfer` library (Table 16-41) contains components for one-dimensional heat transfer with lumped elements. This especially supports modeling of heat transfer in machines provided the parameters of the lumped elements, such as the heat capacity of a part, can be determined by measurements—due to the complex geometries and many materials used in machines, calculating the lumped element parameters from some basic analytic formulas is usually not possible.

Table 16-41. Sublibraries in `Modelica.Thermal.HeatTransfer`.

Name	*Description*
`Examples`	Example models to demonstrate the usage of package Modelica.Thermal.HeatTransfer
`Components`	Lumped thermal components
`Sensors`	Thermal sensors
`Sources`	Thermal sources
`Celsius`	Components with Celsius input and/or output
`Fahrenheit`	Components with Fahrenheit input and/or output
`Rankine`	Components with Rankine input and/or output
`Interfaces`	Connectors and partial models

A rather realistic example is provided in `Examples.Motor` where the heating of an electrical motor is modelled, see Figure 16-32 below.

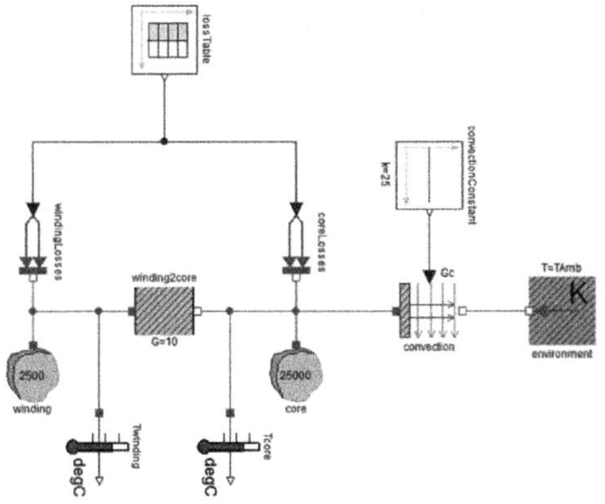

Figure 16-32. The `Modelica.Thermal.HeatTransfer.Examples.Motor` example model.

16.15 ThermoSysPro Library

ThermoSysPro is a library for the modeling and simulation of power plants and energy systems. It provides components in various disciplines related to the modeling of power plants and energy systems. The library contains the sublibraries listed in Table 16-42.

Table 16-42. Sublibraries in `ThermoSysPro` library.

Name	*Description*
`UsersGuide`	ThermoSysPro Licence and Users Guide
`Combustion`	Combustion library
`Correlations`	Fluid correlation library
`ElectroMechanics`	Electro-mechanics components library
`FlueGases`	Flue gases components library
`Functions`	General purpose functions
`HeatNetworksCooling`	Heat network cooling library
`InstrumentationAndControl`	Instrumentation and control library
`MultiFluids`	Multi-fluids components library
`Properties`	Fluids properties library
`Solar`	Solar components library
`Thermal`	Thermal components library
`Units`	Additional SI and non-SI units
`WaterSolution`	Water solution components library
`WaterSteam`	Water/steam components library
`Examples`	

16.15.1 ThermoSysPro.Examples

The main ThermoSysPro example model is the combined cycle power plant depicted in Figure 16-33.

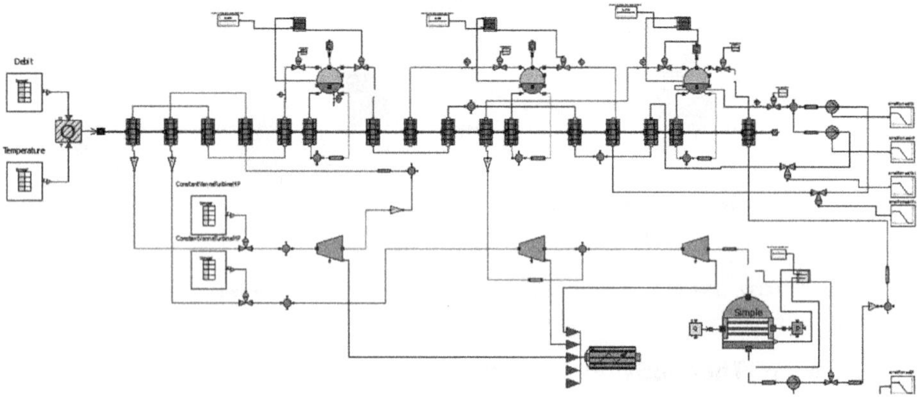

Figure 16-33. `ThermoSysPro` example model `CombinedCyclePowerPlant.CombinedCycle_TripTAC`

16.16 ThermoPower Library

The ThermoPower library is an open-source Modelica library for the dynamic modeling of thermal power plants and energy conversion systems. It provides basic components for system-level modeling, in particular for the study of control systems in traditional and innovative power plants and energy conversion systems.

It has been applied to the dynamic modelling of steam generators, combined-cycle power plants, third- and fourth-generation nuclear power plants, direct-steam generation solar plants, organic Rankine cycle plants, and cryogenic circuits for nuclear fusion applications.

The ThermoPower library uses the medium models provided by the Modelica.Media library (Section 16.13, page 958). The library contains the sublibraries listed in Table 16-43.

Table 16-43. Sublibraries in `ThermoPower` library.

Name	*Description*
`System`	System wide properties
`Icons`	Icons for ThermoPower library
`Functions`	Miscellaneous functions
`Electrical`	Simplified models of electric power components
`Choices`	Choice enumerations for ThermoPower models
`Examples`	Application examples
`Gas`	Models of components with ideal gases as working fluid
`GasExtra`	
`Media`	Medium models for the ThermoPower library

Old	Old models
PowerPlants	Models of thermoelectrical power plants components
Test	Test cases for the ThermoPower models
Thermal	Thermal models of heat transfer
Water	Models of components with water/steam as working fluid
HydraulicConductance	
HydraulicResistance	
PerUnit	
Density	generic start value
LiquidDensity	start value for liquids
GasDensity	start value for gases/vapours
AbsoluteTemperature	generic temperature
AbsolutePressure	generic pressure

16.16.1 ThermoPower Example Models

The library contains the example models listed in Table 16-44.

Table 16-44. Example models in the ThermoPower library.

Name	*Description*
CISE	CISE plant models
HRB	Heat recovery boiler models
RankineCycle	Steam power plant
BraytonCycle	Gas power plant

The gas power plant example model is depicted in Figure 16-34 below.

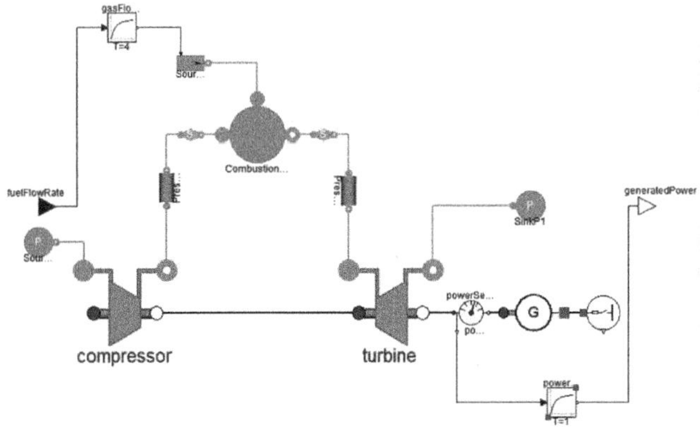

Figure 16-34. Gas turbine with generator and network, the example model ThermoPower.Examples.BraytonCycle.Plant.

16.17 PowerSystems Library

The `PowerSystems` library is intended to model electrical power systems at different levels of detail both in transient and steady-state mode. The version 0.2 described here is an early version. This library might eventually become part of MSL. It contains the sublibraries listed in Table 16-45.

Table 16-45. Sublibraries in the `PowerSystems` library.

Name	*Description*
`AC1ph_DC`	AC 1-phase and DC components from Spot AC1ph_DC
`AC3ph`	AC three phase components from Spot ACdqo
`Basic`	Basic utility classes
`Blocks`	Blocks
`Common`	Common components
`Control`	Control blocks
`Examples`	
`Generic`	Simple components for basic investigations
`Interfaces`	
`Mechanics`	Mechanical components
`PhaseSystems`	Phase systems used in power connectors
`Semiconductors`	Semiconductors
`System`	System reference
`Test`	

16.17.1 PowerSystems.Examples.PowerWorld

This `PowerWorld` example model models a control area for power distribution in island mode, that is, without connection to a larger net. It contains the following consumers and producers:

- A city with a load of about 1000 MW, that is, 1 million inhabitants.
- A thermal power plant with 800 MW nominal power, 60 MW for secondary frequency control and 40 MW for primary frequency control.
- A wind park with a max power of 300 MW.
- A hydro plant providing: 50 MW base load using a river turbine, ±25 MW pumping power to support the day/night load cycle, up to 200 MW peak power on demand.

The model is depicted in Figure 16-35 below.

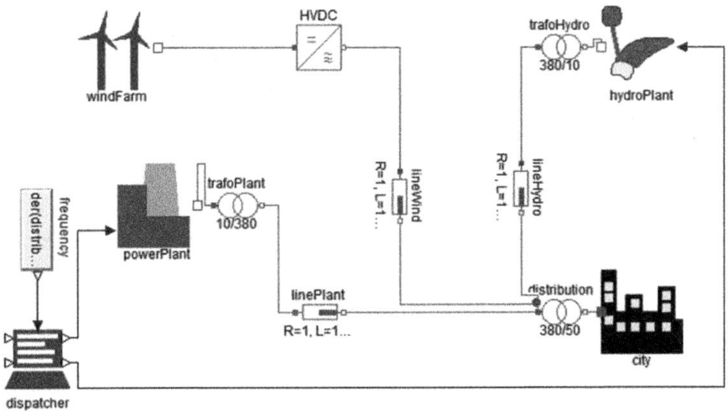

Figure 16-35. The `PowerSystems.PowerWorld` model of electrical power in an island with a city, a thermal power plant, a wind park and a hydro plant.

16.18 PNLib—Extended Hybrid Petri Net (xHPN) Library

PNLib is a Petri Net library that offers powerful modeling with a significantly extended Petri Net formalism called Extended Hybrid Petri Net (xHPN) compared to the normal Petri Nets, for which a basic introduction is given in Section 13.3.6, page 666.

The extensions include for example the combination of three different kinds of transitions—discrete, stochastic, and continuous transitions, and both discrete and continuous places. This library won the first prize in 2012 Modelica Library contest and effectively replaces previous Modelica Petri Net libraries.

The library is very powerful, universal, and generic, which makes it suitable for modeling and simulation of nearly all kinds of processes, such as business processes, production processes, logistic processes, work flows, traffic flows, data flows, multi-processor systems, communication protocols, and so on.

The Extended Hybrid Petri Net (xHPN) formalism consists of:

- three different kinds of *processes*, called *transitions*: discrete, stochastic, and continuous transition,
- two different states, called *places*: discrete and continuous places, and
- four different *arcs*: normal, inhibition, test, and read arc.

The formalism is supported in the PNLib library by models for places, transitions, and arcs:

- a discrete (PD) and a continuous place (PC),
- a discrete (TD), a stochastic (TS), and a continuous transitions (TC), and
- a test (TA), an inhibitor (IA), and a read arc (RA); the *normal* arc is represented by standard Modelica connections.

The main package PNlib is divided into the following subpackages:

- `Interfaces`: contains the connectors of the Petri net component models.
- `Blocks`: contains blocks with specific procedures that are used in the Petri net component models.
- `Functions`: contains functions with specific algorithmic procedures which are used in the Petri net component models.
- `Constants`: contains constants which are used in the Petri net component models.
- `Models`: contains several examples and offers the possibility to structure further Petri net models.

Places, transitions, and arcs in the library are represented by the icons depicted in Figure 16-36. The discrete place is represented by a circle and the continuous place by a double circle. The transitions are boxes which are black for discrete transitions, black with a white triangle for stochastic transitions, and white for continuous transitions. The test arc is represented by a dashed arc, the inhibitor arc by an arc with a white circle at its end, and the read arc by an arc with a black square at its end.

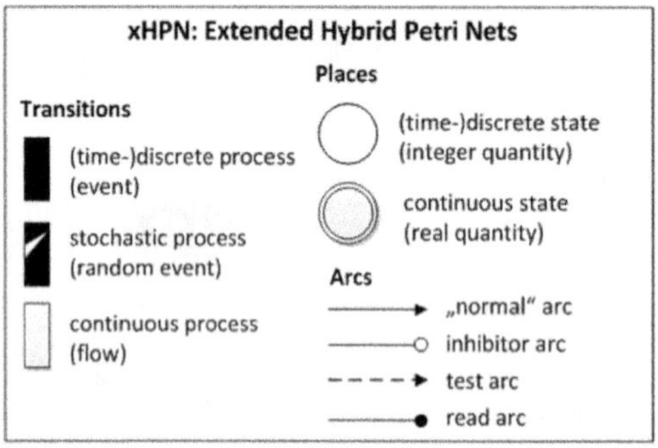

Figure 16-36. Places, transitions and arcs with corresponding icons in the PNLib library.

Discrete places contain an integer quantity, called *tokens* or *marks* while continuous places contain a non-negative real quantity. These marks initiate transitions to *fire* according to specific conditions. These firings lead to changes of the marks in the connected places.

Discrete transitions are provided with *delays* and *firing conditions* and fire first when the associated delay is passed and the conditions are fulfilled. These fixed delays can be replaced by exponentially distributed random values, then, the corresponding transition is called *stochastic transition*. Thereby, the characteristic parameter λ of the exponential distribution can depend functionally on the markings of several places and is recalculated at each point in time when the respective transition becomes active or when one or more markings of involved places change. Based on the characteristic parameter, the next *putative firing time* $\tau = time + Exp(\lambda)$ of the transition can be evaluated and it fires when this point in time is reached.

Both discrete and stochastic transitions *fire* by removing the arc weight from all input places and adding the arc weight to all output places. On the contrary, the firing of continuous transitions takes places as a continuous flow determined by the *firing speed* which can depend functionally on markings and/or time.

Places and transitions are connected by *normal arcs* which are weighted by integer and non-negative real numbers, respectively. However, also functions can be written at the arcs depending on the current markings of the places and/or time. Places can also be connected to transitions by *test*, *inhibition*, and *read arcs*. Then their markings do not change during the firing process. In the case of test and inhibitor arcs, the markings are only read to influence the time of firing while read arcs only indicate the usage of the marking in the transition, e.g. for firing conditions or speed functions.

If a place is connected to a transition by a test arc, the marking of the place must be greater than the arc weight to enable firing. If a place is connected to a transition by an inhibitor arc, the marking of the place must be less than the arc weight to enable firing. In both cases the markings of the places are not changed by fining. To summarize, an Extended Hybrid Petri Net (xHPN) has the following properties:

- It has discrete and continuous places.
- It has discrete, stochastic, and continuous transitions.
- Places can be connected to transitions by normal, test, inhibitor, and read arcs while transitions can only be connected to places by normal arcs.

- Arc weights can be functions depending on markings and/or time.
- Discrete place must be input as well as output of continuous transitions with arcs of same weights,
- Places can be provided with minimum and maximum capacities.
- Discrete transitions can be provided with delays.
- Stochastic transitions can be provided with hazard functions depending on markings.
- Continuous transitions can be provided with maximum speed function depending on markings and/or time.
- All transitions can be provided with additional firing conditions depending on all possible model variables.

16.18.1.1 Connectors

The `PNlib` contains four different kinds of connectors: `PlaceOut`, `PlaceIn`, `TransitionOut`, and `TransitionIn`. The connectors `PlaceOut` and `PlaceIn` are part of place models and connect them to output and input transitions, respectively. Similarly, `TransitionOut` and `TransitionIn` are connectors of the transition model and connect them to output and input places, respectively. Figure 16-37 shows which connector belongs to which Petri net component model.

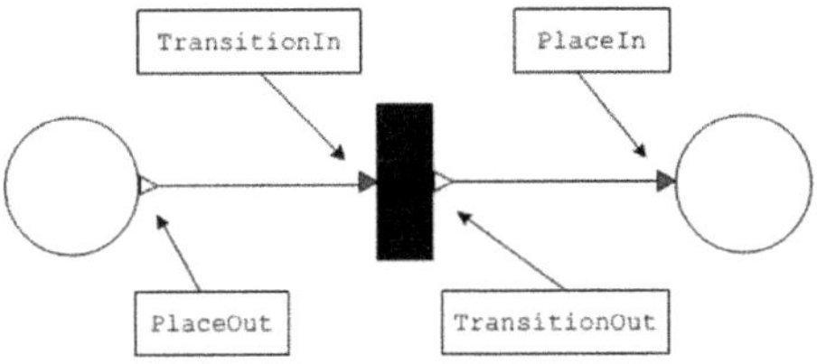

Figure 16-37. Connectors of the `PNLib` library.

The connectors of the Petri net component models are vectors to enable the connection to an arbitrary number of input and output components. Therefore, the dimension parameters `nIn` and `nOut` are declared in the place and transition models with the `connectorSizing` annotation.

16.18.1.2 Example of Business Process with Requests and Orders

The PNLib library is very suitable for describing business processes that involve a sequence of activities or tasks which have to be carried out in order to achieve a particular business goal, for example, a service or product for a particular customer. One example is the model `PNLib.Models.PNproBP` which is partly depicted in Figure 16-38. A related example of a very simple queuing job shop system using simple normal Petri Nets is described in Section 13.3.6.6, page 672.

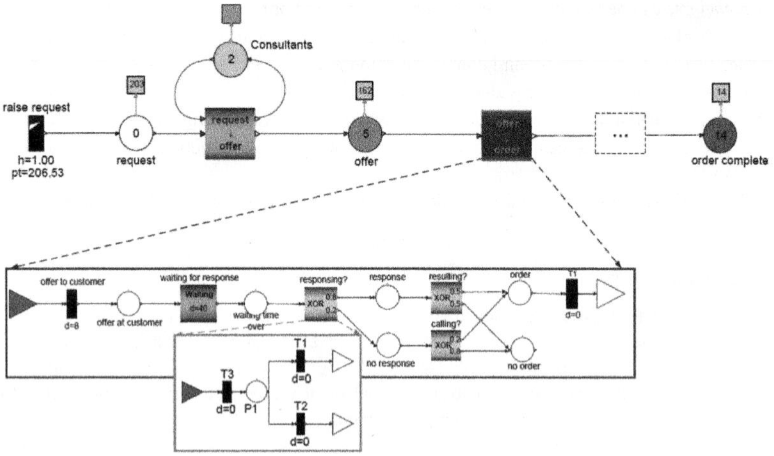

Figure 16-38. Part of a PNLib business process example model `PNLib.Models.PNproBP`.

16.19 BioChem—Biochemical Pathway Library

The design idea behind the `BioChem` library is to create a general purpose Modelica library for modeling, simulation and visualization of biological and biochemical systems. The classes implemented in the `BioChem` library describe substances and reactions that can take place in-between these substances in a diverse number of biochemical pathways.

Since the design objective for `BioChem` was to provide properties and attributes that are common in biological and biochemical systems the library contains several packages holding classes and partial models. The classes can be used as they are in sublibraries to `BioChem`, while the partial models must be further extended to fully functional models.

The library contains the sublibraries listed in Table 16-46.

Table 16-46. Sublibraries in the `BioChem` library.

Name	*Description*
`Math`	
`Icons`	Icons
`Compartments`	Different types of compartments used in the package
`Constants`	Mathematical constants and constants of nature
`Examples`	Some examples of BioChem models
`Interfaces`	Connection points and icons used in the BioChem package
`Reactions`	Reaction edges
`Substances`	Reaction nodes
`Units`	Units used in BioChem

16.19.1 Biochem.Interfaces

This subpackage contains partial models that can be used as building blocks for components such as different types of substances, compartments, and reactions. The models are designed to make it easy to create new customized components as well as to make these components possible to translate to and from SBML. The package contains the following subpackages:

- `Compartments` - Properties used when creating different compartments.
- `Nodes` - Connection points used as interfaces between different components.
- `Reactions` - Building blocks for reactions.
- `Substances` - Basic substance types.

16.19.2 Biochem.Examples

This sublibrary contains several examples, including the model depicted in Figure 16-39, which is a model of the first steps of a metabolic insulin signaling pathway.

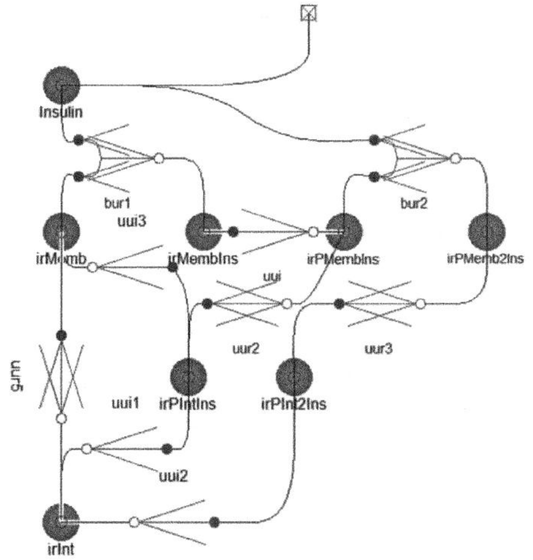

Figure 16-39. The `Biochem.Examples.InsulinSignaling_Sedaghat` metabolic signaling pathway model.

16.20 OpenHydraulics Library

The library `OpenHydraulics` is a free Modelica package providing components describing one-dimensional fluid flow in hydraulic circuits. The library is under development. The version available in October 2013 has very simple oil models and need to be expanded to reflect properties of commonly uses oils.

The library contains the sublibraries listed in Table 16-47.

Table 16-47. Sublibraries in the `OpenHydraulics` library.

Name	*Description*

UsersGuide	User's Guide
Examples	Comprehensive examples of how the Hydraulics library can be used
Basic	Models of basic physical phenomena relevant to the hydraulics domain
Components	Models for typical hydraulic components
Circuits	A collection of simple and complex hydraulic circuits
Fluids	Models of hydraulic fluids
DevelopmentTests	Models used for unit testing during development
Interfaces	Interface definitions for the Hydraulics library
Types	Type definitions that are not part of SIunits
Utilities	Utility models to construct fluid components (should not be used directly)

16.20.1 OpenHydraulics.Basic

The OpenHydraulics/Basic package (Table 16-48) includes models of basic physical phenomena relevant to the hydraulics domain. These basic models are used in the components package to model actual hydraulic components.

Table 16-48. Basic hydraulic model elements in the `OpenHydraulics` library.

Name	*Description*
GenericPressureLoss	
LaminarRestriction	
SharpEdgedOrifice	Sudden expansion in flow diameter from port_a to port_b
SuddenExpansion	Sudden expansion in flow diameter from port_a to port_b
VariableFlow	Controllable flow (independent of pressure)
VariableLaminarRestriction	
VariableRestriction	Flow loss due to controllable restriction
VariableRestrictionSeriesValve	Flow loss due to controllable restriction with series check valves
WallFriction	
FluidPower2MechTrans	
FluidPower2MechRotConst	Ideal constant displacement pump with mechanical connector for the shaft
FluidPower2MechRotVar	Ideal variable displacement pump with mechanical connector for the shaft
AirChamber	
ConstPressureSource	Boundary pressure and temperature source
ConstVolumeSource	Boundary pressure source
VarPressureSource	Boundary pressure and temperature source
VarVolumeSource	Boundary volume flow and temperature source
OpenTank	Boundary pressure, temperature and mass fraction source
VolumeClosed	A constant compressible volume

VolumeOpen	An open constant-pressure volume
BaseClasses	Base classes for flow models

16.20.2 OpenHydraulics.Components

The OpenHydraulics.Components subpackage includes models for typical hydraulic components in the following subpackages:

- Cylinders - Properties used when creating different compartments.
- Lines - Connection points used as interfaces between different components.
- MotorPumps - Building blocks for reactions.
- Sensors - Basic substance types.
- Valves - Basic substance types.
- Volumes - Basic substance types.

16.20.3 OpenHydraulics.Examples

The main example is currently a digging cycle simulation model as depicted in Figure 16-40, page 971.

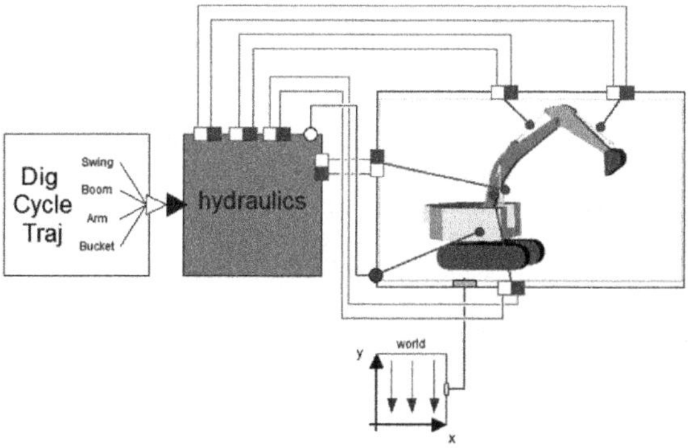

Figure 16-40. The OpenHydraulics.Examples.DigCycleSimulation digging cycle simulation model.

16.21 BondLib and the SystemDynamics Library World3 Model

The BondLib library is designed as a graphical equation-based library for modeling physical systems using the bond graph metaphor, but still using Modelica. The library contains the sublibraries listed in Table 16-49.

Table 16-49. Sublibraries in the BondLib library.

Name	*Description*
Introduction	An introduction to bond graph modeling
Connectors	Bond graph connectors
Bonds	Causal and a-causal bonds

`Basic`	Basic bond graph elements
`Advanced`	Advanced bond graph elements
`Wrapping`	Wrapping bond graphs
`Electrical`	The electrical library
`Hydraulic`	The hydraulic library
`Mechanical`	The mechanical libraries
`Thermal`	The thermal library
`Encapsulating`	Encapsulating bond graphs
`SystemDynamics`	The System Dynamics library
`Examples`	Examples
`Literature`	Literature

16.21.1 SystemDynamics Library

The `SystemDynamics` library has been designed as a graphical equation-based library for modeling mass and information flows in a continuous-time system using Prof. Jay Forrester's System Dynamics metaphor. The library occurs both as an independent library and as a sub-library of Bondlib. Two separate and independent versions of this library had originally been created by Dr. Stefan Fabricius and by Prof. François Cellier and his students. These have been merged into a single version that has furthermore been enhanced as well.

System Dynamics offers a fairly low-level graphical interface, not much different from a block diagram. The fact that continuous systems contain differential equations is hidden from the user by talking about levels, that is, quantities that can accumulate (state variables), and rates, that is, quantities that influence the accumulation and/or depletion of levels (state derivatives).

The System Dynamics modeling metaphor is widely used especially by researchers in the life sciences and social sciences. The library contains the sublibraries listed in Table 16-50.

Table 16-50. Sublibraries in the `SystemDynamics` library.

Name	*Description*
`UsersGuide`	User's Guide
`Interfaces`	Connectors and partial models of the System Dynamics methodology
`Auxiliary`	Auxiliary elements of the System Dynamics methodology
`Functions`	Functions of the System Dynamics methodology
`Groupers`	Groupers of the System Dynamics methodology
`Levels`	Levels of the System Dynamics methodology
`Rates`	Rates of the System Dynamics methodology
`Sensors`	System Dynamics sensors
`Sources`	Sources and sinks of the System Dynamics methodology
`IndustrialDynamics`	Factory models
`PopulationDynamics`	Ecological models
`WorldDynamics`	World models
`IntroductoryExamples`	Introductory example codes of the System Dynamics methodology

16.21.1.1 SystemDynamics.WorldDynamics.World3

This model is represented as a Modelica package that implements Dennis (and Dana) Meadows' WORLD3 model as described in their 1972 book *Limits to Growth: A Report for the Club of Rome's Project on the Predicament of Mankind.* The book has seen two later editions, one published in 1992 (20-year edition), and the most recent one published in 2004 (30-year edition). Each of these new editions was accompanied by an updated model. The model contained in this Modelica `World3` version is the newest model discussed in the 2004 edition *Limits to Growth: The 30-Year Update*.

A short description and discussion of the Modelica `World3` model is in Section 15.4.2.7, page 846. Figure 16-41 below shows the kind of block diagrams that are constructed using the `SystemDynamics` library, here the arable land submodel in `World3`.

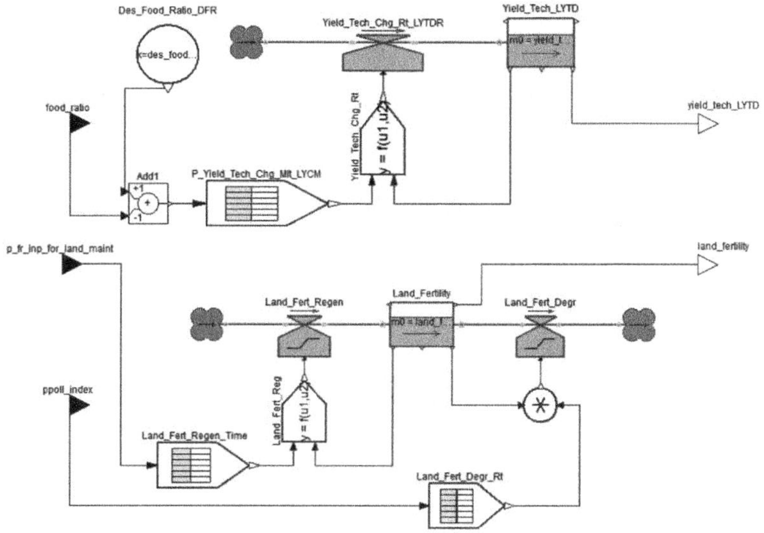

Figure 16-41. The `SystemDynamics.World3.Arable_Land_Dynamics` submodel.

16.22 Summary

This chapter has described the Modelica library structure, the version available at the Modelica Association web page at the time of this writing, including the Modelica standard library (MSL) version 3.2.1. The set of available libraries is growing quickly. However, the existing Modelica standard sublibraries are rather well-tested and have so far mostly gone through small evolutionary enhancements. For this reason the presentation of the now existing Modelica standard libraries will valid to a large extent, even some time into the future.

16.23 Literature

Essentially all text in this chapter has been reproduced with minor adaptations from the documentation of the corresponding free Modelica libraries. These libraries, including both documentation and source code, can be found on the Modelica web site, `www.modelica.org`. Documentation for several commercial libraries is also available on the Modelica web site. The respective (main) authors of the libraries described in this chapter are mentioned in the rest of this section.

Table 16-1 and Table 16-7 were created by Martin Otter and have been reused from (Modelica Association 2013). The material in Table 16-2, Table 16-3, Table 16-4, Table 16-5, Table 16-6 is primarily from the Modelica.org web page.

The constant definitions, with name, value, and description, in the `Modelica.Constants` package are from the following source: (Mohr and Taylor 2000). For more information on units and unit conversion, see (Cardarelli 1997).

The Modelica.Blocks library has been written by Martin Otter and the Modelica.Math library by Martin Otter and Marcus Baur.

The Modelica electrical analog library and its usage is described in (Clauss, Schneider, Leitner, and Schwarz 2000). The Modelica electrical digital library was authored by Christoph Clauß, André Schneider, and Ulrich Donath.

The Modelica_StateGraph2 library is described in detail in (Otter, Malmheden, Elmqvist, Mattsson, Johnsson 2009).

Basic equations and methods behind the MultiBody library can be found in (Otter 1995; Otter, Elmqvist, and Cellier 1996), and multi-body systems theory in general in (Shabana, 1998). The current Modelica.Mechanics.MultiBody library is also described in (Otter, Elmqvist, and Mattsson 2003).

The Media and Fluid libraries and their background are described in (Casella, Otter, Proelss, Richter and Tummescheit 2006; Elmqvist, Tummescheit, Otter 2003; Franke, Casella, Sielemann, Proelss, Otter, Wetter 2009; Franke, Casella, Otter, Sielemann, Elmqvist, Mattsson, and Olsson 2009). These libraries are partly based on experience from the earlier ThermoFluid library (Tummescheit, Eborn, and Wagner 2000; Tummescheit 2002; Tummescheit, and Eborn 2002).

The ThermoSysPro library with its combined cycle power plant application is described in (El Hefni, Bouskela, and Lebreton 2011; El Hefni, Bouskela, and Gentilini 2012).

The ThermoPower library on power plant simulation is described in (Casella and Leva 2003; Casella and Leva 2006).

The OpenHydraulics library has been developed by Chris Paredis and his students Jonathan Jobe, Thomas Johnson, Ben Lee.

There is not as yet a complete Modelica library available for electric power systems, but there is one preliminary version of a library called PowerSystems under development by Rüdiger Franke. This is based on, generalizes, and replaces the SPOT library (Wiesmann 2003). Modeling of electromagnetic transients in power systems is described in (Bachmann and Wiesmann 2000).

The advanced Petri Net library PNLib is described in (Proß 2013) and (Proß and Bachmann 2012).

The BioChem library was initially created by Emma Larsdotter Nilsson at Linköping University 2003-2005 (Larsdotter-Nilsson and Fritzson 2003). The current version of the library was further developed 2006 by Erik Ulfhielm at Linköping University and by MathCore Engineering AB during 2007-2009. The model using BioChem depicted in Figure 16-39 is a model of the first steps of a metabolic insulin signaling pathway based on the model by (Sedaghat et al. 2002).

A Modelica flight dynamics library is presented in (Moormann and Looye 2002).

Bondlib is described in (Cellier and Nebot 2005). The SystemDynamics library is based on theory from (Fisher 2007) and (Forrester 1971).

The World3 system dynamics model in Modelica available in the SystemDynamics library is briefly described in (Cellier 2008). It is a Modelica translation made by Cellier from the original model in STELLA by Meadows et al described in detail in (Meadows, Behrens II, Meadows, Naill, Randers 1974).

The limits of growth and interpretations of simulations of the World3 model are presented in (Meadows, Meadows, Randers, Behrens III 1972; Meadows, Randers, and Meadows 2004).

Part IV

Technology and Tools

Chapter 17

A Mathematical Representation for Modelica Models

At the beginning of this book, in Section 2.20 on page 63, we briefly explained how a Modelica model is translated into a basic mathematical representation in terms of a flat system of *differential and algebraic equations* (DAEs) before being able to simulate the model. This translation process elaborates on the internal model representation by performing analysis and type checking, inheritance and expansion of base classes, modifications and redeclarations, conversion of connect-equations to basic equations, and so on. The result of this analysis and translation process is a flat set of equations, including conditional equations, as well as constants, variables, and function definitions. The term *flat* means that the object-oriented structure has been broken down to a flat representation where no trace of the object hierarchy remains apart from dot notation within names.

However, since discrete and hybrid modeling constructs are an important part of Modelica, a continuous DAE representation is not enough, since discrete variables and discrete state transitions now belong to the basic mathematical state space model for Modelica. This model formalism is called *hybrid DAEs*, that is, hybrid differential and algebraic equations. This is analogous to similar definitions for other modeling formalisms, for example, the finite state automata and DEVS formalisms described in Sections 13.3.5 and 658, respectively, of Chapter 13.

17.1 Defining Hybrid DAEs—a Hybrid Mathematical Representation

To make the hybrid DAE representation easier to understand, first recall the basic ODE *state space* explicit form of the *equations* for continuous systems, previously presented in Section 2.20.1 on page 64 in Chapter 2, and in Section 12.8.1 on page 588 in Chapter 12. In the special case of an equation system on explicit state space form a DAE system reduces to an ODE system.

Here $x(t)$ is the set of *state variables*, that is, for an ODE the variables for which time derivatives occur in the model, $u(t)$ represents the input variables, and $y(t)$ represents the output variables and/or algebraic variables. The time dependency of these variables is made explicit by showing these variables as functions of time. The ODE explicit state space form is as follows:

$$\begin{aligned} \dot{x}(t) &= \hat{f}(x(t),u(t)) \\ y(t) &= \hat{g}(x(t),u(t)) \end{aligned} \qquad (17\text{-}1)$$

Here $\hat{f}(t)$ and $\hat{g}(t)$ are vector-valued functions, and $x(t)$, $y(t)$, $u(t)$ are vectors:

$$x(t)=\begin{pmatrix}x_1(t)\\ \vdots\\ x_n(t)\end{pmatrix},\quad y(t)=\begin{pmatrix}y_1(t)\\ \vdots\\ y_r(t)\end{pmatrix},\quad u(t)=\begin{pmatrix}u_1(t)\\ \vdots\\ u_m(t)\end{pmatrix} \tag{17-2}$$

By rearranging the terms we obtain the more general *DAE implicit form,* where $f(t)=\hat{f}(x(t),u(t))-\dot{x}(t)$, and $g(t)=\hat{g}(x(t),u(t))-y(t)$. Also, for a DAE, $y(t)$ also includes algebraic variables as well as output variables, which means that we need to add a possible dependency on $y(t)$ in $f(t)$.

$$\begin{aligned} f(x(t),\dot{x}(t),u(t),y(t))&=0\\ g(x(t),u(t),y(t))&=0 \end{aligned} \tag{17-3}$$

There is also a rather common *semiexplicit* form of DAE:

$$\begin{aligned} \dot{x}(t)&=f(x(t),y(t),u(t))\\ y(t)&=g(x(t),u(t)) \end{aligned} \tag{17-4}$$

Note that for a DAE it is usually not true that the state variables are those for which time derivatives occur. since the DAE contains algebraic constraints which reduce the degrees of freedom of the model, the number of state variables is often fewer than the number of variables that appear differentiated. Moreover, some state variables may be purely algebraic variables, possibly including discrete-time variables.

17.1.1 Continuous-Time Behavior

Now we want to formulate the continuous part of the *hybrid DAE* system of equations including discrete variables. This is done by adding a vector $q(t_e)$ of *discrete-time variables* and the corresponding predecessor variable vector $q_{pre}(t_e)$ denoted by `pre(q)` in Modelica. For discrete variables we use t_e instead of t to indicate that such variables may only change value at event time points denoted t_e, that is, the variables $q(t_e)$ and $q_{pre}(t_e)$ behave as constants between events.

We also make the constant vector p of *parameters and constants* explicit in the equations, and make the time t explicit. The vector $c(t_e)$ of condition expressions, for example, from the conditions of `if` constructs and `when` constructs, evaluated at the most recent event at time t_e is also included since such conditions are referenced in conditional equations. We obtain the following *continuous DAE* system of equations that describe the system behavior *between* events:

$$\begin{aligned} f(x(t),\dot{x}(t),u(t),y(t),t,q(t_e),q_{pre}(t_e),p,c(t_e))&=0 \qquad (a)\\ g(x(t),u(t),y(t),t,q(t_e),q_{pre}(t_e),p,c(t_e))&=0 \qquad (b) \end{aligned} \tag{17-5}$$

17.1.2 Discrete-Time Behavior

Discrete time behavior is closely related to the notion of an event. Events can occur asynchronously, and affect the system one at time, causing a sequence of state transitions. An event occurs when any of conditions $c(t_e)$ (defined below) of conditional equations changes value from `false` to `true`. We say that an event becomes *enabled* at the time t_e, if and only if, for any sufficiently small value of ε, $c(t_e-\varepsilon)$ is `false` and $c(t_e+\varepsilon)$ is `true`. An enabled event is *fired*, that is, some behavior associated with the event is executed, often causing a discontinuous state transition. Firing of an event may cause other conditions to switch from `false` to `true`. In fact, events are fired until a stable situation is reached when all the condition expressions are `false`.

Discontinuous changes of continuous dynamic variables $x(t)$ can be caused by so-called `reinit` equations in Modelica, which for the sake of simplicity are excluded from the equation representations discussed in this chapter.

However, there are also state changes caused by equations defining the values of the *discrete* variables $q(t_e)$, which may change value *only* at events, with event times denoted t_e. Such discrete variables obtain their value at events, for example, by solving equations in when-equations or evaluating assignments in when-statements. The instantaneous equations defining discrete variables in when-equations are restricted to particularly simple syntactic forms (Section 8.3.5, page 357), for example, *var* = *expr*;. These restrictions are imposed by the Modelica language in order to easily determine which discrete variables are defined by solving the equations in a when-equation.

Such equations can be directly converted to equations in assignment form, that is, assignment statements, with fixed causality from the right-hand side to the left-hand side. Regarding algorithmic when-statements, for example, Section 9.2.10, page 433, that define discrete variables, such definitions are always done through assignments. Therefore we can in both cases express the equations defining discrete variables as *assignments* in the vector equation (17-5a), where the vector-valued *function* f_q specifies the right-hand side expressions of those *assignments to discrete variables*.

$$q(t_e) := f_q(x(t_e), \dot{x}(t_e), u(t_e), y(t_e), t_e, q_{pre}(t_e), p, c(t_e)) \qquad (17\text{-}6)$$

The last argument $c(t_e)$ is made explicit for convenience. It is strictly speaking not necessary since the expressions in $c(t_e)$ could have been incorporated directly into f_q. The vector $c(t_e)$ contains all `Boolean` condition expressions evaluated at the most recent *event* at time t_e. It is defined by the following vector assignment equation with the right-hand side given by the vector-valued function f_e. This function has as arguments the subset of the discrete variables having `Boolean` type, that is, $q^B(t_e)$ and $q^B_{pre}(t_e)$, the subset of `Boolean` parameters or constants, p^B, and a vector $rel(v(t))$ evaluated at time t_e, containing the elementary relational expressions from the model. The vector of condition expressions $c(t_e)$ is defined by the following equation in assignment form:

$$c(t_e) := f_e(q^B(t_e), q^B_{pre}(t_e), p^B, rel(v(t_e))) \qquad (17\text{-}7)$$

Here $rel(v(t)) = rel(\mathtt{cat}(1, x(t), \dot{x}(t), u(t), y(t), t, q(t_e), q_{pre}(t_e), p))$, a `Boolean`-typed vector-valued function containing the relevant elementary *relational expressions* from the model, excluding relations enclosed by `noEvent`(). The argument $v(t) = \{v_1, v_2, ...\}$ is a vector containing all scalar elements of the argument vectors. This can be expressed using the Modelica concatenation function `cat` applied to the vectors, for example, $v(t) = cat(1, x, \dot{x}, u, y, \{t\}, q(t_e), q_{pre}(t_e), p)$. For example, if $rel(v(t)) = \{v_1 > v_2, v_3 >= 0, v_4 < 5, v_6 <= v_7, v_{12} = 133\}$ where $v(t) = \{v_1, v_2, v_3, v_4, v_6, v_7, v_{12}\}$, then it might be the case that $c(t) = \{v_1 > v_2$ `and` $v_3 >= 0, v_{10}$, not v_{11}, $v_4 < 5$ `or` $v_6 <= v_7, v_{12} = 133\}$, where v_{10}, v_{11} are `Boolean` variables and v_1, v_2, v_3, v_4, v_6, v_7 might be `Real` variables, whereas v_{12} might be an `Integer` variable.

17.1.3 The Complete Hybrid DAE

The total equation system consisting of the combination of (17-5), (17-6), and (17-7) is the desired *hybrid DAE* equation representation for Modelica models, consisting of *differential*, *algebraic*, and *discrete* equations.

This framework describes a system where the state evolves in two ways: continuously in time by changing the values of $x(t)$, and by instantaneous changes in the total state represented by the variables $x(t)$, $y(t)$, and $q(t)$. Instantaneous state changes occur at events triggered when some of the conditions $c(t_e)$ change value from `false` to `true`. The set of *state varibles* from which other variables are computed is selected from the set of dynamic variables $x(t)$, algebraic varibles $y(t)$, and discrete-time variables $q(t)$.

Below we summarize the notation used in the above equations, with time dependencies stated explicitly for all time-dependent variables by the arguments t or t_e (also compare Section 12.6.1, page 584):

- $p = \{p_1, p_2, ...\}$, a vector containing the Modelica variables declared as `parameter` or `constant` i.e., variables without any time dependency.
- t, the Modelica variable `time`, the independent variable of type `Real` implicitly occurring in all Modelica models.
- $x(t)$, the vector of dynamic variables of the model, i.e., variables of type `Real` that also appear differentiated, meaning that `der()` is applied to them somewhere in the model.
- $\dot{x}(t)$, the differentiated vector of dynamic variables of the model.
- $u(t)$, a vector of input variables, that is, not dependent on other variables, of type `Real`. These also belong to the set of algebraic variables since they do not appear differentiated.
- $y(t)$, a vector of Modelica variables of type `Real` which do not fall into any other category. Output variables are included among these, which together with $u(t)$ are algebraic variables since they do not appear differentiated.
- $q(t_e)$, a vector of discrete-time Modelica variables of type `discrete Real`, `Boolean`, `Integer` or `String`. These variables change their value only at event instants, that is, at points t_e in time.
- $q_{pre}(t_e)$, the values of q immediately before the current event occurred, that is, at time t_e.
- $c(t_e)$, a vector containing all `Boolean` condition expressions evaluated at the most recent *event* at time t_e. This includes conditions from all if-equations/statements and if-expressions from the original model as well as those generated during the conversion of when-equations and when-statements (see Section 8.3.5, page 357, and Section 9.2.10).
- $rel(v(t)) = rel(cat(1, x, \dot{x}, u, y, \{t\}, q(t_e), q_{pre}(t_e), p))$, a `Boolean` vector valued function containing the relevant elementary relational expressions from the model, excluding relations enclosed by `noEvent()`. The argument $v(t) = \{v_1, v_2, ...\}$ is a vector containing all elements in the vectors $x, \dot{x}, u, y, \{t\}, q(t_e), q_{pre}(t_e), p$. This can be expressed using the Modelica concatenation function `cat` applied to these vectors; $rel(v(t)) = \{v_1 > v_2, v_3 >= 0, v_4 < 5, v_6 <= v_7, v_{12} = 133\}$ is one possible example.
- $f(...)$, the function that defines the differential equations $f(...) = 0$ in (17-5a) of the system of equations.
- $g(...)$, the function that defines the algebraic equations $g(...) = 0$ in (17-5b) of the system of equations.
- $f_q(...)$, the function that defines the difference equations for the discrete variables $q := f_q(...)$, i.e., (17-6) in the system of equations.
- $f_e(...)$, the function that defines the event conditions $c := f_e(...)$, that is, (17-7) in the system of equations.

For simplicity, the special cases involving the `noEvent()` operator and the `reinit()` operator are not contained in the above equations and are not discussed below.

17.1.4 Hybrid DAEs Expressed in Modelica

To understand how hybrid DAEs are expressed in Modelica it is useful to recall once more the *process* of translating a Modelica model to a flat hybrid DAE. Three of the most important tasks in this translation process are the following:

- Expansion and elaboration of inherited base classes.
- Parameterization of base classes, local classes, and variable declarations.
- Generation of equations from `connect` statements.

The result is a "flat Modelica source code" variant of a flat hybrid DAE, in which long variable names with dot notation are allowed. This dot notation is derived from the flattened hierarchical structure (see the simple circuit example in Section 2.20 on page 63 in Chapter 2). However, this representation also contains declarations of variables, constants, and parameters in addition to the equations themselves.

Moreover, the term "equation" is interpreted in a rather general sense since sets of assignment statements can be viewed as subsystems of equations. This is possible since executing a set of assignments is equivalent to solving a corresponding subsystem of equations provided that there are no side effects, which is the case in Modelica. Function definitions in elaborated form, that is, with possible inheritance and modification operations, etc. expanded and elaborated, are kept as whole declarations without being broken down into pieces. Thus, the Modelica flat hybrid DAE form consists of the following kinds of items:

- Declarations of variables, parameters, and constants with the appropriate basic types, prefixes, and attributes (such as for "`parameter Integer k`").
- *Declaration equations*, for example, "`y=8.5`" from declarations such as "`parameter Real y=8.5`".
- *Equations* from equation sections, including both normal equations and *conditional equations* involving if-expressions or if-equations/statements.
- *Function calls* where each call is treated as a *set of equations* involving all the input and all the result variables of the function call. For such a call the number of equations is equal to the number of basic result variables of the called function.
- *Algorithm sections*, where each section is treated as a set of equations. The number of conceptual equations corresponding to an algorithm section equals the number of different variables assigned in the algorithm section.
- *When-equations* or *when-statements*, where each of these is treated as a set of conditional equations. The number of equations in such a set equals the number of variables assigned in the corresponding when-statement, or the number variables solved for in the when-equation.

The flat hybrid DAE representation is a system of equations where some equations are conditionally active, that is, are included in the equation solution process only if certain conditions are true. For example, instantaneous equations within a when-equation are included only when the corresponding when-condition becomes `true`. Thus, the total system of equations may include discontinuities and may have a varying set of *active equations*, being controlled by a discrete-event-handling system.

The equation system might include multiple events, corresponding to groups of conditional equations, that may become active at the *same time instant*. This topic was previously discussed in Section 13.2.6.7. In this case the events must be fired in some *sequence*, which means that the equation solver must choose the order in which these groups of equations should be activated during the solution process. In many cases, the order in which simultaneously enabled events are fired is not significant because different events may affect different parts of the model without any direct interaction. However, it is easy to find models where the order is significant.

Modelica prescribes a *deterministic* ordering of simultaneous events in order to have the property that different simulations of the same model will give the same result. Another possibility would be to have a *nondeterministic* ordering, i.e., the order is picked at random, with the sometimes-problematic property that different simulations may give different results. However, despite the deterministic ordering it is still possible to obtain random orderings by explicit modeling using probability distribution functions as in the queuing examples presented earlier in Section 13.3.4.2.

17.1.5 Structural Time Invariance of Modelica Hybrid DAEs

The Modelica hybrid DAE representation we have just presented is *structurally time invariant*, which means that the set of variables and the set of equations are *fixed* over time. It is *not* possible to add new equations at run time during simulation. One example is that the number of equations generated by a for-loop equation (see Section 8.3.2, page 352), must be known at compile time, requiring the loop bounds to be of at most parameter variability.

Parameters that may influence the structure of the equation system before simulation starts are sometimes called *structural parameters* (see also Section 3.11.2). The reason is that they may influence the structure of the equation system, for example, in terms of the number of equations in the model. An example is a for-equation (Section 8.3.2, page 352) which expands into a number of simple equations, where the number is determined by a parameter expression. However, despite the fixed total set of equations, the set of *active equations* can vary at *run time* since conditional equations can be turned on and off.

Structural time invariance is an *advantage* in the sense that the whole model can be analyzed and compiled *before* being executed. This enables the localization of errors in the model before starting execution, as well as generating efficient code from the model utilizing the fact that all variables and equations are known to the Modelica compiler. This property is well in line with our *declarative* object-oriented mathematical modeling approach where objects are explicitly declared and can be analyzed and reasoned about.

On the other hand, structural time invariance is a *disadvantage* in the sense that objects cannot be created at run-time after the start of simulation. This is in contrast to many other object-oriented languages where dynamic object creation is standard procedure.

The modeling style with dynamic object creation is common in applications such as queuing systems and job shop systems, where objects arrive, are processed, and leave the system. Fortunately, structural time invariance does not prevent modeling those kinds of applications in Modelica. The maximum number of objects that can be simultaneously active in a modeled system, sometimes known as the buffer capacity of the system, can be declared beforehand. These objects in the buffer are initially not active. The arrival of an object is represented as an activation of one of the predeclared objects, whereas an object leaving the system is represented as a deactivation of an existing object. In this sense the structural time invariance of Modelica hybrid DAEs is not a serious disadvantage.

It might be possible to define a more flexible variant of Modelica hybrid DAEs that keeps all the advantages of the current representation in terms of being declarative, possible to analyze, and possible to transform and compile to highly performing code, while supporting a somewhat more flexible modeling style, for example, regarding "dynamic" creation and construction of objects. Such an enhancement might not even require any changes in the basic hybrid DAE representation, but rather extensions in the Modelica language definition.

17.1.6 A DAE Example Subjected to BLT Partitioning

In this section we provide a small example with both differential, algebraic, hybrid, and nonlinear equations, in order to illustrate the different forms of equations.

An inertial mass is rotated by influencing its angular acceleration. The electromecanical `EMF` component transforms the rotational mechanical energy into electrical energy that is absorbed by a simple electrical circuit consisting of an inductor `ind` and two resistors, `R1` and `R2`, connected in series. As output of the model we are interested in measuring the voltage between node (1) and node (2) of the electrical circuit with the help of a voltage sensor component `vsens` (see Figure 17-1).

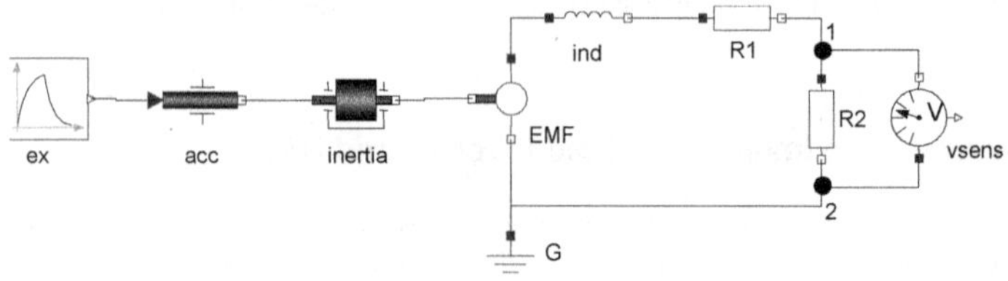

Figure 17-1. Small DAE example model called Generator.

The corresponding Modelica code is:

```
model Generator
  import Modelica.Mechanics.Rotational;
```

```
    import Modelica.Electrical.Analog;
    import Modelica.Blocks.
    Rotational.Accelerate          acc;
    Rotational.Inertia             inertia;
    Analog.Basic.EMF               EMF(k=-1);
    Analog.Basic.Inductor          ind(L=0.1);
    Analog.Basic.Resistor          R1;
    Analog.Basic.Resistor          R2;
    Analog.Basic.Ground            G;
    Analog.Sensors.VoltageSensor vsens;
    Blocks.Sources.Exponentials   ex(riseTime=2,riseTimeConst=1);
  equation
    connect(acc.flange_b, inertia.flange_a);
    connect(inertia.flange_b, EMF.flange_b);
    connect(EMF.p, ind.p);
    connect(ind.n, R1.p);
    connect(EMF.n, G.p);
    connect(EMF.n, R2.n);
    connect(R1.n, R2.p);
    connect(R2.p, vsens.n);
    connect(R2.n, vsens.p);
    connect(ex.y, acc.acceleration);
  end Generator;
```

We simulate the model as usual and show plots of a few variables in Figure 17-2.

```
  simulate(Generator, stopTime=10);
plot({ex.y,vsens.v,inertia.w}, xrange={0,7});
```

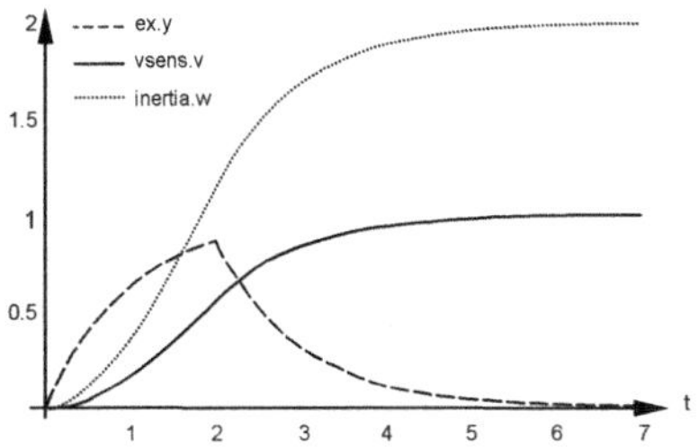

Figure 17-2. Plots of the variables ex.y, vsens.v, and inertia.w of the DAE example model.

17.1.6.1 Kinds of Variables

The different kinds of variables according to the previously defined notation can be extracted from the flattened model:

- p = {acc.phi_start, acc.w_start, inertia.J, EMF.k, ind.L, R1.R, R2.R, ex.outMax, ex.riseTime, ex.riseTimeConst ,ex.fallTimeConst, ex.offset, ex.startTime}
- $x(t)$ = {acc.phi, acc.w, inertia.phi, inertia.w, EMF.flange_b.phi}
- $\dot{x}(t)$ = {acc.phi, acc.w, inertia.phi, inertia.w, EMF.flange_b.phi}
- $u(t)$ = {G.p.v, vsens.p.i, vsens.n.i, ex.y_riseTime}
- $y(t)$ = {acc.phi, acc.w, acc.a, acc.flange_b.phi, acc.flange_b.tau, acc.acceleration, inertia.phi, inertia.flange_a.phi, inertia.flange_a.tau, inertia.flange_b.phi, inertia.flange_b.tau, inertia.w, inertia.a,

```
EMF.v ,EMF.i, EMF.w, EMF.p.v, EMF.p.i, EMF.n.v ,EMF.n.i,
EMF.flange_b.phi, EMF.flange_b.tau, ind.v, ind.i, ind.p.v, ind.p.i,
ind.n.v, ind.n.i ,R1.v, R1.i, R1.p.v, R1.p.i, R1.n.v, R1.n.i, R2.v,
R2.i, R2.p.v, R2.p.i, R2.n.v, R2.n.i, G.p.v, G.p.i, vsens.p.v,
vsens.p.i, vsens.n.v, vsens.n.i,
vsens.y, vsens.v, ex.y, ex.y, ex.y_riseTime}
```

- $c(t_e) =$ `{ time < ex.startTime, time < ex.startTime+ex.riseTime }`

17.1.6.2 Flattened Form

We extract the equations of the model, flatten the structure, and substitute named constants and parameters for their values, obtaining the following total system of equations:

```
eq 0:     ex.fallTimeConst-ex.riseTimeConst = 0
eq 1:     ex.y-acc.acceleration = 0
eq 2:     acc.flange_b.tau+inertia.flange_a.tau = 0
eq 3:     inertia.flange_a.phi-acc.flange_b.phi = 0
eq 4:     ind.n.v-R1.p.v = 0
eq 5:     R1.p.i+ind.n.i = 0
eq 6:     vsens.n.v-R1.n.v = 0
eq 7:     R2.p.v-R1.n.v = 0
eq 8:     R1.n.i+R2.p.i+vsens.n.i = 0
eq 9:     ind.p.v-EMF.p.v = 0
eq 10:    EMF.p.i+ind.p.i = 0
eq 11:    vsens.p.v-EMF.n.v = 0
eq 12:    R2.n.v-EMF.n.v = 0
eq 13:    G.p.v-EMF.n.v = 0
eq 14:    EMF.n.i+G.p.i+R2.n.i+vsens.p.i = 0
eq 15:    EMF.flange_b.tau+inertia.flange_b.tau = 0
eq 16:    inertia.flange_b.phi-EMF.flange_b.phi = 0
eq 17:    ex.y = ex.p_offset+(
          if time < ex.startTime then 0
          else if time < ex.startTime + ex.riseTime then
              ex.outMax*(1-exp(-(time-ex.startTime)/ex.riseTimeConst))
          else ex.y_riseTime*exp(-(time-ex.p_startTime-
                                      ex.riseTime)/ex.fallTimeConst)
          );

eq 18:    ex.y_riseTime-ex.outMax+ex.outMax*exp(
                              ex.riseTime/ex.riseTimeConst) = 0
eq 19:    ex.y-ex.y = 0
eq 20:    vsens.v-vsens.y = 0
eq 21:    vsens.v-vsens.p.v+vsens.n.v = 0
eq 22:    vsens.n.i = 0
eq 23:    vsens.p.i = 0
eq 24:    G.p.v = 0
eq 25:    R2.R*R2.i-R2.v = 0
eq 26:    R2.i-R2.p.i = 0
eq 27:    -R2.p.i-R2.n.i = 0
eq 28:    R2.v-R2.p.v+R2.n.v = 0
eq 29:    R1.R*R1.i-R1.v = 0
eq 30:    R1.i-R1.p.i = 0
eq 31:    -R1.p.i-R1.n.i = 0
eq 32:    R1.v-R1.p.v+R1.n.v = 0
eq 33:    ind.L*der(ind.i)-ind.v = 0
eq 34:    ind.i-ind.p.i = 0
eq 35:    -ind.p.i-ind.n.i = 0
eq 36:    ind.v-ind.p.v+ind.n.v = 0
eq 37:    EMF.flange_b.tau+EMF.k*EMF.i = 0
```

```
eq 38:     EMF.k*EMF.w-EMF.v = 0
eq 39:     EMF.w-der(EMF.flange_b.phi) = 0
eq 40:     EMF.i-EMF.p.i = 0
eq 41:     -EMF.p.i-EMF.n.i = 0
eq 42:     EMF.v-EMF.p.v+EMF.n.v = 0
eq 43:     inertia.J*inertia.a-inertia.flange_a.tau-inertia.flange_b.tau = 0
eq 44:     inertia.a-der(inertia.w) = 0
eq 45:     inertia.w-der(inertia.phi) = 0
eq 46:     inertia.flange_b.phi-inertia.phi = 0
eq 47:     inertia.flange_a.phi-inertia.phi = 0
eq 48:     acc.a-acc.acceleration = 0
eq 49:     acc.a-der(acc.w) = 0
eq 50:     acc.w-der(acc.phi) = 0
eq 51:     acc.phi-acc.flange_b.phi = 0
```

The trivial zero identities below are excluded in the following:

```
Vsens.n.i  = 0
Vsens.p.i  = 0
G.p.v      = 0
-EMF.n.v   = 0
vsens.p.v  = 0
R2.n.v     = 0
```

17.1.6.3 BLT Partitioned Form

According to the procedure for simulating Modelica models (Section 18.1, page 993), the remaining equations are transformed into Block Lower Triangular (BLT) form by symbolically sorting the equations using Tarjans algorithm (see Section 17.1.7, page 989). This enables efficient solution of sparse equation systems by reducing the number of variables that need to be handled by the numerical solver. The total system of equations can then be solved by solving each block sequentially. The BLT decomposition leads to 30 blocks for this model:

- 6 DAE blocks, including ODEs and pure algebraic equations.
- 22 linear equation blocks, one equation per block.
- 1 nonlinear equation block with one equation.
- 1 hybrid block.

The system is partitioned as follows:

```
block 1 Nonlinear equation: ex.y.riseTime-ex.outMax+ex.outMax*exp(-
                              ex.riseTime/ex.riseTimeConst) = 0
block 2 Hybrid equation:   ex.y = ex.offset+(
                              0 = if time < ex.startTime then 0
                           else if time < ex.startTime + ex.riseTime then
                                     ex.outMax*(1-exp(-(time-
                                     ex.startTime)/ex.riseTimeConst))
                            else ex.y_riseTime*exp(-(time-ex.startTime-
                                     ex.riseTime)/ex.fallTimeConst)
                           );

block 3  Linear equation:    ex.y-ex.y = 0
block 4  Linear equation:    ex.y-acc.acceleration  = 0
block 5  Linear equation:    acc.a-acc.acceleration = 0
block 6  Linear equation:    acc.a-der(acc.w) = 0
block 7  DAE:                acc.w-der(acc.phi) = 0
block 8  Linear equation:    acc.phi-acc.flange_b.phi = 0
block 9  Linear equation:    inertia.flange_a.phi-acc.flange_b.phi = 0
block 10 Linear equation:    inertia.flange_a.phi-inertia.phi = 0
```

```
block 11 Linear equation:   inertia.flange_b.phi-inertia.phi = 0
block 12  Linear equation:  inertia.flange_b.phi-EMF.flange_b.phi = 0
block 13  DAE:             EMF.w-der(EMF.flange_b.phi) = 0
block 14  Linear equation:  EMF.k*EMF.w-EMF.v = 0
block 15  Linear equation:  EMF.v-EMF.p.v = 0
block 16  Linear equation:  ind.p.v-EMF.p.v = 0
block 17  DAE:                R1.i-R1.p.i = 0
                              R1.R*R1.i-R1.v = 0
                              R1.v-R1.p.v+R1.n.v = 0
                              ind.n.v-R1.p.v = 0
                              ind.v-ind.p.v+ind.n.v = 0
                              ind.L*der(ind.i)-ind.v = 0
                              ind.i-ind.p.i = 0
                              -ind.p.i-ind.n.i = 0
                              R1.p.i+ind.n.i = 0
                              -R1.p.i-R1.n.i = 0
                              R1.n.i+R2.p.i = 0
                              R2.i-R2.p.i = 0
                              R2.R*R2.i-R2.v = 0
                              R2.v-R2.p.v = 0
                              R2.p.v-R1.n.v = 0
block 18: Linear equation:  vsens.n.v-R1.n.v = 0
block 19: Linear equation:  vsens.v+vsens.n.v = 0
block 20: Linear equation:  vsens.v-vsens.y = 0
block 21: Linear equation:  EMF.p.i+ind.p.i = 0
block 22: Linear equation:  -EMF.p.i-EMF.n.i = 0
block 23: Linear equation:  -R2.p.i-R2.n.i = 0
block 24: Linear equation:  EMF.n.i+G.p.i+R2.n.i = 0
block 25: Linear equation:  MF.i-EMF.p.i = 0
block 26: Linear equation:  EMF.flange_b.tau+EMF.k*EMF.i = 0
block 27: Linear equation:  inertia.w-der(inertia.phi) = 0
block 28: Linear equation:  inertia.a-der(inertia.w) = 0
block 29: Linear equation:  EMF.flange_b.tau+inertia.flange_b.tau
block 30: Linear equation:  inertia.J*inertia.a-inertia.flange_a.tau-
                                       inertia.flange_b.tau = 0
block 31: Linear equation:  acc.flange_b.tau+inertia.flange_a.tau = 0
block 32: Linear equation:  ex.fallTimeConst-ex.riseTimeConst = 0
```

The block lower triangular form is clearly visible in the right matrix of Figure 17-1. For this model there is only one nontrivial strongly connected component (block 17) containing 15 equations.

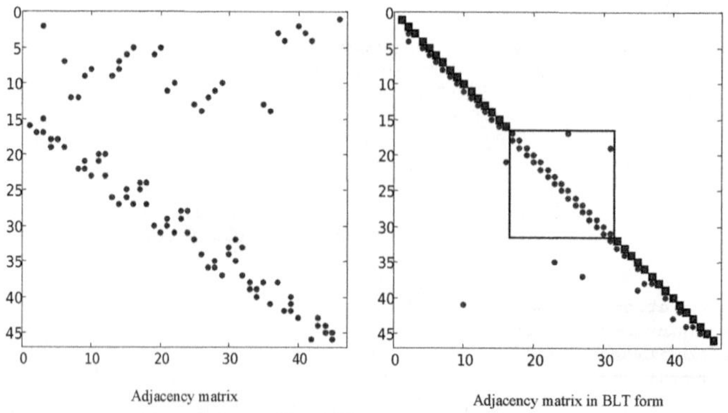

Figure 17-3. Equation adjacency matrix, before, and after BLT (Block Lower Triangular) partitioning. Equations are on the vertical axis, whereas variables are on the horizontal axis.

17.1.7 Tarjan's Algorithm to Generate the BLT Form

We briefly present Tarjan's graph theoretic algorithm to perform topological sorting of an equation system into the block lower triangular (BLT) form, using the small DAE example system presented in Figure 17-4a, with its associated adjacency the matrix with equations on the vertical axis and variables on the horizontal axis. Figure 17-4c shows a bipartite graph representation (see Section 18.2.4.2, page 1007) of the same equation system.

The final BLT form of the equation system, which is the desired result of the BLT transformation, is presented in Figure 17-4b including a small strongly connected component—a block consisting of equations 3 and 4, which is a *simultaneous system of equations*—also called an *algebraic loop*.

Also note that clocked partitions need not be sorted with respect to each other (Section 13.6.13.1, page 715).

$$
\begin{aligned}
f_1(z_3,z_4) &= 0\\
f_2(z_2) &= 0\\
f_3(z_2,z_3,z_5) &= 0\\
f_4(z_1,z_2) &= 0\\
f_5(z_1,z_3,z_5) &= 0
\end{aligned}
$$

$$
\begin{array}{cc} & z_1\ z_2\ z_3\ z_4\ z_5 \\ S_1 = & \begin{pmatrix} 0&0&1&1&0\\ 0&1&0&0&0\\ 0&1&1&0&1\\ 1&1&0&0&0\\ 1&0&1&0&1 \end{pmatrix} \end{array}
$$

(a)

$$
\begin{aligned}
f_2(\underline{z_2}) &= 0\\
f_4(\underline{z_1},z_2) &= 0\\
f_3(z_2,\underline{z_3},\underline{z_5}) &= 0\\
f_5(z_1,\underline{z_3},\underline{z_5}) &= 0\\
f_1(z_3,\underline{z_4}) &= 0
\end{aligned}
$$

$$
\begin{array}{cc} & z_2\ z_1\ z_3\ z_5\ z_4 \\ S_2 = & \begin{pmatrix} \mathbf{1}&0&0&0&0\\ 1&\mathbf{1}&0&0&0\\ 1&0&\boxed{\mathbf{1}&\mathbf{1}}&0\\ 0&1&\boxed{\mathbf{1}&\mathbf{1}}&0\\ 0&0&1&0&\mathbf{1} \end{pmatrix} \end{array}
$$

(b)

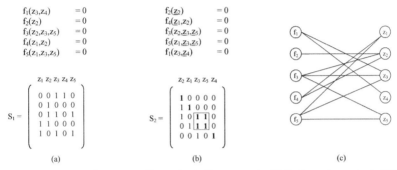

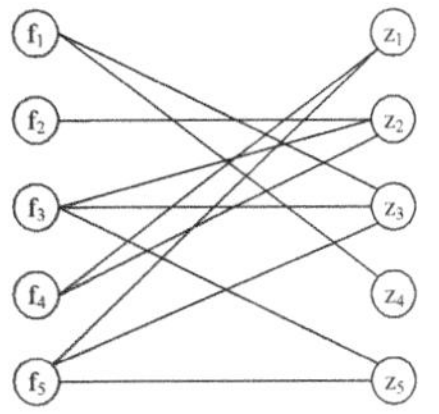

(c)

Figure 17-4. (**a**) Equation system with associated adjacency matrix. (**b**) Goal equation system in BLT form after topological sorting using Tarjan's algorithm. (**c**) Bipartite graph representation of the initial form of the equation system (a) with equations on the left nodes and the variables on the right nodes, to be subject to topological sorting.

Certain prerequisites have to be handled before running Tarjan's algorithm. The situation is actually the following:

1. First we need to compute a *matching* of which variable is used in solving which equation (see Section 18.2.4.3, page 1008).
2. A transformation called *index reduction* (also Section 18.2.4.3) may need to symbolically differentiate certain equations.
3. Finally, Tarjan's algorithm is used to sort the equation system and find the strongly connected components (also called algebraic loops).

The process of running a matching algorithm is depicted in Figure 17-5.

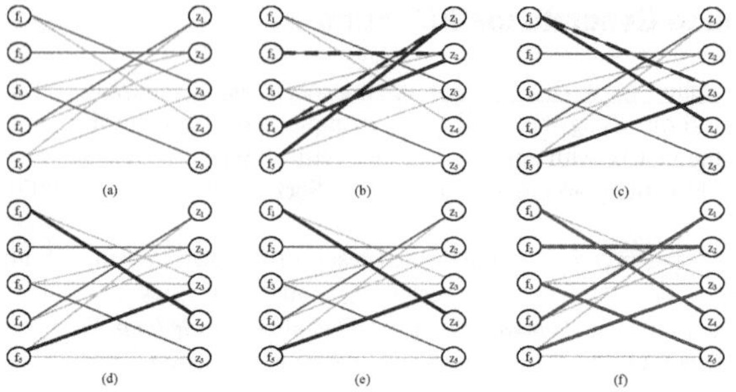

Figure 17-5. Running a matching algorithm on the test problem.

We apply Tarjan's algorithm on the test problem, shown in Figure 17-6.

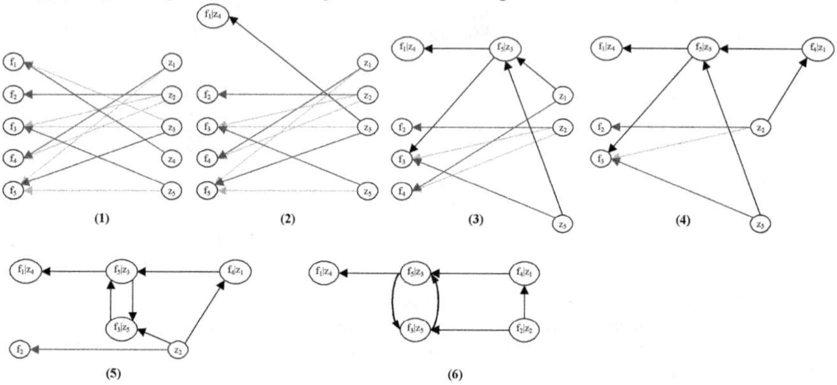

Figure 17-6. The 6 steps needed by Tarjan's algorithm on finding the strongly connected components starting from a bipartite graph (1) for this example. The final form is shown in (6) with one strongly connected component consisting of two nodes.

Tarjan's algorithm for topological sorting starting from the graph with the matching produced in Figure 17-5 is presented below in pseudocode.

Algorithm 17-1: Tarjan's algorithm for finding strongly connected components in a graph

```
 i          := 0;                  // global variable
 number   := zeros(n,1);         // global variable
 lowlink  := zeros(n,1);         // root of strong component
 <empty stack>                   // stack is global

for w in 1:n
  if number(w) == 0              // Main program for visiting each not yet
    strongConnect(w);            // visited node through the recursive procedure
  end if                         // strongConnect()
end for

procedure strongConnect(v)
 i            := i+1;
 number(v)   := i;
 lowlink(v)  := i;
 <put v on stack>
```

```
for <all w directly reachable from v>
  if number(w) == 0          // (v,w) is a tree arc
    strongConnect(w);
    lowlink(v) := min(lowlink(v),lowlink(w))
  else if number(w) < number(v)    // (v,w) is a frond or cross link
    if <w is on stack>
      lowlink(v) := min(lowlink(v), number(w));
    end if
  end if
end for

if lowlink(v) == number(v)    // v is the root of a strong component
  while <w on top of stack satisfies number(w) >= number(v)>
    <delete w from stack and put w in current component>
  end while
end if
```

17.2 Summary

In previous chapters, (Chapter 2 and Chapter 12), we mentioned equation representations such as ODEs and DAEs which are only valid for continuous-time models.

Here we defined the full Hybrid DAE equation representation which is the mathematical basis for equation systems resulting from arbitrary Modelica models, being able to handle both continuous-time, discrete-time, and hybrid models. The Hybrid DAE representation was illustrated by a model example resulting in both continuous-time and discrete-time variables, differential equations, algebraic equations, hybrid equations, as well as both linear and nonlinear subsystems of equations. The example is transformed into a flat Hybrid DAE equation system form, then subject to BLT-partitioning using Tarjan's algorithm, which is briefly described at the end of the chapter.

17.3 Literature

The section on mathematical properties of hybrid DAEs in (Modelica Association 2003) gives a short definition of Modelica hybrid DAEs that is the basis for the definitions in this chapter. Analogous definitions for the Omola language are presented in (Andersson 1994). Tarjans algorithm for finding strongly connected components in graphs is described in (Tarjan 1972). A description of BLT partitioning and equation assignment is also available in part 4 of (Otter 1999b). A general and very comprehensive overview of methods for simulation is available in (Cellier and Kofman 2006).

Chapter 18

Techniques and Research

This chapter gives short overviews of three topics:

- Numeric and symbolic techniques for simulating Modelica models
- Some current work on Modelica language extensions
- A selection of ongoing Modelica-related research

The numeric and symbolic techniques build on the general hybrid DAE equation representation and block lower triangular form (BLT) decomposition described in Chapter 17, page 979.

The described preliminary designs for some Modelica language extensions include specification of model configurations or variants.

The research presented includes methods to find and correct errors and inconsistencies in models, thereby enhancing ease-of-use, performance enhancements of Modelica simulations by the use of parallel computers for example, via the GRID, gray-box model identification, model verification, and model diagnosis.

18.1 Overview of the Process of Simulating Modelica Models

As briefly described in Section 2.20, page 63, and depicted in Figure 18-1, the simulation of a Modelica model uses a combination of symbolic and numeric techniques.

A Modelica compiler typically first transforms a Modelica simulation model into a so-called "flat" model consisting of the equations and algorithm sections as well as variable declarations and functions of all used model components of the simulation model. This is done by the following steps:

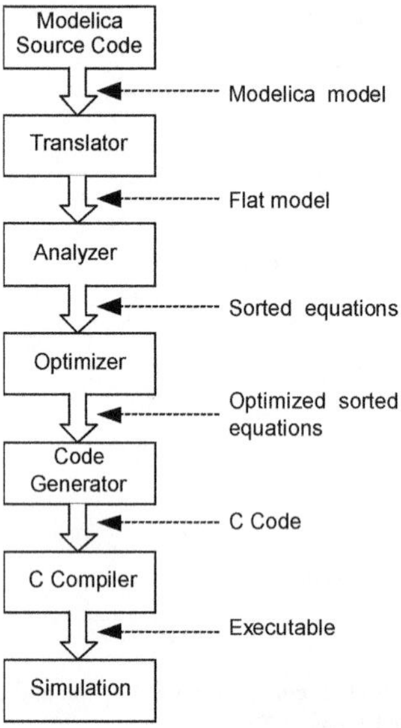

Figure 18-1. The stages of translating and executing a Modelica model. Also in Figure 2-29.

- Expanding all class definitions including expanding inheritance and modifications. This includes adding the equations and assignment statements of the expanded classes for every instance of the model.
- Replacing all connect-equations by the corresponding expanded equations of the connection set (Section 5.7.8, page 219).
- Mapping all algorithm sections to equation sets. For example, an algorithm section can conceptually be viewed as a function call of an implicitly defined function containing the algorithm section (Section 2.14.6, page 54).
- Mapping all when-clauses to equation sets, for example, `when x>2 then v1=expr1;` ... can conceptually be expanded to equations in non-standard Modelica: `b=x>2; v=if edge(b) then expr1 else pre(v1);` ...

The resulting hybrid DAE equation representation for Modelica models (Section 17.1.4, page 982) consists of the combination of three kinds of equations: ordinary differential equations (17-5), algebraic equaitons (17-6), and discrete equations (17-7), see Section 17.1.3, page 981.

This hybrid DAE is transformed and symbolically optimized to enable more efficient and numerically stable simulation, as described briefly below (Section 18.1.1, page 994).

Finally, the symbolically optimized hybrid DAE is solved (Section 18.2.5, page 1010) using numerical methods and handling events.

18.1.1 Symbolic Simplification of Modelica Models for Efficient Solution

As mentioned in Chapter 17, in the general case a Modelica model results in a hybrid DAE equation system (Section 17.1, page 979). Simulating a Modelica model in general requires solving such a system. This is nontrivial for several reasons:

- The equations contain not only `Real` but also `Boolean` , `Integer` and enumeration unknowns.
- The object-oriented nature of Modelica models, typically consisting of many connected components, causes the flattened hybrid DAE equation system to be quite sparse. Many equations include just a few variables out of the thousands of variables in typical models.
- Many Modelica models, especially those that model mechanical or mechatronic systems, have a high value (e.g., 2 or 3) of the so-called DAE index (see Section 18.2.3, page 1003), which causes numerical difficulties for DAE solvers that cannot be fixed even by using short step sizes.
- The object-oriented and component-based properties of Modelica make it fairly easy for the user to construct quite large models, even up to several hundred thousand equations and variables. Such large models pose special demands on the solution techniques.

Many of these difficulties can be resolved by symbolically transforming the system of equations before using a numerical solver. In Section 2.20.2, page 66, and in Section 17.1.6, page 984, we briefly describe the method of symbolically performing BLT-*partitioning*, or topological sorting, of the equation system using Tarjan's algorithm. This algorithm finds the strongly connected components containing interdependent equations, that is, subsystems of simultaneous equations.

The partitioning of the equation system enables efficient solution of sparse equation systems by reducing the number of variables that need to be handled by the numerical solver in each subsystem of equations.

The BLT partitioning also simplifies the solution of equations with mixed `Real`, `Integer`, `Boolean`, and `enumeration` unknowns, since in many cases the `Boolean`, `Integer`, and `enumeration` unknowns can be computed by just a forward evaluation sequence. In other cases (e.g., for ideal diodes, Coulomb friction elements) special heuristic algorithms need to be used.

Certain subsystems of simultaneous equations found by the BLT algorithm are *linear* and can be solved by a standard linear equation solver. Other subsystems are *nonlinear* systems of equations.

Note that clocked base-partitions need not be sorted with respect to each other (Section 13.6.13.1, page 715) since their inputs are known when handling a clock tick event and do not change during solution of clocked equations. However, the equations within a base-clock partition still need to be sorted.

A technique called *tearing* can in many cases further reduce the size and improve performance when solving such a nonlinear subsystem of equations. The tearing technique enables the equations corresponding to a subsystem to be solved sequentially but iteratively by finding a tearing variable and starting from an initial guess for the value of this variable. The process is in general not guaranteed to converge, but usually does.

The need for numeric differentiation by numeric DAE solvers can be reduced or eliminated by employing Pantelides algorithm for *index reduction* (see Section 18.2.4, page 1007) by symbolically transforming the equation system into a form that has lower index. Such a transformed equation system with at most index 1 can be handled by standard numerical DAE solvers such as DASSL (see Section 18.2.2.2), and in some cases even by fairly simple ODE solution methods.

18.2 Simulation Techniques—Solving Equation Systems

As stated previously, there are three different kinds of equation systems resulting from the translation of a Modelica model to a flat set of equations, from the simplest to the most complicated and powerful:

- ODEs—Ordinary differential equations for continuous-time problems
- DAEs—Differential algebraic equations for continuous-time problems
- Hybrid DAEs—Hybrid differential algebraic equations for mixed continuous-discrete problems

In the following, we present a short overview of methods to solve these kinds of equation systems. However, remember that these representations are strongly interrelated: an ODE is a special case of DAE without algebraic equations, whereas a DAE is a special case of hybrid DAEs without discrete or conditional equations. We should also point out that in certain cases a Modelica model results in one of the following two forms of purely algebraic equation systems, which can be viewed as DAEs without a differential equation part:

- Linear algebraic equation systems
- Nonlinear algebraic equation systems

However, rather than representing a whole Modelica model, such algebraic equation systems are usually subsystems of equations resulting from the previously mentioned BLT-partitioning of the total equation system.

We start our solution method overview with a presentation of some well-known methods for solving ODEs.

18.2.1 Numerical Solution of Ordinary Differential Equations

As stated earlier (e.g., equation (17-1), Section 17.1, page 979), an ordinary differential equation system on explicit form can be expressed as follows:

$$\begin{aligned} \dot{x}(t) &= \hat{f}(x(t), u(t)) \\ y(t) &= g(x(t), u(t)) \end{aligned} \tag{18-1}$$

Since in this representation the output $y(t)$ is not needed to compute the state vector $x(t)$ we can ignore the second equation when solving for $x(t)$. The input vector $u(t)$ is independent of $x(t)$. Its effect can be directly incorporated into $\hat{f}$, thereby providing a slightly different function f in the following simplified equation, together with an initial condition at t=0:

$$\begin{aligned} \dot{x}(t) &= f(t, x(t)) \\ x(0) &= x_0 \end{aligned} \tag{18-2}$$

Numerical solution methods to solve ODEs like (18-2) are often called *integration methods* since (18-2) can be solved directly by integration:

$$x(t) = \int_0^t f(s, x(s))\, ds \tag{18-3}$$

18.2.1.1 The Explicit and Implicit Euler Methods

Consider once more the ordinary differential equation (18-2) on explicit form. Starting at $x(0) = x_0$, we would like to numerically compute an approximation to $x(t)$ as a series of values $x(t_0), x(t_1), .. x(t_n)$, and so on. The simplest numerical approximation of the derivative $\dot{x}(t)$ is the following, called the Euler approximation:

$$\dot{x}(t_n) \approx \frac{x_{n+1} - x_n}{h}; \qquad h = t_{n+1} - t_n \tag{18-4}$$

Using the fact that $\dot{x}(t_n) = f(t_n, x_n)$, obtained from (18-2), we derive the *explicit Euler* ODE *solution method* by substituting into (18-4):

$$x(t_{n+1}) \approx x(t_n) + h \cdot f(t_n, x_n) \tag{18-5}$$

It is called *explicit* since the value $x(t_{n+1})$ is explicitly computed from the values at the previous time step. This formula can also be derived as an integration formula by approximating the function f by the fixed value $f(t_n, x_n)$ in the interval (t_n, t_{n+1}):

$$x(t_{n+1}) = x(t_n) + \int_{t_n}^{t_{n+1}} f(t,x(t))dt \approx x(t_n) + h \cdot f(t_n, x_n) \tag{18-6}$$

Another possibility is to use a variant of (18-4) to approximate the derivative at the upper end of the step:

$$\dot{x}(t_{n+1}) \approx \frac{x_{n+1} - x_n}{h} \tag{18-7}$$

Performing a similar substitution as for (18-5) gives the *implicit Euler* ODE *solution method*:

$$x(t_{n+1}) \approx x(t_n) + h \cdot f(t_{n+1}, x_{n+1}) \tag{18-8}$$

In this case a small equation system has to be solved at each step.

18.2.1.2 Multistep Methods

The Euler method given in (18-5) and (18-6) is an example of a one-step method, since the next value depends on one previous value. In general, a numerical method for solving differential equations can be denoted a *k-step method* if it depends on *k* (previous) values:

$$x_{n+1} = H(t, x_{n-k+1}, x_{n-k+2}, \ldots, x_n, x_{n+1}) \tag{18-9}$$

The method is called *explicit* if the next value x_{n+1} only depends on previous values. It is an *implicit method* if the function *H* on the right-hand side also includes x_{n+1}. In that case a small equation system has to be solved at each step. Euler's method is an explicit one-step method.

18.2.1.3 Local Error

The global error is the deviation $x(t_n) - x_n$ between the exact and approximate value for $x(t)$. This absolute difference is hard to compute; therefore the one-step or local error e_n is often used instead:

$$e_n = x_{n+1} - x_n = H(t, x_{n-k}, x_{n-k+1}, \ldots, x_{n-1}, x_n) \tag{18-10}$$

This is the error from one step, assuming that all information from previous steps is exact.

18.2.1.4 Stability

Keeping the error within bounds is not the only criterion for a numerical method. Each numerical method for solving differential equations has a region of stability. If the step size *h* is small enough to be within the region of stability, the method is stable; otherwise the computation becomes unstable and strange oscillations appear. Explicit methods have smaller regions of stability than implicit methods.

It is instructive to take a look at the solution of a small test problem:

```
model ErrStab
  Real z(start=1);
equation
  der(z) = -5*(time+1)*z^(2)+5/(time+1)-1/(time+1)^(2);
end ErrStab;
```

We simulate the problem twice, using Euler's method with two different step sizes, *h*=0.21 and *h*=0.19, respectively, employing the Mathematica command interface to Wolfram SystemModeler:

```
simEuler1= Simulate[ErrStab,{t,0,24},Method->Euler, IntervalLength->0.21];
simEuler2= Simulate[ErrStab,{t,0,24},Method->Euler, IntervalLength->0.19];
```

We compare the results in a plot depicted in Figure 18-2.

```
PlotSimulation[z[t],{t,0,24}, SimulationResult->{simEuler1,simEuler2}];
```

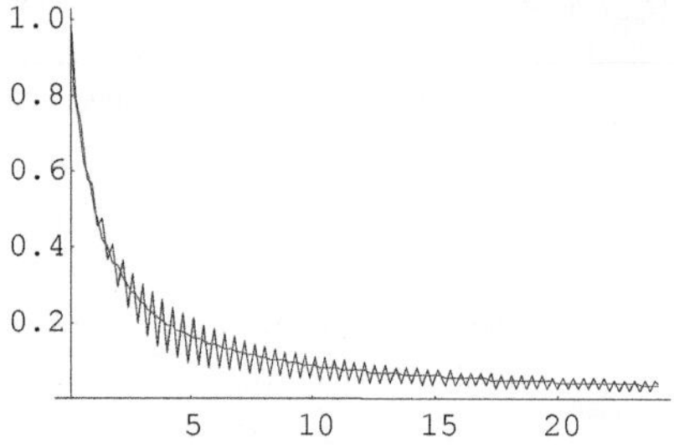

Figure 18-2. Solving the same problem using the Euler method with different step sizes h=0.19 (stable), and h=0.20 (oscillations).

The result is rather dramatic. Even though the difference in step size is quite small the behavior differs substantially. The reason is that the step size is outside the region of *absolute stability* for the solver. It is important to understand that the absolute stability restriction is indeed a stability, not an accuracy, requirement.

For the smaller step size, h=0.19, the solution is stable, but the question is how accurate is it. Therefore, let us compare the solution for this simulation with the exact answer. The equation (18-11) is identical to the differential equation in the `ErrStab` model apart from a time offset of 1:

$$\dot{z} = -5tz^2 + \frac{5}{t} - \frac{1}{t^2}, \qquad z(1) = 1 \tag{18-11}$$

This is one of the rare cases for which an exact analytical solution is available:

$$z(t) = \frac{1}{t} \tag{18-12}$$

Before comparing the results in a plot, we perform a simulation with a much smaller step size and hopefully a smaller error:

```
simEuler3 = Simulate[ErrStab,{t,0,24},Method->Euler,IntervalLength->10^-4];
```

We compare both solutions, `simEuler2` with h=0.19 and `simEuler3` with h=10^{-4}, to the exact solution (see Figure18-2):

```
PlotSimulation[1/t - z[t-1], {t, 1, 25}, SimulationResult->{simEuler2}];
PlotSimulation[1/t - z[t-1], {t, 1, 25}, SimulationResult->{simEuler3}];
```

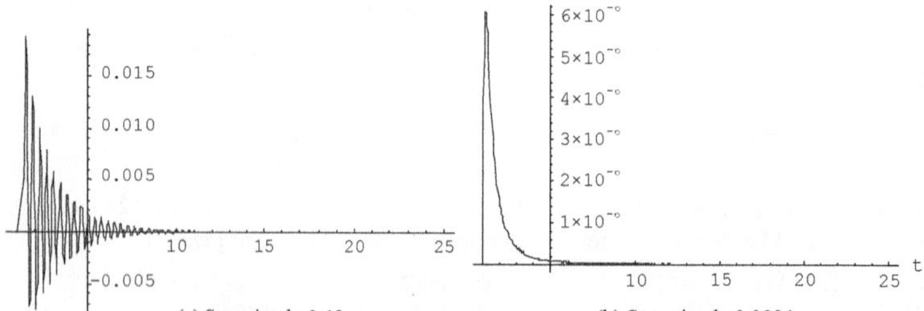

(a) Step size h=0.19 (b) Step size h=0.0001

Figure 18-3. Comparing the exact solution to numerical solutions with step sizes (a) h=0.19 and (b) h=0.0001.

As expected, decreasing the step size to $h=10^{-4}$ gives a much smaller error on the order of 10^{-6}, whereas the previous step length $h=0.19$ gives an error on the order of 0.01. However, decreasing the step size increases the computational work. Also, decreasing the step size too much is not always feasible when using DAE solvers, as we shall see further on.

18.2.1.5 Stiff Differential Equations

Stiff differential equations have solutions with greatly varying time scales. For example, if we model the bouncing ball problem previously presented in Section 2.15, page 55, as a pure continuous-time problem instead of a hybrid continuous-discrete problem, we may have something close to a stiff model.

The reason is the following: while the ball is moving in space it is described by a rather slowly varying function. However, when it touches the ground it bounces and changes speed and direction very suddenly. Large forces cause high accelerations and sudden changes. This effect is described by quickly varying functions for the position, speed, and acceleration of the ball. The solver must take very small steps to accurately compute this part of the behavior. On the other hand, rather long steps were satisfactory while the ball was moving freely in space. Thus, solvers for stiff problems are often adaptive, that is, the step size can be varied during solution.

However, there is one more requirement for a stiff model: a slowly varying dynamic component in the solution should be present at the same time as the quickly varying component, for example, for the ball when it bounces. One example is a bearing ball, which rotates (relatively slowly) around the bearing axis along with the bearing, and at the same time bounces against the cage walls of the bearing.

18.2.1.6 The Runge-Kutta Methods

The simplest Runge-Kutta ODE integration method can be derived by combining numerical integration with the Euler approximation. If we integrate equation (18-2) over the interval (t_n, t_{n+1}) we obtain:

$$x(t_{n+1}) = x(t_n) + \int_{t_n}^{t_{n+1}} f(t, x(t))dt \tag{18-13}$$

Approximating the integral by the value of f at the midpoint of the integration interval, $f(t = t_n + \frac{h}{2})$, multiplied by the length h of the interval gives:

$$x_{n+1} = x_n + h \cdot f(t_n + \tfrac{h}{2}, x(t_n + \tfrac{h}{2})) \tag{18-14}$$

The value $x(t_n + \frac{h}{2})$ is unknown, but can be computed using the Euler approximation:

$$x(t_n + \tfrac{h}{2}) \approx t_n + \tfrac{h}{2} \cdot f(t_n, x_n) \tag{18-15}$$

We substitute (18-15) into (18-14):

$$\begin{aligned} x_{n+1} &= x_n + h \cdot k_2 \\ k_1 &= f(t_n, x_n) \\ k_2 &= f(t_n + \tfrac{h}{2}, x_n + \tfrac{h}{2} \cdot k_1) \end{aligned} \tag{18-16}$$

If we make a series expansion we can show that the local error $x(t_{n+1}) - x_{n+1}$ is $O(h^3)$, that is, a factor of h smaller than the error using Euler's method. In general, a Runge-Kutta method is described by the following equations:

$$\begin{aligned}
x_{n+1} &= x_n + h\cdot(b_1k_1 + \ldots + b_sk_s)\\
k_1 &= f(t_n, x_n)\\
k_2 &= f(t_n + c_2\cdot h, x_n + h\cdot a_{21}\cdot k_1)\\
k_3 &= f(t_n + c_3\cdot h, x_n + h\cdot(a_{31}\cdot k_1 + a_{32}\cdot k_2))\\
&\vdots\\
k_s &= f(t_n + c_s\cdot h, x_n + h\cdot(a_{s1}\cdot k_1 + \ldots + a_{s,s-1}\cdot k_{s-1}))
\end{aligned} \tag{18-17}$$

The number s and the different coefficients are chosen depending on the desired order of accuracy p and/or computational efficiency. A common choice of coefficients is the following: the number of coefficients s=4, the order p=4, and all coefficients except the following equal to zero: $c_2 = 1/2$, $c_3 = 1/2$, $c_4 = 1$, $a_{21} = 1/2$, $a_{32} = 1/2$, $a_{43} = 1$, $b_1 = 1/6$, $b_2 = 2/6$, $b_3 = 2/6$, $b_4 = 1/6$. The coefficients are chosen to give the method the desired accuracy level, i.e.:

$$x(t_{n+1}) - x_{n+1} = O(h^{p+1}) \tag{18-18}$$

18.2.1.7 The Adams Methods

The Adams methods are multistep methods—compute the next step based on a number of previous steps. The coefficients b_i are chosen to give the maximum accuracy for the given number of terms. The *explicit* variant of the method, often called Adams-Bashforth, is specified by (18-19):

$$x_n = x_{n-1} + \sum_{i=1}^{k} b_i f_{n-i} \qquad f_j = f(t_j, x_j) \tag{18-19}$$

The explicit methods combine the values f_n from the preceding k steps. The formulas for the simplest explicit cases follow below:

$$\begin{aligned}
k = 1:&\quad x_n = x_{n-1} + f_{n-1}\,h\\
k = 2:&\quad x_n = x_{n-1} + (3f_{n-1} - f_{n-2})\tfrac{h}{2}\\
k = 3:&\quad x_n = x_{n-1} + (23f_{n-1} - 16f_{n-2} + 5f_{n-3})\tfrac{h}{12}\\
k = 4:&\quad x_n = x_{n-1} + (55f_{n-1} - 59f_{n-2} + 37f_{n-3} - 9f_{n-4})\tfrac{h}{12}
\end{aligned} \tag{18-20}$$

The *implicit* variant, called Adams-Moulton, is specified as follows:

$$x_n = x_{n-1} + \sum_{i=0}^{k-1} b_i f_{n-i} \qquad f_j = f(t_j, x_j) \tag{18-21}$$

The implicit method uses values x_n and f_n from the k most recent steps, including the current step since $f_n = f(t_n, x_n)$. The simplest implicit formulas are given below:

$$\begin{aligned}
k = 1:&\quad x_n = x_{n-1} + f_n\,h\\
k = 2:&\quad x_n = x_{n-1} + (f_n + f_{n-1})\tfrac{h}{2}\\
k = 3:&\quad x_n = x_{n-1} + (5f_n + 8f_{n-1} - f_{n-2})\tfrac{h}{12}\\
k = 4:&\quad x_n = x_{n-1} + (9f_n + 19f_{n-1} - 5f_{n-2} + f_{n-3})\tfrac{h}{24}
\end{aligned} \tag{18-22}$$

18.2.1.8 LSODE1, LSODE2, and LSODAR ODE Solvers

LSODE1 is a multistep method that uses Adams-Bashforth-Moulton (ABM) formulas. The method varies the step size and the order of the methods to efficiently meet the error tolerance. The method is similar to DEABM (see below) but generally uses a lower order and smaller step size to integrate the system.

DEABM is often more efficient if high accuracy is needed. This method is suitable for non-stiff problems. A related method called LSODE2 should be used instead if the problem is stiff.

LSODE2 is a multistep BDF method (Backward Difference Formulas). The BDF methods have wide stability regions and are therefore good choices for stiff problems. LSODE2 also uses a Nordseick representation of the fixed step size BDF formula.

LSODAR is a combination of LSODE1 and 2 together with a root solver to handle discrete events. The method starts with LSODE1 and then switches to the stiff solver if any stiffness is detected. For non-stiff problems the solution is very similar to using LSODE1.

18.2.1.9 DEABM ODE Solver

DEABM is another multistep method that uses Adams-Bashforth-Moulton (ABM) formulas. The method varies the step size and the order of the methods to efficiently meet the error tolerance. It uses divided differences to represent the ABM formulas and is considered more stable than the LSODE implementation of ABM formulas. This is a good choice when high accuracy is needed. The method uses higher orders of the ABM formulas and longer step sizes than LSODE1.

18.2.2 Solution of Differential Algebraic Equations (DAEs)

As we have seen in the previous sections, when solving an ordinary differential equation (ODE) the problem is to compute, that is, to *integrate*, the continuous-time state variables from their derivatives. In the case of ODEs on explicit state space form such as equations (18-1) and (18-2) this is fairly straightforward since the expressions for the derivatives to be integrated are defined by the ODE right-hand side expressions.

However, as we have stated previously, a general DAE system on implicit form such as (18-23) below typically also includes algebraic equations (18-23b) that express algebraic constraints between nondifferentiated variables:

$$\begin{aligned} g(x(t),\dot{x}(t),y(t),u(t)) &= 0 \qquad (a) \\ h(x(t),u(t),y(t)) &= 0 \qquad (b) \end{aligned} \tag{18-23}$$

Here $x(t)$ is the set of unknown differentiated state variables, $u(t)$ are the inputs, and $y(t)$ the algebraic variables that do not appear differentiated. Both parts of (18-23) can be combined into a more compact DAE form with a single vector-valued function F:

$$F(x(t),\dot{x}(t),y(t),u(t)) = 0 \tag{18-24}$$

The main difference compared to solving an ODE is that solving a DAE may also include *differentiation*, that is, calculating the derivatives of certain variables. The reason differentiation may be necessary is that the algebraic equations in many cases express *constraints* between certain state variables in the vector $x(t)$, but not necessarily directly between their derivatives.

However, even though the derivatives are not present in the algebraic constraints, they might be implicitly constrained. For example, $x_1 = x_2$ implies $\dot{x}_1 = \dot{x}_2$. Therefore certain constraint equations have to be differentiated to make the constraints explicit in order to directly influence the numerical solver.

The differential *index* of a general DAE system is the minimum number of times that certain equations in the system need to be differentiated to reduce the system to a set of ODEs, which can then be solved by the usual ODE solvers. Even if the system has a higher index it can sometimes be solved directly by numerical methods. We will discuss this topic in more detail in Section 18.2.3.

18.2.2.1 Numerical DAE Solvers May Fail

For DAE systems with index greater than 1, numerical methods may converge poorly, may converge to the wrong solutions, or may not converge at all. As we have seen, higher index DAE systems may have hidden algebraic constraints between the dependent variables and/or derivatives. Hidden algebraic constraints complicate the problem of providing proper initial conditions for the system and also present difficulties for numerical integration methods.

The main cause of these problems is that the differentiation needed by DAE solvers is a numerically sensitive operation in contrast to integration, which is usually stable. Numerical instabilities and loss of precision can easily occur. It does not help to increase precision by decreasing step sizes as we do for ODEs. The reason is that the error in differentiation will increase with decreasing step sizes due to roundoff errors and inaccurate solutions of algebraic equations in previous steps. Such problems might introduce large artificial variations in the solution, for example, if some part of the system model caused a drastic reduction in step size.

For these reasons there exists no general-purpose numerical DAE solver for DAEs with index higher than 1, even though there are certain numerical DAE solvers for index 2 DAEs with special structure.

This might be a serious situation since many natural models result in DAEs of index 2 or index 3. Fortunately, mixed symbolic-numerical techniques can help, as will be described further on. The DAE system can be symbolically transformed into an equivalent low index DAE through so-called *index reduction* before the numerical solution process is started.

18.2.2.2 The DASSL DAE Solver

When the simulation problem is a DAE the method of choice is DASSL (Differential Algebraic System Solver) by Petzold 1982, and continuously improved. This is the default solver used by several Modelica environments. It uses a BDF (Backward Difference Formulas) scheme to solve the DAE, and has been proved very stable and reliable for most DAE problems. A special version of DASSL, DASSLRT with a root solver, can be called when events occur in the simulated model; see also Section 18.2.5.5 on crossing functions. Newer versions of DASSLRT exist, e.g. the root-finding DAE solver called DASKR included in the latest version of DASPK3.0. Since DASSL uses a BDF formula it can also be used for certain stiff (see Section 18.2.1.5) ODE problems. However, the error formulas in the method are adapted for DAE problems. Therefore it might be better, for example, to use a solver such as LSODE2 for stiff ODE problems if problems arise when using DASSL.

18.2.2.3 Mixed Symbolic and Numerical Solution of DAEs

A mixed symbolic and numerical approach to solution of DAEs avoids the problems of numerical differentiation. The DAE is transformed to a lower index problem by using index reduction. The standard mixed symbolic and numerical approach contains the following steps:

1. Use Pantelides algorithm (see Section 18.2.4.3) to determine how many times each equation has to be differentiated to reduce the *index* to one or zero.
2. Perform *index reduction* of the DAE by analytical symbolic differentiation of certain equations and by applying the method of dummy derivatives (see Section 18.2.4.1).
3. Select the state variables to be used for solving the reduced problem. These can be either selected statically during compilation, or in some cases selected dynamically during simulation.
4. Use a numerical ODE or DAE solver to solve the reduced problem.

In the following we will discuss the notions of index and index reduction in some more detail.

18.2.3 The Notion of DAE Index

From the preceding discussion we can draw the conclusion that index is an important property of DAE systems. Consider once more a DAE system on the general form:

$$F(x(t), \dot{x}(t), y(t), u(t)) = 0 \tag{18-25}$$

We assume that this system is solvable with a continuous solution, given an appropriate initial solution. There are several definitions of DAE *index* in the literature, of which the following, also called *differential index*, is informally defined as follows:

- The index of a DAE system (18-25) is the minimum number of times certain equations in the DAE must be differentiated in order to solve $\dot{x}(t)$ as a function of $x(t)$, $y(t)$, and $u(t)$, i.e., to transform the problem into ODE explicit state space form.

The index gives a classification of DAEs with respect to their numerical properties and can be seen as a measure of the distance between the DAE and the corresponding ODE.

An ODE system on explicit state space form is of index 0 since it is already in the desired form:

$$\dot{x}(t) = f(t, x(t)) \tag{18-26}$$

The following *semiexplicit* form of DAE system is of index 1 under certain conditions:

$$\begin{aligned} \dot{x}(t) &= f(t, x(t), y(t)) && (a) \\ 0 &= g(t, x(t), y(t)) && (b) \end{aligned} \tag{18-27}$$

The condition is that the Jacobian of g with respect to y, $(\partial g / \partial y)$—usually a matrix—see (18-29), is *nonsingular* and therefore has a well-defined inverse. This means that in principle $y(t)$ can be solved as a function of $x(t)$ and substituted into (18-27a) to get state-space form. The solution procedure involves differentiating (18-27b) to get (18-28a), solving for $\dot{y}$, (18-28b), and finally integrating $\dot{y}$ to obtain the y to be substituted.

$$\begin{aligned} 0 &= \left(\frac{\partial g}{\partial y}\right)\dot{y} + \left(\frac{\partial g}{\partial x}\right)\dot{x} + \frac{\partial g}{\partial t} && (a) \\ \dot{y} &= -\left(\frac{\partial g}{\partial y}\right)^{-1}\left(\frac{\partial g}{\partial x}\right)\cdot\dot{x} - \left(\frac{\partial g}{\partial y}\right)^{-1}\frac{\partial g}{\partial t} && (b) \end{aligned} \tag{18-28}$$

The Jacobian of g with respect to y is defined as follows:

$$\left(\frac{\partial g}{\partial y}\right) = \begin{pmatrix} \frac{\partial g_1}{\partial y_1} & \frac{\partial g_1}{\partial y_2} & \cdots & \frac{\partial g_1}{\partial y_r} \\ \frac{\partial g_2}{\partial y_1} & \frac{\partial g_2}{\partial y_2} & \cdots & \frac{\partial g_2}{\partial y_r} \\ \vdots & \vdots & \ddots & \\ \frac{\partial g_s}{\partial y_1} & \frac{\partial g_s}{\partial y_2} & \cdots & \frac{\partial g_s}{\partial y_r} \end{pmatrix} \quad \text{where} \quad y = \begin{pmatrix} y_1 \\ y_2 \\ \vdots \\ y_r \end{pmatrix}, \quad g = \begin{pmatrix} g_1 \\ g_2 \\ \vdots \\ g_s \end{pmatrix} \tag{18-29}$$

A DAE system in the general form (18-25) may have higher index than 1. Mechanical models often lead to index 3 DAE systems as exemplified in Section 18.2.3.3. We conclude:

- There is no need for symbolic differentiation of equations in a DAE system if it is possible to determine the *highest-order derivatives* as continuous functions of time and lower derivatives using stable numerical methods. In this case the index is at most 1.

- The index is zero for such a DAE system if there are no algebraic variables.

A perhaps even simpler way of stating the *high index* property of a DAE system, allowing for the case when certain variables have a derivative of order higher than 1:

- A DAE system has high index if it is necessary to differentiate certain equations when solving for the highest-order derivatives of the variables.

18.2.3.1 Higher Index Problems Are Natural in Component-Based Models

The index of a DAE system is not a property of the modeled system but the *property* of a *particular model representation*, and therefore a function of the modeling methodology. A natural object-oriented component-based methodology with reuse and connections between physical objects leads to high index in the general case[21]. The reason is the constraint equations resulting from setting variables equal across connections between separate objects.

Since the index is not a property of the modeled system it is possible to reduce the index by symbolic manipulations. High index indicates that the model has algebraic relations between differentiated state variables implied by algebraic relations between those state variables. By using knowledge about the particular modeling domain it is often possible to manually eliminate a number of differentiated variables, and thus reduce the index. However, this violates the object-oriented component-based modeling methodology for physical modeling that we want to support.

We conclude that high index models are natural, and that automatic index reduction is necessary to support a general object-oriented component-based modeling methodology with a high degree of reuse.

18.2.3.2 Example of High-Index Electrical Model

As an example of high index that is caused by connection of model components, consider the electrical circuit in Figure 2-21a, which consists of two connected identical subcircuits each containing one resistor and one capacitor. We will show that this system leads to a DAE with index 2. Interestingly enough, Figure 2-21b shows an equivalent transformed circuit with an index 1 DAE where we have used the usual rules for connecting resistors and capacitors in parallel, illustrating the fact that a problem can be transformed from index 2 to index 1.

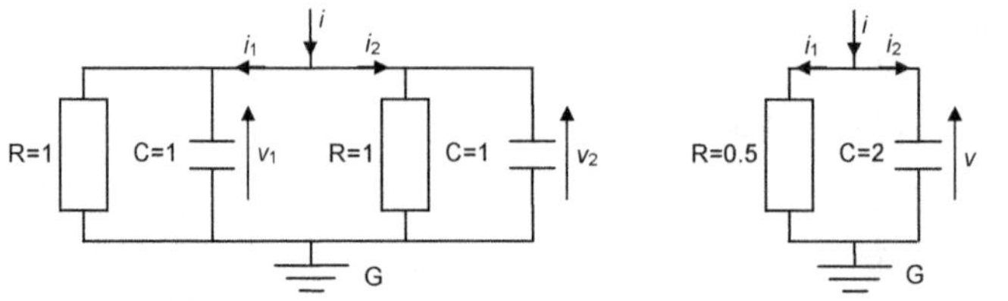

(a) Circuit model with an index 2 DAE system (b) Equivalent circuit model with an index 1 DAE system

Figure 18-4. A circuit model (a) resulting in an index 2 DAE, vs. an equivalent circuit (b) giving rise to an index 1 DAE. Both circuits are driven by a current *i*, which is a known function of time.

To begin the analysis of the circuit depicted in Figure 18-4a, we first recall the constitutive equations relating voltage and current for resistors and capacitors:

$$v = R \cdot i$$
$$\dot{v} = C \cdot i \tag{18-30}$$

[21] However, it is possible to avoid high index in certain application domains by careful manual control of model formulation and by avoiding certain connections. However, this limits reuse of component models.

By using these equations to compute the currents through the resistor and the capacitor in the *left* part of the circuit, we obtain the following equation since the sum of the two currents is equal to i_1:

$$\dot{v}_1 + v_1 - i_1 = 0 \tag{18-31}$$

Analogously, the circuit in the *right* part of Figure 18-4a is described by essentially the same equation:

$$\dot{v}_2 + v_2 - i_2 = 0 \tag{18-32}$$

The connections between the left and right parts of the circuit are reflected in the following constraint equations:

$$\begin{aligned} v_1 - v_2 &= 0 \qquad (a) \\ i_1 + i_2 &= i \qquad (b) \end{aligned} \tag{18-33}$$

The complete DAE system then becomes:

$$\begin{aligned} \dot{v}_1 + v_1 - i_1 &= 0 \\ \dot{v}_2 + v_2 - i_2 &= 0 \\ v_1 - v_2 &= 0 \\ i_1 + i_2 &= i \end{aligned} \tag{18-34}$$

We differentiate the constraint equation (18-33a) between the state variables, $v_1 - v_2 = 0$, to make this constraint explicit also for the differentiated state variables, and replace the original constraint by the differentiated one. The resulting DAE system (18-35) is of index 1 since it has the form (18-27) and is theoretically possible to solve for v_1 and v_2. Thus the original system (18-34) is of index 2.

$$\begin{aligned} \dot{v}_1 + v_1 - i_1 &= 0 \\ \dot{v}_2 + v_2 - i_2 &= 0 \\ \dot{v}_1 - \dot{v}_2 &= 0 \\ i_1 + i_2 &= i \end{aligned} \tag{18-35}$$

This model results in the following sets of variables, including two state variables:

$x(t) = \{v_1, v_2\}$, $y(t) = \{i_1, i_2\}$, $u(t) = \{i\}$

The new index 1 DAE system (18-35), with consistent the initial values, is mathematically equivalent to the original problem (18-34). Unfortunately, due to numerical imprecision in the solver there is *no* guarantee that a numerical solution to (18-35) will fulfill the original constraint $v_1 - v_2 = 0$ in (18-34). Thus we need improved methods for reducing the index of a DAE system, to which we will return in Section 18.2.4.

For comparison, we also derive the equations for the RC circuit in Figure 18-4b, using the usual rules for connecting resistors and capacitors in parallel:

$$\begin{aligned} R_{parallel} &= \frac{R_1 \cdot R_2}{R_1 + R_2} = 0.5 \\ C_{parallel} &= C_1 + C_2 = 2 \end{aligned} \tag{18-36}$$

Here only one state variable is needed. The system is of index 1 since it has the form (18-27):

$$
\begin{aligned}
2\dot{v} + 0.5v - i &= 0\\
i_1 + i_2 - i &= 0\\
v &= 0.5 i_1
\end{aligned}
\tag{18-37}
$$

This model results in the following sets of variables, including one state variable:

$x(t) = \{v_1\}$, $y(t) = \{i_1, i_2\}$, $u(t)=\{i\}$

18.2.3.3 Examples of High-Index Mechanical Models

As an example from the mechanical application domain, consider a classical planar pendulum depicted and described in Section 12.7.3–12.7.4, page 586.

Using Newton's second law to describe the dynamics of the pendulum results in a nonlinear second-order differential equation system:

$$m\ddot{x} = -\frac{x}{L}F; \quad m\ddot{y} = -\frac{y}{L}F - mg \tag{18-38}$$

where F is the force in the rod, g is the gravitational acceleration, and x,y are the coordinates of the mass m. In order to fully specify the physical system the following geometrical constraint needs to be added:

$$x^2 + y^2 = L^2 \tag{18-39}$$

Combining the differential equations from (18-38) and (18-39) we obtain the DAE system of (18-40) below. The geometric constraint does not contain the higher-order derivatives $\ddot{x}, \ddot{y}$ and F. The length constraint equation needs to be differentiated, which yields the system of equations presented in (18-41).

The equation system obtained still does not contain the highest derivates and therefore needs to be differentiated once more, resulting in (18-42). In conclusion, the equation system (18-40) has been differentiated twice in order to get the DAE system down to index 1. Therefore the differential index of the system is equal to 3.

$$
\begin{aligned}
m\ddot{x} &= -\frac{x}{L}F\\
m\ddot{y} &= -\frac{y}{L}F - mg\\
x^2 + y^2 &= L^2
\end{aligned}
\tag{18-40}
$$

$$
\begin{aligned}
m\ddot{x} &= -\frac{x}{L}F\\
m\ddot{y} &= -\frac{y}{L}F - mg\\
2x\dot{x} + 2y\dot{y} &= 0
\end{aligned}
\tag{18-41}
$$

$$
\begin{aligned}
m\ddot{x} &= -\frac{x}{L}F\\
m\ddot{y} &= -\frac{y}{L}F - mg\\
2\dot{x}\dot{x} + 2\dot{y}\dot{y} + 2x\ddot{x} + 2y\ddot{y} &= 0
\end{aligned}
\tag{18-42}
$$

As mentioned regarding the electrical example in the previous section, a transformed index 1 DAE system such as (18-42) is not quite suitable for numerical solvers since the solution tends to drift away from the original constraint (18-39). Fortunately, the method of dummy derivatives described in the next section can help.

In general, mechanical models often lead to index 3 problems when some kind constraint is involved. Consider a mass, m, at a position x, subject to a force F. Its motion is described by Newton's second law:

$$m \cdot \ddot{x} = F \tag{18-43}$$

In robotics and many other mechanical problems the position is constrained to be on a certain trajectory $x_R(t)$:

$$x = x_R(t) \tag{18-44}$$

To calculate the force F, the equation $x = x_R(t)$ needs to be differentiated twice, that is, a high-index problem.

18.2.4 Index Reduction

We have informally shown some examples of reducing the index of a DAE system. However, we need general algorithms to be able to handle DAEs resulting from object-oriented models in general. The following two algorithms in combination compute the index and transform DAE systems to low-index system by index reduction.

- Pantelides' algorithm can be used to *compute the index* and to determine which constraint equations should be differentiated, and how many times each equation has to be differentiated in order to reduce the index to one or zero.
- The method of *dummy derivatives* for *index reduction* augments the DAE system with differentiated versions of equations, and replaces some of the differentiated variables with new algebraic variables called dummy derivatives.

Before going into detail about Pantelides' algorithm, which is based on graph-theoretical methods, we briefly present an example of using the method of dummy derivatives for index reduction.

18.2.4.1 The Method of Dummy Derivatives for Index Reduction

In two of the previous examples of DAE systems, Sections 18.2.3.2 and 18.2.3.3, we reduce the DAE index by replacing certain constraint equations by their differentiated counterparts. Such transformed DAE systems are mathematically equivalent to the original versions but have numerical difficulties since the numerical solution tends to drift and thereby not fulfill the original constraint equations.

Such problems are largely avoided by the method of *dummy derivatives* mentioned above, which *augments* the DAE system with differentiated versions of constraint equations, that is, keeps the original constraint equations, and also *replaces* some differentiated variables with new algebraic variables. In the example DAE system (18-34) we first augment the system with a differentiated version of the third equation instead of replacing it, producing the following *overdetermined* system:

$$\begin{aligned}\dot{v}_1 + v_1 - i_1 &= 0\\ \dot{v}_2 + v_2 - i_2 &= 0\\ v_1 - v_2 &= 0\\ \dot{v}_1 - \dot{v}_2 &= 0\\ i_1 + i_2 &= i\end{aligned} \tag{18-45}$$

The system is overdetermined since we have 5 equations and 4 variables. To add one additional variable we select one of the derivatives of the differentiated constraint equation to be replaced in all equations by a new variable called v_{d2}, known as a dummy derivative—hence the name of the method.

$$\begin{aligned}\dot{v}_1 + v_1 - i_1 &= 0\\ v_{d2} + v_2 - i_2 &= 0\\ v_1 - v_2 &= 0\\ \dot{v}_1 - v_{d2} &= 0\\ i_1 + i_2 &= i\end{aligned} \tag{18-46}$$

This new equation system is *well determined* with 5 equations and 5 variables, and has index 1.

18.2.4.2 Bipartite Graphs

Pantelides' algorithm and the dummy derivatives index reduction method use a so-called bipartite graph representation of equation systems. A bipartite graph representation has the following characteristics:

- A set of nodes representing equations.

- A set of nodes representing variables.
- A set of edges between equation nodes and variable nodes, where there is an edge between an equation node and a variable node if the variable or its derivative is present in the equation.

The bipartite graph representation of the pendulum example is depicted in Figure 18-5. Since Modelica only supports syntax for the first-order derivatives we have rewritten equations (18-40) by introducing v_x and v_y for the velocity components.

$$m\dot{v}_x = -\frac{x}{L}F$$

$$m\dot{v}_y = -\frac{y}{L}F - mg$$

$$x^2 + y^2 = L^2$$

$$\dot{x} = v_x$$

$$\dot{y} = v_y$$

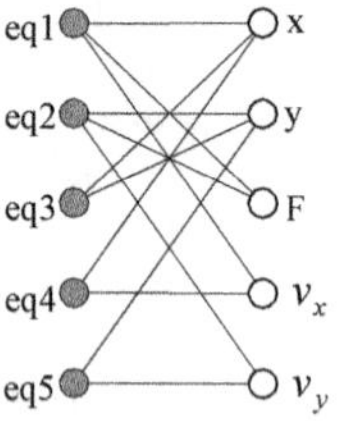

Figure 18-5. Pendulum model equations and the corresponding bipartite graph.

Now we will use this bipartite graph representation when computing the DAE index.

18.2.4.3 Structural DAE Index and Pantelides' Algorithm

The structural index is a computationally efficient alternative to the previously presented differential index definition of DAE index. Computing the structural index is reduced to the problem of finding maximum weighted matchings of different cardinalities in the bipartite graphs that represent the DAE systems. This method is used by Pantelides' algorithm. The following definition of the structural index is closely related to Pantelides' algorithm:

- The *structural index* i_{str} of a DAE is the minimum number of times that any subset of equations in the DAE is differentiated using Pantelides' algorithm.

Now, a method that computes or approximates the index based only on structural information needs to be provided. The algorithm for computing the structural index starts by constructing the bipartite graph representation of the DAE system. When considering the bipartite graph representation of the DAE system the numerical values of the coefficients are ignored (e.g., in an expression k*vx, the coefficient k is ignored when constructing the graph). We have the following definitions:

- A matching M_G^n of size n associated to the bipartite graph G is a set of n edges in the graph G where no two edges have a common end node.
- A perfect matching M_G^n covers all nodes in G, that is, all nodes are connected by exactly one edge.
- A weight w_{ij} is assigned to each edge (v_i, u_j) in the graph G, where the weight is the order of the highest derivative of the variable u_j present in the equation v_i.
- The weight $w(M)$ of a bipartite matching M is defined as the sum of the weights w_{ij} of all edges included in the matching.

An algorithm for computing the structural index and performing index reduction is presented below.

Algorithm 18-1: Computing the Structural Index of a DAE and performing index reduction.

Input Data: DAE system of differential algebraic equations
Result: The numerical value of the structural index $i_{str}(G)$
begin:
- Create a bipartite graph representation G of the DAE system.

- Assign a weight to each edge (v_s,u_t) in the graph G, where the weight is the order of the highest derivative of the variable u_t present in the equation v_s.
- Find all perfect matchings M_k of size *n* in the bipartite graph G.
  - $maxM_G^n = \max(w(M_k))$, where $w(M_k) = \sum_{(i,j)\in M_k} w_{ij}$ for all edges (*i*,*j*) in M_k
- Find all matchings M_k of size *n*-1 in the bipartite graph G.
  - $maxM_G^{n-1} = \max(w(M_k))$, where $w(M_k) = \sum_{(i,j)\in M_k} w_{ij}$ for all edges (*i*,*j*) in M_k
- Compute the structural index as $i_{str}(G) = maxM_G^{n-1} - maxM_G^n + 1$
- **while**($i_{str}(G) > 1$) **do**
  - Differentiate the equation corresponding to the equation node that is not covered by the maximum weighted matching M_k of size *n*-1.
  - Increase the weights of all adjacent edges of the differentiated equation node with 1.
  - Recompute the maximum weighted matching M_k of size *n*-1.
  - Decrement the structural index $i_{str}(G) = i_{str}(G) - 1$

  end while

end.

Let us now consider the bipartite graph shown in Figure 18-6a associated to the DAE from (18-40) and below:

$$
\begin{aligned}
m\ddot{x} &= -\frac{x}{L}F && \text{(eq1)} \\
m\ddot{y} &= -\frac{y}{L}F - mg && \text{(eq2)} \\
x^2 + y^2 &= L^2 && \text{(eq3)}
\end{aligned}
\qquad (18\text{-}47)
$$

Since the highest derivatives $\ddot{x}, \ddot{y}$, of second order, are present in the first and the second equation we assign a weight of 2 to the edges (eq1, *x*) and (eq2, *y*). One perfect matching containing the edges is depicted with thick lines in Figure 18-6b, the other in Figure 18-6c. Edges with weights of 2 because of $\ddot{x}, \ddot{y}$ have weight labels; all other weights are zero. Both perfect matchings have the same total weight = 0+2+0 =2, i.e., the maximum total weight $maxM_G^3 = 2$.

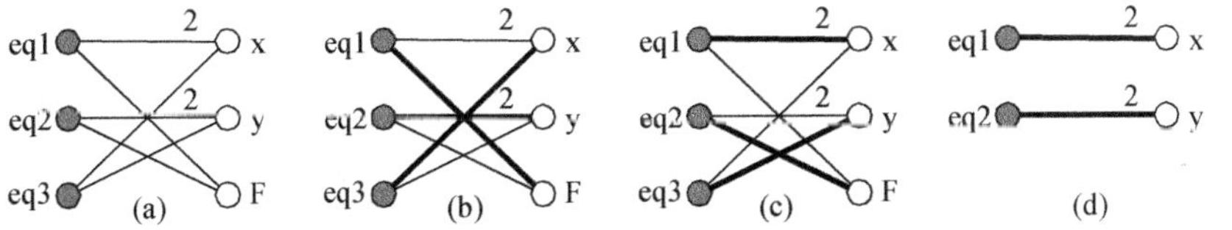

Figure 18-6. (a) Bipartite graph for the DAE system (18-40). (b) Perfect matching of size 3 of the bipartite graph. (c) The other perfect matching of size 3 of the bipartite graph. (d) Matching of size 2 where equation eq3 and variable F have been eliminated from the bipartite graph.

The maximum weighted matching of cardinality equal to 2 is shown in Figure 18-6c and has a total weight equal to 4. The structural index is computed as part of the results from Algorithm 18-1:

$$i_{str}(G) = \max(w(M_G^{n-1})) - \max(w(M_G^n)) + 1 = 4 - 2 + 1 = 3$$

The value corresponds to the previous value for the differential index.

If we differentiate equation (*eq*3) in (18-47), create a bipartite graph, and recompute the structural index we obtain the value 2 as it should be since the index has been reduced by one.

18.2.5 Simulation of Hybrid Models Based on Solving Hybrid DAEs

A Modelica *simulation problem* in the general case is a Modelica *model* that can be reduced to a hybrid DAE as described in 17.1, page 979, in the form of equations (17-5), (17-6), and (17-7), together with additional constraints on variables and their derivatives called *initial conditions*. This is a generalization compared to a simple simulation problem such as the simple circuit problem shown in Section 2.20.1, page 64, that can be expressed as ODEs. If Modelica in the future is extended with partial differential equations (PDEs), the set of additional constraints will also include boundary conditions.

The initial conditions prescribe initial start values of variables and/or their derivatives at simulation time=0 (e.g., expressed by the Modelica `start` attribute value of variables, with the attribute `fixed = true`), or default estimates of start values (the `start` attribute value with `fixed = false`).

The simulation problem is *well defined* provided that the following conditions hold:

- The total model system of equations is consistent and neither underdetermined nor overdetermined.
- The initial conditions are consistent and determine initial values for all variables.
- The model is specific enough to define a unique solution from the start simulation time t_0 to some end simulation time t_1.

The initial conditions of the simulation problem are often specified interactively by the user in the simulation tool, for example, through menus and forms, or alternatively as default `start` attribute values in the simulation code. More complex initial conditions can be specified through `initial equation` sections in Modelica.

18.2.5.1 Hybrid DAE Solution Algorithm—Event Iteration

The general structure of the *hybrid DAE solution algorithm* is presented in Figure 18-7, emphasizing the main structure rather than details.

First, a consistent set of *initial values* needs to be found based on the given constraints, which often requires the solution of an equation system consisting of the initial constraints.

However, note that equations in clocked partitions need not be sorted with respect to each other (Section 13.6.13.1, page 715) since their inputs are known when handling a clock tick event and do not change during solution of clocked equations. Instead the clocked partitions can be solved independently with respect to each other and before event-handling and solution of the unclocked equations.

Then the hybrid DAE solver checks whether any *event conditions* [$c(t_e)$, Section 17.1.2, page 980] in when-equations, when-statements, if-expressions, etc. have become `true` and therefore should trigger events. If there is no event, the *continuous DAE solver* is used to numerically solve the DAE until an event occurs or we have reached the end of the prescribed simulation time.

If the conditions for an event are fulfilled, the *event is fired*, that is, the conditional equations associated with the event are activated and solved together with all other active equations. This means that the variables affected by the event are determined, and new values are computed for these variables. Then a new initial value problem has to be solved to find a consistent set of initial values for *restarting* the continuous DAE solver, since there might have been discontinuous changes to both discrete-time and continuous-time variables at the event. This is called the *restart problem*. Of course, firing an event and solving the restart problem may change the values of variables, which in turn causes other event conditions to become `true` and fire the associated events.

This iterative process of firing events and solving restart problems is called *event iteration*, which must terminate before restarting the continuous DAE solver. See also short notes on event iteration in Section 6.14.2.1, page 296, Section 13.2.6.7, page 623, and Section 18.2.5.3, page 1012. Event iteration is an example of a so-called fixed-point iteration procedure, that is, a procedure assumed to converge to a fixed point.

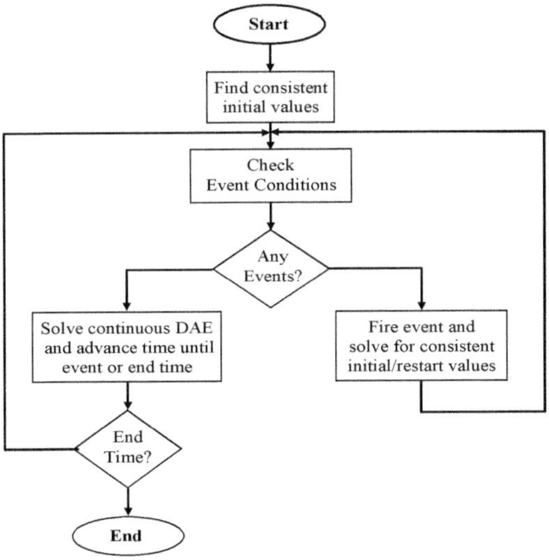

Figure 18-7. General structure of hybrid DAE solution algorithm.

The overall structure of the hybrid DAE solution algorithm is displayed in Figure 18-7 and summarized below:

1. Solve an *initialization value problem* of finding a consistent set of initial values before starting solution of the continuous part, equation (17-5) on page 980, of the hybrid DAE.
2. If there are equations in clocked partitions these partitions are solved independently with respect to each other and before event-handling and solution of the unclocked continuous-time and discrete-time equations.
3. Solve the *continuous DAE part* (17-5) of the hybrid DAE using a numerical DAE solver. During this phase the values of the discrete variables q as well as the values of the conditions c from the when-equations, -statements, if-expressions, and so on, of the model are kept constant. Therefore the functions $f(...)$ and $g(...)$ in (17-5) are continuous functions of continuous variables, which fulfills the basic requirements of continuous DAE solvers.
4. During solution of the continuous DAE, all relations $rel(...)$ occurring in the conditions c are constantly *monitored*. If one of the relations changes value causing a condition to change value from `false` to `true`, the exact time instant of the change is determined, the continuous DAE solution process is halted, and an event is triggered.
5. At an event instant, when an event has been fired, the total system of *active* equations (17-5), (17-6), and (17-7) (Section 17.1.3, page 981) is a mixed set of *algebraic* equations, which is solved for unknowns of type `Real`, `Boolean`, and `Integer`.
6. After the processing of an event, the algorithm continues with step (1) of solving the restart problem of finding a consistent set of initial values. After this step solving the continuous part of the hybrid DAE is restarted if the check in (4) does not indicate new events to be processed in (5).

Note that if a discrete-time variable `v`, which only changes at events, and its predecessor value `pre(v)` are only used in when-equations or when-statements, the Modelica compiler might mask event iteration for the variable `v` since `v` cannot change during event iteration. It is a "quality of implementation" of a Modelica tool to find the minimal loops for event iteration, i.e., not all parts of the model need to be reevaluated

18.2.5.2 Varying Structure of the Active Part of the Hybrid DAE

Even though the total hybrid DAE system of equations is structurally time invariant, that is, the set of variables and the set of equations is fixed over time, it is the case that conditional equations in hybrid DAEs can be activated and deactivated. This means that some variables in the state vectors x and q as well as certain equations can be disabled or deactivated at run-time during simulation, as well as enabled or activated. Such activation or deactivation is caused by events. A disabled variable is kept constant whereas a disabled equation is removed from the total system of active equations that is currently solved. Thus the *active part* of the hybrid DAE can be *structurally dynamic*, i.e., at run-time change the number of *active* variables and equations in the DAE.

18.2.5.3 Finding Consistent Initial Values at Start or Restart

As we have stated briefly above, at the start of the simulation, or at restart after handling an event, it is required to find a consistent set of initial values or restart values of the variables of the hybrid DAE equation system before starting continuous DAE solution process.

At the *start* of the simulation these conditions are given by the initial conditions of the problems (including `start` attribute equations, equations in `initial equation` sections, and so on; see Section 8.4, page 363) together with the system of equations defined by (17-5), (17-6), and (17-7) (see page 981). The user specifies the initial time of the simulation, t_0, and initial values or guesses of initial values of some of the continuous variables, derivatives, and discrete-time variables so that the algebraic part of the equation system can be solved at the initial time $t=t_0$ for all the remaining unknown initial values.

At *restart* after an event, the conditions are given by the *new values* of variables that have changed at the event, together with the current values of the remaining variables, and the system of equations (17-5), (17-6), and (17-7). The goal is the same as in the initial case, to solve for the new values of the remaining variables.

In both of the above cases, that is, at events, including the initial event representing the start of simulation, the process of finding a consistent set of initial values at start or restart is performed by the following iterative procedure, called *event iteration*:

Known variables: x, u, t, p

Unknown variables: $\dot{x}, y, q, q_{pre}, c$

```
loop
   Solve the equation system (1) for the unknowns, with q_pre fixed;
   if  q = q_pre then exit loop;
   q_pre := q;
end loop
```

In the above pseudocode we use the notation q_{pre} corresponding to `pre`(q) in Modelica.

18.2.5.4 Detecting Events During Continuous-time Simulation

Event conditions c are `Boolean` expressions (condition expressions $c(t_e)$, Section 17.1.2, page 980, or Real elementary relations, Section 6.11.1, page 287) depending on discrete-time or continuous-time model variables. As soon as an event condition changes from `false` to `true`, the event occurs. It is useful to divide the set of event conditions into two groups: conditions which depend only on discrete-time variables and therefore may change only when an event is fired, and conditions which also depend on continuous-time variables and may change at any time during the solution of the continuous part of the DAE. We call the first group *discrete-time conditions*, and the second group *continuous-time conditions*.

The first group causes no particular problems. The discrete-time conditions are checked after each event when the discrete-time variables might have changed. If some of the conditions change from `false` to `true`, the corresponding events are simply fired.

The continuous-time conditions, however, are more complicated to handle. Each `Boolean` event condition needs to be converted into a continuous function that can be evaluated and monitored along with the continuous-time DAE solution process. Most numerical software, including DAE solution algorithms, is designed to efficiently detect when the values of specified expressions cross zero.

18.2.5.5 Crossing Functions

To be able to detect when `Boolean` conditions become `true`, we convert each continuous-time `Boolean` event condition into a so-called *crossing function*. Such a function of time crosses zero when the `Boolean` condition changes from `false` to `true`. For example, the simple condition expression `y>53` changes from `false` to `true` when `y-53` *crosses* zero from being less than zero to being greater than zero, as depicted in Figure 18-8. The body of the corresponding crossing function is simply `y-53`.

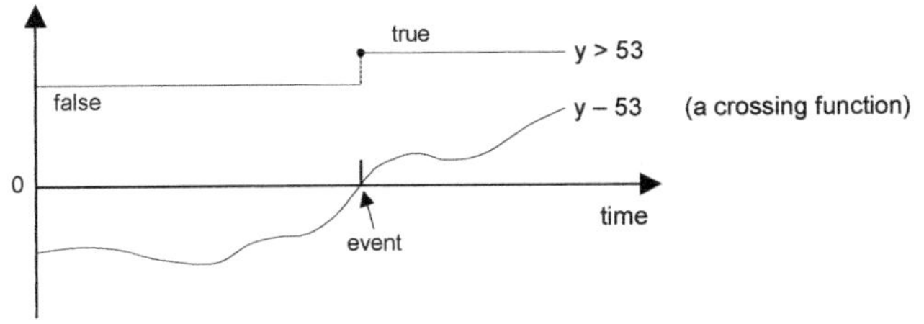

Figure 18-8. A boolean condition expression `y>53`, with its corresponding crossing function `y-53` that crosses zero at the event, thereby determining the time of the event.

The decision to react on changes of event conditions in Modelica from `false` to `true` rather than from `true` to `false` is arbitrary; it could also have been the other way around.

18.2.5.6 Shattering—The Zeno Effect

An interesting phenomenon called shattering, or the Zeno effect, occurs for certain models (e.g., our well-known bouncing ball example, Section 2.15, page 55) where events caused by continuous-time conditions becoming true may occur arbitrarily close to each other. In the bouncing ball example the bouncing events occur closer and closer in time—which eventually causes problems for the Modelica crossing function event detection mechanism since some small "epsilon" step size is needed (floating point precision is always limited) to detect when the crossing function switches from being negative to positive.

In our Modelica bouncing ball example, after some time (depending on the simulator), the ball falls through the ground. The reason for this behavior of the simulator is that the crossing function mechanism needs to determine the time instant when the height becomes negative. However, in order to detect this zero crossing the crossing function need to be computed also for a height of the ball that is actually not zero but a small negative number, say -1.e-10. After restart, the ball velocity of the ball may be so small that it never reaches the height=0 boundary and therefore no new event is generated. As a result, the ball flies a little bit higher, say up to -0.5e-10 and then falls down through the ground.

18.2.5.7 Solution of Mixed Systems of Algebraic Equations

The Modelica language allows mixed algebraic systems of equations where the unknown variables are of type Real, Integer, Boolean, or an enumeration. These systems of equations can be solved by a global fixed-point iteration scheme, similarly to event iteration, by fixing the Boolean, Integer, and/or enumeration unknowns during one iteration. It is a quality of implementation of a Modelica environment to solve these systems more efficiently, for example, by applying the fixed-point iteration scheme to a subset of the model equations. (?? give a reference to the solution scheme)

18.2.6 State Variable Selection for Efficient Simulation

In Section 18.2.2 we stated that the continuous-time part of a Modelica model can be represented as a differential algebraic equation system (DAE), (18-23), also shown here for convenience:

$$\begin{aligned} &g(x(t),\dot{x}(t),y(t),u(t)) = 0 \\ &h_1(x(t),u(t),y(t)) = 0 \end{aligned} \qquad (18\text{-}48)$$

where $x(t)$ is the set of dynamic variables, $u(t)$ represents the input variables, and $y(t)$ represents the output variables and/or algebraic variables.

At least conceptually this DAE is transformed into ODE explicit state space form, e.g. (2-4) in Chapter 2 and (18-49) below, to simplify solution:

$$\begin{aligned} &\dot{x}(t) = f(x(t),u(t)) \\ &y(t) = h_2(x(t),u(t)) \end{aligned} \qquad (18\text{-}49)$$

However, for a DAE not all dynamic variables are needed in the iterative numerical solution of the equation system. There is a vector of *state variables* $x_s(t)$, which is a subset of the vector $x(t)$, possibly extended by some algebraic variables from $y(t)$. The state variables are *independent* of each other, whereas the remaining *dependent* dynamic variables $x_d(t)$ and remaning dependent algebraic variabales $y_d(t)$ can be computed from the state variables.

In Chapter 2 we illustrated this transformation for the simple circuit model (see Section 2.20.1, page 64). We summarize our definition of state variables:

- The set of *state variables*, $x_s(t)$, is a subset of dynamic and algebraic variables that are "independent" of each other. The remaining *dependent* variables should be *directly computable* from the state variables.

There are two important reasons for partitioning the equation system based on state variables:

- Increased performance, since iterative numerical solution involving a small set of state variables is usually much faster than for a large number of variables.
- Increased numerical stability with the right choice of state variables.

Modelica environments usually have support for automatic selection of state variables. The selection is static if it does not change during simulation. Certain environments also have dynamic automatic selection, that is, the set of variables in $x_s(t)$ can vary dynamically over time. Automatic selection of state variables is usually both efficient and reliable. Users should not in general need to bother about state variable selection.

However, there are certain situations where it is valuable to be able to manually influence the state variable selection, as will be discussed in the next section.

18.2.6.1 Manual State Selection Using the stateSelect Attribute

As we remarked previously, both the efficiency and the numerical stability of a simulation is influenced by the selected set of state variables.

The user has the possibility to manually influence the choice of state variables via the `stateSelect` attribute available for all variables of `Real` type. This attribute has a default value

StateSelect.default. It is an instance of the predefined StateSelect enumeration type with five different enumeration values, which is defined as follows including informative comment strings:

```
type StateSelect = enumeration(
  never    "Do not use as state at all.",
  avoid    "Use as state, if it cannot be avoided (but only if variable appears differentiated and no other
                potential state with attribute default, prefer, or always can be selected).",
  default  "Use as state if appropriate, but only if variable appears differentiated.",
  prefer   "Prefer it as state over those having the default value
                (also variables can be selected, which do not appear differentiated).",
  always   "Do use it as a state."
);
```

For example, a variable x which we would like to influence regarding selection as a state variable can be declared with a modification of the stateSelect attribute. The choice StateSelect.prefer will increase its chances to be selected:

```
Real x(stateSelect = StateSelect.prefer);
```

The different alternatives in the StateSelect enumeration type have the following meaning:

- never—a variable with this stateSelect value will *never* be selected as a state variable.
- avoid—the variable should be avoided as a state variable, i.e., it is selected as a state variable only if it appears differentiated and there is no configuration of state variables without it with default, prefer, or always attribute values.
- default—this is the *default* for all Real variables, and means that a variable *might be* a state variable if its derivative appears in the model. However, the variable does not necessarily become a state variable—this depends on the automatic state selection by the Modelica tool.
- prefer—the variable is *preferably selected* as a state variable over those that have the attribute value default, avoid, or never. Note that the variable does *not* need to appear *differentiated* in the model in order to be used as a state variable.
- always—the variable will *always* be selected as a state variable.

There are several situations where manual state selection might be appropriate to avoid certain problems or to improve performance. Here we mention a few such cases:

- *Numerical cancellation*—if there are both variables with relative quantities and variables with large absolute values, for example, absolute angle and relative angle, it is best to choose the variables with relative quantities as state variables by using StateSelect.prefer. The absolute variables can be computed from the relative ones, whereas the other way around can lead to numerical cancellation from differences between almost equal large numbers.
- *Function inversion*—by using StateSelect.prefer for variables that usually occur as inputs to certain functions, for example, thermodynamic property functions, we can avoid numerical function inversion and thereby increase performance.
- *Expensive dynamic state selection*—for example, in 3D mechanical systems with kinematic loops a static selection of state variables is not possible and dynamic state selection is often necessary to avoid singularities. However, for many common systems there is a known set of state variables that gives efficient computation and avoid singularities. For example, regarding mechanical joints the relative position and velocity variables of the driving mechanism is such a stable selection that can be chosen by using StateSelect.always.
- *Secondary sensor variables*—adding secondary sensor variables just for measurement, for example to compute the velocity which is the derivative of the position, should not influence the selection of the set of state variables. Therefore sensor variables might be marked by the attribute value StateSelect.avoid.

However, in general the best advice is to let state selection be done automatically. Only if there are good reasons in special situations, should we use manual state selection. It is recommended not to use the state selection attribute values `StateSelect.never` and `StateSelect.always` in Modelica library classes, since it is hard to predict in what context a library class will be used.

18.3 Selected Modelica-Related Research and Language Design

The following is a short overview of a selection of Modelica-related research activities and current work on certain language extensions. The overview is by no means complete, and is by necessity and laziness biased toward activities in which the author of this book is involved.

18.3.1 Debugging Equation-Based Models

The development of today's complex products requires integrated environments and equation-based object-oriented declarative languages such as Modelica for modeling and simulation. The increased ease of use, the high level of abstraction, and the expressivity of such languages are very attractive properties. However, these attractive properties come with the drawback that programming and modeling errors are often hard to find.

To address these issues we develop tools for static (compile-time) and dynamic (run-time) debugging methods for Modelica models including a debugger prototype that addresses several of those problems. The goal is an integrated debugging framework that combines classical debugging techniques with special techniques for equation-based languages partly based on graph visualization and interaction. An earlier static debugger addressed the problem of detecting the origin of over-constrained or under-constrained systems of equations.

The static transformational debugging functionality addresses the problem that model compilers are optimized so heavily that it is hard to tell the origin of an equation during runtime. This work implements a method that is efficient with less than one percent overhead, yet manages to keep track of all the transformations/operations that the compiler performs on the model.

Modelica models often contain functions and algorithm sections with algorithmic code. The fraction of algorithmic code is increasing since Modelica, in addition to equation-based modeling, is also used for embedded system control code as well as symbolic model transformations in applications using the MetaModelica language extension.

The new OpenModelica dynamic algorithmic code debugger (Figure 19-5, page 1039) is the first Modelica debugger which can operate without high-level code instrumentation. Instead, it communicates with a low-level C-language symbolic debugger to directly extract information from a running executable, set and remove breakpoints, etc. This is made possible by the new bootstrapped OpenModelica compiler which keeps track of a detailed mapping from the high level Modelica code down to the generated C code compiled to machine code.

The dynamic algorithmic code debugger is operational, supports both standard Modelica data structures and tree/list data structures, and operates efficiently on large applications such as the OpenModelica compiler with more than 100 000 lines of code.

The attractive properties of high-level, object-oriented, equation-based languages come with the drawback that programming and modeling errors are often hard to find. For example, in order to simulate models efficiently, Modelica simulation tools perform a a large number of symbolic manipulation in order to reduce the complexity of models and prepare them for efficient simulation. By removing redundancy, the generation of simulation code and the simulation itself can be sped up significantly. The cost of this performance gain is error-messages that are not very user-friendly due to symbolic manipulation, renaming and reordering of variables and equations. For example, the following error message says nothing about the variables involved or its origin:

```
Error solving nonlinear system 2
time = 0.002
residual[0] = 0.288956,  x[0] = 1.105149
residual[1] = 17.000400, x[1] = 1.248448
```

It is usually hard for a typical user of the Modelica tool to determine which symbolic manipulations have been performed and why. If the tool only emits a binary executable this is almost impossible. Even if the tool emits source code in some programming language (typically C), it is still quite hard to know what kind of equation system you have ended up with. This makes it difficult to understand where the model can be changed in order to improve the speed or stability of the simulation. Some tools allow the user to export the description of the translated system of equations, but this is not enough. After symbolic manipulation, the resulting equations no longer need to contain the same variables or structure as the original equations.

This work develops a combination of static and dynamic debugging techniques to address these problems. The dynamic (run-time) debugging allows interactive inspection of large executable models, stepping through algorithmic parts of the models, setting breakpoints, inspecting and modifying data structures and the execution stack.

The static (compile-time) transformational debugging efficiently traces the symbolic transformations throughout the model compilation process and provides explanations regarding to origin of problematic code. A typical Modelica compiler frontend transforms the source model to flat equations involving a new symbolic manipulations such as simplifications and constant expression evaluation. The compiler backend may perform equation system optimization that changes structure, replace variables, symbolically differentiates equations, and so on. The debugger uses this to trace a run-time error position to the source code (Figure 18-9).

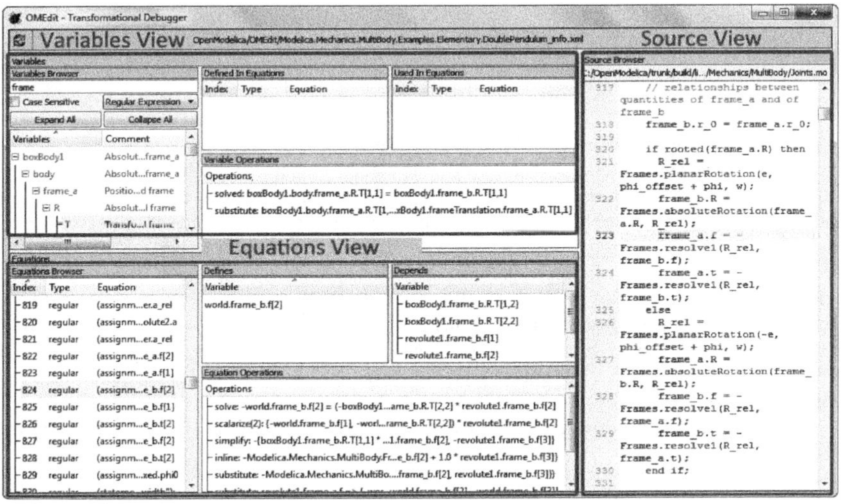

Figure 18-9. The OpenModelica equation model debugger viewed from OMEdit.

We show a small example of how the debugger can trace symbolic operations, based on the following two equations in the original model:

```
0 = y + der(x * time * z);
z = 1.0;
```

The final transformed equation result that is used for the actual executing simulation appears as follows:

```
der(x) = ((-y) - x) / time
```

Even for this small example it is difficult to understand the relation from this equation to the original source equations. Fortunately, the debugger explains the chain of transformations:

(1) substitution:

```
y + der(x * (time * z))
=>
y + der(x * (time * 1.0))
```

(2) simplify:

```
y + der(x * (time * 1.0))
=>
y + der(x * time)
```

(3) expand derivative (symbolic diff):

```
y + der(x * time)
=>
y + (x + der(x) * time)
```

(4) solve:

```
0.0 = y + (x + der(x) * time)
=>
der(x) = ((-y) - x) / time
```

An integrated debugger approach (Figure 18-10) is currently being developed where the origin mapping provided by the static transformational debugging is used by the dynamic debugger to relate run-time errors to the original model sources. During the simulation phase, the user discovers an error in the plotted results, or an irrecoverable error is triggered by the run-time simulation code. In the former case, the user marks either the entire plot of the variable that presents the error or parts of it and starts the debugging framework. The debugger presents an interactive dependency graph with respect to the variable with the wrong value or the expression where the fault occurred. The dependency edges in interactive dependency graph are computed using the transformation tracing previously mentioned. The nodes in the graph consist of all the equations, functions, parameter value definitions, and inputs that were used to calculate the wrong variable value, starting from the known values of states, parameters and time.

In the future, declarative debugging methods that semi-automatically locate bugs may also be included into this debugger.

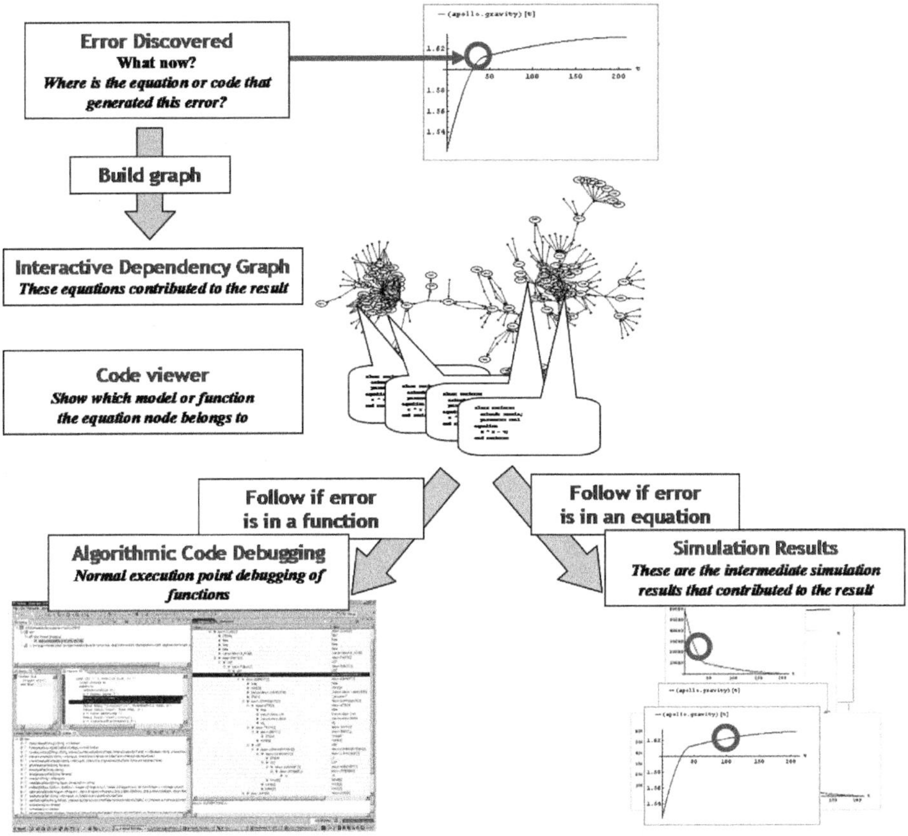

Figure 18-10. Overview of the integrated debugging approach.

18.3.2 Functional Safety

Functional safety is a key concern in almost all industrial sectors, including vehicles, medical equipment, and power plants. The functional correctness of a component is the guarantee that the component behaves the way it should and fulfills all the functional requirements of the system. In order to ensure the functional correctness of a component it is currently necessary to perform a series of rigorous tests on the target device in the appropriate environment context. Skipping this manual phase and allowing for a component to be tested in an early phase, based on a model of its design specification without an actual hardware implementation, would make a significant contribution to reducing the labor, time, and money required to develop the component.

In our approach to Functional Safety verification such aspects are integrated into a model-based development framework (Figure 18-11 left) developed in OpenModelica (Section 19.3.1, page 1035).

Both model components and requirements are modeled by model classes in an integrated model. Requirements are simply a special kind of model that formalize what is required from one component by another in order to perform the task correctly. These components are interconnected through their interfaces. Based on such an integrated model, a dependency graph is generated by analyzing the relations of the functionality provided to the different components of the model according to the specifications by the requirement model components.

Probabilities are then introduced at the leaf nodes. An inference is performed over the Bayesian Network which supports analysis how the whole system is affected by a failure. The acronyms AVA, UNA and NF in the tree nodes represent Available, Unavailable and No Fault respectively. In the scenario in (Figure 18-11 right), the probability of a component's success and failure is analyzed based on fault injection in leaf nodes. Thus in (Figure 18-11 right) a fault has been injected into the Magnetic Valve node which lies at the bottom right of the figure. After inference it is possible to see that the fault is propagated to all the nodes that are dependent on the Magnetic Valve node.

Based on the inference from the Bayesian Network the FMEA table can be generated with the following information: Failed Component, Failure Mode, Potential Effect of Failure and Severity of the Failure. Such a table helps the designers or engineers to adapt their design in order to prevent the possibility of the failure mode.

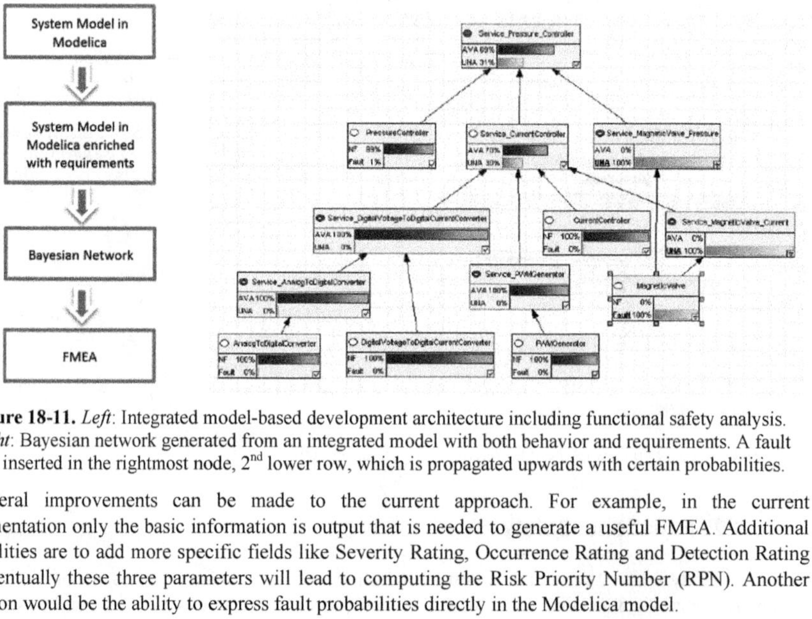

Figure 18-11. *Left*: Integrated model-based development architecture including functional safety analysis. *Right*: Bayesian network generated from an integrated model with both behavior and requirements. A fault was inserted in the rightmost node, 2nd lower row, which is propagated upwards with certain probabilities.

Several improvements can be made to the current approach. For example, in the current implementation only the basic information is output that is needed to generate a useful FMEA. Additional possibilities are to add more specific fields like Severity Rating, Occurrence Rating and Detection Rating and eventually these three parameters will lead to computing the Risk Priority Number (RPN). Another extension would be the ability to express fault probabilities directly in the Modelica model.

18.3.3 Cyber-Physical Hardware-Software Modeling with ModelicaML

One of the most important current paradigm shifts occurring in the design of products may well be the adoption of common system models, as a foundation for product/system design. This allows for a much more effective product development process since a system can be tested in all stages of design. Thus, an integrated holistic environment approach of model-driven development (Figure 18-12) generalizes model-driven approaches to include most aspects of product development. The key concepts are:

- A holistic whole-product cyber-physical model-driven rapid development and design environment for both software and hardware, also including support for product business processes.
- Standardized model representation of products primarily based on open standards such as Modelica and UML.

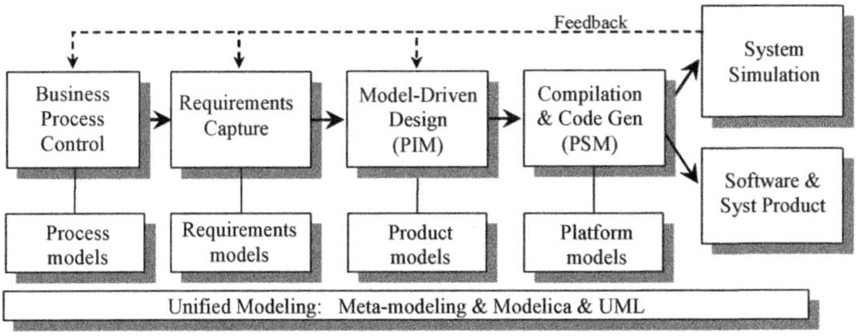

Figure 18-12. Vision of unified modeling framework for cyber-physical model-driven product development from platform independent models (PIM) to platform specific models (PSM).

The OPENPROD project, running 2009-2012, realized a large-scale prototype of such an integrated model-based framework, of which ModelicaML (Section 18.3.3.1, page 1021) and OpenModelica (Section 19.3, page 1033) were important components.

18.3.3.1 Integrated UML-Modelica for Cyber-Physical Whole-Product Modeling

Complex products are increasingly made of both software and hardware components which are closely interacting. Thus, modeling tools and processes need to support co-design of software and hardware in an integrated way. Currently, UML is the dominant graphical modeling notation for software, whereas Modelica is the major object-oriented mathematical modeling language for component-oriented modeling of complex physical systems, e.g., systems containing mechanical, electrical, electronic, hydraulic, thermal, control, electric power or process-oriented subcomponents.

For these reasons we developed the first generation prototype UML-Modelica-SysML integrated modeling environment as a ModelicaML profile integrated in Eclipse as a plug-in. The first generation profile reuses some artifacts from the System Modeling Language (SysML) profile, and combines the major UML diagrams with Modelica graphic connection diagrams. Requirement, equation, and simulation diagrams are also supported in an integrated way.

The second generation ModelicaML profile prototype (Figure 19-7, page 1040) is more comprehensive and more precisely defined. It is based directly on UML and Modelica, implemented using the Papyrus UML tool, generates executable Modelica code, and also supports activity diagrams, state machines, and requirements diagrams. It is possible to model integrated cyber-physical software/hardware models, specify requirements, generate executable Modelica code, and simulate the model while verifying (Section 18.3.4, page 1021) if the requirements are fulfilled or violated.

A related effort called SysML-for-Modelica performed by the OMG SysML-Modelica task force is to define an executable SysML subset with precise semantics by mapping it to Modelica. A version of this mapping has been defined and accepted by OMG as a new standard.

18.3.4 Requirement Verification

What kind of artifacts is required for design verification? The main purpose of design verification is to collect evidence that a given design will satisfy the requirements imposed. Naturally, there will be system designs to be modeled. Furthermore, to determine whether a given system design violates an individual requirement, natural-language requirements will need to be formalized in order to be processable by computers and usable for simulations.

It is crucial to separate the experimental description from the system model. To analyze designs under different conditions, deterministic scenarios will need to be modeled. This is the minimum set of modeling artifacts that is required for design verification. Let us list these modeling artifacts and briefly define their purpose:

- *Requirement Model*: Each requirement is represented by a model that indicates requirement violation at any simulated time instant.
- *System Design Model*: A particular design alternative or version is represented by a model to be used for verification against requirements.
- *Scenario Model:* Scenario defines the course of actions to be simulated. It emulates the user or external events that will be experienced by the system.
- *Verification Model*: Requirements, design alternatives, and scenarios can be combined in different ways. Such combinations are called *verification models*. They are used to perform design verification and to report on requirement violations.

Figure 18-13 shows the basic steps of the vVDR method, the roles involved, and the artifacts created. The nature of this approach is iterative.

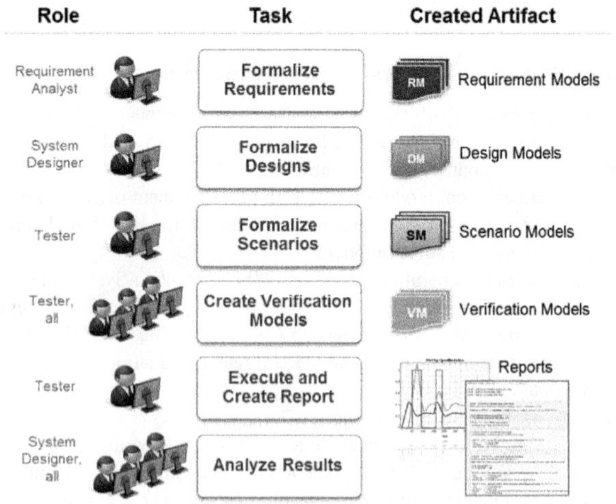

Figure 18-13. Overview of the vVDR method for virtual Verification of Designs against Requirements.

The sequential presentation from Figure 18-13 should merely indicate that typically first the system development process requirements are elicited, then designs are produced, and finally tests are defined. However, in a concurrent engineering environment these activities may overlap and be rerun iteratively.

Figure 18-14 shows the flow of information in the vVDR method for virtual Verification of Designs against Requirements. Requirement models are the output of the *formalize requirements* activity and are the input to the *formalize designs* activity. Design and requirement models are the input to the *formalize scenarios* activity that outputs scenario models. All models are the input to the *create verification models* activity, which outputs verification models to be used for analysis in the *execute and create report* step.

Finally the report generated together with all the generated models become, the input into the *analyze results* activity, not shown in Figure 18-14.

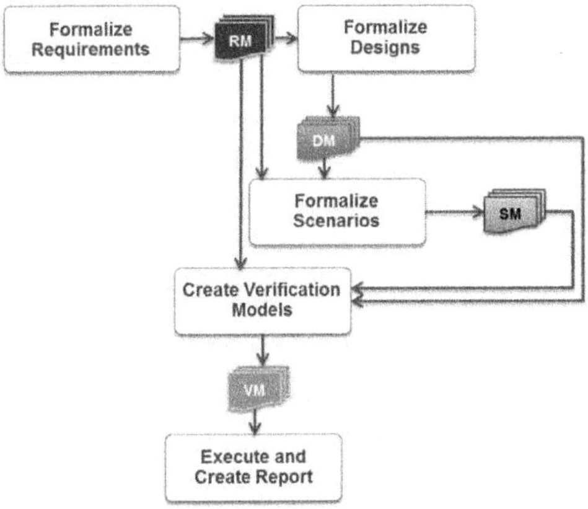

Figure 18-14. Information flow in the vVDR method .

Based on this and related work there is ongoing work, at the time of this writing in the MODRIO project, on integrating such requirement specifications into the Modelica language standard.

18.3.5 Automatic Generation of Parallel Code from Modelica

Using parallel computers is one way of speeding up simulations. However, to actually achieve speed-up the code must be parallelized—divided into tasks which can run mostly in parallel.

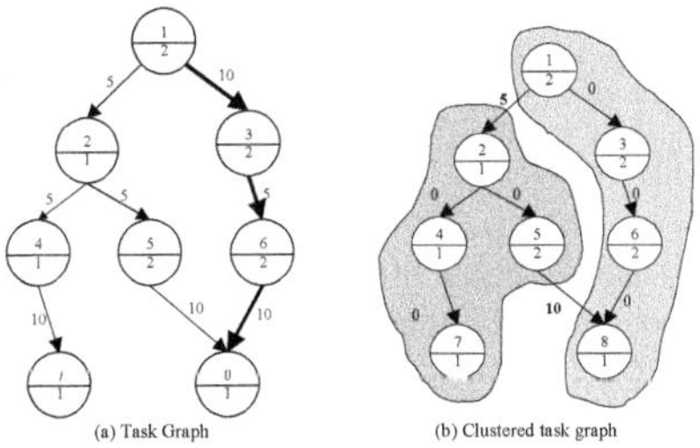

Figure 18-15. (a) Task graph with communication cost on the edges, node number in the upper half of a circular node and node, computation cost in the lower half. (b) Clustered task graph where the tasks have been clustered into two groups with zero internal communication cost and two remaining communication edges between the clusters.

Another important condition for speed-up is that costly communication between the tasks is minimized. The ratio of work to communication must be sufficiently high. If the amount of work in certain tasks is too small they need to be clustered into bigger tasks, provided that the communication to other tasks is not increased. An example of a task graph together with a clustered version of the same task graph is depicted in Figure 18-15.

Which parts of the simulation code contain code that can be parallelized? There are essentially three kinds of functional parallelism in an ODE/DAE equation-based simulation:

- Parallelism over the numerical *method*. A small amount of parallelism can be extracted from certain numerical solvers, e.g. Runge-Kutta solvers.
- Parallelism over *time*. This is mostly applicable to discrete simulations and to a much lesser extent to continuous simulations which develop sequentially over time.
- Parallelism over the *system* of equations, which is the approach taken in Figure 18-15. This means parallelizing the right-hand sides, that is, the code in the function f in an ODE system and the function g in a DAE system (for example, see equation (17-5)).

In Figure 18-15, the automatic parallelizer builds a detailed task graph of all arithmetic operations and function calls in the right-hand sides. The edges represent data-flow dependences. The most difficult problem in this automatic parallelization effort is to find good algorithms for task clustering combined with good task scheduling. Task duplication can also be used to avoid some communication.

Two other approaches to parallelism in Modelica are:

- *Coarse-grained parallelism*, by manually partitioning a model into parts connected by weak coupling, e.g., through TLM connections or similar mechanisms. This allows the computations in the model parts to be de-coupled to some extent, and also run different solvers at different rates. For example, each model partition can be allocated to a processor and run in parallel for some time before needing to synchronize with the rest of the model.
- *Data parallelism*, which concerns performing the same operations on many data elements, which typically occur in large arrays. A Modelica language extension called ParModelica for data-parallel algorithmic programming with Modelica has been designed and implemented in OpenModelica, compiling to multi-core GPUs or CPUs.

For example, data parallelism can be exploited using ParModelica with parallel loops, parallel functions, and allocation of variables at the best place in the memory hierarchy. Two small examples of ParModelica programs are shown below. The first is a parallel matrix multiplication using a parallel `parfor` loop :

```
parfor i in 1:m loop
  for j in 1:pm loop
    ptemp := 0;
    for h in 1:pm loop
      ptemp := multiply(pA[i,h], pB[h,j])+ptemp; // multiply may be parallel
    end for;
    pC[i,j] := ptemp;
  end for;
end parfor;
```

This example shows the ability to declare variables at different places of the OpenCL memory hierarchy: in the host memory, in the global memory, or in the local memory.

```
function parvar
protected
  Integer m = 1000;          // Host Scalar
  Integer A[m,m];            // Host Matrix
  Integer B[m,m];            // Host Matrix
  // global and local device memories
  parglobal Integer pm;      // Global Scalar
  parglobal Integer pA[m,m];// Global Matrix
  parglobal Integer pB[m,m];// Global Matrix
  parlocal  Integer pn;      // Local Scalar
  parlocal  Integer pS[m];   // Local Array
end parvar;
```

The left-hand side of Figure 18-16 shows an NVIDIA GPU architecture suitable for data-parallel programming. The right part of the same figure shows the speedup of matrix multiplication programmed in ParModelica and executed on both a multi-core CPU and a GPU for different problem sizes.

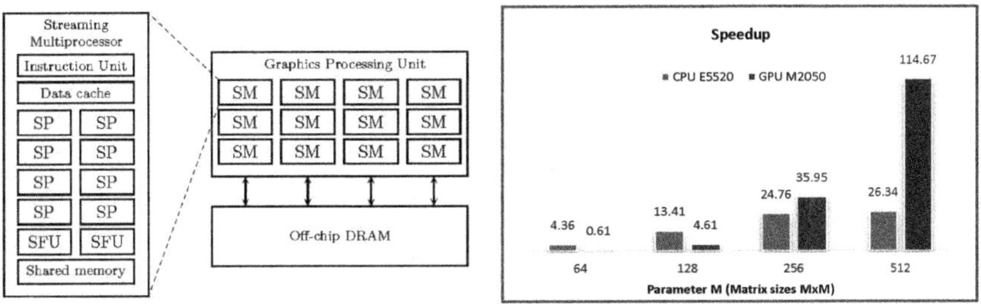

Figure 18-16. *Left*: Simplified schematic of NVIDIA GPU architecture, consisting of a set of Streaming Multiprocessors (SM), each containing a number of Scalar Processors (SP) with fast private memory and on-ship local shared memory. The GPU also has off-chip DRAM. *Right*: Speedup for matrix multiplication written in ParModelica, Intel 16-core CPU and Nvidia 448 core GPU.

18.3.6 Meta-Modeling and Meta-Programming

Meta-programming is programming for the sake of constructing and modifying programs. Meta-modeling is to use a modeling language to model another language, for example, its semantics (Section 19.3.5, page 1045). Several research activities and results related to this topic are part of the MetaModelica language design, implementation, and use (Section 6.15, page 296). A closely related effort in the same area is the MKL language (Modeling Kernel Language). The idea is to define a small kernel language and be able to express most other modeling language constructs in a library using kernel language primitives.

18.3.7 Summary

As indicated in the introduction, this chapter covers three topics: numeric and symbolic techniques for simulation, i.e. solution of equation systems, for example, resulting from Modelica models, some Modelica language extension design activities, and a selection of ongoing Modelica-related research.

We started the presentation by an introductory discussion of numeric and symbolic solution techniques. Then followed an overview of basic numeric ODE solution techniques, followed by DAE solution techniques building on the ODE techniques. We discussed the index of DAE systems, where high index can lead numerical problems. Symbolic techniques for index computation and index reduction were also presented based on bipartite graph representations of equation systems. Then we presented an algorithm skeleton for solving hybrid DAE systems including automatic detection and handling of events together with solution of the continuous part of the DAE system between events. We also discussed automatic and manual selection of state variables when solving DAEs.

Finally, research activities were presented in debugging, functional safety, cyber-physical hardware-software modeling, requirement verification, automatic generation of parallel code, meta-modeling and meta-programming.

18.4 Literature

Here we have grouped the literature references for this chapter according to topic. First we present the references for numerical methods, graphic algorithms, and symbolic manipulation and analysis of equation systems:

- Numerical methods and solution methods—a short introduction to the solution of ODEs is given in (Ljung and Glad 1994), whereas a more in depth presentation is given in (Brenan, Campbell, and Petzold 1989; Hairer, Nørsett, and Wanner 1991). Stiff solvers and models are covered in (Aiken 1985), and methods for stiff and DAE problems in (Hairer and Wanner 1991). Using explicit and implicit Euler methods for Modelica, as well as the mixed mode integration technique, are discussed in (Schiela and Olsson 2000). Sparse Matrix methods are covered by (Duff, Erisman, and Reid 1986). A set of common ODE solvers—ODEPACK—is presented in (Hindmarsh 1983). The DAE solver DASSL is described in (Petzold 1982). The DSBLOCK format for interfacing to several solvers is first presented in (Otter 1992). A very comprehensive overview of numeric and symbolic methods for simulation is available in (Cellier and Kofman 2006).
- Graph algorithms and theory is presented in (Dolan and Aldous 1993; Gibbons 1985; Gilli and Garbely 1996; Murota, 1987; Murota, 2000; Nuutila and Soisalon-Soininen 1993). Tarjans algorithm for finding strongly connected components in graphs is described in (Tarjan 1972). Bipartite graph coverings and matchings are described in (Dulmage and Mendelsohn 1963; Hopcroft and Karp 1973; Uno 1997; Uno 2001).
- Symbolic manipulation, analysis of equations, and symbolic/numeric solution methods is presented in (Leitold and Katalin 2001; Maffezzoni, Girelli, Lluka 1996; Mah 1990; Ramirez 1998; Ramos, Ángel, and Ignasi 1998; Unger, Kröner, and Marquardt 1995). The notion of DAE index is presented in (Günter and Feldmann 1995; Reissig, Martinson, and Barton 2000). Work on index for partial differential equations has recently appeared (Martinson and Barton 2000), (Elmqvist 2003b). Tearing is discussed in (Mah 1990; Elmqvist and Otter 1994). Dynamic state selection is described in (Mattsson, Olsson, and Elmqvist 2000). A very comprehensive overview of numeric and symbolic methods for simulation is available in (Cellier and Kofman 2006).

Some of the ongoing work on extending the Modelica language and related technology is presented in the following articles:

- Meta-programming, i.e., programming for the sake of constructing and modifying programs, is a common use of Lisp systems (Sandewall 1978; Steele 1990), and Mathematica (Wolfram 1997). Meta programming in general is discussed in (Sheard 2001). Ongoing work regarding meta programming of Modelica models is described in (Aronsson, Fritzson, Saldamli, Bunus, and Nyström 2003). The MetaModelica language extension is presented in more detail in (Fritzson, Pop, and Aronsson 2005; Pop and Fritzson 2006; Fritzson and Pop 2011; Fritzson, Pop, and Sjölund 2011). The compilation of the whole OpenModelica compiler using itself (i.e., bootstrapping) is described in (Sjölund, Fritzson, and Pop 2011; Sjölund, Fritzson, and Pop 2014).

Literature references and further reading on the research topics mentioned in this chapter are listed below:

- Declarative debugging for Modelica is first described in (Bunus and Fritzson 2003b) whereas such debugging for other languages is presented in (Shapiro 1982; Fritzson 1993) (Fritzson, Shahmehri, Kamkar, and Gyimothy 1992; Kamkar 1993; Nilsson and Fritzson 1994; Shahmehri, Kamkar and Fritzson 1995; Nilsson 1998). Static debugging of over-constrained and under-constrained equation systems in Modelica: (Bunus and Fritzson 2002a; Bunus and Fritzson 2002b; Bunus 2002; Bunus and Fritzson 2002c; Bunus and Fritzson 2003a; Bunus 2004).
- Integrated debugging, algorithmic Modelica debugging, and transformational debugging are described in ( ).
- Hardware-Software cyber-physical modeling, for example, with ModelicaML— There are two generations of the ModelicaML UML-Modelica profile and Eclipse plug-in. The first generation which partially integrates SysML and Modelica is described in (Pop, Akhvlediani, and Fritzson 2007a; Pop, Akhvlediani, and Fritzson 2007b; Pop, Băluță, and Fritzson 2007; Pop 2008; Süss, Fritzson, and Pop 2008). The second generation includes integrated UML-Modelica software-hardware modeling, simulation, requirement modeling and verification (Schamai 2009; Schamai, Fritzson, Paredis, and Pop 2009; Schamai, Helle, Fritzson, and Paredis 2010; Myers, Schamai,

and Fritzson 2011; Schamai, Fritzson, Paredis, and Helle 2012; Liang, Schamai, Rogovchenko, Sadeghi, Nyberg, Fritzson 2012; Tundis, Rogovchenko-Buffoni, Fritzson, and Garro 2013; Tundis, Rogovchenko-Buffoni, Fritzson, Garro, and Nyberg 2013; Schamai 2013). Compiling UML State machines to Modelica: (Schamai, Pohlmann, Fritzson, Paredis, Helle, Strobel 2010; Schamai, Fritzson, and Paredis 2013; Schamai 2013). Information about Papyrus is found at (Eclipse-Papyrus 2013). Hardware-software co-modeling with Modelica and Behavior trees: (Myers, Fritzson, and Dromey 2008; Myers, Fritzson, and Dromey 2011; Myers, Schamai, and Fritzson 2011), and the Behavior tree approach in (Dromey 2003). The OMG SysML-for-Modelica is described in (Paredis, Bernard, Burkhart, de Koning, Friedenthal, Fritzson, Rouquette, and Schamai 2010; OMG SyM 2012). Model-based product development and the OPENPROD project (Fritzson 2010; ITEA2-OPENPROD 2012; ITEA2-OPENPROD 2013; ITEA2-MODRIO 2013).

- Semantics specification and generation of compilers for modeling languages and Modelica—See (Kahn 1987; Pettersson 1999; Fritzson 1998; Kågedal and Fritzson 1998; Fritzson, Pop, and Aronsson 2005; Pop and Fritzson 2006; Pop and Fritzson 2007; Broman and Fritzson 2007; Fritzson, Pop, Broman, and Aronsson 2009; Broman and Fritzson 2008; Broman and Fritzson 2009; Broman 2010; Fritzson and Pop 2011; Fritzson, Pop, and Sjölund 2011; Broman, Fritzson, Hedin, Åkesson 2012; Fritzson and Pop 2014).
- Parallel simulation—Automatic parallelization of systems of equations and expression trees in equation-based Modelica models is described in (Aronsson and Fritzson 2002; Aronsson 2002; Aronsson and Fritzson 2003; Aronsson and Fritzson 2004; Aronsson and Fritzson 2005; Aronsson 2006; Lundvall and Fritzson 2007a; Lundvall and Fritzson 2007b; Lundvall and Fritzson 2007c; Lundvall, Stavåker, Fritzson, and Kessler 2008a; Lundvall, Stavåker, Fritzson, and Kessler 2008b; Lundvall and Fritzson 2009; Maggio, Stavåker, Donida, Casella, Fritzson 2009; Casella 2013).
- Parallel simulation—data-parallel methods (Stavåker, Rolls, Guo, Fritzson, and Scholz 2010; Östlund, Stavåker, and Fritzson 2010; Stavåker and Fritzson 2010; Moghadam, Gebremedhin, Stavåker, and Fritzson 2011; Gebremedhin, Moghadam, Fritzson, and Stavåker 2012).
- Parallel simulation—manual parallelization, for example, the ParModelica language extension (Gebremedhin, Moghadam, Fritzson, Stavåker 2012), and the NestStepModelica language extension (Kessler and Fritzson 2006). The BEAST simulator is described in (Fritzson, Fritzson, Nordling, and Persson 1997; Nordling 1996; Nordling 2003). Explicit coarse-grained parallelization of partitioned Modelica models, for example, using TLM connectors, is described in (Nyström and Fritzson 2006; Sjölund, Braun, Fritzson, and Krus 2010; Kessler, Schamai, Fritzson 2010; Sjölund, Gebremedhin, and Fritzson 2013).
- Functional safety; uncertainty in models – Functional safety and FMEA computations from models: (Hossain, Nyberg, Rogovchenko and Fritzson 2012; Hossain, Rogovchenko, Nyberg, and Fritzson 2012; Rogovchenko-Buffoni, Tundis, Hossain, Nyberg, and Fritzson 2013, Tundis, Rogovchenko-Buffoni, Garro, Nyberg, and Fritzson 2013). Uncertainties in Modelica models: (Bouskela, Jardin, Benjelloun-Touimi, Aronsson, and Fritzson 2011)
- Verification—model checking, that is, static compile-time model verification: (Clarke, Grumberg, and Peled 2000), and verification in hardware design (Kern and Greenstreet 1999). For dynamic verification against scenarios, see ModelicaML.
- System identification in general including grey box identification—(Ljung 1999), and identification for linear DAEs (Gerdin, Glad, Ljung 2003).
- Diagnosis—a Modelica-like language extended with uncertainty interval computations is described in (Lunde 2000). Some approaches to model-based diagnosis in automotive applications are given in (Nyberg and Nielsen 1997; Frisk and Nyberg 2001; Nyberg 2002).

Chapter 19

Environments

Several programming environments are currently available for the design and simulation of Modelica models. Certain environments also have facilities for post-processing results of simulations, 3D visualization of mechanical systems simulation, CAD integration, special support for real-time and hardware-in-the-loop simulation, and support for integrated modeling, simulation, post processing, and documentation. The first full Modelica environment to appear was Dymola, soon followed by MathModelica, renamed in 2012 to Wolfram SystemModeler.

The OpenModelica environment was the first open source Modelica environment. Its development started in 1997 resulting in the release of a flattening front end for a core subset of Modelica 1.0 in 1998. After a pause of four years, the open source development resumed in 2002. The Open Source Modelica Consortium, which supports the long-term development of OpenModelica, was created in 2007, initially with seven founding organizations. The scope and intensity of the open source development has gradually increased. A the time of this writing, the consortium has forty-five supporting organizational members.

19.1 General Background

Traditionally, simulation and accompanying activities have been expressed using heterogeneous media and tools, with a mixture of manual and computer-supported activities:

- A simulation model is traditionally designed on paper using traditional mathematical notation.
- Simulation programs are written in a low-level programming language and stored on text files.
- Input and output data, if stored at all, are saved in proprietary formats needed for particular applications and numerical libraries.
- Documentation is written on paper or in separate files that are not integrated with the program files.
- The graphical results are printed on paper or saved using proprietary formats.

When the result of the research and experiments, such as a scientific paper or engineering design report, is written, the user normally gathers together input data, algorithms, output data and its visualizations as well as notes and descriptions. One of the major problems in simulation development environments is that gathering and maintaining correct versions of all these components from various files and formats is difficult and error-prone.

A general vision of a solution to this set of problems is to provide an integrated computer-supported modeling and simulation environment that enables the user to work effectively and flexibly with simulations. Users will then be able to prepare and run simulations as well as investigate simulation results. Several auxiliary activities accompany simulation experiments: requirements are specified, models are designed, documentation is associated with appropriate places in the models, input and output data as well as possible constraints on such data are documented and stored together with the simulation model. The user should be able to reproduce experimental results. Therefore, input data and parts of output data as well as the experimenter's notes should be stored for future analysis.

19.1.1 Integrated Interactive Programming Environments

An integrated interactive modeling and simulation environment is a special case of programming environments with applications in modeling and simulation. Thus, it should fulfill the requirements both from general integrated interactive environments and from the application area of modeling and simulation mentioned in the previous section.

The main idea of an integrated programming environment in general is that a number of programming support functions should be available within the same tool in a well-integrated way. This means that the functions should operate on the same data and program representations, exchange information when necessary, resulting in an environment that is both powerful and easy to use. An environment is interactive and incremental if it gives quick feedback, for example, without recomputing everything from scratch, and maintains a dialogue with the user, including preserving the state of previous interactions with the user. Interactive environments are typically both more productive and more fun to use than non-interactive ones.

There are many things that one wants a programming environment to do for the programmer or modeler, particularly if it is interactive. What functionality should be included? Comprehensive software development environments are expected to provide support for the major development phases, such as:

- Requirements analysis
- Design
- Implementation
- Maintenance

A pure programming environment can be somewhat more restrictive and need not necessarily support early phases such as requirements analysis, but it is an advantage if such facilities are also included. The main point is to provide as much computer support as possible for different aspects of systems development, to free the developer from mundane tasks so that more time and effort can be spent on the essential issues. The following is a partial list of integrated programming environment facilities, some of which are already mentioned in (Sandewall 1978), that should be provided for the programmer or modeler:

- Administration and configuration management of program modules and classes, and different versions of these.
- Administration and maintenance of test examples and their correct results.
- Administration and maintenance of formal or informal documentation of program parts, and automatic generation of documentation from programs.
- Support for a given programming methodology, for example, top-down or bottom-up. For example, if a top-down approach should be encouraged, it is natural for the interactive environment to maintain successive composition steps and mutual references between those.
- Support for the interactive session. For example, previous interactions should be saved in an appropriate way so that the user can refer to previous commands or results, go back and edit those, and possibly re-execute.
- Enhanced editing support, performed by an editor that knows about the syntactic structure of the language. It is an advantage if the system allows editing of the program in different views. For example, editing of the overall system structure can be done in the graphical view, whereas editing of detailed properties can be done in the textual view.
- Cross-referencing and query facilities, to help the user understand interdependences between parts of large systems.

- Flexibility and extensibility, for example, mechanisms to extend the syntax and semantics of the programming language representation and the functionality built into the environment.
- Accessible internal representation of programs. This is often a prerequisite to the extensibility requirement. An accessible internal representation means that there is a well-defined representation of programs that are represented in data structures of the programming language itself, so that user-written programs may inspect the structure and generate new programs. This property is also known as the principle of program-data equivalence.

19.1.2 Integrated Computational Documents

There is currently a strong trend in integrating documents and computation. This is most visible in web technology where computational facilities are increasingly being embedded within web pages. However, facilities for user programming and mathematical modeling are still largely absent in web pages.

19.1.2.1 Interactive Notebooks with Literate Programming

Mathematica pioneered the idea and implementation of active interactive electronic notebooks. The Mathematica notebook facility is an interactive WYSIWYG (What-You-See-Is-What-You-Get) realization of Literate Programming, a form of programming where programs are integrated with documentation in the same document. The original implementation of Literate Programming was a noninteractive system integrated with the document processing system LaTex.

Mathematica has one of few interactive WYSIWYG systems so far realized for Literate Programming, which also might be called Literate Modeling. Such documents that may contain technical computations and text, as well as graphics. Hence, these documents are suitable to be used for simulation scripting, model documentation and storage, model analysis and control system design, etc.

Later, several other computer algebra software product makers have included variants of electronic notebooks in their products. More recently an open source simple notebook facility for literate Modelica modeling called OMNotebook has been developed for the OpenModelica environment. This includes the DrModelica notebook document within which most Modelica examples in this book can be run interactively.

19.1.2.2 Tree Structured Hierarchical Document Representation

Traditional documents, for example, books and reports, essentially always have a hierarchical structure. They are divided into sections, subsections, paragraphs, and so on. Both the document itself and its sections usually have headings as labels for easier navigation. This kind of structure is also reflected in electronic notebooks. Every notebook corresponds to one document (one file) and contains a tree structure of cells. A cell can have different kinds of contents, and can even contain other cells. The notebook hierarchy of cells thus reflects the hierarchy of sections and subsections in a traditional document.

One idea is to store Modelica packages including documentation and test cases as notebooks, for example, as in Figure 19-1. This is useful primarily as interactive teaching material, which was pioneered by Mathematica notebooks in teaching mathematics but also for subjects like physics. The possibility of embedding cells with Modelica models in notebooks was part of the earlier MathModelica environment, and is still supported by the OpenModelica notebook facility. The current Wolfram SystemModeler tool supports cells with Mathematica programs, model analysis and simulation commands, but not Modelica models which instead are kept in separate files.

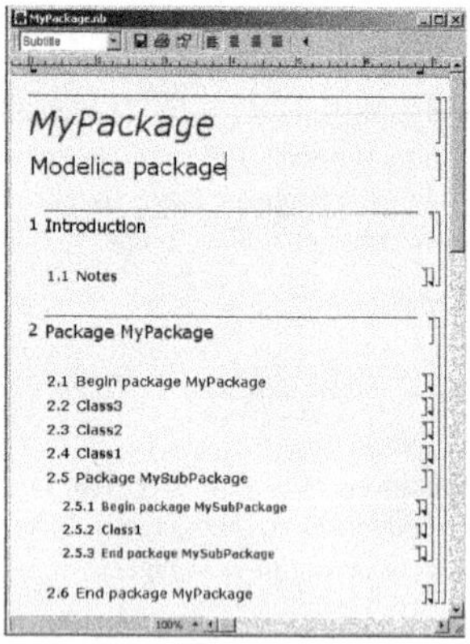

(a)

```
package MyPackage
  model class3
  ...
  end class3;
  model class2 ...
  model class1 ...
  package MySubPackage
    model class1
    ...
    end class1;
  end MySubPackage;
end MyPackage;
```

(b)

Figure 19-1. The package `MyPackage` in a Mathematica notebook (a) and as Modelica text (b).

19.1.2.3 Program Cells, Documentation Cells, and Graphic Cells

A Mathematica notebook cell can include other cells and/or arbitrary text or graphics. In particular a cell can include a code fragment or a graph with computational results.The contents of cells can for example include one of the following forms, a subset of what is actually provided:

- Executable Mathematica programs and fragments which can be used for analysis, compilation and execution of simulation models.
- Mathematical formulas in the traditional mathematical twodimensional syntax.
- Text/documentation, for example, used as comments to executable formal model specifications.
- Dialogue forms for specification and modification of input data.
- Result tables. The results can be automatically represented in (live) tables, which can even be automatically updated after recomputation.
- Graphical result representation, for example, with 2D vector and raster graphics as well as 3D vector and surface graphics.
- 2D structure graphs, that for example are used for various model structure visualizations such as connection diagrams and data structure diagrams.

The less powerful OMNotebook notebook facility in OpenModelica supports a few of these representations, for example, cells with executable Modelica model classes, commands, documentation, pictures, and 2D graphs.

19.1.3 Vision of Integrated Interactive Environment for Modeling and Simulation

Our vision for an integrated interactive modeling and simulation environment is to fulfill essentially all the requirements for general integrated interactive environments combined with the specific needs for modeling and simulation environments, for example:

- Specification of requirements, expressed as documentation and/or mathematics
- Design of the mathematical model

- Symbolic transformations of the mathematical model
- A uniform general language for model design, mathematics, and transformations
- Automatic generation of efficient simulation code
- Execution of simulations
- Evaluation and documentation of numerical experiments
- Graphical presentation

Our vision for, and design of, the earlier MathModelica environment and later the OpenModelica environment was to a large extent inspired by earlier experience in research and development of integrated incremental programming environments, for example, the DICE system and the ObjectMath environment, together with many years of intensive use of advanced integrated interactive environments such as the InterLisp system and Mathematica. The InterLisp system was actually one of the first really powerful integrated environments, and still beats many current programming environments in terms of powerful facilities available to the programmer. It was also the first environment that used graphical window systems in an effective way, even before the Smalltalk environment and the Macintosh window system appeared.

Mathematica is a more recently developed integrated interactive programming environment with many similarities to InterLisp, containing comprehensive programming and documentation facilities, accessible intermediate representation with program-data equivalence, graphics, and support for mathematics and computer algebra. Mathematica is more developed than InterLisp in several areas, for example, syntax, documentation, and pattern-matching, but at the time of this writing was slightly less developed than several Eclipse-based environments in programming support facilities such as object oriented programming and modeling. The advanced facilities provided by Mathematica was the reason to make it an important part of the MathModelica environment. More recently the MathModelica environment was further developed into the current Wolfram SystemModeler.

19.2 Common Characteristics

Most Modelica environments have a number of common characteristics. Models need to be entered and edited, translated to a form that can be executed/simulated, and equation systems to be solved. Therefore, essentially all Modelica environments contain variants of the following modules:

- *A Modelica compiler or interpreter*, translating Modelica to some interpreted form such as byte code or abstract syntax trees, or to a compiled language such as C, C++, etc., which is further translated into executable machine code by standard compilers.
- *An execution and run-time module*. This module executes executable code from translated Modelica expressions, functions, and equations. The module include numerical solvers for solution of the resulting equation system as well as event handling facilities for the discrete and hybrid parts of the Modelica language.
- *An editor for textual model editing*. This can be any standard text editor, or a special-purpose built-in text editor.
- *A graphical model editor*. This is a graphical connection editor for component based model design by connecting instances of Modelica classes.

19.3 OpenModelica

The computational and simulation goals of the OpenModelica tool development include, but are not limited to, the following:

- Providing a complete open source Modelica-based industrial-strength implementation of the Modelica language, including modeling and simulation of equation-based models, system optimization, and additional facilities in the programming/modeling environment.
- Providing an interactive computational environment for the Modelica language. It turns out that with support of appropriate tools and libraries, Modelica is very well suited as a computational language for development and execution of both low level and high level numerical algorithms, e.g. for control system design and for solving nonlinear equation systems.

The research related goals and issues of the OpenModelica open source implementation of a Modelica environment include, but are not limited to, the following:

- Development of a *complete formal specification* and *reference implementation* of Modelica, including both static and dynamic semantics. Such a specification can be used to assist current and future Modelica implementers by providing a semantic reference, as a kind of reference implementation.
- *Language design*, for example, to further *extend the scope* of the language, e.g. for use in diagnosis, structural analysis, system identification, integrated product development with requirement verification, etc., as well as modeling problems that require partial differential equations.
- *Language design* to *improve abstract properties* such as expressiveness, orthogonality, declarativity, reuse, configurability, architectural properties, and so on.
- *Improved implementation techniques*, for example, to enhance the performance of compiled Modelica code by generating code for parallel hardware.
- *Improved debugging* support for equation based languages such as Modelica, to make them even easier to use.
- *Improved optimization support*, with integrated optimization and modeling/simulation. Two kinds: parameter-sweep optimization based on multiple simulations; direct *dynamic optimization* of a goal function without lots of simulations, for example, using collocation or multiple shooting.
- *Easy-to-use* specialized high-level (graphical) *user interfaces* for certain application domains.
- *Visualization* and animation techniques for interpretation and presentation of results.
- *Integrated requirement modeling and verification support.* This includes the ability to enter requirements formalized in a kind of Modelica style, and to verify that the requirements are fulfilled for selected models under certain usage scenarios.

The OpenModelica effort started by developing an rather complete formal specification of the Modelica language. This specification was developed in *Operational Semantics*, which still is the most popular and widely used semantics specification formalism in the programming language community. It was initially used as input for automatic generation of the Modelica translator implementations which are part of the OpenModelica environment. The RML compiler generation tool (our implementation of Operational Semantics) was used for this task.

However, inspired by our vision of integrated interactive environments (Section 19.1.1, page 1030) with self-specification of programs and data, and integrated modeling and simulation environments (Section 19.1.3, page 1032), in 2005 we designed and implemented an extension to Modelica called MetaModelica (Section 6.15, page 296 and Section 19.3.4, page 1044) in order to support language modeling and specification (including modeling itself) in addition to the usual physical systems modeling applications of Modelica.

This language extension has a Modelica-style syntax but was initially implemented on top of the RML compiler kernel. The declarative specification language primitives in RML with single-assignment pattern equations, possibly recursive case records (in MetaModelica called uniontypes) and match expressions, fit well into Modelica since it is a declarative equation-based language. In 2006 our whole formal specification of Modelica static and translational semantics, at that time about 50,000 lines, was automatically translated into MetaModelica. After that, all further development of the symbolic processing parts of the OpenModelica compiler (the run-time parts were mainly written in C), was done in MetaModelica.

At the same time we embarked on an effort to completely integrate the MetaModelica language extension into the Modelica language and the OpenModelica compiler. This would enable us to support both Modelica and MetaModelica by the same compiler, to allow modeling the Modelica tool and the OpenModelica compiler using its own language, to get rid of the limitations of the RML compiler kernel and the need to support two compilers, and to base additional tools such as our Modelica debugger on a single compiler.

Such an ability of a compiler to compile itself is called compiler *bootstrapping*. This development turned out to be more difficult and time-consuming than initially expected; moreover, developers were not available for a few years due resource limitations and other priorities. Finally, bootstrapping of the whole OpenModelica compiler was achieved in 2011. Two years later, in 2013, all our OpenModelica compiler development was shifted to the new bootstrapped compiler, after automatic memory reclamation (garbage collection), separate compilation, and a new efficient debugger had been achieved for our new compiler platform.

19.3.1 The OpenModelica Environment

At the time of this writing, the interactive OpenModelica environment consists of the following components:

- *A graphical and textual model editor*, `OMEdit`. This is a graphical connection editor for component based model design by connecting instances of Modelica classes. The editor also provides text editing. Moreover, the OMEdit GUI provides a graphical user interface to simulation and plotting (`OMPlot`).
- *An interactive session handler*, `OMShell`, that parses and interprets commands (Section E.1, page 1119) and Modelica expressions for evaluation. The session handler also contains simple history facilities, and completion of file names and certain identifiers in commands. There is also a Python variant of the interactive session handler that supports the same commands in Python (Section E.2, page 1133).
- *A Modelica compiler*, `OMC`, translating Modelica to lower level code such as C code, with a symbol table containing definitions of models, functions, and variables. Such definitions can be predefined, user-defined, or obtained from libraries.
- *An execution and run-time module*. This module currently executes compiled binary code from translated models and functions. It includes numerical solvers as well as event handling facilities for the discrete and hybrid parts of the Modelica language.
- *Textual model editors*. Any text editor can be used. Among the OpenModelica tools, text editing of models is supported by `OMEdit`, by the OpenModelica MDT Eclipse plug-in, and by the interactive electronic book `OMNotebook`.
- *An interactive electronic book*, `OMNotebook`. This tool provides an active electronic book facility supporting chapters, sections, execution of simulation models, plotting, etc. One book, DrModelica, for teaching Modelica to the beginner, is automatically opened by default. The user can define his/her own books. This tool is useful for developing interactive course material.
- *An optimization module using parameter sweeps*, called `OMOptim`. This tool performs optimizations by running several simulations for different parameter settings while searching for the optimum value of a user-specified goal function.

- *A dynamic optimization module.* Direct optimization (without running lots of simulations) of a whole solution trajectory using collocation or multiple shooting. A goal function can be formulated to be optimized under the constraints of a selected model.
- *ModelicaML Eclipse plug-in.* This plug-in contains a Modelica-UML profile that allows integrated requirement verification and cyber-physical hardware-software modeling by combining hardware modeling in Modelica with software modeling using UML The tool contains a UML to Modelica translator that makes it possible to simulate combined UML-Modelica models. Moreover, automatic (dynamic) verification of formalized requirements against selected scenarios is supported. See also Section 19.3.1.5, page 1039, and Section 18.3.3, page 1020.
- *MDT Eclipse plug-in.* The MDT (Modelica Development Tooling) Eclipse plug-in for Modelica library and model compiler textual development, project support, cross referencing, building executables, debugging, etc.
- *3D animation visualization.* This is provided by a library, Modelica3D, which is distributed together with OpenModelica.
- *FMI Import and Export.* A model (including models from other tools, even non-Modelica ones) can be imported or exported according to the FMI (Functional Mockup Interface) standard.
- *MetaModelica language extension.* This is used for modeling/specification of languages (including the Modelica language) and for Modelica programming of model transformations. Related to this, there are ongoing discussions in the Modelica Design group about possible extensions to the Modelica language which would enable definition some language constructs in a Modelica core library instead of being hardcoded in the compiler.
- *ParModelica language extension.* This is used for explicit algorithmic parallel Modelica programming with compilation to both multi-core CPU platforms and GPGPU platforms (including NVIDIA).

An interactive session with examples of using OpenModelica can be found in Section E.1.3, page 1129.

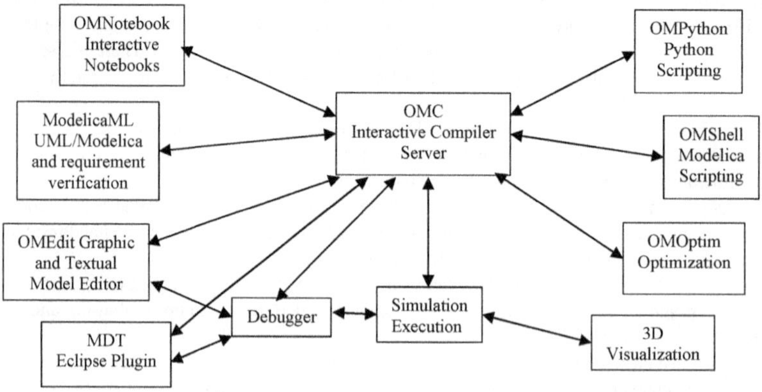

Figure 19-2. The architecture of the OpenModelica environment. Arrows denote data and control flow.

19.3.1.1 OMC – the OpenModelica Model Compiler

OMC is the OpenModelica compiler that translates Modelica models into C code (or Java or C# code using experimental code generators), which is compiled and executed to perform simulations. See Sections 19.3.2, 19.3.3, 19.3.4, and 19.3.5 for various aspects regarding the compilation process and generating the OpenModelica compiler from formal specifications in RML (earlier) or MetaModelica (currently). See also Section 6.15296, page 296, for an overview of the MetaModelica language. At the time of this writing, the OpenModelica compiler (OMC) is generated from a specification of about twohundred thousand lines of MetaModelica. Moreover, OMC is able to compile itself, that is, it is bootstrapped.

19.3.1.2 OMEdit – the OpenModelica Graphical Model Editor and Simulator

OMedit is the OpenModelica graphic model editor (Figure 19-3). In addition to graphic model editing and browsing, it also provides model text editing, simulation, and plotting capabilities.

It is possible to re-run a simulation without re-compilation, e.g., after changing parameter settings for non-structural parameters (Section 17.1.5, page 983). This can be done by popping up a re-simulation menu by right-clicking on the simulation result in the plot variable browser as shown in (Figure 19-3).

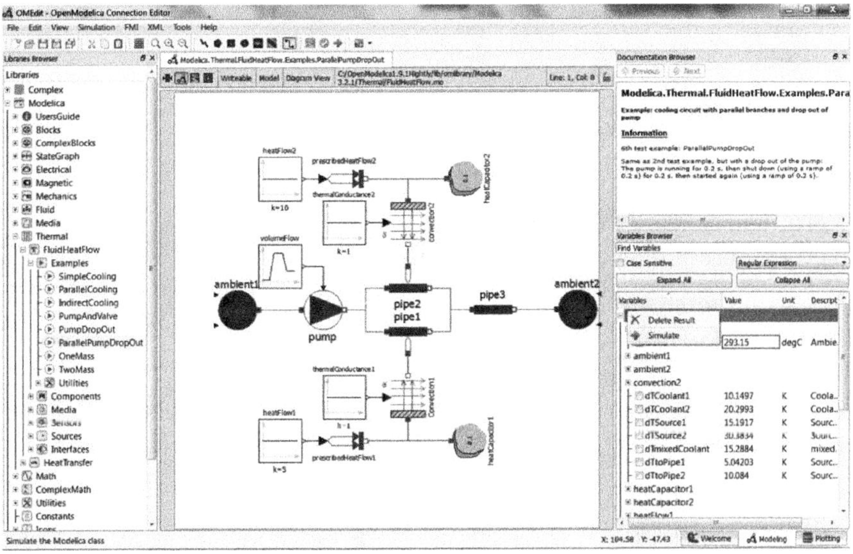

Figure 19-3. OMEdit on the `Modelica.Thermal.FluidHeatFlow.Examples.ParallelPumpDropOut` model. *Center*: Model connection diagram. *Upper right*: information window. *Lower right*: plot variable browser will a small popup re-simulate menu on top.

Using OMEdit to perform simulations and plot simulation results is depicted in Figure 19-4 below.

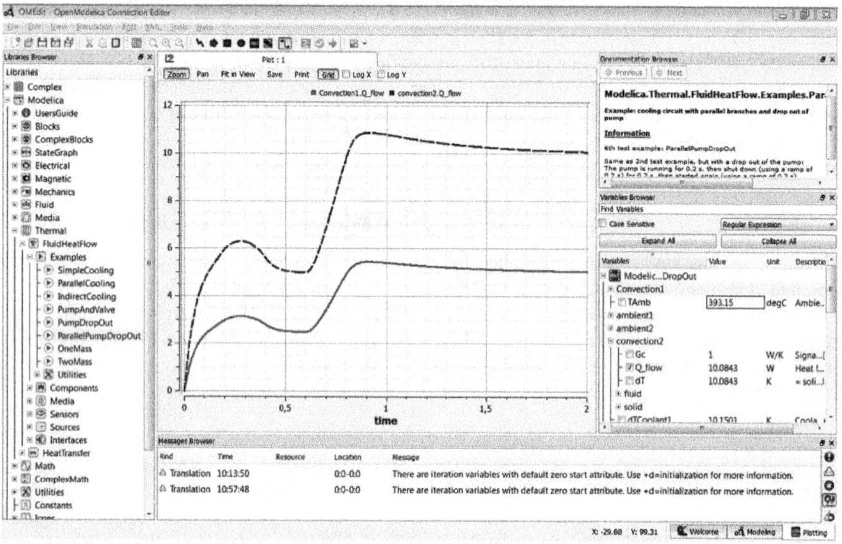

Figure 19-4. Plotting simulation results using OMEdit. *Upper right*: information window. *Lower right*: plot variable browser. *Bottom*: message browser window.

19.3.1.3 The OpenModelica Debugger

The OpenModelica debugger (Figure 19-5, Figure 18-9) is available for use either from OMEdit or from the MDT Eclipse plug-in. The debugger provides traditional debugging of the algorithmic part of Modelica, such as setting breakpoints, starting and stopping execution, single-stepping, inspecting and changing variables, inspecting all kinds of standard Modelica data structures as well as MetaModelica data structures such as trees and lists. It also provides additional capabilities for debugging equation-based models, such as showing and explaining the symbolic transformations performed on selected equations on the way to executable simulation code (Section 18.3.1, page 1016). Moreover, a performance analyzer tool is also included in OpenModelica and integrated with the debugger.

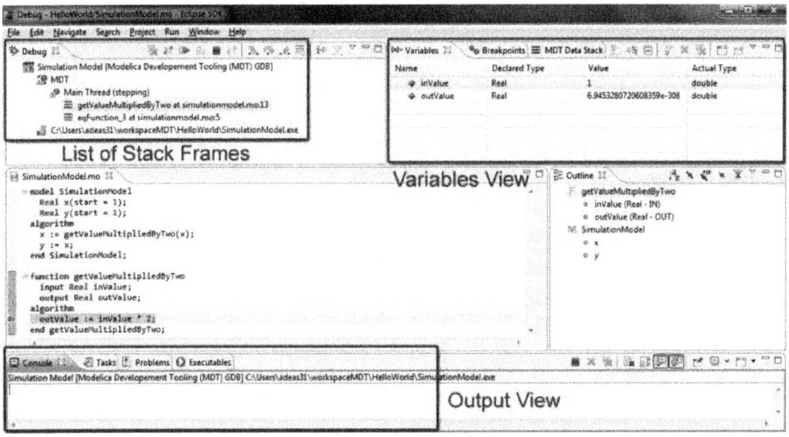

Figure 19-5. The OpenModelica algorithmic code debugger viewed from the MDT Eclipse plug-in. A breakpoint has been set in the function which is called from the small model called SimulationModel.

19.3.1.4 OMNotebook and DrModelica

OMNotebook (Figure 19-6) is book-like interactive user interface to OpenModelica primarily intended for teaching and course material. It supports sections and subsections to any level, hiding and showing sections and cells, interactive evaluation and simulation of Modelica models and plotting results.

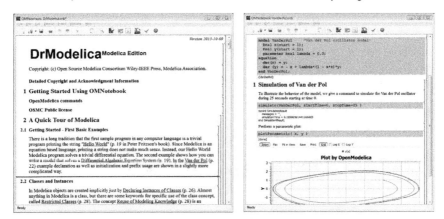

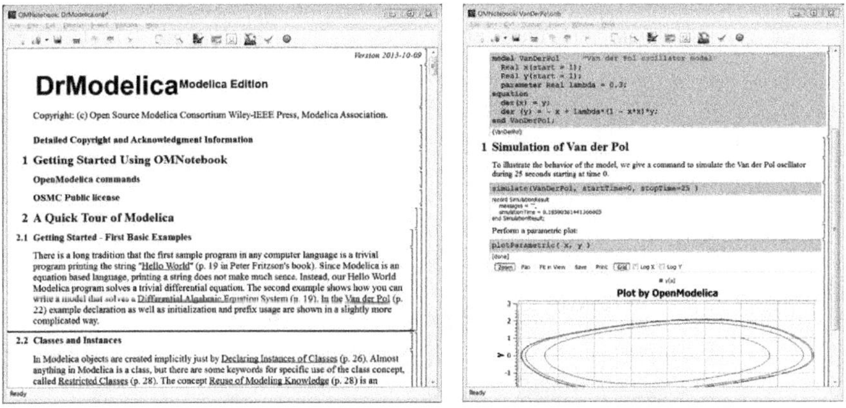

Figure 19-6. The OMNotebook electronic notebook showing part of the DrModelica document (course-material) for learning Modelica. *Left*: The DrModelica document start page. *Right*: The `VanDerPol` sub-document showing a cell with a Modelica model, simulation commands, and plot results.

19.3.1.5 ModelicaML Modelica-UML Profile and Requirement Verification

ModelicaML (Figure 19-7) is an Eclipse plug-in and Modelica-UML profile for the description of system architecture and system dynamic behavior. It is based on an extended subset of the OMG Unified Modeling Language (UML) as well as Modelica, and is designed for Modelica code generation from graphical models such as state machines and activity diagrams, supporting hardware/software co-modeling and system requirement verification against selected scenarios.

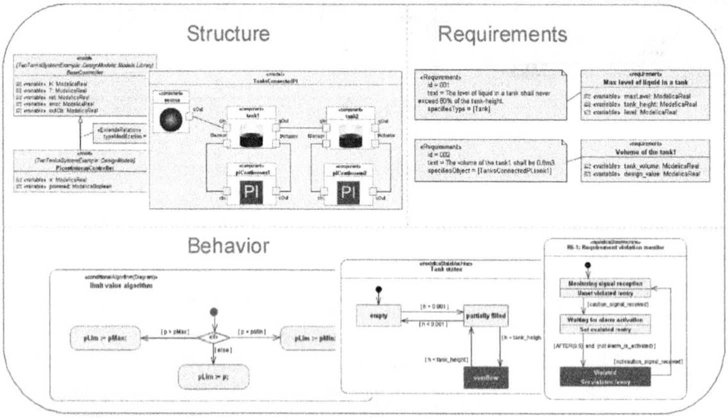

Figure 19-7. The ModelicaML Eclipse plug-in and UML-Modelica profile for integrated software-hardware modeling and requirements verification.

19.3.1.6 MDT (Modelica Development Tooling) Eclipse Plug-in

The MDT (Modelica Development Tooling) Eclipse plug-in is an Eclipse-based textual development environment for Modelica and MetaModelica. It provides the usual facilities for software development such as browsing, building, cross referencing, syntax checking, and showing useful information such as types, function signatures, etc.

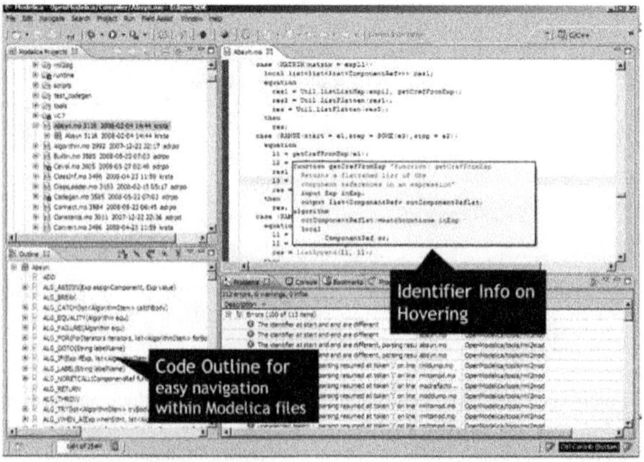

Figure 19-8. The OpenModelica MDT (Modelica Development Tooling) Eclipse plug-in.

MDT is primarily used for development of medium to large scale Modelica projects, such as Modelica libraries written in standard Modelica and the OpenModelica compiler (currently containing more than 200 packages) written in MetaModelica.

19.3.1.7 PySimulator for Post-processing and Analysis

PySimulator is a post-processing and analysis package in Python, for browsing, plotting, analysis, scripting, etc. It uses the OpenModelica OMPython subsystem to communicate with the OpenModelica compiler for simulation and access to model information.

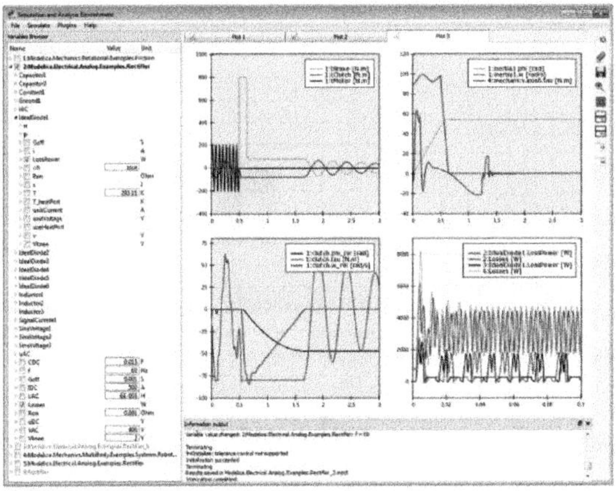

Figure 19-9. The PySimulator analysis and post-processing package, developed by DLR and distributed together with OpenModelica.

19.3.1.8 Design Optimization

Two forms of design optimization tool support are available with OpenModelica: a) the traditional parameter sweep static design optimization using many simulation runs, or b) direct dynamic optimization of a full trajectory. The first method is supported by the OMOptim tool (Figure 19-10).

The second approach, dynamic optimization, formulates an optimization problem directly on a whole trajectory which is divided into trajectory segments (Figure 19-11, left) whose shapes are determined by coefficients which are initially not determined.

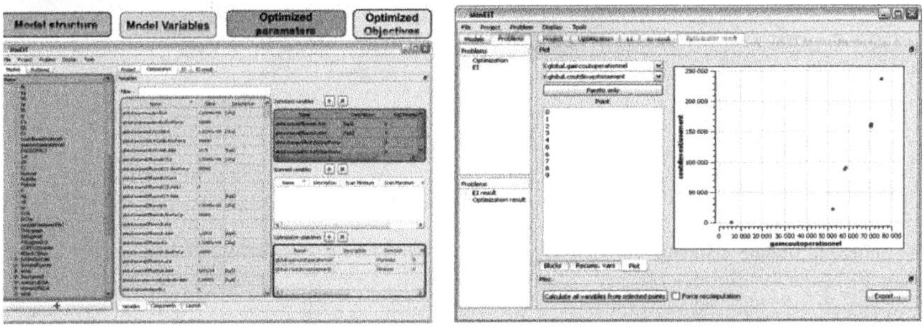

Figure 19-10. The OpenModelica OMOptim tool for parameter sweep optimization. *Left*: selecting variables, objectives, parameters. *Right*: A result plot with a Pareto optimization of two goal functions.

During the optimization process these coefficients are gradually assigned values which make the trajectory segments adjust shape and join into a single trajectory with a shape that optimizes the goal function under the constraints of fulfilling the model equations. Figure 19-11 (right) shows the relative speedup of performing dynamic optimization of a goal function for a small `BatchReactor` model using parallel versions of the dynamic optimization methods multiple shooting and multiple collocation running on a multi-core computer. The Ipopt software is used for part of the optimization mechanism.

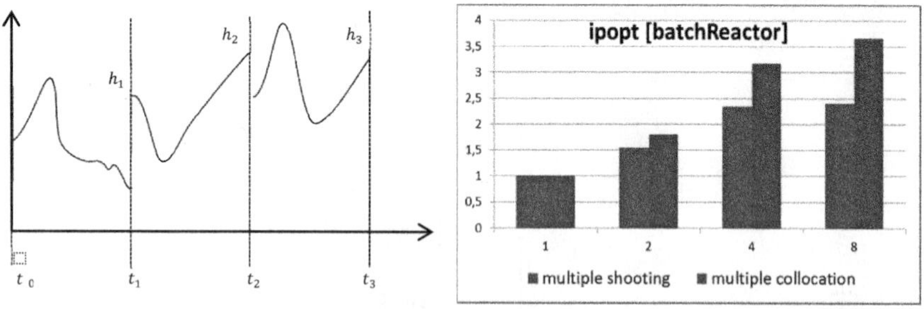

Figure 19-11. *Left*: Dynamic optimization formulates the whole trajectory in terms of trajectory segments whose shapes are adjusted during optimization. *Right*: Relative speedups and computation times of the complete dynamic optimization process for the `BatchReactor` example model using parallel multiple shooting or multiple collocation in OpenModelica on 1, 2, 4, and 8 cores.

19.3.1.9 3D Visualization

Three dimensional visualization and animation can be performed in conjunction with simulation by using the Modelica3D library. Objects are assigned 3D shapes. Their position and orientation can change over time as a result of the simulation.

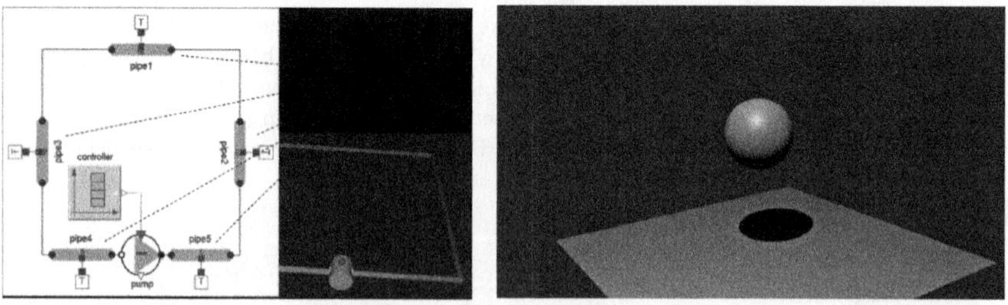

Figure 19-12. Examples of using the Modelica3D library with OpenModelica. *Left*: A 2D and 3D plot of a simple pipe network. *Right*: A 3D image of a bouncing ball.

19.3.2 The Modelica Model Translation Process

The Modelica model translation process by the OpenModelica compiler is schematically depicted in Figure 19-13 below. See also Section 2.20, page 63. The Modelica source code is first translated to a so-called flat model. This phase includes type checking, performing all object-oriented operations such as inheritance, modifications etc., and fixing package inclusion and lookup as well as import statements. The flat model includes a set of equations declarations and functions, with all object-oriented structure removed apart from dot notation within names. This process is a *partial symbolic instantiation* of the model (code instantiation), called *elaboration* in subsequent sections.

The next two phases, the equation analyzer and equation optimizer, are necessary for compiling models containing equations. Finally, C code is generated which is fed through a C compiler (or alternatively Java or C# code and corresponding compilers in experimental versions of the code generator) to produce executable code.

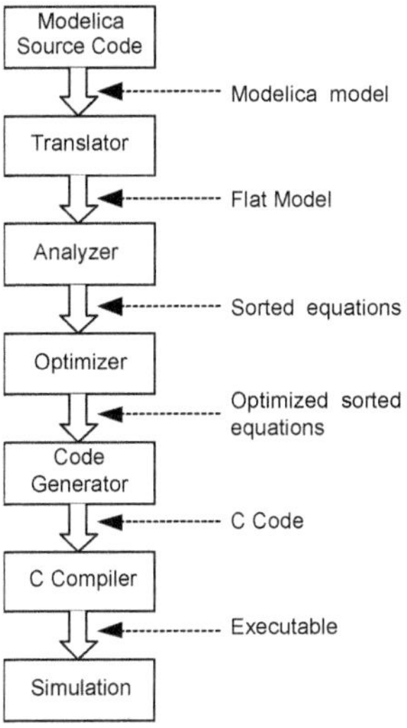

Figure 19-13. Translation stages from Modelica code to executing simulation. The optimizer stage is improving the code but not really optimizing it in the mathematical sense.

19.3.3 Modelica Static and Dynamic Semantics

The complete semantics, that is, meaning, of the constructs in any programming language, also including the Modelica language, is usually divided into two major parts:

- Static semantics
- Dynamic semantics

The *static semantics* specifies compile time issues. These include static type checking, equivalence between different representations of the program and the expansion/flattening of the model into a form with inheritance and modifications expanded, elaboration of the object-oriented model representation, conversion between different levels of the intermediate form, and so on. Such a static semantics is currently given by our formal specification of Modelica.

It should be noted that the semantics specification for an equation based language such as Modelica differs from semantics specifications of ordinary programming languages, since Modelica equation based models are not programs in the usual sense. Instead Modelica is primarily a modeling language (specification language) used to specify relations between different objects in the modeled system.

The *dynamic semantics* specifies the run-time behavior including the equation solving process during the simulation, execution of algorithmic code, and additional run-time aspects of the execution process. We do not currently have a formal specification of the Modelica dynamic semantics, but intend to develop such a specification in the future. The current dynamic run-time behavior is based on hand implementation in the C programming language (or in C# and Java) of the primitives referred to by the Modelica low level DAE equation form intermediate representation.

19.3.3.1 An Example Translation of Models into Equations.

As an example, the Modelica model `B` below is translated into equations, where model `B` refers to model `A`:

```
model A
  Real  x,y;
equation
  x = 2 * y;
end A;

model B
  A     a;
  Real  x[10];
equation
  x[5] = a.y;
end B;
```

The resulting equations appear as follows:

```
B.a.x  = 2 * B.a.y
B.x[5] = B.a.y
```

The object-oriented structure is mostly lost which is why we talk about a flat set of equations, but the variable names in the equations still give a hint about their origin.

What the translator actually does is translating from the Modelica source code to an internal representation of the resulting set of equations. This internal representation is then further translated, for example, to C code. For functions, declarations, and interactively entered expressions, the C code can be generated fairly directly, whereas for equations several symbolic optimization stages must be applied before generating the C code. See also examples in Section 2.20, page 63 and Section 17.1.6, page 984:

19.3.4 Automatic Generation and Formal Specification of Translators

The implementation of compilers and interpreters for nontrivial languages is a complex and error prone process, if done by hand. Therefore, formalisms and generator tools have been developed that allow automatic generation of compilers and interpreters from formal specifications. This offers two major advantages:

- *High level descriptions* of language properties, rather than detailed programming of the translation.
- *High degree of correctness* of generated implementations. The high level specifications are more concise and easier to read than a detailed implementation in some programming language

The *syntax* of a programming language is conveniently described by a *grammar* in a common format, such as BNF, and the structure of the lexical entities, usually called *tokens*, are easily described by *regular expressions*. However, when it comes to the semantics of a programming or modeling language, things are not so straightforward.

The *semantics* of the language describes the “meaning” of any particular program written in the language, that is, what should happen when the program is executed, or evaluated in some form.

Many programming language semantic definitions are given by a standard text written in English which tries to give a complete and unambiguous specification of the language. Unfortunately, this is often not enough. Natural language is inherently not very exact, and it is hard to make sure that all special cases are covered. One of the most important requirements of a language specification is that two different language implementers should be able to read the specification and make implementations that interpret the specification in the same way. This implies that the specification must be exact and unambiguous.

For this reason, formalisms for writing formal specifications of languages have been invented. These formalisms allow for a mathematical semantic description, which as a consequence is exact, unambiguous and easier to verify. One of the most widely used formalisms for specifying semantics is called *Operational Semantics*. A computer processable Operational Semantics specification language called RML for Relational Meta Language, with a compiler generation tool, was previously been developed by Peter Fritzson's group at Linköping university. It was initially used for the formal specification of Modelica in the OpenModelica project.

19.3.4.1 Compiler Generation

Writing a good compiler is not easy. This makes automatic compiler generation from language specifications very interesting. If a language specification is written in a formal manner, all the information needed to build the compiler is already available in a machine-understandable form. Writing the formal semantics for a language can even be regarded as the high-level programming of a compiler.

The different phases of the compilation process are shown in Figure 19-14. More specifically, it shows the translation process of a Modelica translator, which compiles, or rather translates, the Modelica source file. All the parts of the compiler can be specified in a formal manner, using different formalisms such as *regular expressions*, *BNF grammars*, and *Operational Semantics* specifications expressed in MetaModelica. At all stages, there is a tool to convert the formalism into an executable compiler module.

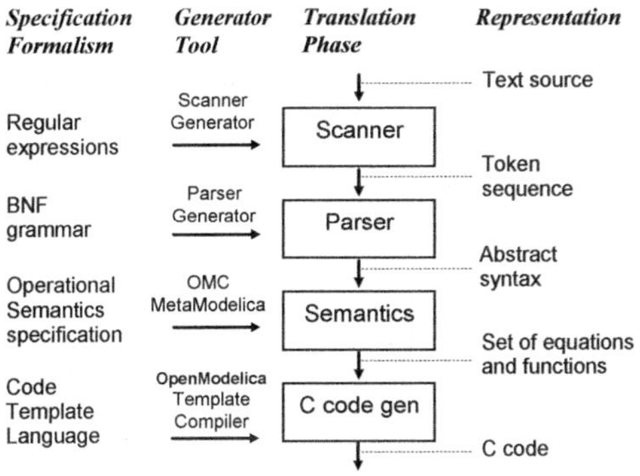

Figure 19-14. Phases in generating the OpenModelica compiler modules from different kinds of specifications. The semantics module performs elaboration of the models including type checking and expansion of class structures, resulting in a set of equations, algorithms and functions.

19.3.5 The Formal Specification of Modelica in MetaModelica

We have previously mentioned that a compiler generation system and language called RML was initially used to produce the OpenModelica compiler from an Operational Semantics language specification. This specification was later automatically translated from RML to MetaModelica syntax. Since fall 2006 the Modelica language specification has been developed in MetaModelica. See Section 6.15296, page 296, for an overview of the MetaModelica language

The generated compiler is produced in ANSI C with a translation speed and quality comparable to hand-written translators.

The specification (i.e., the source code of the compiler written in MetaModelica) is separated into a number of modules, to separate different stages of the translation, and to make it more manageable. This section will very briefly cover some of the most important parts of the specification. In all, the specification currently (2013) contains more than one hundred fifty thousand lines of code.

19.3.5.1 Parsing and Abstract Syntax

The parser is generated from a grammar by a parser generator tool. This parser builds an abstract syntax tree (AST) from the source file, using the AST data types in a MetaModelica module called `Absyn`. The parsing stage is not really part of the semantic description, but is of course necessary to build a real translator.

19.3.5.2 Rewriting the AST

The abstract syntax tree (AST) closely corresponds to the parse tree and keeps the structure of the source file. This has several disadvantages when it comes to translating the program, and especially if the translation rules should be easy to read for a human. For this reason a preparatory translation pass is introduced which translates the AST into an intermediate form, called `SCode`, also a tree structrue. Besides some minor simplifications the `SCode` structure differs from the AST in a number of respects, including the following:

- All variables are described separately. In the source and in the AST several variables in a class definition can be declared at once, as in `Real x, y[17];`. In the `SCode` this is represented as two unrelated declarations, as if it had been written `Real x; Real y[17];`.
- Class declaration sections. In a Modelica class declaration the public, protected, equation and algorithm sections may be included in any number and in any order, with an implicit public section first. In the `SCode` these sections are collected so that all public and protected sections are combined into one section, while keeping the order of the elements. The information about which elements were in a protected section is stored with the element itself.

One might have thought that more work could be done at this stage, like analyzing expression types and resolving names. But due to the nature of the Modelica language, the only way to know anything about how the names will be resolved during elaboration is to do a more or less full elaboration. It is possible to analyze a class declaration and find out what the parts of the declaration would mean if the class was to be elaborated as-is, but since it is possible to modify much of the class while elaborating it that analysis would not be of much use.

19.3.5.3 Elaboration and Instantiation

To be executed, classes in a model need to be instantiated, that is, (code) and data objects are created according to the class declaration. There are two phases of instantiation:

- The symbolic, or compile time, phase of instantiation (code instantiation) is usually called *elaboration* or *flattening*. No data objects are created during this phase. Instead the symbolic internal representation of the model to be executed/simulated is transformed, by performing inheritance operations, modification operations, aggregation operations, and so on.
- The creation of the data object, usually called *instantiation* (data instantiation) in ordinary object-oriented terminology. This can be done either at compile time or at run-time depending on the circumstances and choice of implementation.

The central part of the translation is the code symbolic instantiation or *elaboration* of the model. The convention is that the topmost model in model instance hiearchy implicitly given in the source file is elaborated, which means that the equations in that model declaration, and all its subcomponents, are computed and collected.

The elaboration of a class is done by looking at the class definition, elaborating all subcomponents and collecting all equations, functions, and algorithms. To accomplish this, the translator needs to keep track of the class context. The context includes the lexical scope of the class definition. This constitutes the *environment* which includes the variables and classes declared previously in the same scope as the current class, and its parent scope, and all enclosing scopes. The other part of the context is the current set of modifiers which modify things like parameter values or redeclare subcomponents.

```
model M
  constant Real c = 5;
  model Foo
    parameter Real p = 3;
  Real x;
  equation
    x = p * sin(time) + c;
    end Foo;

  Foo f(p = 17);
end M;
```

In the example above, elaborating the model `M` means elaborating its subcomponent `f`, which is of type `Foo`. While elaborating `f` the current environment is the parent environment, which includes the constant `c`. The current set of modifications is (`p = 17`), which means that the parameter `p` in the instance `f` will be 17 rather than 3.

19.3.6 Summary of OpenModelica

The first version of the OpenModelica environment was to a large extent based on a Modelica compiler automatically generated from a formal Operational Semantics specification of Modelica. This formal specification was later converted into a specification in the MetaModelica language with a Modelica-style syntax. However, the tool still supports optionally writing operational semantics in its traditional rule-based syntax, which is internally converted to the MetaModelica representation.

The current implementation of MetaModelica is integrated with Modelica in the OpenModelica compiler which is bootstrapped, that is, it can model itself and compile itself. Later extensions to the OpenModelica tool environment are: a graphical connection editor and text editor (OMedit), a Modelica debugger, an Eclipse plugin (MDT), a free electronic notebook (OMNotebook), an UML-Modelica profile and Eclipse plugin (ModelicaML) for hardware-software integrated modeling and requirements verification, and a subsystem for model-based optimization (OMOptim).

19.4 Wolfram SystemModeler

Wolfram SystemModeler, previously called MathModelica, together with Mathematica is an integrated interactive development environment for advanced system modeling and simulation. The environment integrates Modelica-based modeling and simulation with graphic design, advanced scripting facilities, integration of program code, test cases, graphics, and documentation. Mathematical type setting and symbolic formula manipulation are provided via the integration with Mathematica. The user interface consists of a graphical model editor and electronic Mathematica notebooks.

The model editor is a graphical user interface in which models can be assembled using model components from a number of Modelica libraries. Mathematica notebooks are interactive documents that combine simulation and technical computations with text, graphics, tables, code, and other elements, i.e., so called literate programming. The accessible Mathematica internal form allows the user to extend the system with new functionality, as well as performing queries on the model representation and write scripts for automatic model generation. Furthermore, extensibility of syntax and semantics provides additional flexibility in adapting to unforeseen user needs.

19.4.1 Mathematica and Modelica

It turns out that Mathematica is an integrated programming environment that fulfils many of our requirements of an integrated interactive modeling and simulation environment. However, by itself, Mathematica previously lacked object-oriented modeling and structuring facilities of models as well as generation of efficient simulation code needed for effective modeling and simulation of large systems.

These modeling and simulation facilities are now integrated with Mathematica by the Wolfram SystemModeler, which provides access to the Modelica language and the Modelica Standard Library. Mathematica provides a structured representation of mathematics and facilities for programming symbolic transformations, whereas the Modelica provides language elements and structuring facilities for object-oriented component based modeling.

The current Wolfram SystemModeler system builds on experience from the design of its immediate predecessor the MathModelica environment, the earlier ObjectMath modeling language and environment integrated with Mathematica, as well as results from object-oriented modeling languages and systems such as Dymola and Omola, which together with ObjectMath and a few other object-oriented modeling languages have provided the basis for the design of Modelica.

The ObjectMath environment was originally designed as an object-oriented extension of Mathematica augmented with efficient code generation and a graphic class browser. The Wolfram SystemModeler product is a successor of the MathModelica product which in many ways can be seen as a logical successor to the ObjectMath research prototype.

19.4.2 The Wolfram SystemModeler Integrated Interactive Environment

The Wolfram SystemModeler system consists of three major subsystems that are used during different phases of the modeling and simulation process, as depicted in Figure 19-15 below.

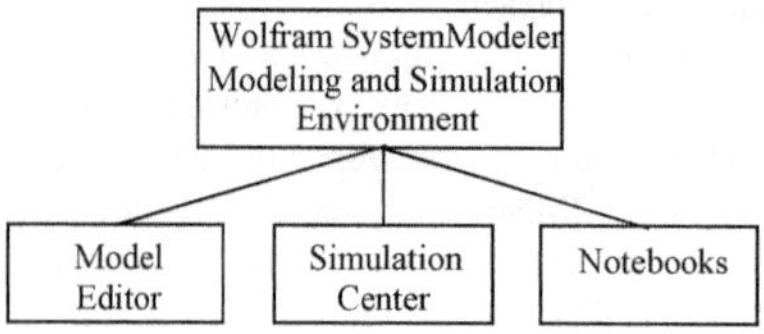

Figure 19-15. The Wolfram System Modeler (WSM) system architecture.

These subsystems are the following:

- The WSM graphic *Model Editor* used for design of models from library components.
- The interactive Mathematica *Notebook* facility, for literate programming, documentation, running simulations, scripting, graphics, and symbolic mathematics with Mathematica coupling.
- The WSM *Simulation Center*, for specifying parameters, running simulations, and plotting curves and 3D graphics.

A key aspect of Wolfram SystemModeler is that the modeling and simulation is done integrated with the Mathematica environment. This does not only give access to the Notebook user interface but also to thousands of available functions and many application packages, as well as the ability of communicating with other programs and import and export of different data formats.

These capabilities make Wolfram SystemModeler more of a complete workbench for the researcher and innovative engineer than just a modeling and simulation tool. Once a model has been developed there is often a need for further analysis such as linearization, sensitivity analysis, transfer function computations, control system design, parametric studies, Monte Carlo simulations, and so on.

19.4.3 Graphic Model Editor

The Wolfram SystemModeler (WSM) *Model Editor* is a graphical user interface for model diagram construction by "drag-and-drop" of model classes from the Modelica Standard Library or from user defined component libraries, visually represented as graphic icons in the editor. A screen shot of the Model Editor is shown in Figure 19-16. At the left the model library and class browser window is visible from which the user can drag models and drop them on the drawing area in the middle of the tool.

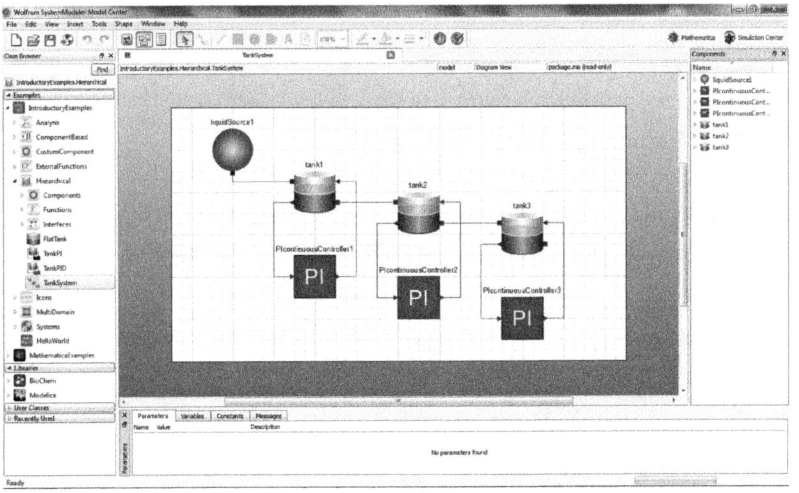

Figure 19-16. The WSM Graphic Model Editor with the class browser to the left, the graphic editing area in the middle and the instance component browser to the right. Courtesy Wolfram MathCore AB.

The Model Editor depicted in Figure 19-16 is implemented based on the Qt graphical library, which means that it is portable to the Linux, Unix, and MacinTosh platforms.

The Model Editor can be viewed as a user interface for graphical programming in Modelica. Its basic functionality consists of selection of components from libraries, connection of components in model diagrams, and entering parameter values for different components.

For large and complex models, it is important to be able to intuitively navigate quickly through component hierarchies. The Model Editor supports such navigation in several ways. A model diagram can be browsed and zoomed.

19.4.3.1 Simulation Center

The WSM *Simulation Center* is a subsystem for running simulations, setting initial values and model parameters, plotting results, and so on. These facilities are accessible via a graphic user interface accessible through the Simulation Center window (Figure 19-17). However, remember that it is also possible to run simulations from the textual user interface available in the Mathematica notebooks (Section E.3, page 1137), and below (Section 19.4.5.1, page 1052).

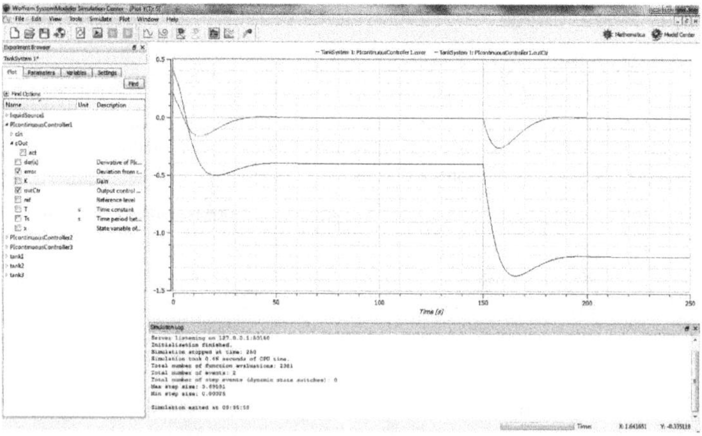

Figure 19-17. The WSM Simulation Center window with a diagram windown containing plots of the signals `inertial.flange_a.tau` and `inertial.w` selected in the subwindow menus.

If a model parameter or initial value has been changed, it is possible to rerun the simulation without rebuilding the executable code if the changed parameter does not influence the equation structure, that is, the parameter is not a structural parameter (Section 17.1.5, page 983).

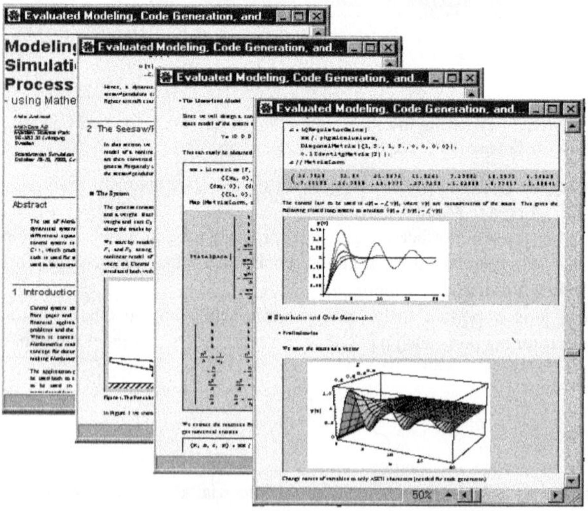

Figure 19-18. Examples of Mathematica notebooks including some Modelica simulations.

19.4.4 Mathematics with 2D-syntax, Greek letters, and Equations

The syntactic facilities of Mathematica allows writing formulas in the standard mathematical notation, for example, well-known from textbooks in mathematics and physics. Certain parts of the Mathematica language syntax are however a bit unusual compared to many common programming languages. The reason for this design choice is to make it possible to use implied multiplication in purely textual Mathematica syntax. The following three syntactic features are unusual:

- Implied multiplication is allowed, that is, a space between two expressions, for example, `x` and `f(x)`, means multiplication just as in mathematics. A multiplication operator * can be used if desired, but is optional.
- Square brackets are used around the arguments at function calls. Round parentheses are only used for grouping of expressions. The exception is `TraditionalForm`, see below.
- Support for two-dimensional mathematical syntactic notation such as integrals, division bars, square roots, matrices, etc.

The reason for the unusual choice of square brackets around function arguments is that the implied multiplication makes the interpretation of round parenthesis ambiguous. For example, `f(x+1)` can be interpreted either as a function call to `f` with the argument `x+1`, or `f` multiplied by `(x+1)`. The integral in the cell below contains examples of both implied multiplication and two-dimensional integral syntax. The cell style is called `StandardForm` in Mathematica and is used for mathematics in Mathematica syntax:

$$\int \frac{x f[x]}{1 + x^2 + x^3} dx$$

There is also a purely textual input form using a linear sequence of characters. All mathematics can also be represented in this syntax. The above example in this textual format appears as follows:

```
Integrate[(x*f[x])/(1 + x^2 + x^3), x]
```

Finally, there is also a cell format called `TraditionalForm` which is very close to traditional mathematical syntax, avoiding the square brackets. The above-mentioned syntactic ambiguities can usually be avoided if the formula is first entered using one of the above input forms, and then converted to `TraditionalForm`:

$$\int \frac{x f(x)}{x^3 + x^2 + 1} dx$$

MathModelica, the predecessor of the Wolfram SystemModeler environment, also supported Mathematica-style syntax of Modelica models. Figure 19-19 shows a small example of a Modelica model class `SimpleDAE` represented in the Mathematica style syntax of Modelica that allows greek characters and two-dimensional syntax. The apostrophe (') is used for the derivatives just as in traditional mathematics, corresponding to the Modelica `der()` operator.

```
Model[SimpleDAE
  Real β₁;
  Real x₂;
  Equation[
```

$$\frac{\beta_1'}{1+(\beta_1')^2} + \frac{\sin[x_2']}{1+(\beta_1')^2} + \beta_1 x_2 + \beta_1 == 1;$$

$$\sin[\beta_1'] - \frac{x_2'}{1+(\beta_1')^2} - 2\beta_1 x_2 + \beta_1 == 0;$$

```
]]
```

Figure 19-19. The `SimpleDAE` Modelica model in Mathematica style syntax using the earlier MathModelica environment.

Even though Wolfram SystemModeler does not support Mathematica-style representation of full Modelica models, the equations from a Modelica model can be imported into a Mathematica representation using the `WSMModelData` command (Section E.3, page 1137), and further processed using the symbolic capabilities of Mathematica.

19.4.5 Advanced Plotting and Interpolating Functions

This section illustrates the flexible usage of simulation results represented as Mathematica interpolating functions, both for further computations that may include simulation results in expressions, and for simple and advanced plotting in 1D, 2D and 3D. The simple bouncing ball model, Section 2.15, page 55, also shown below, is used in some of the following simulation and plotting examples.

```
model BouncingBall "Simple model of a bouncing ball"
  constant Real g = 9.81     "Gravity constant";
  parameter Real c = 0.9     "Coefficient of restitution";
  parameter Real radius=0.1  "Radius of the ball";
  Real height(start = 1)     "Height of the ball center";
  Real velocity(start = 0)   "Velocity of the ball";
equation
  der(height) = velocity;
  der(velocity) = -g;
  when height <= radius then
    reinit(velocity,-c*pre(velocity));
  end when;
end BouncingBall;
```

19.4.5.1 Interpolating Function Representation of Simulation Results

The following simulation of the above `BouncingBall` model (after loading it into WSM) is done for a short time period using very few (11) points:

```
res1 = WSMSimulate["BouncingBall",{0,0.5}, NumberOfIntervals->10]
```

The results returned by WSM`Simulate` are represented by an access descriptor or handle, here `res1`. Relevant variables can be extracted from this handle, for example, `height`, `radius`, and so on, in the following way:

```
{h,radius} = res1[{"height","radius"}]
```

Each result variable from the simulation is a function of time, represented as an interpolating function, here assigned to the Mathematica variables `h` and `radius`.

Working with simulation result datasets in Mathematica is made in a very convenient way using the Mathematica `InterpolatingFunction` mechanism that encapsulates the data into a function object and provides interpolation so that the data acts as a regular function.

The interpolation function can now be used in any computation in Mathematica. First we just access its value at time 0.2:

```
h[0.2]
```

We can also evaluate the derivative of the function `h` at the time `0.2`, getting the result `-1.962`:

```
h'[0.2]
-1.962
```

In this case, Mathematica made the differentiation of the `InterpolatingFunction` object `h` using the derivative operator `'`. Normally the derivatives of the simulation variables are also available in the simulation data. To make the naming more consistent with the current Modelica model, we assign the variable `height`:

```
height = h
```

Then we can write the following and get the same result:

```
height'[0.2]
-1.962
```

Now we perform a new simulation with a different parameter setting, with the result denoted by `res2`:

```
res2 = WSMSimulate["BouncingBall",{0,0.5}, NumberOfIntervals->10,
             ParameterValues-> {c->0.95}];
```

```
{height2,radius2} = res2[{"height","radius"}]
```

Having the previous height curve represented as the function object `height` we can easily compute the difference of the curves between the simulations, for example, using a plot expression `height2[t]-height[t]`.

19.4.5.2 Plotting Interpolating Function Expressions

First we simulate the bouncing ball for eight seconds and store the results in the variable `res1` for subsequent use in the plotting examples.

```
res1 = WSMSimulate["BouncingBall",{0,8}];
```

```
{height,radius} = res1[{"height","radius"}]
```

Since Mathematica represents simulation results as interpolating functions, these functions can be embedded in expressions such as `height[t]+`$\sqrt{3}$ and `Abs[velocity[t]]` in Mathematica syntax. Plotting several arbitrary functions can be done using a list `{...}` of function expressions instead of a single expression:

```
Plot[{height[t]+√3 ,Abs[velocity[t]]} {t,0,8}]
```

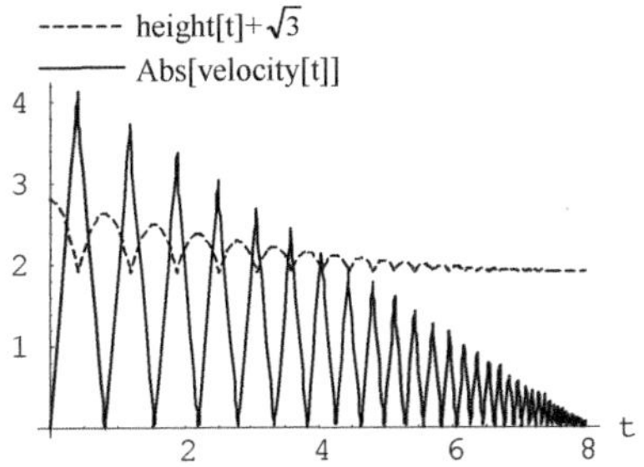

Figure 19-20. Plotting arbitrary functions in the same diagram.

Parametric plots can be done using `ParametricPlot`:

```
ParametricPlot[height[t],velocity[t], {t,0,8}]
```

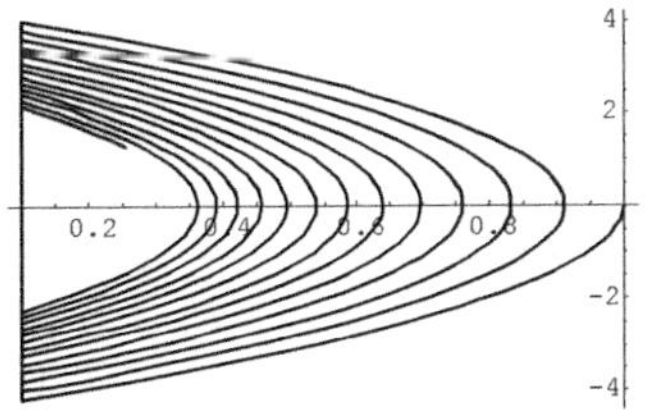

Figure 19-21. A parametric plot.

In the following 3D plot example, we use the Rossler attractor to show the `ParametricPlot3D` command. The Rossler attractor is named after Otto Rossler from his work in chemical kinetics. The system is described by three coupled nonlinear differential equations, where `a`, `b`, and `c` are constants. The attractor never forms limit circles nor does it ever reach a steady state. The equations in standard mathematical syntax appear as follows:

$$\frac{dx}{dt} = -y - x$$

$$\frac{dy}{dt} = x + \alpha y$$

$$\frac{dz}{dt} = \beta + (x - \gamma)z$$

The corresponding Modelica model using a, b, c instead of greek letters is:

```
model Rossler
  Real x(start=1);
  Real y(start=3);
  Real z(start=0);
  parameter Real a(start=0.2);
  parameter Real b(start=0.2);
  parameter Real c(start=8);
equation
  der(x)= -y - z;
  der(y)= x + a*y;
  der(z)= b + x*z - c*z;
end Rossler;
```

The model is simulated using different initial values. Changing these can considerably influence the appearance of the attractor. We simulate and specify the computation of 1000 data points (default is 500):

```
res = WSMSimulate["Rossler", {0,40}, InitialValues -> {x-> 2, y -> 2.5,
     z -> 0}, NumberOfIntervals->1000];
```

```
{x,y,z} = res[{"x","y","z"}]
```

The Rossler attractor is easy to plot using ParametricPlot3D:

```
ParametricPlot3D[{x[t], y[t], z[t]},{t,0,40}, AxesLabel->{X,Y,Z}];
```

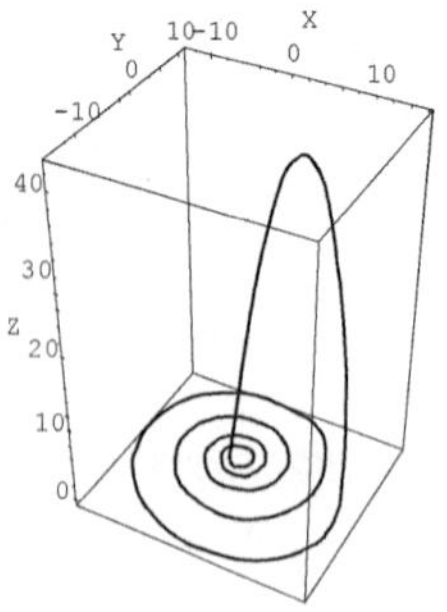

Figure 19-22. 3-D parametric plot of curve with many data points from the Rossler attractor simulation.

19.4.6 Summary of Wolfram SystemModeler

This overview has presented a number of important issues concerning integrated interactive programming environments, especially with respect to the Mathematica and Wolfram SystemModeler environment for object-oriented modeling and simulation.

One of the current strong trends in software systems is the ongoing unification of documents and software. Everything will eventually be integrated into a uniform, to some extent XML-based, representation. The integration of documents, model code, graphics, and so on, in the Mathematica and Wolfram SystemModeler environment is one example of this trend.

19.5 The Dymola Environment

Dymola—Dynamic Modeling Laboratory—is a comprehensive, industrial-strength modeling and simulation environment for Modelica, with special emphasis on efficient real-time simulation. One of the main application areas is simulation in the automotive industry, for example, hardware-in-the-loop simulation of automatic gearboxes and other vehicle subsystems.

The history of Dymola goes back to 1978 when Hilding Elmqvist presented his Ph.D. thesis on methods for component-based modeling and simulation with acausal equations and automatic symbolic manipulation of equation systems into a state space form suitable for numerical solvers. His thesis also described a small modeling language called Dymola, meaning Dynamic Modeling Language. However, at that time the computational power and memory capacity of computers was too limited to use these methods on most realistic industrial problems.

Eventually the capacity of computers increased enough to resume the development of Dymola. In 1992 Hilding Elmqvist founded the Dynasim company. A new and extended version of the Dymola language and tool soon appeared, including full object orientation together with support for discrete event and hybrid simulation.

When the design of the Modelica language had matured enough the Dymola tool was enhanced with support for the Modelica modeling language, which eventually replaced the Dymola language as the standard modeling language of the tool. A new interpretation of Dymola was coined—Dynamic Modeling Laboratory.

The structure of the Dymola tool is similar to the previously presented OpenModelica and Wolfram SystemModeler environments. It contains the following main parts:

- A Modelica compiler including a symbolic optimizer to reduce the size of equation systems.
- A simulation run-time system including a numeric solver for hybrid DAE equation systems.
- A graphic user Interface including a connection editor.
- A text editor for editing Modelica models.

Here we will just take a brief look at some aspects of the Dymola environment regarding the most recent version, Dymola 2014. The description is not complete and is shorter than for the previous two environments—not because there is less material to present—but primarily because this author has not been involved in the development of Dymola, in contrast to the case for OpenModelica and Wolfram SystemModeler (earlier called MathModelica). Additional information regarding Dymola is available in the Dymola user's manual and in a number of papers mentioned in the Dymola references section at the end of this chapter.

19.5.1 Graphical and Textual User Interface

The Dymola environment includes both a graphical connection editor and a text editor, depicted in Figure 19-23, as well as tree browsers for the package/class hierarchy and the instance (component) hierarchy.

The following are a few characteristics of the user interface:

- Both tree browsers (for the package hierarchy and the instance and extends hierarchy) can display small icons at the left of corresponding names of classes and components. A class icon can be dragged from the package hierarchy browser into the graphical connection editor where it will appear as an icon representing an instance, or into the text editor window where it will appear as text.

- The icon representation can be created with the built-in graphical editor which allows insertion of graphical elements such as lines, rectangles, ellipses, polygons, and text strings. Import of scalable bitmaps created by other tools is also possible.
- The hierarchical structure of a model is shown in the component hierarchy browser.
- A built-in text editor for editing models is available. This editor offers syntax highlighting, for example, to show different colors for keywords, type names, and variable names in declarations.

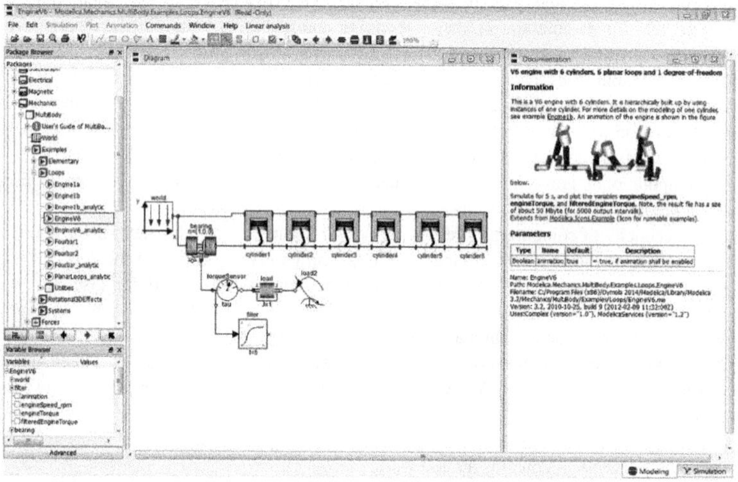

Figure 19-23. The Dymola 2014 graphical user interface. Courtesy Dassault Systèmes.

19.5.2 Real-Time Hardware-in-the-loop Simulation

One of the most powerful features of Dymola is real-time simulation. This is commonly used for hardware-in-the-loop simulation, that is, when a hardware component is replaced by a component with similar properties, but simulated in software using a computer.

However, multi-domain hierarchical modeling often leads to stiff equation systems, for which the solutions contain both slowly varying and fast varying parts. The usual use of the explicit Euler method (Section 18.2.1.1) when real-time constraints are imposed does not work well since it requires a too small step size causing a too large computational effort. Unfortunately, the explicit Euler method becomes unstable if the step size is increased too much. The solution is to use the implicit Euler method instead, which however requires the solution of a small nonlinear equation system at each step, which usually is too computationally intensive.

Fortunately the method of in-line integration can help in these cases. Instead of calling a separate solver to perform the integration, the discretization formulas of the integration method are expanded in-line together with the model equations. The whole equation system is symbolically reduced to a more efficient form, which in many cases dramatically increases the efficiency of solving the nonlinear system at each integration step.

19.5.3 Clocked Synchronous Modeling and Simulation

Dymola was the first Modelica tool to support clocked synchronous modeling and simulation (Section 13.6, page 694), and at the time of this writing still is the only Modelica tool to support that.

The clocked constructs are particularly useful when modeling clocked digital control systems. All simulations of models with clocked language constructs in this book have been done using Dymola.

19.5.4 Other Facilities

Dymola also contain a number of additional facilities not described here, including a 3D graphic animation option, integration with CVS to support version handling, and so on.

19.6 Summary

We started this chapter with a generic description of the structure and parts of typical Modelica modeling and simulation environments. The first environment to be presented was the OpenModelica environment, an open-source effort partly based on generation of its model compiler from a formal specification, first in operational semantics, later in MetaModelica—see a separate summary in Section 19.3.6, page 1047. The second environment to be described was Wolfram SystemModeler—an environment emphasizing integration, interactivity, and extensibility with unification between documentation and code and accessible internal representation—see as separate summary in Section 19.4.6, page 1054. The third and final environment to be briefly described was Dymola, emphasizing high performance real-time simulation.

19.7 Literature

This section provides literature references related to three Modelica environments for modeling and simulation: OpenModelica, Wolfram SystemModeler (before 2012 called MathModelica), and Dymola. During recent years additional Modelica modeling and simulation tools have been developed, which are not described here. See the Modelica Association web page www.modelica.org for up-to-date references to those environments.

Common Background

The integrated programming environment aspects of our design of the *MathModelica* environment (from 2012 developed into the *Wolfram SystemModeler*) and the *OpenModelica environment* have their roots and inspiration from interactive programming environments for languages such as Lisp with the InterLisp system: (Teitelman 1969; Teitelman 1974; Teitelman 1977), common principles and experience of early interactive Lisp environments as described in (Sandewall 1978), interactive and incremental Pascal with the DICE system: (Fritzson 1983; Fritzson 1984), Smalltalk-80: (Goldberg and Robson 1989), Mathematica: (Wolfram 1988; Wolfram 1997), interactive environment generation and Simula: (Hedin and Magnusson 1988; Lindskov, Knudsen, Lehrmann-Madsen, and Magnusson 1993).

OpenModelica

The literature references for OpenModelica have been organized according to topic and/or subsystem:

OpenModelica Environment as a whole—This is described in several overview papers, including: (Fritzson, Aronsson, Lundvall, Nyström, Pop, Saldamli, Broman 2005; Aronsson, Lundvall, Nyström, Pop, Saldamli, and Broman 2006; Fritzson 2010; Fritzson 2011)

OpenModelica Compiler (OMC)— The overall architecture is described in the OpenModelica system documentation (OSMC 2013). A few separate aspects are covered, e.g., event handling (Lundvall, and Fritzson 2005), bootstrapping of the compiler (Sjölund, Fritzson, and Pop 2011; Sjölund, Fritzson, and Pop 2014), compiler backend modularity (Frenkel, Kunze, Fritzson, Sjölund, Pop, and Braun 2011), benchmark suite (Frenkel, Schubert, Kunze, Fritzson, Sjölund, and Pop 2011), matching algorithms (Frenkel, Kunze, and Fritzson 2011), Jacobian computation for fast simulation (Braun, Ochel, and Bachmann 2011; Braun,Yances, Link, and Bachmann 2012), and initialization of hybrid models (Ochel and Bachmann 2013). Some related compiler functionality: comment and indentation preserving unparsing (Fritzson, Pop, Norling, and Blom 2008), the OpenModelica text template language Susan (Fritzson, Privitzer, Sjölund, and Pop 2009), the OpenModelica Java external function interface (Sjölund and Fritzson 2009).

Generating the OpenModelica Compiler from specifications—The OpenModelica model compiler for the Modelica language is automatically generated from a formal specification of Modelica. Initially this specification was developed in the big-step *Operational Semantics* formalism, also called *Natural Semantics*. Tool support was 1997- 2005 provided by the RML compiler, but during 2006-2013 by a separate MetaModelica compiler which reuses the RML backend but has a different frontend. From late fall 2013 the bootstrapped OpenModelica compiler (OMC) has replaced the old MetaModelica compiler for generating the compiler implementation since it includes efficient support for MetaModelica (Fritzson, Pop, and Aronsson 2005; Pop and Fritzson 2006; Fritzson and Pop 2011; Fritzson, Pop, and Sjölund 2011). Operational Semantics/Natural semantics, the RML tool and language and some use for Modelica compiler generation are described in (Kahn 1987; Pettersson 1999; Fritzson 1998; Kågedal and Fritzson 1998; Pop and Fritzson 2006; Pop and Fritzson 2007; Fritzson, Pop, Broman, and Aronsson 2009; Broman, Fritzson, Hedin, Åkesson 2012; Fritzson and Pop 2014). The earlier generation of the OpenModelica translator from Operational Semantics/Natural Semantics in the RML form as well as other aspects of the environment are briefly described in (Kågedal and Fritzson 1998; Fritzson, Aronsson, Bunus, Engelson, Johansson, Karström, Saldamli 2002; Aronsson, Fritzson, Saldamli, and Bunus 2002). A related approach in the sense of using a formal specification language, but using a partial specification of VHDL-AMS in denotational semantics instead of natural semantics is described in (Breuer, Madrid, Bowen, France, Petrie, and Kloos 1999). The ANTLR parser generator currently used for the OpenModelica compiler frontend is described in (Schaps 1999), whereas the OMCCp parser generator with better error handling which might be used in the future for OMC is described in (Palanisamy, Pop, Sjölund, and Fritzson 2014).

OMEdit— The graphic connection editor and its integration with electronic notebooks is described in (Asghar, Tariq, Torabzadeh-Tari, Fritzson, Pop, Sjölund, Vasaiely, and Schamai 2011).

Debugger—Three main versions of the OpenModelica debugger have been developed for both Modelica and MetaModelica, with successively increasing performance and scope: (Pop and Fritzson 2005; Pop, Akhvlediani, and Fritzson 2007; Asghar, Pop, Sjölund, and Fritzson 2012; Pop, Sjölund, Asghar, Fritzson, Casella 2012). Some parts of the RML (operational semantics) debugger (Pop and Fritzson 2005) were adapted and reused for the first OpenModelica debugger.

Performance Analyzer—The OpenModelica performance analyzer, which can be used for both real-time and non-real-time simulations, is described in Section 4.3 of (Huhn, Sjölund, Chen, Schulze, and Fritzson 2011) and in Chapter 9 of the OpenModelica 1.9.0 User's Guide (OSMC 2013).

MDT (Modelica Development Tooling) Eclipse plug-in—This tool is described in (Pop, Fritzson, Remar, Jagudin, and Akhvlediani 2006; Jagudin, Remar, Pop, and Fritzson 2006; Pop 2008).

ModelicaML—There are two generations of the ModelicaML UML-Modelica profile and Eclipse plug-in. The first generation which partially integrates SysML and Modelica is described in (Pop, Akhvlediani, and Fritzson 2007a; Pop, Akhvlediani, and Fritzson 2007b; Pop, Băluţă, and Fritzson 2007; Pop 2008). The second ModelicaML is much further developed and provides integrated UML-Modelica software-hardware modeling, simulation, requirement modeling and verification (Schamai 2009; Schamai, Fritzson, Paredis, and Pop 2009; Paredis, Bernard, Burkhart, de Koning, Friedenthal, Fritzson, Rouquette, and Schamai 2010; Schamai, Helle, Fritzson, and Paredis 2010; Myers, Schamai, and Fritzson 2011;

Schamai, Fritzson, Paredis, and Helle 2012; Liang, Schamai, Rogovchenko, Sadeghi, Nyberg, Fritzson 2012; Schamai 2013). Information about Papyrus is found at (Eclipse-Papyrus 2013).

Optimization Tools—The OMOptim subsystem for parameter sweep optimization is described in (Thieriot, Nemer, Torabzadeh-Tari, Fritzson, Singh, and Kocherry 2011). A parallel version of the built-in OpenModelica dynamic optimizer with collocation and multiple shooting is presented in (Bachmann, Ochel, Ruge, Gebremedhin, Fritzson, Nezhadali, Eriksson, Sivertsson 2012). Dynamic optimization is also available in OpenModelica via XML export to CaSADi (Shitahun, Ruge, Gebremedhin, Bachmann, Eriksson, Andersson, Diehl, Fritzson 2013). The first dynamic optimizer using collocation together with Modelica models is described in (Åkesson 2007). On-line dynamic optimization using Modelica models is described in (Franke 2002; Franke, Rode, and Krüger 2003).

ParModelica Language Extension—See (Gebremedhin, Moghadam, Fritzson, Stavåker 2012).

MetaModelica Language Extension—This is presented in (Fritzson, Pop, and Aronsson 2005; Pop and Fritzson 2006; Fritzson and Pop 2011; Fritzson, Pop, and Sjölund 2011).

OMPython and PySimulator—OMPython provides Python scripting of all OpenModelica API commands (Section E.2, page 1133). Note that the use of Modelica as a scripting language is already supported by OMC. The design, usage, and initial implementation of OMPython is described in (Ganeson, Fritzson, Rogovchenko, Asghar, Sjölund, and Pfeiffer 2012). The PySimulator subsystem is presented in (Pfeiffer, Hellerer, Hartweg, Otter, and Reiner 2012). An old example without OMPython usage for Monte Carlo simulation is described in (Torabzadeh-Tari, Fritzson, Sjölund, Pop 2009).

3D Visualization—An early version of 3D visualization and animation with OpenModelica is described in (Eriksson, Magnusson, Fritzson, and Pop 2008). The current 3D visualization and animation mechanism uses the Modelica3D library (Höger, Mehlhase, Nytsch-Geusen, Isakovic, and Kubiak 2012).

OMNotebook—The OpenModelica version of electronic notebook called OMNotebook is described in (Fernström, Axelsson, Fritzson, Sandholm, and Pop 2006; Asghar, Tariq, Torabzadeh-Tari, Fritzson, Pop, Sjölund, Vasaiely, and Schamai 2011). Applications and extensions of this notebook tool are presented in (Sandholm, Fritzson, Arora, Delp, Petersson, and Rose 2007; Torabzadeh-Tari, Fritzson, Pop, and Sjölund 2010; Torabzadeh-Tari, Sjölund, Pop, and Fritzson 2011; Torabzadeh-Tari, Remala, Sjölund, Pop, and Fritzson 2011; Torabzadeh-Tari, Hossain, Fritzson, and Richter 2011).

Wolfram SystemModeler and MathModelica

Documentation for the *Wolfram SystemModeler* environment is available in (Wolfram Research 2013). Before 2012, the previous version of this environment was called MathModelica which is described in detail in (Fritzson 2006). Older versions are presented in (Fritzson, Engelson, and Gunnarsson 1998; Fritzson, Gunnarsson, and Jirstrand 2002).

The immediate predecessor of the MathModelica environment is the ObjectMath language and environment, described in (Fritzson, Viklund, Herber, Fritzson 1992; Fritzson, Viklund, Fritzson, and Herber 1995; Viklund and Fritzson 1995), based on an analysis of the needs for high-level computational modeling and simulation tools in (Fritzson, Fritzson 1992). MathCode – a productized code generator from the ObjectMath environment is described in (Fritzson 1998; Fritzson, Engelson, and Sheshadri 2008).

The early ObjectMath prototype also lead to the development of BEAST (Bearing Simulation Tool), an object-oriented simulation tool capable of execution on parallel processors described in (Fritzson, Nordling 1995; Fritzson, Fritzson, Nordling, and Persson 1997; Nordling 2003). Successive versions of the MathModelica environment are described in (Fritzson, Engelson, and Gunnarsson 1998; Jirstrand, Gunnarsson, and Fritzson 1999; Jirstrand 2000; Fritzson, Jirstrand, and Gunnarsson 2002). Some versions of MathModelica use Visio, (Visio 2001), for implementing the graphical user interface (GUI), other versions base the GUI on the QT (Dalheimer 2002) library. The used parser generator PCCTS is described in (Parr 1997).

The interactive integrated capabilities of MathModelica (from 2012 developed into Wolfram SystemModeler) of combining programs, documentation, and graphics in a live document are partly related to early work on (noninteractive) literate programming in the LaTeX document processing system,

(Knuth 1984; Knuth 1994), but mostly to the interactive Mathematica environment with its notebooks, also used for teaching mathematics (Davis, Porta, and Uhl 1994).

The DrModelica electronic notebook document was first made using Mathematica notebooks in MathModelica, later using the OpenModelica tool OMNotebook, with the examples and exercises of this book. It was also been inspired by DrScheme (Felleisen, Findler, Flatt, and Krishnamurthi 1998) and DrJava (Allen, Cartwright, and Stoler 2002), and is somewhat related to the idea of elucidative programming (Nørmark 2000). The first version of DrModelica is described in (Lengquist-Sandelin and Monemar 2003; Lengquist-Sandelin, Monemar, Fritzson, and Bunus 2003).

Dymola

The current *Dymola* environment, interpreted as the *Dynamic Modeling Laboratory*, with Modelica as its modeling language, is for example described in (Dassault Systèmes 2013; Brück, Elmqvist, Mattsson, and Olsson 2002), and in a book draft (Elmqvist, Otter, Mattsson, and Olsson 2002). Dynamic selection of states in Dymola is presented in (Mattsson, Olsson, and Elmqvist 2000). The techniques for fast real-time and hardware-in-the-loop simulation supported by Dymola are discussed in (Elmqvist, Mattsson, and Olsson 2002), partly based on earlier work on inline integration (Elmqvist, Cellier, and Otter 1995). Mixed-mode integration is described in (Shiela and Olsson 2000). Initialization of DAEs in Modelica, implemented in Dymola, is presented in (Mattsson, Elmqvist, Otter, and Olsson 2002). The old Dymola, meaning the Dynamic Modeling language, one of the most important predecessors of the Modelica language, is briefly described in Appendix F.1.1, page 1149, and in more detail in (Elmqvist 1978; Cellier 1991; Elmqvist, Brück, and Otter 1996). Hybrid capabilities were introduced in 1993 as described in (Elmqvist, Cellier, and Otter 1993). Some of the ideas for information zooming and graphic capabilities in Dymola were already prototyped in the Lics system (Elmqvist and Mattsson 1982).

Appendix A

Glossary

algorithm section: Part of a class definition consisting of the keyword `algorithm` followed by a sequence of statements. Like an equation, an algorithm section relates variables, that is, constrains the values that these variables can take simultaneously. In contrast to an equation section, an algorithm section distinguishes inputs from outputs: An algorithm section specifies how to compute output variables as a function of given input variables. (See Section 2.14.1, page 49 or Section 9.2.1, page 423.)

array or **array variable**: A variable that contains array elements. For an array, the ordering of its elements matters: The kth element in the sequence of elements of an array x is the array element with index `k`, denoted `x[k]`. All elements of an array have the same type. An array element may again be an array, i.e. arrays can be nested. An array element is hence referenced using n indices in general, where n is the number of dimensions of the array. Special cases are matrix (n=2) and vector (n=1). Array integer indices start with 1, not zero, that is, the lower bound is 1. (See Section 2.13, page 47 or Chapter 7, page 311.)

array constructor: An array can be built using the array-function—with the shorthand curly braces {a, b, ...}, and can also include an iterator to build an array of expressions. (See Section 2.13, page 47 or Section 7.2, page 315.)

array element: An element contained in an array. An array element has no identifier. Instead array elements are referenced by array access expressions called indices that use enumeration values or positive integer index values. (See Section 2.13, page 47 or Section 7.4, page 321.)

assignment: A statement of the form `x := expr`. The expression `expr` must not have higher variability than x. (See Section 2.14.1, page 49 or Section 9.2.3, page 425.)

attribute: A property (or kind of record field) contained in a scalar variable, such as `min`, `max`, and `unit`. All attributes are predefined and attribute values can only be defined using a modification, such as in `Real x(unit="kg")`. Attributes cannot be accessed using dot notation, and are not constrained by equations and algorithm sections. For example, in `Real x(unit="kg") = y;` only the values of `x` and `y` are declared to be equal, but not their unit attributes, nor any other attribute of `x` and `y`. (See Section 2.3.5, page 30 or Section 3.9, page 93.)

base class: Class A is called a base class of B if class B extends class A. This relation is specified by an extends clause in B or in one of B's base classes. A class inherits all elements from its base classes, and may modify all non-final elements inherited from base classes. (See Section 4.1, page 136.)

binding equation: Either a declaration equation or an element modification for the value of the variable. A variable with a binding equation has its value bound to some expression. (See Section 2.6, page 33 or Section 8.2, page 349.)

class: A description that generates an object called instance. The description consists of a class definition, a modification environment that modifies the class definition, an optional list of dimension expressions if the class is an array class, and a lexically enclosing class for all classes. (See Section 2.3, page 26 or Chapter 3, page 79.)

class type or **inheritance interface**: Property of a class, consisting of a number of attributes and a set of public or protected elements consisting of element name, element type, and element attributes. (See Section 3.18.2, page 117.)

connector: An instance of a connector class. A connector acts like an interface or port to an object/instance, to which other connectors can be connected. (See Section 5.2, page 188.)

connection: A coupling between two connectors. (See Section 5.3, page 190.)

constant: A constant is a variable declared with the prefix `constant`. Such a variable does not change value. There is also another but similar kind of constant called parameter. Constants and parameters are very similar, but also have the following differences: a named constant with prefix `constant`, but *not* with prefix `parameter`, can be defined in a package, can be imported from a package (Section 10.2.1, page 497), and can be accessed by nested lookup (Section 3.16.1, page 109) from inside a subclass to the class where the constant is defined. (See Section 2.1.3, page 24.)

component: Used in the Modelica Language Specification with the same meaning as *instance* or variable. Since component with that meaning is non-standard terminology not used outside the Modelica community, *instance* is used instead in this book.

component expression: Used in the Modelica Language Specification with the same meaning as *instance expression* in this book. Since component with that meaning is non-standard terminology not used outside the Modelica community, instance expression is used in this book.

declaration assignment: Assignment of the form `x := expression` defined by a variable declaration in a function. This is similar to a declaration equation, but different since an assigned variable usually can be assigned multiple times. (See Section 2.14.3, page 51 or Section 9.3.1, page 438.)

declaration equation: Equation of the form `x = expression` defined by a component declaration. The expression must not have higher variability than the declared component x. Unlike other equations, a declaration equation can be overridden (replaced or removed) by an element modification. (See Section 2.6, page 33 or Section 8.2, page 349.)

derived class or **subclass**: Class B is called derived from A, if B extends A. (See Section 2.4, page 30 or Section 4.1, page 136.)

element: Part of a class definition, one of: class definition, instance declaration, or extends clause. Instance declarations and class definitions are called named elements. An element is either inherited from a base class or local. (See Chapter 3, page 79.)

element modification: Part of a modification, overrides the declaration equation in the class used by the instance generated by the modified element. Example: `vcc(unit="V")=1000`. (See Section 2.6, page 33 or Section 4.2, page 148.)

element redeclaration: Part of a modification, replaces one of the named elements possibly used to build the instance generated by the element that contains the redeclaration. Example: `redeclare type Voltage = Real(unit="V")` replaces `type Voltage`. (See Section 2.5, page 31 or Section 4.3, page 156.)

encapsulated: A class prefix that makes the class not depend on where it is placed in the package-hierarchy, since its lookup is stopped at the class boundary. (See Section 2.16, page 58, Section 3.11.8, page 104 or Section 10.3.2.1, page 502 and Section 10.4.4, page 510.)

equation: An equality relation that is part of a class definition. A scalar equation relates scalar variables, that is, constrains the values that these variables can take simultaneously. When n-1 variables of an equation containing n variables are known, the value of the nth variable can be inferred (solved for). In contrast to a statement in an algorithm section, an equation does not define for which of its variable it is to be solved. Special cases are: initial equations, instantaneous equations, declaration equations. (See Section 2.6, page 33 or Chapter 8, page 347.)

event: Something that occurs instantaneously at a specific time or when a specific condition occurs. Events are for example defined by the condition occurring in a when clause, if clause, or if expression. (See Section 2.15, page 55 or Section 13.2, page 593.)

expandable connector: A connector that automatically expands to include all fields of connected connectors. Flexible construction of information buses is the key idea behind the `expandable connector` construct. An expandable connector acts like an information bus since it is intended for connection to many kinds of components. To make this possible, it automatically expands the expandable connector type to accommodate all the components connected to it with their different interfaces. If an element with a certain name and type is not present, it is added. All variables/fields in an expandable connector are seen as connector instances even if they are not declared as such, i.e., it is possible to connect to for example, a `Real` variable. The syntax of an expandable connector class declaration is simple, just put the `expandable` keyword in front of the `connector` keyword. (See Section 5.9, page 238.)

expression: A term built from operators, function references, variables / named constants, or variable references (referring to variables) and literals. Each expression has a type and a variability. (See Section 2.1.1, page 22, Section 2.1.3, page 24 or Chapter 6, page 267.)

extends clause: An unnamed element of a class definition that uses a name and an optional modification to specify inheritance of a base class of the class defined using the class definition. (See Section 2.4, page 30 or Section 4.1, page 136.)

flattening: The computation that creates a flattened class of a given class, where all inheritance, modification, etc. has been performed and all names resolved, consisting of a flat set of equations, algorithm sections, component declarations, and functions. (See Section 2.20.1, page 64 or Section 3.16.2, page 109.)

function: A class of the specialized class function. (See Section 2.14.3, page 51 or Section 9.3, page 438.)

function subtype: Asub is a function subtype of A iff Asub is a subtype of A and the additional formal parameters of function Asub that are not in function A are defined in such a way (e.g., additional formal parameters need to have default values), that Asub can be called at places where A is called. (See Section 3.19.6, page 130.)

identifier: An atomic (not composed) name. Example: `Resistor` (See Section 2.1.1, page 22 for names of variables or Section 6.3.1, page 268.)

index or **subscript**: An expression, typically of Integer type or the colon symbol (:), used to reference an element (or a range of elements) of an array. (See Section 2.13, page 47 or Section 7.4, page 321)

inheritance interface or **class type**: Property of a class, consisting of a number of attributes and a set of public or protected elements consisting of element name, element type, and element attributes. (See Section 2.4, page 30 or Section 3.18.2, page 117.)

instance: The object generated by a class. The same as component in the Modelica Language Specification (MLS). Here instance is used since the use of the word component in MLS is nonstandard terminology and is also sometimes confusing since models in libraries are often referred to as component models or just components. An instance contains zero or more variables or instances (i.e., components), equations, algorithms, and local classes. An instance has a type. Basically, two instances have same type, if their important attributes are the same and their public components and classes have pair wise equal identifiers and types. More specific type equivalence definitions are given, for example, for functions. (See Section 2.13, page 47 or Section 3.2, page 80.)

instance expression: An *instance expression* (currently called component expression in the Modelica Language Specification) is an expression with some restrictions, that is, it does not refer to instances of models with equations, only models without equations. (See Section 13.6.11, page 713.)

instantaneous: An equation or statement is instantaneous if it holds only at events, that is, at single points in time. The equations and statements of a when-clause are instantaneous. (See Section 2.15, page 55, Section 8.3.5, page 357, or Section 13.2.6, page 613.)

left limit: For an unclocked discrete-time variable `y` at an event, the *left limit* of the value of y at the event is the *value* of `y` *immediately preceding* the event, that is, taking the limit value of `y` while letting time t approach time t_{event} from the left. *Between* events the left limit of `v` is the *same* value as `v`. The left limit of `v` is the same as `pre(y)`, see Figure 13-16, page 609, and Figure 13-17, page 609.

literal: A real, integer, Boolean, enumeration, or string constant value, that is, a literal. Used to build expressions. (See Section 2.1.3, page 24.)

matrix: An array where the number of dimensions is 2. (See Section 2.13, page 47 or Section 7.1, page 311.)

modification or **modifier**: Part of an element. Modifies the instance generated by that element. A modification or modifier contains element modifications and element redeclarations. (Section 2.3.4, page 29 or Section 4.2, page 148.)

name: Sequence of one or more identifiers separated by dots. Used to reference a class or an instance. A class name is resolved in the scope of a class, which defines a set of visible classes. Example name: `Ele.Resistor`. (See Section 2.16, page 58 or Section 3.2, page 80.)

operator record: A record with user-defined operations; defining, for example, multiplication and addition. (See Section 2.14.4, page 52 or Section 9.5.2, page 483.)

parameter: A parameter is a variable declared with the prefix `parameter`. Such a variable does not change value during simulation, but can be assigned a value immediately before simulation (interactively or by a computation, for example, by calling a function). There is also another but similar kind of variable called *constant*. Constants and parameters are very similar, but also have the following differences: a named constant with prefix `constant`, but *not* with prefix `parameter`, can be defined in a package, can be imported from a package (Section 10.2.1, page 497), and can be accessed by nested lookup (Section 3.16.1, page 109) from inside a subclass to the class where the constant is defined. (See Section 2.1.3, page 24.)

parameter—structural parameter: Some parameter "constants" may be *structural parameters*, that is, parameters whose values influence the structure of the model, that is, the set of active equations. (See Section 17.1.5, page 983.)

partial: A class that is incomplete and cannot be instantiated in a simulation model; useful, for example, as a base-class. (See Section 2.9, page 43 or Section 3.11.7, page 104.)

plug-compatible subtype: A type A is a plug-compatible subtype of type B iff A is a subtype of B, and all public components present in A but not in B must be default-connectable. This is used to avoid introducing, via a redeclaration, an unconnected connector in the object/class of type A at a level where a connection is not possible. (See Section 3.19.5, page 127)

predefined type: One of the built-in types `Real`, `Boolean`, `Integer`, `String` and types defined as `enumeration` types. The attribute declarations of the predefined types define attributes such as `min`, `max`, and `unit`. (See Section 2.1.1, page 22 or Section 3.9, page 93.)

prefix: Property of an element of a class definition which can be present or not be present, for example, `final`, `public`, `flow`. (See Section 3.11, page 98.)

real elementary relation: The numerical solution process is halted and an event occurs whenever a Real elementary relation, e.g., `x > 2`, changes its value. The value of such a relation can only be changed at event instants. During the numerical solution process a Real elementary relation has the constant value of the relation from the most recent event instant. (See Section 6.11.1, page 287.)

redeclaration: A modifier with the keyword `redeclare` that changes a replaceable element. (See Section 2.5, page 31 or Section 4.3, page 156.)

replaceable: An element that can be replaced by a different element having a compatible type. (See Section 2.5, page 31 or Section 4.4, page 168.)

scalar or **scalar variable**: A variable that is not an array. (See Section 2.1.1, page 22 and Section 2.13, page 47 or Section 3.10, page 97.)

simple type: Real, Boolean, integer, string and enumeration types. (See Section 2.1.1, page 22, Section or Section 3.9, page 93.)

simulation model: A model which is intended for simulation and fulfills certain conditions which are necessary but not sufficient for simulation (See Section 8.9.2.2, page 390 or Section 3.11.3, page 101). See also the notion of *structurally non-singular*, which is a necessary condition for simulation.

specialized class: One of model, connector, package, record, operator record, block, function, operator function, or type. The class specialization represents assertions regarding the content of the class and restrict its use in other classes, as well as providing enhancements compared to the basic class concept. For example, a class having the package class specialization must only contain classes and constants. (See Section 2.3.3, page 29 or Section 3.8, page 87.)

stream connector: A connector concept for fluid systems. For some fluid applications involving bi-directional flows of matter with associated properties the standard connector approach gives rise to problematic nonlinear systems of equations with Boolean unknowns for the flow directions and singularities around zero flow. To solve the abovementioned problems, the concept of stream connector has been introduced in Modelica. It introduces a third kind of variable in connectors, so-called stream variables, in addition to flow and potential variables. The stream connector concept includes a prefix keyword stream, only used in front of stream variables in stream connector definitions, a built-in operator inStream(c.v), and a built-in operator actualStream(c.v). See Section 5.10, page 245.

structurally non-singular: A system of equations is considered structurally non-singular if it has the same number of equations as variables, and if there exists a perfect matching of the corresponding bipartite graph (Section 17.1.7, page 989) of the equation system or alternatively a BLT-transformation of the corresponding adjacency matrix (Section 17.1.7, page 989) of the equation system. An equation system that is structurally non-singular may still be numerically singular and thus impossible to solve/simulate.

subtype: Relation between types. A is a subtype of B iff a number of properties of A and B are the same and all important elements of B have corresponding elements in A with the same names and their types being subtypes of corresponding element types in B. (See Section 3.18, page 115, and Section 3.19.3, page 125.)

supertype: Relation between types. The inverse of subtype. A is a subtype of B means that B is a supertype or base type of A. (See Section 2.4, page 30 or Section 3.18, page 115, and Section 3.19.3, page 125.)

type: Property of an instance, expression, consisting of a number of attributes and a set of public elements consisting of element name, element type, and element attributes. Note: The concept of class type is a property of a class definition and also includes protected elements. Class type is used in certain subtype relationships, e.g., regarding inheritance. (See Section 3.18, page 115.)

variability: Property of an expression, which can have one of the following four values:

- *continuous*: an expression that may change its value at any point in time.

• *discrete*: may change its value only at events during simulation. Can be clocked or unclocked.
• *unclocked discrete*: may change its value only at unclocked events during simulation.
• *clocked discrete*: may change its value only at clock tick events during simulation.
•*parameter*: constant during the entire simulation, but can be changed before each simulation and appears in tool menus. The default parameter values of models are often non-physical and are recommended to be changed before simulation.
• *constant*: constant during the entire simulation; can be used and defined in a package.
Assignments x := expr and binding equations x = expr must satisfy a variability constraint: The expression must not have a higher variability than variable x. (See Section 2.1.4, page 25 or Section 6.8.1.3, page 278.)

variable: An instance (object) generated by a variable or constant declaration. Special kinds of variables are scalars, arrays, and attributes. (See Section 2.1.1, page 22, Section 2.3.1, page 27 or Section 3.3, page 80.)

variable declaration: An element of a class definition that generates a variable, parameter, or constant. A variable declaration specifies (1) a variable name, that is, an identifier, (2) the class to be flattened in order to generate the variable, and (3) an optional Boolean parameter expression. Generation of the variable is suppressed if this parameter expression evaluates to false. A variable declaration may be overridden by an element redeclaration. (See Section 2.1.1, page 22, Section 2.3.1, page 27, Section 2.1.3, page 24 or Section 3.10, page 97.)

variable reference: An expression containing a sequence of identifiers and indices. A variable reference is equivalent to the referenced object. A variable reference is resolved (evaluated) in the scope of a class (or expression for the case of a local iterator variable). A scope defines a set of visible variables and classes. Example reference: `Ele.Resistor.u[21].r` (See Section 2.1.1, page 22, and Section 2.13, page 47 or Section 6.3, page 268.)

vector: An array where the number of dimensions is 1. (See Section 2.13, page 47 or Section 7.1, page 311.)

Literature

This glossary has been slightly adapted from the Modelica language specification 3.2 (Modelica Association 2010). The first version of the glossary was developed by Jakob Mauss. The current version contains contributions from many Modelica Association members.

Appendix B

Modelica Formal Syntax

B.1 Lexical Conventions

The following syntactic meta symbols are used (extended BNF—Backus Naur Form):

```
[ ]  optional
{ }  repeat zero or more times
|    or
```

The following lexical units are defined. The ones in boldface are the ones used in the grammar, the rest are just internal to the definition of other lexical units.

```
IDENT = NONDIGIT { DIGIT | NONDIGIT } | Q-IDENT
Q-IDENT  = "'" ( Q-CHAR | S-ESCAPE ) { Q-CHAR | S-ESCAPE } "'"
NONDIGIT = "_" | letters "a" to "z" | letters "A" to "Z"
STRING = """ { S-CHAR | S-ESCAPE } """
```

`S-CHAR` = any member of the Unicode character set except double-quote `"""`, and backslash `"\"`. Unicode is defined at http://www.unicode.org; see also briefly Section 6.1, page 267, regarding the character set and Section 10.3.3, page 503, for storing as UTF-8 on files in the file system.

```
Q-CHAR = NONDIGIT | DIGIT | "!" | "#" | "$" | "%" | "&" | "(" | ")" | "*" |
"+" | "," |
        "-" | "." | "/" | ":" | ";" | "<" | ">" | "=" | "?" | "@" | "[" |
"]" | "^" |
        "{" | "}"  | "|" | "~" | " "
S-ESCAPE = "\'" | "\"" | "\?" | "\\" |
           "\a" | "\b" | "\f" | "\n" | "\r" | "\t" | "\v"
DIGIT = "0" | "1" | "2" | "3" | "4" | "5" | "6" | "7" | "8" | "9"
UNSIGNED_INTEGER = DIGIT { DIGIT }
UNSIGNED_NUMBER = UNSIGNED_INTEGER [ "." [ UNSIGNED_INTEGER ] ]
        [ ( "e" | "E" ) [ "+" | "-" ] UNSIGNED_INTEGER ]
```

Notes: The single quotes are part of a quoted identifier. E.g. 'x' and x are different lexical `IDENTs`.

String constant concatenation `"a" "b"` becoming `"ab"` (as in C) is replaced by the `"+"` operator in Modelica.

Modelica uses the same comment syntax as C++ and Java (i.e., `//` signals the start of a line comment and `/*....*/` is a multi-line comment). Comments may contain any Unicode character. Modelica also has structured comments in the form of annotations and string comments.

Description strings (= production "`string_comment`" in the grammar) and strings in annotations (= `STRING` with production `annotation` in the grammar) may contain any member of the Unicode character set. All other strings have to contain only the subset of Unicode characters identical with the 7-bit US-ASCII character set. As a consequence, operators like ">" or "<", and external functions only operate on ASCII strings and not on Unicode strings. Within a description string the tags `<HTML>` and `</HTML>` or `<html>` and `</html>` optionally define begin and end of content that is HTML encoded.

In the Grammar below, boldface words denote keywords of the Modelica language. Keywords are reserved words and may not be used as identifiers, with the exception of `initial` which is a keyword in section headings, but it is also possible to call the function `initial`(), and `end` which is used to denote the upper dimension size bound in array slices in addition to being used as a keyword in `end while`, `end if`, and `end for`.

B.2 Modelica Grammar

B.2.1 Stored Definition – Within

```
stored_definition:
   [ within [ name ] ";" ]
   { [ final ] class_definition ";" }
```

B.2.2 Class Definition

```
class_definition :
   [ encapsulated ] class_prefixes
   class_specifier

class_prefixes :
   [ partial ]
   ( class | model | [ operator ] record | block |
     [ expandable ] connector | type |
     package | [ ( pure | impure ) ] [ operator ] function | operator )

class_specifier :
   long_class_specifier | short_class_specifier | der_class_specifier

long_class_specifier :
     IDENT string_comment composition end IDENT
   | extends IDENT [ class_modification ] string_comment composition
           end IDENT

short_class_specifier :
     IDENT "=" base_prefix name [ array_subscripts ]
               [ class_modification ] comment
   | IDENT "=" enumeration "(" ( [enum_list] | ":" ) ")" comment

der_class_specifier:
     IDENT "=" der "(" name "," IDENT { "," IDENT } ")" comment

base_prefix :
       type_prefix

enum_list    : enumeration_literal { "," enumeration_literal}

enumeration_literal : IDENT comment

composition  :
   element_list
   { public element_list |
     protected element_list |
     equation_section |
     algorithm_section
   }
   [ external [ language_specification ]
              [ external_function_call ] [ annotation ] ";" ]
   [ annotation  ";" ]

language_specification :
   STRING
```

```
external_function_call :
   [ component_reference "=" ]
   IDENT "(" [ expression_list ] ")"

element_list :
   { element ";" }

element :
   import_clause |
   extends_clause |
   [ redeclare ]
   [ final ]
   [ inner ] [ outer ]
   ( ( class_definition | component_clause) |
     replaceable ( class_definition | component_clause)
        [constraining_clause comment])

import_clause :
   import ( IDENT "=" name | name ["." ( "*" | "{" import_list "}" ) ] )
comment

import_list :
   IDENT [ "," import_list ]
```

B.2.3 Extends

```
extends_clause :
   extends name [ class_modification ] [annotation]

constraining_clause :
   constrainedby name [ class_modification ]
```

B.2.4 Component Clause

```
component_clause:
   type_prefix type_specifier [ array_subscripts ] component_list

type_prefix :
   [ flow | stream ]
   [ discrete | parameter | constant ] [ input | output ]

type_specifier :
   name

component_list :
   component_declaration { "," component_declaration }

component_declaration :
   declaration [ condition_attribute ] comment

condition_attribute:
   if expression

declaration :
   IDENT [ array_subscripts ] [ modification ]
```

B.2.5 Modification

```
modification :
   class_modification [ "=" expression ]
 | "=" expression
 | ":=" expression

class_modification :
   "(" [ argument_list ] ")"

argument_list :
   argument { "," argument }

argument :
   element_modification_or_replaceable
 | element_redeclaration

element_modification_or_replaceable:
  [ each ] [ final ] ( element_modification | element_replaceable)

element_modification :
  name [ modification ] string_comment

element_redeclaration :
   redeclare [ each ] [ final ]
( ( short_class_definition | component_clause1) | element_replaceable )

element_replaceable:
  replaceable ( short_class_definition | component_clause1)
        [constraining_clause]

component_clause1 :
   type_prefix type_specifier component_declaration1

component_declaration1 :
   declaration comment

short_class_definition :
   class_prefixes short_class_specifier
```

B.2.6 Equations

```
equation_section :
  [ initial ] equation { equation ";" }

algorithm_section :
  [ initial ] algorithm { statement ";" }

equation :
  ( simple_expression "=" expression
    | if equation
    | for equation
    | connect clause
    | when equation
    | name function_call_args )
  comment

statement :
  ( component_reference ( ":=" expression | function_call_args )
```

```
        | "(" output_expression_list ")" ":=" component_reference
function_call_args
      | break
      | return
      | if_statement
      | for_statement
      | while_statement
      | when_statement )
   comment

if equation :
     if expression then
        { equation ";" }
     { elseif expression then
        { equation ";" }
     }
     [ else
        { equation ";" }
     ]
     end if

if_statement :
     if expression then
        { statement ";" }
     { elseif expression then
        { statement ";" }
     }
     [ else
        { statement ";" }
     ]
     end if

for equation :
   for for_indices loop
        { equation ";" }
   end for

for_statement :
   for for_indices loop
        { statement ";" }
   end for

for_indices :
   for_index {"," for_index}

for_index:
   IDENT [ in expression ]

while_statement :
   while expression loop
        { statement ";" }
   end while

when equation :
   when expression then
        { equation ";" }
   { elsewhen expression then
        { equation ";" } }
   end when
   when expression then
```

```
when_statement :
    { statement ";" }
  { elsewhen expression then
    { statement ";" } }
  end when

connect_clause :
  connect "(" component_reference "," component_reference ")"
```

B.2.7 Expressions

```
expression :
   simple_expression
 | if expression then expression { elseif expression then expression }
   else expression

simple_expression :
   logical_expression [ ":" logical_expression [ ":" logical_expression ] ]

logical_expression :
   logical_term { or logical_term }

logical_term :
   logical_factor { and logical_factor }

logical_factor :
   [ not ] relation

relation :
   arithmetic_expression [ rel_op arithmetic_expression ]

rel_op :
   "<" | "<=" | ">" | ">=" | "==" | "<>"

arithmetic_expression :
   [ add_op ] term { add_op term }

add_op :
   "+" | "-" | ".+" | ".-"

term :
   factor { mul_op factor }

mul_op :
   "*" | "/" | ".*" | "./"

factor :
   primary [ ("^" | ".^") primary ]

primary :
   UNSIGNED_NUMBER
 | STRING
 | false
 | true
 | ( name | der | initial ) function_call_args
 | component_reference
 | "(" output_expression_list ")"
 | "[" expression_list { ";" expression_list } "]"
 | "{" function_arguments "}"
 | end
```

```
name :
   [ "." ] IDENT { "." IDENT }

component_reference :
   [ "." ] IDENT [ array_subscripts ] { "." IDENT [ array_subscripts ] }

function_call_args :
   "(" [ function_arguments ] ")"

function_arguments :
   function_argument [ "," function_arguments | for for_indices ]
 | named_arguments


named_arguments: named_argument [ "," named_arguments ]

named_argument: IDENT "=" function_argument

function_argument :
   function name "(" [ named_arguments ] ")" | expression

output_expression_list:
   [ expression ] { "," [ expression ] }

expression_list :
   expression { "," expression }

array_subscripts :
   "[" subscript { "," subscript } "]"

subscript :
   ":" | expression

comment :
   string_comment [ annotation ]

string_comment :
   [ STRING { "+" STRING } ]

annotation :
   annotation class_modification
```

B.3 MetaModelica 2.0 Grammar Extensions

B.3.1 ClassDefinition

```
class definition :
        [encapsulated][package][IDENT]restriction class_specifier
      | restriction class_specifier

restriction :
      [partial] | uniontype | [pure | impure] function |
       type | record

class_specifier :
      long_class_specifier | short_class_specifier

long_class_specifier :
     IDENT [string_comment] composition end IDENT

short_class_specifier :
```

Same as in standard Modelica, see Section B.2.2 Class Definition.

```
string_comment :
```

Same as in standard Modelica, see Section B.2.7 Expressions.

```
composition :
```

Same as in standard Modelica, see Section B.2.2 Class Definition.

B.3.2 Component Clause

```
component_clause :
     type_prefix type_specifier [array_subscripts]component_list

type_prefix :
     [input | output]| [parameter | discrete | constant]

type_specifier :
```

Same as in standard Modelica, see Section B.2.4 Component Clause.

```
component_list :
```

Same as in standard Modelica, see Section B.2.4 Component Clause.

B.3.3 Modification

```
modification :
```

Same as in standard Modelica, see Section B.2.5 Modification.

B.3.4 Algorithm

```
algorithm_section :
     algorithm { algorithm_statements ";" }

algorithm_statements :
```

Same as in standard Modelica, see Section B.2.6 Equations.

B.3.5 Equation

```
equationsection :
    equation { equation_statements ";" }

equation_statements :
```

Same as in standard Modelica, see Section B.2.6 Equations.

B.3.6 Expressions

```
expression :
      simple_expression
    | matchstatements

simple_expression :
```

same as in Standard Modelica, see Section B.2.7 Expressions.

```
matchstatements :
     match expression [matchlocal] cases end match
   | matchcontinue expression [matchlocal] cases end matchcontinue

matchlocal :
    [local element_list]

cases :
    case casearg [equationsection] then expression ";"
  | else [equationsection] then expression ";"

casearg :
   expression

element_list :
```

Same as in standard Modelica, see Section B.2.2 Class Definition.

B.4 Optimization Grammar Extensions

B.4.1 ClassDefinition

```
class_definition :
     restriction class_attribute class_specifier

restriction :
     optimization

class_attribute :
     IDENT { "(" named_arguments ")" } end IDENT

class_specifier :
     [string_comment] classparts
```

```
classparts :
     element_list
       {
        public element_item
      | protected element_item
      | equation equation_section }
element_list :
```
Same as in standard Modelica, see Section B.2.2 Class Definition.

```
string_comment :
```
Same as in standard Modelica, see Section B.2.7 Expressions.

```
named_arguments :
```
Same as in standard Modelica, see Section B.2.7 Expressions.

B.4.2 Component Clause

```
component_clause :
        type_prefix type_specifier [array_subscripts] component_list

type_prefix :
        [input | output]| [parameter | discrete | constant]

type_specifier :
```
Same as in standard Modelica, see Section B.2.4 Component Clause.

```
component_list :
```
Same as in standard Modelica, see Section B.2.4 Component Clause.

B.4.3 Modification

```
modification :
```
Same as in standard Modelica, see Section B.2.4 B.2.4 Component Clause.

B.4.4 Equation

```
equationsection :
    equation { equation_statements ";" }

equation_statements :
```
Same as in standard Modelica, see Section B.2.6 Equations.

B.4.5 Expression

```
expression :
```
Same as standard Modelica, see Section B.2.7 Expressions.

B.5 ParModelica Grammar Extensions

B.5.1 Class Definition

```
class_definition :
        [encapsulated][package][IDENT]restriction class_specifier
       | restriction class_specifier

restriction :
       model | block | [parallel | parkernel] function


class_specifier :
       long_class_specifier

long_class_specifier :
       IDENT [string_comment] classparts end IDENT

classparts :
       element_list
        {
          public element_item
        | protected element_item
        | algorithm algorithm_section
        | equation equation_section
          }

element_list :
```

Same as in standard Modelica, see Section B.2.2 Class Definition.

```
string_comment :
```

Same as in standard Modelica, see Section B.2.7 Expressions.

B.5.2 Component clause

```
component_clause  :
       type_prefix type_specifier [array_subscripts] component_list

type_prefix :
        [parlocal | parglobal]|[input | output]
       |[parameter | discrete | constant]

type_specifier :
```

Same as in standard Modelica, see Section B.2.4 Component Clause.

```
component_list :
```

Same as in standard Modelica, see Section B.2.4 Component Clause.

B.5.3 Modification

```
modification :
```

Same as in standard Modelica,refer section A.6.5 “Modification”.

B.5.4 Algorithm

```
algorithm_section :
       algorithm { algorithm_statements ";" }

algorithm_statements :
        parfor_algorithm
      | modelica_algorithm_constructs

modelica_algorithm_constructs :
```
Same as in standard Modelica, see Section B.2.6 Equations.

```
parfor_algorithm :
       parfor for_indices loop
       { algorithm_section }
       end parfor

for_indices :
       for_indices {"," for_index}

for_index :
       IDENT [ in expression ]
```

B.5.5 Equation

```
equationsection :
    equation { equation_statements ";" }

equation_statements :
       parfor_equation
     | modelica_equation_constructs

modelica_equation_constructs :
```
Same as in standard Modelica, see Section B.2.6 Equations.

```
parfor_equation :
     parfor for_indices loop
      { equationsection}
     end parfor

for_indices :
     for_indices {"," for_index}

for_index :
     IDENT [ in expression ]
```

B.5.6 Expressions

```
expression :
```
Same as in standard Modelica, see Section B.2.7 Expressions.

Appendix C

Solutions to Exercises

Chapter 2

Exercise 2–1:

A *class* is a fundamental unit of modeling in Modelica, providing the structure for an object. Classes can contain equations, where the computations are performed.

Since `x + y = sum` is an equation and not an assignment, the equation can also be written as sum `= x + y` without changing the meaning of the expression.

```
class Add
  parameter Integer x = 1;
  parameter Integer y = 2;
  Real sum;
equation
  sum = x + y;
end Add;
```

Exercise 2–2:

Instances are notions of classes and objects.

```
class DogInst
  Dog d;
end DogInst;

class DogTim
  Dog t(name="Tim");
end DogTim;
```

Exercise 2–3:

```
function Average
  input Real a;
  input Real b;
  output Real result;
algorithm
  result := (a + b) / 2;
end Average;

class AverageTest
  Real res;
equation
  res = Average(4, 6);
end AverageTest;
```

Exercise 2–4:

partial class introduces a datatype. A partial class is incomplete, so you cannot create an instance of it.

class introduces a variant.

extends connects a variant to a datatype.

Exercise 2–5:

```
record Bicycle
  Boolean has_wheels = true;
  Integer nrOfWheels = 2;
end Bicycle;

class ChildrensBike
  extends Bicycle;
  Boolean forKids = true;
end ChildrensBike;
```

Exercise 2–6:

```
class Birthyear
  parameter Integer thisYear = 2002;
  // Declaration equation
  parameter Integer age;
protected
  Integer birthYear;
equation
  birthYear = thisYear - age;
  // Normal equation
end Birthyear;

class MartinsBirthyear
Birthyear martinsBirthyear(age = 30);
  // Modification equation
end MartinsBirthyear;
```

Exercise 2–7:

There are more variables than equations, which is typical for partial classes; the keyword partial is therefore missing.

Exercise 2–8:

```
record Test
  Boolean[2] truthvalues = {false, true};
  Integer[5] ints = {13, 2, 5, 4, 87};
  String[3, 4] strings = {{"blue", "Martin",
                          "yellow", "cake"},
                {"Anna", "sun", "star", "heaven"},
                {"candy", "Sofia", "sweet",
"Balthasar"}};
  Real[1, 5] reals = {{4.3, 7.132, 6.5, 4.0, 2.1}};
end Test;
```

Exercise 2–9:

Yes. (You didn't think so, did you?)

Exercise 2–10:

```
class Average
  parameter Real a;
  parameter Real b;
  Real result;
algorithm
  result := (a + b) / 2;
end Average;

class AverageInst
  Average aver(a = 15, b = 23);
end AverageInst;
```

Exercise 2–11:

Note that the sum is calculated in an equation section to show that it is possible to mix algorithm and equation sections in a class.

```
class AverageExtended
  parameter Real a;
  parameter Real b;
  parameter Real c;
  parameter Real d;
  Real sum;
  Real aver;
  Real nrOfVariables = 4;
equation
  sum = a + b + c + d;
algorithm
  aver := sum / nrOfVariables;
end AverageExtended;

class AverageExtInst
  AverageExtended aver(a = 15, b = 23);
end AverageExtInst;
```

Exercise 2–12:

```
class Lights
  Integer switch;
  Boolean off = true;
equation
  if off then
    switch = 0;
  else
    switch = 1;
  end if;
end Lights;

class LightSwitch
  Boolean on;
equation
  when sample(5, 5) then
    if rem(time, 5) == 0 then
      on = true;
    else
      on = false;
    end if;
  end when;
end LightSwitch;
```

Exercise 2–13:

A *package* is a restricted and enhanced class that is primarily used to manage name spaces and organize Modelica code. A package has the restrictions of only containing declarations of classes, including all kinds of restricted classes, and constants. Variable declarations are not allowed.

```
package MyPackage
  function division
    input Real a;
    input Real b;
    output Real result;
  algorithm
    result := a / b;
  end division;
  constant Integer k = 5;
end MyPackage;

class MyPackInst
  Real x = MyPackage.division(10, 5);
end MyPackInst;
```

Chapter 3

Exercise 3–1:

```
class Multiply
  parameter Real x = 2;
  parameter Real y = 3;
  Real product;
equation
  product = x*y;
end Multiply;

model Multiply
  parameter Real x = 2;
  parameter Real y = 3;
  Real product;
equation
  product = x*y;
end Multiply;
```

Exercise 3–2:

```
function AddTen
  input Real x;
  output Real result;
algorithm
  result := x + 10;
end AddTen;

class AddTenCall
  Real res;
equation
  res = AddTen(3.5);
end AddTenCall;
```

Exercise 3–3:

```
class Addition
  class Add
    Real x = 1;
    Real y = 2;
    Real z;
  equation
    x + y = z;
  end Add;
end Addition;
```

Exercise 3–4:

```
class StudentInst
  Student s;
end StudentInst;

class StudentAlice
  Student stud(name = "Alice", nrOfBooks = 65);
end StudentAlice;

class StudentBurt
  Student stud(name = "Burt", nrOfBooks = 32);
end StudentBurt;
```

Exercise 3–5:

A *variable* is a place to store a piece of information. Just as you might store a friend's phone number in your own memory, you can store this information in a computer's memory. Variables are your way of accessing your computer's memory.

There are two different kinds of variables, *discrete-time* and *continuous-time* variables. Discrete-time variables change value only at event instants, whereas continuous-time variables may change value both between and at events.

A parameter is a special kind of constant, which is implemented as a static variable that is initialized once and never changes its value during a specific execution.

Exercise 3–6:

```
class Matrices
  parameter Real m1[2, 3];
  // A matrix with two rows and three columns
  parameter Real m2[5];
  // An array with 5 elements
  Real m3[1, 6];
  // A matrix with one row and six columns constant
  Real[2, 1] m4 = {{4}, {7}};
  //Matrix with two rows and one column
end Matrices;
```

Exercise 3–7:

If nothing is specified, the default start value of all numerical variables is zero, apart from function results and local variables where it is unspecified. Other start values can be specified by setting the start attribute of instance variables. You can also set the initial value like this:

```
when (initial())
  x_dot = -5;
end when;


class Variables
  Real length1(start = 3.5);        // Initial value 3.5
  Real length2(start = 2.0);        // Initial value 2
  Real length3;   // Initial value 0 or (start = 0)
end Variables;
```

Exercise 3–8:

```
record Dog
  Integer nrOfLegs = 4;
  String name = "dog";
end Dog;
```

Exercise 3–9:

A *type* can conceptually be viewed as a set of values. If x has the type Real, this means that x belongs to the set of values represented by the type Real.

The *subtype* relation between types is analogous to the subset relation between sets. If a type A1 is a subtype of A, the set of values corresponding to type A1 is a subset of the set of values corresponding to type A.

The *supertype* relation is the inverse of the subtype relation.

```
class Room
  Real length     = 5;
  Real width      = 4.3;
  Real height     = 2.1;
end Room;
```

Exercise 3–10:

```
class Access
  parameter Real a;
  Real b;
  Real c;
protected
  Integer d, e;
equation
  b = 2.0;
  c = 1.3;
  d = 5;
  e = 7;
end Access;


class AccessInst
  Access acc(a = 7.4);
end AccessInst;
```

Chapter 4

Exercise 4–1:

```
class Bird
  extends Animal;
  Integer wings = 2;
  Integer legs  = 2;
  Boolean CanFly = true;
end Bird;
```

`talks` still have the value `false`.

Exercise 4–2:

```
partial class Vehicle
  Real speed;
end Vehicle;


class Car
  extends Vehicle;
  Real motorEffect;
end Car;


class Boat
  extends Vehicle;
  Real boatWeight;
end Boat;


class Train
  extends Vehicle;
  Real nrOfCarriages;
end Train;

class Bicycle
  extends Vehicle;
  Real NrOfGears;
end Bicycle;


class TrainInst
  Train superTrain(nrOfCarriages = 55);
end TrainInst;
```

Exercise 4–3:

```
class Person
  String name;
  Real weight;
protected
  Integer ID;
end Person;


class Employed
  extends Person;
protected
  Real salary;
end Employed;


class Programmer
  extends Employed;
  String favProgLang;
  Boolean drinksJoltCola;
end Programmer;
```

- `salary` and `ID` are protected variables in `Employed`.
- In the class `Employed2` `name`, `weight`, `salary` and `ID` are protected variables.

Exercise 4–4:

A *modifier* modifies one or more declaration(s) from an inherited class by changing some aspect(s) of the inherited declarations.

```
class Test
  parameter Integer test(start = 3, min = -22,
                    fixed = true);
end Test;
```

Exercise 4–5:

```
class ModArray
  Integer A1[5](fixed = true);
  // Modifies the fixed value for the whole array
  Boolean truthvalues[2](start = {false, false});
  // Modifies the start value for the whole array
  Real A2[2,2](unit[1,2] = "kV");
  /* Modifies the start value for a certain place in the
  matrix */
  Integer A3[2,3](start = {{1, 0, 5}, {}});
  /* Modifies the start value for the first row in the
  matrix */
  String A4[2,2](start = {{"Pippi", "Pippi"},
                          {"Pippi", "Pippi"}});
end ModArray;
```

Exercise 4–7:

```
class Temperature
  parameter Real temp(unit = "degC");
end Temperature;

class Temp20 = Temperature(temp = 20);

model Temp20b
  extends Temperature(temp = 20);
end Temp20b;
```

Exercise 4–8:

```
class Today
  Date date(dayName(nameOfDay = "Wednesday"), date = 2,
  month = "October", year = 2002);
  LunchAppointment lunchApp(lunchTime = 12,
  lunchDate =    "Frederick");
end Today;

class Tomorrow
  Date date(dayName.nameOfDay = "Thursday", date = 3,
  month = "October", year = 2002);
  LunchAppointment lunchApp(lunchTime = 12, lunchDate =
  "Steven");
end Tomorrow;
```

Exercise 4–9:

```
class Point
  parameter Real x;
  parameter Real y;
  parameter Real z;
end Point;

class Redeclaration
  replaceable Point P(x = 1, y = 2, z = 3);
end Redeclaration;

class MyPoint
  extends Point(z = 4);
end MyPoint;

class PointRed
  Redeclaration myPoint(redeclare MyPoint P);
end PointRed;
```

No, because then MyPoint would not be a subclass of Point.

Exercise 4–10:

```
class A
  parameter Real salt;
end A;

class Asub          // Asub is a subtype of A
  extends A(salt = 20);
  parameter Real pepper;
  parameter Real basil;
end Asub;

class AInst
  replaceable A a(salt = 100);
end AInst;
```

The result after redeclaration is: `Asub a(salt = 1, pepper = 2)`

```
class AIred
  extends AInst(redeclare Asub a(pepper = 200));
end AIred;

class AIred2
  AInst t(redeclare Asub a(pepper = 200));
end AIred2
```

Exercise 4–11:

```
class MoreRed
  parameter Real v1[3];
  parameter Real v2[:];
  Integer x = 2;
end MoreRed;
```

Notice that you don't need the keyword replaceable for v1 and v2.

```
class MoreRed2 = MoreRed(redeclare parameter Integer x,
                         redeclare parameter Real v1[5],
                         redeclare parameter Real v2[12]);
```

Exercise 4–12:

```
class Bananas
  Banana lightBanana(unit = "g");       // Correct
  Banana swedishBanana(fixed = true);
  // Error, since fixed is declared final
end Bananas;
```

Exercise 4–13:

- It is a way of expressing classes or programs as generic patterns.
- Because instead of writing many similar pieces of code with essentially the same structure, you can directly express the general structure and provide the specific information as parameters.

Chapter 5

Exercise 5–2:

Inside connectors are `C1.y`, `C2.u`, `C3.u`. Outside connectors are `C1.u`, `C2.y`, `C3.y`.

The following connection equations are generated:

`C1.y = C2.y = C3.u`

Exercise 5–3:

The models including instances `m5` and `m6` with resistors in parallel:

```
model Resistor
  outer Pin ntop, pbot;
end Resistor;

model NResistors
  inner Pin   ntop, pbot;
  Pin         n, p;
  parameter Integer n=0;
  Resistor    rs[n];
equation
  connect(n, ntop);
  connect(p, pbot);
end NResistors;

model Env
  NResistors m5(n=5), m6(n=6);
end Env;
```

Exercise 5–4:

An expandable connector is a connector that expands to accommodate all the variables within the connectors connected to it.

When two or more expandable connectors are connected, each is augmented with the variables that are only declared in the other connector(s). This is very useful for modeling information buses.

An expandable connector cannot directly contain flow variables, however it can contain connectors with flow variables

Chapter 6

Exercise 6–1:

- A *keyword* is a reserved word.
- Because they are reserved for constructing elements in the Modelica language, they cannot be used as identifiers.
- For example: `end, class, and, connect, else` and `parameter`. But there are over 40 of them, so you can find many more.
- `Real, Integer, Boolean and String.`
- An unnamed constant that has different form depending on their type.
- `true`, one of the two boolean literal values.

- The freedom of the expression to change value during simulation.
- The degrees of variability are constant, parameter, unclocked discrete-time, clocked discrete-time, and continuous-time variability.
    - Constant expressions have constant variability, i.e., never change value. In constant expressions the time derivative is equal to zero.
    - Parameter expressions have parameter variability, remain constant during time-dependent simulation, and have time derivative equal to zero.
    - Discrete-time expressions:
        - They have discrete-time variability meaning that they are piecewise constant and change their values only at event instants during simulation.
        - Time derivative is equal to zero.
        - These expressions may include constant or parameter expressions or discrete-time variables, as well as applications of operators and functions with discrete-time arguments.
        - Unclocked discrete-time – values are defined at any time. Clocked discrete-time values are defined and change only at clock tick events.
    - Continuous-time expressions:
        - They have continuous-time variability and may change their values at any time during simulation.
        - They may include constant, parameter, and discrete-time expressions as well as continuous-time Real variables, as well as applications of operators and functions.

Exercise 6–2:

The constant `m` cannot be set to a nonconstant value, in this case `h + 28`.

```
class Happy
  Boolean right(fixed = true);
  parameter Integer h = 15;
  constant Integer m = h + 28;
  parameter Real k = 32;
end Happy;
```

Exercise 6–3:

The first one is allowed because an integer can be converted to a real implicitly.

However the conversion from `Real` to `Integer` needs to be explicit, hence the second statement is incorrect. It can be changed to `Integer i1= integer(r)+5;`

Exercise 6–4:

A conditional expression in Modelica returns one of several values depending on one or more condition(s).

```
der(x) =
  if (a > 0) then x elseif (a == 0) then 0 else -x;
```

The two forms (statement, expression) are equivalent.

Chapter 7

Exercise 7–1:

```
record Matrix
  Real m1[7] = {17.1, 62.7, 7.5, 37.0, 25, 4.121,
  12.333336};
  Integer m2[4, 2] = {{44, 5}, {2, 800}, {7, 23},
  {2032, 77}};
  String[1, 5] m3 = {{"Magnus", "circle", "boy",
  "Marina", "Miranda"}};
  String m4[:];
  Boolean m5[:, 2];
  Boolean m6[0];
end Matrix;
```

Exercise 7–2:

The expanded type is `Student[42, 35]`.

Exercise 7–3:

- A range vector is a vector containing a range of numeric values increasing or decreasing by a fixed increment or decrement value for each additional element.
- {5, 10, 15, 20, 25}

Exercise 7–4:

- v1 has the value {3, 4, 5, 6, 7, 8}
- v2 has the value {-20, -19, -18, -17, -16, -15, -14, -13, -12, -11}
- v3 has the value {11.3, 12.3, 13.3, 14.3, 15.3}
- v4 is an empty vector
- v5 has the value {1.1, 2.1, 3.1}

These vectors are just examples of how the vectors can be constructed. There is more than one solution to every vector.

```
class RangeVectors2
  Real        v1[5]        = 15.0 : 3 : 27.0;
  Real        v2[3]        = -6.5 : -2 : -10.5;
  Integer v3[0];
end RangeVectors2;
```

Exercise 7–5:

- The arrays that are concatenated must have the same number of dimensions.
- The concatenation dimension k, that is used, must exist.
- Arrays must have identical dimension sizes with the exception of the size of dimension k
- Argument arrays must have equivalent maximally expanded element types, where the element type of the result array is the element type of the maximally expanded type of the arguments.
- array1 has the result {{22, 34, 15}, {66, 78, 52}}
- array2 has the result {{22, 34, 15}, {66, 78, 52}}
- array3 has the result {{11, 12}, {13, 14}}
- array4 has the result {{7, 2}, {5, 42}, {24, 74}}
- array5 has the result {{7, 2}, {5, 42}, {24, 74}}
- array6 has the result {{1, 2}, {11, 12}, {13, 14}, {3, 4}}
- array7 has the result {{1, 2, 35, 73}, {72, 51, 12, 23}}

These are examples of how you could concatenate the arrays in the exercise.

```
class MyArrayConcat
  Real[2, 2] myArray1 = cat(1, {{1, 2}}, {{11, 12}});
  Real[1, 4] myArray2 = cat(2, {{1, 2}}, {{11, 12}});
  Real[2, 4] myArray3 = cat(2, [21, 32, 43; 66, 77, 55],
  [12; 24]);
  Real[4, 2] myArray4 = cat(1, [10, 40; 55, 78],
  [20, 50; 31, 22]);
end MyArrayConcat;
```

- myArray1 has the result {{1, 2}, {11, 12}}
- myArray2 has the result {{1, 2, 11, 12}}
- myArray3 has the result {{21, 32, 43, 12}, {66, 77, 55, 24}}
- myArray4 has the result {{10, 40}, {55, 78}, {20, 50}, {31, 22}}

Exercise 7–6:

This is an example of how you could concatenate the arrays in the exercise.

```
class MoreConcat
  Real[1, 2, 1] a1 = {{{1}, {2}}};
  Real[1, 2, 2] a2 = {{{3, 4}, {5, 6}}};
  Real[1, 2, 3] a3 = {{{7, 8, 9}, {10, 11, 12}}};
  Real[1, 2, 6] aReady;
equation
  aReady = cat(3, a1, a2, a3);
end MoreConcat;
```

- aReady has the result {{1, 3, 4, 7, 8, 9}, {2, 5, 6, 10, 11, 12}}

Exercise 7–7:

```
class ArrayIndexing
  Real array1[2, 3];
  Real array2[2, 3];
algorithm
  array1 := fill(1, 2, 3);
  array2 := fill(1, 2, 3);
  array1[1,1] := 10;
  array1[2,1] := 23;
  array2[2,1] := 100;
  array2[2,2] := 100;
  array2[2,3] := 100;
end ArrayIndexing;
```

- The result of array2 {{10, 1, 1}, {23, 1, 1}}
- The result of array2 {{1, 1, 1}, {100, 100, 100}}

```
class ArrayIndexing2
  Real array1[2, 2] = fill(9, 2, 2);
  Real array2[2, 4] = fill(7, 2, 4);
  Real v1[2] = {2, 20};
  Real v2[4] = {6, 7, 8, 9};
  Real array1[2] = v1;
end ArrayIndexing2;
```

- The result of array1 is {{9, 9}, {2, 20}}
- The result of array2 {{7, 7, 7, 7}, {6, 7, 8, 9}}

```
class Slice
  Real[3, 3] V = {{22, 14, 71}, {33, 41, 17},
                  {44, 11, 77}};
  Real[3, 2] W = {{12, 13}, {23, 88}, {99, 43}};
  Real[5]         Y = {23, 24, 25, 26, 27};
  Real v1[3] = V[:, 1];
  Real v2[3] = V[3, :];
  Real v3[1] = V[3, {2}];
  Real v4[3] = W[:, 2];
  Real v5[2] = Y[{1, 2}];
  Real v6[2] = W[3, {1, 2}];
  Real v7[2] = V[3, 1:2];
  Real v8[2] = Y[3:4];
  Real v9[3] = Y[1:2:5];
end Slice;
```

- v1 gets the value {22, 33, 44}.
- v2 gets the third row of V, i.e., the vector {44, 11, 77}.
- v3 gets the second element (in brackets) in the third row in V, i.e., {11}.
- v4 gets the second row of W, i.e., {13, 88, 43}
- v5 gets the first and second elements of Y, i.e., {23, 24}
- v6 gets the first and second elements on the third row of W, i.e., {99, 43}
- v7 gets the first and second elements of the third row of V, i.e., {44, 11, 77}
- v8 gets the 3:rd through 4:th elements of Y as {25, 26}
- v9 gets the 1:st to 5:th elements step 2 elements as {23, 25, 27}

Exercise 7–8:

```
class Concatenate
  Real[1, 2] A = [50, 32];
  Real[2, 1] B = [3; 7];
  Real[5]     a = {4, 9, 7, 5, 2};
  Real[1, 3] V1 = [A, 60];
  Real[1, 4] V2 = [V1, 50];
  Real[1, 3] V3 = cat(2, A, {{20}});
  Real[3, 1] V4 = [B; 60];
  Real[3, 1] V5 = cat(1, B, {{20}});
  Real[6] v = cat(1, a, {18});
end Concatenate;
```

i)	The result is {50, 32, 60}
ii)	The result is {50, 32, 60, 50}
iii)	The result is {50, 32, 20}
iv)	The result is {{3}, {7}, {60}}
v)	The result is {{3}, {7}, {20}}
vi)	The result is {4, 9, 7, 5, 2, 18}

Exercise 7–9:

- No; elementwise operations for the combination of an array and a scalar operand are not defined for addition.
- No; elementwise operations for the combination of an array and a scalar operand are not defined for subtraction.
- Oh, yes! The result is {22, 28, 24}.

Exercise 7–10:

```
class MatrixMultiplication
  Real M1[2, 3] = [2, 3, 4; 5, 6, 7];
  Real M2[3, 2] = [5, 6; 3, 2; 1, 7];
  Real prod[2, 2];
equation
  prod = M1*M2;
end MatrixMultiplication;
```

Exercise 7–11:

- The result of mult1 is 4.
- The result of mult1 is {8, 8}.
- The result of mult1 is {{4, 4}, {4, 4}}.
- The result of mult1 is {84}.
- Oh, yes! The result is {4, 3.5, 2.5, 4.25, 3}.
- No; Elementwise operations for dividing a scalar operand with an array are not defined for division.

```
class Exponent
  Real m[2, 2];
equation
  m = {{1, 3}, {4, 5}} ^ 2;
end Exponent;
```

The result is {{13, 18}, {24, 37}}.

Chapter 8

Exercise 8–1:

- Equations are more powerful than assignments, since one equation can express several different assignments.
- A declaration equation is the equation used when declaring a variable, usually constants or parameters.

Such equations are actually required for constants, but are optional for parameters. It is also possible to specify a declaration equation for a normal state variable, but this will make the variable behave as a kind of constant.

- Modifier equations occur, for example, in a variable declaration when there is a need to modify the default value of an attribute of the variable. A modifier equation replaces the declaration equation, if present, for an attribute of the specific type.

Exercise 8–2:

```
class Repetitive
  Integer rep[7];
equation
  for i in 1:7 loop
    rep[i] = 15;
  end for;
end Repetitive;

class RepetitiveWithoutFor
  Integer rep[7];
equation
  rep[1] = 15;
  rep[2] = 15;
  rep[3] = 15;
  rep[4] = 15;
  rep[5] = 15;
  rep[6] = 15;
  rep[7] = 15;
end RepetitiveWithoutFor;
```

Exercise 8–3:

```
class Repeat
  Integer repeater[4];
equation
  for i in 1:4 loop
    repeater[i] = i + 3;
  end for;
end Repeat;

function Rapper
  input Integer rap[:];
  output Integer sum = 0;
algorithm
  for i in 1:size(rap,1) loop
    sum := sum + rap[i];
  end for;
end Rapper;

class RapperInst
  Integer x;
equation
  x = Rapper({1, 2, 3, 4});
end RapperInst;
```

Exercise 8–4:

It is not good from the programmer's point of view. The variable inside the for-clause is hidden, which is all right, but they are by the programmer easily mixed together.

Exercise 8–5:

- A hybrid model is a model with mixed continuous and discrete parts.
- Well, the thing is that one can use both constructs for hybrid models. The if-equations may contain continuous-time expressions and when-equations may contain only discrete-time expressions.

Exercise 8–6:

```
function MatrixAddition
  input Integer matrix1[:, :];
  input Integer matrix2[:, :];
  output Integer matrixSum[2, 2];
algorithm
  for i in 1:size(matrix1, 1) loop
    for j in 1:size(matrix2, 2) loop
      matrixSum[i, j] := matrix1[i, j] + matrix2[i, j];
    end for;
  end for;
end MatrixAddition;

class MatrixAdditionCall
  Real[2, 2] MA = MatrixAddition([1, 2; 3, 4],
                                 [1, 2; 3, 4]);
end MatrixAdditionCall;
```

Chapter 9

Exercise 9–1:

```
function Sum
  input Real[:] x;
  output Real sum;
algorithm
  for i in 1:size(x,1) loop
    sum := sum + x[i];
  end for;
end Sum;

function Average
  input Real[:] x;
  output Real average;
protected
  Real sum;
algorithm
  average := Sum(x) / size(x,1);
end Average;

class LargestAverage
  parameter Integer[:] A1 = {1, 2, 3, 4, 5};
  parameter Integer[:] A2 = {7, 8, 9};
  Real averageA1, averageA2;
  Boolean A1Largest(start = false);
algorithm
  averageA1 := Average(A1);
  averageA2 := Average(A2);
  if averageA1 > averageA2 then
    A1Largest := true;
  else
    A1Largest := false;
  end if;
end LargestAverage;
```

Exercise 9–2:

Loop through all elements in the array except the first. The smallest value is initially the first value in the array.

```
class FindSmallest
  Real A[:];
  Real smallest;
  Integer place;
algorithm
  smallest := A[1];
  place := 1;
  for i in 2:size(A, 1) loop
    if A[i] < smallest then
      smallest := A[i];
      place := i;
    end if;
  end for;
end FindSmallest;

class FindSmallestElement
  FindSmallest findsmallest(A={9, 5, 8, 7, 2, 4});
end FindSmallestElement;
```

Exercise 9–3:

If the operator abs is used outside a when clause, state events are triggered. If this is not desired, the noEvent function can be applied to it.

```
class SumCalculation
  constant Real e = 0.000001;
  Real sum(start = 0);
  Real next(start = 1.0);
  Integer k(start = 1);
```

```
  Integer posneg(start = 1); // if the sign is + or -
algorithm
  while noEvent(abs(next)) >= e loop
    sum := sum + next;  // Add the sum to the next term
    k := k + 1;      // calculate a new next
    posneg := - posneg;
    next := posneg/(k*k);
  end while;
end SumCalculation;
```

Exercise 9–4:

```
class LightSwitch
  Boolean on;
algorithm
  when sample(5, 5) then
    if rem(time, 5) == 0 then
      on := true;
    else
      on := false;
    end if;
  end when;
end LightSwitch;


class LightSwitchExtended
  Boolean on;
algorithm
  when time < 5 or time >= 25 then
    on := false;
  elsewhen sample(5, 1) then
    if rem(time, 5) == 0 then
      on := true;
    else
      on := false;
    end if;
  end when;
end LightSwitchExtended;
```

Exercise 9–5:

```
model BilliardBalls
  parameter Real c = 0.9; // Elasticity constant of balls
  Real position1(start = 1);   // Position of ball 1
  Real position2(start = 10);  // Position of ball 2
  Real velocity1(start = 10);  // Velocity of ball 1
  Real velocity2(start = -15); // Velocity of ball 2
equation
  der(position1) = velocity1;
  der(position2) = velocity2;
  der(velocity1) = 0;
  der(velocity2) = 0;
algorithm
  when position1 >= position2 then
    reinit(velocity1, -c*velocity1);
    reinit(velocity2, -c*velocity2);
  end when;
end BilliardBalls;
```

Exercise 9–6:

```
function NFaculty
  input Integer n;
algorithm
  for i in 2:n loop
    fak := i*fak;
  end for;
end NFaculty;


class NFacultyCall
  Real n = NFaculty(4);
end NFacultyCall;
```

Exercise 9–7:

```
function FindName
  input String nameArray[:];
  output Integer fak = 1;
  input String name;
  output Integer index;
protected
  Integer i, length = size(nameArray, 1);
algorithm
  index := -1;
  i := 1;
  while index == -1 and i<length loop
    if nameArray[i] == name then
      index := i;
    end if;
    i := i + 1;
  end while;
  assert(index<>-1, "FindName: Failed");
end FindName;


class TestFindName
  Integer findLisp;
  String nameArray[:] = {"C++", "Lisp", "Java", "Ada",
  "Modelica"};
  String lisp = "Lisp";
equation
  findLisp = FindName(nameArray, lisp);
end TestFindName;


class TestFindName2
  Integer findPascal;
  String nameArray[:] = {"C++", "Lisp", "Java", "Ada",
  "Modelica"};
  String pascal = "Pascal";
equation
  findPascal = FindName(nameArray, pascal);
end TestFindName2;
```

Exercise 9–8:

```
function ScalarProduct
  input Integer V1[:];
  input Integer V2[size(V1,1)];
  output Integer scalarProduct;
algorithm
  scalarProduct := V1*V2;
end ScalarProduct;


class Orthogonal
  Integer V1[:] = {1, 2, 3};
  Integer V2[:] = {-3, 0, 1};
  Integer scalarProduct;
  Boolean orthogonal;
algorithm
  scalarProduct := ScalarProduct(V1, V2);
  if scalarProduct == 0 then
    orthogonal := true;
  end if;
end Orthogonal;
```

Chapter 10

Exercise 10–1:

- A package is simply a container or name space for names of classes, functions, constants, and other allowed definitions. A package is also one of the restricted classes.
- Adding the word encapsulated to the package keeps the package well structured as well as being easier to understand and maintain.

Exercise 10–2:

```
package Geometry
  constant Real PI = 3.1415926536;
  type Distance = Real(unit = "m");

  function RectangleArea
    input Distance B;
    input Distance H;
    output Distance area;
  algorithm
    area := B*H;
  end RectangleArea;

  function TriangleArea
    input Distance B;
    input Distance H;
    output Distance area;
  algorithm
    area := RectangleArea(B, H)/2;
  end TriangleArea;

  function CirclePerimeter
    input Distance radius;
    output Distance perimeter;
  algorithm
    perimeter := 2*PI*radius;
  end CirclePerimeter;

  function CircleArea
    input Distance radius;
    output Distance area;
  algorithm
    area := PI*radius^2;
  end CircleArea;

end Geometry;
```

```
class GeometryUser
  Geometry.Distance rectangleArea     =
  Geometry.RectangleArea(4, 5);
  Geometry.Distance triangleArea      =
  Geometry.TriangleArea(4, 5);
  Geometry.Distance circlePerimeter =
  Geometry.CirclePerimeter(3.5);
  Geometry.Distance circleArea        =
  Geometry.CircleArea(3.5);
end GeometryUser;
```

Exercise 10–3:

There are many factors to consider when designing a package, for example, the name of the package or the structuring of the package into subpackages. Other factors that are important to consider are reusability and encapsulation of the package as well as considering dependencies on other packages.

Exercise 10–4:

- A generic package is a package with some kind of formal parameter, e.g. a replaceable type.
- A local package is simply a package that is declared directly inside a class that is not a package.
- Yes, there actually is. A nonencapsulated package is a package declared without the prefix encapsulated. Also large encapsulated packages, containing protected declarations, can be internally structured into nonencapsulated packages.
- That is because used declarations may not be available in the new location for that certain subclass. When copying or moving an encapsulated package or class, at most the import statements inside this package or class, including subpackages and local classes, need to be updated.

Exercise 10–5:

Yes, as a matter of fact it is possible to inherit packages.

```
class GeometryUser
  extends Geometry;
  Distance rectangleArea = RectangleArea(4, 5);
  Distance rectangleArea = TriangleArea(4, 5);
  Distance circlePerimeter = CirclePerimeter(3.5);
  Distance circleArea = CircleArea(3.5);
end GeometryUser;
```

Chapter 11

Exercise 11–1:

```
type Acceleration = Real(final unit="m/s2");
```

Exercise 11–2:

Annotations can be placed at the end of class definitions, and at the end of variable declarations, import clauses, equations, and statements.

Chapter 12

Exercise 12–1:

Top-down modeling starts by defining the overall system structure, perhaps with few details, and progressively expanding the design by adding models and more details for the sub-systems, until a complete model is achieved.

Bottom up modeling starts by designing the low-level component models. These are are used as building blocks for more complex models which might be sub-systems of the final application. Eventually this process leads to the modeling of the whole system.

Exercise 12–2:

It should be easy and natural to connect components. Component interfaces should be designed to facilitate reuse of existing model components in class libraries. These rules sound simple, however they require a lot of careful design in practice.

Exercise 12–3:

It is much easier to compose a component-baed model with other models, and to reuse and extend a component-based model.

Chapter 13

Exercise 13–1:

A system with more equations than unknowns is over-constrained and a system with more unknowns than equations is under-constrained.

Exercise 13–2:

```
class ex2  "unclocked version"
  Real x(start=1);
  Boolean clk;
equation
  clk = sample(0,3);
  when clk then
    x = pre(x)+2;
  end when;
end ex2;

class ex2  "clocked version"
  discrete Real xclocked(start=1);
  Real x;
  Boolean clk;
equation
  clk = Clock(3);
  when clk then
    xclocked = previous(xclocked)+2;
  end when;
  x = hold(xclocked);
end ex2;
```

Exercise 13–3:

For an unclocked discrete-time variable y at an event, `pre(y)` is the value of y immediately preceding the event. Between events `pre(y)` is the same as y.

The function call `previous(y)` gives the predecessor value of a clocked discrete-time variable y, i.e., its value at the previous clock tick event.

Exercise 13–4:

The model is incorrect because two equations with conflicting values can be valid at the same time. Instead `elsewhen` should be used to define a priority between the events.

Exercise 13–5:

```
class exercise5
  parameter Integer level;
  Boolean clk;
  Boolean signal;
  Integer y;
equation
  clk = sample(0,2);
  if(time >=20 and time <= 80 and (y >= level)) then
    signal = true;
  else
    signal = false;
  end if;
end exercise5;
```

Exercise 13–6:

Hybrid systems are systems that contain both continuous-time and discrete-time parts.

A bouncing ball is an example of a hybrid system.

Appendix D

Modelica Standard Library Samples

This appendix shows samples of source code from a few of the mostly used sub-libraries in the Modelica Standard Library.

The package `Modelica` is a standardized and pre-defined package that is developed together with the Modelica language from the Modelica Association, see http://www.Modelica.org. It is also called the *Modelica Standard Library*. It provides constants, types, connectors, partial models and model components in various disciplines.

The Modelica package is free software and can be redistributed and/or modified under the terms of the Modelica License displayed at the front pages of this book.

The version reproduced in this appendix contains sample pieces of the Modelica standard library in the form it was available in September 2013, MSL 3.2.1.

The Modelica package consists of a number of subpackages, which are presented in Chapter 16, page 909.

The Modelica package contains documentation and a users guide.The Examples packages in the various libraries, demonstrate how to use the components of the corresponding sublibrary.

In the `Modelica` package the following conventions are used:

- Class and instance names are usually written in upper and lower case letters, e.g., `ElectricCurrent`. An underscore may be used in names. However, it has to be taken into account that the last underscore in a name might indicate that the following characters are rendered as a subscript. Example: `pin_a` may be rendered as $\texttt{pin}_{\texttt{a}}$.
- Class names start always with an upper case letter, with the exception of functions, which start with a lower case letter.
- Instance names, i.e., names of component instances and of variables (with the exception of constants), start usually with a lower case letter with only a few exceptions if this is common sense (such as T for a temperature variable).
- Constant names, i.e., names of variables declared with the "constant" prefix, follow the usual naming conventions (= upper and lower case letters) and start usually with an upper case letter, e.g., UniformGravity, SteadyState.
- The two connectors of a domain that have identical declarations and different icons are usually distinguished by _a, _b or _p, _n, e.g., Flange_a, Flange_b, HeatPort_a, HeatPort_b.
- A connector class has the instance name definition in the diagram layer and not in the icon layer
- A package XXX has its interface definitions in subpackage XXX.Interfaces, e.g., Electrical.Interfaces.
- Preferred instance names for connectors:

  p,n: positive and negative side of a partial model.

  a,b: side "a" and side "b" of a partial model

  (i.e., connectors are completely equivalent).

Modelica.Constants

Mathematical constants and constants of nature

This package provides often needed constants from mathematics, machine dependent constants and constants from nature. The latter constants (name, value, description) are from the following source:

Peter J. Mohr and Barry N. Taylor (1999):

CODATA Recommended Values of the Fundamental Physical Constants: 1998. Journal of Physical and Chemical Reference Data, Vol. 28, No. 6, 1999 and Reviews of Modern Physics, Vol. 72, No. 2, 2000. See also http://physics.nist.gov/cuu/Constants/

Main Author: Martin Otter.

Types and constants

```
package Constants

"Library of mathematical constants and constants of
 nature (e.g., pi, eps, R, sigma)"

import SI = Modelica.SIunits;
import NonSI = Modelica.SIunits.Conversions.NonSIunits;

extends Modelica.Icons.Package;

// Mathematical constants
final constant Real e=Modelica.Math.exp(1.0);
final constant Real pi=2*Modelica.Math.asin(1.0);
  // 3.14159265358979;
final constant Real D2R=pi/180 "Degree to Radian";
final constant Real R2D=180/pi "Radian to Degree";
final constant Real gamma=0.57721566490153286060
  "see http://en.wikipedia.org/wiki/Euler_constant";

// Machine dependent constants
final constant Real eps=ModelicaServices.Machine.eps
  "Biggest number such that 1.0 + eps = 1.0";
final constant Real small=ModelicaServices.Machine.small
  "Smallest number such that small and -small are
   representable on the machine";
final constant Real inf=ModelicaServices.Machine.inf
  "Biggest Real number such that inf and -inf are
   representable on the machine";
final constant Integer Integer_inf=
  ModelicaServices.Machine.Integer_inf
  "Biggest Integer number such that Integer_inf and -
   Integer_inf are representable on the machine";

// Constants of nature
// (name, value, description from
  http://physics.nist.gov/cuu/Constants/)
final constant SI.Velocity c=299792458
  "Speed of light in vacuum";
final constant SI.Acceleration g_n=9.80665
  "Standard acceleration of gravity on earth";
final constant Real G(final unit="m3/(kg.s2)")=6.6742e-11
  "Newtonian constant of gravitation";
final constant SI.FaradayConstant F = 9.64853399e4
  "Faraday constant, C/mol";
final constant Real h(final unit="J.s") = 6.6260693e-34
  "Planck constant";
final constant Real k(final unit="J/K") = 1.3806505e-23
  "Boltzmann constant";
final constant Real R(final unit="J/(mol.K)") = 8.314472
  "Molar gas constant";
final constant Real sigma(final unit="W/(m2.K4)")=
  5.670400e-8   "Stefan-Boltzmann constant";
final constant Real N_A(final unit="1/mol")= 6.0221415e23
  "Avogadro constant";
final constant Real mue_0(final unit="N/A2") = 4*pi*1.e-7
  "Magnetic constant";
final constant Real epsilon_0(final unit="F/m") =
  1/(mue_0*c*c)  "Electric constant";
final constant NonSI.Temperature_degC T_zero=-273.15
  "Absolute zero temperature";

end Constants;
```

Modelica.SIunits

Type definitions based on SI units according to ISO 31-1992

This package provides predefined types, such as Mass, Length, Time, based on the international standard on units:

ISO 31-1992 "General principles concerning quantities, units and symbols"

ISO 1000-1992 "SI units and recommendations for the use of their multiples and of certain other units".

For more information on units, see also the book of Francois Cardarelli "Scientific Unit Conversion - A Practical Guide to Metrication" (Springer 1997).

The following conventions are used in this package:

Modelica quantity names are defined according to the recommendations of ISO 31. Some of these name are rather long, such as "ThermodynamicTemperature". Shorter alias names are defined, e.g., "type Temp_K = ThermodynamicTemperature;".

Modelica units are defined according to the SI base units without multiples (only exception "kg").

For some quantities, more convenient units for an engineer are defined as "displayUnit", i.e., the default unit for display purposes (e.g., displayUnit="deg" for quantity="Angle").

The type name is identical to the quantity name, following the convention of type names.

All quantity and unit attributes are defined as final in order that they cannot be redefined to another value.

Similiar quantities, such as "Length, Breadth, Height, Thickness, Radius" are defined as the same quantity (here: "Length").

The ordering of the type declarations in this package follows ISO 31:

Chapter 1: Space and Time
Chapter 2: Periodic and Related Phenomena
Chapter 3: Mechanics
Chapter 4: Heat
Chapter 5: Electricity and Magnetism
Chapter 6: Light and Related Electro-Magnetic Radiations
Chapter 7: Acoustics
Chapter 8: Physical Chemistry
Chapter 9: Atomic and Nuclear Physics
Chapter 10: Nuclear Reactions and Ionizing Radiations
Chapter 11: (not defined in ISO 31-1992)
Chapter 12: Characteristic Numbers
Chapter 13: Solid State Physics

Conversion functions between SI and non-SI units are available in subpackage Conversions.

Main Author: Martin Otter

Types and constants

```
type Angle = Real (
  final quantity="Angle",
  final unit="rad",
  displayUnit="deg");
type SolidAngle = Real (
  final quantity="SolidAngle", final unit="sr");
type Length = Real (final quantity="Length",
  final unit="m");
type PathLength = Length;
type Position = Length;
type Distance = Length (min=0);
type Breadth = Length(min=0);
type Height = Length(min=0);
type Thickness = Length(min=0);
type Radius = Length(min=0);
type Diameter = Length(min=0);
type Area = Real (final quantity="Area",
  final unit="m2");
type Volume = Real (final quantity="Volume",
  final unit="m3");
type Time = Real (final quantity="Time",
  final unit="s");
type Duration = Time;
type AngularVelocity = Real (
    final quantity="AngularVelocity",
    final unit="rad/s");
```

```
type AngularAcceleration = Real (
  final quantity="AngularAcceleration",
  final unit="rad/s2");
type Velocity = Real (final quantity="Velocity",
  final unit="m/s");
type Acceleration = Real (final quantity="Acceleration",
final unit="m/s2");

// Periodic and related phenomens (chapter 2 of ISO 31-
1992)
type Period = Real (final quantity="Time",
final unit="s");
type Frequency = Real (final quantity="Frequency",
final unit="Hz");
type AngularFrequency = Real (
  final quantity="AngularFrequency",
  final unit="rad/s");
type Wavelength = Real (final quantity="Wavelength",
final unit="m");
type Wavelenght = Wavelength;
// For compatibility reasons only
type WaveNumber = Real (final quantity="WaveNumber",
final unit="m-1");
type CircularWaveNumber = Real (final
quantity="CircularWaveNumber", final unit=
           "rad/m");
type AmplitudeLevelDifference = Real (final quantity=
        "AmplitudeLevelDifference", final unit="dB");
type PowerLevelDifference = Real (final
quantity="PowerLevelDifference",
    final unit="dB");
type DampingCoefficient = Real (final
quantity="DampingCoefficient", final unit=
        "s-1");
type LogarithmicDecrement = Real (final
quantity="LogarithmicDecrement",
    final unit="1/S");
type AttenuationCoefficient = Real (final
quantity="AttenuationCoefficient",
    final unit="m-1");
type PhaseCoefficient = Real (final
quantity="PhaseCoefficient", final unit=
      "m-1");
type PropagationCoefficient = Real (final
quantity="PropagationCoefficient",
    final unit="m-1");
// added to ISO-chapter
type Damping = DampingCoefficient;

// Mechanics (chapter 3 of ISO 31-1992)
type Mass = Real (
  quantity="Mass",
  final unit="kg",
  min=0);
type Density = Real (
  final quantity="Density",
  final unit="kg/m3",
  displayUnit="g/cm3",
  min=0.0);
type RelativeDensity = Real (
  final quantity="RelativeDensity",
  final unit="1",
  min=0.0);
type SpecificVolume = Real (
  final quantity="SpecificVolume",
  final unit="m3/kg",
  min=0.0);
type LinearDensity = Real (
  final quantity="LinearDensity",
  final unit="kg/m",
  min=0);
type SurfaceDensity = Real (
  final quantity="SurfaceDensity",
  final unit="kg/m2",
  min=0);
type Momentum = Real (final quantity="Momentum", final
unit="kg.m/s");
type Impulse = Real (final quantity="Impulse", final
unit="N.s");
type AngularMomentum = Real (final
quantity="AngularMomentum", final unit=
       "kg.m2/s");
type AngularImpulse = Real (final
quantity="AngularImpulse", final unit=
       "N.m.s");
type MomentOfInertia = Real (final
quantity="MomentOfInertia", final unit=
       "kg.m2");
type Inertia = MomentOfInertia;
type Force = Real (final quantity="Force",
  final unit="N");
type TranslationalSpringConstant=Real(
  final quantity="TranslationalSpringConstant",
  final unit="N/m");
type TranslationalDampingConstant=Real(
  final quantity="TranslationalDampingConstant",
  final unit="N.s/m");
type Weight = Force;
type Torque = Real (final quantity="Torque",
  final unit="N.m");
type ElectricalTorqueConstant = Real(
  final quantity="ElectricalTorqueConstant",
  final unit= "N.m/A");
type MomentOfForce = Torque;
type ImpulseFlowRate = Real (
  final quantity="ImpulseFlowRate", final unit="N");
type AngularImpulseFlowRate = Real (final quantity =
  "AngularImpulseFlowRate", final unit= "N.m");
type RotationalSpringConstant=Real(final quantity=
  "RotationalSpringConstant", final unit="N.m/rad");
type RotationalDampingConstant=Real(final quantity=
  "RotationalDampingConstant", final unit="N.m.s/rad");
type Pressure = Real (
    final quantity="Pressure",
    final unit="Pa",
    displayUnit="bar");
type AbsolutePressure = Pressure (min=0.0, nominal= 1e5);
type PressureDifference = Pressure;
type BulkModulus = AbsolutePressure;
type Stress = Real (final unit="Pa");
type NormalStress = Stress;
type ShearStress = Stress;
type Strain = Real (final quantity="Strain",
  final unit="1");
type LinearStrain = Strain;
type ShearStrain = Strain;
type VolumeStrain = Real (final quantity="VolumeStrain",
  final unit="1");
type PoissonNumber = Real (final
quantity="PoissonNumber", final unit="1");
type ModulusOfElasticity = Stress;
type ShearModulus = Stress;
type SecondMomentOfArea = Real (final quantity=
  "SecondMomentOfArea", final unit="m4");
type SecondPolarMomentOfArea = SecondMomentOfArea;
type SectionModulus = Real (final
  quantity="SectionModulus", final unit="m3");
type CoefficientOfFriction = Real (final quantity=
  "CoefficientOfFriction",final unit="1");
type DynamicViscosity = Real (
    final quantity="DynamicViscosity",
    final unit="Pa.s",
    min=0);
type KinematicViscosity = Real (
    final quantity="KinematicViscosity",
    final unit="m2/s",
    min=0);
type SurfaceTension = Real (final
quantity="SurfaceTension", final unit="N/m");
type Work = Real (final quantity="Work", final unit="J");
type Energy = Real (final quantity="Energy",
  final unit="J");
type EnergyDensity = Real (
  final quantity="EnergyDensity", final unit="J/m3");
type PotentialEnergy = Energy;
type KineticEnergy = Energy;
type Power = Real (final quantity="Power",
  final unit="W");
type EnergyFlowRate = Power;
type EnthalpyFlowRate = Real (final quantity=
  "EnthalpyFlowRate", final unit="W");
type Efficiency = Real (
    final quantity="Efficiency",
    final unit="1",
    min=0);
type MassFlowRate = Real (quantity="MassFlowRate",
  final unit="kg/s");
type VolumeFlowRate = Real (final quantity=
  "VolumeFlowRate", final unit= "m3/s");
// added to ISO-chapter 3
type MomentumFlux = Real (final quantity="MomentumFlux",
  final unit="N");
type AngularMomentumFlux = Real (final
  quantity="AngularMomentumFlux", final unit="N.m");

// Heat (chapter 4 of ISO 31-1992)
type ThermodynamicTemperature = Real (
    final quantity="ThermodynamicTemperature",
    final unit="K",
    min = 0.0,
    start = 288.15,
    nominal = 300,
    displayUnit="degC")
  "Absolute temperature (use type TemperatureDifference
   for relative temperatures)"

annotation(absoluteValue=true);
type Temp_K = ThermodynamicTemperature;
type Temperature = ThermodynamicTemperature;
type TemperatureDifference = Real (
    final quantity="ThermodynamicTemperature",
    final unit="K") annotation(absoluteValue=false);
type Temp_C =
  SIunits.Conversions.NonSIunits.Temperature_degC;
```

```
type TemperatureSlope = Real (final quantity=
  "TemperatureSlope",  final unit="K/s");
type LinearTemperatureCoefficient = Real(final quantity =
  "LinearTemperatureCoefficient", final unit="1/K");
type QuadraticTemperatureCoefficient = Real(final
  quantity = "QuadraticTemperatureCoefficient",
  final unit="1/K2");
type LinearExpansionCoefficient = Real (final quantity=
        "LinearExpansionCoefficient", final unit="1/K");
type CubicExpansionCoefficient = Real (final quantity=
        "CubicExpansionCoefficient", final unit="1/K");
type RelativePressureCoefficient = Real (final quantity=
        "RelativePressureCoefficient", final unit="1/K");
type PressureCoefficient = Real (final quantity=
"PressureCoefficient", final unit= "Pa/K");
type Compressibility = Real (final quantity=
  "Compressibility", final unit= "1/Pa");
type IsothermalCompressibility = Compressibility;
type IsentropicCompressibility = Compressibility;
type Heat = Real (final quantity="Energy",
  final unit="J");
type HeatFlowRate = Real (final quantity="Power",
  final unit="W");
type HeatFlux = Real (final quantity="HeatFlux",
  final unit="W/m2");
type DensityOfHeatFlowRate = Real (final quantity=
  "DensityOfHeatFlowRate",final unit="W/m2");
type ThermalConductivity = Real (final quantity=
  "ThermalConductivity", final unit="W/(m.K)");
type CoefficientOfHeatTransfer = Real (final quantity=
  "CoefficientOfHeatTransfer", final unit="W/(m2.K)");
type SurfaceCoefficientOfHeatTransfer =
  CoefficientOfHeatTransfer;
type ThermalInsulance = Real (final quantity=
  "ThermalInsulance", final unit="m2.K/W");
type ThermalResistance = Real (final quantity=
  "ThermalResistance", final unit="K/W");
type ThermalConductance = Real (final quantity=
  "ThermalConductance", final unit="W/K");
type ThermalDiffusivity = Real (final quantity=
  "ThermalDiffusivity", final unit="m2/s");
type HeatCapacity = Real (final quantity="HeatCapacity",
  final unit="J/K");
type SpecificHeatCapacity = Real (final quantity=
  "SpecificHeatCapacity",final unit="J/(kg.K)");
type SpecificHeatCapacityAtConstantPressure =
  SpecificHeatCapacity;
type SpecificHeatCapacityAtConstantVolume =
  SpecificHeatCapacity;
type SpecificHeatCapacityAtSaturation =
  SpecificHeatCapacity;
type RatioOfSpecificHeatCapacities = Real (final
  quantity="RatioOfSpecificHeatCapacities",
  final unit="1");
type IsentropicExponent = Real (final quantity=
  "IsentropicExponent", final unit="1");
type Entropy = Real (final quantity="Entropy",
  final unit="J/K");
type EntropyFlowRate = Real (final quantity=
  "EntropyFlowRate", final unit="J/(K.s)");
type SpecificEntropy = Real (final quantity=
  "SpecificEntropy",final unit="J/(kg.K)");
type InternalEnergy = Heat;
type Enthalpy = Heat;
type HelmholtzFreeEnergy = Heat;
type GibbsFreeEnergy = Heat;
type SpecificEnergy = Real (final quantity=
  "SpecificEnergy", final unit="J/kg");
type SpecificInternalEnergy = SpecificEnergy;
type SpecificEnthalpy = SpecificEnergy;
type SpecificHelmholtzFreeEnergy = SpecificEnergy;
type SpecificGibbsFreeEnergy = SpecificEnergy;
type MassieuFunction = Real (final quantity=
  "MassieuFunction", final unit="J/K");
type PlanckFunction = Real (final quantity=
  "PlanckFunction", final unit="J/K");
// added to ISO-chapter 4
type DerDensityByEnthalpy = Real (final unit="kg.s2/m5");
type DerDensityByPressure = Real (final unit="s2/m2");
type DerDensityByTemperature = Real (final unit=
  "kg/(m3.K)");
type DerEnthalpyByPressure = Real (final unit=
  "J.m.s2/kg2");
type DerEnergyByDensity = Real (final unit="J.m3/kg");
type DerEnergyByPressure = Real (final unit="J.m.s2/kg");
type DerPressureByDensity = Real (final unit="Pa.m3/kg");
type DerPressureByTemperature = Real (final unit="Pa/K");

// Electricity and Magnetism (chapter 5 of ISO 31-1992)
type ElectricCurrent = Real (final quantity=
  "ElectricCurrent", final unit="A");
type Current = ElectricCurrent;
type CurrentSlope = Real(final quantity="CurrentSlope",
  final unit="A/s");
type ElectricCharge = Real (final quantity=
  "ElectricCharge", final unit="C");
type Charge = ElectricCharge;
type VolumeDensityOfCharge = Real (
    final quantity="VolumeDensityOfCharge",
    final unit="C/m3",
    min=0);
type SurfaceDensityOfCharge = Real (
    final quantity="SurfaceDensityOfCharge",
    final unit="C/m2",
    min=0);
type ElectricFieldStrength = Real (final quantity=
  "ElectricFieldStrength",final unit="V/m");
type ElectricPotential = Real (final
quantity="ElectricPotential", final unit="V");
type Voltage = ElectricPotential;
type PotentialDifference = ElectricPotential;
type ElectromotiveForce = ElectricPotential;
type VoltageSecond = Real (final quantity=
  "VoltageSecond", final unit="V.s") "Voltage second";
type VoltageSlope = Real(final quantity="VoltageSlope",
  final unit="V/s");
type ElectricFluxDensity = Real (final quantity=
  "ElectricFluxDensity", final unit="C/m2");
type ElectricFlux = Real (final quantity="ElectricFlux",
  final unit="C");
type Capacitance = Real (
    final quantity="Capacitance",
    final unit="F",
    min=0);
type CapacitancePerArea = Real (
  final quantity= "CapacitancePerArea",
  final unit="F/m2") "Capacitance per area";
type Permittivity = Real (
    final quantity="Permittivity",
    final unit="F/m",
    min=0);
type PermittivityOfVacuum = Permittivity;
type RelativePermittivity = Real (final quantity=
  "RelativePermittivity",final unit="1");
type ElectricSusceptibility = Real (final quantity=
  "ElectricSusceptibility",  final unit="1");
type ElectricPolarization = Real (final quantity=
  "ElectricPolarization",final unit="C/m2");
type Electrization = Real (final quantity=
  "Electrization", final unit="V/m");
type ElectricDipoleMoment = Real (final quantity=
  "ElectricDipoleMoment", final unit="C.m");
type CurrentDensity = Real (final quantity=
  "CurrentDensity", final unit="A/m2");
type LinearCurrentDensity = Real (final quantity=
  "LinearCurrentDensity",final unit="A/m");
type MagneticFieldStrength = Real (final quantity=
  "MagneticFieldStrength",final unit="A/m");
type MagneticPotential = Real (final quantity=
  "MagneticPotential", final unit="A");
type MagneticPotentialDifference = Real (final quantity=
  "MagneticPotential", final unit="A");
type MagnetomotiveForce = Real (final quantity=
  "MagnetomotiveForce", final unit="A");
type CurrentLinkage = Real (final quantity=
  "CurrentLinkage", final unit="A");
type MagneticFluxDensity = Real (final quantity=
  "MagneticFluxDensity", final unit="T");
type MagneticFlux = Real (final quantity="MagneticFlux",
  final unit="Wb");
type MagneticVectorPotential = Real (final quantity=
  "MagneticVectorPotential",final unit="Wb/m");
type Inductance = Real (
    final quantity="Inductance",
    final unit="H");
type SelfInductance = Inductance(min=0);
type MutualInductance = Inductance;
type CouplingCoefficient = Real (final quantity=
  "CouplingCoefficient", final unit="1");
type LeakageCoefficient = Real (final quantity=
  "LeakageCoefficient", final unit="1");
type Permeability = Real (final quantity="Permeability",
  final unit="H/m");
type PermeabilityOfVacuum = Permeability;
type RelativePermeability = Real (final quantity=
  "RelativePermeability",final unit="1");
type MagneticSusceptibility = Real (final quantity=
  "Magnetic Susceptibility",final unit="1");
type ElectromagneticMoment = Real (final quantity=
  "ElectromagneticMoment",  final unit="A.m2");
type MagneticDipoleMoment = Real (final
quantity="MagneticDipoleMoment",
     final unit="Wb.m");
type Magnetization = Real (final quantity=
  "Magnetization", final unit="A/m");
type MagneticPolarization = Real (final quantity=
  "MagneticPolarization",final unit="T");
type ElectromagneticEnergyDensity = Real (final quantity=
  "EnergyDensity",final unit="J/m3");
type PoyntingVector = Real (final quantity=
  "PoyntingVector", final unit=  "W/m2");
type Resistance = Real (
    final quantity="Resistance",
    final unit="Ohm");
```

```
type Resistivity = Real (final quantity="Resistivity",
  final unit="Ohm.m");
type Conductivity = Real (final quantity="Conductivity",
  final unit="S/m");
type Reluctance = Real (final quantity="Reluctance",
  final unit="H-1");
type Permeance = Real (final quantity="Permeance",
  final unit="H");
type PhaseDifference = Real (
    final quantity="Angle",
    final unit="rad",
    displayUnit="deg");
type Impedance = Resistance;
type ModulusOfImpedance = Resistance;
type Reactance = Resistance;
type QualityFactor = Real (final quantity=
  "QualityFactor", final unit="1");
type LossAngle = Real (
    final quantity="Angle",
    final unit="rad",
    displayUnit="deg");
type Conductance = Real (
    final quantity="Conductance",
    final unit="S");
type Admittance = Conductance;
type ModulusOfAdmittance = Conductance;
type Susceptance = Conductance;
type InstantaneousPower = Real (final quantity="Power",
  final unit="W");
type ActivePower = Real (final quantity="Power",
  final unit="W");
type ApparentPower = Real (final quantity="Power",
  final unit="VA");
type ReactivePower = Real (final quantity="Power",
  final unit="var");
type PowerFactor = Real (final quantity="PowerFactor",
  final unit="1");

// added to ISO-chapter 5
type Transconductance = Real (final quantity=
  "Transconductance", final unit="A/V2");
type InversePotential = Real (final quantity=
  "InversePotential", final unit="1/V");
type ElectricalForceConstant = Real (
     final quantity="ElectricalForceConstant",
     final unit = "N/A");

// Light and Related Electromagnetic Radiations (chapter
6 of ISO 31-1992)"
type RadiantEnergy = Real (final quantity="Energy",
  final unit="J");
type RadiantEnergyDensity = Real (final quantity=
  "EnergyDensity", final unit="J/m3");
type SpectralRadiantEnergyDensity = Real (final quantity=
   "SpectralRadiantEnergyDensity", final unit="J/m4");
type RadiantPower = Real (final quantity="Power",
  final unit="W");
type RadiantEnergyFluenceRate = Real (final quantity=
        "RadiantEnergyFluenceRate", final unit="W/m2");
type RadiantIntensity = Real (final quantity=
  "RadiantIntensity", final unit= "W/sr");
type Radiance = Real (final quantity="Radiance",
  final unit="W/(sr.m2)");
type RadiantExtiance = Real (final quantity=
  "RadiantExtiance", final unit="W/m2");
type Irradiance = Real (final quantity="Irradiance",
  final unit="W/m2");
type Emissivity = Real (final quantity="Emissivity",
  final unit="1");
type SpectralEmissivity = Real (final quantity=
  "SpectralEmissivity", final unit= "1");
type DirectionalSpectralEmissivity = Real (final
  quantity="DirectionalSpectralEmissivity",
  final unit="1");
type LuminousIntensity = Real (final quantity=
  "LuminousIntensity", final unit="cd");
type LuminousFlux = Real (final quantity="LuminousFlux",
  final unit="lm");
type QuantityOfLight = Real (final quantity=
  "QuantityOfLight", final unit="lm.s");
type Luminance = Real (final quantity="Luminance",
  final unit="cd/m2");
type LuminousExitance = Real (final quantity=
  "LuminousExitance", final unit="lm/m2");
type Illuminance = Real (final quantity="Illuminance",
  final unit="lx");
type LightExposure = Real (final quantity=
  "LightExposure", final unit="lx.s");
type LuminousEfficacy = Real (final quantity=
  "LuminousEfficacy", final unit="lm/W");
type SpectralLuminousEfficacy = Real (final quantity=
  "SpectralLuminousEfficacy", final unit="lm/W");
type LuminousEfficiency = Real (final quantity=
  "LuminousEfficiency", final unit= "1");
type SpectralLuminousEfficiency = Real (final quantity=
  "SpectralLuminousEfficiency", final unit="1");
type CIESpectralTristimulusValues = Real (final quantity=
       "CIESpectralTristimulusValues", final unit="1");
type ChromaticityCoordinates = Real (final quantity=
  "CromaticityCoordinates", final unit="1");
type SpectralAbsorptionFactor = Real (final quantity=
        "SpectralAbsorptionFactor", final unit="1");
type SpectralReflectionFactor = Real (final quantity=
        "SpectralReflectionFactor", final unit="1");
type SpectralTransmissionFactor = Real (final quantity=
        "SpectralTransmissionFactor", final unit="1");
type SpectralRadianceFactor = Real (final quantity=
  "SpectralRadianceFactor",  final unit="1");
type LinearAttenuationCoefficient = Real (final quantity=
        "AttenuationCoefficient", final unit="m-1");
type LinearAbsorptionCoefficient = Real (final quantity=
        "LinearAbsorptionCoefficient", final unit="m-1");
type MolarAbsorptionCoefficient = Real (final quantity=
  "MolarAbsorptionCoefficient", final unit="m2/mol");
type RefractiveIndex = Real (final quantity=
  "RefractiveIndex", final unit="1");

// Acoustics (chapter 7 of ISO 31-1992)
type StaticPressure = AbsolutePressure;
type SoundPressure = StaticPressure;
type SoundParticleDisplacement = Real (final quantity=
  "Length", final unit="m");
type SoundParticleVelocity = Real (final quantity=
  "Velocity", final unit="m/s");
type SoundParticleAcceleration = Real (final quantity=
  "Acceleration", final unit= "m/s2");
type VelocityOfSound = Real (final quantity="Velocity",
  final unit="m/s");
type SoundEnergyDensity = Real (final quantity=
  "EnergyDensity", final unit="J/m3");
type SoundPower = Real (final quantity="Power",
  final unit="W");
type SoundIntensity = Real (final quantity=
  "SoundIntensity", final unit="W/m2");
type AcousticImpedance = Real (final quantity=
  "AcousticImpedance", final unit="Pa.s/m3");
type SpecificAcousticImpedance = Real (final quantity=
  "SpecificAcousticImpedance", final unit="Pa.s/m");
type MechanicalImpedance = Real (final quantity=
   "MechanicalImpedance", final unit="N.s/m");
type SoundPressureLevel = Real (final quantity=
  "SoundPressureLevel", final unit="dB");
type SoundPowerLevel = Real (final quantity=
 "SoundPowerLevel", final unit="dB");
type DissipationCoefficient = Real (final quantity=
  "DissipationCoefficient",final unit="1");
type ReflectionCoefficient = Real (final quantity=
  "ReflectionCoefficient",final unit="1");
type TransmissionCoefficient = Real (final quantity=
  "TransmissionCoefficient", final unit="1");
type AcousticAbsorptionCoefficient = Real (
  final quantity="AcousticAbsorptionCoefficient",
  final unit="1");
type SoundReductionIndex = Real (final quantity=
  "SoundReductionIndex", final unit="dB");
type EquivalentAbsorptionArea = Real (final quantity=
  "Area", final unit="m2");
type ReverberationTime = Real (final quantity="Time",
  final unit="s");
type LoudnessLevel = Real (final quantity=
  "LoudnessLevel", final unit="phon");
type Loudness = Real (final quantity="Loudness",
  final unit="sone");
type LoundnessLevel = Real (final
quantity="LoundnessLevel", final unit=
  "phon") "Obsolete type, use LoudnessLevel instead!";
type Loundness = Real (final quantity="Loundness", final
  unit="sone")  "Obsolete type, use Loudness instead!";

// Physical chemistry and molecular physics (chapter 8 of
ISO 31-1992)
type RelativeAtomicMass = Real (final quantity=
  "RelativeAtomicMass", final unit="1");
type RelativeMolecularMass = Real (final quantity=
  "RelativeMolecularMass",final unit="1");
type NumberOfMolecules = Real (final quantity=
  "NumberOfMolecules", final unit="1");
type AmountOfSubstance = Real (
    final quantity="AmountOfSubstance",
    final unit="mol",
    min=0);
type MolarMass = Real (final quantity="MolarMass",
  final unit="kg/mol",min=0);
type MolarVolume = Real (final quantity="MolarVolume",
  final unit="m3/mol", min=0);
type MolarDensity = Real (final quantity="MolarDensity",
  unit="mol/m3");
type MolarEnergy = Real (final quantity="MolarEnergy",
  final unit="J/mol", nominal=2e4);
type MolarInternalEnergy = MolarEnergy;
type MolarHeatCapacity = Real (final quantity=
  "MolarHeatCapacity", final unit="J/(mol.K)");
type MolarEntropy = Real (final quantity="MolarEntropy",
  final unit="J/(mol.K)");
```

```
type MolarEnthalpy = MolarEnergy;
type MolarFlowRate = Real (
  final quantity="MolarFlowRate", final unit=  "mol/s");
type NumberDensityOfMolecules = Real (final quantity=
        "NumberDensityOfMolecules", final unit="m-3");
type MolecularConcentration = Real (final quantity=
  "MolecularConcentration",final unit="m-3");
type MassConcentration = Real (final quantity=
  "MassConcentration", final unit="kg/m3");
type MassFraction = Real (final quantity="MassFraction",
  final unit="1",  min=0, max=1);
type Concentration = Real (final quantity=
  "Concentration", final unit="mol/m3");
type VolumeFraction = Real (final quantity=
  "VolumeFraction", final unit="1");
type MoleFraction = Real (final quantity="MoleFraction",
  final unit="1",  min = 0, max = 1);
type ChemicalPotential = Real (final quantity=
  "ChemicalPotential", final unit=  "J/mol");
type AbsoluteActivity = Real (final quantity=
  "AbsoluteActivity", final unit=  "1");
type PartialPressure = AbsolutePressure;
type Fugacity = Real (final quantity="Fugacity",
  final unit="Pa");
type StandardAbsoluteActivity = Real (final quantity=
        "StandardAbsoluteActivity", final unit="1");
type ActivityCoefficient = Real (final quantity=
  "ActivityCoefficient", final unit="1");
type ActivityOfSolute = Real (final quantity=
  "ActivityOfSolute", final unit="1");
type ActivityCoefficientOfSolute = Real (final quantity=
  "ActivityCoefficientOfSolute", final unit="1");
type StandardAbsoluteActivityOfSolute = Real (
  final quantity= "StandardAbsoluteActivityOfSolute",
  final unit="1");
type ActivityOfSolvent = Real (final quantity=
  "ActivityOfSolvent", final unit="1");
type OsmoticCoefficientOfSolvent = Real (final quantity=
  "OsmoticCoefficientOfSolvent", final unit="1");
type StandardAbsoluteActivityOfSolvent = Real (
  final quantity= "StandardAbsoluteActivityOfSolvent",
  final unit="1");
type OsmoticPressure = Real (
    final quantity="Pressure",
    final unit="Pa",
    displayUnit="bar",
    min=0);
type StoichiometricNumber = Real (final quantity=
  "StoichiometricNumber",final unit="1");
type Affinity = Real (final quantity="Affinity",
  final unit="J/mol");
type MassOfMolecule = Real (final quantity="Mass",
  final unit="kg");
type ElectricDipoleMomentOfMolecule = Real (
  final quantity= "ElectricDipoleMomentOfMolecule",
  final unit="C.m");
type ElectricPolarizabilityOfAMolecule = Real (
  final quantity= "ElectricPolarizabilityOfAMolecule",
  final unit="C.m2/V");
type MicrocanonicalPartitionFunction = Real (
  final quantity= "MicrocanonicalPartitionFunction",
  final unit="1");
type CanonicalPartitionFunction = Real (final quantity=
  "CanonicalPartitionFunction", final unit="1");
type GrandCanonicalPartitionFunction = Real (
  final quantity=  "GrandCanonicalPartitionFunction",
  final unit="1");
type MolecularPartitionFunction = Real (final quantity=
   "MolecularPartitionFunction", final unit="1");
type StatisticalWeight = Real (final quantity=
  "StatisticalWeight", final unit="1");
type MeanFreePath = Length;
type DiffusionCoefficient = Real (final quantity=
  "DiffusionCoefficient",final unit="m2/s");
type ThermalDiffusionRatio = Real (final quantity=
  "ThermalDiffusionRatio",final unit="1");
type ThermalDiffusionFactor = Real (final quantity=
  "ThermalDiffusionFactor",final unit="1");
type ThermalDiffusionCoefficient = Real (final quantity=
  "ThermalDiffusionCoefficient", final unit="m2/s");
type ElementaryCharge = Real (final quantity=
  "ElementaryCharge", final unit= "C");
type ChargeNumberOfIon = Real (final quantity=
  "ChargeNumberOfIon", final unit="1");
type FaradayConstant = Real (final quantity=
  "FaradayConstant", final unit="C/mol");
type IonicStrength = Real (final quantity=
  "IonicStrength", final unit="mol/kg");
type DegreeOfDissociation = Real (final quantity=
  "DegreeOfDissociation",final unit="1");
type ElectrolyticConductivity = Real (final quantity=
  "ElectrolyticConductivity", final unit="S/m");
type MolarConductivity = Real (final quantity=
  "MolarConductivity", final unit="S.m2/mol");
type TransportNumberOfIonic = Real (final quantity=
  "TransportNumberOfIonic", final unit="1");

// Atomic and Nuclear Physics (chapter 9 of ISO 31-1992)
type ProtonNumber = Real (final quantity="ProtonNumber",
  final unit="1");
type NeutronNumber = Real (final quantity=
  "NeutronNumber", final unit="1");
type NucleonNumber = Real (final quantity=
  "NucleonNumber", final unit="1");
type AtomicMassConstant = Real (final quantity="Mass",
  final unit="kg");
type MassOfElectron = Real (final quantity="Mass",
  final unit="kg");
type MassOfProton = Real (final quantity="Mass",
  final unit="kg");
type MassOfNeutron = Real (final quantity="Mass",
  final unit="kg");
type HartreeEnergy = Real (final quantity="Energy",
  final unit="J");
type MagneticMomentOfParticle = Real (final quantity=
  "MagneticMomentOfParticle", final unit="A.m2");
type BohrMagneton = MagneticMomentOfParticle;
type NuclearMagneton = MagneticMomentOfParticle;
type GyromagneticCoefficient = Real (final quantity=
  "GyromagneticCoefficient", final unit="A.m2/(J.s)");
type GFactorOfAtom = Real (final quantity=
  "GFactorOfAtom", final unit="1");
type GFactorOfNucleus = Real (final quantity=
  "GFactorOfNucleus", final unit="1");
type LarmorAngularFrequency = Real (final quantity=
  "AngularFrequency", final unit="s-1");
type NuclearPrecessionAngularFrequency = Real (final
  quantity="AngularFrequency", final unit="s-1");
type CyclotronAngularFrequency = Real (final quantity=
  "AngularFrequency", final unit="s-1");
type NuclearQuadrupoleMoment = Real (final quantity=
  "NuclearQuadrupoleMoment",final unit="m2");
type NuclearRadius = Real (final quantity="Length",
  final unit="m");
type ElectronRadius = Real (final quantity="Length",
  final unit="m");
type ComptonWavelength = Real (final quantity="Length",
  final unit="m");
type MassExcess = Real (final quantity="Mass",
  final unit="kg");
type MassDefect = Real (final quantity="Mass",
  final unit="kg");
type RelativeMassExcess = Real (final quantity=
  "RelativeMassExcess", final unit="1");
type RelativeMassDefect = Real (final quantity=
  "RelativeMassDefect", final unit="1");
type PackingFraction = Real (final quantity=
  "PackingFraction", final unit="1");
type BindingFraction = Real (final quantity=
  "BindingFraction", final unit="1");
type MeanLife = Real (final quantity="Time",
  final unit="s");
type LevelWidth = Real (final quantity="LevelWidth",
  final unit="J");
type Activity = Real (final quantity="Activity",
  final unit="Bq");
type SpecificActivity = Real (final quantity=
  "SpecificActivity", final unit="Bq/kg");
type DecayConstant = Real (final quantity=
  "DecayConstant", final unit="s-1");
type HalfLife = Real (final quantity="Time",
  final unit="s");
type AlphaDisintegrationEnergy = Real (final quantity=
  "Energy", final unit= "J");
type MaximumBetaParticleEnergy = Real (final quantity=
  "Energy", final unit="J");
type BetaDisintegrationEnergy = Real (final quantity=
  "Energy", final unit="J");

// Nuclear Reactions and Ionizing Radiations (chapter 10
of ISO 31-1992)
type ReactionEnergy = Real (final quantity="Energy",
  final unit="J");
type ResonanceEnergy = Real (final quantity="Energy",
  final unit="J");
type CrossSection = Real (final quantity="Area",
  final unit="m2");
type TotalCrossSection = Real (final quantity="Area",
  final unit="m2");
type AngularCrossSection = Real (final quantity=
  "AngularCrossSection", final unit=  "m2/sr");
type SpectralCrossSection = Real (final quantity=
  "SpectralCrossSection", final unit="m2/J");
type SpectralAngularCrossSection = Real (final quantity=
  "SpectralAngularCrossSection", final unit="m2/(sr.J)");
type MacroscopicCrossSection = Real (final quantity=
  "MacroscopicCrossSection",  final unit="m-1");
type TotalMacroscopicCrossSection = Real (final quantity=
  "TotalMacroscopicCrossSection", final unit="m-1");
type ParticleFluence = Real (final quantity=
  "ParticleFluence", final unit=  "m-2");
type ParticleFluenceRate = Real (final quantity=
  "ParticleFluenceRate", final unit="s-1.m2");
type EnergyFluence = Real (final quantity=
```

```
  "EnergyFluence", final unit="J/m2");
type EnergyFluenceRate = Real (final quantity=
  "EnergyFluenceRate", final unit="W/m2");
type CurrentDensityOfParticles = Real (
 final quantity= "CurrentDensityOfParticles",
  final unit="m-2.s-1");
type MassAttenuationCoefficient = Real (
  final quantity= "MassAttenuationCoefficient",
  final unit="m2/kg");
type MolarAttenuationCoefficient = Real (final quantity=
  "MolarAttenuationCoefficient", final unit="m2/mol");
type AtomicAttenuationCoefficient = Real (final quantity=
  "AtomicAttenuationCoefficient", final unit="m2");
type HalfThickness = Real (final quantity="Length",
  final unit="m");
type TotalLinearStoppingPower = Real (final quantity=
  "TotalLinearStoppingPower", final unit="J/m");
type TotalAtomicStoppingPower = Real (final quantity=
  "TotalAtomicStoppingPower", final unit="J.m2");
type TotalMassStoppingPower = Real (final quantity=
  "TotalMassStoppingPower", final unit="J.m2/kg");
type MeanLinearRange = Real (final quantity="Length",
  final unit="m");
type MeanMassRange = Real (
  final quantity="MeanMassRange", final unit="kg/m2");
type LinearIonization = Real (
  final quantity="LinearIonization", final unit= "m-1");
type TotalIonization = Real (final quantity=
  "TotalIonization", final unit="1");
type Mobility = Real ( final quantity=
  "Mobility", final unit="m2/(V.s)");
type IonNumberDensity = Real (final quantity=
  "IonNumberDensity", final unit="m-3");
type RecombinationCoefficient = Real (final quantity=
  "RecombinationCoefficient", final unit="m3/s");
type NeutronNumberDensity = Real (final quantity=
  "NeutronNumberDensity", final unit="m-3");
type NeutronSpeed = Real (final quantity=
  "Velocity", final unit="m/s");
type NeutronFluenceRate = Real (final quantity=
  "NeutronFluenceRate", final unit="s-1.m-2");
type TotalNeutronSourceDensity = Real (final quantity=
  "TotalNeutronSourceDesity", final unit="s-1.m-3");
type SlowingDownDensity = Real (final quantity=
  "SlowingDownDensity", final unit="s-1.m-3");
type ResonanceEscapeProbability = Real (final quantity=
  "ResonanceEscapeProbability", final unit="1");
type Lethargy = Real (final quantity="Lethargy",
  final unit="1");
type SlowingDownArea = Real (final quantity="Area",
  final unit="m2");
type DiffusionArea = Real (final quantity="Area",
  final unit="m2");
type MigrationArea = Real (final quantity="Area",
  final unit="m2");
type SlowingDownLength = Real (final quantity="SLength",
  final unit="m");
type DiffusionLength = Length;
type MigrationLength = Length;
type NeutronYieldPerFission = Real (final quantity=
  "NeutronYieldPerFission", final unit="1");
type NeutronYieldPerAbsorption = Real (final quantity=
  "NeutronYieldPerAbsorption", final unit="1");
type FastFissionFactor = Real (final quantity=
  "FastFissionFactor", final unit="1");
type ThermalUtilizationFactor = Real (final quantity=
  "ThermalUtilizationFactor", final unit="1");
type NonLeakageProbability = Real (final quantity=
  "NonLeakageProbability", final unit="1");
type Reactivity = Real (final quantity="Reactivity",
  final unit="1");
type ReactorTimeConstant = Real (final quantity="Time",
  final unit="s");
type EnergyImparted = Real (final quantity="Energy",
  final unit="J");
type MeanEnergyImparted = Real (final quantity="Energy",
  final unit="J");
type SpecificEnergyImparted = Real (final quantity=
  "SpecificEnergy", final unit="Gy");
type AbsorbedDose = Real (final quantity="AbsorbedDose",
  final unit="Gy");
type DoseEquivalent = Real (final quantity=
  "DoseEquivalent", final unit="Sv");
type AbsorbedDoseRate = Real (final quantity=
  "AbsorbedDoseRate", final unit="Gy/s");
type LinearEnergyTransfer = Real (final quantity=
  "LinearEnergyTransfer", final unit="J/m");
type Kerma = Real (final quantity="Kerma",
  final unit="Gy");
type KermaRate = Real (final quantity="KermaRate",
  final unit="Gy/s");
type MassEnergyTransferCoefficient = Real (
  final quantity="MassEnergyTransferCoefficient",
  final unit="m2/kg");
type Exposure = Real (final quantity="Exposure",
  final unit="C/kg");
type ExposureRate = Real (final quantity="ExposureRate",
  final unit="C/(kg.s)");

// chapter 11 is not defined in ISO 31-1992

// Characteristic Numbers (chapter 12 of ISO 31-1992)
type ReynoldsNumber = Real (final quantity=
  "ReynoldsNumber", final unit="1");
type EulerNumber = Real (final quantity=
  "EulerNumber", final unit="1");
type FroudeNumber = Real (final quantity="FroudeNumber",
  final unit="1");
type GrashofNumber = Real (final quantity=
  "GrashofNumber", final unit="1");
type WeberNumber = Real (final quantity="WeberNumber",
  final unit="1");
type MachNumber = Real (final quantity="MachNumber",
  final unit="1");
type KnudsenNumber = Real (final quantity=
  "KnudsenNumber", final unit="1");
type StrouhalNumber = Real (final quantity=
  "StrouhalNumber", final unit="1");
type FourierNumber = Real (final quantity=
  "FourierNumber", final unit="1");
type PecletNumber = Real (final quantity="PecletNumber",
  final unit="1");
type RayleighNumber = Real (final quantity=
  "RayleighNumber", final unit="1");
type NusseltNumber = Real (final quantity=
  "NusseltNumber", final unit="1");
type BiotNumber = NusseltNumber;
// The Biot number (Bi) is used when
// the Nusselt number is reserved
// for convective transport of heat.
type StantonNumber = Real (final quantity=
  "StantonNumber", final unit="1");
type FourierNumberOfMassTransfer = Real (final quantity=
  "FourierNumberOfMassTransfer", final unit="1");
type PecletNumberOfMassTransfer = Real (final quantity=
  "PecletNumberOfMassTransfer", final unit="1");
type GrashofNumberOfMassTransfer = Real (final quantity=
  "GrashofNumberOfMassTransfer", final unit="1");
type NusseltNumberOfMassTransfer = Real (final quantity=
  "NusseltNumberOfMassTransfer", final unit="1");
type StantonNumberOfMassTransfer = Real (final quantity=
  "StantonNumberOfMassTransfer", final unit="1");
type PrandtlNumber = Real (final quantity=
  "PrandtlNumber", final unit="1");
type SchmidtNumber = Real (final quantity=
  "SchmidtNumber", final unit="1");
type LewisNumber = Real (final quantity="LewisNumber",
  final unit="1");
type MagneticReynoldsNumber = Real (final quantity=
  "MagneticReynoldsNumber", final unit="1");
type AlfvenNumber = Real (final quantity="AlfvenNumber",
  final unit="1");
type HartmannNumber = Real (final quantity=
  "HartmannNumber", final unit="1");
type CowlingNumber = Real (final quantity=
  "CowlingNumber", final unit="1");

// Solid State Physics (chapter 13 of ISO 31-1992)
type BraggAngle = Angle;
type OrderOfReflexion = Real (final quantity=
  "OrderOfReflexion", final unit=
      "1");
type ShortRangeOrderParameter = Real (final quantity=
  "RangeOrderParameter", final unit="1");
type LongRangeOrderParameter = Real (final quantity=
  "RangeOrderParameter", final unit="1");
type DebyeWallerFactor = Real (final quantity=
  "DebyeWallerFactor", final unit="1");
type CircularWavenumber = Real (final quantity=
  "CircularWavenumber", final unit="m-1");
type FermiCircularWavenumber = Real (final quantity=
  "FermiCircularWavenumber", final unit="m-1");
type DebyeCircularWavenumber = Real (final quantity=
  "DebyeCircularWavenumber", final unit="m-1");
type DebyeCircularFrequency = Real (final quantity=
  "AngularFrequency", final unit="s-1");
type DebyeTemperature = ThermodynamicTemperature;
type SpectralConcentration = Real (final quantity=
  "SpectralConcentration", final unit="s/m3");
type GrueneisenParameter = Real (final quantity=
  "GrueneisenParameter", final unit="1");
type MadelungConstant = Real (final quantity=
  "MadelungConstant", final unit="1");
type DensityOfStates = Real (final quantity=
  "DensityOfStates", final unit="J-1/m-3");
type ResidualResistivity = Real (final quantity=
  "ResidualResistivity", final unit="Ohm.m");
type LorenzCoefficient = Real (final quantity=
  "LorenzCoefficient", final unit="V2/K2");
type HallCoefficient = Real (final quantity=
  "HallCoefficient", final unit="m3/C");
type ThermoelectromotiveForce = Real (final quantity=
  "ThermoelectromotiveForce", final unit="V");
type SeebeckCoefficient = Real (final quantity=
```

```
  "SeebeckCoefficient", final unit="V/K");
type PeltierCoefficient = Real (final quantity=
  "PeltierCoefficient", final unit="V");

type ThomsonCoefficient = Real (final quantity=
  "ThomsonCoefficient", final unit="V/K");
type RichardsonConstant = Real (final quantity=
  "RichardsonConstant", final unit="A/(m2.K2)");
type FermiEnergy = Real (final quantity="Energy",
  final unit="eV");
type GapEnergy = Real (final quantity="Energy",
  final unit="eV");
type DonorIonizationEnergy = Real (final quantity=
  "Energy", final unit="eV");
type AcceptorIonizationEnergy = Real (final quantity=
  "Energy", final unit="eV");
type ActivationEnergy = Real (final quantity="Energy",
  final unit="eV");
type FermiTemperature = ThermodynamicTemperature;
type ElectronNumberDensity = Real (final quantity=
  "ElectronNumberDensity", final unit="m-3");
type HoleNumberDensity = Real (final quantity=
  "HoleNumberDensity", final unit="m-3");
type IntrinsicNumberDensity = Real (final quantity=
  "IntrinsicNumberDensity",final unit="m-3");
type DonorNumberDensity = Real (final quantity=
  "DonorNumberDensity", final unit="m-3");
type AcceptorNumberDensity = Real (final quantity=
  "AcceptorNumberDensity", final unit="m-3");
type EffectiveMass = Mass;
type MobilityRatio = Real (final quantity=
  "MobilityRatio", final unit="1");
type RelaxationTime = Time;
type CarrierLifeTime = Time;
type ExchangeIntegral = Real (final quantity="Energy",
  final unit="eV");
type CurieTemperature = ThermodynamicTemperature;
type NeelTemperature = ThermodynamicTemperature;
type LondonPenetrationDepth = Length;
type CoherenceLength = Length;
type LandauGinzburgParameter = Real (final quantity=
  "LandauGinzburgParameter", final unit="1");
type FluxiodQuantum = Real (final quantity=
  "FluxiodQuantum", final unit="Wb");
type TimeAging = Real (final quantity=
  "1/Modelica.SIunits.Time",final unit="1/s");
type ChargeAging = Real (
  final quantity="1/Modelica.SIunits.ElectricCharge",
  final unit="1/(A.s)");

 // Other types not defined in ISO 31-1992
type PerUnit = Real(unit = "1");

 // Complex types for electrical systems (not defined in
ISO 31-1992)
operator record ComplexCurrent =
  Complex(redeclare Modelica.SIunits.Current re,
          redeclare Modelica.SIunits.Current im)
  "Complex electrical current";
operator record ComplexCurrentSlope =
  Complex(redeclare Modelica.SIunits.CurrentSlope re,
          redeclare Modelica.SIunits.CurrentSlope im)
  "Complex current slope";
operator record ComplexCurrentDensity =
  Complex(redeclare Modelica.SIunits.CurrentDensity re,
          redeclare Modelica.SIunits.CurrentDensity im)
  "Complex electrical current density";
operator record ComplexElectricPotential =
  Complex(
    redeclare Modelica.SIunits.ElectricPotential re,
    redeclare Modelica.SIunits.ElectricPotential im)
  "Complex electric potential";
operator record ComplexPotentialDifference =
  Complex(
    redeclare Modelica.SIunits.PotentialDifference re,
    redeclare Modelica.SIunits.PotentialDifference im)
  "Complex electric potential difference";
operator record ComplexVoltage =
  Complex(redeclare Modelica.SIunits.Voltage re,
          redeclare Modelica.SIunits.Voltage im)
  "Complex electrical voltage";
operator record ComplexVoltageSlope =
  Complex(redeclare Modelica.SIunits.VoltageSlope re,
          redeclare Modelica.SIunits.VoltageSlope im)
  "Complex voltage slope";
operator record ComplexElectricFieldStrength =
  Complex(
    redeclare Modelica.SIunits.ElectricFieldStrength re,
    redeclare Modelica.SIunits.ElectricFieldStrength im)
  "Complex electric field strength";
operator record ComplexElectricFluxDensity =
  Complex(
    redeclare Modelica.SIunits.ElectricFluxDensity re,
    redeclare Modelica.SIunits.ElectricFluxDensity im)
  "Complex electric flux density";
operator record ComplexElectricFlux =
  Complex(redeclare Modelica.SIunits.ElectricFlux re,
          redeclare Modelica.SIunits.ElectricFlux im)
  "Complex electric flux";
operator record ComplexMagneticFieldStrength =
  Complex(
    redeclare Modelica.SIunits.MagneticFieldStrength re,
    redeclare Modelica.SIunits.MagneticFieldStrength im)
  "Complex magnetic field strength";
operator record ComplexMagneticPotential =
  Complex(
    redeclare Modelica.SIunits.MagneticPotential re,
    redeclare Modelica.SIunits.MagneticPotential im)
  "Complex magnetic potential";
operator record ComplexMagneticPotentialDifference =
  Complex(
    redeclareModelica.SIunits.MagneticPotentialDifference
     re,
   redeclare Modelica.SIunits.MagneticPotentialDifference
     im)
  "Complex magnetic potential difference";
operator record ComplexMagnetomotiveForce =
  Complex(
    redeclare Modelica.SIunits.MagnetomotiveForce re,
    redeclare Modelica.SIunits.MagnetomotiveForce im)
  "Complex magneto motive force";
operator record ComplexMagneticFluxDensity =
  Complex(
    redeclare Modelica.SIunits.MagneticFluxDensity re,
    redeclare Modelica.SIunits.MagneticFluxDensity im)
  "Complex magnetic flux density";
operator record ComplexMagneticFlux =
  Complex(redeclare Modelica.SIunits.MagneticFlux re,
          redeclare Modelica.SIunits.MagneticFlux im)
  "Complex magnetic flux";
operator record ComplexReluctance =
  Complex(redeclare Modelica.SIunits.Reluctance re,
          redeclare Modelica.SIunits.Reluctance im)
"Complex reluctance"

end SIunits;
```

Modelica.SIunits.Conversions

Conversion functions to/from non SI units and type definitions of non SI units

This subpackage provides conversion functions from the non SI Units defined in package Modelica.SIunits.Conversions.NonSIunits to the corresponding SI Units defined in package Modelica.SIunits and vice versa. It is recommended to use these functions in the following way:

```
  import SI = Modelica.SIunits;
  import Modelica.SIunits.Conversions.*;
     ...
  // convert 25 degree Celsius to Kelvin
  parameter SI.Temperature      T    = from_degC(25);
  // convert 180 degree to radian
  parameter SI.Angle            phi = from_deg(180);
// convert 3600 revolutions per minutes
// to radian per seconds
  parameter SI.AngularVelocity w    = from_rpm(3600);
```

Below two functions are shown as examples. The subpackage contains about 36 conversion functions.

Modelica.SIunits.Conversions.to_degC

Convert from Kelvin to °Celsius

```
function to_degC "Convert from Kelvin to degCelsius"
  extends Modelica.SIunits.Icons.Conversion;
  input Temperature Kelvin "Kelvin value";
  output NonSIunits.Temperature_degC Celsius
    "Celsius value";
algorithm
  Celsius := Kelvin + Modelica.Constants.T_zero;
  annotation (Inline=true);
end to_degC;
```

Modelica.SIunits.Conversions.from_degC

Convert from °Celsius to Kelvin

```
function from_degC "Convert from °Celsius to Kelvin"
  extends Modelica.SIunits.Icons.Conversion;
  input NonSIunits.Temperature_degC Celsius
    "Celsius value";
  output Temperature Kelvin "Kelvin value";
algorithm
  Kelvin := Celsius - Modelica.Constants.T_zero;
  annotation (Inline=true);
end from_degC;
```

Modelica.Math

Main Author: Martin Otter.

Author of the random subpackage: Hubertus Tummescheit.

This package contains the basic mathematical functions which are used by calling them directly with a full name (e.g. y = Modelica.Math.asin(0.5), or by short name y=asin(0.5)). An overview of the contents of this package including its subpackages is available in Section 16.2, page 920. Below the source code of selected `Modelica.Math` functions are shown

Modelica.Math.sin

Sine

```
function sin "Sine"
  extends Modelica.Math.Icons.AxisLeft;
  input Modelica.SIunits.Angle u;
  output Real y;
external "builtin" y = sin(u);
end sin;
```

Modelica.Math.cos

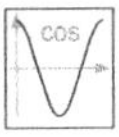

Cosine

```
function cos "cosine"
  extends Modelica.Math.Icons.AxisLeft;
  input SI.Angle u;
  output Real y;
external "builtin" y = cos(u) ;
end cos;
```

Modelica.Math.tan

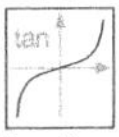

Tangent (u shall not be -pi/2, pi/2, 3*pi/2, ...)

```
function tan "Tangent (u shall not be -pi/2, pi/2,
3*pi/2, ...)"
  extends Modelica.Math.Icons.AxisCenter;
  input SI.Angle u;
  output Real y;
  external "builtin" y = tan(u) ;
end tan;
```

Modelica.Math.asin

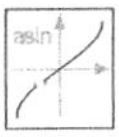

Inverse sine (-1 <= u <= 1)

```
function asin "inverse sine (-1 <= u <= 1)"
  extends Modelica.Math.Icons.AxisCenter;
  input Real u;
  output SI.Angle y;
external "builtin" y = asin(u) ;
end asin;
```

Modelica.Math.acos

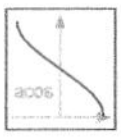

Inverse cosine (-1 <= u <= 1)

```
function acos "inverse cosine (-1 <= u <= 1)"
  extends Modelica.Math.Icons.AxisCenter;
  input Real u;
  output SI.Angle y;
external "builtin" y = acos(u) ;
end acos;
```

Modelica.Math.atan

Inverse tangent

```
function atan "inverse tangent"
  extends Modelica.Math.Icons.AxisCenter;
  input Real u;
  output SI.Angle y;
  external "builtin" y = atan(u) ;
end atan;
```

Modelica.Math.atan2

Four-quadrant inverse tangent

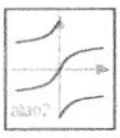

`y = atan2(u1,u2)` computes y such that `tan(y) = u1/u2` and y is in the range `-pi < y < pi`. `u2` may be zero, provided `u1` is not zero.

```
function atan2 "four quadrant inverse tangent"
  extends Modelica.Math.Icons.AxisCenter;
  input Real u1;
  input Real u2;
  output SI.Angle y;
external "builtin" y = atan2(u1,u2) ;
end atan2;
```

Modelica.Math.sinh

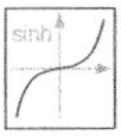

Hyperbolic sine

```
function sinh "hyperbolic sine"
  extends Modelica.Math.Icons.AxisCenter;
  input Real u;
  output Real y;
  external "builtin" y = sinh(u) ;
end sinh;
```

Modelica.Math.cosh

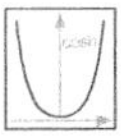

Hyperbolic cosine

```
function cosh "hyperbolic cosine"
  extends Modelica.Math.Icons.AxisCenter;
  input Real u;
  output Real y;
external "builtin" y = cosh(u) ;
end cosh;
```

Modelica.Math.tanh

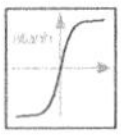

Hyperbolic tangent

```
function tanh "hyperbolic tangent"
  extends Modelica.Math.Icons.AxisCenter;
  input Real u;
  output Real y;
external "builtin" y = tanh(u) ;
end tanh;
```

Modelica.Math.exp

Exponential, base e

```
function exp "exponential, base e"
  extends Modelica.Math.Icons.AxisCenter;
  input Real u;
  output Real y;
  external "builtin" y = exp(u) ;
end exp;
```

Modelica.Math.log

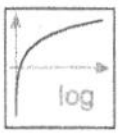

Natural (base e) logarithm (u shall be > 0)

```
function log "natural (base e) logarithm (u shall be >
0)"
  extends Modelica.Math.Icons.AxisLeft;
  input Real u;
  output Real y;
external "builtin" y = log(u) ;
end log;
```

Modelica.Math.log10

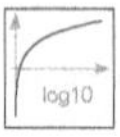

Base 10 logarithm (u shall be > 0)

```
function log10 "base 10 logarithm (u shall be > 0)"
  extends Modelica.Math.Icons.AxisLeft;
  input Real u;
  output Real y;
  external "builtin" y = log10(u) ;
end log10;
```

Modelica.Math.Random

This `Random` package is not yet part of the Modelica standard library but in this book placed as a preliminary subpackage of Math containing the following two random distribution functions random() for uniform distributions and normalvariate() for Normal distribution.

Package header:

```
package Random
  import Modelica.Math; // import might not be needed
  constant Real NV_MAGICCONST=4*exp(-0.5)/sqrt(2.0);
  type Seed = Real[3];
```

Modelica.Math.Random.random

Uniform distribution random function

Distribution uniform between 0 and 1.

```
function random "input random number generator with
external storage of the seed"
  input Seed si "input random seed";
  output Real x "uniform random variate between 0 and 1";
  output Seed so "output random seed";
algorithm
  so[1] := abs(rem((171 * si[1]),30269));
  so[2] := abs(rem((172 * si[2]),30307));
  so[3] := abs(rem((170 * si[3]),30323));
  // zero is a poor Seed, therfore substitute 1;
  if so[1] == 0 then
    so[1] := 1;
  end if;
  if so[2] == 0 then
    so[2] := 1;
  end if;
  if so[3] == 0 then
    so[3] := 1;
  end if;
  x := rem((so[1]/30269.0 +so[2]/30307.0 +
   so[3]/30323.0),1.0);
end random;
```

Modelica.Math.Random.normalvariate

Normal distribution random function

```
function normalvariate "normally distributed random
variable"
  input Real mu "mean value";
  input Real sigma "standard deviation";
  input Seed si "input random seed";
  output Real x "gaussian random variate";
  output Seed so "output random seed";
protected
  Seed s1, s2;
  Real z, zz, u1, u2;
  Boolean break=false;
algorithm
  s1 := si;
  u2 := 1;
  while not break loop
    (u1,s2) := random(s1);
    (u2,s1) := random(s2);
    z := NV_MAGICCONST*(u1-0.5)/u2;
    zz := z*z/4.0;
    break := zz <= (- Math.log(u2));
  end while;
  x := mu + z*sigma;
  so := s1;
end normalvariate;
```

Modelica.Blocks

Main Author: Martin Otter.

This library contains input/output blocks to build block diagrams.

See Section 16.8, page 936, for an overview of this library.

Modelica.Blocks.Interfaces

This package contains interface definitions for *continuous* input/output blocks. In particular it includes the following *connector* classes:

RealInput	Connector with one input signal of type Real.
RealOutput	Connector with one output signal of type Real.
BooleanInput	Connector with one input signal of type Boolean.
BooleanOutput	Connector with one output signal of type Boolean.
IntegerInput	Connector with one input signal of type Integer.
IntegerOutput	Connector with one output signal of type Integer.

See Section 16.8.2, page 937, for an overview of this library.

A few models from the library are shown below:

Modelica.Blocks.Interfaces.RealInput

Connector with one input signal of type Real

```
connector RealInput = input Real
"Connector with one input signal of type Real";
```

Modelica.Blocks.Interfaces.RealOutput

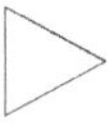

Connector with one output signal of type Real

```
connector RealOutput = output Real
"Connector with one output signal of type Real";
```

Modelica.Blocks.Interfaces.BooleanInput

Connector with one input signal of type Boolean

```
connector BooleanInput = input Boolean
  "Connector with one input signal of type Boolean";
```

Modelica.Blocks.Interfaces.BooleanOutput

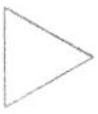

Connector with one output signal of type Boolean

```
connector BooleanOutput = output Boolean
  "Connector with one output signal of type Boolean";
```

Modelica.Blocks.Interfaces.SO

Single Output continuous control block

```
partial block SO "Single Output continuous control block"
  extends Modelica.Blocks.Icons.Block;
  RealOutput y "Connector of Real output signal";
end SO;
```

Modelica.Blocks.Interfaces.MO

Multiple Output continuous control block

```
partial block MO "Multiple Output continuous control
block"
  extends Modelica.Blocks.Icons.Block;
  parameter Integer nout(min = 1) = 1 "Number of
outputs";
  RealOutput y[nout] "Connector of Real output signals"
a;
end MO;
```

Modelica.Blocks.Interfaces.SISO

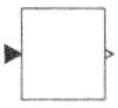

Single Input Single Output continuous control block

```
partial block SISO
  "Single Input Single Output continuous control block"
  extends Modelica.Blocks.Icons.Block;
  RealInput u "Connector of Real input signal";
  RealOutput y "Connector of Real output signal";
end SISO;
```

Modelica.Blocks.Interfaces.SI2SO

2 Single Input/1 Single Output continuous control block

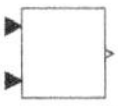

Block has two input vectors u1 and u2 and one output vector y. All signals are scalar.

```
partial block SI2SO
  "2 Single Input / 1 Single Output continuous control
block"
  extends Modelica.Blocks.Icons.Block;
  RealInput u1 "Connector of Real input signal 1";
  RealInput u2 "Connector of Real input signal 2";
  RealOutput y "Connector of Real output signal";
end SI2SO;
```

Modelica.Blocks.Interfaces.MISO

Multiple Input Single Output continuous control block

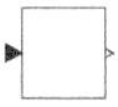

Block has a vector of continuous input signals and one continuous output signal.

```
partial block MISO
  "Multiple Input Single Output continuous control block"
  extends Modelica.Blocks.Icons.Block;
  parameter Integer nin = 1 "Number of inputs";
  RealInput u[nin] "Connector of Real input signals";
  RealOutput y "Connector of Real output signal";
end MISO;
```

Modelica.Blocks.Interfaces.MIMO

Multiple Input Multiple Output continuous control block

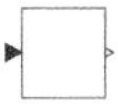

Block has a continuous input and a continuous output signal vector. The signal sizes of the input and output vector may be different.

```
partial block MIMO
  "Multiple Input Multiple Output continuous control
block"
  extends Modelica.Blocks.Icons.Block;
  parameter Integer nin=1 "Number of inputs";
  parameter Integer nout=1 "Number of outputs";
  RealInput u[nin] "Connector of Real input signals";
  RealOutput y[nout]
    "Connector of Real output signals";
end MIMO;
```

Modelica.Blocks.Interfaces.MIMOs

Multiple Input Multiple Output continuous control block with same number of inputs and outputs

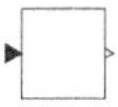

Block has a continuous input and a continuous output signal vector where the signal sizes of the input and output vector are identical.

```
partial block MIMOs
  "Multiple Input Multiple Output continuous control
block with same number of inputs and outputs"
  extends Modelica.Blocks.Icons.Block;
  parameter Integer n=1 "Number of inputs (= number of
outputs)";
  RealInput u[n] "Connector of Real input signals";
  RealOutput y[n] "Connector of Real output signals";
end MIMOs;
```

Modelica.Blocks.Interfaces.MI2MO

2 Multiple Input/Multiple Output continuous control block

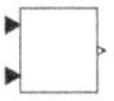

Block has two Input vectors u1 and u2 and one output vector y. All vectors have the same number of elements.

```
partial block MI2MO "2 Multiple Input / Multiple Output
continuous control block"
  extends Modelica.Blocks.Icons.Block;
  parameter Integer n=1
    "Dimension of input and output vectors.";
  RealInput u1[n] "Connector 1 of Real input signals";
  RealInput u2[n] "Connector 2 of Real input signals";
  RealOutput y[n] "Connector of Real output signals";
end MI2MO;
```

Modelica.Blocks.Interfaces.SignalSource

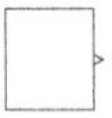

Base class for continuous signal source

```
partial block SignalSource
"Base class for continuous signal source"
  extends SO;
  parameter Real offset=0 "offset of output signal";
  parameter SIunits.Time startTime=0
    "output = offset for time < startTime";
end SignalSource;
```

Modelica.Blocks.Interfaces.SVcontrol

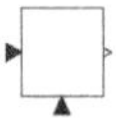

Single-variable continuous controller

```
partial block SVcontrol
"Single-Variable continuous controller"
  extends Modelica.Blocks.Icons.Block;;
  input RealInput u_s "Connector of setpoint input
signal";
  RealInput u_m
    "Connector of measurement input signal";
  RealOutput y "Connector of actuator output signal";
end SVcontrol;
```

Modelica.Blocks.Interfaces.MVcontrol

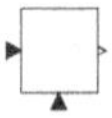

Multivariable continuous controller

```
partial block MVcontrol
"Multi-Variable continuous controller"
  extends Modelica.Blocks.Icons.Block;
  parameter Integer nu_s=1 "Number of setpoint inputs";
  parameter Integer nu_m=1
    "Number of measurement inputs";
  parameter Integer ny=1 "Number of actuator outputs";
  RealInput u_s[nu_s]
    "Connector of setpoint input signals";
  RealInput u_m[nu_m]
    "Connector of measurement input signals";
  RealOutput y[ny]
    "Connector of actuator output signals";
end MVcontrol;
```

Modelica.Blocks.Interfaces.BooleanBlockIcon

Basic graphical layout of Boolean block

```
partial block BooleanBlockIcon "This icon will be removed
in future Modelica versions, use
Modelica.Blocks.Icons.BooleanBlock instead."
end BooleanBlockIcon;
```

Modelica.Blocks.Interfaces.BooleanSISO

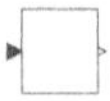

Single Input Single Output control block with signals of type Boolean

```
partial block BooleanSISO "Single Input Single Output
control block with signals of type Boolean"
  extends Modelica.Blocks.Icons.BooleanBlock;
public
  BooleanInput u "Connector of Boolean input signal";
  BooleanOutput y "Connector of Boolean output signal";
end BooleanSISO;
```

Modelica.Blocks.Interfaces.BooleanSignalSource

Base class for Boolean signal sources

```
partial block BooleanSignalSource
  "Base class for Boolean signal sources"
  extends Modelica.Blocks.Icons.BooleanBlock;
  BooleanOutput y "Connector of Boolean output signal";
end BooleanSignalSource;
```

Modelica.Blocks.Interfaces.MI2BooleanMOs

2 Multiple Input/Boolean Multiple Output block with same signal lengths

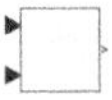

Block has two Boolean input vectors u1 and u2 and one Boolean output vector y. All vectors have the same number of elements.

```
partial block MI2BooleanMOs "2 Multiple Input / Boolean
Multiple Output block with same signal lengths"
  extends BooleanBlockIcon;
  parameter Integer n=1
    "Dimension of input and output vectors.";
  RealInput u1[n]
    "Connector 1 of Boolean input signals";
  RealInput u2[n]
    "Connector 2 of Boolean input signals";
  BooleanOutput y[n]
    "Connector of Boolean output signals";
end MI2BooleanMOs;
```

Modelica.Blocks.Interfaces.IntegerInput

Connector with one input signal of type Integer

```
connector IntegerInput = input Integer
"Connector with input signals of type Integer";
```

Modelica.Blocks.Interfaces.IntegerOutput

Connector with one output signal of type Integer

```
connector IntegerOutput = output Integer
"Connector with output signals of type Integer";
```

Modelica.Blocks.Continuous

This subpackage contains basic *continuous* input/output blocks. See Section 16.8.3, page 940, for an overview of this sublibrary. Source code for selected models is included below.

Modelica.Blocks.Continuous.Integrator

Output the integral of the input signals

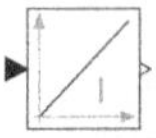

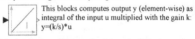

This blocks computes output y (element-wise) as integral of the input u multiplied with the gain k: y=(k/s)*u

```
block Integrator "Output the integral of the input
signals"
  import Modelica.Blocks.Types.Init;
  parameter Real k(unit = "1") = 1 "Integrator gain";
  /* InitialState is the default, because it was the
     default in Modelica 2.2 and therefore this setting
     is backward compatible
  */
  parameter Modelica.Blocks.Types.Init initType =
  Modelica.Blocks.Types.Init.InitialState
    "Type of initialization (1: no init, 2: steady state,
    3,4: initial output)";
  parameter Real y_start = 0
    "Initial or guess value of output (= state)";
  extends Interfaces.SISO(y(start = y_start));
initial equation
  if initType == Init.SteadyState then
    der(y) = 0;
  elseif initType == Init.InitialState or initType ==
Init.InitialOutput then
    y = y_start;
  else
  end if;
equation
  der(y) = k * u;
end Integrator;
```

Modelica.Blocks.Continuous.LimIntegrator

Integrator with limited values of the outputs

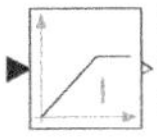

This blocks computes y (element-wise) as integral of the input u multiplied with the gain k. If the integral reaches a given upper or lower limit and the input will drive the integral outside of this bound, the integration is halted and only restarted if the input drives the integral away from the bounds.

```
block LimIntegrator "Integrator with limited values of
the outputs"
  import Modelica.Blocks.Types.Init;
  parameter Real k(unit = "1") = 1 "Integrator gain";
  parameter Real outMax(start = 1)
    "Upper limit of output";
  parameter Real outMin = -outMax
    "Lower limit of output";
  parameter Modelica.Blocks.Types.Init initType =
    Modelica.Blocks.Types.Init.InitialState
    "Type of initialization (1: no init, 2: steady state,
    3/4: initial output)" ;
  parameter Boolean limitsAtInit = true
    "= false, if limits are ignored during initialization
    (i.e., der(y)=k*u)";
  parameter Real y_start = 0 "Initial or guess value of
    output (must be in the limits outMin .. outMax)";
  parameter Boolean strict = false
    "= true, if strict limits with noEvent(..)";
  extends Interfaces.SISO(y(start = y_start));
initial equation
  if initType == Init.SteadyState then
    der(y) = 0;
  elseif initType == Init.InitialState or initType ==
Init.InitialOutput then
    y = y_start;
  else
  end if;
equation
  if initial() and not limitsAtInit then
    der(y) = k * u;
    assert(y >= outMin - 0.001 * abs(outMax - outMin) and
      y <= outMax + 0.001 * abs(outMax - outMin),
      "LimIntegrator: During initialization the limits
      have been ignored.\n" + "However, the result is
      that the output y is not within the required
      limits:\n" + "  y = " + String(y) + ", outMin = " +
      String(outMin) + ", outMax = " + String(outMax));
  elseif strict then
    der(y) = noEvent(if y < outMin and k * u < 0 or y >
      outMax and k * u > 0 then 0 else k * u);
  else
    der(y) = if y < outMin and k * u < 0 or y > outMax
      and k * u > 0 then 0 else k * u;
  end if;
end LimIntegrator;
```

Modelica.Blocks.Continuous.Derivative

Approximated derivative block

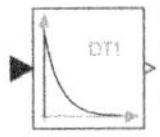

This block defines the transfer function between the input u and the output y element-wise as *approximated derivative*: y = ((k * s) / (T * s + 1)) * u

If you would like to be able to change easily between different transfer functions (FirstOrder, SecondOrder, ...) by changing parameters, use the general block TransferFunction instead and model a derivative block with parameters b = {k,0}, a = {T, 1}.

```
block Derivative "Approximated derivative block"
  import Modelica.Blocks.Types.Init;
  parameter Real k(unit = "1") = 1 "Gains";
  parameter SIunits.Time T(min =
    Modelica.Constants.small) = 0.01 "Time constants (T>0
    required; T=0 is ideal derivative block)";
  parameter Modelica.Blocks.Types.Init initType =
    Modelica.Blocks.Types.Init.NoInit "Type of
    initialization (1: no init, 2: steady state, 3:
    initial state, 4: initial output)" ;
  parameter Real x_start = 0
    "Initial or guess value of state" ;
  parameter Real y_start = 0
    "Initial value of output (= state)" ;
  extends Interfaces.SISO;
  output Real x(start = x_start) "State of block";
protected
  parameter Boolean zeroGain = abs(k) <
    Modelica.Constants.eps;
initial equation
  if initType == Init.SteadyState then
    der(x) = 0;
  elseif initType == Init.InitialState then
    x = x_start;
  elseif initType == Init.InitialOutput then
    if zeroGain then
      x = u;
    else
      y = y_start;
    end if;
  else
  end if;
equation
  der(x) = if zeroGain then 0 else (u - x) / T;
  y = if zeroGain then 0 else k / T * (u - x);
end Derivative;
```

Modelica.Blocks.Continuous.FirstOrder

First-order transfer function block (= 1 pole)

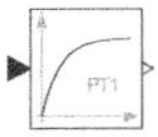

This blocks defines the transfer function between the input u and the output y (element-wise) as first order system: y = (k / (T * s + 1)) * u

If you would like to be able to change easily between different transfer functions (FirstOrder, SecondOrder, ...) by changing parameters, use the general block TransferFunction instead and model a first order SISO system with parameters b = {k}, a = {T, 1}.

```
block FirstOrder
"First order transfer function block (= 1 pole)"
  import Modelica.Blocks.Types.Init;
  parameter Real k(unit = "1") = 1 "Gain";
  parameter SIunits.Time T(start = 1) "Time Constant";
  parameter Modelica.Blocks.Types.Init initType =
    Modelica.Blocks.Types.Init.NoInit "Type of
    initialization (1: no init, 2: steady state, 3/4:
    initial output)";
  parameter Real y_start = 0 "Initial or guess value of
    output (= state)";
  extends Interfaces.SISO(y(start = y_start));
initial equation
  if initType == Init.SteadyState then
    der(y) = 0;
  elseif initType == Init.InitialState or initType ==
  Init.InitialOutput then
    y = y_start;
  else
  end if;
equation
  der(y) = (k * u - y) / T;
end FirstOrder;
```

Modelica.Blocks.Continuous.SecondOrder

Second-order transfer function block (= 2 poles)

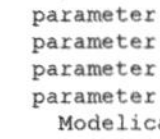

This blocks defines the transfer function between the input u and the output y (element-wise) as second order system: y = (k / ((s / w)^2 + 2*D*(s / w) + 1)) * u

If you would like to be able to change easily between different transfer functions (FirstOrder, SecondOrder, ...) by changing parameters, use the general model class TransferFunction instead and model a second order SISO system with parameters b = {k}, a = {1/w^2, 2*D/w, 1}.

```
block SecondOrder
"Second order transfer function block (= 2 poles)"
  import Modelica.Blocks.Types.Init;
  parameter Real k(unit = "1") = 1 "Gain";
  parameter Real w(start = 1) "Angular frequency";
  parameter Real D(start = 1) "Damping";
  parameter Modelica.Blocks.Types.Init initType =
    Modelica.Blocks.Types.Init.NoInit "Type of
    initialization (1: no init, 2: steady state, 3/4:
    initial output)" ;
  parameter Real y_start = 0 "Initial or guess value of
    output (= state)";
  parameter Real yd_start = 0 "Initial or guess value of
    derivative of output (= state)";
  extends Interfaces.SISO(y(start = y_start));
  output Real yd(start = yd_start) "Derivative of y";
initial equation
  if initType == Init.SteadyState then
    der(y) = 0;
    der(yd) = 0;
  elseif initType == Init.InitialState or initType ==
Init.InitialOutput then
    y = y_start;
    yd = yd_start;
  else
```

```
  end if;
equation
  der(y) = yd;
  der(yd) = w * (w * (k * u - y) - 2 * D * yd);
end SecondOrder;
```

Modelica.Blocks.Continuous.PI

Proportional-Integral controller

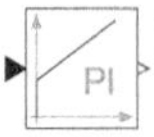

This blocks defines the transfer function between the input u and the output y (element-wise) as PI system:

$$y = k * (1 + (1 / T*s)) * u$$

$$= k * ((T*s + 1) / (T*s)) * u$$

If you would like to be able to change easily between different transfer functions (FirstOrder, SecondOrder, ...) by changing parameters, use the general model class TransferFunction instead and model a PI SISO system with parameters b = {k*T, k}, a = {T, 0}.

```
block PI "Proportional-Integral controller"
  import Modelica.Blocks.Types.Init;
  parameter Real k(unit = "1") = 1 "Gain";
  parameter SIunits.Time T(start = 1, min =
    Modelica.Constants.small) "Time Constant (T>0
    required)";
  parameter Modelica.Blocks.Types.Init initType =
    Modelica.Blocks.Types.Init.NoInit "Type of
    initialization (1: no init, 2: steady state, 3:
    initial state, 4: initial output)";
  parameter Real x_start = 0
    "Initial or guess value of state" ;
  parameter Real y_start = 0 "Initial value of output";
  extends Interfaces.SISO;
  output Real x(start = x_start) "State of block";
initial equation
  if initType == Init.SteadyState then
    der(x) = 0;
  elseif initType == Init.InitialState then
    x = x_start;
  elseif initType == Init.InitialOutput then
    y = y_start;
  else
  end if;
equation
  der(x) = u / T;
  y = k * (x + u);
end PI;
```

Modelica.Blocks.Continuous.PID

PID controller in additive description form

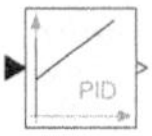

This is the text-book version of a PID-controller. For a more practically useful PID-controller, use block LimPID.

```
block PID
"PID-controller in additive description form"
  import Modelica.Blocks.Types.InitPID;
  import Modelica.Blocks.Types.Init;
  extends Interfaces.SISO;
  parameter Real k(unit = "1") = 1 "Gain";
  parameter SIunits.Time Ti(min =
    Modelica.Constants.small, start = 0.5) "Time Constant
    of Integrator";
  parameter SIunits.Time Td(min = 0, start = 0.1)
    "Time Constant of Derivative block";
  parameter Real Nd(min = Modelica.Constants.small) = 10
    "The higher Nd, the more ideal the derivative block";
  parameter Modelica.Blocks.Types.InitPID initType =
Modelica.Blocks.Types.InitPID.DoNotUse_InitialIntegratorS
    tate"Type of initialization (1: no init, 2: steady
    state,3: initial state, 4: initial output)";
  parameter Real xi_start = 0 "Initial or guess value
    value for integrator output (= integrator state)";
  parameter Real xd_start = 0 "Initial or guess value for
    state of derivative block";
  parameter Real y_start = 0 "Initial value of output";
  constant SI.Time unitTime = 1;
  Blocks.Math.Gain P(k = 1)
    "Proportional part of PID controller";
  Blocks.Continuous.Integrator I(k = unitTime / Ti,
    y_start = xi_start, initType = if initType ==
    InitPID.SteadyState then Init.SteadyState else if
    initType == InitPID.InitialState or initType ==
    InitPID.DoNotUse_InitialIntegratorState then
    Init.InitialState else Init.NoInit) "Integral part of
    PID controller";
  Blocks.Continuous.Derivative D(k = Td / unitTime, T =
    max([Td / Nd,100 * Modelica.Constants.eps]), x_start
    = xd_start, initType = if initType ==
    InitPID.SteadyState or initType ==
    InitPID.InitialOutput then Init.SteadyState else if
    initType == InitPID.InitialState then
    Init.InitialState else Init.NoInit) "Derivative part
    of PID controller";
  Blocks.Math.Gain Gain(k = k) "Gain of PID controller";
  Blocks.Math.Add3 Add ;
initial equation
  if initType == InitPID.InitialOutput then
    y = y_start;
  end if;
equation
  connect(u,P.u);
  connect(u,I.u);
  connect(u,D.u);
  connect(P.y,Add.u1);
  connect(I.y,Add.u2);
  connect(D.y,Add.u3);
  connect(Add.y,Gain.u);
  connect(Gain.y,y);
end PID;
```

Modelica.Blocks.Continuous.LimPID

PID controller with limited output, anti-windup compensation and setpoint weighting

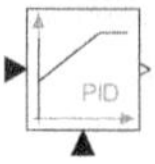

This is a PID controller incorporating several practical aspects. It is designed according to Chapter 3 of the book by K. Astroem and T. Haegglund: *PID Controllers: Theory, Design, and Tuning*, 2nd edition, 1995.

Besides the additive *proportional*, *integral*, and *derivative* part of this controller, the following practical aspects are included:

- The output of this controller is limited. If the controller is in its limits, antiwindup compensation is activated to drive the integrator state to zero.
- The high-frequency gain of the derivative part is limited to avoid excessive amplification of measurement noise.
- Setpoint weighting is present, which allows weighting the setpoint in the proportional and the derivative part independently from the measurement. The controller will respond to load disturbances and measurement noise independently of this setting (parameters wp, wd). However, setpoint changes will depend on this setting. For example, it is useful to set the setpoint weight wd for the derivative part to zero, if steps may occur in the setpoint signal.

```
block LimPID "PID controller with limited output, anti-
windup compensation and setpoint weighting"
  import Modelica.Blocks.Types.InitPID;
  import Modelica.Blocks.Types.Init;
  import Modelica.Blocks.Types.SimpleController;
  extends Interfaces.SVcontrol;
  output Real controlError = u_s - u_m
    "Control error (set point - measurement)";
  parameter .Modelica.Blocks.Types.SimpleController
    controllerType =
    Modelica.Blocks.Types.SimpleController.PID
    "Type of controller";
  parameter Real k(min = 0, unit = "1") = 1
    "Gain of controller";
  parameter SIunits.Time Ti(min =
    Modelica.Constants.small) = 0.5 "Time constant of
    Integrator block";
  parameter SIunits.Time Td(min = 0) = 0.1
    "Time constant of Derivative block";
  parameter Real yMax(start = 1) "Upper limit of output";
  parameter Real yMin = -yMax "Lower limit of output";
  parameter Real wp(min = 0) = 1
    "Set-point weight for Proportional block (0..1)";
  parameter Real wd(min = 0) = 0 "Set-point weight for
Derivative block (0..1)";
  parameter Real Ni(min = 100 * Modelica.Constants.eps) =
    0.9 "Ni*Ti is time constant of anti-windup
    compensation";
  parameter Real Nd(min = 100 * Modelica.Constants.eps)=
    10 "The higher Nd, the more ideal the derivative
    block";
  parameter .Modelica.Blocks.Types.InitPID initType =
.Modelica.Blocks.Types.InitPID.DoNotUse_InitialIntegrator
 State "Type of initialization (1: no init, 2: steady
 state, 3: initial state, 4: initial output)";
  parameter Real xi_start = 0 "Initial or guess value for
    integrator output (= integrator state)";
```

```
  parameter Real xd_start = 0 "Initial or guess value for
    state of derivative block";
  parameter Real y_start = 0 "Initial value of output";
  constant SI.Time unitTime = 1 ;
  Blocks.Math.Add addP(k1 = wp, k2 = -1);
  Blocks.Math.Add addD(k1 = wd, k2 = -1);
  Blocks.Math.Gain P(k = 1);
  Blocks.Continuous.Integrator I(k = unitTime / Ti,
    y_start = xi_start, initType = if initType ==
    InitPID.SteadyState then Init.SteadyState else if
    initType == InitPID.InitialState or initType ==
    InitPID.DoNotUse_InitialIntegratorState then
    Init.InitialState else Init.NoInit) if with_I;
  Blocks.Continuous.Derivative D(k = Td / unitTime, T =
    max([Td / Nd,0.00000000000001]), x_start = xd_start,
    initType = if initType == InitPID.SteadyState or
    initType == InitPID.InitialOutput then
    Init.SteadyState else if initType ==
    InitPID.InitialState then Init.InitialState else
    Init.NoInit);
  Blocks.Math.Gain gainPID(k = k);
  Blocks.Math.Add3 addPID ;
  Blocks.Math.Add3 addI(k2 = -1) ;
  Blocks.Math.Add addSat(k1 = +1, k2 = -1);
  Blocks.Math.Gain gainTrack(k = 1 / (k * Ni)) ;
  Blocks.Nonlinear.Limiter limiter(uMax = yMax, uMin =
    yMin, strict = strict, limitsAtInit = limitsAtInit);
protected
  parameter Boolean with_I = controllerType ==
    SimpleController.PI or controllerType ==
    SimpleController.PID;
  parameter Boolean with_D = controllerType ==
    SimpleController.PD or controllerType ==
    SimpleController.PID;
public
  Sources.Constant Dzero(k = 0);
  Sources.Constant Izero(k = 0);
initial equation
  if initType == InitPID.InitialOutput then
    gainPID.y = y_start;
  end if;
equation
  assert(yMax >= yMin, "LimPID: Limits must be
    consistent. However, yMax (=" + String(yMax) + ") <
    yMin (=" + String(yMin) + ")");
  if initType == InitPID.InitialOutput and (y_start <
  yMin or y_start > yMax) then
    Modelica.Utilities.Streams.error("LimPID: Start value
    y_start (=" + String(y_start) + ") is outside of the
    limits of yMin (=" + String(yMin) + ") and yMax (=" +
    String(yMax) + ")");
  end if;
  assert(limitsAtInit or not limitsAtInit and y >= yMin
    and y <= yMax, "LimPID: During initialization the
    limits have been switched off.\n" + "After
    initialization, the output y (=" + String(y) + ") is
    outside of the limits of yMin (=" + String(yMin) + ")
    and yMax (=" + String(yMax) + ")");
  connect(u_s,addP.u1);
  connect(u_s,addD.u1);
  connect(u_s,addI.u1);
  connect(addP.y,P.u);
  connect(addD.y,D.u);
  connect(addI.y,I.u);
  connect(P.y,addPID.u1;
  connect(D.y,addPID.u2);
  connect(I.y,addPID.u3);
  connect(addPID.y,gainPID.u);
  connect(gainPID.y,addSat.u2);
  connect(gainPID.y,limiter.u);
  connect(limiter.y,addSat.u1);
  connect(limiter.y,y);
  connect(addSat.y,gainTrack.u);
  connect(gainTrack.y,addI.u3);
  connect(u_m,addP.u2);
  connect(u_m,addD.u2);
  connect(u_m,addI.u2);
  connect(Dzero.y,addPID.u2);
  connect(Izero.y,addPID.u3);
end LimPID;
```

Modelica.Blocks.Continuous.TransferFunction

Linear transfer function

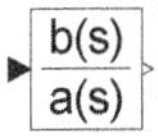

This block defines the transfer function between the input u and the output y as (nb = dimension of b, na = dimension of a):

$$y(s) = \frac{b[1]*s^{\wedge}[nb-1] + b[2]*s^{\wedge}[nb-2] + \ldots + b[nb]}{a[1]*s^{\wedge}[na-1] + a[2]*s^{\wedge}[na-2] + \ldots + a[na]} * u(s)$$

State variables *x* are defined according to *controller canonical* form. Initial values of the states can be set as start values of *x*.

```
block TransferFunction "Linear transfer function"
  import Modelica.Blocks.Types.Init;
  extends Interfaces.SISO;
  parameter Real b[:] = {1} "Numerator coefficients of
    transfer function (e.g., 2*s+3 is specified as
    {2,3})";
  parameter Real a[:] = {1} "Denominator coefficients of
    transfer function (e.g., 5*s+6 is specified as
    {5,6})";
  parameter Modelica.Blocks.Types.Init initType =
    Modelica.Blocks.Types.Init.NoInit "Type of
    initialization (1: no init, 2: steady state, 3:
    initial state, 4: initial output)";
  parameter Real x_start[size(a, 1) - 1] = zeros(nx)
    "Initial or guess values of states";
  parameter Real y_start = 0 "Initial value of output
    (derivatives of y are zero upto nx-1-th derivative)";
  output Real x[size(a, 1) - 1](start = x_start) "State
    of transfer function from controller canonical form";
protected
  parameter Integer na = size(a, 1)
    "Size of Denominator of transfer function.";
  parameter Integer nb = size(b, 1)
    "Size of Numerator of transfer function.";
  parameter Integer nx = size(a, 1) - 1;
  parameter Real bb[:] = vector([zeros(max(0, na - nb),
    1);b]);
  parameter Real d = bb[1] / a[1];
  parameter Real a_end = if a[end] > 100 *
    Modelica.Constants.eps * sqrt(a * a) then a[end] else
    1.0;
  Real x_scaled[size(x, 1)] "Scaled vector x";
initial equation
  if initType == Init.SteadyState then
    der(x_scaled) = zeros(nx);
  elseif initType == Init.InitialState then
    x_scaled = x_start * a_end;
  elseif initType == Init.InitialOutput then
    y = y_start;
    der(x_scaled[2:nx]) = zeros(nx - 1);
  else
  end if;
equation
  assert(size(b, 1) <= size(a, 1), "Transfer function is
not proper");
  if nx == 0 then
    y = d * u;
  else
    der(x_scaled[1]) = (-a[2:na] * x_scaled + a_end * u)
    / a[1];
    der(x_scaled[2:nx]) = x_scaled[1:nx - 1];
    y = (bb[2:na] - d * a[2:na]) * x_scaled / a_end + d *
u;
    x = x_scaled / a_end;
  end if;
end TransferFunction;
```

Modelica.Blocks.Continuous.StateSpace

Linear state space system

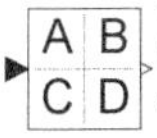

The State Space block defines the relation between the input u and the output y in state space form:

der(x) = A * x + B * u, y = C * x + D * u

The input is a vector of length nu, the output is a vector of length ny, and nx is the number of states. Accordingly,

A has the dimension: A(nx,nx),
B has the dimension: B(nx,nu),
C has the dimension: C(ny,nx),
D has the dimension: D(ny,nu)

```
block StateSpace "Linear state space system"
  import Modelica.Blocks.Types.Init;
  parameter Real A[:,size(A, 1)] = [1,0;0,1] "Matrix A
    of state space model (e.g., A=[1, 0; 0, 1])";
  parameter Real B[size(A, 1),:] = [1;1]
    "Matrix B of state space model (e.g., B=[1; 1])";
  parameter Real C[:,size(A, 1)] = [1,1]
    "Matrix C of state space model (e.g., C=[1, 1])";
  parameter Real D[size(C, 1),size(B, 2)] = zeros(size(C,
    1), size(B, 2)) "Matrix D of state space model";
  parameter Modelica.Blocks.Types.Init initType =
Modelica.Blocks.Types.Init.NoInit "Type of initialization
(1: no init, 2: steady state, 3: initial state, 4:
initial output)";
  parameter Real x_start[nx] = zeros(nx)
    "Initial or guess values of states";
  parameter Real y_start[ny] = zeros(ny)
    "Initial values of outputs (remaining states are in
    steady state if possible)";
```

```
  extends Interfaces.MIMO(final nin = size(B, 2),
    final nout = size(C, 1));
  output Real x[size(A, 1)](start = x_start)
    "State vector";
protected
  parameter Integer nx = size(A, 1) "number of states";
  parameter Integer ny = size(C, 1) "number of outputs";
initial equation
  if initType == Init.SteadyState then
    der(x) = zeros(nx);
  elseif initType == Init.InitialState then
    x = x_start;
  elseif initType == Init.InitialOutput then
    x = Modelica.Math.Matrices.equalityLeastSquares(A, -B
    * u, C, y_start - D * u);
  else
  end if;
equation
  der(x) = A * x + B * u;
  y = C * x + D * u;
end StateSpace;
```

Modelica.Blocks.Nonlinear

This subpackage contains *discontinuous* and *nondifferentiable algebraic* input/output blocks. See Section 16.8.4, page 940, for an overview of this package. Two models from the sublibrary are shown below:

Modelica.Blocks.Nonlinear.Limiter

Limit the range of a signal

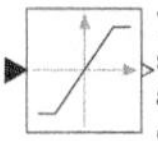

The Limiter block passes its input signal as output signal as long as the input is within the specified upper and lower limits. If this is not the case, the corresponding limits are passed as output.

```
block Limiter "Limit the range of a signal"
  parameter Real uMax(start = 1)
    "Upper limits of input signals";
  parameter Real uMin = -uMax
    "Lower limits of input signals";
  parameter Boolean strict = false
    "= true, if strict limits with noEvent(..)";
  parameter Boolean limitsAtInit = true
    "= false, if limits are ignored during initialization
    (i.e., y=u)";
  extends Interfaces.SISO;
equation
  assert(uMax >= uMin, "Limiter: Limits must be
    consistent. However, uMax (=" + String(uMax) + ") <
    uMin (=" + String(uMin) + ")");
  if initial() and not limitsAtInit then
    y = u;
    assert(u >= uMin - 0.01 * abs(uMin) and u <= uMax +
      0.01 * abs(uMax), "Limiter: During initialization
      the limits have been ignored.\n" + "However, the
      result is that the input u is not within the
      required limits:\n" + "  u = " + String(u) + ",
      uMin = " + String(uMin) + ", uMax = "String(uMax));
  elseif strict then
    y = smooth(0, noEvent(if u > uMax then uMax else if u
      < uMin then uMin else u));
  else
    y = smooth(0, if u > uMax then uMax else if u < uMin
then uMin else u);
  end if;
end Limiter;
```

Modelica.Blocks.Nonlinear.DeadZone

Provide a region of zero output

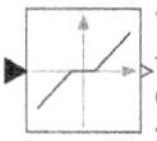

The DeadZone block defines a region of zero output. If the input is within `uMin ... uMax`, the output is zero. Outside of this zone, the output is a linear function of the input with a slope of 1.

```
block DeadZone "Provide a region of zero output"
   parameter Real uMax(start = 1) "Upper limits of dead
zones";
  parameter Real uMin = -uMax
    "Lower limits of dead zones";
  parameter Boolean deadZoneAtInit = true
    "= false, if dead zone is ignored during
    initialization (i.e., y=u)";
  extends Interfaces.SISO;
equation
  assert(uMax >= uMin, "DeadZone: Limits must be
    consistent. However, uMax (=" + String(uMax) + ") <
    uMin (=" + String(uMin) + ")");
  if initial() and not deadZoneAtInit then
    y = u;
  else
    y = smooth(0, if u > uMax then u - uMax else if u <
      uMin then u - uMin else 0);
  end if;
end DeadZone;
```

Modelica.Blocks.Math

This subpackage contains basic *mathematical operations*, such as summation and multiplication, and basic *mathematical functions*, such as *sqrt* and *sin*, as input/output blocks. See Section 16.8.5, page 940, for an overview of this package.

Modelica.Blocks.Sources

This subpackage contains *source* components, i.e., blocks which have only output signals. These blocks are used as signal generators. See Section 16.8.8, page 944, for an overview of this package. A selection of component models is shown below.

Modelica.Blocks.Sources.Clock

Generate actual time signals

```
block Clock "Generate actual time signals"
  parameter Modelica.SIunits.Time offset = 0
    "Offset of output signal";
  parameter Modelica.SIunits.Time startTime = 0
    "Output = offset for time < startTime";
  extends Interfaces.SO;
equation
  y = offset + (if time < startTime then 0 else time -
    startTime);
end Clock;
```

Modelica.Blocks.Sources.Step

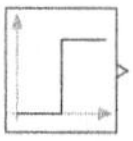

Generate step signals of type Real

```
block Step "Generate step signals of type Real"
  parameter Real height = 1 "Height of step";
  extends Interfaces.SignalSource;
equation
  y = offset + (if time < startTime then 0 else height);
end Step;
```

Modelica.Blocks.Sources.Ramp

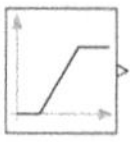

Generate ramp signals

```
block Ramp "Generate ramp signals"
  parameter Real height=1 "Heights of ramps";
  parameter Modelica.SIunits.Time duration(min = 0.0,
start = 2) "Duration of ramp (= 0.0 gives a Step)";
parameter Real offset=0 "Offsets of output signals";
  parameter SIunits.Time startTime=0
    "Output = offset for time < startTime";
  extends Interfaces.SO;
equation
  y = offset + (if time < startTime then 0
    else if time < (startTime + duration)
    then (time - startTime)*height/duration else height);
end Ramp;
```

Modelica.Blocks.Sources.Sine

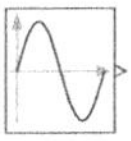

Generate sine signals

```
block Sine "Generate sine signals"
  parameter Real amplitude = 1 "Amplitude of sine wave";
  parameter SIunits.Frequency freqHz(start = 1)
    "Frequency of sine wave";
  parameter SIunits.Angle phase = 0 "Phase of sine wave";
  parameter Real offset = 0 "Offset of output signal";
  parameter SIunits.Time startTime = 0 "Output = offset
    for time < startTime";
  extends Interfaces.SO;
protected
  constant Real pi = Modelica.Constants.pi;
equation
  y = offset + (if time < startTime then 0 else amplitude
    * Modelica.Math.sin(2 * pi * freqHz * (time -
    startTime) + phase));
end Sine;
```

Modelica.Blocks.Sources.ExpSine

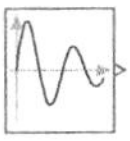

Generate exponentially damped sine signals

```
block ExpSine "Generate exponentially damped sine
signals"
  parameter Real amplitude = 1 "Amplitude of sine wave";
  parameter SIunits.Frequency freqHz(start = 2)
    "Frequency of sine wave";
  parameter SIunits.Angle phase = 0 "Phase of sine wave";
  parameter SIunits.Damping damping(start = 1)
    "Damping coefficient of sine wave";
  parameter Real offset = 0 "Offset of output signal";
  parameter SIunits.Time startTime = 0
    "Output = offset for time < startTime";
  extends Interfaces.SO;
protected
  constant Real pi = Modelica.Constants.pi;
equation
  y = offset + (if time < startTime then 0 else amplitude
    * Modelica.Math.exp(-(time - startTime) * damping) *
  Modelica.Math.sin(2 * pi * freqHz * (time -
    startTime) + phase));
end ExpSine;
```

Modelica.Blocks.Sources.Exponentials

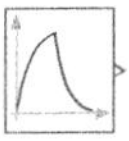

Generate a rising and falling exponential signal

```
model Exponentials
"Generate a rising and falling exponential signal"
  parameter Real outMax = 1
    "Height of output for infinite riseTime";
  parameter SIunits.Time riseTime(min = 0, start = 0.5)
    "Rise time";
  parameter SIunits.Time riseTimeConst(min =
    Modelica.Constants.small) = 0.1 "Rise time constant;
    rising is defined as outMax*(1-exp(-
    riseTime/riseTimeConst))";
  parameter SIunits.Time fallTimeConst(min =
  Modelica.Constants.small) = riseTimeConst
    "Fall time constant";
  parameter Real offset = 0 "Offset of output signal";
  parameter SIunits.Time startTime = 0
    "Output = offset for time < startTime";
  extends Interfaces.SO;
protected
  Real y_riseTime;
equation
  y_riseTime = outMax * (1 - Modelica.Math.exp(-riseTime
    / riseTimeConst));
  y = offset + (if time < startTime then 0 else if time <
     startTime + riseTime then outMax * (1 -
     Modelica.Math.exp(-(time - startTime) /
     riseTimeConst)) else y_riseTime *
     Modelica.Math.exp(-(time - startTime - riseTime) /
     fallTimeConst));
end Exponentials;
```

Modelica.Blocks.Sources.Pulse

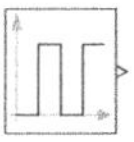

Generate pulse signals of type Real

```
block Pulse "Generate pulse signals of type Real"
  parameter Real amplitude = 1 "Amplitude of pulse";
  parameter Real width(final min =
    Modelica.Constants.small, final max = 100) = 50
   "Width of pulse in % of period";
  parameter Modelica.SIunits.Time period(final min =
    Modelica.Constants.small, start = 1)
    "Time for one period";
  parameter Integer nperiod = -1 "Number of periods (< 0
    means infinite number of periods)";
  parameter Real offset = 0 "Offset of output signals";
  parameter Modelica.SIunits.Time startTime = 0
    "Output = offset for time < startTime";
  extends Modelica.Blocks.Interfaces.SO;
protected
  Modelica.SIunits.Time T_width = period * width / 100;
  Modelica.SIunits.Time T_start "Start time of current
period";
  Integer count "Period count";
initial algorithm
  count:=integer((time - startTime) / period);
  T_start:=startTime + count * period;
equation
  when integer((time - startTime) / period) > pre(count)
  then
    count = pre(count) + 1;
    T_start = time;
  end when;
  y = offset + (if time < startTime or nperiod == 0 or
    nperiod > 0 and count >= nperiod then 0 else if time
    < T_start + T_width then amplitude else 0);
end Pulse;
```

Modelica.Blocks.Sources.SawTooth

Generate saw tooth signals

```
block SawTooth "Generate saw tooth signals"
  parameter Real amplitude = 1 "Amplitude of saw tooth";
  parameter SIunits.Time period(final min =
    Modelica.Constants.small, start = 1)
    "Time for one period";
  parameter Integer nperiod = -1 "Number of periods (< 0
    means infinite number of periods)";
  parameter Real offset = 0 "Offset of output signals";
  parameter SIunits.Time startTime = 0
    "Output = offset for time < startTime";
  extends Interfaces.SO;
protected
  SIunits.Time T_start(final start = startTime) "Start
time of current period";
  Integer count "Period count";
initial algorithm
  count:=integer((time - startTime) / period);
  T_start:=startTime + count * period;
equation
  when integer((time - startTime) / period) > pre(count)
  then
    count = pre(count) + 1;
    T_start = time;
  end when;
  y = offset + (if time < startTime or nperiod == 0 or
    nperiod > 0 and count >= nperiod then 0 else
  amplitude * (time - T_start) / period);
end SawTooth;
```

Modelica.Blocks.Sources.Trapezoid

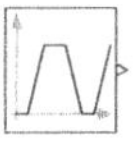

Generate trapezoidal signals of type Real

```
block Trapezoid "Generate trapezoidal signals of type
Real"
  parameter Real amplitude = 1 "Amplitude of trapezoid";
  parameter SIunits.Time rising(final min = 0) = 0
    "Rising duration of trapezoid";
  parameter SIunits.Time width(final min = 0) = 0.5
    "Width duration of trapezoid";
  parameter SIunits.Time falling(final min = 0) = 0
   "Falling duration of trapezoid";
  parameter SIunits.Time period(final min =
    Modelica.Constants.small, start = 1)
```

```
    "Time for one period";
  parameter Integer nperiod = -1 "Number of periods (< 0
    means infinite number of periods)";
  parameter Real offset = 0 "Offset of output signal";
  parameter SIunits.Time startTime = 0
    "Output = offset for time < startTime";
  extends Interfaces.SO;
protected
  parameter SIunits.Time T_rising = rising
    "End time of rising phase within one period";
  parameter SIunits.Time T_width = T_rising + width
    "End time of width phase within one period";
  parameter SIunits.Time T_falling = T_width + falling
    "End time of falling phase within one period";
  SIunits.Time T_start "Start time of current period";
  Integer count "Period count";
initial algorithm
  count:=integer((time - startTime) / period);
  T_start:=startTime + count * period;
equation
  when integer((time - startTime) / period) > pre(count)
  then
    count = pre(count) + 1;
    T_start = time;
  end when;
  y = offset + (if time < startTime or nperiod == 0 or
    nperiod > 0 and count >= nperiod then 0 else if time
    < T_start + T_rising then amplitude * (time -
    T_start) / rising else if time < T_start + T_width
    then amplitude else if time < T_start + T_falling
    then amplitude * (T_start + T_falling - time) /
    falling else 0);
end Trapezoid;
```

Modelica.Blocks.Sources.BooleanConstant

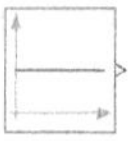

Generate constant signals of type Boolean

```
block BooleanConstant
"Generate constant signals of type Boolean"
  parameter Boolean k=true "Constant output values";
  extends Interfaces.partialBooleanSource;
equation
  y = k;
end BooleanConstant;
```

Modelica.Blocks.Sources.BooleanStep

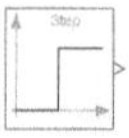

Generate step signals of type Boolean

```
block BooleanStep "Generate step signals of type Boolean"
  parameter Modelica.SIunits.Time startTime = 0
    "Time instant of step start";
  parameter Boolean startValue = false
    "Output before startTime";
  extends Interfaces.partialBooleanSource;
equation
  y = if time >= startTime then not startValue else
     startValue;
end BooleanStep;
```

Modelica.Blocks.Sources.BooleanPulse

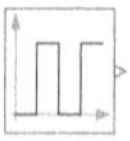

Generate pulse signals of type Boolean

```
block BooleanPulse "Generate pulse signals of type
Boolean"
  parameter Real width(final min =
Modelica.Constants.small, final max = 100) = 50 "Width of
pulse in % of period";
  parameter Modelica.SIunits.Time period(final min =
Modelica.Constants.small, start = 1) "Time for one
period";
  parameter Modelica.SIunits.Time startTime = 0 "Time
instant of first pulse";
  extends
Modelica.Blocks.Interfaces.partialBooleanSource;
protected
  parameter Modelica.SIunits.Time Twidth = period * width
/ 100 "width of one pulse" annotation(HideResult = true);
  discrete Modelica.SIunits.Time pulsStart "Start time of
pulse" annotation(HideResult = true);
initial equation
  pulsStart = startTime;
equation
  when sample(startTime, period) then
    pulsStart = time;
  end when;
  y = time >= pulsStart and time < pulsStart + Twidth;
end BooleanPulse;
```

Modelica.Electrical

Modelica.ElectricalMain Authors: Christoph Clauß and André Schneider.

This library contains electrical components to build up analog and digital circuits.

See Section 16.6, page 929, for an overview of this library. Source code for selected models is included below.

Modelica.Electrical.Analog

This subpackage contains packages for analog electrical components: See Section 16.6.1, page 929, for an overview of this library. Source code for selected models is included below.

Modelica.Electrical.Analog.Interfaces

This subpackage contains connectors and interfaces (partial models) for analog electrical components. See Section 0, page 930, for an overview of this sublibrary. Source code for selected models is included below.

Modelica.Electrical.Analog.Interfaces.Pin

Pin of an electrical component

```
connector Pin "Pin of an electrical component"
  Modelica.SIunits.Voltage v "Potential at the pin" a;
  flow Modelica.SIunits.Current i
    "Current flowing into the pin";
end Pin;
```

Modelica.Electrical.Analog.Interfaces.PositivePin

Positive pin of an electric component

Connectors `PositivePin` and `NegativePin` are nearly identical. The only difference is that the icons are different in order to more easily identify the pins of a component. Usually, connector `PositivePin` is used for the positive and connector `NegativePin` for the negative pin of an electrical component.

```
connector PositivePin "Positive pin of an electric
component"
  Modelica.SIunits.Voltage v "Potential at the pin" a;
  flow Modelica.SIunits.Current i
    "Current flowing into the pin";
end PositivePin;
```

Modelica.Electrical.Analog.Interfaces.NegativePin

Negative pin of an electric component

Connectors `PositivePin` and `NegativePin` are nearly identical. The only difference is that the icons are different in order to more easily identify the pins of a component. Usually, connector `PositivePin` is used for the positive and connector `NegativePin` for the negative pin of an electrical component.

```
connector NegativePin "Negative pin of an electric
component"
  Modelica.SIunits.Voltage v "Potential at the pin" a;
  flow Modelica.SIunits.Current i
    "Current flowing into the pin";
end NegativePin;
```

Modelica.Electrical.Analog.Interfaces.TwoPin

Component with one electrical port

```
partial model TwoPin "Component with two electrical pins"
  SI.Voltage v
    "Voltage drop between the two pins (= p.v - n.v)";
  PositivePin p "Positive pin Positive pin (potential p.v
    > n.v for positive voltage drop v)";
  NegativePin n "Negative pin";
equation
  v = p.v - n.v;
end TwoPin;
```

Modelica.Electrical.Analog.Interfaces.OnePort

Component with two electrical pins p and n and current i from p to n

Superclass of elements which have *two* electrical pins: the positive pin connector p, and the negative pin connector n. It is assumed that the current flowing into pin p is identical to the current flowing out of pin n. This current is provided explicitly as current i.

```
partial model OnePort
"Component with two electrical pins p and n and current i
from p to n"
  SI.Voltage v
    "Voltage drop between the two pins (= p.v - n.v)";
  SI.Current i "Current flowing from pin p to pin n";
  PositivePin p "Positive pin Positive pin (potential p.v
    > n.v for positive voltage drop v)";
  NegativePin n "Negative pin";
equation
  v = p.v - n.v;
  0 = p.i + n.i;
  i = p.i;
end OnePort;
```

Modelica.Electrical.Analog.Interfaces.TwoPort

Component with two electrical ports, including current

```
partial model TwoPort
"Component with two electrical ports, including current"
  SI.Voltage v1 "Voltage drop over the left port";
  SI.Voltage v2 "Voltage drop over the right port";
  SI.Current i1 "Current flowing from pos. to neg. pin of
    the left port";
  SI.Current i2 "Current flowing from pos. to neg. pin of
    the right port";
  PositivePin p1 "Positive pin of the left port
   (potential p1.v > n1.v for positive voltage drop v1)";
  NegativePin n1 "Negative pin of the left port";
  PositivePin p2 "Positive pin of the right port
   (potential p2.v > n2.v for positive voltage drop v2)";
  NegativePin n2 "Negative pin of the right port";
equation
  v1 = p1.v - n1.v;
  v2 = p2.v - n2.v;
  0 = p1.i + n1.i;
  0 = p2.i + n2.i;
  i1 = p1.i;
  i2 = p2.i;
end TwoPort;
```

Modelica.Electrical.Analog.Interfaces.AbsoluteSensor

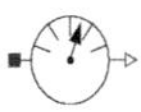

Base class to measure the absolute value of a pin variable

```
partial model AbsoluteSensor
"Base class to measure the absolute value of a pin
variable"
  extends Modelica.Icons.RotationalSensor;
  Interfaces.PositivePin p "Pin to be measured";
  Modelica.Blocks.Interfaces.RealOutput y "Measured
    quantity as Real output signal";
end AbsoluteSensor;
```

Modelica.Electrical.Analog.Interfaces.RelativeSensor

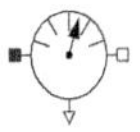

Base class to measure a relative variable between two pins

```
partial model RelativeSensor
"Base class to measure a relative variable between two
pins"
  extends Modelica.Icons.RotationalSensor;
  Interfaces.PositivePin p "Positive pin";
  Interfaces.NegativePin n "Negative pin";
  Modelica.Blocks.Interfaces.RealOutput y "Measured
   quantity as Real output signal";
end RelativeSensor;
```

Modelica.Electrical.Analog.Interfaces.VoltageSource

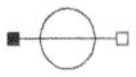

Interface for voltage sources

```
partial model VoltageSource "Interface for voltage
sources"
  extends OnePort;
  parameter SI.Voltage offset=0 "Voltage offset";
  parameter SI.Time startTime=0 "Time offset";
  replaceable Modelica.Blocks.Interfaces.SignalSource
signalSource(final offset=offset,
      final startTime=startTime);
equation
  v = signalSource.y;
end VoltageSource;
```

Modelica.Electrical.Analog.Interfaces.CurrentSource

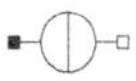

Interface for current sources

```
partial model CurrentSource "Interface for current
sources"
  extends OnePort;
  parameter SI.Current offset=0 "Current offset";
  parameter SI.Time startTime=0 "Time offset";
  replaceable Modelica.Blocks.Interfaces.SignalSource
signalSource(final offset=offset,
      final startTime=startTime);
equation
  i = signalSource.y;
end CurrentSource;
```

Modelica.Electrical.Analog.Basic

This subpackage contains basic analog electrical components. See Section 16.6.1.3, page 931, for an overview of this sublibrary. Source code for selected models is included below.

Modelica.Electrical.Analog.Basic.Ground

Ground node

Ground of an electrical circuit. The potential at the ground node is zero. Every electrical circuit has to contain at least one ground object.

```
model Ground "Ground node"
  Interfaces.Pin p;
equation
  p.v = 0;
end Ground;
```

Modelica.Electrical.Analog.Basic.Resistor

Ideal linear electrical resistor

The linear resistor connects the branch voltage *v* with the branch current i by i*R = v.

The Resistance R is allowed to be positive, zero, or negative.

```
model Resistor "Ideal linear electrical resistor"
  parameter Modelica.SIunits.Resistance R(start = 1)
    "Resistance at temperature T_ref";
  parameter Modelica.SIunits.Temperature T_ref = 300.15
    "Reference temperature";
  parameter Modelica.SIunits.LinearTemperatureCoefficient
    alpha = 0 "Temperature coefficient of resistance
    (R_actual = R*(1 + alpha*(T_heatPort - T_ref))";
  extends Modelica.Electrical.Analog.Interfaces.OnePort;
  extends
Modelica.Electrical.Analog.Interfaces.ConditionalHeatPort
(T = T_ref);
  Modelica.SIunits.Resistance R_actual "Actual resistance
    = R*(1 + alpha*(T_heatPort - T_ref))";
equation
  assert(1 + alpha * (T_heatPort - T_ref) >=
    Modelica.Constants.eps, "Temperature outside scope of
    model!");
  R_actual = R * (1 + alpha * (T_heatPort - T_ref));
  v = R_actual * i;
  LossPower = v * i;
end Resistor;
```

Modelica.Electrical.Analog.Basic.Conductor

Ideal linear electrical conductor

The linear conductor connects the branch voltage v with the branch current `I` by `i=v*G`. The Conductance G is allowed to be positive, zero, or negative.

```
model Conductor "Ideal linear electrical conductor"
  parameter Modelica.SIunits.Conductance G(start = 1)
    "Conductance at temperature T_ref";
  parameter Modelica.SIunits.Temperature T_ref = 300.15
    "Reference temperature";
  parameter Modelica.SIunits.LinearTemperatureCoefficient
    alpha = 0 "Temperature coefficient of conductance
   (G_actual = G_ref/(1 + alpha*(T_heatPort - T_ref))";
  extends Modelica.Electrical.Analog.Interfaces.OnePort;
  extends
Modelica.Electrical.Analog.Interfaces.ConditionalHeatPort
(T = T_ref);
  Modelica.SIunits.Conductance G_actual "Actual
   conductance = G_ref/(1 + alpha*(T_heatPort - T_ref))";
equation
  assert(1 + alpha * (T_heatPort - T_ref) >=
    Modelica.Constants.eps, "Temperature outside scope of
    model!");
  G_actual = G / (1 + alpha * (T_heatPort - T_ref));
  i = G_actual * v;
  LossPower = v * i;
end Conductor;
```

Modelica.Electrical.Analog.Basic.Capacitor

Ideal linear electrical capacitor

The linear capacitor connects the branch voltage *v* with the branch current `i` by `i = C * dv/dt`. The Capacitance `C` is allowed to be positive, zero, or negative.

```
model Capacitor "Ideal linear electrical capacitor"
  extends Interfaces.OnePort(v(start = 0));
  parameter SI.Capacitance C(start = 1) "Capacitance";
equation
  i = C*der(v);
end Capacitor;
```

Modelica.Electrical.Analog.Basic.Inductor

Ideal linear electrical inductor

The linear inductor connects the branch voltage *v* with the branch current `i` by `v = L * di/dt`. The Inductance `L` is allowed to be positive, zero, or negative.

The left port current is zero. Any voltage gain can be chosen.model Inductor "Ideal linear electrical inductor"

```
model Inductor "Ideal linear electrical inductor"
  extends Interfaces.OnePort(i(start = 0));
  parameter SI.Inductance L(start = 1) "Inductance";
equation
  L*der(i) = v;
end Inductor;
```

Modelica.Electrical.Analog.Basic.Transformer

Transformer with two ports

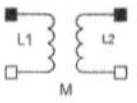

The transformer is a two port. The left port voltage `v1`, left port current `i1`, right port voltage `v2`, and right port current `i2` are connected by the following relation:

$$\begin{pmatrix} v_1 \\ v_2 \end{pmatrix} = \begin{pmatrix} L_1 & M \\ M & L_2 \end{pmatrix} \begin{pmatrix} i_1' \\ i_2' \end{pmatrix}$$

`L1`, `L2`, and `M` are the primary, secondary, and coupling inductances resp.

```
model Transformer "Transformer with two ports"
  extends Interfaces.TwoPort(i1(start = 0), i2(
    start = 0));
  parameter SI.Inductance L1(start = 1)
    "Primary inductance";
  parameter SI.Inductance L2(start = 1)
    "Secondary inductance";
  parameter SI.Inductance M(start = 1)
    "Coupling inductance";
  Real dv;
equation
  v1 = L1 * der(i1) + M * der(i2);
  /* Original equation:
       v2 = M*der(i1) + L2*der(i2);
     If L1 = L2 = M, then this model has one state less.
     However,it might be difficult for a tool to detect
     this. For this reason the model is defined with a
     relative potential:
  */
  dv = (L1 - M) * der(i1) + (M - L2) * der(i2);
  v2 = v1 - dv;
end Transformer;
```

Modelica.Electrical.Analog.Basic.Gyrator

Gyrator

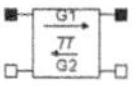

A gyrator is a two-port element defined by the following equations:

```
i1 =  G2 * v2
i2 = -G1 * v1
```

where the constants `G1`, `G2` are called the gyration conductance.

```
model Gyrator "Gyrator"
  extends Interfaces.TwoPort;
  parameter SI.Conductance G1(start = 1)
    "Gyration conductance";
  parameter SI.Conductance G2(start = 1)
    "Gyration conductance";
equation
  i1 = G2*v2;
  i2 = -G1*v1;
end Gyrator;
```

Modelica.Electrical.Analog.Basic.EMF

Electromotoric force (electric/mechanic transformer)

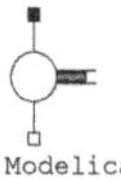

EMF transforms electrical energy into rotational mechanical energy. It is used as basic building block of an electrical motor. The mechanical connector `flange_b` can be connected to elements of the `Modelica.Mechanics.Rotational library`. `flange_b.tau` is the cut-torque, `flange_b.phi` is the angle at the rotational connection.

```
model EMF
"Electromotoric force (electric/mechanic transformer)"
  parameter Boolean useSupport = false "= true, if
    support flange enabled, otherwise implicitly
    grounded";
  parameter SI.ElectricalTorqueConstant k(start = 1)
    "Transformation coefficient";
  SI.Voltage v "Voltage drop between the two pins";
  SI.Current i "Current flowing from positive to negative
    pin";
  SI.Angle phi "Angle of shaft flange with respect to
    support (= flange.phi - support.phi)";
  SI.AngularVelocity w "Angular velocity of flange
    relative to support";
  Interfaces.PositivePin p;
  Interfaces.NegativePin n;
  Modelica.Mechanics.Rotational.Interfaces.Flange_b
    flange;
  Mechanics.Rotational.Interfaces.Support support if
    useSupport "Support/housing of emf shaft";
protected
  Mechanics.Rotational.Components.Fixed fixed if not
    useSupport;
  Mechanics.Rotational.Interfaces.InternalSupport
    internalSupport(tau = -flange.tau);
equation
  v = p.v - n.v;
  0 = p.i + n.i;
  i = p.i;
  phi = flange.phi - internalSupport.phi;
  w = der(phi);
  k * w = v;
  flange.tau = -k * i;
  connect(internalSupport.flange,support);
  connect(internalSupport.flange,fixed.flange);
end EMF;
```

Modelica.Electrical.Analog.Ideal

This subpackage contains ideal electrical analog components. See Section 16.6.1.4, page 933, for an overview of this sublibrary. Source code for selected models is included below.

Modelica.Electrical.Analog.Ideal.IdealThyristor

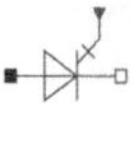

Ideal thyristor

The ideal thyristor model which is open(off), if the voltage drop is less than 0 or both the thyristor already open (off = true) and fire is false closed (not off), if both the voltage drop is greater or equal 0 and either the thyristor was already closed (off=false) or fire is true.

```
model IdealThyristor "Ideal thyristor"
  extends Modelica.Electrical.Analog.Interfaces.OnePort;
  parameter Modelica.SIunits.Resistance Ron(final
    min = 0) = 0.00001 "Closed thyristor resistance";
  parameter Modelica.SIunits.Conductance Goff(final
    min = 0) = 0.00001 "Opened thyristor conductance";
  parameter Modelica.SIunits.Voltage Vknee(final
    min = 0, start = 0) "Forward threshold voltage";
  extends
Modelica.Electrical.Analog.Interfaces.ConditionalHeatPort
(final T = 293.15);
  Boolean off(start = true) "Switching state";
  Modelica.Blocks.Interfaces.BooleanInput fire;
protected
  Real s(final unit = "1") "Auxiliary variable:
    if on then current, if opened then voltage";
  constant Modelica.SIunits.Voltage unitVoltage = 1;
  constant Modelica.SIunits.Current unitCurrent = 1;
equation
  off = s < 0 or pre(off) and not fire;
  v = s * unitCurrent * (if off then 1 else Ron) + Vknee;
  i = s * unitVoltage * (if off then Goff else 1) + Goff
    * Vknee;
  LossPower = v * i;
end IdealThyristor;
```

Modelica.Electrical.Analog.Ideal.IdealGTOThyristor

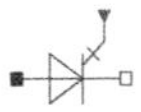

Ideal GTO thyristor

The ideal GTO thyristor model which is open (off), if the voltage drop is less than 0 or fire is false closed (not off), if the voltage drop is greater or equal 0 and fire is true.

```
model IdealGTOThyristor "Ideal GTO thyristor"
  extends Modelica.Electrical.Analog.Interfaces.OnePort;
  parameter Modelica.SIunits.Resistance Ron(final
    min = 0) = 0.00001 "Closed thyristor resistance";
  parameter Modelica.SIunits.Conductance Goff(final
    min = 0) = 0.00001 "Opened thyristor conductance";
  parameter Modelica.SIunits.Voltage Vknee(final
    min = 0, start = 0) "Forward threshold voltage";
  extends
Modelica.Electrical.Analog.Interfaces.ConditionalHeatPort
(final T = 293.15);
  Boolean off(start = true) "Switching state";
  Modelica.Blocks.Interfaces.BooleanInput fire;
protected
  Real s(final unit = "1") "Auxiliary variable:
    if on then current, if opened then voltage";
  constant Modelica.SIunits.Voltage unitVoltage = 1;
  constant Modelica.SIunits.Current unitCurrent = 1;
equation
  off = s < 0 or not fire;
  v = s * unitCurrent * (if off then 1 else Ron) + Vknee;
  i = s * unitVoltage * (if off then Goff else 1) + Goff
    * Vknee;
  LossPower = v * i;
end IdealGTOThyristor;
```

Modelica.Electrical.Analog.Ideal.IdealCommutingSwitch

Ideal commuting switch

The commuting switch has a positive pin p and two negative pins n1 and n2. The switching behaviour is controlled by the input signal control. If control is true, the pin p is connected with the negative pin n2. Otherwise, the pin p is connected to the negative pin n1. In order to prevent singularities during switching, the opened switch has a (very low) conductance Goff and the closed switch has a (very low) resistance Ron.The limiting case is also allowed, i.e., the resistance Ron of the closed switch could be exactly zero and the conductance Goff of the open switch could be also exactly zero. Note, there are circuits, where a description with zero Ron or zero Goff is not possible. Note, in case of useHeatPort=true the temperature dependence of the electrical behavior is not modelled. The parameters are not temperature dependent.

```
model IdealCommutingSwitch "Ideal electrical switch"
  parameter SI.Resistance Ron(final min = 0) = 0.00001
    "Closed switch resistance";
  parameter SI.Conductance Goff(final min = 0) = 0.00001
    "Opened switch conductance";
  extends
Modelica.Electrical.Analog.Interfaces.ConditionalHeatPort
(final T = 293.15);
  Interfaces.PositivePin p;
  Interfaces.NegativePin n2;
  Interfaces.NegativePin n1;
  Modelica.Blocks.Interfaces.BooleanInput control
    "true => p--n2 connected, false => p--n1 connected";
protected
  Real s1(final unit = "1");
  Real s2(final unit = "1") "Auxiliary variables";
  constant Modelica.SIunits.Voltage unitVoltage = 1 ;
  constant Modelica.SIunits.Current unitCurrent = 1 ;
equation
  0 = p.i + n2.i + n1.i;
  p.v - n1.v = s1 * unitCurrent * (if control then 1 else
    Ron);
  n1.i = -s1 * unitVoltage * (if control then Goff else
    1);
  p.v - n2.v = s2 * unitCurrent * (if control then Ron
    else 1);
  n2.i = -s2 * unitVoltage * (if control then 1 else
    Goff);
  LossPower = p.i * p.v + n1.i * n1.v + n2.i * n2.v;
end IdealCommutingSwitch;
```

Modelica.Electrical.Analog.Ideal.ControlledIdealCommutingSwitch

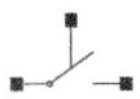

The commuting switch has a positive pin p and two negative pins n1 and n2.The switching behaviour is controlled by the control pin.

If its voltage exceeds the value of the parameter level, the pin p is connected with the negative pin n2. Otherwise, the pin p is connected the negative pin n1. In order to prevent singularities during switching, the opened switch has a (very low) conductance Goff and the closed switch has a (very low) resistance Ron.The limiting case is also allowed, i.e., the resistance Ron of the closed switch could be exactly zero and the conductance Goff of the open switch could be also exactly zero. Note, there are circuits, where a description with zero Ron or zero Goff is not possible. Please note: In case of useHeatPort=true the temperature dependence of the electrical behavior is not modelled. The parameters are not temperature dependent.

```
model ControlledIdealCommutingSwitch
  parameter SI.Voltage level = 0.5 "Switch level";
  parameter SI.Resistance Ron(final min = 0) = 0.00001
    "Closed switch resistance";
  parameter SI.Conductance Goff(final min = 0) = 0.00001
    "Opened switch conductance";
  extends
Modelica.Electrical.Analog.Interfaces.ConditionalHeatPort
(final T = 293.15);
  Interfaces.PositivePin p;
  Interfaces.NegativePin n2;
  Interfaces.NegativePin n1;
  Interfaces.Pin control "Control pin: if control.v >
    level p--n2 connected, otherwise p--n1 connected";
protected
  Real s1(final unit = "1");
  Real s2(final unit = "1") "Auxiliary variables";
  constant Modelica.SIunits.Voltage unitVoltage = 1;
  constant Modelica.SIunits.Current unitCurrent = 1;
equation
  control.i = 0;
  0 = p.i + n2.i + n1.i;
  p.v - n1.v = s1 * unitCurrent * (if control.v > level
    then 1 else Ron);
  n1.i = -s1 * unitVoltage * (if control.v > level
    then Goff else 1);
  p.v - n2.v = s2 * unitCurrent * (if control.v > level
    then Ron else 1);
  n2.i = -s2 * unitVoltage * (if control.v > level then 1
    else Goff);
  LossPower = p.i * p.v + n1.i * n1.v + n2.i * n2.v;
end ControlledIdealCommutingSwitch;
```

Modelica.Electrical.Analog.Ideal.IdealOpAmp

Ideal opamp (norator-nullator pair)

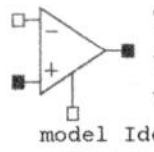

The ideal OpAmp is a two-port. The left port is fixed to v1=0 and i1=0 (nullator). At the right port both any voltage v2 and any current i2 are possible (norator).

```
model IdealOpAmp "Ideal operational amplifier (norator-
nullator pair)"
  SI.Voltage v1 "Voltage drop over the left port";
```

```
    SI.Voltage v2 "Voltage drop over the right port";
    SI.Current i1 "Current flowing from pos. to neg. pin
      of the left port";
    SI.Current i2 "Current flowing from pos. to neg. pin
      of the right port";
    Interfaces.PositivePin p1
      "Positive pin of the left port";
    Interfaces.NegativePin n1
      "Negative pin of the left port";
    Interfaces.PositivePin p2
      "Positive pin of the right port";
    Interfaces.NegativePin n2
      "Negative pin of the right port";
  equation
    v1 = p1.v - n1.v;
    v2 = p2.v - n2.v;
    0 = p1.i + n1.i;
    0 = p2.i + n2.i;
    i1 = p1.i;
    i2 = p2.i;
  v1 = 0;
  i1 = 0;
  i2 = p2.i;
  v1 = 0;
  i1 = 0;
end IdealOpAmp;
```

Modelica.Electrical.Analog.Ideal.IdealDiode

Ideal electrical diode

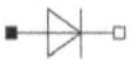

Ideal electrical diode. This is an ideal switch which is open, when it is reversed biased (voltage drop < 0), and which is closed, when it is conducting (current > 0). In order to prevent singularities during switching, the opened diode has a high resistance and the closed diode has a low resistance. If the actual circuit has an appropriate structure, the limiting case is also allowed, i.e., the resistance of the closed diode could be exactly zero and the conductance of the open diode could be also exactly zero (i.e., the resistance is infinity). Note, there are circuits where a description with zero/infinity resistances is not possible.

```
model IdealDiode "Ideal electrical diode"
  extends Modelica.Electrical.Analog.Interfaces.OnePort;
  parameter Modelica.SIunits.Resistance Ron(
    final min = 0) = 0.00001 "Forward state-on
    differential resistance (closed diode resistance)";
  parameter Modelica.SIunits.Conductance Goff(
    final min = 0) = 0.00001 "Backward state-off
    conductance (opened diode conductance)";
  parameter Modelica.SIunits.Voltage Vknee(final
    min = 0, start = 0) "Forward threshold voltage";
  extends
Modelica.Electrical.Analog.Interfaces.ConditionalHeatPort
;
  Boolean off(start = true) "Switching state";
protected
  Real s(start = 0, final unit = "1") "Auxiliary variable
   for actual position on the ideal diode
   characteristic";
  /* s = 0: knee point
     s < 0: below knee point, diode conducting
     s > 0: above knee point, diode locking */
  constant Modelica.SIunits.Voltage unitVoltage = 1;
  constant Modelica.SIunits.Current unitCurrent = 1;
equation
  off = s < 0;
  v = s * unitCurrent * (if off then 1 else Ron) + Vknee;
  i = s * unitVoltage * (if off then Goff else 1) + Goff
    * Vknee;
  LossPower = v * i;
end IdealDiode;
```

Modelica.Electrical.Analog.Ideal.IdealTransformer

Ideal electrical transformer

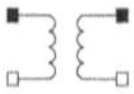

The ideal transformer is an ideal two-port resistive circuit element which is characterized by the following two equations:

```
  v1 =  n * v2
  i2 = -n * i1
```

where n is a real number called the turns ratio.

```
model IdealTransformer "Ideal transformer core with or
without magnetization"
  extends Modelica.Electrical.Analog.Interfaces.TwoPort;
  parameter Real n(start = 1)
    "Turns ratio primary:secondary voltage";
  parameter Boolean considerMagnetization = false
    "Choice of considering magnetization";
  parameter Modelica.SIunits.Inductance Lm1(start = 1)
    "Magnetization inductance w.r.t. primary side";
protected
  Modelica.SIunits.Current im1 "Magnetization current
    w.r.t. primary side";
  Modelica.SIunits.MagneticFlux psim1 "Magnetic flux
    w.r.t. primary side";
equation
  im1 = i1 + i2 / n;
  if considerMagnetization then
    psim1 = Lm1 * im1;
    v1 = der(psim1);
  else
    psim1 = 0;
    im1 = 0;
  end if;
  v1 = n * v2;
end IdealTransformer;
```

Modelica.Electrical.Analog.Ideal.IdealGyrator

Ideal gyrator

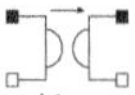

A gyrator is an ideal two-port element defined by the following equations:

```
  i1 =  G * v2
  i2 = -G * v1
```

where the constant G is called the gyration conductance.

```
model IdealGyrator "Ideal gyrator"
  extends Interfaces.TwoPort;
  parameter SI.Conductance G(start = 1)
    "Gyration conductance";
equation
  i1 = G * v2;
  i2 = -G * v1;
end IdealGyrator;
```

Modelica.Electrical.Analog.Ideal.Idle

Idle branch

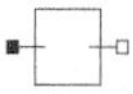

The model Idle is a simple idle running branch

```
model Idle "Idle branch"
  Interfaces.OnePort;
equation
  i = 0;
end Idle;
```

Modelica.Electrical.Analog.Ideal.Short

Short cut branch

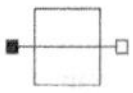

The model Short is a simple short cut branch

```
model Short "Short cut branch"
  Interfaces.OnePort;
equation
  v = 0;
end Short;
```

Modelica.Electrical.Analog.Sensors

This subpackage contains potential, voltage, and current sensors. See Section 16.6.1.5, page 934, for an overview of this sublibrary. Source code for selected models is included below.

Modelica.Electrical.Analog.Sensors.PotentialSensor

Sensor to measure the potential

```
model PotentialSensor "Sensor to measure the potential"
  extends Modelica.Icons.RotationalSensor;
  Interfaces.PositivePin p "pin to be measured";
  Modelica.Blocks.Interfaces.RealOutput phi(unit = "V")
    "Absolute voltage potential as output signal";
equation
  p.i = 0;
  phi = p.v;
end PotentialSensor;
```

Modelica.Electrical.Analog.Sensors.VoltageSensor

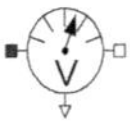

Sensor to measure the voltage between two pins

```
model VoltageSensor "Sensor to measure the voltage
between two pins"
  extends Modelica.Icons.RotationalSensor;
  Interfaces.PositivePin p "positive pin";
  Interfaces.NegativePin n "negative pin";
  Modelica.Blocks.Interfaces.RealOutput v(unit = "V")
    "Voltage between pin p and n (= p.v - n.v) as output
    signal";
equation
  p.i = 0;
  n.i = 0;
  v = p.v - n.v;
end VoltageSensor;
```

Modelica.Electrical.Analog.Sensors.CurrentSensor

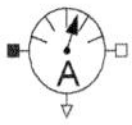

Sensor to measure the current in a branch

```
model CurrentSensor "Sensor to measure the current in
a branch"
  extends Modelica.Icons.RotationalSensor;
  Interfaces.PositivePin p "positive pin";
  Interfaces.NegativePin n "negative pin";
  Modelica.Blocks.Interfaces.RealOutput i(unit = "A")
    "Current in the branch from p to n as output signal";
equation
  p.v = n.v;
  p.i = i;
  n.i = -i;
end CurrentSensor;
```

Modelica.Electrical.Analog.Sources

This subpackage contains time-dependent and controlled voltage and current sources. See Section 16.6.1.6, page 934, for an overview of this sublibrary. Source code for selected models is included below.

Modelica.Electrical.Analog.Sources.SignalVoltage

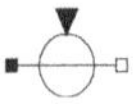

Generic voltage source using the input signal as source voltage

```
model SignalVoltage
  "Generic voltage source using the input signal as
   source voltage"
    Interfaces.PositivePin p;
  Interfaces.NegativePin n;
  Modelica.Blocks.Interfaces.RealInput v(unit = "V")
    "Voltage between pin p and n (= p.v - n.v) as input
     signal";
  SI.Current i "Current flowing from pin p to pin n";
equation
  v = p.v - n.v;
  0 = p.i + n.i;
  i = p.i;
end SignalVoltage;
```

Modelica.Electrical.Analog.Sources.ConstantVoltage

Source for constant voltage

```
model ConstantVoltage "Source for constant voltage"
  parameter SI.Voltage V(start = 1)
    "Value of constant voltage";
  extends Interfaces.OnePort;
equation
  v = V;
end ConstantVoltage;
```

Modelica.Electrical.Analog.Sources.StepVoltage

Step voltage source

```
model StepVoltage "Step voltage source"
  parameter SI.Voltage V(start = 1) "Height of step";
  extends Interfaces.VoltageSource(redeclare
    Modelica.Blocks.Sources.Step signalSource(height =
    V));
end StepVoltage;
```

Modelica.Electrical.Analog.Sources.RampVoltage

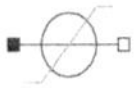

Ramp voltage source

```
model RampVoltage "Ramp voltage source"
  parameter SI.Voltage V(start = 1) "Height of ramp";
  parameter SI.Time duration(min =
    Modelica.Constants.small, start = 2)
    "Duration of ramp";
  extends Interfaces.VoltageSource(redeclare
    Modelica.Blocks.Sources.Ramp signalSource(final
    height = V, final duration = duration));
end RampVoltage;
```

Modelica.Electrical.Analog.Sources.SineVoltage

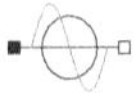

Sine voltage source

```
model SineVoltage "Sine voltage source"
  parameter SI.Voltage V(start = 1)
    "Amplitude of sine wave";
  parameter SI.Angle phase = 0 "Phase of sine wave";
  parameter SI.Frequency freqHz(start = 1)
    "Frequency of sine wave";
  extends Interfaces.VoltageSource(redeclare
    Modelica.Blocks.Sources.Sine signalSource(amplitude =
    V, freqHz = freqHz, phase = phase));
end SineVoltage;
```

Modelica.Electrical.Analog.Sources.ExpSineVoltage

Exponentially damped sine voltage source

```
model ExpSineVoltage "Exponentially damped sine voltage
source"
  parameter SI.Voltage V(start = 1)
    Amplitude of sine wave";
  parameter SI.Frequency freqHz(start = 2)
    "Frequency of sine wave";
  parameter SI.Angle phase = 0 "Phase of sine wave";
  parameter SI.Damping damping(start = 1)
    "Damping coefficient of sine wave";
  extends Interfaces.VoltageSource(redeclare
    Modelica.Blocks.Sources.ExpSine
    signalSource(amplitude = V, freqHz = freqHz, phase =
    phase, damping = damping));
end ExpSineVoltage;
```

Modelica.Electrical.Analog.Sources.ExponentialsVoltage

Rising and falling exponential voltage source

```
model ExponentialsVoltage
  "Rising and falling exponential voltage source"
  parameter Real vMax(start = 1)
    "Upper bound for rising edge";
  parameter SI.Time riseTime(min = 0, start = 0.5)
    "Rise time";
  parameter SI.Time riseTimeConst(min =
    Modelica.Constants.small, start = 0.1) "Rise time
    constant";
  parameter SI.Time fallTimeConst(min =
    Modelica.Constants.small, start = riseTimeConst)
    "Fall time constant";
  extends Interfaces.VoltageSource(redeclare
    Modelica.Blocks.Sources.Exponentials
    signalSource(outMax = vMax, riseTime = riseTime,
    riseTimeConst = riseTimeConst, fallTimeConst =
    fallTimeConst));
end ExponentialsVoltage;
```

Modelica.Electrical.Analog.Sources.PulseVoltage

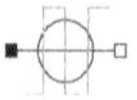

Pulse voltage source

```
model PulseVoltage "Pulse voltage source"
  parameter SI.Voltage V(start = 1) "Amplitude of pulse";
  parameter Real width(final min =
    Modelica.Constants.small, final max = 100, start =
    50) "Width of pulse in % of period";
  parameter SI.Time period(final min =
    Modelica.Constants.small, start = 1) "Time for one
    period";
  extends Interfaces.VoltageSource(redeclare
    Modelica.Blocks.Sources.Pulse signalSource(amplitude
    = V, width = width, period = period));
end PulseVoltage;
```

Modelica.Electrical.Analog.Sources.SawToothVoltage

Sawtooth voltage source

```
model SawToothVoltage "Saw tooth voltage source"
  parameter SI.Voltage V(start = 1)
    "Amplitude of saw tooth";
  parameter SI.Time period(start = 1)
    "Time for one period";
  extends Interfaces.VoltageSource(redeclare
    Modelica.Blocks.Sources.SawTooth
    signalSource(amplitude = V, period = period));
end SawToothVoltage;
```

Modelica.Electrical.Analog.Sources.TableVoltage

Voltage source by linear interpolation in a table

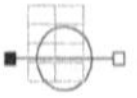

This block generates a voltage source by *linear interpolation* in a table. The time points and voltage values are stored in a matrix *table[i,j]*,

where the first column table[:,1] contains the time points and the second column contains the voltage to be interpolated. The table interpolation has the following properties:

- The time points need to be *monotonically increasing*. *Discontinuities* are allowed, by providing the same time point twice in the table.
- Values *outside* of the table range, are computed by *extrapolation* through the last or first two points of the table.
- If the table has only *one row*, no interpolation is performed and the voltage value is just returned independently of the actual time instant, i.e., this is a constant voltage source.
- Via parameters *startTime* and *offset* the curve defined by the table can be shifted both in time and in the voltage.
- The table is implemented in a numerically sound way by generating *time events* at interval boundaries, in order to not integrate over a discontinuous or nondifferentiable points.

Example:

table = [0 0
1 0
1 1
2 4
3 9
4 16]

If, e.g., `time = 1.0`, the voltage `v = 0.0` (before event), 1.0 (after event)

e.g., `time = 1.5`, the voltage `v = 2.5`,

e.g., `time = 2.0`, the voltage `v = 4.0`,

e.g., `time = 5.0`, the voltage `v = 23.0` (i.e., extrapolation).

```
model TableVoltage
  "Voltage source by linear interpolation in a table"
  parameter Real table[:,:] = [0,0;1,1;2,4] "Table matrix
  (time = first column, voltage = second column)";
  extends Interfaces.VoltageSource(redeclare
    Modelica.Blocks.Sources.TimeTable signalSource(table
    = table));
end TableVoltage;
```

Modelica.Electrical.Analog.Sources.SignalCurrent

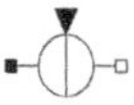

Generic current source using the input signal as source current

```
model SignalCurrent   "Generic current source using the
input signal as source current"
  Interfaces.PositivePin p;
  Interfaces.NegativePin n;
  SI.Voltage v "Voltage drop between the two pins
    (= p.v - n.v)";
  Modelica.Blocks.Interfaces.RealInput i(unit = "A")
    "Current flowing from pin p to pin n as input signal";
equation
  v = p.v - n.v;
  0 = p.i + n.i;
  i = p.i;
end SignalCurrent;
```

Modelica.Electrical.Analog.Sources.ConstantCurrent

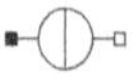

Source for constant current

```
model ConstantCurrent "Source for constant current"
    parameter SI.Current I(start = 1)
      "Value of constant current";
    extends Interfaces.OnePort;
  equation
    i = I;"
end ConstantCurrent;
```

Modelica.Electrical.Analog.Sources.StepCurrent

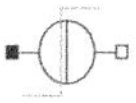

Step current source

```
model StepCurrent "Step current source"
  parameter SI.Current I(start = 1) "Height of step";
  extends Interfaces.CurrentSource(redeclare
    Modelica.Blocks.Sources.Step signalSource(height =
    I));
end StepCurrent;
```

Modelica.Electrical.Analog.Sources.RampCurrent

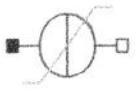

Ramp current source

```
model RampCurrent "Ramp current source"
  parameter SI.Current I(start = 1) "Height of ramp";
  parameter SI.Time duration(min =
    Modelica.Constants.small, start = 2)
    "Duration of ramp";
  extends Interfaces.CurrentSource(redeclare
    Modelica.Blocks.Sources.Ramp signalSource(final
    height = I, final duration = duration));
end RampCurrent;
```

Modelica.Electrical.Analog.Sources.SineCurrent

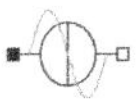

Sine current source

```
model SineCurrent "Sine current source"
  parameter SI.Current I(start = 1)
    "Amplitude of sine wave";
  parameter SI.Angle phase = 0 "Phase of sine wave";
  parameter SI.Frequency freqHz(start = 1)
    "Frequency of sine wave";
  extends Interfaces.CurrentSource(redeclare
    Modelica.Blocks.Sources.Sine signalSource(amplitude =
    I, freqHz = freqHz, phase = phase));
end SineCurrent;
```

Modelica.Electrical.Analog.Sources.ExpSineCurrent

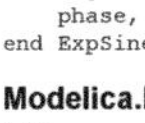

Exponentially damped sine current source

```
model ExpSineCurrent
"Exponentially damped sine current source"
  parameter Real I(start = 1) "Amplitude of sine wave";
  parameter SI.Frequency freqHz(start = 2)
    "Frequency of sine wave";
  parameter SI.Angle phase = 0 "Phase of sine wave";
  parameter SI.Damping damping(start = 1)
    "Damping coefficient of sine wave";
  extends Interfaces.CurrentSource(redeclare
    Modelica.Blocks.Sources.ExpSine
    signalSource(amplitude = I, freqHz = freqHz, phase =
    phase, damping = damping));
end ExpSineCurrent;
```

Modelica.Electrical.Analog.Sources.ExponentialsCurr ont

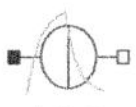

Rising and falling exponential current source

```
model ExponentialsCurrent
"Rising and falling exponential current source"
  parameter Real iMax(start = 1)
    "Upper bound for rising edge";
  parameter SI.Time riseTime(min = 0, start = 0.5)
    "Rise time";
  parameter SI.Time riseTimeConst(min =
    Modelica.Constants.small, start = 0.1)
    "Rise time constant";
  parameter SI.Time fallTimeConst(min =
    Modelica.Constants.small, start = riseTimeConst)
    "Fall time constant";
  extends Interfaces.CurrentSource(redeclare
   Modelica.Blocks.Sources.Exponentials
   signalSource(outMax = iMax, riseTime = riseTime,
   riseTimeConst = riseTimeConst, fallTimeConst =
   fallTimeConst));
end ExponentialsCurrent;
```

Modelica.Electrical.Analog.Sources.PulseCurrent

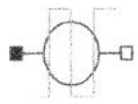

Pulse current source

```
model PulseCurrent "Pulse current source"
  parameter SI.Current I(start = 1) "Amplitude of pulse";
  parameter Real width(final min =
    Modelica.Constants.small, final max = 100, start =
    50) "Width of pulse in % of period";
  parameter SI.Time period(final min =
    Modelica.Constants.small, start = 1)
    "Time for one period";
  extends Interfaces.CurrentSource(redeclare
    Modelica.Blocks.Sources.Pulse signalSource(amplitude
    = I, width = width, period = period));
end PulseCurrent;
```

Modelica.Electrical.Analog.Sources.SawToothCurrent

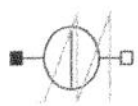

Sawtooth current source

```
model SawToothCurrent "Saw tooth current source"
  parameter SI.Current I(start = 1)
    "Amplitude of saw tooth";
  parameter SI.Time period(start = 1)
    "Time for one period";
  extends Interfaces.CurrentSource(redeclare
    Modelica.Blocks.Sources.SawTooth
    signalSource(amplitude = I, period = period));
end SawToothCurrent;
```

Modelica.Electrical.Analog.Sources.TableCurrent

Current source by linear interpolation in a table

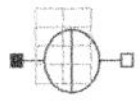

This block generates a current source by *linear interpolation* in a table. The time points and current values are stored in a matrix *table[i,j]*,

where the first column table[:,1] contains the time points and the second column contains the current to be interpolated. The table interpolation has the following properties:

- The time points need to be *monotonically increasing*. *Discontinuities* are allowed, by providing the same time point twice in the table.
- Values *outside* of the table range are computed by *extrapolation* through the last or first two points of the table.
- If the table has only *one row*, no interpolation is performed and the current value is just returned independently of the actual time instant, i.e., this is a constant current source.
- Via parameters *startTime* and *offset* the curve defined by the table can be shifted both in time and in the current.
- The table is implemented in a numerically sound way by generating *time events* at interval boundaries, in order to not integrate over a discontinuous or nondifferentiable points.

```
model TableCurrent
"Current source by linear interpolation in a table"
  parameter Real table[:,:] = [0,0;1,1;2,4]
    "Table matrix (time = first column, current = second
    column)";
  extends Interfaces.CurrentSource(redeclare
    Modelica.Blocks.Sources.TimeTable signalSource(table
    = table));
end TableCurrent;
```

Modelica.Electrical.Analog.Lines

This subpackage contains lossy and lossless transmission lines. See Section 16.6.1.7, page 935, for an overview of this sublibrary. Source code for selected models is included below.

Modelica.Electrical.Analog.Lines.Oline

Lossy transmission line

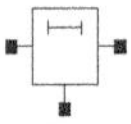

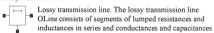

Lossy transmission line. The lossy transmission line OLine consists of segments of lumped resistances and inductances in series and conductances and capacitances that are connected with the reference pin p3. The precision of the model depends on the number N of lumped segments.

```
model OLine "Lossy Transmission Line"
  //extends Interfaces.ThreePol;
  Modelica.Electrical.Analog.Interfaces.Pin p1;
  Modelica.Electrical.Analog.Interfaces.Pin p2;
  Modelica.Electrical.Analog.Interfaces.Pin p3;
  Modelica.SIunits.Voltage v13;
  Modelica.SIunits.Voltage v23;
  Modelica.SIunits.Current i1;
  Modelica.SIunits.Current i2;
  parameter Real r(final min = Modelica.Constants.small,
    unit = "Ohm/m", start = 1) "Resistance per meter";
  parameter Real l(final min = Modelica.Constants.small,
    unit = "H/m", start = 1) "Inductance per meter";
  parameter Real g(final min = Modelica.Constants.small,
    unit = "S/m", start = 1) "Conductance per meter";
  parameter Real c(final min = Modelica.Constants.small,
    unit = "F/m", start = 1) "Capacitance per meter";
  parameter Modelica.SIunits.Length length(final min =
   Modelica.Constants.small, start = 1) "Length of line";
  parameter Integer N(final min = 1, start = 1) "Number
    of lumped segments";
  parameter Modelica.SIunits.LinearTemperatureCoefficient
    alpha_R = 0 "Temperature coefficient of resistance
    (R_actual = R*(1 + alpha*(T_heatPort - T_ref))";
  parameter Modelica.SIunits.LinearTemperatureCoefficient
    alpha_G = 0 "Temperature coefficient of conductance
    (G_actual = G_ref/(1 + alpha*(T_heatPort - T_ref))";
  parameter Boolean useHeatPort = false "=true, if
    HeatPort is enabled";
  parameter Modelica.SIunits.Temperature T = 293.15
    "Fixed device temperature if useHeatPort = false";
  parameter Modelica.SIunits.Temperature T_ref = 300.15;
  Modelica.Thermal.HeatTransfer.Interfaces.HeatPort_a
    heatPort if useHeatPort;
protected
  Modelica.Electrical.Analog.Basic.Resistor R[N + 1](R =
    fill(r * length / (N + 1), N + 1), T_ref =
    fill(T_ref, N + 1), alpha = fill(alpha_R, N + 1),
    useHeatPort = fill(useHeatPort, N + 1), T = fill(T, N
    + 1));
  Modelica.Electrical.Analog.Basic.Inductor L[N + 1](L =
    fill(l * length / (N + 1), N + 1));
  Modelica.Electrical.Analog.Basic.Capacitor C[N](C =
    fill(c * length / N, N));
  Modelica.Electrical.Analog.Basic.Conductor G[N](G =
    fill(g * length / N, N), T_ref = fill(T_ref, N),
    alpha = fill(alpha_G, N), useHeatPort =
    fill(useHeatPort, N), T = fill(T, N));
equation
  v13 = p1.v - p3.v;
  v23 = p2.v - p3.v;
  i1 = p1.i;
  i2 = p2.i;
  connect(p1, R[1].p);
  for i in 1:N loop
  connect(R[i].n, L[i].p);
  connect(L[i].n, C[i].p);
  connect(L[i].n, G[i].p);
  connect(C[i].n, p3);
  connect(G[i].n, p3);
  connect(L[i].n, R[i + 1].p);
  end for;
  connect(R[N + 1].n, L[N + 1].p);
  connect(L[N + 1].n, p2);
  if useHeatPort then
    for i in 1:N + 1 loop
      connect(heatPort,R[i].heatPort);
    end for;
    for i in 1:N loop
      connect(heatPort,G[i].heatPort);
    end for;
  end if;
end OLine;
```

Modelica.Electrical.Analog.Lines.ULine

Lossy RC line

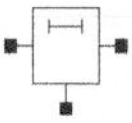

The lossy RC line ULine consists of segments of lumped series resistances and capacitances that are connected with the reference pin p3. The precision of the model depends on the number N of lumped segments.

```
model ULine "Lossy RC Line"
  //extends Interfaces.ThreePol;
  Modelica.Electrical.Analog.Interfaces.Pin p1;
  Modelica.Electrical.Analog.Interfaces.Pin p2;
  Modelica.Electrical.Analog.Interfaces.Pin p3;
  Modelica.SIunits.Voltage v13;
  Modelica.SIunits.Voltage v23;
  Modelica.SIunits.Current i1;
  Modelica.SIunits.Current i2;
  parameter Real r(final min = Modelica.Constants.small,
    unit = "Ohm/m", start = 1) "Resistance per meter";
  parameter Real c(final min = Modelica.Constants.small,
    unit = "F/m", start = 1) "Capacitance per meter";
  parameter Modelica.SIunits.Length length(final min =
   Modelica.Constants.small, start = 1) "Length of line";
  parameter Integer N(final min = 1, start = 1)
    "Number of lumped segments";
  parameter Modelica.SIunits.LinearTemperatureCoefficient
    alpha = 0 "Temperature coefficient of resistance
   (R_actual = R*(1 + alpha*(T_heatPort - T_ref))";
  parameter Boolean useHeatPort = false
    "=true, if HeatPort is enabled";
  parameter Modelica.SIunits.Temperature T = 293.15
    "Fixed device temperature if useHeatPort = false";
  parameter Modelica.SIunits.Temperature T_ref = 300.15;
  Modelica.Thermal.HeatTransfer.Interfaces.HeatPort_a
    heatPort if useHeatPort;
protected
  Modelica.Electrical.Analog.Basic.Resistor R[N + 1](R =
    fill(r * length / (N + 1), N + 1), T_ref =
    fill(T_ref, N + 1), alpha = fill(alpha, N + 1),
    useHeatPort = fill(useHeatPort, N + 1), T = fill(T, N
    + 1));
  Modelica.Electrical.Analog.Basic.Capacitor C[N](C =
    fill(c * length / N, N));
equation
  v13 = p1.v - p3.v;
  v23 = p2.v - p3.v;
  i1 = p1.i;
  i2 = p2.i;
  connect(p1,R[1].p);
  for i in 1:N loop
    connect(R[i].n,R[i + 1].p);
  end for;
  for i in 1:N loop
    connect(R[i].n,C[i].p);
  end for;
  for i in 1:N loop
    connect(C[i].n,p3);
  end for;
  connect(R[N + 1].n,p2);
  if useHeatPort then
    for i in 1:N + 1 loop
      connect(heatPort,R[i].heatPort);
    end for;
  end if;
end ULine;
```

Modelica.Electrical.Analog.-Semiconductors

This subpackage contains semiconductor devices. See Section 16.6.1.8, page 935, for an overview of this sublibrary. Source code for selected models is included below.

Modelica.Electrical.Analog.Semiconductors.Diode

Simple diode

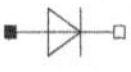

The simple diode is a one port. It consists of the diode itself and a parallel ohmic resistance *R*. The diode formula is: $i = ids\,(e^{v/vt} - 1)$. If the exponent v/vt reaches the limit maxex, the diode characteristic is linearly continued to avoid overflow.

```
model Diode "Simple diode"
  extends Modelica.Electrical.Analog.Interfaces.OnePort;
  parameter SIunits.Current Ids = 0.000001
    "Saturation current";
  parameter SIunits.Voltage Vt = 0.04
    "Voltage equivalent of temperature (kT/qn)";
  parameter Real Maxexp(final
    min = Modelica.Constants.small) = 15
    "Max. exponent for linear continuation";
  parameter SIunits.Resistance R = 100000000.0
    "Parallel ohmic resistance";
  extends
Modelica.Electrical.Analog.Interfaces.ConditionalHeatPort
(T = 293.15);
equation
 i = smooth(1, if v / Vt > Maxexp then
   Ids *(exp(Maxexp) * (1 + v / Vt - Maxexp) - 1) + v / R
   else Ids * (exp(v / Vt) - 1) + v / R);
 LossPower = v * i;
end Diode;
```

Modelica.Electrical.Analog.Semiconductors.PMOS

Simple MOS transistor

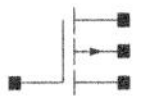

The PMOS model is a simple model of a p-channel metal-oxide semiconductor FET. It differs slightly from the device used in the SPICE simulator. For more details please care for H. Spiro. The model does not consider capacitances. A small fixed drain-source resistance is included (to avoid numerical difficulties).

```
model PMOS "Simple MOS Transistor"
   Interfaces.Pin D "Drain";
   Interfaces.Pin G "Gate";
   Interfaces.Pin S "Source";
   Interfaces.Pin B "Bulk";
  parameter SIunits.Length W = 0.00002 "Width";
  parameter SIunits.Length L = 0.000006 "Length";
  parameter SIunits.Transconductance Beta = 0.0000105
    "Transconductance parameter";
  parameter SIunits.Voltage Vt = -1.0
    "Zero bias threshold voltage";
  parameter Real K2 = 0.41 "Bulk threshold parameter";
  parameter Real K5 = 0.839
    "Reduction of pinch-off region";
  parameter SIunits.Length dW = -0.0000025
    "Narrowing of channel";
  parameter SIunits.Length dL = -0.0000021
    "Shortening of channel";
  parameter SIunits.Resistance RDS = 10000000.0
    "Drain-Source-Resistance";
  extends
Modelica.Electrical.Analog.Interfaces.ConditionalHeatPort
(T = 293.15);
protected
   Real v;
   Real uds;
   Real ubs;
   Real ugst;
   Real ud;
   Real us;
   Real id;
   Real gds;
equation
  assert(L + dL > 0, "PMOS: Effective length must be
    positive");
  assert(W + dW > 0, "PMOS: Effective width  must be
    positive");
  gds = if RDS < 1e-20 and RDS > (-1e-20) then 1e+20
    else 1 / RDS;
  v = Beta * (W + dW) / (L + dL);
  ud = smooth(0, if D.v > S.v then S.v else D.v);
  us = smooth(0, if D.v > S.v then D.v else S.v);
  uds = ud - us;
  ubs = smooth(0, if B.v < us then 0 else B.v - us);
  ugst = (G.v - us - Vt + K2 * ubs) * K5;
  id = smooth(0, if ugst >= 0 then uds * gds else
    if ugst < uds then -v * uds * (ugst - uds / 2) + uds
    * gds else -v * ugst * ugst / 2 + uds * gds);
  G.i = 0;
  D.i = smooth(0, if D.v > S.v then -id else id);
  S.i = smooth(0, if D.v > S.v then id else -id);
  B.i = 0;
  LossPower = D.i * (D.v - S.v);
end PMOS;
```

Modelica.Electrical.Analog.Semiconductors.NMOS

Simple MOS transistor

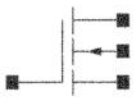

The NMos model is a simple model of an n-channel metal-oxide semiconductor FET. It differs slightly from the device used in the SPICE simulator. For more details please care for H. Spiro. The model does not consider capacitances. A small fixed drain-source resistance is included (to avoid numerical difficulties).

```
model NMOS "Simple MOS Transistor"
   Interfaces.Pin D "Drain";
   Interfaces.Pin G "Gate";
   Interfaces.Pin S "Source";
   Interfaces.Pin B "Bulk";
   parameter SIunits.Length W = 0.00002 "Width";
   parameter SIunits.Length L = 0.000006 "Length";
   parameter SIunits.Transconductance Beta = 0.000041
     "Transconductance parameter";
   parameter SIunits.Voltage Vt = 0.8
     "Zero bias threshold voltage";
   parameter Real K2 = 1.144 "Bulk threshold parameter";
   parameter Real K5 = 0.7311
     "Reduction of pinch-off region";
   parameter SIunits.Length dW = -0.0000025
     "narrowing of channel";
   parameter SIunits.Length dL = -0.0000015
     "shortening of channel";
   parameter SIunits.Resistance RDS = 10000000.0
     "Drain-Source-Resistance";
     extends
Modelica.Electrical.Analog.Interfaces.ConditionalHeatPort
(T = 293.15);
protected
   Real v;
   Real uds;
   Real ubs;
   Real ugst;
   Real ud;
   Real us;
   Real id;
   Real gds;
equation
   assert(L + dL > 0, "NMOS: Effective length must be
     positive");
   assert(W + dW > 0, "NMOS: Effective width  must be
     positive");
   gds = if RDS < 1e-20 and RDS > (-1e-20) then 1e+20
     else 1 / RDS;
   v = Beta * (W + dW) / (L + dL);
   ud = smooth(0, if D.v < S.v then S.v else D.v);
   us = if D.v < S.v then D.v else S.v;
   uds = ud - us;
   ubs = smooth(0, if B.v > us then 0 else B.v - us);
   ugst = (G.v - us - Vt + K2 * ubs) * K5;
   id = smooth(0, if ugst <= 0 then uds * gds
     else if ugst > uds then v * uds * (ugst - uds / 2) +
     uds * gds else v * ugst * ugst / 2 + uds * gds);
   G.i = 0;
   D.i = smooth(0, if D.v < S.v then -id else id);
   S.i = smooth(0, if D.v < S.v then id else -id);
   B.i = 0;
   LossPower = D.i * (D.v - S.v);
end NMOS;
```

Modelica.Electrical.Analog.Semiconductors.NPN

Simple BJT according to Ebers-Moll

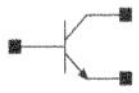

This model is a simple model of a bipolar npn junction transistor according to Ebers-Moll.

```
model NPN "Simple BJT according to Ebers-Moll"
   parameter Real Bf=50 "Forward beta";
   parameter Real Br=0.1 "Reverse beta";
   parameter SIunits.Current Is = 0.0000000000000001
     "Transport saturation current";
   parameter SIunits.InversePotential Vak = 0.02
     "Early voltage (inverse), 1/Volt";
   parameter SIunits.Time Tauf = 0.00000000012
     "Ideal forward transit time";
   parameter SIunits.Time Taur = 0.000000005
     "Ideal reverse transit time";
   parameter SIunits.Capacitance Ccs = 0.000000000001
     "Collector-substrate(ground) cap.";
   parameter SIunits.Capacitance Cje = 0.0000000000004
     "Base-emitter zero bias depletion cap.";
   parameter SIunits.Capacitance Cjc = 0.0000000000005
     "Base-coll. zero bias depletion cap.";
   parameter SIunits.Voltage Phie = 0.8
     "Base-emitter diffusion voltage";
   parameter Real Me = 0.4
     "Base-emitter gradation exponent";
   parameter SIunits.Voltage Phic = 0.8
```

```
    "Base-collector diffusion voltage";
  parameter Real Mc = 0.333
    "Base-collector gradation exponent";
  parameter SIunits.Conductance Gbc = 0.000000000000001
    "Base-collector conductance";
  parameter SIunits.Conductance Gbe = 0.000000000000001
    "Base-emitter conductance";
  parameter SIunits.Voltage Vt = 0.02585
    "Voltage equivalent of temperature";
  parameter Real EMin = -100 "if x < EMin, the exp(x)
    function is linearized";
  parameter Real EMax = 40 "if x > EMax, the exp(x)
    function is linearized";
  parameter Modelica.SIunits.Voltage IC = 0
    "Initial Value";
  parameter Boolean UIC = false;
  extends
Modelica.Electrical.Analog.Interfaces.ConditionalHeatPort
(T = 293.15);
protected
  Real vbc;
  Real vbe;
  Real qbk;
  Real ibc;
  Real ibe;
  Real cbc;
  Real cbe;
  Real ExMin;
  Real ExMax;
  Real Capcje;
  Real Capcjc;
  function pow "Just a helper function for x^y"
    extends Modelica.Icons.Function;
    input Real x;
    input Real y;
    output Real z;
  algorithm
    z:=x ^ y;
  end pow;
public
  Modelica.Electrical.Analog.Interfaces.Pin C
    "Collector";
  Modelica.Electrical.Analog.Interfaces.Pin B "Base";
  Modelica.Electrical.Analog.Interfaces.Pin E "Emitter";
initial equation
  if UIC then
    C.v = IC;
  end if;
equation
  ExMin = exp(EMin);
  ExMax = exp(EMax);
  vbc = B.v - C.v;
  vbe = B.v - E.v;
  qbk = 1 - vbc * Vak;
  ibc = smooth(1, if vbc / Vt < EMin then
    Is * (ExMin * (vbc / Vt - EMin + 1) - 1) + vbc * Gbc
    else if vbc / Vt > EMax then
    Is * (ExMax * (vbc / Vt - EMax + 1) - 1) + vbc * Gbc
    else Is * (exp(vbc / Vt) - 1) + vbc * Gbc);
  ibe = smooth(1, if vbe / Vt < EMin then
    Is * (ExMin * (vbe / Vt - EMin + 1) - 1) + vbe * Gbe
    else if vbe / Vt > EMax then
    Is * (ExMax * (vbe / Vt - EMax + 1) - 1) + vbe * Gbe
    else Is * (exp(vbe / Vt) - 1) + vbe * Gbe);
  Capcjc = smooth(1, if vbc / Phic > 0 then
    Cjc * (1 + Mc * vbc / Phic) else Cjc * pow(1 - vbc /
    Phic, -Mc));
  Capcje = smooth(1, if vbe / Phie > 0 then
    Cje * (1 + Me * vbe / Phie) else Cje * pow(1 - vbe /
    Phie, -Me));
  cbc = smooth(1, if vbc / Vt < EMin then
    Taur * Is / Vt * ExMin * (vbc / Vt - EMin + 1) +
    Capcjc else if vbc / Vt > EMax then
    Taur * Is / Vt * ExMax * (vbc / Vt - EMax + 1) +
    Capcjc else Taur * Is / Vt * exp(vbc / Vt) + Capcjc);
  cbe = smooth(1, if vbe / Vt < EMin then Tauf * Is / Vt
    * ExMin * (vbe / Vt - EMin + 1) + Capcje
    else if vbe / Vt > EMax then Tauf * Is / Vt * ExMax *
    (vbe / Vt - EMax + 1) + Capcje else Tauf * Is / Vt *
     exp(vbe / Vt) + Capcje);
  C.i = (ibe - ibc) * qbk - ibc / Br - cbc * der(vbc) +
    Ccs * der(C.v);
  B.i = ibe / Bf + ibc / Br + cbc * der(vbc) + cbe *
    der(vbe);
  E.i = -B.i - C.i + Ccs * der(C.v);
  LossPower = (C.v - E.v) * (ibe - ibc) * qbk + vbc * ibc
    / Br + vbe * ibe / Bf;
end NPN;
```

Modelica.Electrical.Analog.Examples

This package contains examples for the analog electrical packages. See Section 16.6.1.1, page 930, for an overview of this library. Source code for selected models is included below.

Modelica.Electrical.Analog.Examples.ChuaCircuit

Chua's circuit, ns, V, A

Chua's circuit is the simplest nonlinear circuit which shows chaotic behavior. The circuit consists of linear basic elements (capacitors, resistor, conductor, inductor), and one nonlinear element, which is called Chua's diode. The chaotic behavior is simulated. The simulation end time should be set to 5e4. To get the chaotic behavior please plot `C1.v`. Choose `C2.v` as the independent variable.

```
encapsulated model ChuaCircuit "Chua's circuit, ns, V, A"
  import Modelica.Electrical.Analog.Basic;
  import Modelica.Electrical.Analog.Examples.Utilities;
  import Modleica.Icons;
  extends Icons.Example;
    Basic.Inductor L(L = 18, i(start = 0, fixed = true));
    Basic.Resistor Ro(R = 0.0125);
    Basic.Conductor G(G = 0.565);
    Basic.Capacitor C1(C = 10, v(start = 4,
      fixed = true));
    Basic.Capacitor C2(C = 100, v(start = 0,
      fixed = true));
    Utilities.NonlinearResistor Nr(Ga(min = -1)
      = -0.757576, Gb(min = -1) = -0.409091, Ve = 1);
    Basic.Ground Gnd ;
    v(start=4));
    Modelica.Electrical.Analog.Basic.Capacitor C2(C=100);
  Modelica.Electrical.Analog.Examples.Utilities.
  NonlinearResistor Nr(
  Ga(min=-1) = -0.757576,
  Gb(min=-1) = -0.409091,
  Ve=1);
  Modelica.Electrical.Analog.Basic.Ground Gnd;
equation
  connect(L.p, G.p);
  connect(G.n, Nr.p);
  connect(Nr.n, Gnd.p);
  connect(C1.p, G.n);
  connect(L.n, Ro.p);
  connect(G.p, C2.p);
  connect(C1.n, Gnd.p);
  connect(C2.n, Gnd.p);
  connect(Ro.n, Gnd.p);
end ChuaCircuit;
```

Modelica.Electrical.Analog.Examples.DifferenceAmplifier

It is a simple NPN transistor amplifier circuit. The voltage difference between `R1.p` and `R3.n` is amplified. The output signal is the voltage between `R2.n` and `R4.n`. In this example the voltage at `V1` is amplified because `R3.n` is grounded. The simulation end time should be set to 1e-8. Please plot the input voltage `V1.v`, and the output voltages `R2.n.v`, and `R4.n.v`.

```
encapsulated model DifferenceAmplifier "Simple NPN
transistor amplifier circuit"
  import Modelica.Electrical.Analog.Basic;
  import Modelica.Electrical.Analog.Sources;
  import Modelica.Electrical.Analog.Examples.Utilities;
  import Modelica.Icons;
  extends Icons.Example;
  Sources.ExpSineVoltage V1(V = 0.2,
    freqHz = 200000000.0, damping = 10000000.0);
  Sources.RampVoltage V2(V = 15, duration = 0.000000001);
  Sources.RampCurrent I1(I = 0.16,
    duration = 0.000000001;
  Basic.Resistor R1(R = 0.0001);
  Basic.Resistor R2(R = 100);
  Basic.Resistor R3(R = 0.0001);
  Basic.Resistor R4(R = 100);
  Basic.Capacitor C1(C = 0.0000000001, v(start = 0,
    fixed = true));
  Basic.Capacitor C4(C = 0.0000000001, v(start = 0,
    fixed = true));
  Basic.Capacitor C5(C = 0.0000000001, v(start = 0,
    fixed = true));
  Basic.Capacitor C2(C = 0.0000000001, v(start = 0,
    fixed = true));
  Basic.Capacitor C3(C = 0.0000000001, v(start = 0,
    fixed = true));
  Basic.Ground Gnd1;
  Basic.Ground Gnd9;
  Basic.Ground Gnd3;
  Basic.Ground Gnd2;
  Basic.Ground Gnd6;
  Basic.Ground Gnd7;
  Basic.Ground Gnd8;
  Basic.Ground Gnd5;
  Basic.Ground Gnd4 ;
  Utilities.Transistor Transistor1(ct(v(start = 0,
    fixed = true)));
 Utilities.Transistor Transistor2(ct(v(start = 0,
   fixed = true)));
equation
  connect(V1.n,Gnd1.p);
  connect(C1.n,Gnd2.p);
  connect(I1.n,Gnd7.p);
  connect(C5.n,Gnd8.p);
  connect(C3.n,Gnd5.p);
  connect(R3.n,Gnd4.p);
  connect(C2.n,Gnd3.p);
  connect(C4.p,Gnd6.p);
  connect(I1.p,C5.p);
  connect(R1.p,V1.p);
  connect(R2.p,V2.p);
  connect(R4.p,V2.p);
  connect(V2.n,Gnd9.p);
  connect(R1.n,Transistor1.b);
  connect(Transistor1.b,C1.p);
  connect(Transistor1.c,C2.p);
  connect(R2.n,Transistor1.c);
  connect(Transistor1.e,I1.p);
  connect(Transistor2.b,R3.p);
  connect(Transistor2.b,C3.p);
  connect(C4.n,Transistor2.c);
  connect(R4.n,Transistor2.c);
  connect(C5.p,Transistor2.e);
```

Modelica.Electrical.Analog.Examples.NandGate

CMOS NAND Gate (see Tietze/Schenk, page 157)

The nand gate is a basic CMOS building block. It consists of four CMOS transistors. The output voltage `Nand.y.v` is low if and only if the two input voltages at `Nand.x1.v` and `Nand.x2.v` are both high. In this way the nand functionality is realized. The simulation end time should be set to 1e-7. Please plot the input voltages `Nand.x1.v`, d `Nand.x2.v`, and the output voltage `Nand.y.v`.

```
model NandGate
"CMOS NAND Gate (see Tietze/Schenk, page 157)"
  import Modelica.Electrical.Analog.Basic;
  import Modelica.Electrical.Analog.Sources;
  import Modelica.Electrical.Analog.Examples.Utilities;
  import Modelica.Icons;
  extends Icons.Example;
  Sources.TrapezoidVoltage VIN1(V = 3.5,
    startTime = 0.00000002, rising = 0.000000001,
    width = 0.000000019, falling = 0.000000001, period =
    0.00000004, nperiod = -1);
  Sources.TrapezoidVoltage VIN2(V = 3.5,
    startTime = 0.00000001, rising = 0.000000001,
    width = 0.000000019, falling = 0.000000001,
    period = 0.00000004, nperiod = -1);
  Sources.RampVoltage VDD(V = 5, duration = 0.000000001);
  Basic.Ground Gnd1;
  Basic.Ground Gnd4;
  Basic.Ground Gnd5;  .
  Utilities.Nand Nand(C4(v(start = 0, fixed = true)),
    C7(v(start = 0, fixed = true))) ;
equation
  connect(VDD.n,Gnd1.p);
  connect(VIN1.n,Gnd4.p);
  connect(VIN2.n,Gnd5.p);
  connect(Nand.Vdd,VDD.p);
  connect(VIN1.p,Nand.x1);
  connect(VIN2.p,Nand.x2);
end NandGate;
```

Appendix E

Modelica and Python Scripting

The following are short summaries of scripting commands for three different Modelica environments:

- OpenModelica
- Wolfram SystemModeler
- Dymola

These commands are useful for loading and saving classes, reading and storing data, plotting of results, and various other tasks.

The arguments passed to a scripting function should follow syntactic and typing rules for Modelica and for the scripting function in question. In the following tables, we briefly indicate the types or character of the formal parameters to the functions by the following notation:

- `String` typed argument, e.g. `"hello"`, `"myfile.mo"`.
- `TypeName` – class, package or function name, for example, `MyClass`, `Modelica.Math`.
- `VariableName` – variable name, for example, `v1`, `v2`, `vars1[2].x`, and so on.
- `Integer` or `Real` typed argument, for example, `35`, `3.14`, `xintvariable`.
- `options` – optional parameters with named formal parameter passing.

E.1 OpenModelica Modelica Scripting Commands

The following are brief descriptions of the scripting commands available in the OpenModelica environment.

E.1.1 OpenModelica Basic Commands

This is a selection of the most common commands related to simulation and plotting:

checkModel(className)	Checks a model and returns number of variables and equations. *Inputs*: `TypeName className;` *Outputs*: `String res;`
clear()	Clears everything in OpenModelica compiler and interpreter workspace: symboltable and variables. *Outputs*: `Boolean res;`
getMessagesString()	Returns the current error message. *Outputs*: `String messagesString;`
help()	Display the OpenModelica help text. *Outputs*: `String helpText;`
importFMU(fileName, workDir)	Imports a Functional Mockup Unit. *Inputs*: `String filename; String workdir "./"` "The output directory for imported FMU files. <default> will put the files to current working directory."; *Outputs*: `Boolean res;`
instantiateModel(className)	Flatten model, resulting in a `.mof` file of flattened Modelica.

	Inputs: `TypeName className;` *Outputs*: `String res;`
list(className)	Print class definition. *Inputs*: `TypeName className;` *Outputs*: `String classDef;`
listVariables()	Print user defined variables. *Outputs*: `VariableName res;`
loadFile(fileName)	Load models from file. *Inputs*: `String fileName;` *Outputs*: `Boolean res;`
loadModel(className)	Load the file corresponding to the class, using the Modelica class name to file name mapping to locate the file. *Inputs*: `TypeName className;` *Outputs*: `Boolean res;`

plot(variable, options)	Plot `variable`, which is a single variable name.
	Inputs: `VariableName variable; String title;`
	`Boolean legend; Boolean gridLines;`
	`Real xrange[2]` i.e. `{xmin,xmax};`
	`Real yrange[2]` i.e. `{ymin,ymax};`
	Outputs: `Boolean res;`

plot(variables, options)	Plot `variables`, which is a vector of variable names.
	Inputs: `VariableName variables; String title;`
	`Boolean legend; Boolean gridLines;`
	`Real xrange[2]` i.e. `{xmin,xmax};`
	`Real yrange[2]` i.e. `{ymin,ymax};`
	Outputs: `Boolean res;`

plotParametric(variables1, variables2, options)	Plot each pair of corresponding variables from the vectors of variables `variables1`, `variables2` as a parametric plot. *Inputs*: `VariableName variables1[:]; VariableName variables2[size(variables1,1)]; String title; Boolean legend; Boolean gridLines; Real range[2,2];` *Outputs*: `Boolean res;`
readFile(fileName)	The contents of the given file are returned. Note that if the function fails, the error message is returned as a string instead of multiple outputs or similar. *Inputs*: `String fileName;` *Outputs*: `String content;`
save(className)	Save class definition. *Inputs*: `TypeName className` *Outputs*: `Boolean res;`
saveAll(fileName)	Save the entire loaded AST (Abstract Syntax Tree internal representation of all loaded models) as text to a file. *Inputs*: `String fileName;` *Outputs*: `Boolean res;`
saveModel(fileName, className)	Save class definition in a file. *Inputs*: `String fileName; TypeName className` *Outputs*: `Boolean res;`
saveTotalModel(fileName, className)	Save total class definition into file of a class. *Inputs*: `String fileName; TypeName className` *Outputs*: `Boolean res;`
setDebugFlags(debugFlags)	*Inputs*: `String debugFlags;` *Outputs*: `Boolean res;`
setInitXmlStartValue(fileName, variableName, startValue, outputFile)	Sets the parameter start value in the `model_init.xml` file. No need to recompile the model. *Inputs*: `String fileName; String variableName; String startValue; String outputFile;` *Outputs*: `Boolean success;`
simulate(className, options)	Simulate model, optionally setting simulation values.

	Inputs: `TypeName className; Real startTime; Real stopTime; Integer numberOfIntervals; Real outputInterval; String method; Real tolerance; Real fixedStepSize;` *Outputs*: `SimulationResult simRes;`
typeOf(variableName)	*Inputs*: `VariableName variableName;` *Outputs*: `String res;`
val(var, timepoint)	Returns the value of the variable at a certain time point. *Inputs*: `VariableName var; Real timepoint;` *Outputs*: `Real valAtTime;`

E.1.1 OpenModelica System Commands

This is a selection of common OpenModelica commands related to the operating system:

cd(dir)	Change directory. *Inputs*: `String dir;` *Outputs*: `Boolean res;`
deleteFile(fileName)	Deletes a file with the given name. *Inputs*: `String fileName;` *Outputs*: `Boolean res;`
dirName(path)	Returns the directory name of a file path. *Inputs*: `String path;` *Outputs*: `String dirName;`
runScript(fileName)	Executes the script file given as argument. *Inputs*: `String fileName;` *Outputs*: `Boolean res;`
setLanguageStandard(inVersion)	Sets the Modelica Language Standard. *Inputs*: `String inVersion;` *Outputs*: `Boolean res;`
setModelicaPath(modelicaPath)	Sets the modelica path. See `loadModel()` for a description of what the `MODELICAPATH` is used for. *Inputs*: `String modelicaPath;` *Outputs*: `Boolean res;`
system(fileName)	Execute system command. *Inputs*: `String fileName;` *Outputs*: `Integer res;`
writeFile(fileName, data, optional)	Write the data to file. Returns `true` on success. *Inputs*: `String fileName; String data; Boolean append;` *Outputs*: `Boolean res;`

E.1.2 All OpenModelica API Calls

All OpenModelica API commands shown in alphabetic order:

appendEnvironmentVar(var, value)	Appends a variable to the environment variables list. *Inputs:* `String var; String value;` *Outputs:* `String res;`
baseName(path)	Returns the base name (file part) of a file path. *Inputs:* `String path;` *Outputs:* `String basename;`
cd(dir)	Change directory. *Inputs*: `String dir;` *Outputs*: `Boolean res;`
checkAllModelsRecursive(	Checks all models recursively and returns number of variables and

`className, protected)`	equations. *Inputs*: `TypeName className; Boolean protected` *Outputs*: `String res;`
`checkModel``(className)`	Checks a model and returns number of variables and equations. *Inputs*: `TypeName className;` *Outputs*: `String res;`
`checkSettings``()`	Display some diagnostics. *Outputs*: `CheckSettingsResult res;`
`clear``()`	Clears everything: symboltable and variables. *Outputs*: `Boolean res;`
`clearMessages``()`	Clears the error buffer. *Outputs*: `Boolean res;`
`clearVariables``()`	Clear all user defined variables. *Outputs*: `Boolean res;`
`codeToString``(className)`	Converts to a string after encoding. *Inputs*: `$Code className;` *Outputs*: `String res;`
`compareSimulationResults``( fileName, refFileName, logFileName, refTol, absTol,vars)`	Compares simulation results. *Inputs*: `String fileName; String refFileName; String logFileName; Real refTol; Real absTol; String[:] vars;` *Outputs*: `String res;`
`deleteFile``(fileName)`	Deletes a file with the given name. *Inputs*: `String fileName;` *Outputs*: `Boolean res;`
`dirName``(path)`	Returns the directory name of a file path. *Inputs*: `String path;` *Outputs*: `String dirName;`
`dumpXMLDAE``(className)`	Outputs the DAE system corresponding to a specific model. *Inputs*: `TypeName className;` *Outputs*: `String res;`
`echo``(setEcho)`	echo (false) disables Interactive output, echo(true) enables it again. *Inputs*: `Boolean setEcho;` *Outputs*: `Boolean newEcho;`
`generateCode``(className)`	Generate C-code and compiled into a dll. *Inputs*: `TypeName className;` *Outputs*: `Boolean res;`
`generateHeader``(fileName)`	Generates a C header file containing the external C interface of the MetaModelica uniontypes in the loaded files. This C interface is called by the parser to build nodes for the abstract syntax tree. *Inputs*: `String fileName;` *Outputs*: `Boolean res;`
`getAlgorithmCount``(className)`	Counts the number of Algorithm sections in a class. *Inputs*: `TypeName className;` *Outputs*: `Integer count;`
`getAlgorithmItemsCount``( className)`	Counts the number of Algorithm items in a class. *Inputs*: `TypeName className;` *Outputs*: `Integer count;`
`getAnnotationCount``( className)`	Counts the number of Annotation sections in a class. *Inputs*: `TypeName className;` *Outputs*: `Integer count;`
`getAnnotationVersion``()`	Returns the current annotation version. *Outputs*: `String annotationVersion;`
`getAstAsCorbaString``( fileName)`	Print the whole AST on the CORBA format for records. *Inputs*: `String fileName;` *Outputs*: `String res;`
`getClassComment``(className)`	Returns the class comment. *Inputs*: `TypeName className;` *Outputs*: `String comment;`
`getClassNames``(fileName)`	Returns the list of class names defined in the class. *Inputs*: `String fileName;` *Outputs*: `TypeName classNames;`
`getClassRestriction``(classNam`	Returns the type of class. *Inputs*: `TypeName className;`

e)	*Outputs*: `String restriction;`
getClassInformation(className)	Returns the list containing the information of the class. *Inputs*: `TypeName className;` *Outputs*: `String information;`
getClassesInModelicaPath()	*Outputs*: `String classesInModelicaPath;`
getCompileCommand()	*Outputs*: `String compileCommand;`
getIconAnnotation(className)	Returns the icon representation of the class. *Inputs*: `TypeName className;` *Outputs*: `String out;`
getDiagramAnnotation(className)	Returns the diagram representation of the class. *Inputs*: `TypeName className;` *Outputs*: `String out;`
getParameterName(className)	Returns the list of parameters present in the class. *Inputs*: `TypeName className;` *Outputs*: `String out;`
getParameterValue(className, parameter)	Returns the parameter value. *Inputs*: `TypeName className; String parameter;` *Outputs*: `String value;`
getComponentModifierNames(className)	Returns the list of component modifiers present in the class. *Inputs*: `TypeName className;` *Outputs*: `String out;`
getComponentModifierValue(className, modifier)	Returns the component modifier value. *Inputs*: `TypeName className; String modifier;` *Outputs*: `String value;`
getExtendsModifierNames(className)	Returns the list of extends modifiers present in the class. *Inputs*: `TypeName className;` *Outputs*: `String out;`
getExtendsModifierValue(className, modifier)	Returns the extends modifier value. *Inputs*: `TypeName className; String modifier;` *Outputs*: `String value;`
getDocumentationAnnotation (className)	Returns the documentation annotation defined in the class. *Inputs*: `TypeName className;` *Outputs*: `String out[2] "{info,revision}";`
getEnvironmentVar(var)	Returns the value of the environment variable. *Inputs*: `String var;` *Outputs*: `String value;`
getEquationCount(className)	Counts the number of Equation sections in a class. *Inputs*: `TypeName className;` *Outputs*: `Integer count;`
getEquationItemsCount(className)	Counts the number of Equation items in a class. *Inputs*: `TypeName className;` *Outputs*: `Integer count;`
getErrorString()	Returns the current error message. *Outputs*: `String errorString;`
getImportCount (className)	Counts the number of Import sections in a class. *Inputs*: `TypeName className;` *Outputs*: `Integer count;`
getInitialAlgorithmCount(className)	Counts the number of Initial Algorithm sections in a class. *Inputs*: `TypeName className;` *Outputs*: `Integer count;`
getInitialAlgorithmItemsCount(className)	Counts the number of Initial Algorithm items in a class. *Inputs*: `TypeName className;` *Outputs*: `Integer count;`
getInitialEquationCount(className)	Counts the number of Initial Equation sections in a class. *Inputs*: `TypeName className;` *Outputs*: `Integer count;`
getInitialEquationItemsCount (className)	Counts the number of Initial Equation items in a class. *Inputs*: `TypeName className;` *Outputs*: `Integer count;`
getInstallationDirectoryPath ()	Returns `OPENMODELICAHOME` if it is set; on some platforms the default path is returned if it is not set. *Outputs*: `String installationDirectoryPath;`

getLanguageStandard()	Returns the current Modelica Language Standard in use. *Outputs*: `String outVersion;`
getMessagesString()	Returns the current error message. *Outputs*: `String messagesString;`
getMessagesStringInternal()	Returns Error: message, `TRANSLATION`, Error, code. *Outputs*: `ErrorMessage[:] messagesString;`
getModelicaPath()	Get the Modelica Library Path. *Outputs*: `String modelicaPath;`
getNoSimplify()	Returns true if noSimplify flag is set. *Outputs*: `Boolean res;`
getNthAlgorithm(className, index)	Returns the Nth Algorithm section. *Inputs:* `TypeName className; Integer index;` *Outputs:* `String res;`
getNthAlgorithmItem(className, index)	Returns the Nth Algorithm Item. *Inputs:* `TypeName className; Integer index;` *Outputs:* `String res;`
getNthAnnotationString (className, index)	Returns the Nth Annotation section as string. *Inputs:* `TypeName className; Integer index;` *Outputs:* `String res;`
getNthEquation(className, index)	Returns the Nth Equation section. *Inputs:* `TypeName className; Integer index;` *Outputs:* `String res;`
getNthEquationItem(className)	Returns the Nth Equation Item. *Inputs:* `TypeName className; Integer index;` *Outputs:* `String res;`
getNthImport(className, index)	Returns the Nth Import as string. *Inputs:* `TypeName className; Integer index;` *Outputs:* `String out[3] "{\"Path\",\"Id\",\"Kind\"}";`
getNthInitialAlgorithm(className, index)	Returns the Nth Initial Algorithm section. *Inputs:* `TypeName className; Integer index;` *Outputs:* `String res;`
getNthInitialAlgorithmItem(className, index)	Returns the Nth Initial Algorithm Item. *Inputs:* `TypeName className; Integer index;` *Outputs:* `String res;`
getNthInitialEquation(className, index)	Returns the Nth Initial Equation section. *Inputs:* `TypeName className; Integer index;` *Outputs:* `String res;`
getNthInitialEquationItem(className, index)	Returns the Nth Initial Equation Item. *Inputs:* `TypeName className; Integer index;` *Outputs:* `String res;`
getOrderConnections()	Returns true if orderConnections flag is set. *Outputs*: `Boolean isOrderConnections;`
getPackages(className)	Returns the list of packages defined in the class. *Inputs*: `TypeName className = $Code(AllLoadedClasses);` *Outputs*: `TypeName classNames[:];`
getPlotSilent()	Returns true if plotSilent flag is set. *Outputs*: `Boolean isPlotSilent;`
getSettings()	Returns the settings. *Outputs*: `String settings;`
getShowAnnotations()	*Outputs*: `Boolean show;`
getSourceFile(className)	Returns the filename of the class. *Inputs*: `TypeName className;` *Outputs*: `String filename;`
getTempDirectoryPath()	Returns the current user temporary directory location. *Outputs*: `String tempDirectoryPath;`
getVectorizationLimit()	*Outputs*: `Integer vectorizationLimit;`

getVersion(cl)	Returns the version of the Modelica compiler. *Inputs*: TypeName cl = $Code(OpenModelica); *Outputs*: String version;
help()	Display the OpenModelica help text. *Outputs*: String helpText;
iconv(string, from, to)	Converts one multibyte characters from one character set to another. *Inputs*: String string; String from; String to; *Outputs*: String res;
importFMU(fileName, workDir)	Imports the Functional Mockup Unit. *Inputs*: String filename; String workdir "./" "The output directory for imported FMU files. <default> will put the files to current working directory."; *Outputs*: Boolean res;
instantiateModel(className)	Instantiate model, resulting in a .mof file of flattened Modelica. *Inputs*: TypeName className; *Outputs*: String res;
isModel(className)	Returns true if the given class has restriction model. *Inputs*: TypeName className; *Outputs*: Boolean res;
isPackage(className)	Returns true if the given class is a package. *Inputs*: TypeName className; *Outputs*: Boolean res;
isPartial(className)	Returns true if the given class is partial. *Inputs*: TypeName className; *Outputs*: Boolean res;
list(className)	Print class definition. *Inputs*: TypeName className; *Outputs*: String classDef;
listVariables()	Print user defined variables. *Outputs*: VariableName res;
loadFile(fileName)	Load models from file. *Inputs*: String fileName; *Outputs*: Boolean res;
loadFileInteractive(fileName)	Outputs the class names in the parsed file (top level only). Used by OpenModelica MDT. *Inputs*: String fileName; *Outputs*: TypeName names[:];
loadFileInteractiveQualified (fileName)	Output all the class names in the parsed file fully qualified. *Inputs*: String fileName; *Outputs*: TypeName names[:];
loadModel(className)	Load the file corresponding to the class, using the Modelica class name to file name mapping to locate the file. *Inputs*: TypeName className; *Outputs*: Boolean res;
loadString(data)	Parses the data and merges the resulting AST with the loaded AST. *Inputs*: String data; *Outputs*: TypeName names[:];
parseFile(filename)	Parses the file and returns a list of the classes found in the file. *Inputs*: String filename; *Outputs*: TypeName names[:];
parseString(data)	Parses the string data and returns the list of classes found in data. *Inputs*: String data; *Outputs*: TypeName names[:];
plot(variable, options)	Plots variable, which is a single variable name. *Inputs*: VariableName variable; String title; Boolean legend; Boolean gridLines; Real xrange[2] i.e. {xmin,xmax}; Real yrange[2] i.e. {ymin,ymax}; *Outputs*: Boolean res;
plot(variables, options)	Plots variables, which is a vector of variable names. *Inputs*: VariableName variables; String title;

	`Boolean legend;` `Boolean gridLines;` `Real xrange[2]` i.e., {xmin,xmax}; `Real yrange[2]` i.e., {ymin,ymax}; *Outputs*: `Boolean res;`
plotAll(options)	Plot all variables; It does not accept any variable names as input. *Inputs*: `String title;` `Boolean legend;` `Boolean gridLines;` `Real xrange[2]` i.e., {xmin,xmax}; `Real yrange[2]` i.e., {ymin,ymax}; *Outputs*: `Boolean res;`
plotParametric(variables1, variables2, options)	Plot each pair of corresponding variables from the vectors of variables `variables1`, `variables2` as a parametric plot. *Inputs*: `VariableName variables1[:];` `VariableName variables2[size(variables1,1)];` `String title;` `Boolean legend;` `Boolean gridLines;` `Real range[2,2];` *Outputs*: `Boolean res;`
readFile(fileName)	The contents of the given file are returned. Note that if the function fails, the error message is returned as a string instead of multiple outputs or similar. *Inputs*: `String fileName;` *Outputs*: `String content;`
readFileNoNumeric(fileName)	Returns the contents of the file, with anything resembling a (real) number stripped out, and at the end adding: *Inputs*: `String fileName;` *Outputs*: `String content;`
readFilePostprocessLineDirective(fileName)	Searches lines for the `#modelicaLine` directive. *Inputs*: `String fileName;` *Outputs*: `String res;`
readFileShowLineNumbers(fileName)	Prefixes each line in the file with <n>: where n is the line number. Note: Scales O(n^2) *Inputs*: `String fileName;` *Outputs*: `String res;`
readSimulationResult(fileName, variables, size)	Reads the simulation result for a list of variables and returns a matrix of values (each column as a vector or values for a variable.) Size of result is also given as input. *Inputs*: `String fileName;` `VariableName variables[:];` `Integer size;` *Outputs*: `Real res[size(variables,1),size)];`
readSimulationResultSize(fileName)	The number of intervals that are present in the output file. *Inputs*: `String fileName;` *Outputs*: `Integer size;`
readSimulationResultVars(fileName)	Returns the variables in the simulation file; you can use `val()` and `plot()` commands using these names. *Inputs*: `String fileName;` *Outputs*: `String[:] vars;`
regex(string, re, options)	Sets the error buffer and returns -1 if the regular expression does not compile. *Inputs*: `String string;` `String re;` `Integer maxMatches;` `Boolean extended;` `Boolean caseInsensitive;` *Outputs*: `Integer numMatches;` `String matchedSubstrings[maxMatches];`
regexBool(string, re, options)	Returns true if the string matches the regular expression. *Inputs*: `String string;` `String re;` `Boolean extended;` `Boolean caseInsensitive;` *Outputs*: `Boolean matches;`
regularFileExists(fileName)	Returns the content of the given files. Note that if the function fails, the error message is returned as a string instead of multiple

	outputs or similar. *Inputs*: `String fileName;` *Outputs*: `Boolean res;`
reopenStandardStream(_stream, fileName)	Executes the script file given as argument. *Inputs*: `String fileName; StandardStream _stream;` *Outputs*: `Boolean res;`
runScript(fileName)	Executes the script file given as argument. *Inputs*: `String fileName;` *Outputs*: `Boolean res;`
save(className)	Save class definition. *Inputs*: `TypeName className` *Outputs*: `Boolean res;`
saveAll(fileName)	Save the entire loaded AST to file. *Inputs*: `String fileName;` *Outputs*: `Boolean res;`
saveModel(fileName, className)	Save class definition in a file. *Inputs*: `String fileName; TypeName className` *Outputs*: `Boolean res;`
saveTotalModel(fileName, className)	Save total class definition into file of a class. *Inputs*: `String fileName; TypeName className` *Outputs*: `Boolean res;`
saveTotalSCode(fileName, className)	*Inputs*: `String fileName; TypeName className` *Outputs*: `Boolean res;`
setAnnotationVersion(annotationVersion)	Sets the annotation version. *Inputs*: `String annotationVersion;` *Outputs*: `Boolean res;`
setCXXCompiler(compiler)	*Inputs*: `String compiler;` *Outputs*: `Boolean res;`
setClassComment(className, fileName)	Sets the class comment. *Inputs*: `String fileName; TypeName className` *Outputs*: `Boolean res;`
saveTotalModel(fileName, className)	Save total class definition into file of a class. *Inputs*: `String fileName; TypeName className` *Outputs*: `Boolean res;`
setCompileCommand(compileCommand)	Sets the default Compilation command. *Inputs*: `String compileCommand;` *Outputs*: `Boolean res;`
setCompiler(compiler)	Sets the default C Compiler. *Inputs*: `String compiler;` *Outputs*: `Boolean res;`
setCompilerFlags(compilerFlags)	Sets the compiler flags that are used while compiling the simulation executable. *Inputs*: `String compilerFlags;` *Outputs*: `Boolean res;`
setCompilerPath(compilerPath)	Sets the default compiler location. *Inputs*: `String compilerPath;` *Outputs*: `Boolean res;`
setComponentModifierValue(className, modifier, value)	Sets the component modifier value. *Inputs*: `TypeName className; String modifier; String value;` *Outputs*: `Boolean result;`
setDebugFlags(debugFlags)	Sets the debug flags. For details run "omc +help=debug" on the command line interface. *Inputs*: `String debugFlags;` *Outputs*: `Boolean res;`
setEnvironmentVar(var, value)	Sets an environment variable. *Inputs*: `String var; String value;` *Outputs*: `Boolean res;`
setExtendsModifierValue(className, modifier, value)	Sets the extends modifier value. *Inputs*: `TypeName className; String modifier; String value;` *Outputs*: `Boolean result;`
setIndexReductionMethod(method)	Sets the index reduction method e.g

	setIndexReductionMethod ("dynamicStateSelection"). *Inputs*: String method; *Outputs*: Boolean res;
setInitXmlStartValue(fileName, variableName, startValue, outputFile)	Sets the parameter start value in the model_init.xml file. No need to recompile the model. *Inputs*: String fileName; String variableName; String startValue; String outputFile; *Outputs*: Boolean success;
setInstallationDirectoryPath(debugFlags)	Sets the OPENMODELICAHOME environment variable. *Inputs*: String installationDirectoryPath; *Outputs*: Boolean res;
setLanguageStandard(inVersion)	Sets the Modelica Language Standard. *Inputs*: String inVersion; *Outputs*: Boolean res;
setLinker(linker)	Sets the linker. *Inputs*: String linker; *Outputs*: Boolean res;
setLinkerFlags(linkerFlag)	Sets the linker flag. *Inputs*: String linkerFlag; *Outputs*: Boolean res;
setModelicaPath(modelicaPath)	Sets the modelica path. See *loadModel()* for a description of what the MODELICAPATH is used for. *Inputs*: String modelicaPath; *Outputs*: Boolean res;
setNoSimplify(noSimplify)	Sets the noSimplify flag. *Inputs*: Boolean noSimplify; *Outputs*: Boolean res;
setOrderConnections(debugFlags)	Sets orderering for connect equation. If set, the compiler will order connect equations alphabetically. *Inputs*: Boolean orderConnections; *Outputs*: Boolean res;
setParameterValue(className, parameter, value)	Sets the parameter value in the class, i.e., updates the parameter definition equation. *Inputs*: TypeName className; String parameter; String value; *Outputs*: Boolean result;
setPlotSilent(silent)	Sets the plotSilent flag. If the flag is true show the OMPlot window and pass the arguments to it. If the flag is false don't show OMPlot and just output the list of arguments. The false case is used in OMNotebook where the plot window is not shown; instead the arguments are read and an embedded plot window is created. *Inputs*: Boolean silent; *Outputs*: Boolean res;
setPostOptModules(modules)	Sets the post optimization modules to use in the compiler back end. Use the command "omc +help=optmodules" for more information. Example: setPostOptModules("lateInline", "inlineArrayEqn","removeSimpleEquations") *Inputs*: String module1, module2, ...; *Outputs*: Boolean res;
setPreOptModules(module)	Sets the pre optimization modules to use in the back end. Use the command line command "omc +help=optmodules" for more information. *Inputs*: String module; *Outputs*: Boolean res;
setShowAnnotations()	Show annotations in the flattened code. *Inputs*: Boolean show; *Outputs*: Boolean res;
setSourceFile(className, fileName)	Sets the output file name for the specified class. *Inputs*: TypeName className; String fileName; *Outputs*: Boolean res;
setTempDirectoryPath(tempDirectoryPath)	Sets the current user's temporary directory path. This is not the

	same as the current user's working directory which is set by the `cd()` command. *Inputs*: `String tempDirectoryPath;` *Outputs*: `Boolean res;`
setVectorizationLimit(vectorizationLimit)	Sets scalarization limit. Arrays of size above this limit will not be scalarized, i.e., expanded to a set of scalar elements. *Inputs*: `Integer scalarizationLimit;` *Outputs*: `Boolean res;`
simulate(className, options)	Simulate model, optionally setting simulation values. *Inputs*: `TypeName className; Real startTime; Real stopTime; Integer numberOfIntervals; Real outputInterval; String method; Real tolerance; Real fixedStepSize;` *Outputs*: `SimulationResult simRes;`
stringReplace(str, source, target)	Relace `source` with `target` within `str` producing `res`. *Inputs*: `String str; String source; String target;` *Outputs*: `String res;`
strtok()	Splits the strings at the places given by the token, for example: `strtok("abcbdef","b") => {"a","c","def"}` *Inputs*: `String string; String token;` *Outputs*: `String[:] strings;`
system(fileName)	Execute system command. *Inputs*: `String fileName;` *Outputs*: `Integer res;`
typeNameString(cl)	Converts the qualified class name to string. *Inputs*: `TypeName cl;` *Outputs*: `String out;`
typeNameStrings(cl)	Converts the qualified class name to strings. *Inputs*: `TypeName cl;` *Outputs*: `String out[:];`
typeOf(variableName)	*Inputs*: `VariableName variableName;` *Outputs*: `String res;`
uriToFilename(uri)	Handles modelica:// and file:// URI's. The result is an absolute path on the local system. The result depends on the current MODELICAPATH. Returns the empty string on failure. *Inputs*: `String uri;` *Outputs*: `String fileName;`
val(var, time)	Returns the value of the variable at a certain time point. *Inputs*: `VariableName var; Real time;` *Outputs*: `Real valAtTime;`
writeFile(fileName, data, optional)	Write the data to file. Returns true on success. *Inputs*: `String fileName; String data; Boolean append;` *Outputs*: `Boolean res;`

E.1.3 Examples

The following is an interactive session with the OpenModelica environment including some of the abovementioned commands and examples. First we start the system, and use the command line interface from OMShell, OMNotebook, or command window of some of the other tools. The system responds with a header line:

```
OpenModelica 1.9.0
```

We type in a very small model:

```
>> model test "Testing OpenModelica Scripts" Real x, y; equation x = 5.0; y
= 6.0; end test;
   {test}
```

We give the command to flatten a model:

```
>> instantiateModel(test)
   "class test
       Real x;
       Real y;
     equation
       x = 5.0;
       y = 6.0;
     end test;
  "
```

A range expression is typed in:

```
>> a:=1:10
   {1,2,3,4,5,6,7,8,9,10}
```

It is multiplied by 2:

```
>> a*2
   {2,4,6,8,10,12,14,16,18,20}
```

The variables are cleared:

```
>> clearVariables()
   true
```

We print the loaded class test from its internal representation:

```
>> list(test)
   "class test \"Testing OpenModelica Scripts\"
       Real x;
       Real y;
     equation
       x = 5.0;
       y = 6.0;
     end test;
  "
```

We get the name and other properties of a class:

```
>> getClassNames()
    {test}

>> getClassComment(test)
   "Testing OpenModelica Scripts"

>> isPartial(test)
    false

>> isPackage(test)
    false

>> isModel(test)
    true

>> checkModel(test)
     "Check of test completed successfully.
      Class test has 2 equation(s) and 2 variable(s).
```

```
      2 of these are trivial equation(s).
    "

>> clear()
   true

>> getClassNames()
   {}
```

The common combination of a simulation followed by getting a value and doing a plot:

```
>> simulate(test, stopTime=3.0);

>> val(x , 2.0)
   5.0

>> plot(y)
```

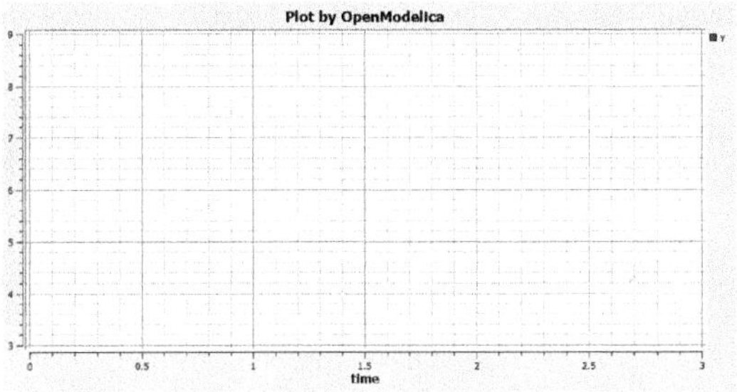


```
>> plotAll()
```

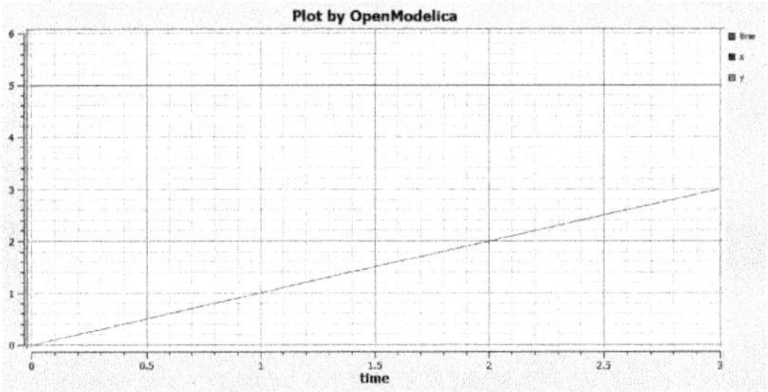

VanDerPol Model and Parametric Plot

```
>> loadFile("C:/OpenModelica1.9.0/share/doc/omc/testmodels/VanDerPol.mo")
   true

>> instantiateModel(VanDerPol)
   "class VanDerPol \"Van der Pol oscillator model\"
     Real x(start = 1.0);
     Real y(start = 1.0);
     parameter Real lambda = 0.3;
   equation
     der(x) = y;
     der(y) = lambda * (1.0 - x ^ 2.0) * y - x;
   end VanDerPol;
  "

>> simulate(VanDerPol);

>> plotParametric(x,y)
```

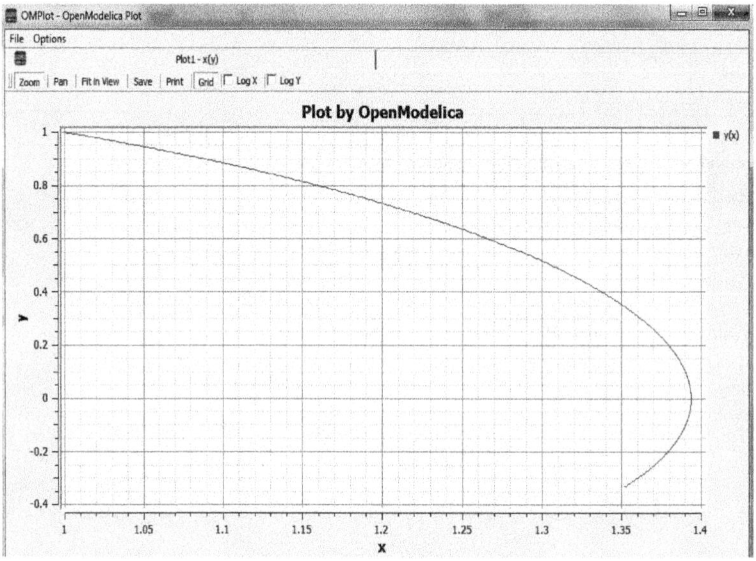

Interactive Function Calls, Reading, and Writing

We enter an assignment of a vector expression, created by the range construction expression 1:12, to be stored in the variable x. The type and the value of the expression is returned.

```
>> x := 1:12
   {1, 2, 3, 4, 5, 6, 7, 8, 9, 10, 11, 12}
```

The function `bubblesort` is called to sort this vector in descending order. The sorted result is returned together with its type. Note that the result vector is of type `Real[:]`, instantiated as `Real[12]`, since this is the declared type of the function result. The input `Integer` vector was automatically converted to a `Real` vector according to the Modelica type coercion rules.

```
>> bubblesort(x)
   {12, 11, 10, 9, 8, 7, 6, 5, 4, 3, 2, 1}
```

Now we want to try another small application, a simplex algorithm for optimization. First read in a small matrix containing coefficients that define a simplex problem to be solved:

```
>> a := read("simplex_in.txt")
   {{-1,-1,-1, 0, 0, 0, 0, 0, 0},
   {-1, 1, 0, 1, 0, 0, 0, 0, 5},
   { 1, 4, 0, 0, 1, 0, 0, 0, 45},
   { 2, 1, 0, 0, 0, 1, 0, 0, 27},
   { 3,-4, 0, 0, 0, 0, 1, 0, 24},
   { 0, 0, 1, 0, 0, 0, 0, 1, 4}}
```

Then call the simplex algorithm implemented as the Modelica function `simplex1`. This function returns four results, which are represented as a tuple of four return values:

```
>> simplex1(a)
   Tuple: 4
   Real[8]: {9, 9, 4, 5, 0, 0, 33, 0}
```

```
  Real: 22
  Integer: 9
  Integer: 3
```

It is possible to compute an expression, for example, `12:-1:1`, and store the result in a file using the `write` command:

```
>> write(12:-1:1,"test.dat")
```

We can read back the stored result from the file into a variable `y`:

```
>> y := read("test.dat")
  Integer[12]: {12, 11, 10, 9, 8, 7, 6, 5, 4, 3, 2, 1}
```

It is also possible to give operating system commands via the `system` utility function. A command is provided as a string argument. The example below shows `system` applied to the Linux command `cat`, which here outputs the contents of the file `bubblesort.mo` to the output stream.

```
>> system("cat bubblesort.mo")
function bubblesort
  input Real[:] x;
  output Real[size(x,1)] y;
protected
  Real t;
algorithm
  y := x;
  for i in 1:size(x,1) loop
    for j in 1:size(x,1) loop
      if y[i] > y[j] then
        t := y[i];
              y[i] := y[j];
                y[j] := t;
      end if;
    end for;
  end for;
end bubblesort;
```

Another built-in command is `cd`, the *change current directory* command. The resulting current directory is returned as a string.

```
>> cd("..")
"/home/petfr/modelica"
```

E.2 OpenModelica Python Scripting Commands

The OpenModelica Python API Interface—OMPython, attempts to mimic the Modelica scripting commands available in the OpenModelica environment, see the table in Section E.1 for available Python scripting commands.

The third party library of OMPython can be created by changing directory to the following:

```
OpenModelicaInstallationDirectory/share/omc/scripts/PythonInterface/
```

and running the command:

```
python setup.py install
```

This will install the OMPython library into the user's Python's third party libraries directory. Now OMPython can be imported and used within Python.

To test the command outputs, simply import the OMPython library from Python and execute the `run()` method of OMPython. The module allows you to interactively send commands to the OMC server and display their output.

For example:

```
C:\>python
  >>> import OMPython
  >>> OMPython.run()
  >> loadModel(Modelica)
     true
```

E.2.1 Examples

The following session in OpenModelica illustrates the use of a few of the above-mentioned functions.

```
>>
loadFile("C:/OpenModelica1.9.0/share/doc/omc/testmodels/BouncingBall.mo")
   true
 >> list(BouncingBall)
   "model BouncingBall
     parameter Real e = 0.7 \"coefficient of restitution\";
     parameter Real g = 9.81 \"gravity acceleration\";
     Real h(start = 1) \"height of ball\";
     Real v \"velocity of ball\";
     Boolean flying(start = true) \"true, if ball is flying\";
     Boolean impact;
     Real v_new;
     Integer foo;
   equation
     impact = h <= 0.0;
     foo = if impact then 1 else 2;
     der(v) = if flying then -g else 0;
     der(h) = v;
     when {h <= 0.0 and v <= 0.0,impact} then
       v_new = if edge(impact) then -e * pre(v) else 0;
       flying = v_new > 0;
       reinit(v, v_new);
     end when;
  end BouncingBall;
  "
 >> getClassNames()
  {'SET1': {'Set1': ['BouncingBall', 'ModelicaServices', 'Complex',
  'Modelica']}}
 >> isPartial(BouncingBall)
   False
 >> isPackage(BouncingBall)
   False
 >> isModel(BouncingBall)
   True
 >> checkModel(BouncingBall)
   "Check of BouncingBall completed successfully.
    Class BouncingBall has 6 equation(s) and 6 variable(s).
    1 of these are trivial equation(s).
    "
 >> getClassRestriction(BouncingBall)
     "model"
 >> getClassInformation(BouncingBall)
 'SET1': {'Values':
['"model","","C:\\\\OpenModelica1.9.0\\\\share\\\\doc\\\\omc
 \\\\testmodels\\\\BouncingBall.mo"']}, 'SET2': {'Set1': [False, False,
False],
 'Set2': ['"writable"', 1, 1, 23, 17]}, 'SET3': {'Set1': [False, False,
False],
```

```
'Set2': ['"writable"', 1, 1, 23, 17]}}
>> existClass(BouncingBall)
True
>> getComponents(BouncingBall)
{'SET1': {}, 'SET2': {'Set4': ['Real', 'v', '"velocity of ball"',
'"public"',
'false', 'false', 'false', 'false', '"unspecified"', '"none"',
'"unspecified"'], 'Set5': ['Boolean', 'flying', '"true', 'if ball is
flying"',
'"public"', 'false','false', 'false', 'false', '"unspecified"', '"none"',
'"unspecified"'], 'Set6':['Boolean', 'impact', '""', '"public"', 'false',
'false', 'false', 'false', '"unspecified"', '"none"', '"unspecified"'],
'Set7':
['Real', 'v_new', '""', '"public"', 'false', 'false', 'false', 'false',
'"unspecified"', '"none"', '"unspecified"'], 'Set1': ['Real',
'e','"coefficient
of restitution"', '"public"', 'false', 'false', 'false', 'false',
'"parameter"', '"none"', '"unspecified"'], 'Set2':['Real', 'g', '"gravit
acceleration"', '"public"', 'false', 'false', 'false', '
   false', '"parameter"', '"none"', '"unspecified"'], 'Set3': ['Real', 'h',
   '"height of ball"', '"public"', 'false', 'false', 'false', 'false',
  '"unspecified"', '"none"', '"unspecified"'], 'Set8': ['Integer', 'foo',
'""',
  '"public"', 'false','false', 'false', 'false', '"unspecified"', '"none"',
  '"unspecified"']}, 'SET3':{}}
>> getConnectionCount(BouncingBall)
   0
>> getNthConnection(BouncingBall)
   1
>> getInheritanceCount(BouncingBall)
   0
>> getComponentModifierValue(BouncingBall,e)
7.5
>> getClassAttributes(BouncingBall)
 {'SET1': {'Elements': {'rec1': {'Properties':
 {'Results': {'comment': '""',
 'restriction': 'MODEL', 'startLine': 1, 'partial': False, 'name':
 '"BouncingBall"','encapsulated': False, 'startColumn': 1, 'readonly':
 '"writable"', 'endColumn': 17, 'file'
 '"C:\\OpenModelica1.9.0\\share\\doc\\omc\\testmodels\\BouncingBall.m
    o"', 'endLine': 23, 'final': False}}}}}}
>> simulate(BouncingBall, stopTime=3.0)
    record SimulationResult
      resultFile =

"C:/Users/alash325/AppData/Local/Temp/OpenModelica/BouncingBall_res.mat",
       simulationOptions = "startTime = 0.0, stopTime = 3.0,
       numberOfIntervals = 500, tolerance = 0.000001, method = 'dassl',
       fileNamePrefix = 'BouncingBall', options = '',
       outputFormat = 'mat', variableFilter = '.*',
        measureTime = false, cflags = '', simflags = ''", messages = "",
     timeFrontend = 0.022458798284363236,
     timeBackend = 0.01647555356928777,
     timeSimCode = 0.005109221712579149,
     timeTemplates = 0.017912705486144133,
     timeCompile = 1.7019944515670637,
     timeSimulation = 0.21892626420791483,
     timeTotal = 1.9834023618418568
     end SimulationResult;
>> plotAll()
   true
```

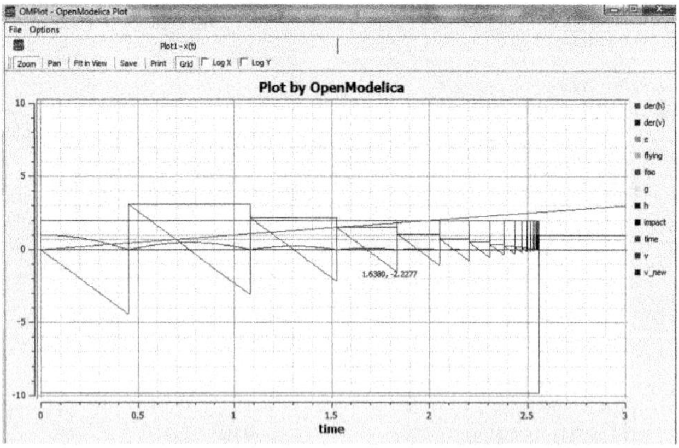

Instead of just giving a `simulate and plot` command, we perform a `runScript` command on a `.mos` (Modelica script) file `sim_BouncingBall.mos` that contains these commands:

```
loadFile("C:/OpenModelica1.9.0/share/doc/omc/testmodels/BouncingBall.mo")
simulate(BouncingBall, stopTime=3.0);
plot({h,flying});
```

The runScript command is:

```
>> runScript("sim_BouncingBall.mos")
   "true
    record SimulationResult
      resultFile =
       "C:/Users/alash325/AppData/Local/Temp/OpenModelica/BouncingBall_res.mat",
       simulationOptions = "startTime = 0.0, stopTime = 3.0, numberOfIntervals =
       500, tolerance = 0.000001, method = 'dassl', fileNamePrefix =
      'BouncingBall', options = '', outputFormat = 'mat', variableFilter = '.*',
        measureTime = false, cflags = '', simflags = ''",
     messages = "",
     timeFrontend = 0.022458798284363236,
     timeBackend = 0.01647555356928777,
     timeSimCode = 0.005109221712579149,
     timeTemplates = 0.017912705486144133,
     timeCompile = 1.7019944515670637,
     timeSimulation = 0.21892626420791483,
     timeTotal = 1.9834023618418568
   end SimulationResult;
true
"
```

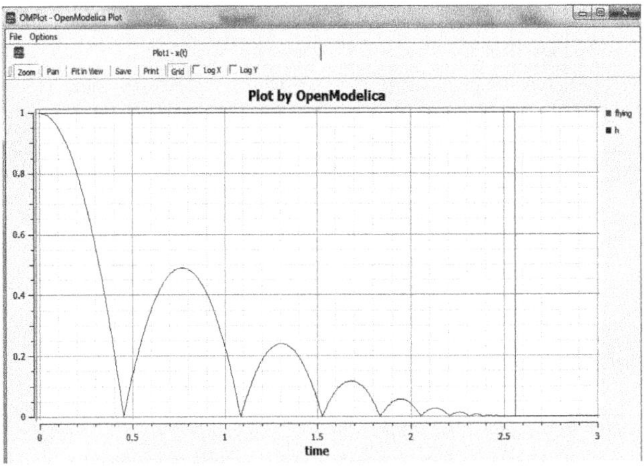


```
>> clear()
 true
>> getClassNames()
     {}
```

E.3 Wolfram SystemModeler Scripting Commands

The following table contains the Mathematica-style Wolfram SystemModeler scripting commands expressed in Mathematica syntax, see also the web page: http://reference.wolfram.com/system-modeler/WSMLink/guide/WSMLink.html. In addition to these, almost a thousand Mathematica commands are available.

Needs["WSMLink`"];	Load the Wolfram SystemModeler Link. This is necessary in order to execute any of the following commands.
WSMModelCenter["optmodelname"]	Open the SystemModeler Model Center with or without loading a specific model. The argument "optmodelname" is optional. Loading a model is necessary before doing simulation or plotting. Loading can be done through the SystemModeler GUI or via this command. Example: WSMModelCenter ["IntroductoryExamples.ComponentBased.BlockCircuit"]
WSMSimulationCenter["optmodelname"]	Open the SystemModeler Simulation Center with or without performing a simulation experiment on a specific model. The argument "optmodelname" is optional. Example: WSMSimulationCenter["IntroductoryExamples.ComponentBased.BlockCircuit"]
WSMSimulate["modelname", {"time1","time2"}, options]	Simulate a model "modelname" over the intervals from "time1" to "time2" and return a WSMSimulationData object. The following optional arguments can be given: WSMInitialValues, WSMInputFunctions, Method, InterpolationOrder, WSMParameterValues
WSMInitialValues->{v1 ->	Sets initial values "vi" to "ai" in the simulation. It is an option

a1,…}	for WSMSimulateSensitivity and WSMSimulate that specifies initial values for variables.
WSMInitialValues->{v1 -> {a1,a2…},…}	Runs simulations in parallel, with "vi" taking initial values "aj". It is an option for WSMSimulateSensitivity and WSMSimulate that specifies initial values for variables.
WSMParameterValues->{p1 -> c1,…}	Sets parameters "pi" to "ci" in the simulation. It is an option for WSMSimulateSensitivity and WSMSimulate that specifies values for parameters.
WSMParameterValues->{pi -> {c1,c2,…},…}	Runs simulations in parallel, with "pi" taking values "cj". It is an option for WSMSimulateSensitivity and WSMSimulate that specifies values for parameters.
WSMInputFunctions->{"var1"-> fun1,…}	It is an option for WSMSimulateSensitivity and WSMSimulate and that specifies values for input variables. It uses fun***i***[t] as the input value for var***i*** at time t.
WSMPlot[sd, {"v1","v2",…}]	Generates a plot of the variables "v_i" from the WSMSimulationData object sd over the simulation interval.
WSMPlot[sd, {"v1","v2",…}, {time1,time2}]	Plot variables over the interval from time1 to time2.
WSMPlot[{sd1,sd2,…}, {"v1","v2",…}]	Plot variables from several simulation objects sd1, sd2, …
WSMSimulateSensitivity["modelname", {time1, time2}, {a,b,…}, options]	Simulates a model and produces its sensitivities to parameters a, b... during the time interval from time1 to time2. The following optional arguments can be given: WSMInitialValues, ,WSMInputFunctions, WSMParameterValues, InterpolationOrder.
WSMFindEquilibrium["modelname", option]	Searches for an equilibrium to the model "modelname". The following optional argument can be given: ModelicaConversion.
WSMFindEquilibrium["modelname", {{{x1, x10}, …}, {{u1, u10}, …},{{y1, y10}, …}}, option]	Searches for an equilibrium, starting from the point xi = xi0, ui = ui0, yi = yi0. The following optional argument can be given: ModelicaConversion.
WSMFindEquilibrium["modelname",{x1 == v1,…}, …]	Searches for an equilibrium, with variable xi, constrained to have the value vi etc.
WSMLinearize["modelname", option]	Gives a linearized state-space to the model "modelname" at equilibrium and returns a StateSpaceModel object. The following optional argument can be given: Method.
WSMLinearize["modelname", {{{x1, x10}, …}, {{u1, u10}, …}}, option]	Linearizes at state values {x10, …} and input values {u10, …}. The following optional argument can be given: Method.
WSMModelData["modelname"]	Gives a formatted summary for the model "modelname".
WSMModelData["modelname", "properties"]	Shows a list of possible properties for the model "modelname".
WSMModelData["modelname", "property", options]	Shows a specified "property" for the model "modelname". The following optional arguments can be given: Method, and ModelicaConversion.
WSMSetValues["modelname", {p1 -> c1,…}]	Sets pi to ci in the modelica model "modelname".

WSMSetValues["modelname", {p1 -> c1,…}, "InitialValues"]	Sets the initial values for pi to ci in the modelica model "modelname".

The following table contains the list of all the kernel commands that can be used in the Kernel Command view of the WSM Model Center.

cd()	Returns the current directory.
cd(dir)	Changes directory to the directory given as a string. *Inputs*: String dir; *Outputs*: Boolean res;
checkModel(classname)	Validates the given class and returns a string with the result. *Inputs*: TypeName className; *Outputs*: String res;
clear()	Clears all class definitions currently loaded.
clearVariables()	Clears all variables defined in the kernel command session.
getVersion()	Returns the version number of the SystemModeler kernel.
instantiateModel(classname)	Performs code instantiation of a class and returns a string containing the flat class definition. *Inputs:* TypeName className; *Outputs:* String res;
list()	Returns a string containing all loaded class definitions.
list(classname)	Returns a string containing the class definition of the named class. *Inputs:* TypeName className; *Outputs:* String classDef;
listVariables()	Returns a vector of the names of the variables currently defined in the kernel session.
loadModel(classname)	Loads the class with the given name from the SystemModeler library path. Use with care as this function does not update the internal structure of Model Center. Loading a class that is already loaded may lead to critical errors. *Inputs:* TypeName className; *Outputs:* String classDef;
loadFile(filename)	Loads the Modelica file with the name given as a string. Use with care as this function does not update the internal structure of Model Center. Loading a class that is already loaded may lead to critical errors. *Inputs:* String fileName; *Outputs:* Boolean res;
readFile(filename)	Loads the file given as a string and returns a string containing the file content. Use with care as this function does not up date the internal structure of Model Center. Loading a class that is already loaded may lead to critical errors. *Inputs:* String fileName; *Outputs:* String content;
timing(expr)	Evaluates the specified expression and returns the elapsed time in seconds.
saveTotalModel(filename, classname)	Saves a total class definition of the named class to the file given as a string. The file will contain all class definitions used by the named class, making it a self-contained file. *Inputs:* String fileName; TypeName className *Outputs:* Boolean res;
typeOf(var)	Returns the type of a kernel session variable as a string. *Inputs:* VariableName variableName; *Outputs:* String res;

E.3.1 Examples

Below follows a few examples of using the scripting commands in Wolfram SystemModeler. The most common case is a `WSMSimulate` followed by a `WSMPlot`.

Mathematica must be running. In a notebook within the Mathematica environment you first start with a `Needs WSMLink` command to activate the link to Wolfram SystemModelier:

```
Needs["WSMLink`"];
```

Then you do a simulation, for example the `HelloWorld` example from the `IntroductoryExamples`:

```
M1 = WSMSimulate["IntroductoryExamples.HelloWorld", {0, 10}];
```

followed by a plot:

```
WSMPlot[M1, {"x"}]
```

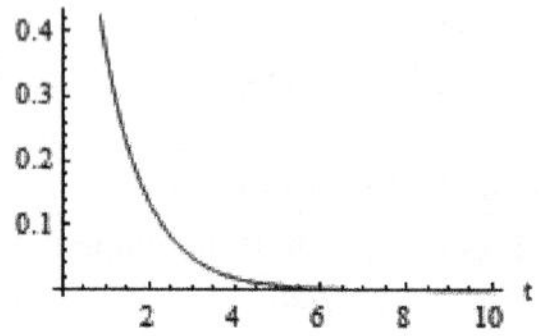

Show a summary of a model:

```
WSMModelData["IntroductoryExamples.HelloWorld"]
```

IntroductoryExamples.HelloWorld

Property	Length
SystemEquations	1
InitialEquations	0
StateVariables	1
AlgebraicVariables	0
InputVariables	0
OutputVariables	0
ParameterValues	0

Show a list of possible properties:

```
WSMModelData["IntroductoryExamples.HelloWorld", "Properties"]
```

```
{AlgebraicVariables, Description, FromModelicaRules, GroupedInitialValues,
 InitialEquations, InitialValues, InputVariables, ModelicaText,
 OutputVariables, ParameterNames, ParameterValues, StateVariables,
 Summary, SummaryTable, SystemEquations, SystemVariables, ToModelicaRules}
```

Use `ModelicaConversion` to see shorter names:

```
WSMModelData["IntroductoryExamples.HelloWorld", "SystemEquations",
             ModelicaConversion -> "Short"]
```

```
{s[1]'[t] == -s[1][t]}
```

Get the rules for converting variables and parameters to and from Modelica form:

```
WSMModelData["IntroductoryExamples.HelloWorld", "ToModelicaRules"]
```

```
{x → x}
```

```
WSMModelData["IntroductoryExamples.HelloWorld", "FromModelicaRules"]
```

```
{x → x}
```

Linearize a DC motor model around an equilibrium:

```
WSMLinearize["MathematicaExamples.Modeling.invertedPendulum.Components.
             DCMotor"]
```

				v
inductor.i	-13.	0.	-1.6	1.
inertia.phi	0.	0.	1.	0.
inertia.w	1.6	0.	0.	0.
w	0.	0.	1.	0.

Find an equilibrium for MixingTank model, starting the search at initial values:

```
mmodel = "MathematicaExamples.Modeling.WaterTanks.MixingTank";
WSMFindEquilibrium[mmodel]
```

```
{{{H, 0.746374}, {Tu, 38.0007}, {Tx, 38.0007}},
 {{u1, 5.21303}, {u2, 3.0807}}, {{y1, 3.73187}, {y2, 3.80007}}}
```

A more advanced example is from the design optimization (Section 15.7, page 869) with a loop of simulations, and the Game of Life model and simulation (Section 13.3.3.1, page 652).

Moreover, the whole Mathematica language is available for advanced scripting.

E.4 Dymola Scripting Commands

These are the Modelica scripting commands available in the Dymola environment:

animationColor(options)	Set animation colors. *Inputs*: Real background[3]; Real selected[3]; Real grid[3]; Real selectedbackground[3]; *Outputs*: Boolean ok;
animationFollow(options)	Set what animation view should follow. *Inputs*: Booleanm followFirst; Boolean followX; Boolean followY; Boolean followZ; Boolean followRotation; *Outputs*: Boolean ok;
animationFrames(options)	Set animation frame properties. *Inputs*: Integer history; Integer interval; Integer delays; *Outputs*: Boolean ok;
animationGrid(grid_square, grid_size)	Set grid size in animation window. *Inputs*: Real grid_square; Real grid_size; *Outputs*: Boolean ok;
animationLightning()	Check animation lighting. *Outputs*: Boolean ok;
animationOnline(options)	Set realtime animation properties. *Inputs*: Boolean onlineAnimation; Boolean realtime; Real scaleFactor; Real loadInterval; *Outputs*: Boolean ok;
animationPerspective(perspective)	Set animation perspective properties. *Inputs*: Real perspective[7]; *Outputs*: Boolean ok;
animationPosition(position)	Set position of animation. *Inputs*: Real position[4]; Integer id; *Outputs*: Boolean ok;
animationRedraw()	Redraw animation window. *Outputs*: Boolean ok;
animationRemove(id)	Remove animation window. *Inputs*: Integer id; *Outputs*: Boolean ok;
animationSelected(options)	Select animation object. *Inputs*: Boolean name; Boolean highlight; Boolean follow; Boolean trace; Integer selected; String selectedName; *Outputs*: Boolean ok;
animationSetup()	Generate script with current setup of animation window. *Outputs*: Boolean ok;
animationSpeed(speed)	Set animation speed. *Inputs*: Real speed; *Outputs*: Boolean ok;
animationSubdivisions(subdivisions)	Set animation subdivision properties. *Inputs*: Integer subdivision[12]; *Outputs*: Boolean ok;
animationTime(timePosition**)**	Set animation time. *Inputs*: Real timePosition; *Outputs*: Boolean ok;
animationTransparency()	Animation transparency. *Outputs*: Boolean ok;
animationTrace()	Animation trace. *Outputs*: Boolean ok;
animationVectorScaling(options)	Set animation scaling properties. *Inputs*: Real force; Real torque; Real velocity; Real acceleration; Real angularvelocity; Real angualracceleration; *Outputs*: Boolean ok;
animationView(view)	Set animation view. *Inputs*: Real view[4,4]; *Outputs*: Boolean ok;
animationViewing(options)	Set properties of animation. *Inputs*: Boolean cylinder;

	Boolean fillmode; Boolean unitcube; Boolean xygrid; Boolean xzgrid; Boolean yzgrid; Boolean perspective; Boolean antialias; *Outputs*: Boolean ok;
cd(dir)	Change directory. *Inputs*: String dir; *Outputs*: Boolean _result;
checkModel(problem)	Instantiate model, optimize equations and report errors. *Inputs*: String problem; *Outputs*: Boolean result;
classDirectory()	Directory containing the class definition, or directory where additional files associated with the class should be stored. *Outputs*: String dir;
clear()	Clears everything, i.e. abstract syntax tree representation of code together with possible user defined variables. *Outputs*: Boolean _result;
clearlog()	Clear the log. *Outputs*: Boolean _result;
closeModel()	Close a model. *Outputs*: Boolean result;
Compile()	Compile default model. *Outputs*: Boolean _result;
Continue()	Continue the default model. *Outputs*: Boolean _result;
createPlot()	Creates plot window.
DefaultModelicaVersion(version, forceUpgrade)	Default Modelica version. *Inputs*: String version; Boolean forceUpgrade;
document(function)	Write calling syntax for named function. *Inputs*: String _function; *Outputs*: Boolean _result;
eraseClasses(classNames_)	Remove classes from symbol table. *Inputs*: String classNames_[:]; *Outputs*: Boolean result;
Execute(file)	Execute file/command. *Inputs*: String file; *Outputs*: Boolean ok;
existTrajectoryNames(fileName, names**)**	Return if names exist in trajectory file. . *Inputs*: String fileName; String names[:]; *Outputs*: String _ exists[size(names, 1)];
exit()	Exit Dymola.
exitDelayed()	Exit Dymola after 5 seconds delay.
experiment(options)	Set default simulation values, e.g. start time, stop time, tolerance, etc. *Inputs*: Real StartTime; Real StopTime; Integer NumberOfIntervals; Real OutputInterval; String Algorithm; Real Tolerance; Real FixedStepSize; *Outputs*: Boolean result;
exportHTMLDirectory(name, directory , options**)**	Export HTML documentation. The library names given in 'listOfLibraries' will be substituted with the corresponding documentation directories in 'listOfLibraryDirectories'. *Inputs*: String name; String directory; String String listOfLibraries[:]; String listOfLibraryDirectories[:]; *Outputs*: Boolean ok;
exportIcon(imageFile, options**)**	Export icon layer to file. *Inputs*: String imageFile; Real width; Real height; *Outputs*: Boolean ok;

exportDiagram(resultFile, option**)**	Export diagram to file. *Inputs*: String resultFile; Real width; Real height; *Outputs*: Boolean ok;
exportInitial(dsName, scriptName, options)	Export initial values to a script file. *Inputs*: String dsName; String scriptName; Boolean exportAllVariables; *Outputs*: Boolean ok;
exportInitialDsin	Generate a copy of internal dsin.txt. *Inputs*: String scriptName; *Outputs*: Boolean ok;
ExportPlotAsImage(fileName, options**)**	Export plot as image in PNG format. *Inputs*: String fileName; Integer id; Boolean includeInLog; *Outputs*: Boolean ok;
help()	List help commands.
importFMU(fileName, options**)**	Imports an FMU. *Inputs*: String fileName; Boolean includeAllVariables; Boolean integrate; Boolean promptReplacement; String packageName; *Outputs*: Boolean result;
importInitial(dsName)	Import initial values as script file. *Inputs*: String dsName; *Outputs*: Boolean ok;
importInitialResult(dsResName**)**	Import start values from ds file. *Inputs*: String dsResName; Real atTime; *Outputs*: Boolean ok;
instantiateModel(problem)	Instantiate model, results in mof file. *Inputs*: String problem; *Outputs*: Boolean result;
interpolateTrajectory(fileName, signals, times)	Read simulation result from file and interpolate values given as a vector of name on time instants given as a vector and return a matrix of interpolated values (one vector for each interpolated variable). *Inputs*: String fileName; String signals[:]; Real times[:]; *Outputs*: Real values[size(signals, 1), size(times, 1)];
linearize()	Linearize default model. *Outputs*: Boolean _result;
linearizeModel(problem, options)	Translate, simulate and linearize model. *Inputs*: String problem; Real startTime; Real stopTime; Integer numberOfIntervals; Real outputInterval; String method ; Real tolerance; Real fixedstepsize; String resultFile; *Outputs*: Boolean result;
list()	Print user defined variables. *Outputs*: Boolean _result;
listfunctions()	List builtin functions on screen. *Outputs*: Boolean _result;
loadAnimation(fileName, options**)**	Load animation .*Inputs*: String fileName; Integer id; Boolean together;
messageBox(message, timeOut, position)	Show message box. *Inputs*: String message; Real timeOut; Real position[2]; *Outputs*: Boolean ok;
messageDialog(message, timeOut, position)	Wait for user input. *Inputs*: String message; Real timeOut; Real position[2]; *Outputs*: Boolean ok;
openModel(path)	Load models from file *path*. *Inputs*: String path; *Outputs*: Boolean result;
openModelFile(model,path)	Load the *file* that contains the *class*. *Inputs*: String model; String path; *Outputs*: Boolean result;

plot(_x)	Plot one or more variables as functions of time. *Inputs*: String _x[:]; *Outputs*: Boolean result;
plotArray(x,y)	Plot the given values as an x-y plot. *Inputs*: Real x[:]; Real y[size(x,1)]; Integer style; String label; *Outputs*: Boolean result;
plotArrays(x,y, options)	Plot the given values as an x-y plot. *Inputs*: Real x[:]; Real y[size(x, 1), :]; Integer style[:]; String legend[:]; *Outputs*: Boolean result;
plotParametricCurve(x,y,s, options)	Plot parametric curve. *Inputs*: Real x[:]; Real y[size(x, 1)]; Real [size(x, 1)]; String legend[:]; *Outputs*: Boolean result;
plotParametricCurves(x,y,s, options**)**	Plot parametric curves. *Inputs*: Real x[:, size(s, 1)]; Real y[size(x, 1), size(s, 1)]; Real s[:]; String legend[:];
plotSetup()	Generate script with current setup of all plot windows. *Outputs*: Boolean ok;
plotSetFilesToKeep()	Plot set files to keep. *Outputs*: Boolean result;
plotSignalOperator(variablePath, signalOperator startTime, stopTime, options)	Plot signal operator in the active diagram of a plot window. *Inputs*: String variablePath; Enumeration signalOperator; Real startTime; Real stopTime; Real period; Integer id; *Outputs*: Boolean result;
plotSignalOperatorHarmonic(variablePath, signalOperator startTime, stopTime, period, intervalLength, window, harmonicNo, options)	Plot signal operator in the active diagram of a plot window. *Inputs*: String variablePath; Enumeration signalOperator; Real startTime; Real stopTime; Real period; Real intervalLength; Integer id; *Outputs*: Boolean result;
plotText(extent,textString, options)	Plot text in the active diagram. *Inputs*: Real extent[2, 2]; String textString; Real fontSize; String fontName; String textStyle; *Outputs*: Boolean result;
plotWindowSetup(_window)	Generate script with current setup of plot window. *Inputs*: Integer _window; *Outputs*: Boolean ok;
printPlot(_x)	Plot and print given variables. *Inputs*: String _x[:]; *Outputs*: Boolean result;
printPlotArray(x, y, style, label)	Plot and print given data. *Inputs*: Real x[:]; Real y[size(x,1)]; Integer style; String label; *Outputs*: Boolean result;
printPlotArrays(x, y, style, lagened)	Plot and print given data. *Inputs*: Real x[:]; Real y[size(x, 1), :]; Integer style[:]; String lagend[:];
ReadAnimationSocket()	Read animation socket. *Outputs*: Boolean ok;
readCSVHeadersInternal(fileName)	Gives headings for csv-files. *Inputs*: String fileName; *Outputs*: String headers[:];
readMATmatrices(fileName)	Gives a table of the matrices found in a mat-file. *Inputs*: String fileName; *Outputs*: String matrices[:, 2];

readMatrix(fileName, modelName,rows,columns)	Read a matrix from a file. *Inputs*: `String fileName; String modelName; Integer rows; Integer columns;` *Outputs*: `Real matrix[rows, columns];`
readMatrixSize(fileName, matrixName)	Read the matrix dimension from a file given a matrix name. *Inputs*: `String fileName; String matrixName;` *Outputs*: `Integer size[2];`
readStringMatrix	
readTrajectory(fileName, signals, size)	Reads the simulation result for a list of variables and returns a matrix of values (each column as a vector or values for a variable.) Size of result is also given as input. *Inputs*: `String fileName; String signals[:] Integer rows;` *Outputs*: `Real values[size(signals,1),rows];`
readTrajectoryNames	
readTrajectorySize(fileName)	Read the size of the trajectory vector from a file. *Inputs*: `String fileName;` *Outputs*: `Integer rows;`
removeMessageBox()	Remove message box. *Outputs*: `Boolean ok;`
removePlots()	Removes all plot windows. *Outputs*: `Boolean ok;`
removeResults()	Removes all results from plot windows. *Outputs*: `Boolean ok;`
RestoreWindow(id, mode, settings)	Restore window setup. *Inputs*: `Integer id; Ineteger mode; String settings;`
RunAnimation(immediate, loadFile, ensureAnimationWindow)	Run animation. *Inputs*: `Boolean immediate; String loadFile; Boolean ensureAnimationWindow;` *Outputs*: `Boolean ok;`
RunScript(_script) *or* @ filename	Executes the script file given as argument. *Inputs*: `String _script;` *Outputs*: `Boolean _result;`
saveEncryptedModel(name, path)	Save an encrypted Modelica-file. *Inputs*: `String name; String path;` *Outputs*: `Boolean _result;`
savelog(logfile)	Save the log to a file. *Inputs*: `String logfile;` *Outputs*: `Boolean _result;`
saveModel(name, path)	Save a Modelica-file. *Inputs*: `String name; String path;` *Outputs*: `Boolean _result;`
saveSettings(fileName, options)	Stores current settings on a file. *Inputs*: `String fileName; Boolean storePlot; Boolean stroeAnimation; Boolean storeSettings; Boolean storeVariables; Boolean storeInitial; Boolean storeAllVariables;` *Outputs*: `Boolean ok;`
saveTotalModel(fileName, modelName)	Save total class definition in file. *Inputs*: `String fileName; String modelName;` *Outputs*: `Boolean result;`
SetVariable(name, val)	Set variable in model. *Inputs*: `String name; Real val;` *Outputs*: `Boolean ok;`
SetDymolaCompiler(compiler, options)	Switch to modeling mode. . *Inputs*: `String compiler; String settings[:];`
ShowComponent(path, components)	Show component. *Inputs*: `String path; String components[:];` *Outputs*: `Boolean ok;`
showMessageWindow(show)	Show/hide log. *Inputs*: `Boolean show;` *Outputs*: `Boolean`

	ok;
simulate()	Simulate the default model. *Outputs*: Boolean _result;
simulateExtendedModel(problem, options)	Simulate a Modelica model. *Inputs*: String problem; Real startTime; Real stopTime; Integer numberOfIntervals; Real outputInterval; String method; Real tolerance; Real fixedstepsize; String resultFile; Boolean result; String initialNames[:]; Real initialValues[size(initialNames,1)]; String finalNames[:]; *Outputs*: Real finalValules[size(finalNames,1)];
simulateModel(problem, options)	Simulate a model. *Inputs*: String problem; Real startTime; Real stopTime; Integer numberOfIntervals; Real outputInterval; String method; Real tolerance; Real fixedstepsize; *Outputs*: Boolean result;
simulateMultiExtendedModel (problem, options)	SimulateMultiExtended a Modelica model. String problem; Real startTime; Real stopTime; Integer numberOfIntervals; Real outputInterval; String method; Real tolerance; Real fixedstepsize; String initialNames[:] ; Real initialValues[:, size(initialNames, 1)]; String finalNames[:]; *Outputs*: Boolean result; Real finalValues[size(initialValues, 1), size(finalNames, 1)];
stopSimulation()	Stop simulation or script execution.
switchLayer(layer)	Switch layer. *Inputs*: Integer layer; Boolean show; *Outputs*: Boolean ok;
switchToModelingMode()	Switch to modeling mode. *Outputs*: Boolean ok;
switchToSimulationMode()	Switch to simulation mode. *Outputs*: Boolean ok;
translateModel(problem)	Instantiate model, optimize equations and *generate* code. *Inputs*: String problem; *Outputs*: Boolean result;
variables()	List variables on screen. *Outputs*: Boolean _result;
vizualize3dModel(problem)	Display a 3D visualization of the latest simulation. *Inputs*: String problem; *Outputs*: Boolean result;
writeCSVFileInternal(fileName, data, options)	Writes a csv file. *Inputs*: String fileName; String headers[:]; Real data[:, size(headers, 1)]; String separator; *Outputs*: Boolean ok;
writeMatrix(fileName, matrixName, matrix)	Write matrix to *file* given a *matrix name* and a *matrix*. *Inputs*: String fileName; String matrixName; Real matrix[:,:]; *Outputs*: Boolean status;
writeTrajectory(fileName, signals, values)	Writes a trajectory file. *Inputs*: String fileName; String signals[:]; String values[:, size(signals, 1)];

E.4.1 Example

Below follows an example of a Dymola script file for the `CoupledClutches` example in the standard Modelica library.

```
// Script generated: 10/11/13 14:00:45

translateModel("Modelica.Mechanics.Rotational.Examples.CoupledClutches")
experiment(StopTime=1.2)
simulate
plot({"J1.w","J2.w","J3.w","J4.w"});
```

Appendix F

Related Equation-Based, Object-Oriented Modeling Languages

In this appendix we give an overview of the languages that have been used as starting point for the Modelica design, that is, Modelica builds upon the experience gained with these languages. Some additional equation-based modeling languages are also briefly presented.

Since the definition of CSSL in 1967, most modeling languages have essentially been block oriented with inputs and outputs. The mathematical models are defined as assignment-like equations for auxiliary variables and derivatives. Physical equations thus need to be transformed to a form suitable for calculations. The only aid in transforming the equations to an algorithm for calculating derivatives is automatic sorting of the equations.

On the contrary, the object oriented modeling languages that constitute the background for development of Modelica all have general equations, that is, *expression* = *expression*, as the basic element. Hierarchical decomposition and reuse are typically supported by some kind of model class. Several languages have provisions to describe physical connection mechanisms, that is, to associate a set of variables with some kind of port. Such ports can be used at higher hierarchical levels when connecting submodels without having to deal with individual variables.

F.1 Language Developments Behind Modelica

The designers of the following object-oriented modeling languages have actively participated creating the Modelica language in part based on experience from these languages.

F.1.1 Dymola Language

Dymola (here meaning Dynamic Modeling Language), introduced in 1978, is based on equations for noncausal modeling, model types for reuse and submodel invocation for hierarchical modeling, and is one of the most important predecessors of Modelica. The Dymola translator utilizes graph theoretical methods for causality assignment, for sorting, (i.e., BLT-partitioning), and for finding minimal systems of simultaneous equations.

Computer algebra is used for solving for the unknowns and to make simplifications of the equations. Constructs for hybrid modeling, including instantaneous equations, were introduced in 1993. Crossing functions for efficient handling of state events are automatically generated. A graphical editor is used to build icons and to make model compositions. Major application areas include multi-body systems, drive-trains, power electronics, thermal systems.

F.1.2 NMF—Neutral Model Format

The Neutral Model Format (NMF) is a language in the Dymola and Omola tradition and was first proposed as a standard to the building and energy systems simulation community in 1989. The language is formally controlled by a committee within ASHRAE (American Society of Heating, Refrigerating and Air-Conditioning Engineers).

Several independently developed NMF tools and model libraries exist, and valuable lessons on language standardization and development of reusable model libraries have been learned. Salient features of NMF are: (1) good support for model documentation, (2) dynamical vector and parameter dimensions (a model can, e.g., calculate required spatial resolution for PDE), (3) full support for calls to foreign models (e.g. legacy or binary Fortran or C models) including foreign model event signals. Inheritance was not present in the original language proposal but was added 1995 to the language specification.

Simulation models can be translated automatically from NMF into the local representation of a particular simulation environment. Several simulation environments have been built around the language. One of these is the IDA Simulation Environment IDA SE, which includes a graphical modeler, an NMF translator, and a solver. In order to illustrate the language a model of a thermal conductance from 1996 is presented below:

```
CONTINUOUS_MODEL  tq_conductance
ABSTRACT  "Linear thermal conductance"
EQUATIONS   /* heat balance */
   0 = - Q + a_u * (T1 - T2);
LINKS
   /* type  name          variables
        TQ   terminal_1   T1, POS_IN Q;
          TQ   terminal_2   T2, POS_OUT Q;
   VARIABLES
   /* type      name    role    description
      Temp       T1      IN      "1st temp"
      Temp       T2      IN      "2nd temp"
      HeatFlux   Q       OUT     "flow from 1 to 2"
PARAMETERS
   /* type      name    role    description
      Area        a     S_P      "cross section area"
      HeatCondA u       S_P      "heat transfer coeff"
      HeatCond   a_u    C_P      "a * u"
PARAMETER_PROCESSING
   a_u := a * u;
   END_MODEL
```

F.1.3 ObjectMath

ObjectMath (Object-Oriented Mathematical Modeling Language) is a high-level programming environment and modeling language designed as an extension to Mathematica. its first version appeared in 1991. The language integrates object-oriented constructs such as classes, and single and multiple inheritance with computer algebra features from Mathematica.

Both equations and assignment statements are included, as well as functions, control structures, and symbolic operations from standard Mathematica. Other features are parameterized classes, named equations that can be specialized at inheritance, hierarchical composition, and dynamic array dimension sizes for multi-dimensional arrays. The environment provides a class browser for the combined inheritance and composition graph and supports generation of efficient code in C++ or Fortran90, as well as an experimental version for generating parallel code.

The user can influence the symbolic transformation of equations or expressions by manually specifying symbolic transformation rules, which also gives an opportunity to control the quality of generated code. The main application area so far has been in mechanical systems modeling and analysis.

F.1.4 Omola

Omola, introduced in 1989, is an object-oriented and equation based modeling language. Models can be decomposed hierarchically with well-defined interfaces that describe interaction. All model components are represented as classes. Inheritance and specialization support easy modification. Omola supports behavioral descriptions in terms of differential-algebraic equations (DAE), ordinary differential equations (ODE) and difference equations. The primitives for describing discrete events allow implementation of high level descriptions as Petri nets and Grafcet. An interactive environment called OmSim supports modeling and simulation: graphical model editor, consistency analysis, symbolic analysis and manipulation to simplify the problem before numerical simulation, ODE and DAE solvers and interactive plotting. Applications of Omola and OmSim include chemical process systems, power generations and power networks.

F.1.5 SIDOPS+

SIDOPS+, introduced in 1997, supports nonlinear multidimensional bond-graph and block-diagram models, which can contain continuous-time parts and discrete-time parts.

The language has facilities for automated modeling support like polymorphic modeling (separation of the interface and the internal description), multiple representations (component graphs, physical concepts like bond graphs or ideal physical models and (acausal) equations or assignment statements), and support for reusability (e.g., documentation fields and physical types). Currently, SIDOPS+ is mainly used in the field of mechatronics and (neural) control. It is the model description language of the package 20-SIM SIDOPS+ is the third generation of SIDOPS which started as a model description language for single-dimensional bond-graph and block-diagram models.

F.1.6 Smile

Smile, introduced in 1995, is an object-oriented, equation-based modeling and simulation environment. The object-oriented and imperative features of Smile's model description language are very similar to Objective-C. Equations may either be specified symbolically or as procedures; external modules can be integrated. Smile also has a dedicated experiment description language. The system consists of translators for the above-mentioned languages, a simulation engine offering several numeric solvers, and components for interactive experimenting, visualization, and optimization. Smile's main application domain traditionally has been the simulation of solar energy equipment and power plants, but thanks to its object-oriented modeling features it is applicable to other classes of complex systems as well.

F.1.7 U.L.M.—ALLAN

The goal of ALLAN, introduced in 1996, is to free engineers from computer science and numerical aspects, and to work towards capitalization and reuse of models. This means noncausal and hierarchical modeling. A graphical representation of the model is associated to the textual representation and can be enhanced by a graphical editor.

A graphical interface is used for hierarchical model assembly. The discrete actions at the interrupts in continuous behavior are managed by events. Automatons (synchronous or asynchronous) are available on events. FORTRAN or C code can be incorporated in the models. Two translators toward the NEPTUNIX and ADASSL (modified DASSLRT) solvers are available. Main application domains are energy systems, car electrical circuits, geology and naval design.

The language U.L.M. was designed in 1993 with the same features as the ALLAN language in a somewhat different implementation. It is a model-exchange language linked to ALLAN. All aspects of modeling are covered by the textual language. There is an emphasis on the separation of the model structure and the model numerical data for reuse purposes. It also has an interesting feature on model validation capitalization.

F.2 Related Languages

Here we describe some related equation-based modeling languages. Some of the early languages have influenced Modelica to some extent, other languages are later developments, or are independent parallel developments.

F.2.1 ASCEND

ASCEND (Advanced System for Computation in ENgineering Design) was developed at Carnegie Mellon University in Pennsylvania, USA to be a rapid model building environment for complex models comprising large sets of nonlinear algebraic equations (Piela 1989, Piela et al. 1991). The language is textual. It supports quantity equations, single inheritance and hierarchical decomposition, but it does not have well defined submodel interfaces. The application domain is chemical process modeling. Later versions support dynamic continuous time modeling.

F.2.2 VHDL-AMS

The VHDL-AMS language, introduced in 1999, is a hardware description language that has been developed to support the modeling of analog, digital, mixed-signal and mixed-technology systems. The language extends the IEEE standard digital design language VHDL (IEEE Std 1076.1-1999) to cover mixed analog and digital systems. It is a large and rich modeling language targeted mainly at the application domain of electronics hardware.

Structuring is done by means of entities and architectures. An entity defines the external view of a component including its parameters (generics), its discrete signal interface and its continuous interface (ports). The architecture associated with an entity describes the implementation which may contain equations (DAEs). As in the case of other equation-based modeling languages the VHDL-AMS language does not specify techniques for the solution of the expressed DAEs, leaving the selection of a suitable numerical method to the simulation environment.

A typical VHDL-AMS simulation framework consists of a compiler and a simulator. The compiler translates the VHDL-AMS source code into an intermediate representation structured as abstract syntax trees with annotated symbol tables and additional semantic information. Similar to other equation-based simulation environments, a hierarchical application model is flattened to a set of discrete and continuous equations.

An analog kernel calculates the analog solutions of the equations at a specified time step by providing an interface to a numerical solver. In this way the original model description is compiled into intermediate object code, linked together with a simulation kernel, and directly executed. The same translation process is also used by the SEAMS VHDL-AMS based simulation framework that incorporates an analyzer, an analog and digital kernel, a code generator, and a compilation module. A design support environment called SIDES (Simulation-Interactive Design Environment System) is attached to SEAMS and includes a GUI viewer, editors, debugging and editing support, library access, and a file and data exchange database to enable all the necessary design environment-simulator interactions.

For reasoning and verification purposes, a denotational semantics of the language has been developed. The general behavior of VHDL-AMS programs is derived by translating the semantics into a prototype simulator implementation. In order to illustrate the syntax of the language, a simple linear resistor model is given below:

```
use electrical_system.all
entity resistor is
  generic(resistance: real);
  port(terminal n1, n2: electrical);
end entity resistor;

architecture signal_flow of resistor is
  quantity vr across ir through n1 to n2;
begin
  ir == vr / resistance;
end architecture signal_flow.
```

F.2.3 The χ Language for Hybrid Systems Simulations

The χ language, introduced in 1999, has been designed with the aim of providing a general language for hybrid system simulations. A χ program consists of processes, systems and function specifications, which are later instantiated by a top-level model. As is the case with most equation-based languages, the top model instance is executed by the simulation environment. A process in χ may have a discrete-event part and/or a continuous-time part and a system may be composed from processes and system instantiations. The continuous-time behavior in χ is expressed with the help of equation statements defined on the local variables of the processes. Model composition in χ is achieved by the use of *channels* in the interface specifications of the sub-models. The *channels* have the same role as connectors in the Modelica language. A process example is given below:

```
proc P =
| [V,x: real] := 0
   , Q: real
   ,b: bool := true
  {
    V' = 2 - Q              //eq0
   ,|Q| Q = sqrt(V)         //eq1
   ,[b -> x' = 1 - x]       //eq2
    | not b -> |x| x = 2 //eq3
    ]
  }
]|
```

F.2.4 gPROMS

gPROMS, introduced in 1992, is a general modeling language for combined lumped and distributed parameter processes described by mixed systems of integral, partial differential, and algebraic equations (IPDAEs). The language is a further development of the Speedup language. The gPROMS language has constructs for certain kinds of partial differential equations. The major application domain is chemical process modeling. The language does not contain constructs for component-based modeling with connectors, and does not support discrete-event modeling.

The modeling language is integrated in a more general simulation system called gPROMS System, 1993, designed to support both continuous and discrete simulation.

The language distinguishes two modeling entities: MODELs (containing DAEs which describes the physical system behavior) and TASKs (containing events representing external actions and disturbances

The language distinguishes two modeling entities: MODELs (containing DAEs which describes the physical system behavior) and TASKs (containing events representing external actions and disturbances imposed on the simulation model). Continuous models and tasks are combined into a single entity called process.

Below we illustrate a lumped parameter model which is defined in gPROMS as follows:

```
MODEL IsothemalFlash
   PARAMETER
      Nocomp  AS    INTEGER
   VARIABLE
      M,    AS ARRAY (Nocomp) OF Holdup
      F,    AS ARRAY (Nocomp) OF Flowrate
      V,L   AS                   Flowrate
      x,y   AS ARRAY (Nocomp) OF MoleFraction
      K     AS ARRAY (Nocomp) OF Kvalue
      ..............................................
   EQUATION
      #Component mass balance
      $M = F - L * x - V * y;
      #Phase equilibrium relationship
      FOR i:= 1 TO Nocomp DO
          K(i) * x(i) = y(i);
      END
      SIGMA(x)=SIGMA(y)=1;
      ..............................................
END #model IsothermalFlash
```

In the above example it can be seen that a MODEL is composed of sections labeled VARIABLE and EQUATION. In the equation section algebraic, differential, and partial differential equations are allowed. The reusability of simulation models described with gPROMS is achieved by hierarchical submodel decomposition and by inheritance.

F.2.5 Abacuss II

Abacuss II (Advanced Batch and Continuous Unsteady State Simulator), introduced in 2002, provides a high-level declarative input language for describing process model simulation. It is an enhanced version of the gPROMS language described by Barton in 1992. The syntax of the Abacuss II language is in the tradition of Pascal and Modula-2. The integrated simulation environment built around the language uses DAEPACK (Differential-Algebraic Equation Package) to perform the required symbolic and numerical calculations.

Abacuss II uses single inheritance, invoked by the keyword INHERITS and the identifier of the parent immediately followed by the identifier of the new model entity. This is illustrated by the following example:

```
MODEL Father
  PARAMETER PI AS REAL DEFAULT 4 * ATAN(1.0)
END

MODEL Child INHERITS Father
  PARAMETER E AS REAL DEFAULT 2.718
END
```

The Child model will inherit all the parameters of the Parent model, and in this particular case Child will contain both PI and E as parameters. Multiple or selective inheritance are not allowed in the language.

The interaction of models with the environment is realized through *stream attributes* that are subsets of the variables describing the time-dependent behavior of the system. Connecting two models in Abacuss is realized by setting up a relationship between stream attributes corresponding to each submodel providing a compressed way of specifying interaction equations among components. The connection relationships need to be declared in the EQUATION section of the model entity. Conditional equations are also allowed to

F.2.6 Cob

Cob, introduced in 2002, is a programming language based on the concept of constrained objects for compositional and declarative modeling of engineering structures. The abstraction models are specified using a declarative object-oriented language. The associated environment includes a graphical editor for developing Cob class definitions, a domain-specific visual interface where already developed components can be combined and a translator, which takes the declarative specification and generates an equivalent CLP(R) (Constraint Logic Program in the Real domain) program.

This translator represents the main difference compared to the other languages and environments in this overview. Instead of generating an imperative equivalent form of the original source code and linking it to numerical solvers, the Cob translator generates an equivalent declarative specification, which is sent to an underlying CLP(R) engine. In this way Cob extends the declarative properties of CLP by introducing object-orientation, conditional constraints and preferences and subsumes the paradigms of CLP and HCLP (hierarchical CLP). By introducing these additional capabilities the applicability of constraint-based languages can easily be extended to engineering applications where components are modeled much more naturally in terms of objects and inheritance hierarchies.

The Cob language is rather expressive compared to the equivalent generated CLP form as seen in the following simple electrical circuit example from (Jayaraman and Tambay 2001).

```
class component
   attributes Real V,I,R
   constraints V=I*R;
   constructors compnent(V1,I1,R1){
      V=V1.  I=I1.  R=R1. }
}
class parallel extends compnent
   attributes compnent [] PC
   constraints
   forall X in PC: X.V = V.
   sum Y in E : Y.I=I.
   sum Z in PC : (1/Z.R)=1/R.
   constructors parallel(B){
      PC=B}
}
```

```
pcomponent([V1, I1, R1], [V, I, R]):-
   V=I*R, V=V1, I=I1, R=R1.
pparallel ([B],[V,I,R,PC]):- PC = B,
   pcomponent(_,[V,I,R]), forall1(PC,X,V)
    N1=I, sum1(PC,N1, Y,I),
    N2=1/R, sum2(PC,N2,Z,R).
forall1([],X,V).
forall1([X|Tail],X,V)):-
   X_V=V, X=[X_V,X_I,X_R],
forall1(Tail,X,V).
sum2([],0,Z,R).
sum2([Z|Tail],(1/Z_R)+Sumrest,Z,R):-
   sum2(Tail,Sumrest,Z,R),
Z=[Z_V,Z_I,Z_R].
sum1([],0,Y,I).
sum2([Y|Tail],(Y_I)+Sumrest,Y,I):-
   sum2(Tail,Sumrest,Y,I),
Y=[Y_V,Y_I,Y_R].
```

The Cob language successfully extends several previous object-oriented constraint imperative languages with *stratified preference logic programs* that allows an efficient simulation of the constraint hierarchies.

F.2.7 Object-Oriented Biomedical System Modeling (OOBSML)

The OOBSML language, introduced in 1999, was developed at Uppsala University Hospital and is aimed at the development of a biomedical continuous system modeling language. It is fully object-oriented and supports model inheritance, encapsulation, and model component instantiation. The language resembles Omola very much.

Besides DAEs, the language also includes formal expressions for documenting models and defining model quantity types and quantity units. It supports explicit definition of model input, output and state quantities, model components, and component connections.

The OOBSML model compiler produces self-contained, independent, executable model components that can be instantiated and used within other OOBSML models and/or stored within model and model

Besides DAEs, the language also includes formal expressions for documenting models and defining model quantity types and quantity units. It supports explicit definition of model input, output and state quantities, model components, and component connections.

The OOBSML model compiler produces self-contained, independent, executable model components that can be instantiated and used within other OOBSML models and/or stored within model and model component libraries. In this way, complex models can be structured as multilevel, multi-component model hierarchies. Technically, the model components produced by the OOBSML compiler are executable computer code objects based on distributed object and object request broker technology. The most basic concept of the OOBSML language is the model concept. A model encapsulates system knowledge and information related to the purpose of modeling such as: input and output quantities, state quantities, types and units, and model behavior represented by algebraic and differential equations.

A simple example of a two compartment model used for medical simulation illustrates the language syntax:

```
model TwoCompWithMetabolism: TwoComp has
  inputs
    meta: reaction_rate [mol/L/h]
  outputs
    Fmeta: substance_flow [mol/h]
  behaviour Dynamic is
  begin
    Np'=Fpo-Fop+Fpe-Fep+Fmeta
    Fmeta=Vmeta *Vp
  end Dynamic
end TwoCompWithMetabolism
```

F.2.8 Ptolemy II

Ptolemy II is an open-source software framework supporting experimentation with actor-oriented design. Actors are software components that execute concurrently and communicate through messages sent via interconnected ports. A model is a hierarchical interconnection of actors.

In Ptolemy II, the semantics of a model is not determined by the framework, but rather by a software component in the model called a director, which implements a model of computation. The Ptolemy Project has developed directors supporting process networks (PN), discrete-events (DE), dataflow (SDF), synchronous/reactive(SR), rendezvous-based models, 3-D visualization, and continuous-time models. Each level of the hierarchy in a model can have its own director, and distinct directors can be composed hierarchically.

A major emphasis of the project has been on understanding the heterogeneous combinations of models of computation realized by these directors. Directors can be combined hierarchically with state machines to make modal models. A hierarchical combination of continuous-time models with state machines yields hybrid systems; a combination of synchronous/reactive with state machines yields StateCharts.

Ptolemy II—Modelica integration has been done, both using FMI (Appendix G, page 1159), and a developed OpenModelica director for Ptolemy II.

F.3 Literature

In the introduction to this appendix, we mention the CSSL definition, described in (Augustin, Fineberg, Johnson, Linebarger, Sansom, and Strauss 1967). A number of object-oriented equation-based modeling languages, whose originators have participated in the design of the Modelica language, are presented in the following references:

- ObjectMath—(Fritzson, Viklund, Herber, Fritzson 1992; Fritzson, Fritzson, Viklund, Herber 1994; Fritzson, Viklund, and Fritzson 1995).
- Omola—(Andersson 1989; Andersson 1992; Mattsson and Andersson 1992; Mattsson, Andersson, and Åström 1993; Andersson 1994).
- Smile—(Kloas, Friesen, and Simons 1995; Ernst, Jähnichen, and Klose 1997).
- SIDOPS+ — (Broenink 1997; Breunese and Broenink 1997).
- ALLAN, U.L.M.—(Jeandel, Boudaud, Ravier, and Bushing 1996).

The following are related equation-based modeling languages:

- ASCEND—(Piela, Epperly, Westerberg, and Westerberg 1991).
- VHDL-AMS—(Frey, Nellayappan, Shanmugasundaram, Mayiladuthurai, Chandrashekar, and Carter 1998; Christen and Bakalar 1999; IEEE Std 1076.1-1999; Schneider, Mades, Glesner, Windisch, and Ecker 2000).
- Abacuss II—the language with applications is described in (Tolsma, Clabaugh, and Barton 2002; Tolsma, and Barton 2000). It is actually an enhanced version of gPROMS as described in (Barton 1992).
- gPROMS—(Barton 1992; Barton and Pantelides 1993; Barton and Pantelides 1994; Oh 1995; Oh and Pantelides 1996).
- The *X* system—(Fábian 1999).
- Cob—(Jayaraman and Tambay 2001; Jayaraman and Tambay 2002).
- OOBSML—(Hakman and Groth 1999; Hakman 2000).
- Ptolemy and Ptolemy II—(Lee 2001; Lee 2002; Eker, Janneck, Lee, Liu, Liu, Ludvig, Sachs, and Xiong 2003; Brooks and Lee 2010). Ptolemy II – OpenModelica integration is described in (Mana 2013; Mizraei, Buffoni, and Fritzson 2013). Almost all text in Section F.2.8 has been cited from the Ptolemy II home page (Ptolemy II, 2013).

Appendix G

FMI—Functional Mockup Interface

This appendix contains a short overview of the Functional Mockup Interface (FMI) standard, version 2.0 RC1 based on the definition in (FMI 2013). FMI is a tool independent standard to support both model exchange and co-simulation of dynamic models using a combination of xml files and C code (either compiled in DLL/shared libraries or in source code). The first version, FMI 1.0, was published in 2010. The FMI development was initiated by Daimler AG with the goal to improve the exchange of simulation models between suppliers and OEMs.

At the time of this writing, development of the standard continues through the participation of many companies and research institutes. FMI 1.0 is supported by a large number of tools and is used by automotive and nonautomotive organizations throughout Europe, Asia, and North America.

On the Downloads page (https://www.fmi-standard.org/downloads), the FMI 2.0 specification, as well as supporting C-header and xml schema files, and an FMI compliance checker are provided. In addition, sample models (exported from different tools in FMI format) are provided to assist tool vendors to ensure compatibility with other tools, as well as a test suite to check whether connected FMUs are appropriately handled by a tool.

G.1 Summary

This appendix gives a short overview description of the Functional Mock-up Interface (FMI), version 2.0, which supports the following:

- exchange of dynamic models between tools
- defining tool coupling for dynamic system simulation environments

FMI for Model Exchange

The intention of FMI for Model Exchange is that a modeling environment can generate C code of a dynamic system model that can be utilized by other modeling and simulation environments. Models are described by differential, algebraic and discrete equations with time-, state- and step-events. If the C code describes a continuous system, then this system is solved with the integrators of the environment where it is used. The models to be treated by this interface can be large for usage in offline or online simulation, or can be used in embedded control systems on micro-processors.

FMI for Co-Simulation

The intention of FMI for Co-Simulation is to provide an interface standard for coupling of simulation tools in a co-simulation environment. The data exchange between subsystems is restricted to discrete communication points. In the time between two communication points, the subsystems are solved independently from each other by their individual solver. Master algorithms control the data exchange between subsystems and the synchronization of all simulation solvers (slaves). Both, rather simple master algorithms, as well as more sophisticated ones are supported. Note, that the master algorithm itself is not part of the FMI standard.

FMI Common Concepts

The two interface standards have many parts in common. In particular, it is possible to utilize several instances of a model and/or a co-simulation tool and to connect them together. The interfaces are independent of the target environment because no header files are used that depend on the target environment (with exception of the data types of the target platform). This allows generating one dynamic link library that can be utilized in any environment on the same platform. A model, a co-simulation slave or the coupling part of a tool, is distributed in one zip file called FMU (Functional Mock-up Unit) that contains several files:

- An XML file contains the definition of all exposed variables in the FMU and other static information. It is then possible to run the FMU on a target system without this information, in other words with no unnecessary overhead.
- All needed model equations or the access to co-simulation tools are provided with a small set of easy to use C functions. A new caching technique allows a more efficient evaluation of the model equations than in other approaches. These C functions can either be provided in source and/or binary form. Binary forms for different platforms can be included in the same FMU zip file.
- The model equations or the co-simulation tool can be either provided directly in the FMU, or the FMU contains only a generic communication module that communicates with an external tool that evaluates or simulates the model. In the XML file information about the capabilities of the FMU are present, for example to characterize the ability of a co-simulation slave to support advanced master algorithms such as the usage of variable communication step sizes, higher order signal extrapolation, or others.
- Further data can be included in the FMU zip file, especially a model icon (bitmap file), documentation files, maps and tables needed by the FMU, and/or all object libraries or dynamic link libraries that are utilized.

A growing set of tools supports FMI. The actual list of tools is available at: https://www.fmi-standard.org

About FMI 2.0

This version 2.0 is a major enhancement compared to FMI 1.0, where the FMI 1.0 Model Exchange and Co-Simulation standards have been merged, and many improvements have been incorporated, often due to practical experience when using the FMI 1.0 standards. New features are usually optional (need neither be supported by the tool that exports an FMU, nor by the tool that imports an FMU). Details are provided in appendix A.3.1. The appendix of the FMI 1.0 specification has been mostly moved in an extended and improved form to a companion document "FunctionalMockupInterface-ImplementationHints.pdf" where practical information for the implementation of the FMI standard is provided.

G.2 Overview

G.2.1 FMI Interfaces and FMU Structure

The FMI (Functional Mock-up Interface) defines an interface to be implemented by an executable called FMU (Functional Mock-up Unit). The FMI functions are used (called) by a simulation environment to create one or more instances of the FMU and to simulate them, typically together with other models. An FMU may either have its own solvers (FMI for Co-Simulation, Section G.4, page 1165) or require the simulation environment to perform numerical integration (FMI for Model Exchange, Section G.3, page 1164). The goal of this interface is that the calling of an FMU in a simulation environment is reasonably simple. No provisions are provided in this document how to generate an FMU from a modeling environment. Hints for implementation can be found in the companion document "FunctionalMockupInterface-ImplementationHints.pdf".

The FMI for Model Exchange interface defines an interface to the model of a dynamic system described by differential, algebraic and discrete-time equations and to provide an interface to evaluate these equations as needed in different simulation environments, as well as in embedded control systems, with explicit or implicit integrators and fixed or variable step size. The interface is designed to allow the description of large models.

The FMI for Co-Simulation interface is designed both for the coupling of simulation tools (simulator coupling, tool coupling), and coupling with subsystem models, which have been exported by their simulators together with its solvers as runnable code. The goal is to compute the solution of time dependent coupled systems consisting of subsystems that are continuous in time (model components that are described by differential-algebraic equations) or time-discrete (model components that are described by difference equations, for example discrete controllers). In a block representation of the coupled system, the subsystems are represented by blocks with (internal) state variables x(t) that are connected to other subsystems (blocks) of the coupled problem by subsystem inputs u(t) and subsystem outputs y(t).

In case of tool coupling, the modular structure of coupled problems is exploited in all stages of the simulation process beginning with the separate model setup and pre-processing for the individual subsystems in different simulation tools. During time integration, the simulation is again performed independently for all subsystems restricting the data exchange between subsystems to discrete communication points. Finally, also the visualization and post-processing of simulation data is done individually for each subsystem in its own native simulation tool.

The two interfaces have large parts in common. In particular:

- FMI Application Programming Interface (C)

All needed equations or tool coupling computations are evaluated by calling standardized "C" functions. "C" is used, because it is the most portable programming language today and is the only programming language that can be utilized in all embedded control systems.

- FMI Description Schema (XML)

The schema defines the structure and content of an XML file generated by a modeling environment. This XML file contains the definition of all variables of the FMU in a standardized way. It is then possible to run the C code in an embedded system without the overhead of the variable definition (the alternative would be to store this information in the C code and access it via function calls, but this is neither practical for embedded systems nor for large models).

Furthermore, the variable definition is a complex data structure and tools should be free how to represent this data structure in their programs. The selected approach allows a tool to store and access the variable definitions (without any memory or efficiency overhead of standardized access functions) in the programming language of the simulation environment, such as C++, C#, Java, or Python.

Note, there are many free and commercial libraries in different programming languages to read XML files into an appropriate data structure, see for example http://en.wikipedia.org/wiki/XML#Parsers, and especially the efficient open source parser SAX (http://sax.sourceforge.net/, http://en.wikipedia.org/wiki/Simple_API_for_XML).

An FMU (in other words a model without integrators, a runnable model with integrators, or a tool coupling interface) is distributed in one zip file. The zip file contains:

- The FMI Description File (in XML format).
- The C sources of the FMU, including the needed run-time libraries used in the model, and/or binaries for one or several target machines, such as Windows dynamic link libraries (.dll) or Linux shared object libraries (.so). The latter solution is especially used if the FMU provider wants to hide the source code to secure the contained know-how or to allow a fully automatic import of the

FMU in another simulation environment. An FMU may contain physical parameters or geometrical dimensions, which should not be open. On the other hand, some functionality requires source code.

- Additional FMU data (like tables, maps) in FMU specific file formats.

A schematic view of an FMU is shown in the next figure:

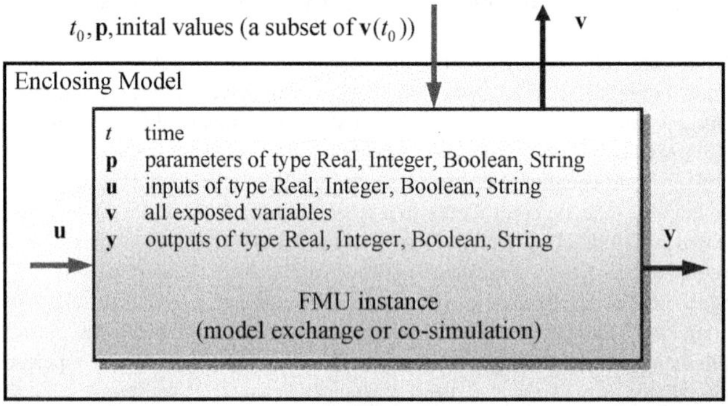

Figure G-1: Data flow between the environment and an FMU. For details, see chapters 3 and 4. Blue arrows: Information provided by the FMU. Red arrows: Information provided to the FMU.

Publications available for FMI are available from https://www.fmi-standard.org/literature, especially Blochwitz et.al. 2011 and 2012.

G.2.2 FMI Properties and Guiding Ideas

In this section properties are listed and some principles are defined that guided the low-level design of the FMI. This shall increase self-consistency of the interface functions. The listed issues are presented starting from high-level properties to low-level implementation issues:

Expressivity: The FMI provides the necessary features that Modelica®, Simulink® and SIMPACK® models can be transformed to an FMU.

Stability: FMI is expected to be supported by many simulation tools worldwide. Implementing such support is a major investment for tool vendors. Stability and backwards compatibility of the FMI has therefore high priority. To support this, the FMI defines "capability flags" that will be used by future versions of the FMI to extend and improve the FMI in a backwards compatible way, whenever feasible.

Implementation: FMUs can be written manually or can be generated automatically from a modeling environment. Existing manually coded models can be transformed manually to a model according to the FMI standard.

Processor independence: It is possible to distribute an FMU without knowing the target processor. This allows to run an FMU on a PC, a Hardware-in-the-Loop simulation platform or as part of the controller software of an ECU, for example, as part of an AUTOSAR SWC. Keeping the FMU independent of the target processor increases the usability of the FMU and is even required by the AUTOSAR software component model. Implementation: using a textual FMU (distribute the C source of the FMU).

Simulator independence: It is possible to compile, link and distribute an FMU without knowing the target simulator. Reason: The standard would be much less attractive otherwise, unnecessarily restricting the later use of an FMU at compile time and forcing users to maintain simulator specific variants of an FMU. Implementation: using a binary FMU. When generating a binary FMU, for example, a Windows dynamic link library (.dll) or a Linux shared object library (.so), the target operating system and eventually the target processor must be known. However, no run-time libraries, source files or header files of the target simulator are needed to generate the binary FMU. As a result, the binary FMU can be executed by any simulator running on the target platform (provided the necessary licenses are available, if required from the model or from the used run-time libraries).

Small run-time overhead: Communication between an FMU and a target simulator through the FMI does not introduce significant run time overhead. This is achieved by a new caching technique (to avoid computing the same variables several times) and by exchanging vectors instead of scalar quantities.

Small footprint: A compiled FMU (the executable) is small. Reason: An FMU may run on an ECU (Electronic Control Unit, for example a microprocessor), and ECUs have strong memory limitations. This is achieved by storing signal attributes (names, units, etc.) and all other static information not needed for model evaluation in a separate text file (= Model Description File) that is not needed on the microprocessor where the executable might run.

Hide data structure: The FMI for Model Exchange does not prescribe a data structure (a C struct) to represent a model. Reason: the FMI standard shall not unnecessarily restrict or prescribe a certain implementation of FMUs or simulators (whoever holds the model data), to ease implementation by different tool vendors.

Support many and nested FMUs: A simulator may run many FMUs in a single simulation run and/or multiple instances of one FMU. The inputs and outputs of these FMUs can be connected with direct feed through. Moreover, an FMU may contain nested FMUs.

Numerical Robustness: The FMI standard allows that problems which are numerically critical (for example time and state events, multiple sample rates, stiff problems) can be treated in a robust way.

Hide cache: A typical FMU will cache computed results for later reuse. To simplify usage and to reduce error possibilities by a simulator, the caching mechanism is hidden from the usage of the FMU for the following reasons. First, the FMI should not force an FMU to implement a certain caching policy. Second, this helps to keep the FMI simple. Implementation: The FMI provides explicit methods (called by the FMU environment) for setting properties that invalidate cached data. An FMU that chooses to implement a cache may maintain a set of "dirty" flags, hidden from the simulator. A get method, for example, to a state, will then either trigger a computation, or return cached data, depending on the value of these flags.

Support numerical solvers: A typical target simulator will use numerical solvers. These solvers require vectors for states, derivatives and zero-crossing functions. The FMU directly fills the values of such vectors provided by the solvers. Reason: minimize execution time. The exposure of these vectors conflicts somewhat with the 'hide data structure' requirement, but the efficiency gain justifies this.

Explicit signature: The intended operations, argument types and return values are made explicit in the signature. For example an operator (such as "compute_derivatives") is not passed as an int argument but a special function is called for this. The "const" prefix is used for any pointer that should not be changed, including "const char*" instead of "char*". Reason: the correct use of the FMI can be checked at compile time and allows calling of the C code in a C++ environment (which is much stricter on "const" as C is). This will help to develop FMUs that use the FMI in the intended way.

Few functions: The FMI consists of a few, "orthogonal" functions, avoiding redundant functions that could be defined in terms of others. Reason: This leads to a compact, easy to use, and hence attractive API with a compact documentation.

Error handling: All FMI methods use a common set of methods to communicate errors.

Allocator must free: All memory (and other resources) allocated by the FMU are freed (released) by the FMU. Likewise, resources allocated by the simulator are released by the simulator. Reason: this helps to prevent memory leaks and runtime errors due to incompatible runtime environments for different components.

Immutable strings: All strings passed as arguments or returned are read-only and must not be modified by the receiver. Reason: This eases the reuse of strings.

Use C: The FMI is encoded using C, not C++. To avoid problems with compiler and linker dependent behavior, run FMU on embedded target.

This version of the functional mockup interface does not have the following desirable properties. They might be added in a future version:

- The FMI for Model Exchange is for ordinary differential equations in state space form (ODE). It is not for a general differential-algebraic equation system. However, algebraic equation systems inside the FMU are supported (for example the FMU can report to the environment to re-run the current step with a smaller step size since a solution could not be found for an algebraic equation system).
- Special features as might be useful for multi-body system programs, like SIMPACK, are not included.
- The interface is for simulation and for embedded systems. Properties that might be additionally needed for trajectory optimization, for example derivatives of the model with respect to parameters during continuous integration, are not included.
- No explicit definition of the variable hierarchy in the XML file.
- The number of states and number of event indicators are fixed for an FMU and cannot be changed.

G.3 FMI for Model Exchange

This section briefly describes the interface to access the equations of a dynamic system from a C program. A schematic view of a model in "FMI for Model Exchange" format is shown in Figure G-2.

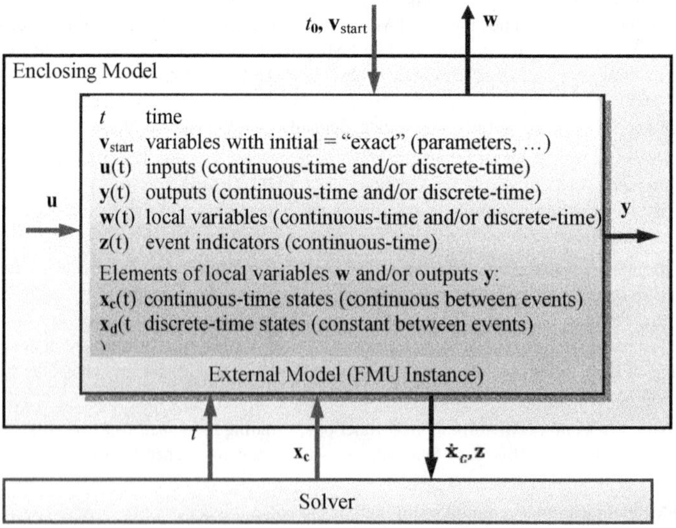

Figure G-2: Data flow between the environment and an FMU for Model Exchange. Blue arrows: Information provided by the FMU. Red arrows: Information provided to the FMU. $\mathbf{v}_{start}, \mathbf{u}, \mathbf{y}, \mathbf{w}, \mathbf{x}_d$ are of type Real, Integer, Boolean, String; $t, \mathbf{x}_c, \mathbf{z}$ are of type Real.

The goal of the Model Exchange interface is to numerically solve a system of differential, algebraic and discrete-time equations. In this version of the interface, ordinary differential equations in state space form with events are handled (abbreviated as "hybrid ODE"). Algebraic equation systems might be contained inside the FMU. Also, the FMU might consist of discrete-time equations only, for example describing a sampled-data controller.

G.4 FMI for Co-Simulation

This chapter defines the Functional Mock-up Interface (FMI) for the coupling of two or more simulation models in a co-simulation environment (FMI for Co-Simulation). Co-simulation is a rather general approach to the simulation of coupled technical systems and coupled physical phenomena in engineering with focus on non-stationary (time-dependent) problems.

FMI for Co-Simulation is designed both for coupling with subsystem models, which have been exported by their simulators together with its solvers as runnable code (Figure G-3), and for coupling of simulation tools (simulator coupling, tool coupling (Figure G-4 and Figure G-5).

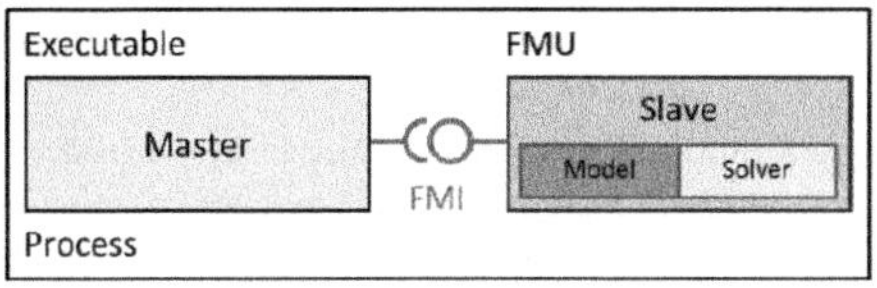

Figure G-3: Co-simulation with generated code on a single computer.
(for simplicity shown for one slave only).

Figure G-4 shows tool coupling on a single computer.

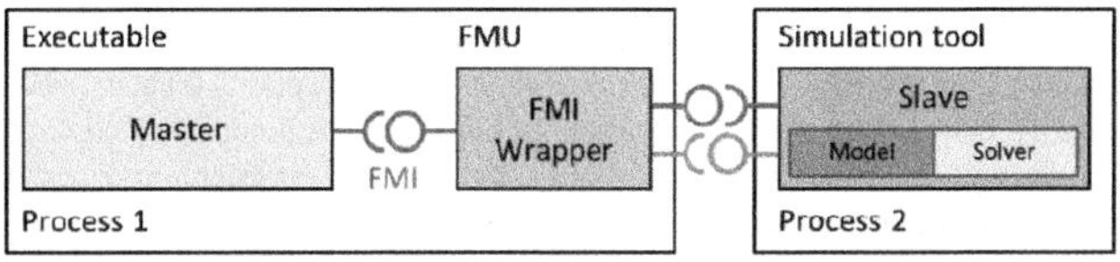

Figure G-4: Co-simulation with tool coupling on a single computer .
(for simplicity shown for one slave only).

In the tool-coupling case the FMU implementation wraps the FMI function calls, to API calls which are provided by the simulation tool (for example a COM or CORBA API). Additionally to the FMU the simulation tool is needed to run a co-simulation.

In its most general form, a tool coupling based co-simulation is implemented on distributed hardware with subsystems being handled by different computers with maybe different OS (cluster computer, computer farm, computers at different locations). The data exchange and communication between the subsystems is typically done using one of the network communication technologies (for example MPI, TCP/IP). The definition of this communication layer is not part of the FMI standard. However distributed co-simulation scenarios can be implemented using FMI as shown in Figure G-5.

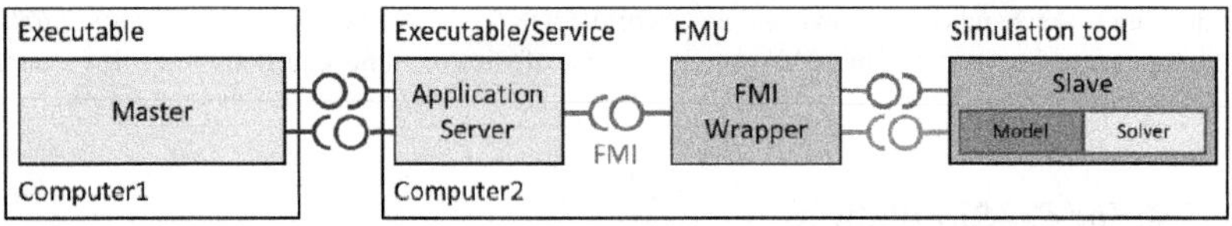

Figure G-5: Distributed co-simulation infrastructure (for simplicity shown for one slave only).

The master has to implement the communication layer. Additional parameters for establishing the network communication (for example identification of the remote computer, port numbers, user account) are to be set via the GUI of the master. These data are not transferred via the FMI API.

G.4.1 FMI Basic Mathematical Description

Co-simulation exploits the modular structure of coupled problems in all stages of the simulation process beginning with the separate model setup and preprocessing for the individual subsystems in different simulation tools (which can be powerful simulators as well as simple C programs).

During time integration, the simulation is again performed independently for all subsystems restricting the data exchange between subsystems to discrete communication points tc_i. For simulator coupling, also the visualization and post-processing of simulation data is done individually for each subsystem in its own native simulation tool. In different contexts, the communication points tc_i, the communication steps Co-simulation exploits the modular structure of coupled problems in all stages of the simulation process beginning with the separate model setup and preprocessing for the individual *subsystems* in different *simulation tools* (which can be powerful simulators as well as simple C programs).

During time integration, the simulation is again performed independently for all subsystems restricting the data exchange between subsystems to discrete *communication points* tc_i. For simulator coupling, also the visualization and post-processing of simulation data is done individually for each subsystem in its own native simulation tool. In different contexts, the communication points tc_i, the *communication steps* $tc_i \rightarrow tc_{i+1}$ and the *communication step sizes* $hc_i := tc_{i+1} - tc_i$ are also known as sampling points (synchronization points), macro steps and sampling rates, respectively. The term "communication point" in FMI for Co-Simulation refers to the communication between subsystems in a co-simulation environment and should not be mixed with the output points for saving simulation results to file.

FMI for Co-Simulation provides an interface standard for the solution of time dependent *coupled systems* consisting of subsystems that are continuous in time (model components that are described by instationary differential equations) or time-discrete (model components that are described by difference equations like, for example discrete controllers). In a block representation of the coupled system, the subsystems are represented by blocks with (internal) *state variables* $x(t)$ that are connected to other subsystems (blocks) of the coupled problem by *subsystem inputs* $u(t)$ and *subsystem outputs* $y(t)$. In this framework, the physical connections between subsystems are represented by mathematical coupling conditions between the inputs $u(t)$ and the outputs $y(t)$ of all subsystems, *Kübler and Schiehlen (2000)*.

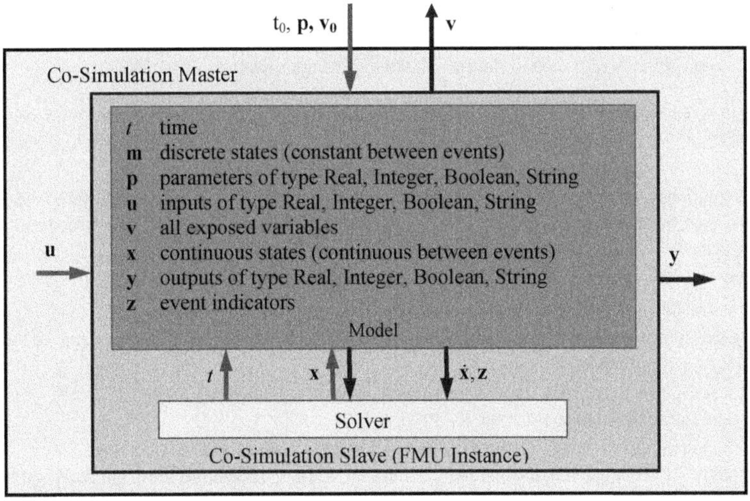

Figure G-6: Data flow at communication points.

For co-simulation, two basic groups of functions have to be realized:

- functions for the data exchange between subsystems
- functions for algorithmic issues to synchronize the simulation of *all* subsystems and to proceed in communication steps $tc_i \rightarrow tc_{i+1}$ from initial time $tc_0 := t_{start}$ to end time $tc_N := t_{stop}$

In FMI for Co-Simulation, both functions are implemented in one software component, the co-simulation *master*. The data exchange between the subsystems (*slaves*) is handled via the master only. There is no direct communication between the slaves. The master functionality can be implemented by a special software tool (a separate simulation backplane) or by one of the involved simulation tools. In its most general form, the coupled system may be simulated in *nested* co-simulation environments and FMI for Co-Simulation applies to each level of the hierarchy.

FMI for Co-Simulation defines interface routines for the communication between the master and all slaves (subsystems) in a co-simulation environment. The most common master algorithm stops at each communication point tc_i the simulation (time integration) of all slaves, collects the outputs $y(tc_i)$ from all subsystems, evaluates the subsystem inputs $u(tc_i)$, distributes these subsystem inputs to the slaves and continues the (co-)simulation with the next communication step $tc_i \rightarrow tc_{i+1} = tc_i + hc$ with fixed communication step size hc. In each slave, an appropriate solver is used to integrate one of the subsystems for a given communication step $tc_i \rightarrow tc_{i+1}$. The most simple co-simulation algorithms approximate the (unknown) subsystem inputs $u(t)$, $(t > tc_i)$ by frozen data $u(tc_i)$ for $tc_i \leq t < tc_{i+1}$. FMI for Co-Simulation supports this classical brute force approach as well as more sophisticated master algorithms. FMI for Co-Simulation is designed to support a very general class of master algorithms but it does *not* define the master algorithm itself.

The ability of slaves to support more sophisticated master algorithms is characterized by a set of *capability flags* inside the XML description of the slave. Typical examples are:

- the ability to handle variable communication step sizes hc_i,
- the ability to repeat a rejected communication step $tc_i \rightarrow tc_{i+1}$ with reduced communication step size,

- the ability to provide derivatives w.r.t. time of outputs to allow interpolation,
- or the ability to provide Jacobians.

FMI for Co-Simulation is restricted to slaves with the following properties:

- All calculated values $v(t)$ are time dependent functions within an a priori defined time interval $t_{start} \leq t \leq t_{stop}$ (provided `stopTimeDefined = fmiTrue` when calling `fmiSetupExperiment`).
- All calculations (simulations) are carried out with increasing time in general. The current time t is running step by step from t_{start} to t_{stop}. The algorithm of the slave may have the property to be able to repeat the simulation of parts of $[t_{start}, t_{stop}]$ or the whole time interval $[t_{start}, t_{stop}]$.
- The slave can be given a time value tc_i, $t_{start} \leq tc_i \leq t_{stop}$.
- The slave is able to interrupt the simulation when tc_i is reached.
- During the interrupted simulation the slave (and its individual solver) can receive values for inputs $u(tc_i)$ and send values of outputs $y(tc_i)$.
- Whenever the simulation in a slave is interrupted, a new time value tc_{i+1}, $tc_i \leq tc_{i+1} \leq t_{stop}$ can be given to simulate the time subinterval $tc_i < t \leq tc_{i+1}$
- The subinterval length hc_i is the communication step size of the ith communication step, $hc_i = tc_{i+1} - tc_i$. In general, the communication step size can be positive, zero, but not negative.

FMI for Co-Simulation allows a co-simulation flow which starts with instantiation and initialization (all slaves are prepared for computation, the communication links are established), followed by simulation (the slaves are forced to simulate a communication step), and finishes with shutdown. In detail the flow is defined in the state machine of the calling sequences from master to slave.

The slave simulators are seen by the master simulator as purely sampled-data systems. Such a sampled-data system can be

- A "real" sampled-data system (so a sampled discrete controller; the inputs and outputs can be of type Real, Integer, Boolean, String, or enumeration. Variables of this type are defined with `variability = "discrete"`; the smallest sample period as accessible by the outside of the FMU is defined by attribute `stepSize` in element `DefaultExperiment`).
- A hybrid ODE that is integrated between communication points (known as "sampled access to time continuous systems") where internal events may occur and be handled, but events are not visible from the outside of the FMU. It is assumed here that all inputs and all outputs of this hybrid ODE are Real signals (defined with `variability = "continuous"`),
- A combination of the systems above.

The communication between the master and a slave takes only place at a discrete set of time instants, called *communication points*.

G.5 Literature

The main reference to the Functional Mockup Interface 2.0 is (Modelica Association Project FMI 2013) from which all text and all figures in this appendix has been cited. However, note that the FMI 2.0 definition document provides much more information than what has been presented here.

Apart from the FMI 2.0 definition document, the following publications provide additional information: (Blochwitz, Otter, Akesson, Arnold, Clauß, Elmqvist, Friedrich, Junghanns, Mauss, Neumerkel, Olsson, and Viel 2012; Åkesson, Braun, Lindholm, and Bachmann 2012; Benveniste,

Caillaud, and Pouzet 2010; Kübler and Schiehlen 2000; Lee and Zheng 2007; Pouzet 2006; ITEA2-MODELISAR 2009).

A related but different approach to numerically stable co-simulation using TLM-connectors is described in (Siemers, Fritzson, and Fritzson 2006). Secure co-simulation is described in (Norling, Broman, Fritzson, Siemers, and Fritzson 2007). A general FMU interface for Modelica is described in (Chen, Huhn, and Fritzson 2011).

References

3Dsystems Inc., Stereo Lithography Interface Specification—The STL format, 2000.

Abadi, M., and Luca Cardelli. *A Theory of Objects*. Springer Verlag, 1996.

Adams, Jeanne C., Walter S. Brainerd, Jeanne T. Martin, Brian T. Smith, Jerrold L. Wagener. *Fortran 90 Handbook, Complete ANSI/ISO Reference*, McGraw Hill, 1992.

Åhlander, Krister. *An Object-Oriented Framework for PDE Solvers* Ph.D. thesis, Dept. of Scientific Computing, Uppsala University, Sweden, 1999.

Ahmed, Nafeez. Nasa-funded study: industrial civilisation headed for 'irreversible collapse'?. In *Guardian*, http://www.theguardian.com/environment/earth-insight/2014/mar/14/nasa-civilisation-irreversible-collapse-study-scientists March 26, 2014.

Aiken, Richard C. (ed.). *Stiff Computation*. Oxford University Press, 1985.

Åkesson, Johan. Tools and Languages for Optimization of Large-Scale Systems. PhD thesis ISRN LUTFD2/TFRT-1081-SE, Department of Automatic Control, Lund University, Sweden, November 2007.

Åkesson, Johan., Willy Braun, Lindholm P., and Bernhard Bachmann. Generation of Sparse Jacobians for the Functional Mockup Interface 2.0. 9th International Modelica Conference, Munich, 2012.

Allen, Eric, Robert Cartwright, and Brian Stoler. DrJava: A Lightweight Pedagogic Environment for Java. In *Proceedings of the 33rd ACM Technical Symposium on Computer Science Education (SIGCSE 2002)*, Northern Kentucky—The Southern Side of Cincinnati, USA, Feb. 27–Mar. 3, 2002.

Ames, Willam F. *Numerical Methods for Partial Differential Equations*, Academic Press, 1992.

Andersson, Anders, and Peter Fritzson. Models for Distributed Real-Time Simulation in a Vehicle Co-Simulator Setup. In *Proceedings of the 5th International Workshop on Equation-Based Object-Oriented Modeling Languages and Tools, (EOOLT'2013)*, Published by Linköping University Electronic Press, www.ep.liu.se, Nottingham, UK, April 19, 2013.

Andersson, Mats. An Object-Oriented Modeling Environment. In *Proceedings of Simulation Methodologies, Languages, and Architectures and AI and Graphics for Simulation*, pp. 77–82, Society for Computer Simulation International, European Simulation Multiconference, 1989.

Andersson, Mats. Combined Object-Oriented Modelling in Omola. In Stephenson (ed.), *Proceedings of the 1992 European Simulation Multiconference (ESM'92)*, York, UK, Society for Computer Simulation International, June 1992.

Andersson, Mats. *Object-Oriented Modeling and Simulation of Hybrid Systems*. Ph.D. thesis, Department of Automatic Control, Lund Institute of Technology, Lund, Sweden, 1994.

Andreasson, Jonas, and Jonas Jarlmark. Modularized Tyre Modeling in Modelica. In *Proceedings of the 2nd International Modelica Conference*, Oberpfaffenhofen, Germany, Mar. 18–19, 2002.

Arnold, Ken, and James Gosling. *The Java Programming Language*. Addison-Wesley, 6th printing, Nov. 1999.

Aronsson, Peter, and Peter Fritzson. Multiprocessor Scheduling of Simulation Code from Modelica Models. In *Proceedings of the 2nd International Modelica Conference*, Oberpfaffenhofen, Germany, Mar. 18–19, 2002.

Aronsson, Peter. *Automatic Parallelization of Simulation Code from Equation Based Languages*. Licentiate thesis, No. 933, Department of Computer and Information Science, Linköpings universitet Sweden, Apr., 2002.

Aronsson, Peter, Peter Fritzson, Levon Saldamli, and Peter Bunus. Incremental Declaration Handling in Open Source Modelica. In *Proceedings of the 43rd Scandinavian Conference on Simulation and Modeling* (SIMS2002), available at www.scansims.org. Oulu, Finland. Sept. 26–25, 2002.

Aronsson, Peter and Peter Fritzson. Task Merging and Replication Using Graph Rewriting. In *Proceedings of the 10th International Workshop on Compilers for Parallel Computers*, Amsterdam, The Netherlands, Jan 8–10, 2003.

Aronsson, Peter, Peter Fritzson, Levon Saldamli, Peter Bunus, and Kaj Nyström. Meta Programming and Function Overloading in OpenModelica. In *Proc. of Modelica'2003*, Linköping, Sweden, (www.modelica.org), Nov 2003.

Aronsson, Peter, and Peter Fritzson. A Task Merging Technique for Parallelization of Modelica Models. In *Proceedings of the 4th International Modelica Conference*, Hamburg, Germany, March 7-8, 2005.

Aronsson, Peter. *Automatic Parallelization of Equation-Based Simulation Programs*. Ph.D. Thesis, Linköping University, Sweden. www.ep.liu.se., Dissertation No. 1022. June 14, 2006.

Asghar, Adeel, Sonia Tariq, Mohsen Torabzadeh-Tari, Peter Fritzson, Adrian Pop, Martin Sjölund, Parham Vasaiely, and Wladimir Schamai. An Open Source Modelica Graphic Editor Integrated with Electronic Notebooks and Interactive Simulation. In *Proceedings of the 8th International Modelica Conference* (Modelica'2011), Dresden, Germany, March.20-22, 2011.

Asghar, Adeel, Adrian Pop, Martin Sjölund, and Peter Fritzson. Efficient Debugging of Large Algorithmic Modelica Applications. In *Proc. of MATHMOD 2012 - 7th Vienna International Conference on Mathematical Modelling*, Vienna University of Technology, Vienna, Austria, February 15 - 17, 2012.

Åström, Karl-Johan, Hilding Elmqvist, and Sven-Erik Mattsson. Evolution of Continuous-Time Modeling and Simulation. In Zobel and Moeller (eds.), *Proceedings of the 12th European Simulation Multiconference (ESM'98)*, pp. 9–18, Society for Computer Simulation International, Manchester, U.K., 1998.

Augustin, Donald C., Mark S. Fineberg, Bruce B. Johnson, Robert N. Linebarger, F. John Sansom, and Jon C. Strauss. The SCi Continuous System Simulation Language (CSSL). *Simulation*, no 9, pp. 281–303, 1967.

Assmann, Uwe. *Invasive Software Composition*. Springer Verlag, 1993.

Bachmann, Bernhard, and Hans-Jürg Wiesmann. Advanced Modeling of Electromagnetic Transients in Power Systems. In *Proceedings of Modelica Workshop 2000*. Lund University, Lund, Sweden. Oct. 23–24, 2000.

Bachmann, Bernhard, Peter Aronsson, and Peter Fritzson. Robust Initialization of Differential Algebraic Equations. In *Proceedings of the 5th International Modelica Conference* (Modelica'2006), Vienna, Austria, Sept. 4-5, 2006.

Bachmann, Bernhard (ed.). *Proceedings of the 6th International Modelica Conference*. Available at www.modelica.org. Bielefeld University, Bielefeld, Germany, March 3–4, 2008.

Bachmann, Bernhard, Lennart Ochel, Vitalij Ruge, Mahder Gebremedhin, Peter Fritzson, Vaheed Nezhadali, Lars Eriksson, Martin Sivertsson. Parallel Multiple-Shooting and Collocation Optimization with OpenModelica. In *Proceedings of the 9th International Modelica Conference* (Modelica'2012), Munich, Germany, Sept.3-5, 2012.

Barton, Paul Inigo and Costas Pantelides, The Modelling of Combined Discrete/Continuous Processes. *AIChemE Journal* 40, pp. 996–979, 1994.

Barton, Paul Inigo, and Costas Pantelides. gPROMS – A Combined Discrete/Continuous Modelling Environment for Chemical Processing Systems. In *Proceedings of International. Conf. Simul. Engg. Educ.*, The Society for Computer Simulation, Simulation Series, 25, 25–34, 1993.

Barton, Paul Inigo. *The Modelling and Simulation of Combined Discrete/Continuous Processes*. PhD. Thesis, Department of Chemical Engineering, Imperial College of Science, Technology and Medicine, University of London, 1992.

Batteh, John, and Michael Tiller. A Modular Model Architecture in Modelica for Rapid Virtual Prototyping of Conventional and Hybrid Ground Vehicles. In *Proceedings of the 2009 Ground Vehicle Systems Engineering and Technology Symposium (GVSETS)*, 2009.

Beater, Peter. Modeling and Digital Simulation of Hydraulic Systems in Design and Engineering Education using Modelica and HyLib. In *Proceedings of Modelica Workshop 2000*. Lund University, Lund, Sweden. Oct. 23–24, 2000.

Beeck, von der, Michael. A Comparison of Statecharts Variants. In *Formal Techniques in Real-Time and Fault-Tolerant Systems*, LNCS 863, pages 128-148, Springer, 1994.

Benveniste, Albert, Paul Caspi, Stephen A. Edwards, Nicolas Halbwachs, Paul Le Guernic, and Robert de Simone. The Synchronous Languages Twelve Years Later. *In Proc. of the IEEE*, Vol., 91, No. 1, 2003.

Benveniste Albert., Caillaud B., Pouzet Marc. The Fundamentals of Hybrid Systems Modelers. In 49th IEEE International Conference on Decision and Control (CDC), Atlanta, Georgia, USA, December 15-17, 2010. http://www.di.ens.fr/~pouzet/bib/cdc10.pdf

Berners-Lee, Tim, R. Fielding, and Larry Masinter. Uniform Resource Identifier (URI) Generic Syntax. RFC3986, January 2005. http://tools.ietf.org/html/rfc3986 Accessed May 2011.

Bergero, Federico, Xenofon Floros, Joaquín Fernández, Ernesto Kofman, François E. Cellier. Simulating Modelica models with a Stand-Alone Quantized State Systems Solver. In *Proceedings of 9th International Modelica Conference*, Munich, Germany, Sept. 3-5, 2012.

Birtwistle, G.M., Ole Johan Dahl, B. Myhrhaug, and Kristen Nygaard. *SIMULA BEGIN*. Auerbach Publishers, Inc., 1973.

Blochwitz, Torsten, Martin Otter, Johan Akesson, Martin Arnold, Christoph Clauß, Hilding Elmqvist, Markus Friedrich, Andreas Junghanns, Jakob Mauss, Dietmar Neumerkel, Hans Olsson, Antoine Viel. Functional Mockup Interface 2.0: The

Standard for Tool independent Exchange of Simulation Models. http://dx.doi.org/10.3384/ecp12076173, In *Proceedings of 9th International Modelica Conference*, Munich, Germany, 2012.

Booch, Grady. *Object Oriented Design with Applications*. Benjamin/Cummings, 1991.

Booch, Grady. *Object-Oriented Analysis and Design*, ISBN: 0-805-35340-2. Addison-Wesley, 1994.

Bouskela, Daniel, Audrey Jardin, Zakia Benjelloun-Touimi, Peter Aronsson, and Peter Fritzson. Modelling of Uncertainties with Modelica. In *Proceedings of the 8th International Modelica Conference* (Modelica'2011), Dresden, Germany, March.20-22, 2011.

Brander, James A. and M. Scott Taylor. The Simple Economics of Easter Island: A Ricardo-Malthus Model of Renewable Resource Use. *The American Economic Review*, 88(1):119-138, 1998.

Braun, Willi, Stephanie Gallardo Yances, Kilian Link, and Bernhard Bachmann. Fast Simulation of Fluid Models with Solored Jacobians. In *Proceedings of the 9th International Modelica Conference* (Modelica'2012), www.ep.liu.se, Munich, Germany, Sept.3-5, 2012.

Braun, Willi, Lennart Ochel, and Bernhard Bachmann. Symbolically Derived Jacobians using Automatic Differentiation – Enhancement of the Openmodelica Compiler. In *Proceedings of the 8th International Modelica Conference* (Modelica'2011), www.ep.liu.se, Dresden, Germany, March.20-22, 2011.

Brenan, K., S. Campbell, and L. Petzold. *Numerical Solution of Initial-Value Problems in Ordinary Differential-Algebraic Equations*. North Holland Publishing, co., New York, 1989.

Breuer, P.T., N.M. Madrid, J.P. Bowen, R. France, M.L Petrie, and C.D. Kloos. Reasoning about VHDL and VHDL-AMS Using Denotational Semantics. In *Proceedings of Design, Automation and Test in Europe Conference and Exhibition*, pp. 346–352, 1999.

Breunese, A.P.J., and J.F. Broenink. Modeling Mechatronic Systems Using the SIDOPS+ Language, *Proceedings of ICBGM'97, 3rd International Conference on Bond Graph Modeling and Simulation*, Phoenix, Arizona, SCS Publishing, San Diego, California, Simulation Series, Vol. 29, no. 1, ISBN 1-56555-050-1, pp. 301–306. See also http://www.rt.el.utwente.nl/proj/modsim/modsim.htm, Jan. 12–15, 1997.

Broenink, J.F. Modelling, Simulation, and Analysis with 20-sim. *Journal A, Benelux Quarterly Journal on Automatic Control*, 38:3, pp. 20–25. Special issue on Computer-Aided Control System Design, (CACSD), 1997.

Broman, David, and Peter Fritzson. Type Safety of Equation-Based Object-Oriented Modeling Languages. PLDI '06: Poster session at the ACM SIGPLAN 2006 Conference on Programming Language Design and Implementation (PLDI), Ottawa, Canada, June, 2006.

Broman, David, and Peter Fritzson, and Sebastien Furic. Types in the Modelica Language. In *Proceedings of the 5th International Modelica Conference* (Modelica'2006), Vienna, Austria, Sept. 4-5, 2006.

Broman, David, Kaj Nyström, and Peter Fritzson. Determining Over- and Under-Constrained Systems of Equations using Structural Constraint Delta. In *Proceedings of the 4th Int. Conf. on Generative Programming and Component Engineering* (GPCE2006), Portland, Oregon, Oct 22-26, 2006.

Broman, David, and Peter Fritzson. Abstract Syntax Can Make the Definition of Modelica Less Abstract. In *Proceedings of the 1st International Workshop on Equation-Based Object-Oriented Languages and Tools, (EOOLT'2007)*, Berlin, July 30, 2007. Published by Linköping University Electronic Press, http://www.ep.liu.se/ecp/024/, July 2007.

Broman, David, Peter Aronsson, and Peter Fritzson. Design Considerations for Dimensional Inference and Unit Consistency Checking in Modelica. In *Proceedings of the 6th International Modelica Conference* (Modelica'2008), Bielefeld, Germany, March.3-4, 2008.

Broman, David, and Peter Fritzson. Higher Order Acausal Models. In *Proceedings of the 2nd International Workshop on Equation-Based Object-Oriented Languages and Tools, (EOOLT'2008)*, Pathos, Cyprus, July 8, 2008. Published by Linköping University Electronic Press, http://www.ep.liu.se/ecp/024/, July 2008.

Broman, David, and Peter Fritzson. Higher Order Acausal Models. *Simulation News Europe*, Vol 19, No 1. ISSN 0929-2268. April 2009.

Broman, David. *Meta-Languages and Semantics for Equation-Based Modeling and Simulation*. Ph.D. Thesis, Linköping University. www.ep.liu.se, Dissertation No. 1333. Oct. 1, 2010.

Broman, David, Peter Fritzson, Görel Hedin, and Johan Åkesson. A comparison of two metacompilation approaches to implementing a complex domain-specific language. In *Proc. of 27th Annual ACM Symposium on Applied Computing* SAC'2012 (www.acm.org/conferences/sac/sac2012/). Pages 1919-1921. Trento, Italy, March 26-30, 2012.

Brooks, Christopher and Edward A. Lee. Ptolemy II - Heterogeneous Concurrent Modeling and Design in Java. Poster presented at the 2010 Berkeley EECS Annual Research Symposium (BEARS). http://ptolemy.berkeley.edu/ptolemyII/ February 11, 2010.

Brück, Dag, Hilding Elmqvist, Sven-Erik Mattsson, and Hans Olsson. Dymola for Multi-Engineering Modeling and Simulation. In *Proceedings of the 2nd International Modelica Conference*, Oberpfaffenhofen, Germany, Mar. 18–19, 2002.

Bunus, Peter, Vadim Engelson, and Peter Fritzson. Mechanical Models Translation and Simulation in Modelica. In *Proceedings of Modelica Workshop 2000*, Lund University, Lund, Sweden, Oct. 23–24, 2000.

Bunus, Peter and Peter Fritzson. DEVS-Based Multi-Formalism Modeling and Simulation in Modelica. In *Proceedings of the 2000 Summer Computer Simulation Conference*. Vancouver, B.C., Canada, July 16–20, 2000.

Bunus, Peter, and Peter Fritzson. A Debugging Scheme for Declarative Equation Based Modeling Languages. In *Proceedings of Fourth International Symposium on Practical Aspects of Declarative Languages*, Portland, Oregon, USA, Jan. 19–20, 2002. LNCS 2257, Springer Verlag, 2002.

Bunus, Peter, and Peter Fritzson. Methods for Structural Analysis and Debugging of Modelica Models. In *Proceedings of the 2nd International Modelica Conference*, Oberpfaffenhofen, Germany, Mar. 18–19, 2002a.

Bunus, Peter. *Debugging and Structural Analysis of Declarative Equation-Based Languages*. Licentiate thesis, Department of Computer and Information Science, Linköping University, Sept. 2002.

Bunus, Peter and Peter Fritzson. Semantics Guided Filtering of Combinatorial Graph Transformations in Declarative Equation-Based Languages. In *Proceedings of the 2nd International Workshop on Source Code Analysis and Manipulation* (*SCAM2002*), Montreal, Canada, Oct. 1, 2002b.

Bunus, Peter, and Peter Fritzson. Automated Static Analysis of Equation-Based Components. Submitted to *Simulation: Transactions of the Society for Modeling and Simulation International*, 2003c.

Bunus, Peter, and Peter Fritzson. Semi-Automatic Fault Localization and Behaviour Verification for Physical System Simulation Models. In *Proceedings of the 18th IEEE International Conference on Automated Software Engineering*, Montreal, Canada, October 6-10, 2003.

Bunus, Peter. *Debugging Techniques for Equation-Based Languages*. Ph.D. Thesis, Linköping University, Sweden. Dissertation No. 873, June 2004.

Bunus, Peter, Peter Fritzson. Automated Static Analysis of Equation-Based Components. *SIMULATION: Transactions of The Society for Modeling and Simulation Internationa*l. Special issue on Component-based Modeling & Simulation. Vol 80:8, 2004.

Cardarelli, Francois. *Scientific Unit Conversion—A Practical Guide to Metrication*. Springer, 1997.

Casella, Francesco, and Alberto Leva. Modelica Open Library for Power Plant Simulation: Design and Experimental Validation. In *Proceedings of the Modelica 2003 Conference*, editor: P. Fritzson, Linköping, Sweden, Nov 3–4, 2003.

Casella, Francesco, Martin Otter, Katrin Proelss, Christoph Richter, Hubertus Tummescheit: The Modelica Fluid and Media Library for Modeling of Incompressible and Compressible Thermo-Fluid Pipe Networks. In *Proceedings of the Modelica 2006 Conference*, Vienna, September 2006.

Casella, Francesco, and Alberto Leva. Modelling of Thermo-Hydraulic Power Generation Processes Using Modelica. *Mathematical and Computer Modeling of Dynamical* Systems, Vol. 12, No 1, pp. 19-33, Feb. 2006.

Casella, Francesco (ed.). *Proceedings of the 7th International Modelica Conference*. Available at www.modelica.org. Como, Italy, March 3–4, 2009.

Casella, Francesco. On the Formulation of Steady-State Initialization Problems in Object-Oriented Models of Closed Thermo-Hydraulic Systems. In *Proceedings of 9th International Modelica Conference*, Munich, Germany, Sept. 3-5, 2012.

Casella, Francesco. A Strategy for Parallel Simulation of Declarative Object-Oriented Models of Generalized Physical Networks. In *Proceedings of the 5th International Workshop on Equation-Based Object-Oriented Modeling Languages and Tools, (EOOLT'2013)*, Published by Linköping University Electronic Press, www.ep.liu.se, Nottingham, UK, April 19, 2013.

Cellier, Francois E. *Combined Continuous/Discrete System Simulation by Use of Digital Computers: Techniques and Tools*. Ph.D. thesis, ETH, 1979.

Cellier, Francois E., *Continuous System Modelling*, Springer Verlag, Berlin, 1991.

Cellier, Francois and A. Nebot, The Modelica Bond Graph Library, In *Proc. 4th Modelica Conference*, Hamburg, Germany, 2005.

Cellier, François E, and Ernesto Kofman. *Continuous System Simulation*. Springer, 2006.

Cellier, François. World3 in Modelica: Creating System Dynamics Models in the Modelica Framework. In *Proceedings of the 6th International Modelica Conference*, Bielefeld, Germany. 2008.

Cellier, Francois, Peter Fritzson, Edward Lee, and David Broman. (Editors). *Proceedings of the 4th International Workshop on Equation-Based Object-Oriented Languages and Tools*, (EOOLT'2011), Zürich, Switzerland, Sept 5, 2011. Published by Linköping University Electronic Press, http://www.ep.liu.se/ecp_home/index.en.aspx?issue=056, Sept, 2011.

Christen, E. and K. Bakalar. *VHDL-AMS—A Hardware Description Language for Analog and Mixed-Signal Applications*. IEEE Transactions on Circuits and Systems II: Analog and Digital Signal Processing. Vol. 46, Issue 10, pp. 1263–1272, Oct. 1999.

Chen, Wuzhu, Michaela Huhn, and Peter Fritzson. A General FMU Interface for Modelica. In *Proceedings of the 4th International Workshop on Equation-Based Object-Oriented Modeling Languages and Tools, (EOOLT'2011)*, Zürich, Switzerland, Sept 5, 2011. Published by Linköping University Electronic Press, www.ep.liu.se, Sept 2011

Clarke, E., O. Grumberg, and D. A. Peled. *Model Checking*. MIT Press, 2000.

Clauss, Christoph, A. Schneider, T. Leitner, and Peter Schwarz. Modelling of Electrical Circuits with Modelica. In *Proceedings of Modelica Workshop 2000*, Lund University, Lund, Sweden, Oct. 23–24, 2000.

Clauss, Christoph, and Peter Beater. Multidomain Systems: Electronic, Hydraulic, and Mechanical Subsystems of a Universal Testing Machine Modeled with Modelica. In *Proceedings of the 2nd International Modelica Conference*, Oberpfaffenhofen, Germany, Mar. 18–19, 2002.

Clauss, Christoph (ed.). *Proceedings of the 8th International Modelica Conference*. Available at www.modelica.org. Dresden, Germany, March 20–22, 2011.

Colaco, Jean-Louis, and Marc Pouzet. Clocks as First Class Abstract Types. In *Proceedings of the Third International Conference on Embedded Software (EMSOFT'03)*, Philadelphia, Pennsylvania, USA, October 2003.

Crane, Michelle, and Juergen Dingel. UML vs. classical vs. Rhapsody statecharts: Not all models are created equal. In *Proc. 8th International Conf. on Model Driven Engineering Languages and Systems*, 97-112. Springer, Oct. 2005.

Dalheimer, Mattias K. *Programming with Qt*. (Also reference documentation at http://doc.trolltech.com/3.1/). O'Reilly, 2002.

Dassault Systèmes. Dymola. CATIA Systems Engineering – Dymola. 2013.http://www.3ds.com/products/catia/portfolio/dymola (accessed April 23, 2013).

Davis, Bill, Horacio Porta, and Jerry Uhl. *Calculus & Mathematica Vector Calculus: Measuring in Two and Three Dimensions*. Addison-Wesley, 1994.

Dolan, A., and J. Aldous. *Networks and Algorithms—An Introductory Approach*. John Wiley & Sons, England, 1993.

Dromey, Geoff. From Requirements to Design: Formalizing the Key Steps. In Software Engineering and Formal Methods, 2-11. IEEE, 2003.

Duff, Iain S., Albert M. Erisman, and John K. Reid. *Direct Methods for Sparse Matrices*. Clarendon Press, Oxford, 1986.

Dulmage, A.L., and N.S. Mendelsohn. Coverings of Bipartite Graphs. *Canadian J. Math.*, 10, pp. 517–534, 1963.

Dynasim AB. *Dymola—Dynamic Modeling Laboratory, Users Manual*, Dynasim AB, Research Park Ideon, SE-223 70, Lund, Sweden, Changed 2010 to Dassault Systemes Sweden. Web pages, www.Dymola.com, www.3ds.com, 2010.

Dynasim AB. Home page, www.dynasim.se. Dynasim AB, Research Park Ideon, SE-223 70, Lund, Sweden, 2003.

Eclipse-Papyrus. Papyrus. 2013. www.eclipse.org/papyrus/ (accessed April 23, 2013).

Edelfeldt, Stina, and Peter Fritzson. Evaluation and Comparison of Models and Modelling Tools Simulating Nitrogen Processes in Treatment Wetlands. *Simulation Modelling Practice and Theory*. Vol 16, No 1, pp 26–49, Published by Elsevier. January 2008.

Eker, Johan, Jorn Janneck, Edward A. Lee, Jie Liu, Xiaojun Liu, Jozsef Ludvig, Sonia Sachs, Yuhong Xiong. Taming heterogeneity - the Ptolemy approach, Proceedings of the IEEE, 91(1):127-144, January 2003. http://ptolemy.berkeley.edu/ptolemyII/

El Hefni, Baligh, Daniel Bouskela, and Grégory Lebreton. Dynamic modelling of a Combined Cycle Power Plant with ThermoSysPro. In *Proceedings of the 8th Modelica Conference*, Dresden, Germany, March 20-22, 2011.

El Hefni, Baligh, Daniel Bouskela, and Guillaume Gentilini. Dynamic modelling of a Condenser/Water Heater with the ThermoSysPro Library. In *Proceedings of the 9th International Modelica Conference*, Munich, Germany, September 3-5, 2012.

Elmqvist, Hilding. *A Structured Model Language for Large Continuous Systems*. Ph.D. thesis, TFRT-1015, Department of Automatic Control, Lund Institute of Technology, Lund, Sweden, 1978.

Elmqvist, Hilding, and Sven-Erik Mattsson. A Graphical Approach to Documentation and Implementation of Control Systems. In *Proceedings of the Third IFAC/IFIP Symposium on Software for Computer Control* (*SOCOCO'82*), Madrid, Spain. Pergamon Press, Oxford, U.K., 1982.

Elmqvist, Hilding, Francois Cellier, and Martin Otter. Object-Oriented Modeling of Hybrid Systems. In *Proceedings of the European Simulation Symposium* (*ESS'93*). Society of Computer Simulation, 1993.

Elmqvist, Hilding, and Martin Otter. Methods for Tearing Systems of Equations in Object-Oriented Modeling. In *Proceedings of the European Simulation Multiconference, (ESM'94)*, pp. 326–334, Barcelona, Spain, SCS, Society for Computer Simulation, June 1994.

Elmqvist, Hilding, Francois Cellier, and Martin Otter. Inline Integration: A New Mixed Symbolic/Numeric Approach for Solving Differential-Algebraic Equation Systems. In *Proceedings of the European Simulation MultiConference*, Prague, June, 1995.

Elmqvist, Hilding, Dag Bruck, and Martin Otter. *Dymola—User's Manual*. Dynasim AB, Research Park Ideon, SE-223 70, Lund, Sweden, 1996.

Elmqvist, Hilding, and Sven-Erik Mattsson. Modelica: The Next Generation Modeling Language—An International Design Effort. In *Proceedings of First World Congress of System Simulation*, Singapore, Sept. 1–3, 1997.

Elmqvist, Hilding, Sven-Erik Mattsson, and Martin Otter. Modelica—A Language for Physical System Modeling, Visualization and Interaction. In *Proceedings of the 1999 IEEE Symposium on Computer-Aided Control System Design (CACSD'99)*, Hawaii, Aug. 22–27, 1999.

Elmqvist, Hilding. Private communication on the history of equations, 2000.

Elmqvist, Hilding, Sven-Erik Mattsson, and Martin Otter. Object-Oriented and Hybrid Modeling in Modelica. *Journal Européen des Systèmes Automatisés*, 35:1, 2001.

Elmqvist, Hilding, Martin Otter, Sven-Erik Mattsson, and Hans Olsson. *Modeling, Simulation, and Optimization with Modelica and Dymola*. Book draft, 246 pages. Dynasim AB, Research Park Ideon, SE-223 70, Lund, Sweden, Oct. 2002.

Elmqvist, Hilding, Sven-Erik Mattsson, and Hans Olsson. New Methods for Hardware-in-the-Loop Simulation of Stiff Models. In *Proceedings of the 2nd International Modelica Conference*, Oberpfaffenhofen, Germany, Mar. 18–19, 2002.

Elmqvist, Hilding. PDEs in Present Modelica. Design document, Modelica Association, August, 2003a.

Elmqvist, Hilding. Index Reduction for Partial Differential Algebraic Equations. Paper draft, Modelica Association, August, 2003b.

Elmqvist, Hilding, Hubertus Tummescheit, Martin Otter. Object-Oriented Modeling of Thermo-Fluid Systems. *Proceedings of the Modelica 2003 Conference*, editor: P. Fritzson, Linköping, Sweden, Nov 3–4, 2003.

Elmqvist Hilding, Martin Otter, Dan Henriksson, Bernhard Thiele, Sven Erik Mattsson. Modelica for Embedded Systems. In *Proceedings of the 7th International Modelica Conference* (Modelica'2009), Available at www.modelica.org, Como, Italy, September.20-22, 2009.

Elmqvist, Hilding, Fabien Gaucher, Sven-Erik Mattsson, and Francois Dupont. State Machines in Modelica. In *Proceedings of 9th International Modelica Conference*, Munich, Germany, Sept. 3-5, 2012.

Elmqvist, Hilding, Martin Otter, and Sven-Erik Mattsson. Fundamentals of Synchronous Control in Modelica. In *Proceedings of 9th International Modelica Conference*, Munich, Germany, Sept 3-5, 2012.

Engelson, Vadim, Håkan Larsson, and Peter Fritzson. A Design, Simulation, and Visualization Environment for Object-Oriented Mechanical and Multi-Domain Models in Modelica. In *Proceedings of the IEEE International Conference on Information Visualization*, pp. 188–193, London, July 14–16, 1999.

Engelson, Vadim. *Tools for Design, Interactive Simulation, and Visualization of Object-Oriented Models in Scientific Computing*. Ph.D. thesis, Dept. of Computer and Information Science, Linköping University, Linköping, Sweden, 2000.

Equa AB. Home page: www.equa.se, 2003.

Ernst, Thilo, Stephan Jähnichen, and Matthias Klose. The Architecture of the Smile/M Simulation Environment. *In Proceedings 15th IMACS World Congress on Scientific Computation, Modelling and Applied Mathematics*, Vol. 6, Berlin, Germany, pp. 653–658. See also http://www.first.gmd.de/smile/smile0.html, 1997.

Eriksson, Henrik, Henrik Magnusson, Peter Fritzson, and Adrian Pop. 3D Animation and Programmable 2D Graphics for Visualization of Simulations in OpenModelica. In *Proceedings of the 49th Scandinavian Conference on Simulation and Modeling* (SIMS'2008), available at www.scan-sims.org. Oslo, Norway. October 7-8, 2008.

Fábian, Georgina. *A Language and Simulator for Hybrid Systems*. Ph.D. Thesis, Technische Universiteit Eindhoven, The Netherlands, 1999.

Fauvel, John, Raymond Flood, Michael Shortland, and Robin Wilson. *LET NEWTON BE! A New Perspective on His Life and Works. Oxford University Press*. 2nd edition. ISBN 0-19-853924-X. 1990.

Felleisen, Matthias, Robert Bruce Findler, Matthew Flatt, and Shiram Krishnamurthi. The DrScheme Project: An Overview. In *Proceedings of the ACM SIGPLAN 1998 Conference on Programming Language Design and Implementation (PLDI'98)*, Montreal, Canada, June 17–19, 1998.

Felgner, F., S. Agustina, R. Cladera Bohigas, R. Merz, and L. Litz. Simulation of Thermal Building Behavior in Modelica. In *Proceedings of the 2nd International Modelica Conference*, Oberpfaffenhofen, Germany, Mar. 18–19, 2002.

Fernström, Anders, Ingemar Axelsson, Peter Fritzson, Anders Sandholm, and Adrian Pop. OMNotebook – Interactive WYSIWYG Book Software for Teaching Programming. In *Proc. of the Workshop on Developing Computer Science Education – How Can It Be Done*?. www.openmodelica.org, Linköping University, Dept. Computer & Inf. Science, Linköping, Sweden, March 10, 2006.

Ferreira, J.A., de Oliveira, J.E. Modeling Hybrid Systems Using Statecharts and Modelica. In Proceedings of the 7th IEEE International Conference on Emerging Technologies and Factory Automation, Barcelona, Spain, 18–21 Oct. 1999.

Ferretti, Giovanni, G. Magnani, P. Rocco, L. Bonometti, and M. Maraglino. Simulating Permanent Magnet Brushless Motors in Dymola. In *Proceedings of the 2nd International Modelica Conference*, Oberpfaffenhofen, Germany. Mar. 18–19, 2002.

Fisher, D.M. *Modeling Dynamic Systems: Lessons for a First Course*. 2nd Edition, ISEE Systems. 2007.

Forget, Julien, Frédéric Boniol, David Lesens, and Claire Pagetti. A Multi-Periodic Synchronous Data-Flow Language. In *Proc. of 11th IEEE High Assurance Systems Engineering Symposium (HASE'08)*, Nanjing, China, pp. 251-260. Dec. 3-5 2008.

Forrester, J.W. *Principles of Systems*. 387p. Pegasus Communications, 1971.

Franke, Rüdiger. Formulation of Dynamic Optimization Problems Using Modelica and their Efficient Solution. In *Proceedings of the 2nd International Modelica Conference*, Oberpfaffenhofen, Germany, Mar. 18–19, 2002.

Franke, Rüdiger, Manfred Rode, and Klaus Krüger. On-line Optimization of Drum Boiler Startup. In *Proceedings of the Modelica'2003 Conference*, Linköping, Sweden, November 2003.

Franke, Rüdiger, Francesco Casella, Martin Otter, Michael Sielemann, Hilding Elmqvist, Sven Erik Mattson, and Hans Olsson. Stream Connectors – An Extension of Modelica for Device-Oriented Modeling of Convective Transport Phenomena. In *Proceedings of the 7th International Modelica Conference* (Modelica'2009), Available at www.modelica.org, Como, Italy, September.20-22, 2009.

Franke, Rüdiger, Francesco Casella, Michael Sielemann, Katrin Proelss, Martin Otter, and Michael Wetter. Standardization of Thermo-Fluid Modeling in Modelica.Fluid. In *Proceedings of the 7th International Modelica Conference* (Modelica'2009), Available at www.modelica.org, Como, Italy, September.20-22, 2009.

Freiseisen, Wolfgang, Robert Keber, Wilhelm Medetz, Petru Pau, and Dietmar Stelzmueller. Using Modelica for Testing Embedded Systems. In *Proceedings of the 2nd International Modelica Conference*, Oberpfaffenhofen, Germany, Mar. 18–19, 2002.

Frenkel, Jens, Günter Kunze, Peter Fritzson, Martin Sjölund, Adrian Pop, and Willi Braun. Towards a Modular and Accessible Modelica Compiler Backend. In *Proceedings of the 8th International Modelica Conference* (Modelica'2011), Dresden, Germany, March.20-22, 2011.

Frenkel, Jens, Christian Schubert, Günter Kunze, Peter Fritzson, Martin Sjölund, and Adrian Pop. Towards a Benchmark Suite for Modelica Compilers: Large Models. In *Proceedings of the 8th International Modelica Conference* (Modelica'2011), Dresden, Germany, March.20-22, 2011.

Frenkel, Jens, Günter Kunze, and Peter Fritzson. Survey of appropriate matching algorithms for large scale systems of differential algebraic equations. In *Proceedings of the 9th International Modelica Conference* (Modelica'2012), Munich, Germany, Sept.3-5, 2012.

Frey, P. K., Nellayappan, V. Shanmugasundaram, R.S. Mayiladuthurai, C.L. Chandrashekar, and H.W. Carter. SEAMS: Simulation Environment for VHDL-AMS. In *Proceedings of Winter Simulation Conference*, Dec. 13–16, Washington, D.C., USA. Vol. 1, pp. 539–546, 1998.

Fritzson, Dag, Peter Fritzson, Lars Viklund, and Johan Herber. Object-Oriented Mathematical Modelling—Applied to Machine Elements. *Computers and Structures*, 51:3, pp. 241–253, Pergamon Press, 1994.

Fritzson, Dag, and Patrik Nordling. Solving Ordinary Differential Equations on Parallel Computers Applied to Dynamic Rolling Bearing Simulation. In *Parallel Programming and Applications*, P. Fritzson, and L. Finmo (eds.), IOS Press, 1995.

Fritzson, Dag, Peter Fritzson, Patrik Nordling, and Tommy Persson. Rolling Bearing Simulation on MIMD Computers, *International Journal of Supercomputer Applications and High Performance Computing* 4, 1997.

Fritzson, Peter, and Karl-Fredrik Berggren. Pseudo-Potential Calculations for Expanded Crystalline Mercury, *Journal of Solid State Physics*, 1976.

Fritzson, Peter. Symbolic Debugging through Incremental Compilation in an Integrated Environment, *Journal of Systems and Software*, 3, pp. 285–294, 1983.

Fritzson, Peter. *Towards a Distributed Programming Environment based on Incremental Compilation*. Ph.D. thesis, 161 pages. Dissertation no. 109, Linköping University, Apr. 13, 1984.

Fritzson, Peter, and Dag Fritzson. The Need for High-Level Programming Support in Scientific Computing—Applied to Mechanical Analysis. *Computers and Structures*, 45:2, pp. 387–295, 1992.

Fritzson, Peter, Lars Viklund, Johan Herber, and Dag Fritzson. Industrial Application of Object-Oriented Mathematical Modeling and Computer Algebra in Mechanical Analysis, In *Proc. of TOOLS EUROPE'92*, Dortmund, Germany, Mar. 30–Apr. 2. Prentice Hall, 1992.

Fritzson Peter, Nahid Shahmehri, Mariam Kamkar, and Tibor Gyimothy. Generalized Algorithmic Debugging and Testing, *ACM Letters on Programming Languages and Systems*, 1:4; pp. 303–322, Dec. 1992.

Fritzson, Peter (ed.). *Proceedings of AADEBUG'93—The 1st International Workshop on Automated and Algorithmic Debugging*, Springer Verlag, LNCS 749, Linköping University, Linköping, Sweden, May 3–5, 1993.

Fritzson, Peter, Lars Viklund, Dag Fritzson, and Johan Herber. High Level Mathematical Modeling and Programming in Scientific Computing, *IEEE Software*, pp. 77–87, July 1995.

Fritzson, Peter. *Efficient Language Implementation by Natural Semantics and RML*. www.ida.liu.se/labs/pelab/rml. Book draft, 1998.

Fritzson, Peter, and Vadim Engelson. Modelica—A Unified Object-Oriented Language for System Modeling and Simulation. *Proceedings of the 12th European Conference on Object-Oriented Programming* (*ECOOP'98*), Brussels, Belgium, July 20–24, 1998.

Fritzson, Peter. *MathCode C++*. MathCore Publishing (www.mathcore.com), 165 pages, Sept. 1998.

Fritzson, Peter, Vadim Engelson, and Johan Gunnarsson. An Integrated Modelica Environment for Modeling, Documentation and Simulation. In *Proceedings of Summer Computer Simulation Conference '98*, Reno, Nevada, USA, July 19–22, 1998.

Fritzson, Peter (ed.). *Proceedings of SIMS'99—The 1999 Conference of the Scandinavian Simulation Society*. Available at www.scansims.org. Linköping, Sweden, Oct. 18–19, 1999.

Fritzson, Peter (ed.). *Proceedings of Modelica 2000 Workshop*. Available at www.modelica.org. Lund University, Lund, Sweden, Oct. 23–24, 2000.

Fritzson, Peter, and Peter Bunus. Modelica—A General Object-Oriented Language for Continuous and Discrete-Event System Modeling and Simulation. *Proceedings of the 35th Annual Simulation Symposium*, San Diego, California, Apr. 14–18. Published by IEEE, 2002.

Fritzson, Peter, Peter Aronsson, Peter Bunus, Vadim Engelson, Henrik Johansson, Andreas Karström, and Levon Saldamli. The Open Source Modelica Project. In *Proceedings of the 2nd International Modelica Conference*, Oberpfaffenhofen, Germany, Mar. 18–19, 2002.

Fritzson Peter, Mats Jirstrand, and Johan Gunnarsson. MathModelica—An Extensible Modeling and Simulation Environment with Integrated Graphics and Literate Programming. At www.ida.liu.se/labs/pelab/modelica/. In *Proceedings of the 2nd International Modelica Conference*, Oberpfaffenhofen, Germany, Mar. 18–19, 2002.

Fritzson, Peter (ed.). *Proceedings of the 3rd International Modelica Conference*. Available at www.modelica.org. Linköping University, Linköping, Sweden, Nov 3–4, 2003.

Fritzson, Peter. *Principles of Object Oriented Modeling and Simulation with Modelica 2.1*, 940 pages, ISBN 0-471-471631, Wiley-IEEE Press. Feb. 2004.

Fritzson, Peter, Adrian Pop, and Peter Aronsson. Towards Comprehensive Meta-Modeling and Meta-Programming Capabilities in Modelica. In *Proceedings of the 4th International Modelica Conference*, Hamburg, Germany, March 7-8, 2005.

Fritzson, Peter. (Editor). *Proceedings of the 4rd International Conference on Modeling and Simulation in Biology, Medicine, and Biomedical Engineering* (BioMedSim'2005), Linköping University, Linköping, Sweden. May 26-27, 2005.

Fritzson, Peter. (Editor). *Proceedings of the 2nd Conference on Modeling and Simulation for Safety and Security* (SimSafe'2005), Linköping University, Linköping, Sweden. May 30, 2005.

Fritzson, Peter, Peter Aronsson, Håkan Lundvall, Kaj Nyström, Adrian Pop, Levon Saldamli, David Broman. The OpenModelica Modeling, Simulation, and Development Environment. In *Proceedings of the 46th Conference on Simulation and Modelling of the Scandinavian Simulation Society* (SIMS2005), Trondheim, Norway, October 13-14, 2005.

Fritzson, Peter, Peter Aronsson, Håkan Lundvall, Kaj Nyström, Adrian Pop, Levon Saldamli, and David Broman. The OpenModelica Modeling, Simulation, and Software Development Environment. www.openmodelica.org. In *Simulation News Europe*, 44/45, December 2005.

Fritzson, Peter. MathModelica - An Object Oriented Mathematical Modeling and Simulation Environment. *Mathematica Journal*, Vol 10, Issue 1. February. 2006.

Fritzson, Peter, Peter Aronsson, Håkan Lundvall, Kaj Nyström, Adrian Pop, Levon Saldamli, and David Broman. OpenModelica – A Free Open-Source Environment for System Modeling, Simulation, and Teaching. Invited paper. In *Proceedings of IEEE International Symposium on Computer-Aided Control Systems Design (CACSD)*, Technische Universität München, Germany, October 4-6, 2006.

Fritzson, Peter, Francois Cellier, and Christoph Nytsch Geusen. (Editors). *Proceedings of the 1st International Workshop on Equation-Based Object-Oriented Languages and Tools*, (EOOLT'2007), in conjunction with ECOOP, Berlin, July 30, 2007. Published by Linköping University Electronic Press, http://www.ep.liu.se/ecp/024/, July, 2007.

Fritzson, Peter, Adrian Pop, Kristoffer Norling, and Mikael Blom. Comment- and Indentation Preserving Refactoring and Unparsing for Modelica. In *Proceedings of the 6th International Modelica Conference* (Modelica'2008), Bielefeld, Germany, March.3-4, 2008.

Fritzson, Peter, Francois Cellier, and David Broman. (Editors). *Proceedings of the 2nd International Workshop on Equation-Based Object-Oriented Languages and Tools,* (EOOLT'2008), in conjunction with ECOOP, Paphos, Cyprus, July 8, 2008. Published by Linköping University Electronic Press, http://www.ep.liu.se/ecp/029/, July, 2008.

Fritzson, Peter, Vadim Engelson, and Krishnamurthy Sheshadri. MathCode: A System for C++ or Fortran Code Generation from Mathematica. *Mathematica Journal*, Vol 10, Issue 4,. November. 2008.

Fritzson, Peter, Adrian Pop, David Broman, Peter Aronsson. Formal Semantics Based Translator Generation and Tool Development in Practice. In *Proceedings of 20th Australian Software Engineering Conference (ASWEC 2009)*, Gold Coast, Queensland, Australia, April 14 – 17, 2009.

Fritzson, Peter, Pavol Privitzer, Martin Sjölund, and Adrian Pop. Towards a Text Generation Template Language for Modelica. In *Proceedings of the 7th International Modelica Conference* (Modelica'2009), Como, Italy, September.20-22, 2009.

Fritzson, Peter. Integrated UML-Modelica Model-Based Product Development for Embedded Systems in OPENPROD. In *Proceedings of the 1st Workshop on Hands-on Platforms and tools for model-based engineering of Embedded Systems* (Hopes'2010), Paris, In conjunction with ECMFA 2010, www.ecmfa-2010.org, June 15, 2010.

Fritzson, Peter, Edward Lee, Francois Cellier, and David Broman. (Editors). *Proceedings of the 3rd International Workshop on Equation-Based Object-Oriented Languages and Tools*, (EOOLT'2010), in conjunction with MODELS, Oslo, Norway, Oct 3, 2010. Published by Linköping University Electronic Press, http://www.ep.liu.se/ecp_home/index.en.aspx?issue=047, Oct, 2010.

Fritzson, Peter. The Modelica Object-Oriented Equation-Based Language and its OpenModelica Environment with MetaModeling, Interoperability, and Parallel Execution. In *Proc. of 2nd Int. Conf. on Simulation, Programming, and Modeling for Autonomous Robots* (SIMPAR 2010). Invited paper and talk. Darmstadt, Germany, Nov 15-18, 2010. Published by Springer Verlag, LNCS/LNAI 6472, 2010.

Fritzson, Peter, and Adrian Pop. *Meta-Programming and Language Modeling with MetaModelica 1.0.* Technical reports in Computer and Information Science, No 9, Linköping University Electronic Press, http://www.ep.liu.se/PubList/ Default.aspx?SeriesID=2550, January 2011.

Fritzson, Peter, Adrian Pop, and Martin Sjölund. *Towards Modelica 4 Meta-Programming and Language Modeling with MetaModelica 2.0.* Technical reports in Computer and Information Science, No 10, Linköping University Electronic Press, http://www.ep.liu.se/PubList/ Default.aspx?SeriesID=2550, February 2011.

Fritzson, Peter. Modelica - A Cyber-physical Modeling Language and the OpenModelica Environment. In *Proceedings of the 7th International Wireless Communications and Mobile Computing Conference*, IWCMC 2011, pages 1648–1653, IEEE, Istanbul, Turkey, July 4-8, 2011.

Fritzson, Peter. Introduction to Modeling and Simulation of Technical and Physical Systems with Modelica. 232 pages, ISBN: 978-1-1180-1068-6, Wiley-IEEE Press, September, 2011.

Fritzson, Peter, and Adrian Pop. *Efficient Language Implementation by Operational Semantics and RML.* Research Report, www.ep.liu.se, 2014.

Frisk, Erik, and Mattias Nyberg. A Minimal Polynomial Basis Solution to Residual Generation for Fault Diagnosis in Linear Systems, *Automatica,* 37:9, pp. 1417–1424, Sept. 2001.

Fuchs, H.U. *Dynamics of Heat.* Springer Verlag, 1996.

Färnqvist, Daniel, Katrin Strandemar, Karl Henrik Johansson, and Joao Pedro Hespanha. Hybrid Modeling of Communication Networks Using Modelica. In *Proceedings of the 2nd International Modelica Conference,* Oberpfaffenhofen, Germany, Mar. 18–19, 2002.

Ganeson, Anand, Peter Fritzson, Olena Rogovchenko, Adeel Asghar, Martin Sjölund, and Andreas Pfeiffer. An OpenModelica Python Interface and its use in PySimulator. In *Proceedings of the 9th International Modelica Conference* (Modelica'2012), Munich, Germany, Sept.3-5, 2012.

Gebremedhin, Mahder, Afshin Hemmati Moghadam, Peter Fritzson, and Kristian Stavåker. A Data-Parallel Algorithmic Modelica Extension for Efficient Execution on Multi-Core Platforms. http://dx.doi.org/10.3384/ecp12076393, In *Proceedings of the 9th International Modelica Conference* (Modelica'2012), Munich, Germany, Sept.3-5, 2012.

Gerdin, Markus, Torkel Glad, and Lennart Ljung. Parameter Estimation in Linear Differential-Algebraic Equations. *Proceedings of the 13th IFAC Symposium on System Identification*, pp. 1530-1535, Rotterdam, The Netherlands, Aug. 2003.

Gibbons, A. *Algorithmic Graph Theory*. Cambridge University Press, 1985.

Gilli, Manfred, and Myriam Garbely. Matchings, Covers, and Jacobian Matrices, *Journal of Economic Dynamics and Control*, 20, pp. 1541–1556, 1996.

Glover, David M. Lectures on Finite Differencing Techniques, Section 11.5 Numerical Diffusion. http://w3eos.whoi.edu/12.747/notes/lect11-12/lectno11-12.html 2002. Accessed October 20, 2013.

Goldberg, Adele, and David Robson. *Smalltalk-80, The Language*. Addison-Wesley, 1989.

Gustafsson, Bertil, Heinz-Otto Kreiss, and Joseph Oliger. *Time Dependent Problems and Difference Methods*. John Wiley & Sons, New York, 1995.

Gottwald, S., W. Gellert (Contributor), and H. Kuestner (Contributor). *The VNR Concise Encyclopedia of Mathematics*. Second edition, ISBN 0-442-20590-2, Van Nostrand Reinhold, New York, 1989.

Günther, M., and U. Feldmann. The DAE-Index in Electric Circuit Simulation. *Mathematics and Computers in Simulation*, 39, pp. 573–582, 1995.

Hairer, E., S.P. Nørsett, and G. Wanner. *Solving Ordinary Differential Equations I. Nonstiff Problems*. Springer Series in Computational Mathematics, 2nd ed. 1992.

Hairer, E., and G. Wanner. *Solving Ordinary Differential Equations II. Stiff and Differential-Algebraic Problems*. Springer Series in Computational Mathematics, 1st ed. 1991.

Hakman, Mikael, and Torgny Groth. Object-Oriented Biomedical System Modelling—The Language, *Computer Methods and Programs in Biomedicine*, 60:3, pp. 153–181, Nov. 1999.

Hakman, Mikael. *Methods and Tools for Object-Oriented Modeling and Knowledge-Based Simulation of Complex Biomedical Systems*. Ph.D. thesis, Uppsala University, 2000.

Halbwachs, Nicolas. *Synchronous Programming of Reactive Systems*. Kluwer Academic, 174 pages, ISBN 0-7923-9311-2, 1993.

Harbison, S.P., and Guy L. Steele Jr. *C, A Reference Manual*. Prentice Hall, Englewood Cliffs, NJ, 3rd ed., 1991.

Harel, David. A Visual Formalism for Complex Systems. www.inf.ed.ac.uk/teaching/courses/seoc1/-2005_2006/resources/statecharts.pdf, In *Science of Computer Programming* 8 No. 3, 231-274. 1987.

Harel, David, and Hillel Kugler. The Rhapsody semantics of statecharts (or, on the executable core of the UML). In *Integration of Software Specification Techniques for Applications in Engineering*, 325-354. Springer Berlin Heidelberg, 2004.

Hedin, Görel, and Boris Magnusson. **The Mjølner Environment: Direct Interaction with Abstractions. *Proceedings of European Conference on Object-Oriented Programming (ECOOP '88)* Oslo, Norway, LNCS 322, pp. 41–54, Springer Verlag, Aug. 1988.**

Hellgren, Jonas. Modeling of Hybrid Electric Vehicles in Modelica for Virtual Prototyping. *Proceedings of the 2nd International Modelica Conference*, Oberpfaffenhofen, Germany, Mar. 18–19, 2002.

Henshaw, William D. Overture Documentation: LLNL Overlapping Grid Project. At http://www.llnl.gov/CASC/Overture/henshaw/overtureDocumentation/overtureDocumentation.html, 2000.

Hindmarsh, A.C. ODEPACK, A Systematized Collection of ODE Solvers, In R. S. Stepleman et al. (eds.), *Scientific Computing*, North-Holland, Amsterdam, 1983. Also Vol. 1 of *IMACS Transactions on Scientific Computation*, pp. 55–64, The Solver is available from http://www.netlib.org/odepack/index.html.

Höger, Christoph, Alexandra Mehlhase, Christoph Nytsch-Geusen, Karsten Isakovic, Rick Kubiak (2012). Modelica3D - Platform Independent Simulation Visualization. In *Proceedings of the 9th International Modelica Conference*, Munich, Germany, September 3-5, 2012.

Holman, J.P. *Heat Transfer*, 8th ed. McGraw-Hill, New York, 1997.

Hopcroft, J.E. and R.M. Karp. An $n^{5/2}$ Algorithm for Maximum Matchings in Bipartite Graphs. *SIAM Journal of Computing*, 2:4, pp. 225–231, Dec. 1973.

Hossain, Muhammed Zoheb, Mattias Nyberg, Olena Rogovchenko and Peter Fritzson. Computerized Model Based Functional Safety Analysis. In *Proc. of MATHMOD 2012 - 7th Vienna International Conference on Mathematical Modelling*, Vienna University of Technology, Vienna, Austria, February 15 - 17, 2012.

Hossain, Muhammed Zoheb, Olena Rogovchenko, Mattias Nyberg, and Peter Fritzson. An Integrated Toolchain for Model Based Functional Safety Analysis. In P*roceedings of The International Workshop on Applied Modelling and Simulation (WAMS 2012)*, Rome, Italy, Sept 24-27, 2012.

Hudak, Paul. Conception, Evolution, and Application of Functional Programming Languages. *ACM Computing Surveys*, 21:3, pp. 359–411, Sept. 1989.

Hudak, Paul. The Haskell School of Expression. New York: Cambridge University Press. ISBN: 0521644089. Year 2000.

Huhn, Michaela, Martin Sjölund, Wuzhu Chen, Christan Schulze, and Peter Fritzson. Tool Support for Modelica Real-time Models. In *Proceedings of the 8th International Modelica Conference* (Modelica'2011), Dresden, Germany, March.20-22, 2011.

Hyötyniemi, Heikki. Towards New Languages for Systems Modeling. In *Proceedings of SIMS 2002*, Oulu, Finland, available at www.scansims.org, Sept. 26–27, 2002.

Idebrant, Andreas. Personal Communication on a Gas Turbine Library in Modelica. MathCore Engineering AB, Teknikringen 1B, SE-583 30 Linköping, Sweden, www.mathcore.com. (see also Proceedings of Modelica'2003). May 2003.

IEEE Std 1076.1-1999. IEEE Computer Society Design Automation Standards Committee, USA. *IEEE Standard VHDL Analog and Mixed-Signal Extensions*, Dec. 23, 1999.

IEEE. Std 610.3-1989. *IEEE Standard Glossary of Modeling and Simulation Terminology*, 1989

IEEE Std 610.12-1990. *IEEE Standard Glossary of Software Engineering Terminology*, 1990.

ISO 31/0-1992. General Principles Concerning Quantities, Units and Symbols, 1992.

ISO 1000-1992. SI Units and Recommendations for the Use of Their Multiples and of Certain Other Units, 1992.

ITEA2-MODRIO. MODRIO – Model-Driven Systems in Operation.
http://www.itea2.org/project/index/view/?project=10114, Accessed October 2013.

ITEA2-OPENPROD. Open Model-Driven Whole-Product Development. 2013. www.ida.liu.se/labs/pelab/OpenProd/ (accessed May 12, 2012).

ITEA2-OPENPROD. OPENPROD - Open Model-Driven Whole-Product Development.
http://www.itea2.org/project/index/view?project=1132, Accessed October 2013.

ITEA2-MODELISAR: MODELISAR WP2 Glossary and Abbreviations. Version 1.0, June 9, 2009.

Jacobson, V., and R. Braden. TCP Extensions for Long-Delay Paths. RFC 1072, TCP SACK. Network Working Group, At http://www.faqs.org/rfcs/rfc1072.html. Oct. 1988.

Jagudin, Elmir, Andreas Remar, Adrian Pop, and Peter Fritzson. OpenModelica MDT Eclipse Plugin for Modelica Development, Code Browsing, and Simulation. In *Proceedings of the 47th Conference on Simulation and Modelling of the Scandinavian Simulation Society* (SIMS2006), Helsingfors, Finland, Sept. 28-29, 2006.

Jardin, Audrey, Daniel Bouskela, Thuy Nguyen, and Nancy Ruel. Modelling of System Properties in a Modelica Framework. In *Proceedings of 8th International Modelica Conference 2011*. Dresden, Germany, 2011.

Jayaraman, B., and P. Tambay. Semantics and Applications of Constrained Objects. Technical Report 2001-15 at Department of Computer Science and Engineering, State University of New York at Buffalo, Oct. 12, 2001.

Jayaraman, B., and P. Tambay. Modeling Engineering Structures with Constrained Objects. In *Proceedings of International Symposium on Practical Applications of Declarative Languages,* Portland, Oregon, pp. 28–46, LNCS 2257, Springer-Verlag, Jan. 2002.

Jeandel, A., F. Boudaud, P. Ravier, and A. Bushing. U.L.M: Un Language de Modélisation (A Modelling Language). In *Proceedings of the CESA'96 IMACS Multiconference.* IMACS, Lille, France, 1996.

Jensen, Jakob Munch, and Hubertus Tummescheit. Moving Boundary Models for Dynamic Simulation of Two-Phase Flows. In *Proceedings of the 2nd International Modelica Conference*, Oberpfaffenhofen, Germany, Mar. 18–19, 2002.

Jirstrand, Mats, Johan Gunnarsson, and Peter Fritzson. MathModelica—A New Modeling and Simulation Environment for Modelica. In *Proceedings of the 3rd International Mathematica Symposium* (*IMS'99*), Linz, Austria, Aug. 1999.

Jirstrand, Mats. MathModelica—A Full System Simulation Tool. In *Proceedings of Modelica Workshop 2000*, Lund University, Lund, Sweden, Oct. 23–24, 2000.

Johansson, Olof, Adrian Pop, and Peter Fritzson. Engineering Design Tool Standards and Interfacing Possibilities to Modelica Simulation Tools. In *Proceedings of the 5th International Modelica Conference* (Modelica'2006), Vienna, Austria, Sept. 4-5, 2006.

Jonasson, Jonas, Hilding Elmqvist, Sven-Erik Mattsson, and Hans Olsson. One-dimensional PDEs in Modelica. Design document, Modelica Association, February 2003.

Kern, Christoph, and Mark R. Greenstreet. Formal Verification in Hardware Design: A Survey, *ACM Transactions on Design Automation of Electronic Systems*, 4:2, pp. 123–193, Apr. 1999.

Kessler, Christoph, and Peter Fritzson. NestStepModelica – Mathematical Modeling and Bulk-Synchronous Parallel Simulation. In *Proc. of PARA'06*, Umeå, June 19-20, 2006. Published in Lecture Notes of Computer Science (LNCS), Vol 4699, pp 1006-1015, Springer Verlag, 2006.

Kessler, Christoph, Wladimir Schamai, and Peter Fritzson. Platform-independent Modeling of Explicitly Parallel Programs. PARS'10: 23rd PARS-Workshop on parallel Systems and Algorithms, Hannover, Germany, Feb. 2010. In: M. Beigl and F.

Cazorla-Almeida (Eds.): *ARCS'10 Workshop Proceedings*, ISBN 978-3-8007-3222-7, VDE-Verlag Berlin/Offenbach, Germany, pp. 83--93. Also in: *PARS-Mitteilungen* 27: 73-83, ISSN 0177-0454, Sep. 2010.

Kloas, M., V. Friesen, and M. Simons. Smile—A Simulation Environment for Energy Systems. In Sydow (ed.), *Proceedings of the 5th Inteernational IMACS-Symposium on Systems Analysis and Simulation* (*SAS'95*), Vol. 18–19 of Systems Analysis Modelling Simulation, pp. 503–506. Gordon and Breach Publishers, 1995.

Knuth, Donald E. Literate Programming. *The Computer Journal*, NO27(2), pp. 97–111, May 1984.

Knuth, Donald E., and Silvio Levy. *The Cweb System of Structured Documentation/Version 3.0.* Addison-Wesley, 1994.

Kral, Christian, and Anton Haumer (eds.). *Proceedings of the 6th International Modelica Conference*. Available at www.modelica.org. Vienna, Austria, Sept 4-6, 2006.

Kågedal, David, and Peter Fritzson. Generating a Modelica Compiler from Natural Semantics Specifications. In *Proceedings of the Summer Computer Simulation Conference '98*, Reno, Nevada, USA, July 19–22 1998.

Kahn, Gilles. *Natural Semantics*. In *Proc. of the Symposium on Theoretical Aspects on Computer Science* (*STACS'87*), LNCS 247, pp. 22–39. Springer-Verlag, 1987.

Kamkar, Mariam. *Interprocedural Dynamic Slicing with Applications to Debugging and Testing*. Ph.D. thesis, Department of Computer Science, Linköping University, Linköping, Sweden, 1993.

Kübler R., Schiehlen, W. Two methods of simulator coupling. Mathematical and Computer Modeling of Dynamical Systems 6 pp. 93-113, 2000.

Langtangen, Hans Petter, *Computational Partial Differential Equations—Numerical Methods and Diffpack Programming.* Springer-Verlag, 1999a—begin

Larsdotter Nilsson, Emma, and Peter Fritzson. Simulating Willow Productivity Using Modelica. In *Proceedings of the 3rd Conference on Modeling and Simulation in Biology*, Department of Medicine and Biomedical Engineering, University of Balamand, Lebanon, May 27–30, 2003.

Larsdotter Nilsson, Emma, and Peter Fritzson. BioChem - A Biological and Chemical Library for Modelica In *Proceedings of the 3rd International Modelica Conference*, pp. 215-220, November 3-4, Linköping, Sweden, 2003.

Larsson, Jonas, and Petter Krus. A Framework for Generating Efficient Simulation Code from Declarative Models. In *Proceedings of ASME International Mechanical Engineering Congress*, Washington D.C., USA, Nov. 16–21, 2003.

Larsson, Mats. ObjectStab—A Modelica Library for Power System Stability Studies. In *Proceedings of Modelica Workshop 2000*, Lund University, Lund, Sweden, Oct. 23–24, 2000.

Lee, Edward A. Overview of the Ptolemy Project, Technical Memorandum UCB/ERL M01/11, http://ptolemy.eecs.berkeley.edu/, University of California, Berkeley, Mar. 6, 2001.

Lee, Edward A. Embedded Software. In M. Zelkowitz (ed.) *Advances in Computers*, Vol. 56, Academic Press, London, 2002.

Lee Edward.A., Zheng H. Leveraging Synchronous Language Principles for Heterogeneous Modeling and Design of Embedded Systems. http://ptolemy.eecs.berkeley.edu/publications/papers/07/unifying/LeeZheng_SRUnifying.pdf EMSOFT'07, Salzburg, Austria, Sept. 30 - Oct. 3, 2007.

Leitold, Adrien, and Hangos M. Katalin. Structural Solvability of Dynamic Process Models, *Journals of Computers and Chemical Engineering*, 25, pp. 1633–1646, 2001.

Lengquist Sandelin, Eva-Lena, and Susanna Monemar. DrModelica—An Experimental Computer-Based Teaching Material for Modelica. Master's thesis, LITH-IDA-Ex03/3, Department of Computer and Information Science, Linköping University, Linköping, Sweden, 2003.

Lengquist Sandelin, Eva-Lena, Susanna Monemar, Peter Fritzson, and Peter Bunus. DrModelica—A Web-Based Teaching Environment for Modelica. In *Proceedings of the 44th Scandinavian Conference on Simulation and Modeling (SIMS'2003)*, available at www.scansims.org. Västerås, Sweden, Sept. 18–19, 2003.

Lengquist-Sandelin, Eva-Lena, Susanna Monemar, Peter Fritzson, and Peter Bunus. DrModelica - An Interactive Tutoring Environment for Modelica. In *Proceedings of the 3rd International Modelica Conference*, Nov. 3-4, Linköping, Sweden, 2003.

Lengquist-Sandelin, Eva-Lena, Susanna Monemar, Peter Fritzson, and Peter Bunus: DrModelica - An Interactive Environment for Learning Modelica and Modeling using MathModelica. In *Proceedings of ISCS'2003*, Cefalu, Sicily, Italy, Nov 28-29, 2003.

Liang, Feng, Wladimir Schamai, Olena Rogovchenko, Sara Sadeghi, Mattias Nyberg, Peter Fritzson. Model-based Requirement Verification: A Case Study. http://dx.doi.org/10.3384/ecp12076385, In *Proceedings of the 9th International Modelica Conference* (Modelica'2012), Munich, Germany, Sept.3-5, 2012.

Lindskov, J., M. Knudsen, O. Löfgren, Ole Lehrmann-Madsen, and Boris Magnusson (Eds.). *Object-Oriented Environments - The Mjølner Approach.* Prentice Hall, 1993.

Linnemann, H., De Hoogh, J., Keyzer, M., and Van Heemst, H. MOIRA-Model of International Relations in Agriculture, North-Holland Publishing Co. Amsterdam. 1979.

Lipsey R.G., P. O. Steiner, and D. D. Purvis. Economics, 3th ed, Harper, New York, 1997.

Ljung, Lennart, and Torkel Glad. *Modeling of Dynamic Systems*, 350 pages. Prentice Hall, 1994.

Ljung, Lennart. *System identification—Theory for the User*, 2nd ed. Prentice Hall, 1999.

Lotka, Alfred J. *Elements of Mathematical Biology*. Dover Publications, New York, 1956.

Louden, Kenneth C. *Programming Languages, Principles and Practice*, ISBN 0-534-93277-0. PWS Publishing Company, Boston, 1993.

Looye, Gertjan, Michael Thümmel, Matthias Kurze, Martin Otter, and Johann Bals. Nonlinear Inverse Models for Control. In *Proceedings of 4th International Modelica Conference*, www.modelica.org, Hamburg, March 7-8, 2005.

Lunde, Karin. *Object-Oriented Modeling in Model-Based Diagnosis*. In *Proceedings of Modelica Workshop 2000*, Lund, Sweden, Oct. 23–24, 2000.

Lunde, Karin, Hilding Elmqvist, Hans Olsson, Martin Otter, and Peter Fritzson. Layers Design Proposals for Modelica Design. Modelica Association, February and June, 2003.

Lundvall, Håkan, and Peter Fritzson. Modeling Concurrent Activities and Resource Sharing in Modelica. In *Proceedings of the 44th Scandinavian Conference on Simulation and Modeling (SIMS'2003)*, available at www.scansims.org. Västerås, Sweden, Sept. 18–19, 2003.

Lundvall, Håkan, Peter Bunus, Peter Fritzson. Towards Automatic Generation of Model Checkable Code from Modelica. In *Proceedings of the 45th Conference on Simulation and Modelling of the Scandinavian Simulation Society (SIMS2004)*, Copenhagen, Denmark, 23-24 September 2004.

Lundvall, Håkan, and Peter Fritzson. Event Handling in the OpenModelica Compiler and Run-time System. In *Proceedings of the 46th Conference on Simulation and Modelling of the Scandinavian Simulation Society* (SIMS2005), Trondheim, Norway, October 13-14, 2005.

Lundvall, Håkan, and Peter Fritzson. Automatic Parallelization of Object Oriented Models across Method and System. In *Proceedings of the EuroSim Congress*, Ljubljana, Sept 9-13, 2007.

Lundvall, Håkan and Peter Fritzson. Automatic Parallelization of Object Oriented Models Executed with Inline Solvers. In *Proceedings of EuroPvm/Parsim*, Springer Verlag LNCS, Volume 4757, 2007. See also http://pvmmpi07.lri.fr/parsim07.html. Paris, France, Sept 30 – Oct 3, 2007.

Lundvall, Håkan and Peter Fritzson. Automatic Parallelization of Mathematical Models Solved with Inlined Runge-Kutta Solvers. In *Proceedings of the 48th Scandinavian Conference on Simulation and Modeling* (SIMS'2007), available at www.scan-sims.org and http://www.ep.liu.se. Göteborg, Sweden. October 30-31, 2007.

Lundvall, Håkan, Kristian Stavåker, Peter Fritzson, and Christoph Kessler. Automatic Parallelization of Simulation Code for Equation-based Models with Software Pipelining and Measurements on Three Platforms. *Computer Architecture News*. Special Issue MCC08 – Multi-Core Computing 2008. Volume 36, Number 5. Published by ACM, Special Interest Group on Computer Architecture. December 2008.

Lundvall, Håkan, Kristian Stavåker, Peter Fritzson, and Christoph Kessler. Automatic Parallelization of Simulation Code for Equation based Models with Software Pipelining and Measurements on Three Platforms. In *Proc. of the 1st Swedish Workshop on Multi-Core Computing (MCC-08)*, Ronneby, November 27-28, 2008.

Lundvall, Håkan, and Peter Fritzson. Automatic Parallelization using Pipelining for Equation-Based Simulation Languages. In proceedings of the *14th Workshop on Compilers for Parallel Computing (CPC'2009)*, Zurich, Switzerland, Jan 7-9, 2009.

Maffezzoni C., R. Girelli, and P. Lluka. Generating Efficient Computational Procedures from Declarative Models, *Simulation Practice and Theory*, 4, pp. 303–317, 1996.

Maggio, Martina, Kristian Stavåker, Filippo Donida, Francesco Casella, Peter Fritzson. Parallel Simulation of Equation-based Object-Oriented Models with Quantized State Systems on a GPU. In *Proceedings of the 7th International Modelica Conference* (Modelica'2009), Como, Italy, September.20-22, 2009.

Mah, Richard. *Chemical Process Structures and Information Flows*. Butterworths Series in Chemical Engineering, Butterworths, 1990.

Malthus, Thomas. An Essay on the Principle of Population. 1798. Reprint. Amherst, NY: Prometheus Books (1998). Also reprint,Vol. 1. Cosimo, Inc., 2013. On-line version with comments: http://www.econlib.org/library/Malthus/malPlong.html

Martinson, W.S. and P.I. Barton. A Differentiation Index for Partial Differential-Algebraic Equations. *SIAM J. Sci. Comput.*, 21, pp. 2295-2315, 2000.

Mascolo, S., C. Casetti, M. Gerla, S. S. Lee, and M. Sanadidi. TCP Westwood. *Congestion Control with Faster Recovery*. UCLA CSD TR #200017, Computer Science Department – UCLA, Los Angeles, CA, 90024. www.cs.ucla.edu/NRU/hpi/ccpw, 2001.

MathCore Engineering AB. Home page: www.mathcore.com. MathCore Engineering AB, Teknikringen 1B, SE-583 30 Linköping, Sweden, 2003.

MathWorks Inc. *Simulink User's Guide*, 2001

MathWorks Inc. *MATLAB User's Guide*, 2002.

Mattsson, Sven-Erik, and Mats Andersson. The Ideas Behind Omola. In *Proceedings of the 1992 IEEE Symposium on Computer-Aided Control System Design (CADCS '92)*, Napa, California, Mar. 1992.

Mattsson, Sven-Erik, and Gustaf Söderlind. Index Reduction in Differential-Algebraic Equations Using Dummy Derivatives, *SIAM Journal on Scientific Computing*, Vol. 14, pp. 677–692, 1993.

Mattsson, Sven-Erik, Mats Andersson, and Karl-Johan Åström. Object-Oriented Modelling and Simulation. In Linkens (ed.), *CAD for Control Systems*, Chapter 2, pp. 31–69. Marcel Dekker, New York, 1993.

Mattsson, Sven-Erik, Hans Olsson, and Hilding Elmqvist. Dynamic Selection of States in Dymola. In *Proceedings of Modelica Workshop 2000*, Lund University, Lund, Sweden, Oct. 23–24, 2000.

Meadows, Donella, Denis Meadows, Jorgen Randers, and W.W. Behrens III. *Limits to Growth: A Report for the Club of Rome's Project on the Predicament of Mankind.* 205p. Universe Books, New York, 1972.

Meadows, Donella, W.W. Behrens III, Denis Meadows, R.F. Naill, Jorgen Randers, and E.K.O. Zahn. *Dynamics of Growth in a Finite World.* 637p. Wright-Allen Press, 1974.

Meadows, Donella, Jorgen Randers, and Denis Meadows. *Limits to Growth: The 30-Year Update.* 368p. Chelsea Green, 2004.

Meyer, Bertrand. *Object-Oriented Software Construction*, 2nd ed, Prentice-Hall, Englewood Cliffs, 1997.

Michael, Gerhard. (ed.) *Biochemical Pathways—An Atlas of Biochemistry and Molecular Biology.* Wiley, Heidelberg, 1999.

Milner, Robert, Mads Tofte, Robert Harper, and David MacQueen, The Definition of Standard ML - Revised. MIT Press. ISBN: 0-262-63181-4. Year 1997.

Mitchell, Edward E.L., and Joseph S. Gauthier. *ACSL: Advanced Continuous Simulation Language—User Guide and Reference Manual.* Mitchell & Gauthier Assoc., Concord, Mass, 1986.

Mirzaei, Mana. Integration of OpenModelica into the Multi-Paradigm Modeling Environment Ptolemy II. Master Thesis. Linköping University, December, 2013.

Mizraei, Mana, Lena Buffoni, and Peter Fritzson. Integration of OpenModelica in Ptolemy II. Submitted to Modelica'2014. December 2013.

Modelica Association. *Modelica—A Unified Object-Oriented Language for Physical Systems Modeling: Tutorial and Design Rationale Version 1.0*, Sept. 1997.

Modelica Association. *Modelica—A Unified Object-Oriented Language for Physical Systems Modeling: Tutorial, Version 1.4.* Available at http://www.modelica.org, Dec. 15, 2000.

Modelica Association. *Modelica—A Unified Object-Oriented Language for Physical Systems Modeling: Language Specification Version 2.1.* Available at http://www.modelica.org, June 6, 2003.

Modelica Association. *Modelica—A Unified Object-Oriented Language for Physical Systems Modeling: Language Specification Version 3.2.* Available at http://www.modelica.org, March, 2010.

Modelica Association. *Modelica—A Unified Object-Oriented Language for Physical Systems Modeling: Language Specification Version 3.3.* Available at http://www.modelica.org, May, 2012.

Modelica Association. *Modelica—A Unified Object-Oriented Language for Physical Systems Modeling: Language Specification Version 3.2 rev 2.* Available at http://www.modelica.org, August, 2013.

Modelica Assocation. Home page: www.modelica.org. Last accessed Nov. 2013.

Modelica Association Project FMI. Functional Mock-up Interface for Model Exchange and Co-Simulation. Vers. 2.0 Release Candidate 1. www.fmi-standard.org. Accessed October 18, 2013.

Mohr, Peter J., and Barry N. Taylor. CODATA Recommended Values of the Fundamental Physical Constants: 1998, *Journal of Physical and Chemical Reference Data*, 28:6, 1999, and *Reviews of Modern Physics*, 72:2, 2000. See also http://physics.nist.gov/cuu/Constants/.

Moghadam, Afshin Hemmati, Mahder Gebremedhin, Kristian Stavåker, and Peter Fritzson. Simulation and Benchmarking of Modelica Models on Multi-core Architectures with Explicit Parallel Algorithmic Language Extensions. In *Proceedings of the Fourth Swedish Workshop on Multicore Computing (MCC'2011)*, Linköping, Sweden, Nov 23-25, 2011.

Moormann, Dieter, and G. Looye. The Modelica Flight Dynamics Library. In *Proceedings of the 2nd International Modelica Conference*, Oberpfaffenhofen, Germany, Mar. 18–19, 2002.

Mossberg, Eva, Kurt Otto, and Michael Thuné. Object-Oriented Software Tools for the Construction of Preconditioners, *Scientific Programming*, 6, pp. 285–295, 1997.

Mosterman, P.J., Martin Otter, and Hilding Elmqvist. Modeling Petri Nets as Local Constraint Equations for Hybrid Systems Using Modelica. In *Proceedings of Summer Computer Simulation Conference '98*, Reno, Nevada, USA, pp. 314–319. July 19–22, 1998.

Motesharrei, Safa, Jorge Rivas, and Eugenia Kalnay. A Minimal Model for Human and Nature Interaction. Department of Atmospheric and Oceanic Sciences, University of Maryland, 2012.

Motesharrei, Safa, Jorge Rivas, and Eugenia Kalnay. A Minimal Model for Human and Nature Interaction. Accepted for publication in the journal *Ecological Economics*. 2014.

Murota, Kazuo. *System Analysis by Graphs and Matroids—Structural Solvability and Controllability*. Springer Verlag, Berlin, 1987.

Murota, Kazuo. *Matrices and Matroids for System Analysis*. Springer Verlag, Berlin, 2000.

Myers, Colin, Chris Clack, and Ellen Poon. *Programming with Standard ML*. Prentice Hall. 1993.

Myers, Toby, Peter Fritzson, and Geoff Dromey. Seamlessly Integrating Software & Hardware Modelling for Large-Scale Systems. In *Proceedings of the 2nd International Workshop on Equation-Based Object-Oriented Languages and Tools, (EOOLT'2008)*, Pathos, Cyprus, July 8, 2008. Published by Linköping University Electronic Press, http://www.ep.liu.se/ecp/024/, July 2008.

Myers, Toby, Peter Fritzson, and Geoff Dromey. Co-Modeling: From Requirements to an Integrated Software/Hardware Model. *IEEE Computer*, May 2011.

Myers, Toby, Wladimir Schamai, and Peter Fritzson. Comodeling Revisited: Execution of Behavior Trees in Modelica. In *Proceedings of the 4th International Workshop on Equation-Based Object-Oriented Modeling Languages and Tools, (EOOLT'2011)*, Zürich, Switzerland, Published by Linköping University Electronic Press, www.ep.liu.se, Sept 5, 2011.

Newman, Charles, John Batteh, and Michael Tiller. Spark-Ignited-Engine Cycle Simulation in Modelica. In *Proceedings of the 2nd International Modelica Conference*, Oberpfaffenhofen, Germany, Mar. 18–19, 2002.

Nilsson, Bernt. *Object-Oriented Modeling of Chemical Processes*. Ph.D. thesis, ISRN LUTFD2/TFRT-1041-SE, Dept. of Automatic Control, Lund Institute of Technology, Lund, Sweden, 1993.

Nilsson, Henrik, and Peter Fritzson: Declarative Algorithmic Debugging for Lazy Functional Languages. In *Journal of Functional Programming*, 4:3 pp. 337–370, July 1994.

Nilsson, Henrik. *Declarative Debugging for Lazy Functional Languages*. Ph.D. thesis, Department of Computer and Information Science, Linköping University, 1998.

Nilsson, Henrik. (Editor). *Proceedings of the 5th International Workshop on Equation-Based Object-Oriented Languages and Tools*, (EOOLT'2013), Nottingham, UK, April 19, 2013. Published by Linköping University Electronic Press, http://www.ep.liu.se/ecp_home/index.en.aspx?issue=084, April, 2013.

Nordling, Patrik. *The Simulation of Rolling Bearing Dynamics on Parallel Computers*. Licentiate Thesis 558, Linköping University, Linköping, Sweden, 1996. PhD thesis draft: Parallel Simulation of Rolling Bearing Multibody System Dynamics, fall 2003.

Norling, Kristoffer, David Broman, Peter Fritzson, Alexander Siemers, and Dag Fritzson. Secure Distributed Co-Simulation over Wide Area Networks. In *Proceedings of the 48th Scandinavian Conference on Simulation and Modeling* (SIMS'2007), available at www.scan-sims.org and http://www.ep.liu.se. Göteborg, Sweden. October 30-31, 2007.

Noronha-Sannervik, Angela, Henrik Eckersten, Theo Verwijst, and Nils-Erik Nordh. Simulating Willow Productivity Based on Radiation Use Efficiency, Shoot Mortality, and Shoot Age. In *Proceedings of SIMS 2002*, available at www.scansims.org. Oulu, Finland, Sept. 26–27, 2002.

Noronha-Sannervik, Angela. Private communication on willow productivity data. Nov. 2002.

Nuutila, Esko, and Eljas Soisalon-Soininen. On Finding the Strongly Connected Components in a Directed Graph, *Information Processing Letters*, 49, pp. 9–14, 1993.

Nyberg, Mattias, and Lars Nielsen. Model Based Diagnosis for the Air Intake System of the SI-Engine, *SAE Transactions, Journal of Commercial Vehicles*, 106, pp. 9–20, 1997.

Nyberg, Mattias. Model-Based Diagnosis of an Automotive Engine Using Several Types of Fault Models, *IEEE Transaction on Control Systems Technology*, 10:5, pp. 679–689. Sept. 2002.

Nyström, Kaj, and Peter Fritzson. Parallel Simulation with Transmission Lines in Modelica. In *Proceedings of the 5th International Modelica Conference* (Modelica'2006), Vienna, Austria, Sept. 4-5, 2006.

Nørmark, Kurt. Requirements for an Elucidative Programming Environment. In *Proceedings of the International Workshop on Program Comprehension (IWPC'2000)*, Limerick, Ireland, June 2000.

ObjectMath Home page: http://www.ida.liu.se/labs/pelab/omath.

OCaml. Objective Caml 3.12.0 installation notes. Aug, 2010. http://caml.inria.fr

Ochel, Lennart, and Bernhard Bachmann. Initialization of Equation-Based Hybrid Models within OpenModelica. In *Proceedings of the 5th International Workshop on Equation-Based Object-Oriented Modeling Languages and Tools, (EOOLT'2013)*, Published by Linköping University Electronic Press, www.ep.liu.se, Nottingham, UK, April 19, 2013.

Odersky, Martin, Lex Spoon, and Bill Venners. Programming in Scala. Artima Press, 2008.

Oh, Min. *Modelling and Simulation of Combined Lumped and Distributed Processes*. Ph.D. thesis, University of London, 1995.

Oh, Min, and Costas Pantelides. A Modelling and Simulation Language for Combined Lumped and Distributed Parameter System, *Computers & Chemical Engineering*, 20:6–7, pp. 611–633, June 1996.

Olsson, Hans, Martin Otter, Sven Erik Mattsson, and Hilding Elmqvist. Balanced Models in Modelica 3.0 for Increased Model Quality. In *Proceedings of the 6th International Modelica Conference* (Modelica'2008), Bielefeld, Germany, March.3-4, 2008.

Olsson, Karl-Olof, and Håkan Wettergren. Maskindynamik. (In Swedish.) ISBN 91-44-01349-3. Studentlitteratur, 2000.

OMG. SysML-Modelica Transformation. Version 1.0. 2012.

OpenModelica home page: http://www.openmodelica.org. Accessed October 2013.

Open Source Modelica Consortium (OSMC). OpenModelica User's Guide 1.9.0. www.openmodelica.org. October 2013.

Open Source Modelica Consortium (OSMC). OpenModelica System Documentation 1.9.0. www.openmodelica.org. October 2013.

Östlund, Per, Kristian Stavåker, and Peter Fritzson. Parallel Simulation of Equation-Based Models on CUDA-Enabled GPUs. In Proc. of Parallel/High-Performance Object-Oriented Scientific Computing, (POOSC'10), In conjuction with SPLASH 2010 http://splashcon.org, Reno-Tahoe, Nevada, USA, October 18, 2010.

Otter, Martin. DSBlock: A Neutral Description of Dynamic Systems, *Open CACSD Electronic Newsletter*, 1:3, 1992.

Otter, Martin. *Objektorientierte Modellierung mechatronischer Systeme am beispiel geregelter Roboter*. Dissertation (in German), Fortshrittberichte VDI, Reihe 20, Nr 147, 1995.

Otter, Martin, Hilding Elmqvist, and Francois Cellier. Modeling of Multibody Systems with the Object-Oriented Modeling Language Dymola, *Nonlinear Dynamics*, 9, pp. 91-112. Kluwer Academic Publishers, 1996.

Otter, Martin, Hilding Elmqvist, and Sven-Erik Mattsson. Proposal for Overdetermined Connector Handling for Modelica Design. Modelica Association. June, 2003.

Otter, Martin, C. Schlegel, and Hilding Elmqvist. Modeling and Real-Time Simulation of an Automatic Gearbox Using Modelica. In *Proceedings of ESS'97—European Simulation Symposium*, Passau, Oct. 19–23, 1997.

Otter, Martin, Hilding Elmqvist, and Sven-Erik Mattsson. Hybrid Modeling in Modelica Based on the Synchronous Data Flow Principle. In *Proceedings of the 1999 IEEE Symposium on Computer-Aided Control System Design (CACSD'99)*, Hawaii, Aug. 22–27, 1999.

Otter, Martin. Objektorientierte Modellierung Physikalischer Systeme, Teil 1: Übersicht. In *Automatisierungstechnik*, 47:1, pp. A1–A4. 1999 (In German.) The first in a series of 17 articles. 1999.

Otter, Martin, Mike Dempsey, and Clemens Schlegel. Package PowerTrain: A Modelica Library for Modeling and Simulation of Vehicle Power Trains. In *Proceedings of Modelica Workshop 2000*, Lund University, Lund, Sweden, Oct. 23–24, 2000.

Otter, Martin (ed.) *Proceedings of the 2nd International Modelica Conference*. Available at www.modelica.org. Oberpfaffenhofen, Germany, Mar. 18–19, 2002.

Otter, Martin. Personal communication on an example of an overdetermined connector kinematic loop. Modelica Association, June 2003.

Otter, Martin, Hilding Elmqvist, and Sven-Erik Mattsson. Proposal for Overdetermined Connector Handling. Design document, Modelica Association, June, 2003a.

Otter, Martin, Hilding Elmqvist, and Sven-Erik Mattsson. The New Modelica MultiBody Library. *Proceedings of the 3rd International Modelica Conference*, available at www.modelica.org. Linköping, Sweden, Nov 3-4, 2003.

Otter, Martin, Martin Malmheden, Hilding Elmqvist, Sven Erik Mattson, and Charlotta Johnsson. A New Formalism for Modeling of Reactive and Hybrid Systems. Linköping University Electronic Press. ISBN 978-91-7393-513-5. ISSN 1650-3740, In *Proceedings of the 7th International Modelica Conference*, Como, Italy, Sept. 20-22, 2009.

Otter, Martin, Bernhard Thiele, and Hilding Elmqvist. A Library for Synchronous Control Systems in Modelica. In *Proceedings of 9th International Modelica Conference*, Munich, Germany, Sept 3-5, 2012.

Otter, Martin, and Dirk Zimmer (eds.). *Proceedings of the 9th International Modelica Conference*. Available at www.modelica.org. Munich, Germany, September 3–5, 2012.

Pantelides, Costas. The Consistent Initialization of Differential Algebraic Systems, *SIAM Journal on Scientific and Statistical Computing*. 9: 2 pp. 213–231, http://epubs.siam.org/doi/abs/10.1137/0909014, Mar. 1988.

Paredis, Christjaan, Yves Bernard, Roger Burkhart, Hans-Peter de Koning, Sanford Friedenthal, Peter Fritzson, Nicolas Rouquette, and Wladimir Schamai, An Overview of the SysML-Modelica Transformation Specification, In *Proceedings of the 2010 INCOSE International Symposium*, Chicago, Illinois, USA, July 12-15, 2010.

Parnas, David L. On the Criteria to Be Used in Decomposing Systems into Modules, *Communications of the ACM*, 15:12, pp. 1053–1058, Dec. 1972.

Parr, Terence J. *Language Translation Using PCCTS & C++*. A Reference Guide, Automata Publishing Company, 1997.

PELAB. Somewhat old page on Modelica Research at PELAB, Programming Environment Laboratory, Dept. of Computer and Information Science, Linköping University, Sweden, www.ida.liu.se/labs/pelab/modelica. Last accessed 2012.

Pelchen, Christoph, Christian Schweiger, and Martin Otter. Modeling and Simulating the Efficiency of Gearboxes and of Planetary Gearboxes. In *Proceedings of the 2nd International Modelica Conference*, Oberpfaffenhofen, Germany, Mar. 18–19, 2002.

Pereira-Remelhe, Manuel A. Combining Discrete Event Models and Modelica—General Thoughts and a Special Modeling Environment. In *Proceedings of the 2nd International Modelica Conference*, Oberpfaffenhofen, Germany. Mar. 18–19, 2002.

Peterson, James L. *Petri Net Theory and the Modeling of Systems*. Prentice Hall, 1981.

Petersson, Mikael. *Compiling Natural Semantics*, Lecture Notes in Computer Science, LNCS 1549. Springer Verlag, 1999.

Petzold, L.R. A Description of DASSL: A Differential/Algebraic System Solver. In *Proceedings of the 10th IMACS World Congress*, Montreal, Aug. 8–13, 1982.

Pfeiffer, Andreas, Matthias Hellerer, Stefan Hartweg, Martin Otter, and Matthias Reiner. PySimulator – A Simulation and Analysis Environment in Python with Plugin Infrastructure. In *Proceedings of the 9th International Modelica Conference* (Modelica'2012), Munich, Germany, Sept.3-5, 2012.

Piela, P.C., T.G. Epperly, K.M. Westerberg, and A.W. Westerberg. ASCEND—An Object-Oriented Computer Environment for Modeling and Analysis: The Modeling Language, *Computers and Chemical Engineering*, Web page: (http://www.cs.cmu.edu/~ascend/Home.html), 15:1, pp. 53–72, 1991.

Pixmap. The Pixmap bitmap format, supported e.g by the Qt library, see www.trolltech.com. The Unix xpm command for reading/writing Pixmap format, see http://koala.ilog.fr/lehors/xpm.html. 2003.

Pop, Adrian, and Peter Fritzson: A Portable Debugger for Algorithmic Modelica Code. In *Proceedings of the 4th International Modelica Conference*, Hamburg, Germany, March 7-8, 2005.

Pop, Adrian, and Peter Fritzson. Debugging Natural Semantics Specifications. In *Proceedings of the 6:th International Symposium on Automated and Analysis-Driven Debugging* (AADEBUG'2005), Monterey, California, September 19-21, 2005.

Pop, Adrian, and Peter Fritzson. An Eclipse-based Integrated Environment for Developing Executable Structural Operational Semantics Specifications. Published electronically at www.entcs.org in *Proceedings of Structural Operational Semantics 2006* – A Satellite Workshop of CONCUR 2006. Bonn, Germany, Aug 26, 2006.

Pop, Adrian, Peter Fritzson, Andreas Remar, Elmir Jagudin, and David Akhvlediani. OpenModelica Development Environment with Eclipse Integration for Browsing, Modeling, and Debugging. In *Proceedings of the 5th International Modelica Conference* (Modelica'2006), Vienna, Austria, Sept. 4-5, 2006.

Pop, Adrian, and Peter Fritzson. MetaModelica: A Unified Equation-Based Semantical and Mathematical Modeling Language. In *Proceedings of Joint Modular Languages Conference 2006* (JMLC2006) LNCS Springer Verlag. Jesus College, Oxford, England, Sept 13-15, 2006.

Pop, Adrian and Peter Fritzson. An Eclipse-based Integrated Environment for Developing Executable Structural Operational Semantics Specifications. *Electronic Notes in Theoretical Computer Science* (ENTCS), Vol 175, pp 71–75. ISSN:1571-0661. May 2007.

Pop, Adrian, David Akhvlediani, and Peter Fritzson. Towards Unified System Modeling with the ModelicaML UML Profile. In *Proceedings of the 1st International Workshop on Equation-Based Object-Oriented Languages and Tools, (EOOLT'2007)*, Berlin, July 30, 2007. Published by Linköping University Electronic Press, http://www.ep.liu.se/ecp/024/, July 2007.

Pop, Adrian, David Akhvlediani, and Peter Fritzson. Towards Unified System Modeling with the ModelicaML UML Profile. *Simulation News Europe*, Vol 17, No 2. ISSN 0929-2268. Sept 2007.

Pop, Adrian, David Akhvlediani, and Peter Fritzson. Towards Run-time Debugging of Equation-based Object-oriented Languages. In *Proceedings of the 48th Scandinavian Conference on Simulation and Modeling* (SIMS'2007), available at www.scan-sims.org and http://www.ep.liu.se. Göteborg, Sweden. October 30-31, 2007.

Pop, Adrian, Vasile Băluţă, and Peter Fritzson .Eclipse Support for Design and Requirements Engineering Based on ModelicaML. In *Proceedings of the 48th Scandinavian Conference on Simulation and Modeling* (SIMS'2007), available at www.scan-sims.org and http://www.ep.liu.se. Göteborg, Sweden. October 30-31, 2007.

Pop, Adrian, David Akhvlediani, Peter Fritzson: Integrated UML and Modelica System Modeling with ModelicaML in Eclipse, In *Proceedings of the 11th IASTED International Conference on Software Engineering and Applications (SEA 2007)*, Cambridge, MA, USA, November 19-21, 2007.

Pop, Adrian, Kristian Stavåker, and Peter Fritzson. Exception Handling for Modelica. In *Proceedings of the 6th International Modelica Conference* (Modelica'2008), Bielefeld, Germany, March.3-4, 2008.

Pop, Adrian. *Integrated Model-Driven Development Environments for Equation-Based Object-Oriented Languages*. Ph.D. Thesis, Linköping University, Sweden. www.ep.liu.se, Dissertation No. 1183, June 5, 2008.

Pop, Adrian, Martin Sjölund, Adeel Asghar, Peter Fritzson, Francesco Casella. Static and Dynamic Debugging of Modelica Models. In *Proceedings of the 9th International Modelica Conference* (Modelica'2012), Munich, Germany, Sept.3-5, 2012.

Potter, Merle C., and Craig W. Somerton. *Schaum's Outline of Theory and Problems of Thermodynamics for Engineers*. Schaum's Outlines Series, ISBN 0-07-050707-4. McGraw-Hill. 1993.

Pouzet, Marc. *Lucid Synchrone, Version 3.0, Tutorial and Reference Manual*. http://www.di.ens.fr/~pouzet/lucid-synchrone/, 2006.

Pouzet, Marc, et al. The Lucid-Synchrone Bibliography. http://www.di.ens.fr/~pouzet/lucid-synchrone/papers/lucy.html Accessed September 2013.

Proß, Sabrina, and Bernhard Bachmann. PNlib - An Advanced Petri Net Library for Hybrid Process Modeling. In *Proceedings of 9th International Modelica Conference*, Munich, Germany, Sept. 3-5, 2012.

Proß, Sabina. *Hybrid Modeling and Optimization of Biological Processes*. PhD thesis. Faculty of Technology, Bielefeld University, Germany, http://pub.uni-bielefeld.de/publication/2562185, 2013.

Ptolemy II. Ptolemy II Home Page. http://ptolemy.berkeley.edu/ptolemyII/, Accessed November 2013.

Ramirez, Vicente Rico. *Representation, Analysis and Solution of Conditional Models in an Equation-Based Environment*. Ph.D. thesis, Carnegie Mellon University, Pittsburgh, Pennsylvania, Aug. 1998.

Ramos, Juan José, Piera Miquel Àngel, and Serra Ignasi. The Use of Physical Knowledge to Guide Formula Manipulation in System Modeling, *Simulation Practice and Theory*, 6: 3, pp. 243-254, Mar. 15, 1998.

Pfeiffer, F., and C. Glocker. *Multibody Dynamics with Unilateral Contacts*. John Wiley & Sons, New York, 1996.

Pritsker, A., and B. Alan. *The GASP IV Simulation Language*. John Wiley & Sons, New York, 1974.

Reissig, Günter, Wade Martinson, and Paul Barton. DAE of Index 1 Might Have an Arbitrary High Structural Index, *SIAM J. Sci. Comput.* 21:6, pp. 1987–1990, 2000.

Rogovchenko-Buffoni, Lena, Andrea Tundis, Muhammed Zoheb Hossain, Mattias Nyberg, and Peter Fritzson. An Integrated Toolchain for Model Based Functional Safety Analysis. Accepted to *Journal of Computational Science*, June, 2013.

Rumbaugh, J.M., M. Blaha, W. Premerlain, F. Eddy, and W. Lorensen. *Object Oriented Modeling and Design*. Prentice-Hall, 1991.

Sahlin, Per., and E.F. Sowell. A Neutral Format for Building Simulation Models. In *Proceedings of the Conference on Building Simulation*, IBPSA, Vancouver, Canada, 1989.

Sahlin Per., A. Bring, and K. Kolsaker. Future Trends of the Neutral Model Format. In *Proceedings of the Conference on Building Simulation*, IBPSA, Madison, WI, USA, Aug, 1995.

Sahlin, Per. *Modelling and Simulation Methods for Modular Continuous Systems in Buildings*. Ph.D. thesis, Department of Building Science, Royal Institute of Technology Stockholm, Sweden, May 1996.

Sahlin, Per., A. Bring, and E.F. Sowell. *The Neutral Model Format for Building Simulation, Version 3.02*. Technical Report, Department of Building Sciences, Royal Institute of Technology, Stockholm, Sweden, June 1996.

Saldamli, Levon, and Peter Fritzson. A Modelica-Based Language for Object-Oriented Modeling with Partial Differential Equations. In *Proceedings of the 4th International EuroSim Congress*, Delft, The Netherlands, June 26–29, 2001.

Saldamli, Levon, Peter Fritzson, and Bernhard. Bachmann. Extending Modelica for Partial Differential Equations. In *Proceedings of the 2nd International Modelica Conference*, Oberpfaffenhofen, Germany, Mar. 18–19, 2002.

Saldamli, Levon. PDEModelica—Towards a High-Level Language for Modeling with Partial Differential Equations. Licentiate thesis, Department of Computer and Information Science, Linköping University, Dec. 2002.

Saldamli, Levon, and Peter Fritzson. Discussion of PDE Specification in Modelica. Design document, Modelica Association, June 2003.

Saldamli, Levon, and Peter Fritzson. Field Type and Field Constructor in Modelica. In *Proceedings of the 45th Conference on Simulation and Modelling of the Scandinavian Simulation Society (SIMS2004)*, Sept 23-24, Copenhagen, Denmark, 2004.

Saldamli, Levon. *PDEModelica - A High-Level Language for Modeling with Partial Differential Equations*. Ph.D. Thesis, Linköping University, Sweden. www.ep.liu.se., Dissertation No. 1022. May 15, 2006.

Sandewall, Erik. Programming in an Interactive Environment: The "LISP" Experience, *Computing Surveys*, 10:1, Mar. 1978.

Sandholm, Anders, Peter Fritzson, Varun Arora, Scott Delp, Göran Petersson, and Jessica Rose. The Gait E-Book - Development of Effective Participatory Learning using Simulation and Active Electronic Books. In *Proceedings of the 11th Mediterranean Conference on Medical and Biological Engineering and Computing (Medicon'2007)*, Ljubljana, Slovenia, June 26 - 30, 2007.

Sargent, R.W.H., and Westerberg, A.W. Speed-Up in Chemical Engineering Design, *Transaction Institute in Chemical Engineering*, 1964.

SBML. Systems Biology Markup Language. Level 1 and Level 2. http://www.sbwsbml.org/sbml/docs/index.html. 2003.

Schamai, Wladimir. Modelica Modeling Language (ModelicaML) – A UML Profile for Modelica. Technical Report. Linköping University Electronic Press, www.ep.liu.se, 2009.

Schamai, Wladimir, Peter Fritzson, Chris Paredis, and Adrian Pop. Towards Unified System Modeling and Simulation with ModelicaML: Modeling of Executable Behavior Using Graphical Notations. In *Proceedings of the 7th International Modelica Conference* (Modelica'2009), Como, Italy, September.20-22, 2009.

Schamai, Wladimir, Uwe Pohlmann, Peter Fritzson, Christiaan J.J. Paredis, Philipp Helle, and Carsten Strobel. Execution of UML State Machines Using Modelica. In *Proceedings of the 3rd International Workshop on Equation-Based Object-Oriented Modeling Languages and Tools, (EOOLT'2010)*, Published by Linköping University Electronic Press, www.ep.liu.se, In conjunction with MODELS'2010, Oslo, Norway, Oct 3, 2010.

Schamai, Wladimir, Philipp Helle, Peter Fritzson, and Christiaan Paredis. Virtual Verification of System Designs against System Requirements. In *Proc. of 3rd International Workshop on Model Based Architecting and Construction of Embedded Systems (ACES'2010*). In conjunction with MODELS'2010. Oslo, Norway, Oct 4, 2010.

Schamai, Wladimir, Peter Fritzson, Christiaan J.J. Paredis, and Philipp Helle. ModelicaML Value Bindings for Automated Model Composition. In *Proc. of Symposium on Theory of Modeling and Simulatio*n (TMS/DEVS 2012). Orlando, Florida, USA, March 26-29, 2012.

Schamai, Wladimir, Peter Fritzson, and Chris JJ Paredis. Translation of UML State Machines to Modelica: Handling Semantic Issues. doi: 10.1177/0037549712470296. In *SIMULATION – Transactions of the The Society of Modeling and Simulation International*. Volume 89 Issue 4, April 2013.

Schamai, Wladimir. ModelicaML - UML Profile for Modelica. 2013. ModelicaML web page. www.openmodelica.org/modelicaml, Accessed April 23, 2013.

Schamai, Wladimir. *Model-Based Verification of Dynamic System Behavior against Requirements - Method, Language, and Tool*. Ph.D. Thesis, Linköping University, Sweden. www.ep.liu.se. Dissertation No. 1547. Nov. 12, 2013.

Schaps, Gary L. Compiler Construction with ANTLR and Java. Dr. Dobb's Journal, Mar. 1999.

Schiela, Anton, and Hans Olsson. Mixed-Mode Integration for Real-Time Simulation. In *Proceedings of Modelica Workshop 2000*, Lund University, Lund, Sweden, Oct 23–24, 2000.

Schmitz, Gerhard (ed.). *Proceedings of the 4th International Modelica Conference*. Available at www.modelica.org. Technical University Hamburg-Harburg, Germany, March 7–8, 2005.

Schneider, T., J. Mades, M. Glesner, A. Windisch, and W. Ecker. An Open VHDL-AMS Simulation Framework. In *Proceedings of 2000 IEEE/ACM International Workshop on Behavioral Modeling and Simulation*, pp. 89–94, Orlando, FL, USA, Oct. 19–20, 2000.

Sedaghat, A., A. Sherman, and J. Quon, Michael. A mathematical model of metabolic insulin signaling. *American Journal of Physiology - Endocrinology and Metabolism*, 283:1048-1101, July 2002.

Shabana, Ahmed A. *Dynamics of Multibody Systems*, 2nd ed. Cambridge University Press, 1998.

Shahmehri, Nahid, Mariam Kamkar, and Peter Fritzson. Usability Criteria for Automated Debugging Systems, *Journal of Systems and Software*, pp. 55–70, Oct. 1995.

Shapiro, Ehud Y. *Algorithmic Program Debugging*. MIT Press, May 1982.

Sheard, Tim. Accomplishments and Research Challenges in Meta-programming. In *Proceedings of the International Workshop on Semantics, Applications and Implementation of Program Generation (SAIG01)*, LNCS 2196, Springer Verlag. Florence, Italy, 2001.

Sheshadri, Krishnamurthyn, and Peter Fritzson. A Mathematica-based PDE Solver Generator. *Proceedings of SIMS'99*, pp 66-78, Conference of the Scandinavian Simulation Society, Linköping, Sweden, September 1999.

Sheshadri, Krishnamurthyn, and Peter Fritzson. A General Symbolic PDE-Solver Generator—Explicit Schemes, *Scientific Programming*, 11: 1, 2003a.

Sheshadri, Krishnamurthyn, and Peter Fritzson. A General Symbolic PDE Solver Generator—Beyond Explicit Schemes. *Scientific Programming*, 11:2, 2003b.

Sheshadri, Krishnamurthyn, and Peter Fritzson. A Symbolic PDE Solver Generator—Finite Elements. Submitted to *Scientific Programming*, 2003c.

Sheshadri, Krishnamurthy, and Peter Fritzson. MathPDE: A Package to Solve PDEs. *Mathematica Journal*, December 2011. http://www.mathematica-journal.com/2011/12/mathpde-a-package-to-solve-pdes-by-finite-differences/

Shitahun, Alachew, Vitalij Ruge, Mahder Gebremedhin, Bernhard Bachmann, Lars Eriksson, Joel Andersson, Moritz Diehl, Peter Fritzson. Model-Based Optimization with OpenModelica and CasADi. www.openmodelica.org. In Proc. of IFAC Conference in Tokyo, Sept. 2013.

Shumate, Ken, and Marilyn Keller. *Software Specification and Design: A Disciplined Approach for Real-Time Systems*. John Wiley & Sons, New York, 1992.

Sielemann, Michael. *Device-Oriented Modeling and Simulation in Aircraft Energy Systems Design*. Ph.D. thesis, http://doku.b.tu-harburg.de/volltexte/2013/1208/, Technical University of Hamburg-Harburg, May 2012.

Sielemann, Michael. Probability-One Homotopy for Robust Initialization of Differential-Algebraic Equations. In *Proceedings of 9th International Modelica Conference*, Munich, Germany, Sept. 3-5, 2012.

Siemers, Alexander, Dag Fritzson, and Peter Fritzson. Meta-Modeling for Multi-Physics Co-Simulations applied for OpenModelica. In *Proceedings of International Congress on Methodologies for Emerging Technologies in Automation* (ANIPLA2006), Rome, Italy, November 13-15, 2006.

Sjöberg, Jonas, Fredrik Fyhr, and Tomas Grönstedt. Estimating Parameters in Physical Models Using MathModelica. In *Proceedings of the 2nd International Modelica Conference*, Oberpfaffenhofen, Germany, Mar. 18–19, 2002.

Sjölund, Martin, and Peter Fritzson. An OpenModelica Java External Function Interface Supporting MetaProgramming. In *Proceedings of the 7th International Modelica Conference* (Modelica'2009), Como, Italy, September.20-22, 2009.

Sjölund, Martin, Robert Braun, Peter Fritzson and Petter Krus. Towards Efficient Distributed Simulation in Modelica using Transmission Line Modeling. In *Proceedings of the 3rd International Workshop on Equation-Based Object-Oriented Modeling Languages and Tools, (EOOLT'2010)*, Published by Linköping University Electronic Press, www.ep.liu.se, In conjunction with MODELS'2010, Oslo, Norway, Oct 3, 2010.

Sjölund, Martin, Peter Fritzson, and Adrian Pop. Bootstrapping a Modelica Compiler aiming at Modelica 4. In *Proceedings of the 8th International Modelica Conference* (Modelica'2011), Dresden, Germany, March.20-22, 2011.

Sjölund, Martin, Peter Fritzson and Adrian Pop. Bootstrapping a Compiler for an Equation-Based Object-Oriented Language. DOI: 10.4173/mic.2014.1.1. *Modeling, Identification and Control*, Vol 35, No 1, pp 1-19, 2014.

Sjölund, Martin, and Peter Fritzson. Debugging Symbolic Transformations in Equation Systems. In *Proceedings of the 4th International Workshop on Equation-Based Object-Oriented Modeling Languages and Tools, (EOOLT'2011)*, Zürich, Switzerland, Sept 5, 2011. Published by Linköping University Electronic Press, www.ep.liu.se, Sept 2011.

Sjölund, Martin, Mahder Gebremedhin, and Peter Fritzson. Parallelizing Equation-Based Models for Simulation on Multi-Core Platforms by Utilizing Model Structure. In *Proceedings of the 17th International Workshop on Compilers for Parallel Computing* (CPC 2013), Lyon, France, http://labexcompilation.ens-lyon.fr/cpc2013/program, July 3-5, 2013.

Stavåker, Kristian, Adrian Pop, and Peter Fritzson. Compiling and Using Pattern Matching in Modelica. In *Proceedings of the 6th International Modelica Conference* (Modelica'2008), Bielefeld, Germany, March.3-4, 2008.

Stavåker, Kristian, Daniel Rolls, Jing Guo, Peter Fritzson, and Sven-Bodo Scholz. Compilation of Modelica Array Computations into Single Assignment C for Efficient Execution on CUDA-enabled GPUs. In *Proceedings of the 3rd International Workshop on Equation-Based Object-Oriented Modeling Languages and Tools, (EOOLT'2010,* Published by Linköping University Electronic Press, Oslo, Norway, Oct 3, 2010 www.ep.liu.se, In conjunction with MODELS'2010, Oslo, Norway, Oct 3, 2010.

Stavåker, Kristian, and Peter Fritzson. Generation of Simulation Code from Equation-Based Models for Execution on CUDA-Enabled GPUs. In *Proc. of the Third Swedish Workshop on Multi-Core Computing*. Göteborg, Sweden, Nov 18-19, 2010.

Stavåker, Kristian, Staffan Ronnås, Martin Wlotzska, Vincent Heuveline, and Peter Fritzson. PDE Modeling with Modelica via FMI Import of HiFlow3 C++ Components. www.scansims.org. In Proc. of the Scandinavian Conference on Modeling and Simulation (SIMS'2013), June 2013.

Steele, Guy. *Common Lisp the Language,* 2nd Edition. Digital Press. 1990.

Stevens, Richard, Peter Brook, Ken Jackson, and Stuart Arnold. *Systems Engineering: Cooping with Complexity*. Prentice-Hall, U.K., 1998.

Süss, Jörn Guy, Peter Fritzson, Adrian Pop, and Luke Wildman. Towards Integrated Model-Driven Testing of SCADA Systems Using the Eclipse Modeling Framework and Modelica. In *Proceedings of 19th Australian Software Engineering Conference (ASWEC 2008)*, Perth, Western Australia, March 25 – 28, 2008.

Süss, Jörn Guy, Peter Fritzson, and Adrian Pop. The Impreciseness of UML and Implications for ModelicaML. In *Proceedings of the 2nd International Workshop on Equation-Based Object-Oriented Languages and Tools, (EOOLT'2008)*, Pathos, Cyprus, July 8, 2008. Published by Linköping University Electronic Press, http://www.ep.liu.se/ecp/024/, July 2008.

Szyperski, Clemens. *Component Software—Beyond Object-Oriented Programming*. Addison-Wesley, 1997.

Tarjan, R.E. Depth First Search and Linear Graph Algorithms, *SIAM Journal of Computting*, 1, pp. 146–160, 1972.

Teitelman, Warren. Toward a Programming Laboratory. In *Proc. of First Int. Jt. Conf. on Artificial Intelligence*, 1969.

Teitelman, Warren. *INTERLISP Reference Manual*. Xerox Palo Alto Research Center, Palo Alto, CA, 1974.

Teitelman, Warren. A Display Oriented Programmer's Assistant, *Computer*, pp. 39–50 Aug. 1977.

Thieriot, Hubert, Maroun Nemer, Mohsen Torabzadeh-Tari, Peter Fritzson, Rajiv Singh, and John John Kocherry. Towards Design Optimization with OpenModelica Emphasizing Parameter Optimization with Genetic Algorithms. In *Proceedings of the 8th International Modelica Conference* (Modelica'2011), Dresden, Germany, March.20-22, 2011.

Thomas, Philip. *Simulation of Industrial Processes for Control Engineers*. Butterworth-Heinemann, 390 pages, ISBN 0-7506-4161-4, 1999.

Tiller, Michael. *Introduction to Physical Modeling with Modelica*. Kluwer Academic Publishers, 2001.

Tiller, Michael, William E. Tobler, and Ming Kuang. Evaluating Engine Contributions to HEV Driveline Vibrations. In *Proceedings of the 2nd International Modelica Conference*, Oberpfaffenhofen, Germany, Mar. 18–19, 2002.

Tolsma, John E., and Paul I. Barton. DAEPACK: An Open Modeling Environment for Legacy Model, *Journal of Industrial & Engineering Chemistry Research*, 39:6, pp. 1826–1839, 2000.

Tolsma, John E., Jerry Clabaugh, and Paul I. Barton. *Abacuss II: Advanced Modeling Environment and Embedded Simulator,* and *Abacuss II Syntax Manual*. Available at http://yoric.mit.edu/abacuss2/abacuss2.html and .../syntax.html. Massachusetts Institute of Technology, Chemical Engineering System Research Group, 2002.

Torabzadeh-Tari, Mohsen, Peter Fritzson, Martin Sjölund, Adrian Pop. OpenModelica-Python Interoperability. Applied to Monte Carlo Simulation. In *Proceedings of the 50th Scandinavian Conference on Simulation and Modeling* (SIMS'2009), available at www.scan-sims.org. Fredericia, Denmark. October 7-8, 2009.

Torabzadeh-Tari, Mohsen, Peter Fritzson, Adrian Pop, and Martin Sjölund. Generalization of an Active Electronic Notebook for Teaching Multiple Programming Languages, In *Proceedings of EDUCON2010*, IEEE, Madrid, April 14-16, 2010.

Torabzadeh-Tari, Mohsen, Zoheb Hossain, Peter Fritzson, and Thomas Richter. OMWeb – Virtual Web-based Remote Laboratory for Modelica in Engineering Courses. In *Proceedings of the 8th International Modelica Conference* (Modelica'2011), Dresden, Germany, March.20-22, 2011.

Torabzadeh-Tari, Mohsen, Martin Sjölund, Adrian Pop, and Peter Fritzson. DrControl: An Interactive Course Material for Teaching Control Engineering. In *Proceedings of the 8th International Modelica Conference* (Modelica'2011), Dresden, Germany, March.20-22, 2011.

Torabzadeh-Tari, Mohsen, Jhansi Reddy Remala, Martin Sjölund, Adrian Pop, and Peter Fritzson. OMSketch — Graphical Sketching in the OpenModelica Interactive Book, OMNotebook. In *Proceedings of the 52th Scandinavian Conference on Simulation and Modeling* (SIMS'2011), available at www.scan-sims.org. Västerås. Sweden, Sept 29-30, 2011.

Tummescheit, Hubertus, Jonas Eborn, and Falko Jens Wagner. Development of a Modelica Base Library for Modeling of Thermo-Hydraulic Systems. In *Proceedings of Modelica Workshop 2000*, Lund University, Lund, Sweden, Oct. 23–24, 2000.

Tummescheit, Hubertus, and Jonas Eborn. Chemical Reaction Modeling with ThermoFluid/MF and MultiFlash. In *Proceedings of the 2nd International Modelica Conference*, Oberpfaffenhofen, Germany, Mar. 18–19, 2002.

Tummescheit, Hubertus. *Design and Implementation of Object-Oriented Model Libraries Using Modelica*. Ph.D. thesis, Dept. of Automatic Control, Lund University, 257 pages, ISSN 0280-5316. 2002.

Tummescheit, Hubertus, and Jonas Eborn. Thermofluid library web page http://www.sf.net/projects/thermofluid. 2003.

Tundis, Andrea, Lena Rogovchenko-Buffoni, Peter Fritzson, and Alfredo Garro. Modeling System Requirements in Modelica: Definition and Comparison of Candidate Approaches. In *Proceedings of the 5th International Workshop on Equation-Based Object-Oriented Modeling Languages and Tools, (EOOLT'2013)*, Published by Linköping University Electronic Press, www.ep.liu.se, Nottingham, UK, April 19, 2013.

Tundis, Andrea, Lena Rogovchenko-Buffoni, Peter Fritzson, Alfredo Garro, Mattias Nyberg, Requirement Verification and Dependency Tracing During Simulation in Modelica, In *Proc. of EUROSIM Congress on Modelling and Simulation*, September 10-12, Wales (UK).

Tundis, Andrea, Lena Rogovchenko-Buffoni, Alfredo Garro, Mattias Nyberg, and Peter Fritzson. Performing Fault Tree Analysis of a Modelica-Based System Design Through a Probability Model. In *Proc. of Workshop on Applied Modeling and Simulation* (WAMS2013), Buenos Aires (Argentina), November 24-27, 2013.

Unger, J., A. Kröner, and W. Marquardt. Structural Analysis of Differential Algebraic Equation Systems—Theory and Applications, *Computers Chem. Engng.* 19:18, pp. 867-882, 1995.

Uno, Takeaki. Algorithms for Enumerating All Perfect, Maximum and Maximal Matchings in Bipartite Graphs. In *Proceedings of 8th Annual International Symposium on Algorithms and Computation (ISAAC '97)*, Singapore, Dec. 17–19, 1997.

Uno, Takeaki. A Fast Algorithm for Enumerating Bipartite Perfect Matchings. In *Proceeding of 12th Annual International Symposium on Algorithms and Computation (ISAAC2001)*, LNCS 2223, pp. 367–379, Springer-Verlag, 2001.

Viklund, Lars, and Peter Fritzson. ObjectMath—An Object-Oriented Language and Environment for Symbolic and Numerical Processing in Scientific Computing, *Scientific Programming*, Vol. 4, pp. 229–250, 1995.

Voit, Eberhard O. *Computational Analysis of Biochemical Systems: A Practical Guide for Biochemists and Molecular Biologists*, Cambridge Univ. Press, 2000.

Volterra, V. Variations and Fluctuations of the Number of Individuals in Animal Species Living Together, *J. du Conseil*, Vol. II, 1928.

Wiesmann, Hans-Jürg. Private communication regarding the SPOT library, and Modelica array concatenation and construction. ABB Corp. Research, Segelhof, CH-5405 Baden, Schweiz. hans-juerg.wiesmann@ch.abb.com, 2001.

Wikipedia. ANSI-C format string placeholders. http://en.wikipedia.org/wiki/Printf_format_string#Format_placeholders Accessed October 2013.

Wikipedia-URI. Uniform Resource Identifier. http://en.wikipedia.org/wiki/Uniform_Resource_Identifier. Accessed April 2011.

Wikipedia-Resource. Resource (Web). http://en.wikipedia.org/wiki/Resource_(Web). Accessed April 2011.

Wikipedia-URI-Scheme. http://en.wikipedia.org/wiki/URI_scheme. Accessed April 2011.

Visio. http://www.microsoft.com/office/visio/, 2001.

Wolfram Research. Wolfram System Modeler. 2013. http://www.wolfram.com/system-modeler/ Accessed April 2013.

Wolfram, Stephen. *Mathematica—A System for Doing Mathematics by Computer*. Addison-Wesley, 1988.

Wolfram, Stephen. *The Mathematica Book*. Wolfram Media Inc, 1997.

Wolfram, Stephen. *A New Kind of Science*. Wolfram Media Inc, 2002.

Wrangsjö, Andreas, Peter Fritzson, and K. Sheshadri. Transforming Systems of PDEs for Efficient Numerical Solution. Available at http://south.rotol.ramk.fi/~keranen/IMS99/paper7/Transformations.pdf. In *Proceedings of the International Mathematica Symposium (IMS99)*, Linz, Austria, 1999.

Zeigler B.P. *Multifaceted Modeling and Discrete Event Simulation*. Academic Press, London, 1984.

Zeigler B.P. *Object-Oriented Simulation with Hierarchical, Modular Models*, Academic Press London, 1990.

Index